Collins

Collins
Thesaurus
A –Z

William Collins' dream of knowledge for all began with the publication of his first book in 1819. A self-educated mill worker, he not only enriched millions of lives, but also founded a flourishing publishing house. Today, staying true to this spirit, Collins books are packed with inspiration, innovation, and practical expertise. They place you at the centre of a world of possibility and give you exactly what you need to explore it.

Language is the key to this exploration, and at the heart of Collins Dictionaries is language as it is really used. New words, phrases, and meanings spring up every day, and all of them are captured and analysed by the Collins Word Web. Constantly updated, and with over 2.5 billion entries, this living language resource is unique to our dictionaries.

Words are tools for life. And a Collins Dictionary makes them work for you.

Collins. Do more.

Collins
Thesaurus
A–Z

HarperCollins Publishers
Westerhill Road
Bishopbriggs
Glasgow
G64 2QT

This edition 2008

© HarperCollins Publishers 1997, 2003, 2006, 2008

ISBN 978-0-00-723700-5

Collins® and Bank of English® are registered
trademarks of HarperCollins Publishers Limited

www.collinslanguage.com

A catalogue record for this book is
available from the British Library

Typeset by Wordcraft, Glasgow

Printed and bound at
Thomson Press (India) Ltd.

Acknowledgements
We would like to thank those authors and
publishers who kindly gave permission for
copyright material to be used in the Collins
Word Web. We would also like to thank Times
Newspapers Ltd for providing valuable data.

Editorial Staff

Contents

Introduction

When this thesaurus was first published in 1997, it proved to be an immensely popular language resource. This new edition has been completely revised to give you even more ways of expanding your vocabulary and adding richness and variety to your language, and has a clear and attractive layout which highlights the many extra features.

The headword list has been selected on the basis of frequency as verified by the Collins Word Web, which means that the entry words given are those most likely to be looked up by the user. The key synonym for each sense is shown first, which not only offers you the most helpful alternative but also lets you identify the sense in question at a glance. Other synonyms are arranged in order of their frequency of occurrence, with the more literary or unfamiliar ones coming towards the end.

The thesaurus offers extensive coverage of English as a world language, with words and phrases from all over the English-speaking world making this a truly international language resource.

A wide range of phrases and idioms is also included, both as lookup points and as alternatives, to add colour and interest to your language.

Illustrative examples, taken from the Collins Word Web, are included wherever an entry word has more than one sense. These not only help you to identify the sense, but show how the word is used in real English.

As well as generous synonym lists, key antonyms are included for many entry words. But this new edition gives you much more than just a wide choice of synonyms and antonyms.

The "related words" feature enables you to find information such as adjectives, collective nouns, manias, and phobias connected with many main entry words. Such words are usually hard to find unless you already have an idea of what the related word might be, but by looking up, for instance, the entry for **spider**, you will find that fear of spiders is **arachnophobia**. The arrangement of such words under the main entry word lets you go to it straight away.

Informative and comprehensive subject word lists provide a wealth of material connected with many entry words. For example, look up the entry **orchestra** and you will find a list of **instruments in a full orchestra**. As well as hundreds of such lists, the new Word Power supplement gives you another, uniquely practical, kind of language help. It lists famous people such as actors, artists, composers, politicians, and writers, all arranged by their occupations. It also lists geographical information such as countries, capitals, currencies, and political parties, arranged by subject. It is therefore a source of invaluable information for solving general-knowledge clues in crosswords and puzzles, and for boosting home study.

Helpful Word Power notes are also included at many entries. These give advice on good English and help you to avoid some of the more common language mistakes. Panel entries such as **business jargon, clichés and pompous expressions, text message symbols and abbreviations,** and **top ten mistakes in English** give you an added dimension of language help.

All these features mean that this new edition is a treasury of useful and practical words and information, arranged in the most helpful way possible.

Features of the Thesaurus

Entry words •——— **bedrock** 1 = <u>first principle</u>, rule, basis, basics, principle, essentials, roots, core, fundamentals, cornerstone, nuts and bolts (*informal*), sine qua non (*Latin*), rudiment ...*Mutual trust is the bedrock of a relationship...*

Foreign words and phrases

2 = <u>bottom</u>, bed, foundation, underpinning, rock bottom, substructure, substratum ...*It took five years to drill down to bedrock...*

Related words expand your vocabulary •——— **bee**

> (Related Words)

adjective: apian
collective nouns: swarm, grist
habitation: hive, apiary
➤ **ants, bees and wasps** ——————— **Cross references**

Labels identify areas of usage •——— **beef** (*Slang*) = <u>complaint</u>, dispute, grievance, —— problem, grumble, criticism, objection, dissatisfaction, annoyance, grouse, gripe (*informal*), protestation, grouch (*informal*), remonstrance

Synonyms offer a wide range of alternatives

Key synonyms given first •——— **beer** = <u>ale</u>, brew, swipes (*Brit. slang*), wallop (*Brit. slang*), hop juice, amber fluid *or* nectar (*Austral. — informal*)

International English from all regions of the world where English is spoken

beetle
➤ **beetles**

Beetles

ambrosia beetle	churchyard beetle
Asiatic beetle	click beetle, snapping
bacon beetle	beetle, *or* skipjack
bark beetle	cockchafer, May beetle,
bee beetle	*or* May bug
black beetle	Colorado beetle *or*
blister beetle	potato beetle
bloody-nosed beetle	curculio
boll weevil	deathwatch beetle
bombardier beetle	devil's coach-horse
burying beetle *or*	diving beetle
sexton	dor
cabinet beetle	dung beetle *or* chafer
cardinal beetle	elater
carpet beetle *or* (*U.S.*)	firefly
carpet bug	flea beetle
carrion beetle	furniture beetle
chafer	glow-worm
Christmas beetle *or* king	gold beetle *or* goldbug
beetle	goldsmith beetle

Subject word lists add an extra dimension to your vocabulary

Features of the Thesaurus

befit = <u>be appropriate for</u>, become, suit, be fitting for, be suitable for, be seemly for, behove (*U.S.*) —————• **Regional labels**

beguile 1 = <u>charm</u>, please, attract, delight, occupy, cheer, fascinate, entertain, absorb, entrance, win over, amuse, divert, distract, enchant, captivate, solace, allure, bewitch, mesmerize, engross, enrapture, tickle the fancy of …*His paintings beguiled the Prince of Wales*…
2 = <u>fool</u>, trick, take in, cheat, con (*informal*), mislead, impose on, deceive, dupe, gull (*archaic*), delude, bamboozle, hoodwink, take for a ride (*informal*), befool …*He used his newspapers to beguile his readers*… [OPPOSITE⟩ enlighten

Illustrative examples from real English show how the entry word is used •

Opposites given for many key words •

Idioms and phrases add colour to your language

Labels identify areas of usage

beguiling = <u>charming</u>, interesting, pleasing, attractive, engaging, lovely, entertaining, pleasant, intriguing, diverting, delightful, irresistible, enchanting, seductive, captivating, enthralling, winning, eye-catching, alluring, bewitching, delectable, winsome, likable *or* likeable

behalf
[PHRASES] **on something** *or* **someone's behalf** *or* **on behalf of something** *or* **someone 1** = <u>as a representative of</u>, representing, in the name of, as a spokesperson for …*She made an emotional public appeal on her son's behalf*… …*On behalf of my wife and myself, I'd like to thank you all*… **2** = <u>for the benefit of</u>, for the sake of, in support of, on the side of, in the interests of, on account of, for the good of, in defence of, to the advantage of, for the profit of …*The honour recognizes work done on behalf of classical theatre*…

Fixed phrases •

Sense numbers

Word Power

behalf – *On behalf of* is sometimes wrongly used as an alternative to *on the part of*. The distinction is that *on behalf of someone* means 'for someone's benefit' or 'representing someone', while *on the part of someone* can be roughly paraphrased as 'by someone'.

Word power notes give advice on good English

Lists in the Thesaurus

Lists in the Thesaurus

Lists in the Thesaurus

Lists in the Thesaurus

Lists in the Thesaurus

Lists in the Thesaurus

Lists in the Thesaurus

A a

aback
PHRASES take someone aback = <u>surprise</u>, throw, shock, stun, confuse, astonish, stagger, startle, bewilder, astound, disconcert, bowl over (*informal*), stupefy, floor (*informal*), knock for six, dumbfound, leave open-mouthed, nonplus, flabbergast (*informal*)

abandon **VERB**
1 = <u>leave</u>, strand, ditch, leave behind, walk out on, forsake, jilt, run out on, throw over, turn your back on, desert, dump, leave high and dry, leave in the lurch …*He claimed that his parents had abandoned him…*
2 = <u>stop</u>, drop, give up, halt, cease, cut out, pack in (*Brit. informal*), discontinue, leave off, desist from …*The authorities have abandoned any attempt to distribute food…* **OPPOSITE** continue
3 = <u>give up</u>, resign from, yield, surrender, relinquish, renounce, waive, cede, forgo, abdicate …*efforts to persuade him to abandon his claim to the presidency…* **OPPOSITE** keep
4 = (takes *ship* as object) <u>evacuate</u>, quit, withdraw from, vacate, depart from …*The crew prepared to abandon ship…* **OPPOSITE** maintain
NOUN = <u>recklessness</u>, dash, wildness, wantonness, unrestraint, careless freedom …*He has splashed money around with gay abandon…* **OPPOSITE** restraint

abandoned
1 = <u>unoccupied</u>, empty, deserted, vacant, derelict, uninhabited …*abandoned buildings that become a breeding ground for crime…* **OPPOSITE** occupied
2 = <u>deserted</u>, dropped, rejected, neglected, stranded, ditched, discarded, relinquished, left, forsaken, cast off, jilted, cast aside, cast out, cast away …*a newsreel of abandoned children suffering from cold and hunger…*
3 = <u>uninhibited</u>, wild, uncontrolled, unbridled, unrestrained, unconstrained …*people who enjoy wild, abandoned lovemaking…* **OPPOSITE** inhibited

abandonment
1 = <u>desertion</u>, leaving, forsaking, jilting …*memories of her father's complete abandonment of her…*
2 = <u>evacuation</u>, leaving, quitting, departure, withdrawal …*the abandonment of two North Sea oilfields…*
3 = <u>stopping</u>, cessation, discontinuation …*Rain forced the abandonment of the next day's competitions…*
4 = <u>renunciation</u>, giving up, surrender, waiver, abdication, cession, relinquishment …*their abandonment of the policy…*

abate
1 = <u>decrease</u>, decline, relax, ease, sink, fade, weaken, diminish, dwindle, lessen, slow, wane, subside, ebb, let up, slacken, attenuate, taper off …*The storms soon abated…* **OPPOSITE** increase
2 = <u>reduce</u>, slow, relax, ease, relieve, moderate, weaken, dull, diminish, decrease, lessen, alleviate, quell, mitigate, attenuate …*a government programme to abate greenhouse gas emissions…* **OPPOSITE** increase

abatement
1 = <u>decrease</u>, slowing, decline, easing, sinking, fading, weakening, relaxation, dwindling, lessening, waning, subsiding, ebbing, cessation, let-up, slackening, diminution, tapering off, attenuation …*Demand for the product shows no sign of abatement…*
2 = <u>reduction</u>, slowing, relief, easing, weakening, dulling, decrease, lessening, cutback, quelling, moderation, remission, slackening, mitigation, diminution, curtailment, alleviation, attenuation, extenuation …*noise abatement…*

abattoir = <u>slaughterhouse</u>, shambles, butchery

abbey = <u>monastery</u>, convent, priory, cloister, nunnery, friary

abbreviate = <u>shorten</u>, reduce, contract, trim, cut, prune, summarize, compress, condense, abridge **OPPOSITE** expand

abbreviated = <u>shortened</u>, shorter, reduced, brief, potted, trimmed, pruned, cut, summarized, compressed, concise, condensed, abridged **OPPOSITE** expanded

abbreviation = <u>shortening</u>, reduction, résumé, trimming, summary, contraction, compression, synopsis, précis, abridgment

---

Abbreviations http://www.acronymfinder.com/

Classified advertisements

Abbreviation	Meaning
AMC *or* amc	all mod cons
deps	deposit
exc *or* excl	excluding
f/f	furnished flat
GCH	gas central heating
inc *or* incl	including
pcm	per calendar month
pw	per week

Lonely hearts column abbreviations

Abbreviation	Meaning
GSOH	good sense of humour
GWM	gay white male
LTR	long term relationship
NS *or* N/S	non-smoker
SOH	sense of humour
SWF	single white female
VGSOH	very good sense of humour
WLTM	would like to meet
WSOH	wicked *or* weird sense of humour
1-2-1	one-to-one

abdicate 1 = <u>resign</u>, retire, quit, step down (*informal*) …*The last French king abdicated in 1848*… 2 = <u>give up</u>, yield, hand over, surrender, relinquish, renounce, waive, vacate, cede, abjure …*Edward chose to abdicate the throne, rather than give Mrs Simpson up*… 3 = <u>renounce</u>, give up, abandon, surrender, relinquish, waive, forgo, abnegate …*Many parents simply abdicate all responsibility for their children*…

abdication 1 = <u>resignation</u>, quitting, retirement, retiral (*chiefly Scot.*) …*the abdication of Edward VIII*… 2 = <u>giving up</u>, yielding, surrender, waiving, renunciation, cession, relinquishment …*Edward was titled Duke of Windsor after his abdication of the throne*… 3 = <u>renunciation</u>, giving up, surrender, abandonment, waiver, abnegation, relinquishment …*There had been a complete abdication of responsibility*…

abdomen = <u>stomach</u>, guts (*slang*), belly, tummy (*informal*), midriff, midsection

(Related Words)
adjective: abdominal

abdominal = <u>gastric</u>, intestinal, visceral

abduct = <u>kidnap</u>, seize, carry off, run off with, run away with, make off with, snatch (*slang*)

abduction = <u>kidnapping</u>, seizure, carrying off

aberrant 1 = <u>abnormal</u>, odd, strange, extraordinary, curious, weird, peculiar, eccentric, queer, irregular, erratic, deviant, off-the-wall (*slang*), oddball (*informal*), anomalous, untypical, wacko (*slang*), outré …*His rages and aberrant behaviour worsened*… 2 = <u>depraved</u>, corrupt, perverted, perverse, degenerate, deviant, debased, debauched …*aberrant sexual crimes*…

aberration = <u>anomaly</u>, exception, defect, abnormality, inconsistency, deviation, quirk, peculiarity, divergence, departure, irregularity, incongruity

abet 1 = <u>help</u>, aid, encourage, sustain, assist, uphold, back, second, incite, egg on, succour …*We shall strike hard at terrorists and those who abet them*… 2 = <u>encourage</u>, further, forward, promote, urge, boost, prompt, spur, foster, incite, connive at …*The media have abetted the feeling of unreality*…

abetting = <u>help</u>, backing, support, aid, assistance, encouragement, abetment, abettal

abeyance
PHRASES **in abeyance** = <u>shelved</u>, pending, on ice (*informal*), in cold storage (*informal*), hanging fire, suspended

abhor = <u>hate</u>, loathe, despise, detest, shrink from, shudder at, recoil from, be repelled by, have an aversion to, abominate, execrate, regard with repugnance *or* horror OPPOSITE> love

abhorrent = <u>hateful</u>, hated, offensive, disgusting, horrible, revolting, obscene, distasteful, horrid, repellent, obnoxious, despicable, repulsive, heinous, odious, repugnant, loathsome, abominable, execrable, detestable

abide VERB 1 = <u>tolerate</u>, suffer, accept, bear, endure, brook, hack (*slang*), put up with, take, stand, stomach, thole (*Scot.*) …*I can't abide people who can't make up their minds*… 2 = <u>last</u>, continue, remain, survive, carry on, endure, persist, keep on …*to make moral judgements on the basis of what is eternal and abides*…
PHRASES **abide by something** = <u>obey</u>, follow, agree to, carry out, observe, fulfil, stand by, act on, comply with, hold to, heed, submit to, conform to, keep to, adhere to, mind …*They have got to abide by the rules*…

abiding = <u>enduring</u>, lasting, continuing, remaining, surviving, permanent, constant, prevailing, persisting, persistent, eternal, tenacious, firm, fast, everlasting, unending, unchanging OPPOSITE> brief

ability 1 = <u>capability</u>, power, potential, facility, capacity, qualification, competence, proficiency, competency, potentiality …*No one had faith in his ability to do the job*… OPPOSITE> inability 2 = <u>skill</u>, talent, know-how (*informal*), gift, expertise, faculty, flair, competence, energy, accomplishment, knack, aptitude, proficiency, dexterity, cleverness, potentiality, adroitness, adeptness …*Her drama teacher spotted her ability*…

abject 1 = <u>wretched</u>, miserable, hopeless, dismal, outcast, pitiful, forlorn, deplorable, pitiable …*Both of them died in abject poverty*… 2 = <u>servile</u>, humble, craven, cringing, fawning, submissive, grovelling, subservient, slavish, mean, low, obsequious …*He sounded abject and eager to please*… OPPOSITE> dignified 3 = <u>despicable</u>, base, degraded, worthless, vile, sordid, debased, reprehensible, contemptible, dishonourable, ignoble, detestable, scungy (*Austral. & N.Z.*) …*the kind of abject low-life that preys on children*…

ablaze 1 = <u>on fire</u>, burning, flaming, blazing, fiery, alight, aflame, afire …*Shops, houses and vehicles were ablaze*… 2 = <u>bright</u>, brilliant, flashing, glowing, sparkling, illuminated, gleaming, radiant, luminous, incandescent, aglow …*The chamber was ablaze with light*… 3 = <u>passionate</u>, excited, stimulated, fierce, enthusiastic, aroused, animated, frenzied, fervent, impassioned, fervid …*He was ablaze with enthusiasm*…

able = <u>capable</u>, experienced, fit, skilled, expert, powerful, masterly, effective, qualified, talented, gifted, efficient, clever, practised, accomplished, competent, skilful, adept, masterful, strong, proficient, adroit, highly endowed OPPOSITE> incapable

able-bodied = <u>strong</u>, firm, sound, fit, powerful, healthy, strapping, hardy, robust, vigorous, sturdy, hale, stout, staunch, hearty, lusty, right as rain (*Brit. informal*), tough, capable, sturdy, Herculean, fighting fit, sinewy, fit as a fiddle OPPOSITE> weak

abnormal = <u>unusual</u>, different, odd, strange, surprising, extraordinary, remarkable, bizarre, unexpected, curious, weird, exceptional, peculiar, eccentric, unfamiliar, queer, irregular, phenomenal, uncommon, erratic, monstrous, singular, unnatural, deviant, unconventional, off-the-wall (*slang*), oddball (*informal*), out of the ordinary, left-field (*informal*), anomalous, atypical, aberrant, untypical, wacko (*slang*), outré OPPOSITE> normal

abnormality 1 = <u>strangeness</u>, deviation, eccentricity, aberration, peculiarity, idiosyncrasy, irregularity, weirdness, singularity, oddness, waywardness, unorthodoxy, unexpectedness, queerness, unnaturalness, bizarreness, unusualness, extraordinariness, aberrance, atypicalness, uncommonness, untypicalness, curiousness …*Further scans are required to confirm any abnormality…*
2 = <u>anomaly</u>, flaw, rarity, deviation, oddity, aberration, exception, peculiarity, deformity, monstrosity, irregularity, malformation …*Genetic abnormalities are usually associated with paternal DNA…*

abnormally = <u>unusually</u>, oddly, strangely, extremely, exceptionally, extraordinarily, overly, excessively, peculiarly, particularly, bizarrely, disproportionately, singularly, fantastically, unnaturally, uncannily, inordinately, uncommonly, prodigiously, freakishly, atypically, subnormally, supernormally

abode = <u>home</u>, house, quarters, lodging, pad (*slang*), residence, habitat, dwelling, habitation, domicile, dwelling place

abolish = <u>do away with</u>, end, destroy, eliminate, shed, cancel, axe (*informal*), get rid of, ditch (*slang*), dissolve, junk (*informal*), suppress, overturn, throw out, discard, wipe out, overthrow, void, terminate, drop, trash (*slang*), repeal, eradicate, put an end to, quash, extinguish, dispense with, revoke, stamp out, obliterate, subvert, jettison, repudiate, annihilate, rescind, exterminate, invalidate, bring to an end, annul, nullify, blot out, expunge, abrogate, vitiate, extirpate OPPOSITE> establish

abolition = <u>eradication</u>, ending, end, withdrawal, destruction, removal, overturning, wiping out, overthrow, voiding, extinction, repeal, elimination, cancellation, suppression, quashing, termination, stamping out, subversion, extermination, annihilation, blotting out, repudiation, erasure, annulment, obliteration, revocation, effacement, nullification, abrogation, rescission, extirpation, invalidation, vitiation, expunction

abominable = <u>detestable</u>, shocking, terrible, offensive, foul, disgusting, horrible, revolting, obscene, vile, horrid, repellent, atrocious, obnoxious, despicable, repulsive, base, heinous, hellish, odious, hateful, repugnant, reprehensible, loathsome, abhorrent, contemptible, villainous, nauseous, wretched, accursed, execrable, godawful (*slang*) OPPOSITE> pleasant

abomination 1 = <u>outrage</u>, bête noire, horror, evil, shame, plague, curse, disgrace, crime, atrocity, torment, anathema, barbarism, bugbear …*What is happening is an abomination…*
2 = <u>hatred</u>, hate, horror, disgust, dislike, loathing, distaste, animosity, aversion, revulsion, antagonism, antipathy, enmity, ill will, animus, abhorrence,

repugnance, odium, detestation, execration …*He had become an object of abomination…*

aboriginal = <u>indigenous</u>, first, earliest, original, primary, ancient, native, primitive, pristine, primordial, primeval, autochthonous

aborigine = <u>original inhabitant</u>, native, aboriginal, indigene

abort 1 = <u>terminate</u> (*a pregnancy*), miscarry …*the latest date at which a foetus can be aborted…*
2 = <u>stop</u>, end, finish, check, arrest, halt, cease, bring *or* come to a halt *or* standstill, axe (*informal*), pull up, terminate, call off, break off, cut short, pack in (*Brit. informal*), discontinue, desist …*The take-off was aborted…*

abortion 1 = <u>termination</u>, miscarriage, feticide, aborticide, deliberate miscarriage …*They had been going out a year when she had an abortion…*
2 = <u>failure</u>, disappointment, fiasco, misadventure, monstrosity, vain effort …*the abortion of the original nuclear project…*

abortive = <u>failed</u>, failing, useless, vain, unsuccessful, idle, ineffective, futile, fruitless, unproductive, ineffectual, miscarried, unavailing, bootless

abound VERB = <u>be plentiful</u>, thrive, flourish, be numerous, proliferate, be abundant, be thick on the ground, superabound …*Stories abound about when he was in charge…*
PHRASES **abound in** *or* **with something** = <u>overflow with</u>, be packed with, teem with, be crowded with, swell with, crawl with, swarm with, be jammed with, be infested with, be thronged with, luxuriate with …*In troubled times, the roads abounded with highwaymen and brigands… …Venice abounds in famous hotels…*

about PREPOSITION **1** = <u>regarding</u>, on, re, concerning, touching, dealing with, respecting, referring to, relating to, concerned with, connected with, relative to, with respect to, as regards, anent (*Scot.*) …*She knew a lot about food…*
2 = <u>around</u>, over, through, round, throughout, all over …*For 18 years, he wandered about Germany, Switzerland and Italy…*
3 = <u>round</u>, around …*She threw her arms about him…*
4 = <u>near</u>, around, close to, bordering, nearby, beside, close by, adjacent to, just round the corner from, in the neighbourhood of, alongside of, contiguous to, within sniffing distance of (*informal*), at close quarters to, a hop, skip and a jump away from (*informal*) …*The restaurant is somewhere about here…*
ADVERB **1** = <u>approximately</u>, around, almost, nearing, nearly, approaching, close to, roughly, just about, more or less, in the region of, in the vicinity of, not far off …*The rate of inflation is running at about 2.7 per cent…*
2 = <u>everywhere</u>, around, all over, here and there, on all sides, in all directions, to and fro, from place to place, hither and thither …*The house isn't big enough with three children running about…*
ADJECTIVE = <u>around</u>, present, active, stirring, in motion, astir …*There were a lot of people about…*

PHRASES **about to** = <u>on the point of</u>, ready to, intending to, on the verge *or* brink of ... *I think he's about to leave...*

about-turn NOUN = <u>change of direction</u>, reverse, reversal, turnaround, U-turn, right about (turn), about-face, volte-face, turnabout ...*The decision was seen as an about-turn for the government...*

VERB = <u>change direction</u>, reverse, about-face, volte-face, face the opposite direction, turn about *or* around, turn through 180 degrees, do *or* perform a U-turn *or* volte-face ...*She about-turned abruptly and left...*

above PREPOSITION 1 = <u>over</u>, upon, beyond, on top of, exceeding, higher than, atop ...*He lifted his arms above his head...* OPPOSITE under

2 = <u>senior to</u>, over, ahead of, in charge of, higher than, surpassing, superior to, more powerful than ...*the people above you in the organization...* OPPOSITE subordinate to

3 = <u>before</u>, more than, rather than, beyond, instead of, sooner than, in preference to ...*I want to be honest, above everything else...*

ADVERB = <u>overhead</u>, upward, in the sky, on high, in heaven, atop, aloft, up above, skyward ...*A long scream sounded from somewhere above...*

ADJECTIVE = <u>preceding</u>, earlier, previous, prior, foregoing, aforementioned, aforesaid ...*Write to the above address...*

(*Related Words*)
prefixes: super-, supra-, sur-

abrasion 1 (*Medical*) = <u>graze</u>, scratch, trauma (*Pathology*), scrape, scuff, chafe, surface injury ...*He had severe abrasions to his right cheek...*

2 = <u>rubbing</u>, wear, scratching, scraping, grating, friction, scouring, attrition, corrosion, wearing down, erosion, scuffing, chafing, grinding down, wearing away, abrading ...*The sole of the shoe should be designed to take constant abrasion...*

abrasive ADJECTIVE 1 = <u>harsh</u>, cutting, biting, tough, sharp, severe, bitter, rough, hard, nasty, cruel, annoying, brutal, stern, irritating, unpleasant, grating, abusive, galling, unkind, hurtful, caustic, vitriolic, pitiless, unfeeling, comfortless ...*She was unrepentant about her abrasive remarks...*

2 = <u>rough</u>, scratching, scraping, grating, scuffing, chafing, scratchy, frictional, erosive ...*an all-purpose non-abrasive cleaner...*

NOUN = <u>scourer</u>, grinder, burnisher, scarifier, abradant ...*Avoid abrasives, which can damage the tiles...*

abreast ADVERB = <u>alongside</u>, level, beside, in a row, side by side, neck and neck, shoulder to shoulder ...*a group of youths riding four abreast...*

PHRASES **abreast of** = <u>informed about</u>, in touch with, familiar with, acquainted with, up to date with, knowledgeable about, conversant with, up to speed with (*informal*), in the picture about, *au courant* with, *au fait* with, keeping your finger on the pulse of ...*We'll keep you abreast of developments...*

abridge = <u>shorten</u>, reduce, contract, trim, clip, diminish, decrease, abstract, digest, cut down, cut back, cut, prune, concentrate, lessen, summarize, compress, curtail, condense, abbreviate, truncate, epitomize, downsize, précis, synopsize (*U.S.*) OPPOSITE expand

abridged = <u>shortened</u>, shorter, reduced, brief, potted (*informal*), trimmed, diminished, pruned, summarized, cut, compressed, curtailed, concise, condensed, abbreviated OPPOSITE expanded

abroad 1 = <u>overseas</u>, out of the country, beyond the sea, in foreign lands ...*About 65 per cent of our sales come from abroad...*

2 = <u>about</u>, everywhere, circulating, at large, here and there, current, all over, in circulation ...*There is still a feeling abroad that this change must be recognised...*

abrupt 1 = <u>sudden</u>, unexpected, hurried, rapid, surprising, quick, swift, rash, precipitate, hasty, impulsive, headlong, unforeseen, unanticipated ...*His abrupt departure is bound to raise questions...* OPPOSITE slow

2 = <u>curt</u>, direct, brief, sharp, rough, short, clipped, blunt, rude, tart, impatient, brisk, concise, snappy, terse, gruff, succinct, pithy, brusque, offhand, impolite, monosyllabic, ungracious, discourteous, uncivil, unceremonious, snappish ...*He was abrupt to the point of rudeness...* OPPOSITE polite

3 = <u>steep</u>, sharp, sheer, sudden, precipitous ...*narrow valleys and abrupt hillsides...* OPPOSITE gradual

4 = <u>uneven</u>, broken, irregular, disconnected, jerky, discontinuous ...*the rather abrupt patting she displayed...*

abruptly 1 = <u>suddenly</u>, short, unexpectedly, all of a sudden, hastily, precipitately, all at once, hurriedly ...*He stopped abruptly and looked my way...* OPPOSITE gradually

2 = <u>curtly</u>, bluntly, rudely, briskly, tersely, shortly, sharply, brusquely, gruffly, snappily ...*'Good night then,' she said abruptly...* OPPOSITE politely

abscess = <u>boil</u>, infection, swelling, blister, ulcer, inflammation, gathering, whitlow, blain, carbuncle, pustule, bubo, furuncle (*Pathology*), gumboil, parulis (*Pathology*)

abscond = <u>escape</u>, flee, get away, bolt, fly, disappear, skip, run off, slip away, clear out, flit (*informal*), make off, break free *or* out, decamp, hook it (*slang*), do a runner (*slang*), steal away, sneak away, do a bunk (*Brit. slang*), fly the coop (*U.S. & Canad. informal*), skedaddle (*informal*), take a powder (*U.S. & Canad. slang*), go on the lam (*U.S. & Canad. slang*), make your getaway, make *or* effect your escape

absence 1 = <u>time off</u>, leave, break, vacation, recess, truancy, absenteeism, nonappearance, nonattendance ...*A bundle of letters had arrived for me in my absence...*

2 = <u>lack</u>, deficiency, deprivation, omission, scarcity, want, need, shortage, dearth, privation, unavailability, nonexistence ...*In the absence of a will, the courts decide who the guardian is...*

absent ADJECTIVE 1 = <u>away</u>, missing, gone, lacking, elsewhere, unavailable, not present, truant, nonexistent, nonattendant ...*He has been absent from* *his desk for two weeks…* OPPOSITE present

2 = absent-minded, blank, unconscious, abstracted, vague, distracted, unaware, musing, vacant, preoccupied, empty, absorbed, bemused, oblivious, dreamy, daydreaming, faraway, unthinking, heedless, inattentive, unheeding …*'Nothing,' she said in an absent way…* OPPOSITE alert

PHRASES **absent yourself** = stay away, withdraw, depart, keep away, truant, abscond, play truant, slope off (*informal*), bunk off (*slang*), remove yourself …*He pleaded guilty to absenting himself without leave…*

absentee = nonattender, stay-at-home, truant, no-show, stayaway

absent-minded = forgetful, absorbed, abstracted, vague, absent, distracted, unaware, musing, preoccupied, careless, bemused, oblivious, dreamy, faraway, engrossed, unthinking, neglectful, heedless, inattentive, unmindful, unheeding, apt to forget, in a brown study, ditzy *or* ditsy (*slang*) OPPOSITE alert

absolute 1 = complete, total, perfect, entire, pure, sheer, utter, outright, thorough, downright, consummate, unqualified, full-on (*informal*), out-and-out, unadulterated, unmitigated, dyed-in-the-wool, thoroughgoing, unalloyed, unmixed, arrant, deep-dyed (*usually derogatory*) …*A sick person needs to have absolute trust in a doctor…*

2 = supreme, sovereign, unlimited, ultimate, full, utmost, unconditional, unqualified, predominant, superlative, unrestricted, pre-eminent, unrestrained, tyrannical, peerless, unsurpassed, unquestionable, matchless, peremptory, unbounded …*He ruled with absolute power…*

3 = autocratic, supreme, unlimited, autonomous, arbitrary, dictatorial, all-powerful, imperious, domineering, tyrannical, despotic, absolutist, tyrannous, autarchical …*the doctrine of absolute monarchy…*

4 = definite, sure, certain, positive, guaranteed, actual, assured, genuine, exact, precise, decisive, conclusive, unequivocal, unambiguous, infallible, categorical, unquestionable, dinkum (*Austral. & N.Z. informal*) …*He brought the absolute proof that we needed…*

absolutely 1 = completely, totally, perfectly, quite, fully, entirely, purely, altogether, thoroughly, wholly, utterly, consummately, every inch, to the hilt, a hundred per cent, one hundred per cent, unmitigatedly, lock, stock and barrel …*She is absolutely right…* OPPOSITE somewhat

2 = definitely, surely, certainly, clearly, obviously, plainly, truly, precisely, exactly, genuinely, positively, decidedly, decisively, without doubt, unquestionably, undeniably, categorically, without question, unequivocally, conclusively, unambiguously, beyond any doubt, infallibly …*'It's worrying, isn't it?' 'Absolutely.'…*

absolution = forgiveness, release, freedom, liberation, discharge, amnesty, mercy, pardon, indulgence, exemption, acquittal, remission, vindication, deliverance, dispensation, exoneration, exculpation, shriving, condonation

absolve = excuse, free, clear, release, deliver, loose, forgive, discharge, liberate, pardon, exempt, acquit, vindicate, remit, let off, set free, exonerate, exculpate OPPOSITE condemn

absorb 1 = soak up, drink in, devour, suck up, receive, digest, imbibe, ingest, osmose …*Refined sugars are absorbed into the bloodstream very quickly…*

2 = engross, hold, involve, fill, arrest, fix, occupy, engage, fascinate, preoccupy, engulf, fill up, immerse, rivet, captivate, monopolize, enwrap …*a second career which absorbed her more completely than acting ever had…*

absorbed = engrossed, lost, involved, fixed, concentrating, occupied, engaged, gripped, fascinated, caught up, intrigued, wrapped up, preoccupied, immersed, riveted, captivated, enthralled, rapt, up to your ears

absorbent = porous, receptive, imbibing, spongy, permeable, absorptive, blotting, penetrable, pervious, assimilative

absorbing = fascinating, interesting, engaging, gripping, arresting, compelling, intriguing, enticing, preoccupying, enchanting, seductive, riveting, captivating, alluring, bewitching, engrossing, spellbinding OPPOSITE boring

absorption 1 = soaking up, consumption, digestion, sucking up, osmosis …*Vitamin C increases absorption of iron…*

2 = immersion, holding, involvement, concentration, occupation, engagement, fascination, preoccupation, intentness, captivation, raptness …*He was struck by the artists' total absorption in their work…*

abstain from = refrain from, avoid, decline, give up, stop, refuse, cease, do without, shun, renounce, eschew, leave off, keep from, forgo, withhold from, forbear, desist from, deny yourself, kick (*informal*) OPPOSITE abandon yourself

abstention 1 = abstaining, non-voting, refusal to vote …*Abstention is traditionally high in Columbia…*

2 = abstinence, refraining, avoidance, forbearance, eschewal, desistance, nonindulgence …*The goal is complete abstention from all mind-altering substances…*

abstinence = abstention, continence, temperance, self-denial, self-restraint, forbearance, refraining, avoidance, moderation, sobriety, asceticism, teetotalism, abstemiousness, soberness OPPOSITE self-indulgence

abstract ADJECTIVE = theoretical, general, complex, academic, intellectual, subtle, profound, philosophical, speculative, unrealistic, conceptual, indefinite, deep, separate, occult, hypothetical, generalized, impractical, arcane, notional, abstruse, recondite, theoretic, conjectural, unpractical, nonconcrete …*starting with a few abstract principles…* OPPOSITE actual

NOUN = summary, résumé, outline, extract, essence, summing-up, digest, epitome, rundown, condensation, compendium, synopsis, précis, recapitulation, review, abridgment …*If you want to submit a paper, you must supply an abstract…*

OPPOSITE expansion

VERB = <u>extract</u>, draw, pull, remove, separate, withdraw, isolate, pull out, take out, take away, detach, dissociate, pluck out …*The author has abstracted poems from earlier books*… OPPOSITE add

abstracted = <u>preoccupied</u>, withdrawn, remote, absorbed, intent, absent, distracted, unaware, wrapped up, bemused, immersed, oblivious, dreamy, daydreaming, faraway, engrossed, rapt, absent-minded, heedless, inattentive, distrait, woolgathering

abstraction 1 = <u>concept</u>, thought, idea, view, theory, impression, formula, notion, hypothesis, generalization, theorem, generality …*Is it worth fighting in the name of an abstraction?*…
2 = <u>absent-mindedness</u>, musing, preoccupation, daydreaming, vagueness, remoteness, absence, inattention, dreaminess, obliviousness, absence of mind, pensiveness, woolgathering, distractedness, bemusedness …*He noticed her abstraction and asked, 'What's bothering you?'*…

absurd = <u>ridiculous</u>, crazy (*informal*), silly, incredible, outrageous, foolish, unbelievable, daft (*informal*), hilarious, ludicrous, meaningless, unreasonable, irrational, senseless, preposterous, laughable, funny, stupid, farcical, illogical, incongruous, comical, zany, idiotic, nonsensical, inane, dumb-ass (*slang*) OPPOSITE sensible

absurdity = <u>ridiculousness</u>, nonsense, folly, stupidity, foolishness, silliness, idiocy, irrationality, incongruity, meaninglessness, daftness (*informal*), senselessness, illogicality, ludicrousness, unreasonableness, preposterousness, farcicality, craziness (*informal*), bêtise (*rare*), farcicalness, illogicalness

absurdly = <u>ridiculously</u>, incredibly, unbelievably, foolishly, ludicrously, unreasonably, incongruously, laughably, irrationally, implausibly, preposterously, illogically, inanely, senselessly, idiotically, inconceivably, farcically

abundance 1 = <u>plenty</u>, heap (*informal*), bounty, exuberance, profusion, plethora, affluence, fullness, opulence, plenitude, fruitfulness, copiousness, ampleness, cornucopia, plenteousness, plentifulness …*a staggering abundance of food*… OPPOSITE shortage
2 = <u>wealth</u>, money, funds, capital, cash, riches, resources, assets, fortune, possessions, prosperity, big money, wad (*U.S. & Canad. slang*), affluence, big bucks (*informal, chiefly U.S.*), opulence, megabucks (*U.S. & Canad. slang*), tidy sum (*informal*), lucre, pretty penny (*informal*), pelf …*What customers want is a display of lushness and abundance*…

abundant = <u>plentiful</u>, full, rich, liberal, generous, lavish, ample, infinite, overflowing, exuberant, teeming, copious, inexhaustible, bountiful, luxuriant, profuse, rank, well-provided, well-supplied, bounteous, plenteous OPPOSITE scarce

abundantly = <u>plentifully</u>, greatly, freely, amply, richly, liberally, fully, thoroughly, substantially, lavishly, extensively, generously, profusely, copiously, exuberantly, in plentiful supply, luxuriantly,

unstintingly, bountifully, bounteously, plenteously, in great *or* large numbers OPPOSITE sparsely

abuse NOUN 1 = <u>maltreatment</u>, wrong, damage, injury, hurt, harm, spoiling, bullying, exploitation, oppression, imposition, mistreatment, manhandling, ill-treatment, rough handling …*an investigation into alleged child abuse*…
2 = <u>insults</u>, blame, slights, curses, put-downs, libel, censure, reproach, scolding, defamation, indignities, offence, tirade, derision, slander, rudeness, vilification, invective, swear words, opprobrium, insolence, upbraiding, aspersions, character assassination, disparagement, vituperation, castigation, contumely, revilement, traducement, calumniation …*I was left shouting abuse as the car sped off*…
3 = <u>misuse</u>, corruption, perversion, misapplication, misemployment, misusage …*an abuse of power*…
VERB 1 = <u>ill-treat</u>, wrong, damage, hurt, injure, harm, mar, oppress, maul, molest, impose upon, manhandle, rough up, brutalize, maltreat, handle roughly, knock about *or* around …*She had been abused by her father*… OPPOSITE care for
2 = <u>insult</u>, injure, offend, curse, put down, smear, libel, slate (*informal, chiefly Brit.*), slag (off) (*slang*), malign, scold, swear at, disparage, castigate, revile, vilify, slander, defame, upbraid, slight, inveigh against, call names, traduce, calumniate, vituperate …*He alleged that he was verbally abused by other soldiers*… OPPOSITE praise

abusive 1 = <u>violent</u>, wild, rough, cruel, savage, brutal, vicious, destructive, harmful, maddened, hurtful, unrestrained, impetuous, homicidal, intemperate, raging, furious, injurious, maniacal …*her cruel and abusive husband*… OPPOSITE kind
2 = <u>insulting</u>, offensive, rude, degrading, scathing, maligning, scolding, affronting, contemptuous, disparaging, castigating, reviling, vilifying, invective, scurrilous, defamatory, insolent, derisive, censorious, slighting, libellous, upbraiding, vituperative, reproachful, slanderous, traducing, opprobrious, calumniating, contumelious …*He was alleged to have used abusive language*… OPPOSITE complimentary

abut = <u>adjoin</u>, join, touch, border, neighbour, link to, attach to, combine with, connect with, couple with, communicate with, annex, meet, unite with, verge on, impinge, append, affix to

abysmal = <u>dreadful</u>, bad, terrible, awful, appalling, dismal, dire, ghastly, hideous, atrocious, godawful (*informal*)

abyss = <u>chasm</u>, gulf, split, crack, gap, pit, opening, breach, hollow, void, gorge, crater, cavity, ravine, cleft, fissure, crevasse, bottomless depth, abysm

academic ADJECTIVE 1 = <u>scholastic</u>, school, university, college, educational, campus, collegiate …*the country's richest and most famous academic institutions*…
2 = <u>scholarly</u>, learned, intellectual, literary, erudite, highbrow, studious, lettered …*The author has settled for a more academic approach*…
3 = <u>theoretical</u>, ideal, abstract, speculative, hypothetical, impractical, notional, conjectural

…These arguments are purely academic…
NOUN = <u>scholar</u>, intellectual, don, student, master, professor, fellow, pupil, lecturer, tutor, scholastic, bookworm, man of letters, egghead (*informal*), savant, academician, acca (*Austral. slang*), bluestocking (*usually disparaging*), schoolman *…He is an academic who believes in winning through argument…*

academy = <u>college</u>, school, university, institution, institute, establishment, seminary, centre of learning

accede to 1 = <u>agree to</u>, accept, grant, endorse, consent to, give in to, surrender to, yield to, concede to, acquiesce in, assent to, comply with, concur to *…Why didn't he accede to our demands at the outset?…*
2 (takes *throne* as object) = <u>inherit</u>, come to, assume, succeed, come into, attain, succeed to (*as heir*), enter upon, fall heir to *…when Henry VIII acceded to the throne…*

accelerate 1 = <u>increase</u>, grow, advance, extend, expand, build up, strengthen, raise, swell, intensify, enlarge, escalate, multiply, inflate, magnify, proliferate, snowball *…Growth will accelerate to 2.9 per cent next year…* OPPOSITE> fall
2 = <u>expedite</u>, press, forward, promote, spur, further, stimulate, hurry, step up (*informal*), speed up, facilitate, hasten, precipitate, quicken *…The government is to accelerate its privatisation programme…* OPPOSITE> delay
3 = <u>speed up</u>, speed, advance, quicken, get under way, gather momentum, get moving, pick up speed, put your foot down (*informal*), open up the throttle, put on speed *…Suddenly the car accelerated…* OPPOSITE> slow down

acceleration = <u>hastening</u>, hurrying, stepping up (*informal*), expedition, speeding up, stimulation, advancement, promotion, spurring, quickening

accent **NOUN** = <u>pronunciation</u>, tone, articulation, inflection, brogue, intonation, diction, modulation, elocution, enunciation, accentuation *…He has developed a slight American accent…*
VERB = <u>emphasize</u>, stress, highlight, underline, bring home, underscore, accentuate, give emphasis to, call *or* draw attention to *…She had a round face accented by a little white cap…*

accentuate = <u>emphasize</u>, stress, highlight, accent, underline, bring home, underscore, foreground, give emphasis to, call *or* draw attention to OPPOSITE> minimize

accept 1 = <u>receive</u>, take, gain, pick up, secure, collect, have, get, obtain, acquire *…All old clothes will be gratefully accepted by the organizers…*
2 = <u>take on</u>, try, begin, attempt, bear, assume, tackle, acknowledge, undertake, embark on, set about, commence, avow, enter upon *…Everyone told me I should accept the job…* OPPOSITE> reject
3 = <u>acknowledge</u>, believe, allow, admit, adopt, approve, recognize, yield, concede, swallow (*informal*), buy (*slang*), affirm, profess, consent to, buy into (*slang*), cooperate with, take on board, accede, acquiesce, concur with *…I do not accept that there is*

any kind of crisis in the industry…
4 = <u>stand</u>, take, experience, suffer, bear, allow, weather, cope with, tolerate, sustain, put up with, wear (*Brit. slang*), stomach, endure, undergo, brook, hack (*slang*), abide, withstand, bow to, yield to, countenance, like it or lump it (*informal*) *…Urban dwellers have to accept noise as part of city life…*

acceptability = <u>adequacy</u>, fitness, suitability, propriety, appropriateness, admissibility, permissibility, acceptableness, satisfactoriness OPPOSITE> unacceptability

acceptable 1 = <u>satisfactory</u>, fair, all right, suitable, sufficient, good enough, standard, adequate, so-so (*informal*), tolerable, up to scratch (*informal*), passable, up to the mark *…There was one restaurant that looked acceptable…* OPPOSITE> unsatisfactory
2 = <u>pleasant</u>, pleasing, welcome, satisfying, grateful, refreshing, delightful, gratifying, agreeable, pleasurable *…a most acceptable present…*

acceptance 1 = <u>accepting</u>, taking, receiving, obtaining, acquiring, reception, receipt *…The party is being downgraded by its acceptance of secret donations…*
2 = <u>acknowledgement</u>, agreement, belief, approval, recognition, admission, consent, consensus, adoption, affirmation, assent, credence, accession, approbation, concurrence, accedence, stamp *or* seal of approval *…a theory that is steadily gaining acceptance…*
3 = <u>taking on</u>, admission, assumption, acknowledgement, undertaking, avowal *…a letter of acceptance…*
4 = <u>submission</u>, yielding, resignation, concession, compliance, deference, passivity, acquiescence *…He thought about it for a moment, then nodded his reluctant acceptance…*

accepted = <u>agreed</u>, received, common, standard, established, traditional, confirmed, regular, usual, approved, acknowledged, recognized, sanctioned, acceptable, universal, authorized, customary, agreed upon, time-honoured OPPOSITE> unconventional

access 1 = <u>admission</u>, entry, passage, entrée, admittance, ingress *…The facilities have been adapted to give access to wheelchair users…*
2 = <u>entrance</u>, road, door, approach, entry, path, gate, opening, way in, passage, avenue, doorway, gateway, portal, passageway *…a courtyard with a side access to the rear gardens…*

accessibility 1 = <u>approachability</u>, availability, readiness, nearness, handiness *…the town's accessibility to the city…*
2 = <u>availability</u>, possibility, attainability, obtainability *…growing fears about the cost and accessibility of health care…*

accessible = <u>handy</u>, near, nearby, at hand, within reach, at your fingertips, at your fingertips, reachable, achievable, get-at-able (*informal*), a hop, skip and a jump away OPPOSITE> inaccessible

accession
PHRASES **accession to** = <u>succession to</u>, attainment of, inheritance of, elevation to, taking up of,

assumption of, taking over of, taking on of

accessory NOUN 1 = extra, addition, supplement, convenience, attachment, add-on, component, extension, adjunct, appendage, appurtenance ...*an exclusive range of bathroom accessories...*
2 = accomplice, partner, ally, associate (*in crime*), assistant, helper, colleague, collaborator, confederate, henchman, abettor ...*She was charged with being an accessory to the embezzlement of funds...*
ADJECTIVE = supplementary, extra, additional, accompanying, secondary, subordinate, complementary, auxiliary, abetting, supplemental, contributory, ancillary ...*Minerals are accessory food factors required in maintaining health...*

accident 1 = crash, smash, wreck, collision, pile-up (*informal*), smash-up (*informal*) ...*She was involved in a serious car accident last week...*
2 = misfortune, blow, disaster, tragedy, setback, calamity, mishap, misadventure, mischance, stroke of bad luck ...*5,000 people die every year because of accidents in the home...*
3 = chance, fortune, luck, fate, hazard, coincidence, fluke, fortuity ...*She discovered the problem by accident...*

accidental 1 = unintentional, unexpected, incidental, unforeseen, unintended, unplanned, unpremeditated ...*The jury returned a verdict of accidental death...* OPPOSITE deliberate
2 = chance, random, casual, unintentional, unintended, unplanned, fortuitous, inadvertent, serendipitous, unlooked-for, uncalculated, contingent ...*His hand brushed against hers; it could have been accidental...*

accidentally = unintentionally, casually, unexpectedly, incidentally, by accident, by chance, inadvertently, unwittingly, randomly, unconsciously, by mistake, haphazardly, fortuitously, adventitiously OPPOSITE deliberately

acclaim VERB = praise, celebrate, honour, cheer, admire, hail, applaud, compliment, salute, approve, congratulate, clap, pay tribute to, commend, exalt, laud, extol, crack up (*informal*), eulogize ...*He was acclaimed as the country's greatest modern painter...*
NOUN = praise, honour, celebration, approval, tribute, applause, cheering, clapping, ovation, accolades, plaudits, kudos, commendation, exaltation, approbation, acclamation, eulogizing, panegyric, encomium ...*She won critical acclaim for her performance...* OPPOSITE criticism

acclaimed = celebrated, famous, acknowledged, praised, outstanding, distinguished, admired, renowned, noted, highly rated, eminent, revered, famed, illustrious, well received, much vaunted, highly esteemed, much touted, well thought of, lionized, highly thought of OPPOSITE criticized

accolade 1 = honour, award, recognition, tribute ...*the ultimate accolade in the sciences...*
2 = praise, approval, acclaim, applause, compliment, homage, laud (*literary*), eulogy, congratulation, commendation, acclamation (*formal*), recognition,

tribute, ovation, plaudit ...*We're always pleased to receive accolades from our guests...*

accommodate 1 = house, put up, take in, lodge, board, quarter, shelter, entertain, harbour, cater for, billet ...*Students are accommodated in homes nearby...*
2 = help, support, aid, encourage, assist, befriend, cooperate with, abet, lend a hand to, lend a helping hand to, give a leg up to (*informal*) ...*He has never made an effort to accommodate photographers...*
3 = adapt, match, fit, fashion, settle, alter, adjust, modify, compose, comply, accustom, reconcile, harmonize ...*She walked slowly to accommodate herself to his pace...*

accommodating = obliging, willing, kind, friendly, helpful, polite, cooperative, agreeable, amiable, courteous, considerate, hospitable, unselfish, eager to please, complaisant OPPOSITE unhelpful

accommodation 1 = housing, homes, houses, board, quartering, quarters, digs (*Brit. informal*), shelter, sheltering, lodging(s), dwellings ...*The government is to provide accommodation for 3000 homeless people...*
2 = adaptation, change, settlement, compromise, composition, adjustment, transformation, reconciliation, compliance, modification, alteration, conformity ...*Religions have to make accommodations with larger political structures...*

accompaniment 1 = backing music, backing, support, obbligato ...*He sang to the musical director's piano accompaniment...*
2 = supplement, extra, addition, extension, companion, accessory, complement, decoration, frill, adjunct, appendage, adornment ...*The recipe makes a good accompaniment to ice-cream...*

accompany 1 = go with, lead, partner, protect, guide, attend, conduct, escort, shepherd, convoy, usher, chaperon ...*Ken agreed to accompany me on a trip to Africa...*
2 = occur with, belong to, come with, supplement, coincide with, join with, coexist with, go together with, follow, go cheek by jowl with ...*This volume of essays was designed to accompany an exhibition...*

accompanying = additional, added, extra, related, associate, associated, joint, fellow, connected, attached, accessory, attendant, complementary, supplementary, supplemental, concurrent, concomitant, appended

accomplice = partner in crime, ally, associate, assistant, companion, accessory, comrade, helper, colleague, collaborator, confederate, henchman, coadjutor, abettor

accomplish = realize, produce, effect, finish, complete, manage, achieve, perform, carry out, conclude, fulfil, execute, bring about, attain, consummate, bring off (*informal*), do, effectuate OPPOSITE fail

accomplished = skilled, able, professional, expert, masterly, talented, gifted, polished, practised, cultivated, skilful, adept, consummate, proficient

OPPOSITE⟩ unskilled

accomplishment 1 = <u>achievement</u>, feat, attainment, act, stroke, triumph, coup, exploit, deed …*The accomplishments of the past year are quite extraordinary…*
2 *often plural* = <u>talent</u>, ability, skill, gift, achievement, craft, faculty, capability, forte, attainment, proficiency …*She can now add basketball to her list of accomplishments…*
3 = <u>accomplishing</u>, effecting, finishing, carrying out, achievement, conclusion, bringing about, execution, completion, realization, fulfilment, attainment, consummation …*His function is vital to the accomplishment of the mission…*

accord NOUN 1 = <u>treaty</u>, contract, agreement, arrangement, settlement, pact, deal (*informal*) …*The party was made legal under the 1991 peace accords…*
2 = <u>sympathy</u>, agreement, concert, harmony, accordance, unison, rapport, conformity, assent, unanimity, concurrence …*I found myself in total accord…* OPPOSITE⟩ conflict
VERB = <u>grant</u>, give, award, render, assign, present with, endow with, bestow on, confer on, vouchsafe, impart with …*On his return home, the government accorded him the rank of Colonel…* OPPOSITE⟩ refuse
PHRASES **accord with something** = <u>agree with</u>, match, coincide with, fit with, square with, correspond with, conform with, concur with, tally with, be in tune with (*informal*), harmonize with, assent with … *Such an approach accords with the principles of Socialist ideology…*

accordance
PHRASES **in accordance with** = <u>in agreement with</u>, consistent with, in harmony with, in concert with, in sympathy with, in conformity with, in assent with, in congruence with

accordingly 1 = <u>consequently</u>, so, thus, therefore, hence, subsequently, in consequence, ergo, as a result …*We have different backgrounds. Accordingly we will have different futures…*
2 = <u>appropriately</u>, correspondingly, properly, suitably, fitly …*It is a difficult job and they should be paid accordingly…*

accost = <u>confront</u>, challenge, address, stop, approach, oppose, halt, greet, hail, solicit (*as a prostitute*), buttonhole

account NOUN 1 = <u>description</u>, report, record, story, history, detail, statement, relation, version, tale, explanation, narrative, chronicle, portrayal, recital, depiction, narration …*He gave a detailed account of what had happened that night…*
2 = <u>importance</u>, standing, concern, value, note, benefit, use, profit, worth, weight, advantage, rank, import, honour, consequence, substance, merit, significance, distinction, esteem, usefulness, repute, momentousness …*These obscure little groups were of no account in national politics…*
PLURAL NOUN (*Commerce*) = <u>ledgers</u>, books, charges, bills, statements, balances, tallies, invoices, computations …*He kept detailed accounts…*
VERB 1 = <u>consider</u>, rate, value, judge, estimate, think,

hold, believe, count, reckon, assess, weigh, calculate, esteem, deem, compute, gauge, appraise, regard as …*The first day of the event was accounted a success…*
PHRASES **account for something** 1 = <u>constitute</u>, make, make up, compose, comprise …*Computers account for 5% of the country's electricity consumption…* 2 = <u>explain</u>, excuse, justify, clarify, give a reason for, give an explanation for, illuminate, clear up, answer for, rationalize, elucidate …*How do you account for the company's high staff turnover?…* 3 = <u>put out of action</u>, kill, destroy, put paid to, incapacitate …*The squadron accounted for seven enemy aircraft in the first week…* ◆ **on account of** = <u>by reason of</u>, because of, owing to, on the basis of, for the sake of, on the grounds of …*He declined to give the speech on account of a sore throat…*

accountability = <u>responsibility</u>, liability, culpability, answerability, chargeability

accountable = <u>answerable</u>, subject, responsible, obliged, liable, amenable, obligated, chargeable

accountant = <u>auditor</u>, book-keeper, bean counter (*informal*)

accounting = <u>accountancy</u>, auditing, book-keeping

accoutrements = <u>paraphernalia</u>, fittings, dress, material, clothing, stuff, equipment, tackle, gear, things, kit, outfit, trimmings, fixtures, array, decorations, baggage, apparatus, furnishings, trappings, garb, adornments, ornamentation, bells and whistles, impedimenta, appurtenances, equipage

accredit 1 = <u>approve</u>, support, back, commission, champion, favour, guarantee, promote, recommend, appoint, recognize, sanction, advocate, license, endorse, warrant, authorize, ratify, empower, certify, entrust, vouch for, depute …*The degree programme is fully accredited by the Institute of Engineers…*
2 = <u>attribute</u>, credit, assign, ascribe, trace to, put down to, lay at the door of …*The discovery of runes is, in Norse mythology, accredited to Odin…*

accredited = <u>authorized</u>, official, commissioned, guaranteed, appointed, recognized, sanctioned, licensed, endorsed, empowered, certified, vouched for, deputed, deputized

accrue = <u>accumulate</u>, issue, increase, grow, collect, gather, flow, build up, enlarge, follow, ensue, pile up, amass, spring up, stockpile

accumulate = <u>build up</u>, increase, grow, be stored, collect, gather, pile up, amass, stockpile, hoard, accrue, cumulate OPPOSITE⟩ disperse

accumulation 1 = <u>collection</u>, increase, stock, store, mass, build-up, pile, stack, heap, rick, stockpile, hoard …*accumulations of dirt…*
2 = <u>growth</u>, collection, gathering, build-up, aggregation, conglomeration, augmentation …*The rate of accumulation decreases with time…*

accuracy = <u>exactness</u>, precision, fidelity, authenticity, correctness, closeness, truth, verity, nicety, veracity, faithfulness, truthfulness, niceness, exactitude, strictness, meticulousness, carefulness, scrupulousness, preciseness, faultlessness, accurateness OPPOSITE⟩ inaccuracy

accurate 1 = <u>precise</u>, right, close, regular, correct, careful, strict, exact, faithful, explicit, authentic, spot-on, just, clear-cut, meticulous, truthful, faultless, scrupulous, unerring, veracious ...*This is the most accurate description of the killer to date...* OPPOSITE inaccurate
2 = <u>correct</u>, right, true, exact, faithful, spot-on (*Brit. informal*), faultless, on the money (*U.S.*) ...*Their prediction was accurate...*

accurately 1 = <u>precisely</u>, rightly, correctly, closely, carefully, truly, properly, strictly, literally, exactly, faithfully, meticulously, to the letter, justly, scrupulously, truthfully, authentically, unerringly, faultlessly, veraciously ...*The test can accurately predict what a bigger explosion would do...*
2 = <u>exactly</u>, rightly, closely, correctly, definitely, truly, properly, precisely, nicely, strictly, faithfully, explicitly, unequivocally, scrupulously, truthfully ...*His concept of 'power' could be more accurately described as 'control'...*

accusation = <u>charge</u>, complaint, allegation, indictment, impeachment, recrimination, citation, denunciation, attribution, imputation, arraignment, incrimination

accuse 1 = <u>point a</u> *or* <u>the finger at</u>, blame for, denounce, attribute to, hold responsible for, impute blame to ...*He accused her of having an affair with another man...* OPPOSITE exonerate
2 = <u>charge with</u>, indict for, impeach for, arraign for, cite, tax with, censure with, incriminate for, recriminate for ...*Her assistant was accused of theft and fraud by the police...* OPPOSITE absolve

accustom = <u>familiarize</u>, train, coach, discipline, adapt, instruct, make used, school, season, acquaint, inure, habituate, acclimatize, make conversant

accustomed 1 = <u>used</u>, trained, familiar, disciplined, given to, adapted, acquainted, in the habit of, familiarized, seasoned, inured, habituated, exercised, acclimatized ...*I was accustomed to being the only child amongst adults...* OPPOSITE unaccustomed
2 = <u>usual</u>, established, expected, general, common, standard, set, traditional, normal, fixed, regular, ordinary, familiar, conventional, routine, everyday, customary, habitual, wonted ...*He took up his accustomed position at the fire...* OPPOSITE unusual

ace NOUN 1 (*Cards, dice, etc.*) = <u>one</u>, single point ...*the ace of hearts...*
2 (*Informal*) = <u>expert</u>, star, champion, authority, winner, professional, master, pro (*informal*), specialist, genius, guru, buff (*informal*), wizard (*informal*), whizz (*informal*), virtuoso, connoisseur, hotshot (*informal*), past master, dab hand (*Brit. informal*), maven (*U.S.*) ...*former motor-racing ace Stirling Moss...*
ADJECTIVE (*Informal*) = <u>great</u>, good, brilliant, mean (*slang*), fine, champion, expert, masterly, wonderful, excellent, cracking (*Brit. informal*), outstanding, superb, fantastic (*informal*), tremendous (*informal*), marvellous (*informal*), terrific (*informal*), mega (*slang*), awesome (*slang*), dope (*slang*), admirable, virtuoso, first-rate, brill (*informal*), bitchin', chillin' (*U.S. slang*), booshit (*Austral. slang*), exo (*Austral. slang*), sik

(*Austral. slang*) ...*It's been a while since I've seen a really ace film...*

acerbic = <u>sharp</u>, cutting, biting, severe, acid, bitter, nasty, harsh, stern, rude, scathing, acrimonious, barbed, unkind, unfriendly, sarcastic, sardonic, caustic, churlish, vitriolic, trenchant, acrid, brusque, rancorous, mordant, mordacious

ache VERB 1 = <u>hurt</u>, suffer, burn, pain, smart, sting, pound, throb, be tender, twinge, be sore ...*Her head was hurting and she ached all over...*
2 = <u>suffer</u>, hurt, grieve, sorrow, agonize, be in pain, go through the mill (*informal*), mourn, feel wretched ...*It must have been hard to keep smiling when his heart was aching...*
NOUN 1 = <u>pain</u>, discomfort, suffering, hurt, smart, smarting, cramp, throb, throbbing, irritation, tenderness, pounding, spasm, pang, twinge, soreness, throe (*rare*) ...*You feel nausea and aches in your muscles...*
2 = <u>anguish</u>, suffering, pain, torture, distress, grief, misery, mourning, torment, sorrow, woe, heartache, heartbreak ...*Nothing could relieve the terrible ache of fear...*
3 = <u>longing</u>, need, hope, wish, desire, urge, yen (*informal*), pining, hunger, craving, yearning, itch, thirst, hankering ...*an overwhelming ache for support from others...*
PHRASES **ache for something** *or* **someone** = <u>long for</u>, want, desire, hope for, dream of, pine, covet, wish for, yearn for, lust for, thirst for, hunger for, crave for, hanker for, itch for, set your heart on, eat your heart out over ... *She still ached for the lost intimacy of marriage...*

achievable = <u>attainable</u>, obtainable, winnable, reachable, realizable, within your grasp, graspable, gettable, acquirable, possible, accessible, probable, feasible, practicable, accomplishable

achieve = <u>accomplish</u>, reach, fulfil, finish, complete, gain, perform, earn, do, get, win, carry out, realize, obtain, conclude, acquire, execute, bring about, attain, consummate, procure, bring off (*informal*), effectuate, put the tin lid on

achievement 1 = <u>accomplishment</u>, effort, feat, deed, stroke, triumph, coup, exploit, act, attainment, feather in your cap ...*a conference celebrating women's achievements...*
2 = <u>fulfilment</u>, effecting, performance, production, execution, implementation, completion, accomplishment, realization, attainment, acquirement, carrying out *or* through ...*It is the achievement of these goals that will bring lasting peace...*

achiever = <u>success</u>, winner, dynamo, high-flyer, doer, go-getter (*informal*), organizer, active person, overachiever, man *or* woman of action, wheeler-dealer (*informal*)

aching 1 = <u>painful</u>, suffering, hurting, tired, smarting, pounding, raw, tender, sore, throbbing, harrowing, inflamed, excruciating, agonizing ...*The aching joints and fever should last no longer than a few days...*

2 = <u>longing</u>, anxious, eager, pining, hungering, craving, yearning, languishing, thirsting, ardent, avid, wishful, wistful, hankering, desirous …*He has an aching need for love…*

acid 1 = <u>sour</u>, sharp, tart, pungent, biting, acidic, acerbic, acrid, acetic, vinegary, acidulous, acidulated, vinegarish, acerb …*These wines are rather hard, and somewhat acid…* OPPOSITE sweet
2 = <u>sharp</u>, cutting, biting, severe, bitter, harsh, stinging, scathing, acrimonious, barbed, pungent, hurtful, sarcastic, sardonic, caustic, vitriolic, acerbic, trenchant, mordant, mordacious …*a comedy told with compassion and acid humour…* OPPOSITE kindly

acidity = <u>sourness</u>, bitterness, sharpness, pungency, tartness, acerbity, acridness, acidulousness, acridity, vinegariness, vinegarishness

acknowledge 1 = <u>admit</u>, own up, allow, accept, reveal, grant, declare, recognize, yield, concede, confess, disclose, affirm, profess, divulge, accede, acquiesce, 'fess up (*U.S. slang*) …*He acknowledged that he was a drug addict…* OPPOSITE deny
2 = <u>greet</u>, address, notice, recognize, salute, nod to, accost, tip your hat to …*He saw her but refused to even acknowledge her…* OPPOSITE snub
3 = <u>reply to</u>, answer, notice, recognize, respond to, come back to, react to, write back to, retort to …*They sent me a postcard acknowledging my request…* OPPOSITE ignore

acknowledged = <u>accepted</u>, admitted, established, confirmed, declared, approved, recognized, well-known, sanctioned, confessed, authorized, professed, accredited, agreed upon

acknowledgement *or* **acknowledgment 1** = <u>recognition</u>, allowing, understanding, yielding, profession, admission, awareness, acceptance, confession, realization, accession, acquiescence …*He appreciated her acknowledgement of his maturity…*
2 = <u>greeting</u>, welcome, notice, recognition, reception, hail, hailing, salute, salutation …*He smiled in acknowledgement and gave her a bow…*
3 = <u>appreciation</u>, answer, thanks, credit, response, reply, reaction, recognition, gratitude, indebtedness, thankfulness, gratefulness …*Grateful acknowledgement is made for permission to reprint…*

acme = <u>height</u>, top, crown, summit, peak, climax, crest, optimum, high point, pinnacle, culmination, zenith, apex, apogee, vertex OPPOSITE depths

acolyte 1 = <u>follower</u>, fan, supporter, pupil, convert, believer, admirer, backer, partisan, disciple, devotee, worshipper, apostle, cohort (*chiefly U.S.*), adherent, henchman, habitué, votary …*To his acolytes, he is known simply as 'The Boss'…*
2 = <u>attendant</u>, assistant, follower, helper, altar boy …*When they reached the shrine, acolytes removed the pall…*

acquaint = <u>tell</u>, reveal, advise, inform, communicate, disclose, notify, enlighten, divulge, familiarize, apprise, let (someone) know

acquaintance 1 = <u>associate</u>, contact, ally, colleague, comrade, confrère …*He exchanged a few words with the man, an old acquaintance of his…* OPPOSITE intimate
2 = <u>relationship</u>, association, exchange, connection, intimacy, fellowship, familiarity, companionship, social contact, cognizance, conversance, conversancy …*He becomes involved in a real murder mystery through his acquaintance with a police officer…* OPPOSITE unfamiliarity

acquainted
PHRASES **acquainted with** = <u>familiar with</u>, aware of, in on, experienced in, conscious of, informed of, alive to, privy to, knowledgeable about, versed in, conversant with, apprised of, cognizant of, up to speed with, *au fait* with

acquiesce = <u>submit</u>, agree, accept, approve, yield, bend, surrender, consent, tolerate, comply, give in, conform, succumb, go along with, bow to, cave in (*informal*), concur, assent, capitulate, accede, play ball (*informal*), toe the line, hoist the white flag OPPOSITE resist

acquiescence = <u>agreement</u>, yielding, approval, acceptance, consent, harmony, giving in, submission, compliance, obedience, conformity, assent, accession, concord, concurrence

acquire = <u>get</u>, win, buy, receive, land, score (*slang*), gain, achieve, earn, pick up, bag, secure, collect, gather, realize, obtain, attain, amass, procure, come into possession of OPPOSITE lose

acquisition 1 = <u>acquiring</u>, gaining, achievement, procurement, attainment, acquirement, obtainment …*the President's recent acquisition of a helicopter…*
2 = <u>purchase</u>, buy, investment, property, gain, prize, asset, possession …*her latest acquisition, a bright red dress…*

acquisitive = <u>greedy</u>, grabbing, grasping, hungry, selfish, avid, predatory, rapacious, avaricious, desirous, covetous OPPOSITE generous

acquit VERB = <u>clear</u>, free, release, deliver, excuse, relieve, discharge, liberate, vindicate, exonerate, absolve, exculpate …*He was acquitted of disorderly behaviour by magistrates…* OPPOSITE find guilty
PHRASES **acquit yourself** = <u>behave</u>, bear yourself, conduct yourself, comport yourself …*Most men acquitted themselves well throughout the action…*

acquittal = <u>clearance</u>, freeing, release, relief, liberation, discharge, pardon, setting free, vindication, deliverance, absolution, exoneration, exculpation

acrid 1 = <u>pungent</u>, biting, strong, burning, sharp, bitter, harsh, stinging, irritating, caustic, astringent, vitriolic, highly flavoured, acerb …*The room filled with the acrid smell of tobacco…*
2 = <u>harsh</u>, cutting, biting, sharp, bitter, nasty, acrimonious, caustic, vitriolic, trenchant, mordant, mordacious …*He is soured by acrid memories he has dredged up…*

acrimonious = <u>bitter</u>, cutting, biting, sharp, severe, hostile, crabbed, sarcastic, embittered, caustic, petulant, spiteful, churlish, astringent, vitriolic, acerbic, trenchant, irascible, testy, censorious, rancorous, mordant, peevish, splenetic, mordacious

OPPOSITE good-tempered

acrimony = <u>bitterness</u>, harshness, rancour, ill will, virulence, sarcasm, pungency, asperity, tartness, astringency, irascibility, peevishness, acerbity, churlishness, trenchancy, mordancy **OPPOSITE** goodwill

acrobat = <u>gymnast</u>, balancer, tumbler, tightrope walker, rope walker, funambulist

across **PREPOSITION** 1 = <u>over</u>, on the other or far side of, past, beyond …*Anyone from the houses across the road could see him*…
2 = <u>throughout</u>, over, all over, right through, all through, covering, straddling, everywhere in, through the whole of, from end to end of, over the length and breadth of …*The film opens across America in December*…
ADVERB = <u>from side to side</u>, athwart, transversely, crossways or crosswise …*Trim toenails straight across using nail clippers*…

across the board = <u>general</u>, full, complete, total, sweeping, broad, widespread, comprehensive, universal, blanket, thorough, wholesale, panoramic, indiscriminate, all-inclusive, wall-to-wall, all-embracing, overarching, all-encompassing, thoroughgoing, without exception or omission **OPPOSITE** limited

act **VERB** 1 = <u>do something</u>, perform, move, function, go about, conduct yourself, undertake something …*I have no reason to doubt that the bank acted properly*…
2 = <u>play</u>, seem to be, pose as, pretend to be, posture as, imitate, sham, feign, characterize, enact, personify, impersonate, play the part of …*They were just acting tough*…
3 = <u>perform</u>, mimic, mime …*She told her parents of her desire to act*…
NOUN 1 = <u>deed</u>, action, step, performance, operation, doing, move, blow, achievement, stroke, undertaking, exploit, execution, feat, accomplishment, exertion …*My insurance covers acts of sabotage*…
2 = <u>pretence</u>, show, front, performance, display, attitude, pose, stance, fake, posture, façade, sham, veneer, counterfeit, feigning, affectation, dissimulation …*His anger was real. It wasn't just an act*…
3 = <u>law</u>, bill, measure, resolution, decree, statute, ordinance, enactment, edict …*an Act of Parliament*…
4 = <u>performance</u>, show, turn, production, routine, presentation, gig (*informal*), sketch …*Numerous bands are playing, as well as comedy acts*…
PHRASES **act for someone** = <u>stand in for</u>, serve, represent, replace, substitute for, cover for, take the place of, fill in for, deputize for, function in place of … *Because we travel so much, we asked a broker to act for us*… ◆ **act on** or **upon something** 1 = <u>obey</u>, follow, carry out, observe, embrace, execute, comply with, heed, conform to, adhere to, abide by, yield to, act upon, be ruled by, act in accordance with, do what is expected …*A patient will usually listen to the doctor's advice and act on it*… 2 = <u>affect</u>, change, influence, impact, transform, alter, modify …*The drug acts very fast on the central nervous system*… ◆ **act up** = <u>misbehave</u>, carry on, cause trouble, mess about, be naughty, horse around (*informal*), give trouble, give someone grief (*Brit. & S. African*), give bother …*I could hear him acting up downstairs*…

acting **NOUN** = <u>performance</u>, playing, performing, theatre, dramatics, portraying, enacting, portrayal, impersonation, characterization, stagecraft …*She has returned home to pursue her career in acting*…
ADJECTIVE = <u>temporary</u>, substitute, intervening, interim, provisional, surrogate, stopgap, pro tem …*The new acting President has a reputation for being independent*…

action **NOUN** 1 = <u>deed</u>, move, act, performance, blow, exercise, achievement, stroke, undertaking, exploit, feat, accomplishment, exertion …*He was the sort of man who didn't like his actions questioned*…
2 = <u>measure</u>, act, step, operation, manoeuvre …*The government is taking emergency action to deal with the crisis*…
3 = <u>lawsuit</u>, case, cause, trial, suit, argument, proceeding, dispute, contest, prosecution, litigation …*a libel action brought by one of the country's top bureaucrats*…
4 = <u>energy</u>, activity, spirit, force, vitality, vigour, liveliness, vim …*Hollywood is where the action is now*…
5 = <u>effect</u>, working, work, force, power, process, effort, operation, activity, movement, influence, functioning, motion, exertion …*Her description of the action of poisons is very accurate*…
6 = <u>battle</u>, war, fight, fighting, conflict, clash, contest, encounter, combat, engagement, hostilities, warfare, fray, skirmish, sortie, affray …*Ten soldiers were wounded in action*…
PLURAL NOUN = <u>behaviour</u>, ways, bearing, conduct, manners, manner, demeanour, deportment, comportment …*He showed no remorse for his actions*…

activate = <u>start</u>, move, trigger (off), stimulate, turn on, set off, initiate, switch on, propel, rouse, prod, get going, mobilize, kick-start (*informal*), set in motion, impel, galvanize, set going, actuate **OPPOSITE** stop

activation = <u>start</u>, triggering, turning on, switching on, animation, arousal, initiation, mobilization, setting in motion, actuation

active 1 = <u>busy</u>, involved, occupied, engaged, tiring, lively, energetic, bustling, restless, on the move, strenuous, tireless, on the go (*informal*) …*Having an active youngster about the house can be quite wearing*… **OPPOSITE** sluggish
2 = <u>energetic</u>, strong, spirited, quick, vital, alert, dynamic, lively, vigorous, potent, animated, vibrant, forceful, nimble, diligent, industrious, sprightly, vivacious, on the go (*informal*), alive and kicking, spry, full of beans (*informal*), bright-eyed and bushy-tailed (*informal*) …*the tragedy of an active mind trapped by failing physical health*… **OPPOSITE** inactive
3 = <u>enthusiastic</u>, committed, engaged, enterprising, devoted, activist, aggressive, ambitious, hard-working, forward, militant, energetic, assertive, forceful,

zealous, industrious ...*We should play an active role in politics*...
4 = in operation, working, live, running, moving, acting, functioning, stirring, at work, in business, in action, operative, in force, effectual, astir ...*Guerrilla groups are active in the province*...

activist = militant, partisan, organizer, warrior

activity 1 = action, work, life, labour, movement, energy, exercise, spirit, enterprise, motion, bustle, animation, vigour, hustle, exertion, hurly-burly, liveliness, activeness ...*There is an extraordinary level of activity in the market*... OPPOSITE inaction
2 = pursuit, act, project, scheme, task, pleasure, interest, enterprise, undertaking, occupation, hobby, deed, endeavour, pastime, avocation ...*Activities range from canoeing to birdwatching*...

actor *or* **actress** = performer, player, artiste, leading man *or* lady, Thespian, luvvie (*informal*), trouper, thesp (*informal*), play-actor, dramatic artist, tragedian *or* tragedienne ...*You have to be a very good actor to play that part*...
➤ **WORD POWER SUPPLEMENT actors**

Word Power

actor/actress – The use of *actress* is now very much on the decline, and women who work in the profession invariably prefer to be referred to as *actors*.

---

actual 1 = genuine, real, true, confirmed, authentic, verified, truthful, bona fide, dinkum (*Austral. & N.Z. informal*) ...*They are using local actors or the actual people involved*... OPPOSITE unreal
2 = real, substantial, concrete, definite, tangible ...*She had written some notes, but she hadn't started the actual work*... OPPOSITE theoretical
➤ **actually**

actuality 1 = reality, truth, substance, verity, materiality, realness, substantiality, factuality, corporeality ...*It exists in dreams rather than actuality*...
2 = fact, truth, reality, verity ...*You may theorise, but we are concerned with actualities*...

actually = really, in fact, indeed, essentially, truly, literally, genuinely, in reality, in truth, in actuality, in point of fact, veritably, as a matter of fact

---

Word Power

actually – The words *actual* and *actually* are often used when speaking, but should only be used in writing where they add something to the meaning of a sentence. For example, in the sentence *he actually rather enjoyed the film*, the word *actually* is only needed if there was originally some doubt as to whether he would enjoy it.

---

acumen = judgment, intelligence, perception, wisdom, insight, wit, ingenuity, sharpness, cleverness,

keenness, shrewdness, discernment, perspicacity, sagacity, smartness, smarts (*slang, chiefly U.S.*), astuteness, acuteness, perspicuity

acute 1 = serious, important, dangerous, critical, crucial, alarming, severe, grave, sudden, urgent, decisive ...*The war aggravated an acute economic crisis*...
2 = sharp, shooting, powerful, violent, severe, intense, overwhelming, distressing, stabbing, cutting, fierce, piercing, racking, exquisite, poignant, harrowing, overpowering, shrill, excruciating ...*His back is arched as if in acute pain*...
3 = perceptive, sharp, keen, smart, sensitive, clever, subtle, piercing, penetrating, discriminating, discerning, ingenious, astute, intuitive, canny, incisive, insightful, observant, perspicacious ...*His relaxed exterior hides an extremely acute mind*... OPPOSITE slow

adage = saying, motto, maxim, proverb, dictum, precept, by-word, saw, axiom, aphorism, apophthegm

adamant = determined, firm, fixed, stiff, rigid, set, relentless, stubborn, uncompromising, insistent, resolute, inflexible, unrelenting, inexorable, unyielding, intransigent, immovable, unbending, obdurate, unshakable OPPOSITE flexible

adapt 1 = adjust, change, match, alter, modify, accommodate, comply, conform, reconcile, harmonize, familiarize, habituate, acclimatize ...*Things will be different and we will have to adapt*...
2 = convert, change, prepare, fit, fashion, make, shape, suit, qualify, transform, alter, modify, tailor, remodel, tweak (*informal*), metamorphose, customize ...*Shelves were built to adapt the library for use as an office*...

adaptability = flexibility, versatility, resilience, variability, convertibility, plasticity, malleability, pliability, changeability, pliancy, adjustability, compliancy, modifiability, adaptableness, alterability

adaptable 1 = flexible, variable, versatile, resilient, easy-going, changeable, modifiable, conformable ...*They are adaptable foragers that can survive on a wide range of foods*...
2 = adjustable, flexible, compliant, malleable, pliant, plastic, modifiable, alterable ...*He hopes to make the workforce more adaptable and skilled*...

adaptation 1 = acclimatization, naturalization, habituation, familiarization, accustomedness ...*Most creatures are capable of adaptation when necessary*...
2 = conversion, change, shift, variation, adjustment, transformation, modification, alteration, remodelling, reworking, refitting ...*He won two awards for his screen adaptation of the play*...

add VERB **1** = count up, total, reckon, sum up, compute, add up, tot up ...*Banks add all the interest and other charges together*... OPPOSITE take away
2 = include, attach, supplement, increase by, adjoin, annex, amplify, augment, affix, append, enlarge by ...*He wants to add a huge sports complex to the hotel*...
PHRASES **add to something** = increase, boost,

expand, strengthen, enhance, step up (*informal*), intensify, raise, advance, spread, extend, heighten, enlarge, escalate, multiply, inflate, magnify, amplify, augment, proliferate ...*Smiles and cheerful faces added to the general gaiety*... ◆ **add up 1** = <u>count up</u>, add, total, count, reckon, calculate, sum up, compute, tally, tot up, add together ...*More than a quarter of seven-year-olds cannot add up properly*... **2** = <u>make sense</u>, hold up, be reasonable, ring true, be plausible, stand to reason, hold water, bear examination, bear investigation ...*They arrested her because her statements did not add up*... ◆ **add up to something** = <u>mean</u>, reveal, indicate, imply, amount to, signify ...*All this adds up to very bad news for the car industry*...

addict 1 = <u>junkie</u> (*informal*), abuser, user (*informal*), druggie (*informal*), freak (*informal*), fiend (*informal*), mainliner (*slang*), smackhead (*slang*), space cadet (*slang*), pill-popper (*informal*), head (*slang*), pothead (*slang*), dope-fiend (*slang*), cokehead (*slang*), acidhead (*slang*), hashhead (*slang*) ...*He's only 24 years old and a drug addict*... **2** = <u>fan</u>, lover, nut (*slang*), follower, enthusiast, freak (*informal*), admirer, buff (*informal*), junkie (*informal*), devotee, fiend (*informal*), adherent, rooter (*U.S.*), zealot, groupie (*slang*), aficionado ...*She's a TV addict and watches as much as she can*...

(*Related Words*)
suffix: -holic

addicted
PHRASES **addicted to** = <u>hooked on</u>, dependent on, inclined to, prone to, accustomed to (*slang*), habituated to

(*Related Words*)
suffix: -holic

addiction 1 = <u>dependence</u>, need, habit, weakness, obsession, attachment, craving, vulnerability, subordination, enslavement, subservience, overreliance ...*She helped him fight his drug addiction*... **2** *with* **to** = <u>love of</u>, passion for, attachment to, fondness for, zeal for, fervour for, ardour for ...*I've developed an addiction to rollercoasters*...

addictive = <u>habit-forming</u>, compelling, compulsive, causing addiction *or* dependency, moreish *or* morish (*informal*)

addition NOUN **1** = <u>extra</u>, supplement, complement, adjunct, increase, gain, bonus, extension, accessory, additive, appendix, increment, appendage, addendum ...*This book is a worthy addition to the series*... **2** = <u>inclusion</u>, adding, increasing, extension, attachment, adjoining, insertion, incorporation, annexation, accession, affixing, augmentation ...*It was completely refurbished with the addition of a picnic site*... OPPOSITE removal **3** = <u>counting up</u>, totalling, reckoning, summing up, adding up, computation, totting up, summation ...*simple addition and subtraction problems*... OPPOSITE subtraction

PHRASES **in addition to** = <u>as well as</u>, along with, on top of, besides, to boot, additionally, over and above, to say nothing of, into the bargain ...*There's a postage and packing fee in addition to the repair charge*...

additional = <u>extra</u>, more, new, other, added, increased, further, fresh, spare, supplementary, auxiliary, ancillary, appended

additive = <u>added ingredient</u>, artificial *or* synthetic ingredient, E number, extra, supplement

addled = <u>confused</u>, silly, foolish, at sea, bewildered, mixed-up, muddled, perplexed, flustered, befuddled

address NOUN **1** = <u>direction</u>, label, inscription, superscription ...*The address on the envelope was illegible*... **2** = <u>location</u>, home, place, house, point, position, situation, site, spot, venue, lodging, pad (*slang*), residence, dwelling, whereabouts, abode, locus, locale, domicile ...*The workmen had gone to the wrong address at the wrong time*... **3** = <u>speech</u>, talk, lecture, discourse, sermon, dissertation, harangue, homily, oration, spiel (*informal*), disquisition ...*He had scheduled an address to the people for that evening*...
VERB **1** = <u>give a speech to</u>, talk to, speak to, lecture, discourse, harangue, give a talk to, spout to, hold forth to, expound to, orate to, sermonize to ...*He will address a conference on human rights next week*... **2** = <u>speak to</u>, talk to, greet, hail, salute, invoke, communicate with, accost, approach, converse with, apostrophize ...*The two ministers did not address each other directly*...
PHRASES **address yourself to something** = <u>concentrate on</u>, turn to, focus on, take up, look to, undertake, engage in, take care of, attend to, knuckle down to, devote yourself to, apply yourself to ...*We have addressed ourselves to the problem of ethics throughout*...

adept ADJECTIVE = <u>skilful</u>, able, skilled, expert, masterly, practised, accomplished, versed, masterful, proficient, adroit, dexterous ...*He is an adept guitar player*... OPPOSITE unskilled
NOUN = <u>expert</u>, master, genius, buff (*informal*), whizz (*informal*), hotshot (*informal*), rocket scientist (*informal, chiefly U.S.*), dab hand (*Brit. informal*), maven (*U.S.*) ...*He was an adept at getting people to talk confidentially to him*...

adequacy = <u>sufficiency</u>, capability, competence, suitability, tolerability, fairness, commensurateness, requisiteness, satisfactoriness

adequate 1 = <u>passable</u>, acceptable, middling, average, fair, ordinary, moderate, satisfactory, competent, mediocre, so-so (*informal*), tolerable, up to scratch (*informal*), presentable, unexceptional ...*One in four people are without adequate homes*... OPPOSITE inadequate **2** = <u>sufficient</u>, enough, capable, suitable, requisite ...*an amount adequate to purchase another house*... OPPOSITE insufficient

adherent NOUN = <u>supporter</u>, fan, advocate, follower, admirer, partisan, disciple, protagonist, devotee,

henchman, hanger-on, upholder, sectary
…*Communism was gaining adherents in Latin America*… OPPOSITE> opponent
ADJECTIVE = <u>adhering</u>, holding, sticking, clinging, sticky, tacky, adhesive, tenacious, glutinous, gummy, gluey, mucilaginous …*an adherent bandage*…

adhere to 1 = <u>follow</u>, keep, maintain, respect, observe, be true, fulfil, obey, heed, keep to, abide by, be loyal, mind, be constant, be faithful …*All members adhere to a strict code of practice*…
2 = <u>be faithful</u>, follow, support, respect, observe, be true, obey, be devoted, be attached, keep to, be loyal …*He urged them to adhere to the values of Islam*…
3 = <u>stick to</u>, attach to, cling to, unite to, glue to, fix to, fasten to, hold fast to, paste to, cement to, cleave to, glue on to, stick fast to, cohere to …*Small particles adhere to the seed*…

adhesion = <u>sticking</u>, grip, attachment, cohesion, coherence, adherence, adhesiveness

> ### *Word Power*
> **adhesion** – *Adhesion* is preferred when talking about sticking or holding fast in a physical sense and a useful alternative that could be used here is *sticking*. The word *adherence*, although close in meaning, would be the preferred word when talking about principles, rules and values.

adhesive NOUN = <u>glue</u>, cement, gum, paste, mucilage …*Glue the mirror in with a strong adhesive*…
ADJECTIVE = <u>sticky</u>, holding, sticking, attaching, clinging, adhering, tacky, cohesive, tenacious, glutinous, gummy, gluey, mucilaginous …*adhesive tape*…

ad hoc ADJECTIVE = <u>makeshift</u>, emergency, improvised, impromptu, expedient, stopgap, jury-rigged (*chiefly Nautical*) …*An ad hoc committee was set up to examine the problem*… OPPOSITE> permanent
ADVERB = <u>for present purposes</u>, when needed, as the need arises …*Most programs have commonsense built in ad hoc*…

adjacent ADJECTIVE = <u>adjoining</u>, neighbouring, nearby, abutting …*The fire quickly spread to adjacent shops*… OPPOSITE> far away
PREPOSITION *with* **to** = <u>next to</u>, touching, close to, neighbouring, beside, near to, adjoining, bordering on, next door to, abutting, cheek by jowl with, alongside of, contiguous to, within sniffing distance of (*informal*), proximate to …*offices adjacent to the museum*…

adjoin = <u>connect with</u> *or* <u>to</u>, join, neighbour (on), link with, attach to, combine with, couple with, communicate with, touch on, border on, annex, approximate, unite with, verge on, impinge on, append, affix to, interconnect with

adjoining = <u>connecting</u>, nearby, joined, joining, touching, bordering, neighbouring, next door, adjacent, interconnecting, abutting, contiguous

adjourn = <u>postpone</u>, delay, suspend, interrupt, put off, stay, defer, recess, discontinue, put on the back burner (*informal*), prorogue, take a rain check on (*U.S. & Canad. informal*) OPPOSITE> continue

adjournment = <u>postponement</u>, delay, suspension, putting off, stay, recess, interruption, deferment, deferral, discontinuation, prorogation

adjudge = <u>judge</u>, determine, declare, decide, assign, pronounce, decree, apportion, adjudicate

adjudicate = <u>judge</u>, decide, determine, settle, referee, umpire, mediate, adjudge, arbitrate

adjudication = <u>judgment</u>, finding, ruling, decision, settlement, conclusion, verdict, determination, arbitration, pronouncement, adjudgment

adjudicator = <u>judge</u>, referee, umpire, arbiter, arbitrator, moderator

adjunct = <u>addition</u>, supplement, accessory, complement, auxiliary, add-on, appendage, addendum, appurtenance

adjust 1 = <u>adapt</u>, change, settle, convert, alter, accommodate, dispose, get used, accustom, conform, reconcile, harmonize, acclimatize, familiarize yourself, attune …*I felt I had adjusted to the idea of being a mother very well*…
2 = <u>change</u>, order, reform, fix, arrange, alter, adapt, revise, modify, set, regulate, amend, reconcile, remodel, redress, rectify, recast, customize, make conform …*To attract investors the country has adjusted its tax laws*…
3 = <u>modify</u>, arrange, fix, tune (up), alter, adapt, remodel, tweak (*informal*), customize …*Liz adjusted her mirror and edged the car out*…

adjustable = <u>alterable</u>, flexible, adaptable, malleable, movable, tractable, modifiable, mouldable

adjustment 1 = <u>alteration</u>, setting, change, ordering, fixing, arrangement, tuning, repair, conversion, modifying, adaptation, modification, remodelling, redress, refinement, rectification …*A technician made an adjustment to a smoke machine at the back*…
2 = <u>acclimatization</u>, settling in, orientation, familiarization, change, regulation, settlement, amendment, reconciliation, adaptation, accustoming, revision, modification, naturalization, acculturation, harmonization, habituation, acclimation, inurement …*He will need a period of adjustment*…

administer 1 = <u>manage</u>, run, control, rule, direct, handle, conduct, command, govern, oversee, supervise, preside over, be in charge of, superintend …*Next summer's exams will be straightforward to administer*…
2 = <u>dispense</u>, give, share, provide, apply, distribute, assign, allocate, allot, dole out, apportion, deal out …*Sister came to watch the nurses administer the drugs*…
3 = <u>execute</u>, do, give, provide, apply, perform, carry out, impose, realize, implement, enforce, render, discharge, enact, dispense, mete out, bring off …*He is shown administering most of the blows*…

administration 1 = <u>management</u>, government, running, control, performance, handling, direction,

conduct, application, command, provision, distribution, governing, administering, execution, overseeing, supervision, manipulation, governance, dispensation, superintendence ...*Standards in the administration of justice have degenerated...*
2 = <u>directors</u>, board, executive(s), bosses (*informal*), management, employers, directorate ...*They would like the college administration to exert more control...*
3 = <u>government</u>, authority, executive, leadership, ministry, regime, governing body ...*He served in posts in both the Ford and Carter administrations...*

administrative = <u>managerial</u>, executive, management, directing, regulatory, governmental, organizational, supervisory, directorial, gubernatorial (*chiefly U.S.*)

administrator = <u>manager</u>, head, official, director, officer, executive, minister, boss (*informal*), agent, governor, controller, supervisor, bureaucrat, superintendent, gaffer (*informal, chiefly Brit.*), organizer, mandarin, functionary, overseer, baas (*S. African*)

admirable = <u>praiseworthy</u>, good, great, fine, capital, noted, choice, champion, prime, select, wonderful, excellent, brilliant, rare, cracking (*Brit. informal*), outstanding, valuable, superb, distinguished, superior, sterling, worthy, first-class, notable, sovereign, dope (*slang*), world-class, exquisite, exemplary, first-rate, superlative, commendable, top-notch (*informal*), brill (*informal*), laudable, meritorious, estimable, tiptop, A1 *or* A-one (*informal*), bitchin' (*U.S. slang*), chillin' (*U.S. slang*), booshit (*Austral. slang*), exo (*Austral. slang*), sik (*Austral. slang*) [OPPOSITE] deplorable

admiration = <u>regard</u>, surprise, wonder, respect, delight, pleasure, praise, approval, recognition, affection, esteem, appreciation, amazement, astonishment, reverence, deference, adoration, veneration, wonderment, approbation

admire **1** = <u>respect</u>, value, prize, honoured, praise, appreciate, esteem, approve of, revere, venerate, take your hat off to, have a good *or* high opinion of, think highly of ...*He admired the way she had coped with life...* [OPPOSITE] despise
2 = <u>adore</u>, like, love, desire, take to, go for, fancy (*Brit. informal*), treasure, worship, cherish, glorify, look up to, dote on, hold dear, be captivated by, have an eye for, find attractive, idolize, take a liking to, be infatuated with, be enamoured of, lavish affection on ...*I admired her when I first met her and I still think she's marvellous...*
3 = <u>marvel at</u>, look at, appreciate, delight in, gaze at, wonder at, be amazed by, take pleasure in, gape at, be awed by, goggle at, be filled with surprise by ...*We took time to stop and admire the view...*

admirer **1** = <u>fan</u>, supporter, follower, enthusiast, partisan, disciple, buff (*informal*), protagonist, devotee, worshipper, adherent, votary ...*He was an admirer of her grandmother's paintings...*
2 = <u>suitor</u>, lover, boyfriend, sweetheart, beau, wooer ...*He was the most persistent of her admirers...*

admissible = <u>permissible</u>, allowed, permitted, acceptable, tolerated, tolerable, passable, allowable [OPPOSITE] inadmissible

admission **1** = <u>admittance</u>, access, entry, introduction, entrance, acceptance, initiation, entrée, ingress ...*There have been increases in hospital admissions of children...*
2 = <u>confession</u>, admitting, profession, declaration, revelation, concession, allowance, disclosure, acknowledgement, affirmation, unburdening, avowal, divulgence, unbosoming ...*She wanted an admission of guilt from her father...*

admit **1** = <u>confess</u>, own up, confide, profess, own up, come clean (*informal*), avow, come out of the closet, sing (*slang, chiefly U.S.*), cough (*slang*), spill your guts (*slang*), 'fess up (*U.S. slang*) ...*Two-thirds of them admit to buying drink illegally...*
2 = <u>allow</u>, agree, accept, reveal, grant, declare, acknowledge, recognize, concede, disclose, affirm, divulge ...*I am willing to admit that I do make mistakes...* [OPPOSITE] deny
3 = <u>let in</u>, allow, receive, accept, introduce, take in, initiate, give access to, allow to enter ...*Security personnel refused to admit him or his wife...* [OPPOSITE] keep out

admittance = <u>access</u>, entry, way in, passage, entrance, reception, acceptance

admittedly = <u>it must be admitted</u>, certainly, undeniably, it must be said, to be fair *or* honest, avowedly, it cannot be denied, it must be allowed, confessedly, it must be confessed, allowedly

admonish **1** = <u>reprimand</u>, caution, censure, rebuke, scold, berate, check, chide, tear into (*informal*), tell off (*informal*), reprove, upbraid, read the riot act to someone, carpet (*informal*), chew out (*U.S. & Canad. informal*), tear someone off a strip (*Brit. informal*), give someone a rocket (*Brit. & N.Z. informal*), slap someone on the wrist, rap someone over the knuckles ...*They admonished me for taking risks with my health...* [OPPOSITE] praise
2 = <u>advise</u>, suggest, warn, urge, recommend, counsel, caution, prescribe, exhort, enjoin, forewarn ...*Your doctor may one day admonish you to improve your posture...*

admonition = <u>reprimand</u>, warning, advice, counsel, caution, rebuke, reproach, scolding, berating, chiding, telling off (*informal*), upbraiding, reproof, remonstrance

ado = <u>fuss</u>, to-do, trouble, delay, bother, stir, confusion, excitement, disturbance, bustle, flurry, agitation, commotion, pother

adolescence = <u>teens</u>, youth, minority, boyhood, girlhood, juvenescence

adolescent [ADJECTIVE] **1** = <u>young</u>, growing, junior, teenage, juvenile, youthful, childish, immature, boyish, undeveloped, girlish, puerile, in the springtime of life ...*adolescent rebellion...*
2 = <u>teenage</u>, young, teen (*informal*), juvenile, youthful, immature ...*An adolescent boy should have an adult in whom he can confide...*
[NOUN] = <u>teenager</u>, girl, boy, kid (*informal*), youth, lad,

minor, young man, youngster, young woman, juvenile, young person, lass, young adult …*Adolescents are happiest with small groups of close friends*…

adopt 1 = <u>take on</u>, follow, support, choose, accept, maintain, assume, select, take over, approve, appropriate, take up, embrace, engage in, endorse, ratify, become involved in, espouse …*Pupils should be helped to adopt a positive approach*…
2 = <u>take in</u>, raise, nurse, mother, rear, foster, bring up, take care of …*There are hundreds of people desperate to adopt a child*… OPPOSITE abandon

adoption 1 = <u>fostering</u>, adopting, taking in, fosterage …*They gave their babies up for adoption*…
2 = <u>embracing</u>, choice, taking on, taking up, support, taking over, selection, approval, following, assumption, maintenance, acceptance, endorsement, appropriation, ratification, approbation, espousal …*the adoption of Japanese management practices*…

adorable = <u>lovable</u>, pleasing, appealing, dear, sweet, attractive, charming, precious, darling, fetching, delightful, cute, captivating, cutesy (*informal, chiefly U.S.*) OPPOSITE hateful

adoration = <u>love</u>, honour, worship, worshipping, esteem, admiration, reverence, estimation, exaltation, veneration, glorification, idolatry, idolization

adore = <u>love</u>, honour, admire, worship, esteem, cherish, bow to, revere, dote on, idolize OPPOSITE hate

adoring = <u>admiring</u>, loving, devoted, worshipping, fond, affectionate, ardent, doting, venerating, enamoured, reverential, reverent, idolizing, adulatory OPPOSITE hating

adorn = <u>decorate</u>, enhance, deck, trim, grace, array, enrich, garnish, ornament, embellish, emblazon, festoon, bedeck, beautify, engarland

adornment 1 = <u>decoration</u>, trimming, supplement, accessory, ornament, frill, festoon, embellishment, frippery …*A building without any adornment or decoration*…
2 = <u>beautification</u>, decorating, decoration, embellishment, ornamentation …*Cosmetics are used for adornment*…

adrift ADJECTIVE 1 = <u>drifting</u>, afloat, cast off, unmoored, aweigh, unanchored …*They were spotted adrift in a dinghy*…
2 = <u>aimless</u>, goalless, directionless, purposeless …*She had the growing sense that she was adrift and isolated*…
ADVERB = <u>wrong</u>, astray, off course, amiss, off target, wide of the mark …*They are trying to place the blame for a policy that has gone adrift*…

adroit = <u>skilful</u>, able, skilled, expert, bright (*informal*), clever, apt, cunning, ingenious, adept, deft, nimble, masterful, proficient, artful, quick-witted, dexterous OPPOSITE unskilful

adulation = <u>extravagant flattery</u>, worship, fawning, sycophancy, fulsome praise, blandishment, bootlicking (*informal*), servile flattery OPPOSITE ridicule

adult NOUN = <u>grown-up</u>, mature person, person of

mature age, grown *or* grown-up person, man *or* woman …*Children under 14 must be accompanied by an adult*…
ADJECTIVE 1 = <u>fully grown</u>, mature, grown-up, of age, ripe, fully fledged, fully developed, full grown …*a pair of adult birds*…
2 = <u>pornographic</u>, blue, dirty, offensive, sexy, erotic, porn (*informal*), obscene, taboo, filthy, indecent, sensual, hard-core, lewd, carnal, porno (*informal*), X-rated (*informal*), salacious, prurient, smutty …*She was the adult film industry's hottest property*…

adulterer *or* **adulteress** = <u>cheat</u> (*informal*), love rat (*Journalistic slang*), love cheat (*Journalistic slang*), fornicator

adulterous = <u>unfaithful</u>, cheating (*informal*), extramarital, fornicating, unchaste

adultery = <u>unfaithfulness</u>, infidelity, cheating (*informal*), fornication, playing the field (*slang*), extramarital sex, playing away from home (*slang*), illicit sex, unchastity, extramarital relations, extracurricular sex (*informal*), extramarital congress, having an affair *or* a fling OPPOSITE faithfulness

advance VERB 1 = <u>progress</u>, proceed, go ahead, move up, come forward, go forward, press on, gain ground, make inroads, make headway, make your way, cover ground, make strides, move onward …*Rebel forces are advancing on the capital*… OPPOSITE retreat
2 = <u>accelerate</u>, speed, promote, hurry (up), step up (*informal*), hasten, precipitate, quicken, bring forward, push forward, expedite, send forward …*Too much protein in the diet may advance the ageing process*…
3 = <u>improve</u>, rise, grow, develop, reform, pick up, progress, thrive, upgrade, multiply, prosper, make strides …*The country has advanced from a rural society to an industrial power*…
4 = <u>suggest</u>, offer, present, propose, allege, cite, advocate, submit, prescribe, put forward, proffer, adduce, offer as a suggestion …*Many theories have been advanced as to why this is*… OPPOSITE withhold
5 = <u>lend</u>, loan, accommodate someone with, supply on credit …*I advanced him some money, which he promised to repay*… OPPOSITE withhold payment
NOUN 1 = <u>down payment</u>, increase (*in price*), credit, loan, fee, deposit, retainer, prepayment …*She was paid a £100,000 advance for her next two novels*…
2 = <u>attack</u>, charge, strike, rush, assault, raid, invasion, offensive, onslaught, advancement, foray, incursion, forward movement, onward movement …*They simulated an advance on enemy positions*…
3 = <u>improvement</u>, development, gain, growth, breakthrough, advancement, step, headway, inroads, betterment, furtherance, forward movement, amelioration, onward movement …*Air safety has not improved since the advances of the 1970s*…
ADJECTIVE = <u>prior</u>, early, previous, beforehand …*The event received little advance publicity*…
PHRASES **in advance** = <u>beforehand</u>, earlier, ahead, previously, in the lead, in the forefront …*The subject of the talk is announced a week in advance*…

advanced = <u>sophisticated</u>, foremost, modern,

revolutionary, up-to-date, higher, leading, recent, prime, forward, ahead, supreme, extreme, principal, progressive, paramount, state-of-the-art, avant-garde, precocious, pre-eminent, up-to-the-minute, ahead of the times OPPOSITE> backward

advancement 1 = promotion, rise, gain, growth, advance, progress, improvement, betterment, preferment, amelioration ...*He cared little for social advancement*...
2 = progress, advance, headway, forward movement, onward movement ...*her work for the advancement of the status of women*...

advantage 1 = benefit, use, start, help, service, aid, profit, favour, asset, assistance, blessing, utility, boon, ace in the hole, ace up your sleeve ...*A good crowd will be a definite advantage to the team*... OPPOSITE> disadvantage
2 = lead, control, edge, sway, dominance, superiority, upper hand, precedence, primacy, pre-eminence ...*Men have created an economic position of advantage over women*...
3 = superiority, good, worth, gain, comfort, welfare, enjoyment, mileage (*informal*) ...*The great advantage of home-grown fruit is its magnificent flavour*...

advantageous 1 = beneficial, useful, valuable, helpful, profitable, of service, convenient, worthwhile, expedient ...*Free exchange of goods was advantageous to all*... OPPOSITE> unfavourable
2 = superior, dominating, commanding, dominant, important, powerful, favourable, fortuitous ...*She was determined to prise what she could from an advantageous situation*...

advent = coming, approach, appearance, arrival, entrance, onset, occurrence, visitation

adventure NOUN 1 = venture, experience, chance, risk, incident, enterprise, speculation, undertaking, exploit, fling, hazard, occurrence, contingency, caper, escapade ...*I set off for a new adventure in the US on the first day of the year*...
2 = excitement, action, passion, thrill, enthusiasm, fever, warmth, flurry, animation, ferment, commotion, elation, discomposure ...*A feeling of adventure and excitement*...
VERB = venture, risk, brave, dare ...*The group has adventured as far as the Alps*...

adventurer 1 = mercenary, rogue, gambler, speculator, opportunist, charlatan, fortune-hunter ...*ambitious political adventurers*...
2 = venturer, hero, traveller, heroine, wanderer, voyager, daredevil, soldier of fortune, swashbuckler, knight-errant ...*A round-the-world adventurer was killed when her plane crashed*...

adventurous = daring, dangerous, enterprising, bold, risky, rash, have-a-go (*informal*), hazardous, reckless, audacious, intrepid, foolhardy, daredevil, headstrong, venturesome, adventuresome, temerarious (*rare*) OPPOSITE> cautious

adversary = opponent, rival, opposer, enemy, competitor, foe, contestant, antagonist OPPOSITE> ally

adverse 1 = harmful, damaging, conflicting,

dangerous, opposite, negative, destructive, detrimental, hurtful, antagonistic, injurious, inimical, inopportune, disadvantageous, unpropitious, inexpedient ...*The decision would have no adverse effect on the investigation*... OPPOSITE> beneficial
2 = unfavourable, bad, threatening, hostile, unfortunate, unlucky, ominous, unfriendly, untimely, unsuited, ill-suited, inopportune, disadvantageous, unseasonable ...*Despite the adverse conditions, the road was finished in just eight months*...
3 = negative, opposing, reluctant, hostile, contrary, dissenting, unwilling, unfriendly, unsympathetic, ill-disposed ...*Wine lakes and butter mountains have drawn considerable adverse publicity*...

adversity = hardship, trouble, distress, suffering, trial, disaster, reverse, misery, hard times, catastrophe, sorrow, woe, misfortune, bad luck, deep water, calamity, mishap, affliction, wretchedness, ill-fortune, ill-luck

advert (*Brit. informal*) = advertisement, bill, notice, display, commercial, ad (*informal*), announcement, promotion, publicity, poster, plug (*informal*), puff, circular, placard, blurb

advertise = publicize, promote, plug (*informal*), announce, publish, push (*informal*), display, declare, broadcast, advise, inform, praise, proclaim, puff, hype, notify, tout, flaunt, crack up (*informal*), promulgate, make known, apprise, beat the drum (*informal*), blazon, bring to public notice

advertisement = advert (*Brit. informal*), bill, notice, display, commercial, ad (*informal*), announcement, promotion, publicity, poster, plug (*informal*), puff, circular, placard, blurb

advice 1 = guidance, help, opinion, direction, suggestion, instruction, counsel, counselling, recommendation, injunction, admonition ...*Don't be afraid to ask for advice when ordering a meal*...
2 = instruction, notification, view, information, warning, teaching, notice, word, intelligence ...*Most have now left the country on the advice of their governments*...

advisable = wise, seemly, sound, suggested, fitting, fit, politic, recommended, appropriate, suitable, sensible, proper, profitable, desirable, apt, prudent, expedient, judicious OPPOSITE> unwise

advise 1 = recommend, suggest, urge, counsel, advocate, caution, prescribe, commend, admonish, enjoin ...*I would strongly advise against it*...
2 = notify, tell, report, announce, warn, declare, inform, acquaint, make known, apprise, let (someone) know ...*I must advise you of my decision to retire*...

adviser = counsellor, authority, teacher, coach, guide, lawyer, consultant, solicitor, counsel, aide, tutor, guru, mentor, helper, confidant, right-hand man

advisory = advising, helping, recommending, counselling, consultative

advocacy = recommendation, support, defence, championing, backing, proposal, urging, promotion, campaigning for, upholding, encouragement, justification, argument for, advancement, pleading

---

Terms of affection

angel	doll	munchkin	sugar
babe *or* babes	flower	muppet	sweetheart
baby	fluffy bunny	pepperpot	sweetie pie
bean	goose	pet	sweets
beloved	honey	petal	tiger
bunnykins	honey bunny	pet lamb	toots
chicken	kitten	poppet	treacle
chicken bunny	kitty *or* kitty cat	precious	treasure
darling	lamb	princess	truelove
dear	little one *or* little 'un	pumpkin	weasel
dearest	love	puppy	
dearheart	loved one	pussycat	
dear one	lover	star	

---

for, propagation, espousal, promulgation, boosterism, spokesmanship

advocate VERB = <u>recommend</u>, support, champion, encourage, propose, favour, defend, promote, urge, advise, justify, endorse, campaign for, prescribe, speak for, uphold, press for, argue for, commend, plead for, espouse, countenance, hold a brief for (*informal*) ...*He advocates fewer government controls on business*... OPPOSITE> oppose
NOUN **1** = <u>supporter</u>, spokesman, champion, defender, speaker, pleader, campaigner, promoter, counsellor, backer, proponent, apostle, apologist, upholder, proposer ...*He was a strong advocate of free market policies*...
2 (*Law*) = <u>lawyer</u>, attorney, solicitor, counsel, barrister ...*When she became an advocate there were only a few women practising*...

aegis = <u>support</u>, backing, wing, favour, protection, shelter, sponsorship, patronage, advocacy, auspices, guardianship

aesthetic = <u>ornamental</u>, artistic, pleasing, pretty, fancy, enhancing, decorative, tasteful, beautifying, nonfunctional

affable = <u>friendly</u>, kindly, civil, warm, pleasant, mild, obliging, benign, gracious, benevolent, good-humoured, amiable, courteous, amicable, cordial, sociable, genial, congenial, urbane, approachable, good-natured OPPOSITE> unfriendly

affair 1 = <u>matter</u>, thing, business, question, issue, happening, concern, event, subject, project, activity, incident, proceeding, circumstance, episode, topic, undertaking, transaction, occurrence ...*The government has mishandled the whole affair*...
2 = <u>relationship</u>, romance, intrigue, fling, liaison, flirtation, amour, dalliance ...*A married male supervisor was carrying on an affair with a colleague*...

affect[1] **1** = <u>influence</u>, involve, concern, impact, transform, alter, modify, change, manipulate, act on, sway, prevail over, bear upon, impinge upon ...*Millions of people have been affected by the drought*...
2 = <u>emotionally move</u>, touch, upset, overcome, stir, disturb, perturb, impress on, tug at your heartstrings (*often facetious*) ...*He loved his sister, and her loss clearly still affects him*...

➤ **effect**

affect[2] = <u>put on</u>, assume, adopt, pretend, imitate, simulate, contrive, aspire to, sham, counterfeit, feign ...*He listened to them, affecting an amused interest*...

affectation = <u>pretence</u>, show, posing, posturing, act, display, appearance, pose, façade, simulation, sham, pretension, veneer, artifice, mannerism, insincerity, pretentiousness, hokum (*slang, chiefly U.S. & Canad.*), artificiality, fakery, affectedness, assumed manners, false display, unnatural imitation

affected 1 = <u>pretended</u>, artificial, contrived, put-on, assumed, mannered, studied, precious, stiff, simulated, mincing, sham, unnatural, pompous, pretentious, counterfeit, feigned, spurious, conceited, insincere, camp (*informal*), la-di-da (*informal*), arty-farty (*informal*), phoney *or* phony (*informal*) ...*She passed by with an affected air and a disdainful look*... OPPOSITE> genuine
2 = <u>touched</u>, influenced, concerned, troubled, damaged, hurt, injured, upset, impressed, stirred, altered, changed, distressed, stimulated, melted, impaired, afflicted, deeply moved ...*Staff at the hospital were deeply affected by the tragedy*... OPPOSITE> untouched

affecting = <u>emotionally moving</u>, touching, sad, pathetic, poignant, saddening, pitiful, pitiable, piteous

affection = <u>fondness</u>, liking, feeling, love, care, desire, passion, warmth, attachment, goodwill, devotion, kindness, inclination, tenderness, propensity, friendliness, amity
➤ **terms of affection**

affectionate = <u>fond</u>, loving, kind, caring, warm, friendly, attached, devoted, tender, doting, warm-hearted OPPOSITE> cool

affiliate = <u>associate</u>, unite, join, link, ally, combine, connect, incorporate, annex, confederate, amalgamate, band together

affiliated = <u>associated</u>, united, joined, linked, allied, connected, incorporated, confederated, amalgamated, federated, conjoined

affiliation = <u>association</u>, union, joining, league, relationship, connection, alliance, combination, coalition, merging, confederation, incorporation, amalgamation, banding together

affinity 1 = <u>attraction</u>, liking, leaning, sympathy,

inclination, rapport, fondness, partiality ...*There is a natural affinity between the two*... OPPOSITE hostility
2 = similarity, relationship, relation, connection, alliance, correspondence, analogy, resemblance, closeness, likeness, compatibility, kinship ...*The two plots share certain obvious affinities*... OPPOSITE difference

affirm 1 = declare, state, maintain, swear, assert, testify, pronounce, certify, attest, avow, aver, asseverate, avouch ...*'The place is a dump,' she affirmed*... OPPOSITE deny
2 = confirm, prove, sanction, endorse, ratify, verify, validate, bear out, substantiate, corroborate, authenticate ...*Everything I had accomplished seemed to affirm that opinion*... OPPOSITE refute

affirmation 1 = declaration, statement, assertion, oath, certification, pronouncement, avowal, asseveration, averment ...*The ministers issued a robust affirmation of their faith in the system*...
2 = confirmation, testimony, ratification, attestation, avouchment ...*The high turnout was an affirmation of the importance of the election*...

affirmative = agreeing, confirming, positive, approving, consenting, favourable, concurring, assenting, corroborative OPPOSITE negative

affix = attach, add, join, stick on, bind, put on, tag, glue, paste, tack, fasten, annex, append, subjoin OPPOSITE remove

afflict = torment, trouble, pain, hurt, wound, burden, distress, rack, try, plague, grieve, harass, ail, oppress, beset, smite

affliction = misfortune, suffering, trouble, trial, disease, pain, distress, grief, misery, plague, curse, ordeal, sickness, torment, hardship, sorrow, woe, adversity, calamity, scourge, tribulation, wretchedness

affluence = wealth, riches, plenty, fortune, prosperity, abundance, big money, exuberance, profusion, big bucks (*informal, chiefly U.S.*), opulence, megabucks (*U.S. & Canad. slang*), pretty penny (*informal*), wad (*U.S. & Canad. slang*)

affluent = wealthy, rich, prosperous, loaded (*slang*), well-off, opulent, well-heeled (*informal*), well-to-do, moneyed OPPOSITE poor

afford 1 = have the money for, manage, bear, pay for, spare, stand, stretch to ...*The arts should be available at prices people can afford*...
2 = bear, stand, sustain, allow yourself ...*We cannot afford to wait*...
3 = give, offer, provide, produce, supply, grant, yield, render, furnish, bestow, impart ...*The room afforded fine views of the city*...

affordable = inexpensive, fair, cheap, reasonable, moderate, modest, low-price, low-cost, economical OPPOSITE expensive

affront VERB = offend, anger, provoke, outrage, insult, annoy, vex, displease, pique, put *or* get your back up, slight ...*One example that particularly affronted him was at the world championships*...
NOUN = insult, wrong, injury, abuse, offence, slight, outrage, provocation, slur, indignity, slap in the face

(*informal*), vexation ...*She has taken my enquiry as a personal affront*...

affronted = offended, cross, angry, upset, slighted, outraged, insulted, annoyed, stung, incensed, indignant, irate, miffed (*informal*), displeased, peeved (*informal*), piqued, tooshie (*Austral. slang*)

afloat 1 = floating, on the surface, buoyant, keeping your head above water, unsubmerged ...*Three hours is a long time to try and stay afloat*... OPPOSITE sunken
2 = solvent, in business, above water ...*Efforts were being made to keep the company afloat*... OPPOSITE bankrupt

afoot = going on, happening, current, operating, abroad, brewing, hatching, circulating, up (*informal*), about, in preparation, in progress, afloat, in the wind, on the go (*informal*), astir

afraid 1 = scared, frightened, nervous, anxious, terrified, shaken, alarmed, startled, suspicious, intimidated, fearful, cowardly, timid, apprehensive, petrified, panicky, panic-stricken, timorous, faint-hearted ...*She did not seem at all afraid*... ...*He's afraid to sleep in his own bedroom*... OPPOSITE unafraid
2 = reluctant, slow, frightened, scared, unwilling, backward, hesitant, recalcitrant, loath, disinclined, unenthusiastic, indisposed ...*He seems to live in an ivory tower, afraid to enter the real world*...
3 = sorry, apologetic, regretful, sad, distressed, unhappy ...*I'm afraid I can't help you*... OPPOSITE pleased

afresh = again, newly, once again, once more, over again, anew

after PREPOSITION **1** = at the end of, following, subsequent to ...*After breakfast she phoned for a taxi*... OPPOSITE before
2 = following, chasing, pursuing, on the hunt for, on the tail of (*informal*), on the track of ...*People were after him for large amounts of money*...
ADVERB = following later, next, succeeding, afterwards, subsequently, thereafter ...*tomorrow, or the day after*...
Related Words
prefix: post-

after-effect *usually plural* = consequence, wake, trail, aftermath, hangover (*informal*), spin-off, repercussion, afterglow, aftershock, delayed response

aftermath = effects, end, results, wake, consequences, outcome, sequel, end result, upshot, aftereffects

afterwards *or* **afterward** = later, after, then, after that, subsequently, thereafter, following that, at a later date *or* time

again ADVERB **1** = once more, another time, anew, afresh ...*He kissed her again*...
2 = also, in addition, moreover, besides, furthermore ...*And again, that's probably part of the progress of technology*...
PHRASES **there again** *or* **then again** = on the other hand, in contrast, on the contrary, conversely ...*They may agree, but there again, they may not*...

against 1 = <u>beside</u>, on, up against, in contact with, abutting, close up to …*She leaned against him*…
2 = <u>opposed to</u>, anti (*informal*), opposing, counter, contra (*informal*), hostile to, in opposition to, averse to, opposite to, not in accord with …*She was very much against commencing the treatment*…
3 = <u>in opposition to</u>, resisting, versus, counter to, in the opposite direction of …*swimming upstream against the current*…
4 = <u>in preparation for</u>, in case of, in anticipation of, in expectation of, in provision for …*You'll need insurance against fire, flood and breakage*…

> **Related Words**

prefixes : anti-, contra-, counter-

age NOUN 1 = <u>years</u>, days, generation, lifetime, stage of life, length of life, length of existence …*He's very confident for his age*…
2 = <u>old age</u>, experience, maturity, completion, seniority, fullness, majority, maturation, senility, decline (*of life*), advancing years, declining years, senescence, full growth, matureness …*Perhaps he has grown wiser with age*… OPPOSITE youth
3 = <u>time</u>, day(s), period, generation, era, epoch …*the age of steam and steel*…
PLURAL NOUN (*Informal*) = <u>a long time</u> or <u>while</u>, years, centuries, for ever (*informal*), aeons, donkey's years (*informal*), yonks (*informal*), a month of Sundays (*informal*), an age or eternity …*The bus took ages to arrive*…
VERB 1 = <u>grow old</u>, decline, weather, fade, deteriorate, wither …*He seemed to have aged in the last few months*…
2 = <u>mature</u>, season, condition, soften, mellow, ripen …*Whisky loses strength as it ages*…

aged = <u>old</u>, getting on, grey, ancient, antique, elderly, past it (*informal*), age-old, antiquated, hoary, superannuated, senescent, cobwebby OPPOSITE young

ageing or **aging** ADJECTIVE = <u>growing old</u> or <u>older</u>, declining, maturing, deteriorating, mellowing, in decline, senile, long in the tooth, senescent, getting on or past it (*informal*) …*He lives with his ageing mother*…
NOUN = <u>growing old</u>, decline, decay, deterioration, degeneration, maturation, senility, senescence …*degenerative diseases and premature ageing*…

ageless = <u>eternal</u>, enduring, abiding, perennial, timeless, immortal, unchanging, deathless, unfading OPPOSITE momentary

agency 1 = <u>business</u>, company, office, firm, department, organization, enterprise, establishment, bureau …*a successful advertising agency*…
2 (*Old-fashioned*) = <u>medium</u>, work, means, force, power, action, operation, activity, influence, vehicle, instrument, intervention, mechanism, efficiency, mediation, auspices, intercession, instrumentality …*a negotiated settlement through the agency of the UN*…

agenda = <u>programme</u>, list, plan, schedule, diary, calendar, timetable

agent 1 = <u>representative</u>, deputy, substitute, advocate, rep (*informal*), broker, delegate, factor, negotiator, envoy, trustee, proxy, surrogate, go-between, emissary …*You are buying direct, rather than through an agent*…
2 = <u>author</u>, officer, worker, actor, vehicle, instrument, operator, performer, operative, catalyst, executor, doer, perpetuator …*They regard themselves as the agents of change in society*…
3 = <u>force</u>, means, power, cause, instrument …*the bleaching agent in white flour*…

aggravate 1 = <u>make worse</u>, exaggerate, intensify, worsen, heighten, exacerbate, magnify, inflame, increase, add insult to injury, fan the flames of …*Stress and lack of sleep can aggravate the situation*… OPPOSITE improve
2 (*Informal*) = <u>annoy</u>, bother, provoke, needle (*informal*), irritate, tease, hassle (*informal*), gall, exasperate, nettle, pester, vex, irk, get under your skin (*informal*), get on your nerves (*informal*), nark (*Brit., Austral., & N.Z. slang*), get up your nose (*informal*), be on your back (*slang*), rub (someone) up the wrong way (*informal*), get in your hair (*informal*), get on your wick (*Brit. slang*) …*What aggravates you most about this country?*… OPPOSITE please

aggravating 1 (*Informal*) = <u>annoying</u>, provoking, irritating, teasing, galling, exasperating, vexing, irksome …*You don't realise how aggravating you can be*…
2 = <u>worsening</u>, exaggerating, intensifying, heightening, exacerbating, magnifying, inflaming …*Stress is a frequent aggravating factor*…

aggravation 1 (*Informal*) = <u>annoyance</u>, grief (*informal*), teasing, irritation, hassle (*informal*), provocation, gall, exasperation, vexation, irksomeness …*I just couldn't take the aggravation*…
2 = <u>worsening</u>, heightening, inflaming, exaggeration, intensification, magnification, exacerbation …*Any aggravations of the injury would keep him out of the match*…

aggregate NOUN = <u>total</u>, body, whole, amount, collection, mass, sum, combination, pile, mixture, bulk, lump, heap, accumulation, assemblage, agglomeration …*society viewed as an aggregate of individuals*…
ADJECTIVE = <u>collective</u>, added, mixed, combined, collected, corporate, assembled, accumulated, composite, cumulative …*the rate of growth of aggregate demand*…
VERB = <u>combine</u>, mix, collect, assemble, heap, accumulate, pile, amass …*We should never aggregate votes to predict results under another system*…

aggregation = <u>collection</u>, body, mass, combination, pile, mixture, bulk, lump, heap, accumulation, assemblage, agglomeration

aggression 1 = <u>hostility</u>, malice, antagonism, antipathy, aggressiveness, ill will, belligerence, destructiveness, malevolence, pugnacity …*Aggression is by no means a male-only trait*…
2 = <u>attack</u>, campaign, injury, assault, offence, raid, invasion, offensive, onslaught, foray, encroachment …*the threat of massive military aggression*…

aggressive 1 = <u>hostile</u>, offensive, destructive, belligerent, unkind, unfriendly, malevolent, contrary, antagonistic, pugnacious, bellicose, quarrelsome, aggers (*Austral. slang*), biffo (*Austral. slang*), inimical, rancorous, ill-disposed …*Some children are much more aggressive than others*… OPPOSITE〉 friendly
2 = <u>forceful</u>, powerful, convincing, effective, enterprising, dynamic, bold, militant, pushing, vigorous, energetic, persuasive, assertive, zealous, pushy (*informal*), in-your-face (*slang*) …*He is respected as a very competitive and aggressive executive*… OPPOSITE〉 submissive

aggressor = <u>attacker</u>, assaulter, invader, assailant

aggrieved = <u>hurt</u>, wronged, injured, harmed, disturbed, distressed, unhappy, afflicted, saddened, woeful, peeved (*informal*), ill-used

aghast = <u>horrified</u>, shocked, amazed, stunned, appalled, astonished, startled, astounded, confounded, awestruck, horror-struck, thunder-struck

agile 1 = <u>nimble</u>, active, quick, lively, swift, brisk, supple, sprightly, lithe, limber, spry, lissom(e) …*He is not as strong and agile as he was at 20*… OPPOSITE〉 slow
2 = <u>acute</u>, sharp, quick, bright (*informal*), prompt, alert, clever, lively, nimble, quick-witted …*She was quick-witted, and had an extraordinarily agile mind*…

agility 1 = <u>nimbleness</u>, activity, suppleness, quickness, swiftness, liveliness, briskness, litheness, sprightliness, spryness …*She blinked in surprise at his agility*…
2 = <u>acuteness</u>, sharpness, alertness, cleverness, quickness, liveliness, promptness, quick-wittedness, promptitude …*His intellect and mental agility have never been in doubt*…

agitate 1 = <u>stir</u>, beat, mix, shake, disturb, toss, rouse, churn …*Gently agitate the water with a paintbrush*…
2 = <u>upset</u>, worry, trouble, disturb, excite, alarm, stimulate, distract, rouse, ruffle, inflame, incite, unnerve, disconcert, disquiet, fluster, perturb, faze, work someone up, give someone grief (*Brit. & S. African*) …*The thought of them inheriting all these things agitated her*… OPPOSITE〉 calm

agitated = <u>upset</u>, worried, troubled, disturbed, shaken, excited, alarmed, nervous, anxious, distressed, rattled (*informal*), distracted, uneasy, unsettled, worked up, ruffled, unnerved, disconcerted, disquieted, edgy, flustered, perturbed, on edge, fazed, ill at ease, hot under the collar (*informal*), in a flap (*informal*), hot and bothered (*informal*), antsy (*informal*), angsty, all of a flutter (*informal*), discomposed OPPOSITE〉 calm

agitation 1 = <u>turbulence</u>, rocking, shaking, stirring, stir, tossing, disturbance, upheaval, churning, convulsion …*Temperature is a measure of agitation of molecules*…
2 = <u>turmoil</u>, worry, trouble, upset, alarm, confusion, excitement, disturbance, distraction, upheaval, stimulation, flurry, outcry, clamour, arousal, ferment, disquiet, commotion, fluster, lather (*informal*), incitement, tumult, discomposure, tizzy, tizz or tiz-woz

(*informal*) …*She was in a state of emotional agitation*…

agitator = <u>troublemaker</u>, revolutionary, inciter, firebrand, instigator, demagogue, rabble-rouser, agent provocateur, stirrer (*informal*)

ago = <u>previously</u>, back, before, since, earlier, formerly

> ## *Word Power*
>
> **ago** – Although *since* can be used as a synonym of *ago* in certain contexts, the use of *ago* and *since* together, as in *it's ten years ago since he wrote that novel*, is redundant. Instead, it would be correct to use *it is ten years since he wrote that novel*, or *it is ten years ago that he wrote that novel.*

agonize = <u>suffer</u>, labour, worry, struggle, strain, strive, writhe, be distressed, be in agony, go through the mill, be in anguish

agonized = <u>tortured</u>, suffering, wounded, distressed, racked, tormented, anguished, broken-hearted, grief-stricken, wretched

agonizing = <u>painful</u>, bitter, distressing, harrowing, heartbreaking, grievous, excruciating, hellish, heart-rending, gut-wrenching, torturous

agony = <u>suffering</u>, pain, distress, misery, torture, discomfort, torment, hardship, woe, anguish, pangs, affliction, throes

agrarian = <u>agricultural</u>, country, land, farming, rural, rustic, agrestic OPPOSITE〉 urban

agree VERB 1 = <u>concur</u>, engage, be as one, sympathize, assent, see eye to eye, be of the same opinion, be of the same mind …*I'm not sure I agree with you*… OPPOSITE〉 disagree
2 = <u>correspond</u>, match, accord, answer, fit, suit, square, coincide, tally, conform, chime, harmonize …*His second statement agrees with the facts*…
3 = <u>suit</u>, get on, be good for, befit …*I don't think the food here agrees with me*…
PHRASES **agree on something** = <u>shake hands on</u>, reach agreement on, settle on, negotiate, work out, arrive at, yield to, thrash out, accede to, concede to …*The warring sides have agreed on a ceasefire*…
♦ **agree to something** = <u>consent to</u>, grant, approve, permit, accede to, assent to, acquiesce to, comply to, concur to …*All 100 senators agreed to postponement*…

agreeable 1 = <u>pleasant</u>, pleasing, satisfying, acceptable, delightful, enjoyable, gratifying, pleasurable, congenial, to your liking, to your taste, likable *or* likeable …*more agreeable and better paid occupations*… OPPOSITE〉 unpleasant
2 = <u>pleasant</u>, nice, friendly, sociable, affable, congenial, good-natured, likable *or* likeable …*I've gone out of my way to be agreeable to his friends*…
3 = <u>consenting</u>, willing, agreeing, approving, sympathetic, complying, responsive, concurring, amenable, in accord, well-disposed, acquiescent …*She was agreeable to the project*…

agreed ADJECTIVE = <u>settled</u>, given, established,

guaranteed, fixed, arranged, definite, stipulated, predetermined ...*There is a discount if goods do not arrive by the agreed time*... OPPOSITE indefinite
INTERJECTION = <u>all right</u>, done, settled, it's a bargain or deal, O.K. or okay (*informal*), you're on (*informal*) ...*That means we move out today. Agreed?*...

agreement 1 = <u>treaty</u>, contract, bond, arrangement, alliance, deal (*informal*), understanding, settlement, bargain, pact, compact, covenant, entente ...*a new defence agreement*...
2 = <u>concurrence</u>, harmony, compliance, union, agreeing, concession, consent, unison, assent, concord, acquiescence ...*The talks ended in acrimony rather than agreement*... OPPOSITE disagreement
3 = <u>correspondence</u>, agreeing, accord, similarity, consistency, analogy, accordance, correlation, affinity, conformity, compatibility, congruity, suitableness ...*The results are generally in agreement with these figures*... OPPOSITE difference

agricultural = <u>farming</u>, country, rural, rustic, agrarian, agronomic, agronomical, agrestic

agriculture = <u>farming</u>, culture, cultivation, husbandry, tillage, agronomy, agronomics

aground = <u>beached</u>, grounded, stuck, shipwrecked, foundered, stranded, ashore, marooned, on the rocks, high and dry

ahead 1 = <u>in front</u>, on, forwards, in advance, onwards, towards the front, frontwards ...*He looked straight ahead*...
2 = <u>at an advantage</u>, in advance, in the lead ...*Children in smaller classes were 1.5 months ahead in reading*...
3 = <u>in the lead</u>, winning, leading, at the head, to the fore, at an advantage ...*Australia were ahead throughout the game*...
4 = <u>in front</u>, before, in advance, onwards, in the lead, in the vanguard ...*You go on ahead. I'll catch you up later*...

aid NOUN 1 = <u>help</u>, backing, support, benefit, favour, relief, promotion, assistance, encouragement, helping hand, succour ...*He was forced to turn to his former enemy for aid*... OPPOSITE hindrance
2 = <u>helper</u>, supporter, assistant, aide, adjutant, aide-de-camp, second, abettor ...*A young woman employed as an aid spoke hesitantly*...
VERB 1 = <u>help</u>, second, support, serve, sustain, assist, relieve, avail, subsidize, abet, succour, be of service to, lend a hand to, give a leg up to (*informal*) ...*a software system to aid managers in decision-making*... OPPOSITE hinder
2 = <u>promote</u>, help, further, forward, encourage, favour, facilitate, pave the way for, expedite, smooth the path of, assist the progress of ...*Calcium may aid the prevention of colon cancer*...

aide = <u>assistant</u>, supporter, deputy, attendant, helper, henchman, right-hand man, adjutant, second, helpmate, coadjutor (*rare*)

ail 1 (*Literary*) = <u>trouble</u>, worry, bother, distress, pain, upset, annoy, irritate, sicken, afflict, be the matter with ...*a debate on what ails the industry*...

2 = <u>be ill</u>, be sick, be unwell, feel unwell, be indisposed, be or feel off colour ...*He is said to be ailing at his home in the country*...

ailing 1 = <u>weak</u>, failing, poor, flawed, unstable, feeble, unsatisfactory, deficient, unsound ...*A rise in overseas sales is good news for the ailing economy*...
2 = <u>ill</u>, suffering, poorly, diseased, sick, weak, crook (*Austral. & N.Z. informal*), feeble, invalid, debilitated, sickly, unwell, infirm, off colour, under the weather (*informal*), indisposed ...*She stopped working to care for her ailing mother*...

ailment = <u>illness</u>, disease, complaint, disorder, sickness, affliction, malady, infirmity, lurgy (*informal*)

aim VERB 1 = <u>try for</u>, want, seek, work for, plan for, strive, aspire to, wish for, have designs on, set your sights on ...*He was aiming for the 100 metres world record*...
2 = <u>point</u>, level, train, direct, sight, take aim (at) ...*He was aiming the rifle at me*...
NOUN = <u>intention</u>, end, point, plan, course, mark, goal, design, target, wish, scheme, purpose, direction, desire, object, objective, ambition, intent, aspiration, Holy Grail (*informal*) ...*a research programme that has failed to achieve its aim*...

aimless = <u>purposeless</u>, random, stray, pointless, erratic, wayward, frivolous, chance, goalless, haphazard, vagrant, directionless, unguided, undirected OPPOSITE purposeful

air NOUN 1 = <u>wind</u>, blast, breath, breeze, puff, whiff, draught, gust, waft, zephyr, air-current, current of air ...*Draughts help to circulate air*...
2 = <u>atmosphere</u>, sky, heavens, aerosphere ...*They fired their guns in the air*...
3 = <u>tune</u>, song, theme, melody, strain, lay, aria ...*an old Irish air*...
4 = <u>manner</u>, feeling, effect, style, quality, character, bearing, appearance, look, aspect, atmosphere, tone, mood, impression, flavour, aura, ambience, demeanour, vibe (*slang*) ...*The meal gave the occasion an almost festive air*...
PLURAL NOUN = <u>affectation</u>, arrogance, pretensions, pomposity, swank (*informal*), hauteur, haughtiness, superciliousness, affectedness ...*We're poor and we never put on airs*...
VERB 1 = <u>publicize</u>, tell, reveal, exhibit, communicate, voice, express, display, declare, expose, disclose, proclaim, utter, circulate, make public, divulge, disseminate, ventilate, make known, give vent to, take the wraps off ...*The whole issue was thoroughly aired at the meeting*...
2 = <u>ventilate</u>, expose, freshen, aerate ...*Once a week she cleaned and aired each room*...
(Related Words)
adjective: aerial

airborne = <u>flying</u>, floating, soaring, in the air, hovering, gliding, in flight, on the wing, wind-borne, volitant

aircraft = <u>plane</u>, jet, aeroplane, airliner, airplane (*U.S. & Canad.*), kite (*Brit. slang*), flying machine

airfield = <u>airport</u>, airstrip, aerodrome, landing strip, air station, airdrome (*U.S.*)

airily = <u>light-heartedly</u>, happily, blithely, gaily, animatedly, breezily, jauntily, buoyantly, high-spiritedly

airing 1 = <u>ventilation</u>, drying, freshening, aeration …*Open the windows and give the bedroom a good airing*…
2 = <u>exposure</u>, display, expression, publicity, vent, utterance, dissemination …*We feel able to talk about sex, but money rarely gets an airing*…

airless = <u>stuffy</u>, close, heavy, stifling, oppressive, stale, breathless, suffocating, sultry, muggy, unventilated OPPOSITE airy

airplane (*U.S. & Canad.*) = <u>plane</u>, aircraft, jet, aeroplane, airliner, kite (*Brit. slang*), flying machine

airport = <u>airfield</u>, aerodrome, airdrome (*U.S.*)

airy 1 = <u>well-ventilated</u>, open, light, fresh, spacious, windy, lofty, breezy, uncluttered, draughty, gusty, blowy …*The bathroom is light and airy*… OPPOSITE stuffy
2 = <u>light-hearted</u>, light, happy, gay, lively, cheerful, animated, merry, upbeat (*informal*), buoyant, graceful, cheery, genial, high-spirited, jaunty, chirpy (*informal*), sprightly, debonair, nonchalant, blithe, frolicsome …*He sailed past, giving them an airy wave of the hand*… OPPOSITE gloomy
3 = <u>insubstantial</u>, imaginary, visionary, flimsy, fanciful, ethereal, immaterial, illusory, wispy, weightless, incorporeal, vaporous …*'launch aid', an airy euphemism for more state handouts*… OPPOSITE real

aisle = <u>passageway</u>, path, lane, passage, corridor, alley, gangway

ajar = <u>open</u>, gaping, agape, partly open, unclosed

akin
PHRASES **akin to** = <u>similar to</u>, like, related to, corresponding to, parallel to, comparable to, allied with, analogous to, affiliated with, of a piece with, kin to, cognate with, congenial with, connected with *or* to

alacrity = <u>eagerness</u>, enthusiasm, willingness, readiness, speed, zeal, gaiety, alertness, hilarity, cheerfulness, quickness, liveliness, briskness, promptness, avidity, joyousness, sprightliness OPPOSITE reluctance

alarm NOUN 1 = <u>fear</u>, horror, panic, anxiety, distress, terror, dread, dismay, fright, unease, apprehension, nervousness, consternation, trepidation, uneasiness …*The news was greeted with alarm by MPs*… OPPOSITE calmness
2 = <u>danger signal</u>, warning, bell, alert, siren, alarm bell, hooter, distress signal, tocsin …*As soon as the door opened he heard the alarm go off*…
VERB = <u>frighten</u>, shock, scare, panic, distress, terrify, startle, rattle, dismay, daunt, unnerve, terrorize, put the wind up (*informal*), give (someone) a turn (*informal*), make (someone's) hair stand on end …*We could not see what had alarmed him*… OPPOSITE calm

alarmed = <u>frightened</u>, troubled, shocked, scared, nervous, disturbed, anxious, distressed, terrified, startled, dismayed, uneasy, fearful, daunted,

unnerved, apprehensive, in a panic OPPOSITE calm

alarming = <u>frightening</u>, shocking, scaring, disturbing, distressing, terrifying, appalling, startling, dreadful, horrifying, menacing, intimidating, dismaying, scary (*informal*), fearful, daunting, fearsome, unnerving, hair-raising, bloodcurdling

albeit = <u>even though</u>, though, although, even if, notwithstanding, tho' (*U.S. or poetic*)

album 1 = <u>record</u>, recording, CD, single, release, disc, waxing (*informal*), LP, vinyl, EP, forty-five, platter (*U.S. slang*), seventy-eight, gramophone record, black disc …*He has a large collection of albums and cassettes*…
2 = <u>book</u>, collection, scrapbook …*She showed me her photo album*…

alchemy = <u>magic</u>, witchcraft, wizardry, sorcery

alcohol 1 = <u>drink</u>, spirits, liquor, intoxicant, juice (*informal*), booze (*informal*), the bottle (*informal*), grog (*informal, chiefly Austral. & N.Z.*), the hard stuff (*informal*), strong drink, Dutch courage (*informal*), firewater, John Barleycorn, hooch *or* hootch (*informal, chiefly U.S. & Canad.*) …*No alcohol is allowed on the premises*…
2 = <u>ethanol</u>, ethyl alcohol …*Products for dry skin have little or no alcohol*…
(Related Words)
fondness for: dipsomania

alcoholic NOUN = <u>drunkard</u>, drinker, drunk, boozer (*informal*), toper, soak (*slang*), lush (*slang*), sponge (*informal*), carouser, sot, tippler, wino (*informal*), inebriate, dipsomaniac, hard drinker, tosspot (*informal*), alky (*slang*), alko *or* alco (*Austral. slang*) …*He admitted publicly that he was an alcoholic*…
ADJECTIVE = <u>intoxicating</u>, hard, strong, stiff, brewed, fermented, distilled, vinous, inebriating, spirituous, inebriant …*tea, coffee, and alcoholic beverages*…

alcove = <u>recess</u>, corner, bay, niche, bower, compartment, cubicle, nook, cubbyhole

alert ADJECTIVE 1 = <u>attentive</u>, careful, awake, wary, vigilant, perceptive, watchful, ready, on the lookout, circumspect, observant, on guard, wide-awake, on your toes, on the watch, keeping a weather eye on, heedful …*He had been spotted by an alert neighbour*… OPPOSITE careless
2 = <u>quick-witted</u>, spirited, quick, bright, sharp, active, lively, brisk, on the ball (*informal*), nimble, agile, sprightly, bright-eyed and bushy-tailed (*informal*) …*His grandfather is still alert at 93*…
NOUN = <u>warning</u>, signal, alarm, siren …*Due to a security alert, the train did not stop at our station*… OPPOSITE all clear
VERB = <u>warn</u>, signal, inform, alarm, notify, tip off, forewarn …*I was hoping he'd alert the police*… OPPOSITE lull

alertness = <u>watchfulness</u>, vigilance, agility, wariness, quickness, liveliness, readiness, circumspection, attentiveness, spiritedness, briskness, nimbleness, perceptiveness, carefulness, sprightliness, promptitude, activeness, heedfulness

alias NOUN = <u>pseudonym</u>, pen name, assumed name, stage name, nom de guerre, nom de plume …*He had* *rented a house using an alias*…

ADVERB = <u>also known as</u>, otherwise, also called, otherwise known as, a.k.a. (*informal*) …*Richard Thorp, alias Alan Turner*…

alibi = <u>excuse</u>, reason, defence, explanation, plea, justification, pretext

alien **ADJECTIVE** **1** = <u>foreign</u>, outside, strange, imported, overseas, unknown, exotic, unfamiliar, not native, not naturalized …*They were afraid of the presence of alien troops in the region*…
2 = <u>strange</u>, new, foreign, novel, remote, unknown, exotic, unfamiliar, estranged, outlandish, untried, unexplored …*His work offers an insight into an alien culture*… **OPPOSITE** similar
NOUN = <u>foreigner</u>, incomer, immigrant, stranger, outsider, newcomer, asylum seeker, outlander …*The woman had hired an illegal alien for child care*…
OPPOSITE citizen
PHRASES **alien to** = <u>unfamiliar to</u>, opposed to, contrary to, separated from, conflicting with, incompatible with, inappropriate to, repugnant to, adverse to …*Such an attitude is alien to most businessmen*…

alienate **VERB** = <u>antagonize</u>, anger, annoy, offend, irritate, hassle (*informal*), gall, repel, estrange, lose the affection of, disaffect …*The government cannot afford to alienate either group*…
PHRASES **alienate someone from something** = <u>estrange</u>, separate, divide, divorce, divert, break off, set against, disunite, part, drive apart, make hostile, disaffect, set at odds, make unfriendly … *His ex-wife was determined to alienate him from his two boys*…

alienation = <u>estrangement</u>, setting against, divorce, withdrawal, separation, turning away, indifference, breaking off, diversion, rupture, disaffection, remoteness

alight¹ **1** = <u>get off</u>, descend, get down, disembark, dismount …*Two men alighted from the vehicle*…
2 = <u>land</u>, light, settle, come down, descend, perch, touch down, come to rest …*A thrush alighted on a branch of the pine tree*… **OPPOSITE** take off

alight² **ADJECTIVE** = <u>lit up</u>, bright, brilliant, shining, illuminated, fiery …*Her face was alight with happiness*…
PHRASES **set alight** = <u>set on fire</u>, ignite, set ablaze, light, set burning, set aflame, set blazing, set flaming, set flaring …*The rioters set several buildings alight*…

align **1** = <u>ally</u>, side, join, associate, affiliate, cooperate, sympathize …*The prime minister is aligning himself with the liberals*…
2 = <u>line up</u>, even, order, range, sequence, regulate, straighten, coordinate, even up, make parallel, arrange in line …*A tripod would be useful to align and steady the camera*…

alignment **1** = <u>alliance</u>, union, association, agreement, sympathy, cooperation, affiliation …*His alignment with the old administration cost him the election*…
2 = <u>lining up</u>, line, order, ranging, arrangement, evening, sequence, regulating, adjustment,

coordination, straightening up, evening up …*a link between the alignment of the planets and events on earth*…

alike **ADJECTIVE** = <u>similar</u>, close, the same, equal, equivalent, uniform, parallel, resembling, identical, corresponding, akin, duplicate, analogous, homogeneous, of a piece, cut from the same cloth, like two peas in a pod …*We are very alike*… **OPPOSITE** different
ADVERB = <u>similarly</u>, identically, equally, uniformly, correspondingly, analogously …*They even dressed alike*… **OPPOSITE** differently

alive **1** = <u>living</u>, breathing, animate, having life, subsisting, existing, functioning, alive and kicking, in the land of the living (*informal*) …*She does not know if he is alive or dead*… **OPPOSITE** dead
2 = <u>in existence</u>, existing, functioning, active, operative, in force, on-going, prevalent, existent, extant …*Factories are trying to stay alive by cutting costs*… **OPPOSITE** inoperative
3 = <u>lively</u>, spirited, active, vital, alert, eager, quick, awake, vigorous, cheerful, energetic, animated, brisk, agile, perky, chirpy (*informal*), sprightly, vivacious, full of life, spry, full of beans (*informal*), zestful …*I never expected to feel so alive in my life again*… **OPPOSITE** dull
4 *with* **to** = <u>aware of</u>, sensitive to, susceptible to, alert to, eager for, awake to, cognizant of, sensible of …*You must be alive to the opportunity!*…

all **PRONOUN** **1** = <u>the whole amount</u>, everything, the whole, the total, the sum, the total amount, the aggregate, the totality, the sum total, the entirety, the entire amount, the complete amount …*I'd spent all I had, every last penny*…
2 = <u>every</u>, each, every single, every one of, each and every …*There is built-in storage space in all bedrooms*…
ADJECTIVE = <u>complete</u>, greatest, full, total, perfect, entire, utter …*In all fairness, she isn't dishonest*…
ADVERB = <u>completely</u>, totally, fully, entirely, absolutely, altogether, wholly, utterly …*I ran away and left her all alone*…

> *Related Words*

prefixes : pan-, panto-

allay = <u>reduce</u>, quiet, relax, ease, calm, smooth, relieve, check, moderate, dull, diminish, compose, soften, blunt, soothe, subdue, lessen, alleviate, appease, quell, mitigate, assuage, pacify, mollify

allegation = <u>claim</u>, charge, statement, profession, declaration, plea, accusation, assertion, affirmation, deposition, avowal, asseveration, averment

allege = <u>claim</u>, hold, charge, challenge, state, maintain, advance, declare, assert, uphold, put forward, affirm, profess, depose, avow, aver, asseverate **OPPOSITE** deny

alleged = <u>claimed</u>, supposed, declared, assumed, so-called, apparent, rumoured, stated, described, asserted, designated, presumed, affirmed, professed, reputed, hypothetical, putative, presupposed, averred, unproved

allegedly = <u>supposedly</u>, apparently, reportedly, by all accounts, reputedly, purportedly

allegiance = <u>loyalty</u>, duty, obligation, devotion, fidelity, homage, obedience, adherence, constancy, faithfulness, troth (*archaic*), fealty OPPOSITE> disloyalty

allegorical = <u>symbolic</u>, figurative, symbolizing, emblematic, parabolic

allegory = <u>symbol</u>, story, tale, myth, symbolism, emblem, fable, parable, apologue

allergic 1 = <u>sensitive</u>, affected by, susceptible, sensitized, hypersensitive ...*I'm allergic to cats*...
2 (*Informal*) = <u>averse</u>, opposed, hostile, loath, disinclined, antipathetic ...*He was allergic to risk*...

allergy 1 = <u>sensitivity</u>, reaction, susceptibility, antipathy, hypersensitivity, sensitiveness ...*Food allergies result in many and varied symptoms*...
2 with to (*Informal*) = <u>dislike of</u>, hatred of, hostility to *or* towards, aversion to, loathing of, disgust of, antipathy towards, animosity towards, displeasure of, antagonism towards, distaste of, enmity towards, opposition towards, repugnance of, disinclination towards ...*I developed an allergy to the company of couples*...

alleviate = <u>ease</u>, reduce, relieve, moderate, smooth, dull, diminish, soften, check, blunt, soothe, subdue, lessen, lighten, quell, allay, mitigate, abate, slacken, assuage, quench, mollify, slake, palliate
➤ **ameliorate**

alley = <u>passage</u>, walk, lane, pathway, alleyway, passageway, backstreet

alliance = <u>union</u>, league, association, agreement, marriage, connection, combination, coalition, treaty, partnership, federation, pact, compact, confederation, affinity, affiliation, confederacy, concordat OPPOSITE> division

allied 1 = <u>united</u>, joined, linked, related, married, joint, combined, bound, integrated, unified, affiliated, leagued, confederate, amalgamated, cooperating, in league, hand in glove (*informal*), in cahoots (*U.S. informal*) ...*forces from three allied nations*...
2 = <u>connected</u>, joined, linked, tied, related, associated, syndicated, affiliated, kindred ...*doctors and other allied medical professionals*...

all-important = <u>essential</u>, central, significant, key, necessary, vital, critical, crucial, pivotal, momentous, consequential

allocate = <u>assign</u>, grant, distribute, designate, set aside, earmark, give out, consign, allow, budget, allot, mete, share out, apportion, appropriate

allocation 1 = <u>allowance</u>, share, measure, grant, portion, quota, lot, ration, stint, stipend ...*During rationing we had a sugar allocation*...
2 = <u>assignment</u>, allowance, rationing, allotment, apportionment, appropriation ...*Town planning and land allocation had to be co-ordinated*...

allot = <u>assign</u>, allocate, designate, set aside, earmark, mete, share out, apportion, budget, appropriate

allotment 1 = <u>plot</u>, patch, tract, kitchen garden ...*He was just back from a hard morning's toil on his allotment*...
2 = <u>assignment</u>, share, measure, grant, allowance, portion, quota, lot, ration, allocation, stint, appropriation, stipend, apportionment ...*His meagre allotment of gas had to be saved for emergencies*...

allotted = <u>assigned</u>, given, allocated, designated, set aside, earmarked, apportioned

all-out *or* **all out** ADJECTIVE = <u>total</u>, full, complete, determined, supreme, maximum, outright, thorough, unlimited, full-scale, optimum, exhaustive, resolute, full-on (*informal*), unrestrained, unremitting, thoroughgoing, unstinted ...*He launched an all-out attack on his critics*... OPPOSITE> half-hearted
ADVERB = <u>energetically</u>, hard, strongly, sharply, heavily, severely, fiercely, vigorously, intensely, violently, powerfully, forcibly, forcefully, with all your might, with might and main ...*We will be going all out to make sure it doesn't happen again*...

allow VERB **1** = <u>permit</u>, approve, enable, sanction, endure, license, brook, endorse, warrant, tolerate, put up with (*informal*), authorize, stand, suffer, bear ...*Smoking will not be allowed*... OPPOSITE> prohibit
2 = <u>let</u>, permit, sanction, authorize, license, tolerate, consent to, countenance, concede to, assent to, give leave to, give the green light for, give a blank cheque to ...*He allows her to drive his Mercedes 300SE*... OPPOSITE> forbid
3 = <u>give</u>, provide, grant, spare, devote, assign, allocate, set aside, deduct, earmark, remit, allot ...*Please allow 28 days for delivery*...
4 = <u>acknowledge</u>, accept, admit, grant, recognize, yield, concede, confess, acquiesce ...*He allows that the development may result in social inequality*...
PHRASES **allow for something** = <u>take something into account</u>, consider, plan for, accommodate, provide for, arrange for, foresee, make provision for, make allowances for, make concessions for, keep something in mind, set something aside for, take something into consideration ...*You have to allow for a certain amount of error*...

allowable = <u>permissible</u>, all right, approved, appropriate, suitable, acceptable, tolerable, admissible, sufferable, sanctionable

allowance 1 = <u>portion</u>, lot, share, amount, measure, grant, pension, subsidy, quota, allocation, stint, annuity, allotment, remittance, stipend, apportionment ...*He lives on an allowance of £70 a week*...
2 = <u>pocket money</u>, grant, fee, payment, consideration, ration, handout, remittance ...*The boy was given an allowance for his own needs*...
3 = <u>concession</u>, discount, reduction, repayment, deduction, rebate ...*those earning less than the basic tax allowance*...

alloy = <u>mixture</u>, combination, compound, blend, hybrid, composite, amalgam, meld, admixture ...*Bronze is an alloy of copper and tin*...
➤ **alloys**

all right ADJECTIVE **1** = <u>satisfactory</u>, O.K. *or* okay (*informal*), average, fair, sufficient, standard, acceptable, good enough, adequate, so-so (*informal*),

Alloys   http://chemistry.about.com/od/metalsalloys/

Alnico®	cupronickel	misch metal	platiniridium
amalgam	Duralumin®	Monel *or* Monell metal	soft solder
austenitic stainless steel	electrum	Nichrome®	speculum metal
Babbit metal	ferrochromium	nickel silver	steel
bell bronze	ferromanganese	nimonic alloy	Stellite®
bell metal	ferromolybdenum	ormolu	sterling silver
billon	ferronickel	oroide	terne
brass	ferrosilicon	osmiridium	tombac *or* tambac
brazing solder	Invar®	permalloy	type metal
Britannia metal	kamacite	pewter	white gold
bronze	magnolia metal	phosphor bronze	zircalloy
chromel	magnox	pinchbeck	
constantan	Manganin®	platina	

up to scratch (*informal*), passable, up to standard, up to the mark, unobjectionable …'*How was the school you attended?' 'It was all right.'…* OPPOSITE unsatisfactory

2 = <u>well</u>, O.K. *or* okay (*informal*), strong, whole, sound, fit, safe, healthy, hale, unharmed, out of the woods, uninjured, unimpaired, up to par …*Are you all right now?…* OPPOSITE ill

ADVERB = <u>satisfactorily</u>, O.K. *or* okay (*informal*), reasonably, well enough, adequately, suitably, acceptably, passably, unobjectionably …*Things have thankfully worked out all right…*
➤ **alright**

allude to = <u>refer to</u>, suggest, mention, speak of, imply, intimate, hint at, remark on, insinuate, touch upon
➤ **elude**

allure NOUN – <u>attractiveness</u>, appeal, charm, attraction, lure, temptation, glamour, persuasion, enchantment, enticement, seductiveness …*It's a game that has really lost its allure…*

VERB = <u>attract</u>, persuade, charm, win over, tempt, lure, seduce, entice, enchant, lead on, coax, captivate, beguile, cajole, decoy, inveigle …*The dog was allured by the smell of roasting meat…*

alluring = <u>attractive</u>, fascinating, enchanting, seductive, tempting, sexy, intriguing, fetching, glamorous, captivating, beguiling, bewitching, come-hither OPPOSITE unattractive

allusion = <u>reference</u>, mention, suggestion, hint, implication, innuendo, intimation, insinuation, casual remark, indirect reference

ally NOUN = <u>partner</u>, friend, colleague, associate, mate, accessory, comrade, helper, collaborator, accomplice, confederate, co-worker, bedfellow, cobber (*Austral. or old-fashioned N.Z. informal*), coadjutor, abettor …*He is a close ally of the Prime Minister…* OPPOSITE opponent

PHRASES **ally yourself with something** or **someone** = <u>unite with</u>, join, associate with, connect, unify, league, affiliate with, collaborate with, join forces with, confederate, band together with, join battle with …*He will have to ally himself with the new movement…*

almighty 1 = <u>all-powerful</u>, supreme, absolute, unlimited, invincible, omnipotent …*Let us now*

confess our sins to Almighty God… OPPOSITE powerless

2 (*Informal*) = <u>great</u>, terrible, enormous, desperate, severe, intense, awful, loud, excessive …*I had the most almighty row with the waitress…* OPPOSITE slight

almost = <u>nearly</u>, about, approaching, close to, virtually, practically, roughly, all but, just about, not quite, on the brink of, not far from, approximately, well nigh, as good as

alms (*Old-fashioned*) = <u>donation</u>, relief, gift, charity, bounty, benefaction

aloft ADJECTIVE = <u>in the air</u>, up, higher, above, overhead, in the sky, on high, high up, up above …*Four of the nine balloons were still aloft the next day…*

ADVERB = <u>upward</u>, skyward, heavenward …*He lifted the cup aloft…*

alone ADJECTIVE **1** = <u>solitary</u>, isolated, sole, separate, apart, abandoned, detached, by yourself, unattended, unaccompanied, out on a limb, unescorted, on your tod (*slang*) …*He was all alone in the middle of the hall…* OPPOSITE accompanied

2 = <u>lonely</u>, abandoned, deserted, isolated, solitary, estranged, desolate, forsaken, forlorn, destitute, lonesome, friendless …*Never in her life had she felt so alone…*

ADVERB **1** = <u>solely</u>, only, individually, singly, exclusively, uniquely …*You alone should determine what is right for you…*

2 = <u>by yourself</u>, independently, unaided, unaccompanied, without help, on your own, unassisted, without assistance, under your own steam …*He was working alone, and did not have an accomplice…* OPPOSITE with help

aloof = <u>distant</u>, cold, reserved, cool, formal, remote, forbidding, detached, indifferent, chilly, unfriendly, unsympathetic, uninterested, haughty, unresponsive, supercilious, unapproachable, unsociable, standoffish OPPOSITE friendly

aloud = <u>out loud</u>, clearly, plainly, distinctly, audibly, intelligibly

alphabet = <u>letters</u>, script, writing system, syllabary
➤ **alphabets**

already = <u>before now</u>, before, previously, at present, by now, by then, even now, by this time, just now, by that time, heretofore, as of now

alright
➤ all right

Word Power

alright – The single-word form *alright* is still considered by many people to be wrong or less acceptable than *all right*. This is borne out by the data in the Bank of English, which suggests that the two-word form is about twenty times commoner than the alternative spelling.

---

also = <u>and</u>, too, further, plus, along with, in addition, as well, moreover, besides, furthermore, what's more, on top of that, to boot, additionally, into the bargain, as well as

alter 1 = <u>modify</u>, change, reform, shift, vary, transform, adjust, adapt, revise, amend, diversify, remodel, tweak (*informal*), recast, reshape, metamorphose, transmute …*They have never altered their programmes*…
2 = <u>change</u>, turn, vary, transform, adjust, adapt, metamorphose …*Little had altered in the village*…

alteration 1 = <u>change</u>, adjustment, shift, amendment, conversion, modification …*Making some simple alterations to your diet will make you feel fitter*…
2 = <u>adjustment</u>, change, amendment, variation, conversion, transformation, adaptation, difference, revision, modification, remodelling, reformation, diversification, metamorphosis, variance, reshaping, transmutation …*Her jacket and skirt were still awaiting alteration*…

altercation = <u>argument</u>, row, clash, disagreement, dispute, controversy, contention, quarrel, squabble, wrangle, bickering, discord, dissension

alternate VERB 1 = <u>interchange</u>, change, alter, fluctuate, intersperse, take turns, oscillate, chop and change, follow one another, follow in turn …*Her gentle moods alternated with calmer states*…
2 = <u>intersperse</u>, interchange, exchange, swap, stagger, rotate …*Now you just alternate layers of that mixture and eggplant*…
ADJECTIVE 1 = <u>alternating</u>, interchanging, every other, rotating, every second, sequential …*They were streaked with alternate bands of colour*…
2 = <u>substitute</u>, alternative, other, different, replacement, complementary …*alternate forms of medical treatment*…
3 (*U.S.*) = <u>alternative</u>, unusual, abnormal, irregular, unconventional, off-the-wall (*slang*), unorthodox, heterodox, uncustomary …*an alternate lifestyle*…
NOUN (*U.S.*) = <u>substitute</u>, reserve, deputy, relief, replacement, stand-by, makeshift …*In most jurisdictions, twelve jurors and two alternates are chosen*…

alternating = <u>interchanging</u>, changing, shifting, swinging, rotating, fluctuating, occurring by turns, oscillating, vacillating, seesawing

alternative NOUN = <u>substitute</u>, choice, other (*of two*), option, preference, recourse …*New treatments may provide an alternative to painkillers*…
ADJECTIVE = <u>different</u>, other, substitute, alternate …*There were alternative methods of transport available*…

alternatively = <u>or</u>, instead, otherwise, on the other hand, if not, then again, as an alternative, by way of alternative, as another option

although = <u>though</u>, while, even if, even though, whilst, albeit, despite the fact that, notwithstanding, even supposing, tho' (*U.S. or poetic*)

altitude = <u>height</u>, summit, peak, elevation, loftiness

altogether 1 = <u>absolutely</u>, quite, completely, totally, perfectly, fully, thoroughly, wholly, utterly, downright, one hundred per cent (*informal*), undisputedly, lock, stock and barrel …*She wasn't altogether sorry to be leaving*…
2 = <u>completely</u>, all, fully, entirely, comprehensively, thoroughly, wholly, every inch, one hundred per cent (*informal*), in every respect …*The choice of language is altogether different*… OPPOSITE partially
3 = <u>on the whole</u>, generally, mostly, in general, collectively, all things considered, on average, for the most part, all in all, on balance, in toto (*Latin*), as a whole …*Altogether, it was a delightful town garden*…
4 = <u>in total</u>, in all, all told, taken together, in sum, everything included, in toto (*Latin*) …*Altogether seven inmates escaped*…

Word Power

altogether – The single-word form *altogether* should not be used as an alternative to *all together* because the meanings are very distinct. *Altogether* is an adverb meaning 'absolutely' or, in a different sense, 'in total'. *All together*, however, means 'all at the same time' or 'all in the same place'. The distinction can be seen in the following example: *altogether there were six or seven families sharing the flat's facilities* means 'in total', while *there were six or seven families all together in one flat*, means 'all crowded in together'.

---

altruism = <u>selflessness</u>, charity, consideration, goodwill, generosity, self-sacrifice, philanthropy, benevolence, magnanimity, humanitarianism, unselfishness, beneficence, charitableness, greatheartedness, bigheartedness OPPOSITE self-interest

altruistic = <u>selfless</u>, generous, humanitarian, charitable, benevolent, considerate, self-sacrificing, philanthropic, unselfish, public-spirited OPPOSITE self-interested

always 1 = <u>habitually</u>, regularly, every time, inevitably, consistently, invariably, aye (*Scot.*), perpetually, without exception, customarily, unfailingly, on every occasion, day in, day out …*Always lock your garage*… OPPOSITE seldom
2 = <u>forever</u>, ever, for keeps, eternally, for all time, evermore, for good and all (*informal*), till the cows come

Alphabets http://www.omniglot.com/writing/alphabets.htm

Related vocabulary

Cyrillic	Kufic or Cufic	logogram or logograph
hiragana	Latin	Nagari
kana	lexigraphy	Roman
kanji	Linear A	
katakana	Linear B	

Arabic letters

ا	alif	د	dāl	ض	ḍād	ك	kāf
ب	bā	ذ	dhāl	ط	ṭā	ل	lām
ت	tā	ر	rā	ظ	ẓā	م	mīm
ث	thā	ز	zā	ع	'ain	ن	nūn
ج	jīm	س	sīn	غ	ghain	ه	hā
ح	ḥā	ش	shīn	ف	fā	و	wāw
خ	khā	ص	ṣād	ق	qāf	ي	yā

Greek letters

A,α	alpha	K,κ	kappa	Ψ,ψ	psi
B,β	beta	Λ,λ	lambda	P,ρ	rho
X,χ	chi	M,μ	mu	Σ,σ	sigma
Δ,δ	delta	N,ν	nu	T,τ	tau
E,ε	epsilon	Ω,ω	omega	Θ,θ	theta
H,η	eta	O,o	omicron	Y,υ	upsilon
Γ,γ	gamma	Φ,φ	phi	Ξ,ξ	xi
I,ι	iota	Π,π	pi	Z,ζ	zeta

Hebrew letters

א	aleph	ק	koph or qoph	שׁ	shin
ע	ayin or ain	ל	lamed or lamedh	שׂ	sin
ב	beth	מ	mem	ת	tav or taw
ד	daleth or daled	נ	nun	ט	teth
ג	gimel	פ	pe	ו	vav or waw
ה	he	ר	resh	י	yod or yodh
ח	heth or cheth	צ	sadhe, sade, or tsade	ז	zayin
כ	kaph	ס	samekh		

Communications code words for the alphabet

Alpha	Juliet	Sierra
Bravo	Kilo	Tango
Charlie	Lima	Uniform
Delta	Mike	Victor
Echo	November	Whiskey
Foxtrot	Oscar	X-Ray
Golf	Papa	Yankee
Hotel	Quebec	Zulu
India	Romeo	

home (*informal*), everlastingly, till the end of time, till Doomsday ...*We will always remember his generosity...*
3 = <u>continually</u>, constantly, all the time, forever, repeatedly, aye (*Scot.*), endlessly, persistently, eternally, perpetually, incessantly, interminably, unceasingly, everlastingly, in perpetuum (*Latin*) ...*She was always moving things around...*

amalgam = <u>combination</u>, mixture, compound, blend, union, composite, fusion, alloy, amalgamation, meld, admixture

amalgamate = <u>combine</u>, unite, ally, compound, blend, incorporate, integrate, merge, fuse, mingle, alloy, coalesce, meld, commingle, intermix OPPOSITE> divide

amalgamation = <u>combination</u>, union, joining, mixing, alliance, coalition, merger, mixture, compound, blend, integration, composite, fusion, mingling, alloy, amalgamating, incorporation, amalgam, meld, admixture, commingling

amass = <u>collect</u>, gather, assemble, compile, accumulate, aggregate, pile up, garner, hoard, scrape together, rake up, heap up

amateur = <u>nonprofessional</u>, outsider, layman, dilettante, layperson, non-specialist, dabbler

amateurish = <u>unprofessional</u>, amateur, crude, bungling, clumsy, inexpert, unaccomplished, unskilful OPPOSITE> professional

amaze = <u>astonish</u>, surprise, shock, stun, alarm, stagger, startle, bewilder, astound, daze, confound, stupefy, flabbergast, bowl someone over (*informal*), boggle someone's mind, dumbfound

amazement = <u>astonishment</u>, surprise, wonder, shock, confusion, admiration, awe, marvel, bewilderment, wonderment, perplexity, stupefaction

amazing = <u>astonishing</u>, striking, surprising, brilliant, stunning, impressive, overwhelming, staggering, sensational (*informal*), bewildering, breathtaking, astounding, eye-opening, wondrous (*archaic or literary*), mind-boggling, jaw-dropping, stupefying

ambassador = <u>representative</u>, minister, agent, deputy, diplomat, envoy, consul, attaché, emissary, legate, plenipotentiary

ambience = <u>atmosphere</u>, feel, setting, air, quality, character, spirit, surroundings, tone, mood, impression, flavour, temper, tenor, aura, complexion, vibes (*slang*), vibrations (*slang*), milieu

ambiguity = <u>vagueness</u>, doubt, puzzle, uncertainty, obscurity, enigma, equivocation, inconclusiveness, indefiniteness, dubiety, dubiousness, tergiversation, indeterminateness, equivocality, doubtfulness, equivocacy

ambiguous = <u>unclear</u>, puzzling, uncertain, obscure, vague, doubtful, dubious, enigmatic, indefinite, inconclusive, cryptic, indeterminate, equivocal, Delphic, oracular, enigmatical, clear as mud (*informal*) OPPOSITE> clear

ambition 1 = <u>goal</u>, end, hope, design, dream, target, aim, wish, purpose, desire, intention, objective, intent, aspiration, Holy Grail (*informal*) ...*His ambition is to sail round the world...*

2 = <u>enterprise</u>, longing, drive, fire, spirit, desire, passion, enthusiasm, warmth, striving, initiative, aspiration, yearning, devotion, zeal, verve, zest, fervour, eagerness, gusto, hankering, get-up-and-go (*informal*), ardour, keenness, avidity, fervency ...*a mixture of ambition and ruthlessness...*

ambitious 1 = <u>enterprising</u>, spirited, keen, active, daring, eager, intent, enthusiastic, hopeful, striving, vigorous, aspiring, energetic, adventurous, avid, zealous, intrepid, resourceful, purposeful, desirous ...*He's a very ambitious lad...* OPPOSITE> unambitious
2 = <u>demanding</u>, trying, hard, taxing, difficult, challenging, tough, severe, impressive, exhausting, exacting, bold, elaborate, formidable, energetic, strenuous, pretentious, arduous, grandiose, industrious ...*Their goal was extraordinarily ambitious...* OPPOSITE> modest

ambivalence = <u>indecision</u>, doubt, opposition, conflict, uncertainty, contradiction, wavering, fluctuation, hesitancy, equivocation, vacillation, irresolution

ambivalent = <u>undecided</u>, mixed, conflicting, opposed, uncertain, doubtful, unsure, contradictory, wavering, unresolved, fluctuating, hesitant, inconclusive, debatable, equivocal, vacillating, warring, irresolute OPPOSITE> definite

amble = <u>stroll</u>, walk, wander, ramble, meander, saunter, dawdle, mosey (*informal*)

ambush VERB = <u>trap</u>, attack, surprise, deceive, dupe, ensnare, waylay, ambuscade, bushwhack (*U.S.*) ...*Rebels ambushed and killed 10 patrolmen...*
NOUN = <u>trap</u>, snare, attack, lure, waylaying, ambuscade ...*A policeman has been shot dead in an ambush...*

ameliorate = <u>improve</u>, better, benefit, reform, advance, promote, amend, elevate, raise, mend, mitigate, make better, assuage, meliorate

---

Word Power

ameliorate – *Ameliorate* is sometimes confused with *alleviate* but the words are not synonymous. *Ameliorate* comes ultimately from the Latin for 'better', and means 'to improve'. The nouns it typically goes with are *condition*, and *situation*. *Alleviate* means 'to lessen', and frequently occurs with *poverty*, *suffering*, *pain*, *symptoms*, and *effects*. Occasionally *ameliorate* is used with *effects* and *poverty* where the other verb may be more appropriate.

---

amenable = <u>receptive</u>, open, susceptible, responsive, agreeable, compliant, tractable, acquiescent, persuadable, able to be influenced OPPOSITE> stubborn

amend VERB = <u>change</u>, improve, reform, fix, correct, repair, edit, alter, enhance, update, revise, modify, remedy, rewrite, mend, rectify, tweak (*informal*), ameliorate, redraw ...*The committee put forward proposals to amend the penal system...*
PLURAL NOUN (usually in *make amends*) = <u>compensation</u>, apology, restoration, redress,

reparation, indemnity, restitution, atonement, recompense, expiation, requital …*He wanted to make amends for causing their marriage to fail…*

amendment 1 = <u>addition</u>, change, adjustment, attachment, adaptation, revision, modification, alteration, remodelling, reformation, clarification, adjunct, addendum …*an amendment to the defence bill…*
2 = <u>change</u>, improvement, repair, edit, remedy, correction, revision, modification, alteration, mending, enhancement, reform, betterment, rectification, amelioration, emendation …*We are making a few amendments to the document…*

amenity 1 = <u>facility</u>, service, advantage, comfort, convenience …*The hotel amenities include a health club and banqueting rooms…*
2 = <u>refinement</u>, politeness, affability, amiability, courtesy, mildness, pleasantness, suavity, agreeableness, complaisance …*A man of little amenity…* OPPOSITE> rudeness

America
➤ **English and American equivalences**
American ADJECTIVE = <u>Yankee</u> or <u>Yank</u>, U.S. …*the American ambassador at the UN…*
NOUN = <u>Yankee</u> or <u>Yank</u>, Yankee Doodle …*The 1990 Nobel Prize for medicine was won by two Americans…*

amiable = <u>pleasant</u>, kind, kindly, pleasing, friendly, attractive, engaging, charming, obliging, delightful, cheerful, benign, winning, agreeable, good-humoured, lovable, sociable, genial, affable, congenial, winsome, good-natured, sweet-tempered, likable or likeable OPPOSITE> unfriendly

amicable = <u>friendly</u>, kindly, brotherly, civil, neighbourly, peaceful, polite, harmonious, good-humoured, amiable, courteous, cordial, sociable, fraternal, peaceable OPPOSITE> unfriendly

amid or **amidst 1** = <u>during</u>, among, at a time of, in an atmosphere of …*He cancelled a foreign trip amid growing concerns of a domestic crisis…*
2 = <u>in the middle of</u>, among, surrounded by, amongst, in the midst of, in the thick of …*a tiny bungalow amid clusters of trees…*

amiss ADJECTIVE = <u>wrong</u>, mistaken, confused, false, inappropriate, rotten, incorrect, faulty, inaccurate, unsuitable, improper, defective, out of order, awry, erroneous, untoward, fallacious …*Their instincts warned them something was amiss…* OPPOSITE> right
PHRASES **take something amiss** = <u>as an insult</u>, wrongly, as offensive, out of turn …*He took it amiss when I asked to speak to someone else…*

ammunition = <u>munitions</u>, rounds, shot, shells, powder, explosives, cartridges, armaments, materiel, shot and shell

amnesty = <u>general pardon</u>, mercy, pardoning, immunity, forgiveness, reprieve, oblivion, remission (*of penalty*), clemency, dispensation, absolution, condonation

amok or **amuck**
PHRASES **run amok** = <u>go mad</u>, go wild, turn violent, go berserk, lose control, go insane, go into a frenzy

among or **amongst 1** = <u>in the midst of</u>, with, together with, in the middle of, amid, surrounded by, amidst, in the thick of …*They walked among the crowds in the large town square…*
2 = <u>in the group of</u>, one of, part of, included in, in the company of, in the class of, in the number of …*Among the speakers was the new American ambassador…*
3 = <u>between</u>, to …*Most of the furniture was distributed among friends…*
4 = <u>with one another</u>, mutually, by all of, by the whole of, by the joint action of …*The directors have been arguing amongst themselves…*

amoral = <u>unethical</u>, nonmoral, unvirtuous

> ### Word Power
>
> **amoral** – *Amoral* is sometimes confused with *immoral*. The *a-* at the beginning of the word means 'without' or 'lacking', so the word is properly used of people who have no moral code, or about places or situations where moral considerations do not apply: *the film was violent and amoral*. In contrast *immoral* should be used to talk about the breaking of moral rules, as in: *drug dealing is the most immoral and evil of all human activities*.

amorous = <u>loving</u>, in love, tender, passionate, fond, erotic, affectionate, ardent, impassioned, doting, enamoured, lustful, attached, lovesick, amatory OPPOSITE> cold

amorphous = <u>shapeless</u>, vague, irregular, nondescript, indeterminate, unstructured, nebulous, formless, inchoate, characterless, unformed, unshaped, unshapen OPPOSITE> definite

amount NOUN **1** = <u>quantity</u>, lot, measure, size, supply, mass, volume, capacity, extent, bulk, number, magnitude, expanse …*I still do a certain amount of work for them…*
2 = <u>total</u>, whole, mass, addition, sum, lot, extent, aggregate, entirety, totality, sum total …*If you always pay the full amount, this won't affect you…*
PHRASES **amount to something 1** = <u>add up to</u>, mean, total, equal, constitute, comprise, aggregate, purport, be equivalent to …*The banks have what amounts to a monopoly…* **2** = <u>come to</u>, become, grow to, develop into, advance to, progress to, mature into …*My music teacher said I'd never amount to anything…*

> ### Word Power
>
> **amount** – Although it is common to use a plural noun after *amount of*, for example in *the amount of people* and *the amount of goods*, this should be avoided. Preferred alternatives would be to use *quantity*, as in *the quantity of people*, or *number*, as in *the number of goods*.

amour = <u>love affair</u>, relationship, affair, romance, intrigue, liaison, affaire de coeur (*French*)

English and American equivalences

English	American	English	American
aeroplane	airplane	handbag	purse
American football	football	hessian	burlap
antenatal	prenatal	high street	main street
aubergine	egg plant	holiday	vacation
autumn	fall	indicator	blinker
bad-tempered	mean	invigilator	proctor
banknote	bill	ironmonger	hardware store
bat	paddle	jam	jelly
benefit	welfare	janitor	caretaker
bin or dustbin	trashcan	lawyer	attorney
biscuit	cookie	lift	elevator
black pudding	blood sausage	mangetout	snowpea
blinds	shades	mate	friend
bonnet (car)	hood	merry-go-round	carousel
boot (car)	trunk	methylated spirits	denatured alcohol
braces (teeth)	retainer	mince	ground beef
braces (lingerie)	suspenders	minim	half note
breve	double whole note	nappy	diaper
broad bean	fava bean	neat (of drinks)	straight
building society	savings and loan	noughts and crosses	tick-tack-toe
burgle	burglarize	nursery	kindergarten
candy floss	cotton candy	off licence	liquor store
car	automobile	paraffin	kerosene
car park	parking lot	pavement	sidewalk
chemist	drug store	pepper	bell pepper
chips	French fries	petrol	gas or gasoline
clothes peg	clothes pin	plait	braid
coffin	casket	plasterboard	dry lining
condom	rubber	plot	lot
cornflour	corn starch	porridge	oatmeal
courgette	zucchini	postcode	zip code
crisps	chips or potato chips	postman	mail man
crossroads	intersection	pub or public house	bar
crotchet	quarter note	public school	private school
current account	checking account	purse	pocketbook
curtains	drapes	pushchair	stroller
cutlery	flatware or silverware	quaver	eighth note
CV	résumé	quilt or eiderdown	comforter
dialing code	area code	railway	railroad
dinner jacket	tuxedo	receptionist	desk clerk
double cream	heavy cream	reverse charge	collect
drapery	dry goods	ring road	beltway
draughts	checkers	roll or bap	bun
drawing pin	thumb tack	rubber	eraser
dressing gown	robe	rubbish	trash or garbage
dummy	pacifier or soother	semibreve	whole note
engaged tone	busy signal	semi-detached	duplex
estate agent	realtor	semiquaver	sixteenth note
estate car	station wagon	shop	store
fire lighter	fire starter	silencer	muffler
first floor	second floor	skip	dumpster
flat	apartment	skirting board	baseboard
flick knife	switch blade	sleeper (railway)	tie
football	soccer	slowcoach	slowpoke
foyer	lobby	soft drink	soda
fringe	bangs	spanner	wrench
garden	yard	spring onion or salad onion	scallion
gear lever	stick shift	state school	public school
goose pimples	goose bumps	stream	creek
ground floor	first floor	surgical spirit	rubbing alcohol
hair grip	bobby pin	sweet	candy
hairpin bend	switchback	tap	faucet

English and American equivalences (continued)

English	American	English	American
tarmac	asphalt	tram	streetcar
telegram	wire	trousers	pants
thread	cotton	turn up	cuff
tights	pantihose	VAT	sales tax
timber	lumber	vest	undershirt
torch	flashlight	waistcoast	vest
town centre	downtown	windscreen	windshield
trainers	sneakers	http://esl.about.com/library/weekly/aa110698.htm	

amphibian

Amphibians

axolotl	midwife toad
brown-striped frog (Austral.)	mud puppy
	natterjack
bullfrog	newt or (dialect or archaic) eft
caecilian	
cane toad (Austral.)	olm
congo eel or snake	pipa or Surinam toad
eft	Queensland cane toad
frog or (Caribbean) crapaud	salamander
	siren
Goliath frog	toad or (Caribbean) crapaud
hairy frog	
hellbender	tree frog
hyla	http://www.amphibiaweb.org/ www.livingunderworld.org/gallery

ample 1 = <u>plenty of</u>, great, rich, liberal, broad, generous, lavish, spacious, abounding, abundant, plentiful, expansive, copious, roomy, unrestricted, voluminous, capacious, profuse, commodious, plenteous ...*The design gave ample space for a good-sized kitchen...* OPPOSITE insufficient
2 = <u>large</u>, great, big, full, wide, broad, extensive, generous, abundant, voluminous, bountiful ...*a young mother with a baby resting against her ample bosom...*

amplification 1 = <u>increase</u>, boosting, stretching, strengthening, expansion, extension, widening, raising, heightening, deepening, lengthening, enlargement, intensification, magnification, dilation, augmentation ...*a voice that needed no amplification...*
2 = <u>explanation</u>, development, expansion, supplementing, fleshing out, elaboration, rounding out, augmentation, expatiation ...*They demanded amplification of the imprecise statement...*

amplify 1 = <u>expand</u>, raise, extend, boost, stretch, strengthen, increase, widen, intensify, heighten, deepen, enlarge, lengthen, magnify, augment, dilate ...*The music was amplified with microphones...* OPPOSITE reduce
2 = <u>go into detail</u>, develop, explain, expand, supplement, elaborate, augment, flesh out, round out, enlarge on, expatiate ...*Intelligent guesswork must be used to amplify the facts...* OPPOSITE simplify

amplitude 1 = <u>extent</u>, reach, range, size, mass, sweep, dimension, bulk, scope, width, magnitude, compass, greatness, breadth, expanse, vastness, spaciousness, bigness, largeness, hugeness, capaciousness ...*a man of great amplitude...*
2 = <u>fullness</u>, abundance, richness, plethora, profusion, completeness, plenitude, copiousness, ampleness ...*The character comes to imply an amplitude of meanings...*

amply = <u>fully</u>, well, greatly, completely, richly, liberally, thoroughly, substantially, lavishly, extensively, generously, abundantly, profusely, copiously, plentifully, unstintingly, bountifully, without stinting, plenteously, capaciously OPPOSITE insufficiently

amputate = <u>cut off</u>, remove, separate, sever, curtail, truncate, lop off

amuck
➤ **amok**

amuse 1 = <u>entertain</u>, please, delight, charm, cheer, tickle, gratify, beguile, enliven, regale, gladden ...*The thought seemed to amuse him...* OPPOSITE bore
2 = <u>occupy</u>, interest, involve, engage, entertain, absorb, divert, engross ...*Put a selection of toys in his cot to amuse him if he wakes early...*

amusement 1 = <u>enjoyment</u>, delight, entertainment, cheer, laughter, mirth, hilarity, merriment, gladdening, beguilement, regalement ...*He watched with amusement to see the child so absorbed...* OPPOSITE boredom
2 = <u>diversion</u>, interest, sport, pleasing, fun, pleasure, recreation, entertainment, gratification ...*It's unacceptable to keep animals confined for our amusement...*
3 = <u>pastime</u>, game, sport, joke, entertainment, hobby, recreation, distraction, diversion, lark, prank ...*People had very few amusements to choose from in those days...*

amusing = <u>funny</u>, humorous, gratifying, laughable, farcical, comical, droll, interesting, pleasing, charming, cheering, entertaining, comic, pleasant, lively, diverting, delightful, enjoyable, cheerful, witty, merry, gladdening, facetious, jocular, rib-tickling, waggish OPPOSITE boring

anaemic 1 = <u>pale</u>, weak, dull, frail, feeble, wan, sickly, bloodless, colourless, infirm, pallid, ashen, characterless, enervated, like death warmed up (informal) ...*Losing a lot of blood makes you tired and anaemic...* OPPOSITE rosy
2 = <u>weak</u>, feeble ...*We will see some economic recovery, but it will be very anaemic...*

anaesthetic NOUN = <u>painkiller</u>, narcotic, sedative, opiate, anodyne, analgesic, soporific, stupefacient, stupefactive …*The operation is carried out under general anaesthetic…*

ADJECTIVE = <u>pain-killing</u>, dulling, numbing, narcotic, sedative, opiate, deadening, anodyne, analgesic, soporific, sleep-inducing, stupefacient, stupefactive …*They are rendered unconscious by anaesthetic darts…*

analogous = <u>similar</u>, like, related, equivalent, parallel, resembling, alike, corresponding, comparable, akin, homologous OPPOSITE different

> ### Word Power
> **analogous** – The correct word to use after *analogous* is *to*, not *with* – for example: *swimming has no event that is analogous to the 100 metres in athletics* (not *analogous with the 100 metres in athletics*).

analogy = <u>similarity</u>, relation, comparison, parallel, correspondence, resemblance, correlation, likeness, equivalence, homology, similitude

analyse 1 = <u>examine</u>, test, study, research, judge, estimate, survey, investigate, interpret, evaluate, inspect, work over …*This book teaches you to analyse causes of stress in your life…*
2 = <u>break down</u>, consider, study, separate, divide, resolve, dissolve, dissect, think through, assay, anatomize …*We haven't had time to analyse those samples yet…*

analysis 1 = <u>study</u>, reasoning, opinion, judgment, interpretation, evaluation, estimation, dissection …*We did an analysis of the way they have spent money in the past…*
2 = <u>examination</u>, test, division, inquiry, investigation, resolution, interpretation, breakdown, scanning, separation, evaluation, scrutiny, sifting, anatomy, dissolution, dissection, assay, perusal, anatomization …*They collect blood samples for analysis at the laboratory…*

analytical *or* **analytic** = <u>rational</u>, questioning, testing, detailed, searching, organized, exact, precise, logical, systematic, inquiring, diagnostic, investigative, dissecting, explanatory, discrete, inquisitive, interpretive, studious, interpretative, expository

anarchic = <u>lawless</u>, rioting, confused, disordered, revolutionary, chaotic, rebellious, riotous, disorganized, misruled, ungoverned, misgoverned OPPOSITE law-abiding

anarchist = <u>revolutionary</u>, rebel, terrorist, insurgent, nihilist

anarchy = <u>lawlessness</u>, revolution, riot, disorder, confusion, chaos, rebellion, misrule, disorganization, misgovernment OPPOSITE order

anathema = <u>abomination</u>, bête noire, enemy, pariah, bane, bugbear

anatomy 1 = <u>structure</u>, build, make-up, frame, framework, composition …*He had worked extensively on the anatomy of living animals…*

2 = <u>examination</u>, study, division, inquiry, investigation, analysis, dismemberment, dissection …*a troubling essay on the anatomy of nationhood…*

ancestor = <u>forefather</u>, predecessor, precursor, forerunner, forebear, antecedent, progenitor OPPOSITE descendant

ancestral = <u>inherited</u>, hereditary, patriarchal, antecedent, forefatherly, genealogical, lineal, ancestorial

ancestry = <u>origin</u>, house, family, line, race, stock, blood, ancestors, descent, pedigree, extraction, lineage, forebears, antecedents, parentage, forefathers, genealogy, derivation, progenitors

anchor NOUN = <u>mooring</u>, hook (*Nautical*), bower (*Nautical*), kedge, drogue, sheet anchor …*We lost our anchor, which caused the boat to drift…*

VERB 1 = <u>moor</u>, harbour, dock, tie up, drop anchor, kedge, drop the hook, cast anchor, let go the anchor, lay anchor, come to anchor …*We could anchor off the pier…*
2 = <u>secure</u>, tie, fix, bind, chain, attach, bolt, fasten, affix …*The child's seatbelt was not properly anchored in the car…*

anchorage = <u>berth</u>, haven, port, harbour, dock, quay, dockage, moorage, harbourage

ancient 1 = <u>classical</u>, old, former, past, bygone, primordial, primeval, olden …*They believed ancient Greece and Rome were vital sources of learning…*
2 = <u>very old</u>, early, aged, antique, obsolete, archaic, age-old, bygone, antiquated, hoary, olden, superannuated, antediluvian, timeworn, old as the hills …*ancient rites…*
3 = <u>old-fashioned</u>, past, dated, outdated, obsolete, out of date, old-time, archaic, unfashionable, antiquated, outmoded, passé, musty, old hat, behind the times, fusty, superannuated, out of style, obsolescent, square (*informal*), cobwebby, démodé (*French*), out of the ark (*informal*), oldfangled, (old-)fogeyish …*He produced articles and stories on his ancient typewriter…* OPPOSITE up-to-date

ancillary = <u>supplementary</u>, supporting, extra, additional, secondary, subsidiary, accessory, subordinate, auxiliary, contributory OPPOSITE major

and 1 = <u>also</u>, including, along with, together with, in addition to, as well as …*When he returned, she and her boyfriend had already gone…*
2 = <u>moreover</u>, plus, furthermore …*These airlines fly to isolated places. And business travellers use them…*

> ### Word Power
> **and** – The forms *try and do something* and *wait and do something* should only be used in informal or spoken English. In more formal writing, use *try to* and *wait to*, for example: *we must try to prevent this happening* (not *try and prevent*).

androgynous = <u>hermaphrodite</u>, bisexual, androgyne, hermaphroditic, epicene

android (*Science fiction*) = <u>robot</u>, automaton,

humanoid, cyborg, mechanical man, bionic man *or* woman

anecdote = <u>story</u>, tale, sketch, short story, yarn, reminiscence, urban myth, urban legend

anew = <u>again</u>, once again, once more, over again, from the beginning, from scratch, another time, afresh

angel 1 = <u>divine messenger</u>, spirit, cherub, archangel, seraph, spiritual being, guardian spirit ...*a choir of angels*...
2 (*Informal*) = <u>dear</u>, ideal, beauty, saint, treasure, darling, dream, jewel, gem, paragon ...*Thank you. You're an angel*...

angelic 1 = <u>pure</u>, beautiful, lovely, innocent, entrancing, virtuous, saintly, adorable, beatific ...*an angelic little face*...
2 = <u>heavenly</u>, celestial, ethereal, cherubic, seraphic ...*angelic choirs*... OPPOSITE demonic

anger NOUN = <u>rage</u>, passion, outrage, temper, fury, resentment, irritation, wrath, indignation, annoyance, agitation, ire, antagonism, displeasure, exasperation, irritability, spleen, pique, ill temper, vehemence, vexation, high dudgeon, ill humour, choler ...*He cried with anger and frustration*... OPPOSITE calmness
VERB = <u>enrage</u>, provoke, outrage, annoy, offend, excite, irritate, infuriate, hassle (*informal*), aggravate (*informal*), incense, fret, gall, madden, exasperate, nettle, vex, affront, displease, rile, pique, get on someone's nerves (*informal*), antagonize, get someone's back up, put someone's back up, nark (*Brit., Austral., & N.Z. slang*), make someone's blood boil, get in someone's hair (*informal*), get someone's dander up (*informal*) ...*The decision to allow more construction angered the residents*... OPPOSITE soothe

angle NOUN 1 = <u>gradient</u>, bank, slope, incline, inclination ...*The boat was leaning at a 30-degree angle*...
2 = <u>intersection</u>, point, edge, corner, knee, bend, elbow, crook, crotch, nook, cusp ...*brackets to adjust the steering wheel's angle*...
3 = <u>point of view</u>, position, approach, direction, aspect, perspective, outlook, viewpoint, slant, standpoint, take (*informal*), side ...*He was considering the idea from all angles*...
PHRASES **angle for something** = <u>seek</u>, scheme, look for, hunt, invite, be after (*informal*), try for, aim for, contrive, fish for, solicit, set your sights on, cast about *or* around for ...*It sounds as if he's just angling for sympathy*...

angler = <u>fisherman</u>, fisher, piscator *or* piscatrix

angling = <u>fishing</u>

angry = <u>furious</u>, cross, heated, mad (*informal*), raging, provoked, outraged, annoyed, passionate, irritated, raving, hacked (off) (*U.S. slang*), choked, infuriated, hot, incensed, enraged, ranting, exasperated, irritable, resentful, nettled, snappy, indignant, irate, tumultuous, displeased, uptight (*informal*), riled, up in arms, incandescent, ill-tempered, irascible, antagonized, waspish, piqued, hot under the collar (*informal*), on the warpath, hopping mad (*informal*),

foaming at the mouth, choleric, splenetic, wrathful, at daggers drawn, in high dudgeon, as black as thunder, ireful, tooshie (*Austral. slang*), off the air (*Austral. slang*) OPPOSITE calm

> *Word Power*
>
> **angry** – Some people feel it is more correct to talk about being *angry with* someone than being *angry at* them. In British English, *angry with* is still more common than *angry at*, but *angry at* is used more commonly in American English.

angst = <u>anxiety</u>, worry, distress, torment, unease, apprehension, agitation, malaise, perturbation, vexation, fretfulness, disquietude, inquietude OPPOSITE peace of mind

anguish = <u>suffering</u>, pain, torture, distress, grief, misery, agony, torment, sorrow, woe, heartache, heartbreak, pang, throe

anguished = <u>suffering</u>, wounded, tortured, distressed, tormented, afflicted, agonized, grief-stricken, wretched, brokenhearted

angular = <u>skinny</u>, spare, lean, gaunt, bony, lanky, scrawny, lank, rangy, rawboned, macilent (*rare*)

animal NOUN 1 = <u>creature</u>, beast, brute ...*He was attacked by wild animals*...
2 = <u>brute</u>, devil, monster, savage, beast, bastard (*informal, offensive*), villain, barbarian, swine (*informal*), wild man ...*He was an animal in his younger days*...
ADJECTIVE = <u>physical</u>, gross, fleshly, bodily, sensual, carnal, brutish, bestial ...*When he was drunk, he showed his animal side*...
(Related Words)
prefix: zoo-
➤ **amphibians** ➤ **animals** ➤ **birds** ➤ **dinosaurs** ➤ **fish** ➤ **insects** ➤ **invertebrates** ➤ **mammals** ➤ **reptiles**

animate ADJECTIVE = <u>living</u>, live, moving, alive, breathing, alive and kicking ...*the study of animate and inanimate aspects of the natural world*...
VERB = <u>enliven</u>, encourage, excite, urge, inspire, stir, spark, move, fire, spur, stimulate, revive, activate, rouse, prod, quicken, incite, instigate, kick-start (*informal*), impel, energize, kindle, embolden, liven up, breathe life into, invigorate, gladden, gee up, vitalize, vivify, inspirit ...*There was little about the game to animate the crowd*... OPPOSITE inhibit

animated = <u>lively</u>, spirited, quick, excited, active, vital, dynamic, enthusiastic, passionate, vivid, vigorous, energetic, vibrant, brisk, buoyant, ardent, airy, fervent, zealous, elated, ebullient, sparky, sprightly, vivacious, gay, alive and kicking, full of beans (*informal*), zestful OPPOSITE listless

animation = <u>liveliness</u>, life, action, activity, energy, spirit, passion, enthusiasm, excitement, pep, sparkle, vitality, vigour, zeal, verve, zest, fervour, high spirits, dynamism, buoyancy, elation, exhilaration, gaiety, ardour, vibrancy, brio, zing (*informal*), vivacity,

Animals

Related words

ant	formic	fish	piscine *or* icthyoid	parrot	psittacine
ass	asinine	fowl	gallinaceous	peacock	pavonine
bear	ursine	fox	vulpine	pig	porcine
bee	apian	goat	caprine *or* hircine	puffin	alcidine
bird	avian *or* ornithic	goose	anserine *or*	seal	phocine
bull	taurine		anserous	sheep	ovine
cat	feline	gull	larine	snake	serpentine,
crab	cancroid	hare	leporine		anguine,
crow	corvine	hawk	accipitrine		ophidian, *or*
deer	cervine	horse	equine		colubrine
dog	canine	lion	leonine	swallow	hirundine
dove	columbine	lynx	lyncean	wasp	vespine
eagle	aquiline	mite *or* tick	acaroid	wolf	lupine
elephant	elephantine	monkey	simian		
falcon	falconine	ox	bovine		

Collective animals

antelopes	herd	gnats	swarm *or* cloud	ponies	herd
apes	shrewdness	goats	herd *or* tribe	porpoises	school *or* gam
asses	pace *or* herd	goldfinches	charm	poultry	run
badgers	cete	grouse	brood, covey, *or*	pups	litter
bears	sloth		pack	quails	bevy
bees	swarm *or* grist	gulls	colony	rabbits	nest
birds	flock,	hares	down *or* husk	racehorses	field *or* string
	congregation,	hawks	cast	ravens	unkindness
	flight, *or* volery	hens	brood	roes	bevy
bitterns	sedge *or* siege	herons	sedge *or* siege	rooks	building *or*
boars	sounder	herrings	shoal *or* glean		clamour
bucks	brace *or* lease	hounds	pack, mute, *or*	ruffs	hill
buffaloes	herd		cry	seals	herd *or* pod
capercailzies	tok	insects	swarm	sheep	flock
cats	clowder	kangaroos	troop	sheldrakes	dopping
cattle	drove *or* herd	kittens	kindle	snipe	walk *or* wisp
choughs	chattering	lapwings	desert	sparrows	host
colts	rag	larks	exaltation	starlings	murmuration
coots	covert	leopards	leap	swallows	flight
cranes	herd, sedge, *or*	lions	pride *or* troop	swans	herd *or* bevy
	siege	mallards	sord *or* sute	swifts	flock
crows	murder	mares	stud	swine	herd, sounder, *or*
cubs	litter	martens	richesse		dryft
curlews	herd	moles	labour	teal	bunch, knob, *or*
curs	cowardice	monkeys	troop		spring
deer	herd	mules	barren	whales	school, gam, *or*
dolphins	school	nightingales	watch		run
doves	flight *or* dule	owls	parliament	whelps	litter
ducks	paddling *or* team	oxen	yoke, drove,	whiting	pod
dunlins	flight		team, *or* herd	wigeon	bunch,
elk	gang	partridges	covey		company, knob,
fish	shoal, draught,	peacocks	muster		*or* flight
	haul, run, *or*	pheasants	nye *or* nide	wildfowl	plump, sord, *or*
	catch	pigeons	flock *or* flight		sute
flies	swarm *or* grist	pigs	litter	wolves	pack, rout, *or*
foxes	skulk	plovers	stand *or* wing		herd
geese	gaggle *or* skein	pochards	flight, rush,	woodcocks	fall
giraffes	herd		bunch, *or* knob		

Habitations

ant	ant hill *or* formicary	fish	redd	rook	rookery
badger	set *or* sett	fox	earth	seal	sealery
beaver	lodge	otter	holt	squirrel	drey *or* dray
bee	hive *or* apiary	pig	sty	termite	termitarium
bird	nest	puffin	puffinry	wasp	vespiary *or* bike
eagle	aerie *or* eyrie	rabbit	warren		

Animals (continued) http://animaldiversity.ummz.umich.edu/site/index.html

Male

ass	jack	fowl	cock	peafowl	peacock
bird	cock	fox	dog	pig	boar
cat	tom	goat	billy *or* buck	rabbit	buck
deer	hart *or* stag	goose	gander	reindeer	buck
donkey	jack	hare	buck	ruff	ruff
duck	drake	horse	stallion	sheep	ram *or* tup
elephant	bull	kangaroo	buck *or* old man	swan	cob
falcon	tercel *or* tiercel	lobster	cock	weasel	whittret
ferret	hob	ox	bull	whale	bull

Female

ass	jenny	goat	nanny	rabbit	doe
bird	hen	hare	doe	ruff	reeve
cat	tabby	horse	mare	sheep	ewe
deer	doe *or* hind	leopard	leopardess	swan	pen
dog	bitch	lion	lioness	tiger	tigress
donkey	jenny	lobster	hen	whale	cow
elephant	cow	mink	sow	wolf	bitch
ferret	gill *or* jill	ox	cow	wren	jenny
fowl	hen	peafowl	peahen		
fox	vixen	pig	sow		

Young

bear	cub	falcon	eyas	owl	owlet
bird	chick, fledg(e)ling, *or* nestling	ferret	kit	ox	calf
		fish	fry *or* fingerling	pig	piglet
butterfly	caterpillar, chrysalis, *or* chrysalid	frog	tadpole	pigeon	squab
		fox	kit *or* cub	salmon	alevin, grilse, parr, *or* smolt
		goat	kid *or* yeanling		
cat	kitten	goose	gosling	seal	pup
cod	codling	hare	leveret	sheep	lamb *or* yeanling
deer	fawn	herring	alevin, brit, *or* sparling	sprat	brit
dog	pup *or* puppy			swan	cygnet
duck	duckling	horse	foal, colt, *or* filly	tiger	cub
eagle	eaglet	kangaroo	joey	toad	tadpole
eel	elver *or* grig	lion	cub	whale	calf
elephant	calf	moth	caterpillar	wolf	cub *or* whelp

ebullience, briskness, airiness, sprightliness, pizzazz *or* pizazz (*informal*)

animosity = hostility, hate, hatred, resentment, bitterness, malice, antagonism, antipathy, enmity, acrimony, rancour, bad blood, ill will, animus, malevolence, virulence, malignity OPPOSITE friendliness

animus = ill will, hate, hostility, hatred, resentment, bitterness, malice, animosity, antagonism, antipathy, enmity, acrimony, rancour, bad blood, malevolence, virulence, malignity

annals = records, history, accounts, registers, journals, memorials, archives, chronicles

annex 1 = seize, take over, appropriate, acquire, occupy, conquer, expropriate, arrogate ...*Rome annexed the Nabatean kingdom in 106 AD*...
2 = join, unite, add, connect, attach, tack, adjoin, fasten, affix, append, subjoin ...*A gate goes through to the annexed garden*... OPPOSITE detach

annexation = seizure, takeover, occupation, conquest, appropriation, annexing, expropriation, arrogation

annexe 1 = extension, wing, ell, supplementary building ...*They are planning to set up a museum in an annexe to the theatre*...
2 = appendix, addition, supplement, attachment, adjunct, addendum, affixment ...*The annexe lists and discusses eight titles*...

annihilate = destroy, abolish, wipe out, erase, eradicate, extinguish, obliterate, liquidate, root out, exterminate, nullify, extirpate, wipe from the face of the earth

annihilation = destruction, wiping out, abolition, extinction, extinguishing, liquidation, rooting out, extermination, eradication, erasure, obliteration, nullification, extirpation

anniversary = jubilee, remembrance, commemoration

Anniversaries

Year	Traditional	Modern
1st	Paper	Clocks
2nd	Cotton	China
3rd	Leather	Crystal, glass
4th	Linen (silk)	Electrical appliances
5th	Wood	Silverware
6th	Iron	Wood
7th	Wool (copper)	Desk sets
8th	Bronze	Linen, lace
9th	Pottery (china)	Leather
10th	Tin (aluminium)	Diamond jewellery
11th	Steel	Fashion jewellery, accessories
12th	Silk	Pearls *or* coloured gems
13th	Lace	Textile, furs
14th	Ivory	Gold jewellery
15th	Crystal	Watches
20th	China	Platinum
25th	Silver	Sterling silver
30th	Pearl	Diamond
35th	Coral (jade)	Jade
40th	Ruby	
45th	Sapphire	
50th	Gold	
55th	Emerald	
60th	Diamond	

---

annotate = <u>make notes on</u>, explain, note, illustrate, comment on, interpret, gloss, footnote, commentate, elucidate, make observations on

annotation = <u>note</u>, comment, explanation, observation, interpretation, illustration, commentary, gloss, footnote, exegesis, explication, elucidation

announce 1 = <u>make known</u>, tell, report, reveal, publish, declare, advertise, broadcast, disclose, intimate, proclaim, trumpet, make public, publicize, divulge, promulgate, propound, shout from the rooftops (*informal*) ...*She was planning to announce her engagement to Peter...* OPPOSITE⟩ keep secret
2 = <u>be a sign of</u>, signal, herald, warn of, signify, augur, harbinger, presage, foretell, portend, betoken ...*The doorbell of the shop announced the arrival of a customer...*

announcement 1 = <u>statement</u>, communication, broadcast, explanation, publication, declaration, advertisement, testimony, disclosure, bulletin, communiqué, proclamation, utterance, intimation, promulgation, divulgence ...*There has been no formal announcement by either government...*
2 = <u>declaration</u>, report, reporting, publication, revelation, disclosure, proclamation, intimation, promulgation, divulgence ...*the announcement of their engagement...*

announcer = <u>presenter</u>, newscaster, reporter, commentator, broadcaster, newsreader, master of ceremonies, anchor man, anchor

annoy = <u>irritate</u>, trouble, bore, anger, harry, bother, disturb, provoke, get (*informal*), bug (*informal*),

needle (*informal*), plague, tease, harass, hassle (*informal*), aggravate (*informal*), badger, gall, madden, ruffle, exasperate, nettle, molest, pester, vex, displease, irk, bedevil, rile, peeve, get under your skin (*informal*), get on your nerves (*informal*), nark (*Brit., Austral., & N.Z. slang*), get up your nose (*informal*), give someone grief (*Brit. & S. African*), make your blood boil, rub someone up the wrong way (*informal*), get your goat (*slang*), get in your hair (*informal*), get on your wick (*Brit. slang*), get your dander up (*informal*), get your back up, incommode, put your back up OPPOSITE⟩ soothe

annoyance 1 = <u>irritation</u>, trouble, anger, bother, grief (*informal*), harassment, disturbance, hassle (*informal*), nuisance, provocation, displeasure, exasperation, aggravation, vexation, bedevilment ...*To her annoyance the stranger did not go away...*
2 = <u>nuisance</u>, bother, pain (*informal*), bind (*informal*), bore, drag (*informal*), plague, tease, pest, gall, pain in the neck (*informal*) ...*Snoring can be more than an annoyance...*

annoyed = <u>irritated</u>, bothered, harassed, hassled (*informal*), aggravated (*informal*), maddened, ruffled, exasperated, nettled, vexed, miffed (*informal*), displeased, irked, riled, harried, peeved (*informal*), piqued, browned off (*informal*)

annoying = <u>irritating</u>, boring, disturbing, provoking, teasing, harassing, aggravating, troublesome, galling, maddening, exasperating, displeasing, bedevilling, peeving (*informal*), irksome, bothersome, vexatious OPPOSITE⟩ delightful

annual 1 = <u>once a year</u>, yearly ...*the annual conference of the trade union movement...*
2 = <u>yearlong</u>, yearly ...*annual costs, £1,600...*

annually 1 = <u>once a year</u>, yearly, each year, every year, per year, by the year, every twelve months, per annum, year after year ...*Companies report to their shareholders annually...*
2 = <u>per year</u>, yearly, each year, every year, by the year, per annum ...*They hire 300 staff annually...*

annul = <u>invalidate</u>, reverse, cancel, abolish, void, repeal, recall, revoke, retract, negate, rescind, nullify, obviate, abrogate, countermand, declare *or* render null and void OPPOSITE⟩ restore

anodyne ADJECTIVE = <u>bland</u>, dull, boring, insipid, unexciting, uninspiring, uninteresting, mind-numbing (*informal*) ...*Their quarterly meetings were anodyne affairs...*
NOUN = <u>painkiller</u>, narcotic, palliative, analgesic, pain reliever ...*Leisure is a kind of anodyne...*

anoint 1 = <u>smear</u>, oil, rub, grease, spread over, daub, embrocate ...*He anointed my forehead with oil...*
2 = <u>consecrate</u>, bless, sanctify, hallow, anele (*archaic*) ...*The Pope has anointed him as Archbishop...*

anomalous = <u>unusual</u>, odd, rare, bizarre, exceptional, peculiar, eccentric, abnormal, irregular, inconsistent, off-the-wall (*slang*), incongruous, deviating, oddball (*informal*), atypical, aberrant, outré OPPOSITE⟩ normal

anomaly = <u>irregularity</u>, departure, exception,

abnormality, rarity, inconsistency, deviation, eccentricity, oddity, aberration, peculiarity, incongruity

anon (*Archaic or literary*) = <u>soon</u>, presently, shortly, promptly, before long, forthwith, betimes (*archaic*), erelong (*archaic or poetic*), in a couple of shakes (*informal*)

anonymity 1 = <u>namelessness</u>, innominateness …*Both mother and daughter have requested anonymity…* 2 = <u>unremarkability</u> or <u>unremarkableness</u>, characterlessness, unsingularity …*the anonymity of the rented room…*

anonymous 1 = <u>unnamed</u>, unknown, unidentified, nameless, unacknowledged, incognito, unauthenticated, innominate …*You can remain anonymous if you wish…* OPPOSITE> identified 2 = <u>unsigned</u>, uncredited, unattributed, unattested …*I heard that an anonymous note was actually being circulated…* OPPOSITE> signed 3 = <u>nondescript</u>, impersonal, faceless, colourless, undistinguished, unexceptional, characterless …*It's nice to stay in a home rather than an anonymous holiday flat…*

answer VERB 1 = <u>reply</u>, explain, respond, resolve, acknowledge, react, return, retort, rejoin, refute …*He paused before answering…* OPPOSITE> ask 2 = <u>satisfy</u>, meet, serve, fit, fill, suit, solve, fulfil, suffice, measure up to …*We must ensure we answer real needs…* NOUN 1 = <u>reply</u>, response, reaction, resolution, explanation, plea, comeback, retort, report, return, defence, acknowledgement, riposte, counterattack, refutation, rejoinder …*Without waiting for an answer, he turned and went in…* OPPOSITE> question 2 = <u>solution</u>, resolution, explanation …*Simply marking an answer wrong will not help the student…* 3 = <u>remedy</u>, solution, vindication …*Prison is not the answer for most young offenders…* PHRASES **answer for something** 1 = <u>be responsible for</u>, be to blame for, be liable for, be accountable for, take the rap for (*slang*), be answerable for, be chargeable for …*That child's mother has a lot to answer for…* 2 = <u>pay for</u>, suffer for, atone for, make amends for …*He must be made to*

answer for his terrible crimes… ♦ **answer someone back** = <u>be impertinent</u>, argue, dispute, disagree, retort, contradict, rebut, talk back, be cheeky …*I always answered my parents back when I thought they were wrong…* ♦ **answer to someone** = <u>be responsible to</u>, obey, work under, be ruled by, be managed by, be subordinate to, be accountable to, be answerable to …*He answers to a boss he has met once in 18 months…*

answerable *usually with **for** or **to*** = <u>responsible</u>, to blame, liable, accountable, amenable, chargeable, subject

ant

> Related Words

habitation : ant hill

➤ **ants, bees, and wasps**

antagonism = <u>hostility</u>, competition, opposition, conflict, rivalry, contention, friction, discord, antipathy, dissension OPPOSITE> friendship

antagonist = <u>opponent</u>, rival, opposer, enemy, competitor, contender, foe, adversary

antagonistic = <u>hostile</u>, opposed, resistant, at odds, incompatible, set against, averse, unfriendly, at variance, inimical, antipathetic, ill-disposed

> ### Word Power
>
> **antagonistic** – A useful synonym for *antagonistic*, for example in *public opinion is antagonistic to nuclear energy*, is *averse*. However, this alternative should be used with care as a very common error is to confuse it with *adverse*. *Averse* is usually followed by *to* and is meant to convey a strong dislike or hostility towards something, normally expressed by a person or people. *Adverse* is wrong in this context and should be used in relation to conditions or results: *adverse road conditions.*

antagonize = <u>annoy</u>, anger, insult, offend, irritate, alienate, hassle (*informal*), aggravate (*informal*), gall, repel, estrange, get under your skin (*informal*), get on your nerves (*informal*), nark (*Brit., Austral., & N.Z. slang*), get up your nose (*informal*), be on your back

Ants, bees, and wasps   http://faunanet.gov.au/wos/group.cfm?Group_ID=27

Amazon ant	gall wasp	mud dauber
ant *or* (*archaic or dialect*) emmet	honeypot ant *or* honey ant	native bee *or* sugarbag fly
army ant *or* legionary ant	honeybee *or* hive bee	Pharaoh ant
bee	horntail *or* wood wasp	policeman fly
blue ant	ichneumon fly *or* ichneumon	ruby-tail wasp
bulldog ant, bull ant, *or* (*Austral.*) bull Joe	wasp	sand wasp
	killer bee	Sirex wasp
bumblebee *or* humblebee	kootchar	slave ant
carpenter bee	leafcutter ant	spider-hunting wasp
cicada hunter	leafcutter bee	termite *or* white ant
cuckoo bee	mason bee	velvet ant
digger wasp	mason wasp	wasp
driver ant	minga	wood ant
flower wasp	mining bee	yellow jacket

(*slang*), rub (someone) up the wrong way (*informal*), disaffect, get in your hair (*informal*), get on your wick (*Brit. slang*) OPPOSITE> pacify

anteater

Anteaters and other edentates

aardvark
anteater
armadillo
echidna *or* spiny anteater
numbat *or* banded anteater
pangolin *or* scaly anteater
sloth *or* ai
tamandu, tamandua, *or* lesser anteater

animaldiversity.ummz.
umich.edu/site/
accounts/information/
Myrmecophagidae

---

antecedent ADJECTIVE = <u>preceding</u>, earlier, former, previous, prior, preliminary, foregoing, anterior, precursory ...*They were allowed to take account of antecedent legislation*... OPPOSITE> subsequent
PLURAL NOUN **1** = <u>ancestors</u>, family, line, stock, blood, descent, extraction, ancestry, forebears, forefathers, genealogy, progenitors ...*a Frenchman with Irish antecedents*...
2 = <u>past</u>, history, background ...*a series of conditions or antecedents which may have contributed to the situation*...

anterior 1 = <u>front</u>, forward, fore, frontward ...*the left anterior descending artery*...
2 = <u>earlier</u>, former, previous, prior, preceding, introductory, foregoing, antecedent ...*memories of our anterior existences*...

anthem = <u>song of praise</u>, carol, chant, hymn, psalm, paean, chorale, canticle

anthology = <u>collection</u>, choice, selection, treasury, digest, compilation, garland, compendium, miscellany, analects

anticipate 1 = <u>expect</u>, predict, forecast, prepare for, look for, hope for, envisage, foresee, bank on, apprehend, foretell, think likely, count upon ...*We could not have anticipated the result of our campaigning*...
2 = <u>await</u>, look forward to, count the hours until ...*We are all eagerly anticipating the next match*...

Word Power

anticipate – The Bank of English reveals that the use of *anticipate* and *expect* as synonyms is well established. However, although both words relate to a person's knowledge of something that will happen in the future, there are subtle differences in meaning that should be understood when choosing which word to use. *Anticipate* means that someone foresees an event and has prepared for it, while expect means 'to regard something as probable', but does not necessarily suggest the state of being prepared. Similarly, using *foresee* as a synonym of *anticipate*, as in *they failed to foresee the vast explosion in commercial revenue which would follow*, is not entirely appropriate.

---

anticipation = <u>expectancy</u>, hope, expectation, apprehension, foresight, premonition, preconception, foretaste, prescience, forethought, presentiment

anticlimax = <u>disappointment</u>, letdown, comedown (*informal*), bathos OPPOSITE> climax

antics = <u>clowning</u>, tricks, stunts, mischief, larks, capers, pranks, frolics, escapades, foolishness, silliness, playfulness, skylarking, horseplay, buffoonery, tomfoolery, monkey tricks

antidote = <u>remedy</u>, cure, preventive, corrective, neutralizer, nostrum, countermeasure, antitoxin, antivenin, counteragent

antipathy = <u>hostility</u>, opposition, disgust, dislike, hatred, loathing, distaste, animosity, aversion, antagonism, enmity, rancour, bad blood, incompatibility, ill will, animus, repulsion, abhorrence, repugnance, odium, contrariety OPPOSITE> affinity

antiquated = <u>obsolete</u>, old, aged, ancient, antique, old-fashioned, elderly, dated, past it (*informal*), out-of-date, archaic, outmoded, passé, old hat, hoary, superannuated, antediluvian, outworn, cobwebby, old as the hills OPPOSITE> up-to-date

antique NOUN = <u>period piece</u>, relic, bygone, heirloom, collector's item, museum piece, object of virtu ...*a genuine antique*...
ADJECTIVE **1** = <u>vintage</u>, classic, antiquarian, olden ...*antique silver jewellery*...
2 = <u>old-fashioned</u>, old, aged, ancient, remote, elderly, primitive, outdated, obsolete, archaic, bygone, primordial, primeval, immemorial, superannuated ...*Their aim is to break taboos and change antique laws*...

antiquity 1 = <u>distant past</u>, ancient times, time immemorial, olden days ...*famous monuments of classical antiquity*...
2 = <u>old age</u>, age, oldness, ancientness, elderliness ...*a town of great antiquity*...
3 = <u>antique</u>, ruin, relic ...*collectors of Roman antiquities*...

antiseptic ADJECTIVE = <u>hygienic</u>, clean, pure, sterile, sanitary, uncontaminated, unpolluted, germ-free, aseptic ...*These herbs have strong antiseptic qualities*... OPPOSITE> unhygienic
NOUN = <u>disinfectant</u>, purifier, bactericide, germicide ...*She bathed the cut with antiseptic*...

antisocial *or* **anti-social 1** = <u>unsociable</u>, reserved, retiring, withdrawn, alienated, unfriendly, uncommunicative, misanthropic, asocial ...*a generation of teenagers who will become aggressive and antisocial*... OPPOSITE> sociable
2 = <u>disruptive</u>, disorderly, hostile, menacing, rebellious, belligerent, antagonistic, uncooperative ...*Playing these games can lead to anti-social behaviour*...

antithesis 1 = <u>opposite</u>, contrast, reverse, contrary, converse, inverse, antipode ...*They are the antithesis of the typical married couple*...
2 = <u>contrast</u>, opposition, contradiction, reversal, inversion, contrariety, contraposition ...*the antithesis between instinct and reason*...

anxiety = <u>uneasiness</u>, concern, care, worry, doubt, tension, alarm, distress, suspicion, angst, unease, apprehension, misgiving, suspense, nervousness, disquiet, trepidation, foreboding, restlessness, solicitude, perturbation, watchfulness, fretfulness, disquietude, apprehensiveness, dubiety OPPOSITE> confidence

anxious 1 = <u>eager</u>, keen, intent, yearning, impatient, itching, ardent, avid, expectant, desirous ...*He is anxious that there should be no delay...* OPPOSITE> reluctant
2 = <u>uneasy</u>, concerned, worried, troubled, upset, careful, wired (*slang*), nervous, disturbed, distressed, uncomfortable, tense, fearful, unsettled, restless, neurotic, agitated, taut, disquieted, apprehensive, edgy, watchful, jittery (*informal*), perturbed, on edge, ill at ease, twitchy (*informal*), solicitous, overwrought, fretful, on tenterhooks, in suspense, hot and bothered, unquiet (*chiefly literary*), like a fish out of water, antsy (*informal*), angsty, on pins and needles, discomposed ...*He admitted he was still anxious about the situation...* OPPOSITE> confident

apace (*Literary*) = <u>quickly</u>, rapidly, swiftly, speedily, without delay, at full speed, expeditiously, posthaste, with dispatch

apart 1 = <u>to pieces</u>, to bits, asunder, into parts ...*He took the clock apart to see what was wrong with it...*
2 = <u>away from each other</u>, distant from each other ...*They live 25 miles apart...*
3 = <u>aside</u>, away, alone, independently, separately, singly, excluded, isolated, cut off, to one side, to yourself, by itself, aloof, to itself, by yourself, out on a limb ...*He saw her standing some distance apart...*
4 with *from* = <u>except for</u>, excepting, other than, excluding, besides, not including, aside from, but, save, bar, not counting ...*The room was empty apart from one man seated beside the fire...*

apartment 1 (*U.S.*) = <u>flat</u>, room, suite, compartment, penthouse, crib ...*She has her own apartment and her own car...*
2 = <u>rooms</u>, quarters, chambers, accommodation, living quarters ...*the private apartments of the Prince of Wales at St James's Palace...*

apathetic = <u>uninterested</u>, passive, indifferent, sluggish, unmoved, stoic, stoical, unconcerned, listless, cold, cool, impassive, unresponsive, phlegmatic, unfeeling, unemotional, torpid, emotionless, insensible OPPOSITE> interested

apathy = <u>lack of interest</u>, indifference, inertia, coolness, passivity, coldness, stoicism, nonchalance, torpor, phlegm, sluggishness, listlessness, unconcern, insensibility, unresponsiveness, impassivity, passiveness, impassibility, unfeelingness, emotionlessness, uninterestedness OPPOSITE> interest

ape = <u>imitate</u>, copy, mirror, echo, mock, parrot, mimic, parody, caricature, affect, counterfeit

aperture = <u>opening</u>, space, hole, crack, gap, rent, passage, breach, slot, vent, rift, slit, cleft, eye, chink, fissure, orifice, perforation, eyelet, interstice

apex 1 = <u>culmination</u>, top, crown, height, climax, highest point, zenith, apogee, acme ...*At the apex of the party was the central committee...* OPPOSITE> depths
2 = <u>highest point</u>, point, top, tip, summit, peak, crest, pinnacle, vertex ...*She led me up a gloomy corridor to the apex of the pyramid...* OPPOSITE> lowest point

aphorism = <u>saying</u>, maxim, gnome, adage, proverb, dictum, precept, axiom, apothegm, saw

aphrodisiac NOUN = <u>love potion</u>, philtre ...*Asparagus is reputed to be an aphrodisiac...*
ADJECTIVE = <u>erotic</u> or <u>erotical</u>, exciting, stimulating, arousing, venereal ...*plants with aphrodisiac qualities...*

apiece = <u>each</u>, individually, separately, for each, to each, respectively, from each, severally OPPOSITE> all together

aplenty ADJECTIVE = <u>in plenty</u>, to spare, galore, in abundance, in quantity, in profusion, à gogo (*informal*) ...*There were problems aplenty, and it was an uncomfortable evening...*
ADVERB = <u>plentifully</u>, in abundance, abundantly, in quantity, in plenty, copiously, plenteously ...*Wickets continued to fall aplenty...*

aplomb = <u>self-possession</u>, confidence, stability, self-confidence, composure, poise, coolness, calmness, equanimity, balance, self-assurance, sang-froid, level-headedness OPPOSITE> self-consciousness

apocalypse = <u>destruction</u>, holocaust, havoc, devastation, carnage, conflagration, cataclysm

---

Four Horsemen of the Apocalypse

white – Christ	black – Famine
red – War	pale – Death

---

apocryphal = <u>dubious</u>, legendary, doubtful, questionable, mythical, spurious, fictitious, unsubstantiated, equivocal, unverified, unauthenticated, uncanonical OPPOSITE> factual

apogee = <u>highest point</u>, top, tip, crown, summit, height, peak, climax, crest, pinnacle, culmination, zenith, apex, acme, vertex

apologetic = <u>regretful</u>, sorry, rueful, contrite, remorseful, penitent

apologize = <u>say sorry</u>, express regret, ask forgiveness, make an apology, beg pardon, say you are sorry

apology NOUN = <u>regret</u>, explanation, excuse, confession, extenuation ...*We received a letter of apology...*
PHRASES **apology for something** or **someone** = <u>mockery of</u>, excuse for, imitation of, caricature of, travesty of, poor substitute for ...*What an apology for a leader!...*

apostle 1 = <u>evangelist</u>, herald, missionary, preacher, messenger, proselytizer ...*the twelve apostles...*
2 = <u>supporter</u>, champion, advocate, pioneer, proponent, propagandist, propagator ...*They present themselves as apostles of free trade...*
➤ **the twelve disciples**

The Twelve Apostles

Andrew	Jude
Bartholomew	Matthew
James	Peter
James	Philip
John	Simon
Judas	Thomas

---

apotheosis = <u>deification</u>, elevation, exaltation, glorification, idealization, idolization

appal = <u>horrify</u>, shock, alarm, frighten, scare, terrify, outrage, disgust, dishearten, revolt, intimidate, dismay, daunt, sicken, astound, harrow, unnerve, petrify, scandalize, make your hair stand on end (*informal*)

appalled = <u>horrified</u>, shocked, stunned, alarmed, frightened, scared, terrified, outraged, dismayed, daunted, astounded, unnerved, disquieted, petrified, disheartened

appalling 1 = <u>horrifying</u>, shocking, terrible, alarming, frightening, scaring, awful, terrifying, horrible, grim, dreadful, intimidating, dismaying, horrific, fearful, daunting, dire, astounding, ghastly, hideous, shameful, harrowing, vile, unnerving, petrifying, horrid, unspeakable, frightful, nightmarish, abominable, disheartening, godawful (*slang*), hellacious (*U.S. slang*) ...*They have been living under the most appalling conditions*... OPPOSITE> reassuring
2 = <u>awful</u>, terrible, tremendous, distressing, horrible, dreadful, horrendous, ghastly, godawful (*slang*) ...*I've got the most appalling headache*...

apparatus 1 = <u>organization</u>, system, network, structure, bureaucracy, hierarchy, setup (*informal*), chain of command ...*a massive bureaucratic apparatus*...
2 = <u>equipment</u>, machine, tackle, gear, means, materials, device, tools, implements, mechanism, outfit, machinery, appliance, utensils, contraption (*informal*) ...*He was rescued by firemen wearing breathing apparatus*...

apparel (*Old-fashioned*) = <u>clothing</u>, dress, clothes, equipment, gear (*informal*), habit, outfit, costume, threads (*slang*), array (*poetic*), garments, robes, trappings, attire, garb, accoutrements, vestments, raiment (*archaic or poetic*), schmutter (*slang*), habiliments

apparent 1 = <u>seeming</u>, supposed, alleged, outward, exterior, superficial, ostensible, specious ...*I was a bit depressed by our apparent lack of progress*... OPPOSITE> actual
2 = <u>obvious</u>, marked, clear, plain, visible, bold, patent, evident, distinct, open, understandable, manifest, noticeable, blatant, conspicuous, overt, unmistakable, palpable, undeniable, discernible, salient, self-evident, indisputable, much in evidence, undisguised, unconcealed, indubitable, staring you in the face (*informal*), plain as the nose on your face ...*The presence of a star is already apparent in the early film*... OPPOSITE> unclear

apparently = <u>seemingly</u>, outwardly, ostensibly, speciously

apparition = <u>ghost</u>, spirit, shade (*literary*), phantom, spectre, spook (*informal*), wraith, chimera, revenant, visitant, eidolon

appeal VERB = <u>plead</u>, call, ask, apply, refer, request, sue, lobby, pray, beg, petition, solicit, implore, beseech, entreat, importune, adjure, supplicate ...*The UN has appealed for help from the international community*... OPPOSITE> refuse
NOUN 1 = <u>plea</u>, call, application, request, prayer, petition, overture, invocation, solicitation, entreaty, supplication, suit, cry from the heart, adjuration ...*The government issued a last-minute appeal to him to return*... OPPOSITE> refusal
2 = <u>attraction</u>, charm, fascination, charisma, beauty, attractiveness, allure, magnetism, enchantment, seductiveness, interestingness, engagingness, pleasingness ...*It was meant to give the party greater public appeal*... OPPOSITE> repulsiveness
PHRASES **appeal to someone** = <u>attract</u>, interest, draw, please, invite, engage, charm, fascinate, tempt, lure, entice, enchant, captivate, allure, bewitch ...*The idea appealed to him*...

appealing = <u>attractive</u>, inviting, engaging, charming, winning, desirable, endearing, alluring, winsome, prepossessing OPPOSITE> repellent

appear 1 = <u>seem</u>, be clear, be obvious, be evident, look (like *or* as if), be apparent, be plain, be manifest, be patent ...*It appears that some missiles have been moved*...
2 = <u>look (like</u> *or* <u>as if)</u>, seem, occur, look to be, come across as, strike you as ...*She did her best to appear more confident than she felt*...
3 = <u>come into view</u>, emerge, occur, attend, surface, come out, turn out, arise, turn up, be present, loom, show (*informal*), issue, develop, arrive, show up (*informal*), come to light, crop up (*informal*), materialize, come forth, come into sight, show your face ...*A woman appeared at the far end of the street*... OPPOSITE> disappear
4 = <u>come into being</u>, come out, be published, be developed, be created, be invented, become available, come into existence ...*a poem which appeared in his last collection of verse*...
5 = <u>perform</u>, play, act, enter, come on, take part, play a part, be exhibited, come onstage ...*She appeared in several of his plays*...

appearance 1 = <u>look</u>, face, form, air, figure, image, looks, bearing, aspect, manner, expression, demeanour, mien (*literary*) ...*He had the appearance of a college student*...
2 = <u>arrival</u>, appearing, presence, turning up, introduction, showing up (*informal*), emergence, advent ...*The sudden appearance of a few bags of rice could start a riot*...
3 = <u>impression</u>, air, front, image, illusion, guise, façade, pretence, veneer, semblance, outward show ...*They gave the appearance of being on both sides*...

appease 1 = <u>pacify</u>, satisfy, calm, soothe, quiet, placate, mollify, conciliate ...*The offer has not appeased separatists...* OPPOSITE anger
2 = <u>ease</u>, satisfy, calm, relieve, diminish, compose, quiet, blunt, soothe, subdue, lessen, alleviate, lull, quell, allay, mitigate, assuage, quench, tranquillize ...*Cash is on hand to appease mounting frustration...*

appeasement 1 = <u>pacification</u>, compromise, accommodation, concession, conciliation, acceding, propitiation, mollification, placation ...*He denies there is a policy of appeasement...*
2 = <u>easing</u>, relieving, satisfaction, softening, blunting, soothing, quieting, lessening, lulling, quelling, solace, quenching, mitigation, abatement, alleviation, assuagement, tranquillization ...*the appeasement of terror...*

appellation (*Formal*) = <u>name</u>, term, style, title, address, description, designation, epithet, sobriquet

append (*Formal*) = <u>add</u>, attach, join, hang, adjoin, fasten, annex, tag on, affix, tack on, subjoin OPPOSITE detach

appendage = <u>attachment</u>, addition, supplement, accessory, appendix, auxiliary, affix, ancillary, adjunct, annexe, addendum, appurtenance

appendix = <u>supplement</u>, add-on, postscript, adjunct, appendage, addendum, addition, codicil

appetite 1 = <u>hunger</u> ...*a slight fever, headache and loss of appetite...*
2 = <u>desire</u>, liking, longing, demand, taste, passion, stomach, hunger, willingness, relish, craving, yearning, inclination, zeal, zest, propensity, hankering, proclivity, appetence, appetency ...*our growing appetite for scandal...* OPPOSITE distaste

appetizer = <u>hors d'oeuvre</u>, titbit, antipasto, canapé

applaud 1 = <u>clap</u>, encourage, praise, cheer, hail, acclaim, laud, give (someone) a big hand ...*The audience laughed and applauded...* OPPOSITE boo
2 = <u>praise</u>, celebrate, approve, acclaim, compliment, salute, commend, extol, crack up (*informal*), big up (*slang, chiefly Caribbean*), eulogize ...*He should be applauded for his courage...* OPPOSITE criticize

applause = <u>ovation</u>, praise, cheering, cheers, approval, acclaim, clapping, accolade, big hand, commendation, hand-clapping, approbation, acclamation, eulogizing, plaudit

appliance = <u>device</u>, machine, tool, instrument, implement, mechanism, apparatus, gadget, waldo

applicable = <u>appropriate</u>, fitting, fit, suited, useful, suitable, relevant, to the point, apt, pertinent, befitting, apposite, apropos, germane, to the purpose OPPOSITE inappropriate

applicant = <u>candidate</u>, entrant, claimant, suitor, petitioner, aspirant, inquirer, job-seeker, suppliant, postulant

application 1 = <u>request</u>, claim, demand, appeal, suit, inquiry, plea, petition, requisition, solicitation ...*His application for membership was rejected...*
2 = <u>relevance</u>, use, value, practice, bearing, exercise, purpose, function, appropriateness, aptness, pertinence, appositeness, germaneness ...*Students

learned the practical application of the theory...*
3 = <u>effort</u>, work, study, industry, labour, trouble, attention, struggle, pains, commitment, hard work, endeavour, dedication, toil, diligence, perseverance, travail (*literary*), attentiveness, assiduity, blood, sweat, and tears (*informal*) ...*his immense talent and unremitting application...*

apply VERB **1** = <u>request</u>, seek, appeal, put in, petition, inquire, solicit, claim, sue, requisition, make application ...*I am continuing to apply for jobs...*
2 = <u>be relevant</u>, concern, relate, refer, be fitting, be appropriate, be significant, fit, suit, pertain, be applicable, bear upon, appertain ...*The rule applies where a person owns stock in a company...*
3 = <u>use</u>, exercise, carry out, employ, engage, implement, practise, execute, assign, administer, exert, enact, utilize, bring to bear, put to use, bring into play ...*The government appears to be applying the same principle...*
4 = <u>put on</u>, work in, cover with, lay on, paint on, anoint, spread on, rub in, smear on, shampoo in, bring into contact with ...*Applying the dye can be messy, particularly on long hair...*
PHRASES **apply yourself to something** = <u>work hard at</u>, concentrate on, study at, pay attention to, try at, commit yourself to, buckle down to (*informal*), be assiduous in, devote yourself to, be diligent in, dedicate yourself to, make an effort at, address yourself to, be industrious in, persevere at *or* with ...*He had applied himself to this task with considerable energy...*

appoint 1 = <u>assign</u>, name, choose, commission, select, elect, install, delegate, nominate ...*It made sense to appoint a banker to this job...* OPPOSITE fire
2 = <u>decide</u>, set, choose, establish, determine, settle, fix, arrange, specify, assign, designate, allot ...*We met at the time appointed...* OPPOSITE cancel

appointed 1 = <u>decided</u>, set, chosen, established, determined, settled, fixed, arranged, assigned, designated, allotted ...*The appointed hour for the ceremony was drawing near...*
2 = <u>assigned</u>, named, chosen, commissioned, selected, elected, installed, delegated, nominated ...*The recently appointed captain led by example in the first game...*
3 = <u>equipped</u>, provided, supplied, furnished, fitted out ...*beautiful, well-appointed houses...*

appointment 1 = <u>selection</u>, naming, election, choosing, choice, commissioning, delegation, nomination, installation, assignment, allotment, designation ...*his appointment as foreign minister in 1985...*
2 = <u>job</u>, office, position, post, situation, place, station, employment, assignment, berth (*informal*) ...*He is to take up an appointment as a researcher with the Society...*
3 = <u>meeting</u>, interview, date, session, arrangement, consultation, engagement, fixture, rendezvous, tryst (*archaic*), assignation ...*She has an appointment with her accountant...*
4 = <u>appointee</u>, candidate, representative, delegate,

nominee, office-holder ...*He is the new appointment at RSA*...

apportion = <u>divide</u>, share, deal, distribute, assign, allocate, dispense, give out, allot, mete out, dole out, measure out, parcel out, ration out

apposite = <u>appropriate</u>, fitting, suited, suitable, relevant, proper, to the point, apt, applicable, pertinent, befitting, apropos, germane, to the purpose, appertaining OPPOSITE> inappropriate

appraisal 1 = <u>assessment</u>, opinion, estimate, judgment, evaluation, estimation, sizing up (*informal*), recce (*slang*) ...*Self-appraisal is never easy*...
2 = <u>valuation</u>, pricing, rating, survey, reckoning, assay ...*He has resisted being drawn into the business of cost appraisal*...

appraise = <u>assess</u>, judge, review, estimate, survey, price, rate, value, evaluate, inspect, gauge, size up (*informal*), eye up, assay, recce (*slang*)

Word Power

appraise – *Appraise is sometimes used where apprise is meant: both patients had been fully apprised* (not *appraised*) *of the situation.* This may well be due to the fact that *appraise* is considerably more common, and that people therefore tend to associate this meaning mistakenly with a word they know better.

appreciable = <u>significant</u>, marked, obvious, considerable, substantial, visible, evident, pronounced, definite, noticeable, clear-cut, discernible, measurable, material, recognizable, detectable, perceptible, distinguishable, ascertainable, perceivable OPPOSITE> insignificant

appreciably = <u>significantly</u>, obviously, definitely, considerably, substantially, evidently, visibly, markedly, noticeably, palpably, perceptively, measurably, recognizably, discernibly, detectably, distinguishably, perceivably, ascertainably

appreciate 1 = <u>enjoy</u>, like, value, regard, respect, prize, admire, treasure, esteem, relish, cherish, savour, rate highly ...*Anyone can appreciate our music*... OPPOSITE> scorn
2 = <u>be aware of</u>, know, understand, estimate, realize, acknowledge, recognize, perceive, comprehend, take account of, be sensitive to, be conscious of, sympathize with, be alive to, be cognizant of ...*She never really appreciated the depth of the conflict*... OPPOSITE> be unaware of
3 = <u>be grateful</u>, be obliged, be thankful, give thanks, be indebted, be in debt, be appreciative ...*I'd appreciate it if you didn't mention that*... OPPOSITE> be ungrateful for
4 = <u>increase</u>, rise, grow, gain, improve, mount, enhance, soar, inflate ...*There is little confidence that houses will appreciate in value*... OPPOSITE> fall

appreciation 1 = <u>admiration</u>, liking, respect, assessment, esteem, relish, valuation, enjoyment, appraisal, estimation, responsiveness ...*He whistled in appreciation*...
2 = <u>gratitude</u>, thanks, recognition, obligation, acknowledgment, indebtedness, thankfulness, gratefulness ...*the gifts presented to them in appreciation of their work*... OPPOSITE> ingratitude
3 = <u>awareness</u>, understanding, regard, knowledge, recognition, perception, sympathy, consciousness, sensitivity, realization, comprehension, familiarity, mindfulness, cognizance ...*They have a strong appreciation of the importance of economic incentives*... OPPOSITE> ignorance
4 = <u>increase</u>, rise, gain, growth, inflation, improvement, escalation, enhancement ...*You have to take capital appreciation of the property into account*... OPPOSITE> fall
5 = <u>review</u>, report, notice, analysis, criticism, praise, assessment, recognition, tribute, evaluation, critique, acclamation ...*I had written an appreciation of his work for a magazine*...

appreciative 1 = <u>enthusiastic</u>, understanding, pleased, aware, sensitive, conscious, admiring, sympathetic, supportive, responsive, knowledgeable, respectful, mindful, perceptive, in the know (*informal*), cognizant, regardful ...*There is a murmur of appreciative laughter*...
2 = <u>grateful</u>, obliged, thankful, indebted, beholden ...*We are very appreciative of their support*...

apprehend 1 = <u>arrest</u>, catch, lift (*slang*), nick (*slang, chiefly Brit.*), capture, seize, run in (*slang*), take, nail (*informal*), bust (*informal*), collar (*informal*), pinch (*informal*), nab (*informal*), take prisoner, feel your collar (*slang*) ...*Police have not apprehended her killer*... OPPOSITE> release
2 = <u>understand</u>, know, think, believe, imagine, realize, recognize, appreciate, perceive, grasp, conceive, comprehend, get the message, get the picture ...*Only now can I begin to apprehend the power of these forces*... OPPOSITE> be unaware of

apprehension 1 = <u>anxiety</u>, concern, fear, worry, doubt, alarm, suspicion, dread, unease, mistrust, misgiving, disquiet, premonition, trepidation, foreboding, uneasiness, pins and needles, apprehensiveness ...*It reflects real anger and apprehension about the future*... OPPOSITE> confidence
2 = <u>arrest</u>, catching, capture, taking, seizure ...*information leading to the apprehension of the alleged killer*... OPPOSITE> release
3 = <u>awareness</u>, understanding, knowledge, intelligence, ken, perception, grasp, comprehension ...*the sudden apprehension of something*... OPPOSITE> incomprehension

apprehensive = <u>anxious</u>, concerned, worried, afraid, alarmed, nervous, suspicious, doubtful, uneasy, fearful, neurotic, disquieted, foreboding, twitchy (*informal*), mistrustful, antsy (*informal*) OPPOSITE> confident

apprentice = <u>trainee</u>, student, pupil, novice, beginner, learner, neophyte, tyro, probationer OPPOSITE> master

apprenticeship = <u>traineeship</u>, probation, studentship, novitiate *or* noviciate

apprise = <u>make aware</u>, tell, warn, advise, inform, communicate, notify, enlighten, acquaint, give notice, make cognizant
➤ **appraise**

approach VERB **1** = <u>move towards</u>, come to, reach, near, advance, catch up, meet, come close, gain on, converge on, come near, push forward, draw near, creep up on ...*When I approached they fell silent*...
2 = <u>make a proposal to</u>, speak to, apply to, appeal to, proposition, solicit, sound out, make overtures to, make advances to, broach the matter with ...*When he approached me about the job, my first reaction was disbelief*...
3 = <u>set about</u>, tackle, undertake, embark on, get down to, launch into, begin work on, commence on, make a start on, enter upon ...*The bank has approached the issue in a practical way*...
4 = <u>approximate</u>, touch, be like, compare with, resemble, come close to, border on, verge on, be comparable to, come near to ...*They race at speeds approaching 200mph*...
NOUN **1** = <u>advance</u>, coming, nearing, appearance, arrival, advent, drawing near ...*At their approach the little boy ran away and hid*...
2 = <u>access</u>, way, drive, road, passage, entrance, avenue, passageway ...*The path serves as an approach to the boat house*...
3 *often plural* = <u>proposal</u>, offer, appeal, advance, application, invitation, proposition, overture ...*There had already been approaches from interested buyers*...
4 = <u>way</u>, means, course, style, attitude, method, technique, manner, procedure, mode, modus operandi ...*We will be exploring different approaches to information-gathering*...
5 = <u>approximation</u>, likeness, semblance ...*the nearest approach to an apology we have so far heard*...

approachable 1 = <u>friendly</u>, open, cordial, sociable, affable, congenial ...*We found him very approachable and easy to talk to*... OPPOSITE⟩ unfriendly
2 = <u>accessible</u>, attainable, reachable, get-at-able (*informal*), come-at-able (*informal*) ...*It is approachable on foot for only a few hours a day*... OPPOSITE⟩ inaccessible

appropriate ADJECTIVE = <u>suitable</u>, right, fitting, fit, suited, correct, belonging, relevant, proper, to the point, in keeping, apt, applicable, pertinent, befitting, well-suited, well-timed, apposite, apropos, opportune, becoming, seemly, felicitous, germane, to the purpose, appurtenant, congruous ...*It is appropriate that Irish names dominate the list*... OPPOSITE⟩ unsuitable
VERB **1** = <u>seize</u>, take, claim, assume, take over, acquire, confiscate, annex, usurp, impound, pre-empt, commandeer, take possession of, expropriate, arrogate ...*Several other newspapers have appropriated the idea*... OPPOSITE⟩ relinquish
2 = <u>allocate</u>, allow, budget, devote, assign, designate, set aside, earmark, allot, share out, apportion ...*He is sceptical that Congress will appropriate more money for this*... OPPOSITE⟩ withhold
3 = <u>steal</u>, take, nick (*slang, chiefly Brit.*), pocket, pinch

(*informal*), pirate, poach, swipe (*slang*), lift (*informal*), heist (*U.S. slang*), embezzle, blag (*slang*), pilfer, misappropriate, snitch (*slang*), purloin, filch, plagiarize, thieve, peculate ...*What do they think about your appropriating their music and culture?*...

appropriateness = <u>suitability</u>, fitness, relevance, correctness, felicity, rightness, applicability, timeliness, aptness, pertinence, fittingness, seemliness, appositeness, properness, germaneness, opportuneness, becomingness, congruousness, felicitousness, well-suitedness

appropriation 1 = <u>setting aside</u>, assignment, allocation, earmarking, allotment, apportionment ...*The government raised defence appropriations by 12 per cent*...
2 = <u>seizure</u>, taking, takeover, assumption, annexation, confiscation, commandeering, expropriation, pre-emption, usurpation, impoundment, arrogation ...*fraud and illegal appropriation of land*...

approval 1 = <u>consent</u>, agreement, sanction, licence, blessing, permission, recommendation, concession, confirmation, mandate, endorsement, leave, compliance, the go-ahead (*informal*), countenance, ratification, the green light, assent, authorization, validation, acquiescence, imprimatur, concurrence, O.K. *or* okay (*informal*) ...*The proposed modifications met with widespread approval*...
2 = <u>favour</u>, liking, regard, respect, praise, esteem, acclaim, appreciation, encouragement, admiration, applause, commendation, approbation, good opinion ...*an obsessive drive to win his father's approval*... OPPOSITE⟩ disapproval

approve VERB = <u>agree to</u>, second, allow, pass, accept, confirm, recommend, permit, sanction, advocate, bless, endorse, uphold, mandate, authorize, ratify, go along with, subscribe to, consent to, buy into (*informal*), validate, countenance, rubber stamp, accede to, give the go-ahead to (*informal*), give the green light to, assent to, concur in, O.K. *or* okay (*informal*) ...*MPs approved the bill by a majority of 97*... OPPOSITE⟩ veto
PHRASES **approve of something** *or* **someone** = <u>favour</u>, like, support, respect, praise, appreciate, agree with, admire, endorse, esteem, acclaim, applaud, commend, be pleased with, have a good opinion of, regard highly, think highly of ...*Not everyone approves of the festival*...

approving = <u>favourable</u>, admiring, applauding, respectful, appreciative, commendatory, acclamatory

approximate ADJECTIVE = <u>rough</u>, close, general, near, estimated, loose, vague, hazy, sketchy, amorphous, imprecise, inexact, almost exact, almost accurate ...*The times are approximate only*... OPPOSITE⟩ exact
VERB = <u>resemble</u>, reach, approach, touch, come close to, border on, come near, verge on ...*Something approximating a just outcome will be ensured*...

approximately = <u>almost</u>, about, around, generally, nearly, close to, relatively, roughly, loosely, just about, more or less, in the region of, in the vicinity of, not far off, in the neighbourhood of

approximation 1 = likeness, approach, correspondence, resemblance, semblance …*That's a fair approximation of the way the next boss will be chosen…*
2 = guess, estimate, conjecture, estimation, guesswork, rough idea, rough calculation, ballpark figure (*informal*), ballpark estimate (*informal*) …*That's an approximation, but my guess is there'll be a reasonable balance…*

a priori = deduced, deductive, inferential

apron = pinny, overall, pinafore (*informal*)

apropos PREPOSITION = concerning, about, re, regarding, respecting, on the subject of, in respect of, as to, with reference to, in re, in the matter of, as regards, in *or* with regard to …*All my suggestions apropos the script were accepted…*
ADJECTIVE = appropriate, right, seemly, fitting, fit, related, correct, belonging, suitable, relevant, proper, to the point, apt, applicable, pertinent, befitting, apposite, opportune, germane, to the purpose …*It was a verse from the book of Job. Very apropos…*

apt 1 = appropriate, timely, right, seemly, fitting, fit, related, correct, belonging, suitable, relevant, proper, to the point, applicable, pertinent, befitting, apposite, apropos, opportune, germane, to the purpose …*The words of this report are as apt today as they were in 1929…* OPPOSITE inappropriate
2 = inclined, likely, ready, disposed, prone, liable, given, predisposed, of a mind …*She was apt to raise her voice and wave her hands about…*
3 = gifted, skilled, expert, quick, bright, talented, sharp, capable, smart, prompt, clever, intelligent, accomplished, ingenious, skilful, astute, adroit, teachable …*She was never a very apt student…* OPPOSITE slow

aptitude = gift, ability, talent, capacity, intelligence, leaning, bent, tendency, faculty, capability, flair, inclination, disposition, knack, propensity, proficiency, predilection, cleverness, proclivity, quickness, giftedness, proneness, aptness

arable = productive, fertile, fruitful, fecund, cultivable, farmable, ploughable, tillable

arbiter 1 = judge, referee, umpire, arbitrator, adjudicator …*the court's role as arbiter in the law-making process…*
2 = authority, expert, master, governor, ruler, dictator, controller, lord, pundit …*Sequins have often aroused the scorn of arbiters of taste…*

arbitrary 1 = random, chance, optional, subjective, unreasonable, inconsistent, erratic, discretionary, personal, fanciful, wilful, whimsical, capricious …*Arbitrary arrests were common…* OPPOSITE logical
2 = dictatorial, absolute, unlimited, uncontrolled, autocratic, dogmatic, imperious, domineering, unrestrained, overbearing, tyrannical, summary, magisterial, despotic, high-handed, peremptory, tyrannous …*the virtually unlimited arbitrary power of slave owners…*

arbitrate = decide, judge, determine, settle, referee, umpire, mediate, adjudicate, adjudge, pass judgment, sit in judgment

arbitration = decision, settlement, judgment, determination, adjudication, arbitrament

arbitrator = judge, referee, umpire, arbiter, adjudicator

arc = curve, bend, bow, arch, crescent, half-moon

arcade = gallery, mall, cloister, portico, colonnade, covered walk, peristyle

arcane = mysterious, secret, hidden, esoteric, occult, recondite, cabbalistic

arch¹ NOUN 1 = archway, curve, dome, span, vault …*The theatre is located under old railway arches in the East End…*
2 = curve, bend, bow, crook, arc, hunch, sweep, hump, curvature, semicircle …*Train the cane supports to form an arch…*
VERB = curve, bridge, bend, bow, span, arc …*the domed ceiling arching overhead…*

arch² = playful, joking, teasing, humorous, sly, mischievous, saucy, tongue-in-cheek, jesting, jokey, pert, good-natured, roguish, frolicsome, waggish …*a slighty amused, arch expression…*

archaic 1 = old, ancient, antique, primitive, bygone, olden (*archaic*) …*archaic sculpture and porcelain…* OPPOSITE modern
2 = old-fashioned, obsolete, out of date, antiquated, outmoded, passé, old hat, behind the times, superannuated …*These archaic practices are advocated by people of limited outlook…* OPPOSITE up-to-date

arched = curved, domed, vaulted

archer = bowman (*archaic*), toxophilite (*formal*)

archetypal *or* **archetypical** = typical, standard, model, original, normal, classic, ideal, exemplary, paradigmatic, prototypal, prototypic *or* prototypical

archetype = prime example, standard, model, original, pattern, classic, ideal, norm, form, prototype, paradigm, exemplar

architect 1 = designer, planner, draughtsman, master builder …*Employ an architect to make sure the plans comply with regulations…*
2 = creator, father, shaper, engineer, author, maker, designer, founder, deviser, planner, inventor, contriver, originator, prime mover, instigator, initiator …*the country's chief architect of economic reform…*

architecture 1 = design, planning, building, construction, architectonics …*He studied architecture and design at college…*
2 = construction, design, style …*a fine example of Moroccan architecture…*
3 = structure, design, shape, make-up, construction, framework, layout, anatomy …*the architecture of muscle fibres…*
➤ **architectural styles**

archive NOUN = record office, museum, registry, repository …*I decided I would go to the archive and look up the issue…*
PLURAL NOUN = records, papers, accounts, rolls, documents, files, registers, deeds, chronicles, annals

Architectural styles http://www.greatbuildings.com/

Art Deco	Early Christian	Jacobean	postmodernist
Art Nouveau	Early English	Louis Quatorze	Queen-Anne
Baroque	Edwardian	Louis Quinze	Regency
Bauhaus	Elizabethan	Louis Seize	Renaissance
brutalist	Empire	Louis Treize	Rococo
Byzantine	Federation	Mannerist	Roman
churrigueresque *or*	functionalism	moderne	Romanesque
churrigueresco	Georgian	Moorish *or* Morisco	Saracen
classical	Gothic	Mudéjar	Saxon
colonial	Gothic Revival	neoclassicist	transition *or* transitional
Composite	Greek Revival	new brutalist	Tudor
Corinthian	International Style *or*	Norman	Tuscan
Decorated	Modernist	Palladian	Victorian
Doric	Ionic	perpendicular	

…the archives of the Imperial War Museum…

arctic (*Informal*) = freezing, cold, frozen, icy, chilly, frosty, glacial, frigid, gelid, frost-bound, cold as ice

Arctic = polar, far-northern, hyperborean

ardent 1 = enthusiastic, keen, eager, avid, zealous, keen as mustard …*an ardent opponent of the war…* OPPOSITE indifferent

2 = passionate, warm, spirited, intense, flaming, fierce, fiery, hot, fervent, impassioned, ablaze, lusty, vehement, amorous, hot-blooded, warm-blooded, fervid …*an ardent lover…* OPPOSITE cold

ardour 1 = passion, feeling, fire, heat, spirit, intensity, warmth, devotion, fervour, vehemence, fierceness …*the sexual ardour had cooled…*

2 = enthusiasm, zeal, eagerness, earnestness, keenness, avidity …*my ardour for football…*

arduous = difficult, trying, hard, tough, tiring, severe, painful, exhausting, punishing, harsh, taxing, heavy, steep, formidable, fatiguing, rigorous, troublesome, gruelling, strenuous, onerous, laborious, burdensome, backbreaking, toilsome OPPOSITE easy

area 1 = region, land, quarter, division, sector, district, stretch, territory, zone, plot, province, patch, neighbourhood, sphere, turf (*U.S. slang*), realm, domain, tract, locality, neck of the woods (*informal*) …*the large number of community groups in the area…*

2 = part, section, sector, portion …*You will notice that your baby has two soft areas on its head…*

3 = range, reach, size, sweep, extent, scope, sphere, domain, width, compass, breadth, parameters (*informal*), latitude, expanse, radius, ambit …*Although large in area, the flat did not have many rooms…*

4 = realm, part, department, field, province, arena, sphere, domain …*She wanted to be involved in every area of my life…*

arena 1 = ring, ground, stage, field, theatre, bowl, pitch, stadium, enclosure, park (*U.S. & Canad.*), coliseum, amphitheatre …*the largest indoor sports arena in the world…*

2 = scene, world, area, stage, field, theatre, sector, territory, province, forum, scope, sphere, realm, domain …*He has no intention of withdrawing from the political arena…*

arguably = possibly, potentially, conceivably, plausibly, feasibly, questionably, debatably, deniably, disputably, contestably, controvertibly, dubitably, refutably

argue VERB 1 = quarrel, fight, row, clash, dispute, disagree, feud, squabble, spar, wrangle, bicker, have an argument, cross swords, be at sixes and sevens, fight like cat and dog, go at it hammer and tongs, bandy words, altercate …*They were still arguing. I could hear them down the road…*

2 = discuss, debate, dispute, thrash out, exchange views on, controvert …*The two of them were arguing this point…*

3 = claim, question, reason, challenge, insist, maintain, hold, allege, plead, assert, contend, uphold, profess, remonstrate, expostulate …*His lawyers are arguing that he is unfit to stand trial…*

4 = demonstrate, show, suggest, display, indicate, imply, exhibit, denote, evince …*I'd like to argue In a framework that is less exaggerated…*

PHRASES **argue someone into something** = persuade someone to, convince someone to, talk someone into, prevail upon someone to, talk someone round to …*Eventually they argued me into going…*

argument 1 = reason, case, reasoning, ground(s), defence, excuse, logic, justification, rationale, polemic, dialectic, line of reasoning, argumentation …*There's a strong argument for lowering the price…*

2 = debate, questioning, claim, row, discussion, dispute, controversy, pleading, plea, contention, assertion, polemic, altercation, remonstrance, expostulation, remonstration …*The issue has caused heated political argument…*

3 = quarrel, fight, row, clash, dispute, controversy, disagreement, misunderstanding, feud, barney (*informal*), squabble, wrangle, bickering, difference of opinion, tiff, altercation …*She got into a heated argument with a stranger…* OPPOSITE agreement

argumentative = quarrelsome, contrary, contentious, belligerent, combative, opinionated, litigious, disputatious OPPOSITE easy-going

arid 1 = dry, desert, dried up, barren, sterile, torrid, parched, waterless, moistureless …*the arid zones of the country…* OPPOSITE lush

2 = boring, dull, tedious, dreary, dry, tiresome, lifeless,

colourless, uninteresting, flat, uninspired, vapid, spiritless, jejune, as dry as dust …*She had given him the only joy his arid life had ever known*… OPPOSITE> exciting

arise 1 = <u>happen</u>, start, begin, follow, issue, result, appear, develop, emerge, occur, spring, set in, stem, originate, ensue, come about, commence, come to light, emanate, crop up (*informal*), come into being, materialize …*if a problem arises later in pregnancy*… 2 (*Old-fashioned*) = <u>get to your feet</u>, get up, rise, stand up, spring up, leap up …*I arose from the chair and left*…
3 = <u>get up</u>, wake up, awaken, get out of bed …*He arose at 6:30 a.m. as usual*…
4 = <u>ascend</u>, rise, lift, mount, climb, tower, soar, move upward …*the flat terrace, from which arises the volume of the house*…

aristocracy = <u>upper class</u>, elite, nobility, gentry, peerage, ruling class, patricians, upper crust (*informal*), noblesse (*literary*), haut monde (*French*), patriciate, body of nobles OPPOSITE> commoners

aristocrat = <u>noble</u>, lord, lady, peer, patrician, grandee, nobleman, aristo (*informal*), childe (*archaic*), noblewoman, peeress

aristocratic 1 = <u>upper-class</u>, lordly, titled, gentle (*archaic*), elite, gentlemanly, noble, patrician, blue-blooded, well-born, highborn …*a wealthy, aristocratic family*… OPPOSITE> common
2 = <u>refined</u>, fine, polished, elegant, stylish, dignified, haughty, courtly, snobbish, well-bred …*He laughed it off with aristocratic indifference*… OPPOSITE> vulgar

arm¹ 1 = <u>upper limb</u>, limb, appendage …*She stretched her arms out*…
2 = <u>branch</u>, part, office, department, division, section, wing, sector, extension, detachment, offshoot, subdivision, subsection …*the research arm of Congress*…
3 = <u>authority</u>, might, force, power, strength, command, sway, potency …*Local people say the long arm of the law was too heavy-handed*…

arm² VERB 1 = <u>equip</u>, provide, supply, outfit, rig, array, furnish, issue with, deck out, accoutre …*She had armed herself with a loaded rifle*…
2 = <u>provide</u>, prime, prepare, protect, guard, strengthen, outfit, equip, brace, fortify, forearm, make ready, gird your loins …*She armed herself with all the knowledge she could gather*…
PLURAL NOUN = <u>weapons</u>, guns, firearms, weaponry, armaments, ordnance, munitions, instruments of war …*The organization has an extensive supply of arms*…

armada = <u>fleet</u>, navy, squadron, flotilla

armaments = <u>weapons</u>, arms, guns, ammunition, weaponry, ordnance, munitions, materiel

armed = <u>carrying weapons</u>, provided, prepared, supplied, ready, protected, guarded, strengthened, equipped, primed, arrayed, furnished, fortified, in arms, forearmed, fitted out, under arms, girded, rigged out, tooled up (*slang*), accoutred

armistice = <u>truce</u>, peace, ceasefire, suspension of hostilities

armour = <u>protection</u>, covering, shield, sheathing, armour plate, chain mail, protective covering

armoured = <u>protected</u>, mailed, reinforced, toughened, bulletproof, armour-plated, steel-plated, ironclad, bombproof

armoury or (*U.S.*) **armory** = <u>arsenal</u>, magazine, ammunition dump, arms depot, ordnance depot

army 1 = <u>soldiers</u>, military, troops, armed force, legions, infantry, military force, land forces, land force, soldiery …*After returning from abroad, he joined the army*…
2 = <u>vast number</u>, host, gang, mob, flock, array, legion, swarm, sea, pack, horde, multitude, throng …*data collected by an army of volunteers*…

aroma = <u>scent</u>, smell, perfume, fragrance, bouquet, savour, odour, redolence

aromatic = <u>fragrant</u>, perfumed, spicy, savoury, pungent, balmy, redolent, sweet-smelling, sweet-scented, odoriferous OPPOSITE> smelly

around PREPOSITION 1 = <u>surrounding</u>, about, enclosing, encompassing, framing, encircling, on all sides of, on every side of, environing …*a prosperous suburb built around a new mosque*…
2 = <u>approximately</u>, about, nearly, close to, roughly, just about, in the region of, circa (*used with dates*), in the vicinity of, not far off, in the neighbourhood of …*My salary was around £19,000*…
ADVERB 1 = <u>everywhere</u>, about, throughout, all over, here and there, on all sides, in all directions, to and fro …*What are you doing following me around?*…
2 = <u>near</u>, close, nearby, handy, at hand, close by, close at hand …*It's important to have lots of people around*…

(*Related Words*)

prefix: circum-

Word Power

around – In American English, *around* is used more often than *round* as an adverbial and preposition, except in a few fixed phrases such as *all year round*. In British English, *round* is more commonly used as an adverb than *around*.

---

arousal = <u>stimulation</u>, movement, response, reaction, excitement, animation, stirring up, provocation, inflammation, agitation, exhilaration, incitement, enlivenment

arouse 1 = <u>stimulate</u>, encourage, inspire, prompt, spark, spur, foster, provoke, rouse, stir up, inflame, incite, instigate, whip up, summon up, whet, kindle, foment, call forth …*His work has aroused intense interest*… OPPOSITE> quell
2 = <u>inflame</u>, move, warm, excite, spur, provoke, animate, prod, stir up, agitate, quicken, enliven, goad, foment …*He apologized, saying this subject always aroused him*…
3 = <u>awaken</u>, wake up, rouse, waken …*We were aroused from our sleep by a knocking at the door*…

arraign = <u>accuse</u>, charge, prosecute, denounce,

indict, impeach, incriminate, call to account, take to task

arrange 1 = <u>plan</u>, agree, prepare, determine, schedule, organize, construct, devise, contrive, fix up …*She arranged an appointment for Friday afternoon…*
2 = <u>put in order</u>, group, form, order, sort, class, position, range, file, rank, line up, organize, set out, sequence, exhibit, sort out (*informal*), array, classify, tidy, marshal, align, categorize, systematize …*He started to arrange the books in piles…* OPPOSITE> disorganize
3 = <u>adapt</u>, score, orchestrate, harmonize, instrument …*The songs were arranged by a well-known pianist…*

arrangement 1 *often plural* = <u>plan</u>, planning, provision, preparation …*I am in charge of all the travel arrangements…*
2 = <u>agreement</u>, contract, settlement, appointment, compromise, deal (*informal*), pact, compact, covenant …*The caves can be visited only by prior arrangement…*
3 = <u>display</u>, grouping, system, order, ordering, design, ranging, structure, rank, organization, exhibition, line up, presentation, array, marshalling, classification, disposition, alignment, setup (*informal*) …*an imaginative flower arrangement…*
4 = <u>adaptation</u>, score, version, interpretation, instrumentation, orchestration, harmonization …*an arrangement of a well-known piece by Mozart…*

array NOUN 1 = <u>arrangement</u>, show, order, supply, display, collection, exhibition, line-up, mixture, parade, formation, presentation, spectacle, marshalling, muster, disposition …*the markets with their wonderful arrays of fruit and vegetables…*
2 (*Poetic*) = <u>clothing</u>, dress, clothes, threads (*slang*), garments, apparel, attire, garb, finery, regalia, raiment (*archaic or poetic*), schmutter (*slang*) …*Bathed, dressed in his finest array, he was ready…*
VERB 1 = arrange, show, group, order, present, range, display, line up, sequence, parade, exhibit, unveil, dispose, draw up, marshal, lay out, muster, align, form up, place in order, set in line (*Military*) …*Here are arrayed such 20th century relics as Madonna's bustier…*
2 = <u>dress</u>, supply, clothe, wrap, deck, outfit, decorate, equip, robe, get ready, adorn, apparel (*archaic*), festoon, attire, fit out, garb, bedeck, caparison, accoutre …*a priest arrayed in white vestments…*

arrest VERB 1 = <u>capture</u>, catch, lift (*slang*), nick (*slang, chiefly Brit.*), seize, run in (*slang*), nail (*informal*), bust (*informal*), collar (*informal*), take, detain, pinch (*informal*), nab (*informal*), apprehend, take prisoner, take into custody, lay hold of …*Seven people were arrested for minor offences…* OPPOSITE> release
2 = <u>stop</u>, end, hold, limit, check, block, slow, delay, halt, stall, stay, interrupt, suppress, restrain, hamper, inhibit, hinder, obstruct, retard, impede …*The new rules could arrest the development of good research…* OPPOSITE> speed up
3 = <u>fascinate</u>, hold, involve, catch, occupy, engage, grip, absorb, entrance, intrigue, rivet, enthral, mesmerize, engross, spellbind …*As he reached the hall, he saw what had arrested her…*
NOUN 1 = <u>capture</u>, bust (*informal*), detention, seizure,

apprehension …*information leading to the arrest of the bombers…* OPPOSITE> release
2 = <u>stoppage</u>, halt, suppression, obstruction, inhibition, blockage, hindrance …*a cardiac arrest…* OPPOSITE> acceleration

arresting = <u>striking</u>, surprising, engaging, dramatic, stunning, impressive, extraordinary, outstanding, remarkable, noticeable, conspicuous, salient, jaw-dropping OPPOSITE> unremarkable

arrival 1 = <u>appearance</u>, coming, arriving, entrance, advent, materialization …*the day after his arrival…*
2 = <u>coming</u>, happening, taking place, dawn, emergence, occurrence, materialization …*They celebrated the arrival of the New Year…*
3 = <u>newcomer</u>, arriver, incomer, visitor, caller, entrant, comer, visitant …*A high proportion of the new arrivals are skilled professionals…*

arrive VERB 1 = <u>come</u>, appear, enter, turn up, show up (*informal*), materialize, draw near …*Fresh groups of guests arrived…* OPPOSITE> depart
2 = <u>occur</u>, happen, take place, ensue, transpire, fall, befall …*They needed to be much further forward before winter arrived…*
3 (*Informal*) = <u>succeed</u>, make it (*informal*), triumph, do well, thrive, flourish, be successful, make good, prosper, cut it (*informal*), reach the top, become famous, make the grade (*informal*), get to the top, crack it (*informal*), hit the jackpot (*informal*), turn out well, make your mark (*informal*), achieve recognition, do all right for yourself (*informal*) …*These are cars which show you've arrived…*
PHRASES **arrive at something** = <u>reach</u>, make, get to, enter, land at, get as far as …*She arrived at the airport early this morning…*

arrogance = <u>conceit</u>, pride, swagger, pretension, presumption, bluster, hubris, pomposity, insolence, hauteur, pretentiousness, high-handedness, haughtiness, loftiness, imperiousness, pompousness, superciliousness, lordliness, conceitedness, contemptuousness, scornfulness, uppishness (*Brit. informal*), disdainfulness, overweeningness OPPOSITE> modesty

arrogant = <u>conceited</u>, lordly, assuming, proud, swaggering, pompous, pretentious, stuck up (*informal*), cocky, contemptuous, blustering, imperious, overbearing, haughty, scornful, puffed up, egotistical, disdainful, self-important, presumptuous, high-handed, insolent, supercilious, high and mighty (*informal*), overweening, immodest, swollen-headed, bigheaded (*informal*), uppish (*Brit. informal*) OPPOSITE> modest

arrow 1 = <u>dart</u>, flight, reed (*archaic*), bolt, shaft (*archaic*), quarrel …*warriors armed with bows and arrows…*
2 = <u>pointer</u>, indicator, marker …*A series of arrows point the way to his grave…*

arsenal = <u>armoury</u>, stock, supply, store, magazine, stockpile, storehouse, ammunition dump, arms depot, ordnance depot

art 1 = <u>artwork</u>, style of art, fine art, creativity …*the*

Art styles and movements

abstract expressionism	cubism	modernism	Pre-Raphaelite
abstractionism	Dada *or* Dadaism	Nabis	realism
Art Deco	De Stijl	naturalism	rococo
Arte Povera	divisionism	Nazarene	Romanesque
Art Nouveau	expressionism	neoclassicism	romanticism
Barbizon School	Fauvism	neoimpressionism	Suprematism
baroque	futurism	neoplasticism	surrealism
Der Blaue Reiter	Gothic	op art	symbolism
Brücke	Impressionism	pointillism	synthetism
classicism	Jugendstil	pop art	ukiyo-e
conceptual art	mannerism	postimpressionism	vorticism
constructivism	minimal art	postmodernism	

first exhibition of such art in the West…

2 = <u>skill</u>, knowledge, method, facility, craft, profession, expertise, competence, accomplishment, mastery, knack, ingenuity, finesse, aptitude, artistry, artifice (*archaic*), virtuosity, dexterity, cleverness, adroitness …*the art of seduction and romance…*

➤ **art styles and movements**

artful 1 = <u>cunning</u>, designing, scheming, sharp, smart, clever, subtle, intriguing, tricky, shrewd, sly, wily, politic, crafty, foxy, deceitful …*the smiles and artifices of a subtly artful woman…* OPPOSITE> straightforward

2 = <u>skilful</u>, masterly, smart, clever, subtle, ingenious, adept, resourceful, proficient, adroit, dexterous …*There is also an artful contrast of shapes…* OPPOSITE> clumsy

Arthurian

Arthurian Legend

http://www.arthuriana.co.uk/
http://members.cox.net/academia/labelle.html

Characters in Arthurian legend

Arthur	Launfal
Bedivere	Merlin
Bors	Modred
Caradoc	Morgan Le Fay
Elaine	Nimue
Galahad	Parsifal *or* Perceval
Gareth (of Orkney)	Tristan *or* Tristram
Gawain *or* Gawayne	Uther Pendragon
Igraine	Viviane *or* the Lady of
Lancelot *or* Launcelot	the Lake
du Lac	

Places in Arthurian legend

Astolat	Glastonbury
Avalon	Lyonnesse
Camelot	Tintagel

article 1 = <u>feature</u>, story, paper, piece, item, creation, essay, composition, discourse, treatise …*a newspaper article…*

2 = <u>thing</u>, piece, unit, item, object, device, tool, implement, commodity, gadget, utensil …*household articles…*

3 = <u>clause</u>, point, part, heading, head, matter, detail, piece, particular, division, section, item, passage, portion, paragraph, proviso …*article 50 of the UN charter…*

articulate ADJECTIVE = <u>expressive</u>, clear, effective, vocal, meaningful, understandable, coherent, persuasive, fluent, eloquent, lucid, comprehensible, communicative, intelligible …*She is an articulate young woman…* OPPOSITE> incoherent

VERB **1** = <u>express</u>, say, tell, state, word, speak, declare, phrase, communicate, assert, pronounce, utter, couch, put across, enunciate, put into words, verbalize, asseverate …*He failed to articulate an overall vision…*

2 = <u>pronounce</u>, say, talk, speak, voice, utter, enunciate, vocalize, enounce …*He articulated each syllable…*

articulation 1 = <u>expression</u>, delivery, pronunciation, saying, talking, voicing, speaking, utterance, diction, enunciation, vocalization, verbalization …*an actor able to sustain clear articulation over long periods…*

2 = <u>voicing</u>, statement, expression, verbalization …*a way of restricting their articulation of grievances…*

3 = <u>joint</u>, coupling, jointing, connection, hinge, juncture …*The articulation of different modes of production…*

artifice 1 = <u>cunning</u>, scheming, trick, device, craft, tactic, manoeuvre, deception, hoax, expedient, ruse, guile, trickery, duplicity, subterfuge, stratagem, contrivance, chicanery, wile, craftiness, artfulness, slyness, machination …*His photographs are full of artifice…*

2 = <u>cleverness</u>, skill, facility, invention, ingenuity, finesse, inventiveness, deftness, adroitness …*a combination of theatrical artifice and dazzling cinematic movement…*

artificial 1 = <u>synthetic</u>, manufactured, plastic, man-made, non-natural …*free from artificial additives and flavours…*

2 = <u>insincere</u>, forced, affected, assumed, phoney *or* phony (*informal*), put on, false, pretended, hollow, contrived, unnatural, feigned, spurious, meretricious …*The voice was affected, the accent artificial…* OPPOSITE> genuine

3 = <u>fake</u>, mock, imitation, bogus, simulated, phoney *or* phony (*informal*), sham, pseudo (*informal*), fabricated, counterfeit, spurious, ersatz, specious …*The sauce was glutinous and tasted artificial…* OPPOSITE> authentic

artillery = <u>big guns</u>, battery, cannon, ordnance, gunnery, cannonry

artisan = <u>craftsman</u>, technician, mechanic,

journeyman, artificer, handicraftsman, skilled workman

artist = <u>creator</u>, master, maker, craftsman, artisan (*obsolete*), fine artist

➤ **WORD POWER SUPPLEMENT artists**

artiste = <u>performer</u>, player, entertainer, Thespian, trouper, play-actor

artistic 1 = <u>creative</u>, cultured, original, sensitive, sophisticated, refined, imaginative, aesthetic, discerning, eloquent, arty (*informal*) ...*They encourage boys to be sensitive and artistic*... OPPOSITE untalented
2 = <u>beautiful</u>, fine, pleasing, lovely, creative, elegant, stylish, cultivated, imaginative, decorative, aesthetic, exquisite, graceful, expressive, ornamental, tasteful ...*an artistic arrangement*... OPPOSITE unattractive

artistry = <u>skill</u>, art, style, taste, talent, craft, genius, creativity, touch, flair, brilliance, sensibility, accomplishment, mastery, finesse, craftsmanship, proficiency, virtuosity, workmanship, artistic ability

artless 1 = <u>natural</u>, simple, fair, frank, plain, pure, open, round, true, direct, genuine, humble, straightforward, sincere, honest, candid, unaffected, upfront (*informal*), unpretentious, unadorned, guileless, uncontrived, undesigning ...*his artless air and charming smile*... OPPOSITE artificial
2 = <u>unskilled</u>, awkward, crude, primitive, rude, bungling, incompetent, clumsy, inept, untalented, maladroit ...*a spiritless and artless display of incompetence*... OPPOSITE artful

arty (*Informal*) = <u>artistic</u>, arty-farty (*informal*), arty-crafty (*informal*)

as CONJUNCTION = <u>when</u>, while, just as, at the time that, during the time that ...*All eyes were on him as he continued*...
PREPOSITION **1** = <u>in the role of</u>, being, under the name of, in the character of ...*I had natural ability as a footballer*...
2 = <u>in the way that</u>, like, in the manner that ...*Behave towards them as you would like to be treated*...
3 = <u>since</u>, because, seeing that, considering that, on account of the fact that ...*This is important as it sets the mood for the day*...
PHRASES **as for** *or* **to** = <u>with regard to</u>, about, re, concerning, regarding, respecting, relating to, with respect to, on the subject of, with reference to, in reference to, in the matter of, apropos of, as regards, anent (*Scot.*) ...*As for giving them guns, I don't think that's a very good idea*... ♦ **as it were** = <u>in a way</u>, to some extent, so to speak, in a manner of speaking, so to say ...*I understood the words, but I didn't, as it were, understand the question*...

ascend 1 = <u>climb</u>, scale, mount, go up ...*I held her hand as we ascended the steps*... OPPOSITE go down
2 = <u>slope upwards</u>, come up, rise up ...*A number of steps ascend from the cobbled street*... OPPOSITE slope downwards
3 = <u>move up</u>, rise, go up ...*Keep the drill centred as it ascends and descends in the hole*... OPPOSITE move down

4 = <u>float up</u>, rise, climb, tower, go up, take off, soar, lift off, fly up ...*They ascended 55,900 feet in their balloon*... OPPOSITE descend

ascendancy *or* **ascendence** = <u>influence</u>, power, control, rule, authority, command, reign, sovereignty, sway, dominance, domination, superiority, supremacy, mastery, dominion, upper hand, hegemony, prevalence, pre-eminence, predominance OPPOSITE inferiority

ascendant *or* **ascendent** ADJECTIVE = <u>influential</u>, controlling, ruling, powerful, commanding, supreme, superior, dominant, prevailing, authoritative, predominant, uppermost, pre-eminent ...*Radical reformers are once more ascendant*...
PHRASES **in the ascendant** = <u>rising</u>, increasing, growing, powerful, mounting, climbing, dominating, commanding, supreme, dominant, influential, prevailing, flourishing, ascending, up-and-coming, on the rise, uppermost, on the way up ...*Geography, drama, art and English are in the ascendant*...

ascension 1 = <u>rise</u>, rising, mounting, climb, ascending, ascent, moving upwards ...*the resurrection and ascension of Jesus Christ*...
2 = <u>succession</u>, taking over, assumption, inheritance, elevation, entering upon ...*fifteen years after his ascension to the throne*...

ascent 1 = <u>climbing</u>, scaling, mounting, climb, clambering, ascending, ascension ...*He led the first ascent of K2*...
2 = <u>upward slope</u>, rise, incline, ramp, gradient, rising ground, acclivity ...*It was a tough course over a gradual ascent*...
3 = <u>rise</u>, rising, climb, ascension, upward movement ...*He pressed the button and the elevator began its slow ascent*...

ascertain = <u>find out</u>, learn, discover, determine, confirm, settle, identify, establish, fix, verify, make certain, suss (out) (*slang*), ferret out

ascetic NOUN = <u>recluse</u>, monk, nun, abstainer, hermit, anchorite, self-denier ...*He left the luxuries of court for a life as an ascetic*... OPPOSITE hedonist
ADJECTIVE = <u>self-denying</u>, severe, plain, harsh, stern, rigorous, austere, Spartan, self-disciplined, celibate, puritanical, frugal, abstemious, abstinent ...*priests practising an ascetic life*... OPPOSITE self-indulgent

ascribe = <u>attribute</u>, credit, refer, charge, assign, put down, set down, impute

---

Word Power

ascribe – *Ascribe* is sometimes used where *subscribe* is meant: *I do not subscribe* (not *ascribe*) *to this view of music.*

---

asexual = <u>sexless</u>, neutral, neuter

ashamed 1 = <u>embarrassed</u>, sorry, guilty, upset, distressed, shy, humbled, humiliated, blushing, self-conscious, red-faced, chagrined, flustered, mortified, sheepish, bashful, prudish, crestfallen, discomfited, remorseful, abashed, shamefaced, conscience-stricken, discountenanced ...*She was ashamed that* *she looked so shabby…* OPPOSITE> proud

2 = <u>reluctant</u>, afraid, embarrassed, scared, unwilling, loath, disinclined …*Women are often ashamed to admit they are being abused…*

ashen = <u>pale</u>, white, grey, wan, livid, pasty, leaden, colourless, pallid, anaemic, ashy, like death warmed up (*informal*) OPPOSITE> rosy

ashore = <u>on land</u>, on the beach, on the shore, aground, to the shore, on dry land, shorewards, landwards

aside ADVERB = <u>to one side</u>, away, alone, separately, apart, alongside, beside, out of the way, on one side, to the side, in isolation, in reserve, out of mind …*She closed the book and laid it aside…*

NOUN = <u>interpolation</u>, remark, parenthesis, digression, interposition, confidential remark …*She mutters an aside to the camera…*

ask **1** = <u>inquire</u>, question, quiz, query, interrogate …*'How is Frank?' he asked…* OPPOSITE> answer

2 = <u>request</u>, apply to, appeal to, plead with, demand, urge, sue, pray, beg, petition, crave, solicit, implore, enjoin, beseech, entreat, supplicate …*We had to ask him to leave…*

3 = <u>invite</u>, bid, summon …*She asked me back to her house…*

askance **1** = <u>suspiciously</u>, doubtfully, dubiously, sceptically, disapprovingly, distrustfully, mistrustfully …*They have always looked askance at the western notion of democracy…*

2 = <u>out of the corner of your eye</u>, sideways, indirectly, awry, obliquely, with a side glance …*'Do you play chess?' he asked, looking askance at me…*

askew ADJECTIVE = <u>crooked</u>, awry, oblique, lopsided, off-centre, cockeyed (*informal*), skewwhiff (*Brit. informal*) …*She stood there, hat askew…* OPPOSITE> straight

ADVERB = <u>crookedly</u>, to one side, awry, obliquely, off-centre, aslant …*Some of the doors hung askew…* OPPOSITE> straight

asleep = <u>sleeping</u>, napping, dormant, crashed out (*slang*), dozing, slumbering, snoozing (*informal*), fast asleep, sound asleep, out for the count, dead to the world (*informal*), in a deep sleep

aspect **1** = <u>feature</u>, point, side, factor, angle, characteristic, facet …*Climate affects every aspect of our lives…*

2 = <u>position</u>, view, situation, scene, bearing, direction, prospect, exposure, point of view, outlook …*The house has a south-west aspect…*

3 = <u>appearance</u>, look, air, condition, quality, bearing, attitude, cast, manner, expression, countenance, demeanour, mien (*literary*) …*The snowy tree assumed a dumb, lifeless aspect…*

aspirant NOUN = <u>candidate</u>, applicant, hopeful, aspirer, seeker, suitor, postulant …*He is among the few aspirants with administrative experience…*

ADJECTIVE = <u>hopeful</u>, longing, ambitious, eager, striving, aspiring, endeavouring, wishful …*aspirant politicians…*

aspiration = <u>aim</u>, longing, end, plan, hope, goal, design, dream, wish, desire, object, intention, objective, ambition, craving, endeavour, yearning, eagerness, Holy Grail (*informal*), hankering

aspire to = <u>aim for</u>, desire, pursue, hope for, long for, crave, seek out, wish for, dream about, yearn for, hunger for, hanker after, be eager for, set your heart on, set your sights on, be ambitious for

aspiring = <u>hopeful</u>, longing, would-be, ambitious, eager, striving, endeavouring, wannabe (*informal*), wishful, aspirant

ass **1** = <u>donkey</u>, moke (*slang*), jennet …*She was led up to the sanctuary on an ass…*

2 = <u>fool</u>, dope (*informal*), jerk (*slang, chiefly U.S. & Canad.*), idiot, plank (*Brit. slang*), berk (*Brit. slang*), wally (*slang*), prat (*slang*), charlie (*Brit. informal*), plonker (*slang*), coot, geek (*slang*), twit (*informal, chiefly Brit.*), bonehead (*slang*), dunce, oaf, simpleton, airhead (*slang*), jackass, dipstick (*Brit. slang*), gonzo (*slang*), schmuck (*U.S. slang*), dork (*slang*), nitwit (*informal*), dolt, blockhead, ninny, divvy (*Brit. slang*), pillock (*Brit. slang*), halfwit, nincompoop, dweeb (*U.S. slang*), putz (*U.S. slang*), fathead (*informal*), weenie (*U.S. informal*), eejit (*Scot. & Irish*), dumb-ass (*slang*), numpty (*Scot. informal*), doofus (*slang, chiefly U.S.*), daftie (*informal*), nerd *or* nurd (*slang*), numbskull *or* numskull, twerp *or* twirp (*informal*), dorba *or* dorb (*Austral. slang*), bogan (*Austral. slang*) …*He was regarded as a pompous ass…*

(**Related Words**)
adjective : asinine
male : jack
female : jenny

assail **1** = <u>criticize</u>, abuse, blast, put down, malign, berate, revile, vilify, tear into (*informal*), diss (*slang, chiefly U.S.*), impugn, go for the jugular, lambast(e) …*These newspapers assail the government each day…*

2 = <u>attack</u>, charge, assault, invade, set about, beset, fall upon, set upon, lay into (*informal*), maltreat, belabour …*He was assailed by a young man with a knife…*

assailant = <u>attacker</u>, assaulter, invader, aggressor, assailer

assassin = <u>murderer</u>, killer, slayer, liquidator, executioner, hit man (*slang*), eliminator (*slang*), hatchet man (*slang*)

assassinate = <u>murder</u>, kill, eliminate (*slang*), take out (*slang*), terminate, hit (*slang*), slay, blow away (*slang, chiefly U.S.*), liquidate

assassination = <u>murder</u>, killing, slaughter, purge, hit (*slang*), removal, elimination (*slang*), slaying, homicide, liquidation

assault NOUN = <u>attack</u>, campaign, strike, rush, storm, storming, raid, invasion, charge, offensive, onset, onslaught, foray, incursion, act of aggression, inroad …*The rebels are poised for a new assault…* OPPOSITE> defence

VERB = <u>strike</u>, attack, beat, knock, punch, belt (*informal*), bang, batter, clip (*informal*), slap, bash (*informal*), deck (*slang*), sock (*slang*), chin (*slang*), smack, thump, set about, lay one on (*slang*), clout (*informal*), cuff, flog, whack, lob, beset, clobber (*slang*), smite (*archaic*), wallop (*informal*), swat, fall upon, set upon, lay into (*informal*), tonk (*slang*), lambast(e), belabour ...*The gang assaulted him with iron bars*...

assay = <u>analyse</u>, examine, investigate, assess, weigh, evaluate, inspect, try, appraise

assemblage = <u>group</u>, company, meeting, body, crowd, collection, mass, gathering, rally, assembly, flock, congregation, accumulation, multitude, throng, conclave, aggregation, convocation

assemble 1 = <u>gather</u>, meet, collect, rally, flock, accumulate, come together, muster, convene, congregate, foregather ...*There was nowhere for students to assemble before classes*... OPPOSITE> scatter
2 = <u>bring together</u>, collect, gather, rally, summon, accumulate, round up, marshal, come together, muster, convene, amass, congregate, call together, foregather, convoke ...*The assembled multitude cheered as the leaders arrived*...
3 = <u>put together</u>, make, join, set up, manufacture, build up, connect, construct, erect, piece together, fabricate, fit together ...*She was trying to assemble the bomb when it went off*... OPPOSITE> take apart

assembly 1 = <u>gathering</u>, group, meeting, body, council, conference, crowd, congress, audience, collection, mass, diet, rally, convention, flock, company, house, congregation, accumulation, multitude, throng, synod, hui (*N.Z.*), assemblage, conclave, aggregation, convocation ...*He waited until quiet settled on the assembly*...
2 = <u>putting together</u>, joining, setting up, manufacture, construction, building up, connecting, erection, piecing together, fabrication, fitting together ...*workers in car assembly plants*...

assent NOUN = <u>agreement</u>, accord, sanction, approval, permission, acceptance, consent, compliance, accession, acquiescence, concurrence ...*He gave his assent to the proposed legislation*... OPPOSITE> refusal
PHRASES **assent to something** = <u>agree to</u>, allow, accept, grant, approve, permit, sanction, O.K., comply with, go along with, subscribe to, consent to, say yes to, accede to, fall in with, acquiesce in, concur with, give the green light to ...*I assented to the publisher's request to write this book*...

assert VERB 1 = <u>state</u>, argue, maintain, declare, allege, swear, pronounce, contend, affirm, profess, attest, predicate, postulate, avow, aver, asseverate, avouch (*archaic*) ...*He asserted that the bill violated the First Amendment*... OPPOSITE> deny
2 = <u>insist upon</u>, stress, defend, uphold, put forward, vindicate, press, stand up for ...*The republics began asserting their right to govern themselves*... OPPOSITE> retract
PHRASES **assert yourself** = <u>be forceful</u>, put your foot down (*informal*), put yourself forward, make your presence felt, exert your influence ...*He's speaking up and asserting himself much more now*...

assertion 1 = <u>statement</u>, claim, allegation, profession, declaration, contention, affirmation, pronouncement, avowal, attestation, predication, asseveration ...*assertions that the recession is truly over*...
2 = <u>insistence</u>, defence, stressing, maintenance, vindication ...*They have made the assertion of ethnic identity possible*...

assertive = <u>confident</u>, firm, demanding, decided, forward, can-do (*informal*), positive, aggressive, decisive, forceful, emphatic, insistent, feisty (*informal, chiefly U.S. & Canad.*), pushy (*informal*), in-your-face (*Brit. slang*), dogmatic, strong-willed, domineering, overbearing, self-assured OPPOSITE> meek

assertiveness = <u>confidence</u>, insistence, aggressiveness, firmness, decisiveness, dogmatism, forcefulness, positiveness, pushiness (*informal*), forwardness, self-assuredness, decidedness, domineeringness OPPOSITE> meekness

assess 1 = <u>judge</u>, determine, estimate, fix, analyse, evaluate, rate, value, check out, compute, gauge, weigh up, appraise, size up (*informal*), eye up ...*The test was to assess aptitude rather than academic achievement*...
2 = <u>evaluate</u>, rate, tax, value, demand, estimate, fix, impose, levy ...*What is the assessed value of the property?*...

assessment 1 = <u>judgment</u>, analysis, determination, evaluation, valuation, appraisal, estimation, rating, opinion, estimate, computation ...*He was remanded to a mental hospital for assessment*...
2 = <u>evaluation</u>, rating, rate, charge, tax, demand, fee, duty, toll, levy, tariff, taxation, valuation, impost ...*inflated assessments of mortgaged property*...

asset NOUN = <u>benefit</u>, help, service, aid, advantage, strength, resource, attraction, blessing, boon, good point, strong point, ace in the hole, feather in your cap, ace up your sleeve ...*Her leadership qualities were the greatest asset to the party*... OPPOSITE> disadvantage
PLURAL NOUN = <u>property</u>, goods, means, holdings, money, funds, effects, capital, riches, finance, reserves, resources, estate, wealth, valuables, possessions ...*By 1989 the group had assets of 3.5 billion francs*...

assiduous = <u>diligent</u>, constant, steady, hard-working, persistent, attentive, persevering, laborious, industrious, indefatigable, studious, unflagging, untiring, sedulous, unwearied OPPOSITE> lazy

assign 1 = <u>give</u>, set, grant, allocate, give out, consign, allot, apportion ...*Later in the year, she'll assign them research papers*...
2 = <u>allocate</u>, give, determine, fix, appoint, distribute, earmark, mete ...*He assigned her all his land*...
3 = <u>select for</u>, post, commission, elect, appoint, delegate, nominate, name, designate, choose for, stipulate for ...*Did you choose this country or were you simply assigned here?*...
4 = <u>attribute</u>, credit, put down, set down, ascribe, accredit ...*Assign the letters of the alphabet their numerical values*...

assignment 1 = <u>task</u>, work, job, charge, position, post, commission, exercise, responsibility, duty, mission, appointment, undertaking, occupation, chore ...*The course involves written assignments and* *practical tests…*

2 = <u>selection</u>, choice, option, appointment, delegation, nomination, designation …*I only ever take photos on assignment…*

3 = <u>giving</u>, issuing, grant, distribution, allocation, earmarking, allotment, designation, consignment, dealing out, assignation (*Law, chiefly Scot.*), apportionment …*The state prohibited the assignment of licences to competitors…*

assimilate 1 = <u>adjust</u>, fit, adapt, accommodate, accustom, conform, mingle, blend in, become like, homogenize, acclimatize, intermix, become similar, acculturate …*They had been assimilated into the nation's culture…*

2 = <u>learn</u>, absorb, take in, incorporate, digest, imbibe (*literary*), ingest …*My mind could only assimilate one possibility at a time…*

assist 1 = <u>help</u>, back, support, further, benefit, aid, encourage, work with, work for, relieve, collaborate with, cooperate with, abet, expedite, succour, lend a hand to, lend a helping hand to, give a leg up to (*informal*) …*They decided to assist me with my chores…*

2 = <u>facilitate</u>, help, further, serve, aid, forward, promote, promote, boost, ease, sustain, reinforce, speed up, pave the way for, make easy, expedite, oil the wheels, smooth the path of, assist the progress of …*a chemical that assists in the manufacture of proteins…* OPPOSITE> hinder

assistance = <u>help</u>, backing, service, support, benefit, aid, relief, boost, promotion, cooperation, encouragement, collaboration, reinforcement, helping hand, sustenance, succour, furtherance, abetment OPPOSITE> hindrance

assistant = <u>helper</u>, partner, ally, colleague, associate, supporter, deputy, subsidiary, aide, aider, second, accessory, attendant, backer, protagonist, collaborator, accomplice, confederate, auxiliary, henchman, right-hand man, adjutant, helpmate, coadjutor (*rare*), abettor, cooperator

associate VERB **1** = <u>connect</u>, couple, league, link, mix, relate, pair, ally, identify, unite, join, combine, attach, affiliate, fasten, correlate, confederate, yoke, affix, lump together, cohere, mention in the same breath, conjoin, think of together …*We've got the idea of associating progress with the future…* OPPOSITE> separate

2 = <u>socialize</u>, mix, hang (*informal, chiefly U.S.*), accompany, hang out (*informal*), run around (*informal*), mingle, be friends, befriend, consort, hang about, hobnob, fraternize …*They found out they'd been associating with a murderer…* OPPOSITE> avoid

NOUN = <u>partner</u>, friend, ally, colleague, mate (*informal*), companion, comrade, affiliate, collaborator, confederate, co-worker, workmate, main man (*slang, chiefly U.S.*), cobber (*Austral. or old-fashioned N.Z. informal*), confrère, compeer …*the restaurant owner's business associates…*

associated = <u>connected</u>, united, joined, leagued, linked, tied, related, allied, combined, involved, bound, syndicated, affiliated, correlated, confederated, yoked

association 1 = <u>group</u>, company, club, order, union, class, society, league, band, set, troop, pack, camp, collection, gathering, organization, circle, corporation, alliance, coalition, partnership, federation, bunch, formation, faction, cluster, syndicate, congregation, batch, confederation, cooperative, fraternity, affiliation, posse (*slang*), clique, confederacy, assemblage …*the British Olympic Association…*

2 = <u>friendship</u>, relationship, link, tie, relations, bond, connection, partnership, attachment, intimacy, liaison, fellowship, affinity, familiarity, affiliation, companionship, comradeship, fraternization …*The association between the two companies stretches back 30 years…*

3 = <u>connection</u>, union, joining, linking, tie, mixing, relation, bond, pairing, combination, mixture, blend, identification, correlation, linkage, yoking, juxtaposition, lumping together, concomitance …*the association of the colour black with death…*

assorted = <u>various</u>, different, mixed, varied, diverse, diversified, miscellaneous, sundry, motley, variegated, manifold, heterogeneous OPPOSITE> similar

assortment = <u>variety</u>, choice, collection, selection, mixture, diversity, array, jumble, medley, mixed bag (*informal*), potpourri, mélange (*French*), miscellany, mishmash, farrago, hotchpotch, salmagundi, pick 'n' mix

assuage 1 = <u>relieve</u>, ease, calm, moderate, temper, soothe, lessen, alleviate, lighten, allay, mitigate, quench, palliate …*She was trying to assuage her guilt…* OPPOSITE> increase

2 = <u>calm</u>, still, quiet, relax, satisfy, soften, soothe, appease, lull, pacify, mollify, tranquillize …*The meat they'd managed to procure assuaged their hunger…* OPPOSITE> provoke

assume 1 = <u>presume</u>, think, believe, expect, accept, suppose, imagine, suspect, guess (*informal, chiefly U.S. & Canad.*), take it, fancy, take for granted, infer, conjecture, postulate, surmise, presuppose …*It is a mistake to assume that the two are similar…* OPPOSITE> know

2 = <u>take on</u>, begin, accept, manage, bear, handle, shoulder, take over, don, acquire, put on, take up, embrace, undertake, set about, attend to, take responsibility for, embark upon, enter upon …*He will assume the role of Chief Executive…*

3 = <u>simulate</u>, affect, adopt, put on, imitate, mimic, sham, counterfeit, feign, impersonate …*He assumed an air of superiority…*

4 = <u>take over</u>, take, appropriate, acquire, seize, hijack, confiscate, wrest, usurp, lay claim to, pre-empt, commandeer, requisition, expropriate, arrogate …*If there is no president, power will be assumed by extremist forces…* OPPOSITE> give up

assumed = <u>false</u>, affected, made-up, pretended, fake, imitation, bogus, simulated, sham, counterfeit, feigned, spurious, fictitious, make-believe, pseudonymous, phoney *or* phony (*informal*) OPPOSITE> real

assumption 1 = <u>presumption</u>, theory, opinion, belief, guess, expectation, fancy, suspicion, premise, acceptance, hypothesis, anticipation, inference, conjecture, surmise, supposition, presupposition, premiss, postulation …*They are wrong in their assumption that we are all alike*…

2 = taking on, managing, handling, shouldering, putting on, taking up, takeover, acquisition, undertaking, embracing, acceptance, adoption, entering upon …*He is calling for 'a common assumption of responsibility'*…

3 = seizure, taking, takeover, acquisition, appropriation, wresting, confiscation, commandeering, expropriation, pre-empting, usurpation, arrogation …*the government's assumption of power*…

assurance 1 = promise, statement, guarantee, commitment, pledge, profession, vow, declaration, assertion, oath, affirmation, protestation, word, word of honour …*an assurance that other forces will not move into the territory*… OPPOSITE▷ lie

2 = confidence, conviction, courage, certainty, self-confidence, poise, assertiveness, security, faith, coolness, nerve, aplomb, boldness, self-reliance, firmness, self-assurance, certitude, sureness, self-possession, positiveness, assuredness …*He led the orchestra with assurance*… OPPOSITE▷ self-doubt

assure 1 = convince, encourage, persuade, satisfy, comfort, prove to, reassure, soothe, hearten, embolden, win someone over, bring someone round …*'Everything's going to be okay,' he assured me*…

2 = make certain, ensure, confirm, guarantee, secure, make sure, complete, seal, clinch …*Last night's victory has assured their promotion*…

3 = promise to, pledge to, vow to, guarantee to, swear to, attest to, confirm to, certify to, affirm to, give your word to, declare confidently to …*We can assure you of our best service at all times*…

assured 1 = confident, certain, positive, bold, poised, assertive, complacent, fearless, audacious, pushy (*informal*), brazen, self-confident, self-assured, self-possessed, overconfident, dauntless, sure of yourself …*He was much more assured than in recent appearances*… OPPOSITE▷ self-conscious

2 = certain, sure, ensured, confirmed, settled, guaranteed, fixed, secure, sealed, clinched, made certain, sound, in the bag (*slang*), dependable, beyond doubt, irrefutable, unquestionable, indubitable …*Our victory is assured; nothing can stop us*… OPPOSITE▷ doubtful

astonish = amaze, surprise, stun, stagger, bewilder, astound, daze, confound, stupefy, boggle the mind, dumbfound, flabbergast (*informal*)

astonished = amazed, surprised, staggered, bewildered, astounded, dazed, stunned, confounded, perplexed, gobsmacked (*informal*), dumbfounded, flabbergasted (*informal*), stupefied

astonishing = amazing, striking, surprising, brilliant, stunning, impressive, overwhelming, staggering, startling, sensational (*informal*), bewildering, breathtaking, astounding, eye-opening, wondrous (*archaic or literary*), jaw-dropping, stupefying

astonishment = amazement, surprise, wonder,

confusion, awe, consternation, bewilderment, wonderment, stupefaction

astound = amaze, surprise, overwhelm, astonish, stagger, bewilder, daze, confound, stupefy, stun, take your breath away, boggle the mind, dumbfound, flabbergast (*informal*)

astounding = amazing, striking, surprising, brilliant, impressive, astonishing, staggering, sensational (*informal*), bewildering, stunning, breathtaking, wondrous (*archaic or literary*), jaw-dropping, stupefying

astray ADJECTIVE *or* ADVERB = off the right track, adrift, off course, off the mark, amiss …*Many items of mail being sent to her have gone astray*…

PHRASES **lead someone astray** = lead into sin, lead into error, lead into bad ways, lead into wrong … *The judge thought he'd been led astray by others*…

astringent 1 = contractive, contractile, styptic …*an astringent lotion*…

2 = severe, strict, exacting, harsh, grim, stern, hard, rigid, rigorous, stringent, austere, caustic, acerbic …*an astringent satire on Hollywood*…

astrology = stargazing, astromancy, horoscopy
➤ **zodiac**

astronaut = space traveller, cosmonaut, spaceman, spacewoman, space pilot

astronomical *or* **astronomic** = huge, great, giant, massive, vast, enormous, immense, titanic, infinite, gigantic, monumental, colossal, boundless, galactic, Gargantuan, immeasurable

astronomy
➤ **planets** ➤ **stars and constellations**

astute = intelligent, politic, bright, sharp, keen, calculating, clever, subtle, penetrating, knowing, shrewd, cunning, discerning, sly, on the ball (*informal*), canny, perceptive, wily, crafty, artful, insightful, foxy, adroit, sagacious OPPOSITE▷ stupid

asunder ADVERB *or* ADJECTIVE (*Literary*) = to pieces, apart, torn, rent, to bits, to shreds, in pieces, into pieces

asylum 1 (*Old-fashioned*) = mental hospital, hospital, institution, psychiatric hospital, madhouse (*informal*), funny farm (*facetious*), loony bin (*slang*), nuthouse (*slang*), rubber room (*U.S. slang*), laughing academy (*U.S. slang*) …*He spent the rest of his life in a mental asylum*…

2 = refuge, security, haven, safety, protection, preserve, shelter, retreat, harbour, sanctuary …*He applied for asylum after fleeing his home country*…

atheism = nonbelief, disbelief, scepticism, infidelity, paganism, unbelief, freethinking, godlessness, irreligion, heathenism

atheist = nonbeliever, pagan, sceptic, disbeliever, heathen, infidel, unbeliever, freethinker, irreligionist

athlete = sportsperson, player, runner, competitor, contender, sportsman, contestant, gymnast, games player, sportswoman

athletic ADJECTIVE = fit, strong, powerful, healthy, active, trim, strapping, robust, vigorous, energetic, muscular, sturdy, husky (*informal*), lusty, herculean, sinewy, brawny, able-bodied, well-proportioned ...*He was tall, with an athletic build*... OPPOSITE feeble

PLURAL NOUN = sports, games, races, exercises, contests, sporting events, gymnastics, track and field events, games of strength ...*intercollegiate athletics*...

Athletic events www.iaaf.org

100 metres	hammer
110 metres hurdles	heptathlon
200 metres	high jump
400 metres	javelin
400 metres hurdles	long jump
800 metres	marathon
1500 metres	orienteering
3000 metres	pentathlon
5000 metres	pole vault
10 000 metres	relay
cross-country	shot put
running	steeplechase
decathlon	triathlon
discus	triple jump
half marathon	walking

---

atmosphere 1 = air, sky, heavens, aerosphere ...*These gases pollute the atmosphere of towns and cities*...

2 = feeling, feel, air, quality, character, environment, spirit, surroundings, tone, mood, climate, flavour, aura, ambience, vibes (*slang*) ...*The muted decor adds to the relaxed atmosphere*...

Regions of the atmosphere

ionosphere
mesosphere
ozone layer *or* ozonosphere
stratosphere
thermosphere
troposphere

---

atom = particle, bit, spot, trace, scrap, molecule, grain, dot, fragment, fraction, shred, crumb, mite, jot, speck, morsel, mote, whit, tittle, iota, scintilla (*rare*)

atone *usually with* **for** = make amends, pay for, compensate for, make up for, redress, answer for, recompense for, do penance for, make reparation for, make redress for

atonement = amends, payment, compensation, satisfaction, redress, reparation, restitution, penance, recompense, expiation, propitiation

atrocious 1 (*Informal*) = shocking, terrible, appalling, horrible, horrifying, grievous, execrable, detestable ...*The food here is atrocious*... OPPOSITE fine

2 = cruel, savage, brutal, vicious, ruthless, infamous, monstrous, wicked, barbaric, inhuman, diabolical, heinous, flagrant, infernal, fiendish, villainous, nefarious, godawful (*slang*), hellacious (*U.S. slang*) ...*The treatment of the prisoners was atrocious*... OPPOSITE kind

atrocity 1 = act of cruelty, wrong, crime, horror, offence, evil, outrage, outrage, cruelty, brutality, obscenity, wrongdoing, enormity, monstrosity, transgression, abomination, barbarity, villainy ...*Those who committed this atrocity should be punished*...

2 = cruelty, wrong, horror, brutality, wrongdoing, enormity, savagery, ruthlessness, wickedness, inhumanity, infamy, transgression, barbarity, viciousness, villainy, baseness, monstrousness, heinousness, nefariousness, shockingness, atrociousness, fiendishness, barbarousness, grievousness, villainousness ...*stomach-churning tales of atrocity and massacre*...

atrophy **VERB** **1** = waste away, waste, shrink, diminish, deteriorate, decay, dwindle, wither, wilt, degenerate, shrivel ...*His muscle atrophied, and he was left lame*...

2 = decline, waste, fade, shrink, diminish, deteriorate, dwindle, wither, wilt, degenerate, shrivel, waste away ...*If you let your mind stagnate, this talent will atrophy*...

NOUN **1** = wasting away, decline, wasting, decay, decaying, withering, deterioration, meltdown (*informal*), shrivelling, degeneration, diminution ...*exercises to avoid atrophy of cartilage*...

2 = wasting, decline, decay, decaying, withering, deterioration, meltdown (*informal*), shrivelling, degeneration, diminution, wasting away ...*levels of consciousness which are in danger of atrophy*...

attach **VERB** **1** = affix, stick, secure, bind, unite, add, join, couple, link, tie, fix, connect, lash, glue, adhere, fasten, annex, truss, yoke, append, make fast, cohere, subjoin ...*Attach labels to things before you file them away*... OPPOSITE detach

2 = ascribe, connect, attribute, assign, place, associate, lay on, accredit, invest with, impute ...*They have attached much significance to your visit*...

PHRASES **attach yourself to** *or* **be attached to something** = join, accompany, associate with, combine with, join forces with, latch on to, unite with, sign up with, become associated with, sign on with, affiliate yourself with ...*He attached himself to a group of poets known as the Martians*...

attached **ADJECTIVE** = spoken for, married, partnered, engaged, accompanied ...*I wondered if he was attached*...

PHRASES **attached to** = fond of, devoted to, affectionate towards, full of regard for ...*She is very attached to her family and friends*...

attachment 1 = fondness, liking, feeling, love, relationship, regard, bond, friendship, attraction, loyalty, affection, devotion, fidelity, affinity, tenderness, reverence, predilection, possessiveness, partiality ...*As a teenager she formed a strong attachment to one of her teachers*... OPPOSITE aversion

2 = accessory, fitting, extra, addition, component, extension, supplement, fixture, auxiliary, adaptor *or* adapter, supplementary part, add-on, adjunct, appendage, accoutrement, appurtenance ...*Some models come with attachments for dusting*...

attack `VERB` 1 = <u>assault</u>, strike (at), mug, set about, ambush, assail, tear into, fall upon, set upon, lay into (*informal*) …*He bundled her into a hallway and brutally attacked her*… `OPPOSITE` defend
2 = <u>invade</u>, occupy, raid, infringe, charge, rush, storm, encroach …*The infantry's aim was to slow attacking forces*…
3 = <u>criticize</u>, blame, abuse, blast, pan (*informal*), condemn, knock (*informal*), slam (*slang*), put down, slate (*informal*), have a go (at) (*informal*), censure, malign, berate, disparage, revile, vilify, tear into (*informal*), slag off (*Brit. slang*), diss (*slang, chiefly U.S.*), find fault with, impugn, go for the jugular, lambast(e), pick holes in, excoriate, bite someone's head off, snap someone's head off, pick to pieces …*He publicly attacked the people who've been calling for a secret ballot*…
`NOUN` 1 = <u>assault</u>, charge, campaign, strike, rush, raid, invasion, offensive, aggression, blitz, onset, onslaught, foray, incursion, inroad …*a campaign of air attacks on strategic targets*… `OPPOSITE` defence
2 = <u>criticism</u>, panning (*informal*), slating (*informal*), censure, disapproval, slagging (*slang*), abuse, knocking (*informal*), bad press, vilification, denigration, calumny, character assassination, disparagement, impugnment …*He launched an attack on businesses for failing to invest*…
3 = <u>bout</u>, fit, access, spell, stroke, seizure, spasm, convulsion, paroxysm …*It brought on an attack of asthma*…

attacker = <u>assailant</u>, assaulter, raider, intruder, invader, aggressor, mugger

attain 1 = <u>obtain</u>, get, win, reach, effect, land, score (*slang*), complete, gain, achieve, earn, secure, realize, acquire, fulfil, accomplish, grasp, reap, procure …*He's halfway to attaining his pilot's licence*…
2 = <u>reach</u>, achieve, realize, acquire, arrive at, accomplish …*attaining a state of calmness and confidence*…

attainable = <u>achievable</u>, possible, likely, potential, accessible, probable, at hand, feasible, within reach, practicable, obtainable, reachable, realizable, graspable, gettable, procurable, accomplishable `OPPOSITE` unattainable

attainment 1 = <u>achievement</u>, getting, winning, reaching, gaining, obtaining, acquisition, feat, completion, reaping, accomplishment, realization, fulfilment, arrival at, procurement, acquirement …*the attainment of independence*…
2 = <u>skill</u>, art, ability, talent, gift, achievement, capability, competence, accomplishment, mastery, proficiency …*their educational attainments*…

attempt `VERB` = <u>try</u>, seek, aim, struggle, tackle, take on, experiment, venture, undertake, essay, strive, endeavour, have a go at (*informal*), make an effort, make an attempt, have a crack at, have a shot at (*informal*), try your hand at, do your best to, jump through hoops (*informal*), have a stab at (*informal*), take the bit between your teeth …*We attempted to do something like that here*…
`NOUN` 1 = <u>try</u>, go (*informal*), shot (*informal*), effort,

trial, bid, experiment, crack (*informal*), venture, undertaking, essay, stab (*informal*), endeavour …*a deliberate attempt to destabilize defence*…
2 = <u>attack</u>, assault …*an attempt on the life of the Prime Minister*…

attempted = <u>tried</u>, ventured, undertaken, endeavoured, assayed

attend `VERB` 1 = <u>be present</u>, go to, visit, be at, be there, be here, frequent, haunt, appear at, turn up at, patronize, show up at (*informal*), show yourself, put in an appearance at, present yourself at …*Thousands of people attended the funeral*… `OPPOSITE` be absent
2 = <u>pay attention</u>, listen, follow, hear, mark, mind, watch, note, regard, notice, observe, look on, heed, take to heart, pay heed, hearken (*archaic*) …*I'm not sure what he said – I wasn't attending*… `OPPOSITE` ignore
3 = <u>escort</u>, conduct, guard, shadow, accompany, companion, shepherd, convoy, usher, squire, chaperon …*horse-drawn coaches attended by liveried footmen*…
`PHRASES` **attend to someone** = <u>look after</u>, help, mind, aid, tend, nurse, care for, take care of, minister to, administer to …*The main thing is to attend to the injured*… ◆ **attend to something** = <u>apply yourself to</u>, concentrate on, look after, take care of, see to, get to work on, devote yourself to, occupy yourself with …*You had better attend to the matter in hand*…

attendance 1 = <u>presence</u>, being there, attending, appearance …*Her attendance at school was sporadic*…
2 = <u>turnout</u>, audience, gate, congregation, house, crowd, throng, number present …*Some estimates put attendance at 60,000*…

attendant `NOUN` = <u>assistant</u>, guide, guard, servant, companion, aide, escort, follower, steward, waiter, usher, warden, helper, auxiliary, custodian, page, menial, concierge, underling, lackey, chaperon, flunky …*He was working as a car-park attendant*…
`ADJECTIVE` = <u>accompanying</u>, related, associated, accessory, consequent, resultant, concomitant …*His victory, and all the attendant publicity, were deserved*…

attention `NOUN` 1 = <u>thinking</u>, thought, mind, notice, consideration, concentration, observation, scrutiny, heed, deliberation, contemplation, thoughtfulness, attentiveness, intentness, heedfulness …*He turned his attention to the desperate state of housing in the province*…
2 = <u>care</u>, support, concern, treatment, looking after, succour, ministration …*a demanding baby who wants attention 24 hours a day*…
3 = <u>awareness</u>, regard, notice, recognition, consideration, observation, consciousness …*Let me draw your attention to some important issues*… `OPPOSITE` inattention
`PLURAL NOUN` = <u>courtesy</u>, compliments, regard, respect, care, consideration, deference, politeness, civility, gallantry, mindfulness, assiduities …*He was flattered by the attentions of a younger woman*… `OPPOSITE` discourtesy

attentive 1 = <u>intent</u>, listening, concentrating, careful,

alert, awake, mindful, watchful, observant, studious, on your toes, heedful, regardful ...*I wish you would be more attentive to detail...* OPPOSITE heedless
2 = <u>considerate</u>, kind, civil, devoted, helpful, obliging, accommodating, polite, thoughtful, gracious, conscientious, respectful, courteous, gallant ...*At parties he is always attentive to his wife...* OPPOSITE neglectful

attenuate = <u>weaken</u>, reduce, contract, lower, diminish, decrease, dilute, lessen, sap, water down, adulterate, enfeeble, enervate, devaluate

attenuated 1 = <u>slender</u>, extended, thinned, slimmed, refined, stretched out, lengthened, drawn out, spun out, elongated, rarefied ...*rounded arches and attenuated columns...*
2 = <u>weakened</u>, reduced, contracted, lowered, diminished, decreased, dilute, diluted, lessened, devalued, sapped, watered down, adulterated, enfeebled, enervated ...*The vaccination contains attenuated strains of the target virus...*

attest = <u>testify</u>, show, prove, confirm, display, declare, witness, demonstrate, seal, swear, exhibit, warrant, assert, manifest, give evidence, invoke, ratify, affirm, certify, verify, bear out, substantiate, corroborate, bear witness, authenticate, vouch for, evince, aver, adjure OPPOSITE disprove

attic = <u>loft</u>, garret, roof space

attire = <u>clothes</u>, wear, dress, clothing, gear (*informal*), habit, uniform, outfit, costume, threads (*slang*), array (*poetic*), garments, robes, apparel, garb, accoutrements, raiment (*archaic or poetic*), vestment, schmutter (*slang*), habiliments

attitude 1 = <u>opinion</u>, thinking, feeling, thought, view, position, approach, belief, mood, perspective, point of view, stance, outlook, viewpoint, slant, frame of mind ...*the general change in attitude towards them...*
2 = <u>manner</u>, air, condition, bearing, aspect, carriage, disposition, demeanour, mien (*literary*) ...*He has a gentle attitude...*
3 = <u>position</u>, bearing, pose, stance, carriage, posture ...*scenes of the king in various attitudes of worshipping...*

attorney = <u>lawyer</u>, solicitor, counsel, advocate, barrister, counsellor, legal adviser

attract 1 = <u>allure</u>, interest, draw, invite, persuade, engage, charm, appeal to, fascinate, win over, tempt, lure (*informal*), induce, incline, seduce, entice, enchant, endear, lead on, coax, captivate, beguile, cajole, bewitch, decoy, inveigle, pull, catch (someone's) eye ...*Summer attracts visitors to the countryside...* OPPOSITE repel
2 = <u>pull</u>, draw, magnetize ...*Anything with strong gravity attracts other things to it...*

attraction 1 = <u>appeal</u>, interest, draw, pull (*informal*), come-on (*informal*), charm, incentive, invitation, lure, bait, temptation, fascination, attractiveness, allure, inducement, magnetism, enchantment, endearment, enticement, captivation, temptingness, pleasingness ...*It was never a physical attraction, just a meeting of minds...*
2 = <u>pull</u>, draw, magnetism ...*the gravitational attraction of the Sun...*

attractive 1 = <u>seductive</u>, charming, tempting, interesting, pleasing, pretty, fair, beautiful, inviting, engaging, likable *or* likeable, lovely, winning, sexy (*informal*), pleasant, handsome, fetching, good-looking, glamorous, gorgeous, magnetic, cute, irresistible, enticing, provocative, captivating, beguiling, alluring, bonny, winsome, comely, prepossessing ...*He was always very attractive to women...* OPPOSITE unattractive
2 = <u>appealing</u>, pleasing, inviting, fascinating, tempting, enticing, agreeable, irresistable ...*Co-operation was more than just an attractive option...* OPPOSITE unappealing

attributable = <u>ascribable</u>, accountable, applicable, traceable, explicable, assignable, imputable, blamable *or* blameable, placeable, referable *or* referrable

attribute VERB = <u>ascribe</u>, apply, credit, blame, refer, trace, assign, charge, allocate, put down, set down, allot, impute ...*They attribute their success to external causes such as luck...*
NOUN = <u>quality</u>, point, mark, sign, note, feature, property, character, element, aspect, symbol, characteristic, indication, distinction, virtue, trait, hallmark, facet, quirk, peculiarity, idiosyncrasy ...*He has every attribute a footballer could want...*

attribution = <u>ascription</u>, charge, credit, blame, assignment, attachment, placement, referral, assignation, imputation

attrition = <u>wearing down</u>, harrying, weakening, harassment, thinning out, attenuation, debilitation

attuned = <u>accustomed</u>, adjusted, coordinated, in tune, in harmony, in accord, harmonized, familiarized, acclimatized

atypical = <u>unusual</u>, exceptional, uncommon, singular, deviant, unconventional, unique, unorthodox, uncharacteristic, out of the ordinary, unrepresentative, out of keeping, uncustomary, nonconforming, unconforming OPPOSITE normal

auburn NOUN *or* ADJECTIVE = <u>reddish-brown</u>, tawny, russet, henna, rust-coloured, copper-coloured, chestnut-coloured, Titian red, nutbrown
➤ **shades of red**

audacious 1 = <u>daring</u>, enterprising, brave, bold, risky, rash, adventurous, reckless, courageous, fearless, intrepid, valiant, daredevil, death-defying, dauntless, venturesome ...*an audacious plan to win the presidency...* OPPOSITE timid
2 = <u>cheeky</u>, presumptuous, impertinent, insolent, impudent, forward, fresh (*informal*), assuming, rude, defiant, brazen, in-your-face (*Brit. slang*), shameless, sassy (*U.S. informal*), pert, disrespectful ...*Audacious thieves stole her car from under her nose...* OPPOSITE tactful

audacity 1 = <u>daring</u>, nerve, courage, guts (*informal*), bravery, boldness, recklessness, face (*informal*), front, enterprise, valour, fearlessness, rashness, adventurousness, intrepidity, audaciousness, dauntlessness, venturesomeness ...*I was shocked at*

the audacity of the gangsters…
2 = <u>cheek</u>, nerve, defiance, gall (*informal*), presumption, rudeness, chutzpah (*U.S. & Canad. informal*), insolence, impertinence, neck (*informal*), impudence, effrontery, brass neck (*Brit. informal*), shamelessness, sassiness (*U.S. informal*), forwardness, pertness, audaciousness, disrespectfulness …*He had the audacity to look at his watch while I was talking…*

audible = <u>clear</u>, distinct, discernible, detectable, perceptible, hearable OPPOSITE> inaudible

audience **1** = <u>spectators</u>, company, house, crowd, gathering, gallery, assembly, viewers, listeners, patrons, congregation, turnout, onlookers, throng, assemblage …*The entire audience broke into loud applause…*
2 = <u>public</u>, market, following, fans, devotees, fanbase, aficionados …*She began to find a receptive audience for her work…*
3 = <u>interview</u>, meeting, hearing, exchange, reception, consultation …*The Prime Minister will seek an audience with the Queen today…*

audit (*Accounting*) VERB = <u>inspect</u>, check, review, balance, survey, examine, investigate, go through, assess, go over, evaluate, vet, verify, appraise, scrutinize, inquire into …*Each year they audit our accounts and certify them as true and fair…*
NOUN = <u>inspection</u>, check, checking, review, balancing, search, survey, investigation, examination, scan, scrutiny, supervision, surveillance, look-over, verification, once-over (*informal*), checkup, superintendence …*The bank is carrying out an internal audit…*

augment = <u>increase</u>, grow, raise, extend, boost, expand, add to, build up, strengthen, enhance, reinforce, swell, intensify, heighten, enlarge, multiply, inflate, magnify, amplify, dilate OPPOSITE> diminish

augur = <u>bode</u>, promise, predict, herald, signify, foreshadow, prophesy, harbinger, presage, prefigure, portend, betoken, be an omen of

august = <u>noble</u>, great, kingly, grand, excellent, imposing, impressive, superb, distinguished, magnificent, glorious, splendid, elevated, eminent, majestic, dignified, regal, stately, high-ranking, monumental, solemn, lofty, exalted

aura = <u>air</u>, feeling, feel, quality, atmosphere, tone, suggestion, mood, scent, aroma, odour, ambience, vibes (*slang*), vibrations (*slang*), emanation

auspices = <u>support</u>, backing, control, charge, care, authority, championship, influence, protection, guidance, sponsorship, supervision, patronage, advocacy, countenance, aegis

auspicious = <u>favourable</u>, timely, happy, promising, encouraging, bright, lucky, hopeful, fortunate, prosperous, rosy, opportune, propitious, felicitous OPPOSITE> unpromising

austere **1** = <u>stern</u>, hard, serious, cold, severe, formal, grave, strict, exacting, harsh, stiff, forbidding, grim, rigorous, solemn, stringent, inflexible, unrelenting, unfeeling …*an austere, distant, cold person…* OPPOSITE> kindly

2 = <u>plain</u>, simple, severe, spare, harsh, stark, bleak, subdued, economical, Spartan, unadorned, unornamented …*The church was austere and simple…* OPPOSITE> luxurious
3 = <u>ascetic</u>, strict, continent, exacting, rigid, sober, economical, solemn, Spartan, unrelenting, self-disciplined, puritanical, chaste, strait-laced, abstemious, self-denying, abstinent …*The life of the troops was comparatively austere…* OPPOSITE> abandoned

austerity **1** = <u>plainness</u>, economy, simplicity, severity, starkness, spareness, Spartanism …*abandoned buildings with a classical austerity…*
2 = <u>asceticism</u>, economy, rigidity, abstinence, self-discipline, chastity, sobriety, continence, puritanism, solemnity, self-denial, strictness, abstemiousness, chasteness, exactingness, Spartanism …*the years of austerity which followed the war…*

authentic **1** = <u>real</u>, true, original, actual, pure, genuine, valid, faithful, undisputed, veritable, lawful, on the level (*informal*), bona fide, dinkum (*Austral. & N.Z. informal*), pukka, the real McCoy, true-to-life …*patterns for making authentic border-style clothing…* OPPOSITE> fake
2 = <u>accurate</u>, true, certain, reliable, legitimate, authoritative, factual, truthful, dependable, trustworthy, veracious …*authentic details about the birth of the organization…* OPPOSITE> fictitious

authenticate **1** = <u>verify</u>, guarantee, warrant, authorize, certify, avouch …*All the antiques have been authenticated…* OPPOSITE> invalidate
2 = <u>vouch for</u>, confirm, endorse, validate, attest …*He authenticated the accuracy of various details…*

authenticity **1** = <u>genuineness</u>, purity, realness, veritableness …*Some factors have cast doubt on the statue's authentcity…*
2 = <u>accuracy</u>, truth, certainty, validity, reliability, legitimacy, verity, actuality, faithfulness, truthfulness, dependability, trustworthiness, authoritativeness, factualness …*The film's authenticity of detail has impressed critics…*

author **1** = <u>writer</u>, composer, novelist, hack, creator, columnist, scribbler, scribe, essayist, wordsmith, penpusher, littérateur, man *or* woman of letters …*She's the author of the book 'Give your Child Music'…*
2 = <u>creator</u>, father, parent, mother, maker, producer, framer, designer, founder, architect, planner, inventor, mover, originator, prime mover, doer, initiator, begetter, fabricator …*the authors of the plan…*

authoritarian ADJECTIVE = <u>strict</u>, severe, absolute, harsh, rigid, autocratic, dictatorial, dogmatic, imperious, domineering, unyielding, tyrannical, disciplinarian, despotic, doctrinaire …*There was a coup to restore authoritarian rule…* OPPOSITE> lenient
NOUN = <u>disciplinarian</u>, dictator, tyrant, despot, autocrat, absolutist …*He became an overly strict authoritarian…*

authoritative **1** = <u>commanding</u>, lordly, masterly, imposing, dominating, confident, decisive, imperative, assertive, autocratic, dictatorial, dogmatic, imperious, self-assured, peremptory …*He has a deep,* *authoritative voice*... OPPOSITE timid

2 = <u>official</u>, approved, sanctioned, legitimate, sovereign, authorized, commanding ...*The first authoritative study was published in 1840...* OPPOSITE unofficial

3 = <u>reliable</u>, learned, sound, true, accurate, valid, scholarly, faithful, authentic, definitive, factual, truthful, veritable, dependable, trustworthy ...*The evidence she uses is highly authoritative...* OPPOSITE unreliable

authority 1 *usually plural* = <u>powers that be</u>, government, police, officials, the state, management, administration, the system, the Establishment, Big Brother (*informal*), officialdom ...*This was a pretext for the authorities to cancel the elections...*

2 = <u>prerogative</u>, right, influence, might, force, power, control, charge, rule, government, weight, strength, direction, command, licence, privilege, warrant, say-so, sway, domination, jurisdiction, supremacy, dominion, ascendancy, mana (*N.Z.*) ...*The judge has no authority to order a second trial...*

3 = <u>expert</u>, specialist, professional, master, ace (*informal*), scholar, guru, buff (*informal*), wizard, whizz (*informal*), virtuoso, connoisseur, arbiter, hotshot (*informal*), fundi (*S. African*) ...*He's an authority on Russian affairs...*

4 = <u>command</u>, power, control, rule, management, direction, grasp, sway, domination, mastery, dominion ...*He has no natural authority...*

5 = <u>permission</u>, leave, permit, sanction, licence, approval, go-ahead (*informal*), liberty, consent, warrant, say-so, tolerance, justification, green light, assent, authorization, dispensation, carte blanche, a blank cheque, sufferance ...*He must first be given authority from his own superiors...*

authorization = <u>permission</u>, right, leave, power, authority, ability, strength, permit, sanction, licence, approval, warrant, say-so, credentials, a blank cheque

authorize 1 = <u>empower</u>, commission, enable, entitle, mandate, accredit, give authority to ...*They authorized him to use force if necessary...*

2 = <u>permit</u>, allow, suffer, grant, confirm, agree to, approve, sanction, endure, license, endorse, warrant, tolerate, ratify, consent to, countenance, accredit, vouch for, give leave, give the green light for, give a blank cheque to, give authority for ...*We are willing to authorize a police raid...* OPPOSITE forbid

authorized = <u>official</u>, commissioned, approved, licensed, ratified, signed and sealed

autobiography = <u>life story</u>, record, history, résumé, memoirs

autocracy = <u>dictatorship</u>, tyranny, despotism, absolutism

autocrat = <u>dictator</u>, tyrant, despot, absolutist

autocratic = <u>dictatorial</u>, absolute, unlimited, all-powerful, imperious, domineering, tyrannical, despotic, tyrannous

automatic 1 = <u>mechanical</u>, robot, automated, mechanized, push-button, self-regulating, self-propelling, self-activating, self-moving, self-acting

...*Modern trains have automatic doors...* OPPOSITE done by hand

2 = <u>involuntary</u>, natural, unconscious, mechanical, spontaneous, reflex, instinctive, instinctual, unwilled ...*the automatic body functions, such as breathing...* OPPOSITE conscious

3 = <u>inevitable</u>, certain, necessary, assured, routine, unavoidable, inescapable ...*They should face an automatic charge of manslaughter...*

autonomous = <u>self-ruling</u>, free, independent, sovereign, self-sufficient, self-governing, self-determining

autonomy = <u>independence</u>, freedom, sovereignty, self-determination, self-government, self-rule, self-sufficiency, home rule OPPOSITE dependency

autopsy = <u>postmortem</u>, dissection, postmortem examination, necropsy

auxiliary ADJECTIVE **1** = <u>supplementary</u>, reserve, emergency, substitute, secondary, back-up, subsidiary, fall-back ...*auxiliary fuel tanks...*

2 = <u>supporting</u>, helping, aiding, assisting, accessory, ancillary ...*the army and auxiliary forces...* OPPOSITE primary

NOUN = <u>helper</u>, partner, ally, associate, supporter, assistant, companion, accessory, subordinate, protagonist, accomplice, confederate, henchman ...*a nursing auxiliary...*

avail NOUN = <u>benefit</u>, use, help, good, service, aid, profit, advantage, purpose, assistance, utility, effectiveness, mileage (*informal*), usefulness, efficacy ...*His efforts were to no avail...*

PHRASES **avail yourself of something** = <u>make use of</u>, use, employ, exploit, take advantage of, profit from, make the most of, utilize, have recourse to, turn to account ...*Guests should feel at liberty to avail themselves of your facilities...*

availability = <u>accessibility</u>, readiness, handiness, attainability, obtainability

available = <u>accessible</u>, ready, to hand, convenient, handy, vacant, on hand, at hand, free, applicable, to be had, achievable, obtainable, on tap (*informal*), attainable, attainable, at your fingertips, at your disposal, ready for use OPPOSITE in use

avalanche 1 = <u>snow-slide</u>, landslide, landslip, snow-slip ...*Four people died when an avalanche buried them alive last week...*

2 = <u>large amount</u>, barrage, torrent, deluge, inundation ...*He was greeted with an avalanche of publicity...*

avant-garde = <u>progressive</u>, pioneering, way-out (*informal*), experimental, innovative, unconventional, far-out (*slang*), ground-breaking, innovatory OPPOSITE conservative

avarice = <u>greed</u>, meanness, penny-pinching, parsimony, acquisitiveness, rapacity, cupidity, stinginess, covetousness, miserliness, greediness, niggardliness, graspingness, close-fistedness, penuriousness OPPOSITE liberality

avenge = <u>get revenge for</u>, revenge, repay, retaliate for, take revenge for, hit back for, requite, pay (someone) back for, get even for (*informal*), even the score for, get your own back for, take vengeance for, take satisfaction for, pay (someone) back in his *or* her own coin for

---

Word Power

avenge – In the past it was considered incorrect to use *avenge* with *yourself*, but this use is now acceptable and relatively common: *she was determined to avenge herself upon this monster.*

---

avenue = <u>street</u>, way, course, drive, road, pass, approach, channel, access, entry, route, path, passage, entrance, alley, pathway, boulevard, driveway, thoroughfare

average NOUN = <u>standard</u>, normal, usual, par, mode, mean, rule, medium, norm, run of the mill, midpoint ...*The pay is about the average for a service industry*...
ADJECTIVE 1 = <u>usual</u>, common, standard, general, normal, regular, ordinary, typical, commonplace, unexceptional ...*The average man burns 2000 calories a day*... OPPOSITE> unusual
2 = <u>mean</u>, middle, medium, intermediate, median ...*Of the US's million millionaires, the average age was 63*... OPPOSITE> minimum
3 = <u>mediocre</u>, fair, ordinary, moderate, pedestrian, indifferent, not bad, middling, insignificant, so-so (*informal*), banal, second-rate, middle-of-the-road, tolerable, run-of-the-mill, passable, undistinguished, uninspired, unexceptional, bog-standard (*Brit. & Irish slang*), no great shakes (*informal*), fair to middling (*informal*) ...*I was only average academically*...
VERB = <u>make on average</u>, be on average, even out to, do on average, balance out to ...*pay increases averaging 9.75%*...
PHRASES **on average** = <u>usually</u>, generally, normally, typically, for the most part, as a rule ...*On average we would be spending $200 a day*...

averse = <u>opposed</u>, reluctant, hostile, unwilling, backward, unfavourable, loath, disinclined, inimical, indisposed, antipathetic, ill-disposed OPPOSITE> favourable

aversion = <u>hatred</u>, hate, horror, disgust, hostility, opposition, dislike, reluctance, loathing, distaste, animosity, revulsion, antipathy, repulsion, abhorrence, disinclination, repugnance, odium, detestation, indisposition OPPOSITE> love

avert 1 = <u>ward off</u>, avoid, prevent, frustrate, fend off, preclude, stave off, forestall ...*A fresh tragedy was narrowly averted yesterday*...
2 = <u>turn away</u>, turn, turn aside ...*He kept his eyes averted*...

aviation = <u>flying</u>, flight, aeronautics, powered flight

aviator = <u>pilot</u>, flyer, airman, airwoman, aeronaut

avid 1 = <u>enthusiastic</u>, keen, devoted, intense, eager, passionate, ardent, fanatical, fervent, zealous, keen as mustard ...*an avid collector of art*... OPPOSITE> indifferent
2 = <u>insatiable</u>, hungry, greedy, thirsty, grasping, voracious, acquisitive, ravenous, rapacious, avaricious, covetous, athirst ...*He was avid for wealth*...

avoid 1 = <u>prevent</u>, stop, frustrate, hamper, foil, inhibit, head off, avert, thwart, intercept, hinder, obstruct, impede, ward off, stave off, forestall, defend against ...*He had to take emergency action to avoid a disaster*...
2 = <u>refrain from</u>, bypass, dodge, eschew, escape, duck (out of) (*informal*), fight shy of, shirk from ...*He managed to avoid giving them an idea of what he was up to*...
3 = <u>keep away from</u>, dodge, shun, evade, steer clear of, sidestep, circumvent, bypass, slip through the net, body-swerve (*Scot.*), give a wide berth to ...*He had ample time to swerve and avoid the woman*...

avoidable 1 = <u>preventable</u>, stoppable, avertible *or* avertable ...*The tragedy was entirely avoidable*...
OPPOSITE> unpreventable
2 = <u>escapable</u>, evadable ...*Smoking is an avoidable cause of disease and death*... OPPOSITE> inevitable

avoidance 1 = <u>refraining</u>, dodging, shirking, eschewal ...*tax avoidance*...
2 = <u>prevention</u>, safeguard, precaution, anticipation, thwarting, elimination, deterrence, forestalling, prophylaxis, preclusion, obviation ...*Improve your health by stress avoidance*...

avow = <u>state</u>, maintain, declare, allege, recognize, swear, assert, proclaim, affirm, profess, aver, asseverate

avowed = <u>declared</u>, open, admitted, acknowledged, confessed, sworn, professed, self-proclaimed

await 1 = <u>wait for</u>, expect, look for, look forward to, anticipate, stay for ...*Little was said as we awaited the arrival of the chairman*...
2 = <u>be in store for</u>, wait for, be ready for, lie in wait for, be in readiness for ...*A nasty surprise awaited them*...

awake ADJECTIVE = <u>not sleeping</u>, sleepless, wide-awake, aware, waking, conscious, aroused, awakened, restless, restive, wakeful, bright-eyed and bushy-tailed ...*I don't stay awake at night worrying about that*... OPPOSITE> asleep
VERB 1 = <u>wake up</u>, come to, wake, stir, awaken, rouse ...*I awoke to the sound of the wind in the trees*...
2 = <u>alert</u>, excite, stimulate, provoke, revive, arouse, activate, awaken, fan, animate, stir up, incite, kick-start (*informal*), enliven, kindle, breathe life into, call forth, vivify ...*He had awoken interest in the sport again*...
PHRASES **awake to** = <u>alert to</u>, aware of, on the lookout for, alive to, attentive to, on the alert for, observant of, watchful of, on guard to, on your toes to, heedful of, vigilant of ...*They are awake to the challenge of stemming the exodus*...
➤ **wake**

awaken 1 = <u>stimulate</u>, excite, provoke, activate, alert, animate, fan, stir up, incite, kick-start (*informal*), enliven, kindle, breathe life into, call forth, vivify ...*The aim was to awaken an interest in foreign cultures*...
2 = <u>awake</u>, wake, revive, arouse, rouse ...*He was snoring when I awakened him*...
➤ **wake**

award NOUN 1 = <u>prize</u>, gift, trophy, decoration, grant, bonsela (*S. African*) …*She presented a bravery award to the schoolgirl*…

2 = grant, subsidy, scholarship, hand-out, endowment, stipend …*this year's annual pay award*…

3 (*Law*) = settlement, payment, compensation …*workmen's compensation awards*…

4 = giving, presentation, allotment, bestowal, conferment, conferral …*the award of the man of the match trophy*…

VERB **1** = present with, give, grant, gift, distribute, render, assign, decree, hand out, confer, endow, bestow, allot, apportion, adjudge …*She was awarded the prize for both films*…

2 = grant, give, render, assign, decree, accord, confer, adjudge …*The contract has been awarded to a British shipyard*…

aware **ADJECTIVE** = informed, enlightened, knowledgeable, learned, expert, versed, up to date, in the picture, in the know (*informal*), erudite, well-read, au fait (*French*), in the loop, well-briefed, au courant (*French*), clued-up (*informal*) …*They are politically very aware*… **OPPOSITE** ignorant

PHRASES **aware of** = knowing about, familiar with, conscious of, wise to (*slang*), alert to, mindful of, acquainted with, alive to, awake to, privy to, hip to (*slang*), appreciative of, attentive to, conversant with, apprised of, cognizant of, sensible of …*They are well aware of the dangers*…

awareness

PHRASES **awareness of** = knowledge of, understanding of, appreciation of, recognition of, attention to, perception of, consciousness of, acquaintance with, enlightenment with, sensibility to, realization of, familiarity with, mindfulness of, cognizance of, sentience of

awash **1** = flooded, drowned, engulfed, submerged, immersed, afloat, inundated, deluged, submersed …*The bathroom floor was awash*…

2 = overburdened, overwhelmed, swamped …*a company which is awash with cash*…

away **ADJECTIVE** = absent, out, gone, elsewhere, abroad, not there, not here, not present, on vacation, not at home …*She was away on a business trip*…

ADVERB **1** = off, elsewhere, abroad, hence, from here …*She drove away before he could speak again*…

2 = aside, out of the way, to one side …*I put my journal away and prepared for bed*…

3 = at a distance, far, apart, remote, isolated …*They live thirty miles away from town*…

4 = continuously, repeatedly, relentlessly, incessantly, interminably, unremittingly, uninterruptedly …*He would work away on his computer well into the night*…

awe **NOUN** = wonder, fear, respect, reverence, horror, terror, dread, admiration, amazement, astonishment, veneration …*She gazed in awe at the great stones*… **OPPOSITE** contempt

VERB = impress, amaze, stun, frighten, terrify, cow, astonish, horrify, intimidate, daunt …*I am still awed by his courage*…

awed = impressed, shocked, amazed, afraid, stunned, frightened, terrified, cowed, astonished, horrified, intimidated, fearful, daunted, dumbfounded, wonder-struck

awe-inspiring = impressive, striking, wonderful, amazing, stunning (*informal*), magnificent, astonishing, intimidating, awesome, daunting, breathtaking, fearsome, wondrous (*archaic or literary*), jaw-dropping **OPPOSITE** unimpressive

awesome = awe-inspiring, striking, shocking, imposing, terrible, amazing, stunning, wonderful, alarming, impressive, frightening, awful, overwhelming, terrifying, magnificent, astonishing, horrible, dreadful, horrifying, intimidating, fearful, daunting, breathtaking, majestic, solemn, fearsome, wondrous (*archaic or literary*), redoubtable, jaw-dropping, stupefying

awestruck or **awe-stricken** = impressed, shocked, amazed, stunned, afraid, frightened, terrified, cowed, astonished, horrified, intimidated, fearful, awed, daunted, awe-inspired, dumbfounded, struck dumb, wonder-struck

awful **1** = disgusting, terrible, tremendous, offensive, gross, nasty, foul, horrible, dreadful, unpleasant, revolting, stinking, sickening, hideous, vulgar, vile, distasteful, horrid, frightful, nauseating, odious, repugnant, loathsome, abominable, nauseous, detestable, godawful (*slang*), hellacious (*U.S. slang*), festy (*Austral. slang*), yucko (*Austral. slang*) …*an awful smell of paint*…

2 = bad, poor, terrible, appalling, foul, rubbish (*slang*), dreadful, unpleasant, dire, horrendous, ghastly, from hell (*informal*), atrocious, deplorable, abysmal, frightful, hellacious (*U.S. slang*) …*Even if the weather's awful there's still lots to do*… **OPPOSITE** wonderful

3 = shocking, serious, alarming, distressing, dreadful, horrifying, horrific, hideous, harrowing, gruesome …*Her injuries were massive; it was awful*…

4 = unwell, poorly (*informal*), ill, terrible, sick, ugly, crook (*Austral. & N.Z. informal*), unhealthy, unsightly, queasy, out of sorts (*informal*), off-colour, under the weather (*informal*), green about the gills …*I looked awful and felt quite sleepy*…

awfully **1** (*Informal*) = very, extremely, terribly, exceptionally, quite, very much, seriously (*informal*), greatly, immensely, exceedingly, excessively, dreadfully …*That caramel looks awfully good*…

2 = badly, woefully, dreadfully, inadequately, disgracefully, wretchedly, unforgivably, shoddily, reprehensibly, disreputably …*I played awfully, and there are no excuses*…

awhile = for a while, briefly, for a moment, for a short time, for a little while

---

Word Power

awhile – *Awhile*, written as a single word, is an adverb meaning 'for a period of time'. It can only be used with a verb, for example: *he stood awhile in thought*. It is quite commonly written by mistake instead of the noun *a while*, meaning 'a period of time', so take care not to confuse the two parts of speech: *I thought about that for a while* (not *awhile*).

awkward 1 = <u>embarrassing</u>, difficult, compromising, sensitive, embarrassed, painful, distressing, delicate, uncomfortable, tricky, trying, humiliating, unpleasant, sticky (*informal*), troublesome, perplexing, disconcerting, inconvenient, thorny, untimely, ill at ease, discomfiting, ticklish, inopportune, toe-curling (*slang*), barro (*Austral. slang*), cringeworthy (*Brit. informal*) ...*There was an awkward moment when people had to decide where to stand...* OPPOSITE comfortable

2 = <u>inconvenient</u>, difficult, troublesome, cumbersome, unwieldy, unmanageable, clunky (*informal*), unhandy ...*It was heavy enough to make it awkward to carry...* OPPOSITE convenient

3 = <u>clumsy</u>, stiff, rude, blundering, coarse, bungling, lumbering, inept, unskilled, bumbling, unwieldy, ponderous, ungainly, gauche, gawky, uncouth, unrefined, artless, inelegant, uncoordinated, graceless, cack-handed (*informal*), unpolished, clownish, oafish, inexpert, maladroit, ill-bred, all thumbs, ungraceful, skill-less, unskilful, butterfingered (*informal*), unhandy, ham-fisted *or* ham-handed (*informal*), unco (*Austral. slang*) ...*She made an awkward gesture with her hands...* OPPOSITE graceful

4 = <u>uncooperative</u>, trying, difficult, annoying, unpredictable, unreasonable, stubborn, troublesome, perverse, prickly, exasperating, irritable, intractable, vexing, unhelpful, touchy, obstinate, obstructive, bloody-minded (*Brit. informal*), vexatious, hard to handle, disobliging ...*She's got to an age where she's being awkward...*

awkwardness 1 = <u>clumsiness</u>, stiffness, rudeness, coarseness, ineptness, ill-breeding, artlessness, gaucheness, inelegance, gaucherie, gracelessness, oafishness, gawkiness, uncouthness, maladroitness, ungainliness, clownishness, inexpertness, uncoordination, unskilfulness, unskilledness ...*He displayed all the awkwardness of adolescence...*

2 = <u>embarrassment</u>, difficulty, discomfort, delicacy, unpleasantness, inconvenience, stickiness (*informal*), painfulness, ticklishness, uphill (*S. African*), thorniness, inopportuneness, perplexingness, untimeliness ...*It*

was a moment of some awkwardness in our relationship...

awry ADVERB *or* ADJECTIVE 1 = <u>wrong</u>, amiss ...*a plan that had gone awry...*

2 = <u>askew</u>, to one side, off course, out of line, obliquely, unevenly, off-centre, cockeyed (*informal*), out of true, crookedly, skew-whiff (*informal*) ...*He was concerned that his hair might go awry...*

3 = <u>askew</u>, twisted, crooked, to one side, uneven, off course, out of line, asymmetrical, off-centre, cockeyed (*informal*), misaligned, out of true, skew-whiff (*informal*) ...*His dark hair was all awry...*

axe NOUN = <u>hatchet</u>, chopper, tomahawk, cleaver, adze ...*She took an axe and wrecked the car...*

VERB 1 (*Informal*) = <u>abandon</u>, end, pull, eliminate, cancel, scrap, wind up, turn off (*informal*), relegate, cut back, terminate, dispense with, discontinue, pull the plug on ...*Community projects are being axed by the government...*

2 (*Informal*) = <u>dismiss</u>, fire (*informal*), sack (*informal*), remove, get rid of, discharge, throw out, oust, give (someone) their marching orders, give the boot to (*slang*), give the bullet to (*Brit. slang*), give the push to ...*She was axed by the Edinburgh club in October after her comments about a referee...*

PHRASES **an axe to grind** = <u>pet subject</u>, grievance, ulterior motive, private purpose, personal consideration, private ends ...*I've got no axe to grind with him...* ♦ **the axe** (*Informal*) = <u>the sack</u> (*informal*), dismissal, discharge, wind-up, the boot (*slang*), cancellation, cutback, termination, the chop (*slang*), the (old) heave-ho (*informal*), the order of the boot (*slang*) ...*one of the four doctors facing the axe...*

axiom = <u>principle</u>, fundamental, maxim, gnome, adage, postulate, dictum, precept, aphorism, truism, apophthegm

axis = <u>pivot</u>, shaft, axle, spindle, centre line

axle = <u>shaft</u>, pin, rod, axis, pivot, spindle, arbor, mandrel

azure NOUN *or* ADJECTIVE = <u>sky blue</u>, blue, clear blue, ultramarine, cerulean, sky-coloured

➤ **shades of blue**

B b

baas (*S. African*) = <u>master</u>, boss (*informal*), chief, ruler, commander, head, overlord, overseer

babble `VERB` **1** = <u>gabble</u>, chatter, gush, spout, waffle (*informal, chiefly Brit.*), splutter, gaggle, burble, prattle, gibber, rabbit on (*Brit. informal*), jabber, prate …*They all babbled simultaneously…*
2 = <u>gurgle</u>, lap, bubble, splash, murmur, ripple, burble, plash …*a brook babbling only yards from the door…*
`NOUN` **1** = <u>gabble</u>, chatter, burble, prattle, blabber …*He couldn't make himself heard above the babble…*
2 = <u>gibberish</u>, waffle (*informal, chiefly Brit.*), drivel, twaddle …*lots of babble about strategies and tactics…*

babe = <u>baby</u>, child, innocent, infant, bairn (*Scot.*), tacker (*Austral. slang*), suckling, newborn child, babe in arms, nursling

baby `NOUN` = <u>child</u>, infant, babe, wean (*Scot.*), little one, bairn (*Scot.*), suckling, newborn child, babe in arms, sprog (*slang*), neonate, rug rat (*slang*), ankle-biter (*Austral. slang*), tacker (*Austral. slang*) …*My wife has just had a baby…*
`ADJECTIVE` = <u>small</u>, little, minute, tiny, mini, wee, miniature, dwarf, diminutive, petite, midget, teeny, pocket-sized, undersized, teeny-weeny, Lilliputian, teensy-weensy, pygmy *or* pigmy …*Serve with baby new potatoes…*
`VERB` = <u>spoil</u>, pamper, cosset, coddle, pet, humour, indulge, spoon-feed, mollycoddle, overindulge, wrap up in cotton wool (*informal*) …*He'd always babied her…*

back `NOUN` **1** = <u>spine</u>, backbone, vertebrae, spinal column, vertebral column …*Three of the victims were shot in the back…*
2 = <u>rear</u>, back end …*a room at the back of the shop…* `OPPOSITE` front
3 = <u>reverse</u>, rear, other side, wrong side, underside, flip side, verso …*Send your answers on the back of a postcard…*
`ADJECTIVE` **1** = <u>rear</u> …*a path leading to the back garden…* `OPPOSITE` front
2 = <u>rearmost</u>, hind, hindmost …*She could remember sitting in the back seat of their car…*
3 = <u>previous</u>, earlier, former, past, elapsed …*A handful of back copies will give an indication of property prices…* `OPPOSITE` future
4 = <u>tail</u>, end, rear, posterior …*They had transmitters taped to their back feathers…*
`VERB` **1** = <u>support</u>, help, second, aid, champion, encourage, favour, defend, promote, sanction, sustain, assist, advocate, endorse, side with, stand up for, espouse, stand behind, countenance, abet, stick up for (*informal*), take up the cudgels for …*He is backed by the civic movement…* `OPPOSITE` oppose
2 = <u>subsidize</u>, help, support, finance, sponsor, assist, underwrite …*Murjani backed him to start the new company…*
`PHRASES` **back down** = <u>give in</u>, collapse, withdraw, yield, concede, submit, surrender, comply, cave in (*informal*), capitulate, accede, admit defeat, back-pedal …*It's too late now to back down…* ◆ **back out** = <u>withdraw</u>, retire, give up, pull out, retreat, drop out, renege, cop out (*slang*), chicken out (*informal*), detach yourself …*I've already promised I'll go – I can't back out now…* ◆ **back someone up** = <u>support</u>, second, aid, assist, stand by, bolster …*The girl denied being there, and the men backed her up…* ◆ **behind someone's back** = <u>secretly</u>, covertly, surreptitiously, furtively, conspiratorially, sneakily, deceitfully …*You enjoy her hospitality, and then criticize her behind her back…*

(Related Words)
adjective: dorsal

backbone **1** = <u>spinal column</u>, spine, vertebrae, vertebral column …*She doubled over, snapping her backbone and breaking her arm…*
2 = <u>foundation</u>, support, base, basis, mainstay, bedrock …*the economic backbone of the nation…*
3 = <u>strength of character</u>, will, character, bottle (*Brit. slang*), resolution, resolve, nerve, daring, courage, determination, guts, pluck, stamina, grit, bravery, fortitude, toughness, tenacity, willpower, mettle, boldness, firmness, spunk (*informal*), fearlessness, steadfastness, moral fibre, hardihood, dauntlessness …*You might be taking drastic measures and you've got to have the backbone to do that…*

backer **1** = <u>supporter</u>, second, ally, angel (*informal*), patron, promoter, subscriber, underwriter, helper, benefactor …*I was looking for a backer to assist me in the attempted buy-out…*
2 = <u>advocate</u>, supporter, patron, sponsor, promoter, protagonist …*He became a backer of reform at the height of the crisis…*

backfire = <u>fail</u>, founder, flop (*informal*), rebound, fall through, fall flat, boomerang, miscarry, misfire, go belly-up (*slang*), turn out badly, meet with disaster

background **1** = <u>upbringing</u>, history, culture, environment, tradition, circumstances, breeding, milieu …*Moulded by his background, he could not escape traditional values…*
2 = <u>experience</u>, grounding, education, preparation, qualifications, credentials …*His background was in engineering…*
3 = <u>circumstances</u>, history, conditions, situation, atmosphere, environment, framework, ambience, milieu, frame of reference …*The meeting takes place against a background of political violence…*

backing **1** = <u>support</u>, seconding, championing, promotion, sanction, approval, blessing, encouragement, endorsement, patronage,

accompaniment, advocacy, moral support, espousal
…*He said the president had the full backing of his
government*…
2 = <u>assistance</u>, support, help, funds, aid, grant,
subsidy, sponsorship, patronage …*She brought her
action with the financial backing of the BBC*…

backlash = <u>reaction</u>, response, resistance,
resentment, retaliation, repercussion, counterblast,
counteraction, retroaction

backlog = <u>build-up</u>, stock, excess, accumulation,
accretion

backside (*Informal*) = <u>buttocks</u>, behind (*informal*),
seat, bottom, rear, tail (*U.S.*), cheeks (*informal*), butt
(*U.S. & Canad. informal*), bum (*Brit. slang*), buns (*U.S.
slang*), rump, rear end, posterior, haunches,
hindquarters, derrière (*euphemistic*), tush, fundament,
gluteus maximus (*Anatomy*), coit (*Austral. slang*),
nates (*technical name*), jacksy (*Brit. slang*), keister *or*
keester (*slang, chiefly U.S.*)

backtrack 1 = <u>retract</u>, withdraw, retreat, draw back,
recant …*The finance minister backtracked on his
decision*…
2 = <u>retrace your steps</u>, go back, reverse, retreat, move
back, back-pedal …*We had to backtrack to the corner
and cross the street*…

backup 1 = <u>support</u>, backing, help, aid, reserves,
assistance, reinforcement, auxiliaries …*There's no
emergency backup immediately available if something
goes wrong*…
2 = <u>substitute</u>, reserve, relief, stand-in, replacement,
stand-by, understudy, second string, locum …*He was
added to the squad as a backup*…

backward 1 = <u>reverse</u>, inverted, inverse, back to
front, rearward …*He did a backward flip* [OPPOSITE]
forward
2 = <u>underdeveloped</u>, undeveloped …*We need to
accelerate the pace of change in our backward
country*…
3 = <u>slow</u>, behind, stupid, retarded, deficient,
underdeveloped, subnormal, half-witted,
behindhand, slow-witted …*I was slow to walk and my
parents thought I was backward*…

backwardness 1 = <u>lack of development</u>,
underdevelopment …*I was astonished at the
backwardness of our country at the time*…
2 = <u>slowness</u>, learning difficulties,
underdevelopment, retardation, arrested
development …*Her parents were concerned about her
backwardness in practical and physical activities*…
[OPPOSITE] brightness

backwards *or* **backward** = <u>towards the rear</u>,
behind you, in reverse, rearwards

backwoods = <u>sticks</u> (*informal*), outback, back
country (*U.S.*), back of beyond, backlands (*U.S.*)

bacteria = <u>microorganisms</u>, viruses, bugs (*slang*),
germs, microbes, pathogens, bacilli

> ## Word Power
>
> **bacteria** – *Bacteria* is a plural noun. It is
> therefore incorrect to talk about *a bacteria*,
> even though this is quite commonly heard,
> especially in the media. The correct singular is
> *a bacterium*.

bad [ADJECTIVE] **1** = <u>harmful</u>, damaging, dangerous,
disastrous, destructive, unhealthy, detrimental,
hurtful, ruinous, deleterious, injurious,
disadvantageous …*Divorce is bad for children*…
[OPPOSITE] beneficial
2 = <u>severe</u>, serious, terrible, acute, extreme, intense,
painful, distressing, fierce, harsh …*The pain is often so
bad she wants to scream*…
3 = <u>poor</u>, unsound …*Of course politicians will
sometimes make bad decisions*…
4 = <u>unfavourable</u>, troubling, distressing, unfortunate,
grim, discouraging, unpleasant, gloomy, adverse
…*The closure of the project is bad news for her staff*…
5 = <u>inferior</u>, poor, inadequate, pathetic, faulty, duff
(*Brit. informal*), unsatisfactory, mediocre, defective,
second-class, deficient, imperfect, second-rate,
shoddy, low-grade, erroneous, substandard, low-rent
(*informal, chiefly U.S.*), two-bit (*U.S. & Canad. slang*),
crappy (*slang*), end-of-the-pier (*Brit. informal*), poxy
(*slang*), dime-a-dozen (*informal*), bush-league
(*Austral. & N.Z. informal*), tinhorn (*U.S. slang*), half-pie
(*N.Z. informal*), bodger *or* bodgie (*Austral. slang*),
strictly for the birds (*informal*) …*Many old people in
Britain are living in bad housing*… [OPPOSITE]
satisfactory
6 = <u>incompetent</u>, poor, useless, incapable, unfit,
inexpert …*He was a bad driver*…
7 = <u>grim</u>, severe, hard, tough, harsh, unpleasant
…*Being unable to hear doesn't seem as bad as being
unable to see*…
8 = <u>wicked</u>, criminal, evil, corrupt, worthless, base, vile,
immoral, delinquent, sinful, depraved, debased,
amoral, egregious, villainous, unprincipled, iniquitous,
nefarious, dissolute, maleficent …*I was selling drugs,
but I didn't think I was a bad person*… [OPPOSITE]
virtuous
9 = <u>naughty</u>, defiant, perverse, wayward, mischievous,
wicked, unruly, impish, undisciplined, roguish,
disobedient …*You are a bad boy for repeating what I
told you*… [OPPOSITE] well-behaved
10 = <u>guilty</u>, sorry, ashamed, apologetic, rueful,
sheepish, contrite, remorseful, regretful, shamefaced,
conscience-stricken …*You don't have to feel bad
about relaxing*…
11 = <u>injured</u>, damaged, diseased, hurt, sick, disabled,
ailing, lame, unhealthy, dicky (*Brit. informal*) …*He has
a bad back so we have a hard bed*…
12 = <u>rotten</u>, off, rank, sour, rancid, mouldy, fetid,
putrid, festy (*Austral. slang*) …*They bought so much
beef that some went bad*…
[PHRASES] **not bad** (*Informal*) = <u>O.K.</u> *or* okay, fine,
middling, average, fair, all right, acceptable, moderate,
adequate, respectable, satisfactory, so-so, tolerable,

passable, fair to middling (*informal*) ... *These are not bad for cheap shoes...*

baddie *or* **baddy** = <u>villain</u>, criminal, rogue, bad guy, scoundrel, miscreant, antihero, evildoer OPPOSITE> goodie *or* goody

badge 1 = <u>image</u>, brand, stamp, identification, crest, emblem, insignia ...*a badge depicting a party leader...*
2 = <u>mark</u>, sign, token ...*sporting a sword as their badge of citizenship...*

badger = <u>pester</u>, worry, harry, bother, bug (*informal*), bully, plague, hound, get at, harass, nag, hassle (*informal*), chivvy, importune, bend someone's ear (*informal*), be on someone's back (*slang*)

(Related Words)
habitation: set *or* sett

badly 1 = <u>poorly</u>, incorrectly, carelessly, inadequately, erroneously, imperfectly, ineptly, shoddily, defectively, faultily ...*I was angry because I played so badly...* OPPOSITE> well
2 = <u>severely</u>, greatly, deeply, seriously, gravely, desperately, sorely, dangerously, intensely, painfully, acutely, exceedingly ...*It was a gamble that went badly wrong...*
3 = <u>unfavourably</u>, unsuccessfully ...*The male sex comes out of the film very badly...*

badness = <u>wickedness</u>, wrong, evil, corruption, sin, impropriety, immorality, villainy, naughtiness, sinfulness, foulness, baseness, rottenness, vileness, shamefulness OPPOSITE> virtue

bad-tempered = <u>irritable</u>, cross, angry, tense, crabbed, fiery, grumbling, snarling, prickly, exasperated, edgy, snappy, sullen, touchy, surly, petulant, sulky, ill-tempered, irascible, cantankerous, tetchy, ratty (*Brit. & N.Z. informal*), tooshie (*Austral. slang*), testy, fretful, grouchy (*informal*), querulous, peevish, crabby, huffy, dyspeptic, choleric, splenetic, crotchety (*informal*), oversensitive, snappish, ill-humoured, liverish, narky (*Brit. slang*), out of humour OPPOSITE> good-tempered

baffle = <u>puzzle</u>, beat (*slang*), amaze, confuse, stump, bewilder, astound, elude, confound, perplex, disconcert, mystify, flummox, boggle the mind of, dumbfound OPPOSITE> explain

baffling = <u>puzzling</u>, strange, confusing, weird, mysterious, unclear, bewildering, elusive, enigmatic, perplexing, incomprehensible, mystifying, inexplicable, unaccountable, unfathomable OPPOSITE> understandable

bag NOUN = <u>sack</u>, container, poke (*Scot.*), sac, receptacle ...*She left the hotel carrying a shopping bag...*
VERB 1 = <u>get</u>, take, land, score (*slang*), gain, pick up, capture, acquire, get hold of, come by, procure, make sure of, win possession of ...*The smart ones will have already bagged their seats...*
2 = <u>catch</u>, get, kill, shoot, capture, acquire, trap ...*Bag a rabbit for supper...*

baggage = <u>luggage</u>, things, cases, bags, equipment, gear, trunks, suitcases, belongings, paraphernalia,

accoutrements, impedimenta

baggy = <u>loose</u>, hanging, slack, loosened, bulging, not fitting, sagging, sloppy, floppy, billowing, roomy, slackened, ill-fitting, droopy, oversize, not tight OPPOSITE> tight

bail¹ *or* **bale** = <u>scoop</u>, empty, dip, ladle, drain off ...*We kept her afloat for a couple of hours by bailing frantically...*

bail² NOUN (*Law*) = <u>security</u>, bond, guarantee, pledge, warranty, surety, guaranty ...*He was freed on bail pending an appeal...*
PHRASES **bail out** = <u>escape</u>, withdraw, get away, retreat, make your getaway, break free *or* out, make *or* effect your escape ...*The pilot bailed out safely...*
♦ **bail something** *or* **someone out** (*Informal*) = <u>save</u>, help, free, release, aid, deliver, recover, rescue, get out, relieve, liberate, salvage, set free, save the life of, extricate, save (someone's) bacon (*Brit. informal*) ...*They will discuss how to bail the economy out of its slump...*

bait NOUN = <u>lure</u>, attraction, incentive, carrot (*informal*), temptation, bribe, magnet, snare, inducement, decoy, carrot and stick, enticement, allurement ...*bait to attract audiences for advertisements...*
VERB = <u>tease</u>, provoke, annoy, irritate, guy (*informal*), bother, needle (*informal*), plague (*informal*), mock, rag, rib (*informal*), wind up (*Brit. slang*), hound, torment, harass, ridicule, taunt, hassle (*informal*), aggravate (*informal*), badger, gall, persecute, pester, goad, irk, bedevil, take the mickey out of (*informal*), chaff, gibe, get on the nerves of (*informal*), nark (*Brit., Austral., & N.Z. slang*), be on the back of (*slang*), get in the hair of (*informal*), get *or* take a rise out of ...*He delighted in baiting his mother...*

baked = <u>dry</u>, desert, seared, dried up, scorched, barren, sterile, arid, torrid, desiccated, sun-baked, waterless, moistureless

bakkie (*S. African*) = <u>truck</u>, pick-up, van, lorry, pick-up truck

balance VERB 1 = <u>stabilize</u>, level, steady ...*He balanced a football on his head...* OPPOSITE> overbalance
2 = <u>offset</u>, match, square, make up for, compensate for, counteract, neutralize, counterbalance, even up, equalize, counterpoise ...*Balance spicy dishes with mild ones...*
3 = <u>weigh</u>, consider, compare, estimate, contrast, assess, evaluate, set against, juxtapose ...*She carefully tried to balance religious sensitivities against democratic freedom...*
4 (*Accounting*) = <u>calculate</u>, rate, judge, total, determine, estimate, settle, count, square, reckon, work out, compute, gauge, tally ...*He balanced his budget by rigid control over public expenditure...*
NOUN 1 = <u>equilibrium</u>, stability, steadiness, evenness, equipoise, counterpoise ...*The medicines you are currently taking could be affecting your balance...* OPPOSITE> instability
2 = <u>stability</u>, equanimity, constancy, steadiness ...*the*

ecological balance of the forest…
3 = <u>parity</u>, equity, fairness, impartiality, equality, correspondence, equivalence …*her ability to maintain the political balance…*
4 = <u>remainder</u>, rest, difference, surplus, residue …*They were due to pay the balance on delivery…*
5 = <u>composure</u>, stability, restraint, self-control, poise, self-discipline, coolness, calmness, equanimity, self-restraint, steadiness, self-possession, self-mastery, strength of mind *or* will …*a balance of mind…*

balanced = <u>unbiased</u>, just, fair, equal, objective, neutral, detached, open-minded, equitable, impartial, disinterested, even-handed, nonpartisan, unprejudiced, without fear or favour, nondiscriminating <u>OPPOSITE</u> biased

balance sheet = <u>statement</u>, report, account, budget, ledger, financial statement, credits and debits sheet

balcony 1 = <u>terrace</u>, veranda …*He appeared on a second floor balcony to appeal to the crowd to be calm…*
2 = <u>upper circle</u>, gods, gallery …*We took our seats in the balcony…*

bald 1 = <u>hairless</u>, bare, shorn, clean-shaven, tonsured, depilated, glabrous (*Biology*), baldheaded, baldpated …*The man's bald head was beaded with sweat…*
2 = <u>plain</u>, direct, simple, straight, frank, severe, bare, straightforward, blunt, rude, outright, downright, forthright, unadorned, unvarnished, straight from the shoulder …*The bald truth is that he's just not happy…*

balding = <u>losing your hair</u>, receding, thin on top, becoming bald

baldness = <u>hairlessness</u>, alopecia (*Pathology*), baldheadedness, baldpatedness, glabrousness (*Biology*)

bale
  ➤ **bail¹**

baleful = <u>menacing</u>, threatening, dangerous, frightening, evil, deadly, forbidding, intimidating, harmful, sinister, ominous, malignant, hurtful, vindictive, pernicious, mournful, malevolent, noxious, venomous, ruinous, intimidatory, minatory, maleficent, bodeful, louring *or* lowering, minacious <u>OPPOSITE</u> friendly

balk *or* **baulk** *often with* ***at*** = <u>recoil</u>, resist, hesitate, dodge, falter, evade, shy away, flinch, quail, shirk, shrink, draw back, jib <u>OPPOSITE</u> accept

ball 1 = <u>sphere</u>, drop, globe, pellet, orb, globule, spheroid …*a golf ball…*
2 = <u>projectile</u>, shot, missile, bullet, ammunition, slug, pellet, grapeshot …*A cannon ball struck the ship…*

ballast = <u>counterbalance</u>, balance, weight, stability, equilibrium, sandbag, counterweight, stabilizer

ballgame
  ➤ **ballgames**

balloon = <u>expand</u>, rise, increase, extend, swell, blow up, enlarge, inflate, bulge, billow, dilate, be inflated, puff out, become larger, distend, bloat, grow rapidly

ballot = <u>vote</u>, election, voting, poll, polling, referendum, show of hands

balm 1 = <u>ointment</u>, cream, lotion, salve, emollient, balsam, liniment, embrocation, unguent …*The balm is very soothing…*
2 = <u>comfort</u>, support, relief, cheer, consolation, solace, palliative, anodyne, succour, restorative, curative …*This place is a balm to the soul…*

balmy 1 = <u>mild</u>, warm, calm, moderate, pleasant, clement, tranquil, temperate, summery …*a balmy summer's evening…* <u>OPPOSITE</u> rough
2 ➤ **barmy**

bamboozle (*Informal*) **1** = <u>cheat</u>, do (*informal*), kid (*informal*), skin (*slang*), trick, fool, take in (*informal*), con (*informal*), stiff, sting (*informal*), mislead, rip off (*slang*), thwart, deceive, fleece, hoax, defraud, dupe, beguile, gull (*archaic*), delude, swindle, stitch up (*slang*), victimize, hoodwink, double-cross (*informal*), diddle (*informal*), take for a ride (*informal*), do the dirty on (*Brit. informal*), bilk, pull a fast one on (*informal*), cozen …*He was bamboozled by con men…*
2 = <u>puzzle</u>, confuse, stump, baffle, bewilder, confound, perplex, mystify, befuddle, flummox, nonplus …*He bamboozled Mercer into defeat…*

ban VERB **1** = <u>prohibit</u>, black, bar, block, restrict, veto, forbid, boycott, suppress, outlaw, banish, disallow, proscribe, debar, blackball, interdict …*Last year arms sales were banned…* <u>OPPOSITE</u> permit
2 = <u>bar</u>, prohibit, exclude, forbid, disqualify, preclude, debar, declare ineligible …*He was banned from driving for three years…*
NOUN = <u>prohibition</u>, block, restriction, veto, boycott, embargo, injunction, censorship, taboo, suppression, stoppage, disqualification, interdiction, interdict, proscription, disallowance …*The General also lifted a ban on political parties…* <u>OPPOSITE</u> permission

banal = <u>unoriginal</u>, stock, ordinary, boring, tired, routine, dull, everyday, stereotypical, pedestrian,

---

Ballgames

American football	bumble-puppy	hockey	punchball
Australian Rules	Canadian football	hurling	pushball
badminton	crazy golf	korfball	pyramid
bagatelle	croquet	lacrosse	rounders
bar billiards	fives	netball	snooker
baseball	football *or* (U.S.) soccer	paintball	squash
billiards	goalball	piggy in the middle	Subbuteo®
boules	golf	pinball	tennis
bowling	handball	pocket billiards	volleyball

commonplace, mundane, tedious, vanilla (*slang*), dreary, stale, tiresome, monotonous, humdrum, threadbare, trite, unimaginative, uneventful, uninteresting, clichéd, old hat, mind-numbing, hackneyed, ho-hum (*informal*), vapid, repetitious, wearisome, platitudinous, cliché-ridden, unvaried OPPOSITE original

banality 1 = unoriginality, triviality, vapidity, triteness …*the banality of life*…
2 = cliché, commonplace, platitude, truism, bromide (*informal*), trite phrase …*His ability to utter banalities never ceased to amaze me*…

band¹ NOUN 1 = ensemble, group, orchestra, combo …*Local bands provide music for dancing*…
2 = gang, company, group, set, party, team, lot, club, body, association, crowd, troop, pack, camp, squad, crew (*informal*), assembly, mob, horde, troupe, posse (*informal*), clique, coterie, bevy …*bands of government soldiers*…
PHRASES **band together** = unite, group, join, league, ally, associate, gather, pool, merge, consolidate, affiliate, collaborate, join forces, cooperate, confederate, pull together, join together, federate, close ranks, club together …*People living in a foreign city band together for company*…

band² 1= headband, tie, strip, ribbon, fillet …*She was wearing a trouser suit and a band around her forehead*…
2 = bandage, tie, binding, strip, belt, strap, cord, swathe, fetter …*He placed a metal band around the injured kneecap*…

bandage NOUN = dressing, plaster, compress, gauze …*His chest was swathed in bandages*…
VERB = dress, cover, bind, swathe …*Apply a dressing to the wound and bandage it*…

bandit = robber, gunman, crook, outlaw, pirate, raider, gangster, plunderer, mugger (*informal*), hijacker, looter, highwayman, racketeer, desperado, marauder, brigand, freebooter, footpad

bandy = exchange, trade, pass, throw, truck, swap, toss, shuffle, commute, interchange, barter, reciprocate

bane = plague, bête noire, trial, disaster, evil, ruin, burden, destruction, despair, misery, curse, pest, torment, woe, nuisance, downfall, calamity, scourge, affliction OPPOSITE blessing

bang NOUN 1 = explosion, report, shot, pop, clash, crack, blast, burst, boom, slam, discharge, thump, clap, thud, clang, peal, detonation …*I heard four or five loud bangs*…
2 = blow, hit, box, knock, stroke, punch, belt (*informal*), rap, bump, bash (*informal*), sock (*slang*), smack, thump, buffet, clout (*informal*), cuff, clump (*slang*), whack, wallop (*informal*), slosh (*Brit. slang*), tonk (*informal*), clomp (*slang*) …*a nasty bang on the head*…
VERB 1 = resound, beat, crash, burst, boom, echo, drum, explode, thunder, thump, throb, thud, clang …*The engine spat and banged*…
2 = bump, knock, elbow, jostle …*I didn't mean to bang into you*…
3 *often with* **on** = hit, pound, beat, strike, crash, knock, belt (*informal*), hammer, slam, rap, bump, bash (*informal*), thump, clatter, pummel, tonk (*informal*) …*We could bang on the desks and shout until they let us out*…
ADVERB = exactly, just, straight, square, squarely, precisely, slap, smack, plumb (*informal*) …*bang in the middle of the track*…

banish 1 = exclude, bar, ban, dismiss, expel, throw out, oust, drive away, eject, evict, shut out, ostracize …*I was banished from the small bedroom upstairs*…
2 = expel, transport, exile, outlaw, deport, drive away, expatriate, excommunicate …*He was banished from England*… OPPOSITE admit
3 = get rid of, remove, eliminate, eradicate, shake off, dislodge, see the back of …*a public investment programme intended to banish the recession*…

banishment = expulsion, exile, dismissal, removal, discharge, transportation, exclusion, deportation, eviction, ejection, extrusion, proscription, expatriation, debarment

banisters = railing, rail, balustrade, handrail, balusters

bank¹ NOUN 1 = financial institution, repository, depository …*I had money in the bank*…
2 = store, fund, stock, source, supply, reserve, pool, reservoir, accumulation, stockpile, hoard, storehouse …*one of the largest data banks in the world*…
VERB = deposit, keep, save …*The agency has banked your cheque*…
PHRASES **bank on something** = rely on, trust (in), depend on, look to, believe in, count on, be sure of, lean on, be confident of, have confidence in, swear by, reckon on, repose trust in …*She is clearly banking on her past to be the meal ticket for her future*…
♦ **bank with someone** = deal with, do business with …*My husband has banked with them since before the war*…

bank² NOUN 1 = side, edge, margin, shore, brink, lakeside, waterside …*an old warehouse on the banks of the canal*…
2 = mound, banking, rise, hill, mass, pile, heap, ridge, dune, embankment, knoll, hillock, kopje *or* koppie (*S. African*) …*resting indolently upon a grassy bank*…
3 = mass, accumulation …*a bank of fog off the north-east coast*…
VERB = tilt, tip, pitch, heel, slope, incline, slant, cant, camber …*A single-engine plane took off and banked above the highway*…

bank³ = row, group, line, train, range, series, file, rank, arrangement, sequence, succession, array, tier …*The typical labourer now sits in front of a bank of dials*…

bankrupt = insolvent, broke (*informal*), spent, ruined, wiped out (*informal*), impoverished, beggared, in the red, on the rocks, destitute, gone bust (*informal*), in receivership, gone to the wall, in the hands of the receivers, on your uppers, in queer street OPPOSITE solvent

bankruptcy = insolvency, failure, crash, disaster,

ruin, liquidation, indebtedness

banner = <u>flag</u>, standard, colours, jack, placard, pennant, ensign, streamer, pennon

banquet = <u>feast</u>, spread (*informal*), dinner, meal, entertainment, revel, blowout (*slang*), repast, slap-up meal (*Brit. informal*)

banter NOUN = <u>joking</u>, kidding (*informal*), ribbing (*informal*), teasing, jeering, mockery, derision, jesting, chaff, pleasantry, repartee, wordplay, badinage, chaffing, raillery, persiflage ...*She heard them exchanging good-natured banter*...
VERB = <u>joke</u>, kid (*informal*), rib (*informal*), tease, taunt, jeer, josh (*slang, chiefly U.S. & Canad.*), jest, take the mickey (*informal*), chaff ...*They shared a cocktail and bantered easily*...

baptism 1 (*Christianity*) = <u>christening</u>, sprinkling, purification, immersion ...*We are at a site of baptism, a place of worship*...
2 = <u>initiation</u>, beginning, debut, introduction, admission, dedication, inauguration, induction, inception, rite of passage, commencement, investiture, baptism of fire, instatement ...*The new boys face a tough baptism against Leeds*...

baptize 1 (*Christianity*) = <u>christen</u>, cleanse, immerse, purify, besprinkle ...*I think your mother was baptized a Catholic*...
2 = <u>initiate</u>, admit, introduce, invest, recruit, enrol, induct, indoctrinate, instate ...*baptized into the Church of England*...

bar NOUN 1 = <u>public house</u>, pub (*informal, chiefly Brit.*), counter, inn, local (*Brit. informal*), lounge, saloon, tavern, canteen, watering hole (*facetious slang*), boozer (*Brit., Austral., & N.Z. informal*), roadhouse, hostelry (*archaic or facetious*), alehouse (*archaic*), taproom ...*the city's most popular country and western bar*...
2 = <u>rod</u>, staff, stick, stake, rail, pole, paling, shaft, baton, mace, batten, palisade, crosspiece ...*a crowd throwing stones and iron bars*...
3 = <u>obstacle</u>, block, barrier, hurdle, hitch, barricade, snag, deterrent, obstruction, stumbling block, impediment, hindrance, interdict ...*one of the fundamental bars to communication*... OPPOSITE> aid
VERB 1 = <u>lock</u>, block, secure, chain, attach, anchor, bolt, blockade, barricade, fortify, fasten, latch, obstruct, make firm, make fast ...*For added safety, bar the door to the kitchen*...
2 = <u>block</u>, restrict, hold up, restrain, hamper, thwart, hinder, obstruct, impede, shut off ...*He stepped in front of her, barring her way*...
3 = <u>exclude</u>, ban, forbid, prohibit, keep out of, disallow, shut out of, ostracize, debar, blackball, interdict, black ...*They have been barred from the country since 1982*... OPPOSITE> admit

barb 1 = <u>point</u>, spur, spike, thorn, bristle, quill, prickle, tine, prong ...*Apply gentle pressure on the barb with the point of the pliers*...
2 = <u>dig</u>, abuse, slight, insult, put-down, snub, sneer, scoff, rebuff, affront, slap in the face (*informal*), gibe, aspersion ...*The barb stung her exactly the way he hoped it would*...

barbarian NOUN 1 = <u>savage</u>, monster, beast, brute, yahoo, swine, ogre, sadist ...*Our maths teacher was a bully and a complete barbarian*...
2 = <u>lout</u>, hooligan, illiterate, vandal, yahoo, bigot, philistine, ned (*Scot. slang*), hoon (*Austral. & N.Z.*), cougan (*Austral. slang*), scozza (*Austral. slang*), bogan (*Austral. slang*), ruffian, ignoramus, boor, lowbrow, vulgarian ...*The visitors looked upon us all as barbarians*...
ADJECTIVE = <u>uncivilized</u>, wild, rough, savage, crude, primitive, vulgar, illiterate, barbaric, philistine, uneducated, unsophisticated, barbarous, boorish, uncouth, uncultivated, lowbrow, uncultured, unmannered ...*rude and barbarian people*...
OPPOSITE> civilized

barbaric 1 = <u>brutal</u>, fierce, cruel, savage, crude, vicious, ruthless, coarse, vulgar, heartless, inhuman, merciless, bloodthirsty, remorseless, barbarous, pitiless, uncouth ...*a particularly barbaric act of violence*...
2 = <u>uncivilized</u>, wild, savage, primitive, rude, barbarian, barbarous ...*a prehistoric and barbaric world*... OPPOSITE> civilized

barbarism = <u>cruelty</u>, outrage, atrocity, brutality, savagery, ruthlessness, wickedness, inhumanity, barbarity, viciousness, coarseness, crudity, monstrousness, heinousness, fiendishness, barbarousness

barbarity = <u>viciousness</u>, horror, atrocity, cruelty, brutality, ferocity, savagery, ruthlessness, inhumanity

barbarous 1 = <u>uncivilized</u>, wild, rough, gross, savage, primitive, rude, coarse, vulgar, barbarian, philistine, uneducated, brutish, unsophisticated, uncouth, uncultivated, unpolished, uncultured, unmannered ...*He thought the poetry of Whitman barbarous*...
2 = <u>brutal</u>, cruel, savage, vicious, ruthless, ferocious, monstrous, barbaric, heartless, inhuman, merciless, remorseless, pitiless ...*It was a barbarous attack on a purely civilian train*...

barbed 1 = <u>cutting</u>, pointed, biting, critical, acid, hostile, nasty, harsh, savage, brutal, searing, withering, scathing, unkind, hurtful, belittling, sarcastic, caustic, scornful, vitriolic, trenchant, acrid, catty (*informal*), mordant, mordacious ...*barbed comments*...
2 = <u>spiked</u>, pointed, toothed, hooked, notched, prickly, jagged, thorny, pronged, spiny, snaggy ...*The factory was surrounded by barbed wire*...

bard (*Archaic or literary*) = <u>poet</u>, singer, rhymer, minstrel, lyricist, troubadour, versifier

bare 1 = <u>naked</u>, nude, stripped, exposed, uncovered, shorn, undressed, divested, denuded, in the raw (*informal*), disrobed, unclothed, buck naked (*slang*), unclad, scuddy (*slang*), without a stitch on (*informal*), in the bare scud (*slang*), naked as the day you were born (*informal*) ...*She seemed unaware that she was bare*... OPPOSITE> dressed
2 = <u>simple</u>, basic, severe, spare, stark, austere, spartan, unadorned, unfussy, unvarnished, unembellished, unornamented, unpatterned ...*bare wooden floors*...

OPPOSITE ▷ adorned

3 = <u>empty</u>, wanting, mean, lacking, deserted, vacant, void, scarce, barren, uninhabited, unoccupied, scanty, unfurnished ...*a bare, draughty interviewing room*...
OPPOSITE ▷ full

4 = <u>plain</u>, hard, simple, cold, basic, essential, obvious, sheer, patent, evident, stark, manifest, bald, literal, overt, unembellished ...*reporters were given nothing but the bare facts*...

barely = <u>only just</u>, just, hardly, scarcely, at a push, almost not OPPOSITE ▷ completely

bargain NOUN **1** = <u>good buy</u>, discount purchase, good deal, good value, steal (*informal*), snip (*informal*), giveaway, cheap purchase ...*At this price the wine is a bargain*...
2 = <u>agreement</u>, deal (*informal*), understanding, promise, contract, negotiation, arrangement, settlement, treaty, pledge, convention, transaction, engagement, pact, compact, covenant, stipulation ...*The treaty was based on a bargain between the governments*...
VERB **1** = <u>haggle</u>, deal, sell, trade, traffic, barter, drive a hard bargain ...*Shop in small local markets and don't be afraid to bargain*...
2 = <u>negotiate</u>, deal, contract, mediate, covenant, stipulate, arbitrate, transact, cut a deal ...*They prefer to bargain with individual clients, for cash*...
PHRASES **bargain for** or **on something** = <u>anticipate</u>, expect, look for, imagine, predict, plan for, forecast, hope for, contemplate, be prepared for, foresee, foretell, count upon ...*He didn't bargain on an undercover investigation*... ...*The effects of this policy were more than they had bargained for*...

barge NOUN = <u>canal boat</u>, lighter, narrow boat, scow, flatboat ...*He lives on a barge and only works when he has to*...
PHRASES **barge in (on something** or **someone)** (*Informal*) = <u>interrupt</u>, break in (on), muscle in (on) (*informal*), intrude (on), infringe (on), burst in (on), butt in (on), impose yourself (on), force your way in (on), elbow your way in (on) ...*He just barged in on us while we were having a private conversation*... ...*Sorry to barge in like this, but I need your advice*... ◆ **barge into someone** = <u>bump into</u>, drive into, press, push against, shoulder, thrust, elbow into, shove into, collide with, jostle with, cannon into ...*He would barge into them and kick them in the shins*...

bark¹ VERB **1** = <u>yap</u>, bay, howl, snarl, growl, yelp, woof ...*Don't let the dogs bark*...
2 = <u>shout</u>, snap, yell, snarl, growl, berate, bawl, bluster, raise your voice ...*I didn't mean to bark at you*...
NOUN = <u>yap</u>, bay, howl, snarl, growl, yelp, woof ...*The Doberman let out a string of roaring barks*...

bark² NOUN = <u>covering</u>, casing, cover, skin, protection, layer, crust, housing, cortex (*Anatomy, botany*), rind, husk ...*The spice comes from the inner bark of the tree*...
VERB = <u>scrape</u>, skin, strip, rub, scratch, shave, graze, scuff, flay, abrade ...*She barked her shin off the edge of the drawer*...

barmy or **balmy** (*Slang*) **1** = <u>stupid</u>, bizarre, foolish,

silly, daft (*informal*), irresponsible, irrational, senseless, preposterous, impractical, idiotic, inane, fatuous, dumb-ass (*slang*) ...*This policy is absolutely barmy*...
2 = <u>insane</u>, odd, crazy, stupid, silly, nuts (*slang*), loony (*slang*), nutty (*slang*), goofy (*informal*), idiotic, loopy (*informal*), crackpot (*informal*), out to lunch (*informal*), dippy, out of your mind, gonzo (*slang*), doolally (*slang*), off your trolley (*slang*), round the twist (*Brit. slang*), up the pole (*informal*), off your rocker (*slang*), off the air (*Austral. slang*), wacko or whacko (*informal*) ...*He used to say I was barmy, and that really got to me*... OPPOSITE ▷ sane

baroque = <u>ornate</u>, fancy, bizarre, elegant, decorated, elaborate, extravagant, flamboyant, grotesque, convoluted, flowery, rococo, florid, bedecked, overelaborate, overdecorated

barrack (*Informal*) = <u>heckle</u>, abuse, mock, bait, criticize, boo, taunt, jeer, shout down, diss (*slang, chiefly U.S.*)

barracks = <u>camp</u>, quarters, garrison, encampment, billet, cantonment, casern

barrage 1 = <u>bombardment</u>, attack, bombing, assault, shelling, battery, volley, blitz, salvo, strafe, fusillade, cannonade, curtain of fire ...*a barrage of anti-aircraft fire*...
2 = <u>torrent</u>, attack, mass, storm, assault, burst, stream, hail, outburst, rain, spate, onslaught, deluge, plethora, profusion ...*a barrage of angry questions from the floor*...

barren 1 = <u>desolate</u>, empty, desert, waste ...*the Tibetan landscape of the high barren mountains*...
2 = <u>unproductive</u>, dry, useless, fruitless, arid, unprofitable, unfruitful ...*He also wants to use water to irrigate barren desert land*... OPPOSITE ▷ fertile
3 = <u>dull</u>, boring, commonplace, tedious, dreary, stale, lacklustre, monotonous, uninspiring, humdrum, uninteresting, vapid, unrewarding, as dry as dust ...*My life has become barren*... OPPOSITE ▷ interesting
4 (*Old-fashioned*) = <u>infertile</u>, sterile, childless, unproductive, nonproductive, infecund, unprolific ...*a three-year-old barren mare*...

barricade NOUN = <u>barrier</u>, wall, railing, fence, blockade, obstruction, rampart, fortification, bulwark, palisade, stockade ...*Large areas of the city have been closed off by barricades*...
VERB = <u>bar</u>, block, defend, secure, lock, bolt, blockade, fortify, fasten, latch, obstruct ...*The doors had been barricaded*...

barrier = <u>barricade</u>, wall, bar, block, railing, fence, pale, boundary, obstacle, ditch, blockade, obstruction, rampart, bulwark, palisade, stockade

barter = <u>trade</u>, sell, exchange, switch, traffic, bargain, swap, haggle, drive a hard bargain

base¹ NOUN **1** = <u>bottom</u>, floor, lowest part, deepest part ...*Line the base and sides of a 20cm deep round cake tin with paper*... OPPOSITE ▷ top
2 = <u>support</u>, stand, foot, rest, bed, bottom, foundation, pedestal, groundwork ...*The mattress is best on a solid bed base*...
3 = <u>foundation</u>, institution, organization,

establishment …*The family base was crucial to my development*…

4 = <u>centre</u>, post, station, camp, settlement, headquarters, starting point …*Gunfire was heard at an army base close to the airport*…

5 = <u>home</u>, house, territory, pad (*slang*), residence, home ground, abode, stamping ground, dwelling place …*For most of the spring and early summer her base was in Scotland*…

6 = <u>essence</u>, source, basis, concentrate, root, core, extract …*Oils may be mixed with a base and massaged into the skin*…

   VERB 1 = <u>ground</u>, found, build, rest, establish, depend, root, construct, derive, hinge …*He based his conclusions on the evidence given by the prisoners*…

2 = <u>place</u>, set, post, station, establish, fix, locate, install, garrison …*We will base ourselves in the town*…

base² = <u>dishonourable</u>, evil, corrupt, infamous, disgraceful, vulgar, shameful, vile, immoral, scandalous, wicked, sordid, abject, despicable, depraved, ignominious, disreputable, contemptible, villainous, ignoble, discreditable, scungy (*Austral. & N.Z.*) …*Love has the power to overcome the baser emeotions*… **OPPOSITE** honourable

baseless = <u>unfounded</u>, false, fabricated, unconfirmed, spurious, unjustified, unproven, unsubstantiated, groundless, unsupported, trumped up, without foundation, unjustifiable, uncorroborated, ungrounded, without basis **OPPOSITE** well-founded

bash (*Informal*) **NOUN** = <u>attempt</u>, go (*informal*), try, shot (*informal*), bid, crack (*informal*), stab (*informal*) …*He's prepared to have a bash at discussing it intelligently*…

  VERB = <u>hit</u>, break, beat, strike, knock, smash, punch, belt (*informal*), crush, deck (*slang*), batter, slap, sock (*slang*), chin (*slang*), smack, thump, clout (*informal*), whack (*informal*), biff (*slang*), clobber (*slang*), wallop (*informal*), slosh (*Brit. slang*), tonk (*informal*), lay one on (*slang*) …*If he tries to bash you he'll have to bash me as well*…

bashful = <u>shy</u>, reserved, retiring, nervous, modest, shrinking, blushing, constrained, timid, self-conscious, coy, reticent, self-effacing, diffident, sheepish, mousy, timorous, abashed, shamefaced, easily embarrassed, overmodest **OPPOSITE** forward

basic **ADJECTIVE** 1 = <u>fundamental</u>, main, key, essential, primary, vital, principal, constitutional, cardinal, inherent, elementary, indispensable, innate, intrinsic, elemental, immanent …*Access to justice is a basic right*…

2 = <u>vital</u>, needed, important, key, necessary, essential, primary, crucial, fundamental, elementary, indispensable, requisite …*shortages of even the most basic foodstuffs*…

3 = <u>essential</u>, central, key, vital, fundamental, underlying, indispensable …*There are certain ethical principles that are basic to all the great religions*… **OPPOSITE** secondary

4 = <u>main</u>, key, essential, primary …*There are three basic types of tea*…

5 = <u>plain</u>, simple, classic, severe, straightforward, Spartan, uncluttered, unadorned, unfussy, bog-standard (*informal*), unembellished …*the extremely basic hotel room*…

  PLURAL NOUN = <u>essentials</u>, facts, principles, fundamentals, practicalities, requisites, nuts and bolts (*informal*), hard facts, nitty-gritty (*informal*), rudiments, brass tacks (*informal*), necessaries …*Let's get down to basics and stop horsing around*…

basically = <u>essentially</u>, firstly, mainly, mostly, principally, fundamentally, primarily, at heart, inherently, intrinsically, at bottom, in substance, au fond (*French*)

basis 1 = <u>arrangement</u>, way, system, footing, agreement …*We're going to be meeting there on a regular basis*…

2 = <u>foundation</u>, support, base, ground, footing, theory, bottom, principle, premise, groundwork, principal element, chief ingredient …*The UN plan is a possible basis for negotiation*…

bask **VERB** = <u>lie</u>, relax, lounge, sprawl, loaf, lie about, swim in, sunbathe, recline, loll, laze, outspan (*S. African*), warm yourself, toast yourself …*Crocodiles bask on the small sandy beaches*…

  PHRASES **bask in** = <u>enjoy</u>, relish, delight in, savour, revel in, wallow in, rejoice in, luxuriate in, indulge yourself in, take joy in, take pleasure in *or* from …*He smiled and basked in her approval*…

bass = <u>deep</u>, low, resonant, sonorous, low-pitched, deep-toned

bastion = <u>stronghold</u>, support, defence, rock, prop, refuge, fortress, mainstay, citadel, bulwark, tower of strength, fastness

bat

Bats www.batworld.org	
barbastelle	insectivorous bat
false vampire	kalong
flying fox	noctule
fruit bat	pipistrelle
hammerhead	serotine
horseshoe bat	vampire bat

batch = <u>group</u>, set, lot, crowd, pack, collection, quantity, bunch, accumulation, assortment, consignment, assemblage, aggregation

bath **NOUN** = <u>wash</u>, cleaning, washing, soaping, shower, soak, cleansing, scrub, scrubbing, bathe, shampoo, sponging, douse, douche, ablution …*Have a bath every morning*…

  VERB = <u>clean</u>, wash, soap, shower, soak, cleanse, scrub, bathe, tub, sponge, rinse, douse, scrub down, lave (*archaic*) …*Don't feel you have to bath your child every day*…

bathe **VERB** 1 = <u>swim</u> …*small ponds for the birds to bathe in*…

2 = <u>wash</u>, clean, bath, soap, shower, soak, cleanse, scrub, tub, sponge, rinse, scrub down, lave (*archaic*) …*Back home, Shirley plays with, feeds and bathes the baby*…

3 = <u>cleanse</u>, clean, wash, soak, rinse …*She paused long enough to bathe her blistered feet…*
4 = <u>cover</u>, flood, steep, engulf, immerse, overrun, suffuse, wash over …*The arena was bathed in warm sunshine…*
NOUN (*Brit.*) = <u>swim</u>, dip, dook (*Scot.*) …*an early-morning bathe…*

bathroom = <u>lavatory</u>, toilet, loo (*Brit. informal*), washroom, can (*U.S. & Canad. slang*), john (*slang, chiefly U.S. & Canad.*), head(s) (*Nautical slang*), shower, convenience (*chiefly Brit.*), bog (*slang*), bogger (*Austral. slang*), brasco (*Austral. slang*), privy, cloakroom (*Brit.*), latrine, rest room, powder room, crapper (*taboo slang*), dunny (*Austral. or old-fashioned N.Z.*), water closet, khazi (*slang*), comfort station (*U.S.*), pissoir (*French*), Gents *or* Ladies, little boy's room *or* little girl's room (*informal*), (public) convenience, W.C.

baton = <u>stick</u>, club, staff, stake, pole, rod, crook, cane, mace, wand, truncheon, sceptre

battalion = <u>company</u>, army, force, team, host, division, troop, brigade, regiment, legion, contingent, squadron, military force, horde, multitude, throng

batten¹ *usually with* **down** = <u>fasten</u>, unite, fix, secure, lock, bind, chain, connect, attach, seal, tighten, anchor, bolt, clamp down, affix, nail down, make firm, make fast, fasten down …*The roof was never securely battened down…*

batten²
PHRASES **batten on something** *or* **someone** = <u>thrive</u>, grow, develop, gain, advance, succeed, get on, boom, do well, flourish, bloom, wax, prosper, burgeon, fatten, grow rich …*battening on fears about mass immigration and unemployment…*

batter 1 = <u>beat</u>, hit, strike, knock, assault, smash, punch, belt (*informal*), deck (*slang*), bang, bash (*informal*), lash, thrash, pound, lick (*informal*), buffet, flog, maul, pelt, clobber (*slang*), smite, wallop (*informal*), pummel, tonk (*informal*), cudgel, thwack (*informal*), lambast(e), belabour, dash against, beat the living daylights out of, lay one on (*slang*), drub …*He battered her around the head…*
2 = <u>damage</u>, destroy, hurt, injure, harm, ruin, crush, mar, wreck, total (*slang*), shatter, weaken, bruise, demolish, shiver, trash (*slang*), maul, mutilate, mangle, mangulate (*Austral. slang*), disfigure, deface, play (merry) hell with (*informal*) …*a storm that's been battering the Northeast coastline…*

battered 1 = <u>beaten</u>, injured, harmed, crushed, bruised, squashed, beat-up (*informal*), manhandle, black-and-blue, ill-treated, maltreated …*research into the experiences of battered women…*
2 = <u>damaged</u>, broken-down, wrecked, beat-up (*informal*), ramshackle, dilapidated …*a battered leather suitcase…*

battery 1 = <u>artillery</u>, ordnance, gunnery, gun emplacement, cannonry …*They stopped beside a battery of abandoned guns…*
2 = <u>series</u>, set, course, chain, string, sequence, suite, succession …*We give a battery of tests to each patient…*

3 (*Criminal law*) = <u>beating</u>, attack, assault, aggression, thumping, onslaught, physical violence …*He has served three years for assault and battery…*

battle NOUN **1** = <u>fight</u>, war, attack, action, struggle, conflict, clash, set-to (*informal*), encounter, combat, scrap (*informal*), biffo (*Austral. slang*), engagement, warfare, fray, duel, skirmish, head-to-head, tussle, scuffle, fracas, scrimmage, sparring match, bagarre (*French*), melee *or* mêlée …*a gun battle between police and drug traffickers…* OPPOSITE peace
2 = <u>conflict</u>, campaign, struggle, debate, clash, dispute, contest, controversy, disagreement, crusade, strife, head-to-head, agitation …*a renewed political battle over their attitude to Europe…*
3 = <u>campaign</u>, war, drive, movement, push, struggle …*the battle against crime…*
VERB **1** = <u>wrestle</u>, war, fight, argue, dispute, contest, combat, contend, feud, grapple, agitate, clamour, scuffle, lock horns …*Many people battled with police…*
2 = <u>struggle</u>, work, labour, strain, strive, go for it (*informal*), toil, make every effort, go all out (*informal*), bend over backwards (*informal*), go for broke (*slang*), bust a gut (*informal*), give it your best shot (*informal*), break your neck (*informal*), exert yourself, make an all-out effort (*informal*), work like a Trojan, knock yourself out (*informal*), do your damnedest (*informal*), give it your all (*informal*), rupture yourself (*informal*) …*Doctors battled throughout the night to save her life…*
➤ **famous battles**

battle cry 1 = <u>slogan</u>, motto, watchword, catch phrase, tag-line, catchword …*the ideological battle cry of Hong Kong…*
2 = <u>war cry</u>, rallying cry, war whoop …*He screamed out a battle cry and charged…*

battlefield = <u>battleground</u>, front, field, combat zone, field of battle

battleship = <u>warship</u>, gunboat, man-of-war, ship of the line, capital ship

batty = <u>crazy</u>, odd, mad, eccentric, bats (*slang*), nuts (*slang*), barking (*slang*), peculiar, daft (*informal*), crackers (*Brit. slang*), queer (*informal*), insane, lunatic, loony (*slang*), barmy (*slang*), off-the-wall (*slang*), touched, nutty (*slang*), potty (*Brit. informal*), oddball (*informal*), off the rails, cracked (*slang*), bonkers (*slang, chiefly Brit.*), cranky (*U.S., Canad., & Irish informal*), dotty (*slang, chiefly Brit.*), loopy (*informal*), crackpot (*informal*), out to lunch (*informal*), barking mad (*slang*), out of your mind, outré, gonzo (*slang*), screwy (*informal*), doolally (*slang*), off your trolley (*slang*), off the air (*Austral. slang*), round the twist (*Brit. slang*), up the pole (*informal*), off your rocker (*slang*), not the full shilling (*informal*), as daft as a brush (*informal, chiefly Brit.*), wacko *or* whacko (*slang*)

bauble = <u>trinket</u>, ornament, trifle, toy, plaything, bagatelle, gimcrack, gewgaw, knick-knack, bibelot, kickshaw

bawdy = <u>rude</u>, blue, dirty, gross, crude, erotic, obscene, coarse, filthy, indecent, vulgar, improper,

Famous battles

Aboukir Bay *or* Abukir Bay	1798	Guadalcanal	1942–3	Plataea	479 B.C.		
Actium	31 B.C.	Hastings	1066	Poltava	1709		
Agincourt	1415	Hohenlinden	1800	Prestonpans	1745		
Alamo	1836	Imphal	1944	Pydna	168 B.C.		
Arnhem	1944	Inkerman	1854	Quatre Bras	1815		
Atlantic	1939–45	Issus	333 B.C.	Ramillies	1706		
Austerlitz	1805	Jemappes	1792	Roncesvalles	778		
Balaklava *or* Balaclava	1854	Jena	1806	Sadowa *or* Sadová	1866		
Bannockburn	1314	Killiecrankie	1689	Saint–Mihiel	1918		
Barnet	1471	Kursk	1943	Salamis	480 B.C.		
Bautzen	1813	Ladysmith	1899–1900	Sedgemoor	1685		
Belleau Wood	1918	Le Cateau	1914	Sempach	1386		
Blenheim	1704	Leipzig	1813	Shiloh	1862		
Borodino	1812	Lepanto	1571	Shipka Pass	1877–78		
Bosworth Field	1485	Leyte Gulf	1944	Somme	1916; 1918		
Boyne	1690	Little Bighorn	1876	Stalingrad	1941–42		
Britain	1940	Lützen	1632	Stamford Bridge	1066		
Bulge	1944–45	Manassas	1861; 1862	Stirling Bridge	1297		
Bull Run	1861–62	Mantinea *or* Mantineia	418 B.C.; 362 B.C.	Tannenberg	1410; 1914		
Bunker Hill	1775	Marathon	490 B.C.	Tewkesbury	1471		
Cannae	216 B.C.	Marengo	1800	Thermopylae	480 B.C.		
Crécy	1346	Marston Moor	1644	Tobruk	1941; 1942		
Culloden	1746	Missionary Ridge	1863	Trafalgar	1805		
Dien Bien Phu	1954	Navarino	425 B.C.	Trenton	1776		
Edgehill	1642	Omdurman	1898	Verdun	1916		
El Alamein	1942	Passchendaele	1917	Vitoria	1813		
Falkirk	1298; 1746	Philippi	42 B.C.	Wagram	1809		
Flodden	1513	Plains of Abraham	1759	Waterloo	1815		
Gettysburg	1863	Plassey	1757	Ypres	1914; 1915; 1917; 1918		
				Zama	202 B.C.		

steamy (*informal*), pornographic, raunchy (*U.S. slang*), suggestive, racy, lewd, risqué, X-rated (*informal*), salacious, prurient, lascivious, smutty, lustful, lecherous, ribald, libidinous, licentious, indelicate, near the knuckle (*informal*), indecorous OPPOSITE clean

bawl 1 = shout, call, scream, roar, yell, howl, bellow, bay, clamour, holler (*informal*), raise your voice, halloo, hollo, vociferate ...*They were shouting and bawling at each other*...
2 = cry, weep, sob, wail, whine, whimper, whinge (*informal*), keen, greet (*Scot. or archaic*), squall, blubber, snivel, shed tears, yowl, mewl, howl your eyes out ...*One of the toddlers was bawling, and another had a runny nose*...

bay¹ = inlet, sound, gulf, entrance, creek, cove, fjord, arm (of the sea), bight, ingress, natural harbour, sea loch (*Scot.*), firth *or* frith (*Scot.*) ...*a short ferry ride across the bay*...
➤ WORD POWER SUPPLEMENT bays

bay² = recess, opening, corner, niche, compartment, nook, alcove, embrasure ...*Someone had placed the device in a loading bay behind the shop*...

bay³ VERB = howl, cry, roar (*used of hounds*), bark, lament, cry out, wail, growl, bellow, quest, bell, clamour, yelp ...*A dog suddenly howled, baying at the moon*...
NOUN = cry, bell, roar (*used of hounds*), quest, bark, lament, howl, wail, growl, bellow, clamour, yelp ...*She trembled at the bay of the dogs*...

PHRASES **at bay** = away, off, at arm's length ...*Eating oranges keeps colds at bay*...

bayonet = stab, cut, wound, knife, slash, pierce, run through, spear, transfix, impale, lacerate, stick

bazaar 1 = market, exchange, fair, marketplace, mart ...*He was a vendor in Egypt's open-air bazaar*...
2 = fair, fête, gala, festival, garden party, bring-and-buy ...*a church bazaar*...

be 1 = be alive, live, exist, survive, breathe, last, be present, continue, endure, be living, be extant, happen ...*It hurt so badly he wished to cease to be*...
2 = take place, happen, occur, arise, come about, transpire (*informal*), befall, come to pass ...*The film's premiere is next week*...
3 = remain, last, stand, continue, stay, endure, prevail, persist, abide, bide ...*How long have you been here?*...

beach = shore, coast, sands, margin, strand, seaside, shingle, lakeside, water's edge, lido, foreshore, seashore, plage, littoral, sea (*chiefly U.S.*)

beached = stranded, grounded, abandoned, deserted, wrecked, ashore, marooned, aground, high and dry

beacon = signal, sign, rocket, beam, flare, lighthouse, bonfire, watchtower, smoke signal, pharos, signal fire

bead NOUN = drop, tear, bubble, pearl, dot, drip, blob, droplet, globule, driblet ...*beads of blood*...
PLURAL NOUN = necklace, pearls, pendant, choker, necklet, chaplet ...*baubles, bangles and beads*...

beady = <u>bright</u>, powerful, concentrated, sharp, intense, shining, glittering, gleaming, glinting

beak 1 = <u>bill</u>, nib, neb (*archaic or dialect*), mandible …*a black bird with a yellow beak…*
2 (*Slang*) = <u>nose</u>, snout, hooter (*slang*), snitch (*slang*), conk (*slang*), neb (*archaic or dialect*), proboscis, schnozzle (*slang, chiefly U.S.*) …*his sharp, aristocratic beak…*

beam VERB **1** = <u>smile</u>, grin …*She beamed at her friend with undisguised admiration…*
2 = <u>transmit</u>, show, air, broadcast, cable, send out, relay, televise, radio, emit, put on the air …*The interview was beamed live across America…*
3 = <u>radiate</u>, flash, shine, glow, glitter, glare, gleam, emit light, give off light …*A sharp white spotlight beamed down on a small stage…*
NOUN **1** = <u>ray</u>, bar, flash, stream, glow, radiation, streak, emission, shaft, gleam, glint, glimmer …*a beam of light…*
2 = <u>rafter</u>, support, timber, spar, plank, girder, joist …*The ceilings are supported by oak beams…*
3 = <u>smile</u>, grin …*She knew he had news, because of the beam on his face…*

beaming 1 = <u>smiling</u>, happy, grinning, pleasant, sunny, cheerful, cheery, joyful, chirpy (*informal*), light-hearted …*his mother's beaming eyes…*
2 = <u>radiating</u>, bright, brilliant, flashing, shining, glowing, sparkling, glittering, gleaming, glimmering, radiant, glistening, scintillating, burnished, lustrous …*An engraved and beaming sun rose out of the sea…*

bear VERB **1** = <u>carry</u>, take, move, bring, lift, transfer, conduct, transport, haul, transmit, convey, relay, tote (*informal*), hump (*Brit. slang*), lug …*a surveyor and his assistant bearing a torch…* OPPOSITE put down
2 = <u>support</u>, shoulder, sustain, endure, uphold, withstand, bear up under …*The ice was not thick enough to bear the weight of marching men…* OPPOSITE give up
3 = <u>display</u>, have, show, hold, carry, possess, exhibit …*notepaper bearing the President's seal…*
4 = <u>suffer</u>, feel, experience, go through, sustain, stomach, endure, undergo, admit, brook, hack (*slang*), abide, put up with (*informal*) …*He bore his sufferings manfully…*
5 = <u>bring yourself to</u>, allow, accept, permit, endure, tolerate (*informal*), countenance …*He can't bear to talk about it, even to me…*
6 = <u>produce</u>, develop, generate, yield, bring forth …*The plants grow and start to bear fruit…*
7 = <u>give birth to</u>, produce, deliver, breed, bring forth, beget …*She bore a son called Karl…*
8 = <u>exhibit</u>, hold, maintain, entertain, harbour, cherish …*She bore no ill will. If they didn't like her, too bad…*
9 = <u>conduct</u>, carry, move, deport …*There was elegance and simple dignity in the way he bore himself…*
PHRASES **bear down on someone** = <u>advance on</u>, attack, approach, move towards, close in on, converge on, move in on, come near to, draw near to …*A group of half a dozen men entered the pub and bore down on her…* ◆ **bear down on something** or **someone**

= <u>press down</u>, push, strain, crush, compress, weigh down, encumber …*She felt as if a great weight was bearing down on her shoulders…* ◆ **bear on something** = <u>be relevant to</u>, involve, concern, affect, regard, refer to, be part of, relate to, belong to, apply to, be appropriate, befit, pertain to, touch upon, appertain to …*The remaining 32 examples do not bear on our problem…* ◆ **bear something out** = <u>support</u>, prove, confirm, justify, endorse, uphold, vindicate, validate, substantiate, corroborate, legitimize …*His photographs do not quite bear this out…* ◆ **bear with someone** = <u>be patient with</u>, suffer, wait for, hold on (*informal*), stand by, tolerate, put up with (*informal*), make allowances for, hang fire …*If you'll bear with me, Frank, I can explain everything…*

bearable = <u>tolerable</u>, acceptable, sustainable, manageable, passable, admissible, supportable, endurable, sufferable OPPOSITE intolerable

beard = <u>whiskers</u>, bristles, stubble, five-o'clock shadow

bearded = <u>unshaven</u>, hairy, whiskered, stubbly, bushy, shaggy, hirsute, bristly, bewhiskered

bearer 1 = <u>agent</u>, carrier, courier, herald, envoy, messenger, conveyor, emissary, harbinger …*I hate to be the bearer of bad news…*
2 = <u>carrier</u>, runner, servant, porter …*a flag bearer…*
3 = <u>payee</u>, beneficiary, consignee …*the chief cashier's promise to pay the bearer…*

bearing NOUN **1** *usually with* **on** *or* **upon** = <u>relevance</u>, relation, application, connection, import, reference, significance, pertinence, appurtenance …*My father's achievements don't have any bearing on what I do…* OPPOSITE irrelevance
2 = <u>manner</u>, attitude, conduct, appearance, aspect, presence, behaviour, tone, carriage, posture, demeanour, deportment, mien, air, comportment …*She later wrote warmly of his bearing and behaviour…*
3 (*Nautical*) = <u>position</u>, course, direction, point of compass …*I'm flying on a bearing of ninety-three degrees…*
PLURAL NOUN = <u>way</u>, course, position, situation, track, aim, direction, location, orientation, whereabouts …*I lost my bearings and was just aware of cars roaring past…*

bearish (*Stock Exchange*) = <u>falling</u>, declining, slumping

beast 1 = <u>animal</u>, creature, brute …*the threats our ancestors faced from wild beasts…*
2 = <u>brute</u>, monster, savage, barbarian, fiend, swine, ogre, ghoul, sadist …*a sex beast who subjected two sisters to a terrifying ordeal…*

beastly 1 = <u>unpleasant</u>, mean, terrible, awful, nasty, foul, rotten, horrid, disagreeable, irksome …*The weather was beastly…* OPPOSITE pleasant
2 (*Informal*) = <u>cruel</u>, mean, nasty, harsh, savage, brutal, coarse, monstrous, malicious, insensitive, sadistic, unfriendly, unsympathetic, uncaring, spiteful, thoughtless, brutish, barbarous, unfeeling, inconsiderate, bestial, uncharitable, unchristian, hardhearted …*He must be wondering why everyone is*

being so beastly to him... OPPOSITE humane

beat VERB **1** = batter, break, hit, strike, knock, punch, belt (*informal*), whip, deck (*slang*), bruise, bash (*informal*), sock (*slang*), lash, chin (*slang*), pound, smack, thrash, cane, thump, lick (*informal*), buffet, clout (*informal*), flog, whack (*informal*), maul, clobber (*slang*), wallop (*informal*), tonk (*informal*), cudgel, thwack (*informal*), lambast(e), lay one on (*slang*), drub ...*They were beaten to death with baseball bats*...
2 = pound, strike, hammer, batter, thrash, pelt ...*The rain was beating on the window pains*...
3 = throb, pulse, tick, thump, tremble, pound, quake, quiver, vibrate, pulsate, palpitate ...*I felt my heart beat faster*...
4 = hit, strike, bang ...*When you beat the drum, you feel good*...
5 = flap, thrash, flutter, agitate, wag, swish ...*Its wings beat slowly*...
6 = defeat, outdo, trounce, overcome, stuff (*slang*), master, tank (*slang*), crush, overwhelm, conquer, lick (*informal*), undo, subdue, excel, surpass, overpower, outstrip, clobber (*slang*), vanquish, outrun, subjugate, run rings around (*informal*), wipe the floor with (*informal*), knock spots off (*informal*), make mincemeat of (*informal*), pip at the post, outplay, blow out of the water (*slang*), put in the shade (*informal*), bring to their knees ...*She was easily beaten into third place*...
NOUN **1** = throb, pounding, pulse, thumping, vibration, pulsating, palpitation, pulsation ...*He could hear the beat of his heart*...
2 = route, way, course, rounds, path, circuit ...*I was a relatively new PC on the beat, stationed in Hendon*...
PHRASES **beat it** (*Slang*) = go away, leave, depart, get lost (*informal*), shoo, exit, go to hell (*informal*), hook it (*slang*), scarper (*Brit. slang*), pack your bags (*informal*), make tracks, hop it (*slang*), scram (*informal*), get on your bike (*Brit. slang*), skedaddle (*informal*), sling your hook (*Brit. slang*), vamoose (*slang, chiefly U.S.*), voetsek (*S. African offensive*) ...*Beat it before it's too late*...
♦ **beat someone up** = assault (*Informal*), attack, batter, thrash, set about, do over (*Brit., Austral., & N.Z. slang*), work over (*slang*), clobber (*slang*), assail, set upon, lay into (*informal*), put the boot in (*slang*), lambast(e), duff up (*Brit. slang*), beat the living daylights out of (*informal*), knock about *or* around, fill in (*Brit. slang*) ...*Then they actually beat her up as well*...

beaten 1 = well-trodden, worn, trodden, trampled, well-used, much travelled ...*Before you is a well-worn path of beaten earth*...
2 = stirred, mixed, whipped, blended, whisked, frothy, foamy ...*Cool a little and slowly add the beaten eggs*...
3 = shaped, worked, formed, stamped, hammered, forged ...*brightly painted beaten metal*...
4 = defeated, overcome, frustrated, overwhelmed, cowed, thwarted, vanquished, disheartened ...*They had looked a beaten side with just seven minutes left*...

beating 1 = thrashing, hiding (*informal*), belting (*informal*), whipping (*slang*), slapping, tanning, lashing, smacking, caning, pasting (*slang*), flogging, drubbing, corporal punishment, chastisement ...*the savage beating of a suspect by police officers*...
2 = defeat, ruin, overthrow, pasting (*slang*), conquest, rout, downfall ...*A beating at Wembley would be too much of a trauma for them*...

beau (*Chiefly U.S.*) = boyfriend, man, guy (*informal*), date, lover, young man, steady, escort, admirer, fiancé, sweetheart, suitor, swain, toy boy, leman (*archaic*), fancy man (*slang*)

beautiful = attractive, pretty, lovely, stunning (*informal*), charming, tempting, pleasant, handsome, fetching, good-looking, gorgeous, fine, pleasing, fair, magnetic, delightful, cute, exquisite, enticing, seductive, graceful, captivating, appealing, radiant, alluring, drop-dead (*slang*), ravishing, bonny, winsome, comely, prepossessing ...*a beautiful red-haired woman kneeling at her mother's feet*...
OPPOSITE ugly

beautify = make beautiful, enhance, decorate, enrich, adorn, garnish, ornament, gild, embellish, grace, festoon, bedeck, glamorize

beauty 1 = attractiveness, charm, grace, bloom, glamour, fairness, elegance, symmetry, allure, loveliness, handsomeness, pulchritude, comeliness, exquisiteness, seemliness ...*an area of outstanding natural beauty*... OPPOSITE ugliness
2 = good-looker, looker (*informal, chiefly U.S.*), lovely (*slang*), sensation, dazzler, belle, goddess, Venus, peach (*informal*), cracker (*slang*), wow (*slang, chiefly U.S.*), dolly (*slang*), knockout (*informal*), heart-throb, stunner (*informal*), charmer, smasher (*informal*), humdinger (*slang*), glamour puss ...*She is known as a great beauty*...
3 = advantage, good, use, benefit, profit, gain, asset, attraction, blessing, good thing, utility, excellence, boon ...*the beauty of such water-based minerals*...
OPPOSITE disadvantage

beaver
PHRASES **beaver away** = work, sweat, slave, persist, graft (*informal*), toil, slog (away), persevere, plug away (*informal*), drudge, hammer away, peg away, exert yourself, break your back, keep your nose to the grindstone

(Related Words)
habitation : lodge

becalmed = still, stuck, settled, stranded, motionless

because CONJUNCTION = since, as, in that ...*They could not obey the command because they had no ammunition*...
PHRASES **because of** = as a result of, on account of, by reason of, thanks to, owing to ...*He failed because of a lack of money*...

Word Power

because – The phrase *on account of* can provide a useful alternative to *because of* in writing. It occurs relatively infrequently in spoken language, where it is sometimes followed by a clause, as in *on account of I don't do drugs*. However, this use is considered nonstandard.

beckon 1 = <u>gesture</u>, sign, wave, indicate, signal, nod, motion, summon, gesticulate ...*He beckoned to the waiter*...
2 = <u>lure</u>, call, draw, pull, attract, invite, tempt, entice, coax, allure ...*All the attractions of the peninsula beckon*...

become `VERB` **1** = <u>come to be</u>, develop into, be transformed into, grow into, change into, evolve into, alter to, mature into, metamorphose into, ripen into ...*After leaving school, he became a professional footballer*...
2 = <u>suit</u>, fit, enhance, flatter, ornament, embellish, grace, harmonize with, set off ...*Does khaki become you?*...
`PHRASES` **become of something** or **someone** = <u>happen to</u>, befall, betide ...*What will become of him?*...

becoming 1 = <u>flattering</u>, pretty, attractive, enhancing, neat, graceful, tasteful, well-chosen, comely ...*Softer fabrics are much more becoming than stiffer ones*... `OPPOSITE` unflattering
2 = <u>appropriate</u>, right, seemly, fitting, fit, correct, suitable, decent, proper, worthy, in keeping, compatible, befitting, decorous, comme il faut (*French*), congruous, meet (*archaic*) ...*This behaviour is not becoming among our politicians*... `OPPOSITE` inappropriate

bed `NOUN` **1** = <u>bedstead</u>, couch, berth, cot (*informal*), bunk (*informal*), pallet, divan ...*She went in to her bedroom and lay down on the bed*...
2 = <u>plot</u>, area, row, strip, patch, ground, land, garden, border ...*beds of strawberries and rhubarb*...
3 = <u>bottom</u>, ground, floor ...*the bare bed of a dry stream*...
4 = <u>base</u>, footing, basis, bottom, foundation, underpinning, groundwork, bedrock, substructure, substratum ...*a sandstone bed*...
`VERB` = <u>fix</u>, set, found, base, plant, establish, settle, root, sink, insert, implant, embed ...*The slabs can then be bedded on mortar to give rigid paving*...
`PHRASES` **bed down** = <u>sleep</u>, lie down, retire, turn in (*informal*), settle down, kip (*Brit. slang*), hit the hay (*slang*) ...*They bedded down in the fields*...

bedclothes = <u>bedding</u>, covers, sheets, blankets, linen, pillow, quilt, duvet, pillowcase, bed linen, coverlet, eiderdown

bedding = <u>bedclothes</u>, covers, sheets, blankets, linen, pillow, quilt, duvet, pillowcase, bed linen, coverlet, eiderdown

bedeck = <u>decorate</u>, grace, trim, array, enrich, adorn, garnish, ornament, embellish, festoon, beautify, bedight (*archaic*), bedizen (*archaic*), engarland

bedevil = <u>plague</u>, worry, trouble, frustrate, torture, irritate, torment, harass, hassle (*informal*), aggravate (*informal*), afflict, pester, vex, irk

bedlam = <u>pandemonium</u>, noise, confusion, chaos, turmoil, clamour, furore, uproar, commotion, rumpus, babel, tumult, hubbub, ruction (*informal*), hullabaloo, hue and cry, ruckus (*informal*)

bedraggled = <u>messy</u>, soiled, dirty, disordered, stained, dripping, muddied, muddy, drenched, ruffled, untidy, sodden, sullied, dishevelled, rumpled, unkempt, tousled, disarranged, disarrayed

bedridden = <u>confined to bed</u>, confined, incapacitated, laid up (*informal*), flat on your back

bedrock 1 = <u>first principle</u>, rule, basis, basics, principle, essentials, roots, core, fundamentals, cornerstone, nuts and bolts (*informal*), sine qua non (*Latin*), rudiment ...*Mutual trust is the bedrock of a relationship*...
2 = <u>bottom</u>, bed, foundation, underpinning, rock bottom, substructure, substratum ...*It took five years to drill down to bedrock*...

bee
(*Related Words*)
adjective: apian
collective nouns: swarm, grist
habitation: hive, apiary
➤ **ants, bees and wasps**

beef (*Slang*) = <u>complaint</u>, dispute, grievance, problem, grumble, criticism, objection, dissatisfaction, annoyance, grouse, gripe (*informal*), protestation, grouch (*informal*), remonstrance

beefy (*Informal*) = <u>brawny</u>, strong, powerful, athletic, strapping, robust, hefty (*informal*), muscular, sturdy, stalwart, bulky, burly, stocky, hulking, well-built, herculean, sinewy, thickset `OPPOSITE` scrawny

beehive = <u>hive</u>, colony, comb, swarm, honeycomb, apiary

beer = <u>ale</u>, brew, swipes (*Brit. slang*), wallop (*Brit. slang*), hop juice, amber fluid or nectar (*Austral. informal*)

beetle
➤ **beetles**

befall (*Archaic or literary*) = <u>happen to</u>, fall upon, occur in, take place in, ensue in, transpire in (*informal*), materialize in, come to pass in

befit = <u>be appropriate for</u>, become, suit, be fitting for, be suitable for, be seemly for, behove (*U.S.*)

befitting = <u>appropriate to</u>, right for, suitable for, fitting for, fit for, becoming to, seemly for, proper for, apposite to, meet (*archaic*) `OPPOSITE` unsuitable for

before `PREPOSITION` **1** = <u>earlier than</u>, ahead of, prior to, in advance of ...*Annie was born a few weeks before Christmas*... `OPPOSITE` after
2 = <u>in front of</u>, ahead of, in advance of, to the fore of ...*They stopped before a large white villa*...
3 = <u>in the presence of</u>, in front of ...*The Government will appear before the committee*...
4 = <u>ahead of</u>, in front of, in advance of ...*I saw before me an idyllic life*...
`ADVERB` **1** = <u>previously</u>, earlier, sooner, in advance, formerly ...*The war had ended only a month or so before*... `OPPOSITE` after
2 = <u>in the past</u>, earlier, once, previously, formerly, at one time, hitherto, beforehand, a while ago, heretofore, in days or years gone by ...*I've been here before*...
(*Related Words*)
prefixes: ante-, fore-, pre-

Beetles

www.ent.iastate.edu/imagegal/coleoptera/
http://www.zin.ru/Animalia/Coleoptera/eng/
http://www.insects.org/entophiles/index.html

ambrosia beetle	churchyard beetle	goliath beetle	rose chafer *or* rose
Asiatic beetle	click beetle, snapping	ground beetle	beetle
bacon beetle	beetle, *or* skipjack	Hercules beetle	rove beetle
bark beetle	cockchafer, May beetle,	huhu	scarab
bee beetle	*or* May bug	Japanese beetle	scavenger beetle
black beetle	Colorado beetle *or*	June bug, June beetle,	snapping beetle
blister beetle	potato beetle	May bug, *or* May beetle	snout beetle
bloody-nosed beetle	curculio	ladybird *or* (*U.S. &*	soldier beetle
boll weevil	deathwatch beetle	*Canad.*) ladybug	Spanish fly
bombardier beetle	devil's coach-horse	larder beetle	stag beetle
burying beetle *or*	diving beetle	leaf beetle	tiger beetle
sexton	dor	leather beetle	timberman beetle
cabinet beetle	dung beetle *or* chafer	longicorn (beetle) *or*	tortoise beetle
cardinal beetle	elater	long-horned beetle	vedalia
carpet beetle *or* (*U.S.*)	firefly	May beetle, cockchafer,	water beetle
carpet bug	flea beetle	*or* June bug	weevil *or* snout beetle
carrion beetle	furniture beetle	museum beetle	weevil, pea weevil, *or*
chafer	glow-worm	oil beetle	bean weevil
Christmas beetle *or* king	gold beetle *or* goldbug	pill beetle	whirligig beetle
beetle	goldsmith beetle	rhinoceros beetle	

---

beforehand = <u>in advance</u>, before, earlier, already, sooner, ahead, previously, in anticipation, before now, ahead of time

befriend = <u>make friends with</u>, back, help, support, benefit, aid, encourage, welcome, favour, advise, sustain, assist, stand by, uphold, side with, patronize, succour

befuddle = <u>confuse</u>, puzzle, baffle, bewilder, muddle, daze, perplex, mystify, disorient, faze, stupefy, flummox, bemuse, intoxicate `OPPOSITE`▷ make clear

befuddled = <u>confused</u>, upset, puzzled, baffled, at sea, bewildered, muddled, dazed, perplexed, taken aback, intoxicated, disorientated, disorganized, muzzy (*U.S. informal*), groggy (*informal*), flummoxed, woozy (*informal*), at sixes and sevens, fuddled, inebriated, thrown off balance, discombobulated (*informal, chiefly U.S. & Canad.*), not with it (*informal*), not knowing if you are coming or going

beg 1 = <u>implore</u>, plead with, beseech, desire, request, pray, petition, conjure, crave, solicit, entreat, importune, supplicate, go on bended knee to …*I begged him to come back to England with me*…
2 = <u>scrounge</u>, bum (*informal*), blag (*slang*), touch (someone) for (*slang*), mooch (*slang*), cadge, forage for, hunt around (for), sponge on (someone) for, freeload (*slang*), seek charity, call for alms, solicit charity …*I was surrounded by people begging for food*… `OPPOSITE`▷ give
3 = <u>dodge</u>, avoid, get out of, duck (*informal*), hedge, parry, shun, evade, elude, fudge, fend off, eschew, flannel (*Brit. informal*), sidestep, shirk, equivocate, body-swerve (*Scot.*) …*The research begs a number of questions*…

beget (*Old-fashioned*) **1** = <u>cause</u>, bring, produce, create, effect, lead to, occasion, result in, generate, provoke, induce, bring about, give rise to, precipitate, incite, engender …*Poverty begets debt*…
2 = <u>father</u>, breed, generate, sire, get, propagate, procreate …*He wanted to beget an heir*…

beggar `NOUN` = <u>tramp</u>, bankrupt, bum (*informal*), derelict, drifter, down-and-out, pauper, vagrant, hobo (*chiefly U.S.*), vagabond, bag lady (*chiefly U.S.*), dosser (*Brit. slang*), derro (*Austral. slang*), starveling …*Now I am a beggar, having lost everything except life*…
`VERB` = <u>defy</u>, challenge, defeat, frustrate, foil, baffle, thwart, withstand, surpass, elude, repel …*The statistics beggar belief*…

begin 1 = <u>start</u>, commence, proceed …*He stood up and began to walk around the room*… `OPPOSITE`▷ stop
2 = <u>commence</u>, start, initiate, embark on, set about, instigate, inaugurate, institute, make a beginning, set on foot …*The US wants to begin talks immediately*…
3 = <u>start talking</u>, start, initiate, commence, begin business, get *or* start the ball rolling …*He didn't know how to begin*…
4 = <u>come into existence</u>, start, appear, emerge, spring, be born, arise, dawn, be developed, be created, originate, commence, be invented, become available, crop up (*informal*), come into being …*It began as a local festival*…
5 = <u>emerge</u>, start, spring, stem, derive, issue, originate …*The fate line begins close to the wrist*… `OPPOSITE`▷ end

beginner = <u>novice</u>, student, pupil, convert, recruit, amateur, initiate, newcomer, starter, trainee, apprentice, cub, fledgling, learner, freshman, neophyte, tyro, probationer, greenhorn (*informal*), novitiate, tenderfoot, proselyte `OPPOSITE`▷ expert

beginning 1 = <u>start</u>, opening, break (*informal*), chance, source, opportunity, birth, origin, introduction, outset, starting point, onset, overture, initiation, inauguration, inception, commencement, opening move …*Think of this as a new beginning*… `OPPOSITE`▷ end
2 = <u>outset</u>, start, opening, birth, onset, prelude, preface, commencement, kickoff (*informal*) …*The question was raised at the beginning of this chapter*…

3 = <u>origins</u>, family, beginnings, stock, birth, roots, heritage, descent, pedigree, extraction, ancestry, lineage, parentage, stirps ...*His views come from his own humble beginnings*...

begrudge 1 = <u>resent</u>, envy, grudge, be jealous of ...*I certainly don't begrudge him the Nobel Prize*...
2 = <u>be bitter about</u>, object to, be angry about, give reluctantly, bear a grudge about, be in a huff about, give stingily, have hard feelings about ...*She spends £2,000 a year on it and she doesn't begrudge a penny*...

beguile 1 = <u>charm</u>, please, attract, delight, occupy, cheer, fascinate, entertain, absorb, entrance, win over, amuse, divert, distract, enchant, captivate, solace, allure, bewitch, mesmerize, engross, enrapture, tickle the fancy of ...*His paintings beguiled the Prince of Wales*...
2 = <u>fool</u>, trick, take in, cheat, con (*informal*), mislead, impose on, deceive, dupe, gull (*archaic*), delude, bamboozle, hoodwink, take for a ride (*informal*), befool ...*He used his newspapers to beguile his readers*... OPPOSITE enlighten

beguiling = <u>charming</u>, interesting, pleasing, attractive, engaging, lovely, entertaining, pleasant, intriguing, diverting, delightful, irresistible, enchanting, seductive, captivating, enthralling, winning, eye-catching, alluring, bewitching, delectable, winsome, likable *or* likeable

behalf
PHRASES **on something** *or* **someone's behalf** *or* **on behalf of something** *or* **someone 1** = <u>as a representative of</u>, representing, in the name of, as a spokesperson for ...*She made an emotional public appeal on her son's behalf*... ...*On behalf of my wife and myself, I'd like to thank you all*... **2** = <u>for the benefit of</u>, for the sake of, in support of, on the side of, in the interests of, on account of, for the good of, in defence of, to the advantage of, for the profit of ...*The honour recognizes work done on behalf of classical theatre*...

> ### *Word Power*
>
> **behalf** – *On behalf of* is sometimes wrongly used as an alternative to *on the part of*. The distinction is that *on behalf of someone* means 'for someone's benefit' or 'representing someone', while *on the part of someone* can be roughly paraphrased as 'by someone'.

behave 1 = <u>act</u>, react, conduct yourself, acquit yourself, comport yourself ...*He'd behaved badly*...
2 *often reflexive* = <u>be well-behaved</u>, be good, be polite, mind your manners, keep your nose clean, act correctly, act politely, conduct yourself properly ...*Sit down and behave yourself*... ...*You have to behave*... OPPOSITE misbehave

behaviour 1 = <u>conduct</u>, ways, actions, bearing, attitude, manner, manners, carriage, demeanour, deportment, mien (*literary*), comportment ...*He was asked to explain his extraordinary behaviour*...
2 = <u>action</u>, working, running, performance, operation,

practice, conduct, functioning ...*This process modifies the cell's behaviour*...

behead = <u>decapitate</u>, execute, guillotine, truncate, decollate (*archaic*)

behest
PHRASES **at someone's behest** = <u>at someone's command</u>, by someone's order, at someone's demand, at someone's wish, by someone's decree, at someone's bidding, at someone's instruction, by someone's mandate, at someone's dictate, at someone's commandment

behind PREPOSITION **1** = <u>at the rear of</u>, at the back of, at the heels of ...*They were parked behind the truck*...
2 = <u>after</u>, following ...*Keith wandered along behind him*...
3 = <u>supporting</u>, for, backing, on the side of, in agreement with ...*He had the state's judicial power behind him*...
4 = <u>causing</u>, responsible for, the cause of, initiating, at the bottom of, to blame for, instigating ...*I'd like to know who was behind this plot*...
5 = <u>later than</u>, after ...*The work is 22 weeks behind schedule*...
ADVERB **1** = <u>the back</u>, the rear ...*She was attacked from behind*...
2 = <u>after</u>, next, following, afterwards, subsequently, in the wake (of) ...*The troopers followed behind*... OPPOSITE in advance of
3 = <u>behind schedule</u>, delayed, running late, behind time ...*The accounts are more than three months behind*... OPPOSITE ahead
4 = <u>overdue</u>, in debt, in arrears, behindhand ...*They were falling behind with their mortgage payments*...
NOUN (*Informal*) = <u>bottom</u>, seat, bum (*Brit. slang*), butt (*U.S. & Canad. informal*), buns (*U.S. slang*), buttocks, rump, posterior, tail (*informal*), derrière (*euphemistic*), tush (*U.S. slang*), jacksy (*Brit. slang*) ...*jeans that actually flatter your behind*...

behold (*Archaic or literary*) = <u>look at</u>, see, view, eye, consider, study, watch, check, regard, survey, witness, clock (*Brit. slang*), examine, observe, perceive, gaze, scan, contemplate, check out (*informal*), inspect, discern, eyeball (*slang*), scrutinize, recce (*slang*), get a load of (*informal*), take a gander at (*informal*), take a dekko at (*Brit. slang*), feast your eyes upon

beholden = <u>indebted</u>, bound, owing, grateful, obliged, in debt, obligated, under obligation

beige NOUN *or* ADJECTIVE = <u>fawn</u>, coffee, cream, sand, neutral, mushroom, tan, biscuit, camel, buff, cinnamon, khaki, oatmeal, ecru, café au lait (*French*)
➤ **shades of brown** ➤ **shades of yellow**

being NOUN **1** = <u>individual</u>, thing, body, animal, creature, human being, beast, mortal, living thing ...*beings from outer space*...
2 = <u>life</u>, living, reality, animation, actuality ...*the complex process by which the novel is brought into being*... OPPOSITE nonexistence
3 = <u>soul</u>, spirit, presence, substance, creature, essence, organism, entity ...*The music seemed to touch his very being*...

belated = <u>late</u>, delayed, overdue, late in the day, tardy, behind time, unpunctual, behindhand

belch 1 = <u>burp</u>, eructate, eruct ...*He covered his mouth with his hand and belched discreetly...*
2 = <u>emit</u>, discharge, erupt, send out, throw out, vent, vomit, issue, give out, gush, eject, diffuse, emanate, exude, give off, exhale, cast out, disgorge, give vent to, send forth, spew forth, breathe forth ...*Tired old trucks belched black smoke...*

beleaguered 1 = <u>harassed</u>, troubled, plagued, tormented, hassled (*informal*), aggravated (*informal*), badgered, persecuted, pestered, vexed, put upon ...*There have been seven attempts against the beleaguered government...*
2 = <u>besieged</u>, surrounded, blockaded, encompassed, beset, encircled, assailed, hemmed in, hedged in, environed ...*The rebels continue to push their way towards the beleaguered capital...*

belie 1 = <u>misrepresent</u>, disguise, conceal, distort, misinterpret, falsify, gloss over ...*Her looks belie her 50 years...*
2 = <u>disprove</u>, deny, expose, discredit, contradict, refute, repudiate, negate, invalidate, rebut, give the lie to, make a nonsense of, gainsay (*archaic or literary*), prove false, blow out of the water (*slang*), controvert, confute ...*The facts of the situation belie his testimony...*

belief 1 = <u>trust</u>, confidence, conviction, reliance ...*a belief in personal liberty...* OPPOSITE disbelief
2 = <u>faith</u>, principles, doctrine, ideology, creed, dogma, tenet, credence, credo ...*He refuses to compete on Sundays because of his religious beliefs...*
3 = <u>opinion</u>, feeling, idea, view, theory, impression, assessment, notion, judgment, point of view, sentiment, persuasion, presumption ...*It is my belief that a common ground can be found...*

believable = <u>credible</u>, possible, likely, acceptable, reliable, authentic, probable, plausible, imaginable, trustworthy, creditable OPPOSITE unbelievable

believe VERB **1** = <u>think</u>, consider, judge, suppose, maintain, estimate, imagine, assume, gather, guess (*informal, chiefly U.S. & Canad.*), reckon, conclude, deem, speculate, presume, conjecture, postulate, surmise ...*I believe you have something of mine...*
2 = <u>accept</u>, hold, buy (*slang*), trust, credit, depend on, rely on, swallow (*informal*), count on, buy into (*slang*), have faith in, swear by, be certain of, be convinced of, place confidence in, presume true, take as gospel, take on (*U.S.*) ...*Don't believe what you read in the papers...* OPPOSITE disbelieve
PHRASES **believe in someone** = <u>trust in</u>, have faith in, place reliance on, place your trust in, pin your faith on, place confidence in ...*If you believe in yourself you can succeed...* ♦ **believe in something** = <u>advocate</u>, champion, approve of, swear by ...*He believed in marital fidelity...*

believer = <u>follower</u>, supporter, convert, disciple, protagonist, devotee, worshipper, apostle, adherent, zealot, upholder, proselyte OPPOSITE sceptic

belittle = <u>run down</u>, dismiss, diminish, put down, underestimate, discredit, ridicule, scorn, rubbish (*informal*), degrade, minimize, downgrade, undervalue, knock (*informal*), deride, malign, detract from, denigrate, scoff at, disparage, decry, sneer at, underrate, deprecate, depreciate, defame, derogate OPPOSITE praise

belle = <u>beauty</u>, looker (*informal*), lovely, good-looker, goddess, Venus, peach (*informal*), cracker (*informal*), stunner (*informal*), charmer

bellicose = <u>aggressive</u>, offensive, hostile, destructive, defiant, provocative, belligerent, combative, antagonistic, pugnacious, hawkish, warlike, quarrelsome, militaristic, sabre-rattling, jingoistic, warmongering

belligerence = <u>aggressiveness</u>, hostility, animosity, antagonism, destructiveness, pugnacity, combativeness, offensiveness, unfriendliness

belligerent ADJECTIVE = <u>aggressive</u>, hostile, contentious, combative, unfriendly, antagonistic, pugnacious, argumentative, bellicose, quarrelsome, aggers (*Austral. slang*), biffo (*Austral. slang*), litigious ...*He was almost back to his belligerent mood of twelve months ago...* OPPOSITE friendly
NOUN = <u>fighter</u>, battler, militant, contender, contestant, combatant, antagonist, warring nation, disputant ...*The belligerents were due to settle their differences...*

bellow VERB = <u>shout</u>, call, cry (out), scream, roar, yell, howl, shriek, clamour, bawl, holler (*informal*) ...*He bellowed the information into the telephone...*
NOUN = <u>shout</u>, call, cry, scream, roar, yell, howl, shriek, bell, clamour, bawl ...*a bellow of tearful rage...*

belly = <u>stomach</u>, insides (*informal*), gut, abdomen, tummy, paunch, vitals, breadbasket (*slang*), potbelly, corporation (*informal*)

belong = <u>go with</u>, fit into, be part of, relate to, attach to, be connected with, pertain to, have as a proper place

belonging = <u>fellowship</u>, relationship, association, loyalty, acceptance, attachment, inclusion, affinity, rapport, affiliation, kinship

belongings = <u>possessions</u>, goods, things, effects, property, stuff, gear, paraphernalia, personal property, accoutrements, chattels, goods and chattels

beloved = <u>dear</u>, loved, valued, prized, dearest, sweet, admired, treasured, precious, darling, worshipped, adored, cherished, revered

below PREPOSITION **1** = <u>under</u>, underneath, lower than ...*The boat dipped below the surface of the water...*
2 = <u>less than</u>, lower than ...*Night temperatures can drop below 15 degrees Celsius...*
3 = <u>subordinate to</u>, subject to, inferior to, lesser than ...*white-collar staff below chief officer level...*
ADVERB **1** = <u>lower</u>, down, under, beneath, underneath ...*Spread out below was a huge crowd...*
2 = <u>beneath</u>, following, at the end, underneath, at the bottom, further on ...*Please write to me at the address below...*

belt NOUN **1** = <u>waistband</u>, band, sash, girdle, girth, cummerbund, cincture ...*He wore a belt with a large brass buckle...*

2 = <u>conveyor belt</u>, band, loop, fan belt, drive belt ...*The turning disc is connected by a drive belt to an electric motor...*

3 (*Geography*) = <u>zone</u>, area, region, section, sector, district, stretch, strip, layer, patch, portion, tract ...*a belt of trees...*

PHRASES **below the belt** (*Informal*) = <u>unfair</u>, foul, crooked (*informal*), cowardly, sly, fraudulent, unjust, dishonest, deceptive, unscrupulous, devious, unethical, sneaky, furtive, deceitful, surreptitious, dishonourable, unsporting, unsportsmanlike, underhanded, not playing the game (*informal*) ...*Do you think it's a bit below the belt, what they're doing?...*

bemoan = <u>lament</u>, regret, complain about, rue, deplore, grieve for, weep for, bewail, cry over spilt milk, express sorrow about, moan over

bemused = <u>puzzled</u>, stunned, confused, stumped, baffled, at sea, bewildered, muddled, preoccupied, dazed, perplexed, mystified, engrossed, clueless, stupefied, nonplussed, absent-minded, flummoxed, half-drunk, fuddled

bench **NOUN** 1 = <u>seat</u>, stall, pew ...*He sat down on a park bench...*

2 = <u>worktable</u>, stand, table, counter, slab, trestle table, workbench ...*the laboratory bench...*

PHRASES **the bench** = <u>court</u>, judge, judges, magistrate, magistrates, tribunal, judiciary, courtroom ...*It shows how seriously the bench viewed these offences...*

benchmark = <u>reference point</u>, gauge, yardstick, measure, level, example, standard, model, reference, par, criterion, norm, touchstone

bend **VERB** 1 = <u>twist</u>, turn, wind, lean, hook, bow, curve, arch, incline, arc, deflect, warp, buckle, coil, flex, stoop, veer, swerve, diverge, contort, inflect, incurvate ...*Bend the bar into a horseshoe...*

2 = <u>submit</u>, yield, bow, surrender, give in, give way, cede, capitulate, resign yourself ...*Congress has to bend to his will...*

3 = <u>force</u>, direct, influence, shape, persuade, compel, mould, sway ...*He's very decisive. You cannot bend him...*

NOUN = <u>curve</u>, turn, corner, hook, twist, angle, bow, loop, arc, zigzag, camber ...*The crash occurred on a sharp bend...*

beneath **PREPOSITION** 1 = <u>under</u>, below, underneath, lower than ...*She found pleasure in sitting beneath the trees...* **OPPOSITE** over

2 = <u>inferior to</u>, below ...*She decided he was beneath her...*

3 = <u>unworthy of</u>, unfitting for, unsuitable for, inappropriate for, unbefitting ...*Many find themselves having to take jobs far beneath them...*

ADVERB = <u>underneath</u>, below, in a lower place ...*On a shelf beneath he spotted a photo album...*

(*Related Words*)

prefix: sub-

benefactor = <u>supporter</u>, friend, champion,

defender, sponsor, angel (*informal*), patron, promoter, contributor, backer, helper, subsidizer, philanthropist, upholder, well-wisher

beneficial = <u>favourable</u>, useful, valuable, helpful, profitable, benign, wholesome, advantageous, expedient, salutary, healthful, serviceable, salubrious, gainful **OPPOSITE** harmful

beneficiary 1 = <u>recipient</u>, receiver, payee, assignee, legatee ...*The main beneficiaries of pension equality so far have been men...*

2 = <u>heir</u>, inheritor ...*a sole beneficiary of a will...*

benefit **NOUN** 1 = <u>good</u>, use, help, profit, gain, favour, utility, boon, mileage (*informal*), avail ...*I'm a great believer in the benefits of this form of therapy...* **OPPOSITE** harm

2 = <u>advantage</u>, interest, aid, gain, favour, assistance, betterment ...*This could now work to his benefit...*

VERB 1 = <u>profit from</u>, make the most of, gain from, do well out of, reap benefits from, turn to your advantage ...*Both sides have benefited from the talks...*

2 = <u>help</u>, serve, aid, profit, improve, advance, advantage, enhance, assist, avail ...*a variety of government schemes benefiting children...* **OPPOSITE** harm

benevolence = <u>kindness</u>, understanding, charity, grace, sympathy, humanity, tolerance, goodness, goodwill, compassion, generosity, indulgence, decency, altruism, clemency, gentleness, philanthropy, magnanimity, fellow feeling, beneficence, kindliness, kind-heartedness **OPPOSITE** ill will

benevolent = <u>kind</u>, good, kindly, understanding, caring, liberal, generous, obliging, sympathetic, humanitarian, charitable, benign, humane, compassionate, gracious, indulgent, amiable, amicable, lenient, cordial, considerate, affable, congenial, altruistic, philanthropic, bountiful, beneficent, well-disposed, kind-hearted, warm-hearted, bounteous, tender-hearted

benighted = <u>uncivilized</u>, crude, primitive, backward, uncultivated, unenlightened

benign 1 = <u>benevolent</u>, kind, kindly, warm, liberal, friendly, generous, obliging, sympathetic, favourable, compassionate, gracious, amiable, genial, affable, complaisant ...*Critics of the scheme take a less benign view...* **OPPOSITE** unkind

2 (*Medical*) = <u>harmless</u>, innocent, superficial, innocuous, curable, inoffensive, not dangerous, remediable ...*It wasn't cancer, only a benign tumour...* **OPPOSITE** malignant

3 = <u>favourable</u>, good, encouraging, warm, moderate, beneficial, clement, advantageous, salutary, auspicious, propitious ...*relatively benign economic conditions...* **OPPOSITE** unfavourable

bent **ADJECTIVE** 1 = <u>misshapen</u>, twisted, angled, bowed, curved, arched, crooked, crippled, distorted, warped, deformed, tortuous, disfigured, out of shape ...*The trees were all bent and twisted from the wind...* **OPPOSITE** straight

2 = <u>stooped</u>, bowed, arched, hunched, stooping ...*a bent, frail, old man*...
NOUN = <u>inclination</u>, ability, taste, facility, talent, leaning, tendency, preference, faculty, forte, flair, knack, penchant, bag (*slang*), propensity, aptitude, predisposition, predilection, proclivity, turn of mind ...*his bent for natural history*...
PHRASES **bent on** = <u>intent on</u>, set on, fixed on (*informal*), predisposed to, resolved on, insistent on ...*He's bent on suicide*...

bequeath **1** = <u>leave</u>, will, give, grant, commit, transmit, hand down, endow, bestow, entrust, leave to by will ...*He bequeathed all his silver to his children*...
2 = <u>give</u>, offer, accord, grant, afford, contribute, yield, lend, pass on, transmit, confer, bestow, impart ...*It is true that colonialism did not bequeath much to Africa*...

bequest = <u>legacy</u>, gift, settlement, heritage, trust, endowment, estate, inheritance, dower, bestowal

berate = <u>scold</u>, rebuke, reprimand, reproach, blast, carpet (*informal*), put down, criticize, slate (*informal, chiefly Brit.*), censure, castigate, revile, chide, harangue, tear into (*informal*), tell off (*informal*), rail at, read the riot act to, reprove, upbraid, slap on the wrist, lambast(e), bawl out (*informal*), excoriate, rap over the knuckles, chew out (*U.S. & Canad. informal*), tear (someone) off a strip (*Brit. informal*), give a rocket (*Brit. & N.Z. informal*), vituperate **OPPOSITE** praise

bereavement = <u>loss</u>, death, misfortune, deprivation, affliction, tribulation

bereft
PHRASES **bereft of** = <u>deprived of</u>, without, minus, lacking in, devoid of, cut off from, parted from, sans (*archaic*), robbed of, empty of, denuded of

berg (*S. African*) = <u>mountain</u>, peak, mount, height, ben (*Scot.*), horn, ridge, fell (*Brit.*), alp, pinnacle, elevation, eminence

berserk = <u>crazy</u>, wild, mad, frantic, ape (*slang*), insane, barro (*Austral. slang*), off the air (*Austral. slang*)

berth **NOUN** **1** = <u>bunk</u>, bed, cot (*Nautical*), hammock, billet ...*Golding booked a berth on the first boat he could*...
2 (*Nautical*) = <u>anchorage</u>, haven, slip, port, harbour, dock, pier, wharf, quay ...*A ship has applied to leave its berth*...
VERB (*Nautical*) = <u>anchor</u>, land, dock, moor, tie up, drop anchor ...*The ship berthed in New York*...

beseech = <u>beg</u>, ask, petition, call upon, plead with, solicit, implore, entreat, importune, adjure, supplicate

beset = <u>plague</u>, trouble, embarrass, torture, haunt, torment, harass, afflict, badger, perplex, pester, vex, entangle, bedevil

besetting = <u>chronic</u>, persistent, long-standing, prevalent, habitual, ingrained, deep-seated, incurable, deep-rooted, inveterate, incorrigible, ineradicable

beside **PREPOSITION** = <u>next to</u>, near, close to, neighbouring, alongside, overlooking, next door to, adjacent to, at the side of, abreast of, cheek by jowl with ...*On the table beside an empty plate was a pile of books*...

PHRASES **beside yourself** = <u>distraught</u>, desperate, mad, distressed, frantic, frenzied, hysterical, insane, crazed, demented, unbalanced, uncontrolled, deranged, berserk, delirious, unhinged, very anxious, overwrought, apoplectic, out of your mind, at the end of your tether ...*He was beside himself with anxiety*...

Word Power

beside – People occasionally confuse *beside* and *besides*. *Besides* is used for mentioning something that adds to what you have already said, for example: *I didn't feel like going and besides, I had nothing to wear. Beside* usually means *next to or at the side of something or someone*, for example: *he was standing beside me* (not *besides me*).

---

besides **PREPOSITION** = <u>apart from</u>, barring, excepting, other than, excluding, as well (as), in addition to, over and above ...*I think she has many good qualities besides being beautiful*...
ADVERB = <u>also</u>, too, further, otherwise, in addition, as well, moreover, furthermore, what's more, into the bargain ...*Besides, today's young people have grown up knowing only a Conservative government*...
▶ **beside**

besiege **1** = <u>harass</u>, worry, trouble, harry, bother, disturb, plague, hound, hassle (*informal*), badger, pester, importune, bend someone's ear (*informal*), give someone grief (*Brit. & S. African*), beleaguer ...*She was besieged by the press and the public*...
2 = <u>surround</u>, confine, enclose, blockade, encompass, beset, encircle, close in on, hem in, shut in, lay siege to, hedge in, environ, beleaguer, invest (*rare*) ...*The main part of the army moved to besiege the town*...

besotted = <u>infatuated</u>, charmed, captivated, beguiled, doting, smitten, bewitched, bowled over (*informal*), spellbound, enamoured, hypnotized, swept off your feet

bespeak **1** = <u>indicate</u>, show, suggest, evidence, reveal, display, predict, imply, exhibit, proclaim, signify, denote, testify to, foretell, evince, betoken ...*His large ears bespeak his ability to hear all*...
2 = <u>engage</u>, solicit, prearrange, order beforehand ...*I'm already bespoken to take you tomorrow morning*...

best **ADJECTIVE** **1** = <u>finest</u>, leading, chief, supreme, principal, first, foremost, superlative, pre-eminent, unsurpassed, most accomplished, most skilful, most excellent ...*He was the best player in the world for most of the 1950s*...
2 = <u>most fitting</u>, right, most desirable, most apt, most advantageous, most correct ...*the best way to end the long-running war*...
NOUN **1** = <u>finest</u>, top, prime, pick, choice, favourite, flower, cream, elite, crème de la crème (*French*) ...*We only offer the best to our clients*...
2 = <u>utmost</u>, most, greatest, hardest, highest endeavour ...*You must do your best to protect yourselves*...
ADVERB = <u>most highly</u>, most fully, most deeply ...*The*

thing I liked best about the show was the music...

bestow = present, give, accord, award, grant, commit, hand out, lavish, confer, endow, entrust, impart, allot, honour with, apportion OPPOSITE obtain

best-seller = success, hit (*informal*), winner, smash (*informal*), sensation, blockbuster (*informal*), wow (*slang*), market leader, smash hit (*informal*), chart-topper (*informal*), runaway success, number one OPPOSITE failure

best-selling = successful, top, hit (*informal*), smash (*informal*), flourishing, lucrative, smash-hit (*informal*), chart-topping (*informal*), moneymaking, number one, highly successful

bet VERB = gamble, chance, stake, venture, hazard, speculate, punt (*chiefly Brit.*), wager, put money, risk money, pledge money, put your shirt *...I bet on a horse called Premonition...*
NOUN = gamble, risk, stake, venture, pledge, speculation, hazard, flutter (*informal*), ante, punt, wager, long shot *...He made a 30 mile trip to the casino to place a bet...*

betray 1 = be disloyal to, break with, grass on (*Brit. slang*), dob in (*Austral. slang*), double-cross (*informal*), stab in the back, be unfaithful to, sell down the river (*informal*), grass up (*slang*), shop (*slang, chiefly Brit.*), put the finger on (*informal*), inform on *or* against *...He might be seen as having betrayed his mother...*
2 = give away, tell, show, reveal, expose, disclose, uncover, manifest, divulge, blurt out, unmask, lay bare, tell on, let slip, evince *...She studied his face, but it betrayed nothing...*

betrayal = disloyalty, sell-out (*informal*), deception, treason, treachery, trickery, duplicity, double-cross (*informal*), double-dealing, breach of trust, perfidy, unfaithfulness, falseness, inconstancy OPPOSITE loyalty

better ADVERB 1 = to a greater degree, more completely, more thoroughly *...I like your interpretation better than the one I was taught...*
2 = in a more excellent manner, more effectively, more attractively, more advantageously, more competently, in a superior way *...If we had played better we might have won...* OPPOSITE worse
ADJECTIVE 1 = underline{well}, stronger, improving, progressing, recovering, healthier, cured, mending, fitter, fully recovered, on the mend (*informal*), more healthy, less ill *...He is better now...* OPPOSITE worse
2 = superior, finer, worthier, higher-quality, surpassing, preferable, more appropriate, more useful, more valuable, more suitable, more desirable, streets ahead, more fitting, more expert *...I've been able to have a better car than I otherwise could have...* OPPOSITE inferior
VERB 1 = beat, top, exceed, excel, surpass, outstrip, outdo, improve on *or* upon, cap (*informal*) *...He bettered the old record of 4 minutes 24...*
2 = improve, further, raise, forward, reform, advance, promote, correct, enhance, upgrade, amend, mend, rectify, augment, ameliorate, meliorate *...Our parents came here with the hope of bettering themselves...*

OPPOSITE worsen
PHRASES **get the better of someone** = defeat, beat, surpass, triumph over, outdo, trounce, outwit, best, subjugate, prevail over, outsmart (*informal*), get the upper hand, score off, run rings around (*informal*), wipe the floor with (*informal*), make mincemeat of (*informal*), blow out of the water (*slang*) *...He usually gets the better of them...*

betterment = improvement, gain, advancement, enhancement, edification, amelioration, melioration

between = amidst, among, mid, in the middle of, betwixt
(*Related Words*)
prefix: inter-

> ## Word Power
> **between** – After *distribute* and words with a similar meaning, *among* should be used rather than *between*: *share out the sweets among the children* (not *between the children*, unless there are only two children).

beverage = drink, liquid, liquor, refreshment, draught, bevvy (*dialect*), libation (*facetious*), thirst quencher, potable, potation

bevy = group, company, set, party, band, crowd, troop, pack, collection, gathering, gang, bunch (*informal*), cluster, congregation, clump, troupe, posse (*slang*), clique, coterie, assemblage

beware 1 = be careful, look out, watch out, be wary, be cautious, take heed, guard against something *...Beware, this recipe is not for slimmers...*
2 = avoid, mind, shun, refrain from, steer clear of, guard against *...Beware using plastic cards in foreign cash machines...*

bewilder = confound, surprise, stun, confuse, puzzle, baffle, mix up, daze, perplex, mystify, stupefy, befuddle, flummox, bemuse, dumbfound, nonplus, flabbergast (*informal*)

bewildered = confused, surprised, stunned, puzzled, uncertain, startled, baffled, at sea, awed, muddled, dizzy, dazed, perplexed, disconcerted, at a loss, mystified, taken aback, speechless, giddy, disorientated, bamboozled (*informal*), nonplussed, flummoxed, at sixes and sevens, thrown off balance, discombobulated (*informal, chiefly U.S. & Canad.*)

bewildering = confusing, surprising, amazing, stunning, puzzling, astonishing, staggering, baffling, astounding, perplexing, mystifying, stupefying

bewitch = enchant, attract, charm, fascinate, absorb, entrance, captivate, beguile, allure, ravish, mesmerize, hypnotize, cast a spell on, enrapture, spellbind OPPOSITE repulse

bewitched = enchanted, charmed, transformed, fascinated, entranced, possessed, captivated, enthralled, beguiled, ravished, spellbound, mesmerized, enamoured, hypnotized, enraptured, under a spell

beyond 1 = on the other side of, outwith (*Scot.*)

...*They heard footsteps in the main room, beyond a door*...

2 = <u>after</u>, over, past, above ...*Few jockeys continue riding beyond the age of forty*...

3 = <u>past</u>, outwith (*Scot.*) ...*His interests extended beyond the fine arts*...

4 = <u>except for</u>, but, save, apart from, other than, excluding, besides, aside from ...*I knew nothing beyond a few random facts*...

5 = <u>exceeding</u>, surpassing, superior to, out of reach of ...*What he had done was beyond my comprehension*...

6 = <u>outside</u>, over, above, outwith (*Scot.*) ...*The situation was beyond her control*...

bias NOUN **1** = <u>prejudice</u>, leaning, bent, tendency, inclination, penchant, intolerance, bigotry, propensity, favouritism, predisposition, nepotism, unfairness, predilection, proclivity, partiality, narrow-mindedness, proneness, one-sidedness ...*There were fierce attacks on the BBC for alleged political bias*... OPPOSITE impartiality

2 = <u>slant</u>, cross, angle, diagonal line ...*The fabric, cut on the bias, hangs as light as a cobweb*...

VERB = <u>influence</u>, colour, weight, prejudice, distort, sway, warp, slant, predispose ...*We mustn't allow it to bias our teaching*...

biased = <u>prejudiced</u>, weighted, one-sided, partial, distorted, swayed, warped, slanted, embittered, predisposed, jaundiced

Bible
➤ Bible

bicker = <u>quarrel</u>, fight, argue, row (*informal*), clash, dispute, scrap (*informal*), disagree, fall out (*informal*), squabble, spar, wrangle, cross swords, fight like cat and dog, go at it hammer and tongs, altercate OPPOSITE agree

bid NOUN **1** = <u>attempt</u>, try, effort, venture, undertaking, go (*informal*), shot (*informal*), stab (*informal*), crack (*informal*), endeavour ...*a bid to silence its critics*...

2 = <u>offer</u>, price, attempt, amount, advance, proposal, sum, tender, proposition, submission ...*He made an agreed takeover bid of £351 million*...

VERB **1** = <u>make an offer</u>, offer, propose, submit, tender, proffer ...*She wanted to bid for it*...

2 = <u>wish</u>, say, call, tell, greet ...*I bade her goodnight*...

3 = <u>tell</u>, call, ask, order, charge, require, direct, desire, invite, command, summon, instruct, solicit, enjoin ...*I dare say he did as he was bidden*...

bidding **1** = <u>order</u>, call, charge, demand, request, command, instruction, invitation, canon, beck, injunction, summons, behest, beck and call ...*the bidding of his backbenchers*...

2 = <u>offer</u>, proposal, auction, tender ...*The bidding starts at £2 million*...

big **1** = <u>large</u>, great, huge, giant, massive, vast, enormous, considerable, substantial, extensive, immense, spacious, gigantic, monumental, mammoth, bulky, burly, colossal, stellar (*informal*), prodigious, hulking, ponderous, voluminous, elephantine, ginormous (*informal*), humongous *or* humungous (*U.S. slang*), sizable *or* sizeable

...*Australia's a big country*... OPPOSITE small

2 = <u>important</u>, serious, significant, grave, urgent, paramount, big-time (*informal*), far-reaching, momentous, major league (*informal*), weighty ...*Her problem was just too big for her to tackle on her own*... OPPOSITE unimportant

3 = <u>powerful</u>, important, prime, principal, prominent, dominant, influential, paramount, eminent, puissant ...*Their father was very big in the army*...

4 = <u>grown-up</u>, adult, grown, mature, elder, full-grown ...*He's a big boy now*... OPPOSITE young

5 = <u>generous</u>, good, princely, noble, heroic, gracious, benevolent, disinterested, altruistic, unselfish, magnanimous, big-hearted ...*They describe him as an idealist with a big heart*...

big-head (*Informal*) = <u>boaster</u>, know-all (*informal*), swaggerer, self-seeker, egomaniac, egotist, braggart, braggadocio, narcissist, swell-head (*informal*), blowhard (*informal*), self-admirer

big-headed = <u>boastful</u>, arrogant, swaggering, bragging, cocky, vaunting, conceited, puffed-up, bumptious, immodest, crowing, overconfident, vainglorious, swollen-headed, egotistic, full of yourself, too big for your boots *or* breeches

bigot = <u>fanatic</u>, racist, extremist, sectarian, maniac, fiend (*informal*), zealot, persecutor, dogmatist

bigoted = <u>intolerant</u>, twisted, prejudiced, biased, warped, sectarian, dogmatic, opinionated, narrow-minded, obstinate, illiberal OPPOSITE tolerant

bigotry = <u>intolerance</u>, discrimination, racism, prejudice, bias, ignorance, injustice, sexism, unfairness, fanaticism, sectarianism, racialism, dogmatism, provincialism, narrow-mindedness, mindlessness, pig-ignorance (*slang*) OPPOSITE tolerance

bigwig (*Informal*) = <u>important person</u>, somebody, celebrity, heavyweight (*informal*), notable, big name, mogul, big gun (*informal*), dignitary, celeb (*informal*), big shot (*informal*), personage, nob (*slang*), big cheese (*slang, old-fashioned*), big noise (*informal*), big hitter (*informal*), heavy hitter (*informal*), panjandrum, notability, V.I.P. OPPOSITE nonentity

bile = <u>bitterness</u>, anger, hostility, resentment, animosity, venom, irritability, spleen, acrimony, pique, nastiness, rancour, virulence, asperity, ill humour, irascibility, peevishness, churlishness

bill¹ NOUN **1** = <u>charges</u>, rate, costs, score, account, damage (*informal*), statement, reckoning, expense, tally, invoice, note of charge ...*They couldn't afford to pay the bills*...

2 = <u>act of parliament</u>, measure, proposal, piece of legislation, projected law ...*The bill was opposed by a large majority*...

3 = <u>list</u>, listing, programme, card, schedule, agenda, catalogue, inventory, roster, syllabus ...*He is topping the bill at a dusk-to-dawn party*...

4 = <u>advertisement</u>, notice, poster, leaflet, bulletin, circular, handout, placard, handbill, playbill ...*A sign forbids the posting of bills*...

VERB **1** = <u>charge</u>, debit, invoice, send a statement to,

Bible

Books of the Bible (Old Testament)

Genesis	1 Kings	Ecclesiastes	Obadiah
Exodus	2 Kings	Song of Solomon	Jonah
Leviticus	1 Chronicles	Isaiah	Micah
Numbers	2 Chronicles	Jeremiah	Nahum
Deuteronomy	Ezra	Lamentations	Habakkuk
Joshua	Nehemiah	Ezekiel	Zephaniah
Judges	Esther	Daniel	Haggai
Ruth	Job	Hosea	Zechariah
1 Samuel	Psalms	Joel	Malachi
2 Samuel	Proverbs	Amos	

Books of the Bible (New Testament)

Matthew	2 Corinthians	1 Timothy	2 Peter
Mark	Galatians	2 Timothy	1 John
Luke	Ephesians	Titus	2 John
John	Philippians	Philemon	3 John
Acts	Colossians	Hebrews	Jude
Romans	1 Thessalonians	James	Revelation
1 Corinthians	2 Thessalonians	1 Peter	

Books of the Bible (Apocrypha)

Tobit	Wisdom	Daniel, Bel and the Snake
Judith	Ecclesiasticus	Song of the Three
1 Maccabees	Baruch	Esdras
2 Maccabees	Daniel and Susanna	Manasseh

Characters in the Bible

Aaron	David	Isaac	Leah
Abednego	Deborah	Isaiah	Levi
Abel	Delilah	Ishmael	Lot
Abigail	Dinah	Issachar	Lot's wife
Abraham	Dives	Jacob	Luke
Absalom	Dorcas	Jael	Magus
Achitophel or	Elias	James	Malachi
Ahithophel	Elijah	Japheth	Manasseh
Adam	Elisha	Jehoshaphat	Mark
Ahab	Enoch	Jehu	Martha
Ahasuerus	Enos	Jephthah or Jephte	Mary
Ammon	Ephraim	Jeremiah	Mary Magdalene
Amos	Esau	Jeroboam	Matthew
Ananias	Esther	Jesse	Matthias
Andrew	Eve	Jesus Christ	Melchior
Asher	Ezekiel	Jethro	Melchizedek or
Balaam	Ezra	Jezebel	Melchisedech
Balthazar	Gabriel	Joab	Meshach
Barabbas	Gad	Job	Methuselah
Bartholomew	Gideon	Joel	Micah
Baruch	Gilead	John	Midian
Bathsheba	Gog and Magog	John the Baptist	Miriam
Beelzebub	Goliath	Jonah or Jonas	Mordecai
Belial	Good Samaritan	Jonathan	Moses
Belshazzar	Habakkuk	Joseph	Nabonidus
Benjamin	Hagar	Joshua	Naboth
Boanerges	Haggai	Josiah	Nahum
Boaz	Ham	Jubal	Naomi
Caiaphas	Hannah	Judah	Naphtali
Cain	Herod	Judas Iscariot	Nathan
Caspar	Hezekiah	Jude	Nathanael
Cush or Kush	Hiram	Judith	Nebuchadnezzar or
Dan	Holofernes	Laban	Nebuchadrezzar
Daniel	Hosea	Lazarus	Nehemiah

Characters in the Bible (continued) http://www.biblegateway.com/

Nicodemus	Rebecca	Simeon	Zacharias, Zachariah, *or*
Nimrod	Reuben	Simon	Zachary
Noah	Ruth	Solomon	Zebedee
Obadiah	Salome	Susanna	Zebulun
Paul	Samson	Tetragrammaton	Zechariah
Peter	Samuel	Thaddeus *or* Thadeus	Zedekiah
Philip	Sarah	Thomas	Zephaniah
Potiphar	Saul	Tobit	Zilpah
Prodigal Son	Seth	Tubal-cain	
Queen of Sheba	Shadrach	Uriah	
Rachel	Shem	Virgin Mary	

Place names in the Bible

Aceldama	Cana	Gomorrah *or* Gomorrha	On
Antioch	Canaan	Goshen	Ophir
Aram	Capernaum	Horeb	Rabbath Ammon
Ararat	Eden	Jericho	Samaria
Arimathaea *or*	Galilee	Jerusalem	Shiloh
Arimathea	Garden of Eden	Judaea *or* Judea	Shinar
Babel	Gath	Judah	Shittim
Bashan	Gaza	land of milk and honey	Sodom
Bethesda	Gehenna	land of Nod	Tadmor
Bethlehem	Gethsemane	Moab	Tophet *or* Topheth
Calvary	Golgotha	Nazareth	wilderness

send an invoice to …*Are you going to bill me for this?*…

2 = <u>advertise</u>, post, announce, push (*informal*), declare, promote, plug (*informal*), proclaim, tout, flaunt, publicize, crack up (*informal*), give advance notice of …*They bill it as Britain's most exciting museum*…

bill² = <u>beak</u>, nib, neb (*archaic or dialect*), mandible …*Its legs and feet are grey, its bill brownish-yellow*…

billet [VERB] = <u>quarter</u>, post, station, locate, install, accommodate, berth, garrison …*The soldiers were billeted in private homes*…
[NOUN] = <u>quarters</u>, accommodation, lodging, barracks …*We hid the radio in Hut 10, which was our billet*…

billow [VERB] = <u>surge</u>, roll, expand, swell, balloon, belly, bulge, dilate, puff up, bloat …*the billowing sails*…
[NOUN] = <u>surge</u>, wave, flow, rush, flood, cloud, gush, deluge, upsurge, outpouring, uprush …*billows of almost solid black smoke*…

bind [VERB] **1** = <u>oblige</u>, make, force, require, engage, compel, prescribe, constrain, necessitate, impel, obligate …*The treaty binds them to respect their neighbour's independence*…
2 = <u>tie</u>, unite, join, stick, secure, attach, wrap, rope, knot, strap, lash, glue, tie up, hitch, paste, fasten, truss, make fast …*Bind the ends of the card together with thread*… [OPPOSITE] untie
3 = <u>restrict</u>, limit, handicap, confine, detain, restrain, hamper, inhibit, hinder, impede, hem in, keep within bounds *or* limits …*All are bound by the same strict etiquette*…
4 = <u>fuse</u>, join, stick, bond, cement, adhere …*These compounds bind with genetic material in the liver*…
5 = <u>bandage</u>, cover, dress, wrap, swathe, encase …*Her mother bound the wound with a rag soaked in iodine*…

[NOUN] (*Informal*) = <u>nuisance</u>, inconvenience, hassle (*informal*), drag (*informal*), spot (*informal*), difficulty, bore, dilemma, pest, hot water (*informal*), uphill (*S. African*), predicament, annoyance, quandary, pain in the neck (*informal*), pain in the backside, pain in the butt (*informal*) …*It is expensive to buy and a bind to carry home*…

binding = <u>compulsory</u>, necessary, mandatory, imperative, obligatory, conclusive, irrevocable, unalterable, indissoluble [OPPOSITE] optional

binge (*Informal*) = <u>bout</u>, session, spell, fling, feast, stint, spree, orgy, bender (*informal*), jag (*slang*), beano (*Brit. slang*), blind (*slang*)

biography = <u>life story</u>, life, record, account, profile, memoir, CV, life history, curriculum vitae

bird = <u>feathered friend</u>, fowl, songbird
> **Related Words**
adjective: avian
male: cock
female: hen
young: chick, fledg(e)ling, nestling
collective nouns: flock, flight
habitation: nest
> birds > birds of prey > seabirds > types of fowl

bird of prey
> **Related Words**
adjective: raptorial
> birds of prey

birth 1 = <u>childbirth</u>, delivery, nativity, parturition …*She weighed 5lb 7oz at birth*… [OPPOSITE] death
2 = <u>beginning</u>, start, rise, source, origin, emergence, outset, genesis, initiation, inauguration, inception, commencement, fountainhead …*the birth of popular*

Birds

Types of bird

accentor
amazon
ani
apostle bird *or* happy
 family bird
avadavat *or* amadavat
avocet
axebird
babbler
Baltimore oriole
barbet
beccafico
bee-eater
bellbird *or* (*Austral.*)
 koromako *or*
 makomako
bird of paradise
bishopbird
bittern
blackbird
blackcap
blackcock
black grouse
blackpoll
bluebird
blue grouse
blue jay
bluethroat
bluetit
boatbill *or* boat-billed
 heron
bobolink
bobwhite
bokmakierie
boobook
bowerbird
brain-fever bird *or*
 (*Austral.*) pallid cuckoo
brambling
broadbill
brolga, Australian crane,
 or (*Austral.*) native
 companion
budgerigar *or* (*Austral.*)
 zebra parrot
bulbul
bullfinch
bunting
bush shrike
bushtit
bush wren
bustard *or* (*Austral.*)
 plain turkey, plains
 turkey, *or* wild turkey
button quail *or* (*Austral.*)
 bustard quail
cacique
canary
Cape Barren goose
Cape pigeon
capercaillie *or*
 capercailzie

Cape sparrow
capuchin
cardinal *or* cardinal
 grosbeak
carrion crow
cassowary
catbird
chaffinch
chat
chickadee
chicken *or* (*Austral.*
 informal*) chook
chiffchaff
chimney swallow *or*
 chimney swift
chipping sparrow
chough
chuck-will's-widow
chukar
cliff swallow
coal tit *or* coletit
cockatiel, cockateel, *or*
 cockatoo-parrot
cockatoo
cock-of-the-rock
collared dove
coly *or* mousebird
conure
coppersmith
coquette
corella
corn bunting
corncrake
cotinga *or* chatterer
coucal, pheasant coucal,
 or swamp pheasant
cowbird
crake
crane
crested tit
crocodile bird
crombec
crossbill
crow *or* (*Scot.*) corbie
cuckoo
cuckoo-shrike
cumulet
curassow
curlew
currawong *or* bell
 magpie
dabchick
darter, anhinga, *or*
 snakebird
demoiselle (crane) *or*
 Numidian crane
diamond bird *or*
 pardalote
dipper *or* water ouzel
diver
dollarbird
dotterel *or* dottrel

dove *or* (*archaic or poetic*)
 culver
dowitcher
drongo
dunlin *or* red-backed
 sandpiper
egret
emperor penguin
emu
emu-wren
fantail
fernbird
fieldfare
fig-bird
finch
finfoot
firebird
firecrest
flamingo
flower-pecker
flycatcher
francolin
friarbird
frogmouth
galah *or* (*Austral.*) galar
 or gillar
gang-gang
gnatcatcher
go-away bird
godwit
goldcrest
golden oriole
goldfinch
Gouldian finch, painted
 finch, *or* purple-
 breasted finch
grackle *or* crow
 blackbird
grassfinch
grassquit
great crested grebe *or*
 loon
great northern diver
great tit
grebe
greenfinch
green leek
greenlet
greenshank
green woodpecker
grey-crowned babbler,
 happy family bird,
 Happy Jack, *or* parson
 bird
grey warbler *or* riroriro
grosbeak
grouse
guan
guinea fowl
hadedah
hawfinch
hazelhen

hedge sparrow *or*
 dunnock
helldiver, pie-billed
 grebe, *or* dabchick
hen harrier *or* (*U.S. &*
 Canad.) marsh harrier
heron
hill myna
hoatzin *or* hoactzin
homing pigeon
honey creeper
honeyeater
honey guide
honeysucker
hooded crow
hoopoe
hornbill
house martin
house sparrow
hummingbird *or*
 trochilus
ibis
jabiru *or* (*Austral.*)
 policeman bird
jacamar
jaçana *or* lily-trotter
jackdaw
jacksnipe
Jacobin
jaeger
Java sparrow
jay
junco
jungle fowl
kagu
kaka
kakapo
kea
killdeer
kingbird
kingfisher
king penguin
kiwi *or* apteryx
knot
koel *or* (*Austral.*) black
 cuckoo *or* cooee bird
kokako
kookaburra, laughing
 jackass, *or* (*Austral.*)
 bushman's clock,
 settler's clock, goburra,
 or great brown
 kingfisher
kotuku
Lahore
lapwing *or* green plover
lark
limpkin *or* courlan
linnet
locust bird
loggerhead shrike
longspur

Types of bird (continued)

long-tailed tit
lorikeet
lory
lourie
lovebird
lyrebird or (Austral.)
 buln-buln
macaw
magpie or (Austral.)
 piping shrike or piping
 crow-shrike
magpie lark or (Austral.)
 mudlark, Murray
 magpie, mulga, or
 peewit
Major Mitchell or
 Leadbeater's cockatoo
makomako
marabou
marsh tit
martin
meadowlark
meadow pipit
metallic starling or
 shining starling
minivet
mistle thrush or missel
 thrush
mistletoe bird
mockingbird
monal or monaul
motmot or sawbill
mourning dove
myna, mynah, or mina
nighthawk, bullbat, or
 mosquito hawk
night heron
nightingale
nightjar, (U.S. &
 Canad.) goatsucker, or
 (Austral.) nighthawk
noddy
noisy friarbird or
 leatherhead
noisy miner or (Austral.)
 micky or soldier bird
notornis
nun
nutcracker
nuthatch
oil bird or guacharo
oriole
ortolan or ortolan
 bunting
ostrich
ouzel or ousel
ovenbird
oxpecker or tick-bird
parakeet or parrakeet
pardalote
parrot
partridge
peacock
peafowl

peewit
pelican
penguin
phalarope
pheasant
pied goose or magpie
 goose
pied wagtail
pigeon
pipit or (N.Z.) pihoihoi
pitta
plover
pratincole
ptarmigan
puffbird
puffin
pukeko
purple gallinule
pyrrhuloxia
quail
quarrian or quarrion
quetzal
racket-tail
rail
rainbow bird
rainbow lorikeet
raven
red-backed shrike
redbreast
red grouse
red-legged partridge
redpoll
redshank
redstart
redwing
reedbird
reed bunting
reedling or bearded tit
reed warbler
regent-bird or regent
 bowerbird
regent honeyeater
rhea or American ostrich
ricebird
riflebird
rifleman
ringed plover
ring-necked pheasant
ringneck parrot, Port
 Lincoln parrot, or buln-
 buln
ring ouzel
roadrunner or chaparral
 cock
robin or robin redbreast
rock dove or rock
 pigeon
rockhopper
roller
rook
rosella
rosy finch
ruff
ruffed grouse

runt
saddleback
saddlebill or jabiru
sage grouse
sanderling
sandgrouse
sand martin
sandpiper
sapsucker
satin bowerbird
Scandaroon
scarlet tanager
scrub bird
sedge warbler
seriema
serin
sheathbill
shoebill
shore bird or (Brit.)
 wader
shrike or butcherbird
sicklebill
silver-eye
siskin or (formerly)
 aberdevine
sitella or tree-runner
skimmer
skylark
snipe
snow bunting
snowy egret
solitaire
song sparrow
song thrush or mavis
sora
sparrow
spoonbill
spotted crake or
 (Austral.) water crake
spotted flycatcher
spotted sandpiper or
 (U.S.) peetweet
squacco
starling
stilt
stint
stock dove
stonechat
stone curlew or thick-
 knee
stork
sugar bird
sulphur-crested
 cockatoo or white
 cockatoo
sunbird
sun bittern
superb blue wren
superb lyrebird
surfbird
swallow
swift
swiftlet
swordbill

tailorbird
takahe
tanager
tattler
tawny pippit
tern
thornbill
thrasher
thrush or (poetic) throstle
tit
titmouse
tody
topknot pigeon
toucan
touraco, turaco, or
 plantain-eater
towhee
tragopan
tree creeper
tree sparrow
trochilus
trogon
tropicbird
troupial
trumpeter
tui or parson bird
turtledove
twite
umbrella bird
veery
verdin
wader or wading bird
wagtail
wall creeper
warbler
water rail
water thrush
wattlebird
waxbill
waxwing
weaverbird or weaver
weka, Maori hen, or
 wood hen
wheatear
whimbrel
whinchat
whip bird
whippoorwill
white-eye or (N.Z.)
 blighty, silvereye, or
 waxeye
whitethroat
whooping crane
willet
willow grouse
willow tit
willow warbler
wonga-wonga or wonga
 pigeon
woodchat or woodchat
 shrike
woodcock
wood ibis
woodlark

Types of bird (continued) http://www.bsc-eoc.org/avibase/avibase.jsp?lang=EN&pg=home

woodpecker	woodswallow	wryneck
wood pigeon, ringdove, cushat,	wood warbler	yellowhammer
(*Scot.*) cushie-doo, *or* (*English*	wren	yellowtail *or* yellowtail kingfisher
dialect) quist	wrybill	zebra finch

Extinct birds

archaeopteryx	great auk	moa	solitaire
archaeornis	huia	notornis	
dodo	ichthyornis	passenger pigeon	

democracy…

3 = <u>ancestry</u>, line, race, stock, blood, background, breeding, strain, descent, pedigree, extraction, lineage, forebears, parentage, genealogy, derivation …*men of low birth*…

(**Related Words**)

adjective : natal

bisect = <u>cut in two</u>, cross, separate, split, halve, cut across, intersect, cut in half, split down the middle, divide in two, bifurcate

bisexual = <u>bi</u> (*slang*), ambidextrous (*slang*), swinging both ways (*slang*), AC/DC (*slang*)

bit¹ 1 = <u>slice</u>, segment, fragment, crumb, mouthful, small piece, morsel …*a bit of cake*…

2 = <u>piece</u>, scrap, small piece …*crumpled bits of paper*…

3 = <u>jot</u>, whit, tittle, iota …*All it required was a bit of work*…

4 = <u>part</u>, moment, period …*The best bit was the car chase*…

5 = <u>little while</u>, time, second, minute, moment, spell, instant, tick (*Brit. informal*), jiffy (*informal*) …*Let's wait a bit*…

bit² NOUN = <u>curb</u>, check, brake, restraint, snaffle …*The horse can be controlled by a snaffle bit and reins*…

PHRASES **take the bit in** *or* **between your teeth** = <u>get to grips with something</u>, get stuck in (*informal*), tackle something, get down to something, set about something, make a start on something …*I got the bit between my teeth and did my best*…

bitchy (*Informal*) = <u>spiteful</u>, mean, nasty, cruel, vicious, malicious, barbed, vindictive, malevolent, venomous, snide, rancorous, catty (*informal*), backbiting, shrewish, ill-natured, vixenish OPPOSITE nice

bite VERB **1** = <u>nip</u>, cut, tear, wound, grip, snap, crush, rend, pierce, champ, pinch, chew, crunch, clamp, nibble, gnaw, masticate …*Llamas won't bite or kick*…

2 = <u>eat</u>, burn, smart, sting, erode, tingle, eat away, corrode, wear away …*nylon biting into the flesh*…

NOUN **1** = <u>snack</u>, food, piece, taste, refreshment, mouthful, morsel, titbit, light meal …*a bite to eat*…

2 = <u>wound</u>, sting, pinch, nip, prick …*The boy had suffered a snake bite but he made a quick recovery*…

3 = <u>edge</u>, interest, force, punch (*informal*), sting, zest, sharpness, keenness, pungency, incisiveness, acuteness …*The novel seems to lack bite and tension*…

4 = <u>kick</u> (*informal*), edge, punch (*informal*), spice, relish, zest, tang, sharpness, piquancy, pungency, spiciness …*I'd have preferred a bit more bite and not so much sugar*…

biting 1 = <u>piercing</u>, cutting, cold, sharp, freezing, frozen, bitter, raw, chill, harsh, penetrating, arctic, nipping, icy, blighting, chilly, wintry, gelid, cold as ice …*a raw, biting northerly wind*…

2 = <u>sarcastic</u>, cutting, sharp, severe, stinging, withering, scathing, acrimonious, incisive, virulent, caustic, vitriolic, trenchant, mordant, mordacious …*This was the most biting criticism made against her*…

bitter 1 = <u>grievous</u>, hard, severe, distressing, fierce, harsh, cruel, savage, ruthless, dire, relentless, poignant, ferocious, galling, unrelenting, merciless, remorseless, gut-wrenching, vexatious, hard-hearted …*the scene of bitter fighting*… OPPOSITE pleasant

2 = <u>resentful</u>, hurt, wounded, angry, offended, sour, put out, sore, choked, crabbed, acrimonious, aggrieved, sullen, miffed (*informal*), embittered, begrudging, peeved (*informal*), piqued, rancorous …*She is said to be very bitter about the way she was sacked*… OPPOSITE happy

3 = <u>freezing</u>, biting, severe, intense, raw, fierce, chill, stinging, penetrating, arctic, icy, polar, Siberian, glacial, wintry …*a night in the bitter cold*… OPPOSITE mild

4 = <u>sour</u>, biting, sharp, acid, harsh, unpleasant, tart, astringent, acrid, unsweetened, vinegary, acidulated, acerb …*The leaves taste rather bitter*… OPPOSITE sweet

bitterly 1 = <u>grievously</u>, harshly, cruelly, savagely, terribly, ruthlessly, mercilessly, distressingly …*a bitterly fought football war*…

2 = <u>resentfully</u>, sourly, sorely, tartly, grudgingly, sullenly, testily, acrimoniously, caustically, mordantly, irascibly …*They bitterly resented their loss of power*…

3 = <u>intensely</u>, freezing, severely, fiercely, icy, bitingly …*It's been bitterly cold here in Moscow*…

bitterness 1 = <u>resentment</u>, hurt, anger, hostility, indignation, animosity, venom, acrimony, pique, rancour, ill feeling, bad blood, ill will, umbrage, vexation, asperity …*I still feel bitterness and anger*…

2 = <u>sourness</u>, acidity, sharpness, tartness, acerbity, vinegariness …*the strength and bitterness of the drink*…

bizarre = <u>strange</u>, odd, unusual, extraordinary, fantastic, curious, weird, way-out (*informal*), peculiar, eccentric, abnormal, ludicrous, queer (*informal*), irregular, rum (*Brit. slang*), uncommon, singular, grotesque, perplexing, uncanny, mystifying, off-the-wall (*slang*), outlandish, comical, oddball (*informal*), off the rails, zany, unaccountable, off-beat, left-field (*informal*), freakish, wacko (*slang*), outré, cockamamie (*slang, chiefly U.S.*) OPPOSITE> normal

black ADJECTIVE **1** = <u>dark</u>, raven, ebony, sable, jet, dusky, pitch-black, inky, swarthy, stygian, coal-black, pitchy, murky ...*He had thick black hair...* OPPOSITE> light

2 = <u>gloomy</u>, sad, depressing, distressing, horrible, grim, bleak, hopeless, dismal, ominous, sombre, morbid, mournful, morose, lugubrious, joyless, funereal, doleful, cheerless ...*After the tragic death of her son, she fell into a black depression...* OPPOSITE> happy

3 = <u>terrible</u>, bad, devastating, tragic, fatal, unfortunate, dreadful, destructive, unlucky, harmful, adverse, dire, catastrophic, hapless, detrimental, untoward, ruinous, calamitous, cataclysmic, ill-starred, unpropitious, ill-fated, cataclysmal ...*He had just undergone one of the blackest days of his political career...*

4 = <u>wicked</u>, bad, evil, corrupt, vicious, immoral, depraved, debased, amoral, villainous, unprincipled, nefarious, dissolute, iniquitous, irreligious, impious, unrighteous ...*the blackest laws in the country's history...* OPPOSITE> good

5 = <u>angry</u>, cross, furious, hostile, sour, menacing, moody, resentful, glowering, sulky, baleful, louring *or* lowering ...*a black look on your face...* OPPOSITE> happy

6 = <u>dirty</u>, soiled, stained, filthy, muddy, blackened, grubby, dingy, grimy, sooty, mucky, scuzzy (*slang, chiefly U.S.*), begrimed, festy (*Austral. slang*), mud-encrusted, miry ...*The whole front of him was black with dirt...* OPPOSITE> clean

PHRASES **black out** = <u>pass out</u>, drop, collapse, faint, swoon, lose consciousness, keel over (*informal*), flake out (*informal*), become unconscious ...*He felt so ill that he blacked out...* ◆ **black something out** = <u>darken</u>, cover, shade, conceal, obscure, eclipse, dim, blacken, obfuscate, make dark, make darker, make dim ...*The whole city is blacked out at night...* ◆ **in the black** = <u>in credit</u>, solid, solvent, in funds, financially sound, without debt, unindebted ...*Until he's in the black we certainly can't afford to get married...*

Word Power

black – When referring to people with dark skin, the adjective *black* or *Black* is used. For people of the US whose origins lie in Africa, the preferred term is *African American*.

Shades from black to white

ash	pearl
black	pewter
charcoal	pitch-black
cream	platinum
ebony	putty
eggshell	raven
grey	sable
gunmetal	silver
iron	slate
ivory	steel grey
jet	stone
off-white	white
oyster white	

blacken **1** = <u>darken</u>, deepen, grow black ...*He watched the blackening clouds move in...*

2 = <u>make dark</u>, shadow, shade, obscure, overshadow, make darker, make dim ...*The smoke blackened the sky like the apocalypse...*

3 = <u>discredit</u>, stain, disgrace, smear, knock (*informal*), degrade, rubbish (*informal*), taint, tarnish, censure, slur, slag (off) (*slang*), malign, reproach, denigrate, disparage, decry, vilify, slander, sully, dishonour, defile, defame, bad-mouth (*slang, chiefly U.S. & Canad.*), traduce, bring into disrepute, smirch, calumniate ...*They're trying to blacken our name...*

blacklist = <u>exclude</u>, bar, ban, reject, rule out, veto, boycott, embargo, expel, vote against, preclude, disallow, repudiate, proscribe, ostracize, debar, blackball

black magic = <u>witchcraft</u>, magic, witching, voodoo, the occult, wizardry, enchantment, sorcery, occultism, incantation, black art, witchery, necromancy, diabolism, sortilege

blackmail NOUN = <u>threat</u>, intimidation, ransom, compulsion, protection (*informal*), coercion, extortion, pay-off (*informal*), shakedown, hush money (*slang*), exaction ...*It looks like the pictures were being used for blackmail...*

VERB = <u>threaten</u>, force, squeeze, compel, exact, intimidate, wring, coerce, milk, wrest, dragoon, extort, bleed (*informal*), press-gang, hold to ransom ...*I thought he was trying to blackmail me into saying whatever he wanted...*

blackness = <u>darkness</u>, shade, gloom, dusk, obscurity, nightfall, murk, dimness, murkiness, duskiness, shadiness, melanism, swarthiness, inkiness, nigrescence, nigritude (*rare*) OPPOSITE> light

blackout **1** = <u>noncommunication</u>, secrecy, censorship, suppression, radio silence ...*a media blackout...*

2 = <u>power cut</u>, power failure ...*an electricity blackout...*

3 = <u>unconsciousness</u>, collapse, faint, oblivion, swoon (*literary*), loss of consciousness, syncope (*Pathology*) ...*I suffered a blackout which lasted for several minutes...*

black sheep = <u>disgrace</u>, rebel, maverick, outcast, renegade, dropout, prodigal, individualist, nonconformist, ne'er-do-well, reprobate, wastrel, bad egg (*old-fashioned informal*)

blame VERB 1 = <u>hold responsible</u>, accuse, denounce, indict, impeach, incriminate, impute, recriminate, point a *or* the finger at …*They blamed the army for most of the atrocities…* OPPOSITE absolve
2 = <u>attribute to</u>, credit to, assign to, put down to, impute to …*The police blamed the explosion on terrorists…*
3 (used in negative constructions) = <u>criticize</u>, charge, tax, blast, condemn, put down, disapprove of, censure, reproach, chide, admonish, tear into (*informal*), find fault with, reprove, upbraid, lambast(e), reprehend, express disapprobation of …*I do not blame them for trying to make some money…* OPPOSITE praise
NOUN = <u>responsibility</u>, liability, rap (*slang*), accountability, onus, culpability, answerability …*Bad women never take the blame for anything…* OPPOSITE praise

blameless = <u>innocent</u>, clear, clean, upright, stainless, honest, immaculate, impeccable, virtuous, faultless, squeaky-clean, unblemished, unsullied, uninvolved, unimpeachable, untarnished, above suspicion, irreproachable, guiltless, unspotted, unoffending OPPOSITE guilty

blanch = <u>turn pale</u>, fade, pale, drain, bleach, wan, whiten, go white, become pallid, become *or* grow white

bland 1 = <u>dull</u>, boring, weak, plain, flat, commonplace, tedious, vanilla (*informal*), dreary, tiresome, monotonous, run-of-the-mill, uninspiring, humdrum, unimaginative, uninteresting, insipid, unexciting, ho-hum (*informal*), vapid, unstimulating, undistinctive …*It's easy on the ear but bland and forgettable…* OPPOSITE exciting
2 = <u>tasteless</u>, weak, watered-down, insipid, flavourless, thin, unstimulating, undistinctive …*It tasted bland and insipid, like warmed card…*

blank ADJECTIVE 1 = <u>unmarked</u>, white, clear, clean, empty, plain, bare, void, spotless, unfilled, uncompleted …*He tore a blank page from his notebook…* OPPOSITE marked
2 = <u>expressionless</u>, empty, dull, vague, hollow, vacant, lifeless, deadpan, straight-faced, vacuous, impassive, inscrutable, inane, wooden, poker-faced (*informal*) …*He gave him a blank look…* OPPOSITE expressive
3 = <u>puzzled</u>, lost, confused, stumped, doubtful, baffled, stuck, at sea, bewildered, muddled, mixed up, confounded, perplexed, disconcerted, at a loss, mystified, clueless, dumbfounded, nonplussed, uncomprehending, flummoxed …*Abbot looked blank. 'I don't follow, sir.'…*
4 = <u>absolute</u>, complete, total, utter, outright, thorough, downright, consummate, unqualified, out and out, unmitigated, unmixed …*a blank refusal to attend…*
NOUN 1 = <u>empty space</u>, space, gap …*Put a word in each blank to complete the sentence…*
2 = <u>void</u>, vacuum, vacancy, emptiness, nothingness, vacuity, tabula rasa …*Everything was a complete blank…*

blanket NOUN 1 = <u>cover</u>, rug, coverlet, afghan …*There was an old blanket in the trunk of my car…*
2 = <u>covering</u>, cover, bed, sheet, coating, coat, layer, film, carpet, cloak, mantle, thickness …*The mud disappeared under a blanket of snow…*
VERB = <u>coat</u>, cover, hide, surround, cloud, mask, conceal, obscure, eclipse, cloak …*More than a foot of snow blanketed parts of Michigan…*
ADJECTIVE = <u>comprehensive</u>, full, complete, wide, sweeping, broad, extensive, wide-ranging, thorough, inclusive, exhaustive, all-inclusive, all-embracing …*the blanket coverage of the Olympics…*

blare = <u>blast</u>, scream, boom, roar, thunder, trumpet, resound, hoot, toot, reverberate, sound out, honk, clang, peal

blarney = <u>flattery</u>, coaxing, exaggeration, fawning, adulation, wheedling, spiel, sweet talk (*informal*), flannel (*Brit. informal*), soft soap (*informal*), sycophancy, servility, obsequiousness, cajolery, blandishment, fulsomeness, toadyism, overpraise, false praise, honeyed words

blasé = <u>nonchalant</u>, cool, bored, distant, regardless, detached, weary, indifferent, careless, lukewarm, glutted, jaded, unmoved, unconcerned, impervious, uncaring, uninterested, apathetic, offhand, world-weary, heedless, satiated, unexcited, surfeited, cloyed OPPOSITE interested

blasphemous = <u>irreverent</u>, cheeky (*informal*), contemptuous, profane, disrespectful, godless, ungodly, sacrilegious, irreligious, impious OPPOSITE reverent

blasphemy = <u>irreverence</u>, swearing, cursing, indignity (*to God*), desecration, sacrilege, profanity, impiety, profanation, execration, profaneness, impiousness

blast NOUN 1 = <u>explosion</u>, crash, burst, discharge, blow-up, eruption, detonation …*250 people were killed in the blast…*
2 = <u>gust</u>, rush, storm, breeze, puff, gale, flurry, tempest, squall, strong breeze …*Blasts of cold air swept down from the mountains…*
3 = <u>blare</u>, blow, scream, trumpet, wail, resound, clamour, hoot, toot, honk, clang, peal …*The buzzer suddenly responded in a long blast of sound…*
VERB 1 = <u>blow up</u>, bomb, destroy, burst, ruin, break up, explode, shatter, demolish, rupture, dynamite, put paid to, blow sky-high …*The explosion blasted out the external supporting wall…*
2 = <u>criticize</u>, attack, put down, censure, berate, castigate, tear into (*informal*), flay, rail at, lambast(e), chew out (*U.S. & Canad. informal*) …*They have blasted the report…*

blasted (*Informal*), confounded, hateful, infernal, detestable

blast-off = <u>launch</u>, launching, take off, discharge, projection, lift-off, propelling, sendoff

blatant = <u>obvious</u>, open, clear, plain, naked, sheer, patent, evident, pronounced, straightforward, outright, glaring, manifest, bald, transparent, noticeable, conspicuous, overt, unmistakable, flaunting, palpable, undeniable, brazen, flagrant, indisputable, ostentatious, unmitigated, cut-and-dried (informal), undisguised, obtrusive, unsubtle, unconcealed OPPOSITE subtle

blaze VERB 1 = burn, glow, flare, flicker, be on fire, go up in flames, be ablaze, fire, flash, flame ...The log fire was blazing merrily...
2 = shine, flash, beam, glow, flare, glare, gleam, shimmer, radiate ...The gardens blazed with colour...
3 = flare up, rage, boil, explode, fume, seethe, be livid, be incandescent ...His dark eyes were blazing with anger...
NOUN 1 = inferno, fire, flames, bonfire, combustion, conflagration ...Two firemen were hurt in a blaze which swept through a tower block...
2 = flash, glow, glitter, flare, glare, gleam, brilliance, radiance ...I wanted the front garden to be a blaze of colour...

blazing 1 = burning, flashing, flaming, glowing, gleaming, on fire, fiery, alight, scorching, smouldering, ablaze, aflame, afire ...a blazing fire...
2 = shining, brilliant, flashing, glowing, sparkling, illuminated, gleaming, radiant, luminous, incandescent, aglow, coruscating ...the blazing, brilliant rays of a new dawn...
3 = furious, excited, angry, raging, passionate, fuming, frenzied, incensed, enraged, seething, fervent, impassioned, wrathful ...My husband has just had a blazing row with his boss...

bleach = lighten, wash out, blanch, peroxide, whiten, blench, etiolate

bleached = whitened, faded, lightened, washed-out, etiolated, stone-washed, peroxided, achromatic

bleak 1 = dismal, black, dark, depressing, grim, discouraging, gloomy, hopeless, dreary, sombre, unpromising, disheartening, joyless, cheerless, comfortless ...The immediate outlook remains bleak... OPPOSITE cheerful
2 = exposed, open, empty, raw, bare, stark, barren, desolate, gaunt, windswept, weather-beaten, unsheltered ...The island's pretty bleak... OPPOSITE sheltered
3 = stormy, cold, severe, bitter, rough, harsh, chilly, windy, tempestuous, intemperate ...The weather can be quite bleak on the coast...

bleary = dim, blurred, fogged, murky, fuzzy, watery, misty, hazy, foggy, blurry, ill-defined, indistinct, rheumy

bleed 1 = lose blood, flow, weep, trickle, gush, exude, spurt, shed blood ...The wound was bleeding profusely...
2 = blend, run, meet, unite, mix, combine, flow, fuse, mingle, converge, ooze, seep, amalgamate, meld, intermix ...The two colours will bleed into each other...
3 (Informal) = extort, milk, squeeze, drain, exhaust, fleece ...They mean to bleed the British to the utmost...

blemish NOUN 1 = mark, line, spot, scratch, bruise, scar, blur, defect, flaw, blot, smudge, imperfection, speck, blotch, disfigurement, pock, smirch ...the blemish on his face... OPPOSITE perfection
2 = defect, fault, weakness, stain, disgrace, deficiency, shortcoming, taint, inadequacy, dishonour, demerit ...the one blemish on an otherwise resounding success...
VERB = dishonour, mark, damage, spot, injure, ruin, mar, spoil, stain, blur, disgrace, impair, taint, tarnish, blot, smudge, disfigure, sully, deface, blotch, besmirch, smirch ...He wasn't about to blemish that pristine record... ...Nobody wanted to blemish his reputation at that time... OPPOSITE enhance

blend VERB 1 = mix, join, combine, compound, incorporate, merge, put together, fuse, unite, mingle, alloy, synthesize, amalgamate, interweave, coalesce, intermingle, meld, intermix, commingle, commix ...Blend the ingredients until you have a smooth cream...
2 = go well, match, fit, suit, go with, correspond, complement, coordinate, tone in, harmonize, cohere ...Make sure all the patches blend together...
3 = combine, mix, link, integrate, merge, put together, fuse, unite, synthesize, marry, amalgamate ...a band that blended jazz, folk and classical music...
NOUN = mixture, cross, mix, combination, compound, brew, composite, union, fusion, synthesis, alloy, medley, concoction, amalgam, amalgamation, meld, mélange (French), conglomeration, admixture ...He makes up his own blends of flour...

bless 1 = sanctify, dedicate, ordain, exalt, anoint, consecrate, hallow, invoke happiness on ...Bless this couple and their loving commitment to one another... OPPOSITE curse
2 = endow, give to, provide for, grant for, favour, grace, bestow to ...If God has seen fit to bless you with this gift, you should use it... OPPOSITE afflict
3 = praise, thank, worship, glorify, magnify, exalt, extol, pay homage to, give thanks to ...Let us bless God for so uniting our hearts...

blessed 1 = endowed, supplied, granted, favoured, lucky, fortunate, furnished, bestowed, jammy (Brit. slang) ...He's the son of a doctor, and well blessed with money...
2 = happy, contented, glad, merry, heartening, joyous, joyful, blissful ...The birth of a healthy baby is a truly blessed event...
3 = holy, sacred, divine, adored, revered, hallowed, sanctified, beatified ...After the ceremony, they were declared 'blessed'...

blessing 1 = benefit, help, service, profit, gain, advantage, favour, gift, windfall, kindness, boon, good fortune, bounty, godsend, manna from heaven ...the blessings of prosperity... OPPOSITE disadvantage
2 = approval, backing, support, agreement, regard, favour, sanction, go-ahead (informal), permission, leave, consent, mandate, endorsement, green light, ratification, assent, authorization, good wishes, acquiescence, approbation, concurrence, O.K. or okay (informal) ...They gave their formal blessing to the idea... OPPOSITE disapproval

3 = <u>benediction</u>, grace, dedication, thanksgiving, invocation, commendation, consecration, benison …*He said the blessing after taking the bread…* `OPPOSITE` curse

blight `NOUN` **1** = <u>curse</u>, suffering, evil, depression, corruption, distress, pollution, misery, plague, hardship, woe, misfortune, contamination, adversity, scourge, affliction, bane, wretchedness …*urban blight and unacceptable poverty…* `OPPOSITE` blessing
2 = <u>disease</u>, plague, pest, fungus, contamination, mildew, contagion, infestation, pestilence, canker, cancer …*the worst year of the potato blight…*
`VERB` = <u>frustrate</u>, destroy, ruin, crush, mar, dash, wreck, spoil, crool *or* cruel (*Austral. slang*), scar, undo, mess up, annihilate, nullify, put a damper on …*families whose lives were blighted by unemployment…*

blind **1** = <u>sightless</u>, unsighted, unseeing, eyeless, visionless, stone-blind …*How would you describe colour to a blind person?…* `OPPOSITE` sighted
2 *often with* **to** = <u>unaware of</u>, unconscious of, deaf to, ignorant of, indifferent to, insensitive to, oblivious of, unconcerned about, inconsiderate of, neglectful of, heedless of, insensible of, unmindful of, disregardful of …*All the time I was blind to your suffering…* `OPPOSITE` aware
3 = <u>unquestioning</u>, prejudiced, wholesale, indiscriminate, uncritical, unreasoning, undiscriminating …*her blind faith in the wisdom of the church…*
4 = <u>hidden</u>, concealed, obscured, dim, unseen, tucked away …*a blind corner…* `OPPOSITE` open
5 = <u>dead-end</u>, closed, dark, obstructed, leading nowhere, without exit …*a dusty hotel room overlooking a blind alley…*
6 = <u>unthinking</u>, wild, violent, rash, reckless, irrational, hasty, senseless, mindless, uncontrollable, uncontrolled, unchecked, impetuous, intemperate, unconstrained …*The poor man went into a blind panic…*
➤ **disabled**

blinding **1** = <u>bright</u>, brilliant, intense, shining, glowing, blazing, dazzling, vivid, glaring, gleaming, beaming, effulgent, bedazzling …*the blinding lights of the delivery room…*
2 = <u>amazing</u>, striking, surprising, stunning, impressive, astonishing, staggering, sensational (*informal*), breathtaking, wondrous (*archaic or literary*), jaw-dropping …*waiting for a blinding revelation that never came…*

blindly **1** = <u>thoughtlessly</u>, carelessly, recklessly, indiscriminately, unreasonably, impulsively, senselessly, heedlessly, regardlessly …*Don't just blindly follow what the banker says…*
2 = <u>wildly</u>, aimlessly, madly, frantically, confusedly …*Panicking blindly they stumbled towards the exit…*

blink `VERB` **1** = <u>flutter</u>, wink, bat …*She was blinking her eyes rapidly…*
2 = <u>flash</u>, flicker, sparkle, wink, shimmer, twinkle, glimmer, scintillate …*Green and yellow lights blinked on the surface of the harbour…*
`PHRASES` **on the blink** (*Slang*) = <u>not working</u>

(properly), faulty, defective, playing up, out of action, malfunctioning, out of order, on the fritz (*U.S. slang*) …*an old TV that's on the blink…*

blinkered = <u>narrow-minded</u>, narrow, one-sided, prejudiced, biased, partial, discriminatory, parochial, constricted, insular, hidebound, one-eyed, lopsided `OPPOSITE` broad-minded

bliss **1** = <u>joy</u>, ecstasy, euphoria, rapture, nirvana, felicity, gladness, blissfulness, delight, pleasure, heaven, satisfaction, happiness, paradise …*It was a scene of such domestic bliss…* `OPPOSITE` misery
2 = <u>beatitude</u>, ecstasy, exaltation, blessedness, felicity, holy joy …*the bliss beyond the now…*

blissful **1** = <u>delightful</u>, pleasing, satisfying, heavenly (*informal*), enjoyable, gratifying, pleasurable …*There's nothing more blissful than lying by that pool…*
2 = <u>happy</u>, joyful, satisfied, ecstatic, joyous, euphoric, rapturous …*a blissful smile…*

blister = <u>sore</u>, boil, swelling, cyst, pimple, wen, blain, carbuncle, pustule, bleb, furuncle (*Pathology*)

blitz = <u>attack</u>, strike, assault, raid, offensive, onslaught, bombardment, bombing campaign, blitzkrieg

blizzard = <u>snowstorm</u>, storm, tempest

bloated **1** = <u>puffed up</u>, swollen, blown-up, enlarged, inflated, puffy, dilated, distended, turgid, tumescent, tumid …*His face was bloated…* `OPPOSITE` shrivelled
2 = <u>too full</u>, swollen up …*Diners do not want to leave the table feeling bloated…*

blob = <u>drop</u>, ball, mass, pearl, lump, bead, dab, droplet, globule, glob, dewdrop

bloc = <u>group</u>, union, league, ring, alliance, coalition, axis, combine

block `NOUN` **1** = <u>piece</u>, bar, square, mass, cake, brick, lump, chunk, cube, hunk, nugget, ingot …*a block of ice…*
2 = <u>obstruction</u>, bar, barrier, obstacle, impediment, hindrance …*a block to peace…*
`VERB` **1** = <u>obstruct</u>, close, stop, cut off, plug, choke, clog, shut off, stop up, bung up (*informal*) …*When the shrimp farm is built it will block the stream…* `OPPOSITE` clear
2 = <u>obscure</u>, bar, cut off, interrupt, obstruct, get in the way of, shut off …*a row of spruce trees that blocked his view…*
3 = <u>shut off</u>, stop, bar, cut off, head off, hamper, obstruct, get in the way of …*The police officer blocked his path…*

blockade = <u>stoppage</u>, block, barrier, restriction, obstacle, barricade, obstruction, impediment, hindrance, encirclement

blockage = <u>obstruction</u>, block, blocking, stoppage, impediment, occlusion

bloke (*Informal*) = <u>man</u>, person, individual, customer (*informal*), character (*informal*), guy (*informal*), fellow, punter (*informal*), chap, boy, bod (*informal*)

blonde *or* **blond** **1** = <u>fair</u>, light, light-coloured, flaxen …*The baby had blonde curls…*
2 = <u>fair-haired</u>, golden-haired, tow-headed …*She was tall, blonde and attractive…*

blood NOUN 1 = lifeblood, gore, vital fluid …*an inherited defect in the blood…*

2 = family, relations, birth, descent, extraction, ancestry, lineage, kinship, kindred …*He was of noble blood, and an officer…*

PHRASES **bad blood** = hostility, anger, offence, resentment, bitterness, animosity, antagonism, enmity, bad feeling, rancour, hard feelings, ill will, animus, dudgeon (*archaic*), disgruntlement, chip on your shoulder …*There is, it seems, some bad blood between them…*

Blood cells

phagocytic white blood cell	macrocyte
erythrocyte	microcyte
haemocyte	poikilocyte
leucocyte	polymorph
lymphocyte	reticulocyte

---

bloodless = pale, white, wan, sickly, pasty, colourless, pallid, anaemic, ashen, chalky, sallow, ashy, like death warmed up (*informal*)

bloodshed = killing, murder, massacre, slaughter, slaying, carnage, butchery, blood-letting, blood bath

bloodthirsty = cruel, savage, brutal, vicious, ruthless, ferocious, murderous, heartless, inhuman, merciless, cut-throat, remorseless, warlike, barbarous, pitiless

bloody 1 = cruel, fierce, savage, brutal, vicious, ferocious, cut-throat, warlike, barbarous, sanguinary …*Forty-three demonstrators were killed in bloody chaos…*

2 = bloodstained, raw, bleeding, blood-soaked, blood-spattered …*His fingers were bloody and cracked…*

bloody-minded (*Brit. informal*) = difficult, contrary, annoying, awkward, unreasonable, stubborn, perverse, exasperating, intractable, unhelpful, obstructive, cussed (*informal*), uncooperative, disobliging OPPOSITE helpful

bloom NOUN 1 = flower, bud, blossom …*Harry carefully plucked the bloom…*

2 = prime, flower, beauty, height, peak, flourishing, maturity, perfection, best days, heyday, zenith, full flowering …*in the full bloom of youth…*

3 = glow, flush, blush, freshness, lustre, radiance, rosiness …*The skin loses its youthful bloom…* OPPOSITE pallor

VERB 1 = flower, blossom, open, bud …*This plant blooms between May and June…* OPPOSITE wither

2 = grow, develop, wax …*She bloomed into an utterly beautiful creature…*

3 = succeed, flourish, thrive, prosper, fare well …*Not many economies bloomed in 1990…* OPPOSITE fail

blossom NOUN = flower, bloom, bud, efflorescence, floret …*the blossoms of plants, shrubs and trees…*

VERB 1 = bloom, grow, develop, mature …*Why do some people take longer than others to blossom?…*

2 = succeed, progress, thrive, flourish, prosper …*His musical career blossomed…*

3 = flower, bloom, bud …*Rain begins to fall and peach trees blossom…*

blot NOUN 1 = disgrace, spot, fault, stain, scar, defect, flaw, taint, blemish, demerit, smirch, blot on your escutcheon …*a blot on the reputation of the architectural profession…*

2 = spot, mark, patch, smear, smudge, speck, blotch, splodge, stain …*an ink blot…*

VERB = soak up, take up, absorb, dry up …*Blot any excess oils with a tissue…*

PHRASES **blot something out** 1 = obliterate, hide, shadow, disguise, obscure, blur, eclipse, block out, efface, obfuscate …*The victim's face was blotted out by a camera blur…* 2 = erase, cancel, excise, obliterate, expunge …*He is blotting certain memories out…*

blotch = mark, spot, patch, splash, stain, blot, smudge, blemish, splodge, smirch, smutch

blow¹ VERB 1 = move, carry, drive, bear, sweep, fling, whisk, buffet, whirl, waft …*The wind blew her hair back from her forehead…*

2 = be carried, hover, flutter, flit, flitter …*Leaves were blowing around in the wind…*

3 = exhale, breathe, pant, puff, breathe out, expel air …*Take a deep breath and blow…*

4 = play, sound, pipe, trumpet, blare, toot …*A saboteur blew a horn to distract the hounds…*

PHRASES **blow over** = die down, end, pass, finish, cease, be forgotten, subside …*Wait, and it'll blow over…* ◆ **blow someone away** 1 = bowl over, amaze, stun, stagger, astound, electrify (*informal*), stupefy, flabbergast …*She just totally blew me away with her singing…* 2 = open fire on, kill, blast (*slang*), bring down, zap (*slang*), pick off, pump full of lead (*slang*) …*He'd like to get hold of a gun and blow them all away…* ◆ **blow something out** = put out, extinguish, snuff out …*I blew out the candle…* ◆ **blow something up** 1 = explode, bomb, blast, dynamite, detonate, blow sky-high …*He was jailed for forty-five years for trying to blow up a plane…* 2 = inflate, pump up, fill, expand, swell, enlarge, puff up, distend …*Other than blowing up a tyre I haven't done any car maintenance…* 3 = exaggerate, heighten, enlarge on, inflate, embroider, magnify, amplify, overstate, embellish, blow out of (all) proportion, make a mountain out of a molehill, make a production out of, make a federal case of (*U.S. informal*), hyperbolize …*Newspapers blew up the story…* 4 = magnify, increase, extend, stretch, expand, widen, broaden, lengthen, amplify, elongate, dilate, make larger …*The image is blown up on a large screen…* ◆ **blow up** 1 = explode, burst, go off, shatter, erupt, detonate …*The bomb blew up as they slept…* 2 (*Informal*) = lose your temper, rage, erupt, lose it (*informal*), crack up (*informal*), see red (*informal*), lose the plot (*informal*), become angry, go ballistic (*slang, chiefly U.S.*), hit the roof (*informal*), blow a fuse (*slang, chiefly U.S.*), fly off the handle (*informal*), become enraged, go off the deep end (*informal*), wig out (*slang*), go up the wall (*slang*), go crook (*Austral. & N.Z. slang*), flip your lid (*slang*), blow your top …*I'm sorry I blew up at you…* 3 = flare up, widen, heighten, enlarge, broaden, magnify …*The scandal blew up into a major political furore*… ◆ **blow your top** (*Informal*) = <u>lose your temper</u>, explode, blow up (*informal*), lose it (*informal*), see red (*informal*), lose the plot (*informal*), have a fit (*informal*), throw a tantrum, fly off the handle (*informal*), go spare (*Brit. slang*), fly into a temper, flip your lid (*slang*), do your nut (*Brit. slang*) …*I just asked him why he was late and he blew his top*…

blow² 1 = <u>knock</u>, stroke, punch, belt (*informal*), bang, rap, bash (*informal*), sock (*slang*), smack, thump, buffet, clout (*informal*), whack (*informal*), wallop (*informal*), slosh (*Brit. slang*), tonk (*informal*), clump (*slang*), clomp (*slang*) …*He went off to hospital after a blow to the face*…

2 = <u>setback</u>, shock, upset, disaster, reverse, disappointment, catastrophe, misfortune, jolt, bombshell, calamity, affliction, whammy (*informal, chiefly U.S.*), choker (*informal*), sucker punch, bummer (*slang*), bolt from the blue, comedown (*informal*) …*The ruling comes as a blow to environmentalists*…

blow-out 1 (*Slang*) = <u>binge</u> (*informal*), party, feast, rave (*Brit. slang*), spree, beano (*Brit. slang*), rave-up (*Brit. slang*), carousal, carouse, hooley *or* hoolie (*chiefly Irish & N.Z.*) …*Once in a while we had a major blow-out*…

2 = <u>puncture</u>, burst, flat, flat tyre …*A lorry travelling south had a blow-out and crashed*…

bludge (*Austral. & N.Z. informal*) = <u>slack</u>, skive (*Brit. informal*), idle, shirk, gold-brick (*U.S. slang*), bob off (*Brit. slang*), scrimshank (*Brit. military slang*)

bludgeon VERB 1 = <u>club</u>, batter, beat, strike, belt (*informal*), clobber (*slang*), pound, cosh (*Brit.*), cudgel …*A wealthy businessman has been found bludgeoned to death*…

2 = <u>bully</u>, force, cow, intimidate, railroad (*informal*), hector, coerce, bulldoze (*informal*), dragoon, steamroller, browbeat, tyrannize …*His relentless aggression bludgeons you into seeing his point*…

NOUN = <u>club</u>, stick, baton, truncheon, cosh (*Brit.*), cudgel, shillelagh, bastinado …*I rather feel that the bludgeon has replaced the rapier*…

blue ADJECTIVE 1 = <u>depressed</u>, low, sad, unhappy, fed up, gloomy, dismal, melancholy, glum, dejected, despondent, downcast, down in the dumps (*informal*), down in the mouth, low-spirited, down-hearted …*There's no earthly reason for me to feel so blue*… OPPOSITE> happy

2 = <u>smutty</u>, dirty, naughty, obscene, indecent, vulgar,

lewd, risqué, X-rated (*informal*), bawdy, near the knuckle (*informal*) …*a secret stash of porn mags and blue movies*… OPPOSITE> respectable

PLURAL NOUN = <u>depression</u>, gloom, melancholy, unhappiness, despondency, the hump (*Brit. informal*), dejection, moodiness, low spirits, the dumps (*informal*), doldrums, gloominess, glumness …*Interfering in-laws are the prime sources of the blues*…

➤ **shades of blue**

blueprint 1 = <u>scheme</u>, plan, design, system, idea, programme, proposal, strategy, pattern, suggestion, procedure, plot, draft, outline, sketch, proposition, prototype, layout, pilot scheme …*the blueprint of a new plan of economic reform*…

2 = <u>plan</u>, scheme, project, pattern, draft, outline, sketch, layout …*The documents contain a blueprint for a nuclear device*…

bluff¹ NOUN = <u>deception</u>, show, lie, fraud, fake, sham, pretence, deceit, bravado, bluster, humbug, subterfuge, feint, mere show …*The letter was a bluff*…

VERB = <u>deceive</u>, lie, trick, fool, pretend, cheat, con, fake, mislead, sham, dupe, feign, delude, humbug, bamboozle (*informal*), hoodwink, double-cross (*informal*), pull the wool over someone's eyes …*He tried to bluff his way through another test and failed it*…

bluff² NOUN = <u>precipice</u>, bank, peak, cliff, ridge, crag, escarpment, promontory, scarp …*a high bluff over the Congaree River*…

ADJECTIVE = <u>hearty</u>, open, frank, blunt, sincere, outspoken, honest, downright, cordial, genial, affable, ebullient, jovial, plain-spoken, good-natured, unreserved, back-slapping …*a man with a bluff exterior*… OPPOSITE> tactful

blunder NOUN = <u>mistake</u>, slip, fault, error, boob (*Brit. slang*), oversight, gaffe, slip-up (*informal*), indiscretion, impropriety, howler (*informal*), bloomer (*Brit. informal*), clanger (*informal*), faux pas, boo-boo (*informal*), gaucherie …*I think he made a tactical blunder*… OPPOSITE> correctness

VERB 1 = <u>make a mistake</u>, blow it (*slang*), err, slip up (*informal*), cock up (*Brit. slang*), miscalculate, foul up, drop a clanger (*informal*), put your foot in it (*informal*), drop a brick (*Brit. informal*), screw up (*informal*) …*No doubt I had blundered again*… OPPOSITE> be correct

2 = <u>stumble</u>, fall, reel, stagger, flounder, lurch, lose

---

Shades of blue

aqua	duck-egg blue	Oxford blue	sky blue
aquamarine	electric blue	peacock blue	steel blue
azure	gentian blue	periwinkle	teal
Cambridge blue	heliotrope	perse	turquoise
cerulean	indigo	petrol blue	ultramarine
clear blue	lapis lazuli	pewter	Wedgwood blue
cobalt blue	midnight blue	royal blue	
Copenhagen blue	navy blue	sapphire	
cyan	Nile blue	saxe blue	

your balance ...*He had blundered into the table, upsetting the flowers*...

blunt ADJECTIVE **1** = <u>frank</u>, forthright, straightforward, explicit, rude, outspoken, bluff, downright, upfront (*informal*), trenchant, brusque, plain-spoken, tactless, impolite, discourteous, unpolished, uncivil, straight from the shoulder ...*She is blunt about her personal life*... OPPOSITE tactful

2 = <u>dull</u>, rounded, dulled, edgeless, unsharpened ...*a blunt object*... OPPOSITE sharp

VERB = <u>dull</u>, weaken, soften, numb, dampen, water down, deaden, take the edge off ...*Our appetite was blunted by the beer*... OPPOSITE stimulate

blur NOUN = <u>haze</u>, confusion, fog, obscurity, dimness, cloudiness, blear, blurredness, indistinctness ...*Her face is a blur*...

VERB **1** = <u>become indistinct</u>, soften, become vague, become hazy, become fuzzy ...*If you move your eyes and your head, the picture will blur*...

2 = <u>obscure</u>, make indistinct, mask, soften, muddy, obfuscate, make vague, befog, make hazy ...*Scientists are trying to blur the distinction between these questions*...

blurred = <u>indistinct</u>, faint, vague, unclear, dim, fuzzy, misty, hazy, foggy, blurry, out of focus, ill-defined, lacking definition

blush VERB = <u>turn red</u>, colour, burn, flame, glow, flush, crimson, redden, go red (as a beetroot), turn scarlet ...*I blushed scarlet at my stupidity*... OPPOSITE turn pale

NOUN = <u>reddening</u>, colour, glow, flush, pink tinge, rosiness, ruddiness, rosy tint ...*A blush spread over Brenda's cheeks*...

bluster VERB = <u>boast</u>, swagger, talk big (*slang*) ...*He was still blustering, but there was panic in his eyes*...

NOUN = <u>hot air</u>, boasting, bluff, swagger, swaggering (*informal*), bravado, bombast ...*the bluster of their campaign*...

blustery = <u>gusty</u>, wild, violent, stormy, windy, tempestuous, inclement, squally, blusterous

board NOUN **1** = <u>plank</u>, panel, timber, slat, piece of timber ...*The floor was draughty bare boards*...

2 = <u>council</u>, directors, committee, congress, ministry, advisers, panel, assembly, chamber, trustees, governing body, synod, directorate, quango, advisory group, conclave ...*the US National Transportation Safety Board*...

3 = <u>meals</u>, provisions, victuals, daily meals ...*Free room and board are provided for all hotel staff*...

VERB = <u>get on</u>, enter, mount, embark, entrain, embus, enplane ...*I boarded the plane bound for England*... OPPOSITE get off

boast VERB **1** = <u>brag</u>, crow, vaunt, bluster, talk big (*slang*), blow your own trumpet, show off, be proud of, flaunt, congratulate yourself on, flatter yourself, pride yourself on, skite (*Austral. & N.Z. informal*) ...*She boasted about her achievements*... OPPOSITE cover up

2 = <u>possess</u>, offer, present, exhibit ...*The houses boast the latest energy-saving technology*...

NOUN = <u>bragging</u>, vaunting, rodomontade (*literary*),

gasconade (*rare*) ...*He was asked about earlier boasts of a quick victory*... OPPOSITE disclaimer

boat NOUN = <u>vessel</u>, ship, craft, barge (*informal*), barque (*poetic*) ...*One of the best ways to see the area is in a small boat*...

PHRASES **in the same boat** = <u>in the same situation</u>, alike, even, together, equal, on a par, on equal or even terms, on the same or equal footing ...*The police and I were in the same boat*... ♦ **miss the boat** = <u>miss your chance</u> or <u>opportunity</u>, miss out, be too late, lose out, blow your chance (*informal*) ...*Big name companies have missed the boat*... ♦ **push the boat out** = <u>celebrate</u>, party, have a fling, go the whole hog (*informal*), go on a bender (*informal*), put the flags out, kill the fatted calf, go on a beano (*Brit. slang*) ...*I earn enough to push the boat out now and again*... ♦ **rock the boat** = <u>cause trouble</u>, protest, object, dissent, make waves (*informal*), throw a spanner in the works, upset the apple cart ...*I said I didn't want to rock the boat in any way*...

➤ **boats and ships**

bob VERB = <u>bounce</u>, duck, leap, hop, weave, skip, jerk, wobble, quiver, oscillate, waggle ...*Balloons bobbed about in the sky*...

PHRASES **bob up** = <u>spring up</u>, rise, appear, emerge, surface, pop up, jump up, bounce up ...*They will bob up like corks as they cook*...

bode = <u>augur</u>, portend, threaten, predict, signify, foreshadow, presage, betoken, be an omen, forebode

bodily = <u>physical</u>, material, actual, substantial, fleshly, tangible, corporal, carnal, corporeal

body 1 = <u>physique</u>, build, form, figure, shape, make-up, frame, constitution ...*The largest organ in the body is the liver*...

2 = <u>torso</u>, trunk ...*Cross your upper leg over your body*...

3 = <u>corpse</u>, dead body, remains, stiff (*slang*), relics, carcass, cadaver ...*His body lay in state*...

4 = <u>organization</u>, company, group, society, league, association, band, congress, institution, corporation, federation, outfit (*informal*), syndicate, bloc, confederation ...*the police representative body*...

5 = <u>main part</u>, matter, material, mass, substance, bulk, essence ...*the preface, followed by the main body of the article*...

6 = <u>expanse</u>, mass, sweep ...*It is probably the most polluted body of water in the world*...

7 = <u>mass</u>, company, press, army, host, crowd, majority, assembly, mob, herd, swarm, horde, multitude, throng, bevy ...*The great body of people moved slowly forward*...

8 = <u>consistency</u>, substance, texture, density, richness, firmness, solidity, viscosity ...*a dry wine, with good body*...

(*Related Words*)

adjectives: corporal, physical

➤ **blood cells** ➤ **bones** ➤ **glands** ➤ **muscles**
➤ **parts of the body** ➤ **parts of the ear**
➤ **parts of the eye** ➤ **parts of the heart**
➤ **teeth**

Boats and ships

airboat	drifter	longship	ship of the line
aircraft carrier	dromond *or* dromon	lugger	sidewheeler
auxiliary	E-boat	man-of-war *or* man o'	skiff
banker	factory ship	war	skipjack
barge	faltboat	maxi	sloop
barque	felucca	merchantman	speedboat
barquentine *or*	ferry	minehunter	square-rigger
barquantine	fireboat	minelayer	steamboat
bateau	fishing boat	minesweeper	steamer
bathyscaph,	flatboat	monitor	steamship
bathyscaphe, *or*	flotel *or* floatel	monohull	stern-wheeler
bathyscape	flyboat	motorboat	submarine
battlecruiser	fore-and-after	MTB (motor torpedo	supertanker
battleship	foyboat	boat)	surfboat
Bermuda rig	freighter	multihull	swamp boat
boatel	frigate	MY *or* motor yacht	tall ship
brigantine	galleas	narrow boat	tanker
bulk carrier	galleon	nuggar	tartan
bumboat	galley	outboard	tender
cabin cruiser	gig	outrigger	threedecker
canal boat	gondola	oysterman	torpedo boat
canoe	gunboat	packet boat	torpedo-boat destroyer
caravel *or* carvel	hooker	paddle steamer	towboat
carrack	houseboat	pink	trawler
catamaran	hoy	pocket battleship	trimaran
catboat	hydrofoil	polacre *or* polacca	trireme
caïque	hydroplane	powerboat	troopship
clipper	icebreaker	proa *or* prau	tub
coble	ice yacht *or* scooter	PT boat	tug *or* tugboat
cockboat *or* cockleboat	Indiaman	púcán	U-boat
cockleshell	ironclad	punt	umiak *or* oomiak
coracle	jet-boat	quinquereme	vaporetto
corvette	jolly boat	raft	vedette
crabber	junk	randan	VJ (vaucluse junior)
cruiser	kayak	revenue cutter	warship
cutter	keelboat	rowboat	weathership
destroyer	ketch	rowing boat	whaler
destroyer escort	laker	sailing boat *or* (*U.S. &*	wherry
dhow	landing craft	*Canad.*) sailboat	windjammer
dinghy	lapstrake *or* lapstreak	scow	xebec, zebec, *or* zebeck
dogger	launch	schooner	yacht
dory	lifeboat	scull	yawl
dreadnought *or*	lightship	sealer	
dreadnaught	liner	shallop	
dredger	longboat	shell	

boffin (*Brit. informal*) = expert, authority, brain(s) (*informal*), intellectual, genius, guru, inventor, thinker, wizard, mastermind, intellect, egghead, wonk (*informal*), brainbox, bluestocking (*usually disparaging*), maven (*U.S.*), fundi (*S. African*)

bog NOUN = marsh, moss (*Scot. & Northern English dialect*), swamp, slough, wetlands, fen, mire, quagmire, morass, marshland, peat bog …*We walked steadily across moor and bog*…
PHRASES **bog something** *or* **someone down** = hold up, stick, delay, halt, stall, slow down, impede, slow up …*The talks have become bogged down with the issue of military reform*…

bogey 1 = bugbear, bête noire, horror, nightmare, bugaboo …*Age is another bogey for actresses*…
2 = spirit, ghost, phantom, spectre, spook (*informal*), apparition, imp, sprite, goblin, bogeyman, hobgoblin, eidolon …*It was no bogey, no demon*…

boggle = confuse, surprise, shock, stun, stagger, bewilder, astound, daze, confound, stupefy, dumbfound

bogus = fake, false, artificial, forged, dummy, imitation, sham, fraudulent, pseudo (*informal*), counterfeit, spurious, ersatz, phoney *or* phony (*informal*) OPPOSITE genuine

Bohemian ADJECTIVE *often not cap.*
= unconventional, alternative, artistic, exotic, way-out (*informal*), eccentric, avant-garde, off-the-wall (*slang*), unorthodox, arty (*informal*), oddball (*informal*), offbeat, left bank, nonconformist, outré …*bohemian pre-war poets*… OPPOSITE conventional
NOUN *often not cap.* = nonconformist, rebel, radical, eccentric, maverick, hippy, dropout, individualist,

Parts of the body http://www.innerbody.com/htm/body.html

Part of the body	Technical name	Related adjective	Part of the body	Technical name	Related adjective
abdomen	—	abdominal	gall bladder	—	—
adenoids	pharyngeal tonsil	adenoid or adenoidal	gland	—	adenoid
			glottis	—	glottic
alimentary canal	—	—	groin	—	inguinal
ankle	talus	—	gullet	oesophagus	oesophageal
anus	—	anal	gum	gingiva	gingival
appendix	vermiform appendix	appendicular	hamstring	—	popliteal
			hard palate	—	—
arm	brachium	brachial	hair	—	—
armpit	axilla	axillary	half-moon	lunula or lunule	—
artery	—	arterial	hand	manus	manual
back	—	dorsal	head	caput	capital
belly	venter	ventral	heart	—	cardiac
bladder	urinary bladder	vesical	heel	—	—
blood	—	haemal, haemic, or haematic	hip	—	—
			ileum	—	ileac or ileal
			inner ear or internal ear	labyrinth	—
bone	os	osseous, osteal, or osteoid	instep	—	—
			intestine	—	alvine
brain	encephalon	cerebral	jaw	—	gnathic or gnathal
breast	—	—			
buttocks	nates	natal or gluteal	jejunum	—	jejunal
			jugular vein	—	—
caecum	—	caecal	kidney	—	renal or nephritic
calf	—	—			
capillary	—	capillary	knee	genu	genicular
cervix	—	cervical	knuckle	—	—
cheek	gena	genal	labia majora	—	labial
chest	—	pectoral	labia minora	—	labial
chin	—	genial or mental	large intestine	—	—
			leg	crus	crural
clitoris	—	clitoral	lip	—	labial
colon	—	colonic	liver	—	hepatic
duodenum	—	duodenal	loin	lumbus	lumbar
ear	—	aural	lung	—	pulmonary
elbow	—	—	lymph cell	lymphocyte	—
epiglottis	—	epiglottal	lymph node	—	—
external ear	auricle or pinna	—	midriff	diaphragm	—
eye	—	ocular or ophthalmic	mons pubis	—	—
			mons veneris	—	—
eyebrow	—	superciliary	mouth	—	stomatic
eyelash	cilium	ciliary	nape	nucha	nuchal
eyelid	—	palpebral	navel or omphalos	umbilicus	umbilical
Fallopian tube	oviduct	oviducal or oviductal	neck	cervix	cervical
finger	—	digital	nerve	—	neural
fingernail	—	ungual or ungular	nerve cell	neuron or neurone	neuronic
			nipple or teat	mamilla or papilla	mamillary
fist	—	—	nose	—	nasal
follicle	—	follicular	nostril	naris	narial or narine
fontanelle or (chiefly U.S.) fontanel	—	—	occiput	—	occipital
			ovary	—	ovarian
foot	pes	pedal	pancreas	—	pancreatic
forearm	—	cubital	penis	—	penile
forehead	—	frontal	pharynx	—	pharyngeal
foreskin	prepuce	preputial	pubes	—	pubic

Parts of the body (continued)

Part of the body	Technical name	Related adjective	Part of the body	Technical name	Related adjective
rectum	—	rectal	toenail	—	ungual or ungular
red blood cell	erythrocyte	erythrocytic			
ribcage	—	—	tongue	lingua	lingual or glottic
scalp	—	—			
scrotum	—	scrotal	tonsil	—	tonsillar or tonsillary
shin	—	—			
shoulder	—	—	torso	—	—
side	—	—	transverse colon	—	—
skin	cutis	cutaneous	trunk	—	—
small intestine	—	—	umbilical cord	umbilicus	—
soft palate	—	—	ureter	—	ureteral or ureteric
sole	—	plantar			
spleen	—	lienal or splenetic	urethra	—	urethral
			vagina	—	vaginal
stomach	—	gastric	vein	vena	venous
tear duct	lacrimal duct	—	vocal cords	glottis	glottal
temple	—	temporal	voice box	larynx	laryngeal
tendon	—	—	vulva	—	vulval, vulvar, or vulvate
testicle	—	testicular			
thigh	—	femoral or crural			
			waist	—	—
thorax	—	thoracic	white blood cell	leucocyte	leucocytic
throat	—	guttural, gular, or jugular	windpipe	trachea	tracheal or tracheate
			womb	uterus	uterine
thumb	pollex	pollical	wrist	carpus	
toe	—	—			

beatnik, iconoclast ...*I am a bohemian. I have no roots*...

boil¹ **VERB** **1** = <u>simmer</u>, bubble, foam, churn, seethe, fizz, froth, effervesce ...*I stood in the kitchen, waiting for the water to boil*...
2 = <u>be furious</u>, storm, rage, rave, fume, be angry, crack up (*informal*), see red (*informal*), go ballistic (*slang, chiefly U.S.*), be indignant, fulminate, foam at the mouth (*informal*), blow a fuse (*slang, chiefly U.S.*), fly off the handle (*informal*), go off the deep end (*informal*), wig out (*slang*), go up the wall (*slang*) ...*She was boiling with anger*...
PHRASES **boil something down** = <u>reduce</u>, concentrate, precipitate (*Chemistry*), thicken, condense, decoct ...*He boils down red wine and uses what's left*...

boil² = <u>pustule</u>, gathering, swelling, blister, blain, carbuncle, furuncle (*Pathology*) ...*a boil on her nose*...

boiling **1** = <u>very hot</u>, hot, burning, baking, tropical, roasting, blistering, scorching, torrid, sultry, sweltering ...*It's boiling in here*...
2 = <u>furious</u>, angry, fuming, choked, infuriated, incensed, enraged, indignant, incandescent, on the warpath, foaming at the mouth, fit to be tied (*slang*), tooshie (*Austral. slang*), off the air (*Austral. slang*) ...*She was boiling with rage*...

boisterous **1** = <u>unruly</u>, wild, disorderly, loud, noisy, wayward, rowdy, wilful, riotous, unrestrained, rollicking, impetuous, rumbustious, uproarious, obstreperous, clamorous ...*a boisterous but good-natured crowd*... **OPPOSITE** self-controlled
2 = <u>stormy</u>, rough, raging, turbulent, tumultuous, tempestuous, blustery, gusty, squally ...*The boisterous wind had been making the sea increasingly choppy*... **OPPOSITE** calm

bold **1** = <u>fearless</u>, enterprising, brave, daring, heroic, adventurous, courageous, gritty, gallant, gutsy (*slang*), audacious, intrepid, valiant, plucky, undaunted, unafraid, unflinching, dauntless, lion-hearted, valorous ...*She becomes a bold, daring rebel*... **OPPOSITE** timid
2 = <u>impudent</u>, forward, fresh (*informal*), confident, rude, cheeky, brash, feisty (*informal, chiefly U.S. & Canad.*), saucy, pushy (*informal*), brazen, in-your-face (*Brit. slang*), shameless, sassy (*U.S. informal*), unabashed, pert, insolent, barefaced, spirited, forceful ...*Men do not like girls who are too bold*... **OPPOSITE** shy
3 = <u>bright</u>, conspicuous, strong, striking, loud, prominent, lively, pronounced, colourful, vivid, flashy, eye-catching, salient, showy ...*bold, dramatic colours*... **OPPOSITE** soft

bolster = <u>support</u>, help, aid, maintain, boost, strengthen, assist, prop, reinforce, hold up, cushion, brace, shore up, augment, buttress, buoy up, give a leg up to (*informal*)

bolt **NOUN** **1** = <u>pin</u>, rod, peg, rivet ...*details right down to the dimensions of nuts and bolts*...

Bones

Bone	Nontechnical name	Bone	Nontechnical name
astragalus	anklebone	metatarsus	—
calcaneus	heel bone	occipital bone	—
carpal	wrist	parietal bone	—
carpus	wrist	patella	kneecap
clavicle	collarbone	pelvis	—
coccyx	—	phalanx	—
costa	rib	pubis	—
cranium	brainpan	radius	—
cuboid	—	rib	—
ethmoid	—	sacrum	—
femur	thighbone	scapula	shoulder blade
fibula	—	skull	—
frontal bone	—	sphenoid	—
hallux	—	spinal column *or* spine	backbone
humerus	—	stapes	stirrup
hyoid	—	sternum	breastbone
ilium	—	talus	anklebone
incus	anvil	tarsal	—
innominate bone	hipbone	tarsus	—
ischium	—	temporal bone	—
malleus	hammer	tibia	shinbone
mandible	lower jawbone	ulna	—
maxilla	upper jawbone	vertebra	—
metacarpal	—	vertebral column	backbone
metatarsal	—	zygomatic bone	cheekbone

2 = bar, catch, lock, latch, fastener, sliding bar …*I heard him slide the bolt across the door…*

3 = arrow, missile, shaft, dart, projectile …*He pulled the crossbow bolt from his head…*

4 = dash, race, flight, spring, rush, rush, bound, sprint, dart, spurt …*a bolt for freedom…*

VERB **1** = lock, close, bar, secure, fasten, latch …*He reminded her to lock and bolt the kitchen door behind her…*

2 – dash, run, fly, spring, jump, rush, bound, leap, sprint, hurtle …*I made some excuse and bolted towards the exit…*

3 = gobble, stuff, wolf, cram, gorge, devour, gulp, guzzle, swallow whole …*Don't bolt your food…*

bomb NOUN = explosive, charge, mine, shell, missile, device, rocket, grenade, torpedo, bombshell, projectile …*There were two bomb explosions in the city overnight…*

VERB = blow up, attack, destroy, assault, shell, blast, blitz, bombard, torpedo, open fire on, strafe, fire upon, blow sky-high …*Airforce jets bombed the city at night…*

bombard 1 = attack, assault, batter, barrage, besiege, beset, assail …*The media bombards all of us with images of violence and drugs and sex…*

2 = bomb, shell, blast, blitz, open fire, strafe, fire upon …*Rebel artillery units have regularly bombarded the airport…*

bombardment = bombing, attack, fire, assault, shelling, blitz, barrage, flak, strafe, fusillade, cannonade

bombast = pomposity, ranting, bragging, hot air (*informal*), bluster, grandiosity, braggadocio, grandiloquence, rodomontade (*literary*), gasconade (*rare*), extravagant boasting, magniloquence

bombastic = grandiloquent, inflated, ranting, windy, high-flown, pompous, grandiose, histrionic, wordy, verbose, declamatory, fustian, magniloquent

bona fide = genuine, real, true, legal, actual, legitimate, authentic, honest, veritable, lawful, on the level (*informal*), kosher (*informal*), dinkum (*Austral. & N.Z. informal*), the real McCoy OPPOSITE bogus

bond NOUN **1** = tie, union, coupling, link, association, relation, connection, alliance, attachment, affinity, affiliation …*the bond that linked them…*

2 = fastening, band, tie, binding, chain, cord, shackle, fetter, manacle …*He managed to break free of his bonds…*

3 = agreement, word, promise, contract, guarantee, pledge, obligation, compact, covenant …*I'm not about to betray my bond with my brother…*

VERB **1** = form friendships, connect …*They all bonded while working together…*

2 = fix, hold, bind, connect, glue, gum, fuse, stick, paste, fasten …*Strips of wood are bonded together and moulded by machine…*

bondage = slavery, imprisonment, captivity, confinement, yoke, duress, servitude, enslavement, subjugation, serfdom, subjection, vassalage, thraldom, enthralment

bone
➤ bones

bonny (*Scot. & Northern English dialect*) = beautiful, pretty, fair, sweet, appealing, attractive, lovely, charming, handsome, good-looking, gorgeous, radiant, alluring, comely

bonus 1 = <u>extra</u>, benefit, commission, prize, gift, reward, premium, dividend, hand-out, perk (*Brit. informal*), bounty, gratuity, honorarium ...*a special end-of-year bonus...*
2 = <u>advantage</u>, benefit, gain, extra, plus, asset, perk (*Brit. informal*), icing on the cake ...*Anything else would be a bonus...*

bony = <u>thin</u>, lean, skinny, angular, gaunt, skeletal, haggard, emaciated, scrawny, undernourished, cadaverous, rawboned, macilent (*rare*)

book NOUN 1 = <u>work</u>, title, volume, publication, manual, paperback, textbook, tract, hardback, tome ...*a book about witches...*
2 = <u>notebook</u>, album, journal, diary, pad, record book, Filofax (*trademark*), notepad, exercise book, jotter, memorandum book ...*I had several names in my little black book that I called regularly...*
VERB = <u>reserve</u>, schedule, engage, line up, organize, charter, arrange for, procure, make reservations ...*She booked herself a flight home last night...*
PHRASES **book in** = <u>register</u>, enter, enrol ...*He was happy to book in at the Royal Pavilion Hotel...*

booking (*Chiefly Brit.*) = <u>reservation</u>, date, appointment

bookish = <u>studious</u>, learned, academic, intellectual, literary, scholarly, erudite, pedantic, well-read, donnish

booklet = <u>brochure</u>, leaflet, hand-out, pamphlet, folder, mailshot, handbill

boom NOUN 1 = <u>expansion</u>, increase, development, growth, advance, jump, boost, improvement, spurt, upsurge, upturn, upswing ...*an economic boom...* OPPOSITE decline
2 = <u>bang</u>, report, shot, crash, clash, blast, burst, explosion, roar, thunder, rumble, clap, peal, detonation ...*The stillness of the night was broken by the boom of a cannon...*
VERB 1 = <u>increase</u>, flourish, grow, develop, succeed, expand, strengthen, do well, swell, thrive, intensify, prosper, burgeon, spurt ...*Lipstick sales have boomed even more...* OPPOSITE fall
2 = <u>bang</u>, roll, crash, blast, echo, drum, explode, roar, thunder, rumble, resound, reverberate, peal ...*Thunder boomed like battlefield cannons over Crooked Mountain...*

boomerang = <u>rebound</u>, backfire, come home to roost

booming 1 = <u>loud</u>, echoing, thundering, bellowing, resounding, deafening, resonant, sonorous, stentorian ...*The ginger man had a large booming voice...*
2 = <u>flourishing</u>, successful, expanding, doing well, thriving, blooming, mushrooming, prospering, rampant, burgeoning, on the up and up (*Brit.*) ...*It has a booming tourist industry...*

boon 1 = <u>benefit</u>, advantage, blessing, godsend, gift ...*This battery booster is a boon for photographers...*
2 = <u>gift</u>, present, grant, favour, donation, hand-out, gratuity, benefaction ...*She begged him to grant her one boon...*

boorish = <u>loutish</u>, gross, crude, rude, hick (*informal, chiefly U.S. & Canad.*), coarse, vulgar, rustic, barbaric, churlish, uneducated, bearish, uncouth, unrefined, uncivilized, clownish, oafish, ill-bred, lubberly OPPOSITE refined

boost VERB = <u>increase</u>, develop, raise, expand, add to, build up, heighten, enlarge, inflate, magnify, amplify, augment, jack up ...*They need to take action to boost sales...* OPPOSITE decrease
NOUN 1 = <u>rise</u>, increase, advance, jump, addition, improvement, expansion, upsurge, upturn, increment, upswing, upward turn ...*The paper is enjoying a boost in circulation...* OPPOSITE fall
2 = <u>encouragement</u>, help ...*It did give me a boost to win such an event...*

boot VERB = <u>kick</u>, punt, put the boot in(to) (*slang*), drop-kick ...*One guy booted the door down...*
PHRASES **boot someone out** (*Informal*) = <u>dismiss</u>, sack (*informal*), expel, throw out, oust, relegate, kick out, eject, kiss off (*slang, chiefly U.S. & Canad.*), show someone the door, give someone the boot (*slang*), give (someone) their marching orders, give someone the bullet (*Brit. slang*), give someone the bum's rush (*slang*), throw out on your ear (*informal*), give someone the heave or push (*informal*) ...*Schools are booting out record numbers of unruly pupils...*

bootleg = <u>illicit</u>, illegal, outlawed, pirate, unofficial, black-market, unlicensed, under-the-table, unauthorized, contraband, hooky (*slang*), under-the-counter OPPOSITE official

booty = <u>plunder</u>, winnings, gains, haul, spoils, prey, loot, takings, pillage, swag (*slang*), boodle (*slang, chiefly U.S.*)

booze (*Informal*) NOUN = <u>alcohol</u>, drink, spirits, juice (*informal*), the bottle (*informal*), liquor, grog (*informal, chiefly Austral. & N.Z.*), the hard stuff (*informal*), strong drink, intoxicant, firewater, John Barleycorn, hooch or hootch (*informal, chiefly U.S. & Canad.*) ...*empty bottles of booze...*
VERB = <u>drink</u>, indulge, get drunk, tipple, imbibe, tope, carouse, bevvy (*dialect*), get plastered, drink like a fish, get soused, get tanked up (*informal*), go on a binge or bender (*informal*), hit the booze or bottle (*informal*) ...*a load of drunken businessmen who had been boozing all afternoon...*

boozer (*Informal*) 1 = <u>pub</u>, local (*Brit. informal*), bar (*informal, chiefly Brit.*), inn, tavern, public house, watering hole (*facetious slang*), roadhouse, hostelry, alehouse (*archaic*), taproom ...*She once caught him in a boozer with another woman...*
2 = <u>drinker</u>, toper, drunk, soak (*slang*), alcoholic, lush (*slang*), drunkard, sot, tippler, wino (*informal*), alko or alco (*Austral. slang*), inebriate ...*We always thought he was a bit of a boozer...*

border NOUN 1 = <u>frontier</u>, line, marches, limit, bounds, boundary, perimeter, borderline, borderland ...*Clifford is enjoying life north of the border...*
2 = <u>edge</u>, lip, margin, skirt, verge, rim, hem, brim, flange ...*pillowcases trimmed with a hand-crocheted border...*
VERB = <u>edge</u>, bound, decorate, trim, fringe, rim, hem ...*white sand bordered by palm trees and tropical*

flowers…

PHRASES **border on something** = <u>come close to</u>, approach, be like, resemble, be similar to, approximate, come near …*The atmosphere borders on the surreal…*

borderline = <u>marginal</u>, bordering, doubtful, peripheral, indefinite, indeterminate, equivocal, inexact, unclassifiable

bore[1] = <u>drill</u>, mine, sink, tunnel, pierce, penetrate, burrow, puncture, perforate, gouge out …*Get the special drill bit to bore the correct-size hole…*

bore[2] VERB = <u>tire</u>, exhaust, annoy, fatigue, weary, wear out, jade, wear down, be tedious, pall on, send to sleep …*Dickie bored him all through the meal with stories of the Navy…* OPPOSITE excite
NOUN = <u>nuisance</u>, pain (*informal*), drag (*informal*), headache (*informal*), yawn (*informal*), anorak (*informal*), pain in the neck (*informal*), dullard, dull person, tiresome person, wearisome talker …*He's a bore and a fool…*

bored = <u>fed up</u>, tired, hacked (off) (*U.S. slang*), wearied, weary, uninterested, sick and tired (*informal*), listless, browned-off (*informal*), brassed off (*Brit. slang*), ennuied

boredom = <u>tedium</u>, apathy, doldrums, weariness, monotony, dullness, sameness, ennui, flatness, world-weariness, tediousness, irksomeness OPPOSITE excitement

boring = <u>uninteresting</u>, dull, tedious, stale, tiresome, monotonous, old, dead, flat, routine, humdrum, insipid, mind-numbing, unexciting, ho-hum (*informal*), repetitious, wearisome, unvaried

born = <u>brought into this world</u>, delivered …*She was born in London on April 29, 1923…*

Word Power

born – This word is spelled without an *e*: *a new baby was born*. The word *borne*, spelled with an *e*, is the past participle of the verb *bear*: *he had borne his ordeal with great courage*, not *he had born his ordeal with great courage*.

---

borrow 1 = <u>take on loan</u>, touch (someone) for (*slang*), scrounge (*informal*), blag (*slang*), mooch (*slang*), cadge, use temporarily, take and return …*Can I borrow a pen please?…* OPPOSITE lend
2 = <u>steal</u>, take, use, copy, adopt, appropriate, acquire, pinch (*informal*), pirate, poach, pilfer, filch, plagiarize …*I borrowed his words for my book's title…*

bosom NOUN 1 = <u>breast</u>, chest, front, bust, teats, thorax …*On my bosom laid her weeping head…*
2 = <u>midst</u>, centre, heart, protection, circle, shelter …*He went back to the snug bosom of his family…*
3 = <u>heart</u>, feelings, spirit, soul, emotions, sympathies, sentiments, affections …*Something gentle seemed to move in her bosom…*
ADJECTIVE = <u>intimate</u>, close, warm, dear, friendly, confidential, cherished, boon, very dear …*They were bosom friends…*

boss NOUN = <u>manager</u>, head, leader, director, chief, executive, owner, master, governor (*informal*), employer, administrator, supervisor, superintendent, gaffer (*informal, chiefly Brit.*), foreman, overseer, kingpin, big cheese (*slang, old-fashioned*), baas (*S. African*), numero uno (*informal*), Mister Big (*slang, chiefly U.S.*) …*He cannot stand his boss…*
PHRASES **boss someone around** (*Informal*) = <u>order around</u>, dominate, bully, intimidate, oppress, dictate to, terrorize, put upon, push around (*slang*), browbeat, ride roughshod over, tyrannize, rule with an iron hand …*He started bossing people around and I didn't like it…*

bossy (*Informal*) = <u>domineering</u>, lordly, arrogant, authoritarian, oppressive, hectoring, autocratic, dictatorial, coercive, imperious, overbearing, tyrannical, despotic, high-handed

botch VERB = <u>spoil</u>, mar, bungle, fumble, screw up (*informal*), mess up, cock up (*Brit. slang*), mismanage, muff, make a nonsense of (*informal*), bodge (*informal*), make a pig's ear of (*informal*), flub (*U.S. slang*), crool or cruel (*Austral. slang*) …*It's a silly idea, and he has botched it…*
NOUN = <u>mess</u>, failure, blunder, miscarriage, bungle, bungling, fumble, hash, cock-up (*Brit. slang*), pig's ear (*informal*), pig's breakfast (*informal*) …*I rather made a botch of that whole thing…*

bother VERB 1 = <u>trouble</u>, concern, worry, upset, alarm, disturb, distress, annoy, dismay, gall, disconcert, vex, perturb, faze, put *or* get someone's back up …*That kind of jealousy doesn't bother me…*
2 = <u>pester</u>, plague, irritate, put out, harass, nag, hassle (*informal*), inconvenience, molest, breathe down someone's neck, get on your nerves (*informal*), nark (*Brit., Austral., & N.Z. slang*), bend someone's ear (*informal*), give someone grief (*Brit. & S. African*), get on your wick (*Brit. slang*) …*I don't know why he bothers me with this kind of rubbish…* OPPOSITE help
NOUN = <u>trouble</u>, problem, worry, difficulty, strain, grief (*Brit. & S. African*), fuss, pest, irritation, hassle (*informal*), nuisance, flurry, uphill (*S. African*), inconvenience, annoyance, aggravation, vexation …*Most men hate the bother of shaving…* OPPOSITE help

bottleneck = <u>block</u>, hold-up, obstacle, congestion, obstruction, impediment, blockage, snarl-up (*informal, chiefly Brit.*), (traffic) jam

bottle shop (*Austral. & N.Z.*) = <u>off-licence</u> (*Brit.*), liquor store (*U.S. & Canad.*), bottle store (*S. African*), package store (*U.S. & Canad.*), offie *or* offy (*Brit. informal*)

bottle store (*S. African*) = <u>off-licence</u> (*Brit.*), liquor store (*U.S. & Canad.*), bottle shop (*Austral. & N.Z.*), package store (*U.S. & Canad.*), offie *or* offy (*Brit. informal*)

bottom NOUN 1 = <u>lowest part</u>, base, foot, bed, floor, basis, foundation, depths, support, pedestal, deepest part …*He sat at the bottom of the stairs…* OPPOSITE top
2 = <u>underside</u>, sole, underneath, lower side …*the bottom of their shoes…*
3 = <u>buttocks</u>, behind (*informal*), rear, butt (*U.S. &*

Canad. informal), bum (*Brit. slang*), buns (*U.S. slang*), backside, rump, seat, tail (*informal*), rear end, posterior, derrière (*euphemistic*), tush (*U.S. slang*), fundament, jacksy (*Brit. slang*) ...*She moved her large bottom on the window-seat...*

4 = <u>basis</u>, base, cause, ground, heart, source, principle, root, origin, core, substance, essence, provenance, derivation, mainspring ...*I have to get to the bottom of this mess...*

ADJECTIVE = <u>lowest</u>, last, base, ground, basement, undermost ...*the bottom drawer of the cupboard...*
OPPOSITE> higher

bottomless **1** = <u>unlimited</u>, endless, infinite, limitless, boundless, inexhaustible, immeasurable, unbounded, illimitable ...*She does not have a bottomless purse...*
2 = <u>deep</u>, profound, yawning, boundless, unfathomable, immeasurable, fathomless, abyssal ...*His eyes were like bottomless brown pools...*

bounce VERB **1** = <u>rebound</u>, return, thump, recoil, ricochet, spring back, resile ...*The ball bounced past the right-hand post...*
2 = <u>bound</u>, spring, jump, leap, skip, caper, prance, gambol, jounce ...*Moira bounced into the office...*
3 (*Slang*) = <u>throw out</u>, fire (*informal*), turn out, expel, oust, relegate, kick out (*informal*), drive out, eject, evict, boot out (*informal*), show someone the door, give someone the bum's rush (*slang*), throw out on your ear (*informal*) ...*He was bounced from two programmes for unbecoming conduct...*
NOUN **1** = <u>springiness</u>, give, spring, bound, rebound, resilience, elasticity, recoil ...*the pace and steep bounce of the pitch...*
2 (*Informal*) = <u>life</u>, go (*informal*), energy, pep, sparkle, zip (*informal*), vitality, animation, vigour, exuberance, dynamism, brio, vivacity, liveliness, vim (*slang*), lustiness, vivaciousness ...*the natural bounce of youth...*

bouncing = <u>lively</u>, healthy, thriving, blooming, robust, vigorous, energetic, perky, sprightly, alive and kicking, fighting fit, full of beans (*informal*), fit as a fiddle (*informal*), bright-eyed and bushy-tailed

bouncy **1** = <u>lively</u>, active, enthusiastic, energetic, bubbly, exuberant, irrepressible, ebullient, perky, chirpy (*informal*), sprightly, vivacious, effervescent, chipper (*informal*), full of beans (*informal*), zestful, full of pep (*informal*), bright-eyed and bushy-tailed ...*She was bouncy and full of energy...* OPPOSITE> listless
2 = <u>springy</u>, flexible, elastic, resilient, rubbery, spongy ...*a bouncy chair...* OPPOSITE> flat

bound¹ **1** = <u>compelled</u>, obliged, forced, committed, pledged, constrained, obligated, beholden, duty-bound ...*All members are bound by an oath of secrecy...*
2 = <u>tied</u>, fixed, secured, attached, lashed, tied up, fastened, trussed, pinioned, made fast ...*Her arms were bound to her sides...*
3 = <u>certain</u>, sure, fated, doomed, destined ...*There are bound to be price increases next year...*

bound² **1** = <u>surround</u>, confine, enclose, terminate, encircle, circumscribe, hem in, demarcate, delimit ...*the trees that bounded the car park...*

2 = <u>limit</u>, fix, define, restrict, confine, restrain, circumscribe, demarcate, delimit ...*Our lives are bounded by work, family and television...*

bound³ VERB = <u>leap</u>, bob, spring, jump, bounce, skip, vault, pounce ...*He bounded up the steps and pushed the bell of the door...*
NOUN = <u>leap</u>, bob, spring, jump, bounce, hurdle, skip, vault, pounce, caper, prance, lope, frisk, gambol ...*With one bound Jack was free...*

boundary **1** = <u>frontier</u>, edge, border, march, barrier, margin, brink ...*Drug traffickers operate across national boundaries...*
2 = <u>edges</u>, limits, bounds, pale, confines, fringes, verges, precinct, extremities ...*the western boundary of the wood...*
3 = <u>dividing line</u>, borderline ...*the boundary between childhood and adulthood...*

boundless = <u>unlimited</u>, vast, endless, immense, infinite, untold, limitless, unending, inexhaustible, incalculable, immeasurable, unbounded, unconfined, measureless, illimitable OPPOSITE> limited

bounds PLURAL NOUN = <u>boundary</u>, line, limit, edge, border, march, margin, pale, confine, fringe, verge, rim, perimeter, periphery ...*The bounds of the empire continued to expand...*
PHRASES **out of bounds** = <u>forbidden</u>, barred, banned, not allowed, vetoed, prohibited, taboo, off-limits (*chiefly U.S. military*), verboten (*German*) ...*Tibet was now virtually out of bounds to foreign journalists...*

bountiful (*Literary*) **1** = <u>plentiful</u>, generous, lavish, ample, prolific, abundant, exuberant, copious, luxuriant, bounteous, plenteous ...*The land is bountiful and no one starves...*
2 = <u>generous</u>, kind, princely, liberal, charitable, hospitable, prodigal, open-handed, unstinting, beneficent, bounteous, munificent, ungrudging ...*Their bountiful host was bringing brandy, whisky and liqueurs...*

bounty (*Literary*) **1** = <u>generosity</u>, charity, assistance, kindness, philanthropy, benevolence, beneficence, liberality, almsgiving, open-handedness, largesse *or* largess ...*The aid organization would not allow such bounty...*
2 = <u>abundance</u>, plenty, exuberance, profusion, affluence, plenitude, copiousness, plenteousness ...*autumn's bounty of fruits, seeds and berries...*
3 = <u>reward</u>, present, grant, prize, payment, gift, compensation, bonus, premium, donation, recompense, gratuity, meed (*archaic*), largesse *or* largess ...*They paid bounties for people to give up their weapons...*

bouquet **1** = <u>bunch of flowers</u>, spray, garland, wreath, posy, buttonhole, corsage, nosegay, boutonniere ...*a bouquet of dried violets...*
2 = <u>aroma</u>, smell, scent, perfume, fragrance, savour, odour, redolence ...*a Sicilian wine with a light red colour and a bouquet of cloves...*

bourgeois = <u>middle-class</u>, traditional, conventional, materialistic, hidebound, Pooterish

bout **1** = <u>period</u>, time, term, fit, session, stretch, spell,

turn, patch, interval, stint …*I was suffering with a bout of nerves…*
2 = round, run, course, series, session, cycle, sequence, stint, spree …*The latest bout of violence has claimed ten lives…*
3 = fight, match, battle, competition, struggle, contest, set-to, encounter, engagement, head-to-head, boxing match …*This will be his eighth title bout in 19 months…*

bovine = dull, heavy, slow, thick, stupid, dull, dense, sluggish, lifeless, inactive, inert, lethargic, dozy (*Brit. informal*), listless, unresponsive, stolid, torpid, slothful

bow¹ VERB = bend, bob, nod, incline, stoop, droop, genuflect, make obeisance …*He bowed slightly before taking her bag…*
NOUN = bending, bob, nod, inclination, salaam, obeisance, kowtow, genuflection …*I gave a theatrical bow and waved…*
PHRASES **bow out** = give up, retire, withdraw, get out, resign, quit, pull out, step down (*informal*), back out, throw In the towel, cop out (*slang*), throw In the sponge, call it a day *or* night …*He bowed out gracefully when his successor was appointed…* ◆ **bow to something** *or* **someone** = give in to, accept, comply with, succumb to, submit to, surrender to, yield to, defer to, concede to, acquiesce to, kowtow to …*She is having to bow to their terms…*

bow² (*Nautical*) = prow, head, stem, fore, beak …*spray from the ship's bow…*

bowed = bent, lowered, angled, curved, arched, inclined, crooked, hunched, stooped, procumbent
OPPOSITE upright

bowels 1 = guts, insides (*informal*), intestines, innards (*informal*), entrails, viscera, vitals …*Snatched sandwiches and junk food had cemented his bowels…*
2 = depths, hold, middle, inside, deep, interior, core, belly, midst, remotest part, deepest part, furthest part, innermost part …*deep in the bowels of the earth…*

bower = arbour, grotto, alcove, summerhouse, shady recess, leafy shelter

bowl¹ = basin, plate, dish, vessel …*Put all the ingredients into a large bowl…*

bowl² VERB **1** = throw, hurl, launch, cast, pitch, toss, fling, chuck (*informal*), lob (*informal*) …*He bowled each ball so well that we won two matches…*
2 = drive, shoot, speed, tear, barrel (along) (*informal, chiefly U.S. & Canad.*), trundle …*It felt just like old times, to bowl down to Knightsbridge…*
PHRASES **bowl someone over 1** = knock down, fell, floor, deck (*slang*), overturn, overthrow, bring down …*People clung to trees as the flash flood bowled them over…* **2** (*Informal*) = surprise, amaze, stun, overwhelm, astonish, stagger, startle, astound, take (someone) aback, stupefy, strike (someone) dumb, throw off balance, sweep off your feet, dumbfound …*I was bowled over by India…*

box¹ NOUN = container, case, chest, trunk, pack, package, carton, casket, receptacle, ark (*dialect*), portmanteau, coffret, kist (*Scot. & Northern English*

dialect*) …*They sat on wooden boxes…*
VERB = pack, package, wrap, encase, bundle up …*He boxed the test pieces and shipped them back to Berlin…*
PHRASES **box something** *or* **someone in** = confine, contain, surround, trap, restrict, isolate, cage, enclose, restrain, imprison, shut up, incarcerate, hem in, shut in, coop up …*He was boxed in with 300 metres to go…*

box² **1** = fight, spar, exchange blows …*At school I boxed and played rugby…*
2 = punch, hit, strike, belt (*informal*), deck (*slang*), slap, sock (*slang*), buffet, clout (*informal*), cuff, whack (*informal*), wallop (*informal*), chin (*slang*), tonk (*informal*), thwack (*informal*), lay one on (*slang*) …*They slapped my face and boxed my ears…*

boxer = fighter, pugilist, prizefighter, sparrer

boxing = prizefighting, the ring, sparring, fisticuffs, the fight game (*informal*), pugilism

Boxing weights

	Amateur	Professional
Light flyweight	48 kg	49 kg
Flyweight	51 kg	51 kg
Bantamweight	54 kg	53.5 kg
Featherweight	57 kg	57 kg
Junior lightweight	—	59 kg
Lightweight	60 kg	61 kg
Light welterweight	63.5 kg	63.5 kg
Welterweight	67 kg	66.6 kg
Light middleweight	71 kg	70 kg
Middleweight	75 kg	72.5 kg
Light heavyweight	81 kg	79 kg
Cruiserweight	—	88.5 kg
Heavyweight	91 kg	+88.5 kg
Superheavyweight	+91 kg	—

boy = lad, kid (*informal*), youth, fellow, youngster, chap (*informal*), schoolboy, junior, laddie (*Scot.*), stripling

boycott = embargo, reject, snub, refrain from, spurn, blacklist, black, cold-shoulder, ostracize, blackball
OPPOSITE support

boyfriend = sweetheart, man, lover, young man, steady, beloved, valentine, admirer, suitor, beau, date, swain, toy boy, truelove, leman (*archaic*), inamorato

boyish = youthful, young, innocent, adolescent, juvenile, childish, immature

brace VERB **1** = steady, support, balance, secure, stabilize …*He braced his back against the wall…*
2 = support, strengthen, steady, prop, reinforce, hold up, tighten, shove, bolster, fortify, buttress, shove up …*The lights showed the old timbers, used to brace the roof…*
NOUN = support, stay, prop, bracer, bolster, bracket, reinforcement, strut, truss, buttress, stanchion …*She wears a neck brace…*

bracing = refreshing, fresh, cool, stimulating, reviving, lively, crisp, vigorous, rousing, brisk, uplifting, exhilarating, fortifying, chilly, rejuvenating, invigorating, energizing, healthful, restorative, tonic, rejuvenative OPPOSITE tiring

brag = boast, crow, swagger, vaunt, bluster, talk big (*slang*), blow your own trumpet, blow your own horn (*U.S. & Canad.*)

braid = interweave, weave, lace, intertwine, plait, entwine, twine, ravel, interlace

brain NOUN 1 = cerebrum, mind, grey matter (*informal*) ...*The eye grows independently of the brain...*
2 (*Informal*) = intellectual, genius, scholar, sage, pundit, mastermind, intellect, prodigy, highbrow, egghead (*informal*), brainbox, bluestocking (*usually disparaging*) ...*I've never been much of a brain myself...*
PLURAL NOUN = intelligence, mind, reason, understanding, sense, capacity, smarts (*slang, chiefly U.S.*), wit, intellect, savvy (*slang*), nous (*Brit. slang*), suss (*slang*), shrewdness, sagacity ...*They were not the only ones to have brains and ambition...*
Related Words
adjective: cerebral

brainwashing = indoctrination, conditioning, persuasion, re-education

brainwave = idea, thought, bright idea, stroke of genius

brainy (*Informal*) = intelligent, quick, bright, sharp, brilliant, acute, smart, alert, clever, rational, knowing, quick-witted

brake NOUN = control, check, curb, restraint, constraint, rein ...*Illness had put a brake on his progress...*
VERB = slow, decelerate, reduce speed ...*She braked to a halt and switched off...*

branch NOUN 1 = bough, shoot, arm, spray, limb, sprig, offshoot, prong, ramification ...*the low, overhanging branches of a giant pine tree...*
2 = office, department, unit, wing, chapter, bureau, local office ...*The local branch is handling the accounts...*
3 = division, part, section, subdivision, subsection ...*He had a fascination for submarines and joined this branch of the service...*
4 = discipline, section, subdivision ...*an experimental branch of naturopathic medicine...*
PHRASES **branch out** = expand, diversify ...*I continued studying moths, and branched out to other insects...*

brand NOUN 1 = trademark ...*a supermarket's own brand...*
2 = label, mark, sign, stamp, symbol, logo, trademark, marker, hallmark, emblem ...*The brand on the barrel stood for Elbert Anderson and Uncle Sam...*
3 = stigma, mark, stain, disgrace, taint, slur, blot, infamy, smirch ...*the brand of shame...*
VERB 1 = stigmatize, mark, label, expose, denounce, disgrace, discredit, censure, pillory, defame ...*I was instantly branded as a rebel...*
2 = mark, burn, label, stamp, scar ...*The owner couldn't be bothered to brand the cattle...*

brandish = wave, raise, display, shake, swing, exhibit, flourish, wield, flaunt

brash = bold, forward, rude, arrogant, cocky, pushy (*informal*), brazen, presumptuous, impertinent, insolent, impudent, bumptious, cocksure, overconfident, hubristic, full of yourself OPPOSITE timid

brassy 1 = strident, loud, harsh, piercing, jarring, noisy, grating, raucous, blaring, shrill, jangling, dissonant, cacophonous ...*Musicians blast their brassy jazz from street corners...*
2 = brazen, forward, bold, brash, saucy, pushy (*informal*), pert, insolent, impudent, loud-mouthed, barefaced ...*Alec and his brassy blonde wife...*
3 = flashy, loud, blatant, vulgar, gaudy, garish, jazzy (*informal*), showy, obtrusive ...*A woman with big brassy ear-rings...* OPPOSITE discreet

brat = youngster, kid (*informal*), urchin, imp, rascal, spoilt child, devil, puppy (*informal*), cub, scallywag (*informal*), whippersnapper, guttersnipe

bravado = swagger, boast, boasting, swaggering, vaunting, bluster, swashbuckling, bombast, braggadocio, boastfulness, fanfaronade (*rare*)

brave ADJECTIVE = courageous, daring, bold, heroic, adventurous, gritty, fearless, resolute, gallant, gutsy (*slang*), audacious, intrepid, valiant, plucky, undaunted, unafraid, unflinching, dauntless, lion-hearted, valorous ...*brave people who dare to challenge the tyrannical regimes...* OPPOSITE timid
VERB = confront, face, suffer, challenge, bear, tackle, dare, endure, defy, withstand, stand up to ...*She had to brave his anger and confess...* OPPOSITE give in to

bravery = courage, nerve, daring, pluck, spirit, bottle (*Brit. slang*), guts (*informal*), grit, fortitude, heroism, mettle, boldness, bravura, gallantry, valour, spunk (*informal*), hardiness, fearlessness, intrepidity, indomitability, hardihood, dauntlessness, doughtiness, pluckiness, lion-heartedness OPPOSITE cowardice

bravo = congratulations, well done

bravura = brilliance, energy, spirit, display, punch (*informal*), dash, animation, vigour, verve, panache, boldness, virtuosity, élan, exhibitionism, brio, ostentation

brawl NOUN = fight, battle, row (*informal*), clash, disorder, scrap (*informal*), fray, squabble, wrangle, skirmish, scuffle, punch-up (*Brit. informal*), free-for-all (*informal*), fracas, altercation, rumpus, broil, tumult, affray (*Law*), shindig (*informal*), donnybrook, ruckus (*informal*), scrimmage, shindy (*informal*), biffo (*Austral. slang*), bagarre (*French*), melee *or* mêlée ...*He had been in a drunken street brawl...*
VERB = fight, battle, scrap (*informal*), wrestle, wrangle, tussle, scuffle, go at it hammer and tongs, fight like Kilkenny cats, altercate ...*Gangs of youths brawled in the street...*

brawn = muscle, might, power, strength, muscles, beef (*informal*), flesh, vigour, robustness, muscularity, beefiness (*informal*), brawniness

bray VERB 1 = neigh, bellow, screech, heehaw ...*The donkey brayed and tried to bolt...*

2 = <u>roar</u>, trumpet, bellow, hoot …*Neil brayed with angry laughter*…

NOUN **1** = <u>neigh</u>, bellow, screech, heehaw …*It was a strange laugh, like the bray of a donkey*…

2 = <u>roar</u>, cry, shout, bellow, screech, hoot, bawl, harsh sound …*She cut him off with a bray of laughter*…

brazen **ADJECTIVE** = <u>bold</u>, forward, defiant, brash, saucy, audacious, pushy (*informal*), shameless, unabashed, pert, unashamed, insolent, impudent, immodest, barefaced, brassy (*informal*) …*She's just a brazen hussy*… **OPPOSITE** shy

PHRASES **brazen it out** = <u>be unashamed</u>, persevere, be defiant, confront something, be impenitent, outface, outstare …*As for the scandal, he is as determined as ever to brazen it out*…

breach **1** = <u>nonobservance</u>, abuse, violation, infringement, trespass, disobedience, transgression, contravention, infraction, noncompliance …*The congressman was accused of a breach of secrecy laws*… **OPPOSITE** compliance

2 = <u>disagreement</u>, difference, division, separation, falling-out (*informal*), quarrel, alienation, variance, severance, disaffection, schism, parting of the ways, estrangement, dissension …*the breach between Tito and Stalin*…

3 = <u>opening</u>, crack, break, hole, split, gap, rent, rift, rupture, aperture, chasm, cleft, fissure …*A large battering ram hammered a breach in the wall*…

▶ **breech**

bread **1** = <u>food</u>, provisions, fare, necessities, subsistence, kai (*N.Z. informal*), nourishment, sustenance, victuals, nutriment, viands, aliment …*I go to work, I put bread on the table, I pay the mortgage*…

2 (*Slang*) = <u>money</u>, funds, cash, finance, necessary (*informal*), silver, tin (*slang*), brass (*Northern English dialect*), dough (*slang*), dosh (*Brit. & Austral. slang*), needful (*informal*), shekels (*informal*), dibs (*slang*), ackers (*slang*), spondulicks (*slang*), rhino (*Brit. slang*) …*a period in which you could earn your bread by the sweat of your brow*…

breadth **1** = <u>width</u>, spread, beam, span, latitude, broadness, wideness …*The breadth of the whole camp was 400 metres*…

2 = <u>extent</u>, area, reach, range, measure, size, scale, spread, sweep, scope, magnitude, compass, expanse, vastness, amplitude, comprehensiveness, extensiveness …*The breadth of his knowledge filled me with admiration*…

break **VERB** **1** = <u>shatter</u>, separate, destroy, split, divide, crack, snap, smash, crush, fragment, demolish, sever, trash (*slang*), disintegrate, splinter, smash to smithereens, shiver …*He fell through the window, breaking the glass*… **OPPOSITE** repair

2 = <u>fracture</u>, crack, smash …*She broke her leg in a skiing accident*…

3 = <u>burst</u>, tear, split …*The bandage must be put on when the blister breaks*…

4 = <u>disobey</u>, breach, defy, violate, disregard, flout, infringe, contravene, transgress, go counter to, infract (*Law*) …*We didn't know we were breaking the law*… **OPPOSITE** obey

5 = <u>stop</u>, cut, check, suspend, interrupt, cut short, discontinue …*He aims to break the vicious cycle*…

6 = <u>disturb</u>, interrupt …*The noise broke my concentration*…

7 = <u>end</u>, stop, cut, drop, give up, abandon, suspend, interrupt, terminate, put an end to, discontinue, pull the plug on …*They have yet to break the link with the trade unions*…

8 = <u>weaken</u>, undermine, cow, tame, subdue, demoralize, dispirit …*He never let his jailers break him*…

9 = <u>ruin</u>, destroy, crush, humiliate, bring down, bankrupt, degrade, impoverish, demote, make bankrupt, bring to ruin …*The newspapers can make or break you*…

10 = <u>pause</u>, stop briefly, stop, rest, halt, cease, take a break, have a breather (*informal*) …*They broke for lunch*…

11 = <u>interrupt</u>, stop, suspend …*We broke our journey at a small country hotel*…

12 = <u>cushion</u>, reduce, ease, moderate, diminish, temper, soften, lessen, alleviate, lighten …*She was saved by bushes which broke her fall*…

13 = <u>be revealed</u>, come out, be reported, be published, be announced, be made public, be proclaimed, be let out, be imparted, be divulged, come out in the wash …*He resigned his post as Bishop when the scandal broke*…

14 = <u>reveal</u>, tell, announce, declare, disclose, proclaim, divulge, make known …*I worried for ages and decided I had better break the news*…

15 = <u>beat</u>, top, better, exceed, go beyond, excel, surpass, outstrip, outdo, cap (*informal*) …*The film has broken all box office records*…

16 (always used of *dawn*) = <u>happen</u>, appear, emerge, occur, erupt, burst out, come forth suddenly …*They continued their search as dawn broke*…

NOUN **1** = <u>fracture</u>, opening, tear, hole, split, crack, gap, rent, breach, rift, rupture, gash, cleft, fissure …*a break in the earth's surface*…

2 = <u>interval</u>, pause, recess, interlude, intermission, entr'acte …*They always play that music during the break*…

3 = <u>holiday</u>, leave, vacation, time off, recess, awayday …*They are currently taking a short break in Spain*…

4 (*Informal*) = <u>stroke of luck</u>, chance, opportunity, advantage, fortune, opening …*The rain was a lucky break for the American*…

5 = <u>breach</u>, split, dispute, separation, rift, rupture, alienation, disaffection, schism, estrangement …*There is some threat of a break in relations between them*…

PHRASES **break away** = <u>get away</u>, escape, flee, run away, break free, break loose, make your escape …*I broke away from him and rushed out into the hall*…

◆ **break down** **1** = <u>stop working</u>, stop, seize up, conk out (*informal*), go kaput (*informal*), go phut, cark it (*Austral. & N.Z. slang*) …*Their car broke down*…

2 = <u>fail</u>, collapse, fall through, be unsuccessful, come unstuck, run aground, come to grief, come a cropper (*informal*), turn out badly …*Paola's marriage broke down*… **3** = <u>be overcome</u>, crack up (*informal*), go to

pieces ...*The young woman broke down and cried*...
◆ **break free of something** *or* **someone** = escape (from), leave, withdraw from, extricate yourself from, free yourself of, disentangle yourself from ...*his inability to break free of his marriage*...
◆ **break in 1** = break and enter, enter, gain access ...*The thief had broken in through a first-floor window*... **2** = interrupt, intervene, interfere, intrude, burst in, interject, butt in, barge in, interpose, put your oar in, put your two cents in (*U.S. slang*) ...*Suddenly, O'Leary broke in with a suggestion*... ◆ **break into something 1** = burgle ...*In this country a house is broken into every 24 seconds*... **2** = begin, start, burst into, give way to, commence, launch into, embark upon ...*The moment she was out of sight she broke into a run*... ◆ **break off** = stop talking, pause, stumble, falter, fumble, hem and haw *or* hum and haw ...*He broke off in mid-sentence*... ◆ **break out 1** = begin, start, happen, occur, arise, set in, commence, spring up ...*He was 29 when war broke out*... **2** = escape, flee, bolt, burst out, get free, break loose, abscond, do a bunk (*Brit. slang*) ...*The two men broke out and cut through a perimeter fence*... **3** = erupt, gush, flare up, burst out, burst forth, pour forth ...*A line of sweat broke out on her forehead*... ◆ **break someone in** = initiate, train, accustom, habituate ...*The band are breaking in a new backing vocalist*... ◆ **break something in** = prepare, condition, tame ...*I'm breaking in these new boots*... ◆ **break something off** = detach, separate, divide, cut off, pull off, sever, part, remove, splinter, tear off, snap off ...*He broke off a large piece of the clay*... ◆ **break something up** = stop, end, suspend, disrupt, dismantle, disperse, terminate, disband, diffuse ...*Police used tear gas to break up a demonstration*... ◆ **break through** = succeed, make it (*informal*), achieve, do well, flourish, cut it (*informal*), get to the top, crack it (*informal*), make your mark (*informal*), shine forth ...*There is still scope for new writers to break through*... ◆ **break through something** = penetrate, go through, get past, burst through ...*Protesters tried to break through a police cordon*... ◆ **break up 1** = finish, be suspended, adjourn, recess ...*The meeting broke up half an hour later*... **2** = split up, separate, part, divorce, end a relationship ...*My girlfriend and I have broken up*... **3** = scatter, separate, divide, dissolve ...*The crowd broke up reluctantly*... ◆ **break with something** *or* **someone** = separate from, drop (*informal*), reject, ditch (*slang*), renounce, depart from, break away from, part company with, repudiate, jilt ...*It was a tough decision for him to break with Leeds*...

breakage = break, cut, tear, crack, rent, breach, fracture, rift, rupture, cleft, fissure

breakaway = rebel, revolutionary, rebellious, dissenting, insurgent, seceding, secessionist, heretical, mutinous, insubordinate, insurrectionary, schismatic

breakdown 1 = collapse, crackup (*informal*) ...*They often seem depressed and close to breakdown*... **2** = analysis, classification, dissection, categorization, detailed list, itemization ...*The organisers were given a

breakdown of the costs*...

breaker = wave, roller, comber, billow, white horse, whitecap

break-in = burglary, robbery, breaking and entering

breakneck = dangerous, rapid, excessive, rash, reckless, precipitate, headlong, express

breakthrough = development, advance, progress, improvement, discovery, find, finding, invention, step forward, leap forwards, turn of events, quantum leap

break-up 1 = separation, split, divorce, breakdown, ending, parting, breaking, splitting, wind-up, rift, disintegration, dissolution, termination ...*a marital break-up*...
2 = dissolution, division, splitting, disintegration ...*the break-up of British Rail*...

breakwater = sea wall, spur, mole, jetty, groyne

breast NOUN = heart, feelings, thoughts, soul, being, emotions, core, sentiments, seat of the affections ...*Happiness flowered in her breast*...
PLURAL NOUN = bosom(s), front, chest, bust ...*a skimpy top which barely covered her breasts*...
(Related Words)
adjective: mammary

breath 1 = inhalation, breathing, pant, gasp, gulp, wheeze, exhalation, respiration ...*He took a deep breath and began to climb the stairs*...
2 = gust, sigh, puff, flutter, flurry, whiff, draught, waft, zephyr, slight movement, faint breeze ...*Not even a breath of wind stirred the pine branches*...
3 = trace, suggestion, hint, whisper, suspicion, murmur, undertone, intimation ...*It was left to her to add a breath of common sense*...
4 = odour, smell, aroma, whiff, vapour, niff (*Brit. slang*) ...*A breath of cooking smell crept to her from the kitchen*...
5 = rest, breather ...*He had to stop for breath*...
6 = life, energy, existence, vitality, animation, life force, lifeblood ...*Here is no light, no breath, no warm flesh*...

breathe 1 = inhale and exhale, pant, gasp, puff, gulp, wheeze, respire, draw in breath ...*Always breathe through your nose*...
2 = whisper, say, voice, express, sigh, utter, articulate, murmur ...*He never breathed a word about our conversation*...
3 = instil, inspire, pass on, inject, impart, infuse, imbue ...*It is the readers who breathe life into a newspaper*...

breather (*Informal*) = rest, break, halt, pause, recess, breathing space, breath of air

breathless 1 = out of breath, winded, exhausted, panting, gasping, choking, gulping, wheezing, out of whack (*informal*), short-winded ...*I was a little breathless and my heartbeat was fast*...
2 = excited, anxious, curious, eager, enthusiastic, impatient, agog, on tenterhooks, in suspense ...*We were breathless with anticipation*...

breathtaking = amazing, striking, exciting, brilliant, dramatic, stunning (*informal*), impressive, thrilling, overwhelming, magnificent, astonishing, sensational, awesome, wondrous (*archaic or literary*), awe-inspiring, jaw-dropping, heart-stirring

breech

> ### *Word Power*
>
> **breech** – *Breech* is sometimes wrongly used as a verb where *breach* is meant: *he admitted he had breached* (not *breeched*) *the rules.*

breed NOUN **1** = variety, race, stock, type, species, strain, pedigree ...*rare breeds of cattle...*
2 = kind, sort, type, variety, brand, stamp ...*the new breed of walking holidays...*
VERB **1** = rear, tend, keep, raise, maintain, farm, look after, care for, bring up, nurture, nourish ...*He lived alone, breeding horses and dogs...*
2 = reproduce, multiply, propagate, procreate, produce offspring, bear young, bring forth young, generate offspring, beget offspring, develop ...*Frogs will usually breed in any convenient pond...*
3 = produce, cause, create, occasion, generate, bring about, arouse, originate, give rise to, stir up ...*If they are unemployed it's bound to breed resentment...*

breeding = refinement, style, culture, taste, manners, polish, grace, courtesy, elegance, sophistication, delicacy, cultivation, politeness, civility, gentility, graciousness, urbanity, politesse

breeze NOUN = light wind, air, whiff, draught, gust, waft, zephyr, breath of wind, current of air, puff of air, capful of wind ...*a cool summer breeze...*
VERB = sweep, move briskly, pass, trip, sail, hurry, sally, glide, flit ...*Lopez breezed into the room...*

breezy 1 = carefree, casual, lively, sparkling, sunny, informal, cheerful, animated, upbeat (*informal*), buoyant, airy, easy-going, genial, jaunty, chirpy (*informal*), sparky, sprightly, vivacious, debonair, blithe, free and easy, full of beans (*informal*), light, light-hearted ...*his bright and breezy personality...*
OPPOSITE serious
2 = windy, fresh, airy, blustery, blowing, gusty, squally, blowy, blusterous ...*The day was breezy and warm...*
OPPOSITE calm

brevity 1 = shortness, transience, impermanence, ephemerality, briefness, transitoriness ...*The bonus of this homely soup is the brevity of its cooking time...*
2 = conciseness, economy, crispness, concision, terseness, succinctness, curtness, pithiness ...*The brevity of the letter concerned me...* OPPOSITE wordiness

brew VERB **1** = boil, make, soak, steep, stew, infuse (*tea*) ...*He brewed a pot of coffee...*
2 = make, ferment, prepare by fermentation ...*I brew my own beer...*

3 = underline{start}, develop, gather, foment ...*At home a crisis was brewing...*
4 = develop, form, gather, foment ...*We'd seen the storm brewing when we were out on the boat...*
NOUN = drink, preparation, mixture, blend, liquor, beverage, infusion, concoction, fermentation, distillation ...*a mild herbal brew...*

bribe NOUN = inducement, incentive, pay-off (*informal*), graft (*informal*), sweetener (*slang*), kickback (*U.S.*), sop, backhander (*slang*), enticement, hush money (*slang*), payola (*informal*), allurement, corrupting gift, reward for treachery ...*He was being investigated for receiving bribes...*
VERB = buy off, reward, pay off (*informal*), lure, corrupt, get at, square, suborn, grease the palm *or* hand of (*slang*), influence by gifts, oil the palm of (*informal*) ...*The company bribed the workers to be quiet...*

bribery = corruption, graft (*informal*), inducement, buying off, payola (*informal*), crookedness (*informal*), palm-greasing (*slang*), subornation

bric-a-brac = knick-knacks, ornaments, trinkets, baubles, curios, objets d'art (*French*), gewgaws, bibelots, kickshaws, objects of virtu

bridal = matrimonial, marriage, wedding, marital, bride's, nuptial, conjugal, spousal, connubial, hymeneal

bride = wife, newly-wed, marriage partner

bridegroom = husband, groom, newly-wed, marriage partner

bridge NOUN **1** = arch, span, viaduct, flyover, overpass ...*He walked over the railway bridge...*
2 = link, tie, bond, connection ...*They saw themselves as a bridge to peace...*
VERB **1** = span, cross, go over, cross over, traverse, reach across, extend across, arch over ...*a tree used to bridge the river...*
2 = underline{reconcile}, unite, resolve ...*She bridged the gap between pop music and opera...*
➤ bridges

bridle NOUN = rein, curb, control, check, restraint, trammels ...*She dismounted and took her horse's bridle...*
VERB **1** = get angry, draw (yourself) up, bristle, seethe, see red, be infuriated, rear up, be indignant, be maddened, raise your hackles, get your dander up (*slang*), get your back up ...*He bridled at the shortness of her tone...*
2 = curb, control, master, govern, moderate, restrain, rein, subdue, repress, constrain, keep in check, check,

> ## *Bridges*
>
> | | | |
> |---|---|---|
> | Brooklyn Bridge | Humber Bridge | Bridge of Sighs |
> | Clifton Suspension Bridge | London Bridge | Skye Bridge |
> | Forth Railway Bridge | Millennium Bridge | Sydney Harbour Bridge |
> | Forth Road Bridge | Oakland Bay Bridge | Tower Bridge |
> | Gateshead Millennium Bridge | Rainbow Bridge | Tyne Bridge |
> | Golden Gate Bridge | Rialto Bridge | Waterloo Bridge |
> | Halfpenny Bridge | Severn Bridge | Westminster Bridge |

keep a tight rein on, keep on a string ...*I must learn to bridle my tongue*...

brief ADJECTIVE **1** = short, fast, quick, temporary, fleeting, swift, short-lived, little, hasty, momentary, ephemeral, quickie (*informal*), transitory ...*This time their visit is brief*... OPPOSITE⟩ long

2 = concise, short, limited, to the point, crisp, compressed, terse, curt, laconic, succinct, clipped, pithy, thumbnail, monosyllabic ...*Write a very brief description of a typical problem*... OPPOSITE⟩ long

3 = curt, short, sharp, blunt, abrupt, brusque ...*He was brief, rapid, decisive*...

VERB = inform, prime, prepare, advise, fill in (*informal*), instruct, clue in (*informal*), gen up (*Brit. informal*), put in the picture (*informal*), give a rundown, keep (someone) posted, give the gen (*Brit. informal*) ...*A spokesman briefed reporters*...

NOUN **1** = summary, résumé, outline, sketch, abstract, summing-up, digest, epitome, rundown, synopsis, précis, recapitulation, abridgment ...*He gives me my first brief of the situation*...

2 = case, defence, argument, data, contention ...*a lawyer's brief*...

briefing **1** = conference, meeting, priming ...*They're holding a press briefing tomorrow*...

2 = instructions, information, priming, directions, instruction, preparation, guidance, preamble, rundown ...*The Chancellor gives a twenty-minute briefing to his backbenchers*...

briefly **1** = quickly, shortly, precisely, casually, temporarily, abruptly, hastily, briskly, momentarily, hurriedly, curtly, summarily, fleetingly, cursorily ...*He smiled briefly*...

2 = in outline, in brief, in passing, in a nutshell, concisely, in a few words ...*There are four alternatives; they are described briefly below*...

brigade **1** = corps, company, force, unit, division, troop, squad, crew, team, outfit, regiment, contingent, squadron, detachment ...*the men of the Seventh Armoured Brigade*...

2 = group, party, body, band, camp, squad, organization, crew, bunch (*informal*) ...*the healthy-eating brigade*...

bright **1** = vivid, rich, brilliant, intense, glowing, colourful, highly-coloured ...*a bright red dress*...

2 = shining, flashing, beaming, glowing, blazing, sparkling, glittering, dazzling, illuminated, gleaming, shimmering, twinkling, radiant, luminous, glistening, resplendent, scintillating, lustrous, lambent, effulgent ...*Newborns hate bright lights and loud noises*...

3 = intelligent, smart, clever, knowing, thinking, quick, aware, sharp, keen, acute, alert, rational, penetrating, enlightened, apt, astute, brainy, wide-awake, clear-headed, perspicacious, quick-witted ...*I was convinced that he was brighter than average*... OPPOSITE⟩ stupid

4 = clever, brilliant, smart, sensible, cunning, ingenious, inventive, canny ...*There are lots of books crammed with bright ideas*...

5 = cheerful, happy, glad, lively, jolly, merry, upbeat (*informal*), joyous, joyful, genial, chirpy (*informal*),

sparky, vivacious, full of beans (*informal*), gay, light-hearted ...*The boy was so bright and animated*...

6 = promising, good, encouraging, excellent, golden, optimistic, hopeful, favourable, prosperous, rosy, auspicious, propitious, palmy ...*Both had successful careers and the future looked bright*...

7 = sunny, clear, fair, pleasant, clement, lucid, cloudless, unclouded ...*the bright winter sky*... OPPOSITE⟩ cloudy

brighten **1** = cheer up, rally, take heart, perk up, buck up (*informal*), become cheerful ...*Seeing him, she seemed to brighten a little*... OPPOSITE⟩ become gloomy

2 = light up, shine, glow, gleam, clear up, lighten, enliven ...*Her tearful eyes brightened with interest*... OPPOSITE⟩ dim

3 = enliven, animate, make brighter, vitalize ...*Planted tubs brightened the area outside the door*...

4 = become brighter, light up, glow, gleam, clear up ...*The sky above the ridge of the mountains brightened*...

brightness **1** = vividness, intensity, brilliance, splendour, resplendence ...*You'll be impressed with the brightness of the colors*...

2 = intelligence, intellect, brains (*informal*), awareness, sharpness, alertness, cleverness, quickness, acuity, brain power, smarts (*slang, chiefly U.S.*), smartness ...*Her brightness seemed quite intimidating to me*...

brilliance *or* **brilliancy** **1** = cleverness, talent, wisdom, distinction, genius, excellence, greatness, aptitude, inventiveness, acuity, giftedness, braininess ...*His brilliance and genius will always remain*... OPPOSITE⟩ stupidity

2 = brightness, blaze, intensity, sparkle, glitter, dazzle, gleam, sheen, lustre, radiance, luminosity, vividness, resplendence, effulgence, refulgence ...*the brilliance of the sun on the water*... OPPOSITE⟩ darkness

3 = splendour, glamour, grandeur, magnificence, éclat, gorgeousness, illustriousness, pizzazz *or* pizazz (*informal*), gilt ...*The opera house was perfection, all brilliance and glamour*...

brilliant **1** = intelligent, sharp, intellectual, alert, clever, quick, acute, profound, rational, penetrating, discerning, inventive, astute, brainy, perspicacious, quick-witted ...*She had a brilliant mind*... OPPOSITE⟩ stupid

2 = expert, masterly, talented, gifted, accomplished ...*a brilliant pianist*... OPPOSITE⟩ untalented

3 = splendid, grand, famous, celebrated, rare, supreme, outstanding, remarkable, superb, magnificent, sterling, glorious, exceptional, notable, renowned, heroic, admirable, eminent, sublime, illustrious ...*a brilliant success*...

4 = bright, shining, intense, sparkling, glittering, dazzling, vivid, radiant, luminous, ablaze, resplendent, scintillating, lustrous, coruscating, refulgent ...*The event was held in brilliant sunshine*... OPPOSITE⟩ dark

brim NOUN = rim, edge, border, lip, margin, verge, brink, flange ...*The toilet was full to the brim with insects*...

VERB 1 = <u>be full</u>, spill, well over, run over, overflow, spill over, brim over ...*They are brimming with confidence*...

2 = <u>fill</u>, well over, fill up, overflow ...*Michael looked at him imploringly, his eyes brimming with tears*...

brine = <u>salt water</u>, saline solution, pickling solution

bring **VERB** 1 = <u>fetch</u>, take, carry, bear, transfer, deliver, transport, import, convey ...*My father brought home a book for me*...

2 = <u>take</u>, guide, conduct, accompany, escort, usher ...*I brought him inside and dried him off*...

3 = <u>cause</u>, produce, create, effect, occasion, result in, contribute to, inflict, wreak, engender ...*The revolution brought more trouble than it was worth*...

4 = <u>make</u>, force, influence, convince, persuade, prompt, compel, induce, move, dispose, sway, prevail on or upon ...*I could not even bring myself to enter the house*...

5 = <u>earn</u>, return, produce, net, command, yield, gross, fetch ...*This brings her the benefit of a higher rate of interest*...

PHRASES **bring someone up** = <u>rear</u>, raise, support, train, develop, teach, nurse, breed, foster, educate, care for, nurture ...*She brought up four children*...

♦ **bring something about** = <u>cause</u>, produce, create, effect, manage, achieve, occasion, realize, generate, accomplish, give rise to, make happen, effectuate, bring to pass ...*The two sides are attempting to bring about fundamental changes*...

♦ **bring something down** 1 = <u>overturn</u>, reduce, undermine, overthrow, abase ...*They were threatening to bring down the government*... 2 = <u>reduce</u>, cut, drop, lower, slash, decrease ...*The air fares war will bring down prices*... 3 = <u>cut down</u>, level, fell, hew, lop, raze ...*The lumberjacks brought the tree down*... 4 = <u>demolish</u>, level, destroy, dismantle, flatten, knock down, pull down, tear down, bulldoze, raze ...*Such forces would normally bring the building down*...

♦ **bring something in** 1 = <u>introduce</u>, start, found, launch, establish, set up, institute, organize, pioneer, initiate, usher in, inaugurate ...*They brought in a controversial law*... 2 = <u>produce</u>, return, net, realize, generate, be worth, yield, gross, fetch, accrue ...*The business brings in about £24,000 a year*... ♦ **bring something off** = <u>accomplish</u>, achieve, perform, carry out, succeed, execute, discharge, pull off, carry off, bring to pass ...*They were about to bring off an even bigger coup*... ♦ **bring something up**= <u>mention</u>, raise, introduce, point out, refer to, allude to, broach, call attention to, speak about or of ...*Why are you bringing that up now?*...

brink = <u>edge</u>, point, limit, border, lip, margin, boundary, skirt, frontier, fringe, verge, threshold, rim, brim

brio = <u>energy</u>, spirit, enthusiasm, dash, pep, zip (*informal*), animation, vigour, verve, zest, panache, gusto, get-up-and-go (*informal*), élan, vivacity, liveliness

brisk 1 = <u>quick</u>, lively, energetic, active, vigorous, animated, bustling, speedy, nimble, agile, sprightly, vivacious, spry ...*The horse broke into a brisk trot*...

OPPOSITE slow

2 = <u>short</u>, sharp, brief, blunt, rude, tart, abrupt, no-nonsense, terse, gruff, pithy, brusque, offhand, monosyllabic, ungracious, uncivil, snappish ...*She attempted to reason with him in a rather brisk fashion*...

3 = <u>invigorating</u>, fresh, biting, sharp, keen, stimulating, crisp, bracing, refreshing, exhilarating, nippy ...*The breeze was cool, brisk and invigorating*...

OPPOSITE tiring

briskly 1 = <u>quickly</u>, smartly, promptly, rapidly, readily, actively, efficiently, vigorously, energetically, pronto (*informal*), nimbly, posthaste ...*Eve walked briskly down the corridor*...

2 = <u>rapidly</u>, quickly, apace, pdq (*slang*) ...*A trader said gold was selling briskly on the local market*...

3 = <u>brusquely</u>, firmly, decisively, incisively ...*'Anyhow,' she added briskly, 'it's none of my business.'*...

bristle **NOUN** = <u>hair</u>, spine, thorn, whisker, barb, stubble, prickle ...*two days' growth of bristles*...

VERB 1 = <u>stand up</u>, rise, prickle, stand on end, horripilate ...*It makes the hair on the nape of my neck bristle*...

2 = <u>be angry</u>, rage, seethe, flare up, bridle, see red, be infuriated, spit (*informal*), go ballistic (*slang, chiefly U.S.*), be maddened, wig out (*slang*), get your dander up (*slang*) ...*He bristled with indignation*...

3 = <u>abound</u>, crawl, be alive, hum, swarm, teem, be thick ...*The country bristles with armed groups*...

Briton = <u>Brit</u> (*informal*), limey (*U.S. & Canad. slang*), Britisher, pommy or pom (*Austral. & N.Z. slang*), Anglo-Saxon

brittle 1 = <u>fragile</u>, delicate, crisp, crumbling, frail, crumbly, breakable, shivery, friable, frangible, shatterable ...*Pine is brittle and breaks easily*...

OPPOSITE tough

2 = <u>tense</u>, nervous, edgy, stiff, wired (*slang*), irritable, curt ...*a brittle man*...

broach 1 = <u>bring up</u>, approach, introduce, mention, speak of, talk of, open up, hint at, touch on, raise the subject of ...*Eventually I broached the subject of her early life*...

2 = <u>open</u>, crack, pierce, puncture, uncork ...*He would ask the landlord to broach a new barrel of wine*...

broad 1 = <u>wide</u>, large, ample, generous, expansive ...*His shoulders were broad and his waist narrow*...

2 = <u>large</u>, huge, comfortable, vast, extensive, ample, spacious, expansive, roomy, voluminous, capacious, uncrowded, commodious, beamy (*of a ship*), sizable or sizeable ...*a broad expanse of lawn*... **OPPOSITE** narrow

3 = <u>full</u>, general, comprehensive, complete, wide, global, catholic, sweeping, extensive, wide-ranging, umbrella, thorough, unlimited, inclusive, far-reaching, exhaustive, all-inclusive, all-embracing, overarching, encyclopedic ...*A broad range of issues was discussed*...

4 = <u>universal</u>, general, common, wide, sweeping, worldwide, widespread, wide-ranging, far-reaching ...*a film with broad appeal*...

5 = <u>general</u>, loose, vague, approximate, indefinite, ill-

defined, inexact, nonspecific, unspecific, undetailed
...*a broad outline of the Society's development*...

6 = <u>clear</u>, open, full, plain ...*Militants shot a man dead in broad daylight today*...

7 = <u>vulgar</u>, blue, dirty, gross, crude, rude, naughty, coarse, indecent, improper, suggestive, risqué, boorish, uncouth, unrefined, ribald, indelicate, near the knuckle (*informal*), indecorous, unmannerly ...*Use wit rather than broad humour*...

broadcast NOUN = <u>transmission</u>, show, programme, telecast ...*a broadcast on the national radio*...
VERB **1** = <u>transmit</u>, show, send, air, radio, cable, beam, send out, relay, televise, disseminate, put on the air ...*CNN also broadcasts programmes in Europe*...
2 = <u>make public</u>, report, announce, publish, spread, advertise, proclaim, circulate, disseminate, promulgate, shout from the rooftops (*informal*) ...*Don't broadcast your business outside the family*...

broaden = <u>expand</u>, increase, develop, spread, extend, stretch, open up, swell, supplement, widen, enlarge, augment OPPOSITE restrict

broadly 1 = <u>in general</u>, largely, generally, mainly, widely, mostly, on the whole, predominantly, in the main, for the most part ...*He broadly got what he wanted out of his meeting*...
2 = <u>widely</u>, greatly, hugely, vastly, extensively, expansively ...*Charles grinned broadly*...
3 = <u>generally</u>, commonly, widely, universally, popularly ...*This gives children a more broadly based education*... OPPOSITE narrowly

broadside = <u>attack</u>, criticism, censure, swipe, denunciation, diatribe, philippic

brochure = <u>booklet</u>, advertisement, leaflet, hand-out, circular, pamphlet, folder, mailshot, handbill

broekies (*S. African informal*) = <u>underpants</u>, pants, briefs, drawers, knickers, panties, boxer shorts, Y-fronts (*trademark*), underdaks (*Austral. slang*)

broke (*Informal*) = <u>penniless</u>, short, ruined, bust (*informal*), bankrupt, impoverished, in the red, cleaned out (*slang*), insolvent, down and out, skint (*Brit. slang*), strapped for cash (*informal*), dirt-poor (*informal*), flat broke (*informal*), penurious, on your uppers, stony-broke (*Brit. slang*), in queer street, without two pennies to rub together (*informal*), without a penny to your name OPPOSITE rich

broken 1 = <u>interrupted</u>, disturbed, incomplete, erratic, disconnected, intermittent, fragmentary, spasmodic, discontinuous ...*nights of broken sleep*...
2 = <u>imperfect</u>, halting, hesitating, stammering, disjointed ...*Eric could only respond in broken English*...
3 = <u>smashed</u>, destroyed, burst, shattered, fragmented, fractured, demolished, severed, ruptured, rent, separated, shivered ...*Damp air came through the broken window*...
4 = <u>defective</u>, not working, ruined, imperfect, out of order, not functioning, on the blink (*slang*), on its last legs, kaput (*informal*) ...*a broken guitar and a rusty snare drum*...
5 = <u>violated</u>, forgotten, ignored, disregarded, not kept, infringed, retracted, disobeyed, dishonoured, transgressed, traduced ...*History is made up of broken promises*...
6 = <u>defeated</u>, beaten, crushed, humbled, crippled, tamed, subdued, oppressed, overpowered, vanquished, demoralized, browbeaten ...*He looked a broken man*...

broken-down = <u>not in working order</u>, old, worn out, out of order, dilapidated, not functioning, out of commission, on the blink (*slang*), inoperative, kaput (*informal*), in disrepair, on the fritz (*U.S. slang*)

broken-hearted = <u>heartbroken</u>, devastated, disappointed, despairing, miserable, choked, desolate, mournful, prostrated, grief-stricken, sorrowful, wretched, disconsolate, inconsolable, crestfallen, down in the dumps (*informal*), heart-sick

broker = <u>dealer</u>, marketer, agent, trader, supplier, merchant, entrepreneur, negotiator, chandler, mediator, intermediary, wholesaler, middleman, factor, purveyor, go-between, tradesman, merchandiser

bronze = <u>reddish-brown</u>, copper, tan, rust, chestnut, brownish, copper-coloured, yellowish-brown, reddish-tan, metallic brown
➤ **shades of brown**

bronzed = <u>tanned</u>, brown, suntanned, sunburnt

brood NOUN **1** = <u>offspring</u>, young, issue, breed, infants, clutch, hatch, litter, chicks, progeny ...*The last brood of the pair was hatched*...
2 = <u>children</u>, family, offspring, progeny, nearest and dearest, flesh and blood ...*She flew to the defence of her brood*...
VERB = <u>think</u>, obsess, muse, ponder, fret, meditate, agonize, mull over, mope, ruminate, eat your heart out, dwell upon, repine ...*She constantly broods about her family*...

brook¹ = <u>stream</u>, burn (*Scot. & Northern English*), rivulet, gill (*dialect*), beck, watercourse, rill, streamlet, runnel (*literary*) ...*He threw the hatchet in the brook*...

brook² = <u>tolerate</u>, stand, allow, suffer, accept, bear, stomach, endure, swallow, hack (*slang*), abide, put up with (*informal*), withstand, countenance, support, thole (*dialect*) ...*The army will brook no weakening of its power*...

brothel = <u>whorehouse</u>, red-light district, bordello, cathouse (*U.S. slang*), house of ill repute, knocking shop (*slang*), bawdy house (*archaic*), house of prostitution, bagnio, house of ill fame, stews (*archaic*)

brother 1 = <u>male sibling</u> ...*Have you got any brothers and sisters?*...
2 = <u>comrade</u>, partner, colleague, associate, mate, pal (*informal*), companion, cock (*Brit. informal*), chum (*informal*), fellow member, confrère, compeer ...*their freedom-loving brothers*...
3 = <u>monk</u>, cleric, friar, monastic, religious, regular ...*priests and religious brothers*...

(*Related Words*)
adjective: fraternal

brotherhood 1 = <u>fellowship</u>, kinship, companionship, comradeship, friendliness, camaraderie, brotherliness …*He believed in socialism and the brotherhood of man*…

2 = association, order, union, community, society, league, alliance, clan, guild, fraternity, clique, coterie …*a secret international brotherhood*…

brotherly = fraternal, friendly, neighbourly, sympathetic, affectionate, benevolent, kind, amicable, altruistic, philanthropic

brow 1 = forehead, temple …*She wrinkled her brow inquisitively*…

2 = top, summit, peak, edge, tip, crown, verge, brink, rim, crest, brim …*He climbed to the brow of the hill*…

brown ADJECTIVE **1** = brunette, dark, bay, coffee, chocolate, brick, toasted, ginger, rust, chestnut, hazel, dun, auburn, tawny, umber, donkey brown, fuscous …*her deep brown eyes*…

2 = tanned, browned, bronze, bronzed, tan, dusky, sunburnt …*rows of bodies slowly going brown in the sun*…

VERB = fry, cook, grill, sear, sauté …*He browned the chicken in a frying pan*…

➤ **shades of brown**

browse 1 = skim, scan, glance at, survey, look through, look round, dip into, leaf through, peruse, flip through, examine cursorily …*There are plenty of biographies for him to browse*…

2 = graze, eat, feed, crop, pasture, nibble …*three red deer stags browsing 50 yards from my lodge*…

bruise NOUN = discoloration, mark, injury, trauma (*Pathology*), blemish, black mark, contusion, black-and-blue mark …*How did you get that bruise on your cheek?*…

VERB **1** = hurt, injure, mark, blacken …*I had only bruised my knee*…

2 = damage, mark, mar, blemish, discolour …*Be sure to store them carefully or they'll get bruised*…

3 = injure, hurt, pain, wound, slight, insult, sting, offend, grieve, displease, rile, pique …*Men's egos are so easily bruised*…

bruiser (*Informal*) = tough, heavy (*slang*), rough (*informal*), bully, thug, gorilla (*informal*), hard man, rowdy, tough guy, hoodlum, bully boy, ruffian, roughneck (*slang*)

bruising NOUN = discoloration, marking, swelling, contusion, ecchymosis …*She had quite a severe bruising and a cut lip*…

ADJECTIVE = hard, tough, violent, rough, fierce, ferocious, rumbustious …*a bruising battle over civil rights*…

brunt = full force, force, pressure, violence, shock, stress, impact, strain, burden, thrust

brush¹ NOUN **1** = broom, sweeper, besom …*Scrub lightly with a brush, then rinse*…

2 = conflict, fight, clash, set-to (*informal*), scrap (*informal*), confrontation, skirmish, tussle, fracas, spot of bother (*informal*), slight engagement …*It is his third brush with the law in less than a year*…

3 = encounter, meeting, confrontation, rendezvous …*the trauma of a brush with death*…

VERB **1** = clean, wash, polish, buff …*Have you brushed your teeth?*…

2 = touch, come into contact with, sweep, kiss, stroke, glance, flick, scrape, graze, caress …*I felt her hair brushing the back of my shoulder*…

PHRASES **brush someone off** (*Slang*) = ignore, cut, reject, dismiss, slight, blank (*slang*), put down, snub, disregard, scorn, disdain, spurn, rebuff, repudiate, disown, cold-shoulder, kiss off (*slang, chiefly U.S. & Canad.*), send to Coventry …*She just brushed me off*…

◆ **brush something aside** = dismiss, ignore, discount, override, disregard, sweep aside, have no time for, kiss off (*slang, chiefly U.S. & Canad.*) …*He brushed aside my views on politics*… ◆ **brush something up** or **brush up on something** = revise, study, go over, cram, polish up, read up on, relearn, bone up on (*informal*), refresh your memory …*I had hoped to brush up my Spanish*…

brush² = shrubs, bushes, scrub, underwood, undergrowth, thicket, copse, brushwood …*a meadow of low brush and grass*…

brusque = curt, short, sharp, blunt, tart, abrupt, hasty, terse, surly, gruff, impolite, monosyllabic, discourteous, unmannerly OPPOSITE ▷ polite

brutal 1 = cruel, harsh, savage, grim, vicious, ruthless, ferocious, callous, sadistic, heartless, atrocious, inhuman, merciless, cold-blooded, inhumane, brutish, bloodthirsty, remorseless, barbarous, pitiless,

---

Shades of brown

almond	chestnut	khaki	seal brown
amber	chocolate	liver	sepia
auburn	cinnabar	mahogany	sienna
bay	cinnamon	mocha	sorrel
beige	cocoa	mousy	tan
biscuit	coffee	mushroom	taupe
bisque	copper	neutral	tawny
bistre	cream	nutbrown	teak
bronze	drab	nutmeg	terracotta
buff	dun	oatmeal	tortoiseshell
burnt sienna	ecru	oxblood	umber
burnt umber	fawn	russet	walnut
butternut	ginger	rust	
café au lait	hazel	sable	
camel	henna	sand	

uncivilized, hard-hearted …*He was the victim of a very brutal murder*… OPPOSITE kind

2 = harsh, tough, severe, rough, rude, indifferent, insensitive, callous, merciless, unconcerned, uncaring, gruff, bearish, tactless, unfeeling, impolite, uncivil, unmannerly …*She spoke with a brutal honesty*… OPPOSITE sensitive

3 = bestial, animal, beastly, crude, coarse, sensual, brute, carnal, brutish …*a kind of frank and brutal passion*…

brutality = cruelty, atrocity, ferocity, savagery, ruthlessness, barbarism, inhumanity, barbarity, viciousness, brutishness, bloodthirstiness, savageness

brutally = cruelly, fiercely, savagely, ruthlessly, viciously, mercilessly, ferociously, remorselessly, in cold blood, callously, murderously, pitilessly, heartlessly, inhumanly, barbarously, brutishly, barbarically, hardheartedly

brute NOUN **1** = savage, devil, monster, beast, barbarian, fiend, swine, ogre, ghoul, sadist …*a drunken brute*…

2 = beast, animal, creature, wild animal …*a big brute of a dog*…

ADJECTIVE = physical, bodily, mindless, instinctive, senseless, unthinking …*He used brute force to take control*…

brutish = coarse, stupid, gross, cruel, savage, crude, vulgar, barbarian, crass, boorish, uncouth, loutish, subhuman, swinish

bubble NOUN = air ball, drop, bead, blister, blob, droplet, globule, vesicle …*a bubble of gas trapped under the surface*…

PLURAL NOUN = foam, fizz, froth, lather, suds, spume, effervescence, head …*With bubbles and boats, children love bathtime*…

VERB **1** = boil, seethe …*Heat the seasoned stock until it is bubbling*…

2 = foam, fizz, froth, churn, agitate, percolate, effervesce …*The fermenting wine bubbled over the top*…

3 = gurgle, splash, murmur, trickle, ripple, babble, trill, burble, lap, purl, plash …*He looked at the stream bubbling through the trees nearby*…

bubbly 1 = lively, happy, excited, animated, merry, bouncy, elated, sparky, alive and kicking, full of beans (*informal*) …*a bubbly girl who likes to laugh*…

2 = frothy, sparkling, fizzy, effervescent, carbonated, foamy, sudsy, lathery …*a nice hot bubbly bath*…

buccaneer = pirate, privateer, corsair, freebooter, sea-rover

buck NOUN (*Archaic*) = gallant, blood, spark, blade, beau, dandy, fop, popinjay, coxcomb …*He'd been a real hellraiser as a young buck*…

PHRASES **buck something** or **someone up** = cheer up, encourage, brighten, hearten, enliven, perk up, gladden, gee up, inspirit, jolly along (*informal*) …*The aim was to buck up their spirits*…

buckle NOUN = fastener, catch, clip, clasp, hasp …*He wore a belt with a large brass buckle*…

VERB **1** = fasten, close, secure, hook, clasp …*A man

came out buckling his belt*…

2 = distort, bend, warp, crumple, contort …*A freak wave had buckled the deck*…

3 = collapse, bend, twist, fold, give way, subside, cave in, crumple …*His right leg buckled under him*…

PHRASES **buckle down** (*Informal*) = apply yourself, set to, fall to, pitch in, get busy, get cracking (*informal*), exert yourself, put your shoulder to the wheel …*I just buckled down and got on with playing*…

bud NOUN = shoot, branch, sprout, twig, sprig, offshoot, scion …*The first buds appeared on the trees*…

VERB = develop, grow, shoot, sprout, burgeon, burst forth, pullulate …*The leaves were budding on the trees now*…

Buddhism

Schools of Buddhism

Foism	Pure Land Buddhism
Geluk	Rinjai
Hinayana	Sakya
Jodo	Soka Gakkai
Kagyü	Soto
Lamaism	Tendai
Mahayana	Theravada
Nichiren	Vajrayana
Nyingma	Zen

budding = developing, beginning, growing, promising, potential, flowering, burgeoning, fledgling, embryonic, nascent, incipient, germinal

buddy (*Chiefly U.S. & Canad.*) = friend, mate (*informal*), pal, companion, comrade, chum (*informal*), crony, main man (*slang, chiefly U.S.*), homeboy (*slang, chiefly U.S.*), cobber (*Austral. or old-fashioned N.Z. informal*)

budge 1 = yield, change, bend, concede, surrender, comply, give way, capitulate …*Both sides say they will not budge*…

2 = persuade, influence, convince, sway …*The Prime Minister was not to be budged by the verbal assault*…

3 = move, roll, slide, stir, give way, change position …*The snake still refused to budge*…

4 = dislodge, move, push, roll, remove, transfer, shift, slide, stir, propel …*I pulled and pulled but I couldn't budge it*…

budget NOUN = allowance, means, funds, income, finances, resources, allocation …*A designer would be beyond their budget*…

VERB = plan, estimate, allocate, cost, ration, apportion, cost out …*I'm learning how to budget my finances*…

buff¹ ADJECTIVE = fawn, cream, tan, beige, yellowish, ecru, straw-coloured, sand-coloured, yellowish-brown, biscuit-coloured, camel-coloured, oatmeal-coloured …*a buff envelope*…

VERB = polish, clean, smooth, brush, shine, rub, wax, brighten, burnish …*He was already buffing the car's hubs*…

PHRASES **in the buff** = naked, bare, nude, in the raw

Bugs http://www.insects.org/entophiles/index.html

bedbug *or* (*Southern U.S.*) chinch	leaf-hopper
cicada *or* cicala	Maori bug
damsel bug	mealy bug
debris bug	pond-skater, water strider, *or* water skater
froghopper, spittle insect, *or* spittle bug	shield bug *or* stink bug
harlequin bug	water boatman
kissing bug	water bug
lace bug	water scorpion

(*informal*), unclothed, in the altogether (*informal*), buck naked (*slang*), unclad, in your birthday suit (*informal*), scuddy (*slang*), without a stitch on (*informal*), with bare skin, in the bare scud (*slang*) …*My character had to appear in the buff for some scenes*…
➤ **shades of brown** ➤ **shades of yellow**

buff² (*Informal*) = expert, fan, addict, enthusiast, freak (*informal*), admirer, whizz (*informal*), devotee, connoisseur, fiend (*informal*), grandmaster, hotshot (*informal*), aficionado, wonk (*informal*), maven (*U.S.*), fundi (*S. African*) …*She is a real film buff*…

buffer = safeguard, screen, shield, cushion, intermediary, bulwark

buffet¹ 1 = smorgasbord, counter, cold table …*A cold buffet had been laid out in the dining room*…
2 = snack bar, café, cafeteria, brasserie, salad bar, refreshment counter …*We sat in the station buffet sipping tea*…

buffet² = knock, push, bang, rap, slap, bump, smack, shove, thump, cuff, jolt, wallop (*informal*), box …*Their plane had been severely buffeted by storms*…

buffoon = clown, fool, comic, comedian, wag, joker, jester, dag (*N.Z. informal*), harlequin, droll, silly billy (*informal*), joculator *or* (*fem.*) joculatrix

bug NOUN 1 (*Informal*) = illness, disease, complaint, virus, infection, disorder, disability, sickness, ailment, malaise, affliction, malady, lurgy (*informal*) …*I think I've got a bit of a stomach bug*…
2 = fault, failing, virus, error, defect, flaw, blemish, imperfection, glitch, gremlin …*There is a bug in the software*…
3 (*Informal*) = mania, passion, rage, obsession, craze, fad, thing (*informal*) …*I've definitely been bitten by the gardening bug*…
VERB 1 = tap, eavesdrop, listen in on, wiretap …*He heard they were planning to bug his office*…
2 (*Informal*) = annoy, bother, disturb, needle (*informal*), plague, irritate, harass, hassle (*informal*), aggravate (*informal*), badger, gall, nettle, pester, vex, irk, get under your skin (*informal*), get on your nerves (*informal*), nark (*Brit., Austral., & N.Z. slang*), get up your nose (*informal*), be on your back (*slang*), get in your hair (*informal*), get on your wick (*Brit. slang*) …*I only did it to bug my parents*…
➤ **bugs**

build VERB 1 = construct, make, raise, put up, assemble, erect, fabricate, form …*Developers are now proposing to build a hotel on the site*… OPPOSITE demolish

2 = establish, start, begin, found, base, set up, institute, constitute, initiate, originate, formulate, inaugurate …*I wanted to build a relationship with my team*… OPPOSITE finish
3 = develop, increase, improve, extend, strengthen, intensify, enlarge, amplify, augment …*Diplomats hope the meetings will build mutual trust*… OPPOSITE decrease
NOUN = physique, form, body, figure, shape, structure, frame …*the smallness of his build*…
PHRASES **build something up** = increase, develop, improve, extend, expand, add to, strengthen, enhance, reinforce, intensify, heighten, fortify, amplify, augment …*We can build up speed gradually and safely*… ◆ **build something** *or* **someone up** = hype, promote, advertise, boost, plug (*informal*), spotlight, publicize …*The media will report on it and the tabloids will build it up*…

building = structure, house, construction, dwelling, erection, edifice, domicile, pile
➤ **buildings and monuments**

build-up 1 = increase, development, growth, expansion, accumulation, enlargement, escalation, upsurge, intensification, augmentation …*a build-up of troops*…
2 = accumulation, accretion …*a build-up of gases in the city's sewers*…
3 = hype, promotion, publicity, plug (*informal*), puff, razzmatazz (*slang*), brouhaha, ballyhoo (*informal*) …*the build-up for the film*…

built-in = essential, integral, included, incorporated, inherent, implicit, in-built, intrinsic, inseparable, immanent

bulbous = bulging, rounded, swelling, swollen, bloated, convex

bulge VERB 1 = swell out, project, expand, swell, stand out, stick out, protrude, puff out, distend, bag …*He bulges out of his black T-shirt*…
2 = stick out, stand out, protrude …*His eyes seemed to bulge like those of a toad*…
NOUN 1 = lump, swelling, bump, projection, hump, protuberance, protrusion …*Why won't those bulges on your hips and thighs go?*… OPPOSITE hollow
2 = increase, rise, boost, surge, intensification …*a bulge in aircraft sales*…

bulk NOUN 1 = size, volume, dimensions, magnitude, substance, vastness, amplitude, immensity, bigness, largeness, massiveness …*the shadowy bulk of an ancient barn*…
2 = weight, size, mass, heaviness, poundage,

Buildings and monuments

Admiralty House	Eiffel Tower	Longleat House
Althorp House	Elysées Palace	Louvre
Alhambra	Empire State Building	Masada
Angel of the North	Forbidden City	Mansion House
Arc de Triomphe	Hampton Court Palace	Monument
Barbican	Hermitage	Nelson's Column
Beehive	Holyroodhouse	Pentagon
Big Ben	Houses of Parliament	Saint James's Palace
Blenheim Palace	Kaaba	Scone Palace
Buckingham Palace	Kensington Palace	Taj Mahal
Cenotaph	Knossos	Tower of London
Charminar	Kremlin	Vatican
Cleopatra's Needle	Lambeth Palace	Palace of Versailles
Crystal Palace	Lateran	Westminster Abbey
Edinburgh Castle	Leaning Tower of Pisa	White House

---

portliness …*Despite his bulk he moved lightly on his feet*…

3 = majority, mass, most, body, quantity, best part, major part, lion's share, better part, generality, preponderance, main part, plurality, nearly all, greater number …*The vast bulk of imports and exports is carried by sea*…

PHRASES **bulk large** = be important, dominate, loom, stand out, loom large, carry weight, preponderate, threaten …*Propaganda bulks large in their plans*…

Word Power

bulk – The use of a plural noun after *bulk*, as in sense 3, although common, is considered by some to be incorrect and should be avoided. This usage is most commonly encountered, according to the Bank of English, when referring to *funds* and *profits*: *the bulk of our profits stem from the sale of beer*. The synonyms *majority* and *most* would work better in this context.

---

bulky = large, big, huge, heavy, massive, enormous, substantial, immense, mega (*slang*), very large, mammoth, colossal, cumbersome, weighty, hulking, unwieldy, ponderous, voluminous, unmanageable, elephantine, massy, ginormous (*informal*), humongous *or* humungous (*U.S. slang*) OPPOSITE> small

bulldoze **1** = demolish, level, destroy, flatten, knock down, tear down, raze …*She defeated developers who wanted to bulldoze her home*…
2 = push, force, drive, thrust, shove, propel …*He bulldozed through the Tigers' defence*…
3 (*Informal*) = force, bully, intimidate, railroad (*informal*), cow, hector, coerce, dragoon, browbeat, put the screws on …*My parents tried to bulldoze me into going to college*…

bullet = projectile, ball, shot, missile, slug, pellet

bulletin = report, account, statement, message, communication, announcement, dispatch, communiqué, notification, news flash

bully NOUN = persecutor, tough, oppressor, tormentor, bully boy, browbeater, coercer, ruffian, intimidator …*I fell victim to the office bully*…
VERB **1** = persecute, intimidate, torment, hound, oppress, pick on, victimize, terrorize, push around (*slang*), ill-treat, ride roughshod over, maltreat, tyrannize, overbear …*I wasn't going to let him bully me*…
2 = force, coerce, railroad (*informal*), bulldoze (*informal*), dragoon, pressurize, browbeat, cow, hector, press-gang, domineer, bullyrag …*She used to bully me into doing my schoolwork*…

bulwark **1** = fortification, defence, bastion, buttress, rampart, redoubt, outwork …*a bulwark against the English*…
2 = defence, support, safeguard, security, guard, buffer, mainstay …*a bulwark of democracy*…

bumbling = clumsy, awkward, blundering, bungling, incompetent, inefficient, lumbering, inept, maladroit, unco (*Austral. slang*) OPPOSITE> efficient

bump VERB **1** = knock, hit, strike, crash, smash, slam, bang …*He bumped his head on the low beam*…
2 = jerk, shake, bounce, rattle, jar, jog, lurch, jolt, jostle, jounce …*We left the road again and bumped over the mountainside*…
NOUN **1** = knock, hit, blow, shock, impact, rap, collision, thump …*Small children often cry after a minor bump*…
2 = thud, crash, knock, smash, bang, smack, thump, clump, wallop (*informal*), clunk, clonk …*I felt a little bump and knew instinctively what had happened*…
3 = lump, swelling, bulge, hump, node, nodule, protuberance, contusion …*She got a large bump on her forehead*…

PHRASES **bump into someone** (*Informal*) = meet, encounter, come across, run into, run across, meet up with, chance upon, happen upon, light upon …*I happened to bump into Mervyn Johns in the hallway*…
♦ **bump someone off** (*Slang*) = murder, kill, assassinate, remove, do in (*slang*), eliminate, take out (*slang*), wipe out (*informal*), dispatch, finish off, do away with, blow away (*slang, chiefly U.S.*), knock off (*slang*), liquidate, rub out (*U.S. slang*) …*They will probably bump you off anyway*…

bumper = <u>exceptional</u>, excellent, exo (*Austral. slang*), massive, unusual, mega (*slang*), jumbo (*informal*), abundant, whacking (*informal, chiefly Brit.*), spanking (*informal*), whopping (*informal*), bountiful

bumpy 1 = <u>uneven</u>, rough, pitted, irregular, rutted, lumpy, potholed, knobby ...*bumpy cobbled streets*...
2 = <u>jolting</u>, jarring, bouncy, choppy, jerky, bone-breaking, jolty ...*a hot and bumpy journey across the desert*...

bunch NOUN 1 = <u>group</u>, band, crowd, party, team, troop, gathering, crew (*informal*), gang, knot, mob, flock, swarm, multitude, posse (*informal*), bevy ...*The players were a great bunch*...
2 = <u>bouquet</u>, spray, sheaf ...*He had left a huge bunch of flowers in her hotel room*...
3 = <u>cluster</u>, clump ...*She had fallen asleep clutching a fat bunch of grapes*...
PHRASES **bunch together** or **up** = <u>group</u>, crowd, mass, collect, assemble, cluster, flock, herd, huddle, congregate ...*People bunched up at all the exits*...

bundle NOUN = <u>bunch</u>, group, collection, mass, pile, quantity, stack, heap, rick, batch, accumulation, assortment ...*He gathered the bundles of clothing into his arms*...
VERB = <u>push</u>, thrust, shove, throw, rush, hurry, hasten, jostle, hustle ...*They bundled him into a taxi*...
PHRASES **bundle someone up** = <u>wrap up</u>, swathe, muffle up, clothe warmly ...*Harry greeted them bundled up in a long coat and a fur hat*... ♦ **bundle something up** = <u>package</u>, tie, pack, bind, wrap, tie up, bale, fasten, truss, tie together, palletize ...*possessions bundled up and carried in weary arms*...

bungle = <u>mess up</u>, blow (*slang*), ruin, spoil, blunder, fudge, screw up (*informal*), botch, cock up (*Brit. slang*), miscalculate, make a mess of, mismanage, muff, foul up, make a nonsense of (*informal*), bodge (*informal*), make a pig's ear of (*informal*), flub (*U.S. slang*), crool or cruel (*Austral. slang*), louse up (*slang*) OPPOSITE accomplish

bungling = <u>incompetent</u>, blundering, awkward, clumsy, inept, botching, cack-handed (*informal*), maladroit, ham-handed (*informal*), unskilful, ham-fisted (*informal*), unco (*Austral. slang*)

bunk¹
PHRASES **do a bunk** (*Brit. slang*) = <u>run away</u>, flee, bolt, clear out (*informal*), beat it (*slang*), abscond, decamp, do a runner (*slang*), run for it (*informal*), cut and run (*informal*), scram (*informal*), fly the coop (*U.S. & Canad. informal*), skedaddle (*informal*), take a powder (*U.S. & Canad. slang*), take it on the lam (*U.S. & Canad. slang*) ...*His live-in lover has done a bunk because he won't marry her*...

bunk² or **bunkum** (*Informal*) = <u>nonsense</u>, rubbish, rot, crap (*slang*), garbage (*informal*), trash, hot air (*informal*), tosh (*slang, chiefly Brit.*), bilge (*informal*), twaddle, tripe (*informal*), guff (*slang*), havers (*Scot.*), moonshine, baloney (*informal*), hogwash, bizzo (*Austral. slang*), bull's wool (*Austral. & N.Z. slang*), hokum (*slang, chiefly U.S. & Canad.*), piffle (*informal*), tomfoolery, poppycock (*informal*), balderdash, bosh (*informal*), eyewash (*informal*), kak (*S. African taboo*

slang), stuff and nonsense, hooey (*slang*), tommyrot, horsefeathers (*U.S. slang*), tarradiddle ...*Henry Ford's opinion that 'history is bunk'*...

buoy NOUN = <u>float</u>, guide, signal, marker, beacon ...*We released the buoy and drifted back on the tide*...
PHRASES **buoy someone up** = <u>encourage</u>, support, boost, cheer, sustain, hearten, cheer up, keep afloat, gee up ...*They are buoyed up by a sense of hope*...

buoyancy 1 = <u>floatability</u>, lightness, weightlessness ...*Air can be pumped into the diving suit to increase buoyancy*...
2 = <u>cheerfulness</u>, bounce (*informal*), pep, animation, good humour, high spirits, zing (*informal*), liveliness, spiritedness, cheeriness, sunniness ...*a mood of buoyancy and optimism*...

buoyant 1 = <u>cheerful</u>, happy, bright, lively, sunny, animated, upbeat (*informal*), joyful, carefree, bouncy, breezy, genial, jaunty, chirpy (*informal*), sparky, vivacious, debonair, blithe, full of beans (*informal*), peppy (*informal*), light-hearted ...*She was in a buoyant mood*... OPPOSITE gloomy
2 = <u>floating</u>, light, floatable ...*a small and buoyant boat*...

burden NOUN 1 = <u>trouble</u>, care, worry, trial, weight, responsibility, stress, strain, anxiety, sorrow, grievance, affliction, onus, albatross, millstone, encumbrance ...*Her illness will be an impossible burden on him*...
2 = <u>load</u>, weight, cargo, freight, bale, consignment, encumbrance ...*She heaved her burden into the back*...
VERB = <u>weigh down</u>, worry, load, tax, strain, bother, overwhelm, handicap, oppress, inconvenience, overload, saddle with, encumber, trammel, incommode ...*We decided not to burden him with the news*...
(*Related Words*)
adjective: onerous

burdensome = <u>troublesome</u>, trying, taxing, difficult, heavy, crushing, exacting, oppressive, weighty, onerous, irksome

bureau 1 = <u>agency</u> ...*the foreign employment bureau*...
2 = <u>office</u>, department, section, branch, station, unit, division, subdivision ...*the paper's Washington bureau*...
3 = <u>desk</u>, writing desk ...*A simple writing bureau sat in front of the window*...

bureaucracy 1 = <u>government</u>, officials, authorities, administration, ministry, the system, civil service, directorate, officialdom, corridors of power ...*State bureaucracies tend to stifle enterprise and initiative*...
2 = <u>red tape</u>, regulations, officialdom, officialese, bumbledom ...*People complain about having to deal with too much bureaucracy*...

bureaucrat = <u>official</u>, minister, officer, administrator, civil servant, public servant, functionary, apparatchik, office-holder, mandarin

burglar = <u>housebreaker</u>, thief, robber, pilferer, filcher, cat burglar, sneak thief, picklock

burglary = <u>breaking and entering</u>, housebreaking,

break-in

burial = funeral, interment, burying, obsequies, entombment, inhumation, exequies, sepulture

burial ground = graveyard, cemetery, churchyard, necropolis, golgotha (*rare*), God's acre

buried 1= absorbed, engrossed, preoccupied, lost, committed, concentrating, occupied, devoted, caught up, intent, immersed, rapt …*She was buried in a book*…
2 = hidden, covered …*buried treasure*…

burlesque NOUN = parody, mockery, satire, caricature, send-up (*Brit. informal*), spoof (*informal*), travesty, takeoff (*informal*) …*The book read like a black comic burlesque*…
ADJECTIVE = satirical, comic, mocking, mock, farcical, travestying, ironical, parodic, mock-heroic, caricatural, hudibrastic …*a trio of burlesque stereotypes*…

burly = brawny, strong, powerful, big, strapping, hefty, muscular, sturdy, stout, bulky, stocky, hulking, beefy (*informal*), well-built, thickset OPPOSITE scrawny

burn 1 = be on fire, blaze, be ablaze, smoke, flame, glow, flare, flicker, go up in flames …*I suddenly realized the blanket was burning*…
2 = set on fire, light, ignite, kindle, incinerate, reduce to ashes …*He found out he'd won the Lottery, but he'd burnt the ticket*…
3 = underline{scorch}, toast, sear, char, singe, brand …*I burnt the toast*…
4 = sting, hurt, smart, tingle, bite, pain …*When you go to the toilet, it burns and stings*…
5 = be passionate, blaze, be excited, be aroused, be inflamed …*The young boy was burning with a fierce ambition*…
6 = underline{seethe}, fume, be angry, simmer, smoulder …*He was burning with rage*…

burning 1 = intense, passionate, earnest, eager, frantic, frenzied, ardent, fervent, impassioned, zealous, vehement, all-consuming, fervid …*I had a burning ambition to become a journalist*… OPPOSITE mild
2 = blazing, flaming, fiery, ignited, smouldering, glowing, ablaze, in flames, afire …*He was last seen alive as he ran into his burning house*…
3 = flashing, blazing, flaming, gleaming, fiery …*She glared at both of them with burning, reproachful eyes*…
4 = crucial, important, pressing, significant, essential, vital, critical, acute, compelling, urgent …*a burning question*…

burnish 1 = improve, enhance, brighten, refine, cultivate, brush up, touch up, emend …*The company badly needs a president who can burnish its image*…
2 = polish, shine, buff, brighten, rub up, furbish …*His shoes were burnished, his shirt perfectly pressed*… OPPOSITE scuff

burrow NOUN = hole, shelter, tunnel, den, lair, retreat …*a rabbit's burrow*…
VERB 1 = underline{dig}, tunnel, excavate …*The larvae burrow into cracks in the floor*…
2 = delve, search, dig, probe, ferret, rummage, forage, fossick (*Austral. & N.Z.*) …*He burrowed into the pile of charts*…

burst VERB 1 = explode, blow up, break, split, crack, shatter, fragment, shiver, disintegrate, puncture, rupture …*She burst the balloon with a pin*… …*The driver lost control when a tyre burst*…
2 = rush, run, break, break out, erupt, spout, gush forth …*Water burst through the dam and flooded their villages*…
3 = barge, charge, rush, shove …*Gunmen burst into his home and opened fire*…
NOUN 1 = rush, surge, fit, outbreak, outburst, spate, gush, torrent, eruption, spurt, outpouring …*short bursts of activity*…
2 = explosion, crack, blast, blasting, bang, discharge …*a burst of machine-gun fire*…
ADJECTIVE = ruptured, flat, punctured, split, rent …*a burst tyre*…

bury 1 = inter, lay to rest, entomb, sepulchre, consign to the grave, inearth, inhume, inurn …*soldiers who helped to bury the dead*… OPPOSITE dig up
2 = hide, cover, conceal, stash (*informal*), secrete, cache, stow away …*She buried it under some leaves*… OPPOSITE uncover
3 = underline{sink}, embed, immerse, enfold …*She buried her face in the pillows*…
4 = forget, draw a veil over, think no more of, put in the past, not give another thought to …*It is time to bury our past misunderstandings*…
5 = engross, involve, occupy, interest, busy, engage, absorb, preoccupy, immerse …*His reaction was to withdraw, to bury himself in work*…

bush NOUN = shrub, plant, hedge, thicket, shrubbery …*Trees and bushes grow down to the water's edge*…
PHRASES **the bush** = the wilds, brush, scrub, woodland, backwoods, back country (*U.S.*), scrubland, backlands (*U.S.*) …*He was shot dead while travelling in the bush*…

bushy = thick, bristling, spreading, rough, stiff, fuzzy, fluffy, unruly, shaggy, wiry, luxuriant, bristly

busily = actively, briskly, intently, earnestly, strenuously, speedily, purposefully, diligently, energetically, assiduously, industriously

business 1 = trade, selling, trading, industry, manufacturing, commerce, dealings, merchandising …*young people seeking a career in business*…
2 = establishment, company, firm, concern, organization, corporation, venture, enterprise …*The company was a family business*…
3 = profession, work, calling, job, line, trade, career, function, employment, craft, occupation, pursuit, vocation, métier …*May I ask what business you are in?*…
4 = matter, issue, subject, point, problem, question, responsibility, task, duty, function, topic, assignment …*Parenting can be a stressful business*…
5 = concern, affair …*My sex life is my own business*…
➤ **business jargon**

businesslike = efficient, professional, practical, regular, correct, organized, routine, thorough, systematic, orderly, matter-of-fact, methodical, well-ordered, workaday OPPOSITE inefficient

businessman *or* **businesswoman** = executive,

Word Power: Business jargon

Many people find the excessive use of business jargon both irritating and pretentious. It is worth noting that in a recent survey carried out among 500 personnel managers, the use of business jargon and buzz phrases was cited as the number two CV crime, coming second only to poor presentation. It is therefore advisable to avoid using any words or phrases which could be considered as coming into this category; there are other, more general, words or expressions which you can substitute for them, and in doing so, avoid the possibility of annoying your readers or listeners.

Words and phrases to avoid using include:

all on the same page/all singing from the same hymnsheet: a situation in which all the people concerned are working together towards the same goal, and thinking along the same lines.

binary thinker: a person who thinks in absolute terms, and to whom things are either black or white, and everything is a yes-or-no proposition.

bottleneck: a situation in which progress cannot be achieved because one person or factor is causing a hold-up.

brainstorm: a meeting in which people are encouraged to propose any ideas which come to mind, regardless of whether they seem practical or not, in order to encourage creative thinking.

bring someone on board: to get someone involved in a project.

can-do: confident and resourceful in the face of adversity.

deliverable: a manageable target.

downsizing/rationalizing/rightsizing: these are all euphemisms for *sacking* and *redundancies* which fool nobody.

focus group: a group of people gathered by a market research company to discuss and assess a product or service.

goal-oriented: focusing single-mindedly on a goal.

hands-on manager: a manager who likes to get involved in all aspects of the business, at all levels.

in *or* **out of the loop:** being part of, or excluded from, a group of people to whom information is circulated.

learning curve: the rate at which someone learns a new job or skill.

mission statement: an official statement of the aims and objectives of a business or other organisation.

on a go-forward basis: making progress.

open a dialogue: begin discussions.

own a project: be responsible for a project.

point of contact: the person you are supposed to contact to discuss a specific matter or project.

proactive: tending to initiate change rather than simply reacting to events.

push the envelope: to push the boundaries of what is considered possible.

results-driven: concentrating purely on the end result.

sidebar meeting: a meeting to be held later on to discuss a subject which is being postponed from discussion in the current meeting.

take a discussion offline: to decide to discuss something at another time, possibly in a *sidebar meeting*.

team player: a person who works for the general good of the project or business, rather than for personal gain or credit.

think outside the box: to think in an unorthodox, original, and creative way.

touch base with someone: make contact with someone to discuss or report on a specific matter or project.

vis-a-vis: with regard to.

window of opportunity: a brief space of time when something can be done, such as taking advantage of a situation or arranging a meeting with a person who is difficult to get hold of.

worst-case scenario: if the worst comes to the worst.

---

director, manager, merchant, capitalist, administrator, entrepreneur, tycoon, industrialist, financier, tradesman, homme d'affaires (*French*)

bust¹ = bosom, breasts, chest, front ...*Good posture also helps your bust look bigger...*

bust² (*Informal*) **VERB 1** = break, smash, split, burst, shatter, fracture, rupture, break into fragments ...*They will have to bust the door to get him out...*
2 = arrest, catch, lift (*slang*), raid, cop (*slang*), nail (*informal*), collar (*informal*), nab (*informal*), feel your collar (*slang*) ...*They were busted for possession of cannabis...*
NOUN = arrest, capture, raid, cop (*slang*) ...*He was imprisoned after a drug bust...*
PHRASES go bust = go bankrupt, fail, break, be ruined, become insolvent ...*Hundreds of restaurants went bust last year...*

bustle VERB = hurry, tear, rush, dash, scramble, fuss, flutter, beetle, hasten, scuttle, scurry, scamper ...*My mother bustled around the kitchen...* **OPPOSITE** idle
NOUN = activity, to-do, stir, excitement, hurry, fuss, flurry, haste, agitation, commotion, ado, tumult, hurly-burly, pother ...*the hustle and bustle of modern life...* **OPPOSITE** inactivity

bustling = busy, full, crowded, rushing, active, stirring, lively, buzzing, energetic, humming, swarming, thronged, hustling, teeming, astir

busy ADJECTIVE 1 = active, brisk, diligent, industrious, assiduous, rushed off your feet ...*He's a very busy man...* **OPPOSITE** idle
2 = occupied with, working, engaged in, on duty, employed in, hard at work, engrossed in, in harness, on active service ...*Life is what happens to you while you're busy making other plans...* **OPPOSITE**

unoccupied

3 = <u>hectic</u>, full, active, tiring, exacting, energetic, strenuous, on the go (*informal*) ...*I'd had a busy day and was rather tired...*

PHRASES **busy yourself** = <u>occupy yourself</u>, be engrossed, immerse yourself, involve yourself, amuse yourself, absorb yourself, employ yourself, engage yourself, keep busy or occupied ...*He busied himself with the camera...*

but **CONJUNCTION** = <u>however</u>, still, yet, nevertheless ...*'But,' he added, 'the vast majority must accept a common future.'...*

PREPOSITION = <u>except (for)</u>, save, bar, barring, excepting, excluding, with the exception of ...*He was forced to wind up everything but the hotel business...*

ADVERB = <u>only</u>, just, simply, merely ...*St Anton is but a snowball's throw away from Lech...*

butcher **NOUN** = <u>murderer</u>, killer, slaughterer, slayer, destroyer, liquidator, executioner, cut-throat, exterminator ...*Klaus Barbie was known in France as the Butcher of Lyon...*

VERB **1** = <u>slaughter</u>, prepare, carve, cut up, dress, cut, clean, joint ...*Pigs were butchered, hams were hung to dry from the ceiling...*

2 = <u>kill</u>, slaughter, massacre, destroy, cut down, assassinate, slay, liquidate, exterminate, put to the sword ...*Our people are being butchered in their own homes...*

3 = <u>mess up</u>, destroy, ruin, wreck, spoil, mutilate, botch, bodge (*informal*) ...*I am not in Cannes because they butchered my film...*

butchery = <u>slaughter</u>, killing, murder, massacre, bloodshed, carnage, mass murder, blood-letting, blood bath

butt¹ **1** = <u>end</u>, handle, shaft, stock, shank, hilt, haft ...*Troops used tear gas and rifle butts to break up the protests...*

2 = <u>stub</u>, end, base, foot, tip, tail, leftover, fag end (*informal*) ...*He paused to stub out the butt of his cigar...*

butt² = <u>target</u>, victim, object, point, mark, subject, dupe, laughing stock, Aunt Sally ...*He is still the butt of cruel jokes about his humble origins...*

butt³ **VERB** = <u>knock</u>, push, bump, punch, buck, thrust, ram, shove, poke, buffet, prod, jab, bunt ...*The male butted me...*

PHRASES **butt in** **1** = <u>interfere</u>, meddle, intrude, heckle, barge in (*informal*), stick your nose in, put your oar in ...*Nobody asked you to butt in...* **2** = <u>interrupt</u>, cut in, break in, chip in (*informal*), put your two cents in (*U.S. slang*) ...*Could I just butt in here and say something?...*

butt⁴ = <u>cask</u>, drum, barrel, cylinder ...*The hose is great for watering your garden from your water butt...*

butter

PHRASES **butter someone up** = <u>flatter</u>, coax, cajole, pander to, blarney, wheedle, suck up to (*informal*), soft-soap, fawn on or upon, honey up, oil your tongue

butterfly

Related Words
young: caterpillar, chrysalis or chrysalid
enthusiast: lepidopterist
➤ **butterflies and moths**

buttocks = <u>bottom</u>, behind (*informal*), bum (*Brit. slang*), backside (*informal*), seat, rear, tail (*informal*), butt (*U.S. & Canad. informal*), buns (*U.S. slang*), rump, posterior, haunches, hindquarters, derrière (*euphemistic*), tush (*U.S. slang*), fundament, gluteus maximus (*Anatomy*), jacksy (*Brit. slang*)

buttonhole = <u>detain</u>, catch, grab, intercept, accost, waylay, take aside

buttress **NOUN** = <u>support</u>, shore, prop, brace, pier, reinforcement, strut, mainstay, stanchion, stay, abutment ...*a buttress of rock...*

VERB = <u>support</u>, sustain, strengthen, shore, prop, reinforce, back up, brace, uphold, bolster, prop up, shore up, augment ...*His tough line is buttressed by a democratic mandate...*

buxom = <u>plump</u>, ample, voluptuous, busty, well-rounded, curvaceous, comely, bosomy, full-bosomed **OPPOSITE** slender

buy **VERB** = <u>purchase</u>, get, score (*slang*), secure, pay for, obtain, acquire, invest in, shop for, procure ...*He could not afford to buy a house...* **OPPOSITE** sell

NOUN = <u>purchase</u>, deal, bargain, acquisition, steal (*informal*), snip (*informal*), giveaway ...*a good buy...*

PHRASES **buy someone off** = <u>bribe</u>, square, fix (*informal*), pay off (*informal*), lure, corrupt, get at, suborn, grease someone's palm (*slang*), influence by gifts, oil the palm of (*informal*) ...*policies designed to buy off the working-class...*

buzz **VERB** = <u>hum</u>, whizz, drone, whir ...*Attack helicopters buzzed across the city...*

NOUN **1** = <u>hum</u>, buzzing, murmur, drone, whir, bombilation or bombination (*literary*) ...*the irritating buzz of an insect...*

2 (*Informal*) = <u>gossip</u>, news, report, latest (*informal*), word, scandal, rumour, whisper, dirt (*U.S. slang*), gen (*Brit. informal*), hearsay, scuttlebutt (*U.S. slang*) ...*The buzz is that she knows something...*

by **PREPOSITION** **1** = <u>through</u>, under the aegis of, through the agency of ...*The feast was served by his mother and sisters...*

2 = <u>via</u>, over, by way of ...*The train passes by Oxford...*

3 = <u>near</u>, past, along, close to, closest to, neighbouring, next to, beside, nearest to, adjoining, adjacent to ...*She was sitting in a rocking chair by the window...*

ADVERB = <u>nearby</u>, close, handy, at hand, within reach ...*Large numbers of security police stood by...*

PHRASES **by and by** = <u>presently</u>, shortly, soon, eventually, one day, before long, in a while, anon, in the course of time, erelong (*archaic or poetic*) ...*By and by the light gradually grew fainter...*

bygone = <u>past</u>, former, previous, lost, forgotten, ancient, of old, one-time, departed, extinct, gone by, erstwhile, antiquated, of yore, olden, past recall, sunk in oblivion **OPPOSITE** future

bypass **1** = <u>get round</u>, avoid, evade, circumvent,

Butterflies and moths http://tolweb.org/tree?group=Lepidoptera

apollo	gipsy moth	processionary moth
argus	goldtail moth *or* yellowtail	purple emperor
bag moth	(moth)	puss moth
bagworm moth	grass moth	red admiral
bell moth	grayling	red underwing
bogong *or* bugong (moth)	hairstreak	ringlet
brimstone	herald moth	silver-Y
brown-tail moth	hawk moth, sphinx moth, *or*	skipper
buff-tip moth	hummingbird moth	small white
cabbage white	house moth	snout
cactoblastis	Io moth	speckled wood
Camberwell beauty *or* (*U.S.*)	Kentish glory	swallowtail
mourning cloak	kitten moth	swift
cardinal	lackey moth	tapestry moth
carpenter moth	lappet moth	thorn (moth)
carpet moth	large white *or* cabbage white	tiger (moth)
cleopatra	leopard moth	tussock moth
comma butterfly	lobster moth	two-tailed pasha
copper	luna moth	umber (moth)
cecropia moth	magpie moth	vapourer moth
cinnabar	marbled white	wave (moth)
clearwing *or* clearwing moth	monarch	wax moth, honeycomb moth, *or*
Clifden nonpareil	mother-of-pearl moth	bee moth
codlin(g) moth	Mother Shipton	wall brown
death's-head moth	old lady	white
drinker moth *or* drinker	orange-tip	white admiral
egger *or* eggar	painted lady	winter moth
ermine moth *or* ermine	peacock butterfly	yellow
festoon	peppered moth	yellow underwing
ghost moth	privet hawk	

outmanoeuvre, body-swerve (*Scot.*) …*Regulators worry that controls could easily be bypassed…*
2 = go round, skirt, circumvent, depart from, deviate from, pass round, detour round …*Money for new roads to bypass cities…* OPPOSITE⟩ cross

bystander = onlooker, passer-by, spectator, witness, observer, viewer, looker-on, watcher, eyewitness
OPPOSITE⟩ participant

byword = saying, slogan, motto, maxim, gnome, adage, proverb, epithet, dictum, precept, aphorism, saw, apophthegm

C c

cab = <u>taxi</u>, minicab, taxicab, hackney, hackney carriage

cabal 1 = <u>clique</u>, set, party, league, camp, coalition, faction, caucus, junta, coterie, schism, confederacy, conclave …*He had been chosen by a cabal of fellow senators*…
2 = <u>plot</u>, scheme, intrigue, conspiracy, machination …*The left saw it as a bourgeois cabal*…

cabin 1 = <u>room</u>, berth, quarters, compartment, deckhouse …*The steward showed her to a small cabin*…
2 = <u>hut</u>, shed, cottage, lodge, cot (*archaic*), shack, chalet, shanty, hovel, bothy …*a log cabin in the woods*…

cabinet 1 = <u>cupboard</u>, case, locker, dresser, closet, press, chiffonier …*a display cabinet with gleaming trophies*…
2 *often cap.* = <u>council</u>, committee, administration, ministry, assembly, board …*The radically-changed Cabinet of the Prime Minister includes eight new ministers*…

cache = <u>store</u>, fund, supply, reserve, treasury, accumulation, stockpile, hoard, stash (*informal*)

cackle VERB = <u>laugh</u>, giggle, chuckle …*The old lady cackled with glee*…
NOUN = <u>laugh</u>, giggle, chuckle …*He let out a brief cackle of triumph*…

cacophony = <u>discord</u>, racket, din, dissonance, disharmony, stridency

cad (*Old-fashioned, informal*) = <u>scoundrel</u> (*slang*), rat (*informal*), bounder (*old-fashioned Brit. slang*), cur, knave, rotter (*slang, chiefly Brit.*), heel, scumbag (*slang*), churl, dastard (*archaic*)

cadence 1 = <u>intonation</u>, accent, inflection, modulation …*He recognised the Polish cadences in her voice*…
2 = <u>rhythm</u>, beat, measure (*Prosody*), metre, pulse, throb, tempo, swing, lilt …*There was a sudden shift in the cadence of the music*…

café = <u>snack bar</u>, restaurant, cafeteria, coffee shop, brasserie, coffee bar, tearoom, lunchroom, eatery *or* eaterie

cage NOUN = <u>enclosure</u>, pen, coop, hutch, pound, corral (*U.S.*) …*I hate to see animals being kept in cages*…
VERB = <u>shut up</u>, confine, restrain, imprison, lock up, mew, incarcerate, fence in, impound, coop up, immure, pound …*Don't you think it's cruel to cage wild creatures?*…

cagey *or* **cagy** (*Informal*) = <u>guarded</u>, reserved, careful, cautious, restrained, wary, discreet, shrewd, wily, reticent, noncommittal, chary OPPOSITE careless

cajole = <u>persuade</u>, tempt, lure, flatter, manoeuvre, seduce, entice, coax, beguile, wheedle, sweet-talk (*informal*), inveigle

cake NOUN = <u>block</u>, bar, slab, lump, cube, loaf, mass …*He bought a cake of soap*…
VERB = <u>solidify</u>, dry, consolidate, harden, thicken, congeal, coagulate, ossify, encrust …*The blood had begun to cake and turn brown*…

calamitous = <u>disastrous</u>, terrible, devastating, tragic, fatal, deadly, dreadful, dire, catastrophic, woeful, ruinous, cataclysmic OPPOSITE fortunate

calamity = <u>disaster</u>, tragedy, ruin, distress, reverse of fortune, hardship, catastrophe, woe, misfortune, downfall, adversity, scourge, mishap, affliction, trial, tribulation, misadventure, cataclysm, wretchedness, mischance OPPOSITE benefit

calculate 1 = <u>work out</u>, value, judge, determine, estimate, count, reckon, weigh, consider, compute, rate, gauge, enumerate, figure …*From this we can calculate the total mass in the galaxy*…
2 = <u>plan</u>, design, aim, intend, frame, arrange, formulate, contrive …*Its twin engines were calculated to give additional safety*…

calculated = <u>deliberate</u>, planned, considered, studied, intended, intentional, designed, aimed, purposeful, premeditated OPPOSITE unplanned

calculating = <u>scheming</u>, designing, sharp, shrewd, cunning, contriving, sly, canny, devious, manipulative, crafty, Machiavellian OPPOSITE direct

calculation 1 = <u>computation</u>, working out, reckoning, figuring, estimate, forecast, judgment, estimation, result, answer …*He made a quick calculation on a scrap of paper*…
2 = <u>planning</u>, intention, deliberation, foresight, contrivance, forethought, circumspection, premeditation …*an act of cold, unspeakably cruel calculation*…

calibrate = <u>measure</u>, gauge

calibre *or* (*U.S.*) **caliber** 1 = <u>worth</u>, quality, ability, talent, gifts, capacity, merit, distinction, faculty, endowment, stature …*I was impressed by the high calibre of the candidates*…
2 = <u>standard</u>, level, quality, grade …*The calibre of the teaching here is very high*…
3 = <u>diameter</u>, bore, gauge, measure …*Next morning she was arrested and a .44 calibre revolver was found in her possession*…

call VERB 1 = <u>name</u>, entitle, dub, designate, term, style, label, describe as, christen, denominate …*They called their daughter Mischa*…
2 = <u>consider</u>, think, judge, estimate, describe as, refer to as, regard as …*His own party called him a traitor*…
3 = <u>cry</u>, announce, shout, scream, proclaim, yell, cry out, whoop …*'Boys!' she called, 'Dinner's ready!'*…
OPPOSITE whisper

4 = <u>phone</u>, contact, telephone, ring (up) (*informal, chiefly Brit.*), give (someone) a bell (*Brit. slang*) …*Will you call me as soon as you hear anything?…*
5 = <u>hail</u>, address, summon, contact, halloo …*He called me over the tannoy…*
6 = <u>summon</u>, gather, invite, rally, assemble, muster, convene, convoke, collect …*The group promised to call a meeting of shareholders…* OPPOSITE dismiss
7 = <u>waken</u>, arouse, awaken, rouse …*I'm late for work! Why didn't you call me earlier?…*
NOUN **1** = <u>visit</u> …*He decided to pay a call on Mr Cummings…*
2 = <u>request</u>, order, demand, appeal, notice, command, announcement, invitation, plea, summons, supplication …*There was a call by the trade unions for members to stay home for the duration of the strike…*
3 (usually used in a negative construction) = <u>need</u>, cause, reason, grounds, occasion, excuse, justification, claim …*There was no call for him to talk to you like he did…*
4 = <u>attraction</u>, draw, pull (*informal*), appeal, lure, attractiveness, allure, magnetism …*a sailor who could not resist the call of the sea…*
5 = <u>cry</u>, shout, scream, yell, whoop …*He heard calls coming from the cellar…* OPPOSITE whisper
PHRASES **call for someone** = <u>fetch</u>, pick up, collect, uplift (*Scot.*) …*I shall call for you at 7 o'clock…* ♦ **call for something 1** = <u>demand</u>, order, request, insist on, cry out for …*They angrily called for his resignation…* **2** = <u>require</u>, need, involve, demand, occasion, entail, necessitate …*It's a situation that calls for a blend of delicacy and force…* ♦ **call on someone 1** = <u>request</u>, ask, bid, invite, appeal to, summon, invoke, call upon, entreat, supplicate …*He was frequently called on to resolve conflicts…* **2** = <u>visit</u>, look up, drop in on, look in on, see …*I'm leaving early tomorrow to call on a friend…* ♦ **call someone up 1** = <u>telephone</u>, phone, ring (*chiefly Brit.*), buzz (*informal*), dial, call up, give (someone) a ring (*informal, chiefly Brit.*), put a call through to, give (someone) a call, give (someone) a buzz (*informal*), give (someone) a bell (*Brit. slang*), give someone a tinkle (*Brit. informal*), get on the blower to (*informal*) …*He called me up to ask how I was…* **2** = <u>enlist</u>, draft, recruit, muster …*The United States has called up some 150,000 military reservists…*

calling = <u>profession</u>, work, business, line, trade, career, mission, employment, province, occupation, pursuit, vocation, walk of life, life's work, métier

callous = <u>heartless</u>, cold, harsh, hardened, indifferent, insensitive, hard-boiled (*informal*), unsympathetic, uncaring, soulless, hard-bitten, unfeeling, obdurate, case-hardened, hardhearted OPPOSITE compassionate

callousness = <u>heartlessness</u>, insensitivity, hardness, coldness, harshness, obduracy, soullessness, hardheartedness, obdurateness

callow = <u>inexperienced</u>, juvenile, naïve, immature, raw, untried, green, unsophisticated, puerile, guileless, jejune, unfledged

calm ADJECTIVE **1** = <u>cool</u>, relaxed, composed, sedate, undisturbed, collected, unmoved, dispassionate, unfazed (*informal*), impassive, unflappable (*informal*), unruffled, unemotional, self-possessed, imperturbable, equable, keeping your cool, unexcited, unexcitable, as cool as a cucumber …*Try to keep calm and just tell me what happened…* OPPOSITE excited
2 = <u>still</u>, quiet, smooth, peaceful, mild, serene, tranquil, placid, halcyon, balmy, restful, windless, pacific …*The normally calm waters of Mururoa lagoon heaved and frothed…* OPPOSITE rough
NOUN **1** = <u>peacefulness</u>, peace, serenity, calmness …*He felt a sudden sense of calm and contentment…*
2 = <u>stillness</u>, peace, quiet, hush, serenity, tranquillity, repose, calmness, peacefulness …*the rural calm of Grand Rapids, Michigan…*
3 = <u>peace</u>, calmness …*Church leaders have appealed for calm…* OPPOSITE disturbance
VERB **1** = <u>soothe</u>, settle, quiet, relax, appease, still, allay, assuage, quieten …*She had a drink to calm her nerves…* OPPOSITE excite
2 = <u>placate</u>, hush, pacify, mollify …*Officials hoped this action would calm the situation…* OPPOSITE aggravate

calmly = <u>coolly</u>, casually, sedately, serenely, nonchalantly, impassively, dispassionately, placidly, unflinchingly, equably, imperturbably, tranquilly, composedly, collectedly, self-possessedly

camaraderie = <u>comradeship</u>, fellowship, brotherhood, companionship, togetherness, esprit de corps, good-fellowship, companionability

camouflage NOUN **1** = <u>protective colouring</u>, mimicry, false appearance, deceptive markings …*Many animals employ camouflage to hide from predators…*
2 = <u>disguise</u>, front, cover, screen, blind, mask, cloak, guise, masquerade, subterfuge, concealment …*Her merrymaking was only a camouflage to disguise her grief…*
VERB = <u>disguise</u>, cover, screen, hide, mask, conceal, obscure, veil, cloak, obfuscate …*This is another clever attempt to camouflage reality…* OPPOSITE reveal

camp¹ = <u>camp site</u>, tents, encampment, bivouac, camping ground, cantonment (*Military*) …*The camp was in a densely-forested area…*

camp² (*Informal*) = <u>affected</u>, mannered, artificial, posturing, ostentatious, effeminate, campy (*informal*), camped up (*informal*), poncy (*slang*) …*Alan Rickman gives a wonderfully camp performance as Professor Snape…*

campaign 1 = <u>drive</u>, appeal, movement, push (*informal*), offensive, crusade …*A new campaign has begun to encourage more people to become blood donors…*
2 = <u>operation</u>, drive, attack, movement, push, offensive, expedition, crusade, jihad …*The General's campaign against the militia has so far failed…*

campaigner = <u>demonstrator</u>, champion, advocate, activist, reformer, crusader

canal = <u>waterway</u>, channel, passage, conduit, duct, watercourse

➤ WORD POWER SUPPLEMENT canals

cancel VERB 1 = call off, drop, abandon, forget about ...*The foreign minister has cancelled his visit to Washington*...

2 = annul, abolish, repeal, abort, quash, do away with, revoke, repudiate, rescind, obviate, abrogate, countermand, eliminate ...*Her insurance had been cancelled by the company*...

PHRASES **cancel something out** = counterbalance, offset, make up for, compensate for, redeem, neutralize, nullify, obviate, balance out ...*These two opposing factors tend to cancel each other out*...

cancellation 1 = abandonment, abandoning ...*No reason has been given for the cancellation of the event*...

2 = annulment, abolition, repeal, elimination, quashing, revocation ...*a march by groups calling for the cancellation of Third World debt*...

cancer 1 = growth, tumour, carcinoma (*Pathology*), malignancy ...*Ninety percent of lung cancers are caused by smoking*...

2 = evil, corruption, rot, sickness, blight, pestilence, canker ...*There's a cancer in the system*...

(Related Words)

prefix : carcino-

candid 1 = honest, just, open, truthful, fair, plain, straightforward, blunt, sincere, outspoken, downright, impartial, forthright, upfront (*informal*), unequivocal, unbiased, guileless, unprejudiced, free, round, frank ...*a candid account of her life as a drug addict*... OPPOSITE > diplomatic

2 = informal, impromptu, uncontrived, unposed ...*There are also some candid pictures taken when he was young*...

candidate = contender, competitor, applicant, nominee, entrant, claimant, contestant, suitor, aspirant, possibility, runner

candour = honesty, simplicity, fairness, sincerity, impartiality, frankness, directness, truthfulness, outspokenness, forthrightness, straightforwardness, ingenuousness, artlessness, guilelessness, openness, unequivocalness, naïveté OPPOSITE > dishonesty

cannabis = marijuana, pot (*slang*), dope (*slang*), hash (*slang*), blow (*slang*), smoke (*informal*), stuff (*slang*), leaf (*slang*), tea (*U.S. slang*), grass (*slang*), chronic (*U.S. slang*), weed (*slang*), hemp, gage (*U.S. dated slang*), hashish, mary jane (*U.S. slang*), ganja, bhang, kif, sinsemilla, dagga (*S. African*), charas

cannon = gun, big gun, artillery piece, field gun, mortar

canny = shrewd, knowing, sharp, acute, careful, wise, clever, subtle, cautious, prudent, astute, on the ball (*informal*), artful, judicious, circumspect, perspicacious, sagacious, worldly-wise OPPOSITE > inept

canon 1 = rule, standard, principle, regulation, formula, criterion, dictate, statute, yardstick, precept ...*These measures offended all the accepted canons of political economy*...

2 = list, index, catalogue, syllabus, roll ...*the body of work which constitutes the canon of English literature as taught in schools*...

canopy = awning, covering, shade, shelter, sunshade

cant[1] 1 = hypocrisy, pretence, lip service, humbug, insincerity, pretentiousness, sanctimoniousness, pious platitudes, affected piety, sham holiness ...*Politicians are holding forth with their usual hypocritical cant*...

2 = jargon, slang, vernacular, patter, lingo, argot ...*He resorted to a lot of pseudo-psychological cant to confuse me*...

cant[2] = tilt, angle, slope, incline, slant, bevel, rise ...*The helicopter canted inward towards the landing area*...

cantankerous = bad-tempered, contrary, perverse, irritable, crusty, grumpy, disagreeable, cranky (*U.S., Canad., & Irish informal*), irascible, tetchy, ratty (*Brit. & N.Z. informal*), testy, quarrelsome, waspish, grouchy (*informal*), peevish, crabby, choleric, crotchety (*informal*), ill-humoured, captious, difficult OPPOSITE > cheerful

canter VERB = jog, lope ...*The competitors cantered into the arena*...

NOUN = jog, lope, easy gait, dogtrot ...*He set off at a canter*...

canvass 1 = campaign, solicit votes, electioneer ...*I'm canvassing for the Labour Party*...

2 = poll, study, examine, investigate, analyse, scan, inspect, sift, scrutinize ...*The survey canvassed the views of almost 80 economists*...

canyon = gorge, pass, gulf, valley, clough (*dialect*), gully, ravine, defile, gulch (*U.S.*), coulee (*U.S.*)

cap 1 (*Informal*) = beat, top, better, exceed, eclipse, lick (*informal*), surpass, transcend, outstrip, outdo, run rings around (*informal*), put in the shade, overtop ...*He always has to cap everyone else's achievements*...

2 = top, cover, crown ...*home-made scones capped with cream*...

3 = complete, finish, crown ...*Our team's victory capped a perfect day*...

capability = ability, means, power, potential, facility, capacity, qualification(s), faculty, competence, proficiency, wherewithal, potentiality OPPOSITE > inability

capable 1 = able, fitted, suited, adapted, adequate ...*Such a weapon would be capable of firing conventional or nuclear shells*... OPPOSITE > incapable

2 = accomplished, experienced, masterly, qualified, talented, gifted, efficient, clever, intelligent, competent, apt, skilful, adept, proficient ...*She's a very capable administrator*... OPPOSITE > incompetent

capacious = spacious, wide, broad, vast, substantial, comprehensive, extensive, generous, ample, expansive, roomy, voluminous, commodious, sizable *or* sizeable OPPOSITE > limited

capacity 1 = ability, power, strength, facility, gift, intelligence, efficiency, genius, faculty, capability, forte, readiness, aptitude, aptness, competence *or* competency ...*Our capacity for giving care, love and attention is limited*...

2 = size, room, range, space, volume, extent,

dimensions, scope, magnitude, compass, amplitude …*an aircraft with a bomb-carrying capacity of 454 kg…*

3 = <u>function</u>, position, role, post, appointment, province, sphere, service, office …*She was visiting in her official capacity as co-chairperson…*

cape = <u>headland</u>, point, head, peninsula, ness (*archaic*), promontory

caper **VERB** = <u>dance</u>, trip, spring, jump, bound, leap, bounce, hop, skip, romp, frolic, cavort, frisk, gambol …*The children were capering about, shouting and laughing…*

NOUN = <u>escapade</u>, sport, stunt, mischief, lark (*informal*), prank, jest, practical joke, high jinks, antic, jape, shenanigan (*informal*) …*Jack would have nothing to do with such childish capers…*

capital **NOUN** = <u>money</u>, funds, stock, investment(s), property, cash, finance, finances, financing, resources, assets, wealth, principal, means, wherewithal …*The company is having difficulties in raising capital…*

ADJECTIVE (*Old-fashioned*) – <u>first-rate</u>, fine, excellent, superb, sterling, splendid, world-class …*They had a capital time in London…*

➤ **WORD POWER SUPPLEMENT capital cities**

capitalism = <u>private enterprise</u>, free enterprise, private ownership, laissez faire *or* laisser faire

capitalize **VERB** = <u>sell</u>, put up for sale, trade, dispose of …*The company will be capitalized at £2 million…*

PHRASES **capitalize on something** = <u>take advantage of</u>, exploit, benefit from, profit from, make the most of, gain from, cash in on (*informal*) …*The rebels seemed to be trying to capitalize on the public's discontent…*

capitulate = <u>give in</u>, yield, concede, submit, surrender, comply, give up, come to terms, succumb, cave in (*informal*), relent **OPPOSITE** resist

capitulation = <u>surrender</u>, yielding, submission, cave-in (*informal*)

caprice = <u>whim</u>, notion, impulse, freak, fad, quirk, vagary, whimsy, humour, fancy, fickleness, inconstancy, fitfulness, changeableness

capricious = <u>unpredictable</u>, variable, unstable, inconsistent, erratic, quirky, fickle, impulsive, mercurial, freakish, fitful, inconstant **OPPOSITE** consistent

capsize = <u>overturn</u>, turn over, invert, tip over, keel over, turn turtle, upset

capsule **1** = <u>pill</u>, tablet, lozenge, bolus …*You can also take red ginseng in convenient capsule form…*

2 (*Botany*) = <u>pod</u>, case, shell, vessel, sheath, receptacle, seed case …*Each flower is globular, with an egg-shaped capsule…*

captain **1** = <u>leader</u>, boss, master, skipper, chieftain, head, number one (*informal*), chief …*He is a former English cricket captain…*

2 = <u>commander</u>, officer, skipper, (senior) pilot …*a beefy German sea captain…*

captivate = <u>charm</u>, attract, fascinate, absorb, entrance, dazzle, seduce, enchant, enthral, beguile,

allure, bewitch, ravish, enslave, mesmerize, ensnare, hypnotize, enrapture, sweep off your feet, enamour, infatuate **OPPOSITE** repel

captive **ADJECTIVE** = <u>confined</u>, caged, imprisoned, locked up, enslaved, incarcerated, ensnared, subjugated, penned, restricted …*Her heart had begun to pound inside her chest like a captive animal…*

NOUN = <u>prisoner</u>, hostage, convict, prisoner of war, detainee, internee …*He described the difficulties of surviving for four months as a captive…*

captivity = <u>confinement</u>, custody, detention, imprisonment, incarceration, internment, durance (*archaic*), restraint

captor = <u>jailer</u> *or* gaoler, guard, keeper, custodian

capture **VERB** = <u>catch</u>, arrest, take, bag, secure, seize, nail (*informal*), collar (*informal*), nab (*informal*), apprehend, lift (*slang*), take prisoner, take into custody, feel your collar (*slang*) …*The police gave chase and captured him as he was trying to escape…*
OPPOSITE release

NOUN = <u>arrest</u>, catching, trapping, imprisonment, seizure, apprehension, taking, taking captive …*The shooting happened while the man was trying to evade capture…*

car **1** = <u>vehicle</u>, motor, wheels (*informal*), auto (*U.S.*), automobile, jalopy (*informal*), motorcar, machine …*They arrived by car…*

2 (*U.S. & Canad.*) = <u>(railway) carriage</u>, coach, cable car, dining car, sleeping car, buffet car, van …*Tour buses have replaced railway cars…*

carcass **1** = <u>body</u>, remains, corpse, skeleton, dead body, cadaver (*Medical*) …*A cluster of vultures crouched on the carcass of a dead buffalo…*

2 = <u>remains</u>, shell, framework, debris, remnants, hulk …*At one end of the camp lies the carcass of an aircraft which crashed in the mountains…*

cardinal = <u>principal</u>, first, highest, greatest, leading, important, chief, main, prime, central, key, essential, primary, fundamental, paramount, foremost, preeminent **OPPOSITE** secondary

care **VERB** = <u>be concerned</u>, mind, bother, be interested, be bothered, give a damn, concern yourself …*a company that cares about the environment…*

NOUN **1** = <u>custody</u>, keeping, control, charge, management, protection, supervision, guardianship, safekeeping, ministration …*the orphans who were in her care…*

2 = <u>caution</u>, attention, regard, pains, consideration, heed, prudence, vigilance, forethought, circumspection, watchfulness, meticulousness, carefulness …*I chose my words with care…* **OPPOSITE** carelessness

3 = <u>worry</u>, concern, pressure, trouble, responsibility, stress, burden, anxiety, hardship, woe, disquiet, affliction, tribulation, perplexity, vexation …*He never seemed to have a care in the world…* **OPPOSITE** pleasure

PHRASES **care for someone** **1** = <u>look after</u>, mind, tend, attend, nurse, minister to, watch over …*They*

hired a nurse to care for her... 2 = <u>love</u>, desire, be fond of, want, prize, find congenial ...He wanted me to know that he still cared for me... ◆ **care for something** or **someone** = <u>like</u>, enjoy, take to, relish, be fond of, be keen on, be partial to ...I don't care for seafood very much... ◆ **take care of** 1 = <u>look after</u>, mind, watch, protect, tend, nurse, care for, provide for, supervise, attend to, keep an eye on, take charge of ...There was no-one else to take care of their children... 2 = <u>deal with</u>, manage, cope with, see to, handle ...Leave me to take care of this problem...

career NOUN 1 = <u>occupation</u>, calling, employment, pursuit, vocation, livelihood, life's work ...She is now concentrating on a career as a fashion designer... 2 = <u>progress</u>, course, path, procedure, passage ...The club has had an interesting, if chequered, career... VERB = <u>rush</u>, race, speed, tear, dash, barrel (along) (informal, chiefly U.S. & Canad.), bolt, hurtle, burn rubber (informal) ...The car went careering off down the track...

carefree = <u>untroubled</u>, happy, cheerful, careless, buoyant, airy, radiant, easy-going, cheery, breezy, halcyon, sunny, jaunty, chirpy (informal), happy-go-lucky, blithe, insouciant, light-hearted OPPOSITE unhappy

careful 1 = <u>cautious</u>, painstaking, scrupulous, fastidious, circumspect, punctilious, chary, heedful, thoughtful, discreet ...One has to be extremely careful when dealing with these people... OPPOSITE careless 2 = <u>thorough</u>, full, particular, accurate, precise, intensive, in-depth, meticulous, conscientious, attentive, exhaustive, painstaking, scrupulous, assiduous ...He decided to prosecute her after careful consideration of all the facts... OPPOSITE casual 3 = <u>prudent</u>, sparing, economical, canny, provident, frugal, thrifty ...Train your children to be careful with their pocket-money...

careless 1 = <u>slapdash</u>, irresponsible, sloppy (informal), cavalier, offhand, neglectful, slipshod, lackadaisical, inattentive ...He pleaded guilty to careless driving... OPPOSITE careful 2 = <u>negligent</u>, hasty, unconcerned, cursory, perfunctory, thoughtless, indiscreet, unthinking, forgetful, absent-minded, inconsiderate, heedless, remiss, incautious, unmindful ...She's careless about her personal hygiene... OPPOSITE careful 3 = <u>nonchalant</u>, casual, offhand, artless, unstudied ...With a careless flip of his wrists, he sent the ball on its way... OPPOSITE careful

carelessness = <u>negligence</u>, neglect, omission, indiscretion, inaccuracy, irresponsibility, slackness, inattention, sloppiness (informal), laxity, thoughtlessness, laxness, remissness

caress VERB = <u>stroke</u>, cuddle, fondle, pet, embrace, hug, nuzzle, neck (informal), kiss ...They kissed and caressed one another... NOUN = <u>stroke</u>, pat, kiss, embrace, hug, cuddle, fondling ...Margaret held my arm in a gentle caress...

caretaker NOUN = <u>warden</u>, keeper, porter, superintendent, curator, custodian, watchman, janitor,

concierge ...The caretaker sleeps in the building all night... ADJECTIVE = <u>temporary</u>, holding, short-term, interim ...The administration intends to hand over power to a caretaker government...

cargo = <u>load</u>, goods, contents, shipment, freight, merchandise, baggage, ware, consignment, tonnage, lading

caricature NOUN = <u>parody</u>, cartoon, distortion, satire, send-up (Brit. informal), travesty, takeoff (informal), lampoon, burlesque, mimicry, farce ...The poster showed a caricature of Hitler with a devil's horns and tail... VERB = <u>parody</u>, take off (informal), mock, distort, ridicule, mimic, send up (Brit. informal), lampoon, burlesque, satirize ...Her political career has been caricatured in the newspapers...

caring = <u>compassionate</u>, loving, kindly, warm, soft, sensitive, tender, sympathetic, responsive, receptive, considerate, warmhearted, tenderhearted, softhearted, touchy-feely (informal)

carnage = <u>slaughter</u>, murder, massacre, holocaust, havoc, bloodshed, shambles, mass murder, butchery, blood bath

carnal = <u>sexual</u>, animal, sexy (informal), fleshly, erotic, sensual, randy (informal, chiefly Brit.), steamy (informal), raunchy (slang), sensuous, voluptuous, lewd, wanton, amorous, salacious, prurient, impure, lascivious, lustful, lecherous, libidinous, licentious, unchaste

carnival = <u>festival</u>, fair, fête, celebration, gala, jubilee, jamboree, Mardi Gras, revelry, merrymaking, fiesta, holiday

carnivore
➤ **carnivores**

carol = <u>song</u>, noel, hymn, Christmas song, canticle

carouse = <u>drink</u>, booze (informal), revel, imbibe, quaff, pub-crawl (informal, chiefly Brit.), bevvy (dialect), make merry, bend the elbow (informal), roister

carp = <u>find fault</u>, knock (informal), complain, beef (slang), criticize, nag, censure, reproach, quibble, cavil, pick holes, kvetch (U.S. slang) OPPOSITE praise

carpenter = <u>joiner</u>, cabinet-maker, woodworker

carping = <u>fault-finding</u>, critical, nagging, picky (informal), nit-picking (informal), hard to please, cavilling, captious

carriage 1 = <u>vehicle</u>, coach, trap, gig, cab, wagon, hackney, conveyance ...He followed in an open carriage drawn by six gray horses... 2 = <u>transportation</u>, transport, delivery, conveying, freight, conveyance, carrying ...It costs £10.86 for one litre, including carriage... 3 = <u>bearing</u>, posture, gait, deportment, air ...Her legs were long and fine, her hips slender, her carriage graceful...
➤ **carriages and carts**

carry VERB 1 = <u>convey</u>, take, move, bring, bear, lift, transfer, conduct, transport, haul, transmit, fetch, relay, cart, tote (informal), hump (Brit. slang), lug ...He

Carnivores http://www.ucmp.berkeley.edu/mammal/carnivora/carnivora.html

aardwolf	ferret	lynx	rooikat
arctic fox	fox	margay	sable
badger	genet *or* genette	marten	sea otter
bear	giant panda	meerkat	serval
binturong	grey fox	mink	silver fox
black bear	grey wolf *or* timber wolf	mongoose	skunk
bobcat	grison	mountain lion	sloth bear
brown bear	grizzly bear *or* grizzly	ocelot	snow leopard *or* ounce
cacomistle *or* cacomixle	hog badger	otter	stoat
caracal *or* desert lynx	hognosed skunk	otter shrew	stone marten
cat *see* **breeds of cat**	hyena *or* hyaena	palm civet	strandwolf
catamount,	ichneumon	panda	sun bear
catamountain, *or* cat-o'-	jackal	panther	swift fox *or* kit fox
mountain	jaguar	pine marten *or* sweet	tayra
cheetah *or* chetah	jaguarondi, jaguarundi,	marten	teledu
cinnamon bear	*or* (*Austral.*) eyra	polar bear *or* (*N. Canad.*)	tiger
civet	kinkajou, honey bear, *or*	nanook	tiger cat
corsac	potto	polecat	timber wolf
coyote *or* prairie wolf	Kodiak bear	prairie dog	weasel
dhole	kolinsky	puma *or* cougar	wolf
dingo *or* (*Austral.*) native	laughing hyena *or*	raccoon, racoon, *or* coon	wolverine, glutton, *or*
dog *or* warrigal	spotted hyena	raccoon dog	carcajou
dog *see* **breeds of dog**	leopard *or* panther	rasse	zibeline
ermine	linsang	ratel	zibet
fennec	lion	red fox	zorilla *or* zorille

carried the plate through to the dining room...
2 = <u>transport</u>, take, transfer, transmit ...*The ship can carry seventy passengers...*
3 = <u>support</u>, stand, bear, maintain, shoulder, sustain, hold up, suffer, uphold, bolster, underpin ...*This horse can't carry your weight...*
4 = <u>transmit</u>, transfer, spread, pass on ...*Frogs eat pests which carry diseases...*
5 = <u>publish</u>, include, release, display, print, broadcast, communicate, disseminate, give ...*Several magazines carried the story...*
6 = <u>win</u>, gain, secure, capture, accomplish ...*It was this point of view that carried the day...*
PHRASES **carry on 1** = <u>continue</u>, last, endure, persist, keep going, persevere ...*Her bravery has given him the will to carry on...* **2** (*Informal*) = <u>make a fuss</u>, act up (*informal*), misbehave, create (*slang*), raise Cain ...*She was yelling and screaming and carrying on like an idiot...* ◆ **carry something on** = <u>engage in</u>, conduct, carry out, undertake, embark on, enter into ...*The consulate will carry on a political dialogue...*
◆ **carry something out** = <u>perform</u>, effect, achieve, realize, implement, fulfil, accomplish, execute, discharge, consummate, carry through ...*Commitments have been made with very little intention of carrying them out...*
carry-on (*Informal, chiefly Brit.*) = <u>fuss</u>, disturbance, racket, fracas, commotion, rumpus, tumult, hubbub, shindy (*informal*)
cart
➤ **carriages and carts**
carton = <u>box</u>, case, pack, package, container
cartoon 1 = <u>drawing</u>, parody, satire, caricature, comic strip, takeoff (*informal*), lampoon, sketch ...*The*

newspaper printed a cartoon depicting the president as a used car salesman...*
2 = <u>animation</u>, animated film, animated cartoon ...*the X-rated TV cartoon, South Park...*
cartridge 1 = <u>shell</u>, round, charge ...*Gun and cartridge manufacturers will lose money if the game laws are amended...*
2 = <u>container</u>, case, magazine, cassette, cylinder, capsule ...*Change the filter cartridge as often as instructed by the manufacturer...*
carve 1 = <u>sculpt</u>, form, cut, chip, sculpture, whittle, chisel, hew, fashion ...*One of the prisoners has carved a beautiful chess set...*
2 = <u>etch</u>, engrave, inscribe, fashion, slash ...*He carved his name on his desk...*
carving = <u>sculpture</u>
cascade **NOUN** = <u>waterfall</u>, falls, torrent, flood, shower, fountain, avalanche, deluge, downpour, outpouring, cataract ...*She stood still for a moment under the cascade of water...*
VERB = <u>flow</u>, fall, flood, pour, plunge, surge, spill, tumble, descend, overflow, gush, teem, pitch ...*A waterfall cascades down the cliff from the hills...*
case¹ 1 = <u>situation</u>, event, circumstance(s), state, position, condition, context, dilemma, plight, contingency, predicament ...*In extreme cases, insurance companies can prosecute for fraud...*
2 = <u>instance</u>, example, occasion, specimen, occurrence ...*Some cases of arthritis respond to a gluten-free diet...*
3 (*Law*) = <u>lawsuit</u>, process, trial, suit, proceedings, dispute, cause, action ...*He lost his case at the European Court of Human Rights...*
case² 1 = <u>cabinet</u>, box, chest, holder ...*There was a*

Carriages and carts

barouche	chariot	gig	rockaway
brake	clarence	Gladstone	sledge
britzka	coach	hansom	spider phaeton *or* spider
brougham	Conestoga wagon	herdic	stagecoach
buckboard	coupe	jaunting car *or* jaunty	sulky
buggy	covered wagon	car	surrey
cab	curricle	landau	tandem
cabriolet	dogcart	phaeton	tarantass
calash *or* calèche	drag	post chaise	tilbury
Cape cart	droshky	prairie schooner	troika
cariole *or* carriole	equipage	pung	victoria
carriage	fiacre	quadriga	vis-à-vis
carryall	fly	randem	wagon
cart	four-in-hand	ratha	wagonette
chaise	gharry	rig	wain

ten-foot long stuffed alligator in a glass case...

2 = <u>container</u>, compact, capsule, carton, cartridge, canister, casket, receptacle ...*She held up a blue spectacle case...*

3 = <u>suitcase</u>, bag, grip, trunk, holdall, portmanteau, valise ...*The porter brought my cases down and called for a taxi...*

4 = <u>crate</u>, box ...*The winner will receive a case of champagne...*

5 = <u>covering</u>, casing, cover, shell, wrapping, jacket, envelope, capsule, folder, sheath, wrapper, integument ...*Vanilla is the seed case of a South American orchid...*

cash = <u>money</u>, change, funds, notes, ready (*informal*), the necessary (*informal*), resources, currency, silver, bread (*slang*), coin, tin (*slang*), brass (*Northern English dialect*), dough (*slang*), rhino (*Brit. slang*), banknotes, bullion, dosh (*Brit. & Austral. slang*), wherewithal, coinage, needful (*informal*), specie, shekels (*informal*), dibs (*slang*), ready money, ackers (*slang*), spondulicks (*slang*)

cashier[1] = <u>teller</u>, accountant, clerk, treasurer, bank clerk, purser, bursar, banker ...*The cashier said that he would fetch the manager...*

cashier[2] = <u>dismiss</u>, discharge, expel, cast off, drum out, give the boot to (*slang*) ...*Many officers were cahiered on political grounds...*

casing = <u>covering</u>, case, cover, shell, container, integument

cask = <u>barrel</u>, drum, cylinder, keg

casket = <u>box</u>, case, chest, coffer, ark (*dialect*), jewel box, kist (*Scot. & Northern English dialect*)

cast NOUN **1** = <u>actors</u>, company, players, characters, troupe, dramatis personae ...*The show is very amusing and the cast are excellent...*

2 = <u>type</u>, turn, sort, kind, style, stamp ...*Hers was an essentially optimistic cast of mind...*

VERB **1** = <u>choose</u>, name, pick, select, appoint, assign, allot ...*He has been cast in the lead role of the new Pinter play...*

2 = <u>bestow</u>, give, level, accord, direct, confer ...*He cast a stern glance at the two men...*

3 = <u>give out</u>, spread, deposit, shed, distribute, scatter,

emit, radiate, bestow, diffuse ...*The moon cast a bright light over the yard...*

4 = <u>throw</u>, project, launch, pitch, shed, shy, toss, thrust, hurl, fling, chuck (*informal*), sling, lob, impel, drive, drop ...*She took a pebble and cast it into the water...*

5 = <u>mould</u>, set, found, form, model, shape ...*This statue of Neptune is cast in bronze...*

PHRASES **cast someone down** = <u>discourage</u>, depress, desolate, dishearten, dispirit, deject ...*I am not too easily cast down by changes of fortune...*

caste = <u>class</u>, order, race, station, rank, status, stratum, social order, lineage

castigate = <u>reprimand</u>, blast, carpet (*informal*), put down, criticize, lash, slate (*informal, chiefly Brit.*), censure, rebuke, scold, berate, dress down (*informal*), chastise, chasten, tear into (*informal*), diss (*slang, chiefly U.S.*), read the riot act, slap on the wrist, lambast(e), bawl out (*informal*), excoriate, rap over the knuckles, haul over the coals (*informal*), chew out (*U.S. & Canad. informal*), tear (someone) off a strip (*Brit. informal*), give a rocket (*Brit. & N.Z. informal*)

cast-iron = <u>certain</u>, established, settled, guaranteed, fixed, definite, copper-bottomed, idiot-proof

castle = <u>fortress</u>, keep, palace, tower, peel, chateau, stronghold, citadel, fastness

➤ **WORD POWER SUPPLEMENT castles**

castrate = <u>neuter</u>, unman, emasculate, geld

casual **1** = <u>careless</u>, relaxed, informal, indifferent, unconcerned, apathetic, blasé, offhand, nonchalant, insouciant, lackadaisical ...*an easy-going young man with a casual approach to life...* OPPOSITE serious

2 = <u>chance</u>, unexpected, random, accidental, incidental, unforeseen, unintentional, fortuitous (*informal*), serendipitous, unpremeditated ...*It was just a casual meeting...* OPPOSITE planned

3 = <u>informal</u>, leisure, sporty, non-dressy ...*I bought casual clothes for the weekend...* OPPOSITE formal

casualty **1** = <u>fatality</u>, death, loss, wounded ...*Troops fired on the demonstrators, causing many casualties...*

2 = <u>victim</u>, sufferer ...*The company has been one of the greatest casualties of the recession...*

cat = <u>feline</u>, pussy (*informal*), moggy (*slang*), puss (*informal*), ballarat (*Austral. informal*), tabby

adjective : feline
male : tom
female : tabby
young : kitten

Breeds of cat
http://www.catsinfo.com/profiles.html

Abyssinian	Persian
Angora	ragdoll
Bengal leopard	Rex
Burmese	Russian blue
colourpoint *or* (*U.S.*)	Siamese
Himalayan	tabby
Havana	tortoiseshell
Maine coon	Turkish
Manx	

---

cataclysm = disaster, collapse, catastrophe, upheaval, debacle, devastation, calamity

cataclysmic = disastrous, devastating, catastrophic, calamitous

catalogue *or* (*U.S.*) **catalog** NOUN = list, record, schedule, index, register, directory, inventory, gazetteer ...*One of the authors of the catalogue is the Professor of Art History...*
VERB = list, file, index, register, classify, inventory, tabulate, alphabetize ...*The Royal Greenwich Observatory was founded to observe and catalogue the stars...*

catapult NOUN = sling, slingshot (*U.S.*), trebuchet, ballista ...*They were hit twice by missiles fired from a catapult...*
VERB = shoot, pitch, plunge, toss, hurl, propel, hurtle, heave ...*He was catapulted into the side of the van...*

cataract 1 (*Medical*) = opacity (*of the eye*) ...*a battle with blindness caused by cataracts...*
2 = waterfall, falls, rapids, cascade, torrent, deluge, downpour, Niagara ...*There was an impressive cataract at the end of the glen...*

catastrophe = disaster, tragedy, calamity, meltdown (*informal*), cataclysm, trouble, trial, blow, failure, reverse, misfortune, devastation, adversity, mishap, affliction, whammy (*informal, chiefly U.S.*), bummer (*slang*), mischance, fiasco

catastrophic = disastrous, devastating, tragic, calamitous, cataclysmic

catch VERB 1 = capture, arrest, trap, seize, nail (*informal*), nab (*informal*), snare, lift (*slang*), apprehend, ensnare, entrap, feel your collar (*slang*) ...*Police say they are confident of catching the killer...*
OPPOSITE free
2 = trap, capture, snare, entangle, ensnare, entrap ...*The locals were encouraged to catch and kill the birds...*
3 = seize, get, grab, snatch ...*I jumped up to catch the ball and fell over...*
4 = grab, take, grip, seize, grasp, clutch, lay hold of ...*He knelt beside her and caught her hand in both of his...* OPPOSITE release
5 = discover, surprise, find out, expose, detect, catch in the act, take unawares ...*He caught a youth breaking into his car...*
6 = contract, get, develop, suffer from, incur, succumb to, go down with ...*The more stress you are under, the more likely you are to catch a cold...* OPPOSITE escape
NOUN 1 = fastener, hook, clip, bolt, latch, clasp, hasp, hook and eye, snib (*Scot.*), sneck (*dialect, chiefly Scot. & Northern English*) ...*Always fit windows with safety locks or catches...*
2 (*Informal*) = drawback, trick, trap, disadvantage, hitch, snag, stumbling block, fly in the ointment ...*It sounds too good to be true – what's the catch?...*
OPPOSITE advantage
PHRASES **catch on** 1 (*Informal*) = understand, see, find out, grasp, see through, comprehend, twig (*Brit. informal*), get the picture, see the light of day ...*He tried to explain it to me, but it took me a while to catch on...* 2 = become popular, take off, become trendy, come into fashion ...*The idea has been around for ages without catching on...*

catching = infectious, contagious, transferable, communicable, infective, transmittable OPPOSITE non-infectious

catchphrase = slogan, saying, quotation, motto

catchy = memorable, haunting, unforgettable, captivating

categorical = absolute, direct, express, positive, explicit, unconditional, emphatic, downright, unequivocal, unqualified, unambiguous, unreserved OPPOSITE vague

category = class, grouping, heading, head, order, sort, list, department, type, division, section, rank, grade, classification

cater
PHRASES **cater for something** *or* **someone** 1 = provide for, supply, provision, purvey, victual ...*Thirty restaurants and hotels catered for the event...* 2 = take into account, consider, bear in mind, make allowance for, have regard for ...*We have to cater for the demands of the marketplace...* ♦ **cater to something** *or* **someone** = indulge, spoil, minister to, pamper, gratify, pander to, coddle, mollycoddle ...*His parents spoil him and cater to his every whim...*

catharsis = release, cleansing, purging, purification

catholic = wide, general, liberal, global, varied, comprehensive, universal, world-wide, tolerant, eclectic, all-inclusive, ecumenical, all-embracing, broad-minded, unbigoted, unsectarian OPPOSITE limited

cattle = cows, stock, beasts, livestock, bovines
adjective : bovine
collective nouns : drove, herd
➤ **cattle**

caucus = group, division, section, camp, sector, lobby, bloc, contingent, pressure group, junta

cause NOUN 1 = origin, source, agency, spring, agent, maker, producer, root, beginning, creator, genesis, originator, prime mover, mainspring ...*Smoking is the biggest preventable cause of death and disease...*

Cattle   http://www.ansi.okstate.edu/breeds/cattle/

Breeds of cattle

Aberdeen Angus	Devon	Holstein	Norwegian Red
Africander	dexter	Illawarra (shorthorn)	Red Poll *or* Red Polled
Alderney	Durham	Jersey	Santa Gertrudis
Ayrshire	Friesian	Kerry	shorthorn
Blonde d'Aquitaine	Galloway	kyloe	Simmental
Brown Swiss	Gelbvieh	Limousin	Sussex
Belted Galloway	Guernsey	longhorn	Texas longhorn
cattalo *or* catalo	Hereford	Meuse-Rhine-Ijssel	
Charolais *or* Charollais	Highland	Normandy	

Cattle and other artiodactyls

addax	chevrotain *or* mouse	Kashmir goat	reindeer
alpaca *or* alpacca	deer	klipspringer	rhebok *or* reebok
antelope	Chinese water deer	kob	Rocky Mountain goat
aoudad	cow *see* **breeds of**	kongoni	roe deer
argali *or* argal	**cattle**	kouprey	sable antelope
ariel	deer	kudu *or* koodoo	saiga
axis (*plural* axises) *or*	dik-dik	llama	sambar *or* sambur
chital	dromedary	markhor *or* markhoor	sassaby
babirusa	duiker *or* duyker	marshbuck	serow
Bactrian camel	eland	moose	sheep *or* (*Austral. slang*)
bharal	elk	mouflon *or* moufflon	jumbuck *see* **breeds of**
bison	gaur	mountain goat	**sheep**
blacktail	gayal	mule deer	sika
blaubok	gazelle	muntjac, muntjak, *or*	springbok
blesbok	gemsbok	barking deer	stag
boar	gerenuk	musk deer	steenbok
boer goat	giraffe *or* (*obsolete*)	nilgai, nilghau, *or*	tahr *or* thar
bongo	camelopard	nylghau	takin
bontebok	gnu	nyala	vicuña *or* vicuna
brocket	goa	okapi	wapiti
bubal *or* bubalis	goat	oribi	wart hog
buffalo	goral	oryx	waterbuck
bull *see* **breeds of**	grysbok	ox *see* **breeds of cattle**	water buffalo, water ox,
cattle	guanaco	peccary	*or* carabao
bushbuck *or* boschbok	harnessed antelope	Père David's deer	white-tailed deer
bushpig	hartebeest *or* hartbeest	pig *see* **breeds of pig**	wild boar
camel *or* (*Anglo-Indian*)	hippopotamus	pronghorn	wildebeest
oont	ibex	pudu	yak
Cape buffalo	impala	razorback	zebu
caribou	Jacob *or* Jacob sheep	red deer	zo *or* zho, *or* dzo
chamois *or* izard	karakul *or* caracul	reedbuck *or* nagor	

OPPOSITE result

2 = <u>reason</u>, call, need, grounds, basis, incentive, motive, motivation, justification, inducement ...*There is obvious cause for concern*...

3 = <u>aim</u>, movement, purpose, principle, object, ideal, enterprise, end ...*His comments have done nothing to help the cause of peace*...

VERB = <u>produce</u>, begin, create, effect, lead to, occasion, result in, generate, provoke, compel, motivate, induce, bring about, give rise to, precipitate, incite, engender ...*I don't want to cause any trouble*... **OPPOSITE** prevent

caustic 1 = <u>burning</u>, corrosive, corroding, astringent, vitriolic, acrid ...*This substance is caustic; use gloves when handling it*...

2 = <u>sarcastic</u>, biting, keen, cutting, severe, stinging, scathing, acrimonious, pungent, vitriolic, trenchant, mordant ...*He was well known for his abrasive wit and*

caustic comments... **OPPOSITE** kind

caution **NOUN** **1** = <u>care</u>, discretion, heed, prudence, vigilance, alertness, forethought, circumspection, watchfulness, belt and braces, carefulness, heedfulness ...*Drivers are urged to exercise extreme caution in icy weather*... **OPPOSITE** carelessness

2 = <u>reprimand</u>, warning, injunction, admonition ...*The others got off with a caution but I was fined*...

VERB **1** = <u>warn</u>, urge, advise, alert, tip off, forewarn, put you on your guard ...*Banks caution young couples against opening joint bank accounts*...

2 = <u>reprimand</u>, warn, admonish, give an injunction to ...*The two men were cautioned but the police say they will not be charged*...

cautious = <u>careful</u>, guarded, alert, wary, discreet, tentative, prudent, vigilant, watchful, judicious, circumspect, cagey (*informal*), on your toes, chary, belt-and-braces, keeping a weather eye on OPPOSITE careless

cautiously = carefully, alertly, discreetly, tentatively, warily, prudently, judiciously, guardedly, circumspectly, watchfully, vigilantly, cagily (*informal*), mindfully

cavalcade = parade, train, procession, march-past

cavalier = offhand, lordly, arrogant, lofty, curt, condescending, haughty, scornful, disdainful, insolent, supercilious

cavalry = horsemen, horse, mounted troops OPPOSITE infantrymen

cave = hollow, cavern, grotto, den, cavity

caveat = warning, caution, admonition, qualification, proviso, reservation, condition

cavern = cave, hollow, grotto, underground chamber

cavernous = vast, wide, huge, enormous, extensive, immense, spacious, expansive, capacious, commodious

cavity = hollow, hole, gap, pit, dent, crater

cavort = frolic, sport, romp, caper, prance, frisk, gambol

cease 1 = stop, end, finish, be over, come to an end, peter out, die away ...*Almost miraculously, the noise ceased*... OPPOSITE start
2 = discontinue, end, stop, fail, finish, give up, conclude, suspend, halt, terminate, break off, refrain, leave off, give over (*informal*), bring to an end, desist, belay (*Nautical*) ...*A small number of firms have ceased trading*... OPPOSITE begin

ceaseless = continual, constant, endless, continuous, eternal, perennial, perpetual, never-ending, interminable, incessant, everlasting, unending, unremitting, nonstop, untiring OPPOSITE occasional

cede = surrender, grant, transfer, abandon, yield, concede, hand over, relinquish, renounce, make over, abdicate

celebrate 1 = rejoice, party, enjoy yourself, carouse, live it up (*informal*), whoop it up (*informal*), make merry, paint the town red (*informal*), go on a spree, put the flags out, roister, kill the fatted calf ...*I was in a mood to celebrate*...
2 = commemorate, honour, observe, toast, drink to, keep ...*Tom celebrated his birthday two days ago*...
3 = perform, observe, preside over, officiate at, solemnize ...*Pope John Paul celebrated mass today in a city in central Poland*...
4 = praise, honour, commend (*informal*), glorify, publicize, exalt, laud, extol, eulogize ...*a festival to celebrate the life and work of this great composer*...

celebrated = renowned, popular, famous, outstanding, distinguished, well-known, prominent, glorious, acclaimed, notable, eminent, revered, famed, Illustrious, pre-eminent, lionized OPPOSITE unknown

celebration 1 = party, festival, gala, jubilee, festivity, rave (*Brit. slang*), beano (*Brit. slang*), revelry, red-letter day, rave-up (*Brit. slang*), merrymaking, carousal, -fest (*in combination*), hooley or hoolie (*chiefly Irish & N.Z.*)

...*There was a celebration in our house that night*...
2 = commemoration, honouring, remembrance ...*This was not a memorial service but a celebration of his life*...
3 = performance, observance, solemnization ...*the celebration of Mass in Latin*...

celebrity 1 = personality, name, star, superstar, big name, dignitary, luminary, bigwig (*informal*), celeb (*informal*), face (*informal*), big shot (*informal*), personage, megastar (*informal*), V.I.P. ...*At the age of twelve, he was already a celebrity*... OPPOSITE nobody
2 = fame, reputation, honour, glory, popularity, distinction, prestige, prominence, stardom, renown, pre-eminence, repute, éclat, notability ...*She has finally achieved celebrity after 25 years as an actress*... OPPOSITE obscurity

celestial 1 = astronomical, planetary, stellar, astral, extraterrestrial ...*the clusters of celestial bodies in the ever-expanding universe*...
2 = heavenly, spiritual, divine, eternal, sublime, immortal, supernatural, astral, ethereal, angelic, godlike, seraphic ...*gods and other celestial beings*...

celibacy = chastity, purity, virginity, continence, singleness

celibate = chaste, single, pure, virgin, continent

cell 1 = room, chamber, lock-up, compartment, cavity, cubicle, dungeon, stall ...*They took her back to the cell, and just left her there to die*...
2 = unit, group, section, core, nucleus, caucus, coterie ...*the abolition of Communist Party cells in all work places*...

cement NOUN 1 = mortar, plaster, paste ...*The stone work has all been pointed with cement*...
2 = sealant, glue, gum, adhesive, binder ...*Stick the pieces on with tile cement*...
VERB = stick, join, bond, attach, seal, glue, plaster, gum, weld, solder ...*Most artificial joints are cemented into place*...

cemetery = graveyard, churchyard, burial ground, necropolis, God's acre

censor = expurgate, cut, blue-pencil, bowdlerize

censorship = expurgation, blue pencil, purgation, bowdlerization *or* bowdlerisation, sanitization *or* sanitisation

censure VERB = criticize, blame, abuse, condemn, carpet (*informal*), denounce, put down, slate (*informal, chiefly U.S.*), rebuke, reprimand, reproach, scold, berate, castigate, chide, tear into (*informal*), diss (*slang, chiefly U.S.*), blast, read the riot act, reprove, upbraid, slap on the wrist, lambast(e), bawl out (*informal*), excoriate, rap over the knuckles, chew out (*U.S. & Canad. informal*), tear (someone) off a strip (*Brit. informal*), give (someone) a rocket (*Brit. & N.Z. informal*), reprehend ...*I would not presume to censure him for his views*... OPPOSITE applaud
NOUN = disapproval, criticism, blame, condemnation, rebuke, reprimand, reproach, dressing down (*informal*), stick (*slang*), stricture, reproof, castigation, obloquy, remonstrance ...*It is a controversial policy which has attracted international censure*... OPPOSITE

approval

central 1 = <u>inner</u>, middle, mid, interior …*She had a house in central London*… OPPOSITE outer
2 = <u>main</u>, chief, key, essential, primary, principal, fundamental, focal …*The Poll Tax was a central part of Mrs Thatcher's reform of local government*… OPPOSITE minor

centralize = <u>unify</u>, concentrate, incorporate, compact, streamline, converge, condense, amalgamate, rationalize

centre NOUN = <u>middle</u>, heart, focus, core, nucleus, hub, pivot, kernel, crux, bull's-eye, midpoint …*A large wooden table dominates the centre of the room*… OPPOSITE edge
VERB = <u>focus</u>, concentrate, cluster, revolve, converge …*All his thoughts are centred on himself*… …*Our efforts centre on helping patients to overcome illness*…

centrepiece = <u>focus</u>, highlight, hub, star

ceremonial ADJECTIVE = <u>formal</u>, public, official, ritual, stately, solemn, liturgical, courtly, ritualistic …*He represented the nation on ceremonial occasions*… OPPOSITE informal
NOUN = <u>ritual</u>, ceremony, rite, formality, solemnity …*It is difficult to imagine a more impressive ceremonial*…

ceremony 1 = <u>ritual</u>, service, rite, observance, commemoration, solemnities …*The flag was blessed in a ceremony in the local cathedral*…
2 = <u>formality</u>, ceremonial, propriety, decorum, formal courtesy …*He was crowned with great ceremony*…

certain 1 = <u>sure</u>, convinced, positive, confident, satisfied, assured, free from doubt …*She's absolutely certain she's going to make it as a singer*… OPPOSITE unsure
2 = <u>bound</u>, sure, fated, destined …*They say he's certain to get a nomination for best supporting actor*… OPPOSITE unlikely
3 = <u>inevitable</u>, unavoidable, inescapable, inexorable, ineluctable …*They intervened to save him from certain death*…
4 = <u>known</u>, true, positive, plain, ascertained, unmistakable, conclusive, undoubted, unequivocal, undeniable, irrefutable, unquestionable, incontrovertible, indubitable …*One thing is certain – they have the utmost respect for each other*… OPPOSITE doubtful
5 = <u>fixed</u>, decided, established, settled, definite …*He has to pay a certain sum in child support every month*… OPPOSITE indefinite
6 = <u>particular</u>, special, individual, specific …*A certain person has been looking for you*…

certainly = <u>definitely</u>, surely, truly, absolutely, undoubtedly, positively, decidedly, without doubt, unquestionably, undeniably, without question, unequivocally, indisputably, assuredly, indubitably, doubtlessly, come hell or high water, irrefutably

certainty 1 = <u>confidence</u>, trust, faith, conviction, assurance, certitude, sureness, positiveness …*I have said with absolute certainty that there will be no change of policy*… OPPOSITE doubt
2 = <u>inevitability</u> …*There is too little certainty about the

outcome yet*… OPPOSITE uncertainty
3 = <u>fact</u>, truth, reality, sure thing (*informal*), surety, banker …*A general election became a certainty three weeks ago*…

certificate = <u>document</u>, licence, warrant, voucher, diploma, testimonial, authorization, credential(s)

certify = <u>confirm</u>, show, declare, guarantee, witness, assure, endorse, testify, notify, verify, ascertain, validate, attest, corroborate, avow, authenticate, vouch for, aver

cessation = <u>ceasing</u>, ending, break, halt, halting, pause, suspension, interruption, respite, standstill, stoppage, termination, let-up (*informal*), remission, abeyance, discontinuance, stay

chafe 1 = <u>rub</u>, scratch, scrape, rasp, abrade …*The shorts were chafing my thighs*…
2 = <u>be annoyed</u>, rage, fume, be angry, fret, be offended, be irritated, be incensed, be impatient, be exasperated, be inflamed, be ruffled, be vexed, be narked (*Brit., Austral., & N.Z. slang*) …*He chafed at having to take orders from someone else*…

chaff = <u>husks</u>, remains, refuse, waste, hulls, rubbish, trash, dregs

chagrin NOUN = <u>annoyance</u>, embarrassment, humiliation, dissatisfaction, disquiet, displeasure, mortification, discomfiture, vexation, discomposure …*Much to his chagrin, she didn't remember him at all*…
VERB = <u>annoy</u>, embarrass, humiliate, disquiet, vex, displease, mortify, discomfit, dissatisfy, discompose …*He was chagrined at missing such an easy goal*…

chain NOUN 1 = <u>tether</u>, coupling, link, bond, shackle, fetter, manacle …*The dogs were growling and pulling at their chains*…
2 = <u>series</u>, set, train, string, sequence, succession, progression, concatenation …*a horrific chain of events*…
VERB = <u>bind</u>, confine, restrain, handcuff, shackle, tether, fetter, manacle …*We were kept in a cell, chained to the wall*…

chairman *or* **chairwoman** 1 = <u>director</u>, president, chief, executive, chairperson …*I had done business with the company's chairman*…
2 = <u>master of ceremonies</u>, spokesman, chair, speaker, MC, chairperson …*The chairman declared the meeting open*…

Word Power

chairman/chairwoman – The general trend of nonsexist language is to find a term which can apply to both sexes equally, as in the use of *actor* to refer to both men and women. *Chairman* can seem inappropriate when applied to a woman, while *chairwoman* specifies gender, and so, as the entry above illustrates, the terms *chair* and *chairperson* are often preferred as alternatives.

---

chalk up (*Informal*) 1 = <u>score</u>, win, gain, achieve, accumulate, attain …*The team chalked up one win *after another*…

2 = <u>record</u>, mark, enter, credit, register, log, tally …*I just chalked his odd behaviour up to midlife crisis*…

challenge NOUN **1** = <u>dare</u>, provocation, summons to contest …*I like a challenge, and they don't come much bigger than this*…
2 = <u>test</u>, trial, opposition, confrontation, defiance, ultimatum, face-off (*slang*) …*In December, she saw off the first challenge to her leadership*…
VERB **1** = <u>dispute</u>, question, tackle, confront, defy, object to, disagree with, take issue with, impugn …*The move was immediately challenged by the opposition*…
2 = <u>dare</u>, invite, provoke, defy, summon, call out, throw down the gauntlet …*He left a note at the crime scene, challenging detectives to catch him*…
3 = <u>test</u>, try, tax …*a task that would challenge his courage*…
4 = <u>question</u>, interrogate, accost …*The men opened fire after they were challenged by the guard*…

chamber **1** = <u>hall</u>, room …*We are going to be in the council chamber when he speaks*…
2 = <u>council</u>, assembly, legislature, legislative body …*the main political chamber of the Slovenian parliament*…
3 = <u>room</u>, bedroom, apartment, enclosure, cubicle …*We shall dine together in my chamber*…
4 = <u>compartment</u>, hollow, cavity …*The incinerator works by focusing the sun's rays onto a cylindrical glass chamber*…

champion NOUN **1** = <u>winner</u>, hero, victor, conqueror, title holder, warrior …*Kasparov became a world chess champion*…
2 = <u>defender</u>, guardian, patron, backer, protector, upholder, vindicator …*He received acclaim as a champion of the oppressed*…
VERB = <u>support</u>, back, defend, promote, advocate, fight for, uphold, espouse, stick up for (*informal*) …*He passionately championed the poor*…

chance NOUN **1** = <u>probability</u>, odds, possibility, prospect, liability, likelihood …*This partnership has a good chance of success*… OPPOSITE certainty
2 = <u>opportunity</u>, opening, occasion, time, scope, window …*All eligible people will get a chance to vote*…
3 = <u>accident</u>, fortune, luck, fate, destiny, coincidence, misfortune, providence …*I met him quite by chance*… OPPOSITE design
4 = <u>risk</u>, speculation, gamble, hazard …*I certainly think it's worth taking a chance*…
ADJECTIVE = <u>accidental</u>, random, casual, incidental, unforeseen, unintentional, fortuitous, inadvertent, serendipitous, unforeseeable, unlooked-for …*He describes their chance meeting as intense*… OPPOSITE planned
VERB **1** = <u>happen</u> …*A man I chanced to meet proved to be a most unusual character*…
2 = <u>risk</u>, try, stake, venture, gamble, hazard, wager …*No sniper would chance a shot from amongst that crowd*…

(*Related Words*)

adjective: fortuitous

change NOUN **1** = <u>alteration</u>, innovation, transformation, modification, mutation, metamorphosis, permutation, transmutation, difference, revolution, transition …*They are going to have to make some drastic changes*…
2 = <u>variety</u>, break (*informal*), departure, variation, novelty, diversion, whole new ball game (*informal*) …*It makes a nice change to see you in a good mood for once*… OPPOSITE monotony
3 = <u>exchange</u>, trade, conversion, swap, substitution, interchange …*He stuffed a bag with a few changes of clothing*…
VERB **1** = <u>alter</u>, reform, transform, adjust, moderate, revise, modify, remodel, reorganize, restyle, convert …*They should change the law to make it illegal to own replica weapons*… OPPOSITE keep
2 = <u>shift</u>, vary, transform, alter, modify, diversify, fluctuate, mutate, metamorphose, transmute …*We are trying to detect and understand how the climate changes*… OPPOSITE stay
3 = <u>exchange</u>, trade, replace, substitute, swap, interchange …*Can we change it for another if it doesn't work properly?*…

changeable = <u>variable</u>, shifting, mobile, uncertain, volatile, unsettled, unpredictable, versatile, unstable, irregular, erratic, wavering, uneven, unreliable, fickle, temperamental, whimsical, mercurial, capricious, unsteady, protean, vacillating, fitful, mutable, inconstant OPPOSITE constant

channel NOUN **1** = <u>means</u>, way, course, approach, medium, route, path, avenue …*We'll be lodging a complaint through the official channels*…
2 = <u>strait</u>, sound, route, passage, canal, waterway, main …*Oil spilled into the channel following a collision between a tanker and a trawler*…
3 = <u>duct</u>, chamber, artery, groove, gutter, furrow, conduit …*Keep the drainage channel clear*…
VERB = <u>direct</u>, guide, conduct, transmit, convey …*Stephen is channelling all his energies into his novel*…

chant NOUN = <u>song</u>, carol, chorus, melody, psalm …*We were listening to a CD of Gregorian chant*…
VERB = <u>sing</u>, chorus, recite, intone, carol …*Muslims chanted and prayed in the temple*…

chaos = <u>disorder</u>, confusion, mayhem, anarchy, lawlessness, pandemonium, entropy, bedlam, tumult, disorganization OPPOSITE orderliness

chaotic = <u>disordered</u>, confused, uncontrolled, anarchic, tumultuous, lawless, riotous, topsy-turvy, disorganized, purposeless

chap (*Informal*) = <u>fellow</u>, man, person, individual, type, sort, customer (*informal*), character, guy (*informal*), bloke (*Brit. informal*), cove (*slang*), dude (*U.S. & Canad. informal*)

chapter **1** = <u>section</u>, part, stage, division, episode, topic, segment, instalment …*I took the title of this chapter from one of my favorite songs*…
2 = <u>period</u>, time, stage, phase …*It was one of the most dramatic chapters of recent British politics*…

char = <u>scorch</u>, sear, singe

character 1 = <u>personality</u>, nature, make-up, cast, constitution, bent, attributes, temper, temperament, complexion, disposition, individuality, marked traits …*There is a side to his character which you haven't seen yet*…
2 = <u>nature</u>, kind, quality, constitution, calibre …*Moscow's reforms were socialist in character*…
3 (*Informal*) = <u>person</u>, sort, individual, type, guy (*informal*), fellow …*What an unpleasant character he is!*…
4 = <u>reputation</u>, honour, integrity, good name, rectitude …*He's begun a series of attacks on my character*…
5 = <u>role</u>, part, persona …*He plays the film's central character*…
6 = <u>eccentric</u>, card (*informal*), original, nut (*slang*), flake (*slang, chiefly U.S.*), oddity, oddball (*informal*), odd bod (*informal*), queer fish (*Brit. informal*), wacko or whacko (*informal*) …*He'll be sadly missed. He was a real character*…
7 = <u>symbol</u>, mark, sign, letter, figure, type, device, logo, emblem, rune, cipher, hieroglyph …*Chinese characters inscribed on a plaque*…

characteristic NOUN = <u>feature</u>, mark, quality, property, attribute, faculty, trait, quirk, peculiarity, idiosyncrasy …*Genes determine the characteristics of every living thing*…
ADJECTIVE = <u>typical</u>, special, individual, specific, representative, distinguishing, distinctive, peculiar, singular, idiosyncratic, symptomatic …*Windmills are a characteristic feature of the landscape*… OPPOSITE rare

characterize = <u>distinguish</u>, mark, identify, brand, inform, stamp, typify

charade = <u>pretence</u>, farce, parody, pantomime, fake

charge VERB **1** = <u>accuse</u>, indict, impeach, incriminate, arraign …*They have all the evidence required to charge him*… OPPOSITE acquit
2 = <u>attack</u>, assault, assail …*Our general ordered us to charge the enemy*… OPPOSITE retreat
3 = <u>rush</u>, storm, stampede …*He charged into the room*…
4 = <u>fill</u>, load, instil, suffuse, lade …*a performance that was charged with energy*…
NOUN **1** = <u>price</u>, rate, cost, amount, payment, expense, toll, expenditure, outlay, damage (*informal*) …*We can arrange this for a small charge*…
2 = <u>accusation</u>, allegation, indictment, imputation …*They appeared at court to deny charges of murder*… OPPOSITE acquittal
3 = <u>care</u>, trust, responsibility, custody, safekeeping …*I have been given charge of this class*…
4 = <u>duty</u>, office, concern, responsibility, remit …*I did not consider it any part of my charge to come up with marketing ideas*…
5 = <u>ward</u>, pupil, protégé, dependant …*The coach tried to get his charges motivated*…
6 = <u>attack</u>, rush, assault, onset, onslaught, stampede, sortie …*He led the bayonet charge from the front*… OPPOSITE retreat

charisma = <u>charm</u>, appeal, personality, attraction, lure, allure, magnetism, force of personality

charismatic = <u>charming</u>, appealing, attractive, influential, magnetic, enticing, alluring

charitable 1 = <u>benevolent</u>, liberal, generous, lavish, philanthropic, bountiful, beneficent …*He made large donations to numerous charitable organizations*… OPPOSITE mean
2 = <u>kind</u>, understanding, forgiving, sympathetic, favourable, tolerant, indulgent, lenient, considerate, magnanimous, broad-minded …*Some people take a less charitable view of his behaviour*… OPPOSITE unkind

charity 1 = <u>charitable organization</u>, fund, movement, trust, endowment …*The National Trust is a registered charity*…
2 = <u>donations</u>, help, relief, gift, contributions, assistance, hand-out, philanthropy, alms-giving, benefaction, largesse or largess …*My mum was very proud. She wouldn't accept charity*… OPPOSITE meanness
3 = <u>kindness</u>, love, pity, humanity, affection, goodness, goodwill, compassion, generosity, indulgence, bounty, altruism, benevolence, fellow feeling, bountifulness, tenderheartedness …*He had no sense of right and wrong, no charity, no humanity*… OPPOSITE ill will

charlatan = <u>fraud</u>, cheat, fake, sham, pretender, quack, con man (*informal*), impostor, fraudster, swindler, mountebank, grifter (*slang, chiefly U.S. & Canad.*), phoney or phony (*informal*), rorter (*Austral. slang*)

charm NOUN **1** = <u>attraction</u>, appeal, fascination, allure, magnetism, desirability, allurement …*He was a man of great distinction and charm*… OPPOSITE repulsiveness
2 = <u>talisman</u>, trinket, amulet, lucky piece, good-luck piece, fetish …*She wore a silver bracelet hung with charms*…
3 = <u>spell</u>, magic, enchantment, sorcery …*They cross their fingers and spit over their shoulders as a charm against the evil eye*…
VERB **1** = <u>attract</u>, win, please, delight, fascinate, absorb, entrance, win over, enchant, captivate, beguile, allure, bewitch, ravish, mesmerize, enrapture, enamour …*My brother charms everyone he meets*… OPPOSITE repel
2 = <u>persuade</u>, seduce, coax, beguile, cajole, sweet-talk (*informal*) …*I'm sure you'll be able to charm him into taking you*…

charming = <u>attractive</u>, pleasing, appealing, engaging, lovely, winning, pleasant, fetching, delightful, cute, irresistible, seductive, captivating, eye-catching, bewitching, delectable, winsome, likable or likeable OPPOSITE unpleasant

chart NOUN = <u>table</u>, diagram, blueprint, graph, tabulation, plan, map …*The chart below shows the results of our survey*…
VERB **1** = <u>plot</u>, map out, delineate, sketch, draft, graph, tabulate …*These seas have been well charted*…
2 = <u>monitor</u>, follow, record, note, document, register,

trace, outline, log, graph, tabulate ...*Bulletin boards charted each executive's progress...*

charter NOUN **1** = document, right, contract, bond, permit, licence, concession, privilege, franchise, deed, prerogative, indenture ...*In Britain, city status is granted by royal charter...*
2 = constitution, laws, rules, code ...*The Prime Minister also attacked the social charter...*
VERB **1** = hire, commission, employ, rent, lease ...*He chartered a jet to fly her home...*
2 = authorize, permit, sanction, entitle, license, empower, give authority ...*The council is chartered to promote the understanding of British culture throughout the world...*

chase VERB **1** = pursue, follow, track, hunt, run after, course ...*She chased the thief for 100 yards...*
2 = drive away, drive, expel, hound, send away, send packing, put to flight ...*Some farmers chase you off their land quite aggressively...*
3 = rush, run, race, shoot, fly, speed, dash, sprint, bolt, dart, hotfoot ...*They chased down the stairs into the alley...*
NOUN = pursuit, race, hunt, hunting ...*He was arrested after a car chase...*

chasm 1 = gulf, opening, crack, gap, rent, hollow, void, gorge, crater, cavity, abyss, ravine, cleft, fissure, crevasse ...*The chasm was deep and its sides almost vertical...*
2 = gap, division, gulf, split, breach, rift, alienation, hiatus ...*the chasm that separates the rich from the poor...*

chassis = frame, framework, fuselage, bodywork, substructure

chaste 1 = pure, moral, decent, innocent, immaculate, wholesome, virtuous, virginal, unsullied, uncontaminated, undefiled, incorrupt ...*Her character was pure, her thoughts chaste...* OPPOSITE promiscuous
2 = simple, quiet, elegant, modest, refined, restrained, austere, unaffected, decorous ...*Beyond them she could see the dim, chaste interior of the room...*

chasten = subdue, discipline, cow, curb, humble, soften, humiliate, tame, afflict, repress, put in your place

chastise = scold, blame, correct, discipline, lecture, carpet (*informal*), nag, censure, rebuke, reprimand, reproach, berate, tick off (*informal*), castigate, chide, tell off (*informal*), find fault with, remonstrate with, bring (someone) to book, take (someone) to task, reprove, upbraid, bawl out (*informal*), give (someone) a talking-to (*informal*), haul (someone) over the coals (*informal*), chew out (*U.S. & Canad. informal*), give (someone) a dressing-down, give a rocket (*Brit. & N.Z. informal*), give (someone) a row OPPOSITE praise

chastity = purity, virtue, innocence, modesty, virginity, celibacy, continence, maidenhood OPPOSITE promiscuity

chat VERB = talk, gossip, jaw (*slang*), natter, blather, schmooze (*slang*), blether (*Scot.*), shoot the breeze (*U.S. slang*), chew the rag or fat (*slang*) ...*I was just chatting to him the other day...*
NOUN = talk, tête-à-tête, conversation, gossip, heart-to-heart, natter, blather, schmooze (*slang*), blether (*Scot.*), chinwag (*Brit. informal*), confab (*informal*), craic (*Irish informal*) ...*She asked me into her office for a chat...*

chatter VERB = prattle, chat, rabbit on (*Brit. informal*), babble, gab (*informal*), natter, tattle, jabber, blather, schmooze (*slang*), blether (*Scot.*), run off at the mouth (*U.S. slang*), prate, gossip ...*Everyone was chattering away in different languages...*
NOUN = prattle, chat, rabbit (*Brit. informal*), gossip, babble, twaddle, gab (*informal*), natter, tattle, jabber, blather, blether (*Scot.*) ...*She kept up a steady stream of chatter the whole time...*

chatty = talkative, informal, effusive, garrulous, gabby (*informal*), gossipy, newsy (*informal*) OPPOSITE quiet

cheap 1 = inexpensive, sale, economy, reduced, keen, reasonable, bargain, low-priced, low-cost, cut-price, economical, cheapo (*informal*) ...*People want good service at a cheap price... ...Smoke detectors are cheap and easy to put up...* OPPOSITE expensive
2 = inferior, poor, worthless, second-rate, shoddy, tawdry, tatty, trashy, substandard, low-rent (*informal, chiefly U.S.*), two-bit (*U.S. & Canad. slang*), crappy (*slang*), two a penny, rubbishy, dime-a-dozen (*informal*), tinhorn (*U.S. slang*), bodger or bodgie (*Austral. slang*) ...*Don't resort to cheap copies; save up for the real thing...* OPPOSITE good
3 (*Informal*) = despicable, mean, low, base, vulgar, sordid, contemptible, scurvy, scungy (*Austral. & N.Z.*) ...*That was a cheap trick to play on anyone...* OPPOSITE decent

cheapen = degrade, lower, discredit, devalue, demean, belittle, depreciate, debase, derogate

cheat VERB **1** = deceive, skin (*slang*), trick, fool, take in (*informal*), con (*informal*), stiff (*slang*), sting (*informal*), mislead, rip off (*slang*), fleece, hoax, defraud, dupe, beguile, gull (*archaic*), do (*informal*), swindle, stitch up (*slang*), victimize, bamboozle (*informal*), hoodwink, double-cross (*informal*), diddle (*informal*), take for a ride (*informal*), bilk, pull a fast one on (*informal*), finagle (*informal*) ...*He cheated an old woman out of her life savings...*
2 = foil, check, defeat, prevent, frustrate, deprive, baffle, thwart ...*He cheated death when he was rescued from the blazing cottage...*
NOUN = deceiver, sharper, cheater, shark, charlatan, trickster, con man (*informal*), impostor, fraudster, double-crosser (*informal*), swindler, grifter (*slang, chiefly U.S. & Canad.*), rorter (*Austral. slang*), chiseller (*informal*) ...*He's nothing but a rotten cheat...*

check VERB **1** *often with* **out** = examine, test, study, look at, research, note, confirm, investigate, monitor, probe, tick, vet, inspect, look over, verify, work over, scrutinize, make sure of, inquire into, take a dekko at (*Brit. slang*) ...*Check the accuracy of every detail in your CV... ...Get a mechanic to check the car out for you before you buy it...* OPPOSITE overlook
2 = stop, control, limit, arrest, delay, halt, curb, bar,

restrain, inhibit, rein, thwart, hinder, repress, obstruct, retard, impede, bridle, stem the flow of, nip in the bud, put a spoke in someone's wheel ...*Sex education is expected to help check the spread of Aids...* OPPOSITE ▷ further

NOUN **1** = examination, test, research, investigation, inspection, scrutiny, once-over (*informal*) ...*He is being constantly monitored with regular checks on his blood pressure...*

2 = control, limitation, restraint, constraint, rein, obstacle, curb, obstruction, stoppage, inhibition, impediment, hindrance, damper ...*There is no check on the flood of new immigrants arriving in the country...*

cheek (*Informal*) = impudence, face (*informal*), front, nerve, sauce (*informal*), gall (*informal*), disrespect, audacity, neck (*informal*), lip (*slang*), temerity, chutzpah (*U.S. & Canad. informal*), insolence, impertinence, effrontery, brass neck (*Brit. informal*), brazenness, sassiness (*U.S. informal*)

cheeky = impudent, rude, forward, fresh (*informal*), insulting, saucy, audacious, sassy (*U.S. informal*), pert, disrespectful, impertinent, insolent, lippy (*U.S. & Canad. slang*) OPPOSITE ▷ respectful

cheer VERB **1** = applaud, hail, acclaim, clap, hurrah ...*Cheering crowds lined the route...* OPPOSITE ▷ boo

2 = hearten, encourage, warm, comfort, elevate, animate, console, uplift, brighten, exhilarate, solace, enliven, cheer up, buoy up, gladden, elate, inspirit ...*The people around him were cheered by his presence...* OPPOSITE ▷ dishearten

NOUN **1** = applause, ovation, plaudits, acclamation ...*The colonel was rewarded by a resounding cheer from his men...*

2 = cheerfulness, comfort, joy, optimism, animation, glee, solace, buoyancy, mirth, gaiety, merriment, liveliness, gladness, hopefulness, merry-making ...*This news did not bring them much cheer...*

PHRASES **cheer someone up** = comfort, encourage, brighten, hearten, enliven, gladden, gee up, jolly along (*informal*) ...*She chatted away brightly, trying to cheer him up...* ◆ **cheer up** = take heart, rally, perk up, buck up (*informal*) ...*Cheer up, things could be a lot worse...*

cheerful 1 = happy, bright, contented, glad, optimistic, bucked (*informal*), enthusiastic, sparkling, gay, sunny, jolly, animated, merry, upbeat (*informal*), buoyant, hearty, cheery, joyful, genial, jaunty, chirpy (*informal*), sprightly, blithe, light-hearted ...*They are both very cheerful in spite of their circumstances...* OPPOSITE ▷ sad

2 = pleasant, bright, sunny, gay, enlivening ...*The room is bright and cheerful...* OPPOSITE ▷ gloomy

cheerfulness = happiness, good humour, exuberance, high spirits, buoyancy, gaiety, good cheer, gladness, geniality, light-heartedness, jauntiness, joyousness

cheering = encouraging, promising, comforting, reassuring, heartening, auspicious, propitious

cheery = cheerful, happy, pleasant, lively, sunny,

upbeat (*informal*), good-humoured, carefree, breezy, genial, chirpy (*informal*), jovial, full of beans (*informal*)

chemical = compound, drug, substance, synthetic substance, potion

➤ **chemical elements**

chemist = pharmacist, apothecary (*obsolete*), pharmacologist, dispenser

cherish 1 = cling to, prize, treasure, hold dear, cleave to ...*I will cherish the memory of that visit for many years to come...* OPPOSITE ▷ despise

2 = care for, love, support, comfort, look after, shelter, treasure, nurture, cosset, hold dear ...*He genuinely loved and cherished his children...* OPPOSITE ▷ neglect

3 = harbour, nurse, sustain, foster, entertain ...*He cherished an ambition to be an actor...*

chess

> ### Chess
> http://www.princeton.edu/~jedwards/cif/chess.html
>
> | Chess piece | Abbreviation |
> | --- | --- |
> | Bishop | B |
> | King | K |
> | King's bishop | KB |
> | King's knight | KN |
> | King's rook | KR |
> | Knight | N |
> | Pawn | P |
> | Queen | Q |
> | Queen's bishop | QB |
> | Queen's knight | QN |
> | Queen's rook | QR |

chest 1 = breast, front ...*He crossed his arms over his chest...*

2 = box, case, trunk, crate, coffer, ark (*dialect*), casket, strongbox ...*At the very bottom of the chest were his carving tools...*

Related Words

adjective: pectoral

chew VERB = munch, bite, grind, champ, crunch, gnaw, chomp, masticate ...*Be careful to eat slowly and chew your food well...*

PHRASES **chew something over** = consider, weigh up, ponder, mull (over), meditate on, reflect upon, muse on, ruminate, deliberate upon ...*You might want to sit back and chew things over for a while...*

chewy = tough, fibrous, leathery, as tough as old boots

chic = stylish, smart, elegant, fashionable, trendy (*Brit. informal*), up-to-date, modish, à la mode, voguish (*informal*) OPPOSITE ▷ unfashionable

chide (*Old-fashioned*) = scold, blame, lecture, carpet (*informal*), put down, criticize, slate (*informal, chiefly Brit.*), censure, rebuke, reprimand, reproach, berate, tick off (*informal*), admonish, tear into (*informal*), blast, tell off (*informal*), find fault, diss (*slang, chiefly U.S.*), read the riot act, reprove, upbraid, slap on the wrist, lambast(e), bawl out (*informal*), rap over the knuckles, chew out (*U.S. & Canad. informal*), tear (someone) off a strip (*Brit. informal*), give (someone) a

Chemical elements http://www.chemicalelements.com/

Chemical element	Symbol	Atomic number	Chemical element	Symbol	Atomic number
hydrogen	H	1	caesium or (U.S.) cesium	Cs	55
helium	He	2	barium	Ba	56
lithium	Li	3	lanthanum	La	57
beryllium	Be	4	cerium	Ce	58
boron	B	5	praseodymium	Pr	59
carbon	C	6	neodymium	Nd	60
nitrogen	N	7	promethium	Pm	61
oxygen	O	8	samarium	Sm	62
fluorine	F	9	europium	Eu	63
neon	Ne	10	gadolinium	Gd	64
sodium	Na	11	terbium	Tb	65
magnesium	Mg	12	dysprosium	Dy	66
aluminium or (U.S.) aluminum	Al	13	holmium	Ho	67
silicon	Si	14	erbium	Er	68
phosphorus	P	15	thulium	Tm	69
sulphur or (U.S.) sulfur	S	16	ytterbium	Yb	70
chlorine	Cl	17	lutetium or lutecium	Lu	71
argon	Ar	18	hafnium	Hf	72
potassium	K	19	tantalum	Ta	73
calcium	Ca	20	tungsten or wolfram	W	74
scandium	Sc	21	rhenium	Re	75
titanium	Ti	22	osmium	Os	76
vanadium	V	23	iridium	Ir	77
chromium	Cr	24	platinum	Pt	78
manganese	Mn	25	gold	Au	79
iron	Fe	26	mercury	Hg	80
cobalt	Co	27	thallium	Tl	81
nickel	Ni	28	lead	Pb	82
copper	Cu	29	bismuth	Bi	83
zinc	Zn	30	polonium	Po	84
gallium	Ga	31	astatine	At	85
germanium	Ge	32	radon	Rn	86
arsenic	As	33	francium	Fr	87
selenium	Se	34	radium	Ra	88
bromine	Br	35	actinium	Ac	89
krypton	Kr	36	thorium	Th	90
rubidium	Rb	37	protactinium	Pa	91
strontium	Sr	38	uranium	U	92
yttrium	Y	39	neptunium	Np	93
zirconium	Zr	40	plutonium	Pu	94
niobium	Nb	41	americium	Am	95
molybdenum	Mo	42	curium	Cm	96
technetium	Tc	43	berkelium	Bk	97
ruthenium	Ru	44	californium	Cf	98
rhodium	Rh	45	einsteinium	Es	99
palladium	Pd	46	fermium	Fm	100
silver	Ag	47	mendelevium	Md	101
cadmium	Cd	48	nobelium	No	102
indium	In	49	lawrencium	Lr	103
tin	Sn	50	rutherfordium	Rf	104
antimony	Sb	51	dubnium	Db	105
tellurium	Te	52	seaborgium	Sg	106
iodine	I	53	bohrium	Bh	107
xenon	Xe	54	hassium	Hs	108
			meitnerium	Mt	109

rocket (*Brit. & N.Z. informal*), reprehend, give (someone) a row (*Scot. informal*)

chief NOUN = <u>head</u>, leader, director, manager, lord, boss (*informal*), captain, master, governor, commander, principal, superior, ruler, superintendent, chieftain, ringleader, baas (*S. African*) ...*The new leader is the deputy chief of the territory's defence force...* OPPOSITE> subordinate

ADJECTIVE = <u>primary</u> ...*The job went to one of his chief rivals...*, highest, leading, main, prime, capital, central, key, essential, premier, supreme, most important, outstanding, principal, prevailing, cardinal, paramount, big-time (*informal*), foremost, major league (*informal*), predominant, uppermost, pre-eminent, especial ...*Financial stress is acknowledged as a chief reason for divorce*... OPPOSITE minor

chiefly 1 = especially, essentially, principally, primarily, above all ...*We are chiefly concerned with the welfare of the children*...
2 = mainly, largely, usually, mostly, in general, on the whole, predominantly, in the main ...*a committee composed chiefly of grey-haired old gentlemen*...

child 1 = youngster, baby, kid (*informal*), minor, infant, babe, juvenile, toddler, tot, wean (*Scot.*), little one, brat, bairn (*Scot.*), suckling, nipper (*informal*), chit, babe in arms, sprog (*slang*), munchkin (*informal, chiefly U.S.*), rug rat (*slang*), nursling, littlie (*Austral. informal*), ankle-biter (*Austral. slang*), tacker (*Austral. slang*) ...*This film is not suitable for children*...
2 = offspring, issue, descendant, progeny ...*How many children do you have?*...

(Related Words)
adjective: filial
prefix: paedo-

childbirth = child-bearing, labour, delivery, lying-in, confinement, parturition

(Related Words)
adjectives: natal, obstetric

childhood = youth, minority, infancy, schooldays, immaturity, boyhood *or* girlhood

childish 1 = youthful, young, boyish *or* girlish ...*One of his most appealing qualities is his childish enthusiasm*...
2 = immature, silly, juvenile, foolish, trifling, frivolous, infantile, puerile ...*I've never seen such selfish and childish behaviour*... OPPOSITE mature

childlike = innocent, trusting, simple, naive, credulous, artless, ingenuous, guileless, unfeigned, trustful

chill VERB 1 = cool, refrigerate, freeze ...*Chill the fruit salad until serving time*...
2 = dishearten, depress, discourage, dismay, dampen, deject ...*There was a coldness in her voice which chilled him*...
NOUN 1 = coldness, bite, nip, sharpness, coolness, rawness, crispness, frigidity ...*September is here, bringing with it a chill in the mornings*...
2 = shiver, frisson, goose pimples, goose flesh ...*He smiled an odd smile that sent a chill through me*...
ADJECTIVE = chilly, biting, sharp, freezing, raw, bleak, chilly, wintry, frigid, parky (*Brit. informal*) ...*A chill wind was blowing*...

chilly 1 = cool, fresh, sharp, crisp, penetrating, brisk, breezy, draughty, nippy, parky (*Brit. informal*), blowy ...*It was a chilly afternoon*... OPPOSITE warm
2 = unfriendly, hostile, unsympathetic, frigid, unresponsive, unwelcoming, cold as ice ...*I was slightly afraid of his chilly, distant politeness*... OPPOSITE friendly

chime VERB = ring ...*The Guildhall clock chimed three o'clock*...
NOUN = sound, boom, toll, jingle, dong, tinkle, clang,

peal ...*the chime of the Guildhall clock*...

chimera = illusion, dream, fantasy, delusion, spectre, snare, hallucination, figment, ignis fatuus, will-o'-the-wisp

china[1] = pottery, ceramics, ware, porcelain, crockery, tableware, service ...*She collects blue and white china*...

china[2] (*Brit. & S. African informal*) = friend, pal, mate (*informal*), buddy (*informal*), companion, best friend, intimate, cock (*Brit. informal*), close friend, comrade, chum (*informal*), crony, main man (*slang, chiefly U.S.*), soul mate, homeboy (*slang, chiefly U.S.*), cobber (*Austral. or old-fashioned N.Z. informal*), bosom friend, boon companion ...*How are you, my old china?*...

chink = opening, crack, gap, rift, aperture, cleft, crevice, fissure, cranny

chip NOUN 1 = fragment, scrap, shaving, flake, paring, wafer, sliver, shard ...*His eyes gleamed like chips of blue glass*...
2 = scratch, nick, flaw, notch, dent ...*The washbasin had a small chip in it*...
3 = counter, disc, token ...*He gambled all his chips on one number*...
VERB 1 = nick, damage, gash ...*The blow chipped the woman's tooth*...
2 = chisel, whittle ...*a sculptor chipping at a block of marble*...
PHRASES **chip in** (*Informal*) 1 = contribute, pay, donate, subscribe, go Dutch (*informal*) ...*We'll all chip in for the petrol and food*...
2 = interpose, put in, interrupt, interject, butt in, put your oar in ...*He chipped in, 'That's right,' before she could answer*...

chirp = chirrup, pipe, peep, warble, twitter, cheep, tweet

chirpy (*Informal*) = cheerful, happy, bright, enthusiastic, lively, sparkling, sunny, jolly, animated, buoyant, radiant, jaunty, sprightly, in high spirits, blithe, full of beans (*informal*), light-hearted

chivalry 1 = courtesy, politeness, gallantry, courtliness, gentlemanliness ...*He always treated women with old-fashioned chivalry*...
2 = knight-errantry, knighthood, gallantry, courtliness ...*Our story is set in England, in the age of chivalry*...

choice NOUN 1 = range, variety, selection, assortment ...*It's available in a choice of colours*...
2 = selection, preference, election, pick ...*His choice of words made Rodney angry*...
3 = option, say, alternative ...*If I had any choice in the matter, I wouldn't have gone*...
ADJECTIVE = best, bad (*slang*), special, prime, nice, prize, select, excellent, elect, crucial (*slang*), exclusive, elite, superior, exquisite, def (*slang*), booshit (*Austral. slang*), exo (*Austral. slang*), sik (*Austral. slang*), hand-picked, dainty ...*The finest array of choicest foods is to be found within their Food Hall*...

choke 1 = suffocate, stifle, smother, overpower, asphyxiate ...*Dense smoke swirled and billowed, its fumes choking her*...
2 = strangle, throttle, asphyxiate ...*They choked him

with his tie...

3 = block, dam, clog, obstruct, bung, constrict, occlude, congest, close, stop, bar ...*The village roads are choked with traffic...*

choose 1 = pick, take, prefer, select, elect, adopt, opt for, designate, single out, espouse, settle on, fix on, cherry-pick, settle upon, predestine ...*I chose him to accompany me on my trip...* `OPPOSITE` reject
2 = wish, want, desire, see fit ...*You can just take out the interest every year, if you choose...*

choosy (*Informal*) = fussy, particular, exacting, discriminating, selective, fastidious, picky (*informal*), finicky, faddy `OPPOSITE` indiscriminating

chop `VERB` = cut, fell, axe, slash, hack, sever, shear, cleave, hew, lop, truncate ...*We were set to work chopping wood...*
`PHRASES` **chop something up** = cut up, divide, fragment, cube, dice, mince ...*Chop up three firm tomatoes...* ♦ **the chop** (*Slang, chiefly Brit.*) = the sack, sacking (*informal*), dismissal, the boot (*slang*), your cards (*informal*), the axe (*informal*), termination, the (old) heave-ho (*informal*), the order of the boot (*slang*) ...*I was amazed when I got the chop from the team...*

choppy = rough, broken, ruffled, tempestuous, blustery, squally `OPPOSITE` calm

chore = task, job, duty, burden, hassle (*informal*), fag (*informal*), errand, no picnic

chortle `VERB` = chuckle, laugh, cackle, guffaw ...*He began chortling like an idiot...*
`NOUN` = chuckle, laugh, cackle, guffaw ...*The old man broke into a wheezy chortle of amusement...*

chorus `NOUN` **1** = refrain, response, strain, burden ...*Everyone joined in the chorus...*
2 = choir, singers, ensemble, vocalists, choristers ...*The chorus was singing 'The Ode to Joy'...*
`PHRASES` **in chorus** = in unison, as one, all together, in concert, in harmony, in accord, with one voice ...*'Let us in,' they all wailed in chorus...*

christen 1 = baptize, name ...*She was born in March and christened in June...*
2 = name, call, term, style, title, dub, designate ...*a boat which he christened 'the Stray Cat'...*

Christianity
➤ **Christian denominations and sects**

Christmas = festive season, Noël, Xmas (*informal*), Yule (*archaic*), Yuletide (*archaic*)

chronic 1 = persistent, constant, continual, deep-seated, incurable, deep-rooted, ineradicable ...*His drinking has led to chronic cirrhosis of the liver...*
2 (*Informal*) = dreadful, awful, appalling, atrocious, abysmal ...*The programme was chronic, all banal dialogue and canned laughter...*

chronicle `VERB` = record, tell, report, enter, relate, register, recount, set down, narrate, put on record ...*The rise of collectivism in Britain has been chronicled by several historians...*
`NOUN` = record, story, history, account, register, journal, diary, narrative, annals ...*this vast chronicle of Napoleonic times...*

chronicler = recorder, reporter, historian, narrator, scribe, diarist, annalist

chronological = sequential, ordered, historical, progressive, consecutive, in sequence `OPPOSITE` random

chubby = plump, stout, fleshy, tubby, flabby, portly, buxom, roly-poly, rotund, round, podgy `OPPOSITE` skinny

chuck (*Informal*) **1** = throw, cast, pitch, shy, toss, hurl, fling, sling, heave ...*Someone chucked a bottle and it caught me on the side of the head...*
2 often with *away* or *out* = throw out, dump (*informal*), scrap, get rid of, bin (*informal*), ditch (*slang*), junk (*informal*), discard, dispose of, dispense with, jettison ...*Don't just chuck your bottles away – recycle them... ...I chucked a whole lot of old magazines and papers...*
3 = give up or over, leave, stop, abandon, cease, resign from, pack in, jack in ...*Last summer, he chucked his job and went on the road...*
4 (*Austral. & N.Z. informal*) = vomit, throw up (*informal*), spew, heave (*slang*), puke (*slang*), barf (*U.S. slang*), chunder (*slang, chiefly Austral.*), upchuck (*U.S. slang*), do a technicolour yawn, toss your cookies (*U.S. slang*) ...*It smelt so bad I thought I was going to chuck...*

chuckle = laugh, giggle, snigger, chortle, titter

chum (*Informal*) = friend, mate (*informal*), pal (*informal*), companion, cock (*Brit. informal*), comrade, crony, main man (*slang, chiefly U.S.*), cobber (*Austral. or old-fashioned N.Z. informal*)

chummy (*Informal*) = friendly, close, thick (*informal*), pally (*informal*), intimate, affectionate, buddy-buddy (*slang, chiefly U.S. & Canad.*), palsy-walsy (*informal*),

---

Christian denominations and sects

http://www.bbc.co.uk/religion/religions/christianity/

Adventism	Coptic Church	Maronite Church	Quakerism
Amish	Dutch Reformed	Methodism	Roman Catholicism
Anabaptism	Church	Moravian Church	Russian Orthodox
Anglicanism	Eastern Orthodox	Mormons *or* Latter-day	Church
Baptist Church	Church	Saints	Salvation Army
Byzantine Church	Episcopal Church	New Jerusalem Church	Seventh-Day
Calvinism	evangelicalism	Orthodox Church	Adventism
Catholicism	Greek Orthodox	Pentecostalism	Shakerism
Christadelphianism	Church	Plymouth Brethren	Society of Friends
Christian Science	Jehovah's Witnesses	Presbyterianism	Unification Church
Congregationalism	Lutheranism	Protestantism	Unitarianism

matey *or* maty (*Brit. informal*)

chunk = <u>piece</u>, block, mass, portion, lump, slab, hunk, nugget, wad, dollop (*informal*), wodge (*Brit. informal*)

chunky = <u>thickset</u>, stocky, beefy (*informal*), stubby, dumpy ...*The sergeant was a chunky man in his late twenties...*

church = <u>chapel</u>, temple, cathedral, kirk (*Scot.*), minster, basilica, tabernacle, place of worship, house of God

(*Related Words*)

adjective: ecclesiastical

churlish = <u>rude</u>, harsh, vulgar, sullen, surly, morose, brusque, ill-tempered, boorish, uncouth, impolite, loutish, oafish, uncivil, unmannerly OPPOSITE polite

churn 1 = <u>stir up</u>, beat, disturb, swirl, agitate ...*The powerful thrust of the boat's engine churned the water...*
2 = <u>swirl</u>, boil, toss, foam, seethe, froth ...*Churning seas smash against the steep cliffs...*

chute = <u>slope</u>, channel, slide, incline, runway, gutter, trough, ramp

cigarette = <u>fag</u> (*Brit. slang*), smoke, gasper (*slang*), ciggy (*informal*), coffin nail (*slang*), cancer stick (*slang*)

cinema 1 = <u>pictures</u>, movies, picture-house, flicks (*slang*) ...*They decided to spend an evening at the cinema...*
2 = <u>films</u>, pictures, movies, big screen (*informal*), motion pictures, silver screen ...*Contemporary African cinema has much to offer in its vitality and freshness...*

cipher 1 = <u>code</u>, coded message, cryptogram ...*The codebreakers cracked the cipher...*
2 = <u>nobody</u>, nonentity ...*They were little more than ciphers who faithfully carried out the Fuehrer's commands...*

circa = <u>approximately</u>, about, around, roughly, in the region of, round about

circle NOUN 1 = <u>ring</u>, round, band, disc, loop, hoop, cordon, perimeter, halo ...*The flag was red with a large white circle... ...The monument consists of a circle of gigantic stones...*
2 = <u>group</u>, company, set, school, club, order, class, society, crowd, assembly, fellowship, fraternity, clique, coterie ...*a small circle of friends...*
3 = <u>sphere</u>, world, area, range, field, scene, orbit, realm, milieu ...*She moved only in the most exalted circles...*
VERB 1 = <u>go round</u>, ring, surround, belt, curve, enclose, encompass, compass, envelop, encircle, circumscribe, hem in, gird, circumnavigate, enwreath ...*This is the ring road that circles the city...*
2 = <u>wheel</u>, spiral, revolve, rotate, whirl, pivot ...*There were two helicopters circling around...*

circuit 1 = <u>course</u>, round, tour, track, route, journey ...*I get asked this question a lot when I'm on the lecture circuit...*
2 = <u>racetrack</u>, course, track, racecourse ...*the historic racing circuit at Brooklands...*
3 = <u>lap</u>, round, tour, revolution, orbit, perambulation ...*She made a slow circuit of the room...*

circuitous 1 = <u>indirect</u>, winding, rambling, roundabout, meandering, tortuous, labyrinthine ...*They were taken on a circuitous route home...* OPPOSITE direct
2 = <u>oblique</u>, indirect ...*He has a pedantic and circuitous writing style...*

circular ADJECTIVE 1 = <u>round</u>, ring-shaped, discoid ...*The car turned into a spacious, circular courtyard...*
2 = <u>circuitous</u>, cyclical, orbital ...*Both sides of the river can be explored on this circular walk...*
NOUN = <u>advertisement</u>, notice, ad (*informal*), announcement, advert (*Brit. informal*), press release ...*A circular has been sent to 1,800 newspapers...*

circulate 1 = <u>spread</u>, issue, publish, broadcast, distribute, diffuse, publicize, propagate, disseminate, promulgate, make known ...*Public employees are circulating a petition calling for his reinstatement...*
2 = <u>flow</u>, revolve, rotate, radiate ...*Cooking odours can circulate throughout the entire house...*

circulation 1 = <u>distribution</u>, currency, readership ...*The paper once had the highest circulation of any daily in the country...*
2 = <u>bloodstream</u>, blood flow ...*Anyone with circulation problems should seek medical advice before flying...*
3 = <u>flow</u>, circling, motion, rotation ...*Fit a ventilated lid to allow circulation of air...*
4 = <u>spread</u>, distribution, transmission, dissemination ...*measures inhibiting the circulation of useful information...*

circumference = <u>edge</u>, limits, border, bounds, outline, boundary, fringe, verge, rim, perimeter, periphery, extremity

circumscribe (*Formal*) = <u>restrict</u>, limit, define, confine, restrain, delineate, hem in, demarcate, delimit, straiten

circumspect = <u>cautious</u>, politic, guarded, careful, wary, discriminating, discreet, sage, prudent, canny, attentive, vigilant, watchful, judicious, observant, sagacious, heedful OPPOSITE rash

circumstance 1 *usually plural* = <u>situation</u>, condition, scenario, contingency, state of affairs, lie of the land ...*They say they will never, under any circumstances, be the first to use force...*
2 *usually plural* = <u>detail</u>, fact, event, particular, respect, factor ...*I'm making inquiries about the circumstances of her murder...*
3 *usually plural* = <u>situation</u>, state, means, position, station, resources, status, lifestyle ...*help and support for the single mother, whatever her circumstances...*
4 = <u>chance</u>, the times, accident, fortune, luck, fate, destiny, misfortune, providence ...*These people are innocent victims of circumstance...*

circumstantial 1 = <u>indirect</u>, contingent, incidental, inferential, presumptive, conjectural, founded on circumstances ...*He was convicted on purely circumstantial evidence...*
2 = <u>detailed</u>, particular, specific ...*The reasons for the project collapsing were circumstantial...*

circumvent 1 (*Formal*) = <u>evade</u>, bypass, elude, steer

clear of, sidestep …*Military rulers tried to circumvent the treaty*…
2 = <u>outwit</u>, trick, mislead, thwart, deceive, dupe, beguile, outflank, hoodwink …*It is a veiled attempt to change gun laws by circumventing legislators*…

cistern = <u>tank</u>, vat, basin, reservoir, sink

citadel = <u>fortress</u>, keep, tower, stronghold, bastion, fortification, fastness

citation 1 = <u>commendation</u>, award, mention …*His citation says he showed outstanding and exemplary courage*…
2 = <u>quotation</u>, quote, reference, passage, illustration, excerpt …*The text is full of Biblical citations*…

cite 1 = <u>quote</u>, name, evidence, advance, mention, extract, specify, allude to, enumerate, adduce …*She cites a favourite poem by George Herbert*…
2 (*Law*) = <u>summon</u>, call, subpoena …*The judge ruled a mistrial and cited the prosecutors for gross misconduct*…

citizen = <u>inhabitant</u>, resident, dweller, ratepayer, denizen, subject, freeman, burgher, townsman
(**Related Words**)
adjective : civil

city = <u>town</u>, metropolis, municipality, conurbation, megalopolis
(**Related Words**)
adjective : civic
➤ **WORD POWER SUPPLEMENT capital cities**

civic = <u>public</u>, community, borough, municipal, communal, local

civil 1 = <u>civic</u>, home, political, domestic, interior, municipal …*This civil unrest threatens the economy*…
OPPOSITE > state
2 = <u>polite</u>, obliging, accommodating, civilized, courteous, considerate, affable, courtly, well-bred, complaisant, well-mannered …*He couldn't even bring himself to be civil to Pauline*… **OPPOSITE** > rude

civility = <u>politeness</u>, consideration, courtesy, tact, good manners, graciousness, cordiality, affability, amiability, complaisance, courteousness

civilization 1 = <u>society</u>, people, community, nation, polity …*He believed Western civilization was in grave economic and cultural danger*…
2 = <u>culture</u>, development, education, progress, enlightenment, sophistication, advancement, cultivation, refinement …*a race with an advanced state of civilization*…

civilize = <u>cultivate</u>, improve, polish, educate, refine, tame, enlighten, humanize, sophisticate

civilized 1 = <u>cultured</u>, educated, sophisticated, enlightened, humane …*All truly civilized countries must deplore torture*… **OPPOSITE** > primitive
2 = <u>polite</u>, mannerly, tolerant, gracious, courteous, affable, well-behaved, well-mannered …*Our divorce was conducted in a very civilized manner*…

clad = <u>dressed</u>, clothed, arrayed, draped, fitted out, decked out, attired, rigged out (*informal*), apparelled, accoutred, covered

claim **VERB** **1** = <u>assert</u>, insist, maintain, allege,

uphold, profess, hold …*He claimed that it was a conspiracy against him*…
2 = <u>take</u>, receive, pick up, collect, lay claim to …*Now they are returning to claim what is theirs*…
3 = <u>demand</u>, call for, ask for, insist on …*They intend to claim for damages against the three doctors*…
NOUN **1** = <u>assertion</u>, statement, allegation, declaration, contention, pretension, affirmation, protestation …*He rejected claims that he had had an affair*…
2 = <u>demand</u>, application, request, petition, call …*The office has been dealing with their claim for benefits*…
3 = <u>right</u>, title, entitlement …*The Tudors had a tenuous claim to the monarchy*…

claimant = <u>applicant</u>, pretender, petitioner, supplicant, suppliant

clairvoyant **ADJECTIVE** = <u>psychic</u>, visionary, prophetic, prescient, telepathic, fey, second-sighted, extrasensory, oracular, sibylline …*a fortune-teller who claims to have clairvoyant powers*…
NOUN = <u>psychic</u>, diviner, prophet, visionary, oracle, seer, augur, fortune-teller, soothsayer, sibyl, prophetess, telepath …*You don't need to be a clairvoyant to see how this is going to turn out*…

clamber = <u>climb</u>, scale, scramble, claw, shin, scrabble

clammy 1 = <u>moist</u>, sweating, damp, sticky, sweaty, slimy …*My shirt was clammy with sweat*…
2 = <u>damp</u>, humid, dank, muggy, close …*As you peer down into this pit, the clammy atmosphere rises to meet your skin*…

clamour = <u>noise</u>, shouting, racket, outcry, din, uproar, agitation, blare, commotion, babel, hubbub, brouhaha, hullabaloo, shout

clamp **NOUN** = <u>vice</u>, press, grip, bracket, fastener …*This clamp is ideal for holding frames and other items*…
VERB = <u>fasten</u>, fix, secure, clinch, brace, make fast …*U-bolts are used to clamp the microphones to the pole*…

clan 1 = <u>family</u>, house, group, order, race, society, band, tribe, sept, fraternity, brotherhood, sodality …*A clash had taken place between rival clans*…
2 = <u>group</u>, set, crowd, circle, crew (*informal*), gang, faction, coterie, schism, cabal …*a powerful clan of industrialists from Monterrey*…

clandestine = <u>secret</u>, private, hidden, underground, concealed, closet, covert, sly, furtive, underhand, surreptitious, stealthy, cloak-and-dagger, under-the-counter

clang **VERB** = <u>ring</u>, toll, resound, chime, reverberate, jangle, clank, bong, clash …*A little later the church bell clanged*…
NOUN = <u>ringing</u>, clash, jangle, knell, clank, reverberation, ding-dong, clangour …*He pulled the gates shut with a clang*…

clap 1 = <u>applaud</u>, cheer, acclaim, give (someone) a big hand …*The men danced and the women clapped*… …*People lined the streets to clap the marchers*… **OPPOSITE** > boo
2 = <u>strike</u>, pat, punch, bang, thrust, slap, whack, wallop

(*informal*), thwack …*He clapped me on the back and boomed, 'Well done.'*…

clarification = <u>explanation</u>, interpretation, exposition, illumination, simplification, elucidation

clarify 1 = <u>explain</u>, resolve, interpret, illuminate, clear up, simplify, make plain, elucidate, explicate, clear the air about, throw *or* shed light on …*A bank spokesman was unable to clarify the situation*…
2 = <u>refine</u>, cleanse, purify …*Clarify the butter by bringing it to a simmer in a small pan*…

clarity 1 = <u>clearness</u>, precision, simplicity, transparency, lucidity, explicitness, intelligibility, obviousness, straightforwardness, comprehensibility …*the clarity with which the author explains this technical subject*… [OPPOSITE] obscurity
2 = <u>transparency</u>, clearness …*The first thing to strike me was the incredible clarity of the water*… [OPPOSITE] cloudiness

clash [VERB] **1** = <u>conflict</u>, grapple, wrangle, lock horns, cross swords, war, feud, quarrel …*A group of 400 demonstrators clashed with police*…
2 = <u>disagree</u>, conflict, vary, counter, differ, depart, contradict, diverge, deviate, run counter to, be dissimilar, be discordant …*Don't make policy decisions which clash with company thinking*…
3 = <u>not go</u>, jar, not match, be discordant …*The red door clashed with the pink walls*…
4 = <u>crash</u>, bang, rattle, jar, clatter, jangle, clang, clank …*The golden bangles on her arms clashed and jangled*…
[NOUN] **1** = <u>conflict</u>, fight, brush, confrontation, collision, showdown (*informal*) …*There are reports of clashes between militants and the security forces in the city*…
2 = <u>disagreement</u>, difference, division, argument, dispute, dissent, difference of opinion …*Inside government, there was a clash of views*…

clasp [VERB] = <u>grasp</u>, hold, press, grip, seize, squeeze, embrace, clutch, hug, enfold …*Mary clasped the children to her desperately*…
[NOUN] **1** = <u>grasp</u>, hold, grip, embrace, hug …*He gripped my hand in a strong clasp*…
2 = <u>fastening</u>, catch, grip, hook, snap, pin, clip, buckle, brooch, fastener, hasp, press stud …*She undid the clasp of the hooded cloak she was wearing*…

class [NOUN] **1** = <u>group</u>, grouping, set, order, league, division, rank, caste, status, sphere …*the relationship between different social classes*…
2 = <u>type</u>, set, sort, kind, collection, species, grade, category, stamp, genre, classification, denomination, genus …*The navy is developing a new class of nuclear-powered submarine*…
[VERB] = <u>classify</u>, group, rate, rank, brand, label, grade, designate, categorize, codify …*I would class my garden as being medium in size*…
➤ **family**

classic [ADJECTIVE] **1** = <u>typical</u>, standard, model, regular, usual, ideal, characteristic, definitive, archetypal, exemplary, quintessential, time-honoured, paradigmatic, dinki-di (*Austral. informal*) …*This is a*

classic example of media hype…
2 = <u>masterly</u>, best, finest, master, world-class, consummate, first-rate …*Aldous Huxley's classic work, The Perennial Philosophy*… [OPPOSITE] second-rate
3 = <u>lasting</u>, enduring, abiding, immortal, undying, ageless, deathless …*These are classic designs which will fit in well anywhere*…
[NOUN] = <u>standard</u>, masterpiece, prototype, paradigm, exemplar, masterwork, model …*The album is one of the classics of modern popular music*…

classical = <u>Greek</u>, Roman, Latin, Attic, Grecian, Hellenic, Augustan
➤ **mythology**

classification = <u>categorization</u>, grading, cataloguing, taxonomy, codification, sorting, analysis, arrangement

classify = <u>categorize</u>, sort, file, rank, arrange, grade, catalogue, codify, pigeonhole, tabulate, systematize

classy (*Informal*) = <u>high-class</u>, select, exclusive, superior, elegant, stylish, posh (*informal, chiefly Brit.*), swish (*informal, chiefly Brit.*), up-market, urbane, swanky (*informal*), top-drawer, ritzy (*slang*), high-toned

clause = <u>section</u>, condition, article, item, chapter, rider, provision, passage, point, part, heading, paragraph, specification, proviso, stipulation

claw [NOUN] **1** = <u>nail</u>, talon …*The cat's claws got caught in my clothes*…
2 = <u>pincer</u>, nipper …*The lobster has two large claws*…
[VERB] = <u>scratch</u>, tear, dig, rip, scrape, graze, maul, scrabble, mangle, mangulate (*Austral. slang*), lacerate …*She struck back at him and clawed his arm with her hand*…

clean [ADJECTIVE] **1** = <u>hygienic</u>, natural, fresh, sterile, pure, purified, antiseptic, sterilized, unadulterated, uncontaminated, unpolluted, decontaminated …*Disease is not a problem because clean water is available*… [OPPOSITE] contaminated
2 = <u>spotless</u>, fresh, washed, immaculate, laundered, impeccable, flawless, sanitary, faultless, squeaky-clean, hygienic, unblemished, unsullied, unstained, unsoiled, unspotted …*He wore his cleanest slacks and a navy blazer*… [OPPOSITE] dirty
3 = <u>moral</u>, good, pure, decent, innocent, respectable, upright, honourable, impeccable, exemplary, virtuous, chaste, undefiled …*I want to live a clean life, a life without sin*… [OPPOSITE] immoral
4 = <u>complete</u>, final, whole, total, perfect, entire, decisive, thorough, conclusive, unimpaired …*It is time for a clean break with the past*…
5 = <u>neat</u>, simple, elegant, trim, delicate, tidy, graceful, uncluttered …*I admire the clean lines of Shaker furniture*… [OPPOSITE] untidy
[VERB] = <u>cleanse</u>, wash, bath, sweep, dust, wipe, vacuum, scrub, sponge, rinse, mop, launder, scour, purify, do up, swab, disinfect, deodorize, sanitize …*Her father cleaned his glasses with a paper napkin*… …*It took half an hour to clean the orange powder off the bath*… [OPPOSITE] dirty

clean-cut = <u>neat</u>, trim, tidy, chiselled

cleanliness = cleanness, purity, freshness, whiteness, sterility, spotlessness

cleanse = purify, clear, purge ...*Your body is beginning to cleanse itself of tobacco toxins...* **1** = absolve, clear, purge, purify ...*Confession cleanses the soul...* **2** = clean, wash, scrub, rinse, scour ...*She demonstrated the proper way to cleanse the face...*

cleanser = detergent, soap, solvent, disinfectant, soap powder, purifier, scourer, wash

clear ADJECTIVE **1** = comprehensible, explicit, articulate, understandable, coherent, lucid, user-friendly, intelligible ...*The book is clear, readable and amply illustrated...* OPPOSITE confused **2** = distinct, audible, perceptible ...*He repeated his answer in a clear, firm voice...* OPPOSITE indistinct **3** = obvious, plain, apparent, bold, patent, evident, distinct, pronounced, definite, manifest, blatant, conspicuous, unmistakable, express, palpable, unequivocal, recognizable, unambiguous, unquestionable, cut-and-dried (*informal*), incontrovertible ...*It was a clear case of homicide...* OPPOSITE ambiguous **4** = certain, sure, convinced, positive, satisfied, resolved, explicit, definite, decided ...*It is important to be clear on what the author is saying here...* OPPOSITE confused **5** = transparent, see-through, translucent, crystalline, glassy, limpid, pellucid ...*The water is clear and plenty of fish are visible...* OPPOSITE opaque **6** = unobstructed, open, free, empty, unhindered, unimpeded, unhampered ...*All exits must be kept clear in case of fire or a bomb scare...* OPPOSITE blocked **7** = bright, fine, fair, shining, sunny, luminous, halcyon, cloudless, undimmed, light, unclouded ...*Most places will be dry with clear skies...* OPPOSITE cloudy **8** = untroubled, clean, pure, innocent, stainless, immaculate, unblemished, untarnished, guiltless, sinless, undefiled ...*I can look back on things with a clear conscience...* VERB **1** = unblock, unclog, free, loosen, extricate, disengage, open, disentangle ...*We called in a plumber to clear our blocked sink...* **2** = remove, clean, wipe, cleanse, tidy (up), sweep away ...*Firemen were still clearing rubble from the scene of the explosion...* **3** = brighten, break up, lighten ...*As the weather cleared, helicopters began to ferry the injured to hospital...* **4** = pass over, jump, leap, vault, miss ...*The horse cleared the fence by several inches...* **5** = absolve, acquit, vindicate, exonerate ...*In a final effort to clear her name, she is writing a book...* OPPOSITE blame PHRASES **clear out** (*Informal*) = go away, leave, retire, withdraw, depart, beat it (*slang*), decamp, hook it (*slang*), slope off, pack your bags (*informal*), make tracks, take yourself off, make yourself scarce ...*'Clear out!' he bawled, 'This is private property.'...* ◆ **clear something out 1** = empty, sort, tidy up ...*I took the precaution of clearing out my desk before I left...* **2** = get rid of, remove, dump, dispose of, throw away *or* out ...*It'll take you a month just to clear out all this rubbish...* ◆ **clear something up 1** = tidy (up), order, straighten, rearrange, put in order ...*I told you to clear up your room...* **2** = solve, explain, resolve, clarify, unravel, straighten out, elucidate ...*During dinner the confusion was cleared up...*

clearance 1 = evacuation, emptying, withdrawal, removal, eviction, depopulation ...*By the late fifties, slum clearance was the watchword in town planning...* **2** = permission, consent, endorsement, green light, authorization, blank cheque, go-ahead (*informal*), leave, sanction, O.K. *or* okay (*informal*) ...*He has a security clearance that allows him access to classified information...* **3** = space, gap, margin, allowance, headroom ...*The lowest fixed bridge has 12.8m clearance...*

clear-cut = straightforward, specific, plain, precise, black-and-white, explicit, definite, unequivocal, unambiguous, cut-and-dried (*informal*)

clearing = glade, space, dell

clearly 1 = obviously, undoubtedly, evidently, distinctly, markedly, overtly, undeniably, beyond doubt, incontrovertibly, incontestably, openly ...*He clearly believes that he is in the right...* **2** = legibly, distinctly ...*Write your address clearly on the back of the envelope...* **3** = audibly, distinctly, intelligibly, comprehensibly ...*Please speak clearly after the tone...*

cleave¹ = split, open, divide, crack, slice, rend, sever, part, hew, tear asunder, sunder ...*The axe had cleaved open the back of his skull...*

cleave²
PHRASES **cleave to** = stick to, stand by, cling to, hold to, be devoted to, adhere to, be attached to, abide by, be true to ...*She teaches the principles she has cleaved to for more than 40 years...*

cleft = opening, break, crack, gap, rent, breach, fracture, rift, chink, crevice, fissure, cranny

clemency = mercy, pity, humanity, compassion, kindness, forgiveness, indulgence, leniency, forbearance, quarter

clement = mild, fine, fair, calm, temperate, balmy

clergy = priesthood, ministry, clerics, clergymen, churchmen, the cloth, holy orders, ecclesiastics
⟨ *Related Words* ⟩
adjectives: clerical, pastoral

clergyman = minister, priest, vicar, parson, reverend (*informal*), rabbi, pastor, chaplain, cleric, rector, curate, father, churchman, padre, man of God, man of the cloth, divine

clerical 1 = administrative, office, bureaucratic, secretarial, book-keeping, stenographic ...*The hospital blamed the mix-up on a clerical error...* **2** = ecclesiastical, priestly, pastoral, sacerdotal ...*a clergyman who had failed to carry out his clerical duties...*

clever 1 = intelligent, quick, bright, talented, gifted, keen, capable, smart, sensible, rational, witty, apt, discerning, knowledgeable, astute, brainy (*informal*), quick-witted, sagacious, knowing, deep, expert ...*My sister has always been the clever one in our family...* OPPOSITE> stupid

2 = shrewd, bright, cunning, ingenious, inventive, astute, resourceful, canny ...*It's a very clever idea...* OPPOSITE> unimaginative

3 = skilful, able, talented, gifted, capable, inventive, adroit, dexterous ...*My father was very clever with his hands...* OPPOSITE> inept

cleverness 1 = intelligence, sense, brains, wit, brightness, nous (*Brit. slang*), suss (*slang*), quickness, gumption (*Brit. informal*), sagacity, smartness, astuteness, quick wits, smarts (*slang, chiefly U.S.*) ...*He congratulated himself on his cleverness...*

2 = shrewdness, sharpness, resourcefulness, canniness ...*a policy almost Machiavellian in its cleverness...*

3 = dexterity, ability, talent, gift, flair, ingenuity, adroitness ...*The artist demonstrates a cleverness with colours and textures...*

cliché = platitude, stereotype, commonplace, banality, truism, bromide, old saw, hackneyed phrase, chestnut (*informal*)

➤ **clichés and pompous expressions**

click NOUN = snap, beat, tick, clack ...*I heard a click and then the telephone message started to play...*

VERB **1** = snap, beat, tick, clack ...*Camera shutters clicked all around me...*

2 (*Informal*) = become clear, come home (to), make sense, fall into place ...*When I saw the TV report, it all suddenly clicked...*

3 (*Informal*) = get on, be compatible, hit it off (*informal*), be on the same wavelength, get on like a house on fire (*informal*), take to each other, feel a rapport ...*They clicked immediately; they liked all the same things...*

client = customer, consumer, buyer, patron, shopper, habitué, patient

clientele = customers, market, business, following, trade, regulars, clients, patronage

cliff = rock face, overhang, crag, precipice, escarpment, face, scar, bluff

climactic = crucial, central, critical, peak, decisive, paramount, pivotal

---

Word Power

climatic – *Climatic* is sometimes wrongly used where *climactic* is meant. *Climatic* should be used to talk about things relating to climate; *climactic* is used to describe something which forms a climax: *the climactic moment of the Revolution.*

---

climate 1 = weather, country, region, temperature, clime ...*the hot and humid climate of Cyprus...*

2 = atmosphere, environment, spirit, surroundings, tone, mood, trend, flavour, feeling, tendency, temper, ambience, vibes (*slang*) ...*A major change of political climate is unlikely...*

climax NOUN = culmination, head, top, summit, height, highlight, peak, pay-off (*informal*), crest, high point, zenith, apogee, high spot (*informal*), acme, ne plus ultra (*Latin*) ...*Reaching the Olympics was the climax of her career...*

VERB = culminate, end, finish, conclude, peak, come to a head ...*They did a series of charity events climaxing in a millennium concert...*

climb VERB **1** = ascend, scale, mount, go up, clamber, shin up ...*Climbing the first hill took half an hour...*

2 = clamber, descend, scramble, dismount ...*He climbed down from the cab...*

3 = rise, go up, soar, ascend, fly up ...*The plane took off, lost an engine as it climbed, and crashed just off the runway...*

PHRASES **climb down** = back down, withdraw, yield, concede, retreat, surrender, give in, cave in (*informal*), retract, admit defeat, back-pedal, eat your words, eat crow (*U.S. informal*) ...*He has climbed down on pledges to reduce capital gains tax...*

clinch 1 = secure, close, confirm, conclude, seal,

Word Power: Clichés and pompous expressions

Some people find certain expressions irritating because they make the speaker sound pretentious, they are too wordy, or they are clichés – that is, they have been used so many times that they have lost much of their force and have become annoying. It is best to avoid using any phrases or expressions which could come into this category, and to find less pompous or more original ways of saying what you want to say. Some of the most commonly-encountered are:

after due consideration: try the alternatives *after thinking about it, after giving it some thought, after considering it carefully*

at the end of the day: *in the end, ultimately, finally, at last, eventually*

at this moment or **point in time**: *now, at the moment, currently*

diametrically opposed to: *completely against, anti, in direct opposition to*

in the final analysis: *in the end, ultimately, finally, at last, eventually*

not to put too fine a point on it: *to be blunt, to be honest, to put it bluntly*

in this day and age: *nowadays, these days, today*

the fact of the matter: *the truth, the situation, the facts, the reality*

suffice it to say: *it is enough to say, let us just say*

to the best of your abilities: *as well as you can, as best you can*

verify, sew up (*informal*), set the seal on ...*He is about to clinch a deal with an American engine manufacturer*...
2 = <u>settle</u>, decide, determine, tip the balance ...*Evidently this information clinched the matter*...

cling VERB **1** = <u>clutch</u>, grip, embrace, grasp, hug, hold on to, clasp ...*She had to cling onto the door handle until the pain passed*...
2 = <u>stick to</u>, attach to, adhere to, fasten to, twine round ...*His sodden trousers were clinging to his shins*...
PHRASES **cling to something** = <u>adhere to</u>, maintain, stand by, cherish, abide by, be true to, be loyal to, be faithful to, cleave to ...*They still cling to their beliefs*...

clinical = <u>unemotional</u>, cold, scientific, objective, detached, analytic, impersonal, antiseptic, disinterested, dispassionate, emotionless

clip¹ VERB **1** = <u>trim</u>, cut, crop, dock, prune, shorten, shear, cut short, snip, pare ...*I saw an old man out clipping his hedge*...
2 (*Informal*) = <u>smack</u>, strike, box, knock, punch, belt (*informal*), thump, clout (*informal*), cuff, whack, wallop (*informal*), skelp (*dialect*) ...*I'd have clipped his ear for him if he'd been my kid*...
NOUN **1** (*Informal*) = <u>smack</u>, strike, box, knock, punch, belt (*informal*), thump, clout (*informal*), cuff, whack, wallop (*informal*), skelp (*dialect*) ...*The boy was later given a clip round the ear by his father*...
2 (*Informal*) = <u>speed</u>, rate, pace, gallop, lick (*informal*), velocity ...*They trotted along at a brisk clip*...

clip² = <u>attach</u>, fix, secure, connect, pin, staple, fasten, affix, hold ...*He clipped his flashlight to his belt*...

clipping = <u>cutting</u>, passage, extract, excerpt, piece, article

clique = <u>group</u>, set, crowd, pack, circle, crew (*informal*), gang, faction, mob, clan, posse (*informal*), coterie, schism, cabal

cloak NOUN **1** = <u>cape</u>, coat, wrap, mantle ...*She set out, wrapping her cloak about her*...
2 = <u>covering</u>, layer, blanket, shroud ...*Today most of England will be under a cloak of thick mist*...
3 = <u>disguise</u>, front, cover, screen, blind, mask, shield, cover-up, façade, pretext, smoke screen ...*Individualism is sometimes used as a cloak for self-interest*...
VERB **1** = <u>cover</u>, coat, wrap, blanket, shroud, envelop ...*The coastline was cloaked in fog*...
2 = <u>hide</u>, cover, screen, mask, disguise, conceal, obscure, veil, camouflage ...*He uses jargon to cloak his inefficiency*...

clobber¹ (*Informal*) = <u>batter</u>, beat, assault, smash, bash (*informal*), lash, thrash, pound, beat up (*informal*), wallop (*informal*), pummel, rough up (*informal*), lambast(e), belabour, duff up (*informal*) ...*She clobbered him with a vase*...

clobber² (*Brit. informal*) = <u>belongings</u>, things, effects, property, stuff, gear, possessions, paraphernalia, accoutrements, chattels ...*His house is filled with a load of old clobber*...

clog = <u>obstruct</u>, block, jam, hamper, hinder, impede, bung, stop up, dam up, occlude, congest

cloistered = <u>sheltered</u>, protected, restricted, shielded, confined, insulated, secluded, reclusive, shut off, sequestered, withdrawn, cloistral OPPOSITE public

close¹ VERB **1** = <u>shut</u>, lock, push to, fasten, secure ...*If you are cold, close the window*... OPPOSITE open
2 = <u>shut down</u>, finish, cease, discontinue ...*Many enterprises will be forced to close because of the recession*...
3 = <u>wind up</u>, finish, axe (*informal*), shut down, terminate, discontinue, mothball ...*There are rumours of plans to close the local college*...
4 = <u>block up</u>, bar, seal, shut up ...*The government has closed the border crossing*... OPPOSITE open
5 = <u>end</u>, finish, complete, conclude, wind up, culminate, terminate ...*He closed the meeting with his customary address*... OPPOSITE begin
6 = <u>clinch</u>, confirm, secure, conclude, seal, verify, sew up (*informal*), set the seal on ...*He needs another $30,000 to close the deal*...
7 = <u>come together</u>, join, connect ...*His fingers closed around her wrist*... OPPOSITE separate
NOUN = <u>end</u>, ending, finish, conclusion, completion, finale, culmination, denouement ...*His retirement brings to a close a glorious chapter in British football history*...

close² **1** = <u>near</u>, neighbouring, nearby, handy, adjacent, adjoining, hard by, just round the corner, within striking distance (*informal*), cheek by jowl, proximate, within spitting distance (*informal*), within sniffing distance, a hop, skip and a jump away ...*The plant is close to Sydney airport*... OPPOSITE far
2 = <u>intimate</u>, loving, friendly, familiar, thick (*informal*), attached, devoted, confidential, inseparable, dear ...*She and Linda became very close*... OPPOSITE distant
3 = <u>noticeable</u>, marked, strong, distinct, pronounced ...*There is a close resemblance between them*...
4 = <u>careful</u>, detailed, searching, concentrated, keen, intense, minute, alert, intent, thorough, rigorous, attentive, painstaking, assiduous ...*His recent actions have been the subject of close scrutiny*...
5 = <u>even</u>, level, neck and neck, fifty-fifty (*informal*), evenly matched, equally balanced ...*It is still a close contest between the two leading parties*...
6 = <u>imminent</u>, near, approaching, impending, at hand, upcoming, nigh, just round the corner ...*A White House official said an agreement is close*... OPPOSITE far away
7 = <u>stifling</u>, confined, oppressive, stale, suffocating, stuffy, humid, sweltering, airless, muggy, unventilated, heavy, thick ...*They sat in that hot, close room for two hours*... OPPOSITE airy
8 = <u>accurate</u>, strict, exact, precise, faithful, literal, conscientious ...*The poem is a close translation from the original Latin*...

closed **1** = <u>shut</u>, locked, sealed, fastened ...*Her bedroom door was closed*... OPPOSITE open
2 = <u>shut down</u>, out of business, out of service ...*The airport shop was closed*...
3 = <u>exclusive</u>, select, restricted ...*No-one was

admitted to this closed circle of elite students…
4 = <u>finished</u>, over, ended, decided, settled, concluded, resolved, terminated …*I now consider the matter closed…*

closeness 1 = <u>nearness</u>, proximity, handiness, adjacency …*the closeness of the Chinese mainland to Hong Kong…*
2 = <u>imminence</u>, nearness, impendency …*this ever-present feeling of the closeness of death…*
3 = <u>intimacy</u>, love, devotion, confidentiality, familiarity, dearness, inseparability …*He experienced a lack of closeness to his parents during childhood…*

closet NOUN (*U.S.*) = <u>cupboard</u>, cabinet, recess, cubicle, cubbyhole …*Perhaps there's room in the broom closet…*
ADJECTIVE = <u>secret</u>, private, hidden, unknown, concealed, covert, unrevealed …*He is a closet Fascist…*

closure = <u>closing</u>, end, finish, conclusion, stoppage, termination, cessation

clot NOUN = <u>lump</u>, mass, clotting, curdling, gob, embolism, coagulation, occlusion …*He needed emergency surgery to remove a blood clot from his brain…*
VERB = <u>congeal</u>, thicken, curdle, coalesce, jell, coagulate …*The patient's blood refused to clot…*

cloth = <u>fabric</u>, material, textiles, dry goods, stuff

clothe = <u>dress</u>, outfit, rig, array, robe, drape, get ready, swathe, apparel, attire, fit out, garb, doll up (*slang*), accoutre, cover, deck OPPOSITE undress

clothes = <u>clothing</u>, wear, dress, gear (*informal*), habits, get-up (*informal*), outfit, costume, threads (*slang*), wardrobe, ensemble, garments, duds (*informal*), apparel, clobber (*Brit. slang*), attire, garb, togs (*informal*), vestments, glad rags (*informal*), raiment (*archaic or poetic*), rigout (*informal*)

clothing = <u>clothes</u>, wear, dress, gear (*informal*), habits, get-up (*informal*), outfit, costume, threads (*slang*), wardrobe, ensemble, garments, duds (*informal*), apparel, clobber (*Brit. slang*), attire, garb, togs (*informal*), vestments, glad rags (*informal*), raiment (*archaic or poetic*), rigout (*informal*)

cloud NOUN **1** = <u>mist</u>, fog, haze, obscurity, vapour, nebula, murk, darkness, gloom …*The sun was almost entirely obscured by cloud…*
2 = <u>billow</u>, mass, shower, puff …*The hens darted away on all sides, raising a cloud of dust…*
VERB **1** = <u>confuse</u>, obscure, distort, impair, muddle, disorient …*Perhaps anger has clouded his vision…*
2 = <u>darken</u>, dim, be overshadowed, be overcast …*The sky clouded and a light rain began to fall…*

Types of cloud

http://www.wildwildweather.com/clouds.htm

altocumulus	false cirrus
altostratus	fractocumulus
cirrocumulus	fractostratus
cirrostratus	nimbostratus
cirrus	nimbus
cumulonimbus	stratocumulus
cumulus	stratus

---

cloudy 1 = <u>dull</u>, dark, dim, gloomy, dismal, sombre, overcast, leaden, sunless, louring *or* lowering …*It was a cloudy, windy day…* OPPOSITE clear
2 = <u>opaque</u>, muddy, murky …*She could just barely see him through the cloudy water…*
3 = <u>vague</u>, confused, obscure, blurred, unclear, hazy, indistinct …*The legal position on this issue is very cloudy…* OPPOSITE plain

clout (*Informal*) VERB = <u>hit</u>, strike, punch, deck (*slang*), slap, sock (*slang*), chin (*slang*), smack, thump, cuff, clobber (*slang*), wallop (*informal*), box, wham, lay one on (*slang*), skelp (*dialect*) …*The officer clouted him on the head…*
NOUN **1** = <u>thump</u>, blow, crack, punch, slap, sock (*slang*), cuff, wallop (*informal*), skelp (*dialect*) …*I was half tempted to give them a clout myself…*
2 = <u>influence</u>, power, standing, authority, pull, weight, bottom, prestige, mana (*N.Z.*) …*The two firms wield enormous clout in financial markets…*

cloven = <u>split</u>, divided, cleft, bisected

clown NOUN **1** = <u>comedian</u>, fool, comic, harlequin, joker, jester, prankster, buffoon, pierrot, dolt …*a classic circus clown with a big red nose and baggy suit…*
2 = <u>fool</u>, dope (*informal*), jerk (*slang, chiefly U.S. & Canad.*), idiot, ass, berk (*Brit. slang*), prat (*slang*), moron, twit (*informal, chiefly Brit.*), imbecile (*informal*), ignoramus, jackass, dolt, blockhead, ninny, putz (*U.S. slang*), eejit (*Scot. & Irish*), doofus (*slang, chiefly U.S.*), dorba *or* dorb (*Austral. slang*), bogan (*Austral. slang*), lamebrain (*informal*), numbskull *or* numskull …*I could do a better job than those clowns in Washington…*
VERB *usually with* ***around*** = <u>play the fool</u>, mess about, jest, act the fool, act the goat, play the goat …*Stop clowning around and get some work done…* …*He clowned a lot and antagonized his workmates…*

cloying 1 = <u>sickly</u>, nauseating, icky (*informal*), treacly, oversweet, excessive …*Her cheap, cloying scent enveloped him…*
2 = <u>over-sentimental</u>, sickly, nauseating, mushy, twee, slushy, mawkish, icky (*informal*), treacly, oversweet …*The film is sentimental but rarely cloying…*

club NOUN **1** = <u>association</u>, company, group, union, society, circle, lodge, guild, fraternity, set, order, sodality …*He was a member of the local youth club…*
2 = <u>stick</u>, bat, bludgeon, truncheon, cosh (*Brit.*), cudgel …*Men armed with knives and clubs attacked his home…*
VERB = <u>beat</u>, strike, hammer, batter, bash, clout (*informal*), bludgeon, clobber (*slang*), pummel, cosh (*Brit.*) …*Two thugs clubbed him with baseball bats…*

clue = <u>indication</u>, lead, sign, evidence, tip, suggestion, trace, hint, suspicion, pointer, tip-off, inkling, intimation

clueless = <u>stupid</u>, thick, dull, naive, dim, dense, dumb (*informal*), simple-minded, dozy (*Brit. informal*), simple, slow, witless, dopey (*informal*), moronic, unintelligent, half-witted, slow on the uptake (*informal*)

clump NOUN = <u>cluster</u>, group, bunch, bundle, shock …*There was a clump of trees bordering the side of the road…*
  VERB = <u>stomp</u>, stamp, stump, thump, lumber, tramp, plod, thud, clomp …*They went clumping up the stairs to bed…*

clumsiness 1 = <u>awkwardness</u>, ineptitude, heaviness, ineptness, inelegance, ponderousness, gracelessness, gawkiness, ungainliness …*I was embarrassed by my clumsiness on the dance-floor…*
  OPPOSITE expertise
2 = <u>insensitivity</u>, heavy-handedness, tactlessness, goucheness, lack of tact, uncouthness …*He cursed himself for his clumsiness and insensitivity…*

clumsy 1 = <u>awkward</u>, blundering, bungling, lumbering, inept, bumbling, ponderous, ungainly, gauche, accident-prone, gawky, heavy, uncoordinated, cack-handed (*informal*), inexpert, maladroit, ham-handed (*informal*), like a bull in a china shop, klutzy (*U.S. & Canad. slang*), unskilful, butterfingered (*informal*), ham-fisted (*informal*), unco (*Austral. slang*) …*I'd never seen a clumsier, less coordinated boxer…* OPPOSITE skilful
2 = <u>unwieldy</u>, ill-shaped, unhandy, clunky (*informal*) …*The keyboard is a large and clumsy instrument…*

cluster NOUN = <u>gathering</u>, group, collection, bunch, knot, clump, assemblage …*A cluster of men blocked the doorway…*
  VERB = <u>gather</u>, group, collect, bunch, assemble, flock, huddle …*The passengers clustered together in small groups…*

clutch VERB 1 = <u>hold</u>, grip, embrace, grasp, cling to, clasp …*She was clutching a photograph in her hand…*
2 = <u>seize</u>, catch, grab, grasp, snatch …*I staggered and had to clutch at a chair for support…*
  PLURAL NOUN = <u>power</u>, hands, control, grip, possession, grasp, custody, sway, keeping, claws …*He escaped his captors' clutches by jumping from a moving vehicle…*

clutter NOUN = <u>untidiness</u>, mess, disorder, confusion, litter, muddle, disarray, jumble, hotchpotch …*She preferred her work area to be free of clutter…* OPPOSITE order
  VERB = <u>litter</u>, scatter, strew, mess up …*I don't want to clutter the room up with too much junk…* OPPOSITE tidy

cluttered = <u>untidy</u>, confused, disordered, littered, messy, muddled, jumbled, disarrayed

coach NOUN 1 = <u>instructor</u>, teacher, trainer, tutor, handler …*He has joined the team as a coach…*
2 = <u>bus</u>, charabanc …*I hate travelling by coach…*
  VERB = <u>instruct</u>, train, prepare, exercise, drill, tutor, cram …*He coached me for my French A levels…*

coalesce = <u>blend</u>, unite, mix, combine, incorporate, integrate, merge, consolidate, come together, fuse, amalgamate, meld, cohere

coalition = <u>alliance</u>, union, league, association, combination, merger, integration, compact, conjunction, bloc, confederation, fusion, affiliation, amalgam, amalgamation, confederacy

coarse 1 = <u>rough</u>, crude, unfinished, homespun, impure, unrefined, rough-hewn, unprocessed, unpolished, coarse-grained, unpurified …*He wore a shepherd's tunic of coarse cloth… …a tablespoon of coarse sea salt…* OPPOSITE smooth
2 = <u>vulgar</u>, offensive, rude, indecent, improper, raunchy (*slang*), earthy, foul-mouthed, bawdy, impure, smutty, impolite, ribald, immodest, indelicate …*He has a very coarse sense of humour…*
3 = <u>loutish</u>, rough, brutish, boorish, uncivil …*They don't know how to behave, and are coarse and insulting…* OPPOSITE well-mannered

coast NOUN = <u>shore</u>, border, beach, strand, seaside, coastline, seaboard …*Camp sites are usually situated along the coast…*
  (Related Words)
  adjective : littoral
  VERB = <u>cruise</u>, sail, drift, taxi, glide, freewheel …*I slipped into neutral gear and coasted down the slope…*

coat NOUN 1 = <u>fur</u>, hair, skin, hide, wool, fleece, pelt …*Vitamin B6 is great for improving the condition of dogs' and horses' coats…*
2 = <u>layer</u>, covering, coating, overlay …*The front door needs a new coat of paint…*
  VERB = <u>cover</u>, spread, plaster, smear …*Coat the fish with seasoned flour…*

coating = <u>layer</u>, covering, finish, skin, sheet, coat, dusting, blanket, membrane, glaze, film, varnish, veneer, patina, lamination

coat of arms = <u>heraldry</u>, crest, insignia, escutcheon, blazonry

coax = <u>persuade</u>, cajole, talk into, wheedle, sweet-talk (*informal*), prevail upon, inveigle, soft-soap (*informal*), twist (someone's) arm, flatter, entice, beguile, allure
  OPPOSITE bully

cobber (*Austral. & old-fashioned N.Z. informal*) = <u>friend</u>, pal, mate (*informal*), buddy (*informal*), china (*Brit. & S. African informal*), best friend, intimate, cock (*Brit. informal*), close friend, comrade, chum (*informal*), crony, alter ego, main man (*slang, chiefly U.S.*), soul mate, homeboy (*slang, chiefly U.S.*), bosom friend, boon companion

cock NOUN = <u>cockerel</u>, rooster, chanticleer …*We heard the sound of a cock crowing in the yard…*
  VERB = <u>raise</u>, prick up, perk up …*He suddenly cocked an ear and listened…*

cocktail = <u>mixture</u>, combination, compound, blend, concoction, mix, amalgamation, admixture

cocky¹ = <u>overconfident</u>, arrogant, brash, swaggering, conceited, egotistical, cocksure, swollen-headed, vain, full of yourself OPPOSITE modest …*He was a little cocky because he was winning all the time…*

cocky² or **cockie** (*Austral. & N.Z. informal*) = <u>farmer</u>, smallholder, crofter (*Scot.*), grazier, agriculturalist, rancher, husbandman …*He got some casual work with the cane cockies on Maroochy River…*

cocoon 1 = <u>wrap</u>, swathe, envelop, swaddle, pad …*She lay on the sofa, cocooned in blankets…*
2 = <u>protect</u>, shelter, cushion, insulate, screen …*I was cocooned in my own safe little world…*

coddle = <u>pamper</u>, spoil, indulge, cosset, baby, nurse, pet, wet-nurse (*informal*), mollycoddle

code 1 = <u>principles</u>, rules, manners, custom, convention, ethics, maxim, etiquette, system ...*Writers are expected to observe journalistic ethics and code of conduct...*
2 = <u>cipher</u>, cryptograph ...*They used elaborate secret codes...*

codify = <u>systematize</u>, catalogue, classify, summarize, tabulate, collect, organize

coerce = <u>force</u>, compel, bully, intimidate, railroad (*informal*), constrain, bulldoze (*informal*), dragoon, pressurize, browbeat, press-gang, twist (someone's) arm (*informal*), drive

coercion = <u>force</u>, pressure, threats, bullying, constraint, intimidation, compulsion, duress, browbeating, strong-arm tactics (*informal*)

cogent = <u>convincing</u>, strong, powerful, effective, compelling, urgent, influential, potent, irresistible, compulsive, forceful, conclusive, weighty, forcible

cognition (*Formal*) = <u>perception</u>, reasoning, understanding, intelligence, awareness, insight, comprehension, apprehension, discernment

coherence = <u>consistency</u>, rationality, concordance, consonance, congruity, union, agreement, connection, unity, correspondence

coherent 1 = <u>consistent</u>, reasoned, organized, rational, logical, meaningful, systematic, orderly ...*He has failed to work out a coherent strategy for modernising the service...* OPPOSITE inconsistent
2 = <u>articulate</u>, lucid, comprehensible, intelligible ...*He's so calm when he speaks in public. I wish I could be that coherent...* OPPOSITE unintelligible

cohort 1 (*Chiefly U.S.*) = <u>supporter</u>, partner, associate, mate, assistant, follower, comrade, protagonist, accomplice, sidekick (*slang*), henchman ...*Drake and his cohorts were not pleased at my promotion...*
2 = <u>group</u>, set, band, contingent, batch ...*We now have results for the first cohort of pupils to be assessed...*

coil 1 = <u>wind</u>, twist, curl, loop, spiral, twine ...*He turned off the water and began to coil the hose...*
2 = <u>curl</u>, wind, twist, snake, loop, entwine, twine, wreathe, convolute ...*A python had coiled itself around the branch of the tree...*

coin NOUN = <u>money</u>, change, cash, silver, copper, dosh (*Brit. & Austral. slang*), specie ...*His pocket was full of coins...*
VERB = <u>invent</u>, create, make up, frame, forge, conceive, originate, formulate, fabricate, think up ...*The phrase 'cosmic ray' was coined by R. A. Millikan in 1925...*
(**Related Words**)
enthusiast: numismatist

coincide 1 = <u>occur simultaneously</u>, coexist, synchronize, be concurrent ...*The exhibition coincides with the 50th anniversary of his death...*
2 = <u>agree</u>, match, accord, square, correspond, tally, concur, harmonize ...*a case in which public and private interests coincide...* OPPOSITE disagree

coincidence = <u>chance</u>, accident, luck, fluke, eventuality, stroke of luck, happy accident, fortuity

coincidental = <u>accidental</u>, unintentional, unintended, unplanned, fortuitous, fluky (*informal*), chance, casual OPPOSITE deliberate

cold ADJECTIVE 1 = <u>chilly</u>, biting, freezing, bitter, raw, chill, harsh, bleak, arctic, icy, frosty, wintry, frigid, inclement, parky (*Brit. informal*), cool ...*It was bitterly cold outside...* OPPOSITE hot
2 = <u>freezing</u>, frozen, chilled, numb, chilly, shivery, benumbed, frozen to the marrow ...*I'm hungry, I'm cold and I have nowhere to sleep...*
3 = <u>distant</u>, reserved, indifferent, aloof, glacial, cold-blooded, apathetic, frigid, unresponsive, unfeeling, passionless, undemonstrative, standoffish ...*His wife is a cold, unfeeling woman...* OPPOSITE emotional
4 = <u>unfriendly</u>, indifferent, stony, lukewarm, glacial, unmoved, unsympathetic, apathetic, frigid, inhospitable, unresponsive ...*The president is likely to receive a cold reception when he speaks today...* OPPOSITE friendly
NOUN = <u>coldness</u>, chill, frigidity, chilliness, frostiness, iciness ...*He must have come inside to get out of the cold...*

cold-blooded = <u>callous</u>, cruel, savage, brutal, ruthless, steely, heartless, inhuman, merciless, unmoved, dispassionate, barbarous, pitiless, unfeeling, unemotional, stony-hearted OPPOSITE caring

collaborate 1 = <u>work together</u>, team up, join forces, cooperate, play ball (*informal*), participate ...*The two men collaborated on an album in 1986...*
2 = <u>conspire</u>, cooperate, collude, fraternize ...*He was accused of having collaborated with the secret police...*

collaboration 1 = <u>teamwork</u>, partnership, cooperation, association, alliance, concert ...*There is substantial collaboration with neighbouring departments...*
2 = <u>conspiring</u>, cooperation, collusion, fraternization ...*rumours of his collaboration with the occupying forces during the war...*

collaborator 1 = <u>co-worker</u>, partner, colleague, associate, team-mate, confederate ...*My wife was an important collaborator on the novel...*
2 = <u>traitor</u>, turncoat, quisling, collaborationist, fraternizer ...*Two alleged collaborators were shot dead by masked activists...*

collapse VERB 1 = <u>fall down</u>, fall, give way, subside, cave in, crumple, fall apart at the seams ...*A section of the Bay Bridge had collapsed...*
2 = <u>fail</u>, fold, founder, break down, fall through, come to nothing, go belly-up (*informal*) ...*His business empire collapsed under a massive burden of debt...*
3 = <u>faint</u>, break down, pass out, black out, swoon (*literary*), crack up (*informal*), keel over (*informal*), flake out (*informal*) ...*It's common to see people in the streets collapsing from hunger...*
NOUN 1 = <u>falling down</u>, ruin, falling apart, cave-in, disintegration, subsidence ...*Floods and a collapse of the tunnel roof were a constant risk...*
2 = <u>failure</u>, slump, breakdown, flop, downfall ...*Their economy is teetering on the edge of collapse...*

3 = <u>faint</u>, breakdown, blackout, prostration ...*A few days after his collapse he was sitting up in bed...*

collar (*Informal*) = <u>seize</u>, catch, arrest, appropriate, grab, capture, nail (*informal*), nab (*informal*), apprehend, lay hands on

collate = <u>collect</u>, gather, organize, assemble, compose, adduce, systematize

collateral = <u>security</u>, guarantee, deposit, assurance, surety, pledge

colleague = <u>fellow worker</u>, partner, ally, associate, assistant, team-mate, companion, comrade, helper, collaborator, confederate, auxiliary, workmate, confrère

collect 1 = <u>gather</u>, save, assemble, heap, accumulate, aggregate, amass, stockpile, hoard ...*Two young girls were collecting firewood...* [OPPOSITE] scatter
2 = <u>raise</u>, secure, gather, obtain, acquire, muster, solicit ...*They collected donations for a fund to help the earthquake victims...*
3 = <u>assemble</u>, meet, rally, cluster, come together, convene, converge, congregate, flock together ...*A crowd collected outside...* [OPPOSITE] disperse

collected = <u>calm</u>, together (*slang*), cool, confident, composed, poised, serene, sedate, self-controlled, unfazed (*informal*), unperturbed, unruffled, self-possessed, keeping your cool, unperturbable, as cool as a cucumber [OPPOSITE] nervous

collection 1 = <u>accumulation</u>, set, store, mass, pile, heap, stockpile, hoard, congeries ...*He has gathered a large collection of prints and paintings over the years...*
2 = <u>accumulation</u>, compilation, anthology ...*Two years ago he published a collection of short stories...*
3 = <u>group</u>, company, crowd, gathering, assembly, cluster, congregation, assortment, assemblage ...*A collection of people of all ages assembled to pay their respects...*
4 = <u>gathering</u>, acquisition, accumulation ...*computer systems designed to speed up the collection of information...*
5 = <u>contribution</u>, donation, alms ...*I asked my headmaster if we could arrange a collection for the refugees...*
6 = <u>offering</u>, offertory ...*I put a five-pound note in the church collection...*

collective 1 = <u>joint</u>, united, shared, common, combined, corporate, concerted, unified, cooperative

...*It was a collective decision taken by the full board...* [OPPOSITE] individual
2 = <u>combined</u>, aggregate, composite, cumulative ...*Their collective volume wasn't very large...* [OPPOSITE] separate

collector
➤ **collectors and enthusiasts**

collide 1 = <u>crash</u>, clash, meet head-on, come into collision ...*Two trains collided head-on early this morning...*
2 = <u>conflict</u>, clash, be incompatible, be at variance ...*It is likely that their interests will collide...*

collision 1 = <u>crash</u>, impact, accident, smash, bump, pile-up (*informal*), prang (*informal*) ...*Their van was involved in a collision with a car...*
2 = <u>conflict</u>, opposition, clash, clashing, encounter, disagreement, incompatibility ...*a collision between two strong personalities...*

colloquial = <u>informal</u>, familiar, everyday, vernacular, conversational, demotic, idiomatic

collude = <u>conspire</u>, scheme, plot, intrigue, collaborate, contrive, abet, connive, be in cahoots (*informal*), machinate

collusion = <u>conspiracy</u>, intrigue, deceit, complicity, connivance, secret understanding

colonist = <u>settler</u>, immigrant, pioneer, colonial, homesteader (*U.S.*), colonizer, frontiersman

colonize = <u>settle</u>, populate, put down roots in, people, pioneer, open up

colonnade = <u>cloisters</u>, arcade, portico, covered walk

colony = <u>settlement</u>, territory, province, possession, dependency, outpost, dominion, satellite state, community

colossal = <u>huge</u>, massive, vast, enormous, immense, titanic, gigantic, monumental, monstrous, mammoth, mountainous, stellar (*informal*), prodigious, gargantuan, herculean, elephantine (*informal*), humongous *or* humungous (*U.S. slang*) [OPPOSITE] tiny

colour *or* (*U.S.*) **color** [NOUN] **1** = <u>hue</u>, tone, shade, tint, tinge, tincture, colourway ...*The badges come in twenty different colours and shapes...*
2 = <u>paint</u>, stain, dye, tint, pigment, tincture, coloration, colourwash, colorant ...*the latest range of lip and eye colours...*
3 = <u>rosiness</u>, glow, bloom, flush, blush, brilliance,

Collectors and enthusiasts

ailurophile	cats	herbalist	herbs
arctophile	teddy bears	lepidopterist	moths and butterflies
audiophile	high-fidelity sound reproduction	medallist	medals
automobilist	cars	numismatist	coins
bibliophile	books	oenophile	wine
brolliologist	umbrellas	paranumismatist	coin-like objects
campanologist	bell-ringing	philatelist	stamps
cartophilist	cigarette cards	phillumenist	matchbox labels
cruciverbalist	crosswords	phraseologist	phrases
deltiologist	picture postcards	scripophile	share certificates
discophile	gramophone records	vexillologist	flags
fusilatelist	phonecards	zoophile	animals

redness, vividness, ruddiness ...*There was a touch of colour in her cheeks...*

4 = <u>liveliness</u>, life, interest, excitement, animation, zest ...*The ceremony brought a touch of colour to the normally drab proceedings...*

PLURAL NOUN 1 = <u>flag</u>, standard, banner, emblem, ensign ...*Troops raised the country's colours in a special ceremony...*

2 = <u>nature</u>, quality, character, aspect, personality, stamp, traits, temperament ...*After we were married, he showed his true colours...*

VERB 1 = <u>blush</u>, flush, crimson, redden, go crimson, burn, go as red as a beetroot ...*He couldn't help noticing that she coloured slightly...*

2 = <u>influence</u>, affect, prejudice, distort, pervert, taint, slant ...*The attitude of parents colours the way their children behave...*

3 = <u>exaggerate</u>, disguise, embroider, misrepresent, falsify, gloss over ...*He wrote a highly coloured account of his childhood...*

➤ **shades from black to white** ➤ **shades of blue** ➤ **shades of brown** ➤ **shades of green** ➤ **shades of orange** ➤ **shades of purple** ➤ **shades of red** ➤ **shades of yellow**

colourful 1 = <u>bright</u>, rich, brilliant, intense, vivid, vibrant, psychedelic, motley, variegated, jazzy (*informal*), multicoloured, Day-glo (*trademark*), kaleidoscopic ...*Everyone was dressed in colourful clothes...* OPPOSITE drab

2 = <u>interesting</u>, rich, unusual, stimulating, graphic, lively, distinctive, vivid, picturesque, characterful ...*an irreverent and colourful tale of Restoration England...* OPPOSITE boring

colourless 1 = <u>uncoloured</u>, faded, neutral, bleached, washed out, achromatic ...*a colourless, almost odourless liquid...*

2 = <u>ashen</u>, washed out, wan, sickly, anaemic ...*Her face was colourless, and she was shaking...* OPPOSITE radiant

3 = <u>uninteresting</u>, dull, tame, dreary, drab, lacklustre, vacuous, insipid, vapid, characterless, unmemorable ...*His wife is a drab, colourless little woman...* OPPOSITE interesting

column 1 = <u>pillar</u>, support, post, shaft, upright, obelisk ...*Great stone steps led past Greek columns to the main building...*

2 = <u>line</u>, train, row, file, rank, string, queue, procession, cavalcade ...*There were reports of columns of military vehicles appearing on the streets...*

columnist = <u>journalist</u>, correspondent, editor, reporter, critic, reviewer, gossip columnist, journo (*slang*)

coma = <u>unconsciousness</u>, trance, oblivion, lethargy, stupor, torpor, insensibility

comatose 1 = <u>unconscious</u>, in a coma, out cold, insensible ...*The right side of my brain had been so severely bruised that I was comatose for a month...*

2 = <u>inert</u>, stupefied, out cold, somnolent, torpid, insensible, dead to the world (*informal*), drugged ...*Granpa lies comatose on the sofa...*

comb 1 = <u>untangle</u>, arrange, groom, dress ...*Her reddish hair was cut short and neatly combed...*

2 = <u>search</u>, hunt through, sweep, rake, sift, scour, rummage, ransack, forage, fossick (*Austral. & N.Z.*), go through with a fine-tooth comb ...*Officers combed the woods for the murder weapon...*

combat NOUN = <u>fight</u>, war, action, battle, conflict, engagement, warfare, skirmish ...*Over 16 million men died in combat during the war...* OPPOSITE peace

VERB = <u>fight</u>, battle against, oppose, contest, engage, cope with, resist, defy, withstand, struggle against, contend with, do battle with, strive against ...*new government measures to combat crime...* OPPOSITE support

combatant NOUN = <u>fighter</u>, soldier, warrior, contender, gladiator, belligerent, antagonist, fighting man, serviceman *or* servicewoman ...*His grandfather was a Boer war combatant...*

ADJECTIVE = <u>fighting</u>, warring, battling, conflicting, opposing, contending, belligerent, combative ...*the monitoring of ceasefires between combatant states...*

combative = <u>aggressive</u>, militant, contentious, belligerent, antagonistic, pugnacious, warlike, bellicose, truculent, quarrelsome OPPOSITE nonaggressive

combination 1 = <u>mixture</u>, mix, compound, blend, composite, amalgam, amalgamation, meld, coalescence ...*A combination of factors are to blame...*

2 = <u>association</u>, union, alliance, coalition, merger, federation, consortium, unification, syndicate, confederation, cartel, confederacy, cabal ...*The company's chairman has proposed a merger or other business combination...*

combine 1 = <u>amalgamate</u>, marry, mix, bond, bind, compound, blend, incorporate, integrate, merge, put together, fuse, synthesize ...*Combine the flour with water to make a paste...* OPPOSITE separate

2 = <u>join together</u>, link, connect, integrate, merge, fuse, amalgamate, meld ...*Disease and starvation are combining to kill thousands...*

3 = <u>unite</u>, associate, team up, unify, get together, collaborate, join forces, cooperate, join together, pool resources ...*Different states or groups can combine to enlarge their markets...* OPPOSITE split up

combustible = <u>flammable</u>, explosive, incendiary, inflammable

come VERB 1 = <u>approach</u>, near, advance, move towards, draw near ...*We heard the train coming...* ...*Tom, come here and look at this...*

2 = <u>arrive</u>, move, appear, enter, turn up (*informal*), show up (*informal*), materialize ...*Two police officers came into the hall...* ...*My brother's coming from Canada tomorrow...*

3 = <u>reach</u>, extend, come up to, come as far as ...*The water came to his chest...*

4 = <u>happen</u>, fall, occur, take place, come about, come to pass ...*Saturday's fire-bombing came without warning...*

5 = <u>be available</u>, be made, be offered, be produced, be on offer ...*The wallpaper comes in black and white only...*

PHRASES **come about** = <u>happen</u>, result, occur, take place, arise, transpire (*informal*), befall, come to pass ...*Any possible solution to the Irish question can only come about through dialogue...* ♦ **come across as something** *or* **someone** = <u>seem</u>, look, seem to be, look like, appear to be, give the impression of being, have the *or* every appearance of being, strike you as (being) ...*He came across as an extremely pleasant and charming young man...* ♦ **come across someone** = <u>meet</u>, encounter, run into, bump into (*informal*) ...*I recently came across a college friend in New York...* ♦ **come across something** = <u>find</u>, discover, notice, unearth, stumble upon, hit upon, chance upon, happen upon, light upon ...*He came across the jawbone of a 4.5 million-year-old marsupial...* ♦ **come at someone** = <u>attack</u>, charge, rush, go for, assault, fly at, assail, fall upon, rush at ...*A madman came at him with an axe...* ♦ **come back** = <u>return</u>, reappear, re-enter ...*She came back half an hour later...* ♦ **come between someone** = <u>separate</u>, part, divide, alienate, estrange, set at odds ...*It's difficult to imagine anything coming between them...* ♦ **come by something** = <u>get</u>, win, land, score (*slang*), secure, obtain, acquire, get hold of, procure, take possession of ...*How did you come by that cheque?...* ♦ **come clean about something** (*Informal*) = <u>confess to</u>, admit, reveal, declare, acknowledge, disclose, divulge, own up to, come out of the closet about, spill your guts about (*slang*), 'fess up to (*U.S.*) ...*I thought it best to come clean about our affair...* ♦ **come down 1** = <u>decrease</u>, fall, drop, reduce, go down, diminish, lessen, become lower ...*Interest rates are coming down...* **2** = <u>fall</u>, descend ...*The rain began to come down...* ♦ **come down on someone** = <u>reprimand</u>, blast, carpet (*informal*), put down, criticize, jump on (*informal*), rebuke, dress down (*informal*), tear into (*informal*), diss (*slang, chiefly U.S.*), read the riot act, lambast(e), bawl out (*informal*), rap over the knuckles, chew out (*U.S. & Canad. informal*), tear (someone) off a strip (*Brit. informal*), give (someone) a rocket (*Brit. & N.Z. informal*) ...*If she came down too hard on him, he would rebel...* ♦ **come down on something** (with one or other side of an argument as object) = <u>decide on</u>, choose, favour ...*He clearly came down on the side of the President...* ♦ **come down to something** = <u>amount to</u>, boil down to ...*In the end it all comes down to a matter of personal preference...* ♦ **come down with something** (with illness as object) = <u>catch</u>, get, take, contract, fall victim to, fall ill, be stricken with, take sick, sicken with ...*He came down with chickenpox...* ♦ **come forward** = <u>volunteer</u>, step forward, present yourself, offer your services ...*A witness came forward to say that she had seen him that night...* ♦ **come from something 1** = <u>be from</u>, originate, hail from, be a native of ...*Nearly half the students come from France...* **2** = <u>be obtained from</u>, be from, issue, emerge, flow, arise, originate, emanate ...*Chocolate comes from the cacao tree...* ♦ **come in 1** = <u>arrive</u>, enter, appear, show up (*informal*), cross the threshold ...*They were scared when they first came in...* **2** = <u>finish</u> ...*My horse came in third in the second race...* ♦ **come in for something** (with criticism or blame as object) = <u>receive</u>, get, suffer, endure, be subjected to, bear the brunt of, be the object of ...*The plans have already come in for fierce criticism...* ♦ **come into something** (with money or property as object) = <u>inherit</u>, be left, acquire, succeed to, be bequeathed, fall heir to ...*My father has just come into a fortune...* ♦ **come off** (*Informal*) = <u>succeed</u>, work out, be successful, pan out (*informal*), turn out well ...*It was a good try but it didn't quite come off...* ♦ **come on 1** = <u>progress</u>, develop, improve, advance, proceed, make headway ...*He is coming on very well at the violin...* **2** = <u>begin</u>, appear, take place ...*Winter is coming on...* ♦ **come out 1** = <u>be published</u>, appear, be released, be issued, be launched ...*The book comes out this week...* **2** = <u>be revealed</u>, emerge, be reported, be announced, become apparent, come to light, be divulged ...*The truth is beginning to come out now...* **3** = <u>turn out</u>, result, end up, work out, pan out (*informal*) ...*I'm sure it will come out all right in the end...* ♦ **come out with something** = <u>say</u>, speak, utter, let out ...*Everyone burst out laughing when he came out with this remark...* ♦ **come round** *or* **around 1** = <u>call</u>, visit, drop in, stop by, pop in ...*Beryl came round last night to apologize...* **2** = <u>change your opinion</u>, yield, concede, mellow, relent, accede, acquiesce ...*It looks like they're coming around to our way of thinking... ...Don't worry, she'll come round eventually...* **3** = <u>regain consciousness</u>, come to, recover, rally, revive ...*When I came round I was on the kitchen floor...* ♦ **come through** = <u>succeed</u>, triumph, prevail, make the grade (*informal*) ...*He's putting his job at risk if he doesn't come through...* ♦ **come through something** (with a negative or bad experience as object) = <u>survive</u>, overcome, endure, withstand, weather, pull through ...*We've come through some rough times...* ♦ **come to** = <u>revive</u>, recover, rally, come round, regain consciousness ...*When he came to and raised his head he saw Barney...* ♦ **come to something** = <u>amount to</u>, total, add up to ...*The bill came to over a hundred pounds...* ♦ **come up** = <u>happen</u>, occur, arise, turn up, spring up, crop up ...*Sorry I'm late – something came up at home...* ♦ **come up to something** = <u>measure up to</u>, meet, match, approach, rival, equal, compare with, resemble, admit of comparison with, stand *or* bear comparison with ...*Her work did not come up to his exacting standards...* ♦ **come up with something** = <u>produce</u>, offer, provide, present, suggest, advance, propose, submit, furnish ...*Several members have come up with suggestions of their own...*

comeback 1 (*Informal*) = <u>return</u>, revival, rebound, resurgence, rally, recovery, triumph ...*Sixties singing star Petula Clark is making a comeback...* **2** = <u>response</u>, reply, retort, retaliation, riposte, rejoinder ...*I tried to think of a witty comeback...*

comedian = <u>comic</u>, laugh (*informal*), wit, clown, funny man, humorist, wag, joker, jester, dag (*N.Z.*

informal), card (*informal*)

comedy 1 = <u>light entertainment</u>, sitcom (*informal*) …*Channel Four's comedy, 'Father Ted'*… OPPOSITE> tragedy, soapie

2 = <u>humour</u>, fun, joking, farce, jesting, slapstick, wisecracking, hilarity, witticisms, facetiousness, chaffing …*He and I provided the comedy with songs and monologues*… OPPOSITE> seriousness

comfort NOUN 1 = <u>ease</u>, luxury, wellbeing, opulence …*She had enough money to live in comfort for the rest of her life*…

2 = <u>consolation</u>, cheer, encouragement, succour, help, support, aid, relief, ease, compensation, alleviation …*I tried to find some words of comfort to offer her*… OPPOSITE> annoyance

VERB = <u>console</u>, encourage, ease, cheer, strengthen, relieve, reassure, soothe, hearten, solace, assuage, gladden, commiserate with …*He put his arm round her, trying to comfort her*… OPPOSITE> distress

comfortable 1 = <u>loose-fitting</u>, loose, adequate, ample, snug, roomy, commodious …*Dress in loose comfortable clothes that do not make you feel restricted*… OPPOSITE> tight-fitting

2 = <u>pleasant</u>, homely, easy, relaxing, delightful, enjoyable, cosy, agreeable, restful …*A home should be comfortable and friendly*… OPPOSITE> unpleasant

3 = <u>at ease</u>, happy, at home, contented, relaxed, serene …*Lie down on your bed and make yourself comfortable*… OPPOSITE> uncomfortable

4 (*Informal*) = <u>well-off</u>, prosperous, affluent, well-to-do, comfortably-off, in clover (*informal*) …*She came from a stable, comfortable, middle-class family*…

comforting = <u>consoling</u>, encouraging, cheering, reassuring, soothing, heart-warming, inspiriting OPPOSITE> upsetting

comic ADJECTIVE = <u>funny</u>, amusing, witty, humorous, farcical, comical, light, joking, droll, facetious, jocular, waggish …*The novel is both comic and tragic*… OPPOSITE> sad

NOUN = <u>comedian</u>, funny man, humorist, wit, clown, wag, jester, dag (*N.Z. informal*), buffoon …*At that time he was still a penniless, unknown comic*…

comical = <u>funny</u>, entertaining, comic, silly, amusing, ridiculous, diverting, absurd, hilarious, ludicrous, humorous, priceless, laughable, farcical, whimsical, zany, droll, risible, side-splitting

coming ADJECTIVE 1 = <u>approaching</u>, next, future, near, due, forthcoming, imminent, in store, impending, at hand, upcoming, on the cards, in the wind, nigh, just round the corner …*This obviously depends on the weather in the coming months*…

2 = <u>up-and-coming</u>, future, promising, aspiring …*He is widely regarded as the coming man of Scottish rugby*…

NOUN = <u>arrival</u>, approach, advent, accession …*Most of us welcome the coming of summer*…

command VERB 1 = <u>order</u>, tell, charge, demand, require, direct, bid, compel, enjoin …*He commanded his troops to attack*… OPPOSITE> beg

2 = <u>have authority over</u>, lead, head, control, rule, manage, handle, dominate, govern, administer, supervise, be in charge of, reign over …*the French general who commands the UN troops in the region*… OPPOSITE> be subordinate to

NOUN 1 = <u>order</u>, demand, direction, instruction, requirement, decree, bidding, mandate, canon, directive, injunction, fiat, ultimatum, commandment, edict, behest, precept …*The tanker failed to respond to a command to stop*…

2 = <u>domination</u>, control, rule, grasp, sway, mastery, dominion, upper hand, power, government …*the struggle for command of the air*…

3 = <u>management</u>, power, control, charge, authority, direction, supervision …*In 1942 he took command of 108 Squadron*…

commandeer = <u>seize</u>, appropriate, hijack, confiscate, requisition, sequester, expropriate, sequestrate

commander = <u>leader</u>, director, chief, officer, boss, head, captain, bass (*S. African*), ruler, commander-in-chief, commanding officer, C in C, C.O.

commanding 1 = <u>dominant</u>, controlling, dominating, superior, decisive, advantageous …*Right now you're in a very commanding position*…

2 = <u>authoritative</u>, imposing, impressive, compelling, assertive, forceful, autocratic, peremptory …*The voice at the other end of the line was serious and commanding*… OPPOSITE> unassertive

commemorate = <u>celebrate</u>, remember, honour, recognize, salute, pay tribute to, immortalize, memorialize OPPOSITE> ignore

commemoration 1 = <u>ceremony</u>, tribute, memorial service, testimonial …*A special commemoration for her will be held next week*…

2 = <u>remembrance</u>, honour, tribute …*a march in commemoration of Malcolm X*…

commemorative = <u>memorial</u>, celebratory

commence 1 = <u>embark on</u>, start, open, begin, initiate, originate, instigate, inaugurate, enter upon …*They commenced a systematic search of the area*… OPPOSITE> stop

2 = <u>start</u>, open, begin, go ahead …*The academic year commences at the beginning of October*… OPPOSITE> end

commencement = <u>beginning</u>, start, opening, launch, birth, origin, dawn, outset, onset, initiation, inauguration, inception, embarkation

commend 1 = <u>praise</u>, acclaim, applaud, compliment, extol, approve, big up (*slang, chiefly Caribbean*), eulogize, speak highly of …*She was highly commended for her bravery*… OPPOSITE> criticize

2 = <u>recommend</u>, suggest, approve, advocate, endorse, vouch for, put in a good word for …*I can commend it to you as a sensible course of action*…

commendable = <u>praiseworthy</u>, deserving, worthy, admirable, exemplary, creditable, laudable, meritorious, estimable

commendation = <u>praise</u>, credit, approval, acclaim, encouragement, Brownie points, approbation, acclamation, good opinion, panegyric, encomium

commensurate 1 = equivalent, consistent, corresponding, comparable, compatible, in accord, proportionate, coextensive ...*Employees are paid salaries commensurate with those of teachers...*
2 = appropriate, fitting, fit, due, sufficient, adequate ...*The resources available are in no way commensurate to the need...*

comment VERB **1** = remark, say, note, mention, point out, observe, utter, opine, interpose ...*Stuart commented that this was very true...*
2 *usually with* **on** = remark on, explain, talk about, discuss, speak about, say something about, allude to, elucidate, make a comment on ...*So far Mr Cook has not commented on these reports...*
NOUN **1** = remark, statement, observation ...*He made these comments at a news conference...*
2 = note, criticism, explanation, illustration, commentary, exposition, annotation, elucidation ...*He had added a few comments in the margin...*

commentary 1 = narration, report, review, explanation, description, voice-over ...*He gave the listening crowd a running commentary on the game...*
2 = analysis, notes, review, critique, treatise ...*He will be writing a twice-weekly commentary on American society and culture...*

commentator 1 = reporter, special correspondent, sportscaster, commenter ...*a sports commentator...*
2 = critic, interpreter, annotator ...*He is a commentator on African affairs...*

commercial 1 = mercantile, business, trade, trading, sales ...*In its heyday it was a major centre of commercial activity...*
2 = profitable, popular, in demand, marketable, saleable ...*Whether the project will be a commercial success is still uncertain...*
3 = materialistic, mercenary, profit-making, venal, monetary, exploited, pecuniary ...*There's a feeling among a lot of people that music has become too commercial...*

commiserate *often with* **with** = sympathize, pity, feel for, console, condole

commission VERB = appoint, order, contract, select, engage, delegate, nominate, authorize, empower, depute ...*You can commission them to paint something especially for you...*
NOUN **1** = duty, authority, trust, charge, task, function, mission, employment, appointment, warrant, mandate, errand ...*She approached him with a commission to write the screen play for the film...*
2 = fee, cut, compensation, percentage, allowance, royalties, brokerage, rake-off (*slang*) ...*He got a commission for bringing in new clients...*
3 = committee, board, representatives, commissioners, delegation, deputation, body of commissioners ...*The authorities have been asked to set up a commission to investigate the murders...*

commit VERB **1** = do, perform, carry out, execute, enact, perpetrate ...*I have never committed any crime...*
2 = give, deliver, engage, deposit, hand over, commend, entrust, consign ...*The government have

committed billions of pounds for a programme to reduce acid rain...* OPPOSITE withhold
3 = put in custody, confine, imprison, consign ...*His drinking caused him to be committed to a psychiatric hospital...* OPPOSITE release
PHRASES **commit yourself to something** = pledge to, promise to, bind yourself to, make yourself liable for, obligate yourself to ...*She didn't want to commit herself to working at weekends...*

commitment 1 = dedication, loyalty, devotion, adherence ...*a commitment to the ideals of Bolshevism...* OPPOSITE indecisiveness
2 = responsibility, tie, duty, obligation, liability, engagement ...*I've got too many commitments to take on anything more right now...*
3 = pledge, promise, guarantee, undertaking, vow, assurance, word ...*We made a commitment to keep working together...* OPPOSITE disavowal

committed 1 = dedicated, devoted, loyal, intent, faithful, devout, resolute, adherent, dutiful ...*He said the government remained committed to attaining peace...*
2 = pledged, involved, promised, tied, engaged, obliged, duty-bound ...*It would have meant cancelling several meetings which I was already committed to...*

committee = group, commission, panel, delegation, subcommittee, deputation
➤ **family**

commodity *usually plural* = goods, produce, stock, products, merchandise, wares

common 1 = usual, standard, daily, regular, ordinary, familiar, plain, conventional, routine, frequent, everyday, customary, commonplace, vanilla (*slang*), habitual, run-of-the-mill, humdrum, stock, workaday, bog-standard (*Brit. & Irish slang*), a dime a dozen ...*Earthquakes are fairly common in this part of the world...* OPPOSITE rare
2 = popular, general, accepted, standard, routine, widespread, universal, prevailing, prevalent ...*It is common practice these days to administer vitamin K during childbirth...*
3 = shared, collective ...*They share a common language...*
4 = ordinary, average, simple, typical, undistinguished, dinki-di (*Austral. informal*) ...*He proclaims himself to be the voice of the common man...* OPPOSITE important
5 = vulgar, low, inferior, coarse, plebeian ...*She might be a little common at times, but she was certainly not boring...* OPPOSITE refined
6 = collective, public, community, social, communal ...*social policies which promote the common good...* OPPOSITE personal

commonplace ADJECTIVE = everyday, common, ordinary, widespread, pedestrian, customary, mundane, vanilla (*slang*), banal, run-of-the-mill, humdrum, dime-a-dozen (*informal*) ...*Foreign vacations have become commonplace nowadays...* OPPOSITE rare
NOUN = cliché, platitude, banality, truism ...*It is a

commonplace to say that the poetry of the first world war was greater than that of the second…

common sense = good sense, sound judgment, level-headedness, practicality, prudence, nous (*Brit. slang*), soundness, reasonableness, gumption (*Brit. informal*), horse sense, native intelligence, mother wit, smarts (*slang, chiefly U.S.*), wit

common-sense = sensible, sound, practical, reasonable, realistic, shrewd, down-to-earth, matter-of-fact, sane, astute, judicious, level-headed, hard-headed OPPOSITE> foolish

commotion = disturbance, to-do, riot, disorder, excitement, fuss, turmoil, racket, upheaval, bustle, furore, uproar, ferment, agitation, ado, rumpus, tumult, hubbub, hurly-burly, brouhaha, hullabaloo, hue and cry

communal 1 = community, neighbourhood *…Communal violence broke out in different parts of the country…*
2 = public, shared, general, joint, collective, communistic *…The inmates ate in a communal dining room…* OPPOSITE> private

commune = community, collective, cooperative, kibbutz

commune with 1 = contemplate, ponder, reflect on, muse on, meditate on *…He set off from the lodge to commune with nature…*
2 = talk to, communicate with, discuss with, confer with, converse with, discourse with, parley with *…You can now commune with people from the safety of your PC…*

communicable = infectious, catching, contagious, transferable, transmittable

communicate 1 = contact, talk, speak, phone, correspond, make contact, be in touch, ring up (*informal, chiefly Brit.*), be in contact, get in contact *…They communicated in sign language… …My natural mother has never communicated with me…*
2 = make known, report, announce, reveal, publish, declare, spread, disclose, pass on, proclaim, transmit, convey, impart, divulge, disseminate *…The result will be communicated to parents…* OPPOSITE> keep secret
3 = pass on, transfer, spread, transmit *…typhus, a disease communicated by body lice…*

communication NOUN 1 = contact, conversation, correspondence, intercourse, link, relations, connection *…The problem is a lack of real communication between you…*
2 = passing on, spread, circulation, transmission, disclosure, imparting, dissemination, conveyance *…Treatment involves the communication of information…*
3 = message, news, report, word, information, statement, intelligence, announcement, disclosure, dispatch *…The ambassador has brought with him a communication from the President…*
PLURAL NOUN = connections, travel, links, transport, routes *…Violent rain has caused flooding and cut communications between neighbouring towns…*

communicative = talkative, open, frank, forthcoming, outgoing, informative, candid, expansive, chatty, voluble, loquacious, unreserved OPPOSITE> reserved

communion = affinity, accord, agreement, unity, sympathy, harmony, intercourse, fellowship, communing, closeness, rapport, converse, togetherness, concord

Communion (*Christianity*) = Eucharist, Mass, Sacrament, Lord's Supper

communiqué = announcement, report, bulletin, dispatch, news flash, official communication

communism *usually cap.* = socialism, Marxism, Stalinism, collectivism, Bolshevism, Marxism-Leninism, state socialism, Maoism, Trotskyism, Eurocommunism, Titoism

communist *often cap.* = socialist, Red (*informal*), Marxist, Bolshevik, collectivist

community 1 = society, people, public, association, population, residents, commonwealth, general public, populace, body politic, state, company *…He's well liked by the local community…*
2 = district, area, quarter, region, sector, parish, neighbourhood, vicinity, locality, locality, locale, neck of the woods (*informal*) *…a black township on the outskirts of the mining community…*

commute 1 = travel to and from, shuttle between, travel between, travel back and forth between *…He commutes to London every day…*
2 (*Law*) = reduce, cut, modify, shorten, alleviate, curtail, remit, mitigate *…His death sentence was commuted to life imprisonment…*

commuter = daily traveller, passenger, suburbanite

compact[1] ADJECTIVE 1 = closely packed, firm, solid, thick, dense, compressed, condensed, impenetrable, impermeable, pressed together *…a thick, bare trunk crowned by a compact mass of dark-green leaves…* OPPOSITE> loose
2 = concise, brief, to the point, succinct, terse, laconic, pithy, epigrammatic, pointed *…The strength of the series is in its concise, compact short-story quality…* OPPOSITE> lengthy
VERB = pack closely, stuff, cram, compress, condense, tamp *…The soil settles and is compacted by the winter rain…* OPPOSITE> loosen

compact[2] = agreement, deal, understanding, contract, bond, arrangement, alliance, treaty, bargain, pact, covenant, entente, concordat *…The Pilgrims signed a democratic compact aboard The Mayflower…*

companion 1 = friend, partner, ally, colleague, associate, mate (*informal*), gossip (*archaic*), buddy (*informal*), comrade, accomplice, crony, confederate, consort, main man (*slang, chiefly U.S.*), homeboy (*slang, chiefly U.S.*), cobber (*Austral. or old-fashioned N.Z. informal*) *…He has been her constant companion for the last six years…*
2 = assistant, aide, escort, attendant *…She was employed as companion to a wealthy old lady…*
3 = complement, match, fellow, mate, twin, counterpart *…The book was written as the companion to a trilogy of television documentaries…*

companionship = fellowship, company, friendship, fraternity, rapport, camaraderie, togetherness, comradeship, amity, esprit de corps, conviviality

company 1 = business, firm, association, corporation, partnership, establishment, syndicate, house, concern …*She worked as a secretary in an insurance company…*
2 = group, troupe, set, community, league, band, crowd, camp, collection, gathering, circle, crew, assembly, convention, ensemble, throng, coterie, bevy, assemblage, party, body …*He was a notable young actor in a company of rising stars…*
3 = troop, unit, squad, team …*The division consists of two tank companies and one infantry company…*
4 = companionship, society, presence, fellowship …*I would be grateful for your company on the drive back…*
5 = guests, party, visitors, callers …*Oh, I'm sorry, I didn't realise you had company…*

comparable 1 = equal, equivalent, on a par, tantamount, a match for, proportionate, commensurate, as good as, in a class with …*They should be paid the same wages for work of comparable value… …Farmers were meant to get an income comparable with that of townspeople…* OPPOSITE⟩ unequal
2 = similar, related, alike, corresponding, akin, analogous, of a piece, cognate, cut from the same cloth …*The scoring systems used in the two studies are not directly comparable…*

comparative = relative, qualified, by comparison, approximate

compare VERB = contrast, balance, weigh, set against, collate, juxtapose …*Compare the two illustrations in Fig 60…*
PHRASES **compare to something** = liken to, parallel, identify with, equate to, correlate to, mention in the same breath as …*Commentators compared his work to that of James Joyce…* ◆ **compare with something** = be as good as, match, approach, equal, compete with, come up to, vie, be on a par with, be the equal of, approximate to, hold a candle to, bear comparison, be in the same class as …*The flowers here do not compare with those at home…*

comparison 1 = contrast, distinction, differentiation, juxtaposition, collation …*There are no previous statistics for comparison…*
2 = similarity, analogy, resemblance, correlation, likeness, comparability …*There is no comparison between the picture quality of a video and that of a DVD…*

compartment 1 = section, carriage, berth …*We shared our compartment with a group of businessmen…*
2 = bay, chamber, booth, locker, niche, cubicle, alcove, pigeonhole, cubbyhole, cell …*I put the vodka in the freezer compartment of the fridge…*
3 = category, area, department, division, section, subdivision …*We usually put the mind, the body and the spirit into three separate compartments…*

compass[1] = range, field, area, reach, scope, sphere, limit, stretch, bound, extent, zone, boundary, realm …*Within the compass of a book of this size, such a comprehensive survey is not practicable…*

compass[2]
➤ **compass points**

compassion = sympathy, understanding, charity, pity, humanity, mercy, heart, quarter, sorrow, kindness, tenderness, condolence, clemency, commiseration, fellow feeling, soft-heartedness, tender-heartedness OPPOSITE⟩ indifference

compassionate = sympathetic, kindly, understanding, tender, pitying, humanitarian, charitable, humane, indulgent, benevolent, lenient, merciful, kind-hearted, tender-hearted OPPOSITE⟩

Compass points

Compass Point	Abbreviation	Compass Point	Abbreviation
North	N	South West	SW
North by East	N by E	South West by West	SW by W
North North East	NNE	West South West	WSW
North East by North	NE by N	West by South	W by S
North East	NE	West	W
North East by East	NE by E	West by North	W by N
East North East	ENE	West North West	WNW
East by North	E by N	North West by West	NW by W
East	E	North West	NW
East by South	E by S	North West by North	NW by N
East South East	ESE	North North West	NNW
South East by East	SE by E	North by West	N by W
South East	SE		
South East by South	SE by S		
South South East	SSE	**Cardinal point**	**Related adjective**
South by East	S by E	north	arctic *or* boreal
South	S	east	oriental
South by West	S by W	south	meridional *or* austral
South South West	SSW	west	occidental *or* hesperidan
South West by South	SW by S		

uncaring

compatibility 1 = <u>agreement</u>, consistency, accordance, affinity, conformity, concord, congruity, accord ...*National courts can freeze any law while its compatibility with European Community legislation is tested...*
2 = <u>like-mindedness</u>, harmony, empathy, rapport, single-mindedness, amity, sympathy, congeniality ...*Dating allows people to check out their compatibility before making a commitment to one another...*

compatible 1 = <u>consistent</u>, in keeping, consonant, congenial, congruent, reconcilable, congruous, accordant, agreeable ...*Free enterprise, he argued, was compatible with Russian values and traditions...* [OPPOSITE] inappropriate
2 = <u>like-minded</u>, harmonious, in harmony, in accord, of one mind, of the same mind, en rapport (*French*) ...*She and I are very compatible – we're interested in all the same things...* [OPPOSITE] incompatible

compatriot = <u>fellow countryman</u>, countryman, fellow citizen

compel = <u>force</u>, make, urge, enforce, railroad (*informal*), drive, oblige, constrain, hustle (*slang*), necessitate, coerce, bulldoze (*informal*), impel, dragoon

compelling 1 = <u>convincing</u>, telling, powerful, forceful, conclusive, weighty, cogent, irrefutable ...*He puts forward a compelling argument against the culling of badgers...*
2 = <u>pressing</u>, binding, urgent, overriding, imperative, unavoidable, coercive, peremptory ...*Another, probably more compelling, factor is that of safety...*
3 = <u>fascinating</u>, gripping, irresistible, enchanting, enthralling, hypnotic, spellbinding, mesmeric ...*Her eyes were her best feature, wide-set and compelling...* ...*a violent yet compelling film...* [OPPOSITE] boring

compendium = <u>collection</u>, summary, abstract, digest, compilation, epitome, synopsis, précis

compensate 1 = <u>recompense</u>, repay, refund, reimburse, indemnify, make restitution, requite, remunerate, satisfy, make good ...*To ease financial difficulties, farmers could be compensated for their loss of subsidies...*
2 = <u>make amends</u>, make up for, atone, make it up to someone, pay for, do penance, cancel out, make reparation, make redress ...*She compensated for her burst of anger by doing even more for the children...*
3 = <u>balance</u>, cancel (out), offset, make up for, redress, counteract, neutralize, counterbalance ...*The rewards more than compensated for the inconveniences involved in making the trip...*

compensation 1 = <u>reparation</u>, damages, payment, recompense, indemnification, offset, remuneration, indemnity, restitution, reimbursement, requital ...*He received one year's salary as compensation for loss of office...*
2 = <u>recompense</u>, amends, reparation, restitution, atonement ...*The present she left him was no compensation for her absence...*

compete 1 = <u>contend</u>, fight, rival, vie, challenge, struggle, contest, strive, pit yourself against ...*The stores will inevitably end up competing with each other for increased market shares...*
2 = <u>take part</u>, participate, be in the running, be a competitor, be a contestant, play ...*He has competed twice in the London marathon...*

competence 1 = <u>ability</u>, skill, talent, capacity, expertise, proficiency, competency, capability ...*I regard him as a man of integrity and high professional competence...* [OPPOSITE] incompetence
2 = <u>fitness</u>, suitability, adequacy, appropriateness ...*They questioned her competence as a mother...* [OPPOSITE] inadequacy

competent 1 = <u>able</u>, skilled, capable, clever, endowed, proficient ...*He was a loyal and very competent civil servant...* [OPPOSITE] incompetent
2 = <u>fit</u>, qualified, equal, appropriate, suitable, sufficient, adequate ...*I don't feel competent to deal with a medical emergency...* [OPPOSITE] unqualified

competition 1 = <u>rivalry</u>, opposition, struggle, contest, contention, strife, one-upmanship (*informal*) ...*There's been some fierce competition for the title...*
2 = <u>opposition</u>, field, rivals, challengers ...*In this business you have to stay one step ahead of the competition...*
3 = <u>contest</u>, event, championship, tournament, head-to-head ...*He will be banned from international competitions for four years...*

competitive 1 = <u>cut-throat</u>, aggressive, fierce, ruthless, relentless, antagonistic, dog-eat-dog ...*Modelling is a tough, competitive world...*
2 = <u>ambitious</u>, pushing, opposing, aggressive, vying, contentious, combative ...*He has always been a fiercely competitive player...*

competitor 1 = <u>rival</u>, competition, opposition, adversary, antagonist ...*The bank isn't performing as well as some of its competitors...*
2 = <u>contestant</u>, participant, contender, challenger, entrant, player, opponent ...*One of the oldest competitors in the race won the silver medal...*

compilation = <u>collection</u>, treasury, accumulation, anthology, assortment, assemblage

compile = <u>put together</u>, collect, gather, organize, accumulate, marshal, garner, amass, cull, anthologize

complacency = <u>smugness</u>, satisfaction, gratification, contentment, self-congratulation, self-satisfaction

complacent = <u>smug</u>, self-satisfied, pleased with yourself, resting on your laurels, pleased, contented, satisfied, gratified, serene, unconcerned, self-righteous, self-assured, self-contented [OPPOSITE] insecure

complain = <u>find fault</u>, moan, grumble, whinge (*informal*), beef (*slang*), carp, fuss, bitch (*slang*), groan, grieve, lament, whine, growl, deplore, grouse, gripe (*informal*), bemoan, bleat, put the boot in (*slang*), bewail, kick up a fuss (*informal*), grouch (*informal*), bellyache (*slang*), kvetch (*U.S. slang*)

complaint 1 = <u>protest</u>, accusation, objection, grievance, remonstrance, charge ...*There have been a* *number of complaints about the standard of service…*

2 = <u>grumble</u>, criticism, beef (*slang*), moan, bitch (*slang*), lament, grievance, wail, dissatisfaction, annoyance, grouse, gripe (*informal*), grouch (*informal*), plaint, fault-finding …*I don't have any complaints about the way I've been treated…*

3 = <u>disorder</u>, problem, trouble, disease, upset, illness, sickness, ailment, affliction, malady, indisposition …*Eczema is a common skin complaint…*

complement VERB = <u>enhance</u>, complete, improve, boost, crown, add to, set off, heighten, augment, round off …*Nutmeg complements the flavour of these beans perfectly…*

NOUN **1** = <u>accompaniment</u>, companion, accessory, completion, finishing touch, rounding-off, adjunct, supplement …*The green wallpaper is the perfect complement to the old pine of the dresser…*

2 = <u>total</u>, capacity, quota, aggregate, contingent, entirety …*Each ship had a complement of around a dozen officers and 250 men…*

Word Power

complement – This is sometimes confused with *compliment* but the two words have very different meanings. As the synonyms show, the verb form of *complement* means 'to enhance' and 'to complete' something. In contrast, common synonyms of *compliment* as a verb are *praise*, *commend*, and *flatter*.

complementary = <u>matching</u>, companion, corresponding, compatible, reciprocal, interrelating, interdependent, harmonizing OPPOSITE incompatible

complete ADJECTIVE **1** = <u>total</u>, perfect, absolute, utter, outright, thorough, consummate, out-and-out, unmitigated, dyed-in-the-wool, thoroughgoing, deep-dyed (*usually derogatory*) …*He made me look like a complete idiot…*

2 = <u>whole</u>, full, entire …*A complete tenement block was burnt to the ground…* OPPOSITE partial

3 = <u>entire</u>, full, whole, intact, unbroken, faultless, undivided, unimpaired …*Scientists have found the oldest complete skeleton of an ape-like man…* OPPOSITE incomplete

4 = <u>unabridged</u>, full, entire …*the complete works of Shakespeare…*

5 = <u>finished</u>, done, ended, completed, achieved, concluded, fulfilled, accomplished …*The work of restoring the farmhouse is complete…* OPPOSITE unfinished

6 = <u>perfect</u>, accomplish, finish off, round off, crown, cap …*the stickers needed to complete the collection…* OPPOSITE spoil

VERB **1** = <u>finish</u>, conclude, fulfil, accomplish, do, end, close, achieve, perform, settle, realize, execute, discharge, wrap up (*informal*), terminate, finalize …*He had just completed his first novel…* OPPOSITE start

2 = <u>fill in</u>, fill out …*Simply complete the coupon below…*

completely = <u>totally</u>, entirely, wholly, utterly, quite, perfectly, fully, solidly, absolutely, altogether, thoroughly, in full, every inch, en masse, heart and soul, a hundred per cent, one hundred per cent, from beginning to end, down to the ground, root and branch, in toto (*Latin*), from A to Z, hook, line and sinker, lock, stock and barrel

completion = <u>finishing</u>, end, close, conclusion, accomplishment, realization, fulfilment, culmination, attainment, fruition, consummation, finalization

complex ADJECTIVE **1** = <u>compound</u>, compounded, multiple, composite, manifold, heterogeneous, multifarious …*His complex compositions are built up of many overlapping layers…*

2 = <u>complicated</u>, difficult, involved, mixed, elaborate, tangled, mingled, intricate, tortuous, convoluted, knotty, labyrinthine, circuitous …*in-depth coverage of today's complex issues…* OPPOSITE simple

NOUN **1** = <u>structure</u>, system, scheme, network, organization, aggregate, composite, synthesis …*Our philosophy is a complex of many tightly interrelated ideas…*

2 (*Informal*) = <u>obsession</u>, preoccupation, phobia, fixation, fixed idea, idée fixe (*French*) …*I have never had a complex about my weight…*

Word Power

complex – Although *complex* and *complicated* are close in meaning, care should be taken when using one as a synonym of the other. *Complex* should be used to say that something consists of several parts rather than that it is difficult to understand, analyse, or deal with, which is what *complicated* inherently means. In the following real example a clear distinction is made between the two words: *the British benefits system is phenomenally complex and is administered by a complicated range of agencies.*

complexion **1** = <u>skin</u>, colour, colouring, hue, skin tone, pigmentation …*She had short brown hair and a pale complexion…*

2 = <u>nature</u>, character, make-up, cast, stamp, disposition …*The political complexion of the government has changed…*

3 = <u>perspective</u>, look, light, appearance, aspect, angle, slant …*This latest development puts a different complexion on things…*

complexity = <u>complication</u>, involvement, intricacy, entanglement, convolution

compliance **1** = <u>conformity</u>, agreement, obedience, assent, observance, concurrence …*The company says it is in full compliance with US labor laws…* OPPOSITE disobedience

2 = <u>submissiveness</u>, yielding, submission, obedience, deference, passivity, acquiescence, complaisance, consent …*Suddenly, he hated her for her compliance and passivity…* OPPOSITE defiance

compliant = <u>obedient</u>, willing, accepting, yielding, obliging, accommodating, passive, cooperative, agreeable, submissive, conformist, deferential, acquiescent, complaisant, conformable

complicate = <u>make difficult</u>, confuse, muddle, embroil, entangle, make intricate, involve OPPOSITE⟩ simplify

complicated 1 = <u>involved</u>, difficult, puzzling, troublesome, problematic, perplexing …*The situation in Lebanon is very complicated…* OPPOSITE⟩ simple
2 = <u>complex</u>, involved, elaborate, intricate, Byzantine (*of attitudes, etc.*), convoluted, labyrinthine, interlaced …*a complicated voting system…* OPPOSITE⟩ understandable
➤ **complex**

complication 1 = <u>problem</u>, difficulty, obstacle, drawback, snag, uphill (*S. African*), stumbling block, aggravation …*The age difference was a complication to the relationship…*
2 = <u>complexity</u>, combination, mixture, web, confusion, intricacy, entanglement …*His poetry was characterised by a complication of imagery and ideas…*

complicity = <u>collusion</u>, conspiracy, collaboration, connivance, abetment

compliment NOUN = <u>praise</u>, honour, tribute, courtesy, admiration, bouquet, flattery, eulogy …*She blushed, but accepted the compliment with good grace…* OPPOSITE⟩ criticism
PLURAL NOUN 1 = <u>greetings</u>, regards, respects, good wishes, salutation …*Give my compliments to your lovely wife when you write home…* OPPOSITE⟩ insult
2 = <u>congratulations</u>, praise, commendation …*That was an excellent meal – my compliments to the chef…*
VERB = <u>praise</u>, flatter, salute, congratulate, pay tribute to, commend, laud, extol, crack up (*informal*), pat on the back, sing the praises of, wax lyrical about, big up (*slang, chiefly Caribbean*), speak highly of …*They complimented me on my performance…* OPPOSITE⟩ criticize

---

Word Power

compliment – *Compliment* is sometimes confused with *complement*.

---

complimentary 1 = <u>flattering</u>, approving, appreciative, congratulatory, eulogistic, commendatory …*We often get complimentary remarks regarding the quality of our service…* OPPOSITE⟩ critical
2 = <u>free</u>, donated, courtesy, honorary, free of charge, on the house, gratuitous, gratis …*He had complimentary tickets for the show…*

comply = <u>obey</u>, follow, respect, agree to, satisfy, observe, fulfil, submit to, conform to, adhere to, abide by, consent to, yield to, defer to, accede to, act in accordance with, perform, acquiesce with OPPOSITE⟩ defy

component NOUN = <u>part</u>, piece, unit, item, element, ingredient, constituent …*Enriched uranium is a key component of nuclear weapons…*
ADJECTIVE = <u>constituent</u>, composing, inherent, intrinsic …*Polish workers will now be making component parts for Boeing 757s…*

compose VERB 1 = <u>put together</u>, make up, constitute, comprise, make, build, form, fashion, construct, compound …*They agreed to form a council composed of leaders of the rival factions…* OPPOSITE⟩ destroy
2 = <u>create</u>, write, produce, imagine, frame, invent, devise, contrive …*He started at once to compose a reply to her letter…*
3 = <u>arrange</u>, make up, construct, put together, order, organize …*The drawing is beautifully composed…*
PHRASES **compose yourself** = <u>calm</u>, still, control, settle, collect, quiet, soothe, pull yourself together …*She quickly composed herself before she entered the room…*

composed = <u>calm</u>, together (*slang*), cool, collected, relaxed, confident, poised, at ease, laid-back (*informal*), serene, tranquil, sedate, self-controlled, level-headed, unfazed (*informal*), unflappable, unruffled, self-possessed, imperturbable, unworried, keeping your cool, as cool as a cucumber OPPOSITE⟩ agitated

composer
➤ **WORD POWER SUPPLEMENT composers**

composite ADJECTIVE = <u>compound</u>, mixed, combined, complex, blended, conglomerate, synthesized …*The chassis is made of a complex composite structure incorporating carbon fibre…*
NOUN = <u>compound</u>, blend, conglomerate, fusion, synthesis, amalgam, meld …*Spain is a composite of diverse traditions and people…*

composition 1 = <u>design</u>, form, structure, make-up, organization, arrangement, constitution, formation, layout, configuration …*Materials of different composition absorb and reflect light differently…*
2 = <u>creation</u>, work, piece, production, opus, masterpiece, chef-d'oeuvre (*French*) …*Bach's compositions are undoubtedly among the greatest ever written…*
3 = <u>essay</u>, writing, study, exercise, treatise, literary work …*Write a composition on the subject 'What I Did on My Holidays'…*
4 = <u>arrangement</u>, balance, proportion, harmony, symmetry, concord, consonance, placing …*Let us study the composition of this painting…*
5 = <u>production</u>, creation, making, fashioning, formation, putting together, invention, compilation, formulation …*These plays are arranged in order of their composition…*

compost = <u>fertilizer</u>, mulch, humus

composure = <u>calmness</u>, calm, poise, self-possession, cool (*slang*), ease, dignity, serenity, tranquillity, coolness, aplomb, equanimity, self-assurance, sang-froid, placidity, sedateness OPPOSITE⟩ agitation

compound NOUN = <u>combination</u>, mixture, blend, composite, conglomerate, fusion, synthesis, alloy, medley, amalgam, meld, composition …*Organic compounds contain carbon in their molecules…* OPPOSITE⟩ element
ADJECTIVE = <u>complex</u>, multiple, composite, conglomerate, intricate, not simple …*a tall shrub with*

shiny compound leaves... OPPOSITE> simple
VERB 1 = <u>intensify</u>, add to, complicate, worsen,
heighten, exacerbate, aggravate, magnify, augment,
add insult to injury ...*Additional bloodshed will only
compound the misery...* OPPOSITE> lessen
2 = <u>combine</u>, unite, mix, blend, fuse, mingle,
synthesize, concoct, amalgamate, coalesce,
intermingle, meld ...*An emotion oddly compounded of
pleasure and bitterness flooded over me...* OPPOSITE>
divide

comprehend = <u>understand</u>, see, take in, perceive,
grasp, conceive, make out, discern, assimilate, see the
light, fathom, apprehend, get the hang of (*informal*),
get the picture, know OPPOSITE> misunderstand

comprehensible = <u>understandable</u>, clear, plain,
explicit, coherent, user-friendly, intelligible

comprehension = <u>understanding</u>, grasp,
conception, realization, sense, knowledge,
intelligence, judgment, perception, discernment
OPPOSITE> incomprehension

comprehensive = <u>broad</u>, full, complete, wide,
catholic, sweeping, extensive, blanket, umbrella,
thorough, inclusive, exhaustive, all-inclusive, all-
embracing, overarching, encyclopedic OPPOSITE>
limited

compress 1 = <u>squeeze</u>, crush, squash, constrict,
press, crowd, wedge, cram ...*Poor posture can
compress the body's organs...*
2 = <u>condense</u>, contract, concentrate, compact,
shorten, summarize, abbreviate ...*Textbooks
compressed six millennia of Egyptian history into a few
pages...*

compressed 1 = <u>squeezed</u>, concentrated, compact,
compacted, consolidated, squashed, flattened,
constricted ...*a biodegradable product made from
compressed peat and cellulose...*
2 = <u>reduced</u>, compacted, shortened, abridged ...*All
those three books are compressed into one volume...*

compression = <u>squeezing</u>, pressing, crushing,
consolidation, condensation, constriction

comprise 1 = <u>be composed of</u>, include, contain,
consist of, take in, embrace, encompass, comprehend
...*The exhibition comprises 50 oils and watercolours...*
2 = <u>make up</u>, form, constitute, compose ...*Women
comprise 44% of hospital medical staff...*

Word Power

comprise – The use of *of* after *comprise*
should be avoided: *the library comprises* (not
comprises of) 6,500,000 books and
manuscripts. *Consist*, however, should be
followed by *of* when used in this way: *Her
crew consisted of children from Devon and
Cornwall.*

---

compromise NOUN = <u>give-and-take</u>, agreement,
settlement, accommodation, concession, adjustment,
trade-off, middle ground, half measures ...*Be willing
to make compromises between what your partner
wants and what you want...* OPPOSITE> disagreement

VERB 1 = <u>meet halfway</u>, concede, make concessions,
give and take, strike a balance, strike a happy
medium, go fifty-fifty (*informal*) ...*I don't think we can
compromise on fundamental principles...* OPPOSITE>
disagree
2 = <u>undermine</u>, expose, embarrass, weaken,
prejudice, endanger, discredit, implicate, jeopardize,
dishonour, imperil ...*He had compromised himself by
accepting the money...* OPPOSITE> support

compulsion 1 = <u>urge</u>, need, obsession, necessity,
preoccupation, drive ...*He felt a compulsion to talk
about his ex-wife all the time...*
2 = <u>force</u>, pressure, obligation, constraint, urgency,
coercion, duress, demand ...*Students learn more when
they are in classes out of choice rather than
compulsion...*

compulsive 1 = <u>obsessive</u>, confirmed, chronic,
persistent, addictive, uncontrollable, incurable,
inveterate, incorrigible ...*He is a compulsive liar...*
2 = <u>fascinating</u>, gripping, absorbing, compelling,
captivating, enthralling, hypnotic, engrossing,
spellbinding ...*This really is compulsive reading...*
3 = <u>irresistible</u>, overwhelming, compelling, urgent,
neurotic, besetting, uncontrollable, driving ...*He
seems to have an almost compulsive desire to play
tricks...*

compulsory = <u>obligatory</u>, forced, required, binding,
mandatory, imperative, requisite, de rigueur (*French*)
OPPOSITE> voluntary

compute = <u>calculate</u>, rate, figure, total, measure,
estimate, count, reckon, sum, figure out, add up, tally,
enumerate

computer
(*Related Words*)
prefix: cyber-
➤ **computer parts**

comrade = <u>companion</u>, friend, partner, ally,
colleague, associate, fellow, mate (*informal*), pal
(*informal*), buddy (*informal*), compatriot, crony,
confederate, co-worker, main man (*slang, chiefly U.S.*),
homeboy (*slang, chiefly U.S.*), cobber (*Austral. or old-
fashioned N.Z. informal*), compeer

comradeship = <u>fellowship</u>, solidarity, fraternity,
brotherhood, companionship, camaraderie

con (*Informal*) **VERB** = <u>swindle</u>, trick, cheat, rip off
(*slang*), kid (*informal*), skin (*slang*), stiff (*slang*),
mislead, deceive, hoax, defraud, dupe, gull (*archaic*),
rook (*slang*), humbug, bamboozle (*informal*),
hoodwink, double-cross (*informal*), diddle (*informal*),
take for a ride (*informal*), inveigle, do the dirty on
(*Brit. informal*), bilk, sell a pup, pull a fast one on
(*informal*) ...*He claimed that the businessman had
conned him out of his life savings... ...The British
motorist has been conned by the government...*
NOUN = <u>swindle</u>, trick, fraud, deception, scam (*slang*),
sting (*informal*), bluff ...*I am afraid you have been the
victim of a con...*

concave = <u>hollow</u>, cupped, depressed, scooped,
hollowed, excavated, sunken, indented OPPOSITE>
convex

Computer parts

analogue-digital converter	DVD reader	MP3 player
arithmetic logic unit *or* ALU	DVD writer	multiplexor
cartridge	emulator	optical character reader
case	encoder	optical disk
CD-rewriter	flatbed scanner	optical scanner
CD-Rom drive	floppy disk	port
central processing unit *or* CPU	graphics card	printed circuit board
chip	hard drive	printer
coaxial cable	integrated circuit	processor
console	interface	scanner
control key	joystick	screen
counter	keyboard	SDRAM
daisywheel	laser printer	SIMM
DDR-RAM	LCD panel	sound card
digital audio player	line printer	speaker
digital camera	magnetic tape unit *or* MTU	trackball
digitizer	memory	transistor
DIMM	microprocessor	USB port
disk	modem	visual display unit *or* VDU
disk drive	monitor	webcam
disk unit	motherboard	
DRAM	mouse	

conceal 1 = <u>hide</u>, bury, stash (*informal*), secrete, cover, screen, disguise, obscure, camouflage ...*The device, concealed in a dustbin, was defused by police...* OPPOSITE> reveal
2 = <u>keep secret</u>, hide, disguise, mask, suppress, veil, dissemble, draw a veil over, keep dark, keep under your hat ...*Robert could not conceal his relief...* OPPOSITE> show

concealed = <u>hidden</u>, covered, secret, screened, masked, obscured, covert, unseen, tucked away, secreted, under wraps, inconspicuous

concealment 1 = <u>cover</u>, hiding, camouflage, hiding place ...*The criminals vainly sought concealment from the searchlight...*
2 = <u>cover-up</u>, disguise, keeping secret ...*His concealment of his true motives was masterly...* OPPOSITE> disclosure

concede 1 = <u>admit</u>, allow, accept, acknowledge, own, grant, confess ...*She finally conceded that he was right...* OPPOSITE> deny
2 = <u>give up</u>, yield, hand over, surrender, relinquish, cede ...*The central government has never conceded that territory to the Kurds...* OPPOSITE> conquer

conceit 1 = <u>self-importance</u>, vanity, arrogance, complacency, pride, swagger, narcissism, egotism, self-love, amour-propre, vainglory ...*He knew, without conceit, that he was considered a genius...*
2 (*Archaic*) = <u>image</u>, idea, concept, metaphor, imagery, figure of speech, trope ...*Critics may complain that the novel's central conceit is rather simplistic...*

conceited = <u>self-important</u>, vain, arrogant, stuck up (*informal*), cocky, narcissistic, puffed up, egotistical, overweening, immodest, vainglorious, swollen-headed, bigheaded (*informal*), full of yourself, too big for your boots *or* breeches OPPOSITE> modest

conceivable = <u>imaginable</u>, possible, credible, believable, thinkable OPPOSITE> inconceivable

conceive 1 = <u>imagine</u>, envisage, comprehend, visualize, think, believe, suppose, fancy, appreciate, grasp, apprehend ...*We now cannot conceive of a world without electricity...*
2 = <u>think up</u>, form, produce, create, develop, design, project, purpose, devise, formulate, contrive ...*I began to conceive a plan of attack...*
3 = <u>become pregnant</u>, get pregnant, become impregnated ...*Women should give up alcohol before they plan to conceive...*

concentrate 1 = <u>focus your attention on</u>, focus on, pay attention to, be engrossed in, put your mind to, keep your mind on, apply yourself to, give your mind to, give all your attention to ...*Try to concentrate on what you're doing...* OPPOSITE> pay no attention to
2 = <u>focus</u>, centre, converge, bring to bear ...*We should concentrate our efforts on tackling crime in the inner cities...*
3 = <u>gather</u>, collect, cluster, accumulate, congregate ...*Most poor people are concentrated in this area...* OPPOSITE> scatter

concentrated 1 = <u>condensed</u>, rich, undiluted, reduced, evaporated, thickened, boiled down ...*Sweeten dishes with honey or concentrated apple juice...*
2 = <u>intense</u>, hard, deep, intensive, all-out (*informal*) ...*She makes a concentrated effort to keep her feet on the ground...*

concentration 1 = <u>attention</u>, application, absorption, single-mindedness, intentness ...*His talking kept breaking my concentration...* OPPOSITE> inattention
2 = <u>focusing</u>, centring, consolidation, convergence, bringing to bear, intensification, centralization ...*This*

concentration of effort and resources should not be to the exclusion of everything else...
3 = <u>convergence</u>, collection, mass, cluster, accumulation, aggregation ...*The area has one of the world's greatest concentrations of wildlife...* OPPOSITE scattering

concept = <u>idea</u>, view, image, theory, impression, notion, conception, hypothesis, abstraction, conceptualization

conception 1 = <u>understanding</u>, idea, picture, impression, perception, clue, appreciation, comprehension, inkling ...*He doesn't have the slightest conception of teamwork...*
2 = <u>idea</u>, plan, design, image, concept, notion ...*The symphony is admirable in its conception...*
3 = <u>impregnation</u>, insemination, fertilization, germination ...*Six weeks after conception your baby is the size of your little fingernail...*
4 = <u>origin</u>, beginning, launching, birth, formation, invention, outset, initiation, inception ...*It is six year's since the project's conception...*

concern NOUN 1 = <u>anxiety</u>, fear, worry, distress, unease, apprehension, misgiving, disquiet ...*The move follows growing public concern over the spread of the disease...*
2 = <u>worry</u>, care, anxiety ...*His concern was that people would know that he was responsible...*
3 = <u>affair</u>, issue, matter, consideration ...*Feminism must address issues beyond the concerns of middle-class whites...*
4 = <u>care</u>, interest, regard, consideration, solicitude, attentiveness ...*He had only gone along out of concern for his two grandsons...*
5 = <u>business</u>, job, charge, matter, department, field, affair, responsibility, task, mission, pigeon (*informal*) ...*The technical aspects are not my concern...*
6 = <u>company</u>, house, business, firm, organization, corporation, enterprise, establishment ...*If not a large concern, his business was at least a successful one...*
7 = <u>importance</u>, interest, bearing, relevance ...*The survey's findings are a matter of great concern...*
VERB 1 = <u>worry</u>, trouble, bother, disturb, distress, disquiet, perturb, make uneasy, make anxious ...*It concerned her that Bess was developing a crush on Max...*
2 = <u>be about</u>, cover, deal with, go into, relate to, have to do with ...*The bulk of the book concerns the author's childhood...*
3 = <u>be relevant to</u>, involve, affect, regard, apply to, bear on, have something to do with, pertain to, interest, touch ...*This matter doesn't concern you, so stay out of it...*

concerned 1 = <u>worried</u>, troubled, upset, bothered, disturbed, anxious, distressed, uneasy ...*I've been very concerned about the situation...* OPPOSITE indifferent
2 = <u>caring</u>, attentive, solicitous ...*A concerned friend put a comforting arm around her shoulder...*
3 = <u>involved</u>, interested, active, mixed up, implicated, privy to ...*I believe he was concerned in all those matters you mention... ...It's been a difficult time for all concerned...*

concerning = <u>regarding</u>, about, re, touching, respecting, relating to, on the subject of, as to, with reference to, in the matter of, apropos of, as regards

concert
PHRASES **in concert** = <u>together</u>, jointly, unanimously, in unison, in league, in collaboration, shoulder to shoulder, concertedly

concerted = <u>coordinated</u>, united, joint, combined, collaborative OPPOSITE separate

concession 1 = <u>compromise</u>, agreement, settlement, accommodation, adjustment, trade-off, give-and-take, half measures ...*Britain has made sweeping concessions to China in order to reach a settlement...*
2 = <u>privilege</u>, right, permit, licence, franchise, entitlement, indulgence, prerogative ...*The government has granted concessions to three private telephone companies...*
3 = <u>reduction</u>, saving, grant, discount, allowance ...*tax concessions for mothers who choose to stay at home with their children...*
4 = <u>surrender</u>, yielding, conceding, renunciation, relinquishment ...*He said there'd be no concession of territory...*

conciliation = <u>pacification</u>, reconciliation, disarming, appeasement, propitiation, mollification, soothing, placation

conciliatory = <u>pacifying</u>, pacific, disarming, appeasing, mollifying, peaceable, placatory, soothing

concise = <u>brief</u>, short, to the point, compact, summary, compressed, condensed, terse, laconic, succinct, pithy, synoptic, epigrammatic, compendious OPPOSITE rambling

conclave = (<u>secret</u> or <u>private</u>) <u>meeting</u>, council, conference, congress, session, cabinet, assembly, parley

conclude 1 = <u>decide</u>, judge, establish, suppose, determine, assume, gather, reckon (*informal*), work out, infer, deduce, surmise ...*We concluded that he was telling the truth...*
2 = <u>come to an end</u>, end, close, finish, wind up, draw to a close ...*The evening concluded with dinner and speeches...* OPPOSITE begin
3 = <u>bring to an end</u>, end, close, finish, complete, wind up, terminate, round off ...*They concluded their annual summit meeting today...* OPPOSITE begin
4 = <u>accomplish</u>, effect, settle, bring about, fix, carry out, resolve, clinch, pull off, bring off (*informal*) ...*If the clubs cannot conclude a deal, an independent tribunal will decide...*

conclusion NOUN 1 = <u>decision</u>, agreement, opinion, settlement, resolution, conviction, verdict, judgment, deduction, inference ...*We came to the conclusion that it was too difficult to combine the two techniques...*
2 = <u>end</u>, ending, close, finish, completion, finale, termination, bitter end, result ...*At the conclusion of the programme, viewers were invited to phone in...*
3 = <u>outcome</u>, result, upshot, consequence, sequel, culmination, end result, issue ...*Executives said it was*

the logical conclusion of a process started in 1987...
PHRASES **in conclusion** = <u>finally</u>, lastly, in closing, to sum up ...*In conclusion, walking is a cheap, safe form of exercise...*

conclusive = <u>decisive</u>, final, convincing, clinching, definite, definitive, irrefutable, unanswerable, unarguable, ultimate OPPOSITE inconclusive

concoct = <u>make up</u>, design, prepare, manufacture, plot, invent, devise, brew, hatch, formulate, contrive, fabricate, think up, cook up (*informal*), trump up, project

concoction = <u>mixture</u>, preparation, compound, brew, combination, creation, blend

concord 1 = <u>harmony</u>, accord, peace, agreement, concert, friendship, consensus, goodwill, unison, good understanding, rapport, unanimity, amity ...*A climate of concord and tolerance prevails among the Muslim and Christian Egyptian citizens...*
2 = <u>treaty</u>, agreement, convention, compact, protocol, entente, concordat ...*The Concord of Wittenberg was agreed in 1536...*

concourse 1 = <u>gathering</u> or <u>meeting place</u>, hall, lounge, foyer, rallying point ...*He crossed the station's concourse towards the escalator...*
2 = <u>crowd</u>, collection, gathering, assembly, crush, multitude, throng, convergence, hui (*N.Z.*), assemblage, meeting ...*The streets were filled with a fair concourse of people that night...*

concrete NOUN = <u>cement</u> (*not in technical usage*) ...*The posts have to be set in concrete...*
ADJECTIVE 1 = <u>specific</u>, precise, explicit, definite, clear-cut, unequivocal, unambiguous ...*He had no concrete evidence...* OPPOSITE vague
2 = <u>real</u>, material, actual, substantial, sensible, tangible, factual ...*using concrete objects to teach addition and subtraction...* OPPOSITE abstract

concubine (*Old-fashioned*) = <u>mistress</u>, courtesan, kept woman

concur = <u>agree</u>, accord, approve, assent, accede, acquiesce

concurrent = <u>simultaneous</u>, coexisting, concomitant, contemporaneous, coincident, synchronous, concerted

concussion 1 = <u>shock</u>, brain injury ...*She fell off a horse and suffered a concussion...*
2 = <u>impact</u>, crash, shaking, clash, jarring, collision, jolt, jolting ...*I was blown off the deck by the concussion of the torpedoes...*

condemn 1 = <u>denounce</u>, damn, criticize, disapprove, censure, reprove, upbraid, excoriate, reprehend, blame ...*Political leaders united yesterday to condemn the latest wave of violence...* OPPOSITE approve
2 = <u>sentence</u>, convict, damn, doom, pass sentence on ...*He was condemned to life imprisonment...* OPPOSITE acquit

condemnation = <u>denunciation</u>, blame, censure, disapproval, reproach, stricture, reproof, denouncement

condensation 1 = <u>distillation</u>, precipitation, liquefaction ...*The surface refrigeration allows the*

condensation of water...
2 = <u>abridgment</u>, summary, abstract, digest, contraction, synopsis, précis, encapsulation ...*a condensation of a book that offers ten ways to be a better manager...*

condense 1 = <u>abridge</u>, contract, concentrate, compact, shorten, summarize, compress, encapsulate, abbreviate, epitomize, précis ...*The English translation has been condensed into a single more readable book...* OPPOSITE expand
2 = <u>concentrate</u>, reduce, precipitate (*Chemistry*), thicken, boil down, solidify, coagulate ...*The compressed gas is cooled and condenses into a liquid...* OPPOSITE dilute

condensed 1 = <u>abridged</u>, concentrated, compressed, potted, shortened, summarized, slimmed-down, encapsulated ...*I also produced a condensed version of the paper...*
2 = <u>concentrated</u>, reduced, thickened, boiled down, precipitated (*Chemistry*) ...*condensed milk...*

condescend 1 = <u>patronize</u>, talk down to, treat like a child, treat as inferior, treat condescendingly ...*a writer who does not condescend to his readers...*
2 = <u>deign</u>, see fit, lower yourself, be courteous enough, bend, submit, stoop, unbend (*informal*), vouchsafe, come down off your high horse (*informal*), humble or demean yourself ...*He never condescended to notice me...*

condescending = <u>patronizing</u>, lordly, superior, lofty, snooty (*informal*), snobbish, disdainful, supercilious, toffee-nosed (*slang, chiefly Brit.*), on your high horse (*informal*)

condescension = <u>patronizing attitude</u>, superiority, disdain, haughtiness, loftiness, superciliousness, lordliness, airs

condition NOUN 1 = <u>state</u>, order, shape, nick (*Brit. informal*), trim ...*The two-bedroom chalet is in good condition...*
2 = <u>situation</u>, state, position, status, circumstances, plight, status quo (*Latin*), case, predicament ...*The government has to encourage people to better their condition...*
3 = <u>requirement</u>, terms, rider, provision, restriction, qualification, limitation, modification, requisite, prerequisite, proviso, stipulation, rule, demand ...*They had agreed to a summit subject to certain conditions...*
4 = <u>health</u>, shape, fitness, trim, form, kilter, state of health, fettle, order ...*She was in fine condition for a woman of her age...*
5 = <u>ailment</u>, problem, complaint, weakness, malady, infirmity ...*Doctors suspect he may have a heart condition...*
PLURAL NOUN = <u>circumstances</u>, situation, environment, surroundings, way of life, milieu ...*The conditions in the camp are just awful...*
VERB = <u>train</u>, teach, educate, adapt, accustom, inure, habituate ...*We have been conditioned to believe that it is weak to be scared...*

conditional = <u>dependent</u>, limited, qualified, subject to, contingent, provisional, with reservations ...*They*

have made us a conditional offer... OPPOSITE
unconditional

conditioning = <u>training</u>, education, teaching, accustoming, habituation

condolence = <u>sympathy</u>, pity, compassion, consolation, commiseration, fellow feeling

condom = <u>sheath</u>, safe (*U.S. & Canad. slang*), rubber (*U.S. slang*), blob (*Brit. slang*), scumbag (*U.S. slang*), Frenchie (*slang*), flunky (*slang*), French letter (*slang*), rubber johnny (*Brit. slang*), French tickler (*slang*)

condone = <u>overlook</u>, excuse, forgive, pardon, disregard, turn a blind eye to, wink at, look the other way, make allowance for, let pass OPPOSITE condemn

conducive = <u>favourable</u>, helpful, productive, contributory, calculated to produce, leading, tending

conduct VERB 1 = <u>carry out</u>, run, control, manage, direct, handle, organize, govern, regulate, administer, supervise, preside over ...*I decided to conduct an experiment...*
2 = <u>accompany</u>, lead, escort, guide, attend, steer, convey, usher, pilot ...*He asked if he might conduct us to the ball...*
NOUN 1 = <u>management</u>, running, control, handling, administration, direction, leadership, organization, guidance, supervision ...*Also up for discussion will be the conduct of free and fair elections...*
2 = <u>behaviour</u>, ways, bearing, attitude, manners, carriage, demeanour, deportment, mien (*literary*), comportment ...*Other people judge you by your conduct...*
PHRASES **conduct yourself** = <u>behave yourself</u>, act, carry yourself, acquit yourself, deport yourself, comport yourself ...*The way he conducts himself reflects on the party...*

conduit = <u>passage</u>, channel, tube, pipe, canal, duct, main

confederacy = <u>union</u>, league, alliance, coalition, federation, compact, confederation, covenant, bund

confederate NOUN = <u>associate</u>, partner, ally, colleague, accessory, accomplice, abettor ...*The conspirators were joined by their confederates...*
ADJECTIVE = <u>allied</u>, federal, associated, combined, federated, in alliance ...*We want a confederate Europe...*

confer 1 = <u>discuss</u>, talk, consult, deliberate, discourse, converse, parley ...*He conferred with Hill and the others in his office...*
2 = <u>grant</u>, give, present, accord, award, hand out, bestow, vouchsafe ...*An honorary degree was conferred on him by Newcastle University in 1976...*

conference = <u>meeting</u>, congress, discussion, convention, forum, consultation, seminar, symposium, hui (*N.Z.*), convocation, colloquium

confess 1 = <u>admit</u>, acknowledge, disclose, confide, own up, come clean (*informal*), divulge, blurt out, come out of the closet, make a clean breast of, get (something) off your chest (*informal*), spill your guts (*slang*), 'fess up (*U.S.*), sing (*slang, chiefly U.S.*) ...*He has confessed to seventeen murders... ...She confesses that she only wrote those books for the money...* OPPOSITE

cover up
2 = <u>declare</u>, own up, allow, prove, reveal, grant, confirm, concede, assert, manifest, affirm, profess, attest, evince, aver ...*I must confess I'm not a great sports enthusiast...*

confession = <u>admission</u>, revelation, disclosure, acknowledgment, avowal, divulgence, exposure, unbosoming

confidant *or* **confidante** = <u>close friend</u>, familiar, intimate, crony, alter ego, bosom friend

confide = <u>tell</u>, admit, reveal, confess, whisper, disclose, impart, divulge, breathe

confidence NOUN 1 = <u>trust</u>, belief, faith, dependence, reliance, credence ...*I have every confidence in you...* OPPOSITE distrust
2 = <u>self-assurance</u>, courage, assurance, aplomb, boldness, self-reliance, self-possession, nerve ...*She always thinks the worst of herself and has no confidence whatsoever...* OPPOSITE shyness
3 = <u>secret</u> ...*I'm not in the habit of exchanging confidences with her...*
PHRASES **in confidence** = <u>in secrecy</u>, privately, confidentially, between you and me (and the gatepost), (just) between ourselves ...*I'm telling you all these things in confidence...*

confident 1 = <u>certain</u>, sure, convinced, positive, secure, satisfied, counting on ...*I am confident that everything will come out right in time...* OPPOSITE unsure
2 = <u>self-assured</u>, positive, assured, bold, self-confident, self-reliant, self-possessed, sure of yourself, can-do (*informal*) ...*In time he became more confident and relaxed...* OPPOSITE insecure

confidential 1 = <u>secret</u>, private, intimate, classified, privy, off the record, hush-hush (*informal*) ...*She accused them of leaking confidential information...*
2 = <u>secretive</u>, low, soft, hushed ...*He adopted a confidential tone of voice...*

confidentially = <u>in secret</u>, privately, personally, behind closed doors, in confidence, in camera, between ourselves, sub rosa

configuration = <u>arrangement</u>, form, shape, cast, outline, contour, conformation, figure

confine VERB 1 = <u>imprison</u>, enclose, shut up, intern, incarcerate, circumscribe, hem in, immure, keep, cage ...*He has been confined to his barracks...*
2 = <u>restrict</u>, limit ...*She had largely confined her activities to the world of big business...*
PLURAL NOUN = <u>limits</u>, bounds, boundaries, compass, precincts, circumference, edge, pale ...*The movie is set entirely within the confines of the abandoned factory...*

confined = <u>restricted</u>, small, limited, narrow, enclosed, cramped

confinement 1 = <u>imprisonment</u>, custody, detention, incarceration, internment, porridge (*slang*) ...*She had been held in solitary confinement for four months...*
2 = <u>childbirth</u>, labour, travail, childbed, accouchement (*French*), time ...*His pregnant wife is near her confinement...*

confirm 1 = <u>prove</u>, support, establish, back up, verify, validate, bear out, substantiate, corroborate, authenticate ...*This confirms what I suspected all along...*
2 = <u>ratify</u>, establish, approve, sanction, endorse, authorize, certify, validate, authenticate ...*He is due to be confirmed as President on Friday...*
3 = <u>strengthen</u>, establish, settle, fix, secure, assure, reinforce, clinch, verify, fortify ...*He has confirmed his position as the world's number one snooker player...*

confirmation 1 = <u>proof</u>, evidence, testimony, verification, ratification, validation, corroboration, authentication, substantiation ...*He took her resignation as confirmation of their suspicions...* OPPOSITE> repudiation
2 = <u>affirmation</u>, approval, acceptance, endorsement, ratification, assent, agreement ...*She glanced over at James for confirmation of what she'd said...* OPPOSITE> disapproval

confirmed = <u>long-established</u>, seasoned, rooted, chronic, hardened, habitual, ingrained, inveterate, inured, dyed-in-the-wool

confiscate = <u>seize</u>, appropriate, impound, commandeer, sequester, expropriate OPPOSITE> give back

confiscation = <u>seizure</u>, appropriation, impounding, forfeiture, expropriation, sequestration, takeover

conflagration = <u>fire</u>, blaze, holocaust, inferno, wildfire

conflict NOUN 1 = <u>dispute</u>, difference, opposition, hostility, disagreement, friction, strife, fighting, antagonism, variance, discord, bad blood, dissension, divided loyalties ...*Try to keep any conflict between you and your ex-partner to a minimum...* OPPOSITE> agreement
2 = <u>struggle</u>, battle, clash, strife ...*the anguish of his own inner conflict...*
3 = <u>battle</u>, war, fight, clash, contest, set-to (*informal*), encounter, combat, engagement, warfare, collision, contention, strife, head-to-head, fracas ...*The National Security Council has met to discuss ways of preventing a military conflict...* OPPOSITE> peace
VERB = <u>be incompatible</u>, clash, differ, disagree, contend, strive, collide, be at variance ...*He held firm opinions which sometimes conflicted with my own...* OPPOSITE> agree

conflicting = <u>incompatible</u>, opposed, opposing, clashing, contrary, contradictory, inconsistent, paradoxical, discordant OPPOSITE> agreeing

conform 1 = <u>fit in</u>, follow, yield, adjust, adapt, comply, obey, fall in with, toe the line, follow the crowd, run with the pack, follow convention ...*Children who can't or won't conform are often bullied...*
2 = <u>fulfil</u>, meet, match, suit, satisfy, agree with, obey, abide by, accord with, square with, correspond with, tally with, harmonize with ...*These activities do not conform with diplomatic rules and regulations...*

conformation = <u>shape</u>, build, form, structure, arrangement, outline, framework, anatomy, configuration

conformist = <u>traditionalist</u>, conservative, reactionary, Babbitt (*U.S.*), stickler, yes man, stick-in-the-mud (*informal*), conventionalist

conformity 1 = <u>compliance</u>, agreement, accordance, observance, conformance, obedience ...*The prime minister is, in conformity with the constitution, chosen by the president...*
2 = <u>conventionality</u>, compliance, allegiance, orthodoxy, observance, traditionalism, Babbittry (*U.S.*) ...*Excessive conformity is usually caused by fear of disapproval...*

confound 1 = <u>bewilder</u>, baffle, amaze, confuse, astonish, startle, mix up, astound, perplex, surprise, mystify, flummox, boggle the mind, be all Greek to (*informal*), dumbfound, nonplus, flabbergast (*informal*) ...*For many years medical scientists were confounded by these seemingly contradictory facts...*
2 = <u>disprove</u>, contradict, refute, negate, destroy, ruin, overwhelm, explode, overthrow, demolish, annihilate, give the lie to, make a nonsense of, prove false, blow out of the water (*slang*), controvert, confute ...*The findings confound all the government's predictions...*

confront 1 = <u>tackle</u>, deal with, cope with, brave, beard, face up to, meet head-on ...*We are learning how to confront death...*
2 = <u>trouble</u>, face, afflict, perplex, perturb, bedevil ...*the environmental crisis which confronts us all...*
3 = <u>challenge</u>, face, oppose, tackle, encounter, defy, call out, stand up to, come face to face with, accost, face off (*slang*) ...*She pushed her way through the mob and confronted him face to face...* OPPOSITE> evade

confrontation = <u>conflict</u>, fight, crisis, contest, set-to (*informal*), encounter, showdown (*informal*), head-to-head, face-off (*slang*)

confuse 1 = <u>mix up with</u>, take for, mistake for, muddle with ...*I can't see how anyone could confuse you two with each other...*
2 = <u>bewilder</u>, puzzle, baffle, perplex, mystify, fluster, faze, flummox, bemuse, be all Greek to (*informal*), nonplus ...*Politics just confuses me...*
3 = <u>obscure</u>, cloud, complicate, muddle, darken, make more difficult, muddy the waters ...*His critics accused him of trying to confuse the issue...*

confused 1 = <u>bewildered</u>, puzzled, baffled, at sea, muddled, dazed, perplexed, at a loss, taken aback, disorientated, muzzy (*U.S. informal*), nonplussed, flummoxed, at sixes and sevens, thrown off balance, discombobulated (*informal, chiefly U.S. & Canad.*), not with it (*informal*), not knowing if you are coming or going ...*People are confused about what they should eat to stay healthy...* OPPOSITE> enlightened
2 = <u>disorderly</u>, disordered, chaotic, mixed up, jumbled, untidy, out of order, in disarray, topsy-turvy, disorganized, higgledy-piggledy (*informal*), at sixes and sevens, disarranged, disarrayed ...*Everything lay in a confused heap on the floor... ...The situation remains confused as both sides claim victory...* OPPOSITE> tidy

confusing = <u>bewildering</u>, complicated, puzzling,

misleading, unclear, baffling, muddling, contradictory, ambiguous, inconsistent, perplexing, clear as mud (*informal*) OPPOSITE clear

confusion 1 = bewilderment, doubt, uncertainty, puzzlement, perplexity, mystification, bafflement, perturbation ...*Omissions in my recent article may have caused some confusion...* OPPOSITE enlightenment
2 = disorder, chaos, turmoil, upheaval, muddle, bustle, shambles, disarray, commotion, disorganization, disarrangement ...*The rebel leader seems to have escaped in the confusion...* OPPOSITE order
3 = puzzlement, bewilderment, perplexity, bafflement, mystification, perturbation ...*I left his office in a state of confusion...*

congeal = thicken, set, freeze, harden, clot, stiffen, condense, solidify, curdle, jell, coagulate

congenial = pleasant, kindly, pleasing, friendly, agreeable, cordial, sociable, genial, affable, convivial, companionable, favourable, complaisant

congenital 1 = inborn, innate, inherent, hereditary, natural, constitutional, inherited, inbred ...*When he was 17, he died of congenital heart disease...*
2 (*Informal*) = complete, confirmed, chronic, utter, hardened, thorough, habitual, incurable, inveterate, incorrigible, deep-dyed (*usually derogatory*) ...*He is a congenital liar...*

congested 1 = packed (out), crowded, overcrowded, teeming ...*Some areas are congested with both cars and people...*
2 = clogged, jammed, blocked-up, overfilled, stuffed, packed, crammed, overflowing, stuffed-up ...*The arteries in his neck had become fatally congested...* OPPOSITE clear

congestion = overcrowding, crowding, mass, jam, clogging, bottleneck, snarl-up (*informal, chiefly Brit.*)

conglomerate = corporation, multinational, corporate body, business, association, consortium, aggregate, agglomerate

congratulate = compliment, pat on the back, wish joy to

congratulations PLURAL NOUN = good wishes, greetings, compliments, best wishes, pat on the back, felicitations ...*I offer you my congratulations on your appointment as chairman...*
INTERJECTION = good wishes, greetings, compliments, best wishes, felicitations ...*Congratulations! You have a healthy baby boy...*

congregate = come together, meet, mass, collect, gather, concentrate, rally, assemble, flock, muster, convene, converge, throng, rendezvous, foregather, convoke OPPOSITE disperse

congregation = parishioners, host, brethren, crowd, assembly, parish, flock, fellowship, multitude, throng, laity

congress 1 = meeting, council, conference, diet, assembly, convention, conclave, legislative assembly, convocation ...*A lot has changed since the party congress...*
2 = legislature, house, council, parliament, representatives, delegates, quango, legislative assembly, chamber of deputies ...*It's far from certain that the congress will approve them...*

conical *or* **conic** = cone-shaped, pointed, tapered, tapering, pyramidal, funnel-shaped

conjecture NOUN = guess, theory, fancy, notion, speculation, assumption, hypothesis, inference, presumption, surmise, theorizing, guesswork, supposition, shot in the dark, guesstimate (*informal*) ...*Your assertion is merely a conjecture, not a fact...*
VERB = guess, speculate, surmise, theorize, suppose, imagine, assume, fancy, infer, hypothesize ...*This may or may not be true; we are all conjecturing here...*

conjunction = combination, union, joining, association, coincidence, juxtaposition, concurrence

conjure VERB 1 = produce, generate, bring about, give rise to, make, create, effect, produce as if by magic ...*They managed to conjure up a victory...*
2 *often with* **up** = summon up, raise, invoke, rouse, call upon ...*The ouija board is used to conjure up spirits and communicate with them...*
PHRASES **conjure something up** = bring to mind, recall, evoke, recreate, recollect, produce as if by magic ...*When he closed his eyes, he could conjure up almost every event of his life...*

conjuring = magic, juggling, trickery, sleight of hand, prestidigitation

connect 1 = link, join, couple, attach, fasten, affix, unite ...*You can connect the machine to your hi-fi...* OPPOSITE separate
2 = associate, unite, join, couple, league, link, mix, relate, pair, ally, identify, combine, affiliate, correlate, confederate, lump together, mention in the same breath, think of together ...*There is no evidence to connect him to the robberies... ...I wouldn't have connected the two events if you hadn't said that...*

connected = linked, united, joined, coupled, related, allied, associated, combined, bracketed, affiliated, akin, banded together

connection 1 = association, relationship, link, relation, bond, correspondence, relevance, tie-in, correlation, interrelation ...*There is no evidence of any connection between BSE and the brain diseases recently confirmed in cats...*
2 = communication, alliance, commerce, attachment, intercourse, liaison, affinity, affiliation, union ...*I no longer have any connection with my ex-husband's family...*
3 = link, coupling, junction, fastening, tie ...*Check radiators for small leaks, especially round pipework connections...*
4 = contact, friend, relation, ally, associate, relative, acquaintance, kin, kindred, kinsman, kith ...*She used her connections to full advantage...*
5 = context, relation, reference, frame of reference ...*13 men have been questioned in connection with the murder...*

connivance = collusion, intrigue, conspiring, complicity, abetting, tacit consent, abetment

connive VERB = conspire, scheme, plot, intrigue,

collude ...*Senior politicians connived to ensure that he was not released*...

PHRASES **connive at something** = <u>turn a blind eye to</u>, overlook, pass by, disregard, abet, wink at, look the other way, blink at, be a party to, be an accessory to, be in collusion with, let pass, shut your eyes to, lend yourself to, aid ...*Mr Mandela suggested the government had connived at the violence*...

conniving = <u>scheming</u>, designing, plotting, calculating, conspiring, contriving

connoisseur = <u>expert</u>, authority, judge, specialist, buff (*informal*), devotee, whiz (*informal*), arbiter, aficionado, savant, maven (*U.S.*), appreciator, cognoscente, fundi (*S. African*)

connotation = <u>implication</u>, colouring, association, suggestion, significance, nuance, undertone

connote = <u>imply</u>, suggest, indicate, intimate, signify, hint at, betoken, involve

conquer 1 = <u>seize</u>, obtain, acquire, occupy, overrun, annex, win ...*Early in the eleventh century the whole of England was again conquered by the Vikings*...
2 = <u>defeat</u>, overcome, overthrow, beat, stuff (*slang*), master, tank (*slang*), triumph, crush, humble, lick (*informal*), undo, subdue, rout, overpower, quell, get the better of, clobber (*slang*), vanquish, subjugate, prevail over, checkmate, run rings around (*informal*), wipe the floor with (*informal*), make mincemeat of (*informal*), put in their place, blow out of the water (*slang*), bring to their knees ...*a Navajo myth about a great warrior who conquers the spiritual enemies of his people*... **OPPOSITE** lose to
3 = <u>overcome</u>, beat, defeat, master, rise above, overpower, get the better of, surmount, best ...*I had learned to conquer my fear of spiders*...

conqueror = <u>winner</u>, champion, master, victor, conquistador, lord

conquest 1 = <u>takeover</u>, coup, acquisition, invasion, occupation, appropriation, annexation, subjugation, subjection ...*He had led the conquest of southern Poland in 1939*...
2 = <u>defeat</u>, victory, triumph, overthrow, pasting (*slang*), rout, mastery, vanquishment ...*This hidden treasure charts the brutal Spanish conquest of the Aztecs*...
3 = <u>seduction</u> ...*people who boast about their sexual conquests*...
4 = <u>catch</u>, prize, supporter, acquisition, follower, admirer, worshipper, adherent, fan, feather in your cap ...*He was a womaniser whose conquests included everyone from prostitutes to princesses*...

conscience **NOUN** 1 = <u>principles</u>, scruples, moral sense, sense of right and wrong, still small voice ...*I have battled with my conscience over whether I should send this letter or not*...
2 = <u>guilt</u>, shame, regret, remorse, contrition, self-reproach, self-condemnation ...*She was suffering terrible pangs of conscience about what she had done*...

PHRASES **in all conscience** = <u>in fairness</u>, rightly, certainly, fairly, truly, honestly, in truth, assuredly

...*She could not, in all conscience, back out on her deal with him*...

conscientious = <u>thorough</u>, particular, careful, exact, faithful, meticulous, painstaking, diligent, punctilious **OPPOSITE** careless

conscious 1 *often with of* = <u>aware of</u>, wise to (*slang*), alert to, responsive to, cognizant of, sensible of, clued-up on (*informal*), percipient of ...*She was very conscious of Max studying her*... **OPPOSITE** unaware
2 = <u>deliberate</u>, knowing, reasoning, studied, responsible, calculated, rational, reflective, self-conscious, intentional, wilful, premeditated ...*Make a conscious effort to relax your muscles*... **OPPOSITE** unintentional
3 = <u>awake</u>, wide-awake, sentient, alive ...*She was fully conscious throughout the operation*... **OPPOSITE** asleep

consciousness = <u>awareness</u>, understanding, knowledge, recognition, enlightenment, sensibility, realization, apprehension

consecrate = <u>sanctify</u>, dedicate, ordain, exalt, venerate, set apart, hallow, devote

consecutive = <u>successive</u>, running, following, succeeding, in turn, uninterrupted, chronological, sequential, in sequence, seriatim

consensus = <u>agreement</u>, general agreement, unanimity, common consent, unity, harmony, assent, concord, concurrence

---

Word Power

consensus – The original meaning of the word *consensus* is *a collective opinion*. Because the concept of 'opinion' is contained within this word, a few people argue that the phrase *a consensus of opinion* is incorrect and should be avoided. However, this common use of the word is unlikely to jar with the majority of speakers.

---

consent **NOUN** = <u>agreement</u>, sanction, approval, go-ahead (*informal*), permission, compliance, green light, assent, acquiescence, concurrence, O.K. or okay (*informal*) ...*Can my child be medically examined without my consent?*... **OPPOSITE** refusal
VERB = <u>agree</u>, approve, yield, permit, comply, concur, assent, accede, acquiesce, play ball (*informal*) ...*I was a little surprised when she consented to my proposal*... **OPPOSITE** refuse

consequence **NOUN** 1 = <u>result</u>, effect, outcome, repercussion, end, issue, event, sequel, end result, upshot ...*Her lawyers said she understood the consequences of her actions*...
2 = <u>importance</u>, interest, concern, moment, value, account, note, weight, import, significance, portent ...*This question is of little consequence*...
3 = <u>status</u>, standing, bottom, rank, distinction, eminence, repute, notability ...*He was a sad little man of no consequence*...

PHRASES **in consequence** = <u>consequently</u>, as a result, so, then, thus, therefore, hence, accordingly, for that reason, thence, ergo …*His death was totally unexpected and, in consequence, no plans had been made for his replacement…*

consequent = <u>following</u>, resulting, subsequent, successive, ensuing, resultant, sequential

consequential 1 = <u>resulting</u>, subsequent, successive, ensuing, indirect, consequent, resultant, sequential, following …*The company disclaims any liability for incidental or consequential damages…*
2 = <u>important</u>, serious, significant, grave, far-reaching, momentous, weighty, eventful …*From a medical standpoint, a week is usually not a consequential delay…*

consequently = <u>as a result</u>, thus, therefore, necessarily, hence, subsequently, accordingly, for that reason, thence, ergo

conservation 1 = <u>preservation</u>, saving, protection, maintenance, custody, safeguarding, upkeep, guardianship, safekeeping …*Attention must be paid to the conservation of the environment…*
2 = <u>economy</u>, saving, thrift, husbandry, careful management, thriftiness …*projects aimed at energy conservation…*

conservative ADJECTIVE = <u>traditional</u>, guarded, quiet, conventional, moderate, cautious, sober, reactionary, die-hard, middle-of-the-road, hidebound …*People tend to be more adventurous when they're young and more conservative as they get older…*
OPPOSITE> radical
NOUN = <u>traditionalist</u>, moderate, reactionary, die-hard, middle-of-the-roader, stick-in-the-mud (*informal*) …*The new judge is regarded as a conservative…*
OPPOSITE> radical

Conservative ADJECTIVE = <u>Tory</u>, Republican (*U.S.*), right-wing …*Even among Conservative voters, more than a third disapprove of the tax…*
NOUN = <u>Tory</u>, Republican (*U.S.*), right-winger …*Up to eighty Conservatives are expected to vote against the bill…*

conservatory = <u>greenhouse</u>, hothouse, glasshouse

conserve 1 = <u>save</u>, husband, take care of, hoard, store up, go easy on, use sparingly …*The factory has closed over the weekend to conserve energy…*
OPPOSITE> waste
2 = <u>protect</u>, keep, save, preserve …*an increase in US aid to help developing countries conserve their forests…*

consider 1 = <u>think</u>, see, believe, rate, judge, suppose, deem, view as, look upon, regard as, hold to be, adjudge …*I had always considered myself a strong, competent woman…*
2 = <u>think about</u>, study, reflect on, examine, weigh, contemplate, deliberate, muse, ponder, revolve, meditate, work over, mull over, eye up, ruminate, chew over, cogitate, turn over in your mind …*Consider how much you can afford to pay…*
3 = <u>bear in mind</u>, remember, regard, respect, think about, care for, take into account, reckon with, take into consideration, make allowance for, keep in view …*You have to consider the feelings of those around

you…*

considerable = <u>large</u>, goodly, much, great, marked, comfortable, substantial, reasonable, tidy, lavish, ample, noticeable, abundant, plentiful, tolerable, appreciable, sizable *or* sizeable …*We have already spent a considerable amount of money on repairs…*
OPPOSITE> small

considerably = <u>greatly</u>, very much, seriously (*informal*), significantly, remarkably, substantially, markedly, noticeably, appreciably

considerate = <u>thoughtful</u>, kind, kindly, concerned, obliging, attentive, mindful, unselfish, solicitous
OPPOSITE> inconsiderate

consideration NOUN **1** = <u>thought</u>, study, review, attention, regard, analysis, examination, reflection, scrutiny, deliberation, contemplation, perusal, cogitation …*He said there should be careful consideration of the company's future role…*
2 = <u>thoughtfulness</u>, concern, respect, kindness, friendliness, tact, solicitude, kindliness, considerateness …*Show consideration for other rail travellers…*
3 = <u>factor</u>, point, issue, concern, element, aspect, determinant …*Price was a major consideration in our choice of house…*
4 = <u>payment</u>, fee, reward, remuneration, recompense, perquisite, tip …*He does odd jobs for a consideration…*
PHRASES **take something into consideration** = <u>bear in mind</u>, consider, remember, think about, weigh, take into account, make allowance for, keep in view …*Other factors must also be taken into consideration…*

considering PREPOSITION = <u>taking into account</u>, in the light of, bearing in mind, in view of, keeping in mind, taking into consideration …*The former hostage is in remarkably good shape considering his ordeal…*
ADVERB (*Informal*) = <u>all things considered</u>, all in all, taking everything into consideration, taking everything into account …*I think you've got off very lightly, considering…*

consign 1 = <u>put away</u>, commit, deposit, relegate …*For decades, many of his works were consigned to the basements of museums…*
2 = <u>deliver</u>, ship, transfer, transmit, convey …*He had managed to obtain arms in France and have them safely consigned to America…*

consignment = <u>shipment</u>, delivery, batch, goods

consist
PHRASES **consist in something** = <u>lie in</u>, involve, reside in, be expressed by, subsist, be found *or* contained in …*His work as a consultant consists in advising foreign companies…* ◆ **consist of something** = <u>be made up of</u>, include, contain, incorporate, amount to, comprise, be composed of …*My diet consisted almost exclusively of fruit…*

consistency 1 = <u>agreement</u>, harmony, correspondence, accordance, regularity, coherence, compatibility, uniformity, constancy, steadiness, steadfastness, evenness, congruity …*There's always a

lack of consistency in matters of foreign policy…
2 = <u>texture</u>, density, thickness, firmness, viscosity, compactness …*I added a little milk to mix the dough to the right consistency…*

consistent 1 = <u>steady</u>, even, regular, stable, constant, persistent, dependable, unchanging, true to type, undeviating …*He has never been the most consistent of players…* OPPOSITE erratic
2 = <u>compatible</u>, agreeing, in keeping, harmonious, in harmony, consonant, in accord, congruent, congruous, accordant …*These new goals are not consistent with the existing policies…* OPPOSITE incompatible
3 = <u>coherent</u>, logical, compatible, harmonious, consonant, all of a piece …*A theory should be internally consistent…* OPPOSITE contradictory

consolation = <u>comfort</u>, help, support, relief, ease, cheer, encouragement, solace, succour, alleviation, assuagement

console = <u>comfort</u>, cheer, relieve, soothe, support, encourage, calm, solace, assuage, succour, express sympathy for OPPOSITE distress

consolidate 1 = <u>strengthen</u>, secure, reinforce, cement, fortify, stabilize …*The Prime Minister hopes to consolidate existing trade ties between the two countries…*
2 = <u>combine</u>, unite, join, marry, merge, unify, amalgamate, federate, conjoin …*The state's four higher education boards are to be consolidated…*

consolidation 1 = <u>strengthening</u>, reinforcement, fortification, stabilization …*Change brought about the growth and consolidation of the working class…*
2 = <u>combination</u>, union, association, alliance, merger, federation, amalgamation …*Further consolidations in the industry may follow…*

consort VERB = <u>associate</u>, mix, mingle, hang with (*informal, chiefly U.S.*), go around with, keep company, fraternize, hang about, around *or* out with …*He regularly consorted with drug-dealers…*
NOUN = <u>spouse</u>, wife, husband, partner, associate, fellow, companion, significant other (*U.S. informal*) …*Queen Victoria's consort, Prince Albert…*

conspicuous = <u>obvious</u>, clear, apparent, visible, patent, evident, manifest, noticeable, blatant, discernible, salient, perceptible, easily seen OPPOSITE inconspicuous

conspiracy = <u>plot</u>, scheme, intrigue, collusion, confederacy, cabal, frame-up (*slang*), machination, league

conspirator = <u>plotter</u>, intriguer, conspirer, traitor, schemer

conspire 1 = <u>plot</u>, scheme, intrigue, devise, manoeuvre, contrive, machinate, plan, hatch treason …*I had a persecution complex and thought people were conspiring against me…*
2 = <u>work together</u>, combine, contribute, cooperate, concur, tend, conduce …*History and geography have conspired to bring Greece to a moment of decision…*

constancy 1 = <u>steadiness</u>, stability, regularity, uniformity, perseverance, firmness, permanence

…*Climate reflects a basic struggle between constancy and change…*
2 = <u>faithfulness</u>, loyalty, devotion, fidelity, dependability, trustworthiness, steadfastness …*Even before they were married, she had worried about his constancy…*

constant 1 = <u>continuous</u>, sustained, endless, persistent, eternal, relentless, perpetual, continual, never-ending, habitual, uninterrupted, interminable, unrelenting, incessant, everlasting, ceaseless, unremitting, nonstop …*Women are under constant pressure to be thin…* OPPOSITE occasional
2 = <u>unchanging</u>, even, fixed, regular, permanent, stable, steady, uniform, continual, unbroken, immutable, immovable, invariable, unalterable, unvarying, firm …*The temperature should be kept more or less constant…* OPPOSITE changing
3 = <u>faithful</u>, true, devoted, loyal, stalwart, staunch, dependable, trustworthy, trusty, steadfast, unfailing, tried-and-true …*She couldn't bear the thought of losing her constant companion…* OPPOSITE undependable

constantly = <u>continuously</u>, always, all the time, invariably, continually, aye (*Scot.*), endlessly, relentlessly, persistently, perpetually, night and day, incessantly, nonstop, interminably, everlastingly, morning, noon and night OPPOSITE occasionally

consternation = <u>dismay</u>, shock, alarm, horror, panic, anxiety, distress, confusion, terror, dread, fright, amazement, fear, bewilderment, trepidation

constituent NOUN **1** = <u>voter</u>, elector, member of the electorate …*They plan to consult their constituents before taking action…*
2 = <u>component</u>, element, ingredient, part, unit, factor, principle …*Caffeine is the active constituent of drinks such as tea and coffee…*
ADJECTIVE = <u>component</u>, basic, essential, integral, elemental …*The fuel is dissolved in nitric acid and separated into its constituent parts…*

constitute 1 = <u>represent</u>, be, consist of, embody, exemplify, be equivalent to …*The result of the vote hardly constitutes a victory…*
2 = <u>make up</u>, make, form, compose, comprise …*The country's ethnic minorities constitute 7 per cent of its total population…*
3 = <u>set up</u>, found, name, create, commission, establish, appoint, delegate, nominate, enact, authorize, empower, ordain, depute …*On 6 July a People's Revolutionary Government was constituted…*

constitution 1 = <u>state of health</u>, build, body, make-up, frame, physique, physical condition …*He must have an extremely strong constitution…*
2 = <u>structure</u>, form, nature, make-up, organization, establishment, formation, composition, character, temper, temperament, disposition …*He ran a small research team looking into the chemical constitution of coal…*

constitutional = <u>legitimate</u>, official, legal, chartered, statutory, vested

constrain 1 = <u>restrict</u>, confine, curb, restrain, rein,

constrict, hem in, straiten, check, chain ...*Women are too often constrained by family commitments...*
2 = force, pressure, urge, bind, compel, oblige, necessitate, coerce, impel, pressurize, drive ...*Individuals will be constrained to make many sacrifices for the greater good...*

constraint 1 = restriction, limitation, curb, rein, deterrent, hindrance, damper, check ...*Their decision to abandon the trip was made because of financial constraints...*
2 = force, pressure, necessity, restraint, compulsion, coercion ...*People are not morally responsible for that which they do under constraint or compulsion...*
3 = repression, reservation, embarrassment, restraint, inhibition, timidity, diffidence, bashfulness ...*She feels no constraint in discussing sexual matters...*

constrict 1 = squeeze, contract, narrow, restrict, shrink, tighten, pinch, choke, cramp, strangle, compress, strangulate ...*Severe migraine can be treated with a drug which constricts the blood vessels...*
2 = limit, restrict, confine, curb, inhibit, delimit, straiten ...*Senators crafting the bill were frequently constricted by budget limits...*

constriction = tightness, pressure, narrowing, reduction, squeezing, restriction, constraint, cramp, compression, blockage, limitation, impediment, stricture

construct 1 = build, make, form, create, design, raise, establish, set up, fashion, shape, engineer, frame, manufacture, put up, assemble, put together, erect, fabricate ...*The boxes should be constructed from rough-sawn timber...* OPPOSITE demolish
2 = create, make, form, set up, organize, compose, put together, formulate ...*You will find it difficult to construct a spending plan without first recording your outgoings...*

construction 1 = building, assembly, creation, formation, composition, erection, fabrication ...*With the exception of teak, this is the finest wood for boat construction...*
2 = structure, building, edifice, form, figure, shape ...*The British pavilion is an impressive steel and glass construction...*
3 (*Formal*) = interpretation, meaning, reading, sense, explanation, rendering, take (*informal, chiefly U.S.*), inference ...*He put the wrong construction on what he saw...*

constructive = helpful, positive, useful, practical, valuable, productive OPPOSITE unproductive

construe = interpret, take, read, explain

consult 1 = ask, refer to, turn to, interrogate, take counsel, ask advice of, pick (someone's) brains, question ...*Consult your doctor before undertaking a strenuous exercise programme...*
2 = confer, talk, debate, deliberate, commune, compare notes, consider ...*The umpires consulted quickly...*
3 = refer to, check in, look in ...*He had to consult a pocket dictionary...*

consultant = specialist, adviser, counsellor, authority

consultation 1 = discussion, talk, council, conference, dialogue ...*Next week he'll be in Florida for consultations with President Mitterand...*
2 = meeting, interview, session, appointment, examination, deliberation, hearing ...*A personal diet plan is devised after a consultation with a nutritionist...*

consume 1 = eat, swallow, devour, put away, gobble (up), eat up, guzzle, polish off (*informal*) ...*Andrew would consume nearly two pounds of cheese per day...*
2 = use up, use, spend, waste, employ, absorb, drain, exhaust, deplete, squander, utilize, dissipate, expend, eat up, fritter away ...*Some of the most efficient refrigerators consume 70 percent less electricity than traditional models...*
3 = destroy, devastate, demolish, ravage, annihilate, lay waste ...*Fire consumed the building...*
4 *often passive* = obsess, dominate, absorb, preoccupy, devour, eat up, monopolize, engross ...*I was consumed by fear...*

consumer = buyer, customer, user, shopper, purchaser

consuming = overwhelming, gripping, absorbing, compelling, devouring, engrossing, immoderate

consummate ADJECTIVE **1** = skilled, perfect, supreme, polished, superb, practised, accomplished, matchless ...*He acted the part with consummate skill...*
2 = complete, total, supreme, extreme, ultimate, absolute, utter, conspicuous, unqualified, deep-dyed (*usually derogatory*) ...*He was a consummate liar and exaggerator...*
VERB = complete, finish, achieve, conclude, perform, perfect, carry out, crown, fulfil, end, accomplish, effectuate, put the tin lid on ...*No one has yet been able to consummate a deal...* OPPOSITE initiate

consummation = completion, end, achievement, perfection, realization, fulfilment, culmination

consumption 1 = using up, use, loss, waste, drain, consuming, expenditure, exhaustion, depletion, utilization, dissipation ...*The laws have led to a reduction in fuel consumption...*
2 (*Old-fashioned*) = tuberculosis, atrophy, T.B., emaciation ...*an opera about a prostitute dying of consumption in a garret...*

contact NOUN **1** = communication, link, association, connection, correspondence, intercourse ...*Opposition leaders are denying any contact with the government in Kabul...*
2 = touch, contiguity ...*Hepatitis B virus is spread by contact with infected blood...*
3 = connection, colleague, associate, liaison, acquaintance, confederate ...*Her business contacts described her as 'a very determined lady'...*
VERB = get or be in touch with, call, reach, approach, phone, ring (up) (*informal, chiefly Brit.*), write to, speak to, communicate with, get hold of, touch base with (*U.S. & Canad. informal*) ...*When she first contacted me, she was upset...*

contagion 1 = contamination, infection, corruption, pollution, taint ...*They have been reluctant to admit

AIDS patients because of unfounded fears of contagion…

2 = <u>spread</u>, spreading, communication, passage, proliferation, diffusion, transference, dissemination, dispersal, transmittal …*He continues to isolate his country from the contagion of foreign ideas…*

contagious = <u>infectious</u>, catching, spreading, epidemic, communicable, transmissible

contain 1 = <u>hold</u>, incorporate, accommodate, enclose, have capacity for …*Factory shops contain a wide range of cheap furnishings…*
2 = <u>include</u>, consist of, embrace, comprise, embody, comprehend …*The committee contains 11 Democrats and nine Republicans…*
3 = <u>restrain</u>, control, hold in, curb, suppress, hold back, stifle, repress, keep a tight rein on …*The city authorities said the curfew had contained the violence…*

container = <u>holder</u>, vessel, repository, receptacle

contaminate = <u>pollute</u>, infect, stain, corrupt, taint, sully, defile, adulterate, befoul, soil OPPOSITE> purify

contaminated = <u>polluted</u>, dirtied, poisoned, infected, stained, corrupted, tainted, sullied, defiled, soiled, adulterated

contamination = <u>pollution</u>, dirtying, infection, corruption, poisoning, decay, taint, filth, impurity, contagion, adulteration, foulness, defilement

contemplate 1 = <u>consider</u>, plan, think of, propose, intend, envisage, foresee, have in view *or* in mind …*He contemplated a career as an army medical doctor…*
2 = <u>think about</u>, consider, ponder, mull over, reflect upon, ruminate (upon), meditate on, brood over, muse over, deliberate over, revolve *or* turn over in your mind …*He lay in his hospital bed and cried as he contemplated his future…*
3 = <u>look at</u>, examine, observe, check out (*informal*), inspect, gaze at, behold, eye up, view, study, regard, survey, stare at, scrutinize, eye …*He contemplated his hands thoughtfully…*

contemplation 1 = <u>thought</u>, consideration, reflection, musing, meditation, pondering, deliberation, reverie, rumination, cogitation …*The garden is a place of quiet contemplation…*
2 = <u>observation</u>, viewing, looking at, survey, examination, inspection, scrutiny, gazing at …*He was lost in contemplation of the landscape…*

contemplative = <u>thoughtful</u>, reflective, introspective, rapt, meditative, pensive, ruminative, in a brown study, intent, musing, deep *or* lost in thought

contemporary ADJECTIVE **1** = <u>modern</u>, latest, recent, current, with it (*informal*), trendy (*Brit. informal*), up-to-date, present-day, in fashion, up-to-the-minute, à la mode, newfangled, happening (*informal*), present, ultramodern …*The gallery holds regular exhibitions of contemporary art, sculpture and photography…* OPPOSITE> old-fashioned
2 = <u>coexisting</u>, concurrent, contemporaneous, synchronous, coexistent …*The book draws upon official records and the reports of contemporary*

witnesses…
NOUN = <u>peer</u>, fellow, equal …*a glossary of terms used by Shakespeare and his contemporaries…*

> ## *Word Power*
> **contemporary** – Since *contemporary* can mean either 'of the same period' or 'of the present period', it is best to avoid it where ambiguity might arise, as in *a production of Othello in contemporary dress*. A synonym such as *modern* or *present-day* would clarify if the first sense were being used, while a specific term, such as *Elizabethan*, would be appropriate for the second sense.

contempt = <u>scorn</u>, disdain, mockery, derision, disrespect, disregard OPPOSITE> respect

contemptible = <u>despicable</u>, mean, low, base, cheap, worthless, shameful, shabby, vile, degenerate, low-down (*informal*), paltry, pitiful, abject, ignominious, measly, scurvy, detestable OPPOSITE> admirable

contemptuous = <u>scornful</u>, insulting, arrogant, withering, sneering, cavalier, condescending, haughty, disdainful, insolent, derisive, supercilious, high and mighty, on your high horse (*informal*) OPPOSITE> respectful

contend 1 = <u>argue</u>, hold, maintain, allege, assert, affirm, avow, aver …*The government contends that he is a fundamentalist…*
2 = <u>compete</u>, fight, struggle, clash, contest, strive, vie, grapple, jostle, skirmish …*The two main groups contended for power…*

contender = <u>competitor</u>, rival, candidate, applicant, hopeful, contestant, aspirant

content¹ NOUN **1** = <u>subject matter</u>, ideas, matter, material, theme, text, substance, essence, gist …*She is reluctant to discuss the content of the play…*
2 = <u>amount</u>, measure, size, load, volume, capacity …*Sunflower margarine has the same fat content as butter…*
PLURAL NOUN **1** = <u>constituents</u>, elements, load, ingredients …*Empty the contents of the pan into the sieve…*
2 = <u>subjects</u>, chapters, themes, topics, subject matter, divisions …*There is no initial list of contents at the start of the book…*

content² ADJECTIVE = <u>satisfied</u>, happy, pleased, contented, comfortable, fulfilled, at ease, gratified, agreeable, willing to accept …*I'm perfectly content with the way the campaign has gone…*
NOUN = <u>satisfaction</u>, peace, ease, pleasure, comfort, peace of mind, gratification, contentment …*Once he'd retired, he could potter about the garden to his heart's content…*
PHRASES **content yourself with something** = <u>satisfy yourself with</u>, be happy with, be satisfied with, be content with …*He had to content himself with the knowledge that he had been right…*

contented = <u>satisfied</u>, happy, pleased, content,

comfortable, glad, cheerful, at ease, thankful, gratified, serene, at peace OPPOSITE discontented

contention 1 = <u>assertion</u>, claim, stand, idea, view, position, opinion, argument, belief, allegation, profession, declaration, thesis, affirmation ...*Sufficient research evidence exists to support this contention...*
2 = <u>dispute</u>, hostility, disagreement, feuding, strife, wrangling, discord, enmity, dissension ...*They generally tried to avoid subjects of contention between them...*

contentious = <u>argumentative</u>, wrangling, perverse, bickering, combative, pugnacious, quarrelsome, litigious, querulous, cavilling, disputatious, factious, captious

contentment = <u>satisfaction</u>, peace, content, ease, pleasure, comfort, happiness, fulfilment, gratification, serenity, equanimity, gladness, repletion, contentedness OPPOSITE discontent

contest NOUN 1 = <u>competition</u>, game, match, trial, tournament, head-to-head ...*Few contests in the recent history of British boxing have been as thrilling...*
2 = <u>struggle</u>, fight, battle, debate, conflict, dispute, encounter, controversy, combat, discord ...*a bitter contest over who should control the state's future...*
VERB 1 = <u>compete in</u>, take part in, fight in, go in for, contend for, vie in ...*He quickly won his party's nomination to contest the elections...*
2 = <u>oppose</u>, question, challenge, argue, debate, dispute, object to, litigate, call in *or* into question ...*Your former employer has to reply within 14 days in order to contest the case...*

contestant = <u>competitor</u>, candidate, participant, contender, entrant, player, aspirant

context 1 = <u>circumstances</u>, times, conditions, situation, ambience ...*the historical context in which Chaucer wrote...*
2 = <u>frame of reference</u>, background, framework, relation, connection ...*Without a context, I would have assume it was written by a man...*

continent
➤ **WORD POWER SUPPLEMENT continents**

contingency = <u>possibility</u>, happening, chance, event, incident, accident, emergency, uncertainty, eventuality, juncture

contingent NOUN = <u>group</u>, detachment, deputation, set, body, section, bunch (*informal*), quota, batch ...*There were contingents from the navies of virtually all EC countries...*
ADJECTIVE = <u>chance</u>, random, casual, uncertain, accidental, haphazard, fortuitous ...*these apparently random, contingent and unexplained phenomena...*
PHRASES **contingent on** = <u>dependent on</u>, subject to, controlled by, conditional on ...*Growth is contingent on improved incomes...*

continual 1 = <u>constant</u>, endless, continuous, eternal, perpetual, uninterrupted, interminable, incessant, everlasting, unremitting, unceasing ...*Despite continual pain, he refused all drugs...* OPPOSITE erratic
2 = <u>frequent</u>, regular, repeated, repetitive, recurrent, oft-repeated ...*She suffered continual police*

harassment... OPPOSITE occasional

continually 1 = <u>constantly</u>, always, all the time, forever, aye (*Scot.*), endlessly, eternally, incessantly, nonstop, interminably, everlastingly ...*The large rotating fans whirred continually...*
2 = <u>repeatedly</u>, often, frequently, many times, over and over, again and again, time and (time) again, persistently, time after time, many a time and oft (*archaic or poetic*) ...*He continually changed his mind...*

continuance = <u>perpetuation</u>, lasting, carrying on, keeping up, endurance, continuation, prolongation

continuation 1 = <u>continuing</u>, lasting, carrying on, maintenance, keeping up, endurance, perpetuation, prolongation ...*What we'll see in the future is a continuation of this trend...*
2 = <u>addition</u>, extension, supplement, sequel, resumption, postscript ...*This chapter is a continuation of Chapter 8...*

continue 1 = <u>keep on</u>, go on, maintain, pursue, sustain, carry on, stick to, keep up, prolong, persist in, keep at, persevere, stick at, press on with ...*Outside the hall, people continued their vigil...* OPPOSITE stop
2 = <u>go on</u>, advance, progress, proceed, carry on, keep going ...*As the investigation continued, the plot began to thicken...*
3 = <u>resume</u>, return to, take up again, proceed, carry on, recommence, pick up where you left off ...*She looked up for a moment, then continued drawing...* OPPOSITE stop
4 = <u>remain</u>, last, stay, rest, survive, carry on, live on, endure, stay on, persist, abide ...*For ten days I continued in this state... ...He had hoped to continue as a full-time career officer...* OPPOSITE quit

continuing = <u>lasting</u>, sustained, enduring, ongoing, in progress

continuity = <u>cohesion</u>, flow, connection, sequence, succession, progression, wholeness, interrelationship

continuous = <u>constant</u>, continued, extended, prolonged, unbroken, uninterrupted, unceasing OPPOSITE occasional

contort = <u>twist</u>, knot, distort, warp, deform, misshape

contortion = <u>twist</u>, distortion, deformity, convolution, bend, knot, warp

contour = <u>outline</u>, profile, lines, form, figure, shape, relief, curve, silhouette

contraband = <u>smuggled</u>, illegal, illicit, black-market, hot (*informal*), banned, forbidden, prohibited, unlawful, bootleg, bootlegged, interdicted

contract NOUN = <u>agreement</u>, deal (*informal*), commission, commitment, arrangement, understanding, settlement, treaty, bargain, convention, engagement, pact, compact, covenant, bond, stipulation, concordat ...*The company won a prestigious contract for work on the building...*
VERB 1 = <u>agree</u>, arrange, negotiate, engage, pledge, bargain, undertake, come to terms, shake hands, covenant, make a deal, commit yourself, enter into an agreement ...*He has contracted to lease part of the collection to a museum in Japan...* OPPOSITE refuse

2 = <u>constrict</u>, confine, tighten, shorten, wither, compress, condense, shrivel …*New research shows that an excess of meat and salt can contract muscles*…
3 = <u>tighten</u>, narrow, knit, purse, shorten, pucker …*As we move our bodies, our muscles contract and relax*…
OPPOSITE > stretch
4 = <u>lessen</u>, reduce, shrink, diminish, decrease, dwindle …*Output fell last year and is expected to contract further this year*… OPPOSITE > increase
5 = <u>catch</u>, get, develop, acquire, incur, be infected with, go down with, be afflicted with …*He contracted AIDS from a blood transfusion*… OPPOSITE > avoid

contraction **1** = <u>tightening</u>, narrowing, tensing, shortening, drawing in, constricting, shrinkage …*Cramp is caused by contraction of the muscles*…
2 = <u>abbreviation</u>, reduction, shortening, compression, diminution, constriction, elision …*'It's' is a contraction of 'it is'*…

contradict **1** = <u>dispute</u>, deny, challenge, belie, fly in the face of, make a nonsense of, be at variance with …*We knew she was wrong, but nobody liked to contradict her*… …*His comments contradict remarks he made earlier that day*…
2 = <u>negate</u>, deny, oppose, counter, contravene, rebut, impugn, controvert …*The result appears to contradict a major study carried out last December*… OPPOSITE > confirm

contradiction **1** = <u>conflict</u>, inconsistency, contravention, incongruity, confutation …*They see no contradiction in using violence to bring about a religious state*…
2 = <u>negation</u>, opposite, denial, antithesis …*What he does is a contradiction of what he says*…

contradictory = <u>inconsistent</u>, conflicting, opposed, opposite, contrary, incompatible, paradoxical, irreconcilable, antithetical, discrepant

contraption (*Informal*) = <u>device</u>, instrument, mechanism, apparatus, gadget, contrivance, rig

contrary ADJECTIVE **1** = <u>opposite</u>, different, opposed, clashing, counter, reverse, differing, adverse, contradictory, inconsistent, diametrically opposed, antithetical …*His sister was of the contrary opinion to his*… OPPOSITE > in agreement
2 = <u>perverse</u>, difficult, awkward, wayward, intractable, wilful, obstinate, cussed (*informal*), stroppy (*Brit. slang*), cantankerous, disobliging, unaccommodating, thrawn (*Scot. & Northern English dialect*) …*Why must she always be so contrary?*… OPPOSITE > cooperative
NOUN = <u>opposite</u>, reverse, converse, antithesis …*Let me assure you that the contrary is, in fact, the case*…
PHRASES **on the contrary** = <u>quite the opposite</u> or reverse, on the other hand, in contrast, conversely …*The government must, on the contrary, re-establish its authority*…

contrast NOUN = <u>difference</u>, opposition, comparison, distinction, foil, disparity, differentiation, divergence, dissimilarity, contrariety …*The two women provided a startling contrast in appearance*…
VERB **1** = <u>differentiate</u>, compare, oppose, distinguish, set in opposition …*She contrasted the situation then

with the present crisis*…
2 = <u>differ</u>, be contrary, be distinct, be at variance, be dissimilar …*Johnstone's easy charm contrasted with the prickliness of his boss*…

contravene **1** (*Formal*) = <u>break</u>, violate, go against, infringe, disobey, transgress …*He said the article did not contravene the industry's code of conduct*…
2 = <u>conflict with</u>, cross, oppose, interfere with, thwart, contradict, hinder, go against, refute, counteract …*This deportation order contravenes basic human rights*…

contravention **1** = <u>breach</u>, violation, infringement, trespass, disobedience, transgression, infraction …*They are in direct contravention of the law*…
2 = <u>conflict</u>, interference, contradiction, hindrance, rebuttal, refutation, disputation, counteraction …*He denied that the new laws were a contravention of fundamental rights*…

contribute VERB = <u>give</u>, provide, supply, donate, furnish, subscribe, chip in (*informal*), bestow …*They say they would like to contribute more to charity*…
PHRASES **contribute to something** = <u>be partly responsible for</u>, lead to, be instrumental in, be conducive to, conduce to, help …*Design faults in the boat contributed to the tragedy*…

contribution = <u>gift</u>, offering, grant, donation, input, subscription, bestowal

contributor **1** = <u>donor</u>, supporter, patron, subscriber, backer, bestower, giver …*Redford is the institute's leading financial contributor and is active in fund-raising*…
2 = <u>writer</u>, correspondent, reporter, journalist, freelance, freelancer, journo (*slang*) …*All of the pieces by the magazine's contributors appear anonymously*…

contrite = <u>sorry</u>, humble, chastened, sorrowful, repentant, remorseful, regretful, penitent, conscience-stricken, in sackcloth and ashes

contrition = <u>regret</u>, sorrow, remorse, repentance, compunction, penitence, self-reproach

contrivance **1** = <u>device</u>, machine, equipment, gear, instrument, implement, mechanism, invention, appliance, apparatus, gadget, contraption …*They wear simple clothes and shun modern contrivances*…
2 = <u>stratagem</u>, plan, design, measure, scheme, trick, plot, dodge, expedient, ruse, artifice, machination …*It is nothing more than a contrivance to raise prices*…

contrive **1** = <u>devise</u>, plan, fabricate, create, design, scheme, engineer, frame, manufacture, plot, construct, invent, improvise, concoct, wangle (*informal*) …*The oil companies were accused of contriving a shortage of gasoline to justify price increases*…
2 = <u>manage</u>, succeed, arrange, manoeuvre …*Somehow he contrived to pass her a note without her chaperone seeing it*…

contrived = <u>forced</u>, planned, laboured, strained, artificial, elaborate, unnatural, overdone, recherché
OPPOSITE > natural

control NOUN **1** = <u>power</u>, government, rule, authority, management, direction, command, discipline, guidance, supervision, jurisdiction, supremacy, mastery, superintendence, charge …*The first aim of his government would be to establish control over the republic's territory…*

2 = restraint, check, regulation, brake, limitation, curb …*There are to be tighter controls on land speculation…*

3 = self-discipline, cool, calmness, self-restraint, restraint, coolness, self-mastery, self-command …*He had a terrible temper, and sometimes lost control completely…*

4 = switch, instrument, button, dial, lever, knob …*He adjusted the temperature control…*

PLURAL NOUN = instruments, dash, dials, console, dashboard, control panel …*He died of a heart attack while at the controls of the plane…*

VERB 1 = have power over, lead, rule, manage, boss (*informal*), direct, handle, conduct, dominate, command, pilot, govern, steer, administer, oversee, supervise, manipulate, call the shots, call the tune, reign over, keep a tight rein on, have charge of, superintend, have (someone) in your pocket, keep on a string …*He now controls the largest retail development empire in southern California… …My husband tried to control me in every way…*

2 = limit, restrict, curb, delimit …*The government tried to control rising health-care costs…*

3 = restrain, limit, check, contain, master, curb, hold back, subdue, repress, constrain, bridle, rein in …*Try to control that temper of yours…*

controversial = disputed, contended, contentious, at issue, debatable, polemic, under discussion, open to question, disputable

controversy = argument, debate, row, discussion, dispute, contention, quarrel, squabble, strife, wrangle, wrangling, polemic, altercation, dissension

conundrum = puzzle, problem, riddle, enigma, teaser, poser, brain-teaser (*informal*)

convalesce = recover, rest, rally, rehabilitate, recuperate, improve

convalescence = recovery, rehabilitation, recuperation, return to health, improvement

convalescent = recovering, getting better, recuperating, on the mend, improving, mending

convene 1 = call, gather, assemble, summon, bring together, muster, convoke …*He convened a meeting of all the managers…*

2 = meet, gather, rally, assemble, come together, muster, congregate …*Senior officials convened in London for an emergency meeting…*

convenience **NOUN** **1** = benefit, good, interest, advantage …*He was happy to make a detour for her convenience…*

2 = suitability, fitness, appropriateness, opportuneness …*She was delighted with the convenience of this arrangement…*

3 = usefulness, utility, serviceability, handiness …*The convenience of digital cameras means that more and more people are buying them nowadays…* **OPPOSITE** uselessness

4 = accessibility, availability, nearness, handiness …*They miss the convenience of London's tubes and buses…*

5 = appliance, facility, comfort, amenity, labour-saving device, help …*The chalets have all the modern conveniences…*

PHRASES **at your convenience** = at a suitable time, at your leisure, in your own time, whenever you like, in your spare time, in a spare moment …*Please call me to set up an appointment at your convenience…*

convenient 1 = suitable, fitting, fit, handy, satisfactory …*The family found it more convenient to eat in the kitchen…*

2 = useful, practical, handy, serviceable, labour-saving …*Pre-prepared foods are a tempting and convenient option…* **OPPOSITE** useless

3 = nearby, available, accessible, handy, at hand, within reach, close at hand, just round the corner …*The town is convenient for Heathrow Airport…* **OPPOSITE** inaccessible

4 = appropriate, timely, suited, suitable, beneficial, well-timed, opportune, seasonable, helpful …*She will try to arrange a mutually convenient time for an interview…*

convent = nunnery, religious community, religious house

convention 1 = custom, practice, tradition, code, usage, protocol, formality, etiquette, propriety …*It's just a social convention that men don't wear skirts…*

2 = agreement, contract, treaty, bargain, pact, compact, protocol, stipulation, concordat …*the importance of observing the Geneva convention on human rights…*

3 = assembly, meeting, council, conference, congress, convocation …*I flew to Boston to attend the annual convention of the Parapsychological Association…*

conventional 1 = proper, conservative, correct, formal, respectable, bourgeois, genteel, staid, conformist, decorous, Pooterish …*a respectable married woman with conventional opinions…*

2 = ordinary, standard, normal, regular, usual, vanilla (*slang*), habitual, bog-standard (*Brit. & Irish slang*), common …*the cost of fuel and electricity used by a conventional system…*

3 = traditional, accepted, prevailing, orthodox, customary, prevalent, hidebound, wonted …*The conventional wisdom on these matters is being challenged…*

4 = unoriginal, routine, stereotyped, pedestrian, commonplace, banal, prosaic, run-of-the-mill, hackneyed, vanilla (*slang*) …*This is a rather conventional work by a mediocre author…* **OPPOSITE** unconventional

converge **VERB** = come together, meet, join, combine, gather, merge, coincide, mingle, intersect …*As they flow south, the five rivers converge…*

PHRASES **converge on something** = close in on, arrive at, move towards, home in on, come together at …*Hundreds of coaches will converge on the capital…*

convergence = <u>meeting</u>, junction, intersection, confluence, concentration, blending, merging, coincidence, conjunction, mingling, concurrence, conflux

conversation = <u>talk</u>, exchange, discussion, dialogue, tête-à-tête, conference, communication, chat, gossip, intercourse, discourse, communion, converse, powwow, colloquy, chinwag (*Brit. informal*), confabulation, confab (*informal*), craic (*Irish informal*)

(*Related Words*)
adjective : colloquial

conversational = <u>chatty</u>, informal, communicative, colloquial

converse[1] = <u>talk</u>, speak, chat, communicate, discourse, confer, commune, exchange views, shoot the breeze (*slang, chiefly U.S. & Canad.*) …*They were conversing in German, their only common language*…

converse[2] NOUN = <u>opposite</u>, reverse, contrary, other side of the coin, obverse, antithesis …*If that is true, the converse is equally so*…
ADJECTIVE = <u>opposite</u>, counter, reverse, contrary …*Stress reduction techniques have the converse effect on the immune system*…

conversion 1 = <u>change</u>, transformation, metamorphosis, transfiguration, transmutation, transmogrification (*jocular*) …*the conversion of disused rail lines into cycle routes*…
2 = <u>adaptation</u>, reconstruction, modification, alteration, remodelling, reorganization …*A loft conversion can add considerably to the value of a house*…
3 = <u>reformation</u>, rebirth, change of heart, proselytization …*his conversion to Christianity*…

convert VERB 1 = <u>change</u>, turn, transform, alter, metamorphose, transpose, transmute, transmogrify (*jocular*) …*a handy table which converts into an ironing board*…
2 = <u>adapt</u>, modify, remodel, reorganize, customize, restyle …*By converting the loft, they were able to have two extra bedrooms*…
3 = <u>reform</u>, save, convince, proselytize, bring to God …*I resent religious people who insist on trying to convert others*…
NOUN = <u>neophyte</u>, disciple, proselyte, catechumen …*She was a recent convert to Roman Catholicism*…

convertible = <u>changeable</u>, interchangeable, exchangeable, adjustable, adaptable

convex = <u>rounded</u>, bulging, protuberant, gibbous, outcurved OPPOSITE concave

convey 1 = <u>communicate</u>, impart, reveal, relate, disclose, make known, tell …*I tried to convey the wonder of the experience to my husband*…
2 = <u>carry</u>, transport, move, bring, support, bear, conduct, transmit, fetch …*They borrowed our boats to convey themselves across the river*…

conveyance 1 (*Old-fashioned*) = <u>vehicle</u>, transport …*He had never travelled in such a strange conveyance before*…
2 = <u>transportation</u>, movement, transfer, transport, transmission, carriage, transference …*the conveyance*

of bicycles on Regional Railway trains…

convict VERB = <u>find guilty</u>, sentence, condemn, imprison, pronounce guilty …*There was sufficient evidence to convict him*…
NOUN = <u>prisoner</u>, criminal, con (*slang*), lag (*slang*), villain, felon, jailbird, malefactor …*The prison houses only lifers and convicts on death row*…

conviction 1 = <u>belief</u>, view, opinion, principle, faith, persuasion, creed, tenet …*Their religious convictions prevented them from taking up arms*…
2 = <u>certainty</u>, confidence, assurance, fervour, firmness, earnestness, certitude …*He preaches with conviction*…

convince 1 = <u>assure</u>, persuade, satisfy, prove to, reassure …*I soon convinced him of my innocence*…
2 = <u>persuade</u>, induce, coax, talk into, prevail upon, inveigle, twist (*someone's*) arm, bring round to the idea of …*He convinced her to go ahead and marry Bud*…

> ## Word Power
> **convince** – The use of *convince* to talk about persuading someone to do something is considered by many British speakers to be wrong or unacceptable. It would be preferable to use an alternative such as *persuade* or *talk into*.

convincing = <u>persuasive</u>, credible, conclusive, incontrovertible, telling, likely, powerful, impressive, probable, plausible, cogent OPPOSITE unconvincing

convivial = <u>sociable</u>, friendly, lively, cheerful, jolly, merry, festive, hearty, genial, fun-loving, jovial, back-slapping, gay, partyish (*informal*)

convocation (*Formal*) = <u>meeting</u>, congress, convention, synod, diet, assembly, concourse, council, assemblage, conclave

convoy = <u>escort</u>, conduct, accompany, shepherd, protect, attend, guard, pilot, usher

convulse 1 = <u>shake</u>, twist, agitate, contort …*He let out a cry that convulsed his whole body*…
2 = <u>twist</u>, contort, work …*Olivia's face convulsed in a series of spasms*…

convulsion 1 = <u>spasm</u>, fit, shaking, seizure, contraction, tremor, cramp, contortion, paroxysm …*He fell to the floor in the grip of an epileptic convulsion*…
2 = <u>upheaval</u>, disturbance, furore, turbulence, agitation, commotion, tumult …*It was a decade that saw many great social, economic and political convulsions*…

cookery
(*Related Words*)
adjective : culinary
➤ **cookery terms**

cool ADJECTIVE 1 = <u>cold</u>, chilled, chilling, refreshing, chilly, nippy …*I felt a current of cool air*… OPPOSITE warm
2 = <u>calm</u>, together (*slang*), collected, relaxed, composed, laid-back (*informal*), serene, sedate, self-

Cookery terms   http://www.bbc.co.uk/food/

à la king	corned	jerk	rissole
à la mode	creole	julienne	roast
antipasto	cuisine	knead	roulade
au gratin	cuisine minceur	ladle	roux
au jus	cured	lard	royal icing
au lait	curried	lardon *or* lardoon	salipicon
au naturel	custard	leaven	sauce
bake	dice	liaison	sauté
barbecue *or* (*Austral.*	dough	luau	scramble
slang) barbie	dressing	lyonnaise	season
bard *or* barde	en brochette	macedoine	silver service
baste	en croute	marengo	sippet
batter	entrée	marinade	smoked
blackened	entremets	marinate	soup
blanch	fajita	marmite	steam
boil	farci	mask	stew
boil-in-the-bag	fillet	mash	stock
braise	flambé	médaillons *or*	stroganoff
broth	flour	medallions	supreme
browning	fondue	meunière	sweat
caramelise	fricassee	meze	sweet-and-sour
carbonado	fry	mirepoix	tandoori
casserole	fumet	mornay	tenderize
caterer	garnish	Newburg	teriyaki
chafing dish	gelatine	nouvelle cuisine	tikka
char-grill	ghee	offal	timbale
chasseur	giblets	oven-ready	topping
chef	glacé	panada	undressed
cobbler	glaze	parboil	unleavened
coddle	goujon	Parmentier	unsmoked
colander	goulash	paste	whip
commis	grate	poach	wholemeal *or* (*chiefly*
confectioner	gravy	potage	*U.S. and Canad.*)
consommé	grill	Provençale	wholewheat
cook	hors d'oeuvre	purée	wholemeal flour *or*
cookbook *or* cookery	ice	ragout	(*chiefly U.S. and Canad.*)
book	icing	rijstaffel	Graham flour
cook-chill	jardinière	rise	yeast

controlled, placid, level-headed, dispassionate, unfazed (*informal*), unruffled, unemotional, self-possessed, imperturbable, unexcited ...*He was marvellously cool, smiling as if nothing had happened...* OPPOSITE> agitated

3 = unfriendly, reserved, distant, indifferent, aloof, lukewarm, unconcerned, uninterested, frigid, unresponsive, offhand, unenthusiastic, uncommunicative, unwelcoming, standoffish ...*People found him too cool, aloof and arrogant...* OPPOSITE> friendly

4 = unenthusiastic, indifferent, lukewarm, uninterested, apathetic, unresponsive, unwelcoming ...*The idea met with a cool response...*

5 (*Informal*) = fashionable, with it (*informal*), hip (*slang*), stylish, trendy (*Brit. informal*), chic, up-to-date, urbane, up-to-the-minute, voguish (*informal*), trendsetting ...*He was trying to be really cool and trendy...*

6 = impudent, bold, cheeky, audacious, brazen, shameless, presumptuous, impertinent ...*He displayed a cool disregard for the rules...*

VERB 1 = lose heat, cool off ...*Drain the meat and*

allow it to cool... OPPOSITE> warm (up)

2 = make cool, freeze, chill, refrigerate, cool off ...*Huge fans are used to cool the factory...* OPPOSITE> warm (up)

3 = calm (down), lessen, abate ...*Within a few minutes their tempers had cooled...*

4 = lessen, calm (down), quiet, moderate, temper, dampen, allay, abate, assuage ...*His strange behaviour had cooled her passion...*

NOUN 1 = coldness, chill, coolness ...*She walked into the cool of the hallway...*

2 (*Slang*) = calmness, control, temper, composure, self-control, poise, self-discipline, self-possession ...*She kept her cool and managed to get herself out of the situation...*

coolness 1 = coldness, freshness, chilliness, nippiness ...*He felt the coolness of the tiled floor...* OPPOSITE> warmness

2 = calmness, control, composure, self-control, self-discipline, self-possession, level-headedness, imperturbability, sedateness, placidness ...*They praised him for his coolness under pressure...* OPPOSITE> agitation

3 = <u>unfriendliness</u>, reserve, distance, indifference, apathy, remoteness, aloofness, frigidity, unconcern, unresponsiveness, frostiness, offhandedness ...*She seemed quite unaware of the sudden coolness of her friend's manner...* OPPOSITE friendliness

4 = <u>impudence</u>, audacity, boldness, insolence, impertinence, shamelessness, cheekiness, brazenness, presumptuousness, audaciousness ...*The coolness of his suggestion took her breath away...*

coop NOUN = <u>pen</u>, pound, box, cage, enclosure, hutch, corral (*chiefly U.S. & Canad.*) ...*Behind the house, the pair set up a chicken coop...*

PHRASES **coop someone up** = <u>confine</u>, imprison, shut up, impound, pound, pen, cage, immure ...*He was cooped up in a cell with ten other inmates...*

cooperate **1** = <u>work together</u>, collaborate, coordinate, join forces, conspire, concur, pull together, pool resources, combine your efforts ...*The two parties are cooperating more than they have done in years...* OPPOSITE conflict

2 = <u>help</u>, contribute to, assist, go along with, aid, pitch in, abet, play ball (*informal*), lend a helping hand ...*He agreed to cooperate with the police investigation...* OPPOSITE oppose

cooperation **1** = <u>teamwork</u>, concert, unity, collaboration, give-and-take, combined effort, esprit de corps, concurrence ...*A deal with Japan could open the door to economic cooperation with East Asia...* OPPOSITE opposition

2 = <u>help</u>, assistance, participation, responsiveness, helpfulness ...*The police asked for the public's cooperation in their hunt for the killer...* OPPOSITE hindrance

cooperative **1** = <u>shared</u>, united, joint, combined, concerted, collective, unified, coordinated, collaborative ...*The visit was intended to develop cooperative relations between the countries...*

2 = <u>helpful</u>, obliging, accommodating, supportive, responsive, onside (*informal*) ...*I made every effort to be co-operative...*

coordinate **1** = <u>organize</u>, synchronize, integrate, bring together, mesh, correlate, systematize ...*Officials visited the earthquake zone to coordinate the relief effort...*

2 = <u>match</u>, blend, harmonize ...*She'll show you how to coordinate pattern and colours...*

PHRASES **co-ordinate with something** = <u>go with</u>, match, blend with, harmonize with ...*Choose a fabric that co-ordinates with your colour scheme...*

cope VERB = <u>manage</u>, get by (*informal*), struggle through, rise to the occasion, survive, carry on, make out (*informal*), make the grade, hold your own ...*It was amazing how my mother coped after my father died...*

PHRASES **cope with something** = <u>deal with</u>, handle, struggle with, grapple with, wrestle with, contend with, tangle with, tussle with, weather ...*She has had to cope with losing all her previous status and money...*

copious = <u>abundant</u>, liberal, generous, lavish, full, rich, extensive, ample, overflowing, plentiful, exuberant, bountiful, luxuriant, profuse, bounteous, superabundant, plenteous

cop out (*Slang*) = <u>avoid</u>, dodge, abandon, withdraw from, desert, quit, skip, renounce, revoke, renege, skive (*Brit. slang*), bludge (*Austral. & N.Z. informal*)

cop-out (*Slang*) = <u>pretence</u>, dodge, pretext, fraud, alibi

copulate = <u>have intercourse</u>, have sex

copy NOUN = <u>reproduction</u>, duplicate, photocopy, carbon copy, image, print, fax, representation, fake, replica, imitation, forgery, counterfeit, Xerox (*trademark*), transcription, likeness, replication, facsimile, Photostat (*trademark*) ...*Always keep a copy of everything in your own files...* OPPOSITE original

VERB **1** = <u>reproduce</u>, replicate, duplicate, photocopy, transcribe, counterfeit, Xerox (*trademark*), Photostat (*trademark*) ...*She never participated in copying classified documents for anyone...* OPPOSITE create

2 = <u>imitate</u>, act like, emulate, behave like, follow, repeat, mirror, echo, parrot, ape, mimic, simulate, follow suit, follow the example of ...*We all tend to copy people we admire... ...coquettish gestures which she had copied from actresses in soap operas...*

cord = <u>rope</u>, line, string, twine

cordial **1** = <u>warm</u>, welcoming, friendly, cheerful, affectionate, hearty, agreeable, sociable, genial, affable, congenial, warm-hearted ...*I had never known him to be so chatty and cordial...* OPPOSITE unfriendly

2 = <u>wholehearted</u>, earnest, sincere, heartfelt ...*She didn't bother to hide her cordial dislike of him...*

cordon NOUN = <u>chain</u>, line, ring, barrier, picket line ...*Police formed a cordon between the two crowds...*

PHRASES **cordon something off** = <u>surround</u>, isolate, close off, fence off, separate, enclose, picket, encircle ...*The police cordoned the area off...*

core **1** = <u>centre</u> ...*Lava is molten rock from the earth's core...*

2 = <u>heart</u>, essence, nucleus, kernel, crux, gist, nub, pith ...*He has the ability to get straight to the core of a problem...*

corner NOUN **1** = <u>angle</u>, joint, crook ...*the corner of a door...*

2 = <u>bend</u>, curve ...*He waited until the man had turned the corner...*

3 = <u>space</u>, hole, niche, recess, cavity, hideaway, nook, cranny, hide-out, hidey-hole (*informal*) ...*She hid it away in a corner of her room...*

4 = <u>tight spot</u>, predicament, tricky situation, spot (*informal*), hole (*informal*), hot water (*informal*), pickle (*informal*) ...*He appears to have got himself into a tight corner...*

VERB **1** = <u>trap</u>, catch, run to earth, bring to bay ...*The police moved in with tear gas and cornered him...*

2 (usually with *market* as object) = <u>monopolize</u>, take over, dominate, control, hog (*slang*), engross, exercise or have a monopoly of ...*This restaurant has cornered the market for specialist paellas...*

cornerstone = <u>basis</u>, key, premise, starting point, bedrock

corny (*Slang*) **1** = <u>unoriginal</u>, banal, trite, hackneyed, dull, old-fashioned, stereotyped, commonplace, feeble, stale, old hat ...*I know it sounds corny, but I'm not motivated by money...*
2 = <u>sentimental</u>, mushy (*informal*), maudlin, slushy (*informal*), mawkish, schmaltzy (*slang*) ...*a corny old love song...*

corollary = <u>consequence</u>, result, effect, outcome, sequel, end result, upshot

corporal = <u>bodily</u>, physical, fleshly, anatomical, carnal, corporeal (*archaic*), material

corporate = <u>collective</u>, collaborative, united, shared, allied, joint, combined, pooled, merged, communal

corporation 1 = <u>business</u>, company, concern, firm, society, association, organization, enterprise, establishment, corporate body ...*chairman of a huge multi-national corporation...*
2 = <u>town council</u>, council, municipal authorities, civic authorities ...*The local corporation has given permission for the work to proceed...*

corps = <u>team</u>, unit, regiment, detachment, company, body, band, division, troop, squad, crew, contingent, squadron

corpse = <u>body</u>, remains, carcass, cadaver, stiff (*slang*)

corpus = <u>collection</u>, body, whole, compilation, entirety, oeuvre (*French*), complete works

corral (*U.S. & Canad.*) **NOUN** = <u>enclosure</u>, yard, pen, confine, coop, fold ...*As we neared the corral, the horses pranced and whinnied...*
VERB = <u>enclose</u>, confine, cage, fence in, impound, pen in, coop up ...*The men were corralled into a hastily constructed concentration camp...*

correct **ADJECTIVE 1** = <u>accurate</u>, right, true, exact, precise, flawless, faultless, on the right lines, O.K. *or* okay (*informal*) ...*The information was correct at the time of going to press...* **OPPOSITE** inaccurate
2 = <u>right</u>, standard, regular, appropriate, acceptable, strict, proper, precise ...*The use of the correct procedure is vital...*
3 = <u>proper</u>, seemly, standard, fitting, diplomatic, kosher (*informal*) ...*They refuse to adopt the rules of correct behaviour...* **OPPOSITE** inappropriate
VERB 1 = <u>rectify</u>, remedy, redress, right, improve, reform, cure, adjust, regulate, amend, set the record straight, emend ...*He may need surgery to correct the problem...* **OPPOSITE** spoil
2 = <u>rebuke</u>, discipline, reprimand, chide, admonish, chastise, chasten, reprove, punish ...*He gently corrected me for taking the Lord's name in vain...* **OPPOSITE** praise

correction 1 = <u>rectification</u>, improvement, amendment, adjustment, modification, alteration, emendation ...*He has made several corrections and additions to the document...*
2 = <u>punishment</u>, discipline, reformation, admonition, chastisement, reproof, castigation ...*jails and other places of correction...*

corrective 1 = <u>remedial</u>, therapeutic, palliative, restorative, rehabilitative ...*He has received extensive corrective surgery to his skull...*
2 = <u>disciplinary</u>, punitive, penal, reformatory ...*He was placed in a corrective institution for children...*

correctly = <u>rightly</u>, right, perfectly, properly, precisely, accurately, aright

correctness 1 = <u>truth</u>, accuracy, precision, exactitude, exactness, faultlessness ...*Please check the correctness of the details on this form...*
2 = <u>decorum</u>, propriety, good manners, civility, good breeding, bon ton (*French*) ...*He conducted himself with formal correctness at all times...*

correlate 1 = <u>correspond</u>, parallel, be connected, equate, tie in ...*Obesity correlates with increased risk of heart disease and stroke...*
2 = <u>connect</u>, compare, associate, tie in, coordinate ...*attempts to correlate specific language functions with particular parts of the brain...*

correlation = <u>correspondence</u>, link, relation, connection, equivalence

correspond 1 = <u>be consistent</u>, match, agree, accord, fit, square, coincide, complement, be related, tally, conform, correlate, dovetail, harmonize ...*The two maps of London correspond closely...* **OPPOSITE** differ
2 = <u>communicate</u>, write, keep in touch, exchange letters ...*We corresponded regularly for years...*

correspondence 1 = <u>communication</u>, writing, contact ...*The judges' decision is final and no correspondence will be entered into...*
2 = <u>letters</u>, post, mail ...*He always replied to his correspondence promptly...*
3 = <u>relation</u>, match, agreement, fitness, comparison, harmony, coincidence, similarity, analogy, correlation, conformity, comparability, concurrence, congruity ...*correspondences between Eastern religions and Christianity...*

correspondent 1 = <u>reporter</u>, journalist, contributor, special correspondent, journo (*slang*), hack ...*Here is a special report from our Europe correspondent...*
2 = <u>letter writer</u>, pen friend *or* pen pal ...*He wasn't a good correspondent and only wrote to me once a year...*

corresponding = <u>equivalent</u>, matching, similar, related, correspondent, identical, complementary, synonymous, reciprocal, analogous, interrelated, correlative

corridor = <u>passage</u>, alley, aisle, hallway, passageway

corroborate = <u>support</u>, establish, confirm, document, sustain, back up, endorse, ratify, validate, bear out, substantiate, authenticate **OPPOSITE** contradict

corrode = <u>eat away</u>, waste, consume, corrupt, deteriorate, erode, rust, gnaw, oxidize

corrosive 1 = <u>corroding</u>, wasting, caustic, vitriolic, acrid, erosive ...*Sodium and sulphur are highly corrosive elements...*
2 = <u>cutting</u>, biting, incisive, virulent, sarcastic, caustic, venomous, vitriolic, trenchant, mordant ...*She had a corrosive sense of humour...*

corrugated = <u>furrowed</u>, channelled, ridged, grooved, wrinkled, creased, fluted, rumpled, puckered, crinkled

corrupt ADJECTIVE **1** = dishonest = furrowed, bent (*slang*), crooked (*informal*), rotten, shady (*informal*), fraudulent, unscrupulous, unethical, venal, unprincipled ...*corrupt police officers who took bribes...* OPPOSITE honest
2 = depraved, abandoned, vicious, degenerate, debased, demoralized, profligate, dishonoured, defiled, dissolute ...*the flamboyant and morally corrupt court of Charles the Second...*
3 = distorted, doctored, altered, falsified ...*a corrupt text of a poem by Milton...*
VERB **1** = bribe, square, fix (*informal*), buy off, suborn, grease (someone's) palm (*slang*) ...*The ability to corrupt politicians, policemen, and judges was fundamental to Mafia operations...*
2 = deprave, pervert, subvert, debase, demoralize, debauch ...*Cruelty depraves and corrupts...* OPPOSITE reform
3 = distort, doctor, tamper with ...*Computer hackers often break into important sites to corrupt files...*

corrupted 1 = depraved, abandoned, perverted, warped, degenerate, debased, demoralized, profligate, dishonoured, defiled, debauched, reprobate ...*the corrupted, brutal Duvalier regime...*
2 = contaminated, soiled, dirtied, infected, spoiled, stained, decayed, rotten, polluted, tainted, tarnished, sullied, defiled, adulterated, vitiated, putrefied ...*The body's T cells kill cells corrupted by viruses...*
3 = distorted, altered ...*The computer files had been corrupted during the upgrade...*

corruption 1 = dishonesty, fraud, fiddling (*informal*), graft (*informal*), bribery, extortion, profiteering, breach of trust, venality, shady dealings (*informal*), shadiness ...*He faces 54 charges of corruption and tax evasion...*
2 = depravity, vice, evil, degradation, perversion, decadence, impurity, wickedness, degeneration, immorality, iniquity, profligacy, viciousness, sinfulness, turpitude, baseness ...*It was a society sinking into corruption and vice...*
3 = distortion, doctoring, falsification ...*The name 'Santa Claus' is a corruption of 'Saint Nicholas'...*

corset = girdle, bodice, foundation garment, panty girdle, stays (*rare*)

cortege = procession, train, entourage, cavalcade, retinue, suite

cosmetic = superficial, surface, touching-up, nonessential

cosmic 1 = extraterrestrial, stellar ...*Inside the heliosphere we are screened from cosmic rays...*
2 = universal, general, omnipresent, all-embracing, overarching ...*There are cosmic laws governing our world...*
3 = vast, huge, immense, infinite, grandiose, limitless, measureless ...*It was an understatement of cosmic proportions...*

cosmonaut = astronaut, spaceman, space pilot, space cadet

cosmopolitan = sophisticated, worldly, cultured, refined, cultivated, urbane, well-travelled, worldly-wise OPPOSITE unsophisticated

cosmos = universe, world, creation, macrocosm

cosset = pamper, baby, pet, coddle, mollycoddle, wrap up in cotton wool (*informal*)

cost NOUN **1** = price, worth, expense, rate, charge, figure, damage (*informal*), amount, payment, expenditure, outlay ...*The cost of a loaf of bread has increased five-fold...*
2 = loss, suffering, damage, injury, penalty, hurt, expense, harm, sacrifice, deprivation, detriment ...*a man who always looks after 'number one', whatever the cost to others...*
PLURAL NOUN = expenses, spending, expenditure, overheads, outgoings, outlay, budget ...*The company admits its costs are still too high...*
VERB **1** = sell at, come to, set (someone) back (*informal*), be priced at, command a price of ...*The course is limited to 12 people and costs £50...*
2 = lose, deprive of, cheat of ...*The operation saved his life, but cost him his sight...*
PHRASES **at all costs** = no matter what, regardless, whatever happens, at any price, come what may, without fail ...*We must avoid any further delay at all costs...*

costly 1 = expensive, dear, stiff, excessive, steep (*informal*), highly-priced, exorbitant, extortionate ...*Having curtains professionally made can be costly...* OPPOSITE inexpensive
2 = splendid, rich, valuable, precious, gorgeous, lavish, luxurious, sumptuous, priceless, opulent ...*the exceptionally beautiful and costly cloths made in northern Italy...*
3 = damaging, disastrous, harmful, catastrophic, loss-making, ruinous, deleterious ...*If you follow the procedures correctly you will avoid costly mistakes...*

costume = outfit, dress, clothing, get-up (*informal*), uniform, ensemble, robes, livery, apparel, attire, garb, national dress

cosy 1 = comfortable, homely, warm, intimate, snug, comfy (*informal*), sheltered ...*Guests can relax in the cosy bar before dinner...*
2 = snug, warm, secure, comfortable, sheltered, comfy (*informal*), tucked up, cuddled up, snuggled down ...*I was lying cosy in bed with the Sunday papers...*
3 = intimate, friendly, informal ...*a cosy chat between friends...*

coterie = clique, group, set, camp, circle, gang, outfit (*informal*), posse (*informal*), cabal

cottage = cabin, lodge, hut, shack, chalet, but-and-ben (*Scot.*), cot

couch NOUN = sofa, bed, chesterfield, ottoman, settee, divan, chaise longue, day bed ...*He lay down on the couch...*
VERB = express, word, frame, phrase, utter, set forth ...*This time his proposal was couched as an ultimatum...*

cough VERB = clear your throat, bark, hawk, hack, hem ...*He began to cough violently...*
NOUN = frog *or* tickle in your throat, bark, hack ...*He put a hand over his mouth to cover a cough...*

PHRASES **cough something up** (*Informal*) = <u>fork out</u>, deliver, hand over, surrender, come across (*informal*), shell out (*informal*), ante up (*informal, chiefly U.S.*) ...*I'll have to cough up $10,000 a year for private tuition...*

council 1 = <u>committee</u>, governing body, board, panel, quango ...*The city council has voted almost unanimously in favour of the proposal...*
2 = <u>governing body</u>, house, parliament, congress, cabinet, ministry, diet, panel, assembly, chamber, convention, synod, conclave, convocation, conference ...*The powers of the King had been handed over temporarily to a council of ministers...*

counsel **NOUN** 1 = <u>advice</u>, information, warning, direction, suggestion, recommendation, caution, guidance, admonition ...*He had always been able to count on her wise counsel...*
2 = <u>legal adviser</u>, lawyer, attorney, solicitor, advocate, barrister ...*The defence counsel warned that the judge should stop the trial...*
VERB = <u>advise</u>, recommend, advocate, prescribe, warn, urge, caution, instruct, exhort, admonish ...*My advisors counselled me to do nothing...*

count **VERB** 1 *often with* **up** = <u>add (up)</u>, total, reckon (up), tot up, score, check, estimate, calculate, compute, tally, number, enumerate, cast up ...*I counted the money. It came to more than five hundred pounds...*
2 = <u>matter</u>, be important, cut any ice (*informal*), carry weight, tell, rate, weigh, signify, enter into consideration ...*It's as if your opinions just don't count...*
3 = <u>consider</u>, judge, regard, deem, think of, rate, esteem, look upon, impute ...*I count him as one of my best friends...*
4 = <u>include</u>, number among, take into account *or* consideration ...*The years before their arrival in prison are not counted as part of their sentence...*
NOUN = <u>calculation</u>, poll, reckoning, sum, tally, numbering, computation, enumeration ...*At the last count the police had 247 people in custody...*
PHRASES **count on** *or* **upon something** *or* **someone** = <u>depend on</u>, trust, rely on, bank on, take for granted, lean on, reckon on, take on trust, believe in, pin your faith on ...*We're all counting on you to do the right thing... ...I'm counting on your support...*
◆ **count someone out** (*Informal*) = <u>leave out</u>, except, exclude, disregard, pass over, leave out of account ...*If it means working extra hours, you can count me out...*

countenance **VERB** = <u>tolerate</u>, sanction, endorse, condone, support, encourage, approve, endure, brook, stand for (*informal*), hack (*slang*), put up with (*informal*) ...*He would not countenance his daughter marrying while she was still a student...*
NOUN (*Literary*) = <u>face</u>, features, expression, look, appearance, aspect, visage, mien, physiognomy ...*He met each inquiry with an impassive countenance...*

counter **VERB** 1 = <u>oppose</u>, meet, block, resist, offset, parry, deflect, repel, rebuff, fend off, counteract, ward off, stave off, repulse, obviate, hold at bay ...*They discussed a plan to counter the effects of such a blockade...*
2 = <u>retaliate</u>, return, answer, reply, respond, come back, retort, hit back, rejoin, strike back ...*The union countered with letters rebutting the company's claim...* **OPPOSITE** yield
ADVERB = <u>opposite to</u>, against, versus, conversely, in defiance of, at variance with, contrarily, contrariwise ...*Their findings ran counter to all expectations...* **OPPOSITE** in accordance with
ADJECTIVE = <u>opposing</u>, conflicting, opposed, contrasting, opposite, contrary, adverse, contradictory, obverse, against ...*These charges and counter charges are being exchanged at an important time...* **OPPOSITE** similar

counteract 1 = <u>act against</u>, check, defeat, prevent, oppose, resist, frustrate, foil, thwart, hinder, cross ...*Many countries within the region are planning measures to counteract a missile attack...*
2 = <u>offset</u>, negate, neutralize, invalidate, counterbalance, annul, obviate, countervail ...*pills to counteract high blood pressure...*

counterbalance = <u>offset</u>, balance out, compensate for, make up for, counterpoise, countervail

counterfeit **ADJECTIVE** = <u>fake</u>, copied, false, forged, imitation, bogus, simulated, sham, fraudulent, feigned, spurious, ersatz, phoney *or* phony (*informal*), pseud *or* pseudo (*informal*) ...*He admitted possessing and delivering counterfeit currency...* **OPPOSITE** genuine
NOUN = <u>fake</u>, copy, reproduction, imitation, sham, forgery, phoney *or* phony (*informal*), fraud ...*Levi Strauss says counterfeits of the company's jeans are flooding Europe...* **OPPOSITE** the real thing
VERB = <u>fake</u>, copy, forge, imitate, simulate, sham, fabricate, feign ...*He is alleged to have counterfeited video cassettes...*

counterpart = <u>opposite number</u>, equal, twin, equivalent, peer, match, fellow, mate

countless = <u>innumerable</u>, legion, infinite, myriad, untold, limitless, incalculable, immeasurable, numberless, uncounted, multitudinous, endless, measureless **OPPOSITE** limited

country **NOUN** 1 = <u>nation</u>, state, land, commonwealth, kingdom, realm, sovereign state, people ...*the disputed boundary between the two countries...*
2 = <u>people</u>, community, nation, society, citizens, voters, inhabitants, grass roots, electors, populace, citizenry, public ...*Seventy per cent of this country is opposed to blood sports...*
3 = <u>countryside</u>, rural areas, provinces, outdoors, sticks (*informal*), farmland, outback (*Austral. & N.Z.*), the middle of nowhere, green belt, wide open spaces (*informal*), backwoods, back country (*U.S.*), the back of beyond, bush (*N.Z. & S. African*), backlands (*U.S.*), boondocks (*U.S. slang*) ...*They live somewhere way out in the country...* **OPPOSITE** town
4 = <u>territory</u>, part, land, region, terrain ...*This is some of the best walking country in the district...*
5 = <u>native land</u>, nationality, homeland, motherland, fatherland, patria (*Latin*) ...*I am willing to serve my*

country...

ADJECTIVE = <u>rural</u>, pastoral, rustic, agrarian, bucolic, Arcadian ...*I want to live a simple country life...*
OPPOSITE urban

(*Related Words*)

adjectives : pastoral, rural

► **WORD POWER SUPPLEMENT countries**

countryman **1** = <u>compatriot</u>, fellow citizen ...*He beat his fellow countryman in the final...*
2 = <u>yokel</u>, farmer, peasant, provincial, hick (*informal, chiefly U.S. & Canad.*), rustic, swain, hillbilly, bucolic, country dweller, hayseed (*U.S. & Canad. informal*), clodhopper (*informal*), cockie (*N.Z.*), (country) bumpkin ...*He had the red face of a countryman...*

countryside = <u>country</u>, rural areas, outdoors, farmland, outback (*Austral. & N.Z.*), green belt, wide open spaces (*informal*), sticks (*informal*)

county **NOUN** = <u>province</u>, district, shire ...*He is living now in his mother's home county of Oxfordshire...*
ADJECTIVE (*Informal*) = <u>upper-class</u>, upper-crust (*informal*), tweedy, plummy (*informal*), green-wellie, huntin', shootin', and fishin' (*informal*) ...*They were all upper-crust ladies, pillars of the county set...*

► **WORD POWER SUPPLEMENT counties**

coup = <u>masterstroke</u>, feat, stunt, action, stroke, exploit, manoeuvre, deed, accomplishment, tour de force (*French*), stratagem, stroke of genius

coup d'état = <u>overthrow</u>, takeover, coup, rebellion, putsch, seizure of power, palace revolution

couple **NOUN** = <u>pair</u>, two, brace, span (*of horses or oxen*), duo, twain (*archaic*), twosome ...*There are a couple of police officers standing guard...*
PHRASES **couple something to something** = <u>link to</u>, connect to, pair with, unite with, join to, hitch to, buckle to, clasp to, yoke to, conjoin to ...*The engine is coupled to a semiautomatic gearbox...*

coupon = <u>slip</u>, ticket, certificate, token, voucher, card, detachable portion

courage = <u>bravery</u>, nerve, fortitude, boldness, balls (*taboo slang*), bottle (*Brit. slang*), resolution, daring, guts (*informal*), pluck, grit, heroism, mettle, firmness, gallantry, valour, spunk (*informal*), fearlessness, intrepidity **OPPOSITE** cowardice

courageous = <u>brave</u>, daring, bold, plucky, hardy, heroic, gritty, stalwart, fearless, resolute, gallant, audacious, intrepid, valiant, indomitable, dauntless, ballsy (*taboo slang*), lion-hearted, valorous, stouthearted **OPPOSITE** cowardly

courier **1** = <u>messenger</u>, runner, carrier, bearer, herald, envoy, emissary ...*The cheques were delivered to the bank by a private courier...*
2 = <u>guide</u>, representative, escort, conductor, chaperon, cicerone, dragoman ...*He was a travel courier...*

course **NOUN** **1** = <u>route</u>, way, line, road, track, channel, direction, path, passage, trail, orbit, tack, trajectory ...*For nearly four hours we maintained our course northwards...*
2 = <u>procedure</u>, plan, policy, programme, method, conduct, behaviour, manner, mode, regimen

...Resignation is the only course left open to him...
3 = <u>progression</u>, order, unfolding, development, movement, advance, progress, flow, sequence, succession, continuity, advancement, furtherance, march ...*a series of naval battles which altered the course of history...*
4 = <u>classes</u>, course of study, programme, schedule, lectures, curriculum, studies ...*I'll shortly be beginning a course on the modern novel...*
5 = <u>racecourse</u>, race, circuit, cinder track, lap ...*On the Tour de France, 200 cyclists cover a course of 2,000 miles...*
6 = <u>period</u>, time, duration, term, passing, sweep, passage, lapse ...*In the course of the 1930s steel production in Britain approximately doubled...*
VERB **1** = <u>run</u>, flow, stream, gush, race, speed, surge, dash, tumble, scud, move apace ...*The tears coursed down his cheeks...*
2 = <u>hunt</u>, follow, chase, pursue ...*New muzzling regulations for dogs coursing hares have been introduced...*
PHRASES **in due course** = <u>in time</u>, finally, eventually, in the end, sooner or later, in the course of time ...*I hope that it will be possible in due course...*
♦ **of course** = <u>naturally</u>, certainly, obviously, definitely, undoubtedly, needless to say, without a doubt, indubitably ...*There'll be the usual inquiry, of course...*

court **NOUN** **1** = <u>law court</u>, bar, bench, tribunal, court of justice, seat of judgment ...*At this rate, you could find yourself in court for assault...*
2 = <u>palace</u>, hall, castle, manor ...*She came to visit England, where she was presented at the court of James I...*
3 = <u>royal household</u>, train, suite, attendants, entourage, retinue, cortege ...*tales of King Arthur and his court...*
VERB **1** = <u>cultivate</u>, seek, flatter, solicit, pander to, curry favour with, fawn upon ...*Britain's political parties are courting the vote of the lesbian and gay community...*
2 = <u>invite</u>, seek, attract, prompt, provoke, bring about, incite ...*If he thinks he can remain in power by force he is courting disaster...*
3 = <u>woo</u>, go (out) with, go steady with (*informal*), date, chase, pursue, take out, make love to, run after, walk out with, keep company with, pay court to, set your cap at, pay your addresses to ...*I was courting him at 19 and married him when I was 21...*

courteous = <u>polite</u>, civil, respectful, mannerly, polished, refined, gracious, gallant, affable, urbane, courtly, well-bred, well-mannered **OPPOSITE** discourteous

courtesan (*History*) = <u>mistress</u>, prostitute, whore, call girl, working girl (*facetious slang*), kept woman, harlot, paramour, scarlet woman, fille de joie (*French*)

courtesy **1** = <u>politeness</u>, grace, good manners, civility, gallantry, good breeding, graciousness, affability, urbanity, courtliness ...*He is a gentleman who behaves with the utmost courtesy towards ladies...*

2 = <u>favour</u>, consideration, generosity, kindness, indulgence, benevolence ...*If you're not coming, at least do me the courtesy of letting me know...*

courtier = <u>attendant</u>, follower, squire, train-bearer

courtly = <u>ceremonious</u>, civil, formal, obliging, refined, polite, dignified, stately, aristocratic, gallant, affable, urbane, decorous, chivalrous, highbred

courtship = <u>wooing</u>, courting, suit, romance, engagement, keeping company

courtyard = <u>yard</u>, square, piazza, quadrangle, area, plaza, enclosure, cloister, quad (*informal*), peristyle

cove = <u>bay</u>, sound, creek, inlet, bayou, firth *or* frith (*Scot.*), anchorage

covenant 1 = <u>promise</u>, contract, agreement, commitment, arrangement, treaty, pledge, bargain, convention, pact, compact, concordat, trust ...*the United Nations covenant on civil and political rights...* **2** (*Law*) = <u>deed</u>, contract, bond ...*If you make regular gifts through a covenant we can reclaim the income tax...*

cover VERB **1** = <u>conceal</u>, cover up, screen, hide, shade, curtain, mask, disguise, obscure, hood, veil, cloak, shroud, camouflage, enshroud ...*the black patch which covered his left eye...* OPPOSITE> reveal **2** = <u>clothe</u>, invest, dress, wrap, envelop ...*He covered his head with a turban...* OPPOSITE> uncover **3** = <u>overlay</u>, blanket, eclipse, mantle, canopy, overspread, layer ...*The clouds had spread and nearly covered the entire sky...* **4** = <u>coat</u>, cake, plaster, smear, envelop, spread, encase, daub, overspread ...*She was soaking wet and covered with mud...* **5** = <u>submerge</u>, flood, engulf, overrun, wash over ...*Nearly a foot of water covered the streets...* **6** = <u>travel over</u>, cross, traverse, pass through *or* over, range ...*It would not be easy to cover ten miles on that amount of petrol...* **7** = <u>protect</u>, guard, defend, shelter, shield, watch over ...*You make a run for it and I'll cover you...* **8** = <u>insure</u>, compensate, provide for, offset, balance, make good, make up for, take account of, counterbalance ...*These items are not covered by your medical insurance...* **9** = <u>deal with</u>, refer to, provide for, take account of, include, involve, contain, embrace, incorporate, comprise, embody, encompass, comprehend ...*The law covers four categories of experiments...* OPPOSITE> exclude **10** = <u>consider</u>, deal with, examine, investigate, , detail, describe, survey, refer to, tell of, recount ...*In this lecture, I aim to cover several topics...* **11** = <u>report on</u>, write about, commentate on, give an account of, relate, tell of, narrate, write up ...*He was sent to Italy to cover the World Cup...* **12** = <u>pay for</u>, fund, provide for, offset, be enough for ...*Please send £1.50 to cover postage...* NOUN **1** = <u>protection</u>, shelter, shield, refuge, defence, woods, guard, sanctuary, camouflage, hiding place, undergrowth, concealment ...*There were barren wastes of field with no trees and no cover...* **2** = <u>insurance</u>, payment, protection, compensation,

indemnity, reimbursement ...*Make sure that the firm's accident cover is adequate...* **3** = <u>covering</u>, case, top, cap, coating, envelope, lid, canopy, sheath, wrapper, awning ...*Put a polythene cover over it to protect it from dust...* **4** = <u>bedclothes</u>, bedding, sheets, blankets, quilt, duvet, eiderdown ...*He groaned and slid farther under the covers...* **5** = <u>jacket</u>, case, binding, wrapper ...*a small book with a green cover...* **6** = <u>disguise</u>, front, screen, mask, cover-up, veil, cloak, façade, pretence, pretext, window-dressing, smoke screen ...*The grocery store was just a cover for their betting shop...* PHRASES **cover for someone** = <u>stand in for</u>, take over, substitute, relieve, double for, fill in for, hold the fort for (*informal*) ...*She did not have enough nurses to cover for those who were off sick...* ◆ **cover something up** = <u>conceal</u>, hide, suppress, repress, keep secret, whitewash (*informal*), hush up, sweep under the carpet, draw a veil over, keep silent about, cover your tracks, keep dark, feign ignorance about, keep under your hat (*informal*) ...*They knew they had done something wrong and lied to cover it up...*

coverage = <u>reporting</u>, treatment, analysis, description, reportage

covering NOUN = <u>cover</u>, protection, coating, overlay, housing, casing, top, clothing, wrapping, wrap, shelter, layer, blanket, wrapper ...*Sawdust was used as a hygienic floor covering...* ADJECTIVE = <u>explanatory</u>, accompanying, introductory, descriptive ...*Include a covering letter with your CV...*

covert = <u>secret</u>, private, hidden, disguised, concealed, veiled, sly, clandestine, underhand, unsuspected, surreptitious, stealthy

cover-up = <u>concealment</u>, conspiracy, whitewash (*informal*), complicity, front, smoke screen

covet = <u>long for</u>, desire, fancy (*informal*), envy, crave, aspire to, yearn for, thirst for, begrudge, hanker after, lust after, set your heart on, have your eye on, would give your eyeteeth for

cow = <u>intimidate</u>, daunt, frighten, scare, bully, dismay, awe, subdue, unnerve, overawe, terrorize, browbeat, psych out (*informal*), dishearten

coward = <u>wimp</u>, chicken (*slang*), scaredy-cat (*informal*), sneak (*informal*), pussy (*slang, chiefly U.S.*), yellow-belly (*slang*)

cowardice = <u>faint-heartedness</u>, weakness, softness, fearfulness, pusillanimity, spinelessness, timorousness

cowardly = <u>faint-hearted</u>, scared, spineless, gutless (*informal*), base, soft, yellow (*informal*), weak, chicken (*slang*), shrinking, fearful, craven, abject, dastardly, timorous, weak-kneed (*informal*), pusillanimous, chicken-hearted, lily-livered, white-livered, sookie (*N.Z.*) OPPOSITE> brave

cowboy = <u>cowhand</u>, drover, herder, rancher, stockman, cattleman, herdsman, gaucho (*S. American*), buckaroo (*U.S.*), ranchero (*U.S.*), cowpuncher (*U.S. informal*), broncobuster (*U.S.*), wrangler (*U.S.*)

cower = <u>cringe</u>, shrink, tremble, crouch, flinch, quail, draw back, grovel

coy 1 = <u>modest</u>, retiring, shy, shrinking, arch, timid, self-effacing, demure, flirtatious, bashful, prudish, skittish, coquettish, kittenish, overmodest ...*She was demure without being coy...* OPPOSITE bold

2 = <u>uncommunicative</u>, mum, secretive, reserved, quiet, silent, evasive, taciturn, unforthcoming, tight-lipped, close-lipped ...*The hotel are understandably coy about the incident...*

crack VERB **1** = <u>break</u>, split, burst, snap, fracture, splinter, craze, rive ...*A gas main had cracked under my neighbour's garage... ...Crack the salt crust and you will find the skin just peels off the fish...*

2 = <u>snap</u>, ring, crash, burst, explode, crackle, pop, detonate ...*Thunder cracked in the sky...*

3 (*Informal*) = <u>hit</u>, clip (*informal*), slap, smack, thump, buffet, clout (*informal*), cuff, whack, wallop (*informal*), chop ...*She drew back her fist and cracked him on the jaw... ...He cracked his head on the pavement and was knocked out...*

4 = <u>break</u>, cleave ...*Crack the eggs into a bowl...*

5 = <u>solve</u>, work out, resolve, interpret, clarify, clear up, fathom, decipher, suss (out) (*slang*), get to the bottom of, disentangle, elucidate, get the answer to ...*He has finally cracked the code after years of painstaking research...*

6 = <u>break down</u>, collapse, yield, give in, give way, succumb, lose control, be overcome, go to pieces ...*She's calm and strong, and will not crack under pressure...*

NOUN **1** = <u>break</u>, chink, gap, breach, fracture, rift, cleft, crevice, fissure, cranny, interstice ...*She watched him though a crack in the curtains...*

2 = <u>split</u>, break, chip, breach, fracture, rupture, cleft ...*The plate had a crack in it...*

3 = <u>snap</u>, pop, crash, burst, explosion, clap, report ...*Suddenly there was a loud crack and glass flew into the air...*

4 (*Informal*) = <u>blow</u>, slap, smack, thump, buffet, clout (*informal*), cuff, whack, wallop (*informal*), clip (*informal*) ...*He took a crack on the head during the game...*

5 (*Informal*) = <u>attempt</u>, go (*informal*), try, shot, opportunity, stab (*informal*) ...*I'd love to have a crack at the title next year...*

6 (*Informal*) = <u>joke</u>, dig, insult, gag (*informal*), quip, jibe, wisecrack, witticism, funny remark, smart-alecky remark ...*He made a nasty crack about her weight...*

ADJECTIVE (*Slang*) = <u>first-class</u>, choice, excellent, ace, elite, superior, world-class, first-rate, hand-picked ...*He is said to be a crack shot...*

PHRASES **crack up** (*Informal*) **1** = <u>have a breakdown</u>, collapse, break down, go crazy (*informal*), go berserk, freak out (*informal*), go to pieces, go ape (*slang*), fly off the handle (*informal*), come apart at the seams (*informal*), throw a wobbly (*slang*), go off the deep end (*informal*), go out of your mind, flip your lid (*slang*), go off your rocker (*slang*), go off your head (*slang*) ...*He's going to crack up if he doesn't take a break soon...*

2 = <u>burst out laughing</u>, laugh, fall about (laughing), guffaw, roar with laughter, be in stitches, split your sides ...*We all just cracked up when he told us...*

crackdown = <u>clampdown</u>, crushing, repression, suppression

cracked ADJECTIVE **1** = <u>broken</u>, damaged, split, chipped, flawed, faulty, crazed, defective, imperfect, fissured ...*a cracked mirror...*

2 (*Informal*) = <u>crazy</u>, nuts (*slang*), eccentric, nutty (*slang*), touched, bats (*slang*) (*informal*), daft (*informal*), batty (*slang*), insane, loony (*slang*), off-the-wall (*slang*), oddball (*informal*), loopy (*informal*), crackpot (*informal*), out to lunch (*informal*), round the bend (*slang*), out of your mind, gonzo (*slang*), doolally (*slang*), off your trolley (*slang*), off the air (*Austral. slang*), round the twist (*Brit. slang*), up the pole (*informal*), off your rocker (*slang*), crackbrained, off your head or nut (*slang*), wacko or whacko (*informal*) ...*Everyone in our family's a bit cracked...*

PHRASES **cracked up** = <u>overrated</u>, exaggerated, blown up, hyped (up), puffed up, overpraised ...*Package holidays are not always all they're cracked up to be...*

cradle NOUN **1** = <u>crib</u>, cot, Moses basket, bassinet ...*The baby sleeps in the cradle upstairs...*

2 = <u>birthplace</u>, beginning, source, spring, origin, fount, fountainhead, wellspring ...*New York is the cradle of capitalism...*

VERB = <u>hold</u>, support, rock, nurse, nestle ...*I cradled her in my arms...*

craft 1 = <u>vessel</u>, boat, ship, plane, aircraft, spacecraft, barque ...*Cannabis smuggling by small craft to remote sites is rising...*

2 = <u>occupation</u>, work, calling, business, line, trade, employment, pursuit, vocation, handiwork, handicraft ...*All kinds of traditional crafts are preserved here...*

3 = <u>skill</u>, art, ability, technique, know-how (*informal*), expertise, knack, aptitude, artistry, dexterity, workmanship ...*Lilyanne learned her craft of cooking from her grandmother...*

4 = <u>cunning</u>, ingenuity, guile, cleverness, scheme, subtlety, deceit, ruse, artifice, trickery, wiles, duplicity, subterfuge, contrivance, shrewdness, artfulness ...*They defeated their enemies through craft and cunning...*

craftsman = <u>skilled worker</u>, artisan, master, maker, wright, technician, artificer, smith

craftsmanship = <u>workmanship</u>, technique, expertise, mastery, artistry

crafty = <u>cunning</u>, scheming, sly, devious, knowing, designing, sharp, calculating, subtle, tricky, shrewd, astute, fraudulent, canny, wily, insidious, artful, foxy, deceitful, duplicitous, tricksy, guileful OPPOSITE open

crag = <u>rock</u>, peak, bluff, pinnacle, tor, aiguille

craggy = <u>rocky</u>, broken, rough, rugged, uneven, jagged, stony, precipitous, jaggy (*Scot.*)

cram 1 = <u>stuff</u>, force, jam, ram, shove, compress, compact ...*She pulled off her school hat and crammed it into a wastebasket...*

2 = <u>pack</u>, fill, stuff ...*She crammed her mouth with* nuts...

3 = <u>squeeze</u>, press, crowd, pack, crush, pack in, fill to overflowing, overfill, overcrowd ...*We crammed into my car and set off...*

4 = <u>study</u>, revise, swot, bone up (*informal*), grind, swot up, mug up (*slang*) ...*She was cramming hard for her exam...*

cramp¹ = <u>spasm</u>, pain, ache, contraction, pang, stiffness, stitch, convulsion, twinge, crick, shooting pain ...*She started getting stomach cramps in the morning...*

cramp² = <u>restrict</u>, hamper, inhibit, hinder, check, handicap, confine, hamstring, constrain, obstruct, impede, shackle, circumscribe, encumber ...*Like more and more women, she believes marriage would cramp her style...*

cramped = <u>restricted</u>, confined, overcrowded, crowded, packed, narrow, squeezed, uncomfortable, awkward, closed in, congested, circumscribed, jammed in, hemmed in OPPOSITE〉 spacious

crank (*Informal*) = <u>eccentric</u>, freak (*Informal*), oddball (*informal*), weirdo or weirdie (*informal*), case (*informal*), character (*informal*), nut (*slang*), flake (*slang, chiefly U.S.*), screwball (*slang, chiefly U.S. & Canad.*), odd fish (*informal*), kook (*U.S. & Canad. informal*), queer fish (*Brit. informal*), rum customer (*Brit. slang*), wacko or whacko (*informal*)

cranky (*U.S., Canad., & Irish informal*) = <u>eccentric</u>, wacky (*slang*), oddball (*informal*), freakish, odd, strange, funny (*informal*), bizarre, peculiar, queer (*informal*), rum (*Brit. slang*), quirky, idiosyncratic, off-the-wall (*slang*), freaky (*slang*), outré, wacko or whacko (*informal*)

cranny = <u>crevice</u>, opening, hole, crack, gap, breach, rift, nook, cleft, chink, fissure, interstice

crash NOUN **1** = <u>collision</u>, accident, smash, wreck, prang (*informal*), bump, pile-up (*informal*), smash-up ...*His elder son was killed in a car crash a few years ago...*

2 = <u>smash</u>, clash, boom, smashing, bang, thunder, thump, racket, din, clatter, clattering, thud, clang ...*Two people in the flat recalled hearing a loud crash about 1.30am...*

3 = <u>collapse</u>, failure, depression, ruin, bankruptcy, downfall ...*He predicted correctly that there was going to be a stock market crash...*

VERB **1** = <u>fall</u>, pitch, plunge, sprawl, topple, lurch, hurtle, come a cropper (*informal*), overbalance, fall headlong ...*He lost his balance and crashed to the floor...*

2 = <u>plunge</u>, hurtle, precipitate yourself ...*We heard the sound of an animal crashing through the undergrowth...*

3 = <u>smash</u>, break, break up, shatter, fragment, fracture, shiver, disintegrate, splinter, dash to pieces ...*Her glass fell on the floor and crashed into a thousand pieces...*

4 = <u>collapse</u>, fail, go under, be ruined, go bust (*informal*), fold up, go broke (*informal*), go to the wall, go belly up (*informal*), smash, fold ...*When the market crashed they assumed the deal would be cancelled...*

ADJECTIVE = <u>intensive</u>, concentrated, immediate, urgent, round-the-clock, emergency ...*I might take a crash course in typing...*

PHRASES **crash into** = <u>collide with</u>, hit, bump into, bang into, run into, drive into, plough into, hurtle into ...*His car crashed into the rear of a van...*

crass = <u>insensitive</u>, stupid, gross, blundering, dense, coarse, witless, boorish, obtuse, unrefined, asinine, indelicate, oafish, lumpish, doltish OPPOSITE〉 sensitive

crate NOUN = <u>container</u>, case, box, packing case, tea chest ...*A crane was already unloading crates and pallets...*

VERB = <u>box</u>, pack, enclose, pack up, encase, case ...*The plane had been dismantled, crated, and shipped to London...*

crater = <u>hollow</u>, hole, depression, dip, cavity, shell hole

crave **1** = <u>long for</u>, yearn for, hanker after, be dying for, want, need, require, desire, fancy (*informal*), hope for, cry out for (*informal*), thirst for, pine for, lust after, pant for, sigh for, set your heart on, hunger after, eat your heart out over, would give your eyeteeth for ...*There may be certain times of day when smokers crave a cigarette...*

2 (*Informal*) = <u>beg</u>, ask for, seek, petition, pray for, plead for, solicit, implore, beseech, entreat, supplicate ...*If I may crave your lordship's indulgence, I would like to consult my client...*

craven = <u>cowardly</u>, weak, scared, fearful, abject, dastardly, mean-spirited, timorous, pusillanimous, chicken-hearted, yellow (*informal*), lily-livered

craving = <u>longing</u>, hope, desire, urge, yen (*informal*), hunger, appetite, ache, lust, yearning, thirst, hankering

crawl VERB = <u>creep</u>, slither, go on all fours, move on hands and knees, inch, drag, wriggle, writhe, move at a snail's pace, worm your way, advance slowly, pull or drag yourself along ...*I began to crawl on my hands and knees towards the door...* OPPOSITE〉 run

PHRASES **be crawling with something** = <u>be full of</u>, teem with, be alive with, swarm with, be overrun with (*slang*), be lousy with ...*This place is crawling with police...* ◆ **crawl to someone** = <u>grovel</u>, creep, cringe, fawn, pander to, suck up to someone (*slang*), toady, truckle, lick someone's boots (*slang*), humble yourself, abase yourself ...*I'd have to crawl to her to keep my job...*

craze = <u>fad</u>, thing, fashion, trend, passion, rage, enthusiasm, mode, vogue, novelty, preoccupation, mania, infatuation, the latest thing (*informal*)

crazed = <u>mad</u>, crazy, raving, insane, lunatic, demented, unbalanced, deranged, berserk, unhinged, berko (*Austral. slang*), off the air (*Austral. slang*)

crazy **1** = <u>strange</u>, odd, bizarre, fantastic, silly, weird, ridiculous, outrageous, peculiar, eccentric, rum (*Brit. slang*), oddball (*informal*), cockamamie (*slang, chiefly U.S.*), wacko or whacko (*informal*), off the air (*Austral. slang*) ...*I ignored the crazy guy seated beside me on the bus...* OPPOSITE〉 normal

2 (*Informal*) = <u>ridiculous</u>, wild, absurd, inappropriate, foolish, ludicrous, irresponsible, unrealistic, unwise, senseless, preposterous, potty (*Brit. informal*), short-sighted, unworkable, foolhardy, idiotic, nonsensical, half-baked (*informal*), inane, fatuous, ill-conceived, quixotic, imprudent, impracticable, cockeyed (*informal*), cockamamie (*slang, chiefly U.S.*) ...*I know it sounds a crazy idea, but hear me out...* OPPOSITE sensible

3 = insane, mad, unbalanced, deranged, touched, cracked (*slang*), mental (*slang*), nuts (*slang*), barking (*slang*), daft (*informal*), batty (*slang*), crazed, lunatic, demented, cuckoo (*informal*), barmy (*slang*), off-the-wall (*slang*), off the air (*Austral. slang*), nutty (*slang*), potty (*Brit. informal*), berserk, delirious, bonkers (*slang, chiefly Brit.*), idiotic, unhinged, loopy (*informal*), crackpot (*informal*), out to lunch (*informal*), round the bend (*slang*), barking mad (*slang*), out of your mind, maniacal, not all there (*informal*), doolally (*slang*), off your head (*slang*), off your trolley (*slang*), round the twist (*Brit. slang*), up the pole (*informal*), of unsound mind, not right in the head, off your rocker (*slang*), not the full shilling (*informal*), a bit lacking upstairs (*informal*), as daft as a brush (*informal, chiefly Brit.*), mad as a hatter, mad as a March hare, nutty as a fruitcake (*slang*) ...*If I think about it too much, I'll go crazy... ...some crazy man who had killed his wife and family before committing suicide...* OPPOSITE sane

4 = fanatical, wild (*informal*), mad, devoted, enthusiastic, passionate, hysterical, ardent, very keen, zealous, smitten, infatuated, enamoured ...*He's crazy about football...* OPPOSITE uninterested

➤ **mad**

creak = squeak, grind, scrape, groan, grate, screech, squeal, scratch, rasp

creaky 1 = squeaky, creaking, squeaking, unoiled, grating, rusty, rasping, raspy ...*She pushed open the creaky door...*

2 = old-fashioned, dated, outdated, obsolete, out of date, archaic, antiquated, outmoded, behind the times, obsolescent ...*During his time in office he reformed the creaky tax system...*

cream NOUN **1** = lotion, ointment, oil, essence, cosmetic, paste, emulsion, salve, liniment, unguent ...*Gently apply the cream to the affected areas...*

2 = best, elite, prime, pick, flower, crème de la crème (*French*) ...*The event was attended by the cream of Hollywood society...*

NOUN or ADJECTIVE = off-white, ivory, yellowish-white ...*cream silk stockings...*

➤ **shades from black to white**

creamy 1 = milky, buttery ...*creamy mashed potato...*

2 = smooth, soft, creamed, lush, oily, velvety, rich ...*Whisk the mixture until it is smooth and creamy...*

crease NOUN **1** = fold, ruck, line, tuck, ridge, groove, pucker, corrugation ...*She frowned at the creases in her silk dress...*

2 = wrinkle, line, crow's-foot ...*There were tiny creases at the corner of his eyes...*

VERB **1** = crumple, rumple, pucker, crinkle, fold, ridge, double up, crimp, ruck up, corrugate ...*Most outfits crease a bit when you're travelling... ...Liz sat down*

carefully, so as not to crease her skirt...

2 = wrinkle, crumple, screw up ...*His face creased with mirth...*

create 1 = cause, lead to, occasion, bring about ...*Criticism will only create feelings of failure...*

2 = make, form, produce, develop, design, generate, invent, coin, compose, devise, initiate, hatch, originate, formulate, give birth to, spawn, dream up (*informal*), concoct, beget, give life to, bring into being *or* existence ...*He's creating a whole new language of painting...* OPPOSITE destroy

3 = appoint, make, found, establish, set up, invest, install, constitute ...*They are about to create a scholarship fund for black students...*

creation 1 = universe, world, life, nature, cosmos, natural world, living world, all living things ...*the origin of all creation...*

2 = invention, production, concept, achievement, brainchild (*informal*), concoction, handiwork, pièce de résistance (*French*), magnum opus, chef-d'oeuvre (*French*) ...*The bathroom is entirely my own creation...*

3 = making, generation, formation, conception, genesis ...*the time and effort involved in the creation of a work of art...*

4 = setting up, development, production, institution, foundation, constitution, establishment, formation, laying down, inception, origination ...*He said all sides were committed to the creation of a democratic state...*

creative = imaginative, gifted, artistic, inventive, original, inspired, clever, productive, fertile, ingenious, visionary

creativity = imagination, talent, inspiration, productivity, fertility, ingenuity, originality, inventiveness, cleverness, fecundity

creator 1 = maker, father, author, framer, designer, architect, inventor, originator, initiator, begetter ...*George Lucas, the creator of the Star Wars films...*

2 *usually with cap.* = God, Maker ...*This was the first object placed in the heavens by the Creator...*

creature 1 = living thing, being, animal, beast, brute, critter (*U.S. dialect*), quadruped, dumb animal, lower animal ...*Many cultures believe that every living creature possesses a spirit...*

2 = person, man, woman, individual, character, fellow, soul, human being, mortal, body ...*He is one of the most amiable creatures in existence...*

3 = minion, tool, instrument (*informal*), puppet, cohort (*chiefly U.S.*), dependant, retainer, hanger-on, lackey ...*We are not merely creatures of our employers...*

credence 1 = credibility, credit, plausibility, believability ...*Further studies are needed to lend credence to this notion...*

2 = belief, trust, confidence, faith, acceptance, assurance, certainty, dependence, reliance ...*Seismologists give this idea little credence...*

credentials 1 = qualifications, ability, skill, capacity, fitness, attribute, capability, endowment(s), accomplishment, eligibility, aptitude, suitability ...*He has the right credentials for the job...*

2 = <u>certification</u>, document, reference(s), papers, title, card, licence, recommendation, passport, warrant, voucher, deed, testament, diploma, testimonial, authorization, missive, letters of credence, attestation, letter of recommendation *or* introduction *…He called at Government House to present his credentials…*

credibility = <u>believability</u>, reliability, plausibility, trustworthiness, tenability

credible 1 = <u>believable</u>, possible, likely, reasonable, probable, plausible, conceivable, imaginable, tenable, verisimilar *…This claim seems perfectly credible to me…* OPPOSITE⟩ unbelievable
2 = <u>reliable</u>, honest, dependable, trustworthy, sincere, trusty *…the evidence of credible witnesses…* OPPOSITE⟩ unreliable

credit NOUN **1** = <u>praise</u>, honour, recognition, glory, thanks, approval, fame, tribute, merit, acclaim, acknowledgment, kudos, commendation, Brownie points *…It would be wrong of us to take all the credit for this result…*
2 = <u>source of satisfaction</u> *or* <u>pride</u>, asset, honour, feather in your cap *…He is a credit to his family…*
3 = <u>prestige</u>, reputation, standing, position, character, influence, regard, status, esteem, clout (*informal*), good name, estimation, repute *…His remarks lost him credit with many people…*
4 = <u>belief</u>, trust, confidence, faith, reliance, credence *…At first this theory met with little credit…*
VERB = <u>believe</u>, rely on, have faith in, trust, buy (*slang*), accept, depend on, swallow (*informal*), fall for, bank on *…You can't credit anything he says…*
PHRASES **credit someone with something** = <u>attribute to</u>, assign to, ascribe to, accredit to, impute to, chalk up to (*informal*) *…You don't credit me with any intelligence at all, do you?…* ◆ **credit something to someone** = <u>attribute to</u>, ascribe to, accredit to, impute to, chalk up to (*informal*) *…Although the song is usually credited to Lennon and McCartney, it was written by McCartney alone…* ◆ **on credit** = <u>on account</u>, by instalments, on tick (*informal*), on hire-purchase, on the slate (*informal*), by deferred payment, on (the) H.P. *…They bought most of their furniture on credit…*

creditable = <u>praiseworthy</u>, worthy, respectable, admirable, honourable, exemplary, reputable, commendable, laudable, meritorious, estimable

credulity = <u>gullibility</u>, naïveté *or* naivety, blind faith, credulousness

creed = <u>belief</u>, principles, profession (*of faith*), doctrine, canon, persuasion, dogma, tenet, credo, catechism, articles of faith

creek 1 = <u>inlet</u>, bay, cove, bight, firth *or* frith (*Scot.*) *…The offshore fishermen took shelter from the storm in a creek…*
2 (*U.S., Canad., Austral., & N.Z.*) = <u>stream</u>, brook, tributary, bayou, rivulet, watercourse, streamlet, runnel *…Follow Austin Creek for a few miles…*

creep VERB **1** = <u>crawl</u>, worm, wriggle, squirm, slither, writhe, drag yourself, edge, inch, crawl on all fours *…The rabbit crept off and hid in a hole…*

2 = <u>sneak</u>, steal, tiptoe, slink, skulk, approach unnoticed *…I went back to the hotel and crept up to my room…*
NOUN (*Slang*) = <u>bootlicker</u> (*informal*), sneak, sycophant, crawler (*slang*), toady *…He's a smug, sanctimonious little creep…*
PHRASES **give someone the creeps** (*Informal*) = <u>disgust</u>, frighten, scare, terrify, horrify, repel, repulse, make you wince, make your hair stand on end, make you squirm, make you flinch, make you quail, make you shrink *…I've always hated that painting. It gives me the creeps…*

creeper = <u>climbing plant</u>, runner, vine (*chiefly U.S.*), climber, rambler, trailing plant

creepy (*Informal*) = <u>disturbing</u>, threatening, frightening, terrifying, weird, forbidding, horrible, menacing, unpleasant, scary (*informal*), sinister, ominous, eerie, macabre, nightmarish, hair-raising, awful

crescent NOUN = <u>meniscus</u>, sickle, new moon, half-moon, old moon, sickle-shape *…a flag with a white crescent on a red ground…*
ADJECTIVE = <u>sickle-shaped</u>, curved, arched, semicircular, bow-shaped *…a crescent moon…*

crest 1 = <u>top</u>, summit, peak, ridge, highest point, pinnacle, apex, head, crown, height *…He reached the crest of the hill…*
2 = <u>tuft</u>, crown, comb, plume, mane, tassel, topknot, cockscomb *…Both birds had a dark blue crest…*
3 = <u>emblem</u>, badge, symbol, insignia, charge, bearings, device *…On the wall is the family crest…*

crestfallen = <u>disappointed</u>, depressed, discouraged, dejected, despondent, downcast, disheartened, disconsolate, downhearted, sick as a parrot (*informal*), choked OPPOSITE⟩ elated

crevice = <u>gap</u>, opening, hole, split, crack, rent, fracture, rift, slit, cleft, chink, fissure, cranny, interstice

crew 1 = <u>(ship's) company</u>, hands, (ship's) complement *…These vessels carry small crews of around twenty men…*
2 = <u>team</u>, company, party, squad, gang, corps, working party, posse *…a two-man film crew making a documentary…*
3 (*Informal*) = <u>crowd</u>, set, lot, bunch (*informal*), band, troop, pack, camp, gang, mob, herd, swarm, company, horde, posse (*informal*), assemblage *…a motley crew of college friends…*

crib NOUN **1** = <u>cradle</u>, bed, cot, bassinet, Moses basket *…She placed the baby back in its crib…*
2 (*Informal*) = <u>translation</u>, notes, key, trot (*U.S. slang*) *…Only desperate students take cribs into the exam with them…*
3 = <u>manger</u>, box, stall, rack, bunker *…He claimed the cribs in which the calves were kept had been approved by the RSPCA…*
VERB (*Informal*) = <u>copy</u>, cheat, pirate, pilfer, purloin, plagiarize, pass off as your own work *…He had been caught cribbing in an exam…*

crick (*Informal*) NOUN = <u>spasm</u>, cramp, convulsion, twinge *…I've got a crick in my neck from looking up at*

Cricket terms http://www.channel4.com/sport/cricket/analyst/

appeal	duck	long off	silly mid on
Ashes	edge	long on	silly mid off
bail	extra	maiden (over)	single
ball	extra cover	mid off	six
bat	fast bowler	mid on	slip
batsman	fielder or fieldsman	mid wicket	spin
bouncer or bumper	fine leg	nightwatchman	square leg
boundary	follow on	no ball	stump
bowl	four	off break	stumped
bowled	full toss	off side	sweep
bowler	glance or glide	on side or leg side	swing
bye	googly	opener or opening	test match
catch	gully	batsman	third man
caught	hit wicket	out	twelfth man
century	hook	over	umpire
chinaman	in	pad	wicket
cover point	innings	pitch	wicketkeeper
covers	leg before wicket	pull	wide
crease	leg break	run	yorker
cut	leg bye	run out	
declare	leg slip	seam	
drive	long leg	short leg	

---

the screen…

VERB = <u>rick</u>, jar, wrench …*I cricked my back from sitting in the same position for too long…*

cricket

➤ **cricket terms**

crime 1 = <u>offence</u>, job (*informal*), wrong, fault, outrage, atrocity, violation, trespass, felony, misdemeanour, misdeed, transgression, unlawful act …*He has committed no crime and poses no danger to the public…*
2 = <u>lawbreaking</u>, corruption, delinquency, illegality, wrong, vice, sin, guilt, misconduct, wrongdoing, wickedness, iniquity, villainy, unrighteousness, malefaction …*Much of the city's crime revolves around protection rackets…*

criminal **NOUN** = <u>lawbreaker</u>, convict, con (*slang*), offender, crook (*informal*), lag (*slang*), villain, culprit, sinner, delinquent, felon, con man (*informal*), rorter (*Austral. slang*), jailbird, malefactor, evildoer, transgressor, skelm (*S. African*) …*He was put in a cell with several hardened criminals…*
ADJECTIVE 1 = <u>unlawful</u>, illicit, lawless, wrong, illegal, corrupt, crooked (*informal*), vicious, immoral, wicked, culpable, under-the-table, villainous, nefarious, iniquitous, indictable, felonious, bent (*slang*) …*The entire party cannot be blamed for the criminal actions of a few members…* **OPPOSITE** lawful
2 (*Informal*) = <u>disgraceful</u>, ridiculous, foolish, senseless, scandalous, preposterous, deplorable …*This project is a criminal waste of time and resources…*

criminality = <u>illegality</u>, crime, corruption, delinquency, wrongdoing, lawlessness, wickedness, depravity, culpability, villainy, sinfulness, turpitude

cringe 1 = <u>shrink</u>, flinch, quail, recoil, start, shy, tremble, quiver, cower, draw back, blench …*I cringed in horror…*

2 = <u>wince</u>, squirm, writhe …*The idea makes me cringe…*

crinkle **VERB** = <u>crease</u>, wrinkle, crumple, pucker, fold, curl, crimp …*When she laughs, her eyes crinkle…*
NOUN = <u>crease</u>, wrinkle, crumple, ruffle, twist, fold, curl, rumple, pucker, crimp …*The fabric was smooth, without a crinkle…*

cripple 1 = <u>disable</u>, paralyse, lame, debilitate, mutilate, maim, incapacitate, enfeeble, weaken, hamstring …*He had been warned that another bad fall could cripple him for life…*
2 = <u>damage</u>, destroy, ruin, bring to a standstill, halt, spoil, cramp, impair, put paid to, vitiate, put out of action …*A total cut-off of supplies would cripple the country's economy…* **OPPOSITE** help

crippled = <u>disabled</u>, handicapped, paralysed, lame, deformed, incapacitated, bedridden, housebound, enfeebled

crisis 1 = <u>emergency</u>, plight, catastrophe, predicament, pass, trouble, disaster, mess, dilemma, strait, deep water, meltdown (*informal*), extremity, quandary, dire straits, exigency, critical situation …*Strikes worsened the country's economic crisis…*
2 = <u>critical point</u>, climax, point of no return, height, confrontation, crunch (*informal*), turning point, culmination, crux, moment of truth, climacteric …*The anxiety that had been building within him reached a crisis…*

crisp 1 = <u>firm</u>, crunchy, crispy, crumbly, fresh, brittle, unwilted …*Bake the potatoes till they're nice and crisp…* **OPPOSITE** soft
2 = <u>bracing</u>, fresh, refreshing, brisk, invigorating …*a crisp autumn day…* **OPPOSITE** warm
3 = <u>clean</u>, smart, trim, neat, tidy, orderly, spruce, snappy, clean-cut, well-groomed, well-pressed …*He wore a panama hat and a crisp white suit…*
4 = <u>brief</u>, clear, short, tart, incisive, terse, succinct,

pithy, brusque ...*In a clear, crisp voice, he began his speech*...

criterion = <u>standard</u>, test, rule, measure, principle, proof, par, norm, canon, gauge, yardstick, touchstone, bench mark

---

Word Power

criterion – The word *criteria* is the plural of *criterion* and it is incorrect to use it as an alternative singular form; *these criteria are not valid* is correct, and so is *this criterion is not valid*, but not *this criteria is not valid*.

---

critic 1 = <u>judge</u>, authority, expert, analyst, commentator, pundit, reviewer, connoisseur, arbiter, expositor ...*The New York critics had praised her performance*...
2 attacker, detractor, knocker (*informal*) ...*He became a fierce critic of the tobacco industry*...

critical 1 = <u>crucial</u>, decisive, momentous, deciding, pressing, serious, vital, psychological, urgent, all-important, pivotal, high-priority, now or never ...*The incident happened at a critical point in the campaign*... OPPOSITE> unimportant
2 = <u>grave</u>, serious, dangerous, acute, risky, hairy (*slang*), precarious, perilous ...*Ten of the injured are said to be in a critical condition*... OPPOSITE> safe
3 = <u>disparaging</u>, disapproving, scathing, derogatory, nit-picking (*informal*), censorious, cavilling, fault-finding, captious, carping, niggling ...*He has apologized for critical remarks he made about the referee*... OPPOSITE> complimentary
4 = <u>analytical</u>, penetrating, discriminating, discerning, diagnostic, perceptive, judicious, accurate, precise ...*What is needed is a critical analysis of the evidence*... OPPOSITE> undiscriminating

criticism 1 = <u>fault-finding</u>, censure, disapproval, disparagement, stick (*slang*), knocking (*informal*), panning (*informal*), slamming (*slang*), slating (*informal*), flak (*informal*), slagging (*slang*), strictures, bad press, denigration, brickbats (*informal*), character assassination, critical remarks, animadversion ...*The policy had repeatedly come under strong criticism*...
2 = <u>analysis</u>, review, notice, assessment, judgment, commentary, evaluation, appreciation, appraisal, critique, elucidation ...*Her work includes novels, poetry and literary criticism*...

criticize = <u>find fault with</u>, censure, disapprove of, knock (*informal*), blast, pan (*informal*), condemn, slam (*slang*), carp, put down, slate (*informal*), have a go (at) (*informal*), disparage, tear into (*informal*), diss (*slang, chiefly U.S.*), nag at, lambast(e), pick holes in, pick to pieces, give (someone *or* something) a bad press, pass strictures upon OPPOSITE> praise

critique = <u>essay</u>, review, analysis, assessment, examination, commentary, appraisal, treatise

croak 1 = <u>grunt</u>, squawk, caw ...*Frogs croaked in the reeds*...
2 = <u>rasp</u>, gasp, grunt, wheeze, utter *or* speak harshly, utter *or* speak huskily, utter *or* speak throatily

...*Daniel managed to croak, 'Help me.'*...
3 (*Slang*) = <u>die</u>, expire, pass away, perish, buy it (*U.S. slang*), check out (*U.S. slang*), kick it (*slang*), go belly-up (*slang*), peg out (*informal*), kick the bucket (*informal*), buy the farm (*U.S. slang*), peg it (*informal*), cark it (*Austral. & N.Z. slang*), pop your clogs (*informal*), hop the twig (*informal*) ...*The old man finally croaked at the age of 92*...

crone = <u>old woman</u>, witch, hag, old bag (*derogatory slang*), old bat (*slang*)

crony = <u>friend</u>, china (*Brit. slang*), colleague, associate, mate (*informal*), pal (*informal*), companion, cock (*Brit. informal*), buddy (*informal*), comrade, chum (*informal*), accomplice, ally, sidekick (*slang*), main man (*slang, chiefly U.S.*), homeboy (*slang, chiefly U.S.*), cobber (*Austral. or old-fashioned N.Z. informal*)

crook NOUN (*Informal*) = <u>criminal</u>, rogue, cheat, thief, shark, lag (*slang*), villain, robber, racketeer, fraudster, swindler, knave (*archaic*), grifter (*slang, chiefly U.S. & Canad.*), chiseller (*informal*), skelm (*S. African*) ...*The man is a crook and a liar*...
VERB = <u>bend</u>, hook, angle, bow, curve, curl, cock, flex ...*He crooked his finger at her and said, 'Come here.'*...
ADJECTIVE (*Austral. & N.Z. informal*) = <u>ill</u>, sick, poorly (*informal*), funny (*informal*), weak, ailing, queer, frail, feeble, unhealthy, seedy (*informal*), sickly, unwell, laid up (*informal*), queasy, infirm, out of sorts (*informal*), dicky (*Brit. informal*), nauseous, off-colour, under the weather (*informal*), at death's door, indisposed, peaky, on the sick list (*informal*), green about the gills ...*He admitted to feeling a bit crook*...
PHRASES **go (off) crook** (*Aust. & N.Z. informal*) = <u>lose your temper</u>, be furious, rage, go mad, lose it (*informal*), seethe, crack up (*informal*), see red (*informal*), lose the plot (*informal*), go ballistic (*slang, chiefly U.S.*), blow a fuse (*slang, chiefly U.S.*), fly off the handle (*informal*), be incandescent, go off the deep end (*informal*), throw a fit (*informal*), wig out (*slang*), go up the wall (*slang*), blow your top, lose your rag (*slang*), be beside yourself, flip your lid (*slang*) ...*She went crook when I confessed*...

crooked 1 = <u>bent</u>, twisted, bowed, curved, irregular, warped, deviating, out of shape, misshapen ...*the crooked line of his broken nose*... OPPOSITE> straight
2 = <u>deformed</u>, crippled, distorted, disfigured ...*Whole families went about with crooked legs or twisted shoulders*...
3 = <u>zigzag</u>, winding, twisting, meandering, tortuous ...*men gathered in the bars of the crooked streets*...
4 = <u>at an angle</u>, angled, tilted, to one side, uneven, slanted, slanting, squint, awry, lopsided, askew, asymmetric, off-centre, skewwhiff (*Brit. informal*), unsymmetrical ...*He gave her a crooked grin*...
5 (*Informal*) = <u>dishonest</u>, criminal, illegal, corrupt, dubious, questionable, unlawful, shady (*informal*), fraudulent, unscrupulous, under-the-table, bent (*slang*), shifty, deceitful, underhand, unprincipled, dishonourable, nefarious, knavish ...*She might expose his crooked business deals to the authorities*... OPPOSITE> honest

croon 1 = <u>sing</u>, warble ...*a nightclub singer who* crooned romantic songs…

2 = <u>say softly</u>, breathe, hum, purr …*The man was crooning soft words of encouragement to his wife…*

crop [NOUN] = <u>yield</u>, produce, gathering, fruits, harvest, vintage, reaping, season's growth …*a fine crop of apples…*

[VERB] **1** = <u>harvest</u>, pick, collect, gather, bring in, reap, bring home, garner, mow …*I started cropping my beans in July…*

2 = <u>graze</u>, eat, browse, feed on, nibble …*I let the horse drop his head to crop the grass…*

3 = <u>cut</u>, reduce, trim, clip, dock, prune, shorten, shear, snip, pare, lop …*She cropped her hair and dyed it blonde…*

[PHRASES] **crop up** (*Informal*) = <u>happen</u>, appear, emerge, occur, arise, turn up, spring up …*As we get older health problems often crop up…*

cross [VERB] **1** = <u>go across</u>, pass over, traverse, cut across, move across, travel across …*She was partly to blame for failing to look as she crossed the road…*

2 = <u>span</u>, bridge, ford, go across, extend over …*A bridge crosses the river about half a mile outside the village…*

3 = <u>intersect</u>, meet, intertwine, crisscross …*The two roads cross at this junction…*

4 = <u>oppose</u>, interfere with, hinder, obstruct, deny, block, resist, frustrate, foil, thwart, impede …*He was not a man to cross…*

5 = <u>interbreed</u>, mix, blend, cross-pollinate, crossbreed, hybridize, cross-fertilize, intercross …*These small flowers were later crossed with a white flowering species…*

[NOUN] **1** = <u>crucifix</u> …*She wore a cross on a silver chain…*

2 = <u>trouble</u>, worry, trial, load, burden, grief, misery, woe, misfortune, affliction, tribulation …*My wife is much cleverer than I am; it is a cross I have to bear…*

3 = <u>mixture</u>, combination, blend, amalgam, amalgamation …*The noise that came out was a cross between a laugh and a bark…*

4 = <u>crossbreed</u>, hybrid …*a cross between a collie and a poodle…*

5 = <u>crossroads</u>, crossing, junction, intersection …*Turn left at the cross and go straight on for two miles…*

[ADJECTIVE] = <u>angry</u>, impatient, irritable, annoyed, put out, hacked (off) (*U.S. slang*), crusty, snappy, grumpy, vexed, sullen, surly, fractious, petulant, disagreeable, short, churlish, peeved (*informal*), ill-tempered, irascible, cantankerous, tetchy, ratty (*Brit. & N.Z. informal*), tooshie (*Austral. slang*), testy, fretful, waspish, in a bad mood, grouchy (*informal*), querulous, shirty (*slang, chiefly Brit.*), peevish, splenetic, crotchety (*informal*), snappish, ill-humoured, captious, pettish, out of humour …*Everyone was getting bored and cross…* [OPPOSITE] good-humoured

[PHRASES] **cross something out** or **off** = <u>strike off</u> or <u>out</u>, eliminate, cancel, delete, blue-pencil, score off or out …*He crossed her name off the list…*

cross-examine = <u>question</u>, grill (*informal*), quiz, interrogate, catechize, pump

crotch = <u>groin</u>, lap, crutch

crouch = <u>bend down</u>, kneel, squat, stoop, bow, duck, hunch

crow = <u>gloat</u>, triumph, boast, swagger, brag, glory in, vaunt, bluster, exult, blow your own trumpet

crowd [NOUN] **1** = <u>multitude</u>, mass, assembly, throng, company, press, army, host, pack, mob, flock, herd, swarm, horde, rabble, concourse, bevy …*It took some two hours before the crowd was fully dispersed…*

2 = <u>group</u>, set, lot, circle, gang, bunch (*informal*), clique …*All the old crowd from my university days were there…*

3 = <u>audience</u>, spectators, house, gate, attendance …*When the song finished, the crowd went wild…*

4 = <u>masses</u>, people, public, mob, rank and file, populace, rabble, proletariat, hoi polloi, riffraff, vulgar herd …*You can learn to stand out from the crowd…*

[VERB] **1** = <u>flock</u>, press, push, mass, collect, gather, stream, surge, cluster, muster, huddle, swarm, throng, congregate, foregather …*The hungry refugees crowded around the lorries…*

2 = <u>squeeze</u>, pack, pile, bundle, cram …*Hundreds of people crowded into the building… …A group of journalists were crowded into a minibus…*

3 = <u>congest</u>, pack, cram …*Demonstrators crowded the streets shouting slogans…*

4 (*Informal*) = <u>jostle</u>, batter, butt, push, elbow, shove …*It had been a tense, restless day with people crowding her all the time…*

crowded = <u>packed</u>, full, busy, mobbed, cramped, swarming, overflowing, thronged, teeming, congested, populous, jam-packed, crushed

crown [NOUN] **1** = <u>coronet</u>, tiara, diadem, circlet, coronal (*poetic*), chaplet …*a beautiful woman wearing a golden crown…*

2 = <u>laurel wreath</u>, trophy, distinction, prize, honour, garland, laurels, wreath, kudos …*He won the middleweight crown in 1947…*

3 = <u>high point</u>, head, top, tip, summit, crest, pinnacle, apex …*We stood on the crown of the hill…*

[VERB] **1** invest, honour, install, dignify, ordain, inaugurate …*He had himself crowned as Emperor…*

2 = <u>top</u>, cap, be on top of, surmount …*A rugged castle crowns the cliffs…*

3 = <u>cap</u>, finish, complete, perfect, fulfil, consummate, round off, put the finishing touch to, put the tin lid on, be the climax or culmination of …*The summit was crowned by the signing of the historical treaty…*

4 (*Slang*) = <u>strike</u>, belt (*informal*), bash, hit over the head, box, punch, cuff, biff (*slang*), wallop …*I felt like crowning him with the frying pan…*

[PHRASES] **the Crown 1** = <u>monarch</u>, ruler, sovereign, rex (*Latin*), emperor or empress, king or queen …*loyal subjects of the Crown… 2* = <u>monarchy</u>, sovereignty, royalty …*All treasure trove is the property of the Crown…*

crowning = <u>supreme</u>, final, ultimate, sovereign, paramount, culminating, consummate, mother of all (*informal*), climactic

crucial 1 (*Informal*) = <u>vital</u>, important, pressing, essential, urgent, momentous, high-priority …*the*

most crucial election campaign in years...
2 = critical, central, key, psychological, decisive, pivotal, now or never ...*At the crucial moment, his nerve failed...*

crucify 1 = execute, put to death, nail to a cross ...*the day that Christ was crucified...*
2 (*Slang*) = pan (*informal*), rubbish (*informal*), ridicule, slag (off) (*slang*), lampoon, wipe the floor with (*informal*), tear to pieces ...*She was crucified by the critics for her performance...*
3 = torture, rack, torment, harrow ...*He had been crucified by guilt ever since his child's death...*

crude 1 = rough, undeveloped, basic, outline, unfinished, makeshift, sketchy, unformed ...*a crude way of assessing the risk of heart disease...*
2 = simple, rudimentary, basic, primitive, coarse, clumsy, rough-and-ready, rough-hewn ...*crude wooden carvings...*
3 = vulgar, dirty, rude, obscene, coarse, indecent, crass, tasteless, lewd, X-rated (*informal*), boorish, smutty, uncouth, gross ...*a crude sense of humour...*
OPPOSITE tasteful
4 = unrefined, natural, raw, unprocessed, unpolished, unprepared ...*8.5 million tonnes of crude steel...*
OPPOSITE processed

crudely 1 = roughly, basically, sketchily ...*The donors can be split – a little crudely – into two groups...*
2 = simply, roughly, basically, coarsely, clumsily ...*a crudely carved wooden form...*
3 = vulgarly, rudely, coarsely, crassly, indecently, obscenely, lewdly, impolitely, tastelessly ...*and yet she spoke so crudely...*

cruel 1 = brutal, ruthless, callous, sadistic, inhumane, hard, fell (*archaic*), severe, harsh, savage, grim, vicious, relentless, murderous, monstrous, unnatural, unkind, heartless, atrocious, inhuman, merciless, cold-blooded, malevolent, hellish, depraved, spiteful, brutish, bloodthirsty, remorseless, barbarous, pitiless, unfeeling, hard-hearted, stony-hearted ...*the persecution of prisoners by cruel officers... ...the cruel practice of bullfighting...* **OPPOSITE** kind
2 = bitter, severe, painful, ruthless, traumatic, grievous, unrelenting, merciless, pitiless ...*Fate dealt him a cruel blow...*

cruelly 1 = brutally, severely, savagely, viciously, mercilessly, in cold blood, callously, monstrously, unmercifully, sadistically, pitilessly, spitefully, heartlessly, barbarously ...*Douglas was often treated cruelly by his fellow-pupils...*
2 = bitterly, deeply, severely, mortally, painfully, ruthlessly, mercilessly, grievously, pitilessly, traumatically ...*His life has been cruelly shattered by an event not of his own making...*

cruelty = brutality, spite, severity, savagery, ruthlessness, sadism, depravity, harshness, inhumanity, barbarity, callousness, viciousness, bestiality, heartlessness, spitefulness, bloodthirstiness, mercilessness, fiendishness, hardheartedness

cruise NOUN = sail, voyage, boat trip, sea trip ...*He and his wife were planning to go on a world cruise...*

VERB 1 = sail, coast, voyage ...*She wants to cruise the canals of France in a barge...*
2 = travel along, coast, drift, keep a steady pace ...*A black and white police car cruised past...*

crumb 1 = bit, grain, particle, fragment, shred, speck, sliver, morsel ...*I stood up, brushing crumbs from my trousers...*
2 = morsel, scrap, atom, shred, mite, snippet, sliver, soupçon (*French*) ...*There is one crumb of comfort – at least we've still got each other...*

crumble 1 = disintegrate, collapse, break up, deteriorate, decay, fall apart, perish, degenerate, decompose, tumble down, moulder, go to pieces ...*The chalk cliffs are crumbling... ...Under the pressure, the flint crumbled into fragments...*
2 = crush, fragment, crumb, pulverize, pound, grind, powder, granulate ...*Roughly crumble the cheese into a bowl...*
3 = collapse, break down, deteriorate, decay, fall apart, degenerate, go to pieces, go to wrack and ruin ...*Their economy crumbled under the weight of United Nations sanctions...*

crumbling = disintegrating, collapsing, deteriorating, decaying, eroding, decomposing, mouldering

crumbly = brittle, short (*of pastry*), powdery, friable

crummy (*Slang*) = second-rate, cheap, inferior, substandard, poor, pants (*informal*), miserable, rotten (*informal*), duff (*Brit. informal*), lousy (*slang*), shoddy, trashy, low-rent (*informal, chiefly U.S.*), for the birds (*informal*), third-rate, contemptible, two-bit (*U.S. & Canad. slang*), crappy (*slang*), rubbishy, poxy (*slang*), dime-a-dozen (*informal*), bodger or bodgie (*Austral. slang*), bush-league (*Austral. & N.Z. informal*), tinhorn (*U.S. slang*), of a sort or of sorts, strictly for the birds (*informal*)

crumple 1 = crush, squash, screw up, scrumple ...*She crumpled the paper in her hand...*
2 = crease, wrinkle, rumple, ruffle, pucker ...*She sat down carefully, so as not to crumple her skirt...*
3 = collapse, sink, go down, fall ...*He crumpled to the floor in agony...*
4 = break down, fall, collapse, give way, cave in, go to pieces ...*Sometimes we just crumpled under our grief...*
5 = screw up, pucker ...*She faltered, and then her face crumpled once more...*

crumpled = crushed, wrinkled, creased, ruffled, rumpled, puckered

crunch VERB = chomp, champ, munch, masticate, chew noisily, grind ...*She sucked an ice cube and crunched it loudly...*
NOUN (*Informal*) = critical point, test, crisis, emergency, crux, moment of truth, hour of decision ...*He can rely on my support when the crunch comes...*

crusade NOUN 1 = campaign, drive, movement, cause, push ...*a crusade against racism on the football terraces...*
2 = holy war, jihad ...*He was leading a religious crusade that did not respect national boundaries...*

VERB = <u>campaign</u>, fight, push, struggle, lobby, agitate, work ...*a newspaper that has crusaded against drug traffickers...*

crusader = <u>campaigner</u>, champion, advocate, activist, reformer

crush VERB 1 = <u>squash</u>, pound, break, smash, squeeze, crumble, crunch, mash, compress, press, crumple, pulverize ...*Their vehicle was crushed by an army tank...*
2 = <u>crease</u>, wrinkle, crumple, rumple, scrumple, ruffle ...*I don't want to crush my skirt...*
3 = <u>overcome</u>, overwhelm, put down, subdue, overpower, quash, quell, extinguish, stamp out, vanquish, conquer ...*The military operation was the first step in a plan to crush the uprising...*
4 = <u>demoralize</u>, depress, devastate, discourage, humble, put down (*slang*), humiliate, squash, flatten, deflate, mortify, psych out (*informal*), dishearten, dispirit, deject ...*Listen to criticism but don't be crushed by it...*
5 = <u>squeeze</u>, press, embrace, hug, enfold ...*He crushed her in his arms...*
NOUN = <u>crowd</u>, mob, horde, throng, press, pack, mass, jam, herd, huddle, swarm, multitude, rabble ...*They got separated from each other in the crush...*

crust = <u>layer</u>, covering, coating, incrustation, film, outside, skin, surface, shell, coat, caking, scab, concretion

crustacean

Crustaceans
http://www.crustacea.net/

barnacle	Norway lobster
crab	opossum shrimp
crayfish, crawfish,	oyster crab
(U.S.) or (Austral. &	prawn
N.Z. informal) craw	robber crab
Dublin Bay prawn	sand hopper, beach
freshwater shrimp	flea, *or* sand flea
goose barnacle	sand shrimp
gribble	scorpion
hermit crab	sea spider
horseshoe crab *or*	shrimp
king crab	soft-shell crab
king prawn	spider crab
krill	spiny lobster, rock
land crab	lobster, crawfish, *or*
langoustine	langouste
lobster	water flea

---

crusty 1 = <u>crispy</u>, well-baked, crisp, well-done, brittle, friable, hard, short ...*crusty french loaves...*
2 = <u>irritable</u>, short, cross, prickly, touchy, curt, surly, gruff, brusque, cantankerous, tetchy, ratty (*Brit. & N.Z. informal*), testy, short-tempered, peevish, crabby, choleric, splenetic, ill-humoured, captious, snappish *or* snappy ...*a crusty old colonel with a gruff manner...*

crux = <u>crucial point</u>, heart, core, essence, nub, decisive point

cry VERB 1 = <u>weep</u>, sob, bawl, shed tears, keen, greet (*Scot. or archaic*), wail, whine, whimper, whinge

(*informal*), blubber, snivel, yowl, howl your eyes out ...*I hung up the phone and started to cry...* OPPOSITE laugh
2 = <u>shout</u>, call, scream, roar, hail, yell, howl, call out, exclaim, shriek, bellow, whoop, screech, bawl, holler (*informal*), ejaculate, sing out, halloo, vociferate ...*'You're under arrest!' he cried...* OPPOSITE whisper
3 = <u>beg</u>, plead, pray, clamour, implore, beseech, entreat ...*She screamed and cried for help...*
4 = <u>announce</u>, hawk, advertise, proclaim, bark (*informal*), trumpet, shout from the rooftops (*informal*) ...*In the street below, a peddler was crying his wares...*
NOUN 1 = <u>weep</u>, greet (*Scot. or archaic*), sob, howl, bawl, blubber, snivel ...*Have a good cry if you want to...*
2 = <u>shout</u>, call, scream, roar, yell, howl, shriek, bellow, whoop, screech, hoot, ejaculation, bawl, holler (*informal*), exclamation, squawk, yelp, yoo-hoo ...*Her brother gave a cry of recognition...*
3 = <u>appeal</u>, prayer, plea, petition, entreaty, supplication ...*Many other countries have turned a deaf ear to their cries for help...*
4 = <u>announcement</u>, proclamation ...*the sound of car horns and street cries...*
PLURAL NOUN = <u>weeping</u>, sobbing, bawling, crying, greeting (*Scot. or archaic*), howling, wailing, blubbering, snivelling ...*The baby's cries woke him again...*
PHRASES **cry off** (*Informal*) = <u>back out</u>, withdraw, quit, cop out (*slang*), beg off, excuse yourself ...*She caught flu and had to cry off at the last minute...*

crypt = <u>vault</u>, tomb, catacomb

cryptic = <u>mysterious</u>, dark, coded, puzzling, obscure, vague, veiled, ambiguous, enigmatic, perplexing, arcane, equivocal, abstruse, Delphic, oracular

crystallize 1 = <u>take shape</u>, form, become clear, come together, materialize ...*Now my thoughts really began to crystallize...*
2 = <u>harden</u>, solidify, coalesce, form crystals ...*Keep stirring the mixture or the sugar will crystallize...*

cub = <u>young</u>, baby, offspring, whelp
Related Words
collective noun: litter

cuddle VERB 1 = <u>hug</u>, embrace, clasp, fondle, cosset ...*He cuddled their newborn baby...*
2 = <u>pet</u>, hug, canoodle (*slang*), bill and coo ...*They used to kiss and cuddle in front of everyone...*
PHRASES **cuddle up** = <u>snuggle</u>, nestle ...*My cat cuddled up to me...*

cuddly = <u>soft</u>, plump, buxom, curvaceous, warm

cue = <u>signal</u>, sign, nod, hint, prompt, reminder, suggestion

cuff[1]
PHRASES **off the cuff** (*Informal*) 1 = <u>impromptu</u>, spontaneous, improvised, offhand, unrehearsed, extempore ...*I didn't mean any offence. It was just an off-the-cuff remark...* 2 = <u>without preparation</u>, spontaneously, impromptu, offhand, on the spur of the moment, ad lib, extempore, off the top of your

head …*He was speaking off the cuff when he made this suggestion…*

cuff² **VERB** = smack, hit, thump, punch, box, knock, bat (*informal*), belt (*informal*), slap, clap, clout (*informal*), whack, biff (*slang*), clobber (*slang*) …*He cuffed the child across the head…*

NOUN = smack, blow, knock, punch, thump, box, belt (*informal*), rap, slap, clout (*informal*), whack, biff (*slang*) …*He gave the dog a cuff…*

cul-de-sac = dead end, blind alley

cull = select, collect, gather, amass, choose, pick, pick up, pluck, glean, cherry-pick

culminate = end up, end, close, finish, conclude, wind up, climax, terminate, come to a head, come to a climax, rise to a crescendo

culmination = climax, conclusion, completion, finale, consummation

culpability = blame, responsibility, fault, liability, accountability

culpable = blameworthy, wrong, guilty, to blame, liable, in the wrong, at fault, sinful, answerable, found wanting, reprehensible **OPPOSITE** blameless

culprit = offender, criminal, villain, sinner, delinquent, felon, person responsible, guilty party, wrongdoer, miscreant, evildoer, transgressor

cult 1 = sect, following, body, faction, party, school, church, faith, religion, denomination, clique …*The teenager may have been abducted by a religious cult…*
2 = craze, fashion, trend, fad …*The programme has become something of a cult among thirty-somethings…*
3 = obsession, worship, admiration, devotion, reverence, veneration, idolization …*The cult of personality surrounding pop stars leaves me cold…*

cultivate 1 = farm, work, plant, tend, till, harvest, plough, bring under cultivation …*She cultivated a small garden of her own…*
2 = develop, establish, acquire, foster, devote yourself to, pursue …*Try to cultivate a positive mental attitude…*
3 = court, associate with, seek out, run after, consort with, butter up, dance attendance upon, seek someone's company *or* friendship, take trouble *or* pains with …*He only cultivates people who may be of use to him…*
4 = foster, further, forward, encourage …*She went out of her way to cultivate his friendship…*
5 = improve, better, train, discipline, polish, refine, elevate, enrich, civilize …*My father encouraged me to cultivate my mind…*

cultivated = refined, cultured, advanced, polished, educated, sophisticated, accomplished, discriminating, enlightened, discerning, civilized, genteel, well-educated, urbane, erudite, well-bred

cultivation 1 = farming, working, gardening, tilling, ploughing, husbandry, agronomy …*environments where aridity makes cultivation of the land difficult…*
2 = growing, planting, production, farming …*groups that want a ban on the cultivation of GM crops…*
3 = development, fostering, pursuit, devotion to …*the cultivation of a positive approach to life and health…*
4 = promotion, support, encouragement, nurture, patronage, advancement, advocacy, enhancement, furtherance …*those who devote themselves to the cultivation of the arts…*
5 = refinement, letters, learning, education, culture, taste, breeding, manners, polish, discrimination, civilization, enlightenment, sophistication, good taste, civility, gentility, discernment …*He was a man of cultivation and scholarship…*

cultural 1 = ethnic, national, native, folk, racial …*a deep sense of honour which was part of his cultural heritage…*
2 = artistic, educational, elevating, aesthetic, enriching, broadening, enlightening, developmental, civilizing, edifying, educative …*This holiday was a rich cultural experience…*

culture 1 = the arts …*France's Minister of Culture and Education…*
2 = civilization, society, customs, way of life …*people of different cultures…*
3 = lifestyle, habit, way of life, mores …*Social workers say this has created a culture of dependency…*
4 = refinement, education, breeding, polish, enlightenment, accomplishment, sophistication, good taste, erudition, gentility, urbanity …*He was a well-travelled man of culture and breeding…*

cultured = refined, advanced, polished, intellectual, educated, sophisticated, accomplished, scholarly, enlightened, knowledgeable, well-informed, genteel, urbane, erudite, highbrow, well-bred, well-read **OPPOSITE** uneducated

culvert = drain, channel, gutter, conduit, watercourse

cumbersome 1 = awkward, heavy, hefty (*informal*), clumsy, bulky, weighty, impractical, inconvenient, burdensome, unmanageable, clunky (*informal*) …*Although the machine looks cumbersome, it is easy to use…* **OPPOSITE** easy to use
2 = inefficient, unwieldy, badly organized …*an old and cumbersome computer system…* **OPPOSITE** efficient

cumulative = collective, increasing, aggregate, amassed, accruing, snowballing, accumulative

cunning **ADJECTIVE** 1 = crafty, sly, devious, artful, sharp, subtle, tricky, shrewd, astute, canny, wily, Machiavellian, shifty, foxy, guileful …*He's a cunning, devious, good-for-nothing so-and-so…* **OPPOSITE** frank
2 = ingenious, subtle, imaginative, shrewd, sly, astute, devious, artful, Machiavellian …*I came up with a cunning plan…*
3 = skilful, clever, deft, adroit, dexterous …*The artist's cunning use of light and shadow creates perspective…* **OPPOSITE** clumsy

NOUN 1 = craftiness, guile, trickery, shrewdness, deviousness, artfulness, slyness, wiliness …*an example of the cunning of modern art thieves…* **OPPOSITE** candour
2 = skill, art, ability, craft, subtlety, ingenuity, finesse, artifice, dexterity, cleverness, deftness, astuteness, adroitness …*He tackled the problem with skill and*

cunning… OPPOSITE clumsiness

cup 1 = mug, goblet, chalice, teacup, beaker, demitasse, bowl …*a set of matching cups and saucers…*
2 = trophy …*First prize is a silver cup and a scroll…*

cupboard = cabinet, closet, locker, press

curative = restorative, healing, therapeutic, tonic, corrective, medicinal, remedial, salutary, healthful, health-giving

curb VERB = restrain, control, check, contain, restrict, moderate, suppress, inhibit, subdue, hinder, repress, constrain, retard, impede, stem the flow of, keep a tight rein on …*He must learn to curb that temper of his…*
NOUN = restraint, control, check, brake, limitation, rein, deterrent, bridle …*He called for much stricter curbs on immigration…*

curdle = congeal, clot, thicken, condense, turn sour, solidify, coagulate OPPOSITE dissolve

cure VERB 1 = make better, correct, heal, relieve, remedy, mend, rehabilitate, help, ease …*An operation finally cured his shin injury…*
2 = restore to health, restore, heal …*I was cured almost overnight…*
3 = preserve, smoke, dry, salt, pickle, kipper …*Legs of pork were cured and smoked over the fire…*
NOUN = remedy, treatment, medicine, healing, antidote, corrective, panacea, restorative, nostrum …*There is still no cure for the common cold…*

cure-all = panacea, elixir, nostrum, elixir vitae (*Latin*)

curio = collector's item, antique, trinket, knick-knack, bibelot

curiosity 1 = inquisitiveness, interest, prying, snooping (*informal*), nosiness (*informal*) …*Mr Lim was a constant source of curiosity to his neighbours…*
2 = oddity, wonder, sight, phenomenon, spectacle, freak, marvel, novelty, rarity …*The company is a curiosity in the world of publishing…*
3 = collector's item, trinket, curio, knick-knack, objet d'art (*French*), bibelot …*The mantelpieces and windowsills are adorned with curiosities…*

curious ADJECTIVE 1 = inquisitive, interested, questioning, searching, inquiring, peering, puzzled, peeping, meddling, prying, snoopy (*informal*), nosy (*informal*) …*He was intensely curious about the world around him…* OPPOSITE uninterested
2 = strange, unusual, bizarre, odd, novel, wonderful, rare, unique, extraordinary, puzzling, unexpected, exotic, mysterious, marvellous, peculiar, queer (*informal*), rum (*Brit. slang*), singular, unconventional, quaint, unorthodox …*A lot of curious things have happened here in the past few weeks…*

curl NOUN 1 = ringlet, lock …*a little girl with blonde curls…*
2 = twist, spiral, coil, kink, whorl, curlicue …*A thick curl of smoke rose from the rusty stove…*
3 = crimp, wave, perm, frizz …*She had curled her hair for the event…*
VERB 1 = twirl, turn, bend, twist, curve, loop, spiral, coil, meander, writhe, corkscrew, wreathe …*Smoke*

was curling up the chimney…
2 = wind, entwine, twine …*She curled her fingers round his wrist…*

curly = wavy, waved, curled, curling, fuzzy, kinky, permed, corkscrew, crimped, frizzy

currency 1 = money, coinage, legal tender, medium of exchange, bills, notes, coins …*More people favour a single European currency than oppose it…*
2 = acceptance, exposure, popularity, circulation, vogue, prevalence …*His theory has gained wide currency in America…*
➤ **WORD POWER SUPPLEMENT currencies**

current NOUN 1 = flow, course, undertow, jet, stream, tide, progression, river, tideway …*The swimmers were swept away by the strong current…*
2 = draught, flow, breeze, puff …*I felt a current of cool air blowing in my face…*
3 = mood, feeling, spirit, atmosphere, trend, tendency, drift, inclination, vibe (*slang*), undercurrent …*A strong current of nationalism is running through the country…*
ADJECTIVE 1 = present, fashionable, ongoing, up-to-date, in, now (*informal*), happening (*informal*), contemporary, in the news, sexy (*informal*), trendy (*Brit. informal*), topical, present-day, in fashion, in vogue, up-to-the-minute …*current trends in the music scene…* OPPOSITE out-of-date
2 = prevalent, general, common, accepted, popular, widespread, in the air, prevailing, circulating, going around, customary, rife, in circulation …*the prevailing tide of current opinion…*

curse VERB 1 = swear, cuss (*informal*), blaspheme, use bad language, turn the air blue (*informal*), be foul-mouthed, take the Lord's name in vain …*He was obviously very drunk and cursed continuously at passers-by…*
2 = abuse, damn, scold, swear at, revile, vilify, fulminate, execrate, vituperate, imprecate …*He cursed her for having been so careless…*
3 = put a curse on, damn, doom, jinx, excommunicate, execrate, put a jinx on, accurse, imprecate, anathematize …*I began to think that I was cursed…*
4 = afflict, trouble, burden …*He's always been cursed with a bad memory…*
NOUN 1 = oath, obscenity, blasphemy, expletive, profanity, imprecation, swearword …*He shot her an angry look and a curse…*
2 = malediction, anathema, jinx, hoodoo (*informal*), evil eye, excommunication, imprecation, execration …*He believes someone has put a curse on him…*
3 = affliction, evil, plague, scourge, cross, trouble, disaster, burden, ordeal, torment, hardship, misfortune, calamity, tribulation, bane, vexation …*The curse of alcoholism is a huge problem in Britain…*

cursed = under a curse, damned, doomed, jinxed, bedevilled, fey (*Scot.*), star-crossed, accursed, ill-fated

cursory = brief, passing, rapid, casual, summary, slight, hurried, careless, superficial, hasty, perfunctory, desultory, offhand, slapdash

curt = <u>terse</u>, short, brief, sharp, summary, blunt, rude, tart, abrupt, gruff, brusque, offhand, ungracious, uncivil, unceremonious, snappish

curtail = <u>reduce</u>, cut, diminish, decrease, dock, cut back, shorten, lessen, cut short, pare down, retrench ...*The celebrations had to be curtailed because of bad weather*...

curtain NOUN = <u>hanging</u>, drape (*chiefly U.S.*), portière ...*Her bedroom curtains were drawn*...
PHRASES **curtain something off** = <u>conceal</u>, screen, hide, veil, drape, shroud, shut off ...*The bed was a massive four-poster, curtained off by ragged draperies*...

curvaceous (*Informal*) = <u>shapely</u>, voluptuous, curvy, busty, well-rounded, buxom, full-figures, bosomy, well-stacked (*Brit. slang*), Rubenesque

curvature = <u>curving</u>, bend, curve, arching, arc

curve NOUN = <u>bend</u>, turn, loop, arc, curvature, camber ...*a curve in the road*...
VERB = <u>bend</u>, turn, wind, twist, bow, arch, snake, arc, coil, swerve ...*The track curved away below him*...
(*Related Words*)
adjective: sinuous

curved = <u>bent</u>, rounded, sweeping, twisted, bowed, arched, arced, humped, serpentine, sinuous, twisty

cushion NOUN = <u>pillow</u>, pad, bolster, headrest, beanbag, scatter cushion, hassock ...*Her leg was propped up on two cushions*...
VERB 1 = <u>protect</u>, support, bolster, cradle, buttress ...*The suspension is designed to cushion passengers from the effects of riding over rough roads*...
2 = <u>soften</u>, dampen, muffle, mitigate, deaden, suppress, stifle ...*He spoke gently, trying to cushion the blow of rejection*...

cushy (*Informal*) = <u>easy</u>, soft, comfortable, undemanding, jammy (*Brit. slang*)

custodian = <u>keeper</u>, guardian, superintendent, warden, caretaker, curator, protector, warder, watchman, overseer

custody 1 = <u>care</u>, charge, protection, supervision, preservation, auspices, aegis, tutelage, guardianship, safekeeping, keeping, trusteeship, custodianship ...*I'm taking him to court to get custody of the children*...
2 = <u>imprisonment</u>, detention, confinement, incarceration ...*Three people appeared in court and two of them were remanded in custody*...

custom 1 = <u>tradition</u>, practice, convention, ritual, form, policy, rule, style, fashion, usage, formality, etiquette, observance, praxis, unwritten law ...*The custom of lighting the Olympic flame goes back centuries*...
2 = <u>habit</u>, way, practice, manner, procedure, routine, mode, wont ...*It was his custom to approach every problem cautiously*...
3 = <u>customers</u>, business, trade, patronage ...*Providing discounts is not the only way to win custom*...

customarily = <u>usually</u>, generally, commonly, regularly, normally, traditionally, ordinarily, habitually, in the ordinary way, as a rule

customary 1 = <u>usual</u>, general, common, accepted, established, traditional, normal, ordinary, familiar, acknowledged, conventional, routine, everyday ...*It is customary to offer a drink or a snack to guests*...
OPPOSITE unusual
2 = <u>accustomed</u>, regular, usual, habitual, wonted ...*She took her customary seat behind her desk*...

customer = <u>client</u>, consumer, regular (*informal*), buyer, patron, shopper, purchaser, habitué

customs = <u>import charges</u>, tax, duty, toll, tariff

cut VERB 1 = <u>slit</u>, saw, score, nick, slice, slash, pierce, hack, penetrate, notch ...*You can hear the saw as it cuts through the bone*... ...*Thieves cut a hole in the fence*...
2 = <u>chop</u>, split, divide, slice, segment, dissect, cleave, part ...*Cut the tomatoes into small pieces*...
3 = <u>carve</u>, slice ...*Mr Long was cutting himself a piece of the cake*...
4 = <u>sever</u>, cut in two, sunder ...*I cut the rope with scissors*...
5 = <u>shape</u>, carve, engrave, chisel, form, score, fashion, chip, sculpture, whittle, sculpt, inscribe, hew ...*Geometric motifs are cut into the stone walls*...
6 = <u>slash</u>, nick, wound, lance, gash, lacerate, incise ...*I cut myself shaving*...
7 = <u>clip</u>, mow, trim, dock, prune, snip, pare, lop ...*The previous tenants hadn't even cut the grass*...
8 = <u>trim</u>, shave, hack, snip ...*She cut his ragged hair and shaved off his beard*...
9 = <u>reduce</u>, lower, slim (down), diminish, slash, decrease, cut back, rationalize, ease up on, downsize ...*The first priority is to cut costs*... OPPOSITE increase
10 = <u>abridge</u>, edit, shorten, curtail, condense, abbreviate, précis ...*He has cut the play judiciously*... OPPOSITE extend
11 = <u>delete</u>, take out, excise, edit out, expurgate ...*The audience wants more music and less drama, so we've cut some scenes*...
12 = <u>hurt</u>, wound, upset, sting, grieve, pain, hurt someone's feelings ...*The personal criticism has cut him deeply*...
13 (*Informal*) = <u>ignore</u>, avoid, slight, blank (*slang*), snub, spurn, freeze (someone) out (*informal*), cold-shoulder, turn your back on, send to Coventry, look straight through (someone) ...*She just cut me in the street*... OPPOSITE greet
14 = <u>cross</u>, interrupt, intersect, bisect ...*a straight line that cuts the vertical axis*...
NOUN 1 = <u>incision</u>, nick, rent, stroke, rip, slash, groove, slit, snip ...*The operation involves making several cuts in the cornea*...
2 = <u>gash</u>, nick, wound, slash, graze, laceration ...*He had sustained a cut on his left eyebrow*...
3 = <u>reduction</u>, fall, lowering, slash, decrease, cutback, diminution ...*The economy needs an immediate 2 per cent cut in interest rates*...
4 (*Informal*) = <u>share</u>, piece, slice, percentage, portion, kickback (*chiefly U.S.*), rake-off (*slang*) ...*The lawyers, of course, will take their cut of the profits*...
5 = <u>style</u>, look, form, fashion, shape, mode, configuration ...*The cut of her clothes made her look*

slimmer and taller…

PHRASES **a cut above something** or **someone** (*Informal*) = <u>superior to</u>, better than, more efficient than, more reliable than, streets ahead of, more useful than, more capable than, more competent than …*He's a cut above the usual boys she goes out with…* ◆ **cut and dried** (*Informal*) = <u>clear-cut</u>, settled, fixed, organized, automatic, sorted out (*informal*), predetermined, prearranged …*We are aiming for guidelines, not cut and dried answers…* ◆ **cut in** = <u>interrupt</u>, break in, butt in, interpose …*'That's not true,' the duchess cut in suddenly…* ◆ **cut out for something** = <u>suited</u>, designed, fitted, suitable, adapted, equipped, adequate, eligible, competent, qualified …*She wasn't cut out for motherhood…* ◆ **cut someone down** = <u>kill</u>, take out (*slang*), massacre, slaughter, dispatch, slay (*archaic*), blow away (*slang, chiefly U.S.*), mow down …*He was cut down in a hail of bullets…* ◆ **cut someone down to size** = <u>make (someone) look small</u>, humble, humiliate, bring low, take (someone) down a peg (*informal*), abash, crush, put (someone) in their place, take the wind out of (someone's) sails …*It's high time someone cut that arrogant little creep down to size…* ◆ **cut someone off** 1 = <u>separate</u>, isolate, sever, keep apart …*The exiles had been cut off from all contact with their homeland…* 2 = <u>interrupt</u>, stop, break in, butt in, interpose …*'But sir, I'm under orders to –' Clark cut him off. 'Don't argue with me.'…* 3 = <u>disinherit</u>, renounce, disown …*His father cut him off without a penny…* ◆ **cut someone out** (*Informal*) = <u>exclude</u>, eliminate, oust, displace, supersede, supplant …*He felt that he was being cut out of the decision-making process completely…* ◆ **cut someone up** = <u>slash</u>, injure, wound, knife, lacerate …*They cut him up with a razor…* ◆ **cut something back** 1 = <u>reduce</u>, check, lower, slash, decrease, curb, lessen, economize, downsize, retrench, draw or pull in your horns (*informal*) …*The government has cut back on defence spending…* 2 = <u>trim</u>, prune, shorten …*Cut back the root of the bulb to within half an inch of the base…* ◆ **cut something down** 1 = <u>reduce</u>, moderate, decrease, lessen, lower …*Car owners were asked to cut down their travel…* 2 = <u>fell</u>, level, hew, lop …*A vandal with a chainsaw cut down several trees in the park…* ◆ **cut something off** = <u>discontinue</u>, disconnect, suspend, halt, obstruct, bring to an end …*The rebels have cut off the electricity supply from the capital…* ◆ **cut something out** 1 = <u>remove</u>, extract, censor, delete, edit out …*All the violent scenes had been cut out of the film…* 2 = <u>stop</u>, cease, refrain from, pack in, kick (*informal*), give up, sever …*You can cut that behaviour out right now…* ◆ **cut something up** = <u>chop</u>, divide, slice, carve, dice, mince …*Cut the sausages up and cook them over a medium heat…* ◆ **cut up** = <u>upset</u>, disturbed, distressed, stricken, agitated, heartbroken, desolated, dejected, wretched …*Terry was very cut up by Jim's death…*

cutback = <u>reduction</u>, cut, retrenchment, economy, decrease, lessening

cute = <u>appealing</u>, sweet, attractive, engaging, charming, delightful, lovable, winsome, winning, cutesy (*informal, chiefly U.S.*)

cut-price = <u>cheap</u>, sale, reduced, bargain, cut-rate (*chiefly U.S.*), cheapo (*informal*)

cut-throat 1 = <u>competitive</u>, fierce, ruthless, relentless, unprincipled, dog-eat-dog …*the cut-throat world of international finance…*
2 = <u>murderous</u>, violent, bloody, cruel, savage, ferocious, bloodthirsty, barbarous, homicidal, thuggish, death-dealing …*Captain Hook and his band of cut-throat pirates…*

cutting 1 = <u>hurtful</u>, wounding, severe, acid, bitter, malicious, scathing, acrimonious, barbed, sarcastic, sardonic, caustic, vitriolic, trenchant, pointed …*People make cutting remarks to help themselves feel superior to others…* **OPPOSITE** > kind
2 = <u>piercing</u>, biting, sharp, keen, bitter, raw, chilling, stinging, penetrating, numbing …*a cutting wind…* **OPPOSITE** > pleasant

cycle = <u>series of events</u>, round (*of years*), circle, revolution, rotation

cyclone = <u>typhoon</u>, hurricane, tornado, whirlwind, tempest, twister (*U.S. informal*), storm

cynic = <u>sceptic</u>, doubter, pessimist, misanthrope, misanthropist, scoffer

cynical 1 = <u>sceptical</u>, mocking, ironic, sneering, pessimistic, scoffing, contemptuous, sarcastic, sardonic, scornful, distrustful, derisive, misanthropic …*He has a very cynical view of the world…* **OPPOSITE** > trusting
2 = <u>unbelieving</u>, sceptical, disillusioned, pessimistic, disbelieving, mistrustful …*My experiences have made me cynical about relationships…* **OPPOSITE** > optimistic

cynicism 1 = <u>scepticism</u>, pessimism, sarcasm, misanthropy, sardonicism …*I found Ben's cynicism wearing at times…*
2 = <u>disbelief</u>, doubt, scepticism, mistrust …*This talk betrays a certain cynicism about free trade…*

cyst = <u>sac</u>, growth, blister, wen, vesicle

D d

dab VERB **1** = pat, touch, tap, wipe, blot, swab
…*dabbing her eyes with a tissue*…
2 = apply, daub, stipple …*She dabbed iodine on the cuts*…
NOUN **1** = spot, bit, drop, pat, fleck, smudge, speck, dollop (*informal*), smidgen *or* smidgin (*informal, chiefly U.S. & Canad.*) …*a dab of glue*…
2 = touch, stroke, flick, smudge …*just one dab of the right fragrance*…

dabble *usually with* **in** *or* **with** = play at *or* with, potter, tinker (with), trifle (with), dip into, dally (with)

daft ADJECTIVE (*Informal, chiefly Brit.*)
1 = stupid, simple, crazy, silly, absurd, foolish, giddy, goofy, idiotic, inane, loopy (*informal*), witless, crackpot (*informal*), out to lunch (*informal*), dopey (*informal*), scatty (*Brit. informal*), asinine, gonzo (*slang*), doolally (*slang*), off your head (*informal*), off your trolley (*slang*), up the pole (*informal*), dumb-ass (*slang*), wacko *or* whacko (*slang*), off the air (*Austral. slang*) …*I wasn't so daft as to believe him*…
2 = crazy, mad, mental (*slang*), touched, nuts (*slang*), barking (*slang*), crackers (*Brit. slang*), insane, lunatic, demented, nutty (*slang*), deranged, unhinged, round the bend (*Brit. slang*), barking mad (*slang*), not right in the head, not the full shilling (*informal*), off the air (*Austral. slang*) …*It either sends you daft or kills you*…
PHRASES **daft about** = enthusiastic about, mad about, crazy about (*informal*), doting on, besotted with, sweet on, nuts about (*slang*), potty about (*Brit. informal*), infatuated by, dotty about (*slang, chiefly Brit.*), nutty about (*informal*) …*He's just daft about her*…

dag NOUN (*N.Z. informal*) = joker, comic, wag, wit, comedian, clown, kidder (*informal*), jester, humorist, prankster …*He does all these great impersonations – he's such a dag*…
PHRASES **rattle your dags** (*N.Z. informal*) = hurry up, get a move on, step on it (*informal*), get your skates on (*informal*), make haste …*You'd better rattle your dags and get on with this before the boss gets back*…

dagga (*S. African*) = cannabis, marijuana, pot (*slang*), dope (*slang*), hash (*slang*), black (*slang*), blow (*slang*), smoke (*informal*), stuff (*slang*), leaf (*slang*), tea (*U.S. slang*), grass (*slang*), chronic (*U.S. slang*), weed (*slang*), hemp, gage (*U.S. dated slang*), hashish, mary jane (*U.S. slang*), ganja, bhang, kif, wacky baccy (*slang*), sinsemilla, charas

dagger NOUN = knife, bayonet, dirk, stiletto, poniard, skean …*The man raised his arm and plunged a dagger into her back*…
PHRASES **at daggers drawn** = on bad terms, at odds, at war, at loggerheads, up in arms, at enmity …*She and her mother were at daggers drawn*…

♦ **look daggers at someone** = glare, frown, scowl, glower, look black, lour *or* lower …*The girls looked daggers at me*…

daily ADVERB = every day, day by day, day after day, once a day, per diem …*The shop is open daily*…
ADJECTIVE **1** = everyday, regular, circadian, diurnal, quotidian …*the company's daily turnover*…
2 = day-to-day, common, ordinary, routine, everyday, commonplace, quotidian …*factors which deeply influence daily life*…

dainty **1** = delicate, pretty, charming, fine, elegant, neat, exquisite, graceful, petite …*The girls were dainty and feminine*… OPPOSITE clumsy
2 = delectable, choice, delicious, tender, tasty, savoury, palatable, toothsome …*a dainty morsel*…
3 = particular, nice, refined, fussy, scrupulous, fastidious, choosy, picky (*informal*), finicky, finical …*They cater for a range of tastes, from the dainty to the extravagant*…

dais = platform, stage, podium, rostrum, estrade

dale = valley, glen, vale, dell, dingle, strath (*Scot.*), coomb

dalliance (*Old-fashioned*) **1** = flirtation, coquetry, amorous play …*a politician engaging in sexual dalliance with his colleague*…
2 = dabbling, playing, toying, trifling …*a fashionable dalliance with ideas of liberty and reason*…

dally VERB (*Old-fashioned*) = waste time, delay, fool (about *or* around), linger, hang about, loiter, while away, dawdle, fritter away, procrastinate, tarry, dilly-dally (*informal*), drag your feet *or* heels …*He did not dally long over his meal*… OPPOSITE hurry (up)
PHRASES **dally with someone** = flirt with, tease, lead on, toy with, play around with, fool (about *or* around) with, trifle with, play fast and loose with (*informal*), frivol with (*informal*) …*He was dallying with some floosie*…

dam NOUN = barrier, wall, barrage, obstruction, embankment, hindrance …*They went ahead with plans to build a dam across the river*…
VERB = block up, block, hold in, restrict, check, confine, choke, hold back, barricade, obstruct …*The reservoir was formed by damming the River Blith*…

damage VERB = spoil, hurt, injure, smash, harm, ruin, crush, devastate, mar, wreck, shatter, weaken, gut, demolish, undo, trash (*slang*), total (*slang*), impair, ravage, mutilate, annihilate, incapacitate, raze, deface, play (merry) hell with (*informal*) …*He damaged the car with a baseball bat*… OPPOSITE fix
NOUN **1** = destruction, harm, loss, injury, suffering, hurt, ruin, crushing, wrecking, shattering, devastation, detriment, mutilation, impairment, annihilation, ruination …*There have been many reports of minor damage to buildings*… OPPOSITE improvement

2 (*Informal*) = <u>cost</u>, price, charge, rate, bill, figure, amount, total, payment, expense, outlay ...*What's the damage for these tickets?*...

PLURAL NOUN (*Law*) = <u>compensation</u>, fine, payment, satisfaction, amends, reparation, indemnity, restitution, reimbursement, atonement, recompense, indemnification, meed (*archaic*), requital ...*He was vindicated in court and damages were awarded*...

damaging = <u>harmful</u>, detrimental, hurtful, ruinous, prejudicial, deleterious, injurious, disadvantageous **OPPOSITE** helpful

dame 1 = <u>lady</u>, baroness, dowager, grande dame (*French*), noblewoman, peeress ...*a Dame of the British Empire*...
2 (*Slang, chiefly U.S. and Canad.*) = <u>woman</u>, girl, lady, female, bird, maiden (*archaic*), miss, chick (*slang*), maid (*archaic*), gal (*slang*), lass, lassie (*informal*), wench (*facetious*), charlie (*Austral. slang*), chook (*Austral. slang*) ...*This is one classy dame you've got yourself here*...

damn **VERB** = <u>criticize</u>, condemn, blast, pan (*informal*), slam (*slang*), denounce, put down, slate (*informal*), censure, castigate, tear into (*informal*), diss (*slang, chiefly U.S.*), inveigh against, lambast(e), excoriate, denunciate ...*You can't damn him for his beliefs*... **OPPOSITE** praise
PHRASES **not give a damn** (*Informal*) = <u>not care</u>, not mind, be indifferent, not give a hoot, not care a jot, not give two hoots, not care a whit, not care a brass farthing, not give a tinker's curse *or* damn (*slang*) ...*Frankly, my dear, I don't give a damn*...

damnation (*Theology*) = <u>condemnation</u>, damning, sending to hell, consigning to perdition

damned (*Slang*) = <u>infernal</u>, accursed, detestable, revolting, infamous, confounded, despicable, abhorred, hateful, loathsome, abominable, freaking (*slang, chiefly U.S.*)

damning = <u>incriminating</u>, implicating, condemnatory, dooming, accusatorial, damnatory, implicative

damp **ADJECTIVE** = <u>moist</u>, wet, dripping, soggy, humid, sodden, dank, sopping, clammy, dewy, muggy, drizzly, vaporous ...*damp weather*... ...*She wiped the table with a damp cloth*... **OPPOSITE** dry
NOUN = <u>moisture</u>, liquid, humidity, drizzle, dew, dampness, wetness, dankness, clamminess, mugginess ...*There was damp everywhere in the house*... **OPPOSITE** dryness
VERB = <u>moisten</u>, wet, soak, dampen, lick, moisturize, humidify ...*She damped a hand towel and laid it across her head*...
PHRASES **damp something down** = <u>curb</u>, reduce, check, cool, moderate, dash, chill, dull, diminish, discourage, restrain, inhibit, stifle, allay, deaden, pour cold water on ...*He tried to damp down his panic*...

dampen 1 = <u>reduce</u>, check, moderate, dash, dull, restrain, deter, stifle, lessen, smother, muffle, deaden ...*Nothing seemed to dampen his enthusiasm*...
2 = <u>moisten</u>, wet, spray, make damp, bedew, besprinkle ...*She took the time to dampen a cloth and wash her face*...

damper (*Informal*) = <u>discouragement</u>, cloud, chill, curb, restraint, gloom, cold water (*informal*), pall

dampness = <u>moistness</u>, damp, moisture, humidity, wetness, sogginess, dankness, clamminess, mugginess **OPPOSITE** dryness

dance **VERB 1** = <u>prance</u>, rock, trip, swing, spin, hop, skip, sway, whirl, caper, jig, frolic, cavort, gambol, bob up and down, cut a rug (*informal*) ...*They like to dance to the music on the radio*...
2 = <u>caper</u>, trip, spring, jump, bound, leap, bounce, hop, skip, romp, frolic, cavort, gambol ...*He danced off down the road*...
NOUN = <u>ball</u>, social, hop (*informal*), disco, knees-up (*Brit. informal*), discotheque, dancing party, B and S (*Austral. informal*) ...*She often went to dances and parties in the village*...
➤ **dances**

dancer = <u>ballerina</u>, hoofer (*slang*), Terpsichorean

dandy **NOUN** = <u>fop</u>, beau, swell (*informal*), blood (*rare*), buck (*archaic*), blade (*archaic*), peacock, dude (*U.S. & Canad. informal*), toff (*Brit. slang*), macaroni (*obsolete*), man about town, popinjay, coxcomb ...*a handsome young dandy*...
ADJECTIVE (*Informal*) = <u>excellent</u>, great, fine, capital, splendid, first-rate ...*Everything's fine and dandy*...

danger 1 = <u>jeopardy</u>, vulnerability, insecurity, precariousness, endangerment ...*Your life is in danger*...
2 = <u>hazard</u>, risk, threat, menace, peril, pitfall ...*These roads are a danger to cyclists*...

dangerous = <u>perilous</u>, threatening, risky, hazardous, exposed, alarming, vulnerable, nasty, ugly, menacing, insecure, hairy (*slang*), unsafe, precarious, treacherous, breakneck, parlous (*archaic*), fraught with danger, chancy (*informal*), unchancy (*Scot.*) **OPPOSITE** safe

dangerously 1 = <u>seriously</u>, badly, severely, gravely, critically, acutely, grievously ...*He is dangerously ill*...
2 = <u>perilously</u>, alarmingly, carelessly, precariously, recklessly, daringly, riskily, harmfully, hazardously, unsafely, unsecurely ...*He rushed downstairs dangerously fast*...

dangle 1 = <u>hang</u>, swing, trail, sway, flap, hang down, depend ...*A gold bracelet dangled from his left wrist*...
2 = <u>wave</u>, wiggle, jiggle, joggle ...*He dangled the keys in front of her face*...
3 = <u>offer</u>, flourish, brandish, flaunt, tempt someone with, lure someone with, entice someone with, tantalize someone with ...*They dangled rich rewards before me*...

dangling = <u>hanging</u>, swinging, loose, trailing, swaying, disconnected, drooping, unconnected

dank = <u>damp</u>, dripping, moist, soggy, clammy, dewy

dapper (*only ever used with reference to men, not women*) = <u>neat</u>, nice, smart, trim, stylish, spruce, dainty, natty (*informal*), well-groomed, well turned out, trig (*archaic or dialect*), soigné **OPPOSITE** untidy

dappled = <u>mottled</u>, spotted, speckled, pied, flecked, variegated, checkered, freckled, stippled, piebald, brindled

Dances

allemande	country dance	Lambeth walk	roundelay or roundel
apache dance	courante	lancers	rumba
ballroom dance	czardas	ländler	salsa
barn dance	Dashing White Sergeant	limbo	saltarello
beguine	ecossaise	macarena	samba
belly dance	eightsome reel	malagueña	saraband
black bottom	excuse-me	mambo	saunter
body popping	fan dance	maxixe	schottische
bogle	fandango	mazurka	seguidilla
bolero	farandole	merengue	shake
boogaloo	flamenco	minuet	shimmy
boogie	folk dance	Morisco or Moresco	shuffle
bossa nova	formation dance	morris dance	siciliano
boston	foxtrot	mosh	Sir Roger de Coverley
bourrée	galliard	musette	skank
branle	galop	nautch	snake dance
brawl	gavotte	old-time dance	snowball
break dance	Gay Gordons	one-step	square dance
breakdown	german	palais glide	step dance
buck and wing	ghost dance	paso doble	stomp
bump	gigue	passacaglia	strathspey
bunny hug	gopak	Paul Jones	strip the willow
butterfly	habanera	pavane	sword dance
cachucha	hay or hey	pogo	tambourin
cakewalk	Highland fling	poi dance	tango
calypso	hoedown	polka	tap dance
cancan	hokey cokey	polonaise	tarantella
carioca	hora	pyrrhic	toe dance
carmagnole	hornpipe	quadrille	twist
carol	hula or hula-hula	quickstep	two-step
cha-cha-cha or cha-cha	hustle	redowa	Tyrolienne
chaconne	jig	reel	Virginia reel
charleston	jitterbug	rigadoon or rigaudon	vogueing
clog dance	jive	ring-shout	volta
conga	jota	robot dancing or	waltz
contredanse or	juba	robotics	war dance
contradance	kazachok	ronggeng	Zapata
Cossack dance	kolo	round	
cotillion	lambada	round dance	

dare 1 = risk doing, venture, presume, make bold, hazard doing, brave doing ...*I didn't dare to tell my uncle what had happened...*
2 = challenge, provoke, defy, taunt, goad, throw down the gauntlet ...*She dared me to ask him out...*

daredevil NOUN = adventurer, show-off (*informal*), madcap, desperado, exhibitionist, stunt man, hot dog (*chiefly U.S.*), adrenalin junky (*slang*) ...*a tragic ending for a daredevil whose luck ran out...*
ADJECTIVE = daring, bold, adventurous, reckless, audacious, madcap, death-defying ...*He gets his kicks from daredevil car-racing...*

daring ADJECTIVE = brave, bold, adventurous, rash, have-a-go (*informal*), reckless, fearless, audacious, intrepid, impulsive, valiant, plucky, game (*informal*), daredevil, venturesome ...*a daring rescue attempt...*
OPPOSITE timid
NOUN = bravery, nerve (*informal*), courage, face (*informal*), spirit, bottle (*Brit. slang*), guts (*informal*), pluck, grit, audacity, boldness, temerity, derring-do (*archaic*), spunk (*informal*), fearlessness, rashness, intrepidity ...*His daring may have cost him his life...*

OPPOSITE timidity

dark ADJECTIVE 1 = dim, murky, shady, shadowy, grey, cloudy, dingy, overcast, dusky, unlit, pitch-black, indistinct, poorly lit, sunless, tenebrous, darksome (*literary*), pitchy, unilluminated ...*It was a dark and stormy night...*
2 = black, brunette, ebony, dark-skinned, sable, dusky, swarthy ...*a tall, dark and handsome stranger...*
OPPOSITE fair
3 = evil, foul, horrible, sinister, infamous, vile, satanic, wicked, atrocious, sinful, hellish, infernal, nefarious, damnable ...*magicians who harnessed dark powers...*
4 = secret, deep, hidden, mysterious, concealed, obscure, mystic, enigmatic, puzzling, occult, arcane, cryptic, abstruse, recondite, Delphic ...*the dark recesses of the mind...*
5 = gloomy, sad, grim, miserable, low, bleak, moody, dismal, pessimistic, melancholy, sombre, morbid, glum, mournful, morose, joyless, doleful, cheerless ...*His endless chatter kept me from thinking dark thoughts...* OPPOSITE cheerful
6 = angry, threatening, forbidding, frowning,

ominous, dour, scowling, sullen, glum, glowering, sulky …*He shot her a dark glance*…

NOUN **1** = <u>darkness</u>, shadows, gloom, dusk, obscurity, murk, dimness, semi-darkness, murkiness …*I've always been afraid of the dark*…

2 = <u>night</u>, twilight, evening, evo (*Austral. slang*), dusk, night-time, nightfall …*after dark*…

darken 1 = <u>cloud</u>, shadow, shade, obscure, eclipse, dim, deepen, overshadow, blacken, becloud …*A storm darkened the sky*… OPPOSITE⟩ brighten

2 = <u>make dark</u>, shade, blacken, make darker, deepen …*She darkened her eyebrows with mascara*…

3 = <u>become gloomy</u>, blacken, become angry, look black, go crook (*Austral. & N.Z. slang*), grow troubled …*His face suddenly darkened*… OPPOSITE⟩ become cheerful

4 = <u>sadden</u>, upset, cloud, blacken, cast a pall over, cast a gloom upon …*Nothing was going to darken his mood today*…

darkness = <u>dark</u>, shadows, shade, gloom, obscurity, blackness, murk, dimness, murkiness, duskiness, shadiness

darling NOUN **1** = <u>beloved</u>, love, dear, dearest, angel, treasure, precious, loved one, sweetheart, sweetie, truelove, dear one …*Hello, darling!*…

2 = <u>favourite</u>, pet, spoilt child, apple of your eye, blue-eyed boy, fair-haired boy (*U.S.*) …*He was the darling of the family*…

ADJECTIVE **1** = <u>beloved</u>, dear, dearest, sweet, treasured, precious, adored, cherished, revered …*my darling baby boy*…

2 = <u>adorable</u>, sweet, attractive, lovely, charming, cute, enchanting, captivating …*a perfectly darling little house*…

darn VERB = <u>mend</u>, repair, patch, stitch, sew up, cobble up …*His aunt darned his old socks*…

NOUN = <u>mend</u>, patch, reinforcement, invisible repair …*blue woollen stockings with untidy darns*…

dart 1 = <u>dash</u>, run, race, shoot, fly, speed, spring, tear, rush, bound, flash, hurry, sprint, bolt, hasten, whizz, haste, flit, scoot …*She darted away through the trees*…

2 = <u>shoot</u>, send, cast …*She darted a sly glance at him*…

dash VERB **1** = <u>rush</u>, run, race, shoot, fly, career, speed, spring, tear, bound, hurry, barrel (along) (*informal, chiefly U.S. & Canad.*), sprint, bolt, dart, hasten, scurry, haste, stampede, burn rubber (*informal*), make haste, hotfoot …*Suddenly she dashed out into the garden*… OPPOSITE⟩ dawdle

2 = <u>throw</u>, cast, pitch, slam, toss, hurl, fling, chuck (*informal*), propel, project, sling, lob (*informal*) …*She dashed the doll against the stone wall*…

3 = <u>crash</u>, break, smash, shatter, shiver, splinter …*The waves dashed against the side of the ship*…

4 = <u>disappoint</u>, ruin, frustrate, spoil, foil, undo, thwart, dampen, confound, crool *or* cruel (*Austral. slang*) …*They had their hopes raised and then dashed*…

NOUN **1** = <u>rush</u>, run, race, sprint, bolt, dart, spurt, sortie …*a 160-mile dash to hospital*…

2 = <u>drop</u>, little, bit, shot (*informal*), touch, spot,

suggestion, trace, hint, pinch, sprinkling, tot, trickle, nip, tinge, soupçon (*French*) …*Add a dash of balsamic vinegar*… OPPOSITE⟩ lot

3 (*Old-fashioned*) = <u>style</u>, spirit, flair, flourish, vigour, verve, panache, élan, brio, vivacity …*He played with great fire and dash*…

dashing 1 (*Old-fashioned*) = <u>stylish</u>, smart, elegant, dazzling, flamboyant, sporty, swish (*informal, chiefly Brit.*), urbane, jaunty, dapper, showy …*He looked very dashing in a designer jacket of soft black leather*…

2 = <u>bold</u>, spirited, daring, exuberant, gallant, plucky, swashbuckling, debonair …*the founding father of the dashing air squadron*… OPPOSITE⟩ dull

dastardly (*Old-fashioned*) = <u>despicable</u>, mean, low, base, sneaking, cowardly, craven, vile, abject, sneaky, contemptible, underhand, weak-kneed (*informal*), faint-hearted, spiritless, recreant (*archaic*), caitiff (*archaic*), niddering (*archaic*)

data = <u>information</u>, facts, figures, details, materials, documents, intelligence, statistics, input, gen (*Brit. informal*), dope (*informal*), info (*informal*)

Word Power

data – From a historical point of view only, the word *data* is a plural. In fact, in many cases it is not clear from context if it is being used as a singular or plural, so there is no issue: *when next needed the data can be accessed very quickly*. When it is necessary to specify, the preferred usage nowadays in general language is to treat it as singular, as in: *this data is useful to the government in the planning of housing services*. There are rather more examples in the Bank of English of *these data* than *this data*, with a marked preference for the plural in academic and scientific writing. As regards *data is* versus *data are*, the preference for the plural form overall is even more marked in that kind of writing. When speaking, however, it is best to opt for treating the word as singular, except in precise scientific contexts. The singular form *datum* is comparatively rare in the sense of a single item of data.

---

date NOUN **1** = <u>time</u>, stage, period …*An inquest will be held at a later date*…

2 = <u>appointment</u>, meeting, arrangement, commitment, engagement, rendezvous, tryst, assignation …*He had made a date with the girl*…

3 = <u>partner</u>, escort, friend, steady (*informal*) …*She is his date for the dance*…

VERB **1** = <u>put a date on</u>, determine the date of, assign a date to, fix the period of …*It is difficult to date the relic*…

2 = <u>become dated</u>, become old-fashioned, obsolesce …*It always looks smart and will never date*…

PHRASES **date from** *or* **date back to** (with a *time* or *date* as object) = <u>come from</u>, belong to, originate in, exist from, bear a date of …*The palace dates back to the 16th century*… ♦ **out of date** = <u>old-fashioned</u>, dated, outdated, old, ancient, obsolete, archaic, unfashionable, antiquated, outmoded, passé, behind the times, obsolescent, démodé (*French*), out of the ark (*informal*) ...*Those boots look really out of date now*... ◆ **to date** = up to now, yet, so far, until now, now, as yet, thus far, up to this point, up to the present ...*This is the band's fourth top twenty single to date*...

dated = old-fashioned, outdated, out of date, obsolete, archaic, unfashionable, antiquated, outmoded, passé, out, old hat, untrendy (*Brit. informal*), démodé (*French*), out of the ark (*informal*) OPPOSITE> modern

daub VERB = stain, cover, paint, coat, dirty, plaster, smear, splatter, slap on (*informal*), spatter, sully, deface, smirch, begrime, besmear, bedaub ...*They daubed his home with slogans*...
NOUN = smear, spot, stain, blot, blotch, splodge, splotch, smirch ...*Apply an extra daub of colour*...

daughter = female child, girl, descendant
(*Related Words*)
adjective: filial

daunt = discourage, alarm, shake, frighten, scare, terrify, cow, intimidate, deter, dismay, put off, subdue, overawe, frighten off, dishearten, dispirit OPPOSITE> reassure

daunted = intimidated, alarmed, shaken, frightened, overcome, cowed, discouraged, deterred, dismayed, put off, disillusioned, unnerved, demoralized, dispirited, downcast

daunting = intimidating, alarming, frightening, discouraging, awesome, unnerving, disconcerting, demoralizing, off-putting (*Brit. informal*), disheartening OPPOSITE> reassuring

dawdle 1 = waste time, potter, trail, lag, idle, loaf, hang about, dally, loiter, dilly-dally (*informal*), drag your feet *or* heels ...*They dawdled arm in arm past the shopfronts*... OPPOSITE> hurry
2 = linger, idle, dally, take your time, procrastinate, drag your feet *or* heels ...*I dawdled over a beer*...

dawn NOUN 1 = daybreak, morning, sunrise, dawning, daylight, aurora (*poetic*), crack of dawn, sunup, cockcrow, dayspring (*poetic*) ...*She woke at dawn*...
2 (*Literary*) = beginning, start, birth, rise, origin, dawning, unfolding, emergence, outset, onset, advent, genesis, inception ...*the dawn of the radio age*...
VERB 1 = begin, start, open, rise, develop, emerge, unfold, originate ...*A new era seemed about to dawn*...
2 = grow light, break, brighten, lighten ...*The next day dawned*...
PHRASES **dawn on** *or* **upon someone** = hit, strike, occur to, register (*informal*), become apparent, come to mind, cross your mind, come into your head, flash across your mind ...*Then the chilling truth dawned on me*...

day NOUN 1 = twenty-four hours, working day ...*The conference is on for three days*...
2 = daytime, daylight, daylight hours ...*They sleep during the day*...

3 = date, particular day ...*What day are you leaving?*...
4 = time, age, era, prime, period, generation, heyday, epoch ...*In my day we treated our elders with more respect*...
PHRASES **call it a day** (*Informal*) = stop, finish, cease, pack up (*informal*), leave off, knock off (*informal*), desist, pack it in (*slang*), shut up shop, jack it in, chuck it in (*informal*), give up *or* over ...*Faced with such opposition, he had no choice but to call it a day*... ◆ **day after day** = continually, regularly, relentlessly, persistently, incessantly, nonstop, unremittingly, monotonously, unfalteringly ...*In this job I just do the same thing day after day*... ◆ **day by day** = gradually, slowly, progressively, daily, steadily, bit by bit, little by little, by degrees ...*Day by day, he got weaker*...
(*Related Words*)
adjective: diurnal

daybreak = dawn, morning, sunrise, first light, crack of dawn, break of day, sunup, cockcrow, dayspring (*poetic*)

daydream VERB = fantasize, dream, imagine, envision, stargaze ...*He daydreams of being a famous journalist*...
NOUN = fantasy, dream, imagining, wish, fancy, reverie, pipe dream, fond hope, figment of the imagination, castle in the air *or* in Spain ...*He escaped into daydreams of heroic men and beautiful women*...

daylight NOUN 1 = sunlight, sunshine, light of day ...*Lack of daylight can make people feel depressed*...
2 = daytime, broad daylight, daylight hours ...*It was still daylight but many cars had their headlamps on*...
PHRASES **in broad daylight** = in public, in full view, in the light of day ...*The murder happened in broad daylight*...

day-to-day = everyday, regular, usual, routine, accustomed, customary, habitual, run-of-the-mill, wonted

daze VERB 1 = stun, shock, paralyse, numb, stupefy, benumb ...*The blow caught me on the temple and dazed me*...
2 = confuse, surprise, amaze, blind, astonish, stagger, startle, dazzle, bewilder, astound, perplex, flummox, dumbfound, nonplus, flabbergast (*informal*), befog ...*We were dazed by the sheer size of the spectacle*...
NOUN (usually used in the phrase *in a daze*) = shock, confusion, distraction, trance, bewilderment, stupor, trancelike state ...*I was walking around in a daze*...

dazed = shocked, stunned, confused, staggered, baffled, at sea, bewildered, muddled, numbed, dizzy, bemused, perplexed, disorientated, flabbergasted (*informal*), dopey (*slang*), groggy (*informal*), stupefied, nonplussed, light-headed, flummoxed, punch-drunk, woozy (*informal*), fuddled

dazzle VERB 1 = impress, amaze, fascinate, overwhelm, astonish, awe, overpower, bowl over (*informal*), overawe, hypnotize, stupefy, take your breath away, strike dumb ...*He dazzled her with his knowledge of the world*...

2 = <u>blind</u>, confuse, daze, bedazzle ...*She was dazzled by the lights...*
　NOUN = <u>splendour</u>, sparkle, glitter, flash, brilliance, magnificence, razzmatazz (*slang*), razzle-dazzle (*slang*), éclat ...*The dazzle of stardom and status attracts them...*

dazzling = <u>splendid</u>, brilliant, stunning, superb, divine, glorious, sparkling, glittering, sensational (*informal*), sublime, virtuoso, drop-dead (*slang*), ravishing, scintillating **OPPOSITE** ordinary

dead **ADJECTIVE** **1** = <u>deceased</u>, gone, departed, late, perished, extinct, defunct, passed away, pushing up (the) daisies ...*My husband's been dead for a year now...* **OPPOSITE** alive
2 = <u>inanimate</u>, still, barren, sterile, stagnant, lifeless, inert, uninhabited ...*The polluted and stagnant water seems dead...*
3 = <u>boring</u>, dull, dreary, flat, plain, stale, tasteless, humdrum, uninteresting, insipid, ho-hum (*informal*), vapid, dead-and-alive ...*It was a horrible, dead little town...*
4 = <u>not working</u>, useless, inactive, inoperative ...*This battery's dead...* **OPPOSITE** working
5 = <u>obsolete</u>, old, antique, discarded, extinct, archaic, disused ...*dead languages...*
6 = <u>spiritless</u>, cold, dull, wooden, glazed, indifferent, callous, lukewarm, inhuman, unsympathetic, apathetic, frigid, glassy, unresponsive, unfeeling, torpid ...*He watched the procedure with cold, dead eyes...* **OPPOSITE** lively
7 = <u>numb</u>, frozen, paralysed, insensitive, inert, deadened, immobilized, unfeeling, torpid, insensible, benumbed ...*My arm had gone dead...*
8 (usually used of *centre, silence,* or *stop*) = <u>total</u>, complete, perfect, entire, absolute, utter, outright, thorough, downright, unqualified ...*They hurried about in dead silence...*
9 (*Informal*) = <u>exhausted</u>, tired, worn out, spent, wasted, done in (*informal*), all in (*slang*), drained, wiped out (*informal*), sapped, knackered (*slang*), prostrated, clapped out (*Brit., Austral., & N.Z. informal*), tired out, ready to drop, dog-tired (*informal*), zonked (*slang*), dead tired, dead beat (*informal*), shagged out (*Brit. slang*), worn to a frazzle (*informal*), on your last legs (*informal*), creamcrackered (*Brit. slang*) ...*I must get some sleep – I'm absolutely dead...*
　NOUN = <u>middle</u>, heart, depth, thick, midst ...*in the dead of night...*
　ADVERB (*Informal*) = <u>exactly</u>, quite, completely, totally, directly, perfectly, fully, entirely, absolutely, thoroughly, wholly, utterly, consummately, wholeheartedly, unconditionally, to the hilt, one hundred per cent, unmitigatedly ...*You're dead right...*

deadbeat (*Informal, chiefly U.S. & Canad.*) = <u>layabout</u>, bum (*informal*), waster, lounger, piker (*Austral. & N.Z. slang*), sponge (*informal*), parasite, drone, loafer, slacker (*informal*), scrounger (*informal*), skiver (*Brit. slang*), idler, freeloader (*slang*), good-for-nothing, sponger (*informal*), wastrel, bludger (*Austral. & N.Z. informal*), cadger, quandong (*Austral. slang*)

deaden **1** = <u>reduce</u>, dull, diminish, check, weaken, cushion, damp, suppress, blunt, paralyse, impair, numb, lessen, alleviate, smother, dampen, anaesthetize, benumb ...*He needs morphine to deaden the pain in his chest...*
2 = <u>suppress</u>, reduce, dull, diminish, cushion, damp, mute, stifle, hush, lessen, smother, dampen, muffle, quieten ...*They managed to deaden the sound...*

deadline = <u>time limit</u>, cutoff point, target date *or* time, limit

deadlock **1** = <u>impasse</u>, stalemate, standstill, halt, cessation, gridlock, standoff, full stop ...*Peace talks ended in a deadlock last month...*
2 = <u>tie</u>, draw, stalemate, impasse, standstill, gridlock, standoff, dead heat ...*Larkham broke the deadlock with a late goal...*

deadly **1** = <u>lethal</u>, fatal, deathly, dangerous, devastating, destructive, mortal, murderous, poisonous, malignant, virulent, pernicious, noxious, venomous, baleful, death-dealing, baneful ...*a deadly disease currently affecting dolphins...*
2 = <u>hard</u>, fierce, harsh, cruel, savage, brutal, grim, stern, ruthless, ferocious, unrelenting, merciless, implacable, barbarous, pitiless, unfeeling, unmerciful, unpitying ...*She levelled a deadly look at him...*
3 (*Informal*) = <u>boring</u>, dull, tedious, flat, monotonous, uninteresting, mind-numbing, unexciting, ho-hum (*informal*), wearisome, as dry as dust ...*She found the party deadly...*
4 = <u>accurate</u>, sure, true, effective, exact, reliable, precise, on target, infallible, unerring, unfailing ...*the fastest and most deadly bowlers in the world today...*
5 = <u>deathly</u>, white, pale, ghostly, ghastly, wan, pasty, colourless, pallid, anaemic, ashen, sallow, whitish, cadaverous, waxen, ashy, deathlike, wheyfaced ...*The deadly pallor of her skin...*

deadpan = <u>expressionless</u>, empty, blank, wooden, straight-faced, vacuous, impassive, inscrutable, poker-faced, inexpressive

deaf **1** = <u>hard of hearing</u>, without hearing, stone deaf ...*She is now profoundly deaf...*
2 = <u>oblivious</u>, indifferent, unmoved, unconcerned, unsympathetic, impervious, unresponsive, heedless, unhearing ...*The assembly were deaf to all pleas for financial help...*
　➤ **disabled**

deafen = <u>make deaf</u>, split *or* burst the eardrums

deafening = <u>ear-splitting</u>, intense, piercing, ringing, booming, overpowering, resounding, dinning, thunderous, ear-piercing

deal **NOUN** **1** (*Informal*) = <u>agreement</u>, understanding, contract, business, negotiation, arrangement, bargain, transaction, pact ...*Japan has done a deal with America on rice exports...*
2 = <u>amount</u>, quantity, measure, degree, mass, volume, share, portion, bulk ...*a great deal of money...*
　PHRASES **deal in something** = <u>sell</u>, trade in, stock, traffic in, buy and sell ...*The company deals in antiques...* ◆ **deal something out** = <u>distribute</u>, give, administer, share, divide, assign, allocate,

dispense, bestow, allot, mete out, dole out, apportion ...*a failure to deal out effective punishments to offenders*... ◆ **deal with something** = <u>be concerned with</u>, involve, concern, touch, regard, apply to, bear on, pertain to, be relevant to, treat of ...*the parts of the book which deal with events in Florence*... ◆ **deal with something** *or* **someone 1** = <u>handle</u>, manage, treat, cope with, take care of, see to, attend to, get to grips with, come to grips with ...*the way in which the company deals with complaints*... **2** = <u>behave towards</u>, act towards, conduct yourself towards ...*He's a hard man to deal with*...

dealer = <u>trader</u>, marketer, merchant, supplier, wholesaler, purveyor, tradesman, merchandiser

dealings = <u>business</u>, selling, trading, trade, traffic, truck, bargaining, commerce, transactions, business relations

dear `ADJECTIVE` **1** = <u>beloved</u>, close, valued, favourite, respected, prized, dearest, sweet, treasured, precious, darling, intimate, esteemed, cherished, revered ...*Mrs Cavendish is a dear friend of mine*... `OPPOSITE` hated **2** (*Brit. informal*) = <u>expensive</u>, costly, high-priced, excessive, pricey (*informal*), at a premium, overpriced, exorbitant ...*Don't buy that one – it's too dear*... `OPPOSITE` cheap
`NOUN` = <u>darling</u>, love, dearest, sweet, angel, treasure, precious, beloved, loved one, sweetheart, truelove ...*Yes, my dear*...

dearly (*Formal*) **1** = <u>very much</u>, greatly, extremely, profoundly ...*She would dearly love to marry*... **2** = <u>at great cost</u>, dear, at a high price, at a heavy cost ...*He is paying dearly for his folly*...

dearth = <u>lack</u>, want, need, absence, poverty, shortage, deficiency, famine, inadequacy, scarcity, paucity, insufficiency, sparsity, scantiness, exiguousness

death 1 = <u>dying</u>, demise, bereavement, end, passing, release, loss, departure, curtains (*informal*), cessation, expiration, decease, quietus ...*There had been a death in the family*... `OPPOSITE` birth **2** = <u>destruction</u>, ending, finish, ruin, wiping out, undoing, extinction, elimination, downfall, extermination, annihilation, obliteration, ruination ...*the death of everything he had ever hoped for*... `OPPOSITE` beginning **3** *sometimes capital* = <u>the Grim Reaper</u>, the Dark Angel ...*Carrying a long scythe is the hooded figure of Death*...

(*Related Words*)
adjectives: fatal, lethal, mortal

deathly 1 = <u>deathlike</u>, white, pale, ghastly, wan, gaunt, haggard, bloodless, pallid, ashen, sallow, cadaverous, ashy, like death warmed up (*informal*) ...*the deathly pallor of her cheeks*... **2** = <u>fatal</u>, terminal, deadly, terrible, destructive, lethal, mortal, malignant, incurable, pernicious ...*a deathly illness*...

debacle *or* **débâcle** = <u>disaster</u>, catastrophe, fiasco

debar = <u>bar</u>, exclude, prohibit, black, stop, keep out, preclude, shut out, blackball, interdict, refuse admission to

---

> ### *Word Power*
>
> **debar** – The word *debar* is not synonymous with *disbar*, which should only be used when talking about a barrister, although evidence shows that the two are often confused.

debase 1 (*Formal*) = <u>corrupt</u>, contaminate, devalue, pollute, impair, taint, depreciate, defile, adulterate, vitiate, bastardize ...*He claims that advertising debases the English language*... `OPPOSITE` purify **2** = <u>degrade</u>, reduce, lower, shame, humble, disgrace, humiliate, demean, drag down, dishonour, cheapen, abase ...*I won't debase myself by answering that question*... `OPPOSITE` exalt

debased 1 = <u>corrupt</u>, devalued, reduced, lowered, mixed, contaminated, polluted, depreciated, impure, adulterated ...*a debased form of Buddhism*... **2** = <u>degraded</u>, corrupt, fallen, low, base, abandoned, perverted, vile, sordid, depraved, debauched, scungy (*Austral. & N.Z.*) ...*Such women were seen as morally debased*... `OPPOSITE` virtuous

debatable = <u>doubtful</u>, uncertain, dubious, controversial, unsettled, questionable, undecided, borderline, in dispute, moot, arguable, iffy (*informal*), open to question, disputable

debate `NOUN` = <u>discussion</u>, talk, argument, dispute, analysis, conversation, consideration, controversy, dialogue, contention, deliberation, polemic, altercation, disputation ...*There has been a lot of debate about this point*...
`VERB` **1** = <u>discuss</u>, question, talk about, argue about, dispute, examine, contest, deliberate, contend, wrangle, thrash out, controvert ...*The causes of depression are much debated*... **2** = <u>consider</u>, reflect, think about, weigh, contemplate, deliberate, ponder, revolve, mull over, ruminate, give thought to, cogitate, meditate upon ...*He debated whether to have yet another double vodka*...

debauched = <u>corrupt</u>, abandoned, perverted, degraded, degenerate, immoral, dissipated, sleazy, depraved, wanton, debased, profligate, dissolute, licentious, pervy (*slang*)

debauchery = <u>depravity</u>, excess, lust, revel, indulgence, orgy, incontinence, gluttony, dissipation, licentiousness, intemperance, overindulgence, lewdness, dissoluteness, carousal

debilitate = <u>weaken</u>, exhaust, wear out, sap, incapacitate, prostrate, enfeeble, enervate, devitalize `OPPOSITE` invigorate

debilitating = <u>weakening</u>, tiring, exhausting, draining, fatiguing, wearing, sapping, incapacitating, enervating, enfeebling, devitalizing `OPPOSITE` invigorating

debonair = <u>elegant</u>, charming, dashing, smooth, refined, courteous, affable, suave, urbane, well-bred

debrief = <u>interrogate</u>, question, examine, probe, quiz, cross-examine

debris = <u>remains</u>, bits, pieces, waste, ruins, wreck, rubbish, fragments, litter, rubble, wreckage, brash, detritus, dross

debt NOUN = debit, bill, score, due, duty, commitment, obligation, liability, arrears …*He is still paying off his debts*…

PHRASES **in debt** = owing, liable, accountable, in the red (*informal*), in arrears, beholden, in hock (*informal, chiefly U.S.*) …*You shouldn't borrow more money if you're already in debt*…

debtor = borrower, mortgagor

debunk (*Informal*) = expose, show up, mock, ridicule, puncture, deflate, disparage, lampoon, cut down to size

debut = entrance, beginning, launch, launching, coming out, introduction, presentation, first appearance, initiation, inauguration

decadence = degeneration, decline, corruption, fall, decay, deterioration, dissolution, perversion, dissipation, debasement, retrogression

decadent = degenerate, abandoned, corrupt, degraded, immoral, self-indulgent, depraved, debased, debauched, dissolute OPPOSITE moral

decamp = make off, fly, escape, desert, flee, bolt, run away, flit (*informal*), abscond, hook it (*slang*), sneak off, do a runner (*slang*), scarper (*Brit. slang*), steal away, do a bunk (*Brit. slang*), fly the coop (*U.S. & Canad. informal*), skedaddle (*informal*), hightail it (*informal, chiefly U.S.*), take a powder (*U.S. & Canad. slang*), take it on the lam (*U.S. & Canad. slang*)

decant *Formal* = transfer, tap, drain, pour out, draw off, let flow

decapitate = behead, execute, guillotine

decay VERB 1 = rot, break down, disintegrate, spoil, crumble, deteriorate, perish, degenerate, fester, decompose, mortify, moulder, go bad, putrefy …*The bodies buried in the fine ash slowly decayed*…
2 = decline, sink, break down, diminish, dissolve, crumble, deteriorate, fall off, dwindle, lessen, wane, disintegrate, degenerate …*The work ethic in this country has decayed over the past 30 years*… OPPOSITE grow
NOUN 1 = rot, rotting, deterioration, corruption, mould, blight, perishing, disintegration, corrosion, decomposition, gangrene, mortification, canker, caries, putrefaction, putrescence, cariosity, putridity …*Plaque causes tooth decay and gum disease*…
2 = decline, collapse, deterioration, failing, fading, decadence, degeneration, degeneracy …*problems of urban decay and gang violence*… OPPOSITE growth

decayed = rotten, bad, decaying, wasted, spoiled, perished, festering, decomposed, corroded, unsound, putrid, putrefied, putrescent, carrion, carious

decaying = rotting, deteriorating, disintegrating, crumbling, perishing, wasting away, wearing away, gangrenous, putrefacient

deceased = dead, late, departed, lost, gone, expired, defunct, lifeless, pushing up daisies (*informal*)

deceit = lying, fraud, cheating, deception, hypocrisy, cunning, pretence, treachery, dishonesty, guile,

artifice, trickery, misrepresentation, duplicity, subterfuge, feint, double-dealing, chicanery, wile, dissimulation, craftiness, imposture, fraudulence, slyness, deceitfulness, underhandedness OPPOSITE honesty

deceitful = dishonest, false, deceiving, fraudulent, treacherous, deceptive, hypocritical, counterfeit, crafty, sneaky, illusory, two-faced, disingenuous, untrustworthy, underhand, insincere, double-dealing, duplicitous, fallacious, guileful, knavish (*archaic*)

deceive VERB = take in, trick, fool (*informal*), cheat, con (*informal*), kid (*informal*), stiff (*slang*), sting (*informal*), mislead, betray, lead (someone) on (*informal*), hoax, dupe, beguile, delude, swindle, outwit, ensnare, bamboozle (*informal*), hoodwink, entrap, double-cross (*informal*), take for a ride (*informal*), pull a fast one on (*slang*), cozen, pull the wool over (someone's) eyes …*He has deceived and disillusioned us all*…
PHRASES **be deceived by something** or **someone** = be taken in by, fall for, swallow (*informal*), take the bait, be made a fool of by, be the dupe of, swallow hook, line, and sinker (*informal*) …*I was deceived by her innocent expression*…

decency 1 = propriety, correctness, decorum, fitness, good form, respectability, etiquette, appropriateness, seemliness …*His sense of decency forced him to resign*…
2 = courtesy, grace, politeness, good manners, civility, good breeding, graciousness, urbanity, courteousness, gallantness …*He did not have the decency to inform me of his plans*…

decent 1 = satisfactory, average, fair, all right, reasonable, suitable, sufficient, acceptable, good enough, adequate, competent, ample, tolerable, up to scratch, passable, up to standard, up to the mark …*Nearby there is a village with a decent pub*… OPPOSITE unsatisfactory
2 = proper, becoming, seemly, fitting, fit, appropriate, suitable, respectable, befitting, decorous, comme il faut (*French*) …*They married after a decent interval*… OPPOSITE improper
3 (*Informal*) = good, kind, friendly, neighbourly, generous, helpful, obliging, accommodating, sympathetic, comradely, benign, gracious, benevolent, courteous, amiable, amicable, sociable, genial, peaceable, companionable, well-disposed …*Most people around here are decent folk*…
4 = respectable, nice, pure, proper, modest, polite, chaste, presentable, decorous …*He wanted to marry a decent woman*…

deception 1 = trickery, fraud, deceit, hypocrisy, cunning, treachery, guile, duplicity, insincerity, legerdemain, dissimulation, craftiness, fraudulence, deceitfulness, deceptiveness …*He admitted conspiring to obtain property by deception*… OPPOSITE honesty
2 = trick, lie, fraud, cheat, bluff, sham, snare, hoax, decoy, ruse, artifice, subterfuge, canard, feint, stratagem, porky (*Brit. slang*), pork pie (*Brit. slang*), wile, hokum (*slang, chiefly U.S. & Canad.*), leg-pull (*Brit.*

informal), imposture, snow job (*slang, chiefly U.S. & Canad.*) ...*You've been the victim of a rather cruel deception*...

deceptive 1 = <u>misleading</u>, false, fake, mock, ambiguous, unreliable, spurious, illusory, specious, fallacious, delusive ...*Appearances can be deceptive*...
2 = <u>dishonest</u>, deceiving, fraudulent, treacherous, hypocritical, crafty, sneaky, two-faced, disingenuous, deceitful, untrustworthy, underhand, insincere, duplicitous, guileful ...*Her worst fault is a strongly deceptive streak*...

decide 1 = <u>make a decision</u>, make up your mind, reach *or* come to a decision, end, choose, determine, purpose, elect, conclude, commit yourself, come to a conclusion ...*I can't decide what to do*... OPPOSITE hesitate
2 = <u>resolve</u>, answer, determine, settle, conclude, decree, clear up, ordain, adjudicate, adjudge, arbitrate ...*This is a question that should be decided by government*...
3 = <u>settle</u>, determine, conclude, resolve ...*The goal that decided the match came just before half-time*...

decided 1 = <u>definite</u>, certain, positive, absolute, distinct, pronounced, clear-cut, undisputed, unequivocal, undeniable, unambiguous, indisputable, categorical, unquestionable ...*We were at a decided disadvantage*... OPPOSITE doubtful
2 = <u>determined</u>, firm, decisive, assertive, emphatic, resolute, strong-willed, unhesitating, unfaltering ...*a man of very decided opinions*... OPPOSITE irresolute

decidedly = <u>definitely</u>, clearly, certainly, absolutely, positively, distinctly, downright, decisively, unequivocally, unmistakably

deciding = <u>determining</u>, chief, prime, significant, critical, crucial, principal, influential, decisive, conclusive

decimate = <u>destroy</u>, devastate, wipe out, ravage, eradicate, annihilate, put paid to, lay waste, wreak havoc on

---

Word Power

decimate – This word, which comes from Latin, originally referred to the slaughtering of one in ten soldiers, a practice of the army of Ancient Rome. In current language, however, the meaning of the word has broadened and it is now used not only to describe the destruction of people and animals, but also of institutions: *overseas visitors will stay away in droves, decimating the tourist industry*. Synonyms such as *destroy* (for sense 1) and *reduce* (for sense 2) are appropriate alternatives.

---

decipher 1 = <u>decode</u>, crack, solve, understand, explain, reveal, figure out (*informal*), unravel, suss (out) (*slang*) ...*I'm still no closer to deciphering the code*...
2 = <u>figure out</u>, read, understand, interpret (*informal*), make out, unravel, deduce, construe, suss (out) (*slang*) ...*I can't decipher these notes*...

decision 1 = <u>judgment</u>, finding, ruling, order, result, sentence, settlement, resolution, conclusion, outcome, verdict, decree, arbitration ...*The judge's decision was greeted with dismay*...
2 = <u>decisiveness</u>, purpose, resolution, resolve, determination, firmness, forcefulness, purposefulness, resoluteness, strength of mind *or* will ...*He is very much a man of decision and action*...

decisive 1 = <u>crucial</u>, significant, critical, final, positive, absolute, influential, definite, definitive, momentous, conclusive, fateful ...*his decisive victory in the elections*... OPPOSITE uncertain
2 = <u>resolute</u>, decided, firm, determined, forceful, uncompromising, incisive, trenchant, strong-minded ...*Firm decisive action will be taken to end the incident*... OPPOSITE Indecisive

deck VERB = <u>decorate</u>, dress, trim, clothe, grace, array, garland, adorn, ornament, embellish, apparel (*archaic*), festoon, attire, bedeck, beautify, bedight (*archaic*), bedizen (*archaic*), engarland ...*The house was decked with flowers*...
PHRASES **deck something** *or* **someone out** = <u>dress up</u>, doll up (*slang*), prettify, trick out, rig out, pretty up, prink, tog up *or* out ...*She had decked him out in expensive clothes*...

declaim VERB = <u>speak</u>, lecture, proclaim, recite, rant, harangue, hold forth, spiel (*informal*), orate, perorate ...*He used to declaim verse to us with immense energy*...
PHRASES **declaim against something** *or* **someone** = <u>protest against</u>, attack, rail, denounce, decry, inveigh ...*He declaimed against the injustice of his treatment*...

declaration 1 = <u>announcement</u>, proclamation, decree, notice, manifesto, notification, edict, pronouncement, promulgation, pronunciamento ...*The two countries will sign the declaration of peace tomorrow*...
2 = <u>affirmation</u>, profession, assertion, revelation, disclosure, acknowledgment, protestation, avowal, averment ...*declarations of undying love*...
3 = <u>statement</u>, testimony, deposition, attestation ...*I signed a declaration allowing my doctor to disclose my medical details*...

declare 1 = <u>state</u>, claim, announce, voice, express, maintain, confirm, assert, proclaim, pronounce, utter, notify, affirm, profess, avow, aver, asseverate ...*He declared his intention to become the best golfer in the world*...
2 = <u>testify</u>, state, witness, swear, assert, affirm, certify, attest, bear witness, vouch, give testimony, asseverate ...*They declare that there is no lawful impediment to the marriage*...
3 = <u>make known</u>, tell, reveal, show, broadcast, confess, communicate, disclose, convey, manifest, make public ...*Anyone carrying money into or out of the country must declare it*...

decline VERB 1 = <u>fall</u>, fail, drop, contract, lower, sink, flag, fade, shrink, diminish, decrease, slow down, fall off, dwindle, lessen, wane, ebb, slacken ...*a declining birth rate*... OPPOSITE rise

2 = <u>deteriorate</u>, fade, weaken, pine, decay, worsen, lapse, languish, degenerate, droop ...*Her father's health has declined significantly in recent months...* OPPOSITE improve
3 = <u>refuse</u>, reject, turn down, avoid, deny, spurn, abstain, forgo, send your regrets, say 'no' ...*He declined their invitation...* OPPOSITE accept
NOUN **1** = <u>depression</u>, recession, slump, falling off, downturn, dwindling, lessening, diminution, abatement ...*The first signs of economic decline became visible...* OPPOSITE rise
2 = <u>deterioration</u>, fall, failing, slump, weakening, decay, worsening, descent, downturn, disintegration, degeneration, atrophy, decrepitude, retrogression, enfeeblement ...*Rome's decline in the fifth century...* OPPOSITE improvement

decode 1 = <u>decipher</u>, crack, work out, solve, interpret, unscramble, decrypt, descramble ...*The secret documents were intercepted and decoded...* OPPOSITE encode
2 = <u>understand</u>, explain, interpret, make sense of, construe, decipher, elucidate, throw light on, explicate ...*You don't need to be a genius to decode his work...*

decompose 1 = <u>rot</u>, spoil, corrupt, crumble, decay, perish, fester, corrode, moulder, go bad, putrefy ...*foods which decompose and rot...*
2 = <u>break down</u>, break up, crumble, deteriorate, fall apart, disintegrate, degenerate ...*Plastics take years to decompose...*

decomposition (*Formal*) **1** = <u>rot</u>, corruption, decay, rotting, perishing, mortification, putrefaction, putrescence, putridity ...*The bodies were in an advanced state of decomposition...*
2 = <u>breakdown</u>, disintegration, dissolution, atomization ...*a nuclear reactor which gives complete decomposition and no unwanted byproducts...*

décor *or* **decor** = <u>decoration</u>, colour scheme, ornamentation, furnishing style

decorate 1 = <u>adorn</u>, deck, trim, embroider, garnish, ornament, embellish, festoon, bedeck, beautify, grace, engarland ...*He decorated the box with glitter and ribbons...*
2 = <u>do up</u>, paper, paint, wallpaper, renovate (*informal*), furbish ...*a small, badly decorated office...*
3 = <u>pin a medal on</u>, cite, confer an honour on *or* upon ...*He was decorated for his services to the nation...*

decoration 1 = <u>adornment</u>, trimming, garnishing, enhancement, elaboration, embellishment, ornamentation, beautification ...*He played a part in the decoration of the tree...*
2 = <u>ornament</u>, trimmings, garnish, frill, scroll, spangle, festoon, trinket, bauble, flounce, arabesque, curlicue, furbelow, falderal, cartouch(e) ...*We were putting the Christmas decorations up...*
3 = <u>medal</u>, award, order, star, colours, ribbon, badge, emblem, garter ...*He was awarded several military decorations...*

decorative = <u>ornamental</u>, fancy, pretty, attractive, enhancing, adorning, for show, embellishing, showy, beautifying, nonfunctional, arty-crafty

decorum = <u>propriety</u>, decency, etiquette, breeding, protocol, respectability, politeness, good manners, good grace, gentility, deportment, courtliness, politesse, punctilio, seemliness OPPOSITE impropriety

decoy = <u>lure</u>, attraction, bait, trap, inducement, enticement, ensnarement

decrease VERB **1** = <u>drop</u>, decline, lessen, contract, lower, ease, shrink, diminish, fall off, dwindle, wane, subside, abate, peter out, slacken ...*Population growth is decreasing each year...*
2 = <u>reduce</u>, cut, lower, contract, depress, moderate, weaken, diminish, turn down, slow down, cut down, shorten, dilute, impair, lessen, curtail, wind down, abate, tone down, truncate, abridge, downsize ...*Regular doses of aspirin decrease the risk of heart attack...* OPPOSITE increase
NOUN = <u>lessening</u>, decline, reduction, loss, falling off, downturn, dwindling, contraction, ebb, cutback, subsidence, curtailment, shrinkage, diminution, abatement ...*There has been a decrease in the number of young unemployed people...* OPPOSITE growth

decree NOUN **1** = <u>law</u>, order, ruling, act, demand, command, regulation, mandate, canon, statute, covenant, ordinance, proclamation, enactment, edict, dictum, precept ...*He issued a decree ordering all unofficial armed groups to disband...*
2 = <u>judgment</u>, finding, order, result, ruling, decision, award, conclusion, verdict, arbitration ...*court decrees relating to marital property...*
VERB = <u>order</u>, rule, command, decide, demand, establish, determine, proclaim, dictate, prescribe, pronounce, lay down, enact, ordain ...*He got the two men off the hook by decreeing a general amnesty...*

decrepit 1 = <u>ruined</u>, broken-down, battered, crumbling, run-down, deteriorated, decaying, beat-up (*informal*), shabby, worn-out, ramshackle, dilapidated, antiquated, rickety, weather-beaten, tumbledown ...*The film was shot in a decrepit police station...*
2 = <u>weak</u>, aged, frail, wasted, fragile, crippled, feeble, past it, debilitated, incapacitated, infirm, superannuated, doddering ...*a decrepit old man...*

decry = <u>condemn</u>, blame, abuse, blast, denounce, put down, criticize, run down, discredit, censure, detract, denigrate, belittle, disparage, rail against, depreciate, tear into (*informal*), diss (*slang, chiefly U.S.*), lambast(e), traduce, excoriate, derogate, cry down, asperse

dedicate 1 = <u>devote</u>, give, apply, commit, concern, occupy, pledge, surrender, give over to ...*He dedicated himself to politics...*
2 = <u>offer</u>, address, assign, inscribe ...*This book is dedicated to the memory of my sister...*
3 = <u>consecrate</u>, bless, sanctify, set apart, hallow ...*The church is dedicated to a saint...*

dedicated = <u>committed</u>, devoted, sworn, enthusiastic, single-minded, zealous, purposeful, given over to, wholehearted OPPOSITE indifferent

dedication 1 = <u>commitment</u>, loyalty, devotion, allegiance, adherence, single-mindedness, faithfulness, wholeheartedness, devotedness ...*To be*

successful takes hard work and dedication… OPPOSITE
indifference
2 = inscription, message, address …*His book contains
a dedication to his parents…*
3 = consecration, ordaining, sanctification, hallowing
…*Some 250 guests attended the dedication ceremony
of the church…*
deduce = work out, reason, understand, gather,
conclude, derive, infer, glean
deduct = subtract, remove, take off, withdraw, take
out, take from, take away, reduce by, knock off
(*informal*), decrease by OPPOSITE add
deduction **1** = conclusion, finding, verdict,
judgment, assumption, inference, corollary …*It was a
pretty astute deduction…*
2 = reasoning, thinking, thought, reason, analysis,
logic, cogitation, ratiocination …*'How did you guess?'
'Deduction,' he replied…*
3 = discount, reduction, cut, concession, allowance,
decrease, rebate, diminution …*your gross income,
before tax and insurance deductions…*
4 = subtraction, reduction, allowance, concession
…*the deduction of tax at 20%…*
deed **1** = action, act, performance, achievement,
exploit, feat …*His heroic deeds were celebrated in every
corner of the country…*
2 (*Law*) = document, title, contract, title deed,
indenture …*He asked if I had the deeds to his father's
property…*
deem = consider, think, believe, hold, account, judge,
suppose, regard, estimate, imagine, reckon, esteem,
conceive
deep ADJECTIVE **1** = big, wide, broad, profound,
yawning, cavernous, bottomless, unfathomable,
fathomless, abyssal …*The workers had dug a deep
hole in the centre of the garden…* OPPOSITE shallow
2 = intense, great, serious (*informal*), acute, extreme,
grave, profound, heartfelt, unqualified, abject, deeply
felt, heartrending …*a period of deep personal crisis…*
OPPOSITE superficial
3 = sound, peaceful, profound, unbroken,
undisturbed, untroubled …*He fell into a deep sleep…*
4 = absorbed, lost, gripped, intent, preoccupied,
carried away, immersed, engrossed, rapt …*Before
long we were deep in conversation…*
5 = wise, learned, searching, keen, critical, acute,
profound, penetrating, discriminating, shrewd,
discerning, astute, perceptive, incisive, perspicacious,
sagacious …*She gave him a long deep look…*
OPPOSITE simple
6 = dark, strong, rich, warm, intense, vivid …*rich, deep
colours…* OPPOSITE light
7 = low, booming, bass, full, mellow, resonant,
sonorous, mellifluous, dulcet, low-pitched, full-toned
…*His voice was deep and mellow…* OPPOSITE high
8 = astute, knowing, clever, designing, scheming,
sharp, smart, intelligent, discriminating, shrewd,
cunning, discerning, canny, devious, perceptive,
insidious, artful, far-sighted, far-seeing, perspicacious,
sagacious …*a very deep individual…* OPPOSITE simple
9 = secret, hidden, unknown, mysterious, concealed,

obscure, abstract, veiled, esoteric, mystifying,
impenetrable, arcane, abstruse, recondite …*a deep,
dark secret…*
10 = far, a long way, a good way, miles, deeply, far
down, a great distance …*They travelled deep into the
forest…*
ADVERB = far into, late …*We talked deep into the
night…*
NOUN = middle, heart, midst, dead, thick, culmination
…*in the deep of night…*
PHRASES **the deep** (*Poetic*) = the ocean, the sea, the
waves, the main, the drink (*informal*), the high seas,
the briny (*informal*) …*whales and other creatures of
the deep…*
deepen **1** = intensify, increase, grow, strengthen,
reinforce, escalate, magnify, augment …*Further job
losses deepened the gloom… …Sloane's uneasiness
deepened…*
2 = dig out, excavate, scoop out, hollow out, scrape
out …*The tunnels have been widened and deepened…*
deeply = thoroughly, completely, seriously, sadly,
severely, gravely, profoundly, intensely, to the heart,
passionately, acutely, to the core, feelingly, movingly,
distressingly, to the quick, affectingly
deep-seated or **deep-rooted** = fixed, confirmed,
rooted, settled, entrenched, ingrained, inveterate,
dyed-in-the-wool, ineradicable OPPOSITE superficial
deface = vandalize, damage, destroy, total (*slang*),
injure, mar, spoil, trash (*slang*), impair, tarnish,
obliterate, mutilate, deform, blemish, disfigure, sully
de facto ADJECTIVE = actual, real, existing …*a de facto
recognition of the republic's independence…*
ADVERB = in fact, really, actually, in effect, in reality
…*Unification has now de facto replaced the signing of
such a treaty…*
defamation = slander, smear, libel, scandal, slur,
vilification, opprobrium, denigration, calumny,
character assassination, disparagement, obloquy,
aspersion, traducement
defamatory = slanderous, insulting, abusive,
denigrating, disparaging, vilifying, derogatory,
injurious, libellous, vituperative, calumnious,
contumelious
defame = slander, smear, libel, discredit, knock
(*informal*), rubbish (*informal*), disgrace, blacken, slag
(off) (*slang*), detract, malign, denigrate, disparage,
vilify, dishonour, stigmatize, bad-mouth (*slang, chiefly
U.S. & Canad.*), besmirch, traduce, cast aspersions on,
speak evil of, cast a slur on, calumniate, vituperate,
asperse
default VERB = fail to pay, dodge, evade, rat
(*informal*), neglect, levant (*Brit.*), welch or welsh
(*slang*) …*Many borrowers are defaulting on loans…*
NOUN **1** (usually in phrase *by default* or *in default of*)
= failure , want, lack, fault, absence, neglect, defect,
deficiency, lapse, omission, dereliction …*The other
team failed to turn up so we won by default…*
2 = nonpayment, evasion …*The country can't pay its
foreign debts and default is inevitable…*
defeat VERB **1** = beat, crush, overwhelm, conquer,

stuff (*slang*), master, worst, tank (*slang*), overthrow, lick (*informal*), undo, subdue, rout, overpower, quell, trounce, clobber (*slang*), vanquish, repulse, subjugate, run rings around (*informal*), wipe the floor with (*informal*), make mincemeat of (*informal*), pip at the post, outplay, blow out of the water (*slang*) ...*His guerrillas defeated the colonial army*... OPPOSITE surrender

2 = <u>frustrate</u>, foil, thwart, ruin, baffle, confound, balk, get the better of, forestall, stymie ...*The challenges of constructing such a huge novel almost defeated her*...

NOUN **1** = <u>conquest</u>, beating, overthrow, pasting (*slang*), rout, debacle, trouncing, repulse, vanquishment ...*The vote was seen as something of a defeat for the lobbyists*... OPPOSITE victory

2 = <u>frustration</u>, failure, reverse, disappointment, setback, thwarting ...*the final defeat of all his hopes*...

defeated = <u>beaten</u>, crushed, conquered, worsted, routed, overcome, overwhelmed, thrashed, licked (*informal*), thwarted, overpowered, balked, trounced, vanquished, checkmated, bested OPPOSITE victorious

defeatist NOUN = <u>pessimist</u>, sceptic, scoffer, doubter, quitter, prophet of doom, yielder ...*a defeatist might give up at this point*...

ADJECTIVE = <u>pessimistic</u>, resigned, despairing, hopeless, foreboding, despondent, fatalistic ...*Don't go out there with a defeatist attitude*...

defecate = <u>excrete</u>, eliminate, discharge, evacuate (*Physiology*), crap (*taboo slang*), dump (*slang, chiefly U.S.*), pass a motion, move the bowels, empty the bowels, open the bowels, egest, void excrement

defect NOUN = <u>deficiency</u>, want, failing, lack, mistake, fault, error, absence, weakness, flaw, shortcoming, inadequacy, imperfection, frailty, foible ...*The report pointed out the defects in the present system*...

VERB = <u>desert</u>, rebel, quit, revolt, change sides, apostatize, tergiversate ...*a KGB official who defected in 1963*...

PHRASES **defect from something** or **someone** = <u>leave</u>, abandon, desert, quit, resign from, walk out on (*informal*), break faith with, tergiversate ...*He defected from the party twenty years ago*...

defection = <u>desertion</u>, revolt, rebellion, abandonment, dereliction, backsliding, apostasy

defective 1 = <u>faulty</u>, broken, not working, flawed, imperfect, out of order, on the blink (*slang*) ...*Retailers can return defective merchandise*... OPPOSITE perfect

2 = <u>deficient</u>, lacking, short, inadequate, insufficient, incomplete, scant ...*food which is defective in nutritional quality*... OPPOSITE

defector = <u>deserter</u>, renegade, turncoat, apostate, recreant (*archaic*), runagate (*archaic*), tergiversator

defence or (*U.S.*) **defense** NOUN **1** = <u>protection</u>, cover, security, guard, shelter, refuge, resistance, safeguard, immunity ...*The land was flat, giving no scope for defence*...

2 = <u>armaments</u> ...*Twenty-eight per cent of the federal budget is spent on defense*...

3 = <u>argument</u>, explanation, excuse, plea, apology, justification, vindication, rationalization, apologia, exoneration, exculpation, extenuation ...*a spirited defence of the government's economic progress*...

4 = <u>plea</u> (*Law*), case, claim, pleading, declaration, testimony, denial, alibi, vindication, rebuttal ...*His defence was that records were fabricated by the police*...

PLURAL NOUN = <u>shield</u>, barricade, fortification, bastion, buttress, rampart, bulwark, fastness ...*Soldiers are beginning to strengthen the city's defences*...

defenceless or (*U.S.*) **defenseless** = <u>helpless</u> exposed, vulnerable, naked, endangered, powerless, wide open, unarmed, unprotected, unguarded OPPOSITE safe

defend 1 = <u>protect</u>, cover, guard, screen, secure, preserve, look after, shelter, shield, harbour, safeguard, fortify, ward off, watch over, stick up for (*informal*), keep safe, give sanctuary ...*They defended themselves against some racist thugs*...

2 = <u>support</u>, champion, justify, maintain, sustain, plead for, endorse, assert, stand by, uphold, vindicate, stand up for, espouse, speak up for, stick up for (*informal*) ...*Police chiefs strongly defended police conduct*...

defendant = <u>the accused</u>, respondent, appellant, litigant, prisoner at the bar

defender 1 = <u>supporter</u>, champion, advocate, sponsor, follower, patron, apologist, upholder, vindicator ...*a strong defender of human rights*...

2 = <u>protector</u>, guard, guardian, escort, bodyguard, guardian angel ...*He proclaims himself a defender of the environment*...

defensible 1 = <u>justifiable</u>, right, sound, reasonable, acceptable, sensible, valid, legitimate, plausible, permissible, well-founded, tenable, excusable, pardonable, vindicable ...*Her reasons for action are morally defensible*... OPPOSITE unjustifiable

2 = <u>secure</u>, safe, unassailable, impregnable, holdable ...*the creation of defensible borders*...

defensive 1 = <u>protective</u>, defending, opposing, safeguarding, watchful, on the defensive, on guard ...*hastily organized defensive measures*...

2 uptight (*informal*) ...*She heard the blustering, defensive note in his voice*...

defensively = <u>in self-defence</u>, in defence, suspiciously, on the defensive

defer = <u>postpone</u>, delay, put off, suspend, shelve, set aside, adjourn, hold over, procrastinate, put on ice (*informal*), put on the back burner (*informal*), protract, take a rain check on (*U.S. & Canad. informal*), prorogue

deference 1 = <u>respect</u>, regard, consideration, attention, honour, esteem, courtesy, homage, reverence, politeness, civility, veneration, thoughtfulness ...*Out of deference to his feelings, I refrained from commenting*... OPPOSITE disrespect

2 = <u>obedience</u>, yielding, submission, compliance, capitulation, acquiescence, obeisance, complaisance ...*a chain of social command linked by deference to authority*... OPPOSITE disobedience

deferential = <u>respectful</u>, civil, polite, courteous, considerate, obedient, submissive, dutiful, ingratiating, reverential, obsequious, complaisant, obeisant, regardful

defer to = <u>comply with</u>, give way to, submit to, bow to, give in to, yield to, accede to, capitulate to

defiance = <u>resistance</u>, challenge, opposition, confrontation, contempt, disregard, provocation, disobedience, insolence, insubordination, rebelliousness, recalcitrance, contumacy OPPOSITE obedience

defiant = <u>resisting</u>, challenging, rebellious, daring, aggressive, bold, provocative, audacious, recalcitrant, antagonistic, insolent, mutinous, disobedient, refractory, insubordinate, contumacious OPPOSITE obedient

deficiency 1 = <u>lack</u>, want, deficit, absence, shortage, deprivation, inadequacy, scarcity, dearth, privation, insufficiency, scantiness ...*They did tests for signs of vitamin deficiency*... OPPOSITE sufficiency
2 = <u>failing</u>, fault, weakness, defect, flaw, drawback, shortcoming, imperfection, frailty, demerit ...*the most serious deficiency in their air defence*...

deficient 1 = <u>lacking</u>, wanting, needing, short, inadequate, insufficient, scarce, scant, meagre, skimpy, scanty, exiguous ...*a diet deficient in vitamins*...
2 = <u>unsatisfactory</u>, weak, flawed, inferior, impaired, faulty, incomplete, defective, imperfect ...*deficient landing systems*...

deficit = <u>shortfall</u>, shortage, deficiency, loss, default, arrears

defile 1 = <u>degrade</u>, stain, disgrace, sully, debase, dishonour, besmirch, smirch ...*He felt his father's memory had been defiled by the article*...
2 = <u>desecrate</u>, violate, contaminate, abuse, pollute, profane, dishonour, despoil, treat sacrilegiously ...*Who gave you permission to defile this sacred place?*...
3 = <u>dirty</u>, soil, contaminate, smear, pollute, taint, tarnish, make foul, smirch, befoul ...*piles of old clothes defiled with excrement*...

define 1 = <u>mark out</u>, outline, limit, bound, delineate, circumscribe, demarcate, delimit ...*Armed forces were deployed to define military zones*...
2 = <u>describe</u>, interpret, characterize, explain, spell out, expound ...*How exactly do you define reasonable behaviour?*...
3 = <u>establish</u>, detail, determine, specify, designate ...*The Court must define the limits of its authority*...

definite 1 = <u>specific</u>, exact, precise, clear, particular, express, determined, fixed, black-and-white, explicit, clear-cut, cut-and-dried (*informal*), clearly defined ...*It's too soon to give a definite answer*... OPPOSITE vague
2 = <u>clear</u>, explicit, black-and-white, clear-cut, unequivocal, unambiguous, guaranteed, cut-and-dried (*informal*) ...*We didn't have any definite proof*...
3 = <u>noticeable</u>, marked, clear, decided, striking, noted, particular, obvious, dramatic, considerable, remarkable, apparent, evident, distinct, notable,

manifest, conspicuous ...*There has been a definite improvement*...
4 = <u>certain</u>, decided, sure, settled, convinced, positive, confident, assured ...*She is very definite about her feelings*... OPPOSITE uncertain

> ## Word Power
>
> **definite** – *Definite* and *definitive* should be carefully distinguished. *Definite* indicates precision and firmness, as in *a definite decision*. *Definitive* includes these senses but also indicates conclusiveness. *A definite answer* indicates a clear and firm answer to a particular question; *a definitive answer* implies an authoritative resolution of a complex question.

definitely = <u>certainly</u>, clearly, obviously, surely, easily, plainly, absolutely, positively, decidedly, needless to say, without doubt, unquestionably, undeniably, categorically, without question, unequivocally, unmistakably, far and away, without fail, beyond any doubt, indubitably, come hell or high water (*informal*)

definition 1 = <u>description</u>, interpretation, explanation, clarification, exposition, explication, elucidation, statement of meaning ...*There is no general agreement on a standard definition of sanity*...
2 = <u>sharpness</u>, focus, clarity, contrast, precision, distinctness ...*This printer has excellent definition*...

definitive 1 = <u>final</u>, convincing, absolute, clinching, decisive, definite, conclusive, irrefutable ...*No one has come up with a definitive answer to that question*...
2 = <u>authoritative</u>, greatest, ultimate, reliable, most significant, exhaustive, superlative, mother of all (*informal*) ...*It is still the definitive book on the islands*...

deflate 1 = <u>humiliate</u>, humble, squash, put down (*slang*), disconcert, chasten, mortify, dispirit ...*Her comments deflated him a bit*...
2 = <u>puncture</u>, flatten, empty ...*The vandals had deflated his car's tyres*... OPPOSITE inflate
3 = <u>collapse</u>, go down, contract, empty, shrink, void, flatten ...*The balloon began to deflate*... OPPOSITE expand
4 (*Economics*) = <u>reduce</u>, depress, decrease, diminish, devalue, depreciate ...*artificially deflated prices*...

deflect = <u>turn aside</u>, turn, bend, twist, sidetrack

deflection = <u>deviation</u>, bending, veering, swerving, divergence, turning aside, refraction, declination

deform 1 = <u>disfigure</u>, twist, injure, cripple, ruin, mar, spoil, mutilate, maim, deface ...*Severe rheumatoid arthritis deforms limbs*...
2 = <u>distort</u>, twist, warp, buckle, mangle, contort, gnarl, misshape, malform ...*Plastic deforms when subjected to heat*...

deformation = <u>distortion</u>, warping, contortion, malformation, disfiguration, misshapenness

deformed = <u>distorted</u>, bent, twisted, crooked, crippled, warped, maimed, marred, mangled, disfigured, misshapen, malformed, misbegotten

deformity 1 = abnormality, defect, malformation, disfigurement ...*facial deformities in babies*...
2 = distortion, irregularity, misshapenness, misproportion ...*Bones grind against each other, leading to pain and deformity*...

defraud = cheat, rob, con (*informal*), do (*slang*), skin (*slang*), stiff (*slang*), rip off (*slang*), fleece, swindle, stitch up (*slang*), rook (*slang*), diddle (*informal*), bilk, gyp (*slang*), pull a fast one on (*informal*), cozen

defray (used with *costs* or *expenses* as object) = pay, meet, cover, clear, settle, discharge

defrost = thaw, warm, soften, de-ice, unfreeze OPPOSITE freeze (up)

deft = skilful, able, expert, clever, neat, handy, adept, nimble, proficient, agile, adroit, dexterous OPPOSITE clumsy

defunct = dead, extinct, gone, departed, expired, deceased, obsolete, bygone, nonexistent, not functioning, out of commission, inoperative

defuse 1 = calm, settle, cool, contain, smooth, stabilize, damp down, take the heat *or* sting out of ...*Officials will hold talks aimed at defusing tensions over trade*... OPPOSITE aggravate
2 = deactivate, disable, disarm, make safe ...*Police have defused a bomb*... OPPOSITE activate
► **diffuse**

defy 1 = resist, oppose, confront, face, brave, beard, disregard, stand up to, spurn, flout, disobey, hold out against, put up a fight (against), hurl defiance at, contemn ...*This was the first time that I had dared to defy her*...
2 = challenge, dare, provoke ...*He defied me to come up with a better idea*...
3 = foil, defeat, escape, frustrate, be beyond, baffle, thwart, elude, confound ...*a fragrance that defies description*...

degenerate VERB = decline, slip, sink, decrease, deteriorate, worsen, rot, decay, lapse, fall off, regress, go to pot, retrogress ...*He degenerated into drug and alcohol abuse*...
ADJECTIVE = depraved, base, corrupt, fallen, low, perverted, degraded, degenerated, immoral, decadent, debased, debauched, dissolute, pervy (*slang*) ...*the degenerate attitudes he found among some of his fellow officers*...

degeneration = deterioration, decline, dissolution, descent, regression, dissipation, degeneracy, debasement

degradation 1 = disgrace, shame, humiliation, discredit, ignominy, dishonour, mortification ...*scenes of misery and degradation*...
2 = deterioration, decline, decadence, degeneration, perversion, degeneracy, debasement, abasement ...*the progressive degradation of the state*...

degrade 1 = demean, disgrace, humiliate, injure, shame, corrupt, humble, discredit, pervert, debase, dishonour, cheapen ...*Pornography degrades women*... OPPOSITE ennoble
2 = demote, reduce, lower, downgrade, depose,

cashier ...*He was degraded to a lower rank*... OPPOSITE promote

degraded 1 = humiliated, embarrassed, shamed, mortified, debased, discomfited, abased ...*I felt cheap and degraded by his actions*...
2 = corrupt, low, base, abandoned, vicious, vile, sordid, decadent, despicable, depraved, debased, profligate, disreputable, debauched, dissolute, scungy (*Austral. & N.Z.*) ...*morally degraded individuals*...

degrading = demeaning, lowering, humiliating, disgraceful, shameful, unworthy, debasing, undignified, contemptible, cheapening, dishonourable, infra dig (*informal*)

degree NOUN 1 measure, rate, stage, extent, grade, proportion, gradation ...*They achieved varying degrees of success*...
2 (*Archaic*) = rank, order, standing, level, class, position, station, status, grade, caste, nobility, echelon ...*the fall of a man of high degree and noble character*...
PHRASES **by degrees** = little by little, slowly, gradually, moderately, gently, piecemeal, bit by bit, imperceptibly, inch by inch, unhurriedly ...*The crowd was thinning, but only by degrees*...

dehydrate = dry, evaporate, parch, desiccate, exsiccate

deign = condescend, consent, stoop, see fit, think fit, lower yourself, deem it worthy

deity = god, goddess, immortal, divinity, godhead, divine being, supreme being, celestial being

dejected = downhearted, down, low, blue, sad, depressed, miserable, gloomy, dismal, melancholy, glum, despondent, downcast, morose, disheartened, wretched, disconsolate, crestfallen, doleful, down in the dumps (*informal*), cast down, sick as a parrot (*informal*), woebegone, low-spirited OPPOSITE cheerful

delay VERB 1 = put off, suspend, postpone, stall, shelve, prolong, defer, hold over, temporize, put on the back burner (*informal*), protract, take a rain check on (*U.S. & Canad. informal*) ...*I delayed my departure until she could join me*...
2 = hold up, detain, hold back, stop, arrest, halt, hinder, obstruct, retard, impede, bog down, set back, slow up ...*The passengers were delayed by bad weather*... OPPOSITE speed (up)
3 = linger, lag, loiter, dawdle, tarry, dilly-dally (*informal*), drag your feet *or* heels (*informal*) ...*If he delayed any longer, the sun would be up*...
NOUN 1 = hold-up, wait, check, setback, interruption, obstruction, stoppage, impediment, hindrance ...*Air restrictions might mean delays for Easter holidaymakers*...
2 = dawdling, lingering, loitering, procrastination, tarrying, dilly-dallying (*informal*) ...*We'll send you a quote without delay*...

delaying = hindering, obstructive, halting, procrastinating, retardant, temporizing, moratory

delectable 1 = delicious, tasty, luscious, inviting, satisfying, pleasant, delightful, enjoyable, lush,

enticing, gratifying, dainty, yummy (*slang*), scrumptious (*informal*), appetizing, toothsome, lekker (*S. African slang*), yummo (*Austral. slang*) ...*a delectable dessert...* OPPOSITE> disgusting
2 = charming, pleasant, delightful, agreeable, adorable ...*a delectable young woman in a swimsuit...*

delegate NOUN = representative, agent, deputy, ambassador, commissioner, envoy, proxy, depute (*Scot.*), legate, spokesman *or* spokeswoman ...*The rebels' chief delegate repeated their demands...*
VERB **1** = entrust, transfer, hand over, give, pass on, assign, relegate, consign, devolve ...*Many employers find it hard to delegate duties...*
2 = appoint, commission, select, contract, engage, nominate, designate, mandate, authorize, empower, accredit, depute ...*Officials have been delegated to start work on a settlement...*

delegation 1 = deputation, envoys, contingent, commission, embassy, legation ...*They sent a delegation to the talks...*
2 = commissioning, relegation, assignment, devolution, committal, deputizing, entrustment ...*the delegation of his responsibilities to his assistant...*

delete = remove, cancel, cut out, erase, edit, excise, strike out, obliterate, efface, blot out, cross out, expunge, dele, rub out, edit out, blue-pencil

deliberate ADJECTIVE **1** = intentional, meant, planned, considered, studied, designed, intended, conscious, calculated, thoughtful, wilful, purposeful, premeditated, prearranged, done on purpose ...*The attack was deliberate and unprovoked...* OPPOSITE> accidental
2 = careful, measured, slow, cautious, wary, thoughtful, prudent, circumspect, methodical, unhurried, heedful ...*His movements were gentle and deliberate...* OPPOSITE> hurried
VERB = consider, think, ponder, discuss, debate, reflect, consult, weigh, meditate, mull over, ruminate, cogitate ...*The jury deliberated for two hours before returning with the verdict...*

deliberately = intentionally, on purpose, consciously, emphatically, knowingly, resolutely, pointedly, determinedly, wilfully, by design, studiously, in cold blood, wittingly, calculatingly

deliberation 1 = consideration, thought, reflection, study, speculation, calculation, meditation, forethought, circumspection, cogitation ...*His decision was the result of great deliberation...*
2 = discussion, talk, conference, exchange, debate, analysis, conversation, dialogue, consultation, seminar, symposium, colloquy, confabulation ...*The outcome of the deliberations was inconclusive...*

delicacy 1 = fragility, frailty, brittleness, flimsiness, frailness, frangibility ...*the delicacy of the crystal glasses...*
2 = daintiness, charm, grace, elegance, neatness, prettiness, slenderness, exquisiteness ...*a country where the feminine ideal is delicacy and grace...*
3 = difficulty, sensitivity, stickiness (*informal*), precariousness, critical nature, touchiness, ticklishness ...*the delicacy of the political situation...*

4 = sensitivity, understanding, consideration, judgment, perception, diplomacy, discretion, skill, finesse, tact, thoughtfulness, savoir-faire, adroitness, sensitiveness ...*He's shown considerable delicacy and tact...*
5 = treat, luxury, goody, savoury, dainty, morsel, titbit, choice item, juicy bit, bonne bouche (*French*) ...*course after course of mouthwatering delicacies...*
6 = lightness, accuracy, precision, elegance, sensibility, purity, subtlety, refinement, finesse, nicety, fineness, exquisiteness ...*He played with a superb delicacy of touch...*

delicate 1 = fine, detailed, elegant, exquisite, graceful ...*china with a delicate design...*
2 = subtle, fine, nice, soft, delicious, faint, refined, muted, subdued, pastel, understated, dainty ...*The colours are delicate and tasteful...* OPPOSITE> bright
3 = fragile, weak, frail, brittle, tender, flimsy, dainty, breakable, frangible ...*Although the material looks tough, it is very delicate...*
4 = sickly, weak, ailing, frail, feeble, unhealthy, debilitated, lacklustre, infirm, in poor health, indisposed ...*She was physically delicate and psychologically unstable...* OPPOSITE> strong
5 = difficult, critical, sensitive, complicated, sticky (*informal*), problematic, precarious, thorny, touchy, knotty, ticklish ...*the delicate issue of adoption...*
6 = skilled, accurate, precise, deft ...*A cosmetic surgeon performed the delicate operation...*
7 = fastidious, nice, critical, pure, Victorian, proper, refined, discriminating, stuffy, scrupulous, prim, puritanical, squeamish, prudish, prissy (*informal*), strait-laced, schoolmarmish (*Brit. informal*), old-maidish (*informal*) ...*He didn't want to offend his mother's delicate sensibilities...* OPPOSITE> crude
8 = diplomatic, sensitive, careful, subtle, thoughtful, discreet, prudent, considerate, judicious, tactful ...*a situation which requires delicate handling...* OPPOSITE> insensitive

delicately 1 = finely, lightly, subtly, softly, carefully, precisely, elegantly, gracefully, deftly, exquisitely, skilfully, daintily ...*soup delicately flavoured with nutmeg...*
2 = tactfully, carefully, subtly, discreetly, thoughtfully, diplomatically, sensitively, prudently, judiciously, considerately ...*a delicately-worded memo...*

delicious 1 = delectable, tasty, luscious, choice, savoury, palatable, dainty, mouthwatering, yummy (*slang*), scrumptious (*informal*), appetizing, toothsome, ambrosial, lekker (*S. African slang*), nectareous, yummo (*Austral. slang*) ...*a wide selection of delicious meals to choose from...* OPPOSITE> unpleasant
2 = delightful, pleasing, charming, heavenly, thrilling, entertaining, pleasant, enjoyable, exquisite, captivating, agreeable, pleasurable, rapturous, delectable ...*a delicious feeling of anticipation...* OPPOSITE> unpleasant

delight NOUN = pleasure, joy, satisfaction, comfort, happiness, ecstasy, enjoyment, bliss, felicity, glee, gratification, rapture, gladness ...*To my delight, the* *plan worked perfectly...* OPPOSITE displeasure

VERB = <u>please</u>, satisfy, content, thrill, charm, cheer, amuse, divert, enchant, rejoice, gratify, ravish, gladden, give pleasure to, tickle pink (*informal*) ...*The report has delighted environmentalists...* OPPOSITE displease

PHRASES **delight in** *or* **take (a) delight in something** *or* **someone** = <u>like</u>, love, enjoy, appreciate, relish, indulge in, savour, revel in, take pleasure in, glory in, luxuriate in ...*He delighted in sharing his news...*

delighted = <u>pleased</u>, happy, charmed, thrilled, enchanted, ecstatic, captivated, jubilant, joyous, elated, over the moon (*informal*), overjoyed, rapt, gladdened, cock-a-hoop, blissed out, in seventh heaven, sent

delightful = <u>pleasant</u>, pleasing, charming, engaging, heavenly, thrilling, fascinating, entertaining, amusing, enjoyable, enchanting, captivating, gratifying, agreeable, pleasurable, ravishing, rapturous OPPOSITE unpleasant

delineate 1 = <u>outline</u>, describe, draw, picture, paint, chart, trace, portray, sketch, render, depict, characterize, map out ...*The relationship between Church and State was delineated in a formal agreement...*
2 = <u>determine</u>, define, chart, map out ...*a settlement to delineate the border...*

delinquency = <u>crime</u>, misconduct, wrongdoing, fault, offence, misdemeanour, misdeed, misbehaviour, villainy, lawbreaking

delinquent = <u>criminal</u>, offender, villain, culprit, young offender, wrongdoer, juvenile delinquent, miscreant, malefactor, lawbreaker

delirious 1 = <u>mad</u>, crazy, raving, insane, demented, deranged, incoherent, unhinged, light-headed ...*I was delirious and blacked out several times...* OPPOSITE rational
2 = <u>ecstatic</u>, wild, excited, frantic, frenzied, hysterical, carried away, blissed out, beside yourself, sent, Corybantic ...*He was delirious with joy...* OPPOSITE calm

delirium 1 = <u>madness</u>, raving, insanity, lunacy, derangement ...*In her delirium, she fell to the floor...*
2 = <u>frenzy</u>, passion, rage, fever, fury, ecstasy, hysteria ...*She was in a delirium of panic...*

deliver 1 = <u>bring</u>, carry, bear, transport, distribute, convey, cart ...*The pizza will be delivered in 20 minutes...*
2 *sometimes with* **up** = <u>hand over</u>, present, commit, give up, yield, surrender, turn over, relinquish, make over ...*He was led in handcuffs and delivered over to me...*
3 = <u>give</u>, read, present, announce, publish, declare, proclaim, pronounce, utter, give forth ...*He will deliver a speech about schools...*
4 = <u>strike</u>, give, deal, launch, throw, direct, aim, administer, inflict ...*A single blow had been delivered to the head...*
5 (*Dated*) = <u>release</u>, free, save, rescue, loose, discharge,

liberate, acquit, redeem, ransom, emancipate ...*I thank God for delivering me from that pain...*

deliverance (*Literary*) = <u>release</u>, rescue, liberation, salvation, redemption, ransom, emancipation

delivery 1 = <u>handing over</u>, transfer, distribution, transmission, dispatch, consignment, conveyance, transmittal ...*the delivery of goods and resources...*
2 = <u>consignment</u>, goods, shipment, batch ...*a delivery of fresh eggs...*
3 = <u>speech</u>, speaking, expression, pronunciation, utterance, articulation, intonation, diction, elocution, enunciation, vocalization ...*His speeches were magnificent but his delivery was hopeless...*
4 = <u>childbirth</u>, labour, confinement, parturition ...*She had an easy delivery...*

delude = <u>deceive</u>, kid (*informal*), fool, trick, take in (*informal*), cheat, con (*informal*), mislead, impose on, hoax, dupe, beguile, gull (*archaic*), bamboozle (*informal*), hoodwink, take for a ride (*informal*), pull the wool over someone's eyes, lead up the garden path (*informal*), cozen, misguide

deluge NOUN 1 = <u>rush</u>, flood, avalanche, barrage, spate, torrent ...*a deluge of criticism...*
2 = <u>flood</u>, spate, overflowing, torrent, downpour, cataclysm, inundation ...*A dozen homes were damaged in the deluge...*
VERB 1 = <u>overwhelm</u>, swamp, engulf, overload, overrun, inundate ...*The office was deluged with complaints...*
2 = <u>flood</u>, drown, swamp, submerge, soak, drench, inundate, douse ...*Torrential rain deluged the capital...*

delusion = <u>misconception</u>, mistaken idea, misapprehension, fancy, illusion, deception, hallucination, fallacy, self-deception, false impression, phantasm, misbelief

deluxe *or* **de luxe** = <u>luxurious</u>, grand, select, special, expensive, rich, exclusive, superior, elegant, costly, splendid, gorgeous, sumptuous, plush (*informal*), opulent, palatial, splendiferous (*facetious*)

delve 1 = <u>research</u>, investigate, explore, examine, probe, look into, burrow, dig into ...*She delved into her mother's past...*
2 = <u>rummage</u>, search, look into, burrow, ransack, forage, dig into, fossick (*Austral. & N.Z.*) ...*He delved into his rucksack and pulled out a folder...*

demagogue = <u>agitator</u>, firebrand, haranguer, rabble-rouser, soapbox orator

demand VERB 1 = <u>request</u>, ask (for), order, expect, claim, seek, call for, insist on, exact, appeal for, solicit ...*She demanded an immediate apology...*
2 = <u>challenge</u>, ask, question, inquire ...*'What do you expect me to do about it?' she demanded...*
3 = <u>require</u>, take, want, need, involve, call for, entail, necessitate, cry out for ...*The task demands much patience and hard work...* OPPOSITE provide
NOUN 1 = <u>request</u>, order, charge, bidding ...*He grew ever more fierce in his demands...*
2 = <u>need</u>, want, call, market, claim, requirement, necessity ...*The demand for coal is down...*

`PHRASES` **in demand** = <u>sought after</u>, needed, popular, favoured, requested, in favour, fashionable, well-liked, in vogue, like gold dust ...*He was much in demand as a lecturer...*

demanding 1 = <u>difficult</u>, trying, hard, taxing, wearing, challenging, tough, exhausting, exacting, exigent ...*It is a demanding job...* `OPPOSITE` easy
2 = <u>trying</u>, troublesome, tiresome, imperious, fractious, unmanageable, clamorous, importunate, exigent ...*a very demanding child...*

demarcation 1 = <u>limit</u>, bound, margin, boundary, confine, enclosure, pale ...*The demarcation of the border between the two countries...*
2 = <u>delimitation</u>, division, distinction, separation, differentiation ...*The demarcation of duties became more blurred...*

demean `VERB` = <u>degrade</u>, lower, debase, humble, abase ...*Pornography demeans women...*
`PHRASES` **demean yourself** = <u>lower yourself</u>, humiliate yourself, humble yourself, debase yourself, downgrade yourself, abase yourself, belittle yourself, degrade yourself ...*I wasn't going to demean myself by answering him...*

demeaning = <u>humiliating</u>, degrading, disgraceful, shameful, unworthy, debasing, undignified, contemptible, cheapening, dishonourable, infra dig (*informal*)

demeanour *or* (*U.S.*) **demeanor** = <u>behaviour</u>, air, bearing, conduct, manner, carriage, deportment, mien, comportment

demented = <u>mad</u>, crazy, foolish, daft (*informal*), frenzied, distraught, manic, insane, crazed, lunatic, unbalanced, deranged, idiotic, unhinged, dotty (*slang, chiefly Brit.*), loopy (*informal*), crackpot (*informal*), out to lunch (*informal*), barking mad (*slang*), barking (*slang*), maniacal, gonzo (*slang*), doolally (*slang*), off your trolley (*slang*), up the pole (*informal*), non compos mentis (*Latin*), not the full shilling (*informal*), crackbrained, wacko *or* whacko (*slang*), off the air (*Austral. slang*) `OPPOSITE` sane

demise 1 = <u>failure</u>, end, fall, defeat, collapse, ruin, breakdown, overthrow, downfall, dissolution, termination ...*the demise of the reform movement...*
2 (*Euphemistic*) = <u>death</u>, end, dying, passing, departure, expiration, decease ...*Smoking was the cause of his early demise...*

democracy = <u>self-government</u>, republic, commonwealth, representative government, government by the people

Democrat `ADJECTIVE` = <u>left-wing</u>, Labour ...*Al Gore, the Democrat candidate...*
`NOUN` = <u>left-winger</u> ...*The director of the company has links to the Democrats...*

democratic = <u>self-governing</u>, popular, republican, representative, autonomous, populist, egalitarian

demolish 1 = <u>knock down</u>, level, destroy, ruin, overthrow, dismantle, flatten, trash (*slang*), total (*slang*), tear down, bulldoze, raze, pulverize ...*The building is being demolished to make way for a motorway...* `OPPOSITE` build

2 = <u>destroy</u>, wreck, overturn, overthrow, undo, blow out of the water (*slang*) ...*Their intention was to demolish his reputation...*
3 (*Facetious*) = <u>devour</u>, eat, consume, swallow, bolt, gorge, put away, gobble up, guzzle, polish off (*informal*), gulp down, wolf down, pig out on (*slang*) ...*We demolished a six-pack of beer...*

demolition = <u>knocking down</u>, levelling, destruction, explosion, wrecking, tearing down, bulldozing, razing

demon 1 = <u>evil spirit</u>, devil, fiend, goblin, ghoul, malignant spirit ...*a woman possessed by evil demons...*
2 = <u>wizard</u>, master, ace (*informal*), addict, fanatic, fiend ...*He is a demon for discipline...*
3 = <u>monster</u>, beast, villain, rogue, barbarian, brute, ogre ...*He was a dictator and a demon...*

demonic *or* **demoniac** *or* **demoniacal** 1 = <u>devilish</u>, satanic, diabolical, hellish, infernal, fiendish, diabolic ...*demonic forces...*
2 = <u>frenzied</u>, mad, furious, frantic, hectic, manic, crazed, frenetic, maniacal, like one possessed ...*a demonic drive to succeed...*

demonstrable = <u>provable</u>, obvious, evident, certain, positive, unmistakable, palpable, undeniable, self-evident, verifiable, irrefutable, incontrovertible, axiomatic, indubitable, attestable, evincible

demonstrate 1 = <u>prove</u>, show, establish, indicate, make clear, manifest, evidence, testify to, evince, show clearly ...*You have to demonstrate that you are reliable...*
2 = <u>show</u>, evidence, express, display, indicate, exhibit, manifest, make clear *or* plain ...*Have they demonstrated a commitment to democracy?...*
3 = <u>march</u>, protest, rally, object, parade, picket, say no to, remonstrate, take up the cudgels, express disapproval ...*Vast crowds have been demonstrating against the reforms...*
4 = <u>describe</u>, show, explain, teach, illustrate ...*He demonstrated how to peel and chop garlic...*

demonstration 1 = <u>march</u>, protest, rally, sit-in, parade, procession, demo (*informal*), picket, mass lobby ...*Riot police broke up the demonstration...*
2 = <u>display</u>, show, performance, explanation, description, presentation, demo (*informal*), exposition ...*a cookery demonstration...*
3 = <u>indication</u>, proof, testimony, confirmation, affirmation, validation, substantiation, attestation ...*an unprecedented demonstration of people power...*
4 = <u>exhibition</u>, display, expression, illustration ...*physical demonstrations of affection...*

demoralize = <u>dishearten</u>, undermine, discourage, shake, depress, weaken, rattle (*informal*), daunt, unnerve, disconcert, psych out (*informal*), dispirit, deject `OPPOSITE` encourage

demoralized = <u>disheartened</u>, undermined, discouraged, broken, depressed, crushed, weakened, subdued, unnerved, unmanned, dispirited, downcast, sick as a parrot (*informal*)

demoralizing = <u>disheartening</u>, discouraging, depressing, crushing, disappointing, daunting, dampening, dispiriting OPPOSITE encouraging

demote = downgrade, relegate, degrade, kick downstairs (*slang*), declass, disrate (*Naval*), lower in rank OPPOSITE promote

demur VERB = object, refuse, protest, doubt, dispute, pause, disagree, hesitate, waver, balk, take exception, cavil ...*At first I demurred when he asked me to do it...* NOUN (always used in a negative construction) = objection, protest, dissent, hesitation, misgiving, qualm, scruple, compunction, demurral, demurrer ...*She entered without demur...*

demure (usually used of a young woman) = shy, reserved, modest, retiring, reticent, unassuming, diffident, decorous OPPOSITE brazen

den 1 = lair, hole, shelter, cave, haunt, cavern, hide-out ...*The skunk makes its den in burrows and hollow logs...*
2 (*Chiefly U.S.*) = study, retreat, sanctuary, hideaway, cloister, sanctum, cubbyhole, snuggery ...*The walls of his den were covered in posters...*

denial 1 = negation, dismissal, contradiction, dissent, disclaimer, retraction, repudiation, disavowal, adjuration ...*their previous denial that chemical weapons were being used...* OPPOSITE admission
2 = refusal, veto, rejection, prohibition, rebuff, repulse ...*the denial of visas to international workers...*
3 = renunciation, giving up, rejection, spurning, abstention, abdication, repudiation, forswearing, disavowal, abnegation, relinquishment, eschewal ...*This religion teaches denial of the flesh...*

denigrate = disparage, run down, slag (off) (*slang*), knock (*informal*), rubbish (*informal*), blacken, malign, belittle, decry, revile, vilify, slander, defame, bad-mouth (*slang, chiefly U.S. & Canad.*), besmirch, impugn, calumniate, asperse OPPOSITE praise

denizen = inhabitant, resident, citizen, occupant, dweller

denomination 1 = religious group, belief, sect, persuasion, creed, school ...*Acceptance of women preachers varies from one denomination to another...*
2 = unit, value, size, grade ...*a pile of bank notes, mostly in small denominations...*

denote = indicate, show, mean, mark, express, import, imply, designate, signify, typify, betoken

denouement *or* **dénouement** 1 = climax, conclusion, finale, termination, culmination ...*the book's sentimental denouement...*
2 = outcome, end, result, consequence, resolution, conclusion, end result, upshot ...*an unexpected denouement to the affair...*

denounce 1 = condemn, attack, censure, decry, castigate, revile, vilify, proscribe, stigmatize, impugn, excoriate, declaim against ...*The leaders took the opportunity to denounce the attacks...*
2 = report, dob in (*Austral. slang*) ...*Informers might at any moment denounce them to the authorities...*

dense 1 = thick, close, heavy, solid, substantial, compact, compressed, condensed, impenetrable, close-knit, thickset ...*a large, dense forest...* OPPOSITE thin

2 = heavy, thick, substantial, opaque, impenetrable ...*a dense column of smoke...*
3 = stupid (*Informal*), slow, thick, dull, dumb (*informal*), crass, dozy (*Brit. informal*), dozy (*Brit. informal*), stolid, dopey (*informal*), moronic, obtuse, brainless, blockheaded, braindead (*informal*), dumb-ass (*informal*), dead from the neck up (*informal*), thickheaded, blockish, dim-witted (*informal*), slow-witted, thick-witted ...*He's not a bad man, just a bit dense...* OPPOSITE bright

density 1 = tightness, closeness, thickness, compactness, impenetrability, denseness, crowdedness ...*The region has a high population density...*
2 = mass, body, bulk, consistency, solidity ...*Jupiter's moon Io has a density of 3.5 grams per cubic centimetre...*

dent VERB = make a dent in, press in, gouge, depress, hollow, imprint, push in, dint, make concave ...*The table's brass feet dented the carpet's thick pile...* NOUN = hollow, chip, indentation, depression, impression, pit, dip, crater, ding (*Austral. dated & N.Z. informal*), dimple, concavity ...*There was a dent in the bonnet of the car...*

denude = strip, expose, bare, uncover, divest, lay bare

denunciation 1 = condemnation, criticism, accusation, censure, stick (*slang*), invective, character assassination, stigmatization, castigation, obloquy, denouncement, fulmination ...*a stinging denunciation of his critics...*
2 = implication, accusation, indictment, incrimination, denouncement, inculpation ...*Denunciation by family, friends and colleagues inevitably sowed distrust...*

deny 1 = contradict, oppose, counter, disagree with, rebuff, negate, rebut, refute, gainsay (*archaic or literary*) ...*She denied the accusations...* OPPOSITE admit
2 = renounce, reject, discard, revoke, retract, repudiate, renege, disown, rebut, disavow, recant, disclaim, abjure, abnegate, refuse to acknowledge *or* recognize ...*I denied my parents because I wanted to become someone else...*
3 = refuse, decline, forbid, reject, rule out, veto, turn down, prohibit, withhold, preclude, disallow, negate, begrudge, interdict ...*His ex-wife denies him access to his children...* OPPOSITE permit

deodorant = antiperspirant, disinfectant, deodorizer, fumigant, air freshener

depart VERB 1 = leave, go, withdraw, retire, disappear, quit, retreat, exit, go away, vanish, absent (yourself), start out, migrate, set forth, take (your) leave, decamp, hook it (*slang*), slope off, pack your bags (*informal*), make tracks ...*In the morning Mr McDonald departed for Sydney...* OPPOSITE arrive
2 = deviate, vary, differ, stray, veer, swerve, diverge, digress, turn aside ...*It takes a brave cook to depart radically from the traditional menu...*
VERB (*Chiefly U.S.*)= resign, leave, quit, step down (*informal*), give in your notice, call it a day *or* night, vacate your post ...*A number of staff departed during*

her reign as manager…

departed (*Euphemistic*) = <u>dead</u>, late, deceased, expired, perished

department 1 = <u>section</u>, office, unit, station, division, branch, bureau, subdivision …*He worked in the sales department…*
2 (*Informal*) = <u>area</u>, line, responsibility, function, province, sphere, realm, domain, speciality …*Sorry, I don't know – that's not my department…*

departure 1 = <u>leaving</u>, going, retirement, withdrawal, exit, going away, removal, exodus, leave-taking …*The airline has more than 90 scheduled departures from here each day…* OPPOSITE> arrival
2 = <u>retirement</u>, going, withdrawal, exit, going away, removal …*This would inevitably involve his departure from the post…*
3 = <u>shift</u>, change, difference, variation, innovation, novelty, veering, deviation, branching out, divergence, digression …*This album is a considerable departure from her previous work…*

depend 1 = <u>be determined by</u>, be based on, be subject to, hang on, rest on, revolve around, hinge on, be subordinate to, be contingent on …*What happened later would depend on his talk with her…*
2 = <u>count on</u>, turn to, trust in, bank on, lean on, rely upon, confide in, build upon, calculate on, reckon on …*She assured him that he could depend on her…*

dependable = <u>reliable</u>, sure, responsible, steady, faithful, staunch, reputable, trustworthy, trusty, unfailing OPPOSITE> undependable

dependant *or* (U.S. sometimes **dependent**) = <u>relative</u>, child, minor, subordinate, cohort (*chiefly U.S.*), protégé, henchman, retainer, hanger-on, minion, vassal

> ### Word Power
>
> **dependant** – *Dependant* is the generally accepted correct spelling in British usage for the noun and always refers to people: *if you are single and have no dependants*. The adjective should be spelt *dependent*: *tax allowance for dependent* (not *dependant*) *children*. American usage spells both adjective and noun with an *e* in the last syllable.

dependence 1 = <u>reliance</u>, trust, hope, confidence, belief, faith, expectation, assurance …*the city's traditional dependence on tourism…*
2 = <u>overreliance</u>, need, addiction, reliance, attachment …*Some doctors regard drug dependence as a psychological disorder…*
3 = <u>helplessness</u>, weakness, vulnerability …*the total dependence of her infirm husband…*

dependency 1 = <u>overreliance</u>, attachment …*I am concerned by his dependency on his mother…*
2 = <u>addiction</u>, dependence, craving, need, habit, obsession, enslavement, overreliance …*He began to show signs of alcohol and drug dependency…*

dependent ADJECTIVE = <u>reliant</u>, vulnerable, helpless, powerless, weak, defenceless …*I refuse to be*

dependent, despite having a baby to care for… OPPOSITE> independent

PHRASES **dependent on** *or* **upon** 1 = <u>reliant on</u>, relying on, counting on …*He was dependent on his parents for everything…* 2 = <u>determined by</u>, depending on, subject to, influenced by, relative to, liable to, conditional on, contingent on …*companies whose earnings are largely dependent on foreign economies…*
➤ **dependant**

depict 1 = <u>illustrate</u>, portray, picture, paint, outline, draw, sketch, render, reproduce, sculpt, delineate, limn …*a gallery of pictures depicting famous battles…*
2 = <u>describe</u>, present, represent, detail, outline, sketch, characterize …*Children's books often depict animals as gentle creatures…*

depiction 1 = <u>picture</u>, drawing, image, outline, illustration, sketch, likeness, delineation …*The vase has a depiction of a man playing a lyre…*
2 = <u>representation</u>, description, portrait, illustration, sketch, portrayal …*the depiction of socialists as Utopian dreamers…*

deplete = <u>use up</u>, reduce, drain, exhaust, consume, empty, decrease, evacuate, lessen, impoverish, expend OPPOSITE> increase

depleted = <u>used (up)</u>, drained, exhausted, consumed, spent, reduced, emptied, weakened, decreased, lessened, worn out, depreciated

depletion = <u>using up</u>, reduction, drain, consumption, lowering, decrease, expenditure, deficiency, dwindling, lessening, exhaustion, diminution

deplorable 1 = <u>terrible</u>, distressing, dreadful, sad, unfortunate, disastrous, miserable, dire, melancholy, heartbreaking, grievous, regrettable, lamentable, calamitous, wretched, pitiable …*Many of them work under deplorable conditions…* OPPOSITE> excellent
2 = <u>disgraceful</u>, shameful, scandalous, reprehensible, disreputable, dishonourable, execrable, blameworthy, opprobrious …*Sexual harassment is deplorable…* OPPOSITE> admirable

deplore 1 = <u>disapprove of</u>, condemn, object to, denounce, censure, abhor, deprecate, take a dim view of, excoriate …*He says he deplores violence…*
2 = <u>lament</u>, regret, mourn, rue, bemoan, grieve for, bewail, sorrow over …*They deplored the heavy loss of life in the earthquake…*

deploy (*used of troops or military resources*) = <u>use</u>, station, set up, position, arrange, set out, dispose, utilize, spread out, distribute

deployment (*used of troops or military resources*) = <u>use</u>, stationing, spread, organization, arrangement, positioning, disposition, setup, utilization

deport = <u>expel</u>, exile, throw out, oust, banish, expatriate, extradite, evict, send packing, show you the door

deportation = <u>expulsion</u>, exile, removal, transportation, exclusion, extradition, eviction, ejection, banishment, expatriation, debarment

depose = <u>oust</u>, dismiss, displace, degrade,

downgrade, cashier, demote, dethrone, remove from office

deposit NOUN **1** = <u>down payment</u>, security, stake, pledge, warranty, instalment, retainer, part payment ...*A deposit of £20 is required when ordering...*
2 = <u>accumulation</u>, growth, mass, build-up, layer ...*underground deposits of gold and diamonds...*
3 = <u>sediment</u>, grounds, residue, lees, precipitate, deposition, silt, dregs, alluvium, settlings ...*A powdery deposit had settled at the bottom of the glass...*
VERB **1** = <u>put</u>, place, lay, drop, settle ...*The barman deposited a glass and two bottles of beer in front of him...*
2 = <u>store</u>, keep, put, bank, save, lodge, entrust, consign, hoard, stash (*informal*), lock away, put in storage ...*You are advised to deposit valuables in the hotel safe...*

deposition 1 = <u>sworn statement</u> (*Law*), evidence, testimony, declaration, affidavit ...*The material would be checked against depositions from other witnesses...*
2 = <u>removal</u>, dismissal, ousting, toppling, expulsion, displacement, unseating, dethronement ...*It was this issue which led to the deposition of the leader...*

depository = <u>storehouse</u>, store, warehouse, depot, repository, safe-deposit box

depot 1 = <u>arsenal</u>, warehouse, storehouse, repository, depository, dump ...*a government arms depot...*
2 = <u>bus station</u>, station, garage, terminus ...*She was reunited with her boyfriend in the bus depot...*

deprave = <u>corrupt</u>, pervert, degrade, seduce, subvert, debase, demoralize, debauch, brutalize, lead astray, vitiate

depraved = <u>corrupt</u>, abandoned, perverted, evil, vicious, degraded, vile, degenerate, immoral, wicked, shameless, sinful, lewd, debased, profligate, debauched, lascivious, dissolute, licentious, pervy (*slang*) OPPOSITE moral

depravity = <u>corruption</u>, vice, evil, criminality, wickedness, immorality, iniquity, profligacy, debauchery, viciousness, degeneracy, sinfulness, debasement, turpitude, baseness, depravation, vitiation

deprecate 1 = <u>disapprove of</u>, condemn, object to, protest against, deplore, frown on, take exception to ...*He deprecated this unseemly behaviour...*
2 = <u>disparage</u>, criticize, run down, discredit, scorn, deride, detract, malign, denigrate, belittle, vilify, depreciate, knock (*informal*), diss (*slang, chiefly U.S.*), bad-mouth (*slang, chiefly U.S. & Canad.*), lambast(e) ...*They deprecate him and refer to him as 'a bit of a red'...*
▶ **depreciate**

depreciate 1 = <u>decrease</u>, reduce, lessen, devalue, deflate, lower in value, devaluate ...*The demand for foreign currency depreciates the real value of local currencies...* OPPOSITE augment
2 = <u>lose value</u>, devalue, devaluate ...*Inflation is rising rapidly and the yuan is depreciating...* OPPOSITE appreciate

depreciation = <u>devaluation</u>, fall, drop, depression, slump, deflation

depress 1 = <u>sadden</u>, upset, distress, chill, discourage, grieve, daunt, oppress, desolate, weigh down, cast down, bring tears to your eyes, make sad, dishearten, dispirit, make your heart bleed, aggrieve, deject, make despondent, cast a gloom upon ...*The state of the country depresses me...* OPPOSITE cheer
2 = <u>lower</u>, cut, reduce, diminish, decrease, impair, lessen ...*The stronger currency depressed sales...* OPPOSITE raise
3 = <u>devalue</u>, depreciate, cheapen, devaluate ...*A dearth of buyers has depressed prices...*
4 = <u>press down</u>, push, squeeze, lower, flatten, compress, push down, bear down on ...*He depressed the pedal that lowered the chair...*

depressed 1 = <u>sad</u>, down, low, blue, unhappy, discouraged, fed up, moody, gloomy, pessimistic, melancholy, sombre, glum, mournful, dejected, despondent, dispirited, downcast, morose, disconsolate, crestfallen, doleful, downhearted, heavy-hearted, down in the dumps (*informal*), cheerless, woebegone, down in the mouth (*informal*), low-spirited ...*He seemed somewhat depressed...*
2 = <u>poverty-stricken</u>, poor, deprived, distressed, disadvantaged, run-down, impoverished, needy, destitute, down at heel ...*attempts to encourage investment in depressed areas...*
3 = <u>lowered</u>, devalued, weakened, impaired, depreciated, cheapened ...*We need to prevent further falls in already depressed prices...*
4 = <u>sunken</u>, hollow, recessed, set back, indented, concave ...*Manual pressure is applied to a depressed point on the body...*

depressing = <u>bleak</u>, black, sad, distressing, discouraging, gloomy, daunting, hopeless, dismal, melancholy, dreary, harrowing, saddening, sombre, heartbreaking, dispiriting, disheartening, funereal, dejecting

depression 1 = <u>despair</u>, misery, sadness, dumps (*informal*), the blues, melancholy, unhappiness, hopelessness, despondency, the hump (*Brit. informal*), bleakness, melancholia, dejection, wretchedness, low spirits, gloominess, dolefulness, cheerlessness, downheartedness ...*I slid into a depression and became morbidly fascinated with death...*
2 = <u>recession</u>, slump, economic decline, stagnation, inactivity, hard *or* bad times ...*He never forgot the hardships he witnessed during the depression...*
3 = <u>hollow</u>, pit, dip, bowl, valley, sink, impression, dent, sag, cavity, excavation, indentation, dimple, concavity ...*an area pockmarked by rainfilled depressions...*

deprivation 1 denial, withdrawal, removal, expropriation, divestment, dispossession, deprival ...*Millions suffer from sleep deprivation caused by long work hours...*
2 = want, need, hardship, suffering, distress, disadvantage, oppression, detriment, privation, destitution ...*Single women with children are likely to suffer financial deprivation...*

deprive = dispossess, rob, strip, divest, expropriate, despoil, bereave

deprived = poor, disadvantaged, needy, in need, lacking, bereft, destitute, in want, denuded, down at heel, necessitous OPPOSITE prosperous

depth NOUN 1 = deepness, drop, measure, extent, profundity, profoundness ...*The fish were detected at depths of more than a kilometre...*
2 = strength, intensity, seriousness, severity, extremity, keenness, intenseness ...*I am well aware of the depth of feeling that exists in the town...*
3 = insight, intelligence, wisdom, penetration, profundity, acuity, discernment, perspicacity, sagacity, astuteness, profoundness, perspicuity ...*His writing has a depth that will outlast him...* OPPOSITE superficiality
4 = breadth, degree, magnitude, amplitude ...*We were impressed with the depth of her knowledge...*
5 = intensity, strength, warmth, richness, brightness, vibrancy, vividness ...*The blue base gives the red paint more depth...*
6 = complexity, intricacy, elaboration, obscurity, abstruseness, reconditeness ...*His music lacks depth...*
PLURAL NOUN 1 = deepest part, middle, midst, remotest part, furthest part, innermost part ...*A sound came from the depths of the forest...*
2 = most intense part, pit, void, abyss, chasm, deepest part, furthest part, bottomless depth ...*a man who had plumbed the depths of despair...*
PHRASES **in depth** = thoroughly, completely, fully, comprehensively, extensively, inside out, meticulously, intensively, exhaustively, leaving no stone unturned ...*We will discuss these three areas in depth...*

depute = appoint, choose, commission, select, elect, nominate, assign, charge, mandate, authorize, empower, accredit

deputy NOUN representative = substitute, ambassador, agent, commissioner, delegate, lieutenant, proxy, surrogate, second-in-command, nuncio, legate, vicegerent, number two ...*France's minister for culture and his deputy attended the meeting...*
ADJECTIVE = assistant, subordinate, depute (*Scot.*) ...*the academy's deputy director...*

deranged = mad, crazy, insane, distracted, frantic, frenzied, irrational, maddened, crazed, lunatic, demented, unbalanced, berserk, delirious, unhinged, loopy (*informal*), crackpot (*informal*), out to lunch (*informal*), barking mad (*slang*), barking (*slang*), gonzo (*slang*), doolally (*slang*), off your trolley (*slang*), up the pole (*informal*), not the full shilling (*informal*),

wacko *or* whacko (*slang*), berko (*Austral. slang*), off the air (*Austral. slang*) OPPOSITE sane

derelict ADJECTIVE = abandoned, deserted, ruined, neglected, discarded, forsaken, dilapidated ...*His body was found dumped in a derelict warehouse...*
NOUN 1 = tramp, bum (*informal*), outcast, drifter, down-and-out, vagrant, hobo (*chiefly U.S.*), vagabond, bag lady, dosser (*Brit. slang*), derro (*Austral. slang*) ...*a confused and wizened derelict wandered in off the street...*
2 (only used with *duty*) = negligent, slack, irresponsible, careless, lax, remiss ...*They would be derelict in their duty not to pursue it...*

dereliction 1 = abandonment, desertion, renunciation, relinquishment ...*The previous owners had rescued the building from dereliction...*
2 = (only used with *duty*) = negligence, failure, neglect, evasion, delinquency, abdication, faithlessness, nonperformance, remissness ...*He pleaded guilty to wilful dereliction of duty...*

deride = mock, ridicule, scorn, knock (*informal*), insult, taunt, sneer, jeer, disdain, scoff, detract, flout, disparage, chaff, gibe, pooh-pooh, contemn

derision = mockery, laughter, contempt, ridicule, scorn, insult, sneering, disdain, scoffing, disrespect, denigration, disparagement, contumely, raillery

derisory = ridiculous, insulting, outrageous, ludicrous, preposterous, laughable, contemptible

derivation = origin, source, basis, beginning, root, foundation, descent, ancestry, genealogy, etymology

derivative NOUN = by-product, spin-off, offshoot, descendant, derivation, outgrowth ...*a poppy-seed derivative similar to heroin...*
ADJECTIVE = unoriginal, copied, second-hand, rehashed, imitative, plagiarized, uninventive, plagiaristic ...*their dull, derivative debut album...* OPPOSITE original

derive VERB = obtain, get, receive, draw, gain, collect, gather, extract, elicit, glean, procure ...*He is one of those people who derives pleasure from helping others...*
PHRASES **derive from something** = come from, stem from, arise from, flow from, spring from, emanate from, proceed from, descend from, issue from, originate from ...*The word Druid may derive from 'drus', meaning 'oak tree'...*

derogatory = disparaging, damaging, offensive, slighting, detracting, belittling, unfavourable, unflattering, dishonouring, defamatory, injurious, discreditable, uncomplimentary, depreciative OPPOSITE complimentary

descend VERB 1 = fall, drop, sink, go down, plunge, dive, tumble, plummet, subside, move down ...*Disaster struck as the plane descended through the mist...* OPPOSITE rise
2 alight, dismount ...*The bus stopped and three people descended...*
3 = go down, come down, walk down, move down, climb down ...*Things are cooler and more damp as we descend to the cellar...*

4 = <u>slope</u>, dip, incline, slant, gravitate ...*The path descended steeply to the rushing river...*

PHRASES **be descended from** = <u>originate from</u>, derive from, spring from, proceed from, issue from ...*He was proud to be descended from tradesmen...*

♦ **descend on something** *or* **someone** = <u>attack</u>, assault, raid, invade, swoop, pounce, assail, arrive, come in force ...*Drunken mobs descended on their homes...* ♦ **descend to something** = <u>lower yourself</u>, stoop, condescend, abase yourself ...*She's got too much dignity to descend to writing anonymous letters...*

descendant = <u>successor</u>, child, issue, son, daughter, heir, offspring, progeny, scion, inheritor OPPOSITE ancestor

descent 1 = <u>fall</u>, drop, plunge, coming down, swoop ...*The airplane crashed on its descent into the airport...*
2 = <u>slope</u>, drop, dip, incline, slant, declination, declivity ...*On the descents, cyclists freewheel past cars...*
3 = <u>decline</u>, deterioration, degradation, decadence, degeneration, debasement ...*his swift descent from respected academic to homeless derelict...*
4 = <u>origin</u>, extraction, ancestry, lineage, family tree, parentage, heredity, genealogy, derivation ...*All the contributors were of foreign descent...*

describe 1 = <u>relate</u>, tell, report, present, detail, explain, express, illustrate, specify, chronicle, recount, recite, impart, narrate, set forth, give an account of ...*We asked her to describe what she had seen...*
2 = <u>portray</u>, depict, characterize, define, sketch ...*Even his allies describe him as forceful, aggressive and determined...*
3 = <u>trace</u>, draw, outline, mark out, delineate ...*The ball described a perfect arc across the field...*

description 1 = <u>account</u>, report, explanation, representation, sketch, narrative, portrayal, depiction, narration, characterization, delineation ...*He gave a description of the surgery he was about to perform...*
2 = <u>calling</u>, naming, branding, labelling, dubbing, designation ...*his description of the country as a 'police state'...*
3 = <u>kind</u>, sort, type, order, class, variety, brand, species, breed, category, kidney, genre, genus, ilk ...*Events of this description occurred daily...*

descriptive = <u>graphic</u>, vivid, expressive, picturesque, detailed, explanatory, pictorial, illustrative, depictive

desecrate = <u>profane</u>, dishonour, defile, violate, contaminate, pollute, pervert, despoil, blaspheme, commit sacrilege OPPOSITE revere

desecration = <u>violation</u>, blasphemy, sacrilege, debasement, defilement, impiety, profanation

desert¹ NOUN = <u>wilderness</u>, waste, wilds, wasteland ...*The vehicles have been modified to suit conditions in the desert...*
ADJECTIVE = <u>barren</u>, dry, waste, wild, empty, bare, lonely, solitary, desolate, arid, unproductive, infertile, uninhabited, uncultivated, unfruitful, untilled ...*the desert wastes of Mexico...*

> **WORD POWER SUPPLEMENT deserts**

desert² 1 = <u>abandon</u>, leave, give up, quit (*informal*), withdraw from, move out of, relinquish, renounce, vacate, forsake, go away from, leave empty, relinquish possession of ...*Poor farmers are deserting their fields and looking for jobs...*
2 = <u>leave</u>, abandon, strand, betray, maroon, walk out on (*informal*), forsake, jilt, run out on (*informal*), throw over, leave stranded, leave high and dry, leave (someone) in the lurch ...*Her husband deserted her years ago...* OPPOSITE take care of
3 = <u>abscond</u>, defect, decamp, go over the hill (*Military slang*) ...*He deserted from the army last month...*

deserted 1 = <u>empty</u>, abandoned, desolate, neglected, lonely, vacant, derelict, bereft, unoccupied, godforsaken ...*a deserted town...*
2 = <u>abandoned</u>, neglected, forsaken, lonely, forlorn, cast off, left stranded, left in the lurch, unfriended ...*the image of a wronged and deserted wife...*

deserter = <u>defector</u>, runaway, fugitive, traitor, renegade, truant, escapee, absconder, apostate

desertion 1 = <u>abandonment</u>, betrayal, forsaking, dereliction, relinquishment ...*It was a long time since she'd referred to her father's desertion of them...*
2 = <u>defection</u>, apostasy ...*mass desertion by the electorate...*
3 = <u>absconding</u>, flight, escape (*informal*), evasion, truancy ...*The high rate of desertion has added to the army's woes...*

deserts
PHRASES **just deserts** = <u>due</u>, payment, reward, punishment, right, return, retribution, recompense, come-uppance (*slang*), meed (*archaic*), requital, guerdon (*poetic*)

deserve = <u>merit</u>, warrant, be entitled to, have a right to, win, rate, earn, justify, be worthy of, have a claim to

deserved = <u>well-earned</u>, just, right, meet (*archaic*), fitting, due, fair, earned, appropriate, justified, suitable, merited, proper, warranted, rightful, justifiable, condign

deservedly = <u>rightly</u>, fittingly, fairly, appropriately, properly, duly, justifiably, justly, by rights, rightfully, according to your due, condignly OPPOSITE undeservedly

deserving = <u>worthy</u>, righteous, commendable, laudable, praiseworthy, meritorious, estimable OPPOSITE undeserving

desiccated = <u>dried</u>, dehydrated, dry, powdered

design VERB **1** = <u>plan</u>, describe, draw, draft, trace, outline, invent, devise, sketch, formulate, contrive, think out, delineate ...*They have designed a machine that is both attractive and practical...*
2 = <u>create</u>, make, plan, project, fashion, scheme, propose, invent, devise, tailor, draw up, conceive, originate, contrive, fabricate, think up ...*We may be able to design a course to suit your particular needs...*
3 = <u>intend</u>, mean, plan, aim, purpose ...*a compromise designed to please everyone...*
NOUN **1** = <u>pattern</u>, form, figure, style, shape, organization, arrangement, construction, motif,

configuration ...*The pictures are based on simple geometric designs*...
2 = <u>plan</u>, drawing, model, scheme, draft, outline, sketch, blueprint, delineation ...*They drew up the design in a week*...
3 = <u>intention</u>, end, point, aim, goal, target, purpose, object, objective, intent ...*Is there some design in having him here?*...

designate 1 = <u>name</u>, call, term, style, label, entitle, dub, nominate, christen ...*one man interviewed in our study, whom we shall designate as 'Mr E'*...
2 = <u>specify</u>, describe, indicate, define, characterize, stipulate, denote ...*I live in Exmoor, which is designated as a national park*...
3 = <u>choose</u>, reserve, select, label, flag, tag, assign, allocate, set aside, earmark, mark out, allot, keep back ...*Some of the rooms were designated as offices*...
4 = <u>appoint</u>, name, choose, commission, select, elect, delegate, nominate, assign, depute ...*We need to designate someone as our spokesperson*...

designation 1 = <u>name</u>, title, label, description, denomination, epithet ...*Level 4 alert is a designation reserved for very serious incidents*...
2 = <u>appointment</u>, specification, classification ...*the designation of the city as a centre of culture*...
3 = <u>election</u>, choice, selection, appointment, nomination ...*the designation of Ali as Prophet Muhammad's successor*...

designer 1 = <u>couturier</u>, stylist ...*She is a fashion designer*...
2 = <u>producer</u>, architect, deviser, creator, planner, inventor, artificer, originator ...*Designer Harvey Postlethwaite has rejoined Ferrari*...

designing = <u>scheming</u>, plotting, intriguing, crooked (*informal*), shrewd, conspiring, cunning, sly, astute, treacherous, unscrupulous, devious, wily, crafty, artful, conniving, Machiavellian, deceitful

desirability = <u>worth</u>, value, benefit, profit, advantage, merit, usefulness

desirable 1 = <u>advantageous</u>, useful, valuable, helpful, profitable, of service, convenient, worthwhile, beneficial, preferable, advisable ...*Prolonged negotiation was not desirable*... OPPOSITE disadvantageous
2 pleasing, enviable, to die for (*informal*), covetable ...*desirable commodities such as coffee and sugar*... OPPOSITE unpopular
3 = <u>attractive</u>, appealing, beautiful, winning, interesting, pleasing, pretty, fair, inviting, engaging, lovely, charming, fascinating, sexy (*informal*), handsome, fetching, good-looking, eligible, glamorous, gorgeous, magnetic, cute, enticing, seductive, captivating, alluring, adorable, bonny, winsome, comely, prepossessing ...*the young women whom his classmates thought most desirable*... OPPOSITE unattractive

desire NOUN **1** = <u>wish</u>, want, longing, need, hope, urge, yen (*informal*), hunger, appetite, aspiration, ache, craving, yearning, inclination, thirst, hankering ...*I had a strong desire to help and care for people*...
2 = <u>lust</u>, passion, libido, appetite, lechery, carnality,

lasciviousness, concupiscence, randiness (*informal, chiefly Brit.*), lustfulness ...*Teenage sex may not always come out of genuine desire*...
VERB **1** = <u>want</u>, long for, crave, fancy, hope for, ache for, covet, aspire to, wish for, yearn for, thirst for, hanker after, set your heart on, desiderate ...*He was bored and desired change in his life*...
2 (*Formal*) = <u>request</u>, ask, petition, solicit, entreat, importune ...*His Majesty desires me to make his wishes known to you*...

desired = <u>required</u>, necessary, correct, appropriate, right, expected, fitting, particular, express, accurate, proper, exact

desist = <u>stop</u>, cease, refrain from, end, kick (*informal*), give up, suspend, break off, abstain, discontinue, leave off, have done with, give over (*informal*), forbear, belay (*Nautical*)

desolate ADJECTIVE **1** = <u>uninhabited</u>, deserted, bare, waste, wild, ruined, bleak, solitary, barren, dreary, godforsaken, unfrequented ...*a desolate, godforsaken place*... OPPOSITE Inhabited
2 = <u>miserable</u>, depressed, lonely, gloomy, dismal, melancholy, forlorn, bereft, dejected, despondent, downcast, wretched, disconsolate, down in the dumps (*informal*), cheerless, comfortless, companionless ...*He was desolate without her*... OPPOSITE happy
VERB **1** = <u>deject</u>, depress, distress, discourage, dismay, grieve, daunt, dishearten ...*I was desolated by the news*... OPPOSITE cheer
2 = <u>destroy</u>, ruin, devastate, ravage, lay low, lay waste, despoil, depopulate ...*A great famine desolated the country*...

desolation 1 = <u>misery</u>, distress, despair, gloom, sadness, woe, anguish, melancholy, unhappiness, dejection, wretchedness, gloominess ...*He expresses his sense of desolation without self-pity*...
2 = <u>bleakness</u>, isolation, loneliness, solitude, wildness, barrenness, solitariness, forlornness, desolateness ...*We looked out upon a scene of utter desolation*...
3 = <u>ruin</u>, destruction, havoc, devastation, ruination ...*The army left a trail of desolation and death in its wake*...

despair NOUN = <u>despondency</u>, depression, misery, gloom, desperation, anguish, melancholy, hopelessness, dejection, wretchedness, disheartenment ...*She shook her head in despair at the futility of it all*...
VERB = <u>lose hope</u>, give up, lose heart, be despondent, be dejected ...*He despairs at much of the press criticism*...

despairing = <u>hopeless</u>, desperate, depressed, anxious, miserable, frantic, dismal, suicidal, melancholy, dejected, broken-hearted, despondent, downcast, grief-stricken, wretched, disconsolate, inconsolable, down in the dumps (*informal*), at the end of your tether

despatch
 ► **dispatch**

desperado = <u>criminal</u>, thug, outlaw, villain, gangster, gunman, bandit, mugger (*informal*), cut-throat, hoodlum (*chiefly U.S.*), ruffian, heavy (*slang*), lawbreaker, skelm (*S. African*)

desperate 1 = <u>hopeless</u>, despairing, in despair, forlorn, abject, dejected, despondent, demoralized, wretched, disconsolate, inconsolable, downhearted, at the end of your tether ...*Her people were poor, desperate and starving*...
2 = <u>grave</u>, great, pressing, serious, critical, acute, severe, extreme, urgent, dire, drastic, very grave ...*Troops are needed to get food to people in desperate need*...
3 = <u>last-ditch</u>, dangerous, daring, determined, wild, violent, furious, risky, frantic, rash, hazardous, precipitate, hasty, audacious, madcap, foolhardy, headstrong, impetuous, death-defying ...*a desperate rescue attempt*...

desperately = <u>gravely</u>, badly, seriously, severely, dangerously, perilously

desperation 1 = <u>misery</u>, worry, trouble, pain, anxiety, torture, despair, agony, sorrow, distraction, anguish, unhappiness, heartache, hopelessness, despondency ...*this feeling of desperation and helplessness*...
2 = <u>recklessness</u>, madness, defiance, frenzy, impetuosity, rashness, foolhardiness, heedlessness ...*It was an act of sheer desperation*...

despicable = <u>contemptible</u>, mean, low, base, cheap, infamous, degrading, worthless, disgraceful, shameful, vile, sordid, pitiful, abject, hateful, reprehensible, ignominious, disreputable, wretched, scurvy, detestable, scungy (*Austral. & N.Z.*), beyond contempt OPPOSITE admirable

despise = <u>look down on</u>, loathe, scorn, disdain, spurn, undervalue, deride, detest, revile, abhor, have a down on (*informal*), contemn OPPOSITE admire

despite = <u>in spite of</u>, in the face of, regardless of, even with, notwithstanding, in defiance of, in the teeth of, undeterred by, in contempt of

despondency = <u>dejection</u>, depression, despair, misery, gloom, sadness, desperation, melancholy, hopelessness, the hump (*Brit. informal*), discouragement, wretchedness, low spirits, disconsolateness, dispiritedness, downheartedness

despondent = <u>dejected</u>, sad, depressed, down, low, blue, despairing, discouraged, miserable, gloomy, hopeless, dismal, melancholy, in despair, glum, dispirited, downcast, morose, disheartened, sorrowful, wretched, disconsolate, doleful, downhearted, down in the dumps (*informal*), sick as a parrot (*informal*), woebegone, low-spirited OPPOSITE cheerful

despot = <u>tyrant</u>, dictator, oppressor, autocrat, monocrat

despotic = <u>tyrannical</u>, authoritarian, dictatorial, absolute, arrogant, oppressive, autocratic, imperious, domineering, monocratic

despotism = <u>tyranny</u>, dictatorship, oppression, totalitarianism, autocracy, absolutism, autarchy, monocracy

dessert = <u>pudding</u>, sweet (*informal*), afters (*Brit.*

informal), second course, last course, sweet course

destination = <u>stop</u>, station, haven, harbour, resting-place, terminus, journey's end, landing-place

destined ADJECTIVE = <u>fated</u>, meant, intended, designed, certain, bound, doomed, ordained, predestined, foreordained ...*He feels that he was destined to become a musician*...
PHRASES **destined for** = <u>bound for</u>, booked, directed, scheduled, routed, heading for, assigned, en route, on the road to ...*products destined for the south*...

destiny NOUN **1** = <u>fate</u>, fortune, lot, portion, doom, nemesis, divine decree ...*We are masters of our own destiny*...
2 *usually cap.* = <u>fortune</u>, chance, karma, providence, kismet, predestination, divine will ...*Is it Destiny or accident that brings people together?*...

destitute ADJECTIVE = <u>penniless</u>, poor, impoverished, distressed, needy, on the rocks, insolvent, poverty-stricken, down and out, indigent, impecunious, dirt-poor (*informal*), on the breadline (*informal*), flat broke (*informal*), short, penurious, on your uppers, necessitous, in queer street (*informal*), moneyless, without two pennies to rub together (*informal*) ...*destitute children who live on the streets*...
PHRASES **destitute of** = <u>lacking</u>, wanting, without, in need of, deprived of, devoid of, bereft of, empty of, drained of, deficient in, depleted in ...*a country destitute of natural resources*...

destroy 1 = <u>ruin</u>, smash, crush, waste, devastate, break down, wreck, shatter, gut, wipe out, dispatch, dismantle, demolish, trash (*slang*), total (*slang*), ravage, slay, eradicate, torpedo, extinguish, desolate, annihilate, put paid to, raze, blow to bits, extirpate, blow sky-high ...*The building was completely destroyed*...
2 = <u>slaughter</u>, kill, exterminate ...*The horse had to be destroyed*...

destruction 1 = <u>ruin</u>, havoc, wreckage, crushing, wrecking, shattering, undoing, demolition, devastation, annihilation, ruination ...*the extensive destruction caused by the rioters*...
2 = <u>massacre</u>, overwhelming, slaughter, overthrow, extinction, end, downfall, liquidation, obliteration, extermination, eradication ...*Our objective was the destruction of the enemy forces*...
3 = <u>slaughter</u> ...*the destruction of animals infected with foot-and-mouth disease*...

destructive 1 = <u>devastating</u>, fatal, deadly, lethal, harmful, damaging, catastrophic, detrimental, hurtful, pernicious, noxious, ruinous, calamitous, cataclysmic, baleful, deleterious, injurious, baneful, maleficent ...*the awesome destructive power of nuclear weapons*...
2 = <u>negative</u>, hostile, discouraging, undermining, contrary, vicious, adverse, discrediting, disparaging, antagonistic, derogatory ...*Try to give constructive rather than destructive criticism*...

desultory = <u>random</u>, vague, irregular, loose, rambling, inconsistent, erratic, disconnected, haphazard, cursory, aimless, off and on, fitful, spasmodic, discursive, unsystematic, inconstant, maundering, unmethodical

detach VERB **1** = separate, free, remove, divide, isolate, cut off, sever, loosen, segregate, disconnect, tear off, disengage, disentangle, unfasten, disunite, uncouple, unhitch, disjoin, unbridle ...*Detach the bottom part from the form and keep it for reference...* OPPOSITE attach
2 = free, remove, separate, isolate, cut off, segregate, disengage ...*Gradually my husband detached me from all my friends...*
PHRASES **detach yourself from something** = distance yourself from, disengage yourself from, remove yourself from, separate yourself from, liberate yourself from, disconnect yourself from, disentangle yourself from ...*Try to detach yourself from the problem and be more objective...*

detached 1 = objective, neutral, impartial, reserved, aloof, impersonal, disinterested, unbiased, dispassionate, uncommitted, uninvolved, unprejudiced ...*The piece is written in a detached, precise style...* OPPOSITE subjective
2 = separate, free, severed, disconnected, loosened, discrete, unconnected, undivided, disjoined ...*He lost his sight because of a detached retina...*

detachment 1 = indifference, fairness, neutrality, objectivity, impartiality, coolness, remoteness, nonchalance, aloofness, unconcern, disinterestedness, nonpartisanship ...*her professional detachment...*
2 (*Military*) = unit, party, force, body, detail, squad, patrol, task force ...*a detachment of marines...*

detail NOUN **1** = point, fact, feature, particular, respect, factor, count, item, instance, element, aspect, specific, component, facet, technicality ...*I recall every detail of the party...*
2 = fine point, part, particular, nicety, minutiae, triviality ...*Only minor details now remain to be settled...*
3 (*Military*) = party, force, body, duty, squad, assignment, fatigue, detachment ...*His personal detail totalled sixty men...*
VERB **1** = list, describe, relate, catalogue, portray, specify, depict, recount, rehearse, recite, narrate, delineate, enumerate, itemize, tabulate, particularize ...*The report detailed the human rights abuses committed...*
2 = appoint, name, choose, commission, select, elect, delegate, nominate, assign, allocate, charge ...*He detailed someone to take it to the Incident Room...*
PHRASES **in detail** = comprehensively, completely, fully, thoroughly, extensively, inside out, exhaustively, point by point, item by item ...*Examine the wording in detail before deciding on the final text...*

detailed 1 = comprehensive, full, complete, minute, particular, specific, extensive, exact, thorough, meticulous, exhaustive, all-embracing, itemized, encyclopedic, blow-by-blow, particularized ...*a detailed account of the discussions...* OPPOSITE brief
2 = complicated, involved, complex, fancy, elaborate, intricate, meticulous, convoluted ...*detailed line drawings...*

detain 1 = hold, arrest, confine, restrain, imprison, intern, take prisoner, take into custody, hold in custody ...*He was arrested and detained for questioning...*
2 = delay, keep, stop, hold up, hamper, hinder, retard, impede, keep back, slow up *or* down ...*We won't detain you any further...*

detect 1 = discover, find, reveal, catch, expose, disclose, uncover, track down, unmask ...*equipment used to detect radiation...*
2 = notice, see, spot, catch, note, identify, observe, remark, recognize, distinguish, perceive, scent, discern, ascertain, descry ...*He could detect a certain sadness in her face...*

detection = discovery, exposure, uncovering, tracking down, unearthing, unmasking, ferreting out

detective = investigator, cop (*slang*), copper (*slang*), dick (*slang, chiefly U.S.*), constable, tec (*slang*), private eye, sleuth (*informal*), private investigator, gumshoe (*U.S. slang*), bizzy (*slang*), C.I.D. man

detention = imprisonment, custody, restraint, keeping in, quarantine, confinement, porridge (*slang*), incarceration OPPOSITE release

deter 1 = discourage, inhibit, put off, frighten, intimidate, daunt, hinder, dissuade, talk out of ...*Jail sentences have done nothing to deter the offenders...*
2 = prevent, stop, check, curb, damp, restrain, prohibit, hinder, debar ...*Capital punishment does not deter crime...*

detergent NOUN = cleaner, cleanser ...*He squeezed some detergent over the dishes...*
ADJECTIVE = cleansing, cleaning, purifying, abstergent, detersive ...*low-lather detergent powders...*

deteriorate 1 = decline, worsen, degenerate, slump, degrade, depreciate, go downhill, go to the dogs (*informal*) (*informal*), go to pot ...*There are fears that the situation may deteriorate...* OPPOSITE improve
2 = disintegrate, decay, spoil, fade, break down, weaken, crumble, fall apart, ebb, decompose, wear away, retrogress ...*X-rays are used to prevent fresh food from deteriorating...*

deterioration 1 = decline, fall, drop, slump, worsening, downturn, depreciation, degradation, degeneration, debasement, retrogression, vitiation, dégringolade (*French*) ...*the rapid deterioration in relations between the two countries...*
2 = disintegration, corrosion, atrophy ...*enzymes that cause the deterioration of food...*

determination 1 = resolution, purpose, resolve, drive, energy, conviction, courage, dedication, backbone, fortitude, persistence, tenacity, perseverance, willpower, boldness, firmness, staying power, stubbornness, constancy, single-mindedness, earnestness, obstinacy, steadfastness, doggedness, relentlessness, resoluteness, indomitability, staunchness ...*They acted with great courage and determination...* OPPOSITE indecision
2 = decision, ruling, settlement, resolution, resolve,

conclusion, verdict, judgment ...*A determination will be made as to the future of the treaty...*

determine 1 = <u>affect</u>, control, decide, rule, condition, direct, influence, shape, govern, regulate, ordain ...*What determines whether you are a success or a failure?...*

2 = <u>settle</u>, learn, establish, discover, check, find out, work out, detect, certify, verify, ascertain ...*The investigation will determine what really happened...*

3 = <u>decide on</u>, choose, establish, purpose, fix, elect, resolve ...*The people have a right to determine their own future...*

4 = <u>decide</u>, purpose, conclude, resolve, make up your mind ...*I determined that I would ask him outright...*

determined ADJECTIVE = <u>resolute</u>, firm, dogged, fixed, constant, bold, intent, persistent, relentless, stalwart, persevering, single-minded, purposeful, tenacious, undaunted, strong-willed, steadfast, unwavering, immovable, unflinching, strong-minded ...*He is making a determined effort to regain lost ground...*

PHRASES **determined to** *or* **on** = <u>intent on</u>, set on, bent on ...*His enemies are determined to ruin him...* ...*Are you absolutely determined on this course of action?...*

determining = <u>deciding</u>, important, settling, essential, critical, crucial, decisive, final, definitive, conclusive

deterrent = <u>discouragement</u>, obstacle, curb, restraint, impediment, check, hindrance, disincentive, defensive measures, determent OPPOSITE> incentive

detest = <u>hate</u>, loathe, despise, abhor, be hostile to, recoil from, be repelled by, have an aversion to, abominate, dislike intensely, execrate, feel aversion towards, feel disgust towards, feel hostility towards, feel repugnance towards OPPOSITE> love

dethrone = <u>depose</u>, oust, unseat, uncrown

detonate 1 = <u>set off</u>, trigger, explode, discharge, blow up, touch off ...*The terrorists planted and detonated the bomb...*

2 = <u>explode</u>, blast, discharge, blow up, fulminate ...*an explosive device which detonated last night...*

detonation 1 = <u>explosion</u>, blast, bang, report, boom, discharge, fulmination

2 = <u>blowing-up</u>, explosion, discharge ...*the accidental detonation of nuclear weapons...*

detour = <u>diversion</u>, bypass, deviation, circuitous route, roundabout way, indirect course

detract from 1 = <u>lessen</u>, reduce, diminish, lower, take away from, derogate, devaluate ...*Her faults did not seem to detract from her appeal...* OPPOSITE> enhance

2 = <u>divert</u>, shift, distract, deflect, draw *or* lead away from ...*They can only detract attention from the serious issues...*

> ## Word Power
>
> **detract** – *Detract* is sometimes wrongly used where *distract* is meant: *a noise distracted* (not *detracted*) *my attention.*

detractor = <u>slanderer</u>, belittler, disparager, defamer, traducer, muckraker, scandalmonger, denigrator, backbiter, derogator (*rare*)

detriment = <u>damage</u>, loss, harm, injury, hurt, prejudice, disadvantage, impairment, disservice

detrimental = <u>damaging</u>, destructive, harmful, adverse, pernicious, unfavourable, prejudicial, baleful, deleterious, injurious, inimical, disadvantageous OPPOSITE> beneficial

detritus = <u>debris</u>, remains, waste, rubbish, fragments, litter

devastate 1 = <u>destroy</u>, waste, ruin, sack, wreck, spoil, demolish, trash (*slang*), level, total (*slang*), ravage, plunder, desolate, pillage, raze, lay waste, despoil ...*A fire devastated large parts of the castle...*

2 (*Informal*) = <u>shatter</u>, overwhelm, confound, floor (*informal*) ...*If word of this gets out, it will devastate his family...*

devastating ADJECTIVE 1 = <u>destructive</u>, damaging, catastrophic, harmful, detrimental, pernicious, ruinous, calamitous, cataclysmic, deleterious, injurious, maleficent ...*the devastating force of the floods...*

2 = <u>traumatic</u>, shocking, upsetting, disturbing, painful, scarring ...*The diagnosis was devastating. She had cancer...*

3 = <u>impressive</u>, moving, striking, touching, affecting, grand, powerful, exciting, dramatic, stirring, awesome ...*the most devastating performance of his career...*

4 = <u>savage</u>, cutting, overwhelming, withering, overpowering, satirical, incisive, sardonic, caustic, vitriolic, trenchant, mordant ...*his devastating criticism of the Prime Minister...*

devastation = <u>destruction</u>, ruin, havoc, ravages, demolition, plunder, pillage, desolation, depredation, ruination, spoliation

develop 1 = <u>grow</u>, advance, progress, mature, evolve, flourish, blossom, ripen ...*Children develop at different rates...*

2 = <u>result</u>, follow, arise, issue, happen, spring, stem, derive, break out, ensue, come about, be a direct result of ...*a problem which developed from a leg injury...*

3 = <u>establish</u>, set up, promote, generate, undertake, initiate, embark on, cultivate, instigate, inaugurate, set in motion ...*her dreams of developing her own business...*

4 = <u>form</u>, start, begin, contract, establish, pick up, breed, acquire, generate, foster, originate ...*She developed a taste for expensive nightclubs...*

5 = <u>expand</u>, extend, work out, elaborate, unfold, enlarge, broaden, amplify, augment, dilate upon ...*They allowed me to develop their original idea...*

development 1 = <u>growth</u>, increase, growing,

advance, progress, spread, expansion, extension, evolution, widening, maturing, unfolding, unravelling, advancement, progression, thickening, enlargement …*the development of the embryo*…
2 = establishment, forming, generation, institution, invention, initiation, inauguration, instigation, origination …*the development of new and innovative services*…
3 = event, change, happening, issue, result, situation, incident, circumstance, improvement, outcome, phenomenon, evolution, unfolding, occurrence, upshot, turn of events, evolvement …*There has been a significant development in the case*…

deviant ADJECTIVE = perverted, sick (*informal*), twisted, bent (*slang*), abnormal, queer (*informal, derogatory*), warped, perverse, wayward, kinky (*slang*), devious, deviate, freaky (*slang*), aberrant, pervy (*slang*), sicko (*informal*) …*social reactions to deviant and criminal behaviour*… OPPOSITE normal
NOUN = pervert, freak, queer (*informal, derogatory*), misfit, sicko (*informal*), odd type …*a dangerous deviant who lived rough*…

deviate = differ, vary, depart, part, turn, bend, drift, wander, stray, veer, swerve, meander, diverge, digress, turn aside

deviation = departure, change, variation, shift, alteration, discrepancy, inconsistency, disparity, aberration, variance, divergence, fluctuation, irregularity, digression

device 1 = gadget, machine, tool, instrument, implement, invention, appliance, apparatus, gimmick, utensil, contraption, contrivance, waldo, gizmo *or* gismo (*slang, chiefly U.S. & Canad.*) …*This device can measure minute quantities of matter*…
2 = ploy, scheme, strategy, plan, design, project, shift, trick, manoeuvre, stunt, dodge, expedient, ruse, artifice, gambit, stratagem, wile …*His actions are obviously a device to buy time*…

devil NOUN **1** = evil spirit, demon, fiend, ghoul, hellhound …*the image of devils with horns and cloven hoofs*…
2 = brute, monster, savage, beast, villain, rogue, barbarian, fiend, terror, swine, ogre …*the savage devils who mugged a helpless old woman*…
3 = person, individual, soul, creature, thing, human being, beggar …*I feel sorry for the poor devil who marries you*…
4 = scamp, monkey (*informal*), rogue, imp, rascal, tyke (*informal*), scoundrel, scallywag (*informal*), mischief-maker, whippersnapper, toerag (*slang*), pickle (*Brit. informal*), nointer (*Austral. slang*) …*You cheeky little devil!*…
PHRASES **the Devil** = Satan, Lucifer, Prince of Darkness, Old One, Deuce, Old Gentleman (*informal*), Lord of the Flies, Old Harry (*informal*), Mephistopheles, Evil One, Beelzebub, Old Nick (*informal*), Mephisto, Belial, Clootie (*Scot.*), deil (*Scot.*), Apollyon, Old Scratch (*informal*), Foul Fiend, Wicked One, archfiend, Old Hornie (*informal*), Abbadon …*the eternal conflict between God and the Devil*…

devilish 1 = fiendish, diabolical, wicked, satanic, atrocious, hellish, infernal, accursed, execrable, detestable, damnable, diabolic …*devilish instruments of torture*…
2 = difficult, involved, complex, complicated, baffling, intricate, perplexing, thorny, knotty, problematical, ticklish …*It was a devilish puzzle to solve*…

devious 1 = sly, scheming, calculating, tricky, crooked (*informal*), indirect, treacherous, dishonest, wily, insidious, evasive, deceitful, underhand, insincere, surreptitious, double-dealing, not straightforward …*She tracked down the other woman by devious means*… OPPOSITE straightforward
2 = indirect, roundabout, wandering, crooked, rambling, tortuous, deviating, circuitous, excursive …*He followed a devious route*… OPPOSITE direct

devise = work out, plan, form, design, imagine, frame, arrange, plot, construct, invent, conceive, formulate, contrive, dream up, concoct, think up

devoid *with of* = lacking in, without, free from, wanting in, sans (*archaic*), bereft of, empty of, deficient in, denuded of, barren of

devolution = transfer of power, decentralization, distribution of power, surrender of power, relinquishment of power

devolve = transfer, entrust, consign, depute

devote = dedicate, give, commit, apply, reserve, pledge, surrender, assign, allot, give over, consecrate, set apart

devoted = dedicated, loving, committed, concerned, caring, true, constant, loyal, faithful, fond, ardent, staunch, devout, steadfast OPPOSITE disloyal

devotee 1 = enthusiast, fan, supporter, follower, addict, admirer, buff (*informal*), fanatic, adherent, aficionado …*She is a devotee of Bach's music*…
2 = follower, student, supporter, pupil, convert, believer, partisan, disciple, learner, apostle, adherent, votary, proselyte, catechumen …*devotees of the Hare Krishna movement*…

devotion NOUN **1** = love, passion, affection, intensity, attachment, zeal, fondness, fervour, adoration, ardour, earnestness …*She was flattered by his devotion*…
2 = dedication, commitment, loyalty, allegiance, fidelity, adherence, constancy, faithfulness …*devotion to the cause*… OPPOSITE indifference
3 = worship, reverence, spirituality, holiness, piety, sanctity, adoration, godliness, religiousness, devoutness …*He was kneeling by his bed in an attitude of devotion*… OPPOSITE irreverence
PLURAL NOUN = prayers, religious observance, church service, divine office …*He performs his devotions twice a day*…

devotional = religious, spiritual, holy, sacred, devout, pious, reverential

devour 1 = eat, consume, swallow, bolt, dispatch, cram, stuff, wolf, gorge, gulp, gobble, guzzle, polish off (*informal*), pig out on (*slang*) …*She devoured half an apple pie*…
2 = enjoy, go through, absorb, appreciate, take in, relish, drink in, delight in, revel in, be preoccupied with, feast on, be engrossed by, read compulsively *or*

voraciously …*He devoured 17 novels during his tour of India*…

devouring = <u>overwhelming</u>, powerful, intense, flaming, consuming, excessive, passionate, insatiable

devout 1 = <u>religious</u>, godly, pious, pure, holy, orthodox, saintly, reverent, prayerful …*She was a devout Christian*… <u>OPPOSITE</u> irreverent
2 = <u>sincere</u>, serious, deep, earnest, genuine, devoted, intense, passionate, profound, ardent, fervent, heartfelt, zealous, dinkum (*Austral. & N.Z. informal*) …*a devout opponent of racism*… <u>OPPOSITE</u> indifferent

dexterity 1 = <u>skill</u>, expertise, mastery, touch, facility, craft, knack, finesse, artistry, proficiency, smoothness, neatness, deftness, nimbleness, adroitness, effortlessness, handiness …*He showed great dexterity on the guitar*… <u>OPPOSITE</u> incompetence
2 = <u>cleverness</u>, art, ability, ingenuity, readiness, aptitude, adroitness, aptness, expertness, skilfulness …*the wit and verbal dexterity of the script*…

diabolical 1 (*Informal*) = <u>dreadful</u>, shocking, terrible, appalling, nasty, tricky, unpleasant, outrageous, vile, excruciating, atrocious, abysmal, damnable …*the diabolical treatment of their prisoners*…
2 = <u>wicked</u>, cruel, savage, monstrous, malicious, satanic, from hell (*informal*), malignant, unspeakable, inhuman, implacable, malevolent, hellish, devilish, infernal, fiendish, ungodly, black-hearted, demoniac, hellacious (*U.S. slang*) …*sins committed in a spirit of diabolical enjoyment*…

diagnose = <u>identify</u>, determine, recognize, distinguish, interpret, pronounce, pinpoint

diagnosis 1 = <u>identification</u>, discovery, recognition, detection …*Diagnosis of this disease can be very difficult*…
2 = <u>opinion</u>, conclusion, interpretation, pronouncement …*She needs to have a second test to confirm the diagnosis*…

diagnostic = <u>symptomatic</u>, particular, distinguishing, distinctive, peculiar, indicative, idiosyncratic, recognizable, demonstrative

diagonal = <u>slanting</u>, angled, oblique, cross, crosswise, crossways, cater-cornered (*U.S. informal*), cornerways

diagonally = <u>aslant</u>, obliquely, on the cross, at an angle, crosswise, on the bias, cornerwise

diagram = <u>plan</u>, figure, drawing, chart, outline, representation, sketch, layout, graph

dialect = <u>language</u>, speech, tongue, jargon, idiom, vernacular, brogue, lingo (*informal*), patois, provincialism, localism

dialectic = <u>debate</u>, reasoning, discussion, logic, contention, polemics, disputation, argumentation, ratiocination

dialogue 1 = <u>discussion</u>, conference, exchange, debate, confabulation …*He wants to open a dialogue with the protesters*…
2 = <u>conversation</u>, discussion, communication, discourse, converse, colloquy, confabulation, duologue, interlocution …*Those who witnessed their dialogue spoke of high emotion*…

3 = <u>script</u>, conversation, lines, spoken part …*The play's dialogue is sharp and witty*…

diametrically = <u>completely</u>, totally, entirely, absolutely, utterly

diarrhoea or (*U.S.*) **diarrhea** = <u>the runs</u>, the trots (*informal*), dysentery, looseness, the skits (*informal*), Montezuma's revenge (*informal*), gippy tummy, holiday tummy, Spanish tummy, the skitters (*informal*)

diary 1 = <u>journal</u>, chronicle, day-to-day account …*the most famous descriptive passage in his diary*…
2 = <u>engagement book</u>, Filofax (*trademark*), appointment book …*My diary is pretty full next week*…

diatribe = <u>tirade</u>, abuse, criticism, denunciation, reviling, stricture, harangue, invective, vituperation, stream of abuse, verbal onslaught, philippic

dicey (*Informal, chiefly Brit.*) = <u>dangerous</u>, difficult, tricky, risky, hairy (*slang*), ticklish, chancy (*informal*)

dichotomy = <u>division</u>, split, separation, disjunction

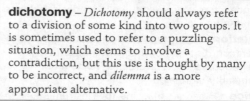

> ### Word Power
> **dichotomy** – <u>Dichotomy</u> should always refer to a division of some kind into two groups. It is sometimes used to refer to a puzzling situation, which seems to involve a contradiction, but this use is thought by many to be incorrect, and *dilemma* is a more appropriate alternative.

dicky (*Brit. informal*) = <u>weak</u>, queer (*informal*), shaky, unreliable, unsteady, unsound, fluttery

dictate <u>VERB</u> = <u>speak</u>, say, utter, read out …*He dictates his novels to his secretary*…
<u>NOUN</u> **1** = <u>command</u>, order, decree, word, demand, direction, requirement, bidding, mandate, injunction, statute, fiat, ultimatum, ordinance, edict, behest …*They must abide by the dictates of the new government*…
2 = <u>principle</u>, law, rule, standard, code, criterion, ethic, canon, maxim, dictum, precept, axiom, moral law …*We have followed the dictates of our consciences*…
<u>PHRASES</u> **dictate to someone** = <u>order (about)</u>, direct, lay down the law, pronounce to …*What gives them the right to dictate to us?*…

dictator = <u>absolute ruler</u>, tyrant, despot, oppressor, autocrat, absolutist, martinet

dictatorial 1 = <u>absolute</u>, unlimited, totalitarian, autocratic, unrestricted, tyrannical, despotic …*He suspended the constitution and assumed dictatorial powers*… <u>OPPOSITE</u> democratic
2 = <u>domineering</u>, authoritarian, oppressive, bossy (*informal*), imperious, overbearing, magisterial, iron-handed, dogmatical …*his dictatorial management style*… <u>OPPOSITE</u> servile

dictatorship = <u>absolute rule</u>, tyranny, totalitarianism, authoritarianism, reign of terror, despotism, autocracy, absolutism

diction = <u>pronunciation</u>, speech, articulation, delivery, fluency, inflection, intonation, elocution, enunciation

dictionary = <u>wordbook</u>, vocabulary, glossary, encyclopedia, lexicon, concordance

dictum 1 = <u>saying</u>, saw, maxim, adage, proverb, precept, axiom, gnome ...*the dictum that it is preferable to be roughly right than precisely wrong...*
2 = <u>decree</u>, order, demand, statement, command, dictate, canon, fiat, edict, pronouncement ...*his dictum that the priority of the government must be the health of the people...*

didactic 1 = <u>instructive</u>, educational, enlightening, moral, edifying, homiletic, preceptive ...*In totalitarian societies, art exists solely for didactic purposes...*
2 = <u>pedantic</u>, academic, formal, pompous, schoolmasterly, erudite, bookish, abstruse, moralizing, priggish, pedagogic ...*He adopts a lofty, didactic tone when addressing women...*

die [VERB] **1** = <u>pass away</u>, depart, expire, perish, buy it (*U.S. slang*), check out (*U.S. slang*), kick it (*slang*), croak (*slang*), give up the ghost, go belly-up (*slang*), snuff it (*slang*), peg out (*informal*), kick the bucket (*slang*), buy the farm (*U.S. slang*), peg it (*informal*), decease, cark it (*Austral. & N.Z. slang*), pop your clogs (*informal*), breathe your last, hop the twig (*slang*) ...*His mother died when he was a child...* [OPPOSITE] live
2 = <u>stop</u>, fail, halt, break down, run down, stop working, peter out, fizzle out, lose power, seize up, conk out (*informal*), go kaput (*informal*), go phut, fade out *or* away ...*The engine coughed, spluttered, and died...*
3 = <u>dwindle</u>, end, decline, pass, disappear, sink, fade, weaken, diminish, vanish, decrease, decay, lapse, wither, wilt, lessen, wane, subside, ebb, die down, die out, abate, peter out, die away, grow less ...*My love for you will never die...* [OPPOSITE] increase
[PHRASES] **be dying for something** = <u>long for</u>, want, desire, crave, yearn for, hunger for, pine for, hanker after, be eager for, ache for, swoon over, languish for, set your heart on ...*I'm dying for a cigarette...* ◆ **be dying of something** (*Informal*) = <u>be overcome with</u>, succumb to, collapse with ...*I'm dying of thirst...*

die-hard *or* **diehard** [NOUN] = <u>reactionary</u>, fanatic, zealot, intransigent, stick-in-the-mud (*informal*), old fogey, ultraconservative ...*He has links with former Communist diehards...*
[ADJECTIVE] = <u>reactionary</u>, uncompromising, inflexible, intransigent, immovable, unreconstructed (*chiefly U.S.*), dyed-in-the-wool, ultraconservative ...*Even their die-hard fans can't pretend this was a good game...*

diet¹ [NOUN] **1** = <u>food</u>, provisions, fare, rations, subsistence, kai (*N.Z. informal*), nourishment, sustenance, victuals, commons, edibles, comestibles, nutriment, viands, aliment ...*Watch your diet – you need plenty of fruit and vegetables...*
2 = <u>fast</u>, regime, abstinence, regimen, dietary regime ...*Have you been on a diet? You've lost a lot of weight...*
[VERB] = <u>slim</u>, fast, lose weight, abstain, eat sparingly ...*Most of us have dieted at some time in our lives...* [OPPOSITE] overindulge

diet² *often cap.* = <u>council</u>, meeting, parliament, sitting, congress, chamber, convention, legislature, legislative assembly ...*The Diet has time to discuss the bill only until the 10th November...*

dieter = <u>slimmer</u>, weight watcher, calorie counter, faster, reducer

differ 1 = <u>be dissimilar</u>, contradict, contrast with, vary, counter, belie, depart from, diverge, negate, fly in the face of, run counter to, be distinct, stand apart, make a nonsense of, be at variance with ...*His story differed from his mother's in several respects...* [OPPOSITE] accord
2 = <u>disagree</u>, clash, dispute, dissent ...*The two leaders have differed on the issue of sanctions...* [OPPOSITE] agree

difference 1 = <u>dissimilarity</u>, contrast, variation, change, variety, exception, distinction, diversity, alteration, discrepancy, disparity, deviation, differentiation, peculiarity, divergence, singularity, particularity, distinctness, unlikeness ...*the vast difference in size...* [OPPOSITE] similarity
2 = <u>remainder</u>, rest, balance, remains, excess ...*They pledge to refund the difference within 48 hours...*
3 = <u>disagreement</u>, conflict, argument, row, clash, dispute, set-to (*informal*), controversy, contention, quarrel, strife, wrangle, tiff, contretemps, discordance, contrariety ...*They are leaning how to resolve their differences...* [OPPOSITE] agreement

different 1 = <u>dissimilar</u>, opposed, contrasting, changed, clashing, unlike, altered, diverse, at odds, inconsistent, disparate, deviating, divergent, at variance, discrepant, streets apart ...*We have totally different views...*
2 = <u>various</u>, some, many, several, varied, numerous, diverse, divers (*archaic*), assorted, miscellaneous, sundry, manifold, multifarious ...*Different countries specialise in different products...*
3 = <u>unusual</u>, unique, special, strange, rare, extraordinary, bizarre, distinctive, something else, peculiar, uncommon, singular, unconventional, out of the ordinary, left-field (*informal*), atypical ...*Try to think of a menu that is interesting and different...*
4 = <u>other</u>, another, separate, individual, distinct, discrete ...*What you do in the privacy of your own home is a different matter...*

> ## *Word Power*
>
> **different** – On the whole, *different from* is preferable to *different to* and *different than*, both of which are considered unacceptable by some people. *Different to* is often heard in British English, but is thought by some people to be incorrect; and *different than*, though acceptable in American English, is often regarded as unacceptable in British English. This makes *different from* the safest option: *this result is only slightly different from that obtained in the US* – or you can rephrase the sentence: *this result differs only slightly from that obtained in the US*.

differential [NOUN] = <u>difference</u>, discrepancy, disparity, amount of difference ...*Industrial wage* *differentials widened…*

ADJECTIVE = <u>distinctive</u>, distinguishing, discriminative, diacritical …*They may be forced to eliminate differential voting rights…*

differentiate 1 = <u>distinguish</u>, separate, discriminate, contrast, discern, mark off, make a distinction, tell apart, set off or apart …*He cannot differentiate between his imagination and the real world…*
2 = <u>make different</u>, separate, distinguish, characterize, single out, segregate, individualize, mark off, set apart …*distinctive policies that differentiate them from the other parties…*
3 = <u>become different</u>, change, convert, transform, alter, adapt, modify …*These ectodermal cells differentiate into two cell types…*

differently = <u>dissimilarly</u>, otherwise, in another way, in contrary fashion OPPOSITE> similarly

difficult 1 = <u>hard</u>, tough, taxing, demanding, challenging, painful, exacting, formidable, uphill, strenuous, problematic, arduous, onerous, laborious, burdensome, wearisome, no picnic (*informal*), toilsome, like getting blood out of a stone …*It is difficult for single mothers to get jobs…* OPPOSITE> easy
2 = <u>problematical</u>, involved, complex, complicated, delicate, obscure, abstract, baffling, intricate, perplexing, thorny, knotty, abstruse, ticklish, enigmatical …*It was a very difficult decision to make…* OPPOSITE> simple
3 = <u>troublesome</u>, trying, awkward, demanding, rigid, stubborn, perverse, fussy, tiresome, intractable, fastidious, fractious, unyielding, obstinate, intransigent, unmanageable, unbending, uncooperative, hard to please, refractory, obstreperous, pig-headed, bull-headed, unaccommodating, unamenable …*I had a feeling you were going to be difficult about this…* OPPOSITE> cooperative
4 = <u>tough</u>, trying, hard, dark, grim, straitened, full of hardship …*These are difficult times…* OPPOSITE> easy

difficulty NOUN 1 = <u>problem</u>, trouble, obstacle, hurdle, dilemma, hazard, complication, hassle (*informal*), snag, uphill (*S. African*), predicament, pitfall, stumbling block, impediment, hindrance, tribulation, quandary, can of worms (*informal*), point at issue, disputed point …*There is only one difficulty. The hardest thing is to leave…*
2 = <u>hardship</u>, labour, pain, strain, awkwardness, painfulness, strenuousness, arduousness, laboriousness …*The injured man mounted his horse with difficulty…*
PHRASES **in difficulty** or **difficulties** = <u>in trouble</u>, in distress, in hot water (*informal*), in a mess, in deep water, in a spot (*informal*), in a fix (*informal*), in a quandary, in a dilemma, in embarrassment, in a jam (*informal*), in dire straits, in a pickle (*informal*), in a tight spot, in perplexity, in a predicament …*Rumours spread about banks being in difficulty…*

diffident = <u>shy</u>, reserved, withdrawn, reluctant, modest, shrinking, doubtful, backward, unsure, insecure, constrained, timid, self-conscious, hesitant, meek, unassuming, unobtrusive, self-effacing,

sheepish, bashful, timorous, unassertive

diffuse VERB = <u>spread</u>, distribute, scatter, circulate, disperse, dispense, dispel, dissipate, propagate, disseminate …*Our aim is to diffuse new ideas obtained from elsewhere…*
ADJECTIVE 1 = <u>spread-out</u>, scattered, dispersed, unconcentrated …*a diffuse community…* OPPOSITE> concentrated
2 = <u>rambling</u>, loose, vague, meandering, waffling (*informal*), long-winded, wordy, discursive, verbose, prolix, maundering, digressive, diffusive, circumlocutory …*His writing is so diffuse that it is almost impossible to understand…* OPPOSITE> concise

---

Word Power

diffuse – This word is quite commonly misused instead of *defuse*, when talking about calming down a situation. However, the words are very different in meaning and should never be used as alternatives to each other.

---

diffusion = <u>spreading</u>, distribution, scattering, circulation, expansion, propagation, dissemination, dispersal, dispersion, dissipation

dig VERB 1 = <u>hollow out</u>, mine, pierce, quarry, excavate, gouge, scoop out …*Dig a large hole and bang the stake in…*
2 = <u>delve</u>, tunnel, burrow, grub …*I changed into clothes more suited to digging…*
3 = <u>turn over</u>, till, break up, hoe …*He was outside digging the garden…*
4 = <u>search</u>, hunt, root, delve, forage, dig down, fossick (*Austral. & N.Z.*) …*He dug around in his pocket for his keys…*
5 = <u>poke</u>, drive, push, stick, punch, stab, thrust, shove, prod, jab …*She dug her nails into his flesh…*
6 (*Informal*) = <u>like</u>, enjoy, go for, appreciate, groove (*dated slang*), delight in, be fond of, be keen on, be partial to …*I really dig this band's energy…*
7 (*Informal*) = <u>understand</u>, follow …*Can you dig what I'm trying to say?…*
NOUN 1 = <u>cutting remark</u>, crack (*slang*), insult, taunt, sneer, jeer, quip, barb, wisecrack (*informal*), gibe …*She couldn't resist a dig at him after his unfortunate performance…*
2 = <u>poke</u>, thrust, butt, nudge, prod, jab, punch …*She silenced him with a sharp dig in the small of the back…*
PLURAL NOUN (*Brit. informal*) = <u>rented accommodation</u>, rooms, quarters, lodgings, rented apartments …*He went to the city and lived in digs…*
PHRASES **dig in** (*Informal*) = <u>begin</u> or <u>start eating</u>, tuck in (*informal*) …*Pull up a chair and dig in…*

digest VERB 1 = <u>ingest</u>, absorb, incorporate, dissolve, assimilate …*She couldn't digest food properly…*
2 = <u>take in</u>, master, absorb, grasp, drink in, soak up, devour, assimilate …*She read everything, digesting every fragment of news…*
NOUN = <u>summary</u>, résumé, abstract, epitome, condensation, compendium, synopsis, précis, abridgment …*a regular digest of environmental*

statistics…

digestion = <u>ingestion</u>, absorption, incorporation, assimilation

(**Related Words**)

adjective : peptic

digit 1 = <u>number</u>, figure, numeral …*Her telephone number differs from mine by one digit…*
2 = <u>finger</u>, toe …*Many animals have five digits…*

dignified = <u>distinguished</u>, august, reserved, imposing, formal, grave, noble, upright, stately, solemn, lofty, exalted, decorous OPPOSITE undignified

dignify = <u>distinguish</u>, honour, grace, raise, advance, promote, elevate, glorify, exalt, ennoble, aggrandize

dignitary = <u>public figure</u>, worthy, notable, high-up (*informal*), bigwig (*informal*), celeb (*informal*), personage, pillar of society, pillar of the church, notability, pillar of the state, V.I.P.

dignity 1 = <u>decorum</u>, breeding, gravity, majesty, grandeur, respectability, nobility, propriety, solemnity, gentility, courtliness, loftiness, stateliness …*Everyone admired her extraordinary dignity and composure…*
2 = <u>self-importance</u>, pride, self-esteem, self-respect, self-regard, self-possession, amour-propre (*French*) …*Admit that you were wrong. You won't lose dignity…*

digress = <u>wander</u>, drift, stray, depart, ramble, meander, diverge, deviate, turn aside, be diffuse, expatiate, go off at a tangent, get off the point *or* subject

dilapidated = <u>ruined</u>, fallen in, broken-down, battered, neglected, crumbling, run-down, decayed, decaying, falling apart, beat-up (*informal*), shaky, shabby, worn-out, ramshackle, in ruins, rickety, decrepit, tumbledown, uncared for, gone to rack and ruin

dilate = <u>enlarge</u>, extend, stretch, expand, swell, widen, broaden, puff out, distend OPPOSITE contract

dilemma NOUN = <u>predicament</u>, problem, difficulty, spot (*informal*), fix (*informal*), mess, puzzle, jam (*informal*), embarrassment, plight, strait, pickle (*informal*), how-do-you-do (*informal*), quandary, perplexity, tight corner *or* spot
PHRASES **on the horns of a dilemma** = <u>between the devil and the deep blue sea</u>, between a rock and a hard place (*informal*), between Scylla and Charybdis …*I found myself on the horns of a dilemma – whatever I did, it would be wrong…*

Word Power

dilemma – The use of *dilemma* to refer to a problem that seems incapable of solution is considered by some people to be incorrect. To avoid this misuse of the word, an appropriate alternative such as *predicament* could be used.

---

dilettante = <u>amateur</u>, aesthete, dabbler, trifler, nonprofessional

diligence = <u>application</u>, industry, care, activity, attention, perseverance, earnestness, attentiveness, assiduity, intentness, assiduousness, laboriousness, heedfulness, sedulousness

diligent = <u>hard-working</u>, careful, conscientious, earnest, active, busy, persistent, attentive, persevering, tireless, painstaking, laborious, industrious, indefatigable, studious, assiduous, sedulous OPPOSITE indifferent

dilute 1 = <u>water down</u>, thin (out), weaken, adulterate, make thinner, cut …*Dilute the syrup well with cooled, boiled water…* OPPOSITE condense
2 = <u>reduce</u>, weaken, diminish, temper, decrease, lessen, diffuse, mitigate, attenuate …*It was a clear attempt to dilute black voting power…* OPPOSITE intensify

diluted = <u>watered down</u>, thinned, weak, weakened, dilute, watery, adulterated, cut (*informal*), wishy-washy (*informal*)

dim ADJECTIVE **1** = <u>dull</u>, weak, pale, muted, subdued, feeble, murky, opaque, dingy, subfusc …*She stood waiting in the dim light…*
2 = <u>poorly lit</u>, dark, gloomy, murky, shady, shadowy, dusky, crepuscular, darkish, tenebrous, unilluminated, caliginous (*archaic*) …*The room was dim and cool and quiet…*
3 = <u>cloudy</u>, grey, gloomy, dismal, overcast, leaden …*a dim February day…* OPPOSITE bright
4 = <u>unclear</u>, obscured, faint, blurred, fuzzy, shadowy, hazy, indistinguishable, bleary, undefined, out of focus, ill-defined, indistinct, indiscernible …*His torch picked out the dim figures…* OPPOSITE distinct
5 = <u>obscure</u>, remote, vague, confused, shadowy, imperfect, hazy, intangible, indistinct …*The era of social activism is all but a dim memory…*
6 = <u>unfavourable</u>, bad, black, depressing, discouraging, gloomy, dismal, sombre, unpromising, dispiriting, disheartening …*The prospects for a peaceful solution are dim…*
7 = <u>stupid</u> (*Informal*), slow, thick, dull, dense, dumb (*informal*), daft (*informal*), dozy (*Brit. informal*), obtuse, unintelligent, asinine, slow on the uptake (*informal*), braindead (*informal*), doltish …*She's not as dim as she seems…* OPPOSITE bright
VERB **1** = <u>turn down</u>, lower, fade, dull, bedim …*Dim the overhead lights…*
2 = <u>grow</u> *or* <u>become faint</u>, fade, dull, grow *or* become dim …*The houselights dimmed…*
3 = <u>darken</u>, dull, cloud over …*The dusk sky dims to a chilly indigo…*

dimension NOUN **1** = <u>aspect</u>, side, feature, angle, facet …*This adds a new dimension to our work…*
2 = <u>extent</u>, size, magnitude, importance, scope, greatness, amplitude, largeness …*She did not understand the dimension of her plight…*
PLURAL NOUN = <u>proportions</u>, range, size, scale, measure, volume, capacity, bulk, measurement, amplitude, bigness …*the grandiose dimensions of the room…*

diminish 1 = <u>decrease</u>, decline, lessen, contract, weaken, shrink, dwindle, wane, recede, subside, ebb, taper, die out, fade away, abate, peter out …*The threat of war has diminished…* OPPOSITE grow
2 = <u>reduce</u>, cut, decrease, lessen, contract, lower, weaken, curtail, abate, retrench …*Federalism is intended to diminish the power of the central state…*

OPPOSITE> increase

3 = belittle, scorn, devalue, undervalue, deride, demean, denigrate, scoff at, disparage, decry, sneer at, underrate, deprecate, depreciate, cheapen, derogate …*He never diminished her in front of other people*…

diminution 1 = decrease, decline, lessening, weakening, decay, contraction, abatement …*a slight diminution in asset value*…

2 = reduction, cut, decrease, weakening, deduction, contraction, lessening, cutback, retrenchment, abatement, curtailment …*The president has accepted a diminution of his original powers*…

diminutive = small, little, tiny, minute, pocket(-sized), mini, wee, miniature, petite, midget, undersized, teeny-weeny, Lilliputian, bantam, teensy-weensy, pygmy *or* pigmy OPPOSITE> giant

din = noise, row, racket, crash, clash, shout, outcry, clamour, clatter, uproar, commotion, pandemonium, babel, hubbub, hullabaloo, clangour OPPOSITE> silence

dine VERB = eat, lunch, feast, sup, chow down (*slang*) …*He dines alone most nights*…

PHRASES **dine on** *or* **off something** = eat, consume, feed on …*I could dine on caviar and champagne for the rest of my life*…

dingy 1 = dull, dark, dim, gloomy, murky, dreary, sombre, drab, colourless, dusky, bedimmed …*He took me to his rather dingy office*…

2 = discoloured, soiled, dirty, shabby, faded, seedy, grimy …*wallpaper with dingy yellow stripes*…

dinkum (*Austral. & N.Z. informal*) = genuine, honest, natural, frank, sincere, candid, upfront (*informal*), artless, guileless

dinky (*Brit. informal*) = cute, small, neat, mini, trim, miniature, petite, dainty, natty (*informal*), cutesy (*informal, chiefly U.S.*)

dinner 1 = meal, main meal, spread (*informal*), repast, blowout (*slang*), collation, refection …*Would you like to stay and have dinner?*…

2 = banquet, feast, blowout (*slang*), repast, beanfeast (*Brit. informal*), carousal …*The annual dinner was held in the spring*…

dinosaur = fuddy-duddy, anachronism, dodo (*informal*), stick-in-the-mud (*informal*), antique (*informal*), fossil (*informal*), relic (*informal*), back number (*informal*)
➤ **dinosaurs**

dint

PHRASES **by dint of** = by means of, using, by virtue of, by force of

diocese = bishopric, see

dip VERB **1** = plunge, immerse, bathe, duck, rinse, douse, dunk, souse …*Dip the food into the sauce*…

2 = drop (down), set, fall, lower, disappear, sink, fade, slump, descend, tilt, subside, sag, droop …*The sun dipped below the horizon*…

3 = slope, drop (down), descend, fall, decline, pitch, sink, incline, drop away …*a path which suddenly dips down into a tunnel*…

NOUN **1** = plunge, ducking, soaking, drenching, immersion, douche, submersion …*Freshen the salad leaves with a quick dip into cold water*…

2 = nod, drop, lowering, slump, sag …*She acknowledged me with a slight dip of the head*…

3 = hollow, hole, depression, pit, basin, dent, trough, indentation, concavity …*Turn right where the road makes a dip*…

4 = mixture, solution, preparation, suspension, infusion, concoction, dilution …*sheep dip*…

PHRASES **dip into something 1** = sample, try, skim, play at, glance at, run over, browse, dabble, peruse …*a chance to dip into a wide selection of books*… **2** = draw upon, use, employ, extract, take from, make use of, fall back on, reach into, have recourse to …*She was forced to dip into her savings*…

diplomacy 1 = statesmanship, statecraft, international negotiation …*Today's resolution is significant for American diplomacy*…

2 = tact, skill, sensitivity, craft, discretion, subtlety, delicacy, finesse, savoir-faire, artfulness …*It took all his powers of diplomacy to get her to return*… OPPOSITE> tactlessness

diplomat = official, ambassador, envoy, statesman, consul, attaché, emissary, chargé d'affaires

diplomatic 1 = consular, official, foreign-office, ambassadorial, foreign-politic …*The two countries have resumed full diplomatic relations*…

2 = tactful, politic, sensitive, subtle, delicate, polite, discreet, prudent, adept, considerate, judicious, treating with kid gloves …*She is very direct. I tend to be more diplomatic*… OPPOSITE> tactless

dire = desperate, pressing, crying, critical, terrible, crucial, alarming, extreme, awful, appalling, urgent, cruel, horrible, disastrous, grim, dreadful, gloomy, fearful, dismal, drastic, catastrophic, ominous, horrid, woeful, ruinous, calamitous, cataclysmic, portentous, godawful (*slang*), exigent, bodeful

direct ADJECTIVE = quickest, shortest …*They took the direct route*…

Dinosaurs http://www.ucmp.berkeley.edu/diapsids/dinosaur.html

allosaur(us)	diplodocus	mosasaur(us)	titanosaur(us)
ankylosaur(us)	dolichosaur(us)	oviraptor	trachodon
apatosaur(us)	dromiosaur(us)	plesiosaur(us)	triceratops
atlantosaur(us)	elasmosaur(us)	pteranodon	tyrannosaur(us)
brachiosaur(us)	hadrosaur(us)	pterodactyl *or* pterosaur	velociraptor
brontosaur(us)	ichthyosaur(us)	protoceratops	
ceratosaur(us)	iguanodon *or*	stegodon *or* stegodont	
compsognathus	iguanodont	stegosaur(us)	
dimetrodon	megalosaur(us)	theropod	

ADVERB 1 = <u>straight</u>, through …*a direct flight from Glasgow…* OPPOSITE circuitous

2 = <u>first-hand</u>, personal, immediate …*He has direct experience of the process…* OPPOSITE indirect

3 = <u>clear</u>, specific, plain, absolute, distinct, definite, explicit, downright, point-blank, unequivocal, unqualified, unambiguous, categorical …*He denied there was a direct connection between the two cases…* OPPOSITE ambiguous

4 = <u>straightforward</u>, open, straight, frank, blunt, sincere, outspoken, honest, matter-of-fact, downright, candid, forthright, truthful, upfront (*informal*), man-to-man, plain-spoken …*He avoided giving a direct answer…* OPPOSITE indirect

5 = <u>verbatim</u>, exact, word-for-word, strict, accurate, faithful, letter-for-letter …*It was a direct quotation from his earlier speech…*

6 = <u>non-stop</u>, straight …*You can fly there direct from Glasgow…*

VERB 1 = <u>aim</u>, point, turn, level, train, focus, fix, cast …*He directed the tiny beam of light at the roof…*

2 = <u>guide</u>, show, lead, point the way, point in the direction of …*A guard directed them to the right…*

3 = <u>control</u>, run, manage, lead, rule, guide, handle, conduct, advise, govern, regulate, administer, oversee, supervise, dispose, preside over, mastermind, call the shots, call the tune, superintend …*He will direct day-to-day operations…*

4 = <u>order</u>, command, instruct, charge, demand, require, bid, enjoin, adjure …*They have been directed to give special attention to poverty…*

5 = <u>address</u>, send, mail, route, label, superscribe …*Please direct your letters to me at this address…*

direction NOUN 1 = <u>way</u>, course, line, road, track, bearing, route, path …*We drove ten miles in the opposite direction…*

2 = <u>tendency</u>, bent, current, trend, leaning, drift, bias, orientation, tack, tenor, proclivity …*They threatened a mass walk-out if the party did not change direction…*

3 = <u>management</u>, government, control, charge, administration, leadership, command, guidance, supervision, governance, oversight, superintendence …*The house was built under the direction of his partner…*

PLURAL NOUN = <u>instructions</u>, rules, information, plan, briefing, regulations, recommendations, indication, guidelines, guidance …*Don't throw away the directions until we've finished cooking…*

directive = <u>order</u>, ruling, regulation, charge, notice, command, instruction, dictate, decree, mandate, canon, injunction, imperative, fiat, ordinance, edict

directly 1 = <u>straight</u>, unswervingly, without deviation, by the shortest route, in a beeline …*The plane will fly the hostages directly back home…*

2 = <u>immediately</u>, promptly, instantly, right away, straightaway, speedily, instantaneously, pronto (*informal*), pdq (*slang*) …*Directly after the meeting, an official appealed on television…*

3 = <u>at once</u>, presently, soon, quickly, as soon as possible, in a second, straightaway, forthwith, posthaste …*He'll be there directly…*

4 = <u>in person</u>, personally …*We could do nothing directly to help them…*

5 = <u>honestly</u>, openly, frankly, plainly, face-to-face, overtly, point-blank, unequivocally, truthfully, candidly, unreservedly, straightforwardly, straight from the shoulder (*informal*), without prevarication …*She explained simply and directly what she hoped to achieve…*

directness = <u>honesty</u>, candour, frankness, sincerity, plain speaking, bluntness, outspokenness, forthrightness, straightforwardness

director = <u>controller</u>, head, leader, manager, chief, executive, chairman, boss (*informal*), producer, governor, principal, administrator, supervisor, organizer, baas (*S. African*)

➤ **WORD POWER SUPPLEMENT film directors**

dirge = <u>lament</u>, requiem, elegy, death march, threnody, dead march, funeral song, coronach (*Scot. & Irish*)

dirt 1 = <u>filth</u>, muck, grime, dust, mud, stain, crap (*taboo slang*), tarnish, smudge, mire, impurity, slob (*Irish*), crud (*slang*), kak (*S. African taboo slang*), grot (*slang*) …*I started to scrub off the dirt…*

2 = <u>soil</u>, ground, earth, clay, turf, clod, loam, loam …*They all sit on the dirt in the shade of a tree…*

dirty **ADJECTIVE** 1 = <u>filthy</u>, soiled, grubby, nasty, foul, muddy, polluted, messy, sullied, grimy, unclean, mucky, grotty (*slang*), grungy (*slang, chiefly U.S. & Canad.*), scuzzy (*slang, chiefly U.S.*), begrimed, festy (*Austral. slang*) …*The woman had matted hair and dirty fingernails…* OPPOSITE clean

2 = <u>dishonest</u>, illegal, unfair, cheating, corrupt, crooked, deceiving, fraudulent, treacherous, deceptive, unscrupulous, crafty, deceitful, double-dealing, unsporting, knavish (*archaic*) …*Their opponents used dirty tactics…* OPPOSITE honest

3 = <u>obscene</u>, rude, coarse, indecent, blue, offensive, gross, filthy, vulgar, pornographic, sleazy, suggestive, lewd, risqué, X-rated (*informal*), bawdy, salacious, smutty, off-colour, unwholesome …*He laughed at their dirty jokes…* OPPOSITE decent

4 = <u>despicable</u>, mean, low, base, cheap, nasty, cowardly, beggarly, worthless, shameful, shabby, vile, sordid, low-down (*informal*), abject, squalid, ignominious, contemptible, wretched, scurvy, detestable, scungy (*Austral. & N.Z.*) …*That was a dirty trick to play…*

VERB = <u>soil</u>, foul, stain, spoil, smear, muddy, pollute, blacken, mess up, smudge, sully, defile, smirch, begrime …*He was afraid the dog's hairs might dirty the seats…* OPPOSITE clean

disability = <u>handicap</u>, affliction, disorder, defect, impairment, disablement, infirmity

disable = <u>handicap</u>, weaken, cripple, damage, hamstring, paralyse, impair, debilitate, incapacitate, prostrate, unman, immobilize, put out of action, enfeeble, render inoperative, render *hors de combat*

disabled = <u>differently abled</u>, physically challenged, handicapped, weakened, crippled, paralysed, lame, mutilated, maimed, incapacitated, infirm, bedridden

OPPOSITE able-bodied

Word Power

disabled – Referring to people with disabilities as *the disabled* can cause offence and should be avoided. Instead, refer to them as people *with disabilities* or *who are physically challenged*, or, possibly, *disabled people* or *differently abled people*. In general, the terms used for disabilities or medical conditions should be avoided as collective nouns for people who have them – so, for example, instead of *the blind*, it is preferable to refer to *sightless people, vision-impaired people*, or *partially-sighted people*, depending on the degree of their condition.

---

disabuse (usually in phrase *disabuse someone of an idea or notion*) = <u>enlighten</u>, correct, set right, open the eyes of, set straight, shatter (someone's) illusions, free from error, undeceive

disadvantage NOUN 1 = <u>drawback</u>, trouble, burden, weakness, handicap, liability, minus (*informal*), flaw, hardship, nuisance, snag, inconvenience, downside, impediment, hindrance, privation, weak point, fly in the ointment (*informal*) ...*They suffer the disadvantage of having been political exiles...* OPPOSITE advantage
2 = <u>harm</u>, loss, damage, injury, hurt, prejudice, detriment, disservice ...*An attempt to prevent an election would be to their disadvantage...* OPPOSITE benefit
PHRASES **at a disadvantage** = <u>exposed</u>, vulnerable, wide open, unprotected, defenceless, open to attack, assailable ...*Children from poor families were at a distinct disadvantage...*

disadvantaged = <u>deprived</u>, struggling, impoverished, discriminated against, underprivileged

disaffected = <u>alienated</u>, resentful, discontented, hostile, estranged, dissatisfied, rebellious, antagonistic, disloyal, seditious, mutinous, uncompliant, unsubmissive

disaffection = <u>alienation</u>, resentment, discontent, hostility, dislike, disagreement, dissatisfaction, animosity, aversion, antagonism, antipathy, disloyalty, estrangement, ill will, repugnance, unfriendliness

disagree VERB 1 = <u>differ (in opinion)</u>, argue, debate, clash, dispute, contest, fall out (*informal*), contend, dissent, quarrel, wrangle, bicker, take issue with, have words (*informal*), cross swords, be at sixes and sevens ...*The two men disagreed about what to do next...* OPPOSITE agree
2 = <u>make ill</u>, upset, sicken, trouble, hurt, bother, distress, discomfort, nauseate, be injurious ...*Orange juice seems to disagree with some babies...*
PHRASES **disagree with something** or **someone** = <u>oppose</u>, object to, dissent from ...*I disagree with drug laws in general...*

disagreeable 1 = <u>nasty</u>, offensive, disgusting, unpleasant, distasteful, horrid, repellent, unsavoury, obnoxious, unpalatable, displeasing, repulsive, objectionable, repugnant, uninviting, yucky *or* yukky (*slang*), yucko (*Austral. slang*) ...*a disagreeable odour...* OPPOSITE pleasant
2 = <u>ill-natured</u>, difficult, nasty, cross, contrary, unpleasant, rude, irritable, unfriendly, bad-tempered, surly, churlish, brusque, tetchy, ratty (*Brit. & N.Z. informal*), peevish, ungracious, disobliging, unlikable *or* unlikeable ...*He's a shallow, disagreeable man...* OPPOSITE good-natured

disagreement NOUN = <u>argument</u>, row, difference, division, debate, conflict, clash, dispute, falling out, misunderstanding, dissent, quarrel, squabble, strife, wrangle, discord, tiff, altercation ...*My instructor and I had a brief disagreement...* OPPOSITE agreement
PHRASES **in disagreement** = <u>at odds</u>, in conflict, at loggerheads, at variance, disunited, at daggers drawn, in disharmony ...*The two sides were locked in disagreement...*

disallow = <u>reject</u>, refuse, ban, dismiss, cancel, veto, forbid, embargo, prohibit, rebuff, repudiate, disown, proscribe, disavow, disclaim, abjure

disappear 1 = <u>vanish</u>, recede, drop out of sight, vanish off the face of the earth, evanesce, be lost to view *or* sight ...*The car drove off and disappeared from sight...* OPPOSITE appear
2 = <u>pass</u>, wane, ebb, fade away ...*The problem should disappear altogether by the age of five...*
3 = <u>flee</u>, bolt, run away, fly, escape, split (*slang*), retire, withdraw, take off (*informal*), get away, vanish, depart, go, make off, abscond, take flight, do a runner (*slang*), scarper (*Brit. slang*), slope off, cut and run (*informal*), beat a hasty retreat, make your escape, make your getaway ...*The prisoner disappeared after being released on bail...*
4 = <u>be lost</u>, be taken, be stolen, go missing, be mislaid ...*My wallet seems to have disappeared...*
5 = <u>cease</u>, end, fade, vanish, dissolve, expire, evaporate, perish, die out, pass away, cease to exist, melt away, leave no trace, cease to be known ...*The immediate threat has disappeared...*

disappearance 1 = <u>vanishing</u>, going, passing, disappearing, fading, melting, eclipse, evaporation, evanescence ...*the gradual disappearance of the pain...*
2 = <u>flight</u>, departure, desertion, disappearing trick ...*his disappearance while out on bail...*
3 = <u>loss</u>, losing, mislaying ...*Police are investigating the disappearance of confidential files...*

disappoint 1 = <u>let down</u>, dismay, fail, dash, disillusion, sadden, vex, chagrin, dishearten, disenchant, dissatisfy, disgruntle ...*He said that he was surprised and disappointed by the decision...*
2 = <u>frustrate</u>, foil, thwart, defeat, baffle, balk ...*His hopes have been disappointed many times before...*

disappointed = <u>let down</u>, upset, distressed, discouraged, depressed, choked, disillusioned, discontented, dejected, disheartened, disgruntled, dissatisfied, downcast, saddened, disenchanted, despondent, downhearted, cast down OPPOSITE satisfied

disappointing = <u>unsatisfactory</u>, inadequate, discouraging, sorry, upsetting, sad, depressing, unhappy, unexpected, pathetic, inferior, insufficient, lame, disconcerting, second-rate, unworthy, not much cop (*Brit. slang*)

disappointment 1 = <u>regret</u>, distress, discontent, dissatisfaction, disillusionment, displeasure, chagrin, disenchantment, dejection, despondency, discouragement, mortification, unfulfilment ...*They expressed their disappointment at what had happened...*
2 = <u>letdown</u>, blow, disaster, failure, setback, fiasco, misfortune, calamity, whammy (*informal, chiefly U.S.*), choker (*informal*), washout (*informal*) ...*The defeat was a bitter disappointment...*
3 = <u>frustration</u>, failure, ill-success ...*There was resentment among the people at the disappointment of their hopes...*

disapproval = <u>displeasure</u>, criticism, objection, condemnation, dissatisfaction, censure, reproach, denunciation, deprecation, disapprobation, stick (*slang*)

disapprove 1 = <u>condemn</u>, object to, dislike, censure, deplore, deprecate, frown on, take exception to, take a dim view of, find unacceptable, have a down on (*informal*), discountenance, look down your nose at (*informal*), raise an *or* your eyebrow ...*My mother disapproved of my working in a pub...* OPPOSITE> approve
2 = <u>turn down</u>, reject, veto, set aside, spurn, disallow ...*The judge disapproved the adoption because of my criminal record...* OPPOSITE> endorse

disapproving = <u>critical</u>, discouraging, frowning, disparaging, censorious, reproachful, deprecatory, condemnatory, denunciatory, disapprobatory OPPOSITE> approving

disarm 1 = <u>demilitarize</u>, disband, demobilize, deactivate ...*The forces in the territory should disarm...*
2 = <u>win over</u>, persuade ...*She did her best to disarm her critics...*

disarmament = <u>arms reduction</u>, demobilization, arms limitation, demilitarization, de-escalation

disarming = <u>charming</u>, winning, irresistible, persuasive, likable *or* likeable

disarray 1 = <u>confusion</u>, upset, disorder, indiscipline, disunity, disharmony, disorganization, unruliness, discomposure, disorderliness ...*The feud has plunged the country into political disarray...* OPPOSITE> order
2 = <u>untidiness</u>, state, mess, chaos, tangle, mix-up, muddle, clutter, shambles, jumble, hotchpotch, hodgepodge (*U.S.*), dishevelment, pig's breakfast (*informal*) ...*He found the room in disarray...* OPPOSITE> tidiness

disaster 1 = <u>catastrophe</u>, trouble, blow, accident, stroke, reverse, tragedy, ruin, misfortune, adversity, calamity, mishap, whammy (*informal, chiefly U.S.*), misadventure, cataclysm, act of God, bummer (*slang*), ruination, mischance ...*the second air disaster in less than two months...*

2 = <u>failure</u>, mess, flop (*informal*), catastrophe, rout, debacle, cock-up (*Brit. slang*), washout (*informal*) ...*The whole production was a disaster...*

disastrous 1 = <u>terrible</u>, devastating, tragic, fatal, unfortunate, dreadful, destructive, unlucky, harmful, adverse, dire, catastrophic, detrimental, untoward, ruinous, calamitous, cataclysmic, ill-starred, unpropitious, ill-fated, cataclysmal ...*the recent, disastrous earthquake...*
2 = <u>unsuccessful</u>, devastating, tragic, calamitous, cataclysmic ...*The team has had another disastrous day...*

disavow = <u>deny</u>, reject, contradict, retract, repudiate, disown, rebut, disclaim, forswear, gainsay (*archaic or literary*), abjure

disband 1 = <u>dismiss</u>, separate, break up, scatter, dissolve, let go, disperse, send home, demobilize ...*All the armed groups will be disbanded...*
2 = <u>break up</u>, separate, scatter, disperse, part company, go (their) separate ways ...*The rebels have agreed to disband by the end of the month...*

disbelief = <u>scepticism</u>, doubt, distrust, mistrust, incredulity, unbelief, dubiety OPPOSITE> belief

disbelieve = <u>doubt</u>, reject, discount, suspect, discredit, not accept, mistrust, not buy (*slang*), repudiate, scoff at, not credit, not swallow (*informal*), give no credence to

disburse = <u>pay out</u>, spend, lay out, fork out (*slang*), expend, shell out (*informal*)

Word Power

disburse – *Disburse* is sometimes wrongly used where *disperse* is meant: *the police used water cannons to disperse* (not *disburse*) *the crowd.*

---

disbursement = <u>payment</u>, spending, expenditure, disposal, outlay

disc *or* **disk** 1 = <u>circle</u>, plate, saucer, discus ...*a revolving disc with replaceable blades...*
2 (*Old-fashioned*) = <u>record</u>, vinyl, gramophone record, phonograph record (*U.S. & Canad.*), platter (*U.S. slang*) ...*This disc includes the piano sonata in C minor...*

Word Power

disc – In British English, the spelling *disc* is generally preferred, except when using the word in its computer senses, where *disk* is preferred. In US English, the spelling *disk* is used for all senses.

---

discard = <u>get rid of</u>, drop, remove, throw away *or* out, reject, abandon, dump (*informal*), shed, scrap, axe (*informal*), ditch (*slang*), junk (*informal*), chuck (*informal*), dispose of, relinquish, dispense with, jettison, repudiate, cast aside OPPOSITE> keep

discern 1 = <u>distinguish</u>, determine, detect, discriminate, pick out, differentiate, make a distinction ...*We've been trying to discern a pattern in his behaviour...*

2 = <u>see</u>, perceive, make out, notice, observe, recognize, behold, catch sight of, suss (out) (*slang*), espy, descry ...*Under the bridge we could just discern a shadowy figure...*

discernible = <u>clear</u>, obvious, apparent, plain, visible, distinct, noticeable, recognizable, detectable, observable, perceptible, distinguishable, appreciable, discoverable

discerning = <u>discriminating</u>, knowing, sharp, critical, acute, sensitive, wise, intelligent, subtle, piercing, penetrating, shrewd, ingenious, astute, perceptive, judicious, clear-sighted, percipient, perspicacious, sagacious

discharge VERB **1** = <u>release</u>, free, clear, liberate, pardon, let go, acquit, allow to go, set free, exonerate, absolve ...*You are being discharged on medical grounds...*
2 = <u>dismiss</u>, sack (*informal*), fire (*informal*), remove, expel, discard, oust, eject, cashier, give (someone) the boot (*slang*), give (someone) the sack (*informal*) ...*the regulation that gay people should be discharged from the military...*
3 = <u>carry out</u>, perform, fulfil, accomplish, do, effect, realize, observe, implement, execute, carry through ...*the quiet competence with which he discharged his many duties...*
4 = <u>pay</u>, meet, clear, settle, square (up), honour, satisfy, relieve, liquidate ...*The goods will be sold in order to discharge the debt...*
5 = <u>pour forth</u>, release, empty, leak, emit, dispense, void, gush, ooze, exude, give off, excrete, disembogue ...*The resulting salty water will be discharged at sea...*
6 = <u>fire</u>, shoot, set off, explode, let off, detonate, let loose (*informal*) ...*He was tried for unlawfully and dangerously discharging a weapon...*
NOUN **1** = <u>release</u>, liberation, clearance, pardon, acquittal, remittance, exoneration ...*The doctors began to discuss his discharge from hospital...*
2 = <u>dismissal</u>, notice, removal, the boot (*slang*), expulsion, the sack (*informal*), the push (*slang*), marching orders (*informal*), ejection, demobilization, kiss-off (*slang, chiefly U.S. & Canad.*), the bum's rush (*slang*), the (old) heave-ho (*informal*), the order of the boot (*slang*), congé, your books *or* cards (*informal*) ...*They face receiving a dishonourable discharge from the Army...*
3 = <u>emission</u>, flow, ooze, secretion, excretion, pus, seepage, suppuration ...*They develop a fever and a watery discharge from the eyes...*
4 = <u>firing</u>, report, shot, blast, burst, explosion, discharging, volley, salvo, detonation, fusillade ...*Where firearms are kept at home, the risk of accidental discharge is high...*
5 = <u>carrying out</u>, performance, achievement, execution, accomplishment, fulfilment, observance ...*free of any influence which might affect the discharge of his duties...*

disciple 1 = <u>apostle</u> ...*Jesus and his disciples...*
2 = <u>follower</u>, student, supporter, pupil, convert, believer, partisan, devotee, apostle, adherent, proselyte, votary, catechumen ...*a major intellectual*

figure with disciples throughout Europe... OPPOSITE teacher
➤ **the twelve apostles**

The Twelve Disciples

Andrew	Jude
Bartholomew	Matthew
James	Peter
James	Philip
John	Simon
Judas	Thomas

disciplinarian = <u>authoritarian</u>, tyrant, despot, stickler, taskmaster, martinet, drill sergeant, strict teacher, hard master

discipline NOUN **1** = <u>control</u>, rule, authority, direction, regulation, supervision, orderliness, strictness ...*the need for strict discipline in military units...*
2 = <u>punishment</u>, penalty, correction, chastening, chastisement, punitive measures, castigation ...*Order and discipline have been placed in the hands of headmasters...*
3 = <u>self-control</u>, control, restraint, self-discipline, coolness, cool, willpower, calmness, self-restraint, orderliness, self-mastery, strength of mind *or* will ...*His image of calm, control and discipline that appealed to voters...*
4 = <u>training</u>, practice, exercise, method, regulation, drill, regimen ...*inner disciplines like transcendental meditation...*
5 = <u>field of study</u>, area, subject, theme, topic, course, curriculum, speciality, subject matter, branch of knowledge, field of inquiry *or* reference ...*appropriate topics for the new discipline of political science...*
VERB **1** = <u>punish</u>, correct, reprimand, castigate, chastise, chasten, penalize, bring to book, reprove ...*He was disciplined by his company, but not dismissed...*
2 = <u>train</u>, control, govern, check, educate, regulate, instruct, restrain ...*I'm very good at disciplining myself...*

disclaim 1 = <u>deny</u>, decline, reject, disallow, retract, repudiate, renege, rebut, disavow, abnegate, disaffirm ...*She disclaims any knowledge of her husband's business activities...*
2 = <u>renounce</u>, reject, abandon, relinquish, disown, abdicate, forswear, abjure ...*the legislation which enabled him to disclaim his title...*

disclaimer = <u>denial</u>, rejection, renunciation, retraction, repudiation, disavowal, abjuration

disclose 1 = <u>make known</u>, tell, reveal, publish, relate, broadcast, leak, confess, communicate, unveil, utter, make public, impart, divulge, out (*informal*), let slip, spill the beans about (*informal*), blow wide open (*slang*), get off your chest (*informal*), spill your guts about (*slang*) ...*Neither side would disclose details of the transaction...* OPPOSITE keep secret
2 = <u>show</u>, reveal, expose, discover, exhibit, unveil, uncover, lay bare, bring to light, take the wraps off

...*clapboard façades that revolve to disclose snug interiors*... OPPOSITE hide

disclosure 1 = <u>revelation</u>, exposé, announcement, publication, leak, admission, declaration, confession, acknowledgment ...*unauthorised newspaper disclosures*...
2 = <u>uncovering</u>, publication, exposure, revelation, divulgence ...*The disclosure of his marriage proposal was badly-timed*...

discolour *or* (*U.S.*) **discolor** 1 = <u>mark</u>, soil, mar, fade, stain, streak, tinge ...*Test first as this cleaner may discolour the fabric*...
2 = <u>stain</u>, fade, streak, rust, tarnish ...*A tooth which has been hit hard may discolour*...

discoloured *or* (*U.S.*) **discolored** = <u>stained</u>, tainted, tarnished, faded, pale, washed out, wan, blotched, besmirched, foxed, etiolated

discomfit = <u>embarrass</u>, unsettle, disconcert, confuse, rattle (*informal*), flurry, ruffle, confound, perplex, unnerve, take aback, fluster, perturb, faze, demoralize, take the wind out of someone's sails, abash, discompose

discomfort NOUN 1 = <u>pain</u>, suffering, hurt, smarting, ache, throbbing, irritation, tenderness, pang, malaise, twinge, soreness ...*He suffered some discomfort, but no real pain*... OPPOSITE comfort
2 = <u>uneasiness</u>, worry, anxiety, doubt, alarm, distress, suspicion, apprehension, misgiving, nervousness, disquiet, agitation, qualms, trepidation, perturbation, apprehensiveness, dubiety, inquietude ...*She heard the discomfort in his voice as he reluctantly agreed*... OPPOSITE reassurance
3 = <u>inconvenience</u>, trouble, difficulty, bother, hardship, irritation, hassle (*informal*), nuisance, uphill (*S. African*), annoyance, awkwardness, unpleasantness, vexation ...*the hazards and discomforts of primitive continental travel*...
VERB = <u>make uncomfortable</u>, worry, trouble, shake, alarm, disturb, distress, unsettle, ruffle, unnerve, disquiet, perturb, discomfit, discompose ...*World leaders will have been greatly discomforted by these events*... OPPOSITE reassure

disconcert = <u>disturb</u>, worry, trouble, upset, confuse, rattle (*informal*), baffle, put off, unsettle, bewilder, shake up (*informal*), undo, flurry, agitate, ruffle, perplex, unnerve, unbalance, take aback, fluster, perturb, faze, flummox, throw off balance, nonplus, abash, discompose, put out of countenance

disconcerted = <u>disturbed</u>, worried, troubled, thrown (*informal*), upset, confused, embarrassed, annoyed, rattled (*informal*), distracted, at sea, unsettled, bewildered, shook up (*informal*), flurried, ruffled, taken aback, flustered, perturbed, fazed, nonplussed, flummoxed, caught off balance, out of countenance

disconcerting = <u>disturbing</u>, upsetting, alarming, confusing, embarrassing, awkward, distracting, dismaying, baffling, bewildering, perplexing, off-putting (*Brit. informal*), bothersome

disconnect 1 = <u>deactivate</u> ...*The device automatically disconnects the ignition*...
2 = <u>cut off</u> ...*The company has disconnected our electricity for non-payment*...
3 = <u>detach</u>, separate, part, divide, sever, disengage, take apart, uncouple ...*He disconnected the bottle from the overhead hook*...

disconnected 1 = <u>unrelated</u> ...*a sequence of utterly disconnected events*...
2 = <u>confused</u>, mixed-up, rambling, irrational, jumbled, unintelligible, illogical, incoherent, disjointed, garbled, uncoordinated ...*a meaningless jumble of disconnected words*...

disconsolate = <u>inconsolable</u>, crushed, despairing, low, sad, unhappy, miserable, gloomy, hopeless, dismal, melancholy, heartbroken, desolate, forlorn, woeful, dejected, grief-stricken, wretched, down in the dumps (*informal*)

discontent = <u>dissatisfaction</u>, unhappiness, displeasure, regret, envy, restlessness, uneasiness, vexation, discontentment, fretfulness

discontented = <u>dissatisfied</u>, complaining, unhappy, miserable, fed up, disgruntled, disaffected, vexed, displeased, fretful, cheesed off (*Brit. slang*), brassed off (*Brit. slang*), with a chip on your shoulder (*informal*) OPPOSITE satisfied

discontinue = <u>stop</u>, end, finish, drop, kick (*informal*), give up, abandon, suspend, quit, halt, pause, cease, axe (*informal*), interrupt, terminate, break off, put an end to, refrain from, leave off, pull the plug on, belay (*Nautical*)

discontinued = <u>stopped</u>, ended, finished, abandoned, halted, terminated, no longer made, given up *or* over

discontinuity = <u>lack of unity</u>, disconnection, incoherence, disunion, lack of coherence, disjointedness, disconnectedness

discord = <u>disagreement</u>, division, conflict, difference, opposition, row, clashing, dispute, contention, friction, strife, wrangling, variance, disunity, dissension, incompatibility, discordance, lack of concord OPPOSITE agreement

discordant 1 = <u>disagreeing</u>, conflicting, clashing, different, opposite, contrary, at odds, contradictory, inconsistent, incompatible, incongruous, divergent ...*He displays attitudes and conduct discordant with his culture*...
2 = <u>harsh</u>, jarring, grating, strident, shrill, jangling, dissonant, cacophonous, inharmonious, unmelodious ...*They produced a discordant sound*...

discount NOUN = <u>deduction</u>, cut, reduction, concession, allowance, rebate, cut price ...*You often get a discount on discontinued goods*...
VERB 1 = <u>mark down</u>, reduce, lower ...*Tour prices are being discounted*...
2 = <u>disregard</u>, reject, ignore, overlook, discard, set aside, dispel, pass over, repudiate, disbelieve, brush off (*slang*), lay aside, pooh-pooh ...*His theory was discounted immediately*...

discourage 1 = <u>dishearten</u>, daunt, deter, crush, put off, depress, cow, dash, intimidate, dismay, unnerve,

unman, overawe, demoralize, cast down, put a damper on, psych out (*informal*), dispirit, deject …*Don't let this setback discourage you*… OPPOSITE> hearten
2 = <u>put off</u>, deter, prevent, dissuade, talk out of, discountenance …*a campaign to discourage children from smoking*… OPPOSITE> encourage

discouraged = <u>put off</u>, deterred, daunted, dashed, dismayed, pessimistic, dispirited, downcast, disheartened, crestfallen, sick as a parrot (*informal*)

discouragement 1 = <u>deterrent</u>, opposition, obstacle, curb, check, setback, restraint, constraint, impediment, hindrance, damper, disincentive …*Uncertainty is one of the major discouragements to investment*…
2 = <u>depression</u>, disappointment, despair, pessimism, hopelessness, despondency, loss of confidence, dejection, discomfiture, low spirits, downheartedness …*There's a sense of discouragement creeping into the workforce*…

discouraging = <u>disheartening</u>, disappointing, depressing, daunting, dampening, unfavourable, off-putting (*Brit. informal*), dispiriting, unpropitious

discourse 1 = <u>conversation</u>, talk, discussion, speech, communication, chat, dialogue, converse …*a tradition of political discourse*…
2 = <u>speech</u>, talk, address, essay, lecture, sermon, treatise, dissertation, homily, oration, disquisition …*He responds with a lengthy discourse on deployment strategy*…

discover 1 = <u>find out</u>, see, learn, reveal, spot, determine, notice, realize, recognize, perceive, detect, disclose, uncover, discern, ascertain, suss (out) (*slang*), get wise to (*informal*) …*As he discovered, she had a brilliant mind*…
2 = <u>find</u>, come across, uncover, unearth, turn up, dig up, come upon, bring to light, light upon …*His body was discovered on a roadside outside the city*…
3 = <u>invent</u>, design, pioneer, devise, originate, contrive, conceive of …*Scientists discovered a way of forming the image in a thin layer on the surface*…

discoverer 1 = <u>explorer</u>, pioneer …*the myth of the heroic discoverer*…
2 = <u>inventor</u>, author, originator, initiator …*the discoverer of carbon-dioxide lasers*…

discovery 1 = <u>finding out</u>, news, announcement, revelation, disclosure, realization …*the discovery that his wife was HIV positive*…
2 = <u>invention</u>, launch, institution, introduction, pioneering, innovation, initiation, inauguration, induction, coinage, origination …*the discovery of new forensic techniques*…
3 = <u>breakthrough</u>, find, finding, development, advance, leap, coup, invention, step forward, godsend, quantum leap …*In that year, two momentous discoveries were made*…
4 = <u>finding</u>, turning up, locating, revelation, uncovering, disclosure, detection, espial …*the discovery of a mass grave in the south-west of the country*…

discredit VERB **1** = <u>disgrace</u>, blame, shame, smear, stain, humiliate, degrade, taint, slur, detract from, disparage, vilify, slander, sully, dishonour, stigmatize, defame, bring into disrepute, bring shame upon …*He says his accusers are trying to discredit him*… OPPOSITE> honour
2 = <u>dispute</u>, question, challenge, deny, reject, discount, distrust, mistrust, repudiate, cast doubt on or upon, disbelieve, pooh-pooh …*They realized there would be problems in discrediting the evidence*…
NOUN = <u>disgrace</u>, scandal, shame, disrepute, smear, stigma, censure, slur, ignominy, dishonour, imputation, odium, ill-repute, aspersion …*His actions have brought discredit on the whole regiment*… OPPOSITE> honour

discredited = <u>rejected</u>, exposed, exploded, discarded, obsolete, refuted, debunked, outworn

discreet = <u>tactful</u>, diplomatic, politic, reserved, guarded, careful, sensible, cautious, wary, discerning, prudent, considerate, judicious, circumspect, sagacious OPPOSITE> tactless
➤ **discrete**

discrepancy = <u>disagreement</u>, difference, variation, conflict, contradiction, inconsistency, disparity, variance, divergence, dissonance, incongruity, dissimilarity, discordance, contrariety

discrete = <u>separate</u>, individual, distinct, detached, disconnected, unattached, discontinuous

> ## *Word Power*
>
> **discrete** – This word is quite often used by mistake where *discreet* is intended: *reading is a set of discrete skills*; *she was discreet* (not *discrete*) *about the affair.*

discretion 1 = <u>tact</u>, care, consideration, judgment, caution, diplomacy, good sense, prudence, acumen, wariness, discernment, circumspection, sagacity, carefulness, judiciousness, heedfulness …*He conducted the whole affair with the utmost discretion*… OPPOSITE> tactlessness
2 = <u>choice</u>, will, wish, liking, mind, option, pleasure, preference, inclination, disposition, predilection, volition …*She was given the money to use at her own discretion*…

discretionary = <u>optional</u>, arbitrary (*Law*), unrestricted, elective, open to choice, nonmandatory

discriminate VERB = <u>differentiate</u>, distinguish, discern, separate, assess, evaluate, tell the difference, draw a distinction …*He is incapable of discriminating between a good idea and a bad one*…
PHRASES **discriminate against someone** = <u>treat differently</u>, single out, victimize, disfavour, treat as inferior, show bias against, show prejudice against …*They believe the law discriminates against women*…

discriminating = <u>discerning</u>, particular, keen, critical, acute, sensitive, refined, cultivated, selective, astute, tasteful, fastidious OPPOSITE> undiscriminating

discrimination 1 = <u>prejudice</u>, bias, injustice, intolerance, bigotry, favouritism, unfairness, inequity

...measures to counteract racial discrimination...
2 = <u>discernment</u>, taste, judgment, perception, insight, penetration, subtlety, refinement, acumen, keenness, sagacity, acuteness, clearness *...He praised our taste and discrimination...*

discriminatory = <u>prejudiced</u>, biased, partial, weighted, favouring, one-sided, partisan, unjust, preferential, prejudicial, inequitable

discuss = <u>talk about</u>, consider, debate, review, go into, examine, argue about, thrash out, ventilate, reason about, exchange views on, deliberate about, weigh up the pros and cons of, converse about, confer about

discussion 1 = <u>talk</u>, debate, argument, conference, exchange, review, conversation, consideration, dialogue, consultation, seminar, discourse, deliberation, symposium, colloquy, confabulation *...There was a discussion about the wording of the report...*
2 = <u>examination</u>, investigation, analysis, scrutiny, dissection *...For a discussion of biology and sexual politics, see chapter 4...*

disdain NOUN = <u>contempt</u>, dislike, scorn, arrogance, indifference, sneering, derision, hauteur, snobbishness, contumely, haughtiness, superciliousness *...She looked at him with disdain...*
VERB = <u>scorn</u>, reject, despise, slight, disregard, spurn, undervalue, deride, look down on, belittle, sneer at, pooh-pooh, contemn, look down your nose at (*informal*), misprize *...a political leader who disdained the compromises of politics...*

disdainful = <u>contemptuous</u>, scornful, arrogant, superior, proud, sneering, aloof, haughty, derisive, supercilious, high and mighty (*informal*), hoity-toity (*informal*), turning up your nose (at), on your high horse (*informal*), looking down your nose (at)

disease 1 = <u>illness</u>, condition, complaint, upset, infection, disorder, sickness, ailment, affliction, malady, infirmity, indisposition, lurgy (*informal*) *...illnesses such as heart disease...*
2 = <u>evil</u>, disorder, plague, curse, cancer, blight, contamination, scourge, affliction, bane, contagion, malady, canker *...the disease of racism eating away at the core of our society...*

diseased = <u>unhealthy</u>, sick, infected, rotten, ailing, tainted, sickly, unwell, crook (*Austral. & N.Z. informal*), unsound, unwholesome

disembark = <u>land</u>, get off, alight, arrive, step out of, go ashore

disembodied = <u>ghostly</u>, phantom, spectral

disenchanted = <u>disillusioned</u>, disappointed, soured, cynical, indifferent, sick of, let down, blasé, jaundiced, undeceived

disenchantment = <u>disillusionment</u>, disappointment, disillusion, rude awakening

disengage 1 = <u>release</u>, free, separate, ease, liberate, loosen, set free, extricate, untie, disentangle, unloose, unbridle *...He gently disengaged himself from his sister's tearful embrace...*
2 = <u>detach</u>, withdraw *...More vigorous action is*

needed to force the army to disengage...*

disengaged = <u>unconnected</u>, separate, apart, detached, unattached

disengagement = <u>disconnection</u>, withdrawal, separation, detachment, disentanglement

disentangle 1 = <u>resolve</u>, clear (up), work out, sort out, clarify, simplify *...The author brilliantly disentangles complex debates...*
2 = <u>free</u>, separate, loose, detach, sever, disconnect, extricate, disengage *...They are looking at ways to disentangle him from this situation...*
3 = <u>untangle</u>, unravel, untwist, unsnarl *...The rope could not be disentangled and had to be cut...*

disfigure 1 = <u>damage</u>, scar, mutilate, maim, injure, wound, deform *...These items could be used to injure or disfigure someone...*
2 = <u>mar</u>, distort, blemish, deface, make ugly, disfeature *...ugly new houses which disfigure the countryside...*

disgorge discharge, send out, expel, throw out, vent, throw up, eject, spout, spew, belch, send forth

disgrace NOUN **1** = <u>shame</u>, contempt, discredit, degradation, disrepute, ignominy, dishonour, infamy, opprobrium, odium, disfavour, obloquy, disesteem *...I have brought disgrace upon my family...* OPPOSITE> honour
2 = <u>scandal</u>, stain, stigma, blot, blemish *...the disgrace of having an illegitimate child...*
VERB = <u>shame</u>, stain, humiliate, discredit, degrade, taint, sully, dishonour, stigmatize, defame, abase, bring shame upon *...These soldiers have disgraced their regiment...* OPPOSITE> honour

disgraced = <u>shamed</u>, humiliated, discredited, branded, degraded, mortified, in disgrace, dishonoured, stigmatized, under a cloud, in the doghouse (*informal*)

disgraceful = <u>shameful</u>, shocking, scandalous, mean, low, infamous, degrading, unworthy, ignominious, disreputable, contemptible, dishonourable, detestable, discreditable, blameworthy, opprobrious

disgruntled = <u>discontented</u>, dissatisfied, annoyed, irritated, put out, hacked (off) (*U.S. slang*), grumpy, vexed, sullen, displeased, petulant, sulky, peeved, malcontent, testy, peevish, huffy, cheesed off (*Brit. slang*)

disguise NOUN = <u>costume</u>, get-up (*informal*), mask, camouflage, false appearance *...a ridiculous disguise...*
VERB = <u>hide</u>, cover, conceal, screen, mask, suppress, withhold, veil, cloak, shroud, camouflage, keep secret, hush up, draw a veil over, keep dark, keep under your hat *...He made no attempt to disguise his contempt...*

disguised 1 = <u>in disguise</u>, masked, camouflaged, undercover, incognito, unrecognizable *...a disguised bank robber...*
2 = <u>false</u>, assumed, pretend, artificial, forged, fake, mock, imitation, sham, pseudo (*informal*), counterfeit, feigned, phoney *or* phony (*informal*) *...Their HQ used to be a disguised builders' yard...*

disgust NOUN 1 = loathing, revulsion, hatred, dislike, nausea, distaste, aversion, antipathy, abomination, repulsion, abhorrence, repugnance, odium, detestation, hatefulness ...*A look of disgust came over his face...* OPPOSITE liking
2 = outrage, shock, anger, hurt, fury, resentment, wrath, indignation ...*Colleagues last night spoke of their disgust at the decision...*
VERB = sicken, outrage, offend, revolt, put off, repel, nauseate, gross out (*U.S. slang*), turn your stomach, fill with loathing, cause aversion ...*He disgusted everyone with his boorish behaviour...* OPPOSITE delight

disgusted 1 = outraged, appalled, offended, sickened, scandalized ...*I'm disgusted with the way that he was treated...*
2 = sickened, repelled, repulsed, nauseated ...*squeamish men who are disgusted by the idea of menstruation...*

disgusting 1 = sickening, foul, revolting, gross, nasty, stinking, vulgar, vile, distasteful, repellent, obnoxious, objectionable, nauseating, odious, hateful, repugnant, loathsome, abominable, nauseous, grotty (*slang*), detestable, cringe-making (*Brit. informal*), noisome, yucky *or* yukky (*slang*), festy (*Austral. slang*), yucko (*Austral. slang*) ...*The curry was disgusting...*
2 = appalling, shocking, terrible, awful, offensive, dreadful, horrifying, dismaying, dire ...*It's a disgusting waste of money...*

dish NOUN 1 = bowl, plate, platter, salver ...*Pile the potatoes into a warm serving dish...*
2 = food, fare, recipe ...*There are plenty of vegetarian dishes to choose from...*
PHRASES **dish something out** (*Informal*) = distribute, assign, allocate, designate, set aside, hand out, earmark, inflict, mete out, dole out, share out, apportion ...*The council wants to dish the money out to specific projects...* ♦ **dish something up** = serve up, serve, produce, present, hand out, ladle out, spoon out ...*They dished up the next course...*

disharmony = discord, conflict, clash, friction, discordance, disaccord, inharmoniousness

disheartened = discouraged, depressed, crushed, dismayed, choked, daunted, dejected, dispirited, downcast, crestfallen, downhearted, sick as a parrot (*informal*)

dishevelled *or* (*U.S.*) **disheveled** = untidy, disordered, messy, ruffled, rumpled, bedraggled, unkempt, tousled, hanging loose, blowsy, uncombed, disarranged, disarrayed, frowzy OPPOSITE tidy

dishonest = deceitful, corrupt, crooked (*informal*), designing, lying, bent (*slang*), false, unfair, cheating, deceiving, shady (*informal*), fraudulent, treacherous, deceptive, unscrupulous, crafty, swindling, disreputable, untrustworthy, double-dealing, unprincipled, mendacious, perfidious, untruthful, guileful, knavish (*archaic*) OPPOSITE honest

dishonesty = deceit, fraud, corruption, cheating, graft (*informal*), treachery, trickery, criminality, duplicity, falsehood, chicanery, falsity, sharp practice, perfidy, mendacity, fraudulence, crookedness, wiliness, unscrupulousness, improbity

dishonour *or* (*U.S.*) **dishonor** VERB = disgrace, shame, discredit, corrupt, degrade, blacken, sully, debase, debauch, defame, abase ...*It would dishonour my family if I didn't wear the veil...* OPPOSITE respect
NOUN = disgrace, scandal, shame, discredit, degradation, disrepute, reproach, ignominy, infamy, opprobrium, odium, disfavour, abasement, obloquy ...*You have brought dishonour on a fine and venerable institution...* OPPOSITE honour

disillusion = shatter your illusions, disabuse, bring down to earth, open the eyes of, disenchant, undeceive

disillusioned = disenchanted, disappointed, enlightened, indifferent, disabused, sadder and wiser, undeceived

disillusionment = disenchantment, disappointment, disillusion, enlightenment, rude awakening, lost innocence

disincentive = discouragement, deterrent, impediment, damper, dissuasion, determent

disinclined = reluctant, unwilling, averse, opposed, resistant, hesitant, balking, loath, not in the mood, indisposed, antipathetic

disinfect = sterilize, purify, decontaminate, clean, cleanse, fumigate, deodorize, sanitize OPPOSITE contaminate

disinfectant = antiseptic, sterilizer, germicide, sanitizer

disintegrate = break up, crumble, fall apart, separate, shatter, splinter, break apart, fall to pieces, go to pieces, disunite

disinterest = indifference, apathy, lack of interest, disregard, detachment, absence of feeling

disinterested 1 = impartial, objective, neutral, detached, equitable, impersonal, unbiased, even-handed, unselfish, uninvolved, unprejudiced, free from self-interest ...*Scientists are expected to be impartial and disinterested...* OPPOSITE biased
2 = indifferent, apathetic, uninterested ...*We had become jaded, disinterested and disillusioned...*

> ## Word Power
>
> **disinterested** – *Disinterested* is now so commonly used to mean 'not interested' that to avoid ambiguity it is often advisable to replace it by a synonym when the meaning intended is 'impartial, unbiased'. In the Bank of English about 10% of the examples of the word occur followed by *in*, and overall about a third of examples are of this usage.

disjointed 1 = incoherent, confused, disordered, rambling, disconnected, unconnected, loose, aimless, fitful, spasmodic ...*his disjointed drunken ramblings...*
2 = disconnected, separated, divided, split, displaced, dislocated, disunited ...*our increasingly fragmented and disjointed society...*

dislike VERB = hate, object to, loathe, despise, shun,

scorn, disapprove of, detest, abhor, recoil from, take a dim view of, be repelled by, be averse to, disfavour, have an aversion to, abominate, have a down on (*informal*), disrelish, have no taste *or* stomach for, not be able to bear *or* abide *or* stand ...*We don't serve liver often because so many people dislike it...* OPPOSITE> like
NOUN = <u>hatred</u>, disgust, hostility, loathing, disapproval, distaste, animosity, aversion, antagonism, displeasure, antipathy, enmity, animus, disinclination, repugnance, odium, detestation, disapprobation ...*The two women viewed each other with dislike and suspicion...* OPPOSITE> liking

dislocate 1 = <u>put out of joint</u>, disconnect, disengage, unhinge, disunite, disjoint, disarticulate ...*She had dislocated her shoulder in the fall...*
2 = <u>disrupt</u>, disturb, disorder ...*The strike was designed to dislocate the economy...*

dislocation 1 = <u>disruption</u>, disorder, disturbance, disarray, disorganization ...*The refugees have suffered a total dislocation of their lives...*
2 = <u>putting out of joint</u>, unhinging, disengagement, disconnection, disarticulation ...*He suffered a double dislocation of his left ankle...*

dislodge 1 = <u>displace</u>, remove, disturb, dig out, uproot, extricate, disentangle, knock loose ...*Use a hoof pick to dislodge stones and dirt from your horse's feet...*
2 = <u>oust</u>, remove, expel, throw out, displace, topple, force out, eject, depose, unseat ...*The leader cannot dislodge her this time...*

disloyal = <u>treacherous</u>, false, unfaithful, subversive, two-faced, faithless, untrustworthy, perfidious, apostate, traitorous OPPOSITE> loyal

disloyalty = <u>treachery</u>, infidelity, breach of trust, double-dealing, falsity, perfidy, unfaithfulness, falseness, betrayal of trust, inconstancy, deceitfulness, breaking of faith, Punic faith

dismal 1 = <u>bad</u>, awful, dreadful, rotten (*informal*), terrible, poor, dire, duff (*Brit. informal*), abysmal, frightful, godawful (*slang*) ...*the country's dismal record in the Olympics...*
2 = <u>sad</u>, gloomy, melancholy, black, dark, depressing, discouraging, bleak, dreary, sombre, forlorn, despondent, lugubrious, sorrowful, wretched, funereal, cheerless, dolorous ...*You can't occupy yourself with dismal thoughts all the time...* OPPOSITE> happy
3 = <u>gloomy</u>, depressing, dull, dreary, lugubrious, cheerless ...*The main part of the hospital is pretty dismal...* OPPOSITE> cheerful

dismantle = <u>take apart</u>, strip, demolish, raze, disassemble, unrig, take to pieces *or* bits

dismay NOUN 1 = <u>alarm</u>, fear, horror, panic, anxiety, distress, terror, dread, fright, unease, apprehension, nervousness, agitation, consternation, trepidation, uneasiness ...*They reacted to the news with dismay...*
2 = <u>disappointment</u>, upset, distress, frustration, dissatisfaction, disillusionment, chagrin, disenchantment, discouragement, mortification

...*Much to her dismay, he did not call...*
VERB 1 = <u>alarm</u>, frighten, scare, panic, distress, terrify, appal, startle, horrify, paralyse, unnerve, put the wind up (someone) (*informal*), give (someone) a turn (*informal*), affright, fill with consternation ...*The committee was dismayed by what it had been told...*
2 = <u>disappoint</u>, upset, sadden, dash, discourage, put off, daunt, disillusion, let down, vex, chagrin, dishearten, dispirit, disenchant, disgruntle ...*He was dismayed to learn that she was already married...*

dismember = <u>cut into pieces</u>, divide, rend, sever, mutilate, dissect, dislocate, amputate, disjoint, anatomize, dislimb

dismiss 1 = <u>reject</u>, disregard, spurn, repudiate, pooh-pooh ...*He dismissed the reports as mere speculation...*
2 = <u>banish</u>, drop, dispel, shelve, discard, set aside, eradicate, cast out, lay aside, put out of your mind ...*I dismissed the thought from my mind...*
3 = <u>sack</u>, fire (*informal*), remove (*informal*), axe (*informal*), discharge, oust, lay off, kick out (*informal*), cashier, send packing (*informal*), give notice to, kiss off (*slang, chiefly U.S. & Canad.*), give (someone) their marching orders, give (someone) the push (*informal*), give (someone) the elbow, give the boot to (*slang*), give the bullet to (*Brit. slang*) ...*the power to dismiss civil servants who refuse to work...*
4 = <u>let go</u>, free, release, discharge, dissolve, liberate, disperse, disband, send away ...*Two more witnesses were called, heard and dismissed...*

dismissal = <u>the sack</u>, removal, discharge, notice, the boot (*slang*), expulsion (*informal*), the push (*slang*), marching orders (*informal*), kiss-off (*slang, chiefly U.S. & Canad.*), the bum's rush (*slang*), the (old) heave-ho (*informal*), the order of the boot (*slang*), your books *or* cards (*informal*)

dismount = <u>get off</u>, descend, get down, alight, light

disobedience = <u>defiance</u>, mutiny, indiscipline, revolt, insubordination, waywardness, infraction, recalcitrance, noncompliance, unruliness, nonobservance

disobey 1 = <u>defy</u>, ignore, rebel, resist, disregard, refuse to obey, dig your heels in (*informal*), go counter to ...*a naughty boy who often disobeyed his mother...*
2 = <u>infringe</u>, defy, refuse to obey, flout, violate, contravene, overstep, transgress, go counter to ...*He was forever disobeying the rules...*

disorder 1 = <u>illness</u>, disease, complaint, condition, sickness, ailment, affliction, malady, infirmity, indisposition ...*a rare nerve disorder that can cause paralysis of the arms...*
2 = <u>untidiness</u>, mess, confusion, chaos, muddle, state, clutter, shambles, disarray, jumble, irregularity, disorganization, hotchpotch, derangement, hodgepodge (*U.S.*), pig's breakfast (*informal*), disorderliness ...*The emergency room was in disorder...*
3 = <u>disturbance</u>, fight, riot, turmoil, unrest, quarrel, upheaval, brawl, clamour, uproar, turbulence, fracas, commotion, rumpus, tumult, hubbub, shindig

(*informal*), hullabaloo, scrimmage, unruliness, shindy (*informal*), bagarre (*French*), biffo (*Austral. slang*) ...*He called on the authorities to stop public disorder...*

disordered = <u>untidy</u>, confused, muddled, all over the place, displaced, out of place, jumbled, misplaced, dislocated, deranged, in a mess, disorganized, in confusion, higgledy-piggledy (*informal*), disarranged, disarrayed, out of kilter

disorderly 1 = <u>untidy</u>, confused, chaotic, messy, irregular, jumbled, indiscriminate, shambolic (*informal*), disorganized, higgledy-piggledy (*informal*), unsystematic ...*The desk was covered in a disorderly jumble of old papers...* OPPOSITE> tidy
2 = <u>unruly</u>, disruptive, rowdy, turbulent, unlawful, stormy, rebellious, boisterous, tumultuous, lawless, riotous, unmanageable, ungovernable, refractory, obstreperous, indisciplined ...*disorderly conduct...*

disorganized = <u>muddled</u>, confused, disordered, shuffled, chaotic, jumbled, haphazard, unorganized, unsystematic, unmethodical

disorientate *or* **disorient** = <u>confuse</u>, upset, perplex, dislocate, cause to lose your bearings

disorientated *or* **disoriented** = <u>confused</u>, lost, unsettled, bewildered, mixed up, perplexed, all at sea

disown = <u>deny</u>, reject, abandon, renounce, disallow, retract, repudiate, cast off, rebut, disavow, disclaim, abnegate, refuse to acknowledge *or* recognize

disparage = <u>run down</u>, dismiss, put down, criticize, underestimate, discredit, ridicule, scorn, minimize, disdain, undervalue, deride, slag (off) (*slang*), knock (*informal*), blast, rubbish (*informal*), malign, detract from, denigrate, belittle, decry, underrate, vilify, slander, deprecate, depreciate, tear into (*informal*), diss (*slang, chiefly U.S.*), defame, bad-mouth (*slang, chiefly U.S. & Canad.*), lambast(e), traduce, derogate, asperse

disparaging = <u>contemptuous</u>, damaging, critical, slighting, offensive, insulting, abusive, scathing, dismissive, belittling, unfavourable, derogatory, unflattering, scornful, disdainful, defamatory, derisive, libellous, slanderous, deprecatory, uncomplimentary, fault-finding, contumelious OPPOSITE> complimentary

disparate = <u>different</u>, contrasting, unlike, contrary, distinct, diverse, at odds, dissimilar, discordant, at variance, discrepant

disparity = <u>difference</u>, gap, inequality, distinction, imbalance, discrepancy, incongruity, unevenness, dissimilarity, disproportion, unlikeness, dissimilitude

dispassionate 1 = <u>unemotional</u>, cool, collected, calm, moderate, composed, sober, serene, unmoved, temperate, unfazed (*informal*), unruffled, imperturbable, unexcited, unexcitable ...*He spoke in a flat dispassionate tone...* OPPOSITE> emotional
2 = <u>objective</u>, fair, neutral, detached, indifferent, impartial, impersonal, disinterested, unbiased, uninvolved, unprejudiced ...*We try to be dispassionate about the cases we bring...* OPPOSITE> biased

dispatch *or* **despatch** VERB **1** = <u>send</u>, transmit, forward, express, communicate, consign, remit ...*He dispatched a telegram...*

2 = <u>kill</u>, murder, destroy, do in (*slang*), eliminate (*slang*), take out (*slang*), execute, butcher, slaughter, assassinate, slay, finish off, put an end to, do away with, blow away (*slang, chiefly U.S.*), liquidate, annihilate, exterminate, take (someone's) life, bump off (*slang*) ...*They may catch him and dispatch him immediately...*
3 = <u>carry out</u>, perform, fulfil, effect, finish, achieve, settle, dismiss, conclude, accomplish, execute, discharge, dispose of, expedite, make short work of (*informal*) ...*He dispatched his business...*
NOUN **1** = <u>message</u>, news, report, story, letter, account, piece, item, document, communication, instruction, bulletin, communiqué, missive ...*This dispatch from our West Africa correspondent...*
2 = <u>speed</u>, haste, promptness, alacrity, rapidity, quickness, swiftness, briskness, expedition, celerity, promptitude, precipitateness ...*He feels we should act with despatch...*

dispel = <u>drive away</u>, dismiss, eliminate, resolve, scatter, expel, disperse, banish, rout, allay, dissipate, chase away

dispensation 1 = <u>exemption</u>, licence, exception, permission, privilege, relaxation, immunity, relief, indulgence, reprieve, remission ...*The committee were not prepared to grant special dispensation...*
2 = <u>distribution</u>, supplying, dealing out, appointment, endowment, allotment, consignment, disbursement, apportionment, bestowal, conferment ...*the dispensation of justice...*

dispense VERB **1** = <u>distribute</u>, assign, allocate, allot, mete out, dole out, share out, apportion, deal out, disburse ...*They had already dispensed £40,000 in grants...*
2 = <u>prepare</u>, measure, supply, mix ...*a store licensed to dispense prescriptions...*
3 = <u>administer</u>, direct, operate, carry out, implement, undertake, enforce, execute, apply, discharge ...*High Court judges dispensing justice round the country...*
4 = <u>exempt</u>, except, excuse, release, relieve, reprieve, let off (*informal*), exonerate ...*No-one is dispensed from collaborating in this task...*
PHRASES **dispense with something** *or* **someone 1** = <u>do away with</u>, ignore, give up, cancel, abolish, omit, disregard, pass over, brush aside, forgo, render needless ...*We'll dispense with formalities...*
2 = <u>do without</u>, get rid of, dispose of, relinquish, shake off ...*Up at the lectern he dispensed with his notes...*

dispersal 1 = <u>scattering</u>, spread, distribution, dissemination, dissipation ...*the plants' mechanisms of dispersal of their spores...*
2 = <u>spread</u>, broadcast, circulation, diffusion, dissemination ...*the dispersal of this notably negative attitude...*

disperse 1 = <u>scatter</u>, spread, distribute, circulate, strew, diffuse, dissipate, disseminate, throw about ...*Intense currents disperse the sewage...*
2 = <u>break up</u>, separate, dismiss, disappear, send off, vanish, scatter, dissolve, rout, dispel, disband, part company, demobilize, go (their) separate ways ...*The*

crowd dispersed peacefully… OPPOSITE⟩ gather
3 = <u>dissolve</u>, disappear, vanish, evaporate, break up, dissipate, melt away, evanesce …*The fog dispersed and I became aware of the sun*…
➤ **disburse**

dispirited = <u>disheartened</u>, depressed, discouraged, down, low, sad, gloomy, glum, dejected, in the doldrums, despondent, downcast, morose, crestfallen, sick as a parrot (*informal*)

dispiriting = <u>disheartening</u>, disappointing, depressing, crushing, discouraging, daunting, sickening, saddening, demoralizing OPPOSITE⟩ reassuring

displace 1 = <u>replace</u>, succeed, take over from, supersede, oust, usurp, supplant, take the place of, crowd out, fill *or* step into (someone's) boots …*These factories have displaced tourism*…
2 = <u>force out</u>, turn out, expel, throw out, oust, unsettle, kick out (*informal*), eject, evict, dislodge, boot out (*informal*), dispossess, turf out (*informal*) …*In Europe alone, 30 million people were displaced*…
3 = <u>move</u>, shift, disturb, budge, misplace, disarrange, derange …*A strong wind is all it would take to displace the stones*…
4 = <u>remove</u>, fire (*informal*), dismiss, sack (*informal*), discharge, oust, depose, cashier, dethrone, remove from office …*They displaced him in a coup*…

display VERB **1** = <u>show</u>, present, exhibit, unveil, open to view, take the wraps off, put on view …*The cabinets display seventeenth-century porcelain*…
OPPOSITE⟩ conceal
2 = <u>expose</u>, show, reveal, bare, exhibit, uncover, lay bare, expose to view …*She displayed her wound*…
3 = <u>demonstrate</u>, show, reveal, register, expose, disclose, betray, manifest, divulge, make known, evidence, evince …*It was unlike him to display his feelings*…
4 = <u>show off</u>, parade, exhibit, sport (*informal*), flash (*informal*), boast, flourish, brandish, flaunt, vaunt, make a (great) show of, disport, make an exhibition of …*She does not have to display her charms*…
NOUN **1** = <u>proof</u>, exhibition, demonstration, evidence, expression, exposure, illustration, revelation, testimony, confirmation, manifestation, affirmation, substantiation …*an outward display of affection*…
2 = <u>exhibition</u>, show, demonstration, presentation, showing, array, expo (*informal*), exposition …*a display of your work*…
3 = <u>ostentation</u>, show, dash, flourish, fanfare, pomp …*He embraced it with such confidence and display*…
4 = <u>show</u>, exhibition, demonstration, parade, spectacle, pageant, pageantry …*a dazzling dance display*…

displease = <u>annoy</u>, upset, anger, provoke, offend, irritate, put out, hassle (*informal*), aggravate (*informal*), incense, gall, exasperate, nettle, vex, irk, rile, pique, nark (*Brit., Austral., & N.Z. slang*), dissatisfy, put your back up

displeasure = <u>annoyance</u>, anger, resentment, irritation, offence, dislike, wrath, dissatisfaction, disapproval, indignation, distaste, pique, vexation,

disgruntlement, disfavour, disapprobation OPPOSITE⟩ satisfaction

disposable 1 = <u>throwaway</u>, paper, nonreturnable …*disposable nappies for babies up to 8lb*…
2 = <u>available</u>, expendable, free for use, consumable, spendable, at your service …*He had little disposable income*…

disposal NOUN = <u>throwing away</u>, dumping (*informal*), scrapping, removal, discarding, clearance, jettisoning, ejection, riddance, relinquishment …*the disposal of radioactive waste*…
PHRASES **at your disposal** = <u>available</u>, ready, to hand, accessible, convenient, handy, on hand, at hand, obtainable, on tap, expendable, at your fingertips, at your service, free for use, ready for use, consumable, spendable …*Do you have this information at your disposal?*…

dispose VERB **1** = <u>arrange</u>, put, place, group, set, order, stand, range, settle, fix, rank, distribute, array …*He was preparing to dispose his effects about the room*…
2 = <u>lead</u>, move, condition, influence, prompt, tempt, adapt, motivate, bias, induce, incline, predispose, actuate …*theologies which dispose their adherents to fanaticism*…
PHRASES **dispose of someone** = <u>kill</u>, murder, destroy, do in (*slang*), take out (*slang*), execute, slaughter, dispatch, assassinate, slay, do away with, knock off (*slang*), liquidate, neutralize, exterminate, take (someone's) life, bump off (*slang*), wipe from the face of the earth (*informal*) …*theologies which dispose their adherents to fanaticism*… ◆ **dispose of something 1** = <u>get rid of</u>, destroy, dump (*informal*), scrap, bin (*informal*), junk (*informal*), chuck (*informal*), discard, unload, dispense with, jettison, get shot of, throw out *or* away …*Fold up the nappy and dispose of it*… **2** = <u>deal with</u>, manage, treat, handle, settle, cope with, take care of, see to, finish with, attend to, get to grips with …*the manner in which you disposed of the that problem*… **3** = <u>give</u>, give up, part with, bestow, transfer, make over …*He managed to dispose of more money and goods*…

disposed = <u>inclined</u>, given, likely, subject, ready, prone, liable, apt, predisposed, tending towards, of a mind to

disposition 1 = <u>character</u>, nature, spirit, make-up, constitution, temper, temperament …*his friendly and cheerful disposition*…
2 = <u>tendency</u>, inclination, propensity, habit, leaning, bent, bias, readiness, predisposition, proclivity, proneness …*They show no disposition to take risks*…
3 = <u>arrangement</u>, grouping, ordering, organization, distribution, disposal, placement …*the disposition of walls and entrances*…
4 = <u>control</u>, management, direction, regulation, disposal …*to oversee the disposition of funds*…

dispossess = <u>strip</u>, deprive

dispossessed = <u>destitute</u>, landless

disproportionate = <u>excessive</u>, too much, unreasonable, uneven, unequal, unbalanced, out of proportion, inordinate, incommensurate

disprove = <u>prove false</u>, discredit, refute, contradict, negate, invalidate, rebut, give the lie to, make a nonsense of, blow out of the water (*slang*), controvert, confute OPPOSITE> prove

dispute NOUN **1** = <u>disagreement</u>, conflict, argument, falling out, dissent, friction, strife, discord, altercation …*There has been much dispute over the ownership of the lease*…
2 = <u>argument</u>, row, clash, controversy, disturbance, contention, feud, quarrel, brawl, squabble, wrangle, difference of opinion, tiff, dissension, shindig (*informal*), shindy (*informal*), bagarre (*French*) …*The dispute between them is settled*…
VERB **1** = <u>contest</u>, question, challenge, deny, doubt, oppose, object to, contradict, rebut, impugn, controvert, call in *or* into question …*He disputed the allegations*…
2 = <u>argue</u>, fight, clash, row, disagree, fall out (*informal*), contend, feud, quarrel, brawl, squabble, spar, wrangle, bicker, have an argument, cross swords, be at sixes and sevens, fight like cat and dog, go at it hammer and tongs, altercate …*Whole towns disputed with neighboring villages over boundaries*…

disqualification = <u>ban</u>, exclusion, elimination, rejection, ineligibility, debarment, disenablement, disentitlement

disqualified = <u>eliminated</u>, knocked out, out of the running, debarred, ineligible

disqualify = <u>ban</u>, rule out, prohibit, preclude, debar, declare ineligible, disentitle

disquiet NOUN = <u>uneasiness</u>, concern, fear, worry, alarm, anxiety, distress, unrest, angst, nervousness, trepidation, foreboding, restlessness, fretfulness, disquietude …*There is growing public disquiet*…
VERB = <u>make uneasy</u>, concern, worry, trouble, upset, bother, disturb, distress, annoy, plague, unsettle, harass, hassle (*informal*), agitate, vex, perturb, discompose, incommode …*He's obviously disquieted by the experience*…

disquieting = <u>worrying</u>, troubling, upsetting, disturbing, distressing, annoying, irritating, unsettling, harrowing, unnerving, disconcerting, vexing, perturbing, bothersome

disregard VERB = <u>ignore</u>, discount, take no notice of, overlook, neglect, pass over, turn a blind eye to, disobey, laugh off, make light of, pay no attention to, pay no heed to, leave out of account, brush aside *or* away …*He disregarded the advice of his executives*…
OPPOSITE> pay attention to
NOUN = <u>ignoring</u>, neglect, contempt, indifference, negligence, disdain, disrespect, heedlessness …*a callous disregard for human life*…

disrepair NOUN = <u>dilapidation</u>, collapse, decay, deterioration, ruination …*The house was in a bad state of disrepair*…
PHRASES **in disrepair** = <u>out of order</u>, broken, decayed, worn-out, decrepit, not functioning, out of commission, on the blink (*slang*), bust (*informal*), kaput (*informal*) …*Everything was in disrepair*…

disreputable = <u>discreditable</u>, mean, low, base, shocking, disorderly, notorious, vicious, infamous, disgraceful, shameful, vile, shady (*informal*), scandalous, ignominious, contemptible, louche, unprincipled, dishonourable, opprobrious OPPOSITE> respectable

disrepute = <u>discredit</u>, shame, disgrace, unpopularity, ignominy, dishonour, infamy, disfavour, ill repute, obloquy, ill favour, disesteem

disrespect = <u>contempt</u>, cheek, disregard, rudeness, lack of respect, irreverence, insolence, impertinence, impudence, discourtesy, incivility, impoliteness, lese-majesty, unmannerliness OPPOSITE> respect

disrespectful = <u>contemptuous</u>, insulting, rude, cheeky, irreverent, bad-mannered, impertinent, insolent, impolite, impudent, discourteous, uncivil, ill-bred

disrupt **1** = <u>interrupt</u>, stop, upset, hold up, interfere with, unsettle, obstruct, cut short, intrude on, break up *or* into …*Anti-war protests disrupted the debate*…
2 = <u>disturb</u>, upset, confuse, disorder, spoil, unsettle, agitate, disorganize, disarrange, derange, throw into disorder …*The drought has disrupted agricultural production*…

disruption = <u>disturbance</u>, disorder, confusion, interference, disarray, interruption, stoppage, disorderliness

disruptive = <u>disturbing</u>, upsetting, disorderly, unsettling, troublesome, unruly, obstreperous, troublemaking OPPOSITE> well-behaved

dissatisfaction = <u>discontent</u>, frustration, resentment, regret, distress, disappointment, dismay, irritation, unhappiness, annoyance, displeasure, exasperation, chagrin

dissatisfied = <u>discontented</u>, frustrated, unhappy, disappointed, fed up, disgruntled, not satisfied, unfulfilled, displeased, unsatisfied, ungratified OPPOSITE> satisfied

dissect **1** = <u>cut up</u> *or* apart, dismember, lay open, anatomize …*We dissected a frog in biology*…
2 = <u>analyse</u>, study, investigate, research, explore, break down, inspect, scrutinize …*People want to dissect his work*…

dissection **1** = <u>cutting up</u>, anatomy, autopsy, dismemberment, postmortem (examination), necropsy, anatomization …*a growing supply of corpses for dissection*…
2 = <u>analysis</u>, examination, breakdown, research, investigation, inspection, scrutiny …*the dissection of my proposals*…

disseminate = <u>spread</u>, publish, broadcast, distribute, scatter, proclaim, circulate, sow, disperse, diffuse, publicize, dissipate, propagate, promulgate

dissemination = <u>spread</u>, publishing, broadcasting, publication, distribution, circulation, diffusion, propagation, promulgation

dissension = <u>disagreement</u>, conflict, dissent, dispute, contention, quarreling, friction, strife, discord, discordance, conflict of opinion

dissent NOUN = disagreement, opposition, protest, resistance, refusal, objection, discord, demur, dissension, dissidence, nonconformity, remonstrance ...*He has responded harshly to any dissent...* OPPOSITE assent

PHRASES **dissent from something** = disagree with, object to, protest against, refuse to accept ...*No one dissents from the decision to unify...*

dissenter = objector, dissident, nonconformist, protestant, disputant

dissenting = disagreeing, protesting, opposing, conflicting, differing, dissident

dissertation = thesis, essay, discourse, critique, exposition, treatise, disquisition

disservice = wrong, injury, harm, injustice, disfavour, unkindness, bad turn, ill turn OPPOSITE good turn

dissident NOUN = protester, rebel, dissenter, demonstrator, agitator, recusant, protest marcher ...*political dissidents...*

ADJECTIVE = dissenting, disagreeing, nonconformist, heterodox, schismatic, dissentient ...*links with a dissident group...*

dissimilar = different, unlike, various, varied, diverse, assorted, unrelated, disparate, miscellaneous, sundry, divergent, manifold, heterogeneous, mismatched, multifarious, not similar, not alike, not capable of comparison OPPOSITE alike

dissipate 1 = disappear, fade, vanish, dissolve, disperse, evaporate, diffuse, melt away, evanesce ...*The tension in the room had dissipated...*
2 = squander, spend, waste, consume, run through, deplete, expend, fritter away, misspend ...*Her father had dissipated her inheritance...*

dissipated 1 = debauched, abandoned, self-indulgent, profligate, intemperate, dissolute, rakish ...*He was still handsome though dissipated...*
2 = squandered, spent, wasted, exhausted, consumed, scattered ...*A lot of it has simply been dissipated...*

dissociate or **disassociate** VERB = separate, distance, divorce, isolate, detach, segregate, disconnect, set apart ...*how to dissociate emotion from reason...*

PHRASES **dissociate yourself from something** or **someone** = break away from, part company with, break off relations with ...*He dissociated himself from his former friends...*

dissociation = separation, break, division, distancing, divorce, isolation, segregation, detachment, severance, disengagement, disconnection, disunion

dissolution 1 = ending, end, finish, conclusion, suspension, dismissal, termination, adjournment, disbandment, discontinuation ...*He stayed on until the dissolution of the firm...* OPPOSITE union
2 = breaking up, parting, divorce, separation, disintegration ...*the dissolution of a marriage...*
3 = corruption, excess, indulgence, depravity, debauchery, gluttony, dissipation, licentiousness, intemperance, overindulgence, wantonness,

dissoluteness ...*the corruption of manners, and dissolution of life...*

dissolve VERB 1 = melt, soften, thaw, flux, liquefy, deliquesce ...*Heat gently until the sugar dissolves...*
2 = end, dismiss, suspend, axe (*informal*), break up, wind up, overthrow, terminate, discontinue, dismantle, disband, disunite ...*The King agreed to dissolve the present commission...*
3 = disappear, fade, vanish, break down, crumble, disperse, dwindle, evaporate, disintegrate, perish, diffuse, dissipate, decompose, melt away, waste away, evanesce ...*His new-found optimism dissolved...*

PHRASES **dissolve into** or **in something** (with *tears* or *laughter* as object) = break into, burst into, give way to, launch into ...*She dissolved into tears...*

dissonance 1 = disagreement, variance, discord, dissension ...*Bring harmony out of dissonance...*
2 = discordance, discord, jangle, cacophony, jarring, harshness, lack of harmony, unmelodiousness ...*a jumble of silence and dissonance...*

distance NOUN 1 = space, length, extent, range, stretch, gap, interval, separation, span, width ...*They measured the distance between the island and the shore...*
2 = remoteness ...*The distance wouldn't be a problem...*
3 = aloofness, reserve, detachment, restraint, indifference, stiffness, coolness, coldness, remoteness, frigidity, uninvolvement, standoffishness ...*There were periods of distance, of coldness...*

PHRASES **go the distance** = finish, stay the course, complete, see through, bring to an end ...*Riders are determined to go the distance...* ♦ **in the distance** = far off, far away, on the horizon, afar, yonder ...*We suddenly saw her in the distance...*

distant 1 = far-off, far, remote, removed, abroad, out-of-the-way, far-flung, faraway, outlying, afar ...*the war in that distant land...* OPPOSITE close
2 = faint, vague, dim, uncertain, obscure, hazy, indistinct ...*Last year's drought is a distant memory...*
3 = remote, slight ...*He's a distant relative...*
4 = reserved, cold, withdrawn, cool, formal, remote, stiff, restrained, detached, indifferent, aloof, unfriendly, reticent, haughty, unapproachable, standoffish ...*He's direct and courteous, but distant...* OPPOSITE friendly
5 = faraway, blank, abstracted, vague, absorbed, distracted, unaware, musing, vacant, preoccupied, bemused, oblivious, dreamy, daydreaming, absent-minded, inattentive ...*There was a distant look in her eyes...*

distaste = dislike, horror, disgust, loathing, aversion, revulsion, displeasure, antipathy, abhorrence, disinclination, repugnance, odium, disfavour, detestation, disrelish

distasteful = unpleasant, offensive, obscene, undesirable, unsavoury, obnoxious, unpalatable, displeasing, repulsive, objectionable, disagreeable, repugnant, loathsome, abhorrent, nauseous, uninviting OPPOSITE enjoyable

distil 1 = purify, refine, evaporate, condense,

sublimate, vaporize ...*When water is used it must be distilled*...

2 = <u>extract</u>, express, squeeze, obtain, take out, draw out, separate out, press out ...*The oil is distilled from the berries*...

distillation = <u>essence</u>, extract, elixir, spirit, quintessence

distinct 1 = <u>different</u>, individual, separate, disconnected, discrete, dissimilar, unconnected, unattached ...*The book is divided into two distinct parts*... OPPOSITE> similar

2 = <u>striking</u>, sharp, dramatic, stunning (*informal*), outstanding, bold, noticeable, well-defined ...*to impart a distinct flavour with a minimum of cooking fat*...

3 = <u>definite</u>, marked, clear, decided, obvious, sharp, plain, apparent, patent, evident, black-and-white, manifest, noticeable, conspicuous, clear-cut, unmistakable, palpable, recognizable, unambiguous, observable, perceptible, appreciable ...*There was a distinct change in her attitude*... OPPOSITE> vague

distinction 1 = <u>difference</u>, contrast, variation, differential, discrepancy, disparity, deviation, differentiation, fine line, distinctness, dissimilarity ...*There were obvious distinctions between the two*...

2 = <u>excellence</u>, note, quality, worth, account, rank, reputation, importance, consequence, fame, celebrity, merit, superiority, prominence, greatness, eminence, renown, repute ...*He is a composer of distinction and sensitivity*...

3 = <u>feature</u>, quality, characteristic, name, mark, individuality, peculiarity, singularity, distinctiveness, particularity ...*He has the distinction of being their greatest living writer*...

4 = <u>merit</u>, credit, honour, integrity, excellence, righteousness, rectitude, uprightness ...*She had served her country with distinction and strength*...

distinctive = <u>characteristic</u>, special, individual, specific, unique, typical, extraordinary, distinguishing, peculiar, singular, idiosyncratic OPPOSITE> ordinary

distinctly 1 = <u>definitely</u>, clearly, obviously, sharply, plainly, patently, manifestly, decidedly, markedly, noticeably, unmistakably, palpably ...*two distinctly different sectors*...

2 = <u>clearly</u>, plainly, precisely ...*'If I may speak, gentlemen,' he said distinctly*...

distinguish 1 = <u>differentiate</u>, determine, separate, discriminate, decide, judge, discern, ascertain, tell the difference, make a distinction, tell apart, tell between ...*Could he distinguish right from wrong?*...

2 = <u>characterize</u>, mark, separate, single out, individualize, set apart ...*one of the things that distinguishes artists from other people*...

3 = <u>make out</u>, recognize, perceive, know, see, tell, pick out, discern ...*He could distinguish voices*...

distinguishable 1 = <u>recognizable</u>, noticeable, conspicuous, discernible, obvious, evident, manifest, perceptible, well-marked ...*This port is distinguishable by its colour*...

2 = <u>conspicuous</u>, clear, strong, bright, plain, bold,

pronounced, colourful, vivid, eye-catching, salient ...*Already shapes were more distinguishable*...

distinguished = <u>eminent</u>, great, important, noted, famous, celebrated, well-known, prominent, esteemed, acclaimed, notable, renowned, prestigious, elevated, big-time (*informal*), famed, conspicuous, illustrious, major league (*informal*) OPPOSITE> unknown

distinguishing = <u>characteristic</u>, marked, distinctive, typical, peculiar, differentiating, individualistic

distort 1 = <u>misrepresent</u>, twist, bias, disguise, pervert, slant, colour, misinterpret, falsify, garble ...*The media distorts reality*...

2 = <u>deform</u>, bend, twist, warp, buckle, mangle, mangulate (*Austral. slang*), disfigure, contort, gnarl, misshape, malform ...*Make sure the image isn't distorted by lumps and bumps*...

distorted 1 = <u>misrepresented</u>, twisted, false, coloured, one-sided, biased, partial, perverted, slanted, garbled ...*These figures give a distorted view*...

2 = <u>deformed</u>, bent, twisted, crooked, irregular, warped, buckled, disfigured, contorted, misshapen ...*His face was distorted but recognizable*...

distortion 1 = <u>misrepresentation</u>, bias, slant, perversion, falsification, colouring ...*He accused reporters of wilful distortion*...

2 = <u>deformity</u>, bend, twist, warp, buckle, contortion, malformation, crookedness, twistedness ...*the gargoyle-like distortion of her face*...

distract 1 = <u>divert</u>, sidetrack, draw away, turn aside, lead astray, draw *or* lead away from ...*Video games sometimes distract him from his homework*...

2 = <u>amuse</u>, occupy, entertain, beguile, engross ...*I took out a book and tried to distract myself*...

3 = <u>agitate</u>, trouble, disturb, confuse, puzzle, torment, bewilder, madden, confound, perplex, disconcert, derange, discompose ...*Another story of hers distracts me*...

➤ **detract**

distracted 1 = <u>agitated</u>, troubled, confused, puzzled, at sea, bewildered, bemused, confounded, perplexed, flustered, in a flap (*informal*) ...*At work, he thought about her all day. He was distracted*...

2 = <u>frantic</u>, wild, mad, crazy, desperate, raving, frenzied, distraught, insane, deranged, grief-stricken, overwrought, at the end of your tether ...*My father was distracted by grief*...

distracting = <u>disturbing</u>, bothering, confusing, dismaying, bewildering, disconcerting, perturbing, off-putting (*Brit. informal*)

distraction 1 = <u>disturbance</u>, interference, diversion, interruption ...*Total concentration is required with no distractions*...

2 = <u>entertainment</u>, recreation, amusement, diversion, pastime, divertissement, beguilement ...*every conceivable distraction from shows to bouncy castles*...

3 = <u>frenzy</u>, desperation, mania, insanity, delirium, derangement ...*A very clingy child can drive a parent to distraction*...

distraught = <u>frantic</u>, wild, desperate, mad, anxious, distressed, raving, distracted, hysterical, worked-up, agitated, crazed, overwrought, out of your mind, at the end of your tether, wrought-up, beside yourself

distress NOUN **1** = <u>suffering</u>, pain, worry, anxiety, torture, grief, misery, agony, sadness, discomfort, torment, sorrow, woe, anguish, heartache, affliction, desolation, wretchedness ...*Her mouth grew stiff with pain and distress...*
2 = <u>need</u>, suffering, trouble, trial, difficulties, poverty, misery, hard times, hardship, straits, misfortune, adversity, calamity, affliction, privation, destitution, ill-fortune, ill-luck, indigence ...*There was little support to help them in their distress...*
VERB = <u>upset</u>, worry, trouble, pain, wound, bother, disturb, dismay, grieve, torment, harass, afflict, harrow, agitate, sadden, perplex, disconcert, agonize, fluster, perturb, faze, throw (someone) off balance ...*I did not want to frighten or distress her...*

distressed **1** = <u>upset</u>, worried, troubled, anxious, distracted, tormented, distraught, afflicted, agitated, saddened, wretched ...*I felt distressed about my problem...*
2 = <u>poverty-stricken</u>, poor, impoverished, needy, destitute, indigent, down at heel, straitened, penurious ...*investment in the nation's distressed areas...*

distressing = <u>upsetting</u>, worrying, disturbing, painful, affecting, sad, afflicting, harrowing, grievous, hurtful, lamentable, heart-breaking, nerve-racking, gut-wrenching, distressful

distribute **1** = <u>hand out</u>, dispense, give out, dish out (*informal*), disseminate, deal out, disburse, pass round ...*Students shouted slogans and distributed leaflets...*
2 = <u>circulate</u>, deliver, convey ...*to distribute a national newspaper...*
3 = <u>share</u>, give, deal, divide, assign, administer, allocate, dispose, dispense, allot, mete out, dole out, apportion, measure out ...*He began to distribute jobs among his friends...*
4 = <u>spread</u>, scatter, disperse, diffuse, disseminate, strew ...*Break the exhibition up and distribute it around existing museums...*

distribution **1** = <u>delivery</u>, mailing, transport, transportation, handling ...*He admitted there had been problems with distribution...*
2 = <u>sharing</u>, division, assignment, rationing, allocation, partition, allotment, dispensation, apportionment ...*a more equitable distribution of wealth...*
3 = <u>spreading</u>, circulation, diffusion, scattering, propagation, dissemination, dispersal, dispersion ...*There will be a widespread distribution of leaflets...*
4 = <u>spread</u>, organization, arrangement, location, placement, disposition ...*those who control the distribution of jobs...*

district = <u>area</u>, community, region, sector, quarter, ward, parish, neighbourhood, vicinity, locality, locale, neck of the woods (*informal*)

distrust VERB = <u>suspect</u>, doubt, discredit, be wary of, wonder about, mistrust, disbelieve, be suspicious of, be sceptical of, misbelieve ...*I don't have any reason to distrust them...* OPPOSITE trust
NOUN = <u>suspicion</u>, question, doubt, disbelief, scepticism, mistrust, misgiving, qualm, wariness, lack of faith, dubiety ...*an atmosphere of distrust...*
OPPOSITE trust

distrustful = <u>suspicious</u>, doubting, wary, cynical, doubtful, sceptical, uneasy, dubious, distrusting, disbelieving, leery (*slang*), mistrustful, chary

disturb **1** = <u>interrupt</u>, trouble, bother, startle, plague, disrupt, put out, interfere with, rouse, hassle, inconvenience, pester, intrude on, butt in on ...*I didn't want to disturb you...*
2 = <u>upset</u>, concern, worry, trouble, shake, excite, alarm, confuse, distress, distract, dismay, unsettle, agitate, ruffle, confound, unnerve, vex, fluster, perturb, derange, discompose ...*He had been disturbed by the news of the attack...* OPPOSITE calm
3 = <u>muddle</u>, disorder, mix up, mess up, disorganize, jumble up, disarrange ...*His notes had not been disturbed...*

disturbance **1** = <u>disorder</u>, bother (*informal*), turmoil, riot, upheaval, fray, brawl, uproar, agitation, fracas, commotion, rumpus, tumult, hubbub, shindig (*informal*), ruction (*informal*), ruckus (*informal*), shindy (*informal*) ...*During the disturbance, three men were hurt...*
2 = <u>upset</u>, bother, disorder, confusion, distraction, intrusion, interruption, annoyance, agitation, hindrance, perturbation, derangement ...*The home would cause less disturbance than a school...*
3 = <u>disorder</u>, upset, problem, trouble ...*Poor educational performance is linked to emotional disturbances...*

disturbed **1** (*Psychiatry*) = <u>unbalanced</u>, troubled, disordered, unstable, neurotic, upset, deranged, unsound, maladjusted ...*The murderer was apparently mentally disturbed...* OPPOSITE balanced
2 = <u>worried</u>, concerned, troubled, upset, bothered, nervous, anxious, uneasy, agitated, disquieted, apprehensive, antsy (*informal*), angsty (*informal*) ...*I was disturbed to find that the dog was dead...*
OPPOSITE calm

disturbing = <u>worrying</u>, troubling, upsetting, alarming, frightening, distressing, startling, discouraging, dismaying, unsettling, harrowing, agitating, disconcerting, disquieting, perturbing

disunity = <u>disagreement</u>, split, breach, dissent, rupture, alienation, variance, discord, schism, estrangement, dissension, discordance

ditch NOUN = <u>channel</u>, drain, trench, dyke, furrow, gully, moat, watercourse ...*The car went out of control and ended up in a ditch...*
VERB **1** (*Slang*) = <u>get rid of</u>, dump (*informal*), scrap, bin (*informal*), junk (*informal*), chuck (*informal*), discard, dispose of, dispense with, jettison, cast off, throw out or overboard ...*I decided to ditch the sofa bed...*
2 (*Slang*) = <u>leave</u>, drop, abandon, dump (*informal*), axe (*informal*), get rid of, bin (*informal*), chuck (*informal*), forsake, jilt ...*I can't bring myself to ditch*

him…

dither (*Chiefly Brit.*) **VERB** = vacillate, hesitate, waver, haver, falter, hum and haw, faff about (*Brit. informal*), shillyshally (*informal*), swither (*Scot.*) …*We're still dithering over whether to get married…* **OPPOSITE** decide
NOUN = flutter, flap (*informal*), fluster, bother, stew (*informal*), twitter (*informal*), tizzy (*informal*), pother, tiz-woz (*informal*) …*I am in such a dither I forget to put the water in…*

diva = singer, opera singer, prima donna

dive **VERB** 1 = plunge, drop, jump, pitch, leap, duck, dip, descend, plummet …*He tried to escape by diving into a river…*
2 = go underwater, submerge …*They are diving to collect marine organisms…*
3 = nose-dive, fall, plunge, crash, pitch, swoop, plummet …*His monoplane stalled and dived into the ground…*
NOUN 1 = plunge, spring, jump, leap, dash, header (*informal*), swoop, lunge, nose dive …*He made a sudden dive for his legs…*
2 (*Slang*) = sleazy bar, joint (*slang*), honky-tonk (*U.S. slang*) …*We've played in all the dives about here…*

diverge 1 = separate, part, split, branch, divide, fork, divaricate …*The aims of the partners began to diverge…*
2 = conflict, differ, disagree, dissent, be at odds, be at variance …*Theory and practice sometimes diverged…*
3 = deviate, depart, stray, wander, meander, turn aside …*a course that diverged from the coastline…*
4 = digress, stray, deviate, digress, ramble, get sidetracked, go off at a tangent, get off the point …*The manuscripts diverged from the original…*

divergence = difference, varying, departure, disparity, deviation, separation

divergent = different, conflicting, differing, disagreeing, diverse, separate, varying, variant, diverging, dissimilar, deviating

---

Word Power

divergent – Some people dislike the use of *divergent* in this sense, preferring synonyms such as *different* or *differing*.

---

diverse 1 = various, mixed, varied, diversified, assorted, miscellaneous, several, sundry, motley, manifold, heterogeneous, of every description …*shops selling a diverse range of gifts…*
2 = different, contrasting, unlike, varying, differing, separate, distinct, disparate, discrete, dissimilar, divergent, discrepant …*Their attitudes were refreshingly diverse…*

diversify = vary, change, expand, transform, alter, spread out, branch out

diversion 1 = distraction, deviation, deflection, digression …*The whole argument is a diversion…*
2 = pastime, play, game, sport, delight, pleasure, entertainment, hobby, relaxation, recreation, enjoyment, distraction, amusement, gratification,

divertissement, beguilement …*Finger-painting is an excellent diversion…*
3 (*Chiefly Brit.*) = detour, deviation, circuitous route, roundabout way, indirect course …*They turned back because of traffic diversions…*
4 (*Chiefly Brit.*) = deviation, change, departure, variation, straying, divergence, digression …*a diversion from his fantasy-themed movies…*

diversity 1 = difference, diversification, variety, divergence, multiplicity, heterogeneity, variegation, diverseness …*the cultural diversity of British society…*
2 = range, variety, sweep, scope, field, sphere, compass, assortment, medley, amplitude, ambit …*as great a diversity of genetic material as possible…*

divert 1 = redirect, switch, avert, deflect, deviate, sidetrack, turn aside …*A new bypass will divert traffic from the A13…*
2 = distract, shift, deflect, detract, sidetrack, lead astray, draw *or* lead away from …*They want to divert the attention of the people from the real issues…*
3 = entertain, delight, amuse, please, charm, gratify, beguile, regale …*diverting her with jokes and fiery arguments…*

diverting = entertaining, amusing, enjoyable, fun, pleasant, humorous, beguiling

divest 1 = deprive, strip, dispossess, despoil …*They were divested of all their personal possessions…*
2 = strip, remove, take off, undress, denude, disrobe, unclothe …*the formalities of divesting her of her coat…*

divide **VERB** 1 = separate, part, split, cut (up), sever, shear, segregate, cleave, subdivide, bisect, sunder …*the artificial line that divided the city…* **OPPOSITE** join
2 *sometimes with* **up** = share, distribute, allocate, portion, dispense, allot, mete, dole out, apportion, deal out, measure out, divvy (up) (*informal*) …*Divide the soup among four bowls…*
3 = split, break up, alienate, embroil, come between, disunite, estrange, sow dissension, cause to disagree, set at variance *or* odds, set *or* pit against one another …*She has done more to divide the group than anyone else…*
PHRASES **divide something up** = group, sort, separate, arrange, grade, classify, categorize …*The idea is to divide up the country into four sectors…*

dividend = bonus, share, cut (*informal*), gain, extra, plus, portion, divvy (*informal*)

divination = prediction, divining, prophecy, presage, foretelling, clairvoyance, fortune-telling, prognostication, augury, soothsaying, sortilege

divine **ADJECTIVE** 1 = heavenly, spiritual, holy, immortal, supernatural, celestial, angelic, superhuman, godlike, cherubic, seraphic, supernal (*literary*), paradisaical …*a gift from divine beings…*
2 = sacred, religious, holy, spiritual, blessed, revered, venerable, hallowed, consecrated, sanctified …*the message of the Divine Book…*
3 (*Informal*) = wonderful, perfect, beautiful, excellent, lovely, stunning (*informal*), glorious, marvellous,

splendid, gorgeous, delightful, exquisite, radiant, superlative, ravishing ...*You look simply divine*...
NOUN = priest, minister, vicar, reverend, pastor, cleric, clergyman, curate, churchman, padre (*informal*), holy man, man of God, man of the cloth, ecclesiastic, father confessor ...*He had the air of a divine*...
VERB 1 = guess, understand, suppose, suspect, perceive, discern, infer, deduce, apprehend, conjecture, surmise, foretell, intuit, prognosticate ...*He had tried to divine her intentions*...
2 = dowse (for water or minerals) ...*I was divining for water*...

divinity 1 = theology, religion, religious studies ...*He entered university to study arts and divinity*...
2 = godliness, holiness, sanctity, godhead, divine nature, godhood ...*a lasting faith in the divinity of Christ's word*...
3 = deity, spirit, genius, guardian spirit, daemon, god or goddess ...*The three statues are Roman divinities*...

division 1 = separation, dividing, splitting up, detaching, partition, cutting up, bisection ...*a division into two independent factions*...
2 = sharing, sharing, distribution, assignment, rationing, allocation, allotment, apportionment ...*the division of labour between workers and management*...
3 = disagreement, split, breach, feud, rift, rupture, abyss, chasm, variance, discord, difference of opinion, estrangement, disunion ...*the division between the prosperous west and the impoverished east*... **OPPOSITE** unity
4 = dividing line, border, boundary, divide, partition, demarcation, divider ...*the division between North and South Korea*...
5 = department, group, head, sector, branch, subdivision ...*the sales division*...
6 = part, bit, piece, section, sector, class, category, segment, portion, fraction, compartment ...*Each was divided into several divisions*...

divisive = disruptive, unsettling, alienating, troublesome, controversial, contentious

divorce **NOUN** 1 = separation, split, break-up, parting, split-up, rift, dissolution, severance, estrangement, annulment, decree nisi, disunion ...*Numerous marriages now end in divorce*...
2 = breach, break, split, falling-out (*informal*), disagreement, feud, rift, bust-up (*informal*), rupture, abyss, chasm, schism, estrangement ...*a divorce between the government and trade unions*...
VERB 1 = separate, split up, part company, annul your marriage, dissolve your marriage ...*My parents divorced when I was young*...
2 = separate, divide, isolate, detach, distance, sever, disconnect, dissociate, set apart, disunite, sunder ...*We have been able to divorce sex from reproduction*...

divulge = make known, tell, reveal, publish, declare, expose, leak, confess, exhibit, communicate, spill (*informal*), disclose, proclaim, betray, uncover, impart, promulgate, let slip, blow wide open (*slang*), get off your chest (*informal*), cough (*slang*), out (*informal*),

spill your guts about (*slang*) **OPPOSITE** keep secret

dizzy 1 = giddy, faint, light-headed, swimming, reeling, staggering, shaky, wobbly, off balance, unsteady, vertiginous, woozy (*informal*), weak at the knees ...*She felt slightly dizzy*...
2 = confused, dazzled, at sea, bewildered, muddled, bemused, dazed, disorientated, befuddled, light-headed, punch-drunk, fuddled ...*Her wonderful dark good looks and wit made me dizzy*...
3 (*Informal*) = scatterbrained, silly, foolish, frivolous, giddy, capricious, forgetful, flighty, light-headed, scatty (*Brit. informal*), empty-headed, bird-brained (*informal*), featherbrained, ditzy *or* ditsy (*slang*) ...*a charmingly dizzy grandmother*...
4 = steep, towering, soaring, lofty, sky-high, vertiginous ...*I escalated to the dizzy heights*...

do **VERB** 1 = perform, work, achieve, carry out, produce, effect, complete, conclude, undertake, accomplish, execute, discharge, pull off, transact ...*I was trying to do some work*...
2 = behave, act, conduct yourself, deport yourself, bear yourself, acquit yourself ...*I go where I will and I do as I please*...
3 = make, prepare, fix, arrange, look after, organize, be responsible for, see to, get ready, make ready ...*I'll do the dinner, you can help*...
4 = solve, work out, resolve, figure out, decode, decipher, puzzle out ...*I could have done the crossword*...
5 = get on, manage, fare, proceed, make out, prosper, get along ...*She did well at school*...
6 = present, give, show, act, produce, stage, perform, mount, put on ...*I've always wanted to do a show on his life*...
7 = be adequate, be enough, be sufficient, answer, serve, suit, content, satisfy, suffice, be of use, pass muster, cut the mustard, fill the bill (*informal*), meet requirements ...*A plain old 'I love you' won't do*...
8 (*Informal*) = cheat, trick, con (*informal*), skin (*slang*), stiff (*slang*), deceive, fleece, hoax, defraud, dupe, swindle, diddle (*informal*), take (someone) for a ride (*informal*), pull a fast one on (*informal*), cozen ...*I'll tell you how they did me*...
9 = produce, make, create, develop, turn out, manufacture, construct, invent, put together, originate, fabricate ...*The company have done a range of tops*...
10 (*Informal*) = visit, tour in *or* around, look at, cover, explore, take in (*informal*), stop in, journey through *or* around, travel in *or* around ...*Families doing Europe can hire one of these motor-homes*...
NOUN (*Informal, chiefly Brit. & N.Z.*) = party, gathering, function, social, event, affair, at-home, occasion, celebration, reception, bash (*informal*), rave (*Brit. slang*), get-together (*informal*), festivity, knees-up (*Brit. informal*), beano (*Brit. slang*), social gathering, shindig (*informal*), soirée, rave-up (*Brit. slang*), hooley *or* hoolie (*chiefly Irish & N.Z.*) ...*They always have all-night dos there*...

PHRASES **do away with someone** = kill, murder, do in (*slang*), destroy, take out (*slang*), dispatch, slay, blow away (*slang, chiefly U.S.*), knock off (*slang*), liquidate, exterminate, take (someone's) life, bump off (*slang*) ...*He tried to do away with her...* ♦ **do away with something** = get rid of, remove, eliminate, axe (*informal*), abolish, junk (*informal*), pull, chuck (*informal*), discard, put an end to, dispense with, discontinue, put paid to, pull the plug on ...*They must do away with nuclear weapons altogether...* ♦ **do for something** or **someone** (*Informal*) = destroy, kill, finish (off), defeat, ruin, shatter, undo, slay, annihilate ...*They did for him in the end...* ♦ **do someone in** (*Slang*) **1** = kill, murder, destroy, eliminate (*slang*), take out (*slang*), execute, butcher, slaughter, dispatch, assassinate, slay, do away with, blow away (*slang, chiefly U.S.*), knock off (*slang*), liquidate, annihilate, neutralize, take (someone's) life, bump off (*slang*) ...*Whoever did him in removed a brave man...* **2** = exhaust, tire, drain, shatter (*informal*), weaken, fatigue, weary, fag (*informal*), sap, wear out, tire out, knacker (*slang*) ...*The Christmas thing kind of did me in...* ♦ **do without something** or **someone** = manage without, give up, dispense with, forgo, kick (*informal*), sacrifice, abstain from, get along without ...*This is something we cannot do without...* ♦ **do's and don'ts** (*Informal*) = rules, code, regulations, standards, instructions, customs, convention, usage, protocol, formalities, etiquette, p's and q's, good or proper behaviour ...*Please advise me on the do's and dont's...*

docile = obedient, manageable, compliant, amenable, submissive, pliant, tractable, biddable, ductile, teachable (*rare*) OPPOSITE> difficult

dock¹ NOUN = port, haven, harbour, pier, wharf, quay, waterfront, anchorage ...*He brought his boat right into the dock at Southampton...*
VERB **1** = moor, land, anchor, put in, tie up, berth, drop anchor ...*The vessel is about to dock in Singapore...*
2 (*of spacecraft*) = link up, unite, join, couple, rendezvous, hook up ...*The shuttle is scheduled to dock with the space station...*

dock² **1** = cut, reduce, decrease, diminish, lessen ...*He threatened to dock her fee...* OPPOSITE> increase
2 = deduct, subtract ...*He had a point docked for insulting his opponent...*
3 = cut off, crop, clip, shorten, curtail, cut short ...*It is an offence for an unqualified person to dock a dog's tail...*

docket NOUN = label, bill, ticket, certificate, tag, voucher, tab, receipt, tally, chit, chitty, counterfoil ...*The clerk asked me to sign the docket...*
VERB = file, index, register ...*The Court has 1,400 appeals on its docket...*

doctor NOUN = physician, medic (*informal*), general practitioner, medical practitioner, G.P. ...*Do not stop the treatment without consulting your doctor...*
VERB **1** = change, alter, interfere with, disguise, pervert, fudge, tamper with, tinker with, misrepresent, falsify, meddle with, mess about with ...*They doctored the photograph...*
2 = add to, spike, cut, mix something with something,

dilute, water down, adulterate ...*He had doctored her milk...*

doctrinaire **1** = dogmatic, rigid, fanatical, inflexible ...*forty-five years of doctrinaire Stalinism...*
2 = impractical, theoretical, speculative, ideological, unrealistic, hypothetical, unpragmatic ...*It is a doctrinaire scheme...*

doctrine = teaching, principle, belief, opinion, article, concept, conviction, canon, creed, dogma, tenet, precept, article of faith

document NOUN = paper, form, certificate, report, record, testimonial, authorization, legal form ...*The foreign minister signed the document today...*
VERB = support, back up, certify, verify, detail, instance, validate, substantiate, corroborate, authenticate, give weight to, particularize ...*The effects of smoking have been well documented...*

doddle (*Brit. informal*) = piece of cake, picnic (*informal*), child's play (*informal*), pushover (*slang*) (*informal*), no sweat (*slang*), cinch (*slang*), cakewalk (*informal*), money for old rope, bludge (*Austral. & N.Z. informal*)

dodge VERB **1** = duck, dart, swerve, sidestep, shoot, shift, turn aside, body-swerve (*Scot.*) ...*We dodged behind a pillar...*
2 = evade, avoid, escape, get away from, elude, body-swerve (*Scot.*), slip through the net of ...*Thieves dodged the security system in the shop...*
3 = avoid, hedge, parry, get out of, evade, shirk ...*He has repeatedly dodged the question...*
NOUN = trick, scheme, ploy, trap, device, fraud, con (*slang*), manoeuvre, deception, scam (*slang*), gimmick, hoax, wheeze (*Brit. slang*), deceit, ruse, artifice, subterfuge, canard, feint, stratagem, contrivance, machination ...*It was probably just a dodge to stop you going away...*

dodgy **1** (*Brit., Austral., & N.Z*) = nasty, offensive, unpleasant, revolting, distasteful, repellent, unsavoury, obnoxious, repulsive, objectionable, repugnant ...*He was a bit of a dodgy character...*
2 (*Brit., Austral., & N.Z.*) = risky, difficult, tricky, dangerous, delicate, uncertain, problematic(al), unreliable, dicky (*Brit. informal*), dicey (*informal, chiefly Brit.*), ticklish, chancy (*informal*) ...*Predicting voting trends is a dodgy business...*
3 = second rate, poor, inferior, mediocre, shoddy, low-grade, low-quality, substandard, for the birds (*informal*), pants (*slang*), end-of-the-pier (*Brit. informal*), rubbishy, bush-league (*Austral. & N.Z. informal*), half-pie (*N.Z. informal*), bodger or bodgie (*Austral. slang*) ...*cheap hotels and dodgy food...*

doer = achiever, organizer, powerhouse (*slang*), dynamo, live wire (*slang*), go-getter (*informal*), active person, wheeler-dealer (*informal*)

doff **1** = tip, raise, remove, lift, take off ...*The peasants doffed their hats...*
2 = take off, remove, shed, discard, throw off, cast off, slip out of, slip off ...*He doffed his shirt and jeans...*

dog NOUN **1** = hound, canine, bitch, puppy, pup, mongrel, tyke, mutt (*slang*), pooch (*slang*), cur, man's

best friend, kuri *or* goorie (*N.Z.*), brak (*S. African*)
...*Outside a dog was barking*...
2 (*Informal*) = scoundrel, villain, cur, heel (*slang*),
knave (*archaic*), blackguard ...*Out of my sight, you
dog!*...
VERB 1 = plague, follow, trouble, haunt, hound,
torment, afflict ...*His career has been dogged by bad
luck*...
2 = pursue, follow, track, chase, shadow, harry, tail
(*informal*), trail, hound, stalk, go after, give chase to
...*The three creatures had dogged him from hut to
hut*...
PHRASES dog-eat-dog = ruthless, fierce, vicious,
ferocious, cut-throat, with no holds barred ...*TV is a
dog-eat-dog business*... ◆ **go to the dogs**
(*Informal*) = deteriorate, degenerate, be in decline, go
downhill (*informal*), go down the drain, go to pot, go
to ruin ...*The country is going to the dogs*...

(**Related Words**)

adjective : canine
female : bitch
young : pup, puppy

> **breeds of dog**

dogged = determined, steady, persistent, stubborn,
firm, staunch, persevering, resolute, single-minded,
tenacious, steadfast, unyielding, obstinate,
indefatigable, immovable, stiff-necked, unshakable,
unflagging, pertinacious **OPPOSITE** irresolute

dogma = doctrine, teachings, principle, opinion,
article, belief, creed, tenet, precept, credo, article of
faith

dogmatic 1 = opinionated, arrogant, assertive,
arbitrary, emphatic, downright, dictatorial, imperious,
overbearing, categorical, magisterial, doctrinaire,
obdurate, peremptory ...*His dogmatic style deflects
opposition*...
2 = doctrinal, authoritative, categorical, canonical,
oracular, ex cathedra ...*Dogmatic socialism does not
offer a magic formula*...

doing NOUN 1 = carrying out *or* through,
performance, execution, implementation ...*Nothing
deflates impossibility like the doing of it*...
2 = handiwork, act, action, achievement, exploit, deed
...*It was all her doing*...

Breeds of dog http://www.dog-breeds.co.uk/

affenpinscher	bull terrier	Italian greyhound	Rhodesian ridgeback
Afghan hound	cairn terrier *or* cairn	Jack Russell (terrier)	Rottweiler
Airedale terrier	chihuahua	Japanese spaniel	rough collie
Akita	chow-chow *or* chow	Japanese tosa	Saint Bernard *or* St.
Alaskan malamute	clumber spaniel	keeshond	Bernard
Alpine spaniel	cocker spaniel	kelpie	Saluki *or* Persian
Alsatian *or* German	collie	Kerry blue terrier	greyhound
shepherd	corgi *or* Welsh corgi	King Charles spaniel	Samoyed
Australian cattle dog,	Cuban bloodhound	komondor	schipperke
blue cattle dog, *or*	dachshund	Labrador retriever,	schnauzer
(Queensland) blue	Dalmatian *or* (*formerly*)	Labrador, *or* lab	Scottish, Scotch, *or*
heeler	carriage dog *or* coach	Lakeland terrier	(*formerly*) Aberdeen
Australian terrier	dog	Lhasa apso	terrier *or* Scottie
Australian silky terrier	Dandie Dinmont	malamute *or* malemute	Sealyham terrier
or Sydney silky	(terrier)	Maltese	setter
barb	deerhound	Manchester terrier *or*	Shetland sheepdog *or*
basenji	Doberman pinscher *or*	black-and-tan terrier	sheltie
basset hound	Doberman	mastiff	shih-tzu
beagle	Egyptian basset	Mexican hairless	Skye terrier
bearded collie	elkhound *or* Norwegian	Newfoundland	spaniel
Bedlington terrier	elkhound	Norfolk springer spaniel	spitz
Belvoir hound	English setter	Norfolk terrier	springer spaniel
Bichon Frise	Eskimo dog	Norwich terrier	Staffordshire bull terrier
Blenheim spaniel	field spaniel	Old English sheepdog	staghound
bloodhound,	foxhound	otterhound	Sussex spaniel
sleuthhound, *or* sleuth	fox terrier	papillon	talbot
blue Gascon hound	French bulldog	Pekingese	terrier
Border collie	golden retriever	pit bull terrier *or*	vizsla
Border terrier	Gordon setter	American pit bull	water spaniel
borzoi *or* Russian	Great Dane	terrier	Weimaraner
wolfhound	greyhound	pointer	Welsh terrier
Boston terrier *or* bull	griffon	Pomeranian	West Highland white
terrier	harrier	poodle	terrier
bouvier	Highland terrier	pug	whippet
boxer	husky	puli	wire-haired terrier
briard	Irish setter *or* red setter	Pyrenean mountain dog	wolfhound
Bruxellois	Irish terrier	raccoon dog *or*	Yorkshire terrier
bulldog	Irish water spaniel	coonhound	
bull mastiff	Irish wolfhound	retriever	

PLURAL NOUN = <u>deeds</u>, actions, exploits, concerns, events, affairs, happenings, proceedings, transactions, dealings, goings-on (*informal*) ...*the everyday doings of a group of schoolchildren*...

doldrums
PHRASES **the doldrums** = <u>blues</u>, depression, dumps (*informal*), gloom, boredom, apathy, inertia, stagnation, inactivity, tedium, dullness, the hump (*Brit. informal*), ennui, torpor, lassitude, listlessness

dole NOUN = <u>share</u>, grant, gift, allowance, portion, donation, quota, parcel, handout, modicum, pittance, alms, gratuity ...*They hold out fragile arms for a dole of food*...
PHRASES **dole something out** = <u>give out</u>, share, deal out, distribute, divide, assign, administer, allocate, hand out, dispense, allot, mete, apportion ...*I began to dole out the money*...

dollop = <u>lump</u>, blob, helping, serving, portion, scoop, gob

dolphin
(*Related Words*)
collective noun: school
➤ **whales and dolphins**

domain 1 = <u>area</u>, field, department, discipline, sphere, realm, speciality ...*the great experimenters in the domain of art*...
2 = <u>sphere</u>, area, field, concern, scene, sector, territory, province, realm ...*This sort of information should be in the public domain*...
3 = <u>kingdom</u>, lands, region, territory, estate, province, empire, realm, dominion, demesne, policies (*Scot.*) ...*the mighty king's domain*...
4 (*N.Z.*) = <u>public park</u>, park, recreation ground, garden, pleasure garden ...*The domain includes a Victorian gazebo and riverside grotto*...

domestic ADJECTIVE 1 = <u>home</u>, internal, native, indigenous, not foreign ...*sales in the domestic market*...
2 = <u>household</u>, home, family, private, domiciliary ...*a plan for sharing domestic chores*...
3 = <u>home-loving</u>, homely, housewifely, stay-at-home, domesticated ...*She was kind and domestic*...
4 = <u>domesticated</u>, trained, tame, house, pet, house-trained ...*a domestic cat*...
NOUN = <u>servant</u>, help, maid, woman (*informal*), daily, char (*informal*), charwoman, daily help ...*She worked for 10 or 15 years as a domestic*...

domesticate 1 = <u>tame</u>, break, train, house-train, gentle ...*We domesticated the dog*...
2 = <u>naturalize</u>, accustom, familiarize, habituate, acclimatize ...*New World peoples domesticated a cornucopia of plants*...

domesticated 1 = <u>tame</u>, broken (in), tamed ...*our domesticated animals and plants*... OPPOSITE wild
2 = <u>home-loving</u>, homely, domestic, housewifely, house-trained (*jocular*) ...*I have never been very domesticated*...

domesticity = <u>home life</u>, housekeeping, domestication, homemaking, housewifery, home-lovingness

dominance = <u>control</u>, government, power, rule, authority, command, sway, domination, supremacy, mastery, ascendancy, paramountcy

dominant 1 = <u>main</u>, chief, primary, outstanding, principal, prominent, influential, prevailing, paramount, prevalent, predominant, pre-eminent ...*She was a dominant figure in the film industry*...
OPPOSITE minor
2 = <u>controlling</u>, leading, ruling, commanding, supreme, governing, superior, presiding, authoritative, ascendant ...*controlled by the dominant class*...

dominate 1 = <u>prevail over</u>, eclipse, overshadow, cloud, overrule, detract from, outshine ...*countries where war dominates life*...
2 = <u>control</u>, lead, rule, direct, master, govern, monopolize, tyrannize, have the upper hand over, lead by the nose (*informal*), overbear, have the whip hand over, domineer, keep under your thumb ...*He denied that his country wants to dominate Europe*...
3 have the upper hand, rule the roost ...*Usually, one partner dominates*...
4 = <u>tower above</u>, overlook, survey, stand over, loom over, stand head and shoulders above, bestride ...*The building dominates this whole place*...

domination = <u>control</u>, power, rule, authority, influence, command, sway, dictatorship, repression, oppression, suppression, supremacy, mastery, tyranny, ascendancy, subordination, despotism, subjection

domineering = <u>overbearing</u>, arrogant, authoritarian, oppressive, autocratic, masterful, dictatorial, coercive, bossy (*informal*), imperious, tyrannical, magisterial, despotic, high-handed, iron-handed OPPOSITE submissive

dominion 1 = <u>control</u>, government, power, rule, authority, command, sovereignty, sway, domination, jurisdiction, supremacy, mastery, ascendancy, mana (*N.Z.*) ...*They believe they have dominion over us*...
2 = <u>kingdom</u>, territory, province, country, region, empire, patch, turf (*U.S. slang*), realm, domain ...*The Republic is a dominion of the Brazilian people*...

don = <u>put on</u>, get into, dress in, pull on, change into, get dressed in, clothe yourself in, slip on *or* into

donate = <u>give</u>, present, contribute, grant, commit, gift, hand out, subscribe, endow, chip in (*informal*), bestow, entrust, impart, bequeath, make a gift of

donation = <u>contribution</u>, gift, subscription, offering, present, grant, hand-out, boon, alms, stipend, gratuity, benefaction, largesse *or* largess

done ADJECTIVE 1 = <u>finished</u>, completed, accomplished, over, through, ended, perfected, realized, concluded, executed, terminated, consummated, in the can (*informal*) ...*By evening the work is done, and just in time*...
2 = <u>cooked</u>, ready, cooked enough, cooked to a turn, cooked sufficiently ...*When the cake is done, remove it from the oven*...
3 = <u>acceptable</u>, proper, conventional, protocol, de rigueur (*French*) ...*It simply isn't done*...
INTERJECTION = <u>agreed</u>, you're on (*informal*), O.K. *or*

okay (*informal*), it's a bargain, it's a deal ...*'You lead and we'll look for it.' – 'Done.'*...

PHRASES **done for** = finished (*Informal*), lost, beaten, defeated, destroyed, ruined, broken, dashed, wrecked, doomed, foiled, undone ...*I thought we were all done for...* ◆ **done in** or **up** (*Informal*) = exhausted, bushed (*informal*), all in (*slang*), worn out, dead (*informal*), knackered (*slang*), clapped out (*Austral. & N.Z. informal*), tired out, ready to drop, dog-tired (*informal*), zonked (*slang*), dead beat (*informal*), fagged out (*informal*), worn to a frazzle (*informal*), on your last legs, creamcrackered (*Brit. slang*) ...*You must be really done in...* ◆ **have** or **be done with something** or **someone** = be through with, give up, be finished with, throw over, wash your hands of, end relations with ...*Let us have done with him...*

donor = giver, contributor, benefactor, philanthropist, grantor (*Law*), donator, almsgiver **OPPOSITE** recipient

doom **NOUN** 1 = destruction, ruin, catastrophe, death, downfall ...*his warnings of impending doom...*
2 = fate, destiny, fortune, lot ...*They are said to have lured sailors to their doom...*
VERB = condemn, sentence, consign, foreordain, destine, predestine, preordain ...*Some suggest the leisure park is doomed to failure...* = condemn

doomed = hopeless, condemned, ill-fated, fated, unhappy, unfortunate, cursed, unlucky, blighted, hapless, bedevilled, luckless, ill-starred, star-crossed, ill-omened

door **NOUN** = opening, entry, entrance, exit, doorway, ingress, egress ...*I was knocking at the front door...*
PHRASES **out of doors** = in the open air, outside, outdoors, out, alfresco ...*The weather was fine for working out of doors...* ◆ **show someone the door** = throw out, remove, eject, evict, turn out, bounce (*slang*), oust, drive out, boot out (*informal*), ask to leave, show out, throw out on your ear (*informal*) ...*Would they forgive him or show him the door?...*

do-or-die = desperate, risky, hazardous, going for broke, win-or-bust, death-or-glory, kill-or-cure

dope **NOUN** 1 (*Slang*) = drugs, narcotics, opiates, dadah (*Austral. slang*) ...*A man asked them if they wanted to buy some dope...*
2 (*Informal*) = idiot, fool, jerk (*slang, chiefly U.S. & Canad.*), plank (*Brit. slang*), charlie (*Brit. informal*), berk (*Brit. slang*), wally (*slang*), prat (*slang*), plonker (*slang*), coot, geek (*slang*), twit (*informal, chiefly Brit.*), dunce, oaf, simpleton, dimwit (*informal*), dipstick (*Brit. slang*), gonzo (*slang*), schmuck (*U.S. slang*), dork (*slang*), nitwit (*informal*), dolt, blockhead, divvy (*Brit. slang*), pillock (*Brit. slang*), dweeb (*U.S. slang*), putz (*U.S. slang*), fathead (*informal*), eejit (*Scot. & Irish*), dumb-ass (*slang*), numpty (*Scot. informal*), lamebrain (*informal*), nerd or nurd (*slang*), numbskull or numskull, dorba or dorb (*Austral. slang*), bogan (*Austral. slang*) ...*I don't feel I'm such a dope...*
3 (*Informal*) = information, facts, details, material, news, intelligence, gen (*Brit. informal*), info (*informal*), inside information, lowdown (*informal*) ...*They had plenty of dope on him...*

VERB = drug, doctor, knock out, inject, sedate, stupefy, anaesthetize, narcotize ...*I'd been doped with Somnolin...*

dopey or **dopy** 1 = drowsy, dazed, groggy (*informal*), drugged, muzzy, stupefied, half-asleep, woozy (*informal*) ...*The medicine always made him feel dopey...*
2 (*Informal*) = stupid, simple, slow, thick, silly, foolish, dense, dumb (*informal*), senseless, goofy (*informal*), idiotic, dozy (*Brit. informal*), asinine, dumb-ass (*slang*) ...*I was so dopey I believed him...*

dormant = latent, inactive, lurking, quiescent, unrealized, unexpressed, inoperative

dorp (*S. African*) = town, village, settlement, municipality

dose 1 = measure, amount, allowance, portion, prescription, ration, draught, dosage, potion ...*A dose of penicillin can wipe out infection...*
2 = quantity, amount, lot, measure, supply, portion ...*a healthy dose of self-confidence...*

dot **NOUN** = spot, point, mark, circle, atom, dab, mite, fleck, jot, speck, full stop, speckle, mote, iota ...*a small black dot in the middle...*
VERB = spot, stud, fleck, speckle ...*Small coastal towns dotted the area...*
PHRASES **on the dot** = on time, promptly, precisely, exactly (*informal*), to the minute, on the button (*informal*), punctually ...*At nine o'clock on the dot, they arrived...*

dote on or **upon** = adore, prize, treasure, admire, hold dear, idolize, lavish affection on

doting = adoring, devoted, fond, foolish, indulgent, lovesick

dotty (*Slang, chiefly Brit.*) = crazy, touched, peculiar, eccentric, batty (*slang*), off-the-wall (*slang*), potty (*Brit. informal*), oddball (*informal*), loopy (*informal*), crackpot (*informal*), out to lunch (*informal*), outré, doolally (*slang*), off your trolley (*slang*), up the pole (*informal*), wacko or whacko (*slang*), off the air (*Austral. slang*)

double **ADJECTIVE** 1 coupled, doubled, paired, twin, duplicate, in pairs, binate (*Botany*) ...*a pair of double doors into the room...*
2 = deceitful, false, fraudulent, deceiving, treacherous, dishonest, deceptive, hypocritical, counterfeit, two-faced, disingenuous, insincere, double-dealing, duplicitous, perfidious, knavish (*archaic*), Janus-faced ...*a woman who had lived a double life...*
3 = dual, enigmatic, cryptic, twofold, Delphic, enigmatical ...*The book has a double meaning...*
VERB 1 = multiply by two, duplicate, increase twofold, repeat, enlarge, increase twofold, magnify ...*They need to double the number of managers...*
2 = fold up or over ...*He doubled the sheet back upon itself...*
NOUN = twin, lookalike, spitting image, copy, fellow, mate, counterpart, clone, replica, ringer (*slang*), impersonator (*informal*), dead ringer (*slang*), Doppelgänger, duplicate ...*Your mother sees you as her double...*

PHRASES **at** *or* **on the double** = <u>at once</u>, now, immediately, directly, quickly, promptly, right now, straight away, right away, briskly, without delay, pronto (*informal*), at full speed, in double-quick time, this instant, this very minute, pdq (*slang*), posthaste, tout de suite (*French*) …*Come to my office, please, on the double…* ◆ **double as something** or **someone** = <u>function as</u>, serve as …*The military greatcoat doubled as a bedroll…*

double-cross = <u>betray</u>, trick, cheat, mislead, two-time (*informal*), defraud, swindle, hoodwink, sell down the river (*informal*), cozen

doubly = <u>twice as</u>, in two ways, twofold, as much again, in double measure

doubt **NOUN** 1 = <u>uncertainty</u>, confusion, hesitation, dilemma, scepticism, misgiving, suspense, indecision, bewilderment, lack of confidence, hesitancy, perplexity, vacillation, lack of conviction, irresolution, dubiety …*They were troubled and full of doubt…* **OPPOSITE** certainty

2 = <u>suspicion</u>, scepticism, distrust, fear, apprehension, mistrust, misgivings, disquiet, qualms, incredulity, lack of faith …*Where there is doubt, may we bring faith…* **OPPOSITE** belief

VERB 1 = <u>be uncertain</u>, be sceptical, be dubious …*They doubted whether that could happen…*

2 = <u>waver</u>, hesitate, vacillate, sway, fluctuate, dither (*chiefly Brit.*), haver, oscillate, chop and change, blow hot and cold (*informal*), keep changing your mind, shillyshally (*informal*), be irresolute *or* indecisive, swither (*Scot.*) …*Stop doubting and start loving…*

3 = <u>disbelieve</u>, question, suspect, query, distrust, mistrust, lack confidence in, misgive …*I have no reason to doubt his word…* **OPPOSITE** believe

PHRASES **no doubt** = <u>certainly</u>, surely, probably, admittedly, doubtless, assuredly, doubtlessly …*No doubt I'm biased…*

Word Power

doubt – In affirmative sentences, *whether* was in the past the only word considered acceptable for linking the verb *doubt* to a following clause, for example *I doubt whether he will come*. Nowadays, *doubt if* and *doubt that* are both considered acceptable alternatives to *doubt whether*. In negative sentences, use *that* after *doubt*, for example *I don't doubt that he is telling the truth*. The old-fashioned form *not doubt but that*, as in *I do not doubt but that he is telling the truth*, is now rarely used and sounds very stiff and formal.

---

doubter = <u>sceptic</u>, questioner, disbeliever, agnostic, unbeliever, doubting Thomas

doubtful 1 = <u>unlikely</u>, unclear, dubious, unsettled, dodgy (*Brit., Austral., & N.Z. informal*), questionable, ambiguous, improbable, indefinite, unconfirmed, inconclusive, debatable, indeterminate, iffy (*informal*), equivocal, inexact …*It seemed doubtful that he would move at all…* **OPPOSITE** certain

2 = <u>unsure</u>, uncertain, hesitant, suspicious, hesitating,

sceptical, unsettled, tentative, wavering, unresolved, perplexed, undecided, unconvinced, vacillating, leery (*slang*), distrustful, in two minds (*informal*), irresolute …*Why did he sound so doubtful?…* **OPPOSITE** certain

3 = <u>questionable</u>, suspect, suspicious, crooked, dubious, dodgy (*Brit., Austral., & N.Z. informal*), slippery, shady (*informal*), unscrupulous, fishy (*informal*), shifty, disreputable, untrustworthy …*They all seemed of very doubtful character…*

Word Power

doubtful – In the past, *whether* was the only word considered acceptable for linking the adjective *doubtful* in the sense of 'improbable' to a following clause, for example *it is doubtful whether he will come*. Nowadays, however, *doubtful if* and *doubtful that* are also considered acceptable.

---

doubtless = <u>probably</u>, presumably, most likely

doughty (*Old-fashioned*) = <u>intrepid</u>, brave, daring, bold, hardy, heroic, courageous, gritty, fearless, resolute, gallant, valiant, redoubtable, dauntless, valorous, stouthearted

dour = <u>gloomy</u>, forbidding, grim, sour, dismal, dreary, sullen, unfriendly, morose **OPPOSITE** cheery

douse *or* **dowse** 1 = <u>put out</u>, smother, blow out, extinguish, snuff (out) …*The crew began to douse the fire…*

2 = <u>drench</u>, soak, steep, saturate, duck, submerge, immerse, dunk, souse, plunge into water …*They doused him in petrol…*

dovetail = <u>correspond</u>, match, agree, accord, coincide, tally, conform, harmonize

dowdy = <u>frumpy</u>, old-fashioned, shabby, drab, tacky (*U.S. informal*), unfashionable, dingy, frumpish, ill-dressed, frowzy **OPPOSITE** chic

down **ADJECTIVE** = <u>depressed</u>, low, sad, blue, unhappy, discouraged, miserable, fed up, dismal, pessimistic, melancholy, glum, dejected, despondent, dispirited, downcast, morose, disheartened, crestfallen, downhearted, down in the dumps (*informal*), sick as a parrot (*informal*), low-spirited …*The old man sounded really down…*

VERB 1 (*Informal*) = <u>swallow</u>, drink (down), drain, gulp (down), put away, toss off …*We downed several bottles of local wine…*

2 = <u>bring down</u>, fell, knock down, throw, trip, floor, tackle, deck (*slang*), overthrow, prostrate …*A bank guard shot him and downed him…*

down-and-out **ADJECTIVE** = <u>destitute</u>, ruined, impoverished, derelict, penniless, dirt-poor (*informal*), flat broke (*informal*), on your uppers (*informal*), without two pennies to rub together (*informal*) …*He looked unshaven, shabby and down-and-out…*

NOUN = <u>tramp</u>, bum (*informal*), beggar, derelict, outcast, pauper, vagrant, vagabond, bag lady, dosser (*Brit. slang*), derro (*Austral. slang*) …*some poor down-and-out in need of a meal…*

downbeat (*Informal*) 1 = <u>low-key</u>, muted, subdued,

sober, sombre ...*The headlines were suitably downbeat...*
2 = gloomy, negative, depressed, pessimistic, unfavourable ...*They found him in gloomy, downbeat mood...* OPPOSITE cheerful

downcast = dejected, sad, depressed, unhappy, disappointed, discouraged, miserable, dismayed, choked, daunted, dismal, despondent, dispirited, disheartened, disconsolate, crestfallen, down in the dumps (*informal*), cheerless, sick as a parrot (*informal*) OPPOSITE cheerful

downfall = ruin, fall, destruction, collapse, breakdown, disgrace, overthrow, descent, undoing, comeuppance (*slang*), comedown

downgrade 1 = demote, degrade, take down a peg (*informal*), lower *or* reduce in rank ...*His superiors downgraded him...* OPPOSITE promote
2 = run down, denigrate, disparage, detract from, decry ...*He was never one to downgrade his talents...*

downmarket = second-rate, cheap, inferior, tacky (*informal*), shoddy, low-grade, tawdry, low-quality, two-bit (*U.S. & Canad. slang*), cheap and nasty (*informal*), lowbrow, bush-league (*Austral. & N.Z. informal*), bodger *or* bodgie (*Austral. slang*) OPPOSITE first-rate

downpour = rainstorm, flood, deluge, torrential rain, cloudburst, inundation

downright = complete, absolute, utter, total, positive, clear, plain, simple, explicit, outright, blatant, unequivocal, unqualified, out-and-out, categorical, undisguised, thoroughgoing, arrant, deep-dyed (*usually derogatory*)

downside = drawback, disadvantage, snag, problem, trouble, minus (*informal*), flip side, other side of the coin (*informal*), bad *or* weak point OPPOSITE benefit

down-to-earth = sensible, practical, realistic, common-sense, matter-of-fact, sane, no-nonsense, hard-headed, unsentimental, plain-spoken

downtrodden = oppressed, abused, exploited, subservient, subjugated, tyrannized

downward = descending, declining, heading down, earthward

doze VERB = nap, sleep, slumber, nod, kip (*Brit. slang*), snooze (*informal*), catnap, drowse, sleep lightly, zizz (*Brit. informal*) ...*For a while she dozed fitfully...*
NOUN = nap, kip (*Brit. slang*), snooze (*informal*), siesta, little sleep, catnap, forty winks (*informal*), shuteye (*slang*), zizz (*Brit. informal*) ...*After lunch I had a doze...*

dozy 1 = drowsy, sleepy, dozing, nodding, half asleep ...*Eating too much makes me dozy...*
2 (*Brit. informal*) = stupid, simple, slow, silly, daft (*informal*), senseless, goofy (*informal*), witless, not all there, slow-witted ...*He called me a dozy cow...*

drab = dull, grey, gloomy, dismal, dreary, shabby, sombre, lacklustre, flat, dingy, colourless, uninspired, vapid, cheerless OPPOSITE bright

draconian *sometimes cap.* = severe, hard, harsh, stern, drastic, stringent, punitive, austere, pitiless

draft NOUN **1** = outline, plan, sketch, version, rough, abstract, delineation, preliminary form ...*I rewrote his first draft...*
2 = money order, bill (of exchange), cheque, postal order ...*The money was payable by a draft...*
VERB = outline, write, plan, produce, create, design, draw, frame, compose, devise, sketch, draw up, formulate, contrive, delineate ...*He drafted a standard letter...*

drag VERB **1** = pull, draw, haul, trail, tow, tug, jerk, yank, hale, lug ...*He got up and dragged his chair towards the table...*
2 = lag, trail, linger, loiter, straggle, dawdle, hang back, tarry, draggle ...*I was dragging behind...*
3 = go slowly, inch, creep, crawl, advance slowly ...*The minutes dragged past...*
NOUN (*Slang*) = nuisance, pain (*informal*), bore, bother, pest, hassle (*informal*), inconvenience, annoyance, pain in the neck, pain in the backside, pain in the butt (*informal*) ...*Shopping for clothes is a drag...*
PHRASES **drag on** = last, continue, carry on, remain, endure, persist, linger, abide ...*The conflict has dragged on for two years...* ◆ **drag yourself** = go slowly, creep, crawl, inch, shuffle, shamble, limp along, move at a snail's pace, advance slowly ...*I managed to drag myself to the surgery...*

dragoon = force, drive, compel, bully, intimidate, railroad (*informal*), constrain, coerce, impel, strong-arm (*informal*), browbeat

drain VERB **1** = remove, draw, empty, withdraw, milk, tap, pump, bleed, evacuate ...*machines to drain water out of the mines...*
2 = empty ...*I didn't know what we would find when we drained the pool...*
3 = flow out, leak, discharge, trickle, ooze, seep, exude, well out, effuse ...*The water drained away...*
4 = drink up, swallow, finish, put away, quaff, gulp down ...*She drained the contents of her glass and refilled it...*
5 = exhaust, tire, wear out, strain, weaken, fatigue, weary, debilitate, prostrate, tax, tire out, enfeeble, enervate ...*My emotional turmoil has drained me...*
6 = consume, waste, exhaust, empty, deplete, use up, sap, dissipate, swallow up ...*Deficits drain resources from the pool of national savings...*
NOUN **1** = sewer, channel, pipe, sink, outlet, ditch, trench, conduit, duct, culvert, watercourse ...*He built his own house and laid his own drains...*
2 = reduction, strain, drag, expenditure, exhaustion, sapping, depletion ...*This has been a big drain on resources...*
PHRASES **down the drain** = gone, lost, wasted, ruined, gone for good ...*His public image is down the drain...*

drainage = sewerage, waste, sewage, seepage

dram = measure, shot (*informal*), drop, glass, tot, slug, snort (*slang*), snifter (*informal*)

drama 1 = play, show, stage show, stage play, dramatization, theatrical piece ...*He acted in radio dramas...*

2 = <u>theatre</u>, acting, dramatic art, stagecraft, dramaturgy, Thespian art ...*He knew nothing of Greek drama...*

3 = <u>excitement</u>, crisis, dramatics, spectacle, turmoil, histrionics, theatrics ...*the drama of a hostage release...*

➤ **WORD POWER SUPPLEMENT drama**

dramatic 1 = <u>exciting</u>, emotional, thrilling, tense, startling, sensational, breathtaking, electrifying, melodramatic, climactic, high-octane (*informal*), shock-horror (*facetious*), suspenseful ...*He witnessed many dramatic escapes...*

2 = <u>theatrical</u>, Thespian, dramaturgical, dramaturgic ...*a dramatic arts major in college...*

3 = <u>expressive</u> ...*She lifted her hands in a dramatic gesture...*

4 = <u>powerful</u>, striking, stunning (*informal*), impressive, effective, vivid, jaw-dropping ...*the film's dramatic special effects...* <u>OPPOSITE</u> ordinary

dramatist = <u>playwright</u>, screenwriter, scriptwriter, dramaturge

dramatize = <u>exaggerate</u>, overdo, overstate, lay it on (thick) (*slang*), play-act, play to the gallery, make a performance of

drape 1 = <u>cover</u>, wrap, fold, array, adorn, swathe ...*He draped himself in the flag...*

2 = <u>hang</u>, drop, dangle, suspend, lean, droop, let fall ...*She draped her arm over the back of the couch...*

drastic = <u>extreme</u>, strong, radical, desperate, severe, harsh, dire, forceful

draught 1 = <u>breeze</u>, current, movement, flow, puff, influx, gust, current of air ...*Block draughts around doors and windows...*

2 = <u>drink</u> ...*He took a draught of beer...*

draw <u>VERB</u> **1** = <u>sketch</u>, design, outline, trace, portray, paint, depict, mark out, map out, delineate ...*Draw a rough design for a logo...*

2 = <u>pull</u>, drag, haul, tow, tug ...*He drew his chair nearer the fire...*

3 = <u>inhale</u>, breathe in, pull, inspire, suck, respire ...*He paused, drawing a deep breath...*

4 = <u>extract</u>, take, remove, drain ...*They still have to draw their water from wells...*

5 = <u>choose</u>, pick, select, take, single out ...*We drew the winning name...*

6 = <u>deduce</u>, make, get, take, derive, infer ...*He draws two conclusions from this...*

7 = <u>attract</u>, engage ...*He wanted to draw attention to their plight...*

8 = <u>entice</u>, bring in ...*The game is currently drawing huge crowds...*

<u>NOUN</u> **1** = <u>tie</u>, deadlock, stalemate, impasse, dead heat ...*The game ended in a draw...*

2 (*Informal*) = <u>appeal</u>, interest, pull (*informal*), charm, attraction, lure, temptation, fascination, attractiveness, allure, magnetism, enchantment, enticement, captivation, temptingness ...*The draw of India lies in its beauty...*

<u>PHRASES</u> **draw back** = <u>recoil</u>, withdraw, retreat, shrink, falter, back off, shy away, flinch, retract, quail,

start back ...*I drew back with a horrified scream...*

◆ **draw on** *or* **upon something** = <u>make use of</u>, use, employ, rely on, exploit, extract, take from, fall back on, have recourse to ...*He drew on his experience as a yachtsman...* ◆ **draw something out** = <u>stretch out</u>, extend, lengthen, elongate, attenuate ...*She drew the speech out interminably...* ◆ **draw something up** = <u>draft</u>, write, produce, create, prepare, frame, compose, formulate, contrive ...*They drew up a formal agreement...* ◆ **draw up** = <u>halt</u>, stop, pull up, stop short, come to a stop ...*A police car drew up at the gate...*

drawback = <u>disadvantage</u>, trouble, difficulty, fault, handicap, obstacle, defect, deficiency, flaw, hitch, nuisance, snag, downside, stumbling block, impediment, detriment, imperfection, hindrance, fly in the ointment (*informal*) <u>OPPOSITE</u> advantage

drawing = <u>picture</u>, illustration, representation, cartoon, sketch, portrayal, depiction, study, outline, delineation

drawl = <u>draw out</u>, extend, prolong, lengthen, drag out, protract

drawn = <u>tense</u>, worn, strained, stressed, tired, pinched, fatigued, harassed, fraught, sapped, harrowed, haggard

dread <u>VERB</u> = <u>fear</u>, shrink from, cringe at the thought of, quail from, shudder to think about, have cold feet about (*informal*), anticipate with horror, tremble to think about ...*I'm dreading Christmas this year...*

<u>NOUN</u> = <u>fear</u>, alarm, horror, terror, dismay, fright, apprehension, consternation, trepidation, apprehensiveness, affright ...*She thought with dread of the cold winters to come...*

<u>ADJECTIVE</u> (*Literary*) = <u>frightening</u>, terrible, alarming, awful, terrifying, horrible, dreadful, dreaded, dire, frightful ...*the dread phrase 'politically correct'...*

dreadful 1 = <u>terrible</u>, shocking, awful, alarming, distressing, appalling, tragic, horrible, formidable, fearful, dire, horrendous, hideous, monstrous, from hell (*informal*), grievous, atrocious, frightful, godawful (*slang*), hellacious (*U.S. slang*) ...*They told us the dreadful news...*

2 = <u>serious</u>, terrible, awful, appalling, horrendous, monstrous, unspeakable, abysmal ...*We've made a dreadful mistake...*

3 = <u>awful</u>, terrible, ghastly, grim, horrendous, frightful, godawful (*slang*), like death warmed up (*informal*) ...*I feel absolutely dreadful...*

dreadfully 1 = <u>extremely</u>, very, terribly, greatly, badly, deeply, very much, desperately, exceptionally, immensely, tremendously, awfully (*informal*), exceedingly, excessively ...*He looks dreadfully ill...*

2 = <u>terribly</u>, badly, horribly, awfully, alarmingly, woefully, appallingly, wickedly, shockingly, frightfully, disgracefully, horrendously, monstrously, wretchedly, abysmally, unforgivably, reprehensibly, disreputably ...*She has behaved dreadfully...*

dream <u>NOUN</u> **1** = <u>vision</u>, illusion, delusion, hallucination, reverie ...*I had a dream that I was in an old house...*

2 = <u>ambition</u>, wish, fantasy, desire, Holy Grail (*informal*), pipe dream …*My dream is to have a house in the country*…

3 = <u>daydream</u> …*I wandered around in a kind of dream*…

4 = <u>delight</u>, pleasure, joy, beauty, treasure, gem, marvel, pearler (*Austral. slang*) …*This cart really is a dream to drive*…

VERB **1** = <u>have dreams</u>, hallucinate …*She dreamt about her baby*…

2 = <u>daydream</u>, stargaze, build castles in the air *or* in Spain …*She spent most of her time looking out of the window and dreaming*…

PHRASES **dream of something** *or* **someone** = <u>daydream about</u>, fantasize about …*She dreamed of going to work overseas*… ◆ **dream something up** = <u>invent</u>, create, imagine, devise, hatch, contrive, concoct, think up, cook up (*informal*), spin …*I dreamed up a plan*…

dreamer = <u>idealist</u>, visionary, daydreamer, utopian, theorizer, fantasizer, romancer, Don Quixote, escapist, Walter Mitty, fantasist, fantast

dreamy 1 = <u>vague</u>, abstracted, absent, musing, preoccupied, daydreaming, faraway, pensive, in a reverie, with your head in the clouds …*His face assumed a dreamy expression*…

2 = <u>relaxing</u>, calming, romantic, gentle, soothing, lulling …*a dreamy, delicate song*…

3 = <u>impractical</u>, vague, imaginary, speculative, visionary, fanciful, quixotic, dreamlike, airy-fairy …*full of dreamy ideals*… OPPOSITE realistic

dreary 1 = <u>dull</u>, boring, tedious, routine, drab, tiresome, lifeless, monotonous, humdrum, colourless, uneventful, uninteresting, mind-numbing, ho-hum (*informal*), wearisome, as dry as dust …*They live such dreary lives*… OPPOSITE exciting

2 = <u>dismal</u>, depressing, bleak, sad, lonely, gloomy, solitary, melancholy, sombre, forlorn, glum, mournful, lonesome, downcast, sorrowful, wretched, joyless, funereal, doleful, cheerless, drear, comfortless …*A dreary little town in the Midwest*…

dredge up (*Informal*) = <u>dig up</u>, raise, rake up, discover, uncover, draw up, unearth, drag up, fish up

dregs 1 = <u>sediment</u>, grounds, lees, waste, deposit, trash, residue, scum, dross, residuum, scourings, draff …*He drained the dregs from his cup*…

2 = <u>scum</u>, outcasts, rabble, down-and-outs, good-for-nothings, riffraff, canaille (*French*), ragtag and bobtail …*the dregs of society*…

drench = <u>soak</u>, flood, wet, duck, drown, steep, swamp, saturate, inundate, souse, imbrue

dress NOUN **1** = <u>frock</u>, gown, garment, robe …*She was wearing a black dress*…

2 = <u>clothing</u>, clothes, gear (*informal*), costume, threads (*slang*), garments, apparel, attire, garb, togs, raiment (*archaic or poetic*), vestment, schmutter (*slang*), habiliment …*a well-groomed gent in smart dress and specs*…

VERB **1** = <u>put on clothes</u>, don clothes, slip on *or* into something …*He told her to wait while he dressed*… OPPOSITE undress

2 = <u>clothe</u> …*We dressed the baby in a warm outfit*…

3 = <u>bandage</u>, treat, plaster, bind up …*I dressed her wounds*…

4 = <u>decorate</u>, deck, adorn, trim, array, drape, ornament, embellish, festoon, bedeck, furbish, rig out …*advice on how to dress a Christmas tree*…

5 = <u>arrange</u>, do (up), groom, set, prepare, comb (out), get ready …*He's so careless about dressing his hair*…

PHRASES **dress someone down** = <u>reprimand</u> (*Informal*), rebuke, scold, berate, castigate, tear into (*informal*), tell off (*informal*), read the riot act, reprove, upbraid, slap on the wrist, carpet (*informal*), bawl out (*informal*), rap over the knuckles, haul over the coals, chew out (*U.S. & Canad. informal*), tear (someone) off a strip (*Brit. informal*), give a rocket (*Brit. & N.Z. informal*) …*He dressed them down in public*… ◆ **dress up 1** = <u>put on fancy dress</u>, wear a costume, disguise yourself …*She dressed up as a witch*… **2** = <u>dress formally</u>, dress for dinner, doll yourself up (*slang*), put on your best bib and tucker (*informal*), put on your glad rags (*informal*) …*She did not feel obliged to dress up for the cameras*…

dressmaker = <u>seamstress</u>, tailor, couturier, sewing woman, modiste

dribble 1 = <u>run</u>, drip, trickle, drop, leak, ooze, seep, fall in drops …*Sweat dribbled down his face*…

2 = <u>drool</u>, drivel, slaver, slobber, drip saliva …*She's dribbling on her collar*…

drift VERB **1** = <u>float</u>, go (aimlessly), bob, coast, slip, sail, slide, glide, meander, waft, be carried along, move gently …*We proceeded to drift along the river*…

2 = <u>wander</u>, stroll, stray, roam, meander, rove, range, straggle, traipse (*informal*), stravaig (*Scot. & Northern English dialect*), peregrinate …*People drifted around the room*…

3 = <u>stray</u>, wander, roam, meander, digress, get sidetracked, go off at a tangent, get off the point …*I let my attention drift*…

4 = <u>pile up</u>, gather, accumulate, amass, bank up …*The snow, except where it drifted, was only calf-deep*…

NOUN **1** = <u>shift</u>, movement, gravitation …*the drift towards the cities*…

2 = <u>pile</u>, bank, mass, heap, mound, accumulation …*A boy was trapped in a snow drift*…

3 = <u>meaning</u>, point, gist, aim, direction, object, import, intention, implication, tendency, significance, thrust, tenor, purport …*She was beginning to get his drift*…

drifter = <u>wanderer</u>, bum (*informal*), tramp, itinerant, vagrant, hobo (*U.S.*), vagabond, rolling stone, bag lady (*chiefly U.S.*), derro (*Austral. slang*)

drill NOUN **1** = <u>bit</u>, borer, gimlet, rotary tool, boring tool …*pneumatic drills*…

2 = <u>training</u>, exercise, discipline, instruction, preparation, repetition …*A local army base teaches them military drill*…

3 = <u>practice</u> …*a fire drill*…

VERB **1** = <u>bore</u>, pierce, penetrate, sink in, puncture, perforate …*I drilled five holes at equal distance*…

2 = <u>train</u>, coach, teach, exercise, discipline, practise, instruct, rehearse …*He drills the choir to a high* *standard…*

drink VERB 1 = <u>swallow</u>, drain, sip, suck, gulp, sup, swig (*informal*), swill, guzzle, imbibe, quaff, partake of, toss off …*He drank his cup of tea…*

2 = <u>booze</u> (*informal*), tipple, tope, hit the bottle (*informal*), bevvy (*dialect*), bend the elbow (*informal*), go on a binge *or* bender (*informal*) …*He was smoking and drinking too much…*

NOUN 1 = <u>glass</u>, cup, swallow, sip, draught, gulp, swig (*informal*), taste, tipple, snifter (*informal*), noggin …*a drink of water…*

2 = <u>beverage</u>, refreshment, potion, liquid, thirst quencher …*Can I offer you a drink?…*

3 = <u>alcohol</u>, booze (*informal*), liquor, spirits, the bottle (*informal*), Dutch courage, hooch *or* hootch (*informal, chiefly U.S. & Canad.*) …*Too much drink is bad for your health…*

PHRASES **drink something in** = <u>absorb</u>, take in, digest, pay attention to, soak up, devour, assimilate, be fascinated by, imbibe …*She stood drinking in the view…* ◆ **drink to something** *or* **someone** = <u>toast</u>, salute, pledge the health of …*Let's drink to his memory…* ◆ **the drink** (*Informal*) = <u>the sea</u>, the main, the deep, the ocean, the briny (*informal*) …*His plane went down in the drink…*

drinker = <u>alcoholic</u>, drunk, boozer (*informal*), soak (*slang*), lush (*slang*), toper, sponge (*informal*), guzzler, drunkard, sot, tippler, wino (*informal*), inebriate, dipsomaniac, bibber, alko *or* alco (*Austral. slang*)

drip VERB = <u>drop</u>, splash, sprinkle, trickle, dribble, exude, drizzle, plop …*a cloth that dripped pink drops upon the floor…*

NOUN 1 = <u>drop</u>, bead, trickle, dribble, droplet, globule, pearl, driblet …*Drips of water rolled down his uniform…*

2 (*Informal*) = <u>weakling</u>, wet (*Brit. informal*), weed (*informal*), softie (*informal*), mummy's boy (*informal*), namby-pamby, ninny, milksop …*The kid is a drip!…*

drive VERB 1 = <u>go (by car)</u>, ride (by car), motor, travel by car …*I drove into town and went for dinner…*

2 = <u>operate</u>, manage, direct, guide, handle, steer …*Don't expect to be able to drive a car or operate machinery…*

3 = <u>push</u>, propel …*pistons that drive the wheels…*

4 = <u>thrust</u>, push, sink, dig, hammer, plunge, stab, ram …*I used the sledgehammer to drive the pegs in…*

5 = <u>herd</u>, urge, impel …*The shepherds drove the sheep up to pasture…*

6 = <u>force</u>, press, prompt, spur, compel, motivate, oblige, railroad (*informal*), prod, constrain, prick, coerce, goad, impel, dragoon, actuate …*Depression drove him to attempt suicide…*

7 = <u>work</u>, overwork, overburden …*For the next six years he drove himself mercilessly…*

NOUN 1 = <u>run</u>, ride, trip, journey, spin (*informal*), hurl (*Scot.*), outing, excursion, jaunt …*We might go for a drive on Sunday…*

2 = <u>initiative</u>, push (*informal*), energy, enterprise, ambition, pep, motivation, zip (*informal*), vigour, get-up-and-go (*informal*) …*He is best remembered for his drive and enthusiasm…*

3 = <u>campaign</u>, push (*informal*), crusade, action, effort, appeal, advance, surge …*the drive towards democracy…*

PHRASES **drive at something** (*Informal*) = <u>mean</u>, suggest, intend, refer to, imply, intimate, get at, hint at, have in mind, allude to, insinuate …*He wasn't sure what she was driving at…*

drivel NOUN = <u>nonsense</u>, rubbish, garbage (*informal*), rot, crap (*slang*), trash, bunk (*informal*), blah (*slang*), hot air (*informal*), tosh (*slang, chiefly Brit.*), waffle (*informal, chiefly Brit.*), prating, pap, bilge (*informal*), twaddle, tripe (*informal*), dross, gibberish, guff (*slang*), moonshine, hogwash, hokum (*slang, chiefly U.S. & Canad.*), piffle (*informal*), poppycock (*informal*), balderdash, bosh (*informal*), eyewash (*informal*), tommyrot, horsefeathers (*U.S. slang*), bunkum *or* buncombe (*chiefly U.S.*), bizzo (*Austral. slang*), bull's wool (*Austral. & N.Z. slang*) …*What absolute drivel!…*

VERB = <u>babble</u>, ramble, waffle (*informal, chiefly Brit.*), gab (*informal*), gas (*informal*), maunder, blether, prate …*I drivelled on about the big race that day…*

driving = <u>forceful</u>, sweeping, dynamic, compelling, vigorous, energetic, galvanic

drizzle NOUN = <u>fine rain</u>, Scotch mist, smir (*Scot.*) …*The drizzle had stopped and the sun was breaking through…*

VERB = <u>rain</u>, shower, spit, spray, sprinkle, mizzle (*dialect*), spot *or* spit with rain …*It was starting to drizzle…*

droll = <u>amusing</u>, odd, funny, entertaining, comic, ridiculous, diverting, eccentric, ludicrous, humorous, quaint, off-the-wall (*slang*), laughable, farcical, whimsical, comical, oddball (*informal*), risible, jocular, clownish, waggish

drone¹ = <u>parasite</u>, skiver (*Brit. slang*), idler, lounger, leech, loafer, couch potato (*slang*), scrounger (*informal*), sponger (*informal*), sluggard, bludger (*Austral. & N.Z. informal*), quandong (*Austral. slang*) …*A few are dim-witted drones, but most are talented…*

drone² VERB = <u>hum</u>, buzz, vibrate, purr, whirr, thrum …*An invisible plane drones through the night sky…*

NOUN = <u>hum</u>, buzz, purr, vibration, whirr, whirring, thrum …*the constant drone of the motorway…*

PHRASES **drone on** = <u>speak monotonously</u>, drawl, chant, spout, intone, talk interminably …*Her voice droned on…*

droning 1 = <u>humming</u>, buzzing, vibrating, purring, whirring, thrumming …*the droning sound of a plane overhead…*

2 = <u>monotonous</u>, boring, tedious, drawling, soporific …*the minister's relentlessly droning voice…*

drool 1 = <u>dribble</u>, drivel, salivate, slaver, slobber, water at the mouth …*The dog was drooling on my shoulder…*

2 often with **over** = <u>gloat over</u>, pet, gush, make much of, rave about (*informal*), dote on, slobber over …*Fashion editors drooled over every item…*

droop 1 = <u>sag</u>, drop, hang (down), sink, bend, dangle, fall down …*a young man with a drooping moustache…*

2 = <u>flag</u>, decline, fade, slump, diminish, wither, wilt, languish ...*Support for him is beginning to droop amongst voters...* •

droopy = <u>sagging</u>, limp, wilting, stooped, floppy, drooping, languid, flabby, languorous, pendulous, lassitudinous

drop [VERB] **1** = <u>fall</u>, lower, decline, diminish ...*Temperatures can drop to freezing at night...*
2 *often with* **away** = <u>decline</u>, fall, sink ...*The ground dropped away steeply...*
3 = <u>plunge</u>, fall, dive, tumble, descend, plummet ...*Part of an aeroplane had dropped out of the sky and hit me...*
4 = <u>drip</u>, trickle, dribble, fall in drops ...*He felt hot tears dropping onto his fingers...*
5 = <u>sink</u>, fall, descend, droop ...*She let her head drop...*
6 = <u>set down</u>, leave, deposit, unload, let off ...*He dropped me outside the hotel...*
7 = <u>quit</u>, give up, abandon, cease, axe (*informal*), kick (*informal*), terminate, relinquish, remit, discontinue, forsake ...*He was told to drop the idea...*
8 = <u>abandon</u>, desert, forsake, repudiate, leave, jilt, throw over ...*He has dropped those friends who used to drink with him...*
[NOUN] **1** = <u>decrease</u>, fall, cut, lowering, decline, reduction, slump, fall-off, downturn, deterioration, cutback, diminution, decrement ...*He was prepared to take a drop in wages...*
2 = <u>droplet</u>, bead, globule, bubble, pearl, drip, driblet ...*a drop of blue ink...*
3 = <u>dash</u>, shot (*informal*), spot, taste, trace, pinch, sip, tot, trickle, nip, dab, mouthful ...*I'll have a drop of that milk...*
4 = <u>fall</u>, plunge, descent, abyss, chasm, precipice ...*There was a sheer drop just outside my window...*
[PHRASES] **drop by** *or* **in (on)** (*Informal*) = <u>visit</u>, call, stop, turn up, look up, call in, look in (on), go and see, pop in (*informal*) ...*I'll drop in on my way home...*
♦ **drop off 1** = <u>fall asleep</u>, nod (off), doze (off), snooze (*informal*), catnap, drowse, have forty winks (*informal*) ...*I was just dropping off...* **2** = <u>decrease</u>, lower, decline, shrink, diminish, fall off, dwindle, lessen, wane, subside, slacken ...*The toll of casualties has dropped off sharply...* ♦ **drop out** = <u>leave</u>, stop, give up, withdraw, quit, pull out, back out, renege, throw in the towel, cop out (*slang*), fall by the wayside ...*He went to university, but dropped out after a year...* ♦ **drop out of something** = <u>discontinue</u>, give up, abandon, quit, cease, terminate, forsake ...*She had a troubled childhood and dropped out of high school...* ♦ **drop someone off** = <u>set down</u>, leave, deliver, let off, allow to alight ...*I'm going to drop you off and pick you up myself...*

droppings = <u>excrement</u>, crap (*taboo slang*), stool, manure, dung, faeces, guano, excreta, doo-doo (*informal*), ordure, kak (*S. African taboo slang*)

dross = <u>rubbish</u>, remains, refuse, lees, waste, debris, crust, impurity, scum, dregs

drought 1 = <u>water shortage</u>, dryness, dry weather, dry spell, aridity, drouth (*Scot.*), parchedness

...*Drought and famines have killed up to two million people...* [OPPOSITE] flood
2 = <u>shortage</u>, lack, deficit, deficiency, want, need, shortfall, scarcity, dearth, insufficiency ...*The Western world was suffering through the oil drought...* [OPPOSITE] abundance

drove *often plural* = <u>herd</u>, company, crowds, collection, gathering, mob, flocks, swarm, horde, multitude, throng

drown 1 = <u>go down</u>, go under ...*He drowned during a storm...*
2 = <u>drench</u>, flood, soak, steep, swamp, saturate, engulf, submerge, immerse, inundate, deluge ...*The country would be drowned in blood...*
3 = <u>overwhelm</u>, overcome, wipe out, overpower, obliterate, swallow up ...*His words were soon drowned by amplified police sirens...*

drowsiness = <u>sleepiness</u>, tiredness, lethargy, torpor, sluggishness, languor, somnolence, heavy eyelids, doziness, torpidity [OPPOSITE] wakefulness

drowsy 1 = <u>sleepy</u>, tired, lethargic, heavy, nodding, dazed, dozy, comatose, dopey (*slang*), half asleep, somnolent, torpid ...*He felt pleasantly drowsy...* [OPPOSITE] awake
2 = <u>peaceful</u>, quiet, sleepy, soothing, lulling, dreamy, restful, soporific ...*The drowsy air hummed with bees...*

drubbing = <u>beating</u>, defeat, hammering (*informal*), pounding, whipping, thrashing, licking (*informal*), pasting (*slang*), flogging, trouncing, clobbering (*slang*), walloping (*informal*), pummelling

drudge = <u>menial</u>, worker, servant, slave, toiler, dogsbody (*informal*), plodder, factotum, scullion (*archaic*), skivvy (*chiefly Brit.*), maid *or* man of all work

drudgery = <u>labour</u>, grind (*informal*), sweat (*informal*), hard work, slavery, chore, fag (*informal*), toil, slog, donkey-work, sweated labour, menial labour, skivvying (*Brit.*)

drug [NOUN] **1** = <u>medication</u>, medicine, remedy, physic, medicament ...*The drug will treat those infected...*
2 = <u>dope</u> (*slang*), narcotic (*slang*), stimulant, opiate, dadah (*Austral. slang*) ...*the problem of drug abuse...*
[VERB] = <u>knock out</u>, dope (*slang*), numb, deaden, stupefy, anaesthetize ...*They drugged the guard dog...*

(**Related Words**)
combining form: pharmaco-

drug addict = <u>junkie</u> (*informal*), tripper (*informal*), crack-head (*informal*), acid head (*informal*), dope-fiend (*slang*), hop-head (*informal*), head (*informal*)

drugged = <u>stoned</u>, high (*informal*), flying (*slang*), bombed (*slang*), tripping (*informal*) (*slang*), wasted (*slang*), smashed (*slang*), wrecked (*slang*), turned on (*slang*), out of it (*slang*), doped (*slang*), under the influence (*informal*), on a trip (*informal*), spaced out (*slang*), comatose, stupefied, out of your mind (*slang*), zonked (*slang*), out to it (*Austral. & N.Z. slang*)

drum [VERB] = <u>pound</u>, beat, tap, rap, lash, thrash, tattoo, throb, pulsate, reverberate ...*Rain drummed on the roof of the car...*

PHRASES **drum something into someone** = drive into, hammer into, instil into, din into, harp on about to ...*Examples were drummed into students' heads*... ♦ **drum something up** = seek, attract, request, ask for, obtain, bid for, petition, round up, solicit, canvass ...*drumming up business*...

drunk ADJECTIVE = intoxicated, loaded (*slang, chiefly U.S. & Canad.*), tight (*informal*), canned (*slang*), flying (*slang*), bombed (*slang*), stoned (*slang*), wasted (*slang*), smashed (*slang*), steaming (*slang*), wrecked (*slang*), soaked (*informal*), out of it (*slang*), plastered (*slang*), drunken, blitzed (*slang*), lit up (*slang*), merry (*Brit. informal*), stewed (*slang*), pickled (*informal*), bladdered (*slang*), under the influence (*informal*), sloshed (*slang*), tipsy, maudlin, well-oiled (*slang*), legless (*informal*), paralytic (*informal*), tired and emotional (*euphemistic*), steamboats (*Scot. slang*), tiddly (*slang, chiefly Brit.*), zonked (*slang*), blotto (*slang*), fuddled, inebriated, out to it (*Austral. & N.Z. slang*), scottish, tanked up (*slang*), bacchic, half seas over (*informal*), bevvied (*dialect*), babalas (*S. African*), fu' (*Scot.*), pie-eyed (*slang*) ...*I got drunk and had to be carried home*...
NOUN = drunkard, alcoholic, lush (*slang*), boozer (*informal*), toper, sot, soak (*slang*), wino (*informal*), inebriate, alko *or* alco (*Austral. slang*) ...*A drunk lay in the alley*...

drunkard = drunk, alcoholic, soak (*slang*), drinker, lush (*slang*), carouser, sot, tippler, toper, wino (*informal*), dipsomaniac, alko *or* alco (*Austral. slang*)

drunken 1 = intoxicated, smashed (*slang*), drunk, flying (*slang*), bombed (*slang*), wasted (*slang*), steaming (*slang*), wrecked (*slang*), out of it (*slang*), boozing (*informal*), blitzed (*slang*), lit up (*slang*), bladdered (*slang*), under the influence (*informal*), tippling, toping, red-nosed, legless (*informal*), paralytic (*informal*), steamboats (*Scot. slang*), zonked (*slang*), bibulous, blotto (*slang*), inebriate, out to it (*Austral. & N.Z. slang*), sottish, Brahms and Liszt (*slang*), bevvied (*dialect*), (gin-)sodden ...*Drunken yobs smashed shop windows*...
2 = boozy, dissipated (*informal*), riotous, debauched, dionysian, orgiastic, bacchanalian, bacchic, saturnalian ...*A loud, drunken party was raging nearby*...

drunkenness = intoxication, alcoholism, intemperance, inebriation, dipsomania, tipsiness, insobriety, bibulousness, sottishness

dry ADJECTIVE 1 = dehydrated, dried-up, arid, torrid, parched, desiccated, waterless, juiceless, sapless, moistureless ...*a hard, dry desert landscape*...
OPPOSITE wet
2 = dried, crisp, withered, brittle, shrivelled, crispy, parched, dessicated, sun-baked ...*She heard the rustle of dry leaves*...
3 = thirsty, parched ...*She was suddenly dry*...
4 = sarcastic, cutting, sharp, keen, cynical, low-key, sly, sardonic, deadpan, droll, ironical, quietly humorous ...*He is renowned for his dry wit*...
5 = dull, boring, tedious, commonplace, dreary, tiresome, monotonous, run-of-the-mill, humdrum,

unimaginative, uninteresting, mind-numbing, ho-hum (*informal*) ...*The work was very dry and dull*...
OPPOSITE interesting
6 = plain, simple, bare, basic, pure, stark, unembellished ...*an infuriating list of dry facts and dates*...
VERB 1 = drain, make dry ...*Wash and dry the lettuce*...
2 *often with* **out** = dehydrate, make dry, desiccate, sear, parch, dehumidify ...*They bought a machine to dry the wood and cut costs*... OPPOSITE wet
PHRASES **dry up** *or* **out** = become dry, harden, wither, mummify, shrivel up, wizen ...*The pollen dries up and becomes hard*...

dryness 1 = aridity, drought, dehydration, aridness, dehumidification, waterlessness, moisturelessness, parchedness ...*the parched dryness of the air*...
2 = thirstiness, thirst, parchedness ...*Symptoms include dryness of the mouth*...

dual = twofold, double, twin, matched, coupled, paired, duplicate, binary, duplex

duality = dualism, dichotomy, polarity, doubleness, biformity, duplexity

dub = name, call, term, style, label, nickname, designate, christen, denominate

dubious 1 = suspect, suspicious, crooked, dodgy (*Brit., Austral., & N.Z. informal*), questionable, unreliable, shady (*informal*), unscrupulous, fishy (*informal*), disreputable, untrustworthy, undependable ...*dubious business dealings*...
OPPOSITE trustworthy
2 = unsure, uncertain, suspicious, hesitating, doubtful, sceptical, tentative, wavering, hesitant, undecided, unconvinced, iffy (*informal*), leery (*slang*), distrustful, in two minds (*informal*) ...*My parents were a bit dubious about it all*... OPPOSITE sure
3 = doubtful, questionable, ambiguous, debatable, moot, arguable, equivocal, open to question, disputable ...*This is a very dubious honour*...

duck 1 = bob, drop, lower, bend, bow, dodge, crouch, stoop ...*He ducked in time to save his head from the blow*...
2 (*Informal*) = dodge, avoid, escape, evade, elude, sidestep, circumvent, shirk, body-swerve (*Scot.*) ...*He had ducked the confrontation*...
3 = dunk, wet, plunge, dip, submerge, immerse, douse, souse ...*She splashed around in the pool trying to duck him*...

duct = pipe, channel, passage, tube, canal, funnel, conduit

dud (*Informal*) ADJECTIVE broken, failed, damaged, bust (*informal*), not working, useless, flawed, impaired, duff (*Brit. informal*), worthless, defective, imperfect, malfunctioning, out of order, unsound, not functioning, valueless, on the blink, inoperative, kaput (*informal*) ...*He replaced a dud valve*...
NOUN 1 = imitation, copy, reproduction, hoax, forgery, phoney *or* phony (*informal*) ...*The mine was a dud*...
2 = failure, flop (*informal*), washout (*informal*), clinker (*slang, chiefly U.S.*), clunker (*informal*) ...*He's been a

dud from day one…

due ADJECTIVE **1** = expected, scheduled, expected to
arrive …*The results are due at the end of the month…*
2 = fitting, deserved, appropriate, just, right,
becoming, fit, justified, suitable, merited, proper,
obligatory, rightful, requisite, well-earned, bounden
…*Treat them with due attention…*
3 = payable, outstanding, owed, owing, unpaid, in
arrears …*I've got a tax rebate due…*
ADVERB = directly, dead, straight, exactly,
undeviatingly …*They headed due north…*
NOUN = right(s), privilege, deserts, merits, prerogative,
comeuppance (*informal*) …*No doubt he felt it was his
due…*
PLURAL NOUN = membership fee, charges, fee,
contribution, levy …*paid for out of membership
dues…*

> ### *Word Power*
>
> **due** – For years people have been debating
> the use of *due to* in the sense 'because of'.
> Purists claimed that a sentence such as *the late
> arrival of the 10.15 train from Guildford is due to
> snow on the lines* was correct, while *the trains
> are running late due to snow on the lines* was
> incorrect. Their reasoning was that as an
> adjective, *due* should modify a noun, as it does
> in the first sentence (the train's late *arrival* was
> *due to* the snow); but in the second sentence
> there is no specific noun that the word *due*
> can be said to modify. Few people nowadays
> would object strongly to the use of *due* in the
> second sentence, but if you want to avoid any
> possibility of this, you may find it preferable
> to replace it with an alternative that is not the
> subject of debate, such as *because of.*

duel NOUN **1** = single combat, affair of honour …*He
killed a man in a duel…*
2 = contest, fight, competition, clash, encounter,
engagement, rivalry …*sporadic artillery duels…*
VERB = fight, struggle, clash, compete, contest,
contend, vie with, lock horns …*We duelled for two
years…*

duff (*Brit., Austral., & N.Z. informal*) = bad, poor,
useless, pathetic, inferior, worthless, unsatisfactory,
defective, deficient, imperfect, substandard, low-rent
(*informal, chiefly U.S.*), poxy (*slang*), pants (*informal*),
bodger *or* bodgie (*Austral. slang*)

duffer (*Informal*) = clot, blunderer (*Brit. informal*),
booby, clod, oaf, bungler, galoot (*slang, chiefly U.S.*),
lubber, lummox (*informal*)

dulcet = sweet, pleasing, musical, charming,
pleasant, honeyed, delightful, soothing, agreeable,
harmonious, melodious, mellifluous, euphonious,
mellifluent

dull ADJECTIVE **1** = boring, tedious, dreary, flat, dry,
plain, commonplace, tiresome, monotonous, prosaic,
run-of-the-mill, humdrum, unimaginative, dozy,
uninteresting, mind-numbing, ho-hum (*informal*),
vapid, as dry as dust …*They can both be rather dull…*
OPPOSITE exciting

2 = lifeless, dead, heavy, slow, indifferent, sluggish,
insensitive, apathetic, listless, unresponsive,
passionless, insensible …*We all feel dull and sleepy
between 1 and 3pm…* OPPOSITE lively
3 = drab, faded, muted, subdued, feeble, murky,
sombre, toned-down, subfusc …*The stamp was a dull
blue colour…*
4 = cloudy, dim, gloomy, dismal, overcast, leaden,
turbid …*It's always dull and raining…* OPPOSITE bright
5 = muted, faint, suppressed, subdued, stifled,
indistinct …*The coffin was closed with a dull thud…*
6 = blunt, dulled, blunted, not keen, not sharp,
edgeless, unsharpened …*using the dull edge of her
knife…* OPPOSITE sharp
VERB **1** = relieve, blunt, lessen, moderate, soften,
alleviate, allay, mitigate, assuage, take the edge off,
palliate …*They gave him morphine to dull the pain…*
2 = cloud over, darken, grow dim, become cloudy
…*Her eyes dulled and she gazed blankly…*
3 = dampen, reduce, check, depress, moderate,
discourage, stifle, lessen, smother, sadden, dishearten,
dispirit, deject …*Her illness failed to dull her
optimism…*

dullness 1 = tediousness, monotony, banality,
flatness, dreariness, vapidity, insipidity …*the dullness
of their routine life…* OPPOSITE interest
2 = stupidity, thickness, slowness, dimness,
obtuseness, doziness (*Brit. informal*), dim-wittedness,
dopiness (*slang*) …*his dullness of mind…* OPPOSITE
intelligence
3 = drabness, greyness, dimness, gloominess,
dinginess, colourlessness …*the dullness of an old
painting…* OPPOSITE brilliance

duly 1 = properly, fittingly, correctly, appropriately,
accordingly, suitably, deservedly, rightfully,
decorously, befittingly …*He duly apologized for his
behaviour…*
2 = on time, promptly, in good time, punctually, at
the proper time …*The engineer duly arrived, expecting
to have to repair the boiler…*

dumb 1 = unable to speak, mute …*a young deaf and
dumb man…* OPPOSITE articulate
2 = silent, mute, speechless, inarticulate, tongue-tied,
wordless, voiceless, soundless, at a loss for words,
mum …*We were all struck dumb for a minute…*
3 (*Informal*) = stupid, thick, dull, foolish, dense, dozy
(*Brit. informal*), dim, obtuse, unintelligent, asinine,
braindead (*informal*), dim-witted (*informal*) …*I came
up with this dumb idea…* OPPOSITE clever

dumbfounded = amazed, stunned, astonished,
confused, overcome, overwhelmed, staggered,
thrown, startled, at sea, dumb, bewildered,
astounded, breathless, confounded, taken aback,
speechless, bowled over (*informal*), gobsmacked (*Brit.
slang*), flabbergasted (*informal*), nonplussed, lost for
words, flummoxed, thunderstruck, knocked sideways
(*informal*), knocked for six (*informal*)

dummy NOUN **1** = model, figure, mannequin, form,
manikin, lay figure …*a shop-window dummy…*
2 = imitation, copy, duplicate, sham, counterfeit,
replica …*The police video camera was a dummy…*

3 (*Slang*) = <u>fool</u>, jerk (*slang, chiefly U.S. & Canad.*), idiot, plank (*Brit. slang*), charlie (*Brit. informal*), berk (*Brit. slang*), wally (*slang*), prat (*slang*), plonker (*slang*), coot, geek (*slang*), dunce, oaf, simpleton, dullard, dimwit (*informal*), dipstick (*Brit. slang*), gonzo (*slang*), schmuck (*U.S. slang*), dork (*slang*), nitwit (*informal*), dolt, blockhead, divvy (*Brit. slang*), pillock (*Brit. slang*), dweeb (*U.S. slang*), fathead (*informal*), weenie (*U.S. informal*), eejit (*Scot. & Irish*), dumb-ass (*slang*), numpty (*Scot. informal*), doofus (*slang, chiefly U.S.*), lamebrain (*informal*), nerd *or* nurd (*slang*), numbskull *or* numskull, dorba *or* dorb (*Austral. slang*), bogan (*Austral. slang*) …*He's no dummy, this guy*…
ADJECTIVE 1 = <u>imitation</u>, false, fake, artificial, mock, bogus, simulated, sham, phoney *or* phony (*informal*) …*Soldiers were still using dummy guns*…
2 = <u>practice</u>, trial, mock, simulated …*They do a dummy run with the brakes*…

dump VERB 1 = <u>drop</u>, deposit, throw down, let fall, fling down …*We dumped our bags on the table*…
2 = <u>get rid of</u>, tip, discharge, dispose of, unload, jettison, empty out, coup (*Scot.*), throw away *or* out …*Untreated sewage is dumped into the sea*…
3 = <u>scrap</u>, axe (*informal*), get rid of, abolish, junk (*informal*), put an end to, discontinue, jettison, put paid to …*Ministers believed it was vital to dump the tax*…
NOUN 1 = <u>rubbish tip</u>, tip, junkyard, rubbish heap, refuse heap …*The walled garden was used as a dump*…
2 (*Informal*) = <u>pigsty</u>, hole (*informal*), joint (*slang*), slum, shack, shanty, hovel …*'What a dump!' she said*…

dumps
PHRASES down in the dumps = <u>down</u>, low, blue, sad, unhappy, low-spirited, discouraged, fed up, moody, pessimistic, melancholy, glum, dejected, despondent, dispirited, downcast, morose, crestfallen, downhearted

dumpy = <u>podgy</u>, homely, short, plump, squat, stout, chunky, chubby, tubby, roly-poly, pudgy, squab, fubsy (*archaic or dialect*)

dunce = <u>simpleton</u>, moron, duffer (*informal*), bonehead (*slang*), loon (*informal*), goose (*informal*), ass, donkey, oaf, dullard, dimwit (*informal*), ignoramus, nitwit (*informal*), dolt, blockhead, halfwit, nincompoop, fathead (*informal*), dunderhead, lamebrain (*informal*), thickhead, numbskull *or* numskull

dungeon = <u>prison</u>, cell, cage, vault, lockup, oubliette, calaboose (*U.S. informal*), donjon, boob (*Austral. slang*)

dunny (*Austral. & old-fashioned N.Z. informal*) = <u>toilet</u>, lavatory, bathroom, loo (*Brit. informal*), W.C., bog (*slang*), Gents *or* Ladies, can (*U.S. & Canad. slang*), john (*slang, chiefly U.S. & Canad.*), head(s) (*Nautical slang*), throne (*informal*), closet, privy, cloakroom (*Brit.*), urinal, latrine, washroom, powder room, crapper (*taboo slang*), water closet, khazi (*slang*), pissoir (*French*), little boy's room *or* little girl's room (*informal*), (public) convenience, bogger (*Austral. slang*), brasco (*Austral. slang*)

dupe VERB = <u>deceive</u>, trick, cheat, con (*informal*), kid (*informal*), rip off (*slang*), hoax, defraud, beguile, gull (*archaic*), delude, swindle, outwit, bamboozle (*informal*), hoodwink, take for a ride (*informal*), pull a fast one on (*informal*), cozen …*Some of the offenders duped the psychologists*…
NOUN 1 = <u>victim</u>, mug (*Brit. slang*), sucker (*slang*), pigeon (*slang*), sap (*slang*), gull, pushover (*slang*), fall guy (*informal*), simpleton …*an innocent dupe in a political scandal*…
2 = <u>puppet</u>, tool, instrument, pawn, stooge (*slang*), cat's-paw …*He was accused of being a dupe of the communists*…

duplicate VERB 1 = <u>repeat</u>, reproduce, echo, copy, clone, replicate …*Scientists hope the work done can be duplicated elswhere*…
2 = <u>copy</u>, photocopy, Xerox (*trademark*), Photostat (*trademark*) …*He was duplicating some articles*…
ADJECTIVE = <u>identical</u>, matched, matching, twin, corresponding, twofold …*a duplicate copy*…
NOUN 1 = <u>copy</u>, facsimile …*I've lost my card and have to get a duplicate*…
2 = <u>photocopy</u>, copy, reproduction, replica, Xerox (*trademark*), carbon copy, Photostat (*trademark*) …*Enclosed is a duplicate of the invoice we sent you last month*…

duplicity = <u>deceit</u>, fraud, deception, hypocrisy, dishonesty, guile, artifice, falsehood, double-dealing, chicanery, perfidy, dissimulation **OPPOSITE** honesty

durable 1 = <u>hard-wearing</u>, strong, tough, sound, substantial, reliable, resistant, sturdy, long-lasting …*Fine bone china is strong and durable*… **OPPOSITE** fragile
2 = <u>enduring</u>, lasting, permanent, continuing, firm, fast, fixed, constant, abiding, dependable, unwavering, unfaltering …*We were unable to establish any durable agreement*…

duration = <u>length</u>, time, period, term, stretch, extent, spell, span

duress (usually in phrase *under duress*) = <u>pressure</u>, threat, constraint, compulsion, coercion

dusk 1 = <u>twilight</u>, evening, evo (*Austral. slang*), nightfall, sunset, dark, sundown, eventide, gloaming (*Scot. or poetic*) …*We arrived home at dusk*… **OPPOSITE** dawn
2 (*Poetic*) = <u>shade</u>, darkness, gloom, obscurity, murk, shadowiness …*She turned and disappeared into the dusk*…

dusky 1 = <u>dim</u>, twilight, shady, shadowy, gloomy, murky, cloudy, overcast, crepuscular, darkish, twilit, tenebrous, caliginous (*archaic*) …*He was walking down the road one dusky evening*…
2 = <u>dark</u>, swarthy, dark-complexioned …*I could see dusky girls with flowers about their necks*…

dust NOUN 1 = <u>grime</u>, grit, powder, powdery dirt …*I could see a thick layer of dust on the stairs*…
2 = <u>earth</u>, ground, soil, dirt …*Your trousers will get dirty if you sit down in the dust*…
3 = <u>particles</u>, fine fragments …*The air was black with coal dust*…

VERB = sprinkle, cover, powder, spread, spray, scatter, sift, dredge ...*Lightly dust the fish with flour...*
PHRASES **bite the dust** (*Informal*) = fail, flop (*informal*), fall through, be unsuccessful, go down, founder, fall flat, come to nothing, fizzle out (*informal*), come unstuck, run aground, come to grief, come a cropper (*informal*), go up in smoke, go belly-up (*slang*), come to naught, not make the grade (*informal*), meet with disaster ...*Her first marriage bit the dust because of irreconcilable differences...*

dusty 1 = dirty, grubby, unclean, unswept, undusted ...*The books looked dusty and unused...*
2 = powdery, sandy, chalky, crumbly, granular, friable ...*Inside the box was only a dusty substance...*

dutiful = conscientious, devoted, obedient, respectful, compliant, submissive, docile, deferential, reverential, filial, punctilious, duteous (*archaic*)
OPPOSITE disrespectful

duty **NOUN** 1 = responsibility, job, task, work, calling, business, service, office, charge, role, function, mission, province, obligation, assignment, pigeon (*informal*), onus ...*My duty is to look after the animals...*
2 = tax, customs, toll, levy, tariff, excise, due, impost ...*Duty on imports would also be reduced...*
PHRASES **be the duty of** *or* **be someone's duty** = be up to (*informal*), rest with, behove (*archaic*), be (someone's) pigeon (*Brit. informal*), be incumbent upon, devolve upon ...*It is the duty of the state to maintain the educational system...* ◆ **off duty** = off work, off, free, on holiday, at leisure ...*I'm off duty...* ◆ **on duty** = at work, busy, engaged, on active service ...*Extra staff had been put on duty...*

dwarf **VERB** 1 = tower above *or* over, dominate, overlook, stand over, loom over, stand head and shoulders above ...*The huge sign dwarfed his figure...*
2 = eclipse, tower above *or* over, put in the shade, diminish ...*completely dwarfing the achievements of others...*
ADJECTIVE = miniature, small, baby, tiny, pocket, dwarfed, diminutive, petite, bonsai, pint-sized, undersized, teeny-weeny, Lilliputian, teensy-weensy ...*dwarf shrubs...*
NOUN = gnome, midget, Lilliputian, Tom Thumb, munchkin (*informal, chiefly U.S.*), homunculus, manikin, hop-o'-my-thumb, pygmy *or* pigmy ...*With the aid of magic the dwarfs created a wonderful rope...*

Snow White's seven dwarfs

Bashful	Happy
Doc	Sleepy
Dopey	Sneezy
Grumpy	

---

dwell **VERB** (*Formal, literary*) = live, stay, reside, rest, quarter, settle, lodge, abide, hang out (*informal*), sojourn, establish yourself ...*He dwells in the mountains...*
PHRASES **dwell on** *or* **upon something** = go on about, emphasize (*informal*), elaborate on, linger over, harp on about, be engrossed in, expatiate on, continue to think about, tarry over ...*I'd rather not dwell on the past...*

dwelling (*Formal, literary*) = home, house, residence, abode, quarters, establishment, lodging, pad (*slang*), habitation, domicile, dwelling house

dwindle = lessen, fall, decline, contract, sink, fade, weaken, shrink, diminish, decrease, decay, wither, wane, subside, ebb, die down, die out, abate, shrivel, peter out, die away, waste away, taper off, grow less
OPPOSITE increase

dye **VERB** = colour, stain, tint, tinge, pigment, tincture ...*The woman spun and dyed the wool...*
NOUN = colouring, colour, pigment, stain, tint, tinge, colorant ...*bottles of hair dye...*

dying 1 = near death, going, failing, fading, doomed, expiring, ebbing, near the end, moribund, fading fast, in extremis (*Latin*), at death's door, not long for this world, on your deathbed, breathing your last ...*He is a dying man...*
2 = final, last, parting, departing ...*the dying wishes of her mother...*
3 = failing, declining, sinking, foundering, diminishing, decreasing, dwindling, subsiding ...*Shipbuilding is a dying business...*

dynamic = energetic, spirited, powerful, active, vital, driving, electric, go-ahead, lively, magnetic, vigorous, animated, high-powered, forceful, go-getting (*informal*), tireless, indefatigable, high-octane (*informal*), zippy (*informal*), full of beans (*informal*)
OPPOSITE apathetic

dynamism = energy, go (*informal*), drive, push (*informal*), initiative, enterprise, pep, zip (*informal*), vigour, zap (*slang*), get-up-and-go (*informal*), brio, liveliness, forcefulness

dynasty = empire, house, rule, regime, sovereignty

E e

each `DETERMINER` = every, every single …*Each book is beautifully illustrated…*
`PRONOUN` = every one, all, each one, each and every one, one and all …*Three doctors each had a different diagnosis…*
`ADVERB` = apiece, individually, singly, for each, to each, respectively, per person, from each, per head, per capita …*The children were given one each…*

Word Power

each – *Each* is a singular pronoun and should be used with a singular verb – for example, *each of the candidates was interviewed separately* (not *were interviewed separately*).

---

eager 1 = anxious, keen, raring, hungry, intent, yearning, impatient, itching, thirsty, zealous …*Robert was eager to talk about life in the Army…* `OPPOSITE` unenthusiastic
2 = keen, interested, earnest, intense, enthusiastic, passionate, ardent, avid (*informal*), fervent, zealous, fervid, keen as mustard, bright-eyed and bushy-tailed (*informal*) …*He looked at the crowd of eager faces around him…* `OPPOSITE` uninterested

eagerness 1 = longing, anxiety, hunger, yearning, zeal, impatience, impetuosity, avidity …*an eagerness to learn…*
2 = passion, interest, enthusiasm, intensity, fervour, ardour, earnestness, keenness, heartiness, thirst, intentness …*the voice of a woman speaking with breathless eagerness…*

ear `NOUN` 1 = sensitivity, taste, discrimination, appreciation, musical perception …*He has a fine ear for music…*
2 = attention, hearing, regard, notice, consideration, observation, awareness, heed …*The lobbyists have the ear of influential western leaders…*
`PHRASES` **lend an ear** = listen, pay attention, heed, take notice, pay heed, hearken (*archaic*), give ear …*Please lend an ear for a moment or two…*

(Related Words)
adjective: aural
➤ **parts of the ear**

early `ADVERB` 1 = in good time, beforehand, ahead of schedule, in advance, with time to spare, betimes (*archaic*) …*She arrived early to get a good seat…*
`OPPOSITE` late
2 = too soon, before the usual time, prematurely, ahead of time …*The snow came early that year…*
`OPPOSITE` late
`ADJECTIVE` 1 = first, opening, earliest, initial, introductory …*the book's early chapters…*
2 = premature, forward, advanced, untimely, unseasonable …*I decided to take early retirement…*
`OPPOSITE` belated
3 = primitive, first, earliest, young, original, undeveloped, primordial, primeval …*early man's cultural development…* `OPPOSITE` developed

earmark 1 = set aside, reserve, label, flag, tag, allocate, designate, mark out, keep back …*Extra money has been earmarked for the new projects…*
2 = mark out, identify, designate …*The pit was one of the 31 earmarked for closure by the Trade and Industry Secretary…*

earn 1 = be paid, make, get, receive, draw, gain, net, collect, bring in, gross, procure, clear, get paid, take home …*The dancers can earn up to £130 for each session…*
2 = deserve, win, gain, attain, justify, merit, warrant, be entitled to, reap, be worthy of …*Companies must earn a reputation for honesty…*

earnest 1 = serious, keen, grave, intense, steady, dedicated, eager, enthusiastic, passionate, sincere, thoughtful, solemn, ardent, fervent, impassioned, zealous, staid, keen as mustard …*Ella was a pious, earnest young woman…* `OPPOSITE` frivolous
2 = determined, firm, dogged, constant, urgent, intent, persistent, ardent, persevering, resolute, heartfelt, zealous, vehement, wholehearted …*Despite their earnest efforts, they failed to win support…*
`OPPOSITE` half-hearted

earnestness 1 = seriousness, resolution, passion, enthusiasm, warmth, gravity, urgency, zeal, sincerity, fervour, eagerness, ardour, keenness …*He spoke with intense earnestness…*
2 = determination, resolve, urgency, zeal, ardour, vehemence …*the earnestness of their struggle for freedom…*

earnings = income, pay, wages, revenue, reward,

Parts of the ear   http://webschoolsolutions.com/patts/systems/ear.htm

ancus	incus	saccule
auditory nerve	malleus	semicircular canals
cochlea	meatus *or* auditory canal	stapes
eardrum, tympanic membrane, *or* tympanum	organ of Corti	tragus
	oval window	utricle
ear lobe	pinna	
Eustachian tube	round window	

proceeds, salary, receipts, return, remuneration, takings, stipend, take-home pay, emolument, gross pay, net pay

earth 1 = <u>world</u>, planet, globe, sphere, orb, earthly sphere, terrestrial sphere ...*The space shuttle returned safely to earth today...*
2 = <u>ground</u>, land, dry land, terra firma ...*The earth shook under our feet...*
3 = <u>soil</u>, ground, land, dust, mould, clay, dirt, turf, sod, silt, topsoil, clod, loam ...*The road winds through parched earth, scrub and cactus...*

> **Related Words**

adjective: terrestrial

Layers of the earth's crust

asthenosphere	oceanic crust
basement	sima
continental crust	sial
lithosphere	transition zone
lower mantle	upper mantle
Mohorovičić discontinuity	

---

earthenware = <u>crockery</u>, pots, ceramics, pottery, terracotta, crocks, faience, maiolica

earthly 1 = <u>worldly</u>, material, physical, secular, mortal, mundane, terrestrial, temporal, human, materialistic, profane, telluric, sublunary, non-spiritual, tellurian, terrene ...*They lived in an earthly paradise...*
OPPOSITE> spiritual
2 = <u>sensual</u>, worldly, base, physical, gross, low, fleshly, bodily, vile, sordid, carnal ...*He has forsworn all earthly pleasures for the duration of a season...*
3 (*Informal*) = <u>possible</u>, likely, practical, feasible, conceivable, imaginable ...*What earthly reason would they have for lying?...*

earthy 1 = <u>direct</u>, simple, natural, plain, rough, straightforward, robust, down-to-earth, frank, uninhibited, unsophisticated, unrefined ...*Denise was a warm, earthy peasant woman with a lively spirit...*
2 = <u>crude</u>, coarse, raunchy (*slang*), lusty, bawdy, ribald ...*his extremely earthy brand of humour...*
3 = <u>claylike</u>, soil-like ...*Strong, earthy colours add to the effect...*

ease NOUN 1 = <u>straightforwardness</u>, simplicity, readiness ...*For ease of reference, only the relevant extracts of the regulations are included...*
2 = <u>comfort</u>, luxury, leisure, relaxation, prosperity, affluence, rest, repose, restfulness ...*She lived a life of ease...* OPPOSITE> hardship
3 = <u>peace of mind</u>, peace, content, quiet, comfort, happiness, enjoyment, serenity, tranquillity, contentment, calmness, quietude ...*Qigong exercises promote ease of mind and body...* OPPOSITE> agitation
4 = <u>naturalness</u>, informality, freedom, liberty, unaffectedness, unconstraint, unreservedness, relaxedness ...*Co-stars particularly appreciate his ease on the set...* OPPOSITE> awkwardness
▪ VERB 1 = <u>relieve</u>, calm, moderate, soothe, lessen,

alleviate, appease, lighten, lower, allay, relax, still, mitigate, assuage, pacify, mollify, tranquillize, palliate ...*I gave him some brandy to ease the pain...* OPPOSITE> aggravate
2 = <u>reduce</u>, moderate, weaken, diminish, decrease, slow down, dwindle, lessen, die down, abate, slacken, grow less, de-escalate ...*The heavy snow had eased a little...*
3 = <u>move carefully</u>, edge, guide, slip, inch, slide, creep, squeeze, steer, manoeuvre ...*I eased my way towards the door...*
4 = <u>facilitate</u>, further, aid, forward, smooth, assist, speed up, simplify, make easier, expedite, lessen the labour of ...*The information pack is designed to ease the process of making a will...* OPPOSITE> hinder
PHRASES **with ease** = <u>effortlessly</u>, simply, easily, readily, without trouble, with no difficulty ...*Anne was capable of passing her exams with ease...*

easily 1 = <u>without a doubt</u>, clearly, surely, certainly, obviously, definitely, plainly, absolutely, undoubtedly, unquestionably, undeniably, unequivocally, far and away, indisputably, beyond question, indubitably, doubtlessly ...*It could easily be another year before we see any change...*
2 = <u>without difficulty</u>, smoothly, readily, comfortably, effortlessly, simply, with ease, straightforwardly, without trouble, standing on your head, with your eyes closed *or* shut ...*Wear clothes you can remove easily...*

easy 1 = <u>simple</u>, straightforward, no trouble, not difficult, effortless, painless, clear, light, uncomplicated, child's play (*informal*), plain sailing, undemanding, a pushover (*slang*), a piece of cake (*informal*), no bother, a bed of roses, easy-peasy (*slang*) ...*This is not an easy task...* OPPOSITE> hard
2 = <u>untroubled</u>, contented, relaxed, satisfied, calm, peaceful, serene, tranquil, quiet, undisturbed, unworried ...*I was not altogether easy in my mind about this decision...*
3 = <u>relaxed</u>, friendly, open, natural, pleasant, casual, informal, laid-back (*informal*), graceful, gracious, unaffected, easy-going, affable, unpretentious, unforced, undemanding, unconstrained, unceremonious ...*She laughed and joked and made easy conversation with everyone...* OPPOSITE> stiff
4 = <u>carefree</u>, comfortable, pleasant, leisurely, well-to-do, trouble-free, untroubled, cushy (*informal*), unworried, easeful ...*She has had a very easy life...* OPPOSITE> difficult
5 = <u>tolerant</u>, light, liberal, soft, flexible, mild, laid-back (*informal*), indulgent, easy-going, lenient, permissive, unoppressive ...*I guess we've always been too easy with our children...* OPPOSITE> strict
6 (*Informal*) = <u>accommodating</u>, yielding, manageable, easy-going, compliant, amenable, submissive, docile, pliant, tractable, biddable ...*'Your father was not an easy child,' she told me...* OPPOSITE> difficult
7 = <u>vulnerable</u>, soft, naive, susceptible, gullible, exploitable ...*She was an easy target for con-men...*
8 = <u>leisurely</u>, relaxed, comfortable, moderate, unhurried, undemanding ...*the easy pace set by*

pilgrims heading to Canterbury…

easy-going = <u>relaxed</u>, easy, liberal, calm, flexible, mild, casual, tolerant, laid-back (*informal*), indulgent, serene, lenient, carefree, placid, unconcerned, amenable, permissive, happy-go-lucky, unhurried, nonchalant, insouciant, even-tempered, easy-peasy (*slang*) OPPOSITE tense

eat 1 = <u>consume</u>, swallow, chew, scoff (*slang*), devour, munch, tuck into (*informal*), put away, gobble, polish off (*informal*), wolf down …*She was eating a sandwich…*
2 = <u>have a meal</u>, lunch, breakfast, dine, snack, feed, graze (*informal*), have lunch, have dinner, have breakfast, nosh (*slang*), take food, have supper, break bread, chow down (*slang*), take nourishment …*Let's go out to eat…*

eavesdrop = <u>listen in</u>, spy, overhear, bug (*informal*), pry, tap in, snoop (*informal*), earwig (*informal*)

ebb VERB **1** = <u>flow back</u>, go out, withdraw, sink, retreat, fall back, wane, recede, fall away …*We hopped from rock to rock as the tide ebbed from the causeway…*
2 = <u>decline</u>, drop, sink, flag, weaken, shrink, diminish, decrease, deteriorate, decay, dwindle, lessen, subside, degenerate, fall away, fade away, abate, peter out, slacken …*There were occasions when my enthusiasm ebbed…*
NOUN **1** = <u>flowing back</u>, going out, withdrawal, retreat, wane, waning, regression, low water, low tide, ebb tide, outgoing tide, falling tide, receding tide …*We decided to leave on the ebb at six o'clock next morning…*
2 = <u>decline</u>, drop, sinking, flagging, weakening, decrease, decay, dwindling, lessening, deterioration, fading away, petering out, slackening, degeneration, subsidence, shrinkage, diminution …*the ebb of her creative powers…*

ebony = <u>black</u>, dark, jet, raven, sable, pitch-black, jet-black, coal-black
➤ shades from black to white

ebullient = <u>exuberant</u>, excited, enthusiastic, buoyant, exhilarated, elated, irrepressible, vivacious, effervescent, effusive, in high spirits, zestful

eccentric ADJECTIVE = <u>odd</u>, strange, bizarre, weird, peculiar, abnormal, queer (*informal*), irregular, uncommon, quirky, singular, unconventional, idiosyncratic, off-the-wall (*slang*), outlandish, whimsical, rum (*Brit. slang*), capricious, anomalous, freakish, aberrant, wacko (*slang*), outré …*an eccentric character who wears a beret and sunglasses…*
OPPOSITE normal
NOUN = <u>crank</u> (*informal*), character (*informal*), nut (*slang*), freak (*informal*), flake (*slang, chiefly U.S.*), oddity, oddball (*informal*), loose cannon, nonconformist, wacko (*slang*), case (*informal*), screwball (*slang, chiefly U.S. & Canad.*), card (*informal*), odd fish (*informal*), kook (*U.S. & Canad. informal*), queer fish (*Brit. informal*), rum customer (*Brit. slang*), weirdo *or* weirdie (*informal*) …*My other friend was a real English eccentric…*

eccentricity 1 = <u>oddity</u>, peculiarity, strangeness, irregularity, weirdness, singularity, oddness, waywardness, nonconformity, capriciousness, unconventionality, queerness (*informal*), bizarreness, whimsicality, freakishness, outlandishness …*She is unusual to the point of eccentricity…*
2 = <u>foible</u>, anomaly, abnormality, quirk, oddity, aberration, peculiarity, idiosyncrasy …*We all have our little eccentricities…*

ecclesiastical = <u>clerical</u>, religious, church, churchly, priestly, spiritual, holy, divine, pastoral, sacerdotal

echelon = <u>level</u>, place, office, position, step, degree, rank, grade, tier, rung

echo NOUN **1** = <u>reverberation</u>, ringing, repetition, answer, resonance, resounding …*He heard nothing but the echoes of his own voice in the cave…*
2 = <u>copy</u>, reflection, clone, reproduction, imitation, duplicate, double, reiteration …*Their cover version is just a pale echo of the real thing…*
3 = <u>reminder</u>, suggestion, trace, hint, recollection, vestige, evocation, intimation …*The accident has echoes of past disasters…*
VERB **1** = <u>reverberate</u>, repeat, resound, ring, resonate …*The distant crash of bombs echoes through the whole city…*
2 = <u>recall</u>, reflect, copy, mirror, resemble, reproduce, parrot, imitate, reiterate, ape …*Many phrases in the last chapter echo earlier passages…*

eclectic = <u>diverse</u>, general, broad, varied, comprehensive, extensive, wide-ranging, selective, diversified, manifold, heterogeneous, catholic, all-embracing, liberal, many-sided, multifarious, dilettantish

eclipse NOUN **1** = <u>obscuring</u>, covering, blocking, shading, dimming, extinction, darkening, blotting out, occultation …*a total eclipse of the sun…*
2 = <u>decline</u>, fall, loss, failure, weakening, deterioration, degeneration, diminution …*the eclipse of the influence of the Republican party in West Germany…*
VERB **1** = <u>surpass</u>, exceed, overshadow, excel, transcend, outdo, outclass, outshine, leave *or* put in the shade (*informal*) …*The gramophone was eclipsed by the compact disc…*
2 = <u>obscure</u>, cover, block, cloud, conceal, dim, veil, darken, shroud, extinguish, blot out …*The sun was eclipsed by the moon…*

economic 1 = <u>financial</u>, business, trade, industrial, commercial, mercantile …*The pace of economic growth is picking up…*
2 = <u>monetary</u>, financial, material, fiscal, budgetary, bread-and-butter (*informal*), pecuniary …*Their country faces an economic crisis…*
3 = <u>profitable</u>, successful, commercial, rewarding, productive, lucrative, worthwhile, viable, solvent, cost-effective, money-making, profit-making, remunerative …*The service will make surfing the Web an economic proposition…*
4 (*Informal*) = <u>economical</u>, fair, cheap, reasonable, modest, low-priced, inexpensive …*The new process is more economic but less environmentally friendly…*

economical 1 = economic, fair, cheap, reasonable, modest, low-priced, inexpensive ...*It is more economical to wash a full load*... OPPOSITE expensive
2 = thrifty, sparing, careful, prudent, provident, frugal, parsimonious, scrimping, economizing ...*ideas for economical housekeeping*... OPPOSITE extravagant
3 = efficient, sparing, cost-effective, money-saving, time-saving, work-saving, unwasteful ...*the practical, economical virtues of a small hatchback*... OPPOSITE wasteful

economics = finance, commerce, the dismal science

economy 1 = financial system, financial state ...*Africa's most industrialized economy*...
2 = thrift, saving, restraint, prudence, providence, husbandry, retrenchment, frugality, parsimony, thriftiness, sparingness ...*They have achieved quite remarkable effects with great economy of means*...

ecstasy = rapture, delight, joy, enthusiasm, frenzy, bliss, trance, euphoria, fervour, elation, rhapsody, exaltation, transport, ravishment OPPOSITE agony

ecstatic = rapturous, entranced, enthusiastic, frenzied, joyous, fervent, joyful, elated, over the moon (*informal*), overjoyed, blissful, delirious, euphoric, enraptured, on cloud nine (*informal*), cock-a-hoop, blissed out, transported, rhapsodic, sent, walking on air, in seventh heaven, floating on air, in exaltation, in transports of delight

ecumenical = unifying, universal, non-denominational, non-sectarian, general

eddy NOUN = swirl, whirlpool, vortex, undertow, tideway, counter-current, counterflow ...*the swirling eddies of the fast-flowing river*...
VERB = swirl, turn, roll, spin, twist, surge, revolve, whirl, billow ...*The dust whirled and eddied in the sunlight*...

edge NOUN 1 = border, side, line, limit, bound, lip, margin, outline, boundary, fringe, verge, brink, threshold, rim, brim, perimeter, contour, periphery, flange ...*She was standing at the water's edge*...
2 = verge, point, brink, threshold ...*They have driven the rhino to the edge of extinction*...
3 = advantage, lead, dominance, superiority, upper hand, head start, ascendancy, whip hand ...*This could give them the edge over their oppponents*...
4 = power, interest, force, bite, effectiveness, animation, zest, incisiveness, powerful quality ...*Featuring new bands gives the show an edge*...
5 = sharpness, point, sting, urgency, bitterness, keenness, pungency, acuteness ...*There was an unpleasant edge to her voice*...
VERB 1 = inch, ease, creep, worm, slink, steal, sidle, work, move slowly ...*He edged closer to the door*...
2 = border, shape, bind, trim, fringe, rim, hem, pipe ...*a chocolate brown jacket edged with yellow*...
PHRASES **on edge** = tense, excited, wired (*slang*), nervous, eager, impatient, irritable, apprehensive, edgy, uptight (*informal*), ill at ease, twitchy (*informal*), tetchy, on tenterhooks, keyed up, antsy (*informal*) ...*Ever since their arrival she had felt on edge*...

edgy = nervous, wired (*slang*), anxious, tense, neurotic, irritable, touchy, uptight (*informal*), on edge, nervy (*Brit. informal*), ill at ease, restive, twitchy (*informal*), irascible, tetchy, on tenterhooks, keyed up, antsy (*informal*), on pins and needles

edible = safe to eat, harmless, wholesome, palatable, digestible, eatable, comestible (*rare*), fit to eat, good OPPOSITE inedible

edict = decree, law, act, order, ruling, demand, command, regulation, dictate, mandate, canon, manifesto, injunction, statute, fiat, ordinance, proclamation, enactment, dictum, pronouncement, ukase (*rare*), pronunciamento

edifice = building, house, structure, construction, pile, erection, habitation

edify = instruct, school, teach, inform, guide, improve, educate, nurture, elevate, enlighten, uplift

edifying = instructive, improving, inspiring, elevating, enlightening, uplifting, instructional

edit 1 = revise, check, improve, correct, polish, adapt, rewrite, censor, condense, annotate, rephrase, redraft, copy-edit, emend, prepare for publication, redact ...*The publisher has the right to edit the book once it has been written*...
2 = put together, select, arrange, organize, assemble, compose, rearrange, reorder ...*She has edited a collection of essays*...
3 = be in charge of, control, direct, be responsible for, be the editor of ...*I used to edit the college paper in the old days*...

edition = version, copy, issue, programme (*TV, Radio*), printing, volume, impression, publication, number

educate = teach, school, train, coach, develop, improve, exercise, inform, discipline, rear, foster, mature, drill, tutor, instruct, cultivate, enlighten, civilize, edify, indoctrinate

educated 1 = cultured, lettered, intellectual, learned, informed, experienced, polished, literary, sophisticated, refined, cultivated, enlightened, knowledgeable, civilized, tasteful, urbane, erudite, well-bred ...*He is an educated, amiable and decent man*... OPPOSITE uncultured
2 = taught, schooled, coached, informed, tutored, instructed, nurtured, well-informed, well-read, well-taught ...*The country's workforce is well educated and diligent*... OPPOSITE uneducated

education 1 = teaching, schooling, training, development, coaching, improvement, discipline, instruction, drilling, tutoring, nurture, tuition, enlightenment, erudition, indoctrination, edification ...*institutions for the care and education of children*...
2 = learning, schooling, culture, breeding, scholarship, civilization, cultivation, refinement ...*a man with little education*...

educational 1 = academic, school, learning, teaching, scholastic, pedagogical, pedagogic ...*the British educational system*...
2 = instructive, useful, cultural, illuminating, enlightening, informative, instructional, didactic, edifying, educative, heuristic ...*The kids had an

enjoyable and educational day…

educator = <u>teacher</u>, professor, lecturer, don, coach, guide, fellow, trainer, tutor, instructor, mentor, schoolteacher, pedagogue, edifier, educationalist *or* educationist, schoolmaster *or* schoolmistress, master *or* mistress

eerie = <u>uncanny</u>, strange, frightening, ghostly, weird, mysterious, scary (*informal*), sinister, uneasy, fearful, awesome, unearthly, supernatural, unnatural, spooky (*informal*), creepy (*informal*), spectral, eldritch (*poetic*), preternatural

efface = <u>obliterate</u>, remove, destroy, cancel, wipe out, erase, eradicate, excise, delete, annihilate, raze, blot out, cross out, expunge, rub out, extirpate

effect NOUN **1** = <u>result</u>, consequence, conclusion, outcome, event, issue, aftermath, fruit, end result, upshot …*the psychological effects of head injuries…*
2 = <u>impression</u>, feeling, impact, influence …*The whole effect is cool, light and airy…*
3 = <u>purpose</u>, meaning, impression, sense, import, drift, intent, essence, thread, tenor, purport …*He told me to get lost, or words to that effect…*
4 = <u>implementation</u>, force, action, performance, operation, enforcement, execution …*We are now resuming diplomatic relations with Syria with immediate effect…*
PLURAL NOUN = <u>belongings</u>, goods, things, property, stuff, gear, furniture, possessions, trappings, paraphernalia, personal property, accoutrements, chattels, movables …*His daughters came to collect his effects…*
VERB = <u>bring about</u>, make, cause, produce, create, complete, achieve, perform, carry out, fulfil, accomplish, execute, initiate, give rise to, consummate, actuate, effectuate …*Prospects for effecting real political change have taken a step backward…*
PHRASES **in effect** = <u>in fact</u>, really, actually, essentially, virtually, effectively, in reality, in truth, as good as, in actual fact, to all intents and purposes, in all but name, in actuality, for practical purposes …*The deal would create, in effect, the world's biggest airline…*
♦ **put, bring** *or* **carry into effect** = <u>implement</u>, perform, carry out, fulfil, enforce, execute, bring about, put into action, put into operation, bring into force …*a decree bringing these political reforms into effect…* ♦ **take** *or* **come into effect** = <u>produce results</u>, work, begin, come into force, become operative …*The ban takes effect from July…* ♦ **to good effect** = <u>successfully</u>, effectively, productively, fruitfully …*Mr Morris feels the museum is using advertising to good effect…* ♦ **to no effect** = <u>unsuccessfully</u>, in vain, to no avail, without success, pointlessly, ineffectively, to no purpose, with no use …*Mr Charles made a formal complaint to the manager, to no effect…*

> ## Word Power
>
> **effect** – It is quite common for the verb *effect* to be mistakenly used where *affect* is intended. *Effect* is relatively uncommon and rather formal, and is a synonym of 'bring about'. Conversely, the noun *effect* is quite often mistakenly written with an initial *a*. The following are correct: *the group is still recovering from the effects of the recession; they really are powerless to effect any change*. The next two examples are incorrect: *the full affects of the shutdown won't be felt for several more days; men whose lack of hair doesn't effect their self-esteem.*

effective **1** = <u>efficient</u>, successful, useful, active, capable, valuable, helpful, adequate, productive, operative, competent, serviceable, efficacious, effectual …*Antibiotics are effective against this organism…* OPPOSITE ineffective
2 = <u>powerful</u>, strong, convincing, persuasive, telling, impressive, compelling, potent, forceful, striking, emphatic, weighty, forcible, cogent …*You can't make an effective argument if all you do is stridently voice your opinion…* OPPOSITE weak
3 = <u>virtual</u>, essential, practical, implied, implicit, tacit, unacknowledged …*They have had effective control of the area…*
4 = <u>in operation</u>, official, current, legal, real, active, actual, in effect, valid, operative, in force, in execution …*The new rules will become effective in the next few days…* OPPOSITE inoperative

effectiveness = <u>power</u>, effect, efficiency, success, strength, capability, use, validity, usefulness, potency, efficacy, fruitfulness, productiveness

effeminate = <u>womanly</u>, affected, camp (*informal*), soft, weak, feminine, unmanly, sissy, effete, foppish, womanish, wussy (*slang*), womanlike, poofy (*slang*), wimpish *or* wimpy (*informal*) OPPOSITE manly

effervescent **1** = <u>fizzy</u>, bubbling, sparkling, bubbly, foaming, fizzing, fermenting, frothing, frothy, aerated, carbonated, foamy, gassy …*an effervescent mineral water…* OPPOSITE still
2 = <u>lively</u>, excited, dynamic, enthusiastic, sparkling, energetic, animated, merry, buoyant, exhilarated, bubbly, exuberant, high-spirited, irrepressible, ebullient, chirpy, vital, scintillating, vivacious, zingy (*informal*) …*an effervescent blonde actress…* OPPOSITE dull

effete = <u>weak</u>, cowardly, feeble, ineffectual, decrepit, spineless, enfeebled, weak-kneed (*informal*), enervated, overrefined, chicken-hearted, wimpish *or* wimpy (*informal*)

efficacy = <u>effectiveness</u>, efficiency, power, value, success, strength, virtue, vigour, use, usefulness, potency, fruitfulness, productiveness, efficaciousness

efficiency **1** = <u>effectiveness</u>, power, economy, productivity, organization, efficacy, cost-effectiveness, orderliness …*ways to increase agricultural efficiency…*
2 = <u>competence</u>, ability, skill, expertise, capability,

readiness, professionalism, proficiency, adeptness, skilfulness ...*her efficiency as a manager*...

efficient 1 = <u>effective</u>, successful, structured, productive, powerful, systematic, streamlined, cost-effective, methodical, well-organized, well-planned, labour-saving, effectual ...*an efficient form of contraception*... OPPOSITE> inefficient
2 = <u>competent</u>, able, professional, capable, organized, productive, skilful, adept, ready, proficient, businesslike, well-organized, workmanlike ...*a highly efficient worker*... OPPOSITE> incompetent

effigy = <u>likeness</u>, figure, image, model, guy, carving, representation, statue, icon, idol, dummy, statuette

effluent = <u>waste</u>, discharge, flow, emission, sewage, pollutant, outpouring, outflow, exhalation, issue, emanation, liquid waste, efflux, effluvium, effluence

effort 1 = <u>attempt</u>, try, endeavour, shot (*informal*), bid, essay, go (*informal*), stab (*informal*) ...*He made no effort to hide*...
2 = <u>exertion</u>, work, labour, trouble, force, energy, struggle, stress, application, strain, striving, graft, toil, hard graft, travail (*literary*), elbow grease (*facetious*), blood, sweat, and tears (*informal*) ...*A great deal of effort had been put into the planning*...
3 = <u>achievement</u>, act, performance, product, job, production, creation, feat, deed, accomplishment, attainment ...*The gallery is showcasing her latest efforts*...

effortless 1 = <u>easy</u>, simple, flowing, smooth, graceful, painless, uncomplicated, trouble-free, facile, undemanding, easy-peasy (*slang*), untroublesome, unexacting ...*In a single effortless motion, he scooped Frannie into his arms*... OPPOSITE> difficult
2 = <u>natural</u>, simple, spontaneous, instinctive, intuitive ...*She liked him above all for his effortless charm*...

effusive = <u>demonstrative</u>, enthusiastic, lavish, extravagant, overflowing, gushing, exuberant, expansive, ebullient, free-flowing, unrestrained, talkative, fulsome, profuse, unreserved

egg NOUN = <u>ovum</u>, gamete, germ cell ...*a baby bird hatching from its egg*...
PHRASES **egg someone on** = <u>incite</u>, push, encourage, urge, prompt, spur, provoke, prod, goad, exhort ...*She was egging him on to fight*...

egocentric = <u>self-centred</u>, vain, selfish, narcissistic, self-absorbed, egotistical, inward looking, self-important, self-obsessed, self-seeking, egoistic, egoistical

egotism *or* **egoism** = <u>self-centredness</u>, self-esteem, vanity, superiority, self-interest, selfishness, narcissism, self-importance, self-regard, self-love, self-seeking, self-absorption, self-obsession, egocentricity, egomania, self-praise, vainglory, self-conceit, self-admiration, conceitedness

ejaculate 1 = <u>have an orgasm</u>, come (*taboo slang*), climax, emit semen ...*a tendency to ejaculate quickly*...
2 = <u>discharge</u>, release, emit, shoot out, eject, spurt ...*sperm ejaculated by the male during sexual intercourse*...

3 (*Literary*) = <u>exclaim</u>, declare, shout, call out, cry out, burst out, blurt out ...*'Good God!' Liz ejaculated*...

ejaculation = <u>discharge</u>, release, emission, ejection

eject 1 = <u>throw out</u>, remove, turn out, expel (*slang*), exile, oust, banish, deport, drive out, evict, boot out (*informal*), force to leave, chuck out (*informal*), bounce, turf out (*informal*), give the bum's rush (*slang*), show someone the door, throw someone out on their ear (*informal*) ...*He was forcibly ejected from the restaurant*...
2 = <u>dismiss</u>, sack (*informal*), fire (*informal*), remove, get rid of, discharge, expel, throw out, oust, kick out (*informal*) ...*He was ejected from his first job for persistent latecoming*...
3 = <u>discharge</u>, expel, emit, give off ...*He fired a single shot, then ejected the spent cartridge*...
4 = <u>bail out</u>, escape, get out ...*The pilot ejected from the plane and escaped injury*...

ejection 1 = <u>expulsion</u>, removal, ouster (*Law*), deportation, eviction, banishment, exile ...*the ejection of hecklers at the meeting*...
2 = <u>dismissal</u>, sacking (*informal*), firing (*informal*), removal, discharge, the boot (*slang*), expulsion, the sack (*informal*), dislodgement ...*These actions led to his ejection from office*...
3 = <u>emission</u>, throwing out, expulsion, spouting, casting out, disgorgement ...*the ejection of an electron by an atomic nucleus*...

eke out VERB = <u>be sparing with</u>, stretch out, be economical with, economize on, husband, be frugal with ...*I had to eke out my redundancy money for about ten weeks*...
PHRASES **eke out a living** = <u>support yourself</u>, survive, get by, make ends meet, scrimp, save, scrimp and save ...*people trying to eke out a living in forest areas*...

elaborate ADJECTIVE 1 = <u>complicated</u>, detailed, studied, laboured, perfected, complex, careful, exact, precise, thorough, intricate, skilful, painstaking ...*an elaborate research project*...
2 = <u>ornate</u>, detailed, involved, complex, fancy, complicated, decorated, extravagant, intricate, baroque, ornamented, fussy, embellished, showy, ostentatious, florid ...*a designer known for his elaborate costumes*... OPPOSITE> plain
VERB 1 = <u>develop</u>, improve, enhance, polish, complicate, decorate, refine, garnish, ornament, flesh out ...*The plan was elaborated by five members of the council*...
2 = <u>expand (upon)</u>, extend, enlarge (on), amplify, embellish, flesh out, add detail (to) ...*A spokesman declined to elaborate on the statement*... OPPOSITE> simplify

élan = <u>style</u>, spirit, dash, flair, animation, vigour, verve, zest, panache, esprit, brio, vivacity, impetuosity

elapse = <u>pass</u>, go, go by, lapse, pass by, slip away, roll on, slip by, roll by, glide by

elastic 1 = <u>flexible</u>, yielding, supple, rubbery, pliable, plastic, springy, pliant, tensile, stretchy, ductile, stretchable ...*Work the dough until it is slightly* *elastic...* OPPOSITE> rigid

2 = adaptable, yielding, variable, flexible, accommodating, tolerant, adjustable, supple, complaisant ...*an elastic interpretation of the rules...* OPPOSITE> inflexible

elasticity 1 = flexibility, suppleness, plasticity, give (*informal*), pliability, ductility, springiness, pliancy, stretchiness, rubberiness ...*Daily facial exercises help to retain the skin's elasticity...*

2 = adaptability, accommodation, flexibility, tolerance, variability, suppleness, complaisance, adjustability, compliantness ...*the elasticity of demand for this commodity...*

elated = joyful, excited, delighted, proud, cheered, thrilled, elevated, animated, roused, exhilarated, ecstatic, jubilant, joyous, over the moon (*informal*), overjoyed, blissful, euphoric, rapt, gleeful, sent, puffed up, exultant, in high spirits, on cloud nine (*informal*), cock-a-hoop, blissed out, in seventh heaven, floating *or* walking on air OPPOSITE> dejected

elation = joy, delight, thrill, excitement, ecstasy, bliss, euphoria, glee, rapture, high spirits, exhilaration, jubilation, exaltation, exultation, joyfulness, joyousness

elbow NOUN = joint, turn, corner, bend, angle, curve ...*The boat was moored at the elbow of the river...* VERB = push, force, crowd, shoulder, knock, bump, shove, nudge, jostle, hustle ...*They elbowed me out of the way...* PHRASES **at your elbow** = within reach, near, to hand, handy, at hand, close by ...*the whisky glass that was forever at his elbow...*

elder ADJECTIVE = older, first, senior, first-born, earlier born ...*the elder of her two daughters...* NOUN **1** = older person, senior ...*Nowadays the young have no respect for their elders...*

2 (*Presbyterianism*) = church official, leader, office bearer, presbyter ...*He is now an elder of the village church...*

elect VERB **1** = vote for, choose, pick, determine, select, appoint, opt for, designate, pick out, settle on, decide upon ...*The people have voted to elect a new president...*

2 = choose, decide, prefer, select, opt ...*Those electing to smoke will be seated at the rear...* ADJECTIVE **1** = selected, chosen, picked, choice, preferred, select, elite, hand-picked ...*one of the elect few permitted to enter...*

2 = future, to-be, coming, next, appointed, designate, prospective ...*the date when the president-elect takes office...*

election 1 = vote, poll, ballot, determination, referendum, franchise, plebiscite, show of hands ...*Poland's first fully free elections for more than fifty years...*

2 = appointment, choosing, picking, choice, selection ...*the election of the Labour government in 1964...*

elector = voter, chooser, selector, constituent, member of the electorate, member of a constituency, enfranchised person

electric 1 = electric-powered, powered, cordless, battery-operated, electrically-charged, mains-operated ...*her electric guitar...*

2 = charged, exciting, stirring, thrilling, stimulating, dynamic, tense, rousing, electrifying ...*The atmosphere in the hall was electric...*

electrify 1 = thrill, shock, excite, amaze, stir, stimulate, astonish, startle, arouse, animate, rouse, astound, jolt, fire, galvanize, take your breath away ...*The spectators were electrified by his courage...* OPPOSITE> bore

2 = wire up, wire, supply electricity to, convert to electricity ...*The west-coast line was electrified as long ago as 1974...*

elegance = style, taste, beauty, grace, dignity, sophistication, grandeur, refinement, polish, gentility, sumptuousness, courtliness, gracefulness, tastefulness, exquisiteness

elegant 1 = stylish, fine, beautiful, sophisticated, delicate, artistic, handsome, fashionable, refined, cultivated, chic, luxurious, exquisite, nice, discerning, graceful, polished, sumptuous, genteel, choice, tasteful, urbane, courtly, modish, comely, à la mode ...*Patricia looked as beautiful and elegant as always...* OPPOSITE> inelegant

2 = ingenious, simple, effective, appropriate, clever, neat, apt ...*The poem impressed me with its elegant simplicity...*

elegiac (*Literary*) = lamenting, sad, melancholy, nostalgic, mournful, plaintive, melancholic, sorrowful, funereal, valedictory, keening, dirgeful, threnodial, threnodic

elegy = lament, requiem, dirge, plaint (*archaic*), threnody, keen, funeral song, coronach (*Scot. & Irish*), funeral poem

element NOUN **1** = component, part, feature, unit, section, factor, principle, aspect, foundation, ingredient, constituent, subdivision ...*one of the key elements of the UN's peace plan...*

2 = group, faction, clique, set, party, circle ...*The government must weed out criminal elements from the security forces...*

3 = trace, suggestion, hint, dash, suspicion, tinge, smattering, soupçon ...*There is an element of truth in his accusation...* PLURAL NOUN = weather conditions, climate, the weather, wind and rain, atmospheric conditions, powers of nature, atmospheric forces ...*The area is exposed to the elements...* PHRASES **be in your element** = be in a situation you enjoy, be in your natural environment, be in familiar surroundings ...*My stepmother was in her element, organizing everyone...*

elemental 1 = basic, essential, principal, fundamental, elementary ...*the elemental theory of music...*

2 = primal, original, primitive, primordial ...*the elemental powers of the universe...*

3 = atmospheric, natural, meteorological ...*the elemental forces that shaped this rugged Atlantic* *coast...*

elementary 1 = <u>basic</u>, essential, primary, initial, fundamental, introductory, preparatory, rudimentary, elemental, bog-standard (*informal*) ...*Literacy now includes elementary computer skills...* OPPOSITE advanced
2 = <u>simple</u>, clear, easy, plain, straightforward, rudimentary, uncomplicated, facile, undemanding, unexacting ...*elementary questions designed to test numeracy...* OPPOSITE complicated

elevate 1 = <u>promote</u>, raise, advance, upgrade, exalt, kick upstairs (*informal*), aggrandize, give advancement to ...*He was elevated to the post of Prime Minister...*
2 = <u>increase</u>, lift, raise, step up, intensify, move up, hoist, raise high ...*Emotional stress can elevate blood pressure...*
3 = <u>raise</u>, lift, heighten, uplift, hoist, lift up, raise up, hike up, upraise ...*Jack elevated the gun at the sky...*
4 = <u>cheer</u>, raise, excite, boost, animate, rouse, uplift, brighten, exhilarate, hearten, lift up, perk up, buoy up, gladden, elate ...*She bought some new clothes, but they failed to elevate her spirits...*

elevated 1 = <u>exalted</u>, high, important, august, grand, superior, noble, dignified, high-ranking, lofty ...*His new job has given him a certain elevated status...*
2 = <u>high-minded</u>, high, fine, grand, noble, inflated, dignified, sublime, lofty, high-flown, pompous, exalted, bombastic ...*the magazine's elevated tone...* OPPOSITE humble
3 = <u>raised</u>, high, lifted up, upraised ...*an elevated platform on the stage...*

elevation 1 = <u>side</u>, back, face, front, aspect ...*the addition of a two-storey wing on the north elevation...*
2 = <u>altitude</u>, height ...*We're at an elevation of about 13,000 feet above sea level...*
3 = <u>promotion</u>, upgrading, advancement, exaltation, preferment, aggrandizement ...*celebrating his elevation to the rank of Prime Minister...*
4 = <u>rise</u>, hill, mountain, height, mound, berg (*S. African*), high ground, higher ground, eminence, hillock, rising ground, acclivity ...*The resort is built on an elevation overlooking the sea...*

elicit 1 = <u>bring about</u>, cause, derive, bring out, evoke, give rise to, draw out, bring forth, bring to light, call forth ...*He was hopeful that his request would elicit a positive response...*
2 = <u>obtain</u>, extract, exact, evoke, wrest, draw out, extort, educe ...*the question of how far police should go to elicit a confession...*

eligible 1 = <u>entitled</u>, fit, qualified, suited, suitable ...*You could be eligible for a university scholarship...* OPPOSITE ineligible
2 = <u>available</u>, free, single, unmarried, unattached ...*Britain's most eligible bachelor...*

eliminate 1 = <u>remove</u>, end, stop, withdraw, get rid of, abolish, cut out, dispose of, terminate, banish, eradicate, put an end to, do away with, dispense with, stamp out, exterminate, get shot of, wipe from the face of the earth ...*The Act has not eliminated discrimination in employment...*
2 = <u>knock out</u>, drop, reject, exclude, axe (*informal*), get rid of, expel, leave out, throw out, omit, put out, eject ...*I was eliminated from the 400 metres in the semifinals...*
3 (*Slang*) = <u>murder</u>, kill, do in (*slang*), take out (*slang*), terminate, slay, blow away (*slang, chiefly U.S.*), liquidate, annihilate, exterminate, bump off (*slang*), rub out (*U.S. slang*), waste (*informal*) ...*They claimed that 87,000 'reactionaries' had been eliminated...*

elite NOUN = <u>aristocracy</u>, best, pick, elect, cream, upper class, nobility, gentry, high society, crème de la crème (*French*), flower, nonpareil ...*a government comprised mainly of the elite...* OPPOSITE rabble
ADJECTIVE = <u>leading</u>, best, finest, pick, choice, selected, elect, crack (*slang*), supreme, exclusive, privileged, first-class, foremost, first-rate, pre-eminent, most excellent ...*the elite troops of the President's bodyguard...*

elitist ADJECTIVE = <u>snobbish</u>, exclusive, superior, arrogant, selective, pretentious, stuck-up (*informal*), patronizing, condescending, snooty (*informal*), uppity, high and mighty (*informal*), hoity-toity (*informal*), high-hat (*informal, chiefly U.S.*), uppish (*Brit. informal*) ...*He described skiing as an elitist sport...*
NOUN = <u>snob</u>, highbrow, prig, social climber ...*He was an elitist who had no time for the masses...*

elixir 1 = <u>panacea</u>, cure-all, nostrum, sovereign remedy ...*a magical elixir of eternal youth...*
2 = <u>syrup</u>, essence, solution, concentrate, mixture, extract, potion, distillation, tincture, distillate ...*For severe teething pains, try an infant paracetamol elixir...*

elliptical or **elliptic** 1 = <u>oval</u>, egg-shaped, ovoid, ovate, ellipsoidal, oviform ...*the moon's elliptical orbit...*
2 = <u>oblique</u>, concentrated, obscure, compact, indirect, ambiguous, concise, condensed, terse, cryptic, laconic, abstruse, recondite ...*elliptical references to matters best not discussed in public...*

elongate = <u>lengthen</u>, extend, stretch (out), make longer

elongated = <u>extended</u>, long, stretched

elope = <u>run away</u>, leave, escape, disappear, bolt, run off, slip away, abscond, decamp, sneak off, steal away, do a bunk (*informal*)

eloquence 1 = <u>fluency</u>, effectiveness, oratory, expressiveness, persuasiveness, forcefulness, gracefulness, powerfulness ...*the eloquence with which he delivered his message...*
2 = <u>expressiveness</u>, significance, meaningfulness, pointedness ...*the eloquence of his gestures...*

eloquent 1 = <u>silver-tongued</u>, moving, powerful, effective, stirring, articulate, persuasive, graceful, forceful, fluent, expressive, well-expressed ...*He made a very eloquent speech at the dinner...* OPPOSITE inarticulate
2 = <u>expressive</u>, telling, pointed, revealing, significant, pregnant, vivid, meaningful, indicative, suggestive ...*Her only reply was an eloquent glance at the clock...*

elsewhere = <u>in</u> *or* <u>to another place</u>, away, abroad, hence (*archaic*), somewhere else, not here, in other places, in *or* to a different place

elucidate = <u>clarify</u>, explain, illustrate, interpret, make clear, unfold, illuminate, spell out, clear up, gloss, expound, make plain, annotate, explicate, shed *or* throw light upon

elude 1 = <u>evade</u>, escape, lose, avoid, flee, duck (*informal*), dodge, get away from, shake off, run away from, circumvent, outrun, body-swerve (*Scot.*) ...*The thieves managed to elude the police for months...*
2 = <u>escape</u>, baffle, frustrate, puzzle, stump, foil, be beyond (someone), thwart, confound ...*The appropriate word eluded him...*

> ## *Word Power*
>
> **elude** – *Elude* is sometimes wrongly used where *allude* is meant: *he was alluding* (not *eluding*) *to his previous visit to the city.*

elusive 1 = <u>difficult to catch</u>, tricky, slippery, difficult to find, evasive, shifty ...*I had no luck in tracking down this elusive man...*
2 = <u>indefinable</u>, puzzling, fleeting, subtle, baffling, indefinite, transient, intangible, indescribable, transitory, indistinct ...*an attempt to recapture an elusive memory...*
3 = <u>evasive</u>, puzzling, misleading, baffling, ambiguous, fraudulent, deceptive, illusory, equivocal, fallacious, unspecific, oracular, elusory ...*an elusive answer...*

> ## *Word Power*
>
> **elusive** – The spelling of *elusive*, as in *a shy, elusive character*, should be noted. This adjective derives from the verb *elude*, and should not be confused with the rare word *illusive* meaning 'not real' or 'based on illusion'.

emaciated = <u>skeletal</u>, thin, weak, lean, pinched, skinny, wasted, gaunt, bony, haggard, atrophied, scrawny, attenuate, attenuated, undernourished, scraggy, half-starved, cadaverous, macilent (*rare*)

emanate 1 = <u>give out</u>, send out, emit, radiate, exude, issue, give off, exhale, send forth ...*He emanated sympathy...*
2 = <u>flow</u>, emerge, spring, proceed, arise, stem, derive, originate, issue, come forth ...*The aroma of burning wood emanated from the stove...*

emancipate = <u>free</u>, release, liberate, set free, deliver, discharge, let out, let loose, untie, unchain, enfranchise, unshackle, disencumber, unfetter, unbridle, disenthral, manumit OPPOSITE> enslave

emancipation = <u>liberation</u>, freedom, freeing, release, liberty, discharge, liberating, setting free, letting loose, untying, deliverance, unchaining, manumission, enfranchisement, unshackling, unfettering OPPOSITE> slavery

emasculate = <u>weaken</u>, soften, cripple, impoverish, debilitate, reduce the power of, enfeeble, make feeble, enervate, deprive of force

embalm = <u>preserve</u>, lay out, mummify

embargo NOUN = <u>ban</u>, bar, block, barrier, restriction, boycott, restraint, check, prohibition, moratorium, stoppage, impediment, blockage, hindrance, interdiction, interdict, proscription ...*The UN has imposed an arms embargo against the country...*
VERB = <u>block</u>, stop, bar, ban, restrict, boycott, check, prohibit, impede, blacklist, proscribe, ostracize, debar, interdict ...*They embargoed oil shipments to the US...*

embark VERB = <u>go aboard</u>, climb aboard, board ship, step aboard, go on board, take ship ...*They embarked on the battle cruiser HMS Renown...* OPPOSITE> get off
PHRASES **embark on something** = <u>begin</u>, start, launch, enter, engage, take up, set out, undertake, initiate, set about, plunge into, commence, broach ...*He is embarking on a new career as a writer...*

embarrass = <u>shame</u>, distress, show up (*informal*), humiliate, disconcert, chagrin, fluster, mortify, faze, discomfit, make uncomfortable, make awkward, discountenance, nonplus, abash, discompose, make ashamed, put out of countenance

embarrassed = <u>ashamed</u>, upset, shamed, uncomfortable, shown-up, awkward, abashed, humiliated, uneasy, unsettled, self-conscious, thrown, disconcerted, red-faced, chagrined, flustered, mortified, sheepish, discomfited, discountenanced, caught with egg on your face, not know where to put yourself, put out of countenance

embarrassing = <u>humiliating</u>, upsetting, compromising, shaming, distressing, delicate, uncomfortable, awkward, tricky, sensitive, troublesome, shameful, disconcerting, touchy, mortifying, discomfiting, toe-curling (*slang*), cringe-making (*Brit. informal*), cringeworthy (*Brit. informal*), barro (*Austral. slang*)

embarrassment NOUN 1 = <u>shame</u>, distress, showing up (*informal*), humiliation, discomfort, unease, chagrin, self-consciousness, awkwardness, mortification, discomfiture, bashfulness, discomposure ...*We apologise for any embarrassment this statement may have caused...*
2 = <u>problem</u>, difficulty, nuisance, source of trouble, thorn in your flesh ...*The poverty figures were an embarrassment to the president...*
3 = <u>predicament</u>, problem, difficulty (*informal*), mess, jam (*informal*), plight, scrape (*informal*), pickle (*informal*) ...*He is in a state of temporary financial embarrassment...*
PHRASES **an embarrassment of riches** = <u>overabundance</u>, excess, surplus, glut, profusion, surfeit, superabundance, superfluity ...*The art gallery has an embarrassment of riches, with nowhere to put most of them...*

embed *or* **imbed** = <u>fix</u>, set, plant, root, sink, lodge, insert, implant, drive in, dig in, hammer in, ram in

embellish 1 = <u>decorate</u>, enhance, adorn, dress, grace, deck, trim, dress up, enrich, garnish, ornament, gild, festoon, bedeck, tart up (*slang*), beautify ...*The*

boat was embellished with red and blue carvings…
2 = <u>elaborate</u>, colour, exaggerate, dress up, embroider, varnish …*He embellished the story with invented dialogue and extra details…*

embellishment 1 = <u>decoration</u>, garnishing, ornament, gilding, enhancement, enrichment, adornment, ornamentation, trimming, beautification …*Florence is full of buildings with bits of decoration and embellishment…*
2 = <u>elaboration</u>, exaggeration, embroidery …*I lack the story-teller's gift of embellishment…*

embers = <u>cinders</u>, ashes, residue, live coals

embezzle = <u>misappropriate</u>, steal, appropriate, rob, pocket, nick (*slang, chiefly Brit.*), pinch (*informal*), rip off (*slang*), siphon off, pilfer, purloin, filch, help yourself to, thieve, defalcate (*Law*), peculate

embezzlement = <u>misappropriation</u>, stealing, robbing, fraud, pocketing, theft, robbery, nicking (*slang, chiefly Brit.*), pinching (*informal*), appropriation, siphoning off, thieving, pilfering, larceny, purloining, filching, pilferage, peculation, defalcation (*Law*)

embittered = <u>resentful</u>, angry, acid, bitter, sour, soured, alienated, disillusioned, disaffected, venomous, rancorous, at daggers drawn (*informal*), nursing a grudge, with a chip on your shoulder (*informal*)

emblazon = <u>decorate</u>, show, display, present, colour, paint, illuminate, adorn, ornament, embellish, blazon

emblem 1 = <u>crest</u>, mark, design, image, figure, seal, shield, badge, insignia, coat of arms, heraldic device, sigil (*rare*) …*the emblem of the Red Cross…*
2 = <u>representation</u>, symbol, mark, sign, type, token …*The eagle was an emblem of strength and courage…*

emblematic *or* **emblematical 1** = <u>symbolic</u>, significant, figurative, allegorical …*Dogs are emblematic of faithfulness…*
2 = <u>characteristic</u>, representative, typical, symptomatic …*This comment is emblematic of his no-nonsense approach to life…*

embodiment = <u>personification</u>, example, model, type, ideal, expression, symbol, representation, manifestation, realization, incarnation, paradigm, epitome, incorporation, paragon, perfect example, exemplar, quintessence, actualization, exemplification, reification

embody 1 = <u>personify</u>, represent, express, realize, incorporate, stand for, manifest, exemplify, symbolize, typify, incarnate, actualize, reify, concretize …*Jack Kennedy embodied all the hopes of the 1960s…*
2 = <u>incorporate</u>, include, contain, combine, collect, concentrate, organize, take in, integrate, consolidate, bring together, encompass, comprehend, codify, systematize …*The proposal has been embodied in a draft resolution…*

embolden = <u>encourage</u>, cheer, stir, strengthen, nerve, stimulate, reassure, fire, animate, rouse, inflame, hearten, invigorate, gee up, make brave, give courage, vitalize, inspirit

embrace VERB **1** = <u>hug</u>, hold, cuddle, seize, squeeze, grasp, clasp, envelop, encircle, enfold, canoodle

(*slang*), take *or* hold in your arms …*Penelope came forward and embraced her sister…*
2 = <u>accept</u>, support, receive, welcome, adopt, grab, take up, seize, make use of, espouse, take on board, welcome with open arms, avail yourself of, receive enthusiastically …*He embraces the new information age…*
3 = <u>include</u>, involve, cover, deal with, contain, take in, incorporate, comprise, enclose, provide for, take into account, embody, encompass, comprehend, subsume …*a theory that would embrace the whole field of human endeavour…*
NOUN = <u>hug</u>, hold, cuddle, squeeze, clinch (*slang*), clasp, canoodle (*slang*) …*a young couple locked in a passionate embrace…*

embroil = <u>involve</u>, complicate, mix up, implicate, entangle, mire, ensnare, encumber, enmesh

embryo 1 = <u>foetus</u>, unborn child, fertilized egg …*The embryo lives in the amniotic cavity…*
2 = <u>germ</u>, beginning, source, root, seed, nucleus, rudiment …*The League of Nations was the embryo of the UN…*

embryonic = <u>rudimentary</u>, early, beginning, primary, budding, fledgling, immature, seminal, nascent, undeveloped, incipient, inchoate, unformed, germinal
OPPOSITE advanced

emerge 1 = <u>come out</u>, appear, come up, surface, rise, proceed, arise, turn up, spring up, emanate, materialize, issue, come into view, come forth, become visible, manifest yourself …*He was waiting outside as she emerged from the building…* OPPOSITE withdraw
2 = <u>become apparent</u>, develop, come out, turn up, become known, come to light, crop up, transpire, materialize, become evident, come out in the wash …*Several interesting facts emerged from his story…*

emergence 1 = <u>coming</u>, development, arrival, surfacing, rise, appearance, arising, turning up, issue, dawn, advent, emanation, materialization …*the emergence of new democracies in Central Europe…*
2 = <u>disclosure</u>, publishing, broadcasting, broadcast, publication, declaration, revelation, becoming known, becoming apparent, coming to light, becoming evident …*Following the emergence of new facts, the conviction was quashed…*

emergency NOUN = <u>crisis</u>, danger, difficulty, accident, disaster, necessity, pinch, plight, scrape (*informal*), strait, catastrophe, predicament, calamity, extremity, quandary, exigency, critical situation, urgent situation …*He has the ability to deal with emergencies quickly…*
ADJECTIVE **1** = <u>urgent</u>, crisis, immediate …*She made an emergency appointment…*
2 = <u>alternative</u>, extra, additional, substitute, replacement, temporary, makeshift, stopgap …*The plane is carrying emergency supplies…*

emergent = <u>developing</u>, coming, beginning, rising, appearing, budding, burgeoning, fledgling, nascent, incipient

emigrate = <u>move abroad</u>, move, relocate, migrate,

remove, resettle, leave your country

emigration = <u>departure</u>, removal, migration, exodus, relocation, resettlement

eminence 1 = <u>prominence</u>, reputation, importance, fame, celebrity, distinction, note, esteem, rank, dignity, prestige, superiority, greatness, renown, pre-eminence, repute, notability, illustriousness ...*pilots who achieved eminence in the aeronautical world...*
2 = <u>high ground</u>, bank, rise, hill, summit, height, mound, elevation, knoll, hillock, kopje *or* koppie (*S. African*) ...*The house is built on an eminence, and has a pleasing prospect...*

eminent = <u>prominent</u>, high, great, important, noted, respected, grand, famous, celebrated, outstanding, distinguished, well-known, superior, esteemed, notable, renowned, prestigious, elevated, paramount, big-time (*informal*), foremost, high-ranking, conspicuous, illustrious, major league (*informal*), exalted, noteworthy, pre-eminent OPPOSITE> unknown

emissary = <u>envoy</u>, agent, deputy, representative, ambassador, diplomat, delegate, courier, herald, messenger, consul, attaché, go-between, legate

emission = <u>giving off</u> *or* out, release, shedding, leak, radiation, discharge, transmission, venting, issue, diffusion, utterance, ejaculation, outflow, issuance, ejection, exhalation, emanation, exudation

emit 1 = <u>give off</u>, release, shed, leak, transmit, discharge, send out, throw out, vent, issue, give out, radiate, eject, pour out, diffuse, emanate, exude, exhale, breathe out, cast out, give vent to, send forth ...*The stove emitted a cloud of evil-smelling smoke...* OPPOSITE> absorb
2 = <u>utter</u>, produce, voice, give out, let out ...*Polly blinked and emitted a small cry...*

emotion 1 = <u>feeling</u>, spirit, soul, passion, excitement, sensation, sentiment, agitation, fervour, ardour, vehemence, perturbation ...*Her voice trembled with emotion...*
2 = <u>instinct</u>, sentiment, sensibility, intuition, tenderness, gut feeling, soft-heartedness ...*the split between reason and emotion...*

emotional 1 = <u>psychological</u>, private, personal, hidden, spiritual, inner ...*Victims are left with emotional problems that can last for life...*
2 = <u>moving</u>, touching, affecting, exciting, stirring, thrilling, sentimental, poignant, emotive, heart-rending, heart-warming, tear-jerking (*informal*) ...*It was a very emotional moment...*
3 = <u>passionate</u>, enthusiastic, sentimental, fiery, feeling, susceptible, responsive, ardent, fervent, zealous, temperamental, excitable, demonstrative, hot-blooded, fervid, touchy-feely (*informal*) ...*I don't get as emotional as I once did...* OPPOSITE> dispassionate
4 = <u>emotive</u>, sensitive, controversial, delicate, contentious, heated, inflammatory, touchy ...*Selling ivory from elephants is a very emotional issue...*

Word Power

emotional – Although *emotive* can be used as a synonym of *emotional*, as in sense 4, there are differences in meaning that should first be understood. *Emotional* is the more general and neutral word for referring to anything to do with the emotions and emotional states. *Emotive* has the more restricted meaning of 'tending to arouse emotion', and is often associated with issues, subjects, language, and words. However, since *emotional* can also mean 'arousing emotion', with certain nouns it is possible to use either word, depending on the slant one wishes to give: *an emotive/emotional appeal on behalf of the disadvantaged young.*

---

emotive 1 = <u>sensitive</u>, controversial, delicate, contentious, inflammatory, touchy ...*Embryo research is an emotive subject...*
2 = <u>moving</u>, touching, affecting, emotional, exciting, stirring, thrilling, sentimental, poignant, heart-rending, heart-warming, tear-jerking (*informal*) ...*He made an emotive speech to his fans...*

empathize
PHRASES **empathize with** = <u>identify with</u>, understand, relate to, feel for, sympathize with, have a rapport with, feel at one with, be on the same wavelength as

emphasis 1 = <u>importance</u>, attention, weight, significance, stress, strength, priority, moment, intensity, insistence, prominence, underscoring, pre-eminence ...*Too much emphasis is placed on research...*
2 = <u>stress</u>, accent, accentuation, force, weight ...*The emphasis is on the first syllable of the word...*

emphasize 1 = <u>highlight</u>, stress, insist, underline, draw attention to, dwell on, underscore, weight, play up, make a point of, give priority to, press home, give prominence to, prioritize ...*I should emphasize that nothing has been finally decided as yet...* OPPOSITE> minimize
2 = <u>stress</u>, accent, accentuate, lay stress on, put the accent on ...*'That's up to you,' I said, emphasizing the 'you'...*

emphatic 1 = <u>forceful</u>, decided, certain, direct, earnest, positive, absolute, distinct, definite, vigorous, energetic, unmistakable, insistent, unequivocal, vehement, forcible, categorical ...*His response was immediate and emphatic...* OPPOSITE> hesitant
2 = <u>significant</u>, marked, strong, striking, powerful, telling, storming (*informal*), impressive, pronounced, decisive, resounding, momentous, conclusive ...*Yesterday's emphatic victory was their fifth in succession...* OPPOSITE> insignificant

empire 1 = <u>kingdom</u>, territory, province, federation, commonwealth, realm, domain, imperium (*rare*) ...*the fall of the Roman empire...*
2 = <u>organization</u>, company, business, firm, concern, corporation, consortium, syndicate, multinational, conglomeration ...*control of a huge publishing*

empire…

(**Related Words**)

adjective : imperial

empirical *or* **empiric** = <u>first-hand</u>, direct, observed, practical, actual, experimental, pragmatic, factual, experiential OPPOSITE> hypothetical

employ 1 = <u>hire</u>, commission, appoint, take on, retain, engage, recruit, sign up, enlist, enrol, have on the payroll …*The company employs 18 staff…*
2 = <u>use</u>, apply, exercise, exert, make use of, utilize, ply, bring to bear, put to use, bring into play, avail yourself of …*the approaches and methods we employed in this study…*
3 = <u>spend</u>, fill, occupy, involve, engage, take up, make use of, use up …*Your time could be usefully employed in attending to business matters…*

employed 1 = <u>working</u>, in work, having a job, in employment, in a job, earning your living …*He was employed on a part-time basis…* OPPOSITE> out of work
2 = <u>busy</u>, active, occupied, engaged, hard at work, in harness, rushed off your feet …*You have enough work to keep you fully employed…* OPPOSITE> idle

employee = <u>worker</u>, labourer, workman, staff member, member of staff, hand, wage-earner, white-collar worker, blue-collar worker, hired hand, job-holder, member of the workforce

employer 1 = <u>boss</u> (*informal*), manager, head, leader, director, chief, executive, owner, owner, master, chief executive, governor (*informal*), skipper, managing director, administrator, patron, supervisor, superintendent, gaffer (*informal, chiefly Brit.*), foreman, proprietor, manageress, overseer, kingpin, honcho (*informal*), big cheese (*slang, old-fashioned*), baas (*S. African*), numero uno (*informal*), Mister Big (*slang, chiefly U.S.*) …*It is a privilege to work for such an excellent employer…*
2 = <u>company</u>, business, firm, organization, establishment, outfit (*informal*) …*Shorts is Ulster's biggest private-sector employer…*

employment 1 = <u>job</u>, work, business, position, trade, post, situation, employ, calling, profession, occupation, pursuit, vocation, métier …*She was unable to find employment in the area…*
2 = <u>taking on</u>, commissioning, appointing, hire, hiring, retaining, engaging, appointment, recruiting, engagement, recruitment, enlisting, enrolling, enlistment …*a ban on the employment of children under the age of nine…*
3 = <u>use</u>, application, exertion, exercise, utilization …*the widespread employment of 'smart' bombs in this war…*

emporium (*Old-fashioned*) = <u>shop</u>, market, store, supermarket, outlet, warehouse, department store, mart, boutique, bazaar, retail outlet, superstore, hypermarket

empower 1 = <u>authorize</u>, allow, commission, qualify, permit, sanction, entitle, delegate, license, warrant, give power to, give authority to, invest with power …*The army is now empowered to operate on a shoot-to-kill basis…*

2 = <u>enable</u>, equip, emancipate, give means to, enfranchise …*empowering the underprivileged by means of education…*

emptiness 1 = <u>futility</u>, banality, worthlessness, hollowness, pointlessness, meaninglessness, barrenness, senselessness, aimlessness, purposelessness, unsatisfactoriness, valuelessness …*suffering from feelings of emptiness and depression…*
2 = <u>meaninglessness</u>, vanity, banality, frivolity, idleness, unreality, silliness, triviality, ineffectiveness, cheapness, insincerity, worthlessness, hollowness, inanity, unsubstantiality, trivialness, vainness …*the unsoundness and emptiness of his beliefs…*
3 = <u>void</u>, gap, vacuum, empty space, nothingness, blank space, free space, vacuity …*She wanted a man to fill the emptiness in her life…*
4 = <u>bareness</u>, waste, desolation, destitution, blankness, barrenness, desertedness, vacantness …*the emptiness of the desert…*
5 = <u>blankness</u>, vacancy, vacuity, impassivity, vacuousness, expressionlessness, stoniness, unintelligence, absentness, vacantness …*There was an emptiness about her eyes, as if she were in a state of shock…*

empty ADJECTIVE 1 = <u>bare</u>, clear, abandoned, deserted, vacant, free, void, desolate, destitute, uninhabited, unoccupied, waste, unfurnished, untenanted, without contents …*The room was bare and empty…* OPPOSITE> full
2 = <u>meaningless</u>, cheap, hollow, vain, idle, trivial, ineffective, futile, insubstantial, insincere …*His father said he was going to beat him, but he knew it was an empty threat…*
3 = <u>worthless</u>, meaningless, hollow, pointless, unsatisfactory, futile, unreal, senseless, frivolous, fruitless, aimless, inane, valueless, purposeless, otiose, bootless …*My life was hectic but empty before I met him…* OPPOSITE> meaningful
4 = <u>blank</u>, absent, vacant, stony, deadpan, vacuous, impassive, expressionless, unintelligent …*She saw the empty look in his eyes as he left…*
5 (*Informal*) = <u>hungry</u>, unfilled, famished, starving (*informal*), unfed …*Never drink on an empty stomach…*
VERB 1 = <u>clear</u>, drain, gut, void, unload, pour out, unpack, unburden, remove the contents of …*I emptied the ashtray…* OPPOSITE> fill
2 = <u>exhaust</u>, consume the contents of, void, deplete, use up …*Cross emptied his glass with one swallow…* OPPOSITE> replenish
3 = <u>evacuate</u>, clear, vacate …*a bore who could empty a room in two minutes just by talking about his therapy…*

emulate = <u>imitate</u>, follow, copy, mirror, echo, mimic, take after, follow in the footsteps of, follow the example of, take a leaf out of someone's book, model yourself on

emulation = <u>imitation</u>, following, copying, mirroring, reproduction, mimicry

enable 1 = <u>allow</u>, permit, facilitate, empower, give

someone the opportunity, give someone the means
...*The new test should enable doctors to detect the
disease early...* OPPOSITE prevent
2 = <u>authorize</u>, allow, commission, permit, qualify,
sanction, entitle, license, warrant, empower, give
someone the right ...*The authorities have refused
visas to enable them to enter the country...* OPPOSITE
stop

enact 1 = <u>establish</u>, order, pass, command, approve,
sanction, proclaim, decree, authorize, ratify, ordain,
validate, legislate, make law ...*The bill would be
submitted for discussion before being enacted as law...*
2 = <u>perform</u>, play, act, present, stage, represent, put
on, portray, depict, act out, play the part of, appear as
or in, personate ...*She enacted the stories told to her by
her father...*

enactment 1 = <u>passing</u>, legislation, sanction,
approval, establishment, proclamation, ratification,
authorization, validation, making law ...*the
enactment of a Bill of Rights...*
2 = <u>decree</u>, order, law, act, ruling, bill, measure,
command, legislation, regulation, resolution, dictate,
canon, statute, ordinance, commandment, edict,
bylaw ...*enactments which empowered the court to
require security to be given...*
3 = <u>portrayal</u>, staging, performance, playing, acting,
performing, representation, depiction, play-acting,
personation ...*The building was also used for the
enactment of plays...*

enamoured
PHRASES **enamoured with** = <u>in love with</u>, taken
with, charmed by, fascinated by, entranced by, fond
of, enchanted by, captivated by, enthralled by, smitten
with, besotted with, bewitched by, crazy about
(*informal*), infatuated with, enraptured by, wild about
(*informal*), swept off your feet by, nuts on or about
(*slang*)

encampment = <u>camp</u>, base, post, station, quarters,
campsite, bivouac, camping ground, cantonment

encapsulate *or* **incapsulate** = <u>sum up</u>, digest,
summarize, compress, condense, abbreviate,
epitomize, abridge, précis

enchant = <u>fascinate</u>, delight, charm, entrance, dazzle,
captivate, enthral, beguile, bewitch, ravish,
mesmerize, hypnotize, cast a spell on, enrapture,
enamour, spellbind

enchanting = <u>delightful</u>, fascinating, appealing,
attractive, lovely, charming, entrancing, pleasant,
endearing, captivating, alluring, bewitching, ravishing,
winsome, Orphean

enchantment 1 = <u>charm</u>, fascination, delight,
beauty, joy, attraction, bliss, allure, transport, rapture,
mesmerism, ravishment, captivation, beguilement,
allurement ...*The campsite had its own peculiar
enchantment...*
2 = <u>spell</u>, magic, charm, witchcraft, voodoo, wizardry,
sorcery, occultism, incantation, necromancy,
conjuration ...*an effective countercharm against
enchantment by the faerie folk...*

encircle = <u>surround</u>, ring, circle, enclose, encompass,

compass, envelop, girdle, circumscribe, hem in,
enfold, environ, gird in, begird (*poetic*), enwreath

enclose *or* **inclose 1** = <u>surround</u>, cover, circle,
bound, wrap, fence, pound, pen, hedge, confine, close
in, encompass, wall in, encircle, encase, fence in,
impound, circumscribe, hem in, shut in, environ ...*The
land was enclosed by an eight-foot wire fence...*
2 = <u>send with</u>, include, put in, insert ...*I enclose a
cheque for £10...*

encompass 1 = <u>include</u>, hold, involve, cover, admit,
deal with, contain, take in, embrace, incorporate,
comprise, embody, comprehend, subsume ...*His
repertoire encompassed everything from Bach to Scott
Joplin...*
2 = <u>surround</u>, circle, enclose, close in, envelop,
encircle, fence in, ring, girdle, circumscribe, hem in,
shut in, environ, enwreath ...*Egypt is encompassed by
the Mediterranean, Sudan, the Red Sea and Libya...*

encounter VERB **1** = <u>experience</u>, meet, face, suffer,
have, go through, sustain, endure, undergo, run into,
live through ...*Every day we encounter stresses of one
kind or another...*
2 = <u>meet</u>, confront, come across, run into (*informal*),
bump into (*informal*), run across, come upon, chance
upon, meet by chance, happen on or upon ...*Did you
encounter anyone on your walk?...*
3 = <u>battle with</u>, attack, fight, oppose, engage with,
confront, combat, clash with, contend with, strive
against, struggle with, grapple with, face off (*slang*),
do battle with, cross swords with, come into conflict
with, meet head on ...*They were about to cross the
border and encounter Iraqi troops...*
NOUN **1** = <u>meeting</u>, brush, confrontation, rendezvous,
chance meeting ...*an encounter with a remarkable
man...*
2 = <u>battle</u>, fight, action, conflict, clash, dispute,
contest, set to (*informal*), run-in (*informal*), combat,
confrontation, engagement, collision, skirmish, head-
to-head, face-off (*slang*) ...*They were killed in an
encounter with security forces near the border...*

encourage 1 = <u>inspire</u>, comfort, rally, cheer,
stimulate, reassure, animate, console, rouse, hearten,
cheer up, embolden, buoy up, pep up, boost
someone's morale, give hope to, buck up (*informal*),
gee up, lift the spirits of, give confidence to, inspirit
...*When things aren't going well, he always encourages
me...* OPPOSITE discourage
2 = <u>urge</u>, persuade, prompt, spur, coax, incite, egg on,
abet ...*He encouraged her to quit her job...* OPPOSITE
dissuade
3 = <u>promote</u>, back, help, support, increase, further,
aid, forward, advance, favour, boost, strengthen,
foster, advocate, stimulate, endorse, commend,
succour ...*Their task is to encourage private investment
in Russia...* OPPOSITE prevent

encouragement 1 = <u>inspiration</u>, help, support, aid,
favour, comfort, comforting, cheer, cheering,
consolation, reassurance, morale boosting, succour
...*Thanks for all your advice and encouragement...*
2 = <u>urging</u>, prompting, stimulus, persuasion, coaxing,
egging on, incitement ...*She had needed no

encouragement to accept his invitation...
3 = <u>promotion</u>, backing, support, boost, endorsement, stimulation, advocacy, furtherance *...The encouragement of trade will benefit the process of economic reform in China...*

encouraging = <u>promising</u>, good, bright, comforting, cheering, stimulating, reassuring, hopeful, satisfactory, cheerful, favourable, rosy, heartening, auspicious, propitious OPPOSITE> discouraging

encroach = <u>intrude</u>, invade, trespass, infringe, usurp, impinge, trench, overstep, make inroads, impose yourself

encroachment = <u>intrusion</u>, invasion, violation, infringement, trespass, incursion, usurpation, inroad, impingement

encumber **1** = <u>burden</u>, load, embarrass, saddle, oppress, obstruct, retard, weigh down *...The company is still labouring under the debt burden that it was encumbered with in the 1980s...*
2 = <u>hamper</u>, restrict, handicap, slow down, cramp, inhibit, clog, hinder, inconvenience, overload, impede, weigh down, trammel, incommode *...fishermen encumbered with bulky clothing and boots...*

encyclopedic = <u>comprehensive</u>, full, complete, vast, universal, wide-ranging, thorough, in-depth, exhaustive, all-inclusive, all-embracing, all-encompassing, thoroughgoing

end NOUN **1** = <u>close</u>, ending, finish, expiry, expiration *...The report is expected by the end of the year...* OPPOSITE> beginning
2 = <u>conclusion</u>, ending, climax, completion, finale, culmination, denouement, consummation *...His big scene comes towards the end of the film...* OPPOSITE> start
3 = <u>finish</u>, close, stop, resolution, conclusion, closure, wind-up, completion, termination, cessation *...She brought the interview to an abrupt end...*
4 = <u>extremity</u>, limit, edge, border, bound, extent, extreme, margin, boundary, terminus *...Surveillance equipment is placed at both ends of the tunnel...*
5 = <u>tip</u>, point, head, peak, extremity *...He tapped the ends of his fingers together...*
6 = <u>purpose</u>, point, reason, goal, design, target, aim, object, mission, intention, objective, drift, intent, aspiration *...another policy designed to achieve the same end...*
7 = <u>outcome</u>, result, consequence, resolution, conclusion, completion, issue, sequel, end result, attainment, upshot, consummation *...The end justifies the means...*
8 = <u>death</u>, dying, ruin, destruction, passing on, doom, demise, extinction, dissolution, passing away, extermination, annihilation, expiration, ruination *...Soon after we spoke to him, he met a violent end...*
9 = <u>remnant</u>, butt, bit, stub, scrap, fragment, stump, remainder, leftover, tail end, oddment, tag end *...an ashtray overflowing with cigarette ends...*
VERB **1** = <u>stop</u>, finish, complete, resolve, halt, cease, axe (*informal*), dissolve, wind up, terminate, call off, discontinue, put paid to, bring to an end, pull the plug on, call a halt to, nip in the bud, belay (*Nautical*)

...Talks have resumed to try to end the fighting... OPPOSITE> start
2 = <u>finish</u>, close, conclude, wind up, culminate, terminate, come to an end, draw to a close *...The book ends on a lengthy description of Hawaii...* OPPOSITE> begin
3 = <u>destroy</u>, take, kill, abolish, put an end to, do away with, extinguish, annihilate, exterminate, put to death *...I believe you should be free to end your own life...*
PHRASES **end up 1** = <u>finish up</u>, stop, wind up, come to a halt, fetch up (*informal*) *...The car ended up at the bottom of the river...* **2** = <u>turn out to be</u>, finish as, finish up, pan out (*informal*), become eventually *...She could have ended up a millionairess...*

(**Related Words**)
adjectives: final, terminal, ultimate

endanger = <u>put at risk</u>, risk, threaten, compromise, hazard, jeopardize, imperil, put in danger, expose to danger OPPOSITE> save

endear = <u>attract</u>, draw, bind, engage, charm, attach, win, incline, captivate

endearing = <u>attractive</u>, winning, pleasing, appealing, sweet, engaging, charming, pleasant, cute, enticing, captivating, lovable, alluring, adorable, winsome, cutesy (*informal, chiefly U.S.*)

endeavour (*Formal*) VERB = <u>try</u>, labour, attempt, aim, struggle, venture, undertake, essay, strive, aspire, have a go, go for it (*informal*), make an effort, have a shot (*informal*), have a crack (*informal*), take pains, bend over backwards (*informal*), do your best, go for broke (*slang*), bust a gut (*informal*), give it your best shot (*informal*), jump through hoops (*informal*), have a stab (*informal*), break your neck (*informal*), make an all-out effort (*informal*), knock yourself out (*informal*), do your damnedest (*informal*), give it your all (*informal*), rupture yourself (*informal*) *...I will endeavour to rectify the situation...*
NOUN = <u>attempt</u>, try, shot (*informal*), effort, trial, go (*informal*), aim, bid, crack (*informal*), venture, enterprise, undertaking, essay, stab (*informal*) *...His first endeavours in the field were wedding films...*

ended = <u>finished</u>, done, over, through, closed, past, complete, done with, settled, all over (bar the shouting), no more, concluded, accomplished, wrapped-up (*informal*), at an end, finis

ending = <u>finish</u>, end, close, resolution, conclusion, summing up, wind-up, completion, finale, termination, culmination, cessation, denouement, last part, consummation OPPOSITE> start

endless **1** = <u>eternal</u>, constant, infinite, perpetual, continual, immortal, unbroken, unlimited, uninterrupted, limitless, interminable, incessant, boundless, everlasting, unending, ceaseless, inexhaustible, undying, unceasing, unbounded, measureless, unfading *...causing over 25,000 deaths in a seemingly endless war...* OPPOSITE> temporary
2 = <u>interminable</u>, constant, persistent, perpetual, never-ending, incessant, monotonous, overlong *...I am sick to death of your endless complaints...*
3 = <u>continuous</u>, unbroken, uninterrupted, undivided,

without end ...*an endless conveyor belt*...

endorse *or* **indorse** 1 = <u>approve</u>, back, support, champion, favour, promote, recommend, sanction, sustain, advocate, warrant, prescribe, uphold, authorize, ratify, affirm, approve of, subscribe to, espouse, vouch for, throw your weight behind ...*I can endorse this statement wholeheartedly*...
2 = <u>sign</u>, initial, countersign, sign on the back of, superscribe, undersign ...*The payee must endorse the cheque*...

endorsement *or* **indorsement** = <u>approval</u>, backing, support, championing, favour, promotion, sanction, recommendation, acceptance, agreement, warrant, confirmation, upholding, subscription, fiat, advocacy, affirmation, ratification, authorization, seal of approval, approbation, espousal, O.K. *or* okay (*informal*)

endow 1 = <u>provide</u>, favour, grace, bless, supply, furnish, enrich, endue ...*He was endowed with wealth, health and a good intellect*...
2 = <u>finance</u>, fund, pay for, award, grant, invest in, confer, settle on, bestow, make over, bequeath, purvey, donate money to ...*The ambassador has endowed a public-service fellowship programme*...
3 = <u>imbue</u>, steep, bathe, saturate, pervade, instil, infuse, permeate, impregnate, inculcate ...*Herbs have been used for centuries to endow a whole range of foods with subtle flavours*...

endowment 1 = <u>provision</u>, fund, funding, award, income, grant, gift, contribution, revenue, subsidy, presentation, donation, legacy, hand-out, boon, bequest, stipend, bestowal, benefaction, largesse *or* largess ...*The company gave the Oxford Union a generous £1m endowment*...
2 *often plural* = <u>talent</u>, power, feature, quality, ability, gift, capacity, characteristic, attribute, qualification, genius, faculty, capability, flair, aptitude ...*individuals with higher-than-average intellectual endowments*...

endurance 1 = <u>staying power</u>, strength, resolution, resignation, determination, patience, submission, stamina, fortitude, persistence, tenacity, perseverance, toleration, sufferance, doggedness, stickability (*informal*), pertinacity ...*a test of endurance*...
2 = <u>permanence</u>, stability, continuity, duration, continuation, longevity, durability, continuance, immutability, lastingness ...*The book is about the endurance of the class system in Britain*...

endure 1 = <u>experience</u>, suffer, bear, weather, meet, go through, encounter, cope with, sustain, brave, undergo, withstand, live through, thole (*Scot.*) ...*He'd endured years of pain and sleepless nights because of arthritis*...
2 = <u>put up with</u>, stand, suffer, bear, allow, accept, stick (*slang*), take (*informal*), permit, stomach, swallow, brook, tolerate, hack (*slang*), abide, submit to, countenance, stick out (*informal*), take patiently ...*I simply can't endure another moment of her company*...
3 = <u>last</u>, live, continue, remain, stay, hold, stand, go on, survive, live on, prevail, persist, abide, be durable, wear well ...*Somehow the language endures and continues to survive to this day*...

enduring = <u>long-lasting</u>, lasting, living, continuing, remaining, firm, surviving, permanent, constant, steady, prevailing, persisting, abiding, perennial, durable, immortal, steadfast, unwavering, immovable, imperishable, unfaltering ◖OPPOSITE◗ brief

enemy = <u>foe</u>, rival, opponent, the opposition, competitor, the other side, adversary, antagonist ◖OPPOSITE◗ friend
◖ *Related Words* ◗
adjective: inimical

energetic 1 = <u>forceful</u>, strong, determined, powerful, storming (*informal*), active, aggressive, dynamic, vigorous, potent, hard-hitting, high-powered, strenuous, punchy (*informal*), forcible, high-octane (*informal*) ...*an energetic public-relations campaign*...
2 = <u>lively</u>, spirited, active, dynamic, vigorous, animated, brisk, tireless, bouncy, indefatigable, alive and kicking, zippy (*informal*), full of beans (*informal*), bright-eyed and bushy-tailed (*informal*) ...*Two-year-olds can be incredibly energetic*... ◖OPPOSITE◗ lethargic
3 = <u>strenuous</u>, hard, taxing, demanding, tough, exhausting, vigorous, arduous ...*an energetic exercise routine*...

energize 1 = <u>stimulate</u>, drive, stir, motivate, activate, animate, enthuse, quicken, enliven, galvanize, liven up, pep up, invigorate, vitalize, inspirit ...*their ability to energize their followers*...
2 = <u>stimulate</u>, operate, trigger, turn on, start up, activate, switch on, kick-start, electrify, actuate ...*When energized, the coil creates an electromagnetic force*...

energy 1 = <u>strength</u>, might, force, power, activity, intensity, stamina, exertion, forcefulness ...*He was saving his energy for the big race in Belgium*...
2 = <u>liveliness</u>, life, drive, fire, spirit, determination, pep, go (*informal*), zip (*informal*), vitality, animation, vigour, verve, zest, resilience, get-up-and-go (*informal*), élan, brio, vivacity, vim (*slang*) ...*At 65 years old, her energy and looks are wonderful*...
3 = <u>power</u> ...*Oil shortages have brought an energy crisis*...

enfold *or* **infold** 1 = <u>wrap</u>, surround, enclose, wrap up, encompass, shroud, immerse, swathe, envelop, sheathe, enwrap ...*Wood was comfortably enfolded in a woolly dressing-gown*...
2 = <u>embrace</u>, hold, fold, hug, cuddle, clasp ...*He enfolded her gently in his arms*...

enforce 1 = <u>carry out</u>, apply, implement, fulfil, execute, administer, put into effect, put into action, put into operation, put in force ...*The measures are being enforced by Interior Ministry troops*...
2 = <u>impose</u>, force, require, urge, insist on, compel, exact, oblige, constrain, coerce ...*They tried to limit the cost by enforcing a low-tech specification*...

enforced = <u>imposed</u>, required, necessary, compelled, dictated, prescribed, compulsory, mandatory, constrained, ordained, obligatory, unavoidable, involuntary

enforcement 1 = <u>administration</u>, carrying out,

application, prosecution, execution, implementation, reinforcement, fulfilment ...*the adequate enforcement of the law...*
2 = <u>imposition</u>, requirement, obligation, insistence, exaction ...*the stricter enforcement of speed limits for vehicles...*

engage 1 *with in* = <u>participate in</u>, join in, take part in, undertake, practise, embark on, enter into, become involved in, set about, partake of ...*They continue to engage in terrorist activities...*
2 = <u>captivate</u>, win, draw, catch, arrest, fix, attract, capture, charm, attach, fascinate, enchant, allure, enamour ...*He engaged us with tales of his adventures...*
3 = <u>occupy</u>, involve, draw, busy, grip, absorb, tie up, preoccupy, immerse, engross ...*He tried to engage me in conversation...*
4 = <u>employ</u>, commission, appoint, take on, hire, retain, recruit, enlist, enrol, put on the payroll ...*We have been able to engage some staff...* OPPOSITE> dismiss
5 = <u>book</u>, reserve, secure, hire, rent, charter, lease, prearrange ...*He managed to engage a room for the night...*
6 = <u>interlock</u>, join, interact, mesh, interconnect, dovetail ...*Press the lever until you hear the catch engage...*
7 = <u>set going</u>, apply, trigger, activate, switch on, energize, bring into operation ...*Show me how to engage the four-wheel drive...*
8 (*Military*) = <u>begin battle with</u>, attack, take on, encounter, combat, fall on, battle with, meet, fight with, assail, face off (*slang*), wage war on, join battle with, give battle to, come to close quarters with ...*They could engage the enemy beyond the range of the torpedoes...*

engaged 1 = <u>occupied</u>, working, involved, committed, employed, busy, absorbed, tied up, preoccupied, engrossed ...*the various projects he was engaged on...*
2 = <u>betrothed</u>, promised, pledged, affianced, promised in marriage ...*He was engaged to Miss Julia Boardman...* OPPOSITE> unattached
3 = <u>in use</u>, busy, tied up, unavailable ...*We tried to phone you back but the line was engaged...* OPPOSITE> free

engagement 1 = <u>appointment</u>, meeting, interview, date, commitment, arrangement, rendezvous ...*He had an engagement at a restaurant in Greek Street at eight...*
2 = <u>betrothal</u>, marriage contract, troth (*archaic*), agreement to marry ...*I've broken off my engagement to Arthur...*
3 = <u>battle</u>, fight, conflict, action, struggle, clash, contest, encounter, combat, confrontation, skirmish, face-off (*slang*) ...*The constitution prevents them from military engagement on foreign soil...*
4 = <u>participation</u>, joining, taking part, involvement ...*his proactive engagement in the peace process...*
5 = <u>job</u>, work, post, situation, commission, employment, appointment, gig (*informal*), stint ...*her first official engagement as Miss World...*

engaging = <u>charming</u>, interesting, pleasing, appealing, attractive, lovely, fascinating, entertaining, winning, pleasant, fetching (*informal*), delightful, cute, enchanting, captivating, agreeable, lovable, winsome, cutesy (*informal, chiefly U.S.*), likable *or* likeable
OPPOSITE> unpleasant

engender 1 = <u>produce</u>, make, cause, create, lead to, occasion, excite, result in, breed, generate, provoke, induce, bring about, arouse, give rise to, precipitate, incite, instigate, foment, beget ...*Insults engender hatred against those who indulge in them...*
2 = <u>breed</u>, father, create, generate, conceive, give birth to, spawn, sire, propagate, bring forth, beget, procreate, give life to ...*the desire to engender children...*

engine = <u>machine</u>, motor, mechanism, generator, dynamo

engineer NOUN **1** = <u>designer</u>, producer, architect, developer, deviser, creator, planner, inventor, stylist, artificer, originator, couturier ...*He is a fully qualified civil engineer...*
 2 = <u>worker</u>, specialist, operator, practitioner, operative, driver, conductor, technician, handler, skilled employee ...*They sent a service engineer to repair the disk drive...*
VERB **1** = <u>design</u>, plan, create, construct, devise, originate ...*Many of Kuwait's freeways were engineered by W. S. Atkins...*
2 = <u>bring about</u>, plan, control, cause, effect, manage, set up (*informal*), scheme, arrange, plot, manoeuvre, encompass, mastermind, orchestrate, contrive, concoct, wangle (*informal*), finagle (*informal*) ...*Some people believe that his murder was engineered by Stalin...*

English
➤ **top ten mistakes in English**

engrained
➤ **ingrained**

engrave = <u>carve</u>, cut, etch, inscribe, chisel, incise, chase, enchase (*rare*), grave (*archaic*)

engraved = <u>fixed</u>, set, printed, impressed, lodged, embedded, imprinted, etched, ingrained, infixed

engraving 1 = <u>print</u>, block, impression, carving, etching, inscription, plate, woodcut, dry point ...*the engraving of Shakespeare at the front of the book...*
2 = <u>cutting</u>, carving, etching, inscribing, chiselling, inscription, chasing, dry point, enchasing (*rare*) ...*Glass engraving has increased in popularity over recent years...*

engrossed = <u>absorbed</u>, lost, involved, occupied, deep, engaged, gripped, fascinated, caught up, intrigued, intent, preoccupied, immersed, riveted, captivated, enthralled, rapt

engrossing = <u>absorbing</u>, interesting, arresting, engaging, gripping, fascinating, compelling, intriguing, riveting, captivating, enthralling

engulf *or* **ingulf 1** = <u>immerse</u>, bury, flood (out), plunge, consume, drown, swamp, encompass, submerge, overrun, inundate, deluge, envelop, swallow up ...*The flat was engulfed in flames...*

Word Power: Top Ten Mistakes in English

There are certain mistakes which are very commonly made in English. Some, such as errors in punctuation or spelling, occur only in written English, and some are regarded as being more acceptable in spoken than in written English. Others were once considered to be serious grammatical mistakes, but have gradually become accepted by all but the strictest of language purists. Here are ten of the most frequently-made mistakes in English:

1 Misuse of apostrophes:

An apostrophe is used in one of three ways:

- to indicate possession, when it is added to the end of a word and followed by an **'s**, as in *the dragon's lair; children's programmes.* If a plural word already ends in **'s'**, the apostrophe follows that letter, as in *our parents' generation; seven years' hard work.*

- to show where a letter or letters have been omitted, as in *drum'n'bass; What's happening?; nine o'clock; We've only just begun.*

- It is also acceptable, though not obligatory, to use an apostrophe to form the plural of a number, letter, or symbol, as in *P's and Q's; 7's; £'s.* Many people either wrongly omit the apostrophe altogether where there should be one, or they put it in the wrong place. Others make the mistake of using an apostrophe where none is needed, most commonly to form plurals (*a kilo of tomatoes* is correct, but *a kilo of tomato's* is not) or to form possessive pronouns (*I'm a huge fan of hers* is correct, but not *I'm a huge fan of her's*).

2 Confusion of *their*, *there*, and *they're*:

Their refers to something belonging to or connected with people or things which have already been mentioned: *It wasn't their fault.* **There** means **at that place**: *I'm going there tomorrow.* **They're** is a shortened way of saying **they are** (note the apostrophe which indicates that a letter has been omitted): *They're very unhappy.*

3 Confusion of *its* and *it's*:

Its refers to something belonging to or relating to a thing which has already been mentioned: *The baby threw its rattle out of the pram.*

It's is a shortened way of saying **it is** or **it has** (note the apostrophe which indicates that a letter has been omitted): *It's a lovely day; it's been a great weekend.*

4 Confusion of *your* and *you're*:

Your means belonging to you: *Don't forget your keys.* **You're** is a shortened way of saying **you are** (note the apostrophe which indicates that a letter has been omitted): *You're kidding!*

5 Dangling modifiers:

A modifier is a word or phrase which adds some further information about another word. For example, **garage** is a modifer of **door** in **garage door,** because it tells you something specific about the door. Many people make the mistake of using a modifier phrase in such a way that there is no word in the sentence which it can sensibly modify, so that it "dangles": for example, in the sentence *Flying over Switzerland, the Alps appeared awesome*, there is no word to which *flying* can sensibly refer – the sentence seems to be saying that the Alps were flying, rather than the speaker or speakers! The sentence needs to be reworded to make the sense clear:
As we flew over Switzerland, the Alps appeared awesome.

6 Double negatives:

When you use two negatives in the same sentence, far from making what you are saying more emphatically negative, they have the opposite effect, and make a positive. So avoid using a sentence like *There isn't no milk in the fridge* if what you are trying to say is that the fridge has no milk in it; *There isn't any milk in the fridge* is correct, as is *There is no milk in the fridge.*

7 Agreement between nouns and verbs:

If the subject of a sentence is singular, it needs a singular verb; if the subject is plural, it should have a plural verb. Make the subject and verb agree regardless of any phrases or clauses which happen to come between them: *We are just leaving; A knife and fork were already laid out on the table* (note that a plural verb is needed here because there are two subjects, joined by *and*). A collective noun such as *family* or *team* usually takes a singular verb: *The team has played well this season.*

8 Comparatives and superlatives:

The endings **-er** and **-est** can be added to most shorter adjectives to form their comparative and superlative: *His job is tough; your job is tougher; my job is the toughest.* Most adjectives with more than one syllable, and most adverbs, use **more** and **most**, or **less** and **least**, instead of **-er** and **-est** to form comparatives and superlatives: *She is beautiful; my sister is more/less beautiful; our cousin is the most/least beautiful.* A common mistake is to combine the two ways of forming comparatives and superlatives, as in *I've got a more faster car than you*, or to use **-er**

Word Power: Top Ten Mistakes in English (continued)

or **-est** where **more** or **most** should be used, as in *Your outfit is beautifuller than mine.*

9 Split infinitives:

An infinitive of a verb is the form which includes **to**, as in *to be, or not to be.* It used to be considered a serious grammatical mistake to split an infinitive, that is, to insert a word or words (usually an adverb) between the **to** and the other part of the verb, as in *He decided to firmly deal with the offenders.* It is true that a split infinitive may result in a clumsy-sounding sentence, as it does in this case – *He decided to deal firmly with the offenders* sounds much more natural – but this alone is not enough to justify the total condemnation which the split infinitive still provokes from some language purists. Indeed, trying to avoid a split infinitive may result in a very artificial and awkward-sounding sentence, as in *He decided really to try next time*; the most natural place for the adverb to go here is in the split-infinitive position, *He decided to really try next time.* There is therefore a strong case for saying, as many people do, that the split infinitive

is a matter of style rather than a grammatical error, and may be used as and when appropriate. However, many writers prefer to avoid it in formal English, because people with a more traditional view of grammar are still likely to consider this construction as incorrect.

10 Ending a sentence with a preposition:

It used to be considered incorrect to end a sentence with a preposition, as in *New York is a place I'd love to go to.* This practice has gradually gained widespread acceptance, and is no longer regarded as a serious grammatical error. In fact, in many contexts, it is the preferred form, since it results in a more natural-sounding sentence – Winston Churchill once famously made fun of purists who condemned the practice by saying, *"This is the sort of English up with which I will not put,"* proving how awkward a sentence could sound if you stuck rigidly to the rule! However, since traditionalists are still likely to consider the practice incorrect, it is better to avoid ending a sentence with a preposition unless it would otherwise sound awkward.

---

2 = <u>overwhelm</u>, overcome, crush, absorb, swamp, engross ...*He was engulfed by a feeling of emptiness*...

enhance = <u>improve</u>, better, increase, raise, lift, boost, add to, strengthen, reinforce, swell, intensify, heighten, elevate, magnify, augment, exalt, embellish, ameliorate OPPOSITE> reduce

enhancement = <u>improvement</u>, strengthening, heightening, enrichment, increment, embellishment, boost, betterment, augmentation, amelioration

enigma = <u>mystery</u>, problem, puzzle, riddle, paradox, conundrum, teaser

enigmatic *or* **enigmatical** = <u>mysterious</u>, puzzling, obscure, baffling, ambiguous, perplexing, incomprehensible, mystifying, inexplicable, unintelligible, paradoxical, cryptic, inscrutable, unfathomable, indecipherable, recondite, Delphic, oracular, sphinxlike OPPOSITE> straightforward

enjoin **1** = <u>order</u>, charge, warn, urge, require, direct, bid, command, advise, counsel, prescribe, instruct, call upon ...*She enjoined me strictly not to tell anyone else*... **2** (*Law*) = <u>prohibit</u>, bar, ban, forbid, restrain, preclude, disallow, proscribe, interdict, place an injunction on ...*the government's attempt to enjoin the publication of the book*...

enjoy VERB **1** = <u>take pleasure in</u> *or* <u>from</u>, like, love, appreciate, relish, delight in, revel in, be pleased with, be fond of, be keen on, rejoice in, be entertained by, find pleasure in, find satisfaction in, take joy in ...*He enjoys playing cricket*... OPPOSITE> hate **2** = <u>have</u>, use, own, experience, possess, have the benefit of, reap the benefits of, have the use of, be blessed *or* favoured with ...*The average German will enjoy 40 days' paid holiday this year*...

PHRASES **enjoy yourself** = <u>have a good time</u>, be happy, have fun, have a field day (*informal*), have a ball (*informal*), live life to the full, make merry, let your hair down ...*He's too busy enjoying himself to get much work done*...

enjoyable = <u>pleasurable</u>, good, great, fine, pleasing, nice, satisfying, lovely, entertaining, pleasant, amusing, delicious, delightful, gratifying, agreeable, delectable, to your liking OPPOSITE> unpleasant

enjoyment **1** – <u>pleasure</u>, liking, fun, delight, entertainment, joy, satisfaction, happiness, relish, recreation, amusement, indulgence, diversion, zest, gratification, gusto, gladness, delectation, beer and skittles (*informal*) ...*She ate with great enjoyment*... **2** = <u>benefit</u>, use, advantage, favour, possession, blessing ...*the enjoyment of equal freedom by all*...

enlarge VERB **1** = <u>expand</u>, increase, extend, add to, build up, widen, intensify, blow up (*informal*), heighten, broaden, inflate, lengthen, magnify, amplify, augment, make bigger, elongate, make larger ...*plans to enlarge the park into a 30,000 all-seater stadium*... OPPOSITE> reduce **2** = <u>grow</u>, increase, extend, stretch, expand, swell, wax, multiply, inflate, lengthen, diffuse, elongate, dilate, become bigger, puff up, grow larger, grow bigger, become larger, distend, bloat ...*The glands in the neck may enlarge*... PHRASES **enlarge on something** = <u>expand on</u>, develop, add to, fill out, elaborate on, flesh out, expatiate on, give further details about ...*I wish to enlarge on the statement I made yesterday*...

enlighten = <u>inform</u>, tell, teach, advise, counsel, educate, instruct, illuminate, make aware, edify, apprise, let know, cause to understand

enlightened = <u>informed</u>, aware, liberal, reasonable, educated, sophisticated, refined, cultivated, open-minded, knowledgeable, literate, broad-minded OPPOSITE ignorant

enlightenment = <u>understanding</u>, information, learning, education, teaching, knowledge, instruction, awareness, wisdom, insight, literacy, sophistication, comprehension, cultivation, refinement, open-mindedness, edification, broad-mindedness

enlist 1 = <u>join up</u>, join, enter (into), register, volunteer, sign up, enrol ...*He enlisted as a private in the Mexican War*...
2 = <u>recruit</u>, secure, gather, take on, hire, sign up, call up, muster, mobilize, conscript ...*Three thousand men were enlisted*...
3 = <u>obtain</u>, get, gain, secure, engage, procure ...*I had to enlist the help of several neighbours to clear the mess*...

enliven = <u>cheer up</u>, excite, inspire, cheer, spark, enhance, stimulate, wake up, animate, fire, rouse, brighten, exhilarate, quicken, hearten, perk up, liven up, buoy up, pep up, invigorate, gladden, vitalize, vivify, inspirit, make more exciting, make more lively OPPOSITE subdue

en masse = <u>all together</u>, together, as one, as a whole, ensemble, as a group, in a group, all at once, in a mass, as a body, in a body

enmity = <u>hostility</u>, hate, spite, hatred, bitterness, friction, malice, animosity, aversion, venom, antagonism, antipathy, acrimony, rancour, bad blood, ill will, animus, malevolence, malignity OPPOSITE friendship

ennoble 1 = <u>dignify</u>, honour, enhance, elevate, magnify, raise, glorify, exalt, aggrandize ...*the fundamental principles of life which ennoble mankind*...
2 = <u>raise to the peerage</u>, kick upstairs (*informal*), make noble ...*He had been ennobled for arranging a government loan in 1836*...

ennui (*Literary*) = <u>boredom</u>, dissatisfaction, tiredness, the doldrums, lethargy, tedium, lassitude, listlessness

enormity 1 (*Informal*) = <u>hugeness</u>, extent, magnitude, greatness, vastness, immensity, massiveness, enormousness, extensiveness ...*He was appalled by the enormity of the task ahead of him*...
2 = <u>wickedness</u>, disgrace, atrocity, depravity, viciousness, villainy, turpitude, outrageousness, baseness, vileness, evilness, monstrousness, heinousness, nefariousness, atrociousness ...*the enormity of the crime they had committed*...
3 = <u>atrocity</u>, crime, horror, evil, outrage, disgrace, monstrosity, abomination, barbarity, villainy ...*the horrific enormities perpetrated on the islanders*...

enormous = <u>huge</u>, massive, vast, extensive, tremendous, gross, excessive, immense, titanic, jumbo (*informal*), gigantic, monstrous, mammoth, colossal, mountainous, stellar (*informal*), prodigious, gargantuan, elephantine, astronomic, ginormous (*informal*), Brobdingnagian, humongous *or* humungous (*U.S. slang*) OPPOSITE tiny

enough DETERMINER = <u>sufficient</u>, adequate, ample, abundant, as much as you need, as much as is necessary ...*They had enough money for a one-way ticket*...
PRONOUN = <u>sufficiency</u>, plenty, sufficient, abundance, adequacy, right amount, ample supply ...*I hope you brought enough for everyone*...
ADVERB = <u>sufficiently</u>, amply, fairly, moderately, reasonably, adequately, satisfactorily, abundantly, tolerably, passably ...*Do you think sentences for criminals are tough enough already?*...

enquire
➤ **inquire**

enquiry
➤ **inquiry**

enrage = <u>anger</u>, provoke, irritate, infuriate, aggravate (*informal*), incense, gall, madden, inflame, exasperate, incite, antagonize, make you angry, nark (*Brit., Austral., & N.Z. slang*), make your blood boil, get your back up, make you see red (*informal*), put your back up OPPOSITE calm

enraged = <u>furious</u>, cross, wild, angry, angered, mad (*informal*), raging, irritated, fuming, choked, infuriated, aggravated (*informal*), incensed, inflamed, exasperated, very angry, irate, livid (*informal*), incandescent, on the warpath, fit to be tied (*slang*), boiling mad, raging mad, tooshie (*Austral. slang*), off the air (*Austral. slang*)

enraptured = <u>enchanted</u>, delighted, charmed, fascinated, absorbed, entranced, captivated, transported, enthralled, beguiled, bewitched, ravished, spellbound, enamoured

enrich 1 = <u>enhance</u>, develop, improve, boost, supplement, refine, cultivate, heighten, endow, augment, ameliorate, aggrandize ...*Vivid fantasies can enrich your sex life*...
2 = <u>make rich</u>, make wealthy, make affluent, make prosperous, make well-off ...*He enriched himself at the expense of others*...

enrol 1 = <u>enlist</u>, register, be accepted, be admitted, join up, matriculate, put your name down for, sign up or on ...*To enrol for the conference, fill in the attached form*...
2 = <u>recruit</u>, take on, engage, enlist ...*I thought I'd enrol you with an art group at the school*...

enrolment = <u>enlistment</u>, admission, acceptance, engagement, registration, recruitment, matriculation, signing on *or* up

en route = <u>on</u> *or* <u>along the way</u>, travelling, on the road, in transit, on the journey

ensemble 1 = <u>group</u>, company, band, troupe, cast, orchestra, chorus, supporting cast ...*an ensemble of young musicians*...
2 = <u>collection</u>, set, body, whole, total, sum, combination, entity, aggregate, entirety, totality, assemblage, conglomeration ...*The state is an ensemble of political and social structures*...
3 = <u>outfit</u>, suit, get-up (*informal*), costume ...*a dashing ensemble in navy and white*...

enshrine = <u>preserve</u>, protect, treasure, cherish,

revere, exalt, consecrate, embalm, sanctify, hallow, apotheosize

ensign = <u>flag</u>, standard, colours, banner, badge, pennant, streamer, jack, pennon

enslave = <u>subjugate</u>, bind, dominate, trap, suppress, enthral, yoke, tyrannize, sell into slavery, reduce to slavery, enchain

ensnare = <u>trap</u>, catch, capture, seize, snarl, embroil, net, snare, entangle, entrap, enmesh

ensue = <u>follow</u>, result, develop, succeed, proceed, arise, stem, derive, come after, issue, befall, flow, come next, come to pass (*archaic*), supervene, be consequent on, turn out *or* up OPPOSITE> come first

ensure *or* **insure** 1 = <u>make certain</u>, guarantee, secure, make sure, confirm, warrant, certify ...*Steps must be taken to ensure this never happens again...*
2 = <u>protect</u>, defend, secure, safeguard, guard, make safe ...*The plan is aimed at ensuring the future of freshwater fish species...*

entail = <u>involve</u>, require, cause, produce, demand, lead to, call for, occasion, need, impose, result in, bring about, give rise to, encompass, necessitate

entangle 1 = <u>tangle</u>, catch, trap, twist, knot, mat, mix up, snag, snarl, snare, jumble, ravel, trammel, enmesh ...*The door handle had entangled itself with the strap of her bag...* OPPOSITE> disentangle
2 = <u>embroil</u>, involve, complicate, mix up, muddle, implicate, bog down, enmesh ...*Bureaucracy can entangle ventures for months...*

entanglement 1 = <u>affair</u>, involvement, romance, intrigue, fling, liaison, love affair, amour, illicit romance ...*a romantic entanglement...*
2 = <u>difficulty</u>, mess, confusion, complication, mix-up, muddle, predicament, imbroglio ...*trying to do his job without the usual bureaucratic entanglements...*
3 = <u>becoming entangled</u>, mix-up, becoming enmeshed, becoming ensnared, becoming jumbled, entrapment, snarl-up (*informal, chiefly Brit.*), ensnarement ...*Many dolphins are accidentally killed through entanglement in fishing equipment...*

enter 1 = <u>come</u> *or* <u>go in</u> *or* into, arrive, set foot in somewhere, cross the threshold of somewhere, make an entrance ...*He entered and stood near the door...* OPPOSITE> exit
2 = <u>penetrate</u>, get in, insert into, pierce, pass into, perforate ...*The bullet entered his right eye...*
3 = <u>join</u>, start work at, begin work at, sign up for, enrol in, become a member of, enlist in, commit yourself to ...*He entered the company as a junior trainee...* OPPOSITE> leave
4 = <u>participate in</u>, join (in), be involved in, get involved in, play a part in, partake in, associate yourself with, start to be in ...*A million young people enter the labour market each year...*
5 = <u>begin</u>, start, take up, move into, set about, commence, set out on, embark upon ...*I have entered a new phase in my life...*
6 = <u>compete in</u>, contest, take part in, join in, fight, sign up for, go in for ...*As a boy he entered many music competitions...*

7 = <u>record</u>, note, register, log, list, write down, take down, inscribe, set down, put in writing ...*Prue entered the passage in her notebook, then read it aloud again...*
8 = <u>submit</u>, offer, present, table, register, lodge, tender, put forward, proffer ...*I entered a plea of guilty to the charges...*

enterprise 1 = <u>firm</u>, company, business, concern, operation, organization, establishment, commercial undertaking ...*There are plenty of small industrial enterprises...*
2 = <u>venture</u>, operation, project, adventure, undertaking, programme, pursuit, endeavour ...*Horse breeding is a risky enterprise...*
3 = <u>initiative</u>, energy, spirit, resource, daring, enthusiasm, push (*Informal*), imagination, drive, pep, readiness, vigour, zeal, ingenuity, originality, eagerness, audacity, boldness, get-up-and-go (*informal*), alertness, resourcefulness, gumption (*informal*), adventurousness, imaginativeness ...*His trouble is that he lacks enterprise...*

enterprising = <u>resourceful</u>, original, spirited, keen, active, daring, alert, eager, bold, enthusiastic, vigorous, imaginative, energetic, adventurous, ingenious, up-and-coming, audacious, zealous, intrepid, venturesome

entertain 1 = <u>amuse</u>, interest, please, delight, occupy, charm, enthral, cheer, divert, recreate (*rare*), regale, give pleasure to ...*He entertained us with anecdotes about his job...*
2 = <u>show hospitality to</u>, receive, accommodate, treat, put up, lodge, be host to, have company of, invite round, ask round, invite to a meal, ask for a meal ...*I don't really like to entertain guests any more...*
3 = <u>consider</u>, support, maintain, imagine, think about, hold, foster, harbour, contemplate, conceive of, ponder, cherish, bear in mind, keep in mind, think over, muse over, give thought to, cogitate on, allow yourself to consider ...*I wouldn't entertain the idea of doing such a job...*

entertaining = <u>enjoyable</u>, interesting, pleasing, funny, charming, cheering, pleasant, amusing, diverting, delightful, witty, humorous, pleasurable, recreative (*rare*)

entertainment 1 = <u>enjoyable</u>, fun, pleasure, leisure, satisfaction, relaxation, recreation, enjoyment, distraction, amusement, diversion ...*I play the piano purely for my own entertainment...*
2 = <u>pastime</u>, show, sport, performance, play, treat, presentation, leisure activity, beer and skittles ...*He organized entertainments and events for elderly people...*

enthral = <u>engross</u>, charm, grip, fascinate, absorb, entrance, intrigue, enchant, rivet, captivate, beguile, ravish, mesmerize, hypnotize, enrapture, hold spellbound, spellbind

enthralling = <u>engrossing</u>, charming, gripping, fascinating, entrancing, compelling, intriguing, compulsive, enchanting, riveting, captivating, beguiling, mesmerizing, hypnotizing, spellbinding

enthusiasm 1 = <u>keenness</u>, interest, passion, excitement, warmth, motivation, relish, devotion, zeal, zest, fervour, eagerness, ardour, vehemence, earnestness, zing (*informal*), avidity …*Her lack of enthusiasm filled me with disappointment*…
2 = <u>interest</u>, passion, rage, hobby, obsession, craze, fad (*informal*), mania, hobbyhorse …*the current enthusiasm for skateboarding*…

enthusiast = <u>fan</u>, supporter, lover, follower, addict, freak (*informal*), admirer, buff (*informal*), fanatic, devotee, fiend (*informal*), adherent, zealot, aficionado

enthusiastic = <u>keen</u>, earnest, spirited, committed, excited, devoted, warm, eager, lively, passionate, vigorous, ardent, hearty, exuberant, avid, fervent, zealous, ebullient, vehement, wholehearted, full of beans (*informal*), fervid, keen as mustard, bright-eyed and bushy-tailed (*informal*) OPPOSITE> apathetic

entice = <u>lure</u>, attract, invite, persuade, draw, tempt, induce, seduce, lead on, coax, beguile, allure, cajole, decoy, wheedle, prevail on, inveigle, dangle a carrot in front of

enticing = <u>attractive</u>, appealing, inviting, charming, fascinating, tempting, intriguing, irresistible, persuasive, seductive, captivating, beguiling, alluring OPPOSITE> unattractive

entire 1 = <u>continuous</u>, unified, unbroken, uninterrupted, undivided …*He had spent his entire life in China as a doctor*…
2 = <u>whole</u>, full, complete, total, gross …*The entire family was killed in the crash*…
3 = <u>absolute</u>, full, total, utter, outright, thorough, unqualified, unrestricted, undiminished, unmitigated, unreserved …*He assured me of his entire confidence in me*…
4 = <u>intact</u>, whole, perfect, unmarked, unbroken, sound, unharmed, undamaged, without a scratch, unmarred …*No document is entire, and it is often unclear in what order the pieces fit together*…

entirely 1 = <u>completely</u>, totally, perfectly, absolutely, fully, altogether, thoroughly, wholly, utterly, every inch, without exception, unreservedly, in every respect, without reservation, lock, stock and barrel …*The two cases are entirely different*… OPPOSITE> partly
2 = <u>only</u>, exclusively, solely …*The whole episode was entirely my fault*…

entirety = <u>whole</u>, total, sum, unity, aggregate, totality

entitle 1 = <u>give the right to</u>, allow, enable, permit, sanction, license, qualify for, warrant, authorize, empower, enfranchise, make eligible …*Your contract entitles you to a full refund*…
2 = <u>call</u>, name, title, term, style, label, dub, designate, characterize, christen, give the title of, denominate …*an instrumental piece entitled 'Changing States'*…

entity 1 = <u>thing</u>, being, body, individual, object, presence, existence, substance, quantity, creature, organism …*the concept of the earth as a living entity*…
2 = <u>essential nature</u>, being, existence, essence, quintessence, real nature, quiddity (*Philosophy*) …*key

periods of national or cultural entity and development*…

entomb = <u>bury</u>, inter, lay to rest, sepulchre, place in a tomb, inhume, inurn

entourage = <u>retinue</u>, company, following, staff, court, train, suite, escort, cortege

entrails = <u>intestines</u>, insides (*informal*), guts, bowels, offal, internal organs, innards (*informal*), vital organs, viscera

entrance¹ 1 = <u>way in</u>, opening, door, approach, access, entry, gate, passage, avenue, doorway, portal, inlet, ingress, means of access …*He drove in through a side entrance*… OPPOSITE> exit
2 = <u>appearance</u>, coming in, entry, arrival, introduction, ingress …*The audience chanted his name as he made his entrance*… OPPOSITE> exit
3 = <u>admission</u>, access, entry, entrée, admittance, permission to enter, ingress, right of entry …*Hewitt gained entrance to the house by pretending to be a heating engineer*…

entrance² 1 = <u>enchant</u>, delight, charm, absorb, fascinate, dazzle, captivate, transport, enthral, beguile, bewitch, ravish, gladden, enrapture, spellbind …*She entranced the audience with her classical Indian singing*… OPPOSITE> bore
2 = <u>mesmerize</u>, bewitch, hypnotize, put a spell on, cast a spell on, put in a trance …*The sailors were entranced by the voices of the sirens*…

entrant 1 = <u>newcomer</u>, novice, initiate, beginner, trainee, apprentice, convert, new member, fresher, neophyte, tyro, probationer …*the newest entrant to the political scene*…
2 = <u>competitor</u>, player, candidate, entry, participant, applicant, contender, contestant …*All items submitted for the competition must be the entrant's own work*…

entrap NOUN = <u>trick</u>, lure, seduce, entice, deceive, implicate, lead on, embroil, beguile, allure, entangle, ensnare, inveigle, set a trap for, enmesh …*She was trying to entrap him into marriage*…
VERB = <u>catch</u>, net, capture, trap, snare, entangle, ensnare …*The whale's mouth contains filters which entrap plankton*…

entreaty = <u>plea</u>, appeal, suit, request, prayer, petition, exhortation, solicitation, supplication, importunity, earnest request

entrench = <u>fix</u>, set, establish, plant, seat, settle, root, install, lodge, anchor, implant, embed, dig in, ensconce, ingrain

entrenched *or* **intrenched** = <u>fixed</u>, set, firm, rooted, well-established, ingrained, deep-seated, deep-rooted, indelible, unshakeable, ineradicable

entrepreneur = <u>businessman</u> *or* <u>businesswoman</u>, tycoon, director, executive, contractor, industrialist, financier, speculator, magnate, impresario, business executive

entrust *or* **intrust 1** = <u>give custody of</u>, trust, deliver, commit, delegate, hand over, turn over, confide, commend, consign …*her reluctance to entrust her children to the care of someone else*…
2 = <u>assign</u>, charge, trust, invest, authorize …*They are

prepared to entrust him with the leadership of the party…

entry 1 = <u>admission</u>, access, entrance, admittance, entrée, permission to enter, right of entry …*Entry to the museum is free…*
2 = <u>coming in</u>, entering, appearance, arrival, entrance …*He made his triumphal entry into Mexico…* OPPOSITE exit
3 = <u>introduction</u>, presentation, initiation, inauguration, induction, debut, investiture …*The time has come to prepare her for her entry into society…*
4 = <u>record</u>, listing, account, note, minute, statement, item, registration, memo, memorandum, jotting …*Her diary entry for that day records his visit…*
5 = <u>competitor</u>, player, attempt, effort, candidate, participant, challenger, submission, entrant, contestant …*The winner was selected from hundreds of entries…*
6 = <u>way in</u>, opening, door, approach, access, gate, passage, entrance, avenue, doorway, portal, inlet, passageway, ingress, means of access …*A lorry blocked the entry to the school…*

entwine *or* **intwine** = <u>twist</u>, surround, embrace, weave, knit, braid, encircle, wind, intertwine, interweave, plait, twine, ravel, interlace, entwist (*archaic*) OPPOSITE disentangle

enumerate 1 = <u>list</u>, tell, name, detail, relate, mention, quote, cite, specify, spell out, recount, recite, itemize, recapitulate …*She enumerated all the reasons why she wanted to leave him…*
2 = <u>count</u>, calculate, sum up, total, reckon, compute, add up, tally, number …*They enumerated the casualties…*

enunciate 1 = <u>pronounce</u>, say, speak, voice, sound, utter, articulate, vocalize, enounce (*formal*) …*She enunciated each word slowly and carefully…*
2 = <u>state</u>, declare, proclaim, pronounce, publish, promulgate, propound …*He was always ready to enunciate his views to anyone who would listen…*

envelop = <u>enclose</u>, cover, hide, surround, wrap around, embrace, blanket, conceal, obscure, veil, encompass, engulf, cloak, shroud, swathe, encircle, encase, swaddle, sheathe, enfold, enwrap

envelope = <u>wrapping</u>, casing, case, covering, cover, skin, shell, coating, jacket, sleeve, sheath, wrapper

enveloping = <u>enclosing</u>, surrounding, concealing, encompassing, shrouding, encircling, all-embracing, enfolding

enviable = <u>desirable</u>, favoured, privileged, fortunate, lucky, blessed, advantageous, to die for (*informal*), much to be desired, covetable OPPOSITE undesirable

envious = <u>covetous</u>, jealous, grudging, malicious, resentful, green-eyed, begrudging, spiteful, jaundiced, green with envy

environment 1 = <u>surroundings</u>, setting, conditions, situation, medium, scene, circumstances, territory, background, atmosphere, context, habitat, domain, milieu, locale …*The children were brought up in completely different environments…*
2 = <u>habitat</u>, home, surroundings, territory, terrain,

locality, natural home …*the maintenance of a safe environment for marine mammals…*

environmental = <u>ecological</u>, green

environmentalist = <u>conservationist</u>, ecologist, green, friend of the earth

environs = <u>surrounding area</u>, surroundings, district, suburbs, neighbourhood, outskirts, precincts, vicinity, locality, purlieus

envisage 1 = <u>imagine</u>, contemplate, conceive (of), visualize, picture, fancy, think up, conceptualize …*I can't envisage being married to someone like him…*
2 = <u>foresee</u>, see, expect, predict, anticipate, envision …*Scientists envisage a major breakthrough in the next few years…*

envision = <u>conceive of</u>, expect, imagine, predict, anticipate, see, contemplate, envisage, foresee, visualize

envoy 1 = <u>ambassador</u>, minister, diplomat, emissary, legate, plenipotentiary …*A French envoy arrived in Beirut on Sunday…*
2 = <u>messenger</u>, agent, deputy, representative, delegate, courier, intermediary, emissary …*the Secretary General's personal envoy…*

envy NOUN = <u>covetousness</u>, spite, hatred, resentment, jealousy, bitterness, malice, ill will, malignity, resentfulness, enviousness (*informal*) …*He admitted his feelings of envy towards his brother…*
VERB 1 = <u>be jealous (of)</u>, resent, begrudge, be envious (of) …*I have a famous brother and a lot of people envy me for that…*
2 = <u>covet</u>, desire, crave, aspire to, yearn for, hanker after …*He envied Caroline her peace of mind…*

ephemeral – <u>transient</u>, short, passing, brief, temporary, fleeting, short-lived, fugitive, flitting, momentary, transitory, evanescent, impermanent, fugacious OPPOSITE eternal

epidemic NOUN 1 = <u>outbreak</u>, plague, growth, spread, scourge, contagion …*A flu epidemic is sweeping through Britain…*
2 = <u>spate</u>, plague, outbreak, wave, rash, eruption, upsurge …*an epidemic of racist crimes…*
ADJECTIVE = <u>widespread</u>, wide-ranging, general, sweeping, prevailing, rampant, prevalent, rife, pandemic …*The abuse of crack has reached epidemic proportions in the US in recent years…*

epilogue = <u>conclusion</u>, postscript, coda, afterword, concluding speech OPPOSITE prologue

episode 1 = <u>event</u>, experience, happening, matter, affair, incident, circumstance, adventure, business, occurrence, escapade …*an unfortunate and rather sordid episode in my life…*
2 = <u>instalment</u>, part, act, scene, section, chapter, passage …*The final episode will be shown next Saturday…*
3 = <u>period</u>, attack, spell, phase, bout …*He suffered three episodes of depression in two years…*

episodic 1 = <u>irregular</u>, occasional, sporadic, intermittent …*episodic attacks of fever…*
2 = <u>irregular</u>, rambling, disconnected, anecdotal, disjointed, wandering, discursive, digressive …*an*

episodic narrative of unrelated characters…

epistle = <u>letter</u>, note, message, communication, missive

epitaph = <u>commemoration</u>, inscription, elegy, engraving, obituary

epithet = <u>name</u>, title, description, tag, nickname, designation, appellation, sobriquet, moniker *or* monicker (*slang*), obscenity, blasphemy, swear word, imprecation

epitome = <u>personification</u>, essence, embodiment, type, representation, norm, archetype, exemplar, typical example, quintessence

epitomize = <u>typify</u>, represent, illustrate, embody, exemplify, symbolize, personify, incarnate

epoch = <u>era</u>, time, age, period, date, aeon

equal `ADJECTIVE` 1 = <u>identical</u>, the same, matched, matching, like, equivalent, uniform, alike, corresponding, tantamount, one and the same, proportionate, commensurate …*a population having equal numbers of men and women…* `OPPOSITE` unequal
2 = <u>fair</u>, just, impartial, egalitarian, unbiased, even-handed, equable …*Women demand equal rights with men…* `OPPOSITE` unfair
3 = <u>even</u>, balanced, fifty-fifty (*informal*), evenly matched, evenly balanced, evenly proportioned …*an equal contest…* `OPPOSITE` uneven
4 *with* **to** = <u>capable of</u>, up to, ready for, suitable for, fit for, strong enough for, good enough for, sufficient for, adequate for, competent to …*She wanted to show she was equal to any test they gave her…*
`NOUN` = <u>match</u>, equivalent, fellow, twin, mate, peer, parallel, counterpart, compeer …*She was one of the boys, their equal…*
`VERB` 1 = <u>amount to</u>, make, come to, total, balance, agree with, level, parallel, tie with, equate, correspond to, be equal to, square with, be tantamount to, equalize, tally with, be level with, be even with …*The average pay rise equalled 1.41 times inflation…*
`OPPOSITE` be unequal to
2 = <u>be equal to</u>, match, reach, rival, come up to, be level with, be even with …*The victory equalled Scotland's best in history…*
3 = <u>be as good as</u>, match, compare with, equate with, measure up to, be as great as …*No amount of money can equal memories like that…*

equality 1 = <u>fairness</u>, equal opportunity, equal treatment, egalitarianism, fair treatment, justness …*the principle of racial equality…* `OPPOSITE` inequality
2 = <u>sameness</u>, balance, identity, similarity, correspondence, parity, likeness, uniformity, equivalence, evenness, coequality, equatability …*They advocate the unconditional equality of incomes…* `OPPOSITE` disparity

equalize 1 = <u>make equal</u>, match, level, balance, square, equal, smooth, equate, standardize, even out, even up, regularize, make level …*Such measures are needed to equalize wage rates between countries…*
2 = <u>draw level</u>, level the score, square the score, make the score level …*Brazil equalized with only 16 minutes*

remaining…

equanimity = <u>composure</u>, peace, calm, poise, serenity, tranquillity, coolness, aplomb, calmness, phlegm, steadiness, presence of mind, sang-froid, self-possession, placidity, level-headedness, imperturbability

equate 1 = <u>identify</u>, associate, connect, compare, relate, mention in the same breath, think of in connection with, think of together …*I equate suits with power and authority…*
2 = <u>make equal</u>, match, balance, square, even up, equalize …*relying on arbitrage to equate prices between the various stock exchanges…*
3 = <u>be equal to</u>, match, pair, parallel, agree with, compare with, offset, tally, liken, be commensurate with, correspond with *or* to …*the maximum compensation available, equating to six months' wages…*

equation = <u>equating</u>, match, agreement, balancing, pairing, comparison, parallel, equality, correspondence, likeness, equivalence, equalization

equestrian = <u>riding</u>, mounted, horse riding
➤ **equestrianism**

equilibrium 1 = <u>stability</u>, balance, symmetry, steadiness, evenness, equipoise, counterpoise …*For the economy to be in equilibrium, income must equal expenditure…*
2 = <u>composure</u>, calm, stability, poise, serenity, coolness, calmness, equanimity, steadiness, self-possession, collectedness …*I paused and took deep breaths to restore my equilibrium…*

equip 1 = <u>supply</u>, provide for, stock, dress, outfit, arm, rig, array, furnish, endow, attire, fit out, deck out, kit out, fit up, accoutre …*The country did not have the funds to equip the reserve army properly…*
2 = <u>prepare</u>, qualify, educate, get ready, endow …*Our aim is to provide courses which equip students for future employment…*

equipment = <u>apparatus</u>, stock, supplies, material, stuff, tackle, gear, tools, provisions, kit, rig, baggage, paraphernalia, accoutrements, appurtenances, equipage

equitable = <u>even-handed</u>, just, right, fair, due, reasonable, proper, honest, impartial, rightful, unbiased, dispassionate, proportionate, unprejudiced, nondiscriminatory

equity = <u>fairness</u>, justice, integrity, honesty, fair play, righteousness, impartiality, rectitude, reasonableness, even-handedness, fair-mindedness, uprightness, equitableness `OPPOSITE` unfairness

equivalence = <u>equality</u>, correspondence, agreement, similarity, identity, parallel, match, parity, conformity, likeness, sameness, parallelism, evenness, synonymy, alikeness, interchangeableness

equivalent `NOUN` = <u>equal</u>, counterpart, correspondent, twin, peer, parallel, match, opposite number …*the civil administrator of the West Bank and his equivalent in Gaza…*
`ADJECTIVE` = <u>equal</u>, even, same, comparable, parallel, identical, alike, corresponding, correspondent,

---

Equestrianism

Equestrian events and sports

Ascot	Grand National	nursery stakes	races, the
Badminton	gymkhana	Oaks	Saint Leger
buckjumping	harness racing	One Thousand Guineas	showjumping
cavalcade	horse racing	picnic race	steeplechase
claiming race	hunt	plate	sweepstake or (esp. U.S.)
classic	joust	point-to-point	sweepstakes
Derby	jump-off	polo	three-day eventing
dressage	Kentucky Derby	puissance	Two Thousand Guineas
eventing	meeting	race meeting	

Classic English horse races

Race	Course	Distance
One Thousand Guineas (fillies)	Newmarket	one mile
Two Thousand Guineas (colts)	Newmarket	one mile
Derby (colts)	Epsom	one and a half miles
the Oaks (fillies)	Epsom	one and a half miles

Types of jump

brush and rails	hog's back	planks	wall
double oxer	narrow stile	post and rails	water jump
gate	parallel poles	triple bars	

---

synonymous, of a kind, tantamount, interchangeable, of a piece with, commensurate, homologous ...*A unit of alcohol is equivalent to a glass of wine...* OPPOSITE> different

equivocal = ambiguous, uncertain, misleading, obscure, suspicious, vague, doubtful, dubious, questionable, ambivalent, indefinite, evasive, oblique, indeterminate, prevaricating, oracular OPPOSITE> clear

era = age, time, period, stage, date, generation, cycle, epoch, aeon, day *or* days

eradicate = wipe out, eliminate, remove, destroy, get rid of, abolish, erase, excise, extinguish, stamp out, obliterate, uproot, weed out, annihilate, put paid to, root out, efface, exterminate, expunge, extirpate, wipe from the face of the earth

eradication = wiping out, abolition, destruction, elimination, removal, extinction, extermination, annihilation, erasure, obliteration, effacement, extirpation, expunction

erase 1 = delete, cancel out, wipe out, remove, eradicate, excise, obliterate, efface, blot out, expunge ...*They are desperate to erase the memory of their defeat...*
2 = rub out, remove, wipe out, delete, scratch out ...*She erased the words from the blackboard...*

erect VERB 1 = build, raise, set up, lift, pitch, mount, stand up, rear, construct, put up, assemble, put together, elevate ...*Demonstrators have erected barricades in the roads...* OPPOSITE> demolish
2 = found, establish, form, create, set up, institute, organize, put up, initiate ...*the edifice of free trade which has been erected since the war...*
ADJECTIVE = upright, raised, straight, standing, stiff, firm, rigid, vertical, elevated, perpendicular, pricked-up ...*Her head was erect and her back was straight...*

OPPOSITE> bent

erection 1 (*Slang*) = hard-on, erect penis ...*As he disrobed, his erection became obvious...*
2 = building, setting-up, manufacture, construction, assembly, creation, establishment, elevation, fabrication ...*the erection of temporary fencing to protect hedges under repair...*

ergo = therefore, so, then, thus, hence, consequently, accordingly, for that reason, in consequence

erode 1 = disintegrate, crumble, deteriorate, corrode, break up, grind down, waste away, wear down *or* away ...*By 1980, Miami beach had all but totally eroded...*
2 = destroy, consume, spoil, crumble, eat away, corrode, break up, grind down, abrade, wear down *or* away ...*Once exposed, soil is quickly eroded by wind and rain...*
3 = weaken, destroy, undermine, diminish, impair, lessen, wear away ...*His fumbling of the issue of reform has eroded his authority...*

erosion 1 = disintegration, deterioration, corrosion, corrasion, wearing down *or* away, grinding down ...*erosion of the river valleys...*
2 = deterioration, wearing, undermining, destruction, consumption, weakening, spoiling, attrition, eating away, abrasion, grinding down, wearing down *or* away ...*an erosion of moral standards...*

erotic = sexual, sexy (*informal*), crude, explicit, rousing, sensual, seductive, vulgar, stimulating, steamy (*informal*), suggestive, aphrodisiac, voluptuous, carnal, titillating, bawdy, lustful, sexually arousing, erogenous, amatory

err 1 = make a mistake, mistake, go wrong, blunder, slip up (*informal*), misjudge, be incorrect, be inaccurate, miscalculate, go astray, be in error, put

your foot in it (*informal*), misapprehend, blot your copybook (*informal*), drop a brick *or* clanger (*informal*) ...*The contractors seriously erred in their original estimates*...
2 = <u>sin</u>, fall, offend, lapse, trespass, do wrong, deviate, misbehave, go astray, transgress, be out of order, blot your copybook (*informal*) ...*If he errs again, he will be severely punished*...

errand = <u>job</u>, charge, commission, message, task, mission

errant = <u>sinning</u>, offending, straying, wayward, deviant, erring, aberrant

erratic = <u>unpredictable</u>, variable, unstable, irregular, shifting, eccentric, abnormal, inconsistent, uneven, unreliable, wayward, capricious, desultory, changeable, aberrant, fitful, inconstant [OPPOSITE] regular

erroneous = <u>incorrect</u>, wrong, mistaken, false, flawed, faulty, inaccurate, untrue, invalid, unfounded, spurious, amiss, unsound, wide of the mark, inexact, fallacious [OPPOSITE] correct

error = <u>mistake</u>, slip, fault, blunder, flaw, boob (*Brit. slang*), delusion, oversight, misconception, fallacy, inaccuracy, howler (*informal*), bloomer (*Brit. informal*), boner (*slang*), miscalculation, misapprehension, solecism, erratum

ersatz = <u>artificial</u>, substitute, pretend, fake, imitation, synthetic, bogus, simulated, sham, counterfeit, spurious, phoney *or* phony (*informal*)

erstwhile = <u>former</u>, old, late, previous, once, past, ex (*informal*), one-time, sometime, bygone, quondam

erudite = <u>learned</u>, lettered, cultured, educated, scholarly, cultivated, knowledgeable, literate, well-educated, well-read [OPPOSITE] uneducated

erudition = <u>learning</u>, education, knowledge, scholarship, letters, lore, academic knowledge

erupt **1** = <u>explode</u>, blow up, flare up, emit lava ...*The volcano erupted in 1980*...
2 = <u>discharge</u>, expel, vent, emit, vomit, eject, spout, throw off, spit out, pour forth, spew forth *or* out ...*Those volcanoes erupt not lava but liquid sulphur*...
3 = <u>gush</u>, burst out, be ejected, burst forth, pour forth, belch forth, spew forth *or* out ...*Lava erupted from the volcano and flowed over the ridge*...
4 = <u>start</u>, break out, began, explode, flare up, burst out, boil over ...*Heavy fighting erupted again two days after the cease-fire*...
5 (*Medical*) = <u>break out</u>, appear, flare up ...*My skin erupted in pimples*...

eruption **1** = <u>explosion</u>, discharge, outburst, venting, ejection ...*the volcanic eruption of Tambora in 1815*...
2 = <u>flare-up</u>, outbreak, sally ...*the sudden eruption of violence on the streets of the city*...
3 (*Medical*) = <u>inflammation</u>, outbreak, rash, flare-up ...*an unpleasant eruption of boils*...

escalate **1** = <u>grow</u>, increase, extend, intensify, expand, surge, be increased, mount, heighten ...*Unions and management fear the dispute could escalate*... [OPPOSITE] decrease
2 = <u>increase</u>, develop, extend, intensify, expand, build

up, step up, heighten, enlarge, magnify, amplify ...*Defeat could cause one side or the other to escalate the conflict*... [OPPOSITE] lessen

escalation = <u>increase</u>, rise, build-up, expansion, heightening, developing, acceleration, upsurge, intensification, amplification

escapade = <u>adventure</u>, fling, stunt, romp, trick, scrape (*informal*), spree, mischief, lark (*informal*), caper, prank, antic

escape [VERB] **1** = <u>get away</u>, flee, take off, fly, bolt, skip, slip away, abscond, decamp, hook it (*slang*), do a runner (*slang*), do a bunk (*Brit. slang*), fly the coop (*U.S. & Canad. informal*), make a break for it, slip through your fingers, skedaddle (*informal*), take a powder (*U.S. & Canad. slang*), make your getaway, take it on the lam (*U.S. & Canad. slang*), break free *or* out, make *or* effect your escape, run away *or* off ...*A prisoner has escaped from a jail in Northern England*...
2 = <u>avoid</u>, miss, evade, dodge, shun, elude, duck, steer clear of, circumvent, body-swerve (*Scot.*) ...*He was lucky to escape serious injury*...
3 = <u>be forgotten by</u>, be beyond (someone), baffle, elude, puzzle, stump ...*an actor whose name escapes me for the moment*...
4 = <u>leak out</u>, flow out, drain away, discharge, gush out, emanate, seep out, exude, spurt out, spill out, pour forth ...*Leave a vent open to let some of the moist air escape*...
[NOUN] **1** = <u>getaway</u>, break, flight, break-out, bolt, decampment ...*He made his escape from the country*...
2 = <u>avoidance</u>, evasion, circumvention, elusion ...*his narrow escape from bankruptcy*...
3 = <u>relaxation</u>, relief, recreation, distraction, diversion, pastime ...*For me television is an escape*...
4 = <u>leak</u>, emission, discharge, outpouring, gush, spurt, outflow, leakage, drain, seepage, issue, emanation, efflux, effluence, outpour ...*You should report any suspected gas escape immediately*...

eschew = <u>avoid</u>, give up, abandon, have nothing to do with, shun, elude, renounce, refrain from, forgo, abstain from, fight shy of, forswear, abjure, kick (*informal*), swear off, give a wide berth to, keep *or* steer clear of

escort [NOUN] **1** = <u>guard</u>, protection, safeguard, bodyguard, company, train, convoy, entourage, retinue, cortege ...*He arrived with a police escort*...
2 = <u>companion</u>, partner, attendant, guide, squire (*rare*), protector, beau, chaperon ...*My sister needed an escort for a company dinner*...
[VERB] = <u>accompany</u>, lead, partner, conduct, guide, guard, shepherd, convoy, usher, squire, hold (someone's) hand, chaperon ...*I escorted him to the door*...

esoteric = <u>obscure</u>, private, secret, hidden, inner, mysterious, mystical, mystic, occult, arcane, cryptic, inscrutable, abstruse, recondite, cabbalistic

especially **1** = <u>notably</u>, largely, chiefly, mainly, mostly, principally, strikingly, conspicuously, outstandingly ...*The group is said to be gaining* support, especially in the rural areas...

2 = <u>very</u>, specially, particularly, signally, extremely, remarkably, unusually, exceptionally, extraordinarily, markedly, supremely, uncommonly ...*Giving up smoking can be especially difficult...*

3 = <u>particularly</u>, expressly, exclusively, precisely, specifically, uniquely, peculiarly, singularly ...*The system we design will be especially for you...*

espionage = <u>spying</u>, intelligence, surveillance, counter-intelligence, undercover work

espouse = <u>support</u>, back, champion, promote, maintain, defend, adopt, take up, advocate, embrace, uphold, stand up for

espy = <u>catch sight of</u>, see, discover, spot, notice, sight, observe, spy, perceive, detect, glimpse, make out, discern, behold, catch a glimpse of, descry

essay NOUN **1** = <u>composition</u>, study, paper, article, piece, assignment, discourse, tract, treatise, dissertation, disquisition ...*He was asked to write an essay about his home town...*
2 (*Formal*) – <u>attempt</u>, go (*informal*), try, effort, shot (*informal*), trial, struggle, bid, test, experiment, crack (*informal*), venture, undertaking, stab (*informal*), endeavour, exertion ...*His first essay in running a company was a disaster...*
VERB (*Formal*) = <u>attempt</u>, try, test, take on, undertake, strive for, endeavour, have a go at, try out, have a shot at (*informal*), have a crack at (*informal*), have a bash at (*informal*) ...*He essayed a smile, but it was a dismal failure...*

essence NOUN **1** = <u>fundamental nature</u>, nature, being, life, meaning, heart, spirit, principle, soul, core, substance, significance, entity, bottom line, essential part, kernel, crux, lifeblood, pith, quintessence, basic characteristic, quiddity ...*Some claim that Ireland's very essence is expressed through its language...*
2 = <u>concentrate</u>, spirits, extract, elixir, tincture, distillate ...*Add a few drops of vanilla essence...*
PHRASES **in essence** = <u>essentially</u>, materially, virtually, basically, fundamentally, in effect, substantially, in the main, to all intents and purposes, in substance ...*In essence, we share the same ideology...* ◆ **of the essence** = <u>vitally important</u>, essential, vital, critical, crucial, key, indispensable, of the utmost importance ...*Time is of the essence with this project...*

essential ADJECTIVE **1** = <u>vital</u>, important, needed, necessary, critical, crucial, key, indispensable, requisite, vitally important ...*It is absolutely essential that we find this man quickly...* OPPOSITE unimportant
2 = <u>fundamental</u>, main, basic, radical, key, principal, constitutional, cardinal, inherent, elementary, innate, intrinsic, elemental, immanent ...*Two essential elements must be proven: motive and opportunity...* OPPOSITE secondary
3 = <u>concentrated</u>, extracted, refined, volatile, rectified, distilled ...*essential oils used in aromatherapy...*
NOUN = <u>prerequisite</u>, principle, fundamental, necessity, must, basic, requisite, vital part, sine qua non (*Latin*), rudiment ...*the essentials of everyday life, such as food and water...*

establish **1** = <u>set up</u>, found, start, create, institute, organize, install, constitute, inaugurate ...*They established the school in 1989...*
2 = <u>prove</u>, show, confirm, demonstrate, ratify, certify, verify, validate, substantiate, corroborate, authenticate ...*An autopsy was being done to establish the cause of death...*
3 = <u>secure</u>, form, base, ground, plant, settle, fix, root, implant, entrench, ensconce, put down roots ...*He has established himself as a pivotal figure in US politics...*

establishment NOUN **1** = <u>creation</u>, founding, setting up, foundation, institution, organization, formation, installation, inauguration, enactment ...*discussions to explore the establishment of diplomatic relations...*
2 = <u>organization</u>, company, business, firm, house, concern, operation, structure, institution, institute, corporation, enterprise, outfit (*informal*), premises, setup (*informal*) ...*Shops and other commercial establishments remained closed today...*
3 = <u>office</u>, house, building, plant, quarters, factory ...*a scientific research establishment...*
PHRASES **the Establishment** = <u>the authorities</u>, the system, the powers that be, the ruling class, the established order, institutionalized authority ...*the revolution against the Establishment...*

estate **1** = <u>lands</u>, property, area, grounds, domain, manor, holdings, demesne ...*a shooting party on his estate in Yorkshire...*
2 = <u>area</u>, centre, park, development, site, zone, plot ...*an industrial estate...*
3 (*Law*) = <u>property</u>, capital, assets, fortune, goods, effects, wealth, possessions, belongings ...*His estate was valued at £100,000...*

esteem NOUN = <u>respect</u>, regard, honour, consideration, admiration, reverence, estimation, veneration ...*He is held in high esteem by his colleagues...*
VERB = <u>respect</u>, admire, think highly of, like, love, value, prize, honour, treasure, cherish, revere, reverence, be fond of, venerate, regard highly, take off your hat to ...*a scholar whom he highly esteemed...*

estimate VERB **1** = <u>calculate roughly</u>, value, guess, judge, reckon, assess, evaluate, gauge, number, appraise ...*His personal riches were estimated at over £8 million...*
2 = <u>think</u>, believe, consider, rate, judge, hold, rank, guess, reckon, assess, conjecture, surmise ...*Officials estimate it will be two days before electricity is restored to the island...*
NOUN **1** = <u>approximate calculation</u>, guess, reckoning, assessment, judgment, evaluation, valuation, appraisal, educated guess, guesstimate (*informal*), rough calculation, ballpark figure (*informal*), approximate cost, approximate price, ballpark estimate (*informal*), appraisement ...*This figure is five times the original estimate...*
2 = <u>assessment</u>, opinion, belief, appraisal, evaluation, conjecture, appraisement, judgment, estimation, surmise ...*I was wrong in my estimate of his*

capabilities...

estimation 1 = <u>opinion</u>, view, regard, belief, honour, credit, consideration, judgment, esteem, evaluation, admiration, reverence, veneration, good opinion, considered opinion ...*He has gone down considerably in my estimation*...
2 = <u>estimate</u>, reckoning, assessment, appreciation, valuation, appraisal, guesstimate (*informal*), ballpark figure (*informal*) ...*estimations of pre-tax profits of £12.5 million*...

estrangement = <u>alienation</u>, parting, division, split, withdrawal, break-up, breach, hostility, separation, withholding, disaffection, disunity, dissociation, antagonization

estuary = <u>inlet</u>, mouth, creek, firth, fjord

et cetera = <u>and so on</u>, and so forth, etc.

Word Power

etc – The literal meaning of the Latin phrase *et cetera* is 'and other things'. The use of *and* in a list ending with *et cetera*, as in *we bought bread, cheese, butter, and et cetera*, is therefore redundant. Nor is there ever any need to repeat the phrase *et cetera* for emphasis at the end of a list. Such repetition, as in *he bought paper, ink, notebooks, et cetera, et cetera* is very informal and should not be used in writing or formal speaking.

---

etch 1 = <u>engrave</u>, cut, impress, stamp, carve, imprint, inscribe, furrow, incise, ingrain ...*a simple band of heavy gold etched with runes*...
2 = <u>corrode</u>, eat into, burn into ...*The acid etched holes in the surface*...

etching = <u>print</u>, impression, carving, engraving, imprint, inscription

eternal 1 = <u>everlasting</u>, lasting, permanent, enduring, endless, perennial, perpetual, timeless, immortal, unending, unchanging, immutable, indestructible, undying, without end, unceasing, imperishable, deathless, sempiternal (*literary*) ...*the quest for eternal youth*... <u>OPPOSITE</u> transitory
2 = <u>interminable</u>, constant, endless, abiding, infinite, continual, immortal, never-ending, everlasting, ceaseless, unremitting, deathless ...*In the background was that eternal humming noise*... <u>OPPOSITE</u> occasional

eternity 1 (*Theology*) = <u>the afterlife</u>, heaven, paradise, the next world, the hereafter ...*I have always found the thought of eternity terrifying*...
2 = <u>perpetuity</u>, immortality, infinity, timelessness, endlessness, infinitude, time without end ...*the idea that our species will survive for all eternity*...
3 = <u>ages</u>, years, an age, centuries, for ever (*informal*), aeons, donkey's years (*informal*), yonks (*informal*), a month of Sundays (*informal*), a long time *or* while, an age *or* eternity ...*The war went on for an eternity*...

ethereal 1 = <u>delicate</u>, light, fine, subtle, refined, exquisite, tenuous, dainty, rarefied ...*gorgeous, hauntingly ethereal melodies*...

2 = <u>insubstantial</u>, light, fairy, aerial, airy, intangible, rarefied, impalpable ...*the ethereal world of romantic fiction*...
3 = <u>spiritual</u>, heavenly, unearthly, sublime, celestial, unworldly, empyreal ...*the ethereal realm of the divine*...

ethical 1 = <u>moral</u>, behavioural ...*the ethical dilemmas of genetic engineering*...
2 = <u>right</u>, morally right, morally acceptable, good, just, fitting, fair, responsible, principled, correct, decent, proper, upright, honourable, honest, righteous, virtuous ...*Would it be ethical to lie to save a person's life?*... <u>OPPOSITE</u> unethical

ethics = <u>moral code</u>, standards, principles, morals, conscience, morality, moral values, moral principles, moral philosophy, rules of conduct, moral beliefs

ethnic *or* **ethnical** = <u>cultural</u>, national, traditional, native, folk, racial, genetic, indigenous

ethos = <u>spirit</u>, character, attitude, beliefs, ethic, tenor, disposition

etiquette = <u>good</u> *or* <u>proper behaviour</u>, manners, rules, code, customs, convention, courtesy, usage, protocol, formalities, propriety, politeness, good manners, decorum, civility, politesse, p's and q's, polite behaviour

eulogy = <u>praise</u>, tribute, acclaim, compliment, applause, accolade, paean, commendation, exaltation, glorification, acclamation, panegyric, encomium, plaudit, laudation

euphoria = <u>elation</u>, joy, ecstasy, bliss, glee, rapture, high spirits, exhilaration, jubilation, intoxication, transport, exaltation, joyousness <u>OPPOSITE</u> despondency

Europe
➤ WORD POWER SUPPLEMENT European Union

evacuate 1 = <u>remove</u>, clear, withdraw, expel, move out, send to a safe place ...*18,000 people have been evacuated from the city*...
2 = <u>abandon</u>, leave, clear, desert, quit, depart (from), withdraw from, pull out of, move out of, relinquish, vacate, forsake, decamp from ...*The residents have evacuated the area*...

evacuation 1 = <u>removal</u>, departure, withdrawal, clearance, flight, expulsion, exodus ...*an evacuation of the city's four million inhabitants*...
2 = <u>abandonment</u>, withdrawal from, pulling out, moving out, clearance from, vacation from ...*the mass evacuation of Srebrenica*...

evade 1 = <u>avoid</u>, escape, dodge, get away from, shun, elude, eschew, steer clear of, sidestep, circumvent, duck, shirk, slip through the net of, escape the clutches of, body-swerve (*Scot.*) ...*He managed to evade the police for six months*... <u>OPPOSITE</u> face
2 = <u>avoid answering</u>, parry, circumvent, fend off, balk, cop out of (*slang*), fence, fudge, hedge, prevaricate, flannel (*Brit. informal*), beat about the bush about, equivocate ...*Mr Archer denied that he was evading the question*...

evaluate = <u>assess</u>, rate, value, judge, estimate, rank, reckon, weigh, calculate, gauge, weigh up, appraise, size up (*informal*), assay

evaluation = <u>assessment</u>, rating, judgment, calculation, valuation, appraisal, estimation

evangelical *or* **evangelistic** = <u>crusading</u>, converting, missionary, zealous, revivalist, proselytizing, propagandizing

evaporate 1 = <u>disappear</u>, vaporize, dematerialize, evanesce, melt, vanish, dissolve, disperse, dry up, dispel, dissipate, fade away, melt away ...*Moisture is drawn to the surface of the fabric so that it evaporates...*
2 = <u>dry up</u>, dry, dehydrate, vaporize, desiccate ...*The water is evaporated by the sun...*
3 = <u>fade away</u>, disappear, fade, melt, vanish, dissolve, disperse, dissipate, melt away ...*My anger evaporated and I wanted to cry...*

evaporation 1 = <u>vaporization</u>, vanishing, disappearance, dispelling, dissolution, fading away, melting away, dispersal, dissipation, evanescence, dematerialization ...*The cooling effect is caused by the evaporation of sweat on the skin...*
2 = <u>drying up</u>, drying, dehydration, desiccation, vaporization ...*an increase in evaporation of both lake and ground water...*

evasion 1 = <u>avoidance</u>, escape, dodging, shirking, cop-out (*slang*), circumvention, elusion ...*an evasion of responsibility...*
2 = <u>deception</u>, shuffling, cunning, fudging, pretext, ruse, artifice, trickery, subterfuge, equivocation, prevarication, sophistry, evasiveness, obliqueness, sophism ...*They face accusations from the Opposition Party of evasion and cover-up...*

evasive 1 = <u>deceptive</u>, misleading, indirect, cunning, slippery, tricky, shuffling, devious, oblique, shifty, cagey (*informal*), deceitful, dissembling, prevaricating, equivocating, sophistical, casuistic, casuistical ...*He was evasive about the circumstances of their first meeting...* <u>OPPOSITE</u> straightforward
2 = <u>avoiding</u>, escaping, circumventing ...*Four high-flying warplanes had to take evasive action...*

eve 1 = <u>night before</u>, day before, vigil ...*the eve of his 27th birthday...*
2 = <u>brink</u>, point, edge, verge, threshold ...*when Europe stood on the eve of war in 1914...*

even ADVERB 1 = <u>despite</u>, in spite of, disregarding, notwithstanding, in spite of the fact that, regardless of the fact that ...*He kept calling me, even though he was married...*
2 = <u>all the more</u>, much, still, yet, to a greater extent, to a greater degree ...*Stan was speaking even more slowly than usual...*
ADJECTIVE 1 = <u>regular</u>, stable, constant, steady, smooth, uniform, unbroken, uninterrupted, unwavering, unvarying, metrical ...*It is important to have an even temperature when you work...* OPPOSITE variable
2 = <u>level</u>, straight, flat, plane, smooth, true, steady, uniform, parallel, flush, horizontal, plumb ...*The tables are fitted with a glass top to provide an even surface...* OPPOSITE uneven

3 = <u>equal</u>, like, the same, matching, similar, uniform, parallel, identical, comparable, commensurate, coequal ...*Divide the dough into 12 even pieces...* OPPOSITE unequal
4 = <u>equally matched</u>, level, tied, drawn, on a par, neck and neck, fifty-fifty (*informal*), equalized, all square, equally balanced ...*It was an even game...* OPPOSITE ill-matched
5 = <u>square</u>, quits, on the same level, on an equal footing ...*You don't owe me anything now. We're even...*
6 = <u>calm</u>, stable, steady, composed, peaceful, serene, cool, tranquil, well-balanced, placid, undisturbed, unruffled, imperturbable, equable, even-tempered, unexcitable, equanimous ...*Normally Rose had an even temper; she was rarely irritable...* OPPOSITE excitable
7 = <u>fair</u>, just, balanced, equitable, impartial, disinterested, unbiased, dispassionate, fair and square, unprejudiced ...*We all have an even chance of winning...* OPPOSITE unfair
PHRASES **even as** = <u>while</u>, just as, whilst, at the time that, at the same time as, exactly as, during the time that ...*Even as she said this, she knew it was not quite true...* ◆ **even so** = <u>nevertheless</u>, still, however, yet, despite that, in spite of (that), nonetheless, all the same, notwithstanding that, be that as it may ...*The bus was half empty. Even so, he came and sat next to me...* ◆ **even something out** = <u>make</u> *or* <u>become level</u>, align, level, square, smooth, steady, flatten, stabilize, balance out, regularize ...*Rates of house price inflation have evened out between the North and South of the country...* ◆ **even something up** = <u>equalize</u>, match, balance, equal ...*These missiles would help to even up the balance of power...* ◆ **even the score** = <u>pay (someone) back</u>, repay, get even (*informal*), reciprocate, equalize, requite, get your own back, settle the score, take vengeance, take an eye for an eye, give tit for tat, return like for like ...*If one partner has an extramarital affair, the other may want to even the score...* ◆ **get even** (*Informal*) = <u>pay back</u>, repay, reciprocate, even the score, requite, get your own back, settle the score, take vengeance, take an eye for an eye, be revenged *or* revenge yourself, give tit for tat, pay (someone) back in their own coin, return like for like ...*I'm going to get even if it's the last thing I do...*

even-handed = <u>fair</u>, just, balanced, equitable, impartial, disinterested, unbiased, fair and square, unprejudiced

evening = <u>dusk</u> (*archaic*), night, sunset, twilight, sundown, eve, vesper (*archaic*), eventide (*archaic or poetic*), gloaming (*Scot. or poetic*), e'en (*archaic or poetic*), close of day, crepuscule, even, evo (*Austral. slang*)

event NOUN 1 = <u>incident</u>, happening, experience, matter, affair, occasion, proceeding, fact, business, circumstance, episode, adventure, milestone, occurrence, escapade ...*in the wake of recent events in Europe...*
2 = <u>competition</u>, game, tournament, contest, bout

...*major sporting events*...

PHRASES **in any event** *or* **at all events** = whatever happens, regardless, in any case, no matter what, at any rate, come what may ...*It is not going to be an easy decision, in any event*... ◆ **in the event of** = in the eventuality of, in the situation of, in the likelihood of ...*The bank will make an immediate refund in the event of any error*...

eventful = exciting, active, busy, dramatic, remarkable, historic, full, lively, memorable, notable, momentous, fateful, noteworthy, consequential
OPPOSITE> dull

eventual = final, later, resulting, future, overall, concluding, ultimate, prospective, ensuing, consequent

eventuality = possibility, event, likelihood, probability, case, chance, contingency

eventually = in the end, finally, one day, after all, some time, ultimately, at the end of the day, in the long run, sooner or later, some day, when all is said and done, in the fullness of time, in the course of time

ever 1 = at any time, at all, in any case, at any point, by any chance, on any occasion, at any period ...*Don't you ever talk to me like that again!*...
2 = always, for ever, at all times, relentlessly, eternally, evermore, unceasingly, to the end of time, everlastingly, unendingly, aye (*Scot.*) ...*Mother, ever the peacemaker, told us to stop fighting*...
3 = constantly, continually, endlessly, perpetually, incessantly, unceasingly, unendingly ...*They grew ever further apart as time went on*...

everlasting 1 = eternal, endless, abiding, infinite, perpetual, timeless, immortal, never-ending, indestructible, undying, imperishable, deathless ...*The icon embodies a potent symbol of everlasting life*... OPPOSITE> transitory
2 = continual, constant, endless, continuous, never-ending, interminable, incessant, ceaseless, unremitting, unceasing ...*I'm tired of your everlasting bickering*...

every = each, each and every, every single

everybody = everyone, each one, the whole world, each person, every person, all and sundry, one and all
➤ everyone

everyday 1 = daily, day-to-day, diurnal, quotidian ...*opportunities for improving fitness in your everyday routine*... OPPOSITE> occasional
2 = ordinary, common, usual, familiar, conventional, routine, dull, stock, accustomed, customary, commonplace, mundane, vanilla (*slang*), banal, habitual, run-of-the-mill, unimaginative, workaday, unexceptional, bog-standard (*Brit. & Irish slang*), common or garden (*informal*), dime-a-dozen (*informal*), wonted ...*an exhilarating escape from the drudgery of everyday life*... OPPOSITE> unusual

everyone = everybody, each one, the whole world, each person, every person, all and sundry, one and all

---

Word Power

everyone – *Everyone* and *everybody* are interchangeable, and can be used as synonyms of each other in any context. Care should be taken, however, to distinguish between *everyone* as a single word and *every one* as two words, the latter form correctly being used to refer to each individual person or thing in a particular group: *every one of them is wrong.*

---

everything = all, the whole, the total, the lot, the sum, the whole lot, the aggregate, the entirety, each thing, the whole caboodle (*informal*), the whole kit and caboodle (*informal*)

everywhere 1 = all over, all around, the world over, high and low, in each place, in every nook and cranny, far and wide *or* near, to *or* in every place ...*I looked everywhere but I couldn't find him*...
2 = all around, all over, in each place, in every nook and cranny, ubiquitously, far and wide *or* near, to *or* in every place ...*There were clothes scattered around everywhere*...

evict = expel, remove, turn out, put out, throw out, oust, kick out (*informal*), eject, dislodge, boot out (*informal*), force to leave, dispossess, chuck out (*informal*), show the door (to), turf out (*informal*), throw on to the streets

eviction = expulsion, removal, clearance, ouster (*Law*), ejection, dispossession, dislodgement

evidence NOUN 1 = proof, grounds, data, demonstration, confirmation, verification, corroboration, authentication, substantiation ...*There is no evidence to support this theory*...
2 = sign(s), mark, suggestion, trace, indication, token, manifestation ...*Police said there was no evidence of a struggle*...
3 = testimony, statement, witness, declaration, submission, affirmation, deposition, avowal, attestation, averment ...*Forensic scientists will be called to give evidence*...
VERB = show, prove, reveal, display, indicate, witness, demonstrate, exhibit, manifest, signify, denote, testify to, evince ...*He still has a lot to learn, as is evidenced by his recent behaviour*...

evident = obvious, clear, plain, apparent, visible, patent, manifest, tangible, noticeable, blatant, conspicuous, unmistakable, palpable, salient, indisputable, perceptible, incontrovertible, incontestable, plain as the nose on your face
OPPOSITE> hidden

evidently 1 = obviously, clearly, plainly, patently, undoubtedly, manifestly, doubtless, without question, unmistakably, indisputably, doubtlessly, incontrovertibly, incontestably ...*He had evidently just woken up*...
2 = apparently, it seems, seemingly, outwardly, it would seem, ostensibly, so it seems, to all appearances ...*Ellis evidently wished to negotiate downwards, after Atkinson had set the guidelines*...

evil NOUN **1** = <u>wickedness</u>, bad, wrong, vice, corruption, sin, wrongdoing, depravity, immorality, iniquity, badness, viciousness, villainy, sinfulness, turpitude, baseness, malignity, heinousness, maleficence ...*We are being attacked by the forces of evil...*
2 = <u>harm</u>, suffering, pain, hurt, misery, sorrow, woe ...*those who see television as the root of all evil...*
3 = <u>act of cruelty</u>, crime, ill, horror, outrage, cruelty, brutality, misfortune, mischief, affliction, monstrosity, abomination, barbarity, villainy ...*Racism is one of the greatest evils in the world...*
ADJECTIVE **1** = <u>wicked</u>, bad, wrong, corrupt, vicious, vile, malicious, base, immoral, malignant, sinful, unholy, malevolent, heinous, depraved, villainous, nefarious, iniquitous, reprobate, maleficent ...*the country's most evil criminals...*
2 = <u>harmful</u>, painful, disastrous, destructive, dire, catastrophic, mischievous, detrimental, hurtful, woeful, pernicious, ruinous, sorrowful, deleterious, injurious, baneful (*archaic*) ...*Few people would not condemn slavery as evil...*
3 = <u>demonic</u>, satanic, diabolical, hellish, devilish, infernal, fiendish ...*This place is said to be haunted by an evil spirit...*
4 = <u>offensive</u>, nasty, foul, unpleasant, vile, noxious, disagreeable, putrid, pestilential, mephitic ...*There was an evil stench in the room...*
5 = <u>unfortunate</u>, unlucky, unfavourable, ruinous, calamitous, inauspicious ...*people of honour who happen to have fallen upon evil times...*

evince (*Formal*) = <u>show</u>, evidence, reveal, establish, express, display, indicate, demonstrate, exhibit, make clear, manifest, signify, attest, bespeak, betoken, make evident

evoke **1** = <u>arouse</u>, cause, excite, stimulate, induce, awaken, give rise to, stir up, rekindle, summon up ...*The programme has evoked a storm of protest...* OPPOSITE suppress
2 = <u>provoke</u>, produce, elicit, call to mind, call forth, educe (*rare*) ...*Hearing these songs can still evoke strong memories and emotions...*

evolution **1** = <u>rise</u>, development, adaptation, natural selection, Darwinism, survival of the fittest, evolvement ...*the evolution of plants and animals...*
2 = <u>development</u>, growth, advance, progress, working out, expansion, extension, unfolding, progression, enlargement, maturation, unrolling ...*a crucial period in the evolution of modern physics...*

evolve **1** = <u>develop</u>, metamorphose, adapt yourself ...*Modern birds evolved from dinosaurs...*
2 = <u>grow</u>, develop, advance, progress, mature ...*Popular music evolved from folk songs...*
3 = <u>work out</u>, develop, progress, expand, elaborate, unfold, enlarge, unroll ...*He evolved a working method from which he has never departed...*

exacerbate = <u>make worse</u>, excite, provoke, irritate, intensify, worsen, infuriate, aggravate (*informal*), enrage, madden, inflame, exasperate, vex, embitter, add insult to injury, fan the flames of, envenom

exact ADJECTIVE **1** = <u>accurate</u>, very, correct, true, particular, right, express, specific, careful, precise, identical, authentic, faithful, explicit, definite, orderly, literal, unequivocal, faultless, on the money (*U.S.*), unerring, veracious ...*I can't remember the exact words he used...* OPPOSITE approximate
2 = <u>meticulous</u>, severe, careful, strict, exacting, precise, rigorous, painstaking, scrupulous, methodical, punctilious ...*She is very punctual and very exact in her duties...*
VERB **1** = <u>demand</u>, claim, require, call for, force, impose, command, squeeze, extract, compel, wring, wrest, insist upon, extort ...*He has exacted a high price for his co-operation...*
2 = <u>inflict</u>, apply, impose, administer, mete out, deal out ...*She exacted a terrible revenge on her attackers...*

exacting **1** = <u>demanding</u>, hard, taxing, difficult, tough, painstaking ...*He was not well enough to carry out such an exacting task...* OPPOSITE easy
2 = <u>strict</u>, severe, harsh, stern, rigid, rigorous, stringent, oppressive, imperious, unsparing ...*Our new manager has very exacting standards...*

exactly ADVERB **1** = <u>accurately</u>, correctly, definitely, truly, precisely, strictly, literally, faithfully, explicitly, rigorously, unequivocally, scrupulously, truthfully, methodically, unerringly, faultlessly, veraciously ...*Can you describe exactly what he looked like?...*
2 = <u>precisely</u>, just, expressly, prompt (*informal*), specifically, bang on (*informal*), to the letter, on the button (*informal*) ...*He arrived at exactly five o'clock...*
INTERJECTION = <u>precisely</u>, yes, quite, of course, certainly, indeed, truly, that's right, absolutely, spot-on (*Brit. informal*), just so, quite so, ya (*S. African*), as you say, you got it (*informal*), assuredly, yebo (*S. African informal*) ...*'We don't know the answer to that.' – 'Exactly. So shut up and stop speculating.'...*
PHRASES **not exactly** (*Ironical*) = <u>not at all</u>, hardly, not really, not quite, certainly not, by no means, in no way, not by any means, in no manner ...*Sailing is not exactly a cheap hobby...*

exaggerate = <u>overstate</u>, emphasize, enlarge, inflate, embroider, magnify, overdo, amplify, exalt, embellish, overestimate, overemphasize, pile it on about (*informal*), blow up out of all proportion, lay it on thick about (*informal*), lay it on with a trowel about (*informal*), make a production (out) of (*informal*), make a federal case of (*U.S. informal*), hyperbolize

exaggerated = <u>overstated</u>, extreme, excessive, over the top (*informal*), inflated, extravagant, overdone, tall (*informal*), amplified, hyped, pretentious, exalted, overestimated, overblown, fulsome, hyperbolic, highly coloured, O.T.T. (*slang*)

exaggeration = <u>overstatement</u>, inflation, emphasis, excess, enlargement, pretension, extravagance, hyperbole, magnification, amplification, embellishment, exaltation, pretentiousness, overemphasis, overestimation OPPOSITE understatement

exalt **1** = <u>praise</u>, acclaim, applaud, pay tribute to, bless, worship, magnify (*archaic*), glorify, reverence, laud, extol, crack up (*informal*), pay homage to, idolize, apotheosize, set on a pedestal ...*This book*

exalts her as a genius…
2 = <u>uplift</u>, raise, lift, excite, delight, inspire, thrill, stimulate, arouse, heighten, elevate, animate, exhilarate, electrify, fire the imagination of, fill with joy, elate, inspirit …*Great music exalts the human spirit…*

exaltation 1 = <u>elation</u>, delight, joy, excitement, inspiration, ecstasy, stimulation, bliss, transport, animation, elevation, rapture, exhilaration, jubilation, exultation, joyousness …*The city was swept up in the mood of exaltation…*
2 = <u>praise</u>, tribute, worship, acclaim, applause, glory, blessing, homage, reverence, magnification, apotheosis, glorification, acclamation, panegyric, idolization, extolment, lionization, laudation …*The poem is an exaltation of love…*

exalted 1 = <u>high-ranking</u>, high, grand, honoured, intellectual, noble, prestigious, august, elevated, eminent, dignified, lofty …*I seldom move in such exalted circles…*
2 = <u>noble</u>, ideal, superior, elevated, intellectual, uplifting, sublime, lofty, high-minded …*I don't think of poetry as an exalted calling, as some poets do…*
3 = <u>elated</u>, excited, inspired, stimulated, elevated, animated, uplifted, transported, exhilarated, ecstatic, jubilant, joyous, joyful, over the moon (*informal*), blissful, rapturous, exultant, in high spirits, on cloud nine (*informal*), cock-a-hoop, in seventh heaven, inspirited …*She had the look of someone exalted by an excess of joy…*

examination 1 = <u>checkup</u>, analysis, going-over (*informal*), exploration, health check, check, medical, once-over (*informal*) …*a routine medical examination…*
2 = <u>exam</u>, test, research, paper, investigation, practical, assessment, quiz, evaluation, oral, appraisal, catechism …*accusations of cheating in school examinations…*

examine 1 = <u>inspect</u>, test, consider, study, check, research, review, survey, investigate, explore, probe, analyse, scan, vet, check out, ponder, look over, look at, sift through, work over, pore over, appraise, scrutinize, peruse, take stock of, assay, recce (*slang*), look at carefully, go over *or* through …*He examined her passport and stamped it…*
2 = <u>check</u>, analyse, check over …*The doctor examined her, but could find nothing wrong…*
3 = <u>test</u>, question, assess, quiz, evaluate, appraise, catechize …*the pressures of being judged and examined by our teachers…*
4 = <u>question</u>, quiz, interrogate, cross-examine, grill (*informal*), give the third degree to (*informal*) …*I was called and examined as a witness…*

example NOUN **1** = <u>instance</u>, specimen, case, sample, illustration, case in point, particular case, particular instance, typical case, exemplification, representative case …*examples of sexism and racism in the police force…*
2 = <u>illustration</u>, model, ideal, standard, norm, precedent, pattern, prototype, paradigm, archetype, paragon, exemplar …*This piece is a perfect example of*

symphonic construction…
3 = <u>warning</u>, lesson, caution, deterrent, admonition …*We were punished as an example to others…*
PHRASES **for example** = <u>as an illustration</u>, like, such as, for instance, to illustrate, by way of illustration, exempli gratia (*Latin*), e.g., to cite an instance …*You could, for example, walk instead of taking the car…*

exasperate = <u>irritate</u>, anger, provoke, annoy, rouse, infuriate, hassle (*informal*), exacerbate, aggravate (*informal*), incense, enrage, gall, madden, inflame, bug (*informal*), nettle, get to (*informal*), vex, embitter, irk, rile (*informal*), pique, rankle, peeve (*informal*), needle (*informal*), get on your nerves (*informal*), try the patience of, nark (*Brit., Austral., & N.Z. slang*), get in your hair (*informal*), get on your wick (*Brit. slang*) OPPOSITE calm

exasperating = <u>irritating</u>, provoking, annoying, infuriating, aggravating (*informal*), galling, maddening, vexing, irksome, enough to drive you up the wall (*informal*), enough to try the patience of a saint

exasperation = <u>irritation</u>, anger, rage, fury, wrath, provocation, passion, annoyance, ire (*literary*), pique, aggravation (*informal*), vexation, exacerbation

excavate 1 = <u>dig up</u>, mine, dig, tunnel, scoop, cut, hollow, trench, burrow, quarry, delve, gouge …*A team of archaeologists is excavating the site…*
2 = <u>unearth</u>, expose, uncover, dig out, exhume, lay bare, bring to light, bring to the surface, disinter …*They have excavated the fossil remains of a prehistoric man…*

excavation = <u>hole</u>, mine, pit, ditch, shaft, cutting, cut, hollow, trench, burrow, quarry, dig, trough, cavity, dugout, diggings

exceed 1 = <u>surpass</u>, better, pass, eclipse, beat, cap (*informal*), top, be over, be more than, overtake, go beyond, excel, transcend, be greater than, outstrip, outdo, outreach, be larger than, outshine, surmount, be superior to, outrun, run rings around (*informal*), outdistance, knock spots off (*informal*), put in the shade (*informal*) …*His performance exceeded all expectations…*
2 = <u>go over the limit of</u>, go beyond, overstep, go beyond the bounds of …*This programme exceeded the bounds of taste and decency…*

exceeding = <u>extraordinary</u>, great, huge, vast, enormous, superior, excessive, exceptional, surpassing, superlative, pre-eminent, streets ahead

exceedingly = <u>extremely</u>, very, highly, greatly, especially, hugely, seriously (*informal*), vastly, unusually, enormously, exceptionally, extraordinarily, excessively, superlatively, inordinately, to a fault, to the nth degree, surpassingly

excel VERB = <u>be superior</u>, better, pass, eclipse, beat, top, cap (*informal*), exceed, go beyond, surpass, transcend, outdo, outshine, surmount, run rings around (*informal*), put in the shade (*informal*), outrival …*Few dancers have excelled her in virtuosity…*
PHRASES **excel in** *or* **at something** = <u>be good at</u>, be master of, predominate in, shine at, be proficient

in, show talent in, be skilful at, have (something) down to a fine art, be talented at ...*She excelled at outdoor sports*...

excellence = high quality, worth, merit, distinction, virtue, goodness, perfection, superiority, purity, greatness, supremacy, eminence, virtuosity, transcendence, pre-eminence, fineness

excellent = outstanding, good, great, fine, prime, capital, noted, choice, champion, cool (*informal*), select, brilliant, very good, cracking (*Brit. informal*), crucial (*slang*), mean (*slang*), superb, distinguished, fantastic, magnificent, superior, sterling, worthy, first-class, marvellous, exceptional, terrific, splendid, notable, mega (*slang*), topping (*Brit. slang*), sovereign, dope (*slang*), world-class, exquisite, admirable, exemplary, wicked (*slang*), first-rate, def (*slang*), superlative, top-notch (*informal*), brill (*informal*), pre-eminent, meritorious, estimable, tiptop, bodacious (*slang, chiefly U.S.*), boffo (*slang*), jim-dandy (*slang*), A1 or A-one (*informal*), bitchin' (*U.S. slang*), chillin' (*U.S. slang*), booshit (*Austral. slang*), exo (*Austral. slang*), sik (*Austral. slang*) OPPOSITE terrible

except or **except for** PREPOSITION = apart from, but for, saving, bar, barring, excepting, other than, excluding, omitting, with the exception of, aside from, save (*archaic*), not counting, exclusive of ...*I don't drink, except for the occasional glass of wine*...
VERB = exclude, rule out, leave out, omit, disregard, pass over ...*Men are such swine (present company excepted, of course)*...

exception NOUN = special case, departure, freak, anomaly, inconsistency, deviation, quirk, oddity, peculiarity, irregularity ...*an exception to the usual rule*...
PHRASES **take exception to something** = object to, disagree with, take offence at, take umbrage at, be resentful of, be offended at, demur at, quibble at ...*I take exception to being checked up on like this*...

exceptional 1 = remarkable, special, excellent, extraordinary, outstanding, superior, first-class, marvellous, notable, phenomenal, first-rate, prodigious, unsurpassed, one in a million, bodacious (*slang, chiefly U.S.*), unexcelled ...*His piano playing is exceptional*... OPPOSITE average
2 = unusual, special, odd, strange, rare, extraordinary, unprecedented, peculiar, abnormal, irregular, uncommon, inconsistent, singular, deviant, anomalous, atypical, aberrant ...*The courts hold that this case is exceptional*... OPPOSITE ordinary

excerpt NOUN = extract, part, piece, section, selection, passage, portion, fragment, quotation, citation, pericope ...*an excerpt from Tchaikovsky's 'Nutcracker'*...
VERB = extract, take, select, quote, cite, pick out, cull ...*The readings were excerpted from his autobiography*...

excess NOUN 1 = surfeit, surplus, overdose, overflow, overload, plethora, glut, overabundance, superabundance, superfluity ...*Avoid an excess of sugar in your diet*... OPPOSITE shortage
2 = overindulgence, extravagance, profligacy, debauchery, dissipation, intemperance, indulgence, prodigality, extreme behaviour, immoral behaviour, dissoluteness, immoderation, exorbitance, unrestraint ...*He had led a life of excess*... OPPOSITE moderation
ADJECTIVE = spare, remaining, extra, additional, surplus, unwanted, redundant, residual, leftover, superfluous, unneeded ...*After cooking the fish, pour off any excess fat*...

excessive 1 = immoderate, too much, enormous, extreme, exaggerated, over the top (*slang*), extravagant, needless, unreasonable, disproportionate, undue, uncontrolled, superfluous, prodigal, unrestrained, profligate, inordinate, fulsome, intemperate, unconscionable, overmuch, O.T.T. (*slang*) ...*the alleged use of excessive force by police*...
2 = inordinate, unfair, unreasonable, disproportionate, undue, unwarranted, exorbitant, over the odds, extortionate, immoderate ...*banks which cripple their customers with excessive charges*...

exchange VERB = interchange, change, trade, switch, swap, truck, barter, reciprocate, bandy, give to each other, give to one another ...*We exchanged addresses*...
NOUN 1 = conversation, talk, word, discussion, chat, dialogue, natter, powwow ...*I had a brief exchange with him before I left*...
2 = interchange, dealing, trade, switch, swap, traffic, trafficking, truck, swapping, substitution, barter, bartering, reciprocity, tit for tat, quid pro quo ...*a free exchange of information*...
3 = market, money market, Bourse ...*the Stock Exchange*...

excise[1] = tax, duty, customs, toll, levy, tariff, surcharge, impost ...*Smokers will be hit by increases in tax and excise*...

excise[2] 1 = delete, cut, remove, erase, destroy, eradicate, strike out, exterminate, cross out, expunge, extirpate, wipe from the face of the earth ...*a crusade to excise racist and sexist references in newspapers*...
2 = cut off or out or away, remove, take out, extract ...*She has already had one skin cancer excised*...

excitable = nervous, emotional, violent, sensitive, tense, passionate, volatile, hasty, edgy, temperamental, touchy, mercurial, uptight (*informal*), irascible, testy, hot-headed, hot-tempered, quick-tempered, highly strung OPPOSITE calm

excite 1 = thrill, inspire, stir, stimulate, provoke, awaken, animate, move, fire, rouse, exhilarate, agitate, quicken, inflame, enliven, galvanize, foment ...*I only take on work that excites me*...
2 = arouse, stimulate, provoke, evoke, rouse, stir up, fire, elicit, work up, incite, instigate, whet, kindle, waken ...*The proposal failed to excite our interest*...
3 = titillate, thrill, stimulate, turn on (*slang*), arouse, get going (*informal*), electrify ...*Try exciting your partner with a little bondage*...

excited 1 = thrilled, stirred, stimulated, enthusiastic, high (*informal*), moved, wild, aroused, awakened, animated, roused, tumultuous, aflame ...*He was so excited he could hardly speak*...
2 = agitated, worried, stressed, alarmed, nervous,

disturbed, tense, flurried, worked up, feverish, overwrought, hot and bothered (*informal*), discomposed ...*There's no need to get so excited...*

excitement 1 = <u>exhilaration</u>, action, activity, passion, heat, thrill, adventure, enthusiasm, fever, warmth, flurry, animation, furore, ferment, agitation, commotion, elation, ado, tumult, perturbation, discomposure ...*The audience was in a state of great excitement...*
2 = <u>pleasure</u>, thrill, sensation, stimulation, tingle, kick (*informal*) ...*The game had its challenges, excitements and rewards...*

exciting 1 = <u>stimulating</u>, inspiring, dramatic, gripping, stirring, thrilling, moving, sensational, rousing, exhilarating, electrifying, intoxicating, rip-roaring (*informal*) ...*the most exciting adventure of their lives...* OPPOSITE boring
2 = <u>titillating</u>, stimulating, sexy (*informal*), arousing, erotic, provocative ...*fantasizing about a sexually exciting scene...*

exclaim = <u>cry out</u>, call, declare, cry, shout, proclaim, yell, utter, call out, ejaculate, vociferate

exclamation = <u>cry</u>, call, shout, yell, outcry, utterance, ejaculation, expletive, interjection, vociferation

exclude 1 = <u>keep out</u>, bar, ban, veto, refuse, forbid, boycott, embargo, prohibit, disallow, shut out, proscribe, black, refuse to admit, ostracize, debar, blackball, interdict, prevent from entering ...*The Academy excluded women from its classes...* OPPOSITE let in
2 = <u>omit</u>, reject, eliminate, rule out, miss out, leave out, preclude, repudiate ...*Vegetarians exclude meat products from their diet...* OPPOSITE include
3 = <u>eliminate</u>, reject, ignore, rule out, except, leave out, set aside, omit, pass over, not count, repudiate, count out ...*We can't exclude the possibility of suicide...*

exclusion 1 = <u>ban</u>, bar, veto, refusal, boycott, embargo, prohibition, disqualification, interdict, proscription, debarment, preclusion, forbiddance, nonadmission ...*They demand the exclusion of former communists from political life...*
2 = <u>elimination</u>, exception, missing out, rejection, leaving out, omission, repudiation ...*the exclusion of dairy products from your diet...*

exclusive ADJECTIVE 1 = <u>select</u>, fashionable, stylish, private, limited, choice, narrow, closed, restricted, elegant, posh (*informal, chiefly Brit.*), chic, selfish, classy (*slang*), restrictive, aristocratic, high-class, swish (*informal, chiefly Brit.*), up-market, snobbish, top-drawer, ritzy (*slang*), high-toned, clannish, discriminative, cliquish ...*He is a member of Britain's most exclusive club...* OPPOSITE unrestricted
2 = <u>sole</u>, only, full, whole, single, private, complete, total, entire, unique, absolute, undivided, unshared ...*We have exclusive use of a 60-foot boat...* OPPOSITE shared
3 = <u>entire</u>, full, whole, complete, total, absolute, undivided ...*She wants her father's exclusive attention...*

4 = <u>limited</u>, unique, restricted, confined, peculiar ...*Infatuations are not exclusive to the very young...*
PHRASES **exclusive of** = <u>except for</u>, excepting, excluding, ruling out, not including, omitting, not counting, leaving aside, debarring ...*All charges are exclusive of value added tax...*

excommunicate = <u>expel</u>, ban, remove, exclude, denounce, banish, eject, repudiate, proscribe, cast out, unchurch, anathematize

excrement = <u>faeces</u>, crap (*taboo slang*), dung, stool, droppings, motion, mess (*especially of a domestic animal*), defecation, excreta, ordure, kak (*S. African taboo slang*), night soil

excrete = <u>defecate</u>, discharge, expel, evacuate, crap (*taboo slang*), eliminate, void, eject, exude, egest

excruciating = <u>agonizing</u>, acute, severe, extreme, burning, violent, intense, piercing, racking, searing, tormenting, exquisite, harrowing, unbearable, insufferable, torturous, unendurable

excursion = <u>trip</u>, airing, tour, journey, outing, expedition, ramble, day trip, jaunt, pleasure trip

excuse NOUN 1 = <u>justification</u>, reason, explanation, defence, grounds, plea, apology, pretext, vindication, mitigation, mitigating circumstances, extenuation ...*There is no excuse for what he did...* OPPOSITE accusation
2 = <u>pretext</u>, evasion, pretence, cover-up, expedient, get-out, cop-out (*slang*), subterfuge ...*It was just an excuse to get out of going to school...*
3 (*Informal*) = <u>poor substitute</u>, apology, mockery, travesty ...*He is a pathetic excuse for a father...*
VERB 1 = <u>justify</u>, explain, defend, vindicate, condone, mitigate, apologize for, make excuses for ...*I know you're upset but that doesn't excuse your behaviour...* OPPOSITE blame
2 = <u>forgive</u>, pardon, overlook, tolerate, indulge, acquit, pass over, turn a blind eye to, exonerate, absolve, bear with, wink at, make allowances for, extenuate, exculpate ...*He's a total bastard – excuse me for swearing...*
3 = <u>free</u>, relieve, liberate, exempt, release, spare, discharge, let off, absolve ...*She was excused from her duties for the day...* OPPOSITE convict

execute 1 = <u>put to death</u>, kill, shoot, hang, behead, decapitate, guillotine, electrocute ...*His father had been executed for treason...*
2 = <u>carry out</u>, effect, finish, complete, achieve, realize, do, implement, fulfil, enforce, accomplish, render, discharge, administer, prosecute, enact, consummate, put into effect, bring off ...*We are going to execute our campaign plan to the letter...*
3 = <u>perform</u>, do, carry out, accomplish ...*The landing was skilfully executed...*

execution 1 = <u>killing</u>, hanging, the death penalty, the rope, capital punishment, beheading, the electric chair, the guillotine, the noose, the scaffold, electrocution, decapitation, the firing squad, necktie party (*informal*) ...*He was sentenced to execution by lethal injection...*
2 = <u>carrying out</u>, performance, operation,

administration, achievement, effect, prosecution, rendering, discharge, enforcement, implementation, completion, accomplishment, realization, enactment, bringing off, consummation ...*the unquestioning execution of his orders*...
3 = <u>performance</u>, style, delivery, manner, technique, mode, presentation, rendition ...*his masterly execution of a difficult piece*...

executioner = <u>hangman</u>, firing squad, headsman, public executioner, Jack Ketch

executive NOUN **1** = <u>administrator</u>, official, director, manager, chairman, managing director, controller, chief executive officer, senior manager, chairwoman, chairperson ...*Her husband is a senior bank executive*...
2 = <u>administration</u>, government, directors, management, leadership, hierarchy, directorate ...*the executive of the National Union of Students*...
ADJECTIVE = <u>administrative</u>, controlling, directing, governing, regulating, decision-making, managerial ...*He sits on the executive committee of the company*...

exemplar 1 = <u>model</u>, example, standard, ideal, criterion, paradigm, epitome, paragon ...*They viewed their new building as an exemplar of taste*...
2 = <u>example</u>, instance, illustration, type, specimen, prototype, typical example, representative example, exemplification ...*One of the wittiest exemplars of the technique was M.C. Escher*...

exemplary 1 = <u>ideal</u>, good, fine, model, excellent, sterling, admirable, honourable, commendable, laudable, praiseworthy, meritorious, estimable, punctilious ...*He showed outstanding and exemplary courage in the face of danger*...
2 = <u>typical</u>, representative, characteristic, illustrative ...*an exemplary case of how issues of this sort can be resolved*...
3 = <u>warning</u>, harsh, cautionary, admonitory, monitory ...*He demanded exemplary sentences for those behind the violence*...

exemplify = <u>show</u>, represent, display, demonstrate, instance, illustrate, exhibit, depict, manifest, evidence, embody, serve as an example of

exempt ADJECTIVE = <u>immune</u>, free, excepted, excused, released, spared, clear, discharged, liberated, not subject to, absolved, not liable to ...*Men in college were exempt from military service*... OPPOSITE liable
VERB = <u>grant immunity</u>, free, except, excuse, release, spare, relieve, discharge, liberate, let off, exonerate, absolve ...*Companies with fewer than 55 employees would be exempted from these requirements*...

exemption = <u>immunity</u>, freedom, privilege, relief, exception, discharge, release, dispensation, absolution, exoneration

exercise VERB **1** = <u>put to use</u>, use, apply, employ, practise, exert, enjoy, wield, utilize, bring to bear, avail yourself of ...*They are merely exercising their right to free speech*...
2 = <u>train</u>, work out, practise, drill, keep fit, inure, do exercises ...*She exercises two or three times a week*...
3 = <u>worry</u>, concern, occupy, try, trouble, pain, disturb,

burden, distress, preoccupy, agitate, perplex, vex, perturb ...*an issue that has long exercised the finest scientific minds*...
NOUN **1** = <u>use</u>, practice, application, operation, employment, discharge, implementation, enjoyment, accomplishment, fulfilment, exertion, utilization ...*Leadership does not rest on the exercise of force alone*...
2 = <u>exertion</u>, training, activity, action, work, labour, effort, movement, discipline, toil, physical activity ...*Lack of exercise can lead to feelings of depression and exhaustion*...
3 = <u>manoeuvre</u>, campaign, operation, movement, deployment ...*a missile being used in a military exercise*...
4 = <u>task</u>, problem, lesson, assignment, work, schooling, practice, schoolwork ...*Try working through the opening exercises in this chapter*...

exert VERB = <u>apply</u>, use, exercise, employ, wield, make use of, utilize, expend, bring to bear, put forth, bring into play ...*He exerted all his considerable charm to get her to agree*...
PHRASES **exert yourself** = <u>make an effort</u>, work, labour, struggle, strain, strive, endeavour, go for it (*informal*), try hard, toil, bend over backwards (*informal*), do your best, go for broke (*slang*), bust a gut (*informal*), spare no effort, make a great effort, give it your best shot (*informal*), break your neck (*informal*), apply yourself, put yourself out, make an all-out effort (*informal*), get your finger out (*Brit. informal*), pull your finger out (*Brit. informal*), knock yourself out (*informal*), do your damnedest (*informal*), give it your all (*informal*), rupture yourself (*informal*) ...*He never exerts himself for other people*...

exertion 1 = <u>effort</u>, action, exercise, struggle, industry, labour, trial, pains, stretch, strain, endeavour, toil, travail (*literary*), elbow grease (*facetious*) ...*panting from the exertion of climbing the stairs*...
2 = <u>use</u>, exercise, application, employment, bringing to bear, utilization ...*the exertion of legislative power*...

exhale 1 = <u>breathe out</u>, breathe, expel, blow out, respire ...*Hold your breath for a moment and exhale*...
2 = <u>give off</u>, emit, steam, discharge, send out, evaporate, issue, eject, emanate ...*The craters exhale water, carbon dioxide, and sulphur dioxide*...

exhaust 1 = <u>tire out</u>, tire, fatigue, drain, disable, weaken, cripple, weary, sap, wear out, debilitate, prostrate, enfeeble, make tired, enervate ...*The effort of speaking had exhausted him*...
2 = <u>use up</u>, spend, finish, consume, waste, go through, run through, deplete, squander, dissipate, expend ...*We have exhausted almost all our food supplies*...

exhausted 1 = <u>worn out</u>, tired out, drained, spent, beat (*slang*), bushed (*informal*), dead (*informal*), wasted, done in (*informal*), weak, all in (*slang*), disabled, crippled, fatigued, wiped out (*informal*), sapped, debilitated, jaded, knackered (*slang*), prostrated, clapped out (*Brit., Austral., & N.Z. informal*), effete, enfeebled, enervated, ready to drop, dog-tired (*informal*), zonked (*slang*), dead tired, dead beat (*informal*), shagged out (*Brit. slang*), fagged out (*informal*), worn to a frazzle (*informal*), on your last legs (*informal*), creamcrackered (*Brit. slang*), out on your feet (*informal*) ...*She was too exhausted even to think clearly...* OPPOSITE> invigorated

2 = used up, consumed, spent, finished, gone, depleted, dissipated, expended, at an end ...*Mining companies are shutting down operations as the coal supply is exhausted...* OPPOSITE> replenished

exhausting = tiring, hard, testing, taxing, difficult, draining, punishing, crippling, fatiguing, wearying, gruelling, sapping, debilitating, strenuous, arduous, laborious, enervating, backbreaking

exhaustion 1 = tiredness, fatigue, weariness, lassitude, feebleness, prostration, debilitation, enervation ...*He is suffering from nervous exhaustion...*

2 = depletion, emptying, consumption, using up ...*the exhaustion of the country's resources...*

exhaustive = thorough, detailed, complete, full, total, sweeping, comprehensive, extensive, intensive, full-scale, in-depth, far-reaching, all-inclusive, all-embracing, encyclopedic, thoroughgoing OPPOSITE> superficial

exhibit VERB **1** = show, reveal, display, demonstrate, air, evidence, express, indicate, disclose, manifest, evince, make clear *or* plain ...*He has exhibited signs of anxiety and stress...*

2 = display, show, present, set out, parade, unveil, flaunt, put on view ...*Her work was exhibited in the best galleries in Europe...*

NOUN **1** = object, piece, model, article, illustration ...*He showed me round the exhibits in the museum...*

2 = exhibition, show, fair, display, spectacle, expo (*informal*), exposition ...*the 8th international exhibit of agricultural technology...*

exhibition 1 = show, display, exhibit, showing, fair, representation, presentation, spectacle, showcase, expo (*informal*), exposition ...*an exhibition of expressionist art...*

2 = display, show, performance, demonstration, airing, revelation, manifestation ...*He treated the fans to an exhibition of power and speed...*

exhilarate = excite, delight, cheer, thrill, stimulate, animate, exalt, lift, enliven, invigorate, gladden, elate, inspirit, pep *or* perk up

exhilarating = exciting, thrilling, stimulating, breathtaking, cheering, exalting, enlivening, invigorating, gladdening, vitalizing, exhilarant

exhilaration = excitement, delight, joy, happiness, animation, high spirits, elation, mirth, gaiety, hilarity, exaltation, cheerfulness, vivacity, liveliness, gladness, joyfulness, sprightliness, gleefulness OPPOSITE> depression

exhort (*Formal*) = urge, warn, encourage, advise, bid, persuade, prompt, spur, press, counsel, caution, call upon, incite, goad, admonish, enjoin, beseech, entreat

exhortation (*Formal*) = urging, warning, advice, counsel, lecture, caution, bidding, encouragement, sermon, persuasion, goading, incitement, admonition,

beseeching, entreaty, clarion call, enjoinder (*rare*)

exhume (*Formal*) = dig up, unearth, disinter, unbury, disentomb OPPOSITE> bury

exile NOUN **1** = banishment, expulsion, deportation, eviction, separation, ostracism, proscription, expatriation ...*During his exile, he began writing books...*

2 = expatriate, refugee, outcast, émigré, deportee ...*the release of all political prisoners and the return of exiles...*

VERB = banish, expel, throw out, deport, oust, drive out, eject, expatriate, proscribe, cast out, ostracize ...*Dante was exiled from Florence in 1302 because of his political activities...*

exiled = banished, deported, expatriate, outcast, refugee, ostracized, expat

exist 1 = live, be present, be living, last, survive, breathe, endure, be in existence, be, be extant, have breath ...*Many people believe that the Loch Ness Monster does exist...*

2 = occur, happen, stand, remain, obtain, be present, prevail, abide ...*the social climate which existed 20 years ago...*

3 = survive, stay alive, make ends meet, subsist, eke out a living, scrape by, scrimp and save, support yourself, keep your head above water, get along *or* by ...*the problems of having to exist on unemployment benefit...*

Word Power

exist – Although *be extant* is given as a synonym of *exist*, according to some, *extant* should properly only be used where there is a connotation of survival, often against all odds: *the oldest extant document dates from 1492.* Using *extant* where the phrase *in existence* can be substituted, would in this view be incorrect: *in existence* (not *extant*) *for nearly 15 years, they have been consistently one of the finest rock bands on the planet.* In practice, however, the distinct meanings of the two phrases often overlap: *these beasts, the largest primates on the planet and the greatest of the great apes, are man's closest living relatives and the only extant primates with which we share close physical characteristics.*

---

existence 1 = reality, being, life, survival, duration, endurance, continuation, subsistence, actuality, continuance ...*Public worries about accidents are threatening the very existence of the nuclear power industry...*

2 = life, situation, way of life, life style ...*the man who rescued her from her wretched existence...*

3 = creation, life, the world, reality, the human condition, this mortal coil ...*pondering the mysteries of existence...*

existent = in existence, living, existing, surviving, around, standing, remaining, present, current, alive, enduring, prevailing, abiding, to the fore (*Scot.*), extant

existing = in existence, living, present, surviving,

remaining, available, alive, in operation, extant, alive and kicking OPPOSITE gone

exit NOUN **1** = <u>way out</u>, door, gate, outlet, doorway, vent, gateway, escape route, passage out, egress ...*We headed quickly for the fire exit...* OPPOSITE entry
2 = <u>departure</u>, withdrawal, retreat, farewell, going, retirement, goodbye, exodus, evacuation, decamping, leave-taking, adieu ...*She made a dignified exit...*
VERB = <u>depart</u>, leave, go out, withdraw, retire, quit, retreat, go away, say goodbye, bid farewell, make tracks, take your leave, go offstage (*Theatre*) ...*He exited without saying goodbye...* OPPOSITE enter

exodus = <u>departure</u>, withdrawal, retreat, leaving, flight, retirement, exit, migration, evacuation

exonerate = <u>acquit</u>, clear, excuse, pardon, justify, discharge, vindicate, absolve, exculpate

exorbitant = <u>excessive</u>, high, expensive, extreme, ridiculous, outrageous, extravagant, unreasonable, undue, preposterous, unwarranted, inordinate, extortionate, unconscionable, immoderate OPPOSITE reasonable

exorcise *or* **exorcize** **1** = <u>drive out</u>, expel, cast out, adjure ...*He tried to exorcise the pain of his childhood trauma...*
2 = <u>purify</u>, free, cleanse ...*They came to our house and exorcized me...*

exorcism = <u>driving out</u>, cleansing, expulsion, purification, deliverance, casting out, adjuration

exotic **1** = <u>unusual</u>, different, striking, strange, extraordinary, bizarre, fascinating, curious, mysterious, colourful, glamorous, peculiar, unfamiliar, outlandish ...*his striking and exotic appearance...* OPPOSITE ordinary
2 = <u>foreign</u>, alien, tropical, external, extraneous, naturalized, extrinsic, not native ...*travelling around the globe to collect rare and exotic plant species...*

expand VERB **1** = <u>get bigger</u>, increase, grow, extend, swell, widen, blow up, wax, heighten, enlarge, multiply, inflate, thicken, fill out, lengthen, fatten, dilate, become bigger, puff up, become larger, distend ...*Water expands as it freezes...* OPPOSITE contract
2 = <u>make bigger</u>, increase, develop, extend, widen, blow up, heighten, enlarge, multiply, broaden, inflate, thicken, fill out, lengthen, magnify, amplify, augment, dilate, make larger, distend, bloat, protract ...*We can expand the size of the image...* OPPOSITE reduce
3 = <u>spread (out)</u>, open (out), stretch (out), unfold, unravel, diffuse, unfurl, unroll, outspread ...*The flowers fully expand at night...*
PHRASES **expand on something** = <u>go into detail about</u>, embellish, elaborate on, develop, flesh out, expound on, enlarge on, expatiate on, add detail to ...*He expanded on some remarks he made in his last speech...*

expanse = <u>area</u>, range, field, space, stretch, sweep, extent, plain, tract, breadth

expansion **1** = <u>increase</u>, development, growth, spread, diffusion, magnification, multiplication, amplification, augmentation ...*the rapid expansion of private health insurance...*

2 = <u>enlargement</u>, inflation, increase, growth, swelling, unfolding, expanse, unfurling, opening out, distension ...*Slow breathing allows for full expansion of the lungs...*

expansive **1** = <u>wide</u>, broad, extensive, spacious, sweeping ...*an expansive grassy play area...*
2 = <u>comprehensive</u>, extensive, broad, wide, widespread, wide-ranging, thorough, inclusive, far-reaching, voluminous, all-embracing ...*the book's expansive coverage of this period...*
3 = <u>talkative</u>, open, friendly, outgoing, free, easy, warm, sociable, genial, affable, communicative, effusive, garrulous, loquacious, unreserved ...*He became more expansive as he began to relax...*

expatriate NOUN = <u>exile</u>, refugee, emigrant, émigré ...*British expatriates in Spain...*
ADJECTIVE = <u>exiled</u>, refugee, banished, emigrant, émigré, expat ...*The military is preparing to evacuate women and children of expatriate families...*

expect **1** = <u>think</u>, believe, suppose, assume, trust, imagine, reckon, forecast, calculate, presume, foresee, conjecture, surmise, think likely ...*We expect the talks will continue until tomorrow...*
2 = <u>anticipate</u>, look forward to, predict, envisage, await, hope for, contemplate, bargain for, look ahead to ...*I wasn't expecting to see you today...*
3 = <u>require</u>, demand, want, wish, look for, call for, ask for, hope for, insist on, count on, rely upon ...*He expects total obedience and blind loyalty from his staff...*

expectancy **1** = <u>likelihood</u>, prospect, tendency, outlook, probability ...*the average life expectancy of the British male...*
2 = <u>expectation</u>, hope, anticipation, waiting, belief, looking forward, assumption, prediction, probability, suspense, presumption, conjecture, surmise, supposition ...*The atmosphere here at the stadium is one of expectancy...*

expectant **1** = <u>expecting</u>, excited, anticipating, anxious, ready, awaiting, eager, hopeful, apprehensive, watchful, in suspense ...*She turned to me with an expectant look on her face...*
2 = <u>pregnant</u>, expecting (*informal*), gravid, enceinte ...*antenatal classes for expectant mothers...*

expectation **1** = <u>projection</u>, supposition, assumption, calculation, belief, forecast, assurance, likelihood, probability, presumption, conjecture, surmise, presupposition ...*Sales of the car have far exceeded expectations...*
2 = <u>anticipation</u>, hope, possibility, prospect, chance, fear, promise, looking forward, excitement, prediction, outlook, expectancy, apprehension, suspense ...*His nerves tingled with expectation...*
3 = <u>requirement</u>, demand, want, wish, insistence, reliance ...*Sometimes people have unreasonable expectations of the medical profession...*

expected = <u>anticipated</u>, wanted, promised, looked-for, predicted, forecast, awaited, hoped-for, counted on, long-awaited

expecting = <u>pregnant</u>, with child, expectant, in the club (*Brit. slang*), in the family way (*informal*), gravid, enceinte

expediency *or* **expedience** = suitability, benefit, fitness, utility, effectiveness, convenience, profitability, practicality, usefulness, prudence, pragmatism, propriety, desirability, appropriateness, utilitarianism, helpfulness, advisability, aptness, judiciousness, properness, meetness, advantageousness

expedient NOUN = means, measure, scheme, method, resource, resort, device, manoeuvre, expediency, stratagem, contrivance, stopgap ...*I reduced my spending by the simple expedient of destroying my credit cards*...
ADJECTIVE = advantageous, effective, useful, profitable, fit, politic, appropriate, practical, suitable, helpful, proper, convenient, desirable, worthwhile, beneficial, pragmatic, prudent, advisable, utilitarian, judicious, opportune ...*It might be expedient to keep this information to yourself*... OPPOSITE unwise

expedite (*Formal*) = speed (up), forward, promote, advance, press, urge, rush, assist, hurry, accelerate, dispatch, facilitate, hasten, precipitate, quicken
OPPOSITE hold up

expedition 1 = journey, exploration, mission, voyage, tour, enterprise, undertaking, quest, trek ...*Byrd's 1928 expedition to Antarctica*...
2 = team, crew, party, group, company, travellers, explorers, voyagers, wayfarers ...*Forty-three members of the expedition were killed*...
3 = trip, tour, outing, excursion, jaunt ...*We went on a shopping expedition*...

expel 1 = throw out, exclude, ban, bar, dismiss, discharge, relegate, kick out (*informal*), ask to leave, send packing, turf out (*informal*), black, debar, drum out, blackball, give the bum's rush (*slang*), show you the door, throw out on your ear (*informal*) ...*secondary school students expelled for cheating in exams*... OPPOSITE let in
2 = banish, exile, oust, deport, expatriate, evict, force to leave, proscribe ...*An American academic was expelled from the country yesterday*... OPPOSITE take in
3 = drive out, discharge, throw out, force out, let out, eject, issue, dislodge, spew, belch, cast out ...*Poisonous gas is expelled into the atmosphere*...

expend (*Formal*) 1 = use (up), employ, go through (*informal*), exhaust, consume, dissipate ...*the number of calories you expend through exercise*...
2 = spend, pay out, lay out (*informal*), fork out (*slang*), shell out, disburse ...*the amount of money expended on this project so far*...

expendable = dispensable, unnecessary, unimportant, replaceable, nonessential, inessential
OPPOSITE indispensable

expenditure 1 = spending, payment, expense, outgoings, cost, charge, outlay, disbursement ...*The government should reduce their expenditure on defence*...
2 = consumption, use, using, application, output ...*The rewards justified the expenditure of effort*...

expense NOUN = cost, charge, expenditure, payment, spending, output, toll, consumption, outlay, disbursement ...*She has refurbished the whole place at vast expense*...
PHRASES **at the expense of** = with the sacrifice of, with the loss of, at the cost of, at the price of ...*The company has increased productivity at the expense of safety*...

expensive = costly, high-priced, lavish, extravagant, rich, dear, stiff, excessive, steep (*informal*), pricey, overpriced, exorbitant OPPOSITE cheap

experience NOUN 1 = knowledge, understanding, practice, skill, evidence, trial, contact, expertise, know-how (*informal*), proof, involvement, exposure, observation, participation, familiarity, practical knowledge ...*He lacks experience of international rugby*...
2 = event, affair, incident, happening, test, trial, encounter, episode, adventure, ordeal, occurrence ...*It was an experience I would not like to go through again*...
VERB = undergo, have, know, feel, try, meet, face, suffer, taste, go through, observe, sample, encounter, sustain, perceive, endure, participate in, run into, live through, behold, come up against, apprehend, become familiar with ...*couples who have experienced the trauma of divorce*...

experienced 1 = knowledgeable, trained, professional, skilled, tried, tested, seasoned, expert, master, qualified, familiar, capable, veteran, practised, accomplished, competent, skilful, adept, well-versed ...*a team made up of experienced professionals*...
OPPOSITE inexperienced
2 = worldly-wise, knowing, worldly, wise, mature, sophisticated ...*Perhaps I'm a bit more experienced about life than you are*...

experiment NOUN 1 = test, trial, investigation, examination, venture, procedure, demonstration, observation, try-out, assay, trial run, scientific test, dummy run ...*a proposed new law banning animal experiments*...
2 = research, investigation, analysis, observation, research and development, experimentation, trial and error ...*The only way to find out is by experiment*...
VERB = test, investigate, trial, research, try, examine, pilot, sample, verify, put to the test, assay ...*Scientists have been experimenting with a new drug*...

experimental 1 = test, trial, pilot, preliminary, provisional, tentative, speculative, empirical, exploratory, trial-and-error, fact-finding, probationary ...*The technique is still in the experimental stages*...
2 = innovative, new, original, radical, creative, ingenious, avant-garde, inventive, ground-breaking ...*He writes bizarre and highly experimental music*...

expert NOUN = specialist, authority, professional, master, pro (*informal*), ace (*informal*), genius, guru, pundit, buff (*informal*), wizard, adept, whizz (*informal*), maestro, virtuoso, connoisseur, hotshot (*informal*), past master, dab hand (*Brit. informal*), wonk (*informal*), maven (*U.S.*), fundi (*S. African*) ...*an expert in computer graphics*... OPPOSITE amateur

ADJECTIVE = <u>skilful</u>, trained, experienced, able, professional, skilled, master, masterly, qualified, talented, outstanding, clever, practised, accomplished, handy, competent, apt, adept, knowledgeable, virtuoso, deft, proficient, facile, adroit, dexterous ...*The faces of the waxworks are modelled by expert sculptors*... **OPPOSITE** > unskilled

expertise = <u>skill</u>, knowledge, know-how (*informal*), facility, grip, craft, judgment, grasp, mastery, knack, proficiency, dexterity, cleverness, deftness, adroitness, aptness, expertness, knowing inside out, ableness, masterliness, skilfulness

expiration = <u>expiry</u>, end, finish, conclusion, close, termination, cessation

expire 1 = <u>become invalid</u>, end, finish, conclude, close, stop, run out, cease, lapse, terminate, come to an end, be no longer valid ...*He continued to live in the States after his visa had expired*...
2 = <u>die</u>, decease, depart, buy it (*U.S. slang*), check out (*U.S. slang*), perish, kick it (*slang*), croak (*slang*), go belly-up (*slang*), snuff it (*informal*), peg out (*informal*), kick the bucket (*informal*), peg it (*informal*), depart this life, meet your maker, cark it (*Austral. & N.Z. slang*), pop your clogs (*informal*), pass away *or* on ...*He expired in excruciating agony*...

expiry = <u>expiration</u>, ending, end, conclusion, close, demise, lapsing, lapse, termination, cessation

explain 1 = <u>make clear</u> *or* plain, describe, demonstrate, illustrate, teach, define, solve, resolve, interpret, disclose, unfold, clarify, clear up, simplify, expound, elucidate, put into words, throw light on, explicate (*formal*), give the details of ...*He explained the process to us in simple terms*...
2 = <u>account for</u>, excuse, justify, give a reason for, give an explanation for ...*Can you explain why you didn't telephone me?*...

explanation 1 = <u>reason</u>, meaning, cause, sense, answer, account, excuse, motive, justification, vindication, mitigation, the why and wherefore ...*The president has given no explanation for his behaviour*...
2 = <u>description</u>, report, definition, demonstration, teaching, resolution, interpretation, illustration, clarification, exposition, simplification, explication, elucidation ...*his lucid explanation of the mysteries of cricket*...

explanatory = <u>descriptive</u>, interpretive, illustrative, interpretative, demonstrative, justifying, expository, illuminative, elucidatory, explicative

explicit 1 = <u>clear</u>, obvious, specific, direct, certain, express, plain, absolute, exact, precise, straightforward, definite, overt, unequivocal, unqualified, unambiguous, categorical ...*He left explicit instructions on how to set the video timer*... **OPPOSITE** > vague
2 = <u>frank</u>, direct, open, specific, positive, plain, patent, graphic, distinct, outspoken, upfront (*informal*), unambiguous, unrestricted, unrestrained, uncensored, unreserved ...*songs containing explicit references to sexual activity*... **OPPOSITE** > indirect

explode 1 = <u>blow up</u>, erupt, burst, go off, shatter,

shiver ...*They were clearing up when the second bomb exploded*...
2 = <u>detonate</u>, set off, discharge, let off ...*The first test atomic bomb was exploded in the New Mexico desert*...
3 = <u>lose your temper</u>, rage, erupt, blow up (*informal*), lose it (*informal*), crack up (*informal*), see red (*informal*), lose the plot (*informal*), become angry, have a fit (*informal*), go ballistic (*slang, chiefly U.S.*), hit the roof (*informal*), throw a tantrum, blow a fuse (*slang, chiefly U.S.*), go berserk (*slang*), go mad (*slang*), fly off the handle (*informal*), go spare (*Brit. slang*), become enraged, go off the deep end (*informal*), go up the wall (*slang*), blow your top (*informal*), go crook (*Austral. & N.Z. slang*), fly into a temper, flip your lid (*slang*), do your nut (*Brit. slang*) ...*He exploded with rage at the accusation*...
4 = <u>increase</u>, grow, develop, extend, advance, shoot up, soar, boost, expand, build up, swell, step up (*informal*), escalate, multiply, proliferate, snowball, aggrandize ...*The population has exploded in the last twenty years*...
5 = <u>disprove</u>, discredit, refute, belie, demolish, repudiate, put paid to, invalidate, debunk, prove impossible, prove wrong, give the lie to, blow out of the water (*slang*) ...*an article which explodes the myth that thin equals sexy*...

exploit **VERB** 1 = <u>take advantage of</u>, abuse, use, manipulate, milk, misuse, dump on (*slang, chiefly U.S.*), ill-treat, play on *or* upon ...*Casual workers are being exploited for slave wages*...
2 = <u>make the best use of</u>, use, make use of, utilize, cash in on (*informal*), capitalize on, put to use, make capital out of, use to advantage, use to good advantage, live off the backs of, turn to account, profit by *or* from ...*The opposition are exploiting the situation to their advantage*...
NOUN = <u>feat</u>, act, achievement, enterprise, adventure, stunt, deed, accomplishment, attainment, escapade ...*His wartime exploits were made into a TV series*...

exploitation 1 = <u>misuse</u>, abuse, manipulation, imposition, using, ill-treatment ...*the exploitation of working women*...
2 = <u>capitalization</u>, utilization, using to good advantage, trading upon ...*the exploitation of the famine by local politicians*...

exploration 1 = <u>expedition</u>, tour, trip, survey, travel, journey, reconnaissance, recce (*slang*) ...*We devoted a week to the exploration of the Mayan sites of Copan*...
2 = <u>investigation</u>, study, research, survey, search, inquiry, analysis, examination, probe, inspection, scrutiny, once-over (*informal*) ...*an exploration of Celtic mythology*...

exploratory = <u>investigative</u>, trial, searching, probing, experimental, analytic, fact-finding

explore 1 = <u>travel around</u>, tour, survey, scout, traverse, range over, recce (*slang*), reconnoitre, case (*slang*), have *or* take a look around ...*We explored the old part of the town*...
2 = <u>investigate</u>, consider, research, survey, search, prospect, examine, probe, analyse, look into, inspect, work over, scrutinize, inquire into ...*The film explores

the relationship between artist and instrument…

explosion 1 = <u>blast</u>, crack, burst, bang, discharge, report, blowing up, outburst, clap, detonation …*Three people were killed in a bomb explosion in London today…*
2 = <u>increase</u>, rise, development, growth, boost, expansion, enlargement, escalation, upturn …*a population explosion…*
3 = <u>outburst</u>, fit, storm, attack, surge, flare-up, eruption, paroxysm …*His reaction was an explosion of anger…*
4 = <u>outbreak</u>, flare-up, eruption, upsurge …*an explosion of violence in the country's capital…*

explosive NOUN = <u>bomb</u>, mine, shell, missile, rocket, grenade, charge, torpedo, incendiary …*A large quantity of arms and explosives was seized…*
ADJECTIVE **1** = <u>unstable</u>, dangerous, volatile, hazardous, unsafe, perilous, combustible, inflammable …*Highly explosive gas is naturally found in coal mines…*
2 = <u>sudden</u>, rapid, marked, unexpected, startling, swift, abrupt …*the explosive growth of computer networks…*
3 = <u>dangerous</u>, worrying, strained, anxious, charged, ugly, tense, hazardous, stressful, perilous, nerve-racking, overwrought …*a potentially explosive situation…*
4 = <u>fiery</u>, violent, volatile, stormy, touchy, vehement …*He inherited his father's explosive temper…*

exponent 1 = <u>advocate</u>, champion, supporter, defender, spokesman, spokeswoman, promoter, backer, spokesperson, proponent, propagandist, upholder …*a leading exponent of genetic engineering…*
2 = <u>performer</u>, player, interpreter, presenter, executant …*the great exponent of Bach, Glenn Gould…*

expose VERB **1** = <u>uncover</u>, show, reveal, display, exhibit, present, unveil, manifest, lay bare, take the wraps off, put on view …*He pulled up his t-shirt, exposing his white belly…* OPPOSITE > hide
2 = <u>reveal</u>, disclose, uncover, air, detect, betray, show up, denounce, unearth, let out, divulge, unmask, lay bare, make known, bring to light, out (*informal*), smoke out, blow wide open (*slang*) …*After the scandal was exposed, he committed suicide…* OPPOSITE > keep secret
3 = <u>make vulnerable</u>, risk, subject, endanger, hazard, leave open, jeopardize, put at risk, imperil, lay open …*people exposed to high levels of radiation…*
PHRASES **expose someone to something** = <u>introduce to</u>, acquaint with, bring into contact with, familiarize with, make familiar with, make conversant with …*when women from these societies become exposed to Western culture…*

exposé = <u>exposure</u>, revelation, uncovering, disclosure, divulgence

exposed 1 = <u>unconcealed</u>, revealed, bare, exhibited, unveiled, shown, uncovered, on display, on show, on view, laid bare, made manifest …*Skin cancer is most likely to occur on exposed parts of the body…*
2 = <u>unsheltered</u>, open, unprotected, open to the elements …*This part of the coast is very exposed…*
3 = <u>vulnerable</u>, open, subject, in danger, liable, susceptible, wide open, left open, laid bare, in peril, laid open …*The troops are exposed to attack by the enemy…*

exposition 1 = <u>explanation</u>, account, description, interpretation, illustration, presentation, commentary, critique, exegesis, explication, elucidation …*Her speech was an exposition of her beliefs in freedom and justice…*
2 = <u>exhibition</u>, show, fair, display, demonstration, presentation, expo (*informal*) …*an art exposition…*

exposure 1 = <u>vulnerability</u>, subjection, susceptibility, laying open …*Exposure to lead is known to damage the brains of young children…*
2 = <u>hypothermia</u>, frostbite, extreme cold, intense cold …*Two people died of exposure in Chicago overnight…*
3 = <u>revelation</u>, exposé, uncovering, disclosure, airing, manifestation, detection, divulging, denunciation, unmasking, divulgence …*the exposure of Anthony Blunt as a former Soviet spy…*
4 = <u>publicity</u>, promotion, attention, advertising, plugging (*informal*), propaganda, hype, pushing, media hype …*The candidates have been getting a lot of exposure on TV…*
5 = <u>uncovering</u>, showing, display, exhibition, baring, revelation, presentation, unveiling, manifestation …*a bodice allowing full exposure of the breasts…*
6 = <u>contact</u>, experience, awareness, acquaintance, familiarity …*Repeated exposure to the music reveals its hidden depths…*

expound = <u>explain</u>, describe, illustrate, interpret, unfold, spell out, set forth, elucidate, explicate (*formal*)

express VERB **1** = <u>state</u>, communicate, convey, articulate, say, tell, put, word, speak, voice, declare, phrase, assert, pronounce, utter, couch, put across, enunciate, put into words, give voice to, verbalize, asseverate …*He expressed grave concern at their attitude…*
2 = <u>show</u>, indicate, exhibit, demonstrate, reveal, disclose, intimate, convey, testify to, depict, designate, manifest, embody, signify, symbolize, denote, divulge, bespeak, make known, evince …*He expressed his anger in a destructive way…*
ADJECTIVE **1** = <u>explicit</u>, clear, direct, precise, pointed, certain, plain, accurate, exact, distinct, definite, outright, unambiguous, categorical …*The ship was sunk on express orders from the Prime Minister…*
2 = <u>specific</u>, exclusive, particular, sole, special, deliberate, singular, clear-cut, especial …*I bought the camera with the express purpose of taking nature photos…*
3 = <u>fast</u>, direct, quick, rapid, priority, prompt, swift, high-speed, speedy, quickie (*informal*), nonstop, expeditious …*A special express service is available…*

expression 1 = <u>statement</u>, declaration, announcement, communication, mention, assertion, utterance, articulation, pronouncement, enunciation, verbalization, asseveration …*From Cairo came*

expressions of regret at the attack...
2 = <u>indication</u>, demonstration, exhibition, display, showing, show, sign, symbol, representation, token, manifestation, embodiment ...*We attended as an expression of solidarity...*
3 = <u>look</u>, countenance, face, air, appearance, aspect, mien (*literary*) ...*He sat there with a sad expression on his face...*
4 = <u>intonation</u>, style, delivery, phrasing, emphasis, execution, diction ...*She puts a lot of expression into her playing...*
5 = <u>phrase</u>, saying, word, wording, term, language, speech, remark, maxim, idiom, adage, choice of words, turn of phrase, phraseology, locution, set phrase ...*He uses some remarkably coarse expressions...*

expressionless = <u>blank</u>, empty, deadpan, straight-faced, wooden, dull, vacuous, inscrutable, poker-faced (*informal*)

expressive 1 = <u>vivid</u>, strong, striking, telling, moving, lively, sympathetic, energetic, poignant, emphatic, eloquent, forcible ...*She had a small, expressive face...* OPPOSITE impassive
2 = <u>meaningful</u>, indicative, suggestive, demonstrative, revealing, significant, allusive ...*All his poems are expressive of his love for nature...*

expressly 1 = <u>explicitly</u>, clearly, plainly, absolutely, positively, definitely, outright, manifestly, distinctly, decidedly, categorically, pointedly, unequivocally, unmistakably, in no uncertain terms, unambiguously ...*He had expressly forbidden her to go out on her own...*
2 = <u>specifically</u>, specially, especially, particularly, purposely, exclusively, precisely, solely, exactly, deliberately, intentionally, on purpose ...*Bleasdale had written the role expressly for this actor...*

expropriate (*Formal*) = <u>seize</u>, take, appropriate, confiscate, assume, take over, take away, commandeer, requisition, arrogate

expropriation (*Formal*) = <u>seizure</u>, takeover, impounding, confiscation, commandeering, requisitioning, sequestration, disseisin (*Law*)

expulsion 1 = <u>ejection</u>, exclusion, dismissal, removal, exile, discharge, eviction, banishment, extrusion, proscription, expatriation, debarment, dislodgment ...*Her behaviour led to her expulsion from school...*
2 = <u>discharge</u>, emptying, emission, voiding, spewing, secretion, excretion, ejection, seepage, suppuration ...*the expulsion of waste products from the body...*

expunge (*Formal*) = <u>erase</u>, remove, destroy, abolish, cancel, get rid of, wipe out, eradicate, excise, delete, extinguish, strike out, obliterate, annihilate, efface, exterminate, annul, raze, blot out, extirpate

exquisite 1 = <u>beautiful</u>, elegant, graceful, pleasing, attractive, lovely, charming, comely ...*She has exquisite manners...* OPPOSITE unattractive
2 = <u>fine</u>, beautiful, lovely, elegant, precious, delicate, dainty ...*The natives brought exquisite beadwork to sell...*
3 = <u>intense</u>, acute, severe, sharp, keen, extreme, piercing, poignant, excruciating ...*His words gave her exquisite pain...*
4 = <u>refined</u>, cultivated, discriminating, sensitive, polished, selective, discerning, impeccable, meticulous, consummate, appreciative, fastidious ...*The house was furnished with exquisite taste...*
5 = <u>excellent</u>, fine, outstanding, superb, choice, perfect, select, delicious, divine, splendid, admirable, consummate, flawless, superlative, incomparable, peerless, matchless ...*The hotel features friendly staff and exquisite cuisine...* OPPOSITE imperfect

extant = <u>in existence</u>, existing, remaining, surviving, living, existent, subsisting, undestroyed

Word Power

extant – Used carefully, the word *extant* describes something that has survived, often against all odds. It therefore carries a slightly more specific meaning than *in existence*, and should not be considered as being automatically interchangeable with this phrase. For example, you might say *the oldest extant document dates from 1492*; but *in existence* (not *extant*) *for 15 years, they are still one of the most successful bands in the world*. In many contexts, however, these ideas overlap, leaving the writer to decide whether *extant* or *in existence* best expresses the intended meaning.

extend 1 = <u>spread out</u>, reach, stretch, continue, carry on ...*The territory extends over one fifth of Canada's land mass...*
2 = <u>stretch</u>, stretch out, spread out, unfurl, straighten out, unroll ...*Stand straight with your arms extended at your sides...*
3 = <u>last</u>, continue, go on, stretch, carry on ...*His playing career extended from 1894 to 1920...*
4 = <u>protrude</u>, project, stand out, bulge, stick out, hang, overhang, jut out ...*His legs extended from the bushes...*
5 = <u>reach</u>, spread, go as far as ...*His possessiveness extends to people as well as property...*
6 = <u>widen</u>, increase, develop, expand, spread, add to, enhance, supplement, enlarge, broaden, diversify, amplify, augment ...*They have added three new products to extend their range...* OPPOSITE reduce
7 = <u>make longer</u>, prolong, lengthen, draw out, spin out, elongate, drag out, protract ...*They have extended the deadline by 24 hours...* OPPOSITE shorten
8 = <u>offer</u>, give, hold out, present, grant, advance, yield, reach out, confer, stretch out, stick out, bestow, impart, proffer, put forth ...*'I'm Chuck,' the man said, extending his hand...* OPPOSITE withdraw

extended 1 = <u>lengthened</u>, long, prolonged, protracted, stretched out, drawn-out, unfurled, elongated, unrolled ...*He and Naomi spent an extended period getting to know one another...*
2 = <u>broad</u>, wide, expanded, extensive, widespread, comprehensive, large-scale, enlarged, far-reaching ...*a tribal society grouped in huge extended families...*
3 = <u>outstretched</u>, conferred, stretched out, proffered

...She found herself kissing the old lady's extended hand...

extension 1 = annexe, wing, addition, supplement, branch, appendix, add-on, adjunct, appendage, ell, addendum *...the new extension to London's National Gallery...*
2 = lengthening, extra time, continuation, postponement, prolongation, additional period of time, protraction *...He has been granted a six-month extension to his visa...*
3 = development, expansion, widening, increase, stretching, broadening, continuation, enlargement, diversification, amplification, elongation, augmentation *...Russia is contemplating the extension of its territory...*

extensive ADJECTIVE = large, considerable, substantial, spacious, wide, sweeping, broad, expansive, capacious, commodious *...This 18th century manor house is set in extensive grounds...*
2 = comprehensive, complete, thorough, lengthy, long, wide, wholesale, pervasive, protracted, all-inclusive *...The story received extensive coverage in the Times...* OPPOSITE restricted
3 = great, large, huge, extended, vast, widespread, comprehensive, universal, large-scale, far-reaching, prevalent, far-flung, all-inclusive, voluminous, humongous *or* humungous (*U.S. slang*) *...The blast caused extensive damage...* OPPOSITE limited

extent 1 = magnitude, amount, degree, scale, level, measure, stretch, quantity, bulk, duration, expanse, amplitude *...The full extent of the losses was revealed yesterday...*
2 = size, area, range, length, reach, bounds, sweep, sphere, width, compass, breadth, ambit *...an estate about seven or eight acres in extent...*

exterior NOUN = outside, face, surface, covering, finish, skin, appearance, aspect, shell, coating, façade, outside surface *...The exterior of the building was a masterpiece of architecture...*
ADJECTIVE = outer, outside, external, surface, outward, superficial, outermost *...The exterior walls were made of pre-formed concrete...* OPPOSITE inner

exterminate = destroy, kill, eliminate, abolish, eradicate, annihilate, extirpate

extermination = destruction, murder, massacre, slaughter, killing, wiping out, genocide, elimination, mass murder, annihilation, eradication, extirpation

external 1 = outer, outside, surface, apparent, visible, outward, exterior, superficial, outermost *...the external surface of the wall...* OPPOSITE internal
2 = foreign, international, alien, exotic, exterior, extraneous, extrinsic *...the commissioner for external affairs...* OPPOSITE domestic
3 = outside, visiting, independent, extramural *...The papers are checked by external examiners...* OPPOSITE inside

extinct 1 = dead, lost, gone, vanished, defunct *...It is 250 years since the wolf became extinct in Britain...* OPPOSITE living
2 = obsolete, abolished, void, terminated, defunct

...Herbalism had become an all but extinct skill in the Western World...
3 = inactive, extinguished, doused, out, snuffed out, quenched *...The island's tallest volcano is long extinct...*

extinction = dying out, death, destruction, abolition, oblivion, extermination, annihilation, eradication, obliteration, excision, extirpation

extinguish 1 = put out, stifle, smother, blow out, douse, snuff out, quench *...It took about 50 minutes to extinguish the fire...*
2 = destroy, end, kill, remove, eliminate, obscure, abolish, suppress, wipe out, erase, eradicate, annihilate, put paid to, exterminate, expunge, extirpate *...The message extinguished her hopes of Richard's return...*

extol = praise, acclaim, applaud, pay tribute to, celebrate, commend, magnify (*archaic*), glorify, exalt, laud, crack up (*informal*), sing the praises of, eulogize, cry up, panegyrize

extort = extract, force, squeeze, exact, bully, bleed (*informal*), blackmail, wring, coerce, wrest

extortion = blackmail, force, oppression, compulsion, coercion, shakedown (*U.S. slang*), rapacity, exaction

extortionate 1 = exorbitant, excessive, outrageous, unreasonable, inflated, extravagant, preposterous, sky-high, inordinate, immoderate *...the extortionate price of designer clothes...* OPPOSITE reasonable
2 = grasping, hard, severe, exacting, harsh, rigorous, oppressive, rapacious, blood-sucking (*informal*), usurious *...people who have entered into extortionate credit transactions...*

extra ADJECTIVE **1** = additional, more, new, other, added, further, fresh, accessory, supplementary, auxiliary, add-on, supplemental, ancillary *...Extra staff have been taken on to cover busy periods...* OPPOSITE vital
2 = surplus, excess, reserve, spare, unnecessary, redundant, needless, unused, leftover, superfluous, extraneous, unneeded, inessential, supernumerary, supererogatory *...This exercise will help you burn up any extra calories...*
NOUN = addition, bonus, supplement, accessory, complement, add-on, affix, adjunct, appendage, addendum, supernumerary, appurtenance *...Optional extras including cooking tuition...* OPPOSITE necessity
ADVERB **1** = in addition, additionally, over and above *...You may be charged extra for this service...*
2 = exceptionally, very, specially, especially, particularly, extremely, remarkably, unusually, extraordinarily, uncommonly *...Try extra hard to be nice to him...*

extract VERB **1** = obtain, take out, distil, squeeze out, draw out, express, separate out, press out *...Citric acid can be extracted from the juice of oranges...*
2 = take out, draw, pull, remove, withdraw, pull out, bring out *...He extracted a small notebook from his pocket...*

3 = <u>pull out</u>, remove, take out, draw, uproot, pluck out, extirpate ...*She has to have a tooth extracted at 3 today...*
4 = <u>elicit</u>, get, obtain, force, draw, gather, derive, exact, bring out, evoke, reap, wring, glean, coerce, wrest ...*He tried to extract further information from the witness...*
5 = <u>select</u>, quote, cite, abstract, choose, cut out, reproduce, cull, copy out ...*material extracted from a range of texts...*
◾NOUN **1** = <u>passage</u>, selection, excerpt, cutting, clipping, abstract, quotation, citation ...*He read us an extract from his latest novel...*
2 = <u>essence</u>, solution, concentrate, juice, distillation, decoction, distillate ...*fragrances taken from plant extracts...*

> ## Word Power
>
> **extract** – People sometimes use *extract* where *extricate* would be better. Although both words can refer to a physical act of removal from a place, *extract* has a more general sense than *extricate*. *Extricate* has additional overtones of 'difficulty', and is most commonly used with reference to getting a person – particularly *yourself* – out of a situation. So, for example, you might say *he will find it difficult to extricate himself* (not *extract himself*) *from this situation*.

extraction 1 = <u>origin</u>, family, ancestry, descent, race, stock, blood, birth, pedigree, lineage, parentage, derivation ...*He married a young lady of Indian extraction...*
2 = <u>taking out</u>, drawing, pulling, withdrawal, removal, uprooting, extirpation ...*the extraction of wisdom teeth...*
3 = <u>distillation</u>, separation, derivation ...*High temperatures are used during the extraction of cooking oils...*

extraneous 1 = <u>nonessential</u>, unnecessary, extra, additional, redundant, needless, peripheral, supplementary, incidental, superfluous, unneeded, inessential, adventitious, unessential ...*Just give me the basic facts, with no extraneous details...*
2 = <u>irrelevant</u>, inappropriate, unrelated, unconnected, immaterial, beside the point, impertinent, inadmissible, off the subject, inapplicable, inapt, inapposite ...*Let's not allow ourselves to be sidetracked by extraneous questions...*

extraordinary 1 = <u>remarkable</u>, special, wonderful, outstanding, rare, amazing, fantastic, astonishing, marvellous, exceptional, notable, serious (*informal*), phenomenal, singular, wondrous (*archaic or literary*), out of this world (*informal*), extremely good ...*He is an extraordinary musician...* ◄OPPOSITE► unremarkable
2 = <u>unusual</u>, surprising, odd, strange, unique, remarkable, bizarre, curious, weird, unprecedented, peculiar, unfamiliar, uncommon, unheard-of, unwonted ...*What an extraordinary thing to happen!...* ◄OPPOSITE► ordinary

extravagance 1 = <u>overspending</u>, squandering, profusion, profligacy, wastefulness, waste, lavishness, prodigality, improvidence ...*He was accused of gross mismanagement and financial extravagance...*
2 = <u>luxury</u>, treat, indulgence, extra, frill, nonessential ...*Her only extravagance was shoes...*
3 = <u>excess</u>, folly, exaggeration, absurdity, recklessness, wildness, dissipation, outrageousness, unreasonableness, preposterousness, immoderation, exorbitance, unrestraint ...*the ridiculous extravagance of his claims...*

extravagant 1 = <u>wasteful</u>, excessive, lavish, prodigal, profligate, spendthrift, imprudent, improvident ...*his extravagant lifestyle...* ◄OPPOSITE► economical
2 = <u>overpriced</u>, expensive, costly ...*Her aunt gave her an uncharacteristically extravagant gift...*
3 = <u>exorbitant</u>, excessive, steep (*informal*), unreasonable, inordinate, extortionate ...*hotels charging extravagant prices...* ◄OPPOSITE► reasonable
4 = <u>excessive</u>, exaggerated, outrageous, wild, fantastic, absurd, foolish, over the top (*slang*), unreasonable, preposterous, fanciful, unrestrained, inordinate, outré, immoderate, O.T.T. (*slang*) ...*He was extravagant in his admiration of Lillie...* ◄OPPOSITE► moderate
5 = <u>showy</u>, elaborate, flamboyant, impressive, fancy, flashy, ornate, pretentious, grandiose, gaudy, garish, ostentatious ...*The couple wed in extravagant style in 1995...* ◄OPPOSITE► restrained

extravaganza = <u>spectacular</u>, show, spectacle, display, pageant, flight of fancy

extreme ◾ADJECTIVE **1** = <u>great</u>, high, highest, greatest, worst, supreme, acute, severe, maximum, intense, ultimate, utmost, mother of all (*informal*), uttermost ...*people living in extreme poverty...* ◄OPPOSITE► mild
2 = <u>severe</u>, radical, strict, harsh, stern, rigid, dire, drastic, uncompromising, unbending ...*The scheme was rejected as being too extreme...*
3 = <u>radical</u>, unusual, excessive, exceptional, exaggerated, outrageous, over the top (*slang*), unreasonable, uncommon, unconventional, fanatical, zealous, out-and-out, inordinate, egregious, intemperate, immoderate, O.T.T. (*slang*) ...*his extreme political views...* ◄OPPOSITE► moderate
4 = <u>farthest</u>, furthest, far, final, last, ultimate, remotest, terminal, utmost, far-off, faraway, outermost, most distant, uttermost ...*the room at the extreme end of the corridor...* ◄OPPOSITE► nearest
◾NOUN = <u>limit</u>, end, edge, opposite, pole, ultimate, boundary, antithesis, extremity, acme ...*a 'middle way' between the extremes of success and failure...*

extremely = <u>very</u>, highly, greatly, particularly, severely, terribly, ultra, utterly, unusually, exceptionally, extraordinarily, intensely, tremendously, markedly, awfully (*informal*), acutely, exceedingly, excessively, inordinately, uncommonly, to a fault, to the nth degree, to *or* in the extreme

extremist ◾NOUN = <u>radical</u>, activist, militant, enthusiast, fanatic, devotee, die-hard, bigot, zealot, energumen ...*Police believe the bombing was the work of left-wing extremists...*

ADJECTIVE = <u>extreme</u>, wild, mad, enthusiastic, passionate, frenzied, obsessive, fanatical, fervent, zealous, bigoted, rabid, immoderate, overenthusiastic *…The riots were organized by extremist groups…*

extremity **NOUN** 1 = <u>limit</u>, end, edge, border, top, tip, bound, minimum, extreme, maximum, pole, margin, boundary, terminal, frontier, verge, brink, rim, brim, pinnacle, termination, nadir, zenith, apex, terminus, apogee, farthest point, furthest point, acme *…a small port on the north-western extremity of the island…*
2 = <u>depth</u>, height, excess, climax, consummation, acuteness *…his lack of restraint in the extremity of his grief…*
3 = <u>crisis</u>, trouble, emergency, disaster, setback, pinch, plight, hardship, adversity, dire straits, exigency, extreme suffering *…Even in extremity, she never lost her sense of humour…*
PLURAL NOUN = <u>hands and feet</u>, limbs, fingers and toes *…Rheumatoid arthritis affects the extremities and limbs…*

extricate 1 = <u>withdraw</u>, relieve, free, clear, deliver, liberate, wriggle out of, get (someone) off the hook (*slang*), disembarrass *…an attempt to extricate himself from his financial difficulties…*
2 = <u>free</u>, clear, release, remove, rescue, get out, disengage, disentangle *…Emergency workers tried to extricate the survivors from the wreckage…*
➤ **extract**

extrovert or **extroverted** **ADJECTIVE** = <u>sociable</u>, social, lively, outgoing, hearty, exuberant, amiable, gregarious *…His extrovert personality won him many friends…* **OPPOSITE** introverted
NOUN = <u>outgoing person</u>, mingler, socializer, mixer, life and soul of the party *…He was a showman, an extrovert who revelled in controversy…* **OPPOSITE** introvert

exuberance 1 = <u>high spirits</u>, energy, enthusiasm, vitality, life, spirit, excitement, pep, animation, vigour, zest, eagerness, buoyancy, exhilaration, cheerfulness, brio, vivacity, ebullience, liveliness, effervescence, sprightliness *…Her burst of exuberance overwhelmed me…*
2 = <u>luxuriance</u>, abundance, richness, profusion, plenitude, lushness, superabundance, lavishness, rankness, copiousness *…the exuberance of plant life in the region…*

exuberant 1 = <u>high-spirited</u>, spirited, enthusiastic, lively, excited, eager, sparkling, vigorous, cheerful, energetic, animated, upbeat (*informal*), buoyant, exhilarated, elated, ebullient, chirpy (*informal*), sprightly, vivacious, effervescent, full of life, full of beans (*informal*), zestful *…Our son was a highly active and exuberant little person…* **OPPOSITE** subdued
2 = <u>luxuriant</u>, rich, lavish, abundant, lush, overflowing, plentiful, teeming, copious, profuse, superabundant, plenteous *…hillsides ablaze with exuberant flowers and shrubs…*
3 = <u>fulsome</u>, excessive, exaggerated, lavish, overdone, superfluous, prodigal, effusive *…exuberant praise…*

exude 1 = <u>radiate</u>, show, display, exhibit, manifest,

emanate *…She exudes an air of confidence…*
2 = <u>emit</u>, leak, discharge, ooze, emanate, issue, secrete, excrete *…Nearby was a factory which exuded a pungent smell…*
3 = <u>seep</u>, leak, sweat, bleed, weep, trickle, ooze, emanate, issue, filter through, well forth *…the fluid that exudes from the cane toad's back…*

exult 1 = <u>be joyful</u>, be delighted, rejoice, be overjoyed, celebrate, be elated, be jubilant, jump for joy, make merry, be in high spirits, jubilate *…He seemed calm, but inwardly he exulted…*
2 = <u>revel</u>, glory in, boast, crow, taunt, brag, vaunt, drool, gloat, take delight in *…He was still exulting over his victory…*

exultant = <u>joyful</u>, delighted, flushed, triumphant, revelling, rejoicing, jubilant, joyous, transported, elated, over the moon (*informal*), overjoyed, rapt, gleeful, exulting, cock-a-hoop

eye **NOUN** 1 = <u>eyeball</u>, optic (*informal*), peeper (*slang*), orb (*poetic*), organ of vision, organ of sight *…He is blind in one eye…*
2 *often plural* = <u>eyesight</u>, sight, vision, observation, perception, ability to see, range of vision, power of seeing *…her sharp eyes and acute hearing…*
3 = <u>appreciation</u>, taste, recognition, judgment, discrimination, perception, discernment *…He has an eye for talent…*
4 = <u>observance</u>, observation, supervision, surveillance, attention, notice, inspection, heed, vigil, watch, lookout, vigilance, alertness, watchfulness *…He played under his grandmother's watchful eye…*
5 = <u>centre</u>, heart, middle, mid, core, nucleus *…the eye of the hurricane…*
VERB = <u>look at</u>, view, study, watch, check, regard, survey, clock (*Brit. slang*), observe, stare at, scan, contemplate, check out (*informal*), inspect, glance at, gaze at, behold (*archaic or literary*), eyeball (*slang*), scrutinize, peruse, get a load of (*informal*), take a dekko at (*Brit. slang*), have or take a look at *…We eyed each other thoughtfully…*
PHRASES **an eye for an eye** = <u>retaliation</u>, justice, revenge, vengeance, reprisal, retribution, requital, lex talionis *…His philosophy was an eye for an eye and a tooth for a tooth…* ◆ **close** or **shut your eyes to something** = <u>ignore</u>, reject, overlook, disregard, pass over, turn a blind eye to, take no notice of, be oblivious to, pay no attention to, turn your back on, turn a deaf ear to, bury your head in the sand *…They just closed their eyes to what was going on…* ◆ **eye something** or **someone up** = <u>ogle</u>, leer at, make eyes at, give (someone) the (glad) eye *…My brother is forever eyeing up women in the street…* ◆ **in** or **to someone's eyes** = <u>in the opinion of</u>, in the mind of, from someone's viewpoint, in the judgment of, in someone's point of view, in the belief of *…He was, in their eyes, a sensible and reliable man…* ◆ **keep an eye** or **your eye on someone** or **something** = <u>watch</u>, supervise, observe, monitor, regard, survey, guard, look after, look out for, pay attention to, watch over, scrutinize, keep tabs on (*informal*), keep under surveillance, keep in view, watch like a hawk *…You*

can't keep an eye on your children 24 hours a day…
◆ **see eye to eye** = <u>agree</u>, accord, get on, fall in, coincide, go along, subscribe to, be united, jibe (*informal*), concur, harmonize, speak the same language, be on the same wavelength, be of the same mind, be in unison …*They saw eye to eye on almost every aspect of the production…* ◆ **set, clap** or **lay eyes on someone** or **something** = <u>see</u>, meet, notice, observe, encounter, come across, run into, behold …*I haven't set eyes on him for years…*
◆ **up to your eyes** = <u>very busy</u>, overwhelmed, caught up, inundated, wrapped up in, engaged, flooded out, fully occupied, up to here, up to your elbows …*I am up to my eyes in work just now…*

(**Related Words**)
adjectives : ocular, ophthalmic, optic
➤ **parts of the eye**
eye-catching = <u>striking</u>, arresting, attractive, dramatic, spectacular, captivating, showy
eyesight = <u>vision</u>, sight, observation, perception, ability to see, range of vision, power of seeing, power of sight
eyesore = <u>mess</u>, blight, blot, blemish, sight (*informal*), horror, disgrace, atrocity, ugliness, monstrosity, disfigurement
eyewitness = <u>observer</u>, witness, spectator, looker-on, viewer, passer-by, watcher, onlooker, bystander

---

Parts of the eye http://webschoolsolutions.com/patts/systems/eye.htm

aqueous humour	conjunctiva	lens	retinal vessels
blind spot	cornea	ocular muscle	rod
choroid *or* chorioid	eyeball	optic nerve	sclera
ciliary body	fovea	pupil	suspensory ligament
cone	iris	retina	vitreous body

F f

fable 1 = <u>legend</u>, myth, parable, allegory, story, tale, apologue …*Each tale has the timeless quality of fable…*
2 = <u>fiction</u>, lie, fantasy, myth, romance, invention, yarn (*informal*), fabrication, falsehood, fib, figment, untruth, fairy story (*informal*), urban myth, white lie, tall story (*informal*), urban legend …*Is reincarnation fact or fable?…* OPPOSITE fact

fabled = <u>legendary</u>, fictional, famed, mythical, storied, famous, fabulous

fabric 1 = <u>cloth</u>, material, stuff, textile, web …*small squares of red cotton fabric…*
2 = <u>framework</u>, structure, make-up, organization, frame, foundations, construction, constitution, infrastructure …*The fabric of society has been deeply damaged…*
3 = <u>structure</u>, foundations, construction, framework, infrastructure …*Condensation will eventually cause the fabric of the building to rot away…*

fabricate 1 = <u>make up</u>, invent, concoct, falsify, form, coin, devise, forge, fake, feign, trump up …*All four claim that officers fabricated evidence against them…*
2 = <u>manufacture</u>, make, build, form, fashion, shape, frame, construct, assemble, erect …*All the tools are fabricated from high quality steel…*

fabrication 1 = <u>forgery</u>, lie, fiction, myth, fake, invention, fable, concoction, falsehood, figment, untruth, porky (*Brit. slang*), fairy story (*informal*), pork pie (*Brit. slang*), cock-and-bull story (*informal*) …*She described the interview with her as a 'complete fabrication'…*
2 = <u>manufacture</u>, production, construction, assembly, erection, assemblage, building …*More than 200 improvements were made in the design and fabrication of the shuttle…*

fabulous 1 (*Informal*) = <u>wonderful</u>, excellent, brilliant, superb, spectacular, fantastic (*informal*), marvellous, sensational (*informal*), first-rate, brill (*informal*), magic (*informal*), out-of-this-world (*informal*) …*The scenery and weather were fabulous…* OPPOSITE ordinary
2 = <u>astounding</u>, amazing, extraordinary, remarkable, incredible, astonishing, legendary, immense, unbelievable, breathtaking, phenomenal, inconceivable …*You'll be entered in our free draw to win this fabulous prize…*
3 = <u>legendary</u>, imaginary, mythical, fictitious, made-up, fantastic, invented, unreal, mythological, apocryphal …*The chimaera of myth is a fabulous beast made up of the parts of other animals…*

façade 1 = <u>front</u>, face, exterior, frontage …*the façade of the building…*
2 = <u>show</u>, front, appearance, mask, exterior, guise, pretence, veneer, semblance …*They hid the troubles plaguing their marriage behind a façade of family togetherness…*

face NOUN 1 = <u>countenance</u>, features, kisser (*slang*), profile, dial (*Brit. slang*), mug (*slang*), visage, physiognomy, lineaments, phiz *or* phizog (*slang*) …*She had a beautiful face…*
2 = <u>expression</u>, look, air, appearance, aspect, countenance …*He was walking around with a sad face…*
3 = <u>side</u>, front, cover, outside, surface, aspect, exterior, right side, elevation, facet, vertical surface …*He climbed 200 feet up the cliff face…*
4 (*Informal*) = <u>impudence</u>, front, confidence, audacity, nerve, neck (*informal*), sauce (*informal*), cheek (*informal*), assurance, gall (*informal*), presumption, boldness, chutzpah (*U.S. & Canad. informal*), sass (*U.S. & Canad. informal*), effrontery, brass neck (*Brit. informal*), sassiness (*U.S. informal*) …*I haven't the face to borrow off him…*
VERB 1 = <u>look onto</u>, overlook, be opposite, look out on, front onto, give towards *or* onto …*The garden faces south…*
2 = <u>confront</u>, meet, encounter, deal with, oppose, tackle, cope with, experience, brave, defy, come up against, be confronted by, face off (*slang*) …*He looked relaxed and calm as he faced the press…*
3 *often with* up to = <u>accept</u>, deal with, tackle, acknowledge, cope with, confront, come to terms with, meet head-on, reconcile yourself to …*You must face the truth that the relationship has ended…*
PHRASES **face to face** = <u>facing</u>, tête-à-tête, opposite, confronting, eyeball to eyeball, in confrontation, à deux (*French*), vis-à-vis …*It would have been their first face to face encounter…* ◆ **fly in the face of something** = <u>defy</u>, oppose, disregard, go against, flout, rebel against, disobey, act in defiance of …*He said that the decision flew in the face of natural justice…* ◆ **make** *or* **pull a face at someone** = <u>scowl</u>, frown, pout, grimace, smirk, moue (*French*) …*She made a face at him behind his back…* ◆ **on the face of it** = <u>to all appearances</u>, apparently, seemingly, outwardly, at first sight, at face value, to the eye …*On the face of it, that seems to make sense…* ◆ **put on a brave face** = <u>appear cheerful</u>, air, take courage, grin and bear it (*informal*), look cheerful, keep your chin up (*informal*), not show your disappointment …*Friends will see you are putting on a brave face…* ◆ **show your face** = <u>turn up</u>, come, appear, be seen, show up (*informal*), put in *or* make an appearance, approach …*I felt I ought to show my face at her father's funeral…* ◆ **to your face** = <u>directly</u>, openly, straight, in person, in your presence …*Her opponent called her a liar to her face…*

faceless = <u>impersonal</u>, remote, unknown, unidentified, anonymous

facelift 1 = <u>renovation</u>, improvement, restoration, refurbishing, modernization, redecoration …*Nothing*

gives a room a faster facelift than a coat of paint...
2 = <u>cosmetic surgery</u>, plastic surgery *...She once threw a party to celebrate her facelift...*

facet 1 = <u>aspect</u>, part, face, side, phase, angle *...The caste system shapes nearly every facet of Indian life...*
2 = <u>face</u>, side, surface, plane, slant *...The stones shone back at her, a thousand facets of light in their white-gold settings...*

facile 1 = <u>superficial</u>, shallow, slick, glib, hasty, cursory *...I hated him making facile suggestions when I knew the problem was extremely complex...*
2 = <u>effortless</u>, easy, simple, quick, ready, smooth, skilful, adept, fluent, uncomplicated, proficient, adroit, dexterous, light *...His facile win tells us he's in form...* OPPOSITE difficult

facilitate = <u>further</u>, help, forward, promote, ease, speed up, pave the way for, make easy, expedite, oil the wheels of, smooth the path of, assist the progress of OPPOSITE hinder

facility 1 *often plural* = <u>amenity</u>, means, aid, opportunity, advantage, resource, equipment, provision, convenience, appliance *...What recreational facilities are now available?...*
2 = <u>opportunity</u>, possibility, convenience *...The bank will not extend the borrowing facility...*
3 = <u>ability</u>, skill, talent, gift, craft, efficiency, knack, fluency, proficiency, dexterity, quickness, adroitness, expertness, skilfulness *...They shared a facility for languages...*
4 = <u>ease</u>, readiness, fluency, smoothness, effortlessness *...He had always spoken with facility...* OPPOSITE difficulty

facing = <u>opposite</u>, fronting, partnering

facsimile = <u>copy</u>, print, carbon, reproduction, replica, transcript, duplicate, photocopy, Xerox (*trademark*), carbon copy, Photostat (*trademark*), fax

fact NOUN **1** = <u>truth</u>, reality, gospel (truth), certainty, verity, actuality, naked truth *...How much was fact and how much fancy no one knew...* OPPOSITE fiction
2 = <u>detail</u>, point, feature, particular, item, specific, circumstance *...The lorries always left in the dead of night when there were few witnesses around to record the fact...*
3 = <u>event</u>, happening, act, performance, incident, deed, occurrence, fait accompli (*French*) *...He was sure the gun was planted after the fact...*
PLURAL NOUN = <u>information</u>, details, data, the score (*informal*), gen (*Brit. informal*), info (*informal*), the whole story, ins and outs, the lowdown (*informal*) *...There is so much information you can find the facts for yourself...*
PHRASES **in fact** = <u>actually</u>, really, indeed, truly, in reality, in truth, to tell the truth, in actual fact, in point of fact *...That sounds rather simple, but in fact it's very difficult...*

faction 1 = <u>group</u>, set, party, division, section, camp, sector, minority, combination, coalition, gang, lobby, bloc, contingent, pressure group, caucus, junta, clique, coterie, schism, confederacy, splinter group, cabal, ginger group *...A peace agreement will be signed by*

the leaders of the country's warring factions...
2 = <u>dissension</u>, division, conflict, rebellion, disagreement, friction, strife, turbulence, variance, discord, infighting, disunity, sedition, tumult, disharmony, divisiveness *...Faction and self-interest appear to be the norm...* OPPOSITE agreement

factor = <u>element</u>, thing, point, part, cause, influence, item, aspect, circumstance, characteristic, consideration, component, determinant

> ### *Word Power*
>
> **factor** – In strict usage, *factor* should only be used to refer to something which contributes to a result. It should not be used to refer to a part of something, such as a plan or arrangement; more appropriate alternatives to *factor* in this sense are words such as *component* or *element*.

factory = <u>works</u>, plant, mill, workshop, assembly line, shop floor, manufactory (*obsolete*)

factual = <u>true</u>, objective, authentic, unbiased, close, real, sure, correct, genuine, accurate, exact, precise, faithful, credible, matter-of-fact, literal, veritable, circumstantial, unadorned, dinkum (*Austral. & N.Z. informal*), true-to-life OPPOSITE fictitious

faculty NOUN **1** = <u>ability</u>, power, skill, facility, talent, gift, capacity, bent, capability, readiness, knack, propensity, aptitude, dexterity, cleverness, adroitness, turn *...A faculty for self-preservation is necessary when you have friends like hers...* OPPOSITE failing
2 = <u>department</u>, school, discipline, profession, branch of learning *...the Faculty of Social and Political Sciences...*
3 = <u>teaching staff</u>, staff, teachers, professors, lecturers (*chiefly U.S.*) *...The faculty agreed on a change in the requirements...*
PLURAL NOUN = <u>powers</u>, reason, senses, intelligence, wits, capabilities, mental abilities, physical abilities *...He was drunk and not in control of his faculties...*

fad = <u>craze</u>, fashion, trend, fancy, rage, mode, vogue, whim, mania, affectation

fade 1 = <u>become pale</u>, dull, dim, bleach, wash out, blanch, discolour, blench, lose colour, lose lustre, decolour *...All colour fades, especially under the impact of direct sunlight...*
2 = <u>make pale</u>, dull, dim, bleach, wash out, blanch, discolour, decolour *...Even a soft light fades the carpets in a room...*
3 = <u>grow dim</u>, dim, fade away, become less loud *...The sound of the last bomber's engines faded into the distance...*
4 = <u>dwindle</u>, disappear, vanish, melt away, fall, fail, decline, flag, dissolve, dim, disperse, wither, wilt, wane, perish, ebb, languish, die out, droop, shrivel, die away, waste away, vanish into thin air, become unimportant, evanesce, etiolate *...She had a way of fading into the background when things got rough...*

faded = <u>discoloured</u>, pale, bleached, washed out, dull, dim, indistinct, etiolated, lustreless

fading = <u>declining</u>, dying, disappearing, vanishing, decreasing, on the decline

faeces = <u>excrement</u>, stools, excreta, bodily waste, dung, droppings, ordure

fail `VERB` **1** = <u>be unsuccessful</u>, founder, fall flat, come to nothing, fall, miss, go down, break down, flop (*informal*), be defeated, fall short, fall through, fall short of, fizzle out (*informal*), come unstuck, run aground, miscarry, be in vain, misfire, fall by the wayside, go astray, come to grief, come a cropper (*informal*), bite the dust, go up in smoke, go belly-up (*slang*), come to naught, lay an egg (*slang, chiefly U.S. & Canad.*), go by the board, not make the grade (*informal*), go down like a lead balloon (*informal*), turn out badly, fall flat on your face, meet with disaster, be found lacking *or* wanting ...*He was afraid the revolution they had started would fail*... `OPPOSITE` succeed
2 = <u>disappoint</u>, abandon, desert, neglect, omit, let down, forsake, turn your back on, be disloyal to, break your word, forget ...*We waited twenty-one years, don't fail us now*...
3 = <u>stop working</u>, stop, die, give up, break down, cease, stall, cut out, malfunction, conk out (*informal*), go on the blink (*informal*), go phut ...*The lights mysteriously failed*...
4 = <u>wither</u>, perish, sag, droop, waste away, shrivel up ...*In fact many food crops failed because of the drought*...
5 = <u>go bankrupt</u>, crash, collapse, fold (*informal*), close down, go under, go bust (*informal*), go out of business, be wound up, go broke (*informal*), go to the wall, go into receivership, go into liquidation, become insolvent, smash ...*So far this year, 104 banks have failed*...
6 = <u>decline</u>, fade, weaken, deteriorate, dwindle, sicken, degenerate, fall apart at the seams, be on your last legs (*informal*) ...*He was 58 and his health was failing rapidly*...
7 = <u>give out</u>, disappear, fade, dim, dwindle, wane, gutter, languish, peter out, die away, grow dim, sink ...*Here in the hills, the light failed more quickly*...
`PHRASES` **without fail** = <u>without exception</u>, regularly, constantly, invariably, religiously, unfailingly, conscientiously, like clockwork, punctually, dependably ...*He attended every meeting without fail*...

failing `NOUN` = <u>shortcoming</u>, failure, fault, error, weakness, defect, deficiency, lapse, flaw, miscarriage, drawback, misfortune, blemish, imperfection, frailty, foible, blind spot ...*He had invented an imaginary son, in order to make up for his real son's failings*...
`OPPOSITE` strength
`PREPOSITION` = <u>in the absence of</u>, lacking, in default of ...*Find someone who will let you talk things through, or failing that, write down your thoughts*...

failure **1** = <u>lack of success</u>, defeat, collapse, abortion, wreck, frustration, breakdown, overthrow, miscarriage, fiasco, downfall ...*The policy is doomed to failure*... `OPPOSITE` success
2 = <u>loser</u>, disappointment, no-good, flop (*informal*), write-off, incompetent, no-hoper (*chiefly Austral.*), dud (*informal*), clinker (*slang, chiefly U.S.*), black sheep, washout (*informal*), clunker (*informal*), dead duck (*slang*), ne'er-do-well, nonstarter ...*I just felt I had*

been a failure in my personal life...
3 = <u>negligence</u>, neglect, deficiency, default, shortcoming, omission, oversight, dereliction, nonperformance, nonobservance, nonsuccess, remissness ...*They didn't prove his case of a failure of duty*... `OPPOSITE` observance
4 = <u>breakdown</u>, stalling, cutting out, malfunction, crash, disruption, stoppage, mishap, conking out (*informal*) ...*There were also several accidents mainly caused by engine failures on take-off*...
5 = <u>failing</u>, deterioration, decay, loss, decline ...*He was being treated for kidney failure*...
6 = <u>bankruptcy</u>, crash, collapse, ruin, folding (*informal*), closure, winding up, downfall, going under, liquidation, insolvency ...*Business failures rose 16% last month*... `OPPOSITE` prosperity

faint `ADJECTIVE` **1** = <u>dim</u>, low, light, soft, thin, faded, whispered, distant, dull, delicate, vague, unclear, muted, subdued, faltering, hushed, bleached, feeble, indefinite, muffled, hazy, ill-defined, indistinct ...*He became aware of the soft, faint sounds of water dripping*... `OPPOSITE` clear
2 = <u>slight</u>, weak, feeble, unenthusiastic, remote, slim, vague, slender ...*She made a faint attempt at a laugh*...
3 = <u>timid</u>, weak, feeble, lame, unconvincing, unenthusiastic, timorous, faint-hearted, spiritless, half-hearted, lily-livered ...*He let his arm flail out in a faint attempt to strike her*... `OPPOSITE` brave
4 = <u>dizzy</u>, giddy, light-headed, vertiginous, weak, exhausted, fatigued, faltering, wobbly, drooping, languid, lethargic, muzzy, woozy (*informal*), weak at the knees, enervated ...*Other signs of angina are nausea, feeling faint and shortness of breath*...
`OPPOSITE` energetic
`VERB` = <u>pass out</u>, black out, lose consciousness, keel over (*informal*), fail, go out, collapse, fade, weaken, languish, swoon (*literary*), flake out (*informal*) ...*I thought he'd faint when I kissed him*...
`NOUN` = <u>blackout</u>, collapse, coma, swoon (*literary*), unconsciousness, syncope (*Pathology*) ...*She slumped on the ground in a faint*...

faintly **1** = <u>slightly</u>, rather, a little, somewhat, dimly ...*She felt faintly ridiculous*...
2 = <u>softly</u>, weakly, feebly, in a whisper, indistinctly, unclearly ...*The voice came faintly back to us across the water*...

fair¹ `ADJECTIVE` **1** = <u>unbiased</u>, impartial, even-handed, unprejudiced, just, clean, square, equal, objective, reasonable, proper, legitimate, upright, honourable, honest, equitable, lawful, trustworthy, on the level (*informal*), disinterested, dispassionate, above board, according to the rules ...*I wanted them to get a fair deal*... `OPPOSITE` unfair
2 = <u>respectable</u>, middling, average, reasonable, decent, acceptable, moderate, adequate, satisfactory, not bad, mediocre, so-so (*informal*), tolerable, passable, O.K. *or* okay (*informal*), all right ...*He had a fair command of English*...
3 = <u>light</u>, golden, blonde, blond, yellowish, fair-haired, light-coloured, flaxen-haired, towheaded, tow-haired ...*She had bright eyes and fair hair*...

4 = <u>light-complexioned</u>, white, pale ...*It's important to protect my fair skin from the sun...*

5 = <u>fine</u>, clear, dry, bright, pleasant, sunny, favourable, clement, cloudless, unclouded, sunshiny ...*Weather conditions were fair...*

6 = <u>beautiful</u>, pretty, attractive, lovely, handsome, good-looking, bonny, comely, beauteous, well-favoured ...*Faint heart never won fair lady...* OPPOSITE ugly

PHRASES **fair and square** = <u>honestly</u>, straight, legally, on the level (*informal*), by the book, lawfully, above board, according to the rules, without cheating ...*We were beaten fair and square...*

fair² = <u>carnival</u>, show, market, fête, festival, exhibition, mart, expo (*informal*), bazaar, exposition, gala ...*The date for the fair has been changed...*

fairly 1 = <u>equitably</u>, objectively, legitimately, honestly, justly, lawfully, without prejudice, dispassionately, impartially, even-handedly, without bias ...*They solved their problems quickly and fairly...*

2 = <u>moderately</u>, rather, quite, somewhat, reasonably, adequately, pretty well, tolerably, passably ...*We did fairly well...*

3 = <u>positively</u>, really, simply, absolutely, in a manner of speaking, veritably ...*He fairly flew across the room...*

4 = <u>deservedly</u>, objectively, honestly, justifiably, justly, impartially, equitably, without fear or favour, properly ...*It can no doubt be fairly argued that he is entitled to every penny...*

fair-minded = <u>impartial</u>, just, fair, reasonable, open-minded, disinterested, unbiased, even-handed, unprejudiced

fairness = <u>impartiality</u>, justice, equity, legitimacy, decency, disinterestedness, uprightness, rightfulness, equitableness

fairy = <u>sprite</u>, elf, brownie, hob, pixie, puck, imp, leprechaun, peri, Robin Goodfellow

fairy tale *or* **fairy story 1** = <u>folk tale</u>, romance, traditional story ...*She was like a princess in a fairy tale...*

2 = <u>lie</u>, fantasy, fiction, invention, fabrication, untruth, porky (*Brit. slang*), pork pie (*Brit. slang*), urban myth, tall story, urban legend, cock-and-bull story (*informal*) ...*Many of those who write books lie much more than those who tell fairy tales...*

faith 1 = <u>confidence</u>, trust, credit, conviction, assurance, dependence, reliance, credence ...*She had placed a great deal of faith in him...* OPPOSITE distrust

2 = <u>religion</u>, church, belief, persuasion, creed, communion, denomination, dogma ...*England shifted officially from a Catholic to a Protestant faith in the 16th century...* OPPOSITE agnosticism

faithful ADJECTIVE **1** = <u>loyal</u>, true, committed, constant, attached, devoted, dedicated, reliable, staunch, truthful, dependable, trusty, steadfast, unwavering, true-blue, immovable, unswerving ...*Older Americans are among this country's most faithful voters... ...She had remained faithful to her husband...* OPPOSITE disloyal

2 = <u>accurate</u>, just, close, true, strict, exact, precise ...*His screenplay is faithful to the novel...*

PHRASES **the faithful** = <u>believers</u>, brethren, followers, congregation, adherents, the elect, communicants ...*The faithful revered him then as a prophet...*

faithfulness = <u>loyalty</u>, devotion, fidelity, constancy, dependability, trustworthiness, fealty, adherence

faithless = <u>disloyal</u>, unreliable, unfaithful, untrustworthy, doubting, false, untrue, treacherous, dishonest, fickle, perfidious, untruthful, traitorous, unbelieving, inconstant, false-hearted, recreant (*archaic*)

fake ADJECTIVE = <u>artificial</u>, false, forged, counterfeit, affected, assumed, put-on, pretend (*informal*), mock, imitation, sham, pseudo (*informal*), feigned, pinchbeck, phoney *or* phony (*informal*) ...*The bank manager is said to have issued fake certificates...* OPPOSITE genuine

NOUN **1** = <u>forgery</u>, copy, fraud, reproduction, dummy, imitation, hoax, counterfeit ...*It is filled with famous works of art, and every one of them is a fake...*

2 = <u>charlatan</u>, deceiver, sham, quack, mountebank, phoney *or* phony (*informal*) ...*She denied claims that she is a fake...*

VERB **1** = <u>forge</u>, copy, reproduce, fabricate, counterfeit, falsify ...*faked evidence...*

2 = <u>sham</u>, affect, assume, put on, pretend, simulate, feign, go through the motions of ...*He faked nonchalance...*

fall VERB **1** = <u>drop</u>, plunge, tumble, plummet, trip, settle, crash, collapse, pitch, sink, go down, come down, dive, stumble, descend, topple, subside, cascade, trip over, drop down, nose-dive, come a cropper (*informal*), keel over, go head over heels ...*Her father fell into the sea after a massive heart attack...* OPPOSITE rise

2 = <u>decrease</u>, drop, decline, go down, flag, slump, diminish, fall off, dwindle, lessen, subside, ebb, abate, depreciate, become lower ...*Her weight fell to under seven stones...* OPPOSITE increase

3 = <u>be overthrown</u>, be taken, surrender, succumb, yield, submit, give way, capitulate, be conquered, give in *or* up, pass into enemy hands ...*The town fell to Croatian forces...* OPPOSITE triumph

4 = <u>be killed</u>, die, be lost, perish, be slain, be a casualty, meet your end ...*Another wave of troops followed the first, running past those who had fallen...* OPPOSITE survive

5 = <u>occur</u>, happen, come about, chance, take place, fall out, befall, come to pass ...*Easter falls in early April...*

NOUN **1** = <u>drop</u>, slip, plunge, dive, spill, tumble, descent, plummet, nose dive ...*The helmets are designed to withstand impacts equivalent to a fall from a bicycle...*

2 = <u>decrease</u>, drop, lowering, decline, reduction, slump, dip, falling off, dwindling, lessening, diminution, cut ...*There was a sharp fall in the value of the pound...*

3 = <u>collapse</u>, defeat, surrender, downfall, death, failure, ruin, resignation, destruction, overthrow, submission, capitulation ...*the fall of Rome...*

4 = <u>slope</u>, incline, descent, downgrade, slant, declivity ...*a fall of 3.5 kilometres...*

PLURAL NOUN = <u>waterfall</u>, rapids, cascade, cataract, linn (*Scot.*), force (*Northern English dialect*) ...*The falls have always been an insurmountable obstacle for salmon and sea trout...*

PHRASES **fall apart 1** = <u>break up</u>, crumble, disintegrate, fall to bits, go to seed, come apart at the seams, break into pieces, go *or* come to pieces, shatter ...*The work was never finished and bit by bit the building fell apart...* **2** = <u>break down</u>, dissolve, disperse, disband, lose cohesion ...*The national coalition fell apart five weeks ago...* **3** = <u>go to pieces</u>, break down, crack up (*informal*), have a breakdown, crumble ...*I was falling apart...* ◆ **fall asleep** = <u>drop off</u> (*informal*), go to sleep, doze off, nod off (*informal*), go out like a light ...*I was again able to go to bed and fall asleep...* ◆ **fall away 1** = <u>slope</u>, drop, go down, incline, incline downwards ...*On either side of the tracks the ground fell away sharply...* **2** = <u>decrease</u>, drop, diminish, fall off, dwindle, lessen ...*Demand began to fall away...* ◆ **fall back** = <u>retreat</u>, retire, withdraw, move back, recede, pull back, back off, recoil, draw back ...*The congregation fell back from them as they entered...* ◆ **fall back on something** *or* **someone** = <u>resort to</u>, have recourse to, employ, turn to, make use of, call upon, press into service ...*When necessary, instinct is the most reliable resource you can fall back on...* ◆ **fall behind 1** = <u>lag</u>, trail, be left behind, drop back, get left behind, lose your place ...*The horse fell behind on the final furlong...* **2** = <u>be in arrears</u>, be late, not keep up ...*He faces losing his home after falling behind with the payments...* ◆ **fall down** = <u>fail</u>, disappoint, go wrong, fall short, fail to make the grade, prove unsuccessful ...*That is where his argument falls down...* ◆ **fall for someone** = <u>fall in love with</u>, become infatuated with, be smitten by, be swept off your feet by, desire, fancy (*Brit. informal*), succumb to the charms of, lose your head over ...*I just fell for him right away...* ◆ **fall for something** = <u>be fooled by</u>, be deceived by, be taken in by, be duped by, buy (*slang*), accept, swallow (*informal*), take on board, give credence to ...*It was just a line to get you out of here, and you fell for it!...* ◆ **fall foul of something** *or* **someone** = <u>come into conflict with</u>, brush with, have trouble with, cross swords with, run foul of, make an enemy of ...*Women who fall foul of the law are viewed as wicked...* ◆ **fall in** = <u>collapse</u>, sink, cave in, crash in, fall to the ground, fall apart at the seams, come down about your ears ...*Part of my bedroom ceiling has fallen in...* ◆ **fall in love with someone** = <u>lose your heart (to)</u>, fall (for), become infatuated (with), be smitten by, fancy (*Brit. informal*), become attached to, take a fancy to, become fond of, become enamoured of, be swept off your feet (by), conceive an affection for ...*You fall in love with a man for God knows what reasons...* ◆ **fall in with someone** = <u>make friends with</u>, go around with, become friendly with, hang about with (*informal*) ...*At University he had fallen in with a small clique of literature students...* ◆ **fall in with something** = <u>go along with</u>, support, accept, agree

with, comply with, submit to, yield to, buy into (*informal*), cooperate with, assent, take on board, concur with ...*Her reluctance to fall in with his plans led to trouble...* ◆ **fall off 1** = <u>tumble</u>, topple, plummet, be unseated, come a cropper *or* purler (*informal*), take a fall *or* tumble ...*He fell off at the second fence...* **2** = <u>decrease</u>, drop, reduce, decline, fade, slump, weaken, shrink, diminish, dwindle, lessen, wane, subside, fall away, peter out, slacken, tail off (*informal*), ebb away, go down *or* downhill ...*Unemployment is rising again and retail buying has fallen off...* ◆ **fall on** *or* **upon something** *or* **someone** = <u>attack</u>, assault, snatch, assail, tear into (*informal*), lay into, descend upon, pitch into (*informal*), belabour, let fly at, set upon *or* about ...*They fell upon the enemy from the rear...* ◆ **fall out** (*Informal*) = <u>argue</u>, fight, row, clash, differ, disagree, quarrel, squabble, have a row, have words, come to blows, cross swords, altercate ...*She fell out with her husband...* ◆ **fall short** = <u>be lacking</u>, miss, fail, disappoint, be wanting, be inadequate, be deficient, fall down on (*informal*), prove inadequate, not come up to expectations *or* scratch (*informal*) ...*His achievements are bound to fall short of his ambitions...* ◆ **fall through** = <u>fail</u>, be unsuccessful, come to nothing, fizzle out (*informal*), miscarry, go awry, go by the board ...*The deal fell through...* ◆ **fall to someone** = <u>be the responsibility of</u>, be up to, come down to, devolve upon ...*It fell to me to get rid of them...* ◆ **fall to something** = <u>begin</u>, start, set to, set about, commence, apply yourself to ...*They fell to fighting among themselves...*

fallacy = <u>error</u>, mistake, illusion, flaw, deception, delusion, inconsistency, misconception, deceit, falsehood, untruth, misapprehension, sophistry, casuistry, sophism, faultiness

fallen 1 = <u>killed</u>, lost, dead, slaughtered, slain, perished ...*Work began on establishing the cemeteries as permanent memorials to our fallen servicemen...* **2** (*Old-fashioned*) = <u>dishonoured</u>, lost, loose, shamed, ruined, disgraced, immoral, sinful, unchaste ...*She would be thought of as a fallen woman...*

fallible = <u>imperfect</u>, weak, uncertain, ignorant, mortal, frail, erring, prone to error OPPOSITE infallible

fallow 1 = <u>uncultivated</u>, unused, undeveloped, unplanted, untilled ...*The fields lay fallow...* **2** = <u>inactive</u>, resting, idle, dormant, inert ...*There followed something of a fallow period...*

false ADJECTIVE **1** = <u>incorrect</u>, wrong, mistaken, misleading, faulty, inaccurate, invalid, improper, unfounded, erroneous, inexact ...*This resulted in false information being entered...* OPPOSITE correct **2** = <u>untrue</u>, fraudulent, unreal, concocted, fictitious, trumped up, fallacious, untruthful, truthless ...*You do not know whether what you are told is true or false...* OPPOSITE true **3** = <u>artificial</u>, forged, fake, mock, reproduction, synthetic, replica, imitation, bogus, simulated, sham, pseudo (*informal*), counterfeit, feigned, spurious, ersatz, pretended ...*He paid for a false passport...* OPPOSITE real

4 = <u>treacherous</u>, lying, deceiving, unreliable, two-timing (*informal*), dishonest, deceptive, hypocritical, unfaithful, two-faced, disloyal, unsound, deceitful, faithless, untrustworthy, insincere, double-dealing, dishonourable, duplicitous, mendacious, perfidious, treasonable, traitorous, inconstant, delusive, false-hearted ...*She was a false friend, envious of her lifestyle and her life with her husband...* OPPOSITE loyal
PHRASES **play someone false** = <u>deceive</u>, cheat, betray, double-cross, stab in the back, sell down the river (*informal*), give the Judas kiss to ...*I'm afraid he's been playing us all false...*

falsehood 1 = <u>untruthfulness</u>, deception, deceit, dishonesty, prevarication, mendacity, dissimulation, perjury, inveracity (*rare*) ...*She called the verdict a victory of truth over falsehood...*
2 = <u>lie</u>, story, fiction, fabrication, fib, untruth, porky (*Brit. slang*), pork pie (*Brit. slang*), misstatement ...*He accused them of knowingly spreading falsehoods about him...*

falsify = <u>alter</u>, forge, fake, tamper with, doctor, cook (*slang*), distort, pervert, belie, counterfeit, misrepresent, garble, misstate

falter 1 = <u>hesitate</u>, delay, waver, vacillate, break ...*I have not faltered in my quest for a new future...* OPPOSITE persevere
2 = <u>tumble</u>, shake, tremble, totter ...*As he neared the house, he faltered...*
3 = <u>stutter</u>, pause, stumble, hesitate, stammer, speak haltingly ...*Her voice faltered and she had to stop a moment to control it...*

faltering = <u>hesitant</u>, broken, weak, uncertain, stumbling, tentative, stammering, timid, irresolute

fame = <u>prominence</u>, glory, celebrity, stardom, name, credit, reputation, honour, prestige, stature, eminence, renown, repute, public esteem, illustriousness OPPOSITE obscurity

famed = <u>renowned</u>, celebrated, recognized, well-known, acclaimed, widely-known

familiar ADJECTIVE **1** = <u>well-known</u>, household, everyday, recognized, common, stock, domestic, repeated, ordinary, conventional, routine, frequent, accustomed, customary, mundane, recognizable, common or garden (*informal*) ...*They are already familiar faces on our TV screens...* OPPOSITE unfamiliar
2 = <u>friendly</u>, close, dear, intimate, confidential, amicable, chummy (*informal*), buddy-buddy (*slang, chiefly U.S. & Canad.*), palsy-walsy (*informal*) ...*the old familiar relationship...* OPPOSITE formal
3 = <u>relaxed</u>, open, easy, friendly, free, near, comfortable, intimate, casual, informal, amicable, cordial, free-and-easy, unreserved, unconstrained, unceremonious, hail-fellow-well-met ...*the comfortable, familiar atmosphere...*
4 = <u>disrespectful</u>, forward, bold, presuming, intrusive, presumptuous, impudent, overfamiliar, overfree ...*The driver of that taxi-cab seemed to me familiar to the point of impertinence...*
PHRASES **familiar with** = <u>acquainted with</u>, aware of, introduced to, conscious of, at home with, no stranger to, informed about, abreast of, knowledgeable about, versed in, well up in, proficient in, conversant with, on speaking terms with, in the know about, *au courant* with, *au fait* with ...*only too familiar with the problems...*

familiarity 1 = <u>acquaintance</u>, experience, understanding, knowledge, awareness, grasp, acquaintanceship ...*The enemy would always have the advantage of familiarity with the rugged terrain...* OPPOSITE unfamiliarity
2 = <u>friendliness</u>, friendship, intimacy, closeness, freedom, ease, openness, fellowship, informality, sociability, naturalness, absence of reserve, unceremoniousness ...*Close personal familiarity between councillors and staff can prove embarrassing...* OPPOSITE formality
3 = <u>disrespect</u>, forwardness, overfamiliarity, liberties, liberty, cheek, presumption, boldness ...*He had behaved with undue and oily familiarity...* OPPOSITE respect

familiarize = <u>accustom</u>, instruct, habituate, make used to, school, season, train, prime, coach, get to know (about), inure, bring into common use, make conversant

family 1 = <u>relations</u>, people, children, issue, relatives, household, folk (*informal*), offspring, descendants, brood, kin, nuclear family, progeny, kindred, next of kin, kinsmen, ménage, kith and kin, your nearest and dearest, kinsfolk, your own flesh and blood ...*His family are completely behind him, whatever he decides...*
2 = <u>children</u>, kids (*informal*), offspring, little ones, munchkins (*informal, chiefly U.S.*), littlies (*Austral. informal*) ...*Are you going to have a family?...*
3 = <u>ancestors</u>, forebears, parentage, forefathers, house, line, race, blood, birth, strain, tribe, sept, clan, descent, dynasty, pedigree, extraction, ancestry, lineage, genealogy, line of descent, stemma, stirps ...*Her family came to Los Angeles at the turn of the century...*
4 = <u>species</u>, group, class, system, order, kind, network, genre, classification, subdivision, subclass ...*foods in the cabbage family, such as Brussels sprouts...*
(Related Words)
adjective: familial

Word Power

family – Some careful writers insist that a singular verb should always be used with collective nouns such as *government*, *team*, *family*, *committee*, and *class*, for example: *the class is doing a project on Vikings*; *the company is mounting a big sales campaign*. In British usage, however, a plural verb is often used with a collective noun, especially where the emphasis is on a collection of individual objects or people rather than a group regarded as a unit: *the family are all on holiday*. The most important thing to remember is never to treat the same collective noun as both singular and plural in the same sentence: *the family is well and sends its best wishes* or *the family are well and send their best wishes*, but not *the family is well and send their best wishes*.

family tree = <u>lineage</u>, genealogy, line of descent, ancestral tree, line, descent, pedigree, extraction, ancestry, blood line, stemma, stirps

famine = <u>hunger</u>, want, starvation, deprivation, scarcity, dearth, destitution

famous = <u>well-known</u>, celebrated, acclaimed, notable, noted, excellent, signal, honoured, remarkable, distinguished, prominent, glorious, legendary, renowned, eminent, conspicuous, illustrious, much-publicized, lionized, far-famed OPPOSITE> unknown

fan¹ NOUN = <u>blower</u>, ventilator, air conditioner, vane, punkah (*in India*), blade, propeller …*He cools himself with an electric fan*…
VERB 1 = <u>blow</u>, cool, refresh, air-condition, ventilate, air-cool, winnow (*rare*) …*She fanned herself with a piece of cardboard*…
2 = <u>stimulate</u>, increase, excite, provoke, arouse, rouse, stir up, work up, agitate, whip up, add fuel to the flames, impassion, enkindle …*economic problems which often fan hatred*…
PHRASES **fan out** = <u>spread out</u>, spread, lay out, disperse, unfurl, open out, space out …*The main body of troops fanned out to the west*…

fan² = <u>supporter</u>, lover, follower, enthusiast, addict, freak (*informal*), admirer, buff (*informal*), devotee, fiend (*informal*), adherent, zealot, groupie (*slang*), aficionado, rooter (*U.S.*) …*As a boy he was a Manchester United fan*…

fanatic = <u>extremist</u>, activist, militant, addict, enthusiast, buff (*informal*), visionary, devotee, bigot, zealot, energumen

fanatical = <u>obsessive</u> burning, wild, mad, extreme, enthusiastic, passionate, frenzied, visionary, fervent, zealous, bigoted, rabid, immoderate, overenthusiastic

fanaticism = <u>immoderation</u>, enthusiasm, madness, devotion, dedication, zeal, bigotry, extremism, infatuation, single-mindedness, zealotry, obsessiveness, monomania, overenthusiasm

fancier = <u>expert</u>, amateur, breeder, connoisseur, aficionado

fanciful = <u>unreal</u>, wild, ideal, romantic, fantastic, curious, fabulous, imaginative, imaginary, poetic, extravagant, visionary, fairy-tale, mythical, whimsical, capricious, chimerical OPPOSITE> unimaginative

fancy ADJECTIVE 1 = <u>elaborate</u>, decorated, decorative, extravagant, intricate, baroque, ornamented, ornamental, ornate, elegant, fanciful, embellished …*It was packaged in a fancy plastic case with attractive graphics*… OPPOSITE> plain
2 = <u>expensive</u>, high-quality, classy, flashy, swish (*informal*), showy, ostentatious …*They sent me to a fancy private school*…
NOUN 1 = <u>whim</u>, thought, idea, desire, urge, notion, humour, impulse, inclination, caprice …*His interest was just a passing fancy*…
2 = <u>delusion</u>, dream, vision, fantasy, nightmare, daydream, chimera, phantasm …*His book is a bold surrealist mixture of fact and fancy*…
VERB 1 = <u>wish for</u>, want, desire, would like, hope for,

dream of, relish, long for, crave, be attracted to, yearn for, thirst for, hanker after, have a yen for …*I just fancied a drink*…
2 = (*informal*) = <u>be attracted to</u>, find attractive, desire, lust after, like, prefer, favour, take to, go for, be captivated by, have an eye for, have a thing about (*informal*), have eyes for, take a liking to …*I think he thinks I fancy him*…
3 = <u>suppose</u>, think, believe, imagine, guess (*informal, chiefly U.S. & Canad.*), reckon, conceive, infer, conjecture, surmise, think likely, be inclined to think …*She fancied he was trying to hide a smile*…
PHRASES **fancy yourself** = <u>think you are God's gift</u>, have a high opinion of yourself, think you are the cat's whiskers …*She really fancies herself in that new outfit*… ◆ **take a fancy to something** or **someone** = <u>start liking</u>, like, want, be fond of, hanker after, have a partiality for …*Sylvia took quite a fancy to him*…

fanfare = <u>trumpet call</u>, flourish, trump (*archaic*), tucket (*archaic*), fanfaronade

fang = <u>tooth</u>, tusk

fantasize = <u>daydream</u>, imagine, invent, romance, envision, hallucinate, see visions, live in a dream world, build castles in the air, give free rein to the imagination

fantastic 1 (*Informal*) = <u>wonderful</u>, great, excellent, very good, mean (*slang*), topping (*Brit. slang*), cracking (*Brit. informal*), crucial (*slang*), smashing (*informal*), superb, tremendous (*informal*), magnificent, marvellous, terrific (*informal*), sensational (*informal*), mega (*slang*), awesome (*slang*), dope (*slang*), world-class, first-rate, def (*slang*), brill (*informal*), out of this world (*informal*), boffo (*slang*), jim-dandy (*slang*), bitchin' (*U.S. slang*), chillin' (*U.S. slang*), booshit (*Austral. slang*), exo (*Austral. slang*), sik (*Austral. slang*) …*I have a fantastic social life*… OPPOSITE> ordinary
2 (*Informal*) = <u>enormous</u>, great, huge, vast, severe, extreme, overwhelming, tremendous, immense …*fantastic amounts of money*…
3 = <u>strange</u>, bizarre, weird, exotic, peculiar, imaginative, queer, grotesque, quaint, unreal, fanciful, outlandish, whimsical, freakish, chimerical, phantasmagorical …*outlandish and fantastic images*…
4 = <u>implausible</u>, unlikely, incredible, absurd, irrational, preposterous, capricious, cock-and-bull (*informal*), cockamamie (*slang, chiefly U.S.*), mad …*He had cooked up some fantastic story about how the ring had come into his possession*…

fantasy or (*Archaic*) **phantasy** 1 = <u>daydream</u>, dream, wish, fancy, delusion, reverie, flight of fancy, pipe dream …*Everyone's had a fantasy about winning the lottery*…
2 = <u>imagination</u>, fancy, invention, creativity, originality …*a world of imagination and fantasy*…

far ADVERB 1 = <u>a long way</u>, miles, deep, a good way, afar, a great distance …*They came from far away*…
2 = <u>much</u>, greatly, very much, extremely, significantly, considerably, decidedly, markedly, incomparably …*He was a far better cook than Amy*…

ADJECTIVE *often with* *off* = <u>remote</u>, distant, far-flung, faraway, long, removed, out-of-the-way, far-off, far-removed, outlying, off the beaten track ...*people in far off lands...* **OPPOSITE** near

PHRASES **by far** *or* **far and away** = <u>very much</u>, easily, immeasurably, by a long way, incomparably, to a great degree, by a long shot, by a long chalk (*informal*), by a great amount ...*by far the most successful...* ◆ **far and wide** = <u>extensively</u>, everywhere, worldwide, far and near, widely, broadly, in all places, in every nook and cranny, here, there and everywhere ...*His fame spread far and wide...* ◆ **far from** = <u>not at all</u>, not, by no means, absolutely not ...*She is far from happy...* ◆ **so far** **1** = <u>up to a point</u>, to a certain extent, to a limited extent ...*Their loyalty only went so far...* **2** = <u>up to now</u>, to date, until now, thus far, up to the present ...*So far, they have had no success...*

faraway **1** = <u>distant</u>, far, remote, far-off, far-removed, far-flung, outlying, beyond the horizon ...*They had just returned from faraway places...*
2 = <u>dreamy</u>, lost, distant, abstracted, vague, absent ...*She smiled with a faraway look in her eyes...*

farce **1** = <u>comedy</u>, satire, slapstick, burlesque, buffoonery, broad comedy ...*The plot often borders on farce...*
2 = <u>mockery</u>, joke, nonsense, parody, shambles, sham, absurdity, travesty, ridiculousness ...*The election was a farce, as only 22% of voters cast their ballots...*

farcical **1** = <u>ludicrous</u>, ridiculous, diverting, absurd, preposterous, laughable, nonsensical, derisory, risible ...*a farcical nine months' jail sentence...*
2 = <u>comic</u>, funny, amusing, slapstick, droll, custard-pie ...*from farcical humour to deepest tragedy...*

fare **NOUN** **1** = <u>charge</u>, price, ticket price, transport cost, ticket money, passage money ...*He could barely afford the railway fare...*
2 = <u>food</u>, meals, diet, provisions, board, commons, table, feed, menu, rations, tack (*informal*), kai (*N.Z. informal*), nourishment, sustenance, victuals, nosebag (*slang*), nutriment, vittles (*obsolete or dialect*), eatables ...*traditional Portuguese fare...*
3 = <u>passenger</u>, customer, pick-up (*informal*), traveller ...*The taxi driver picked up a fare...*
VERB **1** = <u>get on</u>, do, manage, make out, prosper, get along ...*He was not faring well...*
2 *used impersonally* = <u>happen</u>, go, turn out, proceed, pan out (*informal*) ...*The show fared quite well...*

farewell **INTERJECTION** = <u>goodbye</u>, bye (*informal*), so long, see you, take care, good morning, bye-bye (*informal*), good day, all the best, good night, good evening, good afternoon, see you later, ciao (*Italian*), have a nice day (*U.S.*), adieu (*French*), au revoir (*French*), be seeing you, auf Wiedersehen (*German*), adios (*Spanish*), mind how you go ...*'Farewell, lad, and may we meet again soon.'...*
NOUN = <u>goodbye</u>, parting, departure, leave-taking, adieu, valediction, sendoff (*informal*), adieux *or* adieus ...*a touching farewell...*

far-fetched = <u>unconvincing</u>, unlikely, strained, fantastic, incredible, doubtful, unbelievable, dubious, unrealistic, improbable, unnatural, preposterous, implausible, hard to swallow (*informal*), cock-and-bull (*informal*) **OPPOSITE** believable

farm **NOUN** = <u>smallholding</u>, holding, ranch (*chiefly U.S. & Canad.*), farmstead, land, station (*Austral. & N.Z.*), acres, vineyard, plantation, croft (*Scot.*), grange, homestead, acreage ...*We have a small farm...*
VERB = <u>cultivate</u>, work, plant, operate, till the soil, grow crops on, bring under cultivation, keep animals on, practise husbandry ...*They had farmed the same land for generations...*

farmer = <u>agriculturist</u>, yeoman, smallholder, crofter (*Scot.*), grazier, agriculturalist, rancher, agronomist, husbandman, cockie *or* cocky (*Austral. & N.Z. informal*)

farming = <u>agriculture</u>, cultivation, husbandry, land management, agronomy, tilling

far-out = <u>strange</u>, wild, unusual, bizarre, weird, avant-garde, unconventional, off-the-wall (*slang*), outlandish, outré, advanced

far-reaching = <u>extensive</u>, important, significant, sweeping, broad, widespread, pervasive, momentous

far-sighted = <u>prudent</u>, acute, wise, cautious, sage, shrewd, discerning, canny, provident, judicious, prescient, far-seeing, politic

farther

Word Power

farther – *Farther, farthest, further,* and *furthest* can all be used to refer to literal distance, but *further* and *furthest* are used for figurative senses denoting greater or additional amount, time, etc.: *further to my letter. Further* and *furthest* are also preferred for figurative distance.

---

farthest
► **farther**

fascinate = <u>entrance</u>, delight, charm, absorb, intrigue, enchant, rivet, captivate, enthral, beguile, allure, bewitch, ravish, transfix, mesmerize, hypnotize, engross, enrapture, interest greatly, enamour, hold spellbound, spellbind, infatuate **OPPOSITE** bore

fascinated = <u>entranced</u>, charmed, absorbed, very interested, captivated, hooked on, enthralled, beguiled, smitten, bewitched, engrossed, spellbound, infatuated, hypnotized, under a spell

fascinating = <u>captivating</u>, engaging, gripping, compelling, intriguing, very interesting, irresistible, enticing, enchanting, seductive, riveting, alluring, bewitching, ravishing, engrossing **OPPOSITE** boring

fascination = <u>attraction</u>, pull, spell, magic, charm, lure, glamour, allure, magnetism, enchantment, sorcery

Fascism *sometimes not cap.* = <u>authoritarianism</u>, dictatorship, totalitarianism, despotism, autocracy, absolutism, Hitlerism

fashion **NOUN** **1** = <u>style</u>, look, trend, rage, custom, convention, mode, vogue, usage, craze, fad, latest style, prevailing taste, latest ...*I wore short skirts, as* *was the fashion…*

2 = <u>method</u>, way, style, approach, manner, mode …*We must go about this in an organised fashion…*

VERB **1** = <u>make</u>, shape, cast, construct, work, form, create, design, manufacture, forge, mould, contrive, fabricate …*The desk was fashioned out of oak…*

2 = <u>fit</u>, adapt, tailor, suit, adjust, accommodate …*dresses fashioned to hide the bulges…*

PHRASES **after a fashion** = <u>to some extent</u>, somehow, in a way, moderately, to a certain extent, to a degree, somehow or other, in a manner of speaking …*He knew the way, after a fashion…*

fashionable = <u>popular</u>, in fashion, trendy (*Brit. informal*), cool (*slang*), in (*informal*), latest, happening (*informal*), current, modern, with it (*informal*), usual, smart, hip (*slang*), prevailing, stylish, chic, up-to-date, customary, genteel, in vogue, all the rage, up-to-the-minute, modish, à la mode, voguish (*informal*), trendsetting, all the go (*informal*) **OPPOSITE** unfashionable

fast¹ **ADJECTIVE** **1** = <u>quick</u>, flying, winged, rapid, fleet, hurried, accelerated, swift, speedy, brisk, hasty, nimble, mercurial, sprightly, nippy (*Brit. informal*) …*She walked at a fast pace…* **OPPOSITE** slow

2 = <u>fixed</u>, firm, sound, stuck, secure, tight, jammed, fortified, fastened, impregnable, immovable …*He held the gate fast…* **OPPOSITE** unstable

3 = <u>dissipated</u>, wild, exciting, loose, extravagant, reckless, immoral, promiscuous, giddy, self-indulgent, wanton, profligate, impure, intemperate, dissolute, rakish, licentious, gadabout (*informal*) …*He experimented with drugs and the fast life…*

4 = <u>close</u>, lasting, firm, permanent, constant, devoted, loyal, faithful, stalwart, staunch, steadfast, unwavering …*The men had always been fast friends…*

ADVERB **1** = <u>quickly</u>, rapidly, swiftly, hastily, hurriedly, speedily, presto, apace, in haste, like a shot (*informal*), at full speed, hell for leather (*informal*), like lightning, hotfoot, like a flash, at a rate of knots, like the clappers (*Brit. informal*), like a bat out of hell (*slang*), pdq (*slang*), like nobody's business (*informal*), posthaste, like greased lightning (*informal*), with all haste …*He drives terrifically fast…* **OPPOSITE** slowly

2 = <u>firmly</u>, staunchly, resolutely, steadfastly, determinedly, unwaveringly, unchangeably …*We can only try to hold fast to our principles…*

3 = <u>securely</u>, firmly, tightly, fixedly …*She held fast to the stair rail…*

4 = <u>fixedly</u>, firmly, soundly, deeply, securely, tightly …*The tanker is stuck fast on the rocks…*

5 = <u>recklessly</u>, wildly, loosely, extravagantly, promiscuously, rakishly, intemperately …*He lived fast and died young…*

fast² **VERB** = <u>go hungry</u>, abstain, go without food, deny yourself, practise abstention, refrain from food or eating …*She had fasted to lose weight…*

NOUN = <u>fasting</u>, diet, abstinence …*The fast is broken, traditionally with dates and water…*

fasten **1** = <u>secure</u>, close, lock, chain, seal, bolt, do up …*He fastened the door behind him…*

2 = <u>tie</u>, bind, lace, tie up …*The dress fastens down the*

back…

3 = <u>fix</u>, join, link, connect, grip, attach, anchor, affix, make firm, make fast …*Use screws to fasten the shelf to the wall…*

4 = <u>concentrate</u>, focus, fix …*Her thoughts fastened on one event…*

5 = <u>direct</u>, aim, focus, fix, concentrate, bend, rivet …*They fastened their gaze on the table and did not look up…*

fastening = <u>tie</u>, union, coupling, link, linking, bond, joint, binding, connection, attachment, junction, zip, fusion, clasp, concatenation, ligature, affixation

fastidious = <u>particular</u>, meticulous, fussy, overdelicate, difficult, nice, critical, discriminating, dainty, squeamish, choosy, picky (*informal*), hard to please, finicky, punctilious, pernickety, hypercritical, overnice **OPPOSITE** careless

fat **ADJECTIVE** **1** = <u>overweight</u>, large, heavy, plump, gross, stout, obese, fleshy, beefy (*informal*), tubby, portly, roly-poly, rotund, podgy, corpulent, elephantine, broad in the beam (*informal*), solid …*I can eat what I like without getting fat…* **OPPOSITE** thin

2 = <u>large</u>, rich, substantial, thriving, flourishing, profitable, productive, lucrative, fertile, lush, prosperous, affluent, fruitful, cushy (*slang*), jammy (*Brit. slang*), remunerative …*They are set to make a fat profit…* **OPPOSITE** scanty

3 = <u>fatty</u>, greasy, lipid, adipose, oleaginous, suety, oily …*Most heart cases are the better for cutting out fat meat…* **OPPOSITE** lean

NOUN = <u>fatness</u>, flesh, bulk, obesity, cellulite, weight problem, flab, blubber, paunch, fatty tissue, adipose tissue, corpulence, beef (*informal*) …*ways of reducing body fat…*

PHRASES **fat chance** = <u>no chance</u>, a slim chance, very little chance, not much chance …*You've got fat chance of getting there on time…*

fatal **1** = <u>disastrous</u>, devastating, crippling, lethal, catastrophic, ruinous, calamitous, baleful, baneful …*It dealt a fatal blow to his chances…* **OPPOSITE** minor

2 = <u>decisive</u>, final, determining, critical, crucial, fateful …*putting off that fatal moment…*

3 = <u>lethal</u>, deadly, mortal, causing death, final, killing, terminal, destructive, malignant, incurable, pernicious …*She had suffered a fatal heart attack…* **OPPOSITE** harmless

fatalism = <u>resignation</u>, acceptance, passivity, determinism, stoicism, necessitarianism, predestinarianism

fatality = <u>casualty</u>, death, loss, victim

fate **1** = <u>destiny</u>, chance, fortune, luck, the stars, weird (*archaic*), providence, nemesis, kismet, predestination, divine will …*I see no use quarrelling with fate…*

2 = <u>fortune</u>, destiny, lot, portion, cup, horoscope …*No man chooses his fate…*

3 = <u>outcome</u>, future, destiny, end, issue, upshot …*What will be the fate of the elections?…*

4 = <u>downfall</u>, end, death, ruin, destruction, doom, demise …*This new proposal seems doomed to the same fate…*

fated = <u>destined</u>, doomed, predestined, preordained, foreordained, pre-elected

fateful 1 = <u>crucial</u>, important, significant, critical, decisive, momentous, portentous ...*What changed for him in that fateful year?*... OPPOSITE> unimportant
2 = <u>disastrous</u>, fatal, deadly, destructive, lethal, ominous, ruinous ...*He had sailed on his third and fateful voyage*...

Fates, the

The Fates

Atropos   Lachesis
Clotho

---

father NOUN **1** = <u>daddy</u> (*informal*), dad (*informal*), male parent, patriarch, pop (*U.S. informal*), governor (*informal*), old man (*Brit. informal*), pa (*informal*), old boy (*informal*), papa (*old-fashioned informal*), sire, pater, biological father, foster father, begetter, paterfamilias, birth father ...*He was a good father to my children*...
2 = <u>founder</u>, author, maker, architect, creator, inventor, originator, prime mover, initiator ...*He was the father of modern photography*...
3 *usually cap.* = <u>priest</u>, minister, vicar, parson, pastor, cleric, churchman, padre (*informal*), confessor, abbé, curé, man of God ...*The prior, Father Alessandro, came over to talk to them*...
4 *usually plural* = <u>forefather</u>, predecessor, ancestor, forebear, progenitor ...*land of my fathers*...
5 *usually plural* (usually found in phrase *city fathers*) = <u>leader</u>, senator, elder, patron, patriarch, guiding light, city father ...*City fathers tried to revive the town's economy*...
VERB **1** = <u>sire</u>, parent, conceive, bring to life, beget, procreate, bring into being, give life to, get ...*He fathered at least three children*...
2 = <u>originate</u>, found, create, establish, author, institute, invent, engender ...*He fathered the modern computer*...
(Related Words)
adjective: paternal

fatherland = <u>homeland</u>, motherland, old country, native land, land of your birth, land of your fathers

fatherly = <u>paternal</u>, kind, kindly, tender, protective, supportive, benign, affectionate, indulgent, patriarchal, benevolent, forbearing

fathom = <u>understand</u>, grasp, comprehend, interpret, get to the bottom of

fatigue NOUN = <u>tiredness</u>, lethargy, weariness, ennui, heaviness, debility, languor, listlessness, overtiredness ...*Those affected suffer extreme fatigue*... OPPOSITE> freshness
VERB = <u>tire</u>, exhaust, weaken, weary, drain, fag (out) (*informal*), whack (*Brit. informal*), wear out, jade, take it out of (*informal*), poop (*informal*), tire out, knacker (*slang*), drain of energy, overtire ...*It fatigues me to list them all*... OPPOSITE> refresh

fatigued = <u>tired</u>, exhausted, weary, tired out, bushed (*informal*), wasted, all in (*slang*), fagged (out)

(*informal*), whacked (*Brit. informal*), jaded, knackered (*slang*), clapped out (*Austral. & N.Z. informal*), overtired, zonked (*slang*), dead beat (*informal*), jiggered (*informal*), on your last legs, creamcrackered (*Brit. informal*)

fatten 1 = <u>grow fat</u>, spread, expand, swell, thrive, broaden, thicken, put on weight, gain weight, coarsen, become fat, become fatter ...*The creature continued to grow and fatten*...
2 *often with* **up** = <u>feed up</u>, feed, stuff, build up, cram, nourish, distend, bloat, overfeed ...*They fattened up ducks and geese*...

fatty = <u>greasy</u>, fat, creamy, oily, adipose, oleaginous, suety, rich

fatuous = <u>foolish</u>, stupid, silly, dull, absurd, dense, ludicrous, lunatic, mindless, idiotic, vacuous, inane, witless, puerile, moronic, brainless, asinine, weak-minded, dumb-ass (*slang*)

fault NOUN **1** = <u>responsibility</u>, liability, guilt, accountability, culpability ...*It was all my fault we quarrelled*...
2 = <u>mistake</u>, slip, error, offence, blunder, lapse, negligence, omission, boob (*Brit. slang*), oversight, slip-up, indiscretion, inaccuracy, howler (*informal*), glitch (*informal*), error of judgment, boo-boo (*informal*) ...*It was a genuine fault*...
3 = <u>failing</u>, lack, weakness, defect, deficiency, flaw, drawback, shortcoming, snag, blemish, imperfection, Achilles heel, weak point, infirmity, demerit ...*His manners always made her blind to his faults*... OPPOSITE> strength
4 = <u>misdeed</u>, failing, wrong, offence, sin, lapse, misconduct, wrongdoing, trespass, frailty, misdemeanour, delinquency, transgression, peccadillo ...*Hypocrisy is one fault of which he cannot be accused*...
VERB = <u>criticize</u>, blame, complain, condemn, moan about, censure, hold (someone) responsible, hold (someone) accountable, find fault with, call to account, impugn, find lacking, hold (someone) to blame ...*You can't fault them for lack of invention*...
PHRASES **at fault** = <u>guilty</u>, responsible, to blame, accountable, in the wrong, culpable, answerable, blamable ...*He didn't accept that he was at fault*...
♦ **find fault with something** or **someone** = <u>criticize</u>, complain about, whinge about (*informal*), whine about (*informal*), quibble, diss (*slang, chiefly U.S.*), carp at, take to task, pick holes in, grouse about (*informal*), haul over the coals (*informal*), pull to pieces ...*I do tend to find fault with everybody*... ♦ **to a fault** = <u>excessively</u>, overly (*U.S.*), unduly, ridiculously, in the extreme, needlessly, out of all proportion, preposterously, overmuch, immoderately ...*He was generous to a fault*...

faultless = <u>flawless</u>, model, perfect, classic, correct, accurate, faithful, impeccable, exemplary, foolproof, unblemished

faulty 1 = <u>defective</u>, damaged, not working, malfunctioning, broken, bad, flawed, impaired, imperfect, blemished, out of order, on the blink ...*They will repair the faulty equipment*...

2 = <u>incorrect</u>, wrong, flawed, inaccurate, bad, weak, invalid, erroneous, unsound, imprecise, fallacious …*Their interpretation was faulty*…

faux pas = <u>gaffe</u>, blunder, indiscretion, impropriety, bloomer (*Brit. informal*), boob (*Brit. slang*), clanger (*informal*), solecism, breach of etiquette, gaucherie

favour NOUN **1** = <u>approval</u>, grace, esteem, goodwill, kindness, friendliness, commendation, partiality, approbation, kind regard …*They viewed him with favour*… OPPOSITE▷ disapproval
2 = <u>favouritism</u>, preference, bias, nepotism, preferential treatment, partisanship, jobs for the boys (*informal*), partiality, one-sidedness …*employers to show favour to women and racial minorities*…
3 = <u>support</u>, backing, aid, championship, promotion, assistance, patronage, espousal, good opinion …*He wanted to win the favour of the voters*…
4 = <u>good turn</u>, service, benefit, courtesy, kindness, indulgence, boon, good deed, kind act, obligement (*Scot. or archaic*) …*I've come to ask for a favour*… OPPOSITE▷ wrong
5 = <u>memento</u>, present, gift, token, souvenir, keepsake, love-token …*place cards and wedding favours*…
VERB **1** = <u>prefer</u>, opt for, like better, incline towards, choose, pick, desire, select, elect, adopt, go for, fancy, single out, plump for, be partial to …*She favours community activism over legislation*… OPPOSITE▷ object to
2 = <u>indulge</u>, reward, spoil, esteem, side with, pamper, befriend, be partial to, smile upon, pull strings for (*informal*), have in your good books, treat with partiality, value …*There was good reason for favouring him*…
3 = <u>support</u>, like, back, choose, champion, encourage, approve, fancy, advocate, opt for, subscribe to, commend, stand up for, espouse, be in favour of, countenance, patronize …*He favours greater protection of the environment*… OPPOSITE▷ oppose
4 = <u>help</u>, benefit, aid, advance, promote, assist, accommodate, facilitate, abet, succour, do a kindness to …*Circumstances favoured them*…
5 = <u>oblige</u>, please, honour, accommodate, benefit …*The beautiful girls would favour me with a look*…
PHRASES **in favour of** = <u>for</u>, backing, supporting, behind, pro, all for (*informal*), on the side of, right behind …*They were in favour of the decision*…

favourable 1 = <u>positive</u>, kind, understanding, encouraging, welcoming, friendly, approving, praising, reassuring, enthusiastic, sympathetic, benign, commending, complimentary, agreeable, amicable, well-disposed, commendatory …*He made favourable comments about her work*… OPPOSITE▷ disapproving
2 = <u>affirmative</u>, agreeing, confirming, positive, assenting, corroborative …*He expects a favourable reply*…
3 = <u>advantageous</u>, timely, good, promising, fit, encouraging, fair, appropriate, suitable, helpful, hopeful, convenient, beneficial, auspicious, opportune, propitious …*favourable weather conditions*… OPPOSITE▷ disadvantageous

favourably 1 = <u>positively</u>, well, enthusiastically, helpfully, graciously, approvingly, agreeably, with approval, without prejudice, genially, with approbation, in a kindly manner, with cordiality …*He responded favourably to my suggestions*…
2 = <u>advantageously</u>, well, fortunately, conveniently, profitably, to your advantage, auspiciously, opportunely …*They are far more favourably placed than their opponents*…

favourite ADJECTIVE = <u>preferred</u>, favoured, best-loved, most-liked, special, choice, dearest, pet, esteemed, fave (*informal*) …*Her favourite writer is Charles Dickens*…
NOUN = <u>darling</u>, pet, preference, blue-eyed boy (*informal*), pick, choice, dear, beloved, idol, fave (*informal*), teacher's pet, the apple of your eye …*He was a favourite of the King*…

favouritism = <u>bias</u>, preference, nepotism, preferential treatment, partisanship, jobs for the boys (*informal*), partiality, one-sidedness OPPOSITE▷ impartiality

fawn[1] = <u>beige</u>, neutral, buff, yellowish-brown, greyish-brown …*She put on a light fawn coat*…
➤ **shades of brown**

fawn[2] *usually with* **on** *or* **upon** *or* **over** = <u>ingratiate yourself</u>, court, flatter, pander to, creep, crawl, kneel, cringe, grovel, curry favour, toady, pay court, kowtow, bow and scrape, dance attendance, truckle, be obsequious, be servile, lick (someone's) boots …*People fawn on you when you're famous*…

fawning = <u>obsequious</u>, crawling, flattering, cringing, abject, grovelling, prostrate, deferential, sycophantic, servile, slavish, bowing and scraping, bootlicking (*informal*)

fear NOUN **1** = <u>dread</u>, horror, panic, terror, dismay, awe, fright, tremors, qualms, consternation, alarm, trepidation, timidity, fearfulness, blue funk (*informal*), apprehensiveness, cravenness …*I shivered with fear at the sound of gunfire*…
2 = <u>bugbear</u>, bête noire, horror, nightmare, anxiety, terror, dread, spectre, phobia, bogey, thing (*informal*) …*Flying was his greatest fear*…
3 = <u>anxiety</u>, concern, worry, doubt, nerves (*informal*), distress, suspicion, willies (*informal*), creeps (*informal*), butterflies (*informal*), funk (*informal*), angst, unease, apprehension, misgiving(s), nervousness, agitation, foreboding(s), uneasiness, solicitude, blue funk (*informal*), heebie-jeebies (*informal*), collywobbles (*informal*), disquietude …*His fear might be groundless*…
4 = <u>awe</u>, wonder, respect, worship, dread, reverence, veneration …*There is no fear of God before their eyes*…
VERB **1** = <u>be afraid of</u>, dread, be scared of, be frightened of, shudder at, be fearful of, be apprehensive about, tremble at, be terrified by, have a horror of, take fright at, have a phobia about, have qualms about, live in dread of, be in a blue funk about (*informal*), have butterflies in your stomach about (*informal*), shake in your shoes about …*If people fear you they respect you*…

2 = <u>worry</u>, suspect, anticipate, be afraid, expect, foresee, apprehend ...*She feared she was coming down with flu...*

3 = <u>revere</u>, respect, reverence, venerate, stand in awe of ...*They feared God in a way which most modern men can hardly imagine...*

4 = <u>regret</u>, feel, suspect, have a feeling, have a hunch, have a sneaking suspicion, have a funny feeling ...*I fear that a land war now looks probable...*

PHRASES **fear for something** or **someone** = <u>worry about</u>, be concerned about, be anxious about, tremble for, be distressed about, feel concern for, be disquieted over ...*He fled, saying he feared for his life...*

fearful 1 = <u>scared</u>, afraid, alarmed, frightened, nervous, terrified, apprehensive, petrified, jittery (*informal*) ...*They were fearful that the fighting might spread...* OPPOSITE> unafraid

2 = <u>timid</u>, afraid, frightened, scared, alarmed, wired (*slang*), nervous, anxious, shrinking, tense, intimidated, uneasy, neurotic, hesitant, apprehensive, jittery (*informal*), panicky, nervy (*Brit. informal*), diffident, jumpy, timorous, pusillanimous, faint-hearted ...*I had often been very fearful and isolated...* OPPOSITE> brave

3 = <u>frightful</u>, shocking, terrible, awful, distressing, appalling, horrible, grim, dreadful, horrific, dire, horrendous, ghastly, hideous, monstrous, harrowing, gruesome, grievous, unspeakable, atrocious, hair-raising, hellacious (*U.S. slang*) ...*The earthquake was a fearful disaster...*

fearfully 1 = <u>nervously</u>, uneasily, timidly, apprehensively, diffidently, in fear and trembling, timorously, with bated breath, with many misgivings *or* forebodings, with your heart in your mouth ...*Softly, fearfully, he stole from the room...*

2 = <u>very</u>, terribly, horribly, tremendously, awfully, exceedingly, excessively, dreadfully, frightfully ...*This dress is fearfully expensive...*

fearless = <u>intrepid</u>, confident, brave, daring, bold, heroic, courageous, gallant, gutsy (*slang*), valiant, plucky, game (*informal*), doughty, undaunted, indomitable, unabashed, unafraid, unflinching, dauntless, lion-hearted, valorous

fearsome = <u>formidable</u>, alarming, frightening, awful, terrifying, appalling, horrifying, menacing, dismaying, awesome, daunting, horrendous, unnerving, hair-raising, awe-inspiring, baleful, hellacious (*U.S. slang*)

feasibility = <u>possibility</u>, viability, usefulness, expediency, practicability, workability

feasible = <u>practicable</u>, possible, reasonable, viable, workable, achievable, attainable, realizable, likely OPPOSITE> impracticable

feast NOUN 1 = <u>banquet</u>, repast, spread (*informal*), dinner, entertainment, barbecue, revel, junket, beano (*Brit. slang*), blowout (*slang*), carouse, slap-up meal (*Brit. informal*), beanfeast (*Brit. informal*), jollification, carousal, festive board, treat ...*Lunch was a feast of meat, vegetables, cheese, and wine...*

2 = <u>festival</u>, holiday, fête, celebration, holy day, red-letter day, religious festival, saint's day, -fest, gala day

...*The feast of passover began last night...*

3 = <u>treat</u>, delight, pleasure, enjoyment, gratification, cornucopia ...*Chicago provides a feast for the ears of any music lover...*

VERB = <u>eat your fill</u>, wine and dine, overindulge, eat to your heart's content, stuff yourself, consume, indulge, gorge, devour, pig out (*slang*), stuff your face (*slang*), fare sumptuously, gormandize ...*We feasted on cakes and ice cream...*

PHRASES **feast your eyes on something** or **someone** = <u>look at with delight</u>, gaze at, devour with your eyes ...*She stood feasting her eyes on the view...*

feat = <u>accomplishment</u>, act, performance, achievement, enterprise, undertaking, exploit, deed, attainment, feather in your cap

feather NOUN = <u>plume</u> ...*a purple hat with a green feather...*
PLURAL NOUN = <u>plumage</u>, plumes, down ...*black ostrich feathers...*

feathery = <u>downy</u>, soft, feathered, fluffy, plumed, wispy, plumy, plumate *or* plumose (*Botany & Zoology*), light

feature NOUN 1 = <u>aspect</u>, quality, characteristic, attribute, point, mark, property, factor, trait, hallmark, facet, peculiarity ...*The gardens are a special feature of this property...*

2 = <u>article</u>, report, story, piece, comment, item, column ...*a special feature on breast cancer research...*

3 = <u>highlight</u>, draw, attraction, innovation, speciality, specialty, main item, crowd puller (*informal*), special attraction, special ...*the most striking feature of the whole garden...*

PLURAL NOUN = <u>face</u>, countenance, physiognomy, lineaments ...*She arranged her features in a bland expression...*

VERB 1 = <u>spotlight</u>, present, promote, set off, emphasize, play up, accentuate, foreground, call attention to, give prominence to, give the full works (*slang*) ...*This event features a stunning catwalk show...*

2 = <u>star</u>, appear, headline, participate, play a part ...*She featured in a Hollywood film...*

febrile (*Formal*) = <u>feverish</u>, hot, fevered, flushed, fiery, inflamed, delirious, pyretic (*Medical*)

feckless = <u>irresponsible</u>, useless, hopeless, incompetent, feeble, worthless, futile, ineffectual, aimless, good-for-nothing, shiftless, weak

federation = <u>union</u>, league, association, alliance, combination, coalition, partnership, consortium, syndicate, confederation, amalgamation, confederacy, entente, Bund (*German*), copartnership, federacy

fed up = <u>cheesed off</u>, down, depressed, bored, tired, annoyed, hacked (off) (*U.S. slang*), weary, gloomy, blue, dismal, discontented, dissatisfied, glum, sick and tired (*informal*), browned-off (*informal*), down in the mouth (*informal*), brassed off (*Brit. slang*)

fee = <u>charge</u>, pay, price, cost, bill, account, payment, wage, reward, hire, salary, compensation, toll, remuneration, recompense, emolument, honorarium, meed (*archaic*)

feeble 1 = <u>weak</u>, failing, exhausted, weakened, delicate, faint, powerless, frail, debilitated, sickly, languid, puny, weedy (*informal*), infirm, effete, enfeebled, doddering, enervated, etiolated, shilpit (*Scot.*) ...*He was old and feeble*... OPPOSITE strong
2 = <u>inadequate</u>, weak, pathetic, insufficient, incompetent, ineffective, inefficient, lame, insignificant, ineffectual, indecisive ...*He said the Government had been feeble*...
3 = <u>unconvincing</u>, poor, thin, weak, slight, tame, pathetic, lame, flimsy, paltry, flat ...*This is a feeble argument*... OPPOSITE effective

feed VERB 1 = <u>cater for</u>, provide for, nourish, provide with food, supply, sustain, nurture, cook for, wine and dine, victual, provision ...*Feeding a hungry family is expensive*...
2 = <u>graze</u>, eat, browse, pasture ...*The cows stopped feeding*...
3 = <u>eat</u>, drink milk, take nourishment ...*When a baby is thirsty, it feeds more often*...
4 = <u>supply</u>, take, send, carry, convey, impart ...*blood vessels that feed blood to the brain*...
5 = <u>disclose</u>, give, tell, reveal, supply, communicate, pass on, impart, divulge, make known ...*He fed information to a rival company*...
6 = <u>encourage</u>, boost, fuel, strengthen, foster, minister to, bolster, fortify, augment, make stronger ...*Wealth is feeding our obsession with house prices*...
NOUN 1 = <u>food</u>, fodder, forage, silage, provender, pasturage ...*a crop grown for animal feed*...
2 (*Informal*) = <u>meal</u>, spread (*informal*), dinner, lunch, tea, breakfast, feast, supper, tuck-in (*informal*), nosh (*slang*), repast, nosh-up (*Brit. slang*) ...*She's had a good feed*...
PHRASES **feed on something** = <u>live on</u>, depend on, devour, exist on, partake of, subsist on ...*The insects breed and feed on particular cacti*...

feel VERB 1 = <u>experience</u>, suffer, bear, go through, endure, undergo, have a sensation of, have ...*He was still feeling pain from a stomach injury*...
2 = <u>touch</u>, handle, manipulate, run your hands over, finger, stroke, paw, maul, caress, fondle ...*The doctor felt his head*...
3 = <u>be aware of</u>, have a sensation of, be sensible of, enjoy ...*He felt her leg against his*...
4 = <u>perceive</u>, sense, detect, discern, know, experience, notice, observe ...*He felt something was nearby*...
5 = <u>grope</u>, explore, fumble, sound ...*He felt his way down the wooden staircase*...
6 = <u>sense</u>, be aware, be convinced, have a feeling, have the impression, intuit, have a hunch, feel in your bones ...*I feel that he still misses her*...
7 = <u>believe</u>, consider, judge, deem, think, hold, be of the opinion that ...*They felt that the police could not guarantee their safety*...
8 = <u>seem</u>, appear, strike you as ...*The air feels wet and cold on these evenings*...
9 = <u>notice</u>, note, observe, perceive, detect, discern ...*The charity is still feeling the effects of revelations about its former president*...
NOUN 1 = <u>texture</u>, finish, touch, surface, surface quality ...*a crisp papery feel*...
2 = <u>impression</u>, feeling, air, sense, quality, atmosphere, mood, aura, ambience, vibes (*slang*) ...*He wanted to get the feel of the place*...
PHRASES **feel for someone** = <u>feel compassion for</u>, pity, feel sorry for, sympathize with, be moved by, be sorry for, empathize, commiserate with, bleed for, feel sympathy for, condole with ...*I really felt for her*...
♦ **feel like something** = <u>want</u>, desire, would like, fancy, wish for, could do with, feel the need for, feel inclined, feel up to, have the inclination for ...*I feel like a little exercise*...

feeler
PHRASES **put out feelers** = <u>make an approach to</u>, probe, test the water, make overtures, make a trial, launch a trial balloon

feeling NOUN 1 = <u>emotion</u>, sentiment ...*Strong feelings of pride welled up in me*...
2 = <u>opinion</u>, view, attitude, belief, point of view, instinct, inclination ...*She has strong feelings about the growth in violence*...
3 = <u>passion</u>, heat, emotion, intensity, warmth, sentimentality ...*a voice that trembles with feeling*...
4 = <u>ardour</u>, love, care, affection, warmth, tenderness, fondness, fervour ...*He never lost his feeling for her*...
5 = <u>sympathy</u>, understanding, concern, pity, appreciation, sensitivity, compassion, sorrow, sensibility, empathy, fellow feeling ...*He felt a rush of feeling for the woman*...
6 = <u>sensation</u>, sense, impression, awareness ...*Focus on the feeling of relaxation*...
7 = <u>sense of touch</u>, sense, perception, sensation, feel, touch ...*After the accident he had no feeling in his legs*...
8 = <u>impression</u>, idea, sense, notion, suspicion, consciousness, hunch, apprehension, inkling, presentiment ...*I have a feeling that everything will come right for us*...
9 = <u>atmosphere</u>, mood, aura, ambience, feel, air, quality, vibes (*slang*) ...*a feeling of opulence and grandeur*...
PLURAL NOUN = <u>emotions</u>, ego, self-esteem, sensibilities, susceptibilities, sensitivities ...*He was afraid of hurting my feelings*...
PHRASES **bad feeling** = <u>hostility</u>, anger, dislike, resentment, bitterness, distrust, enmity, ill feeling, ill will, upset ...*There's been some bad feeling between them*... ♦ **fellow feeling** = <u>sympathy</u>, understanding, concern, care, pity, compassion, feeling, empathy ...*There is genuine fellow feeling for the victims*...

feign = <u>pretend</u>, affect, assume, put on, devise, forge, fake, imitate, simulate, sham, act, fabricate, counterfeit, give the appearance of, dissemble, make a show of

feigned = <u>pretended</u>, affected, assumed, false, artificial, fake, imitation, simulated, sham, pseudo (*informal*), fabricated, counterfeit, spurious, ersatz, insincere

feint = <u>bluff</u>, manoeuvre, dodge, mock attack, play, blind, distraction, pretence, expedient, ruse, artifice, gambit, subterfuge, stratagem, wile

felicity 1 = <u>happiness</u>, joy, ecstasy, bliss, delectation, blessedness, blissfulness ...*a period of domestic felicity*...
2 = <u>aptness</u>, grace, effectiveness, suitability, propriety, appropriateness, applicability, becomingness, suitableness ...*his felicity of word and phrase*...

feline 1 = <u>catlike</u>, leonine ...*a black, furry, feline creature*...
2 = <u>graceful</u>, flowing, smooth, elegant, sleek, slinky, sinuous, stealthy ...*He moves with feline pace*...

fell 1 = <u>cut down</u>, cut, level, demolish, flatten, knock down, hew, raze ...*Badly infected trees should be felled*...
2 = <u>knock down</u>, floor, flatten, strike down, prostrate, deck (*slang*) ...*A blow on the head felled him*...

fellow [ADJECTIVE] = <u>co-</u>, similar, related, allied, associate, associated, affiliated, akin, like ...*My fellow inmates treated me with kindness*...
[NOUN] 1 (*Old-fashioned*) = <u>man</u>, boy, person, individual, customer (*informal*), character, guy (*informal*), bloke (*Brit. informal*), punter (*informal*), chap (*informal*) ...*He appeared to be a fine fellow*...
2 = <u>associate</u>, colleague, peer, co-worker, member, friend, partner, equal, companion, comrade, crony, compeer ...*He stood out from all his fellows at work*...

fellowship 1 = <u>society</u>, club, league, association, organization, guild, fraternity, brotherhood, sisterhood, order, sodality ...*the National Youth Fellowship*...
2 = <u>camaraderie</u>, intimacy, communion, familiarity, brotherhood, companionship, sociability, amity, kindliness, fraternization, companionability, intercourse ...*a sense of community and fellowship*...

feminine 1 = <u>womanly</u>, pretty, soft, gentle, tender, modest, delicate, graceful, girlie, girlish, ladylike ...*the ideal of feminine beauty*... [OPPOSITE] masculine
2 = <u>effeminate</u>, camp (*informal*), weak, unmanly, effete, womanish, unmasculine ...*men with feminine gestures*...

femininity = <u>womanliness</u>, delicacy, softness, womanhood, gentleness, girlishness, feminineness, muliebrity

fen = <u>marsh</u>, moss (*Scot.*), swamp, bog, slough, quagmire, holm (*dialect*), morass

fence [NOUN] = <u>barrier</u>, wall, defence, guard, railings, paling, shield, hedge, barricade, hedgerow, rampart, palisade, stockade, barbed wire ...*They climbed over the fence into the field*...
[VERB] *often with* **in** *or* **off** = <u>enclose</u>, surround, bound, hedge, pound, protect, separate, guard, defend, secure, pen, restrict, confine, fortify, encircle, coop, impound, circumscribe ...*He intends to fence in about 100 acres of land*...
[PHRASES] **sit on the fence** = <u>be uncommitted</u>, be uncertain, be undecided, vacillate, be in two minds, blow hot and cold (*informal*), be irresolute, avoid committing yourself ...*He is sitting on the fence,*

refusing to commit himself...

fend
[PHRASES] **fend for yourself** = <u>look after yourself</u>, support yourself, sustain yourself, take care of yourself, provide for yourself, make do, make provision for yourself, shift for yourself ...*He was just left to fend for himself*... ♦ **fend something** *or* **someone off** 1 = <u>deflect</u>, resist, parry, avert, ward off, stave off, turn aside, hold *or* keep at bay ...*He fended off questions from the Press*... 2 = <u>beat off</u>, resist, parry, avert, deflect, repel, drive back, ward off, stave off, repulse, keep off, turn aside, hold *or* keep at bay ...*He raised his hand to fend off the blow*...

feral 1 = <u>wild</u>, untamed, uncultivated, undomesticated, unbroken ...*There are many feral cats roaming the area*...
2 = <u>savage</u>, fierce, brutal, ferocious, fell, wild, vicious, bestial ...*the feral scowl of the young street mugger*...

ferment [NOUN] = <u>commotion</u>, turmoil, unrest, turbulence, trouble, heat, excitement, glow, fever, disruption, frenzy, stew, furore, uproar, agitation, tumult, hubbub, brouhaha, imbroglio, state of unrest ...*The country is in a state of political ferment*...
[OPPOSITE] tranquillity
[VERB] 1 = <u>brew</u>, froth, concoct, effervesce, work, rise, heat, boil, bubble, foam, seethe, leaven ...*red wine made from grapes left to ferment for three weeks*...
2 = <u>stir up</u>, excite, provoke, rouse, agitate, inflame, incite ...*They tried to ferment political unrest*...
3 = <u>smoulder</u>, seethe, fester, heat, boil, foment ...*His anger still ferments after a decade*...
➤ **foment**

ferocious 1 = <u>fierce</u>, violent, savage, ravening, predatory, feral, rapacious, wild ...*By its nature a lion is ferocious*... [OPPOSITE] gentle
2 = <u>cruel</u>, bitter, brutal, vicious, ruthless, relentless, barbaric, merciless, brutish, bloodthirsty, barbarous, pitiless, tigerish ...*Fighting has been ferocious*...

ferocity = <u>savagery</u>, violence, cruelty, brutality, ruthlessness, inhumanity, wildness, barbarity, viciousness, fierceness, rapacity, bloodthirstiness, savageness, ferociousness

ferry [NOUN] = <u>ferry boat</u>, boat, ship, passenger boat, packet boat, packet ...*They crossed the river by ferry*...
[VERB] = <u>transport</u>, bring, carry, ship, take, run, shuttle, convey, chauffeur ...*They ferried in more soldiers to help with the search*...

fertile = <u>productive</u>, rich, flowering, lush, fat, yielding, prolific, abundant, plentiful, fruitful, teeming, luxuriant, generative, fecund, fruit-bearing, flowing with milk and honey, plenteous [OPPOSITE] barren

fertility = <u>fruitfulness</u>, abundance, richness, fecundity, luxuriance, productiveness

fertilization = <u>insemination</u>, propagation, procreation, implantation, pollination, impregnation

fertilize 1 = <u>inseminate</u>, impregnate, pollinate, make pregnant, fructify, make fruitful, fecundate ...*sperm levels needed to fertilize the egg*...
2 = <u>enrich</u>, feed, compost, manure, mulch, top-dress, dress ...*grown in recently fertilized soil*...

fertilizer = <u>compost</u>, muck, manure, dung, guano, marl, bone meal, dressing

fervent = <u>ardent</u>, earnest, enthusiastic, fervid, passionate, warm, excited, emotional, intense, flaming, eager, animated, fiery, ecstatic, devout, heartfelt, impassioned, zealous, vehement, perfervid (*literary*) OPPOSITE apathetic

---

Word Power

fervid – Care should be taken when using *fervid* as an alternative to *fervent*. Although both come from the same root and share the meaning 'intense, ardent', *fervent* has largely positive connotations, and is associated with hopes, wishes, and beliefs, or admirers, supporters, and fans. Apart from being used less often than *fervent*, *fervid* is chiefly negative: *in the fervid politics of New York city*. A *fervent kiss* from an admirer would probably be welcome; a *fervid* one would not.

---

fervour = <u>ardour</u>, passion, enthusiasm, excitement, intensity, warmth, animation, zeal, eagerness, vehemence, earnestness, fervency

fester 1 = <u>intensify</u>, gall, smoulder, chafe, irk, rankle, aggravate ...*Resentments are starting to fester...*
2 = <u>putrefy</u>, decay, become infected, become inflamed, suppurate, ulcerate, maturate, gather ...*The wound is festering and gangrene has set in...*

festering 1 = <u>venomous</u>, vicious, smouldering, virulent, black-hearted ...*recrimination and festering resentment...*
2 = <u>septic</u>, infected, poisonous, inflamed, pussy, suppurating, ulcerated, purulent, maturating, gathering ...*afflicted by festering sores...*

festival 1 = <u>celebration</u>, fair, carnival, gala, treat, fête, entertainment, jubilee, fiesta, festivities, jamboree, -fest, field day ...*The Festival will provide spectacles like river pageants...*
2 = <u>holy day</u>, holiday, feast, commemoration, feast day, red-letter day, saint's day, fiesta, fête, anniversary ...*the Jewish festival of the Passover...*

festive = <u>celebratory</u>, happy, holiday, carnival, jolly, merry, gala, hearty, jubilant, cheery, joyous, joyful, jovial, convivial, gleeful, back-slapping, Christmassy, mirthful, sportive, light-hearted, festal, gay OPPOSITE mournful

festivity 1 = <u>merrymaking</u>, fun, pleasure, amusement, mirth, gaiety, merriment, revelry, conviviality, joviality, joyfulness, jollification, sport ...*There was a general air of festivity and abandon...*
2 *often plural* = <u>celebration</u>, party, festival, entertainment, rave (*Brit. slang*), beano (*Brit. slang*), fun and games, rave-up (*Brit. slang*), jollification, festive event, carousal, festive proceedings, hooley *or* hoolie (*chiefly Irish & N.Z.*) ...*The festivities included a firework display...*

festoon VERB = <u>decorate</u>, deck, array, drape, garland, swathe, bedeck, wreathe, beribbon, engarland, hang ...*The temples are festooned with lights...*

NOUN = <u>decoration</u>, garland, swathe, wreath, swag, lei, chaplet ...*festoons of laurel and magnolia...*

fetch VERB 1 = <u>bring</u>, pick up, collect, go and get, get, carry, deliver, conduct, transport, go for, obtain, escort, convey, retrieve ...*She fetched a towel from the bathroom...*
2 = <u>sell for</u>, make, raise, earn, realize, go for, yield, bring in ...*The painting is expected to fetch two million pounds...*
PHRASES **fetch up** = <u>end up</u>, reach, arrive, turn up, come, stop, land, halt, finish up ...*We eventually fetched up at their house...*

fetching = <u>attractive</u>, sweet, charming, enchanting, fascinating, intriguing, cute, enticing, captivating, alluring, winsome

fête *or* **fete** NOUN = <u>fair</u>, festival, gala, bazaar, garden party, sale of work ...*The Vicar is organizing a church fete...*
VERB = <u>entertain</u>, welcome, honour, make much of, wine and dine, hold a reception for (someone), lionize, bring out the red carpet for (someone), kill the fatted calf for (someone), treat ...*The actress was fêted at a special dinner...*

fetish 1 = <u>fixation</u>, obsession, mania, thing (*informal*), idée fixe (*French*) ...*I've got a bit of a shoe fetish...*
2 = <u>talisman</u>, amulet, cult object ...*Tribal elders carried the sacred fetishes...*

fetter VERB 1 = <u>restrict</u>, bind, confine, curb, restrain, hamstring, hamper, encumber, clip someone's wings, trammel, straiten ...*He would not be fettered by bureaucracy...*
2 = <u>chain</u>, tie, tie up, shackle, hobble, hold captive, manacle, gyve (*archaic*), put a straitjacket on ...*My foes fettered me hand and foot...*
PLURAL NOUN 1 = <u>restraints</u>, checks, curbs, constraints, captivity, obstructions, bondage, hindrances ...*without the fetters of restrictive rules...*
2 = <u>chains</u>, bonds, irons, shackles, manacles, leg irons, gyves (*archaic*), bilboes ...*He saw a boy in fetters in the dungeon...*

feud NOUN = <u>hostility</u>, row, conflict, argument, faction, falling out, disagreement, rivalry, contention, quarrel, grudge, strife, bickering, vendetta, discord, enmity, broil, bad blood, estrangement, dissension ...*a long and bitter feud between families...*
VERB = <u>quarrel</u>, row, clash, dispute, fall out, contend, brawl, war, squabble, duel, bicker, be at odds, be at daggers drawn ...*He feuded with his ex-wife...*

fever 1 = <u>ague</u>, high temperature, feverishness, pyrexia (*Medical*) ...*Symptoms of the disease include fever and weight loss...*
2 = <u>excitement</u>, heat, passion, intensity, flush, turmoil, ecstasy, frenzy, ferment, agitation, fervour, restlessness, delirium ...*I got married in a fever of excitement...*
(Related Words)
adjective : febrile

feverish *or* **fevered** 1 = <u>frantic</u>, excited, desperate, distracted, frenzied, impatient, obsessive, restless, agitated, frenetic, overwrought ...*a state of feverish* excitement... OPPOSITE > calm

2 = <u>hot</u>, burning, flaming, fevered, flushed, hectic, inflamed, febrile, pyretic (*Medical*) ...*She looked feverish, her eyes glistened*...

few DETERMINER = <u>not many</u>, one or two, hardly any, scarcely any, rare, thin, scattered, insufficient, scarce, scant, meagre, negligible, sporadic, sparse, infrequent, scanty, inconsiderable ...*In some districts there are few survivors*... OPPOSITE > many
PRONOUN = <u>a small number</u>, a handful, a sprinkling, a scattering, some, scarcely any ...*A strict diet is appropriate for only a few*...
PHRASES **few and far between** = <u>scarce</u>, rare, unusual, scattered, irregular, uncommon, in short supply, hard to come by, infrequent, thin on the ground, widely spaced, seldom met with ...*Successful women politicians were few and far between*...

fiancé *or* **fiancée** = <u>husband-</u> *or* <u>wife-to-be</u>, intended, betrothed, prospective spouse, future husband *or* wife

fiasco = <u>flop</u>, failure, disaster, ruin, mess (*informal*), catastrophe, rout, debacle, cock-up (*Brit. slang*), washout (*informal*)

fib = <u>lie</u>, story, fiction, untruth, whopper (*informal*), porky (*Brit. slang*), pork pie (*Brit. slang*), white lie, prevarication

fibre NOUN = <u>thread</u>, strand, filament, tendril, pile, texture, staple, wisp, fibril ...*a variety of coloured fibres*...
PHRASES **moral fibre** = <u>strength of character</u>, strength, resolution, resolve, stamina, backbone, toughness ...*They all lacked courage, backbone or moral fibre*...

fickle = <u>capricious</u>, variable, volatile, unpredictable, unstable, unfaithful, temperamental, mercurial, unsteady, faithless, changeable, quicksilver, vacillating, fitful, flighty, blowing hot and cold, mutable, irresolute, inconstant OPPOSITE > constant

fiction **1** = <u>tale</u>, story, novel, legend, myth, romance, fable, storytelling, narration, creative writing, work of imagination ...*She is a writer of historical fiction*...
2 = <u>imagination</u>, fancy, fantasy, creativity ...*a story of truth or fiction*...
3 = <u>lie</u>, fancy, fantasy, invention, improvisation, fabrication, concoction, falsehood, untruth, porky (*Brit. slang*), pork pie (*Brit. slang*), urban myth, tall story, urban legend, cock and bull story (*informal*), figment of the imagination ...*Total recycling is a fiction*...

fictional = <u>imaginary</u>, made-up, invented, legendary, unreal, nonexistent

fictitious **1** = <u>false</u>, made-up, bogus, untrue, non-existent, fabricated, counterfeit, feigned, spurious, apocryphal ...*a source of fictitious rumours*...
OPPOSITE > true
2 = <u>imaginary</u>, imagined, made-up, assumed, invented, artificial, improvised, mythical, unreal, fanciful, make-believe ...*Persons portrayed in this production are fictitious*...

fiddle VERB **1** *usually with* **with** = <u>fidget</u>, play, finger,

toy, tamper, trifle, mess about *or* around ...*She fiddled with a pen on the desk*...
2 *usually with* **with** = <u>tinker</u>, adjust, interfere, mess about *or* around ...*He fiddled with the radio dial*...
3 (*Informal*) = <u>cheat</u>, cook (*informal*), fix, manoeuvre (*informal*), graft (*informal*), diddle (*informal*), wangle (*informal*), gerrymander, finagle (*informal*) ...*Stop fiddling your expenses account*...
NOUN **1** (*Brit. informal*) = <u>fraud</u>, racket, scam (*slang*), piece of sharp practice, fix, sting (*informal*), graft (*informal*), swindle, wangle (*informal*) ...*legitimate businesses that act as a cover for tax fiddles*...
2 = <u>violin</u> ...*He played the fiddle at local dances*...

fiddling = <u>trivial</u>, small, petty, trifling, insignificant, unimportant, pettifogging, futile

fidelity **1** = <u>loyalty</u>, faith, integrity, devotion, allegiance, constancy, faithfulness, dependability, trustworthiness, troth (*archaic*), fealty, staunchness, devotedness, lealty (*archaic or Scot.*), true-heartedness ...*I had to promise fidelity to the Queen*...
OPPOSITE > disloyalty
2 = <u>accuracy</u>, precision, correspondence, closeness, adherence, faithfulness, exactitude, exactness, scrupulousness, preciseness ...*the fidelity of these early documents*... OPPOSITE > inaccuracy

fidget = <u>move restlessly</u>, fiddle (*informal*), bustle, twitch, fret, squirm, chafe, jiggle, jitter (*informal*), be like a cat on hot bricks (*informal*), worry

field NOUN **1** = <u>meadow</u>, land, green, lea (*poetic*), pasture, mead (*archaic*), greensward (*archaic or literary*) ...*They went for walks together in the fields*...
2 = <u>speciality</u>, line, area, department, environment, territory, discipline, province, pale, confines, sphere, domain, specialty, sphere of Influence, purview, metier, sphere of activity, bailiwick, sphere of interest, sphere of study ...*They are both experts in their field*...
3 = <u>line</u>, reach, range, limits, bounds, sweep, scope ...*Our field of vision is surprisingly wide*...
4 = <u>competitors</u>, competition, candidates, runners, applicants, entrants, contestants ...*The two most experienced athletes led the field*...
VERB **1** (*Informal*) = <u>deal with</u>, answer, handle, respond to, reply to, deflect, turn aside ...*He fielded questions from journalists*...
2 (*Sport*) = <u>retrieve</u>, return, stop, catch, pick up ...*He fielded the ball and threw it at the wicket*...

fiend **1** = <u>brute</u>, monster, savage, beast, degenerate, barbarian, ogre, ghoul ...*a saint to his parents and a fiend to his children*...
2 (*Informal*) = <u>enthusiast</u>, fan, addict, freak (*informal*), fanatic, maniac, energumen ...*a strong-tea fiend*...
3 = <u>demon</u>, devil, evil spirit, hellhound ...*She is a fiend incarnate, leading these people to eternal damnation*...

fiendish **1** = <u>clever</u>, brilliant, imaginative, shrewd, cunning, ingenious ...*a fiendish plan*...
2 = <u>difficult</u>, involved, complex, puzzling, baffling, intricate, thorny, knotty ...*It is a fiendish question without an easy answer*...
3 = <u>wicked</u>, cruel, savage, monstrous, malicious, satanic, malignant, unspeakable, atrocious, inhuman, diabolical, implacable, malevolent, hellish, devilish,

infernal, accursed, ungodly, black-hearted, demoniac
…*a fiendish act of wickedness*…

fierce 1 = <u>ferocious</u>, wild, dangerous, cruel, savage, brutal, aggressive, menacing, vicious, fiery, murderous, uncontrollable, feral, untamed, barbarous, fell (*archaic*), threatening, baleful, truculent, tigerish, aggers (*Austral. slang*), biffo (*Austral. slang*) …*the teeth of some fierce animal*… OPPOSITE gentle
2 = <u>intense</u>, strong, keen, passionate, relentless, cut-throat …*He inspires fierce loyalty in his friends*…
3 = <u>stormy</u>, strong, powerful, violent, intense, raging, furious, howling, uncontrollable, boisterous, tumultuous, tempestuous, blustery, inclement …*Two climbers were trapped by a fierce storm*… OPPOSITE tranquil

fiercely = <u>ferociously</u>, savagely, passionately, furiously, viciously, menacingly, tooth and nail, in a frenzy, like cat and dog, frenziedly, tigerishly, with no holds barred, tempestuously, with bared teeth, uncontrolledly

fiery 1 = <u>burning</u>, flaming, glowing, blazing, on fire, red-hot, ablaze, in flames, aflame, afire …*People set up fiery barricades*…
2 = <u>excitable</u>, violent, fierce, passionate, irritable, impetuous, irascible, peppery, hot-headed, choleric …*a red-head's fiery temper*…

fiesta = <u>carnival</u>, party, holiday, fair, fête, festival, celebration, feast, revel, jubilee, festivity, jamboree, Mardi Gras, revelry, Saturnalia, saint's day, merrymaking, carousal, bacchanal *or* bacchanalia, gala

fight VERB 1 = <u>oppose</u>, campaign against, dispute, contest, resist, defy, contend, withstand, stand up to, take issue with, make a stand against …*She devoted her life to fighting poverty*…
2 = <u>strive</u>, battle, push, struggle, contend …*He had to fight hard for his place in the team*…
3 = <u>battle</u>, assault, combat, war with, go to war, do battle, wage war, take up arms, bear arms against, engage in hostilities, carry on war, engage …*The Sioux fought other tribes for territorial rights*…
4 = <u>engage in</u>, conduct, wage, pursue, carry on …*They fought a war against injustice*…
5 = <u>take the field</u>, cross swords, taste battle …*He fought in the war and was taken prisoner*…
6 = <u>brawl</u>, clash, scrap (*informal*), exchange blows, struggle, row, tilt, wrestle, feud, grapple, tussle, joust, come to blows, lock horns, fight like Kilkenny cats …*a lot of unruly drunks fighting*…
7 = <u>quarrel</u>, argue, row, dispute, fall out (*informal*), squabble, wrangle, bicker …*She was always arguing and fighting with him*…
8 = <u>box</u>, spar with, exchange blows with …*I'd like to fight him for the title*…
NOUN 1 = <u>battle</u>, campaign, movement, struggle …*I will continue the fight for justice*…
2 = <u>conflict</u>, war, action, clash, contest, encounter, brush, combat, engagement, hostilities, skirmish, passage of arms …*They used to be allies in the fight against the old Communist regime*…
3 = <u>brawl</u>, set-to (*informal*), riot, scrap (*informal*),

confrontation, rumble (*U.S. & N.Z. slang*), fray, duel, skirmish, head-to-head, tussle, scuffle, free-for-all (*informal*), fracas, altercation, dogfight, joust, dissension, affray (*Law*), shindig (*informal*), scrimmage, sparring match, exchange of blows, shindy (*informal*), melee *or* mêlée, biffo (*Austral. slang*) …*He got a bloody nose in a fight*…
4 = <u>row</u>, argument, dispute, quarrel, squabble …*He had a big fight with his Dad last night*…
5 = <u>match</u>, contest, bout, battle, competition, struggle, set-to, encounter, engagement, head-to-head, boxing match …*The referee stopped the fight in the second round*…
6 = <u>resistance</u>, spirit, pluck, militancy, mettle, belligerence, will to resist, gameness, pluckiness …*We had a lot of fight in us*…
PHRASES **fight shy of something** = <u>avoid</u>, shun, steer clear of, duck out of (*informal*), keep at arm's length, hang back from, keep aloof from …*It's no use fighting shy of publicity*…

fighter 1 = <u>combatant</u>, battler, militant, contender, contestant, belligerent, antagonist, disputant …*She's a real fighter and has always defied the odds*…
2 = <u>boxer</u>, wrestler, bruiser (*informal*), pugilist, prize fighter …*a tough little street fighter*…
3 = <u>soldier</u>, warrior, fighting man, man-at-arms …*His guerrillas are widely accepted as some of the best fighters in the Afghan resistance*…

fighting = <u>battle</u>, war, conflict, combat, hostilities, warfare, bloodshed

figment = <u>invention</u>, production, fancy, creation, fiction, fable, improvisation, fabrication, falsehood

figurative = <u>symbolical</u>, representative, abstract, allegorical, typical, tropical (*Rhetoric*), imaginative, ornate, descriptive, fanciful, pictorial, metaphorical, flowery, florid, poetical, emblematical OPPOSITE literal

figure NOUN 1 = <u>digit</u>, character, symbol, number, numeral, cipher …*deduct the second figure from the first*…
2 = <u>outline</u>, form, shape, shadow, profile, silhouette …*A figure appeared in the doorway*…
3 = <u>shape</u>, build, body, frame, proportions, chassis (*slang*), torso, physique …*Take pride in your health and your figure*…
4 = <u>personage</u>, force, face (*informal*), leader, person, individual, character, presence, somebody, personality, celebrity, worthy, notable, big name, dignitary, notability …*The movement is supported by key figures*…
5 = <u>diagram</u>, drawing, picture, illustration, representation, sketch, emblem …*Figure 26 shows a small circular garden of herbs*…
6 = <u>design</u>, shape, pattern, device, motif, depiction …*The impulsive singer had the figure cut into his shaven hair*…
7 = <u>price</u>, cost, value, amount, total, sum …*It's hard to put a figure on the damage*…
VERB 1 = <u>make sense</u>, follow, be expected, add up, go without saying, seem reasonable …*When I finished, he said, 'Yeah. That figures'*…
2 *usually with in* = <u>feature</u>, act, appear, contribute to,

be included, be mentioned, play a part, be featured, have a place in, be conspicuous ...*I didn't figure in his plans...*
3 = <u>calculate</u>, work out, compute, tot up, add, total, count, reckon, sum, tally ...*Figure the interest rate...*
PHRASES **figure on something** (*U.S. informal*) = <u>plan on</u>, depend on, rely on, count on, bargain on ...*I never figured on that scenario...* ◆ **figure out** = <u>calculate</u>, reckon, work out, compute ...*I want to figure out how much it'll cost...* ◆ **figure something** or **someone out** = <u>understand</u>, make out, fathom, make head or tail of (*informal*), see, solve, resolve, comprehend, make sense of, decipher, think through, suss (out) (*slang*) ...*How do you figure that out?... ...I can't figure that guy out at all...*

figurehead = <u>nominal head</u>, leader in name only, titular head, front man, name, token, dummy, puppet, mouthpiece, cipher, nonentity, straw man (*chiefly U.S.*), man of straw

figure of speech = <u>expression</u>, image, turn of phrase, trope
➤ **figures of speech**

filament = <u>strand</u>, string, wire, fibre, thread, staple, wisp, cilium (*Biology & Zoology*), fibril, pile

file¹ **NOUN** **1** = <u>folder</u>, case, portfolio, binder ...*a file of insurance papers...*
2 = <u>dossier</u>, record, information, data, documents, case history, report, case ...*We have files on people's tax details...*
3 = <u>line</u>, row, chain, string, column, queue, procession ...*A file of soldiers, spaced and on both sides...*
VERB **1** = <u>arrange</u>, order, classify, put in place, slot in (*informal*), categorize, pigeonhole, put in order ...*Papers are filed alphabetically...*
2 = <u>register</u>, record, enter, log, put on record ...*They have filed formal complaints...*
3 = <u>march</u>, troop, parade, walk in line, walk behind one another ...*They filed into the room and sat down...*

file² = <u>smooth</u>, shape, polish, rub, refine, scrape, rasp, burnish, rub down, abrade ...*shaping and filing nails...*

filibuster **NOUN** = <u>obstruction</u>, delay, postponement, hindrance, procrastination ...*The Senator used a filibuster to stop the bill...*
VERB = <u>obstruct</u>, prevent, delay, put off, hinder, play for time, procrastinate ...*They threatened to filibuster until senate adjourns...*

filigree = <u>wirework</u>, lace, lattice, tracery, lacework

fill **VERB** **1** = <u>top up</u>, fill up, make full, become full, brim over ...*While the bath was filling, he undressed...*
2 = <u>swell</u>, expand, inflate, become bloated, extend, balloon, fatten ...*Your lungs fill with air...*
3 = <u>pack</u>, crowd, squeeze, cram, throng ...*Thousands of people filled the streets...*
4 = <u>stock</u>, supply, store, pack, load, furnish, replenish ...*I fill the shelves in a supermarket until 12pm...*
5 = <u>plug</u>, close, stop, seal, cork, bung, block up, stop up ...*Fill the holes with plaster...*
6 = <u>saturate</u>, charge, pervade, permeate, imbue,

impregnate, suffuse, overspread ...*The barn was filled with the smell of hay...*
7 = <u>fulfil</u>, hold, perform, carry out, occupy, take up, execute, discharge, officiate ...*She filled the role of diplomat's wife for many years...*
8 *often with* **up** = <u>satisfy</u>, stuff, gorge, glut, satiate, sate ...*They filled themselves with chocolate cake...*
PHRASES **fill in for someone** = <u>replace</u>, represent, substitute for, cover for, take over from, act for, stand in for, sub for, deputize for ...*relief employees who fill in for workers while on break...* ◆ **fill someone in** (*Informal*) = <u>inform</u>, acquaint, advise of, apprise of, bring up to date with, update with, put wise to (*slang*), give the facts or background of ...*I'll fill him in on the details...* ◆ **fill something in** = <u>complete</u>, answer, fill up, fill out (*U.S.*) ...*Fill in the coupon and send it to the above address...* ◆ **your fill** = <u>sufficient</u>, enough, plenty, ample, all you want, a sufficiency ...*We have had our fill of disappointments...*

filling **NOUN** = <u>stuffing</u>, padding, filler, wadding, inside, insides, contents, innards (*informal*) ...*Make the filling from down or feathers...*
ADJECTIVE = <u>satisfying</u>, heavy, square, substantial, ample ...*a well-spiced and filling meal...*

fillip = <u>boost</u>, push, spur, spice, incentive, stimulus, prod, zest, goad

film **NOUN** **1** = <u>movie</u>, picture, flick (*slang*), motion picture ...*He appeared in the star role of the film...*
2 = <u>cinema</u>, the movies ...*Film is a business with limited opportunities for actresses...*
3 = <u>layer</u>, covering, cover, skin, coating, coat, dusting, tissue, membrane, scum, gauze, integument, pellicle ...*The sea is coated with a film of sewage...*
4 = <u>haze</u>, cloud, blur, mist, veil, opacity, haziness, mistiness ...*There was a sort of film over my eyes...*
VERB **1** = <u>photograph</u>, record, shoot, video, videotape, take ...*We filmed the scene in one hour...*
2 = <u>adapt for the screen</u>, make into a film ...*He filmed her life story...*
　　　Related Words
　　　adjective: cinematic

filter **VERB** **1** = <u>purify</u>, treat, strain, refine, riddle, sift, sieve, winnow, filtrate, screen ...*The best prevention for cholera is to filter water...*
2 = <u>trickle</u>, leach, seep, percolate, well, escape, leak, penetrate, ooze, dribble, exude ...*Water filtered through the peat...*
NOUN = <u>sieve</u>, mesh, gauze, strainer, membrane, riddle, sifter ...*a paper coffee filter...*

filth **1** = <u>dirt</u>, refuse, pollution, muck, garbage, sewage, contamination, dung, sludge, squalor, grime, faeces, slime, excrement, nastiness, carrion, excreta, crud (*slang*), foulness, putrefaction, ordure, defilement, kak (*S. African taboo slang*), grot (*slang*), filthiness, uncleanness, putrescence, foul matter ...*tons of filth and sewage...*
2 = <u>obscenity</u>, corruption, pornography, indecency, impurity, vulgarity, smut, vileness, dirty-mindedness ...*The dialogue was all filth and innuendo...*

filthy **1** = <u>dirty</u>, nasty, foul, polluted, vile, squalid, slimy, unclean, putrid, faecal, scummy, scuzzy (*slang,*

Word Power: Figures of speech

Writers and speakers often use figures of speech for effect, or to make what they are saying or writing more interesting. Here are the figures of speech you are most likely to come across:

alliteration: the use of the same sound at the beginning of several words or syllables, as in *Round the rugged rock the ragged rascal ran.*

analogy: a comparison between two things, made to show a similarity between them: *He made an analogy between an atom and the solar system.*

antithesis: the juxtaposition of contrasting ideas or words to produce an effect of balance: *My words fly up, my thoughts remain below.*

apostrophe: as well as referring to a punctuation mark, the word *apostrophe* has a second meaning; it is a rhetorical digression from a speech, especially to an imaginary or absent person, or to a personification (see **personification** below): *Beethoven, you'd be turning in your grave if you knew how they were murdering your Ninth Symphony!*

circumlocution *or* **periphrasis:** two words used to describe an indirect way of expressing something, for example saying *I don't think the two events are entirely unconnected* instead of the more direct *I think the two events are connected.*

climax: a rhetorical device in which a series of sentences, clauses, or phrases are arranged by order of increasing intensity: *Your comments were unnecessary, unhelpful, and downright bad manners.*

emphasis: stress given to a particular syllable, word or phrase in speaking: *Well, I like him even if you don't.*

hyperbaton: a rhetorical device in which the normal order of words is reversed, as in *Now this lifestyle I could definitely get used to!*

hyperbole: a deliberate exaggeration used for effect: *I've told you a million times not to do that.*

inversion: the rhetorical reversal of the normal order of words, as in *Weeping left she sorrowfully.*

irony: the humorous or mildly sarcastic use of words to mean the opposite of what they literally mean: *And you, of course, have never told a lie in your life* (when you are actually saying that the other person has lied, and you know it).

litotes *or* **meiosis:** two words which mean the used of understatement for rhetorical effect, especially using negation with a word instead of using the word's opposite, for example saying *She was not a little upset* instead of *She was very upset.*

malapropism: the unintentional misuse of a word because you have confused it with another word which sounds similar, especially when this creates an amusing effect, as in *He was under the affluence of alcohol* instead of *He was under the influence of alcohol.* This figure of speech gets its name from **Mrs. Malaprop,** a character in Sheridan's play *The Rivals* (1775), who habitually misused words to comic effect.

metaphor: a figure of speech in which a word or phrase is used to refer to an object or action which it does not literally mean, in order to imply a resemblance between them, for example *He is a lion in battle* (meaning he is **like** a lion in battle, not that he actually **is** a lion).

metonymy: the substitution of a word which refers to an attribute of something for the word which means the thing itself, for example *the crown* when used to refer to a monarch (who wears the crown).

onomatopoeia: the formation of a word whose sound imitates the sound of the noise or action it is used to describe, such as *hiss, bubble,* or *thwack.*

oxymoron: an effect in which two contradictory terms are used in conjunction, as in *a living death.*

parenthesis: a phrase, often explanatory or qualifying, which is inserted into a passage with which it is not grammatically connected. It is marked off from the rest of the passage by brackets or dashes, and the brackets used are called **parentheses** (plural form of **parenthesis**), for example *My father (who, incidentally, is an expert in this field) thinks you are mistaken.*

personification *or* **prosopop(o)eia:** two words which mean the representation of an abstract quality or idea in the form of a person, creature, etc., as in *Old Father Time* or *the Grim Reaper.*

pleonasm: the use of more words than necessary to express an idea, as in *a tiny little baby*, where *tiny* and *little* mean the same thing, and a baby is usually little in any case.

repetition: the act of repeating a word or phrase, as in *You should never, never, never play with matches.*

rhetorical question: a question to which no answer is required or expected, used especially for dramatic effect, for example *Who knows how this will end?* (with the implication that nobody knows).

sarcasm: mocking or ironic language used to convey scorn or insult, as in *I don't suppose it occurred to you to check your facts first?*

simile: a figure of speech which expresses the resemblance between one thing and another, usually including the words **like** or **as**: *as light as a feather; This place is like a pigsty.* The difference between a metaphor and a simile is that a simile's wording says that one thing is *like* another, while a metaphor's wording says one thing *is* the other (although it is not supposed to be taken literally).

spoonerism: the transposition of the initial sounds of a pair of words, often with an amusingly ambiguous result, for example *Let's drink a toast to the queer old dean* instead of *Let's drink a toast to the dear old queen.* This figure of speech gets its name from the **Reverend W A Spooner** (1844-1930), an English clergyman renowned for doing this.

synechdoche: a figure of speech in which a part is substituted for a whole, or a whole for a part, as in *50 head of cattle* for *50 cows* (not just their heads), or *the army* for *a soldier*.

tautology: the unnecessary use of words which merely repeat elements of the meaning conveyed by other words already used, for example *Will these supplies be sufficient enough?* instead of *Will these supplies be sufficient?* or *Will these supplies be enough?* (*Sufficient* and *enough* mean the same thing, so only one or the other is needed.)

tmesis: the insertion of a word or words between the parts of another word, as in *I'm abso-bloody-lutely furious!*

zeugma or **syllepsis:** two names for the use of a word to govern or modify two or more words, although it is only appropriate to one of them or it has a different sense with each, for amusing effect, for example *Mr. Pickwick took his hat and his leave* (Charles Dickens) or *She departed in tears and a carriage.*

---

chiefly U.S.), feculent, festy (*Austral. slang*) ...*The water looks stale and filthy...*

2 = <u>grimy</u>, black, muddy, smoky, blackened, grubby, sooty, unwashed, mucky, scuzzy (*slang, chiefly U.S.*), begrimed, mud-encrusted, miry, festy (*Austral. slang*) ...*He always wore a filthy old jacket...*

3 = <u>obscene</u>, foul, corrupt, coarse, indecent, pornographic, suggestive, lewd, depraved, foul-mouthed, X-rated (*informal*), bawdy, impure, smutty, licentious, dirty-minded ...*The play was full of filthy foul language...*

4 = <u>despicable</u>, mean, low, base, offensive, vicious, vile, contemptible, scurvy ...*'You filthy swine!' Penelope shouted...*

final 1 = <u>last</u>, latest, end, closing, finishing, concluding, ultimate, terminal, last-minute, eventual, terminating ...*the final book in the series...* OPPOSITE first

2 = <u>irrevocable</u>, absolute, decisive, definitive, decided, finished, settled, definite, conclusive, irrefutable, incontrovertible, unalterable, determinate ...*The judge's decision is final...*

finale = <u>climax</u>, ending, close, conclusion, culmination, denouement, last part, epilogue, last act, crowning glory, finis OPPOSITE opening

finality = <u>conclusiveness</u>, resolution, decisiveness, certitude, definiteness, irrevocability, inevitableness, unavoidability, decidedness

finalize = <u>complete</u>, settle, conclude, tie up, decide, agree, work out, clinch, wrap up (*informal*), shake hands, sew up (*informal*), complete the arrangements for

finally 1 = <u>eventually</u>, at last, in the end, ultimately, at the last, at the end of the day, in the long run, at length, at the last moment, at long last, when all is said and done, in the fullness of time, after a long time ...*The food finally arrived at the end of the week...*

2 = <u>lastly</u>, in the end, ultimately ...*Finally came the dessert trolley...*

3 = <u>in conclusion</u>, lastly, in closing, to conclude, to sum up, in summary ...*Finally, a word or two of advice...*

4 = <u>conclusively</u>, for good, permanently, for ever, completely, definitely, once and for all, decisively, convincingly, inexorably, irrevocably, for all time, inescapably, beyond the shadow of a doubt ...*Finally draw a line under the affair...*

finance VERB = <u>fund</u>, back, support, pay for, guarantee, float, invest in, underwrite, endow, subsidize, bankroll (*U.S.*), set up in business, provide security for, provide money for ...*new taxes to finance increased military expenditure...*

NOUN = <u>economics</u>, business, money, banking, accounts, investment, commerce, financial affairs, money management ...*a major player in the world of high finance...*

PLURAL NOUN = <u>resources</u>, money, funds, capital, cash, affairs, budgeting, assets, cash flow, financial affairs, money management, wherewithal, financial condition ...*Women manage the day-to-day finances...*

financial = <u>economic</u>, business, money, budgeting, budgetary, commercial, monetary, fiscal, pecuniary

financing = <u>funding</u>, money, support, funds, capital, subsidy, sponsorship, endowment, underwriting, financial support, financial backing

find VERB **1** = <u>discover</u>, turn up, uncover, unearth, spot, expose, come up with, locate, detect, come across, track down, catch sight of, stumble upon, hit upon, espy, ferret out, chance upon, light upon, put your finger on, lay your hand on, run to ground, run to earth, descry ...*The police also found a pistol...* OPPOSITE lose

2 = <u>regain</u>, recover, get back, retrieve, repossess ...*Luckily she found her bag...*

3 = <u>obtain</u>, get, come by, procure, win, gain, achieve, earn, acquire, attain ...*Many people here cannot find*

work…

4 = <u>encounter</u>, meet, recognize …*They found her walking alone on the beach…*

5 = <u>observe</u>, learn, note, discover, notice, realize, remark, come up with, arrive at, perceive, detect, become aware, experience, ascertain …*The study found that heart disease can begin in childhood…*

6 = <u>feel</u>, have, experience, sense, obtain, know …*Could anyone find pleasure in killing this creature?…*

7 = <u>provide</u>, supply, contribute, furnish, cough up (*informal*), purvey, be responsible for, bring …*Their parents can usually find the money for them…*

NOUN = <u>discovery</u>, catch, asset, bargain, acquisition, good buy …*Another lucky find was a pair of candle-holders…*

PHRASES **find someone out** = <u>detect</u>, catch, unmask, rumble (*Brit. informal*), reveal, expose, disclose, uncover, suss (out) (*slang*), bring to light …*I wondered for a moment if she'd found me out…* ◆ **find something out** = <u>learn</u>, discover, realize, observe, perceive, detect, become aware, come to know, note …*It was such a relief to find out that the boy was normal…*

finding *usually plural* = <u>judgment</u>, ruling, decision, award, conclusion, verdict, recommendation, decree, pronouncement

fine¹ 1 = <u>excellent</u>, good, great, striking, choice, beautiful, masterly, select, rare, very good, supreme, impressive, outstanding, magnificent, superior, accomplished, sterling, first-class, divine, exceptional, splendid, world-class, exquisite, admirable, skilful, ornate, first-rate, showy …*This is a fine book…* OPPOSITE poor

2 = <u>satisfactory</u>, good, all right, suitable, acceptable, convenient, agreeable, hunky-dory (*informal*), fair, O.K. *or* okay (*informal*) …*It's fine to ask questions as we go along…*

3 = <u>fine-grained</u>, ground, powdered, powdery, granulated, pulverized …*The ship came to rest on the fine sand…*

4 = <u>thin</u>, small, light, narrow, wispy …*The heat scorched the fine hairs on her arms…*

5 = <u>delicate</u>, light, thin, sheer, lightweight, flimsy, wispy, gossamer, diaphanous, gauzy, chiffony …*Her suit was of a pale grey fine material…* OPPOSITE coarse

6 = <u>stylish</u>, expensive, elegant, refined, tasteful, quality …*We waited in our fine clothes…*

7 = <u>exquisite</u>, delicate, fragile, dainty …*She wears fine jewellery wherever she goes…*

8 = <u>minute</u>, exact, precise, nice …*They are reserving judgement on the fine detail…*

9 = <u>keen</u>, minute, nice, quick, sharp, critical, acute, sensitive, subtle, precise, refined, discriminating, tenuous, fastidious, hairsplitting …*She has a fine eye for detail…*

10 = <u>brilliant</u>, quick, keen, alert, clever, intelligent, penetrating, astute …*He had a fine mind and excellent knowledge…*

11 = <u>sharp</u>, keen, polished, honed, razor-sharp, cutting …*tapering to a fine point…*

12 = <u>good-looking</u>, striking, pretty, attractive, lovely, smart, handsome, stylish, bonny, well-favoured …*You're a very fine woman…*

13 = <u>sunny</u>, clear, fair, dry, bright, pleasant, clement, balmy, cloudless …*I'll do the garden if the weather is fine…* OPPOSITE cloudy

14 = <u>pure</u>, clear, refined, unadulterated, unalloyed, unpolluted, solid, sterling …*a light, fine oil, high in vitamin content…*

fine² NOUN = <u>penalty</u>, damages, punishment, forfeit, financial penalty, amercement (*obsolete*) …*If convicted he faces a fine of one million dollars…* VERB = <u>penalize</u>, charge, punish …*She was fined £300 and banned from driving…*

finery = <u>splendour</u>, trappings, frippery, glad rags (*informal*), gear (*informal*), decorations, ornaments, trinkets, Sunday best, gewgaws, showiness, best bib and tucker (*informal*)

finesse NOUN = <u>skill</u>, style, know-how (*informal*), polish, craft, diplomacy, discretion, sophistication, subtlety, delicacy, tact, cleverness, quickness, savoir-faire, adroitness, artfulness, adeptness …*handling diplomatic challenges with finesse…* VERB = <u>manoeuvre</u>, steer, manipulate, bluff …*a typical politician trying to finesse a sticky situation…*

finger VERB = <u>touch</u>, feel, handle, play with, manipulate, paw (*informal*), maul, toy with, fiddle with (*informal*), meddle with, play about with …*He fingered the few coins in his pocket…* PHRASES **put your finger on something** = <u>identify</u>, place, remember, discover, indicate, recall, find out, locate, pin down, bring to mind, hit upon, hit the nail on the head …*She couldn't quite put her finger on the reason…*

(*Related Words*)
adjective : digital

finish VERB **1** = <u>stop</u>, close, complete, achieve, conclude, cease, accomplish, execute, discharge, culminate, wrap up (*informal*), terminate, round off, bring to a close *or* conclusion …*He was cheered when he finished his speech…* OPPOSITE start

2 = <u>get done</u>, complete, put the finishing touch(es) to, finalize, do, deal with, settle, conclude, fulfil, carry through, get out of the way, make short work of …*They've been working to finish a report this week…*

3 = <u>end</u>, stop, conclude, wind up, terminate …*The teaching day finished at around 4pm…*

4 = <u>consume</u>, dispose of, devour, polish off, drink, eat, drain, get through, dispatch, deplete …*He finished his dinner and left…*

5 = <u>use up</u>, use, spend, empty, exhaust, expend …*Once you have finished all 21 pills, stop for seven days…*

6 = <u>coat</u>, polish, stain, texture, wax, varnish, gild, veneer, lacquer, smooth off, face …*The bowl is finished in a pearlised lustre…*

7 *usually with* **off** = <u>destroy</u>, defeat, overcome, bring down, best, worst, ruin, get rid of, dispose of, rout, put an end to, overpower, annihilate, put paid to, move in for the kill, drive to the wall, administer *or* give the coup de grâce …*I played well but I didn't finish him off…*

8 *usually with* **off** = <u>kill</u>, murder, destroy, do in (*slang*), take out (*slang*), massacre, butcher, slaughter, dispatch, slay, eradicate, do away with, blow away (*slang, chiefly U.S.*), knock off (*slang*), annihilate, exterminate, take (someone's) life, bump off (*slang*) ...*She finished him off with an axe*...
NOUN 1 = <u>end</u>, ending, close, closing, conclusion, run-in, winding up (*informal*), wind-up, completion, finale, termination, culmination, cessation, last stage(s), denouement, finalization ...*I intend to see the job through to the finish*... OPPOSITE> beginning
2 = <u>surface</u>, appearance, polish, shine, grain, texture, glaze, veneer, lacquer, lustre, smoothness, patina ...*The finish of the woodwork was excellent*...

finished 1 = <u>over</u>, done, completed, achieved, through, ended, closed, full, final, complete, in the past, concluded, shut, accomplished, executed, tied up, wrapped up (*informal*), terminated, sewn up (*informal*), finalized, over and done with ...*Finally, last spring, the film was finished*... OPPOSITE> begun
2 = <u>ruined</u>, done for (*informal*), doomed, bankrupt, through, lost, gone, defeated, devastated, wrecked, wiped out, undone, washed up (*informal, chiefly U.S.*), wound up, liquidated ...*'This business is finished,' he said sadly*...

finite = <u>limited</u>, bounded, restricted, demarcated, conditioned, circumscribed, delimited, terminable, subject to limitations OPPOSITE> infinite

fire NOUN **1** = <u>flames</u>, blaze, combustion, inferno, conflagration, holocaust ...*A forest fire is sweeping across the country*...
2 = <u>passion</u>, force, light, energy, heat, spirit, enthusiasm, excitement, dash, intensity, sparkle, life, vitality, animation, vigour, zeal, splendour, verve, fervour, eagerness, dynamism, lustre, radiance, virtuosity, élan, ardour, brio, vivacity, impetuosity, burning passion, scintillation, fervency, pizzazz *or* pizazz (*informal*) ...*His punishing schedule seemed to dim his fire at times*...
3 = <u>bombardment</u>, shooting, firing, shelling, hail, volley, barrage, gunfire, sniping, flak, salvo, fusillade, cannonade ...*His car was raked with fire from automatic weapons*...
VERB 1 = <u>let off</u>, shoot, launch, shell, loose, set off, discharge, hurl, eject, detonate, let loose (*informal*), touch off ...*a huge gun designed to fire nuclear or chemical shells*...
2 = <u>shoot</u>, explode, discharge, detonate, pull the trigger ...*Soldiers fired rubber bullets to disperse crowds*...
3 (*Informal*) = <u>dismiss</u>, sack (*informal*), get rid of, discharge, lay off, make redundant, cashier, give notice, show the door, give the boot (*slang*), kiss off (*slang, chiefly U.S. & Canad.*), give the push, give the bullet (*Brit. slang*), give marching orders, give someone their cards, give the sack to (*informal*) ...*She was sent a letter saying she was fired from her job*...
4 *sometimes with* **up** = <u>inspire</u>, excite, stir, stimulate, motivate, irritate, arouse, awaken, animate, rouse, stir up, quicken, inflame, incite, electrify, enliven, spur on,

galvanize, inspirit, impassion ...*They were fired with an enthusiasm for public speaking*...
5 = <u>set fire to</u>, torch, ignite, set on fire, kindle, set alight, set ablaze, put a match to, set aflame, enkindle, light ...*matches, turpentine and cotton, with which they fired the houses*...
PHRASES on fire 1 = <u>burning</u>, flaming, blazing, alight, ablaze, in flames, aflame, fiery ...*The captain radioed that the ship was on fire*... **2** = <u>ardent</u>, excited, inspired, eager, enthusiastic, passionate, fervent ...*He was on fire, youthfully impatient*...

(Related Words)
fondness for: pyromania

firearm = <u>gun</u>, weapon, handgun, revolver, shooter (*slang*), piece (*slang*), rod (*slang*), pistol, heater (*U.S. slang*)

firebrand = <u>rabble-rouser</u>, activist, incendiary, fomenter, instigator, agitator, demagogue, tub-thumper, soapbox orator

fireworks 1 = <u>pyrotechnics</u>, illuminations, feux d'artifice ...*The rally ended with spectacular fireworks and band music*...
2 (*Informal*) = <u>trouble</u>, row, storm, rage, temper, wax (*informal, chiefly Brit.*), uproar, hysterics, paroxysms, fit of rage ...*The big media companies will be forced to compete, and we should see some fireworks*...

firm¹ 1 = <u>hard</u>, solid, compact, dense, set, concentrated, stiff, compacted, rigid, compressed, inflexible, solidified, unyielding, congealed, inelastic, jelled, close-grained, jellified ...*Fruit should be firm and excellent in condition*... OPPOSITE> soft
2 = <u>secure</u>, strong, fixed, secured, rooted, stable, steady, anchored, braced, robust, cemented, fast, sturdy, embedded, fastened, riveted, taut, stationary, motionless, immovable, unmoving, unshakeable, unfluctuating ...*use a firm platform or a sturdy ladder*... OPPOSITE> unstable
3 = <u>strong</u>, close, tight, steady ...*The quick handshake was firm and cool*...
4 = <u>strict</u>, unwavering, unswerving, unshakeable, constant, stalwart, resolute, inflexible, steadfast, unyielding, immovable, unflinching, unbending, obdurate, unalterable, unfaltering ...*They needed the guiding hand of a firm father figure*...
5 = <u>determined</u>, true, settled, fixed, resolved, strict, definite, set on, adamant, stalwart, staunch, resolute, inflexible, steadfast, unyielding, unwavering, immovable, unflinching, unswerving, unbending, obdurate, unshakeable, unalterable, unshaken, unfaltering ...*He held a firm belief in the afterlife*... OPPOSITE> wavering
6 = <u>definite</u>, hard, clear, confirmed, settled, fixed, hard-and-fast, cut-and-dried (*informal*) ...*firm evidence*...

firm² = <u>company</u>, business, concern, association, organization, house, corporation, venture, enterprise, partnership, establishment, undertaking, outfit (*informal*), consortium, conglomerate ...*The firm's employees were expecting large bonuses*...

firmament (*Literary*) = <u>sky</u>, skies, heaven, heavens, the blue, vault, welkin (*archaic*), empyrean (*poetic*), vault of heaven

firmly 1 = <u>securely</u>, safely, tightly …*The door is locked and the windows are firmly shut*…
2 = <u>immovably</u>, securely, steadily, like a rock, unflinchingly, enduringly, motionlessly, unshakeably …*boards firmly fixed to metal posts in the ground*…
3 = <u>steadily</u>, securely, tightly, unflinchingly …*She held me firmly by the elbow*…
4 = <u>resolutely</u>, strictly, staunchly, steadfastly, determinedly, through thick and thin, with decision, with a rod of iron, definitely, unwaveringly, unchangeably …*Political opinions are firmly held*…

firmness 1 = <u>hardness</u>, resistance, density, rigidity, stiffness, solidity, inflexibility, compactness, fixedness, inelasticity …*the firmness of the ground*…
2 = <u>steadiness</u>, tension, stability, tightness, soundness, tautness, tensile strength, immovability …*testing the firmness of the nearest stakes*…
3 = <u>strength</u>, tightness, steadiness …*He was surprised at the firmness of her grip*…
4 = <u>resolve</u>, resolution, constancy, inflexibility, steadfastness, obduracy, strictness, strength of will, fixity, fixedness, staunchness …*There was no denying his considerable firmness of purpose*…

first ADJECTIVE 1 = <u>earliest</u>, original, primitive, primordial, primeval …*The first men of this race lived like gods*…
2 = <u>initial</u>, opening, earliest, maiden, introductory, pristine …*the first few flakes of snow*…
3 = <u>top</u>, best, winning, premier …*The first prize is thirty-one thousand pounds*…
4 = <u>elementary</u>, key, basic, primary, fundamental, cardinal, rudimentary, elemental …*It is time to go back to first principles*…
5 = <u>foremost</u>, highest, greatest, leading, head, ruling, chief, prime, supreme, principal, paramount, overriding, pre-eminent …*The first priority for development is to defeat inflation*…
ADVERB = <u>to begin with</u>, firstly, initially, at the beginning, in the first place, beforehand, to start with, at the outset, before all else …*I do not remember who spoke first*…
NOUN = <u>novelty</u>, innovation, originality, new experience …*It is a first for New York*…
PHRASES **from the first** = <u>from the start</u>, from the beginning, from the outset, from the very beginning, from the introduction, from the starting point, from the inception, from the commencement, from the word 'go' (*informal*) …*You knew about me from the first, didn't you?*…

first-class *or* **first class** = <u>excellent</u>, great, very good, superb, topping (*Brit. slang*), top, tops (*slang*), bad (*slang*), prime, capital, choice, champion, cool (*informal*), brilliant, crack (*slang*), mean (*slang*), cracking (*Brit. informal*), crucial (*slang*), outstanding, premium, ace (*informal*), marvellous, exceptional, mega (*slang*), sovereign, dope (*slang*), world-class, blue-chip, top-flight, top-class, five-star, exemplary, wicked (*slang*), first-rate, def (*slang*), superlative, second to none, top-notch (*informal*), brill (*informal*), top-drawer, matchless, tiptop, boffo (*slang*), jim-dandy (*slang*), twenty-four carat, A1 *or* A-one (*informal*),

bitchin' (*U.S. slang*), chillin' (*U.S. slang*), booshit (*Austral. slang*), exo (*Austral. slang*), sik (*Austral. slang*)
OPPOSITE terrible

first-hand ADJECTIVE = <u>direct</u>, personal, immediate, face-to-face, straight from the horse's mouth …*He'll get a first-hand briefing on the emergency*…
ADVERB = <u>directly</u>, personally, immediately, face-to-face, straight from the horse's mouth …*I heard all about it first-hand*…

first-rate = <u>excellent</u>, outstanding, first class, exceptional, mean (*slang*), topping (*Brit. slang*), top, tops (*slang*), prime, cool (*informal*), crack (*slang*), cracking (*Brit. informal*), crucial (*slang*), exclusive, superb, mega (*slang*), sovereign, dope (*slang*), world-class, admirable, wicked (*slang*), def (*slang*), superlative, second to none, top-notch (*informal*), brill (*informal*), tiptop, bodacious (*slang, chiefly U.S.*), boffo (*slang*), jim-dandy (*slang*), A1 *or* A-one (*informal*), bitchin' (*U.S. slang*), chillin' (*U.S. slang*), booshit (*Austral. slang*), exo (*Austral. slang*), sik (*Austral. slang*)

fiscal = <u>financial</u>, money, economic, monetary, budgetary, pecuniary, tax

fish VERB 1 = <u>angle</u>, net, cast, trawl …*He learnt to fish in the river Cam*…
2 = <u>look (for)</u>, search, delve, ferret, rummage, fossick (*Austral. & N.Z.*) …*He fished in his pocket for the key*…
PHRASES **fish for something** = <u>seek</u>, look for, angle for, try to get, hope for, hunt for, hint at, elicit, solicit, invite, search for …*She may be fishing for a compliment*… ♦ **fish something out** = <u>pull out</u>, produce, take out, extract, bring out, extricate, haul out, find …*She fished out a pair of his socks*…

> **Related Words**
adjectives: piscine, ichthyoid
young: fry
collective noun: shoal
➤ **fish** ➤ **sharks**

fishy 1 = <u>fishlike</u>, piscine, piscatorial, piscatory …*It hasn't a very strong fishy flavour*…
2 (*Informal*) = <u>suspicious</u>, odd, suspect, unlikely, funny (*informal*), doubtful, dubious, dodgy (*Brit., Austral., & N.Z. informal*), queer, rum (*Brit. slang*), questionable, improbable, implausible, cock-and-bull (*informal*) …*There seems to be something fishy going on*…

fission = <u>splitting</u>, parting, breaking, division, rending, rupture, cleavage, schism, scission

fissure = <u>crack</u>, opening, hole, split, gap, rent, fault, breach, break, fracture, rift, slit, rupture, cleavage, cleft, chink, crevice, cranny, interstice

fit¹ VERB 1 = <u>adapt</u>, fashion, shape, arrange, alter, adjust, modify, tweak (*informal*), customize …*She was having her wedding dress fitted*…
2 = <u>place</u>, position, insert …*She fitted her key in the lock*…
3 = <u>attach</u>, join, connect, interlock …*Fit hinge bolts to give support to the door lock*…
4 = <u>suit</u>, meet, match, belong to, agree with, go with, conform to, correspond to, accord with, be appropriate to, concur with, tally with, dovetail with,

Fish

http://www.fishbase.org/search.cfm
http://www.flmnh.ufl.edu/fish/

Types of fish

alewife
amberjack
anabantid
anabas
anableps
anchoveta
anchovy
angelfish
arapaima
archerfish
argentine
barbel
barracouta or (*Austral.*) hake
barracuda
barramunda
barramundi or (*Austral.*) barra or
 giant perch
bass
batfish
beluga
bib, pout, or whiting pout
bigeye
billfish
bitterling
black bass
black bream
blackfish or (*Austral.*) nigger
bleak
blenny
blindfish
bloodfin
blowfish or (*Austral.*) toado
blue cod, rock cod, or (*N.Z.*)
 rawaru, pakirikiri, or patutuki
bluefin tuna
bluefish or snapper
bluegill
boarfish
bonefish
bonito or (*Austral.*) horse
 mackerel
bony bream
bowfin or dogfish
bream or (*Austral.*) brim
brill
brook trout or speckled trout
brown trout
buffalo fish
bullhead
bull trout
bully or (*N.Z.*) pakoko, titarakura,
 or toitoi
burbot, eelpout, or ling
butterfish
butterfish, greenbone, or (*N.Z.*)
 koaea or marari
butterfly fish
cabezon or cabezone
cabrilla
callop
candlefish or eulachon
capelin or caplin

carp
catfish
cavalla or cavally
cavefish
cero
characin or characid
chimaera
Chinook salmon, quinnat
 salmon, or king salmon
chub
chum
cichlid
cisco or lake herring
climbing fish or climbing perch
clingfish
coalfish or (*Brit.*) saithe or coley
cobia, black kingfish, or sergeant
 fish
cockabully
cod or codfish
coelacanth
coho or silver salmon
coley
conger
coral trout
crappie
croaker
crucian
dab
dace
damselfish
danio
dart
darter
dealfish
dentex
dollarfish
dorado
dory
dragonet
eel or (*N.Z.*) tuna
eelpout
electric eel
fallfish
father lasher or short-spined sea
 scorpion
fighting fish or betta
filefish
flatfish
flathead
flounder or (*N.Z.*) patiki
flying fish
flying gurnard
four-eyed fish
frogfish
garpike, garfish, gar, or (*Austral.*)
 ballahoo
geelbek
gemfish or (*Austral.*) hake
gilthead
goby
golden perch, freshwater bream,

Murray perch, or yellow-belly
goldeye
goldfish
goldsinny or goldfinny
gourami
grayling or (*Austral.*) yarra herring
greenling
grenadier or rat-tail
groper or grouper
grunion
grunt
gudgeon
guitarfish
gunnel
guppy
gurnard or gurnet
gwyniad
haddock
hagfish or hag
hairtail or (*U.S.*) cutlass fish
hake
halfbeak
halibut
hapuku
herring
hogfish
horned pout or brown bullhead
horse mackerel
houndfish
houting
ice fish
jacksmelt
javelin fish or Queensland
 trumpeter
jewelfish
jewfish or (*Austral. informal*) jewie
John Dory
jurel
kahawai, Australian salmon,
 native salmon, salmon trout, or
 bay trout
kelpfish or (*Austral. informal*)
 kelpie
killifish
kingfish
kingklip
kokanee
labyrinth fish
lampern or river lamprey
lamprey or lamper eel
lancet fish
lantern fish
largemouth bass
latimeria
leatherjacket
lemon sole
lepidosiren
ling or (*Austral.*) beardie
lingcod
lionfish
loach
louvar

Types of fish (continued)

luderick or (N.Z.) parore
lumpfish or lumpsucker
lungfish
mackerel or (colloquial) shiner
mangrove Jack
manta, manta ray, devilfish, or
  devil ray
marlin or spearfish
megrim
menhaden
milkfish
miller's thumb
minnow or (Scot.) baggie minnow
mirror carp
moki
molly
monkfish or (U.S.) goosefish
mooneye
moonfish
Moorish idol
moray
morwong, black perch, or (N.Z.)
  porae
mudcat
mudfish
mudskipper
mullet
mulloway
Murray cod
muskellunge, maskalonge,
  maskanonge, or (informal) musky
  or muskie
nannygai or redfish
needlefish
numbfish
oarfish or king of the herrings
oldwife
opah, moonfish, or kingfish
orange chromide
orange roughy
orfe
ouananiche
ox-eye herring
paddlefish
panchax
pandora
paradise fish
parrotfish
pearl perch
perch or (Austral.) redfin
pickerel
pigfish or hogfish
pike, luce, or jackfish
pikeperch
pilchard or (Austral. informal) pillie
pilot fish
pinfish or sailor's choice
pipefish or needlefish
piranha or piraña
plaice
platy
pogge or armed bullhead
pollack or pollock
pollan

pomfret
pompano
porcupine fish or globefish
porgy or pogy
pout
powan or lake herring
puffer or globefish
pumpkinseed
Queensland halibut
Queensland lungfish
rabbitfish
rainbow trout
ray
red cod
red emperor
redfin
redfish
red mullet or (U.S.) goatfish
red salmon
red snapper
remora
ribbonfish
roach
robalo
rock bass
rock cod
rockfish or (formerly) rock salmon
rockling
rosefish
rudd
ruffe, ruff, or pope
runner
salmon
salmon trout
sand dab
sand eel, sand lance, or launce
sardine
sauger
saury or skipper
sawfish
scabbard fish
scad
scaldfish
scat
scorpion fish
sculpin
scup or northern porgy
sea bass
sea bream
sea horse
sea lamprey
sea perch
sea raven
sea robin
sea scorpion
sea snail or snailfish
sea trout
Sergeant Baker
sergeant major
shad
shanny
sheepshead
shiner
shovelnose

Siamese fighting fish
sild
silver belly
silverfish
silverside or silversides
skate
skelly
skipjack or skipjack tuna
sleeper or sleeper goby
smallmouth bass
smelt
smooth hound
snapper, red bream, or (Austral.)
  wollomai or wollamai
snipefish or bellows fish
snoek
snook
sockeye or red salmon
sole
solenette
spadefish
Spanish mackerel or Queensland
  kingfish
spotted mackerel or school
  mackerel
sprat
squeteague
squirrelfish
steelhead
sterlet
stickleback
stingray
stone bass or wreckfish
stonefish
stone roller
sturgeon
sucker
sunfish
surfperch or sea perch
surgeonfish
swordfish
swordtail
tailor
tarakihi or terakihi
tarpon
tarwhine
tautog or blackfish
tench
teraglin
tetra
thornback
threadfin
tilapia
tilefish
toadfish
tommy rough or tommy ruff
topminnow
torsk or (U.S. & Canadian) cusk
trevalla
trevally or samson fish
triggerfish
tripletail
trout
trunkfish, boxfish, or cowfish

Types of fish *(continued)*

tuna *or* tunny	whitebait	wolffish *or* catfish
turbot	whitefish	wrasse
vendace	whiting	yellow jack
wahoo	wirrah	yellowtail
walleye, walleyed pike, *or* dory	witch	zander
weakfish	wobbegong, wobbygong, *or*	
weever	wobegong	

Extinct fish

ceratodus	ostracoderm	placoderm

be consonant with …*Her daughter doesn't fit the current feminine ideal…*

5 = <u>equip</u>, provide, arm, prepare, outfit, accommodate, fit out, kit out, rig out, accoutre …*The bombs were fitted with time devices…*

ADJECTIVE **1** = <u>appropriate</u>, qualified, suitable, competent, right, becoming, meet (*archaic*), seemly, trained, able, prepared, fitting, fitted, ready, skilled, correct, deserving, capable, adapted, proper, equipped, good enough, adequate, worthy, convenient, apt, well-suited, expedient, apposite …*You're not fit to be a mother!…* OPPOSITE inappropriate

2 = <u>healthy</u>, strong, robust, sturdy, well, trim, strapping, hale, in good shape, in good condition, in good health, toned up, as right as rain, in good trim, able-bodied …*It will take a very fit person to beat me…* OPPOSITE unfit

fit² NOUN **1** = <u>seizure</u>, attack, bout, spasm, convulsion, paroxysm …*Once a fit has started there's nothing you can do to stop it…*

2 = <u>bout</u>, burst, outbreak, outburst, spell …*I broke into a fit of giggles…*

PHRASES **have a fit** = <u>go mad</u>, explode, blow up (*informal*), lose it (*informal*), see red (*informal*), lose the plot (*informal*), throw a tantrum, fly off the handle (*informal*), go spare (*Brit. slang*), blow your top (*informal*), fly into a temper, flip your lid (*slang*), do your nut (*Brit. slang*) …*He'd have a fit if he knew what we were up to!…* ◆ **in** *or* **by fits and starts** = <u>spasmodically</u>, sporadically, erratically, fitfully, on and off, irregularly, intermittently, off and on, unsystematically …*Military technology advances by fits and starts…*

fitful = <u>irregular</u>, broken, disturbed, erratic, variable, flickering, unstable, uneven, fluctuating, sporadic, intermittent, impulsive, haphazard, desultory, spasmodic, inconstant OPPOSITE regular

fitfully = <u>irregularly</u>, on and off, intermittently, sporadically, off and on, erratically, in fits and starts, spasmodically, in snatches, desultorily, by fits and starts, interruptedly

fitness 1 = <u>appropriateness</u>, qualifications, adaptation, competence, readiness, eligibility, suitability, propriety, preparedness, applicability, aptness, pertinence, seemliness …*There is a debate about his fitness for the job…*

2 = <u>health</u>, strength, good health, vigour, good

condition, wellness, robustness …*Squash was thought to offer all-round fitness…*

fitted 1 = <u>built-in</u>, permanent …*I've recarpeted our bedroom and added fitted wardrobes…*

2 *often with* **with** = <u>equipped</u>, provided, supplied, set up, appointed, outfitted, furnished, rigged out, accoutred …*Bedrooms are fitted with alarm pull cords…*

fitting NOUN = <u>accessory</u>, part, piece, unit, connection, component, attachment …*brass light fittings…*

PLURAL NOUN = <u>furnishings</u>, extras, equipment, fixtures, appointments, furniture, trimmings, accessories, conveniences, accoutrements, bells and whistles, fitments, appurtenances …*He has made fittings for antique cars…*

ADJECTIVE = <u>appropriate</u>, suitable, proper, apt, right, becoming, meet (*archaic*), seemly, correct, decent, desirable, apposite, decorous, comme il faut (*French*) …*The President's address was a fitting end to the campaign…* OPPOSITE unsuitable

fix VERB **1** = <u>place</u>, join, stick, attach, set, position, couple, plant, link, establish, tie, settle, secure, bind, root, connect, locate, pin, install, anchor, glue, cement, implant, embed, fasten, make fast …*Fix the photo to the card using double-sided tape…*

2 = <u>decide</u>, set, name, choose, limit, establish, determine, settle, appoint, arrange, define, conclude, resolve, arrive at, specify, agree on …*He's fixed a time when I can see him…*

3 = <u>arrange</u>, organize, sort out, see to, fix up, make arrangements for …*I've fixed it for you to see them…*

4 = <u>repair</u>, mend, service, sort, correct, restore, adjust, regulate, see to, overhaul, patch up, get working, put right, put to rights …*If something is broken, we fix it…*

5 = <u>focus</u>, direct at, level at, fasten on, rivet on …*Attention is fixed on the stock market…*

6 (*Informal*) = <u>rig</u>, set up (*informal*), influence, manipulate, bribe, manoeuvre, fiddle (*informal*), pull strings (*informal*) …*They offered players bribes to fix a league match…*

7 = <u>stabilize</u>, set, consolidate, harden, thicken, stiffen, solidify, congeal, rigidify …*Egg yolk is used to fix the pigment…*

NOUN (*Informal*) = <u>mess</u>, spot (*informal*), corner, hole (*slang*), difficulty, jam (*informal*), dilemma, embarrassment, plight, hot water (*informal*), pickle (*informal*), uphill (*S. African*), predicament, difficult situation, quandary, tight spot, ticklish situation

...The government has got itself in a fix...
PHRASES **fix someone up** = provide, supply, accommodate, bring about, furnish, lay on, arrange for ...*We'll fix him up with a job...* ♦ **fix something up** = arrange, plan, settle, fix, organize, sort out, agree on, make arrangements for ...*I fixed up an appointment to see her...*

fixated = obsessed, fascinated, preoccupied, captivated, attached, devoted, absorbed, caught up in, single-minded, smitten, taken up with, besotted, wrapped up in, engrossed, spellbound, infatuated, mesmerized, hypnotized, hung up on (slang), monomaniacal, prepossessed **OPPOSITE** uninterested

fixation = obsession, complex, addiction, hang-up (informal), preoccupation, mania, infatuation, idée fixe (French), thing (informal)

fixed 1 = inflexible, set, steady, resolute, unwavering, unflinching, unblinking, unbending, undeviating ...*people who have fixed ideas about things...* **OPPOSITE** wavering
2 = immovable, set, established, secure, rooted, permanent, attached, anchored, rigid, made fast ...*Nato was concentrating on hitting buildings and other fixed structures...* **OPPOSITE** mobile
3 = agreed, set, planned, decided, established, settled, arranged, resolved, specified, definite ...*The deal was settled at a prearranged fixed price...*
4 = mended, going, sorted, repaired, put right, in working order ...*The vehicle was fixed...*
5 (Informal) = rigged, framed, put-up, manipulated, packed ...*Some races are fixed...*

fizz 1 = bubble, froth, fizzle, effervesce, produce bubbles ...*She was holding a tray of glasses that fizzed...*
2 = sputter, buzz, sparkle, hiss, crackle ...*The engine fizzed and went dead...*

fizzle out (Informal) = die away, fail, collapse, fold (informal), abort, fall through, peter out, come to nothing, miss the mark, end in disappointment

fizzy = bubbly, bubbling, sparkling, effervescent, carbonated, gassy

flab = fat, flesh, flabbiness, fleshiness, weight, beef (informal), heaviness, slackness, plumpness, loose flesh

flabbergasted = astonished, amazed, stunned, overcome, overwhelmed, staggered, astounded, dazed, confounded, disconcerted, speechless, bowled over (informal), gobsmacked (Brit. slang), dumbfounded, nonplussed, lost for words, struck dumb, abashed, rendered speechless

flabby 1 = limp, hanging, loose, slack, unfit, sagging, sloppy, baggy, floppy, lax, drooping, flaccid, pendulous, toneless, yielding ...*bulging thighs and flabby stomach...* **OPPOSITE** firm
2 = weak, ineffective, feeble, impotent, wasteful, ineffectual, disorganized, spineless, effete, boneless, nerveless, enervated, wussy (slang), wimpish or wimpy (informal) ...*Many signs of flabby management remain...*

flaccid = limp, soft, weak, loose, slack, lax, drooping, flabby, nerveless

flag¹ **NOUN** = banner, standard, colours, jack, pennant, ensign, streamer, pennon, banderole, gonfalon ...*They raised the white flag in surrender...*
VERB = mark, identify, indicate, label, tab, pick out, note, docket ...*I promise to flag these things more clearly...*
PHRASES **flag something** or **someone down** = hail, stop, signal, salute, wave down ...*They flagged a car down...*

flag² = weaken, fall, die, fail, decline, sink, fade, slump, pine, faint, weary, fall off, succumb, falter, wilt, wane, ebb, sag, languish, abate, droop, peter out, taper off, feel the pace, lose your strength ...*His enthusiasm was in no way flagging...*

flagging = weakening, failing, declining, waning, giving up, tiring, sinking, fading, decreasing, slowing down, deteriorating, wearying, faltering, wilting, ebbing

flagrant = outrageous, open, blatant, barefaced, shocking, crying, enormous, awful, bold, dreadful, notorious, glaring, infamous, scandalous, flaunting, atrocious, brazen, shameless, out-and-out, heinous, ostentatious, egregious, undisguised, immodest, arrant, flagitious **OPPOSITE** slight

flagstone = paving stone, flag, slab, block

flail = thrash, beat, windmill, thresh

flair 1 = ability, feel, talent, gift, genius, faculty, accomplishment, mastery, knack, aptitude ...*She has a flair for languages...*
2 = style, taste, dash, chic, elegance, panache, discernment, stylishness ...*the panache and flair you'd expect...*

flak = criticism, stick (slang), opposition, abuse, complaints, hostility, condemnation, censure, disapproval, bad press, denigration, brickbats (informal), disparagement, fault-finding, disapprobation

flake **NOUN** = chip, scale, layer, peeling, shaving, disk, wafer, sliver, lamina, squama (Biology) ...*flakes of paint...*
VERB = chip, scale (off), peel (off), blister, desquamate ...*Some of the shell had flaked away...*

flamboyance = showiness, show, style, dash, sparkle, chic, flair, verve, swagger, extravagance, panache, pomp, glitz (informal), élan, bravura, swank (informal), theatricality, exhibitionism, brio, ostentation, stylishness, flashiness, flamboyancy, floridity, pizzazz or pizazz (informal) **OPPOSITE** restraint

flamboyant 1 = camp (informal), dashing, theatrical, swashbuckling ...*He was a flamboyant personality...*
2 = showy, rich, elaborate, over the top (informal), extravagant, baroque, ornate, ostentatious, rococo ...*flamboyant architectural paint effects...*
3 = colourful, striking, exciting, brilliant, glamorous, stylish, dazzling, glitzy (slang), showy, florid ...*He wears flamboyant clothes...*

flame **NOUN** 1 = fire, light, spark, glow, blaze, brightness, inferno ...*a huge ball of flame...*

2 = <u>passion</u>, fire, enthusiasm, intensity, affection, warmth, fervour, ardour, keenness, fervency ...*that burning flame of love*...
3 (*Informal*) = <u>sweetheart</u>, partner, lover, girlfriend, boyfriend, beloved, heart-throb (*Brit*.), beau, ladylove ...*She kept inviting his old flame round to their house*...
VERB = <u>burn</u>, flash, shine, glow, blaze, flare, glare ...*His dark eyes flamed with rage*...

flaming 1 = <u>burning</u>, blazing, fiery, ignited, red, brilliant, raging, glowing, red-hot, ablaze, in flames, afire ...*A group followed carrying flaming torches*...
2 = <u>intense</u>, angry, raging, impassioned, hot, aroused, vivid, frenzied, ardent, scintillating, vehement ...*She had a flaming row with her lover*...

flammable = <u>combustible</u>, incendiary, inflammable, ignitable

> ### *Word Power*
>
> **flammable** – *Flammable* and *inflammable* are interchangeable when used of the properties of materials. *Flammable* is, however, often preferred for warning labels as there is less likelihood of misunderstanding (*inflammable* being sometimes taken to mean *not flammable*). *Inflammable* is preferred in figurative contexts: *this could prove to be an inflammable situation*.

flank **NOUN** **1** = <u>side</u>, quarter, hip, thigh, loin, haunch, ham ...*He put his hand on the dog's flank*...
2 = <u>wing</u>, side, sector, aspect ...*The assault element opened up from their right flank*...
VERB = <u>border</u>, line, wall, screen, edge, circle, bound, skirt, fringe, book-end ...*The altar was flanked by two Christmas trees*...

flannel **NOUN** (*Informal*) = <u>waffle</u> (*informal, chiefly Brit*.), flattery, blarney, sweet talk (*U.S. informal*), baloney (*informal*), equivocation, hedging, prevarication, weasel words (*informal, chiefly U.S.*), soft soap (*informal*) ...*He gave me a lot of flannel*...
VERB (*Informal*) = <u>prevaricate</u>, hedge, flatter, waffle (*informal, chiefly Brit*.), blarney, sweet-talk (*informal*), soft-soap (*informal*), equivocate, butter up, pull the wool over (someone's) eyes ...*He flannelled and prevaricated*...

flap **VERB** **1** = <u>flutter</u>, wave, swing, swish, flail ...*Sheets flapped on the clothes line*...
2 = <u>beat</u>, wave, thrash, flutter, agitate, wag, vibrate, shake, thresh ...*The bird flapped its wings furiously*...
3 (*Informal*) = <u>panic</u>, fuss, dither (*chiefly Brit*.) ...*There's no point in you flapping around in the kitchen, making your guest feel uneasy*...
NOUN **1** = <u>cover</u>, covering, tail, fold, skirt, tab, overlap, fly, apron, lapel, lappet ...*He drew back the tent flap and strode out*...
2 = <u>flutter</u>, beating, waving, shaking, swinging, bang, banging, swish ...*the gunshot flap of a topsail*...
3 (*Informal*) = <u>panic</u>, state (*informal*), agitation, commotion, sweat (*informal*), stew (*informal*), dither (*chiefly Brit*.), fluster, twitter (*informal*), tizzy (*informal*) ...*Wherever he goes, there's always a flap*...

flare **NOUN** = <u>flame</u>, burst, flash, blaze, dazzle, glare, flicker ...*The flare of fires lights up the blacked-out streets*...
VERB **1** = <u>blaze</u>, flame, dazzle, glare, flicker, flutter, waver, burn up ...*Camp fires flared like beacons in the dark*...
2 = <u>widen</u>, spread, broaden, spread out, dilate, splay ...*a dress cut to flare from the hips*...
PHRASES **flare up 1** = <u>burn</u>, explode, blaze, be on fire, go up in flames, be alight, flame ...*The fire flared up again*... **2** = <u>erupt</u>, break out, fire up, burst out, boil over ...*People were injured as fighting flared up*... **3** = <u>lose your temper</u>, explode, lose it (*informal*), lose control, lose the plot (*informal*), throw a tantrum, fly off the handle (*informal*), lose your cool (*informal*), blow your top (*informal*), fly into a temper ...*She suddenly lost her temper with me and flared up*... **4** = <u>recur</u>, come back, reappear, come again ...*Old ailments can often flare up again*...

flash **NOUN** **1** = <u>blaze</u>, ray, burst, spark, beam, sparkle, streak, flare, dazzle, shaft, glare, gleam, flicker, shimmer, twinkle, scintillation, coruscation ...*a sudden flash of lightning*...
2 = <u>burst</u>, show, sign, touch, display, rush, demonstration, surge, outbreak, outburst, manifestation ...*The essay could do with a flash of wit*...
VERB **1** = <u>blaze</u>, shine, beam, sparkle, glitter, flare, glare, gleam, light up, flicker, shimmer, twinkle, glint, glisten, scintillate, coruscate ...*Lightning flashed among the distant dark clouds*...
2 = <u>speed</u>, race, shoot, fly, tear, sweep, dash, barrel (along) (*informal, chiefly U.S. & Canad.*), whistle, sprint, bolt, streak, dart, zoom, burn rubber (*informal*) ...*Cars flashed by every few minutes*...
3 (*Informal*) = <u>show quickly</u>, display, expose, exhibit, flourish, show off, flaunt ...*He flashed his official card*...
ADJECTIVE (*Informal*) = <u>ostentatious</u>, smart, glamorous, trendy, showy, cheap ...*flash jewellery and watches*...
PHRASES **in a flash** = <u>in a moment</u>, in a second, in an instant, in a split second, in a trice, in a jiffy (*informal*), in the twinkling of an eye, in a twinkling, in two shakes of a lamb's tail (*informal*), in the bat of an eye (*informal*) ...*The answer came to him in a flash*...

flashy = <u>showy</u>, loud, over the top (*informal*), flamboyant, brash, tacky (*informal*), flaunting, glitzy (*slang*), tasteless, naff (*Brit. slang*), gaudy, garish, jazzy (*informal*), tawdry, ostentatious, snazzy (*informal*), glittery, meretricious, cheap and nasty, in poor taste, tinselly **OPPOSITE** plain

flat¹ **ADJECTIVE** **1** = <u>even</u>, level, levelled, plane, smooth, uniform, horizontal, unbroken, planar ...*Sit the cup on a flat surface while measuring*... **OPPOSITE** uneven
2 = <u>horizontal</u>, prone, outstretched, reclining, prostrate, laid low, supine, recumbent, lying full length ...*Two men near him threw themselves flat*... **OPPOSITE** upright
3 = <u>punctured</u>, collapsed, burst, blown out, deflated, empty ...*It was impossible to ride with a flat tyre*...

4 = <u>used up</u>, finished, empty, drained, expired …*The battery was flat*…

5 = <u>absolute</u>, firm, direct, straight, positive, fixed, plain, final, explicit, definite, outright, unconditional, downright, unmistakable, unequivocal, unqualified, out-and-out, categorical, peremptory …*She is likely to give you a flat refusal*…

6 = <u>dull</u>, dead, empty, boring, depressing, pointless, tedious, stale, lacklustre, tiresome, lifeless, monotonous, uninteresting, insipid, unexciting, spiritless …*The past few days have been flat and empty*… OPPOSITE exciting

7 = <u>without energy</u>, empty, weak, tired, depressed, drained, weary, worn out, dispirited, downhearted, tired out …*I've been feeling flat at times*…

8 = <u>monotonous</u>, boring, uniform, dull, tedious, droning, tiresome, unchanging, colourless, toneless, samey (*informal*), uninflected, unvaried …*Her voice was flat, with no hope in it*…

NOUN *often plural* = <u>plain</u>, strand, shallow, marsh, swamp, shoal, lowland, mud flat …*salt marshes and mud flats*…

ADVERB = <u>completely</u>, directly, absolutely, categorically, precisely, exactly, utterly, outright, point blank, unequivocally …*He had turned her down flat*…

PHRASES **flat out** (*Informal*) = <u>at full speed</u>, all out, to the full, hell for leather (*informal*), as hard as possible, at full tilt, at full gallop, posthaste, for all you are worth, under full steam …*Everyone is working flat out*…

flat² = <u>apartment</u>, rooms, quarters, digs, suite, penthouse, living quarters …*She lives with her husband in a flat*…

flatly = <u>absolutely</u>, completely, positively, categorically, unequivocally, unhesitatingly

flatten **1** = <u>level</u>, roll, plaster, squash, compress, trample, iron out, even out, smooth off …*How do you put enough pressure on to the metal to flatten it?*…

2 = <u>destroy</u>, level, ruin, demolish, knock down, pull down, tear down, throw down, bulldoze, raze, remove …*Bombing raids flattened much of the area*…

3 (*Informal*) = <u>knock down</u>, fell, floor, deck (*slang*), bowl over, prostrate, knock off your feet …*I've never seen a woman flatten someone like that!*…

4 (*Informal*) = <u>crush</u>, beat, defeat, trounce, master, worst, overwhelm, conquer, lick (*informal*), undo, subdue, rout, overpower, quell, clobber (*slang*), vanquish, run rings around (*informal*), wipe the floor with (*informal*), make mincemeat of (*informal*), blow out of the water (*slang*) …*In the squash court his aim is to flatten me*…

flatter **1** = <u>praise</u>, compliment, pander to, sweet-talk (*informal*), court, humour, puff, flannel (*Brit. informal*), fawn, cajole, lay it on (thick) (*slang*), wheedle, inveigle, soft-soap (*informal*), butter up, blandish …*I knew he was just flattering me*…

2 = <u>suit</u>, become, enhance, set off, embellish, do something for, show to advantage …*Orange flatters those with golden skin tones*…

flattering **1** = <u>becoming</u>, kind, effective, enhancing, well-chosen …*It wasn't a very flattering photograph*…

OPPOSITE unflattering

2 = <u>ingratiating</u>, complimentary, gratifying, fawning, sugary, fulsome, laudatory, adulatory, honeyed, honey-tongued …*The press was flattering*… OPPOSITE uncomplimentary

flattery = <u>obsequiousness</u>, fawning, adulation, sweet-talk (*informal*), flannel (*Brit. informal*), blarney, soft-soap (*informal*), sycophancy, servility, cajolery, blandishment, fulsomeness, toadyism, false praise, honeyed words

flatulence **1** = <u>wind</u>, borborygmus (*Medical*), eructation …*Avoid any food that causes flatulence*…

2 = <u>pretentiousness</u>, boasting, hot air (*informal*), twaddle, pomposity, bombast, claptrap, empty words, fustian, prolixity, rodomontade, fanfaronade (*rare*) …*so much bloated nationalistic flatulence*…

flaunt = <u>show off</u>, display, boast, parade, exhibit, flourish, brandish, vaunt, make a (great) show of, sport (*informal*), disport, make an exhibition of, flash about

Word Power

flaunt – *Flaunt* is sometimes wrongly used where *flout* is meant: *they must be prevented from flouting* (not *flaunting*) *the law*.

flavour NOUN **1** = <u>taste</u>, seasoning, flavouring, savour, extract, essence, relish, smack, aroma, odour, zest, tang, zing (*informal*), piquancy, tastiness …*The cheese has a strong flavour*… OPPOSITE blandness

2 = <u>quality</u>, feeling, feel, style, property, touch, character, aspect, tone, suggestion, stamp, essence, tinge, soupçon (*French*) …*clothes with a nostalgic Forties flavour*…

VERB = <u>season</u>, spice, add flavour to, enrich, infuse, imbue, pep up, leaven, ginger up, lace …*Flavour dishes with exotic herbs and spices*…

flavouring = <u>essence</u>, extract, zest, tincture, spirit

flaw **1** = <u>weakness</u>, failing, defect, weak spot, spot, fault, scar, blemish, imperfection, speck, disfigurement, chink in your armour …*The only flaw in his character is a short temper*…

2 = <u>crack</u>, break, split, breach, tear, rent, fracture, rift, cleft, crevice, fissure, scission …*a flaw in the rock wide enough for a foot*…

flawed **1** = <u>damaged</u>, defective, imperfect, blemished, broken, cracked, chipped, faulty …*the unique beauty of a flawed object*…

2 = <u>erroneous</u>, incorrect, inaccurate, invalid, wrong, mistaken, false, faulty, untrue, unfounded, spurious, amiss, unsound, wide of the mark, inexact, fallacious …*The tests were seriously flawed*…

flawless **1** = <u>perfect</u>, impeccable, faultless, spotless, unblemished, unsullied …*She has a flawless complexion*…

2 = <u>intact</u>, whole, sound, unbroken, undamaged …*Stained glass craftsmen would always use flawless glass*…

flay **1** = <u>skin</u>, strip, peel, scrape, excoriate, remove the skin from …*to flay the flesh away from his muscles*…

2 = <u>upbraid</u>, slam (*slang*), castigate, revile, tear into (*informal*), diss (*slang, chiefly U.S.*), excoriate, tear a strip off, execrate, pull to pieces (*informal*), give a tongue-lashing, criticize severely ...*The critics flayed him with accusations of misanthropy...*

fleck NOUN = <u>mark</u>, speck, streak, spot, dot, pinpoint, speckle ...*His hair is dark grey with flecks of ginger...*
VERB = <u>speckle</u>, mark, spot, dust, dot, streak, dapple, stipple, mottle, variegate, bespeckle, besprinkle ...*patches of red paint which flecked her blouse...*

fledgling **1** = <u>chick</u>, nestling, young bird ...*The fathers of these fledglings are all dead...*
2 = <u>new</u>, beginning, developing, emerging, amateur, embryonic, probationary ...*advice he gave to fledgling writers...*

flee = <u>run away</u>, leave, escape, bolt, fly, avoid, split (*slang*), take off (*informal*), get away, vanish, depart, run off, shun, make off, abscond, decamp, take flight, hook it (*slang*), do a runner (*slang*), scarper (*Brit. slang*), slope off, cut and run (*informal*), make a run for It, beat a hasty retreat, turn tail, fly the coop (*U.S. & Canad. informal*), make a quick exit, skedaddle (*informal*), make yourself scarce (*informal*), take a powder (*U.S. & Canad. slang*), make your escape, make your getaway, take it on the lam (*U.S. & Canad. slang*), take to your heels

fleece NOUN = <u>wool</u>, hair, coat, fur, coat of wool ...*a blanket of lamb's fleece...*
VERB = <u>cheat</u>, skin (*slang*), steal, rob, con (*informal*), rifle, stiff (*slang*), soak (*U.S. & Canad. slang*), bleed (*informal*), rip off (*slang*), plunder, defraud, overcharge, swindle, rook (*slang*), diddle (*informal*), take for a ride (*informal*), despoil, take to the cleaners (*slang*), sell a pup, cozen, mulct ...*She claims he fleeced her out of thousands of pounds...*

fleet¹ = <u>navy</u>, vessels, task force, squadron, warships, flotilla, armada, naval force, sea power, argosy ...*damage inflicted upon the British fleet...*

fleet² = <u>swift</u>, flying, fast, quick, winged, rapid, speedy, nimble, mercurial, meteoric, nimble-footed ...*He was as fleet as a deer...*

fleeting = <u>momentary</u>, short, passing, flying, brief, temporary, short-lived, fugitive, transient, flitting, ephemeral, transitory, evanescent, fugacious, here today, gone tomorrow OPPOSITE> lasting

flesh NOUN **1** = <u>fat</u>, muscle, beef (*informal*), tissue, body, brawn ...*Illness had wasted the flesh from her body...*
2 = <u>fatness</u>, fat, adipose tissue, corpulence, weight ...*porcine wrinkles of flesh...*
3 = <u>meat</u>, food ...*the pale pink flesh of trout and salmon...*
4 = <u>physical nature</u>, sensuality, physicality, carnality, body, human nature, flesh and blood, animality, sinful nature ...*the sins of the flesh...*
PHRASES **your own flesh and blood** = <u>family</u>, blood, relations, relatives, kin, kindred, kith and kin, blood relations, kinsfolk ...*The kid was his own flesh and blood...*

(**Related Words**)

adjective: carnal

fleshy = <u>plump</u>, fat, chubby, obese, hefty, overweight, ample, stout, chunky, meaty, beefy (*informal*), tubby, podgy, brawny, corpulent, well-padded

flex = <u>bend</u>, contract, stretch, angle, curve, tighten, crook, move

flexibility **1** = <u>elasticity</u>, pliability, springiness, pliancy, tensility, give (*informal*) ...*The flexibility of the lens decreases with age...*
2 = <u>adaptability</u>, openness, versatility, adjustability ...*the flexibility of distance learning...*
3 = <u>complaisance</u>, accommodation, give and take, amenability ...*They should be ready to show some flexibility...*

flexible **1** = <u>pliable</u>, plastic, yielding, elastic, supple, lithe, limber, springy, willowy, pliant, tensile, stretchy, whippy, lissom(e), ductile, bendable, mouldable ...*brushes with long, flexible bristles...* OPPOSITE> rigid
2 = <u>adaptable</u>, open, variable, adjustable, discretionary ...*flexible working hours...* OPPOSITE> inflexible
3 = <u>compliant</u>, accommodating, manageable, amenable, docile, tractable, biddable, complaisant, responsive, gentle ...*Their boss was flexible and lenient...* OPPOSITE> unyielding

flick VERB **1** = <u>jerk</u>, pull, tug, lurch, jolt ...*The man flicked his gun up from beside his thigh...*
2 = <u>strike</u>, tap, jab, remove quickly, hit, touch, stroke, rap, flip, peck, whisk, dab, fillip ...*She flicked a speck of fluff from her sleeve...*
NOUN = <u>tap</u>, touch, sweep, stroke, rap, flip, peck, whisk, jab ...*a flick of a paintbrush...*
PHRASES **flick through something** = <u>browse</u>, glance at, skim, leaf through, flip through, thumb through, skip through ...*She flicked through some magazines...*

flicker VERB **1** = <u>twinkle</u>, flash, sparkle, flare, shimmer, gutter, glimmer ...*Firelight flickered on the faded furnishings...*
2 = <u>flutter</u>, waver, quiver, vibrate ...*Her eyelids flickered then opened...*
NOUN **1** = <u>glimmer</u>, flash, spark, flare, gleam ...*I saw the flicker of flames...*
2 = <u>trace</u>, drop, breath, spark, atom, glimmer, vestige, iota ...*He felt a flicker of regret...*

flickering = <u>wavering</u>, guttering, twinkling, unsteady

flier
➤ flyer

flight¹ **1** = <u>journey</u>, trip, voyage ...*The flight will take four hours...*
2 = <u>aviation</u>, flying, air transport, aeronautics, aerial navigation ...*Supersonic flight could be come a routine form of travel...*
3 = <u>flying</u>, winging, mounting, soaring, ability to fly ...*These hawks are magnificent in flight...*
4 = <u>flock</u>, group, unit, cloud, formation, squadron, swarm, flying group ...*a flight of green parrots...*

flight² NOUN = <u>escape</u>, fleeing, departure, retreat, exit, running away, exodus, getaway, absconding ...*his secret flight into exile...*

PHRASES **put something** *or* **someone to flight** = drive off, scatter, disperse, rout, stampede, scare off, send packing, chase off ...*We were put to flight by a herd of bullocks...* ♦ **take flight** = run away *or* off, flee, bolt, abscond, decamp, do a runner (*slang*), turn tail, do a bunk (*Brit. slang*), fly the coop (*U.S. & Canad. informal*), beat a retreat, light out (*informal*), skedaddle (*informal*), make a hasty retreat, take a powder (*U.S. & Canad. slang*), withdraw hastily, take it on the lam (*U.S. & Canad. slang*) ...*He decided to take flight immediately...*

flighty = frivolous, wild, volatile, unstable, irresponsible, dizzy, fickle, unbalanced, impulsive, mercurial, giddy, capricious, unsteady, thoughtless, changeable, impetuous, skittish, light-headed, harebrained, scatterbrained, ditzy *or* ditsy (*slang*)

flimsy 1 = fragile, weak, slight, delicate, shallow, shaky, frail, superficial, makeshift, rickety, insubstantial, gimcrack, unsubstantial ...*a flimsy wooden door...* OPPOSITE sturdy
2 = thin, light, sheer, transparent, chiffon, gossamer, gauzy ...*a flimsy pink chiffon nightgown...*
3 = unconvincing, poor, thin, weak, inadequate, pathetic, transparent, trivial, feeble, unsatisfactory, frivolous, tenuous, implausible ...*The charges were based on flimsy evidence...*

flinch 1 = wince, start, duck, shrink, cringe, quail, recoil, cower, blench ...*The slightest pressure made her flinch...*
2 *often with* **from** = shy away, shrink, withdraw, flee, retreat, back off, swerve, shirk, draw back, baulk ...*He has never flinched from harsh decisions...*

fling VERB = throw, toss, hurl, chuck (*informal*), launch, cast, pitch, send, shy, jerk, propel, sling, precipitate, lob (*informal*), catapult, heave, let fly ...*The woman flung the cup at him...*
NOUN 1 = binge, good time, bash, bit of fun, party, rave (*Brit. slang*), spree, indulgence (*informal*), beano (*Brit. slang*), night on the town, rave-up (*Brit. slang*), hooley *or* hoolie (*chiefly Irish & N.Z.*) ...*the last fling before you take up a job...*
2 = try, go (*informal*), attempt, shot (*informal*), trial, crack (*informal*), venture, gamble, stab (*informal*), bash (*informal*), whirl (*informal*) ...*the England bowler's chance of a fling at South Africa in the second Test today...*

flip VERB 1 = flick, switch, snap, slick, jerk ...*He walked out, flipping off the lights...*
2 = spin, turn, overturn, turn over, roll over, twist ...*The plane flipped over and burst into flames...*
3 = toss, throw, cast, pitch, flick, fling, sling ...*I flipped a cigarette butt out of the window...*
NOUN = toss, throw, cast, pitch, spin, snap, twist, flick, jerk ...*having gambled all on the flip of a coin...*

flippant = frivolous, rude, cheeky, irreverent, flip (*informal*), superficial, saucy, glib, pert, disrespectful, offhand, impertinent, impudent OPPOSITE serious

flirt VERB 1 = chat up, lead on (*informal*), dally with, make advances at, make eyes at, coquet, philander, make sheep's eyes at ...*He's flirting with all the ladies...*
2 *usually with* **with** = toy with, consider, entertain, play with, dabble in, trifle with, give a thought to, expose yourself to ...*My mother used to flirt with nationalism...*
NOUN = tease, philanderer, coquette, heart-breaker, wanton, trifler ...*She's a born flirt...*

flirtation = teasing, philandering, dalliance, coquetry, toying, intrigue, trifling

flirtatious = teasing, flirty, coquettish, amorous, come-on (*informal*), arch, enticing, provocative, coy, come-hither, sportive

flit = fly, dash, dart, skim, pass, speed, wing, flash, fleet, whisk, flutter

float 1 = glide, sail, drift, move gently, bob, coast, slide, be carried, slip along ...*barges floating quietly by the grassy river banks...*
2 = be buoyant, stay afloat, be *or* lie on the surface, rest on water, hang, hover, poise, displace water ...*Empty things float...* OPPOSITE sink
3 = launch, offer, sell, set up, promote, get going, push off ...*He floated his firm on the Stock Market...* OPPOSITE dissolve

floating 1 = uncommitted, wavering, undecided, indecisive, vacillating, sitting on the fence (*informal*), unaffiliated, independent ...*floating voters appear to have deserted the party...*
2 = free, wandering, variable, fluctuating, unattached, migratory, movable, unfixed ...*a house I shared with a floating population of others...*

flock NOUN 1 = herd, group, flight, drove, colony, gaggle, skein ...*They kept a small flock of sheep...*
2 = crowd, company, group, host, collection, mass, gathering, assembly, convoy, herd, congregation, horde, multitude, throng, bevy ...*his flock of advisors...*
VERB 1 = stream, crowd, mass, swarm, throng ...*The public have flocked to the show...*
2 = gather, group, crowd, mass, collect, assemble, herd, huddle, converge, throng, congregate, troop ...*The crowds flocked around her...*

flog = beat, whip, lash, thrash, whack, scourge, hit hard, trounce, castigate, chastise, flay, lambast(e), flagellate, punish severely

flogging = beating, hiding (*informal*), whipping, lashing, thrashing, caning, scourging, trouncing, flagellation, horsewhipping

flood NOUN 1 = deluge, downpour, flash flood, inundation, tide, overflow, torrent, spate, freshet ...*This is the sort of flood dreaded by cavers...*
2 = torrent, flow, rush, stream, tide, abundance, multitude, glut, outpouring, profusion ...*The administration is trying to stem the flood of refugees...*
3 = series, stream, avalanche, barrage, spate, torrent ...*He received a flood of complaints...*
4 = outpouring, rush, stream, surge, torrent ...*She broke into a flood of tears...*
VERB 1 = immerse, swamp, submerge, inundate, deluge, drown, cover with water ...*The house was flooded...*

2 = <u>pour over</u>, swamp, run over, overflow, inundate, brim over ...*Many streams have flooded their banks...*
3 = <u>engulf</u>, flow into, rush into, sweep into, overwhelm, surge into, swarm into, pour into, gush into ...*Large numbers of immigrants flooded the area...*
4 = <u>saturate</u>, fill, choke, swamp, glut, oversupply, overfill ...*a policy aimed at flooding Europe with exports...*
5 = <u>stream</u>, flow, rush, pour, surge ...*Enquiries flooded in from all over the world...*

(**Related Words**)
adjectives: fluvial, diluvial

floor NOUN **1** = <u>ground</u> ...*He's sitting on the floor watching TV...*
2 = <u>storey</u>, level, stage, tier ...*It's on the fifth floor of the hospital...*
VERB **1** (*Informal*) = <u>disconcert</u>, stump, baffle, confound, beat, throw (*informal*), defeat, puzzle, conquer, overthrow, bewilder, perplex, bowl over (*informal*), faze, discomfit, bring up short, dumbfound, nonplus ...*He was floored by the announcement...*
2 = <u>knock down</u>, fell, knock over, prostrate, deck (*slang*) ...*He was floored twice in the second round...*

flop VERB **1** = <u>slump</u>, fall, drop, collapse, sink, tumble, topple ...*She flopped, exhausted, on to a sofa...*
2 = <u>hang down</u>, hang, dangle, sag, droop, hang limply ...*His hair flopped over his left eye...*
3 (*Informal*) = <u>fail</u>, close, bomb (*U.S. & Canad. slang*), fold (*informal*), founder, fall short, fall flat, come to nothing, come unstuck, misfire, go belly-up (*slang*), go down like a lead balloon (*informal*) ...*The film flopped badly at the box office...* OPPOSITE⟩ succeed
NOUN (*Informal*) = <u>failure</u>, disaster, loser, fiasco, debacle, washout (*informal*), cockup (*Brit. slang*), nonstarter ...*The public decide whether a film is a hit or a flop...* OPPOSITE⟩ success

floppy = <u>droopy</u>, soft, loose, hanging, limp, flapping, sagging, baggy, flip-flop, flaccid, pendulous

floral = <u>flowery</u>, flower-patterned

florid 1 = <u>flowery</u>, high-flown, figurative, grandiloquent, euphuistic ...*a liking for florid writing...*
2 = <u>ornate</u>, busy, flamboyant, baroque, fussy, embellished, flowery, overelaborate ...*the cast-iron fireplace and the florid ceiling...* OPPOSITE⟩ plain
3 = <u>flushed</u>, ruddy, rubicund, high-coloured, high-complexioned, blowsy ...*He was a stout, florid man...* OPPOSITE⟩ pale

flotsam = <u>debris</u>, sweepings, rubbish, junk, wreckage, detritus, odds and ends, jetsam

flounce = <u>bounce</u>, storm, stamp, go quickly, throw, spring, toss, fling, jerk

flounder 1 = <u>falter</u>, struggle, stall, slow down, run into trouble, come unstuck (*informal*), be in difficulties, hit a bad patch ...*The economy was floundering...*
2 = <u>dither</u>, struggle, blunder, be confused, falter, be in the dark, be out of your depth ...*The president is

floundering, trying to jump-start his campaign...*
3 = <u>struggle</u>, struggle, toss, thrash, plunge, stumble, tumble, muddle, fumble, grope, wallow ...*men floundering about in the water...*

Word Power

flounder – *Flounder* is sometimes wrongly used where *founder* is meant: *the project foundered* (not *floundered*) *because of lack of funds.*

---

flourish VERB **1** = <u>thrive</u>, increase, develop, advance, progress, boom, bloom, blossom, prosper, burgeon ...*Business soon flourished...* OPPOSITE⟩ fail
2 = <u>succeed</u>, do well, be successful, move ahead, get ahead, go places (*informal*), go great guns (*slang*), go up in the world ...*On graduation he flourished as a journalist...*
3 = <u>grow</u>, thrive, develop, flower, succeed, get on, bloom, blossom, prosper, bear fruit, be vigorous, be in your prime ...*The plant is flourishing particularly well...*
4 = <u>wave</u>, brandish, sweep, swish, display, shake, swing, wield, flutter, wag, flaunt, vaunt, twirl ...*He flourished his glass to make the point...*
NOUN **1** = <u>wave</u>, sweep, brandish, swish, shaking, swing, dash, brandishing, twirling, twirl, showy gesture ...*with a flourish of his hand...*
2 = <u>show</u>, display, parade, fanfare ...*with a flourish of church bells...*
3 = <u>curlicue</u>, sweep, decoration, swirl, plume, embellishment, ornamentation ...*He underlined his name with a showy flourish...*

flourishing = <u>thriving</u>, successful, doing well, blooming, mushrooming, prospering, rampant, burgeoning, on a roll, going places, going strong, in the pink, in top form, on the up and up (*informal*)

flout = <u>defy</u>, scorn, spurn, scoff at, outrage, insult, mock, scout (*archaic*), ridicule, taunt, deride, sneer at, jeer at, laugh in the face of, show contempt for, gibe at, treat with disdain OPPOSITE⟩ respect
➤ **flaunt**

flow VERB **1** = <u>run</u>, course, rush, sweep, move, issue, pass, roll, flood, pour, slide, proceed, stream, run out, surge, spill, go along, circulate, swirl, glide, ripple, cascade, whirl, overflow, gush, inundate, deluge, spurt, teem, spew, squirt, purl, well forth ...*A stream flowed down into the valley...*
2 = <u>pour</u>, move, sweep, flood, stream, overflow ...*Large numbers of refugees continue to flow into the country...*
3 = <u>issue</u>, follow, result, emerge, spring, pour, proceed, arise, derive, ensue, emanate ...*Undesirable consequences flow from these misconceptions...*
NOUN **1** = <u>stream</u>, current, movement, motion, course, issue, flood, drift, tide, spate, gush, flux, outpouring, outflow, undertow, tideway ...*watching the quiet flow of the olive-green water...*
2 = <u>outpouring</u>, flood, stream, succession, train, plenty, abundance, deluge, plethora, outflow, effusion, emanation ...*the opportunity to control the

flow of information…

flower NOUN **1** = <u>bloom</u>, blossom, efflorescence
…*Each individual flower is tiny…*
2 = <u>elite</u>, best, prime, finest, pick, choice, cream,
height, crème de la crème (*French*), choicest part
…*the flower of American manhood…*
3 = <u>height</u>, prime, peak, vigour, freshness, greatest *or*
finest point …*You are hardly in the first flower of
youth…*
VERB **1** = <u>bloom</u>, open, mature, flourish, unfold,
blossom, burgeon, effloresce …*Several of these plants
will flower this year…*
2 = <u>blossom</u>, grow, develop, progress, mature, thrive,
flourish, bloom, bud, prosper …*Their relationship
flowered…*
(*Related Words*)
adjective : floral
prefix : antho-
➤ **flowers**

flowering = <u>blooming</u>, in flower, in bloom, in
blossom, out, open, ready, blossoming, florescent,
abloom

flowery 1 = <u>floral</u>, flower-patterned …*The baby was
dressed in a flowery jumpsuit…*
2 = <u>ornate</u>, fancy, rhetorical, high-flown, embellished,
figurative, florid, overwrought, euphuistic, baroque
…*They were using uncommonly flowery language…*
OPPOSITE plain

flowing 1 = <u>streaming</u>, rushing, gushing, teeming,
falling, full, rolling, sweeping, flooded, fluid, prolific,
abundant, overrun, brimming over …*fragrance borne
by the swiftly flowing stream…*
2 = <u>sleek</u>, smooth, fluid, unbroken, uninterrupted …*a
smooth flowing line against a cloudless sky…*
3 = <u>fluent</u>, easy, natural, continuous, effortless,
uninterrupted, free-flowing, cursive, rich …*his own
rhetoric and flowing style of delivery…*

fluctuate 1 = <u>change</u>, swing, vary, alter, hesitate,
alternate, waver, veer, rise and fall, go up and down,
ebb and flow, seesaw …*Body temperatures can
fluctuate when you are ill…*
2 = <u>shift</u>, undulate, oscillate, vacillate …*the constantly
fluctuating price of crude oil…*

fluctuation = <u>change</u>, shift, swing, variation,
instability, alteration, wavering, oscillation,
alternation, vacillation, unsteadiness, inconstancy

fluency = <u>ease</u>, control, facility, command, assurance,
readiness, smoothness, slickness, glibness, volubility,
articulateness

fluent = <u>effortless</u>, natural, articulate, well-versed,
glib, facile, voluble, smooth-spoken

fluff NOUN = <u>fuzz</u>, down, pile, dust, fibre, threads, nap,
lint, oose (*Scot.*), dustball …*bits of fluff on the sleeve of
her jumper…*
VERB (*Informal*) = <u>mess up</u>, spoil, bungle, screw up
(*informal*) (*informal*), cock up (*Brit. slang*), foul up
(*informal*), make a nonsense of, be unsuccessful in,
make a mess off, muddle, crool *or* cruel (*Austral. slang*)
…*She fluffed her interview at Oxford…*

fluffy = <u>soft</u>, fuzzy, feathery, downy, fleecy, flossy

fluid NOUN = <u>liquid</u>, solution, juice, liquor, sap …*Make
sure that you drink plenty of fluids…*
ADJECTIVE **1** = <u>flowing</u>, easy, natural, smooth, elegant,
graceful, fluent, effortless, feline, sinuous …*long fluid
dresses… …His painting became more fluid…*
2 = <u>changeable</u>, mobile, flexible, volatile, unstable,
adjustable, fluctuating, indefinite, shifting, floating,
adaptable, mercurial, protean, mutable …*The
situation is extremely fluid…* OPPOSITE fixed
3 = <u>liquid</u>, running, flowing, watery, molten, melted,
runny, liquefied, in solution, aqueous …*List the fluid
and cellular components of blood…* OPPOSITE solid

fluke = <u>stroke of luck</u>, accident, coincidence, chance
occurrence, chance, stroke, blessing, freak, windfall,
quirk, lucky break, serendipity, quirk of fate, fortuity,
break

flunk (*Informal*) = <u>fail</u>, screw up (*informal*), flop in
(*informal*), plough (*Brit. slang*), be unsuccessful in, not
make the grade at (*informal*), not come up to scratch
in (*informal*), not come up to the mark in (*informal*)

flurry 1 = <u>commotion</u>, stir, bustle, flutter, to-do,
excitement, hurry, fuss, disturbance, flap, whirl, furore,
ferment, agitation, fluster, ado, tumult …*There was a
flurry of excitement…*
2 = <u>burst</u>, spell, bout, outbreak, spurt …*a flurry of
diplomatic activity…*
3 = <u>gust</u>, shower, gale, swirl, squall, storm …*A flurry of
snowflakes was scudding by the window…*

flush¹ VERB **1** = <u>blush</u>, colour, burn, flame, glow,
crimson, redden, suffuse, turn red, go red, colour up,
go as red as a beetroot …*He turned away, his face
flushing…*
2 *often with* ***out*** = <u>cleanse</u>, wash out, swab, rinse out,
flood, drench, syringe, swill, hose down, douche
…*Flush the eye with clean cold water…*
3 = <u>expel</u>, drive, eject, dislodge …*Flush the contents
down the lavatory…*
NOUN **1** = <u>blush</u>, colour, glow, reddening, redness,
rosiness …*There was a slight flush on his cheeks…*
2 = <u>bloom</u>, glow, vigour, freshness …*the first flush of
young love…*

flush² ADJECTIVE **1** = <u>level</u>, even, true, flat, square,
plane …*Make sure the tile is flush with the surrounding
tiles…*
2 (*Informal*) = <u>wealthy</u>, rich, rolling (*slang*), well-off, in
the money (*informal*), in funds, well-heeled
(*informal*), replete, moneyed, well-supplied …*Many
developing countries were flush with dollars…*
3 = <u>affluent</u>, liberal, generous, lavish, abundant,
overflowing, plentiful, prodigal, full …*If we're feeling
flush we'll give them champagne…*
ADVERB = <u>level</u>, even, touching, squarely, in contact,
hard (against) …*The edges fit flush with the walls…*

flush³ *often with* ***out*** = <u>drive out</u>, force, dislodge, put
to flight, start, discover, disturb, uncover, rouse …*They
flushed them out of their hiding places…*

flushed 1 *often with* ***with*** = <u>exhilarated</u>, excited,
aroused, elated, high (*informal*), inspired, thrilled,
animated, enthused, intoxicated …*She was flushed
with the success of the venture…*

Flowers http://www.lovetoknow.com/Flowers/flowers.htm

acacia	delphinium	narcissus
acanthus	digitalis	nasturtium
African violet	dog rose	old man's beard
aloe	edelweiss	orchid
alyssum	eglantine	oxeye daisy
amaranth	forget-me-not	oxlip
amaryllis	foxglove	oxtongue
anemone	freesia	pansy
arbutus	geranium	passionflower
asphodel	gilliflower *or* gillyflower	peony *or* paeony
aspidistra	gladiolus	petunia
aster	godetia	phlox
aubrietia, aubrieta, *or* aubretia	grape hyacinth	pimpernel
azalea	groundsel	pink
babe-in-a-cradle	guelder-rose	poppy
begonia	gypsophila	primrose
betony	harebell	primula
bignonia	heartsease *or* heart's-ease	ragged robin
black-eyed Susan	heliotrope	ragweed
bluebell	hellebore	rose
bog asphodel	hemlock	saffron
bougainvillea	hibiscus	samphire
burdock	hollyhock	saxifrage
Busy Lizzie	hyacinth	scarlet pimpernel
buttercup	hydrangea	snapdragon
cactus	iris	snowdrop
calendula	jasmine	speedwell
camellia	jonquil	stock
camomile *or* chamomile	larkspur	(Sturt's) desert pea
cardinal flower	lavender	sunflower
carnation	lily	sweetbrier
celandine	lily of the valley	sweet pea
Christmas cactus	lobelia	sweet william
chrysanthemum	London pride	tiger lily
clematis	lotus	tulip
clianthus	love-in-idleness	valerian
columbine	love-lies-bleeding	verbena
Cooktown orchid	lupin	violet
cornflower	magnolia	wallflower
cotoneaster	mallow	water lily
cowslip	mandrake	willowherb
crocus	marguerite	wintergreen
cyclamen	marigold	wisteria
daffodil	marjoram	wood anemone
dahlia	meadowsweet	woodbine
daisy	monkshood	yarrow
dandelion	Michaelmas daisy	zinnia
deadly nightshade	morning-glory	

2 = <u>blushing</u>, red, hot, burning, embarrassed, glowing, rosy, crimson, feverish, ruddy, rubicund ...*Young girls with flushed faces pass by...*

fluster = <u>upset</u>, bother, disturb, ruffle, heat, excite, confuse, hurry, rattle (*informal*), bustle, hassle (*informal*), flurry, agitate, confound, unnerve, perturb, throw off balance, make nervous

fluted = <u>grooved</u>, channelled, furrowed, corrugated

flutter [VERB] **1** = <u>beat</u>, bat, flap, tremble, shiver, flicker, ripple, waver, fluctuate, agitate, ruffle, quiver, vibrate, palpitate ...*a butterfly fluttering its wings...*
2 = <u>flit</u>, hover, flitter ...*The birds were fluttering among the trees...*
[NOUN] **1** = <u>tremor</u>, tremble, shiver, shudder, palpitation

...*She felt a flutter of trepidation in her stomach...*
2 = <u>vibration</u>, twitching, quiver, quivering ...*loud twittering and a desperate flutter of wings...*
3 = <u>agitation</u>, state (*informal*), confusion, excitement, flap (*informal*), tremble, flurry, dither (*chiefly Brit.*), commotion, fluster, tumult, perturbation, state of nervous excitement ...*She was in a flutter...*

flux 1 = <u>instability</u>, change, transition, unrest, modification, alteration, mutation, fluctuation, mutability ...*a period of economic flux...*
2 = <u>flow</u>, movement, motion, fluidity ...*the flux of cosmic rays...*

fly¹ [VERB] **1** = <u>take wing</u>, soar, glide, take to the air, wing, mount, sail, hover, flutter, flit ...*The bird flew* away…

2 = <u>pilot</u>, control, operate, steer, manoeuvre, navigate, be at the controls, aviate …*He flew a small plane to Cuba…*

3 = <u>airlift</u>, send by plane, take by plane, take in an aircraft …*The relief supples are being flown from Pisa…*

4 = <u>flutter</u>, wave, float, flap …*A flag was flying on the new HQ…*

5 = <u>display</u>, show, flourish, brandish …*He sailed in a ship flying a red flag…*

6 = <u>rush</u>, race, shoot, career, speed, tear, dash, hurry, barrel (along) (*informal, chiefly U.S. & Canad.*), sprint, bolt, dart, zoom, hare (*Brit. informal*), hasten, whizz (*informal*), scoot, scamper, burn rubber (*informal*), be off like a shot (*informal*) …*I flew downstairs…*

7 = <u>pass swiftly</u>, pass, glide, slip away, roll on, flit, elapse, run its course, go quickly …*We walked and the time flew by…*

8 = <u>leave</u>, disappear, get away, depart, run, escape, flee, take off, run from, shun, clear out (*informal*), light out (*informal*), abscond, decamp, take flight, do a runner (*slang*), run for it, cut and run (*informal*), fly the coop (*U.S. & Canad. informal*), beat a retreat, make a quick exit, make a getaway, show a clean pair of heels, skedaddle (*informal*), hightail (*informal, chiefly U.S.*), take a powder (*U.S. & Canad. slang*), hasten away, make your escape, take it on the lam (*U.S. & Canad. slang*), take to your heels …*I'll have to fly…*

PHRASES **let fly** (*Informal*) = <u>lose your temper</u>, lash out, burst forth, keep nothing back, give free rein, let (someone) have it …*She let fly with a string of obscenities…* ◆ **let something fly** = <u>throw</u>, launch, cast, hurl, shoot, fire, fling, chuck (*informal*), sling, lob (*informal*), hurtle, let off, heave …*The midfielder let fly a powerful shot…*

fly²

PHRASES **fly in the ointment** = <u>problem</u>, difficulty, rub, flaw, hitch, drawback, snag, small problem

Related Words

collective noun: swarm

➤ **flies**

fly³ (*Slang, chiefly Brit.*) = <u>cunning</u>, knowing, sharp,

smart, careful, shrewd, astute, on the ball (*informal*), canny, wide-awake, nobody's fool, not born yesterday …*He is devious and very fly…*

flyer or **flier** **1** (*Old-fashioned*) = <u>pilot</u>, aeronaut, airman *or* airwoman, aviator *or* aviatrix …*escape lines for shot-down allied flyers…*

2 = <u>air traveller</u>, air passenger …*regular business flyers…*

3 = <u>handbill</u>, bill, notice, leaf, release, literature (*informal*), leaflet, advert (*Brit. informal*), circular, booklet, pamphlet, handout, throwaway (*U.S.*), promotional material, publicity material …*posters, newsletters and flyers…*

4 = <u>jump</u>, spring, bound, leap, hurdle, vault, jeté, flying *or* running jump …*At this point he took a flyer off the front…*

flying **1** = <u>airborne</u>, waving, winging, floating, streaming, soaring, in the air, hovering, flapping, gliding, fluttering, wind-borne, volitant …*a species of flying insect…*

2 = <u>fast</u>, running, express, speedy, winged, mobile, rapid, fleet, mercurial …*He made a flying start to the final…*

3 = <u>hurried</u>, brief, rushed, fleeting, short-lived, hasty, transitory, fugacious …*I paid a flying visit to the capital…*

foam **NOUN** = <u>froth</u>, spray, bubbles, lather, suds, spume, head …*The water curved round the rock in bursts of foam…*

VERB = <u>bubble</u>, boil, fizz, froth, lather, effervesce …*We watched the water foam and bubble…*

fob

PHRASES **fob someone off** = <u>put off</u>, deceive, appease, flannel (*Brit. informal*), give (someone) the run-around (*informal*), stall, equivocate with …*I've asked her but she fobs me off with excuses…* ◆ **fob something off on someone** = <u>pass off</u>, dump, get rid of, inflict, unload, foist, palm off …*He likes to fob his work off on others…*

focus **VERB** **1** = <u>concentrate</u>, centre, spotlight, zero in on (*informal*), meet, join, direct, aim, pinpoint, converge, rivet, bring to bear, zoom in …*The summit is expected to focus on arms control…*

Flies http://www.cirrusimage.com/flies.htm

antlion *or* antlion fly	chalcid *or* chalcid fly	grannom	robber fly, bee killer, *or* assassin fly
aphid *or* plant louse	cluster fly	greenbottle	
aphis	crane fly *or* (*Brit.*) daddy-longlegs	green blowfly *or* (*Austral. informal*) blue-arsed fly	sandfly
apple blight *or* American blight	damselfly		scorpion fly
bee fly	dobsonfly	greenfly	screwworm fly
beetfly *or* mangold fly	dragonfly *or* (*colloquial*) devil's darning-needle	horsefly *or* cleg	silverhorn
blackfly *or* bean aphid		housefly	snake fly
blowfly, bluebottle, *or* (*Austral. informal*) blowie	drosophila, fruit fly, *or* vinegar fly	hover fly	stable fly
	fly	lacewing	stonefly
botfly	frit fly	lantern fly	tachina fly
buffalo gnat *or* black fly	fruit fly	mayfly *or* dayfly	tsetse fly *or* tzetze fly
bulb fly	gadfly	Mediterranean fruit fly *or* Medfly	vinegar fly
bushfly	gallfly	needle fly	warble fly
carrot fly	gnat	onion fly	whitefly
			willow fly

2 = fix, train, direct, aim ...*He focused the binoculars on the boat*...
NOUN **1** = centre, focal point, central point, core, bull's eye, centre of attraction, centre of activity, cynosure ...*The children are the focus of her life*...
2 = focal point, heart, target, headquarters, hub, meeting place ...*The focus of the campaign for Black rights*...
PHRASES **in focus** = clear, sharp, distinct, crisp, sharp-edged, sharply defined ...*Pictures should be in focus*... ◆ **out of focus** = blurred, obscure, unclear, fuzzy, hazy, muzzy, ill-defined, indistinct ...*Some of the pictures are out of focus*...

fodder = feed, food, rations, tack (*informal*), foodstuff, kai (*N.Z. informal*), forage, victuals, provender, vittles (*obsolete or dialect*)

foe = enemy, rival, opponent, adversary, antagonist, foeman (*archaic*) OPPOSITE friend

fog NOUN **1** = mist, gloom, haze, smog, murk, miasma, murkiness, peasouper (*informal*) ...*The crash happened In thick fog*...
2 = stupor, confusion, trance, daze, haze, disorientation ...*He was in a fog when he got up*...
VERB **1** *sometimes with* **up** = mist over *or* up, cloud over, steam up, become misty ...*The windows fogged immediately*...
2 = daze, cloud, dim, muddle, blind, confuse, obscure, bewilder, darken, perplex, stupefy, befuddle, muddy the waters, obfuscate, blear, becloud, bedim ...*His mind was fogged with fatigue*...

foggy 1 = misty, grey, murky, cloudy, obscure, blurred, dim, hazy, nebulous, indistinct, soupy, smoggy, vaporous, brumous (*rare*) ...*Conditions were damp and foggy this morning*... OPPOSITE clear
2 = unclear, confused, clouded, stupid, obscure, vague, dim, bewildered, muddled, dazed, cloudy, stupefied, indistinct, befuddled, dark ...*My foggy brain sifted through the possibilities*... OPPOSITE sharp

foible = idiosyncrasy, failing, fault, weakness, defect, quirk, imperfection, peculiarity, weak point, infirmity

foil¹ = thwart, stop, check, defeat, disappoint, counter, frustrate, hamper, baffle, elude, balk, circumvent, outwit, nullify, checkmate, nip in the bud, put a spoke in (someone's) wheel (*Brit.*) ...*A brave police chief foiled an armed robbery*...

foil² = complement, setting, relief, contrast, background, antithesis ...*A cold beer is the perfect foil for a curry*...

foist
PHRASES **foist something** *or* **someone off on someone** = unload, get rid of, pass off, palm off ...*No wonder she was so keen to foist him off on us*... ◆ **foist something on** *or* **upon someone** = force ...*I don't foist my beliefs on other people*...

fold VERB **1** = bend, double, gather, tuck, overlap, crease, pleat, intertwine, double over, turn under ...*He folded the paper carefully*...
2 (*Informal*) = go bankrupt, close, fail, crash, collapse, founder, shut down, go under, be ruined, go bust (*informal*), go to the wall, go belly-up (*slang*) ...*The company folded in 1990*...
3 = wrap, envelop, entwine, enfold ...*He folded her in his arms*...
4 = wrap up, wrap, enclose, envelop, do up, enfold ...*an object folded neatly in tissue-paper*...
NOUN = crease, turn, gather, bend, layer, overlap, wrinkle, pleat, ruffle, furrow, knife-edge, double thickness, folded portion ...*Make another fold and turn the ends together*...

folder = file, portfolio, envelope, dossier, binder

folk 1 = people, persons, humans, individuals, men and women, human beings, humanity, inhabitants, mankind, mortals ...*the innate reserve of country folk*...
2 *usually plural* = family, parents, relations, relatives, tribe, clan, kin, kindred ...*I've been avoiding my folks lately*...

follow VERB **1** = accompany, attend, escort, come after, go behind, tag along behind, bring up the rear, come behind, come *or* go with, tread on the heels of ...*Please follow me, madam*...
2 = pursue, track, dog, hunt, chase, shadow, tail (*informal*), trail, hound, stalk, run after ...*I think we're being followed*... OPPOSITE avoid
3 = come after, go after, come next ...*the rioting and looting that followed the verdict*... OPPOSITE precede
4 = result, issue, develop, spring, flow, proceed, arise, ensue, emanate, be consequent, supervene ...*If the explanation is right, two things will follow*...
5 = obey, observe, comply with, adhere to, mind, watch, note, regard, stick to, heed, conform to, keep to, pay attention to, be guided by, toe the line, act according to, act in accordance with, give allegiance to ...*Take care to follow the instructions*... OPPOSITE ignore
6 = copy, imitate, emulate, mimic, model, adopt, live up to, take a leaf out of someone's book, take as an example, pattern yourself upon ...*He did not follow his example in taking drugs*...
7 = succeed, replace, come after, take over from, come next, supersede, supplant, take the place of, step into the shoes of ...*He followed his father and became a surgeon*...
8 = understand, get, see, catch, realize, appreciate, take in, grasp, catch on (*informal*), keep up with, comprehend, fathom, get the hang of (*informal*), get the picture ...*Can you follow the plot so far?*...
9 = keep up with, support, be interested in, cultivate, be devoted to, be a fan of, keep abreast of, be a devotee *or* supporter of ...*the millions of people who follow football*...
PHRASES **follow something through** = complete, conclude, pursue, see through, consummate, bring to a conclusion ...*They have been unwilling to follow through their ideas*...

follower 1 = supporter, fan, representative, convert, believer, admirer, backer, partisan, disciple, protagonist, devotee, worshipper, apostle, pupil, cohort (*chiefly U.S.*), adherent, henchman, groupie (*slang*), habitué, votary ...*violent clashes between followers of the two organisations*... OPPOSITE leader

2 = <u>attendant</u>, assistant, companion, helper, sidekick (*slang*), henchman, retainer (*History*), hanger-on, minion, lackey ...*a London gangster and his two thuggish followers*... OPPOSITE opponent

following ADJECTIVE **1** = <u>next</u>, subsequent, successive, ensuing, coming, later, succeeding, specified, consequent, consequential ...*We went to dinner the following evening*...
2 = <u>coming</u>, about to be mentioned ...*Write down the following information*...
NOUN = <u>supporters</u>, backing, public, support, train, fans, audience, circle, suite, patronage, clientele, entourage, coterie, retinue ...*Rugby League enjoys a huge following*...

folly = <u>foolishness</u>, bêtise (*rare*), nonsense, madness, stupidity, absurdity, indiscretion, lunacy, recklessness, silliness, idiocy, irrationality, imprudence, rashness, imbecility, fatuity, preposterousness, daftness (*informal*), desipience OPPOSITE wisdom

foment = <u>stir up</u>, raise, encourage, promote, excite, spur, foster, stimulate, provoke, brew, arouse, rouse, agitate, quicken, incite, instigate, whip up, goad, abet, sow the seeds of, fan the flames

> ## *Word Power*
>
> **foment** – Both *foment* and *ferment* can be used to talk about stirring up trouble: *he was accused of fomenting/fermenting unrest*. Only *ferment* can be used intransitively or as a noun: *his anger continued to ferment* (not *foment*); *rural areas were unaffected by the ferment in the cities*.

fond ADJECTIVE **1** = <u>loving</u>, caring, warm, devoted, tender, adoring, affectionate, indulgent, doting, amorous ...*She gave him a fond smile*... OPPOSITE indifferent
2 = <u>unrealistic</u>, empty, naive, vain, foolish, deluded, indiscreet, credulous, overoptimistic, delusive, delusory, absurd ...*My fond hope is that we'll be ready on time*... OPPOSITE sensible
PHRASES **fond of 1** = <u>attached to</u>, in love with, keen on, attracted to, having a soft spot for, enamoured of ...*I am very fond of Michael*... **2** = <u>keen on</u>, into (*informal*), hooked on, partial to, having a soft spot for, having a taste for, addicted to, having a liking for, predisposed towards, having a fancy for ...*He was fond of marmalade*...

fondle = <u>caress</u>, pet, cuddle, touch gently, pat, stroke, dandle

fondly 1 = <u>lovingly</u>, tenderly, affectionately, amorously, dearly, possessively, with affection, indulgently, adoringly ...*Their eyes met fondly across the table*...
2 = <u>unrealistically</u>, stupidly, vainly, foolishly, naively, credulously ...*I fondly imagined my life could be better*...

fondness 1 = <u>devotion</u>, love, affection, warmth, attachment, kindness, tenderness, care ...*a great fondness for children*... OPPOSITE dislike
2 = <u>liking</u>, love, taste, fancy, attraction, weakness,

preference, attachment, penchant, susceptibility, predisposition, soft spot, predilection, partiality ...*I've always had a fondness for jewels*...

food = <u>nourishment</u>, cooking, provisions, fare, board, commons, table, eats (*slang*), stores, feed, diet, meat, bread, menu, tuck (*informal*), tucker (*Austral. & N.Z. informal*), rations, nutrition, cuisine, tack (*informal*), refreshment, scoff (*slang*), nibbles, grub (*slang*), foodstuffs, subsistence, kai (*N.Z. informal*), larder, chow (*informal*), sustenance, nosh (*slang*), daily bread, victuals, edibles, comestibles, provender, nosebag (*slang*), pabulum (*rare*), nutriment, vittles (*obsolete or dialect*), viands, aliment, eatables (*slang*), survival rations

(*Related Words*)
adjective: alimentary
noun: gastronomy

fool NOUN **1** = <u>simpleton</u>, idiot, mug (*Brit. slang*), berk (*Brit. slang*), charlie (*Brit. informal*), silly, goose (*informal*), dope (*informal*), jerk (*slang, chiefly U.S. & Canad.*), dummy (*slang*), ass (*U.S. & Canad. taboo slang*), clot (*Brit. informal*), plank (*Brit. slang*), sap (*slang*), wally (*slang*), illiterate, prat (*slang*), plonker (*slang*), coot, moron, nit (*informal*), git (*Brit. slang*), geek (*slang*), twit (*informal, chiefly Brit.*), bonehead (*slang*), chump (*informal*), dunce, imbecile (*informal*), loon, clod, cretin, oaf, bozo (*U.S. slang*), dullard, dimwit (*informal*), ignoramus, dumbo (*slang*), jackass, dipstick (*Brit. slang*), gonzo (*slang*), schmuck (*U.S. slang*), dork (*slang*), nitwit (*informal*), dolt, blockhead, ninny, divvy (*Brit. slang*), bird-brain (*informal*), pillock (*Brit. slang*), halfwit, nincompoop, dweeb (*U.S. slang*), putz (*U.S. slang*), fathead (*informal*), weenie (*U.S. informal*), schlep (*U.S. slang*), eejit (*Scot. & Irish*), dumb-ass (*slang*), pea-brain (*slang*), dunderhead, numpty (*Scot. informal*), doofus (*slang, chiefly U.S.*), lamebrain (*informal*), mooncalf, thickhead, clodpate (*archaic*), nerd *or* nurd (*slang*), numbskull *or* numskull, twerp *or* twirp (*informal*), dorba *or* dorb (*Austral. slang*), bogan (*Austral. slang*) ...*He'd been a fool to get involved with her*... OPPOSITE genius
2 = <u>dupe</u>, butt, mug (*Brit. slang*), sucker (*slang*), gull (*archaic*), stooge (*slang*), laughing stock, pushover (*informal*), fall guy (*informal*), chump (*informal*), greenhorn (*informal*), easy mark (*informal*) ...*He feels she has made a fool of him*...
3 = <u>jester</u>, comic, clown, harlequin, motley, buffoon, pierrot, court jester, punchinello, joculator *or (fem.)* joculatrix, merry-andrew ...*Every good court has its resident fool*...
VERB = <u>deceive</u>, cheat, mislead, delude, kid (*informal*), trick, take in, con (*informal*), stiff (*slang*), have (someone) on, bluff, hoax, dupe, beguile, gull (*archaic*), swindle, make a fool of, bamboozle, hoodwink, take for a ride (*informal*), put one over on (*informal*), play a trick on, pull a fast one on (*informal*) ...*Art dealers fool a lot of people*...
PHRASES **fool around** *or* **about 1** = <u>mess about</u>, sleep around (*informal*), womanize (*informal*), philander, flirt, court, toy, trifle, mess about, mess around, dally, coquet ...*Her husband was fooling*

around... **2** (*Informal*) = <u>mess about</u>, hang around, idle, waste time, lark, play about, dawdle, kill time, fool about, play the fool, act the fool, footle (*informal*) *...Stop fooling about...* ◆ **fool around with something** (*Informal*) = <u>play around with</u>, play with, tamper with, toy with, mess around with, meddle with, trifle with, fiddle around with (*informal*), monkey around with *...He was fooling around with his cot, and he fell out of bed...*

foolhardy = <u>rash</u>, risky, irresponsible, reckless, precipitate, unwise, impulsive, madcap, impetuous, hot-headed, imprudent, incautious, venturesome, venturous, temerarious OPPOSITE cautious

foolish **1** = <u>unwise</u>, silly, absurd, rash, unreasonable, senseless, short-sighted, ill-advised, foolhardy, nonsensical, inane, indiscreet, ill-judged, ill-considered, imprudent, unintelligent, asinine, injudicious, incautious *...It would be foolish to raise hopes unnecessarily...* OPPOSITE sensible
2 = <u>silly</u>, stupid, mad, daft (*informal*), simple, weak, crazy, ridiculous, dumb (*informal*), ludicrous, senseless, barmy (*slang*), potty (*Brit. informal*), goofy (*informal*), idiotic, half-baked (*informal*), dotty (*slang*), inane, fatuous, loopy (*informal*), witless, crackpot (*informal*), moronic, brainless, half-witted, imbecilic, off your head (*informal*), braindead (*informal*), harebrained, as daft as a brush (*informal, chiefly Brit.*), dumb-ass (*slang*), doltish *...How foolish I was not to have seen my doctor earlier...*

foolishly = <u>unwisely</u>, stupidly, mistakenly, absurdly, like a fool, idiotically, incautiously, imprudently, ill-advisedly, indiscreetly, short-sightedly, injudiciously, without due consideration

foolishness **1** = <u>stupidity</u>, irresponsibility, recklessness, idiocy, weakness, absurdity, indiscretion, silliness, inanity, imprudence, rashness, foolhardiness, folly, bêtise (*rare*) *...the foolishness of dangerously squabbling politicians...*
2 = <u>nonsense</u>, carrying-on (*informal, chiefly Brit.*), rubbish, trash, bunk (*informal*), claptrap (*informal*), rigmarole, foolery, bunkum *or* buncombe (*chiefly U.S.*) *...I don't have time to listen to this foolishness...*

foolproof = <u>infallible</u>, certain, safe, guaranteed, never-failing, unassailable, sure-fire (*informal*), unbreakable

football
➤ **football**

footing **1** = <u>basis</u>, foundation, foothold, base position, ground, settlement, establishment, installation, groundwork *...a sounder financial footing for the future...*
2 = <u>relationship</u>, terms, position, basis, state, standing, condition, relations, rank, status, grade *...They are trying to compete on an equal footing...*
3 = <u>foothold</u>, hold, grip, toehold, support *...He lost his footing and slid into the water...*

footpath (*Austral.*) = <u>pavement</u>, sidewalk (*U.S. & Canad.*)

footstep **1** = <u>step</u>, tread, footfall *...I heard footsteps outside...*

2 = <u>footprint</u>, mark, track, trace, outline, imprint, indentation, footmark *...people's footsteps in the snow...*

footwear = <u>footgear</u>, boots, shoes, slippers, sandals

forage VERB = <u>search</u>, hunt, scavenge, cast about, seek, explore, raid, scour, plunder, look round, rummage, ransack, scrounge (*informal*), fossick (*Austral. & N.Z.*) *...They were forced to forage for clothes and fuel...*
NOUN (*for cattle, etc.*) = <u>fodder</u>, food, feed, foodstuffs, provender *...forage needed to feed one cow and its calf...*

foray = <u>raid</u>, sally, incursion, inroad, attack, assault, invasion, swoop, reconnaissance, sortie, irruption

forbearance **1** = <u>patience</u>, resignation, restraint, tolerance, indulgence, long-suffering, moderation, self-control, leniency, temperance, mildness, lenity, longanimity (*rare*) *...a high degree of tolerance and forbearance...* OPPOSITE impatience
2 = <u>abstinence</u>, refraining, avoidance *...forbearance from military action...*

forbid = <u>prohibit</u>, ban, disallow, proscribe, exclude, rule out, veto, outlaw, inhibit, hinder, preclude, make illegal, debar, interdict OPPOSITE permit

---

Word Power

forbid – Traditionally, it has been considered more correct to talk about *forbidding someone to do something*, rather than *forbidding someone from doing something*. Recently, however, the *from* option has become generally more acceptable, so that *he was forbidden to come in* and *he was forbidden from coming in* may both now be considered correct.

---

forbidden = <u>prohibited</u>, banned, vetoed, outlawed, taboo, out of bounds, proscribed, verboten (*German*)

forbidding = <u>threatening</u>, severe, frightening, hostile, grim, menacing, sinister, daunting, ominous, unfriendly, foreboding, baleful, bodeful OPPOSITE inviting

force VERB **1** = <u>compel</u>, make, drive, press, pressure, urge, overcome, oblige, railroad (*informal*), constrain, necessitate, coerce, impel, strong-arm (*informal*), dragoon, pressurize, press-gang, put the squeeze on (*informal*), obligate, twist (someone's) arm, put the screws on (*informal*), bring pressure to bear upon *...They forced him to work for them at gun point...*
2 = <u>impose</u>, foist *...To force this agreement on the nation is wrong...*
3 = <u>push</u>, thrust, propel *...They forced her head under the icy waters, drowning her...*
4 = <u>break open</u>, blast, wrench, prise, wrest, use violence on *...The police forced the door of the flat and arrested him...*
5 = <u>extort</u>, drag, exact, wring *...using torture to force a confession out of a suspect...* OPPOSITE coax
NOUN **1** = <u>compulsion</u>, pressure, violence, enforcement, constraint, oppression, coercion, duress, arm-twisting (*informal*) *...calls for the siege to be*

Football

Terms used in (Association) Football http://www.fifa.com/fifa/history_E.html

aggregate (score)	goalpost *or* post	playoff
back	half	professional foul
ballplayer	halfback	promotion
ballwinner	half time	red card
booking *or* caution	half way line	referee
breakaway	handball	relegation
cap	indirect free kick	reserves
catenaccio	inside left	right back
centre circle	inside right	Route One
centre forward	inswinger	save
centre half	international	score draw
clearance	kick off	sending-off *or* ordering-off
cross	lay off	SFA
crossbar *or* bar	left back	shot
corner (kick)	linesman	six-yard line
cut out	long ball	sliding tackle
defender	mark	stoppage time *or* injury time
derby	midfield	striker
direct free kick	midfielder	square
dribble	nil	substitute
dummy	non-league	sweeper
extra time	nutmeg	tackle
FA	offside	target man
FIFA	offside trap	throw in
finishing	onside	total football
forward	one-two	touchline
foul	outside left	transfer
free kick	outside right	trap
fullback	own goal	UEFA
full time	pass	wall
goal	pass-back	wall pass
goal area *or* six-yard box	penalty (kick) *or* spot kick	wing
goalkeeper *or* goalie	penalty area *or* penalty box	winger
goal kick *or* bye kick	penalty shoot-out	yellow card
goal net *or* net	penalty spot	

Terms used in Australian Rules Football http://afl.com.au/

Australian Football League *or* AFL	forward pocket	rove
back pocket	free kick	rover
behind *or* point	goal	rub out
behind line	goal umpire	ruck
behind post	guernsey	ruckrover
boundary	half-back	scrimmage
eighteen, the	half-forward	shepherd
field umpire	handball	shirt front
flank	interchange	stab kick
footy, Aussie Rules, *or* (*jocular*)	mark	stanza
aerial ping-pong	nineteenth man	throw in
follower	quarter	twentieth man

Terms used in American Football http://www.nfl.com/

backfield	field goal	lineman
blitz	football *or* pigskin	offense
block	fullback	overtime
center	gridiron	pass
complete	guard	play
cornerback	halfback	point after
defense	incomplete	punt
defensive back	interception	punter
defensive end	kicker	quarterback
down	line *or* line of scrimmage	run *or* rush
end zone	line backer	running back

Terms used in American Football (continued)

sack	shotgun	tackle
safety	snap	tight end
scrimmage	special team	
secondary	Super Bowl	

---

ended by force...

2 = <u>power</u>, might, pressure, energy, stress, strength, impact, muscle, momentum, impulse, stimulus, vigour, potency, dynamism, life ...*slamming the door behind her with all her force*... OPPOSITE weakness

3 = <u>influence</u>, power, effect, authority, weight, strength, punch (*informal*), significance, effectiveness, validity, efficacy, soundness, persuasiveness, cogency, bite ...*He changed our world through the force of his ideas*...

4 = <u>intensity</u>, vigour, vehemence, fierceness, drive, emphasis, persistence ...*She took a step back from the force of his rage*...

5 = <u>army</u>, unit, division, corps, company, body, host, troop, squad, patrol, regiment, battalion, legion, squadron, detachment ...*a pan-European peace-keeping force*...

PHRASES **in force 1** = <u>valid</u>, working, current, effective, binding, operative, operational, in operation, on the statute book ...*The new tax is already in force*... **2** = <u>in great numbers</u>, all together, in full strength ...*Voters turned out in force*...

forced 1 = <u>compulsory</u>, enforced, slave, unwilling, mandatory, obligatory, involuntary, conscripted ...*a system of forced labour*... OPPOSITE voluntary

2 = <u>false</u>, affected, strained, wooden, stiff, artificial, contrived, unnatural, insincere, laboured ...*a forced smile*... OPPOSITE natural

forceful 1 = <u>dynamic</u>, powerful, vigorous, potent, assertive ...*He was a man of forceful character*... OPPOSITE weak

2 = <u>powerful</u>, strong, convincing, effective, compelling, persuasive, weighty, pithy, cogent, telling ...*This is a forceful argument for joining them*...

forcible 1 = <u>violent</u>, armed, aggressive, compulsory, drastic, coercive ...*forcible resettlement of villagers*...

2 = <u>compelling</u>, strong, powerful, effective, active, impressive, efficient, valid, mighty, potent, energetic, forceful, weighty, cogent ...*He is a forcible advocate for the arts*...

forcibly = <u>by force</u>, compulsorily, under protest, against your will, under compulsion, by main force, willy-nilly

forebear = <u>ancestor</u>, father, predecessor, forerunner, forefather, progenitor

foreboding 1 = <u>dread</u>, fear, anxiety, chill, unease, apprehension, misgiving, premonition, presentiment, apprehensiveness ...*an uneasy sense of foreboding*...

2 = <u>omen</u>, warning, prediction, portent, sign, token, foreshadowing, presage, prognostication, augury, foretoken ...*No one paid any attention to their gloomy forebodings*...

forecast NOUN = <u>prediction</u>, projection, anticipation, prognosis, planning, guess, outlook, prophecy,

foresight, conjecture, forewarning, forethought ...*He delivered his election forecast*...

VERB = <u>predict</u>, anticipate, foresee, foretell, call, plan, estimate, calculate, divine, prophesy, augur, forewarn, prognosticate, vaticinate (*rare*) ...*They forecast a defeat for the Prime Minister*...

forefather = <u>ancestor</u>, father, predecessor, forerunner, forebear, progenitor, procreator, primogenitor

forefront = <u>lead</u>, centre, front, fore, spearhead, prominence, vanguard, foreground, leading position, van

forego
➤ **forgo**

foregoing = <u>preceding</u>, former, above, previous, prior, antecedent, anterior, just mentioned, previously stated

foreground 1 = <u>front</u>, focus, forefront ...*the foreground of this boldly painted landscape*...

2 = <u>prominence</u>, limelight, fore, forefront ...*This worry has come to the foreground in recent years*...

foreign 1 = <u>alien</u>, overseas, exotic, unknown, outside, strange, imported, borrowed, remote, distant, external, unfamiliar, far off, outlandish, beyond your ken ...*a foreign language*... OPPOSITE native

2 = <u>unassimilable</u>, external, extraneous, outside ...*rejected the transplanted organ as a foreign object*...

3 = <u>uncharacteristic</u>, inappropriate, unrelated, incongruous, inapposite, irrelevant ...*He fell into a gloomy mood that was usually so foreign to him*...

foreigner = <u>alien</u>, incomer, immigrant, non-native, stranger, newcomer, settler, outlander

(*Related Words*)
fear of: xenophobia

foremost = <u>leading</u>, best, first, highest, front, chief, prime, primary, supreme, initial, most important, principal, paramount, inaugural, pre-eminent, headmost

forerunner 1 = <u>omen</u>, sign, indication, token, premonition, portent, augury, prognostic, foretoken ...*Some respiratory symptoms can be the forerunners of asthma*...

2 = <u>precursor</u>, predecessor, ancestor, prototype, forebear, harbinger, progenitor, herald ...*the forerunners of those who were to support the Nazis*...

foresee = <u>predict</u>, forecast, anticipate, envisage, prophesy, foretell, forebode, vaticinate (*rare*), divine

foreshadow = <u>predict</u>, suggest, promise, indicate, signal, imply, bode, prophesy, augur, presage, prefigure, portend, betoken, adumbrate, forebode

foresight = <u>forethought</u>, prudence, circumspection, far-sightedness, care, provision, caution, precaution, anticipation, preparedness, prescience, premeditation, prevision (*rare*) OPPOSITE> hindsight

forestall = <u>prevent</u>, stop, frustrate, anticipate, head off, parry, thwart, intercept, hinder, preclude, balk, circumvent, obviate, nip in the bud, provide against

forestry = <u>woodcraft</u>, silviculture, arboriculture, dendrology (*Botany*), woodmanship

foretaste = <u>sample</u>, example, indication, preview, trailer, prelude, whiff, foretoken, warning

foretell = <u>predict</u>, forecast, prophesy, portend, call, signify, bode, foreshadow, augur, presage, forewarn, prognosticate, adumbrate, forebode, foreshow, soothsay, vaticinate (*rare*)

forever 1 = <u>evermore</u>, always, ever, for good, for keeps, for all time, in perpetuity, for good and all (*informal*), till the cows come home (*informal*), world without end, till the end of time, till Doomsday ...*We will live together forever*...
2 = <u>constantly</u>, always, all the time, continually, endlessly, persistently, eternally, perpetually, incessantly, interminably, unremittingly, everlastingly ...*He was forever attempting to arrange deals*...

> ## *Word Power*
>
> **forever** – *Forever* and *for ever* can both be used to say that something is without end. For all other meanings, *forever* is the preferred form.

forewarn = <u>alert</u>, advise, caution, tip off, apprise, give fair warning, put on guard, put on the qui vive

foreword = <u>introduction</u>, preliminary, preface, preamble, prologue, prolegomenon

forfeit VERB = <u>relinquish</u>, lose, give up, surrender, renounce, be deprived of, say goodbye to, be stripped of ...*He was ordered to forfeit more than £1.5m in profits*...
NOUN = <u>penalty</u>, fine, damages, forfeiture, loss, mulct, amercement (*obsolete*) ...*That is the forfeit he must pay*...

forfeiture = <u>loss</u>, giving up, surrender, forfeiting, confiscation, sequestration (*Law*), relinquishment

forge 1 = <u>form</u>, build, create, establish, set up, fashion, shape, frame, construct, invent, devise, mould, contrive, fabricate, hammer out, make, work ...*They agreed to forge closer economic ties*...
2 = <u>fake</u>, copy, reproduce, imitate, counterfeit, feign, falsify, coin ...*They discovered forged dollar notes*...
3 = <u>create</u>, make, work, found, form, model, fashion, shape, cast, turn out, construct, devise, mould, contrive, fabricate, hammer out, beat into shape ...*To forge a blade takes great skill*...

forged 1 = <u>fake</u>, copy, false, counterfeit, pretend, artificial, mock, pirated, reproduction, synthetic, imitation, bogus, simulated, duplicate, quasi, sham, fraudulent, pseudo, fabricated, copycat (*informal*), falsified, ersatz, unoriginal, ungenuine, phony *or* phoney (*informal*) ...*She was carrying a forged American passport*... OPPOSITE> genuine
2 = <u>formed</u>, worked, founded, modelled, fashioned, shaped, cast, framed, stamped, crafted, moulded, minted, hammered out, beat out, beaten into shape

...*fifteen tons of forged steel parts*...

forger = <u>counterfeiter</u>, copier, copyist, falsifier, coiner

forgery 1 = <u>falsification</u>, faking, pirating, counterfeiting, fraudulence, fraudulent imitation, coining ...*He was found guilty of forgery*...
2 = <u>fake</u>, imitation, sham, counterfeit, falsification, phoney *or* phony (*informal*) ...*The letter was a forgery*...

forget 1 = <u>fail to remember</u>, not remember, not recollect, let slip from the memory, fail to bring to mind ...*She forgot where she left the car*... OPPOSITE> remember
2 = <u>neglect</u>, overlook, omit, not remember, be remiss, fail to remember ...*Don't forget that all dogs need a supply of water*...
3 = <u>leave behind</u>, lose, lose sight of, mislay ...*I forgot my passport*...
4 = <u>dismiss from your mind</u>, ignore, overlook, stop thinking about, let bygones be bygones, consign to oblivion, put out of your mind ...*I can't forget what happened today*...

forgetful = <u>absent-minded</u>, vague, careless, neglectful, oblivious, lax, negligent, dreamy, slapdash, heedless, slipshod, inattentive, unmindful, apt to forget, having a memory like a sieve OPPOSITE> mindful

forgetfulness = <u>absent-mindedness</u>, oblivion, inattention, carelessness, abstraction, laxity, laxness, dreaminess, obliviousness, lapse of memory, heedlessness, woolgathering

forgive = <u>excuse</u>, pardon, bear no malice towards, not hold something against, understand, acquit, condone, remit, let off (*informal*), turn a blind eye to, exonerate, absolve, bury the hatchet, let bygones be bygones, turn a deaf ear to, accept (someone's) apology OPPOSITE> blame

forgiveness = <u>pardon</u>, mercy, absolution, exoneration, overlooking, amnesty, acquittal, remission, condonation

forgiving = <u>lenient</u>, tolerant, compassionate, clement, patient, mild, humane, gracious, long-suffering, merciful, magnanimous, forbearing, willing to forgive, soft-hearted

forgo *or* **forego** = <u>give up</u>, sacrifice, surrender, do without, kick (*informal*), abandon, resign, yield, relinquish, renounce, waive, say goodbye to, cede, abjure, leave alone *or* out

forgotten = <u>unremembered</u>, lost, past, buried, left behind, omitted, obliterated, bygone, blotted out, consigned to oblivion, past recall, gone (clean) out of your mind

fork = <u>branch</u>, part, separate, split, divide, diverge, subdivide, branch off, go separate ways, bifurcate

forked = <u>branching</u>, split, branched, divided, angled, pronged, zigzag, tined, Y-shaped, bifurcate(d)

forlorn 1 = <u>miserable</u>, helpless, pathetic, pitiful, lost, forgotten, abandoned, unhappy, lonely, homeless, forsaken, bereft, destitute, wretched, disconsolate, friendless, down in the dumps (*informal*), pitiable, cheerless, woebegone, comfortless ...*He looked a* *forlorn figure as he limped off…* OPPOSITE cheerful

2 = <u>abandoned</u>, deserted, ruined, bleak, dreary, desolate, godforsaken, waste …*The once glorious palaces stood empty and forlorn…*

3 = <u>hopeless</u>, useless, vain, pointless, futile, no-win, unattainable, impracticable, unachievable, impossible, not having a prayer …*a forlorn effort to keep from losing my mind…*

form NOUN **1** = <u>type</u>, sort, kind, variety, way, system, order, class, style, practice, method, species, manner, stamp, description …*He contracted a rare form of cancer…*

2 = <u>shape</u>, formation, configuration, construction, cut, model, fashion, structure, pattern, cast, appearance, stamp, mould …*Valleys often take the form of deep canyons…*

3 = <u>structure</u>, plan, order, organization, arrangement, construction, proportion, format, framework, harmony, symmetry, orderliness …*the sustained narrative form of the novel…*

4 = <u>build</u>, being, body, figure, shape, frame, outline, anatomy, silhouette, physique, person …*her petite form and delicate features…*

5 = <u>condition</u>, health, shape, nick (*informal*), fitness, trim, good condition, good spirits, fettle …*He's now fighting his way back to top form…*

6 = <u>document</u>, paper, sheet, questionnaire, application …*You will be asked to fill in an application form…*

7 = <u>procedure</u>, behaviour, manners, etiquette, use, rule, conduct, ceremony, custom, convention, ritual, done thing, usage, protocol, formality, wont, right practice …*a frequent broadcaster on correct form and dress…*

8 = <u>class</u>, year, set, rank, grade, stream …*I was going into the sixth form at school…*

9 = <u>mode</u>, character, shape, appearance, arrangement, manifestation, guise, semblance, design …*The rejoicing took the form of exuberant masquerades…*

VERB **1** = <u>arrange</u>, combine, line up, organize, assemble, dispose, draw up …*He gave orders for the cadets to form into lines…*

2 = <u>make</u>, produce, model, fashion, build, create, shape, manufacture, stamp, construct, assemble, forge, mould, fabricate …*The bowl was formed out of clay…*

3 = <u>constitute</u>, make up, compose, comprise, serve as, make …*Children form the majority of dead and injured…*

4 = <u>establish</u>, start, found, launch, set up, invent, devise, put together, bring about, contrive …*You may want to form a company to buy a joint freehold…*

5 = <u>take shape</u>, grow, develop, materialize, rise, appear, settle, show up (*informal*), accumulate, come into being, crystallize, become visible …*Stalactites and stalagmites began to form…*

6 = <u>draw up</u>, design, devise, formulate, plan, pattern, frame, organize, think up …*She rapidly formed a plan…*

7 = <u>develop</u>, pick up, acquire, cultivate, contract, get

into (*informal*) …*It is easier to form good habits than to break bad ones…*

8 = <u>train</u>, develop, shape, mould, school, teach, guide, discipline, rear, educate, bring up, instruct …*Anger at injustice formed his character…*

PHRASES **off form** = <u>below par</u>, unfit, stale, out of condition, under the weather (*informal*), not up to the mark, not in the pink (*informal*) …*His players were off form and tired…* ◆ **on form** = <u>up to the mark</u>, fit, healthy, in good shape, in good condition, toned up, in good trim …*She was back on form again now…*

formal 1 = <u>serious</u>, stiff, detached, aloof, official, reserved, correct, conventional, remote, exact, precise, starched, prim, unbending, punctilious, ceremonious …*He wrote a very formal letter of apology…* OPPOSITE informal

2 = <u>official</u>, express, explicit, authorized, set, legal, fixed, regular, approved, strict, endorsed, prescribed, rigid, certified, solemn, lawful, methodical, pro forma (*Latin*) …*No formal announcement has been made…*

3 = <u>ceremonial</u>, traditional, solemn, ritualistic, dressy …*They arranged a formal dinner after the play…*

4 = <u>conventional</u>, established, traditional …*He didn't have any formal dance training…*

formality 1 = <u>correctness</u>, seriousness, decorum, ceremoniousness, protocol, etiquette, politesse, p's and q's, punctilio …*Her formality and seriousness amused him…*

2 = <u>convention</u>, form, conventionality, matter of form, procedure, ceremony, custom, gesture, ritual, rite …*The will was read, but it was a formality…*

format = <u>arrangement</u>, form, style, make-up, look, plan, design, type, appearance, construction, presentation, layout

formation 1 = <u>establishment</u>, founding, forming, setting up, starting, production, generation, organization, manufacture, constitution …*the formation of a new government…*

2 = <u>development</u>, shaping, constitution, evolution, moulding, composition, compilation, accumulation, genesis, crystallization …*The formation of my character and temperament…*

3 = <u>arrangement</u>, grouping, figure, design, structure, pattern, rank, organization, array, disposition, configuration …*He was flying in formation with seven other jets…*

formative 1 = <u>developmental</u>, sensitive, susceptible, impressionable, malleable, pliant, mouldable …*She spent her formative years growing up in London…*

2 = <u>determinative</u>, controlling, important, shaping, significant, influential, moulding, decisive, developmental …*a formative influence on his life…*

former 1 = <u>previous</u>, one-time, erstwhile, ex-, late, earlier, prior, sometime, foregoing, antecedent, anterior, quondam, whilom (*archaic*), ci-devant (*French*) …*He pleaded not guilty to murdering his former wife…* OPPOSITE current

2 = <u>past</u>, earlier, long ago, bygone, old, ancient, departed, old-time, long gone, of yore …*Remember him as he was in former years…* OPPOSITE present

3 = <u>aforementioned</u>, above, first mentioned,

aforesaid, preceding, foregoing ...*Most people can be forgiven for choosing the former...*

formerly = <u>previously</u>, earlier, in the past, at one time, before, lately, once, already, heretofore, aforetime (*archaic*)

formidable 1 = <u>difficult</u>, taxing, challenging, overwhelming, staggering, daunting, mammoth, colossal, arduous, very great, onerous, toilsome ...*We have a formidable task ahead of us...* OPPOSITE easy
2 = <u>impressive</u>, great, powerful, tremendous, mighty, terrific, awesome, invincible, indomitable, redoubtable, puissant ...*She looked every bit as formidable as her mother...*
3 = <u>intimidating</u>, threatening, dangerous, terrifying, appalling, horrible, dreadful, menacing, dismaying, fearful, daunting, frightful, baleful, shocking ...*a formidable, well-trained, well-equipped fighting force...* OPPOSITE encouraging

formula 1 = <u>method</u>, plan, policy, rule, principle, procedure, recipe, prescription, blueprint, precept, modus operandi, way ...*The new peace formula means hostilities have ended...*
2 = <u>form of words</u>, code, phrase, formulary, set expression ...*He developed a mathematical formula...*
3 = <u>mixture</u>, preparation, compound, composition, concoction, tincture, medicine ...*bottles of formula...*

formulate 1 = <u>devise</u>, plan, develop, prepare, work out, invent, evolve, coin, forge, draw up, originate, map out ...*He formulated his plan for escape...*
2 = <u>express</u>, detail, frame, define, specify, articulate, set down, codify, put into words, systematize, particularize, give form to ...*I was impressed by how he formulated his ideas...*

forsake 1 = <u>desert</u>, leave, abandon, quit, strand, jettison, repudiate, cast off, disown, jilt, throw over, leave in the lurch ...*I still love him and would never forsake him...*
2 = <u>give up</u>, set aside, relinquish, forgo, kick (*informal*), yield, surrender, renounce, have done with, stop using, abdicate, stop having, turn your back on, forswear ...*She forsook her notebook for new technology...*
3 = <u>abandon</u>, leave, go away from, take your leave of ...*He has no plans to forsake the hills...*

forsaken 1 = <u>abandoned</u>, ignored, lonely, stranded, ditched, left behind, marooned, outcast, forlorn, cast off, jilted, friendless, left in the lurch ...*She felt forsaken and gave up any attempt at order...*
2 = <u>deserted</u>, abandoned, isolated, solitary, desolate, forlorn, destitute, disowned, godforsaken ...*a forsaken church and a derelict hotel...*

fort NOUN = <u>fortress</u>, keep, station, camp, tower, castle, garrison, stronghold, citadel, fortification, redoubt, fastness, blockhouse ...*Soldiers inside the fort are under sustained attack...*
PHRASES **hold the fort** (*Informal*) = <u>take responsibility</u>, cover, stand in, carry on, take over the reins, maintain the status quo, deputize, keep things moving, keep things on an even keel ...*His partner is holding the fort while he is away...*

forte = <u>speciality</u>, strength, talent, strong point, métier, long suit (*informal*), gift OPPOSITE weak point

forth 1 (*Formal or old-fashioned*) = <u>forward</u>, out, away, ahead, onward, outward ...*Go forth into the desert...*
2 = <u>out</u>, into the open, out of concealment ...*He brought forth a small gold amulet...*

forthcoming 1 = <u>approaching</u>, coming, expected, future, imminent, prospective, impending, upcoming ...*his opponents in the forthcoming election...*
2 = <u>available</u>, ready, accessible, at hand, in evidence, obtainable, on tap (*informal*) ...*They promised that the money would be forthcoming...*
3 = <u>communicative</u>, open, free, informative, expansive, sociable, chatty, talkative, unreserved ...*He was very forthcoming in court...*

forthright = <u>outspoken</u>, open, direct, frank, straightforward, blunt, downright, candid, upfront (*informal*), plain-spoken, straight from the shoulder (*informal*) OPPOSITE secretive

forthwith = <u>immediately</u>, directly, instantly, at once, right away, straightaway, without delay, tout de suite (*French*), quickly

fortification 1 = <u>reinforcement</u>, protecting, securing, protection, strengthening, reinforcing, embattlement ...*Europe's fortification of its frontiers...*
2 = <u>defence</u>, keep, protection, castle, fort, fortress, stronghold, bastion, citadel, bulwark, fastness ...*troops stationed just behind the fortification...*
3 = <u>strengthening</u>, supplementing, reinforcement ...*nutrient fortification of food...*

fortify 1 = <u>protect</u>, defend, secure, strengthen, reinforce, support, brace, garrison, shore up, augment, buttress, make stronger, embattle ...*British soldiers working to fortify an airbase...*
2 = <u>strengthen</u>, add alcohol to ...*All sherry is made from wine fortified with brandy...*
3 = <u>sustain</u>, encourage, confirm, cheer, strengthen, reassure, brace, stiffen, hearten, embolden, invigorate ...*The volunteers were fortified by their patriotic belief...* OPPOSITE dishearten

fortitude = <u>courage</u>, strength, resolution, determination, guts (*informal*), patience, pluck, grit, endurance, bravery, backbone, perseverance, firmness, staying power, valour, fearlessness, strength of mind, intrepidity, hardihood, dauntlessness, stoutheartedness

fortress = <u>castle</u>, fort, stronghold, citadel, redoubt, fastness

fortuitous 1 = <u>chance</u>, lucky, random, casual, contingent, accidental, arbitrary, incidental, unforeseen, unplanned ...*a fortuitous quirk of fate...*
2 = <u>lucky</u>, happy, fortunate, serendipitous, providential, fluky (*informal*) ...*It was a fortuitous discovery...*

fortunate 1 = <u>lucky</u>, happy, favoured, bright, golden, rosy, on a roll, jammy (*Brit. slang*), in luck, having a charmed life, born with a silver spoon in your mouth ...*He's has had a very fortunate life...* OPPOSITE unfortunate
2 = <u>well-off</u>, rich, successful, comfortable, wealthy,

prosperous, affluent, opulent, well-heeled (*informal*), well-to-do, sitting pretty (*informal*) ...*the economic burdens placed on less fortunate families*...

3 = providential, auspicious, fortuitous, felicitous, timely, promising, encouraging, helpful, profitable, convenient, favourable, advantageous, expedient, opportune, propitious ...*It was fortunate that the water was shallow*...

fortunately = luckily, happily, as luck would have it, providentially, by good luck, by a happy chance

fortune NOUN 1 = large sum of money, bomb (*Brit. slang*), packet (*slang*), bundle (*slang*), big money, big bucks (*informal, chiefly U.S.*), megabucks (*U.S. & Canad. slang*), an arm and a leg (*informal*), king's ransom, pretty penny (*informal*) ...*Eating out all the time costs a fortune*...

2 = wealth, means, property, riches, resources, assets, pile (*informal*), possessions, treasure, prosperity, mint, gold mine, wad (*U.S. & Canad. slang*), affluence, opulence, tidy sum (*informal*) ...*He made his fortune in car sales*... OPPOSITE poverty

3 = luck, accident, fluke (*informal*), stroke of luck, serendipity, hap (*archaic*), twist of fate, run of luck ...*Such good fortune must be shared with my friends*...

4 = chance, fate, destiny, providence, the stars, Lady Luck, kismet, fortuity ...*He is certainly being smiled on by fortune*...

PLURAL NOUN = destiny, life, lot, experiences, history, condition, success, means, circumstances, expectation, adventures ...*She kept up with the fortunes of the family*...

forum 1 = meeting, conference, assembly, meeting place, court, body, council, parliament, congress, gathering, diet, senate, rally, convention, tribunal (*archaic or literary*), seminar, get-together (*informal*), congregation, caucus (*chiefly U.S. & Canad.*), synod, convergence, symposium, hui (*N.Z.*), moot, assemblage, conclave, convocation, consistory (*in various Churches*), ecclesia (*in Church use*), colloquium, folkmoot (*in medieval England*) ...*a forum where problems could be discussed*...

2 = public square, court, square, chamber, platform, arena, pulpit, meeting place, amphitheatre, stage, rostrum, agora (*in ancient Greece*) ...*Generals appeared before the excited crowds in the Forum*...

forward ADVERB 1 (also **forwards**) = forth, on, ahead, onwards ...*He walked forward into the room*... OPPOSITE backward(s)

2 = on, onward, onwards ...*His work from that time forward was confined to portraits*...

3 = into the open, out, to light, to the front, to the surface, into consideration, into view, into prominence ...*Over the years similar theories have been put forward*...

ADJECTIVE 1 = leading, first, head, front, advance, foremost, fore ...*to allow more troops to move to forward positions*...

2 = future, early, advanced, progressive, premature, prospective, onward, forward-looking ...*The University system requires more forward planning*...

3 = presumptuous, confident, familiar, bold, fresh

(*informal*), assuming, presuming, cheeky, brash, pushy (*informal*), brazen, shameless, sassy (*U.S. informal*), pert, impertinent, impudent, bare-faced, overweening, immodest, brass-necked (*Brit. informal*), overfamiliar, brazen-faced, overassertive ...*He's very forward and confident*... OPPOSITE shy

VERB 1 = further, back, help, support, aid, encourage, speed, advance, favour, promote, foster, assist, hurry, hasten, expedite ...*He forwarded their cause with courage, skill and humour*... OPPOSITE retard

2 = send on, send, post, pass on, ship, route, transmit, dispatch, freight, redirect ...*The document was forwarded to the President*...

fossick (*Austral. & N.Z.*) = search, hunt, explore, ferret, check, forage, rummage

foster 1 = bring up, mother, raise, nurse, look after, rear, care for, take care of, nurture ...*She has fostered more than 100 children*...

2 = develop, support, further, encourage, feed, promote, stimulate, uphold, nurture, cultivate, foment ...*They are keen to foster trading links with the West*... OPPOSITE suppress

3 = cherish, sustain, entertain, harbour, accommodate, nourish ...*She fostered a fierce ambition*...

foul ADJECTIVE 1 = dirty, rank, offensive, nasty, disgusting, unpleasant, revolting, contaminated, rotten, polluted, stinking, filthy, tainted, grubby, repellent, squalid, repulsive, sullied, grimy, nauseating, loathsome, unclean, impure, grotty (*slang*), fetid, grungy (*slang, chiefly U.S. & Canad.*), putrid, malodorous, noisome, scuzzy (*slang, chiefly U.S.*), mephitic, olid, yucky *or* yukky (*slang*), festy (*Austral. slang*), yucko (*Austral. slang*) ...*foul, polluted water*... OPPOSITE clean

2 = obscene, crude, indecent, foul-mouthed, low, blue, dirty, gross, abusive, coarse, filthy, vulgar, lewd, profane, blasphemous, scurrilous, smutty, scatological ...*He was sent off for using foul language*...

3 = stormy, bad, wild, rough, wet, rainy, murky, foggy, disagreeable, blustery ...*The weather was foul, with heavy hail and snow*...

4 = unfair, illegal, dirty, crooked, shady (*informal*), fraudulent, unjust, dishonest, unscrupulous, underhand, inequitable, unsportsmanlike ...*a foul tackle*...

5 = offensive, bad, base, wrong, evil, notorious, corrupt, vicious, infamous, disgraceful, shameful, vile, immoral, scandalous, wicked, sinful, despicable, heinous, hateful, abhorrent, egregious, abominable, dishonourable, nefarious, iniquitous, detestable ...*He is accused of all manner of foul deeds*... OPPOSITE admirable

VERB 1 = dirty, soil, stain, contaminate, smear, pollute, taint, sully, defile, besmirch, smirch, begrime, besmear ...*sea grass fouled with black tar*... OPPOSITE clean

2 = clog, block, jam, choke ...*The pipe was fouled with grain*...

3 = entangle, catch, twist, snarl, ensnare, tangle up ...*The freighter fouled its propeller in fishing nets*...

PHRASES **foul something up** = <u>bungle</u>, spoil, botch, mess up, cock up (*Brit. slang*), make a mess of, mismanage, make a nonsense of, muck up (*slang*), bodge (*informal*), make a pig's ear of (*informal*), put a spanner in the works (*Brit. informal*), flub (*U.S. slang*), crool or cruel (*Austral. slang*) …*There are risks that laboratories may foul up these tests*…

foul play = <u>crime</u>, fraud, corruption, deception, treachery, criminal activity, duplicity, dirty work, double-dealing, skulduggery, chicanery, villainy, sharp practice, perfidy, roguery, dishonest behaviour

found **1** = <u>establish</u>, start, set up, begin, create, institute, organize, construct, constitute, originate, endow, inaugurate, bring into being …*He founded the Centre for Journalism Studies*… **2** = <u>erect</u>, build, construct, raise, settle …*The town was founded in 1610*…

foundation **1** = <u>basis</u>, heart, root, mainstay, beginning, support, ground, rest, key, principle, fundamental, premise, starting point, principal element …*Best friends are the foundation of my life*… **2** *often plural* = <u>substructure</u>, underpinning, groundwork, bedrock, base, footing, bottom …*vertical or lateral support for building foundations*… **3** = <u>setting up</u>, institution, instituting, organization, settlement, establishment, initiating, originating, starting, endowment, inauguration …*the foundation of the modern welfare state*…

founded

PHRASES **founded on** = <u>based on</u>, built on, rooted in, grounded on, established on

founder¹ = <u>initiator</u>, father, establisher, author, maker, framer, designer, architect, builder, creator, beginner, generator, inventor, organizer, patriarch, benefactor, originator, constructor, institutor …*He was the founder of the medical faculty*…

founder² **1** = <u>fail</u>, collapse, break down, abort, fall through, be unsuccessful, come to nothing, come unstuck, miscarry, misfire, fall by the wayside, come to grief, bite the dust, go belly-up (*slang*), go down like a lead balloon (*informal*) …*The talks have foundered*… **2** = <u>sink</u>, go down, be lost, submerge, capsize, go to the bottom …*Three ships foundered in heavy seas*…

> ## Word Power
>
> **founder** – *Founder is sometimes wrongly* used where *flounder* is meant: *this unexpected turn of events left him floundering* (not *foundering*).

fountain **1** = <u>font</u>, spring, reservoir, spout, fount, water feature, well …*In the centre of the courtyard was a round fountain*… **2** = <u>jet</u>, stream, spray, gush …*The volcano spewed a fountain of molten rock*… **3** = <u>source</u>, fount, wellspring, wellhead, beginning, rise, cause, origin, genesis, commencement, derivation, fountainhead …*You are a fountain of ideas*…

fowl

Related Words
male: cock
female: hen
➤ **types of fowl**

foxy = <u>crafty</u>, knowing, sharp, tricky, shrewd, cunning, sly, astute, canny, devious, wily, artful, guileful

foyer = <u>entrance hall</u>, lobby, reception area, vestibule, anteroom, antechamber

fracas = <u>brawl</u>, fight, trouble, row, riot, disturbance, quarrel, uproar, skirmish, scuffle, free-for-all (*informal*), rumpus, aggro (*slang*), affray (*Law*), shindig (*informal*), donnybrook, scrimmage, shindy (*informal*), bagarre (*French*), melee or mêlée, biffo (*Austral. slang*)

fraction **1** = <u>bit</u>, little bit, mite, jot, tiny amount, iota, scintilla …*I opened my eyes a fraction*… **2** = <u>percentage</u>, share, cut, division, section, proportion, slice, ratio, portion, quota, subdivision,

Types of fowl http://www.ansi.okstate.edu/poultry/index.htm

American wigeon *or* baldpate	cock *or* cockerel	megapode	sea duck
Ancona chicken	Dorking chicken	merganser *or* sawbill	shelduck
Andalusian chicken	duck	Minorca chicken	shoveler
Australorp chicken	eider *or* eider duck	moorhen	smew
bantam chicken	Faverolle chicken	Muscovy duck *or* musk duck	snow goose
barnacle goose	gadwall	mute swan	sultan
Bewick's swan	goldeneye	nene	Sumatra chicken
black swan	goosander	New Hampshire chicken	Sussex chicken
blue duck	goose	Orpington chicken	swan
blue goose	greylag *or* greylag goose	paradise duck	teal
Brahma chicken	Hamburg chicken	pintail	trumpeter swan
brush turkey *or* scrub turkey	harlequin duck	Plymouth Rock chicken	turkey
bufflehead	hen	pochard	velvet scoter
Campine chicken	Houdan chicken	redhead	whistling swan
Canada goose	Leghorn chicken	Rhode Island Red chicken	whooper *or* whooper swan
canvasback	magpie goose	ruddy duck	wigeon *or* widgeon
chicken *or* (*Austral. slang*) chook	mallard	scaup *or* scaup duck	wood duck
Cochin chicken	mallee fowl *or* (*Austral.*) gnow	screamer	Wyandotte chicken
	mandarin duck		
	marsh hen		

moiety …*only a small fraction of the cost…*
3 = fragment, part, piece, section, sector, selection, segment …*You will find only a fraction of the collection on display…*

fractious = irritable, cross, awkward, unruly, touchy, recalcitrant, petulant, tetchy, ratty (*Brit. & N.Z. informal*), testy, fretful, grouchy (*informal*), querulous, peevish, refractory, crabby, captious, froward (*archaic*), pettish OPPOSITE affable

fracture NOUN 1 = break, split, crack …*a double fracture of the right arm…*
2 = cleft, opening, split, crack, gap, rent, breach, rift, rupture, crevice, fissure, schism …*large fractures in the crust creating the valleys…*
VERB 1 = break, crack …*You've fractured a rib…*
2 = split, separate, divide, rend, fragment, splinter, rupture …*a society that could fracture along class lines…*

fragile 1 = unstable, weak, vulnerable, delicate, uncertain, insecure, precarious, flimsy …*The fragile government was on the brink of collapse…*
2 = fine, weak, delicate, frail, feeble, brittle, flimsy, dainty, easily broken, breakable, frangible …*Coffee was served to them in cups of fragile china…* OPPOSITE durable
3 = delicate, fine, charming, elegant, neat, exquisite, graceful, petite, dainty …*The haircut emphasised her fragile beauty…*
4 = unwell, poorly, weak, delicate, crook (*Austral. & N.Z. informal*), shaky, frail, feeble, sickly, unsteady, infirm …*He felt irritated and strangely fragile…*

fragility = weakness, delicacy, frailty, infirmity, feebleness, brittleness, frangibility

fragment NOUN = piece, part, bit, scrap, particle, portion, fraction, shiver, shred, remnant, speck, sliver, wisp, morsel, oddment, chip …*She read everything, digesting every fragment of news…*
VERB 1 = break, split, shatter, crumble, shiver, disintegrate, splinter, come apart, break into pieces, come to pieces …*It's an exploded fracture – the bones have fragmented…* OPPOSITE fuse
2 = break up, divide, split up, disunite …*Their country's government has fragmented into disarray…*

fragmentary = incomplete, broken, scattered, partial, disconnected, discrete, sketchy, piecemeal, incoherent, scrappy, disjointed, bitty, unsystematic

fragrance 1 = scent, smell, perfume, bouquet, aroma, balm, sweet smell, sweet odour, redolence, fragrancy …*A shrubby plant with a strong fragrance…* OPPOSITE stink
2 = perfume, scent, cologne, eau de toilette, eau de Cologne, toilet water, Cologne water …*The advertisement is for a male fragrance…*

fragrant = aromatic, perfumed, balmy, redolent, sweet-smelling, sweet-scented, odorous, ambrosial, odoriferous OPPOSITE stinking

frail 1 = feeble, weak, puny, decrepit, infirm …*She lay in bed looking particularly frail…* OPPOSITE strong
2 = flimsy, weak, vulnerable, delicate, fragile, brittle, unsound, wispy, insubstantial, breakable, frangible,

slight …*The frail craft rocked as he clambered in…*

frailty 1 = weakness, susceptibility, fallibility, peccability …*a triumph of will over human frailty…* OPPOSITE strength
2 = infirmity, poor health, feebleness, puniness, frailness …*She died after a long period of increasing frailty…*
3 = fault, failing, vice, weakness, defect, deficiency, flaw, shortcoming, blemish, imperfection, foible, weak point, peccadillo, chink in your armour …*She is aware of his faults and frailties…* OPPOSITE strong point

frame NOUN 1 = mounting, setting, surround, mount …*She kept a picture of her mother in a silver frame…*
2 = casing, framework, structure, shell, system, form, construction, fabric, skeleton, chassis …*He supplied housebuilders with modern timber frames…*
3 = physique, build, form, body, figure, skeleton, anatomy, carcass, morphology …*belts pulled tight against their bony frames…*
VERB 1 = mount, case, enclose …*The picture is now ready to be framed…*
2 = surround, ring, enclose, close in, encompass, envelop, encircle, fence in, hem in …*The swimming pool is framed by tropical gardens…*
3 = devise, plan, form, shape, institute, draft, compose, sketch, forge, put together, conceive, hatch, draw up, formulate, contrive, map out, concoct, cook up, block out …*A convention was set up to frame a constitution…*
PHRASES **frame of mind** = mood, state, spirit, attitude, humour, temper, outlook, disposition, mind-set, fettle …*He was not in the right frame of mind to continue…*

framework 1 = system, plan, order, scheme, arrangement, fabric, schema, frame of reference, the bare bones …*within the framework of federal regulations…*
2 = structure, body, frame, foundation, shell, fabric, skeleton …*wooden shelves on a steel framework…*

France
(*Related Words*)
adjectives: French, Gallic
➤ **administrative regions**

franchise 1 = authorization, right, permit, licence, charter, privilege, prerogative …*the franchise to build and operate the tunnel…*
2 = vote, voting rights, suffrage …*the introduction of universal franchise…*

frank 1 = candid, open, free, round, direct, plain, straightforward, blunt, outright, sincere, outspoken, honest, downright, truthful, forthright, upfront (*informal*), unrestricted, plain-spoken, unreserved, artless, ingenuous, straight from the shoulder (*informal*) …*They had a frank discussion about the issue…* OPPOSITE secretive
2 = unconcealed, open, undisguised, dinkum (*Austral. & N.Z. informal*) …*with frank admiration on his face…*

frankly 1 = honestly, sincerely, in truth, candidly, to tell you the truth, to be frank, to be frank with someone, to be honest …*Quite frankly, I don't care…*

2 = <u>openly</u>, freely, directly, straight, plainly, bluntly, overtly, candidly, without reserve, straight from the shoulder …*The leaders have been speaking frankly about their problems…*

frankness = <u>outspokenness</u>, openness, candour, truthfulness, plain speaking, bluntness, forthrightness, laying it on the line, ingenuousness, absence of reserve

frantic 1 = <u>frenzied</u>, wild, mad, raging, furious, raving, distracted, distraught, berserk, uptight (*informal*), overwrought, at the end of your tether, beside yourself, at your wits' end, berko (*Austral. slang*) …*A bird had been locked in and was now quite frantic…* OPPOSITE▷ calm
2 = <u>hectic</u>, desperate, frenzied, fraught (*informal*), frenetic …*A busy night in the restaurant is frantic in the kitchen…*

fraternity 1 = <u>companionship</u>, fellowship, brotherhood, kinship, camaraderie, comradeship …*He needs the fraternity of others…*
2 = <u>circle</u>, company, set, order, clan, guild …*the spread of stolen guns among the criminal fraternity…*
3 = <u>brotherhood</u>, club, union, society, league, association, sodality …*He joined a college fraternity…*

fraud 1 = <u>deception</u>, deceit, treachery, swindling, guile, trickery, duplicity, double-dealing, chicanery, sharp practice, imposture, fraudulence, spuriousness …*He was jailed for two years for fraud…* OPPOSITE▷ honesty
2 = <u>scam</u>, craft, cheat, sting (*informal*), deception (*slang*), artifice, humbug, canard, stratagems, chicane …*a fraud involving pension and social security claims…*
3 = <u>hoax</u>, trick, cheat, con (*informal*), deception, sham, spoof (*informal*), prank, swindle, ruse, practical joke, joke, fast one (*informal*), imposture …*He never wrote the letter; it was a fraud…*
4 (*Informal*) = <u>impostor</u>, cheat, fake, bluffer, sham, hoax, hoaxer, forgery, counterfeit, pretender, charlatan, quack, fraudster, swindler, mountebank, grifter (*slang, chiefly U.S. & Canad.*), double-dealer, phoney *or* phony (*informal*) …*He believes many psychics are frauds…*

fraudulent = <u>deceitful</u>, false, crooked (*informal*), untrue, sham, treacherous, dishonest, deceptive, counterfeit, spurious, crafty, swindling, double-dealing, duplicitous, knavish, phoney *or* phony (*informal*), criminal OPPOSITE▷ genuine

fraught ADJECTIVE **1** (*Informal*) = <u>tense</u>, trying, difficult, distressing, tricky, emotionally charged …*It has been a somewhat fraught day…*
2 = <u>agitated</u>, wired (*slang*), anxious, distressed, tense, distracted, emotive, uptight (*informal*), emotionally charged, strung-up, on tenterhooks, hag-ridden …*She's depressed, fraught, and exhausted…*
PHRASES **fraught with** = <u>filled with</u>, full of, charged with, accompanied by, attended by, stuffed with, laden with, heavy with, bristling with, replete with, abounding with …*The production has been fraught with problems…*

fray¹ = <u>fight</u>, battle, row, conflict, clash, set-to (*informal*), riot, combat, disturbance, rumble (*U.S. & N.Z. slang*), quarrel, brawl, skirmish, scuffle, rumpus, broil, affray (*Law*), shindig (*informal*), donnybrook, battle royal, ruckus (*informal*), scrimmage, shindy (*informal*), bagarre (*French*), melee *or* mêlée, biffo (*Austral. slang*) …*Today he entered the fray on the side of the moderates…*

fray² = <u>wear thin</u>, wear, rub, fret, wear out, chafe, wear away, become threadbare …*The stitching had begun to fray at the edges…*

frayed 1 = <u>worn</u>, ragged, worn out, tattered, threadbare, worn thin, out at elbows …*a shapeless and frayed jumper…*
2 = <u>strained</u>, stressed, tense, edgy, uptight (*informal*), frazzled …*Nerves are frayed all round…*

freak ADJECTIVE = <u>abnormal</u>, chance, unusual, unexpected, exceptional, unpredictable, queer, erratic, unparalleled, unforeseen, fortuitous, unaccountable, atypical, aberrant, fluky (*informal*), odd, bizarre …*The ferry was hit by a freak wave off the coast…*
NOUN **1** (*Informal*) = <u>enthusiast</u>, fan, nut (*slang*), addict, buff (*informal*), fanatic, devotee, fiend (*informal*), aficionado …*He's a self-confessed computer freak…*
2 = <u>aberration</u>, eccentric, anomaly, abnormality, sport (*Biology*), monster, mutant, oddity, monstrosity, malformation, rara avis (*Latin*), queer fish (*Brit. informal*), teratism …*Not so long ago, transsexuals were regarded as freaks…*
3 = <u>weirdo</u> *or* <u>weirdie</u> (*informal*), eccentric (*informal*), oddity, case (*informal*), character (*informal*), nut (*slang*), flake (*slang, chiefly U.S.*), oddball (*informal*), nonconformist, screwball (*slang, chiefly U.S. & Canad.*), odd fish (*informal*), kook (*U.S. & Canad. informal*), queer fish (*Brit. informal*) …*The cast consisted of a bunch of freaks and social misfits…*

freakish 1 = <u>odd</u>, strange, fantastic, weird, abnormal, monstrous, grotesque, unnatural, unconventional, outlandish, freaky (*slang*), aberrant, outré, malformed, preternatural, teratoid (*Biology*) …*a freakish monstrous thing, something out of a dream…*
2 = <u>whimsical</u>, odd, unpredictable, arbitrary, humorous, erratic, wayward, fanciful, capricious, changeable, fitful, vagarious (*rare*) …*a freakish, extraordinary incident…*

freaky = <u>weird</u>, odd, wild, strange, crazy, bizarre, abnormal, queer, rum (*Brit. slang*), unconventional, far-out (*slang*), freakish

free ADJECTIVE **1** = <u>complimentary</u>, for free (*informal*), for nothing, unpaid, for love, free of charge, on the house, without charge, gratuitous, at no cost, gratis, buckshee (*Brit. slang*) …*The seminars are free, with lunch provided…*
2 = <u>allowed</u>, permitted, unrestricted, unimpeded, open, clear, able, loose, unattached, unregulated, disengaged, untrammelled, unobstructed, unhampered, unengaged …*The government will be free to pursue its economic policies…*
3 = <u>at liberty</u>, loose, liberated, at large, off the hook

(*slang*), on the loose ...*All the hostages are free*...
OPPOSITE> confined

4 = independent, unfettered, unrestrained, uncommitted, footloose, unconstrained, unengaged, not tied down ...*I was young, free and single at the time*...

5 = non-working, leisure, unemployed, idle, unoccupied ...*She spent her free time shopping*...

6 = available, extra, empty, spare, vacant, unused, uninhabited, unoccupied, untaken ...*There's only one seat free on the train*...

7 = generous, willing, liberal, eager, lavish, charitable, hospitable, prodigal, bountiful, open-handed, unstinting, unsparing, bounteous, munificent, big (*informal*) ...*They weren't always so free with their advice*... OPPOSITE> mean

8 = autonomous, independent, democratic, sovereign, self-ruling, self-governing, emancipated, self-determining, autarchic ...*We cannot survive as a free nation*...

9 = relaxed, open, easy, forward, natural, frank, liberal, familiar, loose, casual, informal, spontaneous, laid-back (*informal*), easy-going (*informal*), lax, uninhibited, unforced, free and easy, unbidden, unconstrained, unceremonious ...*a confidential but free manner*... OPPOSITE> formal

VERB **1** = clear, deliver, disengage, cut loose, release, rescue, rid, relieve, exempt, undo, redeem, ransom, extricate, unburden, unshackle ...*It will free us of a whole lot of debt*...

2 = release, liberate, let out, set free, deliver, loose, discharge, unleash, let go, untie, emancipate, unchain, turn loose, uncage, set at liberty, unfetter, disenthrall, unbridle, manumit ...*They are going to free more prisoners*... OPPOSITE> confine

3 = disentangle, extricate, disengage, detach, separate, loose, unfold, unravel, disconnect, untangle, untwist, unsnarl ...*It took firemen two hours to free him*...

ADVERB = freely, easily, loosely, smoothly, idly ...*Two stubby legs swing free*...

PHRASES **free and easy** = relaxed, liberal, casual, informal, tolerant, laid-back (*informal*), easy-going, lax, lenient, uninhibited, unceremonious ...*He had a free and easy approach*... ♦ **free of** or **from** = unaffected by, without, above, lacking (in), beyond, clear of, devoid of, exempt from, immune to, sans (*archaic*), safe from, untouched by, deficient in, unencumbered by, not liable to ...*She retains her slim figure and is free of wrinkles*...

freedom 1 = independence, democracy, sovereignty, autonomy, self-determination, emancipation, self-government, home rule, autarchy ...*They want greater political freedom*...

2 = liberty, release, discharge, emancipation, deliverance, manumission ...*All hostages and detainees would gain their freedom*... OPPOSITE> captivity

3 = exemption, release, relief, privilege, immunity, impunity ...*freedom from government control*...

4 = licence, latitude, a free hand, free rein, play, power, range, opportunity, ability, facility, scope, flexibility,

discretion, leeway, carte blanche, blank cheque, elbowroom ...*freedom to buy and sell at the best price*... OPPOSITE> restriction

5 = openness, ease, directness, naturalness, abandon, familiarity, candour, frankness, informality, casualness, ingenuousness, lack of restraint or reserve, unconstraint ...*His freedom of manner ran contrary to the norm*... OPPOSITE> restraint

free-for-all (*Informal*) = fight, row, riot, brawl, fracas, affray (*Law*), dust-up (*informal*), shindig (*informal*), donnybrook, scrimmage, shindy (*informal*), bagarre (*French*), melee or mêlée, biffo (*Austral. slang*)

freely 1 = abundantly, liberally, lavishly, like water, extravagantly, copiously, unstintingly, with a free hand, bountifully, open-handedly, amply ...*He was spending very freely*...

2 = openly, frankly, plainly, candidly, unreservedly, straightforwardly, without reserve ...*He had someone to whom he could talk freely*...

3 = willingly, readily, voluntarily, spontaneously, without prompting, of your own free will, of your own accord ...*He freely admits he lives for racing*...

4 = easily, cleanly, loosely, smoothly, readily ...*You must allow the clubhead to swing freely*...

5 = without restraint, voluntarily, willingly, unchallenged, as you please, without being forced, without let or hindrance ...*They cast their votes freely*...

freeway (*U.S. & Austral.*) = motorway, autobahn (*German*), autoroute (*French*), autostrada (*Italian*)

freewheel = coast, drift, glide, relax your efforts, rest on your oars, float

freeze 1 = ice over or up, harden, stiffen, solidify, congeal, become solid, glaciate ...*The ground froze solid*...

2 = chill, benumb ...*The cold morning froze my fingers*...

3 = fix, hold, limit, hold up, peg ...*Wages have been frozen and workers laid off*...

4 = suspend, stop, shelve, curb, cut short, discontinue ...*They have already frozen their aid programme*...

freezing 1 = icy, biting, bitter, raw, chill, chilled, penetrating, arctic, numbing, polar, Siberian, frosty, glacial, wintry, parky (*Brit. informal*), cold as ice, frost-bound, cutting ...*a freezing January afternoon*...

2 = frozen, chilled, numb, chilly, very cold, shivery, benumbed, frozen to the marrow ...*You must be freezing!*...

freight 1 = transportation, traffic, delivery, carriage, shipment, haulage, conveyance, transport ...*France derives 16% of revenue from air freight*...

2 = cargo, goods, contents, load, lading, delivery, burden, haul, bulk, shipment, merchandise, bales, consignment, payload, tonnage ...*26 tonnes of freight*...

French = Gallic ...*All the staff are French*...

(*Related Words*)
combining forms: Franco-, Gallo-

frenetic = frantic, wild, excited, crazy, frenzied, distraught, obsessive, fanatical, demented, unbalanced, overwrought, maniacal

frenzied = <u>uncontrolled</u>, wild, excited, mad, crazy, furious, frantic, distraught, hysterical, agitated, frenetic, feverish, rabid, maniacal

frenzy 1 = <u>fit</u>, burst, bout, outburst, spasm, convulsion, paroxysm ...*The country was gripped by a frenzy of nationalism...*
2 = <u>fury</u>, transport, passion, rage, madness, turmoil, distraction, seizure, hysteria, mania, insanity, agitation, aberration, lunacy, delirium, paroxysm, derangement ...*Something like a frenzy enveloped them...* OPPOSITE calm

frequency = <u>recurrence</u>, repetition, constancy, periodicity, commonness, frequentness, prevalence

frequent ADJECTIVE = <u>common</u>, repeated, usual, familiar, constant, everyday, persistent, reiterated, recurring, customary, continual, recurrent, habitual, incessant ...*He is a frequent visitor to the house...* OPPOSITE infrequent
VERB = <u>visit</u>, attend, haunt, be found at, patronize, hang out at (*informal*), visit often, go to regularly, be a regular customer of ...*I hear he frequents that restaurant...* OPPOSITE keep away

frequently = <u>often</u>, commonly, repeatedly, many times, very often, oft (*archaic or poetic*), over and over again, habitually, customarily, oftentimes (*archaic*), not infrequently, many a time, much OPPOSITE infrequently

fresh 1 = <u>additional</u>, more, new, other, added, further, extra, renewed, supplementary, auxiliary ...*He asked the police to make fresh enquiries...*
2 = <u>natural</u>, raw, crude, unsalted, unprocessed, uncured, unpreserved, undried, green ...*A meal with fresh ingredients doesn't take long to prepare...* OPPOSITE preserved
3 = <u>new</u>, original, novel, unusual, latest, different, recent, modern, up-to-date, this season's, unconventional, unorthodox, ground-breaking, left-field (*informal*), new-fangled, modernistic ...*These designers are full of fresh ideas...* OPPOSITE old
4 = <u>invigorating</u>, clear, clean, bright, sweet, pure, stiff, crisp, sparkling, bracing, refreshing, brisk, spanking, unpolluted ...*The air was fresh and she felt revived...* OPPOSITE stale
5 = <u>cool</u>, cold, refreshing, brisk, chilly, nippy ...*The breeze was fresh and from the north...*
6 = <u>vivid</u>, bright, verdant, undimmed, unfaded ...*a semi-circular mosaic, its colours still fresh...* OPPOSITE old
7 = <u>rosy</u>, clear, fair, bright, healthy, glowing, hardy, blooming, wholesome, ruddy, florid, dewy, good ...*His fresh complexion made him look young...* OPPOSITE pallid
8 = <u>lively</u>, rested, bright, keen, vital, restored, alert, bouncing, revived, refreshed, vigorous, energetic, sprightly, invigorated, spry, chipper (*informal*), full of beans (*informal*), like a new man, full of vim and vigour (*informal*), unwearied, bright-eyed and bushy-tailed (*informal*) ...*I nearly always wake up fresh and rested...* OPPOSITE weary
9 = <u>inexperienced</u>, new, young, green, natural, raw, youthful, unqualified, callow, untrained, untried, artless, uncultivated, wet behind the ears ...*The soldiers were fresh recruits...* OPPOSITE experienced
10 = <u>cheeky</u> (*Informal*), bold, brazen, impertinent, forward, familiar, flip (*informal*), saucy, audacious, sassy (*U.S. informal*), pert, disrespectful, presumptuous, insolent, impudent, smart-alecky (*informal*) ...*Don't get fresh with me...* OPPOSITE well-mannered

freshen = <u>refresh</u>, restore, rouse, enliven, revitalize, spruce up, liven up, freshen up, titivate

freshness 1 = <u>novelty</u>, creativity, originality, inventiveness, newness, innovativeness ...*They have a freshness and individuality that others lack...*
2 = <u>cleanness</u>, shine, glow, bloom, sparkle, vigour, brightness, wholesomeness, clearness, dewiness ...*the freshness of early morning...*

fret 1 = <u>worry</u>, anguish, brood, agonize, obsess, lose sleep, upset yourself, distress yourself ...*I was constantly fretting about others' problems...*
2 = <u>annoy</u>, trouble, bother, disturb, distress, provoke, irritate, grieve, torment, harass, nag, gall, agitate, ruffle, nettle, vex, goad, chagrin, irk, rile, pique, peeve (*informal*), rankle with ...*The quickening of time frets me...*

friction 1 = <u>conflict</u>, opposition, hostility, resentment, disagreement, rivalry, discontent, wrangling, bickering, animosity, antagonism, discord, bad feeling, bad blood, dissension, incompatibility, disharmony, dispute ...*There was friction between the children...*
2 = <u>resistance</u>, rubbing, scraping, grating, irritation, erosion, fretting, attrition, rasping, chafing, abrasion, wearing away ...*The pistons are graphite-coated to prevent friction...*
3 = <u>rubbing</u>, scraping, grating, fretting, rasping, chafing, abrasion ...*the friction of his leg against hers...*

friend 1 = <u>companion</u>, pal, mate (*informal*), buddy (*informal*), partner, china (*Brit. & S. African informal*), familiar, best friend, intimate, cock (*Brit. informal*), close friend, comrade, chum (*informal*), crony, alter ego, confidant, playmate, confidante, main man (*slang, chiefly U.S.*), soul mate, homeboy (*slang, chiefly U.S.*), cobber (*Austral. or old-fashioned N.Z. informal*), bosom friend, boon companion, Achates ...*I had a long talk with my best friend...* OPPOSITE foe
2 = <u>supporter</u>, ally, associate, sponsor, advocate, patron, backer, partisan, protagonist, benefactor, adherent, well-wisher ...*the Friends of Birmingham Royal Ballet...*

friendliness = <u>amiability</u>, warmth, sociability, conviviality, neighbourliness, affability, geniality, kindliness, congeniality, companionability, mateyness or matiness (*Brit. informal*), open arms

friendly 1 = <u>amiable</u>, kind, kindly, welcoming, warm, neighbourly, thick (*informal*), attached, pally (*informal*), helpful, sympathetic, fond, outgoing, comradely, confiding, affectionate, receptive, benevolent, attentive, sociable, genial, affable,

fraternal, good, close, on good terms, chummy (*informal*), peaceable, companionable, clubby, well-disposed, buddy-buddy (*slang, chiefly U.S. & Canad.*), palsy-walsy (*informal*), matey *or* maty (*Brit. informal*), on visiting terms ...*He has been friendly to me*...
2 = <u>amicable</u>, warm, familiar, pleasant, intimate, informal, benign, conciliatory, cordial, congenial, convivial ...*a friendly atmosphere*... OPPOSITE> unfriendly

friendship 1 = <u>attachment</u>, relationship, bond, alliance, link, association, tie ...*They struck up a close friendship*...
2 = <u>friendliness</u>, affection, harmony, goodwill, intimacy, affinity, familiarity, closeness, rapport, fondness, companionship, concord, benevolence, comradeship, amity, good-fellowship ...*a whole new world of friendship and adventure*... OPPOSITE> unfriendliness
3 = <u>closeness</u>, love, regard, affection, intimacy, fondness, companionship, comradeship ...*He really values your friendship*...

fright 1 = <u>fear</u>, shock, alarm, horror, panic, terror, dread, dismay, quaking, apprehension, consternation, trepidation, cold sweat, fear and trembling, (blue) funk (*informal*) ...*To hide my fright I asked a question*... OPPOSITE> courage
2 = <u>scare</u>, start, turn, surprise, shock, jolt, the creeps (*informal*), the shivers, the willies (*slang*), the heebie-jeebies (*slang*) ...*The snake gave everyone a fright*...
3 (*Informal*) = <u>sight</u> (*informal*), mess (*informal*), eyesore, scarecrow, frump ...*She looked a fright in a long dark wig*...

frighten = <u>scare</u>, shock, alarm, terrify, cow, appal, startle, intimidate, dismay, daunt, unnerve, petrify, unman, terrorize, scare (someone) stiff, put the wind up (someone) (*informal*), scare the living daylights out of (someone) (*informal*), make your hair stand on end (*informal*), get the wind up, make your blood run cold, throw into a panic, affright (*archaic*), freeze your blood, make (someone) jump out of his skin (*informal*), throw into a fright OPPOSITE> reassure

frightened = <u>afraid</u>, alarmed, scared, terrified, shocked, frozen, cowed, startled, dismayed, unnerved, petrified, flustered, panicky, terrorized, in a panic, scared stiff, in a cold sweat, abashed, terror-stricken, affrighted (*archaic*), in fear and trepidation, numb with fear

frightening = <u>terrifying</u>, shocking, alarming, appalling, startling, dreadful, horrifying, menacing, intimidating, dismaying, scary (*informal*), fearful, daunting, fearsome, unnerving, spooky (*informal*), hair-raising, baleful, spine-chilling, bloodcurdling

frightful 1 = <u>terrible</u>, shocking, alarming, awful, appalling, horrible, grim, terrifying, dreadful, dread, fearful, traumatic, dire, horrendous, ghastly, hideous, harrowing, gruesome, unnerving, lurid, from hell (*informal*), grisly, macabre, petrifying, horrid, unspeakable, godawful (*slang*), hellacious (*U.S. slang*) ...*refugees trapped in frightful conditions*... OPPOSITE> pleasant
2 = <u>dreadful</u>, great, terrible, extreme, awful, annoying,

unpleasant, disagreeable, insufferable ...*He got himself into a frightful muddle*... OPPOSITE> slight

frigid 1 = <u>freezing</u>, cold, frozen, icy, chill, arctic, Siberian, frosty, cool, glacial, wintry, gelid, frost-bound, hyperboreal ...*The water was too frigid to allow him to remain submerged*... OPPOSITE> hot
2 = <u>chilly</u>, formal, stiff, forbidding, rigid, passive, icy, austere, aloof, lifeless, repellent, unresponsive, unfeeling, unbending, unapproachable, passionless, unloving, cold as ice, cold-hearted ...*She replied with a frigid smile*... OPPOSITE> warm

frill NOUN = <u>ruffle</u>, gathering, tuck, ruff, flounce, ruche, ruching, furbelow, purfle ...*net curtains with frills*...
PLURAL NOUN = <u>trimmings</u>, extras, additions, fuss, jazz (*slang*), dressing up, decoration(s), bits and pieces, icing on the cake, finery, embellishments, affectation(s), ornamentation, ostentation, frippery, bells and whistles, tomfoolery, gewgaws, superfluities, fanciness, frilliness, fandangles ...*The booklet restricts itself to facts without frills*...

frilly = <u>ruffled</u>, fancy, lacy, frothy, ruched, flouncy

fringe NOUN **1** = <u>border</u>, edging, edge, binding, trimming, hem, frill, tassel, flounce ...*The jacket had leather fringes*...
2 = <u>edge</u>, limits, border, margin, march, marches, outskirts, perimeter, periphery, borderline ...*They lived together on the fringe of the campus*...
ADJECTIVE = <u>unofficial</u>, alternative, radical, innovative, avant-garde, unconventional, unorthodox ...*numerous fringe meetings held during the conference*...
VERB = <u>border</u>, edge, surround, bound, skirt, trim, enclose, flank ...*Swampy islands of vegetation fringe the coastline*...

fringed 1 = <u>bordered</u>, edged, befringed ...*She wore a fringed scarf*...
2 = <u>edged</u>, bordered, margined, outlined ...*tiny islands fringed with golden sand*...

frisk 1 (*Informal*) = <u>search</u>, check, inspect, run over, shake down (*U.S. slang*), body-search ...*He pushed him against the wall and frisked him*...
2 = <u>frolic</u>, play, sport, dance, trip, jump, bounce, hop, skip, romp, caper, prance, cavort, gambol, rollick, curvet ...*creatures that grunted and frisked about*...

frisky = <u>lively</u>, spirited, romping, playful, bouncy, high-spirited, rollicking, in high spirits, full of beans (*informal*), coltish, kittenish, frolicsome, ludic (*literary*), sportive, full of joie de vivre OPPOSITE> sedate

fritter away = <u>squander</u>, waste, run through, dissipate, misspend, idle away, fool away, spend like water

frivolity = <u>flippancy</u>, fun, nonsense, folly, trifling, lightness, jest, gaiety, silliness, triviality, superficiality, levity, shallowness, childishness, giddiness, flummery, light-heartedness, puerility, flightiness, frivolousness OPPOSITE> seriousness

frivolous 1 = <u>flippant</u>, foolish, dizzy, superficial, silly, flip (*informal*), juvenile, idle, childish, giddy, puerile, flighty, ill-considered, empty-headed, light-hearted, nonserious, light-minded, ditzy *or* ditsy (*slang*) ...*I *was a bit too frivolous to be a doctor…* OPPOSITE > serious

2 = trivial, petty, trifling, unimportant, light, minor, shallow, pointless, extravagant, peripheral, niggling, paltry, impractical, nickel-and-dime (*U.S. slang*), footling (*informal*) …*wasting money on frivolous projects…* OPPOSITE > important

frizzy = tight-curled, crisp, corrugated, wiry, crimped, frizzed

frog

(*Related Words*)

young: tadpole

➤ **amphibians**

frolic VERB = play, romp, lark, caper, cavort, frisk, gambol, make merry, rollick, cut capers, sport …*Tourists sunbathe and frolic in the ocean…*

NOUN = merriment, sport, fun, amusement, gaiety, fun and games, skylarking (*informal*), high jinks, drollery …*Their relationship is never short on fun and frolic…*

front NOUN **1** = head, start, lead, beginning, top, fore, forefront …*Stand at the front of the line…*

2 = exterior, facing, face, façade, frontage, anterior, obverse, forepart …*Attached to the front of the house was a veranda…*

3 = foreground, fore, forefront, nearest part …*the front of the picture…*

4 = front line, trenches, vanguard, firing line, van …*Her husband is fighting at the front…*

5 = appearance, show, face, air, bearing, aspect, manner, expression, exterior, countenance, demeanour, mien …*He kept up a brave front…*

6 (*Informal*) = disguise, cover, blind, mask, cover-up, cloak, façade, pretext …*a front for crime syndicates…*

ADJECTIVE **1** = foremost, at the front …*She is still missing her front teeth…* OPPOSITE > back

2 = leading, first, lead, head, foremost, topmost, headmost …*He is the front runner for the star role…*

VERB = face onto, overlook, look out on, have a view of, look over *or* onto …*Victorian houses fronting onto the pavement…*

PHRASES **in front** = in advance, first, before, leading, ahead, preceding, in the lead, at the head, to the fore, in the van …*Polls show him out in front in the race…*

frontier = border, limit, edge, bound, boundary, confines, verge, perimeter, borderline, dividing line, borderland, marches

frost = hoarfrost, freeze, freeze-up, Jack Frost, rime

frosty 1 = cold, frozen, icy, chilly, wintry, parky (*Brit. informal*) …*sharp, frosty nights…*

2 = icy, ice-capped, icicled, hoar (*rare*), rimy …*a cat lifting its paws off the frosty stones…*

3 = unfriendly, discouraging, icy, frigid, off-putting (*Brit. informal*), unenthusiastic, unwelcoming, standoffish, cold as ice …*He may get a frosty reception…*

froth NOUN = foam, head, bubbles, lather, suds, spume, effervescence, scum …*the froth on the top of a glass of beer…*

VERB = fizz, foam, come to a head, lather, bubble over, effervesce …*The sea froths over my feet…*

frothy 1 = foamy, foaming, bubbly, effervescent, sudsy, spumous, spumescent, spumy …*frothy milk shakes…*

2 = trivial, light, empty, slight, unnecessary, vain, petty, trifling, frivolous, frilly, unsubstantial …*the kind of frothy songs one hears…*

frown VERB = glare, scowl, glower, make a face, look daggers, knit your brows, give a dirty look, lour *or* lower …*He frowned at her anxiously…*

NOUN = scowl, glare, glower, dirty look …*a deep frown on the boy's face…*

PHRASES **frown on** = disapprove of, dislike, discourage, take a dim view of, look askance at, discountenance, view with disfavour, not take kindly to, show disapproval *or* displeasure …*This practice is frowned upon as being wasteful…*

frozen 1 = icy, hard, solid, frosted, arctic, ice-covered, icebound …*the frozen bleakness of the Far North…*

2 = chilled, cold, iced, refrigerated, ice-cold …*frozen desserts like ice cream…*

3 = ice-cold, freezing, numb, very cold, frigid, frozen stiff, chilled to the marrow …*I'm frozen out here…*

4 = motionless, rooted, petrified, stock-still, turned to stone, stopped dead in your tracks …*She was frozen in horror…*

5 = fixed, held, stopped, limited, suspended, pegged (*of prices*) …*Prices would be frozen and wages raised…*

frugal 1 = thrifty, sparing, careful, prudent, provident, parsimonious, abstemious, penny-wise, saving, cheeseparing …*She lives a frugal life…* OPPOSITE > wasteful

2 = meagre, economical, niggardly …*Her diet was frugal…*

fruit 1 = produce, crop, yield, harvest …*The fruit has got a long storage life…*

2 *often plural* = result, reward, outcome, end result, return, effect, benefit, profit, advantage, consequence …*The findings are the fruit of more than three years research…*

fruitful 1 = useful, successful, effective, rewarding, profitable, productive, worthwhile, beneficial, advantageous, well-spent, gainful …*We had a long, fruitful relationship…* OPPOSITE > useless

2 = fertile, fecund, fructiferous …*a landscape that was fruitful and lush…* OPPOSITE > barren

3 = productive, prolific, abundant, plentiful, rich, flush, spawning, copious, profuse, plenteous …*blossoms on a fruitful tree…*

fruition = fulfilment, maturity, completion, perfection, enjoyment, realization, attainment, maturation, consummation, ripeness, actualization, materialization

fruitless = useless, vain, unsuccessful, in vain, pointless, futile, unproductive, abortive, to no avail, ineffectual, unprofitable, to no effect, unavailing, unfruitful, profitless, bootless OPPOSITE > fruitful

fruity 1 = rich, full, mellow …*a lovely, fruity wine…*

2 = resonant, full, deep, rich, vibrant, mellow …*He had a solid, fruity laugh…*

3 (*Informal, chiefly Brit.*) = risqué, indecent, suggestive, racy, blue, hot, sexy, ripe, spicy (*informal*), vulgar, juicy, titillating, bawdy, salacious, smutty, indelicate, near the knuckle (*informal*) ...*She clearly enjoyed the fruity joke*...

frumpy *or* **frumpish** = <u>dowdy</u>, dated, dreary, out of date, drab, unfashionable, dingy, mumsy, badly-dressed

frustrate 1 = <u>discourage</u>, anger, depress, annoy, infuriate, exasperate, dishearten, dissatisfy ...*These questions frustrated me*... OPPOSITE encourage
2 = <u>thwart</u>, stop, check, block, defeat, disappoint, counter, confront, spoil, foil, baffle, inhibit, hobble, balk, circumvent, forestall, neutralize, stymie, nullify, render null and void, crool *or* cruel (*Austral. slang*) ...*The government has deliberately frustrated his efforts*... OPPOSITE further

frustrated = <u>disappointed</u>, discouraged, infuriated, discontented, exasperated, resentful, embittered, irked, disheartened, carrying a chip on your shoulder (*informal*)

frustration 1 = <u>annoyance</u>, disappointment, resentment, irritation, grievance, dissatisfaction, exasperation, vexation ...*a man fed up with the frustrations of everyday life*...
2 = <u>obstruction</u>, blocking, curbing, foiling, failure, spoiling, thwarting, contravention, circumvention, nonfulfilment, nonsuccess ...*the frustration of their plan*...

fudge = <u>misrepresent</u>, avoid, dodge, evade, hedge, stall, fake, flannel (*Brit. informal*), patch up, falsify, equivocate

fuel NOUN **1** = <u>nourishment</u>, food, kai (*N.Z. informal*), sustenance ...*Babies and toddlers need fuel for growth*...
2 = <u>incitement</u>, encouragement, ammunition, provocation, food, material, incentive, fodder ...*His comments are bound to add fuel to the debate*...
VERB = <u>inflame</u>, power, charge, fire, fan, encourage, feed, boost, sustain, stimulate, nourish, incite, whip up, stoke up ...*The economic boom was fuelled by easy credit*...

fugitive = <u>runaway</u>, refugee, deserter, escapee, runagate (*archaic*)

fulfil 1 = <u>carry out</u>, perform, execute, discharge, keep, effect, finish, complete, achieve, conclude, accomplish, bring to completion ...*He is too ill to fulfil his duties*... OPPOSITE neglect
2 = <u>achieve</u>, realize, satisfy, attain, consummate, bring to fruition, perfect ...*He decided to fulfil his dream and go to college*...
3 = <u>satisfy</u>, please, content, cheer, refresh, gratify, make happy ...*After the war, nothing quite fulfilled her*...
4 = <u>comply with</u>, meet, fill, satisfy, observe, obey, conform to, answer ...*All the necessary conditions were fulfilled*...

fulfilment = <u>achievement</u>, effecting, implementation, carrying out *or* through, end, crowning, discharge, discharging, completion, perfection, accomplishment, realization, attainment, observance, consummation

full ADJECTIVE **1** = <u>filled</u>, stocked, brimming, replete, complete, entire, loaded, sufficient, intact, gorged, saturated, bursting at the seams, brimful ...*Repeat the layers until the terrine is full*...
2 = <u>crammed</u>, crowded, packed, crushed, jammed, in use, congested, chock-full, chock-a-block ...*The centre is full beyond capacity*... OPPOSITE empty
3 = <u>occupied</u>, taken, in use, unavailable ...*The cheap seats were all full*...
4 = <u>satiated</u>, satisfied, having had enough, replete, sated ...*It's healthy to stop eating when I'm full*...
5 = <u>extensive</u>, detailed, complete, broad, generous, adequate, ample, abundant, plentiful, copious, plenary, plenteous ...*Full details will be sent to you*... OPPOSITE incomplete
6 = <u>maximum</u>, highest, greatest, top, utmost ...*He revved the engine to full power*...
7 = <u>comprehensive</u>, complete, thorough, exhaustive, all-inclusive, all-embracing, unabridged ...*They can now publish a full list of candidates*...
8 = <u>rounded</u>, strong, rich, powerful, intense, pungent ...*Italian plum tomatoes have a full flavour*...
9 = <u>plump</u>, rounded, voluptuous, shapely, well-rounded, buxom, curvaceous ...*large sizes for ladies with a fuller figure*...
10 = <u>voluminous</u>, large, loose, baggy, billowing, puffy, capacious, loose-fitting, balloon-like ...*My wedding dress has a very full skirt*... OPPOSITE tight
11 = <u>rich</u>, strong, deep, loud, distinct, resonant, sonorous, clear ...*She has a full voice, mine is a bit lighter*... OPPOSITE thin
PHRASES **in full** = <u>completely</u>, fully, in total, without exception, in its entirety, in toto (*Latin*) ...*We will refund your money in full*... ◆ **to the full** = <u>thoroughly</u>, completely, fully, entirely, to the limit, without reservation, to the utmost ...*She has a good mind which should be used to the full*...

full-blooded = <u>wholehearted</u>, full, complete, sweeping, thorough, uncompromising, exhaustive, all-embracing

full-blown 1 = <u>fully developed</u>, total, full-scale, fully fledged, full, whole, developed, complete, advanced, entire, full-sized, fully grown, fully formed ...*You're talking this thing up into a full-blown conspiracy*... OPPOSITE undeveloped
2 = <u>in full bloom</u>, full, flowering, unfolded, blossoming, opened out ...*the faded hues of full-blown roses*...

full-bodied = <u>rich</u>, strong, heavy, heady, mellow, fruity, redolent, full-flavoured, well-matured

fullness 1 = <u>plenty</u>, glut, saturation, sufficiency, profusion, satiety, repletion, copiousness, ampleness, adequateness ...*High fibre diets give the feeling of fullness*...
2 = <u>completeness</u>, wealth, entirety, totality, wholeness, vastness, plenitude, comprehensiveness, broadness, extensiveness ...*She displayed the fullness of her cycling talent*...
3 = <u>roundness</u>, voluptuousness, curvaceousness, swelling, enlargement, dilation, distension,

tumescence ...*I accept my body with all its womanly fullness...*

4 = <u>richness</u>, strength, resonance, loudness, clearness ...*with modest riffs and a fullness in sound...*

full-scale = <u>major</u>, extensive, wide-ranging, all-out, sweeping, comprehensive, proper, thorough, in-depth, exhaustive, all-encompassing, thoroughgoing, full-dress

fully 1 = <u>completely</u>, totally, perfectly, entirely, absolutely, altogether, thoroughly, intimately, wholly, positively, utterly, every inch, heart and soul, to the hilt, one hundred per cent, in all respects, from first to last, lock, stock and barrel ...*She was fully aware of my thoughts...*

2 = <u>in all respects</u>, completely, totally, entirely, altogether, thoroughly, wholly ...*He had still not fully recovered...*

3 = <u>adequately</u>, amply, comprehensively, sufficiently, enough, satisfactorily, abundantly, plentifully ...*These debates are discussed fully later in the book...*

4 = <u>at least</u>, quite, without (any) exaggeration, without a word of a lie (*informal*) ...*He set his sights and let fly from fully 35 yards...*

fully-fledged = <u>experienced</u>, trained, senior, professional, qualified, mature, proficient, time-served

fulsome = <u>extravagant</u>, excessive, over the top, sickening, overdone, fawning, nauseating, inordinate, ingratiating, cloying, insincere, saccharine, sycophantic, unctuous, smarmy (*Brit. informal*), immoderate, adulatory, gross

---

Word Power

fulsome – In journalism, *fulsome* is often used simply to mean 'extremely complimentary' or 'full, rich, or abundant'. In other kinds of writing, however, this word should only be used if you intend to suggest negative overtones of excess or insincerity.

---

fumble 1 = <u>grope</u>, flounder, paw (*informal*), scrabble, feel around ...*She crept from the bed and fumbled for her dressing gown...*

2 = <u>stumble</u>, struggle, blunder, flounder, bumble ...*I fumbled around like an idiot...*

3 = <u>bungle</u>, spoil, botch, mess up, cock up (*Brit. slang*), mishandle, mismanage, muff, make a hash of (*informal*), make a nonsense of, bodge (*informal*), misfield, crool *or* cruel (*Austral. slang*) ...*I'd hate to fumble a chance like this...*

fume VERB = <u>rage</u>, boil, seethe, see red (*informal*), storm, rave, rant, smoulder, crack up (*informal*), go ballistic (*slang, chiefly U.S.*), champ at the bit (*informal*), blow a fuse (*slang, chiefly U.S.*), fly off the handle (*informal*), get hot under the collar (*informal*), go off the deep end (*informal*), wig out (*slang*), go up the wall (*slang*), get steamed up about (*slang*) ...*I fumed when these women did not respond...*

PLURAL NOUN = <u>smoke</u>, gas, exhaust, pollution, haze, vapour, smog, miasma, exhalation, effluvium ...*car exhaust fumes...*

NOUN = <u>stench</u>, stink, whiff (*Brit. slang*), reek, pong (*Brit. informal*), foul smell, niff (*Brit. slang*), malodour, mephitis, fetor, noisomeness ...*stale alcohol fumes...*

fuming = <u>furious</u>, angry, raging, choked, roused, incensed, enraged, seething, up in arms, incandescent, in a rage, on the warpath (*informal*), foaming at the mouth (*informal*), at boiling point (*informal*), all steamed up (*slang*), tooshie (*Austral. slang*)

fun NOUN **1** = <u>amusement</u>, sport, treat, pleasure, entertainment, cheer, good time, recreation, enjoyment, romp, distraction, diversion, frolic, junketing, merriment, whoopee (*informal*), high jinks, living it up, jollity, beer and skittles (*informal*), merrymaking, jollification ...*You still have time to join in the fun...*

2 = <u>joking</u>, clowning, merriment, playfulness, play, game, sport, nonsense, teasing, jesting, skylarking (*informal*), horseplay, buffoonery, tomfoolery, jocularity, foolery ...*There was lots of fun going on last night...*

3 = <u>enjoyment</u>, pleasure, joy, cheer, mirth, gaiety ...*She had a great sense of fun...* OPPOSITE > gloom

ADJECTIVE = <u>enjoyable</u>, entertaining, pleasant, amusing, lively, diverting, witty, convivial ...*It was a fun evening...*

PHRASES **for** *or* **in fun** = <u>for a joke</u>, tongue in cheek, jokingly, playfully, for a laugh, mischievously, in jest, teasingly, with a straight face, facetiously, light-heartedly, roguishly, with a gleam *or* twinkle in your eye ...*Don't say such things, even in fun...* ◆ **make fun of something** *or* **someone** = <u>mock</u>, tease, ridicule, poke fun at, take off, rag, rib (*informal*), laugh at, taunt, mimic, parody, deride, send up (*Brit. informal*), scoff at, sneer at, lampoon, make a fool of, pour scorn on, take the mickey out of (*Brit. informal*), satirize, pull someone's leg, hold up to ridicule, make a monkey of, make sport of, make the butt of, make game of ...*Don't make fun of me!...*

function NOUN **1** = <u>purpose</u>, business, job, concern, use, part, office, charge, role, post, operation, situation, activity, exercise, responsibility, task, duty, mission, employment, capacity, province, occupation, raison d'être (*French*) ...*The main function of merchant banks is to raise capital...*

2 = <u>reception</u>, party, affair, gathering, bash (*informal*), lig (*Brit. slang*), social occasion, soiree, do (*informal*) ...*We were going down to a function in London...*

VERB **1** = <u>work</u>, run, operate, perform, be in business, be in running order, be in operation *or* action, go ...*The authorities say the prison is now functioning properly...*

2 = <u>act</u>, serve, operate, perform, behave, officiate, act the part of, do duty, have the role of, be in commission, be in operation *or* action, serve your turn ...*On weekdays, one third of the room functions as a workspace...*

functional 1 = <u>practical</u>, utility, utilitarian, serviceable, hard-wearing, useful ...*The decor is functional...*

2 = <u>working</u>, operative, operational, in working order, going, prepared, ready, viable, up and running, workable, usable …*We have fully functional smoke alarms on all staircases…*

functionary = <u>officer</u>, official, dignitary, office holder, office bearer, employee

fund `NOUN` 1 = <u>reserve</u>, stock, supply, store, collection, pool, foundation, endowment, tontine …*a scholarship fund for undergraduate students…*
2 = <u>store</u>, stock, source, supply, mine, reserve, treasury, vein, reservoir, accumulation, hoard, repository …*He has an extraordinary fund of energy…*
`PLURAL NOUN` = <u>money</u>, capital, cash, finance, means, savings, necessary (*informal*), resources, assets, silver, bread (*slang*), wealth, tin (*slang*), brass (*Northern English dialect*), dough (*slang*), rhino (*Brit. slang*), the ready (*informal*), dosh (*Brit. & Austral. slang*), hard cash, the wherewithal, needful (*informal*), shekels (*informal*), dibs (*slang*), ready money, ackers (*slang*), spondulicks (*slang*) …*The concert will raise funds for Aids research…*
`VERB` = <u>finance</u>, back, support, pay for, promote, float, endow, subsidize, stake, capitalize, provide money for, put up the money for …*The foundation has funded a variety of faculty programs…*
`PHRASES` **in funds** = <u>finance</u>, flush (*informal*), in the black, solvent, well-off, well-supplied …*I'll pay you back as soon as I'm in funds again…*

fundamental 1 = <u>central</u>, first, most important, prime, key, necessary, basic, essential, primary, vital, radical, principal, cardinal, integral, indispensable, intrinsic …*the fundamental principles of democracy…*
`OPPOSITE` incidental
2 = <u>basic</u>, essential, underlying, organic, profound, elementary, rudimentary …*The two leaders have very fundamental differences…*

fundamentally 1 = <u>basically</u>, at heart, at bottom …*Fundamentally, women like him for his sensitivity…*
2 = <u>essentially</u>, radically, basically, primarily, profoundly, intrinsically …*He disagreed fundamentally with her judgement…*

fundi (*S. African*) = <u>expert</u>, authority, specialist, professional, master, pro (*informal*), ace (*informal*), genius, guru, pundit, buff (*informal*), maestro, virtuoso, boffin (*Brit. informal*), hotshot (*informal*), past master, dab hand (*Brit. informal*), wonk (*informal*), maven (*U.S.*)

funeral = <u>burial</u>, committal, laying to rest, cremation, interment, obsequies, entombment, inhumation

funereal = <u>gloomy</u>, dark, sad, grave, depressing, dismal, lamenting, solemn, dreary, sombre, woeful, mournful, lugubrious, sepulchral, dirge-like, deathlike

funk = <u>chicken out of</u>, dodge, recoil from, take fright, flinch from, duck out of (*informal*), turn tail (*informal*)

funnel 1 = <u>conduct</u>, direct, channel, convey, move, pass, pour, filter …*This device funnels the water from a downpipe into a butt…*
2 = <u>channel</u>, direct, pour, filter, convey …*The centre will funnel money into research…*

funny 1 = <u>humorous</u>, amusing, comical, entertaining, killing (*informal*), rich, comic, silly, ridiculous, diverting, absurd, jolly, witty, hilarious, ludicrous, laughable, farcical, slapstick, riotous, droll, risible, facetious, jocular, side-splitting, waggish, jocose …*I'll tell you a funny story…* `OPPOSITE` unfunny
2 = <u>comic</u>, comical, a scream, a card (*informal*), a caution (*informal*) …*He could be funny when he wanted to be…*
3 = <u>peculiar</u>, odd, strange, unusual, remarkable, bizarre, puzzling, curious, weird, mysterious, suspicious, dubious, queer, rum (*Brit. slang*), quirky, perplexing …*There's something funny about him…*
4 = <u>ill</u>, poorly (*informal*), queasy, sick, odd, crook (*Austral. & N.Z. informal*), ailing, queer, unhealthy, seedy (*informal*), unwell, out of sorts (*informal*), off-colour (*informal*), under the weather (*informal*) …*My head ached and my stomach felt funny…*

furious 1 = <u>angry</u>, mad, raging, boiling, fuming, choked, frantic, frenzied, infuriated, incensed, enraged, maddened, inflamed, very angry, cross, livid (*informal*), up in arms, incandescent, on the warpath (*informal*), foaming at the mouth, wrathful, in high dudgeon, wroth (*archaic*), fit to be tied (*slang*), beside yourself, tooshie (*Austral. slang*) …*He is furious at the way his wife has been treated…* `OPPOSITE` pleased
2 = <u>violent</u>, wild, intense, fierce, savage, turbulent, stormy, agitated, boisterous, tumultuous, vehement, unrestrained, tempestuous, impetuous, ungovernable …*A furious gunbattle ensued…*

furnish 1 = <u>decorate</u>, fit, fit out, appoint, provide, stock, supply, store, provision, outfit, equip, fit up, purvey …*Many proprietors try to furnish their hotels with antiques…*
2 = <u>supply</u>, give, offer, provide, present, reveal, grant, afford, hand out, endow, bestow …*They'll be able to furnish you with the details…*

furniture = <u>household goods</u>, furnishings, fittings, house fittings, goods, things (*informal*), effects, equipment, appointments, possessions, appliances, chattels, movable property, movables

furore = <u>commotion</u>, to-do, stir, excitement, fury, disturbance, flap (*informal*), outburst, frenzy, outcry, uproar, brouhaha, hullabaloo

furrow `NOUN` 1 = <u>groove</u>, line, channel, hollow, trench, seam, crease, fluting, rut, corrugation …*Bike trails crisscrossed the grassy furrows…*
2 = <u>wrinkle</u>, line, crease, crinkle, crow's-foot, gather, fold, crumple, rumple, pucker, corrugation …*Deep furrows marked the corner of his mouth…*
`VERB` = <u>wrinkle</u>, knit, draw together, crease, seam, flute, corrugate …*My bank manager furrowed his brow…*

further *or* **farther** `ADVERB` = <u>in addition</u>, moreover, besides, furthermore, also, yet, on top of, what's more, to boot, additionally, over and above, as well as, into the bargain …*Further, losing one day doesn't mean you won't win the next…*
`ADJECTIVE` = <u>additional</u>, more, new, other, extra, fresh, supplementary …*There was nothing further to be done…*
`VERB` = <u>promote</u>, help, develop, aid, forward, champion, push, encourage, speed, advance, work for, foster, contribute to, assist, plug (*informal*), facilitate,

pave the way for, hasten, patronize, expedite, succour, lend support to ...*Education needn't only be about furthering your career...* OPPOSITE hinder

➤ **farther**

furthermore = moreover, further, in addition, besides, too, as well, not to mention, what's more, to boot, additionally, into the bargain

furthest *or* **farthest** = most distant, extreme, ultimate, remotest, outermost, uttermost, furthermost, outmost

➤ **farthest**

furtive = sly, secret, hidden, sneaking, covert, cloaked, behind someone's back, secretive, clandestine, sneaky, under-the-table, slinking, conspiratorial, skulking, underhand, surreptitious, stealthy OPPOSITE open

fury 1 = anger, passion, rage, madness, frenzy, wrath, ire, red mist (*informal*), impetuosity ...*She screamed, her face distorted with fury...* OPPOSITE calmness
2 = violence, force, power, intensity, severity, turbulence, ferocity, savagery, vehemence, fierceness, tempestuousness ...*We were lashed by the full fury of the elements...* OPPOSITE peace

fuse 1 = join, unite, combine, blend, integrate, merge, put together, dissolve, amalgamate, federate, coalesce, intermingle, meld, run together, commingle, intermix, agglutinate ...*Conception occurs when a single sperm fuses with an egg...* OPPOSITE separate
2 = bond, join, stick, melt, weld, smelt, solder ...*They all fuse into a glassy state...*

fusion = merging, uniting, union, merger, federation, mixture, blend, blending, integration, synthesis, amalgamation, coalescence, commingling, commixture

fuss NOUN 1 = commotion, to-do, worry, upset, bother, stir, confusion, excitement, hurry, flap (*informal*), bustle, flutter, flurry, agitation, fidget, fluster, ado, hue and cry, palaver, storm in a teacup (*Brit.*), pother ...*I don't know what all the fuss is about...*
2 = bother, trouble, struggle, hassle (*informal*), nuisance, inconvenience, hindrance ...*He gets down to work without any fuss...*
3 = complaint, row, protest, objection, trouble, display, argument, difficulty, upset, bother, unrest, hassle (*informal*), squabble, furore, altercation ...*We kicked up a fuss and got an apology...*
VERB = worry, flap (*informal*), bustle, fret, niggle, fidget, chafe, take pains, make a meal of (*informal*), be agitated, labour over, get worked up, get in a stew (*informal*), make a thing of (*informal*) ...*She fussed about getting me a drink...*

fussy 1 = particular, difficult, exacting, discriminating, fastidious, dainty, squeamish, choosy (*informal*), picky (*informal*), nit-picking (*informal*), hard to please, finicky, pernickety, faddish, faddy, old-maidish, old womanish, overparticular ...*She's not fussy about her food...*
2 = overelaborate, busy, cluttered, rococo, overdecorated, overembellished ...*We are not keen on floral patterns and fussy designs...*

futile 1 = useless, vain, unsuccessful, pointless, empty, hollow, in vain, worthless, barren, sterile, fruitless, forlorn, unproductive, abortive, to no avail, ineffectual, unprofitable, valueless, unavailing, otiose, profitless, nugatory, without rhyme or reason, bootless ...*a futile attempt to ward off the blow...* OPPOSITE useful
2 = trivial, pointless, trifling, unimportant ...*She doesn't want to comment. It's too futile...* OPPOSITE important

futility 1 = uselessness, ineffectiveness, pointlessness, fruitlessness, emptiness, hollowness, spitting in the wind, bootlessness ...*the injustice and futility of terrorism...*
2 = triviality, vanity, pointlessness, unimportance ...*a sense of the emptiness and futility of life...*

future NOUN 1 = time to come, hereafter, what lies ahead ...*He made plans for the future...*
2 = prospect, expectation, outlook ...*She has a splendid future in the police force...*
ADJECTIVE = forthcoming, to be, coming, later, expected, approaching, to come, succeeding, fated, ultimate, subsequent, destined, prospective, eventual, ensuing, impending, unborn, in the offing ...*the future King and Queen...* OPPOSITE past

fuzz = fluff, down, hair, pile, fibre, nap, floss, lint

fuzzy 1 = frizzy, fluffy, woolly, downy, flossy, down-covered, linty, napped ...*He is a fierce bearded character with fuzzy hair...*
2 = indistinct, faint, blurred, vague, distorted, unclear, shadowy, bleary, unfocused, out of focus, ill-defined ...*a couple of fuzzy pictures...* OPPOSITE distinct

G g

gadget = <u>device</u>, thing, appliance, machine, tool, implement, invention, instrument, novelty, apparatus, gimmick, utensil, contraption (*informal*), gizmo (*slang, chiefly U.S. & Canad.*), contrivance

gaffe = <u>blunder</u>, mistake, error, indiscretion, lapse, boob (*Brit. slang*), slip-up (*informal*), slip, howler, bloomer (*informal*), clanger (*informal*), faux pas, boo-boo (*informal*), solecism, gaucherie

gag¹ NOUN = <u>muzzle</u>, tie, restraint …*His captors had put a gag of thick leather in his mouth*…
VERB 1 = <u>suppress</u>, silence, subdue, muffle, curb, stifle, muzzle, quieten …*a journalist who claimed he was gagged by his bosses*…
2 = <u>retch</u>, choke, heave …*I knelt by the toilet and gagged*…
PHRASES **be gagging for something** *or* **be gagging to do something** = <u>crave</u>, want, desire, long for, yearn for, be desperate for, cry out for (*informal*), thirst for, hunger for, lust after, be eager for, be dying for, would give your eyeteeth for …*Men everywhere are gagging for a car like this*…

gag² (*Informal*) = <u>joke</u>, crack (*slang*), funny (*informal*), quip, pun, jest, wisecrack (*informal*), sally, witticism …*He made a gag about bald men*…

gaiety 1 = <u>cheerfulness</u>, glee, good humour, buoyancy, happiness, animation, exuberance, high spirits, elation, exhilaration, hilarity, merriment, joie de vivre (*French*), good cheer, vivacity, jollity, liveliness, gladness, effervescence, light-heartedness, joyousness …*There was a bright, infectious gaiety in the children's laughter*… OPPOSITE misery
2 = <u>merrymaking</u>, celebration, revels, festivity, fun, mirth, revelry, conviviality, jollification, carousal …*The mood was one of laughter and gaiety*…

gaily 1 = <u>cheerfully</u>, happily, gleefully, brightly, blithely, merrily, joyfully, cheerily, jauntily, light-heartedly, chirpily (*informal*) …*She laughed gaily*…
2 = <u>colourfully</u>, brightly, vividly, flamboyantly, gaudily, brilliantly, flashily, showily …*gaily painted front doors*…

gain VERB 1 = <u>acquire</u>, get, receive, achieve, earn, pick up, win, secure, collect, gather, obtain, build up, attain, glean, procure …*Students can gain valuable experience doing part-time work*…
2 = <u>profit</u>, make, earn, get, win, clear, land, score (*slang*), achieve, net, bag, secure, collect, gather, realize, obtain, capture, acquire, bring in, harvest, attain, reap, glean, procure …*The company didn't disclose how much it expects to gain from the deal*… OPPOSITE lose
3 = <u>put on</u>, increase in, gather, build up …*Some people gain weight after they give up smoking*…
4 = <u>attain</u>, earn, get, achieve, win, reach, get to, secure, obtain, acquire, arrive at, procure …*Passing exams is no longer enough to gain a place at university*…
NOUN 1 = <u>rise</u>, increase, growth, advance, improvement, upsurge, upturn, increment, upswing …*House prices showed a gain of nearly 8% in June*…
2 = <u>profit</u>, income, earnings, proceeds, winnings, return, produce, benefit, advantage, yield, dividend, acquisition, attainment, lucre, emolument …*He buys art solely for financial gain*… OPPOSITE loss
PLURAL NOUN = <u>profits</u>, earnings, revenue, proceeds, winnings, takings, pickings, booty …*Investors will have their gains taxed as income in future*…
PHRASES **gain on something** *or* **someone** = <u>get nearer to</u>, close in on, approach, catch up with, narrow the gap on …*The car began to gain on the van*… ◆ **gain time** = <u>stall</u>, delay, play for time, procrastinate, temporize, use delaying tactics …*I hoped to gain time by keeping him talking*…

gainful = <u>profitable</u>, rewarding, productive, lucrative, paying, useful, valuable, worthwhile, beneficial, fruitful, advantageous, expedient, remunerative, moneymaking

gainsay = <u>deny</u>, dispute, disagree with, contradict, contravene, rebut, controvert OPPOSITE confirm

gait = <u>walk</u>, step, bearing, pace, stride, carriage, tread, manner of walking

gala NOUN = <u>festival</u>, party, fête, celebration, carnival, festivity, pageant, jamboree …*a gala at the Royal Opera House*…
ADJECTIVE = <u>festive</u>, merry, joyous, joyful, celebratory, convivial, gay, festal …*I want to make her birthday a gala occasion*…

galaxy = <u>star system</u>, solar system, nebula
(*Related Words*)
adjective: galactic

gale 1 = <u>storm</u>, hurricane, tornado, cyclone, whirlwind, blast, gust, typhoon, tempest, squall …*forecasts of fierce gales over the next few days*…
2 (*Informal*) = <u>outburst</u>, scream, roar, fit, storm, shout, burst, explosion, outbreak, howl, shriek, eruption, peal, paroxysm …*gales of laughter from the audience*…

gall VERB = <u>annoy</u>, provoke, irritate, aggravate (*informal*), get (*informal*), trouble, bother, disturb, plague, madden, ruffle, exasperate, nettle, vex, displease, irk, rile (*informal*), peeve (*informal*), get under your skin (*informal*), get on your nerves (*informal*), nark (*Brit., Austral., & N.Z. slang*), get up your nose (*informal*), make your blood boil, rub up the wrong way, get on your wick (*Brit. slang*), get your back up, put your back up …*It was their smugness that galled her most*…
NOUN = <u>growth</u>, lump, excrescence …*The mites live within the galls that are formed on the plant*…

gallant 1 = <u>brave</u>, daring, bold, heroic, courageous, dashing, noble, manly, gritty, fearless, intrepid, valiant, plucky, doughty, dauntless, lion-hearted, valorous, manful, mettlesome ...*gallant soldiers who gave their lives*... OPPOSITE cowardly
2 = <u>courteous</u>, mannerly, gentlemanly, polite, gracious, attentive, courtly, chivalrous ...*He was a thoughtful, gallant and generous man*... OPPOSITE discourteous

gallantry 1 = <u>bravery</u>, spirit, daring, courage, nerve, guts (*informal*), pluck, grit, heroism, mettle, boldness, manliness, valour, derring-do (*archaic*), fearlessness, intrepidity, valiance, courageousness, dauntlessness, doughtiness ...*He was awarded a medal for his gallantry*... OPPOSITE cowardice
2 = <u>courtesy</u>, politeness, chivalry, attentiveness, graciousness, courtliness, gentlemanliness, courteousness ...*He kissed her hand with old-fashioned gallantry*... OPPOSITE discourtesy

galling = <u>annoying</u>, provoking, irritating, aggravating (*informal*), disturbing, humiliating, maddening, exasperating, vexing, displeasing, rankling, irksome, vexatious, nettlesome

gallop 1 = <u>run</u>, race, shoot, career, speed, bolt, stampede ...*The horses galloped away*...
2 = <u>dash</u>, run, race, shoot, fly, career, speed, tear, rush, barrel (along) (*informal, chiefly U.S. & Canad.*), sprint, dart, zoom ...*They were galloping around the garden playing football*...

galore = <u>in abundance</u>, everywhere, to spare, all over the place, aplenty, in great numbers, in profusion, in great quantity, à gogo (*informal*)

galvanize = <u>stimulate</u>, encourage, inspire, prompt, move, fire, shock, excite, wake, stir, spur, provoke, startle, arouse, awaken, rouse, prod, jolt, kick-start, electrify, goad, impel, invigorate

gamble NOUN 1 = <u>risk</u>, chance, venture, lottery, speculation, uncertainty, leap in the dark ...*the President's risky gamble in calling an election*... OPPOSITE certainty
2 = <u>bet</u>, flutter (*informal*), punt (*chiefly Brit.*), wager ...*My father-in-law likes a drink and the odd gamble*...
VERB 1 = <u>take a chance</u>, back, speculate, take the plunge, stick your neck out (*informal*), put your faith or trust in ...*Few firms will be prepared to gamble on new products*...
2 = <u>risk</u>, chance, stake, venture, hazard, wager ...*Are you prepared to gamble your career on this matter?*...
3 = <u>bet</u>, play, game, stake, speculate, back, punt, wager, put money on, have a flutter (*informal*), try your luck, put your shirt on, lay or make a bet ...*John gambled heavily on the horses*...

game¹ NOUN 1 = <u>pastime</u>, sport, activity, entertainment, recreation, distraction, amusement, diversion ...*the game of hide-and-seek*... OPPOSITE job
2 = <u>match</u>, meeting, event, competition, tournament, clash, contest, round, head-to-head ...*We won three games against Australia*...
3 = <u>amusement</u>, joke, entertainment, diversion, lark

...*Some people simply regard life as a game*...
4 = <u>activity</u>, business, line, situation, proceeding, enterprise, undertaking, occupation, pursuit ...*She's new to this game, so go easy on her*...
5 = <u>wild animals</u> or <u>birds</u>, prey, quarry ...*men who shoot game for food*...
6 = <u>scheme</u>, plan, design, strategy, trick, plot, tactic, manoeuvre, dodge, ploy, scam, stratagem ...*All right, what's your little game?*...
ADJECTIVE 1 = <u>willing</u>, prepared, ready, keen, eager, interested, inclined, disposed, up for it (*informal*), desirous ...*He said he's game for a similar challenge next year*...
2 = <u>brave</u>, courageous, dogged, spirited, daring, bold, persistent, gritty, fearless, feisty (*informal, chiefly U.S. & Canad.*), persevering, intrepid, valiant, plucky, unflinching, dauntless ...*They were the only ones game enough to give it a try*... OPPOSITE cowardly

game² = <u>lame</u>, injured, disabled, crippled, defective, bad, maimed, deformed, gammy (*Brit. slang*) ...*a game leg*...

gamut = <u>range</u>, series, collection, variety, lot, field, scale, sweep, catalogue, scope, compass, assortment

gang = <u>group</u>, crowd, pack, company, party, lot, band, crew (*informal*), bunch, mob, horde

gangster = <u>hoodlum</u> (*chiefly U.S.*), crook (*informal*), thug, bandit, heavy (*slang*), tough, hood (*U.S. slang*), robber, gang member, mobster (*U.S. slang*), racketeer, desperado, ruffian, brigand, wise guy (*U.S.*), tsotsi (*S. African*)

gaol
➤ **jail**

gap 1 = <u>opening</u>, space, hole, break, split, divide, crack, rent, breach, slot, vent, rift, aperture, cleft, chink, crevice, fissure, cranny, perforation, interstice ...*the wind tearing through gaps in the window frames*...
2 = <u>interval</u>, pause, recess, interruption, respite, lull, interlude, breathing space, hiatus, intermission, lacuna, entr'acte ...*There followed a gap of four years*...
3 = <u>difference</u>, gulf, contrast, disagreement, discrepancy, inconsistency, disparity, divergence ...*the gap between the poor and the well-off*...

gape 1 = <u>stare</u>, wonder, goggle, gawp (*Brit. slang*), gawk ...*She stopped what she was doing and gaped at me*...
2 = <u>open</u>, split, crack, yawn ...*A hole gaped in the roof*...

gaping = <u>wide</u>, great, open, broad, vast, yawning, wide open, cavernous

garb = <u>clothes</u>, dress, clothing, gear (*slang*), wear, habit, get-up (*informal*), uniform, outfit, costume, threads (*slang*), array, ensemble, garments, robes, duds (*informal*), apparel, clobber (*Brit. slang*), attire, togs (*informal*), vestments, raiment (*archaic*), rigout (*informal*)

garbage 1 = <u>junk</u>, rubbish, litter, trash (*chiefly U.S.*), refuse, waste, sweepings, scraps, debris, muck, filth, swill, slops, offal, detritus, dross, odds and ends, flotsam and jetsam, grot (*slang*), leavings, dreck (*slang, chiefly U.S.*), scourings, offscourings …*rotting piles of garbage…*

2 = nonsense, rot, crap (*slang*), trash, hot air (*informal*), tosh (*informal*), pap, bilge (*informal*), drivel, twaddle, tripe (*informal*), gibberish, guff (*slang*), moonshine, claptrap (*informal*), hogwash, hokum (*slang, chiefly U.S. & Canad.*), codswallop (*Brit. slang*), piffle (*informal*), poppycock (*informal*), balderdash, bosh (*informal*), eyewash (*informal*), kak (*S. African slang*), stuff and nonsense, bunkum *or* buncombe (*chiefly U.S.*), bizzo (*Austral. slang*), bull's wool (*Austral. & N.Z. slang*) …*I personally think the story is complete garbage…*

garbled = jumbled, confused, distorted, mixed up, muddled, incomprehensible, unintelligible

garden = grounds, park, plot, patch, lawn, allotment, yard (*U.S. & Canad.*)

⟮ *Related Words* ⟯
adjective : horticultural

gargantuan = huge, big, large, giant, massive, towering, vast, enormous, extensive, tremendous, immense, mega (*slang*), titanic, jumbo (*informal*), gigantic, monumental, monstrous, mammoth, colossal, mountainous, prodigious, stupendous, elephantine, ginormous (*informal*), Brobdingnagian, humongous *or* humungous (*U.S. slang*) ⟨OPPOSITE⟩ tiny

Word Power

gargantuan – Some people think that *gargantuan* should only be used to describe things connected with food: *a gargantuan meal; his gargantuan appetite.* Nevertheless, the word is now widely used as a synonym of *colossal* or *massive*.

garish = gaudy, bright, glaring, vulgar, brilliant, flash (*informal*), loud, brash, tacky (*informal*), flashy, tasteless, naff (*Brit. slang*), jazzy (*informal*), tawdry, showy, brassy, raffish ⟨OPPOSITE⟩ dull

garland NOUN = wreath, band, bays, crown, honours, loop, laurels, festoon, coronet, coronal, chaplet …*They wore garlands of summer flowers in their hair…*
VERB = adorn, crown, deck, festoon, wreathe …*Players were garlanded with flowers…*

garment *often plural* = clothes, wear, dress, clothing, gear (*slang*), habit, get-up (*informal*), uniform, outfit, costume, threads (*slang*), array, robes, duds (*informal*), apparel, clobber (*Brit. slang*), attire, garb, togs, vestments, articles of clothing, raiment (*archaic*), rigout (*informal*), habiliment

garnish NOUN = decoration, ornament, embellishment, adornment, ornamentation, trimming, trim …*Reserve some watercress for garnish…*
VERB = decorate, adorn, ornament, embellish, deck, festoon, trim, bedeck …*She had prepared the vegetables and was garnishing the roast…* ⟨OPPOSITE⟩ strip

garrison NOUN **1** = troops, group, unit, section, command, armed force, detachment …*a five-hundred man garrison…*
2 = fort, fortress, camp, base, post, station, stronghold, fortification, encampment …*The approaches to the garrison have been heavily mined…*
VERB **1** = occupy, protect, guard, defend, man, supply with troops …*British troops still garrisoned the country…*
2 = station, position, post, mount, install, assign, put on duty …*No other soldiers were garrisoned there…*

garrulous 1 = talkative, gossiping, chattering, babbling, gushing, chatty, long-winded, effusive, gabby (*informal*), prattling, voluble, gossipy, loquacious, verbose, mouthy …*a garrulous old woman…* ⟨OPPOSITE⟩ taciturn
2 = rambling, lengthy, diffuse, long-winded, wordy, discursive, windy, overlong, verbose, prolix, prosy …*boring, garrulous prose…* ⟨OPPOSITE⟩ concise

gas = fumes, vapour
➤ **types of gas**

gash NOUN = cut, tear, split, wound, rent, slash, slit, gouge, incision, laceration …*a long gash just above his right eye…*

Types of gas

acetylene	dichlorodifluoromethane	liquefied petroleum gas (LPG)	producer gas *or* air gas
afterdamp	electrolytic gas		propane
ammonia	ethane	marsh gas	radon
argon	ethylene	methane	sewage gas
arsine	flue gas	methylamine	stibine
biogas	fluorine	methyl bromide	synthetic natural gas (SNG)
butadiene	formaldehyde	methyl chloride	
butane	helium	natural gas	sulphur dioxide
butene	hydrogen	neon	synthesis gas
Calor gas	hydrogen bromide	nitric oxide	tail gas
carbon dioxide *or* carbonic-acid gas	hydrogen chloride	nitrogen	tetrafluoroethene
	hydrogen fluoride	nitrogen dioxide	tetrafluoroethylene
carbon monoxide	hydrogen iodide	nitrous oxide	town gas
chlorine	hydrogen sulphide	oilgas	vinyl chloride
coal gas	ketene	oxygen	water gas
cyanogen	krypton	ozone	xenon
diazomethane	laughing gas *or* nitrous oxide (LNG)	phosgene	
diborane		phosphine	

VERB = <u>cut</u>, tear, split, wound, rend, slash, slit, gouge, lacerate …*He gashed his leg while felling trees…*

gasp **VERB** = <u>pant</u>, blow, puff, choke, gulp, fight for breath, catch your breath …*He gasped for air before being pulled under again…*
NOUN = <u>pant</u>, puff, gulp, intake of breath, sharp intake of breath …*She gave a small gasp of pain…*

gate = <u>barrier</u>, opening, door, access, port (*Scot.*), entrance, exit, gateway, portal, egress

gather 1 = <u>congregate</u>, assemble, get together, collect, group, meet, mass, rally, flock, come together, muster, convene, converge, rendezvous, foregather …*In the evenings, we gathered round the fire and talked…* **OPPOSITE** scatter
2 = <u>assemble</u>, group, collect, round up, marshal, bring together, muster, convene, call together …*He called to her to gather the children together…* **OPPOSITE** disperse
3 = <u>collect</u>, assemble, accumulate, round up, mass, heap, marshal, bring together, muster, pile up, garner, amass, stockpile, hoard, stack up …*She started gathering up her things…*
4 = <u>pick</u>, harvest, pluck, reap, garner, glean …*The people lived by fishing, gathering nuts and fruits, and hunting…*
5 = <u>build up</u>, rise, increase, grow, develop, expand, swell, intensify, wax, heighten, deepen, enlarge, thicken …*Storm clouds were gathering in the distance…*
6 = <u>understand</u>, believe, hear, learn, assume, take it, conclude, presume, be informed, infer, deduce, surmise, be led to believe …*I gather his report is highly critical of the project…*
7 = <u>fold</u>, tuck, pleat, ruffle, pucker, shirr …*Gather the skirt at the waist…*

gathering 1 = <u>assembly</u>, group, crowd, meeting, conference, company, party, congress, mass, rally, convention, knot, flock, get-together (*informal*), congregation, muster, turnout, multitude, throng, hui (*N.Z.*), concourse, assemblage, conclave, convocation …*He spoke today before a large gathering of world leaders…*
2 = <u>collecting</u>, gaining, collection, obtaining, acquisition, roundup, accumulation, stockpiling, attainment, procuring …*a mission to spearhead the gathering of information…*

gauche = <u>awkward</u>, clumsy, inept, unsophisticated, inelegant, graceless, unpolished, uncultured, maladroit, ill-bred, ill-mannered, lacking in social graces **OPPOSITE** sophisticated

gaudy = <u>garish</u>, bright, glaring, vulgar, brilliant, flash (*informal*), loud, brash, tacky (*informal*), flashy, tasteless, jazzy (*informal*), tawdry, showy, gay, ostentatious, raffish **OPPOSITE** dull

gauge **VERB** 1 = <u>measure</u>, calculate, evaluate, value, size, determine, count, weigh, compute, ascertain, quantify …*He gauged the wind at over thirty knots…*
2 = <u>judge</u>, estimate, guess, assess, evaluate, rate, appraise, reckon, adjudge …*See if you can gauge his reaction to the offer…*

NOUN = <u>meter</u>, indicator, dial, measuring instrument …*a temperature gauge…*

gaunt 1 = <u>thin</u>, lean, skinny, skeletal, wasted, drawn, spare, pinched, angular, bony, lanky, haggard, emaciated, scrawny, skin and bone, scraggy, cadaverous, rawboned …*Looking gaunt and tired, he denied there was anything to worry about…* **OPPOSITE** plump
2 = <u>bleak</u>, bare, harsh, forbidding, grim, stark, dismal, dreary, desolate, forlorn …*a large, gaunt, grey house…* **OPPOSITE** inviting

gawky = <u>awkward</u>, clumsy, lumbering, ungainly, gauche, uncouth, loutish, graceless, clownish, oafish, maladroit, lumpish, ungraceful, unco (*Austral. slang*) **OPPOSITE** graceful

gay **ADJECTIVE** 1 = <u>homosexual</u>, camp (*informal*), lesbian, pink (*informal*), queer (*informal, derogatory*), same-sex, sapphic …*The quality of life for gay men has improved over the last decade…*
2 = <u>cheerful</u>, happy, bright, glad, lively, sparkling, sunny, jolly, animated, merry, upbeat (*informal*), buoyant, cheery, joyous, joyful, carefree, jaunty, chirpy (*informal*), vivacious, jovial, gleeful, debonair, blithe, insouciant, full of beans (*informal*), light-hearted …*I am in good health, gay and cheerful…* **OPPOSITE** sad
3 = <u>colourful</u>, rich, bright, brilliant, vivid, flamboyant, flashy, gaudy, garish, showy …*I like gay, vibrant posters…* **OPPOSITE** drab
NOUN = <u>homosexual</u>, lesbian, fairy (*slang*), queer (*informal, derogatory*), faggot (*slang, chiefly U.S. & Canad.*), auntie or aunty (*Austral. slang*), lily (*Austral. slang*) …*Gays have proved themselves to be style leaders…* **OPPOSITE** heterosexual

---

Word Power

gay – By far the most common and up-to-date use of the word *gay* is in reference to being homosexual. Other senses of the word have become uncommon and dated.

---

gaze **VERB** = <u>stare</u>, look, view, watch, regard, contemplate, gape, eyeball (*slang*), ogle, look fixedly …*He gazed reflectively at the fire…*
NOUN = <u>stare</u>, look, fixed look …*She felt uncomfortable under the woman's steady gaze…*

gazette = <u>newspaper</u>, paper, journal, organ, periodical, news-sheet

gear **NOUN** 1 = <u>mechanism</u>, works, action, gearing, machinery, cogs, cogwheels, gearwheels …*The boat's steering gear failed…*
2 = <u>equipment</u>, supplies, tackle, tools, instruments, outfit, rigging, rig, accessories, apparatus, trappings, paraphernalia, accoutrements, appurtenances, equipage …*fishing gear…*
3 = <u>possessions</u>, things, effects, stuff, kit, luggage, baggage, belongings, paraphernalia, personal property, chattels …*They helped us put our gear in the van…*
4 = <u>clothing</u>, wear, dress, clothes, habit, outfit, costume, threads (*slang*), array, garments, apparel,

Gemstones   http://www.gemstone.org/

adularia	citrine	jasper	rose quartz
agate	Colorado ruby	jet	rubellite
alexandrite	Colorado topaz	kunzite	ruby
almandine	corundum	lapis lazuli	sapphire
amazonite	cymophane	liver opal	sard *or* sardine
amethyst	demantoid	Madagascar aquamarine	sardonyx
andalusite	diamond	melanite	smoky quartz
andradite	diopside	moonstone	Spanish topaz
aquamarine	emerald	morganite	spessartite
aventurine, aventurin, *or* avanturine	fire opal	morion	sphene
balas	garnet	moss agate	spinel
beryl	girasol, girosol, *or* girasole	New Zealand greenstone	spodumene
black opal	grossularite	odontolite	staurolite
bloodstone	hawk's-eye	onyx	sunstone
bone turquoise	helidor	opal	titanite
cairngorm	heliotrope	Oriental almandine	topaz
carnelian	hessonite	Oriental emerald	topazolite
cat's-eye	hiddenite	peridot	tourmaline
chalcedony	hyacinth	plasma	turquoise
chrysoberyl	indicolite *or* indigolite	pyrope	uvarovite
chrysolite	jacinth	quartz	vesuvianite
chrysoprase	jadeite *or* jade	rhodolite	water sapphire
			white sapphire

attire, garb, togs, rigout ...*I used to wear trendy gear but it just looked ridiculous...*

VERB with **to** or **towards** = equip, fit, suit, adjust, adapt, rig, tailor ...*Colleges are not always geared towards the needs of mature students...*

gem 1 = precious stone, jewel, stone, semiprecious stone ...*The mask is inset with emeralds and other gems...*
2 = treasure, pick, prize, jewel, flower, pearl, masterpiece, paragon, humdinger (*slang*) ...*Castel Clara was a gem of a hotel...*
➤ **gemstones**

genealogy = ancestry, descent, pedigree, line, origin, extraction, lineage, family tree, parentage, derivation, blood line

general 1 = widespread, accepted, popular, public, common, broad, extensive, universal, prevailing, prevalent ...*Contrary to general opinion, Wiccans are not devil-worshippers...* **OPPOSITE** individual
2 = overall, complete, total, global, comprehensive, blanket, inclusive, all-embracing, overarching ...*His firm took over general maintenance of the park last summer...* **OPPOSITE** restricted
3 = universal, overall, widespread, collective, across-the-board, all-inclusive ...*The figures represent a general decline in unemployment...* **OPPOSITE** exceptional
4 = vague, broad, loose, blanket, sweeping, unclear, inaccurate, approximate, woolly, indefinite, hazy, imprecise, ill-defined, inexact, unspecific, undetailed ...*chemicals called by the general description 'flavour enhancer'...* **OPPOSITE** specific
5 = ordinary, regular, usual, typical, conventional, everyday, customary ...*This book is intended for the general reader rather than the student...* **OPPOSITE** special

generality 1 = generalization, abstraction, sweeping statement, vague notion, loose statement ...*He avoided this tricky question and talked in generalities...*
2 = impreciseness, vagueness, looseness, lack of detail, inexactitude, woolliness, indefiniteness, approximateness, inexactness, lack of preciseness ...*There are problems with this definition, given its level of generality...*

generally 1 = broadly, mainly, mostly, principally, on the whole, predominantly, in the main, for the most part ...*University teachers generally have admitted a lack of enthusiasm about their subjects...*
2 = usually, commonly, typically, regularly, normally, on average, on the whole, for the most part, almost always, in most cases, by and large, ordinarily, as a rule, habitually, conventionally, customarily ...*As women we generally say and feel too much about these things...* **OPPOSITE** occasionally
3 = commonly, widely, publicly, universally, extensively, popularly, conventionally, customarily ...*It is generally believed that drinking red wine in moderation is beneficial...* **OPPOSITE** individually

generate = produce, create, make, form, cause, initiate, bring about, originate, give rise to, engender, whip up **OPPOSITE** end

generation 1 = age group, peer group ...*He's the leading American playwright of his generation...*
2 = age, period, era, time, days, lifetime, span, epoch ...*Within a generation, flight has become popular with many travellers...*

generic = collective, general, common, wide, sweeping, comprehensive, universal, blanket, inclusive, all-encompassing **OPPOSITE** specific

generosity 1 = liberality, charity, bounty, munificence, beneficence, largesse *or* largess ...*There are many stories of his generosity...*
2 = magnanimity, goodness, kindness, benevolence, selflessness, charity, unselfishness, high-mindedness,

nobleness …*his moral decency and generosity of spirit…*

generous 1 = <u>liberal</u>, lavish, free, charitable, free-handed, hospitable, prodigal, bountiful, open-handed, unstinting, beneficent, princely, bounteous, munificent, ungrudging …*He's very generous with his money…* OPPOSITE⟩ mean
2 = <u>magnanimous</u>, kind, noble, benevolent, good, big, high-minded, unselfish, big-hearted, ungrudging …*He was not generous enough to congratulate his successor…*
3 = <u>plentiful</u>, lavish, ample, abundant, full, rich, liberal, overflowing, copious, bountiful, unstinting, profuse, bounteous (*literary*), plenteous …*a room with a generous amount of storage space…* OPPOSITE⟩ meagre

genesis = <u>beginning</u>, source, root, origin, start, generation, birth, creation, dawn, formation, outset, starting point, engendering, inception, commencement, propagation OPPOSITE⟩ end

genial = <u>friendly</u>, kind, kindly, pleasant, warm, cheerful, jolly, hearty, agreeable, cheery, amiable, cordial, affable, congenial, jovial, convivial, good-natured, warm-hearted OPPOSITE⟩ unfriendly

genitals = <u>sex organs</u>, privates, loins, genitalia, private parts, reproductive organs, pudenda
⟨ *Related Words* ⟩
adjective: venereal

genius 1 = <u>brilliance</u>, ability, talent, capacity, gift, bent, faculty, excellence, endowment, flair, inclination, knack, propensity, aptitude, cleverness, creative power …*This is the mark of her genius as a designer…*
2 = <u>master</u>, expert, mastermind, brain (*informal*), buff (*informal*), intellect (*informal*), adept, maestro, virtuoso, whiz (*informal*), hotshot (*informal*), rocket scientist (*informal, chiefly U.S.*), wonk (*informal*), brainbox, maven (*U.S.*), master-hand, fundi (*S. African*) …*a 14-year-old mathematical genius…* OPPOSITE⟩ dunce

genre = <u>type</u>, group, school, form, order, sort, kind, class, style, character, fashion, brand, species, category, stamp, classification, genus, subdivision

genteel = <u>refined</u>, cultured, mannerly, elegant, formal, gentlemanly, respectable, polite, cultivated, courteous, courtly, well-bred, ladylike, well-mannered OPPOSITE⟩ unmannerly

gentility = <u>refinement</u>, culture, breeding, courtesy, elegance, formality, respectability, cultivation, rank, politeness, good manners, good family, blue blood, good breeding, high birth, courtliness, gentle birth

gentle 1 = <u>kind</u>, loving, kindly, peaceful, soft, quiet, pacific, tender, mild, benign, humane, compassionate, amiable, meek, lenient, placid, merciful, kind-hearted, sweet-tempered, tender-hearted …*a quiet and gentle man who liked sports and enjoyed life…* OPPOSITE⟩ unkind
2 = <u>slow</u>, easy, slight, deliberate, moderate, gradual, imperceptible …*His movements were gentle and deliberate…*
3 = <u>moderate</u>, low, light, easy, soft, calm, slight, mild, soothing, clement, temperate, balmy …*The wind had*

dropped to a gentle breeze… OPPOSITE⟩ violent

gentlemanly = <u>chivalrous</u>, mannerly, obliging, refined, polite, civil, cultivated, courteous, gallant, genteel, suave, well-bred, well-mannered

gentleness = <u>tenderness</u>, compassion, kindness, consideration, sympathy, sweetness, softness, mildness, kindliness

gentry = <u>nobility</u>, lords, elite, nobles, upper class, aristocracy, peerage, ruling class, patricians, upper crust (*informal*), gentility, gentlefolk

genuine 1 = <u>authentic</u>, real, original, actual, sound, true, pure, sterling, valid, legitimate, honest, veritable, bona fide, dinkum (*Austral. & N.Z. informal*), the real McCoy …*They are convinced the painting is genuine…* OPPOSITE⟩ counterfeit
2 = <u>heartfelt</u>, sincere, honest, earnest, real, true, frank, unaffected, wholehearted, unadulterated, unalloyed, unfeigned …*There was genuine joy in the room…* OPPOSITE⟩ affected
3 = <u>sincere</u>, straightforward, honest, natural, frank, candid, upfront (*informal*), dinkum (*Austral. & N.Z. informal*), artless, guileless …*She is a very caring and genuine person…* OPPOSITE⟩ hypocritical

genus = <u>type</u>, sort, kind, group, set, order, race, class, breed, category, genre, classification

geography
➤ **geography terms and features**

geology
➤ **geology ➤ layers of the earth's crust**

germ 1 = <u>microbe</u>, virus, bug (*informal*), bacterium, bacillus, microorganism …*a germ that destroyed hundred of millions of lives…*
2 = <u>beginning</u>, root, seed, origin, spark, bud, embryo, rudiment …*The germ of an idea took root in her mind…*

Germany
➤ **administrative regions**
⟨ *Related Words* ⟩
adjective: Teutonic

germinate = <u>sprout</u>, grow, shoot, develop, generate, swell, bud, vegetate

gestation = <u>incubation</u>, development, growth, pregnancy, evolution, ripening, maturation

gesticulate = <u>signal</u>, sign, wave, indicate, motion, gesture, beckon, make a sign

gesture NOUN = <u>sign</u>, action, signal, motion, indication, gesticulation …*She made a menacing gesture with her fist…*
VERB = <u>signal</u>, sign, wave, indicate, motion, beckon, gesticulate …*I gestured towards the boathouse and he looked inside…*

get VERB 1 = <u>become</u>, grow, turn, wax, come to be …*The boys were getting bored…*
2 = <u>persuade</u>, convince, win over, induce, influence, sway, entice, coax, incite, impel, talk into, wheedle, prevail upon …*How did you get him to pose for this picture?…*
3 = <u>arrive</u>, come, reach, make it (*informal*) …*It was dark by the time she got home…*

Geography terms and features http://www.geographynetwork.com

afforestation	eastings	longitude	scree
antipodes	environment	longshore drift	sierra
arête	epicentre	mantle	snow line
atlas	equator	map	southern hemisphere
atmosphere	erosion	meander	South Pole
atoll	escarpment	Mercator projection	spit
basin	estuary	moraine	spring
bay	fault	new town	spur
beach	fell	northern hemisphere	stack
canyon	fjord	northings	steppe
cliff	flood plain	North Pole	subsoil
climate	glaciation	occidental	suburb
col	glacier	ocean	tarn
conservation	glade	Ordnance Survey	temperate
continent	glen	oriental	Third World
continental drift	global warming	ozone layer	topsoil
continental shelf	green belt	permafrost	tor
contour	greenhouse effect	plate tectonics	tropics
conurbation	grid reference	pollution	tsunami
coombe	hanging valley	precipitation	tundra
coral reef	headland	rainforest	urbanization
core	ice cap	rain shadow	veld or veldt
corrie, cirque, or cwm	infrastructure	reef	volcano
crag	International Date Line	relief map	wadi
crater	irrigation	ridge	watercourse
crevasse	isobar	rift valley	water cycle
crust	isobath	rill	waterfall
culvert	isohyet	river basin	watershed
deforestation	isotherm	rivulet	water table
delta	isthmus	salt flat	weathering
desert	jungle	salt lake	wetland
desertification	lagoon	sandbank	whirlpool
dormitory	latitude	sand bar	
dyke	levée	sand dune	
earthquake	loch	savanna or savannah	

4 = <u>manage</u>, fix, succeed, arrange, contrive, wangle (*informal*) ...*How did he get to be the boss of a major company?*...

5 (*Informal*) = <u>annoy</u>, upset, anger, bother, disturb, trouble, bug (*informal*), irritate, aggravate (*informal*), gall, madden, exasperate, nettle, vex, irk, rile, pique, get on your nerves (*informal*), nark (*Brit., Austral., & N.Z. slang*), get up your nose (*informal*), give someone grief (*Brit. & S. African*), make your blood boil, get your goat (*slang*), get on your wick (*Brit. slang*), get your back up ...*What gets me is the attitude of these people*...

6 = <u>obtain</u>, receive, gain, acquire, win, land, score (*slang*), achieve, net, pick up, bag, secure, attain, reap, get hold of, come by, glean, procure, get your hands on, come into possession of ...*The problem was how to get enough food*...

7 = <u>fetch</u>, bring, collect ...*Go and get your Daddy for me*...

8 = <u>understand</u>, follow, catch, see, notice, realize, appreciate, be aware of, take in, perceive, grasp, comprehend, fathom, apprehend, suss (out) (*slang*), get the hang of (*informal*), get your head round ...*You don't seem to get the point*...

9 = <u>catch</u>, develop, contract, succumb to, fall victim to, go down with, come down with, become infected with, be afflicted with, be smitten by ...*When I was five I got measles*...

10 = <u>arrest</u>, catch, grab, capture, trap, seize, take, nail (*informal*), collar (*informal*), nab (*informal*), apprehend, take prisoner, take into custody, lay hold of ...*The police have got the killer*...

11 = <u>contact</u>, reach, communicate with, get hold of, get in touch with ...*We've been trying to get you on the phone all day*...

12 = <u>puzzle</u>, confuse, baffle, bewilder, confound, perplex, mystify, stump, beat (*slang*), flummox, nonplus ...*No, I can't answer that question – you've got me there*...

13 (*Informal*) = <u>move</u>, touch, affect, excite, stir, stimulate, arouse, have an impact on, have an effect on, tug at (someone's) heartstrings (*often facetious*) ...*I don't know what it is about that song, it just gets me*...

PHRASES **get across something** = <u>cross</u>, negotiate, pass over, traverse, ford ...*When we got across the beach, we saw some Spanish guys waiting for us*... ◆ **get ahead** = <u>prosper</u>, advance, progress, succeed, get on, do well, thrive, flourish, be successful, make good, cut it (*informal*), make the grade (*informal*), turn out well, make your mark ...*He wanted safety, security, a home, and a chance to get*

Geology

Geological eras

Cenozoic   Palaeozoic
Mesozoic   Precambrian

Geological periods

Quaternary   Triassic   Silurian
Tertiary   Permian   Ordovician
Cretaceous   Carboniferous   Cambrian
Jurassic   Devonian

Epochs of the Cenozoic era http://www.windows.ucar.edu/tour/link=/earth/geology/geology.html

Holocene   Miocene   Palaeocene
Pleistocene   Oligocene
Pliocene   Eocene

ahead... ♦ **get at someone** 1 = <u>criticize</u>, attack, blame, put down, knock (*informal*), carp, have a go (at) (*informal*), taunt, nag, hassle (*informal*), pick on, disparage, diss (*slang, chiefly U.S.*), find fault with, put the boot into (*slang*), nark (*Brit., Austral., & N.Z. slang*), be on your back (*slang*) ...*His mother doesn't like me, and she gets at me all the time...* 2 = <u>corrupt</u>, influence, bribe, tamper with, buy off, fix (*informal*), suborn ...*He claims these government officials have been got at...* ♦ **get at something** 1 = <u>reach</u>, touch, grasp, get (a) hold of, stretch to ...*The goat was on its hind legs trying to get at the leaves...* 2 = <u>find out</u>, get, learn, reach, reveal, discover, acquire, detect, uncover, attain, get hold of, gain access to, come to grips with ...*We're only trying to get at the truth...* 3 = <u>imply</u>, mean, suggest, hint, intimate, lead up to, insinuate ...*'What are you getting at now?' demanded Rick...* ♦ **get away** = <u>escape</u>, leave, disappear, flee, depart, fly, slip away, abscond, decamp, hook it (*slang*), do a runner (*slang*), slope off, do a bunk (*Brit. slang*), fly the coop (*U.S. & Canad. informal*), skedaddle (*informal*), take a powder (*U.S. & Canad. slang*), make good your escape, make your getaway, take it on the lam (*U.S. & Canad. slang*), break free *or* out, run away *or* off ...*They tried to stop him but he got away...* ♦ **get back** = <u>return</u>, arrive home, come back *or* home ...*It was late when we got back from the hospital...* ♦ **get back at someone** = <u>retaliate</u>, pay (someone) back, hit back at, take revenge on, get even with, strike back at, even the score with, exact retribution on, get your own back on, make reprisal with, be avenged on, settle the score with, give (someone) a taste of his *or* her own medicine, give tit for tat, take *or* wreak vengeance on ...*My wife had left me and I wanted to get back at her...* ♦ **get by** = <u>manage</u>, survive, cope, fare, get through, exist, make out, get along, make do, subsist, muddle through, keep your head above water, make both ends meet ...*I'm a survivor. I'll get by...* ♦ **get in** = <u>arrive</u>, come in, appear, land ...*Our flight got in late...* ♦ **get off** 1 = <u>be absolved</u>, be acquitted, escape punishment, walk (*slang, chiefly U.S.*) ...*He is likely to get off with a small fine...* 2 = <u>leave</u>, go, move, take off (*informal*), depart, slope off, make tracks, set out *or* off ...*I'd like to get off before it starts to get dark...* 3 = <u>descend</u>, leave, exit, step down, alight, disembark, dismount ...*We got off at the next stop...* ♦ **get on** 1 = <u>be friendly</u>, agree, get along, concur, be compatible, hit it off (*informal*), harmonize, be on good terms ...*Do you get on with your neighbours?...* 2 = <u>progress</u>, manage, cope, fare, advance, succeed, make out (*informal*), prosper, cut it (*informal*), get along ...*I asked how he was getting on...* 3 = <u>board</u>, enter, mount, climb, embark, ascend ...*The bus stopped to let the passengers get on...* ♦ **get out** = <u>leave</u>, escape, withdraw, quit, take off (*informal*), exit, go, break out, go away, depart, evacuate, vacate, clear out (*informal*), abscond, decamp, hook it (*slang*), free yourself, do a bunk (*Brit. slang*), extricate yourself, sling your hook (*Brit. slang*) ...*I think we should get out while we still can...* ♦ **get out of something** = <u>avoid</u>, dodge, evade, escape, shirk, body-swerve (*Scot.*) ...*It's amazing what people will do to get out of paying taxes...* ♦ **get over something** 1 = <u>recover from</u>, survive, get better from, come round, bounce back, mend, get well, recuperate, turn the corner, pull through, get back on your feet, feel yourself again, regain your health *or* strength ...*It took me a very long time to get over the shock of her death...* 2 = <u>overcome</u>, deal with, solve, resolve, defeat, master, lick (*informal*), shake off, rise above, get the better of, surmount ...*How would they get over that problem, he wondered?...* 3 = <u>cross</u>, pass, pass over, traverse, get across, move across, ford, go across ...*The travellers were trying to get over the river...* ♦ **get round someone** (*Informal*) = <u>win over</u>, persuade, charm, influence, convince, convert, sway, coax, cajole, wheedle, prevail upon, bring round, talk round ...*Max could always get round his mother...* ♦ **get round something** = <u>overcome</u>, deal with, solve, resolve, defeat, master, bypass, lick (*informal*), shake off, rise above, get the better of, circumvent, surmount ...*No one has found a way of getting round the problem...* ♦ **get something across** = <u>communicate</u>, publish, spread, pass on, transmit, convey, impart, get (something) through, disseminate, bring home, make known, put over, make clear *or* understood ...*I need a better way of getting my message across to people...* ♦ **get something back** = <u>regain</u>, recover, retrieve, take back, recoup, repossess ...*You have 14 days in* which to cancel and get your money back... ◆ **get something over** = communicate, spread, pass on, convey, impart, make known, get or put across, make clear or understood ...We have got the message over to young people that smoking isn't cool... ◆ **get together** = meet, unite, join, collect, gather, rally, assemble, muster, convene, converge, congregate ...This is the only forum where East and West can get together... ◆ **get up** = arise, stand (up), rise, get to your feet ...I got up and walked over to the door...

getaway = escape, break, flight, break-out, decampment

get-together = gathering, party, celebration, reception, meeting, social, function, bash (informal), rave (Brit. slang), festivity, do (informal), knees-up (Brit. informal), beano (Brit. slang), social gathering, shindig (informal), soirée, rave-up (Brit. slang), hooley or hoolie (chiefly Irish & N.Z.)

ghastly = horrible, shocking, terrible, awful, grim, dreadful, horrendous, hideous, from hell (informal), horrid (informal), repulsive, frightful, loathsome, godawful (slang) OPPOSITE lovely

ghost 1 = spirit, soul, phantom, spectre, spook (informal), apparition, wraith, shade (literary), phantasm ...The village is said to be haunted by the ghosts of the dead children...
2 = trace, shadow, suggestion, hint, suspicion, glimmer, semblance ...He gave the ghost of a smile...
(Related Words)
adjective: spectral

ghostly = unearthly, weird, phantom, eerie, supernatural, uncanny, spooky (informal), spectral, eldritch (poetic), phantasmal

ghoulish = macabre, sick (informal), disgusting, hideous, gruesome, grisly, horrid, morbid, unwholesome

giant ADJECTIVE = huge, great, large, vast, enormous, extensive, tremendous, immense, titanic, jumbo (informal), gigantic, monumental, monstrous, mammoth, colossal, mountainous, stellar (informal), prodigious, stupendous, gargantuan, elephantine, ginormous (informal), Brobdingnagian, humongous or humungous (U.S. slang) ...a giant step towards unification... ...a giant oak table... OPPOSITE tiny
NOUN = ogre, monster, titan, colossus, leviathan, behemoth ...a Nordic saga of giants and monsters...

gibber = gabble, chatter, babble, waffle (informal, chiefly Brit.), prattle, jabber, blab, rabbit on (Brit. informal), blather, blabber

gibberish = nonsense, crap (slang), garbage (informal), jargon, hot air (informal), tosh (slang, chiefly Brit.), babble, pap, bilge (informal), drivel, twaddle, tripe (informal), guff (slang), prattle, mumbo jumbo, moonshine, jabber, gabble, gobbledegook (informal), hogwash, hokum (slang, chiefly U.S. & Canad.), blather, double talk, piffle (informal), all Greek (informal), poppycock (informal), balderdash, bosh (informal), yammer (informal), eyewash (informal), tommyrot, horsefeathers (U.S. slang), bunkum or buncombe (chiefly U.S.), bizzo (Austral.

slang), bull's wool (Austral. & N.Z. slang)

gibe
➤ **jibe**

gidday or **g'day** (Austral. & N.Z.) = hello, hi (informal), greetings, how do you do?, good morning, good evening, good afternoon, welcome, kia ora (N.Z.)

giddy 1 = dizzy, reeling, faint, unsteady, light-headed, vertiginous ...He felt giddy and light-headed...
2 = flighty, silly, volatile, irresponsible, reckless, dizzy, careless, frivolous, impulsive, capricious, thoughtless, impetuous, skittish, heedless, scatterbrained, ditzy or ditsy (slang) ...Man is a giddy creature... OPPOSITE serious

gift 1 = donation, offering, present, contribution, grant, legacy, hand-out, endowment, boon, bequest, gratuity, prezzie (informal), bonsela (S. African), largesse or largess ...a gift of $50,000...
2 = talent, ability, capacity, genius, power, bent, faculty, capability, forte, flair, knack, aptitude ...As a youth he discovered a gift for teaching...

gifted = talented, able, skilled, expert, masterly, brilliant, capable, clever, accomplished, proficient, adroit OPPOSITE talentless

gigantic = huge, great, large, giant, massive, vast, enormous, extensive, tremendous, immense, titanic, jumbo (informal), monumental, monstrous, mammoth, colossal, mountainous, stellar (informal), prodigious, stupendous, gargantuan, herculean, elephantine, ginormous (informal), Brobdingnagian, humongous or humungous (U.S. slang) OPPOSITE tiny

giggle VERB = laugh, chuckle, snigger, chortle, titter, twitter, tee-hee ...Both girls began to giggle...
NOUN = laugh, chuckle, snigger, chortle, titter, twitter ...She gave a little giggle...

gimmick = stunt, trick, device, scheme, manoeuvre, dodge, ploy, gambit, stratagem, contrivance

gingerly = cautiously, carefully, reluctantly, suspiciously, tentatively, warily, hesitantly, timidly, circumspectly, cagily (informal), charily OPPOSITE carelessly

gird 1 = girdle, bind, belt ...The other knights urged Galahad to gird on his sword...
2 = surround, ring, pen, enclose, encompass, encircle, hem in, enfold, engird ...a proposal to gird the river with a series of small hydroelectric dams...
3 = prepare, ready, steel, brace, fortify, make or get ready ...They are girding themselves for battle against a new enemy...

girdle NOUN = belt, band, sash, waistband, cummerbund ...These muscles hold in the waist like an invisible girdle...
VERB = surround, ring, bound, enclose, encompass, hem, encircle, fence in, gird ...The old town centre is girdled by a boulevard lined with trees...

girl = female child, schoolgirl, lass, lassie (informal), miss, maiden (archaic), maid (archaic)

girth = size, measure, proportions, dimensions, bulk, measurement(s), circumference

gist = essence, meaning, point, idea, sense, import,

core, substance, drift, significance, nub, pith, quintessence

give [VERB] 1 = <u>perform</u>, do, carry out, execute …*She stretched her arms out and gave a great yawn…*
2 = <u>communicate</u>, announce, publish, transmit, pronounce, utter, emit, issue, be a source of, impart …*He gave no details of his plans…*
3 = <u>produce</u>, make, cause, occasion, engender …*Her visit gave great pleasure to the children…*
4 = <u>present</u>, contribute, donate, provide, supply, award, grant, deliver, commit, administer, furnish, confer, bestow, entrust, consign, make over, hand over or out …*This recipe was given to me years ago…* …*They still give to charity despite hard economic times…* [OPPOSITE] take
5 = <u>collapse</u>, fall, break, sink, bend …*My knees gave under me…*
6 = <u>concede</u>, allow, grant …*You're a bright enough kid, I'll give you that…* •
7 = <u>surrender</u>, yield, devote, hand over, relinquish, part with, cede …*a memorial to a man who gave his life for his country…*
8 = <u>demonstrate</u>, show, offer, provide, evidence, display, indicate, manifest, set forth …*The handout gives all the times of the performances…*
[PHRASES] **give in** = <u>admit defeat</u>, yield, concede, collapse, quit, submit, surrender, comply, succumb, cave in (*informal*), capitulate …*My parents gave in and let me go to the camp…* ◆ **give something away** = <u>reveal</u>, expose, leak, disclose, betray, uncover, let out, divulge, let slip, let the cat out of the bag (*informal*) …*They were giving away company secrets…* ◆ **give something off** or **out** = <u>emit</u>, produce, release, discharge, send out, throw out, vent, exude, exhale …*Natural gas gives off less carbon dioxide than coal…* ◆ **give something out** 1 = <u>distribute</u>, issue, deliver, circulate, hand out, dispense, dole out, pass round …*There were people at the entrance giving out leaflets…* 2 = <u>make known</u>, announce, publish, broadcast, communicate, transmit, utter, notify, impart, disseminate, shout from the rooftops (*informal*) …*He wouldn't give out any information…* ◆ **give something up** 1 = <u>abandon</u>, stop, quit, kick (*informal*), cease, cut out, renounce, leave off, say goodbye to, desist, kiss (something) goodbye, forswear …*I'm trying to give up smoking…*
2 = <u>quit</u>, leave, resign, step down from (*informal*) …*She gave up her job to join her husband's campaign…* 3 = <u>hand over</u>, yield, surrender, relinquish, waive …*The government refused to give up any territory…*

given 1 = <u>specified</u>, particular, specific, designated, stated, predetermined …*the number of accidents at this spot in a given period…*
2 = <u>inclined</u>, addicted, disposed, prone, liable …*I am not very given to emotional displays…*

glacial 1 = <u>icy</u>, biting, cold, freezing, frozen, bitter, raw, chill, piercing, arctic, polar, chilly, frosty, wintry …*The air from the sea felt glacial…*
2 = <u>unfriendly</u>, hostile, cold, icy, frosty, antagonistic, frigid, inimical …*The Duchess gave him a glacial look*

and moved on…

glad 1 = <u>happy</u>, pleased, delighted, contented, cheerful, gratified, joyful, overjoyed, chuffed (*slang*), gleeful …*I'm glad I decided to go after all…* [OPPOSITE] unhappy
2 (*Archaic*) = <u>pleasing</u>, happy, cheering, pleasant, delightful, cheerful, merry, gratifying, cheery, joyous, felicitous …*the bringer of glad tidings…*

gladly 1 = <u>happily</u>, cheerfully, gleefully, merrily, gaily, joyfully, joyously, jovially …*He gladly accepted my invitation…*
2 = <u>willingly</u>, freely, happily, readily, cheerfully, with pleasure, with (a) good grace …*The counsellors will gladly baby-sit during their free time…* [OPPOSITE] reluctantly

glamorous 1 = <u>attractive</u>, beautiful, lovely, charming, entrancing, elegant, dazzling, enchanting, captivating, alluring, bewitching …*some of the world's most beautiful and glamorous women…* [OPPOSITE] unglamorous
2 = <u>exciting</u>, glittering, prestigious, glossy, glitzy (*slang*) …*his glamorous playboy lifestyle…* [OPPOSITE] unglamorous

glamour 1 = <u>charm</u>, appeal, beauty, attraction, fascination, allure, magnetism, enchantment, bewitchment …*Her air of mystery only added to her glamour…*
2 = <u>excitement</u>, magic, thrill, romance, prestige, glitz (*slang*) …*the glamour of show biz…*

glance [VERB] 1 = <u>peek</u>, look, view, check, clock (*Brit. informal*), gaze, glimpse, check out (*informal*), peep, take a dekko at (*Brit. slang*) …*He glanced at his watch…* [OPPOSITE] scrutinize
2 *with* **over, through,** *etc.* = <u>scan</u>, browse, dip into, leaf through, flip through, thumb through, skim through, riffle through, run over or through …*I picked up the book and glanced through it…*
[NOUN] = <u>peek</u>, look, glimpse, peep, squint, butcher's (*Brit. slang*), quick look, gander (*informal*), brief look, dekko (*slang*), shufti (*Brit. slang*) …*She stole a quick glance at her watch…* [OPPOSITE] good look

---

Word Power

glance – Care should be taken not to confuse *glance* and *glimpse*: *he caught a glimpse* (not *glance*) *of her making her way through the crowd; he gave a quick* glance (not *glimpse*) *at his watch.* A *glance* is a deliberate action, while a *glimpse* seems opportunistic.

---

gland
(*Related Words*)
adjective: adenoid
➤ **glands**

glare [VERB] 1 = <u>scowl</u>, frown, glower, look daggers, stare angrily, give a dirty look, lour or lower …*He glared and muttered something…*
2 = <u>dazzle</u>, blaze, flare, flame …*The light was glaring straight into my eyes…*
[NOUN] 1 = <u>scowl</u>, frown, glower, dirty look, black look,

Glands

adrenal gland	lacrimal gland	parathyroid gland	testicle
endocrine gland	liver	pituitary gland	thyroid gland
exocrine gland	mammary gland	prostate	
hypothalamus	mucus gland	salivary gland	
islets of Langerhans *or*	ovary	sebaceous gland	
islands of Langerhans	pancreas	sweat gland	

angry stare, lour *or* lower …*His glasses magnified his irritable glare*…
2 = <u>dazzle</u>, glow, blaze, flare, flame, brilliance …*the glare of a car's headlights*…

glaring 1 = <u>obvious</u>, open, outstanding, patent, visible, gross, outrageous, manifest, blatant, conspicuous, overt, audacious, flagrant, rank, egregious, unconcealed …*I never saw such a glaring example of misrepresentation*… OPPOSITE inconspicuous
2 = <u>dazzling</u>, strong, bright, glowing, blazing …*She was clearly uneasy under the glaring camera lights*… OPPOSITE subdued

glassy 1 = <u>smooth</u>, clear, slick, shiny, glossy, transparent, slippery …*glassy green pebbles*…
2 = <u>expressionless</u>, cold, fixed, empty, dull, blank, glazed, vacant, dazed, lifeless …*There was a remote, glassy look in his eyes*…

glaze NOUN = <u>coat</u>, finish, polish, shine, gloss, varnish, enamel, lacquer, lustre, patina …*hand-painted tiles with decorative glazes*…
VERB = <u>coat</u>, polish, gloss, varnish, enamel, lacquer, burnish, furbish …*After the pots are fired, they are glazed in a variety of colours*…

gleam VERB = <u>shine</u>, flash, glow, sparkle, glitter, flare, shimmer, glint, glimmer, glisten, scintillate …*His red sports car gleamed in the sun*…
NOUN **1** = <u>glimmer</u>, flash, beam, glow, sparkle …*the gleam of the headlights*…
2 = <u>brightness</u>, flash, gloss, brilliance, sheen, lustre …*Her fair hair had a golden gleam*…
3 = <u>trace</u>, ray, suggestion, hint, flicker, glimmer, inkling …*There was a gleam of hope for a peaceful settlement*…

gleaming = <u>shining</u>, bright, brilliant, glowing, sparkling, glimmering, glistening, scintillating, burnished, lustrous OPPOSITE dull

glean = <u>gather</u>, learn, pick up, collect, harvest, accumulate, reap, garner, amass, cull

glee = <u>delight</u>, joy, triumph, exuberance, elation, exhilaration, mirth, hilarity, merriment, exultation, gladness, joyfulness, joyousness OPPOSITE gloom

gleeful = <u>delighted</u>, happy, pleased, cheerful, merry, triumphant, gratified, exuberant, jubilant, joyous, joyful, elated, overjoyed, chirpy (*informal*), exultant, cock-a-hoop, mirthful

glib = <u>smooth</u>, easy, ready, quick, slick, plausible, slippery, fluent, suave, artful, insincere, fast-talking, smooth-tongued OPPOSITE sincere

glide = <u>slip</u>, sail, slide, skim

glimmer VERB = <u>gleam</u>, shine, glow, sparkle, glitter, blink, flicker, shimmer, twinkle, glisten …*The moon glimmered faintly through the mists*…
NOUN **1** = <u>glow</u>, ray, sparkle, gleam, blink, flicker, shimmer, twinkle …*In the east there is the faintest glimmer of light*…
2 = <u>trace</u>, ray, suggestion, hint, grain, gleam, flicker, inkling …*Our last glimmer of hope faded*…

glimpse NOUN = <u>look</u>, sighting, sight, glance, peep, peek, squint, butcher's (*Brit. slang*), quick look, gander (*informal*), brief view, shufti (*Brit. slang*) …*The fans waited outside the hotel to get a glimpse of their heroine*…
VERB = <u>catch sight of</u>, spot, sight, view, clock (*Brit. informal*), spy, espy …*She glimpsed a group of people standing on the bank of a river*…

glint VERB = <u>gleam</u>, flash, shine, sparkle, glitter, twinkle, glimmer …*The sea glinted in the sun*…
NOUN = <u>gleam</u>, flash, shine, sparkle, glitter, twinkle, twinkling, glimmer …*glints of sunlight*…

glisten = <u>gleam</u>, flash, shine, sparkle, glitter, shimmer, twinkle, glint, glimmer, scintillate

glitch = <u>problem</u>, difficulty, fault, flaw, bug (*informal*), hitch, snag, uphill (*S. African*), interruption, blip, malfunction, kink, gremlin, fly in the ointment

glitter VERB = <u>shine</u>, flash, sparkle, flare, glare, gleam, shimmer, twinkle, glint, glimmer, glisten, scintillate …*The palace glittered with lights*…
NOUN **1** = <u>glamour</u>, show, display, gilt, splendour, tinsel, pageantry, gaudiness, showiness …*all the glitter and glamour of a Hollywood premiere*…
2 = <u>sparkle</u>, flash, shine, beam, glare, gleam, brilliance, sheen, shimmer, brightness, lustre, radiance, scintillation …*the glitter of strobe lights and mirror balls*…

gloat = <u>relish</u>, triumph, glory, crow, revel in, vaunt, drool, exult, rub your hands

global 1 = <u>worldwide</u>, world, international, universal, planetary …*a global ban on nuclear testing*…
2 = <u>comprehensive</u>, general, total, thorough, unlimited, exhaustive, all-inclusive, all-encompassing, encyclopedic, unbounded …*a global vision of contemporary society*… OPPOSITE limited

globe = <u>planet</u>, world, earth, sphere, orb

gloom 1 = <u>darkness</u>, dark, shadow, cloud, shade, twilight, dusk, obscurity, blackness, dullness, murk, dimness, murkiness, cloudiness, gloominess, duskiness …*the gloom of a foggy November morning*… OPPOSITE light
2 = <u>depression</u>, despair, misery, sadness, sorrow, blues, woe, melancholy, unhappiness, desolation, despondency, dejection, low spirits, downheartedness …*the deepening gloom over the*

economy... OPPOSITE> happiness

gloomy 1 = <u>dark</u>, dull, dim, dismal, black, grey, obscure, murky, dreary, sombre, shadowy, overcast, dusky ...*Inside it's gloomy after all that sunshine*... OPPOSITE> light
2 = <u>miserable</u>, down, sad, dismal, low, blue, pessimistic, melancholy, glum, dejected, despondent, dispirited, downcast, joyless, downhearted, down in the dumps (*informal*), cheerless, down in the mouth, in low spirits ...*He is gloomy about the fate of the economy*... OPPOSITE> happy
3 = <u>depressing</u>, bad, dismal, dreary, black, saddening, sombre, dispiriting, disheartening, funereal, cheerless, comfortless ...*Officials say the outlook for next year is gloomy*...

glorify 1 = <u>praise</u>, celebrate, magnify, laud, extol, crack up (*informal*), eulogize, sing *or* sound the praises of ...*the banning of songs glorifying war*... OPPOSITE> condemn
2 = <u>worship</u>, honour, bless, adore, revere, exalt, pay homage to, venerate, sanctify, immortalize ...*We are committed to serving the Lord and glorifying his name*... OPPOSITE> dishonour
3 = <u>enhance</u>, raise, elevate, adorn, dignify, magnify, augment, lift up, ennoble, add lustre to, aggrandize ...*They've glorified his job with an impressive title, but he's still just a salesman*... OPPOSITE> degrade

glorious 1 = <u>splendid</u>, beautiful, bright, brilliant, shining, superb, divine, gorgeous, dazzling, radiant, resplendent, splendiferous (*facetious*) ...*a glorious Edwardian opera house*... OPPOSITE> dull
2 = <u>delightful</u>, fine, wonderful, excellent, heavenly (*informal*), marvellous, splendid, gorgeous, pleasurable, splendiferous (*facetious*) ...*We opened the window and let in the glorious evening air*...
3 = <u>illustrious</u>, famous, celebrated, distinguished, noted, grand, excellent, honoured, magnificent, noble, renowned, elevated, eminent, triumphant, majestic, famed, sublime ...*He had a glorious career spanning more than six decades*... OPPOSITE> ordinary

glory NOUN 1 = <u>honour</u>, praise, fame, celebrity, distinction, acclaim, prestige, immortality, eminence, kudos, renown, exaltation, illustriousness ...*He had his moment of glory when he won the London Marathon*... OPPOSITE> shame
2 = <u>splendour</u>, majesty, greatness, grandeur, nobility, pomp, magnificence, pageantry, éclat, sublimity ...*the glory of the royal court*...
3 = <u>beauty</u>, brilliance, lustre, radiance, gorgeousness, resplendence ...*the glory of an autumn sunset*...
4 = <u>worship</u>, praise, blessing, gratitude, thanksgiving, homage, adoration, veneration ...*Glory be to God*...
VERB = <u>triumph</u>, boast, relish, revel, crow, drool, gloat, exult, take delight, pride yourself ...*The workers were glorying in their new-found freedom*...

gloss¹ 1 = <u>shine</u>, gleam, sheen, polish, brilliance, varnish, brightness, veneer, lustre, burnish, patina ...*The rain produced a black gloss on the asphalt*...
2 = <u>façade</u>, show, front, surface, appearance, mask, semblance ...*He tried to put a gloss of respectability on the horrors the regime perpetrated*...

gloss² NOUN = <u>interpretation</u>, comment, note, explanation, commentary, translation, footnote, elucidation ...*A gloss in the margin explains this unfamiliar word*...
VERB = <u>interpret</u>, explain, comment, translate, construe, annotate, elucidate ...*Earlier editors glossed 'drynke' as 'love-potion'*...

glossy = <u>shiny</u>, polished, shining, glazed, bright, brilliant, smooth, sleek, silky, burnished, glassy, silken, lustrous OPPOSITE> dull

glow NOUN 1 = <u>light</u>, gleam, splendour, glimmer, brilliance, brightness, radiance, luminosity, vividness, incandescence, phosphorescence ...*The rising sun cast a golden glow over the fields*... OPPOSITE> dullness
2 = <u>colour</u>, bloom, flush, blush, reddening, rosiness ...*The moisturiser gave my face a healthy glow that lasted all day*... OPPOSITE> pallor
VERB 1 = <u>shine</u>, burn, gleam, brighten, glimmer, smoulder ...*The night lantern glowed softly in the darkness*...
2 = <u>be pink</u>, colour, flush, blush ...*Her freckled skin glowed with health*...
3 = <u>be suffused</u>, thrill, radiate, tingle ...*The expectant mothers positively glowed with pride*...

glower VERB = <u>scowl</u>, glare, frown, look daggers, give a dirty look, lour *or* lower ...*He glowered at me but said nothing*...
NOUN = <u>scowl</u>, glare, frown, dirty look, black look, angry stare, lour *or* lower ...*His frown deepened into a glower of resentment*...

glowing 1 = <u>complimentary</u>, enthusiastic, rave (*informal*), ecstatic, rhapsodic, laudatory, adulatory ...*The premiere of his play received glowing reviews*... OPPOSITE> scathing
2 = <u>aglow</u>, red, bright, beaming, radiant, suffused ...*a happy face, glowing with good health*... OPPOSITE> pale
3 = <u>bright</u>, vivid, vibrant, rich, warm, radiant, luminous ...*stained glass in rich, glowing colours*... OPPOSITE> dull

glue NOUN = <u>adhesive</u>, cement, gum, paste ...*a tube of glue*...
VERB = <u>stick</u>, fix, seal, cement, gum, paste, affix ...*Glue the fabric around the window*...

glum = <u>gloomy</u>, miserable, dismal, down, low, melancholy, dejected, downcast, morose, doleful, downhearted, down in the dumps (*informal*), down in the mouth, in low spirits OPPOSITE> cheerful

glut NOUN = <u>surfeit</u>, excess, surplus, plethora, saturation, oversupply, overabundance, superabundance ...*There's a glut of agricultural products in Western Europe*... OPPOSITE> scarcity
VERB 1 = <u>saturate</u>, flood, choke, clog, overload, inundate, deluge, oversupply ...*Soldiers returning from war had glutted the job market*...
2 = <u>overfill</u>, fill, stuff, cram, satiate ...*The pond was glutted with fish*...

glutinous = <u>sticky</u>, adhesive, cohesive, gooey, viscous, gummy, gluey, viscid

glutton = <u>gourmand</u>, gorger, gannet (*slang*), gobbler, pig (*informal*)

gluttonous = <u>greedy</u>, insatiable, voracious, ravenous, rapacious, piggish, hoggish

gluttony = <u>greed</u>, rapacity, voracity, greediness, voraciousness, piggishness

gnarled 1 = <u>twisted</u>, knotted, contorted, knotty …*a garden full of ancient gnarled trees…*
2 = <u>wrinkled</u>, rough, rugged, leathery …*an old man with gnarled hands…*

gnaw 1 = <u>bite</u>, chew, nibble, munch …*Woodlice attack living plants and gnaw at the stems…*
2 = <u>distress</u>, worry, trouble, harry, haunt, plague, nag, fret …*Doubts were already gnawing away at the back of his mind…*
3 = <u>erode</u>, consume, devour, eat away *or* into, wear away *or* down …*This run of bad luck has gnawed away at his usually optimistic character…*

go VERB 1 = <u>move</u>, travel, advance, journey, proceed, pass, fare (*archaic*), set off …*It took us an hour to go three miles…* OPPOSITE stay
2 = <u>leave</u>, withdraw, depart, move out, decamp, slope off, make tracks …*Come on, let's go…*
3 = <u>lead</u>, run, reach, spread, extend, stretch, connect, span, give access …*There's a mountain road that goes from Blairstown to Millbrook Village…*
4 = <u>elapse</u>, pass, flow, fly by, expire, lapse, slip away …*The week has gone so quickly!…*
5 = <u>be given</u>, be spent, be awarded, be allotted …*The money goes to projects chosen by the Board…*
6 = <u>die</u>, perish, pass away, buy it (*U.S. slang*), expire, check out (*U.S. slang*), kick it (*slang*), croak (*slang*), give up the ghost, snuff it (*informal*), peg out (*informal*), kick the bucket (*slang*), peg it (*informal*), cark it (*Austral. & N.Z. slang*), pop your clogs (*informal*) …*I want you to have my jewellery after I've gone…*
7 = <u>proceed</u>, develop, turn out, work out, fare, fall out, pan out (*informal*) …*She says everything is going smoothly…*
8 = <u>function</u>, work, run, move, operate, perform …*My car isn't going very well at the moment…* OPPOSITE fail
9 = <u>match</u>, blend, correspond, fit, suit, chime, harmonize …*That jacket and those trousers don't really go…*
10 = <u>serve</u>, help, tend …*It just goes to prove you can't trust anyone…*
NOUN 1 = <u>attempt</u>, try, effort, bid, shot (*informal*), crack (*informal*), essay, stab (*informal*), whirl (*informal*), whack (*informal*) …*It took us two goes to get the colour right…*
2 = <u>turn</u>, shot (*informal*), spell, stint …*Whose go is it next?…*
3 (*Informal*) = <u>energy</u>, life, drive, spirit, pep, vitality, vigour, verve, force, get-up-and-go (*informal*), oomph (*informal*), brio, vivacity …*For an old woman she still has a lot of go in her…*
PHRASES **go about something** 1 = <u>tackle</u>, begin, approach, undertake, set about …*I want him back, but I just don't know how to go about it…* 2 = <u>engage in</u>, perform, conduct, pursue, practise, ply, carry on with, apply yourself to, busy *or* occupy yourself with …*We were simply going about our business when we were pounced on by the police…* ◆ **go along with**

something = <u>agree</u>, follow, cooperate, concur, assent, acquiesce …*Whatever the majority decision, I'm prepared to go along with it…* ◆ **go at something** = <u>set about</u>, start, begin, tackle, set to, get down to, wade into, get to work on, make a start on, get cracking on (*informal*), address yourself to, get weaving on (*informal*) …*He went at this unpleasant task with grim determination…* ◆ **go away** = <u>leave</u>, withdraw, exit, depart, move out, go to hell (*informal*), decamp, hook it (*slang*), slope off, pack your bags (*informal*), make tracks, get on your bike (*Brit. slang*), bog off (*Brit. slang*), sling your hook (*Brit. slang*) …*I wish he'd just go away and leave me alone…* ◆ **go back** = <u>return</u> …*I decided to go back to bed…* ◆ **go back on something** = <u>repudiate</u>, break, forsake, retract, renege on, desert, back out of, change your mind about …*The budget crisis has forced the President to go back on his word…* ◆ **go by** = <u>pass</u>, proceed, elapse, flow on, move onward …*My grandmother was becoming more and more frail as time went by…* ◆ **go by something** = <u>obey</u>, follow, adopt, observe, comply with, heed, submit to, be guided by, take as guide …*If they can prove that I'm wrong, then I'll go by what they say…* ◆ **go down** 1 = <u>fall</u>, drop, decline, slump, decrease, fall off, dwindle, lessen, ebb, depreciate, become lower …*Crime has gone down 70 per cent…* 2 = <u>set</u>, sink …*the glow left in the sky after the sun has gone down…* 3 = <u>sink</u>, founder, go under, be submerged …*The ship went down during a training exercise…* ◆ **go far** = <u>be successful</u>, advance, progress, succeed, get on (*informal*), do well, cut it (*informal*), get ahead (*informal*), make your mark, make a name for yourself …*With your talent, you will go far…* ◆ **go for someone** 1 = <u>prefer</u>, like, choose, favour, admire, be attracted to, be fond of, hold with …*I tend to go for large dark men…* 2 = <u>attack</u>, assault, assail, spring upon, rush upon, launch yourself at, set about *or* upon …*Patrick went for him, grabbing him by the throat…* 3 = <u>scold</u>, attack, blast, criticize, flame (*informal*), put down, tear into (*informal*), diss (*slang, chiefly U.S.*), impugn, lambast(e) …*My mum went for me because I hadn't told her where I was going…* ◆ **go in for something** = <u>participate in</u>, pursue, take part in, undertake, embrace, practise, engage in …*They go in for tennis and bowls…* ◆ **go into something** 1 = <u>investigate</u>, consider, study, research, discuss, review, examine, pursue, probe, analyse, look into, delve into, work over, scrutinize, inquire into …*I'd like to go into this matter in a bit more detail…* 2 = <u>enter</u>, begin, participate in …*He has decided to go into the tourism business…* ◆ **go off** 1 = <u>depart</u>, leave, quit, go away, move out, decamp, hook it (*slang*), slope off, pack your bags (*informal*) …*She just went off without saying a word to anyone…* 2 = <u>explode</u>, fire, blow up, detonate …*A gun went off somewhere in the distance…* 3 = <u>sound</u>, ring, toll, chime, peal …*The fire alarm went off…* 4 = <u>take place</u>, happen, occur, come off (*informal*), come about …*The meeting went off all right…* 5 (*Informal*) = <u>go bad</u>, turn, spoil, rot, go stale …*Don't eat that! It's gone off!…* ◆ **go on** 1 = <u>happen</u>, occur, take place …*I don't* know what's going on... **2** = <u>continue</u>, last, stay, proceed, carry on, keep going ...*the necessity for the war to go on...* ◆ **go on about something** = <u>ramble on</u>, carry on, chatter, waffle (*informal, chiefly Brit.*), witter (on) (*informal*), rabbit on (*Brit. informal*), prattle, blether ...*They're always going on about choice and market forces...* ◆ **go on doing something** *or* **go on with something** = <u>continue</u>, pursue, proceed, carry on, stick to, persist, keep on, keep at, persevere, stick at ...*Go on with your work...* ◆ **go out 1** = <u>see someone</u>, court, date (*informal, chiefly U.S.*), woo, go steady (*informal*), be romantically involved with ...*They've been going out for six weeks now...* **2** = <u>be extinguished</u>, die out, fade out ...*The bedroom light went out after a moment...* ◆ **go over something 1** = <u>examine</u>, study, review, revise, inspect, work over ...*An accountant has gone over the books...* **2** = <u>rehearse</u>, read, scan, reiterate, skim over, peruse ...*We went over our lines together before the show...* ◆ **go through something 1** = <u>suffer</u>, experience, bear, endure, brave, undergo, tolerate, withstand ...*He was going through a very difficult time...* **2** = <u>search</u>, look through, rummage through, rifle through, hunt through, fossick through (*Austral. & N.Z.*), ferret about in ...*It was evident that someone had been going through my possessions...* **3** = <u>examine</u>, check, search, explore, look through, work over ...*Going through his list of customers is a massive job...* **4** = <u>use up</u>, exhaust, consume, squander ...*He goes through around £500 a week...* ◆ **go through with something** = <u>carry on</u>, continue, pursue, keep on, persevere ...*Richard pleaded with Belinda not to go through with the divorce...* ◆ **go together 1** = <u>harmonize</u>, match, agree, accord, fit, make a pair ...*Red wine and oysters don't really go together...* **2** (*Informal*) = <u>go out</u>, court, date (*informal, chiefly U.S.*), go steady (*informal*) ...*We met a month ago and we've been going together ever since...* ◆ **go under 1** = <u>fail</u>, die, sink, go down, fold (*informal*), founder, succumb, go bankrupt ...*If one firm goes under it could provoke a cascade of bankruptcies...* **2** = <u>sink</u>, go down, founder, submerge ...*The ship went under, taking with her all her crew...* ◆ **go up** = <u>increase</u>, rise, mount, soar, get higher ...*Interest rates have gone up again...* ◆ **go with something** = <u>match</u>, suit, blend, correspond with, agree with, fit, complement, harmonize ...*Does this tie go with this shirt?...* ◆ **go without something** = <u>be deprived of</u>, want, lack, be denied, do without, abstain, go short, deny yourself ...*I have known what it is like to go without food for days...* ◆ **no go** = <u>impossible</u>, not on (*informal*), vain, hopeless, futile ...*I tried to get him to change his mind, but it was no go...*

goad VERB **1** = <u>provoke</u>, drive, annoy, sting, irritate, lash, harass, hassle (*informal*), nark (*Brit., Austral., & N.Z. slang*), be on your back (*slang*) ...*Charles was forever trying to goad her into losing her temper...* **2** = <u>urge</u>, drive, prompt, spur, stimulate, provoke, arouse, propel, prod, prick, incite, instigate, egg on, exhort, impel ...*He goaded me into taking direct action...*
NOUN = <u>incentive</u>, urge, spur, motivation, pressure,

stimulus, stimulation, impetus, incitement ...*His distrust only acted as a goad to me to prove him wrong...*

go-ahead NOUN (*Informal*) = <u>permission</u>, consent, green light, assent, leave, authorization, O.K. *or* okay (*informal*) ...*Don't do any major repair work until you get the go-ahead from your insurers...*
ADJECTIVE = <u>enterprising</u>, pioneering, ambitious, progressive, go-getting (*informal*), up-and-coming ...*The estate is one of the most go-ahead wine producers in South Africa...*

goal = <u>aim</u>, end, target, purpose, object, intention, objective, ambition, destination, Holy Grail (*informal*)

goat
> Related Words
adjective: caprine
male: billy, buck
female: nanny
young: kid, yeanling
collective nouns: herd, tribe

gob = <u>piece</u>, lump, chunk, hunk, nugget, blob, wad, clod, wodge (*Brit. informal*)

gobble = <u>devour</u>, swallow, gulp, guzzle, wolf, bolt, cram in, gorge on, pig out on (*slang*), stuff yourself with

go-between = <u>intermediary</u>, agent, medium, broker, factor, dealer, liaison, mediator, middleman

god = <u>deity</u>, immortal, divinity, divine being, supreme being
➤ **gods and goddesses** ➤ **the Fates** ➤ **the Graces** ➤ **the Muses**

God
> Related Words
adjective: divine

God-forsaken = <u>desolate</u>, abandoned, deserted, remote, neglected, lonely, bleak, gloomy, backward, dismal, dreary, forlorn, wretched

godless = <u>wicked</u>, depraved, profane, unprincipled, atheistic, ungodly, irreligious, impious, unrighteous

godlike = <u>divine</u>, heavenly, celestial, superhuman

godly = <u>devout</u>, religious, holy, righteous, pious, good, saintly, god-fearing

godsend = <u>blessing</u>, help, benefit, asset, boon

gogga (*S. African*) = <u>insect</u>, bug, creepy-crawly (*Brit. informal*)

goggle = <u>stare</u>, gape, gawp (*slang*), gawk

going-over 1 = <u>examination</u>, study, check, review, survey, investigation, analysis, inspection, scrutiny, perusal ...*Michael was given a complete going-over and was diagnosed with hay fever...*
2 = <u>thrashing</u>, attack, beating, whipping, thumping, pasting (*slang*), buffeting, drubbing (*informal*) ...*The bouncers took him outside and gave him a thorough going-over...*
3 = <u>dressing-down</u>, talking-to (*informal*), lecture, rebuke, reprimand, scolding, chiding, tongue-lashing, chastisement, castigation ...*Our manager gave us a right going-over in the changing room after the game...*

Gods and Goddesses http://www.pantheon.org/

Aztec

Acolmiztli	Huixtocihuatl	Tepeyollotl
Acolnahuacatl	Ilamatecuhtli	Teteo
Amimitl	Innan	Tezcatlipoca
Atl	Itzlacoliuhque	Tlahuixcalpantecuhtli
Atlaua	Itzli	Tlaloc
Camaxtli	Itzpapalotl	Tlaltecuhtli
Centeotl	Ixtlilton	Tlazolteotl
Centzonuitznaua	Macuilxochitl	Tonacatecuhtli
Chalchiuhtlatonal	Malinalxochi	Tonatiuh
Chalchiuhtlicue	Mayahuel	Tzapotla
Chalchiutotolin	Mictlantecihuatl	Tena
Chalmecacihuilt	Mictlantecutli	Tzintetol
Chantico	Mixcoatl	Tzontemoc
Chicomecoatl	Nanauatzin	Uixtociuatl
Chicomexochtli	Omacatl	Xilonen
Chiconahui	Omecihuatl	Xipe Totec
Cihuacoatl	Ometecuhtli	Xippilli
Coatlicue	Patecatl	Xiuhcoatl
Cochimetl	Paynal	Xiuhteuctli
Coyolxauhqui	Quetzalcoatl	Xochipilli
Ehecatl	Tecciztecatl	Xochiquetzal
Huehueteotl	Techalotl	Xolotl
Huitzilopochtli	Techlotl	Yacatecuhtli

Egyptian

Anubis	Maat	Re
Hathor	Osiris	Serapis
Horus	Ptah	Set
Isis	Ra *or* Amen-Ra	Thoth

Greek

Aeolus	winds	Helios	sun
Aphrodite	love and beauty	Hephaestus	fire and metalworking
Apollo	light, youth, and music	Hera	queen of the gods
Ares	war	Hermes	messenger of the gods
Artemis	hunting and the moon	Horae *or* the Hours	seasons
Asclepius	healing	Hymen	marriage
Athene *or* Pallas Athene	wisdom	Hyperion	sun
Bacchus	wine	Hypnos	sleep
Boreas	north wind	Iris	rainbow
Cronos	fertility of the earth	Momus	blame and mockery
Demeter	agriculture	Morpheus	sleep and dreams
Dionysus	wine	Nemesis	vengeance
Eos	dawn	Nike	victory
Eros	love	Pan	woods and shepherds
Fates	destiny	Poseidon	sea and earthquakes
Gaea *or* Gaia	the earth	Rhea	fertility
Graces	charm and beauty	Selene	moon
Hades	underworld	Uranus	sky
Hebe	youth and spring	Zephyrus	west wind
Hecate	underworld	Zeus	king of the gods

Hindu

Agni	Indra	Rama
Brahma	Kali	Siva *or* Shiva
Devi	Kama	Ushas
Durga	Krishna	Varuna
Ganesa	Lakshmi	Vishnu
Hanuman	Maya	

Gods and Goddesses (continued)

Incan

Apo	Ekkeko	Pachacamac
Apocatequil	Huaca	Pariacaca
Apu Illapu	Illapa	Paricia
Apu Punchau	Inti	Punchau
Catequil	Ka-Ata-Killa Kon	Supay
Cavillaca	Mama Allpa	Urcaguary
Chasca	Mama Cocha	Vichama
Chasca Coyllur	Mama Oello	Viracocha
Cocomama	Mama Pacha	Zaramama
Coniraya	Mama Quilla	
Copacati	Manco Capac	

Mayan

Mayan	Backlum Chaam	Hurakan
Ac Yanto	Balam	Itzamna
Acan	Bitol	Itzananohk'u
Acat	Buluc Chabtan	Ix
Ah Bolom Tzacab	Cabaguil	Ixchel or Ix Chebel Yax
Ah Cancum	Cakulha	Ixtab
Ah Chun Caan	Camaxtli	Ixzaluoh
Ah Chuy Kak	Camazotz	Kan
Ah Ciliz	Caprakan	Kan-u-Uayeyab
Ah Cun Can	Cauac	Kan-xib-yui
Ah Cuxtal	Chac	Kianto
Ah Hulneb	Chac Uayab Xoc	K'in
Ah Kin	Chamer	Kinich Ahau
Ah Mun	Chibirias	Kukulcan
Ah Muzencab	Cit Bolon Tum	Mulac
Ah Peku	Cizin	Naum
Ah Puch	Colel Cab	Nohochacyum
Ah Tabai	Colop U Uichkin	Tlacolotl
Ah Uincir Dz'acab	Coyopa	Tohil
Ah Uuc Ticab	Cum Hau	Tzakol
Ahau-Kin	Ekchuah	Votan
Ahmakiq	Ghanan	Xaman Ek
Ahulane	Gucumatz	Yaluk
Ajbit	Hacha'kyum	Yum Caax
Akhushtal	Hun Came	Zotz
Alaghom Naom	Hun Hunahpu	
Alom	Hunab Ku	

Norse

Aegir	Frigg or Frigga	Norns
Aesir	Hel or Hela	Odin or Othin
Balder	Heimdall, Heimdal, or Heimdallr	Thor
Bragi	Idun or Ithunn	Tyr or Tyrr
Frey or Freyr	Loki	Vanir
Freya or Freyja	Njord or Njorth	

Roman

Aesculapius	medicine	Janus	doors and beginnings
Apollo	light, youth, and music	Juno	queen of the gods
Aurora	dawn	Jupiter or Jove	king of the gods
Bacchus	wine	Lares	household
Bellona	war	Luna	moon
Bona Dea	fertility	Mars	war
Ceres	agriculture	Mercury	messenger of the gods
Cupid	love	Minerva	wisdom
Cybele	nature	Neptune	sea
Diana	hunting and the moon	Penates	storeroom
Faunus	forests	Phoebus	sun
Flora	flowers	Pluto	underworld

Roman (continued)

Quirinus	war	Trivia	crossroads
Saturn	agriculture and vegetation	Venus	love
Sol	sun	Victoria	victory
Somnus	sleep	Vulcan	fire and metalworking

---

golden 1 = <u>yellow</u>, bright, brilliant, blonde, blond, flaxen ...*She combed and arranged her golden hair...* OPPOSITE> dark

2 = <u>successful</u>, glorious, prosperous, best, rich, flourishing, halcyon ...*the golden age of American moviemaking...* OPPOSITE> worst

3 = <u>promising</u>, excellent, valuable, favourable, advantageous, auspicious, opportune, propitious ...*There's a golden opportunity for peace which must be seized...* OPPOSITE> unfavourable

➤ **shades of orange** ➤ **shades of yellow**

golf
➤ **golf terms**

gone 1 = <u>missing</u>, lost, away, vanished, absent, astray ...*He's already been gone four hours!...*

2 = <u>used up</u>, spent, finished, consumed ...*After two years, all her money was gone...*

3 = <u>past</u>, over, ended, finished, elapsed ...*Those happy times are gone forever...*

4 = <u>dead</u>, no more, departed, extinct, deceased, defunct ...*The paramedics tried to revive him, but it was too late – he was gone...*

good ADJECTIVE 1 = <u>excellent</u>, great, fine, pleasing, capital, choice, crucial (*slang*), acceptable, pleasant, worthy, first-class, divine, splendid, satisfactory, superb, enjoyable, awesome (*slang*), dope (*slang*), world-class, admirable, agreeable, super (*informal*), pleasurable, wicked (*slang*), bad (*slang*), first-rate, tiptop, bitchin' (*U.S. slang*), booshit (*Austral. slang*), exo (*Austral. slang*), sik (*Austral. slang*) ...*You should read this book – it's really good...* OPPOSITE> bad

2 = <u>proficient</u>, able, skilled, capable, expert, talented, efficient, clever, accomplished, reliable, first-class, satisfactory, competent, thorough, adept, first-rate, adroit, dexterous ...*He is very good at his job...* OPPOSITE> bad

3 = <u>beneficial</u>, useful, healthy, helpful, favourable, wholesome, advantageous, salutary, salubrious ...*Rain water was once considered to be good for the complexion...* OPPOSITE> harmful

4 = <u>honourable</u>, moral, worthy, ethical, upright, admirable, honest, righteous, exemplary, right, virtuous, trustworthy, altruistic, praiseworthy, estimable ...*The president is a good man...* OPPOSITE> bad

5 = <u>well-behaved</u>, seemly, mannerly, proper, polite, orderly, obedient, dutiful, decorous, well-mannered ...*The children have been very good all day...* OPPOSITE> naughty

6 = <u>kind</u>, kindly, friendly, obliging, charitable, humane, gracious, benevolent, merciful, beneficent, well-disposed, kind-hearted ...*It's very good of you to help out at such short notice...* OPPOSITE> unkind

7 = <u>cheerful</u>, happy, pleasant, agreeable, congenial, convivial ...*Everyone was in a pretty good mood...*

8 = <u>true</u>, real, genuine, proper, reliable, dependable, sound, trustworthy, dinkum (*Austral. & N.Z. informal*) ...*She's been a good friend to me over the years...*

9 = <u>full</u>, long, whole, complete, entire, solid, extensive ...*The film lasts a good two and a half hours...* OPPOSITE> scant

10 = <u>considerable</u>, large, substantial, sufficient, adequate, ample ...*A good number of people agree with me...*

11 = <u>valid</u>, convincing, compelling, legitimate, authentic, persuasive, sound, bona fide ...*Can you think of one good reason why I should tell you?...* OPPOSITE> invalid

12 = <u>best</u>, newest, special, finest, nicest, smartest, fancy, most valuable, most precious ...*Try not to get paint on your good clothes...*

13 = <u>sunny</u>, clear, fair, bright, calm, mild, clement, balmy, cloudless ...*If the weather's good tomorrow, we'll go for a picnic...*

14 = <u>edible</u>, untainted, uncorrupted, eatable, fit to eat ...*Is this fish still good, or has it gone off?...* OPPOSITE> bad

15 = <u>convenient</u>, timely, fitting, fit, appropriate, suitable, well-timed, opportune ...*Is this a good time for us to discuss our plans?...* OPPOSITE> inconvenient

NOUN 1 = <u>benefit</u>, interest, gain, advantage, use, service, profit, welfare, behalf, usefulness, wellbeing ...*I'm only doing all this for your own good...* OPPOSITE> disadvantage

2 = <u>virtue</u>, goodness, righteousness, worth, merit, excellence, morality, probity, rectitude, uprightness ...*Good and evil may co-exist within one family...* OPPOSITE> evil

PHRASES **for good** = <u>permanently</u>, finally, for ever, once and for all, irrevocably, never to return, sine die (*Latin*) ...*A few shots of this drug cleared up the disease for good...*

goodbye NOUN = <u>farewell</u>, parting, leave-taking ...*It was a very emotional goodbye...*

INTERJECTION = <u>farewell</u>, see you, see you later, ciao (*Italian*), cheerio, adieu, ta-ta, au revoir (*French*), auf Wiedersehen (*German*), adios (*Spanish*) ...*Well, goodbye and good luck...*

good-humoured = <u>genial</u>, happy, pleasant, cheerful, amiable, affable, congenial, good-tempered

good-looking = <u>attractive</u>, pretty, fair, beautiful, lovely, handsome, gorgeous, bonny, personable, comely, well-favoured

good-natured = <u>amiable</u>, kind, kindly, friendly, generous, helpful, obliging, tolerant, agreeable, benevolent, good-hearted, magnanimous, well-disposed, warm-hearted

goodness 1 = <u>virtue</u>, honour, merit, integrity,

Golf terms http://www.randa.org/flash/rules/PDF/RoG2004.pdf

ace	driver	local rules	score
air shot *or* fresh air shot	driving range	loft	score card
albatross	duff	long iron	scratch
approach	eagle	marker	shaft
apron	fade	match play	shank
back nine	fairway	medal play	short iron
backswing	fluff	medal tee	single
bag	foozle	midiron	slice
ball	fore	nine-hole course	slow play
bandit	four-ball	nineteenth hole	spoon
better-ball	foursome	par	Stableford system
birdie	front nine	pin	stance
blade	gimme	pitch and run	stroke
bogey	green	pitching wedge	stroke play
borrow	green fee	pitch shot	stymie
bunker, trap, *or (esp.*	green keeper	play through	sweetspot
U.S. *& Canad.)* sand	greensome	plus fours	swing
trap	grip	plus twos	take-away
caddie	half	practice swing	tee
caddie car	half shot	pull	thin
carry	handicap	putt	tiger
casual water	hazard	putter	threesome
chip	heel	putting green	top
club	hole	rabbit	trolley
clubhouse	hole in one	recovery	waggle
course	honour	rough	wedge
cup	hook	round	wood
cut	hosel	rub of the green	yips
divot	iron	run	
dormie	ladies' tee	Royal and Ancient *or*	
downswing	lag	R & A	
draw	lie	sand wedge	
drive	links	sclaff	

morality, honesty, righteousness, probity, rectitude, uprightness ...*He retains his faith in human goodness*... OPPOSITE > badness
2 = <u>excellence</u>, value, quality, worth, merit, superiority ...*his total belief in the goodness of socialist society*...
3 = <u>nutrition</u>, benefit, advantage, nourishment, wholesomeness, salubriousness ...*drinks full of natural goodness*...
4 = <u>kindness</u>, charity, humanity, goodwill, mercy, compassion, generosity, friendliness, benevolence, graciousness, beneficence, kindliness, humaneness, kind-heartedness ...*performing actions of goodness towards the poor*...

goods 1 = <u>merchandise</u>, stock, products, stuff, commodities, wares ...*a wide range of consumer goods*...
2 = <u>property</u>, things, effects, gear, furniture, movables, possessions, furnishings, belongings, trappings, paraphernalia, chattels, appurtenances ...*You can give all your unwanted goods to charity*...

goodwill = <u>friendliness</u>, favour, friendship, benevolence, amity, kindliness

gooey 1 = <u>sticky</u>, soft, tacky, viscous, glutinous, gummy, icky (*informal*), gluey, gloopy, gungy ...*a lovely gooey, sticky mess*...
2 = <u>sentimental</u>, romantic, sloppy, soppy, maudlin, syrupy (*informal*), slushy (*informal*), mawkish, tear-jerking (*informal*), icky (*informal*) ...*He wrote me a long, gooey love letter*...

goose
(*Related Words*)
adjective: anserine
male: gander
young: gosling
collective nouns: gaggle, skein

gore¹ = <u>blood</u>, slaughter, bloodshed, carnage, butchery ...*video nasties full of blood and gore*...

gore² = <u>pierce</u>, wound, stab, spit, transfix, impale ...*He was gored to death by a rhinoceros* ...

gorge NOUN = <u>ravine</u>, canyon, pass, clough (*dialect*), chasm, cleft, fissure, defile, gulch ...*a steep path into Crete's Samaria Gorge*...
VERB **1** = <u>overeat</u>, bolt, devour, gobble, wolf, swallow, gulp, guzzle, pig out (*slang*) ...*I could spend all day gorging on chocolate*...
2 *usually reflexive* = <u>stuff</u>, fill, feed, cram, glut, surfeit, satiate, sate ...*Three men were gorging themselves on grouse and watermelon*...

gorgeous 1 = <u>magnificent</u>, grand, beautiful, superb, spectacular, splendid, glittering, dazzling, luxurious, sumptuous, opulent ...*Some of these Renaissance buildings are absolutely gorgeous*... OPPOSITE > shabby
2 = <u>delightful</u>, good, great, grand, wonderful, excellent, brilliant, lovely, fantastic, pleasant, terrific, splendid, enjoyable, super, splendiferous (*facetious*) ...*I've had a gorgeous time today*... OPPOSITE > awful

3 (*Informal*) = beautiful, attractive, lovely, stunning (*informal*), elegant, handsome, good-looking, exquisite, drop-dead (*slang*), ravishing ...*The cosmetics industry uses gorgeous women to sell its products...* OPPOSITE ugly
4 = fine, glorious, sunny ...*It's a gorgeous day...* OPPOSITE dull

gory 1 = grisly, bloody, murderous, bloodthirsty ...*The film is full of gory death scenes...*
2 = bloody, bloodstained, blood-soaked ...*The ambulanceman carefully stripped off his gory clothes...*

gospel 1 = doctrine, news, teachings, message, revelation, creed, credo, tidings ...*He visited the sick and preached the gospel...*
2 = truth, fact, certainty, the last word, verity ...*The results were not to be taken as gospel...*

gossamer = delicate, light, fine, thin, sheer, transparent, airy, flimsy, silky, diaphanous, gauzy

gossip NOUN **1** = idle talk, scandal, hearsay, tittle-tattle, buzz, dirt (*U.S. slang*), jaw (*slang*), gen (*Brit. informal*), small talk, chitchat, blether, scuttlebutt (*U.S. slang*), chinwag (*Brit. informal*) ...*a magazine packed with celebrity gossip...* ...*There has been a lot of gossip about the reasons for his absence...*
2 = busybody, babbler, prattler, chatterbox (*informal*), blether, chatterer, scandalmonger, gossipmonger ...*She was a vicious old gossip...*
VERB = chat, chatter, blather, schmooze (*slang*), jaw (*slang*), dish the dirt (*informal*), blether, shoot the breeze (*slang, chiefly U.S.*), chew the fat or rag (*slang*) ...*We gossiped well into the night...*

gouge VERB = scoop, cut, score, dig (out), scratch, hollow (out), claw, chisel, gash, incise ...*quarries which have gouged great holes in the hills...*
NOUN = gash, cut, scratch, hollow, score, scoop, notch, groove, trench, furrow, incision ...*iron-rimmed wheels digging great gouges into the road's surface...*

gourmet = connoisseur, foodie (*informal*), bon vivant (*French*), epicure, gastronome

govern 1 = rule, lead, control, command, manage, direct, guide, handle, conduct, order, reign over, administer, oversee, supervise, be in power over, call the shots, call the tune, hold sway over, superintend ...*They go to the polls on Friday to choose the people they want to govern their country...*
2 = determine, decide, guide, rule, influence, underlie, sway ...*Marine insurance is governed by a strict series of rules and regulations...*
3 = restrain, control, check, contain, master, discipline, regulate, curb, inhibit, tame, subdue, get the better of, bridle, hold in check, keep a tight rein on ...*Try to govern your temper...*

government 1 = administration, executive, ministry, regime, governing body, powers-that-be ...*The Government has insisted that confidence is needed before the economy can improve...*
2 = rule, state, law, authority, administration, sovereignty, governance, dominion, polity, statecraft ...*our system of government...*
➤ **family**

governmental = administrative, state, political, official, executive, ministerial, sovereign, bureaucratic

governor = leader, administrator, ruler, head, minister, director, manager, chief, officer, executive, boss (*informal*), commander, controller, supervisor, superintendent, mandarin, comptroller, functionary, overseer, baas (*S. African*)

(Related Words)
adjective: gubernatorial

gown = dress, costume, garment, robe, frock, garb, habit

grab = snatch, catch, seize, capture, bag, grip, grasp, clutch, snap up, pluck, latch on to, catch *or* take hold of

grace NOUN **1** = elegance, finesse, poise, ease, polish, refinement, fluency, suppleness, gracefulness ...*He moved with the grace of a trained dancer...* OPPOSITE ungainliness
2 = manners, decency, cultivation, etiquette, breeding, consideration, propriety, tact, decorum, mannerliness ...*He hadn't even the grace to apologize for what he'd done...* OPPOSITE bad manners
3 = indulgence, mercy, pardon, compassion, quarter, charity, forgiveness, reprieve, clemency, leniency ...*He was granted four days' grace to be with his family...*
4 = benevolence, favour, goodness, goodwill, generosity, kindness, beneficence, kindliness ...*It was only by the grace of God that no one died...* OPPOSITE ill will
5 = prayer, thanks, blessing, thanksgiving, benediction ...*Leo, will you say grace?...*
6 = favour, regard, respect, approval, esteem, approbation, good opinion ...*The reasons for his fall from grace are not clear...* OPPOSITE disfavour
VERB **1** = adorn, enhance, decorate, enrich, set off, garnish, ornament, deck, embellish, bedeck, beautify ...*the beautiful old Welsh dresser that graced this homely room...*
2 = honour, favour, distinguish, elevate, dignify, glorify ...*He graced our ceremony with his distinguished presence...* OPPOSITE insult

graceful 1 = elegant, easy, flowing, smooth, fine, pleasing, beautiful, agile, symmetrical, gracile (*rare*) ...*Her movements were so graceful they seemed effortless...* OPPOSITE inelegant
2 = polite, mannerly, charming, gracious, civil, courteous, well-mannered ...*She was calm and graceful under pressure...*

graceless 1 = inelegant, forced, awkward, clumsy, ungainly, unco (*Austral. slang*) ...*a graceless pirouette...*
2 = ill-mannered, crude, rude, coarse, vulgar, rough, improper, shameless, unsophisticated, gauche, barbarous, boorish, gawky, uncouth, loutish, indecorous, unmannerly ...*She couldn't stand his blunt, graceless manner...*

Graces, the (*Greek myth*) = Charities

The Graces
Aglaia   Thalia
Euphrosyne

gracious 1 = <u>courteous</u>, polite, civil, accommodating, kind, kindly, pleasing, friendly, obliging, amiable, cordial, hospitable, courtly, chivalrous, well-mannered ...*He is always a gracious host...* OPPOSITE ungracious

2 = <u>elegant</u>, fine, grand, beautiful, handsome, fashionable, stylish, luxurious, graceful, tasteful ...*a gracious old country house...*

grade VERB = <u>classify</u>, rate, order, class, group, sort, value, range, rank, brand, arrange, evaluate ...*The college does not grade the children's work...*

NOUN 1 = <u>class</u>, condition, quality, brand ...*a good grade of plywood...*

2 = <u>mark</u>, degree, place, order ...*pressure on students to obtain good grades...*

3 = <u>level</u>, position, rank, group, order, class, stage, step, station, category, rung, echelon ...*Staff turnover is high among junior grades...*

PHRASES **make the grade** (*Informal*) = <u>succeed</u>, measure up, win through, pass muster, come up to scratch (*informal*), come through with flying colours, prove acceptable, measure up to expectations ...*She had a strong desire to be a dancer, but failed to make the grade...*

gradient = <u>slope</u>, hill, rise, grade, incline, bank

gradual = <u>steady</u>, even, slow, regular, gentle, moderate, progressive, piecemeal, unhurried OPPOSITE sudden

gradually = <u>steadily</u>, slowly, moderately, progressively, gently, step by step, evenly, piecemeal, bit by bit, little by little, by degrees, piece by piece, unhurriedly, drop by drop

graduate 1 = <u>mark off</u>, grade, proportion, regulate, gauge, calibrate, measure out ...*The volume control knob is graduated from 1 to 11...*

2 = <u>classify</u>, rank, grade, group, order, sort, range, arrange, sequence ...*proposals to introduce an income tax which is graduated...*

graft NOUN 1 = <u>shoot</u>, bud, implant, sprout, splice, scion ...*These plants are propagated by grafts, buds or cuttings...*

2 (*Informal*) = <u>labour</u>, work, industry, effort, struggle, sweat, toil, slog, exertion, blood, sweat, and tears (*informal*) ...*His career has been one of hard graft...*

VERB 1 = <u>join</u>, insert, transplant, implant, splice, affix ...*Pear trees are grafted on quince root-stocks...*

2 = <u>work</u>, labour, struggle, sweat (*informal*), grind (*informal*), slave, strive, toil, drudge ...*I really don't enjoy grafting away in a stuffy office all day...*

grain 1 = <u>seed</u>, kernel, grist ...*a grain of wheat...*

2 = <u>cereal</u>, corn ...*a bag of grain...*

3 = <u>bit</u>, piece, trace, spark, scrap, suspicion, molecule, particle, fragment, atom, ounce, crumb, mite, jot, speck, morsel, granule, modicum, mote, whit, iota ...*a grain of sand...*

4 = <u>texture</u>, pattern, surface, fibre, weave, nap ...*Brush the paint over the wood in the direction of the grain...*

grammar = <u>syntax</u>, rules of language
▶ **grammatical cases**

grammatical = <u>syntactic</u>, linguistic

Grammatical cases

http://www.ucl.ac.uk/internet-grammar/home.htm

ablative	instrumental
accusative	locative
agentive	nominative
dative	objective
elative	oblique
ergative	possessive
genitive	subjective
illative	vocative

---

grand 1 = <u>impressive</u>, great, large, magnificent, striking, fine, princely, imposing, superb, glorious, noble, splendid, gorgeous, luxurious, eminent, majestic, regal, stately, monumental, sublime, sumptuous, grandiose, opulent, palatial, ostentatious, splendiferous (*facetious*) ...*a grand building in the centre of town...* OPPOSITE unimposing

2 = <u>ambitious</u>, great, glorious, lofty, grandiose, exalted, ostentatious ...*He arrived in America full of grand schemes and lofty dreams...*

3 = <u>superior</u>, great, lordly, noble, elevated, eminent, majestic, dignified, stately, lofty, august, illustrious, pompous, pretentious, haughty ...*She's too busy with her grand new friends to bother with us now...*

4 = <u>excellent</u>, great (*informal*), fine, wonderful, very good, brilliant, outstanding, smashing (*informal*), superb, first-class, divine, marvellous (*informal*), terrific (*informal*), splendid, awesome (*slang*), world-class, admirable, super (*informal*), first-rate, splendiferous (*facetious*) ...*He was having a grand time meeting new people...* OPPOSITE bad

5 = <u>chief</u>, highest, lead, leading, head, main, supreme, principal, big-time (*informal*), major league (*informal*), pre-eminent ...*the federal grand jury...* OPPOSITE inferior

grandeur = <u>splendour</u>, glory, majesty, nobility, pomp, state, magnificence, sumptuousness, sublimity, stateliness ...*Only once inside do you appreciate the church's true grandeur...*

grandiose 1 = <u>pretentious</u>, ambitious, extravagant, flamboyant, high-flown, pompous, showy, ostentatious, bombastic ...*Not one of his grandiose plans has ever come to anything...* OPPOSITE unpretentious

2 = <u>imposing</u>, grand, impressive, magnificent, majestic, stately, monumental, lofty ...*the grandiose building which housed the mayor's offices...* OPPOSITE humble

grant NOUN = <u>award</u>, allowance, donation, endowment, gift, concession, subsidy, hand-out, allocation, bounty, allotment, bequest, stipend ...*My application for a grant has been rejected...*

VERB 1 = <u>give</u>, allow, present, award, accord, permit, assign, allocate, hand out, confer on, bestow on, impart on, allot, vouchsafe ...*France has agreed to grant him political asylum...*

2 = <u>accept</u>, allow, admit, acknowledge, concede, cede, accede ...*The magistrates granted that the charity was justified in bringing the action...*

granule = <u>grain</u>, scrap, molecule, particle, fragment, atom, crumb, jot, speck, iota

graphic 1 = <u>vivid</u>, clear, detailed, striking, telling, explicit, picturesque, forceful, expressive, descriptive, illustrative, well-drawn ...*graphic descriptions of violence...* OPPOSITE> vague
2 = <u>pictorial</u>, seen, drawn, visible, visual, representational, illustrative, diagrammatic ...*a graphic representation of how the chemical acts on the body...* OPPOSITE> impressionistic

grapple 1 = <u>deal</u>, tackle, cope, face, fight, battle, struggle, take on, engage, encounter, confront, combat, contend, wrestle, tussle, get to grips, do battle, address yourself to ...*The economy is just one of the problems that the country is grappling with...*
2 = <u>struggle</u>, fight, combat, wrestle, battle, clash, contend, strive, tussle, scuffle, come to grips ...*He grappled desperately with Holmes for control of the weapon...*

grasp VERB 1 = <u>grip</u>, hold, catch, grab, seize, snatch, clutch, clinch, clasp, lay *or* take hold of ...*He grasped both my hands...*
2 = <u>understand</u>, realize, take in, get, see, follow, catch on, comprehend, get the message about, get the picture about, catch *or* get the drift of ...*The Government has not yet grasped the seriousness of the crisis...*
NOUN 1 = <u>grip</u>, hold, possession, embrace, clutches, clasp ...*She slipped her hand from his grasp...*
2 = <u>understanding</u>, knowledge, grip, perception, awareness, realization, mastery, comprehension ...*They have a good grasp of foreign languages...*
3 = <u>reach</u>, power, control, range, sweep, capacity, scope, sway, compass, mastery ...*Peace is now within our grasp...*

grasping = <u>greedy</u>, acquisitive, rapacious, mean, selfish, stingy, penny-pinching (*informal*), venal, miserly, avaricious, niggardly, covetous, tightfisted, close-fisted, snoep (*S. African informal*) OPPOSITE> generous

grate VERB 1 = <u>shred</u>, mince, pulverize ...*Grate the cheese into a mixing bowl...*
2 = <u>scrape</u>, grind, rub, scratch, creak, rasp ...*His chair grated as he got to his feet...*
PHRASES **grate on someone** *or* **grate on someone's nerves** = <u>annoy</u>, irritate, aggravate (*informal*), gall, exasperate, nettle, jar, vex, chafe, irk, rankle, peeve, get under your skin (*informal*), get up your nose (*informal*), get on your nerves (*informal*), nark (*Brit., Austral., & N.Z. slang*), set your teeth on edge, get on your wick (*Brit. slang*), rub you up the wrong way ...*His manner always grated on me...*

grateful = <u>thankful</u>, obliged, in (someone's) debt, indebted, appreciative, beholden

gratification 1 = <u>satisfaction</u>, delight, pleasure, joy, thrill, relish, enjoyment, glee, kick *or* kicks (*informal*) ...*Eventually they recognised him, much to his gratification...* OPPOSITE> disappointment
2 = <u>indulgence</u>, satisfaction, fulfilment ...*the gratification of his every whim...* OPPOSITE> denial

gratify = <u>please</u>, delight, satisfy, thrill, give pleasure,

gladden

grating[1] = <u>grille</u>, grid, grate, lattice, trellis, gridiron ...*an open grating in the sidewalk...*

grating[2] = <u>irritating</u>, grinding, harsh, annoying, jarring, unpleasant, scraping, raucous, strident, squeaky, rasping, discordant, disagreeable, irksome ...*I can't stand that grating voice of his...* OPPOSITE> pleasing

gratitude = <u>thankfulness</u>, thanks, recognition, obligation, appreciation, indebtedness, sense of obligation, gratefulness OPPOSITE> ingratitude

gratuitous = <u>unjustified</u>, unnecessary, needless, unfounded, unwarranted, superfluous, wanton, unprovoked, groundless, baseless, uncalled-for, unmerited, causeless OPPOSITE> justifiable

gratuity = <u>tip</u>, present, gift, reward, bonus, donation, boon, bounty, recompense, perquisite, baksheesh, benefaction, pourboire (*French*), bonsela (*S. African*), largesse *or* largess

grave[1] = <u>tomb</u>, vault, crypt, mausoleum, sepulchre, pit, last resting place, burying place ...*They used to visit her grave twice a year...*
(*Related Words*)
adjective: sepulchral

grave[2] 1 = <u>serious</u>, important, significant, critical, pressing, threatening, dangerous, vital, crucial, acute, severe, urgent, hazardous, life-and-death, momentous, perilous, weighty, leaden, of great consequence ...*He says the situation in his country is very grave...* OPPOSITE> trifling
2 = <u>solemn</u>, sober, gloomy, dull, thoughtful, subdued, sombre, dour, grim-faced, long-faced, unsmiling ...*She could tell by his grave expression that something terrible had happened...* OPPOSITE> carefree

graveyard = <u>cemetery</u>, churchyard, burial ground, charnel house, necropolis, boneyard (*informal*), God's acre (*literary*)

gravitas = <u>seriousness</u>, gravity, solemnity

gravitate with *to* or *towards* = <u>be drawn</u>, move, tend, lean, be pulled, incline, be attracted, be influenced

gravity 1 = <u>seriousness</u>, importance, consequence, significance, urgency, severity, acuteness, moment, weightiness, momentousness, perilousness, hazardousness ...*You don't seem to appreciate the gravity of this situation...* OPPOSITE> triviality
2 = <u>solemnity</u>, gloom, seriousness, gravitas, thoughtfulness, grimness ...*There was an appealing gravity to everything she said...* OPPOSITE> frivolity

graze[1] = <u>feed</u>, crop, browse, pasture ...*cows grazing in a field...*

graze[2] VERB 1 = <u>scratch</u>, skin, bark, scrape, chafe, abrade ...*I had grazed my knees a little...*
2 = <u>touch</u>, brush, rub, scrape, shave, skim, kiss, glance off ...*A bullet had grazed his arm...*
NOUN = <u>scratch</u>, scrape, abrasion ...*He just has a slight graze...*

greasy 1 = <u>fatty</u>, slick, slippery, oily, slimy, oleaginous ...*He propped his elbows upon the greasy counter...*

2 = <u>sycophantic</u>, fawning, grovelling, ingratiating, smooth, slick, oily, unctuous, smarmy (*Brit. informal*), toadying …*She called him 'a greasy little Tory sycophant'*…

great **1** = <u>large</u>, big, huge, vast, enormous, extensive, tremendous, immense, gigantic, mammoth, bulky, colossal, prodigious, stupendous, voluminous, elephantine, ginormous (*informal*), humongous *or* humungous (*U.S. slang*) …*a great hall as long and high as a church*… [OPPOSITE> small

2 = <u>extreme</u>, considerable, excessive, high, decided, pronounced, extravagant, prodigious, inordinate …*I'll take great care of it*… …*That must have taken great effort on his part*…

3 = <u>major</u>, lead, leading, chief, main, capital, grand, primary, principal, prominent, superior, paramount, big-time (*informal*), major league (*informal*) …*the great cultural achievements of the past*…

4 = <u>important</u>, serious, significant, critical, crucial, heavy, grave, momentous, weighty, consequential …*his pronouncements on the great political matters of the age*… [OPPOSITE> unimportant

5 = <u>famous</u>, celebrated, outstanding, excellent, remarkable, distinguished, prominent, glorious, notable, renowned, eminent, famed, illustrious, exalted, noteworthy …*the great American president, Abraham Lincoln*…

6 = <u>expert</u>, skilled, talented, skilful, good, able, masterly, crack (*slang*), superb, world-class, adept, stellar (*informal*), superlative, proficient, adroit …*He was one of the West Indies' greatest cricketers*… [OPPOSITE> unskilled

7 (*Informal*) = <u>excellent</u>, good, fine, wonderful, mean (*slang*), topping (*Brit. slang*), cracking (*Brit. informal*), superb, fantastic (*informal*), tremendous (*informal*), marvellous (*informal*), terrific (*informal*), mega (*slang*), sovereign, awesome (*slang*), dope (*slang*), admirable, first-rate, def (*informal*), brill (*informal*), boffo (*slang*), bitchin', chillin' (*U.S. slang*), booshit (*Austral. slang*), exo (*Austral. slang*), sik (*Austral. slang*) …*It's a great film, you must see it*… [OPPOSITE> poor

8 = <u>very</u>, really, particularly, truly, extremely, awfully (*informal*), exceedingly …*He gave me a great big smile*…

9 = <u>utter</u>, complete, total, absolute, perfect, positive, downright, consummate, unqualified, out-and-out, flagrant, egregious, unmitigated, thoroughgoing, arrant …*You stupid great git!*…

10 = <u>enthusiastic</u>, keen, active, devoted, zealous …*I'm not a great fan of football*…

greatly = <u>very much</u>, much, hugely, vastly, extremely, highly, seriously (*informal*), notably, considerably, remarkably, enormously, immensely, tremendously, markedly, powerfully, exceedingly, mightily, abundantly, by much, by leaps and bounds, to the nth degree

greatness **1** = <u>grandeur</u>, glory, majesty, splendour, power, pomp, magnificence …*the greatness of ancient Rome*…

2 = <u>fame</u>, glory, celebrity, distinction, eminence, note, lustre, renown, illustriousness …*Abraham Lincoln achieved greatness*…

greed *or* **greediness** **1** = <u>gluttony</u>, voracity, insatiableness, ravenousness …*He ate too much out of sheer greed*…

2 = <u>avarice</u>, longing, desire, hunger, craving, eagerness, selfishness, acquisitiveness, rapacity, cupidity, covetousness, insatiableness …*an insatiable greed for power*… [OPPOSITE> generosity

greedy **1** = <u>gluttonous</u>, insatiable, voracious, ravenous, piggish, hoggish …*a greedy little boy who ate too many sweets*…

2 = <u>avaricious</u>, grasping, selfish, insatiable, acquisitive, rapacious, materialistic, desirous, covetous …*He attacked greedy bosses for awarding themselves big pay rises*… [OPPOSITE> generous

Greek [ADJECTIVE] = <u>Hellenic</u> …*his extensive knowledge of Greek antiquity*…
[NOUN] = <u>Hellene</u> …*The ancient Greeks referred to themselves as Hellenes*…

green [ADJECTIVE] **1** = <u>verdant</u>, leafy, grassy …*The city has only thirteen square centimetres of green space for each inhabitant*…

2 = <u>ecological</u>, conservationist, environment-friendly, ecologically sound, eco-friendly, ozone-friendly, non-polluting …*trying to persuade governments to adopt greener policies*…

3 = <u>unripe</u>, fresh, raw, immature …*Pick and ripen any green fruits in a warm dark place*…

4 = <u>inexperienced</u>, new, innocent, raw, naive, ignorant, immature, gullible, callow, untrained, unsophisticated, credulous, ingenuous, unpolished, wet behind the ears (*informal*) …*He was a young lad, very green and immature*…

5 = <u>jealous</u>, grudging, resentful, envious, covetous …*Collectors worldwide will turn green with envy*…

6 = <u>nauseous</u>, ill, sick, pale, unhealthy, wan, under the weather …*By the end of the race the runners would be green with sickness*…

7 with capital = <u>environmentalist</u>, conservationist …*The Greens see themselves as a radical alternative to the two major parties*…

[NOUN] = <u>lawn</u>, common, turf, sward, grassplot …*a pageant on the village green*…

(**Related Words**)
adjective : verdant

Shades of Green

almond green	jade
apple green	lime green
aqua	Lincoln green
aquamarine	Nile green
avocado	olive
celadon	pea green
chartreuse	pine green
citron	pistachio
cyan	sea green
eau de nil	teal
emerald green	turquoise

green light = <u>authorization</u>, sanction, approval, go-ahead (*informal*), blessing, permission, confirmation, clearance, imprimatur, O.K. *or* okay (*informal*)

greet 1 = <u>salute</u>, hail, nod to, say hello to, address, accost, tip your hat to ...*He greeted us with a smile*...
2 = <u>welcome</u>, meet, receive ...*She was waiting at the door to greet her guests*...
3 = <u>receive</u>, take, respond to, react to ...*The European Court's decision has been greeted with dismay*...

greeting NOUN = <u>welcome</u>, reception, hail, salute, address, salutation ...*His greeting was familiar and friendly*...
PLURAL NOUN = <u>best wishes</u>, regards, respects, compliments, good wishes, salutations ...*They exchanged hearty Christmas greetings*...

gregarious = <u>outgoing</u>, friendly, social, cordial, sociable, affable, convivial, companionable OPPOSITE unsociable

grey 1 = <u>dull</u>, dark, dim, gloomy, cloudy, murky, drab, misty, foggy, overcast, sunless ...*It was a grey, wet April Sunday*...
2 = <u>boring</u>, dull, anonymous, faceless, colourless, nondescript, characterless ...*little grey men in suits*...
3 = <u>old</u>, aged, ancient, mature, elderly, venerable, hoary ...*a grey old man*...
4 = <u>pale</u>, wan, livid, bloodless, colourless, pallid, ashen, like death warmed up (*informal*) ...*His face was grey with pain*...
5 = <u>ambiguous</u>, uncertain, neutral, unclear, debatable ...*The whole question of refugees is something of a grey area*...
➤ **shades from black to white**

gridlock 1 = <u>traffic jam</u> ...*The streets are wedged solid with the traffic gridlock*...
2 = <u>deadlock</u>, halt, stalemate, impasse, standstill, full stop ...*He agreed that these policies will lead to a gridlock in the future*...

grief NOUN = <u>sadness</u>, suffering, pain, regret, distress, misery, agony, mourning, sorrow, woe, anguish, remorse, bereavement, heartache, heartbreak, mournfulness ...*Their grief soon gave way to anger*...
OPPOSITE joy
PHRASES **come to grief** (*Informal*) = <u>fail</u>, founder, break down, come unstuck, miscarry, fall flat on your face, meet with disaster ...*So many marriages have come to grief over lack of money*...

grievance = <u>complaint</u>, protest, beef (*slang*), gripe (*informal*), axe to grind, chip on your shoulder (*informal*)

grieve 1 = <u>mourn</u>, suffer, weep, ache, lament, sorrow, wail ...*He's grieving over his dead wife and son*...
2 = <u>sadden</u>, hurt, injure, distress, wound, crush, pain, afflict, upset, agonize, break the heart of, make your heart bleed ...*It grieved me to see him in such distress*... OPPOSITE gladden

grievous 1 = <u>deplorable</u>, shocking, appalling, dreadful, outrageous, glaring, intolerable, monstrous, shameful, unbearable, atrocious, heinous, lamentable, egregious ...*Their loss would be a grievous blow to our engineering industries*... OPPOSITE pleasant
2 = <u>severe</u>, damaging, heavy, wounding, grave,

painful, distressing, dreadful, harmful, calamitous, injurious ...*He survived in spite of suffering grievous injuries*... OPPOSITE mild

grim = <u>terrible</u>, shocking, severe, harsh, forbidding, horrible, formidable, sinister, ghastly, hideous, gruesome (*slang*), grisly, horrid, frightful, godawful

grimace VERB = <u>scowl</u>, frown, sneer, wince, lour *or* lower, make a face *or* faces ...*She started to sit up, grimaced with pain, and sank back*...
NOUN = <u>scowl</u>, frown, sneer, wince, face, wry face ...*He took another drink of his coffee. 'Awful,' he said with a grimace*...

grime = <u>dirt</u>, filth, soot, smut, grot (*slang*)

grimy = <u>dirty</u>, polluted, filthy, soiled, foul, grubby, sooty, unclean, grotty (*slang*), smutty, scuzzy (*slang*), begrimed, festy (*Austral. slang*)

grind VERB 1 = <u>crush</u>, mill, powder, grate, pulverize, pound, kibble, abrade, granulate ...*Grind the pepper in a pepper mill*...
2 = <u>press</u>, push, crush, jam, mash, force down ...*He ground his cigarette under his heel*...
3 = <u>grate</u>, scrape, grit, gnash ...*If you grind your teeth at night, see your dentist*...
4 = <u>sharpen</u>, file, polish, sand, smooth, whet ...*The tip can be ground to a much sharper edge*...
NOUN = <u>hard work</u> (*Informal*), labour, effort, task, sweat (*informal*), chore, toil, drudgery ...*Life continues to be a terrible grind for the ordinary person*...
PHRASES **grind someone down** = <u>oppress</u>, suppress, harass, subdue, hound, bring down, plague, persecute, subjugate, trample underfoot, tyrannize (over) ...*There will always be some bosses who want to grind you down*...

grip VERB 1 = <u>grasp</u>, hold, catch, seize, clutch, clasp, latch on to, take hold of ...*She gripped his hand tightly*...
2 = <u>engross</u>, fascinate, absorb, entrance, hold, catch up, compel, rivet, enthral, mesmerize, spellbind ...*The whole nation was gripped by the dramatic story*...
NOUN 1 = <u>clasp</u>, hold, grasp, handclasp (*U.S.*) ...*His strong hand eased the bag from her grip*...
2 = <u>control</u>, rule, influence, command, power, possession, sway, dominance, domination, mastery ...*The president maintains an iron grip on his country*...
3 = <u>hold</u>, purchase, friction, traction ...*a new kind of rubber which gives tyres a better grip*...
4 = <u>understanding</u>, sense, command, perception, awareness, grasp, appreciation, mastery, comprehension, discernment ...*He has lost his grip on reality*...
PHRASES **come** *or* **get to grips with something** = <u>tackle</u>, deal with, handle, take on, meet, encounter, cope with, confront, undertake, grasp, face up to, grapple with, close with, contend with ...*The government's first task is to get to grips with the economy*...

gripe (*Informal*) VERB = <u>complain</u>, moan, groan, grumble, beef (*slang*), carp, bitch (*slang*), nag, whine, grouse, bleat, grouch (*informal*), bellyache (*slang*), kvetch (*U.S. slang*) ...*He started griping about the*

prices they were charging…
NOUN = complaint, protest, objection, beef (*slang*), moan, grumble, grievance, grouse, grouch (*informal*) …*My only gripe is that just one main course and one dessert were available…*

gripping = fascinating, exciting, thrilling, entrancing, compelling, compulsive, riveting, enthralling, engrossing, spellbinding, unputdownable (*informal*)

grisly = gruesome, shocking, terrible, awful, terrifying, appalling, horrible, grim, dreadful, sickening, ghastly, hideous, macabre, horrid, frightful, abominable, hellacious (*U.S. slang*) OPPOSITE pleasant

> ## *Word Power*
>
> **grisly** – Note the spelling of *grisly* (as in *a grisly murder*). It should be carefully distinguished from the word *grizzly* (as in *a grizzly bear*), which means 'greyish in colour'.

grit NOUN 1 = gravel, sand, dust, pebbles …*He felt tiny bits of grit and sand peppering his knees…*
2 = courage, spirit, resolution, determination, nerve, guts (*informal*), balls (*taboo slang*), pluck, backbone, fortitude, toughness, tenacity, perseverance, mettle, doggedness, hardihood …*He showed grit and determination in his fight back to health…*
VERB = clench, grind, grate, gnash …*Gritting my teeth, I did my best to stifle a sharp retort…*

gritty 1 = rough, sandy, dusty, abrasive, rasping, grainy, gravelly, granular …*She threw a handful of gritty dust into his eyes…*
2 = courageous, game, dogged, determined, tough, spirited, brave, hardy, feisty (*informal, chiefly U.S. & Canad.*), resolute, tenacious, plucky, steadfast, mettlesome …*a gritty determination to get to the top…*

grizzle = whine, fret, whimper, whinge (*informal*), snivel, girn (*Scot.*)

grizzled = grey, greying, grey-haired, grizzly, hoary, grey-headed

groan VERB 1 = moan, cry, sigh …*The man on the floor began to groan with pain…*
2 (*Informal*) = complain, object, moan, grumble, gripe (*informal*), beef (*slang*), carp, bitch (*slang*), lament, whine, grouse, bemoan, whinge (*informal*), grouch (*informal*), bellyache (*slang*) …*His parents were beginning to groan about the cost of it all…*
NOUN 1 = moan, cry, sigh, whine …*She heard him let out a pitiful, muffled groan…*
2 (*Informal*) = complaint, protest, objection, grumble, beef (*slang*), grouse, gripe (*informal*), grouch (*informal*) …*I don't have time to listen to your moans and groans…*

groggy = dizzy, faint, stunned, confused, reeling, shaky, dazed, wobbly, weak, unsteady, muzzy, stupefied, befuddled, punch-drunk, woozy (*informal*)

groom NOUN 1 = stableman, stableboy, hostler *or* ostler (*archaic*) …*He worked as a groom at a stables on Dartmoor…*
2 = newly-wed, husband, bridegroom, marriage

partner …*We toasted the bride and groom…*
VERB 1 = brush, clean, tend, rub down, curry …*The horses were exercised and groomed with special care…*
2 = smarten up, dress, clean, turn out, get up (*informal*), tidy, preen, spruce up, primp, gussy up (*slang, chiefly U.S.*) …*She always appeared perfectly groomed…*
3 = underline{train}, prime, prepare, coach, ready, educate, drill, nurture, make ready …*He was already being groomed for a top job…*

groove = indentation, cut, hollow, score, channel, trench, flute, gutter, trough, furrow, rut

grope = feel, search, fumble, flounder, fish, finger, scrabble, cast about, fossick (*Austral. & N.Z.*)

gross ADJECTIVE 1 = flagrant, obvious, glaring, blatant, serious, shocking, rank, plain, sheer, utter, outrageous, manifest, shameful, downright, grievous, unqualified, heinous, egregious, unmitigated, arrant …*The company were found guilty of gross negligence…* OPPOSITE qualified
2 = vulgar, offensive, crude, rude, obscene, low, coarse, indecent, improper, unseemly, lewd, X-rated (*informal*), impure, smutty, ribald, indelicate …*That's a disgusting thing to say – you're so gross!…* OPPOSITE decent
3 = coarse, crass, tasteless, unsophisticated, ignorant, insensitive, callous, boorish, unfeeling, unrefined, uncultured, undiscriminating, imperceptive …*He is a gross and boorish individual…* OPPOSITE cultivated
4 obese = fat, overweight, great, big, large, heavy, massive, dense, bulky, hulking, corpulent, lumpish …*I've put on so much weight I look totally gross…* OPPOSITE slim
5 = total, whole, entire, aggregate, before tax, before deductions …*Gross sales in June totalled 270 million…* OPPOSITE net
VERB = earn, make, take, bring in, rake in (*informal*) …*So far the films have grossed nearly £290 million…*

grotesque 1 = unnatural, bizarre, weird, odd, strange, fantastic, distorted, fanciful, deformed, outlandish, whimsical, freakish, misshapen, malformed …*statues of grotesque mythical creatures…* OPPOSITE natural
2 = absurd, ridiculous, ludicrous, preposterous, incongruous …*the grotesque disparities between the rich and the poor…* OPPOSITE natural

grouch VERB = complain, moan, grumble, beef (*slang*), carp, bitch (*slang*), whine, grouse, gripe (*informal*), whinge (*informal*), bleat, find fault, bellyache (*slang*), kvetch (*U.S. slang*) …*They grouched about how hard-up they were…*
NOUN 1 = moaner, complainer, grumbler, whiner, grouser, malcontent, curmudgeon, crosspatch (*informal*), crab (*informal*), faultfinder …*He's an old grouch but she puts up with him…*
2 = complaint, protest, objection, grievance, moan, grumble, beef (*slang*), grouse, gripe (*informal*) …*One of their biggest grouches is the new system of payment…*

grouchy = bad-tempered, cross, irritable, grumpy, discontented, grumbling, surly, petulant, sulky, ill-tempered, irascible, cantankerous, tetchy, ratty (*Brit. & N.Z. informal*), testy, querulous, peevish, huffy, liverish

ground NOUN 1 = earth, land, dry land, terra firma …*We slid down the roof and dropped to the ground*…
2 = arena, pitch, stadium, park (*informal*), field, enclosure …*the city's football ground*…
PLURAL NOUN 1 = estate, holding, land, fields, gardens, property, district, territory, domain …*the palace grounds*…
2 = reason, cause, basis, argument, call, base, occasion, foundation, excuse, premise, motive, justification, rationale, inducement …*In the interview he gave some grounds for optimism*…
3 = dregs, lees, deposit, sediment …*Place the coffee grounds in the bottom and pour hot water over them*…
VERB 1 = base, found, establish, set, settle, fix …*Her argument was grounded in fact*…
2 = instruct, train, prepare, coach, teach, inform, initiate, tutor, acquaint with, familiarize with …*Make sure the children are properly grounded in the basics*…

groundless = baseless, false, unfounded, unjustified, unproven, empty, unauthorized, unsubstantiated, unsupported, uncorroborated OPPOSITE well-founded

groundwork = preliminaries, basis, foundation, base, footing, preparation, fundamentals, cornerstone, underpinnings, spadework

group NOUN 1 = crowd, company, party, band, troop, pack, gathering, gang, bunch, congregation, posse (*slang*), bevy, assemblage …*The trouble involved a small group of football supporters*…
2 = band, ensemble, combo …*ELP were the progressive rock group par excellence*…
3 = cluster, collection, formation, clump, aggregation …*a small group of islands off northern Japan*…
VERB 1 = arrange, order, sort, class, range, gather, organize, assemble, put together, classify, marshal, bracket, assort …*The fact sheets are grouped into seven sections*…
2 = unite, associate, gather, cluster, get together, congregate, band together …*We want to encourage them to group together as one big purchaser*…

grouse VERB = complain, moan, grumble, gripe (*informal*), beef (*slang*), carp, bitch (*slang*), whine, whinge (*informal*), bleat, find fault, grouch (*informal*), bellyache (*slang*), kvetch (*U.S. slang*) …*'How come they never tell us what's going on?' he groused*…
NOUN = complaint, protest, objection, moan, grievance, grumble, gripe (*informal*), beef (*slang*), grouch (*informal*) …*There have been grouses about the economy, interest rates and house prices*…

grove = wood, woodland, plantation, covert, thicket, copse, brake, coppice, spinney

grovel = humble yourself, creep, crawl, flatter, fawn, pander, cower, toady, kowtow, bow and scrape, lick someone's boots, demean yourself, abase yourself OPPOSITE hold your head high

grow 1 = develop, fill out, get bigger, get taller …*We stop growing once we reach maturity*… OPPOSITE shrink
2 = get bigger, spread, swell, extend, stretch, expand,

widen, enlarge, multiply, thicken …*An inoperable tumour was growing in his brain*…
3 = spring up, shoot up, develop, flourish, sprout, germinate, vegetate …*The station had roses growing at each end of the platform*…
4 = cultivate, produce, raise, farm, breed, nurture, propagate …*I always grow a few red onions in my allotment*…
5 = become, get, turn, come to be …*He's growing old*…
6 = originate, spring, arise, stem, issue …*The idea for this book grew out of conversations with Philippa Brewster*…
7 = underline{improve}, advance, progress, succeed, expand, thrive, flourish, prosper …*The economy continues to grow*…

grown-up NOUN = adult, man, woman …*Tell a grown-up if you're being bullied*…
ADJECTIVE = mature, adult, of age, fully-grown …*Her grown-up children are all doing well in their chosen careers*…

growth 1 = increase, development, expansion, extension, growing, heightening, proliferation, enlargement, multiplication …*the unchecked growth of the country's population*… OPPOSITE decline
2 = progress, success, improvement, expansion, advance, prosperity, advancement …*enormous economic growth*… OPPOSITE failure
3 = vegetation, development, production, sprouting, germination, shooting …*This helps to encourage new growth and makes the plant flower profusely*…
4 (*Medical*) = tumour, cancer, swelling, lump, carcinoma (*Pathology*), sarcoma (*Medical*), excrescence …*This type of surgery could even be used to extract cancerous growths*…

grub NOUN 1 = larva, maggot, caterpillar …*The grubs do their damage by tunnelling through ripened fruit*…
2 (*Slang*) = food, feed, rations, tack (*informal*), eats (*slang*), kai (*N.Z. informal*), sustenance, nosh (*slang*), victuals, nosebag (*slang*), vittles (*obsolete or dialect*) …*Get yourself some grub and come and sit down*…
VERB 1 = search, hunt, scour, ferret, rummage, forage, fossick (*Austral. & N.Z.*) …*grubbing through piles of paper for his address*…
2 = dig, search, root (*informal*), probe, burrow, rootle (*Brit.*) …*chickens grubbing around in the dirt for food*…

grubby = dirty, soiled, filthy, squalid, messy, shabby, seedy, scruffy, sordid, untidy, grimy, unwashed, unkempt, mucky, smutty, grungy (*slang, chiefly U.S. & Canad.*), slovenly, manky (*Scot. dialect*), scuzzy (*slang*), scungy (*Austral. & N.Z.*), frowzy, besmeared, festy (*Austral. slang*)

grudge NOUN = resentment, bitterness, grievance, malice, hate, spite, dislike, animosity, aversion, venom, antipathy, enmity, rancour, hard feelings, ill will, animus, malevolence …*It was an accident and I bear him no grudge*… OPPOSITE goodwill
VERB = resent, mind, envy, covet, begrudge …*Few seem to grudge him his good fortune*… OPPOSITE welcome

gruelling = exhausting, demanding, difficult, tiring, trying, hard, taxing, grinding, severe, crushing, fierce, punishing, harsh, stiff, brutal, fatiguing, strenuous, arduous, laborious, backbreaking `OPPOSITE` easy

gruesome = <u>horrific</u>, shocking, terrible, awful, horrible, grim, horrifying, fearful, obscene, horrendous, ghastly, hideous, from hell (*informal*), grisly, macabre, horrid, repulsive, repugnant, loathsome, abominable, spine-chilling, hellacious (*U.S. slang*) `OPPOSITE` pleasant

gruff 1 = <u>hoarse</u>, rough, harsh, rasping, husky, low, croaking, throaty, guttural ...*He picked up the phone expecting to hear the chairman's gruff voice*...
`OPPOSITE` mellifluous
2 = <u>surly</u>, rough, rude, grumpy, blunt, crabbed, crusty, sullen, bad-tempered, curt, churlish, brusque, impolite, grouchy (*informal*), ungracious, discourteous, uncivil, ill-humoured, unmannerly, ill-natured ...*His gruff exterior concealed a kind heart*...
`OPPOSITE` polite

grumble `VERB` 1 = <u>complain</u>, moan, gripe (*informal*), whinge (*informal*), beef (*slang*), carp, bitch (*slang*), whine, grouse, bleat, grouch (*informal*), bellyache (*slang*), kvetch (*U.S. slang*), repine ...*'This is very inconvenient,' he grumbled*...
2 = <u>rumble</u>, growl, gurgle ...*His stomach grumbled loudly*...
`NOUN` 1 = <u>complaint</u>, protest, objection, moan, grievance, grouse, gripe (*informal*), grouch (*informal*), beef (*slang*) ...*My grumble is with the structure and organisation of his material*...
2 = <u>rumble</u>, growl, gurgle ...*One could hear, far to the east, a grumble of thunder*...

grumpy = <u>irritable</u>, cross, bad-tempered, grumbling, crabbed, edgy, surly, petulant, ill-tempered, cantankerous, tetchy, ratty (*Brit. & N.Z. informal*), testy, grouchy (*informal*), querulous, peevish, huffy, crotchety (*informal*), liverish

guarantee `VERB` 1 = <u>ensure</u>, secure, assure, warrant, insure, make certain ...*Surplus resources alone do not guarantee growth*...
2 = <u>promise</u>, pledge, undertake, swear ...*We guarantee to refund your money if you are not delighted with your purchase*...
`NOUN` 1 = <u>promise</u>, word, pledge, undertaking, assurance, certainty, covenant, word of honour ...*We can give no guarantee that their demands will be met*...
2 = <u>warranty</u>, contract, bond, guaranty ...*The goods were still under guarantee*...

guarantor = <u>underwriter</u>, guarantee, supporter, sponsor, backer, surety, warrantor

guard `VERB` = <u>protect</u>, watch, defend, secure, police, mind, cover, screen, preserve, shelter, shield, patrol, oversee, safeguard, watch over ...*Gunmen guarded homes near the cemetery*...
`NOUN` 1 = <u>sentry</u>, warder, warden, custodian, watch, patrol, lookout, watchman, sentinel ...*The prisoners overpowered their guards and locked them in a cell*...
2 = <u>escort</u>, patrol, convoy ...*a heavily armed guard of police*...

3 = <u>shield</u>, security, defence, screen, protection, pad, safeguard, bumper, buffer, rampart, bulwark ...*The heater should have a safety guard fitted*...
4 = <u>caution</u>, vigilance, wariness, watchfulness ...*It takes me a long time to drop my guard and get close to people*...
`PHRASES` **off guard** = <u>unprepared</u>, napping, unwary, unready, with your defences down ...*His question had caught me off guard*... ♦ **on (your) guard** = <u>vigilant</u>, cautious, wary, prepared, ready, alert, watchful, on the lookout, circumspect, on the alert, on the qui vive ...*Be on your guard against crooked car dealers*...
(*Related Words*)
adjective: custodial

guarded = <u>cautious</u>, reserved, careful, suspicious, restrained, wary, discreet, prudent, reticent, circumspect, cagey (*informal*), leery (*slang*), noncommittal

guardian = <u>keeper</u>, champion, defender, guard, trustee, warden, curator, protector, warder, custodian, preserver

guerrilla = <u>freedom fighter</u>, partisan, irregular, underground fighter, member of the underground *or* resistance

guess `VERB` 1 = <u>estimate</u>, predict, work out, speculate, fathom, conjecture, postulate, surmise, hazard a guess, hypothesize ...*I can only guess what it cost him to tell you the truth*... `OPPOSITE` know
2 = <u>suppose</u>, think, believe, suspect, judge, imagine, reckon, fancy, conjecture, dare say ...*I guess I'm just being paranoid*...
`NOUN` 1 = <u>estimate</u>, reckoning, speculation, judgment, hypothesis, conjecture, surmise, shot in the dark, ballpark figure (*informal*) ...*He took her pulse and made a guess at her blood pressure*... `OPPOSITE` certainty
2 = <u>supposition</u>, feeling, idea, theory, notion, suspicion, hypothesis ...*My guess is that she's waiting for you to make the first move*...

guesswork = <u>speculation</u>, theory, presumption, conjecture, estimation, surmise, supposition

guest = <u>visitor</u>, company, caller

guff (*Informal*) = <u>nonsense</u>, rubbish, rot, crap (*slang*), garbage (*informal*), trash, hot air (*informal*), tosh (*slang, chiefly Brit.*), pap, bilge (*informal*), humbug, drivel, tripe (*informal*), moonshine, hogwash, hokum (*slang, chiefly U.S. & Canad.*), piffle (*informal*), poppycock (*informal*), balderdash, bosh (*informal*), eyewash (*informal*), kak (*S. African taboo slang*), empty talk, tommyrot, horsefeathers (*U.S. slang*), bunkum *or* buncombe (*chiefly U.S.*), bizzo (*Austral. slang*), bull's wool (*Austral. & N.Z. slang*)

guidance = <u>advice</u>, direction, leadership, instruction, government, help, control, management, teaching, counsel, counselling, auspices

guide `NOUN` 1 = <u>handbook</u>, manual, guidebook, instructions, catalogue ...*Our 10-page guide will help you change your life for the better*...
2 = <u>directory</u>, street map ...*The Rough Guide to Paris lists accommodation for as little as £25 a night*...

3 = <u>escort</u>, leader, controller, attendant, usher, chaperon, torchbearer, dragoman ...*With guides, the journey can be done in fourteen days*...
4 = <u>pointer</u>, sign, signal, mark, key, clue, landmark, marker, beacon, signpost, guiding light, lodestar ...*His only guide was the stars overhead*...
5 = <u>model</u>, example, standard, ideal, master, inspiration, criterion, paradigm, exemplar, lodestar ...*The checklist serves as a guide to students, teachers and parents*...
VERB 1 = <u>lead</u>, direct, escort, conduct, pilot, accompany, steer, shepherd, convoy, usher, show the way ...*He took the bewildered man by the arm and guided him out*...
2 = <u>steer</u>, control, manage, direct, handle, command, manoeuvre ...*He guided his plane down the runway and took off*...
3 = <u>supervise</u>, train, rule, teach, influence, advise, counsel, govern, educate, regulate, instruct, oversee, sway, superintend ...*He should have let his instinct guide him*...

guild = <u>society</u>, union, league, association, company, club, order, organization, corporation, lodge, fellowship, fraternity, brotherhood

guile = <u>cunning</u>, craft, deception, deceit, trickery, duplicity, cleverness, art, gamesmanship (*informal*), craftiness, artfulness, slyness, trickiness, wiliness **OPPOSITE** honesty

guilt 1 = <u>shame</u>, regret, remorse, contrition, guilty conscience, bad conscience, self-reproach, self-condemnation, guiltiness ...*Her emotions went from anger to guilt in the space of a few seconds*... **OPPOSITE** pride
2 = <u>culpability</u>, blame, responsibility, misconduct, delinquency, criminality, wickedness, iniquity, sinfulness, blameworthiness, guiltiness ...*You were never convinced of his guilt, were you?*... **OPPOSITE** innocence

guilty 1 = <u>ashamed</u>, sorry, rueful, sheepish, contrite, remorseful, regretful, shamefaced, hangdog, conscience-stricken ...*When she saw me, she looked extremely guilty*... **OPPOSITE** proud
2 = <u>culpable</u>, responsible, convicted, to blame, offending, erring, at fault, reprehensible, iniquitous, felonious, blameworthy ...*They were found guilty of manslaughter*... ...*The guilty pair were caught red-handed*... **OPPOSITE** innocent

guise 1 = <u>form</u>, appearance, dress, fashion, shape, aspect, mode, semblance ...*He claimed the Devil had appeared to him in the guise of a goat*...
2 = <u>pretence</u>, show, mask, disguise, face, front, aspect, façade, semblance ...*Fascism is on the rise under the guise of conservative politics*...

gulf 1 = <u>bay</u>, bight, sea inlet ...*Hurricane Andrew was last night heading into the Gulf of Mexico*...
2 = <u>chasm</u>, opening, split, gap, rent, breach, separation, void, rift, abyss, cleft ...*the gulf between rural and urban life*...

gullible = <u>trusting</u>, innocent, naive, unsuspecting, green, simple, silly, foolish, unsophisticated, credulous, born yesterday, wet behind the ears (*informal*), easily taken in, unsceptical, as green as grass **OPPOSITE** suspicious

gully = <u>ravine</u>, canyon, gorge, chasm, channel, fissure, defile, watercourse

gulp VERB 1 = <u>swallow</u>, bolt, devour, gobble, knock back (*informal*), wolf, swig (*informal*), swill, guzzle, quaff ...*She quickly gulped her tea*...
2 = <u>gasp</u>, swallow, choke ...*He slumped back, gulping for air*...
NOUN = <u>swallow</u>, draught, mouthful, swig (*informal*) ...*He drank half of his whisky in one gulp*...

gum NOUN = <u>glue</u>, adhesive, resin, cement, paste ...*a pound note that had been torn in half and stuck together with gum*...
VERB = <u>stick</u>, glue, affix, cement, paste, clog ...*a mild infection in which the baby's eyelashes can become gummed together*...

gun = <u>firearm</u>, shooter (*slang*), piece (*slang*), rod (*slang*), heater (*U.S. slang*), handgun
➤ **guns**

gunman = <u>armed man</u>, hit man (*slang*), gunslinger (*U.S. slang*)

gurgle VERB = <u>ripple</u>, lap, bubble, splash, murmur, babble, burble, purl, plash ...*a narrow channel along*

Guns http://dmoz.org/Shopping/Recreation/Guns/

AK-47 *or* Kalashnikov	chokebore	M-16	revolver
anti-aircraft gun *or* ack-ack gun	Colt	machine gun	rifle
Armalite	culverin	Magnum	scatter-gun
arquebus	derringer *or* deringer	matchlock	shotgun
BAR	Enfield rifle	Mauser	six-shooter
Big Bertha	firelock	Maxim gun	Springfield rifle
blunderbuss	flintlock	mitrailleuse	Sten gun
Bofors gun	forty-five	musket	stern-chaser
breech-loader	fusil	muzzle-loader	sub-machine-gun
Bren gun	Garand rifle	Owen gun	Thompson sub-machine gun
Browning	Gatling	petronel	trench mortar
burp gun	howitzer	pistol	Uzi
carbine	Lewis gun	pom-pom	Winchester rifle
carronade	Luger	pump gun	zip gun
chassepot	M-1 rifle	Quaker gun	
	M-14	repeater	

which water gurgles…

NOUN = <u>burble</u>, chuckle, ripple, babble …*There was a gurgle of laughter on the other end of the line…*

guru 1 = <u>authority</u>, expert, leader, master, pundit, arbiter, Svengali, torchbearer, fundi (*S. African*) …*Fashion gurus dictate crazy ideas such as puffball skirts…*
2 = <u>teacher</u>, mentor, sage, master, tutor, mahatma, guiding light, swami, maharishi …*He set himself up as a faith healer and spiritual guru…*

gush **VERB** 1 = <u>flow</u>, run, rush, flood, pour, jet, burst, stream, cascade, issue, spurt, spout …*Piping hot water gushed out of the tap…*
2 = <u>enthuse</u>, rave, spout, overstate, rhapsodize, effuse …*'Oh, you were just brilliant,' she gushed…*
NOUN = <u>stream</u>, flow, rush, flood, jet, burst, issue, outburst, cascade, torrent, spurt, spout, outflow …*I heard a gush of water…*

gust **NOUN** 1 = <u>blast</u>, blow, rush, breeze, puff, gale, flurry, squall …*A gust of wind drove down the valley…*
2 = <u>surge</u>, fit, storm, burst, explosion, gale, outburst, eruption, paroxysm …*A gust of laughter greeted him as he walked into the room…*
VERB = <u>blow</u>, blast, puff, squall …*strong winds gusting up to 164 miles an hour…*

gusto = <u>relish</u>, enthusiasm, appetite, appreciation, liking, delight, pleasure, enjoyment, savour, zeal, verve, zest, fervour, exhilaration, brio, zing (*informal*)
OPPOSITE apathy

gusty = <u>windy</u>, stormy, breezy, blustering, tempestuous, blustery, inclement, squally, blowy

gut **NOUN** = <u>paunch</u> (*Informal*), belly, spare tyre (*Brit. slang*), potbelly …*His gut sagged over his belt…*
PLURAL NOUN 1 = <u>intestines</u>, insides (*informal*), stomach, belly, bowels, inwards, innards (*informal*), entrails …*The crew-men were standing ankle-deep in fish guts…*
2 (*Informal*) = <u>courage</u>, spirit, nerve, daring, pluck, grit, backbone, willpower, bottle (*slang*), audacity, mettle, boldness, spunk (*informal*), forcefulness, hardihood …*The new Chancellor has the guts to push through unpopular tax increases…*
VERB 1 = <u>disembowel</u>, draw, dress, clean, eviscerate

…*It is not always necessary to gut the fish prior to freezing…*
2 = <u>ravage</u>, strip, empty, sack, rifle, plunder, clean out, ransack, pillage, despoil …*The church had been gutted by vandals…*
ADJECTIVE = <u>instinctive</u>, natural, basic, emotional, spontaneous, innate, intuitive, involuntary, heartfelt, deep-seated, unthinking …*At first my gut reaction was to simply walk out of there…*
(**Related Words**)
technical name: viscera
adjective: visceral

gutsy = <u>brave</u>, determined, spirited, bold, have-a-go (*informal*), courageous, gritty, staunch, feisty (*informal, chiefly U.S. & Canad.*), game (*informal*), resolute, gallant, plucky, indomitable, mettlesome

gutter = <u>drain</u>, channel, tube, pipe, ditch, trench, trough, conduit, duct, sluice

guy (*Informal*) = <u>man</u>, person, fellow, lad, cat (*dated slang*), bloke (*Brit. informal*), chap

guzzle = <u>devour</u>, drink, bolt, wolf, cram, gorge, gobble, knock back (*informal*), swill, quaff, tope, pig out on (*slang*), stuff yourself with

gymnastics

Gymnastic events

http://www.fig-gymnastics.com/UrlGrpServer.jser?@_ID=6018&@_TEMPLATE=5991

asymmetric bars	parallel bars
beam	pommel horse
floor exercises	rings
high *or* horizontal bar	rhythmic gymnastics
	side horse vault
horse vault	

Gypsy *or* **Gipsy** = <u>traveller</u>, roamer, wanderer, Bohemian, rover, rambler, nomad, vagrant, Romany, vagabond …*the largest community of Gypsies of any country…*

gyrate = <u>rotate</u>, circle, spin, spiral, revolve, whirl, twirl, pirouette

H h

habit 1 = <u>mannerism</u>, custom, way, practice, manner, characteristic, tendency, quirk, propensity, foible, proclivity …*He has an endearing habit of licking his lips*…
2 = <u>custom</u>, rule, practice, tradition, routine, convention, mode, usage, wont, second nature …*It had become a habit with her to annoy him*…
3 = <u>addiction</u>, weakness, obsession, dependence, compulsion, fixation …*After twenty years as a chain smoker, he has given up the habit*…
4 = <u>dress</u>, costume, garment, apparel, garb, habiliment, riding dress …*She emerged having changed into her riding habit*…

habitat = <u>home</u>, environment, surroundings, element, territory, domain, terrain, locality, home ground, abode, habitation, natural home

habitation 1 = <u>occupation</u>, living in, residence, tenancy, occupancy, residency, inhabitance, inhabitancy …*20 percent of private-rented dwellings are unfit for human habitation*…
2 (*Formal*) = <u>dwelling</u>, home, house, residence, quarters, lodging, pad (*slang*), abode, living quarters, domicile, dwelling house …*Behind the habitations, the sandstone cliffs rose abruptly*…

habitual 1 = <u>customary</u>, normal, usual, common, standard, natural, traditional, fixed, regular, ordinary, familiar, routine, accustomed, wonted …*He soon recovered his habitual geniality*… |OPPOSITE⟩ unusual
2 = <u>persistent</u>, established, confirmed, constant, frequent, chronic, hardened, recurrent, ingrained, inveterate …*three out of four of them would become habitual criminals*… |OPPOSITE⟩ occasional

hack¹ |VERB| 1 = <u>cut</u>, chop, slash, mutilate, mangle, mangulate (*Austral. slang*), gash, hew, lacerate …*He desperately hacked through the undergrowth*… …*Some were hacked to death with machetes*…
2 (*Informal*) = <u>cough</u>, bark, wheeze, rasp …*The patients splutter and hack*…
|NOUN| (*Informal*) = <u>cough</u>, bark, wheeze, rasp …*smoker's hack*…

hack² |NOUN| 1 = <u>reporter</u>, writer, correspondent, journalist, scribbler, contributor, literary hack, penny-a-liner, Grub Street writer …*tabloid hacks, always eager to find victims*…
2 = <u>yes-man</u>, lackey, toady, flunky …*Party hacks from the old days still hold influential jobs*…
|ADJECTIVE| = <u>unoriginal</u>, pedestrian, mediocre, poor, tired, stereotyped, banal, undistinguished, uninspired …*ill-paid lectureships and hack writing*…

hackles
|PHRASES| **raise someone's hackles** *or* **make someone's hackles rise** = <u>anger</u>, annoy, infuriate, cause resentment, rub someone up the wrong way, make someone see red (*informal*), get someone's dander up (*slang*)

hackneyed = <u>clichéd</u>, stock, tired, common, stereotyped, pedestrian, played out (*informal*), commonplace, worn-out, stale, overworked, banal, run-of-the-mill, threadbare, trite, unoriginal, timeworn |OPPOSITE⟩ original

Hades = <u>underworld</u>, hell, nether regions, lower world, infernal regions, realm of Pluto, (the) inferno

hag = <u>witch</u>, virago, shrew, vixen, crone, fury, harridan, beldam (*archaic*), termagant

haggard = <u>gaunt</u>, wasted, drawn, thin, pinched, wrinkled, ghastly, wan, emaciated, shrunken, careworn, hollow-eyed |OPPOSITE⟩ robust

haggle 1 = <u>bargain</u>, barter, beat down, drive a hard bargain, dicker (*chiefly U.S.*), chaffer, palter, higgle …*Ella taught her how to haggle with used furniture dealers*…
2 = <u>wrangle</u>, dispute, quarrel, squabble, bicker …*As the politicians haggle, the violence worsens*…

hail¹ |VERB| 1 = <u>acclaim</u>, honour, acknowledge, cheer, applaud, glorify, exalt …*hailed as the greatest American novelist of his generation*… |OPPOSITE⟩ condemn
2 = <u>salute</u>, call, greet, address, welcome, speak to, shout to, say hello to, accost, sing out, halloo …*I saw him and hailed him*… |OPPOSITE⟩ snub
3 = <u>flag down</u>, summon, signal to, wave down …*I hurried away to hail a taxi*…
|PHRASES| **hail from somewhere** = <u>come from</u>, be in, originate in, be a native of, have your roots in …*The band hail from Glasgow*…

hail² |NOUN| 1 = <u>hailstones</u>, sleet, hailstorm, frozen rain …*a short-lived storm with heavy hail*…
2 = <u>shower</u>, rain, storm, battery, volley, barrage, bombardment, pelting, downpour, salvo, broadside …*The victim was hit by a hail of bullets*…
|VERB| 1 = <u>shower</u>, rain, pelt …*It started to hail, huge great stones*…
2 = <u>rain</u>, batter, barrage, bombard, pelt, rain down on, beat down upon …*Shellfire was hailing down on the city's edge*…

hair |NOUN| = <u>locks</u>, mane, tresses, shock, mop, head of hair …*a girl with long blonde hair*…
|PHRASES| **let your hair down** = <u>let yourself go</u>, relax, chill out (*slang, chiefly U.S.*), let off steam (*informal*), let it all hang out (*informal*), mellow out (*informal*), veg out (*slang, chiefly U.S.*), outspan (*S. African*) …*a time when everyone really lets their hair down*… ♦ **not turn a hair** = <u>remain calm</u>, keep your cool (*slang*), not bat an eyelid, keep your hair on (*Brit. informal*) …*The man didn't turn a hair*… ♦ **split hairs** = <u>quibble</u>, find fault, cavil, overrefine, pettifog …*Don't split hairs. You know what I'm getting at*…

hairdresser = <u>stylist</u>, barber, coiffeur *or* coiffeuse, friseur

hairless = <u>bare</u>, bald, clean-shaven, shorn, beardless, tonsured, depilated, baldheaded, glabrous *or* glabrate (*Biology*)

hair-raising = <u>frightening</u>, shocking, alarming, thrilling, exciting, terrifying, startling, horrifying, scary, breathtaking, creepy, petrifying, spine-chilling, bloodcurdling

hairstyle = <u>haircut</u>, hairdo, coiffure, cut, style

hairy 1 = <u>shaggy</u>, woolly, furry, stubbly, bushy, bearded, unshaven, hirsute, fleecy, bewhiskered, pileous (*Biology*), pilose (*Biology*) ...*I don't mind having a hairy chest, but the stuff on my back is really thick...*
2 (*Slang*) = <u>dangerous</u>, scary, risky, unpredictable, hazardous, perilous ...*His driving was a bit hairy...*

halcyon 1 = <u>happy</u>, golden, flourishing, prosperous, carefree, palmy ...*It was all a far cry from those halcyon days in 1990...*
2 = <u>peaceful</u>, still, quiet, calm, gentle, mild, serene, tranquil, placid, pacific, undisturbed, unruffled ...*The next day dawned sunny with a halcyon blue sky...*

hale (*Old-fashioned*) = <u>healthy</u>, well, strong, sound, fit, flourishing, blooming, robust, vigorous, hearty, in the pink, in fine fettle, right as rain (*Brit. informal*), able-bodied

half NOUN = <u>fifty per cent</u>, equal part ...*A half of the voters have not made up their minds...*
ADJECTIVE = <u>partial</u>, limited, fractional, divided, moderate, halved, incomplete ...*Children received only a half portion...*
ADVERB = <u>partially</u>, partly, incompletely, slightly, all but, barely, in part, inadequately, after a fashion, pretty nearly ...*The vegetables are only half cooked...*
PHRASES **by halves** = <u>incompletely</u>, inadequately, insufficiently, imperfectly, to a limited extent, skimpily, scrappily ...*They rarely do things by halves...*
(*Related Words*)
prefixes: bi-, hemi-, demi-, semi-

half-baked (*Informal*) = <u>stupid</u>, impractical, crazy, silly, foolish, senseless, short-sighted, inane, loopy (*informal*), ill-conceived, crackpot (*informal*), ill-judged, brainless, unformed, poorly planned, harebrained, dumb-ass (*slang*), unthought out *or* through

half-hearted = <u>unenthusiastic</u>, indifferent, apathetic, cool, neutral, passive, lacklustre, lukewarm, uninterested, perfunctory, listless, spiritless OPPOSITE enthusiastic

halfway ADVERB 1 = <u>midway</u>, to the midpoint, to *or* in the middle ...*He was halfway up the ladder...*
2 (*Informal*) = <u>partially</u>, partly, moderately, rather, nearly ...*You need hard currency to get anything halfway decent...*
ADJECTIVE = <u>midway</u>, middle, mid, central, intermediate, equidistant ...*He was third fastest at the halfway point...*
PHRASES **meet someone halfway** = <u>compromise</u>, accommodate, come to terms, reach a compromise, strike a balance, trade off with, find the middle

ground ...*The Democrats are willing to meet the president halfway...*

hall 1 = <u>passage</u>, lobby, corridor, hallway, foyer, entry, passageway, entrance hall, vestibule ...*The lights were on in the hall and in the bedroom...*
2 = <u>meeting place</u>, chamber, auditorium, concert hall, assembly room ...*We filed into the lecture hall...*

hallmark 1 = <u>trademark</u>, indication, badge, emblem, sure sign, telltale sign ...*a technique that has become the hallmark of their films...*
2 (*Brit.*) = <u>mark</u>, sign, device, stamp, seal, symbol, signet, authentication ...*He uses a hallmark on the base of his lamps to distinguish them...*

hallowed = <u>sanctified</u>, holy, blessed, sacred, honoured, dedicated, revered, consecrated, sacrosanct, inviolable, beatified

hallucinate = <u>imagine</u>, trip (*informal*), envision, daydream, fantasize, freak out (*informal*), have hallucinations

hallucination = <u>illusion</u>, dream, vision, fantasy, delusion, mirage, apparition, phantasmagoria, figment of the imagination

hallucinogenic = <u>psychedelic</u>, mind-blowing (*informal*), psychoactive, hallucinatory, psychotropic, mind-expanding

halo = <u>ring of light</u>, aura, corona, radiance, nimbus, halation (*Photography*), aureole *or* aureola

halt VERB 1 = <u>stop</u>, draw up, pull up, break off, stand still, wait, rest, call it a day, belay (*Nautical*) ...*They halted at a short distance from the house...* OPPOSITE continue
2 = <u>come to an end</u>, stop, cease ...*The flow of assistance to refugees has virtually halted...*
3 = <u>hold back</u>, end, check, block, arrest, stem, curb, terminate, obstruct, staunch, cut short, impede, bring to an end, stem the flow, nip in the bud ...*Striking workers halted production at the auto plant yesterday...* OPPOSITE aid
NOUN = <u>stop</u>, end, close, break, stand, arrest, pause, interruption, impasse, standstill, stoppage, termination ...*Air traffic has been brought to a halt...* OPPOSITE continuation

halting = <u>faltering</u>, stumbling, awkward, hesitant, laboured, stammering, imperfect, stuttering

halve 1 = <u>cut in half</u>, reduce by fifty per cent, decrease by fifty per cent, lessen by fifty per cent ...*The work force has been halved in two years...*
2 = <u>split in two</u>, cut in half, bisect, divide in two, share equally, divide equally ...*Halve the pineapple and scoop out the inside...*

hammer VERB 1 = <u>hit</u>, drive, knock, beat, strike, tap, bang ...*Hammer a wooden peg into the hole...*
2 often with *into* = <u>impress upon</u>, repeat, drive home, drum into, grind into, din into, drub into ...*He hammered it into me that I had not become a rotten goalkeeper...*
3 (*Informal*) = <u>defeat</u>, beat, thrash, stuff (*slang*), master, worst, tank (*slang*), lick (*informal*), slate (*informal*), trounce, clobber (*slang*), run rings around (*informal*), wipe the floor with (*informal*), blow out of

the water (*slang*), drub …*He hammered the young left-hander in four straight sets…*

PHRASES **hammer away at something** = <u>work</u>, keep on, persevere, grind, persist, stick at, plug away (*informal*), drudge, pound away, peg away (*chiefly Brit.*), beaver away (*Brit. informal*) …*Palmer kept hammering away at his report…* ◆ **hammer something out** = <u>work out</u>, produce, finish, complete, settle, negotiate, accomplish, sort out, bring about, make a decision, thrash out, come to a conclusion, form a resolution, excogitate …*I think we can hammer out a solution…*

hamper = <u>hinder</u>, handicap, hold up, prevent, restrict, frustrate, curb, slow down, restrain, hamstring, interfere with, cramp, thwart, obstruct, impede, hobble, fetter, encumber, trammel OPPOSITE> help

hamstring = <u>thwart</u>, stop, block, prevent, ruin, frustrate, handicap, curb, foil, obstruct, impede, balk, fetter

hamstrung = <u>incapacitated</u>, disabled, crippled, helpless, paralysed, at a loss, hors de combat (*French*)

hand NOUN 1 = <u>palm</u>, fist, paw (*informal*), mitt (*slang*), hook, meathook (*slang*) …*I put my hand into my pocket…*
2 = <u>influence</u>, part, share, agency, direction, participation …*Did you have a hand in his downfall?…*
3 = <u>assistance</u>, help, aid, support, helping hand …*Come and give me a hand in the garden…*
4 = <u>worker</u>, employee, labourer, workman, operative, craftsman, artisan, hired man, hireling …*He now works as a farm hand…*
5 = <u>round of applause</u>, clap, ovation, big hand …*Let's give 'em a big hand…*
6 = <u>writing</u>, script, handwriting, calligraphy, longhand, penmanship, chirography …*written in the composer's own hand…*
PLURAL NOUN = <u>control</u>, charge, care, keeping, power, authority, command, possession, custody, disposal, supervision, guardianship …*He is leaving his business in the hands of a colleague…*
VERB 1 = <u>give</u>, pass, hand over, present to, deliver …*He handed me a little rectangle of white paper…*
2 = <u>help</u>, guide, conduct, lead, aid, assist, convey …*He handed her into his old Alfa Romeo sports car…*
PHRASES **at hand** = <u>approaching</u>, near, imminent, just round the corner …*His retirement was at hand…* ◆ **at** *or* **on hand** = <u>within reach</u>, nearby, handy, close, available, ready, on tap (*informal*), at your fingertips …*Having the right equipment on hand is enormously helpful…* ◆ **hand in glove** = <u>in association</u>, in partnership, in league, in collaboration, in cooperation, in cahoots (*informal*) …*They work hand in glove with the western intelligence agencies…* ◆ **hand over fist** = <u>swiftly</u>, easily, steadily, by leaps and bounds …*Investors would lose money hand over fist if a demerger went ahead…* ◆ **hand something** *or* **someone over** 1 = <u>give</u>, present, deliver, donate …*He handed over a letter of apology…* 2 = <u>turn over</u>, release, transfer, deliver, yield, surrender …*The American was formally handed over to the ambassador…* ◆ **hand something down** = <u>pass</u>

on *or* <u>down</u>, pass, transfer, bequeath, will, give, grant, gift, endow …*a family heirloom handed down from generation to generation…* ◆ **hand something on** = <u>pass on</u> *or* down, pass, transfer, bequeath, will, give, grant, relinquish …*His chauffeur-driven car will be handed on to his successor…* ◆ **hands down** = <u>easily</u>, effortlessly, with ease, comfortably, without difficulty, with no trouble, standing on your head, with one hand tied behind your back, with no contest, with your eyes closed *or* shut …*We should have won hands down…* ◆ **in hand** 1 = <u>in reserve</u>, ready, put by, available for use …*I'll pay now as I have the money in hand…* 2 = <u>under control</u>, in order, receiving attention …*The organisers say that matters are well in hand…* ◆ **lay hands on someone** 1 = <u>attack</u>, assault, set on, beat up, work over (*slang*), lay into (*informal*) …*The crowd laid hands on him…* 2 = <u>bless</u> (*Christianity*), confirm, ordain, consecrate …*The bishop laid hands on the sick…* ◆ **lay hands on something** = <u>get hold of</u>, get, obtain, gain, grab, acquire, seize, grasp …*the ease with which prisoners can lay hands on drugs…*

(**Related Words**)
adjective : manual

handbook = <u>guidebook</u>, guide, manual, instruction book, Baedeker, vade mecum

handcuff VERB = <u>shackle</u>, secure, restrain, fetter, manacle …*They tried to handcuff him but he fought his way free…*
PLURAL NOUN = <u>shackles</u>, cuffs (*informal*), fetters, manacles, bracelets (*slang*) …*He was led away to jail in handcuffs…*

handful – <u>few</u>, sprinkling, small amount, small quantity, smattering, small number OPPOSITE> a lot

handgun = <u>pistol</u>, automatic, revolver, shooter (*informal*), piece (*U.S. slang*), rod (*U.S. slang*), derringer

handicap NOUN 1 = <u>disability</u>, defect, impairment, physical abnormality …*a child with a medically recognised handicap…*
2 = <u>disadvantage</u>, block, barrier, restriction, obstacle, limitation, hazard, drawback, shortcoming, stumbling block, impediment, albatross, hindrance, millstone, encumbrance …*Being a foreigner was not a handicap…* OPPOSITE> advantage
3 = <u>advantage</u>, penalty, head start …*I see your handicap is down from 16 to 12…*
VERB = <u>hinder</u>, limit, restrict, burden, hamstring, hamper, hold back, retard, impede, hobble, encumber, place at a disadvantage …*Greater levels of stress may seriously handicap some students…* OPPOSITE> help

handicraft = <u>skill</u>, art, craft, handiwork

handily 1 = <u>conveniently</u>, readily, suitably, helpfully, advantageously, accessibly …*He was handily placed to slip the ball home at the far post…*
2 = <u>skilfully</u>, expertly, cleverly, deftly, adroitly, capably, proficiently, dexterously …*In the November election Nixon won handily…*

handiwork = <u>creation</u>, product, production, achievement, result, design, invention, artefact, handicraft, handwork

handkerchief = <u>hanky</u>, tissue (*informal*), mouchoir, snot rag (*slang*), nose rag (*slang*)

handle NOUN = <u>grip</u>, knob, hilt, haft, stock, handgrip, helve …*The handle of a cricket bat protruded from under his arm…*
VERB **1** = <u>manage</u>, deal with, tackle, cope with …*I don't know if I can handle the job…*
2 = <u>deal with</u>, manage, take care of, administer, conduct, supervise …*She handled travel arrangements for the press corps…*
3 = <u>control</u>, manage, direct, operate, guide, use, steer, manipulate, manoeuvre, wield …*One report said the aircraft would become difficult to handle…*
4 = <u>hold</u>, feel, touch, pick up, finger, grasp, poke, paw (*informal*), maul, fondle …*Be careful when handling young animals…*
5 = <u>deal in</u>, market, sell, trade in, carry, stock, traffic in …*Japanese dealers won't handle US cars…*
6 = <u>discuss</u>, report, treat, review, tackle, examine, discourse on …*I think we should handle the story very sensitively…*
PHRASES **fly off the handle** (*Informal*) = <u>lose your temper</u>, explode, lose it (*informal*), lose the plot (*informal*), let fly (*informal*), go ballistic (*slang, chiefly U.S.*), fly into a rage, have a tantrum, wig out (*slang*), lose your cool (*slang*), blow your top, flip your lid (*slang*), hit *or* go through the roof (*informal*) …*He flew off the handle at the slightest thing…*

handling = <u>management</u>, running, treatment, approach, administration, conduct, manipulation

handout 1 *often plural* = <u>charity</u>, dole, alms …*They depended on handouts from the state…*
2 = <u>press release</u>, bulletin, circular, mailshot …*Official handouts described the couple as elated…*
3 = <u>leaflet</u>, literature (*informal*), bulletin, flyer, pamphlet, printed matter …*lectures, handouts, slides and videos…*
4 = <u>giveaway</u>, freebie (*informal*), free gift, free sample …*advertised with publicity handouts…*

hand-picked = <u>selected</u>, chosen, choice, select, elect, elite, recherché OPPOSITE random

handsome 1 = <u>good-looking</u>, attractive, gorgeous, fine, stunning, elegant, personable, nice-looking, dishy (*informal, chiefly Brit.*), comely, fanciable, well-proportioned …*a tall, dark, handsome farmer…* OPPOSITE ugly
2 = <u>generous</u>, large, princely, liberal, considerable, lavish, ample, abundant, plentiful, bountiful, sizable *or* sizeable …*They will make a handsome profit on the property…* OPPOSITE mean

handsomely = <u>generously</u>, amply, richly, liberally, lavishly, abundantly, plentifully, bountifully, munificently

handwriting = <u>writing</u>, hand, script, fist, scrawl, calligraphy, longhand, penmanship, chirography
Related Words
adjective: graphology

handy 1 = <u>useful</u>, practical, helpful, neat, convenient, easy to use, manageable, user-friendly, serviceable …*handy hints on looking after indoor plants… …a*

handy little device… OPPOSITE useless
2 = <u>convenient</u>, close, near, available, nearby, accessible, on hand, at hand, within reach, just round the corner, at your fingertips …*This lively town is handy for Londoners… …Keep a pencil and paper handy…* OPPOSITE inconvenient
3 = <u>skilful</u>, skilled, expert, clever, adept, ready, deft, nimble, proficient, adroit, dexterous …*Are you handy with a needle?…* OPPOSITE unskilled

handyman = <u>odd-jobman</u>, jack-of-all-trades, handy Andy (*informal*), DIY expert

hang VERB **1** = <u>dangle</u>, swing, suspend, be pendent …*I was left hanging by my fingertips…*
2 = <u>lower</u>, suspend, dangle, let down, let droop …*I hung the sheet out of the window at 6am…*
3 = <u>lean</u>, incline, loll, bend forward, bow, bend downward …*He hung over the railing and kicked out with his feet…*
4 = <u>droop</u>, drop, dangle, trail, sag …*the shawl hanging loose from her shoulders…*
5 = <u>decorate</u>, cover, fix, attach, deck, furnish, drape, fasten …*The walls were hung with huge modern paintings…*
6 = <u>execute</u>, lynch, string up (*informal*), gibbet, send to the gallows …*The five were expected to be hanged at 7 am on Tuesday…*
7 = <u>hover</u>, float, drift, linger, remain …*A haze of expensive perfume hangs around her…*
PHRASES **get the hang of something** = <u>grasp</u>, understand, learn, master, comprehend, catch on to, acquire the technique of, get the knack *or* technique …*It's a bit tricky at first till you get the hang of it…*
◆ **hang about** *or* **around** = <u>loiter</u>, frequent, haunt, linger, roam, loaf, waste time, dally, dawdle, skulk, tarry, dilly-dally (*informal*) …*On Saturdays we hang about in the park…* ◆ **hang around with someone** = <u>associate</u>, go around with, mix, hang (*informal, chiefly U.S.*), hang out (*informal*) …*She used to hang around with the boys…* ◆ **hang back** = <u>be reluctant</u>, hesitate, hold back, recoil, demur, be backward …*His closest advisors believe he should hang back no longer…* ◆ **hang fire** = <u>put off</u>, delay, stall, be slow, vacillate, hang back, procrastinate …*I've got to hang fire on that one…* ◆ **hang on** (*Informal*) **1** = <u>wait</u>, stop, hold on, hold the line, remain …*Hang on a sec. I'll come with you…* **2** = <u>continue</u>, remain, go on, carry on, endure, hold on, persist, hold out, persevere, stay the course …*Manchester United hung on to take the Cup…* **3** = <u>grasp</u>, grip, clutch, cling, hold fast …*He hangs on tightly, his arms around my neck…* ◆ **hang on** *or* **upon something 1** = <u>depend</u>, turn, rest, be subject to, hinge, be determined by, be dependent, be conditional, be contingent …*Much hangs on the success of the collaboration…* **2** = <u>listen attentively to</u>, pay attention to, be rapt, give ear to …*a man who knew his listeners were hanging on his every word…* ◆ **hang onto something 1** = <u>retain</u>, keep, maintain, preserve, hold onto, keep possession of …*The President has been trying hard to hang onto power…* **2** = <u>grip</u>, seize, grasp, clutch, hold onto, take hold of, latch onto, hold tightly …*hanging onto his*

legs... ◆ **hang over something** or **someone** = loom, threaten, menace, impend ...*A question mark hangs over many of their futures...*

hanger-on = parasite, follower, cohort (*chiefly U.S.*), leech, dependant, minion, lackey, sycophant, freeloader (*slang*), sponger (*informal*), ligger (*slang*), quandong (*Austral. slang*)

hanging = suspended, swinging, dangling, loose, flopping, flapping, floppy, drooping, unattached, unsupported, pendent

hangout = haunt, joint (*slang*), resort, dive (*slang*), den

hangover = aftereffects, morning after (*informal*), head (*informal*), crapulence

hang-up (*Informal*) = preoccupation, thing (*informal*), problem, block, difficulty, obsession, mania, inhibition, phobia, fixation

hank = coil, roll, length, bunch, piece, loop, clump, skein

hanker after or **for** = desire, want, long for, hope for, crave, covet, wish for, yearn for, pine for, lust after, eat your heart out, ache for, yen for (*informal*), itch for, set your heart on, hunger for or after, thirst for or after

hankering = desire, longing, wish, hope, urge, yen (*informal*), pining, hunger, ache, craving, yearning, itch, thirst

haphazard 1 = unsystematic, disorderly, disorganized, casual, careless, indiscriminate, aimless, slapdash, slipshod, hit or miss (*informal*), unmethodical ...*The investigation does seem haphazard...* [OPPOSITE] systematic
2 = random, chance, accidental, arbitrary, fluky (*informal*) ...*She was trying to connect her life's seemingly haphazard events...* [OPPOSITE] planned

hapless = unlucky, unfortunate, cursed, unhappy, miserable, jinxed, luckless, wretched, ill-starred, ill-fated

happen [VERB] 1 = occur, take place, come about, follow, result, appear, develop, arise, come off (*informal*), ensue, crop up (*informal*), transpire (*informal*), materialize, present itself, come to pass, see the light of day, eventuate ...*We cannot say for sure what will happen...*
2 = chance, turn out (*informal*), have the fortune to be ...*I looked in the nearest paper, which happened to be the Daily Mail...*
3 = befall, overtake, become of, betide ...*It's the best thing that ever happened to me...*
[PHRASES] **happen on** or **upon something** = find, encounter, run into, come upon, turn up, stumble on, hit upon, chance upon, light upon, blunder on, discover unexpectedly ...*He just happened upon a charming guest house...*

happening = event, incident, occasion, case, experience, chance, affair, scene, accident, proceeding, episode, adventure, phenomenon, occurrence, escapade

happily 1 = luckily, fortunately, providentially, favourably, auspiciously, opportunely, propitiously,

seasonably ...*Happily, his neck injuries were not serious...*
2 = joyfully, cheerfully, gleefully, blithely, merrily, gaily, joyously, delightedly ...*Albert leaned back happily and lit a cigarette...*
3 = willingly, freely, gladly, enthusiastically, heartily, with pleasure, contentedly, lief (*rare*) ...*If I've caused any offence, I will happily apologise...*

happiness = pleasure, delight, joy, cheer, satisfaction, prosperity, ecstasy, enjoyment, bliss, felicity, exuberance, contentment, wellbeing, high spirits, elation, gaiety, jubilation, merriment, cheerfulness, gladness, beatitude, cheeriness, blessedness, light-heartedness [OPPOSITE] unhappiness

happy 1 = pleased, delighted, content, contented, thrilled, glad, blessed, blest, sunny, cheerful, jolly, merry, ecstatic, gratified, jubilant, joyous, joyful, elated, over the moon (*informal*), overjoyed, blissful, rapt, blithe, on cloud nine (*informal*), cock-a-hoop, walking on air (*informal*), floating on air ...*I'm just happy to be back running...*
2 = contented, blessed, blest, joyful, blissful, blithe ...*We have a very happy marriage...* [OPPOSITE] sad
3 = fortunate, lucky, timely, appropriate, convenient, favourable, auspicious, propitious, apt, befitting, advantageous, well-timed, opportune, felicitous, seasonable ...*a happy coincidence...* [OPPOSITE] unfortunate

happy-go-lucky = carefree, casual, easy-going, irresponsible, unconcerned, untroubled, nonchalant, blithe, heedless, insouciant, devil-may-care, improvident, light-hearted [OPPOSITE] serious

harangue [VERB] = rant at, address, lecture, exhort, preach to, declaim, hold forth, spout at (*informal*) ...*haranguing her furiously in words she didn't understand...*
[NOUN] = rant, address, speech, lecture, tirade, polemic, broadside, diatribe, homily, exhortation, oration, spiel (*informal*), declamation, philippic ...*a political harangue...*

harass = annoy, trouble, bother, worry, harry, disturb, devil (*informal*), plague, bait, hound, torment, hassle (*informal*), badger, persecute, exasperate, pester, vex, breathe down someone's neck, chivvy (*Brit.*), give someone grief (*Brit. & S. African*), be on your back (*slang*), beleaguer

harassed = hassled, worried, troubled, strained, harried, under pressure, plagued, tormented, distraught (*informal*), vexed, under stress, careworn

harassment = hassle, trouble, bother, grief (*informal*), torment, irritation, persecution (*informal*), nuisance, badgering, annoyance, pestering, aggravation (*informal*), molestation, vexation, bedevilment

harbinger (*Literary*) = sign, indication, herald, messenger, omen, precursor, forerunner, portent, foretoken

harbour [NOUN] 1 = port, haven, dock, mooring, marina, pier, wharf, anchorage, jetty, pontoon, slipway

...The ship was allowed to tie up in the harbour...
2 = <u>sanctuary</u>, haven, shelter, retreat, asylum, refuge, oasis, covert, safe haven, sanctum *...a safe harbour for music rejected by the mainstream...*
VERB 1 = <u>hold</u>, bear, maintain, nurse, retain, foster, entertain, nurture, cling to, cherish, brood over *...He might have been murdered by someone harbouring a grudge...*
2 = <u>shelter</u>, protect, hide, relieve, lodge, shield, conceal, secrete, provide refuge, give asylum to *...harbouring terrorist suspects...*

hard ADJECTIVE **1** = <u>tough</u>, strong, firm, solid, stiff, compact, rigid, resistant, dense, compressed, stony, impenetrable, inflexible, unyielding, rocklike *...He stamped his feet on the hard floor...* OPPOSITE soft
2 = <u>difficult</u>, involved, complex, complicated, puzzling, tangled, baffling, intricate, perplexing, impenetrable, thorny, knotty, unfathomable, ticklish *...That's a very hard question...* OPPOSITE easy
3 = <u>exhausting</u>, tough, exacting, formidable, fatiguing, wearying, rigorous, uphill, gruelling, strenuous, arduous, laborious, burdensome, Herculean, backbreaking, toilsome *...Coping with three babies is very hard work...* OPPOSITE easy
4 = <u>forceful</u>, strong, powerful, driving, heavy, sharp, violent, smart, tremendous, fierce, vigorous, hefty *...He gave her a hard push which toppled her backwards...*
5 = <u>harsh</u>, severe, strict, cold, exacting, cruel, grim, stern, ruthless, stubborn, unjust, callous, unkind, unrelenting, implacable, unsympathetic, pitiless, unfeeling, obdurate, unsparing, affectless, hardhearted *...His father was a hard man...* OPPOSITE kind
6 = <u>grim</u>, dark, painful, distressing, harsh, disastrous, unpleasant, intolerable, grievous, disagreeable, calamitous *...Those were hard times...*
7 = <u>definite</u>, reliable, verified, cold, plain, actual, bare, undeniable, indisputable, verifiable, unquestionable, unvarnished *...He wanted more hard evidence...*
8 = <u>bitter</u>, angry, hostile, resentful, acrimonious, embittered, antagonistic, rancorous *...I struck him, and dismissed him with hard words...*
ADVERB 1 = <u>strenuously</u>, steadily, persistently, earnestly, determinedly, doggedly, diligently, energetically, assiduously, industriously, untiringly *...I'll work hard. I don't want to let him down...*
2 = <u>intently</u>, closely, carefully, sharply, keenly *...You had to listen hard to hear him...*
3 = <u>forcefully</u>, strongly, heavily, sharply, severely, fiercely, vigorously, intensely, violently, powerfully, forcibly, with all your might, with might and main *...I kicked a dustbin very hard and broke my toe...* OPPOSITE softly
4 = <u>with difficulty</u>, painfully, laboriously *...the hard won rights of the working woman...*

hard-bitten (*Informal*) = <u>tough</u>, realistic, cynical, practical, shrewd, down-to-earth, matter-of-fact, hard-nosed (*informal*), hard-headed, unsentimental, hard-boiled (*informal*), case-hardened, badass (*slang, chiefly U.S.*) OPPOSITE idealistic

hard-boiled = <u>tough</u> (*Informal*), practical, realistic, cynical, shrewd, down-to-earth, matter-of-fact, hard-nosed (*informal*), hard-headed, unsentimental, case-hardened, badass (*slang, chiefly U.S.*) OPPOSITE idealistic
hard-core 1 = <u>dyed-in-the-wool</u>, extreme, dedicated, rigid, staunch, die-hard, steadfast, obstinate, intransigent *...a hard-core group of right-wing senators...*
2 = <u>explicit</u>, obscene, pornographic, X-rated (*informal*) *...jailed for peddling hard-core porn videos through the post...*
harden 1 = <u>solidify</u>, set, freeze, cake, bake, clot, thicken, stiffen, crystallize, congeal, coagulate, anneal *...Mould the mixture into shape before it hardens...*
2 = <u>accustom</u>, season, toughen, train, brutalize, inure, habituate, case-harden *...hardened by the rigours of the Siberian steppes...*
3 = <u>reinforce</u>, strengthen, fortify, steel, nerve, brace, toughen, buttress, gird, indurate *...Their action can only serve to harden the attitude of landowners...*
hardened 1 = <u>habitual</u>, set, fixed, chronic, shameless, inveterate, incorrigible, reprobate, irredeemable, badass (*slang, chiefly U.S.*) *...hardened criminals...* OPPOSITE occasional
2 = <u>seasoned</u>, experienced, accustomed, toughened, inured, habituated *...hardened politicians...* OPPOSITE naive
hard-headed = <u>shrewd</u>, tough, practical, cool, sensible, realistic, pragmatic, astute, hard-boiled (*informal*), hard-bitten, level-headed, unsentimental, badass (*slang, chiefly U.S.*) OPPOSITE idealistic
hard-hearted = <u>unsympathetic</u>, hard, cold, cruel, indifferent, insensitive, callous, stony, unkind, heartless, inhuman, merciless, intolerant, uncaring, pitiless, unfeeling, unforgiving, hard as nails, affectless OPPOSITE kind
hardly 1 = <u>barely</u>, only just, scarcely, just, faintly, with difficulty, infrequently, with effort, at a push (*Brit. informal*), almost not *...Nick, on the sofa, hardly slept...* OPPOSITE completely
2 = <u>only just</u>, just, only, barely, not quite, scarcely *...I could hardly see the garden for the fog...*
3 = <u>not at all</u>, not, no way, by no means *...It's hardly surprising his ideas didn't catch on...*
➤ **scarcely**
hard-nosed = <u>tough</u> (*Informal*), practical, realistic, shrewd, pragmatic, down-to-earth, hardline, uncompromising, businesslike, hard-headed, unsentimental, badass (*slang, chiefly U.S.*)
hard-pressed ADJECTIVE **1** = <u>under pressure</u>, pushed (*informal*), harried, in difficulties, up against it (*informal*), with your back to the wall *...Hard-pressed consumers are spending less on luxuries...*
2 = <u>pushed</u> (*informal*), in difficulties, up against it (*informal*) *...This year the airline will be hard-pressed to make a profit...*
hardship = <u>suffering</u>, want, need, trouble, trial, difficulty, burden, misery, torment, oppression, persecution, grievance, misfortune, austerity,

adversity, calamity, affliction, tribulation, privation, destitution OPPOSITE> ease

hard up = <u>poor</u>, broke (*informal*), short, bust (*informal*), bankrupt, impoverished, in the red (*informal*), cleaned out (*slang*), penniless, out of pocket, down and out, skint (*Brit. slang*), strapped for cash (*informal*), impecunious, dirt-poor (*informal*), on the breadline, flat broke (*informal*), on your uppers (*informal*), in queer street, without two pennies to rub together (*informal*), short of cash *or* funds OPPOSITE> wealthy

hardy 1 = <u>strong</u>, tough, robust, sound, fit, healthy, vigorous, rugged, sturdy, hale, stout, stalwart, hearty, lusty, in fine fettle ...*They grew up to be farmers, round-faced and hardy*... OPPOSITE> frail
2 = <u>courageous</u>, brave, daring, bold, heroic, manly, gritty, feisty (*informal, chiefly U.S. & Canad.*), resolute, intrepid, valiant, plucky, valorous, stouthearted ...*A few hardy souls leapt into the encircling seas*... OPPOSITE> feeble

hare
(*Related Words*)
adjective: leporine
male: buck
female: doe
young: leveret
habitation: down, husk
➤ **rabbits and hares**

harem = <u>women's quarters</u>, seraglio, zenana (*in eastern countries*), gynaeceum (*in ancient Greece*)

hark VERB (*Old-fashioned*) = <u>listen</u>, attend, pay attention, hearken (*archaic*), give ear, hear, mark, notice, give heed ...*Hark. I hear the returning footsteps of my love*...
PHRASES **hark back to something 1** = <u>recall</u>, recollect, call to mind, cause you to remember, cause you to recollect ...*pitched roofs, which hark back to the Victorian era*... **2** = <u>return to</u>, remember, recall, revert to, look back to, think back to, recollect, regress to ...*The result devastated me at the time. Even now I hark back to it*...

harlot (*Literary*) = <u>prostitute</u>, tart (*informal*), whore, slag, pro (*slang*), tramp (*slang*) (*Brit. slang*), call girl, working girl (*facetious slang*), slapper (*Brit. slang*), hussy, streetwalker, loose woman, fallen woman, scrubber (*Brit. & Austral. slang*), strumpet

harm VERB **1** = <u>injure</u>, hurt, wound, abuse, molest, ill-treat, maltreat, lay a finger on, ill-use ...*The hijackers seemed anxious not to harm anyone*... OPPOSITE> heal
2 = <u>damage</u>, hurt, ruin, mar, spoil, impair, blemish ...*a warning that the product may harm the environment*...
NOUN **1** = <u>injury</u>, suffering, damage, ill, hurt, distress ...*a release of radioactivity which would cause harm*...
2 = <u>damage</u>, loss, ill, hurt, misfortune, mischief, detriment, impairment, disservice ...*It would probably do the economy more harm than good*... OPPOSITE> good
3 = <u>sin</u>, wrong, evil, wickedness, immorality, iniquity, sinfulness, vice ...*There was no harm in keeping the money*... OPPOSITE> goodness

harmful = <u>damaging</u>, dangerous, negative, evil, destructive, hazardous, unhealthy, detrimental, hurtful, pernicious, noxious, baleful, deleterious, injurious, unwholesome, disadvantageous, baneful, maleficent OPPOSITE> harmless

harmless 1 = <u>safe</u>, benign, wholesome, innocuous, not dangerous, nontoxic, innoxious ...*working at developing harmless substitutes for these gases*... OPPOSITE> dangerous
2 = <u>inoffensive</u>, innocent, innocuous, gentle, tame, unobjectionable ...*He seemed harmless enough*...

harmonious 1 = <u>friendly</u>, amicable, cordial, sympathetic, compatible, agreeable, in harmony, in unison, fraternal, congenial, in accord, concordant, of one mind, en rapport (*French*) ...*the most harmonious European Community summit for some time*... OPPOSITE> unfriendly
2 = <u>compatible</u>, matching, coordinated, correspondent, agreeable, consistent, consonant, congruous ...*a harmonious blend of colours*... OPPOSITE> incompatible
3 = <u>melodious</u>, musical, harmonic, harmonizing, tuneful, concordant, mellifluous, dulcet, sweet-sounding, euphonious, euphonic, symphonious (*literary*) ...*producing harmonious sounds*... OPPOSITE> discordant

harmonize VERB = <u>match</u>, accord, suit, blend, correspond, tally, chime, coordinate, go together, tone in, cohere, attune, be of one mind, be in unison ...*The music had to harmonize with the seasons*...
VERB = <u>coordinate</u>, match, agree, blend, tally, reconcile, attune ...*members have progressed towards harmonizing their economies*...

harmony 1 = <u>accord</u>, order, understanding, peace, agreement, friendship, unity, sympathy, consensus, cooperation, goodwill, rapport, conformity, compatibility, assent, unanimity, concord, amity, amicability, like-mindedness ...*a future in which humans live in harmony with nature*... OPPOSITE> conflict
2 = <u>tune</u>, melody, unison, tunefulness, euphony, melodiousness ...*singing in harmony*... OPPOSITE> discord
3 = <u>balance</u>, consistency, fitness, correspondence, coordination, symmetry, compatibility, suitability, concord, parallelism, consonance, congruity ...*the ordered harmony of the universe*... OPPOSITE> incongruity

harness VERB **1** = <u>exploit</u>, control, channel, apply, employ, utilize, mobilize, make productive, turn to account, render useful ...*the movement's ability to harness the anger of all Ukrainians*...
2 = <u>put in harness</u>, couple, saddle, yoke, hitch up ...*the horses were harnessed to a heavy wagon*...
NOUN = <u>equipment</u>, tackle, gear, tack, trappings ...*Always check that the straps of the harness are properly adjusted*...
PHRASES **in harness 1** = <u>working</u>, together, in a team ...*At Opera North he will be in harness with Paul Daniel*... **2** = <u>at work</u>, working, employed, active, busy, in action ...*The longing for work will return and you*

will be right back in harness...

harp on = <u>go on</u>, reiterate, dwell on, labour, press, repeat, rub in

harried = <u>harassed</u>, worried, troubled, bothered, anxious, distressed, plagued, tormented, hassled (*informal*), agitated, beset, hard-pressed, hag-ridden

harrowing = <u>distressing</u>, disturbing, alarming, frightening, painful, terrifying, chilling, traumatic, tormenting, heartbreaking, excruciating, agonizing, nerve-racking, heart-rending, gut-wrenching

harry = <u>pester</u>, trouble, bother, disturb, worry, annoy, plague, tease, torment, harass, hassle (*informal*), badger, persecute, molest, vex, bedevil, breathe down someone's neck, chivvy, give someone grief (*Brit. & S. African*), be on your back (*slang*), get in your hair (*informal*)

harsh 1 = <u>severe</u>, hard, tough, grim, stark, stringent, austere, Spartan, inhospitable, comfortless ...*Hundreds of political detainees were held under harsh conditions...*
2 = <u>bleak</u>, cold, freezing, severe, bitter, icy ...*The weather grew harsh and unpredictable...*
3 = <u>cruel</u>, savage, brutal, ruthless, relentless, unrelenting, barbarous, pitiless ...*the harsh experience of war...*
4 = <u>hard</u>, sharp, severe, bitter, cruel, stern, unpleasant, abusive, unkind, pitiless, unfeeling ...*He said many harsh and unkind things...* OPPOSITE kind
5 = <u>drastic</u>, hard, severe, stringent, punitive, austere, Draconian, punitory ...*more harsh laws governing the behaviour, status and even clothes of women...*
6 = <u>raucous</u>, rough, jarring, grating, strident, rasping, discordant, croaking, guttural, dissonant, unmelodious ...*It's a pity she has such a loud harsh voice...* OPPOSITE soft

harshly = <u>severely</u>, roughly, cruelly, strictly, grimly, sternly, brutally

harshness = <u>bitterness</u>, acrimony, ill-temper, sourness, asperity, acerbity

harvest NOUN 1 = <u>harvesting</u>, picking, gathering, collecting, reaping, harvest-time ...*300 million tons of grain in the fields at the start of the harvest...*
2 = <u>crop</u>, yield, year's growth, produce ...*a bumper potato harvest...*
VERB 1 = <u>gather</u>, pick, collect, bring in, pluck, reap ...*Many farmers are refusing to harvest the sugar cane...*
2 = <u>collect</u>, get, gain, earn, obtain, acquire, accumulate, garner, amass ...*In his new career he has blossomed and harvested many awards...*

hash
PHRASES **make a hash of something** (*Informal*) = <u>mess up</u>, muddle, bungle, botch, cock up (*Brit. slang*), mishandle, mismanage, make a nonsense of (*informal*), bodge (*informal*), make a pig's ear of (*informal*), flub (*U.S. slang*)

hassle (*Informal*) NOUN = <u>trouble</u>, problem, difficulty, upset, bother, grief (*informal*), trial, struggle, uphill (*S. African*), inconvenience ...*I don't think it's worth the money or the hassle...*

VERB = <u>bother</u>, bug (*informal*), annoy, harry, hound, harass, badger, pester, get on your nerves (*informal*), be on your back (*slang*), get in your hair (*informal*), breath down someone's neck ...*My husband started hassling me...*

hassled = <u>bothered</u>, pressured, worried, stressed, under pressure, hounded, uptight, browbeaten, hunted, hot and bothered

haste NOUN = <u>speed</u>, rapidity, urgency, expedition, dispatch, velocity, alacrity, quickness, swiftness, briskness, nimbleness, fleetness, celerity, promptitude, rapidness ...*Authorities appear to be moving with haste against the three dissidents...* OPPOSITE slowness
PHRASES **in haste** = <u>hastily</u>, rashly, too quickly, impetuously ...*Don't act in haste or be hot-headed...*

hasten 1 = <u>hurry (up)</u>, speed (up), advance, urge, step up (*informal*), accelerate, press, dispatch, precipitate, quicken, push forward, expedite ...*He may hasten the collapse of his own country...* OPPOSITE slow down
2 = <u>rush</u>, run, race, fly, speed, tear (along), dash, hurry (up), barrel (along) (*informal, chiefly U.S. & Canad.*), sprint, bolt, beetle, scuttle, scurry, haste, burn rubber (*informal*), step on it (*informal*), make haste, get your skates on (*informal*) ...*He hastened along the landing to her room...* OPPOSITE dawdle

hastily 1 = <u>quickly</u>, fast, rapidly, promptly, straightaway, speedily, apace, pronto (*informal*), double-quick, hotfoot, pdq (*slang*), posthaste ...*He said goodnight hastily...*
2 = <u>hurriedly</u>, rashly, precipitately, recklessly, too quickly, on the spur of the moment, impulsively, impetuously, heedlessly ...*I decided that nothing should be done hastily...*

hasty 1 = <u>speedy</u>, fast, quick, prompt, rapid, fleet, hurried, urgent, swift, brisk, expeditious ...*They need to make a hasty escape...* OPPOSITE leisurely
2 = <u>brief</u>, short, quick, passing, rushed, fleeting, superficial, cursory, perfunctory, transitory ...*After the hasty meal, they took up their positions...* OPPOSITE long
3 = <u>rash</u>, premature, reckless, precipitate, impulsive, headlong, foolhardy, thoughtless, impetuous, indiscreet, imprudent, heedless, incautious, unduly quick ...*Let's not be hasty...* OPPOSITE cautious

hatch 1 = <u>incubate</u>, breed, sit on, brood, bring forth ...*I transferred the eggs to a hen canary to hatch and rear...*
2 = <u>devise</u>, plan, design, project, scheme, manufacture, plot, invent, put together, conceive, brew, formulate, contrive, dream up (*informal*), concoct, think up, cook up (*informal*), trump up ...*accused of hatching a plot to assassinate the Pope...*

hatchet = <u>axe</u>, machete, tomahawk, cleaver

hate VERB 1 = <u>detest</u>, loathe, despise, dislike, be sick of, abhor, be hostile to, recoil from, be repelled by, have an aversion to, abominate, not be able to bear, execrate ...*Most people hate him, but I don't...* OPPOSITE love

2 = <u>dislike</u>, detest, shrink from, recoil from, have no stomach for, not be able to bear ...*She hated hospitals and dreaded the operation*... OPPOSITE like

3 = <u>be unwilling</u>, regret, be reluctant, hesitate, be sorry, be loath, feel disinclined ...*I hate to admit it, but you were right*...

NOUN = <u>dislike</u>, hostility, hatred, loathing, animosity, aversion, antagonism, antipathy, enmity, abomination, animus, abhorrence, odium, detestation, execration ...*eyes that held a look of hate*... OPPOSITE love

hateful = <u>horrible</u>, despicable, offensive, foul, disgusting, forbidding, revolting, obscene, vile, repellent, obnoxious, repulsive, heinous, odious, repugnant, loathsome, abhorrent, abominable, execrable, detestable OPPOSITE pleasant

hatred = <u>hate</u>, dislike, animosity, aversion, revulsion, antagonism, antipathy, enmity, abomination, ill will, animus, repugnance, odium, detestation, execration OPPOSITE love

haughty – <u>proud</u>, arrogant, lofty, high, stuck up (*informal*), contemptuous, conceited, imperious, snooty (*informal*), scornful, snobbish, disdainful, supercilious, high and mighty (*informal*), overweening, hoity-toity (*informal*), on your high horse (*informal*), uppish (*Brit. informal*) OPPOSITE humble

haul VERB **1** = <u>drag</u>, draw, pull, hale, heave ...*He hauled himself to his feet*...

2 = <u>pull</u>, trail, convey, tow, move, carry, transport, tug, cart, hump (*Brit. slang*), lug ...*A crane hauled the car out of the stream*...

NOUN = <u>yield</u>, gain, spoils, find, catch, harvest, loot, takings, booty ...*The haul was worth £4,000*...

haunt VERB **1** = <u>plague</u>, trouble, obsess, torment, come back to, possess, stay with, recur, beset, prey on, weigh on ...*The decision to leave her children now haunts her*...

2 = <u>visit</u>, hang around *or* about, frequent, linger in, resort to, patronize, repair to, spend time in, loiter in, be a regular in ...*During the day he haunted the town's cinemas*...

3 = <u>appear in</u>, materialize in ...*His ghost is said to haunt some of the rooms*...

NOUN = <u>meeting place</u>, resort, hangout (*informal*), den, rendezvous, stamping ground, gathering place ...*a favourite summer haunt for yachtsmen*...

haunted **1** = <u>possessed</u>, ghostly, cursed, eerie, spooky (*informal*), jinxed ...*a haunted castle*...

2 = <u>preoccupied</u>, worried, troubled, plagued, obsessed, tormented ...*She looked so haunted, I almost didn't recognise her*...

haunting = <u>evocative</u>, poignant, unforgettable, indelible

have VERB **1** = <u>own</u>, keep, possess, hold, retain, occupy, boast, be the owner of ...*I want to have my own business*...

2 = <u>get</u>, obtain, take, receive, accept, gain, secure, acquire, procure, take receipt of ...*When can I have the new car?*...

3 = <u>suffer</u>, experience, undergo, sustain, endure, be suffering from ...*He might be having a heart attack*...

4 = <u>give birth to</u>, bear, deliver, bring forth, beget, bring into the world ...*My wife has just had a baby boy*...

5 = <u>put up with</u> (*informal*), allow, permit, consider, think about, entertain, tolerate ...*I'm not having any of that nonsense*...

6 = <u>experience</u>, go through, undergo, meet with, come across, run into, be faced with ...*Did you have some trouble with your neighbours?*...

PHRASES **have had it** (*Informal*) = <u>be exhausted</u>, be knackered (*Brit. informal*), be finished, be pooped (*U.S. slang*) ...*I've had it. Let's call it a day*... ◆ **have someone on** = <u>tease</u>, kid (*informal*), wind up (*Brit. slang*), trick, deceive, take the mickey, pull someone's leg, play a joke on ...*I thought he was just having me on*... ◆ **have something on 1** = <u>wear</u>, be wearing, be dressed in, be clothed in, be attired in ...*She had on new black shoes*... **2** = <u>have something planned</u>, be committed to, be engaged to, have something on the agenda ...*We have a meeting on that day*... ◆ **have to 1** = <u>must</u>, should, be forced, ought, be obliged, be bound, have got to, be compelled ...*Now, you have to go into town*... **2** = <u>have got to</u>, must ...*That has to be the biggest lie ever told*...

haven 1 = <u>sanctuary</u>, shelter, retreat, asylum, refuge, oasis, sanctum ...*a real haven at the end of a busy working day*...

2 = <u>harbour</u>, port, anchorage, road (*Nautical*) ...*She lay alongside in Largs Yacht Haven for a few days*...

havoc NOUN **1** = <u>devastation</u>, damage, destruction, waste, ruin, wreck, slaughter, ravages, carnage, desolation, rack and ruin, despoliation ...*Rioters caused havoc in the centre of the town*...

2 (*Informal*) = <u>disorder</u>, confusion, chaos, disruption, mayhem, shambles ...*A single mare running loose could cause havoc among otherwise reliable stallions*...

PHRASES **play havoc with something** = <u>wreck</u>, destroy, devastate, disrupt, demolish, disorganize, bring into chaos ...*Drug addiction soon played havoc with his career*...

hawk = <u>peddle</u>, market, sell, push, traffic, tout (*informal*), vend

hawker = <u>pedlar</u>, tout, vendor, travelling salesman, crier, huckster, barrow boy (*Brit.*), door-to-door salesman

haywire 1 = <u>chaotic</u>, confused, disordered, tangled, mixed up, shambolic (*informal*), topsy-turvy, disorganized, disarranged ...*Many Americans think their legal system is haywire*...

2 = <u>out of order</u>, out of commission, on the blink (*slang*), on the fritz (*slang*) ...*Her pacemaker went haywire near hand dryers*...

3 (*of people*) = <u>crazy</u>, wild, mad, potty (*Brit. informal*), berserk, bonkers (*slang, chiefly Brit.*), loopy (*informal*), mad as a hatter, berko (*Austral. slang*), off the air (*Austral. slang*) ...*I went haywire in our first few weeks on holiday*...

hazard NOUN = <u>danger</u>, risk, threat, problem, menace, peril, jeopardy, pitfall, endangerment, imperilment

…a sole that reduces the hazard of slipping on slick surfaces…

`VERB` = jeopardize, risk, endanger, threaten, expose, imperil, put in jeopardy …*He could not believe that the man would have hazarded his grandson…*

`PHRASES` **hazard a guess** = guess, conjecture, suppose, speculate, presume, take a guess …*I would hazard a guess that they'll do fairly well…*

hazardous = dangerous, risky, difficult, uncertain, unpredictable, insecure, hairy (*slang*), unsafe, precarious, perilous, parlous (*archaic or humorous*), dicey (*informal, chiefly Brit.*), fraught with danger, chancy (*informal*) `OPPOSITE` safe

haze = mist, film, cloud, steam, fog, obscurity, vapour, smog, dimness, smokiness

hazy 1 = misty, faint, dim, dull, obscure, veiled, smoky, cloudy, foggy, overcast, blurry, nebulous …*The air was filled with hazy sunshine and frost…* `OPPOSITE` bright 2 = vague, uncertain, unclear, muddled, fuzzy, indefinite, loose, muzzy, nebulous, ill-defined, indistinct …*I have only a hazy memory of what he was like…* `OPPOSITE` clear

head `NOUN` 1 = skull, crown, pate, bean (*U.S. & Canad. slang*), nut (*slang*), loaf (*slang*), cranium, conk (*slang*), noggin, noddle (*informal, chiefly Brit.*) …*She turned her head away from him…*
2 = mind, reasoning, understanding, thought, sense, brain, brains (*informal*), intelligence, wisdom, wits, common sense, loaf (*Brit. informal*), intellect, rationality, grey matter, brainpower, mental capacity …*He was more inclined to use his head…*
3 = ability, mind, talent, capacity, faculty, flair, mentality, aptitude …*I don't have a head for business…*
4 = front, beginning, top, first place, fore, forefront …*the head of the queue…*
5 = forefront, cutting edge, vanguard, van …*his familiar position at the head of his field…*
6 = top, crown, summit, height, peak, crest, pinnacle, apex, vertex …*the head of the stairs…*
7 (*Informal*) = head teacher, principal, headmaster *or* headmistress …*full of admiration for the head and teachers…*
8 = leader, president, director, manager, chief, boss (*informal*), captain, master, premier, commander, principal, supervisor, superintendent, chieftain …*heads of government from more than 100 countries…*
9 = climax, crisis, turning point, culmination, end, conclusion …*These problems came to a head in September…*
10 = source, start, beginning, rise, origin, commencement, well head …*the head of the river…*
11 (*Geography*) = headland, point, cape, promontory, foreland …*a ship off the beach head…*
`ADJECTIVE` = chief, main, leading, first, highest, front, prime, premier, supreme, principal, arch, foremost, pre-eminent, topmost …*I had the head man out from the gas company…*
`VERB` 1 = lead, precede, be the leader of, be *or* go first, be *or* go at the front of, lead the way …*The*

parson, heading the procession, had just turned right…
2 = top, lead, crown, cap …*Running a business heads the list of ambitions among interviewees…*
3 = be in charge of, run, manage, lead, control, rule, direct, guide, command, govern, supervise …*He heads the department's Office of Civil Rights…*
`PHRASES` **go to your head** 1 = intoxicate, befuddle, inebriate, addle, stupefy, fuddle, put (someone) under the table (*informal*) …*That wine was strong, it went to your head…* 2 = make someone conceited, puff someone up, make someone full of themselves …*not a man to let a little success go to his head…* ◆ **head for something** *or* **someone** = make for, aim for, set off for, go to, turn to, set out for, make a beeline for, start towards, steer for …*He headed for the bus stop…* ◆ **head over heels** = completely, thoroughly, utterly, intensely, wholeheartedly, uncontrollably …*head over heels in love…* ◆ **head someone off** = intercept, divert, deflect, cut someone off, interpose, block someone off …*He turned into the hallway and headed her off…* ◆ **head something off** = prevent, stop, avert, parry, fend off, ward off, forestall …*good at spotting trouble on the way and heading it off…* ◆ **put your heads together** (*Informal*) = consult, confer, discuss, deliberate, talk (something) over, powwow, confab (*informal*), confabulate …*Everyone put their heads together and reached an arrangement…*

(*Related Words*)
adjective: capital, cephalic

headache 1 = migraine, head (*informal*), neuralgia, cephalalgia (*Medical*) …*I have had a terrible headache for the past two days…*
2 = problem (*Informal*), worry, trouble, bother, nuisance, inconvenience, bane, vexation …*Their biggest headache is the increase in the price of fuel…*

head-first *or* **head first** 1 = headlong, head foremost …*He has apparently fallen head-first down the stairwell…*
2 = recklessly, rashly, hastily, precipitately, without thinking, carelessly, heedlessly, without forethought …*On arrival he plunged head first into these problems…*

heading 1 = title, name, caption, headline, rubric …*helpful chapter headings…*
2 = category, class, section, division …*There, under the heading of wholesalers, he found it…*

headland = promontory, point, head, cape, cliff, bluff, mull (*Scot.*), foreland, bill

headlong `ADVERB` 1 = hastily, hurriedly, helter-skelter, pell-mell, heedlessly …*He ran headlong for the open door…*
2 = headfirst, head-on, headforemost …*She missed her footing and fell headlong down the stairs…*
3 = rashly, wildly, hastily, precipitately, head first, thoughtlessly, impetuously, heedlessly, without forethought …*Do not leap headlong into decisions…*
`ADJECTIVE` = hasty, reckless, precipitate, dangerous, impulsive, thoughtless, breakneck, impetuous, inconsiderate …*a headlong rush for the exit…*

headmaster or **headmistress** = <u>principal</u>, head, head teacher, rector

> ### *Word Power*
>
> **headmaster/headmistress** – The general trend of nonsexist language is to find a term which can apply to both sexes equally, as in the use of *actor* to refer to both men and women. This being so, *head teacher* is usually preferable to the gender-specific terms *headmaster* and *headmistress*.

headstrong = <u>stubborn</u>, wilful, obstinate, contrary, perverse, unruly, intractable, stiff-necked, ungovernable, self-willed, pig-headed, mulish, froward (*archaic*) OPPOSITE⟩ manageable

headway

PHRASES **make headway** = <u>progress</u>, advance, come *or* get on, gain ground, make inroads (into), cover ground, make strides

heady 1 = <u>exciting</u>, thrilling, stimulating, exhilarating, overwhelming, intoxicating …*in the heady days just after their marriage*…
2 = <u>intoxicating</u>, strong, potent, inebriating, spirituous …*The wine is a heady blend of claret and aromatic herbs*…

heal 1 *sometimes with* **up** = <u>mend</u>, get better, get well, cure, regenerate, show improvement …*The bruising had gone, but it was six months before it all healed*…
2 = <u>cure</u>, restore, mend, make better, remedy, make good, make well …*No doctor has ever healed a broken bone. They just set them*… OPPOSITE⟩ injure
3 = <u>ease</u>, help, soothe, lessen, alleviate, assuage, salve, ameliorate …*the best way to heal a broken heart*…
4 = <u>patch up</u>, settle, reconcile, put right, harmonize, conciliate …*Sophie and her sister have healed the family rift*…

healing 1 = <u>restoring</u>, medicinal, therapeutic, remedial, restorative, curative, analeptic, sanative …*Get in touch with the body's own healing abilities*…
2 = <u>soothing</u>, comforting, gentle, mild, assuaging, palliative, emollient, lenitive, mitigative …*I place my hands on their head in a healing way, and calm them down*…

health 1 = <u>condition</u>, state, form, shape, tone, constitution, fettle …*Although he's old, he's in good health*…
2 = <u>wellbeing</u>, strength, fitness, vigour, good condition, wellness, soundness, robustness, healthiness, salubrity, haleness …*In hospital they nursed me back to health*… OPPOSITE⟩ illness
3 = <u>state</u>, condition, shape …*There's no way to predict the future health of the banking industry*…

healthful = <u>healthy</u>, beneficial, good for you, bracing, nourishing, wholesome, nutritious, invigorating, salutary, salubrious, health-giving

healthy 1 = <u>well</u>, sound, fit, strong, active, flourishing, hardy, blooming, robust, vigorous, sturdy, hale, hearty, in good shape (*informal*), in good condition, in the pink, alive and kicking, fighting fit, in fine form, in fine fettle, hale and hearty, fit as a fiddle (*informal*), right as rain (*Brit. informal*), physically fit, in fine feather …*She had a normal pregnancy and delivered a healthy child*… OPPOSITE⟩ ill
2 = <u>wholesome</u>, beneficial, nourishing, good for you, nutritious, salutary, hygienic, healthful, salubrious, health-giving …*a healthy diet*… OPPOSITE⟩ unwholesome
3 = <u>invigorating</u>, bracing, beneficial, good for you, salutary, healthful, salubrious …*a healthy outdoor pursuit*…

heap NOUN **1** = <u>pile</u>, lot, collection, store, mountain, mass, stack, rick, mound, accumulation, stockpile, hoard, aggregation …*a heap of bricks*…
2 *often plural* (*Informal*) = <u>a lot</u>, lots (*informal*), plenty, masses, load(s) (*informal*), ocean(s), great deal, quantities, tons, stack(s), lashings (*Brit. informal*), abundance, oodles (*informal*) …*You have heaps of time*…
VERB *sometimes with* **up** = <u>pile</u>, store, collect, gather, stack, accumulate, mound, amass, stockpile, hoard, bank …*They were heaping up wood for a bonfire*…
PHRASES **heap something on someone** = <u>load with</u>, burden with, confer on, assign to, bestow on, shower upon …*He heaped scorn on both their methods and motives*…

hear 1 = <u>overhear</u>, catch, detect …*She heard no further sounds*…
2 = <u>listen to</u>, heed, attend to, eavesdrop on, listen in to, give attention to, hearken to (*archaic*), hark to, be all ears for (*informal*) …*You can hear commentary on the match in about half an hour*…
3 (*Law*) = <u>try</u>, judge, examine, investigate …*He had to wait months before his case was heard*…
4 = <u>learn</u>, discover, find out, understand, pick up, gather, be informed, ascertain, be told of, get wind of (*informal*), hear tell (*dialect*) …*He had heard that the trophy had been sold*…

hearing 1 = <u>sense of hearing</u>, auditory perception, ear, aural faculty …*His mind still seemed clear and his hearing was excellent*…
2 = <u>inquiry</u>, trial, investigation, industrial tribunal …*The judge adjourned the hearing until next Tuesday*…
3 = <u>chance to speak</u>, interview, audience, audition …*a means of giving a candidate a fair hearing*…
4 = <u>earshot</u>, reach, range, hearing distance, auditory range …*No one spoke disparagingly of her father in her hearing*…

(**Related Words**)
adjective: audio

hearsay = <u>rumour</u>, talk, gossip, report, buzz, dirt (*U.S. slang*), word of mouth, tittle-tattle, talk of the town, scuttlebutt (*slang, chiefly U.S.*), idle talk, mere talk, on dit (*French*)

heart NOUN **1** = <u>emotions</u>, feelings, sentiments, love, affection …*I phoned him up and poured out my heart*… …*The beauty quickly captured his heart*…
2 = <u>nature</u>, character, soul, constitution, essence, temperament, inclination, disposition …*She loved his

brilliance and his generous heart…
3 = <u>tenderness</u>, feeling(s), love, understanding, concern, sympathy, pity, humanity, affection, compassion, kindness, empathy, benevolence, concern for others *…They are ruthless, formidable, without heart…*
4 = <u>root</u>, core, essence, centre, nucleus, marrow, hub, kernel, crux, gist, central part, nitty-gritty (*informal*), nub, pith, quintessence *…The heart of the problem is supply and demand…*
5 = <u>courage</u>, will, spirit, mind, purpose, bottle (*Brit. informal*), resolution, resolve, nerve, stomach, enthusiasm, determination, guts (*informal*), spine, pluck, bravery, backbone, fortitude, mettle, boldness, spunk (*informal*) *…I did not have the heart or spirit left to jog back to my hotel…*
PHRASES **at heart** = <u>fundamentally</u>, essentially, basically, really, actually, in fact, truly, in reality, in truth, in essence, deep down, at bottom, au fond (*French*) *…He was a very gentle boy at heart…* ◆ **by heart** = <u>from</u> or <u>by memory</u>, verbatim, word for word, pat, word-perfect, by rote, off by heart, off pat, parrot-fashion (*informal*) *…Mack knew this passage by heart…* ◆ **from the bottom of your heart** = <u>deeply</u>, heartily, fervently, heart and soul, devoutly, with all your heart *…thanking you from the bottom of my heart…* ◆ **from the heart** = <u>sincerely</u>, earnestly, in earnest, with all your heart, in all sincerity *…He was clearly speaking from the heart…* ◆ **heart and soul** = <u>completely</u>, entirely, absolutely, wholeheartedly, to the hilt, devotedly *…He is heart and soul a Scot…* ◆ **take heart** = <u>be encouraged</u>, be comforted, cheer up, perk up, brighten up, be heartened, buck up (*informal*), derive comfort *…Investors failed to take heart from the stronger yen…*

Related Words
adjective : cardiac

heartache = <u>sorrow</u>, suffering, pain, torture, distress, despair, grief, agony, torment, bitterness, anguish, remorse, heartbreak, affliction, heartsickness

heartbreak = <u>grief</u>, suffering, pain, despair, misery, sorrow, anguish, desolation

heartbreaking = <u>sad</u>, distressing, tragic, bitter, poignant, harrowing, desolating, grievous, pitiful, agonizing, heart-rending, gut-wrenching OPPOSITE happy

hearten = <u>encourage</u>, inspire, cheer, comfort, assure, stimulate, reassure, animate, console, rouse, incite, embolden, buoy up, buck up (*informal*), raise someone's spirits, revivify, gee up, inspirit

heartfelt = <u>sincere</u>, deep, earnest, warm, genuine, profound, honest, ardent, devout, hearty, fervent, cordial, wholehearted, dinkum (*Austral & N.Z. informal*), unfeigned OPPOSITE insincere

heartily **1** = <u>sincerely</u>, feelingly, deeply, warmly, genuinely, profoundly, cordially, unfeignedly *…He laughed heartily…*
2 = <u>enthusiastically</u>, vigorously, eagerly, resolutely, earnestly, zealously *…I heartily agree with her comments…*

3 = <u>thoroughly</u>, very, completely, totally, absolutely *…We're all heartily sick of all the aggravation…*

heartless = <u>cruel</u>, hard, callous, cold, harsh, brutal, unkind, inhuman, merciless, cold-blooded, uncaring, pitiless, unfeeling, cold-hearted, affectless, hardhearted OPPOSITE compassionate

heart-rending = <u>moving</u>, sad, distressing, affecting, tragic, pathetic, poignant, harrowing, heartbreaking, pitiful, gut-wrenching, piteous

heart-to-heart ADJECTIVE = <u>intimate</u>, honest, candid, open, personal, sincere, truthful, unreserved *…I had a heart-to-heart talk with my mother…* NOUN = <u>tête-à-tête</u>, cosy chat, one-to-one, private conversation, private chat *…I've had a heart-to-heart with him…*

heart-warming = <u>moving</u>, touching, affecting, pleasing, encouraging, warming, rewarding, satisfying, cheering, gratifying, heartening

hearty **1** = <u>friendly</u>, genial, warm, generous, eager, enthusiastic, ardent, cordial, affable, ebullient, jovial, effusive, unreserved, back-slapping *…He was a hearty, bluff, athletic sort of guy…* OPPOSITE cool
2 = <u>wholehearted</u>, sincere, heartfelt, real, true, earnest, genuine, honest, unfeigned *…With the last sentiment, Arnold was in hearty agreement…* OPPOSITE insincere
3 = <u>substantial</u>, filling, ample, square, solid, nourishing, sizable or sizeable *…The men ate a hearty breakfast…*
4 = <u>healthy</u>, well, strong, sound, active, hardy, robust, vigorous, energetic, hale, alive and kicking, right as rain (*Brit. informal*) *…She was still hearty and strong at 120 years and married a third husband at 92…* OPPOSITE frail

heat VERB *sometimes with* **up** = <u>warm (up)</u>, cook, boil, roast, reheat, make hot *…Meanwhile, heat the tomatoes and oil in a pan…* OPPOSITE chill
NOUN **1** = <u>warmth</u>, hotness, temperature, swelter, sultriness, fieriness, torridity, warmness, calefaction *…Leaves drooped in the fierce heat of the sun…* OPPOSITE cold
2 = <u>hot weather</u>, warmth, closeness, high temperature, heatwave, warm weather, hot climate, hot spell, mugginess *…The heat is killing me…*
3 = <u>passion</u>, excitement, intensity, violence, fever, fury, warmth, zeal, agitation, fervour, ardour, vehemence, earnestness, impetuosity *…It was all done in the heat of the moment…* OPPOSITE calmness
PHRASES **get heated up** = <u>get excited</u>, be stimulated, be stirred, become animated, be roused, be inflamed, be inspirited, become impassioned *…I get very heated up when people say that…* ◆ **heat up** **1** = <u>intensify</u>, increase, heighten, deepen, escalate *…The war of words continues to heat up…* **2** = <u>warm up</u>, get hotter, become hot, rise in temperature, become warm, grow hot *…In the summer her mobile home heats up like an oven…*

Related Words
adjectives : thermal, calorific

heated **1** = <u>impassioned</u>, intense, spirited, excited, angry, violent, bitter, raging, furious, fierce, lively, passionate, animated, frenzied, fiery, stormy, vehement, tempestuous ...*It was a very heated argument...* OPPOSITE calm

2 = wound up, worked up, keyed up, het up (*informal*) ...*People get a bit heated about issues like these...*

heathen NOUN **1** (*Old-fashioned*) = pagan, infidel, unbeliever, idolater, idolatress ...*the condescending air of missionaries seeking to convert the heathen...*

2 = barbarian, savage, philistine, oaf, ignoramus, boor ...*She called us all heathens and hypocrites...*

ADJECTIVE **1** (*Old-fashioned*) = pagan, infidel, godless, irreligious, idolatrous, heathenish ...*a heathen temple...*

2 = uncivilized, savage, primitive, barbaric, brutish, unenlightened, uncultured ...*to disappear into the cold heathen north...*

heave 1 = lift, raise, pull (up), drag (up), haul (up), tug, lever, hoist, heft (*informal*) ...*He heaved Barney to his feet...*

2 = throw, fling, toss, send, cast, pitch, hurl, sling ...*Heave a brick at the telly...*

3 = expand, rise, swell, pant, throb, exhale, dilate, palpitate ...*His chest heaved, and he took a deep breath...*

4 = surge, rise, swell, billow ...*The grey seas heaved...*

5 = vomit, be sick, throw up (*informal*), chuck (up) (*slang, chiefly U.S.*), chuck (*Austral. & N.Z. informal*), gag, spew, retch, barf (*U.S. slang*), chunder (*slang, chiefly Austral.*), upchuck (*U.S. slang*), do a technicolour yawn (*slang*), toss your cookies (*U.S. slang*) ...*He gasped and heaved and vomited...*

6 = breathe, sigh, puff, groan, sob, breathe heavily, suspire (*archaic*), utter wearily ...*Mr Collier heaved a sigh and got to his feet...*

heaven NOUN **1** = paradise, next world, hereafter, nirvana (*Buddhism, Hinduism*), bliss, Zion (*Christianity*), Valhalla (*Norse myth*), Happy Valley, happy hunting ground (*Native American legend*), life to come, life everlasting, abode of God, Elysium *or* Elysian fields (*Greek myth*) ...*I believed that when I died I would go to heaven...*

2 (*Informal*) = happiness, paradise, ecstasy, bliss, felicity, utopia, contentment, rapture, enchantment, dreamland, seventh heaven, transport, sheer bliss ...*My idea of heaven is drinking champagne with friends on a sunny day...*

PHRASES **the heavens** (*Old-fashioned*) = sky, ether, firmament, celestial sphere, welkin (*archaic*), empyrean (*poetic*) ...*a detailed map of the heavens...*

heavenly 1 = celestial, holy, divine, blessed, blest, immortal, supernatural, angelic, extraterrestrial, superhuman, godlike, beatific, cherubic, seraphic, supernal (*literary*), empyrean (*poetic*), paradisaical ...*heavenly beings whose function it is to serve God...* OPPOSITE earthly

2 (*Informal*) = wonderful, lovely, delightful, beautiful, entrancing, divine (*informal*), glorious, exquisite, sublime, alluring, blissful, ravishing, rapturous ...*The idea of spending two weeks with him seems heavenly...*

OPPOSITE awful

heavily 1 = excessively, to excess, very much, a great deal, frequently, considerably, copiously, without restraint, immoderately, intemperately ...*Her husband drank heavily and beat her...*

2 = densely, closely, thickly, compactly ...*They can be found in grassy and heavily wooded areas...*

3 = with difficulty, laboriously, slowly, painfully, sluggishly ...*She was breathing heavily with an occasional gasp for air...*

4 = hard, clumsily, awkwardly, weightily ...*A man stumbled heavily against the car...*

heaviness 1 = weight, gravity, ponderousness, heftiness ...*the heaviness of earthbound matter...*

2 = sluggishness, torpor, numbness, dullness, lassitude, languor, deadness ...*There was a heaviness in the air that stunned them...*

3 = sadness, depression, gloom, seriousness, melancholy, despondency, dejection, gloominess, glumness ...*a heaviness in his reply which discouraged further questioning...*

heavy 1 = weighty, large, massive, hefty, bulky, ponderous ...*He was carrying a very heavy load...* OPPOSITE light

2 = intensive, severe, serious, concentrated, fierce, excessive, relentless ...*Heavy fighting has been going on...*

3 = considerable, large, huge, substantial, abundant, copious, profuse ...*There was a heavy amount of traffic on the roads...* OPPOSITE slight

4 = onerous, hard, difficult, severe, harsh, tedious, intolerable, oppressive, grievous, burdensome, wearisome, vexatious ...*They bear a heavy burden of responsibility...* OPPOSITE easy

5 = sluggish, slow, dull, wooden, stupid, inactive, inert, apathetic, drowsy, listless, indolent, torpid ...*I struggle to raise eyelids still heavy with sleep...* OPPOSITE alert

6 = hard, demanding, difficult, physical, strenuous, laborious ...*They employ two full-timers to do the heavy work...*

7 = overcast, dull, gloomy, cloudy, leaden, louring *or* lowering ...*The night sky was heavy with rain clouds...*

8 = humid, close, sticky, oppressive, clammy, airless, muggy ...*The air outside was heavy and moist and sultry...*

9 = sad, depressed, gloomy, grieving, melancholy, dejected, despondent, downcast, sorrowful, disconsolate, crestfallen ...*My parents' faces were heavy with fallen hope...* OPPOSITE happy

10 = sorrowful, sad, gloomy, melancholy, dejected, downcast, grief-stricken, disconsolate ...*He handed over his resignation with a heavy heart...*

11 = serious, grave, solemn, difficult, deep, complex, profound, weighty ...*I don't want any more of that heavy stuff...* OPPOSITE trivial

heavy-handed 1 = oppressive, harsh, Draconian, autocratic, domineering, overbearing ...*heavy-handed police tactics...*

2 = clumsy, awkward, bungling, inept, graceless, inexpert, maladroit, ham-handed (*informal*), like a bull in a china shop (*informal*), ham-fisted (*informal*)

...*She tends to be a little heavy-handed*... OPPOSITE> skilful

heckle = <u>jeer</u>, interrupt, shout down, disrupt, bait, barrack (*informal*), boo, taunt, pester

hectic = <u>frantic</u>, chaotic, frenzied, heated, wild, excited, furious, fevered, animated, turbulent, flurrying, frenetic, boisterous, feverish, tumultuous, flustering, riotous, rumbustious OPPOSITE> peaceful

hector = <u>bully</u>, harass, browbeat, worry, threaten, menace, intimidate, ride roughshod over, bullyrag

hedge NOUN = <u>guard</u>, cover, protection, compensation, shield, safeguard, counterbalance, insurance cover ...*Gold is traditionally a hedge against inflation*...
VERB 1 = <u>prevaricate</u>, evade, sidestep, duck, dodge, flannel (*Brit. informal*), waffle (*informal, chiefly Brit.*), quibble, beg the question, pussyfoot (*informal*), equivocate, temporize, be noncommittal ...*When asked about his involvement, he hedged*...
2 = <u>enclose</u>, edge, border, surround, fence ...*sweeping lawns hedged with floribundas*...
PHRASES **hedge against something** = <u>protect against</u>, insure against, guard against, safeguard against, shield against, cover against, fortify against ...*You can hedge against redundancy or illness with insurance*... ♦ **hedge someone in** = <u>hamper</u>, restrict, handicap, hamstring, hinder, hem in ...*He was hedged in by his own shyness*... ♦ **hedge something** or **someone about** or **around** = <u>restrict</u>, confine, hinder, hem in, hem around, hem about ...*The offer was hedged around by conditions*... ♦ **hedge something in** = <u>surround</u>, enclose, encompass, encircle, ring, fence in, girdle, hem in ...*a steep and rocky footpath hedged in by the shadowy green forest*...

hedonism = <u>pleasure-seeking</u>, gratification, sensuality, self-indulgence, dolce vita, pursuit of pleasure, luxuriousness, sensualism, sybaritism, epicureanism, epicurism

hedonistic = <u>pleasure-seeking</u>, self-indulgent, luxurious, voluptuous, sybaritic, epicurean, bacchanalian

heed (*Formal*) VERB = <u>pay attention to</u>, listen to, take notice of, follow, mark, mind, consider, note, regard, attend, observe, obey, bear in mind, be guided by, take to heart, give ear to ...*Few at the conference in London last week heeded his warning*... OPPOSITE> ignore
NOUN = <u>thought</u>, care, mind, note, attention, regard, respect, notice, consideration, watchfulness ...*He pays too much heed these days to my nephew Tom*... OPPOSITE> disregard

heedless = <u>careless</u>, reckless, negligent, rash, precipitate, oblivious, foolhardy, thoughtless, unthinking, imprudent, neglectful, inattentive, incautious, unmindful, unobservant OPPOSITE> careful

heel NOUN 1 = <u>end</u>, stump, remainder, crust, rump, stub ...*the heel of a loaf of bread*...
2 (*Slang*) = <u>swine</u>, cad (*Brit. informal*), scoundrel, scally (*Northwest English dialect*), bounder (*old-fashioned Brit. slang*), rotter (*slang, chiefly Brit.*), scumbag (*slang*), blackguard ...*Suddenly I feel like a total heel*...
PHRASES **take to your heels** = <u>flee</u>, escape, run away *or* off, take flight, hook it (*slang*), turn tail, show a clean pair of heels, skedaddle (*informal*), vamoose (*slang, chiefly U.S.*) ...*He stood, for a moment, then took to his heels*...

hefty (*Informal*) 1 = <u>big</u>, strong, massive, strapping, robust, muscular, burly, husky (*informal*), hulking, beefy (*informal*), brawny ...*She was quite a hefty woman*... OPPOSITE> small
2 (*Informal*) = <u>forceful</u>, heavy, powerful, vigorous (*slang*) ...*Lambert gave him a hefty shove to send him on his way*... OPPOSITE> gentle
3 = <u>heavy</u>, large, massive, substantial, tremendous, awkward, ample, bulky, colossal, cumbersome, weighty, unwieldy, ponderous ...*The gritty foursome took turns shouldering the hefty load every five minutes*... OPPOSITE> light
4 = <u>large</u>, massive, substantial, excessive, inflated, sizeable, astronomical (*informal*), extortionate ...*A long-distance romance followed with hefty phone bills*...

height 1 = <u>tallness</u>, stature, highness, loftiness ...*Her height is intimidating for some men*... OPPOSITE> shortness
2 = <u>altitude</u>, measurement, highness, elevation, tallness ...*build a wall up to a height of 2 metres*... OPPOSITE> depth
3 = <u>peak</u>, top, hill, mountain, crown, summit, crest, pinnacle, elevation, apex, apogee, vertex ...*From a height, it looks like a desert*... OPPOSITE> valley
4 = <u>culmination</u>, climax, zenith, limit, maximum, ultimate, extremity, uttermost, ne plus ultra (*Latin*), utmost degree ...*He was struck down at the height of his career*... OPPOSITE> low point
(*Related Words*)
fear of: acrophobia

heighten = <u>intensify</u>, increase, add to, improve, strengthen, enhance, sharpen, aggravate, magnify, amplify, augment

heinous = <u>shocking</u>, evil, monstrous, grave, awful, vicious, outrageous, revolting, infamous, hideous, unspeakable, atrocious, flagrant, odious, hateful, abhorrent, abominable, villainous, nefarious, iniquitous, execrable

heir = <u>successor</u>, beneficiary, inheritor, heiress (*fem.*), scion, next in line, inheritress *or* inheritrix (*fem.*)

hell NOUN 1 = <u>the underworld</u>, the abyss, Hades (*Greek myth*), hellfire, the inferno, fire and brimstone, the bottomless pit, Gehenna (*New Testament, Judaism*), the nether world, the lower world, Tartarus (*Greek myth*), the infernal regions, the bad fire (*informal*), Acheron (*Greek myth*), Abaddon, the abode of the damned ...*Don't worry about going to Hell, just be good*...
2 (*Informal*) = <u>torment</u>, suffering, agony, trial, nightmare, misery, ordeal, anguish, affliction, martyrdom, wretchedness ...*the hell of grief and lost love*...

PHRASES **hell for leather** = headlong, speedily, quickly, swiftly, hurriedly, at the double, full-tilt, pell-mell, hotfoot, at a rate of knots, like a bat out of hell (*slang*), posthaste ...*The first horse often goes hell for leather*...

hell-bent = intent (*Informal*), set, determined, settled, fixed, resolved, bent

hellish 1 (*Informal*) = atrocious, terrible, dreadful, cruel, vicious, monstrous, wicked, inhuman, barbarous, abominable, nefarious, accursed, execrable, detestable ...*He was held for three years in hellish conditions*... **OPPOSITE** wonderful
2 = devilish, fiendish, diabolical, infernal, damned, damnable, demoniacal ...*They began to pray, making devilish gestures with a hellish noise*...

hello = hi (*informal*), greetings, how do you do?, good morning, good evening, good afternoon, welcome, kia ora (*N.Z.*), gidday *or* g'day (*Austral. & N.Z.*)

helm **NOUN** (*Nautical*) = tiller, wheel, rudder, steering gear ...*I got into our dinghy while Willis took the helm*...
PHRASES **at the helm** = in charge, in control, in command, directing, at the wheel, in the saddle, in the driving seat ...*He has been at the helm of Lonrho for 31 years*...

help **VERB** **1** *sometimes with out* = aid, back, support, second, encourage, promote, assist, relieve, stand by, befriend, cooperate with, abet, lend a hand, succour, lend a helping hand, give someone a leg up (*informal*) ...*If you're not willing to help me, I'll find somebody who will*... **OPPOSITE** hinder
2 = improve, ease, heal, cure, relieve, remedy, facilitate, alleviate, mitigate, ameliorate ...*A cosmetic measure which will do nothing to help the situation long term*... **OPPOSITE** make worse
3 = assist, aid, support, give a leg up (*informal*) ...*Martin helped Tanya over the rail*...
4 = resist, refrain from, avoid, control, prevent, withstand, eschew, keep from, abstain from, forbear ...*I can't help feeling sorry for the poor man*...
NOUN **1** = assistance, aid, support, service, advice, promotion, guidance, cooperation, helping hand ...*Thanks very much for your help*... **OPPOSITE** hindrance
2 = remedy, cure, relief, corrective, balm, salve, succour, restorative ...*There is no help for him and no doctor on this earth could save him*...
3 = assistant, hand, worker, employee, helper ...*a hired help*...

helper = assistant, partner, ally, colleague, supporter, mate, deputy, second, subsidiary, aide, aider, attendant, collaborator, auxiliary, henchman, right-hand man, adjutant, helpmate, coadjutor, abettor

helpful 1 = cooperative, accommodating, kind, caring, friendly, neighbourly, sympathetic, supportive, benevolent, considerate, beneficent ...*The staff in the London office are helpful*...
2 = useful, practical, productive, profitable, constructive, serviceable ...*The catalog includes helpful information*...
3 = beneficial, advantageous, expedient, favourable ...*It is often helpful to have someone with you when you get bad news*...

helpfulness 1 = cooperation, kindness, support, assistance, sympathy, friendliness, rallying round, neighbourliness, good neighbourliness ...*The level of expertise and helpfulness is higher in small shops*...
2 = usefulness, benefit, advantage ...*the helpfulness of the information pack*...

helping = portion, serving, ration, piece, dollop (*informal*), plateful

helpless 1 = vulnerable, exposed, unprotected, defenceless, abandoned, dependent, stranded, wide open, forlorn, destitute ...*The children were left helpless*... **OPPOSITE** invulnerable
2 = powerless, weak, disabled, incapable, paralysed, incompetent, unfit, feeble, debilitated, impotent, infirm ...*Since the accident I am completely helpless*... **OPPOSITE** powerful

helplessness 1 = vulnerability, weakness, impotence, powerlessness, disability, infirmity, feebleness, forlornness, defencelessness

helter-skelter **ADJECTIVE** = haphazard, confused, disordered, random, muddled, jumbled, topsy-turvy, hit-or-miss, higgledy-piggledy (*informal*) ...*another crisis in his helter-skelter existence*...
ADVERB = wildly, rashly, anyhow, headlong, recklessly, carelessly, pell-mell ...*a panic-stricken crowd running helter-skelter*...

hem **NOUN** = edge, border, margin, trimming, fringe ...*Cut a jagged edge along the hem to give a ragged look*...
PHRASES **hem something** *or* **someone in 1** = surround, edge, border, skirt, confine, enclose, shut in, hedge in, environ ...*Manchester is hemmed in by greenbelt countryside*... **2** = restrict, confine, beset, circumscribe ...*hemmed in by rigid, legal contracts*...

hence = therefore, thus, consequently, for this reason, in consequence, ergo, on that account

henceforth = from now on, in the future, hereafter, hence, hereinafter, from this day forward

henchman = attendant, supporter, heavy (*slang*), associate, aide, follower, subordinate, bodyguard, minder (*slang*), crony, sidekick (*slang*), cohort (*chiefly U.S.*), right-hand man, minion, satellite, myrmidon

henpecked = dominated, subjugated, browbeaten, subject, bullied, timid, cringing, meek, treated like dirt, led by the nose, tied to someone's apron strings **OPPOSITE** domineering

herald **VERB** **1** = indicate, promise, precede, pave the way, usher in, harbinger, presage, portend, foretoken ...*Their discovery could herald a cure for some forms of impotence*...
2 = announce, publish, advertise, proclaim, broadcast, trumpet, publicize ...*Tonight's clash is being heralded as the match of the season*...
NOUN **1** (*Often literary*) = forerunner, sign, signal, indication, token, omen, precursor, harbinger ...*I welcome the report as the herald of more freedom, not*

less…

2 = <u>messenger</u>, courier, proclaimer, announcer, crier, town crier, bearer of tidings …*Jill hovered by the hearth while the herald delivered his news*…

Herculean 1 = <u>arduous</u>, hard, demanding, difficult, heavy, tough, exhausting, formidable, gruelling, strenuous, prodigious, onerous, laborious, toilsome …*Finding a lawyer may seem like a Herculean task*…
2 = <u>strong</u>, muscular, powerful, athletic, strapping, mighty, rugged, sturdy, stalwart, husky (*informal*), sinewy, brawny …*His shoulders were Herculean with long arms*…

Hercules

Labours of Hercules

http://www.perseus.tufts.edu/Hercules/labors.html

the slaying of the Nemean lion
the slaying of the Lernaean hydra
the capture of the hind of Ceryneia
the capture of the wild boar of Erymanthus
the cleansing of the Augean stables
the shooting of the Stymphalian birds
the capture of the Cretan bull
the capture of the horses of Diomedes
the taking of the girdle of Hippolyte
the capture of the cattle of Geryon
the recovery of the golden apples of
  Hesperides
the taking of Cerberus

---

herd NOUN **1** = <u>flock</u>, crowd, collection, mass, drove, crush, mob, swarm, horde, multitude, throng, assemblage, press …*large herds of elephant and buffalo*…
2 (*Often disparaging*) = <u>mob</u>, the masses, rabble, populace, the hoi polloi, the plebs, riffraff …*They are individuals; they will not follow the herd*…
VERB **1** = <u>lead</u>, drive, force, direct, guide, shepherd …*The group was herded onto a bus*…
2 = <u>drive</u>, lead, force, guide, shepherd …*A boy herded sheep down towards the lane*…

hereafter ADVERB = <u>in future</u>, after this, from now on, henceforth, henceforward, hence …*Hereafter for three years my name will not appear at all*…
PHRASES **the hereafter** = <u>afterlife</u>, next world, life after death, future life, the beyond …*belief in the hereafter*…

hereditary 1 = <u>genetic</u>, inborn, inbred, transmissible, inheritable …*In men, hair loss is hereditary*…
2 (*Law*) = <u>inherited</u>, handed down, passed down, willed, family, traditional, transmitted, ancestral, bequeathed, patrimonial …*hereditary peerages*…

heredity = <u>genetics</u>, inheritance, genetic make-up, congenital traits

heresy = <u>unorthodoxy</u>, apostasy, dissidence, impiety, revisionism, iconoclasm, heterodoxy

heretic = <u>nonconformist</u>, dissident, separatist, sectarian, renegade, revisionist, dissenter, apostate, schismatic

heretical 1 = <u>controversial</u>, unorthodox, revisionist, freethinking …*I made a heretical suggestion*…
2 = <u>unorthodox</u>, revisionist, iconoclastic, heterodox, impious, idolatrous, schismatic, freethinking …*The Church regards spirit mediums as heretical*…

heritage = <u>inheritance</u>, legacy, birthright, lot, share, estate, tradition, portion, endowment, bequest, patrimony

hermit = <u>recluse</u>, monk, loner (*informal*), solitary, anchorite, anchoress, stylite, eremite

hero 1 = <u>protagonist</u>, leading man, lead actor, male lead, principal male character …*The hero of Doctor Zhivago dies in 1929*…
2 = <u>star</u>, champion, celebrity, victor, superstar, great man, heart-throb (*Brit.*), conqueror, exemplar, celeb (*informal*), megastar (*informal*), popular figure, man of the hour …*the goalscoring hero of the British hockey team*…
3 = <u>idol</u>, favourite, pin-up (*slang*), fave (*informal*) …*I still remember my boyhood heroes*…

heroic 1 = <u>courageous</u>, brave, daring, bold, fearless, gallant, intrepid, valiant, doughty, undaunted, dauntless, lion-hearted, valorous, stouthearted …*The heroic sergeant risked his life to rescue 29 fishermen*…
OPPOSITE> cowardly
2 = <u>legendary</u>, classical, mythological, Homeric …*another in an endless series of man's heroic myths of his own past*…
3 = <u>epic</u>, grand, classic, extravagant, exaggerated, elevated, inflated, high-flown, grandiose …*a heroic style, with a touch of antiquarian realism*… OPPOSITE> simple

heroine 1 = <u>protagonist</u>, leading lady, diva, prima donna, female lead, lead actress, principal female character …*The heroine is a senior TV executive*…
2 = <u>star</u>, celebrity, goddess, celeb (*informal*), megastar (*informal*), woman of the hour …*The heroine of the day was the winner of the Gold medal*…
3 = <u>idol</u>, favourite, pin-up (*slang*), fave (*informal*) …*I still remember my childhood heroines*…

Word Power

hero – Note that the word *heroine*, meaning 'a female hero', has an *e* at the end. The drug *heroin* is spelled without a final *e*.

---

heroism = <u>bravery</u>, daring, courage, spirit, fortitude, boldness, gallantry, valour, fearlessness, intrepidity, courageousness

hero-worship = <u>admiration</u>, idolization, adulation, adoration, veneration, idealization, putting on a pedestal

hesitant = <u>uncertain</u>, reluctant, shy, halting, doubtful, sceptical, unsure, hesitating, wavering, timid, diffident, lacking confidence, vacillating, hanging back, irresolute, half-hearted OPPOSITE> confident

hesitate 1 = <u>waver</u>, delay, pause, haver (*Brit.*), wait, doubt, falter, be uncertain, dither (*chiefly Brit.*), vacillate, equivocate, temporize, hum and haw, shillyshally (*informal*), swither (*Scot. dialect*) …*She*

hesitated, debating whether to answer the phone...
OPPOSITE be decisive
2 = be reluctant, be unwilling, shrink from, think twice, boggle, scruple, demur, hang back, be disinclined, balk *or* baulk ...*I will not hesitate to take unpopular decisions...* OPPOSITE be determined

hesitation 1 = delay, pausing, uncertainty, stalling, dithering, indecision, hesitancy, doubt, vacillation, temporizing, shilly-shallying, irresolution, hemming and hawing, dubiety ...*After some hesitation, he answered her question...*
2 = reluctance, reservation(s), misgiving(s), ambivalence, qualm(s), unwillingness, scruple(s), compunction, demurral ...*The board said it had no hesitation in rejecting the offer...*

heterogeneous = varied, different, mixed, contrasting, unlike, diverse, diversified, assorted, unrelated, disparate, miscellaneous, motley, incongruous, dissimilar, divergent, manifold, discrepant

hew 1 = cut, chop, axe, hack, split, lop ...*He felled, peeled and hewed his own timber...*
2 (*Old-fashioned*) = carve, make, form, fashion, shape, model, sculpture, sculpt ...*medieval monasteries hewn out of the rockface...*

heyday = prime, time, day, flowering, pink, bloom, high point, zenith, salad days, prime of life

hiatus = pause, break, interval, space, gap, breach, blank, lapse, interruption, respite, chasm, discontinuity, lacuna, entr'acte

hibernate = sleep, lie dormant, winter, overwinter, vegetate, remain torpid, sleep snug

hidden 1 = secret, veiled, dark, mysterious, obscure, mystical, mystic, shrouded, occult, latent, cryptic, hermetic, ulterior, abstruse, recondite, hermetical ...*Uncover hidden meanings and discover special messages...*
2 = concealed, covered, secret, covert, unseen, clandestine, secreted, under wraps, unrevealed ...*The pictures had obviously been taken by a hidden camera...*

hide[1] **1** = conceal, stash (*informal*), secrete, cache, put out of sight ...*He hid the bicycle in the hawthorn hedge...* OPPOSITE display
2 = go into hiding, take cover, keep out of sight, hole up, lie low, go underground, go to ground, go to earth ...*They hid behind a tree...*
3 = keep secret, suppress, withhold, keep quiet about, hush up, draw a veil over, keep dark, keep under your hat ...*I have absolutely nothing to hide, I have done nothing wrong...* OPPOSITE disclose
4 = obscure, cover, screen, bury, shelter, mask, disguise, conceal, eclipse, veil, cloak, shroud, camouflage, blot out ...*The compound was hidden by trees and shrubs...* OPPOSITE reveal

hide[2] = skin, fell, leather, pelt ...*the process of tanning animal hides...*

hideaway = hiding place, haven, retreat, refuge, sanctuary, hide-out, nest, sequestered nook

hidebound = conventional, set, rigid, narrow, puritan, narrow-minded, strait-laced, brassbound, ultraconservative, set in your ways OPPOSITE broad-minded

hideous 1 = ugly, revolting, ghastly, monstrous, grotesque, gruesome, grisly, unsightly, repulsive ...*She saw a hideous face at the window and screamed...* OPPOSITE beautiful
2 = terrifying, shocking, terrible, awful, appalling, disgusting, horrible, dreadful, horrific, obscene, sickening, horrendous, macabre, horrid, odious, loathsome, abominable, detestable, godawful (*slang*) ...*His family was subjected to a hideous attack...*

hideout = hiding place, shelter, den, hideaway, lair, secret place

hiding (*Informal*) = beating, whipping, thrashing, tanning (*slang*), caning, licking (*informal*), flogging, spanking, walloping (*informal*), drubbing, lathering (*informal*), whaling, larruping (*Brit. dialect*)

hierarchy = grading, ranking, social order, pecking order, class system, social stratum

higgledy-piggledy (*Informal*) ADJECTIVE = haphazard, muddled, jumbled, indiscriminate, topsy-turvy, helter-skelter, pell-mell ...*books stacked in higgledy-piggledy piles on the floor...*
ADVERB = haphazardly, all over the place, anyhow, topsy-turvy, helter-skelter, all over the shop (*informal*), pell-mell, confusedly, any old how ...*boulders tossed higgledy-piggledy as though by some giant...*

high ADJECTIVE **1** = tall, towering, soaring, steep, elevated, lofty ...*A house with a high wall around it...* OPPOSITE short
2 = extreme, great, acute, severe, extraordinary, excessive ...*Officials said casualties were high...* OPPOSITE low
3 = strong, violent, extreme, blustery, squally, sharp ...*High winds have knocked down trees and power lines...*
4 = expensive, dear, steep (*informal*), costly, stiff, high-priced, exorbitant ...*I think it's a good buy overall, despite the high price...*
5 = important, leading, ruling, chief, powerful, significant, distinguished, prominent, superior, influential, notable, big-time (*informal*), eminent, major league (*informal*), exalted, consequential ...*Every one of them is controlled by the families of high officials...* OPPOSITE lowly
6 = notable, leading, important, famous, significant, celebrated, outstanding, distinguished, superior, renowned, eminent, exalted, noteworthy, pre-eminent ...*She has always had a high reputation for her excellent stories...*
7 = high-pitched, piercing, shrill, penetrating, treble, soprano, strident, sharp, acute, piping ...*Her high voice really irritated Maria...* OPPOSITE deep
8 = cheerful, excited, merry, exhilarated, exuberant, joyful, bouncy (*informal*), boisterous, elated, light-hearted ...*Her spirits were high with the hope of seeing Nick...* OPPOSITE dejected
9 (*Informal*) = intoxicated, stoned (*slang*), spaced out (*slang*), tripping (*informal*), turned on (*slang*), on a trip

(*informal*), delirious, euphoric, freaked out (*informal*), hyped up (*slang*), zonked (*slang*), inebriated ...*He was too high on drugs and alcohol to remember them...*
10 = luxurious, rich, grand, lavish, extravagant, opulent, hedonistic ...*an emphatic contrast to his Park Avenue high life...*
ADVERB = way up, aloft, far up, to a great height ...*on combat patrol flying high above the landing sites...*
NOUN 1 = peak, height, top, summit, crest, record level, apex ...*Sales of Russian vodka have reached an all-time high...*
2 (*Informal*) = intoxication, trip (*informal*), euphoria, delirium, ecstasy ...*The 'thrill' sought is said to be similar to a drug high...*
PHRASES high and dry = abandoned, stranded, helpless, forsaken, bereft, destitute, in the lurch ...*You could be left high and dry in a strange town...* ◆ **high and low** = everywhere, all over (the place), far and wide, exhaustively, in every nook and cranny ...*I have searched high and low for clothes to fit him...* ◆ **high and mighty** (*Informal*) = self-important, superior, arrogant, stuck-up (*informal*), conceited, imperious, overbearing, haughty, snobbish, disdainful ...*I think you're a bit too high and mighty yourself...* ◆ **high up** = important, prominent, powerful, significant, distinguished, superior, influential, notable, big-time (*informal*), eminent, major league (*informal*), exalted, consequential ...*His cousin is somebody quite high up in the navy...*

highbrow (*Often disparaging*) **ADJECTIVE** = intellectual, cultured, sophisticated, deep, cultivated, brainy (*informal*), highbrowed, bookish ...*He presents his own highbrow literary programme...* **OPPOSITE** unintellectual
NOUN = intellectual, scholar, egghead (*informal*), brain (*informal*), mastermind, Brahmin (*U.S.*), aesthete, savant, brainbox (*slang*) ...*the sniggers of the highbrows...* **OPPOSITE** philistine

high-class = high-quality, top (*slang*), choice, select, exclusive, elite, superior, posh (*informal, chiefly Brit.*), classy (*slang*), top-flight, upper-class, swish (*informal, chiefly Brit.*), first-rate, up-market, top-drawer, ritzy (*slang*), tip-top, high-toned, A1 *or* A-one (*informal*) **OPPOSITE** inferior

higher-up (*Informal*) = superior, senior, manager, director, executive, boss, gaffer (*informal, chiefly Brit.*), baas (*S. African*)

high-flown = extravagant, elaborate, pretentious, exaggerated, inflated, lofty, grandiose, overblown, florid, high-falutin (*informal*), arty-farty (*informal*), magniloquent **OPPOSITE** straightforward

high-handed = dictatorial, domineering, overbearing, arbitrary, oppressive, autocratic, bossy (*informal*), imperious, tyrannical, despotic, peremptory

highlands = uplands, hills, heights, hill country, mountainous region

highlight VERB = emphasize, stress, accent, feature, set off, show up, underline, spotlight, play up, accentuate, foreground, focus attention on, call attention to, give prominence to, bring to the fore ...*Two events have highlighted the tensions in recent days...* **OPPOSITE** play down
NOUN = high point, peak, climax, feature, focus, best part, focal point, main feature, high spot, memorable part ...*one of the highlights of the tournament...* **OPPOSITE** low point

highly 1 = extremely, very, greatly, seriously (*informal*), vastly, exceptionally, extraordinarily, immensely, decidedly, tremendously, supremely, eminently ...*He was a highly successful salesman...*
2 = favourably, well, warmly, enthusiastically, approvingly, appreciatively ...*one of the most highly regarded chefs in the French capital...*

highly-strung = nervous, stressed, tense, sensitive, wired (*slang*), restless, neurotic, taut, edgy, temperamental, excitable, nervy (*Brit. informal*), twitchy (*informal*), on tenterhooks, easily upset, on pins and needles **OPPOSITE** relaxed

high-minded = principled, moral, worthy, noble, good, fair, pure, ethical, upright, elevated, honourable, righteous, idealistic, virtuous, magnanimous **OPPOSITE** dishonourable

high-powered = dynamic, driving, powerful, enterprising, effective, go-ahead, aggressive, vigorous, energetic, forceful, fast-track, go-getting (*informal*), high-octane (*informal*), highly capable

high-pressure (*Informal*) = forceful, aggressive, compelling, intensive, persistent, persuasive, high-powered, insistent, bludgeoning, pushy (*informal*), in-your-face (*slang*), coercive, importunate

high-spirited = lively, spirited, vivacious, vital, daring, dashing, bold, energetic, animated, vibrant, exuberant, bouncy, boisterous, fun-loving, ebullient, sparky, effervescent, alive and kicking, full of life, spunky (*informal*), full of beans (*informal*), frolicsome, mettlesome

hijack = seize, take over, commandeer, expropriate, skyjack

hike NOUN = walk, march, trek, ramble, tramp, traipse, journey on foot ...*a hike around the cluster of hills...*
VERB = walk, march, trek, ramble, tramp, leg it (*informal*), back-pack, hoof it (*slang*) ...*You could hike through the Fish River Canyon...*
PHRASES hike something up = hitch up, raise, lift, pull up, jack up ...*He hiked up his trouser legs...*

hiker = walker, rambler, backpacker, wayfarer, hillwalker

hilarious 1 = funny, entertaining, amusing, hysterical, humorous, exhilarating, comical, side-splitting ...*He had a fund of hilarious tales...*
2 = merry, uproarious, happy, gay, noisy, jolly, joyous, joyful, jovial, rollicking, convivial, mirthful ...*Everyone had a hilarious time...* **OPPOSITE** serious

hilarity = merriment, high spirits, mirth, gaiety, laughter, amusement, glee, exuberance, exhilaration, cheerfulness, jollity, levity, conviviality, joviality, boisterousness, joyousness, jollification

hill 1 = mount, down (*archaic*), fell, height, mound, prominence, elevation, eminence, hilltop, tor, knoll,

hillock, brae (*Scot.*), kopje *or* koppie (*S. African*) ...*They climbed to the top of the hill...*
2 = slope, incline, gradient, rise, climb, brae (*Scot.*), acclivity ...*the shady street that led up the hill to the office building...*

hilly = mountainous, rolling, steep, undulating

hilt NOUN = handle, grip, haft, handgrip, helve ...*the hilt of the small, sharp knife...*
PHRASES **to the hilt** (*Informal*) = fully, completely, totally, entirely, wholly ...*James was overdrawn and mortgaged to the hilt...*

hind = back, rear, hinder, posterior, caudal (*Anatomy*)

hinder = obstruct, stop, check, block, prevent, arrest, delay, oppose, frustrate, handicap, interrupt, slow down, deter, hamstring, hamper, thwart, retard, impede, hobble, stymie, encumber, throw a spanner in the works, trammel, hold up *or* back OPPOSITE help

hindrance = obstacle, check, bar, block, difficulty, drag, barrier, restriction, handicap, limitation, hazard, restraint, hitch, drawback, snag, deterrent, interruption, obstruction, stoppage, stumbling block, impediment, encumbrance, trammel OPPOSITE help

Hinduism

> ### Hindu denominations and sects
> http://www.bbc.co.uk/religion/religions/
> hinduism/index.shtml
>
> | Hare Krishna | Saktas |
> | Saivaism | Vaishnavism |

hinge on = depend on, be subject to, hang on, turn on, rest on, revolve around, be contingent on, pivot on

hint NOUN **1** = clue, mention, suggestion, implication, indication, reminder, tip-off, pointer, allusion, innuendo, inkling, intimation, insinuation, word to the wise ...*I'd dropped a hint about having an exhibition of his work...*
2 *often plural* = advice, help, tip(s), suggestion(s), pointer(s) ...*I'm hoping to get some fashion hints...*
3 = trace, touch, suggestion, taste, breath, dash, whisper, suspicion, tinge, whiff, speck, undertone, soupçon (*French*) ...*I glanced at her and saw no hint of irony on her face...*
VERB *sometimes with **at*** = suggest, mention, indicate, imply, intimate, tip off, let it be known, insinuate, allude to the fact, tip the wink (*informal*) ...*The President hinted he might make some changes in the government...*

hip (*Slang*) = trendy (*Brit. informal*), with it, fashionable, in, aware, informed, wise (*slang*), clued-up (*informal*)

hippy *or* **hippie** = flower child, bohemian, dropout, free spirit, beatnik

hire VERB **1** = employ, commission, take on, engage, appoint, sign up, enlist ...*hired on short-term contracts...*
2 = rent, charter, lease, let, engage ...*To hire a car you must produce a current driving licence...*
NOUN **1** = rental, hiring, rent, lease ...*Fishing tackle is available for hire...*

2 = charge, rental, price, cost, fee ...*Surf board hire is $12 per day...*

hirsute (*Formal*) = hairy, bearded, shaggy, unshaven, bristly, bewhiskered, hispid (*Biology*)

hiss VERB **1** = whistle, wheeze, rasp, whiz, whirr, sibilate ...*The air hissed out of the pipe...*
2 = jeer, mock, ridicule, deride, decry, revile ...*The delegates booed and hissed him...*
NOUN = fizz, buzz, hissing, fizzing, sibilance, sibilation ...*the hiss of a beer bottle opening...*

historian = chronicler, recorder, biographer, antiquarian, historiographer, annalist, chronologist

historic = significant, notable, momentous, famous, celebrated, extraordinary, outstanding, remarkable, ground-breaking, consequential, red-letter, epoch-making OPPOSITE unimportant

> ## Word Power
>
> **historic** – Although *historic* and *historical* are similarly spelt they are very different in meaning and should not be used interchangeably. A distinction is usually made between *historic*, which means 'important' or 'significant', and *historical*, which means 'pertaining to history': *a historic decision*; *a historical perspective*.

historical = factual, real, documented, actual, authentic, chronicled, attested, archival, verifiable OPPOSITE contemporary
➤ **historic**

history 1 = the past, the old days, antiquity, yesterday, the good old days, yesteryear, ancient history, olden days, days of old, days of yore, bygone times ...*Is history about to repeat itself?...*
2 = chronicle, record, story, account, relation, narrative, saga, recital, narration, annals, recapitulation ...*his magnificent history of broadcasting in Canada...*
➤ **history**

histrionic ADJECTIVE = theatrical, affected, dramatic, forced, camp (*informal*), actorly, artificial, unnatural, melodramatic, actressy ...*Dorothea let out a histrionic groan...*
PLURAL NOUN = dramatics, scene, tantrums, performance, temperament, theatricality, staginess ...*When I explained everything, there were no histrionics...*

hit VERB **1** = strike, beat, knock, punch, belt (*informal*), deck (*slang*), bang, batter, clip (*informal*), slap, bash (*informal*), sock (*slang*), chin (*slang*), smack, thump, clout (*informal*), cuff, flog, whack, clobber (*slang*), smite (*archaic*), wallop (*informal*), swat, lay one on (*slang*) ...*She hit him hard across his left arm...*
2 = collide with, run into, bump into, clash with, smash into, crash against, bang into, meet head-on ...*The car hit a traffic sign before skidding out of control...*
3 = affect, damage, harm, ruin, devastate, overwhelm, touch, impact on, impinge on, leave a mark on, make

History
http://www.historyofnations.net/
http://personal.cmich.edu/~loren1mg/world-history.html

Historical characters

Alexander the Great
Alfred the Great
Mark Antony
Attila the Hun
Augustus
Thomas à Becket
Billy the Kid
The Black Prince
Bonnie Prince Charlie (Charles
  Edward Stuart)
Lucrezia Borgia
Boudicca or Boadicea
Brutus
Buddha
Buffalo Bill (William Frederick
  Cody)
Julius Caesar
Catherine the Great
Charlemagne
Winston Churchill
El Cid
Cleopatra
Clive of India
Christopher Columbus
Captain James Cook
Hernando Cortés
Crazy Horse
Davy Crockett
Oliver Cromwell
George Armstrong Custer

Francis Drake
Guy Fawkes
Yuri Gagarin
Mahatma Gandhi
Giuseppe Garibaldi
Genghis Khan
Geronimo
Gordon of Khartoum
Che Guevara
Haile Selassie
Hannibal
Henry VIII
Hereward the Wake
Hiawatha
Wild Bill (James Butler) Hickok
Adolf Hitler
Ivan the Terrible
Jesse James
Jesus
Joan of Arc
Martin Luther King
Lawrence of Arabia
Robert E(dward) Lee
Vladimir Ilyich Lenin
Abraham Lincoln
Martin Luther
Mary, Queen of Scots
Mao Ze Dong or Mao Tse-tung
Marie Antoinette
Mohammed or Muhammad

Montezuma
Benito Mussolini
Napoleon Bonaparte
Horatio Nelson
Florence Nightingale
Captain (Lawrence Edward
  Grace) Oates
Pericles
Marco Polo
Pompey
Walter Raleigh
Grigori Efimovich Rasputin
Richard the Lionheart
Robert the Bruce
Saladin
Robert Falcon Scott
Sitting Bull
Socrates
Joseph Stalin
Tomás de Torquemada
Leon Trotsky
William Wallace
Warwick the Kingmaker
George Washington
Duke of Wellington
William the Conqueror
Orville and Wilbur Wright
Emiliano Zapata

Historical events

Agincourt
Alamo
American Civil War or (chiefly
  U.S.) the War between the
  States
Armistice
Battle of Hastings
Black Death
Bloody Sunday
Boer War
Boston Tea Party
Boxer Rebellion
Charge of the Light Brigade
Civil War
Cold War
Crimean War
Crusades
Cultural Revolution
D-day
Declaration of Independence
Depression
Diet of Worms
Easter Rising
French Revolution

General Strike
Gettysburg Address
Glorious Revolution
Gordon Riots
Great Fire of London
Great Schism
Great Trek
Gunpowder Plot
Hiroshima
Holocaust
Hundred Years War
Hungarian Uprising
Indian Mutiny
Industrial Revolution
Jacobite Rebellion
Korean War
Kristallnacht or Crystal Night
Long March
Magna Carta
Munich Agreement
Night of the Long Knives
Napoleonic Wars
Norman Conquest
Pearl Harbor

Peasants' Revolt
Peterloo Massacre
Potato Famine
Reformation
Reign of Terror
Renaissance
Restoration
Risorgimento
Russian Revolution
Saint Valentine's Day Massacre
South Sea Bubble
Spanish Armada
Spanish Civil War
Spanish Inquisition
Suez Crisis
Thirty Years' War
Tiananmen Square Massacre
Trafalgar
Treaty of Versailles
Vietnam War
Wall Street Crash
Wars of the Roses
Watergate
Waterloo

an impact or impression on ...The big cities have been
hit by a wave of panic-buying... ...the earthquake
which hit northern Peru...

4 = reach, strike, gain, achieve, secure, arrive at,
accomplish, attain ...Oil prices hit record levels

yesterday...

NOUN 1 = shot, blow, impact, collision ...The house
took a direct hit then the rocket exploded...

2 = blow, knock, stroke, belt (informal), rap, slap,
bump, smack, clout (informal), cuff, swipe (informal),

wallop (*informal*) ...*a hit on the head*...

3 = <u>success</u>, winner, triumph, smash (*informal*), sensation, sellout, smasheroo (*informal*) ...*The song became a massive hit in 1945*...

PHRASES **hit it off** (*Informal*) = <u>get on (well) with</u>, take to, click (*slang*), warm to, be on good terms, get on like a house on fire (*informal*) ...*How well did you hit it off with one another?*... ◆ **hit on** or **upon something** = <u>think up</u>, discover, arrive at, guess, realize, invent, come upon, stumble on, chance upon, light upon, strike upon ...*We finally hit on a solution*... ◆ **hit out at something** or **someone** = <u>attack</u>, condemn, denounce, lash out, castigate, rail against, assail, inveigh against, strike out at ...*The President hit out at what he sees as foreign interference*...

hit-and-miss or **hit-or-miss** = <u>haphazard</u>, random, uneven, casual, indiscriminate, cursory, perfunctory, aimless, disorganized, undirected **OPPOSITE** systematic

hitch **NOUN** = <u>problem</u>, catch, trouble, check, difficulty, delay, hold-up, obstacle, hazard, drawback, hassle (*informal*), snag, uphill (*S. African*), stoppage, mishap, impediment, hindrance ...*The five-hour operation went without a hitch*...
VERB **1** (*Informal*) = <u>hitchhike</u>, thumb a lift ...*I hitched a lift into town*...
2 = <u>fasten</u>, join, attach, unite, couple, tie, connect, harness, tether, yoke, make fast ...*We hitched the horse to the cart*...
PHRASES **hitch something up** = <u>pull up</u>, tug, jerk, yank, hoick ...*He hitched his trousers up over his potbelly*...

hither (*Old-fashioned*) = <u>here</u>, over here, to this place, close, closer, near, nearer, nigh (*archaic*)

hitherto (*Formal*) = <u>previously</u>, so far, until now, thus far, up to now, till now, heretofore

hive **1** = <u>colony</u>, swarm ...*the dance performed by honeybees as they returned to the hive*...
2 = <u>centre</u>, hub, powerhouse (*slang*) ...*In the morning the house was a hive of activity*...

hoard **VERB** = <u>save</u>, store, collect, gather, treasure, accumulate, garner, amass, stockpile, buy up, put away, hive, cache, lay up, put by, stash away (*informal*) ...*They've begun to hoard food and gasoline*...
NOUN = <u>store</u>, fund, supply, reserve, mass, pile, heap, fall-back, accumulation, stockpile, stash, cache, treasure-trove ...*a hoard of silver and jewels*...

hoarse = <u>rough</u>, harsh, husky, grating, growling, raucous, rasping, gruff, throaty, gravelly, guttural, croaky **OPPOSITE** clear

hoary **1** = <u>old</u>, aged, ancient, antique, venerable, antiquated ...*the hoary old myth that women are unpredictable*...
2 = <u>white-haired</u>, white, grey, silvery, frosty, grey-haired, grizzled, hoar ...*hoary beards*...

hoax **NOUN** = <u>trick</u>, joke, fraud, con (*informal*), deception, spoof (*informal*), prank, swindle, ruse, practical joke, canard, fast one (*informal*), imposture ...*His claim to have a bomb was a hoax*...

VERB = <u>deceive</u>, trick, fool, take in (*informal*), con (*slang*), wind up (*Brit. slang*), kid (*informal*), bluff, dupe, gull (*archaic*), delude, swindle, bamboozle (*informal*), gammon (*Brit. informal*), hoodwink, take (someone) for a ride (*informal*), befool, hornswoggle (*slang*) ...*He recently hoaxed Nelson Mandela by pretending to be Tony Blair*...

hobble **1** = <u>limp</u>, stagger, stumble, shuffle, falter, shamble, totter, dodder, halt ...*He got up slowly and hobbled over to the table*...
2 = <u>restrict</u>, hamstring, shackle, fetter ...*The poverty of 10 million citizens hobbles our economy*...

hobby = <u>pastime</u>, relaxation, leisure pursuit, sideline, diversion, avocation, favourite occupation, (leisure) activity

hobnob = <u>socialize</u>, mix, associate, hang out (*informal*), mingle, consort, hang about, keep company, fraternize

hog (*Slang*) = <u>monopolize</u>, dominate, tie up, corner, corner the market in, be a dog in the manger

hoist **VERB** = <u>raise</u>, lift, erect, elevate, heave, upraise ...*He hoisted himself to a sitting position*...
NOUN = <u>lift</u>, crane, elevator, winch, tackle ...*It takes three nurses and a hoist to get me into this chair*...

hold **VERB** **1** = <u>carry</u>, keep, grip, grasp, cling to, clasp ...*Hold the baby while I load the car*...
2 = <u>support</u>, take, bear, shoulder, sustain, prop, brace ...*Hold the weight with a straight arm above your head*... **OPPOSITE** give way
3 = <u>embrace</u>, grasp, clutch, hug, squeeze, cradle, clasp, enfold ...*If only he would hold her close to him*...
4 = <u>restrain</u>, constrain, check, bind, curb, hamper, hinder ...*He was held in an arm lock*... **OPPOSITE** release
5 = <u>accommodate</u>, take, contain, seat, comprise, have a capacity for ...*The small bottles don't seem to hold much*...
6 = <u>consider</u>, think, believe, view, judge, regard, maintain, assume, reckon, esteem, deem, presume, entertain the idea ...*She holds that it is not admissible to ordain women*... **OPPOSITE** deny
7 = <u>occupy</u>, have, fill, maintain, retain, possess, hold down (*informal*) ...*She has never held a ministerial post*...
8 = <u>conduct</u>, convene, have, call, run, celebrate, carry on, assemble, preside over, officiate at, solemnize ...*They held frequent consultations concerning technical problems*... **OPPOSITE** cancel
9 = <u>detain</u>, arrest, confine, imprison, impound, pound, hold in custody, put in jail ...*the return of two seamen held on spying charges*... **OPPOSITE** release
10 *sometimes with* **up** = <u>continue</u>, last, remain, stay, wear, resist, endure, persist, persevere ...*Our luck couldn't hold for ever*...
11 = <u>apply</u>, exist, be the case, stand up, operate, be in force, remain true, hold good, remain valid ...*Today, most people think that argument no longer holds*...
NOUN **1** = <u>grip</u>, grasp, clutch, clasp ...*He released his hold on the camera*...
2 = <u>foothold</u>, footing, purchase, leverage, vantage, anchorage ...*The idea didn't really get a hold in this*

country…

3 = <u>control</u>, authority, influence, pull (*informal*), sway, dominance, clout (*informal*), mastery, dominion, ascendancy, mana (*N.Z.*) …*It's always useful to have a hold over people…*

PHRASES **hold back** = <u>desist</u>, forbear, hesitate, stop yourself, restrain yourself, refrain from doing something …*She wanted to say something but held back…* ◆ **hold forth** = <u>speak</u>, go on, discourse, lecture, preach, spout (*informal*), harangue, declaim, spiel (*informal*), descant, orate, speechify …*He is capable of holding forth with great eloquence…* ◆ **hold off** = <u>put off</u>, delay, postpone, defer, avoid, refrain, keep from …*The hospital staff held off taking him in for an X-ray…* ◆ **hold on** = <u>wait (a minute)</u>, hang on (*informal*), sit tight (*informal*), hold your horses (*informal*), just a moment *or* second …*Hold on while I have a look…* ◆ **hold onto something** *or* **someone 1** = <u>grab</u>, hold, grip, clutch, cling to …*He was struggling to hold onto the rock above his head…* **2** = <u>retain</u>, keep, hang onto, not give away, keep possession of …*to enable Spurs to hold onto their striker…* ◆ **hold out** = <u>last</u>, continue, carry on, endure, hang on, persist, persevere, stay the course, stand fast …*He can only hold out for a few more weeks…* ◆ **hold out against something** *or* **someone** = <u>withstand</u>, resist, fend off, keep at bay, fight …*They held out against two companies of troops…* ◆ **hold someone back** = <u>hinder</u>, prevent, restrain, check, hamstring, hamper, inhibit, thwart, obstruct, impede …*Does her illness hold her back from making friends or enjoying life?…* ◆ **hold someone up** = <u>delay</u>, slow down, hinder, stop, detain, retard, impede, set back …*Why were you holding everyone up?…* ◆ **hold something** *or* **someone off** = <u>fend off</u>, repel, rebuff, stave off, repulse, keep off …*holding off a tremendous challenge…* ◆ **hold something back 1** = <u>restrain</u>, check, curb, control, suppress, rein (in), repress, stem the flow of …*Stagnation in home sales is holding back economic recovery…* **2** = <u>withhold</u>, hold in, suppress, stifle, repress, keep the lid on (*informal*), keep back …*You seem to be holding something back…* ◆ **hold something out** = <u>offer</u>, give, present, extend, proffer …*Max held out his cup for a refill…* ◆ **hold something over** = <u>postpone</u>, delay, suspend, put off, defer, adjourn, waive, take a rain check on (*U.S. & Canad. informal*) …*Further voting might be held over until tomorrow…* ◆ **hold something up 1** = <u>display</u>, show, exhibit, flourish, show off, hold aloft, present …*Hold it up so we can see it…* **2** = <u>support</u>, prop, brace, bolster, sustain, shore up, buttress, jack up …*Mills have iron pillars holding up the roof…* **3** = <u>rob</u>, mug (*informal*), stick up (*slang, chiefly U.S.*), waylay …*A thief ran off with hundreds of pounds after holding up a petrol station…* ◆ **hold up** = <u>last</u>, survive, endure, bear up, wear …*Children's wear is holding up well in the recession…* ◆ **hold with something** = <u>approve of</u>, be in favour of, support, subscribe to, countenance, agree to *or* with, take kindly to …*I don't hold with the way they do things nowadays…* ◆ **hold your own** = <u>keep up</u>, do well, hold out, keep pace, stay put, stand firm, hold fast, stand your ground, stick to your guns (*informal*), keep your head above water, maintain your position …*The Frenchman held his own against the challenger…* ◆ **lay hold of something** *or* **someone** = <u>grasp</u>, grab, seize, grip, snatch, get hold of, get …*They laid hold of him with rough hands…*

holder 1 = <u>owner</u>, bearer, possessor, keeper, purchaser, occupant, proprietor, custodian, incumbent …*the holders of the Championship… …the club has 73,500 season-ticket holders…* **2** = <u>case</u>, cover, container, sheath, receptacle, housing …*a toothbrush holder…*

holdings = <u>property</u>, securities, investments, resources, estate, assets, possessions, stocks and shares, land interests

hold-up 1 = <u>robbery</u>, theft, mugging (*informal*), stick-up (*slang, chiefly U.S.*) …*an armed hold-up at a National Australia bank…* **2** = <u>delay</u>, wait, hitch, trouble, difficulty, setback, snag, traffic jam, obstruction, stoppage, bottleneck …*They arrived late due to a motorway hold-up…*

hole NOUN **1** = <u>cavity</u>, depression, pit, hollow, pocket, chamber, cave, shaft, cavern, excavation …*He took a shovel, dug a hole, and buried his possessions…* **2** = <u>opening</u>, split, crack, break, tear, gap, rent, breach, outlet, vent, puncture, aperture, fissure, orifice, perforation …*They got in through a hole in the wall… …kids with holes in the knees of their jeans…* **3** = <u>burrow</u>, nest, den, earth, shelter, retreat, covert, lair …*a rabbit hole…* **4** = <u>fault</u>, error, flaw, defect, loophole, discrepancy, inconsistency, fallacy …*There were some holes in that theory…* **5** (*Informal*) = <u>hovel</u>, dump (*informal*), dive (*slang*), slum, joint (*slang*) …*Why don't you leave this awful hole and come to live with me?…* **6** (*Informal*) = <u>predicament</u>, spot (*informal*), fix (*informal*), mess, jam (*informal*), dilemma, scrape (*informal*), tangle, hot water (*informal*), quandary, tight spot, imbroglio …*He admitted that the government was in 'a dreadful hole'…*

PHRASES **hole up** = <u>hide</u>, shelter, take refuge, go into hiding, take cover, go to earth …*holing up in his Paris flat with the phone off the hook…* ◆ **pick holes in something** = <u>criticize</u>, knock (*informal*), rubbish (*informal*), put down, run down, slate (*informal*), slag (off) (*slang*), denigrate, disprove, disparage, diss (*slang, chiefly U.S.*), find fault with, bad-mouth (*slang, chiefly U.S. & Canad.*), niggle at, cavil at, pull to pieces, asperse …*He then goes on to pick holes in the article…*

holiday 1 = <u>vacation</u>, leave, break, time off, recess, away day …*I've just come back from a holiday in the United States…* **2** = <u>festival</u>, bank holiday, festivity, public holiday, fête, celebration, anniversary, feast, red-letter day, name day, saint's day, gala …*New Year's Day is a public holiday throughout Britain…*

holiness = <u>sanctity</u>, spirituality, sacredness, purity, divinity, righteousness, piety, godliness, saintliness, blessedness, religiousness, devoutness, virtuousness

holler (*Informal*) `VERB` *sometimes with* **out** = <u>yell</u>, call, cry, shout, cheer, roar, hail, bellow, whoop, clamour, bawl, hurrah, halloo, huzzah (*archaic*) ...*He hollered for help...*
`NOUN` = <u>yell</u>, call, cry, shout, cheer, roar, hail, bellow, whoop, clamour, bawl, hurrah, halloo, huzzah (*archaic*) ...*The men were celebrating with drunken whoops and hollers...*

hollow `ADJECTIVE` **1** = <u>empty</u>, vacant, void, unfilled, not solid ...*a hollow cylinder...* `OPPOSITE` solid
2 = <u>sunken</u>, depressed, cavernous, indented, concave, deep-set ...*hollow cheeks...* `OPPOSITE` rounded
3 = <u>worthless</u>, empty, useless, vain, meaningless, pointless, futile, fruitless, specious, Pyrrhic, unavailing ...*Any threat to bring in the police is a hollow one...* `OPPOSITE` meaningful
4 = <u>insincere</u>, false, artificial, cynical, hypocritical, hollow-hearted ...*His hollow laugh had no mirth in it...*
5 = <u>dull</u>, low, deep, flat, rumbling, muted, muffled, expressionless, sepulchral, toneless, reverberant ...*the hollow sound of a gunshot...* `OPPOSITE` vibrant
`NOUN` **1** = <u>cavity</u>, cup, hole, bowl, depression, pit, cave, den, basin, dent, crater, trough, cavern, excavation, indentation, dimple, concavity ...*where water gathers in a hollow and forms a pond...* `OPPOSITE` mound
2 = <u>valley</u>, dale, glen, dell, dingle ...*Locals in the sleepy hollow peered out of their country cottages...* `OPPOSITE` hill
`VERB` *often followed by* **out** = <u>scoop out</u>, dig out, excavate, gouge out, channel, groove, furrow ...*Someone had hollowed out a large block of stone...*

holocaust **1** = <u>devastation</u>, destruction, carnage, genocide, inferno, annihilation, conflagration ...*A nuclear holocaust seemed a very real possibility in the '50s...*
2 = <u>genocide</u>, massacre, carnage, mass murder, annihilation, pogrom ...*a fund for survivors of the holocaust and their families...*

holy **1** = <u>sacred</u>, blessed, hallowed, dedicated, venerable, consecrated, venerated, sacrosanct, sanctified ...*To them, as to all Tibetans, this is a holy place...* `OPPOSITE` unsanctified
2 = <u>devout</u>, godly, religious, pure, divine, faithful, righteous, pious, virtuous, hallowed, saintly, god-fearing ...*The Indians think of him as a holy man...* `OPPOSITE` sinful

homage **1** = <u>respect</u>, honour, worship, esteem, admiration, awe, devotion, reverence, duty, deference, adulation, adoration ...*two marvellous films that pay homage to our literary heritage...* `OPPOSITE` contempt
2 = <u>allegiance</u>, service, tribute, loyalty, devotion, fidelity, faithfulness, obeisance, troth (*archaic*), fealty ...*At his coronation he received the homage of kings...*

home `NOUN` **1** = <u>dwelling</u>, house, residence, abode, habitation, pad (*slang*), domicile, dwelling place ...*the allocation of land for new homes...*
2 = <u>birthplace</u>, household, homeland, home town, homestead, native land ...*She was told to leave home by her father... ...His father worked away from home for many years...*

3 = <u>territory</u>, environment, habitat, range, element, haunt, home ground, abode, habitation, stamping ground ...*threatening the home of the famous African mountain gorillas...*
`ADJECTIVE` = <u>domestic</u>, national, local, central, internal, native, inland ...*Europe's software companies still have a growing home market...*
`PHRASES` **at home 1** = <u>in</u>, present, available ...*Remember I'm not at home to callers...* **2** = <u>at ease</u>, relaxed, comfortable, content, at peace ...*We soon felt quite at home...* ◆ **at home in, on,** *or* **with** = <u>familiar with</u>, experienced in, skilled in, proficient in, conversant with, au fait with, knowledgeable of, well-versed in ...*Graphic artists will feel at home with Photoshop...* ◆ **bring something home to someone** = <u>make clear</u>, emphasize, drive home, press home, impress upon ...*It was to bring home to Americans the immediacy of the crisis...*
➤ **hone**

homeland = <u>native land</u>, birthplace, motherland, fatherland, country of origin, mother country

homeless = <u>destitute</u>, exiled, displaced, dispossessed, unsettled, outcast, abandoned, down-and-out

homely **1** = <u>comfortable</u>, welcoming, friendly, domestic, familiar, informal, cosy, comfy (*informal*), homespun, downhome (*slang, chiefly U.S.*), homelike, homy ...*We try and provide a very homely atmosphere...*
2 = <u>plain</u>, simple, natural, ordinary, modest, everyday, down-to-earth, unaffected, unassuming, unpretentious, unfussy ...*Scottish baking is homely, comforting and truly good...* `OPPOSITE` elaborate
3 (*U.S.*) = <u>unattractive</u>, plain, ugly, not striking, unprepossessing, not beautiful, no oil painting (*informal*), ill-favoured ...*The man was homely and overweight...*

homespun = <u>unsophisticated</u>, homely, plain, rough, rude, coarse, home-made, rustic, artless, inelegant, unpolished

homey (*Chiefly U.S.*) = <u>homely</u>, comfortable, welcoming, domestic, friendly, familiar, cosy, comfy (*informal*), homespun, downhome (*slang, chiefly U.S.*), homelike

homicidal = <u>murderous</u>, deadly, lethal, maniacal, death-dealing

homicide = <u>murder</u>, killing, manslaughter, slaying, bloodshed

homily = <u>sermon</u>, talk, address, speech, lecture, preaching, discourse, oration, declamation

homogeneous *or* **homogenous** = <u>uniform</u>, similar, consistent, identical, alike, comparable, akin, analogous, kindred, unvarying, cognate `OPPOSITE` diverse

homosexual `ADJECTIVE` = <u>gay</u>, lesbian, queer (*informal, derogatory*), camp (*informal*), pink (*informal*), same-sex, homoerotic, sapphic, moffie (*S. African slang*) ...*a homosexual relationship...*
`NOUN` = <u>gay</u>, lesbian, queer (*informal, derogatory*), moffie (*S. African slang*), auntie *or* aunty (*Austral.*

slang), lily (*Austral. slang*) ...*You didn't tell me he was a homosexual...*

Related Words

fear of: homophobia

hone 1 = <u>improve</u>, better, polish, enhance, upgrade, refine, sharpen, augment, help ...*honing the skills of senior managers...*

2 = <u>sharpen</u>, point, grind, edge, file, polish, whet, strop ...*four grinding wheels for honing fine-edged tools...*

Word Power

hone – *Hone is sometimes wrongly used where home is meant: this device makes it easier to home in on (not hone in on) the target.*

---

honest 1 = <u>trustworthy</u>, decent, upright, reliable, ethical, honourable, conscientious, reputable, truthful, virtuous, law-abiding, trusty, scrupulous, high-minded, veracious ...*My dad was the most honest man I have ever met...* OPPOSITE dishonest

2 = <u>open</u>, direct, frank, plain, straightforward, outright, sincere, candid, forthright, upfront (*informal*), undisguised, round, ingenuous, unfeigned ...*I was honest about what I was doing...* OPPOSITE secretive

3 = <u>genuine</u>, real, true, straight, fair, proper, authentic, equitable, impartial, on the level (*informal*), bona fide, dinkum (*Austral. & N.Z. informal*), above board, fair and square, on the up and up, honest to goodness ...*It was an honest mistake on his part...* OPPOSITE false

honestly 1 = <u>ethically</u>, legitimately, legally, in good faith, on the level (*informal*), lawfully, honourably, by fair means, with clean hands ...*charged with failing to act honestly in his duties as an officer...*

2 = <u>frankly</u>, plainly, candidly, straight (out), truthfully, to your face, in plain English, in all sincerity ...*It came as a shock to hear him talk so honestly about an old friend...*

honesty 1 = <u>integrity</u>, honour, virtue, morality, fidelity, probity, rectitude, veracity, faithfulness, truthfulness, trustworthiness, straightness, incorruptibility, scrupulousness, uprightness, reputability ...*It's time for complete honesty from political representatives...*

2 = <u>frankness</u>, openness, sincerity, candour, bluntness, outspokenness, genuineness, plainness, straightforwardness ...*Good communication encourages honesty in a relationship...*

honeyed 1 = <u>flattering</u>, sweet, soothing, enticing, mellow, seductive, agreeable, sweetened, cajoling, alluring, melodious, unctuous, dulcet ...*His gentle manner and honeyed tones reassured Andrew...*

2 (*Poetic*), sweetened, luscious, sugary, syrupy, toothsome ...*I could smell the honeyed ripeness of melons and peaches...*

honorary = <u>nominal</u>, unofficial, titular, ex officio, honoris causa (*Latin*), in name or title only

honour NOUN 1 = <u>integrity</u>, principles, morality, honesty, goodness, fairness, decency, righteousness, probity, rectitude, trustworthiness, uprightness ...*I can no longer serve with honour as a member of your government...* OPPOSITE dishonour

2 = <u>prestige</u>, credit, reputation, glory, fame, distinction, esteem, dignity, elevation, eminence, renown, repute, high standing ...*He brought honour and glory to his country...* OPPOSITE disgrace

3 = <u>title</u>, award, distinction, accolade, decoration, laurel, adornment ...*He was showered with honours – among them an Oscar in 1950...*

4 = <u>reputation</u>, standing, prestige, image, status, stature, good name, kudos, cachet ...*Britain's national honour was at stake...*

5 = <u>acclaim</u>, regard, respect, praise, recognition, compliments, homage, accolades, reverence, deference, adoration, commendation, veneration ...*One grand old English gentleman at least will be received with honour...* OPPOSITE contempt

6 = <u>privilege</u>, credit, favour, pleasure, compliment, source of pride *or* satisfaction ...*Five other cities had been competing for the honour of staging the Games...*

7 (*Old-fashioned*) = <u>virginity</u>, virtue, innocence, purity, modesty, chastity ...*He had fell designs on her honour...*

VERB 1 = <u>acclaim</u>, celebrate, praise, decorate, compliment, commemorate, dignify, commend, glorify, exalt, laud, lionize ...*Two American surgeons were honoured with the Nobel Prize...*

2 = <u>respect</u>, value, esteem, prize, appreciate, admire, worship, adore, revere, glorify, reverence, exalt, venerate, hallow ...*Honour your parents, that's what the Bible says...* OPPOSITE scorn

3 = <u>fulfil</u>, keep, carry out, observe, discharge, live up to, be true to, be as good as (*informal*), be faithful to ...*He had failed to honour his word...*

4 = <u>pay</u>, take, accept, clear, pass, cash, credit, acknowledge ...*The bank refused to honour his cheque...* OPPOSITE refuse

honourable 1 = <u>principled</u>, moral, ethical, just, true, fair, upright, honest, virtuous, trustworthy, trusty, high-minded, upstanding ...*I believe he was an honourable man...*

2 = <u>proper</u>, right, respectable, righteous, virtuous, creditable ...*However, their intentions are honourable...*

3 = <u>prestigious</u>, great, noble, noted, distinguished, notable, renowned, eminent, illustrious, venerable ...*an honourable profession...*

hoodoo (*Informal*) = <u>jinx</u>, curse, bad luck, voodoo, nemesis, hex (*U.S. & Canad. informal*), evil eye, evil star

hoodwink = <u>deceive</u>, trick, fool, cheat, con (*informal*), kid (*informal*), mislead, hoax, dupe, gull (*archaic*), delude, swindle, rook (*slang*), bamboozle (*informal*), take (someone) for a ride (*informal*), lead up the garden path (*informal*), sell a pup, pull a fast one on (*informal*), cozen, befool

hook NOUN = <u>fastener</u>, catch, link, lock, holder, peg, clasp, hasp ...*One of his jackets hung from a hook...*

VERB 1 = <u>fasten</u>, fix, secure, catch, clasp, hasp ...*one of those can openers you hook onto the wall...*

2 = <u>catch</u>, land, trap, entrap ...*Whenever one of us*

hooked a fish, we moved on...

PHRASES **by hook or by crook** = <u>by any means</u>, somehow, somehow or other, someway, by fair means or foul ...*They intend to get their way, by hook or by crook...* ♦ **hook, line, and sinker** (*Informal*) = <u>completely</u>, totally, entirely, thoroughly, wholly, utterly, through and through, lock, stock and barrel ...*We fell for it hook, line, and sinker...* ♦ **off the hook** (*Informal*) = <u>let off</u>, cleared, acquitted, vindicated, in the clear, exonerated, under no obligation, allowed to walk (*slang, chiefly U.S.*) ...*Officials accused of bribery always seem to get off the hook...*

hooked 1 = <u>bent</u>, curved, beaked, aquiline, beaky, hook-shaped, hamate (*rare*), hooklike, falcate (*Biology*), unciform (*Anatomy, etc.*), uncinate (*Biology*) ...*He was tall and thin, with a hooked nose...*
2 (*Informal*) = <u>obsessed</u>, addicted, taken, devoted, turned on (*slang*), enamoured ...*Open this book and read a few pages and you will be hooked...*
3 (*Informal*) = <u>addicted</u>, dependent, using (*informal*), having a habit ...*He spent a number of years hooked on cocaine, heroin and alcohol...*

hooligan = <u>delinquent</u>, tough, vandal, casual, ned (*Scot. slang*), rowdy, hoon (*Austral. & N.Z.*), hoodlum (*chiefly U.S.*), ruffian, lager lout, yob *or* yobbo (*Brit. slang*), cougan (*Austral. slang*), scozza (*Austral. slang*), bogan (*Austral. slang*)

hooliganism = <u>delinquency</u>, violence, disorder, vandalism, rowdiness, loutishness, yobbishness

hoop = <u>ring</u>, band, loop, wheel, round, girdle, circlet

hoot **VERB 1** = <u>toot</u>, sound, blast, blare, beep, honk ...*Somewhere in the distance a siren hooted...*
2 = <u>shout</u>, cry, yell, scream, shriek, whoop ...*Bev hooted with laughter...*
3 = <u>jeer</u>, boo, howl, yell, catcall ...*The protesters chanted, blew whistles and hooted...*
4 = <u>cry</u>, call, screech, tu-whit tu-whoo ...*Out in the garden an owl hooted suddenly...*
NOUN 1 = <u>toot</u>, beep, honk ...*He strode on, ignoring the car, in spite of a further warning hoot...*
2 = <u>cry</u>, shout, howl, scream, shriek, whoop ...*hoots of laughter...*
3 = <u>jeer</u>, yell, boo, catcall ...*His confession was greeted with derisive hoots...*
4 (*Informal*) = <u>laugh</u>, scream (*informal*), caution (*informal*), card (*informal*) ...*He's a hoot, a real character...*

hop **VERB** = <u>jump</u>, spring, bound, leap, skip, vault, caper ...*I hopped down three steps...*
NOUN = <u>jump</u>, step, spring, bound, leap, bounce, skip, vault ...*'This is a catchy rhythm,' he added with a few hops...*

hope **VERB** = <u>believe</u>, expect, trust, rely, look forward to, anticipate, contemplate, count on, foresee, keep your fingers crossed, cross your fingers ...*I hope that the police will take the strongest action against them...*
NOUN = <u>belief</u>, confidence, expectation, longing, dream, desire, faith, ambition, assumption, anticipation, expectancy, light at the end of the tunnel ...*Kevin hasn't given up hope of being fit...*

OPPOSITE despair

hopeful 1 = <u>optimistic</u>, confident, assured, looking forward to, anticipating, buoyant, sanguine, expectant ...*Surgeons were hopeful of saving her sight...* **OPPOSITE** despairing
2 = <u>promising</u>, encouraging, bright, reassuring, cheerful, rosy, heartening, auspicious, propitious ...*hopeful forecasts that the economy will improve...* **OPPOSITE** unpromising

hopefully 1 = <u>optimistically</u>, confidently, expectantly, with anticipation, sanguinely ...*'Am I welcome?' he smiled hopefully...*
2 (*Informal*) = <u>it is hoped</u>, probably, all being well, God willing, conceivably, feasibly, expectedly ...*Hopefully, you won't have any problems after reading this...*

> ## Word Power
>
> **hopefully** – Some people object to the use of *hopefully* as a synonym for the phrase 'it is hoped that' in a sentence such as *hopefully I'll be able to attend the meeting*. This use of the adverb first appeared in America in the 1960s, but it has rapidly established itself elsewhere. There are really no strong grounds for objecting to it, since we accept other sentence adverbials that fulfil a similar function, for example *unfortunately*, which means 'it is unfortunate that' in a sentence such as *unfortunately I won't be able to attend the meeting*.

hopeless 1 = <u>pessimistic</u>, desperate, despairing, forlorn, in despair, abject, dejected, despondent, demoralized, defeatist, disconsolate, downhearted ...*Even able pupils feel hopeless about job prospects...* **OPPOSITE** hopeful
2 = <u>impossible</u>, pointless, futile, useless, vain, forlorn, no-win, unattainable, impracticable, unachievable, not having a prayer ...*I don't believe your situation is as hopeless as you think...*
3 (*Informal*) = <u>no good</u>, inadequate, useless (*informal*), poor, pants (*informal*), pathetic, inferior, incompetent, ineffectual ...*I'd be hopeless at working for somebody else...*
4 = <u>incurable</u>, irreversible, irreparable, lost, helpless, irremediable, past remedy, remediless ...*a hopeless mess...* **OPPOSITE** curable

hopelessly 1 = <u>without hope</u>, desperately, in despair, despairingly, irredeemably, irremediably, beyond all hope ...*hopelessly in love...*
2 = <u>completely</u>, totally, extremely, desperately, terribly, utterly, tremendously, awfully, impossibly, frightfully ...*The story is hopelessly confusing...*

horde = <u>crowd</u>, mob, swarm, press, host, band, troop, pack, crew, drove, gang, multitude, throng

horizon 1 = <u>skyline</u>, view, vista, field *or* range of vision ...*The sun had already sunk below the horizon...*
2 = <u>scope</u>, perspective, range, prospect, stretch, ken, sphere, realm, compass, ambit, purview ...*By embracing other cultures, we actually broaden our horizons...*

horizontal = <u>level</u>, flat, plane, parallel, supine

horny (*Informal*) = <u>aroused</u>, excited, turned on (*slang*), randy (*informal, chiefly Brit.*), raunchy (*slang*), amorous, lustful

horrible 1 (*Informal*) = <u>dreadful</u>, terrible, awful, nasty, cruel, beastly (*informal*), mean, unpleasant, ghastly (*informal*), unkind, horrid, disagreeable ...*a horrible little boy*... OPPOSITE wonderful
2 = <u>terrible</u>, awful, appalling, terrifying, shocking, grim, dreadful, revolting, fearful, obscene, ghastly, hideous, shameful, gruesome, from hell (*informal*), grisly, horrid, repulsive, frightful, heinous, loathsome, abhorrent, abominable, hellacious (*U.S. slang*) ...*Still the horrible shrieking came out of his mouth*...

horrid 1 (*Informal*) = <u>unpleasant</u>, terrible, awful, offensive, nasty, disgusting, horrible, dreadful, obscene, disagreeable, yucky or yukky (*slang*), yucko (*Austral. slang*) ...*What a horrid smell!*...
2 (*Informal*) = <u>nasty</u>, dreadful, horrible, mean, unkind, cruel, beastly (*informal*) ...*I must have been a horrid little girl*...

horrific = <u>horrifying</u>, shocking, appalling, frightening, awful, terrifying, grim, dreadful, horrendous, ghastly, from hell (*informal*), grisly, frightful, hellacious (*U.S. slang*)

horrify 1 = <u>terrify</u>, alarm, frighten, scare, intimidate, petrify, terrorize, put the wind up (*informal*), gross out (*U.S. slang*), make your hair stand on end, affright ...*a crime trend that will horrify all parents*... OPPOSITE comfort
2 = <u>shock</u>, appal, disgust, dismay, sicken, outrage ...*When I saw these figures I was horrified*... OPPOSITE delight

horror 1 = <u>terror</u>, fear, alarm, panic, dread, dismay, awe, fright, apprehension, consternation, trepidation ...*I felt numb with horror*...
2 = <u>hatred</u>, disgust, loathing, aversion, revulsion, antipathy, abomination, abhorrence, repugnance, odium, detestation ...*his horror of death*... OPPOSITE love

horse NOUN = <u>nag</u>, mount, mare, colt, filly, stallion, gelding, jade, pony, yearling, steed (*archaic or literary*), dobbin, moke (*Austral. slang*), hobby (*archaic or dialect*), yarraman or yarramin (*Austral.*), gee-gee (*slang*), cuddy or cuddie (*dialect, chiefly Scot.*), studhorse or stud ...*A small man on a grey horse had appeared*...
PHRASES **horse around** or **about** (*Informal*) = <u>play around</u> or **about**, fool about or around, clown, misbehave, play the fool, roughhouse (*slang*), play the goat, monkey about or around, indulge in horseplay, lark about or around ...*Later that day I was horsing around with Katie*...

Related Words
adjectives: equestrian, equine, horsey
noun: equitation
male: stallion
female: mare
young: foal, colt, filly
fondness for: hippomania

fear of: hippophobia
➤ **equestrianism** ➤ **horses**

horseman = <u>rider</u>, equestrian

hospitable 1 = <u>welcoming</u>, kind, friendly, liberal, generous, gracious, amicable, cordial, sociable, genial, bountiful ...*The locals are hospitable and welcoming*... OPPOSITE inhospitable
2 = <u>receptive</u>, tolerant, responsive, open-minded, amenable, accessible ...*hospitable political environments*... OPPOSITE unreceptive

hospitality = <u>welcome</u>, warmth, kindness, friendliness, sociability, conviviality, neighbourliness, cordiality, heartiness, hospitableness

host¹ or **hostess** NOUN **1** = <u>master of ceremonies</u>, proprietor, innkeeper, landlord or landlady ...*We were greeted by our host, a courteous man in a formal suit*...
2 = <u>presenter</u>, compere (*Brit.*), anchorman or anchorwoman ...*I am host of a live radio programme*...
VERB = <u>present</u>, introduce, compere (*Brit.*), front (*informal*) ...*She also hosts a show on St Petersburg Radio*...

host² **1** = <u>multitude</u>, lot, load (*informal*), wealth, array, myriad, great quantity, large number ...*a whole host of gadgets*...
2 = <u>crowd</u>, army, pack, drove, mob, herd, legion, swarm, horde, throng ...*A host of stars from British stage and screen attended the awards ceremony*...

hostage = <u>captive</u>, prisoner, pledge, pawn, security, surety

hostile 1 = <u>antagonistic</u>, anti (*informal*), opposed, opposite, contrary, inimical, ill-disposed ...*hostile to the idea of foreign intervention*...
2 = <u>unfriendly</u>, belligerent, antagonistic, unkind, malevolent, warlike, bellicose, inimical, rancorous, ill-disposed ...*The Governor faced hostile crowds when he visited the town*... OPPOSITE friendly
3 = <u>inhospitable</u>, adverse, alien, uncongenial, unsympathetic, unwelcoming, unpropitious ...*some of the most hostile climatic conditions in the world*... OPPOSITE hospitable

hostility NOUN **1** = <u>unfriendliness</u>, hatred, animosity, spite, bitterness, malice, venom, antagonism, enmity, abhorrence, malevolence, detestation ...*She looked at Ron with open hostility*... OPPOSITE friendliness
2 = <u>opposition</u>, resentment, antipathy, aversion, antagonism, ill feeling, bad blood, ill-will, animus ...*hostility among traditionalists to this method of teaching history*... OPPOSITE approval
PLURAL NOUN = <u>warfare</u>, war, fighting, conflict, combat, armed conflict, state of war ...*Military chiefs agreed to cease hostilities throughout the country*... OPPOSITE peace

hot ADJECTIVE **1** = <u>heated</u>, burning, boiling, steaming, flaming, roasting, searing, blistering, fiery, scorching, scalding, piping hot ...*Cook the meat quickly on a hot barbecue plate*...
2 = <u>warm</u>, close, stifling, humid, torrid, sultry, sweltering, balmy, muggy ...*It was too hot even for a gentle stroll*... OPPOSITE cold

Horses http://www.ansi.okstate.edu/breeds/horses/

Breeds of horse

Akhal-Teke
American Quarter horse
American Saddle horse
Andalusian
Anglo-Arab
Anglo-Norman
Appaloosa
Arab
Ardennes
Balearic
Barb
Basuto
Batak *or* Deli
boerperd
Beetewk
Brabançon
Breton
Burmese *or* Shan
Cleveland Bay
Clydesdale
Connemara
Criollo
Dales pony
Danish
Dartmoor pony
Don
Dutch Draught
Esthonian, Smudish, *or* Zmudzin
Exmoor
Fell pony
Finnish horse
Fjord pony
Flemish
Friesian
Gelderland
Gidran
Groningen
Gudbrandsdal

Hackney
Hafflinger
Hambletonian
Hanoverian
Highland pony
Holstein
Huçul
Iceland pony
Iomud
Jutland
Kabarda
Karabair
Karabakh
Karadagh
Kathiawari
Kladruber
Klepper
Knabstrup
Konik
Kurdistan pony
Limousin
Lipizzaner *or* Lippizaner
Lokai
Manipur
Marwari
Mecklenburg
Mongolian
Morgan
mustang *or* bronco
New Forest pony
Nonius
North Swedish horse
Oldenburg
Orlov Trotter
Palomino
Percheron
Persian Arab
Pinto

Pinzgauer
Polish Arab
Polish Half-bred
Polish Thoroughbred
Quarter horse
racehorse
Rhenish
Russian saddle horse *or* Orlov
 Rostopchin
Schleswig
Shagya
Shetland pony
Shirazi *or* Gulf Arab
Shire horse
Spanish Jennet *or* Genet
Spiti
Standard Bred
Strelet
Suffolk *or* Suffolk Punch
Swedish Ardennes
Tarbenian
Tarpan
Tennessee Walking Horse *or*
 Walking Horse
Thoroughbred
Timor pony
Trakehner
Turk *or* Turkoman
Viatka
Waler
Welsh Cob
Welsh Mountain pony
Welsh pony
Yamoote
Yorkshire Coach horse
Zeeland horse
Zemaitukas

Types of horse

carthorse
cavalry horse
cayuse
charger
cob
courser
cow pony
crock
destrier
drayhorse
hack
high-stepper
hunter

liberty horse
nag
night horse
packhorse
palfrey
pacer
packhorse
plug
polo pony
pony
racehorse *or* (*Austral. informal*)
 neddy
rip

running mate
saddle horse *or* saddler
screw
show jumper
stalking-horse
stockhorse
sumpter
trooper
warhorse
weed
workhorse

Wild horses

brumby
buckjumper
mustang

Przewalski's horse *or* wild horse
quagga
tarpan

warrigal, warregal, *or* warragul
zebra

Extinct horses

hyracotherium *or* eohippus
merychippus

miohippus
pliohippus

quagga
tarpan

Horses (continued)

Legendary/fictional/historical horses

Bayard
Black Beauty
Black Bess
Boxer
Bucephalus
Champion
El Fideldo
Flicka
Hercules
Incitatus
Mister Ed
Pegasus
Rosinante
Silver
Sleipnir
Traveler
Trigger

Horse colours

albino
bay
black
blue roan
chestnut
claybank
cream
dapple
dapplegrey
dun
fleabitten
grey
mealy
palomino
piebald
pinto
roan
skewbald
sorrel
strawberry roan

Horse markings

blaze
coronet
snip
sock
star
stocking
stripe
white face

Horse gaits

amble
canter
extended trot
gallop
jog trot
lope
pace
prance
rising trot
single-foot or rack
sitting trot
trot
walk

Horse parts

back
bar
barrel
brisket
buttress
cannon bone
chestnut
chin groove
coffin bone
coronet band
counter
coupling
croup or croupe
diagonal
dock
ergot
fetlock joint
flank
forearm
forehand
foreleg
forelock
forequarters
frog
gambrel
gaskin or second thigh
hamstring
haunch
haw
heel
hock
hoof
loins
mane
muzzle
near-fore
near-hind
neck
off-fore
off-hind
pastern
poll
quarter
saddle
shannon or shank
sheath
sole
splint bone
stifle joint
tail
toe
tusk
wall
white line
withers

Horses, rhinos and other perissodactyls

ass
chigetai or dziggetai
donkey
elephant
horse see **breeds of horse**
keitloa
kiang
kulan
mule
onager
rhinoceros
tapir
white elephant
zebra

3 = <u>spicy</u>, pungent, peppery, piquant, biting, sharp, acrid ...*He loved hot curries...* OPPOSITE> mild

4 = <u>intense</u>, passionate, heated, spirited, excited, fierce, lively, animated, ardent, inflamed, fervent, impassioned, fervid ...*The nature of Scottishness is a matter of hot debate in Scotland...*

5 = <u>new</u>, latest, fresh, recent, up to date, just out, up to the minute, bang up to date (*informal*), hot off the press ...*If you hear any hot news, tell me won't you...* OPPOSITE> old

6 = <u>popular</u>, hip, fashionable, cool, in demand, sought-after, must-see, in vogue ...*a ticket for the hottest show in town...* OPPOSITE> unpopular

7 = <u>fierce</u>, intense, strong, keen, competitive, cut-throat ...*hot competition from abroad...*

8 = <u>fiery</u>, violent, raging, passionate, stormy, touchy, vehement, impetuous, irascible ...*His hot temper was making it difficult for others to work with him...* OPPOSITE> calm

PHRASES **hot on the heels of something** or **someone** = shortly after, soon after, immediately after, right after, close behind, straight after, hard on the heels of, directly after ...*The shock news comes hot on the heels of the company axing its site in Scotland...*

hot air = <u>empty talk</u>, rant, guff (*slang*), bombast, wind, gas (*informal*), verbiage, claptrap (*informal*), blather, bunkum (*chiefly U.S.*), blether, bosh (*informal*), tall talk (*informal*)

hotbed = <u>breeding ground</u>, nest, den

hot-headed = <u>volatile</u>, rash, fiery, reckless, precipitate, hasty, unruly, foolhardy, impetuous, hot-tempered, quick-tempered

hothouse = <u>greenhouse</u>, conservatory, glasshouse, orangery

hotly 1 = <u>fiercely</u>, passionately, angrily, vehemently, indignantly, with indignation, heatedly, impetuously ...*The bank hotly denies any wrongdoing...*

2 = <u>closely</u>, enthusiastically, eagerly, with enthusiasm, hotfoot ...*He'd snuck out of America hotly pursued by the CIA...*

hound 1 = <u>harass</u>, harry, bother, provoke, annoy, torment, hassle (*informal*), prod, badger, persecute, pester, goad, keep after ...*hounded by the press...*

2 = <u>force</u>, drive, pressure, push, chase, railroad (*informal*), propel, impel, pressurize ...*hounded out of office...*

> **Related Words**
> *collective noun*: pack

house NOUN **1** = <u>home</u>, residence, dwelling, building, pad (*slang*), homestead, edifice, abode, habitation, domicile ...*her parents' house in Warwickshire...*

2 = <u>household</u>, family, ménage ...*If he set his alarm clock, it would wake the whole house...*

3 = <u>firm</u>, company, business, concern, organization, partnership, establishment, outfit (*informal*) ...*the world's top fashion houses...*

4 = <u>assembly</u>, parliament, Commons, legislative body ...*the joint sessions of the two parliamentary houses...*

5 = <u>restaurant</u>, inn, hotel, pub (*Brit. informal*), tavern,

public house, hostelry ...*The house offers a couple of freshly prepared à la carte dishes...*

6 = <u>dynasty</u>, line, race, tribe, clan, ancestry, lineage, family tree, kindred ...*the Saudi Royal House...*

VERB **1** = <u>accommodate</u>, board, quarter, take in, put up, lodge, harbour, billet, domicile ...*Regrettably we have to house families in these inadequate flats...*

2 = <u>contain</u>, keep, hold, cover, store, protect, shelter ...*The building houses a collection of motorcycles and cars...*

3 = <u>take</u>, accommodate, sleep, provide shelter for, give a bed to ...*The building will house twelve boys and eight girls...*

PHRASES **on the house** = <u>free</u>, for free (*informal*), for nothing, free of charge, gratis, without expense ...*He brought them glasses of champagne on the house...*

household NOUN = <u>family</u>, home, house, ménage, family circle ...*growing up in a male-only household...* ADJECTIVE = <u>domestic</u>, family, domiciliary ...*I always do the household chores first...*

householder = <u>occupant</u>, resident, tenant, proprietor, homeowner, freeholder, leaseholder

housekeeping = <u>household management</u>, homemaking (*U.S.*), home economy, housewifery, housecraft

housing 1 = <u>accommodation</u>, homes, houses, dwellings, domiciles ...*a shortage of affordable housing...*

2 = <u>case</u>, casing, covering, cover, shell, jacket, holder, container, capsule, sheath, encasement ...*Both housings are waterproof to a depth of two metres...*

hovel = <u>hut</u>, hole, shed, cabin, den, slum, shack, shanty

hover 1 = <u>float</u>, fly, hang, drift, be suspended, flutter, poise ...*Beautiful butterflies hovered above the wild flowers...*

2 = <u>linger</u>, loiter, wait nearby, hang about or around (*informal*) ...*Judith was hovering in the doorway...*

3 = <u>waver</u>, alternate, fluctuate, haver (*Brit.*), falter, dither (*chiefly Brit.*), oscillate, vacillate, seesaw, swither (*Scot. dialect*) ...*We hover between great hopes and great fears...*

however = <u>but</u>, nevertheless, still, though, yet, even though, on the other hand, nonetheless, notwithstanding, anyhow, be that as it may

howl VERB **1** = <u>bay</u>, cry, bark, yelp, quest (*used of hounds*) ...*A dog suddenly howled, baying at the moon...*

2 = <u>cry</u>, shout, scream, roar, weep, yell, cry out, wail, shriek, bellow, bawl, yelp ...*The baby was howling for her 3am feed...*

NOUN **1** = <u>baying</u>, cry, bay, bark, barking, yelp, yelping, yowl ...*It was the howl of an animal crying out in hunger...*

2 = <u>cry</u>, scream, roar, bay, wail, outcry, shriek, bellow, clamour, hoot, bawl, yelp, yowl ...*a howl of rage...*

howler (*Informal*) = <u>mistake</u>, error, blunder, boob (*Brit. slang*), bloomer (*Brit. informal*), clanger (*informal*), malapropism, schoolboy howler, booboo

(*informal*)

hub = <u>centre</u>, heart, focus, core, middle, focal point, pivot, nerve centre

hubbub 1 = <u>noise</u>, racket, din, uproar, cacophony, pandemonium, babel, tumult, hurly-burly ...*a hubbub of excited conversation from over a thousand people...*
2 = <u>hue and cry</u>, confusion, disturbance, riot, disorder, clamour, rumpus, bedlam, brouhaha, ruction (*informal*), hullabaloo, ruckus (*informal*) ...*the hubbub over the election...*

hubris = <u>pride</u>, vanity, arrogance, conceit, self-importance, haughtiness, conceitedness

huddle VERB 1 = <u>curl up</u>, crouch, hunch up, nestle, snuggle, make yourself small ...*She sat huddled on the side of the bed, weeping...*
2 = <u>crowd</u>, press, gather, collect, squeeze, cluster, flock, herd, throng ...*strangers huddling together for warmth...*
NOUN 1 = <u>crowd</u>, mass, bunch, cluster, heap, muddle, jumble ...*a huddle of bodies, gasping for air...*
2 (*Informal*) = <u>discussion</u>, conference, meeting, hui (*N.Z.*), powwow, confab (*informal*) ...*He went into a huddle with his lawyers to consider an appeal...*

hue 1 = <u>colour</u>, tone, shade, dye, tint, tinge, tincture ...*The same hue will look different in different lights...*
2 = <u>aspect</u>, light, cast, complexion ...*a comeback of such theatrical hue...*

huff NOUN = <u>sulk</u>, temper, bad mood, passion, rage, pet, pique, foulie (*Austral. slang*) ...*He went into a huff because he lost the game...*
PHRASES **in a huff** = <u>offended</u>, hurt, angered, provoked, annoyed, put out (*informal*), hacked (off) (*U.S. slang*), exasperated, sulking (*informal*), nettled, vexed, miffed (*informal*), irked, riled, peeved, piqued, in high dudgeon ...*She was in a huff about what I'd said...*

hug VERB 1 = <u>embrace</u>, hold (onto), cuddle, squeeze, cling, clasp, enfold, hold close, take in your arms ...*They hugged each other like a couple of lost children...*
2 = <u>clasp</u>, hold (onto), grip, nurse, retain ...*He trudged towards them, hugging a large box...*
3 = <u>follow closely</u>, keep close, stay near, cling to, follow the course of ...*The road hugs the coast for hundreds of miles...*
NOUN = <u>embrace</u>, squeeze, bear hug, clinch (*slang*), clasp ...*She leapt out of the seat, and gave him a hug...*

huge = <u>enormous</u>, great, giant, large, massive, vast, extensive, tremendous, immense, mega (*slang*), titanic, jumbo (*informal*), gigantic, monumental, mammoth, bulky, colossal, mountainous, stellar (*informal*), prodigious, stupendous, gargantuan, elephantine, ginormous (*informal*), Brobdingnagian, humongous *or* humungous (*U.S. slang*) OPPOSITE> tiny

hugely = <u>immensely</u>, enormously, massively, prodigiously, monumentally, stupendously

hui (*N.Z.*) = <u>meeting</u>, gathering, assembly, meet, conference, congress, session, rally, convention, get-together (*informal*), reunion, congregation, conclave,

convocation, powwow

hulk = <u>wreck</u>, shell, hull, shipwreck, frame

hulking = <u>ungainly</u>, massive, lumbering, gross, awkward, clumsy, bulky, cumbersome, overgrown, unwieldy, ponderous, clunky (*informal*), oafish, lumpish, lubberly, unco (*Austral. slang*)

hull NOUN 1 = <u>framework</u>, casing, body, covering, frame, skeleton ...*The hull had suffered extensive damage to the starboard side...*
2 = <u>husk</u>, skin, shell, peel, pod, rind, shuck ...*I soaked the hulls off lima beans...*
VERB = <u>trim</u>, peel, skin, shell, husk, shuck ...*Soak them in water with lemon juice for 30 minutes before hulling...*

hum 1 = <u>drone</u>, buzz, murmur, throb, vibrate, purr, croon, thrum, whir ...*We could hear a buzz, like a bee humming...*
2 (*Informal*) = <u>be busy</u>, buzz, bustle, move, stir, pulse, be active, vibrate, pulsate ...*On Saturday morning, the town hums with activity...*

human ADJECTIVE 1 = <u>mortal</u>, anthropoid, manlike ...*the human body...* OPPOSITE> nonhuman
2 = <u>kind</u>, natural, vulnerable, kindly, understandable, humane, compassionate, considerate, approachable ...*Singapore has a human side too, beside the relentless efficiency...* OPPOSITE> inhuman
NOUN = <u>human being</u>, person, individual, body, creature, mortal, man *or* woman ...*The drug has not yet been tested on humans...* OPPOSITE> nonhuman
(Related Words)
combining form: anthropo-

humane = <u>kind</u>, compassionate, good, kindly, understanding, gentle, forgiving, tender, mild, sympathetic, charitable, benign, clement, benevolent, lenient, merciful, good-natured, forbearing, kind-hearted OPPOSITE> cruel

humanitarian ADJECTIVE 1 = <u>compassionate</u>, charitable, humane, benevolent, altruistic, beneficent ...*They will be released as a humanitarian act...*
2 = <u>charitable</u>, philanthropic, public-spirited ...*a convoy of humanitarian aid from Britain...*
NOUN = <u>philanthropist</u>, benefactor, Good Samaritan, altruist ...*I like to think of myself as a humanitarian...*

humanity NOUN 1 = <u>the human race</u>, man, mankind, people, men, mortals, humankind, Homo sapiens ...*They face charges of committing crimes against humanity...*
2 = <u>human nature</u>, mortality, humanness ...*It made him feel deprived of his humanity...*
3 = <u>kindness</u>, charity, compassion, understanding, sympathy, mercy, tolerance, tenderness, philanthropy, benevolence, fellow feeling, benignity, brotherly love, kind-heartedness ...*His speech showed great humility and humanity...*
PLURAL NOUN = <u>arts</u>, liberal arts, classics, classical studies, literae humaniores ...*The number of students majoring in the humanities has declined...*

humble ADJECTIVE 1 = <u>modest</u>, meek, unassuming, unpretentious, submissive, self-effacing, unostentatious ...*Andy was a humble, courteous and* *gentle man…* OPPOSITE> proud

2 = <u>lowly</u>, common, poor, mean, low, simple, ordinary, modest, obscure, commonplace, insignificant, unimportant, unpretentious, undistinguished, plebeian, low-born *…He came from a fairly humble, poor background…* OPPOSITE> distinguished

3 common, commonplace *…He made his own reflector from a strip of humble kitchen foil…*

VERB = <u>humiliate</u>, shame, disgrace, break, reduce, lower, sink, crush, put down (*slang*), bring down, subdue, degrade, demean, chagrin, chasten, mortify, debase, put (someone) in their place, abase, take down a peg (*informal*), abash *…the little car company that humbled the industry giants…* OPPOSITE> exalt

PHRASES **humble yourself** = <u>humiliate yourself</u>, grovel, eat humble pie, swallow your pride, eat crow (*U.S. informal*), abase yourself, go on bended knee *…He humbled himself and became obedient…*

humbly = <u>meekly</u>, modestly, respectfully, cap in hand, diffidently, deferentially, submissively, unassumingly, obsequiously, subserviently, on bended knee, servilely

humbug = <u>nonsense</u>, rubbish, trash, hypocrisy, cant, baloney (*informal*), claptrap (*informal*), quackery, eyewash (*informal*), charlatanry

humdrum = <u>dull</u>, ordinary, boring, routine, commonplace, mundane, tedious, dreary, banal, tiresome, monotonous, uneventful, uninteresting, mind-numbing, ho-hum (*informal*), repetitious, wearisome, unvaried OPPOSITE> exciting

humid = <u>damp</u>, sticky, moist, wet, steamy, sultry, dank, clammy, muggy OPPOSITE> dry

humidity = <u>damp</u>, moisture, dampness, wetness, moistness, sogginess, dankness, clamminess, mugginess, humidness

humiliate = <u>embarrass</u>, shame, humble, crush, disgrace, put down, subdue, degrade, chagrin, chasten, mortify, debase, discomfit, bring low, put (someone) in their place, take the wind out of someone's sails, abase, take down a peg (*informal*), abash, make (someone) eat humble pie OPPOSITE> honour

humiliating = <u>embarrassing</u>, shaming, humbling, mortifying, crushing, disgracing, degrading, ignominious, toe-curling (*slang*), cringe-making (*Brit. informal*), cringeworthy (*Brit. informal*), barro (*Austral. slang*)

humiliation = <u>embarrassment</u>, shame, disgrace, humbling, put-down, degradation, affront, indignity, chagrin, ignominy, dishonour, mortification, loss of face, abasement, self-abasement

humility = <u>modesty</u>, diffidence, meekness, submissiveness, servility, self-abasement, humbleness, lowliness, unpretentiousness, lack of pride OPPOSITE> pride

humorist = <u>comedian</u>, comic, wit, eccentric, wag, joker, card (*informal*), jester, dag (*N.Z. informal*), funny man

humorous = <u>funny</u>, comic, amusing, entertaining, witty, merry, hilarious, ludicrous, laughable, farcical, whimsical, comical, droll, facetious, jocular, side-splitting, waggish, jocose OPPOSITE> serious

humour NOUN **1** = <u>comedy</u>, funniness, fun, amusement, funny side, jocularity, facetiousness, ludicrousness, drollery, comical aspect *…She couldn't ignore the humour of the situation…* OPPOSITE> seriousness

2 = <u>mood</u>, spirits, temper, disposition, frame of mind *…Could that have been the source of his good humour?…*

3 = <u>joking</u>, jokes, comedy, wit, gags (*informal*), farce, jesting, jests, wisecracks (*informal*), witticisms, wittiness *…The film has lots of adult humour…*

VERB = <u>indulge</u>, accommodate, go along with, spoil, flatter, pamper, gratify, pander to, mollify, cosset, fawn on *…Most of the time he humoured her for an easy life…* OPPOSITE> oppose

humourless = <u>serious</u>, intense, solemn, straight, dry, dour, unfunny, po-faced, unsmiling, heavy-going, unamused, unamusing

hump NOUN = <u>lump</u>, bump, projection, bulge, mound, hunch, knob, protuberance, protrusion *…The path goes over a large hump by a tree…*

VERB (*Informal*) = <u>carry</u>, lug, heave, hoist, shoulder *…Charlie humped his rucksack up the stairs…*

PHRASES **get the hump** (*Brit. informal*) = <u>sulk</u>, mope, be in the doldrums, get the blues, be down in the dumps (*informal*) *…She's always got the hump about something these days…*

hunch NOUN = <u>feeling</u>, idea, impression, suspicion, intuition, premonition, inkling, presentiment *…I had a hunch that we would work well together…*

VERB = <u>crouch</u>, bend, stoop, curve, arch, huddle, draw in, squat, hump *…He hunched over the map to read the small print…*

hunger NOUN **1** = <u>appetite</u>, emptiness, voracity, hungriness, ravenousness *…Hunger is the body's sign that blood sugar is too low…*

2 = <u>starvation</u>, famine, malnutrition, undernourishment *…Three hundred people are dying of hunger every day…*

3 = <u>desire</u>, appetite, craving, yen (*informal*), ache, lust, yearning, itch, thirst, greediness *…He has a hunger for success that seems bottomless…*

PHRASES **hunger for** or **after something** = <u>want</u>, desire, crave, hope for, long for, wish for, yearn for, pine for, hanker after, ache for, thirst after, itch after *…He hungered for adventure…*

hungry 1 = <u>starving</u>, ravenous, famished, starved, empty, hollow, voracious, peckish (*informal, chiefly Brit.*), famishing *…My friend was hungry, so we went to get some food…*

2 = <u>eager</u>, keen, craving, yearning, greedy, avid, desirous, covetous, athirst *…I left Oxford in 1961 hungry to be a critic…*

hunk = <u>lump</u>, piece, chunk, block, mass, wedge, slab, nugget, wodge (*Brit. informal*), gobbet

hunt VERB = <u>stalk</u>, track, chase, pursue, trail, hound, gun for *…Her irate husband was hunting her lover with a gun…*

NOUN = search, hunting, investigation, chase, pursuit, quest ...*The couple had helped in the hunt for the toddlers...*

PHRASES **hunt for something** or **someone** = search for, look for, try to find, seek for, forage for, rummage for, scour for, look high and low, fossick for (*Austral. & N.Z.*), go in quest of, ferret about for ...*A forensic team was hunting for clues...*

hunted = harassed, desperate, harried, tormented, stricken, distraught, persecuted, terror-stricken

hunter = huntsman or huntress, Diana, Orion, Nimrod, jaeger (*rare*), Artemis, sportsman or sportswoman

hurdle 1 = obstacle, block, difficulty, barrier, handicap, hazard, complication, snag, uphill (*S. African*), obstruction, stumbling block, impediment, hindrance ...*The weather will be the biggest hurdle...*
2 = fence, wall, hedge, block, barrier, barricade ...*The horse dived at the hurdle and clipped the top...*

hurl = throw, fling, chuck (*informal*), send, fire, project, launch, cast, pitch, shy, toss, propel, sling, heave, let fly (with)

hurly-burly = commotion, confusion, chaos, turmoil, disorder, upheaval, furore, uproar, turbulence, pandemonium, bedlam, tumult, hubbub, brouhaha **OPPOSITE** order

hurricane = storm, gale, tornado, cyclone, typhoon, tempest, twister (*U.S. informal*), windstorm, willy-willy (*Austral.*)

hurried 1 = hasty, quick, brief, rushed, short, swift, speedy, precipitate, quickie (*informal*), breakneck ...*They had a hurried breakfast, then left...*
2 = rushed, perfunctory, hectic, speedy, superficial, hasty, cursory, slapdash ...*a hurried overnight redrafting of the text...*

hurriedly = hastily, quickly, briskly, speedily, in a rush, at the double, hurry-scurry

hurry **VERB** 1 = rush, fly, dash, barrel (along) (*informal, chiefly U.S. & Canad.*), scurry, scoot, burn rubber (*informal*) ...*Claire hurried along the road...* **OPPOSITE** dawdle
2 = make haste, rush, lose no time, get a move on (*informal*), step on it (*informal*), get your skates on (*informal*) ...*There was no longer any reason to hurry...*
3 *sometimes with **up*** = speed (up), accelerate, hasten, quicken, hustle, urge, push on, goad, expedite ...*The President's attempt to hurry the process of independence...* **OPPOSITE** slow down
NOUN = rush, haste, speed, urgency, bustle, flurry, commotion, precipitation, quickness, celerity, promptitude ...*the hurry of people wanting to get home...* **OPPOSITE** slowness
PHRASES **in a hurry** = quickly, hastily, hurriedly, immediately, rapidly, instantly, swiftly, abruptly, briskly, at speed, speedily, expeditiously, at *or* on the double ...*Troops had left the area in a hurry...*

hurt **VERB** 1 = injure, damage, wound, cut, disable, bruise, scrape, impair, gash ...*He had hurt his back in an accident...* **OPPOSITE** heal

2 = ache, be sore, be painful, burn, smart, sting, throb, be tender ...*His collar bone only hurt when he lifted his arm...*
3 = harm, injure, molest, ill-treat, maltreat, lay a finger on ...*Did they hurt you?...*
4 = upset, distress, pain, wound, annoy, sting, grieve, afflict, sadden, cut to the quick, aggrieve ...*I'll go. I've hurt you enough...*
NOUN 1 = distress, suffering, pain, grief, misery, agony, sadness, sorrow, woe, anguish, heartache, wretchedness ...*I was full of jealousy and hurt...* **OPPOSITE** happiness
2 = harm, trouble, damage, wrong, loss, injury, misfortune, mischief, affliction ...*I am sorry for any hurt that it may have caused...*
ADJECTIVE 1 = injured, wounded, damaged, harmed, cut, scratched, bruised, scarred, scraped, grazed ...*They were dazed but did not seem to be badly hurt...* **OPPOSITE** healed
2 = upset, pained, injured, wounded, sad, crushed, offended, aggrieved, miffed (*informal*), rueful, piqued, tooshie (*Austral. slang*) ...*He gave me a slightly hurt look...* **OPPOSITE** calmed

hurtful = unkind, upsetting, distressing, mean, cutting, damaging, wounding, nasty, cruel, destructive, harmful, malicious, mischievous, detrimental, pernicious, spiteful, prejudicial, injurious, disadvantageous, maleficent

hurtle = rush, charge, race, shoot, fly, speed, tear, crash, plunge, barrel (along) (*informal, chiefly U.S. & Canad.*), scramble, spurt, stampede, scoot, burn rubber (*informal*), rush headlong, go hell for leather (*informal*)

husband **NOUN** = partner, man (*informal*), spouse, hubby (*informal*), mate, old man (*informal*), bridegroom, significant other (*U.S. informal*), better half (*humorous*) ...*Eva married her husband Jack in 1957...*
VERB = conserve, budget, use sparingly, save, store, hoard, economize on, use economically, manage thriftily ...*Husbanding precious resources was part of rural life...* **OPPOSITE** squander

husbandry 1 = farming, agriculture, cultivation, land management, tillage, agronomy ...*The current meagre harvest suggests poor husbandry...*
2 = thrift, economy, good housekeeping, frugality, careful management ...*These people consider themselves adept at financial husbandry...*

hush **VERB** = quieten, still, silence, suppress, mute, muzzle, shush ...*She tried to hush her noisy father...*
NOUN = quiet, silence, calm, still (*poetic*), peace, tranquillity, stillness, peacefulness ...*A hush fell over the crowd...*
PHRASES **hush something up** = cover up, conceal, suppress, sit on (*informal*), squash, smother, keep secret, sweep under the carpet (*informal*), draw a veil over, keep dark ...*The authorities have tried to hush it up...*

hush-hush (*Informal*) = secret, confidential, classified, top-secret, restricted, under wraps

husk = rind, shell, hull, covering, bark, chaff, shuck

husky 1 = hoarse, rough, harsh, raucous, rasping, croaking, gruff, throaty, guttural, croaky …*His voice was husky with grief…*
2 (*Informal*) = muscular, powerful, strapping, rugged, hefty, burly, stocky, beefy (*informal*), brawny, thickset …*a very husky young man, built like a football player…*

hustle 1 = jostle, force, push, crowd, rush, hurry, thrust, elbow, shove, jog, bustle, impel …*The guards hustled Harry out of the car…*
2 = hurry, hasten, get a move on (*informal*) …*You'll have to hustle if you're to get home for supper…*

hut 1 = cabin, shack, shanty, hovel …*a mud hut with no electricity, gas, or running water…*
2 = shed, outhouse, lean-to, lockup …*Never leave a garage or garden hut unlocked…*

hybrid 1 = crossbreed, cross, mixture, compound, composite, mule, amalgam, mongrel, half-breed, half-blood …*a hybrid between watermint and spearmint…* …*best champion Mule or Hybrid…*
2 = mixture, compound, composite, amalgam …*a hybrid of solid and liquid fuel…*

hygiene = cleanliness, sanitation, disinfection, sterility, sanitary measures, hygienics

hygienic = clean, healthy, sanitary, pure, sterile, salutary, disinfected, germ-free, aseptic OPPOSITE⟩ dirty

hymn 1 = religious song, song of praise, carol, chant, anthem, psalm, paean, canticle, doxology …*Readings were accompanied by an old Irish hymn…*
2 = song of praise, anthem, paean …*a hymn to freedom and rebellion…*

hype (*Slang*) = publicity, promotion, build-up, plugging (*informal*), puffing, racket, razzmatazz (*slang*), brouhaha, ballyhoo (*informal*)

hyperbole = exaggeration, hype (*informal*), overstatement, enlargement, magnification, amplification

hypnotic 1 = mesmeric, soothing, narcotic, opiate, soporific, sleep-inducing, somniferous …*The hypnotic state lies between being awake and being asleep…*

2 = mesmerizing, spellbinding, mesmeric …*His songs are often both hypnotic and reassurringly pleasant…*

hypnotize 1 = mesmerize, put in a trance, put to sleep …*The ability to hypnotize yourself can be learnt in a single session…*
2 = fascinate, absorb, entrance, magnetize, spellbind …*He's hypnotized by that black hair and that white face…*

hypochondriac = neurotic, valetudinarian

hypocrisy = insincerity, pretence, deceit, deception, cant, duplicity, dissembling, falsity, imposture, sanctimoniousness, phoniness (*informal*), deceitfulness, pharisaism, speciousness, two-facedness, phariseeism OPPOSITE⟩ sincerity

hypocrite = fraud, deceiver, pretender, charlatan, impostor, pharisee, dissembler, Tartuffe, Pecksniff, Holy Willie, whited sepulchre, phoney *or* phony (*informal*)

hypocritical = insincere, false, fraudulent, hollow, deceptive, spurious, two-faced, deceitful, sanctimonious, specious, duplicitous, dissembling, canting, Janus-faced, pharisaical, phoney *or* phony (*informal*)

hypodermic = syringe, needle, works (*slang*)

hypothesis = theory, premise, proposition, assumption, thesis, postulate, supposition, premiss

hypothetical = theoretical, supposed, academic, assumed, imaginary, speculative, putative, conjectural OPPOSITE⟩ real

hysteria = frenzy, panic, madness, agitation, delirium, hysterics, unreason

hysterical 1 = frenzied, mad, frantic, raving, distracted, distraught, crazed, uncontrollable, berserk, overwrought, convulsive, beside yourself, berko (*Austral. slang*) …*I slapped her because she became hysterical…* OPPOSITE⟩ calm
2 (*Informal*) = hilarious, uproarious, side-splitting, farcical, comical, wildly funny …*a hysterical, satirical revue…* OPPOSITE⟩ serious

ice

PHRASES **break the ice** = <u>kick off</u> (*informal*), lead the way, take the plunge (*informal*), make a start, begin a relationship, initiate the proceedings, start *or* set the ball rolling (*informal*) …*The main purpose of his trip was to break the ice*… ◆ **skate on thin ice** = <u>be at risk</u>, be vulnerable, be unsafe, be in jeopardy, be out on a limb, be open to attack, be sticking your neck out (*informal*) …*I had skated on thin ice for long enough*…

icy 1 = <u>cold</u>, freezing, bitter, biting, raw, chill, chilling, arctic, chilly, frosty, glacial, ice-cold, frozen over, frost-bound …*An icy wind blew across the moor*…
OPPOSITE hot
2 = <u>slippery</u>, glassy, slippy (*informal or dialect*), like a sheet of glass, rimy …*an icy road*…
3 = <u>unfriendly</u>, cold, distant, hostile, forbidding, indifferent, aloof, stony, steely, frosty, glacial, frigid, unwelcoming …*His response was icy*… **OPPOSITE** friendly

idea 1 = <u>plan</u>, scheme, proposal, design, theory, strategy, method, solution, suggestion, recommendation, proposition …*It's a good idea to keep a stock of tins in the cupboard*…
2 = <u>notion</u>, thought, view, understanding, teaching, opinion, belief, conclusion, hypothesis, impression, conviction, judgment, interpretation, sentiment, doctrine, conception, viewpoint …*Some of his ideas about democracy are entirely his own*…
3 = <u>impression</u>, estimate, guess, hint, notion, clue, conjecture, surmise, inkling, approximation, intimation, ballpark figure …*This graph will give you some idea of levels of ability*…
4 = <u>understanding</u>, thought, view, sense, opinion, concept, impression, judgment, perception, conception, abstraction, estimation …*By the end of the week you will have a clearer idea of the system*…
5 = <u>intention</u>, aim, purpose, object, end, plan, reason, goal, design, objective, motive …*The idea is to help lower-income families to buy their homes*…

Word Power

idea – It is usually considered correct to say that someone has *the idea of doing something*, rather than *the idea to do something*. For example, you would say *he had the idea of taking a holiday*, not *he had the idea to take a holiday*.

ideal **NOUN** 1 *often plural* = <u>principle</u>, standard, ideology, morals, conviction, integrity, scruples, probity, moral value, rectitude, sense of duty, sense of honour, uprightness …*The party has drifted too far from its socialist ideals*…
2 = <u>epitome</u>, standard, dream, pattern, perfection, last word, paragon, nonpareil, standard of perfection …*Throughout his career she remained his feminine ideal*…
3 = <u>model</u>, example, criterion, prototype, paradigm, archetype, exemplar …*the ideal of beauty in those days*…
ADJECTIVE 1 = <u>perfect</u>, best, model, classic, supreme, ultimate, archetypal, exemplary, consummate, optimal, quintessential …*She decided I was the ideal person to take over this job*… **OPPOSITE** imperfect
2 = <u>imaginary</u>, impractical, Utopian, romantic, fantastic, fabulous, poetic, visionary, fairy-tale, mythical, unreal, fanciful, unattainable, ivory-towered, imagal (*Psychoanalysis*) …*Their ideal society collapsed around them in revolution*… **OPPOSITE** actual
3 = <u>hypothetical</u>, academic, intellectual, abstract, theoretical, speculative, conceptual, metaphysical, transcendental, notional …*an ideal economic world*…

idealist = <u>romantic</u>, visionary, dreamer, Utopian

idealistic = <u>perfectionist</u>, romantic, optimistic, visionary, Utopian, quixotic, impracticable, starry-eyed **OPPOSITE** realistic

idealize = <u>romanticize</u>, glorify, exalt, worship, magnify, ennoble, deify, put on a pedestal, apotheosize

ideally = <u>in a perfect world</u>, in theory, preferably, if possible, all things being equal, under the best of circumstances, if you had your way, in a Utopia

identical = <u>alike</u>, like, the same, matching, equal, twin, equivalent, corresponding, duplicate, synonymous, indistinguishable, analogous, interchangeable, a dead ringer (*slang*), the dead spit (*informal*), like two peas in a pod **OPPOSITE** different

identifiable = <u>recognizable</u>, noticeable, known, unmistakable, discernible, detectable, distinguishable, ascertainable

identification 1 = <u>discovery</u>, recognition, determining, establishment, diagnosis, confirmation, detection, divination …*Early identification of the disease can prevent death*…
2 = <u>recognition</u>, naming, labelling, distinguishing, cataloguing, classifying, confirmation, pinpointing, establishment of identity …*Officials are awaiting positive identification before proceeding*…
3 = <u>connection</u>, relationship, link, association, tie, partnership, affinity, familiarity, interconnection, interrelation …*There is a close identification of nationhood with language*…
4 = <u>understanding</u>, relationship, involvement, unity, sympathy, empathy, rapport, fellow feeling …*She had an intense identification with animals*…
5 = <u>ID</u>, papers, credentials, licence, warrant, identity card, proof of identity, letters of introduction …*I'll need to see some identification*…

identify VERB 1 = <u>recognize</u>, place, name, remember, spot, label, flag, catalogue, tag, diagnose, classify, make out, pinpoint, recollect, put your finger on (*informal*) ...*I tried to identify her perfume*...
2 = <u>establish</u>, spot, confirm, finger (*informal, chiefly U.S.*), demonstrate, pick out, single out, certify, verify, validate, mark out, substantiate, corroborate ...*Police have already identified around ten suspects*...
PHRASES **identify something** or **someone with something** or **someone** = <u>equate with</u>, associate with, think of in connection with, put in the same category as ...*Audiences identify her with roles depicting sweet, passive women*... ♦ **identify with someone** = <u>relate to</u>, understand, respond to, feel for, ally with, empathize with, speak the same language as, put yourself in the place or shoes of, see through another's eyes, be on the same wavelength as ...*She would only play the role if she could identify with the character*...

identity = <u>individuality</u>, self, character, personality, existence, distinction, originality, peculiarity, uniqueness, oneness, singularity, separateness, distinctiveness, selfhood, particularity

ideology = <u>belief(s)</u>, ideas, principles, ideals, opinion, philosophy, doctrine, creed, dogma, tenets, world view, credence, articles of faith, Weltanschauung (*German*)

idiocy = <u>foolishness</u>, insanity, lunacy, tomfoolery, inanity, imbecility, senselessness, cretinism, fatuity, abject stupidity, asininity, fatuousness OPPOSITE> wisdom

idiom 1 = <u>phrase</u>, expression, turn of phrase, locution, set phrase ...*Proverbs and idioms may become worn with over-use*...
2 = <u>language</u>, talk, style, usage, jargon, vernacular, parlance, mode of expression ...*I was irritated by his use of archaic idiom*...

idiosyncrasy = <u>peculiarity</u>, habit, characteristic, quirk, eccentricity, oddity, mannerism, affectation, trick, singularity, personal trait

idiosyncratic = <u>distinctive</u>, special, individual, typical, distinguishing, distinct, peculiar, individualistic

idiot = <u>fool</u>, jerk (*slang, chiefly U.S. & Canad.*), ass, plank (*Brit. slang*), charlie (*Brit. informal*), berk (*Brit. slang*), wally (*slang*), prat (*slang*), plonker (*slang*), moron, geek (*slang*), twit (*informal, chiefly Brit.*), chump, imbecile, cretin, oaf, simpleton, airhead (*slang*), dimwit (*informal*), dipstick (*Brit. slang*), gonzo (*slang*), schmuck (*U.S. slang*), dork (*slang*), nitwit (*informal*), blockhead, divvy (*Brit. slang*), pillock (*Brit. slang*), halfwit, nincompoop, dweeb (*U.S. slang*), putz (*U.S. slang*), eejit (*Scot. & Irish*), dumb-ass (*slang*), dunderhead, numpty (*Scot. informal*), doofus (*slang, chiefly U.S.*), lamebrain (*informal*), mooncalf, nerd or nurd (*slang*), numbskull or numskull, galah (*Austral. & N.Z. informal*), dorba or dorb (*Austral. slang*), bogan (*Austral. slang*)

idiotic = <u>foolish</u>, crazy, stupid, dumb (*informal*), daft (*informal*), insane, lunatic, senseless, foolhardy, inane, fatuous, loopy (*informal*), crackpot (*informal*), moronic, imbecile, unintelligent, asinine, imbecilic, braindead (*informal*), harebrained, dumb-ass (*slang*), halfwitted OPPOSITE> wise

idle ADJECTIVE 1 = <u>unoccupied</u>, unemployed, redundant, jobless, out of work, out of action, inactive, at leisure, between jobs, unwaged, at a loose end ...*Employees have been idle for almost a month now*... OPPOSITE> occupied
2 = <u>unused</u>, stationary, inactive, out of order, ticking over, gathering dust, mothballed, out of service, out of action or operation ...*Now the machine is lying idle*...
3 = <u>lazy</u>, slow, slack, sluggish, lax, negligent, inactive, inert, lethargic, indolent, lackadaisical, good-for-nothing, remiss, workshy, slothful, shiftless ...*I've never met such an idle bunch of workers!*... OPPOSITE> busy
4 = <u>useless</u>, vain, pointless, hopeless, unsuccessful, ineffective, worthless, futile, fruitless, unproductive, abortive, ineffectual, groundless, of no use, valueless, disadvantageous, unavailing, otiose, of no avail, profitless, bootless ...*It would be idle to pretend the system is worthless*... OPPOSITE> useful
5 = <u>trivial</u>, superficial, insignificant, frivolous, silly, unnecessary, irrelevant, foolish, unhelpful, flippant, puerile, flighty, ill-considered, empty-headed, nugatory ...*He kept up the idle chatter for another five minutes*... OPPOSITE> meaningful
VERB 1 *often with* **away** = <u>fritter</u>, while, waste, fool, lounge, potter, loaf, dally, loiter, dawdle, laze ...*He idled the time away in dreamy thought*...
2 = <u>do nothing</u>, slack, hang out (*informal*), languish, take it easy, shirk, stagnate, mark time, kill time, skive (*Brit. slang*), vegetate, sit back and do nothing, veg out (*slang*), kick your heels, bludge (*Austral. & N.Z. informal*) ...*We spent many hours idling in cafés*...
3 = <u>drift</u>, wander, meander, coast, float, stray, go aimlessly ...*They idled along looking at things*...

idleness 1 = <u>inactivity</u>, unemployment, leisure, inaction, time on your hands ...*Idleness is a very bad thing for human nature*...
2 = <u>loafing</u>, inertia, sloth, pottering, trifling, laziness, time-wasting, lazing, torpor, sluggishness, skiving (*Brit. slang*), vegetating, dilly-dallying (*informal*), shiftlessness ...*Idleness and incompetence are not inbred in our workers*...

idling = <u>loafing</u>, resting, drifting, pottering, taking it easy, dawdling

idly = <u>lazily</u>, casually, passively, languidly, unthinkingly, sluggishly, languorously, lethargically, apathetically, indolently, inertly, lackadaisically, inactively, shiftlessly, slothfully OPPOSITE> energetically

idol 1 = <u>hero</u>, superstar, pin-up, favourite, pet, darling, beloved (*slang*), fave (*informal*) ...*They cheered as they caught sight of their idol*...
2 = <u>graven image</u>, god, image, deity, pagan symbol ...*They shaped the substance into idols that were eaten ceremoniously*...

idolize = <u>worship</u>, love, adore, admire, revere, glorify, exalt, look up to, venerate, hero-worship, deify, bow down before, dote upon, apotheosize, worship to excess

idyllic = <u>heavenly</u>, idealized, ideal, charming, peaceful, pastoral, picturesque, rustic, Utopian, halcyon, out of this world, unspoiled, arcadian

if CONJUNCTION 1 = <u>provided</u>, assuming, given that, providing, allowing, admitting, supposing, granting, in case, presuming, on the assumption that, on condition that, as long as ...*If you would like to make a donation, please enclose a cheque...*
2 = <u>when</u>, whenever, every time, any time ...*She gets very upset if I exclude her from anything...*
3 = <u>whether</u> ...*He asked if I had left with you, and I said no...*
NOUN = <u>doubt</u>, condition, uncertainty, provision, constraint, hesitation, vagueness, stipulation ...*This business is full of ifs...*

iffy = <u>uncertain</u>, doubtful, unpredictable, conditional, undecided, up in the air, problematical, chancy (*informal*), in the lap of the gods

ignite 1 = <u>catch fire</u>, burn, burst into flames, fire, inflame, flare up, take fire ...*The blast was caused by pockets of methane gas which ignited...*
2 = <u>set fire to</u>, light, set alight, torch, kindle, touch off, put a match to (*informal*) ...*The bombs ignited a fire which destroyed some 60 houses...*

ignoble 1 = <u>dishonourable</u>, low, base, mean, petty, infamous, degraded, craven, disgraceful, shabby, vile, degenerate, abject, unworthy, shameless, despicable, heinous, dastardly, contemptible, wretched ...*an ignoble episode from their country's past...*
2 = <u>lowly</u>, mean, low, base, common, peasant, vulgar, plebeian, humble, lowborn (*rare*), baseborn (*archaic*) ...*They wanted to spare him the shame of an ignoble birth...*

ignominious = <u>humiliating</u>, disgraceful, shameful, sorry, scandalous, abject, despicable, mortifying, undignified, disreputable, dishonourable, inglorious, discreditable, indecorous OPPOSITE honourable

ignominy = <u>disgrace</u>, shame, humiliation, contempt, discredit, stigma, disrepute, dishonour, infamy, mortification, bad odour OPPOSITE honour

ignorance 1 = <u>lack of education</u>, stupidity, foolishness, blindness, illiteracy, benightedness, unenlightenment, unintelligence, mental darkness ...*In my ignorance, I had never heard of R and B music...* OPPOSITE knowledge
2 with *of* = <u>unawareness of</u>, inexperience of, unfamiliarity with, innocence of, unconsciousness of, greenness about, oblivion about, nescience of (*literary*) ...*a complete ignorance of non-European history...*

ignorant 1 = <u>uneducated</u>, unaware, naive, green, illiterate, inexperienced, innocent, untrained, unlearned, unread, untutored, uncultivated, wet behind the ears (*informal*), unlettered, untaught, unknowledgeable, uncomprehending, unscholarly, as green as grass ...*They don't ask questions for fear of appearing ignorant...* OPPOSITE educated
2 = <u>insensitive</u>, gross, crude, rude, shallow, superficial, crass ...*Some very ignorant people called me all kinds of names...*
3 with *of* = <u>uninformed of</u>, unaware of, oblivious to, blind to, innocent of, in the dark about, unconscious of, unschooled in, out of the loop of, inexperienced of, uninitiated about, unknowing of, unenlightened about ...*Many people are worryingly ignorant of the facts...* OPPOSITE informed

ignore 1 = <u>pay no attention to</u>, neglect, disregard, slight, overlook, scorn, spurn, rebuff, take no notice of, be oblivious to ...*She said her husband ignored her...* OPPOSITE pay attention to
2 = <u>overlook</u>, discount, disregard, reject, neglect, shrug off, pass over, brush aside, turn a blind eye to, turn a deaf ear to, shut your eyes to ...*Such arguments ignore the important issues...*
3 = <u>snub</u>, cut (*informal*), slight, blank (*slang*), rebuff, cold-shoulder, turn your back on, give (someone) the cold shoulder, send (someone) to Coventry, give (someone) the brush-off ...*I kept sending letters and cards but he just ignored me...*

ilk = <u>type</u>, sort, kind, class, style, character, variety, brand, breed, stamp, description, kidney, disposition

Word Power

ilk – Some people object to the use of the phrase *of that ilk* to mean 'of that type or class', claiming that it arises from a misunderstanding of the original Scottish expression. The Scottish phrase *of that ilk* has a very specific meaning, indicating that the person mentioned is laird of an estate with the same name as his family, for example *Moncrieff of that ilk* (that is, 'Moncrieff, laird of Moncrieff estate'). The more general use is, however, well established and is now generally regarded as acceptable.

ill ADJECTIVE 1 = <u>unwell</u>, sick, poorly (*informal*), diseased, funny (*informal*), weak, crook (*Austral. & N.Z. slang*), ailing, queer, frail, feeble, unhealthy, seedy (*informal*), sickly, laid up (*informal*), queasy, infirm, out of sorts (*informal*), dicky (*Brit. informal*), nauseous, off-colour, under the weather (*informal*), at death's door, indisposed, peaky, on the sick list (*informal*), valetudinarian, green about the gills, not up to snuff (*informal*) ...*He was seriously ill with pneumonia...* OPPOSITE healthy
2 = <u>harmful</u>, bad, damaging, evil, foul, unfortunate, destructive, unlucky, vile, detrimental, hurtful, pernicious, noxious, ruinous, deleterious, injurious, iniquitous, disadvantageous, maleficent ...*ill effects from the contamination of the water...* OPPOSITE favourable
3 = <u>hostile</u>, malicious, acrimonious, cross, harsh, adverse, belligerent, unkind, hurtful, unfriendly, malevolent, antagonistic, hateful, bellicose, cantankerous, inimical, rancorous, ill-disposed ...*He bears no ill feelings towards you...* OPPOSITE kind
4 = <u>bad</u>, threatening, disturbing, menacing, unlucky, sinister, gloomy, dire, ominous, unhealthy,

unfavourable, foreboding, unpromising, inauspicious, unwholesome, unpropitious, bodeful …*His absence preyed on her mind like an ill omen*…
NOUN 1 = problem, trouble, suffering, worry, trial, injury, pain, hurt, strain, harm, distress, misery, hardship, woe, misfortune, affliction, tribulation, unpleasantness …*He is responsible for many of the country's ills*…
2 = harm, suffering, damage, hurt, evil, destruction, grief, trauma, anguish, mischief, malice …*I know it will be difficult for them but I wish them no ill*… **OPPOSITE** good
ADVERB 1 = badly, unfortunately, unfavourably, inauspiciously …*This development may bode ill for the government*…
2 = hardly, barely, scarcely, just, only just, by no means, at a push …*We can ill afford another scandal*… **OPPOSITE** well
3 = underline{illegally}, criminally, unlawfully, fraudulently, dishonestly, illicitly, illegitimately, unscrupulously, foully …*He used his ill-gotten gains to pay for a £360,000 house*…
4 = insufficiently, badly, poorly, inadequately, imperfectly, deficiently …*We were ill-prepared for last year's South Africa tour*…

ill-advised = misguided, inappropriate, foolish, rash, reckless, unwise, short-sighted, unseemly, foolhardy, thoughtless, indiscreet, ill-judged, ill-considered, imprudent, wrong-headed, injudicious, incautious, impolitic, overhasty **OPPOSITE** wise

ill at ease = uncomfortable, nervous, tense, strange, wired (*slang*), disturbed, anxious, awkward, uneasy, unsettled, faltering, unsure, restless, out of place, neurotic, self-conscious, hesitant, disquieted, edgy, on edge, twitchy (*informal*), on tenterhooks, fidgety, unquiet, like a fish out of water, antsy (*informal*), unrelaxed, on pins and needles (*informal*) **OPPOSITE** comfortable

ill-considered = unwise, rash, imprudent, careless, precipitate, hasty, heedless, injudicious, improvident, overhasty

ill-defined = unclear, vague, indistinct, blurred, dim, fuzzy, shadowy, woolly, nebulous **OPPOSITE** clear

illegal = unlawful, banned, forbidden, prohibited, criminal, outlawed, unofficial, illicit, unconstitutional, lawless, wrongful, off limits, unlicensed, under-the-table, unauthorized, proscribed, under-the-counter, actionable (*Law*), felonious **OPPOSITE** legal

illegality = crime, wrong, felony, criminality, lawlessness, illegitimacy, wrongness, unlawfulness, illicitness

illegible = indecipherable, unreadable, faint, crabbed, scrawled, hieroglyphic, hard to make out, undecipherable, obscure **OPPOSITE** legible

illegitimacy 1 = bastardy, bastardism …*Divorce and illegitimacy lead to millions of one-parent families*…
2 = illegality, unconstitutionality, unlawfulness, illicitness, irregularity …*They denounced the illegitimacy and oppressiveness of the regime*…

illegitimate 1 = born out of wedlock, natural, bastard, love, misbegotten (*literary*), baseborn (*archaic*) …*In 1985 the news of his illegitimate child came out*…
2 = unlawful, illegal, illicit, improper, unconstitutional, under-the-table, unauthorized, unsanctioned …*a ruthless and illegitimate regime*… **OPPOSITE** legal
3 = invalid, incorrect, illogical, spurious, unsound …*It is not illegitimate to seek a parallel between the two events*…

ill-fated = doomed, unfortunate, unlucky, unhappy, blighted, hapless, luckless, ill-starred, star-crossed, ill-omened

ill feeling = hostility, resentment, bitterness, offence, indignation, animosity, antagonism, enmity, rancour, bad blood, hard feelings, ill will, animus, dudgeon (*archaic*), chip on your shoulder **OPPOSITE** goodwill

illiberal = intolerant, prejudiced, bigoted, narrow-minded, small-minded, reactionary, hidebound, uncharitable, ungenerous **OPPOSITE** tolerant

illicit 1 = illegal, criminal, prohibited, unlawful, black-market, illegitimate, off limits, unlicensed, unauthorized, bootleg, contraband, felonious …*information about the use of illicit drugs*… **OPPOSITE** legal
2 = forbidden, improper, immoral, wrong, guilty, clandestine, furtive …*He clearly condemns illicit love*…

illiteracy = lack of education, ignorance, benightedness, illiterateness

illiterate = uneducated, ignorant, unlettered, unable to read and write, analphabetic **OPPOSITE** educated

ill-judged = misguided, foolish, rash, unwise, short-sighted, ill-advised, ill-considered, wrong-headed, injudicious, overhasty

ill-mannered = rude, impolite, discourteous, coarse, churlish, boorish, insolent, uncouth, loutish, uncivil, ill-bred, badly behaved, ill-behaved, unmannerly **OPPOSITE** polite

illness = sickness, ill health, malaise, attack, disease, complaint, infection, disorder, bug (*informal*), disability, ailment, affliction, poor health, malady, infirmity, indisposition, lurgy (*informal*)

illogical = irrational, absurd, unreasonable, meaningless, incorrect, faulty, inconsistent, invalid, senseless, spurious, inconclusive, unsound, unscientific, specious, fallacious, sophistical **OPPOSITE** logical

ill-tempered = cross, irritable, grumpy, irascible, sharp, annoyed, impatient, touchy, bad-tempered, curt, spiteful, tetchy, ratty (*Brit. & N.Z. informal*), testy, choleric, ill-humoured, liverish **OPPOSITE** good-natured

ill-treat = abuse, injure, harm, wrong, damage, harry, harass, misuse, oppress, dump on (*slang, chiefly U.S.*), mishandle, maltreat, ill-use, handle roughly, knock about *or* around

ill-treatment = abuse, harm, mistreatment, damage, injury, misuse, ill-use, rough handling

illuminate 1 = light up, light, brighten, irradiate, illumine (*literary*) …*No streetlights illuminate the* street... OPPOSITE darken

2 = <u>explain</u>, interpret, make clear, clarify, clear up, enlighten, shed light on, elucidate, explicate, give insight into ... *The instructors use games to illuminate the subject...* OPPOSITE obscure

3 = <u>decorate</u>, illustrate, adorn, ornament ... *medieval illuminated manuscripts...*

illuminating = <u>informative</u>, revealing, enlightening, helpful, explanatory, instructive OPPOSITE confusing

illumination NOUN **1** = <u>light</u>, lighting, lights, ray, beam, lighting up, brightening, brightness, radiance ...*The only illumination came from a small window above...*

2 = <u>enlightenment</u>, understanding, insight, perception, awareness, revelation, inspiration, clarification, edification ...*No further illumination can be had from this theory...*

PLURAL NOUN = <u>lights</u>, decorations, fairy lights ...*the famous Blackpool illuminations...*

illusion **1** = <u>delusion</u>, misconception, misapprehension, fancy, deception, fallacy, self-deception, false impression, false belief, misbelief ...*No one really has any illusions about winning the war...*

2 = <u>false impression</u>, feeling, appearance, impression, fancy, deception, imitation, sham, pretence, semblance, fallacy ...*Floor-to-ceiling windows give the illusion of extra space...* OPPOSITE reality

3 = <u>fantasy</u>, vision, hallucination, trick, spectre, mirage, semblance, daydream, apparition, chimera, figment of the imagination, phantasm, ignis fatuus, will-o'-the-wisp ...*It creates the illusion of moving around in the computer's graphic environment...*

illusory *or* **illusive** = <u>unreal</u>, false, misleading, untrue, seeming, mistaken, apparent, sham, deceptive, deceitful, hallucinatory, fallacious, chimerical, delusive OPPOSITE real

illustrate **1** = <u>demonstrate</u>, show, exhibit, emphasize, exemplify, explicate ...*The example of the United States illustrates this point...*

2 = <u>explain</u>, describe, interpret, sum up, make clear, clarify, summarize, bring home, point up, make plain, elucidate ...*She illustrates her analysis with extracts from interviews and discussions...*

3 = <u>adorn</u>, ornament, embellish ...*He has illustrated the book with black-and-white photographs...*

illustrated = <u>pictured</u>, decorated, illuminated, embellished, pictorial, with illustrations

illustration **1** = <u>example</u>, case, instance, sample, explanation, demonstration, interpretation, specimen, analogy, clarification, case in point, exemplar, elucidation, exemplification ...*These figures are an illustration of the country's dynamism...*

2 = <u>picture</u>, drawing, painting, image, print, plate, figure, portrait, representation, sketch, decoration, portrayal, likeness, adornment ...*She looked like a princess in a nineteenth century illustration...*

illustrative **1** = <u>representative</u>, typical, descriptive, explanatory, interpretive, expository, explicatory, illustrational ...*The following excerpt is illustrative of*

her interaction with students...

2 = <u>pictorial</u>, graphic, diagrammatic, delineative ...*an illustrative guide to the daily activities of the football club...*

illustrious = <u>famous</u>, great, noted, celebrated, signal, brilliant, remarkable, distinguished, prominent, glorious, noble, splendid, notable, renowned, eminent, famed, exalted OPPOSITE obscure

ill will = <u>hostility</u>, spite, dislike, hatred, envy, resentment, grudge, malice, animosity, aversion, venom, antagonism, antipathy, enmity, acrimony, rancour, bad blood, hard feelings, animus, malevolence, unfriendliness OPPOSITE goodwill

image **1** = <u>thought</u>, idea, vision, concept, impression, perception, conception, mental picture, conceptualization ...*The words 'Côte d'Azur' conjure up images of sun, sea and sand...*

2 = <u>figure of speech</u>, metaphor, simile, conceit, trope ...*The images in the poem illustrate the poet's frame of mind...*

3 = <u>reflection</u>, appearance, likeness, mirror image ...*I peered at my image in the mirror...*

4 = <u>figure</u>, idol, icon, fetish, talisman ...*The polished stone bore the graven image of a snakebird...*

5 = <u>replica</u>, copy, reproduction, counterpart, spit (*informal, chiefly Brit.*), clone, facsimile, spitting image (*informal*), similitude, Doppelgänger, (dead) ringer (*slang*), double ...*The boy is the image of his father...*

6 = <u>picture</u>, photo, photograph, representation, reproduction, snapshot ...*A computer creates an image on the screen...*

imaginable = <u>possible</u>, conceivable, likely, credible, plausible, believable, under the sun, comprehensible, thinkable, within the bounds of possibility, supposable OPPOSITE unimaginable

imaginary = <u>fictional</u>, made-up, invented, supposed, imagined, assumed, ideal, fancied, legendary, visionary, shadowy, unreal, hypothetical, fanciful, fictitious, mythological, illusory, nonexistent, dreamlike, hallucinatory, illusive, chimerical, unsubstantial, phantasmal, suppositious, imagal (*Psychoanalysis*) OPPOSITE real

imagination **1** = <u>creativity</u>, vision, invention, ingenuity, enterprise, insight, inspiration, wit, originality, inventiveness, resourcefulness ...*He has a logical mind and a little imagination...*

2 = <u>mind's eye</u>, fancy ...*Long before I went there, the place was alive in my imagination...*

imaginative = <u>creative</u>, original, inspired, enterprising, fantastic, clever, stimulating, vivid, ingenious, visionary, inventive, fanciful, dreamy, whimsical, poetical OPPOSITE unimaginative

imagine **1** = <u>envisage</u>, see, picture, plan, create, project, think of, scheme, frame, invent, devise, conjure up, envision, visualize, dream up (*informal*), think up, conceive of, conceptualize, fantasize about, see in the mind's eye, form a mental picture of ...*He could not imagine a more peaceful scene...*

2 = <u>believe</u>, think, suppose, assume, suspect, gather, guess (*informal, chiefly U.S. & Canad.*), realize, take it, reckon, fancy, deem, speculate, presume, take for granted, infer, deduce, apprehend, conjecture, surmise ...*I imagine you're referring to me...*

imbalance = <u>unevenness</u>, bias, inequality, unfairness, partiality, disproportion, lopsidedness, top-heaviness, lack of proportion

imbed
➤ **embed**

imbibe (*Formal*) **1** = <u>drink</u>, consume, knock back (*informal*), sink (*informal*), swallow, suck, swig (*informal*), quaff ...*They were used to imbibing enormous quantities of alcohol...*
2 = <u>absorb</u>, receive, take in, gain, gather, acquire, assimilate, ingest ...*He'd imbibed a set of mystical beliefs from the cradle...*

imbue = <u>instil</u>, infuse, steep, bathe, saturate, pervade, permeate, impregnate, inculcate

imitate **1** = <u>copy</u>, follow, repeat, echo, emulate, ape, simulate, mirror, follow suit, duplicate, counterfeit, follow in the footsteps of, take a leaf out of (someone's) book ...*a precedent which may be imitated by other activists...*
2 = <u>do an impression of</u>, take off (*informal*), mimic, do (*informal*), affect, copy, mock, parody, caricature, send up (*Brit. informal*), spoof (*informal*), impersonate, burlesque, personate ...*He screwed up his face and imitated the Colonel...*

imitation NOUN **1** = <u>replica</u>, fake, reproduction, sham, forgery, carbon copy (*informal*), counterfeit, counterfeiting, likeness, duplication ...*the most accurate imitation of Chinese architecture in Europe...*
2 = <u>copying</u>, echoing, resemblance, aping, simulation, mimicry ...*She learned her golf by imitation...*
3 = <u>impression</u>, parody, mockery, takeoff (*informal*), impersonation ...*I could do a pretty good imitation of him...*
ADJECTIVE = <u>artificial</u>, mock, reproduction, dummy, synthetic, man-made, simulated, sham, pseudo (*informal*), ersatz, repro, phoney *or* phony (*informal*) ...*a set of Dickens bound in imitation leather...*
OPPOSITE> real

imitator = <u>impersonator</u>, mimic, impressionist, copycat, echo, follower, parrot (*informal*), copier, carbon copy (*informal*)

immaculate **1** = <u>clean</u>, impeccable, spotless, trim, neat, spruce, squeaky-clean, spick-and-span, neat as a new pin ...*Her front room was kept immaculate...*
OPPOSITE> dirty
2 = <u>pure</u>, perfect, innocent, impeccable, virtuous, flawless, faultless, squeaky-clean, guiltless, above reproach, sinless, incorrupt ...*her immaculate reputation...* OPPOSITE> corrupt
3 = <u>perfect</u>, flawless, impeccable, stainless, faultless, unblemished, unsullied, uncontaminated, unpolluted, untarnished, unexceptionable, undefiled ...*My car's in absolutely immaculate condition...* OPPOSITE> tainted

immaterial = <u>irrelevant</u>, insignificant, unimportant, unnecessary, trivial, trifling, inconsequential, extraneous, inconsiderable, of no importance, of no consequence, inessential, a matter of indifference, of little account, inapposite OPPOSITE> significant

immature **1** = <u>young</u>, adolescent, undeveloped, green, raw, premature, unfinished, imperfect, untimely, unripe, unformed, unseasonable, unfledged ...*The birds were in immature plumage...*
2 = <u>childish</u>, juvenile, infantile, puerile, callow, babyish, wet behind the ears (*informal*), jejune ...*You're just being childish and immature...* OPPOSITE> adult

immaturity **1** = <u>rawness</u>, imperfection, greenness, unpreparedness, unripeness ...*In spite of some immaturity of style, it showed real imagination...*
2 = <u>childishness</u>, puerility, callowness, juvenility, babyishness ...*his immaturity and lack of social skills...*

immeasurable = <u>incalculable</u>, vast, immense, endless, unlimited, infinite, limitless, boundless, bottomless, inexhaustible, unfathomable, unbounded, inestimable, measureless, illimitable OPPOSITE> finite

immediate **1** = <u>instant</u>, prompt, instantaneous, quick, on-the-spot, split-second ...*My immediate reaction was one of disgust...* OPPOSITE> later
2 = <u>current</u>, present, pressing, existing, actual, urgent, on hand, extant ...*The immediate problem is not lack of food, but transportation...*
3 = <u>nearest</u>, next, direct, close, near, adjacent, contiguous, proximate ...*I was seated at his immediate left...* OPPOSITE> far

immediately = <u>at once</u>, now, instantly, straight away, directly, promptly, right now, right away, there and then, speedily, without delay, without hesitation, instantaneously, forthwith, pronto (*informal*), unhesitatingly, this instant, on the nail, this very minute, posthaste, tout de suite (*French*), before you could say Jack Robinson (*informal*)

immemorial = <u>age-old</u>, ancient, long-standing, traditional, fixed, rooted, archaic, time-honoured, of yore, olden (*archaic*)

immense = <u>huge</u>, great, massive, vast, large, giant, enormous, extensive, tremendous, mega (*slang*), titanic, infinite, jumbo (*informal*), very big, gigantic, monumental, monstrous, mammoth, colossal, mountainous, stellar (*informal*), prodigious, interminable, stupendous, king-size, king-sized, immeasurable, elephantine, ginormous (*informal*), Brobdingnagian, illimitable, humongous *or* humungous (*U.S. slang*) OPPOSITE> tiny

immerse **1** = <u>engross</u>, involve, absorb, busy, occupy, engage ...*His commitments did not allow him to immerse himself in family life...*
2 = <u>plunge</u>, dip, submerge, sink, duck, bathe, douse, dunk, submerse ...*The electrodes are immersed in liquid...*

immersed = <u>engrossed</u>, involved, absorbed, deep, busy, occupied, taken up, buried, consumed, wrapped up, bound up, rapt, spellbound, mesmerized, in a brown study

immersion **1** = <u>involvement</u>, concentration, preoccupation, absorption ...*long-term assignments*

that allowed them total immersion in their subjects…
2 = <u>dipping</u>, submerging, plunging, ducking, dousing, dunking …*The wood had become swollen from prolonged immersion…*

immigrant = <u>settler</u>, incomer, alien, stranger, outsider, newcomer, migrant, emigrant

imminent = <u>near</u>, coming, close, approaching, threatening, gathering, on the way, in the air, forthcoming, looming, menacing, brewing, impending, at hand, upcoming, on the cards, on the horizon, in the pipeline, nigh (*archaic*), in the offing, fast-approaching, just round the corner, near-at-hand OPPOSITE remote

immobile = <u>motionless</u>, still, stationary, fixed, rooted, frozen, stable, halted, stiff, rigid, static, riveted, lifeless, inert, at rest, inanimate, immovable, immobilized, at a standstill, unmoving, stock-still, like a statue, immotile OPPOSITE mobile

immobility = <u>stillness</u>, firmness, steadiness, stability, fixity, inertness, immovability, motionlessness, absence of movement

immobilize = <u>paralyse</u>, stop, freeze, halt, disable, cripple, lay up (*informal*), bring to a standstill, put out of action, render inoperative

immoral = <u>wicked</u>, bad, wrong, abandoned, evil, corrupt, vicious, obscene, indecent, vile, degenerate, dishonest, pornographic, sinful, unethical, lewd, depraved, impure, debauched, unprincipled, nefarious, dissolute, iniquitous, reprobate, licentious, of easy virtue, unchaste OPPOSITE moral
➤ **amoral**

immorality = <u>wickedness</u>, wrong, vice, evil, corruption, sin, depravity, iniquity, debauchery, badness, licentiousness, turpitude, dissoluteness OPPOSITE morality

immortal ADJECTIVE **1** = <u>timeless</u>, eternal, everlasting, lasting, traditional, classic, constant, enduring, persistent, abiding, perennial, ageless, unfading …*Wuthering Heights – that immortal love story…* OPPOSITE ephemeral
2 = <u>undying</u>, eternal, perpetual, indestructible, death-defying, imperishable, deathless …*They were considered gods and therefore immortal…* OPPOSITE mortal
NOUN **1** = <u>hero</u>, genius, paragon, great …*They had paid £50 a head just to be in the presence of an immortal…*
2 = <u>god</u>, goddess, deity, Olympian, divine being, immortal being …*In the legend, the fire is supposed to turn him into an immortal…*

immortality 1 = <u>eternity</u>, perpetuity, everlasting life, timelessness, incorruptibility, indestructibility, endlessness, deathlessness …*belief in the immortality of the soul…*
2 = <u>fame</u>, glory, celebrity, greatness, renown, glorification, gloriousness …*Some people want to achieve immortality through their works…*

immovable 1 = <u>fixed</u>, set, fast, firm, stuck, secure, rooted, stable, jammed, stationary, immutable, unbudgeable …*It was declared unsafe because the*

support bars were immovable…
2 = <u>inflexible</u>, adamant, resolute, steadfast, constant, unyielding, unwavering, impassive, obdurate, unshakable, unchangeable, unshaken, stony-hearted, unimpressionable …*On one issue, however, she was immovable…* OPPOSITE flexible

immune
PHRASES **immune from** = <u>exempt from</u>, free from, let off (*informal*), not subject to, not liable to …*Members are immune from prosecution for corruption…* ◆ **immune to 1** = <u>resistant to</u>, free from, protected from, safe from, not open to, spared from, secure against, invulnerable to, insusceptible to …*The blood test will tell whether you are immune to the disease…* **2** = <u>unaffected by</u>, not affected by, invulnerable to, insusceptible to …*He never became immune to the sight of death…*

immunity 1 = <u>exemption</u>, amnesty, indemnity, release, freedom, liberty, privilege, prerogative, invulnerability, exoneration …*The police are offering immunity to witnesses who can help them…*
2 *with* **to** = <u>resistance to</u>, protection from, resilience to, inoculation against, immunization from …*immunity to airborne bacteria…* OPPOSITE susceptibility to

immunize = <u>vaccinate</u>, inoculate, protect, safeguard

immutable = <u>unchanging</u>, fixed, permanent, stable, constant, enduring, abiding, perpetual, inflexible, steadfast, sacrosanct, immovable, ageless, invariable, unalterable, unchangeable, changeless

imp 1 = <u>demon</u>, devil, sprite …*He sees the devil as a little imp with horns…*
2 = <u>rascal</u>, rogue, brat, urchin, minx, scamp, pickle (*Brit. informal*), gamin, nointer (*Austral. slang*) …*I didn't say that, you little imp!…*

impact NOUN **1** = <u>effect</u>, influence, consequences, impression, repercussions, ramifications …*They expect the meeting to have a marked impact on the country's future…*
2 = <u>collision</u>, force, contact, shock, crash, knock, stroke, smash, bump, thump, jolt …*The pilot must have died on impact…*
VERB = <u>hit</u>, strike, crash, clash, crush, ram, smack, collide …*the sharp tinkle of metal impacting on stone…*

impair = <u>worsen</u>, reduce, damage, injure, harm, mar, undermine, weaken, spoil, diminish, decrease, blunt, deteriorate, lessen, hinder, debilitate, vitiate, enfeeble, enervate OPPOSITE improve

impaired = <u>damaged</u>, flawed, faulty, defective, imperfect, unsound

impale = <u>pierce</u>, stick, run through, spike, lance, spear, skewer, spit, transfix

impart 1 = <u>communicate</u>, pass on, convey, tell, reveal, discover, relate, disclose, divulge, make known …*the ability to impart knowledge and command respect…*
2 = <u>give</u>, accord, lend, bestow, offer, grant, afford, contribute, yield, confer …*She managed to impart great elegance to the dress she wore…*

impartial = <u>neutral</u>, objective, detached, just, fair, equal, open-minded, equitable, disinterested, unbiased, even-handed, nonpartisan, unprejudiced, without fear or favour, nondiscriminating OPPOSITE⟩ unfair

impartiality = neutrality, equity, fairness, equality, detachment, objectivity, disinterest, open-mindedness, even-handedness, disinterestedness, dispassion, nonpartisanship, lack of bias OPPOSITE⟩ unfairness

impassable = blocked, closed, obstructed, impenetrable, unnavigable

impasse = deadlock, stalemate, standstill, dead end, standoff, blind alley (*informal*)

impassioned = intense, heated, passionate, warm, excited, inspired, violent, stirring, flaming, furious, glowing, blazing, vivid, animated, rousing, fiery, worked up, ardent, inflamed, fervent, ablaze, vehement, fervid OPPOSITE⟩ cool

impassive = unemotional, unmoved, emotionless, reserved, cool, calm, composed, indifferent, self-contained, serene, callous, aloof, stoical, unconcerned, apathetic, dispassionate, unfazed (*informal*), inscrutable, stolid, unruffled, phlegmatic, unfeeling, poker-faced (*informal*), imperturbable, insensible, impassible (*rare*), unexcitable, insusceptible, unimpressible

impatience 1 = irritability, shortness, edginess, intolerance, quick temper, snappiness, irritableness …*There was a hint of impatience in his tone*… OPPOSITE⟩ patience
2 = eagerness, longing, enthusiasm, hunger, yearning, thirst, zeal, fervour, ardour, vehemence, earnestness, keenness, impetuosity, heartiness, avidity, intentness, greediness …*She showed impatience to continue the climb*…
3 = haste, hurry, impetuosity, rashness, hastiness …*They visited a fertility clinic in their impatience to have a child*…

impatient 1 = cross, tense, annoyed, irritated, prickly, edgy, touchy, bad-tempered, intolerant, petulant, ill-tempered, cantankerous, ratty (*Brit. & N.Z. informal*), hot-tempered, quick-tempered, crotchety (*informal*), ill-humoured, narky (*Brit. slang*), out of humour …*He becomes impatient as the hours pass*…
2 = irritable, fiery, abrupt, hasty, snappy, indignant, curt, vehement, brusque, irascible, testy …*Beware of being too impatient with others*… OPPOSITE⟩ easygoing
3 = eager, longing, keen, hot, earnest, raring, anxious, hungry, intent, enthusiastic, yearning, greedy, restless, ardent, avid, fervent, zealous, chafing, vehement, fretful, straining at the leash, fervid, keen as mustard, like a cat on hot bricks (*informal*), athirst …*They are impatient for jobs and security*… OPPOSITE⟩ calm

impeach = charge, accuse, prosecute, blame, denounce, indict, censure, bring to trial, arraign

impeachment = accusation, prosecution, indictment, arraignment

impeccable = faultless, perfect, pure, exact, precise, exquisite, stainless, immaculate, flawless, squeaky-clean, unerring, unblemished, unimpeachable, irreproachable, sinless, incorrupt OPPOSITE⟩ flawed

impede = hinder, stop, slow (down), check, bar, block, delay, hold up, brake, disrupt, curb, restrain, hamper, thwart, clog, obstruct, retard, encumber, cumber, throw a spanner in the works of (*Brit. informal*) OPPOSITE⟩ help

impediment = obstacle, barrier, check, bar, block, difficulty, hazard, curb, snag, obstruction, stumbling block, hindrance, encumbrance, fly in the ointment, millstone around your neck OPPOSITE⟩ aid

impel = force, move, compel, drive, require, push, influence, urge, inspire, prompt, spur, stimulate, motivate, oblige, induce, prod, constrain, incite, instigate, goad, actuate OPPOSITE⟩ discourage

impending = looming, coming, approaching, near, nearing, threatening, forthcoming, brewing, imminent, hovering, upcoming, on the horizon, in the pipeline, in the offing

impenetrable 1 = impassable, solid, impervious, thick, dense, hermetic, impermeable, inviolable, unpierceable …*The range forms an impenetrable barrier between Europe and Asia*… OPPOSITE⟩ passable
2 = incomprehensible, obscure, baffling, dark, hidden, mysterious, enigmatic, arcane, inexplicable, unintelligible, inscrutable, unfathomable, indiscernible, cabbalistic, enigmatical …*His philosophical work is notoriously impenetrable*… OPPOSITE⟩ understandable

imperative = urgent, essential, pressing, vital, crucial, compulsory, indispensable, obligatory, exigent OPPOSITE⟩ unnecessary

imperceptible = undetectable, slight, subtle, small, minute, fine, tiny, faint, invisible, gradual, shadowy, microscopic, indistinguishable, inaudible, infinitesimal, teeny-weeny, unnoticeable, insensible, impalpable, indiscernible, teensy-weensy, inappreciable OPPOSITE⟩ perceptible

imperceptibly = invisibly, slowly, subtly, little by little, unobtrusively, unseen, by a hair's-breadth, unnoticeably, indiscernibly, inappreciably

imperfect = flawed, impaired, faulty, broken, limited, damaged, partial, unfinished, incomplete, defective, patchy, immature, deficient, rudimentary, sketchy, undeveloped, inexact OPPOSITE⟩ perfect

imperfection 1 = blemish, fault, defect, flaw, stain …*Scanners locate imperfections in the cloth*…
2 = fault, failing, weakness, defect, deficiency, flaw, shortcoming, inadequacy, frailty, foible, weak point …*He concedes that there are imperfections in the socialist system*…
3 = incompleteness, deficiency, inadequacy, frailty, insufficiency …*It is its imperfection that gives it its beauty*… OPPOSITE⟩ perfection

imperial = royal, regal, kingly, queenly, princely, sovereign, majestic, monarchial, monarchal

imperil = endanger, risk, hazard, jeopardize OPPOSITE⟩ protect

imperious = domineering, dictatorial, bossy (*informal*), haughty, lordly, commanding, arrogant, authoritative, autocratic, overbearing, tyrannical, magisterial, despotic, high-handed, overweening, tyrannous

impermanent = <u>temporary</u>, passing, brief, fleeting, elusive, mortal, short-lived, flying, fugitive, transient, momentary, ephemeral, transitory, perishable, fly-by-night (*informal*), evanescent, inconstant, fugacious, here today, gone tomorrow (*informal*)

impersonal 1 = <u>inhuman</u>, cold, remote, bureaucratic …*a large impersonal orphanage…*
2 = <u>detached</u>, neutral, dispassionate, cold, formal, aloof, businesslike …*We must be as impersonal as a surgeon with a knife…* OPPOSITE intimate

impersonate 1 = <u>imitate</u>, pose as (*informal*), masquerade as, enact, ape, act out, pass yourself off as …*He was returned to prison for impersonating a police officer…*
2 = <u>mimic</u>, take off (*informal*), do (*informal*), ape, parody, caricature, do an impression of, personate …*He was a brilliant mimic who could impersonate most of the staff…*

impersonation = <u>imitation</u>, impression, parody, caricature, takeoff (*informal*), mimicry

impertinent 1 = <u>rude</u>, forward, cheeky (*informal*), saucy (*informal*), fresh (*informal*), bold, flip (*informal*), brazen, sassy (*U.S. informal*), pert, disrespectful, presumptuous, insolent, impolite, impudent, lippy (*U.S. & Canad. slang*), discourteous, uncivil, unmannerly …*I don't like strangers who ask impertinent questions…* OPPOSITE polite
2 = <u>inappropriate</u>, irrelevant, incongruous, inapplicable …*Since we already knew this, to tell us again seemed impertinent…* OPPOSITE appropriate

imperturbable = <u>calm</u>, cool, collected, composed, complacent, serene, tranquil, sedate, undisturbed, unmoved, stoic, stoical, unfazed (*informal*), unflappable (*informal*), unruffled, self-possessed, nerveless, unexcitable, equanimous OPPOSITE agitated

impervious *with to* 1 = <u>unaffected by</u>, immune to, unmoved by, closed to, untouched by, proof against, invulnerable to, unreceptive to, unswayable by …*They are impervious to all suggestion of change…*
2 = <u>resistant to</u>, sealed to, impenetrable by, invulnerable to, impassable to, hermetic to, impermeable by, imperviable by …*The floorcovering will need to be impervious to water…*

impetuous = <u>rash</u>, hasty, impulsive, violent, furious, fierce, eager, passionate, spontaneous, precipitate, ardent, impassioned, headlong, unplanned, unbridled, vehement, unrestrained, spur-of-the-moment, unthinking, unpremeditated, unreflecting OPPOSITE cautious

impetus 1 = <u>incentive</u>, push, spur, motivation, impulse, stimulus, catalyst, goad, impulsion …*She needed a new impetus for her talent…*
2 = <u>force</u>, power, energy, momentum …*This decision will give renewed impetus to economic regeneration…*

impinge
PHRASES **impinge on** *or* **upon something** =

invade, violate, encroach on, trespass on, infringe on, make inroads on, obtrude on …*If he were at home all the time he would impinge on my space…* ♦ **impinge on** *or* **upon something** *or* **someone** = <u>affect</u>, influence, relate to, impact on, touch, touch upon, have a bearing on, bear upon …*These cuts have impinged on the region's largest employers…*

impish = <u>mischievous</u>, devilish, roguish, rascally, elfin, puckish, waggish, sportive, prankish

implacable = <u>ruthless</u>, cruel, relentless, uncompromising, intractable, inflexible, unrelenting, merciless, unforgiving, inexorable, unyielding, remorseless, pitiless, unbending, unappeasable OPPOSITE merciful

implant 1 = <u>insert</u>, place, plant, fix, root, sow, graft, embed, ingraft …*Doctors have implanted an artificial heart into a 46-year-old man…*
2 = <u>instil</u>, sow, infuse, inculcate, infix …*His father had implanted in him an ambition to obtain an education…*

implausible = <u>improbable</u>, unlikely, weak, incredible, unbelievable, dubious, suspect, unreasonable, flimsy, unconvincing, far-fetched, cock-and-bull (*informal*)

implement VERB = <u>carry out</u>, effect, carry through, complete, apply, perform, realize, fulfil, enforce, execute, discharge, bring about, enact, put into action *or* effect …*The government promised to implement a new system to control loan institutions…* OPPOSITE hinder
NOUN = <u>tool</u>, machine, device, instrument, appliance, apparatus, gadget, utensil, contraption, contrivance, agent …*writing implements…*

implementation = <u>carrying out</u>, effecting, execution, performance, performing, discharge, enforcement, accomplishment, realization, fulfilment

implicate VERB = <u>incriminate</u>, involve, compromise, embroil, entangle, inculpate …*He didn't find anything in the notebooks to implicate her…* OPPOSITE dissociate
PHRASES **implicate something** *or* **someone in something** = <u>involve in</u>, associate with, connect with, tie up with …*This particular system has been implicated in alcohol effects…*

implicated = <u>involved</u>, suspected, incriminated, under suspicion

implication NOUN 1 = <u>suggestion</u>, hint, inference, meaning, conclusion, significance, presumption, overtone, innuendo, intimation, insinuation, signification …*The implication was obvious: vote for us or you'll be sorry…*
2 = <u>involvement</u>, association, connection, incrimination, entanglement …*Implication in a murder finally brought him to the gallows…*
PLURAL NOUN = <u>consequences</u>, result, developments, ramifications, complications, upshot …*He was acutely aware of the political implications of his decision…*

implicit 1 = <u>implied</u>, understood, suggested, hinted at, taken for granted, unspoken, inferred, tacit, undeclared, insinuated, unstated, unsaid, unexpressed

...*He wanted to make explicit in the film what was implicit in the play...* OPPOSITE> explicit

2 = <u>inherent</u>, contained, underlying, intrinsic, latent, ingrained, inbuilt ...*Implicit in snobbery is a certain timidity*...

3 = <u>absolute</u>, full, complete, total, firm, fixed, entire, constant, utter, outright, consummate, unqualified, out-and-out, steadfast, wholehearted, unadulterated, unreserved, unshakable, unshaken, unhesitating ...*He had implicit faith in the noble intentions of the Emperor*...

implicitly = <u>absolutely</u>, completely, utterly, unconditionally, unreservedly, firmly, unhesitatingly, without reservation

implied = <u>suggested</u>, inherent, indirect, hinted at, implicit, unspoken, tacit, undeclared, insinuated, unstated, unexpressed

implore = <u>beg</u>, beseech, entreat, conjure, plead with, solicit, pray to, importune, crave of, supplicate, go on bended knee to

imply 1 = <u>suggest</u>, hint, insinuate, indicate, signal, intimate, signify, connote, give (someone) to understand ...*Are you implying that I had something to do with this?*...

2 = <u>involve</u>, mean, entail, include, require, indicate, import, point to, signify, denote, presuppose, betoken ...*The meeting in no way implies a resumption of contact with the terrorists*...

> **infer**

impolite = <u>bad-mannered</u>, rude, disrespectful, rough, churlish, boorish, insolent, uncouth, unrefined, loutish, ungentlemanly, ungracious, discourteous, indelicate, uncivil, unladylike, indecorous, ungallant, ill-bred, unmannerly, ill-mannered OPPOSITE> polite

import VERB = <u>bring in</u>, buy in, ship in, land, introduce ...*We spent $5000 million more on importing food than on selling abroad*...

NOUN **1** (*Formal*) = <u>significance</u>, concern, value, worth, weight, consequence, substance, moment, magnitude, usefulness, momentousness ...*Such arguments are of little import*...

2 = <u>meaning</u>, implication, significance, sense, message, bearing, intention, explanation, substance, drift, interpretation, thrust, purport, upshot, gist, signification ...*I have already spoken about the import of his speech*...

importance 1 = <u>significance</u>, interest, concern, matter, moment, value, worth, weight, import, consequence, substance, relevance, usefulness, momentousness ...*Safety is of paramount importance*...

2 = <u>prestige</u>, standing, status, rule, authority, influence, distinction, esteem, prominence, supremacy, mastery, dominion, eminence, ascendancy, pre-eminence, mana (*N.Z.*) ...*He was too puffed up with his own importance to accept the verdict*...

important 1 = <u>significant</u>, critical, substantial, grave, urgent, serious, material, signal, primary, meaningful, far-reaching, momentous, seminal, weighty, of

substance, salient, noteworthy ...*an important economic challenge to the government*... OPPOSITE> unimportant

2 *often with **to*** = <u>valued</u>, loved, prized, dear, essential, valuable, of interest, treasured, precious, esteemed, cherished, of concern, highly regarded ...*Her sons are the most important thing in her life*...

3 = <u>powerful</u>, leading, prominent, commanding, supreme, outstanding, high-level, dominant, influential, notable, big-time (*informal*), foremost, eminent, high-ranking, authoritative, major league (*informal*), of note, noteworthy, pre-eminent ...*an important figure in the media world*...

impose

PHRASES **impose on someone** = <u>intrude on</u>, exploit, take advantage of, use, trouble, abuse, bother, encroach on, horn in (*informal*), trespass on, gate-crash (*informal*), take liberties with, butt in on, presume upon, force yourself on, obtrude on ...*I was afraid you'd think we were imposing on you*...

♦ **impose something on** *or* **upon someone 1** = <u>levy</u>, apply, introduce, put, place, set, charge, establish, lay, fix, institute, exact, decree, ordain ...*They impose fines on airlines who bring in illegal immigrants*... **2** = <u>inflict</u>, force, enforce, visit, press, apply, thrust, dictate, saddle (someone) with, foist ...*Beware of imposing your own tastes on your children*...

imposing = <u>impressive</u>, striking, grand, august, powerful, effective, commanding, awesome, majestic, dignified, stately, forcible OPPOSITE> unimposing

imposition 1 = <u>application</u>, introduction, levying, decree, laying on ...*the imposition of VAT on fuel bills*...

2 = <u>intrusion</u>, liberty, presumption, cheek (*informal*), encroachment ...*I know this is an imposition, but please hear me out*...

3 = <u>charge</u>, tax, duty, burden, levy ...*the Poll Tax and other local government impositions*...

impossibility = <u>hopelessness</u>, inability, impracticability, inconceivability

impossible 1 = <u>not possible</u>, out of the question, impracticable, unfeasible, beyond the bounds of possibility ...*It was impossible to get in because no one knew the password*...

2 = <u>unachievable</u>, hopeless, out of the question, vain, unthinkable, inconceivable, far-fetched, unworkable, implausible, unattainable, unobtainable, beyond you, not to be thought of ...*You shouldn't promise what's impossible*... OPPOSITE> possible

3 = <u>absurd</u>, crazy (*informal*), ridiculous, unacceptable, outrageous, ludicrous, unreasonable, unsuitable, intolerable, preposterous, laughable, farcical, illogical, insoluble, unanswerable, inadmissible, ungovernable ...*The Government was now in an impossible situation*...

impostor = <u>fraud</u>, cheat, fake, impersonator, rogue, deceiver, sham, pretender, hypocrite, charlatan, quack, trickster, knave (*archaic*), phoney *or* phony (*informal*)

impotence = <u>powerlessness</u>, inability, helplessness, weakness, disability, incompetence, inadequacy, paralysis, inefficiency, frailty, incapacity, infirmity, ineffectiveness, uselessness, feebleness, enervation, inefficacy OPPOSITE powerfulness

impotent = <u>powerless</u>, weak, helpless, unable, disabled, incapable, paralysed, frail, incompetent, ineffective, feeble, incapacitated, unmanned, infirm, emasculate, nerveless, enervated OPPOSITE powerful

impoverish 1 = <u>bankrupt</u>, ruin, beggar, break, pauperize ...*a society impoverished by wartime inflation...*
2 = <u>deplete</u>, drain, exhaust, diminish, use up, sap, wear out, reduce ...*Mint impoverishes the soil quickly...*

impoverished 1 = <u>poor</u>, needy, destitute, ruined, distressed, bankrupt, poverty-stricken, indigent, impecunious, straitened, penurious, necessitous, in reduced *or* straitened circumstances ...*The goal is to lure businesses into impoverished areas...* OPPOSITE rich
2 = <u>depleted</u>, spent, reduced, empty, drained, exhausted, played out, worn out, denuded ...*Against the impoverished defence, he poached an early goal...*

impracticable = <u>unfeasible</u>, impossible, out of the question, unworkable, unattainable, unachievable OPPOSITE practicable

impractical 1 = <u>unworkable</u>, impracticable, unrealistic, inoperable, impossible, unserviceable, nonviable ...*With regularly scheduled airlines, sea travel became impractical...* OPPOSITE practical
2 = <u>idealistic</u>, wild, romantic, unrealistic, visionary, unbusinesslike, starry-eyed ...*He's full of wacky, weird and impractical ideas...* OPPOSITE realistic

imprecise = <u>indefinite</u>, estimated, rough, vague, loose, careless, ambiguous, inaccurate, sloppy (*informal*), woolly, hazy, indeterminate, wide of the mark, equivocal, ill-defined, inexact, inexplicit, blurred round the edges OPPOSITE precise

impregnable = <u>invulnerable</u>, strong, secure, unbeatable, invincible, impenetrable, unassailable, indestructible, immovable, unshakable, unconquerable OPPOSITE vulnerable

impregnate 1 = <u>saturate</u>, soak, steep, fill, seep, pervade, infuse, permeate, imbue, suffuse, percolate, imbrue (*rare*) ...*plastic impregnated with a light-absorbing dye...*
2 = <u>inseminate</u>, fertilize, make pregnant, fructify, fecundate, get with child ...*War entailed killing the men and impregnating the women...*

impress VERB = <u>excite</u>, move, strike, touch, affect, influence, inspire, grab (*informal*), amaze, overcome, stir, overwhelm, astonish, dazzle, sway, awe, overawe, make an impression on ...*What impressed him most was their speed...*
PHRASES **impress something on** *or* **upon someone** = <u>stress</u>, bring home to, instil in, drum into, knock into, emphasize to, fix in, inculcate in, ingrain in ...*I've impressed on them the need for professionalism...*

impression NOUN 1 = <u>idea</u>, feeling, thought, sense, opinion, view, assessment, judgment, reaction, belief, concept, fancy, notion, conviction, suspicion, hunch, apprehension, inkling, funny feeling (*informal*) ...*My*

impression is that they are totally out of control...
2 = <u>effect</u>, influence, impact, sway ...*She gave no sign that his charm had made any impression on her...*
3 = <u>imitation</u>, parody, impersonation, mockery, send-up (*Brit. informal*), takeoff (*informal*) ...*He amused us doing impressions of film actors...*
4 = <u>mark</u>, imprint, stamp, stamping, depression, outline, hollow, dent, impress, indentation ...*the world's oldest fossil impressions of plant life...*
PHRASES **make an impression** = <u>cause a stir</u>, stand out, make an impact, be conspicuous, find favour, make a hit (*informal*), arouse comment, excite notice ...*He's certainly made an impression on the interviewing board...*

impressionable = <u>suggestible</u>, vulnerable, susceptible, open, sensitive, responsive, receptive, gullible, ingenuous OPPOSITE blasé

impressive = <u>grand</u>, striking, splendid, good, great (*informal*), fine, affecting, powerful, exciting, wonderful, excellent, dramatic, outstanding, stirring, superb, first-class, marvellous (*informal*), terrific (*informal*), awesome, world-class, admirable, first-rate, forcible OPPOSITE unimpressive

imprint NOUN = <u>mark</u>, print, impression, stamp, indentation ...*the imprint of his little finger...*
VERB = <u>engrave</u>, print, stamp, impress, etch, emboss ...*a racket with the club's badge imprinted on the strings...*

imprison = <u>jail</u>, confine, detain, lock up, constrain, put away, intern, incarcerate, send down (*informal*), send to prison, impound, put under lock and key, immure OPPOSITE free

imprisoned = <u>jailed</u>, confined, locked up, inside (*slang*), in jail, captive, behind bars, put away, interned, incarcerated, in irons, under lock and key, immured

imprisonment = <u>confinement</u>, custody, detention, captivity, incarceration, internment, duress

improbable 1 = <u>doubtful</u>, unlikely, uncertain, unbelievable, dubious, questionable, fanciful, far-fetched, implausible ...*It seems improbable that this year's figure will show a drop...* OPPOSITE probable
2 = <u>unconvincing</u>, weak, unbelievable, preposterous ...*Their marriage seems an improbable alliance...* OPPOSITE convincing

impromptu = <u>spontaneous</u>, improvised, unprepared, off-the-cuff (*informal*), offhand, ad-lib, unscripted, unrehearsed, unpremeditated, extempore, unstudied, extemporaneous, extemporized OPPOSITE rehearsed

improper 1 = <u>inappropriate</u>, unfit, unsuitable, out of place, unwarranted, incongruous, unsuited, ill-timed, uncalled-for, inopportune, inapplicable, unseasonable, inapt, infelicitous, inapposite, malapropos ...*He maintained that he had done nothing improper...* OPPOSITE appropriate
2 = <u>indecent</u>, vulgar, suggestive, unseemly, untoward, risqué, smutty, unbecoming, unfitting, impolite, off-colour, indelicate, indecorous ...*He would never be improper; he is always the perfect gentleman...*

OPPOSITE> decent

3 = <u>incorrect</u>, wrong, inaccurate, false, irregular, erroneous ...*The improper use of medicine can lead to severe adverse reactions...*

impropriety (*Formal*) **1** = <u>indecency</u>, vulgarity, immodesty, bad taste, incongruity, unsuitability, indecorum ...*Inviting him up to your hotel room would smack of impropriety...* OPPOSITE> propriety

2 = <u>lapse</u>, mistake, slip, blunder, gaffe, bloomer (*Brit. informal*), faux pas, solecism, gaucherie ...*He resigned amid allegations of financial impropriety...*

improve 1 = <u>enhance</u>, better, add to, upgrade, amend, mend, augment, embellish, touch up, ameliorate, polish up ...*He improved their house...* OPPOSITE> worsen

2 = <u>get better</u>, pick up, look up (*informal*), develop, advance, perk up, take a turn for the better (*informal*) ...*The weather is beginning to improve...*

3 = <u>recuperate</u>, recover, rally, mend, make progress, turn the corner, gain ground, gain strength, convalesce, be on the mend, grow better, make strides, take on a new lease of life (*informal*) ...*He had improved so much the doctor cut his dosage...*

improvement 1 = <u>enhancement</u>, increase, gain, boost, amendment, correction, heightening, advancement, enrichment, face-lift, embellishment, betterment, rectification, augmentation, amelioration ...*the dramatic improvements in conditions...*

2 = <u>advance</u>, development, progress, recovery, reformation, upswing, furtherance ...*The system we've just introduced has been a great improvement...*

improvisation 1 = <u>invention</u>, spontaneity, ad-libbing, extemporizing ...*Funds were not abundant, and clever improvisation was necessary...*

2 = <u>ad-lib</u> ...*an improvisation on 'Jingle Bells'...*

improvise 1 = <u>devise</u>, contrive, make do, concoct, throw together ...*If you don't have a wok, improvise one...*

2 = <u>ad-lib</u>, invent, vamp, busk, wing it (*informal*), play it by ear (*informal*), extemporize, speak off the cuff (*informal*) ...*Take the story and improvise on it...*

improvised = <u>unprepared</u>, spontaneous, makeshift, spur-of-the-moment, off-the-cuff (*informal*), ad-lib, unrehearsed, extempore, extemporaneous, extemporized

imprudent = <u>unwise</u>, foolish, rash, irresponsible, reckless, careless, ill-advised, foolhardy, indiscreet, unthinking, ill-judged, ill-considered, inconsiderate, heedless, injudicious, incautious, improvident, impolitic, overhasty, temerarious OPPOSITE> prudent

impudence = <u>boldness</u>, nerve (*informal*), cheek (*informal*), face (*informal*), front, neck (*informal*), gall (*informal*), lip (*slang*), presumption, audacity, rudeness, chutzpah (*U.S. & Canad. informal*), insolence, impertinence, effrontery, brass neck (*Brit. informal*), shamelessness, sauciness, brazenness, sassiness (*U.S. informal*), pertness, bumptiousness

impudent = <u>bold</u>, rude, cheeky (*informal*), forward, fresh (*informal*), saucy (*informal*), cocky (*informal*), audacious, brazen, shameless, sassy (*U.S. informal*),

pert, presumptuous, impertinent, insolent, lippy (*U.S. & Canad. slang*), bumptious, immodest, bold-faced OPPOSITE> polite

impulse NOUN **1** = <u>urge</u>, longing, desire, drive, wish, fancy, notion, yen (*informal*), instinct, yearning, inclination, itch, whim, compulsion, caprice ...*He resisted an impulse to smile...*

2 = <u>force</u>, pressure, push, movement, surge, motive, thrust, momentum, stimulus, catalyst, impetus ...*Their impulse of broadcasting was for human rights...*

PHRASES **on impulse** = <u>impulsively</u>, of your own accord, freely, voluntarily, instinctively, impromptu, off the cuff (*informal*), in the heat of the moment, off your own bat, quite unprompted ...*After lunch she decided, on impulse, to take a bath...*

impulsive = <u>instinctive</u>, emotional, unpredictable, quick, passionate, rash, spontaneous, precipitate, intuitive, hasty, headlong, impetuous, devil-may-care, unconsidered, unpremeditated OPPOSITE> cautious

impunity = <u>immunity</u>, freedom, licence, permission, liberty, security, exemption, dispensation, nonliability

impure 1 = <u>unrefined</u>, mixed, alloyed, debased, adulterated, admixed ...*impure diamonds...*

2 = <u>immoral</u>, corrupt, obscene, indecent, gross, coarse, lewd, carnal, X-rated (*informal*), salacious, unclean, prurient, lascivious, smutty, lustful, ribald, immodest, licentious, indelicate, unchaste ...*They say such behaviour might lead to impure temptations...* OPPOSITE> moral

3 = <u>unclean</u>, dirty, foul, infected, contaminated, polluted, filthy, tainted, sullied, defiled, unwholesome, vitiated, festy (*Austral. slang*) ...*They were warned against drinking the impure water from the stream...* OPPOSITE> clean

impurity 1 *often plural* = <u>dirt</u>, pollutant, scum, grime, contaminant, dross, bits, foreign body, foreign matter ...*The air is filtered to remove impurities...*

2 = <u>contamination</u>, infection, pollution, taint, filth, foulness, defilement, dirtiness, uncleanness, befoulment ...*The soap is boiled to remove all traces of impurity...*

3 = <u>immorality</u>, corruption, obscenity, indecency, vulgarity, prurience, coarseness, licentiousness, immodesty, carnality, lewdness, grossness, salaciousness, lasciviousness, unchastity, smuttiness ...*impurity, lust and evil desires...*

impute = <u>attribute</u>, assign, ascribe, credit, refer, accredit

inaccessible = <u>out-of-reach</u>, remote, out-of-the-way, unattainable, impassable, unreachable, unapproachable, un-get-at-able (*informal*) OPPOSITE> accessible

inaccuracy 1 = <u>imprecision</u>, unreliability, incorrectness, unfaithfulness, erroneousness, inexactness ...*He was disturbed by the inaccuracy of the answers...*

2 = <u>error</u>, mistake, slip, fault, defect, blunder, lapse, boob (*Brit. slang*), literal (*Printing*), howler (*informal*), miscalculation, typo (*informal, Printing*), erratum, corrigendum ...*Guard against inaccuracies by* *checking with a variety of sources...*

inaccurate = <u>incorrect</u>, wrong, mistaken, wild, faulty, careless, unreliable, defective, unfaithful, erroneous, unsound, imprecise, wide of the mark, out, inexact, off-base (*U.S. & Canad. informal*), off-beam (*informal*), discrepant, way off-beam (*informal*) OPPOSITE> accurate

inaction = <u>inactivity</u>, inertia, idleness, immobility, torpor, dormancy, torpidity

inactive 1 = <u>unused</u>, idle, dormant, latent, inert, immobile, mothballed, out of service, inoperative, abeyant ...*The satellite has been inactive since its launch two years ago...* OPPOSITE> used
2 = <u>idle</u>, unemployed, out of work, jobless, unoccupied, kicking your heels ...*He has been inactive since last year...* OPPOSITE> employed
3 = <u>lazy</u>, passive, slow, quiet, dull, low-key (*informal*), sluggish, lethargic, sedentary, indolent, somnolent, torpid, slothful ...*He certainly was not politically inactive...* OPPOSITE> active

inactivity = <u>immobility</u>, unemployment, inaction, passivity, hibernation, dormancy OPPOSITE> mobility

inadequacy 1 = <u>shortage</u>, poverty, dearth, paucity, insufficiency, incompleteness, meagreness, skimpiness, scantiness, inadequateness ...*the inadequacy of the water supply...*
2 = <u>incompetence</u>, inability, deficiency, incapacity, ineffectiveness, incompetency, unfitness, inefficacy, defectiveness, inaptness, faultiness, unsuitableness ...*his deep-seated sense of inadequacy...*
3 = <u>shortcoming</u>, failing, lack, weakness, shortage, defect, imperfection ...*He drank heavily in an effort to forget his own inadequacies...*

inadequate 1 = <u>insufficient</u>, short, scarce, meagre, poor, lacking, incomplete, scant, sparse, skimpy, sketchy, insubstantial, scanty, niggardly, incommensurate ...*Supplies of food and medicine are inadequate...* OPPOSITE> adequate
2 = <u>incapable</u>, incompetent, pathetic, faulty, unfitted, defective, unequal, deficient, imperfect, unqualified, not up to scratch (*informal*), inapt ...*She felt quite painfully inadequate in the crisis...* OPPOSITE> capable

inadequately = <u>insufficiently</u>, poorly, thinly, sparsely, scantily, imperfectly, sketchily, skimpily, meagrely

inadvertent = <u>unintentional</u>, accidental, unintended, chance, careless, negligent, unwitting, unplanned, thoughtless, unthinking, heedless, unpremeditated, unheeding

inadvertently = <u>unintentionally</u>, accidentally, by accident, mistakenly, unwittingly, by mistake, involuntarily OPPOSITE> deliberately

inalienable = <u>sacrosanct</u>, absolute, unassailable, inherent, entailed (*Law*), non-negotiable, inviolable, nontransferable, untransferable

inane = <u>senseless</u>, stupid, silly, empty, daft (*informal*), worthless, futile, trifling, frivolous, mindless, goofy (*informal*), idiotic, vacuous, fatuous, puerile, vapid, unintelligent, asinine, imbecilic, devoid of intelligence OPPOSITE> sensible

inanimate = <u>lifeless</u>, inert, dead, cold, extinct, defunct, inactive, soulless, quiescent, spiritless, insensate, insentient OPPOSITE> animate

inaugural = <u>first</u>, opening, initial, maiden, introductory, dedicatory

inaugurate 1 = <u>invest</u>, install, induct, instate ...*The new president will be inaugurated on January 20...*
2 = <u>open</u>, commission, dedicate, ordain ...*A new centre for research was inaugurated today...*
3 = <u>launch</u>, begin, introduce, institute, set up, kick off (*informal*), initiate, originate, commence, get under way, usher in, set in motion ...*They inaugurated the first ever scheduled flights...*

inauguration 1 = <u>investiture</u>, installation, induction ...*the inauguration of the new Governor...*
2 = <u>opening</u>, launch, birth, inception, commencement ...*They later attended the inauguration of the University...*
3 = <u>launch</u>, launching, setting up, institution, initiation ...*the inauguration of monetary union...*

inborn = <u>natural</u>, inherited, inherent, hereditary, instinctive, innate, intuitive, ingrained, congenital, inbred, native, immanent, in your blood, connate

inbred = <u>innate</u>, natural, constitutional, native, ingrained, inherent, deep-seated, immanent

in-built = <u>integral</u>, built-in, incorporated, component

incalculable = <u>vast</u>, enormous, immense, countless, infinite, innumerable, untold, limitless, boundless, inestimable, numberless, uncountable, measureless, without number, incomputable

incandescent = <u>glowing</u>, brilliant, shining, red-hot, radiant, luminous, white-hot, Day-Glo, phosphorescent

incantation = <u>chant</u>, spell, charm, formula, invocation, hex (*U.S. & Canad. informal*), abracadabra, conjuration

incapacitate = <u>disable</u>, cripple, paralyse, scupper (*Brit. slang*), prostrate, immobilize, put someone out of action (*informal*), lay someone up (*informal*)

incapacitated = <u>disabled</u>, unfit, out of action (*informal*), laid up (*informal*), immobilized, indisposed, hors de combat (*French*)

incapacity = <u>inability</u>, weakness, inadequacy, impotence, powerlessness, ineffectiveness, feebleness, incompetency, unfitness, incapability

incapsulate
➤ encapsulate

incarcerate = <u>imprison</u>, confine, detain, lock up, restrict, restrain, intern, send down (*Brit.*), impound, coop up, throw in jail, put under lock and key, immure, jail *or* gaol

incarceration = <u>confinement</u>, restraint, imprisonment, detention, captivity, bondage, internment

incarnate 1 = <u>personified</u>, embodied, typified ...*He referred to her as evil incarnate...*
2 = <u>made flesh</u>, in the flesh, in human form, in bodily form ...*Why should God become incarnate as a male?...*

incarnation = <u>embodiment</u>, manifestation, epitome, type, impersonation, personification, avatar, exemplification, bodily form

incendiary = <u>inflammatory</u>, provocative, subversive, seditious, rabble-rousing, dissentious

incense¹ = <u>perfume</u>, scent, fragrance, bouquet, aroma, balm, redolence ...*an atmospheric place, pungent with incense*...

incense² = <u>anger</u>, infuriate, enrage, excite, provoke, irritate, gall, madden, inflame, exasperate, rile (*informal*), raise the hackles of, nark (*Brit., Austral., & N.Z. slang*), make your blood boil (*informal*), rub you up the wrong way, make your hackles rise, get your hackles up, make you see red (*informal*) ...*This proposal will incense conservation campaigners*...

incensed = <u>angry</u>, mad (*informal*), furious, cross, fuming, choked, infuriated, enraged, maddened, exasperated, indignant, irate, up in arms, incandescent, steamed up (*slang*), hot under the collar (*informal*), on the warpath (*informal*), wrathful, ireful (*literary*), tooshie (*Austral. slang*), off the air (*Austral. slang*)

incentive = <u>inducement</u>, motive, encouragement, urge, come-on (*informal*), spur, lure, bait, motivation, carrot (*informal*), impulse, stimulus, impetus, stimulant, goad, incitement, enticement OPPOSITE> disincentive

inception = <u>beginning</u>, start, rise, birth, origin, dawn, outset, initiation, inauguration, commencement, kickoff (*informal*) OPPOSITE> end

incessant = <u>constant</u>, endless, continuous, persistent, eternal, relentless, perpetual, continual, unbroken, never-ending, interminable, unrelenting, everlasting, unending, ceaseless, unremitting, nonstop, unceasing OPPOSITE> intermittent

incessantly = <u>all the time</u>, constantly, continually, endlessly, persistently, eternally, perpetually, nonstop, ceaselessly, without a break, interminably, everlastingly

incidence = <u>prevalence</u>, frequency, occurrence, rate, amount, degree, extent

incident 1 = <u>disturbance</u>, scene, clash, disorder, confrontation, brawl, uproar, skirmish, mishap, fracas, commotion, contretemps ...*Safety chiefs are investigating the incident*...
2 = <u>adventure</u>, drama, excitement, crisis, spectacle, theatrics ...*The birth was not without incident*...
3 = <u>happening</u>, event, affair, business, fact, matter, occasion, circumstance, episode, occurrence, escapade ...*They have not based it on any incident from the past*...

incidental 1 = <u>secondary</u>, subsidiary, subordinate, minor, occasional, ancillary, nonessential ...*The playing of music proved to be incidental to the main business*... OPPOSITE> essential
2 = <u>accompanying</u>, related, attendant, contingent, contributory, concomitant ...*At the bottom of the bill were various incidental expenses*...

incidentally 1 = <u>by the way</u>, in passing, en passant, parenthetically, by the bye ...*The tower, incidentally,*

dates from the twelfth century...
2 = <u>accidentally</u>, casually, by chance, coincidentally, fortuitously, by happenstance ...*In her denunciation, she incidentally shed some light on another mystery*...

incinerate 1 = <u>burn up</u>, carbonize ...*The government is trying to stop them incinerating their own waste*...
2 = <u>cremate</u>, burn up, reduce to ashes, consume by fire ...*Some of the victims were incinerated*...

incipient = <u>beginning</u>, starting, developing, originating, commencing, embryonic, nascent, inchoate, inceptive

incision = <u>cut</u>, opening, slash, notch, slit, gash

incisive = <u>penetrating</u>, sharp, keen, acute, piercing, trenchant, perspicacious OPPOSITE> dull

incite = <u>provoke</u>, encourage, drive, excite, prompt, urge, spur, stimulate, set on, animate, rouse, prod, stir up, inflame, instigate, whip up, egg on, goad, impel, foment, put up to, agitate for *or* against OPPOSITE> discourage

incitement = <u>provocation</u>, prompting, encouragement, spur, motive, motivation, impulse, stimulus, impetus, agitation, inducement, goad, instigation, clarion call

inclination 1 = <u>desire</u>, longing, wish, need, aspiration, craving, yearning, hankering ...*He had neither the time nor the inclination to think about it*...
2 = <u>tendency</u>, liking, taste, turn, fancy, leaning, bent, stomach, prejudice, bias, affection, thirst, disposition, penchant, fondness, propensity, aptitude, predisposition, predilection, proclivity, partiality, turn of mind, proneness ...*He set out to follow his artistic inclinations*... OPPOSITE> aversion
3 = <u>bow</u>, bending, nod, bowing ...*a polite inclination of his head*...

incline VERB 1 = <u>predispose</u>, influence, tend, persuade, prejudice, bias, sway, turn, dispose ...*the factors which incline us towards particular beliefs*...
2 = <u>bend</u>, lower, nod, bow, stoop, nutate (*rare*) ...*He inclined his head very slightly*...
NOUN = <u>slope</u>, rise, dip, grade, descent, ramp, ascent, gradient, declivity, acclivity ...*He came to a halt at the edge of a steep incline*...

inclined 1 = <u>disposed</u>, given, prone, likely, subject, liable, apt, predisposed, tending towards ...*He was inclined to self-pity*...
2 = <u>willing</u>, minded, ready, disposed, of a mind (*informal*) ...*I am inclined to agree with Alan*...

inclose
➤ enclose

include 1 = <u>contain</u>, involve, incorporate, cover, consist of, take in, embrace, comprise, take into account, embody, encompass, comprehend, subsume ...*The trip was extended to include a few other events*... OPPOSITE> exclude
2 = <u>count</u>, introduce, make a part of, number among ...*I had worked hard to be included in a project like this*...
3 = <u>add</u>, enter, put in, insert ...*You should include details of all your benefits*...

including = <u>containing</u>, with, counting, plus, together with, as well as, inclusive of

inclusion = <u>addition</u>, incorporation, introduction, insertion OPPOSITE exclusion

inclusive = <u>comprehensive</u>, full, overall, general, global, sweeping, all-in, blanket, umbrella, across-the-board, all-together, catch-all (*chiefly U.S.*), all-embracing, overarching, in toto (*Latin*) OPPOSITE limited

incognito = <u>in disguise</u>, unknown, disguised, unrecognized, under an assumed name

incoherent = <u>unintelligible</u>, wild, confused, disordered, wandering, muddled, rambling, inconsistent, jumbled, stammering, disconnected, stuttering, unconnected, disjointed, inarticulate, uncoordinated OPPOSITE coherent

income = <u>revenue</u>, gains, earnings, means, pay, interest, returns, profits, wages, rewards, yield, proceeds, salary, receipts, takings

incoming 1 = <u>arriving</u>, landing, approaching, entering, returning, homeward ...*The airport was closed to incoming flights*... OPPOSITE departing
2 = <u>new</u>, next, succeeding, elected, elect ...*the problems confronting the incoming government*...

incomparable = <u>unequalled</u>, supreme, unparalleled, paramount, superlative, transcendent, unrivalled, inimitable, unmatched, peerless, matchless, beyond compare

incompatibility = <u>inconsistency</u>, conflict, discrepancy, antagonism, incongruity, irreconcilability, disparateness, uncongeniality

incompatible = <u>inconsistent</u>, conflicting, contradictory, unsuitable, disparate, incongruous, discordant, antagonistic, irreconcilable, unsuited, mismatched, discrepant, uncongenial, antipathetic, ill-assorted, inconsonant OPPOSITE compatible

incompetence = <u>ineptitude</u>, inability, inadequacy, incapacity, ineffectiveness, uselessness, insufficiency, ineptness, incompetency, unfitness, incapability, skill-lessness

incompetent = <u>inept</u>, useless, incapable, unable, cowboy (*informal*), floundering, bungling, unfit, unfitted, ineffectual, incapacitated, inexpert, skill-less, unskilful OPPOSITE competent

incomplete = <u>unfinished</u>, partial, insufficient, wanting, short, lacking, undone, defective, deficient, imperfect, undeveloped, fragmentary, unaccomplished, unexecuted, half-pie (*N.Z. informal*) OPPOSITE complete

incomprehensible 1 = <u>unintelligible</u> ...*Her speech was almost incomprehensible*... OPPOSITE comprehensible
2 = <u>obscure</u>, puzzling, mysterious, baffling, enigmatic, perplexing, opaque, impenetrable, inscrutable, unfathomable, above your head, beyond comprehension, all Greek to you (*informal*), beyond your grasp ...*incomprehensible mathematics puzzles*... OPPOSITE understandable

inconceivable = <u>unimaginable</u>, impossible, incredible, staggering (*informal*), unbelievable, unthinkable, out of the question, incomprehensible, unheard-of, mind-boggling (*informal*), beyond belief, unknowable, not to be thought of OPPOSITE conceivable

inconclusive = <u>uncertain</u>, vague, ambiguous, open, indecisive, unsettled, undecided, unconvincing, up in the air (*informal*), indeterminate

incongruity = <u>inappropriateness</u>, discrepancy, inconsistency, disparity, incompatibility, unsuitability, inaptness, inharmoniousness

incongruous = <u>inappropriate</u>, absurd, out of place, conflicting, contrary, contradictory, inconsistent, unsuitable, improper, incompatible, discordant, incoherent, extraneous, unsuited, unbecoming, out of keeping, inapt, disconsonant OPPOSITE appropriate

inconsequential = <u>unimportant</u>, trivial, insignificant, minor, petty, trifling, negligible, paltry, immaterial, measly, inconsiderable, nickel-and-dime (*U.S. slang*), of no significance

inconsiderable = <u>insignificant</u>, small, slight, light, minor, petty, trivial, trifling, negligible, unimportant, small-time (*informal*), inconsequential, exiguous

inconsiderate = <u>selfish</u>, rude, insensitive, self-centred, careless, unkind, intolerant, thoughtless, unthinking, tactless, uncharitable, ungracious, indelicate OPPOSITE considerate

inconsistency 1 = <u>unreliability</u>, instability, unpredictability, fickleness, unsteadiness ...*His worst fault was his inconsistency*...
2 = <u>incompatibility</u>, paradox, discrepancy, disparity, disagreement, variance, divergence, incongruity, contrariety, inconsonance ...*the alleged inconsistencies in his evidence*...

inconsistent 1 = <u>changeable</u>, variable, unpredictable, unstable, irregular, erratic, uneven, fickle, capricious, unsteady, inconstant ...*You are inconsistent and unpredictable*... OPPOSITE consistent
2 = <u>incompatible</u>, conflicting, contrary, at odds, contradictory, in conflict, incongruous, discordant, incoherent, out of step, irreconcilable, at variance, discrepant, inconstant ...*The outburst was inconsistent with the image he had cultivated*... OPPOSITE compatible

inconsolable = <u>heartbroken</u>, devastated, despairing, desolate, wretched, heartsick, brokenhearted, sick at heart, prostrate with grief

inconspicuous 1 = <u>unobtrusive</u>, hidden, unnoticeable, retiring, quiet, ordinary, plain, muted, camouflaged, insignificant, unassuming, unostentatious ...*I'll try to be as inconspicuous as possible*... OPPOSITE noticeable
2 = <u>plain</u>, ordinary, modest, unobtrusive, unnoticeable ...*The studio is an inconspicuous grey building*...

incontrovertible = <u>indisputable</u>, sure, certain, established, positive, undeniable, irrefutable, unquestionable, unshakable, beyond dispute, incontestable, indubitable

inconvenience NOUN 1 = <u>trouble</u>, difficulty, bother,

upset, fuss, disadvantage, disturbance, disruption, drawback, hassle (*informal*), nuisance, downside, annoyance, hindrance, awkwardness, vexation, uphill (*S. African*) ...*We apologize for any inconvenience caused during the repairs*...
2 = <u>awkwardness</u>, unfitness, unwieldiness, cumbersomeness, unhandiness, unsuitableness, untimeliness ...*The expense and inconvenience of PCs means that they will be replaced*...
VERB = <u>trouble</u>, bother, disturb, upset, disrupt, put out, hassle (*informal*), irk, discommode, give (someone) bother *or* trouble, make (someone) go out of his way, put to trouble ...*He promised not to inconvenience them any further*...

inconvenient **1** = <u>troublesome</u>, annoying, awkward, embarrassing, disturbing, unsuitable, tiresome, untimely, bothersome, vexatious, inopportune, disadvantageous, unseasonable ...*It's very inconvenient to have to wait so long*... OPPOSITE convenient
2 = <u>difficult</u>, awkward, unmanageable, cumbersome, unwieldy, unhandy ...*This must be the most inconvenient house ever built*...

incorporate **1** = <u>include</u>, contain, take in, embrace, integrate, embody, encompass, assimilate, comprise of ...*The new cars will incorporate a number of major improvements*...
2 = <u>integrate</u>, include, absorb, unite, merge, accommodate, knit, fuse, assimilate, amalgamate, subsume, coalesce, harmonize, meld ...*The agreement allowed the rebels to be incorporated into the police force*...
3 = <u>blend</u>, mix, combine, compound, consolidate, fuse, mingle, meld ...*Gradually incorporate the olive oil into the dough*...

incorporation = <u>merger</u>, federation, blend, integration, unifying, inclusion, fusion, absorption, assimilation, amalgamation, coalescence

incorrect = <u>false</u>, wrong, mistaken, flawed, faulty, unfitting, inaccurate, untrue, improper, erroneous, out, wide of the mark (*informal*), specious, inexact, off-base (*U.S. & Canad. informal*), off-beam (*informal*), way off-beam (*informal*) OPPOSITE correct

incorrigible = <u>incurable</u>, hardened, hopeless, intractable, inveterate, unreformed, irredeemable

increase VERB **1** = <u>raise</u>, extend, boost, expand, develop, advance, add to, strengthen, enhance, step up (*informal*), widen, prolong, intensify, heighten, elevate, enlarge, multiply, inflate, magnify, amplify, augment, aggrandize ...*The company has increased the price of its cars*... OPPOSITE decrease
2 = <u>grow</u>, develop, spread, mount, expand, build up, swell, wax, enlarge, escalate, multiply, fill out, get bigger, proliferate, snowball, dilate ...*The population continues to increase*... OPPOSITE shrink
NOUN = <u>growth</u>, rise, boost, development, gain, addition, expansion, extension, heightening, proliferation, enlargement, escalation, upsurge, upturn, increment, intensification, augmentation, aggrandizement ...*a sharp increase in productivity*...
PHRASES **on the increase** = <u>growing</u>, increasing, spreading, expanding, escalating, multiplying, developing, on the rise, proliferating ...*Crime is on the increase*...

increasingly = <u>progressively</u>, more and more, to an increasing extent, continuously more

incredible **1** (*Informal*) = <u>amazing</u>, great, wonderful, brilliant, stunning, extraordinary, overwhelming, ace (*informal*), astonishing, staggering, marvellous, sensational (*informal*), mega (*slang*), breathtaking, astounding, far-out (*slang*), prodigious, awe-inspiring, superhuman, rad (*informal*) ...*Thanks, I had an incredible time*...
2 = <u>unbelievable</u>, impossible, absurd, unthinkable, questionable, improbable, inconceivable, preposterous, unconvincing, unimaginable, outlandish, far-fetched, implausible, beyond belief, cock-and-bull (*informal*), not able to hold water ...*Do not dismiss as incredible the stories your children tell you*...

incredulity = <u>disbelief</u>, doubt, scepticism, distrust, unbelief

incredulous = <u>disbelieving</u>, doubting, sceptical, suspicious, doubtful, dubious, unconvinced, distrustful, mistrustful, unbelieving OPPOSITE credulous

increment = <u>increase</u>, gain, addition, supplement, step up, advancement, enlargement, accretion, accrual, augmentation, accruement

incriminate = <u>implicate</u>, involve, accuse, blame, indict, point the finger at (*informal*), stigmatize, arraign, blacken the name of, inculpate

incumbent NOUN = <u>holder</u>, keeper, bearer, custodian ...*The previous incumbent led the party for eleven years*...
ADJECTIVE (*Formal*)= <u>obligatory</u>, required, necessary, essential, binding, compulsory, mandatory, imperative ...*It is incumbent upon all of us to make an extra effort*...

incur = <u>sustain</u>, experience, suffer, gain, earn, collect, meet with, provoke, run up, induce, arouse, expose yourself to, lay yourself open to, bring upon yourself

incurable **1** = <u>fatal</u>, terminal, inoperable, irrecoverable, irremediable, remediless ...*He is suffering from an incurable skin disease*...
2 = <u>incorrigible</u>, hopeless, inveterate, dyed-in-the-wool ...*He's an incurable romantic*...

incursion = <u>foray</u>, raid, invasion, penetration, infiltration, inroad, irruption

indebted = <u>grateful</u>, obliged, in debt, obligated, beholden, under an obligation

indecency = <u>obscenity</u>, impurity, lewdness, impropriety, pornography, vulgarity, coarseness, crudity, licentiousness, foulness, outrageousness, immodesty, grossness, vileness, bawdiness, unseemliness, indelicacy, smuttiness, indecorum OPPOSITE decency

indecent **1** = <u>obscene</u>, lewd, dirty, blue, offensive, outrageous, inappropriate, rude, gross, foul, crude, coarse, filthy, vile, improper, pornographic, salacious, impure, smutty, immodest, licentious, scatological,

indelicate ...*She accused him of making indecent suggestions*... OPPOSITE> decent
2 = <u>unbecoming</u>, unsuitable, vulgar, improper, tasteless, unseemly, undignified, disreputable, unrefined, discreditable, indelicate, indecorous, unbefitting ...*The legislation was drafted with indecent haste*... OPPOSITE> proper

indecision = <u>hesitation</u>, doubt, uncertainty, wavering, ambivalence, dithering (*chiefly Brit.*), hesitancy, indecisiveness, vacillation, shilly-shallying (*informal*), irresolution

indecisive **1** = <u>hesitating</u>, uncertain, wavering, doubtful, faltering, tentative, undecided, dithering (*chiefly Brit.*), vacillating, in two minds (*informal*), undetermined, pussyfooting (*informal*), irresolute ...*He was criticised as a weak and indecisive leader*... OPPOSITE> decisive
2 = <u>inconclusive</u>, unclear, undecided, indefinite, indeterminate ...*An indecisive vote would force a second round of voting*... OPPOSITE> conclusive

indeed **1** = <u>certainly</u>, yes, definitely, surely, truly, absolutely, undoubtedly, positively, decidedly, without doubt, undeniably, without question, unequivocally, indisputably, assuredly, doubtlessly ...*'Did you know him?' 'I did indeed.'*...
2 = <u>really</u>, actually, in fact, certainly, undoubtedly, genuinely, in reality, to be sure, in truth, categorically, verily (*archaic*), in actuality, in point of fact, veritably ...*Later he admitted that the payments had indeed been made*...

indefatigable = <u>tireless</u>, dogged, persevering, patient, relentless, diligent, inexhaustible, unremitting, assiduous, unflagging, untiring, sedulous, pertinacious, unwearying, unwearied

indefensible = <u>unforgivable</u>, wrong, inexcusable, unjustifiable, untenable, unpardonable, insupportable, unwarrantable OPPOSITE> defensible

indefinite **1** = <u>uncertain</u>, general, vague, unclear, unsettled, loose, unlimited, evasive, indeterminate, imprecise, undefined, equivocal, ill-defined, indistinct, undetermined, inexact, unfixed, oracular ...*The trial was adjourned for an indefinite period*... OPPOSITE> settled
2 = <u>unclear</u>, unknown, uncertain, obscure, doubtful, ambiguous, indeterminate, imprecise, undefined, ill-defined, indistinct, undetermined, inexact, unfixed ...*a handsome woman of indefinite age*... OPPOSITE> specific

indefinitely = <u>endlessly</u>, continually, for ever, ad infinitum, sine die (*Latin*), till the cows come home (*informal*)

indelible = <u>permanent</u>, lasting, enduring, ingrained, indestructible, ineradicable, ineffaceable, inexpungible, inextirpable OPPOSITE> temporary

indemnify **1** = <u>insure</u>, protect, guarantee, secure, endorse, underwrite ...*They agreed to indemnify the taxpayers against any loss*...
2 = <u>compensate</u>, pay, reimburse, satisfy, repair, repay, requite, remunerate ...*They don't have the money to indemnify everybody*...

indemnity **1** = <u>insurance</u>, security, guarantee, protection ...*They had failed to take out full indemnity cover*...
2 = <u>compensation</u>, remuneration, reparation, satisfaction, redress, restitution, reimbursement, requital ...*The government paid the family an indemnity for the missing pictures*...
3 (*Law*) = <u>exemption</u>, immunity, impunity, privilege ...*He was offered indemnity from prosecution in return for his evidence*...

indent **1** = <u>notch</u>, cut, score, mark, nick, pink, scallop, dint, serrate ...*the country's heavily indented coastline*...
2 = <u>order</u>, request, ask for, requisition ...*We had to indent for hatchets and torches*...

indentation = <u>notch</u>, cut, nick, depression, pit, dip, bash (*informal*), hollow, dent, jag, dimple

independence = <u>freedom</u>, liberty, autonomy, separation, sovereignty, self-determination, self-government, self-rule, self-sufficiency, self-reliance, home rule, autarchy OPPOSITE> subjugation

independent **1** = <u>separate</u>, unrelated, unconnected, unattached, uncontrolled, unconstrained ...*Two independent studies have been carried out*... OPPOSITE> controlled
2 = <u>self-sufficient</u>, free, liberated, unconventional, self-contained, individualistic, unaided, self-reliant, self-supporting ...*There were benefits to being a single, independent woman*...
3 = <u>self-governing</u>, free, autonomous, separated, liberated, sovereign, self-determining, nonaligned, decontrolled, autarchic ...*a fully independent state*... OPPOSITE> subject

independently = <u>separately</u>, alone, solo, on your own, by yourself, unaided, individually, autonomously, under your own steam

indescribable = <u>unutterable</u>, indefinable, beyond words, ineffable, inexpressible, beyond description, incommunicable, beggaring description

indestructible = <u>permanent</u>, durable, unbreakable, lasting, enduring, abiding, immortal, everlasting, indelible, incorruptible, imperishable, indissoluble, unfading, nonperishable OPPOSITE> breakable

indeterminate = <u>uncertain</u>, indefinite, unspecified, vague, inconclusive, imprecise, undefined, undetermined, inexact, unfixed, unstipulated OPPOSITE> fixed

index = <u>indication</u>, guide, sign, mark, note, evidence, signal, symptom, hint, clue, token

indicate **1** = <u>show</u>, suggest, reveal, display, signal, demonstrate, point to, imply, disclose, manifest, signify, denote, bespeak, make known, be symptomatic of, evince, betoken ...*The survey indicated that most old people are independent*...
2 = <u>imply</u>, suggest, hint, intimate, signify, insinuate, give someone to understand ...*He has indicated that he might resign*...
3 = <u>point to</u>, point out, specify, gesture towards, designate ...*'Sit down,' he said, indicating a chair*...
4 = <u>register</u>, show, record, mark, read, express, display,

demonstrate ...*The gauge indicated that it was boiling...*

indicated = <u>recommended</u>, needed, necessary, suggested, called-for, desirable, advisable

indication = <u>sign</u>, mark, evidence, warning, note, signal, suggestion, symptom, hint, clue, manifestation, omen, inkling, portent, intimation, forewarning

indicative = <u>suggestive</u>, significant, symptomatic, pointing to, exhibitive, indicatory, indicial

indicator = <u>sign</u>, mark, measure, guide, display, index, signal, symbol, meter, gauge, marker, benchmark, pointer, signpost, barometer

indict = <u>charge</u>, accuse, prosecute, summon, impeach, arraign, serve with a summons

indictment = <u>charge</u>, allegation, prosecution, accusation, impeachment, summons, arraignment

indifference 1 = <u>disregard</u>, apathy, lack of interest, negligence, detachment, coolness, carelessness, coldness, nonchalance, callousness, aloofness, inattention, unconcern, absence of feeling, heedlessness ...*his callous indifference to the plight of his son...* OPPOSITE> concern
2 = <u>irrelevance</u>, insignificance, triviality, unimportance ...*They regard dress as a matter of indifference...*

indifferent 1 = <u>unconcerned</u>, distant, detached, cold, cool, regardless, careless, callous, aloof, unimpressed, unmoved, unsympathetic, impervious, uncaring, uninterested, apathetic, unresponsive, heedless, inattentive ...*People have become indifferent to the suffering of others...* OPPOSITE> concerned
2 = <u>mediocre</u>, middling, average, fair, ordinary, moderate, insignificant, unimportant, so-so (*informal*), immaterial, passable, undistinguished, uninspired, of no consequence, no great shakes (*informal*), half-pie (*N.Z. informal*) ...*She had starred in several indifferent movies...* OPPOSITE> excellent

indigenous = <u>native</u>, original, aboriginal, home-grown, autochthonous

indigent (*Formal*) = <u>destitute</u>, poor, impoverished, needy, penniless, poverty-stricken, down and out, in want, down at heel (*informal*), impecunious, dirt-poor, straitened, on the breadline, short, flat broke (*informal*), penurious, necessitous OPPOSITE> wealthy

indigestion = <u>upset stomach</u>, heartburn, dyspepsia, dyspepsy

indignant = <u>resentful</u>, angry, mad (*informal*), heated, provoked, furious, annoyed, hacked (off) (*U.S. slang*), sore (*informal*), fuming (*informal*), choked, incensed, disgruntled, exasperated, irate, livid (*informal*), seeing red (*informal*), miffed (*informal*), riled, up in arms (*informal*), peeved (*informal*), in a huff, hot under the collar (*informal*), huffy (*informal*), wrathful, narked (*Brit., Austral., & N.Z. slang*), in high dudgeon, tooshie (*Austral. slang*), off the air (*Austral. slang*)

indignation = <u>resentment</u>, anger, rage, fury, wrath, ire (*literary*), exasperation, pique, umbrage, righteous anger

indignity = <u>humiliation</u>, abuse, outrage, injury, slight, insult, snub, reproach, affront, disrespect, dishonour, opprobrium, obloquy, contumely

indirect 1 = <u>related</u>, accompanying, secondary, subsidiary, contingent, collateral, incidental, unintended, ancillary, concomitant ...*They are feeling the indirect effects of the recession elsewhere...*
2 = <u>circuitous</u>, winding, roundabout, curving, wandering, rambling, deviant, meandering, tortuous, zigzag, long-drawn-out, circumlocutory ...*The goods went by a rather indirect route...* OPPOSITE> direct

indirectly 1 = <u>by implication</u>, in a roundabout way, circumlocutorily ...*Drugs are indirectly responsible for the violence...*
2 = <u>obliquely</u>, in a roundabout way, evasively, not in so many words, circuitously, periphrastically ...*He referred indirectly to the territorial dispute...*

indiscreet 1 = <u>tactless</u>, foolish, rash, reckless, unwise, hasty, ill-advised, unthinking, ill-judged, ill-considered, imprudent, heedless, injudicious, incautious, undiplomatic, impolitic OPPOSITE> discreet

indiscretion 1 = <u>folly</u>, foolishness, recklessness, imprudence, rashness, tactlessness, gaucherie ...*Occasionally they paid for their indiscretion with their lives...*
2 = <u>mistake</u>, slip, error, lapse, folly, boob (*Brit. slang*), gaffe, bloomer (*Brit. informal*), faux pas ...*rumours of his mother's youthful indiscretions...*

indiscriminate = <u>random</u>, general, wholesale, mixed, sweeping, confused, chaotic, careless, mingled, jumbled, miscellaneous, promiscuous, motley, haphazard, uncritical, aimless, desultory, hit or miss (*informal*), higgledy-piggledy (*informal*), undiscriminating, unsystematic, unselective, undistinguishable, unmethodical OPPOSITE> systematic

indispensable = <u>essential</u>, necessary, needed, key, vital, crucial, imperative, requisite, needful OPPOSITE> dispensable

indistinct 1 = <u>unclear</u>, confused, obscure, faint, blurred, vague, doubtful, ambiguous, fuzzy, shadowy, indefinite, misty, hazy, unintelligible, indistinguishable, indeterminate, bleary, undefined, out of focus, ill-defined, indiscernible ...*The lettering is fuzzy and indistinct...* OPPOSITE> distinct
2 = <u>muffled</u>, confused, faint, dim, weak, indistinguishable, indiscernible ...*the indistinct murmur of voices...*

indistinguishable = <u>identical to</u>, the same as, cut from the same cloth as, like as two peas in a pod to (*informal*)

individual ADJECTIVE 1 = <u>separate</u>, single, independent, isolated, lone, solitary, discrete ...*waiting for the group to decide rather than making individual decisions...* OPPOSITE> collective
2 = <u>unique</u>, special, fresh, novel, exclusive, distinct, singular, idiosyncratic, unorthodox ...*It was all part of her very individual personality...* OPPOSITE> conventional
NOUN = <u>person</u>, being, human, party, body (*informal*), type, unit, character, soul, creature, human being, mortal, personage, living soul ...*the rights and responsibilities of the individual...*

individualism = <u>independence</u>, self-interest, originality, self-reliance, egoism, egocentricity, self-direction, freethinking

individualist = <u>maverick</u>, nonconformist, independent, original, loner, lone wolf, freethinker

individuality = <u>character</u>, personality, uniqueness, distinction, distinctiveness, originality, peculiarity, singularity, separateness, discreteness

individually = <u>separately</u>, independently, singly, one by one, one at a time, severally

indoctrinate = <u>brainwash</u>, school, train, teach, drill, initiate, instruct, imbue

indoctrination = <u>brainwashing</u>, schooling, training, instruction, drilling, inculcation

indomitable = <u>invincible</u>, resolute, steadfast, set, staunch, unbeatable, unyielding, unflinching, unconquerable, untameable <u>OPPOSITE</u> weak

indorse
➤ **endorse**

indorsement
➤ **endorsement**

induce 1 = <u>cause</u>, produce, create, begin, effect, lead to, occasion, generate, provoke, motivate, set off, bring about, give rise to, precipitate, incite, instigate, engender, set in motion ...*an economic crisis induced by high oil prices...* <u>OPPOSITE</u> prevent
2 = <u>persuade</u>, encourage, influence, get, move, press, draw, convince, urge, prompt, sway, entice, coax, incite, impel, talk someone into, prevail upon, actuate ...*I would do anything to induce them to stay...* <u>OPPOSITE</u> dissuade

inducement = <u>incentive</u>, motive, cause, influence, reward, come-on (*informal*), spur, consideration, attraction, lure, bait, carrot (*informal*), encouragement, impulse, stimulus, incitement, clarion call

induct = <u>install</u>, admit, introduce, allow, swear, initiate, inaugurate

induction = <u>installation</u>, institution, introduction, initiation, inauguration, investiture

indulge <u>VERB</u> 1 = <u>gratify</u>, satisfy, fulfil, feed, give way to, yield to, cater to, pander to, regale, gladden, satiate ...*His success has let him indulge his love of expensive cars...*
2 = <u>spoil</u>, pamper, cosset, baby, favour, humour, give in to, coddle, spoon-feed, mollycoddle, fawn on, overindulge ...*He did not agree with indulging children...*
<u>PHRASES</u> **indulge yourself** = <u>treat yourself</u>, splash out, spoil yourself, luxuriate in something, overindulge yourself ...*You can indulge yourself without spending a fortune...*

indulgence 1 = <u>luxury</u>, treat, extravagance, favour, privilege ...*The car is one of my few indulgences...*
2 = <u>leniency</u>, pampering, spoiling, kindness, fondness, permissiveness, partiality ...*The king's indulgence towards his sons angered them...*
3 = <u>intemperance</u>, excess, extravagance, debauchery, dissipation, overindulgence, prodigality,

immoderation, dissoluteness, intemperateness ...*Sadly, constant indulgence can be a costly affair...* <u>OPPOSITE</u> temperance
4 = <u>gratification</u>, satisfaction, fulfilment, appeasement, satiation ...*his indulgence of his gross appetites...*

indulgent = <u>lenient</u>, liberal, kind, kindly, understanding, gentle, tender, mild, fond, favourable, tolerant, gratifying, easy-going, compliant, permissive, forbearing <u>OPPOSITE</u> strict

industrialist = <u>capitalist</u>, tycoon, magnate, boss, producer, manufacturer, baron, financier, captain of industry, big businessman

industrious = <u>hard-working</u>, diligent, active, busy, steady, productive, energetic, conscientious, tireless, zealous, laborious, assiduous, sedulous <u>OPPOSITE</u> lazy

industry 1 = <u>business</u>, production, manufacturing, trade, trading, commerce, commercial enterprise ...*countries where industry is developing rapidly...*
2 = <u>trade</u>, world, business, service, line, field, craft, profession, occupation ...*the textile industry...*
3 = <u>diligence</u>, effort, labour, hard work, trouble, activity, application, striving, endeavour, toil, vigour, zeal, persistence, assiduity, tirelessness ...*No one doubted his industry or his integrity...*

ineffable = <u>indescribable</u>, unspeakable, indefinable, beyond words, unutterable, inexpressible, incommunicable

ineffective 1 = <u>unproductive</u>, useless, futile, vain, unsuccessful, pointless, fruitless, to no avail, ineffectual, unprofitable, to no effect, unavailing, unfruitful, profitless, bootless, inefficacious ...*Reform will continue to be painful and ineffective...* <u>OPPOSITE</u> effective
2 = <u>inefficient</u>, inadequate, useless, poor, weak, pathetic, powerless, unfit, feeble, worthless, inept, impotent, ineffectual ...*They are burdened with an ineffective leader...*

ineffectual 1 = <u>unproductive</u>, useless, ineffective, vain, unsuccessful, pointless, futile, fruitless, to no avail, unprofitable, to no effect, unavailing, unfruitful, profitless, bootless, inefficacious ...*the well-meaning but ineffectual jobs programs of the past...*
2 = <u>inefficient</u>, useless, powerless, poor, weak, inadequate, pathetic, unfit, ineffective, feeble, worthless, inept, impotent ...*The mayor had become ineffectual in the war against drugs...*

inefficiency = <u>incompetence</u>, slackness, sloppiness, disorganization, carelessness

inefficient 1 = <u>wasteful</u>, uneconomical, profligate, ruinous, improvident, unthrifty, inefficacious ...*the inefficient use of funds...*
2 = <u>incompetent</u>, incapable, inept, weak, bungling, feeble, sloppy, ineffectual, disorganized, slipshod, inexpert ...*Some people are very inefficient workers...* <u>OPPOSITE</u> efficient

ineligible = <u>unqualified</u>, ruled out, unacceptable, disqualified, incompetent (*Law*), unfit, unfitted, unsuitable, undesirable, objectionable, unequipped

inept 1 = <u>incompetent</u>, bungling, clumsy, cowboy

(*informal*), awkward, bumbling, gauche, cack-handed (*informal*), inexpert, maladroit, unskilful, unhandy, unworkmanlike ...*He was inept and lacked the intelligence to govern*... OPPOSITE competent
2 = *unsuitable*, inappropriate, out of place, ridiculous, absurd, meaningless, pointless, unfit, improper, inapt, infelicitous, malapropos ...*The Government's inept response turned this into a crisis*... OPPOSITE appropriate

ineptitude = *incompetence*, inefficiency, inability, incapacity, clumsiness, unfitness, gaucheness, inexpertness, unhandiness

inequality = *disparity*, prejudice, difference, bias, diversity, irregularity, unevenness, lack of balance, disproportion, imparity, preferentiality

inert 1 = *inactive*, still, motionless, dead, passive, slack, static, dormant, lifeless, leaden, immobile, inanimate, unresponsive, unmoving, quiescent, torpid, unreactive, slumberous (*chiefly poetic*) ...*He covered the inert body with a blanket*... OPPOSITE moving
2 = *dull*, dry, boring, plain, static, commonplace, tedious, dreary, tiresome, lifeless, monotonous, prosaic, run-of-the-mill, unimaginative, uninteresting, vapid, torpid ...*The novel itself remains oddly inert*...

inertia = *inactivity*, apathy, lethargy, passivity, stillness, laziness, sloth, idleness, stupor, drowsiness, dullness, immobility, torpor, sluggishness, indolence, lassitude, languor, listlessness, deadness, unresponsiveness OPPOSITE activity

inescapable = *unavoidable*, inevitable, certain, sure, fated, destined, inexorable, ineluctable, ineludible (*rare*)

inevitability 1 = *certainty*, fate, shoo-in (*U.S. & Canad.*) ...*Success is an inevitability for us*...
2 = *sureness*, ineluctability, inexorability *or* inexorableness, unavoidability *or* unavoidableness ...*the inevitability of death*...

inevitable = *unavoidable*, inescapable, inexorable, sure, certain, necessary, settled, fixed, assured, fated, decreed, destined, ordained, predetermined, predestined, preordained, ineluctable, unpreventable OPPOSITE avoidable

inevitably = *unavoidably*, naturally, necessarily, surely, certainly, as a result, automatically, consequently, of necessity, perforce, inescapably, as a necessary consequence

inexcusable = *unforgivable*, indefensible, unjustifiable, outrageous, unpardonable, unwarrantable, inexpiable OPPOSITE excusable

inexhaustible 1 = *endless*, infinite, never-ending, limitless, boundless, bottomless, unbounded, measureless, illimitable ...*They seem to have an inexhaustible supply of ammunition*... OPPOSITE limited
2 = *tireless*, undaunted, indefatigable, unfailing, unflagging, untiring, unwearying, unwearied ...*the sound of his inexhaustible voice, still talking*... OPPOSITE tiring

inexorable = *unrelenting*, relentless, implacable, hard, severe, harsh, cruel, adamant, inescapable, inflexible, merciless, unyielding, immovable, remorseless, pitiless, unbending, obdurate, ineluctable, unappeasable OPPOSITE relenting

inexorably = *relentlessly*, inevitably, irresistibly, remorselessly, implacably, unrelentingly

inexpensive = *cheap*, reasonable, low-priced, budget, bargain, modest, low-cost, economical OPPOSITE expensive

inexperience = *unfamiliarity*, ignorance, newness, rawness, greenness, callowness, unexpertness

inexperienced = *new*, unskilled, untrained, green, fresh, amateur, raw, unfamiliar, unused, callow, immature, unaccustomed, untried, unschooled, wet behind the ears (*informal*), unacquainted, unseasoned, unpractised, unversed, unfledged OPPOSITE experienced

inexplicable = *unaccountable*, strange, mysterious, baffling, enigmatic, incomprehensible, mystifying, unintelligible, insoluble, inscrutable, unfathomable, beyond comprehension OPPOSITE explicable

inextricably = *inseparably*, totally, intricately, irretrievably, indissolubly, indistinguishably

infallibility 1 = *supremacy*, perfection, omniscience, impeccability, faultlessness, irrefutability, unerringness ...*exaggerated views of the infallibility of science*...
2 = *reliability*, safety, dependability, trustworthiness, sureness ...*The technical infallibility of their systems is without doubt*...

infallible 1 = *perfect*, impeccable, faultless, unerring, omniscient, unimpeachable ...*She had an infallible eye for style*... OPPOSITE fallible
2 = *sure*, certain, reliable, unbeatable, dependable, trustworthy, foolproof, sure-fire (*informal*), unfailing ...*She hit on an infallible way of staying sober amid a flood of toasts*... OPPOSITE unreliable

infamous = *notorious*, base, shocking, outrageous, disgraceful, monstrous, shameful, vile, scandalous, wicked, atrocious, heinous, odious, hateful, loathsome, ignominious, disreputable, egregious, abominable, villainous, dishonourable, nefarious, iniquitous, detestable, opprobrious, ill-famed, flagitious OPPOSITE esteemed

infamy = *notoriety*, scandal, shame, disgrace, atrocity, discredit, stigma, disrepute, ignominy, dishonour, abomination, opprobrium, villainy, odium, outrageousness, obloquy

infancy 1 = *early childhood*, babyhood ...*the development of the mind from infancy onwards*...
2 = *beginnings*, start, birth, roots, seeds, origins, dawn, early stages, emergence, outset, cradle, inception ...*the infancy of the electronic revolution*... OPPOSITE end

infant NOUN = *baby*, child, babe, toddler, tot, wean (*Scot.*), little one, bairn (*Scot.*), suckling, newborn child, babe in arms, sprog (*slang*), munchkin (*informal, chiefly U.S.*), neonate, rug rat (*slang*), littlie (*Austral. informal*), ankle-biter (*Austral. slang*), tacker (*Austral. slang*) ...*young mums with infants in prams*...

ADJECTIVE = <u>early</u>, new, developing, young, growing, initial, dawning, fledgling, newborn, immature, embryonic, emergent, nascent, unfledged …*The infant company was based in Germany…*

infantile = <u>childish</u>, immature, puerile, babyish, young, weak **OPPOSITE** mature

infatuated = <u>obsessed</u>, fascinated, captivated, possessed, carried away, inflamed, beguiled, smitten (*informal*), besotted, bewitched, intoxicated, crazy about (*informal*), spellbound, enamoured, enraptured, under the spell of, head over heels in love with, swept off your feet

infatuation = <u>obsession</u>, thing (*informal*), passion, crush (*informal*), madness, folly, fixation, foolishness

infect 1 = <u>contaminate</u>, transmit disease to, spread disease to *or* among …*A single mosquito can infect a large number of people…*
2 = <u>pollute</u>, dirty, poison, foul, corrupt, contaminate, taint, defile, vitiate …*The birds infect the milk…*
3 = <u>affect</u>, move, touch, influence, upset, overcome, stir, disturb …*I was infected by her fear…*

infection = <u>disease</u>, condition, complaint, illness, virus, disorder, corruption, poison, pollution, contamination, contagion, defilement, septicity

infectious = <u>catching</u>, spreading, contagious, communicable, poisoning, corrupting, contaminating, polluting, virulent, defiling, infective, vitiating, pestilential, transmittable

infer = <u>deduce</u>, understand, gather, conclude, derive, presume, conjecture, surmise, read between the lines, put two and two together

---

Word Power

infer – The use of *infer* to mean *imply* is becoming more and more common in both speech and writing. There is nevertheless a useful distinction between the two which many people would be in favour of maintaining. To *infer* means 'to deduce', and is used in the construction 'to infer something from something': *I inferred from what she said that she had not been well.* To *imply* means 'to suggest, to insinuate' and is normally followed by a clause: *are you implying that I was responsible for the mistake?*

---

inference = <u>deduction</u>, conclusion, assumption, reading, consequence, presumption, conjecture, surmise, corollary

inferior **ADJECTIVE** 1 = <u>lower</u>, junior, minor, secondary, subsidiary, lesser, humble, subordinate, lowly, less important, menial …*the inferior status of women in many societies…* **OPPOSITE** superior
2 = <u>substandard</u>, bad, poor, mean, worse, poorer, pants (*informal*), flawed, rotten, dire, indifferent, duff (*Brit. informal*), mediocre, second-class, deficient, imperfect, second-rate, shoddy, low-grade, unsound, downmarket, low-rent (*informal, chiefly U.S.*), for the birds (*informal*), wretched, two-bit (*U.S. & Canad. slang*), crappy (*slang*), no great shakes (*informal*),

poxy (*slang*), dime-a-dozen (*informal*), bush-league (*Austral. & N.Z. informal*), not much cop (*Brit. slang*), tinhorn (*U.S. slang*), half-pie (*N.Z. informal*), of a sort *or* of sorts, strictly for the birds (*informal*), bodger *or* bodgie (*Austral. slang*) …*The cassettes were of inferior quality…* **OPPOSITE** excellent
NOUN = <u>underling</u>, junior, subordinate, lesser, menial, minion …*It was a gentleman's duty to be civil, even to his inferiors…*

inferiority = <u>subservience</u>, subordination, lowliness, servitude, abasement, inferior status *or* standing **OPPOSITE** superiority

infernal 1 = <u>damned</u>, malevolent, hellish, devilish, accursed, damnable …*The post office is shut, which is an infernal bore…*
2 = <u>hellish</u>, lower, underworld, nether, Stygian, Hadean, Plutonian, chthonian, Tartarean (*literary*) …*the goddess of the infernal regions…* **OPPOSITE** heavenly

infertile 1 = <u>sterile</u>, barren, infecund …*According to one survey, one woman in eight is infertile…*
2 = <u>barren</u>, unproductive, nonproductive, unfruitful, infecund …*The waste is dumped, making the surrounding land infertile…* **OPPOSITE** fertile

infertility = <u>sterility</u>, barrenness, unproductiveness, unfruitfulness, infecundity

infest = <u>overrun</u>, flood, invade, penetrate, ravage, swarm, throng, beset, permeate

infested = <u>overrun</u>, plagued, crawling, swarming, ridden, alive, ravaged, lousy (*slang*), beset, pervaded, teeming

infidel = <u>unbeliever</u>, sceptic, atheist, heretic, agnostic, heathen, nonconformist, freethinker, nonbeliever

infidelity = <u>unfaithfulness</u>, cheating (*informal*), adultery, betrayal, duplicity, disloyalty, bad faith, perfidy, falseness, faithlessness, false-heartedness

infiltrate = <u>penetrate</u>, pervade, permeate, creep in, percolate, filter through to, make inroads into, sneak in to (*informal*), insinuate yourself, work *or* worm your way into

infinite 1 = <u>vast</u>, enormous, immense, wide, countless, innumerable, untold, stupendous, incalculable, immeasurable, inestimable, numberless, uncounted, measureless, uncalculable …*an infinite variety of landscapes…*
2 = <u>enormous</u>, total, supreme, absolute, all-embracing, unbounded …*With infinite care, he shifted positions…*
3 = <u>limitless</u>, endless, unlimited, eternal, perpetual, never-ending, interminable, boundless, everlasting, bottomless, unending, inexhaustible, immeasurable, without end, unbounded, numberless, measureless, illimitable, without number …*There is an infinite number of atoms…* **OPPOSITE** finite

infinity = <u>eternity</u>, vastness, immensity, perpetuity, endlessness, infinitude, boundlessness

infirm 1 = <u>frail</u>, weak, feeble, failing, ailing, debilitated, decrepit, enfeebled, doddery, doddering …*her ageing, infirm husband…* **OPPOSITE** robust
2 = <u>irresolute</u>, weak, faltering, unstable, shaky,

insecure, wavering, wobbly, indecisive, unsound, vacillating ...*She has little patience with the 'infirm of purpose'*...

inflame 1 = <u>enrage</u>, stimulate, provoke, fire, heat, excite, anger, arouse, rouse, infuriate, ignite, incense, madden, agitate, kindle, rile, foment, intoxicate, make your blood boil, impassion ...*They hold the rebels responsible for inflaming the villagers...* OPPOSITE calm
2 = <u>aggravate</u>, increase, intensify, worsen, exacerbate, fan ...*The shooting has only inflamed passions further*...

inflamed = <u>swollen</u>, sore, red, hot, angry, infected, fevered, festering, chafing, septic

inflammable = <u>flammable</u>, explosive, volatile, incendiary, combustible
➤ **flammable**

inflammation = <u>swelling</u>, soreness, burning, heat, sore, rash, tenderness, redness, painfulness

inflammatory = <u>provocative</u>, incendiary, explosive, fiery, inflaming, insurgent, anarchic, rabid, riotous, intemperate, seditious, rabble-rousing, demagogic, like a red rag to a bull, instigative

inflate 1 = <u>blow up</u>, pump up, swell, balloon, dilate, distend, aerate, bloat, puff up *or* out ...*He jumped into the sea and inflated the liferaft...* OPPOSITE deflate
2 = <u>increase</u>, boost, expand, enlarge, escalate, amplify ...*Promotion can inflate a film's final cost...* OPPOSITE diminish
3 = <u>exaggerate</u>, embroider, embellish, emphasize, enlarge, magnify, overdo, amplify, exalt, overstate, overestimate, overemphasize, blow out of all proportion, aggrandize, hyperbolize ...*Even his war record was fraudulently inflated*...

inflated = <u>exaggerated</u>, excessive, swollen, amplified, hyped, exalted, overblown

inflation = <u>increase</u>, expansion, extension, swelling, escalation, enlargement, intensification

inflection 1 = <u>intonation</u>, stress, emphasis, beat, measure, rhythm, cadence, modulation, accentuation ...*His voice was devoid of inflection*...
2 (*Grammar*) = <u>conjugation</u>, declension ...*At around 2 years, the child adds many grammatical inflections*...

inflexibility = <u>obstinacy</u>, persistence, intransigence, obduracy, fixity, steeliness

inflexible 1 = <u>fixed</u>, set, established, rooted, rigid, immovable, unadaptable ...*He was a man of unchanging habits and an inflexible routine*...
2 = <u>obstinate</u>, strict, relentless, firm, fixed, iron, adamant, rigorous, stubborn, stringent, uncompromising, resolute, steely, intractable, inexorable, implacable, steadfast, hard and fast, unyielding, immutable, immovable, unbending, obdurate, stiff-necked, dyed-in-the-wool, unchangeable, brassbound, set in your ways ...*They viewed him as stubborn, inflexible and dogmatic*... OPPOSITE flexible
3 = <u>stiff</u>, hard, rigid, hardened, taut, inelastic, nonflexible ...*The boot is too inflexible to be comfortable...* OPPOSITE pliable

inflict = <u>impose</u>, exact, administer, visit, apply, deliver, levy, wreak, mete *or* deal out

influence NOUN **1** = <u>control</u>, power, authority, direction, command, domination, supremacy, mastery, ascendancy, mana (*N.Z.*) ...*As he grew older, she had less influence and couldn't control him*...
2 = <u>power</u>, force, authority, pull (*informal*), weight, strength, connections, importance, prestige, clout (*informal*), leverage, good offices ...*They should continue to use their influence for the release of all hostages*...
3 = <u>spell</u>, hold, power, rule, weight, magic, sway, allure, magnetism, enchantment ...*I fell under the influence of a history master*...
VERB **1** = <u>affect</u>, have an effect on, have an impact on, control, concern, direct, guide, impact on, modify, bear upon, impinge upon, act *or* work upon ...*What you eat may influence your risk of getting cancer*...
2 = <u>persuade</u>, move, prompt, urge, counsel, induce, incline, dispose, arouse, sway, rouse, entice, coax, incite, instigate, predispose, impel, prevail upon ...*The conference influenced us to launch the campaign*...
3 = <u>carry weight with</u>, cut any ice with (*informal*), pull strings with (*informal*), bring pressure to bear upon, make yourself felt with ...*Her attempt to influence the Press rebounded*...

influential 1 = <u>important</u>, powerful, moving, telling, leading, strong, guiding, inspiring, prestigious, meaningful, potent, persuasive, authoritative, momentous, weighty ...*one of the most influential books ever written...* OPPOSITE unimportant
2 = <u>instrumental</u>, important, significant, controlling, guiding, effective, crucial, persuasive, forcible, efficacious ...*He had been influential in shaping economic policy*...

influx = <u>arrival</u>, flow, rush, invasion, convergence, inflow, incursion, inundation, inrush

infold
➤ **enfold**

inform VERB **1** = <u>tell</u>, advise, let someone know, notify, brief, instruct, enlighten, acquaint, leak to, communicate to, fill someone in, keep someone posted, apprise, clue someone in (*informal*), put someone in the picture (*informal*), tip someone off, send word to, give someone to understand, make someone conversant (with) ...*They would inform him of any progress they had made*...
2 = <u>infuse</u>, characterize, permeate, animate, saturate, typify, imbue, suffuse ...*All great songs are informed by a certain sadness and tension*...
PHRASES **inform on someone** = <u>betray</u>, report, denounce, shop (*slang, chiefly Brit.*), peach (*slang*), give someone away, incriminate, tell on (*informal*), blow the whistle on (*informal*), grass on (*Brit. slang*), double-cross (*informal*), rat on (*informal*), spill the beans on (*informal*), stab someone in the back, nark (*Brit., Austral., & N.Z. slang*), blab about, squeal on (*slang*), snitch on (*slang*), put the finger on (*informal*), sell someone down the river (*informal*), blow the gaff on (*Brit. slang*), tell all on, inculpate, dob someone in (*Austral. & N.Z. slang*) ...*Somebody must have informed on us*...

informal 1 = <u>natural</u>, relaxed, casual, familiar, unofficial, laid-back, easy-going, colloquial, unconstrained, unceremonious …*She is refreshingly informal…*
2 = <u>relaxed</u>, easy, comfortable, simple, natural, casual, cosy, laid-back (*informal*), mellow, leisurely, easy-going …*The house has an informal atmosphere…* OPPOSITE formal
3 = <u>casual</u>, comfortable, leisure, everyday, simple …*Most of the time she needs informal clothes…*
4 = <u>unofficial</u>, irregular, unconstrained, unceremonious …*an informal meeting of EU ministers…* OPPOSITE official

informality = <u>familiarity</u>, naturalness, casualness, ease, relaxation, simplicity, lack of ceremony

information = <u>facts</u>, details, material, news, latest (*informal*), report, word, message, notice, advice, knowledge, data, intelligence, instruction, counsel, the score (*informal*), gen (*Brit. informal*), dope (*informal*), info (*informal*), inside story, blurb, lowdown (*informal*), tidings, drum (*Austral. informal*)

informative = <u>instructive</u>, revealing, educational, forthcoming, illuminating, enlightening, chatty, communicative, edifying, gossipy, newsy

informed = <u>knowledgeable</u>, up to date, enlightened, learned, primed, posted, expert, briefed, familiar, versed, acquainted, in the picture, up, abreast, in the know (*informal*), erudite, well-read, conversant, au fait (*French*), in the loop, genned up (*Brit. informal*), au courant (*French*), keeping your finger on the pulse

informer = <u>betrayer</u>, grass (*Brit. slang*), sneak, squealer (*slang*), Judas, accuser, stool pigeon, nark (*Brit., Austral., & N.Z. slang*), fizgig (*Austral. slang*)

infrequent = <u>occasional</u>, rare, uncommon, unusual, sporadic, few and far between, once in a blue moon OPPOSITE frequent

infringe VERB = <u>break</u>, violate, contravene, disobey, transgress …*The film exploited his image and infringed his copyright…*
PHRASES **infringe on** *or* **upon something** = <u>intrude on</u>, compromise, undermine, limit, weaken, diminish, disrupt, curb, encroach on, trespass on …*It's starting to infringe on our personal liberties…*

infringement = <u>contravention</u>, breach, violation, trespass, transgression, infraction, noncompliance, nonobservance

infuriate = <u>enrage</u>, anger, provoke, irritate, incense, gall, madden, exasperate, rile, nark (*Brit., Austral., & N.Z. slang*), be like a red rag to a bull, make your blood boil, get your goat (*slang*), make your hackles rise, raise your hackles, get your back up, make you see red (*informal*), put your back up OPPOSITE soothe

infuriating = <u>annoying</u>, irritating, aggravating (*informal*), provoking, galling, maddening, exasperating, irksome, vexatious, pestilential

infuse 1 = <u>fill</u>, charge, inspire, pervade, inundate, imbue, suffuse …*A strange spirit infused the place…*
2 = <u>brew</u>, soak, steep, saturate, immerse, macerate …*teas made by infusing the roots of herbs…*

ingenious = <u>creative</u>, original, brilliant, clever,

masterly, bright, subtle, fertile, shrewd, inventive, skilful, crafty, resourceful, adroit, dexterous OPPOSITE unimaginative

ingenuity = <u>originality</u>, genius, inventiveness, skill, gift, faculty, flair, knack, sharpness, cleverness, resourcefulness, shrewdness, adroitness, ingeniousness OPPOSITE dullness

ingrained *or* **engrained** = <u>fixed</u>, rooted, deep-seated, fundamental, constitutional, inherent, hereditary, in the blood, intrinsic, deep-rooted, indelible, inveterate, inborn, inbred, inbuilt, ineradicable, brassbound

ingratiate
PHRASES **ingratiate yourself with someone** = <u>get on the right side of</u>, court, win over, flatter, pander to, crawl to, play up to, get in with, suck up to (*informal*), curry favour with, grovel to, keep someone sweet, lick someone's boots, fawn to, toady to, seek someone's favour, rub someone up the right way (*informal*), be a yes man to, insinuate yourself with

ingratiating = <u>sycophantic</u>, servile, obsequious, crawling, humble, flattering, fawning, unctuous, toadying, bootlicking (*informal*), timeserving

ingredient = <u>component</u>, part, element, feature, piece, unit, item, aspect, attribute, constituent

ingulf
➤ **engulf**

inhabit = <u>live in</u>, people, occupy, populate, reside in, tenant, lodge in, dwell in, colonize, take up residence in, abide in, make your home in

inhabitant = <u>occupant</u>, resident, citizen, local, native, tenant, inmate, dweller, occupier, denizen, indigene, indweller
➤ **WORD POWER SUPPLEMENT inhabitants**

inhabited = <u>populated</u>, peopled, occupied, held, developed, settled, tenanted, colonized

inhalation = <u>breathing</u>, breath, inspiration, inhaling

inhale = <u>breathe in</u>, gasp, draw in, suck in, respire OPPOSITE exhale

inherent = <u>intrinsic</u>, natural, basic, central, essential, native, fundamental, underlying, hereditary, instinctive, innate, ingrained, elemental, congenital, inborn, inbred, inbuilt, immanent, connate OPPOSITE extraneous

inherit = <u>be left</u>, come into, be willed, accede to, succeed to, be bequeathed, fall heir to

inheritance = <u>legacy</u>, estate, heritage, provision, endowment, bequest, birthright, patrimony

inheritor = <u>heir</u>, successor, recipient, beneficiary, legatee

inhibit 1 = <u>hinder</u>, stop, prevent, check, bar, arrest, frustrate, curb, restrain, constrain, obstruct, impede, bridle, stem the flow of, throw a spanner in the works of, hold back *or* in …*Sugary drinks inhibit digestion…* OPPOSITE further
2 = <u>prevent</u>, stop, bar, frustrate, forbid, prohibit, debar …*The poor will be inhibited from getting the medical care they need…* OPPOSITE allow

inhibited = <u>shy</u>, reserved, guarded, withdrawn,

frustrated, subdued, repressed, constrained, self-conscious, reticent, uptight (*informal*) OPPOSITE> uninhibited

inhibition 1 = shyness, reserve, restraint, hang-up (*informal*), modesty, nervousness, reticence, self-consciousness, timidity, diffidence, bashfulness, mental blockage, timidness ...*They behave with a total lack of inhibition*...
2 = obstacle, check, bar, block, barrier, restriction, hazard, restraint, hitch, drawback, snag, deterrent, obstruction, stumbling block, impediment, hindrance, encumbrance, interdict ...*They cited security fears as a major inhibition to internet shopping*...

inhospitable 1 = bleak, empty, bare, hostile, lonely, forbidding, barren, sterile, desolate, unfavourable, uninhabitable, godforsaken ...*the earth's most inhospitable regions*...
2 = unfriendly, unwelcoming, uncongenial, cool, unkind, xenophobic, ungenerous, unsociable, unreceptive ...*He believed the province to be inhabited by a mean, inhospitable people*... OPPOSITE> hospitable

inhuman = cruel, savage, brutal, vicious, ruthless, barbaric, heartless, merciless, diabolical, cold-blooded, remorseless, barbarous, fiendish, pitiless, unfeeling, bestial OPPOSITE> humane

inhumane = cruel, savage, brutal, severe, harsh, grim, unkind, heartless, atrocious, unsympathetic, hellish, depraved, barbarous, pitiless, unfeeling, uncompassionate

inhumanity = cruelty, atrocity, brutality, ruthlessness, barbarism, viciousness, heartlessness, unkindness, brutishness, cold-bloodedness, pitilessness, cold-heartedness, hardheartedness

inimical = hostile, opposed, contrary, destructive, harmful, adverse, hurtful, unfriendly, unfavourable, antagonistic, injurious, unwelcoming, ill-disposed OPPOSITE> helpful

inimitable = unique, unparalleled, unrivalled, incomparable, supreme, consummate, unmatched, peerless, unequalled, matchless, unsurpassable, nonpareil, unexampled

iniquity = wickedness, wrong, crime, evil, sin, offence, injustice, wrongdoing, misdeed, infamy, abomination, sinfulness, baseness, unrighteousness, heinousness, evildoing OPPOSITE> goodness

initial = opening, first, early, earliest, beginning, primary, maiden, inaugural, commencing, introductory, embryonic, incipient, inchoate, inceptive OPPOSITE> final

initially = at first, first, firstly, originally, primarily, at the start, in the first place, to begin with, at the outset, in the beginning, in the early stages, at *or* in the beginning

initiate VERB 1 = begin, start, open, launch, establish, institute, pioneer, kick off (*informal*), bring about, embark on, originate, set about, get under way, instigate, kick-start, inaugurate, set in motion, trigger off, lay the foundations of, commence on, set going, break the ice on, set the ball rolling on ...*They wanted to initiate a discussion on economics*...

2 = introduce, admit, enlist, enrol, launch, establish, invest, recruit, induct, instate ...*She was initiated as a member of the secret society*...
NOUN = novice, member, pupil, convert, amateur, newcomer, beginner, trainee, apprentice, entrant, learner, neophyte, tyro, probationer, novitiate, proselyte ...*He was an initiate of a Chinese spiritual discipline*...
PHRASES **initiate someone into something** = instruct in, train in, coach in, acquaint with, drill in, make aware of, teach about, tutor in, indoctrinate, prime in, familiarize with ...*I was initiated into the darker side of the work*...

initiation 1 = introduction, installation, inauguration, inception, commencement ...*They announced the initiation of a rural development programme*...
2 = entrance, debut, introduction, admission, inauguration, induction, inception, enrolment, investiture, baptism of fire, instatement ...*This was my initiation into the peace movement*...

initiative 1 = advantage, start, lead, upper hand ...*We have the initiative and we intend to keep it*...
2 = enterprise, drive, push (*informal*), energy, spirit, resource, leadership, ambition, daring, enthusiasm, pep, vigour, zeal, originality, eagerness, dynamism, boldness, inventiveness, get-up-and-go (*informal*), resourcefulness, gumption (*informal*), adventurousness ...*He was disappointed by her lack of initiative*...

inject 1 = vaccinate, shoot (*informal*), administer, jab (*informal*), shoot up (*informal*), mainline (*informal*), inoculate ...*His son was injected with strong drugs*...
2 = introduce, bring in, insert, instil, infuse, breathe, interject ...*She kept trying to inject a little fun into their relationship*...

injection 1 = vaccination, shot (*informal*), jab (*informal*), dose, vaccine, booster, immunization, inoculation ...*They gave me an injection to help me sleep*...
2 = introduction, investment, insertion, advancement, dose, infusion, interjection ...*An injection of cash is needed to fund some of these projects*...

injunction = order, ruling, command, instruction, dictate, mandate, precept, exhortation, admonition

injure 1 = hurt, wound, harm, break, damage, smash, crush, mar, disable, shatter, bruise, impair, mutilate, maim, mangle, mangulate (*Austral. slang*), incapacitate ...*A bomb exploded, seriously injuring five people*...
2 = damage, harm, ruin, wreck, weaken, spoil, impair, crool *or* cruel (*Austral. slang*) ...*Too much stress can injure your health*...
3 = undermine, damage, mar, blight, tarnish, blacken, besmirch, vitiate ...*an attempt to injure another trader's business*...

injured 1 = hurt, damaged, wounded, broken, cut, crushed, disabled, weakened, bruised, scarred, crook (*Austral. & N.Z. slang*), fractured, lamed, mutilated, maimed, mangled ...*The injured man had a superficial stomach wound*...

2 = <u>wronged</u>, abused, harmed, insulted, offended, tainted, tarnished, blackened, maligned, vilified, mistreated, dishonoured, defamed, ill-treated, maltreated, ill-used ...*As yet, there has been no complaint from the injured party...*

3 = <u>upset</u>, hurt, wounded, troubled, bothered, undermined, distressed, unhappy, stung, put out, grieved, hassled (*informal*), disgruntled, displeased, reproachful, cut to the quick ...*compensation for injured feelings...*

injurious = <u>harmful</u>, bad, damaging, corrupting, destructive, adverse, unhealthy, detrimental, hurtful, pernicious, noxious, ruinous, deleterious, iniquitous, disadvantageous, baneful (*archaic*), maleficent, unconducive

injury 1 = <u>wound</u>, cut, damage, slash, trauma (*Pathology*), sore, gash, lesion, abrasion, laceration ...*Four police officers sustained serious injuries in the explosion...*

2 = <u>harm</u>, suffering, damage, ill, hurt, disability, misfortune, affliction, impairment, disfigurement ...*The two other passengers escaped serious injury...*

3 = <u>wrong</u>, abuse, offence, insult, injustice, grievance, affront, detriment, disservice ...*She was awarded £3,500 for injury to her feelings...*

injustice 1 = <u>unfairness</u>, discrimination, prejudice, bias, inequality, oppression, intolerance, bigotry, favouritism, inequity, chauvinism, iniquity, partisanship, partiality, narrow-mindedness, one-sidedness, unlawfulness, unjustness ...*They will continue to fight injustice...* OPPOSITE justice

2 = <u>wrong</u>, injury, crime, abuse, error, offence, sin, grievance, infringement, trespass, misdeed, transgression, infraction, bad *or* evil deed ...*I don't want to do an injustice to what I've recorded...*

inkling = <u>suspicion</u>, idea, hint, suggestion, notion, indication, whisper, clue, conception, glimmering, intimation, faintest *or* foggiest idea

inland = <u>interior</u>, internal, upcountry

inlet = <u>bay</u>, creek, cove, passage, entrance, fjord, bight, ingress, sea loch (*Scot.*), arm of the sea, firth *or* frith (*Scot.*)

innards 1 = <u>intestines</u>, insides (*informal*), guts, entrails, viscera, vitals ...*What happens to the innards of a carcass hung up for butchery?...*

2 = <u>works</u>, mechanism, guts (*informal*) ...*The innards of the PC are built into the desk...*

innate = <u>inborn</u>, natural, inherent, essential, native, constitutional, inherited, indigenous, instinctive, intuitive, intrinsic, ingrained, congenital, inbred, immanent, in your blood, connate OPPOSITE acquired

inner 1 = <u>inside</u>, internal, interior, inward ...*She got up and went into an inner office...* OPPOSITE outer

2 = <u>central</u>, middle, internal, interior ...*I've always taught in inner London...*

3 = <u>intimate</u>, close, personal, near, private, friendly, confidential, cherished, bosom ...*He was part of the Francoist inner circle...*

4 = <u>hidden</u>, deep, secret, underlying, obscure, repressed, esoteric, unrevealed ...*He loves studying chess and discovering its inner secrets...* OPPOSITE obvious

innkeeper = <u>publican</u>, hotelier, mine host, host *or* hostess, landlord *or* landlady

innocence 1 = <u>naiveté</u>, simplicity, inexperience, freshness, credulity, gullibility, ingenuousness, artlessness, unworldliness, guilelessness, credulousness, simpleness, trustfulness, unsophistication, naiveness ...*the sweet innocence of youth...* OPPOSITE worldliness

2 = <u>blamelessness</u>, righteousness, clean hands, uprightness, sinlessness, irreproachability, guiltlessness ...*He claims to have evidence which could prove his innocence...* OPPOSITE guilt

3 = <u>chastity</u>, virtue, purity, modesty, virginity, celibacy, continence, maidenhood, stainlessness ...*She can still evoke the innocence of 14-year-old Juliet...*

4 = <u>ignorance</u>, oblivion, lack of knowledge, inexperience, unfamiliarity, greenness, unawareness, nescience (*literary*) ...*'Maybe innocence is bliss,' he suggested...*

innocent ADJECTIVE **1** = <u>not guilty</u>, in the clear, blameless, clear, clean, honest, faultless, squeaky-clean, uninvolved, irreproachable, guiltless, unoffending ...*The police knew from day one that I was innocent...* OPPOSITE guilty

2 = <u>naive</u>, open, trusting, simple, natural, frank, confiding, candid, unaffected, childlike, gullible, unpretentious, unsophisticated, unworldly, credulous, artless, ingenuous, guileless, wet behind the ears (*informal*), unsuspicious ...*They seemed so young and innocent...* OPPOSITE worldly

3 = <u>harmless</u>, innocuous, inoffensive, well-meant, unobjectionable, unmalicious, well-intentioned ...*It was probably an innocent question, but he got very flustered...* OPPOSITE malicious

4 = <u>pure</u>, stainless, immaculate, moral, virgin, decent, upright, impeccable, righteous, pristine, wholesome, spotless, demure, chaste, unblemished, virginal, unsullied, sinless, incorrupt ...*that innocent virgin, Clarissa...* OPPOSITE impure

NOUN = <u>child</u>, novice, greenhorn (*informal*), babe in arms (*informal*), ingénue *or* (*masc.*) ingénu ...*He was a hopeless innocent where women were concerned...*

PHRASES **innocent of** = <u>free from</u>, clear of, unaware of, ignorant of, untouched by, unfamiliar with, empty of, lacking, unacquainted with, nescient of ...*She was completely natural and innocent of any airs and graces...*

innocuous = <u>harmless</u>, safe, innocent, inoffensive, innoxious

innovation 1 = <u>change</u>, revolution, departure, introduction, variation, transformation, upheaval, alteration ...*technological innovations of the industrial age...*

2 = <u>newness</u>, novelty, originality, freshness, modernism, modernization, uniqueness ...*We must promote originality and encourage innovation...*

innovative = <u>novel</u>, new, original, different, fresh, unusual, unfamiliar, uncommon, inventive, singular, ground-breaking, left-field (*informal*), transformational, variational

innovator = <u>modernizer</u>, introducer, inventor, changer, transformer

innuendo = <u>insinuation</u>, suggestion, hint, implication, whisper, overtone, intimation, imputation, aspersion

innumerable = <u>countless</u>, many, numerous, infinite, myriad, untold, incalculable, numberless, unnumbered, multitudinous, beyond number OPPOSITE> limited

inordinate = <u>excessive</u>, unreasonable, disproportionate, extravagant, undue, preposterous, unwarranted, exorbitant, unrestrained, intemperate, unconscionable, immoderate OPPOSITE> moderate

inorganic = <u>artificial</u>, chemical, man-made, mineral

inquest = <u>inquiry</u>, investigation, probe, inquisition

inquire or **enquire** VERB = <u>ask</u>, question, query, quiz, seek information of, request information of ...*He inquired whether there had been any messages left for him...*
PHRASES **inquire into something** = <u>investigate</u>, study, examine, consider, research, search, explore, look into, inspect, probe into, scrutinize, make inquiries into ...*Inspectors inquired into the affairs of the company...*

inquiring or **enquiring** = <u>inquisitive</u>, interested, curious, questioning, wondering, searching, probing, doubtful, analytical, investigative, nosy (*informal*)

inquiry or **enquiry 1** = <u>question</u>, query, investigation ...*He made some inquiries and discovered she had gone abroad...*
2 = <u>investigation</u>, hearing, study, review, search, survey, analysis, examination, probe, inspection, exploration, scrutiny, inquest ...*a murder inquiry...*
3 = <u>research</u>, investigation, analysis, examination, inspection, exploration, scrutiny, interrogation ...*The investigation has switched to a new line of inquiry...*

inquisition = <u>investigation</u>, questioning, examination, inquiry, grilling (*informal*), quizzing, inquest, cross-examination, third degree (*informal*)

inquisitive = <u>curious</u>, questioning, inquiring, peering, probing, intrusive, prying, snooping (*informal*), scrutinizing, snoopy (*informal*), nosy (*informal*), nosy-parkering (*informal*) OPPOSITE> uninterested

insane 1 = <u>mad</u>, crazy, nuts (*slang*), cracked (*slang*), mental (*slang*), barking (*slang*), crackers (*Brit. slang*), mentally ill, crazed, demented, cuckoo (*informal*), deranged, loopy (*informal*), barking mad (*slang*), out of your mind, gaga (*informal*), screwy (*informal*), doolally (*slang*), off your trolley (*slang*), round the twist (*informal*), of unsound mind, not right in the head, non compos mentis (*Latin*), off your rocker (*slang*), not the full shilling (*informal*), mentally disordered, off the air (*Austral. slang*) ...*Some people simply can't take it and they go insane...* OPPOSITE> sane
2 = <u>stupid</u>, foolish, daft (*informal*), bizarre, irresponsible, irrational, lunatic, senseless, preposterous, impractical, idiotic, inane, fatuous, dumb-ass (*slang*) ...*Listen, this is completely insane...*

OPPOSITE> reasonable
➤ **mad**

insanity 1 = <u>madness</u>, mental illness, dementia, aberration, mental disorder, delirium, craziness, mental derangement ...*a powerful study of a woman's descent into insanity...* OPPOSITE> sanity
2 = <u>stupidity</u>, folly, lunacy, irresponsibility, senselessness, preposterousness ...*the final financial insanity of the decade...* OPPOSITE> sense

---

Word Power

insanity – The word *insane* has a specific legal use, as in *insane and unfit to plead*. The word *insanity*, however, is not acceptable in general mental health contexts, and many of its synonyms, for example *mental derangement*, are also considered inappropriate or offensive. Acceptable terms are *psychiatric disorder* or *psychiatric illness*.

---

insatiable = <u>unquenchable</u>, greedy, voracious, ravenous, rapacious, intemperate, gluttonous, unappeasable, insatiate, quenchless, edacious OPPOSITE> satiable

inscribe 1 = <u>carve</u>, cut, etch, engrave, impress, imprint ...*They read the words inscribed on the walls of the monument...*
2 = <u>dedicate</u>, sign, address ...*The book is inscribed: To John Arlott from Laurie Lee...*

inscription = <u>engraving</u>, words, lettering, label, legend, saying

inscrutable 1 = <u>enigmatic</u>, blank, impenetrable, deadpan, unreadable, poker-faced (*informal*), sphinxlike ...*It is important to keep a straight face and remain inscrutable...* OPPOSITE> transparent
2 = <u>mysterious</u>, incomprehensible, inexplicable, hidden, unintelligible, unfathomable, unexplainable, undiscoverable ...*Even when opened the contents of the package were as inscrutable as ever...* OPPOSITE> comprehensible

insect = <u>bug</u>, creepy-crawly (*Brit. informal*), gogga (*S. African informal*)
(**Related Words**)
adjective: entomic
collective noun: swarm
➤ **ants, bees and wasps** ➤ **beetles** ➤ **bugs**
➤ **butterflies and moths** ➤ **flies** ➤ **insects**

insecure 1 = <u>unconfident</u>, worried, anxious, afraid, shy, uncertain, unsure, timid, self-conscious, hesitant, meek, self-effacing, diffident, unassertive ...*Many women are insecure about their performance as mothers...* OPPOSITE> confident
2 = <u>unsafe</u>, dangerous, exposed, vulnerable, hazardous, wide-open, perilous, unprotected, defenceless, unguarded, open to attack, unshielded, ill-protected ...*Mobile phones are inherently insecure, as anyone can listen in...* OPPOSITE> safe
3 = <u>unreliable</u>, unstable, unsafe, precarious, unsteady, unsound ...*low-paid, insecure jobs...* OPPOSITE> secure
= <u>unreliable</u>

<table>
<tr><td colspan="3">Insects http://www.insects.org/</td></tr>
<tr><td>apple maggot</td><td>flea</td><td>seventeen-year locust or</td></tr>
<tr><td>body louse, cootie (U.S. & N.Z.),</td><td>German cockroach or (U.S.)</td><td> periodical cicada</td></tr>
<tr><td> or (N.Z. slang) kutu</td><td> Croton bug</td><td>sheep ked or sheep tick</td></tr>
<tr><td>bollworm</td><td>grasshopper</td><td>silkworm</td></tr>
<tr><td>booklouse</td><td>katydid</td><td>silverfish</td></tr>
<tr><td>bookworm</td><td>lac insect</td><td>stick insect or (U.S. & Canad.)</td></tr>
<tr><td>bristletail</td><td>locust</td><td> walking stick</td></tr>
<tr><td>cabbageworm</td><td>louse</td><td>sucking louse</td></tr>
<tr><td>caddis worm or caseworm</td><td>mantis or praying mantis</td><td>tent caterpillar</td></tr>
<tr><td>cankerworm</td><td>measuring worm, looper, or</td><td>thrips</td></tr>
<tr><td>cochineal or cochineal insect</td><td> inchworm</td><td>treehopper</td></tr>
<tr><td>cockroach</td><td>midge</td><td>wax insect</td></tr>
<tr><td>cotton stainer</td><td>mole cricket</td><td>web spinner</td></tr>
<tr><td>crab (louse)</td><td>mosquito</td><td>weta</td></tr>
<tr><td>cricket</td><td>nit</td><td>wheel bug</td></tr>
<tr><td>earwig, or (Scot. dialect) clipshears,</td><td>phylloxera</td><td>wireworm</td></tr>
<tr><td> or clipshear</td><td>scale insect</td><td>woodworm</td></tr>
</table>

insecurity 1 = <u>anxiety</u>, fear, worry, uncertainty, unsureness …*She is always assailed by emotional insecurity…* OPPOSITE> confidence
2 = <u>vulnerability</u>, risk, danger, weakness, uncertainty, hazard, peril, defencelessness …*The increase in crime has created feelings of insecurity…* OPPOSITE> safety
3 = <u>instability</u>, uncertainty, unreliability, precariousness, weakness, shakiness, unsteadiness, dubiety, frailness …*the harshness and insecurity of agricultural life…* OPPOSITE> stability

insensitive ADJECTIVE = <u>unfeeling</u>, indifferent, unconcerned, uncaring, tough, hardened, callous, crass, unresponsive, thick-skinned, obtuse, tactless, imperceptive, unsusceptible …*My husband is very insensitive about my problem…* OPPOSITE> sensitive
PHRASES **insensitive to** = <u>unaffected by</u>, immune to, impervious to, dead to, unmoved by, proof against …*He had become insensitive to cold…*

inseparable 1 = <u>devoted</u>, close, intimate, bosom …*The two girls were inseparable…*
2 = <u>indivisible</u>, inalienable, conjoined, indissoluble, inseverable …*He believes liberty is inseparable from social justice…*

insert = <u>put</u>, place, set, position, work in, slip, slide, slot, thrust, stick in, wedge, tuck in

insertion 1 = <u>inclusion</u>, introduction, interpolation …*the first experiment involving the insertion of a new gene…*
2 = <u>insert</u>, addition, inclusion, supplement, implant, inset …*The correction to the text may involve an insertion or a deletion…*

inside NOUN = <u>interior</u>, contents, core, nucleus, inner part, inner side …*Cut off the top and scoop out the inside with a teaspoon…*
PLURAL NOUN (*Informal*) = <u>stomach</u>, gut, guts, belly, bowels, internal organs, innards (*informal*), entrails, viscera, vitals …*My insides ached from eating too much…*
ADJECTIVE 1 = <u>inner</u>, internal, interior, inward, innermost …*four-berth inside cabins with en suite bathrooms…* OPPOSITE> outside
2 = <u>confidential</u>, private, secret, internal, exclusive, restricted, privileged, classified …*The editor denies he had any inside knowledge…*
ADVERB = <u>indoors</u>, in, within, under cover …*They chatted briefly on the doorstep before going inside…*

insidious = <u>stealthy</u>, subtle, cunning, designing, smooth, tricky, crooked, sneaking, slick, sly, treacherous, deceptive, wily, crafty, artful, disingenuous, Machiavellian, deceitful, surreptitious, duplicitous, guileful OPPOSITE> straightforward

insight 1 = <u>understanding</u>, intelligence, perception, sense, knowledge, vision, judgment, awareness, grasp, appreciation, intuition, penetration, comprehension, acumen, discernment, perspicacity …*He was a man of considerable insight and diplomatic skills…*
2 *with* into = <u>understanding of</u>, perception of, awareness of, experience of, description of, introduction to, observation of, judgment of, revelation about, comprehension of, intuitiveness of …*The talk gave us some insight into the work they were doing…*

insightful = <u>perceptive</u>, shrewd, discerning, understanding, wise, penetrating, knowledgeable, astute, observant, perspicacious, sagacious

insignia = <u>badge</u>, symbol, decoration, crest, earmark, emblem, ensign, distinguishing mark

insignificance = <u>unimportance</u>, irrelevance, triviality, pettiness, worthlessness, meaninglessness, inconsequence, immateriality, paltriness, negligibility OPPOSITE> importance

insignificant = <u>unimportant</u>, minor, irrelevant, petty, trivial, meaningless, trifling, meagre, negligible, flimsy, paltry, immaterial, inconsequential, nondescript, measly, scanty, inconsiderable, of no consequence, nonessential, small potatoes, nickel-and-dime (*U.S. slang*), of no account, nugatory, unsubstantial, not worth mentioning, of no moment OPPOSITE> important

insincere = <u>deceitful</u>, lying, false, pretended, hollow, untrue, dishonest, deceptive, devious, hypocritical, unfaithful, evasive, two-faced, disingenuous, faithless, double-dealing, duplicitous, dissembling, mendacious, perfidious, untruthful, dissimulating, Janus-faced OPPOSITE sincere

insinuate = imply, suggest, hint, indicate, intimate, allude

insipid 1 = tasteless, bland, flavourless, watered down, watery, wishy-washy (*informal*), unappetizing, savourless ...*It tasted bland and insipid, like warm cardboard...* OPPOSITE tasty
2 = bland, boring, dull, flat, dry, weak, stupid, limp, tame, pointless, tedious, stale, drab, banal, tiresome, lifeless, prosaic, trite, unimaginative, colourless, uninteresting, anaemic, wishy-washy (*informal*), ho-hum (*informal*), vapid, wearisome, characterless, spiritless, jejune, prosy ...*On the surface she seemed meek, rather bland and insipid... ...They gave an insipid opening performance in a nil-nil draw...* OPPOSITE exciting

insist 1 = persist, press (someone), be firm, stand firm, stand your ground, lay down the law, put your foot down (*informal*), not take no for an answer, brook no refusal, take *or* make a stand ...*I didn't want to join in, but he insisted...*
2 = demand, order, urge, require, command, dictate, entreat ...*I insisted that the fault be repaired...*
3 = assert, state, maintain, hold, claim, declare, repeat, vow, swear, contend, affirm, reiterate, profess, avow, aver, asseverate ...*He insisted that he was acting out of compassion...*

insistence 1 = demand, urging, command, pressing, dictate, entreaty, importunity, insistency ...*She had attended an interview at his insistence...*
2 = assertion, claim, statement, declaration, contention, persistence, affirmation, pronouncement, reiteration, avowal, attestation ...*her insistence that she wanted to dump her raunchy image...*

insistent 1 = emphatic, persistent, demanding, pressing, dogged, urgent, forceful, persevering, unrelenting, peremptory, importunate, exigent ...*He is most insistent on this point...*
2 = persistent, repeated, constant, repetitive, incessant, unremitting ...*the insistent rhythms of dance music...*

insolence = rudeness, cheek (*informal*), disrespect, front, abuse, sauce (*informal*), gall (*informal*), audacity, boldness, chutzpah (*U.S. & Canad. informal*), insubordination, impertinence, impudence, effrontery, backchat (*informal*), incivility, sassiness (*U.S. informal*), pertness, contemptuousness OPPOSITE politeness

insolent = rude, cheeky, impertinent, fresh (*informal*), bold, insulting, abusive, saucy, contemptuous, pert, impudent, uncivil, insubordinate, brazen-faced OPPOSITE polite

insoluble = inexplicable, mysterious, baffling, obscure, mystifying, impenetrable, unaccountable, unfathomable, indecipherable, unsolvable OPPOSITE explicable

insolvency = bankruptcy, failure, ruin, liquidation

insolvent = bankrupt, ruined, on the rocks (*informal*), broke (*informal*), failed, gone bust

(*informal*), in receivership, gone to the wall, in the hands of the receivers, in queer street (*informal*)

insomnia = sleeplessness, restlessness, wakefulness

insouciance = nonchalance, light-heartedness, jauntiness, airiness, breeziness, carefreeness

inspect 1 = examine, check, look at, view, eye, survey, observe, scan, check out (*informal*), look over, eyeball (*slang*), scrutinize, give (something *or* someone) the once-over (*informal*), take a dekko at (*Brit. slang*), go over *or* through ...*Cut the fruit in half and inspect the pips...*
2 = check, examine, investigate, study, look at, research, search, survey, assess, probe, audit, vet, oversee, supervise, check out (*informal*), look over, work over, superintend, give (something *or* someone) the once-over (*informal*), go over *or* through ...*Each hotel is inspected once a year...*

inspection 1 = examination, investigation, scrutiny, scan, look-over, once-over (*informal*) ...*Closer inspection reveals that they are banded with yellow...*
2 = check, search, investigation, review, survey, examination, scan, scrutiny, supervision, surveillance, look-over, once-over (*informal*), checkup, recce (*slang*), superintendence ...*A routine inspection of the vessel turned up 50 kg of the drug...*

inspector = examiner, investigator, supervisor, monitor, superintendent, auditor, censor, surveyor, scrutinizer, checker, overseer, scrutineer

inspiration 1 = imagination, creativity, ingenuity, talent, insight, genius, productivity, fertility, stimulation, originality, inventiveness, cleverness, fecundity, imaginativeness ...*A good way of getting inspiration is by looking at others' work...*
2 = motivation, example, influence, model, boost, spur, incentive, revelation, encouragement, stimulus, catalyst, stimulation, inducement, incitement, instigation, afflatus ...*She was very impressive and a great inspiration to all...* OPPOSITE deterrent
3 = influence, spur, stimulus, muse ...*India's myths and songs are the inspiration for her books...*

inspire 1 = motivate, move, cause, stimulate, encourage, influence, persuade, spur, be responsible for, animate, rouse, instil, infuse, hearten, enliven, imbue, spark off, energize, galvanize, gee up, inspirit, fire *or* touch the imagination of ...*What inspired you to change your name?...* OPPOSITE discourage
2 = give rise to, cause, produce, result in, prompt, stir, spawn, engender ...*His legend would even inspire a song by Simon and Garfunkel...*

inspired 1 = brilliant, wonderful, impressive, exciting, outstanding, thrilling, memorable, dazzling, enthralling, superlative, of genius ...*She produced an inspired performance...*
2 = stimulated, possessed, aroused, uplifted, exhilarated, stirred up, enthused, exalted, elated, galvanized ...*Garcia played like a man inspired...*

inspiring = uplifting, encouraging, exciting, moving, affecting, stirring, stimulating, rousing, exhilarating, heartening OPPOSITE uninspiring

instability 1 = uncertainty, insecurity, weakness,

imbalance, vulnerability, wavering, volatility, unpredictability, restlessness, fluidity, fluctuation, disequilibrium, transience, impermanence, precariousness, mutability, shakiness, unsteadiness, inconstancy ...*unpopular policies which resulted in political instability...* OPPOSITE⟩ stability
2 = imbalance, weakness, volatility, variability, frailty, unpredictability, oscillation, vacillation, capriciousness, unsteadiness, flightiness, fitfulness, changeableness ...*Caligula's inherent mental instability...*

install 1 = set up, put in, place, position, station, establish, lay, fix, locate, lodge ...*They had installed a new phone line in the apartment...*
2 = institute, establish, introduce, invest, ordain, inaugurate, induct, instate ...*A new Catholic bishop was installed yesterday...*
3 = settle, position, plant, establish, lodge, ensconce ...*Before her husband's death she had installed herself in a modern villa...*

installation 1 = setting up, fitting, instalment, placing, positioning, establishment ...*Lives could be saved if installation of alarms was stepped up...*
2 = appointment, ordination, inauguration, induction, investiture, instatement ...*He invited her to attend his installation as chief of his tribe...*
3 (*Military*) = base, centre, post, station, camp, settlement, establishment, headquarters ...*a secret military installation...*

instalment 1 = payment, repayment, part payment ...*The first instalment is payable on application...*
2 = part, section, chapter, episode, portion, division ...*The next instalment deals with the social impact of the war...*

instance NOUN **1** = example, case, occurrence, occasion, sample, illustration, precedent, case in point, exemplification ...*a serious instance of corruption...*
2 = insistence, demand, urging, pressure, stress, application, request, prompting, impulse, behest, incitement, instigation, solicitation, entreaty, importunity ...*The meeting was organised at the instance of two senior ministers...*
VERB = name, mention, identify, point out, advance, quote, finger (*informal, chiefly U.S.*), refer to, point to, cite, specify, invoke, allude to, adduce, namedrop ...*She could have instanced many women who fitted this description...*

instant NOUN **1** = moment, second, minute, shake (*informal*), flash, tick (*Brit. informal*), no time, twinkling, split second, jiffy (*informal*), trice, twinkling of an eye (*informal*), two shakes (*informal*), two shakes of a lamb's tail (*informal*), bat of an eye (*informal*) ...*The pain disappeared in an instant...*
2 = time, point, hour, moment, stage, occasion, phase, juncture ...*At the same instant, he flung open the car door...*
ADJECTIVE **1** = immediate, prompt, instantaneous, direct, quick, urgent, on-the-spot, split-second ...*He had taken an instant dislike to her...*
2 = ready-made, fast, convenience, ready-mixed,

ready-cooked, precooked ...*He was stirring instant coffee into two mugs of hot water...*

instantaneous = immediate, prompt, instant, direct, on-the-spot

instantaneously = immediately, instantly, at once, straight away, promptly, on the spot, forthwith, in the same breath, then and there, pronto (*informal*), in the twinkling of an eye (*informal*), on the instant, in a fraction of a second, posthaste, quick as lightning, in the bat of an eye (*informal*)

instantly = immediately, at once, straight away, now, directly, on the spot, right away, there and then, without delay, instantaneously, forthwith, this minute, pronto (*informal*), posthaste, instanter (*Law*), tout de suite (*French*)

instead ADVERB = rather, alternatively, preferably, in preference, in lieu, on second thoughts ...*Forget about dieting and eat normally instead...*
PHRASES **instead of** = in place of, rather than, in preference to, in lieu of, in contrast with, as an alternative *or* equivalent to ...*She had to spend four months away, instead of the usual two...*

instigate = provoke, start, encourage, move, influence, prompt, trigger, spur, stimulate, set off, initiate, bring about, rouse, prod, stir up, get going, incite, kick-start, whip up, impel, kindle, foment, actuate OPPOSITE⟩ suppress

instigation = prompting, urging, bidding, incentive, encouragement, behest, incitement

instigator = ringleader, inciter, motivator, leader, spur, goad, troublemaker, incendiary, firebrand, prime mover, fomenter, agitator, stirrer (*informal*), mischief-maker

instil *or* **instill** = introduce, implant, engender, infuse, imbue, impress, insinuate, sow the seeds, inculcate, engraft, infix

instinct 1 = natural inclination, feeling, urge, talent, tendency, faculty, inclination, intuition, knack, aptitude, predisposition, sixth sense, proclivity, gut reaction (*informal*), second sight ...*I didn't have a strong maternal instinct...*
2 = talent, skill, gift, capacity, bent, genius, faculty, knack, aptitude ...*She has a natural instinct to perform...*
3 = intuition, feeling, impulse, gut feeling (*informal*), sixth sense ...*I should have gone with my first instinct...*

instinctive = natural, inborn, automatic, unconscious, mechanical, native, inherent, spontaneous, reflex, innate, intuitive, subconscious, involuntary, visceral, unthinking, instinctual, unlearned, unpremeditated, intuitional OPPOSITE⟩ acquired

instinctively = intuitively, naturally, automatically, without thinking, involuntarily, by instinct, in your bones

institute NOUN = establishment, body, centre, school, university, society, association, college, institution, organization, foundation, academy, guild, conservatory, fellowship, seminary, seat of learning

...*a research institute devoted to software programming*...

VERB = establish, start, begin, found, launch, set up, introduce, settle, fix, invest, organize, install, pioneer, constitute, initiate, originate, enact, commence, inaugurate, set in motion, bring into being, put into operation ...*We will institute a number of methods to improve saftey*... **OPPOSITE** end

institution 1 = establishment, body, centre, school, university, society, association, college, institute, organization, foundation, academy, guild, conservatory, fellowship, seminary, seat of learning ...*Class size varies from one type of institution to another*...
2 = custom, practice, tradition, law, rule, procedure, convention, ritual, fixture, rite ...*I believe in the institution of marriage*...
3 = creation, introduction, establishment, investment, debut, foundation, formation, installation, initiation, inauguration, enactment, inception, commencement, investiture ...*the institution of the forty-hour week*...

institutional = conventional, accepted, established, formal, establishment (*informal*), organized, routine, orthodox, bureaucratic, procedural, societal

instruct 1 = order, tell, direct, charge, bid, command, mandate, enjoin ...*They have instructed solicitors to sue for compensation*...
2 = teach, school, train, direct, coach, guide, discipline, educate, drill, tutor, enlighten, give lessons in ...*He instructs family members in nursing techniques*...
3 = tell, advise, inform, counsel, notify, brief, acquaint, apprise ...*Instruct them that they've got three months to get it sorted out*...

instruction **NOUN** 1 = order, ruling, command, rule, demand, direction, regulation, dictate, decree, mandate, directive, injunction, behest ...*No reason for this instruction was given*...
2 = teaching, schooling, training, classes, grounding, education, coaching, lesson(s), discipline, preparation, drilling, guidance, tutoring, tuition, enlightenment, apprenticeship, tutorials, tutelage ...*Each candidate is given instruction in safety*...
PLURAL NOUN = information, rules, advice, directions, recommendations, guidance, specifications ...*This book gives instructions for making a variety of hand creams*...

instructive = informative, revealing, useful, educational, helpful, illuminating, enlightening, instructional, cautionary, didactic, edifying

instructor = teacher, coach, guide, adviser, trainer, demonstrator, tutor, guru, mentor, educator, pedagogue, preceptor (*rare*), master *or* mistress, schoolmaster *or* schoolmistress

instrument 1 = tool, device, implement, mechanism, appliance, apparatus, gadget, utensil, contraption (*informal*), contrivance, waldo ...*a thin tube-like optical instrument*...
2 = agent, means, force, cause, medium, agency, factor, channel, vehicle, mechanism, organ ...*The veto is a traditional instrument for diplomacy*...
3 (*Informal*) = puppet, tool, pawn, toy, creature, dupe,

stooge (*slang*), plaything, cat's-paw ...*The Council was an instrument of Government*...
> **instruments in a full orchestra** > **musical instruments**

instrumental = active, involved, influential, useful, helpful, conducive, contributory, of help *or* service

insubstantial 1 = flimsy, thin, weak, slight, frail, feeble, tenuous ...*Her limbs were insubstantial, almost transparent*... **OPPOSITE** substantial
2 = imaginary, unreal, fanciful, immaterial, ephemeral, illusory, incorporeal, chimerical ...*Their thoughts seemed as insubstantial as smoke*...

insufferable = unbearable, impossible, intolerable, dreadful, outrageous, unspeakable, detestable, insupportable, unendurable, past bearing, more than flesh and blood can stand, enough to test the patience of a saint, enough to try the patience of Job **OPPOSITE** bearable

insufficient = inadequate, incomplete, scant, meagre, short, sparse, deficient, lacking, unqualified, Insubstantial, incommensurate **OPPOSITE** ample

insular = narrow-minded, prejudiced, provincial, closed, limited, narrow, petty, parochial, blinkered, circumscribed, inward-looking, illiberal, parish-pump **OPPOSITE** broad-minded

insulate = isolate, protect, screen, defend, shelter, shield, cut off, cushion, cocoon, close off, sequester, wrap up in cotton wool

insult **VERB** = offend, abuse, injure, wound, slight, outrage, put down, humiliate, libel, snub, slag (off) (*slang*), malign, affront, denigrate, disparage, revile, slander, displease, defame, hurt (someone's) feelings, call names, give offence to ...*I didn't mean to insult you*... **OPPOSITE** praise
NOUN 1 = jibe, slight, put-down, abuse, snub, barb, affront, indignity, contumely, abusive remark, aspersion ...*Some of the officers shouted insults at prisoners on the roof*...
2 = offence, slight, outrage, snub, slur, affront, rudeness, slap in the face (*informal*), kick in the teeth (*informal*), insolence, aspersion ...*Their behaviour was an insult to the people they represented*...
> **insults and terms of abuse**

insulting = offensive, rude, abusive, slighting, degrading, affronting, contemptuous, disparaging, scurrilous, insolent **OPPOSITE** complimentary

insuperable = insurmountable, invincible, impassable, unconquerable **OPPOSITE** surmountable

insurance 1 = assurance, cover, security, protection, coverage, safeguard, indemnity, indemnification ...*You are advised to take out insurance on your lenses*...
2 = protection, security, guarantee, provision, shelter, safeguard, warranty ...*Put something away as insurance against failure of the business*...

insure 1 = assure, cover, protect, guarantee, warrant, underwrite, indemnify ...*We automatically insure your furniture and belongings against fire*...
2 = protect, cover, safeguard ...*He needs to insure himself against ambitious party rivals*...

Musical instruments

accordion	cottage piano	lyre	sitar
aeolian harp	cowbell	mandola	slide guitar
alphorn *or* alpenhorn	crumhorn *or*	mandolin *or* mandoline	snare drum
althorn	krummhorn	maraca	sousaphone
Autoharp	crwth	marimba	Spanish guitar
baby grand	cymbal	mbira	spinet
Bach trumpet	cymbalo	mellophone	square piano
bagpipes	didgeridoo	melodeon *or* melodion	steam organ
balalaika	Dobro	metallophone	steel guitar
bandore	double bass	Moog	stylophone
banjo	double bassoon	mouth organ	synthesizer
barrel organ	drum	musette	syrinx
baryton	drum machine	naker	tabla
bass drum	dulcimer	ngoma	tabor *or* tabour
basset horn	electric guitar	nickelodeon	tambour
bass guitar	electronic organ	nose flute	tamboura
bassoon	English horn	oboe	tambourine
bass viol	euphonium	oboe da caccia	tam-tam
bell	fiddle	oboe d'amore	theorbo
bodhrán	fife	ocarina	Theremin
Böhm flute	flageolet	octachord	timbal *or* tymbal
bombardon	flugelhorn	ondes Martenot	timpani *or* tympani
bongo	flute	ophicleide	tom-tom
boudoir grand	French horn	orchestrina *or*	triangle
bouzouki	gittarone	orchestrion	trigon
bugle	gittern	organ	trombone
calliope	glass harmonica	orpharion	trumpet
carillon	glockenspiel	oud	tuba
castanets	gong	panpipes	tubular bells
celesta *or* celeste	gran cassa	pedal steel guitar	uillean pipes
cello *or* violoncello	grand piano	penny whistle	ukulele *or* ukelele
cembalo	guitar	piano	upright piano
chamber organ	Hammond organ	Pianola	vibraphone
Chapman stick	handbell	piccolo	vihuela
chime	harmonica	pipe	vina
Chinese block	harmonium	player piano	viol
chitarrone	harp	portative organ	viola
cimbalon *or* cymbalon	harpsichord	racket	viola da braccio
cithara *or* kithara	Hawaiian guitar	rebec *or* rebeck	viola da gamba
cittern, cither *or* cithern	helicon	recorder	viola d'amore
clarinet	horn	reco-reco	violin
clarion	hornpipe	reed organ	violone
clarsach	hunting horn	reed pipe	virginal
clave	hurdy-gurdy	regal	vocoder
clavicembalo	idiophone	rote	washboard
clavichord	jew's-harp	sackbut	Welsh harp
clavier	kazoo	samisen	whip
concert grand	kettledrum	sarangi	whistle
concertina	keyboard	sarod	wood block
conga	kit	sarrusophone	Wurlitzer
contrabass	kora	saxhorn	xylophone
contrabassoon	koto	saxophone	xylorimba
cor anglais	lur *or* lure	shawm	zither
cornet	lute	side drum	
cornett	lyra viol	sistrum	

insurgent NOUN = <u>rebel</u>, revolutionary, revolter, rioter, resister, mutineer, revolutionist, insurrectionist ...*The insurgents took control of the main military air base*...
ADJECTIVE = <u>rebellious</u>, revolutionary, mutinous, revolting, riotous, seditious, disobedient, insubordinate, insurrectionary ...*The insurgent leaders were publicly executed*...

insurmountable = <u>insuperable</u>, impossible, overwhelming, hopeless, invincible, impassable, unconquerable

insurrection = <u>rebellion</u>, rising, revolution, riot, coup, revolt, uprising, mutiny, insurgency, putsch, sedition

intact = <u>undamaged</u>, whole, complete, sound,

Insults and terms of abuse

airhead	drip	nitwit (*informal*)
article	dumb-ass (*slang*)	numbskull *or* numskull
berk	dumbo (*slang*)	numpty (*Scot. informal*)
bird-brain (*informal*)	dummy (*slang*)	oaf
bitch	dunce	ogre
blockhead	dweeb (*U.S. slang*)	pea-brain (*slang*)
bonehead (*slang*)	eejit (*Scot. & Irish*)	pillock (*Brit. slang*)
bozo (*U.S. slang*)	fathead (*informal*)	plank (*Brit. slang*)
bushpig	fool	plonker (*slang*)
cabbage	galah (*Austral. & N.Z. informal*)	prat (*slang*)
charlie (*Brit. informal*)	geek (*slang*)	rascal
cheeky monkey	git (*Brit. slang*)	rogue
chicken	goose (*informal*)	scab
chuckie	halfwit	scoundrel
chump (*informal*)	heifer	scrubber
clod	idiot	scutter
clot (*Brit. informal*)	imbecile (*informal*)	simpleton
clown	jerk (*slang, chiefly U.S. & Canad.*)	slag
coot	lamebrain (*informal*)	slapper
cow	loon	tart
cretin	mincer	thickhead
devil	minger	thicko (*Brit. slang*)
dimwit (*informal*)	mong	twerp *or* twirp (*informal*)
dipstick (*Brit. slang*)	moron	twit (*informal, chiefly Brit.*)
divvy (*Brit. slang*)	mug (*Brit. slang*)	wally (*slang*)
donkey	muppet	whore *or* 'ho
doofus (*slang, chiefly U.S.*)	nerd *or* nurd (*slang*)	wimp
dope (*informal*)	nincompoop	wretch
dork (*slang*)	ninny	wuss
doughnut	nit (*informal*)	

perfect, entire, virgin, untouched, unscathed, unbroken, flawless, unhurt, faultless, unharmed, uninjured, unimpaired, undefiled, all in one piece, together, scatheless, unviolated OPPOSITE> damaged

intangible = <u>abstract</u>, vague, invisible, dim, elusive, shadowy, airy, unreal, indefinite, ethereal, evanescent, incorporeal, impalpable, unsubstantial

integral 1 = <u>essential</u>, basic, fundamental, necessary, component, constituent, indispensable, intrinsic, requisite, elemental ...*Rituals form an integral part of any human society...* OPPOSITE> inessential
2 = <u>whole</u>, full, complete, entire, intact, undivided ...*This is meant to be an integral service...* OPPOSITE> partial

integrate = <u>join</u>, unite, combine, blend, incorporate, merge, accommodate, knit, fuse, mesh, assimilate, amalgamate, coalesce, harmonize, meld, intermix OPPOSITE> separate

integrity 1 = <u>honesty</u>, principle, honour, virtue, goodness, morality, purity, righteousness, probity, rectitude, truthfulness, trustworthiness, incorruptibility, uprightness, scrupulousness, reputability ...*I have always regarded him as a man of integrity...* OPPOSITE> dishonesty
2 = <u>unity</u>, unification, cohesion, coherence, wholeness, soundness, completeness ...*Separatist movements are a threat to the integrity of the nation...* OPPOSITE> fragility

intellect 1 = <u>intelligence</u>, mind, reason, understanding, sense, brains (*informal*), judgment

...*Do the emotions develop in parallel with the intellect?...*
2 (*Informal*) = <u>thinker</u>, intellectual, genius, mind, brain (*informal*), intelligence, rocket scientist (*informal, chiefly U.S.*), egghead (*informal*) ...*My boss isn't a great intellect...*

intellectual ADJECTIVE = <u>scholarly</u>, learned, academic, lettered, intelligent, rational, cerebral, erudite, scholastic, highbrow, well-read, studious, bookish ...*They were very intellectual and witty...* OPPOSITE> stupid
NOUN = <u>academic</u>, expert, genius, thinker, master, brain (*informal*), mastermind, maestro, highbrow, rocket scientist (*informal, chiefly U.S.*), egghead (*informal*), brainbox, bluestocking (*usually disparaging*), master-hand, fundi (*S. African*), acca (*Austral. slang*)...*teachers, artists and other intellectuals...* OPPOSITE> idiot

intelligence 1 = <u>intellect</u>, understanding, brains (*informal*), mind, reason, sense, knowledge, capacity, smarts (*slang, chiefly U.S.*), judgment, wit, perception, awareness, insight, penetration, comprehension, brightness, aptitude, acumen, nous (*Brit. slang*), alertness, cleverness, quickness, discernment, grey matter (*informal*), brain power ...*She's a woman of exceptional intelligence...* OPPOSITE> stupidity
2 = <u>information</u>, news, facts, report, findings, word, notice, advice, knowledge, data, disclosure, gen (*Brit. informal*), tip-off, low-down (*informal*), notification ...*a senior officer involved in gathering intelligence...*

OPPOSITE misinformation

intelligent = clever, bright, smart, knowing, quick, sharp, acute, alert, rational, penetrating, enlightened, apt, discerning, knowledgeable, astute, well-informed, brainy (*informal*), perspicacious, quick-witted, sagacious OPPOSITE stupid

intelligentsia = intellectuals, highbrows, literati, masterminds, the learned, eggheads (*informal*), illuminati

intelligible = understandable, clear, distinct, lucid, comprehensible OPPOSITE unintelligible

intemperate = excessive, extreme, over the top (*slang*), wild, violent, severe, passionate, extravagant, uncontrollable, self-indulgent, unbridled, prodigal, unrestrained, tempestuous, profligate, inordinate, incontinent, ungovernable, immoderate, O.T.T. (*slang*) OPPOSITE temperate

intend 1 = plan, mean, aim, determine, scheme, propose, purpose, contemplate, envisage, foresee, be resolved *or* determined, have in mind *or* view ...*She intends to do A levels and go to university...*
2 *often with* **for** = destine, mean, design, earmark, consign, aim, mark out, set apart ...*This money is intended for the development of the tourist industry...*

intended ADJECTIVE = planned, proposed ...*He hoped the sarcasm would have its intended effect...*
NOUN (*Informal*) = betrothed, fiancé *or* fiancée, future wife *or* husband, husband- *or* wife-to-be ...*Attention is turned to the Queen's youngest son and his intended...*

intense 1 = extreme, great, severe, fierce, serious (*informal*), deep, powerful, concentrated, supreme, acute, harsh, intensive, excessive, profound, exquisite, drastic, forceful, protracted, unqualified, agonizing, mother of all (*informal*) ...*He was sweating from the intense heat...* OPPOSITE mild
2 = fierce, close, tough ...*The battle for third place was intense...*
3 = passionate, burning, earnest, emotional, keen, flaming, consuming, fierce, eager, enthusiastic, heightened, energetic, animated, ardent, fanatical, fervent, heartfelt, impassioned, vehement, forcible, fervid ...*She is more adult, and more intense than I had imagined...* OPPOSITE indifferent

---

Word Power

intense – *Intense* is sometimes wrongly used where *intensive* is meant: *the land is under intensive* (not *intense*) *cultivation. Intensely* is sometimes wrongly used where *intently* is meant: *he listened intently* (not *intensely*).

---

intensely 1 = very, highly, extremely, greatly, strongly, severely, terribly, ultra, utterly, unusually, exceptionally, extraordinarily, markedly, awfully (*informal*), acutely, exceedingly, excessively, inordinately, uncommonly, to the nth degree, to *or* in the extreme ...*The fast-food business is intensely competitive...*
2 = intently, deeply, seriously (*informal*), profoundly,

passionately ...*He sipped his drink, staring intensely at me...*

intensify 1 = increase, boost, raise, extend, concentrate, add to, strengthen, enhance, compound, reinforce, step up (*informal*), emphasize, widen, heighten, sharpen, magnify, amplify, augment, redouble ...*They are intensifying their efforts to secure the release of the hostages...* OPPOSITE decrease
2 = escalate, increase, extend, widen, heighten, deepen, quicken ...*The conflict is almost bound to intensify...*

intensity 1 = force, power, strength, severity, extremity, fierceness ...*The attack was anticipated, but its intensity came as a shock...*
2 = passion, emotion, fervour, force, power, fire, energy, strength, depth, concentration, excess, severity, vigour, potency, extremity, fanaticism, ardour, vehemence, earnestness, keenness, fierceness, fervency, intenseness ...*His intensity, and the ferocity of his feelings alarmed me...*

intensive = concentrated, thorough, exhaustive, full, demanding, detailed, complete, serious, concerted, intense, comprehensive, vigorous, all-out, in-depth, strenuous, painstaking, all-embracing, assiduous, thoroughgoing
► **intense**

intent ADJECTIVE = absorbed, focused, fixed, earnest, committed, concentrated, occupied, intense, fascinated, steady, alert, wrapped up, preoccupied, enthralled, attentive, watchful, engrossed, steadfast, rapt, enrapt ...*She looked from one intent face to another...* OPPOSITE indifferent
NOUN = intention, aim, purpose, meaning, end, plan, goal, design, target, object, resolution, resolve, objective, ambition, aspiration ...*a statement of intent on arms control...* OPPOSITE chance
PHRASES **intent on something** = set on, committed to, eager to, bent on, fixated on, hellbent on (*informal*), insistent about, determined about, resolute about, inflexible about, resolved about ...*The rebels are obviously intent on stepping up the pressure...* ♦ **to all intents and purposes** = in effect, essentially, effectively, really, actually, in fact, virtually, in reality, in truth, in actuality, for practical purposes ...*To all intents and purposes he was my father...*
► **intense**

intention = aim, plan, idea, goal, end, design, target, wish, scheme, purpose, object, objective, determination, intent

intentional = deliberate, meant, planned, studied, designed, purposed, intended, calculated, wilful, premeditated, prearranged, done on purpose, preconcerted OPPOSITE unintentional

intentionally = deliberately, on purpose, wilfully, by design, designedly

intently = attentively, closely, hard, keenly, steadily, fixedly, searchingly, watchfully

inter = bury, lay to rest, entomb, sepulchre, consign to the grave, inhume, inurn

intercede = <u>mediate</u>, speak, plead, intervene, arbitrate, advocate, interpose

intercept = <u>catch</u>, take, stop, check, block, arrest, seize, cut off, interrupt, head off, deflect, obstruct

interchange NOUN = <u>exchange</u>, give and take, alternation, reciprocation ...*the interchange of ideas from different disciplines...*
VERB = <u>exchange</u>, switch, swap, alternate, trade, barter, reciprocate, bandy ...*She likes to interchange furniture at home with stock from the shop...*

interchangeable = <u>identical</u>, the same, equivalent, synonymous, reciprocal, exchangeable, transposable, commutable

intercourse 1 = <u>sexual intercourse</u>, sex (*informal*), lovemaking, the other (*informal*), congress, screwing (*taboo slang*), intimacy, shagging (*Brit. taboo slang*), sexual relations, sexual act, nookie (*slang*), copulation, coitus, carnal knowledge, intimate relations, rumpy-pumpy (*slang*), legover (*slang*), coition ...*We didn't have intercourse...*
2 = <u>contact</u>, relationships, communication, association, relations, trade, traffic, connection, truck, commerce, dealings, correspondence, communion, converse, intercommunication ...*There was social intercourse between the old and the young...*

interest NOUN 1 = <u>importance</u>, concern, significance, moment, note, weight, import, consequence, substance, relevance, momentousness ...*Food was of no interest to her at all...* OPPOSITE insignificance
2 = <u>attention</u>, regard, curiosity, notice, suspicion, scrutiny, heed, absorption, attentiveness, inquisitiveness, engrossment ...*They will follow the political crisis with interest...* OPPOSITE disregard
3 *often plural* = <u>hobby</u>, activity, pursuit, entertainment, relaxation, recreation, amusement, preoccupation, diversion, pastime, leisure activity ...*He developed a wide range of sporting interests...*
4 *often plural* = <u>advantage</u>, good, benefit, profit, gain, boot (*dialect*) ...*Did the Directors act in the best interests of their club?...*
5 *often plural* = <u>business</u>, concern, matter, affair ...*The family controls large dairy interests...*
6 = <u>stake</u>, investment ...*The West has an interest in promoting democratic forces...*
VERB 1 = <u>arouse your curiosity</u>, engage, appeal to, fascinate, move, involve, touch, affect, attract, grip, entertain, absorb, intrigue, amuse, divert, rivet, captivate, catch your eye, hold the attention of, engross ...*This part of the book interests me in particular...* OPPOSITE bore
2 *with in* = <u>sell</u>, persuade to buy ...*In the meantime, can I interest you in a new car?...*
PHRASES **in the interest(s) of** = <u>for the sake of</u>, on behalf of, on the part of, to the advantage of ...*We must all work together in the interest of national stability...*

interested 1 = <u>curious</u>, into (*informal*), moved, affected, attracted, excited, drawn, keen, gripped, fascinated, stimulated, intent, responsive, riveted, captivated, attentive ...*He did not look interested...* OPPOSITE uninterested

2 = <u>involved</u>, concerned, affected, prejudiced, biased, partial, partisan, implicated, predisposed ...*All the interested parties finally agreed to the idea...*

interesting = <u>intriguing</u>, fascinating, absorbing, pleasing, appealing, attractive, engaging, unusual, gripping, stirring, entertaining, entrancing, stimulating, curious, compelling, amusing, compulsive, riveting, captivating, enthralling, beguiling, thought-provoking, engrossing, spellbinding OPPOSITE uninteresting

interface NOUN = <u>connection</u>, link, boundary, border, frontier ...*the interface between bureaucracy and the working world...*
VERB = <u>connect</u>, couple, link, combine, join together ...*the way we interface with the environment...*

interfere VERB = <u>meddle</u>, intervene, intrude, butt in, get involved, tamper, pry, encroach, intercede, stick your nose in (*informal*), stick your oar in (*informal*), poke your nose in (*informal*), intermeddle, put your two cents in (*U.S. slang*) ...*Stop interfering and leave me alone!...*
PHRASES **interfere with something** or **someone** = <u>conflict with</u>, affect, get in the way of, check, block, clash, frustrate, handicap, hamper, disrupt, cramp, inhibit, thwart, hinder, obstruct, impede, baulk, trammel, be a drag upon (*informal*) ...*Drug problems frequently interfered with his work...*

interference = <u>intrusion</u>, intervention, meddling, opposition, conflict, obstruction, prying, impedance, meddlesomeness, intermeddling

interfering = <u>meddling</u>, intrusive, prying, obtrusive, meddlesome, interruptive

interim ADJECTIVE = <u>temporary</u>, provisional, makeshift, acting, passing, intervening, caretaker, improvised, transient, stopgap, pro tem ...*an interim report...*
NOUN = <u>interval</u>, meanwhile, meantime, respite, interregnum, entr'acte ...*He was to remain in jail in the interim...*

interior NOUN 1 = <u>inside</u>, centre, heart, middle, contents, depths, core, belly, nucleus, bowels, bosom, innards (*informal*) ...*The boat's interior badly needed painting...*
2 (*Geography*) = <u>heartland</u>, centre, hinterland, upcountry ...*a 5-day hike into the interior...*
ADJECTIVE 1 = <u>inside</u>, internal, inner ...*He turned on the interior light and examined the map...* OPPOSITE exterior
2 = <u>mental</u>, emotional, psychological, private, personal, secret, hidden, spiritual, intimate, inner, inward, instinctive, impulsive ...*the interior life of human beings...*
3 (*Politics*) = <u>domestic</u>, home, national, civil, internal ...*The French Interior Minister has intervened over the scandal...*

interject = <u>interrupt with</u>, put in, interpose, introduce, throw in, interpolate

interjection = <u>exclamation</u>, cry, ejaculation, interpolation, interposition

interloper = <u>trespasser</u>, intruder, gate-crasher

(*informal*), uninvited guest, meddler, unwanted visitor, intermeddler

interlude = <u>interval</u>, break, spell, stop, rest, halt, episode, pause, respite, stoppage, breathing space, hiatus, intermission, entr'acte

intermediary = <u>mediator</u>, agent, middleman, broker, entrepreneur, go-between

intermediate = <u>middle</u>, mid, halfway, in-between (*informal*), midway, intervening, transitional, intermediary, median, interposed

interminable = <u>endless</u>, long, never-ending, dragging, unlimited, infinite, perpetual, protracted, limitless, boundless, everlasting, ceaseless, long-winded, long-drawn-out, immeasurable, wearisome, unbounded OPPOSITE> limited

intermission = <u>interval</u>, break, pause, stop, rest, suspension, recess, interruption, respite, lull, stoppage, interlude, cessation, let-up (*informal*), breathing space, entr'acte

intermittent = <u>periodic</u>, broken, occasional, recurring, irregular, punctuated, sporadic, recurrent, stop-go (*informal*), fitful, spasmodic, discontinuous OPPOSITE> continuous

intern = <u>imprison</u>, hold, confine, detain, hold in custody

internal 1 = <u>domestic</u>, home, national, local, civic, in-house, intramural ...*The country stepped up internal security*...
2 = <u>inner</u>, inside, interior ...*Some of the internal walls are made of plasterboard*... OPPOSITE> external
3 = <u>emotional</u>, mental, private, secret, subjective ...*The personal, internal battle is beautifully portrayed*... OPPOSITE> revealed

international = <u>global</u>, world, worldwide, universal, cosmopolitan, planetary, intercontinental

Internet
PHRASES **the Internet** = <u>the information superhighway</u>, the net (*informal*), the web (*informal*), the World Wide Web, cyberspace
➤ **internet domain names**

interplay = <u>interaction</u>, give-and-take, reciprocity, reciprocation, meshing

interpret 1 = <u>take</u>, understand, read, explain, regard, construe ...*The speech might be interpreted as a coded message*...
2 = <u>translate</u>, convert, paraphrase, adapt, transliterate ...*She spoke little English, so her husband interpreted*...
3 = <u>explain</u>, define, clarify, spell out, make sense of, decode, decipher, expound, elucidate, throw light on, explicate ...*The judge has to interpret the law as it's being passed*...
4 = <u>understand</u>, read, explain, crack, solve, figure out (*informal*), comprehend, decode, deduce, decipher, suss out (*slang*) ...*The pictures are often difficult to interpret*...
5 = <u>portray</u>, present, perform, render, depict, enact, act out ...*Shakespeare, marvellously interpreted by Orson Welles*...

interpretation 1 = <u>explanation</u>, meaning, reading, understanding, sense, analysis, construction,

exposition, explication, elucidation, signification ...*The Opposition put a different interpretation on the figures*...
2 = <u>performance</u>, portrayal, presentation, rendering, reading, execution, rendition, depiction ...*her full-bodied interpretation of the role of Micaela*...
3 = <u>reading</u>, study, review, version, analysis, explanation, examination, diagnosis, evaluation, exposition, exegesis, explication, elucidation ...*the interpretation of the scriptures*...

interpreter = <u>translator</u>, linguist, metaphrast, paraphrast

interrogate = <u>question</u>, ask, examine, investigate, pump, grill (*informal*), quiz, cross-examine, cross-question, put the screws on (*informal*), catechize, give (someone) the third degree (*informal*)

interrogation = <u>questioning</u>, inquiry, examination, probing, grilling (*informal*), cross-examination, inquisition, third degree (*informal*), cross-questioning

interrupt 1 = <u>intrude</u>, disturb, intervene, interfere (with), break in, heckle, butt in, barge in (*informal*), break (someone's) train of thought ...*'Sorry to interrupt, Colonel.'*...
2 = <u>suspend</u>, break, stop, end, cut, stay, check, delay, cease, cut off, postpone, shelve, put off, defer, break off, adjourn, cut short, discontinue ...*He has interrupted his holiday to return to London*...

interrupted = <u>disturbed</u>, broken, incomplete, cut off, uneven, disconnected, intermittent, discontinuous

interruption 1 = <u>disruption</u>, break, halt, obstacle, disturbance, hitch, intrusion, obstruction, impediment, hindrance ...*The sudden interruption stopped her in mid-flow*...
2 = <u>stoppage</u>, stop, pause, suspension, cessation, severance, hiatus, disconnection, discontinuance ...*interruptions in the supply of food and fuel*...

intersect = <u>cross</u>, meet, cut, divide, cut across, bisect, crisscross

intersection = <u>junction</u>, crossing, crossroads

intersperse = <u>scatter</u>, sprinkle, intermix, pepper, interlard, bestrew

interval 1 = <u>period</u>, time, spell, term, season, space, stretch, pause, span ...*There was a long interval of silence*...
2 = <u>break</u>, interlude, intermission, rest, gap, pause, respite, lull, entr'acte ...*During the interval, wine was served*...
3 = <u>delay</u>, wait, gap, interim, hold-up, meanwhile, meantime, stoppage, hiatus ...*the interval between her arrival and lunch*...
4 = <u>stretch</u>, area, space, distance, gap ...*figures separated by intervals of pattern and colour*...

intervene 1 = <u>step in</u> (*informal*), interfere, mediate, intrude, intercede, arbitrate, interpose, take a hand (*informal*) ...*The situation calmed down when police intervened*...
2 = <u>interrupt</u>, involve yourself, put your oar in, interpose yourself, put your two cents in (*U.S. slang*) ...*She intervened and told me to stop it*...
3 = <u>happen</u>, occur, take place, follow, succeed, arise,

Internet domain names

.co	Commercial company (used with country)	.cm	Cameroon
.com	Commercial company	.cn	China
.net	Company *or* organization	.co	Colombia
.org	Organization, usually nonprofit	.cr	Costa Rica
.edu	Educational establishment	.cu	Cuba
.eu	European Union	.cv	Cap Verde
.gov	US government organization	.cx	Christmas Island
.mil	US military	.cy	Cyprus
.int	International organization	.cz	Czech Republic
.arpa	Internet infrastructure	.de	Germany
.aero	Air-transport industry	.dj	Dijibouti
.biz	Business	.dk	Denmark
.coop	Cooperative	.dm	Dominica
.info	General use	.do	Dominican Republic
.museum	Museum	.dz	Algeria
.name	Individual user	.ec	Ecuador
.pro	Professionals (accountants, lawyers, etc.)	.ee	Estonia
		.eg	Egypt
		.eh	Western Sahara
.ac	Ascension Island	.er	Eritrea
.ad	Andorra	.es	Spain
.ae	United Arab Emirates	.et	Ethiopia
.af	Afghanistan	.fi	Finland
.ag	Antigua and Barbuda	.fj	Fiji
.ai	Anguilla	.fk	Falkland Islands (Malvina)
.al	Albania	.fm	Micronesia, Federal State of
.am	Armenia	.fo	Faroe Islands
.an	Netherlands Antilles	.fr	France
.ao	Angola	.ga	Gabon
.aq	Antarctica	.gd	Grenada
.ar	Argentina	.ge	Georgia
.as	American Samoa	.gf	French Guiana
.at	Austria	.gg	Guernsey
.au	Australia	.gh	Ghana
.aw	Aruba	.gi	Gibraltar
.az	Azerbaijan	.gl	Greenland
.ba	Bosnia and Herzegovina	.gm	Gambia
.bb	Barbados	.gn	Guinea
.bd	Bangladesh	.gp	Equatorial Guinea
.be	Belgium	.gr	Greece
.bf	Burkina Faso	.gs	South Georgia and the South Sandwich Islands
.bg	Bulgaria		
.bh	Bahrain	.gt	Guatemala
.bi	Burundi	.gu	Guam
.bj	Benin	.gw	Guinea-Bissau
.bm	Bermuda	.gy	Guyana
.bn	Brunei Darussalam	.hk	Hong Kong
.bo	Bolivia	.hm	Heard and McDonald Islands
.br	Brazil	.hn	Honduras
.bs	Bahamas	.hr	Croatia/Hrvatska
.bt	Bhutan	.ht	Haiti
.bv	Bouvet Island	.hu	Hungary
.bw	Botswana	.id	Indonesia
.by	Belarus	.ie	Ireland
.bz	Belize	.il	Israel
.ca	Canada	.im	Isle of Man
.cc	Cocos (Keeling) Islands	.in	India
.cd	Congo, Democratic Republic of the	.io	British Indian Ocean Territory
.cf	Central African Republic	.iq	Iraq
.cg	Congo, Republic of	.ir	Iran (Islamic Republic of)
.ch	Switzerland	.is	Iceland
.ci	Côte d'Ivoire	.it	Italy
.ck	Cook Islands	.je	Jersey
.cl	Chile	.jm	Jamaica

Internet domain names (continued)

.jo	Jordan	.pr	Puerto Rico
.jp	Japan	.ps	Palestinian Territories
.ke	Kenya	.pt	Portugal
.kg	Kyrgyzstan	.pw	Palau
.kh	Cambodia	.py	Paraguay
.ki	Kiribati	.qa	Qatar
.km	Comoros	.re	Reunion Island
.kn	Saint Kitts and Nevis	.ro	Romania
.kp	Korea, Democratic People's Republic	.ru	Russian Federation
.kr	Korea, Republic of	.rw	Rwanda
.kw	Kuwait	.sa	Saudi Arabia
.ky	Cayman Islands	.sb	Soloman Islands
.kz	Kazakhstan	.sc	Seychelles
.la	Lao People's Democratic Republic	.sd	Sudan
.lb	Lebanon	.se	Sweden
.lc	Saint Lucia	.sg	St. Helena
.li	Liechtenstein	.si	Slovenia
.lk	Sri Lanka	.sj	Svalbard and Jan Mayen Islands
.lr	Liberia	.sk	Slovak Republic
.ls	Lesotho	.sl	Sierra Leone
.lt	Lithuania	.sm	San Marino
.lu	Luxembourg	.sn	Senegal
.lv	Latvia	.so	Somalia
.ly	Libyan Arab Jamahiriya	.sr	Suriname
.ma	Morocco	.st	Sao Tome and Principe
.mc	Monaco	.sv	El Salvador
.md	Moldova, Republic of	.sy	Syrian Arab Republic
.mg	Madagascar	.sz	Swaziland
.mh	Marshall Islands	.tc	Turks and Caicos Islands
.mk	Macedonia, Former Yugoslav Republic	.td	Chad
.ml	Mali	.tf	French Southern Territories
.mm	Myanmar	.tg	Togo
.mn	Mongolia	.th	Thailand
.mo	Macau	.tj	Tajikistan
.mp	Northern Mariana Islands	.tk	Tokelau
.mq	Martinique	.tm	Turkmenistan
.mr	Mauritania	.tn	Tunisia
.ms	Montserrat	.to	Tongo
.mt	Malta	.tp	East Timor
.mu	Mauritius	.tr	Turkey
.mv	Maldives	.tt	Trinidad and Tobago
.mw	Malawi	.tv	Tuvalu
.mx	Mexico	.tw	Taiwan
.my	Malaysia	.tz	Tanzania
.mz	Mozambique	.ua	Ukraine
.na	Namibia	.ug	Uganda
.nc	New Caledonia	.uk	United Kingdom
.ne	Niger	.um	US Minor Outlying Islands
.nf	Norfolk Island	.us	United States
.ng	Nigeria	.uy	Uruguay
.ni	Nicaragua	.uz	Uzbekistan
.nl	Netherlands	.va	Holy See (City Vatican State)
.no	Norway	.vc	Saint Vincent and the Grenadines
.np	Nepal	.ve	Venezuela
.nr	Nauru	.vg	Virgin Islands (British)
.nu	Niue	.vi	Virgin Islands (USA)
.nz	New Zealand	.vn	Vietnam
.om	Oman	.vu	Vanuatu
.pa	Panama	.wf	Wallis and Futuna Islands
.pe	Peru	.ws	Western Samoa
.pf	French Polynesia	.ye	Yemen
.pg	Papua New Guinea	.yt	Mayotte
.ph	Philippines	.yu	Yugoslavia
.pk	Pakistan	.za	South Africa
.pl	Poland	.zm	Zambia
.pm	St. Pierre and Miquelon	.zw	Zimbabwe
.pn	Pitcairn Island		

ensue, befall, materialize, come to pass, supervene ...*The mailboat comes weekly unless bad weather intervenes*...

intervention = <u>mediation</u>, involvement, interference, intrusion, arbitration, conciliation, intercession, interposition, agency

interview NOUN **1** = <u>meeting</u>, examination, evaluation, oral (examination), interrogation ...*When I went for my first job interview I arrived extremely early*...
2 = <u>audience</u>, talk, conference, exchange, dialogue, consultation, press conference ...*There'll be an interview with the Chancellor after the break*...
VERB **1** = <u>examine</u>, talk to, sound out ...*He was among three candidates interviewed for the job*...
2 = <u>question</u>, interrogate, examine, investigate, ask, pump, grill (*informal*), quiz, cross-examine, cross-question, put the screws on (*informal*), catechize, give (someone) the third degree (*informal*) ...*The police interviewed the driver, but they had no evidence to go on*...

interviewer = <u>questioner</u>, reporter, investigator, examiner, interrogator, interlocutor

intestinal = <u>abdominal</u>, visceral, duodenal, gut (*informal*), inner, coeliac, stomachic

intestines = <u>guts</u>, insides (*informal*), bowels, internal organs, innards (*informal*), entrails, vitals
(*Related Words*)
technical name : viscera

intimacy = <u>familiarity</u>, closeness, understanding, confidence, confidentiality, fraternization OPPOSITE aloofness

intimate[1] ADJECTIVE **1** = <u>close</u>, dear, loving, near, warm, friendly, familiar, thick (*informal*), devoted, confidential, cherished, bosom, inseparable, nearest and dearest ...*I discussed this only with my intimate friends*... OPPOSITE distant
2 = <u>private</u>, personal, confidential, special, individual, particular, secret, exclusive, privy ...*He wrote about the intimate details of his family life*... OPPOSITE public
3 = <u>detailed</u>, minute, full, experienced, personal, deep, particular, specific, immediate, comprehensive, exact, elaborate, profound, penetrating, thorough, in-depth, intricate, first-hand, exhaustive ...*He surprised me with his intimate knowledge of the situation*...
4 = <u>cosy</u>, relaxed, friendly, informal, harmonious, snug, comfy (*informal*), warm ...*an intimate candlelit dinner for two*...
NOUN = <u>friend</u>, close friend, buddy (*informal*), mate (*informal*), pal, comrade, chum (*informal*), mucker (*Brit. slang*), crony, main man (*slang, chiefly U.S.*), china (*Brit. slang*), homeboy (*slang, chiefly U.S.*), cobber (*Austral. or old-fashioned N.Z. informal*), bosom friend, familiar, confidant *or* confidante, (constant) companion ...*They are to have an autumn wedding, an intimate of the couple confides*... OPPOSITE stranger

intimate[2] **1** = <u>suggest</u>, indicate, hint, imply, warn, allude, let it be known, insinuate, give (someone) to understand, drop a hint, tip (someone) the wink (*Brit. informal*) ...*He intimated that he was contemplating leaving the company*...
2 = <u>announce</u>, state, declare, communicate, impart, make known ...*He had intimated to them his readiness to come to a settlement*...

intimately 1 = <u>closely</u>, very well, personally, warmly, familiarly, tenderly, affectionately, confidentially, confidingly ...*You have to be willing to get to know your partner intimately*...
2 = <u>fully</u>, very well, thoroughly, in detail, inside out, to the core, through and through ...*a golden age of musicians whose work she knew intimately*...

intimation 1 = <u>hint</u>, warning, suggestion, indication, allusion, inkling, insinuation ...*I did not have any intimation that he was going to resign*...
2 = <u>announcement</u>, notice, communication, declaration ...*their first public intimation of how they will spend the budget*...

intimidate = <u>frighten</u>, pressure, threaten, alarm, scare, terrify, cow, bully, plague, menace, hound, awe, daunt, harass, subdue, oppress, persecute, lean on (*informal*), coerce, overawe, scare off (*informal*), terrorize, pressurize, browbeat, twist someone's arm (*informal*), tyrannize, dishearten, dispirit, affright (*archaic*), domineer

intimidation = <u>bullying</u>, pressure, threat(s), menaces, coercion, arm-twisting (*informal*), browbeating, terrorization

intonation 1 = <u>tone</u>, inflection, cadence, modulation, accentuation ...*His voice had a very slight German intonation*...
2 = <u>incantation</u>, spell, charm, formula, chant, invocation, hex (*U.S. & Canad. informal*), conjuration ...*They could hear strange music and chanting intonations*...

intone = <u>chant</u>, sing, recite, croon, intonate

intoxicated 1 = <u>drunk</u>, tight (*informal*), smashed (*slang*), canned (*slang*), high (*informal*), cut (*Brit. slang*), flying (*slang*), bombed (*slang*), stoned (*slang*), wasted (*slang*), steaming (*slang*), wrecked (*slang*), stiff (*slang*), out of it (*slang*), plastered (*slang*), drunken, blitzed (*slang*), lit up (*slang*), stewed (*slang*), under the influence, tipsy, legless (*informal*), paralytic (*informal*), sozzled (*informal*), steamboats (*Scot. slang*), zonked (*slang*), blotto (*slang*), fuddled, the worse for drink, inebriated, out to it (*Austral. & N.Z. slang*), drunk as a skunk, in your cups (*informal*), half seas over (*Brit. informal*), bevvied (*dialect*), three sheets in the wind (*informal*), babalas (*S. African*) ...*He appeared intoxicated, police said*...
2 = <u>euphoric</u>, excited, exhilarated, high (*informal*), sent (*slang*), stimulated, dizzy, ecstatic, elated, infatuated, enraptured ...*They had become intoxicated by their success*...

intoxicating 1 = <u>alcoholic</u>, strong, intoxicant, spirituous, inebriant ...*intoxicating liquor*...
2 = <u>exciting</u>, thrilling, stimulating, sexy (*informal*), heady, exhilarating ...*The music is pulsating and the atmosphere intoxicating*...

intoxication 1 = <u>drunkenness</u>, inebriation, tipsiness, inebriety, insobriety ...*Intoxication interferes with*

memory and thinking…
2 = <u>excitement</u>, euphoria, elation, exhilaration, infatuation, delirium, exaltation …*the intoxication of greed and success…*

intractable = <u>difficult</u>, contrary, awkward, wild, stubborn, perverse, wayward, unruly, uncontrollable, wilful, incurable, fractious, unyielding, obstinate, intransigent, headstrong, unmanageable, undisciplined, cantankerous, unbending, obdurate, uncooperative, stiff-necked, ungovernable, self-willed, refractory, pig-headed, bull-headed

intransigent = <u>uncompromising</u>, intractable, tough, stubborn, hardline, tenacious, unyielding, obstinate, immovable, unbending, obdurate, stiff-necked, inflexible, unbudgeable `OPPOSITE` compliant

intrenched
➤ **entrenched**

intrepid = <u>fearless</u>, brave, daring, bold, heroic, game (*informal*), have-a-go (*informal*), courageous, stalwart, resolute, gallant, audacious, valiant, plucky, doughty, undaunted, unafraid, unflinching, nerveless, dauntless, lion-hearted, valorous, stouthearted `OPPOSITE` fearful

intricacy = <u>complexity</u>, involvement, complication, elaborateness, obscurity, entanglement, convolutions, involution, intricateness, knottiness

intricate = <u>complicated</u>, involved, complex, difficult, fancy, sophisticated, elaborate, obscure, tangled, baroque, perplexing, tortuous, Byzantine, convoluted, rococo, knotty, labyrinthine, daedal (*literary*) `OPPOSITE` simple

intrigue `NOUN` **1** = <u>plot</u>, scheme, conspiracy, manoeuvre, manipulation, collusion, ruse, trickery, cabal, stratagem, double-dealing, chicanery, sharp practice, wile, knavery, machination …*the plots and intrigues in the novel…*
2 = <u>affair</u>, romance, intimacy, liaison, amour …*She detected her husband in an intrigue with a prostitute…*
`VERB` **1** = <u>interest</u>, fascinate, arouse the curiosity of, attract, charm, rivet, titillate, pique, tickle your fancy …*The novelty of the situation intrigued him…*
2 = <u>plot</u>, scheme, manoeuvre, conspire, connive, machinate …*The main characters spend their time intriguing for control…*

intriguing = <u>interesting</u>, fascinating, absorbing, exciting, engaging, gripping, stirring, stimulating, curious, compelling, amusing, diverting, provocative, beguiling, thought-provoking, titillating, engrossing, tantalizing

intrinsic = <u>essential</u>, real, true, central, natural, basic, radical, native, genuine, fundamental, constitutional, built-in, underlying, inherent, elemental, congenital, inborn, inbred `OPPOSITE` extrinsic

intrinsically = <u>essentially</u>, basically, fundamentally, constitutionally, as such, in itself, at heart, by definition, per se

introduce **1** = <u>bring in</u>, establish, set up, start, begin, found, develop, launch, institute, organize, pioneer, initiate, originate, commence, get going, instigate, phase in, usher in, inaugurate, set in motion, bring into being …*The Government has introduced a number of other money-saving ideas…*
2 = <u>present</u>, acquaint, make known, familiarize, do the honours, make the introduction …*Someone introduced us and I sat next to him…*
3 = <u>announce</u>, present, open, launch, precede, lead into, preface, lead off …*'Health Matters' is introduced by Dick Oliver on the World Service…*
4 = <u>suggest</u>, offer, air, table, advance, propose, recommend, float, submit, bring up, put forward, set forth, ventilate, broach, moot …*She does not abandon her responsibility to introduce new ideas…*
5 = <u>add</u>, insert, inject, throw in (*informal*), infuse, interpose, interpolate …*I wish to introduce a note of cool reason to the discussion…*

introduction **1** = <u>launch</u>, institution, establishment, start, opening, beginning, pioneering, presentation, initiation, inauguration, induction, commencement, instigation …*He is remembered for the introduction of the moving assembly line…* `OPPOSITE` elimination
2 = <u>opening</u>, prelude, preface, lead-in, preliminaries, overture, preamble, foreword, prologue, intro (*informal*), commencement, opening remarks, proem, opening passage, prolegomena, prolegomenon, exordium …*In her introduction to the book she provides a summary of the ideas…* `OPPOSITE` conclusion
3 = <u>insertion</u>, addition, injection, interpolation …*the introduction of air bubbles into the veins…* `OPPOSITE` extraction

introductory **1** = <u>preliminary</u>, elementary, first, early, initial, inaugural, preparatory, initiatory, prefatory, precursory …*an introductory course in religion and theology…* `OPPOSITE` concluding
2 = <u>starting</u>, opening, initial, early …*out on the shelves at an introductory price of £2.99…*

introspection = <u>self-examination</u>, brooding, self-analysis, navel-gazing (*slang*), introversion, heart-searching

introspective = <u>inward-looking</u>, introverted, brooding, contemplative, meditative, subjective, pensive, inner-directed

introverted = <u>introspective</u>, withdrawn, inward-looking, self-contained, self-centred, indrawn, inner-directed

intrude `VERB` = <u>butt in</u>, encroach, push in, obtrude, thrust yourself in *or* forward, put your two cents in (*U.S. slang*) …*He kept intruding with personal questions…*
`PHRASES` **intrude on something** *or* **someone**
1 = <u>interfere with</u>, interrupt, impinge on, encroach on, meddle with, infringe on …*It's annoying when unforeseen events intrude on your day…* **2** = <u>trespass on</u>, invade, infringe on, obtrude on …*They intruded on to the field of play…*

intruder = <u>trespasser</u>, burglar, invader, squatter, prowler, interloper, infiltrator, gate-crasher (*informal*)

intrusion **1** = <u>interruption</u>, interference, infringement, trespass, encroachment …*I hope you don't mind this intrusion…*

2 = <u>invasion</u>, breach, infringement, infiltration, encroachment, infraction, usurpation ...*I felt it was a grotesque intrusion into our lives...*

intrusive 1 = <u>interfering</u>, disturbing, invasive, unwanted, presumptuous, uncalled-for, importunate ...*The cameras were not an intrusive presence...*
2 = <u>pushy</u> (*informal*), forward, interfering, unwanted, impertinent, nosy (*informal*), officious, meddlesome ...*Her bodyguards were less than gentle with intrusive journalists...*

intrust
➤ **entrust**

intuition 1 = <u>instinct</u>, perception, insight, sixth sense, discernment ...*Her intuition was telling her that something was wrong...*
2 = <u>feeling</u>, idea, impression, suspicion, premonition, inkling, presentiment ...*You can't make a case on intuitions, you know...*

intuitive = <u>instinctive</u>, spontaneous, innate, involuntary, instinctual, untaught, unreflecting

intuitively = <u>instinctively</u>, automatically, spontaneously, involuntarily, innately, instinctually

intwine
➤ **entwine**

inundate 1 = <u>overwhelm</u>, flood, swamp, engulf, overflow, overrun, glut ...*Her office was inundated with requests for tickets...*
2 = <u>flood</u>, engulf, submerge, drown, overflow, immerse, deluge ...*Their neighbourhood is being inundated by the rising waters...*

inured = <u>accustomed</u>, hardened, toughened, trained, strengthened, tempered, familiarized, habituated, desensitized, case-hardened, annealed

invade 1 = <u>attack</u>, storm, assault, capture, occupy, seize, raid, overwhelm, violate, conquer, overrun, annex, march into, assail, descend upon, infringe on, burst in on, make inroads on ...*In 1944 the allies invaded the Italian mainland...*
2 = <u>infest</u>, swarm, overrun, flood, infect, ravage, beset, pervade, permeate, overspread ...*Every so often the kitchen would be invaded by ants...*

invader = <u>attacker</u>, raider, plunderer, aggressor, looter, trespasser

invalid¹ [NOUN] = <u>patient</u>, sufferer, convalescent, valetudinarian ...*I hate being treated as an invalid...*
[ADJECTIVE] = <u>disabled</u>, ill, sick, poorly (*informal*), weak, ailing, frail, feeble, sickly, infirm, bedridden, valetudinarian ...*I have an invalid wife and am labelled as a carer...*

invalid² 1 = <u>null and void</u>, void, worthless, untrue, null, not binding, inoperative, nugatory ...*The trial was stopped and the results declared invalid...* [OPPOSITE] valid
2 = <u>unfounded</u>, false, untrue, illogical, irrational, unsound, unscientific, baseless, fallacious, ill-founded ...*Those arguments are rendered invalid by the hard facts...* [OPPOSITE] sound

invalidate = <u>nullify</u>, cancel, annul, undermine, weaken, overthrow, undo, quash, overrule, rescind, abrogate, render null and void [OPPOSITE] validate

invalidity = <u>falsity</u>, fallacy, unsoundness, inconsistency, irrationality, illogicality, speciousness, sophism, fallaciousness

invaluable = <u>precious</u>, valuable, priceless, costly, inestimable, beyond price, worth your *or* its weight in gold [OPPOSITE] worthless

invariably = <u>always</u>, regularly, constantly, every time, inevitably, repeatedly, consistently, ever, continually, aye (*Scot.*), eternally, habitually, perpetually, without exception, customarily, unfailingly, on every occasion, unceasingly, day in, day out

invasion 1 = <u>attack</u>, assault, capture, takeover, raid, offensive, occupation, conquering, seizure, onslaught, foray, appropriation, sortie, annexation, incursion, expropriation, inroad, irruption, arrogation ...*seven years after the Roman invasion of Britain...*
2 = <u>intrusion</u>, breach, violation, disturbance, disruption, infringement, overstepping, infiltration, encroachment, infraction, usurpation ...*Is reading a child's diary a gross invasion of privacy?...*

invective = <u>abuse</u>, censure, tirade, reproach, berating, denunciation, diatribe, vilification, tongue-lashing, billingsgate, vituperation, castigation, obloquy, contumely, philippic(s), revilement

invent 1 = <u>create</u>, make, produce, develop, design, discover, imagine, manufacture, generate, come up with (*informal*), coin, devise, conceive, originate, formulate, spawn, contrive, improvise, dream up (*informal*), concoct, think up ...*He invented the first electric clock...*
2 = <u>make up</u>, devise, concoct, forge, fake, fabricate, feign, falsify, cook up (*informal*), trump up ...*I stood there, trying to invent a plausible excuse...*

invention 1 = <u>creation</u>, machine, device, design, development, instrument, discovery, innovation, gadget, brainchild (*informal*), contraption, contrivance ...*It's been tricky marketing his new invention...*
2 = <u>development</u>, design, production, setting up, foundation, construction, constitution, creation, discovery, introduction, establishment, pioneering, formation, innovation, conception, masterminding, formulation, inception, contrivance, origination ...*fifty years after the invention of the printing press...*
3 = <u>fiction</u>, story, fantasy, lie, yarn, fabrication, concoction, falsehood, fib (*informal*), untruth, urban myth, prevarication, tall story (*informal*), urban legend, figment *or* product of (someone's) imagination ...*The story was undoubtedly pure invention...*
4 = <u>creativity</u>, vision, imagination, initiative, enterprise, inspiration, genius, brilliance, ingenuity, originality, inventiveness, resourcefulness, creativeness, ingeniousness, imaginativeness ...*powers of invention and mathematical ability...*

inventive = <u>creative</u>, original, innovative, imaginative, gifted, inspired, fertile, ingenious, ground-breaking, resourceful [OPPOSITE] uninspired

inventor = <u>creator</u>, father, maker, author, framer, designer, architect, coiner, originator

inventory = list, record, catalogue, listing, account, roll, file, schedule, register, description, log, directory, tally, roster, stock book

inverse 1 = opposite, reverse, reversed, contrary, inverted, converse, transposed ...*The tension grew in inverse proportion to the distance from their destination...*
2 = reverse, opposite, reversed, inverted, transposed ...*The hologram can be flipped to show the inverse image...*

inversion = reversal, opposite, antithesis, transposition, contrary, contrariety, contraposition, transposal, antipode

invert = overturn, upturn, turn upside down, upset, reverse, capsize, transpose, introvert, turn inside out, turn turtle, invaginate (*Pathology*), overset, intussuscept (*Pathology*)

invertebrate
➤ **crustaceans** ➤ **invertebrates** ➤ **snails, slugs and other gastropods** ➤ **spiders and other arachnids**

invest VERB 1 = spend, expend, advance, venture, put in, devote, lay out, sink in, use up, plough in ...*When people buy houses they're investing a lot of money...*
2 = charge, fill, steep, saturate, endow, pervade, infuse, imbue, suffuse, endue ...*The buildings are invested with a nations's history...*
3 = empower, provide, charge, sanction, license, authorize, vest ...*The constitution had invested him with certain powers...*
4 = install, establish, ordain, crown, inaugurate, anoint, consecrate, adopt, induct, enthrone, instate ...*He was invested as a paramount chief of a district tribe...*
PHRASES **invest in something** = buy, get, purchase, score (*slang*), pay for, obtain, acquire, procure ...*Why don't you invest in an ice cream machine?...*

investigate = examine, study, research, consider, go into, explore, search for, analyse, look into, inspect, look over, sift, probe into, work over, scrutinize, inquire into, make inquiries about, enquire into

investigation = examination, study, inquiry, hearing, research, review, search, survey, analysis, probe, inspection, exploration, scrutiny, inquest, fact finding, recce (*slang*)

investigative = fact-finding, researching, investigating, research, inspecting

investigator = examiner, researcher, inspector, monitor, detective, analyser, explorer, reviewer, scrutinizer, checker, inquirer, scrutineer

investment 1 = investing, backing, funding, financing, contribution, speculation, transaction, expenditure, outlay ...*The government introduced tax incentives to encourage investment...*
2 = stake, interest, share, concern, portion, ante (*informal*) ...*an investment of £28 million...*
3 = buy, asset, acquisition, venture, risk, speculation, gamble ...*A small-screen portable TV can be a good investment...*

inveterate 1 = chronic, confirmed, incurable, hardened, established, long-standing, hard-core, habitual, obstinate, incorrigible, dyed-in-the-wool, ineradicable, deep-dyed (*usually derogatory*) ...*an inveterate gambler...*
2 = deep-rooted, entrenched, ingrained, deep-seated, incurable, established ...*the inveterate laziness of these boys...*
3 = staunch, long-standing, dyed-in-the-wool, deep-dyed (*usually derogatory*) ...*the spirit of an inveterate Tory...*

invidious = undesirable, unpleasant, hateful, thankless OPPOSITE⟩ pleasant

invigorating = refreshing, stimulating, bracing, fresh, tonic, uplifting, exhilarating, rejuvenating, energizing, healthful, restorative, salubrious, rejuvenative

invincible = unbeatable, unassailable, indomitable, unyielding, indestructible, impregnable, insuperable, invulnerable, unconquerable, unsurmountable OPPOSITE⟩ vulnerable

invisible 1 = unseen, imperceptible, indiscernible, unseeable, unperceivable ...*The lines were so fine as to be nearly invisible...* OPPOSITE⟩ visible
2 = hidden, concealed, obscured, secret, disguised, inconspicuous, unobserved, unnoticeable, inappreciable ...*The problems of the poor are largely invisible...*

invitation 1 = request, call, invite (*informal*), bidding, summons ...*He received an invitation to lunch...*
2 = inducement, come-on (*informal*), temptation, challenge, provocation, open door, overture, incitement, enticement, allurement ...*Don't leave your bag there – it's an invitation to a thief...*

invite 1 = ask, bid, summon, request the pleasure of (someone's) company ...*She invited him to her birthday party...*
2 = request, seek, look for, call for, ask for, bid for, appeal for, petition, solicit ...*The Department is inviting applications from local groups...*
3 = encourage, attract, cause, draw, lead to, court, ask for (*informal*), generate, foster, tempt, provoke, induce, bring on, solicit, engender, allure, call forth, leave the door open to ...*Their refusal to compromise will invite more criticism from the UN...*

inviting = tempting, appealing, attractive, pleasing, welcoming, warm, engaging, fascinating, intriguing, magnetic, delightful, enticing, seductive, captivating, beguiling, alluring, mouthwatering OPPOSITE⟩ uninviting

invocation 1 = appeal, request, petition, beseeching, solicitation, entreaty ...*an invocation for divine guidance...*
2 = prayer, chant, supplication, orison ...*Please stand for the invocation...*

invoke 1 = apply, use, implement, call in, initiate, resort to, put into effect ...*The judge invoked an international law that protects refugees...*
2 = call upon, appeal to, pray to, petition, conjure,

Invertebrates
Types of invertebrates

http://www.nhm.ac.uk/nature-online/life/insects-spiders/index.html
http://www.nhm.ac.uk/nature-online/life/other-invertebrates/index.html

amoeba *or* (*U.S.*) ameba	horseleech	sea mouse
animalcule *or* animalculum	jellyfish *or* (*Austral. slang*) blubber	sea pen
arrowworm	lancelet *or* amphioxus	sea slater
arthropod	leech	sea squirt
Balmain bug	liver fluke	sea urchin
bardy, bardie, *or* bardi	lugworm, lug, *or* lobworm	seed oyster
bivalve	lungworm	soft-shell (clam)
bladder worm	millipede, millepede, *or* milleped	sponge
blue-ringed octopus	mollusc	squid
box jellyfish *or* (*Austral.*) sea wasp	mussel	starfish
brachiopod *or* lamp shell	octopus *or* devilfish	stomach worm
brandling	otter shell	stony coral
bryozoan *or* (*colloquial*) sea mat	oyster	sunstar
catworm, white worm, *or* white cat	paddle worm	tapeworm
centipede	paper nautilus, nautilus, *or* argonaut	tardigrade *or* water bear
chicken louse	pearly nautilus, nautilus, *or* chambered nautilus	tellin
chiton *or* coat-of-mail shell	piddock	teredo *or* shipworm
clam	pipi *or* ugari	trepang *or* bêche-de-mer
clappy-doo *or* clabby-doo	Portuguese man-of-war *or* (*Austral.*) bluebottle	tube worm
cockle	quahog, hard-shell clam, hard-shell, *or* round clam	tubifex
cone (shell)	ragworm *or* (*U.S.*) clamworm	tusk shell *or* tooth shell
coral	razor-shell *or* (*U.S.*) razor clam	Venus's flower basket
crown-of-thorns (starfish)	red coral *or* precious coral	Venus's-girdle
ctenophore *or* comb jelly	roundworm	Venus shell
cunjevoi *or* cunje	sandworm *or* (*Austral.*) pumpworm	vinegar eel, vinegar worm, *or* eelworm
cuttlefish *or* cuttle	scallop	water louse *or* water slater
daphnia	sea anemone	water measurer
earthworm	sea cucumber	water stick insect
eelworm	sea lily	wheatworm
gaper		whipworm
gapeworm		woodborer
gastropod		worm
Guinea worm		

Extinct invertebrates

ammonite	eurypterid	trilobite
belemnite	graptolite	

solicit, beseech, entreat, adjure, supplicate ...*The great magicians of old invoked their gods with sacrifice...*

involuntary = unintentional, automatic, unconscious, spontaneous, reflex, instinctive, uncontrolled, unthinking, instinctual, blind, unconditioned OPPOSITE voluntary

involve 1 = entail, mean, demand, require, call for, occasion, result in, imply, give rise to, encompass, necessitate ...*Running a kitchen involves a great deal of discipline and speed...*
2 = include, contain, take in, embrace, cover, incorporate, draw in, comprise of, number among ...*The cover-up involved people at the very highest level...*
3 = implicate, tangle, mix up, embroil, link, entangle, incriminate, mire, stitch up (*slang*), enmesh, inculpate (*formal*) ...*I seem to have involved myself in something I don't understand...*
4 = concern, draw in, associate, connect, bear on ...*He started involving me in the more confidential aspects of*

the job...

involved 1 = complicated, complex, intricate, hard, difficult, confused, confusing, sophisticated, elaborate, tangled, bewildering, jumbled, entangled, tortuous, Byzantine, convoluted, knotty, unfathomable, labyrinthine ...*The operation can be quite involved, requiring special procedures...* OPPOSITE straightforward
2 = concerned with, associated with, participating in, connected with, caught up in, occupied by ...*It's an organisation for people involved in agriculture...*
3 = absorbed in, caught up in, lost in, deep in, fascinated by, immersed in, gripped by, captivated by, enthralled by, up to your ears in, wrapped up in ...*She was so involved in her career she had no time for fun...*

involvement = connection, interest, relationship, concern, association, commitment, friendship, attachment ...*He has always felt a deep involvement with animals...*

invulnerable = safe, secure, invincible,

impenetrable, unassailable, indestructible, insusceptible OPPOSITE> vulnerable

inward 1 = <u>incoming</u>, entering, penetrating, inbound, inflowing, ingoing, inpouring ...*a sharp, inward breath like a gasp...*
2 = <u>internal</u>, inner, private, personal, inside, secret, hidden, interior, confidential, privy, innermost, inmost ...*a glow of inward satisfaction...* OPPOSITE> outward

inwardly = <u>privately</u>, secretly, to yourself, within, inside, at heart, deep down, in your head, in your inmost heart

iota = <u>bit</u>, particle, atom, trace, hint, scrap, grain, mite, jot, speck, whit, tittle, scintilla (*rare*)

irascible = <u>bad-tempered</u>, cross, irritable, crabbed, touchy, cantankerous, peppery, tetchy, ratty (*Brit. & N.Z. informal*), testy, short-tempered, hot-tempered, quick-tempered, choleric, narky (*Brit. slang*)

irate = <u>angry</u>, cross, furious, angered, mad (*informal*), provoked, annoyed, irritated, fuming (*informal*), choked, infuriated, incensed, enraged, worked up, exasperated, indignant, livid, riled, up in arms, incandescent, hacked off (*U.S. slang*), piqued, hot under the collar (*informal*), wrathful, fit to be tied (*slang*), as black as thunder, tooshie (*Austral. slang*), off the air (*Austral. slang*)

ire = <u>anger</u>, rage, fury, wrath, passion, indignation, annoyance, displeasure, exasperation, choler

Ireland = <u>Hibernia</u> (*Latin*)

iridescent = <u>shimmering</u>, pearly, opalescent, shot, opaline, prismatic, rainbow-coloured, polychromatic, nacreous

Irish = <u>Hibernian</u>, green

irk = <u>irritate</u>, annoy, aggravate (*informal*), provoke, bug (*informal*), put out (*informal*), gall, ruffle, nettle, vex, rile, peeve (*informal*), get on your nerves (*informal*), nark (*Brit., Austral., & N.Z. slang*), miff (*informal*), be on your back (*slang*), get in your hair (*informal*), rub you up the wrong way (*informal*), put your nose out of joint (*informal*), get your back up, put your back up

irksome = <u>irritating</u>, trying, annoying, aggravating, troublesome, unwelcome, exasperating, tiresome, vexing, disagreeable, burdensome, wearisome, bothersome, vexatious OPPOSITE> pleasant

iron PLURAL NOUN = <u>chains</u>, shackles, fetters, manacles, bonds ...*These people need to be clapped in irons themselves...*
ADJECTIVE 1 = <u>ferrous</u>, ferric, irony ...*The huge iron gate was locked...*
2 = <u>inflexible</u>, hard, strong, tough, steel, rigid, adamant, unconditional, steely, implacable, indomitable, unyielding, immovable, unbreakable, unbending, obdurate ...*a man of icy nerve and iron will...* OPPOSITE> weak
PHRASES **iron something out** = <u>settle</u>, resolve, sort out, eliminate, get rid of, reconcile, clear up, simplify, unravel, erase, eradicate, put right, straighten out, harmonize, expedite, smooth over ...*The various groups had managed to iron out their differences...*

(*Related Words*)
adjectives: ferric, ferrous
combining form: ferro-

ironic *or* **ironical** 1 = <u>sarcastic</u>, dry, sharp, acid, bitter, stinging, mocking, sneering, scoffing, wry, scathing, satirical, tongue-in-cheek, sardonic, caustic, double-edged, acerbic, trenchant, mordant, mordacious ...*At the most solemn moments he would make an ironic remark...*
2 = <u>paradoxical</u>, absurd, contradictory, puzzling, baffling, ambiguous, inconsistent, confounding, enigmatic, illogical, incongruous ...*It's ironic that the sort of people this film celebrates would never watch it...*

irony 1 = <u>sarcasm</u>, mockery, ridicule, bitterness, scorn, satire, cynicism, derision, causticity, mordancy ...*She examined his face for a hint of irony, but found none...*
2 = <u>paradox</u>, ambiguity, absurdity, incongruity, contrariness ...*Opposition parties wasted no time in stressing the irony of the situation...*

irrational 1 = <u>illogical</u>, crazy, silly, absurd, foolish, unreasonable, unwise, preposterous, idiotic, nonsensical, unsound, unthinking, injudicious, unreasoning ...*an irrational fear of science...* OPPOSITE> rational
2 = <u>senseless</u>, wild, crazy, unstable, insane, mindless, demented, aberrant, brainless, off the air (*Austral. slang*) ...*They behaved in such a bizarre and irrational manner...*

irrationality = <u>senselessness</u>, madness, insanity, absurdity, lunacy, lack of judgment, illogicality, unreasonableness, preposterousness, unsoundness, brainlessness

irreconcilable 1 = <u>implacable</u>, uncompromising, inflexible, inexorable, intransigent, unappeasable ...*an irreconcilable clash of personalities...*
2 = <u>incompatible</u>, conflicting, opposed, inconsistent, incongruous, diametrically opposed ...*their irreconcilable points of view...*

irrefutable = <u>undeniable</u>, sure, certain, irresistible, invincible, unassailable, indisputable, unanswerable, unquestionable, incontrovertible, beyond question, incontestable, indubitable, apodictic, irrefragable

irregular ADJECTIVE 1 = <u>variable</u>, inconsistent, erratic, shifting, occasional, random, casual, shaky, wavering, uneven, fluctuating, eccentric, patchy, sporadic, intermittent, haphazard, unsteady, desultory, fitful, spasmodic, unsystematic, inconstant, nonuniform, unmethodical ...*She was suffering from an irregular heartbeat...* OPPOSITE> steady
2 = <u>uneven</u>, broken, rough, twisted, twisting, curving, pitted, ragged, crooked, unequal, jagged, bumpy, lumpy, serpentine, contorted, lopsided, craggy, indented, asymmetrical, serrated, holey, unsymmetrical ...*He had bad teeth, irregular and discoloured...* OPPOSITE> even
3 = <u>inappropriate</u>, unconventional, improper, unethical, odd, unusual, extraordinary, disorderly, exceptional, peculiar, unofficial, abnormal, queer, rum (*Brit. slang*), back-door, unsuitable, unorthodox, out-

of-order, unprofessional, anomalous ...*The minister was accused of irregular business practices*...
4 = <u>unofficial</u>, underground, guerrilla, volunteer, resistance, partisan, rogue, paramilitary, mercenary ...*At least 17 irregular units are involved in the war*...

irregularity **1** = <u>inconsistency</u>, randomness, disorganization, unsteadiness, unpunctuality, haphazardness, disorderliness, lack of method, desultoriness ...*a dangerous irregularity in her heartbeat*...
2 = <u>unevenness</u>, deformity, asymmetry, crookedness, contortion, patchiness, lopsidedness, raggedness, lack of symmetry, spottiness, jaggedness ...*treatment of irregularities of the teeth*...
3 = <u>malpractice</u>, anomaly, breach, abnormality, deviation, oddity, aberration, malfunction, peculiarity, singularity, unorthodoxy, unconventionality ...*charges arising from alleged financial irregularities*...

irregularly = <u>erratically</u>, occasionally, now and again, intermittently, off and on, anyhow, unevenly, fitfully, haphazardly, eccentrically, spasmodically, jerkily, in snatches, out of sequence, by fits and starts, disconnectedly, unmethodically, unpunctually

irrelevance *or* **irrelevancy** = <u>inappropriateness</u>, inapplicability, inaptness, unconnectedness, pointlessness, non sequitur, inconsequence, extraneousness, inappositeness OPPOSITE relevance

irrelevant = <u>unconnected</u>, unrelated, unimportant, inappropriate, peripheral, insignificant, negligible, immaterial, extraneous, beside the point, impertinent, neither here nor there, inapplicable, inapt, inapposite, inconsequent OPPOSITE relevant

irreparable = <u>beyond repair</u>, irreversible, incurable, irretrievable, irrecoverable, irremediable

irreplaceable = <u>indispensable</u>, unique, invaluable, priceless

Irrepressible = <u>unstoppable</u>, buoyant, uncontrollable, boisterous, ebullient, effervescent, unmanageable, unquenchable, bubbling over, uncontainable, unrestrainable, insuppressible

irresistible **1** = <u>overwhelming</u>, compelling, overpowering, urgent, potent, imperative, compulsive, uncontrollable, overmastering ...*It proved an irresistible temptation to go back*...
2 = <u>seductive</u>, inviting, tempting, enticing, provocative, fascinating, enchanting, captivating, beguiling, alluring, bewitching, ravishing ...*The music is irresistible*...
3 = <u>inescapable</u>, inevitable, unavoidable, sure, certain, fated, destined, inexorable, ineluctable ...*They feel the case for change is irresistible*...

irrespective of = <u>despite</u>, in spite of, regardless of, discounting, notwithstanding, without reference to, without regard to

irresponsible = <u>thoughtless</u>, reckless, careless, wild, unreliable, giddy, untrustworthy, flighty, ill-considered, good-for-nothing, shiftless, harebrained, undependable, harum-scarum, scatterbrained, featherbrained OPPOSITE responsible

irreverence = <u>disrespect</u>, cheek (*informal*),

impertinence, sauce (*informal*), mockery, derision, lack of respect, impudence, flippancy, cheekiness (*informal*)

irreverent = <u>disrespectful</u>, cheeky (*informal*), impertinent, fresh (*informal*), mocking, flip (*informal*), saucy, contemptuous, tongue-in-cheek, sassy (*U.S. informal*), flippant, iconoclastic, derisive, impudent OPPOSITE reverent

irreversible = <u>irrevocable</u>, incurable, irreparable, final, unalterable

irrevocable = <u>fixed</u>, settled, irreversible, fated, predetermined, immutable, invariable, irretrievable, predestined, unalterable, unchangeable, changeless, irremediable, unreversible

irrigate = <u>water</u>, wet, moisten, flood, inundate

irritability = <u>bad temper</u>, impatience, ill humour, prickliness, tetchiness, irascibility, peevishness, testiness, touchiness OPPOSITE good humour

irritable = <u>bad-tempered</u>, cross, snappy, hot, tense, crabbed, fiery, snarling, prickly, exasperated, edgy, touchy, petulant, ill-tempered, irascible, cantankerous, tetchy, ratty (*Brit. & N.Z. informal*), testy, fretful, peevish, crabby, dyspeptic, choleric, crotchety (*informal*), oversensitive, snappish, ill-humoured, narky (*Brit. slang*), out of humour OPPOSITE even-tempered

irritate **1** = <u>annoy</u>, anger, bother, provoke, offend, needle (*informal*), harass, infuriate, aggravate (*informal*), incense, fret, enrage, gall, ruffle, inflame, exasperate, nettle, pester, vex, irk, pique, rankle with, get under your skin (*informal*), get on your nerves (*informal*), nark (*Brit., Austral., & N.Z. slang*), drive you up the wall (*slang*), rub you up the wrong way (*informal*), get your goat (*slang*), try your patience, get in your hair (*informal*), get on your wick (*informal*), get your dander up (*informal*), raise your hackles, get your back up, get your hackles up, put your back up ...*Their attitude irritates me*... OPPOSITE placate
2 = <u>inflame</u>, pain, rub, scratch, scrape, grate, graze, fret, gall, chafe, abrade ...*Chillies can irritate the skin*...

irritated = <u>annoyed</u>, cross, angry, bothered, put out, hacked (off) (*U.S. slang*), harassed, impatient, ruffled, exasperated, irritable, nettled, vexed, displeased, flustered, peeved (*informal*), piqued, out of humour, tooshie (*Austral. slang*)

irritating = <u>annoying</u>, trying, provoking, infuriating, upsetting, disturbing, nagging, aggravating (*informal*), troublesome, galling, maddening, disquieting, displeasing, worrisome, irksome, vexatious, pestilential OPPOSITE pleasing

irritation **1** = <u>annoyance</u>, anger, fury, resentment, wrath, gall, indignation, impatience, displeasure, exasperation, chagrin, irritability, ill temper, shortness, vexation, ill humour, testiness, crossness, snappiness, infuriation ...*For the first time he felt irritation at her methods*... OPPOSITE pleasure
2 = <u>nuisance</u>, annoyance, irritant, pain (*informal*), drag (*informal*), bother, plague, menace, tease, pest, hassle, provocation, gall, goad, aggravation (*informal*), pain

in the neck (*informal*), thorn in your flesh ...*Don't allow a minor irritation to mar your ambitions...*

Islam

> *Moslem denominations and sects*
> http://www.bbc.co.uk/religion/religions/islam/index
> Alaouites *or* Alawites
> Druse *or* Druze
> Imami
> Ismaili *or* Isma'ili
> Nizari
> Shiah, Shia *or* Shiite
> Sufism
> Sunni
> Wahhabism *or* Wahabism
> Zaidi

island = <u>isle</u>, inch (*Scot. & Irish*), atoll, holm (*dialect*), islet, ait *or* eyot (*dialect*), cay *or* key

(**Related Words**)

adjective: insular

➤ **WORD POWER SUPPLEMENT islands and island groups**

isolate 1 = <u>separate</u>, break up, cut off, detach, split up, insulate, segregate, disconnect, divorce, sequester, set apart, disunite, estrange ...*This policy could isolate members from the UN security council...*
2 = <u>quarantine</u>, separate, exclude, cut off, detached, keep in solitude ...*Patients will be isolated for one month after treatment...*

isolated 1 = <u>remote</u>, far, distant, lonely, out-of-the-way, hidden, retired, far-off, secluded, inaccessible, faraway, outlying, in the middle of nowhere, off the beaten track, backwoods, godforsaken, incommunicado, unfrequented ...*Many of the refugee areas are in isolated areas...*
2 = <u>single</u>, individual, unique, unusual, sole, random, exceptional, freak, lone, solitary, abnormal, unrelated, anomalous, atypical, untypical ...*The allegations related to an isolated case of cheating...*

isolation = <u>separation</u>, withdrawal, loneliness, segregation, detachment, quarantine, solitude, exile, self-sufficiency, seclusion, remoteness, disconnection, insularity

issue **NOUN** 1 = <u>topic</u>, point, matter, problem, business, case, question, concern, subject, affair, argument, theme, controversy, can of worms (*informal*) ...*Is it right for the Church to express a view on political issues?...*
2 = <u>point</u>, question, concern, bone of contention, matter of contention, point in question ...*I wasn't earning much money, but that was not the issue...*
3 = <u>edition</u>, printing, copy, impression, publication, number, instalment, imprint, version ...*The problem is underlined in the latest issue of the Lancet...*
4 = <u>children</u>, young, offspring, babies, kids (*informal*), seed (*chiefly biblical*), successors, heirs, descendants, progeny, scions ...*He died without issue in 1946...*

OPPOSITE parent
5 = <u>distribution</u>, issuing, supply, supplying, delivery, publication, circulation, sending out, dissemination, dispersal, issuance ...*the issue of supplies to refugees...*
VERB 1 = <u>give out</u>, release, publish, announce, deliver, spread, broadcast, distribute, communicate, proclaim, put out, circulate, emit, impart, disseminate, promulgate, put in circulation ...*He issued a statement denying the allegations...*
2 = <u>emerge</u>, came out, proceed, rise, spring, flow, arise, stem, originate, emanate, exude, come forth, be a consequence of ...*A tinny voice issued from a speaker...*
PHRASES **at issue** = <u>under discussion</u>, in question, in dispute, under consideration, to be decided, for debate ...*The problems of immigration were not the question at issue...* ◆ **take issue with something or someone** = <u>disagree with</u>, question, challenge, oppose, dispute, object to, argue with, take exception to, raise an objection to ...*She might take issue with you on that matter...*

Italy
➤ **administrative regions**

itch **VERB** 1 = <u>prickle</u>, tickle, tingle, crawl ...*When you have hayfever, your eyes and nose stream and itch...*
2 = <u>long</u>, ache, crave, burn, pine, pant, hunger, lust, yearn, hanker ...*I was itching to get involved...*
NOUN 1 = <u>irritation</u>, tingling, prickling, itchiness ...*Scratch my back – I've got an itch...*
2 = <u>desire</u>, longing, craving, passion, yen (*informal*), hunger, lust, yearning, hankering, restlessness ...*an insatiable itch to switch from channel to channel...*

itchy = <u>impatient</u>, eager, restless, unsettled, edgy, restive, fidgety

item 1 = <u>article</u>, thing, object, piece, unit, component ...*The most valuable item on show will be a Picasso...*
2 = <u>matter</u>, point, issue, case, question, concern, detail, subject, feature, particular, affair, aspect, entry, theme, consideration, topic ...*The other item on the agenda is the tour...*
3 = <u>report</u>, story, piece, account, note, feature, notice, article, paragraph, bulletin, dispatch, communiqué, write-up ...*There was an item in the paper about him...*

itemize = <u>list</u>, record, detail, count, document, instance, set out, specify, inventory, number, enumerate, particularize

itinerant = <u>wandering</u>, travelling, journeying, unsettled, Gypsy, roaming, roving, nomadic, migratory, vagrant, peripatetic, vagabond, ambulatory, wayfaring **OPPOSITE** settled

itinerary = <u>schedule</u>, line, programme, tour, route, journey, circuit, timetable

ivory tower = <u>seclusion</u>, remoteness, unreality, retreat, refuge, cloister, sanctum, splendid isolation, world of your own

J j

jab VERB = <u>poke</u>, dig, punch, thrust, tap, stab, nudge, prod, lunge …*a needle was jabbed into the baby's arm*…
NOUN = <u>poke</u>, dig, punch, thrust, tap, stab, nudge, prod, lunge …*He gave me a jab in the side*…

jacket = <u>covering</u>, casing, case, cover, skin, shell, coat, wrapping, envelope, capsule, folder, sheath, wrapper, encasement, housing

jackpot = <u>prize</u>, winnings, award, pool, reward, pot, kitty, bonanza, pot of gold at the end of the rainbow

jack up 1 = <u>hoist</u>, raise, elevate, winch up, lift, rear, uplift, lift up, heave, haul up, hike up, upraise …*They jacked up the car*…
2 = <u>increase</u>, raise, put up, augment, advance, boost, expand, add to, enhance, step up (*informal*), intensify, enlarge, escalate, inflate, amplify …*The company would have to jack up its prices*…

jaded 1 = <u>tired</u>, bored, weary, worn out, done in (*informal*), clapped out (*Brit., Austral., & N.Z. informal*), spent, drained, exhausted, shattered, dulled, fatigued, fed up, wearied, fagged (out) (*informal*), sapped, uninterested, listless, tired-out, enervated, zonked (*slang*), over-tired, ennuied …*We had both become jaded, disinterested and disillusioned*… OPPOSITE fresh
2 = <u>satiated</u>, sated, surfeited, cloyed, gorged, glutted …*scrumptious little things to tickle my jaded palate*…

jagged = <u>uneven</u>, pointed, craggy, broken, toothed, rough, ragged, ridged, spiked, notched, barbed, cleft, indented, serrated, snaggy, denticulate OPPOSITE rounded

jail *or* **gaol** NOUN = <u>prison</u>, penitentiary (*U.S.*), jailhouse (*Southern U.S.*), penal institution, can (*slang*), inside, cooler (*slang*), confinement, dungeon, clink (*slang*), glasshouse (*Military informal*), brig (*chiefly U.S.*), borstal, calaboose (*U.S. informal*), choky (*slang*), pound, nick (*Brit. slang*), stir (*slang*), jug (*slang*), slammer (*slang*), lockup, reformatory, quod (*slang*), poky *or* pokey (*U.S. & Canad. slang*), boob (*Austral. slang*) …*Three prisoners escaped from a jail*…
VERB = <u>imprison</u>, confine, detain, lock up, constrain, put away, intern, incarcerate, send down, send to prison, impound, put under lock and key, immure …*He was jailed for twenty years*…

jailbird *or* **gaolbird** = <u>prisoner</u>, convict, con (*slang*), lag (*slang*), trusty, felon, malefactor, ticket-of-leave man (*Historical*)

jailer *or* **gaoler** = <u>guard</u>, keeper, warden, screw (*slang*), captor, warder, turnkey (*archaic*)

jam NOUN **1** = <u>tailback</u>, queue, hold-up, bottleneck, snarl-up, line, chain, congestion, obstruction, stoppage, gridlock …*a nine-mile traffic jam*…
2 = <u>predicament</u>, tight spot, scrape (*informal*), corner, state, situation, trouble, spot (*informal*), hole (*slang*), fix (*informal*), bind, emergency, mess, dilemma, pinch, plight, strait, hot water, pickle (*informal*), deep water, quandary …*It could get the government out of a jam*…
VERB **1** = <u>pack</u>, force, press, stuff, squeeze, compact, ram, wedge, cram, compress …*He jammed his hands into his pockets*…
2 = <u>crowd</u>, cram, throng, crush, press, mass, surge, flock, swarm, congregate …*In summer, the beach is jammed with day-trippers*…
3 = <u>congest</u>, block, clog, stick, halt, stall, obstruct …*The phone lines are jammed. Everybody wants to talk about it*…

jamboree = <u>festival</u>, party, fête, celebration, blast (*U.S. slang*), rave (*Brit. slang*), carnival, spree, jubilee, festivity, beano (*Brit. slang*), merriment, revelry, carouse, rave-up (*Brit. slang*), carousal, frolic, hooley *or* hoolie (*chiefly Irish & N.Z.*)

jangle VERB = <u>rattle</u>, ring, clash, clatter, chime, ping, vibrate, jingle, ding, clank …*Her necklaces and bracelets jangled as she walked*…
NOUN = <u>clash</u>, clang, cacophony, reverberation, rattle, jar, racket, din, dissonance, clangour …*a jangle of bells*… OPPOSITE quiet

janitor = <u>caretaker</u>, porter, custodian, concierge, doorkeeper

jar¹ = <u>pot</u>, container, flask, receptacle, vessel, drum, vase, jug, pitcher, urn, crock, canister, repository, decanter, carafe, flagon …*We saved each season's harvest in clear glass jars*…

jar² 1 *usually with* **on** = <u>irritate</u>, grind, clash, annoy, offend, rattle, gall, nettle, jangle, irk, grate on, get on your nerves (*informal*), nark (*Brit., Austral., & N.Z. slang*), discompose …*The least bit of discord seemed to jar on his nerves*…
2 *sometimes with* **with** = <u>clash</u>, conflict, contrast, differ, disagree, interfere, contend, collide, oppose …*They had always been complementary and their temperaments seldom jarred*…
3 = <u>jolt</u>, rock, shake, disturb, bump, rattle, grate, agitate, vibrate, rasp, convulse …*The impact jarred his arm, right up to the shoulder*…

jargon = <u>parlance</u>, slang, idiom, patter, tongue, usage, dialect, cant, lingo (*informal*), patois, argot

jaundiced = <u>cynical</u>, bitter, hostile, prejudiced, biased, suspicious, partial, jealous, distorted, sceptical, resentful, envious, bigoted, spiteful, preconceived OPPOSITE optimistic

jaunt = <u>outing</u>, tour, trip, stroll, expedition, excursion, ramble, promenade, airing

jaunty = <u>sprightly</u>, buoyant, carefree, high-spirited, gay, smart, trim, lively, airy, spruce, breezy, perky, sparky, dapper, self-confident, showy OPPOSITE serious

jaw PLURAL NOUN = <u>opening</u>, gates, entrance, aperture, mouth, abyss, maw, orifice, ingress …*He opens the jaws of the furnace with the yank of a lever*… **VERB** (*Informal*) = talk, chat, rabbit (on) (*Brit. informal*), gossip, chatter, spout, babble, natter, schmooze (*slang*), shoot the breeze (*U.S. slang*), run off at the mouth (*slang*), chew the fat *or* rag (*slang*) …*jawing for half an hour with the very affable waiter*…

(Related Words)

technical names: maxilla (upper), mandible (lower)

jazzy = flashy, fancy, snazzy (*informal*), gaudy, wild, smart, lively

jealous 1 = suspicious, suspecting, guarded, protective, wary, doubtful, sceptical, attentive, anxious, apprehensive, vigilant, watchful, zealous, possessive, solicitous, distrustful, mistrustful, unbelieving …*She got insanely jealous and there was a terrible fight*… **OPPOSITE** trusting
2 = envious, grudging, resentful, begrudging, green, intolerant, green-eyed, invidious, green with envy, desirous, covetous, emulous …*I have never sought to make my readers jealous of my megastar lifestyle*… **OPPOSITE** satisfied

jealousy = suspicion, distrust, mistrust, possessiveness, doubt, spite, resentment, wariness, ill-will, dubiety

jeer VERB = mock, hector, deride, heckle, knock (*informal*), barrack, ridicule, taunt, sneer, scoff, banter, flout, gibe, cock a snook at (*Brit.*), contemn (*formal*) …*His motorcade was jeered by angry residents*… **OPPOSITE** cheer
NOUN = mockery, abuse, ridicule, taunt, sneer, hiss, boo, scoff, hoot, derision, gibe, catcall, obloquy, aspersion …*the heckling and jeers of his audience*… **OPPOSITE** applause

jeopardize = endanger, threaten, put at risk, put in jeopardy, risk, expose, gamble, hazard, menace, imperil, put on the line

jeopardy = danger, risk, peril, vulnerability, venture, exposure, liability, hazard, insecurity, pitfall, precariousness, endangerment

jerk VERB = jolt, bang, bump, lurch, shake …*The car jerked to a halt*…
NOUN = lurch, movement, thrust, twitch, jolt, throw …*He indicated the bedroom with a jerk of his head*…

jerky = bumpy, rough, jolting, jumpy, shaky, bouncy, uncontrolled, twitchy, fitful, spasmodic, convulsive, tremulous **OPPOSITE** smooth

jest NOUN = joke, play, crack (*slang*), sally, gag (*informal*), quip, josh (*slang, chiefly U.S. & Canad.*), banter, hoax, prank, wisecrack (*informal*), pleasantry, witticism, jape, bon mot …*It was a jest rather than a reproach*…
VERB = joke, kid (*informal*), mock, tease, sneer, jeer, quip, josh (*slang, chiefly U.S. & Canad.*), scoff, banter, deride, chaff, gibe …*He enjoyed drinking and jesting with his cronies*…

jester 1 = fool, clown, harlequin, zany, madcap, prankster, buffoon, pantaloon, mummer …*a chap dressed as a court jester*…

2 = humorist, comic, wit, comedian, wag, joker, dag (*N.Z. informal*), quipster, joculator *or* (*fem.*) joculatrix …*He is the class jester writ large*…

jet NOUN = stream, current, spring, flow, rush, flood, burst, spray, fountain, cascade, gush, spurt, spout, squirt …*benches equipped with water jets to massage your back and feet*…
VERB 1 = fly, wing, cruise, soar, zoom …*They spend a great deal of time jetting around the world*…
2 = stream, course, issue, shoot, flow, rush, surge, spill, gush, emanated, spout, spew, squirt …*a cloud of white smoke jetted out from the trees*…

jet-black NOUN *or* **ADJECTIVE** = black, jet, raven, ebony, sable, pitch-black, inky, coal-black
➤ shades of black to white

jet-setting = fashionable, rich, sophisticated, trendy (*Brit. informal*), cosmopolitan, well-off, high-society, ritzy (*slang*), trendsetting

jettison 1 = abandon, reject, desert, dump, shed, scrap, throw out, discard, throw away, relinquish, forsake, slough off, throw on the scrapheap …*The government seems to have jettisoned the plan*…
2 = expel, dump, unload, throw overboard, eject, heave …*The crew jettisoned excess fuel and made an emergency landing*…

jetty = pier, dock, wharf, mole, quay, breakwater, groyne

jewel 1 = gemstone, gem, precious stone, brilliant, ornament, trinket, sparkler (*informal*), rock (*slang*) …*a golden box containing precious jewels*…
2 = treasure, wonder, prize, darling, pearl, gem, paragon, pride and joy …*Barbados is a perfect jewel of an island*…

jewellery = jewels, treasure, gems, trinkets, precious stones, ornaments, finery, regalia

jibe *or* **gibe NOUN** = jeer, sneer, dig (*informal*), crack, taunt, snide remark …*a cruel jibe about her weight*…
VERB = jeer, mock, sneer, taunt …*'What's the matter, can't you read?' she jibed*…

jig = skip, bob, prance, jiggle, shake, bounce, twitch, wobble, caper, wiggle, jounce

jiggle 1 = shake, jerk, agitate, joggle …*He jiggled the doorknob noisily*…
2 = jerk, bounce, jog, fidget, shake, twitch, wiggle, jig, shimmy, joggle …*He tapped his feet, hummed tunes and jiggled about*…

jilt = reject, drop, disappoint, abandon, desert, ditch (*slang*), betray, discard, deceive, forsake, throw over, coquette, leave (someone) in the lurch

jingle VERB = ring, rattle, clatter, chime, jangle, tinkle, clink, clank, tintinnabulate …*Her bracelets jingled like bells*…
NOUN 1 = rattle, ringing, tinkle, clang, clink, reverberation, clangour …*the jingle of money in a man's pocket*…
2 = song, tune, melody, ditty, chorus, slogan, verse, limerick, refrain, doggerel …*advertising jingles*…

jinx NOUN = curse, plague, voodoo, nemesis, black magic, hoodoo (*informal*), hex (*U.S. & Canad. informal*), evil eye …*Someone had put a jinx on him*…

VERB = <u>curse</u>, bewitch, hex (*U.S. & Canad. informal*)
...*He's trying to rattle me, he said to himself, trying to jinx me so I can't succeed*...

jitters = <u>nerves</u>, anxiety, butterflies (in your stomach) (*informal*), nervousness, the shakes (*informal*), fidgets, cold feet (*informal*), the willies (*informal*), tenseness, heebie-jeebies (*slang*)

jittery = <u>nervous</u>, anxious, jumpy, twitchy (*informal*), wired (*slang*), trembling, shaky, neurotic, agitated, quivering, hyper (*informal*), fidgety, antsy (*informal*) OPPOSITE> calm

job 1 = <u>position</u>, post, function, capacity, work, posting, calling, place, business, office, trade, field, career, situation, activity, employment, appointment, craft, profession, occupation, placement, vocation, livelihood, métier ...*the pressure of being the first woman in the job*...
2 = <u>task</u>, concern, duty, charge, work, business, role, operation, affair, responsibility, function, contribution, venture, enterprise, undertaking, pursuit, assignment, stint, chore, errand ...*Their main job is to preserve health rather than treat illness*...

jobless = <u>unemployed</u>, redundant, out of work, on the dole (*Brit. informal*), inactive, out of a job, unoccupied, idle

jockey = <u>manoeuvre</u>, manage, engineer, negotiate, trim, manipulate, cajole, insinuate, wheedle, finagle (*informal*)

jog 1 = <u>run</u>, trot, canter, lope, dogtrot ...*He could scarcely jog around the block that first day*...
2 = <u>nudge</u>, push, shake, prod ...*Avoid jogging the camera*...
3 = <u>stimulate</u>, remind, prompt, stir, arouse, activate, nudge, prod ...*Keep a card file on the books you have read to jog your memory later*...

join 1 = <u>enrol in</u>, enter, sign up for, become a member of, enlist in ...*He joined the Army five years ago*...
2 = <u>connect</u>, unite, couple, link, marry, tie, combine, attach, knit, cement, adhere, fasten, annex, add, splice, yoke, append ...*The opened link is used to join the two ends of the chain*... OPPOSITE> detach
3 = <u>meet</u>, touch, border, extend, butt, adjoin, conjoin, reach ...*Allahabad, where the Ganges and the Yamuna rivers join*... OPPOSITE> part

joint ADJECTIVE = <u>shared</u>, mutual, collective, communal, united, joined, allied, combined, corporate, concerted, consolidated, cooperative, reciprocal, collaborative ...*They came to a joint decision as to where they would live*...
NOUN = <u>junction</u>, union, link, connection, knot, brace, bracket, seam, hinge, weld, linkage, intersection, node, articulation, nexus ...*Cut the stem just below a leaf joint*...
(*Related Words*)
adjective : articular

jointly = <u>collectively</u>, together, in conjunction, as one, in common, mutually, in partnership, in league, unitedly OPPOSITE> separately

joke NOUN **1** = <u>jest</u>, gag (*informal*), wisecrack (*informal*), witticism, crack (*informal*), sally, quip, josh

(*slang, chiefly U.S. & Canad.*), pun, quirk, one-liner (*informal*), jape ...*No one told worse jokes than Claus*...
2 = <u>laugh</u>, jest, fun, josh (*slang, chiefly U.S. & Canad.*), lark, sport, frolic, whimsy, jape ...*It was probably just a joke to them, but it wasn't funny to me*...
3 = <u>prank</u>, trick, practical joke, lark (*informal*), caper, frolic, escapade, antic, jape ...*I thought she was playing a joke on me at first but she wasn't*...
4 = <u>laughing stock</u>, butt, clown, buffoon, simpleton ...*That man is just a complete joke*...
VERB = <u>jest</u>, kid (*informal*), fool, mock, wind up (*Brit. slang*), tease, ridicule, taunt, quip, josh (*slang, chiefly U.S. & Canad.*), banter, deride, frolic, chaff, gambol, play the fool, play a trick ...*Don't get defensive, Charlie. I was only joking*...

joker = <u>comedian</u>, comic, wit, clown, wag, kidder (*informal*), jester, prankster, buffoon, trickster, humorist

jokey = <u>playful</u>, funny, amusing, teasing, humorous, mischievous, jesting, wisecracking, droll, facetious, waggish, prankish, nonserious OPPOSITE> humourless

jolly = <u>happy</u>, bright, funny, lively, hopeful, sunny, cheerful, merry, vibrant, hilarious, festive, upbeat (*informal*), bubbly, gay, airy, playful, exuberant, jubilant, cheery, good-humoured, joyous, joyful, carefree, breezy, genial, ebullient, chirpy (*informal*), sprightly, jovial, convivial, effervescent, frolicsome, ludic (*literary*), mirthful, sportive, light-hearted, jocund, gladsome (*archaic*), blithesome OPPOSITE> miserable

jolt VERB **1** = <u>jerk</u>, push, shake, knock, jar, shove, jog, jostle ...*The train jolted into motion*...
2 = <u>surprise</u>, upset, stun, disturb, astonish, stagger, startle, perturb, discompose ...*He was momentarily jolted by the news*...
NOUN **1** = <u>jerk</u>, start, jump, shake, bump, jar, jog, lurch, quiver ...*One tiny jolt could worsen her injuries*...
2 = <u>surprise</u>, blow, shock, setback, reversal, bombshell, thunderbolt, whammy (*informal, chiefly U.S.*), bolt from the blue ...*The campaign came at a time when America needed such a jolt*...

jostle = <u>push</u>, press, crowd, shake, squeeze, thrust, butt, elbow, bump, scramble, shove, jog, jolt, throng, hustle, joggle

jot VERB *usually with* **down** = <u>note down</u>, record, list, note, register, tally, scribble ...*Listen carefully to the instructions and jot them down*...
NOUN = <u>bit</u>, detail, ace, scrap, grain, particle, atom, fraction, trifle, mite, tad (*informal, chiefly U.S.*), speck, morsel, whit, tittle, iota, scintilla, smidgen *or* smidgin (*informal, chiefly U.S. & Canad.*) ...*It doesn't affect my judgement one jot*...

journal 1 = <u>magazine</u>, record, review, register, publication, bulletin, chronicle, gazette, periodical, zine (*informal*) ...*All our results are published in scientific journals*...
2 = <u>newspaper</u>, paper, daily, weekly, monthly, tabloid ...*He was a spokesperson for The New York Times and some other journals*...
3 = <u>diary</u>, record, history, log, notebook, chronicle,

annals, yearbook, commonplace book, daybook ...*On the plane he wrote in his journal...*

journalist = <u>reporter</u>, writer, correspondent, newsman *or* newswoman, stringer, commentator, broadcaster, hack (*derogatory*), columnist, contributor, scribe (*informal*), pressman, journo (*slang*), newshound (*informal*), newspaperman *or* newspaperwoman

journey NOUN **1** = <u>trip</u>, drive, tour, flight, excursion, progress, cruise, passage, trek, outing, expedition, voyage, ramble, jaunt, peregrination, travel ...*a journey from Manchester to Plymouth...*
2 = <u>progress</u>, passage, voyage, pilgrimage, odyssey ...*My films try to describe a journey of discovery...*
VERB = <u>travel</u>, go, move, walk, fly, range, cross, tour, progress, proceed, fare, wander, trek, voyage, roam, ramble, traverse, rove, wend, go walkabout (*Austral.*), peregrinate ...*She has journeyed on horseback through Africa and Turkey...*

joust VERB **1** = <u>compete</u>, fight, contend, vie, struggle, contest, strive, challenge ...*Lawyers joust in the courtroom...*
2 = <u>cross swords</u>, fight, engage, tilt, trade blows, enter the lists, break a lance ...*Knights joust on the field...*
NOUN = <u>duel</u>, match, lists, tournament, set-to, encounter, combat, engagement, tilt, tourney, passage of arms ...*an annual reconstruction of medieval jousts and banquets...*

jovial = <u>cheerful</u>, happy, jolly, animated, glad, merry, hilarious, buoyant, airy, jubilant, cheery, cordial, convivial, blithe, gay, mirthful, jocund, jocose
OPPOSITE > solemn

joy **1** = <u>delight</u>, pleasure, triumph, satisfaction, happiness, ecstasy, enjoyment, bliss, transport, euphoria, festivity, felicity, glee, exuberance, rapture, elation, exhilaration, radiance, gaiety, jubilation, hilarity, exaltation, ebullience, exultation, gladness, joyfulness, ravishment ...*Salter shouted with joy...*
OPPOSITE > sorrow
2 = <u>treasure</u>, wonder, treat, prize, delight, pride, charm, thrill ...*one of the joys of being a chef...*

joyful **1** = <u>pleasing</u>, satisfying, engaging, charming, delightful, enjoyable, gratifying, agreeable, pleasurable ...*Giving birth to a child is both painful and joyful...*
2 = <u>delighted</u>, happy, satisfied, glad, jolly, merry, gratified, pleased, jubilant, elated, over the moon (*informal*), jovial, rapt, enraptured, on cloud nine (*informal*), cock-a-hoop, floating on air, light-hearted, jocund, gladsome (*archaic*), blithesome ...*We're a very joyful people...*

joyless = <u>unhappy</u>, sad, depressing, miserable, gloomy, dismal, dreary, dejected, dispirited, downcast, down in the dumps (*informal*), cheerless

joyous = <u>joyful</u>, cheerful, merry, festive, heartening, rapturous, blithe

jubilant = <u>overjoyed</u>, excited, thrilled, glad, triumphant, rejoicing, exuberant, joyous, elated, over the moon (*informal*), euphoric, triumphal, enraptured, exultant, cock-a-hoop, rhapsodic OPPOSITE > downcast

jubilation = <u>joy</u>, triumph, celebration, excitement, ecstasy, jubilee, festivity, elation, jamboree, exultation

jubilee = <u>celebration</u>, holiday, fête, festival, carnival, festivity, gala

Judaism

Jewish denominations and sects
http://www.bbc.co.uk/religion/religions/judaism/
Chassidism, Chasidism, Hassidism, *or* Hasidism
Conservative Judaism
Liberal Judaism
Orthodox Judaism
Reform Judaism
Zionism

judge NOUN **1** = <u>magistrate</u>, justice, beak (*Brit. slang*), His, Her *or* Your Honour ...*The judge adjourned the hearing until next Tuesday...*
2 = <u>referee</u>, expert, specialist, umpire, mediator, examiner, connoisseur, assessor, arbiter, appraiser, arbitrator, moderator, adjudicator, evaluator, authority ...*A panel of judges is now selecting the finalists...*
3 = <u>critic</u>, assessor, arbiter, appraiser, evaluator ...*I'm a pretty good judge of character...*
VERB **1** = <u>adjudicate</u>, referee, umpire, mediate, officiate, adjudge, arbitrate ...*Entries will be judged in two age categories...*
2 = <u>evaluate</u>, rate, consider, appreciate, view, class, value, review, rank, examine, esteem, criticize, ascertain, surmise ...*It will take a few more years to judge the impact of these ideas...*
3 = <u>estimate</u>, guess, assess, calculate, evaluate, gauge, appraise ...*It is important to judge the weight of your washing load...*
4 = <u>find</u>, rule, pass, pronounce, decree, adjudge ...*He was judged guilty and burned at the stake...*

(*Related Words*)
adjective: judicial

judgment **1** = <u>opinion</u>, view, estimate, belief, assessment, conviction, diagnosis, valuation, deduction, appraisal ...*In your judgement, what has changed over the past few years?...*
2 = <u>verdict</u>, finding, result, ruling, decision, sentence, conclusion, determination, decree, order, arbitration, adjudication, pronouncement ...*The Court is expected to give its judgement within the next ten days...*
3 = <u>sense</u>, common sense, good sense, judiciousness, reason, understanding, taste, intelligence, smarts (*slang, chiefly U.S.*), discrimination, perception, awareness, wisdom, wit, penetration, prudence, sharpness, acumen, shrewdness, discernment, perspicacity, sagacity, astuteness, percipience ...*Publication of the information was a serious error in judgement...*

judgmental = <u>condemnatory</u>, self-righteous, censorious, pharisaic, critical

judicial = <u>legal</u>, official, judiciary, juridical

judicious = <u>sensible</u>, considered, reasonable, discerning, sound, politic, acute, informed, diplomatic, careful, wise, cautious, rational, sober, discriminating, thoughtful, discreet, sage, enlightened, shrewd, prudent, sane, skilful, astute, expedient, circumspect, well-advised, well-judged, sagacious, sapient OPPOSITE injudicious

jug = container, pitcher, urn, carafe, creamer (*U.S. & Canad.*), vessel, jar, crock, ewer

juggle = manipulate, change, doctor (*informal*), fix (*informal*), alter, modify, disguise, manoeuvre, tamper with, misrepresent, falsify

juice 1 = liquid, extract, fluid, liquor, sap, nectar ...*the juice of about six lemons...*
2 = secretion, serum ...*the digestive juices of the human intestinal tract...*

juicy 1 = moist, lush, watery, succulent, sappy ...*a thick, juicy steak...*
2 (*Informal*) = interesting, colourful, sensational, vivid, provocative, spicy (*informal*), suggestive, racy, risqué ...*It provided some juicy gossip for a few days...*

jumble NOUN – muddle, mixture, mess, disorder, confusion, chaos, litter, clutter, disarray, medley, mélange (*French*), miscellany, mishmash, farrago, hotchpotch (*U.S.*), hodgepodge, gallimaufry, pig's breakfast (*informal*), disarrangement ...*a meaningless jumble of words...*
VERB = mix, mistake, confuse, disorder, shuffle, tangle, muddle, confound, entangle, ravel, disorganize, disarrange, dishevel ...*animals whose remains were jumbled together by scavengers and floods...*

jumbo = giant, large, huge, immense, mega (*informal*), gigantic, oversized, elephantine, ginormous (*informal*), humongous *or* humungous (*U.S. slang*) OPPOSITE tiny

jump VERB **1** = leap, dance, spring, bound, bounce, hop, skip, caper, prance, gambol ...*stamping their boots and jumping up and down to knock the snow off...*
2 = vault, clear, hurdle, go over, sail over, hop over ...*He jumped the first fence beautifully...*
3 = spring, bound, leap, bounce ...*She jumped to her feet and ran downstairs...*
4 = recoil, start, jolt, flinch, shake, jerk, quake, shudder, twitch, wince ...*The phone shrilled, making her jump...*
5 = increase, rise, climb, escalate, gain, advance, boost, mount, soar, surge, spiral, hike, ascend ...*The number of crimes jumped by ten per cent last year...*
6 = miss, avoid, skip, omit, evade, digress ...*He refused to jump the queue for treatment at the local hospital...*
NOUN **1** = leap, spring, skip, bound, buck, hop, vault, caper ...*With a few hops and a jump they launched themselves into the air...*
2 = rise, increase, escalation, upswing, advance, boost, elevation, upsurge, upturn, increment, augmentation ...*an eleven per cent jump in profits...*
3 = jolt, start, movement, shock, shake, jar, jerk, lurch, twitch, swerve, spasm ...*When Spider tapped on the window, Miguel gave an involuntary jump...*
4 = hurdle, gate, barrier, fence, obstacle, barricade, rail ...*Hurdlers need to have unnaturally over-flexible knees to clear the jump...*

jumped-up = conceited, arrogant, pompous, stuck-up, cocky, overbearing, puffed up, presumptuous, insolent, immodest, toffee-nosed, self-opinionated, too big for your boots *or* breeches

jumper = sweater, top, jersey, cardigan, woolly, pullover

jumpy = nervous, anxious, tense, shaky, restless, neurotic, agitated, hyper (*informal*), apprehensive, jittery (*informal*), on edge, twitchy (*informal*), fidgety, timorous, antsy (*informal*), wired (*slang*) OPPOSITE calm

juncture = moment, time, point, crisis, occasion, emergency, strait, contingency, predicament, crux, exigency, conjuncture

junior 1 = minor, lower, secondary, lesser, subordinate, inferior ...*a junior minister attached to the prime minister's office...*
2 = younger ...*junior pupils...* OPPOSITE senior

junk = rubbish, refuse, waste, scrap, litter, debris, crap (*slang*), garbage (*chiefly U.S.*), trash, clutter, rummage, dross, odds and ends, oddments, flotsam and jetsam, leavings, dreck (*slang, chiefly U.S.*)

junkie *or* **junky** = addict, user, drug addict, druggie (*informal*), head (*slang*), freak (*informal*), mainliner (*slang*), smackhead (*slang*), pill-popper (*slang*), pothead (*slang*), cokehead (*slang*), acidhead (*slang*), hashhead (*slang*), weedhead (*slang*)

junta = cabal, council, faction, league, set, party, ring, camp, crew, combination, assembly, gang, clique, coterie, schism, confederacy, convocation

jurisdiction 1 = authority, say, power, control, rule, influence, command, sway, dominion, prerogative, mana (*N.Z.*) ...*The British police have no jurisdiction over foreign bank accounts...*
2 = range, area, field, district, bounds, zone, province, circuit, scope, orbit, sphere, compass, dominion ...*matters which lie within his own jurisdiction...*

just ADVERB **1** = recently, lately, only now ...*The two had only just met...*
2 = merely, but, only, simply, solely, no more than, nothing but ...*It's just a suggestion...*
3 = barely, hardly, only just, scarcely, at most, by a whisker, at a push, by the skin of your teeth ...*He could just reach the man's head with his right hand...*
4 = exactly, really, quite, completely, totally, perfectly, entirely, truly, absolutely, precisely, altogether, positively ...*Kiwi fruit are just the thing for a healthy snack...*
ADJECTIVE **1** = fair, good, legitimate, honourable, right, square, pure, decent, upright, honest, equitable, righteous, conscientious, impartial, virtuous, lawful, blameless, unbiased, fair-minded, unprejudiced ...*She fought honestly for a just cause and for freedom...* OPPOSITE unfair
2 = fitting, due, correct, deserved, appropriate, justified, reasonable, suitable, decent, sensible, merited, proper, legitimate, desirable, apt, rightful, well-deserved, condign ...*This cup final is a just reward for all the efforts they have put in...* OPPOSITE inappropriate

PHRASES **just about** = <u>practically</u>, almost, nearly, close to, virtually, all but, not quite, well-nigh ...*He is just about the best golfer in the world*...

> ### *Word Power*
>
> **just** – The expression *just exactly* is considered to be poor style because, since both words mean the same thing, only one or the other is needed. Use *just – it's just what they want –* or *exactly – it's exactly what they want*, but not both together.

justice 1 = <u>fairness</u>, equity, integrity, honesty, decency, impartiality, rectitude, reasonableness, uprightness, justness, rightfulness, right ...*There is no justice in this world!*... OPPOSITE injustice
2 = <u>justness</u>, fairness, legitimacy, reasonableness, right, integrity, honesty, legality, rectitude, rightfulness ...*We must win people round to the justice of our cause*...
3 = <u>judge</u>, magistrate, beak (*Brit. slang*), His, Her *or* Your Honour ...*a justice on the Supreme Court*...

justifiable = <u>reasonable</u>, right, sound, fit, acceptable, sensible, proper, valid, legitimate, understandable, lawful, well-founded, defensible, tenable, excusable, warrantable, vindicable OPPOSITE indefensible

justification = <u>reason</u>, grounds, defence, basis, excuse, approval, plea, warrant, apology, rationale, vindication, rationalization, absolution, exoneration, explanation, exculpation, extenuation

justify = <u>explain</u>, support, warrant, bear out, legitimize, establish, maintain, confirm, defend, approve, excuse, sustain, uphold, acquit, vindicate, validate, substantiate, exonerate, legalize, absolve, exculpate

justly = <u>justifiably</u>, rightly, correctly, properly, legitimately, rightfully, with good reason, lawfully

jut = <u>stick out</u>, project, extend, protrude, poke, bulge, overhang, impend

juvenile NOUN = <u>child</u>, youth, minor, girl, boy, teenager, infant, adolescent ...*The number of juveniles in the general population has fallen*... OPPOSITE adult
ADJECTIVE 1 = <u>young</u>, junior, adolescent, youthful, immature ...*a scheme to lock up persistent juvenile offenders*... OPPOSITE adult
2 = <u>immature</u>, childish, infantile, puerile, young, youthful, inexperienced, boyish, callow, undeveloped, unsophisticated, girlish, babyish, jejune ...*As he gets older he becomes more juvenile*...

juxtaposition = <u>proximity</u>, adjacency, contact, closeness, vicinity, nearness, contiguity, propinquity

K k

kai (*N.Z. informal*) = <u>food</u>, grub (*slang*), provisions, fare, board, commons, eats (*slang*), feed, diet, meat, bread, tuck (*informal*), tucker (*Austral. & N.Z. informal*), rations, nutrition, tack (*informal*), refreshment, scoff (*slang*), nibbles, foodstuffs, nourishment, chow (*informal*), sustenance, nosh (*slang*), daily bread, victuals, edibles, comestibles, provender, nosebag (*slang*), pabulum (*rare*), nutriment, vittles (*obsolete or dialect*), viands, aliment, eatables (*slang*)

kak (*S. African taboo*) **1** = <u>faeces</u>, excrement, stool, muck, manure, dung, droppings, waste matter ...*His shoes were covered in kak*...
2 = <u>rubbish</u>, nonsense, garbage (*informal*), rot, crap (*taboo slang*), drivel, tripe (*informal*), claptrap (*informal*), poppycock (*informal*), pants, bizzo (*Austral. slang*), bull's wool (*Austral. & N.Z. slang*) ...*Now you're just talking kak*...

kaleidoscopic 1 = <u>many-coloured</u>, multi-coloured, harlequin, psychedelic, motley, variegated, prismatic, varicoloured ...*a kaleidoscopic set of bright images*...
2 = <u>changeable</u>, shifting, varied, mobile, variable, fluid, uncertain, volatile, unpredictable, unstable, fluctuating, indefinite, unsteady, protean, mutable, impermanent, inconstant ...*a kaleidoscopic world of complex relationships*...
3 = <u>complicated</u>, complex, confused, confusing, disordered, puzzling, unclear, baffling, bewildering, chaotic, muddled, intricate, jumbled, convoluted, disorganized, disarranged ...*a kaleidoscopic and fractured view of Los Angeles*...

kamikaze = <u>self-destructive</u>, suicidal, foolhardy

keel over 1 = <u>collapse</u>, faint, pass out, black out (*informal*), swoon (*literary*) ...*He keeled over and fell flat on his back*...
2 = <u>capsize</u>, list, upset, founder, overturn, turn over, lean over, tip over, topple over, turn turtle ...*The vessel keeled over towards the murky water*...

keen¹ 1 = <u>eager</u>, earnest, spirited, devoted, intense, fierce, enthusiastic, passionate, ardent, avid, fervent, impassioned, zealous, ebullient, wholehearted, fervid, bright-eyed and bushy-tailed (*informal*) ...*a keen amateur photographer*... OPPOSITE unenthusiastic
2 = <u>earnest</u>, fierce, intense, vehement, burning, flaming, consuming, eager, passionate, heightened, energetic, ardent, fanatical, fervent, impassioned, fervid ...*his keen sense of loyalty*...
3 = <u>sharp</u>, satirical, incisive, trenchant, pointed, cutting, biting, edged, acute, acid, stinging, piercing, penetrating, searing, tart, withering, scathing, pungent, sarcastic, sardonic, caustic, astringent, vitriolic, acerbic, mordant, razor-like, finely honed ...*a keen sense of humour*... OPPOSITE dull
4 = <u>perceptive</u>, quick, sharp, brilliant, acute, smart, wise, clever, subtle, piercing, penetrating, discriminating, shrewd, discerning, ingenious, astute, intuitive, canny, incisive, insightful, observant, perspicacious, sapient ...*a man of keen intellect*... OPPOSITE obtuse
5 = <u>penetrating</u>, clear, powerful, sharp, acute, sensitive, piercing, discerning, perceptive, observant ...*a keen eye for detail*...
6 = <u>intense</u>, strong, fierce, relentless, cut-throat ...*Competition is keen for these awards*...

keen² = <u>lament</u>, cry, weep, sob, mourn, grieve, howl, sorrow, wail, whine, whimper, bewail ...*He tossed back his head and keened*...

keep¹ VERB **1** *usually with* ***from*** = <u>prevent</u>, hold back, deter, inhibit, block, stall, restrain, hamstring, hamper, withhold, hinder, retard, impede, shackle, keep back ...*Embarrassment has kept me from doing all sorts of things*...
2 *sometimes with* ***on*** = <u>continue</u>, go on, carry on, persist in, persevere in, remain ...*I turned back after a while, but he kept walking*...
3 = <u>hold on to</u>, maintain, retain, keep possession of, save, preserve, nurture, cherish, conserve ...*We want to keep as many players as we can*... OPPOSITE lose
4 = <u>store</u>, put, place, house, hold, deposit, pile, stack, heap, amass, stow ...*She kept her money under the mattress*...
5 = <u>carry</u>, stock, have, hold, sell, supply, handle, trade in, deal in ...*The shop keeps specialised books on various aspects of the collection*...
6 = <u>comply with</u>, carry out, honour, fulfil, hold, follow, mind, respect, observe, respond to, embrace, execute, obey, heed, conform to, adhere to, abide by, act upon ...*I'm hoping you'll keep your promise to come for a long visit*... OPPOSITE disregard
7 = <u>support</u>, maintain, sustain, provide for, mind, fund, board, finance, feed, look after, foster, shelter, care for, take care of, nurture, safeguard, cherish, nourish, subsidize ...*She could just about afford to keep her five kids*...
8 = <u>raise</u>, own, maintain, tend, farm, breed, look after, rear, care for, bring up, nurture, nourish ...*This mad writer kept a lobster as a pet*...
9 = <u>manage</u>, run, administer, be in charge (of), rule, direct, handle, govern, oversee, supervise, preside over, superintend ...*His father kept a village shop*...
10 = <u>delay</u>, detain, hinder, impede, stop, limit, check, arrest, curb, constrain, obstruct, retard, set back ...*'Sorry to keep you, Jack.'*... OPPOSITE release
11 = <u>associate with</u>, mix with, mingle with, hang out with (*informal*), hang with (*informal, chiefly U.S.*), be friends with, consort with, run around with (*informal*), hobnob with, socialize with, hang about with, fraternize with ...*I don't like the company you keep*...
NOUN = <u>board</u>, food, maintenance, upkeep, means,

living, support, nurture, livelihood, subsistence, kai (*N.Z. informal*), nourishment, sustenance ...*I need to give my parents money for my keep...*

PHRASES keep at it = <u>persist with it</u>, continue, carry on, keep going, stick with it, stay with it, be steadfast, grind it out, persevere with it, remain with it ...*'Keep at it!' Thade encouraged me...* ◆ **keep something back 1** = <u>hold back</u>, hold, save, set aside, husband, store, retain, preserve, hang on to, conserve, stockpile, hoard, lay up, put by ...*Roughly chop the vegetables, and keep back a few for decoration...* **2** = <u>suppress</u>, hide, reserve, conceal, restrain, cover up, withhold, stifle, censor, repress, smother, muffle, muzzle, keep something under your hat ...*Neither of them is telling the whole truth. They're both keeping something back...* **3** = <u>restrain</u>, control, limit, check, delay, restrict, curb, prohibit, withhold, hold back, constrain, retard, keep a tight rein on ...*I can no longer keep back my tears...* ◆ **keep something up 1** = <u>continue</u>, make, maintain, carry on, persist in, persevere with ...*They can no longer keep up the repayments...* **2** = <u>maintain</u>, sustain, uphold, perpetuate, retain, preserve, prolong ...*keeping up the pressure against the government...* ◆ **keep up** = <u>keep pace</u>, match, compete, contend, emulate, persevere ...*Things are changing so fast, it's hard to keep up...*

keep² = <u>tower</u>, castle, stronghold, dungeon, citadel, fastness, donjon ...*the parts of the keep open to visitors...*

keeper = <u>curator</u>, guardian, steward, superintendent, attendant, caretaker, overseer, preserver ...*the keeper of the library at the V&A...*

keeping **NOUN** = <u>care</u>, keep, charge, trust, protection, possession, maintenance, custody, patronage, guardianship, safekeeping ...*It has been handed over for safe keeping...*

PHRASES in keeping with = <u>in agreement with</u>, consistent with, in harmony with, in accord with, in compliance with, in conformity with, in balance with, in correspondence with, in proportion with, in congruity with, in observance with ...*His office was in keeping with his station and experience...*

keepsake = <u>souvenir</u>, symbol, token, reminder, relic, remembrance, emblem, memento, favour

keg = <u>barrel</u>, drum, vat, cask, firkin, tun, hogshead

ken

PHRASES beyond someone's ken = <u>beyond the knowledge of</u>, beyond the comprehension of, beyond the understanding of, beyond the acquaintance of, beyond the awareness of, beyond the cognizance of ...*beyond the ken of the average layman...*

kernel = <u>essence</u>, core, substance, gist, grain, marrow, germ, nub, pith

key **NOUN 1** = <u>opener</u>, door key, latchkey ...*She reached for her coat and car keys...*
2 = <u>answer</u>, means, secret, solution, path, formula, passage, clue, cue, pointer, sign ...*The key to success is to be ready from the start...*
ADJECTIVE = <u>essential</u>, leading, major, main, important,

chief, necessary, basic, vital, crucial, principal, fundamental, decisive, indispensable, pivotal ...*He is expected to be the key witness at the trial...* **OPPOSITE** minor

keynote = <u>heart</u>, centre, theme, core, substance, essence, marrow, kernel, gist, pith

keystone = <u>basis</u>, principle, core, crux, ground, source, spring, root, motive, cornerstone, lynchpin, mainspring, fundament, quoin

kia ora (*N.Z.*) = <u>hello</u>, hi (*informal*), greetings, gidday or g'day (*Austral. & N.Z.*), how do you do?, good morning, good evening, good afternoon, welcome

kick **VERB 1** = <u>boot</u>, strike, knock, punt, put the boot in(to) (*slang*) ...*The fiery actress kicked him in the shins...*
2 (*Informal*) = <u>give up</u>, break, stop, abandon, quit, cease, eschew, leave off, desist from, end ...*She's kicked her drug habit...*
NOUN 1 (*Informal*) = <u>thrill</u>, glow, buzz (*slang*), tingle, high (*slang*), sensation ...*I got a kick out of seeing my name in print...*
2 (*Informal*) = <u>pungency</u>, force, power, edge, strength, snap (*informal*), punch, intensity, pep, sparkle, vitality, verve, zest, potency, tang, piquancy ...*The coffee had more of a kick than it seemed on first tasting...*
PHRASES kick off (*Informal*) = <u>begin</u>, start, open, commence, launch, initiate, get under way, kick-start, get on the road ...*The shows kick off on October 24th...* ◆ **kick someone out** (*Informal*) = <u>dismiss</u>, remove, reject, get rid of, discharge, expel, oust, eject, evict, toss out, give the boot (*slang*), sack (*informal*), kiss off (*slang, chiefly U.S. & Canad.*), give (someone) their marching orders, give the push, give the bum's rush (*slang*), show you the door, throw you out on your ear (*informal*) ...*They kicked five foreign journalists out of the country...*

kickback = <u>bribe</u>, payoff, backhander (*slang*), enticement, share, cut (*informal*), payment, gift, reward, incentive, graft (*informal*), sweetener (*slang*), inducement, sop, recompense, hush money (*slang*), payola (*informal*), allurement

kick-off (*Informal*) = <u>start</u>, opening, beginning, commencement, outset, starting point, inception

kid¹ (*Informal*) = <u>child</u>, girl, boy, baby, lad, teenager, youngster, infant, adolescent, juvenile, toddler, tot, lass, wean, little one, bairn, stripling, sprog (*slang*), munchkin (*informal, chiefly U.S.*), rug rat (*U.S. & Canad. informal*), littlie (*Austral. informal*), ankle-biter (*Austral. slang*), tacker (*Austral. slang*) ...*All the kids in my class could read...*

kid² = <u>tease</u>, joke, trick, fool, pretend, mock, rag (*Brit.*), wind up (*Brit. slang*), ridicule, hoax, beguile, gull (*archaic*), delude, jest, bamboozle, hoodwink, cozen ...*I'm just kidding...*

kidnap = <u>abduct</u>, remove, steal, capture, seize, snatch (*slang*), hijack, run off with, run away with, make off with, hold to ransom

kill 1 = <u>slay</u>, murder, execute, slaughter, destroy, waste (*informal*), do in (*slang*), take out (*slang*), massacre, butcher, wipe out (*informal*), dispatch, cut down,

erase, assassinate, eradicate, whack (*informal*), do away with, blow away (*slang, chiefly U.S.*), obliterate, knock off (*slang*), liquidate, decimate, annihilate, neutralize, exterminate, croak, mow down, take (someone's) life, bump off (*slang*), extirpate, wipe from the face of the earth (*informal*) ...*More than 1,000 people have been killed by the armed forces...*
2 (*Informal*) = <u>destroy</u>, defeat, crush, scotch, still, stop, total (*slang*), ruin, halt, cancel, wreck, shatter, veto, suppress, dismantle, stifle, trash (*slang*), ravage, eradicate, smother, quash, quell, extinguish, annihilate, put paid to ...*Public opinion may yet kill the proposal...*

killer = <u>murderer</u>, slaughterer, slayer, hit man (*slang*), butcher, gunman, assassin, destroyer, liquidator, terminator, executioner, exterminator

killing NOUN = <u>murder</u>, massacre, slaughter, execution, dispatch, manslaughter, elimination, slaying, homicide, bloodshed, carnage, fatality, liquidation, extermination, annihilation, eradication, butchery, necktie party (*informal*) ...*This is a brutal killing...*
ADJECTIVE **1** (*Informal*) = <u>tiring</u>, hard, testing, taxing, difficult, draining, exhausting, punishing, crippling, fatiguing, gruelling, sapping, debilitating, strenuous, arduous, laborious, enervating, backbreaking ...*He covered the last 300 metres in around 41sec, a killing pace...*
2 = <u>deadly</u>, deathly, dangerous, fatal, destructive, lethal, mortal, murderous, death-dealing ...*Diphtheria was a killing disease...*
PHRASES **make a killing** (*Informal*) = <u>profit</u>, gain, clean up (*informal*), be lucky, be successful, make a fortune, strike it rich (*informal*), make a bomb (*slang*), rake it in (*informal*), had a windfall ...*They have made a killing on the deal...*

killjoy = <u>spoilsport</u>, dampener, damper, wet blanket (*informal*)

kin = <u>family</u>, people, relations, relatives, connections, kindred, kinsmen, kith, kinsfolk

kind¹ 1 = <u>class</u>, sort, type, variety, brand, grade, category, genre, classification, league ...*They developed a new kind of film-making...*
2 = <u>sort</u>, set, type, ilk, family, race, species, breed, genus ...*I hate Lewis and his kind just as much as you do...*
3 = <u>nature</u>, sort, type, manner, style, quality, character, make-up, habit, stamp, description, mould, essence, temperament, persuasion, calibre, disposition ...*Donations came in from all kinds of people...*

> ## *Word Power*
>
> **kind** – It is common in informal speech to combine singular and plural in sentences like *children enjoy those kind of stories*. However, this is not acceptable in careful writing, where the plural must be used consistently: *children enjoy those kinds of stories*.

kind² = <u>considerate</u>, good, loving, kindly, understanding, concerned, friendly, neighbourly,
gentle, generous, mild, obliging, sympathetic, charitable, thoughtful, benign, humane, affectionate, compassionate, clement, gracious, indulgent, benevolent, attentive, amiable, courteous, amicable, lenient, cordial, congenial, philanthropic, unselfish, propitious, beneficent, kind-hearted, bounteous, tender-hearted ...*He was a very kind man, full of common sense...* OPPOSITE unkind

kind-hearted = <u>sympathetic</u>, kind, generous, helpful, tender, humane, compassionate, gracious, amicable, considerate, altruistic, good-natured, tender-hearted OPPOSITE hard-hearted

kindle 1 = <u>arouse</u>, excite, inspire, stir, thrill, stimulate, provoke, induce, awaken, animate, rouse, sharpen, inflame, incite, foment, bestir, enkindle ...*These poems have helped kindle the imagination of generations of children...*
2 = <u>light</u>, start, ignite, fire, spark, torch, inflame, set fire to, set a match to ...*I came in and kindled a fire in the stove...* OPPOSITE extinguish

kindly ADJECTIVE = <u>benevolent</u>, kind, caring, nice, warm, gentle, helpful, pleasant, mild, sympathetic, beneficial, polite, favourable, benign, humane, compassionate, hearty, cordial, considerate, genial, affable, good-natured, beneficent, well-disposed, kind-hearted, warm-hearted ...*He was a stern critic but an extremely kindly man...* OPPOSITE cruel
ADVERB = <u>benevolently</u>, politely, generously, thoughtfully, tenderly, lovingly, cordially, affectionately, helpfully, graciously, obligingly, agreeably, indulgently, selflessly, unselfishly, compassionately, considerately ...*He kindly carried our picnic in a rucksack...* OPPOSITE unkindly

kindness 1 = <u>goodwill</u>, understanding, charity, grace, humanity, affection, patience, tolerance, goodness, compassion, hospitality, generosity, indulgence, decency, tenderness, clemency, gentleness, philanthropy, benevolence, magnanimity, fellow-feeling, amiability, beneficence, kindliness ...*We have been treated with such kindness by everybody...* OPPOSITE malice
2 = <u>good deed</u>, help, service, aid, favour, assistance, bounty, benefaction ...*It would be a kindness to leave her alone...*

kindred NOUN = <u>family</u>, relations, relatives, connections, flesh, kin, lineage, kinsmen, kinsfolk ...*The offender made proper restitution to the victim's kindred...*
ADJECTIVE **1** = <u>similar</u>, like, related, allied, corresponding, affiliated, akin, kin, cognate, matching ...*I recall discussions with her on these and kindred topics...*
2 = <u>like-minded</u>, compatible, understanding, similar, friendly, sympathetic, responsive, agreeable, in tune, congenial, like, companionable ...*We're sort of kindred spirits...*

king = <u>ruler</u>, monarch, sovereign, crowned head, leader, lord, prince, Crown, emperor, majesty, head of state, consort, His Majesty, overlord
(*Related Words*)
adjectives: royal, regal, monarchical

kingdom 1 = <u>country</u>, state, nation, land, division, territory, province, empire, commonwealth, realm, domain, tract, dominion, sovereign state ...*the Kingdom of Denmark...*
2 = <u>domain</u>, territory, province, realm, area, department, field, zone, arena, sphere ...*nature study trips to the kingdom of the polar bear...*

kink 1 = <u>twist</u>, bend, wrinkle, knot, tangle, coil, corkscrew, entanglement, crimp, frizz ...*a tiny black kitten with tufted ears and a kink in her tail...*
2 = <u>quirk</u>, eccentricity, foible, idiosyncrasy, whim, fetish, vagary, singularity, crotchet ...*What kink did he have in his character?...*
3 = <u>flaw</u>, difficulty, defect, complication, tangle, knot, hitch, imperfection ...*working out the kinks of a potential trade agreement...*

kinky 1 (*Slang*) = <u>perverted</u>, warped, deviant, unnatural, degenerated, unsavoury, unhealthy, depraved, licentious, pervy (*slang*) ...*engaging in some kind of kinky sexual activity...*
2 (*Slang*) = <u>weird</u>, odd, strange, bizarre, peculiar, eccentric, queer, quirky, unconventional, off-the-wall (*slang*), outlandish, oddball (*informal*), wacko (*slang*), outré ...*kinky behaviour...*
3 = <u>twisted</u>, curled, curly, frizzy, tangled, coiled, crimped, frizzled ...*He had red kinky hair...*

kinship 1 = <u>relationship</u>, kin, family ties, consanguinity, ties of blood, blood relationship ...*the ties of kinship...*
2 = <u>similarity</u>, relationship, association, bearing, connection, alliance, correspondence, affinity ...*She evidently felt a sense of kinship with the woman...*

kinsman *or* **kinswoman** = <u>relative</u>, relation, blood relative, fellow tribesman, fellow clansman

kiosk = <u>booth</u>, stand, counter, stall, newsstand, bookstall

kiss VERB 1 = <u>peck</u> (*informal*), osculate, snog (*Brit. slang*), neck (*informal*), smooch (*informal*), canoodle (*slang*) ...*She kissed me hard on the mouth...*
2 = <u>brush</u>, touch, shave, scrape, graze, caress, glance off, stroke ...*The wheels of the aircraft kissed the runway...*
NOUN = <u>peck</u> (*informal*), snog (*Brit. slang*), smacker (*slang*), smooch (*informal*), French kiss, osculation ...*I put my arms around her and gave her a kiss...*

kit NOUN 1 = <u>equipment</u>, supplies, materials, tackle, tools, instruments, provisions, implements, rig, apparatus, trappings, utensils, paraphernalia, accoutrements, appurtenances ...*The kit consisted of about twenty cosmetic items...*
2 = <u>gear</u>, things, effects, dress, clothes, clothing, stuff, equipment, uniform, outfit, rig, costume, garments, baggage, equipage ...*I forgot my gym kit...*
PHRASES **kit something** *or* **someone out** *or* **up** = <u>equip</u>, fit, supply, provide with, arm, stock, outfit, costume, furnish, fix up, fit out, deck out, accoutre ...*kitted out with winter coat, skirts, jumpers, nylon stockings...*

kitchen = <u>cookhouse</u>, galley, kitchenette, scullery

knack = <u>skill</u>, art, ability, facility, talent, gift, capacity, trick, bent, craft, genius, expertise, forte, flair, competence, ingenuity, propensity, aptitude, dexterity, cleverness, quickness, adroitness, expertness, handiness, skilfulness OPPOSITE> ineptitude

knackered (*Brit. slang*) 1 = <u>exhausted</u>, worn out, tired out, drained, beat (*slang*), done in (*informal*), all in (*slang*), debilitated, prostrated, enervated, ready to drop, dog-tired (*informal*), zonked (*slang*), dead tired, dead beat (*slang*) ...*I was absolutely knackered at the end of the match...*
2 = <u>broken</u>, not working, out of order, not functioning, done in (*informal*), ruined, worn out, on the blink (*slang*), on its last legs ...*My tape player's knackered...*

knavish (*Old-fashioned*) = <u>dishonest</u>, tricky, fraudulent, deceptive, unscrupulous, rascally, scoundrelly, deceitful, villainous, unprincipled, dishonourable, roguish OPPOSITE> honourable

knead = <u>squeeze</u>, work, massage, manipulate, form, press, shape, stroke, blend, rub, mould

kneel = <u>genuflect</u>, bow, stoop, curtsy *or* curtsey, bow down, kowtow, get down on your knees, make obeisance

knell = <u>ring</u>, sound, toll, chime, clang, peal

knickers = <u>underwear</u>, smalls, briefs, drawers, panties, bloomers

knife NOUN = <u>blade</u>, carver, cutter, cutting tool ...*a knife and fork...*
VERB = <u>cut</u>, wound, stab, slash, thrust, gore, pierce, spear, jab, bayonet, impale, lacerate ...*She was knifed in the back six times...*

knit 1 = <u>join</u>, unite, link, tie, bond, ally, combine, secure, bind, connect, merge, weave, fasten, meld ...*Sport knits the whole family close together...*
2 = <u>heal</u>, unite, join, link, bind, connect, loop, mend, fasten, intertwine, interlace ...*broken bones that have failed to knit...*
3 = <u>furrow</u>, tighten, knot, wrinkle, crease, screw up, pucker, scrunch up ...*They knitted their brows and started to grumble...*

knob = <u>ball</u>, stud, nub, protuberance, boss, bunch, swell, knot, bulk, lump, bump, projection, snag, hump, protrusion, knurl

knock VERB 1 = <u>bang</u>, beat, strike, tap, rap, bash (*informal*), thump, buffet, pummel ...*Knock at my window at eight o'clock and I'll be ready...*
2 = <u>hit</u>, strike, punch, belt (*informal*), deck (*slang*), slap, chin (*slang*), smack, thump, clap, cuff, smite (*archaic*), thwack, lay one on (*slang*) ...*He was mucking around and he knocked her in the stomach...*
3 (*Informal*) = <u>criticize</u>, condemn, put down, run down, abuse, blast, pan (*informal*), slam (*slang*), slate (*informal*), have a go (at) (*informal*), censure, slag (off) (*slang*), denigrate, belittle, disparage, deprecate, diss (*slang, chiefly U.S.*), find fault with, carp at, lambast(e), pick holes in, cast aspersions on, cavil at, pick to pieces, give (someone *or* something) a bad press ...*I'm not knocking them: if they want to do it, it's up to them...*

NOUN 1 = <u>knocking</u>, pounding, beating, tap, hammering, bang, banging, rap, thump, thud …*They heard a knock at the front door…*
2 = <u>bang</u>, blow, impact, jar, collision, jolt, smash …*The bags have tough exterior materials to protect against knocks…*
3 = <u>blow</u>, hit, punch, crack, belt (*informal*), clip, slap, bash, smack, thump, clout (*informal*), cuff, box …*He had taken a knock on the head in training…*
4 (*Informal*) = <u>setback</u>, check, defeat, blow, upset, reverse, disappointment, hold-up, hitch, reversal, misfortune, rebuff, whammy (*informal, chiefly U.S.*), bummer (*slang*) …*The art market has suffered some severe knocks…*
PHRASES **knock about** *or* **around** = <u>wander</u>, travel, roam, rove, range, drift, stray, ramble, straggle, traipse, go walkabout (*Austral.*), stravaig (*Scot. & Northern English dialect*) …*reporters who knock around in troubled parts of the world…* ◆ **knock about** *or* **around with someone** = <u>mix with</u>, associate with, mingle with, hang out with (*informal*), hang with (*informal, chiefly U.S.*), be friends with, consort with, run around with (*informal*), hobnob with, socialize with, accompany, hang about with, fraternize with …*I used to knock about with all the lads…* ◆ **knock off** (*Informal*) = <u>stop work</u>, get out, conclude, shut down, terminate, call it a day (*informal*), finish work, clock off, clock out …*What time do you knock off?…* ◆ **knock someone about** *or* **around** = <u>hit</u>, attack, beat, strike, damage, abuse, hurt, injure, wound, assault, harm, batter, slap, bruise, thrash, beat up (*informal*), buffet, maul, work over (*slang*), clobber (*slang*), mistreat, manhandle, maltreat, lambast(e), slap around (*informal*) …*He started knocking me around…* ◆ **knock someone down** = <u>run over</u>, hit, run down, knock over, mow down …*He died in hospital after being knocked down by a car…* ◆ **knock someone off** (*Slang*) = <u>kill</u>, murder, do in (*slang*), slaughter, destroy, waste (*informal*), take out (*slang*), execute, massacre, butcher, wipe out (*informal*), dispatch, cut down, erase, assassinate, slay, eradicate, whack (*informal*), do away with, blow away (*slang, chiefly U.S.*), obliterate, liquidate, decimate, annihilate, neutralize, exterminate, croak, mow down, take (someone's) life, bump off (*slang*), extirpate, wipe from the face of the earth (*informal*) …*Several people had a motive to knock him off…* ◆ **knock someone out** 1 = <u>floor</u>, knock unconscious, knock senseless, render unconscious, level, stun, daze …*He had never been knocked out in a professional fight…* 2 = <u>eliminate</u>, beat, defeat, trounce, vanquish …*We were knocked out in the quarter-finals…* 3 (*Informal*) = <u>impress</u>, move, strike, touch, affect, influence, excite, inspire, grab (*informal*), stir, overwhelm, sway, make an impression on …*That performance knocked me out…* ◆ **knock something down** = <u>demolish</u>, destroy, flatten, tear down, level, total (*slang*), fell, ruin, dismantle, trash (*slang*), bulldoze, raze, pulverize …*Why doesn't he just knock the wall down?…* ◆ **knock something off** 1 (*Slang*) = <u>steal</u>, take, nick (*slang, chiefly Brit.*), thieve, rob, pinch, cabbage (*Brit. slang*), blag (*slang*), pilfer, purloin, filch …*Cars can be

stolen almost as easily as knocking off a bike…* 2 = <u>remove</u>, take away, deduct, debit, subtract …*I'll knock off another £100 if you pay in cash…*

knockabout = <u>boisterous</u>, riotous, rollicking, rough-and-tumble, rumbustious, rambunctious (*informal*), harum-scarum, farcical, slapstick

knockout 1 = <u>killer blow</u>, coup de grâce (*French*), kayo (*slang*), KO *or* K.O. (*slang*) …*a first-round knockout in Las Vegas…*
2 (*Informal*) = <u>success</u>, hit, winner, triumph, smash, sensation, smash hit, stunner (*informal*), smasheroo (*informal*) …*The first story is a knockout…* **OPPOSITE** failure

knoll = <u>hillock</u>, hill, swell, mound, barrow, hummock

knot **NOUN** 1 = <u>connection</u>, tie, bond, joint, bow, loop, braid, splice, rosette, ligature …*One lace had broken and been tied in a knot…*
2 = <u>group</u>, company, set, band, crowd, pack, squad, circle, crew (*informal*), gang, mob, clique, assemblage …*A little knot of men stood clapping…*
VERB = <u>tie</u>, secure, bind, complicate, weave, loop, knit, tether, entangle …*He knotted the bandanna around his neck…*

knotty 1 = <u>puzzling</u>, hard, difficult, complex, complicated, tricky, baffling, intricate, troublesome, perplexing, mystifying, thorny, problematical …*The new management team faces some knotty problems…*
2 = <u>knotted</u>, rough, rugged, bumpy, gnarled, knobby, nodular …*the knotty trunk of a hawthorn tree…*

know 1 = <u>have knowledge of</u>, see, understand, recognize, perceive, be aware of, be conscious of …*I don't know the name of the place… …I think I know the answer…*
2 = <u>be acquainted with</u>, recognize, associate with, be familiar with, be friends with, be friendly with, have knowledge of, have dealings with, socialize with, fraternize with, be pals with …*Do you two know each other?…* **OPPOSITE** be unfamiliar with
3 *sometimes with **about** or **of*** = <u>be familiar with</u>, experience, understand, ken (*Scot.*), comprehend, fathom, apprehend, have knowledge of, be acquainted with, feel certain of, have dealings in, be versed in …*Hire someone with experience, someone who knows about real estate…* **OPPOSITE** be ignorant of
4 = <u>recognize</u>, remember, identify, recall, place, spot, notice, distinguish, perceive, make out, discern, differentiate, recollect …*Would she know you if she saw you on the street?…*

know-all (*Informal*) = <u>smart aleck</u>, wise guy (*informal*), smarty (*informal*), clever-clogs (*informal*), clever Dick (*informal*), smarty-pants (*informal*), smartarse (*slang*), wiseacre, smarty-boots (*informal*)

know-how (*Informal*) = <u>expertise</u>, experience, ability, skill, knowledge, facility, talent, command, craft, grasp, faculty, capability, flair, knack, ingenuity, aptitude, proficiency, dexterity, cleverness, deftness, savoir-faire, adroitness, ableness

knowing = <u>meaningful</u>, significant, expressive, eloquent, enigmatic, suggestive

knowingly = <u>deliberately</u>, purposely, consciously, intentionally, on purpose, wilfully, wittingly

knowledge 1 = <u>understanding</u>, sense, intelligence, judgment, perception, awareness, insight, grasp, appreciation, penetration, comprehension, discernment ...*the quest for scientific knowledge...*
2 = <u>learning</u>, schooling, education, science, intelligence, instruction, wisdom, scholarship, tuition, enlightenment, erudition ...*She didn't intend to display her knowledge, at least not yet...* OPPOSITE› ignorance
3 = <u>consciousness</u>, recognition, awareness, apprehension, cognition, discernment ...*taken without my knowledge or consent...* OPPOSITE› unawareness
4 = <u>acquaintance</u>, information, notice, intimacy, familiarity, cognizance ...*She disclaims any knowledge of her husband's business concerns...* OPPOSITE› unfamiliarity

knowledgeable 1 = <u>well-informed</u>, acquainted, conversant, au fait (*French*), experienced, understanding, aware, familiar, conscious, in the know (*informal*), cognizant, in the loop, au courant (*French*), clued-up (*informal*) ...*school-age children who were very knowledgeable about soccer...*
2 = <u>intelligent</u>, lettered, learned, educated, scholarly, erudite ...*He was a knowledgeable and well-read man...*

known = <u>famous</u>, well-known, celebrated, popular, common, admitted, noted, published, obvious, familiar, acknowledged, recognized, plain, confessed, patent, manifest, avowed OPPOSITE› unknown

kopje *or* **koppie** (*S. African*) = <u>hill</u>, down (*archaic*), fell, mount, height, mound, prominence, elevation, eminence, hilltop, tor, knoll, hillock, brae (*Scot.*)

kudos = <u>prestige</u>, regard, honour, praise, glory, fame, distinction, esteem, acclaim, applause, plaudits, renown, repute, notability, laudation

L l

label NOUN **1** = <u>tag</u>, ticket, tab, marker, flag, tally, sticker, docket (*chiefly Brit.*) ...*He peered at the label on the bottle*...
2 = <u>epithet</u>, description, classification, characterization ...*Her treatment of her husband earned her the label of the most hated woman in America*...
3 = <u>brand</u>, company, mark, trademark, brand name, trade name ...*designer labels*...
VERB **1** = <u>tag</u>, mark, stamp, ticket, flag, tab, tally, sticker, docket (*chiefly Brit.*) ...*The produce was labelled 'Made in China'*...
2 = <u>brand</u>, classify, describe, class, call, name, identify, define, designate, characterize, categorize, pigeonhole ...*Too often the press are labelled as bad boys*...

laborious 1 = <u>hard</u>, difficult, tiring, exhausting, wearing, tough, fatiguing, uphill, strenuous, arduous, tiresome, onerous, burdensome, herculean, wearisome, backbreaking, toilsome ...*Keeping the garden tidy all year round can be a laborious task*...
OPPOSITE easy
2 = <u>industrious</u>, hard-working, diligent, tireless, persevering, painstaking, indefatigable, assiduous, unflagging, sedulous ...*He was gentle and kindly, living a laborious life in his Paris flat*...
3 (*of literary style, etc.*) = <u>forced</u>, laboured, strained, ponderous, not fluent ...*a laborious prose style*...
OPPOSITE natural

labour NOUN **1** = <u>toil</u>, effort, industry, grind (*informal*), pains, sweat (*informal*), slog (*informal*), exertion, drudgery, travail, donkey-work ...*the labour of seeding, planting and harvesting*... OPPOSITE leisure
2 = <u>workers</u>, employees, workforce, labourers, hands, workmen ...*The country lacked skilled labour*...
3 = <u>work</u>, effort, employment, toil, industry ...*Every man should receive a fair price for the product of his labour*...
4 = <u>childbirth</u>, birth, delivery, contractions, pains, throes, travail, labour pains, parturition ...*By the time she realised she was in labour, it was too late*...
5 = <u>chore</u>, job, task, undertaking ...*The chef looked up from his labours*...
VERB **1** = <u>work</u>, toil, strive, work hard, grind (*informal*), sweat (*informal*), slave, endeavour, plod away, drudge, travail, slog away (*informal*), exert yourself, peg along *or* away (*chiefly Brit.*), plug along *or* away (*informal*) ...*peasants labouring in the fields*... OPPOSITE rest
2 = <u>struggle</u>, work, strain, work hard, strive, go for it (*informal*), grapple, toil, make an effort, make every effort, do your best, exert yourself, work like a Trojan ...*For years he laboured to build a religious community*...
3 = <u>overemphasize</u>, stress, elaborate, exaggerate,

strain, dwell on, overdo, go on about, make a production (out) of (*informal*), make a federal case of (*U.S. informal*) ...*I don't want to labour the point, but there it is*...
4 *usually with* ***under*** = <u>be disadvantaged by</u>, suffer from, be a victim of, be burdened by ...*She laboured under the illusion that I knew what I was doing*...

Labour = <u>left-wing</u>, Democrat (*U.S.*)

laboured 1 = <u>difficult</u>, forced, strained, heavy, awkward ...*From his slow walk and laboured breathing, she realized he was not well*...
2 = <u>contrived</u>, studied, affected, awkward, unnatural, overdone, ponderous, overwrought ...*The prose of his official communications was so laboured, pompous and verbose*...

labourer = <u>worker</u>, workman, working man, manual worker, hand, blue-collar worker, drudge, unskilled worker, navvy (*Brit. informal*), labouring man

labyrinth = <u>maze</u>, jungle, tangle, coil, snarl, entanglement

labyrinthine = <u>mazelike</u>, winding, tangled, intricate, tortuous, convoluted, mazy

lace NOUN **1** = <u>netting</u>, net, filigree, tatting, meshwork, openwork ...*a plain white lace bedspread*...
2 = <u>cord</u>, tie, string, lacing, thong, shoelace, bootlace ...*He was sitting on the bed, tying the laces of an old pair of running shoes*...
VERB **1** = <u>fasten</u>, tie, tie up, do up, secure, bind, close, attach, thread ...*No matter how tightly I lace these shoes, my ankles wobble*...
2 = <u>mix</u>, drug, doctor, add to, spike, contaminate, fortify, adulterate ...*She laced his food with sleeping pills*...
3 = <u>intertwine</u>, interweave, entwine, twine, interlink ...*He took to lacing his fingers together in an attempt to keep his hands still*...

lacerate 1 = <u>tear</u>, cut, wound, rend, rip, slash, claw, maim, mangle, mangulate (*Austral. slang*), gash, jag ...*Its claws lacerated his thighs*...
2 = <u>hurt</u>, wound, rend, torture, distress, torment, afflict, harrow ...*He was born into a family already lacerated with tensions and divisions*...

laceration = <u>cut</u>, injury, tear, wound, rent, rip, slash, trauma (*Pathology*), gash, mutilation

lack NOUN = <u>shortage</u>, want, absence, deficiency, need, shortcoming, deprivation, inadequacy, scarcity, dearth, privation, shortness, destitution, insufficiency, scantiness ...*Despite his lack of experience, he got the job*... OPPOSITE abundance
VERB = <u>miss</u>, want, need, require, not have, be without, be short of, be in need of, be deficient in ...*It lacked the power of the Italian cars*... OPPOSITE have

lackey = <u>hanger-on</u>, fawner, pawn, attendant, tool, instrument, parasite, cohort (*chiefly U.S.*), valet, menial, minion, footman, sycophant, yes-man, manservant, toady, flunky, flatterer, varlet (*archaic*)

lacking = deficient, wanting, needing, missing, inadequate, minus (*informal*), flawed, impaired, sans (*archaic*)

lacklustre = flat, boring, dull, dim, dry, muted, sombre, drab, lifeless, prosaic, leaden, unimaginative, uninspired, unexciting, vapid, lustreless

laconic = terse, short, brief, clipped, to the point, crisp, compact, concise, curt, succinct, pithy, monosyllabic, sentential OPPOSITE long-winded

lacy = filigree, open, fine, sheer, delicate, frilly, gossamer, gauzy, net-like, lace-like, meshy

lad = boy, kid (*informal*), guy (*informal*), youth, fellow, youngster, chap (*informal*), juvenile, shaver (*informal*), nipper (*informal*), laddie (*Scot.*), stripling

laden = loaded, burdened, hampered, weighted, full, charged, taxed, oppressed, fraught, weighed down, encumbered

lady 1 = gentlewoman, duchess, noble, dame, baroness, countess, aristocrat, viscountess, noblewoman, peeress ...*Our governess was told to make sure we knew how to talk like English ladies...*
2 = woman, female, girl, miss, maiden (*archaic*), maid (*archaic*), lass, damsel, lassie (*informal*), charlie (*Austral. slang*), chook (*Austral. slang*) ...*She's a very sweet old lady...*

ladylike = refined, cultured, sophisticated, elegant, proper, modest, respectable, polite, genteel, courtly, well-bred, decorous OPPOSITE unladylike

lag 1 = hang back, delay, drag (behind), trail, linger, be behind, idle, saunter, loiter, straggle, dawdle, tarry, drag your feet (*informal*) ...*The boys crept forward, Roger lagging a little...*
2 = drop, fail, diminish, decrease, flag, fall off, wane, ebb, slacken, lose strength ...*Trade has lagged since the embargo...*

laggard = straggler, lounger, lingerer, piker (*Austral. & N.Z. slang*), snail, saunterer, loafer, loiterer, dawdler, skiver (*Brit. slang*), idler, slowcoach (*Brit. informal*), sluggard, bludger (*Austral. & N.Z. informal*), slowpoke (*U.S. & Canad. informal*)

laid-back = relaxed, calm, casual, together (*slang*), at ease, easy-going, unflappable (*informal*), unhurried, free and easy, easy-peasy (*slang*) OPPOSITE tense

lair 1 = underline{nest}, den, hole, burrow, resting place ...*a fox's lair...*
2 = hide-out (*Informal*), retreat, refuge, den, sanctuary ...*The village was once a pirate's lair...*

laissez-faire *or* **laisser-faire** = nonintervention, free trade, individualism, free enterprise, live and let live

lake = pond, pool, reservoir, loch (*Scot.*), lagoon, mere, lough (*Irish*), tarn
➤ **WORD POWER SUPPLEMENT lakes, lochs, and loughs**

lame 1 = disabled, handicapped, crippled, limping, defective, hobbling, game, halt (*archaic*) ...*He had to*

pull out of the Championships when his horse went lame...
2 = unconvincing, poor, pathetic, inadequate, thin, weak, insufficient, feeble, unsatisfactory, flimsy ...*He mumbled some lame excuse about having gone to sleep...*

lament VERB = bemoan, grieve, mourn, weep over, complain about, regret, wail about, deplore, bewail ...*Ken began to lament the death of his only son...*
NOUN 1 = complaint, moaning, moan, keening, wail, wailing, lamentation, plaint, ululation ...*the professional woman's lament that a woman's judgment is questioned more than a man's...*
2 = dirge, requiem, elegy, threnody, monody, coronach (*Scot. & Irish*) ...*a lament for the late, great Buddy Holly...*

lamentable 1 = regrettable, distressing, tragic, unfortunate, harrowing, grievous, woeful, deplorable, mournful, sorrowful, gut-wrenching ...*This lamentable state of affairs lasted until 1947...*
2 = disappointing, poor, miserable, unsatisfactory, mean, low quality, meagre, pitiful, wretched, not much cop (*Brit. slang*) ...*He admitted he was partly to blame for England's lamentable performance...*

lamentation = sorrow, grief, weeping, mourning, moan, grieving, sobbing, keening, lament, wailing, dirge, plaint, ululation

laminated = covered, coated, overlaid, veneered, faced

lampoon VERB = ridicule, mock, mimic, parody, caricature, send up (*Brit. informal*), take off (*informal*), make fun of, squib, burlesque, satirize, pasquinade ...*He was lampooned for his short stature and political views...*
NOUN = satire, parody, caricature, send-up (*Brit. informal*), takeoff (*informal*), skit, squib, burlesque, pasquinade ...*his scathing lampoons of consumer culture...*

land NOUN 1 = ground, earth, dry land, terra firma ...*It isn't clear whether the plane went down over land or sea...*
2 = soil, ground, earth, clay, dirt, sod, loam ...*a small piece of grazing land...*
3 = countryside, farming, farmland, rural districts ...*Living off the land was hard enough at the best of times...*
4 (*Law*) = property, grounds, estate, acres, real estate, realty, acreage, real property ...*Good agricultural land is in short supply...*
5 = country, nation, region, state, district, territory, province, kingdom, realm, tract, motherland, fatherland ...*America, land of opportunity...*
VERB 1 = arrive, dock, put down, moor, berth, alight, touch down, disembark, come to rest, debark ...*The jet landed after a flight of just under three hours...*
2 (*Informal*) = gain, get, win, score (*slang*), secure, obtain, acquire ...*He landed a place on the graduate training scheme...*
PHRASES **land up** = end up, arrive, turn up, wind up, finish up, fetch up (*informal*) ...*We landed up at the Las Vegas at about 6.30...*

(Related Words)
adjective: terrestrial

landing 1 = <u>coming in</u>, arrival, touchdown, disembarkation, disembarkment …*I had to make a controlled landing into the sea…*
2 = <u>platform</u>, jetty, quayside, landing stage …*Take the bus to the landing…*

landlord 1 = <u>owner</u>, landowner, proprietor, freeholder, lessor, landholder …*His landlord doubled the rent…*
2 = <u>innkeeper</u>, host, hotelier, hotel-keeper …*The landlord refused to serve him because he considered him too drunk…*

landmark 1 = <u>feature</u>, spectacle, monument …*The Ambassador Hotel is a Los Angeles landmark…*
2 = <u>milestone</u>, turning point, watershed, critical point …*a landmark arms control treaty…*
3 = <u>boundary marker</u>, cairn, benchmark, signpost, milepost …*an abandoned landmark on top of Townsville's Castle Hill…*

landscape = <u>scenery</u>, country, view, land, scene, prospect, countryside, outlook, terrain, panorama, vista

landslide = <u>landslip</u>, avalanche, rockfall

lane = <u>road</u>, street, track, path, strip, way, passage, trail, pathway, footpath, passageway, thoroughfare

language 1 = <u>tongue</u>, speech, vocabulary, dialect, idiom, vernacular, patter, lingo (*informal*), patois, lingua franca …*the English language…*
2 = <u>speech</u>, communication, expression, speaking, talk, talking, conversation, discourse, interchange, utterance, parlance, vocalization, verbalization …*Students examined how children acquire language…*
3 = <u>style</u>, wording, expression, phrasing, vocabulary, usage, parlance, diction, phraseology …*a booklet summarising it in plain language…*
➤ **languages**

languid = <u>inactive</u>, lazy, indifferent, lethargic, weary, sluggish, inert, uninterested, listless, unenthusiastic, languorous, lackadaisical, torpid, spiritless OPPOSITE> energetic

languish 1 = <u>decline</u>, waste away, fade away, wither away, flag, weaken, wilt, sicken …*He continues to languish in prison…* OPPOSITE> flourish
2 (*Literary*) = <u>waste away</u>, suffer, rot, be abandoned, be neglected, be disregarded …*New products languish on the drawing board…* OPPOSITE> thrive
3 often with **for** = <u>pine</u>, want, long, desire, sigh, hunger, yearn, hanker, eat your heart out over, suspire …*a bride languishing for a kiss that never comes…*

languishing = <u>fading</u>, failing, declining, flagging, sinking, weakening, deteriorating, withering, wilting, sickening, drooping, droopy, wasting away

lank 1 = <u>limp</u>, lifeless, long, dull, straggling, lustreless …*She ran her fingers through her hair; it felt lank and dirty…*
2 = <u>thin</u>, lean, slim, slender, skinny, spare, gaunt, lanky, emaciated, scrawny, attenuated, scraggy, rawboned …*a lank youth with a ponytail…*

lanky = <u>gangling</u>, thin, tall, spare, angular, gaunt, bony, weedy (*informal*), scrawny, rangy, scraggy, rawboned, loose-jointed OPPOSITE> chubby

lap[1] = <u>circuit</u>, course, round, tour, leg, distance, stretch, circle, orbit, loop …*the last lap of the race…*

lap[2] VERB 1 = <u>ripple</u>, wash, splash, slap, swish, gurgle, slosh, purl, plash …*the water that lapped against the pillars of the pier…*
2 = <u>drink</u>, sip, lick, swallow, gulp, sup …*The kitten lapped milk from a dish…*
PHRASES **lap something up** = <u>relish</u>, like, enjoy, appreciate, delight in, savour, revel in, wallow in, accept eagerly …*They're eager to learn, so they lap it up…*

lapse NOUN 1 = <u>decline</u>, fall, drop, descent, deterioration, relapse, backsliding …*His behaviour showed neither decency or dignity. It was an uncommon lapse…*
2 = <u>mistake</u>, failing, fault, failure, error, slip, negligence, omission, oversight, indiscretion …*The incident was being seen as a serious security lapse…*
3 = <u>interval</u>, break, gap, passage, pause, interruption, lull, breathing space, intermission …*a time lapse between receipt of new information and its publication…*
VERB 1 = <u>slip</u>, fall, decline, sink, drop, slide, deteriorate, degenerate …*Teenagers occasionally find it all too much to cope with and lapse into bad behaviour…*
2 = <u>end</u>, stop, run out, expire, terminate, become obsolete, become void …*Her membership of the Labour Party has lapsed…*

lapsed 1 = <u>expired</u>, ended, finished, run out, invalid, out of date, discontinued, unrenewed …*He returned to the Party after years of lapsed membership…*
2 = <u>backsliding</u>, uncommitted, lacking faith, nonpractising …*She calls herself a lapsed Catholic…*

large ADJECTIVE 1 = <u>big</u>, great, huge, heavy, giant, massive, vast, enormous, tall, considerable, substantial, strapping, immense (*informal*), hefty, gigantic, monumental, bulky, chunky, burly, colossal, hulking, goodly, man-size, brawny, elephantine, thickset, ginormous (*informal*), humongous *or* humungous (*U.S. slang*), sizable *or* sizeable …*He was a large man with a thick square head…* OPPOSITE> small
2 = <u>massive</u>, great, big, huge, giant, vast, enormous, considerable, substantial, immense, tidy (*informal*), jumbo (*informal*), gigantic, monumental, mammoth, colossal, gargantuan, stellar (*informal*), king-size, ginormous (*informal*), humongous *or* humungous (*U.S. slang*), sizable *or* sizeable …*In a large room about a dozen children are sitting on the carpet…* OPPOSITE> small
3 = <u>plentiful</u>, full, grand, liberal, sweeping, broad, comprehensive, extensive, generous, lavish, ample, spacious, abundant, grandiose, copious, roomy, bountiful, capacious, profuse …*The gang finally left with a large amount of cash and jewellery…* OPPOSITE> scanty
PHRASES **at large** 1 = <u>in general</u>, generally, chiefly, mainly, as a whole, in the main …*The public at large*

Languages

www.ilovelanguages.com
www.ethnologue.com
http://www.bbc.co.uk/languages/

African languages

Adamawa	Hottentot	Pondo
Afrikaans	Hutu	Rwanda
Akan	Ibibio or Efik	Sango
Amharic	Ibo or Igbo	Sesotho
Bambara	Kabyle	Shona
Barotse	Kikuyu	Somali
Bashkir	Kingwana	Songhai
Bemba	Kirundi	Sotho
Berber	Kongo	Susu
Chewa	Krio	Swahili
Chichewa	Lozi	Swazi
Coptic	Luba or Tshiluba	Temne
Damara	Luganda	Tigré
Duala	Luo	Tigrinya
Dyula	Malagasy	Tiv
Edo, Bini, or Beni	Malinke or Maninke	Tonga
Ewe	Masai	Tsonga
Fanagalo or Fanakalo	Matabele	Tswana
Fang	Mossi or Moore	Tuareg
Fanti	Nama or Namaqua	Twi or (formerly) Ashanti
Fula, Fulah, or Fulani	Ndebele	Venda
Ga or Gã	Nuba	Wolof
Galla	Nupe	Xhosa
Ganda	Nyanja	Yoruba
Griqua or Grikwa	Nyoro	Zulu
Hausa	Ovambo	
Herero	Pedi or Northern Sotho	

Asian languages

Abkhaz, Abkhazi, or Abkhazian	Gurkhali	Mon
Adygei or Adyghe	Hebrew	Mongol
Afghan	Hindi	Mongolian
Ainu	Hindustani, Hindoostani, or	Moro
Arabic	Hindostani	Naga
Aramaic	Iranian	Nepali
Armenian	Japanese	Nuri
Assamese	Javanese	Oriya
Azerbaijani	Kabardian	Ossetian or Ossetic
Bahasa Indonesia	Kafiri	Ostyak
Balinese	Kalmuck or Kalmyk	Pashto, Pushto, or Pushtu
Baluchi or Balochi	Kannada, Kanarese, or Canarese	Punjabi
Bengali	Kara-Kalpak	Shan
Bihari	Karen	Sindhi
Brahui	Kashmiri	Sinhalese
Burmese	Kazakh or Kazak	Sogdian
Buryat or Buriat	Kazan Tatar	Tadzhiki or Tadzhik
Cantonese	Khalkha	Tagalog
Chukchee or Chukchi	Khmer	Tamil
Chuvash	Kirghiz	Tatar
Chinese	Korean	Telugu or Telegu
Cham	Kurdish	Thai
Circassian	Lahnda	Tibetan
Dinka	Lao	Tungus
Divehi	Lepcha	Turkmen
Dzongka	Malay	Turkoman or Turkman
Evenki	Malayalam or Malayalaam	Uigur or Uighur
Farsi	Manchu	Urdu
Filipino	Mandarin	Uzbek
Gondi	Marathi or Mahratti	Vietnamese
Gujarati or Gujerati	Mishmi	Yakut

Languages (continued)

Australasian languages

Aranda
Beach-la-Mar
Dinka
Fijian
Gurindji
Hawaiian
Hiri Motu
kamilaroi

Krio
Maori
Moriori
Motu
Nauruan
Neo-Melanesian
Papuan
Pintubi

Police Motu
Samoan
Solomon Islands Pidgin
Tongan
Tuvaluan
Warlpiri

Asian languages

Abkhaz, Abkhazi, *or* Abkhazian
Adygei *or* Adyghe
Afghan
Ainu
Arabic
Aramaic
Armenian
Assamese
Azerbaijani
Bahasa Indonesia
Balinese
Baluchi *or* Balochi
Bengali
Bihari
Brahui
Burmese
Buryat *or* Buriat
Cantonese
Chukchee *or* Chukchi
Chuvash
Chinese
Cham
Circassian
Dinka
Divehi
Dzongka
Evenki
Farsi
Filipino
Gondi
Gujarati *or* Gujerati

Gurkhali
Hebrew
Hindi
Hindustani, Hindoostani, *or* Hindostani
Iranian
Japanese
Javanese
Kabardian
Kafiri
Kalmuck *or* Kalmyk
Kannada, Kanarese, *or* Canarese
Kara-Kalpak
Karen
Kashmiri
Kazakh *or* Kazak
Kazan Tatar
Khalkha
Khmer
Kirghiz
Korean
Kurdish
Lahnda
Lao
Lepcha
Malay
Malayalam *or* Malayalaam
Manchu
Mandarin
Marathi *or* Mahratti
Mishmi

Mon
Mongol
Mongolian
Moro
Naga
Nepali
Nuri
Oriya
Ossetian *or* Ossetic
Ostyak
Pashto, Pushto, *or* Pushtu
Punjabi
Shan
Sindhi
Sinhalese
Sogdian
Tadzhiki *or* Tadzhik
Tagalog
Tamil
Tatar
Telugu *or* Telegu
Thai
Tibetan
Tungus
Turkmen
Turkoman *or* Turkman
Uigur *or* Uighur
Urdu
Uzbek
Vietnamese
Yakut

European languages

Albanian
Alemannic
Basque
Bohemian
Bokmål
Breton
Bulgarian
Byelorussian
Castilian
Catalan
Cheremiss *or* Cheremis
Cornish
Croatian
Cymric *or* Kymric
Czech
Danish
Dutch
English

Erse
Estonian
Faeroese
Finnish
Flemish
French
Frisian
Friulian
Gaelic
Gagauzi
Galician
Georgian
German
Greek
Hungarian
Icelandic
Italian
Karelian

Komi
Ladin
Ladino
Lallans *or* Lallan
Lapp
Latvian *or* Lettish
Lithuanian
Lusatian
Macedonian
Magyar
Maltese
Manx
Mingrelian *or* Mingrel
Mordvin
Norwegian
Nynorsk *or* Landsmål
Polish
Portuguese

European languages (continued)

Provençal
Romanian
Romansch or Romansh
Romany or Romanes
Russian
Samoyed
Sardinian

Serbo-Croat or Serbo-Croatian
Shelta
Slovak
Slovene
Sorbian
Spanish
Swedish

Turkish
Udmurt
Ukrainian
Vogul
Votyak
Welsh
Yiddish

North American languages

Abnaki
Aleut or Aleutian
Algonquin or Algonkin
Apache
Arapaho
Assiniboine
Blackfoot
Caddoan
Catawba
Cayuga
Cherokee
Cheyenne
Chickasaw
Chinook
Choctaw
Comanche
Creek
Crow
Delaware
Erie
Eskimo

Fox
Haida
Hopi
Huron
Inuktitut
Iroquois
Kwakiutl
Mahican or Mohican
Massachuset or Massachusetts
Menomini
Micmac
Mixtec
Mohave or Mojave
Mohawk
Narraganset or Narragansett
Navaho or Navajo
Nez Percé
Nootka
Ojibwa
Okanagan, Okanogan, or
  Okinagan

Oneida
Onondaga
Osage
Paiute or Piute
Pawnee
Pequot
Sahaptin, Sahaptan, or Sahaptian
Seminole
Seneca
Shawnee
Shoshone or Shoshoni
Sioux
Tahltan
Taino
Tlingit
Tuscarora
Ute
Winnebago
Zuñi

South American languages

Araucanian
Aymara
Chibchan

Galibi
Guarani
Nahuatl

Quechua, Kechua, or Quichua
Tupi
Zapotec

Ancient languages

Akkadian
Ancient Greek
Anglo-Saxon
Assyrian
Avar
Avestan or Avestic
Aztec
Babylonian
Canaanite
Celtiberian
Chaldee
Edomite
Egyptian
Elamite
Ethiopic
Etruscan
Faliscan
Frankish
Gallo-Romance or Gallo-Roman
Ge'ez
Gothic
Hebrew

Himyaritic
Hittite
Illyrian
Inca
Ionic
Koine
Langobardic
langue d'oc
langue d'oïl
Latin
Libyan
Lycian
Lydian
Maya or Mayan
Messapian or Messapïc
Norn
Old Church Slavonic
Old High German
Old Norse
Old Prussian
Oscan
Osco-Umbrian

Pahlavi or Pehlevi
Pali
Phoenician
Phrygian
Pictish
Punic
Sabaean or Sabean
Sabellian
Sanskrit
Scythian
Sumerian
Syriac
Thracian
Thraco-Phrygian
Tocharian or Tokharian
Ugaritic
Umbrian
Vedic
Venetic
Volscian
Wendish

Languages (continued)

Artificial languages

Esperanto
Ido
interlingua
Volapuk *or* Volapük

Languages groups

Afro-Asiatic
Albanian
Algonquian *or* Algonkian
Altaic
Anatolian
Athapascan, Athapaskan,
 Athabascan, *or* Athabaskan
Arawakan
Armenian
Australian
Austro-Asiatic
Austronesian
Baltic
Bantu
Benue-Congo
Brythonic
Caddoan
Canaanitic
Carib
Caucasian
Celtic
Chadic
Chari-Nile
Cushitic
Cymric
Dardic
Dravidian
East Germanic
East Iranian
Eskimo
Finnic
Germanic
Gur

Hamitic
Hamito-Semitic
Hellenic
Hindustani
Indic
Indo-Aryan
Indo-European
Indo-Iranian
Indo-Pacific
Iranian
Iroquoian
Italic
Khoisan
Kordofanian
Kwa
Malayo-Polynesian
Mande
Mayan
Melanesian
Micronesian
Mongolic
Mon-Khmer
Munda
Muskogean *or* Muskhogean
Na-Dene *or* Na-Déné
Nguni
Niger-Congo
Nilo-Saharan
Nilotic
Norse
North Germanic
Oceanic
Pahari

Pama-Nyungan
Penutian
Polynesian
Rhaetian
Romance
Saharan
Salish *or* Salishan
San
Sanskritic
Semi-Bantu
Semitic
Semito-Hamitic
Shoshonean
Siouan
Sinitic
Sino-Tibetan
Slavonic
Sudanic
Tibeto-Burman
Trans-New Guinea phylum
Tungusic
Tupi-Guarani
Turkic
Ugric
Uralic
Uto-Aztecan
Voltaic
Wakashan
West Atlantic
West Germanic
West Iranian
West Slavonic
Yuman

---

does not seem to want any change... **2** = free, roaming, on the run, fugitive, at liberty, on the loose, unchained, unconfined ...*The man who tried to have her killed is still at large*... ◆ **by and large** = on the whole, generally, mostly, in general, all things considered, predominantly, in the main, for the most part, all in all, as a rule, taking everything into consideration ...*By and large, the papers greet the government's new policy with scepticism*...

largely = mainly, generally, chiefly, widely, mostly, principally, primarily, considerably, predominantly, extensively, by and large, as a rule, to a large extent, to a great extent

large-scale = wide-ranging, global, sweeping, broad, wide, vast, extensive, wholesale, far-reaching

largesse *or* **largess** **1** = generosity, charity, bounty, philanthropy, munificence, liberality, alms-giving, benefaction, open-handedness ...*his most recent act of largesse*...

2 = gift, present, grant, donation, endowment, . bounty, bequest ...*The president has been travelling around the country distributing largesse*...

lark (*Informal*) **NOUN** = prank, game, fun, fling, romp, spree, revel, mischief, caper, frolic, escapade, skylark, gambol, antic, jape, rollick ...*The children thought it was a great lark*...

PHRASES **lark about** = fool around, play around, romp around, have fun, caper, frolic, cavort, gambol, muck around, make mischief, lark around, rollick, cut capers ...*They complained about me larking about when they were trying to concentrate*...

lascivious **1** = lustful, sensual, immoral, randy (*informal, chiefly Brit.*), horny (*slang*), voluptuous, lewd, wanton, salacious, prurient, lecherous, libidinous, licentious, unchaste ...*The man was lascivious, sexually perverted and insatiable*...

2 = bawdy, dirty, offensive, crude, obscene, coarse, indecent, blue, vulgar, immoral, pornographic, suggestive, X-rated (*informal*), scurrilous, smutty, ribald ...*their lewd and lascivious talk*...

lash¹ **VERB** **1** = pound, beat, strike, hammer, drum, smack (*dialect*) ...*The rain was absolutely lashing down*...

2 = censure, attack, blast, put down, criticize, slate

(*informal, chiefly Brit.*), ridicule, scold, berate, castigate, lampoon, tear into (*informal*), flay, upbraid, satirize, lambast(e), belabour …*The report lashes into police commanders for failing to act on intelligence information…*

3 = <u>whip</u>, beat, thrash, birch, flog, lam (*slang*), scourge, chastise, lambast(e), flagellate, horsewhip …*They snatched up whips and lashed the backs of those who had fallen…*

NOUN = <u>blow</u>, hit, strike, stroke, stripe, swipe (*informal*) …*They sentenced him to five lashes for stealing a ham from his neighbour…*

lash² = <u>fasten</u>, join, tie, secure, bind, rope, strap, make fast …*Secure the anchor by lashing it to the rail…*

lass = <u>girl</u>, young woman, miss, bird (*slang*), maiden, chick (*slang*), maid, damsel, colleen (*Irish*), lassie (*informal*), wench (*facetious*), charlie (*Austral. slang*), chook (*Austral. slang*)

last¹ **ADJECTIVE 1** = <u>most recent</u>, latest, previous …*Much has changed since my last visit…*

2 = <u>hindmost</u>, furthest, final, at the end, remotest, furthest behind, most distant, rearmost, aftermost …*She said it was the very last house on the road…* **OPPOSITE** foremost

3 = <u>final</u>, closing, concluding, ultimate, utmost …*the last three pages of the chapter…* **OPPOSITE** first

ADVERB = <u>in</u> or <u>at the end</u>, after, behind, in the rear, bringing up the rear …*I testified last…*

NOUN = <u>end</u>, ending, close, finish, conclusion, completion, finale, termination …*a thriller with plenty of twists to keep you guessing to the last…*

PHRASES **at last** = <u>finally</u>, eventually, in the end, ultimately, at the end of the day, at length, at long last, in conclusion, in the fullness of time …*'All right,' he said at last. 'You may go.'…* ♦ **the last word 1** = <u>final decision</u>, final say, final statement, conclusive comment …*She likes to have the last word in any discussion…* **2** = <u>leading</u>, best, first, highest, finest, cream, supreme, elite, first-class, foremost, first-rate, superlative, pre-eminent, unsurpassed, crème de la crème (*French*), most excellent …*a venue that is the last word in trendiness…*

Word Power

last – Since *last* can mean either *after all others* or *most recent*, it is better to avoid using this word where ambiguity might arise, as in *her last novel. Final* or *latest* should be used as alternatives in such contexts to avoid any possible confusion.

last² = <u>continue</u>, keep, remain, survive, wear, carry on, endure, hold on, persist, keep on, hold out, abide **OPPOSITE** end …*You only need a very small amount, so the tube lasts for ages…*

last-ditch = <u>final</u>, frantic, desperate, struggling, straining, heroic, all-out (*informal*)

lasting = <u>continuing</u>, long-term, permanent, enduring, remaining, eternal, abiding, long-standing, perennial, lifelong, durable, perpetual, long-lasting, deep-rooted, indelible, unending, undying, unceasing **OPPOSITE** passing

lastly = <u>finally</u>, to conclude, at last, in the end, ultimately, all in all, to sum up, in conclusion

latch **NOUN** = <u>fastening</u>, catch, bar, lock, hook, bolt, clamp, hasp, sneck (*dialect*) …*You left the latch off the gate and the dog escaped…*

VERB = <u>fasten</u>, bar, secure, lock, bolt, make fast, sneck (*dialect*) …*He latched the door, tested it and turned round to speak to us…*

late **ADJECTIVE 1** = <u>overdue</u>, delayed, last-minute, belated, tardy, behind time, unpunctual, behindhand …*Steve arrived late…* **OPPOSITE** early

2 = <u>dead</u>, deceased, departed, passed on, old, former, previous, preceding, defunct …*my late husband…* **OPPOSITE** alive

3 = <u>recent</u>, new, advanced, fresh …*some late news just in for the people of Merseyside…* **OPPOSITE** old

ADVERB = <u>behind time</u>, belatedly, tardily, behindhand, dilatorily, unpunctually …*The talks began some fifteen minutes late…* **OPPOSITE** early

lately = <u>recently</u>, of late, just now, in recent times, not long ago, latterly

lateness = <u>delay</u>, late date, retardation, tardiness, unpunctuality, belatedness, advanced hour

latent = <u>hidden</u>, secret, concealed, invisible, lurking, veiled, inherent, unseen, dormant, undeveloped, quiescent, immanent, unrealized, unexpressed **OPPOSITE** obvious

later **ADVERB** = <u>afterwards</u>, after, next, eventually, in time, subsequently, later on, thereafter, in a while, in due course, at a later date, by and by, at a later time …*I'll join you later…*

ADJECTIVE = <u>subsequent</u>, next, following, ensuing …*at a later news conference…*

lateral = <u>sideways</u>, side, flanking, edgeways, sideward

latest = <u>up-to-date</u>, current, fresh, newest, happening (*informal*), modern, most recent, up-to-the-minute

lather **NOUN 1** = <u>froth</u>, soap, bubbles, foam, suds, soapsuds …*He wiped of the lather with a towel…*

2 (*Informal*) = <u>fluster</u>, state (*informal*), sweat, fever, fuss, flap (*informal*), stew (*informal*), dither (*chiefly Brit.*), twitter (*informal*), tizzy (*informal*), pother …*'I'm not going to get into a lather over this defeat,' said the manager…*

VERB = <u>froth</u>, soap, foam …*The shampoo lathers so much it's difficult to rinse it all out…*

latitude = <u>scope</u>, liberty, indulgence, freedom, play, room, space, licence, leeway, laxity, elbowroom, unrestrictedness

latter **PRONOUN** = <u>second</u>, last, last-mentioned, second-mentioned …*He tracked down his cousin and uncle. The latter was sick…*

ADJECTIVE = <u>last</u>, later, latest, ending, closing, final, concluding …*The latter part of the debate concentrated on abortion…* **OPPOSITE** earlier

Word Power

latter – The *latter* should only be used to specify the second of two items, for example in *if I had to choose between the hovercraft and the ferry, I would opt for the latter*. Where there are three or more items, the last can be referred to as *the last-named*, but not *the latter*.

latterly = <u>recently</u>, lately, of late, hitherto

lattice = <u>grid</u>, network, web, grating, mesh, grille, trellis, fretwork, tracery, latticework, openwork, reticulation

laud (*Literary*) = <u>praise</u>, celebrate, honour, acclaim, approve, magnify (*archaic*), glorify, extol, sing *or* sound the praises of

laudable = <u>praiseworthy</u>, excellent, worthy, admirable, of note, commendable, creditable, meritorious, estimable OPPOSITE> blameworthy

laugh VERB = <u>chuckle</u>, giggle, snigger, crack up (*informal*), cackle, chortle, guffaw, titter, roar, bust a gut (*informal*), be convulsed (*informal*), be in stitches, crease up (*informal*), split your sides, be rolling in the aisles (*informal*) ...*He laughed with pleasure when people said he looked like his Dad*...
NOUN 1 = <u>chortle</u>, giggle, chuckle, snigger, guffaw, titter, belly laugh, roar *or* shriek ...*He gave a deep rumbling laugh at his own joke*...
2 (*Informal*) = <u>joke</u>, scream (*informal*), hoot (*informal*), lark, prank ...*Working there's great. It's quite a good laugh actually*...
3 (*Informal*) = <u>clown</u>, character (*informal*), scream (*informal*), comic, caution (*informal*), wit, comedian, entertainer, card (*informal*), wag, joker, hoot (*informal*), humorist ...*He was a good laugh and great to have in the dressing room*...
PHRASES **laugh at something** *or* **someone** = <u>make fun of</u>, mock, tease, ridicule, taunt, jeer, deride, scoff at, belittle, lampoon, take the mickey out of (*informal*), pour scorn on, make a mock of ...*I thought people were laughing at me because I was ugly*...
♦ **laugh something off** = <u>disregard</u>, ignore, dismiss, overlook, shrug off, minimize, brush aside, make light of, pooh-pooh ...*While I used to laugh it off, I'm now getting irritated by it*...

laughable 1 = <u>ridiculous</u>, absurd, ludicrous, preposterous, farcical, nonsensical, derisory, risible, derisive, worthy of scorn ...*He claimed that the allegations were 'laughable'*...
2 = <u>funny</u>, amusing, hilarious, humorous, diverting, comical, droll, mirthful ...*Groucho's laughable view of human pomp*...

laughing stock = <u>figure of fun</u>, target, victim, butt, fair game, Aunt Sally (*Brit.*), everybody's fool

laughter 1 = <u>chuckling</u>, laughing, giggling, chortling, guffawing, tittering, cachinnation ...*Their laughter filled the corridor*...
2 = <u>amusement</u>, entertainment, humour, glee, fun, mirth, hilarity, merriment ...*Pantomime is about bringing laughter to thousands*...

launch VERB 1 = <u>propel</u>, fire, dispatch, discharge, project, send off, set in motion, send into orbit ...*A Delta II rocket was launched from Cape Canaveral early this morning*...
2 = <u>begin</u>, start, open, initiate, introduce, found, set up, originate, commence, get under way, instigate, inaugurate, embark upon ...*The police have launched an investigation into the incident*...
NOUN 1 = <u>propelling</u>, projection, sendoff ...*This morning's launch of the space shuttle Columbia has been delayed*...
2 = <u>beginning</u>, start, introduction, initiation, opening, founding, setting-up, inauguration, commencement, instigation ...*the launch of a campaign to restore law and order*...
PHRASES **launch into something** = <u>start enthusiastically</u>, begin, initiate, embark on, instigate, inaugurate, embark upon ...*He launched into a speech about the importance of new products*...

launder 1 = <u>wash</u>, clean, dry-clean, tub, wash and iron, wash and press ...*She wore a freshly laundered and starched white shirt*...
2 = <u>process</u>, doctor, manipulate ...*The House voted today to crack down on banks that launder drug money*...

laurel
PHRASES **rest on your laurels** = <u>sit back</u>, relax, take it easy, relax your efforts

lavatory = <u>toilet</u>, bathroom, loo (*Brit. informal*), bog (*slang*), can (*U.S. & Canad. slang*), john (*slang, chiefly U.S. & Canad.*), head(s) (*Nautical slang*), throne (*informal*), closet, privy, cloakroom (*Brit.*), urinal, latrine, washroom, powder room, ablutions (*Military Informal*), crapper (*taboo slang*), water closet, khazi (*slang*), pissoir (*French*), Gents *or* Ladies, little boy's room *or* little girl's room (*informal*), (public) convenience, W.C., dunny (*Austral. & old-fashioned N.Z. informal*), bogger (*Austral. slang*), brasco (*Austral. slang*)

lavish ADJECTIVE 1 = <u>grand</u>, magnificent, splendid, lush, abundant, sumptuous, exuberant, opulent, copious, luxuriant, profuse ...*a lavish party to celebrate his fiftieth birthday*... OPPOSITE> stingy
2 = <u>extravagant</u>, wild, excessive, exaggerated, unreasonable, wasteful, prodigal, unrestrained, intemperate, immoderate, improvident, thriftless ...*Critics attack his lavish spending and flamboyant style*... OPPOSITE> thrifty
3 = <u>generous</u>, free, liberal, bountiful, effusive, open-handed, unstinting, munificent ...*American reviewers are lavish in their praise of this book*... OPPOSITE> stingy
VERB = <u>shower</u>, pour, heap, deluge, dissipate ...*The emperor promoted the general and lavished him with gifts*... OPPOSITE> stint

law NOUN 1 = <u>constitution</u>, code, legislation, charter, jurisprudence ...*Obscene and threatening phone calls are against the law*...
2 = <u>statute</u>, act, bill, rule, demand, order, command, code, regulation, resolution, decree, canon, covenant, ordinance, commandment, enactment, edict ...*The law was passed on a second vote*...

3 = <u>principle</u>, standard, code, formula, criterion, canon, precept, axiom ...*inflexible moral laws...*
4 = <u>the legal profession</u>, the bar, barristers ...*a career in law...*
PHRASES lay down the law = <u>be dogmatic</u>, call the shots (*informal*), pontificate, rule the roost, crack the whip, boss around, dogmatize, order about *or* around ...*traditional parents who believed in laying down the law for their offspring...*
(Related Words)
adjectives: legal, judicial

law-abiding = <u>obedient</u>, good, peaceful, honourable, orderly, honest, lawful, compliant, dutiful, peaceable

lawful = <u>legal</u>, constitutional, just, proper, valid, warranted, legitimate, authorized, rightful, permissible, legalized, allowable, licit **OPPOSITE** unlawful

lawless = <u>disorderly</u>, wild, unruly, rebellious, chaotic, reckless, insurgent, anarchic, riotous, unrestrained, seditious, mutinous, insubordinate, ungoverned **OPPOSITE** law-abiding

lawlessness = <u>anarchy</u>, disorder, chaos, reign of terror, mob rule, mobocracy, ochlocracy

lawsuit = <u>case</u>, cause, action, trial, suit, argument, proceedings, dispute, contest, prosecution, legal action, indictment, litigation, industrial tribunal, legal proceedings

lawyer = <u>legal adviser</u>, attorney, solicitor, counsel, advocate, barrister, counsellor, legal representative

lax = <u>slack</u>, casual, careless, sloppy (*informal*), easy-going, negligent, lenient, slapdash, neglectful, slipshod, remiss, easy-peasy (*slang*), overindulgent **OPPOSITE** strict

laxative = <u>purgative</u>, salts, purge, cathartic, physic (*rare*), aperient

lay¹ VERB 1 = <u>place</u>, put, set, spread, plant, establish, settle, leave, deposit, put down, set down, posit ...*Lay a sheet of newspaper on the floor...*
2 = <u>devise</u>, plan, design, prepare, work out, plot, hatch, contrive, concoct ...*They were laying a trap for the kidnapper...*
3 = <u>produce</u>, bear, deposit ...*Freezing weather hampered the hen's ability to lay eggs...*
4 = <u>arrange</u>, prepare, make, organize, position, locate, set out, devise, put together, dispose, draw up ...*The organisers meet in March to lay plans...*
5 = <u>attribute</u>, charge, assign, allocate, allot, ascribe, impute ...*She refused to lay the blame on any one party...*
6 = <u>put forward</u>, offer, present, advance, lodge, submit, bring forward ...*Police have decided not to lay charges over allegations of phone tapping...*
7 = <u>bet</u>, stake, venture, gamble, chance, risk, hazard, wager, give odds ...*I wouldn't lay bets on his remaining manager after the spring...*
PHRASES lay into someone (*Informal*) = <u>attack</u>, hit, set about, hit out at, assail, tear into, pitch into (*informal*), go for the jugular, lambast(e), belabour, lash into, let fly at ...*A mob of women laid into him*

with handbags and pointed shoes... ◆ **lay it on thick** (*Slang*) = <u>exaggerate</u>, flatter, overdo it, lay it on with a trowel (*informal*), overpraise, soft-soap (*informal*) ...*Don't lay it on too thick, but make sure they are flattered...* ◆ **lay off** (*Informal*) = <u>stop</u>, give up, quit, cut it out, leave alone, pack in, abstain, leave off, give over (*informal*), let up, get off someone's back (*informal*), give it a rest (*informal*) ...*He went on attacking her until other passengers arrived and told him to lay off...* ◆ **lay someone off** = <u>dismiss</u>, fire (*informal*), release, drop, sack (*informal*), pay off, discharge, oust, let go, make redundant, give notice to, give the boot to (*slang*), give the sack to (*informal*), give someone their cards ...*100,000 federal workers will be laid off to reduce the deficit...*
◆ **lay someone out** (*Informal*) = <u>knock out</u>, fell, floor, knock unconscious, knock for six, kayo (*slang*) ...*He turned round, marched over to the man, and just laid him out...* ◆ **lay someone up** (*Informal*) = <u>confine (to bed)</u>, hospitalize, incapacitate ...*He was recovering from a knee injury that laid him up for six months...* ◆ **lay something aside** = <u>abandon</u>, reject, dismiss, postpone, shelve, put off, renounce, put aside, cast aside ...*All animosities were laid aside for the moment...* ◆ **lay something bare** = <u>reveal</u>, show, expose, disclose, unveil, divulge ...*The clearing out of disused workshops laid bare thousands of glazed tiles...* ◆ **lay something down 1** = <u>stipulate</u>, state, establish, prescribe, assume, formulate, affirm, ordain, set down, postulate ...*The Companies Act lays down a set of minimum requirements...* **2** = <u>sacrifice</u>, give up, yield, surrender, turn over, relinquish ...*The drug traffickers have offered to lay down their arms...* ◆ **lay something in** = <u>store (up)</u>, collect, build up, accumulate, buy in, amass, stockpile, hoard, stock up, heap up ...*They began to lay in extensive stores of food supplies...* ◆ **lay something on** = <u>provide</u>, prepare, supply, organize, give, cater (for), furnish, purvey ...*They laid on a superb meal...* ◆ **lay something out 1** = <u>arrange</u>, order, design, display, exhibit, put out, spread out ...*She took a deck of cards and began to lay them out...* **2** (*Informal*) = <u>spend</u>, pay, invest, fork out (*slang*), expend, shell out (*informal*), disburse ...*You won't have to lay out a fortune for this dining table...*

Word Power

lay – In standard English, the verb *to lay* (meaning 'to put something somewhere') always needs an object, for example *the Queen laid a wreath*. By contrast, the verb *to lie* is always used without an object, for example *he was just lying there*.

---

lay² 1 = <u>nonclerical</u>, secular, non-ordained, laic, laical ...*He is a Methodist lay preacher and social worker...*
2 = <u>nonspecialist</u>, amateur, unqualified, untrained, inexpert, nonprofessional ...*It is difficult for a lay person to gain access to medical libraries...*

layer 1 = <u>covering</u>, film, cover, sheet, coating, coat, blanket, mantle ...*A fresh layer of snow covered the* *street...*

2 = <u>tier</u>, level, seam, stratum ...*Critics and the public puzzle out the layers of meaning in his photos...*

layman = <u>nonprofessional</u>, amateur, outsider, lay person, non-expert, nonspecialist

layoff = <u>unemployment</u>, firing (*informal*), sacking (*informal*), dismissal, discharge

layout = <u>arrangement</u>, design, draft, outline, format, plan, formation, geography

laze 1 = <u>idle</u>, lounge, hang around, loaf, stand around, loll ...*Fred lazed in an easy chair...*

2 *often with* **away** = <u>kill time</u>, waste time, fritter away, pass time, while away the hours, veg out (*slang, chiefly U.S.*), fool away ...*She lazed away most of the morning...*

laziness = <u>idleness</u>, negligence, inactivity, slowness, sloth, sluggishness, slackness, indolence, tardiness, dilatoriness, slothfulness, do-nothingness, faineance

lazy 1 = <u>idle</u>, inactive, indolent, slack, negligent, inert, remiss, workshy, slothful, shiftless ...*I was too lazy to learn how to read music...* OPPOSITE> industrious

2 = <u>lethargic</u>, languorous, slow-moving, languid, sleepy, sluggish, drowsy, somnolent, torpid ...*We would have a lazy lunch and then lie on the beach in the sun...* OPPOSITE> quick

leach = <u>extract</u>, strain, drain, filter, seep, percolate, filtrate, lixiviate (*Chemistry*)

lead VERB **1** = <u>go in front (of)</u>, head, be in front, be at the head (of), walk in front (of) ...*Tom was leading, a rifle slung over his back...*

2 = <u>guide</u>, conduct, steer, escort, precede, usher, pilot, show the way ...*He led him into the house...*

3 = <u>connect to</u>, link, open onto ...*the doors that led to the yard...*

4 = <u>be ahead (of)</u>, be first, exceed, be winning, excel, surpass, come first, transcend, outstrip, outdo, blaze a trail ...*So far he leads by five games to two...*

5 = <u>command</u>, rule, govern, preside over, head, control, manage, direct, supervise, be in charge of, head up ...*He led the country between 1949 and 1984...*

6 = <u>live</u>, have, spend, experience, pass, undergo ...*She led a normal happy life with her sister and brother...*

7 = <u>result in</u>, cause, produce, contribute, generate, bring about, bring on, give rise to, conduce ...*He warned that a pay rise would lead to job cuts...*

8 = <u>cause</u>, prompt, persuade, move, draw, influence, motivate, prevail, induce, incline, dispose ...*It was not as straightforward as we were led to believe...*

NOUN **1** = <u>first place</u>, winning position, primary position, vanguard, van ...*Labour are still in the lead in the opinion polls...*

2 = <u>advantage</u>, start, advance, edge, margin, winning margin ...*He now has a lead of 30 points...*

3 = <u>example</u>, direction, leadership, guidance, model, pattern ...*the need for the president to give a moral lead...*

4 = <u>clue</u>, tip, suggestion, trace, hint, guide, indication, pointer, tip-off ...*The inquiry team is following up possible leads...*

5 = <u>leading role</u>, principal, protagonist, title role, star part, principal part ...*Two dancers from the Bolshoi Ballet dance the leads...*

6 = <u>leash</u>, line, cord, rein, tether ...*He came out with a little dog on a lead...*

ADJECTIVE = <u>main</u>, prime, top, leading, first, head, chief, premier, primary, most important, principal, foremost ...*Cossiga's reaction is the lead story in the Italian press...*

PHRASES **lead off** = <u>begin</u>, start, open, set out, kick off (*informal*), initiate, commence, get going, get under way, inaugurate, start the ball rolling (*informal*) ...*Whenever there was a dance he and I led off...*

♦ **lead someone on** = <u>entice</u>, tempt, lure, mislead, draw on, seduce, deceive, beguile, delude, hoodwink, inveigle, string along (*informal*) ...*I bet she led him on, but how could he be so weak?...* ♦ **lead up to something** = <u>introduce</u>, approach, prepare for, intimate, pave the way for, prepare the way, make advances, make overtures, work round to ...*I'm leading up to something quite important...*

leaden 1 = <u>grey</u>, dingy, overcast, sombre, lacklustre, dark grey, greyish, lustreless, louring *or* lowering ...*The weather was bitterly cold, with leaden skies...*

2 = <u>laboured</u>, wooden, stiff, sluggish, plodding, stilted, humdrum ...*a leaden English translation from the Latin...*

3 = <u>lifeless</u>, dull, gloomy, dismal, dreary, languid, listless, spiritless ...*the leaden boredom of the Victorian marriage...*

4 = <u>heavy</u>, lead, crushing, oppressive, cumbersome, inert, onerous, burdensome ...*The dull, leaden sickly feeling returned...*

leader = <u>principal</u>, president, head, chief, boss (*informal*), director, manager, chairman, captain, chair, premier, governor, commander, superior, ruler, conductor, controller, counsellor, supervisor, superintendent, big name, big gun (*informal*), chairwoman, chieftain, bigwig (*informal*), ringleader, chairperson, big shot (*informal*), overseer, big cheese (*slang, old-fashioned*), big noise (*informal*), big hitter (*informal*), baas (*S. African*), torchbearer, number one OPPOSITE> follower

leadership 1 = <u>authority</u>, control, influence, command, premiership, captaincy, governance, headship, superintendency ...*He praised her leadership during the crisis...*

2 = <u>guidance</u>, government, authority, management, administration, direction, supervision, domination, directorship, superintendency ...*What most people want to see is determined, decisive action and firm leadership...*

leading = <u>principal</u>, top, major, main, first, highest, greatest, ruling, chief, prime, key, primary, supreme, most important, outstanding, governing, superior, dominant, foremost, pre-eminent, unsurpassed, number one OPPOSITE> minor

leaf NOUN **1** = <u>frond</u>, flag, needle, pad, blade, bract, cotyledon, foliole ...*The leaves of the horse chestnut had already fallen...*

2 = <u>page</u>, sheet, folio ...*He flattened the wrappers and* *put them between the leaves of his book…*

PHRASES **leaf through something** (with *book, magazine* etc. as object) = <u>skim</u>, glance, scan, browse, look through, dip into, flick through, flip through, thumb through, riffle …*Most patients derive enjoyment from leafing through old picture albums…*

◆ **turn over a new leaf** = <u>reform</u>, change, improve, amend, make a fresh start, begin anew, change your ways, mend your ways …*He realized he was in the wrong and promised to turn over a new leaf…*

leaflet = <u>booklet</u>, notice, advert (*Brit. informal*), brochure, bill, circular, flyer, tract, pamphlet, handout, mailshot, handbill

leafy = <u>green</u>, leaved, leafed, shaded, shady, summery, verdant, bosky (*literary*), springlike, in foliage

league **NOUN** 1 = <u>association</u>, union, alliance, coalition, group, order, band, corporation, combination, partnership, federation, compact, consortium, guild, confederation, fellowship, fraternity, confederacy …*the League of Nations…*
2 (*Informal*) = <u>class</u>, group, level, category, ability group …*Her success has taken her out of my league…*
PHRASES **in league with someone** = <u>collaborating with</u>, leagued with, allied with, conspiring with, working together with, in cooperation with, in cahoots with (*informal*), hand in glove with …*He accused the President of being in league with the terrorists…*

leak **VERB** 1 = <u>escape</u>, pass, spill, release, discharge, drip, trickle, ooze, seep, exude, percolate …*The pool's sides had cracked and the water had leaked out…*
2 = <u>disclose</u>, tell, reveal, pass on, give away, make public, divulge, let slip, make known, spill the beans (*informal*), blab (*informal*), let the cat out of the bag, blow wide open (*slang*) …*He revealed who had leaked a confidential police report…*
NOUN 1 = <u>leakage</u>, leaking, discharge, drip, oozing, seepage, percolation …*It's thought a gas leak may have caused the blast…*
2 = <u>hole</u>, opening, crack, puncture, aperture, chink, crevice, fissure, perforation …*a leak in the radiator…*
3 = <u>disclosure</u>, exposé, exposure, admission, revelation, uncovering, betrayal, unearthing, divulgence …*Serious leaks involving national security are likely to be investigated…*

leaky = <u>leaking</u>, split, cracked, punctured, porous, waterlogged, perforated, holey, not watertight

lean[1] **VERB** 1 = <u>bend</u>, tip, slope, incline, tilt, heel, slant …*He leaned forward to give her a kiss…*
2 = <u>rest</u>, prop, be supported, recline, repose …*She was feeling tired and was glad to lean against him…*
3 = <u>tend</u>, prefer, favour, incline, be prone to, gravitate, be disposed to, have a propensity to …*Politically, I lean towards the right…*
PHRASES **lean on someone** = <u>depend on</u>, trust, rely on, cling to, count on, confide in, have faith in …*She leaned on him to help her solve her problems…*

lean[2] = <u>thin</u>, slim, slender, skinny, angular, trim, spare, gaunt, bony, lanky, wiry, emaciated, scrawny, svelte,

lank, rangy, scraggy, macilent (*rare*) **OPPOSITE** fat …*She watched the tall, lean figure step into the car…*

leaning = <u>tendency</u>, liking for, bias, inclination, taste, bent, disposition, penchant, propensity, aptitude, predilection, proclivity, partiality, proneness

leap **VERB** 1 = <u>jump</u>, spring, bound, bounce, hop, skip, caper, cavort, frisk, gambol …*The newsreels show him leaping into the air…*
2 = <u>vault</u>, clear, jump, bound, spring …*He leapt over a wall brandishing a weapon…*
3 = <u>rush</u>, jump, come, reach, arrive at, hurry, hasten, form hastily …*People should not leap to conclusions and blame the pilot…*
4 = <u>increase</u>, advance, soar, surge, rocket, escalate, shoot up …*They leapt to third in the table, 31 points behind the leaders…*
NOUN 1 = <u>jump</u>, spring, bound, hop, skip, vault, caper, frisk …*He took Britain's fifth medal with a leap of 2.37 metres…*
2 = <u>rise</u>, change, increase, soaring, surge, escalation, upsurge, upswing …*The result has been a giant leap in productivity…*
PHRASES **leap at something** = <u>accept eagerly</u>, seize on, jump at …*They leapt at the chance of a cheap holiday in Italy…*

learn 1 = <u>master</u>, grasp, acquire, pick up, take in, attain, become able, familiarize yourself with …*Their children were going to learn English…*
2 = <u>discover</u>, hear, understand, gain knowledge, find out about, become aware, discern, ascertain, come to know, suss (out) (*slang*) …*It was only after his death that she learned of his affair…*
3 = <u>memorize</u>, commit to memory, learn by heart, learn by rote, get (something) word-perfect, learn parrot-fashion, get off pat, con (*archaic*) …*He learned this song as an inmate in a Texas prison…*

learned = <u>scholarly</u>, experienced, lettered, cultured, skilled, expert, academic, intellectual, versed, literate, well-informed, erudite, highbrow, well-read **OPPOSITE** uneducated

learner = <u>student</u>, pupil, scholar, novice, beginner, trainee, apprentice, disciple, neophyte, tyro **OPPOSITE** expert

learning = <u>knowledge</u>, study, education, schooling, research, scholarship, tuition, enlightenment

lease = <u>hire</u>, rent, let, loan, charter, rent out, hire out

leash **NOUN** 1 = <u>lead</u>, line, restraint, cord, rein, tether …*All dogs should be on a leash…*
2 = <u>restraint</u>, hold, control, check, curb …*They have kept the company on a tight leash…*
VERB = <u>tether</u>, control, secure, restrain, tie up, hold back, fasten …*Make sure your dog is leashed and muzzled…*

least **DETERMINER** = <u>smallest</u>, meanest, fewest, minutest, lowest, tiniest, minimum, slightest, minimal …*If you like cheese, go for the ones with the least fat…*
PHRASES **at least** = <u>at the minimum</u>, at the very least, not less than …*Aim to have at least half a pint of milk a day…*

leathery = <u>tough</u>, hard, rough, hardened, rugged,

wrinkled, durable, leathern (*archaic*), coriaceous, leatherlike

leave `VERB` **1** = <u>depart from</u>, withdraw from, go from, escape from, desert, quit, flee, exit, pull out of, retire from, move out of, disappear from, run away from, forsake, flit (*informal*), set out from, go away from, hook it (*slang*), pack your bags (*informal*), make tracks, abscond from, decamp from, sling your hook (*Brit. slang*), slope off from, take your leave of, do a bunk from (*Brit. slang*), take yourself off from (*informal*) ...*Just pack your bags and leave*... ...*He was not allowed to leave the country*... `OPPOSITE` arrive
2 = <u>quit</u>, give up, get out of, resign from, drop out of ...*He left school with no qualifications*...
3 = <u>give up</u>, abandon, desert, dump (*informal*), drop, surrender, ditch (*informal*), chuck (*informal*), discard, relinquish, renounce, jilt (*informal*), cast aside, forbear, leave in the lurch ...*He left me for another woman*... `OPPOSITE` stay with
4 = <u>entrust</u>, commit, delegate, refer, hand over, assign, consign, allot, cede, give over ...*For the moment, I leave you to make all the decisions*...
5 = <u>bequeath</u>, will, transfer, endow, transmit, confer, hand down, devise (*Law*), demise ...*He died two years later, leaving everything to his wife*...
6 = <u>forget</u>, lay down, leave behind, mislay ...*I'd left my raincoat in the restaurant*...
7 = <u>cause</u>, produce, result in, generate, deposit ...*Abuse always leaves emotional scars*...
`NOUN` **1** = <u>holiday</u>, break, vacation, time off, sabbatical, leave of absence, furlough ...*Why don't you take a few days' leave?*...
2 = <u>permission</u>, freedom, sanction, liberty, concession, consent, allowance, warrant, authorization, dispensation ...*an application for leave to appeal against the judge's order*... `OPPOSITE` refusal
3 = <u>departure</u>, parting, withdrawal, goodbye, farewell, retirement, leave-taking, adieu, valediction ...*He thanked them for the pleasure of their company and took his leave*... `OPPOSITE` arrival
`PHRASES` **leave off something** = <u>stop</u>, end, finish, give up, cease, halt, break off, refrain from, abstain from, discontinue, knock off (*informal*), give over (*informal*), kick (*informal*), desist, keep off, belay (*Nautical*) ...*We all left off eating and stood about with bowed heads*... ◆ **leave something** or **someone out** = <u>omit</u>, exclude, miss out, forget, except, reject, ignore, overlook, neglect, skip, disregard, bar, cast aside, count out ...*If you prefer mild flavours, leave out the chilli*...

leave-taking = <u>departure</u>, going, leaving, parting, goodbye, farewell, valediction, sendoff (*informal*)

lecherous = <u>lustful</u>, randy (*informal, chiefly Brit.*), raunchy (*slang*), lewd, wanton, carnal, salacious, prurient, lascivious, libidinous, licentious, lubricious (*literary*), concupiscent, goatish (*archaic or literary*), unchaste, ruttish `OPPOSITE` puritanical

lechery = <u>lustfulness</u>, lust, licentiousness, salaciousness, sensuality, profligacy, debauchery, prurience, womanizing, carnality, lewdness, wantonness, lasciviousness, libertinism, concupiscence, randiness (*informal, chiefly Brit.*), leching (*informal*), rakishness, lubricity, libidinousness, lecherousness

lecture `NOUN` **1** = <u>talk</u>, address, speech, lesson, instruction, presentation, discourse, sermon, exposition, harangue, oration, disquisition ...*In his lecture he covered an enormous variety of topics*...
2 = <u>telling-off</u> (*informal*), rebuke, reprimand, talking-to (*informal*), heat (*slang, chiefly U.S. & Canad.*), going-over (*informal*), wigging (*Brit. slang*), censure, scolding, chiding, dressing-down (*informal*), reproof, castigation ...*Our captain gave us a stern lecture on safety*...
`VERB` **1** = <u>talk</u>, speak, teach, address, discourse, spout, expound, harangue, give a talk, hold forth, expatiate ...*She has lectured and taught all over the world*...
2 = <u>tell off</u> (*informal*), berate, scold, reprimand, carpet (*informal*), censure, castigate, chide, admonish, tear into (*informal*), read the riot act, reprove, bawl out (*informal*), chew out (*U.S. & Canad. informal*), tear (someone) off a strip (*Brit. informal*), give a rocket (*Brit. & N.Z. informal*), give someone a talking-to (*informal*), give someone a dressing-down (*informal*), give someone a telling-off (*informal*) ...*He used to lecture me about getting too much sun*...

ledge = <u>shelf</u>, step, ridge, projection, mantle, sill

lee = <u>shelter</u>, cover, screen, protection, shadow, shade, shield, refuge

leech = <u>parasite</u>, hanger-on, sycophant, freeloader (*slang*), sponger (*informal*), ligger (*slang*), bloodsucker (*informal*), quandong (*Austral. slang*)

leer `VERB` = <u>grin</u>, eye, stare, wink, squint, goggle, smirk, drool, gloat, ogle ...*men standing around, leering at passing females*...
`NOUN` = <u>grin</u>, stare, wink, squint, smirk, drool, gloat, ogle ...*When I asked the clerk for my room key, he gave it to me with a leer*...

leery (*Slang*) = <u>wary</u>, cautious, uncertain, suspicious, doubting, careful, shy, sceptical, dubious, unsure, distrustful, on your guard, chary

lees = <u>sediment</u>, grounds, refuse, deposit, precipitate, dregs, settlings

leeway = <u>room</u>, play, space, margin, scope, latitude, elbowroom

left 1 = <u>left-hand</u>, port, larboard (*Nautical*) ...*She had a pain in her chest, on the left side*...
2 (*of politics*) = <u>socialist</u>, liberal, radical, progressive, left-wing, leftist ...*The play offers a new perspective on left politics*...
Related Words
adjectives: sinister, sinistral

leftover `NOUN` = <u>remnant</u>, leaving, remains, scrap, oddment ...*Refrigerate any leftovers*...
`ADJECTIVE` = <u>surplus</u>, remaining, extra, excess, unwanted, unused, uneaten ...*Leftover chicken makes a wonderful salad*...

left-wing = <u>socialist</u>, communist, red (*informal*), radical, leftist, liberal, revolutionary, militant, Marxist, Bolshevik, Leninist, collectivist, Trotskyite

left-winger = <u>socialist</u>, communist, red (*informal*), radical, revolutionary, militant, Marxist, Bolshevik, Leninist, Trotskyite

leg NOUN **1** = limb, member, shank, lower limb, pin (*informal*), stump (*informal*) ...*He was tapping his walking stick against his leg*...
2 = support, prop, brace, upright ...*His ankles were tied to the legs of the chair*...
3 = stage, part, section, stretch, lap, segment, portion ...*The first leg of the journey was by boat*...
PHRASES **a leg up** = boost, help, support, push, assistance, helping hand ...*The strong balance sheet should give a leg up to profits*... ◆ **leg it** (*Informal*) = run, walk, escape, flee, hurry, run away, make off, make tracks, hotfoot, go on foot, skedaddle (*informal*) ...*He was legging it across the field*... ◆ **not have a leg to stand on** (*Informal*) = have no basis, be vulnerable, be undermined, be invalid, be illogical, be defenceless, lack support, be full of holes ...*It's only my word against his, so I don't have a leg to stand on*... ◆ **on its** or **your last legs** = worn out, dying, failing, exhausted, giving up the ghost, at death's door, about to collapse, about to fail, about to break down ...*By the mid-1980s the copper industry in the US was on its last legs*... ◆ **pull someone's leg** (*Informal*) = tease, joke, trick, fool, kid (*informal*), have (someone) on, rag, rib (*informal*), wind up (*Brit. slang*), deceive, hoax, make fun of, poke fun at, twit, chaff, lead up the garden path ...*Of course I won't tell them; I was only pulling your leg*... ◆ **shake a leg** (*Informal*) = hurry, rush, move it, hasten, get cracking (*informal*), get a move on (*informal*), look lively (*informal*), stir your stumps (*informal*) ...*Come on, shake a leg! We've got loads to do today*... ◆ **stretch your legs** = take a walk, exercise, stroll, promenade, move about, go for a walk, take the air ...*Take regular breaks to stretch your legs*...

legacy = bequest, inheritance, endowment, gift, estate, devise (*Law*), heirloom

legal 1 = judicial, judiciary, forensic, juridical, jurisdictive ...*the British legal system*...
2 = lawful, allowed, sanctioned, constitutional, proper, valid, legitimate, authorized, rightful, permissible, legalized, allowable, within the law, licit ...*What I did was perfectly legal*...

legalistic = hairsplitting, narrow, strict, contentious, literal, narrow-minded, polemical, litigious, disputatious

legality = lawfulness, validity, legitimacy, accordance with the law, permissibility, rightfulness, admissibleness

legalize or **legalise** = permit, allow, approve, sanction, license, legitimate, authorize, validate, legitimize, make legal, decriminalize

legal tender = currency, money, medium, payment, specie

legend 1 = myth, story, tale, fiction, narrative, saga, fable, folk tale, urban myth, urban legend, folk story ...*the legends of ancient Greece*...
2 = celebrity, star, phenomenon, genius, spectacle, wonder, big name, marvel, prodigy, luminary, celeb

(*informal*), megastar (*informal*) ...*the blues legend, B.B. King*...
3 = inscription, title, caption, device, device, motto, rubric ...*a banner bearing the following legend*...

legendary 1 = famous, celebrated, well-known, acclaimed, renowned, famed, immortal, illustrious ...*His political skill is legendary*... OPPOSITE unknown
2 = mythical, fabled, traditional, romantic, fabulous, fanciful, fictitious, storybook, apocryphal ...*The hill is supposed to be the resting place of the legendary King Lud*... OPPOSITE factual

legible = readable, clear, plain, bold, neat, distinct, easy to read, easily read, decipherable

legion NOUN **1** = army, company, force, division, troop, brigade ...*The last of the Roman legions left Britain in AD 410*...
2 = multitude, host, mass, drove, number, horde, myriad, throng ...*His sense of humour won him a legion of friends*...
ADJECTIVE = very many, numerous, countless, myriad, numberless, multitudinous ...*Books on this subject are legion*...

legislate = make laws, establish laws, prescribe, enact laws, pass laws, ordain, codify laws, put laws in force

legislation 1 = law, act, ruling, rule, bill, measure, regulation, charter, statute ...*legislation to protect women's rights*...
2 = lawmaking, regulation, prescription, enactment, codification ...*This can be put right through positive legislation*...

legislative = law-making, parliamentary, congressional, judicial, ordaining, law-giving, juridical, jurisdictive

legislator = lawmaker, parliamentarian, lawgiver

legislature = parliament, house, congress, diet, senate, assembly, chamber, law-making body

legitimate ADJECTIVE **1** = lawful, real, true, legal, acknowledged, sanctioned, genuine, proper, authentic, statutory, authorized, rightful, kosher (*informal*), dinkum (*Austral. & N.Z. informal*), legit (*slang*), licit ...*They have demanded the restoration of the legitimate government*... OPPOSITE unlawful
2 = reasonable, just, correct, sensible, valid, warranted, logical, justifiable, well-founded, admissible ...*That's a perfectly legitimate fear*... OPPOSITE unreasonable
VERB = legitimize, allow, permit, sanction, authorize, legalize, give the green light to, legitimatize, pronounce lawful ...*We want to legitimate this process by passing a law*...

legitimize or **legitimise** = legalize, permit, sanction, legitimate, authorize, give the green light to, pronounce lawful

leisure NOUN = spare, free, rest, holiday, quiet, ease, retirement, relaxation, vacation, recreation, time off, breathing space, spare moments ...*a relaxing way to fill my leisure time*... OPPOSITE work
PHRASES **at your leisure** = in your own (good) time, in due course, at your convenience, unhurriedly, when it suits you, without hurry, at an unhurried

pace, when you get round to it (*informal*) ...*He could read through all the national papers at his leisure*...

leisurely ADJECTIVE = <u>unhurried</u>, relaxed, slow, easy, comfortable, gentle, lazy, laid-back (*informal*), restful ...*Lunch was a leisurely affair*... OPPOSITE hurried
ADVERB = <u>unhurriedly</u>, slowly, easily, comfortably, lazily, at your leisure, at your convenience, lingeringly, indolently, without haste ...*We walked leisurely into the hotel*... OPPOSITE hurriedly

lekker (*S. African slang*) = <u>delicious</u>, tasty, luscious, choice, savoury, palatable, dainty, delectable, mouthwatering, yummy (*slang*), scrumptious (*informal*), appetizing, toothsome, ambrosial, yummo (*Austral. slang*)

lemon
(*Related Words*)
adjectives : citric, citrine, citrous
➤ shades of yellow

lend VERB 1 = <u>loan</u>, advance, sub (*Brit. informal*), accommodate one with ...*I lent him ten pounds to go to the pictures*...
2 = <u>give</u>, provide, add, present, supply, grant, afford, contribute, hand out, furnish, confer, bestow, impart ...*He attended the news conference to lend his support*...
PHRASES **lend itself to something** = <u>be appropriate for</u>, suit, be suitable for, fit, be appropriate to, be adaptable to, present opportunities of, be serviceable for ...*The room itself lends itself well to summer eating with its light airy atmosphere*...

length NOUN 1 = <u>distance</u>, reach, measure, extent, span, longitude ...*It is about a metre in length*...
2 = <u>duration</u>, term, period, space, stretch, span, expanse ...*His film is over two hours in length*...
3 = <u>piece</u>, measure, section, segment, portion ...*a 30ft length of rope*...
4 = <u>lengthiness</u>, extent, elongation, wordiness, verbosity, prolixity, long-windedness, extensiveness, protractedness ...*I hope the length of this letter will make up for my not having written earlier*...
PHRASES **at length** 1 = <u>at last</u>, finally, eventually, in time, in the end, at long last ...*At length, my father went into the house*... 2 = <u>for a long time</u>, completely, fully, thoroughly, for hours, in detail, for ages, in depth, to the full, exhaustively, interminably ...*They spoke at length, reviewing the entire incident*...

lengthen 1 = <u>extend</u>, continue, increase, stretch, expand, elongate, make longer ...*The runway had to be lengthened*... OPPOSITE shorten
2 = <u>protract</u>, extend, prolong, draw out, spin out, make longer ...*They want to lengthen the school day*... OPPOSITE cut down

lengthy 1 = <u>protracted</u>, long, prolonged, very long, tedious, lengthened, diffuse, drawn-out, interminable, long-winded, long-drawn-out, overlong, verbose, prolix ...*the lengthy process of filling out forms*...
2 = <u>very long</u>, rambling, interminable, long-winded, wordy, discursive, extended, overlong, verbose, prolix ...*a lengthy article in the newspaper*... OPPOSITE brief

leniency *or* **lenience** = <u>mercy</u>, compassion, clemency, quarter, pity, tolerance, indulgence, tenderness, moderation, gentleness, forbearance, mildness, lenity

lenient = <u>merciful</u>, sparing, gentle, forgiving, kind, tender, mild, tolerant, compassionate, clement, indulgent, forbearing OPPOSITE severe

leper = <u>outcast</u>, reject, untouchable, pariah, lazar (*archaic*)

lesbian ADJECTIVE = <u>homosexual</u>, gay, les (*slang*), butch (*slang*), sapphic, lesbo (*slang*), tribadic ...*Many of her best friends were lesbian*...
NOUN = <u>lezzie</u> (*slang*), les (*slang*), butch (*slang*), lesbo (*slang*) ...*a youth group for lesbians, gays and bisexuals*...

lesion = <u>injury</u>, hurt, wound, bruise, trauma (*Pathology*), sore, impairment, abrasion, contusion

less DETERMINER = <u>smaller quantity</u>, shorter, slighter, not so much ...*Eat less fat to reduce the risk of heart disease*...
ADVERB = <u>to a smaller extent</u>, little, barely, not much, not so much, meagrely ...*We are eating more and exercising less*...
PREPOSITION = <u>minus</u>, without, lacking, excepting, subtracting ...*Company car drivers will pay ten percent, less tax*...

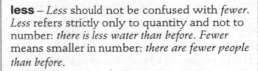

> ## Word Power
>
> **less** – *Less* should not be confused with *fewer*. *Less* refers strictly only to quantity and not to number: *there is less water than before*. *Fewer* means smaller in number: *there are fewer people than before*.

lessen 1 = <u>reduce</u>, lower, diminish, decrease, relax, ease, narrow, moderate, weaken, erode, impair, degrade, minimize, curtail, lighten, wind down, abridge, de-escalate ...*Keep immunisations up to date to lessen the risk of serious illness*... OPPOSITE increase
2 = <u>grow less</u>, diminish, decrease, contract, ease, weaken, shrink, slow down, dwindle, lighten, wind down, die down, abate, slacken ...*The attention she gives him will certainly lessen once the baby is born*...

lessening = <u>reduction</u>, decline, decrease, weakening, slowing down, dwindling, contraction, erosion, waning, ebbing, moderation, let-up (*informal*), petering out, slackening, shrinkage, diminution, abatement, curtailment, minimization, de-escalation

lesser = <u>lower</u>, slighter, secondary, subsidiary, subordinate, inferior, less important OPPOSITE greater

lesson 1 = <u>class</u>, schooling, period, teaching, coaching, session, instruction, lecture, seminar, tutoring, tutorial ...*She took piano lessons*...
2 = <u>example</u>, warning, model, message, moral, deterrent, precept, exemplar ...*There is one lesson to be learned from this crisis*...
3 = <u>exercise</u>, reading, practice, task, lecture, drill, assignment, homework, recitation ...*Now let's look at lesson one*...

4 = <u>Bible reading</u>, reading, text, Bible passage, Scripture passage ...*The Rev. Nicola Judd read the lesson...*

let VERB **1** = <u>enable</u>, make, allow, cause, grant, permit ...*They let him talk...*

2 = <u>allow</u>, grant, permit, warrant, authorize, give the go-ahead, give permission, suffer (*archaic*), give the green light, give leave, give the O.K. or okay (*informal*) ...*Mum didn't let us have sweets very often...*

3 = <u>lease</u>, hire, rent, rent out, hire out, sublease ...*The reasons for letting a house, or part of one, are varied...*

PHRASES **let on** (*Informal*) **1** = <u>reveal</u>, disclose, say, tell, admit, give away, divulge, let slip, make known, let the cat out of the bag (*informal*) ...*He knows who the culprit is, but he is not letting on...*

2 = <u>pretend</u>, make out, feign, simulate, affect, profess, counterfeit, make believe, dissemble, dissimulate ...*He's been knocking on doors, letting on he's selling encyclopedias...* ◆ **let someone down** = <u>disappoint</u>, fail, abandon, desert, disillusion, fall short, leave stranded, leave in the lurch, disenchant, dissatisfy ...*Don't worry, I won't let you down...* ◆ **let someone go** = <u>release</u>, free, let out, allow to leave, set free, allow to escape, turn loose ...*They held him for three hours and then let him go...* ◆ **let someone off** = <u>excuse</u>, release, discharge, pardon, spare, forgive, exempt, dispense, exonerate, absolve, grant an amnesty to ...*The police let him off with a warning...* ◆ **let something** or **someone in** = <u>admit</u>, include, receive, welcome, greet, take in, incorporate, give access to, allow to enter ...*The lattice-work lets in air, but not light...* ◆ **let something down** = <u>deflate</u>, empty, exhaust, flatten, puncture ...*I let the tyres down on his car...* ◆ **let something off 1** = <u>fire</u>, explode, set off, discharge, detonate ...*He had let off fireworks to celebrate the Revolution...* **2** = <u>emit</u>, release, leak, exude, give off ...*They must do it without letting off any fumes...* ◆ **let something out 1** = <u>release</u>, discharge ...*He let out his breath in a long sigh...* **2** = <u>emit</u>, make, produce, give vent to ...*When she saw him, she let out a cry of horror...* **3** = <u>reveal</u>, tell, make known, let slip, leak, disclose, betray, let fall, take the wraps off ...*She let out that she had seen him the night before...* ◆ **let up** = <u>stop</u>, diminish, decrease, subside, relax, ease (up), moderate, lessen, abate, slacken ...*The rain had let up...*

letdown = <u>disappointment</u>, disillusionment, frustration, anticlimax, setback, washout (*informal*), comedown (*informal*), disgruntlement

lethal = <u>deadly</u>, terminal, fatal, deathly, dangerous, devastating, destructive, mortal, murderous, poisonous, virulent, pernicious, noxious, baneful OPPOSITE harmless

lethargic = <u>sluggish</u>, slow, lazy, sleepy, heavy, dull, indifferent, debilitated, inactive, inert, languid, apathetic, drowsy, listless, comatose, stupefied, unenthusiastic, somnolent, torpid, slothful, enervated, unenergetic OPPOSITE energetic

lethargy = <u>sluggishness</u>, inertia, inaction, slowness, indifference, apathy, sloth, stupor, drowsiness, dullness, torpor, sleepiness, lassitude, languor, listlessness, torpidity, hebetude (*rare*) OPPOSITE energy

letter NOUN **1** = <u>message</u>, line, answer, note, reply, communication, dispatch, acknowledgment, billet (*archaic*), missive, epistle ...*I had received a letter from a very close friend...*

2 = <u>character</u>, mark, sign, symbol ...*the letters of the alphabet...*

PLURAL NOUN = <u>learning</u>, education, culture, literature, humanities, scholarship, erudition, belles-lettres ...*bon viveur, man of letters and long-time party supporter...*

PHRASES **to the letter** = <u>precisely</u>, strictly, literally, exactly, faithfully, accurately, word for word, punctiliously ...*She obeyed his instructions to the letter...*

(*Related Words*)

adjective : epistolatory

let-up (*Informal*) = <u>lessening</u>, break, pause, interval, recess, respite, lull, cessation, remission, breathing space, slackening, abatement

level NOUN **1** = <u>position</u>, standard, degree, grade, standing, stage, rank, status ...*in order according to their level of difficulty...*

2 = <u>height</u>, altitude, elevation, vertical position ...*The water came up to her chin and the bubbles were at eye level...*

3 = <u>flat surface</u>, plane, horizontal ...*The horse showed good form on the level...*

ADJECTIVE **1** = <u>equal</u>, in line, aligned, balanced, on a line, at the same height ...*She knelt down so that their eyes were level...*

2 = <u>horizontal</u>, even, flat, plane, smooth, uniform, as flat as a pancake ...*a plateau of level ground...* OPPOSITE slanted

3 = <u>calm</u>, even, regular, stable, steady, unchanging, equable, even-tempered, unvarying ...*He forced his voice to remain level...*

4 = <u>even</u>, tied, equal, drawn, neck and neck, all square, level pegging ...*The teams were level at the end of extra time...*

VERB **1** = <u>equalize</u>, balance, even up ...*He got two goals to level the score...*

2 = <u>destroy</u>, devastate, wreck, demolish, flatten, knock down, pull down, tear down, bulldoze, raze, lay waste to ...*Further tremors could level yet more buildings...* OPPOSITE build

3 = <u>direct</u>, point, turn, train, aim, focus, beam ...*The soldiers level guns at each other along the border...*

4 = <u>flatten</u>, plane, smooth, make flat, even off or out ...*He'd been levelling off the ground before putting up the shed...*

PHRASES **level with someone** (*Informal*) = <u>be honest</u>, be open, be frank, come clean (*informal*), be straightforward, be up front (*slang*), be above board, keep nothing back ...*Levelling with you, I was in two minds before this happened...* ◆ **on the level** (*Informal*) = <u>honest</u>, genuine, sincere, open, straight, fair, square, straightforward, up front (*slang*), dinkum (*Austral. & N.Z. informal*), above board ...*There were *moments where you wondered if anyone was on the level...*

level-headed = <u>calm</u>, balanced, reasonable, composed, together (*slang*), cool, collected, steady, sensible, sane, dependable, unflappable (*informal*), self-possessed, even-tempered

lever NOUN = <u>handle</u>, bar, crowbar, jemmy, handspike *...Robert leaned lightly on the lever and the rock groaned...*
VERB = <u>prise</u>, move, force, raise, pry (*U.S.*), jemmy *...Neighbours eventually levered the door open with a crowbar...*

leverage 1 = <u>influence</u>, authority, pull (*informal*), weight, rank, clout (*informal*), purchasing power, ascendancy *...His position affords him the leverage to get things done through committees...*
2 = <u>force</u>, hold, pull, strength, grip, grasp *...The spade and fork have longer shafts, providing better leverage...*

leviathan = <u>monster</u>, whale, mammoth, Titan, hulk, colossus, behemoth

levy NOUN = <u>tax</u>, fee, toll, tariff, duty, assessment, excise, imposition, impost, exaction *...an annual motorway levy on all drivers...*
VERB = <u>impose</u>, charge, tax, collect, gather, demand, exact *...Taxes should not be levied without the authority of Parliament...*

lewd = <u>indecent</u>, obscene, vulgar, dirty, blue, loose, vile, pornographic, wicked, wanton, X-rated (*informal*), profligate, bawdy, salacious, impure, lascivious, smutty, lustful, libidinous, licentious, unchaste

lexicon = <u>vocabulary</u>, dictionary, glossary, word list, wordbook

liability NOUN 1 = <u>disadvantage</u>, burden, drawback, inconvenience, drag, handicap, minus (*informal*), nuisance, impediment, albatross, hindrance, millstone, encumbrance *...What was once a vote-catching policy is now a political liability...*
2 = <u>responsibility</u>, accountability, culpability, obligation, onus, answerability *...They admit liability, but dispute the amount of his claim...*
PLURAL NOUN = <u>debts</u>, expenditure, debit, arrears, obligations, accounts payable *...The company had liabilities of $250 million...*

liable 1 = <u>likely</u>, tending, inclined, disposed, prone, apt *...Only a small number are liable to harm themselves or others...*
2 = <u>vulnerable</u>, subject, exposed, prone, susceptible, open, at risk of *...These women are particularly liable to depression...*
3 = <u>responsible</u>, accountable, amenable, answerable, bound, obligated, chargeable *...The airline's insurer is liable for damages...*

Word Power

liable – In the past, it was considered incorrect to use *liable* to mean 'probable' or 'likely', as in *it's liable to happen soon*. However, this usage is now generally considered acceptable.

---

liaise = <u>communicate</u>, link up, connect, intermediate, mediate, interchange, hook up, keep contact

liaison 1 = <u>contact</u>, communication, connection, interchange *...Liaison between the police and the art world is vital to combat art crime...*
2 = <u>intermediary</u>, contact, hook-up, go-between *...She acts as a liaison between patients and staff...*
3 = <u>affair</u>, romance, intrigue, fling, love affair, amour, entanglement, illicit romance *...She embarked on a series of sexual liaisons with society figures...*

liar = <u>falsifier</u>, storyteller (*informal*), perjurer, fibber, fabricator, prevaricator

libel NOUN = <u>defamation</u>, slander, misrepresentation, denigration, smear, calumny, vituperation, obloquy, aspersion *...He sued them for libel over the remarks...*
VERB = <u>defame</u>, smear, slur, blacken, malign, denigrate, revile, vilify, slander, traduce, derogate, calumniate, drag (someone's) name through the mud *...The newspaper which libelled him had already offered him compensation...*

liberal 1 = <u>tolerant</u>, enlightened, open-minded, permissive, advanced, catholic, humanitarian, right-on (*informal*), indulgent, easy-going, unbiased, high-minded, broad-minded, unprejudiced, unbigoted, politically correct *or* PC *...She is known to have liberal views on abortion and contraception...* OPPOSITE intolerant
2 = <u>progressive</u>, radical, reformist, libertarian, advanced, right-on (*informal*), forward-looking, humanistic, free-thinking, latitudinarian, politically correct *or* PC *...a liberal democracy with a multiparty political system...* OPPOSITE conservative
3 = <u>abundant</u>, generous, handsome, lavish, ample, rich, plentiful, copious, bountiful, profuse, munificent *...She made liberal use of her older sister's make-up and clothes...* OPPOSITE limited
4 = <u>generous</u>, kind, charitable, extravagant, free-handed, prodigal, altruistic, open-hearted, bountiful, magnanimous, open-handed, unstinting, beneficent, bounteous *...They thanked him for his liberal generosity...* OPPOSITE stingy
5 = <u>flexible</u>, general, broad, rough, free, loose, lenient, not close, inexact, not strict, not literal *...a liberal translation...* OPPOSITE strict

liberalism = <u>progressivism</u>, radicalism, humanitarianism, libertarianism, freethinking, latitudinarianism

liberalize = <u>relax</u>, ease, moderate, modify, stretch, soften, broaden, loosen, mitigate, slacken, ameliorate

liberate = <u>free</u>, release, rescue, save, deliver, discharge, redeem, let out, set free, let loose, untie, emancipate, unchain, unbind, manumit OPPOSITE imprison

liberator = <u>deliverer</u>, saviour, rescuer, redeemer, freer, emancipator, manumitter

liberty NOUN **1** = <u>independence</u>, sovereignty, liberation, autonomy, immunity, self-determination, emancipation, self-government, self-rule …*Such a system would be a blow to the liberty of the people*… **2** = <u>freedom</u>, liberation, redemption, emancipation, deliverance, manumission, enfranchisement, unshackling, unfettering …*Three convictions meant three months' loss of liberty*… OPPOSITE restraint PHRASES **at liberty 1** = <u>free</u>, escaped, unlimited, at large, not confined, untied, on the loose, unchained, unbound …*There is no confirmation that he is at liberty*… **2** = <u>able</u>, free, allowed, permitted, entitled, authorized …*I'm not at liberty to say where it is, because the deal hasn't gone through yet*… ♦ **take liberties** or **a liberty** = <u>not show enough respect</u>, show disrespect, act presumptuously, behave too familiarly, behave impertinently …*She knew she was taking a big liberty in doing this for him without his knowledge*…

libretto = <u>words</u>, book, lines, text, script, lyrics

licence NOUN **1** = <u>certificate</u>, document, permit, charter, warrant …*The painting was returned on a temporary import licence*… **2** = <u>permission</u>, the right, authority, leave, sanction, liberty, privilege, immunity, entitlement, exemption, prerogative, authorization, dispensation, a free hand, carte blanche, blank cheque …*The curfew gave the police licence to hunt people as if they were animals*… OPPOSITE denial **3** = <u>freedom</u>, creativity, latitude, independence, liberty, deviation, leeway, free rein, looseness …*All that stuff about catching a giant fish was just a bit of poetic licence*… OPPOSITE restraint **4** = <u>laxity</u>, abandon, disorder, excess, indulgence, anarchy, lawlessness, impropriety, irresponsibility, profligacy, licentiousness, unruliness, immoderation …*a world of licence and corruption*… OPPOSITE moderation PHRASES **under licence** = <u>with permission</u>, under a charter, under warrant, under a permit, with authorization, under a patent …*They made the Mig-21 jet fighter under licence from Russia*…

license = <u>permit</u>, commission, enable, sanction, allow, entitle, warrant, authorize, empower, certify, accredit, give a blank cheque to OPPOSITE forbid

lick VERB **1** = <u>taste</u>, lap, tongue, touch, wash, brush …*The dog licked the man's hand excitedly*… **2** (*Informal*) = <u>beat</u>, defeat, overcome, best, top, stuff (*slang*), tank (*slang*), undo, rout, excel, surpass, outstrip, outdo, trounce, clobber (*slang*), vanquish, run rings around (*informal*), wipe the floor with (*informal*), blow out of the water (*slang*) …*He might be able to lick us all in a fair fight*… **3** (*of flames*) = <u>flicker</u>, touch, flick, dart, ripple, ignite, play over, kindle …*The fire sent its red tongues licking into the hallway*… NOUN **1** = <u>dab</u>, little, bit, touch, taste, sample, stroke, brush, speck …*It could do with a lick of paint to

brighten up its premises*… **2** (*Informal*) = <u>pace</u>, rate, speed, clip (*informal*) …*an athletic cyclist travelling at a fair lick*…

licking 1 = <u>defeat</u>, beating, pasting (*slang*), trouncing, drubbing …*They gave us a hell of a licking*… **2** = <u>thrashing</u>, beating, hiding (*informal*), whipping, tanning (*slang*), flogging, spanking, drubbing …*If Dad came home and found us, we could expect a licking*…

lie¹ NOUN = <u>falsehood</u>, deceit, fabrication, fib, fiction, invention, deception, untruth, porky (*Brit. slang*), pork pie (*Brit. slang*), white lie, falsification, prevarication, falsity, mendacity …*I've had enough of your lies*… VERB = <u>fib</u>, fabricate, invent, misrepresent, falsify, tell a lie, prevaricate, perjure, not tell the truth, equivocate, dissimulate, tell untruths, not speak the truth, say something untrue, forswear yourself …*If asked, he lies about his age*… PHRASES **give the lie to something** = <u>disprove</u>, expose, discredit, contradict, refute, negate, invalidate, rebut, make a nonsense of, prove false, controvert, confute …*This survey gives the lie to the idea that Britain is moving towards economic recovery*…

(Related Words)
adjective : mendacious

lie² **1** = <u>recline</u>, rest, lounge, couch, sprawl, stretch out, be prone, loll, repose, be prostrate, be supine, be recumbent …*He was lying motionless on his back*… **2** = <u>be placed</u>, be, rest, exist, extend, be situated …*a newspaper lying on a nearby couch*… **3** = <u>be situated</u>, sit, be located, be positioned …*The islands lie at the southern end of the mountain range*… **4** usually with **in** = <u>exist</u>, be present, consist, dwell, reside, pertain, inhere …*The problem lay in the large amounts spent on defence*… **5** = <u>be buried</u>, remain, rest, be, be found, belong, be located, be interred, be entombed …*Here lies Catin, son of Magarus*… **6** usually with **on** or **upon** = <u>weigh</u>, press, rest, burden, oppress …*The pain of losing his younger brother still lies heavy on his mind*…

liege = <u>feudal lord</u>, master, superior, sovereign, chieftain, overlord, seigneur, suzerain

lieu
PHRASES **in lieu of** = <u>instead of</u>, in place of

life NOUN **1** = <u>being</u>, existence, breath, entity, vitality, animation, viability, sentience …*a newborn baby's first minutes of life*… **2** = <u>living things</u>, creatures, wildlife, organisms, living beings …*Is there life on Mars?*… **3** = <u>existence</u>, being, lifetime, time, days, course, span, duration, continuance …*He spent the last fourteen years of his life in retirement*… **4** = <u>way of life</u>, situation, conduct, behaviour, life style …*How did you adjust to college life?*… **5** = <u>liveliness</u>, activity, energy, spirit, go (*informal*), pep, sparkle, vitality, animation, vigour, verve, zest, high spirits, get-up-and-go (*informal*), oomph (*informal*), brio, vivacity …*The town itself was full of life and character*…

6 = <u>biography</u>, story, history, career, profile, confessions, autobiography, memoirs, life story ...*It was his aim to write a life of John Paul Jones*...
7 = <u>spirit</u>, heart, soul, essence, core, lifeblood, moving spirit, vital spark, animating spirit, élan vital (*French*) ...*He's sucked the life out of her*...
8 = <u>person</u>, human, individual, soul, human being, mortal ...*a war in which thousands of lives were lost*...
PHRASES **come to life** = <u>rouse</u>, revive, awaken, become active, become animate, show signs of life ...*Poems which had seemed dull suddenly came to life*... ◆ **for dear life** (*Informal*) = <u>desperately</u>, quickly, vigorously, urgently, intensely, for all you are worth ...*I made for the raft and clung on for dear life*...
◆ **give your life** = <u>lay down your life</u>, die, sacrifice yourself ...*He gave his life to save his family*...
◆ **that's life** = <u>that's the way things are</u>, that's it, that's the way the cookie crumbles (*informal*) ...*'It might never have happened if she hadn't gone back.' 'That's life.'*...

(*Related Words*)
adjectives: animate, vital

lifeblood = <u>animating force</u> = <u>critical</u>, life, heart, inspiration, guts (*informal*), essence, stimulus, driving force, vital spark

lifeless **1** = <u>dead</u>, unconscious, extinct, deceased, cold, defunct, inert, inanimate, comatose, out cold, out for the count, insensible, in a faint, insensate, dead to the world (*informal*) ...*There was no breathing or pulse and he was lifeless*... **OPPOSITE** alive
2 = <u>barren</u>, empty, desert, bare, waste, sterile, unproductive, uninhabited ...*They may appear lifeless, but they provide a valuable habitat for plants and animals*...
3 = <u>dull</u>, cold, flat, hollow, heavy, slow, wooden, stiff, passive, static, pointless, sluggish, lacklustre, lethargic, colourless, listless, torpid, spiritless ...*His novels are shallow and lifeless*... **OPPOSITE** lively

lifelike = <u>realistic</u>, faithful, authentic, natural, exact, graphic, vivid, photographic, true-to-life, undistorted

lifelong = <u>long-lasting</u>, enduring, lasting, permanent, constant, lifetime, for life, persistent, long-standing, perennial, deep-rooted, for all your life

lifetime = <u>existence</u>, time, day(s), course, period, span, life span, your natural life, all your born days

lift **VERB** **1** = <u>raise</u>, pick up, hoist, draw up, elevate, uplift, heave up, buoy up, raise high, bear aloft, upheave, upraise ...*Curious shoppers lifted their children to take a closer look at the parade*... **OPPOSITE** lower
2 = <u>revoke</u>, end, remove, withdraw, stop, relax, cancel, terminate, rescind, annul, countermand ...*The Commission has urged them to lift their ban on imports*... **OPPOSITE** impose
3 = <u>exalt</u>, raise, improve, advance, promote, boost, enhance, upgrade, elevate, dignify, cheer up, perk up, ameliorate, buoy up ...*A brisk walk in the fresh air can lift your mood*... **OPPOSITE** depress
4 = <u>disappear</u>, clear, vanish, disperse, dissipate, rise, be dispelled ...*The fog had lifted and revealed a warm sunny day*...

5 (*Informal*) = <u>steal</u>, take, copy, appropriate, nick (*slang, chiefly Brit.*), pocket, pinch (*informal*), pirate, cabbage (*Brit. slang*), crib (*informal*), half-inch (*old-fashioned slang*), blag (*slang*), pilfer, purloin, plagiarize, thieve ...*The line could have been lifted from a Woody Allen film*...
NOUN **1** = <u>boost</u>, encouragement, stimulus, reassurance, uplift, pick-me-up, fillip, shot in the arm (*informal*), gee-up ...*My selection for the team has given me a tremendous lift*... **OPPOSITE** blow
2 = <u>elevator</u> (*chiefly U.S.*), hoist, paternoster ...*They took the lift to the fourth floor*...
3 = <u>ride</u>, run, drive, transport, hitch (*informal*), car ride ...*He had a car and often gave me a lift home*...
PHRASES **lift off** = <u>take off</u>, be launched, blast off, take to the air ...*The plane lifted off and climbed steeply into the night sky*...

light¹ **NOUN** **1** = <u>brightness</u>, illumination, luminosity, luminescence, ray of light, flash of light, shining, glow, blaze, sparkle, glare, gleam, brilliance, glint, lustre, radiance, incandescence, phosphorescence, scintillation, effulgence, lambency, refulgence ...*Cracks of light filtered through the shutters*... **OPPOSITE** dark
2 = <u>lamp</u>, bulb, torch, candle, flare, beacon, lighthouse, lantern, taper ...*You get into the music and lights, and the people around you*...
3 = <u>match</u>, spark, flame, lighter ...*Have you got a light, anybody?*...
4 = <u>aspect</u>, approach, attitude, context, angle, point of view, interpretation, viewpoint, slant, standpoint, vantage point ...*He has worked hard to portray New York in a better light*...
5 = <u>understanding</u>, knowledge, awareness, insight, information, explanation, illustration, enlightenment, comprehension, illumination, elucidation ...*At last the light dawned. He was going to get married!*... **OPPOSITE** mystery
6 = <u>daybreak</u>, morning, dawn, sun, sunrise, sunshine, sunlight, daylight, daytime, sunbeam, morn (*poetic*), cockcrow, broad day ...*Three hours before first light, he gave orders for the evacuation of the camp*...
ADJECTIVE **1** = <u>bright</u>, brilliant, shining, glowing, sunny, illuminated, luminous, well-lighted, well-lit, lustrous, aglow, well-illuminated ...*Her house is light and airy, crisp and clean*... **OPPOSITE** dark
2 = <u>pale</u>, fair, faded, blonde, blond, bleached, pastel, light-coloured, whitish, light-toned, light-hued ...*The walls are light in colour*... **OPPOSITE** dark
VERB **1** = <u>illuminate</u>, light up, brighten, lighten, put on, turn on, clarify, switch on, floodlight, irradiate, illumine, flood with light ...*The giant moon lit the road brightly*... **OPPOSITE** darken
2 = <u>ignite</u>, inflame, fire, torch, kindle, touch off, set alight, set a match to ...*He hunched down to light a cigarette*... **OPPOSITE** put out
PHRASES **bring something to light** = <u>reveal</u>, expose, unveil, show, discover, disclose, show up, uncover, unearth, lay bare ...*The truth is unlikely to be brought to light by this enquiry*... ◆ **come to light** = <u>be revealed</u>, appear, come out, turn up, be discovered, become known, become apparent, be

disclosed, transpire …*Nothing about this sum has come to light…* ◆ **in the light of something** = considering, because of, taking into account, bearing in mind, in view of, taking into consideration, with knowledge of …*In the light of this information, we can now identify a number of issues…* ◆ **light up** 1 = cheer, shine, blaze, sparkle, animate, brighten, lighten, irradiate …*Sue's face lit up with surprise…* 2 = shine, flash, beam, blaze, sparkle, flare, glare, gleam, flicker …*a keypad that lights up when you pick up the handset…* ◆ **shed** or **throw light on something** = explain, clarify, make clear, clear up, simplify, make plain, elucidate …*A new approach may shed light on the problem…*

Related Words
prefix : photo-

light² ADJECTIVE 1 = insubstantial, thin, delicate, lightweight, easy, slight, portable, buoyant, airy, flimsy, underweight, not heavy, transportable, lightsome, imponderous …*Try to wear light, loose clothes…* OPPOSITE heavy
2 = weak, soft, gentle, moderate, slight, mild, faint, indistinct …*a light breeze…* OPPOSITE strong
3 = crumbly, loose, sandy, porous, spongy, friable …*light, tropical soils…* OPPOSITE hard
4 = digestible, small, restricted, modest, frugal, not rich, not heavy …*wine and cheese or other light refreshment…* OPPOSITE substantial
5 = undemanding, easy, simple, moderate, manageable, effortless, cushy (*informal*), untaxing, unexacting …*He was on the training field for some light work yesterday…* OPPOSITE strenuous
6 = insignificant, small, minute, tiny, slight, petty, trivial, trifling, inconsequential, inconsiderable, unsubstantial …*She confessed her astonishment at her light sentence…* OPPOSITE serious
7 = light-hearted, pleasing, funny, entertaining, amusing, diverting, witty, trivial, superficial, humorous, gay, trifling, frivolous, unserious …*a light entertainment programme…* OPPOSITE serious
8 = carefree, happy, bright, lively, sunny, cheerful, animated, merry, gay, airy, frivolous, cheery, untroubled, blithe, light-hearted …*to finish on a lighter note…*
9 = nimble, graceful, airy, deft, agile, sprightly, lithe, limber, lissom, light-footed, sylphlike …*the light steps of a ballet dancer…* OPPOSITE clumsy
10 = dizzy, reeling, faint, volatile, giddy, unsteady, light-headed …*Her head felt light, and a serene confidence came over her…*

PHRASES **light on** or **upon something** 1 = settle, land, perch, alight …*Her eyes lit on the brandy that he had dropped on the floor…* 2 = come across, find, discover, encounter, stumble on, hit upon, happen upon …*the kind of thing that philosophers lighted upon…* ◆ **light out** (*U.S.*) = run away, escape, depart, make off, abscond, quit, do a runner (*slang*), scarper (*Brit. slang*), do a bunk (*Brit. slang*), fly the coop (*U.S. & Canad. informal*), skedaddle (*informal*), take a powder (*U.S. & Canad. slang*), take it on the lam (*U.S. & Canad. slang*) …*I lit out of the door and never went back*

again…

lighten¹ = brighten, flash, shine, illuminate, gleam, light up, irradiate, become light, make bright …*The sky began to lighten…*

lighten² 1 = ease, relieve, alleviate, allay, reduce, facilitate, lessen, mitigate, assuage …*He felt the need to lighten the atmosphere…* OPPOSITE intensify
2 = cheer, lift, revive, brighten, hearten, perk up, buoy up, gladden, elate …*Here's a little something to lighten your spirits…* OPPOSITE depress
3 = make lighter, ease, disburden, reduce in weight …*Blending with a food processor lightens the mixture…*

light-headed 1 = faint, dizzy, hazy, giddy, delirious, unsteady, vertiginous, woozy (*informal*) …*Your blood pressure will drop and you may feel light-headed…*
2 = frivolous, silly, shallow, foolish, superficial, trifling, inane, flippant, flighty, bird-brained (*informal*), featherbrained, rattlebrained (*slang*) …*a light-headed girl…*

light-hearted = carefree, happy, bright, glad, sunny, cheerful, jolly, merry, upbeat (*informal*), playful, joyous, joyful, genial, chirpy (*informal*), jovial, untroubled, gleeful, happy-go-lucky, gay, effervescent, blithe, insouciant, frolicsome, ludic (*literary*), jocund, blithesome (*literary*) OPPOSITE gloomy

lightly 1 = moderately, thinly, slightly, sparsely, sparingly …*a small and lightly armed UN contingent…* OPPOSITE heavily
2 = gently, softly, slightly, faintly, delicately, gingerly, airily, timidly …*He kissed her lightly on the mouth…* OPPOSITE forcefully
3 = carelessly, indifferently, breezily, thoughtlessly, flippantly, frivolously, heedlessly, slightingly …*'Once a detective always a detective,' he said lightly…* OPPOSITE seriously
4 = easily, simply, readily, effortlessly, unthinkingly, without thought, flippantly, heedlessly …*His allegations cannot be dismissed lightly…* OPPOSITE with difficulty

lightweight 1 = thin, fine, delicate, sheer, flimsy, gossamer, diaphanous, filmy, unsubstantial …*lightweight denim…*
2 = unimportant, shallow, trivial, insignificant, slight, petty, worthless, trifling, flimsy, paltry, inconsequential, undemanding, insubstantial, nickel-and-dime (*U.S. slang*), of no account …*Some of the discussion in the book is lightweight and unconvincing…* OPPOSITE significant

like¹ ADJECTIVE = similar to, same as, allied to, equivalent to, parallel to, resembling, identical to, alike, corresponding to, comparable to, akin to, approximating, analogous to, cognate to …*She's a great friend; we are like sisters…* OPPOSITE different
NOUN = equal, equivalent, parallel, match, twin, counterpart …*We are dealing with an epidemic the like of which we have never seen…* OPPOSITE opposite

Word Power

like – The use of *like* to mean 'such as' was in the past considered undesirable in formal writing, but has now become acceptable, for example in *I enjoy team sports like football and rugby*. However, the common use of *look like* and *seem like* to mean 'look or seem as if' is thought by many people to be incorrect or nonstandard. You might say *it looks as if* (or *as though*) *he's coming*, but it is still wise to avoid *it looks like he's coming*, particularly in formal or written contexts.

like² VERB **1** = <u>enjoy</u>, love, adore (*informal*), delight in, go for, dig (*slang*), relish, savour, revel in, be fond of, be keen on, be partial to, have a preference for, have a weakness for ...*He likes baseball*... OPPOSITE dislike
2 = <u>admire</u>, approve of, appreciate, prize, take to, esteem, cherish, hold dear, take a shine to (*informal*), think well of ...*I like the way this book is set out*...
OPPOSITE dislike
3 = <u>wish</u>, want, choose, prefer, desire, select, fancy, care, feel inclined ...*Would you like to come back for coffee?*...
NOUN *usually plural* = <u>liking</u>, favourite, preference, cup of tea (*informal*), predilection, partiality ...*I know all her likes and dislikes, and her political viewpoints*...

likelihood = <u>probability</u>, chance, possibility, prospect, liability, good chance, strong possibility, reasonableness, likeliness

likely ADJECTIVE **1** = <u>inclined</u>, disposed, prone, liable, tending, apt ...*People are more likely to accept change if they understand it*...
2 = <u>probable</u>, expected, anticipated, odds-on, on the cards, to be expected ...*A 'yes' vote is the likely outcome*...
3 = <u>plausible</u>, possible, reasonable, credible, feasible, believable, verisimilar ...*It's likely that he still loves her*...
4 = <u>appropriate</u>, promising, pleasing, fit, fair, favourite, qualified, suitable, acceptable, proper, hopeful, agreeable, up-and-coming, befitting ...*He seemed a likely candidate to becoming Prime Minister*...
ADVERB = <u>probably</u>, no doubt, presumably, in all probability, like enough (*informal*), doubtlessly, like as not (*informal*) ...*Very likely he'd told them of his business interest*...

Word Power

likely – When using *likely* as an adverb, it is usual to precede it by another, intensifying, adverb such as *very* or *most*, for example *it will most likely rain*. The use of *likely* as an adverb without an intensifier, for example *it will likely rain*, is considered nonstandard in British English, though it is common in colloquial US English.

like-minded = <u>agreeing</u>, compatible, harmonious, in harmony, unanimous, in accord, of one mind, of the same mind, en rapport (*French*)

liken = <u>compare</u>, match, relate, parallel, equate, juxtapose, mention in the same breath, set beside

likeness 1 = <u>resemblance</u>, similarity, correspondence, affinity, similitude ...*These stories have a startling likeness to one another*...
2 = <u>portrait</u>, study, picture, model, image, photograph, copy, counterpart, representation, reproduction, replica, depiction, facsimile, effigy, delineation ...*The museum displays wax likenesses of every US president*...
3 = <u>appearance</u>, form, guise, semblance ...*a disservice in the likeness of a favour*...

likewise 1 = <u>also</u>, too, as well, further, in addition, moreover, besides, furthermore ...*All their attempts were spurned. Similar offers from the right were likewise rejected*...
2 = <u>similarly</u>, the same, in the same way, in similar fashion, in like manner ...*He made donations and encouraged others to do likewise*...

liking = <u>fondness</u>, love, taste, desire, bent, stomach, attraction, weakness, tendency, preference, bias, affection, appreciation, inclination, thirst, affinity, penchant, propensity, soft spot, predilection, partiality, proneness OPPOSITE dislike

lilt = <u>rhythm</u>, intonation, cadence, beat, pitch, swing, sway

limb 1 = <u>part</u>, member, arm, leg, wing, extension, extremity, appendage ...*She stretched out her cramped limbs*...
2 = <u>branch</u>, spur, projection, offshoot, bough ...*the limb of an enormous leafy tree*...

limber ADJECTIVE = <u>pliant</u>, flexible, supple, agile, plastic, graceful, elastic, lithe, pliable, lissom(e), loose-jointed, loose-limbed ...*He bent at the waist to show how limber his long back was*...
PHRASES **limber up** = <u>loosen up</u>, prepare, exercise, warm up, get ready ...*The dancers were limbering up at the back of the hall*... ...*some exercises to limber up the legs*...

limelight = <u>publicity</u>, recognition, fame, the spotlight, attention, prominence, stardom, public eye, public notice, glare of publicity

limit NOUN **1** = <u>end</u>, bound, ultimate, deadline, utmost, breaking point, termination, extremity, greatest extent, the bitter end, end point, cutoff point, furthest bound ...*Her love for him was being tested to its limits*...
2 = <u>boundary</u>, end, edge, border, extent, pale, confines, frontier, precinct, perimeter, periphery ...*the city limits*...
3 = <u>limitation</u>, maximum, restriction, ceiling, restraint ...*He outlined the limits of British power*...
VERB = <u>restrict</u>, control, check, fix, bound, confine, specify, curb, restrain, ration, hinder, circumscribe, hem in, demarcate, delimit, put a brake on, keep within limits, straiten ...*He limited payments on the country's foreign debt*...
PHRASES **the limit** (*Informal*) = <u>the end</u>, it (*informal*), enough, the last straw, the straw that broke the

camel's back ...*Really, Mark, you are the limit!*...

limitation 1 = <u>restriction</u>, control, check, block, curb, restraint, constraint, obstruction, impediment ...*There is to be no limitation on the number of opposition parties*...

2 = <u>weakness</u>, failing, qualification, reservation, defect, disadvantage, flaw, drawback, shortcoming, snag, imperfection ...*This drug has one important limitation*...

limited 1 = <u>restricted</u>, controlled, fixed, defined, checked, bounded, confined, curbed, hampered, constrained, finite, circumscribed ...*They have a limited amount of time to get their point across*...

> OPPOSITE unlimited

2 = <u>narrow</u>, little, small, restricted, slight, inadequate, minimal, insufficient, unsatisfactory, scant ...*The shop has a very limited selection*...

limitless = <u>infinite</u>, endless, unlimited, never-ending, vast, immense, countless, untold, boundless, unending, inexhaustible, undefined, immeasurable, unbounded, numberless, measureless, illimitable, uncalculable

limp¹ VERB = <u>hobble</u>, stagger, stumble, shuffle, halt (*archaic*), hop, falter, shamble, totter, dodder, hirple (*Scot.*) ...*He limped off with a leg injury*...

NOUN = <u>lameness</u>, hobble, hirple (*Scot.*) ...*A stiff knee forced her to walk with a limp*...

limp² **1** = <u>floppy</u>, soft, relaxed, loose, flexible, slack, lax, drooping, flabby, limber, pliable, flaccid ...*The residue can leave the hair limp and dull looking*... OPPOSITE stiff

2 = <u>weak</u>, tired, exhausted, worn out, spent, debilitated, lethargic, enervated ...*He carried her limp body into the room and laid her on the bed*... OPPOSITE strong

limpid 1 = <u>clear</u>, bright, pure, transparent, translucent, crystal-clear, crystalline, pellucid ...*limpid rock-pools*...

2 = <u>understandable</u>, clear, lucid, unambiguous, comprehensible, intelligible, perspicuous ...*The speech was a model of its kind – limpid and unaffected*...

line¹ NOUN **1** = <u>stroke</u>, mark, rule, score, bar, band, channel, dash, scratch, slash, underline, streak, stripe, groove ...*Draw a line down the centre of the page*...

2 = <u>wrinkle</u>, mark, crease, furrow, crow's foot ...*He has a large, generous face with deep lines*...

3 = <u>row</u>, queue, rank, file, series, column, sequence, convoy, procession, crocodile (*Brit.*) ...*Children clutching empty bowls form a line*...

4 = <u>string</u>, cable, wire, strand, rope, thread, cord, filament, wisp ...*a piece of fishing line*...

5 = <u>trajectory</u>, way, course, track, channel, direction, route, path, axis ...*Walk in a straight line*...

6 = <u>outline</u>, shape, figure, style, cut, features, appearance, profile, silhouette, configuration, contour ...*a dress that follows the line of the body*...

7 = <u>boundary</u>, mark, limit, edge, border, frontier, partition, borderline, demarcation ...*the California state line*...

8 (*Military*) = <u>formation</u>, front, position, front line, trenches, firing line ...*the fortification they called the Maginot Line*...

9 = <u>approach</u>, policy, position, way, course, practice, scheme, method, technique, procedure, tactic, avenue, ideology, course of action ...*The government promised to take a hard line on terrorism*...

10 = <u>occupation</u>, work, calling, interest, business, job, area, trade, department, field, career, activity, bag (*slang*), employment, province, profession, pursuit, forte, vocation, specialization ...*What was your father's line of business?*...

11 = <u>lineage</u>, family, breed, succession, race, stock, strain, descent, ancestry, parentage ...*We were part of a long line of artists*...

12 = <u>note</u>, message, letter, memo, report, word, card, e-mail, postcard ...*My phone doesn't work, so drop me a line*...

PLURAL NOUN = <u>principle</u>, plan, example, model, pattern, procedure, convention ...*so-called autonomous republics based on ethnic lines*...

VERB **1** = <u>border</u>, edge, bound, fringe, rank, skirt, verge, rim ...*Thousands of people lined the streets as the procession went by*...

2 = <u>mark</u>, draw, crease, furrow, cut, rule, score, trace, underline, inscribe ...*Her face was lined with concern*...

PHRASES **draw the line at something** = <u>object to</u>, prohibit, stop short at, set a limit at, put your foot down over ...*He declared that he would draw the line at hitting a woman*... ♦ **in line 1** = <u>in alignment</u>, lined, level, true, straight, lined up, in a row, plumb ...*Venus, the Sun and Earth were all in line*... **2** = <u>under control</u>, in order, in check ...*All this was just designed to frighten me and keep me in line*... ♦ **in line for** = <u>due for</u>, being considered for, a candidate for, shortlisted for, in the running for, on the short list for, next in succession to ...*He must be in line for a place in the Guinness Book of Records*... ♦ **in line with** = <u>in accord</u>, in agreement, in harmony, in step, in conformity ...*This is in line with medical opinion*...

♦ **line something up 1** = <u>align</u>, order, range, arrange, sequence, array, regiment, dispose, marshal, straighten, straighten up, put in a line ...*He lined the glasses up behind the bar*... **2** = <u>prepare</u>, schedule, organize, secure, obtain, come up with, assemble, get together, lay on, procure ...*He's lining up a two-week tour for the New Year*... ♦ **line up** = <u>queue up</u>, file, fall in, form a queue, form ranks ...*The senior leaders lined up behind him in orderly rows*...

line² = <u>fill</u>, face, cover, reinforce, encase, inlay, interline, ceil ...*They line their dens with leaves and grass*...

lineage = <u>descent</u>, family, line, succession, house, stock, birth, breed, pedigree, extraction, ancestry, forebears, progeny, heredity, forefathers, genealogy

lined 1 = <u>wrinkled</u>, worn, furrowed, wizened ...*His lined face was that of an old man*...

2 = <u>ruled</u>, feint ...*Take a piece of lined paper*...

line-up = <u>arrangement</u>, team, row, selection, array

linger 1 = <u>continue</u>, last, remain, stay, carry on, endure, persist, abide ...*The guilty feelings lingered*...

2 = <u>hang on</u>, last, survive, cling to life, die slowly ...*He lingered for weeks in a coma...*
3 = <u>stay</u>, remain, stop, wait, delay, lag, hang around, idle, dally, loiter, take your time, wait around, dawdle, hang in the air, procrastinate, tarry, drag your feet *or* heels ...*Customers are welcome to linger over coffee until midnight...*

lingering = <u>slow</u>, prolonged, protracted, long-drawn-out, remaining, dragging, persistent

lingo (*Informal*) = <u>language</u>, jargon, dialect, talk, speech, tongue, idiom, vernacular, patter, cant, patois, argot

link NOUN **1** = <u>connection</u>, relationship, association, tie-up, affinity, affiliation, vinculum ...*the link between smoking and lung cancer...*
2 = <u>relationship</u>, association, tie, bond, connection, attachment, liaison, affinity, affiliation ...*They hope to cement close links with Moscow...*
3 = <u>component</u>, part, piece, division, element, constituent ...*Seafood is the first link in a chain of contaminations...*
VERB **1** = <u>associate</u>, relate, identify, connect, bracket ...*Liver cancer is linked to the hepatitis B virus...*
2 = <u>connect</u>, join, unite, couple, tie, bind, attach, fasten, yoke ...*the Channel Tunnel linking Britain and France...* OPPOSITE> separate

lion = <u>hero</u>, champion, fighter, warrior, conqueror, lionheart, brave person
(*Related Words*)
adjective : leonine
female : lioness
young : cub
collective nouns : pride, troop

lip NOUN **1** = <u>edge</u>, rim, brim, margin, brink, flange ...*the lip of the jug...*
2 (*Slang*) = <u>impudence</u>, rudeness, insolence, impertinence, sauce (*informal*), cheek (*informal*), effrontery, backchat (*informal*), brass neck (*informal*) ...*Enough of that lip if you want me to help you!...*
PHRASES **smack** *or* **lick your lips** = <u>gloat</u>, drool, slaver ...*They licked their lips in anticipation...*
(*Related Words*)
adjective : labial

liquefy = <u>melt</u>, dissolve, thaw, liquidize, run, fuse, flux, deliquesce

liquid NOUN = <u>fluid</u>, solution, juice, liquor, sap ...*Drink plenty of liquid...*
ADJECTIVE **1** = <u>fluid</u>, running, flowing, wet, melted, thawed, watery, molten, runny, liquefied, aqueous ...*Wash in warm water with liquid detergent...*
2 = <u>clear</u>, bright, brilliant, shining, transparent, translucent, limpid ...*a mosaic of liquid cobalts and greens...*
3 = <u>smooth</u>, clear, soft, flowing, sweet, pure, melting, fluent, melodious, mellifluous, dulcet, mellifluent ...*He had a deep liquid voice...*
4 (*of assets*) = <u>convertible</u>, disposable, negotiable, realizable ...*The bank had sufficient liquid assets to continue operating...*

liquidate 1 = <u>dissolve</u>, cancel, abolish, terminate,

annul ...*A unanimous vote was taken to liquidate the company...*
2 = <u>convert to cash</u>, cash, realize, sell off, sell up ...*The company closed down operations and began liquidating its assets...*
3 = <u>kill</u>, murder, remove, destroy, do in (*slang*), silence, eliminate, take out (*slang*), get rid of, wipe out (*informal*), dispatch, finish off, do away with, blow away (*slang, chiefly U.S.*), annihilate, exterminate, bump off (*slang*), rub out (*U.S. slang*) ...*They have not hesitated in the past to liquidate their rivals...*

liquor 1 = <u>alcohol</u>, drink, spirits, booze (*informal*), grog, hard stuff (*informal*), strong drink, Dutch courage (*informal*), intoxicant, juice (*informal*), hooch or hootch (*informal, chiefly U.S. & Canad.*) ...*The room was filled with cases of liquor...*
2 = <u>juice</u>, stock, liquid, extract, gravy, infusion, broth ...*Drain the oysters and retain the liquor...*

list[1] NOUN = <u>inventory</u>, record, listing, series, roll, file, schedule, index, register, catalogue, directory, tally, invoice, syllabus, tabulation, leet (*Scot.*) ...*There were six names on the list...*
VERB = <u>itemize</u>, record, note, enter, file, schedule, index, register, catalogue, write down, enrol, set down, enumerate, note down, tabulate ...*The students were asked to list their favourite sports...*

list[2] VERB = <u>lean</u>, tip, heel, incline, tilt, cant, heel over, careen ...*The ship listed again, and she was thrown back across the bunk...*
NOUN = <u>tilt</u>, leaning, slant, cant ...*The ship's list was so strong that she stumbled...*

listen 1 = <u>hear</u>, attend, pay attention, hark, be attentive, be all ears, lend an ear, hearken (*archaic*), prick up your ears, give ear, keep your ears open, pin back your ears (*informal*) ...*He spent his time listening to the radio...*
2 = <u>pay attention</u>, observe, obey, mind, concentrate, heed, take notice, take note of, take heed of, do as you are told, give heed to ...*When I asked him to stop, he wouldn't listen...*

listless = <u>languid</u>, sluggish, lifeless, lethargic, heavy, limp, vacant, indifferent, languishing, inert, apathetic, lymphatic, impassive, supine, indolent, torpid, inattentive, enervated, spiritless, mopish OPPOSITE> energetic

litany 1 = <u>recital</u>, list, tale, catalogue, account, repetition, refrain, recitation, enumeration ...*She listened to the litany of complaints against her client...*
2 = <u>prayer</u>, petition, invocation, supplication, set words ...*She recited a litany in an unknown tongue...*

literacy = <u>education</u>, learning, knowledge, scholarship, cultivation, proficiency, articulacy, ability to read and write, articulateness

literal 1 = <u>exact</u>, close, strict, accurate, faithful, verbatim, word for word ...*a literal translation...*
2 = <u>unimaginative</u>, boring, dull, down-to-earth, matter-of-fact, factual, prosaic, colourless, uninspired, prosy ...*He is a very literal person...*
3 = <u>actual</u>, real, true, simple, plain, genuine, gospel, bona fide, unvarnished, unexaggerated ...*He was

saying no more than the literal truth…

literally = <u>exactly</u>, really, closely, actually, simply, plainly, truly, precisely, strictly, faithfully, to the letter, verbatim, word for word

literary = <u>well-read</u>, lettered, learned, formal, intellectual, scholarly, literate, erudite, bookish

literate = <u>educated</u>, lettered, learned, cultured, informed, scholarly, cultivated, knowledgeable, well-informed, erudite, well-read

literature 1 = <u>writings</u>, letters, compositions, lore, creative writing, written works, belles-lettres …*classic works of literature…*
2 = <u>information</u>, publicity, leaflet, brochure, circular, pamphlet, handout, mailshot, handbill …*I'm sending you literature from two other companies…*
➤ **figures of speech** ➤ **literature**
➤ **Shakespeare**

lithe = <u>supple</u>, flexible, agile, limber, pliable, pliant, lissom(e), loose-jointed, loose-limbed

litigant = <u>claimant</u>, party, plaintiff, contestant, litigator, disputant

litigation = <u>lawsuit</u>, case, action, process, disputing, prosecution, contending

litigious = <u>contentious</u>, belligerent, argumentative, quarrelsome, disputatious

litter NOUN 1 = <u>rubbish</u>, refuse, waste, fragments, junk, debris, shreds, garbage (*chiefly U.S.*), trash, muck, detritus, grot (*slang*) …*If you see litter in the corridor, pick it up…*
2 = <u>jumble</u>, mess, disorder, confusion, scatter, tangle, muddle, clutter, disarray, untidiness …*He pushed aside the litter of books…*
3 = <u>brood</u>, family, young, offspring, progeny …*a litter of puppies…*
4 = <u>bedding</u>, couch, mulch, floor cover, straw-bed …*The birds scratch through leaf litter on the forest floor…*
5 = <u>stretcher</u>, palanquin …*The Colonel winced as the porters jolted the litter…*
VERB 1 = <u>clutter</u>, mess up, clutter up, be scattered about, disorder, disarrange, derange …*Glass from broken bottles litters the pavement…*
2 = <u>scatter</u>, spread, shower, strew …*Concrete holiday resorts are littered across the mountainside…*

little DETERMINER = <u>not much</u>, small, insufficient, scant, meagre, sparse, skimpy, measly, hardly any …*I had little money and little free time…* OPPOSITE> ample
ADJECTIVE 1 = <u>small</u>, minute, short, tiny, mini, wee, compact, miniature, dwarf, slender, diminutive, petite, dainty, elfin, bijou, infinitesimal, teeny-weeny, Lilliputian, munchkin (*informal, chiefly U.S.*), teensy-weensy, pygmy *or* pigmy …*We sat round a little table…* OPPOSITE> big
2 = <u>young</u>, small, junior, infant, immature, undeveloped, babyish …*When I was little, I was hyperactive…*
3 = <u>unimportant</u>, minor, petty, trivial, trifling, insignificant, negligible, paltry, inconsiderable …*He found himself getting angry over little things…* OPPOSITE> important

4 = <u>short</u>, brief, fleeting, short-lived, passing, hasty, momentary …*She stood up quickly, giving a little cry of astonishment…* OPPOSITE> long
5 = <u>mean</u>, base, cheap, petty, narrow-minded, small-minded, illiberal …*I won't play your little mind-games…*
ADVERB 1 = <u>hardly</u>, barely, not quite, not much, only just, scarcely …*On the way back they spoke very little…* OPPOSITE> much
2 = <u>rarely</u>, seldom, scarcely, not often, infrequently, hardly ever …*We go there very little nowadays…* OPPOSITE> always
NOUN = <u>bit</u>, touch, spot, trace, hint, dash, particle, fragment, pinch, small amount, dab, trifle, tad (*informal, chiefly U.S.*), snippet, speck, modicum …*Don't give me too much. Just a little…* OPPOSITE> lot
PHRASES **a little** = <u>to a small extent</u>, slightly, to some extent, to a certain extent, to a small degree …*I'm getting a little tired of having to correct your mistakes…* ◆ **little by little** = <u>gradually</u>, slowly, progressively, step by step, piecemeal, bit by bit, imperceptibly, by degrees …*Little by little, he was becoming weaker…*

liturgical = <u>ceremonial</u>, ritual, solemn, sacramental, formal, eucharistic

liturgy = <u>ceremony</u>, service, ritual, services, celebration, formula, worship, rite, sacrament, form of worship

live¹ VERB 1 = <u>dwell</u>, board, settle, lodge, occupy, abide, inhabit, hang out (*informal*), stay (*chiefly Scot.*), reside, have as your home, have your home in …*She has lived here for 10 years…*
2 = <u>exist</u>, last, prevail, be, have being, breathe, persist, be alive, have life, draw breath, remain alive …*He's got a terrible disease and will not live long…*
3 = <u>survive</u>, remain alive, feed yourself, get along, make a living, earn a living, make ends meet, subsist, eke out a living, support yourself, maintain yourself …*the last indigenous people to live by hunting…*
4 = <u>thrive</u>, be happy, flourish, prosper, have fun, enjoy life, enjoy yourself, luxuriate, live life to the full, make the most of life …*My friends told me to get out and live a bit…*
PHRASES **live it up** (*Informal*) = <u>enjoy yourself</u>, celebrate, have fun, revel, have a ball (*informal*), push the boat out (*Brit. informal*), paint the town red, make whoopee (*informal*), overindulge yourself …*There's no reason why you couldn't live it up once in a while…*

live² ADJECTIVE 1 = <u>living</u>, alive, breathing, animate, existent, vital, quick (*archaic*) …*tests on live animals…*
2 = <u>active</u>, connected, switched on, unexploded …*A live bomb had earlier been defused…*
3 = <u>topical</u>, important, pressing, current, hot, burning, active, vital, controversial, unsettled, prevalent, pertinent …*Directors' remuneration looks set to become a live issue…*
PHRASES **live wire** (*Informal*) = <u>dynamo</u>, hustler (*U.S. & Canad. slang*), ball of fire (*informal*), life and soul of the party, go-getter (*informal*), self-starter …*My sister's a real live wire, and full of fun…*

livelihood = <u>occupation</u>, work, employment, means,

Literature http://www.bartleby.com/

Literature terms

allegory
alliteration
allusion
amphigory *or* amphigouri
Angry Young Men
anti-hero
antinovel
anti-roman
aphorism
archaism
Augustan
Bakhtinian
bathos
Beat Generation *or* Beats
belles-lettres
belletrist
bibliography
Bildungsroman
black comedy
Bloomsbury group
bodice-ripper
bombast
bowdlerization
Brechtian
bricolage
Byronic
carnivalesque
campus novel
causerie
Celtic Revival
cento
chiller
Ciceronian
classicism
coda
colloquialism
comedy
comedy of manners
commedia dell'arte
conceit
courtly love
cultural materialism
cut-up technique
cyberpunk
death of the author
decadence
deconstruction
denouement
Derridian
dialectic
dialogue
Dickensian
discourse
double entendre
drama
epic
epilogue
epistle
epistolary novel
epitaph
erasure

essay
exegesis
expressionism
fable
fabulist
faction
fantastique
fantasy
feminist theory
festschrift
figure of speech
fin de siècle
foreword
Foucauldian
Futurism
gloss
Gongorism
Gothic
hagiography
Hellenism
hermeneutics
historical novel
historicism
Homeric
Horatian
hudibrastic verse
imagery
interior monologue
intertextuality
invective
Jacobean
Janeite
Johnsonian
journalese
Joycean
Juvenalian
Kafkaesque
kailyard
kenning
kiddy lit
lampoon
Laurentian *or* Lawrentian
legend
literary criticism
littérateur
locus classicus
Lost Generation
magic realism *or* magical realism
marxist theory
maxim
melodrama
metafiction
metalanguage
metaphor
mock-heroic
modernism
motif
myth
mythopoeia
narrative
narratology

narrator
naturalism
new criticism
new historicism
nom de plume
nouveau roman
novel
novelette
novella
onomatopoeia
oxymoron
palindrome
paraphrase
parody
pastiche
pastoral
pathos
picaresque
plagiarism
plot
polemic
pornography
post-colonialism
postmodernism
post-structuralism
post-theory
pot-boiler
queer theory
realism
Restoration comedy
roman
roman à clef
Romanticism
saga
samizdat
satire
science fiction *or* SF
sentimental novel
short story
signifier and signified
simile
sketch
socialist realism
splatterpunk
Spoonerism
story
stream of consciousness
structuralism
Sturm und Drang
subplot
subtext
Surrealism
Swiftian
theme
theory
thesis
tragedy
tragicomedy
trope
verse
vignette

Literature (continued)

Literary characters

Character	Book	Author
Captain Ahab	Moby Dick	Herman Melville
Aladdin	The Arabian Nights' Entertainments	Traditional
Alice	Alice's Adventures in Wonderland, Through the Looking-Glass	Lewis Carroll
Bridget Allworthy	Tom Jones	Henry Fielding
Squire Allworthy	Tom Jones	Henry Fielding
Blanch Amory	Pendennis	William Makepeace Thackeray
Harry Angstrom	Rabbit, Run et al.	John Updike
Artful Dodger	Oliver Twist	Charles Dickens
Jack Aubrey	Master and Commander et al.	Patrick O'Brian
Aunt Polly	Tom Sawyer	Mark Twain
Joe Bagstock	Dombey and Son	Charles Dickens
David Balfour	Kidnapped, Catriona	Robert Louis Stevenson
Mrs. Bardell	The Pickwick Papers	Charles Dickens
Barkis	David Copperfield	Charles Dickens
Jake Barnes	The Sun Also Rises	Ernest Hemingway
Adam Bede	Adam Bede	George Eliot
Seth Bede	Adam Bede	George Eliot
Laura Bell	Pendennis	William Makepeace Thackeray
Elizabeth Bennet	Pride and Prejudice	Jane Austen
Jane Bennet	Pride and Prejudice	Jane Austen
Kitty Bennet	Pride and Prejudice	Jane Austen
Lydia Bennet	Pride and Prejudice	Jane Austen
Mary Bennet	Pride and Prejudice	Jane Austen
Mr. Bennet	Pride and Prejudice	Jane Austen
Mrs. Bennet	Pride and Prejudice	Jane Austen
Edmund Bertram	Mansfield Park	Jane Austen
Julia Bertram	Mansfield Park	Jane Austen
Lady Bertram	Mansfield Park	Jane Austen
Maria Bertram	Mansfield Park	Jane Austen
Sir Thomas Bertram	Mansfield Park	Jane Austen
Tom Bertram	Mansfield Park	Jane Austen
Biddy	Great Expectations	Charles Dickens
Charles Bingley	Pride and Prejudice	Jane Austen
Stephen Blackpool	Hard Times	Charles Dickens
Anthony Blanche	Brideshead Revisited	Evelyn Waugh
Leopold Bloom	Ulysses	James Joyce
Molly Bloom	Ulysses	James Joyce
Mr. Boffin	Our Mutual Friend	Charles Dickens
Mrs. Boffin	Our Mutual Friend	Charles Dickens
Farmer Boldwood	Far from the Madding Crowd	Thomas Hardy
Josiah Bounderby	Hard Times	Charles Dickens
Madeline Bray	Nicholas Nickleby	Charles Dickens
Alan Breck	Kidnapped, Catriona	Robert Louis Stevenson
Sue Bridehead	Jude the Obscure	Thomas Hardy
Miss Briggs	Vanity Fair	William Makepeace Thackeray
Dorothea Brooke	Middlemarch	George Eliot
Mr. Brooke	Middlemarch	George Eliot
Mr. Brownlow	Oliver Twist	Charles Dickens
Daisy Buchanan	The Great Gatsby	F. Scott Fitzgerald
Rosa Bud	Edwin Drood	Charles Dickens
Billy Budd	Billy Budd, Foretopman	Herman Melville
Mr. Bulstrode	Middlemarch	George Eliot
Bumble	Oliver Twist	Charles Dickens
Mrs. Cadwallader	Middlemarch	George Eliot
Carker	Dombey and Son	Charles Dickens
Richard Carstone	Bleak House	Charles Dickens
Sydney Carton	A Tale of Two Cities	Charles Dickens
Mr. Casaubon	Middlemarch	George Eliot
Casby	Little Dorrit	Charles Dickens
Flora Casby	Little Dorrit	Charles Dickens

Literary characters (continued)

Character	Book	Author
Dunstan Cass	Silas Marner	George Eliot
Godfrey Cass	Silas Marner	George Eliot
Lady Castlewood	Henry Esmond	William Makepeace Thackeray
Lord Castlewood	Henry Esmond	William Makepeace Thackeray
Holden Caulfield	The Catcher in the Rye	J. D. Salinger
Chadband	Bleak House	Charles Dickens
Constance Chatterley	Lady Chatterley's Lover	D. H. Lawrence
The Cheeryble Brothers	Nicholas Nickleby	Charles Dickens
Edward Chester	Barnaby Rudge	Charles Dickens
Sir James Chettam	Middlemarch	George Eliot
Chuffey	Martin Chuzzlewit	Charles Dickens
Frank Churchill	Emma	Jane Austen
Jonas Chuzzlewit	Martin Chuzzlewit	Charles Dickens
Martin Chuzzlewit	Martin Chuzzlewit	Charles Dickens
Ada Clare	Bleak House	Charles Dickens
Angel Clare	Tess of the D'Urbervilles	Thomas Hardy
Arthur Clennam	Little Dorrit	Charles Dickens
Humphry Clinker	Humphry Clinker	Tobias Smollett
William Collins	Pride and Prejudice	Jane Austen
Benjy Compson	The Sound and the Fury	William Faulkner
David Copperfield	David Copperfield	Charles Dickens
Emily Costigan	Pendennis	William Makepeace Thackeray
Bob Cratchit	A Christmas Carol	Charles Dickens
Henry Crawford	Mansfield Park	Jane Austen
Mary Crawford	Mansfield Park	Jane Austen
Bute Crawley	Vanity Fair	William Makepeace Thackeray
Miss Crawley	Vanity Fair	William Makepeace Thackeray
Mrs. Bute Crawley	Vanity Fair	William Makepeace Thackeray
Pitt Crawley	Vanity Fair	William Makepeace Thackeray
Rawdon Crawley	Vanity Fair	William Makepeace Thackeray
Sir Pitt Crawley	Vanity Fair	William Makepeace Thackeray
Septimus Crisparkle	Edwin Drood	Charles Dickens
Vincent Crummles	Nicholas Nickleby	Charles Dickens
Jerry Cruncher	A Tale of Two Cities	Charles Dickens
Robinson Crusoe	Robinson Crusoe	Daniel Defoe
Captain Cuttle	Dombey and Son	Charles Dickens
Sebastian Dangerfield	The Ginger Man	J. P. Donleavy
Fitzwilliam Darcy	Pride and Prejudice	Jane Austen
Charles Darnay	A Tale of Two Cities	Charles Dickens
Elinor Dashwood	Sense and Sensibility	Jane Austen
John Dashwood	Sense and Sensibility	Jane Austen
Margaret Dashwood	Sense and Sensibility	Jane Austen
Marianne Dashwood	Sense and Sensibility	Jane Austen
Mrs. Henry Dashwood	Sense and Sensibility	Jane Austen
Dick Datchery	Edwin Drood	Charles Dickens
Fancy Day	Under The Greenwood Tree	Thomas Hardy
Lady Catherine de Bourgh	Pride and Prejudice	Jane Austen
Stephen Dedalus	A Portrait of the Artist as a Young Man, Ulysses	James Joyce
Sir Leicester Dedlock	Bleak House	Charles Dickens
Lady Dedlock	Bleak House	Charles Dickens
Madame Defarge	A Tale of Two Cities	Charles Dickens
Dick Dewy	Under The Greenwood Tree	Thomas Hardy
Mr. Dick	David Copperfield	Charles Dickens
Jim Dixon	Lucky Jim	Kingsley Amis
William Dobbin	Vanity Fair	William Makepeace Thackeray
Mr. Dombey	Dombey and Son	Charles Dickens
Florence Dombey	Dombey and Son	Charles Dickens
Don Quixote	Don Quixote de la Mancha	Miguel de Cervantes
Arabella Donn	Jude the Obscure	Thomas Hardy
Lorna Doone	Lorna Doone	R. D. Blackmore
Amy Dorrit or Little Dorrit	Little Dorrit	Charles Dickens

Literary characters (continued)

Character	Book	Author
Fanny Dorrit	Little Dorrit	Charles Dickens
Tip Dorrit	Little Dorrit	Charles Dickens
William Dorrit	Little Dorrit	Charles Dickens
Edwin Drood	Edwin Drood	Charles Dickens
Bentley Drummle	Great Expectations	Charles Dickens
Catriona Drummond	Catriona	Robert Louis Stevenson
Alec D'Urberville	Tess of the D'Urbervilles	Thomas Hardy
Tess Durbeyfield	Tess of the D'Urbervilles	Thomas Hardy
Catherine Earnshaw	Wuthering Heights	Emily Brontë
Hareton Earnshaw	Wuthering Heights	Emily Brontë
Hindley Earnshaw	Wuthering Heights	Emily Brontë
Anne Elliot	Persuasion	Jane Austen
Elizabeth Elliot	Persuasion	Jane Austen
Sir Walter Elliot	Persuasion	Jane Austen
Em'ly	David Copperfield	Charles Dickens
Eppie	Silas Marner	George Eliot
Esmeralda	Notre Dame de Paris	Victor Hugo
Beatrix Esmond	Henry Esmond	William Makepeace Thackeray
Henry Esmond	Henry Esmond	William Makepeace Thackeray
Estella	Great Expectations	Charles Dickens
Bathsheba Everdene	Far from the Madding Crowd	Thomas Hardy
Jane Eyre	Jane Eyre	Charlotte Brontë
Fagin	Oliver Twist	Charles Dickens
Andrew Fairservice	Rob Roy	Sir Walter Scott
Donald Farfrae	The Mayor of Casterbridge	Thomas Hardy
Jude Fawley	Jude the Obscure	Thomas Hardy
Edward Ferrars	Sense and Sensibility	Jane Austen
Huck *or* Huckleberry Finn	Tom Sawyer, Huckleberry Finn	Mark Twain
Miss Flite	Bleak House	Charles Dickens
Julia Flyte	Brideshead Revisited	Evelyn Waugh
Sebastian Flyte	Brideshead Revisited	Evelyn Waugh
Phileas Fogg	Around the World in Eighty Days	Jules Verne
Man Friday	Robinson Crusoe	Daniel Defoe
Sarah Gamp	Martin Chuzzlewit	Charles Dickens
Joe Gargery	Great Expectations	Charles Dickens
Jay Gatsby	The Great Gatsby	F. Scott Fitzgerald
Walter Gay	Dombey and Son	Charles Dickens
Solomon Gills	Dombey and Son	Charles Dickens
Louisa Gradgrind	Hard Times	Charles Dickens
Thomas Gradgrind	Hard Times	Charles Dickens
Tom Gradgrind	Hard Times	Charles Dickens
Mary Graham	Martin Chuzzlewit	Charles Dickens
Edith Granger	Dombey and Son	Charles Dickens
Dorian Gray	The Picture of Dorian Gray	Oscar Wilde
Mr. Grewgious	Edwin Drood	Charles Dickens
Mrs. Grundy	Speed the Plough	T. Morton
Ben Gunn	Treasure Island	Robert Louis Stevenson
Chris Guthrie	Sunset Song et al.	Lewis Grassic Gibbon
Ham	David Copperfield	Charles Dickens
Richard Hannay	The Thirty-nine Steps et al.	John Buchan
Emma Haredale	Barnaby Rudge	Charles Dickens
John Harmon	Our Mutual Friend	Charles Dickens
James Harthouse	Hard Times	Charles Dickens
Miss Havisham	Great Expectations	Charles Dickens
Sir Mulberry Hawk	Nicholas Nickleby	Charles Dickens
Jim Hawkins	Treasure Island	Robert Louis Stevenson
Bradley Headstone	Our Mutual Friend	Charles Dickens
Heathcliff	Wuthering Heights	Emily Brontë
Uriah Heep	David Copperfield	Charles Dickens
Michael Henchard	The Mayor of Casterbridge	Thomas Hardy
Lizzy Hexam	Our Mutual Friend	Charles Dickens
Betty Higden	Our Mutual Friend	Charles Dickens

Literary characters (continued)

Character	Book	Author
Sherlock Holmes	The Adventures of Sherlock Holmes et al.	Sir Arthur Conan Doyle
Humbert Humbert	Lolita	Vladimir Nabokov
Mr. Hyde	The Strange Case of Dr. Jekyll and Mr. Hyde	Robert Louis Stevenson
Injun Joe	Tom Sawyer	Mark Twain
Ishmael	Moby Dick	Herman Melville
Jaggers	Great Expectations	Charles Dickens
John Jarndyce	Bleak House	Charles Dickens
Bailie Nicol Jarvie	Rob Roy	Sir Walter Scott
John Jasper	Edwin Drood	Charles Dickens
Jeeves	My Man Jeeves et al.	P. G. Wodehouse
Dr. Jekyll	The Strange Case of Dr. Jekyll and Mr. Hyde	Robert Louis Stevenson
Mrs. Jellyby	Bleak House	Charles Dickens
Mrs. Jennings	Sense and Sensibility	Jane Austen
Jim	Huckleberry Finn	Mark Twain
Lord Jim	Lord Jim	Joseph Conrad
Jingle	The Pickwick Papers	Charles Dickens
Jo	Bleak House	Charles Dickens
Cissy Jupe	Hard Times	Charles Dickens
Joseph K.	The Trial	Franz Kafka
George Knightley	Emma	Jane Austen
Krook	Bleak House	Charles Dickens
Kurtz	Heart of Darkness	Joseph Conrad
Will Ladislaw	Middlemarch	George Eliot
Helena Landless	Edwin Drood	Charles Dickens
Neville Landless	Edwin Drood	Charles Dickens
Edgar Linton	Wuthering Heights	Emily Brontë
Isabella Linton	Wuthering Heights	Emily Brontë
Dr. Livesey	Treasure Island	Robert Louis Stevenson
Tertius Lydgate	Middlemarch	George Eliot
Rob Roy Macgregor	Rob Roy	Sir Walter Scott
Randle P. McMurphy	One Flew Over the Cuckoo's Nest	Ken Kesey
Abel Magwitch	Great Expectations	Charles Dickens
Dr. Manette	A Tale of Two Cities	Charles Dickens
Lucie Manette	A Tale of Two Cities	Charles Dickens
Madame Mantalini	Nicholas Nickleby	Charles Dickens
The Marchioness	The Old Curiosity Shop	Charles Dickens
Jacob Marley	A Christmas Carol	Charles Dickens
Philip Marlowe	The Big Sleep et al.	Raymond Chandler
Silas Marner	Silas Marner	George Eliot
Stephen Maturin	Master and Commander et al.	Patrick O'Brian
Oliver Mellors	Lady Chatterley's Lover	D. H. Lawrence
Merdle	Little Dorrit	Charles Dickens
Mrs. Merdle	Little Dorrit	Charles Dickens
Wilkins Micawber	David Copperfield	Charles Dickens
Walter Mitty	The Secret Life of Walter Mitty	James Thurber
Lord Mohun	Henry Esmond	William Makepeace Thackeray
Monks	Oliver Twist	Charles Dickens
Dean Moriarty	On the Road	Jack Kerouac
Professor Moriarty	The Adventures of Sherlock Holmes et al.	Sir Arthur Conan Doyle
Dinah Morris	Adam Bede	George Eliot
Murdstone	David Copperfield	Charles Dickens
Mrs. Grundy	Hard Times	Charles Dickens
Baron Münchhausen	Münchhausen, Baron, Narrative of His Marvellous Travels	R. E. Raspe
Nancy	Oliver Twist	Charles Dickens
Little Nell	The Old Curiosity Shop	Charles Dickens
Captain Nemo	Twenty Thousand Leagues under the Sea	Jules Verne

Literary characters (continued)

Character	Book	Author
Kate Nickleby	Nicholas Nickleby	Charles Dickens
Nicholas Nickleby	Nicholas Nickleby	Charles Dickens
Ralph Nickleby	Nicholas Nickleby	Charles Dickens
Newman Noggs	Nicholas Nickleby	Charles Dickens
Susan Nipper	Dombey and Son	Charles Dickens
Kit Nubbles	The Old Curiosity Shop	Charles Dickens
Gabriel Oak	Far from the Madding Crowd	Thomas Hardy
Glorvina O'Dowd	Vanity Fair	William Makepeace Thackeray
Major O'Dowd	Vanity Fair	William Makepeace Thackeray
Mrs. O'Dowd	Vanity Fair	William Makepeace Thackeray
Francis Osbaldistone	Rob Roy	Sir Walter Scott
Rashleigh Osbaldistone	Rob Roy	Sir Walter Scott
George Osborne	Vanity Fair	William Makepeace Thackeray
Pancks	Little Dorrit	Charles Dickens
Sancho Panza	Don Quixote de la Mancha	Miguel de Cervantes
Sal Paradise	On the Road	Jack Kerouac
Passepartout	Around the World in Eighty Days	Jules Verne
Pecksniff	Martin Chuzzlewit	Charles Dickens
Charity Pecksniff	Martin Chuzzlewit	Charles Dickens
Mercy Pecksniff	Martin Chuzzlewit	Charles Dickens
Peggoty	David Copperfield	Charles Dickens
Arthur Pendennis	Pendennis	William Makepeace Thackeray
Helen Pendennis	Pendennis	William Makepeace Thackeray
Pew	Treasure Island	Robert Louis Stevenson
Samuel Pickwick	The Pickwick Papers	Charles Dickens
Ruth Pinch	Martin Chuzzlewit	Charles Dickens
Tom Pinch	Martin Chuzzlewit	Charles Dickens
Pip *or* Philip Pirrip	Great Expectations	Charles Dickens
Herbert Pocket	Great Expectations	Charles Dickens
Charles Pooter	The Diary of a Nobody	G. and W. Grossmith
Martin Poyser	Adam Bede	George Eliot
Mrs. Poyser	Adam Bede	George Eliot
Fanny Price	Mansfield Park	Jane Austen
J. Alfred Prufrock	Prufrock and Other Observations	T. S. Eliot
Pumblechook	Great Expectations	Charles Dickens
Quasimodo	Notre Dame de Paris	Victor Hugo
Queequeg	Moby Dick	Herman Melville
Daniel Quilp	The Old Curiosity Shop	Charles Dickens
Roderick Random	Roderick Random	Tobias Smollett
Riah	Our Mutual Friend	Charles Dickens
Rogue Riderhood	Our Mutual Friend	Charles Dickens
Fanny Robin	Far from the Madding Crowd	Thomas Hardy
Mr. Rochester	Jane Eyre	Charlotte Brontë
Barnaby Rudge	Barnaby Rudge	Charles Dickens
Lady Russell	Persuasion	Jane Austen
Charles Ryder	Brideshead Revisited	Evelyn Waugh
Tom Sawyer	Tom Sawyer	Mark Twain
Scrooge	A Christmas Carol	Charles Dickens
Amelia Sedley	Vanity Fair	William Makepeace Thackeray
Jos Sedley	Vanity Fair	William Makepeace Thackeray
Tristram Shandy	The Life and Opinions of Tristram Shandy	Laurence Sterne
Becky *or* Rebecca Sharp	Vanity Fair	William Makepeace Thackeray
Bill Sikes	Oliver Twist	Charles Dickens
Long John Silver	Treasure Island	Robert Louis Stevenson
Harold Skimpole	Bleak House	Charles Dickens
Sleary	Hard Times	Charles Dickens
Smike	Nicholas Nickleby	Charles Dickens
Harriet Smith	Emma	Jane Austen
Winston Smith	1984	George Orwell
Augustus Snodgrass	The Pickwick Papers	Charles Dickens
Hetty Sorrel	Adam Bede	George Eliot

Literary characters (continued)

Character	Book	Author
Lady Southdown	Vanity Fair	William Makepeace Thackeray
Mrs. Sparsit	Hard Times	Charles Dickens
Dora Spenlow	David Copperfield	Charles Dickens
Wackford Squeers	Nicholas Nickleby	Charles Dickens
Starbuck	Moby Dick	Herman Melville
Lucy Steele	Sense and Sensibility	Jane Austen
James Steerforth	David Copperfield	Charles Dickens
Lord Steyne	Vanity Fair	William Makepeace Thackeray
Esther Summerson	Bleak House	Charles Dickens
Dick Swiveller	The Old Curiosity Shop	Charles Dickens
Mark Tapley	Martin Chuzzlewit	Charles Dickens
Tartuffe	Tartuffe	Molière
Mr. Tartar	Edwin Drood	Charles Dickens
Tarzan	Tarzan of the Apes	Edgar Rice Burroughs
Becky Thatcher	Tom Sawyer	Mark Twain
Montague Tigg	Martin Chuzzlewit	Charles Dickens
Tiny Tim	A Christmas Carol	Charles Dickens
Mrs. Todgers	Martin Chuzzlewit	Charles Dickens
Toots	Dombey and Son	Charles Dickens
Traddles	David Copperfield	Charles Dickens
Squire Trelawney	Treasure Island	Robert Louis Stevenson
Fred Trent	The Old Curiosity Shop	Charles Dickens
Job Trotter	The Pickwick Papers	Charles Dickens
Betsey Trotwood	David Copperfield	Charles Dickens
Sergeant Troy	Far from the Madding Crowd	Thomas Hardy
Tulkinghorn	Bleak House	Charles Dickens
Tracy Tupman	The Pickwick Papers	Charles Dickens
Thomas Tusher	Henry Esmond	William Makepeace Thackeray
Oliver Twist	Oliver Twist	Charles Dickens
Gabriel Varden	Barnaby Rudge	Charles Dickens
Dolly Varden	Barnaby Rudge	Charles Dickens
Mr. Veneering	Our Mutual Friend	Charles Dickens
Mrs. Veneering	Our Mutual Friend	Charles Dickens
Diggory Venn	Return of the Native	Thomas Hardy
Diana Vernon	Rob Roy	Sir Walter Scott
Rosamond Vincy	Middlemarch	George Eliot
Johann Voss	Voss	Patrick White
Eustacia Vye	Return of the Native	Thomas Hardy
George Warrington	Pendennis	William Makepeace Thackeray
Dr. Watson	The Adventures of Sherlock Holmes et al.	Sir Arthur Conan Doyle
Silas Wegg	Our Mutual Friend	Charles Dickens
Sam Weller	The Pickwick Papers	Charles Dickens
Wemmick	Great Expectations	Charles Dickens
Frank Wentworth	Persuasion	Jane Austen
Agnes Wickfield	David Copperfield	Charles Dickens
George Wickham	Pride and Prejudice	Jane Austen
Damon Wildeve	Return of the Native	Thomas Hardy
Bella Wilfer	Our Mutual Friend	Charles Dickens
John Willoughby	Sense and Sensibility	Jane Austen
Nathaniel Winkle	The Pickwick Papers	Charles Dickens
Dolly Winthrop	Silas Marner	George Eliot
Allan Woodcourt	Bleak House	Charles Dickens
Emma Woodhouse	Emma	Jane Austen
Mr. Woodhouse	Emma	Jane Austen
Bertie Wooster	My Man Jeeves et al.	P. G. Wodehouse
Eugene Wrayburn	Our Mutual Friend	Charles Dickens
Jenny Wren	Our Mutual Friend	Charles Dickens
Clym Yeobright	Return of the Native	Thomas Hardy
Thomasin Yeobright	Return of the Native	Thomas Hardy
Yossarian	Catch-22	Joseph Heller
Yuri Zhivago	Doctor Zhivago	Boris Pasternak
Zorba or Alexis Zorbas	Zorba the Greek	Nikos Kazantzakis

living, job, maintenance, subsistence, bread and butter (*informal*), sustenance, (means of) support, (source of) income

lively 1 = <u>animated</u>, spirited, quick, keen, active, alert, dynamic, sparkling, vigorous, cheerful, energetic, outgoing, merry, upbeat (*informal*), brisk, bubbly, nimble, agile, perky, chirpy (*informal*), sparky, sprightly, vivacious, frisky, gay, alive and kicking, spry, chipper (*informal*), blithe, full of beans (*informal*), frolicsome, full of pep (*informal*), blithesome, bright-eyed and bushy-tailed ...*She had a sweet, lively personality...* OPPOSITE dull
2 = <u>busy</u>, crowded, stirring, buzzing, bustling, moving, eventful ...*lively streets full of bars and cafés...* OPPOSITE slow
3 = <u>vivid</u>, strong, striking, bright, exciting, stimulating, bold, colourful, refreshing, forceful, racy, invigorating ...*toys made with bright and lively colours...* OPPOSITE dull
4 = <u>enthusiastic</u>, strong, keen, stimulating, eager, formidable, vigorous, animated, weighty ...*The newspapers showed a lively interest in European developments...*

liven up 1 = <u>stir</u>, brighten, hot up (*informal*), cheer up, perk up, buck up (*informal*) ...*He livened up after midnight, relaxing a little...*
2 = <u>cheer up</u>, animate, rouse, enliven, perk up, brighten up, pep up, buck up (*informal*), put life into, vitalize, vivify ...*How could we decorate the room to liven it up?...*

livery = <u>costume</u>, dress, clothing, suit, uniform, attire, garb, regalia, vestments, raiment (*archaic or poetic*)

livid 1 (*Informal*) = <u>angry</u>, cross, furious, outraged, mad (*informal*), boiling, fuming, choked, infuriated, incensed, enraged, exasperated, indignant, incandescent, hot under the collar (*informal*), fit to be tied (*slang*), beside yourself, as black as thunder, tooshie (*Austral. slang*), off the air (*Austral. slang*) ...*I am absolutely livid about it...* OPPOSITE delighted
2 = <u>discoloured</u>, angry, purple, bruised, black-and-blue, contused ...*The scarred side of his face was a livid red...*

living NOUN 1 = <u>livelihood</u>, work, job, maintenance, occupation, subsistence, bread and butter (*informal*), sustenance, (means of) support, (source of) income ...*He earns his living doing all kinds of things...*
2 = <u>lifestyle</u>, ways, situation, conduct, behaviour, customs, lifestyle, way of life, mode of living ...*the stresses of modern living...*
ADJECTIVE 1 = <u>alive</u>, existing, moving, active, vital, breathing, lively, vigorous, animated, animate, alive and kicking, in the land of the living (*informal*), quick (*archaic*) ...*All things, whether living or dead, are believed to influence each other...* OPPOSITE dead
2 = <u>current</u>, continuing, present, developing, active, contemporary, persisting, ongoing, operative, in use, extant ...*a living language...* OPPOSITE obsolete

lizard
➤ **reptiles**

load VERB 1 = <u>fill</u>, stuff, pack, pile, stack, heap, cram, freight, lade ...*The three men had finished loading the*
truck...
2 = <u>make ready</u>, charge, prime, prepare to fire ...*I knew how to load and handle a gun...*
NOUN 1 = <u>cargo</u>, lading, delivery, haul, shipment, batch, freight, bale, consignment ...*He drove by with a big load of hay...*
2 = <u>oppression</u>, charge, pressure, worry, trouble, weight, responsibility, burden, affliction, onus, albatross, millstone, encumbrance, incubus ...*High blood pressure imposes an extra load on the heart...*
PHRASES **load someone down** = <u>burden</u>, worry, trouble, hamper, oppress, weigh down, saddle with, encumber, snow under ...*I'm loaded down with work at the moment...*

loaded 1 = <u>laden</u>, full, charged, filled, weighted, burdened, freighted ...*shoppers loaded with bags...*
2 = <u>charged</u>, armed, primed, at the ready, ready to shoot *or* fire ...*He turned up on her doorstep with a loaded gun...*
3 = <u>tricky</u>, charged, sensitive, delicate, manipulative, emotive, insidious, artful, prejudicial, tendentious ...*That's a loaded question...*
4 = <u>biased</u>, weighted, rigged, distorted ...*The press is loaded in favour of the government...*
5 (*Slang*) = <u>rich</u>, wealthy, affluent, well off, rolling (*slang*), flush (*informal*), well-heeled (*informal*), well-to-do, moneyed ...*Her new boyfriend's absolutely loaded...*

loaf[1] 1 = <u>lump</u>, block, cake, cube, slab ...*a loaf of crusty bread...*
2 (*Slang*) = <u>head</u>, mind, sense, common sense, block (*informal*), nous (*Brit. slang*), chump (*Brit. slang*), gumption (*Brit. informal*), noddle (*informal, chiefly Brit.*) ...*You've got to use your loaf in this game...*

loaf[2] = <u>idle</u>, hang around, take it easy, lie around, loiter, loll, laze, lounge around, veg out (*slang, chiefly U.S.*), be indolent ...*She studied, and I just loafed around...*

loafer = <u>idler</u>, lounger, bum (*informal*), piker (*Austral. & N.Z. slang*), drone (*Brit.*), shirker, couch potato (*slang*), time-waster, layabout, skiver (*Brit. slang*), ne'er-do-well, wastrel, bludger (*Austral. & N.Z. informal*), lazybones (*informal*)

loan NOUN = <u>advance</u>, credit, mortgage, accommodation, allowance, touch (*slang*), overdraft ...*They want to make it easier for people to get a loan...*
VERB = <u>lend</u>, allow, credit, advance, accommodate, let out ...*They asked us to loan our boat to them...*

loath *or* **loth** = <u>unwilling</u>, against, opposed, counter, resisting, reluctant, backward, averse, disinclined, indisposed OPPOSITE willing

loathe = <u>hate</u>, dislike, despise, detest, abhor, abominate, have a strong aversion to, find disgusting, execrate, feel repugnance towards, not be able to bear *or* abide

loathing = <u>hatred</u>, hate, horror, disgust, aversion, revulsion, antipathy, abomination, repulsion, abhorrence, repugnance, odium, detestation, execration

loathsome = <u>hateful</u>, offensive, nasty, disgusting, horrible, revolting, obscene, vile, obnoxious, repulsive, nauseating, odious, repugnant, abhorrent, abominable, execrable, detestable, yucky *or* yukky (*slang*), yucko (*Austral. slang*) OPPOSITE⟩ delightful

lob (*Informal*) = <u>throw</u>, launch, toss, hurl, lift, pitch, shy (*informal*), fling, loft

lobby VERB = <u>campaign</u>, press, pressure, push, influence, promote, urge, persuade, appeal, petition, pull strings (*Brit. informal*), exert influence, bring pressure to bear, solicit votes ...*Gun control advocates are lobbying hard for new laws...*
NOUN 1 = <u>pressure group</u>, group, camp, faction, lobbyists, interest group, special-interest group, ginger group ...*Agricultural interests are some of the most powerful lobbies there...*
2 = <u>corridor</u>, hall, passage, entrance, porch, hallway, foyer, passageway, entrance hall, vestibule ...*I met her in the lobby of the museum...*

lobola (*S. African*) = <u>dowry</u>, portion, marriage settlement, dot (*archaic*)

local ADJECTIVE 1 = <u>community</u>, district, regional, provincial, parish, neighbourhood, small-town (*chiefly U.S.*), parochial, parish pump ...*I was going to pop up to the local library...*
2 = <u>confined</u>, limited, narrow, restricted ...*The blockage caused a local infection...*
NOUN = <u>resident</u>, native, inhabitant, character (*informal*), local yokel (*disparaging*) ...*That's what the locals call the place...*

locale = <u>site</u>, place, setting, position, spot, scene, location, venue, locality, locus

locality 1 = <u>neighbourhood</u>, area, region, district, vicinity, neck of the woods (*informal*) ...*Details of the drinking water quality in your locality can be obtained...*
2 = <u>site</u>, place, setting, position, spot, scene, location, locale ...*Such a locality is popularly referred to as a 'hot spot'...*

localize 1 = <u>ascribe</u>, specify, assign, pinpoint, narrow down ...*Examine the area carefully in order to localize the most tender point...*
2 = <u>restrict</u>, limit, contain, concentrate, confine, restrain, circumscribe, delimit ...*There was an attempt to localize the benefits of the university's output...*

locate 1 = <u>find</u>, discover, detect, come across, track down, pinpoint, unearth, pin down, lay your hands on, run to earth *or* ground ...*We've simply been unable to locate him...*
2 = <u>place</u>, put, set, position, seat, site, establish, settle, fix, situate ...*It was voted the best city to locate a business...*

location = <u>place</u>, point, setting, position, situation, spot, venue, whereabouts, locus, locale

lock¹ VERB 1 = <u>fasten</u>, close, secure, shut, bar, seal, bolt, latch, sneck (*dialect*) ...*Are you sure you locked the front door?...*
2 = <u>unite</u>, join, link, engage, mesh, clench, entangle, interlock, entwine ...*He locked his fingers behind his head...*

3 = <u>embrace</u>, press, grasp, clutch, hug, enclose, grapple, clasp, encircle ...*He locked her in a passionate clinch...*
NOUN = <u>fastening</u>, catch, bolt, clasp, padlock ...*He heard her key turning in the lock...*
PHRASES **lock someone out** = <u>shut out</u>, bar, ban, exclude, keep out, debar, refuse admittance to ...*My husband's locked me out...* ♦ **lock someone up** = <u>imprison</u>, jail, confine, cage, detain, shut up, incarcerate, send down (*informal*), send to prison, put behind bars ...*You're mad. You should be locked up...*

lock² = <u>strand</u>, curl, tuft, tress, ringlet ...*She brushed a lock of hair off his forehead...*

lodge NOUN 1 = <u>cabin</u>, house, shelter, cottage, hut, chalet, gatehouse, hunting lodge ...*a ski lodge...*
2 = <u>society</u>, group, club, association, section, wing, chapter, branch, assemblage ...*My father would occasionally go to his Masonic lodge...*
VERB 1 = <u>register</u>, put, place, set, lay, enter, file, deposit, submit, put on record ...*He has four weeks in which to lodge an appeal...*
2 = <u>stay</u>, room, stop, board, reside, sojourn ...*She lodged with a farming family...*
3 = <u>accommodate</u>, house, shelter, put up, entertain, harbour, quarter, billet ...*They questioned me, then lodged me in a children's home...*
4 = <u>stick</u>, remain, catch, implant, come to rest, become fixed, imbed ...*The bullet lodged in the sergeant's leg...*

lodger = <u>tenant</u>, roomer, guest, resident, boarder, paying guest

lodging *often plural* = <u>accommodation</u>, rooms, boarding, apartments, quarters, digs (*Brit. informal*), shelter, residence, dwelling, abode, habitation

lofty 1 = <u>noble</u>, grand, distinguished, superior, imposing, renowned, elevated, majestic, dignified, stately, sublime, illustrious, exalted ...*Amid the chaos, he had lofty aims...* OPPOSITE⟩ humble
2 = <u>high</u>, raised, towering, tall, soaring, elevated, sky-high ...*a light, lofty apartment...* OPPOSITE⟩ low
3 = <u>haughty</u>, lordly, proud, arrogant, patronizing, condescending, snooty (*informal*), disdainful, supercilious, high and mighty (*informal*), toffee-nosed (*slang, chiefly Brit.*) ...*the lofty disdain he often expresses for his profession...* OPPOSITE⟩ modest

log NOUN 1 = <u>stump</u>, block, branch, chunk, trunk, bole, piece of timber ...*He dumped the logs on the big stone hearth...*
2 = <u>record</u>, listing, account, register, journal, chart, diary, tally, logbook, daybook ...*The complaint was recorded in the ship's log...*
VERB = <u>record</u>, report, enter, book, note, register, chart, put down, tally, set down, make a note of ...*Details of the crime are logged in the computer...*

loggerheads
PHRASES **at loggerheads** = <u>quarrelling</u>, opposed, feuding, at odds, estranged, in dispute, at each other's throats, at daggers drawn, at enmity

logic 1 = <u>science of reasoning</u>, deduction, dialectics, argumentation, ratiocination, syllogistic reasoning

...*Students learn philosophy and logic*...

2 = <u>connection</u>, rationale, coherence, relationship, link, chain of thought ...*I don't follow the logic of your argument*...

3 = <u>reason</u>, reasoning, sense, good reason, good sense, sound judgment ...*The plan was based on sound commercial logic*...

logical 1 = <u>rational</u>, clear, reasoned, reasonable, sound, relevant, consistent, valid, coherent, pertinent, well-organized, cogent, well-reasoned, deducible ...*a logical argument*... OPPOSITE illogical

2 = <u>reasonable</u>, obvious, sensible, most likely, natural, necessary, wise, plausible, judicious ...*There was a logical explanation*... OPPOSITE unlikely

logistics = <u>organization</u>, management, strategy, engineering, plans, masterminding, coordination, orchestration

loiter = <u>linger</u>, idle, loaf, saunter, delay, stroll, lag, dally, loll, dawdle, skulk, dilly-dally (*informal*), hang about *or* around

loll 1 = <u>lounge</u>, relax, lean, slump, flop, sprawl, loaf, slouch, recline, outspan (*S. African*) ...*He lolled back in his comfortable chair*...

2 = <u>droop</u>, drop, hang, flop, flap, dangle, sag, hang loosely ...*his tongue lolling out of the side of his mouth*...

lone 1 = <u>solitary</u>, single, separate, one, only, sole, by yourself, unaccompanied ...*a lone woman motorist*...

2 = <u>isolated</u>, deserted, remote, secluded, lonesome, godforsaken ...*a lone tree on a hill*...

loneliness = <u>solitude</u>, isolation, desolation, seclusion, aloneness, dreariness, solitariness, forlornness, lonesomeness, desertedness

lonely 1 = <u>solitary</u>, alone, isolated, abandoned, lone, withdrawn, single, estranged, outcast, forsaken, forlorn, destitute, by yourself, lonesome, friendless, companionless ...*lonely people who just want to talk*... OPPOSITE accompanied

2 = <u>desolate</u>, deserted, remote, isolated, solitary, out-of-the-way, secluded, uninhabited, sequestered, off the beaten track (*informal*), godforsaken, unfrequented ...*dark, lonely streets*... OPPOSITE crowded

loner (*Informal*) = <u>individualist</u>, outsider, solitary, maverick, hermit, recluse, misanthrope, lone wolf

lonesome (*Chiefly U.S. & Canad.*) = <u>lonely</u>, deserted, isolated, lone, gloomy, dreary, desolate, forlorn, friendless, cheerless, companionless

long¹ 1 = <u>elongated</u>, extended, stretched, expanded, extensive, lengthy, far-reaching, spread out ...*Her legs were long and thin*... OPPOSITE short

2 = <u>prolonged</u>, slow, dragging, sustained, lengthy, lingering, protracted, interminable, spun out, long-drawn-out ...*This is a long film, three hours and seven minutes*... OPPOSITE brief

long² = <u>desire</u>, want, wish, burn, dream of, pine, hunger, ache, lust, crave, yearn, covet, itch, hanker, set your heart on, eat your heart out over ...*He longed for the good old days*...

long-drawn-out = <u>prolonged</u>, marathon, lengthy,

protracted, interminable, spun out, dragged out, overlong, overextended

longing NOUN = <u>desire</u>, hope, wish, burning, urge, ambition, hunger, yen (*informal*), hungering, aspiration, ache, craving, yearning, coveting, itch, thirst, hankering ...*He felt a longing for the familiar*... OPPOSITE indifference
ADJECTIVE = <u>yearning</u>, anxious, eager, burning, hungry, pining, craving, languishing, ardent, avid, wishful, wistful, desirous ...*sharp intakes of breath and longing looks*... OPPOSITE indifferent

long-lived = <u>long-lasting</u>, enduring, full of years, old as Methuselah, longevous

long-standing = <u>established</u>, fixed, enduring, abiding, long-lasting, long-lived, long-established, time-honoured

long-suffering = <u>uncomplaining</u>, patient, resigned, forgiving, tolerant, easy-going, stoical, forbearing

long-winded = <u>rambling</u>, prolonged, lengthy, tedious, diffuse, tiresome, wordy, long-drawn-out, garrulous, discursive, repetitious, overlong, verbose, prolix OPPOSITE brief

look VERB **1** = <u>see</u>, view, consider, watch, eye, study, check, regard, survey, clock (*Brit. slang*), examine, observe, stare, glance, gaze, scan, check out (*informal*), inspect, gape, peep, behold (*archaic*), goggle, eyeball (*slang*), scrutinize, ogle, gawp (*Brit. slang*), gawk, recce (*slang*), get a load of (*informal*), take a gander at (*informal*), rubberneck (*slang*), take a dekko at (*Brit. slang*), feast your eyes upon ...*She turned to look at him*...

2 = <u>search</u>, seek, hunt, forage, fossick (*Austral. & N.Z.*) ...*Have you looked on the piano?*...

3 = <u>consider</u>, contemplate ...*Next term we'll be looking at the Second World War period*...

4 = <u>face</u>, overlook, front on, give onto ...*The terrace looks onto the sea*...

5 = <u>hope</u>, expect, await, anticipate, reckon on ...*We're not looking to make a fortune*...

6 = <u>seem</u>, appear, display, seem to be, look like, exhibit, manifest, strike you as ...*She was looking miserable*...

NOUN **1** = <u>glimpse</u>, view, glance, observation, review, survey, sight, examination, gaze, inspection, peek, squint (*informal*), butcher's (*Brit. slang*), gander (*informal*), once-over (*informal*), recce (*slang*), eyeful (*informal*), look-see (*slang*), shufti (*Brit. slang*) ...*She took a last look in the mirror*...

2 = <u>appearance</u>, effect, bearing, face, air, style, fashion, cast, aspect, manner, expression, impression, complexion, guise, countenance, semblance, demeanour, mien (*literary*) ...*They've opted for a rustic look in the kitchen*...

PHRASES **look after something** *or* **someone** = <u>take care of</u>, mind, watch, protect, tend, guard, nurse, care for, supervise, sit with, attend to, keep an eye on, take charge of ...*I love looking after the children*...

♦ **look down on** *or* **upon someone** = <u>disdain</u>, despise, scorn, sneer at, spurn, hold in contempt, treat with contempt, turn your nose up (at) (*informal*), contemn (*formal*), look down your nose at (*informal*), misprize ...*I wasn't successful, so they looked down on me...* ◆ **look forward to something** = <u>anticipate</u>, expect, look for, wait for, await, hope for, long for, count on, count the days until, set your heart on ...*He was looking forward to working with the new Prime Minister...* ◆ **look into something** = <u>investigate</u>, study, research, go into, examine, explore, probe, follow up, check out, inspect, look over, delve into, scrutinize, inquire about, make inquiries about ...*He had once looked into buying an island...* ◆ **look like something** = <u>investigate</u>, echo, take after, remind you of, be the image of, make you think of, put you in mind of ...*They look like stars to the naked eye...* ◆ **look out for something** = <u>be careful of</u>, beware, watch out for, pay attention to, be wary of, be alert to, be vigilant about, keep an eye out for, be on guard for, keep your eyes open for, keep your eyes peeled for, keep your eyes skinned for, be on the qui vive for ...*What are the symptoms to look out for?...* ◆ **look over something** = <u>examine</u>, view, check, monitor, scan, check out (*informal*), inspect, look through, eyeball (*slang*), work over, flick through, peruse, cast an eye over, take a dekko at (*Brit. slang*) ...*He could have looked over the papers in less than ten minutes...* ◆ **look someone up** = <u>visit</u>, call on, go to see, pay a visit to, drop in on (*informal*), look in on ...*She looked up some friends of bygone years...* ◆ **look something up** = <u>research</u>, find, search for, hunt for, track down, seek out ...*I looked up your name and address in the personnel file...* ◆ **look up** = <u>improve</u>, develop, advance, pick up, progress, come along, get better, shape up (*informal*), perk up, ameliorate, show improvement ...*Things are looking up in the computer industry...* ◆ **look up to someone** = <u>respect</u>, honour, admire, esteem, revere, defer to, have a high opinion of, regard highly, think highly of ...*A lot of the younger girls look up to you...*

lookalike = <u>double</u>, twin, clone, replica, spit (*informal, chiefly Brit.*), ringer (*slang*), spitting image (*informal*), dead ringer (*slang*), living image, exact match, spit and image (*informal*)

lookout **1** = <u>watchman</u>, guard, sentry, sentinel, vedette (*Military*) ...*One committed the burglary and the other acted as lookout...*
2 = <u>watch</u>, guard, vigil, qui vive ...*He denied that he had failed to keep a proper lookout during the night...*
3 = <u>watchtower</u>, post, tower, beacon, observatory, citadel, observation post ...*Troops tried to set up a lookout post inside a refugee camp...*
4 (*Informal*) = <u>concern</u>, business, worry, funeral (*informal*), pigeon (*Brit. informal*) ...*It was your lookout if you put your life in danger...*

loom **1** = <u>appear</u>, emerge, hover, take shape, threaten, bulk, menace, come into view, become visible ...*the bleak mountains that loomed out of the blackness...*
2 = <u>overhang</u>, rise, mount, dominate, tower, soar, overshadow, hang over, rise up, overtop ...*He loomed over me...*

loop NOUN = <u>curve</u>, ring, circle, bend, twist, curl, spiral, hoop, coil, loophole, twirl, kink, noose, whorl, eyelet, convolution ...*She reached for a loop of garden hose...*
VERB = <u>twist</u>, turn, join, roll, circle, connect, bend, fold, knot, curl, spiral, coil, braid, encircle, wind round, curve round ...*He looped the rope over the wood...*

loophole = <u>let-out</u>, escape, excuse, plea, avoidance, evasion, pretence, pretext, subterfuge, means of escape

loose ADJECTIVE **1** = <u>free</u>, detached, insecure, unfettered, released, floating, wobbly, unsecured, unrestricted, untied, unattached, movable, unfastened, unbound, unconfined ...*A page came loose and floated onto the tiles...*
2 = <u>slack</u>, easy, hanging, relaxed, loosened, not fitting, sloppy, baggy, slackened, loose-fitting, not tight ...*Wear loose clothes as they're more comfortable...* OPPOSITE tight
3 (*Old-fashioned*) = <u>promiscuous</u>, fast, abandoned, immoral, dissipated, lewd, wanton, profligate, disreputable, debauched, dissolute, libertine, licentious, unchaste ...*casual sex and loose morals...* OPPOSITE chaste
4 = <u>vague</u>, random, inaccurate, disordered, rambling, diffuse, indefinite, disconnected, imprecise, ill-defined, indistinct, inexact ...*We came to some sort of loose arrangement before he went home...* OPPOSITE precise
VERB = <u>free</u>, release, ease, liberate, detach, unleash, let go, undo, loosen, disconnect, set free, slacken, untie, disengage, unfasten, unbind, unloose, unbridle ...*He loosed his grip on the rifle...* OPPOSITE fasten

loosen VERB = <u>untie</u>, undo, release, separate, detach, let out, unstick, slacken, unbind, work free, work loose, unloose ...*He loosened the scarf around his neck...*
PHRASES **loosen up** = <u>relax</u>, chill (*slang*), soften, unwind, go easy (*informal*), lighten up (*slang*), hang loose, outspan (*S. African*), ease up *or* off ...*Relax, smile; loosen up in mind and body...*

loot VERB = <u>plunder</u>, rob, raid, sack, rifle, ravage, ransack, pillage, despoil ...*Gangs began breaking windows and looting shops...*
NOUN = <u>plunder</u>, goods, prize, haul, spoils, booty, swag (*slang*) ...*They steal in order to sell their loot for cash...*

lop = <u>cut</u>, crop, chop, trim, clip, dock, hack, detach, prune, shorten, sever, curtail, truncate

lope = <u>stride</u>, spring, bound, gallop, canter, lollop

lopsided = <u>crooked</u>, one-sided, tilting, warped, uneven, unequal, disproportionate, squint, unbalanced, off balance, awry, askew, out of shape, asymmetrical, cockeyed, out of true, skewwhiff (*Brit. informal*)

lord NOUN **1** = <u>peer</u>, nobleman, count, duke, gentleman, earl, noble, baron, aristocrat, viscount, childe (*archaic*) ...*She married a lord and lives in a huge house in the country...*
2 = <u>ruler</u>, leader, chief, king, prince, master, governor, commander, superior, monarch, sovereign, liege, overlord, potentate, seigneur ...*It was the home of the powerful lords of Baux...*
PHRASES **lord it over someone** = <u>boss around</u> *or* about (*informal*), order around, threaten, bully,

menace, intimidate, hector, bluster, browbeat, ride roughshod over, pull rank on, tyrannize, put on airs, be overbearing, act big (*slang*), overbear, play the lord, domineer ...*Alex seemed to enjoy lording it over the three girls...* ◆ **the Lord** *or* **Our Lord** = <u>Jesus Christ</u>, God, Christ, Messiah, Jehovah, the Almighty, the Galilean, the Good Shepherd, the Nazarene ...*Ask the Lord to help you in your times of trouble...*

lore = <u>traditions</u>, sayings, experience, saws, teaching, beliefs, wisdom, doctrine, mythos, folk-wisdom, traditional wisdom

lose 1 = <u>be defeated</u>, be beaten, lose out, be worsted, come to grief, come a cropper (*informal*), be the loser, suffer defeat, get the worst of, take a licking (*informal*) ...*The government lost the argument over the pace of reform...*
2 = <u>mislay</u>, miss, drop, forget, displace, be deprived of, fail to keep, lose track of, suffer loss, misplace ...*I lost my keys...*
3 = <u>forfeit</u>, miss, fail, yield, default, be deprived of, pass up (*informal*), lose out on (*informal*) ...*He lost his licence...*
4 = <u>waste</u>, consume, squander, drain, exhaust, lavish, deplete, use up, dissipate, expend, misspend ...*He stands to lose millions of pounds...*
5 = <u>stray from</u>, miss, confuse, wander from ...*The men lost their way in a sandstorm...*
6 = <u>escape from</u>, pass, leave behind, evade, lap, duck, dodge, shake off, elude, slip away from, outstrip, throw off, outrun, outdistance, give someone the slip ...*I couldn't lose him, but he couldn't overtake...*

loser = <u>failure</u>, flop (*informal*), underdog, also-ran, no-hoper (*Austral. slang*), dud (*informal*), lemon (*slang*), clinker (*slang, chiefly U.S.*), washout (*informal*), non-achiever

loss NOUN 1 = <u>losing</u>, waste, disappearance, deprivation, squandering, drain, forfeiture ...*The loss of income is about £250 million...* OPPOSITE gain
2 *sometimes plural* = <u>deficit</u>, debt, deficiency, debit, depletion, shrinkage, losings ...*The company will cease operating due to continued losses...* OPPOSITE gain
3 = <u>damage</u>, cost, injury, hurt, harm, disadvantage, detriment, impairment ...*His death is a great loss to us...* OPPOSITE advantage
PLURAL NOUN = <u>casualties</u>, dead, victims, death toll, fatalities, number killed, number wounded ...*Enemy losses were said to be high...*
PHRASES **at a loss** = <u>confused</u>, puzzled, baffled, bewildered, stuck (*informal*), helpless, stumped, perplexed, mystified, nonplussed, at your wits' end ...*I was at a loss for what to do next...*

lost 1 = <u>missing</u>, missed, disappeared, vanished, strayed, wayward, forfeited, misplaced, mislaid ...*a lost book...*
2 = <u>bewildered</u>, confused, puzzled, baffled, helpless, ignorant, perplexed, mystified, clueless (*slang*) ...*I feel lost and lonely in a strange town alone...*
3 = <u>wasted</u>, consumed, neglected, misused, squandered, forfeited, dissipated, misdirected, frittered away, misspent, misapplied ...*a lost*

opportunity...
4 = <u>gone</u>, finished, destroyed, vanished, extinct, defunct, died out ...*The sense of community is lost...*
5 = <u>past</u>, former, gone, dead, forgotten, lapsed, extinct, obsolete, out-of-date, bygone, unremembered ...*the relics of a lost civilization...*
6 = <u>engrossed</u>, taken up, absorbed, entranced, abstracted, absent, distracted, preoccupied, immersed, dreamy, rapt, spellbound ...*She was silent for a while, lost in thought...*
7 = <u>fallen</u>, corrupt, depraved, wanton, abandoned, damned, profligate, dissolute, licentious, unchaste, irreclaimable ...*without honour, without heart, without religion ... a lost woman...*

lot NOUN 1 = <u>bunch</u> (*informal*), group, crowd, crew, set, band, quantity, assortment, consignment ...*We've just sacked one lot of builders...*
2 = <u>destiny</u>, situation, circumstances, fortune, chance, accident, fate, portion, doom, hazard, plight ...*Young people are usually less contented with their lot...*
3 = <u>share</u>, group, set, piece, collection, portion, parcel, batch ...*The receivers are keen to sell the stores as one lot...*
PHRASES **a lot** *or* **lots** 1 = <u>plenty</u>, scores, masses (*informal*), load(s) (*informal*), ocean(s), wealth, piles (*informal*), a great deal, quantities, stack(s), heap(s), a good deal, large amount, abundance, reams (*informal*), oodles (*informal*) ...*A lot of our land is used to grow crops...* 2 = <u>often</u>, regularly, a great deal, frequently, a good deal ...*They went out a lot when they lived in the city...* ◆ **draw lots** = <u>choose</u>, pick, select, toss up, draw straws (*informal*), throw dice, spin a coin ...*Two names were selected by drawing lots...* ◆ **throw in your lot with someone** = <u>join with</u>, support, join forces with, make common cause with, align yourself with, ally *or* align yourself with, join fortunes with ...*He has decided to throw in his lot with the far-right groups...*

loth
➤ **loath**

lotion = <u>cream</u>, solution, balm, salve, liniment, embrocation

lottery 1 = <u>raffle</u>, draw, lotto (*Brit., N.Z., & S. African*), sweepstake ...*the national lottery...*
2 = <u>gamble</u>, chance, risk, venture, hazard, toss-up (*informal*) ...*Which judges are assigned to a case is always a bit of a lottery...*

lotto (*Brit., S. African, & N.Z.*) = <u>lottery</u>, national lottery, draw, raffle, sweepstake

loud 1 = <u>noisy</u>, strong, booming, roaring, piercing, thundering, forte (*Music*), turbulent, resounding, deafening, thunderous, rowdy, blaring, strident, boisterous, tumultuous, vociferous, vehement, sonorous, ear-splitting, obstreperous, stentorian, clamorous, ear-piercing, high-sounding ...*Suddenly there was a loud bang...* OPPOSITE quiet
2 = <u>garish</u>, bold, glaring, flamboyant, vulgar, brash, tacky (*informal*), flashy, lurid, tasteless, naff (*Brit. slang*), gaudy, tawdry, showy, ostentatious, brassy ...*He liked to shock with his gold chains and loud clothes...* OPPOSITE sombre

3 = <u>loud-mouthed</u>, offensive, crude, coarse, vulgar, brash, crass, raucous, brazen (*informal*) ...*I like your manner; loud people are horrible*... OPPOSITE> quiet

loudly = <u>noisily</u>, vigorously, vehemently, vociferously, uproariously, lustily, shrilly, fortissimo (*Music*), at full volume, deafeningly, at the top of your voice, clamorously

lounge VERB = <u>relax</u>, pass time, hang out (*informal*), idle, loaf, potter, sprawl, lie about, waste time, recline, take it easy, saunter, loiter, loll, dawdle, laze, kill time, make yourself at home, veg out (*slang, chiefly U.S.*), outspan (*S. African*), fritter time away ...*They ate and drank and lounged in the shade*...
NOUN = <u>sitting room</u>, living room, parlour, drawing room, front room, reception room, television room ...*They sat before a roaring fire in the lounge*...

louring
➤ **lowering**

lousy 1 (*Slang*) = <u>inferior</u>, bad, poor, terrible, awful, no good, miserable, rotten (*informal*), duff, second-rate, shoddy, low-rent (*informal, chiefly U.S.*), for the birds (*informal*), two-bit (*U.S. & Canad. slang*), slovenly, poxy (*slang*), dime-a-dozen (*informal*), bush-league (*Austral. & N.Z. informal*), not much cop (*Brit. slang*), tinhorn (*U.S. slang*), of a sort *or* of sorts, strictly for the birds (*informal*), bodger *or* bodgie (*Austral. slang*) ...*The menu is limited and the food is lousy*...
2 (*Slang*) = <u>mean</u>, low, base, dirty, vicious, rotten (*informal*), vile, despicable, hateful, contemptible ...*This is just lousy, cheap, fraudulent behaviour from the government*...
3 (*Slang*) with **with** = <u>well-supplied with</u>, rolling in (*slang*), not short of, amply supplied with ...*a hotel lousy with fleas*...

lout = <u>oaf</u>, boor, bear, ned (*Scot. slang*), yahoo, hoon (*Austral. & N.Z. slang*), clod, bumpkin, gawk, dolt, churl, lubber, lummox (*informal*), clumsy idiot, yob *or* yobbo (*Brit. slang*), cougan (*Austral. slang*), scozza (*Austral. slang*), bogan (*Austral. slang*)

lovable *or* **loveable** = <u>endearing</u>, attractive, engaging, charming, winning, pleasing, sweet, lovely, fetching (*informal*), delightful, cute, enchanting, captivating, cuddly, amiable, adorable, winsome, likable *or* likeable OPPOSITE> detestable

love VERB **1** = <u>adore</u>, care for, treasure, cherish, prize, worship, be devoted to, be attached to, be in love with, dote on, hold dear, think the world of, idolize, feel affection for, have affection for, adulate ...*We love each other, and we want to spend our lives together*... OPPOSITE> hate
2 = <u>enjoy</u>, like, desire, fancy, appreciate, relish, delight in, savour, take pleasure in, have a soft spot for, be partial to, have a weakness for ...*We loved the food so much, especially the fish dishes*... OPPOSITE> dislike
3 = <u>cuddle</u>, neck (*informal*), kiss, pet, embrace, caress, fondle, canoodle (*slang*) ...*the loving and talking that marked an earlier stage of the relationship*...
NOUN **1** = <u>passion</u>, liking, regard, friendship, affection, warmth, attachment, intimacy, devotion, tenderness, fondness, rapture, adulation, adoration, infatuation, ardour, endearment, amity ...*Our love for each other*

has been increased by what we've been through together... OPPOSITE> hatred
2 = <u>liking</u>, taste, delight in, bent for, weakness for, relish for, enjoyment, devotion to, penchant for, inclination for, zest for, fondness for, soft spot for, partiality to ...*a love of literature*...
3 = <u>beloved</u>, dear, dearest, sweet, lover, angel, darling, honey, loved one, sweetheart, truelove, dear one, leman (*archaic*), inamorata *or* inamorato ...*Don't cry, my love*... OPPOSITE> enemy
4 = <u>sympathy</u>, understanding, heart, charity, pity, humanity, warmth, mercy, sorrow, kindness, tenderness, friendliness, condolence, commiseration, fellow feeling, soft-heartedness, tender-heartedness ...*a manifestation of his love for his fellow men*...
PHRASES **fall in love with someone** = <u>lose your heart to</u>, fall for, be taken with, take a shine to (*informal*), become infatuated with, fall head over heels in love with, be swept off your feet by, bestow your affections on ...*I fell in love with him the moment I saw him*... ◆ **for love** = <u>without payment</u>, freely, for nothing, free of charge, gratis, pleasurably ...*She does it for love – not money*... ◆ **for love or money** = <u>by any means</u>, ever, under any conditions ...*Replacement parts couldn't be found for love or money*... ◆ **in love** = <u>enamoured</u>, charmed, captivated, smitten, wild (*informal*), mad (*informal*), crazy (*informal*), enthralled, besotted, infatuated, enraptured ...*She had never before been in love*... ◆ **make love** = <u>have sexual intercourse</u>, have sex, go to bed, sleep together, do it (*informal*), mate, have sexual relations, have it off (*slang*), have it away (*slang*) ...*After six months of friendship, one night, they made love*...

Related Words
adjective: amatory

love affair 1 = <u>romance</u>, relationship, affair, intrigue, liaison, amour, affaire de coeur (*French*) ...*a love affair with a married man*...
2 = <u>enthusiasm</u>, love, passion, appreciation, devotion, mania, zest ...*His love affair with France knew no bounds*...

loveless 1 = <u>unloving</u>, hard, cold, icy, insensitive, unfriendly, heartless, frigid, unresponsive, unfeeling, cold-hearted ...*She is in a loveless relationship*...
2 = <u>unloved</u>, disliked, forsaken, lovelorn, friendless, unappreciated, unvalued, uncherished ...*A busy professional life had left her loveless at the age of 30*...

lovelorn = <u>lovesick</u>, mooning, slighted, pining, yearning, languishing, spurned, jilted, moping, unrequited, crossed in love

lovely 1 = <u>beautiful</u>, appealing, attractive, charming, winning, pretty, sweet, handsome, good-looking, exquisite, admirable, enchanting, graceful, captivating, amiable, adorable, comely ...*You look lovely*... OPPOSITE> ugly
2 = <u>wonderful</u>, pleasing, nice, pleasant, engaging, marvellous, delightful, enjoyable, gratifying, agreeable ...*What a lovely surprise!*... OPPOSITE> horrible

lovemaking = <u>sexual intercourse</u>, intercourse, intimacy, sexual relations, the other (*informal*), mating, nookie (*slang*), copulation, coitus, act of love, carnal knowledge, rumpy-pumpy (*slang*), coition, sexual union *or* congress

lover = <u>sweetheart</u>, beloved, loved one, beau, flame (*informal*), mistress, admirer, suitor, swain (*archaic*), woman friend, lady friend, man friend, toy boy, paramour, leman (*archaic*), fancy bit (*slang*), boyfriend *or* girlfriend, fancy man *or* fancy woman (*slang*), fiancé *or* fiancée, inamorata *or* inamorato

loving 1 = <u>affectionate</u>, kind, warm, dear, friendly, devoted, tender, fond, ardent, cordial, doting, amorous, solicitous, demonstrative, warm-hearted ...*a loving husband and father*... OPPOSITE cruel
2 = <u>tender</u>, kind, caring, warm, gentle, sympathetic, considerate ...*The house has been restored with loving care*...

low¹ ADJECTIVE 1 = <u>small</u>, little, short, stunted, squat, fubsy (*archaic or dialect*) ...*She put it down on the low table*... OPPOSITE tall
2 = <u>low-lying</u>, deep, depressed, shallow, subsided, sunken, ground-level ...*The sun was low in the sky*... OPPOSITE high
3 = <u>inexpensive</u>, cheap, reasonable, bargain, moderate, modest, cut-price, economical, bargain-basement ...*The low prices and friendly service made for a pleasant evening out*...
4 = <u>meagre</u>, little, small, reduced, depleted, scant, trifling, insignificant, sparse, paltry, measly ...*They are having to live on very low incomes*... OPPOSITE significant
5 = <u>inferior</u>, bad, poor, inadequate, pathetic, worthless, unsatisfactory, mediocre, deficient, second-rate, shoddy, low-grade, puny, substandard, low-rent (*informal, chiefly U.S.*), half-pie (*N.Z. informal*), bodger *or* bodgie (*Austral. slang*) ...*They criticised staff for the low standard of care*...
6 = <u>quiet</u>, soft, gentle, whispered, muted, subdued, hushed, muffled ...*Her voice was so low he had to strain to catch it*... OPPOSITE loud
7 = <u>dejected</u>, down, blue, sad, depressed, unhappy, miserable, fed up, moody, gloomy, dismal, forlorn, glum, despondent, downcast, morose, disheartened, downhearted, down in the dumps (*informal*), sick as a parrot (*informal*), cheesed off (*informal*), brassed off (*Brit. slang*) ...*'I didn't ask for this job, you know,' he tells friends when he is low*... OPPOSITE happy
8 = <u>coarse</u>, common, rough, gross, crude, rude, obscene, disgraceful, vulgar, undignified, disreputable, unbecoming, unrefined, dishonourable, ill-bred ...*stripteases interspersed with bits of ribald low comedy*...
9 = <u>contemptible</u>, mean, base, nasty, cowardly, degraded, vulgar, vile, sordid, abject, unworthy, despicable, depraved, menial, reprehensible, dastardly, scurvy, servile, unprincipled, dishonourable, ignoble ...*That was a really low trick*... OPPOSITE honourable
10 = <u>lowly</u>, poor, simple, plain, peasant, obscure, humble, meek, unpretentious, plebeian, lowborn ...*a man of low birth and no breeding*...
11 = <u>ill</u>, weak, exhausted, frail, dying, reduced, sinking, stricken, feeble, debilitated, prostrate ...*She's still feeling a bit low after having flu*... OPPOSITE strong
PHRASES **lie low** = <u>hide</u>, lurk, hole up, hide away, keep a low profile, hide out, go underground, skulk, go into hiding, take cover, keep out of sight, go to earth, conceal yourself ...*Far from lying low, he became more outspoken than ever*...

low² = <u>moo</u>, bellow ...*Cattle were lowing in the barns*...

low-down NOUN (*Informal*) = <u>information</u>, intelligence, info (*informal*), inside story, gen (*Brit. informal*), dope (*informal*) ...*We want you to give us the lowdown on your team-mates*...
ADJECTIVE = <u>mean</u>, low, base, cheap (*informal*), nasty, ugly, despicable, reprehensible, contemptible, underhand, scurvy ...*They will stoop to every low-down trick*...

lower ADJECTIVE 1 = <u>subordinate</u>, under, smaller, junior, minor, secondary, lesser, low-level, inferior, second-class ...*the lower ranks of council officers*...
2 = <u>reduced</u>, cut, diminished, decreased, lessened, curtailed, pared down ...*You may get it at a slightly lower price*... OPPOSITE increased
VERB 1 = <u>drop</u>, sink, depress, let down, submerge, take down, let fall, make lower ...*They lowered the coffin into the grave*... OPPOSITE raise
2 = <u>lessen</u>, cut, reduce, moderate, diminish, slash, decrease, prune, minimize, curtail, abate ...*a drug which lowers cholesterol levels*... OPPOSITE increase
3 = <u>demean</u>, humble, disgrace, humiliate, degrade, devalue, downgrade, belittle, condescend, debase, deign, abase ...*Don't lower yourself. Don't be the way they are*...
4 = <u>quieten</u>, soften, hush, tone down ...*He moved closer, lowering his voice*...

lowering *or* **louring** 1 = <u>darkening</u>, threatening, forbidding, menacing, black, heavy, dark, grey, clouded, gloomy, ominous, cloudy, overcast, foreboding ...*a heavy, louring sky*...
2 = <u>glowering</u>, forbidding, grim, frowning, brooding, scowling, sullen, surly ...*We walked in fear of his lowering temperament*...

low-key = <u>subdued</u>, quiet, restrained, muted, played down, understated, muffled, toned down, low-pitched

lowly 1 = <u>lowborn</u> ...*lowly bureaucrats pretending to be senators*..., obscure, subordinate, inferior, mean, proletarian, ignoble, plebeian
2 = <u>unpretentious</u>, common, poor, average, simple, ordinary, plain, modest, homespun ...*He started out as a lowly photographer*...

low-tech = <u>unsophisticated</u>, simple, basic, elementary OPPOSITE high-tech *or* hi-tech

loyal = <u>faithful</u>, true, devoted, dependable, constant, attached, patriotic, staunch, trustworthy, trusty, steadfast, dutiful, unwavering, true-blue, immovable, unswerving, tried and true, true-hearted OPPOSITE disloyal

loyalty = <u>faithfulness</u>, commitment, devotion, allegiance, reliability, fidelity, homage, patriotism, obedience, constancy, dependability, trustworthiness, steadfastness, troth (*archaic*), fealty, staunchness, trueness, trustiness, true-heartedness

lozenge = <u>tablet</u>, pastille, troche, cough drop, jujube

lubricate = <u>oil</u>, grease, smear, smooth the way, oil the wheels, make smooth, make slippery

lucid **1** = <u>clear</u>, obvious, plain, evident, distinct, explicit, transparent, clear-cut, crystal clear, comprehensible, intelligible, limpid, pellucid ...*His prose is always lucid and compelling...* OPPOSITE vague
2 = <u>clear-headed</u>, sound, reasonable, sensible, rational, sober, all there, sane, compos mentis (*Latin*), in your right mind ...*He wasn't very lucid; he didn't quite know where he was...* OPPOSITE confused

luck NOUN **1** = <u>good fortune</u>, success, advantage, prosperity, break (*informal*), stroke of luck, blessing, windfall, good luck, fluke, godsend, serendipity ...*I knew I needed a bit of luck to win...*
2 = <u>fortune</u>, lot, stars, chance, accident, fate, hazard, destiny, hap (*archaic*), twist of fate, fortuity ...*The goal owed more to luck than good planning...*
PHRASES **in luck** = <u>fortunate</u>, successful, favoured, prosperous, rosy, well-off, on a roll, sitting pretty (*informal*), jammy (*Brit. slang*) ...*You're in luck; the doctor's still in...* ◆ **out of luck** = <u>unfortunate</u>, cursed, unlucky, unsuccessful, luckless ...*If you want money, you're out of luck...*

luckily = <u>fortunately</u>, happily, by chance, as luck would have it, fortuitously, opportunely, as it chanced

luckless = <u>unlucky</u>, unfortunate, unsuccessful, hapless, unhappy, disastrous, cursed, hopeless, jinxed, calamitous, ill-starred, star-crossed, unpropitious, ill-fated

lucky **1** = <u>fortunate</u>, successful, favoured, charmed, blessed, prosperous, jammy (*Brit. slang*), serendipitous ...*I consider myself the luckiest man on the face of the earth...* OPPOSITE unlucky
2 = <u>fortuitous</u>, timely, fortunate, auspicious, opportune, propitious, providential, adventitious ...*They are now desperate for a lucky break...* OPPOSITE unlucky

lucrative = <u>profitable</u>, rewarding, productive, fruitful, paying, high-income, well-paid, money-making, advantageous, gainful, remunerative

ludicrous = <u>ridiculous</u>, crazy, absurd, preposterous, odd, funny, comic, silly, laughable, farcical, outlandish, incongruous, comical, zany, nonsensical, droll, burlesque, cockamamie (*slang, chiefly U.S.*) OPPOSITE sensible

lug = <u>drag</u>, carry, pull, haul, tow, yank, hump (*Brit. slang*), heave

luggage = <u>baggage</u>, things, cases, bags, gear, trunks, suitcases, paraphernalia, impedimenta

lugubrious = <u>gloomy</u>, serious, sad, dismal, melancholy, dreary, sombre, woeful, mournful, morose, sorrowful, funereal, doleful, woebegone, dirgelike

lukewarm **1** = <u>tepid</u>, warm, blood-warm ...*Wash your face with lukewarm water...*

2 = <u>half-hearted</u>, cold, cool, indifferent, unconcerned, uninterested, apathetic, unresponsive, phlegmatic, unenthusiastic, laodicean ...*The study received a lukewarm response from the Home Secretary...*

lull NOUN = <u>respite</u>, pause, quiet, silence, calm, hush, tranquillity, stillness, let-up (*informal*), calmness ...*a lull in the conversation...*
VERB = <u>calm</u>, soothe, subdue, still, quiet, compose, hush, quell, allay, pacify, lullaby, tranquillize, rock to sleep ...*It is easy to be lulled into a false sense of security...*

lullaby = <u>cradlesong</u>, berceuse

lumber¹ VERB (*Brit. informal*) = <u>burden</u>, land, load, saddle, impose upon, encumber ...*She was lumbered with a bill for about £90...*
NOUN (*Brit.*) = <u>junk</u>, refuse, rubbish, discards, trash, clutter, jumble, white elephants, castoffs, trumpery ...*The wheels had been consigned to the loft as useless lumber...*

lumber² = <u>plod</u>, shuffle, shamble, trudge, stump, clump, waddle, trundle, lump along ...*He turned and lumbered back to his chair...*

lumbering = <u>awkward</u>, heavy, blundering, bumbling, hulking, unwieldy, ponderous, ungainly, elephantine, heavy-footed, lubberly

luminary = <u>celebrity</u>, star, expert, somebody, lion, worthy, notable, big name, dignitary, leading light, celeb (*informal*), personage, megastar (*informal*), fundi (*S. African*), V.I.P.

luminous **1** = <u>bright</u>, lighted, lit, brilliant, shining, glowing, vivid, illuminated, radiant, resplendent, lustrous, luminescent ...*The luminous dial on the clock showed five minutes to seven...*
2 = <u>clear</u>, obvious, plain, evident, transparent, lucid, intelligible, perspicuous ...*a remarkable woman with a luminous sense of responsibility...*

lump¹ NOUN **1** = <u>piece</u>, group, ball, spot, block, mass, cake, bunch, cluster, chunk, wedge, dab, hunk, nugget, gob, clod, gobbet ...*a lump of wood...*
2 = <u>swelling</u>, growth, bump, tumour, bulge, hump, protuberance, protrusion, tumescence ...*I've got a lump on my shoulder...*
VERB = <u>group</u>, throw, mass, combine, collect, unite, pool, bunch, consolidate, aggregate, batch, conglomerate, coalesce, agglutinate ...*She felt out of place lumped together with alcoholics and hard-drug users...*

lump²
PHRASES **lump it** = <u>put up with it</u>, take it, stand it, bear it, suffer it, hack it (*slang*), tolerate it, endure it, brook it ...*He was going to kick up a fuss, but he realized he'd have to lump it...*

lumpy = <u>bumpy</u>, clotted, uneven, knobbly, grainy, curdled, granular, full of lumps

lunacy **1** = <u>foolishness</u>, madness, folly, stupidity, absurdity, aberration, idiocy, craziness, tomfoolery, imbecility, foolhardiness, senselessness ...*the lunacy of the tax system...* OPPOSITE sense
2 = <u>insanity</u>, madness, mania, dementia, psychosis, idiocy, derangement ...*Lunacy became the official*

explanation for his actions… OPPOSITE sanity

lunatic NOUN = <u>madman</u>, maniac, psychopath, nut (*slang*), loony (*slang*), nutter (*Brit. slang*), nutcase (*slang*), headcase (*informal*), headbanger (*informal*) …*Her son thinks she's a raving lunatic…*
ADJECTIVE = <u>mad</u>, crazy, insane, irrational, nuts (*slang*), barking (*slang*), daft, demented, barmy (*slang*), deranged, bonkers (*slang, chiefly Brit.*), unhinged, loopy (*informal*), crackpot (*informal*), out to lunch (*informal*), barking mad (*slang*), maniacal, gonzo (*slang*), up the pole (*informal*), crackbrained, wacko *or* whacko (*informal*), off the air (*Austral. slang*) …*the operation of the market taken to lunatic extremes…*
➤ **mad**

lunge VERB = <u>pounce</u>, charge, bound, dive, leap, plunge, dash, thrust, poke, jab …*I lunged forward to try to hit him…*
NOUN = <u>thrust</u>, charge, pounce, pass, spring, swing, jab, swipe (*informal*) …*He knocked on the door and made a lunge for her when she opened it…*

lurch 1 = <u>tilt</u>, roll, pitch, list, rock, lean, heel …*As the car sped over a pothole, she lurched forward…*
2 = <u>stagger</u>, reel, stumble, weave, sway, totter …*a drunken yob lurching out of a bar, shouting obscenities…*

lure VERB = <u>tempt</u>, draw, attract, invite, trick, seduce, entice, beckon, lead on, allure, decoy, ensnare, inveigle …*They did not realise that they were being lured into a trap…*
NOUN = <u>temptation</u>, attraction, incentive, bait, carrot (*informal*), magnet, inducement, decoy, enticement, siren song, allurement …*The lure of rural life is proving as strong as ever…*

lurid 1 = <u>sensational</u>, shocking, disgusting, graphic, violent, savage, startling, grim, exaggerated, revolting, explicit, vivid, ghastly, gruesome, grisly, macabre, melodramatic, yellow (*of journalism*), gory, unrestrained, shock-horror (*facetious*) …*lurid accounts of deaths and mutilations…* OPPOSITE mild
2 = <u>glaring</u>, bright, bloody, intense, flaming, vivid, fiery, livid, sanguine, glowering, overbright …*She always painted her toenails a lurid red or orange…* OPPOSITE pale

lurk = <u>hide</u>, sneak, crouch, prowl, snoop, lie in wait, slink, skulk, conceal yourself, move with stealth, go furtively

luscious 1 = <u>sexy</u>, attractive, arousing, erotic, inviting, provocative, seductive, cuddly, sensuous, alluring, voluptuous, kissable, beddable …*a luscious young blonde…*
2 = <u>delicious</u>, sweet, juicy, rich, honeyed, savoury, succulent, palatable, mouth-watering, delectable, yummy (*slang*), scrumptious (*informal*), appetizing, toothsome, yummo (*Austral. slang*) …*luscious fruit…*

lush 1 = <u>abundant</u>, green, flourishing, lavish, dense, prolific, rank, teeming, overgrown, verdant …*the lush green meadows…*
2 = <u>luxurious</u>, grand, elaborate, lavish, extravagant, sumptuous, plush (*informal*), ornate, opulent, palatial, ritzy (*slang*) …*The hotel is lush, plush and very non-*

backpacker…
3 = <u>succulent</u>, fresh, tender, ripe, juicy …*an unusual combination of vegetables and lush fruits…*

lust NOUN 1 = <u>lechery</u>, sensuality, licentiousness, carnality, the hots (*slang*), libido, lewdness, wantonness, salaciousness, lasciviousness, concupiscence, randiness (*informal, chiefly Brit.*), pruriency …*His lust for her grew until it was overpowering…*
2 = <u>desire</u>, longing, passion, appetite, craving, greed, thirst, cupidity, covetousness, avidity, appetence …*It was his lust for glitz and glamour that was driving them apart…*
PHRASES **lust for** *or* **after someone** = <u>desire</u>, want, crave, need, yearn for, covet, slaver over, lech after (*informal*), be consumed with desire for, hunger for *or* after …*Half the campus is lusting after her…*
♦ **lust for** *or* **after something** = <u>desire</u>, crave, yearn for, covet …*She lusted after the Directorship…*

lustful = <u>lascivious</u>, sexy (*informal*), passionate, erotic, craving, sensual, randy (*informal, chiefly Brit.*), raunchy (*slang*), horny (*slang*), hankering, lewd, wanton, carnal, prurient, lecherous, hot-blooded, libidinous, licentious, concupiscent, unchaste

lustre 1 = <u>sparkle</u>, shine, glow, glitter, dazzle, gleam, gloss, brilliance, sheen, shimmer, glint, brightness, radiance, burnish, resplendence, lambency, luminousness …*Gold retains its lustre for far longer than other metals…*
2 = <u>glory</u>, honour, fame, distinction, prestige, renown, illustriousness …*The team is relying too much on names that have lost their lustre…*

lustrous = <u>shining</u>, bright, glowing, sparkling, dazzling, shiny, gleaming, glossy, shimmering, radiant, luminous, glistening, burnished

lusty = <u>vigorous</u>, strong, powerful, healthy, strapping, robust, rugged, energetic, sturdy, hale, stout, stalwart, hearty, virile, red-blooded (*informal*), brawny

luxuriant 1 = <u>lush</u>, rich, dense, abundant, excessive, thriving, flourishing, rank, productive, lavish, ample, fertile, prolific, overflowing, plentiful, exuberant, fruitful, teeming, copious, prodigal, riotous, profuse, fecund, superabundant, plenteous …*wide spreading branches and luxuriant foliage…* OPPOSITE sparse
2 = <u>elaborate</u>, fancy, decorated, extravagant, flamboyant, baroque, sumptuous, ornate, festooned, flowery, rococo, florid, corinthian …*luxuriant draperies and soft sofas…* OPPOSITE plain
➤ **luxurious**

luxuriate 1 = <u>enjoy</u>, delight, indulge, relish, revel, bask, wallow …*Lie back and luxuriate in the scented oil…*
2 = <u>live in luxury</u>, take it easy, live the life of Riley, have the time of your life, be in clover …*He retired to luxuriate in Hollywood…*

luxurious 1 = <u>sumptuous</u>, expensive, comfortable, magnificent, costly, splendid, lavish, plush (*informal*), opulent, ritzy (*slang*), de luxe, well-appointed …*a luxurious hotel…*
2 = <u>self-indulgent</u>, pleasure-loving, sensual,

pampered, voluptuous, sybaritic, epicurean …*She had come to enjoy this luxurious lifestyle*… OPPOSITE⟩ austere

---

Word Power

luxurious – *Luxurious is sometimes wrongly used where luxuriant is meant: he had a luxuriant (not luxurious) moustache; the walls were covered with a luxuriant growth of wisteria.*

---

luxury 1 = <u>opulence</u>, splendour, richness, extravagance, affluence, hedonism, a bed of roses, voluptuousness, the life of Riley, sumptuousness …*She was brought up in an atmosphere of luxury and wealth*… OPPOSITE⟩ poverty
2 = <u>extravagance</u>, treat, extra, indulgence, frill, nonessential …*We never had money for little luxuries*… OPPOSITE⟩ necessity
3 = <u>pleasure</u>, delight, comfort, satisfaction, enjoyment, bliss, indulgence, gratification, wellbeing

…*Relax in the luxury of a Roman-style bath*… OPPOSITE⟩ discomfort

lying NOUN = <u>dishonesty</u>, perjury, deceit, fabrication, guile, misrepresentation, duplicity, fibbing, double-dealing, prevarication, falsity, mendacity, dissimulation, untruthfulness …*Lying is something that I will not tolerate*…
ADJECTIVE = <u>deceitful</u>, false, deceiving, treacherous, dishonest, two-faced, double-dealing, dissembling, mendacious, perfidious, untruthful, guileful …*You lying, cowardly beast!*… OPPOSITE⟩ truthful

lyric 1 (*of poetry*) = <u>songlike</u>, musical, lyrical, expressive, melodic …*His splendid short stories and lyric poetry*…
2 (*of a voice*) = <u>melodic</u>, clear, clear, light, flowing, graceful, mellifluous, dulcet …*her fresh, beautiful, lyric voice*…

lyrical = <u>enthusiastic</u>, emotional, inspired, poetic, carried away, ecstatic, expressive, impassioned, rapturous, effusive, rhapsodic

M m

macabre = <u>gruesome</u>, grim, ghastly, frightening, ghostly, weird, dreadful, unearthly, hideous, eerie, grisly, horrid, morbid, frightful, ghoulish OPPOSITE delightful

Machiavellian = <u>scheming</u>, cynical, shrewd, cunning, designing, intriguing, sly, astute, unscrupulous, wily, opportunist, crafty, artful, amoral, foxy, deceitful, underhand, double-dealing, perfidious

machine 1 = <u>appliance</u>, device, apparatus, engine, tool, instrument, mechanism, gadget, contraption, gizmo (*informal*), contrivance …*I put a coin in the machine and pulled the lever…*
2 = <u>system</u>, agency, structure, organization, machinery, setup (*informal*) …*He has put the party publicity machine behind another candidate…*

machinery 1 = <u>equipment</u>, gear, instruments, apparatus, works, technology, tackle, tools, mechanism(s), gadgetry …*Farmers import most of their machinery and materials…*
2 = <u>administration</u>, system, organization, agency, machine, structure, channels, procedure …*the government machinery and administrative procedures…*

macho = <u>manly</u>, masculine, butch (*slang*), chauvinist, virile, he-man

mad 1 = <u>insane</u>, mental (*slang*), crazy (*informal*), nuts (*slang*), bananas (*slang*), barking (*slang*), raving, distracted, frantic, frenzied, unstable, crackers (*Brit. slang*), batty (*slang*), crazed, lunatic, loony (*slang*), psychotic, demented, cuckoo (*informal*), unbalanced, barmy (*slang*), nutty (*slang*), deranged, delirious, rabid, bonkers (*slang, chiefly Brit.*), flaky (*U.S. slang*), unhinged, loopy (*informal*), crackpot (*informal*), out to lunch (*informal*), round the bend (*Brit. slang*), aberrant, barking mad (*slang*), out of your mind, gonzo (*slang*), screwy (*informal*), doolally (*slang*), off your head (*slang*), off your trolley (*slang*), round the twist (*Brit. slang*), up the pole (*informal*), of unsound mind, as daft as a brush (*informal, chiefly Brit.*), lost your marbles (*informal*), not right in the head, non compos mentis (*Latin*), off your rocker (*slang*), not the full shilling (*informal*), off your nut (*slang*), off your chump (*slang*), wacko *or* whacko (*informal*), off the air (*Austral. slang*) …*the mad old lady down the street…* OPPOSITE sane
2 = <u>foolish</u>, absurd, wild, stupid, daft (*informal*), ludicrous, unreasonable, irrational, unsafe, senseless, preposterous, foolhardy, nonsensical, unsound, inane, imprudent, asinine …*Isn't that a rather mad idea?…* OPPOSITE sensible
3 (*Informal*) = <u>angry</u>, cross, furious, irritated, fuming, choked, infuriated, raging, ape (*slang*), incensed, enraged, exasperated, irate, livid (*informal*), berserk, seeing red (*informal*), incandescent, wrathful, fit to be tied (*slang*), in a wax (*informal, chiefly Brit.*), berko (*Austral. slang*), tooshie (*Austral. slang*), off the air (*Austral. slang*) …*I'm pretty mad about it, I can tell you…* OPPOSITE calm
4 = <u>enthusiastic</u>, wild, crazy (*informal*), nuts (*slang*), keen, hooked, devoted, in love with, fond, daft (*informal*), ardent, fanatical, avid, impassioned, zealous, infatuated, dotty (*slang, chiefly Brit.*), enamoured …*He's mad about you…* OPPOSITE nonchalant
5 = <u>frenzied</u>, wild, excited, energetic, abandoned, agitated, frenetic, uncontrolled, boisterous, full-on (*informal*), ebullient, gay, riotous, unrestrained …*The game is a mad dash against the clock…*

Word Power

mad – *Mad* is often used in informal speech to describe behaviour that is wild or unpredictable, or a person who is behaving in such a way. Care should be taken with this word and with all its synonyms, since many of them can cause great offence. In particular, it is important to avoid the loose use of clinical terms such as *psychotic* unless you are referring seriously to specific psychiatric disorders. In contexts where psychiatric disorders are being discussed, you should avoid labelling people with the name of their condition. For example, instead of describing someone as *psychotic*, you would say they were *having a psychotic episode*; similarly, you would say that someone is *affected by depression*, rather than labelling them *a depressive*. Note that some people also object to the phrase *suffer from* in this context, as in *he suffers from paranoia*, preferring more neutral verbs such as *experience* or *be affected by*. Also avoid using old-fashioned words such as *insane*, *demented*, and *lunatic* with reference to psychiatric disorders. In all contexts, informal and judgmental words such as *mental* and *loony* are to be avoided.

---

madcap ADJECTIVE = <u>reckless</u>, rash, impulsive, ill-advised, wild, crazy, foolhardy, thoughtless, crackpot (*informal*), hot-headed, imprudent, heedless, hare-brained …*They flitted from one madcap scheme to another…*
NOUN = <u>daredevil</u>, tearaway, wild man, hothead …*Madcap Mark Roberts can be seen doing dangerous stunts in the countryside…*

madden = <u>infuriate</u>, irritate, incense, enrage, upset, provoke, annoy, aggravate (*informal*), gall, craze, inflame, exasperate, vex, unhinge, drive you crazy, nark (*Brit., Austral., & N.Z. slang*), drive you round the bend (*Brit. slang*), make your blood boil, drive you to distraction (*informal*), get your goat (*slang*), drive you round the twist (*Brit. slang*), get your dander up (*informal*), make your hackles rise, raise your hackles, drive you off your head (*slang*), drive you out of your mind, get your back up, get your hackles up, make you see red (*informal*), put your back up OPPOSITE⟩ calm

made-up 1 = <u>painted</u>, powdered, rouged, done up ...*heavily made-up face*...
2 = <u>false</u>, invented, imaginary, fictional, untrue, mythical, unreal, fabricated, make-believe, trumped-up, specious ...*It looks like a made-up word to me*...

madly 1 (*Informal*) = <u>passionately</u>, wildly, desperately, intensely, exceedingly, extremely, excessively, to distraction, devotedly ...*She has fallen madly in love with him*...
2 = <u>foolishly</u>, wildly, absurdly, ludicrously, unreasonably, irrationally, senselessly, nonsensically ...*This seemed madly dangerous*...
3 = <u>energetically</u>, quickly, wildly, rapidly, hastily, furiously, excitedly, hurriedly, recklessly, speedily, like mad (*informal*), hell for leather, like lightning, hotfoot, like the clappers (*Brit. informal*), like nobody's business (*informal*), like greased lightning (*informal*) ...*Children ran madly around the tables, shouting and playing*...
4 = <u>insanely</u>, frantically, hysterically, crazily, deliriously, distractedly, rabidly, frenziedly, dementedly ...*He would cackle madly to himself in the small hours*...

madman *or* **madwoman** = <u>lunatic</u>, psycho (*slang*), maniac, loony (*slang*), nut (*slang*), psychotic, psychopath, nutter (*Brit. slang*), nutcase (*slang*), headcase (*informal*), mental case (*slang*), headbanger (*informal*)
➤ **mad**

madness 1 = <u>insanity</u>, mental illness, delusion, mania, dementia, distraction, aberration, psychosis, lunacy, craziness, derangement, psychopathy ...*He was driven to the brink of madness*...
2 = <u>foolishness</u>, nonsense, folly, absurdity, idiocy, wildness, daftness (*informal*), foolhardiness, preposterousness ...*It is political madness*...
3 = <u>frenzy</u>, riot, furore, uproar, abandon, excitement, agitation, intoxication, unrestraint ...*The country was in a state of madness*...

maelstrom 1 = <u>whirlpool</u>, swirl, eddy, vortex, Charybdis (*literary*) ...*a maelstrom of surf and confused seas*...
2 = <u>turmoil</u>, disorder, confusion, chaos, upheaval, uproar, pandemonium, bedlam, tumult ...*Inside, she was a maelstrom of churning emotions*...

maestro = <u>master</u>, expert, genius, virtuoso, wonk (*informal*), fundi (*S. African*)

magazine = <u>journal</u>, paper, publication, supplement, rag (*informal*), issue, glossy (*informal*), pamphlet, periodical, fanzine (*informal*)

magic NOUN **1** = <u>sorcery</u>, wizardry, witchcraft, enchantment, occultism, black art, spells, necromancy, sortilege, theurgy ...*Legends say that Merlin raised the stones by magic*...
2 = <u>conjuring</u>, illusion, trickery, sleight of hand, hocus-pocus, jiggery-pokery (*informal, chiefly Brit.*), legerdemain, prestidigitation, jugglery ...*His secret hobby: performing magic*...
3 = <u>charm</u>, power, glamour, fascination, magnetism, enchantment, allurement ...*The singer believes he can still regain some of his old magic*...
ADJECTIVE = <u>miraculous</u>, entrancing, charming, fascinating, marvellous, magical, magnetic, enchanting, bewitching, spellbinding, sorcerous ...*Then came those magic moments in the rose-garden*...

magician 1 = <u>conjuror</u>, illusionist, prestidigitator ...*It was like watching a magician showing you how he performs a trick*...
2 = <u>sorcerer</u>, witch, wizard, illusionist, warlock, necromancer, thaumaturge (*rare*), theurgist, archimage (*rare*), enchanter *or* enchantress ...*Uther called on Merlin the magician to help him*...
3 = <u>miracle-worker</u>, genius, marvel, wizard, virtuoso, wonder-worker, spellbinder ...*He was a magician with words*...

magisterial = <u>authoritative</u>, lordly, commanding, masterful, imperious OPPOSITE⟩ subservient

magistrate = <u>judge</u>, justice, provost (*Scot.*), bailie (*Scot.*), justice of the peace, J.P.

⟨ **Related Words** ⟩
adjective: magisterial

magnanimous = <u>generous</u>, kind, noble, selfless, big, free, kindly, handsome, charitable, high-minded, bountiful, unselfish, open-handed, big-hearted, unstinting, beneficent, great-hearted, munificent, ungrudging OPPOSITE⟩ petty

magnate = <u>tycoon</u>, leader, chief, fat cat (*slang, chiefly U.S.*), baron, notable, mogul, bigwig (*informal*), grandee, big shot (*informal*), captain of industry, big wheel (*slang*), big cheese (*slang, old-fashioned*), plutocrat, big noise (*informal*), big hitter (*informal*), magnifico, heavy hitter (*informal*), nabob (*informal*), Mister Big (*slang, chiefly U.S.*), V.I.P.

magnetic = <u>attractive</u>, irresistible, seductive, captivating, charming, fascinating, entrancing, charismatic, enchanting, hypnotic, alluring, mesmerizing OPPOSITE⟩ repulsive

magnetism = <u>charm</u>, appeal, attraction, power, draw, pull, spell, magic, fascination, charisma, attractiveness, allure, enchantment, hypnotism, drawing power, seductiveness, mesmerism, captivatingness

magnification 1 = <u>enlargement</u>, increase, inflation, boost, expansion, blow-up (*informal*), intensification, amplification, dilation, augmentation ...*a magnification of the human eye*...
2 = <u>exaggeration</u>, build-up, heightening, deepening, enhancement, aggrandizement ...*the magnification of this character on the screen*...

magnificence = <u>splendour</u>, glory, majesty, grandeur, brilliance, nobility, gorgeousness, sumptuousness, sublimity, resplendence

magnificent 1 = <u>splendid</u>, striking, grand, impressive, august, rich, princely, imposing, elegant,

divine (*informal*), glorious, noble, gorgeous, lavish, elevated, luxurious, majestic, regal, stately, sublime, sumptuous, grandiose, exalted, opulent, transcendent, resplendent, splendiferous (*facetious*) …*a magnificent country house in wooded grounds*…
OPPOSITE ordinary
2 = brilliant, fine, excellent, outstanding, superb, superior, splendid …*She is magnificent at making you feel able to talk*…

magnify 1 = enlarge, increase, boost, expand, intensify, blow up (*informal*), heighten, amplify, augment, dilate …*The telescope magnifies images over 11 times*… OPPOSITE reduce
2 = make worse, exaggerate, intensify, worsen, heighten, deepen, exacerbate, aggravate, increase, inflame, fan the flames of …*Poverty and human folly magnify natural disasters*…
3 = exaggerate, overdo, overstate, build up, enhance, blow up, inflate, overestimate, dramatize, overrate, overplay, overemphasize, blow up out of all proportion, aggrandize, make a production (out) of (*informal*), make a federal case of (*U.S. informal*) …*spend their time magnifying ridiculous details*…
OPPOSITE understate

magnitude 1 = importance, consequence, significance, mark, moment, note, weight, proportion, dimension, greatness, grandeur, eminence …*An operation of this magnitude is going to be difficult*…
OPPOSITE unimportance
2 = immensity, size, extent, enormity, strength, volume, vastness, bigness, largeness, hugeness …*the magnitude of the task confronting them*… OPPOSITE smallness
3 = intensity, measure, capacity, amplitude …*a quake with a magnitude exceeding 5*…

maid 1 = servant, chambermaid, housemaid, menial, handmaiden (*archaic*), maidservant, female servant, domestic (*archaic*), parlourmaid, serving-maid …*A maid brought me breakfast at half past eight*…
2 (*Literary*) = girl, maiden, lass, miss, nymph (*poetic*), damsel, lassie (*informal*), wench …*But can he win back the heart of this fair maid?*…

maiden NOUN (*Literary*) = girl, maid, lass, damsel, miss, virgin, nymph (*poetic*), lassie (*informal*), wench …*stories of brave princes and beautiful maidens*…
ADJECTIVE **1** = first, initial, inaugural, introductory, initiatory …*The Titanic sank on its maiden voyage*…
2 = unmarried, pure, virgin, intact, chaste, virginal, unwed, undefiled …*An elderly maiden aunt had left him £1000*…

mail NOUN **1** = letters, post, packages, parcels, correspondence …*She looked through the mail*…
2 = postal service, post, postal system …*Your cheque is in the mail*…
VERB = post, send, forward, e-mail, dispatch, send by mail *or* post …*He mailed me the contract*…

maim = cripple, hurt, injure, wound, mar, disable, hamstring, impair, lame, mutilate, mangle, incapacitate, put out of action, mangulate (*Austral. slang*)

main ADJECTIVE = chief, leading, major, prime, head, special, central, particular, necessary, essential, premier, primary, vital, critical, crucial, supreme, outstanding, principal, cardinal, paramount, foremost, predominant, pre-eminent …*My main concern now is to protect the children*… OPPOSITE minor
PLURAL NOUN **1** = pipeline, channel, pipe, conduit, duct …*the water supply from the mains*…
2 = cable, line, electricity supply, mains supply …*amplifiers which plug into the mains*…
PHRASES **in the main** = on the whole, generally, mainly, mostly, in general, for the most part …*In the main, children are taboo in the workplace*…

mainly = chiefly, mostly, largely, generally, usually, principally, in general, primarily, above all, substantially, on the whole, predominantly, in the main, for the most part, most of all, first and foremost, to the greatest extent

mainstay = pillar, backbone, bulwark, prop, anchor, buttress, lynchpin, chief support

mainstream = conventional, general, established, received, accepted, central, current, core, prevailing, orthodox OPPOSITE unconventional

maintain 1 = continue, retain, preserve, sustain, carry on, keep, keep up, prolong, uphold, nurture, conserve, perpetuate …*You should always maintain your friendships*… OPPOSITE end
2 = assert, state, hold, claim, insist, declare, allege, contend, affirm, profess, avow, aver, asseverate …*Prosecutors maintain that no deal was made*…
OPPOSITE disavow
3 = look after, care for, take care of, finance, conserve, keep in good condition …*The house costs a fortune to maintain*…

maintenance 1 = upkeep, keeping, care, supply, repairs, provision, conservation, nurture, preservation …*the maintenance of government buildings*…
2 = allowance, living, support, keep, food, livelihood, subsistence, upkeep, sustenance, alimony, aliment …*Absent fathers must pay maintenance for their children*…
3 = continuation, carrying-on, continuance, support, perpetuation, prolongation, sustainment, retainment …*the maintenance of peace and stability in Asia*…

majestic = grand, magnificent, impressive, superb, kingly, royal, august, princely, imposing, imperial, noble, splendid, elevated, awesome, dignified, regal, stately, monumental, sublime, lofty, pompous, grandiose, exalted, splendiferous (*facetious*) OPPOSITE modest

majesty = grandeur, glory, splendour, magnificence, dignity, nobility, sublimity, loftiness, impressiveness, awesomeness, exaltedness OPPOSITE triviality

major 1 = important, vital, critical, significant, great, serious, radical, crucial, outstanding, grave, extensive, notable, weighty, pre-eminent …*Exercise has a major part to play in combating disease*…
2 = main, higher, greater, bigger, lead, leading, head, larger, better, chief, senior, supreme, superior, elder, uppermost …*We heard extracts from three of his*

major works... OPPOSITE minor

majority 1 = <u>most</u>, more, mass, bulk, best part, better part, lion's share, preponderance, plurality, greater number ...*The majority of our customers come from out of town...*

2 = <u>adulthood</u>, maturity, age of consent, seniority, manhood *or* womanhood ...*Once you reach your majority you can do what you please...*

Word Power

majority – *The majority of* should always refer to a countable number of things or people. If you are talking about an amount or quantity, rather than a countable number, use *most of*, as in *most of the harvest was saved* (not *the majority of the harvest was saved*).

---

make VERB **1** = <u>produce</u>, cause, create, effect, lead to, occasion, generate, bring about, give rise to, engender, beget ...*The crash made a noise like a building coming down...*

2 = <u>perform</u>, do, act out, effect, carry out, engage in, execute, prosecute ...*I made a gesture at him and turned away...*

3 = <u>force</u>, cause, press, compel, drive, require, oblige, induce, railroad (*informal*), constrain, coerce, impel, dragoon, pressurize, prevail upon ...*You can't make me do anything...*

4 = <u>appoint</u>, name, select, elect, invest, install, nominate, assign, designate, hire as, cast as, employ as, ordain, vote in as, recruit as, engage as, enlist as ...*They made him transport minister...*

5 = <u>create</u>, build, produce, manufacture, form, model, fashion, shape, frame, construct, assemble, compose, forge, mould, put together, originate, fabricate ...*They now make cars at two plants in Europe...*

6 = <u>enact</u>, form, pass, establish, fix, institute, frame, devise, lay down, draw up ...*The only person who makes rules in this house is me...*

7 = <u>earn</u>, get, gain, net, win, clear, secure, realize, obtain, acquire, bring in, take in, fetch ...*How much money did we make?...*

8 = <u>amount to</u>, total, constitute, add up to, count as, tot up to (*informal*) ...*They are adding three aircraft carriers. That makes six in all...*

9 = <u>get to</u>, reach, catch, arrive at, meet, arrive in time for ...*We made the train, jumping aboard just as it was pulling out... ...We have to make New Orleans by nightfall...*

10 = <u>calculate</u>, judge, estimate, determine, think, suppose, reckon, work out, compute, gauge, count up, put a figure on ...*I make the total for the year as £69,599...*

NOUN = <u>brand</u>, sort, style, model, build, form, mark, kind, type, variety, construction, marque ...*What make of car did he rent?...*

PHRASES **make as if** = <u>pretend</u>, affect, give the impression that, feign, feint, make a show of, act as if *or* though ...*He made as if to chase me...* ◆ **make away** *or* **off with something** = <u>steal</u>, nick (*slang, chiefly Brit.*), pinch (*informal*), nab (*informal*), carry off, swipe (*slang*), knock off (*slang*), pilfer, cart off (*slang*), purloin, filch ...*They tied her up and made away with £2000...* ◆ **make believe** = <u>pretend</u>, play, enact, feign, play-act, act as if *or* though ...*He made believe he didn't understand what I was saying...* ◆ **make do** = <u>manage</u>, cope, improvise, muddle through, get along *or* by, scrape along *or* by ...*It's not going to be easy but I can make do...* ◆ **make for something 1** = <u>head for</u>, aim for, head towards, set out for, be bound for, make a beeline for, steer (a course) for, proceed towards ...*He rose from his seat and made for the door...* **2** = <u>contribute to</u>, produce, further, forward, advance, promote, foster, facilitate, be conducive to ...*A happy parent makes for a happy child...* ◆ **make it** (*Informal*) **1** = <u>succeed</u>, be successful, prosper, be a success, arrive (*informal*), get on, make good, cut it (*informal*), get ahead, make the grade (*informal*), crack it (*informal*), make it big, get somewhere, distinguish yourself ...*I have the talent to make it...* **2** = <u>get better</u>, survive, recover, rally, come through, pull through ...*The nurses didn't think he was going to make it...* ◆ **make off** = <u>flee</u>, clear out (*informal*), abscond, fly, bolt, decamp, hook it (*slang*), do a runner (*slang*), run for it (*informal*), slope off, cut and run (*informal*), beat a hasty retreat, fly the coop (*U.S. & Canad. informal*), make away, skedaddle (*informal*), take a powder (*U.S. & Canad. slang*), take to your heels, run away *or* off ...*They broke free and made off in a stolen car...* ◆ **make out** = <u>fare</u>, manage, do, succeed, cope, get on, proceed, thrive, prosper ...*He wondered how they were making out...* ◆ **make something out 1** = <u>see</u>, observe, distinguish, perceive, recognize, detect, glimpse, pick out, discern, catch sight of, espy, descry ...*I could just make out a tall pale figure...* **2** = <u>understand</u>, see, work out, grasp, perceive, follow, realize, comprehend, fathom, decipher, suss (out) (*slang*), get the drift of ...*It's hard to make out what criteria are used...* **3** = <u>write out</u>, complete, draft, draw up, inscribe, fill in *or* out ...*I'll make out a receipt for you...* **4** = <u>pretend</u>, claim, suggest, maintain, declare, allege, hint, imply, intimate, assert, insinuate, let on, make as if ...*They were trying to make out that I'd done it...* **5** = <u>prove</u>, show, describe, represent, demonstrate, justify ...*You could certainly make out a case for this point of view...* ◆ **make something up** = <u>invent</u>, create, construct, compose, write, frame, manufacture, coin, devise, hatch, originate, formulate, dream up, fabricate, concoct, cook up (*informal*), trump up ...*She made up stories about him...* ◆ **make up** = <u>settle your differences</u>, shake hands, make peace, bury the hatchet, call it quits, forgive and forget, mend fences, become reconciled, declare a truce, be friends again ...*She came back and they made up...* ◆ **make up for something** = <u>compensate for</u>, redress, make amends for, atone for, balance out, offset, expiate, requite, make reparation for, make recompense for ...*The compensation is intended to make up for stress caused...* ◆ **make up something 1** = <u>form</u>, account for, constitute, compose, comprise ...*Women officers make up 13 per cent of the police force...* **2** = <u>complete</u>, meet, supply, fill, round off ...*Some of the* money they receive is in grants; loans make up the rest... ◆ **make up to someone** (*Informal*) = <u>flirt with</u>, be all over, come on to, chase after, court, pursue, woo, run after, chat up (*informal*), curry favour with, make overtures to, make eyes at ...*She watched as her best friend made up to the man she herself loved...* ◆ **make up your mind** = <u>decide</u>, choose, determine, settle on, resolve, make a decision about, come to a decision about, reach a decision about ...*He had already made up his mind which side he was on...*

make-believe NOUN = <u>fantasy</u>, imagination, pretence, charade, unreality, dream, play-acting ...*She squandered her millions on a life of make-believe...* OPPOSITE> reality
ADJECTIVE = <u>imaginary</u>, dream, imagined, made-up, fantasy, pretend, pretended, mock, sham, unreal, fantasized ...*Children withdraw at times into a make-believe world...* OPPOSITE> real

maker = <u>manufacturer</u>, producer, builder, constructor, fabricator

Maker = <u>God</u>, Creator, Prime Mover

makeshift = <u>temporary</u>, provisional, make-do, substitute, jury (*chiefly Nautical*), expedient, rough and ready, stopgap

make-up 1 = <u>cosmetics</u>, paint (*informal*), powder, face (*informal*), greasepaint (*Theatre*), war paint (*informal*), maquillage (*French*) ...*Normally she wore little make-up, but this evening was clearly an exception...*
2 = <u>nature</u>, character, constitution, temperament, make, build, figure, stamp, temper, disposition, frame of mind, cast of mind ...*He became convinced that there was some fatal flaw in his make-up...*
3 = <u>structure</u>, organization, arrangement, form, construction, assembly, constitution, format, formation, composition, configuration ...*the chemical make-up of the atmosphere...*

making NOUN = <u>creation</u>, production, manufacture, construction, assembly, forging, composition, fabrication ...*a book about the making of the movie...*
PLURAL NOUN = <u>beginnings</u>, qualities, potential, stuff, basics, materials, capacity, ingredients, essence, capability, potentiality ...*He had the makings of a successful journalist...*
PHRASES **in the making** = <u>budding</u>, potential, up and coming, emergent, coming, growing, developing, promising, burgeoning, nascent, incipient ...*Her drama teacher says she is a star in the making...*

malady = <u>disease</u>, complaint, illness, disorder, sickness, ailment, affliction, infirmity, ill, indisposition, lurgy (*informal*)

malaise = <u>unease</u>, illness, depression, anxiety, weakness, sickness, discomfort, melancholy, angst, disquiet, doldrums, lassitude, enervation

malcontent NOUN = <u>troublemaker</u>, rebel, complainer, grumbler, grouser, agitator, stirrer (*informal*), mischief-maker, grouch (*informal*), fault-finder ...*Five years ago, a band of malcontents seized power...*

ADJECTIVE = <u>discontented</u>, unhappy, disgruntled, dissatisfied, disgusted, rebellious, resentful, disaffected, restive, unsatisfied, ill-disposed, factious ...*The film follows three malcontent teenagers around Paris...*

male = <u>masculine</u>, manly, macho, virile, manlike, manful OPPOSITE> female

malevolent = <u>spiteful</u>, hostile, vicious, malicious, malign, malignant, vindictive, pernicious, vengeful, hateful (*archaic*), baleful, rancorous, evil-minded, maleficent, ill-natured OPPOSITE> benevolent

malfunction VERB = <u>break down</u>, fail, go wrong, play up (*Brit. informal*), stop working, be defective, conk out (*informal*), develop a fault ...*Radiation can cause microprocessors to malfunction...*
NOUN = <u>fault</u>, failure, breakdown, defect, flaw, impairment, glitch ...*There must have been a computer malfunction...*

malice = <u>spite</u>, animosity, enmity, hate, hatred, bitterness, venom, spleen, rancour, bad blood, ill will, animus, malevolence, vindictiveness, evil intent, malignity, spitefulness, vengefulness, maliciousness

malicious = <u>spiteful</u>, malevolent, malignant, vicious, bitter, resentful, pernicious, vengeful, bitchy (*informal*), hateful, baleful, injurious, rancorous, catty (*informal*), shrewish, ill-disposed, evil-minded, ill-natured OPPOSITE> benevolent

malign VERB = <u>disparage</u>, abuse, run down, libel, knock (*informal*), injure, rubbish (*informal*), smear, blacken (someone's name), slag (off) (*slang*), denigrate, revile, vilify, slander, defame, bad-mouth (*slang, chiefly U.S. & Canad.*), traduce, speak ill of, derogate, do a hatchet job on (*informal*), calumniate, asperse ...*We maligned him dreadfully, assuming the very worst about him...* OPPOSITE> praise
ADJECTIVE = <u>evil</u>, bad, destructive, harmful, hostile, vicious, malignant, wicked, hurtful, pernicious, malevolent, baleful, deleterious, injurious, baneful, maleficent ...*the malign influence jealousy had on their lives...* OPPOSITE> good

malignant 1 (*Medical*) = <u>uncontrollable</u>, dangerous, evil, fatal, deadly, cancerous, virulent, irremediable ...*a malignant breast tumour...*
2 = <u>hostile</u>, harmful, bitter, vicious, destructive, malicious, malign, hurtful, pernicious, malevolent, spiteful, baleful, injurious, inimical, maleficent, of evil intent ...*a malignant minority indulging in crime and violence...* OPPOSITE> benign

malleable 1 = <u>manageable</u>, adaptable, compliant, impressionable, pliable, tractable, biddable, governable, like putty in your hands ...*She was young enough to be malleable...*
2 = <u>workable</u>, soft, plastic, tensile, ductile ...*Silver is the most malleable of all metals...*

malpractice = <u>misconduct</u>, abuse, negligence, mismanagement, misbehaviour, dereliction

mammal
➤ **anteaters and other edentates** ➤ **bats**
➤ **carnivores** ➤ **cattle and other artiodactyls**
➤ **horses, rhinos and other perissodactyls**

➤ **marsupials** ➤ **monkeys, apes and other primates** ➤ **rabbits and hares** ➤ **rodents** ➤ **sea mammals** ➤ **shrews and other insectivores** ➤ **whales and dolphins**

Extinct mammals

http://www.kokogiak.com/megafauna/default.asp

apeman	Irish elk
aurochs	labyrinthodont
australopithecine	mammoth
baluchitherium	mastodon
chalicothere	megathere
creodont	nototherium
dinoceras *or*	quagga
uintathere	sabre-toothed tiger *or*
dinothere	cat
dryopithecine	tarpan
eohippus	titanothere
glyptodont	

---

mammoth = <u>colossal</u>, huge, giant, massive, vast, enormous, mighty, immense, titanic, jumbo (*informal*), gigantic, monumental, mountainous, stellar (*informal*), prodigious, stupendous, gargantuan, elephantine, ginormous (*informal*), Brobdingnagian, humongous *or* humungous (*U.S. slang*) OPPOSITE⟩ tiny

man NOUN **1** = <u>male</u>, guy (*informal*), fellow (*informal*), gentleman, bloke (*Brit. informal*), chap (*Brit. informal*), dude (*U.S. informal*), geezer (*informal*), adult male ...*I had not expected the young man to reappear before evening*...
2 = <u>human</u>, human being, body, person, individual, adult, being, somebody, soul, personage ...*a possible step to sending a man back to the moon*...
3 = <u>mankind</u>, humanity, people, mortals, human race, humankind, Homo sapiens ...*Anxiety is modern man's natural state*...
4 = <u>partner</u>, boy, husband, lover, mate, boyfriend, old man, groom, spouse, sweetheart, beau, significant other (*U.S.*) ...*Does your man cuddle you enough?*...
VERB = <u>staff</u>, people, fill, crew, occupy, garrison, furnish with men ...*Soldiers manned roadblocks in the city*...
PHRASES **to a man** = <u>without exception</u>, as one, every one, unanimously, each and every one, one and all, bar none ...*Economists, almost to a man, were sceptical*...

(Related Words)
adjectives: anthropoid

mana (*N.Z.*) = <u>authority</u>, influence, power, might, force, weight, strength, domination, sway, standing, status, importance, esteem, stature, eminence

manacle NOUN = <u>handcuff</u>, bond, chain, shackle, tie, iron, fetter, gyve (*archaic*) ...*He had a steel-reinforced cell with manacles fixed to the walls*...
VERB = <u>handcuff</u>, bind, confine, restrain, check, chain, curb, hamper, inhibit, constrain, shackle, fetter, tie someone's hands, put in chains, clap *or* put in irons ...*His hands were manacled behind his back*...

manage 1 = <u>be in charge of</u>, run, handle, rule, direct, conduct, command, govern, administer, oversee, supervise, preside over, be head of, call the shots in,

superintend, call the tune in ...*Within two years, he was managing the store*...
2 = <u>organize</u>, use, handle, govern, regulate ...*Managing your time is increasingly important*...
3 = <u>cope</u>, survive, shift, succeed, get on, carry on, fare, get through, make out, cut it (*informal*), get along, make do, get by (*informal*), crack it (*informal*), muddle through ...*How did your mother manage when he left?*...
4 = <u>perform</u>, do, deal with, achieve, carry out, undertake, cope with, accomplish, contrive, finish off, bring about *or* off ...*those who can only manage a few hours of work*...
5 = <u>control</u>, influence, guide, handle, master, dominate, manipulate ...*Her daughter couldn't manage the horse*...
6 = <u>steer</u>, operate, pilot ...*managing a car well in bad conditions*...

manageable = <u>easy</u>, convenient, handy, user-friendly, wieldy OPPOSITE⟩ difficult

management 1 = <u>administration</u>, control, rule, government, running, charge, care, operation, handling, direction, conduct, command, guidance, supervision, manipulation, governance, superintendence ...*the responsibility for its day-to-day management*...
2 = <u>directors</u>, board, executive(s), bosses (*informal*), administration, employers, directorate ...*The management is doing its best to control the situation*...

manager = <u>supervisor</u>, head, director, executive, boss (*informal*), governor, administrator, conductor, controller, superintendent, gaffer (*informal, chiefly Brit.*), proprietor, organizer, comptroller, overseer, baas (*S. African*)

mandate = <u>command</u>, order, charge, authority, commission, sanction, instruction, warrant, decree, bidding, canon, directive, injunction, fiat, edict, authorization, precept

mandatory = <u>compulsory</u>, required, binding, obligatory, requisite OPPOSITE⟩ optional

manfully = <u>bravely</u>, boldly, vigorously, stoutly, hard, strongly, desperately, courageously, stalwartly, powerfully, resolutely, determinedly, heroically, valiantly, nobly, gallantly, like the devil, to the best of your ability, like a Trojan, intrepidly, like one possessed, with might and main

mangle = <u>crush</u>, mutilate, maim, deform, cut, total (*slang*), tear, destroy, ruin, mar, rend, wreck, spoil, butcher, cripple, hack, distort, trash (*slang*), maul, disfigure, lacerate, mangulate (*Austral. slang*)

manhandle 1 = <u>rough up</u>, pull, push, paw (*informal*), maul, handle roughly, knock about *or* around ...*Foreign journalists were manhandled by the police*...
2 = <u>haul</u>, carry, pull, push, lift, manoeuvre, tug, shove, hump (*Brit. slang*), heave ...*The three of us manhandled the dinghy out of the shed*...

manhood = <u>manliness</u>, masculinity, spirit, strength, resolution, courage, determination, maturity, bravery, fortitude, mettle, firmness, virility, valour, hardihood, manfulness

Types of mania

Mania	Meaning	Mania	Meaning
ablutomania	washing	iconomania	icons
agoramania	open spaces	kinesomania	movement
ailuromania	cats	kleptomania	stealing
andromania	men	logomania	talking
Anglomania	England	macromania	becoming larger
anthomania	flowers	megalomania	your own importance
apimania	bees	melomania	music
arithmomania	counting	mentulomania	penises
automania	solitude	micromania	becoming smaller
autophonomania	suicide	monomania	one thing
balletomania	ballet	musicomania	music
ballistomania	bullets	musomania	mice
bibliomania	books	mythomania	lies
chionomania	snow	necromania	death
choreomania	dancing	noctimania	night
chrematomania	money	nudomania	nudity
cremnomania	cliffs	nymphomania	sex
cynomania	dogs	ochlomania	crowds
dipsomania	alcohol	oikomania	home
doramania	fur	oinomania	wine
dromomania	travelling	ophidiomania	reptiles
egomania	your self	orchidomania	testicles
eleuthromania	freedom	ornithomania	birds
entheomania	religion	phagomania	eating
entomomania	insects	pharmacomania	medicines
ergasiomania	work	phonomania	noise
eroticomania	erotica	photomania	light
erotomania	sex	plutomania	great wealth
florimania	plants	potomania	drinking
gamomania	marriage	pyromania	fire
graphomania	writing	scribomania	writing
gymnomania	nakedness	siderodromomania	railway travel
gynomania	women	sitomania	food
hamartiomania	sin	sophomania	your own wisdom
hedonomania	pleasure	thalassomania	the sea
heliomania	sun	thanatomania	death
hippomania	horses	theatromania	theatre
homicidomania	murder	timbromania	stamps
hydromania	water	trichomania	hair
hylomania	woods	verbomania	words
hypnomania	sleep	xenomania	foreigners
ichthyomania	fish	zoomania	animals

mania 1 = <u>obsession</u>, passion, thing (*informal*), desire, rage, enthusiasm, craving, preoccupation, craze, fad (*informal*), fetish, fixation, partiality ...*They had a mania for travelling*...
2 = <u>madness</u>, disorder, frenzy, insanity, dementia, aberration, lunacy, delirium, craziness, derangement ...*the treatment of mania*...
➤ **types of mania**

maniac 1 = <u>madman</u> *or* <u>madwoman</u>, psycho (*slang*), lunatic, loony (*slang*), psychopath, nutter (*Brit. slang*), nutcase (*slang*), headcase (*informal*), headbanger (*informal*) ...*a drug-crazed maniac*...
2 = <u>fanatic</u>, fan, enthusiast, freak (*informal*), fiend (*informal*) ...*big spending football maniacs*...

manifest ADJECTIVE = <u>obvious</u>, apparent, patent, evident, open, clear, plain, visible, bold, distinct, glaring, noticeable, blatant, conspicuous, unmistakable, palpable, salient ...*cases of manifest*

injustice... OPPOSITE concealed
VERB = <u>display</u>, show, reveal, establish, express, prove, declare, demonstrate, expose, exhibit, set forth, make plain, evince ...*He's only convincing when that inner fury manifests itself*... OPPOSITE conceal

manifestation 1 = <u>sign</u>, symptom, indication, mark, example, evidence, instance, proof, token, testimony ...*Different animals have different manifestations of the disease*...
2 = <u>display</u>, show, exhibition, expression, demonstration, appearance, exposure, revelation, disclosure, materialization ...*the manifestation of grief*...

manifold (*Formal*) = <u>numerous</u>, many, various, varied, multiple, diverse, multiplied, diversified, abundant, assorted, copious, multifarious, multitudinous, multifold

manipulate 1 = <u>influence</u> ...*She was unable, for* *once, to manipulate events…*, control, direct, guide, conduct, negotiate, exploit, steer, manoeuvre, do a number on (*chiefly U.S.*), twist around your little finger …*He's a very difficult character. He manipulates people…*

2 = work, use, operate, handle, employ, wield …*The technology uses a pen to manipulate a computer…*

mankind = people, man, humanity, human race, humankind, Homo sapiens

---

Word Power

mankind – Some people object to the use of *mankind* to refer to all human beings on the grounds that it is sexist. A preferable term is *humankind*, which refers to both men and women.

---

manliness = virility, masculinity, manhood, machismo, courage, bravery, vigour, heroism, mettle, boldness, firmness, valour, fearlessness, intrepidity, hardihood

manly = virile, male, masculine, macho, strong, powerful, brave, daring, bold, strapping, hardy, heroic, robust, vigorous, muscular, courageous, fearless, butch (*slang*), resolute, gallant, valiant, well-built, red-blooded (*informal*), dauntless, stout-hearted, valorous, manful OPPOSITE⟩ effeminate

man-made = artificial, manufactured, plastic (*slang*), mock, synthetic, ersatz

manner NOUN **1** = style, way, fashion, method, means, form, process, approach, practice, procedure, habit, custom, routine, mode, genre, tack, tenor, usage, wont …*The manner in which young children are spoken to depends on who is present…*

2 = behaviour, look, air, bearing, conduct, appearance, aspect, presence, tone, demeanour, deportment, mien (*literary*), comportment …*His manner was self-assured and brusque…*

3 = type, form, sort, kind, nature, variety, brand, breed, category …*What manner of place is this?…*

PLURAL NOUN **1** = conduct, bearing, behaviour, breeding, carriage, demeanour, deportment, comportment …*He dressed well and had impeccable manners…*

2 = politeness, courtesy, etiquette, refinement, polish, decorum, p's and q's …*That should teach you some manners…*

3 = protocol, ceremony, customs, formalities, good form, proprieties, the done thing, social graces, politesse …*the morals and manners of a society…*

mannered = affected, put-on, posed, artificial, pseudo (*informal*), pretentious, stilted, arty-farty (*informal*) OPPOSITE⟩ natural

mannerism = habit, characteristic, trait, quirk, peculiarity, foible, idiosyncrasy

manoeuvre VERB **1** = steer, direct, guide, pilot, work, move, drive, handle, negotiate, jockey, manipulate, navigate …*We attempted to manoeuvre the canoe closer to him…*

2 = scheme, plot, plan, intrigue, wangle (*informal*),

machinate …*He manoeuvred his way to the top…*

3 = manipulate, arrange, organize, devise, manage, set up, engineer, fix, orchestrate, contrive, stage-manage …*You manoeuvred things in similar situations in the past…*

NOUN **1** = stratagem, move, plan, action, movement, scheme, trick, plot, tactic, intrigue, dodge, ploy, ruse, artifice, subterfuge, machination …*manoeuvres to block the electoral process…*

2 *often plural* = movement, operation, exercise, deployment, war game …*The camp was used for military manoeuvres…*

mansion = residence, manor, hall, villa, dwelling, abode, habitation, seat

mantle NOUN **1** = covering, cover, screen, cloud, curtain, envelope, blanket, veil, shroud, canopy, pall …*The park looked grim under a mantle of soot and ash…*

2 = cloak, wrap, cape, hood, shawl …*flaxen hair that hung round her shoulders like a silken mantle…*

VERB = cover, hide, blanket, cloud, wrap, screen, mask, disguise, veil, cloak, shroud, envelop, overspread …*Many of the peaks were already mantled with snow…*

manual ADJECTIVE **1** = physical, human, done by hand …*semi-skilled and unskilled manual work…*

2 = hand-operated, hand, non-automatic …*There is a manual pump to get rid of water…*

NOUN = handbook, guide, instructions, bible, guidebook, workbook …*the instruction manual…*

manufacture VERB **1** = make, build, produce, construct, form, create, process, shape, turn out, assemble, compose, forge, mould, put together, fabricate, mass-produce …*The first three models are being manufactured at our factory in Manchester…*

2 = concoct, make up, invent, devise, hatch, fabricate, think up, cook up (*informal*), trump up …*He said the allegations were manufactured on the flimsiest evidence…*

NOUN = making, production, construction, assembly, creation, produce, fabrication, mass-production …*the manufacture of nuclear weapons…*

manufacturer = maker, producer, builder, creator, industrialist, factory-owner, constructor, fabricator

manure = compost, muck, fertilizer, dung, droppings, excrement, ordure

many DETERMINER = numerous, various, varied, countless, abundant, myriad, innumerable, sundry, copious, manifold, umpteen (*informal*), profuse, multifarious, multitudinous, multifold, divers (*archaic*) …*He had many books and papers on the subject…*

PRONOUN = a lot, lots (*informal*), plenty, a mass, scores, piles (*informal*), tons (*informal*), heaps (*informal*), large numbers, a multitude, umpteen (*informal*), a horde, a thousand and one …*Many had avoided the delays by consulting the tourist office…*

PHRASES **the many** = the masses, the people, the crowd, the majority, the rank and file, the multitude, (the) hoi polloi …*It gave power to a few to change the world for the many…*

mar 1 = <u>harm</u>, damage, hurt, spoil, stain, blight, taint, tarnish, blot, sully, vitiate, put a damper on …*A number of problems marred the smooth running of the event…*
2 = <u>ruin</u>, injure, spoil, scar, flaw, impair, mutilate, detract from, maim, deform, blemish, mangle, disfigure, deface …*The scar was discreet enough not to mar his good looks…* OPPOSITE > improve

marauder = <u>raider</u>, outlaw, bandit, pirate, robber, ravager, plunderer, pillager, buccaneer, brigand, corsair, sea wolf, freebooter, reiver (*dialect*)

march VERB **1** = <u>parade</u>, walk, file, pace, stride, tread, tramp, swagger, footslog …*A Scottish battalion was marching down the street…*
2 = <u>walk</u>, strut, storm, sweep, stride, stalk, flounce …*She marched in without even knocking…*
NOUN **1** = <u>walk</u>, trek, hike, tramp, slog, yomp (*Brit. informal*), routemarch …*After a short march, the column entered the village…*
2 = <u>demonstration</u>, parade, procession, demo (*informal*) …*Organisers expect up to 3000 people to join the march…*
3 = <u>progress</u>, development, advance, evolution, progression …*The relentless march of technology…*
PHRASES **on the march** = <u>advancing</u>, marching, progressing, proceeding, on the way, under way, en route, afoot, on your way, astir …*Serbian troops and militia on the march…*

margin 1 = <u>room</u>, space, surplus, allowance, scope, play, compass, latitude, leeway, extra room, elbowroom …*There is very little margin for error in the way the money is collected…*
2 = <u>edge</u>, side, limit, border, bound, boundary, confine, verge, brink, rim, brim, perimeter, periphery …*These islands are on the margins of human habitation…*

marginal 1 = <u>insignificant</u>, small, low, minor, slight, minimal, negligible …*This is a marginal improvement on October…*
2 = <u>borderline</u>, bordering, on the edge, peripheral …*The poor are forced to cultivate marginal lands higher up the mountain…*

marijuana = <u>cannabis</u>, pot (*slang*), weed (*slang*), dope (*slang*), blow (*slang*), smoke (*informal*), stuff (*slang*), leaf (*slang*), tea (*U.S. slang*), grass (*slang*), chronic (*U.S. slang*), hemp, hash (*slang*), gage (*U.S. dated slang*), hashish, mary jane (*U.S. slang*), ganja, bhang, kif, wacky baccy (*slang*), sinsemilla, dagga (*S. African*), charas

marine = <u>nautical</u>, sea, maritime, oceanic, naval, saltwater, seafaring, ocean-going, seagoing, pelagic, thalassic

mariner = <u>sailor</u>, seaman, sea dog, seafarer, hand, salt, tar, navigator, gob (*U.S. slang*), matelot (*slang, chiefly Brit.*), Jack Tar, seafaring man, bluejacket

marital = <u>matrimonial</u>, married, wedded, nuptial, conjugal, spousal, connubial

maritime 1 = <u>nautical</u>, marine, naval, sea, oceanic, seafaring …*the largest maritime museum of its kind…*
2 = <u>coastal</u>, seaside, littoral …*The country has a*

temperate, maritime climate…

mark NOUN **1** = <u>spot</u>, stain, streak, smudge, line, nick, impression, scratch, bruise, scar, dent, blot, blemish, blotch, pock, splotch, smirch …*The dogs rub against the walls and make dirty marks…*
2 = <u>characteristic</u>, feature, symptom, standard, quality, measure, stamp, par, attribute, criterion, norm, trait, badge, hallmark, yardstick, peculiarity …*The mark of a civilized society is that it looks after its weakest members…*
3 = <u>indication</u>, sign, note, evidence, symbol, proof, token …*Shopkeepers closed their shutters as a mark of respect…*
4 = <u>brand</u>, impression, label, stamp, print, device, flag, seal, symbol, token, earmark, emblem, insignia, signet …*Each book was adorned with the publisher's mark at the bottom of the spine…*
5 = <u>impression</u>, effect, influence, impact, trace, imprint, vestiges …*A religious upbringing had left its mark on him…*
6 = <u>target</u>, goal, aim, purpose, end, object, objective …*The second shot missed its mark completely…*
VERB **1** = <u>scar</u>, scratch, dent, imprint, nick, brand, impress, stain, bruise, streak, blot, smudge, blemish, blotch, splotch, smirch …*How do you stop the horses marking the turf?…*
2 = <u>label</u>, identify, brand, flag, stamp, characterize …*The bank marks the cheque 'certified'…*
3 = <u>grade</u>, correct, assess, evaluate, appraise …*He was marking essays in his study…*
4 = <u>distinguish</u>, show, illustrate, exemplify, denote, evince, betoken …*the river which marks the border…*
5 = <u>observe</u>, mind, note, regard, notice, attend to, pay attention to, pay heed to, hearken to (*archaic*) …*Mark my words. He won't last…*
PHRASES **make your mark** = <u>succeed</u>, make it (*informal*), make good, prosper, be a success, achieve recognition, get on in the world, make something of yourself, find a place in the sun, make a success of yourself …*She made her mark in the film industry in the 1960s…*

marked = <u>noticeable</u>, clear, decided, striking, noted, obvious, signal, dramatic, considerable, outstanding, remarkable, apparent, prominent, patent, evident, distinct, pronounced, notable, manifest, blatant, conspicuous, salient OPPOSITE > imperceptible

markedly = <u>noticeably</u>, greatly, clearly, obviously, seriously (*informal*), signally, patently, notably, considerably, remarkably, evidently, manifestly, distinctly, decidedly, strikingly, conspicuously, to a great extent, outstandingly

market NOUN = <u>fair</u>, mart, bazaar, souk (*Arabic*) …*Many traders in the market have special offers today…*
VERB = <u>sell</u>, promote, retail, peddle, vend, offer for sale …*These phones have been marketed here since 1963…*

marketable = <u>sought after</u>, wanted, in demand, saleable, merchantable, vendible

marksman *or* **markswoman** = <u>sharpshooter</u>, good shot, crack shot (*informal*), dead shot (*informal*), deadeye (*informal, chiefly U.S.*)

maroon = <u>abandon</u>, leave, desert, strand, leave high and dry (*informal*), cast away, cast ashore

marriage 1 = <u>wedding</u>, match, nuptials, wedlock, wedding ceremony, matrimony, espousal, nuptial rites ...*When did the marriage take place?*...
2 = <u>union</u>, coupling, link, association, alliance, merger, confederation, amalgamation ...*The merger is an audacious marriage between old and new*...

(Related Words)

adjectives: conjugal, connubial, marital, nuptial

married 1 = <u>wedded</u>, one, united, joined, wed, hitched (*slang*), spliced (*informal*) ...*We have been married for 14 years*...
2 = <u>marital</u>, wifely, husbandly, nuptial, matrimonial, conjugal, spousal, connubial ...*the first ten years of married life*...

marry 1 = <u>tie the knot</u> (*informal*), wed, take the plunge (*informal*), walk down the aisle (*informal*), get hitched (*slang*), get spliced (*informal*), become man and wife, plight your troth (*old-fashioned*) ...*They married a month after they met*...
2 = <u>unite</u>, match, join, link, tie, bond, ally, merge, knit, unify, splice, yoke ...*It will be difficult to marry his two interests – cooking and sport*...

marsh = <u>swamp</u>, moss (*Scot. & Northern English dialect*), bog, slough, fen, quagmire, morass

marshal 1 = <u>conduct</u>, take, lead, guide, steer, escort, shepherd, usher ...*He was marshalling the visitors, showing them where to go*...
2 = <u>arrange</u>, group, order, collect, gather, line up, organize, assemble, deploy, array, dispose, draw up, muster, align ...*The government marshalled its economic resources*...

marsupial
➤ **marsupials**

martial = <u>military</u>, soldierly, brave, heroic, belligerent, warlike, bellicose

martial art
➤ **martial arts**

martyrdom = <u>persecution</u>, suffering, torture, agony, ordeal, torment, anguish OPPOSITE bliss

marvel VERB = <u>be amazed</u>, wonder, gaze, gape, goggle, be awed, be filled with surprise ...*Her fellow workers marvelled at her infinite energy*...
NOUN 1 = <u>wonder</u>, phenomenon, miracle, portent ...*A new technological marvel was invented there – the electron microscope*...
2 = <u>genius</u>, whizz (*informal*), prodigy ...*Her death is a great tragedy. She really was a marvel*...

marvellous = <u>excellent</u>, great (*informal*), mean (*slang*), topping (*Brit. slang*), wonderful, brilliant, bad (*slang*), cracking (*Brit. informal*), amazing, crucial (*slang*), extraordinary, remarkable, smashing (*informal*), superb, spectacular, fantastic (*informal*), magnificent, astonishing, fabulous (*informal*), divine (*informal*), glorious, terrific (*informal*), splendid, sensational (*informal*), mega (*slang*), sovereign, awesome (*slang*), breathtaking, phenomenal, astounding, singular, miraculous, colossal, super

(*informal*), wicked (*informal*), def (*slang*), prodigious, wondrous (*archaic or literary*), brill (*informal*), stupendous, jaw-dropping, bodacious (*slang, chiefly U.S.*), boffo (*slang*), jim-dandy (*slang*), chillin' (*U.S. slang*), booshit (*Austral. slang*), exo (*Austral. slang*), sik (*Austral. slang*) OPPOSITE terrible

masculine 1 = <u>male</u>, manly, mannish, manlike, virile, manful ...*masculine characteristics such as a deep voice and facial hair*...
2 = <u>strong</u>, powerful, bold, brave, strapping, hardy, robust, vigorous, muscular, macho, butch (*slang*), resolute, gallant, well-built, red-blooded (*informal*), stout-hearted ...*an aggressive, masculine image*...

mask NOUN 1 = <u>disguise</u>, visor, vizard (*archaic*), stocking mask, false face, domino (*rare*) ...*a gunman wearing a mask*...
2 = <u>façade</u>, disguise, show, front, cover, screen, blind, cover-up, veil, cloak, guise, camouflage, veneer, semblance, concealment ...*His mask cracked, and she saw an angry and violent man*...
VERB = <u>disguise</u>, hide, conceal, obscure, cover (up), screen, blanket, veil, cloak, mantle, camouflage, enshroud ...*A thick grey cloud masked the sun*...

masquerade VERB = <u>pose</u>, pretend to be, impersonate, profess to be, pass yourself off, simulate, disguise yourself ...*He masqueraded as a doctor and fooled everyone*...
NOUN 1 = <u>pretence</u>, disguise, deception, front (*informal*), cover, screen, put-on (*slang*), mask, cover-up, cloak, guise, subterfuge, dissimulation, imposture ...*He claimed that the elections would be a masquerade*...
2 = <u>masked ball</u>, revel, mummery, fancy dress party, costume ball, masked party ...*A man was killed at the Christmas masquerade*...

mass NOUN 1 = <u>lot</u>, collection, load, combination, pile, quantity, bunch, stack, heap, rick, batch, accumulation, stockpile, assemblage, aggregation, conglomeration ...*On his desk is a mass of books and papers*...
2 = <u>piece</u>, block, lump, chunk, hunk, concretion ...*Cut it up before it cools and sets into a solid mass*...
3 = <u>majority</u>, body, bulk, best part, greater part, almost all, lion's share, preponderance ...*The Second World War involved the mass of the population*...
4 = <u>crowd</u>, group, body, pack, lot, army, host, band, troop, drove, crush, bunch (*informal*), mob, flock, herd, number, horde, multitude, throng, rabble, assemblage ...*A mass of excited people clogged the street*...
5 = <u>size</u>, matter, weight, extent, dimensions, bulk, magnitude, greatness ...*Pluto and Triton have nearly the same mass and density*...
ADJECTIVE = <u>large-scale</u>, general, popular, widespread, extensive, universal, wholesale, indiscriminate, pandemic ...*ideas on combating mass unemployment*...
VERB = <u>gather</u>, assemble, accumulate, collect, rally, mob, muster, swarm, amass, throng, congregate, foregather ...*Shortly after the announcement, police began to mass at the shipyard*...
PHRASES **the masses** = <u>the multitude</u>, the crowd,

Marsupials http://animaldiversity.ummz.umich.edu/site/accounts/information/Metatheria.html

agile wallaby, river wallaby, sandy wallaby, *or* jungle kangaroo
antechinus
antelope kangaroo *or* antilopine wallaby
bandicoot
barred bandicoot *or* marl
Bennett's tree kangaroo *or* tcharibeena
bettong
bilby, rabbit(-eared) bandicoot, long-eared bandicoot, dalgyte, *or* dalgite
bobuck *or* mountain (brushtail) possum
boodie (rat), burrowing rat-kangaroo, Lesueur's rat-kangaroo, tungoo, *or* tungo
boongary *or* Lumholtz's tree kangaroo
bridled nail-tail wallaby *or* merrin
brindled bandicoot *or* northern brown bandicoot
brush-tail(ed) possum
burramys *or* (mountain) pygmy possum
crest-tailed marsupial mouse, Cannings' little dog, *or* mulgara
crescent nail-tail wallaby *or* wurrung
cuscus
dasyurid, dasyure, native cat, marsupial cat, *or* wild cat
desert bandicoot
desert-rat kangaroo
dibbler
diprotodon
dunnart
eastern grey kangaroo, great grey kangaroo, forest kangaroo, *or* (grey) forester
fluffy glider *or* yellow-bellied glider
flying phalanger, flying squirrel, glider, *or* pongo
green ringtail possum *or* toolah
hairy-nosed wombat
hare-wallaby
honey mouse, honey possum, noolbenger, *or* tait
jerboa, jerboa pouched mouse, jerboa kangaroo, *or* kultarr
kangaroo *or* (*Austral. informal*) roo
koala (bear) *or* (*Austral.*) native bear
kowari
larapinta *or* Darling Downs dunnart
Leadbeater's possum *or* fairy possum
lemuroid ringtail possum
long-nosed bandicoot
mardo *or* yellow-footed antechinus
marlu
marsupial mole
marsupial mouse
mongan *or* Herbert River ringtail possum
munning
musky rat-kangaroo
naked-nose wombat

ningaui
northern nail-tail wallaby *or* karrabul
northern native cat *or* satanellus
numbat *or* banded anteater
opossum *or* possum
pademelon *or* paddymelon
parma wallaby
phalanger
pig-footed bandicoot
pitchi-pitchi *or* wuhl-wuhl
platypus, duck-billed platypus, *or* duckbill
potoroo
pretty-face wallaby *or* whiptail wallaby
pygmy glider, feather glider, *or* flying mouse
quenda *or* (southern) brown bandicoot
quokka
quoll
rat kangaroo
red kangaroo *or* plains kangaroo
red(-necked) wallaby, Bennett's wallaby, eastern brush wallaby, rufous wallaby, *or* brush kangaroo
ringtail *or* ringtail(ed) possum
rock wallaby *or* brush-tailed wallaby
rufous rat-kangaroo
scrub wallaby
short-eared bandicoot
short-nosed bandicoot
short-nosed rat kangaroo *or* squeaker
squirrel glider
striped possum
sugar glider
swamp wallaby, black wallaby, *or* black-tailed wallaby
tammar, damar, *or* dama
Tasmanian barred bandicoot *or* Gunn's bandicoot
Tasmanian devil *or* ursine dasyure
thylacine, Tasmanian wolf, *or* Tasmanian tiger
tiger cat *or* spotted native cat
toolache *or* Grey's brush wallaby
tree kangaroo
tuan, phascogale, *or* wambenger
wallaby
wallaroo, uroo,
warabi
western grey kangaroo, black-faced kangaroo, sooty kangaroo, *or* mallee kangaroo
wintarro *or* golden bandicoot
wogoit *or* rock possum
wombat *or* (*Austral.*) badger
woylie *or* brush-tailed bettong
yapok
yallara
yellow-footed rock wallaby *or* ring-tailed rock wallaby

---

the mob, the common people, the great unwashed (*derogatory*), the hoi polloi, the commonalty ...*His music is commercial. It is aimed at the masses...*

massacre NOUN = slaughter, killing, murder, holocaust, carnage, extermination, annihilation, butchery, mass slaughter, blood bath ...*She lost her mother in the massacre...*
VERB = slaughter, kill, murder, butcher, take out (*slang*), wipe out, slay, blow away (*slang, chiefly U.S.*),

annihilate, exterminate, mow down, cut to pieces ...*Troops indiscriminately massacred the defenceless population...*

massage NOUN = rub-down, rubbing, manipulation, kneading, reflexology, shiatsu, acupressure, chiropractic treatment, palpation ...*Massage isn't a long-term cure for stress...*
VERB 1 = rub down, rub, manipulate, knead, pummel, palpate ...*She massaged her foot, which was bruised*

Martial arts http://dir.yahoo.com/Recreation/Sports/Martial_Arts/

aikido	kendo	tae kwon-do
capoeira	kick boxing	tai chi chuan
Crane style kung fu	kung fu	tai chi qi gong
Goju Kai karate	Kyokushinkai karate	Ta Sheng Men *or* Monkey style
Goju Ryu karate	kyudo	kung fu
hapkido	naginata-do	Thai boxing *or* Muay Thai
Hung Gar *or* Tiger style kung fu	ninjitsu *or* ninjutsu	Tomiki aikido
iai-do	Praying Mantis style kung fu	Tukido®
iai-jutsu	Sankukai karate	Wado Ryu karate
Ishin Ryu karate	Shito Ryu karate	Wing Chun *or* Wing Tsun kung
Jeet Kune Do	Shotokai karate	fu
judo	Shotokan karate	yari-jutsu
ju jitsu, jiu jitsu *or* ju-jutsu	Shukokai karate	
karate *or* karate-do	sumo *or* sumo wrestling	

and aching…

2 = <u>manipulate</u>, alter, distort, doctor, cook (*informal*), fix (*informal*), rig, fiddle (*informal*), tamper with, tinker with, misrepresent, fiddle with, falsify …*efforts to massage the unemployment figures…*

massive = <u>huge</u>, great, big, heavy, imposing, vast, enormous, solid, impressive, substantial, extensive, monster, immense, hefty, titanic, gigantic, monumental, whacking (*informal*), mammoth, bulky, colossal, whopping (*informal*), weighty, stellar (*informal*), hulking, ponderous, gargantuan, elephantine, ginormous (*informal*), humongous *or* humungous (*U.S. slang*) OPPOSITE> tiny

master NOUN **1** = <u>lord</u>, ruler, commander, chief, director, manager, boss (*informal*), head, owner, captain, governor, employer, principal, skipper (*informal*), controller, superintendent, overlord, overseer, baas (*S. African*) …*My master ordered me to deliver the message…* OPPOSITE> servant
2 = <u>expert</u>, maestro, pro (*informal*), ace (*informal*), genius, wizard, adept, virtuoso, grandmaster, doyen, past master, dab hand (*Brit. informal*), wonk (*informal*), maven (*U.S.*), fundi (*S. African*) …*He is a master at blocking progress…* OPPOSITE> amateur
3 = <u>teacher</u>, tutor, instructor, schoolmaster, pedagogue, preceptor …*a retired maths master…* OPPOSITE> student
ADJECTIVE = <u>main</u>, principal, chief, prime, grand, great, foremost, predominant …*There's a Georgian four-poster in the master bedroom…* OPPOSITE> lesser
VERB **1** = <u>learn</u>, understand, pick up, acquire, grasp, get the hang of (*informal*), become proficient in, know inside out, know backwards …*Students are expected to master a second language…*
2 = <u>overcome</u>, defeat, suppress, conquer, check, curb, tame, lick (*informal*), subdue, overpower, quash, quell, triumph over, bridle, vanquish, subjugate …*He wanted to master his fears of becoming ill…* OPPOSITE> give in to
3 = <u>control</u>, manage, direct, dominate, rule, command, govern, regulate …*His genius alone has mastered every crisis…*

masterful 1 = <u>skilful</u>, skilled, expert, finished, fine, masterly, excellent, crack (*informal*), supreme, clever, superior, world-class, exquisite, adept, consummate,

first-rate, deft, superlative, adroit, dexterous …*a masterful performance of boxing…* OPPOSITE> unskilled
2 = <u>domineering</u>, authoritative, dictatorial, bossy (*informal*), arrogant, imperious, overbearing, tyrannical, magisterial, despotic, high-handed, peremptory, overweening, self-willed …*Successful businesses need bold, masterful managers…* OPPOSITE> meek

Word Power

masterful – In current usage there is a lot of overlap between the meanings of *masterful* and *masterly*. According to some, the first should only be used where there is a connotation of power and domination, the second where the connotations are of great skill. Nevertheless, as the Bank of English shows, the majority of uses of *masterful* these days relate to the second meaning, as in *musically, it was a masterful display of the folk singer's art*. Anyone wishing to observe the distinction would use only *masterly* in the context just given, and *masterful* in contexts such as: *his need to be masterful with women was extreme; Alec was so masterful that he surprised himself.*

masterly = <u>skilful</u>, skilled, expert, finished, fine, excellent, crack (*informal*), supreme, clever, superior, world-class, exquisite, adept, consummate, first-rate, superlative, masterful, adroit, dexterous
➤ **masterful**

mastermind VERB = <u>plan</u>, manage, direct, organize, devise, conceive, be the brains behind (*informal*) …*The finance minister will continue to mastermind economic reform…*
NOUN = <u>organizer</u>, director, manager, authority, engineer, brain(s) (*informal*), architect, genius, planner, intellect, virtuoso, rocket scientist (*informal, chiefly U.S.*), brainbox …*He was the mastermind behind the plan…*

masterpiece = <u>classic</u>, tour de force (*French*), pièce de résistance (*French*), magnum opus, master work, jewel, chef-d'oeuvre (*French*)

mastery 1 = <u>understanding</u>, knowledge, comprehension, ability, skill, know-how, command, grip, grasp, expertise, prowess, familiarity, attainment, finesse, proficiency, virtuosity, dexterity, cleverness, deftness, acquirement ...*He demonstrated his mastery of political manoeuvring...*

2 = <u>control</u>, authority, command, rule, victory, triumph, sway, domination, superiority, conquest, supremacy, dominion, upper hand, ascendancy, pre-eminence, mana (*N.Z.*), whip hand ...*a region where humans have gained mastery over the major rivers...*

masturbation = <u>self-abuse</u>, onanism, playing with yourself (*slang*), autoeroticism

match NOUN **1** = <u>game</u>, test, competition, trial, tie, contest, fixture, bout, head-to-head ...*He was watching a football match...*

2 = <u>companion</u>, mate, equal, equivalent, counterpart, fellow, complement ...*Moira was a perfect match for him...*

3 = <u>replica</u>, double, copy, twin, equal, spit (*informal, chiefly Brit.*), duplicate, lookalike, ringer (*slang*), spitting image (*informal*), dead ringer (*slang*), spit and image (*informal*) ...*He asked his assistant to look for a match of the vase he broke...*

4 = <u>marriage</u>, union, couple, pair, pairing, item (*informal*), alliance, combination, partnership, duet, affiliation ...*Hollywood's favourite love match foundered on the rocks...*

5 = <u>equal</u>, rival, equivalent, peer, competitor, counterpart ...*I was no match for a man with such power...*

VERB **1** = <u>correspond with</u>, suit, go with, complement, fit with, accompany, team with, blend with, tone with, harmonize with, coordinate with ...*These shoes match your dress...*

2 = <u>tailor</u>, fit, suit, adapt ...*You don't have to match your lipstick to your outfit...*

3 = <u>correspond</u>, agree, accord, square, coincide, tally, conform, match up, be compatible, harmonize, be consonant ...*Their strengths in memory and spatial skills matched...*

4 = <u>pair</u>, unite, join, couple, link, marry, ally, combine, mate, yoke ...*It can take time and money to match buyers and sellers...*

5 = <u>rival</u>, equal, compete with, compare with, emulate, contend with, measure up to ...*We matched them in every department of the game...*

PHRASES **match something** or **someone against something** or **someone** = <u>pit against</u>, set against, play off against, put in opposition to ...*The finals begin today, matching the United States against France...*

matching = <u>identical</u>, like, same, double, paired, equal, toning, twin, equivalent, parallel, corresponding, comparable, duplicate, coordinating, analogous OPPOSITE> different

matchless = <u>unequalled</u>, unique, unparalleled, unrivalled, perfect, supreme, exquisite, consummate, superlative, inimitable, incomparable, unmatched, peerless, unsurpassed OPPOSITE> average

mate NOUN **1** (*Informal*) = <u>friend</u>, pal (*informal*), companion, buddy (*informal*), china (*Brit. slang*), cock (*Brit. informal*), comrade, chum (*informal*), mucker (*Brit. informal*), crony, main man (*slang, chiefly U.S.*), homeboy (*slang, chiefly U.S.*), cobber (*Austral. or old-fashioned N.Z. informal*) ...*A mate of mine used to play soccer for Liverpool...*

2 = <u>partner</u>, lover, companion, spouse, consort, significant other (*U.S. informal*), better half (*humorous*), helpmeet, husband or wife ...*He has found his ideal mate...*

3 = <u>double</u>, match, fellow, twin, counterpart, companion ...*The guest cabin is a mirror image of its mate...*

4 = <u>assistant</u>, subordinate, apprentice, helper, accomplice, sidekick (*informal*) ...*The electrician's mate ignored the red-lettered warning signs...*

5 = <u>colleague</u>, associate, companion, co-worker, fellow-worker, compeer ...*He celebrated with work mates in the pub...*

VERB **1** = <u>pair</u>, couple, breed, copulate ...*They want the males to mate with wild females...*

2 = <u>marry</u>, match, wed, get married, shack up (*informal*) ...*Women typically seek older men with which to mate...*

3 = <u>join</u>, match, couple, pair, yoke ...*The film tries very hard to mate modern with old...*

material NOUN **1** = <u>substance</u>, body, matter, stuff, elements, constituents ...*the decomposition of organic material...*

2 = <u>cloth</u>, stuff, fabric, textile ...*the thick material of her skirt...*

3 = <u>information</u>, work, details, facts, notes, evidence, particulars, data, info (*informal*), subject matter, documentation ...*In my version of the story, I added some new material...*

ADJECTIVE **1** = <u>physical</u>, worldly, solid, substantial, concrete, fleshly, bodily, tangible, palpable, corporeal, nonspiritual ...*the material world...*

2 = <u>relevant</u>, important, significant, essential, vital, key, serious, grave, meaningful, applicable, indispensable, momentous, weighty, pertinent, consequential, apposite, apropos, germane ...*The company failed to disclose material information...*

materialize 1 = <u>occur</u>, happen, take place, turn up, come about, take shape, come into being, come to pass ...*None of the anticipated difficulties materialized...*

2 = <u>appear</u>, arrive, emerge, surface, turn up, loom, show up (*informal*), pop up (*informal*), put in an appearance ...*He materialized at her side, notebook at the ready...*

materially = <u>significantly</u>, much, greatly, considerably, essentially, seriously, gravely, substantially OPPOSITE> insignificantly

maternal = <u>motherly</u>, protective, nurturing, maternalistic

maternity = <u>motherhood</u>, parenthood, motherliness

matey (*Brit. informal*) = <u>friendly</u>, intimate, comradely, thick (*informal*), pally (*informal*), amiable, sociable, chummy (*informal*), free-and-easy, companionable, clubby, buddy-buddy (*slang, chiefly U.S. & Canad.*), hail-fellow-well-met, palsy-walsy (*informal*)

mathematics
➤ **mathematical terms**

matrimonial = <u>marital</u>, married, wedding, wedded, nuptial, conjugal, spousal, connubial, hymeneal

matrimony = <u>marriage</u>, nuptials, wedlock, wedding ceremony, marital rites

matted = <u>tangled</u>, knotted, unkempt, knotty, tousled, ratty, uncombed

matter NOUN **1** = <u>situation</u>, thing, issue, concern, business, question, event, subject, affair, incident, proceeding, episode, topic, transaction, occurrence ...*It was a private matter*...

2 = <u>substance</u>, material, body, stuff ...*A proton is an elementary particle of matter*...

3 = <u>content</u>, sense, subject, argument, text, substance, burden, thesis, purport, gist, pith ...*This conflict forms the matter of the play*...

4 (*Medical*) = <u>pus</u>, discharge, secretion, suppuration, purulence ...*If the wound starts to produce yellow matter, see your doctor*...

5 = <u>importance</u>, interest, moment, note, weight, import, consequence, significance ...*Forget it; it's of no matter*...

VERB = <u>be important</u>, make a difference, count, be relevant, make any difference, mean anything, have influence, carry weight, cut any ice (*informal*), be of consequence, be of account ...*It doesn't matter how long you take*...

matter-of-fact = <u>unsentimental</u>, flat, dry, plain, dull, sober, down-to-earth, mundane, lifeless, prosaic, deadpan, unimaginative, unvarnished, emotionless, unembellished

mature VERB = <u>develop</u>, grow up, bloom, blossom, come of age, become adult, age, reach adulthood, maturate ...*young girls who have not yet matured*...

ADJECTIVE **1** = <u>matured</u>, seasoned, ripe, mellow,

Mathematical terms http://mathworld.wolfram.com/

acute angle	ellipse	node	recurring decimal
addition	equals	nonagon	reflex angle
algorithm *or* algorism	equation	number	remainder
angle	equilateral	numerator	rhombus
arc	even	oblong	right angle
area	exponential	obtuse angle	right-angled triangle
average	factor	octagon	root
axis	factorial	octahedron	scalar
base	formula	odd	scalene
binary	fraction	open set	secant
binomial	frequency	operation	sector
cardinal number	function	operator	semicircle
Cartesian coordinates	graph	ordinal number	set
chord	helix	origin	significant figures
circle	hemisphere	parabola	simultaneous equations
circumference	heptagon	parallel	sine
closed set	hexagon	parallelogram	slide rule
coefficient	hyperbola	pentagon	solid
common denominator	hypotenuse	percentage	sphere
common factor	icosahedron	perfect number	square
complex number	imaginary number	pi	square root
concentric	improper fraction	plus	strange attractor
cone	index	polygon	subset
constant	infinity	polyhedron	subtraction
coordinate *or* co-ordinate	integer	polynomial	sum
	integral	power	surd
cosecant	intersection	prime number	tangent
cosine	irrational number	prism	tetrahedron
cotangent	isosceles	probability	torus
cube	locus	product	trapezium
cube root	logarithm *or* log	proof	triangle
cuboid	lowest common denominator	proper fraction	union
curve		Pythagoras' theorem	universal set
cusp	lowest common multiple	quadrant	value
cylinder		quadratic equation	variable
decagon	Mandelbrot set	quadrilateral	vector
decimal	matrix	quotient	Venn diagram
denary	mean	radian	volume
denominator	median	radius	vulgar fraction
diagonal	minus	ratio	x-axis
diameter	mode	rational number	y-axis
digit	multiplication	real number	z-axis
division	natural logarithm	reciprocal	zero
dodecahedron	natural number	rectangle	

ripened …*grate some mature cheddar cheese*…

2 = <u>grown-up</u>, adult, grown, of age, full-blown, fully fledged, fully-developed, full-grown …*Here is the voice of a mature man, expressing sorrow for a lost ideal*… OPPOSITE immature

maturity 1 = <u>adulthood</u>, majority, completion, puberty, coming of age, fullness, full bloom, full growth, pubescence, manhood *or* womanhood …*Humans experience a delayed maturity compared with other mammals*… OPPOSITE immaturity

2 = <u>ripeness</u>, perfection, maturation …*the dried seeds of peas that have been picked at maturity*…

maudlin = <u>sentimental</u>, tearful, mushy (*informal*), soppy (*Brit. informal*), weepy (*informal*), slushy (*informal*), mawkish, lachrymose, icky (*informal*), overemotional

maul 1 = <u>mangle</u>, claw, lacerate, tear, mangulate (*Austral. slang*) …*He had been mauled by a bear*…

2 = <u>ill-treat</u>, beat, abuse, batter, thrash, beat up (*informal*), molest, work over (*slang*), pummel, manhandle, rough up, handle roughly, knock about *or* around …*The troops were severely mauled before evacuating the island*…

maverick NOUN = <u>rebel</u>, radical, dissenter, individualist, protester, eccentric, heretic, nonconformist, iconoclast, dissentient …*He was too much of a maverick to hold high office*… OPPOSITE traditionalist

ADJECTIVE = <u>rebel</u>, radical, dissenting, individualistic, eccentric, heretical, iconoclastic, nonconformist …*Her maverick behaviour precluded any chance of promotion*…

maw = <u>mouth</u>, crop, throat, jaws, gullet, craw

maxim = <u>saying</u>, motto, adage, proverb, rule, saw, gnome, dictum, axiom, aphorism, byword, apophthegm

maximum ADJECTIVE = <u>greatest</u>, highest, supreme, paramount, utmost, most, maximal, topmost …*The maximum height for a fence here is 2 metres*… OPPOSITE minimal

NOUN = <u>top</u>, most, peak, ceiling, crest, utmost, upper limit, uttermost …*The law provides for a maximum of two years in prison*… OPPOSITE minimum

maybe = <u>perhaps</u>, possibly, it could be, conceivably, perchance (*archaic*), mayhap (*archaic*), peradventure (*archaic*)

mayhem = <u>chaos</u>, trouble, violence, disorder, destruction, confusion, havoc, fracas, commotion

maze = <u>web</u>, puzzle, confusion, tangle, snarl, mesh, labyrinth, imbroglio, convolutions, complex network

meadow = <u>field</u>, pasture, grassland, ley, lea (*poetic*)

meagre = <u>insubstantial</u>, little, small, poor, spare, slight, inadequate, pathetic, slender, scant, sparse, deficient, paltry, skimpy, puny, measly, scanty, exiguous, scrimpy

meal = <u>repast</u>, board, spread (*informal*), snack, something to eat, banquet, dinner, feast, bite to eat (*informal*)

(*Related Words*)

adjective: prandial

mean¹ 1 = <u>signify</u>, say, suggest, indicate, represent, express, stand for, convey, spell out, purport, symbolize, denote, connote, betoken …*The red signal means that you can shoot*…

2 = <u>imply</u>, suggest, intend, indicate, refer to, intimate, get at (*informal*), hint at, have in mind, drive at (*informal*), allude to, insinuate …*What do you think he means by that?*…

3 = <u>presage</u>, promise, herald, foreshadow, augur, foretell, portend, betoken, adumbrate …*An enlarged prostate does not necessarily mean cancer*…

4 = <u>result in</u>, cause, produce, effect, lead to, involve, bring about, give rise to, entail, engender, necessitate …*Trade and product discounts can mean big savings*…

5 = <u>intend</u>, want, plan, expect, design, aim, wish, think, propose, purpose, desire, set out, contemplate, aspire, have plans, have in mind …*I didn't mean to hurt you*…

6 = <u>destine</u>, make, design, suit, fate, predestine, preordain …*He said that we were meant to be together*…

Word Power

mean – In standard British English, *mean* should not be followed by *for* when expressing intention. *I didn't mean this to happen* is acceptable, but not *I didn't mean for this to happen*.

---

mean² 1 = <u>miserly</u>, stingy, parsimonious, niggardly, close (*informal*), near (*informal*), tight, selfish, beggarly, mercenary, skimpy, penny-pinching, ungenerous, penurious, tight-fisted, mingy (*Brit. informal*), snoep (*S. African informal*) …*Don't be mean with the fabric, or the curtains will end up looking skimpy*… OPPOSITE generous

2 = <u>dishonourable</u>, base, petty, degraded, disgraceful, shameful, shabby, vile, degenerate, callous, sordid, abject, despicable, narrow-minded, contemptible, wretched, scurvy, ignoble, hard-hearted, scungy (*Austral. & N.Z.*), low-minded …*Upstaging the bride was a particularly mean trick*… OPPOSITE honourable

3 = <u>malicious</u>, hostile, nasty, sour, unpleasant, rude, unfriendly, bad-tempered, disagreeable, churlish, ill-tempered, cantankerous …*The prison officer described him as the meanest man he'd ever met*… OPPOSITE kind

4 = <u>shabby</u>, poor, miserable, run-down, beggarly, seedy, scruffy, sordid, paltry, squalid, tawdry, low-rent (*informal, chiefly U.S.*), contemptible, wretched, down-at-heel, grungy (*slang, chiefly U.S.*), scuzzy (*slang, chiefly U.S.*) …*He was raised in the mean streets of the central market district*… OPPOSITE superb

5 = <u>lowly</u>, low, common, ordinary, modest, base, obscure, humble, inferior, vulgar, menial, proletarian, undistinguished, servile, ignoble, plebeian, lowborn, baseborn (*archaic*) …*southern opportunists of mean origins*… OPPOSITE noble

mean³ NOUN = <u>average</u>, middle, balance, norm, median, midpoint …*Take a hundred and twenty*

values and calculate the mean…
ADJECTIVE = <u>average</u>, middle, middling, standard, medium, normal, intermediate, median, medial …*the mean score for 26-year-olds…*

meander **VERB** 1 = <u>wind</u>, turn, snake, zigzag …*The river meandered in lazy curves…*
2 = <u>wander</u>, stroll, stray, ramble, stravaig (*Scot. & Northern English dialect*) …*We meandered along the Irish country roads…*
NOUN = <u>curve</u>, bend, turn, twist, loop, coil, zigzag …*The outer bank of a meander in the river…*

meandering = <u>winding</u>, wandering, snaking, tortuous, convoluted, serpentine, circuitous **OPPOSITE** straight

meaning **NOUN** 1 = <u>significance</u>, message, explanation, substance, value, import, implication, drift, interpretation, essence, purport, connotation, upshot, gist, signification …*I became more aware of the symbols and their meanings…*
2 = <u>definition</u>, sense, interpretation, explication, elucidation, denotation …*arguing over the exact meaning of this word or that…*
3 = <u>purpose</u>, point, end, idea, goal, design, aim, object, intention …*Unsure of the meaning of this remark, he remained silent…*
4 = <u>force</u>, use, point, effect, value, worth, consequence, thrust, validity, usefulness, efficacy …*a challenge that gives meaning to life…*
ADJECTIVE = <u>expressive</u>, meaningful, pointed, revealing, significant, speaking, pregnant, suggestive, telltale …*He nodded and gave me a meaning look…*

meaningful 1 = <u>significant</u>, important, serious, material, useful, relevant, valid, worthwhile, purposeful …*a meaningful and constructive dialogue…* **OPPOSITE** trivial
2 = <u>expressive</u>, suggestive, meaning, pointed, speaking, pregnant …*The two men expressed a quick, meaningful look…*

meaningless = <u>nonsensical</u>, senseless, inconsequential, inane, insubstantial **OPPOSITE** worthwhile

meanness 1 = <u>miserliness</u>, parsimony, stinginess, tight-fistedness, niggardliness, selfishness, minginess (*Brit. informal*), penuriousness …*This careful attitude to money can border on meanness…*
2 = <u>pettiness</u>, degradation, degeneracy, wretchedness, narrow-mindedness, shabbiness, baseness, vileness, sordidness, shamefulness, scurviness, abjectness, low-mindedness, ignobility, despicableness, disgracefulness, dishonourableness …*Their meanness of spirit is embarrassing…*
3 = <u>malice</u>, hostility, bad temper, rudeness, nastiness, unpleasantness, ill temper, sourness, unfriendliness, maliciousness, cantankerousness, churlishness, disagreeableness …*There was always a certain amount of cruelty, meanness and villainy…*
4 = <u>shabbiness</u>, squalor, insignificance, pettiness, wretchedness, seediness, tawdriness, sordidness, scruffiness, humbleness, poorness, paltriness, beggarliness, contemptibleness …*the meanness of our surroundings…*

means **PLURAL NOUN** 1 = <u>method</u>, way, course, process, medium, measure, agency, channel, instrument, avenue, mode, expedient …*We do not have the means to fight such a crimewave…*
2 = <u>money</u>, funds, capital, property, riches, income, resources, estate, fortune, wealth, substance, affluence, wherewithal …*He did not have the means to compensate her…*
PHRASES **by all means** = <u>certainly</u>, surely, of course, definitely, absolutely, positively, doubtlessly …*'Can I come and see your house?' 'Yes, by all means.'…* ◆ **by means of** = <u>by way of</u>, using, through, via, utilizing, with the aid of, by dint of …*a course taught by means of lectures and seminars…* ◆ **by no means** = <u>in no way</u>, no way, not at all, definitely not, not in the least, on no account, not in the slightest, not the least bit, absolutely not …*This is by no means out of the ordinary…*

meantime *or* **meanwhile** = <u>at the same time</u>, in the meantime, simultaneously, for the present, concurrently, in the meanwhile

meanwhile *or* **meantime** = <u>for now</u>, in the meantime, for the moment, in the interim, for then, in the interval, in the meanwhile, in the intervening time

measly = <u>meagre</u>, miserable, pathetic, paltry, mean, poor, petty, beggarly, pitiful, skimpy, puny, stingy, contemptible, scanty, miserly, niggardly, ungenerous, mingy (*Brit. informal*), snoep (*S. African informal*)

measurable 1 = <u>perceptible</u>, material, significant, distinct, palpable, discernible, detectable …*Both leaders expect measurable progress…*
2 = <u>quantifiable</u>, material, quantitative, assessable, determinable, computable, gaugeable, mensurable …*measurable quantities such as the number of jobs…*

measure **VERB** = <u>quantify</u>, rate, judge, determine, value, size, estimate, survey, assess, weigh, calculate, evaluate, compute, gauge, mark out, appraise, calibrate …*Measure the length and width of the gap…*
NOUN 1 = <u>quantity</u>, share, amount, degree, reach, range, size, capacity, extent, proportion, allowance, portion, scope, quota, ration, magnitude, allotment, amplitude …*The colonies were claiming a larger measure of self-government…*
2 = <u>standard</u>, example, model, test, par, criterion, norm, benchmark, barometer, yardstick, touchstone, litmus test …*The local elections were seen as a measure of the government's success…*
3 = <u>action</u>, act, step, procedure, means, course, control, proceeding, initiative, manoeuvre, legal action, deed, expedient …*He said stern measures would be taken against the rioters…*
4 = <u>gauge</u>, rule, scale, metre, ruler, yardstick …*a tape measure…*
5 = <u>law</u>, act, bill, legislation, resolution, statute, enactment …*They passed a measure that would give small businesses more benefits…*
PHRASES **for good measure** = <u>in addition</u>, as well, besides, to boot, as an extra, into the bargain, as a bonus …*For good measure, a few details of hotels were included…* ◆ **measure up** = <u>come up to standard</u>,

be fit, be adequate, be capable, be suitable, make the grade (*informal*), be suited, be satisfactory, come up to scratch (*informal*), cut the mustard (*U.S. slang*), fulfil the expectations, fit *or* fill the bill …*I was informed that I didn't measure up…* ◆ **measure up to something** *or* **someone** = achieve, meet, match, rival, equal, compare to, come up to, be equal to, vie with, be on a level with …*It was tiring, always trying to measure up to her high standards…*

measured 1 = steady, even, slow, regular, dignified, stately, solemn, leisurely, sedate, unhurried …*They have to proceed at a measured pace…*
2 = considered, planned, reasoned, studied, calculated, deliberate, sober, premeditated, well-thought-out …*Her more measured approach will appeal to voters…*
3 = quantified, standard, exact, regulated, precise, gauged, verified, predetermined, modulated …*Is the difference in measured intelligence genetic or environmental?…*

measurement 1 = size, length, dimension, area, amount, weight, volume, capacity, extent, height, depth, width, magnitude, amplitude …*Some of the measurements are doubtless inaccurate…*
2 = calculation, assessment, evaluation, estimation, survey, judgment, valuation, appraisal, computation, calibration, mensuration, metage …*Measurement of blood pressure can be undertaken by the practice nurse…*

meat 1 = food, provisions, nourishment, sustenance, eats (*slang*), fare, flesh, rations, grub (*slang*), subsistence, kai (*N.Z. informal*), chow (*informal*), nosh (*slang*), victuals, comestibles, provender, nutriment, viands …*They gave meat and drink to the poor…*
2 = gist, point, heart, core, substance, essence, nucleus, marrow, kernel, nub, pith …*The real meat of the conference was the attempt to agree on minimum standards…*

meaty 1 = substantial, rich, nourishing, hearty …*a lasagne with a meaty sauce…*
2 = brawny, muscular, heavy, solid, strapping, sturdy, burly, husky (*informal*), fleshy, beefy (*informal*), heavily built …*a pleasant lady with meaty arms…*
3 = interesting, rich, significant, substantial, profound, meaningful, pithy …*This time she has been given a more meaty role in the film…*

mechanical 1 = automatic, automated, mechanized, power-driven, motor-driven, machine-driven …*a small mechanical device that taps out the numbers…* OPPOSITE manual
2 = unthinking, routine, automatic, matter-of-fact, cold, unconscious, instinctive, lacklustre, involuntary, impersonal, habitual, cursory, perfunctory, unfeeling, machine-like, emotionless, spiritless …*His retort was mechanical…* OPPOSITE conscious

mechanism 1 = workings, motor, gears, works, action, components, machinery, innards (*informal*) …*the locking mechanism…*
2 = process, workings, way, means, system, performance, operation, medium, agency, method, functioning, technique, procedure, execution,

methodology …*the clumsy mechanism of price controls…*
3 = machine, system, structure, device, tool, instrument, appliance, apparatus, contrivance …*The heat-producing mechanism will switch itself on automatically…*

meddle = interfere, intervene, tamper, intrude, pry, butt in, interpose, stick your nose in (*informal*), put your oar in, intermeddle, put your two cents in (*U.S. slang*)

mediate = intervene, moderate, step in (*informal*), intercede, settle, referee, resolve, umpire, reconcile, arbitrate, interpose, conciliate, make peace, restore harmony, act as middleman, bring to terms, bring to an agreement

mediation = arbitration, intervention, reconciliation, conciliation, good offices, intercession, interposition

mediator = negotiator, arbitrator, judge, referee, advocate, umpire, intermediary, middleman, arbiter, peacemaker, go-between, moderator, interceder, honest broker

medicinal = therapeutic, medical, healing, remedial, restorative, curative, analeptic, roborant, sanative

medicine = remedy, drug, cure, prescription, medication, nostrum, physic, medicament
➤ **medicine**

medieval (*Informal*) = old-fashioned, antique, primitive, obsolete, out-of-date, archaic, prehistoric, antiquated, anachronistic, antediluvian, unenlightened, out of the ark

mediocre = second-rate, average, ordinary, indifferent, middling, pedestrian, inferior, commonplace, vanilla (*slang*), insignificant, so-so (*informal*), banal, tolerable, run-of-the-mill, passable, undistinguished, uninspired, bog-standard (*Brit. & Irish slang*), no great shakes (*informal*), half-pie (*N.Z. informal*), fair to middling (*informal*) OPPOSITE excellent

mediocrity 1 = insignificance, indifference, inferiority, meanness, ordinariness, unimportance, poorness …*She lamented the mediocrity of contemporary literature…*
2 = nonentity, nobody, lightweight (*informal*), second-rater, cipher …*Surrounded by mediocrities, he seemed a towering intellectual…*

meditate VERB = reflect, think, consider, contemplate, deliberate, muse, ponder, ruminate, cogitate, be in a brown study …*I was meditating, and reached a higher state of consciousness…*
PHRASES **meditate on something** = consider, study, contemplate, ponder, reflect on, mull over, think over, chew over, deliberate on, weigh, turn something over in your mind …*He meditated on the problem…*

meditation = reflection, thought, concentration, study, musing, pondering, contemplation, reverie, ruminating, rumination, cogitation, cerebration, a brown study

meditative = reflective, thoughtful, contemplative, studious, pensive, deliberative, ruminative, cogitative

Medicine

Branches of medicine http://www.medhelp.org/

aetiology or etiology	hematology	otolaryngology
anaesthetics	hydrotherapeutics	otology
anaplasty	immunochemistry	paediatrics or (U.S.) pediatrics
anatomy	immunology	pathology
andrology	industrial medicine	periodontics
angiology	internal medicine	pharyngology
audiology	laryngology	physical medicine
aviation medicine	materia medica	physiotherapy or (U.S.)
bacteriology	midwifery	physiatrics
balneology	morbid anatomy	plastic surgery
bioastronautics	myology	posology
biomedicine	neonatology	preventive medicine
cardiology	nephrology	proctology
chiropody	neuroanatomy	psychiatry
dental hygiene or oral hygiene	neuroendocrinology	psychoanalysis
dental surgery	neurology	psychology
dentistry	neuropathology	radiology
dermatology	neurophysiology	rheumatology
diagnostics	neuropsychiatry	rhinology
eccrinology	neurosurgery	serology
electrophysiology	nosology	space medicine
electrotherapeutics	nostology	spare-part surgery
embryology	nuclear medicine	speech therapy
encephalography	nutrition	sports medicine
endocrinology	obstetrics	stomatology
endodontics	odontology	surgery
epidemiology	oncology	symptomatology
exodontics	ophthalmology	syphilology
forensic or legal medicine	optometry	therapeutics
gastroenterology	orthodontics or orthodontia	tocology or tokology
genitourinary medicine	orthopaedics or (U.S.)	toxicology
geratology	orthopedics	trichology
geriatrics	orthoptics	urology
gerontology	orthotics	venereology
gynaecology or (U.S.) gynecology	osteology	veterinary science or medicine
haematology or (U.S.)	osteoplasty	virology

Branches of alternative medicine http://nccam.nih.gov/

acupressure	herbalism	moxibustion
acupuncture	homeopathy or homoeopathy	naturopathy
Alexander technique	hydrotherapy	osteopathy
aromatherapy	hypnosis	radionics
autogenic training	hypnotherapy	reflexology
Bach flower remedy	iridology	shiatsu
biofeedback	kinesiology	
chiropractic	massage	

medium ADJECTIVE = average, mean, middle, middling, fair, intermediate, midway, mediocre, median, medial ...*foods which contain only medium levels of sodium...* OPPOSITE extraordinary

NOUN **1** = spiritualist, seer, clairvoyant, fortune teller, spiritist, channeller ...*Going to see a medium provided a starting point for her...*

2 = middle, mean, centre, average, compromise, middle ground, middle way, midpoint, middle course, middle path ...*It's difficult to strike a happy medium...*

medley = mixture, confusion, jumble, assortment, patchwork, pastiche, mixed bag (*informal*), potpourri, mélange (*French*), miscellany, mishmash, farrago, hotchpotch, hodgepodge, salmagundi, olio,

gallimaufry, omnium-gatherum

meek 1 = submissive, soft, yielding, gentle, peaceful, modest, mild, patient, humble, timid, long-suffering, compliant, unassuming, unpretentious, docile, deferential, forbearing, acquiescent ...*He was a meek, mild-mannered fellow...* OPPOSITE overbearing

2 = spineless, weak, tame, boneless, weak-kneed (*informal*), spiritless, unresisting, wussy (*slang*), wimpish or wimpy (*informal*) ...*He may be self-effacing, but he certainly isn't meek...*

meet 1 = encounter, come across, run into, happen on, find, contact, confront, bump into (*informal*), run across, chance on, come face to face with ...*He's the kindest person I've ever met...* OPPOSITE avoid

2 = <u>gather</u>, collect, assemble, get together, rally, come together, muster, convene, congregate, foregather …*The commission met four times between 1988 and 1991*… OPPOSITE⟩ disperse

3 = <u>fulfil</u>, match (up to), answer, perform, handle, carry out, equal, satisfy, cope with, discharge, comply with, come up to, conform to, gratify, measure up to …*The current arrangements are inadequate to meet our needs*… OPPOSITE⟩ fall short of

4 = <u>experience</u>, face, suffer, bear, go through, encounter, endure, undergo …*Never had she met such spite and pettiness*…

5 = <u>converge</u>, unite, join, cross, touch, connect, come together, link up, adjoin, intersect, abut …*a crossing where four paths meet*… OPPOSITE⟩ diverge

meeting 1 = <u>conference</u>, gathering, assembly, meet, congress, session, rally, convention, get-together (*informal*), reunion, congregation, hui (*N.Z.*), conclave, convocation, powwow …*He travels to London regularly for business meetings*…

2 = <u>encounter</u>, introduction, confrontation, engagement, rendezvous, tryst, assignation …*Thirty-seven years after our first meeting I was back in his studio*…

3 = <u>convergence</u>, union, crossing, conjunction, junction, intersection, concourse, confluence …*the meeting of three streams*…

melancholy ADJECTIVE = <u>sad</u>, down, depressed, unhappy, low, blue, miserable, moody, gloomy, dismal, sombre, woeful, glum, mournful, dejected, despondent, dispirited, melancholic, downcast, lugubrious, pensive, sorrowful, disconsolate, joyless, doleful, downhearted, heavy-hearted, down in the dumps (*informal*), woebegone, down in the mouth, low-spirited …*It was at this time of day that he felt most melancholy*… OPPOSITE⟩ happy
NOUN = <u>sadness</u>, depression, misery, gloom, sorrow, woe, blues, unhappiness, despondency, the hump (*Brit. informal*), dejection, low spirits, gloominess, pensiveness …*He watched the process with an air of melancholy*… OPPOSITE⟩ happiness

melee *or* **mêlée** = <u>fight</u>, fray, brawl, skirmish, tussle, scuffle, free-for-all (*informal*), fracas, set-to (*informal*), rumpus, broil, affray (*Law*), shindig (*informal*), donnybrook, ruction (*informal*), battle royal, ruckus (*informal*), scrimmage, stramash (*Scot.*), shindy (*informal*), bagarre (*French*), biffo (*Austral. slang*)

mellow ADJECTIVE **1** = <u>tuneful</u>, full, rich, soft, melodious, mellifluous, dulcet, well-tuned, euphonic …*the mellow background music*…

2 = <u>full-flavoured</u>, rounded, rich, sweet, smooth, delicate, juicy …*a mellow, well-balanced wine*…

3 = <u>ripe</u>, perfect, mature, ripened, well-matured …*a mellow, creamy Somerset Brie*… OPPOSITE⟩ unripe

4 = <u>relaxed</u>, happy, cheerful, jolly, elevated, merry (*Brit. informal*), expansive, cordial, genial, jovial …*After a few glasses, he was feeling mellow*…
VERB **1** = <u>relax</u>, improve, settle, calm, mature, soften, sweeten …*She has mellowed with age*…

2 = <u>season</u>, develop, improve, perfect, ripen …*Long cooking mellows the flavour beautifully*…

melodramatic = <u>theatrical</u>, actorly, extravagant, histrionic, sensational, hammy (*informal*), actressy, stagy, overemotional, overdramatic

melody 1 = <u>tune</u>, song, theme, refrain, air, music, strain, descant …*a catchy melody with a frenetic beat*…

2 = <u>tunefulness</u>, music, harmony, musicality, euphony, melodiousness …*Her voice was full of melody*…

melt 1 = <u>dissolve</u>, run, soften, fuse, thaw, diffuse, flux, defrost, liquefy, unfreeze, deliquesce …*The snow had melted*…

2 *often with* ***away*** = <u>disappear</u>, fade, vanish, dissolve, disperse, evaporate, evanesce …*When he heard these words, his inner doubts melted away*…

3 = <u>soften</u>, touch, relax, disarm, mollify …*His smile is enough to melt any woman's heart*…

member = <u>representative</u>, associate, supporter, fellow, subscriber, comrade, disciple

membership 1 = <u>participation</u>, belonging, fellowship, enrolment …*his membership of the Communist Party*…

2 = <u>members</u>, body, associates, fellows …*the recent fall in party membership*…

memento = <u>souvenir</u>, trophy, memorial, token, reminder, relic, remembrance, keepsake

memoir = <u>account</u>, life, record, register, journal, essay, biography, narrative, monograph

memoirs = <u>autobiography</u>, diary, life story, life, experiences, memories, journals, recollections, reminiscences

memorable = <u>noteworthy</u>, celebrated, impressive, historic, important, special, striking, famous, significant, signal, extraordinary, remarkable, distinguished, haunting, notable, timeless, unforgettable, momentous, illustrious, catchy, indelible, unfading OPPOSITE⟩ forgettable

memorandum = <u>note</u>, minute, message, communication, reminder, memo, jotting

memorial NOUN **1** = <u>monument</u>, cairn, shrine, plaque, cenotaph …*Every village had its war memorial*…

2 = <u>petition</u>, address, statement, memorandum …*a memorial to the Emperor written in characters of gold*…
ADJECTIVE = <u>commemorative</u>, remembrance, monumental …*A memorial service is being held at St Paul's Church*…

memorize = <u>remember</u>, learn, commit to memory, learn by heart, learn by rote, get by heart, con (*archaic*)

memory 1 = <u>recall</u>, mind, retention, ability to remember, powers of recall, powers of retention …*He had a good memory for faces*…

2 = <u>recollection</u>, reminder, reminiscence, impression, echo, remembrance …*He had happy memories of his father*…

3 = <u>commemoration</u>, respect, honour, recognition, tribute, remembrance, observance …*They held a minute's silence in memory of those who had died*…

menace NOUN **1** = <u>danger</u>, risk, threat, hazard, peril, jeopardy …*In my view you are a menace to the public*…
2 (*Informal*) = <u>nuisance</u>, plague, pest, annoyance, troublemaker, mischief-maker …*Don't be such a menace!*…
3 = <u>threat</u>, warning, intimidation, ill-omen, ominousness, commination …*a pervading sense of menace*…
VERB = <u>bully</u>, threaten, intimidate, terrorize, alarm, frighten, scare, browbeat, utter threats to …*She is being menaced by her sister's boyfriend*…

menacing = <u>threatening</u>, dangerous, alarming, frightening, forbidding, looming, intimidating, ominous, baleful, intimidatory, minatory, bodeful, louring *or* lowering, minacious OPPOSITE encouraging

mend VERB **1** = <u>repair</u>, fix, restore, renew, patch up, renovate, refit, retouch …*They took a long time to mend the roof*…
2 = <u>darn</u>, repair, patch, stitch, sew …*cooking their meals, mending their socks*…
3 = <u>heal</u>, improve, recover, cure, remedy, get better, be all right, be cured, recuperate, pull through, convalesce …*He must have an operation to mend torn knee ligaments*… …*The arm is broken, but you'll mend*…
4 = <u>improve</u>, better, reform, correct, revise, amend, rectify, ameliorate, emend …*There will be disciplinary action if you do not mend your ways*…
PHRASES **on the mend** = <u>convalescent</u>, improving, recovering, getting better, recuperating, convalescing …*The baby had been poorly but was on the mend*…

menial ADJECTIVE = <u>low-status</u>, degrading, lowly, unskilled, low, base, sorry, boring, routine, dull, humble, mean, vile, demeaning, fawning, abject, grovelling, humdrum, subservient, ignominious, sycophantic, servile, slavish, ignoble, obsequious …*low-paid menial jobs such as cleaning*… OPPOSITE high
NOUN = <u>servant</u>, domestic, attendant, lackey, labourer, serf, underling, drudge, vassal (*archaic*), dogsbody (*informal*), flunky, skivvy (*chiefly Brit.*), varlet (*archaic*) …*The name 'beef-eater' was aimed at any well-fed menial*… OPPOSITE master

menstruation = <u>period</u>, menstrual cycle, menses, courses (*Physiology*), flow (*informal*), monthly (*informal*), the curse (*informal*), catamenia (*Physiology*)

mental 1 = <u>intellectual</u>, rational, theoretical, cognitive, brain, conceptual, cerebral …*the mental development of children*…
2 (*Informal*) = <u>insane</u>, mad, disturbed, unstable, mentally ill, lunatic, psychotic, unbalanced, deranged, round the bend (*Brit. slang*), as daft as a brush (*informal, chiefly Brit.*), not right in the head …*I just said to him 'you must be mental!'*…

mentality = <u>attitude</u>, character, personality, psychology, make-up, outlook, disposition, way of thinking, frame of mind, turn of mind, cast of mind

mentally = <u>psychologically</u>, intellectually, rationally, inwardly, subjectively

mention VERB = <u>refer to</u>, point out, acknowledge, bring up, state, report, reveal, declare, cite, communicate, disclose, intimate, tell of, recount, hint at, impart, allude to, divulge, broach, call attention to, make known, touch upon, adduce, speak about *or* of …*She did not mention her mother's absence*…
NOUN **1** *often with* **of** = <u>reference to</u>, announcement, observation, indication, remark on, notification, allusion to …*The statement made no mention of government casualties*…
2 = <u>acknowledgment</u>, recognition, tribute, citation, honourable mention …*Two of the losers deserve special mention*…
PHRASES **not to mention** = <u>to say nothing of</u>, besides, not counting, as well as …*It was both deliberate and malicious, not to mention sick*…

mentor = <u>guide</u>, teacher, coach, adviser, tutor, instructor, counsellor, guru

menu = <u>bill of fare</u>, tariff (*chiefly Brit.*), set menu, table d'hôte, carte du jour (*French*)

mercantile 1 = <u>commercial</u>, business, trade, trading, merchant …*the emergence of a new mercantile class*…
2 = <u>profit-making</u>, money-orientated …*the urban society and its mercantile values*…

mercenary NOUN = <u>hireling</u>, freelance (*History*), soldier of fortune, condottiere (*History*), free companion (*History*) …*In the film he plays a brutish, trigger-happy mercenary*…
ADJECTIVE **1** = <u>greedy</u>, grasping, acquisitive, venal, avaricious, covetous, money-grubbing (*informal*), bribable …*Despite his mercenary motives, he is not a cynic*… OPPOSITE generous
2 = <u>hired</u>, paid, bought, venal …*The mercenary soldier is not a valued creature*…

merchandise NOUN = <u>goods</u>, produce, stock, products, truck, commodities, staples, wares, stock in trade, vendibles …*25% off selected merchandise*…
VERB = <u>trade</u>, market, sell, retail, distribute, deal in, buy and sell, traffic in, vend, do business in …*He advises shops on how to merchandise their wares*…

merchant = <u>tradesman</u>, dealer, trader, broker, retailer, supplier, seller, salesman, vendor, shopkeeper, trafficker, wholesaler, purveyor

merciful = <u>compassionate</u>, forgiving, sympathetic, kind, liberal, soft, sparing, generous, mild, pitying, humane, clement, gracious, lenient, beneficent, forbearing, tender-hearted, benignant OPPOSITE merciless

merciless = <u>cruel</u>, ruthless, hard, severe, harsh, relentless, callous, heartless, unforgiving, fell (*archaic*), inexorable, implacable, unsympathetic, inhumane, barbarous, pitiless, unfeeling, unsparing, hard-hearted, unmerciful, unappeasable, unpitying

mercurial = <u>capricious</u>, volatile, unpredictable, erratic, variable, unstable, fickle, temperamental, impulsive, irrepressible, changeable, quicksilver, flighty, inconstant OPPOSITE consistent

mercy NOUN **1** = <u>compassion</u>, charity, pity,

forgiveness, quarter, favour, grace, kindness, clemency, leniency, benevolence, forbearance …*Neither side showed its prisoners any mercy*… OPPOSITE cruelty

2 = <u>blessing</u>, relief, boon, godsend, piece of luck, benison (*archaic*) …*It was a mercy he'd gone so quickly in the end*…

PHRASES **at the mercy of something** or **someone 1** = <u>defenceless against</u>, subject to, open to, exposed to, vulnerable to, threatened by, susceptible to, prey to, an easy target for, naked before, unprotected against …*Buildings are left to decay at the mercy of vandals and bad weather*… **2** = <u>in the power of</u>, under the control of, in the clutches of, under the heel of …*Servants or slaves were at the mercy of their masters*…

mere 1 = <u>simple</u>, merely, no more than, nothing more than, just, common, plain, pure, pure and simple, unadulterated, unmitigated, unmixed …*It proved to be a mere trick of fate*…

2 = <u>bare</u>, slender, trifling, meagre, just, only, basic, no more than, minimal, scant, paltry, skimpy, scanty …*Cigarettes were a mere 2 cents a packet*…

merge 1 = <u>combine</u>, blend, fuse, amalgamate, unite, join, mix, consolidate, mingle, converge, coalesce, melt into, meld, intermix …*The two countries merged into one*… OPPOSITE separate

2 = <u>join</u>, unite, combine, consolidate, fuse …*He wants to merge the two agencies*… OPPOSITE separate

3 = <u>melt</u>, blend, incorporate, mingle, tone with, be swallowed up by, become lost in …*His features merged into the darkness*…

merger = <u>union</u>, fusion, consolidation, amalgamation, combination, coalition, incorporation

merit NOUN = <u>advantage</u>, value, quality, worth, strength, asset, virtue, good point, strong point, worthiness …*They have been persuaded of the merits of the scheme*…

VERB = <u>deserve</u>, warrant, be entitled to, earn, incur, have a right to, be worthy of, have a claim to …*Such ideas merit careful consideration*…

merited = <u>deserved</u>, justified, warranted, just, earned, appropriate, entitled, rightful, condign, rightly due

merriment = <u>fun</u>, amusement, glee, mirth, sport, laughter, festivity, frolic, gaiety, hilarity, revelry, jollity, levity, liveliness, conviviality, joviality, jocularity, merrymaking

merry ADJECTIVE **1** = <u>cheerful</u>, happy, upbeat (*informal*), carefree, glad, jolly, festive, joyous, joyful, genial, fun-loving, chirpy (*informal*), vivacious, rollicking, convivial, gleeful, blithe, frolicsome, mirthful, sportive, light-hearted, jocund, gay, blithesome …*He was much loved for his merry nature*… OPPOSITE gloomy

2 (*Brit. informal*) = <u>tipsy</u>, happy, elevated (*informal*), mellow, tiddly (*slang, chiefly Brit.*), squiffy (*Brit. informal*) …*After a couple of glasses I was feeling a bit merry*…

PHRASES **make merry** = <u>have fun</u>, celebrate, revel, have a good time, feast, frolic, enjoy yourself, carouse, make whoopee (*informal*) …*Neighbours went out into the streets and made merry together*…

mesh NOUN **1** = <u>net</u>, netting, network, web, tracery …*The ground-floor windows are obscured by wire mesh*…

2 = <u>trap</u>, web, tangle, toils, snare, entanglement …*He lures young talent into his mesh*…

VERB **1** = <u>engage</u>, combine, connect, knit, come together, coordinate, interlock, dovetail, fit together, harmonize …*Their senses of humour meshed perfectly*…

2 = <u>entangle</u>, catch, net, trap, tangle, snare, ensnare, enmesh …*Limes and plane trees meshed in unpruned disorder*…

mesmerize = <u>entrance</u>, fascinate, absorb, captivate, grip, enthral, hypnotize, magnetize, hold spellbound, spellbind

mess NOUN **1** = <u>untidiness</u>, disorder, confusion, chaos, turmoil, litter, clutter, disarray, jumble, disorganization, grot (*slang*), dirtiness …*Linda can't stand mess*…

2 = <u>shambles</u>, botch, hash, cock-up (*Brit. slang*), state, bodge (*informal*), pig's breakfast (*informal*) …*I've made such a mess of my life*…

3 = <u>difficulty</u>, dilemma, plight, spot (*informal*), hole (*informal*), fix (*informal*), jam (*informal*), hot water (*informal*), stew (*informal*), mix-up, muddle, pickle (*informal*), uphill (*S. African*), predicament, deep water, perplexity, tight spot, imbroglio, fine kettle of fish (*informal*) …*I've got myself into a bit of a mess*…

PHRASES **mess about** or **around 1** = <u>potter about</u>, dabble, amuse yourself, footle (*informal*), fool about or around, muck about or around (*informal*), play about or around …*Stop messing about and get on with your work*… …*We were just messing around playing with paint*… **2** = <u>meddle</u>, play, interfere, toy, fiddle (*informal*), tamper, tinker, trifle, fool about or around …*I'd like to know who's been messing about with the pram*… ♦ **mess something up 1** = <u>botch</u>, bungle, make a hash of (*informal*), make a nonsense of, make a pig's ear of (*informal*), cock something up (*Brit. slang*), muck something up (*Brit. slang*), muddle something up …*If I messed it up, I would probably be fired*… **2** = <u>dirty</u>, foul, litter, pollute, clutter, besmirch, disarrange, befoul, dishevel …*I hope they haven't messed up your house*… ♦ **mess with something** or **someone** = <u>interfere</u>, play, fiddle (*informal*), tamper, tinker, meddle …*You are messing with people's religion and they don't like that*…

message NOUN **1** = <u>communication</u>, note, bulletin, word, letter, notice, memo, dispatch, memorandum, communiqué, missive, intimation, tidings …*Would you like to leave a message?*…

2 = <u>point</u>, meaning, idea, moral, theme, import, purport …*The report's message was unequivocal*…

3 (*Scot.*) = <u>errand</u>, job, task, commission, mission …*I was employed to run messages for him in 1957*…

PHRASES **get the message** = <u>understand</u>, see, get it, catch on (*informal*), comprehend, twig (*Brit. informal*), get the point, take the hint …*I think they*

Metals

Metal	Symbol	Metal	Symbol
actinium	Ac	molybdenum	Mo
aluminium	Al	neodymium	Nd
americium	Am	neptunium	Np
antimony	Sb	nickel	Ni
barium	Ba	niobium	Nb
berkelium	Bk	nobelium	No
beryllium	Be	osmium	Os
bismuth	Bi	palladium	Pd
cadmium	Cd	platinum	Pt
caesium *or* (*U.S.*) cesium	Cs	plutonium	Pu
calcium	Ca	polonium	Po
californium	Cf	potassium	K
cerium	Ce	praseodymium	Pr
chromium	Cr	promethium	Pm
cobalt	Co	protactinium	Pa
copper	Cu	radium	Ra
curium	Cm	rhenium	Re
dysprosium	Dy	rhodium	Rh
einsteinium	Es	rubidium	Rb
erbium	Er	ruthenium	Ru
europium	Eu	samarium	Sm
fermium	Fm	scandium	Sc
francium	Fr	silver	Ag
gadolinium	Gd	sodium	Na
gallium	Ga	strontium	Sr
germanium	Ge	tantalum	Ta
gold	Au	technetium	Tc
hafnium	Hf	terbium	Tb
holmium	Ho	thallium	Tl
indium	In	thorium	Th
iridium	Ir	thulium	Tm
iron	Fe	tin	Sn
lanthanum	La	titanium	Ti
lawrencium	Lr	tungsten *or* wolfram	W
lead	Pb	uranium	U
lithium	Li	vanadium	V
lutetium	Lu	ytterbium	Yb
magnesium	Mg	yttrium	Y
manganese	Mn	zinc	Zn
mendelevium	Md	zirconium	Zr
mercury	Hg		

got the message that this attitude is wrong…

messenger = <u>courier</u>, agent, runner, carrier, herald, envoy, bearer, go-between, emissary, harbinger, delivery boy, errand boy

messy 1 = <u>disorganized</u>, sloppy (*informal*), untidy, slovenly …*She was a good, if messy, cook…*
2 = <u>dirty</u>, grubby, grimy, scuzzy (*slang, chiefly U.S.*) …*The work tends to be messy, so wear old clothes…*
3 = <u>untidy</u>, disordered, littered, chaotic, muddled, cluttered, shambolic, disorganized …*Mum made me clean up my messy room…* OPPOSITE tidy
4 = <u>dishevelled</u>, ruffled, untidy, rumpled, bedraggled, unkempt, tousled, uncombed …*She's just an old woman with very messy hair…*
5 = <u>confusing</u>, difficult, complex, confused, tangled, chaotic, tortuous …*Life is a messy and tangled business…*

metal
 ➤ **metals**

Word Power

metal – Care should be taken not to confuse *metal* (a chemical element) with *mettle* (meaning 'courage'). So you would write *this is a real test of the club's mettle* (not *metal*).

metamorphose = <u>transform</u>, change, alter, remake, convert, remodel, mutate, reshape, be reborn, transmute, transfigure, transmogrify (*jocular*), transubstantiate

metamorphosis = <u>transformation</u>, conversion, alteration, change, mutation, rebirth, changeover, transfiguration, transmutation, transubstantiation, transmogrification (*jocular*)

metaphor = <u>figure of speech</u>, image, symbol, analogy, emblem, conceit (*literary*), allegory, trope, figurative expression

metaphorical = <u>figurative</u>, symbolic, emblematic,

allegorical, emblematical, tropical (*Rhetoric*)

metaphysical 1 = <u>abstract</u>, intellectual, theoretical, deep, basic, essential, ideal, fundamental, universal, profound, philosophical, speculative, high-flown, esoteric, transcendental, abstruse, recondite, oversubtle ...*metaphysical questions like personal responsibility for violence...*
2 = <u>supernatural</u>, spiritual, unreal, intangible, immaterial, incorporeal, impalpable, unsubstantial ...*He was moved by a metaphysical sense quite alien to him...*

meteoric = <u>spectacular</u>, sudden, overnight, rapid, fast, brief, brilliant, flashing, fleeting, swift, dazzling, speedy, transient, momentary, ephemeral OPPOSITE> gradual

mete out = <u>distribute</u>, portion, assign, administer, ration, dispense, allot, dole out, share out, apportion, deal out, measure out, parcel out, divide out

method 1 = <u>manner</u>, process, approach, technique, way, plan, course, system, form, rule, programme, style, practice, fashion, scheme, arrangement, procedure, routine, mode, modus operandi ...*new teaching methods...*
2 = <u>orderliness</u>, planning, order, system, form, design, structure, purpose, pattern, organization, regularity ...*They go about their work with method and common sense...*

methodical = <u>orderly</u>, planned, ordered, structured, regular, disciplined, organized, efficient, precise, neat, deliberate, tidy, systematic, meticulous, painstaking, businesslike, well-regulated OPPOSITE> haphazard

meticulous = <u>thorough</u>, detailed, particular, strict, exact, precise, microscopic, fussy, painstaking, perfectionist, scrupulous, fastidious, punctilious OPPOSITE> careless

metropolis = <u>city</u>, town, capital, big city, municipality, conurbation, megalopolis

mettle 1 = <u>courage</u>, spirit, resolution, resolve, life, heart, fire, bottle (*Brit. slang*), nerve, daring, guts (*informal*), pluck, grit, bravery, fortitude, vigour, boldness, gallantry, ardour, valour, spunk (*informal*), indomitability, hardihood, gameness ...*It's the first real test of his mettle this season...*
2 = <u>character</u>, quality, nature, make-up, stamp, temper, kidney, temperament, calibre, disposition ...*He is of a different mettle from the others...*

microbe = <u>microorganism</u>, virus, bug (*informal*), germ, bacterium, bacillus

microscopic = <u>tiny</u>, minute, invisible, negligible, minuscule, imperceptible, infinitesimal, teeny-weeny, teensy-weensy OPPOSITE> huge

midday = <u>noon</u>, twelve o'clock, noonday, noontime, twelve noon, noontide

middle NOUN 1 = <u>centre</u>, heart, inside, thick, core, midst, nucleus, hub, halfway point, midpoint, midsection ...*I was in the middle of the back row...*
2 = <u>waist</u>, gut, belly, tummy (*informal*), waistline, midriff, paunch, midsection ...*At 53, he has a few extra pounds around his middle...*
ADJECTIVE 1 = <u>central</u>, medium, inside, mid,

intervening, inner, halfway, intermediate, median, medial ...*that crucial middle point of the picture...*
2 = <u>intermediate</u>, inside, intervening, inner ...*the middle level of commanding officers...*

middle-class = <u>bourgeois</u>, traditional, conventional, suburban, petit-bourgeois

middleman = <u>intermediary</u>, broker, entrepreneur, distributor, go-between

middling 1 = <u>mediocre</u>, all right, indifferent, so-so (*informal*), unremarkable, tolerable, run-of-the-mill, passable, serviceable, unexceptional, half-pie (*N.Z. informal*), O.K. or okay (*informal*) ...*They enjoyed only middling success until 1963...*
2 = <u>moderate</u>, medium, average, fair, ordinary, modest, adequate, bog-standard (*Brit. & Irish slang*) ...*a man of middling height...*

midget NOUN = <u>dwarf</u>, shrimp (*informal*), gnome, Tom Thumb, munchkin (*informal, chiefly U.S.*), homunculus, manikin, homuncule, pygmy *or* pigmy ...*They used to call him 'midget' or 'shorty' at work...*
ADJECTIVE 1 = <u>baby</u>, small, tiny, miniature, dwarf, teeny-weeny, teensy-weensy ...*an accompaniment of midget roast potatoes...*
2 = <u>diminutive</u>, little, pocket-sized, Lilliputian, dwarfish, pygmy *or* pigmy ...*The part is played by midget actor Warwick Edwards...*

midnight = <u>twelve o'clock</u>, middle of the night, dead of night, twelve o'clock at night, the witching hour

midst NOUN = <u>middle</u>, centre, heart, interior, thick, depths, core, hub, bosom ...*The organisation realised it had a traitor in its midst...*
PHRASES **in the midst of** = <u>among</u>, during, in the middle of, surrounded by, amidst, in the thick of, enveloped by ...*She arrived in the midst of a blizzard...*

midway ADJECTIVE *or* ADVERB = <u>halfway</u>, in the middle of, part-way, equidistant, at the midpoint, betwixt and between

miffed = <u>upset</u>, hurt, annoyed, offended, irritated, put out, hacked (off) (*U.S. slang*), resentful, nettled, aggrieved, vexed, displeased, irked, in a huff, piqued, narked (*Brit., Austral., & N.Z. slang*), tooshie (*Austral. slang*)

might NOUN = <u>power</u>, force, energy, ability, strength, capacity, efficiency, capability, sway, clout (*informal*), vigour, prowess, potency, efficacy, valour, puissance ...*The might of the army could prove a decisive factor...*
PHRASES **with all your might** = <u>forcefully</u>, vigorously, mightily, full force, manfully, full blast, lustily, as hard as possible, as hard as you can ...*She swung the hammer with all her might...*

mightily 1 = <u>very</u>, highly, greatly, hugely, very much, seriously (*informal*), extremely, intensely, decidedly, exceedingly ...*He had given a mightily impressive performance...*
2 = <u>powerfully</u>, vigorously, strongly, forcefully, energetically, with all your strength, with all your might and main ...*She strove mightily to put him from her thoughts...*

mighty **1** = <u>powerful</u>, strong, strapping, robust, hardy, vigorous, potent, sturdy, stout, forceful, stalwart, doughty, lusty, indomitable, manful, puissant ...*a mighty young athlete...* OPPOSITE weak
2 = <u>great</u>, large, huge, grand, massive, towering, vast, enormous, tremendous, immense, titanic, gigantic, monumental, bulky, colossal, stellar (*informal*), prodigious, stupendous, elephantine, ginormous (*informal*), humongous *or* humungous (*U.S. slang*) ...*a land marked with vast lakes and mighty rivers...* OPPOSITE tiny

migrant NOUN = <u>wanderer</u>, immigrant, traveller, gypsy, tinker, rover, transient, nomad, emigrant, itinerant, drifter, vagrant ...*economic migrants and political refugees...*
   ADJECTIVE = <u>itinerant</u>, wandering, drifting, roving, travelling, shifting, immigrant, gypsy, transient, nomadic, migratory, vagrant ...*migrant workers...*

migrate = <u>move</u>, travel, journey, wander, shift, drift, trek, voyage, roam, emigrate, rove

migration = <u>wandering</u>, journey, voyage, travel, movement, shift, trek, emigration, roving

migratory = <u>nomadic</u>, travelling, wandering, migrant, itinerant, unsettled, shifting, gypsy, roving, transient, vagrant, peripatetic

mild **1** = <u>gentle</u>, kind, easy, soft, pacific, calm, moderate, forgiving, tender, pleasant, mellow, compassionate, indulgent, serene, easy-going, amiable, meek, placid, docile, merciful, peaceable, forbearing, equable, easy-oasy (*slang*) ...*He is a mild man, reasonable almost to the point of blandness...* OPPOSITE harsh
2 = <u>temperate</u>, warm, calm, moderate, clement, tranquil, balmy ...*The area is famous for its mild winters...* OPPOSITE cold
3 = <u>bland</u>, thin, smooth, tasteless, insipid, flavourless ...*The cheese has a soft, mild flavour...*
4 = <u>soothing</u>, mollifying, emollient, demulcent, lenitive ...*Wash your face thoroughly with a mild soap...*

milieu = <u>surroundings</u>, setting, scene, environment, element, background, location, sphere, locale, mise en scène (*French*)

militant ADJECTIVE = <u>aggressive</u>, warring, fighting, active, combating, contending, vigorous, assertive, in arms, embattled, belligerent, combative ...*one of the most active militant groups...* OPPOSITE peaceful
   NOUN = <u>activist</u>, radical, fighter, partisan, belligerent, combatant ...*The militants were apparently planning a terrorist attack...*

military ADJECTIVE = <u>warlike</u>, armed, soldierly, martial, soldierlike ...*Military action may become necessary...*
   NOUN = <u>armed forces</u>, forces, services, army ...*Did you serve in the military?...*

militate
   PHRASES **militate against something** = <u>counteract</u>, conflict with, contend with, count against, oppose, counter, resist, be detrimental to, weigh against, tell against
   ► **mitigate**

militia = <u>reserve(s)</u>, National Guard (*U.S.*), Territorial Army (*Brit.*), yeomanry (*History*), fencibles (*History*), trainband (*History*)

milk = <u>exploit</u>, use, pump, squeeze, drain, take advantage of, bleed, impose on, wring, fleece, suck dry
  (Related Words)
  adjectives: lactic, lacteal

milky = <u>white</u>, clouded, opaque, cloudy, alabaster, whitish, milk-white

mill NOUN **1** = <u>grinder</u>, crusher, quern ...*a pepper mill...*
2 = <u>factory</u>, works, shop, plant, workshop, foundry ...*a textile mill...*
   VERB = <u>grind</u>, pound, press, crush, powder, grate, pulverize, granulate, comminute ...*freshly milled black pepper...*
   PHRASES **mill about** *or* **around** = <u>swarm</u>, crowd, stream, surge, seethe, throng ...*Quite a few people were milling about...* ♦ **run of the mill** = <u>commonplace</u>, middling, average, fair, ordinary, routine, everyday, unremarkable, unexceptional, bog-standard (*Brit. & Irish slang*) ...*I was just a very average run of the mill student...*

millstone = <u>burden</u>, weight, load, albatross, drag, affliction, dead weight, encumbrance

mime NOUN = <u>dumb show</u>, gesture, pantomime, mummery ...*Students presented a mime and a puppet show...*
   VERB = <u>act out</u>, represent, gesture, simulate, pantomime ...*She mimed getting up in the morning...*

mimic VERB **1** = <u>imitate</u>, do (*informal*), take off (*informal*), ape, parody, caricature, impersonate ...*He could mimic anybody, reducing his friends to helpless laughter...*
2 = <u>resemble</u>, look like, mirror, echo, simulate, take on the appearance of ...*Don't try to mimic anybody. Just be yourself...*
   NOUN = <u>imitator</u>, impressionist, copycat (*informal*), impersonator, caricaturist, parodist, parrot ...*He's a very good mimic...*

mimicry = <u>imitation</u>, impression, impersonation, copying, imitating, mimicking, parody, caricature, mockery, burlesque, apery

mince **1** = <u>cut</u>, grind, crumble, dice, hash, chop up ...*I'll buy some lean meat and mince it myself...*
2 = <u>posture</u>, pose, ponce (*slang*), attitudinize ...*'Ooh, a sailor!' he minced and she laughed aloud...*
3 = <u>tone down</u>, spare, moderate, weaken, diminish, soften, hold back, extenuate, palliate, euphemize ...*The doctors didn't mince their words, and predicted the worst...*

mincing = <u>affected</u>, nice, camp (*informal*), precious, pretentious, dainty, sissy, effeminate, foppish, poncy (*slang*), arty-farty (*informal*), lah-di-dah (*informal*), niminy-piminy

mind NOUN **1** = <u>brain</u>, head, imagination, psyche, subconscious ...*I'm trying to clear my mind of all this...*
2 = <u>memory</u>, recollection, remembrance, powers of

recollection ...*He spent the next hour going over the trial in his mind*...

3 = attention, thinking, thoughts, concentration ...*My mind was never on my work*...

4 = intelligence, reason, reasoning, understanding, sense, spirit, brain(s) (*informal*), wits, mentality, intellect, grey matter (*informal*), ratiocination ...*an excellent training for the young mind*...

5 = thinker, academic, intellectual, genius, brain (*informal*), scholar, sage, intellect, rocket scientist (*informal, chiefly U.S.*), brainbox, acca (*Austral. slang*) ...*She moved to London, meeting some of the best minds of her time*...

6 = intention, will, wish, desire, urge, fancy, purpose, leaning, bent, notion, tendency, inclination, disposition ...*They could interpret it that way if they'd a mind to*...

7 = sanity, reason, senses, judgment, wits, marbles (*informal*), rationality, mental balance ...*Sometimes I feel I'm losing my mind*...

8 = attitude, view, opinion, belief, feeling, thoughts, judgment, point of view, outlook, sentiment, way of thinking ...*They're all of the same mind*...

VERB 1 = take offence at, dislike, care about, object to, resent, disapprove of, be bothered by, look askance at, be affronted by ...*I hope you don't mind me calling in like this*...

2 = be careful, watch, take care, be wary, be cautious, be on your guard ...*Mind you don't burn those sausages*...

3 = be sure, ensure, make sure, be careful, make certain ...*Mind you don't let the cat out*...

4 = look after, watch, protect, tend, guard, take care of, attend to, keep an eye on, have *or* take charge of ...*Could you mind the shop while I'm out, please?*...

5 = pay attention to, follow, mark, watch, note, regard, respect, notice, attend to, listen to, observe, comply with, obey, heed, adhere to, take heed of, pay heed to ...*You mind what I say now!*...

PHRASES bear *or* **keep something** *or* **someone in mind** = remember, consider, take into account, take note, do not forget, be mindful, make a mental note, be cognizant ...*Bear in mind that petrol stations are scarce in this area*... ♦ **in** *or* **of two minds** = undecided, uncertain, unsure, wavering, hesitant, dithering (*chiefly Brit.*), vacillating, swithering (*Scot.*), shillyshallying (*informal*) ...*I am in two minds about going*... ♦ **make up your mind** = decide, choose, determine, resolve, reach a decision, come to a decision ...*Once he made up his mind to do something there was no stopping him*... ♦ **mind out** = be careful, watch out, take care, look out, beware, pay attention, keep your eyes open, be on your guard ...*Mind out. We're coming in to land!*... ♦ **never mind 1** = forget, don't worry about, pay no attention to, disregard, don't bother about, don't concern yourself about ...*Never mind your shoes. They'll soon dry off*... **2** = forget it, it doesn't matter, don't worry about, it's unimportant, don't give it a second thought ...*'I'm really sorry.' 'Never mind, it happens to me all the time.'*...

Related Words
adjective: mental

mindful = aware, careful, conscious, alert to, sensible, wary, thoughtful, attentive, respectful, watchful, alive to, cognizant, chary, heedful, regardful **OPPOSITE** heedless

mindless 1 = unthinking, gratuitous, thoughtless, careless, oblivious, brutish, inane, witless, heedless, unmindful, dumb-ass (*slang*) ...*blackmail, extortion and mindless violence*... **OPPOSITE** reasoning
2 = unintelligent, stupid, foolish, careless, negligent, idiotic, thoughtless, inane, witless, forgetful, moronic, obtuse, neglectful, asinine, imbecilic, braindead (*informal*), dumb-ass (*slang*), dead from the neck up (*informal*) ...*She wasn't at all the mindless little wife they perceived her to be*...
3 = mechanical, automatic, monotonous, mind-numbing, brainless ...*the mindless repetitiveness of some tasks*...

mind's eye = imagination, head, mind

mine NOUN 1 = pit, deposit, shaft, vein, colliery, excavation, coalfield, lode ...*an explosion at a coal mine*...
2 = source, store, fund, stock, supply, reserve, treasury, wealth, abundance, hoard ...*a mine of information*...
VERB 1 = dig up, extract, quarry, unearth, delve, excavate, hew, dig for ...*Not enough coal to be mined economically*...
2 = lay mines in *or* under, sow with mines ...*The approaches to the garrison have been heavily mined*...

miner = coalminer, pitman (*Brit.*), collier (*Brit.*)
mineral
➤ **minerals**

mingle 1 = mix, combine, blend, merge, unite, join, marry, compound, alloy, interweave, coalesce, intermingle, meld, commingle, intermix, admix ...*Cheers and applause mingled in a single roar*...
OPPOSITE separate
2 = associate, circulate, hang out (*informal*), consort, socialize, rub shoulders (*informal*), hobnob, fraternize, hang about *or* around ...*Guests ate and mingled*...
OPPOSITE dissociate

miniature = small, little, minute, baby, reduced, tiny, pocket, toy, mini, wee, dwarf, scaled-down, diminutive, minuscule, midget, teeny-weeny, Lilliputian, teensy-weensy, pygmy *or* pigmy **OPPOSITE** giant

minimal = minimum, smallest, least, slightest, token, nominal, negligible, least possible, littlest

minimize 1 = reduce, decrease, shrink, diminish, prune, curtail, attenuate, downsize, miniaturize ...*You can minimize these problems with sensible planning*...
OPPOSITE increase
2 = play down, discount, underestimate, belittle, disparage, decry, underrate, deprecate, depreciate, make light *or* little of ...*Some have minimized the importance of these factors*... **OPPOSITE** praise

minimum ADJECTIVE = lowest, smallest, least, slightest, minimal, least possible, littlest ...*He was only five feet nine, the minimum height for a policeman*...

Minerals http://www.minerals.net/index.htm

actinolite
agate
albite
allanite
allophane
alunite
amalgam
amblygonite
analcite *or* analcime
anatase
andalusite
andesine
anglesite
anhydrite
ankerite
annabergite
anorthite
apatite
apophyllite
aragonite
argentite
arsenopyrite
augite
autunite
axinite
azurite
baddeleyite
barytes
bastnaesite *or* bastnasite
bauxite
beryl
biotite
bismuthinite *or* bismuth
 glance
Boehmite
boracite
borax
bornite
braunite
brookite
calaverite
calcite
carnallite
carnotite
cassiterite
celestite *or* celestine
cerargyrite
chabazite
chalcanthite
chalcocite
chalcopyrite
chlorite
chromite
chrysoberyl
chrysotile
cinnabar
clay mineral
cleveite
clinopyroxene
cobaltite *or* cobaltine
colemanite
columbite
cordierite
corundum

cristobalite
crocidolite
crocoite *or* crocoisite
cryolite
cuprite
cyanite
datolite
diallage
diamond
diaspore
diopside
dioptase
dolomite
dumortierite
emery
enstatite
epidote
erythrite
euxenite
fayalite
feldspar *or* felspar
feldspathoid
fluorapatite
fluorspar, fluor *or (U.S.*
 & Canad.) fluorite
forsterite
franklinite
gahnite
galena *or* galenite
garnet
garnierite
gehlenite
germanite
geyserite
gibbsite
glauconite
goethite *or* göthite
graphite
greenockite
gummite
gypsum
halite
harmotome
hematite *or* haematite
hemimorphite
hessite
heulandite
hiddenite
hornblende
hyacinth
hypersthene
illite
ilmenite
jadeite
jarosite
jasper
kainite
kaolinite
kernite
kieserite
kunzite
labradorite
lapis lazuli
lazulite

lazurite
leucite
limonite
magnesite
magnetite
malachite
manganite
marcasite
margarite
massicot
meerschaum
metamict
mica
microcline
millerite
mimetite
molybdenite
monazite
montmorillonite
monzonite
mullite
muscovite
natrolite
nepheline *or* nephelite
nephrite
niccolite
norite
oligoclase
olivenite
olivine
opal
orpiment
orthoclase
ozocerite *or* ozokerite
pentlandite
periclase
perovskite
petuntse *or* petuntze
phenacite *or* phenakite
phosgenite
phosphorite
piedmontite
pinite
pitchblende
pollucite
polybasite
proustite
psilomelane
pyrargyrite
pyrite
pyrolusite
pyromorphite
pyrophyllite
pyroxene
pyroxenite
pyrrhotite *or* pyrrhotine
quartz
realgar
rhodochrosite
rhodonite
rutile
samarskite
saponite
sapphirine

scapolite
scheelite
scolecite
senarmontite
serpentine
siderite
sillimanite
smaltite
smaragdite
smectite
smithsonite
sodalite
sperrylite
sphalerite
sphene
spinel
spodumene
stannite
staurolite
stibnite
stilbite
strontianite
sylvanite
sylvite *or* sylvine
talc
tantalite
tenorite
tetradymite
tetrahedrite
thenardite
thorianite
thorite
tiemannite
topaz
torbernite
tourmaline
tremolite
triphylite
trona
troostite
tungstite
turgite
turquoise
uralite
uraninite
uranite
vanadinite
variscite
vermiculite
vesuvianite
wavellite
willemite
witherite
wolframite
wollastonite
wulfenite
zaratite
zeolite
zincite
zinkenite *or* zinckenite
zircon
zoisite

OPPOSITE › maximum

NOUN = <u>lowest</u>, least, depth, slightest, lowest level, nadir, bottom level …*She has cut her teaching hours to a minimum*…

minion = <u>follower</u>, henchman, underling, lackey, favourite, pet, creature, darling, parasite, cohort (*chiefly U.S.*), dependant, hanger-on, sycophant, yes man, toady, hireling, flunky, flatterer, lickspittle, bootlicker (*informal*)

minister NOUN **1** = <u>official</u>, ambassador, diplomat, delegate, executive, administrator, envoy, cabinet member, office-holder, plenipotentiary …*He concluded a deal with the Danish minister in Washington*…
2 = <u>clergyman</u>, priest, divine, vicar, parson, preacher, pastor, chaplain, cleric, rector, curate, churchman, padre (*informal*), ecclesiastic …*His father was a Baptist minister*…
VERB *often with to* = <u>attend</u>, serve, tend, answer to, accommodate, take care of, cater to, pander to, administer to, be solicitous of …*For 44 years he had ministered to the poor and the sick*…

ministry **1** = <u>department</u>, office, bureau, government department …*the Ministry of Justice*…
2 = <u>administration</u>, government, council, cabinet …*He disclosed that his ministry gave funds to parties in Namibia*…
3 = <u>the priesthood</u>, the church, the cloth, the pulpit, holy orders …*So what prompted him to enter the ministry?*…

minor = <u>small</u>, lesser, subordinate, smaller, light, slight, secondary, petty, inferior, trivial, trifling, insignificant, negligible, unimportant, paltry, inconsequential, inconsiderable, nickel-and-dime (*U.S. slang*) OPPOSITE › major

minstrel = <u>musician</u>, singer, harper, bard, troubadour, songstress, jongleur

mint VERB **1** = <u>make</u>, produce, strike, cast, stamp, punch, coin …*the right to mint coins*…
2 = <u>invent</u>, produce, fashion, make up, construct, coin, devise, forge, fabricate, think up …*The book comprises a lexicon of freshly minted descriptions*…
NOUN = <u>fortune</u>, million, bomb (*Brit. slang*), pile (*informal*), packet (*slang*), bundle (*slang*), heap (*informal*), King's ransom …*They were worth a mint*…
ADJECTIVE = <u>perfect</u>, excellent, first-class, brand-new, fresh, unmarked, undamaged, unblemished, untarnished …*a set of Victorian stamps in mint condition*…

minuscule = <u>tiny</u>, little, minute, fine, very small, miniature, microscopic, diminutive, infinitesimal, teeny-weeny, Lilliputian, teensy-weensy

minute¹ NOUN **1** = <u>sixty seconds</u>, sixtieth of an hour …*A minute later she came to the front door*…
2 = <u>moment</u>, second, bit, shake (*informal*), flash, instant, tick (*Brit. informal*), sec (*informal*), short time, little while, jiffy (*informal*), trice …*I'll be with you in a minute*…
PLURAL NOUN = <u>record</u>, notes, proceedings, transactions, transcript, memorandum …*He'd been

reading the minutes of the last meeting…
PHRASES **any minute** = <u>very soon</u>, any time, at any time, before long, any moment, any second …*It looked as though it might rain any minute*… ♦ **up to the minute** = <u>latest</u>, in, newest, now (*informal*), with it (*informal*), smart, stylish, trendiest, trendy (*Brit. informal*), vogue, up to date, modish, (most) fashionable …*a big range of up-to-the-minute appliances*…

minute² **1** = <u>small</u>, little, tiny, miniature, slender, fine, microscopic, diminutive, minuscule, infinitesimal, teeny-weeny, Lilliputian, teensy-weensy …*Only a minute amount is needed*… OPPOSITE › huge
2 = <u>negligible</u>, slight, petty, trivial, trifling, unimportant, paltry, puny, piddling (*informal*), inconsiderable, picayune (*U.S.*) …*gambling large sums on the minute chance of a big win*… OPPOSITE › significant
3 = <u>precise</u>, close, detailed, critical, exact, meticulous, exhaustive, painstaking, punctilious …*We will have to pore over this report in minute detail*… OPPOSITE › imprecise

minutely = <u>precisely</u>, closely, exactly, in detail, critically, meticulously, painstakingly, exhaustively, with a fine-tooth comb

minutiae = <u>details</u>, particulars, subtleties, trifles, trivia, niceties, finer points, ins and outs

miracle = <u>wonder</u>, phenomenon, sensation, marvel, amazing achievement, astonishing feat

miraculous = <u>wonderful</u>, amazing, extraordinary, incredible, astonishing, marvellous, magical, unbelievable, phenomenal, astounding, inexplicable, wondrous (*archaic or literary*), unaccountable, superhuman OPPOSITE › ordinary

mirage = <u>illusion</u>, vision, hallucination, pipe dream, chimera, optical illusion, phantasm

mire NOUN **1** = <u>mud</u>, dirt, muck, ooze, sludge, slime, slob (*Irish*), gloop (*informal*), grot (*slang*) …*the muck and mire of farmyards*…
2 = <u>swamp</u>, marsh, bog, fen, quagmire, morass, wetland …*Many of those killed were buried in the mire*…
VERB **1** = <u>soil</u>, dirty, muddy, besmirch, begrime, bespatter …*The party has been mired by allegations of sleaze*…
2 = <u>entangle</u>, involve, mix up, catch up, bog down, tangle up, enmesh …*The minister still remains mired in the controversy of the affair*…
PHRASES **in the mire** = <u>in trouble</u>, entangled, in difficulties, encumbered …*We're still in the mire, but I think we're good enough to escape*…

mirror NOUN = <u>looking-glass</u>, glass (*Brit.*), reflector, speculum …*He went into the bathroom and looked in the mirror*…
VERB = <u>reflect</u>, show, follow, match, represent, copy, repeat, echo, parallel, depict, reproduce, emulate …*His own shock was mirrored in her face*…

mirror image = <u>reflection</u>, double, image, copy, twin, representation, clone, replica, likeness, spitting image (*informal*), dead ringer (*informal*), exact likeness

mirth = <u>merriment</u>, amusement, fun, pleasure, laughter, rejoicing, festivity, glee, frolic, sport, gaiety, hilarity, cheerfulness, revelry, jollity, levity, gladness, joviality, jocularity, merrymaking, joyousness

misadventure = <u>misfortune</u>, accident, disaster, failure, reverse, setback, catastrophe, debacle, bad luck, calamity, mishap, bad break (*informal*), ill fortune, ill luck, mischance

misapprehension = <u>misunderstanding</u>, mistake, error, delusion, misconception, fallacy, misreading, false impression, misinterpretation, false belief, misconstruction, wrong idea *or* impression

misappropriate = <u>steal</u>, embezzle, pocket, misuse, swindle, misspend, misapply, defalcate (*Law*)

misbehave = <u>be naughty</u>, be bad, act up (*informal*), muck about (*Brit. slang*), get up to mischief (*informal*), carry on (*informal*), be insubordinate [OPPOSITE] behave

misbehaviour = <u>misconduct</u>, mischief, misdemeanour, shenanigans (*informal*), impropriety, acting up (*informal*), bad behaviour, misdeeds, rudeness, indiscipline, insubordination, naughtiness, monkey business (*informal*), incivility

miscalculate 1 = <u>misjudge</u>, get something wrong, underestimate, underrate, overestimate, overrate *...He has badly miscalculated the mood of the people...*
2 = <u>calculate wrongly</u>, blunder, make a mistake, get it wrong, err, slip up *...The government seems to have miscalculated and bills are higher...*

miscarriage 1 = <u>spontaneous abortion</u>, still birth *...She wanted to get pregnant again after suffering a miscarriage...*
2 = <u>failure</u>, error, breakdown, mismanagement, undoing, thwarting, mishap, botch (*informal*), perversion, misfire, mischance, nonsuccess *...The report concluded that no miscarriage of justice had taken place...*

miscarry 1 = <u>have a miscarriage</u>, lose your baby, have a spontaneous abortion *...Many women who miscarry eventually have healthy babies...*
2 = <u>fail</u>, go wrong, fall through, come to nothing, misfire, go astray, go awry, come to grief, go amiss, go pear-shaped (*informal*), gang agley (*Scot.*) *...My career miscarried when I thought I had everything...*

miscellaneous = <u>mixed</u>, various, varied, diverse, confused, diversified, mingled, assorted, jumbled, sundry, motley, indiscriminate, manifold, heterogeneous, multifarious, multiform

mischief 1 = <u>misbehaviour</u>, trouble, naughtiness, pranks, shenanigans (*informal*), monkey business (*informal*), waywardness, devilment, impishness, roguishness, roguery *...The little lad was always up to some mischief...*
2 = <u>harm</u>, trouble, damage, injury, hurt, evil, disadvantage, disruption, misfortune, detriment *...The conference was a platform to cause political mischief...*

mischievous 1 = <u>naughty</u>, bad, troublesome, wayward, exasperating, playful, rascally, impish, roguish, vexatious, puckish, frolicsome, arch, ludic (*literary*), sportive, badly behaved *...She rocks back and forth on her chair like a mischievous child...*
2 = <u>malicious</u>, damaging, vicious, destructive, harmful, troublesome, malignant, detrimental, hurtful, pernicious, spiteful, deleterious, injurious *...a mischievous campaign by the press...*

misconception = <u>delusion</u>, error, misunderstanding, fallacy, misapprehension, mistaken belief, wrong idea, wrong end of the stick, misconstruction

misconduct = <u>immorality</u>, wrongdoing, mismanagement, malpractice, misdemeanour, delinquency, impropriety, transgression, misbehaviour, dereliction, naughtiness, malfeasance (*Law*), unethical behaviour, malversation (*rare*)

misconstrue = <u>misinterpret</u>, misunderstand, misjudge, misread, mistake, misapprehend, get a false impression of, misconceive, mistranslate, get your lines crossed about, make a wrong interpretation of

misdeed *often plural* = <u>offence</u>, wrong, crime, fault, sin, misconduct, trespass, misdemeanour, transgression, villainy

misdemeanour = <u>offence</u>, misconduct, infringement, trespass, misdeed, transgression, misbehaviour, peccadillo

miserable 1 = <u>down</u>, low, depressed, distressed, gloomy, dismal, afflicted, melancholy, heartbroken, desolate, forlorn, mournful, dejected, broken-hearted, despondent, downcast, sorrowful, wretched, disconsolate, crestfallen, doleful, down in the dumps (*informal*), woebegone, down in the mouth (*informal*) *...She went to bed, miserable and depressed...*
[OPPOSITE] happy
2 = <u>pathetic</u>, low, sorry, disgraceful, mean, shameful, shabby, abject, despicable, deplorable, lamentable, contemptible, scurvy, pitiable, detestable, piteous *...They have so far accepted a miserable 1,100 refugees from the former Yugoslavia...* [OPPOSITE] respectable

miserly = <u>mean</u>, stingy, penny-pinching (*informal*), parsimonious, close, near, grasping, beggarly, illiberal, avaricious, niggardly, ungenerous, covetous, penurious, tightfisted, close-fisted, mingy (*Brit. informal*), snoep (*S. African informal*) [OPPOSITE] generous

misery 1 = <u>unhappiness</u>, distress, despair, grief, suffering, depression, torture, agony, gloom, sadness, discomfort, torment, hardship, sorrow, woe, anguish, melancholy, desolation, wretchedness *...All that money brought nothing but misery...* [OPPOSITE] happiness
2 = <u>poverty</u>, want, need, squalor, privation, penury, destitution, wretchedness, sordidness, indigence *...An elite profited from the misery of the poor...* [OPPOSITE] luxury
3 (*Brit. informal*) = <u>moaner</u>, pessimist, killjoy, spoilsport, grouch (*informal*), prophet of doom, wet blanket (*informal*), sourpuss (*informal*), wowser (*Austral. & N.Z. slang*) *...I'm not such a misery now. I've*

got things sorted out a bit…

4 = <u>misfortune</u>, trouble, trial, disaster, load, burden, curse, ordeal, hardship, catastrophe, sorrow, woe, calamity, affliction, tribulation, bitter pill (*informal*) …*There is no point dwelling on the miseries of the past…*

misfire = <u>fail</u>, go wrong, fall through, miscarry, go pear-shaped (*informal*), fail to go off, go phut (*informal*)

misfit = <u>nonconformist</u>, eccentric, flake (*slang, chiefly U.S.*), oddball (*informal*), fish out of water (*informal*), square peg (in a round hole) (*informal*)

misfortune 1 *often plural* = <u>bad luck</u>, adversity, hard luck, ill luck, infelicity, evil fortune …*She seemed to enjoy the misfortunes of others…*
2 = <u>mishap</u>, loss, trouble, trial, blow, failure, accident, disaster, reverse, tragedy, harm, misery, setback, hardship, calamity, affliction, tribulation, whammy (*informal, chiefly U.S.*), misadventure, bummer (*slang*), mischance, stroke of bad luck, evil chance …*He had had his full share of misfortunes…* OPPOSITE good luck

misgiving = <u>unease</u>, worry, doubt, anxiety, suspicion, uncertainty, reservation, hesitation, distrust, apprehension, qualm, trepidation, scruple, dubiety

misguided = <u>unwise</u>, mistaken, foolish, misled, misplaced, deluded, ill-advised, imprudent, injudicious, labouring under a delusion *or* misapprehension

mishandle = <u>mismanage</u>, bungle, botch, mess up (*informal*), screw (up) (*informal*), make a mess of, muff, make a hash of (*informal*), make a nonsense of, bodge (*informal*), flub (*U.S. slang*)

mishap = <u>accident</u>, disaster, misfortune, stroke of bad luck, adversity, calamity, misadventure, contretemps, mischance, infelicity, evil chance, evil fortune

misinform = <u>mislead</u>, deceive, misdirect, misguide, give someone a bum steer (*informal, chiefly U.S.*)

misinterpret = <u>misunderstand</u>, mistake, distort, misrepresent, misjudge, falsify, pervert, misread, misconstrue, get wrong, misapprehend, misconceive

misjudge = <u>miscalculate</u>, be wrong about, underestimate, underrate, overestimate, overrate, get the wrong idea about

mislay = <u>lose</u>, misplace, miss, be unable to find, lose track of, be unable to put *or* lay your hand on, forget the whereabouts of

mislead = <u>deceive</u>, fool, delude, take someone in (*informal*), bluff, beguile, misdirect, misinform, hoodwink, lead astray, pull the wool over someone's eyes (*informal*), take someone for a ride (*informal*), misguide, give someone a bum steer (*informal, chiefly U.S.*)

misleading = <u>confusing</u>, false, ambiguous, deceptive, spurious, evasive, disingenuous, tricky (*informal*), deceitful, specious, delusive, delusory, sophistical, casuistical, unstraightforward OPPOSITE straightforward

mismatched = <u>incompatible</u>, clashing, irregular, disparate, incongruous, discordant, unsuited, ill-assorted, unreconcilable, misallied

misquote = <u>misrepresent</u>, twist, distort, pervert, muddle, mangle, falsify, garble, misreport, misstate, quote *or* take out of context

misrepresent = <u>distort</u>, disguise, pervert, belie, twist, misinterpret, falsify, garble, misstate

miss¹ VERB **1** = <u>fail to notice</u>, mistake, overlook, pass over …*It's the first thing you see. You can't miss it…*
2 = <u>misunderstand</u>, fail to appreciate …*She seemed to have missed the point…*
3 = <u>long for</u>, wish for, yearn for, want, need, hunger for, pine for, long to see, ache for, feel the loss of, regret the absence of …*Your mum and I are going to miss you at Christmas…*
4 = <u>be late for</u>, fail to catch *or* get …*He missed the last bus home…*
5 = <u>not go to</u>, skip, cut, omit, be absent from, fail to attend, skive off (*informal*), play truant from, bludge (*Austral. & N.Z. informal*), absent yourself from …*We missed our swimming lesson last week…*
6 = <u>avoid</u>, beat, escape, skirt, duck, cheat, bypass, dodge, evade, get round, elude, steer clear of, sidestep, circumvent, find a way round, give a wide berth to …*We left early, hoping to miss the worst of the traffic…*
NOUN = <u>mistake</u>, failure, fault, error, blunder, omission, oversight …*After several more misses, they finally got two arrows in the lion's chest…*

miss² = <u>girl</u>, maiden, maid, schoolgirl, young lady, lass, damsel, spinster, lassie (*informal*) …*She didn't always come over as such a shy little miss…*

misshapen = <u>deformed</u>, twisted, crippled, distorted, ugly, crooked, warped, grotesque, wry, unsightly, contorted, ungainly, malformed, ill-made, unshapely, ill-proportioned

missile = <u>projectile</u>, weapon, shell, rocket

missing = <u>lost</u>, misplaced, not present, gone, left behind, astray, unaccounted for, mislaid, nowhere to be found

mission 1 = <u>assignment</u>, job, labour, operation, work, commission, trip, message (*Scot.*), task, undertaking, expedition, chore, errand …*the most crucial stage of his latest peace mission…*
2 = <u>task</u>, work, calling, business, job, office, charge, goal, operation, commission, trust, aim, purpose, duty, undertaking, pursuit, quest, assignment, vocation, errand …*He viewed his mission in life as protecting the weak from evil…*

missionary = <u>evangelist</u>, preacher, apostle, converter, propagandist, proselytizer

missive = <u>letter</u>, report, note, message, communication, dispatch, memorandum, epistle

mist NOUN = <u>fog</u>, cloud, steam, spray, film, haze, vapour, drizzle, smog, dew, condensation, haar (*Eastern Brit.*), smur *or* smir (*Scot.*) …*Thick mist made flying impossible…*
PHRASES **mist over** *or* **up** = <u>steam (up)</u>, cloud, obscure, blur, fog, film, blear, becloud, befog …*The windscreen was misting over…*

mistake NOUN 1 = error, blunder, oversight, slip, misunderstanding, boob (*Brit. slang*), misconception, gaffe (*informal*), slip-up (*informal*), bloomer (*Brit. informal*), clanger (*informal*), miscalculation, error of judgment, faux pas, false move, boo-boo (*informal*) ...*He says there must have been some mistake*...
2 = oversight, error, slip, inaccuracy, fault, slip-up (*informal*), howler (*informal*), goof, solecism, erratum ...*Spelling mistakes are often just the result of haste*...
VERB 1 = confuse with, accept as, take for, mix up with, misinterpret as, confound with ...*Hayfever is often mistaken for a summer cold*...
2 = misunderstand, misinterpret, misjudge, misread, misconstrue, get wrong, misapprehend, misconceive ...*No one should mistake how serious this issue is*...
PHRASES **make a mistake** = miscalculate, be wrong, blunder, err, boob (*Brit. slang*), slip up (*informal*), misjudge, goof (*informal*), drop a clanger (*informal*), put your foot in it (*informal*), be wide of *or* be off the mark ...*I thought I had made a mistake, so I redid it*...

mistaken 1 = wrong, incorrect, misled, in the wrong, misguided, off the mark, off target, wide of the mark, misinformed, off base (*U.S. & Canad. informal*), barking up the wrong tree (*informal*), off beam (*informal*), getting the wrong end of the stick (*informal*), way off beam (*informal*), labouring under a misapprehension ...*I see I was mistaken about you*... OPPOSITE correct
2 = inaccurate, false, inappropriate, faulty, unfounded, erroneous, unsound, fallacious ...*She obviously had a mistaken view*... OPPOSITE accurate

mistakenly = incorrectly, wrongly, falsely, by mistake, inappropriately, erroneously, in error, inaccurately, misguidedly, fallaciously

mistimed = inopportune, badly timed, inconvenient, untimely, ill-timed, unseasonable, unsynchronized

mistreat = abuse, injure, harm, molest, misuse, maul, manhandle, wrong, rough up, ill-treat, brutalize, maltreat, ill-use, handle roughly, knock about *or* around

mistreatment = abuse, ill-treatment, maltreatment, injury, harm, misuse, mauling, manhandling, roughing up, molestation, unkindness, rough handling, brutalization, ill-usage

mistress = lover, girlfriend, concubine, kept woman, paramour, floozy (*slang*), fancy woman (*slang*), inamorata, doxy (*archaic*), fancy bit (*slang*), ladylove (*rare*)

mistrust NOUN = suspicion, scepticism, distrust, doubt, uncertainty, apprehension, misgiving, wariness, dubiety ...*There was mutual mistrust between the two men*...
VERB = be wary of, suspect, beware, distrust, apprehend, have doubts about ...*You should mistrust all journalists*...

misty = foggy, unclear, murky, fuzzy, obscure, blurred, vague, dim, opaque, cloudy, hazy, overcast, bleary, nebulous, indistinct OPPOSITE clear

misunderstand 1 = misinterpret, misread, get the wrong idea (about), mistake, misjudge, misconstrue, mishear, misapprehend, be at cross-purposes with, misconceive ...*They simply misunderstood him*...
2 = miss the point, get the wrong end of the stick, get your wires crossed, get your lines crossed ...*I think he simply misunderstood*...

misunderstanding 1 = mistake, error, mix-up, misconception, misreading, misapprehension, false impression, misinterpretation, misjudgment, wrong idea, misconstruction ...*Tell them what you want to avoid misunderstandings*...
2 = disagreement, difference, conflict, argument, difficulty, breach, falling-out (*informal*), quarrel, rift, squabble, rupture, variance, discord, dissension ...*a misunderstanding between friends*...

misunderstood = misjudged, misinterpreted, misread, misconstrued, unrecognized, misheard, unappreciated

misuse NOUN 1 = waste, embezzlement, squandering, dissipation, fraudulent use, misemployment, misusage ...*the misuse of public funds*...
2 = abuse, corruption, exploitation ...*the misuse of power*...
3 = misapplication, abuse, illegal use, wrong use ...*the misuse of drugs in sport*...
4 = perversion, distortion, desecration, profanation ...*Fundamentalism is a deplorable misuse of a faith*...
5 = misapplication, solecism, malapropism, catachresis ...*his hilarious misuse of words*...
6 = mistreatment, abuse, harm, exploitation, injury, manhandling, ill-treatment, maltreatment, rough handling, inhumane treatment, cruel treatment, ill-usage ...*the history of the misuse of Aborigines*...
VERB 1 = abuse, misapply, misemploy, prostitute ...*She misused her position in the government*...
2 = waste, squander, dissipate, embezzle, misappropriate ...*The committee has cleared leaders of misusing funds*...
3 = mistreat, abuse, injure, harm, exploit, wrong, molest, manhandle, ill-treat, brutalize, maltreat, ill-use, handle roughly ...*His parents should not have misused him*... OPPOSITE cherish
4 = profane, corrupt, desecrate, pervert ...*breaking a taboo, misusing a sacred ceremony*...

mitigate = ease, moderate, soften, check, quiet, calm, weaken, dull, diminish, temper, blunt, soothe, subdue, lessen, appease, lighten, remit, allay, placate, abate, tone down, assuage, pacify, mollify, take the edge off, extenuate, tranquillize, palliate, reduce the force of OPPOSITE intensify

---

Word Power

mitigate – *Mitigate is sometimes wrongly used where* militate *is meant:* his behaviour militates (*not* mitigates) *against his chances of promotion.*

---

mitigation 1 = extenuation, explanation, excuse ...*In mitigation, the offences were at the lower end of the scale*...

2 = <u>relief</u>, moderation, allaying, remission, diminution, abatement, alleviation, easement, extenuation, mollification, palliation, assuagement ...*the mitigation or cure of a physical or mental condition...*

mix VERB **1** = <u>combine</u>, blend, merge, unite, join, cross, compound, incorporate, put together, fuse, mingle, jumble, alloy, amalgamate, interweave, coalesce, intermingle, meld, commingle, commix ...*Oil and water don't mix... ...Mix the cinnamon with the sugar...*
2 = <u>socialize</u>, associate, hang out (*informal*), mingle, circulate, come together, consort, hobnob, fraternize, rub elbows (*informal*) ...*He mixes with people younger than himself...*
3 *often with* **up** = <u>combine</u>, marry, blend, integrate, amalgamate, coalesce, meld, commix ...*The plan was to mix up office and residential zones...*
NOUN = <u>mixture</u>, combination, blend, fusion, compound, jumble, assortment, alloy, medley, concoction, amalgam, mixed bag (*informal*), meld, melange, miscellany ...*a magical mix of fantasy and reality...*
PHRASES **mix someone up** = <u>bewilder</u>, upset, confuse, disturb, puzzle, muddle, perplex, unnerve, fluster, throw into confusion ...*You're not helping at all, you're just mixing me up even more...* ♦ **mix someone up in something** *usually passive* = <u>entangle</u>, involve, implicate, embroil, rope in ...*He could have got mixed up in the murder...* ♦ **mix something up 1** = <u>confuse</u>, scramble, muddle, confound ...*Depressed people often mix up their words...* **2** = <u>blend</u>, beat, mix, stir, fold ...*Mix up the batter in advance...*

mixed 1 = <u>uncertain</u>, conflicting, confused, doubtful, unsure, muddled, contradictory, ambivalent, indecisive, equivocal ...*I came home from the meeting with mixed feelings...*
2 = <u>varied</u>, diverse, different, differing, diversified, cosmopolitan, assorted, jumbled, disparate, miscellaneous, motley, haphazard, manifold, heterogeneous ...*I found a very mixed group of individuals...* OPPOSITE homogeneous
3 = <u>crossbred</u>, hybrid, mongrel, impure, cross-breed, half-caste, half-breed, interdenominational, interbred ...*a mixed breed dog...* OPPOSITE pure
4 = <u>combined</u>, blended, fused, alloyed, united, compound, incorporated, composite, mingled, amalgamated ...*silver jewellery with mixed metals and semi-precious stones...* OPPOSITE pure

mixed-up = <u>confused</u>, disturbed, puzzled, bewildered, at sea, upset, distraught, muddled, perplexed, maladjusted

mixture 1 = <u>blend</u>, mix, variety, fusion, assortment, combine, brew, jumble, medley, concoction, amalgam, amalgamation, mixed bag (*informal*), meld, potpourri, mélange (*French*), miscellany, conglomeration, hotchpotch, admixture, salmagundi ...*a mixture of spiced, grilled vegetables...*
2 = <u>composite</u>, union, compound, alloy ...*a mixture of concrete and resin...*
3 = <u>cross</u>, combination, blend, association ...*a mixture*

between Reggae, Bhangra, and Soul fusion...
4 = <u>concoction</u>, union, compound, blend, brew, composite, amalgam, conglomeration ...*Prepare the mixture carefully...*

mix-up = <u>confusion</u>, mistake, misunderstanding, mess, tangle, muddle, jumble, fankle (*Scot.*)

moan VERB **1** = <u>groan</u>, sigh, sob, whine, keen, lament, deplore, bemoan, bewail ...*'My head, my head,' she moaned...*
2 (*Informal*) = <u>grumble</u>, complain, groan, whine, beef (*slang*), carp, bitch (*slang*), grouse, gripe (*informal*), whinge (*informal*), bleat, moan and groan, grouch (*informal*) ...*I used to moan if I didn't get at least 8 hours' sleep...*
NOUN **1** = <u>groan</u>, sigh, sob, lament, wail, grunt, whine, lamentation ...*She gave a low choking moan and began to tremble violently...*
2 (*Informal*) = <u>complaint</u>, protest, grumble, beef (*slang*), bitch (*slang*), whine, grouse, gripe (*informal*), grouch (*informal*), kvetch (*U.S. slang*) ...*They have been listening to people's gripes and moans...*

mob NOUN **1** = <u>crowd</u>, pack, collection, mass, body, press, host, gathering, drove, gang, flock, herd, swarm, horde, multitude, throng, assemblage ...*a growing mob of demonstrators...*
2 = <u>masses</u>, rabble, hoi polloi, scum, great unwashed (*informal & derogatory*), riffraff, canaille (*French*), commonalty ...*If they continue like this there is a danger of the mob taking over...*
3 (*Slang*) = <u>gang</u>, company, group, set, lot, troop, crew (*informal*) ...*Can you stop your mob tramping all over the place?...*
VERB **1** = <u>surround</u>, besiege, overrun, jostle, fall on, set upon, crowd around, swarm around ...*Her car was mobbed by the media...*
2 = <u>crowd into</u>, fill, crowd, pack, jam, cram into, fill to overflowing ...*Demonstrators mobbed the streets...*

mobile 1 = <u>movable</u>, moving, travelling, wandering, portable, locomotive, itinerant, peripatetic, ambulatory, motile ...*a four hundred seat mobile theatre...*
2 = <u>changeable</u>, meaning, animated, expressive, eloquent, suggestive, ever-changing ...*She had a mobile, expressive face...*

mobilize 1 = <u>rally</u>, organize, stimulate, excite, prompt, marshal, activate, awaken, animate, muster, foment, put in motion ...*We must try to mobilize international support...*
2 = <u>deploy</u>, prepare, ready, rally, assemble, call up, marshal, muster, call to arms, get *or* make ready ...*The government has mobilized troops to help...*

mock VERB = <u>laugh at</u>, insult, tease, ridicule, taunt, scorn, sneer, scoff, deride, flout, make fun of, wind someone up (*Brit. slang*), poke fun at, chaff, take the mickey out of (*informal*), jeer at, show contempt for, make a monkey out of, laugh to scorn ...*I thought you were mocking me...* OPPOSITE respect
ADJECTIVE = <u>imitation</u>, pretended, artificial, forged, fake, false, faked, dummy, bogus, sham, fraudulent, pseudo (*informal*), counterfeit, feigned, spurious, ersatz, phoney *or* phony (*informal*) ...*'It's tragic,' he*

swooned in mock horror... OPPOSITE> genuine
NOUN = laughing stock, fool, dupe, sport, travesty, jest, Aunt Sally (Brit.) ...She found herself made a mock of...

mockery 1 = derision, contempt, ridicule, scorn, jeering, disdain, scoffing, disrespect, gibes, contumely ...Was there a glint of mockery in his eyes?...
2 = farce, laughing stock, joke, apology (informal), letdown ...This action makes a mockery of the government's plans...

mocking = scornful, insulting, taunting, scoffing, satirical, contemptuous, irreverent, sarcastic, sardonic, derisory, disrespectful, disdainful, derisive, satiric, contumelious

mode 1 = method, way, plan, course, system, form, state, process, condition, style, approach, quality, practice, fashion, technique, manner, procedure, custom, vein ...the capitalist mode of production...
2 = fashion, style, trend, rage, vogue, look, craze ...Their designs were exterminated by the mode for uncluttered space...

model NOUN 1 = representation, image, copy, miniature, dummy, replica, imitation, duplicate, lookalike, facsimile, mock-up ...an architect's model of a wooden house...
2 = pattern, example, design, standard, type, original, ideal, mould, norm, gauge, prototype, paradigm, archetype, exemplar, lodestar ...the Chinese model of economic reform...
3 = version, form, kind, design, style, type, variety, stamp, mode, configuration ...To keep the cost down, opt for a basic model...
4 = sitter, subject, poser ...an artist's model...
5 = mannequin, supermodel, fashion model, clothes horse (informal) ...a top photographic model...
ADJECTIVE 1 = imitation, copy, toy, miniature, dummy, duplicate, facsimile ...a model aeroplane...
2 = ideal, perfect, impeccable, exemplary, consummate, flawless, faultless ...At school she was a model pupil... OPPOSITE> imperfect
3 = archetypal, standard, typical, illustrative, paradigmatic ...The aim is to develop a model farm from which farmers can learn...
VERB 1 = base, shape, plan, found, pattern, mold ...She asked if he had modelled the hero on anyone in particular...
2 = show off (informal) = base, wear, display, sport ...Two boys modelled a variety of clothes from Harrods...
3 = shape, form, design, fashion, cast, stamp, carve, mould, sculpt ...Sometimes she carved wood or modelled clay...

moderate ADJECTIVE 1 = mild, reasonable, controlled, limited, cool, calm, steady, modest, restrained, deliberate, sober, middle-of-the-road, temperate, judicious, peaceable, equable ...He was an easy-going man of very moderate views... OPPOSITE> extreme
2 = average, middling, medium, fair, ordinary, indifferent, mediocre, so-so (informal), passable, unexceptional, fairish, half-pie (N.Z. informal), fair to

middling (informal) ...The drug offered only moderate improvements...
VERB 1 = soften, control, calm, temper, regulate, quiet, diminish, decrease, curb, restrain, tame, subdue, play down, lessen, repress, mitigate, tone down, pacify, modulate, soft-pedal (informal) ...They are hoping that he will be persuaded to moderate his views...
2 = lessen, relax, ease, wane, abate ...The crisis has moderated somewhat... OPPOSITE> intensify
3 = arbitrate, judge, chair, referee, preside, mediate, take the chair ...trying to moderate a quarrel between the two states...

moderation NOUN = restraint, justice, fairness, composure, coolness, temperance, calmness, equanimity, reasonableness, mildness, justness, judiciousness, sedateness, moderateness ...He called on all parties to show moderation...
PHRASES **in moderation** = moderately, within reason, within limits, within bounds, in moderate quantities ...Many of us are able to drink in moderation...

modern 1 = current, present, contemporary, recent, late, present-day, latter-day ...the problem of materialism in modern society...
2 = up-to-date, latest, fresh, new, novel, with it (informal), up-to-the-minute, newfangled, neoteric (rare) ...a more tailored and modern style... OPPOSITE> old-fashioned

modernity = novelty, currency, innovation, freshness, newness, contemporaneity, recentness

modernize = update, renew, revamp, remake, renovate, remodel, rejuvenate, make over, face-lift, bring up to date, rebrand

modest 1 = moderate, small, limited, fair, ordinary, middling, meagre, frugal, scanty, unexceptional ...You don't get rich, but you can earn a modest living from it...
2 = unpretentious, simple, reserved, retiring, quiet, shy, humble, discreet, blushing, self-conscious, coy, meek, reticent, unassuming, self-effacing, demure, diffident, bashful ...He's modest, as well as being a great player...

modesty = reserve, decency, humility, shyness, propriety, reticence, timidity, diffidence, quietness, coyness, self-effacement, meekness, lack of pretension, bashfulness, humbleness, unpretentiousness, demureness, unobtrusiveness, discreetness OPPOSITE> conceit

modicum = little, bit, drop, touch, inch, scrap, dash, grain, particle, fragment, atom, pinch, ounce, shred, small amount, crumb, tinge, mite, tad (informal, chiefly U.S.), speck, iota

modification = change, restriction, variation, qualification, adjustment, revision, alteration, mutation, reformation, refinement, modulation

modify 1 = change, reform, vary, convert, transform, alter, adjust, adapt, revise, remodel, rework, tweak (informal), reorganize, recast, reshape, redo, refashion ...They agreed to modify their recruitment policy...

2 = <u>tone down</u>, limit, reduce, lower, qualify, relax, ease, restrict, moderate, temper, soften, restrain, lessen, abate ...*He had to modify his language considerably*...

modish = <u>fashionable</u>, current, smart, stylish, trendy (*Brit. informal*), in, now (*informal*), with it (*informal*), contemporary, hip (*slang*), vogue, chic, all the rage, up-to-the-minute, à la mode, voguish

modulate = <u>adjust</u>, balance, vary, tone, tune, regulate, harmonize, inflect, attune

modus operandi = <u>procedure</u>, way, system, process, operation, practice, method, technique, praxis

mogul = <u>tycoon</u>, lord, baron, notable, magnate, big gun (*informal*), big shot (*informal*), personage, nob (*slang, chiefly Brit.*), potentate, big wheel (*slang*), big cheese (*slang, old-fashioned*), big noise (*informal*), big hitter (*informal*), heavy hitter (*informal*), nabob (*informal*), bashaw, V.I.P.

moist = <u>damp</u>, wet, dripping, rainy, soggy, humid, dank, clammy, dewy, not dry, drizzly, dampish, wettish

moisten = <u>dampen</u>, water, wet, soak, damp, moisturize, humidify, bedew

moisture = <u>damp</u>, water, liquid, sweat, humidity, dew, perspiration, dampness, wetness, dankness, wateriness

molecule = <u>particle</u>, atom, mite, jot, speck, mote, iota

molest **1** = <u>abuse</u>, attack, hurt, injure, harm, interfere with, assail, accost, manhandle, ill-treat, maltreat ...*He was accused of sexually molesting a colleague*...
2 = <u>annoy</u>, worry, upset, harry, bother, disturb, bug (*informal*), plague, irritate, tease, torment, harass, afflict, badger, persecute, beset, hector, pester, vex ...*He disguised himself to avoid being molested in the street*...

mollify = <u>pacify</u>, quiet, calm, compose, soothe, appease, quell, sweeten, placate, conciliate, propitiate

moment **1** = <u>instant</u>, second, minute, flash, shake (*informal*), tick (*Brit. informal*), no time, twinkling, split second, jiffy (*informal*), trice, two shakes (*informal*), two shakes of a lamb's tail (*informal*), bat of an eye (*informal*) ...*In a moment he was gone*...
2 = <u>time</u>, point, stage, instant, point in time, hour, juncture ...*At this moment a car stopped outside the house*...
3 = <u>importance</u>, concern, value, worth, weight, import, consequence, substance, significance, gravity, seriousness, weightiness ...*I was glad I had nothing of great moment to do that afternoon*...

momentarily = <u>briefly</u>, for a moment, temporarily, for a second, for a minute, for a short time, for an instant, for a little while, for a short while, for the nonce

momentary = <u>short-lived</u>, short, brief, temporary, passing, quick, fleeting, hasty, transitory [OPPOSITE] lasting

momentous = <u>significant</u>, important, serious, vital, critical, crucial, grave, historic, decisive, pivotal, fateful, weighty, consequential, of moment, earth-shaking (*informal*) [OPPOSITE] unimportant

momentum = <u>impetus</u>, force, power, drive, push, energy, strength, thrust, propulsion

monarch = <u>ruler</u>, king *or* queen, sovereign, tsar, potentate, crowned head, emperor *or* empress, prince *or* princess

monarchy **1** = <u>sovereignty</u>, despotism, autocracy, kingship, absolutism, royalism, monocracy ...*a debate on the future of the monarchy*...
2 = <u>kingdom</u>, empire, realm, principality ...*The country was a monarchy until 1973*...

monastery = <u>abbey</u>, house, convent, priory, cloister, religious community, nunnery, friary

monastic = <u>monkish</u>, secluded, cloistered, reclusive, withdrawn, austere, celibate, contemplative, ascetic, sequestered, hermit-like, conventual, cenobitic, coenobitic, cloistral, eremitic, monachal

monetary = <u>financial</u>, money, economic, capital, cash, fiscal, budgetary, pecuniary

money [NOUN] = <u>cash</u>, funds, capital, currency, hard cash, green (*slang*), readies (*informal*), riches, necessary (*informal*), silver, bread (*slang*), coin, tin (*slang*), brass (*Northern English dialect*), loot (*informal*), dough (*slang*), the ready (*informal*), banknotes, dosh (*Brit. & Austral. slang*), lolly (*Brit. slang*), the wherewithal, legal tender, megabucks (*U.S. & Canad. slang*), needful (*informal*), specie, shekels (*informal*), dibs (*slang*), filthy lucre (*facetious*), moolah (*slang*), ackers (*slang*), gelt (*slang, chiefly U.S.*), spondulicks (*slang*), pelf (*contemptuous*), mazuma (*slang, chiefly U.S.*) ...*A lot of money that you pay goes back to the distributor*...
[PHRASES] **in the money** = <u>rich</u>, wealthy, prosperous, affluent, rolling (*slang*), loaded (*slang*), flush (*informal*), well-off, well-heeled (*informal*), well-to-do, on Easy Street (*informal*), in clover (*informal*) ...*If you are lucky, you could be in the money*...

(*Related Words*)
adjective: pecuniary
➤ **WORD POWER SUPPLEMENT currencies**

moneyed *or* **monied** = <u>rich</u>, loaded (*slang*), wealthy, flush (*informal*), prosperous, affluent, well-off, well-heeled (*informal*), well-to-do

money-making = <u>profitable</u>, successful, lucrative, gainful, paying, thriving, remunerative

mongrel [NOUN] = <u>hybrid</u>, cross, half-breed, crossbreed, mixed breed, bigener (*Biology*) ...*They were walking their pet mongrel on the outskirts of the town when it happened*...
[ADJECTIVE] = <u>half-breed</u>, hybrid, crossbred, of mixed breed ...*He was determined to save his mongrel puppy*...

monitor [VERB] = <u>check</u>, follow, record, watch, survey, observe, scan, oversee, supervise, keep an eye on, keep track of, keep tabs on ...*Officials had not been allowed to monitor the voting*...
[NOUN] **1** = <u>guide</u>, observer, supervisor, overseer, invigilator ...*Government monitors will continue to accompany reporters*...
2 = <u>prefect</u> (*Brit.*), head girl, head boy, senior boy, senior girl ...*As a school monitor he set a good*

example…

monk (*Loosely*) = <u>friar</u>, brother, religious, novice, monastic, oblate

Related Words

adjective: monastic

monkey 1 = <u>simian</u>, ape, primate, jackanapes (*archaic*) …*He walked on all fours like a monkey…*
2 = <u>rascal</u>, horror, devil, rogue, imp, tyke, scallywag, mischief maker, scamp, nointer (*Austral. slang*) …*She's such a little monkey…*

Related Words

adjective: simian
collective noun: troop

➤ **monkeys, apes and other primates**

monolithic = <u>huge</u>, giant, massive, imposing, solid, substantial, gigantic, monumental, colossal, impenetrable, intractable, immovable

monologue = <u>speech</u>, lecture, sermon, harangue, soliloquy, oration, spiel (*informal*)

➤ **soliloquy**

monopolize 1 = <u>control</u>, corner, take over, dominate, exercise *or* have a monopoly of …*They are virtually monopolizing the market…*
2 = <u>keep to yourself</u>, corner, hog (*slang*), engross …*He monopolized her totally, to the exclusion of her brothers and sisters…*

monotonous 1 = <u>tedious</u>, boring, dull, repetitive, uniform, all the same, plodding, tiresome, humdrum, unchanging, colourless, mind-numbing, soporific, ho-hum (*informal*), repetitious, wearisome, samey (*informal*), unvaried …*It's monotonous work, like most factory jobs…* OPPOSITE> interesting
2 = <u>toneless</u>, flat, uniform, droning, unchanging, uninflected …*a monotonous voice…* OPPOSITE> animated

monotony = <u>tedium</u>, routine, boredom, dullness, sameness, uniformity, flatness, repetitiveness, tediousness, repetitiousness, colourlessness, tiresomeness

monster NOUN 1 = <u>giant</u>, mammoth, titan, colossus, monstrosity, leviathan, behemoth …*He said he'd hooked a real monster of a fish…*
2 = <u>brute</u>, devil, savage, beast, demon, villain, barbarian, fiend, ogre, ghoul, bogeyman …*You make me sound like an absolute monster!…*

ADJECTIVE = <u>huge</u>, giant, massive, enormous, tremendous, immense, mega (*slang*), titanic, jumbo (*informal*), gigantic, monstrous, mammoth, colossal, stellar (*informal*), stupendous, gargantuan, elephantine, ginormous (*informal*), humongous *or* humungous (*U.S. slang*) …*The film will be a monster hit…*

monstrosity 1 = <u>freak</u>, horror, monster, mutant, ogre, lusus naturae, miscreation, teratism …*The towering figure looked like some monstrosity from a sci-fi movie…*
2 = <u>hideousness</u>, horror, evil, atrocity, abnormality, obscenity, dreadfulness, frightfulness, heinousness, hellishness, loathsomeness …*the monstrosity of Nazism…*

monstrous 1 = <u>outrageous</u>, shocking, evil, horrifying, vicious, foul, cruel, infamous, intolerable, disgraceful, scandalous, atrocious, inhuman, diabolical, heinous, odious, loathsome, devilish, egregious, fiendish, villainous …*She endured his monstrous behaviour for years…* OPPOSITE> decent
2 = <u>huge</u>, giant, massive, great, towering, vast, enormous, tremendous, immense, titanic, gigantic, mammoth, colossal, stellar (*informal*), prodigious, stupendous, gargantuan, elephantine, ginormous (*informal*), humongous *or* humungous (*U.S. slang*) …*They were erecting a monstrous edifice…* OPPOSITE> tiny
3 = <u>unnatural</u>, terrible, horrible, dreadful, abnormal, obscene, horrendous, hideous, grotesque, gruesome, frightful, hellish, freakish, fiendish, miscreated …*the film's monstrous fantasy figure…* OPPOSITE> normal

month = <u>four weeks</u>, thirty days, moon

monument 1 = <u>memorial</u>, cairn, statue, pillar, marker, shrine, tombstone, mausoleum, commemoration, headstone, gravestone, obelisk, cenotaph …*He laid a wreath on a monument near Bayeux…*
2 = <u>testament</u>, record, witness, token, reminder, remembrance, memento …*By his achievements he leaves a fitting monument to his beliefs…*

➤ **buildings and other monuments**

monumental 1 = <u>important</u>, classic, significant, outstanding, lasting, enormous, historic, enduring, memorable, awesome, majestic, immortal,

---

Monkeys, apes and other primates

http://nationalzoo.si.edu/Animals/Primates/Facts/default.cfm

aye-aye	gelada	macaque	sifaka
baboon	gibbon	mandrill	spider monkey
Barbary ape	gorilla	mangabey	squirrel monkey
bonnet monkey	green monkey	marmoset	talapoin
bushbaby *or* galago	grivet	mona	tamarin
capuchin	guenon	monkey *or* (*archaic*)	tana
chacma	guereza	jackanapes	tarsier
chimpanzee *or* chimp	howler monkey	orang-outang, orang-	titi
colobus	indris *or* indri	utan, *or* orang	vervet
douc	langur	proboscis monkey	wanderoo
douroucouli	lemur	rhesus monkey	
drill	loris	saki	
flying lemur *or* colugo	macaco	siamang	

unforgettable, prodigious, stupendous, awe-inspiring, epoch-making …*his monumental work on Chinese astronomy…* OPPOSITE unimportant
2 (*Informal*) = <u>immense</u>, great, massive, terrible, tremendous, horrible, staggering, catastrophic, gigantic, colossal, whopping (*informal*), indefensible, unforgivable, egregious …*It had been a monumental blunder to give him the assignment…* OPPOSITE tiny
3 = <u>commemorative</u>, memorial, monolithic, statuary, funerary …*monumental architecture…*

mood NOUN **1** = <u>state of mind</u>, spirit, humour, temper, vein, tenor, disposition, frame of mind …*He was clearly in a good mood today…*
2 = <u>depression</u>, sulk, bad temper, blues, dumps (*informal*), wax (*informal, chiefly Brit.*), melancholy, doldrums, the hump (*Brit. informal*), bate (*Brit. slang*), fit of pique, low spirits, the sulks, grumps (*informal*), foulie (*Austral. slang*) …*She was obviously in a mood…*
PHRASES **in the mood** = <u>inclined</u>, willing, interested, minded, keen, eager, disposed towards, in the (right) frame of mind, favourable towards …*After all that activity we were in the mood for a good meal…*

moody 1 = <u>changeable</u>, volatile, unpredictable, unstable, erratic, fickle, temperamental, impulsive, mercurial, capricious, unsteady, fitful, flighty, faddish, inconstant …*She was unstable and moody…*
OPPOSITE stable
2 = <u>sulky</u>, cross, wounded, angry, offended, irritable, crabbed, crusty, temperamental, touchy, curt, petulant, ill-tempered, irascible, cantankerous, tetchy, testy, in a huff, short-tempered, waspish, piqued, crabby, huffy, splenetic, crotchety (*informal*), ill-humoured, huffish, tooshie (*Austral. slang*) …*He is a moody man behind that jokey front…* OPPOSITE cheerful
3 = <u>gloomy</u>, sad, miserable, melancholy, frowning, dismal, dour, sullen, glum, introspective, in the doldrums, out of sorts (*informal*), downcast, morose, lugubrious, pensive, broody, crestfallen, doleful, down in the dumps (*informal*), saturnine, down in the mouth (*informal*), mopish, mopy …*Don't go all moody on me!…* OPPOSITE cheerful
4 = <u>sad</u>, gloomy, melancholy, sombre …*melancholy guitars and moody lyrics…*

moon NOUN = <u>satellite</u> …*Neptune's large moon…*
VERB = <u>idle</u>, drift, loaf, languish, waste time, daydream, mope, mooch (*Brit. slang*) …*She was mooning around all morning, doing nothing…*
PHRASES **once in a blue moon** = <u>rarely</u>, almost never, very seldom, hardly ever, scarcely ever …*Once in a blue moon you get some problems…*
(**Related Words**)
adjective : lunar

moor[1] = <u>moorland</u>, fell (*Brit.*), heath, muir (*Scot.*) …*The small town is high up in the moors…*

moor[2] = <u>tie up</u>, fix, secure, anchor, dock, lash, berth, fasten, make fast …*She had moored her boat on the right bank of the river…*

moot VERB = <u>bring up</u>, propose, suggest, introduce, put forward, ventilate, broach …*When the theatre idea was first mooted, I had my doubts…*
ADJECTIVE = <u>debatable</u>, open, controversial, doubtful, unsettled, unresolved, undecided, at issue, arguable, open to debate, contestable, disputable …*How long he'll be able to do so is a moot point…*

mop NOUN **1** = <u>squeegee</u>, sponge, swab …*She was standing outside the door with a mop and bucket…*
2 = <u>mane</u>, shock, mass, tangle, mat, thatch …*He was dark-eyed with a mop of tight curls…*
VERB = <u>clean</u>, wash, wipe, sponge, swab, squeegee …*There was a woman mopping the stairs…*
PHRASES **mop something up 1** = <u>clean up</u>, wash, sponge, mop, soak up, swab, wipe up, sop up …*A waiter mopped up the mess as best he could…*
2 (*Military*) = <u>finish off</u>, clear, account for, eliminate, round up, clean out, neutralize, pacify …*The infantry divisions mopped up remaining centres of resistance…*

mope = <u>brood</u>, moon, pine, hang around, idle, fret, pout, languish, waste time, sulk, be gloomy, eat your heart out, be apathetic, be dejected, be down in the mouth (*informal*), have a long face, wear a long face, go about like a half-shut knife (*informal*)

moral ADJECTIVE **1** = <u>ethical</u>, social, behavioural …*the moral issues involved in 'playing God'…*
2 = <u>psychological</u>, emotional, mental …*He showed moral courage in defending his ideas…*
3 = <u>good</u>, just, right, principled, pure, decent, innocent, proper, noble, ethical, upright, honourable, honest, righteous, virtuous, blameless, high-minded, chaste, upstanding, meritorious, incorruptible …*The committee members are moral, competent people…*
OPPOSITE immoral
NOUN = <u>lesson</u>, meaning, point, message, teaching, import, significance, precept …*The moral of the story is, let the buyer beware…*
PLURAL NOUN = <u>morality</u>, standards, conduct, principles, behaviour, manners, habits, ethics, integrity, mores, scruples …*Western ideas and morals…*

morale = <u>confidence</u>, heart, spirit, temper, self-esteem, team spirit, mettle, esprit de corps

morality 1 = <u>virtue</u>, justice, principles, morals, honour, integrity, goodness, honesty, decency, fair play, righteousness, good behaviour, propriety, chastity, probity, rectitude, rightness, uprightness …*an effort to preserve traditional morality…*
2 = <u>ethics</u>, conduct, principles, ideals, morals, manners, habits, philosophy, mores, moral code …*aspects of Christian morality…*
3 = <u>rights and wrongs</u>, ethics, ethicality …*the morality of blood sports…*

morass 1 = <u>mess</u>, confusion, chaos, jam (*informal*), tangle, mix-up, muddle, quagmire …*I tried to drag myself out of the morass of despair…*
2 = <u>marsh</u>, swamp, bog, slough, fen, moss (*Scot. & Northern English dialect*), quagmire, marshland …*a morass of gooey mud…*

moratorium = <u>postponement</u>, stay, freeze, halt, suspension, respite, standstill

morbid 1 = <u>gruesome</u>, sick, dreadful, ghastly, hideous, unhealthy, grisly, macabre, horrid, ghoulish, unwholesome ...*Some people have a morbid fascination with crime...*

2 = <u>gloomy</u>, brooding, pessimistic, melancholy, sombre, grim, glum, lugubrious, funereal, low-spirited ...*He was in no mood for any morbid introspection...* <u>OPPOSITE</u> cheerful

3 = <u>diseased</u>, sick, infected, deadly, ailing, unhealthy, malignant, sickly, pathological, unsound ...*Uraemia is a morbid condition...* <u>OPPOSITE</u> healthy

more <u>ADJECTIVE</u> = <u>extra</u>, additional, spare, new, other, added, further, fresh, new-found, supplementary ...*Give them a bit more information...*
<u>ADVERB</u> 1 = <u>to a greater extent</u>, longer, better, further, some more ...*When we are tired we feel pain more...*
2 = <u>moreover</u>, also, in addition, besides, furthermore, what's more, on top of that, to boot, into the bargain, over and above that ...*He was blind, and more, his eyepits were scooped hollows...*
➤ **most**

moreover = <u>furthermore</u>, also, further, in addition, too, as well, besides, likewise, what is more, to boot, additionally, into the bargain, withal (*literary*)

moribund = <u>declining</u>, weak, waning, standing still, stagnant, stagnating, on the way out, at a standstill, obsolescent, on its last legs, forceless

morning 1 = <u>before noon</u>, forenoon, morn (*poetic*), a.m. ...*On Sunday morning he was woken by the telephone...*
2 = <u>dawn</u>, sunrise, morrow (*archaic*), first light, daybreak, break of day ...*I started to lose hope of ever seeing the morning...*

moron = <u>fool</u>, idiot, dummy (*slang*), berk (*Brit. slang*), charlie (*Brit. informal*), tosser (*Brit. slang*), dope (*informal*), jerk (*slang, chiefly U.S. & Canad.*), ass, plank (*Brit. slang*), wally (*slang*), prat (*slang*), plonker (*slang*), coot, geek (*slang*), twit (*informal, chiefly Brit.*), bonehead (*slang*), chump, dunce, imbecile, cretin, oaf, simpleton, airhead (*slang*), dimwit (*informal*), dipstick (*Brit. slang*), gonzo (*slang*), schmuck (*U.S. slang*), dork (*slang*), nitwit (*informal*), dolt, blockhead, divvy (*Brit. slang*), pillock (*Brit. slang*), halfwit, dweeb (*U.S. slang*), putz (*U.S. slang*), fathead (*informal*), weenie (*U.S. informal*), eejit (*Scot. & Irish*), dumb-ass (*slang*), dunderhead, numpty (*Scot. informal*), doofus (*slang, chiefly U.S.*), lamebrain (*informal*), mental defective, thickhead, muttonhead (*slang*), nerd *or* nurd (*slang*), numbskull *or* numskull, dorba *or* dorb (*Austral. slang*), bogan (*Austral. slang*)

moronic = <u>idiotic</u>, simple, foolish, mindless, thick, stupid, daft (*informal*), retarded, gormless (*Brit. informal*), brainless, cretinous, unintelligent, dimwitted (*informal*), asinine, imbecilic, braindead (*informal*), mentally defective, dumb-ass (*slang*), doltish, dead from the neck up (*informal*), halfwitted, muttonheaded (*slang*)

morose = <u>sullen</u>, miserable, moody, gloomy, down, low, cross, blue, depressed, sour, crabbed, pessimistic, perverse, melancholy, dour, crusty, glum, surly, mournful, gruff, churlish, sulky, taciturn, ill-tempered, in a bad mood, grouchy (*informal*), down in the dumps (*informal*), crabby, saturnine, ill-humoured, ill-

natured <u>OPPOSITE</u> cheerful

morsel = <u>piece</u>, bite, bit, slice, scrap, part, grain, taste, segment, fragment, fraction, snack, crumb, nibble, mouthful, tad (*informal, chiefly U.S.*), titbit, soupçon (*French*)

mortal <u>ADJECTIVE</u> 1 = <u>human</u>, worldly, passing, earthly, fleshly, temporal, transient, ephemeral, perishable, corporeal, impermanent, sublunary ...*Man is designed to be mortal...*
2 = <u>fatal</u>, killing, terminal, deadly, destructive, lethal, murderous, death-dealing ...*a mortal blow to terrorism...*
3 = <u>unrelenting</u>, bitter, sworn, deadly, relentless, to the death, implacable, out-and-out, irreconcilable, remorseless ...*Broadcasting was regarded as the mortal enemy of live music...*
4 = <u>great</u>, serious, terrible, enormous, severe, extreme, grave, intense, awful, dire, agonizing ...*She lived in mortal fear that one day she would be found out...*
<u>NOUN</u> = <u>human being</u>, being, man, woman, body, person, human, individual, earthling ...*impossible needs for any mere mortal to meet...*

mortality 1 = <u>humanity</u>, transience, impermanence, ephemerality, temporality, corporeality, impermanency ...*The event served as a stark reminder of our mortality...*
2 = <u>death</u>, dying, fatality, loss of life ...*the nation's infant mortality rate...*

mortified = <u>humiliated</u>, embarrassed, shamed, crushed, annoyed, humbled, horrified, put down, put out (*informal*), ashamed, confounded, deflated, vexed, affronted, displeased, chagrined, chastened, discomfited, abashed, put to shame, rendered speechless, made to eat humble pie (*informal*), given a showing-up (*informal*)

mortify 1 = <u>humiliate</u>, disappoint, embarrass, shame, crush, annoy, humble, deflate, vex, affront, displease, chagrin, discomfit, abase, put someone to shame, abash ...*She mortified her family by leaving her husband...*
2 = <u>discipline</u>, control, deny, subdue, chasten, abase ...*The most austere of the Christians felt the need to mortify themselves...*

mortuary = <u>morgue</u>, funeral home (*U.S.*), funeral parlour

Moslem
➤ **Islam**

most = <u>nearly all</u>, the majority, the mass, almost all, the bulk, the lion's share, the preponderance

---

Word Power

most – *More* and *most* should be distinguished when used in comparisons. *More* applies to cases involving two people, objects, etc., *most* to cases involving three or more: *John is the more intelligent of the two; he is the most intelligent of the students.*

---

mostly 1 = <u>mainly</u>, largely, chiefly, principally, primarily, above all, on the whole, predominantly, for the most part, almost entirely ...*I am working with mostly highly motivated people*...

2 = generally, usually, on the whole, most often, as a rule, customarily ...*We mostly go to clubs, or round to a friend's house*...

mote = speck, spot, grain, particle, fragment, atom, mite

moth

(Related Words)

young: caterpillar
enthusiast: lepidopterist
➤ **butterflies and moths**

mother NOUN = female parent, mum (*Brit. informal*), ma (*informal*), mater, dam, old woman (*informal*), mom (*U.S. informal*), mummy (*Brit. informal*), old lady (*informal*), foster mother, birth mother, biological mother ...*Mother and child form a close attachment*...
VERB **1** = give birth to, produce, bear, bring forth, drop ...*She had dreamed of mothering a large family*...

2 = nurture, raise, protect, tend, nurse, rear, care for, cherish ...*She felt a great need to mother him*...
3 = pamper, baby, spoil, indulge, fuss over, cosset, mollycoddle, overprotect ...*Don't mother me!*...
ADJECTIVE = native, natural, innate, inborn, connate ...*He looks on Turkey as his mother country*...

(Related Words)

adjective: maternal

motherly = maternal, loving, kind, caring, warm, comforting, sheltering, gentle, tender, protective, fond, affectionate

motif 1 = design, form, shape, decoration, ornament ...*wallpaper with a rose motif*...
2 = theme, idea, subject, concept, leitmotif ...*the motif of magical apples in fairytales*...

motion NOUN **1** = movement, action, mobility, passing, travel, progress, flow, passage, locomotion, motility, kinesics ...*the laws governing light, sound and motion*...
2 = gesture, sign, wave, signal, gesticulation ...*He made a neat chopping motion with his hand*...
3 = proposal, suggestion, recommendation, proposition, submission ...*The conference is now debating the motion*...
VERB = gesture, direct, wave, signal, nod, beckon, gesticulate ...*She motioned for the doors to be opened*...
PHRASES **in motion 1** = in progress, going on, under way, afoot, on the go (*informal*) ...*His job begins in earnest now that the World Cup is in motion*... **2** = moving, going, working, travelling, functioning, under way, operational, on the move (*informal*) ...*Always stay seated while a bus is in motion*...

(Related Words)

adjective: kinetic

motionless = still, static, stationary, standing, fixed, frozen, calm, halted, paralysed, lifeless, inert, unmoved, transfixed, at rest, immobile, inanimate, at a standstill, unmoving, stock-still OPPOSITE moving

motivate 1 = inspire, drive, stimulate, provoke, lead,

move, cause, prompt, stir, trigger, set off, induce, arouse, prod, get going, instigate, impel, actuate, give incentive to, inspirit ...*His hard work was motivated by a need to achieve*...
2 = stimulate, drive, inspire, stir, arouse, get going, galvanize, incentivize ...*How do you motivate people to work hard and efficiently?*...

motivation 1 = incentive, inspiration, motive, stimulus, reason, spur, impulse, persuasion, inducement, incitement, instigation, carrot and stick ...*Money is my motivation*...
2 = inspiration, drive, desire, ambition, hunger, interest ...*The team may be lacking motivation for next week's game*...

motive NOUN = reason, motivation, cause, ground(s), design, influence, purpose, object, intention, spur, incentive, inspiration, stimulus, rationale, inducement, incitement, mainspring, the why and wherefore ...*Police have ruled out robbery as a motive for the killing*...
ADJECTIVE = moving, driving, motivating, operative, activating, impelling ...*the motive power behind a boxer's punches*...

motley = miscellaneous, mixed, varied, diversified, mingled, unlike, assorted, disparate, dissimilar, heterogeneous OPPOSITE homogeneous

motor car
➤ **car**

mottled = blotchy, spotted, pied, streaked, marbled, flecked, variegated, chequered, speckled, freckled, dappled, tabby, stippled, piebald, brindled

motto = saying, slogan, maxim, rule, cry, formula, gnome, adage, proverb, dictum, precept, byword, watchword, tag-line

mould¹ NOUN **1** = cast, form, die, shape, pattern, stamp, matrix ...*the moulds for the foundry*...
2 = design, line, style, fashion, build, form, cut, kind, shape, structure, pattern, brand, frame, construction, stamp, format, configuration ...*At first sight, he is not cast in the leading man mould*...
3 = nature, character, sort, kind, quality, type, stamp, kidney, calibre, ilk ...*every man of heroic mould who struggles up to eminence*...
VERB **1** = shape, make, work, form, create, model, fashion, cast, stamp, construct, carve, forge, sculpt ...*We moulded a statue out of mud*...
2 = influence, make, form, control, direct, affect, shape ...*The experience has moulded her personality*...

mould² = fungus, blight, mildew, mustiness, mouldiness ...*jars of jam with mould on them*...

moulder = decay, waste, break down, crumble, rot, disintegrate, perish, decompose

mouldy = stale, spoiled, rotting, decaying, bad, rotten, blighted, musty, fusty, mildewed

mound 1 = heap, bing (*Scot.*), pile, drift, stack, rick ...*huge mounds of dirt*...
2 = hill, bank, rise, dune, embankment, knoll, hillock, kopje *or* koppie (*S. African*) ...*We sat on a grassy mound and had our picnic*...
3 (*Archaeology*) = barrow, tumulus ...*an ancient,*

man-made burial mound...

4 = <u>earthwork</u>, rampart, bulwark, motte (*History*) ...*a rough double-moated mound earmarked as an ancient monument...*

mount `VERB` **1** (*Military*) = <u>launch</u>, stage, prepare, deliver, set in motion ...*a security operation mounted by the army...*

2 = <u>increase</u>, build, grow, swell, intensify, escalate, multiply ...*For several hours, tension mounted...* `OPPOSITE` decrease

3 = <u>accumulate</u>, increase, collect, gather, build up, pile up, amass, cumulate ...*The uncollected garbage mounts in the streets...*

4 = <u>ascend</u>, scale, climb (up), go up, clamber up, make your way up ...*He was mounting the stairs to the tower...* `OPPOSITE` descend

5 = <u>get (up) on</u>, jump on, straddle, climb onto, climb up on, hop on to, bestride, get on the back of, get astride ...*He mounted his horse and rode away...* `OPPOSITE` get off

6 = <u>display</u>, set, frame, set off ...*He mounts the work in a frame...*

7 = <u>fit</u>, place, set, position, set up, fix, secure, attach, install, erect, put in place, put in position, emplace ...*The fuel tank is mounted on the side of the truck...*

8 = <u>display</u>, present, stage, prepare, put on, organize, get up (*informal*), exhibit, put on display ...*mounting an exhibition of historical Tiffany jewellery...*

`NOUN` **1** = <u>horse</u>, steed (*literary*) ...*the number of owners who care for older mounts...*

2 = <u>backing</u>, setting, support, stand, base, mounting, frame, fixture, foil ...*Even on a solid mount, any movement nearby may shake the image...*

mountain **1** = <u>peak</u>, mount, height, ben (*Scot.*), horn, ridge, fell (*Brit.*), berg (*S. African*), alp, pinnacle, elevation, Munro, eminence ...*Ben Nevis, Britain's highest mountain...*

2 = <u>heap</u>, mass, masses, pile, a great deal, ton, stack, abundance, mound, profusion, shedload (*Brit. informal*) ...*They are faced with a mountain of bureaucracy...*

➤ **WORD POWER SUPPLEMENT mountains**

mountainous **1** = <u>high</u>, towering, soaring, steep, rocky, highland, alpine, upland ...*a mountainous region...*

2 = <u>huge</u>, great, enormous, mighty, immense, daunting, gigantic, monumental, mammoth, prodigious, hulking, ponderous ...*a plan designed to reduce the company's mountainous debt...* `OPPOSITE` tiny

mourn **1** *often with* ***for*** = <u>grieve for</u>, miss, lament, keen for, weep for, sorrow for, wail for, wear black for ...*She still mourned her father...*

2 = <u>bemoan</u>, rue, deplore, bewail ...*We mourned the loss of our cities...*

mournful **1** = <u>dismal</u>, sad, unhappy, miserable, gloomy, grieving, melancholy, sombre, heartbroken, desolate, woeful, rueful, heavy, downcast, grief-stricken, lugubrious, disconsolate, joyless, funereal, heavy-hearted, down in the dumps (*informal*), cheerless, brokenhearted ...*He looked mournful, even*

near to tears... `OPPOSITE` happy

2 = <u>sad</u>, distressing, unhappy, tragic, painful, afflicting, melancholy, harrowing, grievous, woeful, deplorable, lamentable, plaintive, calamitous, sorrowful, piteous ...*the mournful wail of bagpipes...* `OPPOSITE` cheerful

mourning **1** = <u>grieving</u>, grief, bereavement, weeping, woe, lamentation, keening ...*The period of mourning and bereavement may be long...*

2 = <u>black</u>, weeds, sackcloth and ashes, widow's weeds ...*Yesterday the whole country was in mourning...*

mouth **1** = <u>lips</u>, trap (*slang*), chops (*slang*), jaws, gob (*slang, esp. Brit.*), maw, yap (*slang*), cakehole (*Brit. slang*) ...*She clamped her hand against her mouth...*

2 = <u>entrance</u>, opening, gateway, cavity, door, aperture, crevice, orifice ...*the mouth of the tunnel...*

3 = <u>opening</u>, lip, rim ...*a lit candle stuck in the bottle's mouth...*

4 = <u>inlet</u>, outlet, estuary, firth, outfall, debouchment ...*the mouth of the river...*

5 (*Informal*) = <u>boasting</u>, gas (*informal*), bragging, hot air (*slang*), braggadocio, idle talk, empty talk ...*She is all mouth and no talent...*

(Related Words)

adjectives : oral, oscular

mouthful = <u>taste</u>, little, bite, bit, drop, sample, swallow, sip, sup, spoonful, morsel, forkful

mouthpiece **1** = <u>spokesperson</u>, agent, representative, delegate, spokesman *or* spokeswoman ...*their mouthpiece is the vice-president...*

2 = <u>publication</u>, journal, organ, periodical ...*The newspaper is regarded as a mouthpiece of the ministry...*

movable = <u>portable</u>, mobile, transferable, detachable, not fixed, transportable, portative

move `VERB` **1** = <u>transfer</u>, change, carry, transport, switch, shift, transpose ...*She moved the sheaf of papers into position...*

2 = <u>go</u>, walk, march, advance, progress, shift, proceed, stir, budge, make a move, change position ...*She waited for him to get up, but he didn't move...*

3 = <u>relocate</u>, leave, remove, quit, go away, migrate, emigrate, move house, flit (*Scot. & Northern English dialect*), decamp, up sticks (*Brit. informal*), pack your bags (*informal*), change residence ...*My home is in Yorkshire and I don't want to move...*

4 = <u>drive</u>, lead, cause, influence, persuade, push, shift, inspire, prompt, stimulate, motivate, induce, shove, activate, propel, rouse, prod, incite, impel, set going ...*The hearings moved him to come up with these suggestions...* `OPPOSITE` discourage

5 = <u>touch</u>, affect, excite, impress, stir, agitate, disquiet, make an impression on, tug at your heartstrings (*often facetious*) ...*These stories surprised and moved me...*

6 = <u>propose</u>, suggest, urge, recommend, request, advocate, submit, put forward ...*I moved that the case be dismissed...*

`NOUN` **1** = <u>action</u>, act, step, movement, shift, motion, manoeuvre, deed ...*Daniel's eyes followed her every* *move*...

2 = <u>ploy</u>, action, measure, step, initiative, stroke, tactic, manoeuvre, deed, tack, ruse, gambit, stratagem ...*The cut in interest rates was a wise move*...

3 = <u>transfer</u>, posting, shift, removal, migration, relocation, flit (*Scot. & Northern English dialect*), flitting (*Scot. & Northern English dialect*), change of address ...*He announced his move to Montparnasse in 1909*...

4 = <u>turn</u>, go, play, chance, shot (*informal*), opportunity ...*It's your move, chess fans tell Sports Minister*...

PHRASES **get a move on** = <u>speed up</u>, hurry (up), get going, get moving, get cracking (*informal*), step on it (*informal*), make haste, shake a leg (*informal*), get your skates on (*informal*), stir yourself ...*I'd better get a move on if I want to finish on time*... ◆ **on the move** (*Informal*) **1** = <u>in transit</u>, moving, travelling, journeying, on the road (*informal*), under way, voyaging, on the run, in motion, on the wing ...*My husband and I were always on the move*... **2** = <u>active</u>, moving, developing, advancing, progressing, succeeding, stirring, going forward, astir ...*Aviation is on the move, and many airlines are forming alliances*...

movement **1** = <u>group</u>, party, organization, grouping, front, camp, faction ...*a nationalist movement that's gaining strength*...

2 = <u>campaign</u>, drive, push, crusade ...*He contributed to the Movement for the Ordination of Women*...

3 = <u>move</u>, act, action, operation, motion, gesture, manoeuvre ...*He could watch her every movement*...

4 = <u>activity</u>, moving, stirring, bustle, agitation ...*There was movement behind the door*...

5 = <u>advance</u>, progress, flow, progression ...*the movement of the fish going up river*...

6 = <u>transfer</u>, transportation, displacement ...*the movement of people, goods and services across borders*...

7 = <u>trend</u>, flow, swing, current, tendency ...*the movement towards democracy*...

8 = <u>development</u>, change, shift, variation, fluctuation ...*the meeting seems to have produced no movement on either side*...

9 = <u>progression</u>, advance, progress, breakthrough ...*the participants believed movement forward was possible*...

10 (*Music*) = <u>section</u>, part, division, passage ...*the first movement of Beethoven's 7th symphony*...

movie **NOUN** = <u>film</u>, picture, feature, flick (*slang*), motion picture, moving picture (*U.S.*) ...*That was the first movie he ever made*...

PHRASES **the movies** = <u>the cinema</u>, a film, the pictures (*informal*), the flicks (*slang*), the silver screen (*informal*) ...*He took her to the movies*...

moving **1** = <u>emotional</u>, touching, affecting, exciting, inspiring, stirring, arousing, poignant, emotive, impelling ...*It was a moving moment for them*... **OPPOSITE** unemotional

2 = <u>mobile</u>, running, active, going, operational, in motion, driving, kinetic, movable, motile, unfixed ...*the moving parts in the engine*... **OPPOSITE** stationary

3 = <u>motivating</u>, stimulating, dynamic, propelling, inspirational, impelling, stimulative ...*He has been a moving force in the world of art criticism*...

mow **VERB** = <u>cut</u>, crop, trim, shear, scythe ...*He mowed the lawn and did other routine chores*...

PHRASES **mow something** or **someone down** = <u>massacre</u>, butcher, slaughter, cut down, shoot down, blow away (*slang, chiefly U.S.*), cut to pieces ...*Gunmen mowed down 10 people in the attack*...

much **ADVERB** **1** = <u>greatly</u>, a lot, considerably, decidedly, exceedingly, appreciably ...*My hairstyle has never changed much*... **OPPOSITE** hardly

2 = <u>often</u>, a lot, regularly, routinely, a great deal, frequently, many times, habitually, on many occasions, customarily ...*She didn't see her father much*...

DETERMINER = <u>great</u>, a lot of, plenty of, considerable, substantial, piles of (*informal*), ample, abundant, copious, oodles of (*informal*), plenteous, sizable or sizeable amount ...*They are grown in full sun, without much water*... **OPPOSITE** little

PRONOUN = <u>a lot</u>, plenty, a great deal, lots (*informal*), masses (*informal*), loads (*informal*), tons (*informal*), heaps (*informal*), a good deal, an appreciable amount ...*There was so much to talk about*... **OPPOSITE** little

muck **NOUN** **1** = <u>dirt</u>, mud, filth, crap (*taboo slang*), sewage, ooze, scum, sludge, mire, slime, slob (*Irish*), gunk (*informal*), gunge (*informal*), crud (*slang*), kak (*S. African informal*), grot (*slang*) ...*This congealed muck was interfering with the filter*...

2 = <u>manure</u>, crap (*taboo slang*), dung, ordure ...*He could smell muck and clean fresh hay*...

PHRASES **muck something up** = <u>ruin</u>, bungle, botch, make a mess of, blow (*slang*), mar, spoil, muff, make a nonsense of, bodge (*informal*), make a pig's ear of (*informal*), flub (*U.S. slang*), make a muck of (*slang*), mess something up, screw something up (*informal*), cock something up (*Brit. slang*), crool or cruel (*Austral. slang*) ...*At the 13th hole, I mucked it up*...

mucky = <u>dirty</u>, soiled, muddy, filthy, messy, grimy, mud-caked, bespattered, begrimed, festy (*Austral. slang*)

mud = <u>dirt</u>, clay, ooze, silt, sludge, mire, slime, slob (*Irish*), gloop (*informal*)

muddle **NOUN** = <u>confusion</u>, mess, disorder, chaos, plight, tangle, mix-up, clutter, disarray, daze, predicament, jumble, ravel, perplexity, disorganization, hotchpotch, hodgepodge (*U.S.*), pig's breakfast (*informal*), fankle (*Scot.*) ...*My thoughts are all in a muddle*...

VERB **1** = <u>jumble</u>, confuse, disorder, scramble, tangle, mix up, make a mess of ...*Already some people have begun to muddle the two names*...

2 = <u>confuse</u>, bewilder, daze, confound, perplex, disorient, stupefy, befuddle ...*She felt muddled, and a wave of dizziness swept over her*...

PHRASES **muddle along** or **through** = <u>scrape by</u>, make it, manage, cope, get along, get by (*informal*), manage somehow ...*We will muddle through and just play it day by day*...

muddled 1 = <u>incoherent</u>, confused, loose, vague, unclear, woolly, muddleheaded ...*the muddled thinking of the Government's transport policy...* OPPOSITE clear
2 = <u>bewildered</u>, confused, at sea, dazed, perplexed, disoriented, stupefied, befuddled ...*I'm afraid I'm a little muddled. I don't know where to begin...*
3 = <u>jumbled</u>, confused, disordered, scrambled, tangled, chaotic, messy, mixed-up, disorganized, higgledy-piggledy (*informal*), disarrayed ...*a muddled pile of historical manuscripts...* OPPOSITE orderly

muddy ADJECTIVE 1 = <u>boggy</u>, swampy, marshy, miry, quaggy ...*a muddy track...*
2 = <u>dirty</u>, soiled, grimy, mucky, mud-caked, bespattered, clarty (*Scot. & Northern English dialect*) ...*muddy boots...*
3 = <u>dull</u>, flat, blurred, unclear, smoky, washed-out, dingy, lustreless ...*The paper has turned a muddy colour...*
4 = <u>cloudy</u>, dirty, foul, opaque, impure, turbid ...*He was up to his armpits in muddy water...*
5 = <u>confused</u>, vague, unclear, muddled, fuzzy, woolly, hazy, indistinct ...*Such muddy thinking is typical of those who have always had it easy...*
VERB = <u>smear</u>, soil, dirty, smirch, begrime, bespatter ...*The clothes he was wearing were all muddied...*

muff = <u>botch</u>, bungle, fluff (*informal*), spoil, screw up (*informal*), mess up, cock up (*Brit. slang*), make a mess of, mismanage, make a nonsense of, bodge (*informal*), make a pig's ear of (*informal*), flub (*U.S. slang*), make a muck of (*informal*), crool *or* cruel (*Austral. slang*)

muffle VERB = <u>deaden</u>, suppress, gag, stifle, silence, dull, soften, hush, muzzle, quieten ...*He held a handkerchief over the mouthpiece to muffle his voice...*
VERB *often with* ***up*** = <u>wrap up</u>, cover, disguise, conceal, cloak, shroud, swathe, envelop, swaddle ...*All of us were muffled up in several layers of clothing...*

muffled = <u>indistinct</u>, suppressed, subdued, dull, faint, dim, muted, strangled, stifled

mug[1] = <u>cup</u>, pot, jug, beaker, tankard, stein, flagon, toby jug ...*He had been drinking mugs of coffee to keep himself awake...*

mug[2] 1 = <u>face</u>, features, countenance, visage, clock (*Brit. slang*), kisser (*slang*), dial (*slang*), mush (*Brit. slang*), puss (*slang*), phiz *or* phizog (*Brit. slang*) ...*He managed to get his ugly mug on telly...*
2 = <u>fool</u>, innocent, sucker (*slang*), charlie (*Brit. informal*), gull (*archaic*), chump (*informal*), simpleton, putz (*U.S. slang*), weenie (*U.S. informal*), muggins (*Brit. slang*), easy *or* soft touch (*slang*), dorba *or* dorb (*Austral. slang*), bogan (*Austral. slang*) ...*I feel such a mug for signing the agreement...*

mug[3] VERB = <u>attack</u>, assault, beat up, rob, steam (*informal*), hold up, do over (*Brit., Austral., & N.Z. slang*), work over (*slang*), assail, lay into (*informal*), put the boot in (*slang*), duff up (*Brit. slang*), set about *or* upon ...*I was getting into my car when this guy tried to mug me...*
PHRASES **mug up (on) something** = <u>study</u>, cram (*informal*), bone up on (*informal*), swot up on (*Brit.*

informal), get up (*informal*) ...*It's advisable to mug up on your Spanish before you go...*

mull over = <u>ponder</u>, consider, study, think about, examine, review, weigh, contemplate, reflect on, think over, muse on, meditate on, ruminate on, deliberate on, turn something over in your mind

multiple = <u>many</u>, several, various, numerous, collective, sundry, manifold, multitudinous

multiplicity = <u>number</u>, lot, host, mass, variety, load (*informal*), pile (*informal*), ton, stack, diversity, heap (*informal*), array, abundance, myriad, profusion

multiply 1 = <u>increase</u>, extend, expand, spread, build up, accumulate, augment, proliferate ...*Her husband multiplied his demands on her time...* OPPOSITE decrease
2 = <u>reproduce</u>, breed, propagate ...*These creatures can multiply quickly...*

multitude 1 = <u>great number</u>, lot, host, collection, army, sea, mass, assembly, legion, horde, myriad, concourse, assemblage ...*Addiction to drugs can bring a multitude of other problems...*
2 = <u>crowd</u>, host, mass, mob, congregation, swarm, sea, horde, throng, great number ...*the multitudes that surround the Pope...*
3 = <u>public</u>, mob, herd, populace, rabble, proletariat, common people, hoi polloi, commonalty ...*The hideous truth was hidden from the multitude...*

mum = <u>silent</u>, quiet, dumb, mute, secretive, uncommunicative, unforthcoming, tight-lipped, closemouthed

mumbo jumbo 1 = <u>gibberish</u>, nonsense, jargon, humbug, cant, Greek (*informal*), claptrap (*informal*), gobbledegook (*informal*), rigmarole, double talk ...*It's all full of psychoanalytic mumbo jumbo...*
2 = <u>superstition</u>, magic, ritual, hocus-pocus ...*He dabbled in all sorts of mumbo jumbo...*

munch = <u>chew</u>, champ, crunch, chomp, scrunch, masticate

mundane 1 = <u>ordinary</u>, routine, commonplace, banal, everyday, day-to-day, vanilla (*slang*), prosaic, humdrum, workaday ...*Be willing to do mundane tasks with good grace...* OPPOSITE extraordinary
2 = <u>earthly</u>, worldly, human, material, fleshly, secular, mortal, terrestrial, temporal, sublunary ...*spiritual immortals who had transcended the mundane world...* OPPOSITE spiritual

municipal = <u>civic</u>, city, public, local, community, council, town, district, urban, metropolitan, borough

municipality = <u>town</u>, city, district, borough, township, burgh (*Scot.*), urban community, dorp (*S. African*)

murder NOUN 1 = <u>killing</u>, homicide, massacre, assassination, slaying, bloodshed, carnage, butchery ...*The three accused are charged with attempted murder...*
2 (*Informal*) = <u>agony</u>, misery, hell (*informal*) ...*I've taken three aspirins, but this headache's still absolute murder...*
VERB 1 = <u>kill</u>, massacre, slaughter, assassinate, hit (*slang*), destroy, waste (*informal*), do in (*informal*),

eliminate (*slang*), take out (*slang*), butcher, dispatch, slay, blow away (*slang, chiefly U.S.*), bump off (*slang*), rub out (*U.S. slang*), take the life of, do to death ...*a thriller about two men who murder a third...*

2 = <u>ruin</u>, destroy, mar, spoil, butcher, mangle ...*She murdered the song...*

3 (*Informal*) = <u>beat decisively</u>, thrash, stuff (*slang*), cream (*slang, chiefly U.S.*), tank (*slang*), hammer (*informal*), slaughter, lick (*informal*), wipe the floor with (*informal*), make mincemeat of (*informal*), blow someone out of the water (*slang*), drub, defeat someone utterly ...*The front row murdered the Italians in the scrums...*

murderer = <u>killer</u>, assassin, slayer, butcher, slaughterer, cut-throat, hit man (*slang*)

murderous **1** = <u>deadly</u>, savage, brutal, destructive, fell (*archaic*), bloody, devastating, cruel, lethal, withering, ferocious, cut-throat, bloodthirsty, barbarous, internecine, death-dealing, sanguinary ...*This murderous lunatic could kill them all....*

2 (*Informal*) = <u>unpleasant</u>, difficult, dangerous, exhausting, sapping, harrowing, strenuous, arduous, hellish (*informal*), killing (*informal*) ...*Four games in six days is murderous and most unfair...*

murky **1** = <u>dark</u>, gloomy, dismal, grey, dull, obscure, dim, dreary, cloudy, misty, impenetrable, foggy, overcast, dusky, nebulous, cheerless ...*Their plane crashed in murky weather...* OPPOSITE> bright

2 = <u>dark</u>, obscure, cloudy, impenetrable ...*the deep, murky waters of Loch Ness...*

murmur VERB = <u>mumble</u>, whisper, mutter, drone, purr, babble, speak in an undertone ...*He turned and murmured something to the professor...*

NOUN **1** = <u>whisper</u>, whispering, mutter, mumble, drone, purr, babble, undertone ...*She spoke in a low murmur...*

2 = <u>complaint</u>, word, moan (*informal*), grumble, beef (*slang*), grouse, gripe (*informal*) ...*She was so flattered she paid up without a murmur...*

muscle NOUN **1** = <u>tendon</u>, sinew, muscle tissue, thew ...*He has a strained thigh muscle...*

2 = <u>strength</u>, might, force, power, weight, stamina, potency, brawn, sturdiness ...*The team showed more muscle than mental application...*

PHRASES **muscle in** (*Informal*) = <u>impose yourself</u>, encroach, butt in, force your way in, elbow your way in ...*He complained that they were muscling in on his deal...*

➤ **muscles**

muscular = <u>strong</u>, powerful, athletic, strapping, robust, vigorous, sturdy, stalwart, husky (*informal*), beefy (*informal*), lusty, sinewy, muscle-bound, brawny, powerfully built, thickset, well-knit

muse = <u>ponder</u>, consider, reflect, contemplate, think, weigh up, deliberate, speculate, brood, meditate, mull over, think over, ruminate, cogitate, be lost in thought, be in a brown study

Muses, the

Muses

Calliope	epic poetry
Clio	history
Erato	love poetry
Euterpe	lyric poetry and music
Melpomene	tragedy
Polyhymnia	singing, mime, and sacred dance
Terpsichore	dance and choral song
Thalia	comedy and pastoral poetry
Urania	astronomy

mush **1** = <u>pulp</u>, paste, mash, purée, pap, slush, goo (*informal*) ...*Over-ripe bananas will collapse into a mush in this recipe...*

2 (*Informal*) = <u>sentimentality</u>, corn (*informal*), slush (*informal*), schmaltz (*slang*), mawkishness ...*The lyrics are mush and the melodies banal...*

mushroom = <u>expand</u>, increase, spread, boom, flourish, sprout, burgeon, spring up, shoot up, proliferate, luxuriate, grow rapidly

mushy **1** = <u>soft</u>, squidgy (*informal*), slushy, squashy, squelchy, pulpy, doughy, pappy, semi-liquid, paste-like, semi-solid ...*When the fruit is mushy and cooked, remove from the heat...*

2 (*Informal*) = <u>sentimental</u>, wet (*Brit. informal*), sloppy (*informal*), corny (*slang*), sugary, maudlin, weepy, saccharine, syrupy, slushy (*informal*), mawkish, schmaltzy (*slang*), icky (*informal*), three-hankie (*informal*) ...*Don't go getting all mushy and sentimental...*

music

➤ **music**

musical = <u>melodious</u>, lyrical, harmonious, melodic, lilting, tuneful, dulcet, sweet-sounding, euphonious,

Muscles http://www.bbc.co.uk/science/humanbody/body/factfiles/muscle_anatomy.shtml

accelerator	deltoid	lumbricalis	sartorius
accessorius	depressor	masseter	scalenus
adductor	digrastic	opponent	soleus
agonist	dilator	pectoral	sphincter
antagonist	elevator	peroneal muscle	supinator
arytenoid	erector	pronator	suspensory *or* suspensor
biceps	evertor	psoas	tensor
buccinator	extensor	quadriceps	trapezius
compressor	flexor	rectus	triceps
constrictor	gastrocnemius	retractor	
contractor	gluteus *or* glutaeus	rhomboideus	
corrugator	levator	rotator	

Music http://www.allmusic.com/

Classical music genres

ars antiqua	Gothic	Renaissance
ars nova	impressionist	rococo
baroque	minimalist	romantic
classical	music concrète	salon music
early music	nationalist	serial music
expressionist	neoclassical	twelve-tone *or* dodecaphonic
galant	post-romantic	

Types of composition

air	fantasy *or* fantasia	pavane
albumblatt	farandole	phantasy
allemande	fugue	pibroch
anthem	galliard	polka
aria	galop	polonaise
bagatelle	gavotte	prelude
ballade	gigue	psalm
ballet	grand opera	quadrille
barcarole	hornpipe	quartet
berceuse	humoresque	quintet
bolero	impromptu	raga
bourrée	interlude	reel
canon	lament	Requiem
cantata	ländler	rhapsody
canticle	lied	ricercar *or* ricercare
canzona	madrigal	rigadoon *or* rigadoun
canzone	march	romance
canzonetta	mass	scherzo
capriccio	mazurka	schottische
cavatina	medley	septet
chaconne	minuet	serenade
chorale	motet	sextet
chorus	nocturne	sinfonia concertante
concertante	nonet	sinfonietta
concertino	notturno	Singspiel
concerto	octet	sonata
concerto grosso	opera	sonatina
concertstück	opera buffa	song
contredanse *or* contradance	opera seria	song cycle
czardas	operetta	strathspey
dirge	oratorio	suite
divertimento	overture	symphonic poem
divertissement	partita	symphony
duet	part song	toccata
dumka	passacaglia	tone poem
duo	passepied	trio
ecossaise	Passion	trio sonata
elegy	pastiche	waltz
étude	pastorale	

Popular music types

acid house	Cajun	folk music
acid jazz	calypso	folk rock
acid rock	cool jazz	free jazz
ambient	country and western	funk
bebop	country blues	fusion
bhangra	country rock	gangsta rap
bluebeat	Cu-bop	glam rock
bluegrass	death metal	gospel
blues	disco	Goth
boogie-woogie	Dixieland	grunge
bop	doo-wop	hardbop
bubblegum	dub	hardcore

Popular music types (continued)

harmolodics	New Age	rock
heavy metal	New Country	rockabilly
hip-hop	New Orleans jazz	rock and roll
House	new romantic	salsa
Indie	New Wave	ska
industrial	P-funk	skiffle
jazz	pop	soul
jazz-funk	progressive rock	surf music
jazz-rock	psychobilly	swing
jungle	punk	swingbeat
mainstream jazz	ragga	techno
Merseybeat	rap	thrash metal
modern jazz	rave	trad jazz
Motown	reggae	world music
Muzak	rhythm and blues	zydeco

Expression and tempo instructions

Instruction	Meaning	Instruction	Meaning
accelerando	with increasing speed	lento	slowly
adagio	slowly	maestoso	majestically
agitato	in an agitated manner	marziale	martial
allegretto	fairly quickly or briskly	mezzo	(in combination) moderately
allegro	quickly, in a brisk, lively manner	moderato	at a moderate tempo
		molto	(in combination) very
amoroso	lovingly	non troppo or	(in combination) not too
andante	at a moderately slow tempo	non tanto	much
andantino	slightly faster than andante	pianissimo	very quietly
animato	in a lively manner	piano	softly
appassionato	impassioned	più	(in combination) more
assai	(in combination) very	pizzicato	(in music for stringed
calando	with gradually decreasing		instruments) to be plucked
tone and speed			with the finger
cantabile	in a singing style	poco or un poco	(in combination) a little
con	(in combination) with	pomposo	in a pompous manner
con affeto	with tender emotion	presto	very fast
con amore	lovingly	prestissimo	faster than presto
con anima	with spirit	quasi	(in combination) almost, as
con brio	vigorously		if
con fuoco	with fire	rallentando	becoming slower
con moto	quickly	rubato	with a flexible tempo
crescendo	gradual increase in loudness	scherzando	in jocular style
diminuendo	gradual decrease in loudness	sciolto	free and easy
dolce	gently and sweetly	semplice	simple and unforced
doloroso	in a sorrowful manner	sforzando	with strong initial attack
energico	energetically	smorzando	dying away
espressivo	expressively	sospirando	'sighing', plaintive
forte	loud or loudly	sostenuto	in a smooth and sustained
fortissimo	very loud		manner
furioso	in a frantically rushing manner	sotto voce	extremely quiet
		staccato	(of notes) short, clipped, and
giocoso	merry		separate
grave	solemn and slow	strascinando	stretched out
grazioso	graceful	strepitoso	noisy
lacrimoso	sad and mournful	stringendo	with increasing speed
largo	slowly and broadly	tanto	(in combination) too much
larghetto	slowly and broadly, but less so than largo	tardo	slow
		troppo	(in combination) too much
legato	smoothly and connectedly	vivace	in a brisk lively manner
leggiero	light	volante	'flying', fast and light

euphonic OPPOSITE> discordant

musing = thinking, reflection, meditation, abstraction, contemplation, introspection, reverie, dreaming, day-dreaming, rumination, navel gazing (*slang*), absent-mindedness, cogitation, brown study, cerebration, woolgathering

must¹ = necessity, essential, requirement, duty, fundamental, obligation, imperative, requisite, prerequisite, sine qua non (*Latin*), necessary thing ...*A visit to the motor museum is a must*...

must² = mould, rot, decay, mildew, mustiness, fustiness, fetor, mouldiness ...*The air was heady with the smell of must*...

muster VERB 1 = summon up, collect, call up, marshal ...*Mustering all her strength, she pulled hard on the oars*...
2 = rally, group, gather, assemble, round up, marshal, mobilize, call together ...*The general had mustered his troops north of the border*...
3 = assemble, meet, come together, convene, congregate, convoke ...*They mustered in the open, well wrapped and saying little*...
NOUN = assembly, meeting, collection, gathering, rally, convention, congregation, roundup, mobilization, hui (*N.Z.*), concourse, assemblage, convocation ...*He called a general muster of all soldiers*...
PHRASES **pass muster** = be acceptable, qualify, measure up, make the grade, fill the bill (*informal*), be or come up to scratch ...*I could not pass muster in this language*...

musty = stale, stuffy, airless, decayed, smelly, dank, mouldy, fusty, mildewed, frowsty, mildewy

mutation 1 = anomaly, variation, deviant, freak of nature ...*Scientists have found a genetic mutation that causes the disease*...
2 = change, variation, evolution, transformation, modification, alteration, deviation, metamorphosis, transfiguration ...*I was forced to watch my father's mutation from sober to drunk*...

mute ADJECTIVE 1 = close-mouthed, silent, taciturn, tongue-tied, tight-lipped, unspeaking ...*He was mute, distant and indifferent*...
2 = silent, dumb, unspoken, tacit, wordless, voiceless, unvoiced ...*I threw her a mute look of appeal*...
3 = dumb, speechless, voiceless, unspeaking, aphasic, aphonic ...*The duke's daughter became mute after a shock*...
VERB 1 = tone down, lower, moderate, subdue, dampen, soft-pedal ...*Bush muted his racially moderate views*...
2 = muffle, subdue, moderate, lower, turn down, soften, dampen, tone down, deaden ...*The wooded hillside muted the sounds*...

mutilate 1 = maim, damage, injure, disable, butcher, cripple, hack, lame, cut up, mangle, mangulate (*Austral. slang*), dismember, disfigure, lacerate, cut to pieces ...*He tortured and mutilated six young men*...
2 = distort, cut, damage, mar, spoil, butcher, hack, censor, adulterate, expurgate, bowdlerize ...*The

writer's verdict was that his screenplay had been mutilated*...

mutiny NOUN = rebellion, revolt, uprising, insurrection, rising, strike, revolution, riot, resistance, disobedience, insubordination, refusal to obey orders ...*A series of mutinies in the armed forces destabilized the regime*...
VERB = rebel, revolt, rise up, disobey, strike, resist, defy authority, refuse to obey orders, be insubordinate ...*Units around the city mutinied after receiving no pay*...

mutt 1 = mongrel, dog, hound, tyke, pooch (*informal*), cur ...*He was being harassed by a large, off-the-leash mutt*...
2 = fool, idiot, berk (*Brit. slang*), moron, charlie (*Brit. informal*), jerk (*slang, chiefly U.S. & Canad.*), plank (*Brit. slang*), wally (*slang*), prat (*slang*), plonker (*slang*), coot, geek (*slang*), twit (*informal, chiefly Brit.*), imbecile (*informal*), ignoramus, dipstick (*Brit. slang*), gonzo (*slang*), schmuck (*U.S. slang*), dork (*slang*), dolt, divvy (*Brit. slang*), pillock (*Brit. slang*), dweeb (*U.S. slang*), putz (*U.S. slang*), weenie (*U.S. informal*), eejit (*Scot. & Irish*), dumb-ass (*slang*), dunderhead, numpty (*Scot. informal*), doofus (*slang, chiefly U.S.*), thickhead, nerd or nurd (*slang*), numbskull or numskull, dorba or dorb (*Austral. slang*), bogan (*Austral. slang*) ...*'I'm the mutt of my family,' she declares*...

mutter = grumble, complain, murmur, rumble, whine, mumble, grouse, bleat, grouch (*informal*), talk under your breath

mutual = shared, common, joint, interactive, returned, communal, reciprocal, interchangeable, reciprocated, correlative, requited

Word Power

mutual – *Mutual* is sometimes used, as in *a mutual friend*, to mean 'common to or shared by two or more people'. This use has sometimes been frowned on in the past because it does not reflect the two-way relationship contained in the origins of the word, which comes from Latin *mutuus* meaning 'reciprocal'. However, this usage is very common and is now generally regarded as acceptable.

muzzle NOUN 1 = jaws, mouth, nose, snout ...*The dog presented its muzzle for scratching*...
2 = gag, guard, restraint ...*dogs that have to wear a muzzle*...
VERB = suppress, silence, curb, restrain, choke, gag, stifle, censor ...*He complained of being muzzled by the chairman*...

myopic 1 = narrow-minded, short-sighted, narrow, unimaginative, small-minded, unadventurous, near-sighted ...*The government still has a myopic attitude to spending*...
2 = short-sighted, near-sighted, as blind as a bat (*informal*) ...*Rhinos are thick-skinned, myopic and love to wallow in mud*...

myriad NOUN = <u>multitude</u>, millions, scores, host, thousands, army, sea, mountain, flood, a million, a thousand, swarm, horde …*They face a myriad of problems bringing up children…*
ADJECTIVE = <u>innumerable</u>, countless, untold, incalculable, immeasurable, a thousand and one, multitudinous …*pop culture in all its myriad forms…*

mysterious 1 = <u>strange</u>, unknown, puzzling, curious, secret, hidden, weird, concealed, obscure, baffling, veiled, mystical, perplexing, uncanny, incomprehensible, mystifying, impenetrable, arcane, inexplicable, cryptic, insoluble, unfathomable, abstruse, recondite …*He died in mysterious circustances…* OPPOSITE > clear
2 = <u>secretive</u>, enigmatic, evasive, discreet, covert, reticent, furtive, inscrutable, non-committal, surreptitious, cloak-and-dagger, sphinx-like …*As for his job – well, he was very mysterious about it…*

mystery 1 = <u>puzzle</u>, problem, question, secret, riddle, enigma, conundrum, teaser, poser (*informal*), closed book …*The source of the gunshots still remains a mystery…*
2 = <u>secrecy</u>, uncertainty, obscurity, mystique, darkness, ambiguity, ambiguousness …*It is an elaborate ceremony, shrouded in mystery…*

mystic *or* **mystical** = <u>supernatural</u>, mysterious, transcendental, esoteric, occult, arcane, metaphysical, paranormal, inscrutable, otherworldly, abstruse, cabalistic, preternatural, nonrational

mystify = <u>puzzle</u>, confuse, baffle, bewilder, beat (*slang*), escape, stump, elude, confound, perplex, bamboozle (*informal*), flummox, be all Greek to (*informal*), nonplus, befog

mystique = <u>fascination</u>, spell, magic, charm, glamour, awe, charisma

myth 1 = <u>legend</u>, story, tradition, fiction, saga, fable, parable, allegory, fairy story, folk tale, urban myth, urban legend …*a famous Greek myth…*
2 = <u>illusion</u>, story, fancy, fantasy, imagination, invention, delusion, superstition, fabrication, falsehood, figment, tall story, cock and bull story (*informal*) …*Contrary to popular myth, most women are not spendthrifts…*

mythical 1 = <u>legendary</u>, storied, fabulous, imaginary, fairy-tale, fabled, mythological, storybook, allegorical, folkloric, chimerical …*the mythical beast that had seven or more heads…*
2 = <u>imaginary</u>, made-up, fantasy, invented, pretended, untrue, unreal, fabricated, fanciful, fictitious, make-believe, nonexistent …*They are trying to preserve a mythical sense of nationhood…*

mythological = <u>legendary</u>, fabulous, fabled, traditional, invented, heroic, imaginary, mythical, mythic, folkloric

mythology = <u>legend</u>, myths, folklore, stories, tradition, lore, folk tales, mythos
➤ **Arthurian**

Mythology   http://www.pantheon.org/

Characters in classical mythology

Achilles	Eurydice	Orion
Actaeon	Galatea	Orpheus
Adonis	Ganymede	Pandora
Aeneas	Hector	Paris
Agamemnon	Hecuba	Penelope
Ajax	Helen	Persephone
Amazons	Heracles	Perseus
Andromache	Hercules	Pleiades
Andromeda	Hermaphroditus	Pollux
Antigone	Hippolytus	Polydeuces
Arachne	Hyacinthus	Polyphemus
Argonauts	Icarus	Priam
Ariadne	Io	Prometheus
Atalanta	Ixion	Proserpina
Atlas	Jason	Psyche
Callisto	Jocasta	Pygmalion
Calypso	Leda	Pyramus
Cassandra	Medea	Remus
Cassiopeia	Medusa	Romulus
Castor	Menelaus	Semele
Charon	Midas	sibyl
Circe	Minos	Silenus
Clytemnestra	Muses	Sisyphus
Daedalus	Narcissus	Tantalus
Dido	Niobe	Theseus
Echo	Odysseus	Thisbe
Electra	Oedipus	Tiresias
Europa	Orestes	Ulysses

Mythology (continued)

Characters in Norse mythology

Andvari	Gunnar	Regin
Ask	Gutthorn	Sigmund
Atli	Hreidmar	Sigurd
Brynhild	Lif	Wayland
Fafnir	Lifthrasir	
Gudrun	Mimir	

Places in Norse mythology

Asgard or Asgarth	Jotunheim or Jotunnheim	Utgard
Bifrost	Midgard or Midgarth	Valhalla
Hel or Hela	Niflheim	

Places in classical mythology

Acheron	Helicon	Phlegethon
Colchis	Islands of the Blessed	Styx
Elysium	Lethe	Tartarus
Erebus	Olympus	Thebes
Hades	Parnassus	Troy

Mythological creatures

afreet or afrit	giant	naiad
androsphinx	goblin	Nereid
banshee	Gorgon	nix or nixie
basilisk	gremlin	nymph
behemoth	Grendel	Oceanid
bunyip	griffin, griffon, or gryphon	orc
centaur	hamadryad	oread
Cerberus	Harpy	peri
Charybdis	hippocampus	phoenix
chimera or chimaera	hippogriff or hippogryph	pixie
cockatrice	hobbit	roc
Cyclops	hobgoblin	salamander
dragon	Hydra	satyr
dryad	impundulu	Scylla
dwarf	jinni, jinnee, djinni, or djinny	Siren
Echidna	kelpie	Sphinx
elf	kraken	sylph
erlking	kylin	tokoloshe
fairy	lamia	tricorn
faun	leprechaun	troll
fay	leviathan	unicorn
Fury	mermaid	water nymph
genie	merman	wood nymph
Geryon	Minotaur	

N n

nab = <u>catch</u>, arrest, apprehend, seize, lift (*slang*), nick (*slang, chiefly Brit.*), grab, capture, nail (*informal*), collar (*informal*), snatch, catch in the act, feel your collar (*slang*)

nadir = <u>bottom</u>, depths, lowest point, rock bottom, all-time low [OPPOSITE] height

naff (*Brit. slang*) = <u>bad</u>, poor, inferior, worthless, pants (*slang*), duff (*Brit. informal*), shabby, second-rate, shoddy, low-grade, low-quality, trashy, substandard, for the birds (*informal*), crappy (*slang*), valueless, rubbishy, poxy (*slang*), strictly for the birds (*informal*), twopenny-halfpenny, bodger *or* bodgie (*Austral. slang*) ...*This music is really naff...* [OPPOSITE] excellent

nag¹ [VERB] = <u>scold</u>, harass, badger, pester, worry, harry, plague, hassle (*informal*), vex, berate, breathe down someone's neck, upbraid, chivvy, bend someone's ear (*informal*), be on your back (*slang*), henpeck ...*The more Sarah nagged her, the more stubborn Cissie became...*
[NOUN] = <u>scold</u>, complainer, grumbler, virago, shrew, tartar, moaner, harpy, harridan, termagant, fault-finder ...*My husband calls me a nag if I complain about anything...*

nag² = <u>horse</u> (*U.S.*), hack, jade, plug ...*a bedraggled knight riding a lame, flea-ridden old nag...*

nagging 1 = <u>continuous</u>, persistent, continual, niggling, repeated, constant, endless, relentless, perpetual, never-ending, interminable, unrelenting, incessant, unremitting ...*He complained about a nagging pain between his shoulders...*
2 = <u>scolding</u>, complaining, critical, sharp-tongued, shrewish ...*He tried to ignore the screaming, nagging voice of his wife...*

nail [NOUN] 1 = <u>tack</u>, spike, rivet, hobnail, brad (*technical*) ...*A mirror hung on a nail above the washboard...*
2 = <u>fingernail</u>, toenail, talon, thumbnail, claw ...*Keep your nails short and your hands clean...*
[VERB] 1 = <u>fasten</u>, fix, secure, attach, pin, hammer, tack ...*Frank put the first plank down and nailed it in place...*
2 (*Informal*) = <u>catch</u>, arrest, capture, apprehend, lift (*slang*), trap, nab (*informal*), snare, ensnare, entrap, feel your collar (*slang*) ...*The police have been trying to nail him for years...*

naive *or* **naïve** = <u>gullible</u>, trusting, credulous, unsuspicious, green, simple, innocent, childlike, callow, unsophisticated, unworldly, artless, ingenuous, guileless, wet behind the ears (*informal*), jejune, as green as grass [OPPOSITE] worldly

naivety *or* **naïveté** = <u>gullibility</u>, innocence, simplicity, inexperience, credulity, ingenuousness, artlessness, guilelessness, callowness

naked 1 = <u>nude</u>, stripped, exposed, bare, uncovered, undressed, in the raw (*informal*), starkers (*informal*), stark-naked, unclothed, in the buff (*informal*), in the altogether (*informal*), buck naked (*slang*), undraped, in your birthday suit (*informal*), scuddy (*slang*), without a stitch on (*informal*), in the bare scud (*slang*), naked as the day you were born (*informal*) ...*They stripped him naked... ...A girl was lying on the rug, completely naked...* [OPPOSITE] dressed
2 = <u>defenceless</u>, vulnerable, helpless, wide open, unarmed, unprotected, unguarded ...*The deal leaves the authorities virtually naked...*
3 = <u>undisguised</u>, open, simple, plain, patent, evident, stark, manifest, blatant, overt, unmistakable, unqualified, unadorned, unvarnished, unconcealed ...*Naked aggression could not go unchallenged...* [OPPOSITE] disguised

nakedness 1 = <u>nudity</u>, undress, bareness, deshabille ...*He pulled the blanket over his body to hide his nakedness...*
2 = <u>starkness</u>, simplicity, openness, plainness ...*the nakedness of the emotion expressed in these songs...*

name [NOUN] 1 = <u>title</u>, nickname, designation, appellation, term, handle (*slang*), denomination, epithet, sobriquet, cognomen, moniker *or* monicker (*slang*) ...*I don't even know if Sullivan is his real name...*
2 = <u>reputation</u>, character, honour, fame, distinction, esteem, eminence, renown, repute, note ...*He had made a name for himself as a musician... ...I was forced to pursue this litigation to protect my good name...*
[VERB] 1 = <u>call</u>, christen, baptize, dub, term, style, label, entitle, denominate ...*My mother insisted on naming me Horace...*
2 = <u>nominate</u>, choose, commission, mention, identify, select, appoint, specify, designate ...*The Scots have yet to name their team...*
(Related Words)
adjective: nominal

named 1 = <u>called</u>, christened, known as, dubbed, termed, styled, labelled, entitled, denominated, baptized ...*He was named John...*
2 = <u>nominated</u>, chosen, picked, commissioned, mentioned, identified, selected, appointed, cited, specified, designated, singled out ...*She has been named Business Woman of the Year...*

nameless 1 = <u>unnamed</u>, unknown, obscure, anonymous, unheard-of, undistinguished, untitled ...*They had their cases rejected by nameless officials...*
2 = <u>anonymous</u>, unknown, unnamed, incognito ...*My source of information is a judge who wishes to remain nameless...*
3 = <u>horrible</u>, unspeakable, indescribable, abominable, ineffable, unutterable, inexpressible ...*He was

suddenly seized by a nameless dread…

namely = <u>specifically</u>, that is to say, to wit, i.e., viz.

nap¹ NOUN = <u>sleep</u>, rest, kip (*Brit. slang*), siesta, catnap, forty winks (*informal*), shuteye (*slang*), zizz (*Brit. informal*) …*I think I'll take a little nap for an hour or so…*

VERB = <u>sleep</u>, rest, nod, drop off (*informal*), doze, kip (*Brit. slang*), snooze (*informal*), nod off (*informal*), catnap, drowse, zizz (*Brit. informal*) …*An elderly person may nap during the day…*

nap² = <u>pile</u>, down, fibre, weave, shag, grain …*She buried her face in the towel's soft nap…*

napkin = <u>serviette</u>, cloth

narcissism = <u>egotism</u>, vanity, self-love, self-admiration

narcotic NOUN = <u>drug</u>, anaesthetic, painkiller, sedative, opiate, tranquillizer, anodyne, analgesic …*He appears to be under the influence of some sort of narcotic…*
ADJECTIVE = <u>sedative</u>, calming, dulling, numbing, hypnotic, analgesic, stupefying, soporific, painkilling …*drugs which have a narcotic effect…*

narrate = <u>tell</u>, recount, report, detail, describe, relate, unfold, chronicle, recite, set forth

narration = <u>account</u>, storytelling, telling, reading, relation, explanation, description, recital, voice-over (*in film*)

narrative = <u>story</u>, report, history, detail, account, statement, tale, chronicle

narrator = <u>storyteller</u>, writer, author, reporter, commentator, chronicler, reciter, raconteur

narrow ADJECTIVE 1 = <u>thin</u>, fine, slim, pinched, slender, tapering, attenuated …*a woman with a full bust and hips and a narrow waist…* OPPOSITE broad
2 = <u>limited</u>, restricted, confined, tight, close, near, cramped, meagre, constricted, circumscribed, scanty, straitened, incapacious …*He squeezed his way along the narrow space between the crates…* OPPOSITE wide
3 = <u>insular</u>, prejudiced, biased, partial, reactionary, puritan, bigoted, dogmatic, intolerant, narrow-minded, small-minded, illiberal …*a narrow and outdated view of family life…* OPPOSITE broad-minded
4 = <u>exclusive</u>, limited, select, restricted, confined …*She achieved a fame that transcended the narrow world of avant-garde theatre…*
VERB 1 = <u>restrict</u>, limit, reduce, diminish, constrict, circumscribe, straiten …*I don't want to narrow my options too early on…*
2 = <u>get narrower</u>, taper, shrink, tighten, constrict …*This sign means that the road narrows on both sides…*
PLURAL NOUN = <u>channel</u>, sound, gulf, passage, straits …*The tide was sluicing out through the narrows…*

narrowly 1 = <u>just</u>, barely, only just, scarcely, by the skin of your teeth, by a whisker *or* hair's-breadth …*Five firemen narrowly escaped death…*
2 = <u>closely</u>, keenly, carefully, intently, intensely, fixedly, searchingly …*He frowned and looked narrowly at his colleague…*

narrow-minded = <u>intolerant</u>, conservative, prejudiced, biased, provincial, petty, reactionary, parochial, short-sighted, bigoted, insular, opinionated, small-minded, hidebound, illiberal, strait-laced
OPPOSITE broad-minded

nastiness 1 = <u>spite</u>, malice, venom, unpleasantness, meanness, bitchiness (*slang*), offensiveness, spitefulness …*'You're just like your mother,' he said, with a tone of nastiness in his voice…*
2 = <u>dirt</u>, pollution, filth, squalor, impurity, foulness, defilement …*Much filth and nastiness is spread amongst the huts…*
3 = <u>obscenity</u>, porn (*informal*), pornography, indecency, licentiousness, ribaldry, smuttiness …*Almost every page of the book was filled with this kind of nastiness…*

nasty 1 = <u>unpleasant</u>, ugly, disagreeable …*This divorce could turn nasty…* OPPOSITE pleasant
2 = <u>spiteful</u>, mean, offensive, annoying, vicious, unpleasant, abusive, vile, malicious, bad-tempered, despicable, disagreeable …*He's only nasty to me when there's no-one around to see it…* OPPOSITE pleasant
3 = <u>disgusting</u>, unpleasant, dirty, offensive, foul, horrible, polluted, filthy, sickening, vile, distasteful, repellent, obnoxious, objectionable, disagreeable, nauseating, odious, repugnant, loathsome, grotty (*slang*), malodorous, noisome, unappetizing, yucky *or* yukky (*slang*), festy (*Austral. slang*), yucko (*Austral. slang*) …*It's got a really nasty smell…*
4 = <u>serious</u>, bad, dangerous, critical, severe, painful …*Lili had a nasty chest infection…*
5 = <u>obscene</u>, blue, gross, foul, indecent, pornographic, lewd, impure, lascivious, smutty, ribald, licentious …*There's no need for such nasty language, young man…* OPPOSITE clean

nation 1 = <u>country</u>, state, commonwealth, realm …*Such policies would require unprecedented cooperation between nations…*
2 = <u>public</u>, people, community, society, population …*It was a story that touched the nation's heart…*

national ADJECTIVE 1 = <u>nationwide</u>, state, public, civil, widespread, governmental, countrywide …*major national and international issues…*
2 = <u>ethnic</u>, social …*the national characteristics and history of the country…*
NOUN = <u>citizen</u>, subject, resident, native, inhabitant …*He is in fact a British national and passport holder…*

nationalism = <u>patriotism</u>, loyalty to your country, chauvinism, jingoism, nationality, allegiance, fealty

nationalistic = <u>patriotic</u>, xenophobic, chauvinistic, jingoistic, loyal to your country

nationality 1 = <u>citizenship</u>, birth …*When asked his nationality, he said, 'British'…*
2 = <u>race</u>, nation, ethnic group …*the many nationalities that comprise Ethopia…*

nationwide = <u>national</u>, general, widespread, countrywide, overall

native ADJECTIVE 1 = <u>indigenous</u>, local, aboriginal (*often offensive*) …*a spokeswoman for native peoples around the world…*
2 = <u>mother</u>, indigenous, vernacular …*French is not my*

native tongue...

3 = <u>domestic</u>, local, indigenous, home-made, home-grown, home ...*Several native plants also provide edible berries...*

NOUN = <u>inhabitant</u>, national, resident, citizen, countryman, aborigine (*often offensive*), dweller ...*He was a native of France...*

nativity *usually capital* = <u>birth of Christ</u>, manger scene

natter VERB = <u>gossip</u>, talk, rabbit (on) (*Brit. informal*), jaw (*slang*), chatter, witter (*informal*), prattle, jabber, gabble, blather, blether, shoot the breeze (*informal*), run off at the mouth (*slang*), prate, talk idly, chew the fat *or* rag (*slang*) ...*His mother would natter on the phone for hours...*

NOUN = <u>gossip</u>, talk, conversation, chat, jaw (*slang*), craic (*Irish informal*), gab (*informal*), prattle, jabber, gabble, palaver, blather, chitchat, blether, chinwag (*Brit. informal*), gabfest (*informal, chiefly U.S. & Canad.*), confabulation ...*We must get together some time for a good natter...*

natty = <u>smart</u>, sharp, dashing, elegant, trim, neat, fashionable, stylish, trendy (*Brit. informal*), chic, spruce, well-dressed, dapper, snazzy (*informal*), well-turned-out, crucial (*slang*)

natural 1 = <u>logical</u>, reasonable, valid, legitimate ...*A period of depression is a natural response to bereavement...*

2 = <u>normal</u>, common, regular, usual, ordinary, typical, everyday ...*It's just not natural behaviour for a child of his age...* OPPOSITE abnormal

3 = <u>innate</u>, native, characteristic, indigenous, inherent, instinctive, intuitive, congenital, inborn, immanent, in your blood, essential ...*He has a natural flair for business...*

4 = <u>unaffected</u>, open, frank, genuine, spontaneous, candid, unpretentious, unsophisticated, dinkum (*Austral. & N.Z. informal*), artless, ingenuous, real, simple, unstudied ...*Jan's sister was as natural and friendly as the rest of the family...* OPPOSITE affected

5 = <u>pure</u>, plain, organic, whole, unrefined, unbleached, unpolished, unmixed ...*He prefers to use high quality natural produce...* OPPOSITE processed

naturalism = <u>realism</u>, authenticity, plausibility, verisimilitude, factualism

naturalist = <u>biologist</u>, ecologist, botanist, zoologist

naturalistic 1 = <u>realistic</u>, photographic, kitchen sink, representational, lifelike, warts and all (*informal*), true-to-life, vérité, factualistic ...*These drawings are amongst his most naturalistic...*

2 = <u>lifelike</u>, realistic, real-life, true-to-life ...*Research is needed under rather more naturalistic conditions...*

naturally 1 = <u>of course</u>, certainly, as a matter of course, as anticipated ...*We are naturally concerned about the future...*

2 = <u>typically</u>, simply, normally, spontaneously, customarily ...*A study of yoga leads naturally to meditation...*

nature 1 = <u>creation</u>, world, earth, environment, universe, cosmos, natural world ...*man's ancient sense of kinship with nature...*

2 = <u>flora and fauna</u>, country, landscape, countryside, scenery, natural history ...*an organization devoted to the protection of nature...*

3 = <u>quality</u>, character, make-up, constitution, attributes, essence, traits, complexion, features ...*The protests had been non-political in nature...*

4 = <u>temperament</u>, character, personality, disposition, outlook, mood, humour, temper ...*She trusted people. That was her nature...*

5 = <u>kind</u>, sort, style, type, variety, species, category, description ...*This – and other books of a similar nature – are urgently needed...*

naughty 1 = <u>disobedient</u>, bad, mischievous, badly behaved, wayward, playful, wicked, sinful, fractious, impish, roguish, refractory ...*You naughty boy, you gave me such a fright...* OPPOSITE good

2 = <u>obscene</u>, blue, vulgar, improper, lewd, risqué, X-rated (*informal*), bawdy, smutty, off-colour, ribald ...*saucy TV shows crammed with naughty innuendo...* OPPOSITE clean

nausea 1 = <u>sickness</u>, vomiting, retching, squeamishness, queasiness, biliousness ...*I was overcome with a feeling of nausea...*

2 = <u>disgust</u>, loathing, aversion, revulsion, abhorrence, repugnance, odium ...*She spoke in a little-girl voice which brought on a palpable feeling of nausea...*

nauseate 1 = <u>sicken</u>, turn your stomach ...*The smell of frying nauseated her...*

2 = <u>disgust</u>, offend, horrify, revolt, repel, repulse, gross out (*U.S. slang*) ...*Ugliness nauseates me. I like to have beautiful things around me...*

nauseous 1 = <u>sick</u>, crook (*Austral. & N.Z. informal*) ...*The drugs make me feel nauseous...*

2 = <u>sickening</u>, offensive, disgusting, revolting, distasteful, repulsive, nauseating, repugnant, loathsome, abhorrent, detestable, yucky *or* yukky (*slang*), yucko (*Austral. slang*) ...*The floor was deep with bat dung giving off a nauseous smell...*

nautical = <u>maritime</u>, marine, yachting, naval, seafaring, seagoing

naval = <u>nautical</u>, marine, maritime

navel 1 = <u>bellybutton</u> (*informal*) ...*A small incision is made just below the navel...*

2 = <u>centre</u>, middle, hub, central point ...*The city was once the jewel in the navel of the Gold Coast...*

(*Related Words*)
technical name: umbilicus
adjective: umbilical

navigate 1 = <u>steer</u>, drive, direct, guide, handle, pilot, sail, skipper, manoeuvre ...*He was responsible for safely navigating the ship...*

2 = <u>manoeuvre</u>, drive, direct, guide, handle, pilot ...*He expertly navigated the plane through 45 minutes of fog...*

3 = <u>plot a course</u>, sail, find your way, plan a course ...*They navigated by the sun and stars...*

4 = <u>sail</u>, cruise, manoeuvre, voyage ...*Such boats can be built locally and can navigate on the Nile...*

navigation = <u>sailing</u>, cruising, steering, voyaging, seamanship, helmsmanship

navigator = <u>helmsman</u>, pilot, seaman, mariner

navy = <u>fleet</u>, warships, flotilla, armada

near 1 = <u>close</u>, bordering, neighbouring, nearby, beside, adjacent, adjoining, close by, at close quarters, just round the corner, contiguous, proximate, within sniffing distance (*informal*), a hop, skip and a jump away (*informal*) ...*The town is very near*... ...*Where's the nearest telephone?*... OPPOSITE far

2 = <u>imminent</u>, forthcoming, approaching, looming, impending, upcoming, on the cards (*informal*), nigh, in the offing, near-at-hand, next ...*Departure time was near*... OPPOSITE far-off

3 = <u>intimate</u>, close, related, allied, familiar, connected, attached, akin ...*I have no near relations*... OPPOSITE distant

4 (*Informal*) = <u>mean</u>, stingy, parsimonious, miserly, niggardly, ungenerous, tightfisted, close-fisted ...*They joked about him being so near with his money*...

nearby ADVERB = <u>close at hand</u>, within reach, not far away, at close quarters, just round the corner, proximate, within sniffing distance (*informal*) ...*He might easily have been seen by someone who lived nearby*...
ADJECTIVE = <u>neighbouring</u>, adjacent, adjoining ...*At a nearby table a man was complaining in a loud voice*...

nearing = <u>approaching</u>, coming, advancing, imminent, impending, upcoming

nearly 1 = <u>practically</u>, about, almost, virtually, all but, just about, not quite, as good as, well-nigh ...*The beach was nearly empty*...

2 = <u>almost</u>, about, approaching, roughly, just about, approximately ...*It was already nearly eight o'clock*...

neat 1 = <u>tidy</u>, nice, straight, trim, orderly, spruce, uncluttered, shipshape, spick-and-span ...*Her house was neat and tidy and gleamingly clean*... OPPOSITE untidy

2 = <u>methodical</u>, tidy, systematic, fastidious ...*'It's not like Alf to leave a mess like that,' I remarked, 'He's always so neat.'*... OPPOSITE disorganized

3 = <u>smart</u>, trim, tidy, spruce, dapper, natty (*informal*), well-groomed, well-turned out ...*She always looked neat and well groomed*...

4 = <u>graceful</u>, elegant, adept, nimble, agile, adroit, efficient ...*He had the neat movements of a dancer*... OPPOSITE clumsy

5 = <u>clever</u>, efficient, handy, apt, well-judged ...*It was a neat solution to the problem*... OPPOSITE inefficient

6 = <u>cool</u>, great (*informal*), excellent, brilliant, cracking (*Brit. informal*), smashing (*informal*), superb, fantastic (*informal*), tremendous, ace (*informal*), fabulous (*informal*), marvellous, terrific, awesome (*slang*), mean (*slang*), super (*informal*), brill (*informal*), bodacious (*slang, chiefly U.S.*), boffo (*slang*), chillin' (*U.S. slang*), booshit (*Austral. slang*), exo (*Austral. slang*), sik (*Austral. slang*) ...*I've just had a really neat idea*... OPPOSITE terrible

7 (*of alcoholic drinks*) = <u>undiluted</u>, straight, pure, unmixed ...*He poured himself a glass of neat brandy and swallowed it in one*...

neatly 1 = <u>tidily</u>, nicely, smartly, systematically, methodically, fastidiously ...*He took off his trousers and folded them neatly*...

2 = <u>smartly</u>, elegantly, stylishly, tidily, nattily ...*She was neatly dressed, her hair was tidy and she carried a shoulder-bag*...

3 = <u>gracefully</u>, expertly, efficiently, adeptly, skilfully, nimbly, adroitly, dexterously, agilely ...*He sent the ball over the bar with a neatly executed header*...

4 = <u>cleverly</u>, precisely, accurately, efficiently, aptly, elegantly ...*She neatly summed up a common attitude among many teachers and parents*...

neatness 1 = <u>order</u>, organization, harmony, tidiness, orderliness ...*The grounds were a perfect balance between neatness and natural wildness*...

2 = <u>tidiness</u>, niceness, orderliness, smartness, fastidiousness, trimness, spruceness ...*He was a paragon of neatness and efficiency*...

3 = <u>grace</u>, skill, efficiency, expertise, precision, elegance, agility, dexterity, deftness, nimbleness, adroitness, adeptness, daintiness, gracefulness, preciseness, skilfulness ...*neatness of movement*...

4 = <u>cleverness</u>, efficiency, precision, elegance, aptness ...*He appreciated the neatness of their plan*...

nebulous 1 = <u>vague</u>, confused, uncertain, obscure, unclear, ambiguous, indefinite, hazy, indeterminate, imprecise, indistinct ...*the nebulous concept of 'spirit'*...

2 = <u>obscure</u>, vague, dim, murky, shadowy, cloudy, misty, hazy, amorphous, indeterminate, shapeless, indistinct, unformed ...*We glimpsed a nebulous figure through the mist*...

necessarily 1 = <u>automatically</u>, naturally, definitely, undoubtedly, accordingly, by definition, of course, certainly ...*A higher price does not necessarily guarantee a better product*...

2 = <u>inevitably</u>, of necessity, unavoidably, perforce, incontrovertibly, nolens volens (*Latin*) ...*In any policy area, a number of ministries is necessarily involved*...

necessary 1 = <u>needed</u>, required, essential, vital, compulsory, mandatory, imperative, indispensable, obligatory, requisite, de rigueur (*French*), needful ...*Is your journey really necessary?*... ...*Please make all the necessary arrangements*... OPPOSITE unnecessary

2 = <u>inevitable</u>, certain, unavoidable, inescapable ...*Wastage was no doubt a necessary consequence of war*... OPPOSITE avoidable

necessitate = <u>compel</u>, force, demand, require, call for, oblige, entail, constrain, impel, make necessary

necessity NOUN **1** = <u>need</u>, demand, requirement, exigency, indispensability, needfulness ...*There is agreement on the necessity of reforms*...

2 = <u>essential</u>, need, necessary, requirement, fundamental, requisite, prerequisite, sine qua non (*Latin*), desideratum, want ...*Water is a basic necessity of life*...

3 = <u>inevitability</u>, certainty ...*the ultimate necessity of death*...

4 = <u>poverty</u>, need, privation, penury, destitution, extremity, indigence ...*They were reduced to begging through economic necessity*...

PLURAL NOUN = essentials, needs, requirements, fundamentals ...*They sometimes had to struggle to pay for necessities...*

necropolis = cemetery, graveyard, churchyard, burial ground

need **VERB** 1 = want, miss, require, lack, have to have, demand ...*He desperately needed money...*
2 = require, want, demand, call for, entail, necessitate, have occasion to *or* for ...*The building needs quite a few repairs...*
3 = have to, be obliged to ...*You needn't bother, I'll do it myself...*
NOUN 1 = requirement, demand, essential, necessity, requisite, desideratum ...*the special nutritional needs of children...*
2 = longing, wish, desire, hunger, want ...*The need for revenge kept eating at me...*
3 = necessity, call, demand, requirement, obligation ...*There's no need to call the police...*
4 = emergency, want, necessity, urgency, exigency ...*In her moment of need, her mother was nowhere to be seen...*
5 = poverty, deprivation, destitution, neediness, distress, extremity, privation, penury, indigence, impecuniousness ...*the state of need in Third World countries...*

needed = necessary, wanted, required, lacked, called for, desired

needle = irritate, provoke, annoy, sting, bait, harass, taunt, nag, hassle (*informal*), aggravate (*informal*), prod, gall, ruffle, spur, prick, nettle, goad, irk, rile, get under your skin (*informal*), get on your nerves (*informal*), nark (*Brit., Austral., & N.Z. slang*), get in your hair (*informal*)

needless = unnecessary, excessive, pointless, gratuitous, useless, unwanted, redundant, superfluous, groundless, expendable, uncalled-for, dispensable, nonessential, undesired **OPPOSITE** essential

needlework = embroidery, tailoring, stitching, sewing, needlecraft

needy = poor, deprived, disadvantaged, impoverished, penniless, destitute, poverty-stricken, underprivileged, indigent, down at heel (*informal*), impecunious, dirt-poor, on the breadline (*informal*) **OPPOSITE** wealthy

negate 1 = invalidate, reverse, cancel, wipe out, void, repeal, revoke, retract, rescind, neutralize, annul, nullify, obviate, abrogate, countermand ...*These environmental protection laws could be negated if the European Community decides they interfere with trade...*
2 = deny, oppose, contradict, refute, disallow, disprove, rebut, gainsay (*archaic or literary*) ...*I can neither negate nor affirm this claim...* **OPPOSITE** confirm

negation 1 = opposite, reverse, contrary, contradiction, converse, antithesis, inverse, antonym ...*He repudiates liberty and equality as the negation of order and government...*
2 = denial, refusal, rejection, contradiction, renunciation, repudiation, disavowal, veto ...*She shook her head in a gesture of negation...*

negative **ADJECTIVE** 1 = neutralizing, invalidating, annulling, nullifying, counteractive ...*This will have a very serious negative effect on economic recovery...*
2 = pessimistic, cynical, unwilling, gloomy, antagonistic, jaundiced, uncooperative, contrary ...*There's no point in going along to an interview with a negative attitude...* **OPPOSITE** optimistic
3 = dissenting, contradictory, refusing, denying, rejecting, opposing, resisting, contrary ...*Dr. Velayati gave a vague but negative response...* **OPPOSITE** assenting
NOUN = denial, no, refusal, rejection, contradiction ...*We were fobbed off with a crisp negative...*

neglect **VERB** 1 = disregard, ignore, leave alone, turn your back on, fail to look after ...*The woman denied that she had neglected her child...* **OPPOSITE** look after
2 = shirk, forget, overlook, omit, evade, pass over, skimp, procrastinate over, let slide, be remiss in *or* about ...*If you don't keep an eye on them, children tend to neglect their homework...*
3 = fail, forget, omit ...*She neglected to inform me of her change of plans...*
NOUN 1 = negligence, inattention, unconcern ...*hundreds of orphans, old and handicapped people, some of whom have since died of neglect...* **OPPOSITE** care
2 = shirking, failure, oversight, carelessness, dereliction, forgetfulness, slackness, laxity, laxness, slovenliness, remissness ...*her deliberate neglect of her professional duty...*

neglected 1 = uncared-for, abandoned, underestimated, disregarded, undervalued, unappreciated ...*The fact that he is not coming today makes his grandmother feel neglected...*
2 = run down, derelict, overgrown, uncared-for ...*a neglected house with an overgrown garden...*

negligence = carelessness, failure, neglect, disregard, shortcoming, omission, oversight, dereliction, forgetfulness, slackness, inattention, laxity, thoughtlessness, laxness, inadvertence, inattentiveness, heedlessness, remissness

negligent = careless, slack, thoughtless, unthinking, forgetful, slapdash, neglectful, heedless, slipshod, inattentive, remiss, unmindful, disregardful **OPPOSITE** careful

negligible = insignificant, small, minute, minor, petty, trivial, trifling, unimportant, inconsequential, imperceptible, nickel-and-dime (*U.S. slang*) **OPPOSITE** significant

negotiable 1 = debatable, flexible, unsettled, undecided, open to discussion, discussable *or* discussible ...*The manor is for sale at a negotiable price...*
2 = valid, transferable, transactional ...*The bonds may no longer be negotiable...*

negotiate 1 = bargain, deal, contract, discuss, debate, consult, confer, mediate, hold talks, arbitrate, cut a deal, conciliate, parley, discuss terms ... *The president may be willing to negotiate with the democrats...*

2 = arrange, manage, settle, work out, bring about, transact ... *The local government and the army have negotiated a truce...*

3 = get round, clear, pass, cross, pass through, get over, get past, surmount ... *I negotiated the corner on my motorbike...*

negotiation 1 = bargaining, debate, discussion, transaction, dialogue, mediation, arbitration, wheeling and dealing (*informal*) ... *We have had meaningful negotiations and I believe we are close to a deal...*

2 = arrangement, management, settlement, working out, transaction, bringing about ... *They intend to take no part in the negotiation of a new treaty of union...*

negotiator = mediator, ambassador, diplomat, delegate, intermediary, arbitrator, moderator, honest broker

neighbourhood 1 = district, community, quarter, region, surroundings, locality, locale ... *It seemed like a good neighbourhood to raise my children...*

2 = vicinity, confines, proximity, precincts, environs, purlieus ... *the loss of woodlands in the neighbourhood of large towns...*

neighbouring = nearby, next, near, bordering, surrounding, connecting, adjacent, adjoining, abutting, contiguous, nearest OPPOSITE remote

neighbourly = helpful, kind, social, civil, friendly, obliging, harmonious, amiable, considerate, sociable, genial, hospitable, companionable, well-disposed

nemesis = retribution, fate, destruction, destiny, vengeance

neophyte (*Formal*) = novice, student, pupil, recruit, amateur, beginner, trainee, apprentice, disciple, learner, tyro, probationer, novitiate, proselyte, catechumen

nepotism = favouritism, bias, patronage, preferential treatment, partiality

nerd *or* **nurd** (*Slang*) **1** = bore, obsessive, anorak (*informal*), geek (*informal*), trainspotter (*informal*), dork (*slang*), wonk (*informal*) ... *the outdated notion that users of the Internet are all sad computer nerds...*

2 = fool, weed, drip (*informal*), sap (*slang*), wally (*slang*), sucker (*slang*), wimp (*informal*), booby, prat (*slang*), plonker (*slang*), twit (*informal, chiefly Brit.*), simpleton, dipstick (*Brit. slang*), schmuck (*U.S. slang*), divvy (*Brit. slang*), putz (*U.S. slang*), wuss (*slang*), eejit (*Scot. & Irish*), dumb-ass (*slang*), doofus (*slang, chiefly U.S.*), dorba *or* dorb (*Austral. slang*), bogan (*Austral. slang*) ... *No woman in her right mind would look twice at such a charmless little nerd...*

nerve NOUN **1** = bravery, courage, spirit, bottle (*Brit. slang*), resolution, daring, determination, guts (*informal*), pluck, grit, fortitude, vigour, coolness, balls (*taboo slang*), mettle, firmness, spunk (*informal*), fearlessness, steadfastness, intrepidity, hardihood, gameness ... *I never got up enough nerve to ask her out...* ... *If we keep our nerve, we might be able to bluff it out...*

2 (*Informal*) = impudence, face (*informal*), front, neck (*informal*), sauce (*informal*), cheek (*informal*), brass (*informal*), gall, audacity, boldness, temerity, chutzpah (*U.S. & Canad. informal*), insolence, impertinence, effrontery, brass neck (*Brit. informal*), brazenness, sassiness (*U.S. slang*) ... *He had the nerve to ask me to prove who I was...*

PLURAL NOUN = tension, stress, strain, anxiety, butterflies (in your stomach) (*informal*), nervousness, cold feet (*informal*), heebie-jeebies (*slang*), worry ... *I just played badly. It wasn't nerves...*

PHRASES **nerve yourself** = brace yourself, prepare yourself, steel yourself, fortify yourself, gear yourself up, gee yourself up ... *I nerved myself to face the pain...*

⌐ Related Words ⌐
technical name: neuron *or* neurone
adjective: neural

nerve-racking *or* **nerve-wracking** = tense, trying, difficult, worrying, frightening, distressing, daunting, harassing, stressful, harrowing, gut-wrenching

nervous = apprehensive, anxious, uneasy, edgy, worried, wired (*slang*), tense, fearful, shaky, hysterical, neurotic, agitated, ruffled, timid, hyper (*informal*), jittery (*informal*), uptight (*informal*), flustered, on edge, excitable, nervy (*Brit. informal*), jumpy, twitchy (*informal*), fidgety, timorous, highly strung, antsy (*informal*), toey (*Austral. slang*) OPPOSITE calm

nervous breakdown = collapse, breakdown, crack-up (*informal*), neurasthenia (*obsolete*), nervous disorder

nervousness = anxiety, stress, tension, strain, unease, disquiet, agitation, trepidation, timidity, excitability, perturbation, edginess, worry, jumpiness, antsiness (*informal*)

nervy = anxious, nervous, tense, agitated, wired (*slang*), restless, jittery (*informal*), on edge, excitable, jumpy, twitchy (*informal*), fidgety

nest 1 = refuge, resort, retreat, haunt, den, hideaway ... *He moved into a £2,000-a-month love nest with his blonde mistress...*

2 = hotbed, den, breeding-ground ... *Biarritz was notorious in those days as a nest of spies...*

nest egg = savings, fund(s), store, reserve, deposit, fall-back, cache

nestle = snuggle, cuddle, huddle, curl up, nuzzle

nestling = chick, fledgling, baby bird

net¹ NOUN = mesh, netting, network, web, lattice, lacework, openwork ... *the use of a net in greenhouses to protect crops against insects...*
VERB = catch, bag, capture, trap, nab (*informal*), entangle, ensnare, enmesh ... *Poachers have been netting fish to sell on the black market...*

net² *or* **nett** ADJECTIVE **1** = after taxes, final, clear, take-home ... *At the year end, net assets were £18 million...*

2 = final, closing, ultimate, eventual, conclusive ... *The party made a net gain of 210 seats...*
VERB = earn, make, clear, gain, realize, bring in, accumulate, reap ... *The state government expects to*

net about 1.46 billion rupees…

nether = <u>lower</u>, bottom, beneath, underground, inferior, basal

nettle = <u>irritate</u>, provoke, annoy, gall, sting, aggravate (*informal*), incense, ruffle, exasperate, vex, goad, pique, get on your nerves (*informal*), nark (*Brit., Austral., & N.Z. slang*)

network 1 = <u>web</u>, system, arrangement, grid, mesh, lattice, circuitry, nexus, plexus, interconnection, net …*The uterus is supplied with a network of blood vessels and nerves…*
2 = <u>maze</u>, warren, labyrinth …*Strasbourg, with its rambling network of medieval streets…*

neurosis = <u>obsession</u>, instability, mental illness, abnormality, phobia, derangement, mental disturbance, psychological *or* emotional disorder

neurotic = <u>unstable</u>, nervous, disturbed, anxious, abnormal, obsessive, compulsive, manic, unhealthy, hyper (*informal*), twitchy (*informal*), overwrought, maladjusted ⟨OPPOSITE⟩ rational

neuter = <u>castrate</u>, doctor (*informal*), emasculate, spay, dress, fix (*informal*), geld

neutral 1 = <u>unbiased</u>, impartial, disinterested, even-handed, dispassionate, sitting on the fence, uninvolved, noncommittal, nonpartisan, unprejudiced, nonaligned, unaligned, noncombatant, nonbelligerent …*Those who had decided to remain neutral now found themselves forced to take sides…* ⟨OPPOSITE⟩ biased
2 = <u>expressionless</u>, dull, blank, deadpan, toneless …*He told her about the death, describing the events in as neutral a manner as he could…*
3 = <u>uncontroversial</u> *or* noncontroversial, safe, inoffensive …*Stick to talking about neutral subjects on your first meeting…*
4 = <u>colourless</u>, achromatic …*I tend to wear neutral colours like grey and beige…*

neutrality = <u>impartiality</u>, detachment, noninterference, nonpartisanship, noninvolvement, nonalignment, noninterventionism

neutralize = <u>counteract</u>, cancel, offset, undo, compensate for, negate, invalidate, counterbalance, nullify

never 1 = <u>at no time</u>, not once, not ever …*She was never really well after that…* ⟨OPPOSITE⟩ always
2 = <u>under no circumstances</u>, no way, not at all, on no account, not on your life (*informal*), not on your nelly (*Brit. slang*), not for love nor money (*informal*), not ever …*I would never do anything to hurt him…*

> ## Word Power
> **never** – *Never* is sometimes used in informal speech and writing as an emphatic form of *not*, with simple past tenses of certain verbs: *I never said that* – and in very informal speech as a denial in place of *did not*: *he says I hit him, but I never.* These uses of *never* should be avoided in careful writing.

never-never (*Informal*) = <u>hire-purchase</u> (*Brit.*), H.P.

(*Brit.*)

nevertheless = <u>even so</u>, still, however, yet, regardless, nonetheless, notwithstanding, in spite of that, (even) though, but

new 1 = <u>modern</u>, recent, contemporary, up-to-date, latest, happening (*informal*), different, current, advanced, original, fresh, novel, topical, state-of-the-art, ground-breaking, modish, newfangled, modernistic, ultramodern, all-singing, all-dancing …*a brilliant new invention that puts a world of information at your fingertips…* ⟨OPPOSITE⟩ old-fashioned
2 = <u>brand new</u>, unused …*There are many boats, new and used, for sale…*
3 = <u>extra</u>, more, added, new-found, supplementary …*Many are looking for a new source of income by taking on freelance work…*
4 = <u>unfamiliar</u>, unaccustomed, strange, unknown …*I had been in my new job only a few days… …She was still new to the art of bargaining…*
5 = <u>renewed</u>, changed, improved, restored, altered, rejuvenated, revitalized …*The treatment made him feel like a new man…*

newcomer 1 = <u>new arrival</u>, incomer, immigrant, stranger, foreigner, alien, settler …*He must be a newcomer to town…*
2 = <u>beginner</u>, stranger, outsider, novice, new arrival, parvenu, Johnny-come-lately (*informal*) …*The candidates are all relative newcomers to politics…*

newly = <u>recently</u>, just, lately, freshly, anew, latterly

newness = <u>novelty</u>, innovation, originality, freshness, strangeness, unfamiliarity

(Related Words)
combining form: neo-
fear of: neophobia

news = <u>information</u>, latest (*informal*), report, word, story, release, account, statement, advice, exposé, intelligence, scandal, rumour, leak, revelation, buzz, gossip, dirt (*U.S. slang*), disclosure, bulletin, dispatch, gen (*Brit. informal*), communiqué, hearsay, tidings, news flash, scuttlebutt (*U.S. slang*)

newsworthy = <u>interesting</u>, important, arresting, significant, remarkable, notable, sensational, noteworthy

next ⟨ADJECTIVE⟩ **1** = <u>following</u>, later, succeeding, subsequent …*I caught the next available flight…*
2 = <u>adjacent</u>, closest, nearest, neighbouring, adjoining …*The man in the next chair was asleep…*
⟨ADVERB⟩ = <u>afterwards</u>, then, later, following, subsequently, thereafter …*I don't know what to do next…*

nexus = <u>connection</u>, link, tie, bond, junction, joining

nibble ⟨VERB⟩ = <u>bite</u>, eat, peck, pick at, nip, munch, gnaw …*He started to nibble his biscuit…*
⟨NOUN⟩ = <u>snack</u>, bite, taste, peck, crumb, morsel, titbit, soupçon (*French*) …*We each took a nibble of cheese…*

nice 1 = <u>pleasant</u>, delightful, agreeable, good, attractive, charming, pleasurable, enjoyable …*We had a nice meal with a bottle of champagne…* ⟨OPPOSITE⟩ unpleasant
2 = <u>kind</u>, helpful, obliging, considerate …*It was nice of*

you to go to so much trouble… OPPOSITE▷ unkind
3 = likable *or* likeable, friendly, engaging, charming, pleasant, agreeable, amiable, prepossessing …*I've met your father and I think he's really nice*…
4 = polite, cultured, refined, courteous, genteel, well-bred, well-mannered …*The kids are very well brought up and have nice manners*… OPPOSITE▷ vulgar
5 = precise, fine, careful, strict, accurate, exact, exacting, subtle, delicate, discriminating, rigorous, meticulous, scrupulous, fastidious …*As a politician, he drew a nice distinction between his own opinions and the wishes of the majority*… OPPOSITE▷ vague

nicely 1 = pleasantly, well, delightfully, attractively, charmingly, agreeably, pleasingly, acceptably, pleasurably …*He's just written a book, nicely illustrated and not too technical*… OPPOSITE▷ unpleasantly
2 = kindly, politely, thoughtfully, amiably, courteously …*He treated you very nicely and acted like a decent guy*…
3 = precisely, exactly, accurately, finely, carefully, strictly, subtly, delicately, meticulously, rigorously, scrupulously …*I think this sums up the problem very nicely*… OPPOSITE▷ carelessly
4 = satisfactorily, well, adequately, acceptably, passably …*She has a private income, so they manage very nicely*…

nicety = fine point, distinction, subtlety, nuance, refinement, minutiae

niche 1 = recess, opening, corner, hollow, nook, alcove …*There was a niche in the rock where the path ended*…
2 = position, calling, place, slot (*informal*), vocation, pigeonhole (*informal*) …*Perhaps I will find my niche in a desk job*…

nick VERB **1** (*Slang*) = steal, pinch (*informal*), swipe (*slang*), pilfer, snitch (*slang*) …*We used to nick biscuits from the kitchen*
2 = cut, mark, score, damage, chip, scratch, scar, notch, dent, snick …*A sharp blade is likely to nick the skin and draw blood*…
NOUN = cut, mark, scratch, score, chip, scar, notch, dent, snick …*The barbed wire had left only the tiniest nick below my right eye*…

nickname = pet name, label, diminutive, epithet, sobriquet, familiar name, moniker *or* monicker (*slang*), handle (*slang*)

nifty 1 (*Informal*) = slick, excellent, sharp, smart, clever, neat, stylish …*The film features some nifty special effects*…
2 = agile, quick, swift, skilful, deft …*Knight displayed all the nifty legwork of a champion bowler*…

niggle VERB **1** = bother, concern, worry, trouble, disturb, rankle …*I realise now that the things which used to niggle me didn't really matter*…
2 = criticize, provoke, annoy, plague, irritate, hassle (*informal*), badger, find fault with, nag at, cavil, be on your back (*slang*) …*I don't react any more when opponents try to niggle me*…
NOUN = complaint, moan, grievance, grumble, beef (*slang*), bitch (*slang*), lament, grouse, gripe (*informal*), grouch (*informal*) …*The life we have built together is*

far more important than any minor niggle either of us might have…

niggling 1 = irritating, troubling, persistent, bothersome …*Both players have been suffering from niggling injuries*…
2 = petty, minor, trifling, insignificant, unimportant, fussy, quibbling, picky (*informal*), piddling (*informal*), nit-picking (*informal*), finicky, pettifogging …*They started having tiffs about the most niggling little things*…

nigh ADVERB = almost, about, nearly, close to, practically, approximately …*Accurate earthquake prediction is well nigh impossible*…
ADJECTIVE = near, next, close, imminent, impending, at hand, upcoming …*The end of the world is nigh*…

night = darkness, dark, night-time, dead of night, night watches, hours of darkness
(Related Words)
adjective: nocturnal

nightfall = evening, sunset, twilight, dusk, sundown, eventide, gloaming (*Scot. or poetic*), eve (*archaic*), evo (*Austral. slang*) OPPOSITE▷ daybreak

nightly ADJECTIVE = nocturnal, night-time …*One of the nurses came by on her nightly rounds*…
ADVERB = every night, nights (*informal*), each night, night after night …*She had prayed nightly for his safe return*…

nightmare 1 = bad dream, hallucination, night terror …*Jane did not eat cheese because it gave her nightmares*…
2 = ordeal, trial, hell, horror, torture, torment, tribulation, purgatory, hell on earth …*My years in prison were a nightmare*…

nightmarish = terrifying, frightening, disturbing, appalling, horrible, horrific, ghastly, hideous, harrowing, frightful

nihilism 1 = negativity, rejection, denial, scepticism, cynicism, pessimism, renunciation, atheism, repudiation, agnosticism, unbelief, abnegation …*These disillusioned students embraced agnosticism, atheism, and nihilism*…
2 = anarchy, disorder, lawlessness …*This moral nihilism has proved both irresponsible and politically counter-productive*…

nil 1 = nothing, love, zero, zip (*U.S. slang*) …*The score was 2-nil*…
2 = zero, nothing, none, naught, zilch (*slang*), zip (*U.S. slang*) …*The chances of success are virtually nil*…

nimble 1 = agile, active, lively, deft, proficient, sprightly, nippy (*Brit. informal*), spry, dexterous …*Lily, who was light and nimble on her feet, was learning to tap-dance*… OPPOSITE▷ clumsy
2 = alert, ready, bright (*informal*), sharp, keen, active, smart, quick-witted …*To keep your mind nimble, you must use it*…

nimbus = halo, atmosphere, glow, aura, ambience, corona, irradiation, aureole

nip¹ VERB **1** = pop, go, run, rush, dash …*Could you nip down to the corner shop for some milk?*…
2 = bite, snap, nibble …*She was patting the dog when*

it nipped her finger…

3 = <u>pinch</u>, catch, grip, squeeze, clip, compress, tweak …*He nipped Billy's cheek between two rough fingers…*

PHRASES **nip something in the bud** = <u>thwart</u>, check, frustrate …*It is important to recognize jealousy and to nip it in the bud before it gets out of hand…*

nip² = <u>dram</u>, shot (*informal*), drop, taste, finger, swallow, portion, peg (*Brit.*), sip, draught, sup, mouthful, snifter (*informal*), soupçon (*French*) …*She had a habit of taking an occasional nip from a flask of cognac…*

nipper 1 (*Informal*) = <u>child</u>, girl, boy, baby, kid (*informal*), infant, tot, little one, sprog (*slang*), munchkin (*informal, chiefly U.S.*), rug rat (*slang*), littlie (*Austral. informal*), ankle-biter (*Austral. slang*), tacker (*Austral. slang*) …*I couldn't have been much more than a nipper when you last saw me…*

2 = <u>pincer</u>, claw …*Just inside the ragworm's mouth is a sharp, powerful pair of nippers…*

nipple = <u>teat</u>, breast, udder, tit, pap, papilla, mamilla

nippy 1 = <u>chilly</u>, biting, parky (*Brit. informal*) …*It can get quite nippy in the evenings…*

2 = <u>fast</u> (*Informal*), quick, speedy …*This nippy new car has fold-down rear seats…*

3 = <u>agile</u>, fast, quick, active, lively, nimble, sprightly, spry …*He's nippy, and well suited to badminton…*

nirvana = <u>paradise</u>, peace, joy, bliss, serenity, tranquillity

nitty-gritty = <u>basics</u>, facts, reality, essentials, core, fundamentals, substance, essence, bottom line, crux, gist, nuts and bolts, heart of the matter, ins and outs, brass tacks (*informal*)

no **INTERJECTION** = <u>not at all</u>, certainly not, of course not, absolutely not, never, no way, nay …*'Any problems?' – 'No, everything's fine.'…* **OPPOSITE** yes

NOUN 1 = <u>refusal</u>, rejection, denial, negation, veto …*My answer to that is an emphatic no…* **OPPOSITE** consent

2 = <u>objector</u>, protester, dissident, dissenter …*According to the latest poll, the noes have 50 per cent and the yeses 35 per cent…*

nob (*Slang*) = <u>aristocrat</u>, fat cat (*slang, chiefly U.S.*), toff (*Brit. slang*), bigwig (*informal*), celeb (*informal*), big shot (*informal*), big hitter (*informal*), aristo (*informal*), heavy hitter (*informal*), nabob (*informal*), V.I.P.

nobble 1 (*Brit. slang*) = <u>influence</u>, square, win over, pay off (*informal*), corrupt, intimidate, bribe, get at, buy off, suborn, grease the palm *or* hand of (*slang*) …*The trial was stopped after allegations of attempts to nobble the jury…*

2 (*Brit. slang*) = <u>disable</u>, handicap, weaken, incapacitate …*the drug used to nobble two horses at Doncaster last week…*

3 = <u>thwart</u>, check, defeat, frustrate, snooker, foil, baffle, balk, prevent …*Their plans were nobbled by jealous rivals…*

nobility 1 = <u>aristocracy</u>, lords, elite, nobles, upper class, peerage, ruling class, patricians, high society …*They married into the nobility and entered the highest ranks of society…*

2 = <u>dignity</u>, majesty, greatness, grandeur, magnificence, stateliness, nobleness …*I found Mr. Mandela supremely courteous, with a genuine nobility of bearing…*

3 = <u>integrity</u>, honour, virtue, goodness, honesty, righteousness, probity, rectitude, worthiness, incorruptibility, uprightness …*There can be no doubt about the remarkable strength and nobility of her character…*

noble **ADJECTIVE 1** = <u>worthy</u>, generous, upright, honourable, virtuous, magnanimous …*He was an upright and noble man…* **OPPOSITE** despicable

2 = <u>dignified</u>, great, august, imposing, impressive, distinguished, magnificent, splendid, stately …*She was described by contemporaries as possessing a noble bearing and excellent manners…* **OPPOSITE** lowly

3 = <u>aristocratic</u>, lordly, titled, gentle (*archaic*), patrician, blue-blooded, highborn …*Although he was of noble birth he lived as a poor man…* **OPPOSITE** humble

NOUN = <u>lord</u>, peer, aristocrat, nobleman, aristo (*informal*) …*In those days, many of the nobles and landowners were a law unto themselves…* **OPPOSITE** commoner

nobody **PRONOUN** = <u>no-one</u> …*They were shut away in a little room where nobody could overhear…*

NOUN = <u>nonentity</u>, nothing (*informal*), lightweight (*informal*), zero, cipher …*A man in my position has nothing to fear from a nobody like you…* **OPPOSITE** celebrity

nocturnal = <u>nightly</u>, night, of the night, night-time

nod **VERB 1** = <u>agree</u>, concur, assent, show agreement …*'Are you okay?' I asked. She nodded and smiled…*

2 = <u>incline</u>, bob, bow, duck, dip …*She nodded her head in understanding…*

3 = <u>signal</u>, indicate, motion, gesture …*He lifted his end of the canoe, nodding to me to take up mine…*

4 = <u>salute</u>, acknowledge …*All the girls nodded and said 'Hi'…*

NOUN 1 = <u>signal</u>, sign, motion, gesture, indication …*Then, at a nod from their leader, they all sat…*

2 = <u>salute</u>, greeting, acknowledgment …*I gave him a quick nod of greeting and slipped into the nearest chair…*

node = <u>nodule</u>, growth, swelling, knot, lump, bump, bud, knob, protuberance

noise = <u>sound</u>, talk, row, racket, outcry, clamour, din, clatter, uproar, babble, blare, fracas, commotion, pandemonium, rumpus, cry, tumult, hubbub **OPPOSITE** silence, calm

noisy 1 = <u>rowdy</u>, chattering, strident, boisterous, vociferous, riotous, uproarious, obstreperous, clamorous …*a noisy group of drunken students…* **OPPOSITE** quiet

2 = <u>loud</u>, piercing, deafening, tumultuous, ear-splitting, cacophonous, clamorous …*It may be necessary to ask a neighbour to turn down noisy music…* **OPPOSITE** quiet

nomad = <u>wanderer</u>, migrant, rover, rambler, itinerant, drifter, vagabond

nomadic = <u>wandering</u>, travelling, roaming, migrant, roving, itinerant, migratory, vagrant, peripatetic

nomenclature = <u>terminology</u>, vocabulary, classification, taxonomy, phraseology, locution

nominal 1 = <u>titular</u>, formal, purported, in name only, supposed, so-called, pretended, theoretical, professed, ostensible ...*As he was still not allowed to run a company, his wife became its nominal head...*
2 = <u>token</u>, small, symbolic, minimal, trivial, trifling, insignificant, inconsiderable ...*The ferries carry bicycles for a nominal charge...*

nominate 1 = <u>propose</u>, suggest, recommend, submit, put forward ...*The public will be able to nominate candidates for the awards...*
2 = <u>appoint</u>, name, choose, commission, select, elect, assign, designate, empower ...*It is legally possible for an elderly person to nominate someone to act for them...*

nomination 1 = <u>proposal</u>, suggestion, recommendation ...*a list of nominations for senior lectureships...*
2 = <u>appointment</u>, election, selection, designation, choice ...*On Leo's death there were two main candidates for nomination as his replacement...*

nominee = <u>candidate</u>, applicant, entrant, contestant, aspirant, runner

non-aligned *or* **nonaligned** = <u>neutral</u>, impartial, uninvolved, nonpartisan, noncombatant, nonbelligerent

nonchalance = <u>indifference</u>, insouciance, detachment, unconcern, cool (*slang*), calm, apathy, composure, carelessness, equanimity, casualness, sang-froid, self-possession, dispassion, imperturbability

nonchalant = <u>indifferent</u>, cool, calm, casual, detached, careless, laid-back (*informal*), airy, unconcerned, apathetic, dispassionate, unfazed (*informal*), unperturbed, blasé, offhand, unemotional, insouciant, imperturbable OPPOSITE concerned

non-committal *or* **noncommittal** = <u>evasive</u>, politic, reserved, guarded, careful, cautious, neutral, vague, wary, discreet, tentative, ambiguous, indefinite, circumspect, tactful, equivocal, temporizing, unrevealing

nonconformist *or* **non-conformist** = <u>dissenter</u>, rebel, radical, protester, eccentric, maverick, heretic, individualist, iconoclast, dissentient OPPOSITE traditionalist

nondescript = <u>undistinguished</u>, ordinary, dull, commonplace, unremarkable, run-of-the-mill, uninspiring, indeterminate, uninteresting, featureless, insipid, unexceptional, common *or* garden (*informal*), mousy, characterless, unmemorable, vanilla (*informal*), nothing to write home about OPPOSITE distinctive

none 1 = <u>not any</u>, nothing, zero, not one, nil, no part, not a bit, zilch (*slang, chiefly U.S. & Canad.*), diddly (*U.S. slang*) ...*I turned to bookshops and libraries seeking information and found none...*
2 = <u>no-one</u>, nobody, not one ...*None of us knew what*

to say to her...

nonentity = <u>nobody</u>, lightweight (*informal*), mediocrity, cipher, small fry, unimportant person

nonetheless = <u>nevertheless</u>, however, yet, even so, despite that, in spite of that

non-event *or* **nonevent** = <u>flop</u> (*informal*), failure, disappointment, fiasco, dud (*informal*), washout, clunker (*informal*)

non-existent *or* **nonexistent** = <u>imaginary</u>, imagined, fancied, fictional, mythical, unreal, hypothetical, illusory, insubstantial, hallucinatory OPPOSITE real

nonplussed = <u>taken aback</u>, stunned, confused, embarrassed, puzzled, astonished, stumped, dismayed, baffled, bewildered, astounded, confounded, perplexed, disconcerted, mystified, fazed, dumbfounded, discomfited, flummoxed, discountenanced

nonsense 1 = <u>rubbish</u>, hot air (*informal*), waffle (*informal, chiefly Brit.*), twaddle, pants (*slang*), rot, crap (*slang*), garbage (*informal*), trash, bunk (*informal*), tosh (*slang, chiefly Brit.*), rhubarb, pap, foolishness, bilge (*informal*), drivel, tripe (*informal*), gibberish, guff (*slang*), bombast, moonshine, claptrap (*informal*), hogwash, hokum (*slang, chiefly U.S. & Canad.*), blather, double Dutch (*Brit. informal*), piffle (*informal*), poppycock (*informal*), balderdash, bosh (*informal*), eyewash (*informal*), stuff and nonsense, tommyrot, horsefeathers (*U.S. slang*), bunkum *or* buncombe (*chiefly U.S.*), bizzo (*Austral. slang*), bull's wool (*Austral. & N.Z. slang*) ...*Most orthodox doctors, however, dismiss this theory as complete nonsense...* OPPOSITE sense
2 = <u>idiocy</u>, folly, stupidity, absurdity, silliness, inanity, senselessness, ridiculousness, ludicrousness, fatuity ...*Surely it is an economic nonsense to deplete the world of natural resources...*

nonsensical = <u>senseless</u>, crazy, silly, ridiculous, absurd, foolish, ludicrous, meaningless, irrational, incomprehensible, inane, asinine, cockamamie (*slang, chiefly U.S.*)

non-starter *or* **nonstarter** = <u>dead loss</u>, dud (*informal*), washout (*informal*), no-hoper (*informal*), turkey (*informal*), lemon (*informal*), loser, waste of space *or* time

non-stop *or* **nonstop** ADJECTIVE = <u>continuous</u>, constant, relentless, uninterrupted, steady, endless, unbroken, interminable, incessant, unending, ceaseless, unremitting, unfaltering ...*The training was non-stop and continued for three days...* OPPOSITE occasional
ADVERB = <u>continuously</u>, constantly, steadily, endlessly, relentlessly, perpetually, incessantly, without stopping, ceaselessly, interminably, unremittingly, uninterruptedly, unendingly, unfalteringly, unbrokenly ...*The snow fell non-stop for 24 hours...*

nook = <u>niche</u>, corner, recess, cavity, crevice, alcove, cranny, inglenook (*Brit.*), cubbyhole, opening

noon NOUN = <u>midday</u>, high noon, noonday, noontime, twelve noon, noontide ...*The long day of meetings started at noon...*

ADJECTIVE = <u>midday</u>, noonday, noontime, noontide …*The noon sun was fierce*…

norm **NOUN** = <u>standard</u>, rule, model, pattern, mean, type, measure, average, par, criterion, benchmark, yardstick …*Their actions departed from what she called the commonly accepted norms of behaviour*… **PHRASES** **the norm** = <u>the rule</u>, the average, par for the course, the usual thing …*Families of six or seven were the norm in those days*…

normal 1 = <u>usual</u>, common, standard, average, natural, regular, ordinary, acknowledged, typical, conventional, routine, accustomed, habitual, run-of-the-mill …*The two countries have resumed normal diplomatic relations*… …*The hospital claimed they were simply following their normal procedure*… **OPPOSITE** unusual
2 = <u>sane</u>, reasonable, rational, lucid, well-adjusted, compos mentis (*Latin*), in your right mind, mentally sound, in possession of all your faculties …*Depressed patients are more likely to become ill than normal people*…

normality 1 = <u>regularity</u>, order, routine, ordinariness, naturalness, conventionality, usualness …*A semblance of normality has returned to the city after the attack*…
2 = <u>sanity</u>, reason, balance, rationality, lucidity …*Behind the smiling facade of normality lurked a psychopathic serial killer*…

normally 1 = <u>usually</u>, generally, commonly, regularly, typically, ordinarily, as a rule, habitually …*Normally, the transportation system in Paris carries 950,000 passengers a day*…
2 = <u>as usual</u>, naturally, properly, conventionally, in the usual way …*the failure of the blood to clot normally*…

normative = <u>standardizing</u>, controlling, regulating, prescriptive, normalizing, regularizing

Norse
➤ **mythology**

north **ADJECTIVE** = <u>northern</u>, polar, arctic, boreal, northerly …*On the north side of the mountain*… …*a bitterly cold north wind*…
ADVERB = <u>northward(s)</u>, in a northerly direction …*The hurricane which had destroyed Honolulu was moving north*…

North Star = <u>Pole Star</u>, Polaris, lodestar

nose **NOUN** = <u>snout</u>, bill, beak, hooter (*slang*), snitch (*slang*), conk (*slang*), neb (*archaic or dialect*), proboscis, schnozzle (*slang, chiefly U.S.*) …*She's got funny eyes and a big nose*…
VERB = <u>ease forward</u>, push, edge, shove, nudge …*The car nosed forward out of the drive*… …*Ben drove past them, nosing his car into the garage*…
PHRASES **poke** *or* **stick your nose into something** = <u>pry</u>, interfere, meddle, intrude, snoop (*informal*), be inquisitive …*We don't take kindly to strangers who poke their noses into our affairs*…

(*Related Words*)
adjectives: nasal, rhinal

nosedive **VERB** = <u>drop</u>, plunge, dive, plummet, fall sharply …*The value of the shares nosedived by £2.6*

billion… …*The cockpit was submerged as the plane nosedived into the water*…
NOUN = <u>plunge</u>, drop, dive, plummet, sharp fall …*My career has taken a nosedive in the past year or two*… …*The catamaran sailed over the precipice and plunged into a nosedive*…

nosh (*Slang*) **NOUN** 1 = <u>food</u>, eats (*slang*), fare, grub (*slang*), feed, tack (*informal*), scoff (*slang*), kai (*N.Z. informal*), chow (*informal*), sustenance, victuals, comestibles, nosebag (*slang*), vittles (*obsolete or dialect*), viands …*a restaurant which serves fine wines and posh nosh*…
2 = <u>meal</u>, repast …*We went for a nosh at our local Indian restaurant*…
VERB = <u>eat</u>, consume, scoff (*slang*), devour, feed on, munch, gobble, partake of, wolf down …*Guests mingled in the gardens, sipped wine, and noshed at cabaret tables*… …*sipping enormous bowls of frothy cappuccino and noshing huge slabs of carrot cake*…

nostalgia = <u>reminiscence</u>, longing, regret, pining, yearning, remembrance, homesickness, wistfulness

nostalgic = <u>sentimental</u>, longing, emotional, homesick, wistful, maudlin, regretful

notable **ADJECTIVE** 1 = <u>remarkable</u>, marked, striking, unusual, extraordinary, outstanding, evident, pronounced, memorable, noticeable, uncommon, conspicuous, salient, noteworthy …*The most notable architectural feature of the town is its castle*… **OPPOSITE** imperceptible
2 = <u>prominent</u>, famous, celebrated, distinguished, well-known, notorious, renowned, eminent, pre-eminent …*the notable occultist, Madame Blavatsky*… **OPPOSITE** unknown
NOUN = <u>celebrity</u>, worthy, big name, dignitary, luminary, celeb (*informal*), personage, megastar (*informal*), notability, V.I.P. …*The notables attending included five Senators, two Supreme Court judges and three State Governors*…

notably = <u>remarkably</u>, unusually, distinctly, extraordinarily, markedly, noticeably, strikingly, conspicuously, singularly, outstandingly, uncommonly, pre-eminently, signally …*a notably brave officer who had served under Wolfe at Quebec*…

notation 1 = <u>signs</u>, system, characters, code, symbols, script …*The dot in musical notation symbolizes an abrupt or staccato quality*…
2 = <u>note</u>, record, noting, jotting …*He was checking the readings and making notations on a clipboard*…

notch **NOUN** 1 = <u>level</u> (*Informal*), step, degree, grade, cut (*informal*) …*Average earnings in the economy moved up another notch in August*…
2 = <u>cut</u>, nick, incision, indentation, mark, score, cleft …*The blade had a hole through the middle and a notch on one side*…
VERB = <u>cut</u>, mark, score, nick, scratch, indent …*a bamboo walking stick with a notched handle*…

note **NOUN** 1 = <u>message</u>, letter, communication, memo, memorandum, epistle …*Stevens wrote him a note asking him to come to his apartment*…
2 = <u>record</u>, reminder, memo, memorandum, jotting,

minute ...*I made a note of his address...*

3 = annotation, comment, remark, gloss ...*See note 16 on page 223...*

4 = document, form, record, certificate ...*In the eyes of the law, signing a delivery note is seen as 'accepting' the goods...*

5 = symbol, mark, sign, indication, token ...*He has never been able to read or transcribe musical notes...*

6 = tone, touch, trace, hint, sound ...*I detected a note of bitterness in his voice...*

PLURAL NOUN = jottings, record, impressions, outline, report ...*I want to type up my notes from the meeting...*

VERB 1 = notice, see, observe, perceive ...*Suddenly I noted that the rain had stopped...*

2 = bear in mind, be aware, take into account ...*Please note that there are a limited number of tickets...*

3 = mention, record, mark, indicate, register, remark ...*The report noted a sharp drop in cases of sexually transmitted diseases...*

4 = write down, record, scribble, take down, set down, jot down, put in writing, put down in black and white ...*A policeman was noting the number plates of passing cars...*

PHRASES of note 1 = fame, prestige, eminence, renown, standing, character, reputation, consequence, celebrity ...*Besides being an artist of great note, he can also be a fascinating conversationalist...* **2** = importance, consequence, significance, distinction ...*She has published nothing of note in the last ten years...* ◆ **take note of something** *or* **someone** = notice, note, regard, observe, heed, pay attention to ...*Take note of the weather conditions...*

Musical notes and rests

British name	American name
breve	double-whole note
semibreve	whole note
minim	half note
crotchet	quarter note
quaver	eighth note
semiquaver	sixteenth note
demisemiquaver	thirty-second note
hemidemisemiquaver	sixty-fourth note

---

notebook = notepad, record book, exercise book, jotter, journal, diary, Filofax (*trademark*), memorandum book

noted = famous, celebrated, recognized, distinguished, well-known, prominent, notorious, acclaimed, notable, renowned, eminent, conspicuous, illustrious **OPPOSITE** unknown

noteworthy = remarkable, interesting, important, significant, extraordinary, outstanding, exceptional, notable **OPPOSITE** ordinary

nothing 1 = nought, zero, nil, naught, not a thing, zilch (*slang*), sod all (*slang*), damn all (*slang*), zip (*U.S. slang*) ...*I know nothing of these matters...*

2 = a trifle, no big deal, a mere bagatelle ...*'Thanks*

for all your help.''It was nothing.'...*

3 = nobody, cipher, nonentity ...*I went from being a complete nothing to all of a sudden having people calling me the new star of the Nineties...*

4 = void, emptiness, nothingness, nullity, nonexistence ...*philosophical ideas of the void, the nothing and the 'un-thought'...*

nothingness 1 = oblivion, nullity, nonexistence, nonbeing ...*There might be something beyond the grave, you know, and not just nothingness...*

2 = insignificance, triviality, worthlessness, meaninglessness, unimportance ...*the banal lyrics, clichéd song structures and light, fluffy nothingness of her latest album...*

notice VERB = observe, see, mind, note, spot, remark, distinguish, perceive, detect, heed, discern, behold (*archaic or literary*), mark, eyeball (*slang*) ...*People should not hesitate to contact the police if they notice anything suspicious...* **OPPOSITE** overlook

NOUN 1 = sign, advertisement, poster, placard, warning, bill ...*A few seaside guest houses had 'No Vacancies' notices in their windows...*

2 = notification, warning, advice, intimation, news, communication, intelligence, announcement, instruction, advance warning ...*Unions are requested to give seven days' notice of industrial action...*

3 = review, comment, criticism, evaluation, critique, critical assessment ...*She got some good notices for her performance last night...*

4 = attention, interest, note, regard, consideration, observation, scrutiny, heed, cognizance ...*Nothing that went on in the hospital escaped her notice...* **OPPOSITE** oversight

5 = the sack (*informal*), dismissal, discharge, the boot (*slang*), the push (*slang*), marching orders (*informal*), the (old) heave-ho (*informal*), your books *or* cards (*informal*) ...*They predicted that many teachers would be given their notice by the end of next term...*

noticeable = obvious, clear, striking, plain, bold, evident, distinct, manifest, conspicuous, unmistakable, salient, observable, perceptible, appreciable

notification = announcement, declaration, notice, statement, telling, information, warning, message, advice, intelligence, publication, notifying

notify = inform, tell, advise, alert to, announce, warn, acquaint with, make known to, apprise of

notion 1 = idea, view, opinion, belief, concept, impression, judgment, sentiment, conception, apprehension, inkling, mental image *or* picture, picture ...*I disagree with the notion that violence on TV causes acts of violence in society... ...He has a realistic notion of his capabilities...*

2 = whim, wish, desire, fancy, impulse, inclination, caprice ...*I had a whimsical notion to fly off to Rio that night...*

notional = hypothetical, ideal, abstract, theoretical, imaginary, speculative, conceptual, unreal, fanciful **OPPOSITE** actual

notoriety = infamy, discredit, disrepute, dishonour,

bad reputation, opprobrium, ill repute, obloquy

notorious = <u>infamous</u>, disreputable, opprobrious

notoriously = <u>infamously</u>, disreputably

notwithstanding PREPOSITION = <u>despite</u>, in spite of, regardless of …*He despised Pitt, notwithstanding the similar views they both held…*
ADVERB = <u>nevertheless</u>, however, though, nonetheless …*He doesn't want me there, but I'm going, notwithstanding…*

nought or (*Archaic or literary*) **naught** 1 = <u>zero</u>, nothing, nil …*Properties are graded from nought to ten for energy efficiency…*
2 = <u>nothing</u>, zip (*U.S. slang*), slang, nothingness, nada, zilch, sod all (*slang*), damn all (*slang*) …*All our efforts came to nought…*

nourish 1 = <u>feed</u>, supply, sustain, nurture …*The food the mother eats nourishes both her and her baby…*
2 = <u>encourage</u>, support, maintain, promote, sustain, foster, cultivate …*This attitude has been carefully nourished by a small group of journalists and scholars…*

nourishing = <u>nutritious</u>, beneficial, wholesome, healthful, health-giving, nutritive

nourishment = <u>food</u>, nutrition, sustenance, nutriment, tack (*informal*), kai (*N.Z. informal*), victuals, vittles (*obsolete or dialect*)

novel[1] = <u>story</u>, tale, fiction, romance, narrative …*He had all but finished writing a first novel…*

novel[2] = <u>new</u>, different, original, fresh, unusual, innovative, uncommon, singular, ground-breaking, left-field (*informal*) …*Staging your own murder mystery party is a novel way to entertain a group of friends…* OPPOSITE ordinary

novelist = <u>author</u>, writer
➤ WORD POWER SUPPLEMENT novelists

novelty 1 = <u>newness</u>, originality, freshness, innovation, surprise, uniqueness, strangeness, unfamiliarity …*The radical puritanism of Conceptual art and Minimalism had lost its novelty…*
2 = <u>curiosity</u>, marvel, rarity, oddity, wonder …*In those days a motor car was still a novelty…*
3 = <u>trinket</u>, souvenir, memento, bauble, bagatelle, gimcrack, trifle, gewgaw, knick-knack …*At Easter, we give them plastic eggs filled with small toys, novelties and coins…*

novice 1 = <u>beginner</u>, pupil, amateur, newcomer, trainee, apprentice, learner, neophyte, tyro, probationer, proselyte …*I'm a novice at these things. You're the professional…* OPPOSITE expert
2 = <u>novitiate</u> …*She had entered the monastery as a novice many months previously…*

now ADVERB 1 = <u>nowadays</u>, at the moment, these days …*Beef now costs over 30 roubles a pound…*
2 = <u>immediately</u>, presently (*Scot. & U.S.*), promptly, instantly, at once, straightaway …*Please tell him I need to talk to him now…*
PHRASES **now and then** or **again** = <u>occasionally</u>, sometimes, at times, from time to time, on and off, on occasion, once in a while, intermittently, infrequently, sporadically …*Now and then he would pay us a brief visit…*

nowadays = <u>now</u>, today, at the moment, these days, in this day and age

noxious = <u>harmful</u>, deadly, poisonous, unhealthy, hurtful, pernicious, injurious, unwholesome, noisome, pestilential, insalubrious, foul OPPOSITE harmless

nuance = <u>subtlety</u>, degree, distinction, graduation, refinement, nicety, gradation

nub = <u>gist</u>, point, heart, core, essence, nucleus, kernel, crux, pith

nubile = <u>attractive</u>, sexy (*informal*), desirable, ripe (*informal*), marriageable

nucleus = <u>centre</u>, heart, focus, basis, core, pivot, kernel, nub

nude = <u>naked</u>, stripped, exposed, bare, uncovered, undressed, stark-naked, in the raw (*informal*), disrobed, starkers (*informal*), unclothed, in the buff (*informal*), au naturel (*French*), in the altogether (*informal*), buck naked (*slang*), unclad, undraped, in your birthday suit (*informal*), scuddy (*slang*), without a stitch on (*informal*), in the bare scud (*slang*), naked as the day you were born (*informal*) OPPOSITE dressed

nudge VERB 1 = <u>push</u>, touch, dig, jog, prod, elbow, shove, poke …*'Stop it,' he said, and nudged me in the ribs…*
2 = <u>prompt</u>, influence, urge, persuade, spur, prod, coax, prevail upon …*Bit by bit Bob nudged Fritz into selling his controlling interest…*
NOUN 1 = <u>push</u>, touch, dig, elbow, bump, shove, poke, jog, prod …*She slipped her arm under his and gave him a nudge…*
2 = <u>prompting</u>, push, encouragement, prod …*The challenge appealed to him. All he needed was a little nudge…*

nudity = <u>nakedness</u>, undress, nudism, bareness, deshabille

nugget = <u>lump</u>, piece, mass, chunk, clump, hunk

nuisance = <u>trouble</u>, problem, trial, bore, drag (*informal*), bother, plague, pest, irritation, hassle (*informal*), inconvenience, annoyance, pain (*informal*), pain in the neck (*informal*), pain in the backside (*informal*), pain in the butt (*informal*) OPPOSITE benefit

null
PHRASES **null and void** = <u>invalid</u>, useless, void, worthless, ineffectual, valueless, inoperative

nullify = <u>invalidate</u>, quash, revoke, render null and void, abolish, void, repeal, rescind, annul, abrogate OPPOSITE validate

numb ADJECTIVE 1 = <u>unfeeling</u>, dead, frozen, paralysed, insensitive, deadened, immobilized, torpid, insensible …*His legs felt numb and his toes ached…* OPPOSITE sensitive
2 = <u>stupefied</u>, deadened, unfeeling, insensible …*The mother, numb with grief, had trouble speaking…*
VERB 1 = <u>stun</u>, knock out, paralyse, daze, stupefy …*For a while the shock of his letter numbed her…*
2 = <u>deaden</u>, freeze, dull, paralyse, immobilize, benumb …*The cold numbed my fingers…*

number NOUN 1 = <u>numeral</u>, figure, character, digit, integer ...*None of the doors have numbers on them...*
2 = <u>amount</u>, quantity, collection, total, count, sum, aggregate ...*I have had an enormous number of letters from concerned parents...* OPPOSITE shortage
3 = <u>crowd</u>, horde, multitude, throng ...*People turned out to vote in huge numbers...*
4 = <u>group</u>, company, set, band, crowd, gang, coterie ...*We had a stag night for one of our number who had decided to get married...*
5 = <u>issue</u>, copy, edition, imprint, printing ...*an article which appeared in the summer number of the magazine...*
VERB 1 = <u>amount to</u>, come to, total, add up to ...*They told me that their village numbered 100 or so...*
2 = <u>calculate</u>, account, reckon, compute, enumerate ...*One widely cited report numbered the dead at over 10,000...* OPPOSITE guess
3 = <u>include</u>, count ...*He numbered several Americans among his friends...*

numbered 1 = <u>reckoned</u>, totalled, counted ...*The Liberian army is officially numbered at eight thousand strong...*
2 = <u>limited</u>, restricted, limited in number ...*Her days as leader are numbered...*

numbness 1 = <u>deadness</u>, paralysis, insensitivity, dullness, torpor, insensibility ...*I have recently been suffering from numbness in my fingers and toes...*
2 = <u>torpor</u>, deadness, dullness, stupefaction ...*She swung from emotional numbness to overwhelming fear and back again...*

numeral = <u>number</u>, figure, digit, character, symbol, cipher, integer

numerous = <u>many</u>, several, countless, lots, abundant, plentiful, innumerable, copious, manifold, umpteen (*informal*), profuse, thick on the ground OPPOSITE few

nuptial ADJECTIVE = <u>marital</u>, wedding, wedded, bridal, matrimonial, conjugal, connubial, hymeneal (*poetic*) ...*He had referred to the room as the nuptial chamber...*
PLURAL NOUN = <u>wedding</u>, marriage, matrimony, espousal (*archaic*) ...*couples who never go near a church but insist on their nuptials being celebrated with a traditional church ceremony...*

nurse 1 = <u>look after</u>, treat, tend, care for, take care of, minister to ...*All the years he was sick my mother had nursed him...*
2 = <u>harbour</u>, have, maintain, preserve, entertain, cherish, keep alive ...*He nursed an ambition to lead his own orchestra...*
3 = <u>breast-feed</u>, feed, nurture, nourish, suckle, wet-nurse ...*She did not have enough milk to nurse the infant...*

nursery = <u>crèche</u>, kindergarten, playgroup

nurture VERB 1 = <u>bring up</u>, raise, look after, rear, care for, develop ...*Parents want to know the best way to nurture and raise their children to adulthood...* OPPOSITE neglect
2 = <u>tend</u>, grow, cultivate ...*The modern conservatory is not an environment for nurturing plants...*
NOUN = <u>upbringing</u>, training, education, instruction, rearing, development ...*The human organism learns partly by nature, partly by nurture...*

nut NOUN 1 = <u>kernel</u>, stone, seed, pip ...*Nuts are a good source of vitamin E...*
2 (*Slang*) = <u>madman</u>, eccentric, flake (*slang, chiefly U.S.*), psycho (*slang*), crank (*informal*), lunatic, maniac, loony (*slang*), nutter (*Brit. slang*), oddball (*informal*), crackpot (*informal*), wacko (*slang*), nutcase (*slang*), headcase (*informal*) ...*Some nut with a gun walked in and just opened fire on the diners...*
3 (*Slang*) = <u>head</u>, skull, noggin ...*He took a bottle and smashed me over the nut...*
PHRASES **nuts and bolts** = <u>essentials</u>, basics, fundamentals, nitty-gritty (*informal*), practicalities, ins and outs, details ...*Social skills are the nuts and bolts of social interaction...*

nutrition = <u>food</u>, nourishment, sustenance, nutriment

nutritious = <u>nourishing</u>, beneficial, wholesome, healthful, health-giving, nutritive

nuts (*Slang*) = <u>insane</u>, mad, crazy (*informal*), bananas (*slang*), barking (*slang*), eccentric, batty (*slang*), psycho (*slang*), irrational, loony (*slang*), demented, nutty (*slang*), deranged, loopy (*informal*), out to lunch (*informal*), barking mad (*slang*), gonzo (*slang*), doolally (*slang*), off your trolley (*slang*), up the pole (*informal*), as daft as a brush (*informal, chiefly Brit.*), not the full shilling (*informal*), wacko or whacko (*informal*), off the air (*Austral. slang*)

nuzzle = <u>snuggle</u>, cuddle, nudge, burrow, nestle

nymph 1 = <u>sylph</u>, dryad, naiad, hamadryad, Oceanid (*Greek myth*), oread ...*In the depths of a river, the three water nymphs – the Rhinemaidens – play and sing...*
2 = <u>girl</u>, lass, maiden, maid, damsel ...*They had one daughter, an exquisite nymph named Jacqueline...*

O o

oasis 1 = <u>watering hole</u> …*The province was largely a wasteland with an occasional oasis…*
2 = <u>haven</u>, retreat, refuge, sanctuary, island, resting place, sanctum …*an oasis of peace in a troubled world…*

oath 1 = <u>promise</u>, bond, pledge, vow, word, compact, covenant, affirmation, sworn statement, avowal, word of honour …*a solemn oath by members to help each other…*
2 = <u>swear word</u>, curse, obscenity, blasphemy, expletive, four-letter word, cuss (*informal*), profanity, strong language, imprecation, malediction …*Weller let out a foul oath and hurled himself upon him…*

obedience = <u>compliance</u>, yielding, submission, respect, conformity, reverence, deference, observance, subservience, submissiveness, docility, complaisance, tractability, dutifulness, conformability OPPOSITE> disobedience

obedient = <u>submissive</u>, yielding, compliant, under control, respectful, law-abiding, well-trained, amenable, docile, dutiful, subservient, deferential, tractable, acquiescent, biddable, accommodating, passive, meek, ingratiating, malleable, pliant, unresisting, bootlicking (*informal*), obeisant, duteous OPPOSITE> disobedient

obese = <u>fat</u>, overweight, heavy, solid, gross, plump, stout, fleshy, beefy (*informal*), tubby, portly, outsize, roly-poly, rotund, podgy, corpulent, elephantine, paunchy, well-upholstered (*informal*), Falstaffian OPPOSITE> thin

obesity = <u>fatness</u>, flab, heaviness, a weight problem, grossness, corpulence, beef (*informal*), embonpoint (*French*), rotundity, fleshiness, stoutness, portliness, bulkiness, podginess, tubbiness OPPOSITE> thinness

obey 1 = <u>submit to</u>, surrender (to), give way to, succumb to, bow to, give in to, yield to, serve, cave in to (*informal*), take orders from, do what you are told by …*Cissie obeyed her mother without question…* OPPOSITE> disobey
2 = <u>submit</u>, yield, surrender, give in, give way, succumb, cave in, toe the line, knuckle under (*informal*), do what is expected, come to heel, get into line …*If you love me you will obey…*
3 = <u>carry out</u>, follow, perform, respond to, implement, fulfil, execute, discharge, act upon, carry through …*The commander refused to obey an order…* OPPOSITE> disregard
4 = <u>abide by</u>, keep, follow, comply with, observe, mind, embrace, hold to, heed, conform to, keep to, adhere to, be ruled by …*Most people obey the law…*

object[1] 1 = <u>thing</u>, article, device, body, item, implement, entity, gadget, contrivance …*an object the shape of a coconut…*
2 = <u>purpose</u>, aim, end, point, plan, idea, reason, goal, design, target, principle, function, intention, objective, intent, motive, end in view, end purpose, the why and wherefore …*The object of the exercise is to raise money for charity…*
3 = <u>target</u>, victim, focus, butt, recipient …*She was an object of pity among her friends…*

object[2] 1 with *to* = <u>protest against</u>, oppose, say no to, kick against (*informal*), argue against, draw the line at, take exception to, raise objections to, cry out against, complain against, take up the cudgels against, expostulate against …*A lot of people objected to the plan…* OPPOSITE> accept
2 = <u>disagree</u>, demur, remonstrate, expostulate, express disapproval …*We objected strongly…* OPPOSITE> agree

objection = <u>protest</u>, opposition, complaint, doubt, exception, dissent, outcry, censure, disapproval, niggle (*informal*), protestation, scruple, demur, formal complaint, counter-argument, cavil, remonstrance, demurral OPPOSITE> agreement

objectionable = <u>offensive</u>, annoying, irritating, unacceptable, unpleasant, rude, intolerable, undesirable, distasteful, obnoxious, deplorable, displeasing, unseemly, disagreeable, repugnant, abhorrent, beyond the pale, insufferable, detestable, discourteous, uncivil, unmannerly, exceptionable, dislikable *or* dislikeable OPPOSITE> pleasant

objective NOUN = <u>purpose</u>, aim, goal, end, plan, hope, idea, design, target, wish, scheme, desire, object, intention, ambition, aspiration, Holy Grail (*informal*), end in view, why and wherefore …*His objective was to play golf and win…*
ADJECTIVE 1 = <u>factual</u>, real, circumstantial …*He has no objective evidence to support his claim…*
2 = <u>unbiased</u>, detached, just, fair, judicial, open-minded, equitable, impartial, impersonal, disinterested, even-handed, dispassionate, unemotional, uninvolved, unprejudiced, uncoloured …*I would like your objective opinion on this…* OPPOSITE> subjective

objectively = <u>impartially</u>, neutrally, fairly, justly, without prejudice, dispassionately, with an open mind, equitably, without fear or favour, even-handedly, without bias, disinterestedly, with objectivity *or* impartiality

objectivity = <u>impartiality</u>, detachment, neutrality, equity, fairness, disinterest, open-mindedness, even-handedness, impersonality, disinterestedness, dispassion, nonpartisanship, lack of bias, equitableness OPPOSITE> subjectivity

obligation NOUN 1 = <u>duty</u>, compulsion …*Students usually feel an obligation to attend lectures…*
2 = <u>task</u>, job, duty, work, calling, business, charge, role, function, mission, province, assignment, pigeon

(*informal*), chore ...*I feel that's my obligation, to do whatever is possible*...

3 = responsibility, duty, liability, accountability, culpability, answerability, accountableness ...*I have an ethical and moral obligation to my client*...

4 = contract, promise, agreement, understanding, bond, debt, commitment, engagement ...*The companies failed to meet their obligation to plant new trees*...

PHRASES **under an obligation** = in (someone's) debt, indebted, obliged, grateful, thankful, obligated, beholden, duty-bound, honour-bound, owing a favour ...*I'd rather not be under any obligation to him*...

obligatory **1** = compulsory, required, necessary, essential, binding, enforced, mandatory, imperative, unavoidable, requisite, coercive, de rigueur (*French*) ...*Third-party insurance is obligatory when driving in Italy*... OPPOSITE optional

2 = customary, regular, usual, popular, normal, familiar, conventional, fashionable, bog-standard (*Brit. & Irish slang*) ...*This hotel has every facility, including the obligatory swimming-pool*...

oblige **1** = compel, make, force, require, bind, railroad (*Informal*), constrain, necessitate, coerce, impel, dragoon, obligate ...*This decree obliges unions to delay strikes*...

2 = help, assist, serve, benefit, please, favour, humour, accommodate, indulge, gratify, do someone a service, put yourself out for, do (someone) a favour *or* a kindness, meet the wants *or* needs of ...*He is always ready to oblige journalists with information*... OPPOSITE bother

obliged **1** = forced, required, bound, compelled, obligated, duty-bound, under an obligation, under compulsion, without any option ...*I was obliged to answer their questions*...

2 = grateful, in (someone's) debt, thankful, indebted, appreciative, beholden ...*I am extremely obliged to you*...

obliging = accommodating, kind, helpful, willing, civil, friendly, polite, cooperative, agreeable, amiable, courteous, considerate, hospitable, unselfish, good-natured, eager to please, complaisant OPPOSITE unhelpful

oblique **1** = indirect, implied, roundabout, backhanded, evasive, elliptical, circuitous, circumlocutory, inexplicit, periphrastic ...*It was an oblique reference to his time in prison*... OPPOSITE direct

2 = slanting, angled, sloped, sloping, inclined, tilted, tilting, slanted, diagonal, at an angle, asymmetrical, canted, aslant, slantwise, atilt, cater-cornered (*U.S. informal*) ...*The mountain ridge runs at an oblique angle to the coastline*...

3 = sidelong, sideways, covert, indirect, furtive, surreptitious ...*She gave him an oblique glance*...

obliquely **1** = indirectly, evasively, not in so many words, circuitously, in a roundabout manner *or* way ...*He referred obliquely to a sordid event in her past*...

2 = at an angle, sideways, diagonally, sidelong, aslant, slantwise, aslope ...*The muscle runs obliquely downwards inside the abdominal cavity*...

obliterate **1** = destroy, eliminate, devastate, waste, wreck, wipe out, demolish, ravage, eradicate, desolate, annihilate, put paid to, raze, blow to bits, extirpate, blow sky-high, destroy root and branch, wipe from *or* off the face of the earth ...*Whole villages were obliterated by the fire*... OPPOSITE create

2 = eradicate, remove, eliminate, cancel, get rid of, wipe out, erase, excise, delete, extinguish, root out, efface, blot out, expunge, extirpate ...*He drank to obliterate the memory of what had occurred*...

oblivion **1** = unconsciousness, forgetfulness, senselessness, obliviousness, unawareness, insensibility, (waters of) Lethe ...*He drank himself into oblivion*... OPPOSITE consciousness

2 = neglect, anonymity, insignificance, obscurity, limbo, nothingness, unimportance ...*Most of these performers will fail and sink into oblivion*...

3 = extinction, annihilation, eradication, obliteration ...*An entire section of the town was bombed into oblivion*...

oblivious *usually with* **to** *or* **of** = unaware, unconscious, ignorant, regardless, careless, negligent, blind to, unaffected by, impervious to, forgetful, deaf to, unconcerned about, neglectful, heedless, inattentive, insensible, unmindful, unobservant, disregardful, incognizant OPPOSITE aware

---

Word Power

oblivious – It was formerly considered incorrect to use *oblivious* and *unaware* as synonyms, but this use is now acceptable. When employed with this meaning, *oblivious* should be followed either by *to* or *of*, *to* being much the commoner.

---

obnoxious = loathsome, offensive, nasty, foul, disgusting, unpleasant, revolting, obscene, sickening, vile, horrid, repellent, repulsive, objectionable, disagreeable, nauseating, odious, hateful, repugnant, reprehensible, abhorrent, abominable, insufferable, execrable, detestable, hateable, dislikable *or* dislikeable, yucky *or* yukky (*slang*), yucko (*Austral. slang*) OPPOSITE pleasant

obscene **1** = indecent, dirty, offensive, gross, foul, coarse, filthy, vile, improper, immoral, pornographic, suggestive, blue, loose, shameless, lewd, depraved, X-rated (*informal*), bawdy, salacious, prurient, impure, lascivious, smutty, ribald, unwholesome, scabrous, immodest, licentious, indelicate, unchaste ...*I'm no prude, but I think these photos are obscene*... OPPOSITE decent

2 = offensive, shocking, evil, disgusting, outrageous, revolting, sickening, vile, wicked, repellent, atrocious, obnoxious, heinous, nauseating, odious, loathsome, abominable, detestable ...*It was obscene to spend millions producing unwanted food*...

obscenity **1** = indecency, pornography, impurity, impropriety, vulgarity, smut, prurience, coarseness, crudity, licentiousness, foulness, outrageousness, blueness, immodesty, suggestiveness, lewdness, dirtiness, grossness, vileness, filthiness, bawdiness, unseemliness, indelicacy, smuttiness, salacity …*He justified the use of obscenity on the grounds that it was art*… OPPOSITE decency

2 = swear word, curse, oath, expletive, four-letter word, cuss (*informal*), profanity, vulgarism …*They shouted obscenities at us as we passed*…

3 = atrocity, wrong, horror, offence, evil, outrage, cruelty, brutality, abomination, barbarity, vileness …*the obscenities of civil war*…

obscure ADJECTIVE **1** = unknown, minor, little-known, humble, unfamiliar, out-of-the-way, unseen, lowly, unimportant, unheard-of, unsung, nameless, undistinguished, inconspicuous, unnoted, unhonoured, unrenowned …*The hymn was written by an obscure Greek composer*… OPPOSITE famous

2 = abstruse, involved, complex, confusing, puzzling, subtle, mysterious, deep, vague, unclear, doubtful, mystical, intricate, ambiguous, enigmatic, esoteric, perplexing, occult, opaque, incomprehensible, arcane, cryptic, unfathomable, recondite, clear as mud (*informal*) …*The contract is written in obscure language*… OPPOSITE straightforward

3 = unclear, hidden, uncertain, confused, mysterious, concealed, doubtful, indefinite, indeterminate …*The word is of obscure origin*… OPPOSITE well-known

4 = indistinct, vague, blurred, dark, clouded, faint, dim, gloomy, veiled, murky, fuzzy, shadowy, cloudy, misty, hazy, indistinguishable, indeterminate, dusky, undefined, out of focus, ill-defined, obfuscated, indiscernible, tenebrous …*The hills were just an obscure shape in the mist*… OPPOSITE clear

VERB **1** = obstruct, hinder, block out …*Trees obscured his vision*…

2 = hide, cover (up), screen, mask, disguise, conceal, veil, cloak, shroud, camouflage, envelop, encase, enshroud …*The building is almost completely obscured by a huge banner*… OPPOSITE expose

3 = obfuscate, confuse, cloud, blur, muddy, darken, muddy the waters of, adumbrate, befog, throw a veil over, bedim …*the jargon that frequently obscures legal documents*… OPPOSITE clarify

obscurity **1** = insignificance, oblivion, unimportance, non-recognition, inconsequence, lowliness, inconspicuousness, namelessness, ingloriousness …*His later life was spent in obscurity and loneliness*…

2 = vagueness, complexity, ambiguity, intricacy, incomprehensibility, inexactitude, woolliness, abstruseness, impreciseness, impenetrableness, reconditeness, lack of preciseness …*Hunt was irritated by the obscurity of his reply*… OPPOSITE clarity

3 = darkness, dark, shadows, shade, gloom, haze, blackness, murk, dimness, murkiness, haziness, duskiness, shadiness, shadowiness, indistinctness …*the vast branches vanished into deep indigo obscurity above my head*…

observable = noticeable, clear, obvious, open, striking, apparent, visible, patent, evident, distinct, manifest, blatant, conspicuous, unmistakable, discernible, salient, recognizable, detectable, perceptible, appreciable, perceivable

observance **1** = carrying out of, attention to, performance of, respect for, notice of, honouring of, observation of, compliance with, adherence to, fulfilment of, discharge of, obedience to, keeping of, heeding of, conformity to …*Councils should ensure strict observance of laws*… OPPOSITE disregard for

2 = ceremony, rite, procedure, service, form, act, practice, tradition, celebration, custom, ritual, formality, ceremonial, ordinance, liturgy …*Numerous religious observances set the rhythm of the day*…

observant **1** = attentive, quick, alert, perceptive, concentrating, careful, vigilant, mindful, watchful, wide-awake, sharp-eyed, eagle-eyed, keen-eyed, on your toes, heedful …*An observant doctor can detect depression from expression and posture*… OPPOSITE unobservant

2 = devout, godly, holy, orthodox, pious, obedient, reverent …*This is a profoundly observant Islamic country*…

observation **1** = watching, study, survey, review, notice, investigation, monitoring, attention, consideration, examination, inspection, scrutiny, surveillance, contemplation, cognition, perusal …*careful observation of the movement of the planets*…

2 = comment, finding, thought, note, statement, opinion, remark, explanation, reflection, exposition, utterance, pronouncement, annotation, elucidation, obiter dictum …*This book contains observations about the nature of addiction*…

3 = remark, thought, comment, statement, opinion, reflection, assertion, utterance, animadversion …*Is that a criticism or just an observation?*…

4 = observance of, attention to, compliance with, notice of, honouring of, adherence to, fulfilment of, discharge of, heeding of, carrying out of …*strict observation of oil quotas*…

observe **1** = watch, study, view, look at, note, check, regard, survey, monitor, contemplate, check out (*informal*), look on, keep an eye on (*informal*), gaze at, pay attention to, keep track of, scrutinize, keep tabs on (*informal*), recce (*slang*), keep under observation, watch like a hawk, take a dekko at (*Brit. slang*) …*He studies and observes the behaviour of babies*…

2 = notice, see, note, mark, discover, spot, regard, witness, clock (*Brit. slang*), distinguish, perceive, detect, discern, behold (*archaic or literary*), eye, eyeball (*slang*), peer at, espy, get a load of (*informal*) …*In 1664 Hooke observed a reddish spot on the surface of the planet*…

3 = remark, say, comment, state, note, reflect, mention, declare, opine, pass comment, animadvert …*'I like your hair that way,' he observed*…

4 = comply with, keep, follow, mind, respect, perform, carry out, honour, fulfil, discharge, obey, heed, conform to, adhere to, abide by …*Forcing motorists to observe speed restrictions is difficult*… OPPOSITE disregard

5 = celebrate, keep, commemorate, mark, remember, participate in, solemnize ...*We are observing Christmas quietly this year...*

observer 1 = <u>witness</u>, viewer, spectator, looker-on, watcher, onlooker, eyewitness, bystander, spotter, fly on the wall, beholder ...*A casual observer would have assumed they were lovers...*
2 = <u>commentator</u>, commenter, reporter, special correspondent ...*Political observers believe there may be a general election soon...*
3 = <u>monitor</u>, inspector, watchdog, supervisor, overseer, scrutineer ...*A UN observer should attend the conference...*

obsess = <u>preoccupy</u>, dominate, grip, absorb, possess, consume, rule, haunt, plague, hound, torment, bedevil, monopolize, be on your mind, engross, prey on your mind, be uppermost in your thoughts

obsessed = <u>absorbed</u>, absorbed, dominated, gripped, caught up, haunted, distracted, hung up (*slang*), preoccupied, immersed, beset, in the grip, infatuated, fixated, having a one-track mind |OPPOSITE> indifferent

obsession = <u>preoccupation</u>, thing (*informal*), complex, enthusiasm, addiction, hang-up (*informal*), mania, phobia, fetish, fixation, infatuation, ruling passion, pet subject, hobbyhorse, idée fixe (*French*), bee in your bonnet (*informal*)

obsessive = <u>compulsive</u>, fixed, gripping, consuming, haunting, tormenting, irresistible, neurotic, besetting, uncontrollable, obsessional

obsolete = <u>outdated</u>, old, passé, ancient, antique, old-fashioned, dated, discarded, extinct, past it, out of date, archaic, disused, out of fashion, out, antiquated, anachronistic, outmoded, musty, old hat, behind the times, superannuated, antediluvian, outworn, démodé (*French*), out of the ark (*informal*), vieux jeu (*French*) |OPPOSITE> up-to-date

obstacle 1 = <u>obstruction</u>, block, barrier, hurdle, hazard, snag, impediment, blockage, hindrance ...*She had to navigate her way round trolleys and other obstacles...*
2 = <u>hindrance</u>, check, bar, block, difficulty, barrier, handicap, hurdle, hitch, drawback, snag, deterrent, uphill (*S. African*), obstruction, stumbling block, impediment ...*Overcrowding remains a large obstacle to improving conditions...* |OPPOSITE> help

obstinacy = <u>stubbornness</u>, persistence, tenacity, perseverance, resolution, intransigence, firmness, single-mindedness, inflexibility, obduracy, doggedness, relentlessness, wilfulness, resoluteness, pig-headedness, pertinacity, tenaciousness, mulishness |OPPOSITE> flexibility

obstinate = <u>stubborn</u>, dogged, determined, persistent, firm, perverse, intractable, inflexible, wilful, tenacious, recalcitrant, steadfast, unyielding, opinionated, intransigent, immovable, headstrong, unmanageable, cussed, strong-minded, unbending, obdurate, stiff-necked, unshakable, self-willed, refractory, pig-headed, bull-headed, mulish, contumacious, pertinacious |OPPOSITE> flexible

obstruct 1 = <u>block</u>, close, bar, cut off, plug, choke, clog, barricade, shut off, stop up, bung up (*informal*) ...*Lorries obstructed the road completely...*
2 = <u>hold up</u>, stop, check, bar, block, prevent, arrest, restrict, interrupt, slow down, hamstring, interfere with, hamper, inhibit, clog, hinder, retard, impede, get in the way of, bring to a standstill, cumber ...*Drivers who park illegally obstruct the flow of traffic...*
3 = <u>impede</u>, prevent, frustrate, hold up, slow down, hamstring, interfere with, hamper, hold back, thwart, hinder, retard, get in the way of, trammel, cumber ...*The authorities are obstructing the investigation...* |OPPOSITE> help
4 = <u>obscure</u>, screen, cut off, cover, hide, mask, shield ...*She positioned herself so as not to obstruct his view...*

obstruction 1 = <u>obstacle</u>, bar, block, difficulty, barrier, hazard, barricade, snag, impediment, hindrance ...*drivers parking near his house and causing an obstruction...*
2 = <u>blockage</u>, stoppage, occlusion ...*The boy was suffering from a bowel obstruction...*
3 = <u>hindrance</u>, stop, check, bar, block, difficulty, barrier, restriction, handicap, obstacle, restraint, deterrent, stumbling block, impediment, trammel ...*Americans viewed the army as an obstruction to legitimate economic development...* |OPPOSITE> help

obstructive = <u>unhelpful</u>, difficult, awkward, blocking, delaying, contrary, stalling, inhibiting, restrictive, hindering, uncooperative, disobliging, unaccommodating |OPPOSITE> helpful

obtain 1 = <u>get</u>, gain, acquire, land, net, pick up, bag, secure, get hold of, come by, procure, get your hands on, score (*slang*), come into possession of ...*Evans was trying to obtain a false passport...* |OPPOSITE> lose
2 = <u>achieve</u>, get, gain, realize, accomplish, attain ...*The perfect body has always been difficult to obtain...*
3 (*Formal*) = <u>prevail</u>, hold, stand, exist, be the case, abound, predominate, be in force, be current, be prevalent ...*The longer this situation obtains, the bigger the problems will be...*

obtainable 1 = <u>available</u>, to be had, procurable ...*This herb is obtainable from health food shops...*
2 = <u>attainable</u>, accessible, achievable, at your fingertips, at your disposal, reachable, realizable, gettable, accomplishable ...*That's new information that isn't obtainable by other means...*

obtuse = <u>stupid</u>, simple, slow, thick, dull, dim, dense, dumb (*informal*), sluggish, retarded, simple-minded, dozy (*Brit. informal*), witless, stolid, dopey (*informal*), moronic, brainless, uncomprehending, cretinous, unintelligent, half-witted, slow on the uptake (*informal*), braindead (*informal*), dumb-ass (*informal*), doltish, dead from the neck up (*informal*), boneheaded (*slang*), thickheaded, dull-witted, imperceptive, slow-witted, muttonheaded (*slang*), thick as mince (*Scot. informal*), woodenheaded (*informal*) |OPPOSITE> clever

obviate (*Formal*) = <u>avert</u>, avoid, remove, prevent, counter, do away with, preclude, counteract, ward off, stave off, forestall, render unnecessary

obvious = clear, open, plain, apparent, visible, bold, patent, evident, distinct, pronounced, straightforward, explicit, manifest, transparent, noticeable, blatant, conspicuous, overt, unmistakable, palpable, unequivocal, undeniable, salient, recognizable, unambiguous, self-evident, indisputable, perceptible, much in evidence, unquestionable, open-and-shut, cut-and-dried (*informal*), undisguised, incontrovertible, self-explanatory, unsubtle, unconcealed, clear as a bell, staring you in the face (*informal*), right under your nose (*informal*), sticking out a mile (*informal*), plain as the nose on your face (*informal*) OPPOSITE unclear

obviously 1 = clearly, of course, certainly, needless to say, without doubt, assuredly ...*There are obviously exceptions to this...*
2 = plainly, patently, undoubtedly, evidently, manifestly, markedly, without doubt, unquestionably, undeniably, beyond doubt, palpably, indubitably, incontrovertibly, irrefutably, incontestably ...*She's obviously cleverer than I am...*

occasion NOUN 1 = time, moment, point, stage, incident, instance, occurrence, juncture ...*I often think fondly of an occasion some years ago...*
2 = function, event, affair, do (*informal*), happening, experience, gathering, celebration, occurrence, social occasion ...*It will be a unique family occasion...*
3 = opportunity, chance, time, opening, window ...*It is always an occasion for setting out government policy...*
4 = reason, cause, call, ground(s), basis, excuse, incentive, motive, warrant, justification, provocation, inducement ...*You had no occasion to speak to him like that...*
VERB (*Formal*) = cause, begin, produce, create, effect, lead to, inspire, result in, generate, prompt, provoke, induce, bring about, originate, evoke, give rise to, precipitate, elicit, incite, engender ...*The incident occasioned a full-scale parliamentary row...*

occasional = infrequent, odd, rare, casual, irregular, sporadic, intermittent, few and far between, desultory, periodic OPPOSITE constant

occasionally = sometimes, at times, from time to time, on and off, now and then, irregularly, on occasion, now and again, periodically, once in a while, every so often, at intervals, off and on, (every) now and then OPPOSITE constantly

occult NOUN = magic, witchcraft, sorcery, wizardry, enchantment, occultism, black art, necromancy, theurgy ...*his unhealthy fascination with the occult...*
ADJECTIVE = supernatural, dark, magical, mysterious, psychic, mystical, mystic, unearthly, unnatural, esoteric, uncanny, arcane, paranormal, abstruse, recondite, preternatural, cabbalistic, supranatural ...*organizations which campaign against paganism and occult practices...*

occultism = black magic, magic, witchcraft, wizardry, sorcery, the black arts, necromancy, diabolism, theurgy, supernaturalism

occupancy = occupation, use, residence, holding, term, possession, tenure, tenancy, habitation, inhabitancy

occupant = occupier, resident, tenant, user, holder, inmate, inhabitant, incumbent, dweller, denizen, addressee, lessee, indweller

occupation 1 = job, work, calling, business, line (of work), office, trade, position, post, career, situation, activity, employment, craft, profession, pursuit, vocation, livelihood, walk of life ...*I was looking for an occupation which would allow me to travel...*
2 = hobby, pastime, diversion, relaxation, sideline, leisure pursuit, (leisure) activity ...*Hang-gliding is a dangerous occupation...*
3 = invasion, seizure, conquest, incursion, subjugation, foreign rule ...*the deportation of Jews from Paris during the German occupation...*
4 = occupancy, use, residence, holding, control, possession, tenure, tenancy, habitation, inhabitancy ...*She is seeking an order for 'sole use and occupation' of the house...*

occupied 1 = in use, taken, full, engaged, unavailable ...*three beds, two of which were occupied...*
2 = inhabited, peopled, lived-in, settled, tenanted ...*The house was occupied by successive generations of farmers...* OPPOSITE uninhabited
3 = busy, engaged, employed, working, active, tied up (*informal*), engrossed, hard at work, in harness, hard at it (*informal*), rushed off your feet ...*I forgot about it because I was so occupied with other things...*

occupy 1 = inhabit, own, live in, stay in (*Scot.*), be established in, dwell in, be in residence in, establish yourself in, ensconce yourself in, tenant, reside in, lodge in, take up residence in, make your home, abide in ...*the couple who occupy the flat above mine...* OPPOSITE vacate
2 = invade, take over, capture, seize, conquer, keep, hold, garrison, overrun, annex, take possession of, colonize ...*Alexandretta had been occupied by the French in 1918...* OPPOSITE withdraw
3 = hold, control, dominate, possess ...*Men still occupy more positions of power than women...*
4 = take up, consume, tie up, use up, monopolize, keep busy *or* occupied ...*Her parliamentary career has occupied all of her time...*
5 *often passive* = engage, interest, involve, employ, busy, entertain, absorb, amuse, divert, preoccupy, immerse, hold the attention of, engross, keep busy *or* occupied ...*I had other matters to occupy me that day...*
6 = fill, take up, cover, fill up, utilize, pervade, permeate, extend over ...*The tombs occupy two thirds of the church...*

occur VERB 1 = happen, take place, come about, follow, result, chance, arise, turn up (*informal*), come off (*informal*), ensue, crop up (*informal*), transpire (*informal*), befall, materialize, come to pass (*archaic*), betide, eventuate ...*The deaths occurred when troops tried to disperse the demonstrators...*
2 = exist, appear, be found, develop, obtain, turn up, be present, be met with, manifest itself, present itself,

show itself ...*The disease occurs throughout Africa*...
PHRASES **occur to someone** = <u>come to mind</u>, strike someone, dawn on someone, come to you, spring to mind, cross someone's mind, present itself to someone, enter someone's head, offer itself to someone, suggest itself to someone ...*It didn't occur to me to check my insurance policy*...

Word Power

occur – It is usually regarded as incorrect to talk of pre-arranged events *occurring* or *happening*. For this meaning a synonym such as *take place* would be more appropriate: *the wedding took place* (not *occurred* or *happened*) *in the afternoon.*

---

occurrence 1 = <u>incident</u>, happening, event, fact, matter, affair, proceeding, circumstance, episode, adventure, phenomenon, transaction ...*Traffic jams are now a daily occurrence*...
2 = <u>existence</u>, instance, appearance, manifestation, materialization ...*the greatest occurrence of heart disease in the over-65s*...

odd **ADJECTIVE** 1 = <u>peculiar</u>, strange, unusual, different, funny, extraordinary, bizarre, weird, exceptional, eccentric, abnormal, queer, rum (*Brit. slang*), deviant, unconventional, far-out (*slang*), quaint, kinky (*informal*), off-the-wall (*slang*), outlandish, whimsical, oddball (*informal*), out of the ordinary, offbeat, left-field (*informal*), freakish, freaky (*slang*), wacko (*slang*), outré ...*He'd always been odd, but not to this extent*...
2 = <u>unusual</u>, different, strange, rare, funny (*slang*), extraordinary, remarkable, bizarre, fantastic, curious, weird, exceptional, peculiar, abnormal, queer, irregular, uncommon, singular, uncanny, outlandish, out of the ordinary, freakish, atypical, freaky ...*Something odd began to happen*... **OPPOSITE** normal
3 = <u>occasional</u>, various, varied, random, casual, seasonal, irregular, periodic, miscellaneous, sundry, incidental, intermittent, infrequent ...*He did various odd jobs around the place*... **OPPOSITE** regular
4 = <u>spare</u>, remaining, extra, surplus, single, lone, solitary, uneven, leftover, unmatched, unpaired ...*I found an odd sock in the washing machine*... **OPPOSITE** matched
PHRASES **odd man** or **odd one out** = <u>misfit</u>, exception, outsider, freak, eccentric, maverick, oddball (*informal*), nonconformist, fish out of water (*informal*), square peg in a round hole (*informal*) ...*All my family smoke apart from me – I'm the odd man out*...

oddity 1 = <u>misfit</u>, eccentric, crank (*informal*), nut (*slang*), maverick, flake (*slang, chiefly U.S.*), oddball (*informal*), loose cannon, nonconformist, odd man out, wacko (*slang*), screwball (*slang, chiefly U.S. & Canad.*), card (*informal*), fish out of water, square peg (in a round hole) (*informal*), odd fish (*Brit. informal*), odd bird (*informal*), rara avis, weirdo or weirdie (*informal*) ...*He's a bit of an oddity, but quite harmless*...
2 = <u>strangeness</u>, abnormality, peculiarity, eccentricity, weirdness, singularity, incongruity, oddness, unconventionality, queerness, unnaturalness, bizarreness, freakishness, extraordinariness, outlandishness ...*I was struck by the oddity of this question*...
3 = <u>irregularity</u>, phenomenon, anomaly, freak, abnormality, rarity, quirk, eccentricity, kink, peculiarity, idiosyncrasy, singularity, unorthodoxy, unconventionality ...*the oddities of the Welsh legal system*...

odds **PLURAL NOUN** = <u>probability</u>, chances, likelihood ...*What are the odds of that happening?*...
PHRASES **at odds** 1 = <u>in conflict</u>, arguing, quarrelling, in opposition to, at loggerheads, in disagreement, at daggers drawn, on bad terms ...*He was at odds with his neighbour*... 2 = <u>at variance</u>, conflicting, contrary to, at odds, out of line, out of step, at sixes and sevens (*informal*), not in keeping, out of harmony ...*Her inexperience is at odds with the tale she tells*... ◆ **odds and ends** = <u>scraps</u>, bits, pieces, remains, rubbish, fragments, litter, debris, shreds, remnants, bits and pieces, bric-a-brac, bits and bobs, oddments, odds and sods, leavings, miscellanea, sundry or miscellaneous items ...*She packed her clothes and a few other odds and ends*...

odious = <u>offensive</u>, nasty, foul, disgusting, horrible, unpleasant, revolting, obscene, sickening, vile, horrid, repellent, unsavoury, obnoxious, unpalatable, repulsive, disagreeable, nauseating, hateful, repugnant, loathsome, abhorrent, abominable, execrable, detestable, yucky or yukky (*slang*), yucko (*Austral. slang*) **OPPOSITE** delightful

odour 1 = <u>smell</u>, scent, perfume, fragrance, stink, bouquet, aroma, whiff, stench, pong (*Brit. informal*), niff (*Brit. slang*), redolence, malodour, fetor ...*the faint odour of whisky on his breath*...
2 = <u>atmosphere</u>, feeling, air, quality, spirit, tone, climate, flavour, aura, vibe (*slang*) ...*a tantalising odour of scandal*...

odyssey = <u>journey</u>, tour, trip, passage, quest, trek, expedition, voyage, crusade, excursion, pilgrimage, jaunt, peregrination

of = <u>about</u>, on, concerning, regarding, with respect to, as regards

---

Word Power

of – *Of* is sometimes used instead of *have* in phrases such as *should have, could have,* and *might have*. This is because, when people are speaking, they often drop the *h* at the beginning of *have*, making the word's pronunciation very similar to that of *of*. Using *of* in this way is, however, regarded as nonstandard, and in writing it should definitely be avoided.

---

off **ADVERB** = <u>away</u>, out, apart, elsewhere, aside, hence, from here ...*He went off on his own*...
ADJECTIVE 1 = <u>absent</u>, gone, unavailable, not present, inoperative, nonattendant ...*She was off sick 27 days*

last year…

2 = <u>cancelled</u>, abandoned, postponed, shelved …*Today's game is off…*

3 = <u>bad</u>, rotten, rancid, mouldy, high, turned, spoiled, sour, decayed, decomposed, putrid …*Food starts to smell when it goes off…*

4 = <u>unacceptable</u>, poor, unsatisfactory, disappointing, inadequate, second-rate, shoddy, displeasing, below par, mortifying, substandard, disheartening …*Coming home drunk like that – it's a bit off, isn't it?…*

PHRASES **off and on** = <u>occasionally</u>, sometimes, at times, from time to time, on and off, now and then, irregularly, on occasion, now and again, periodically, once in a while, every so often, intermittently, at intervals, sporadically, every once in a while, (every) now and again …*We lived together, off and on, for two years…*

offbeat = <u>unusual</u>, odd, strange, novel, extraordinary, bizarre, weird, way-out (*informal*), eccentric, queer, rum (*Brit. slang*), uncommon, Bohemian, unconventional, far-out (*slang*), idiosyncratic, kinky (*informal*), off-the-wall (*slang*), unorthodox, oddball (*informal*), out of the ordinary, left-field (*informal*), freaky (*slang*), wacko (*slang*), outré OPPOSITE conventional

offence NOUN **1** = <u>crime</u>, wrong, sin, lapse, fault, violation, wrongdoing, trespass, felony, misdemeanour, delinquency, misdeed, transgression, peccadillo, unlawful act, breach of conduct …*It is a criminal offence to sell goods which are unsafe…*

2 = <u>outrage</u>, shock, anger, trouble, bother, grief (*informal*), resentment, irritation, hassle (*informal*), wrath, indignation, annoyance, ire (*literary*), displeasure, pique, aggravation, hard feelings, umbrage, vexation, wounded feelings …*The book might be published without creating offence…*

3 = <u>insult</u>, injury, slight, hurt, harm, outrage, put-down (*slang*), injustice, snub, affront, indignity, displeasure, rudeness, slap in the face (*informal*), insolence …*His behaviour was an offence to his hosts…*

PHRASES **take offence** = <u>be offended</u>, resent, be upset, be outraged, be put out (*informal*), be miffed (*informal*), be displeased, take umbrage, be disgruntled, be affronted, be piqued, take the needle (*informal*), get riled, take the huff, go into a huff, be huffy …*You're very quick to take offence today…*

offend 1 = <u>distress</u>, upset, outrage, pain, wound, slight, provoke, insult, annoy, irritate, put down, dismay, snub, aggravate (*informal*), gall, agitate, ruffle, disconcert, vex, affront, displease, rile, pique, give offence, hurt (someone's) feelings, nark (*Brit., Austral., & N.Z. slang*), cut to the quick, miff (*informal*), tread on (someone's) toes (*informal*), put (someone's) nose out of joint, put (someone's) back up, disgruntle, get (someone's) goat (*slang*) …*He had no intention of offending the community…* OPPOSITE please

2 = <u>disgust</u>, revolt, turn (someone) off (*informal*), put off, sicken, repel, repulse, nauseate, gross out (*U.S. slang*), make (someone) sick, turn your stomach, be disagreeable to, fill with loathing …*The smell of cigar smoke offends me…*

3 = <u>break the law</u>, sin, err, do wrong, fall, fall from grace, go astray …*alleged criminals who offend while on bail…*

offended = <u>upset</u>, pained, hurt, bothered, disturbed, distressed, outraged, stung, put out (*informal*), grieved, disgruntled, agitated, ruffled, resentful, affronted, miffed (*informal*), displeased, in a huff, piqued, huffy, tooshie (*Austral. slang*)

offender = <u>criminal</u>, convict, con (*slang*), crook, lag (*slang*), villain, culprit, sinner, delinquent, felon, jailbird, wrongdoer, miscreant, malefactor, evildoer, transgressor, lawbreaker

offensive ADJECTIVE **1** = <u>insulting</u>, rude, abusive, embarrassing, slighting, annoying, irritating, degrading, affronting, contemptuous, disparaging, displeasing, objectionable, disrespectful, scurrilous, detestable, discourteous, uncivil, unmannerly …*offensive remarks about minority groups…* OPPOSITE respectful

2 = <u>disgusting</u>, gross, nasty, foul, unpleasant, revolting, stinking, sickening, vile, repellent, unsavoury, obnoxious, unpalatable, objectionable, disagreeable, nauseating, odious, repugnant, loathsome, abominable, grotty (*slang*), detestable, noisome, yucky *or* yukky (*slang*), festy (*Austral. slang*), yucko (*Austral. slang*) …*the offensive smell of manure…* OPPOSITE pleasant

3 = <u>attacking</u>, threatening, aggressive, striking, hostile, invading, combative …*The troops were in an offensive position…* OPPOSITE defensive

NOUN = <u>attack</u>, charge, campaign, strike, push (*informal*), rush, assault, raid, drive, invasion, onslaught, foray, incursion …*The armed forces have launched an offensive to recapture lost ground…*

offer VERB **1** = <u>present with</u>, give, hand, hold out to …*Rhys offered him an apple…*

2 = <u>provide</u>, present, furnish, make available, afford, place at (someone's) disposal …*Western governments have offered aid…* OPPOSITE withhold

3 = <u>volunteer</u>, come forward, offer your services, be at (someone's) service …*Peter offered to help us…*

4 = <u>propose</u>, suggest, advance, extend, submit, put forward, put forth …*They offered no suggestion as to how it might be done…*

5 = <u>give</u>, show, bring, provide, render, impart …*His mother and sister rallied round offering comfort…*

6 = <u>put up for sale</u>, sell, put on the market, put under the hammer …*The house is being offered at 1.5 million pounds…*

7 = <u>bid</u>, submit, propose, extend, tender, proffer …*He offered a fair price for the land…*

NOUN **1** = <u>proposal</u>, suggestion, proposition, submission, attempt at, endeavour, overture …*He has refused all offers of help…*

2 = <u>bid</u>, tender, bidding price …*We've made an offer for the house…*

offering 1 = <u>contribution</u>, gift, donation, present, subscription, hand-out, stipend, widow's mite …*funds from local church offerings…*

2 = <u>sacrifice</u>, tribute, libation, burnt offering, oblation (*in religious contexts*) …*a Shinto ritual in which* *offerings are made to the great Sun…*

offhand ADJECTIVE = <u>casual</u>, informal, indifferent, careless, abrupt, cavalier, aloof, unconcerned, curt, uninterested, glib, cursory, couldn't-care-less, apathetic, perfunctory, blasé, brusque, take-it-or-leave-it (*informal*), nonchalant, lackadaisical, unceremonious, offhanded …*Consumers found the attitude of its staff offhand…* OPPOSITE attentive ● ADVERB = <u>off the cuff</u> (*informal*), spontaneously, impromptu, just like that (*informal*), ad lib, extempore, off the top of your head (*informal*), without preparation, extemporaneously …*I couldn't tell you offhand how long he's worked here…*

office NOUN 1 = <u>place of work</u>, workplace, base, workroom, place of business …*He had an office just big enough for a desk and chair…*
2 = <u>branch</u>, department, division, section, wing, subdivision, subsection …*Downing Street's press office…*
3 = <u>post</u>, place, role, work, business, service, charge, situation, commission, station, responsibility, duty, function, employment, capacity, appointment, occupation …*the honour and dignity of the office of President…* ● PLURAL NOUN = <u>support</u>, help, backing, aid, favour, assistance, intervention, recommendation, patronage, mediation, advocacy, auspices, aegis, moral support, intercession, espousal …*Thanks to his good offices, a home has been found for the birds…*

officer 1 = <u>official</u>, executive, agent, representative, bureaucrat, public servant, appointee, dignitary, functionary, office-holder, office bearer …*a local education authority officer…*
2 = <u>police officer</u>, detective, PC, police constable, police man, police woman …*an officer in the West Midlands police force…*

official ADJECTIVE 1 = <u>authorized</u>, approved, formal, sanctioned, licensed, proper, endorsed, warranted, legitimate, authentic, ratified, certified, authoritative, accredited, bona fide, signed and sealed, ex officio, ex cathedra, straight from the horse's mouth (*informal*) …*An official announcement is expected later today…* OPPOSITE unofficial
2 = <u>formal</u>, prescribed, bureaucratic, ceremonial, solemn, ritualistic …*his official duties…* ● NOUN = <u>officer</u>, executive, agent, representative, bureaucrat, public servant, appointee, dignitary, functionary, office-holder, office bearer …*a senior UN official…*

officiate 1 = <u>preside</u>, conduct, celebrate …*Bishop Silvester officiated at the funeral…*
2 = <u>superintend</u>, supervise, be in charge, run, control, serve, manage, direct, handle, chair, look after, overlook, oversee, preside, take charge, adjudicate, emcee (*informal*) …*He has been chosen to officiate at the cup final…*

offing
PHRASES **in the offing** = <u>imminent</u>, coming, close, near, coming up, gathering, on the way, in the air, forthcoming, looming, brewing, hovering, impending, at hand, upcoming, on the cards, on the horizon, in

the wings, in the pipeline, nigh (*archaic*), in prospect, close at hand, fast-approaching, in the immediate future, just round the corner …*A general amnesty for political prisoners may be in the offing…*

off-key = <u>cacophonous</u>, harsh, jarring, grating, shrill, jangling, discordant, dissonant, inharmonious, unmelodious

offload 1 = <u>get rid of</u>, shift, dump, dispose of, unload, dispense with, jettison, foist, see the back of, palm off …*Prices have been cut by developers anxious to offload unsold apartments…*
2 = <u>unload</u>, take off, transfer, dump, discharge, jettison, unpack, unship, unlade …*The cargo was offloaded in Singapore three days later…*

off-putting (*Informal*) = <u>discouraging</u>, upsetting, disturbing, frustrating, nasty, formidable, intimidating, dismaying, unsettling, daunting, dampening, unnerving, disconcerting, unfavourable, dispiriting, discomfiting

offset = <u>cancel out</u>, balance, set off, make up for, compensate for, redeem, counteract, neutralize, counterbalance, nullify, obviate, balance out, counterpoise, countervail

offshoot = <u>by-product</u>, development, product, branch, supplement, complement, spin-off, auxiliary, adjunct, appendage, outgrowth, appurtenance

offspring 1 = <u>child</u>, baby, kid (*informal*), youngster, infant, successor, babe, toddler, heir, issue, tot, descendant, wean (*Scot.*), little one, brat, bairn (*Scot.*), nipper (*informal*), chit, scion, babe in arms (*informal*), sprog (*slang*), munchkin (*informal, chiefly U.S.*), rug rat (*slang*), littlie (*Austral. informal*), ankle-biter (*Austral. slang*), tacker (*Austral. slang*) …*She was less anxious about her offspring than she had been…* OPPOSITE parent
2 = <u>children</u>, kids (*informal*), young, family, issue, stock, seed (*chiefly biblical*), fry, successors, heirs, spawn, descendants, brood, posterity, lineage, progeny, scions …*Characteristics are often passed from parents to offspring…*

often = <u>frequently</u>, much, generally, commonly, repeatedly, again and again, very often, oft (*archaic or poetic*), over and over again, time and again, habitually, time after time, customarily, oftentimes (*archaic*), not infrequently, many a time, ofttimes (*archaic*) OPPOSITE never

ogle = <u>leer at</u>, stare at, eye up (*informal*), gawp at (*Brit. slang*), give the once-over (*informal*), make sheep's eyes at (*informal*), give the glad eye (*informal*), lech or letch after (*informal*)

ogre 1 = <u>fiend</u>, monster, beast, villain, brute, bogeyman …*Some people think of bank managers as ogres…*
2 = <u>monster</u>, giant, devil, beast, demon, bogey, spectre, fiend, ghoul, bogeyman, bugbear …*an ogre in a fairy tale…*

oil VERB = <u>lubricate</u>, grease, make slippery …*A crew of assistants oiled the mechanism until it worked perfectly…* ● NOUN 1 = <u>lubricant</u>, grease, lubrication, fuel oil …*Her* *car had run out of oil…*

2 = <u>lotion</u>, cream, balm, salve, liniment, embrocation, solution …*sun-tan oil…*

oily **1** = <u>greasy</u>, slick, slimy, fatty, slippery, oleaginous, smeary …*traces of an oily substance…*

2 = <u>sycophantic</u>, smooth, flattering, slick, plausible, hypocritical, fawning, grovelling, glib, ingratiating, fulsome, deferential, servile, unctuous, obsequious, smarmy (*Brit. informal*), mealy-mouthed, toadying …*He asked in an oily voice what he could do for them today…*

ointment = <u>salve</u>, dressing, cream, lotion, balm, lubricant, emollient, liniment, embrocation, unguent, cerate

OK *or* **okay** `ADJECTIVE` (*Informal*) **1** = <u>all right</u>, fine, fitting, fair, in order, correct, approved, permitted, suitable, acceptable, convenient, allowable …*Is it OK if I bring a friend with me?…* `OPPOSITE` unacceptable

2 = <u>fine</u>, good, average, middling, fair, all right, acceptable, adequate, satisfactory, not bad (*informal*), so-so (*informal*), tolerable, up to scratch (*informal*), passable, unobjectionable …*'Did you enjoy the film?' 'It was okay.'…* `OPPOSITE` unsatisfactory

3 = <u>well</u>, all right, safe, sound, healthy, hale, unharmed, uninjured, unimpaired …*Would you go and check the baby's ok?…*

`INTERJECTION` = <u>all right</u>, right, yes, agreed, very good, roger, very well, ya (*S. African*), righto (*Brit. informal*), okey-dokey (*informal*), yebo (*S. African informal*) …*'Shall I ring you later?' – 'OK.'…*

`VERB` = <u>approve</u>, allow, pass, agree to, permit, sanction, second, endorse, authorize, ratify, go along with, consent to, validate, countenance, give the go-ahead, rubber-stamp (*informal*), say yes to, give the green light, assent to, give the thumbs up (*informal*), concur in, give your consent to, give your blessing to …*His doctor wouldn't OK the trip…*

`NOUN` = <u>authorization</u>, agreement, sanction, licence, approval, go-ahead (*informal*), blessing, permission, consent, say-so (*informal*), confirmation, mandate, endorsement, green light, ratification, assent, seal of approval, approbation …*He gave the okay to issue a new press release…*

old **1** = <u>aged</u>, elderly, ancient, getting on, grey, mature, past it (*informal*), venerable, patriarchal, grey-haired, antiquated, over the hill (*informal*), senile, grizzled, decrepit, hoary, senescent, advanced in years, full of years, past your prime …*He was considered too old for the job…* `OPPOSITE` young

2 = <u>tumbledown</u>, ruined, crumbling, decayed, shaky, disintegrating, worn-out, done, tottering, ramshackle, rickety, decrepit, falling to pieces …*a dilapidated old farmhouse…*

3 = <u>worn</u>, ragged, shabby, frayed, cast-off, tattered, tatty, threadbare …*Dress in old clothes for gardening…*

4 = <u>out of date</u>, old-fashioned, dated, passé, antique, outdated, obsolete, archaic, unfashionable, antiquated, outmoded, behind the times, superannuated, out of style, antediluvian, out of the ark (*informal*), démodé (*French*) …*They got rid of all*

their old, outdated office equipment… `OPPOSITE` up-to-date

5 = <u>former</u>, earlier, past, previous, prior, one-time, erstwhile, late, quondam, whilom (*archaic*), ex- …*Mark was heartbroken when Jane returned to her old boyfriend…*

6 = <u>long-standing</u>, established, fixed, enduring, abiding, long-lasting, long-established, time-honoured …*He is an old enemy of mine…*

7 = <u>early</u>, ancient, original, remote, of old, antique, aboriginal, primitive, archaic, gone by, bygone, undeveloped, primordial, primeval, immemorial, of yore, olden (*archaic*), pristine …*How did people manage in the old days before electricity?…*

8 = <u>stale</u>, common, commonplace, worn-out, banal, threadbare, trite, old hat, insipid, hackneyed, overused, repetitious, unoriginal, platitudinous, cliché-ridden, timeworn …*He trotted out all the same old excuses as before…*

9 = <u>long-established</u>, seasoned, experienced, tried, tested, trained, professional, skilled, expert, master, qualified, familiar, capable, veteran, practised, accomplished, vintage, versed, hardened, competent, skilful, adept, knowledgeable, age-old, of long standing, well-versed …*She's an old campaigner at this game…*

10 = <u>customary</u>, established, traditional, conventional, historic, long-established, time-honoured, of long standing …*They dance, and sing the old songs they sang at home…*

➤ **senile**

old-fashioned **1** = <u>out of date</u>, ancient, dated, outdated, unfashionable, antiquated, outmoded, passé, old hat, behind the times, fusty, out of style, démodé (*French*), out of the ark (*informal*), not with it (*informal*), (old-)fogeyish …*She always wears such boring, old-fashioned clothes…* `OPPOSITE` up-to-date

2 = <u>oldfangled</u>, square (*informal*), outdated, old, past, dead, past it (*informal*), obsolete, old-time, archaic, unfashionable, superannuated, obsolescent, out of the ark (*informal*) …*She has some old-fashioned values…*

old man **1** = <u>senior citizen</u>, grandfather (*slang*), patriarch, old age pensioner, old person, old-timer (*U.S.*), elder, elder statesman, wrinkly (*informal*), old codger (*informal*), old stager, greybeard, coffin-dodger (*slang*), oldster (*informal*), O.A.P. (*Brit.*) …*a wizened, bent-over old man…*

2 (*Informal*) = <u>father</u>, pop (*informal*), dad (*informal*), daddy (*informal*), pa (*informal*), old boy (*informal*), papa (*old-fashioned informal*), pater, paterfamilias …*My old man used to work down the mines…*

3 = <u>manager</u>, boss (*informal*), supervisor, governor (*informal*), ganger, superintendent, gaffer (*informal*), foreman, overseer, baas (*S. African*) …*Why's the old man got it in for you?…*

➤ **old person**

old person = <u>senior citizen</u>, senior, retired person, old age pensioner, elder, pensioner (*slang*), coffin-dodger (*slang*), elderly person, O.A.P. (*Brit.*)

Word Power

old person – While not as offensive as *coffin-dodger* and some of the other synonyms listed here, phrases such as *old man*, *old woman*, *old person*, and *elderly person* may still cause offence. It is better to use *senior citizen* or *senior*.

old-time = <u>old-fashioned</u>, traditional, vintage, ancient, antique, old-style, bygone

old woman = <u>senior citizen</u>, old lady, pensioner (*slang*), retired person, old age pensioner, elder, coffin-dodger (*slang*), elderly person, O.A.P. (*Brit.*)
➤ **old person**

old-world = <u>traditional</u>, old-fashioned, picturesque, quaint, archaic, gentlemanly, courteous, gallant, courtly, chivalrous, ceremonious

Olympian 1 = <u>colossal</u>, huge, massive, enormous, tremendous, awesome, gigantic, monumental, mammoth, prodigious …*Getting his book into print has been an Olympian task…*
2 = <u>majestic</u>, kingly, regal, royal, august, grand, princely, imperial, glorious, noble, splendid, elevated, awesome, dignified, regal, stately, sublime, lofty, pompous, grandiose, exalted, rarefied, godlike …*She affects an Olympian disdain for their opinions…*

omen = <u>portent</u>, sign, warning, threat, indication, foreshadowing, foreboding, harbinger, presage, forewarning, writing on the wall, prognostication, augury, prognostic, foretoken

ominous = <u>threatening</u>, menacing, sinister, dark, forbidding, grim, fateful, foreboding, unpromising, portentous, baleful, inauspicious, premonitory, unpropitious, minatory, bodeful OPPOSITE promising

omission 1 = <u>exclusion</u>, removal, leaving out, elimination, deletion, excision, noninclusion …*her omission from the guest list…* OPPOSITE inclusion
2 = <u>gap</u>, space, blank, exclusion, lacuna …*There is one noticeable omission in your article…*
3 = <u>failure</u>, neglect, default, negligence, oversight, carelessness, dereliction, forgetfulness, slackness, laxity, laxness, slovenliness, neglectfulness, remissness …*an injury occasioned by any omission of the defendant…*

omit 1 = <u>leave out</u>, miss (out), drop, exclude, eliminate, skip, give (something) a miss (*informal*) …*Our apologies for omitting your name from the article…* OPPOSITE include
2 = <u>forget</u>, fail, overlook, neglect, pass over, lose sight of, leave (something) undone, let (something) slide …*She had omitted to tell him she was married…*

omnipotence = <u>supremacy</u>, sovereignty, dominance, domination, mastery, primacy, ascendancy, pre-eminence, predominance, invincibility, supreme power, absolute rule, undisputed sway …*leaders who use violent discipline to assert their omnipotence…* OPPOSITE powerlessness

omnipotent = <u>almighty</u>, supreme, invincible, all-powerful OPPOSITE powerless

once ADVERB 1 = <u>on one occasion</u>, one time, one single time …*I only met her once, very briefly…*
2 = <u>at one time</u>, in the past, previously, formerly, long ago, in the old days, once upon a time, in times past, in times gone by …*I lived there once, before I was married…*
CONJUNCTION = <u>as soon as</u>, when, after, the moment, immediately, the instant …*Once she got inside the house, she slammed the door…*
PHRASES **at once** 1 = <u>immediately</u>, now, right now, straight away, directly, promptly, instantly, right away, without delay, without hesitation, forthwith, this (very) minute, pronto (*informal*), this instant, straightway (*archaic*), posthaste, tout de suite (*French*) …*I must go at once…* 2 = <u>simultaneously</u>, together, at the same time, all together, in concert, in unison, concurrently, in the same breath, in chorus, at *or* in one go (*informal*) …*They all started talking at once…*
◆ **once and for all** = <u>for the last time</u>, finally, completely, for good, positively, permanently, for ever, decisively, inexorably, conclusively, irrevocably, for all time, inescapably, with finality, beyond the shadow of a doubt …*We have to resolve this matter once and for all…* ◆ **once in a while** = <u>occasionally</u>, sometimes, at times, from time to time, on and off, irregularly, on occasion, now and again, periodically, every now and then, every so often, at intervals, off and on …*He phones me once in a while…*

oncoming 1 = <u>approaching</u>, advancing, looming, onrushing …*He skidded into the path of an oncoming car…*
2 = <u>forthcoming</u>, coming, approaching, expected, threatening, advancing, gathering, imminent, impending, upcoming, fast-approaching …*the oncoming storm…*

one-horse (*Informal*) (only used to describe *towns*) = <u>small</u>, slow, quiet, minor, obscure, sleepy, unimportant, small-time (*informal*), backwoods, tinpot (*Brit. informal*)

onerous = <u>trying</u>, hard, taxing, demanding, difficult, heavy, responsible, grave, crushing, exhausting, exacting, formidable, troublesome, oppressive, weighty, laborious, burdensome, irksome, backbreaking, exigent OPPOSITE easy

one-sided 1 = <u>unequal</u>, unfair, uneven, unjust, unbalanced, lopsided, inequitable, ill-matched …*It was a totally one-sided competition…* OPPOSITE equal
2 = <u>biased</u>, prejudiced, weighted, twisted, coloured, unfair, partial, distorted, partisan, warped, slanted, unjust, discriminatory, lopsided …*She gave a very one-sided account of the affair…* OPPOSITE unbiased

one-time = <u>former</u>, previous, prior, sometime, late, erstwhile, quondam, ci-devant (*French*), ex-

ongoing = <u>in progress</u>, current, growing, developing, advancing, progressing, evolving, unfolding, unfinished, extant

onlooker = <u>spectator</u>, witness, observer, viewer, looker-on, watcher, eyewitness, bystander

only ADJECTIVE = <u>sole</u>, one, single, individual, exclusive, unique, lone, solitary, one and only …*She was the only* *applicant for the job…*

ADVERB **1** = <u>just</u>, simply, purely, merely, no more than, nothing but, but, at most, at a push …*At the moment it's only a theory…*
2 = <u>hardly</u>, just, barely, only just, scarcely, at most, at a push …*I only have enough money for one ticket…*
3 = <u>exclusively</u>, entirely, purely, solely …*Computers are only for use by class members…*

onset = <u>beginning</u>, start, rise, birth, kick-off (*informal*), outbreak, starting point, inception, commencement **OPPOSITE** end

onslaught = <u>attack</u>, charge, campaign, strike, rush, assault, raid, invasion, offensive, blitz, onset, foray, incursion, onrush, inroad **OPPOSITE** retreat

onus = <u>burden</u>, weight, responsibility, worry, task, stress, load, obligation, liability

onward *or* **onwards** = <u>forward</u>, on, forwards, ahead, beyond, in front, forth

ooze¹ **1** = <u>seep</u>, well, drop, escape, strain, leak, drain, sweat, filter, bleed, weep, drip, trickle, leach, dribble, percolate …*Blood was still oozing from the wound…*
2 = <u>emit</u>, release, leak, sweat, bleed, discharge, drip, leach, give out, dribble, exude, give off, excrete, overflow with, pour forth …*The cut was oozing a clear liquid…*
3 = <u>exude</u>, emit, radiate, display, exhibit, manifest, emanate, overflow with …*Graham positively oozed confidence…*

ooze² = <u>mud</u>, clay, dirt, muck, silt, sludge, mire, slime, slob (*Irish*), gloop (*informal*), alluvium …*He thrust his hand into the ooze and brought out a large toad…*

opaque **1** = <u>cloudy</u>, clouded, dull, dim, muddied, muddy, murky, hazy, filmy, turbid, lustreless …*The bathroom has an opaque glass window…* **OPPOSITE** clear
2 = <u>incomprehensible</u>, obscure, unclear, difficult, puzzling, baffling, enigmatic, perplexing, impenetrable, unintelligible, cryptic, unfathomable, abstruse, obfuscated, beyond comprehension …*the opaque language of the official report…* **OPPOSITE** lucid

open **VERB** **1** = <u>unfasten</u>, unlock, unclasp, throw wide, unbar, unclose …*He opened the window and looked out…* **OPPOSITE** close
2 = <u>unwrap</u>, uncover, undo, unravel, untie, unstrap, unseal, unlace …*The Inspector opened the parcel…* **OPPOSITE** wrap
3 = <u>uncork</u>, crack (open) …*Let's open another bottle of wine…*
4 = <u>unfold</u>, spread (out), expand, stretch out, unfurl, unroll …*When you open the map, you will find it is divided into squares…* **OPPOSITE** fold
5 = <u>clear</u>, unblock …*Police have opened the road again after the crash…* **OPPOSITE** block
6 = <u>undo</u>, loosen, unbutton, unfasten …*He opened his shirt to show me his scar…* **OPPOSITE** fasten
7 = <u>begin business</u> …*The new shopping complex opens tomorrow…*
8 = <u>start</u>, begin, launch, trigger, kick off (*informal*), initiate, commence, get going, instigate, kick-start,

inaugurate, set in motion, get (something) off the ground (*informal*), enter upon …*They are now ready to open negotiations…* **OPPOSITE** end
9 = <u>begin</u>, start, commence …*The service opened with a hymn…* **OPPOSITE** end

ADJECTIVE **1** = <u>unclosed</u>, unlocked, ajar, unfastened, yawning, gaping, unlatched, unbolted, partly open, unbarred, off the latch …*an open door…* **OPPOSITE** closed
2 = <u>unsealed</u>, unstoppered …*an open bottle of milk…* **OPPOSITE** unopened
3 = <u>extended</u>, expanded, unfolded, stretched out, spread out, unfurled, straightened out, unrolled …*A newspaper lay open on the coffee table…* **OPPOSITE** shut
4 = <u>frank</u>, direct, natural, plain, innocent, straightforward, sincere, transparent, honest, candid, truthful, upfront (*informal*), plain-spoken, above board, unreserved, artless, ingenuous, guileless, straight from the shoulder (*informal*) …*She has an open, trusting nature…* **OPPOSITE** sly
5 = <u>obvious</u>, clear, frank, plain, apparent, visible, patent, evident, distinct, pronounced, manifest, transparent, noticeable, blatant, conspicuous, downright, overt, unmistakable, palpable, recognizable, avowed, flagrant, perceptible, much in evidence, undisguised, unsubtle, barefaced, unconcealed …*their open dislike of each other…* **OPPOSITE** hidden
6 = <u>receptive</u>, welcoming, sympathetic, responsive, amenable …*He seems open to suggestions…*
7 = <u>susceptible</u>, subject, exposed, vulnerable, in danger, disposed, liable, wide open, unprotected, at the mercy of, left open, laid bare, an easy target for, undefended, laid open, defenceless against, unfortified …*They left themselves open to accusations of double standards…* **OPPOSITE** defended
8 = <u>unresolved</u>, unsettled, undecided, debatable, up in the air, moot, arguable, yet to be decided …*It is an open question how long his commitment will last…*
9 = <u>clear</u>, free, passable, uncluttered, unhindered, unimpeded, navigable, unobstructed, unhampered …*The emergency services will do their best to keep the highway open…* **OPPOSITE** obstructed
10 = <u>unenclosed</u>, wide, rolling, sweeping, exposed, extensive, bare, spacious, wide-open, undeveloped, uncrowded, unfenced, not built-up, unsheltered …*Police will continue their search of nearby open ground…* **OPPOSITE** enclosed
11 = <u>undone</u>, gaping, unbuttoned, unzipped, agape, unfastened …*Her blouse was open to the waist…* **OPPOSITE** fastened
12 = <u>available</u>, to hand, accessible, handy, vacant, on hand, obtainable, attainable, at your fingertips, at your disposal …*There are a wide range of career opportunities open to young people…*
13 = <u>general</u>, public, free, catholic, broad, universal, blanket, unconditional, across-the-board, unqualified, all-inclusive, unrestricted, overarching, free to all, nondiscriminatory …*an open invitation…* **OPPOSITE** restricted
14 = <u>vacant</u>, free, available, empty, up for grabs

(*informal*), unoccupied, unfilled, unengaged ...*The job is still open*...

15 = <u>generous</u>, kind, liberal, charitable, benevolent, prodigal, bountiful, open-handed, unstinting, beneficent, bounteous, munificent, ungrudging ...*the public's open and generous response to the appeal*...

16 = <u>gappy</u>, loose, lacy, porous, honeycombed, spongy, filigree, fretted, holey, openwork ...*Ciabatta has a distinctive crisp crust and open texture*...

open-air = <u>outdoor</u>, outside, out-of-door(s), alfresco

open-and-shut = <u>straightforward</u>, simple, obvious, routine, clear-cut, foregone, noncontroversial

opening ADJECTIVE = <u>first</u>, early, earliest, beginning, premier, primary, initial, maiden, inaugural, commencing, introductory, initiatory ...*the season's opening game*...
    NOUN **1** = <u>beginning</u>, start, launch, launching, birth, dawn, outset, starting point, onset, overture, initiation, inauguration, inception, commencement, kickoff (*informal*), opening move ...*the opening of peace talks*... OPPOSITE ending
    2 = <u>hole</u>, break, space, tear, split, crack, gap, rent, breach, slot, outlet, vent, puncture, rupture, aperture, cleft, chink, fissure, orifice, perforation, interstice ...*He squeezed through an opening in the fence*... OPPOSITE blockage
    3 = <u>opportunity</u>, chance, break (*informal*), time, place, moment, window, occasion, look-in (*informal*) ...*All she needed was an opening to show her capabilities*...
    4 = <u>job</u>, position, post, situation, opportunity, vacancy ...*We don't have any openings just now, but we'll call you*...

openly **1** = <u>frankly</u>, plainly, in public, honestly, face to face, overtly, candidly, unreservedly, unhesitatingly, forthrightly, straight from the shoulder (*informal*) ...*We can now talk openly about AIDS*... OPPOSITE privately
    2 = <u>blatantly</u>, publicly, brazenly, unashamedly, shamelessly, in full view, flagrantly, unabashedly, wantonly, undisguisedly, without pretence ...*He was openly gay*... OPPOSITE secretly

open-minded = <u>unprejudiced</u>, liberal, free, balanced, catholic, broad, objective, reasonable, enlightened, tolerant, impartial, receptive, unbiased, even-handed, dispassionate, fair-minded, broad-minded, undogmatic OPPOSITE narrow-minded

openness = <u>frankness</u>, honesty, truthfulness, naturalness, bluntness, forthrightness, ingenuousness, artlessness, guilelessness, candidness, freeness, open-heartedness, absence of reserve, candour *or* (*U.S.*) candor, sincerity *or* sincereness, unreservedness

operate **1** = <u>manage</u>, run, direct, handle, govern, oversee, supervise, preside over, be in charge of, call the shots in, superintend, call the tune in ...*Until his death he owned and operated a huge company*...
    2 = <u>function</u>, work, act, be in business, be in action ...*allowing commercial businesses to operate in the country*...
    3 = <u>run</u>, work, use, control, drive, manoeuvre ...*The men were trapped as they operated a tunnelling machine*...
    4 = <u>work</u>, go, run, perform, function ...*the number of fax machines operating around the world*... OPPOSITE break down
    5 = <u>perform surgery</u>, carry out surgery, put someone under the knife (*informal*) ...*The surgeons had to decide quickly whether or not to operate*...

operation NOUN **1** = <u>undertaking</u>, process, affair, organization, proceeding, procedure, coordination ...*A major rescue operation is under way*...
    2 = <u>manoeuvre</u>, campaign, movement, exercise, assault, deployment ...*a full-scale military operation*...
    3 = <u>business</u>, concern, firm, organization, corporation, venture, enterprise ...*The company has converted its mail-order operation into an e-business*...
    4 = <u>surgery</u>, surgical operation, surgical intervention ...*an operation to reduce a bloodclot on the brain*...
    5 = <u>performance</u>, working, running, action, movement, functioning, motion, manipulation ...*Dials monitor every aspect of the operation of the aircraft*...
    6 = <u>effect</u>, force, activity, agency, influence, impact, effectiveness, instrumentality ...*This change is due to the operation of several factors*...
    PHRASES **in operation** = <u>in action</u>, current, effective, going, functioning, active, in effect, in business, operative, in force ...*The night-time curfew remains in operation*...

operational = <u>working</u>, going, running, ready, functioning, operative, viable, functional, up and running, workable, usable, in working order OPPOSITE inoperative

operative ADJECTIVE **1** = <u>in force</u>, current, effective, standing, functioning, active, efficient, in effect, in business, operational, functional, in operation, workable, serviceable ...*The scheme was operative by the end of 1983*... OPPOSITE inoperative
    2 = <u>relevant</u>, important, key, fitting, significant, appropriate, crucial, influential, apt, applicable, indicative, pertinent, apposite, germane ...*A small whisky may help you sleep – 'small' being the operative word*...
    NOUN **1** = <u>worker</u>, hand, employee, mechanic, labourer, workman, artisan, machinist, working man *or* working woman ...*In an automated car plant there is not a human operative to be seen*...
    2 (*U.S. & Canad.*) = <u>spy</u>, secret agent, double agent, secret service agent, undercover agent, mole, foreign agent, fifth columnist, nark (*Brit., Austral., & N.Z. slang*) ...*The CIA wants to protect its operatives*...

operator **1** = <u>worker</u>, hand, driver, mechanic, operative, conductor, technician, handler, skilled employee ...*He first of all worked as a machine operator*...
    2 = <u>contractor</u>, dealer, trader, administrator ...*the country's largest cable TV operator*...
    3 (*Informal*) = <u>manipulator</u>, worker, mover, Machiavellian, mover and shaker, machinator, wheeler-dealer (*informal*), wirepuller ...*one of the shrewdest political operators in the Arab world*...

opiate = <u>narcotic</u>, drug, downer (*slang*), painkiller, sedative, tranquillizer, bromide, anodyne, analgesic, soporific, pacifier, nepenthe

opine (*Formal*) = suggest, say, think, believe, judge, suppose, declare, conclude, venture, volunteer, imply, intimate, presume, conjecture, surmise, ween (*poetic*), give as your opinion

opinion NOUN **1** = belief, feeling, view, idea, theory, notion, conviction, point of view, sentiment, viewpoint, persuasion, conjecture ...*Most who expressed an opinion spoke favourably of him...*
2 = estimation, view, impression, assessment, judgment, evaluation, conception, appraisal, considered opinion ...*That has improved my already favourable opinion of him...*
PHRASES **be of the opinion** = believe, think, hold, consider, judge, suppose, maintain, imagine, guess (*informal, chiefly U.S. & Canad.*), reckon, conclude, be convinced, speculate, presume, conjecture, postulate, surmise, be under the impression ...*Frank is of the opinion that there has been a cover-up...* ◆ **matter of opinion** = debatable point, debatable, open question, open to question, moot point, open for discussion, matter of judgment ...*Whether or not it is a work of art is a matter of opinion...*

opinionated = dogmatic, prejudiced, biased, arrogant, adamant, stubborn, assertive, uncompromising, single-minded, inflexible, bigoted, dictatorial, imperious, overbearing, obstinate, doctrinaire, obdurate, cocksure, pig-headed, self-assertive, bull-headed OPPOSITE open-minded

opponent 1 = adversary, rival, enemy, the opposition, competitor, challenger, foe, contestant, antagonist ...*Mr Kennedy's opponent in the leadership contest...* OPPOSITE ally
2 = opposer, dissident, objector, dissentient, disputant ...*He became an outspoken opponent of the old Soviet system...* OPPOSITE supporter

opportune (*Formal*) = timely, fitting, fit, welcome, lucky, appropriate, suitable, happy, proper, convenient, fortunate, favourable, apt, advantageous, auspicious, fortuitous, well-timed, propitious, heaven-sent, felicitous, providential, seasonable, falling into your lap OPPOSITE inopportune

opportunism = expediency, convenience, exploitation, realism, manipulation, pragmatism, capitalization, realpolitik, utilitarianism, making hay while the sun shines (*informal*), striking while the iron is hot (*informal*), unscrupulousness, Machiavellianism

opportunity = chance, opening, time, turn, hour, break (*informal*), moment, window, possibility, occasion, slot, scope, look-in (*informal*)

oppose = be against, fight (against), check, bar, block, prevent, take on, counter, contest, resist, confront, face, combat, defy, thwart, contradict, withstand, stand up to, hinder, struggle against, obstruct, fly in the face of, take issue with, be hostile to, counterattack, speak (out) against, be in opposition to, be in defiance of, strive against, set your face against, take *or* make a stand against

OPPOSITE support

opposed with *to* **1** = against, anti (*informal*), hostile, adverse, contra (*informal*), in opposition, averse, antagonistic, inimical, (dead) set against ...*I am utterly opposed to any form of terrorism...*
2 = underline{contrary}, opposite, conflicting, opposing, clashing, counter, adverse, contradictory, in opposition, incompatible, antithetical, antipathetic, dissentient ...*people with views almost diametrically opposed to his own...*

opposing 1 = conflicting, different, opposed, contrasting, opposite, differing, contrary, contradictory, incompatible, irreconcilable ...*I have a friend who holds the opposing view...*
2 = rival, warring, conflicting, clashing, competing, enemy, opposite, hostile, combatant, antagonistic, antipathetic ...*The leader said he still favoured a dialogue between the opposing sides...*

opposite PREPOSITION = facing, face to face with, across from, eyeball to eyeball (*informal*) ...*She sat opposite her at breakfast...*
ADJECTIVE **1** = underline{facing}, other, opposing ...*the opposite side of the room...*
2 = different, conflicting, opposed, contrasted, contrasting, unlike, differing, contrary, diverse, adverse, at odds, contradictory, inconsistent, dissimilar, divergent, irreconcilable, at variance, poles apart, diametrically opposed, antithetical, streets apart ...*Everything he does is opposite to what is considered normal behaviour...* OPPOSITE alike
3 = rival, conflicting, opposed, opposing, competing, hostile, antagonistic, inimical ...*They fought on opposite sides during the War of Independence...*
NOUN = reverse, contrary, converse, antithesis, the other extreme, contradiction, inverse, the other side of the coin (*informal*), obverse ...*She's very shy, but her sister is quite the opposite...*

opposition 1 = hostility, resistance, resentment, disapproval, obstruction, animosity, aversion, antagonism, antipathy, obstructiveness, counteraction, contrariety ...*Much of the opposition to this plan has come from the media...* OPPOSITE support
2 = opponent(s), competition, rival(s), enemy, competitor(s), other side, challenger(s), foe, contestant(s), antagonist(s) ...*The team inflicted a crushing defeat on the opposition...*

oppress 1 = subjugate, abuse, suppress, wrong, master, overcome, crush, overwhelm, put down, subdue, overpower, persecute, rule over, enslave, maltreat, hold sway over, trample underfoot, bring someone to heel, tyrannize over, rule with an iron hand, bring someone under the yoke ...*Men still oppress women both physically and socially...* OPPOSITE liberate
2 = depress, burden, discourage, torment, daunt, harass, afflict, sadden, vex, weigh down, dishearten, cast someone down, dispirit, take the heart out of, deject, lie *or* weigh heavy upon, make someone despondent ...*The atmosphere in the room oppressed her...*

oppressed = <u>downtrodden</u>, abused, exploited, subject, burdened, distressed, slave, disadvantaged, helpless, misused, enslaved, prostrate, underprivileged, subservient, subjugated, browbeaten, maltreated, tyrannized, henpecked OPPOSITE liberated

oppression = <u>persecution</u>, control, suffering, abuse, injury, injustice, cruelty, domination, repression, brutality, suppression, severity, tyranny, authoritarianism, harshness, despotism, ill-treatment, subjugation, subjection, maltreatment OPPOSITE justice

oppressive 1 = <u>tyrannical</u>, severe, harsh, heavy, overwhelming, cruel, brutal, authoritarian, unjust, repressive, Draconian, autocratic, inhuman, dictatorial, coercive, imperious, domineering, overbearing, burdensome, despotic, high-handed, peremptory, overweening, tyrannous ...*The new laws will be as oppressive as those they replace...* OPPOSITE merciful
2 – <u>stifling</u>, close, heavy, sticky, overpowering, suffocating, stuffy, humid, torrid, sultry, airless, muggy ...*The oppressive afternoon heat had quite tired him out...*

oppressor = <u>persecutor</u>, tyrant, bully, scourge, tormentor, despot, autocrat, taskmaster, iron hand, slave-driver, harrier, intimidator, subjugator

opt VERB = <u>choose</u>, decide, prefer, select, elect, see fit, make a selection ...*Students can opt to stay in residence...* OPPOSITE reject
PHRASES **opt for something** or **someone** = <u>choose</u>, pick, select, take, adopt, go for, designate, decide on, single out, espouse, fix on, plump for, settle upon, exercise your discretion in favour of ...*You may wish to opt for one method or the other...*

optimistic 1 = <u>hopeful</u>, positive, confident, encouraged, can-do (*informal*), bright, assured, cheerful, rosy, buoyant, idealistic, Utopian, sanguine, expectant, looking on the bright side, buoyed up, disposed to take a favourable view, seen through rose-coloured spectacles ...*Michael was in a jovial and optimistic mood...* OPPOSITE pessimistic
2 = <u>encouraging</u>, promising, bright, good, cheering, reassuring, satisfactory, rosy, heartening, auspicious, propitious ...*an optimistic forecast that the economy would pick up by the end of the year...* OPPOSITE discouraging

optimum or **optimal** = <u>ideal</u>, best, highest, finest, choicest, perfect, supreme, peak, outstanding, first-class, foremost, first-rate, flawless, superlative, pre-eminent, most excellent, A1 or A-one (*informal*), most favourable or advantageous OPPOSITE worst

option = <u>choice</u>, alternative, selection, preference, freedom of choice, power to choose, election

optional = <u>voluntary</u>, open, discretionary, possible, extra, elective, up to the individual, noncompulsory OPPOSITE compulsory

opulence 1 = <u>luxury</u>, riches, wealth, splendour, prosperity, richness, affluence, voluptuousness, lavishness, sumptuousness, luxuriance ...*the opulence of the hotel's sumptuous interior...*
2 = <u>wealth</u>, means, riches (*informal*), capital, resources, assets, fortune, substance, prosperity, affluence, easy circumstances, prosperousness ...*He is surrounded by possessions which testify to his opulence...* OPPOSITE poverty

opulent 1 = <u>luxurious</u>, expensive, magnificent, costly, splendid, lavish, sumptuous, plush (*informal*), ritzy (*slang*), de luxe, well-appointed ...*an opulent lifestyle...*
2 = <u>rich</u>, wealthy, prosperous, propertied, loaded (*slang*), flush (*informal*), affluent, well-off, well-heeled (*informal*), well-to-do, moneyed, filthy rich, stinking rich (*informal*), made of money (*informal*) ...*the spoilt child of an opulent father...* OPPOSITE poor

opus = <u>work</u>, piece, production, creation, composition, work of art, brainchild, oeuvre (*French*)

oracle 1 = <u>prophet</u>, diviner, sage, seer, clairvoyant, augur, soothsayer, sibyl, prophesier ...*Ancient peoples consulted the oracle and the shaman for advice...*
2 = <u>prophecy</u>, vision, revelation, forecast, prediction, divination, prognostication, augury, divine utterance ...*Aeneas had begged the Sybil to speak her oracle in words...*
3 = <u>authority</u>, judge, expert, source, professional, master, specialist, adviser, scholar, guru, mentor, pundit, wizard, mastermind, connoisseur, arbiter, high priest, horse's mouth, fundi (*S. African*) ...*He is the oracle on modern etiquette...*

oral = <u>spoken</u>, vocal, verbal, unwritten, viva voce

orange

Shades of orange

amber	ochre
burnt sienna	peach
gold	tangerine
grenadine	terracotta

oration = <u>speech</u>, talk, address, lecture, discourse, harangue, homily, spiel (*informal*), disquisition, declamation

orator = <u>public speaker</u>, speaker, lecturer, spokesperson, declaimer, rhetorician, Cicero, spieler (*informal*), word-spinner, spokesman or spokeswoman

oratory = <u>rhetoric</u>, eloquence, public speaking, speech-making, expressiveness, fluency, a way with words, declamation, speechifying, grandiloquence, spieling (*informal*)

orb = <u>sphere</u>, ball, circle, globe, round

orbit NOUN 1 = <u>path</u>, course, track, cycle, circle, revolution, passage, rotation, trajectory, sweep, ellipse, circumgyration ...*the point at which the planet's orbit is closest to the sun...*
2 = <u>sphere of influence</u>, reach, range, influence, province, scope, sphere, domain, compass, ambit ...*Eisenhower acknowledged that Hungary lay within the Soviet orbit...*
VERB = <u>circle</u>, ring, go round, compass, revolve around, encircle, circumscribe, gird, circumnavigate

…the first satellite to orbit the Earth…

orchestra

> ## Instruments in a full orchestra
>
> http://www.mti.dmu.ac.uk/~ahugill/manual/
>
> | | |
> |---|---|
> | violin | french horn |
> | viola | trumpet |
> | double bass | tuba |
> | piano | trombone |
> | harp | timpani |
> | piccolo | gong |
> | flute | bass-drum |
> | oboe | xylophone |
> | cor anglais | celesta |
> | contra-bassoon | snare drum |
> | bassoon | tubular bells |
> | clarinet | |

orchestrate 1 = <u>organize</u>, plan, run, set up, arrange, be responsible for, put together, see to (*informal*), marshal, coordinate, concert, stage-manage …*The colonel orchestrated the rebellion from inside his army jail…*
2 = <u>score</u>, set, arrange, adapt …*He was orchestrating the first act of his opera…*

ordain 1 = <u>appoint</u>, call, name, commission, select, elect, invest, install, nominate, anoint, consecrate, frock …*Her brother was ordained as a priest in 1982…*
2 (*Formal*) = <u>order</u>, will, rule, demand, require, direct, establish, command, dictate, prescribe, pronounce, lay down, decree, instruct, enact, legislate, enjoin …*He ordained that women should be veiled in public…*
3 = <u>predestine</u>, fate, intend, mark out, predetermine, foreordain, destine, preordain …*His future seemed ordained right from the start…*

ordeal = <u>hardship</u>, trial, difficulty, test, labour, suffering, trouble(s), nightmare, burden, torture, misery, agony, torment, anguish, toil, affliction, tribulation(s), baptism of fire [OPPOSITE] pleasure

order [VERB] 1 = <u>command</u>, instruct, direct, charge, demand, require, bid, compel, enjoin, adjure …*Williams ordered him to leave…* [OPPOSITE] forbid
2 = <u>decree</u>, rule, demand, establish, prescribe, pronounce, ordain …*The President has ordered a full investigation…* [OPPOSITE] ban
3 = <u>request</u>, ask (for), book, demand, seek, call for, reserve, engage, apply for, contract for, solicit, requisition, put in for, send away for …*I often order goods over the Internet these days…*
4 = <u>arrange</u>, group, sort, class, position, range, file, rank, line up, organize, set out, sequence, catalogue, sort out, classify, array, dispose, tidy, marshal, lay out, tabulate, systematize, neaten, put in order, set in order, put to rights …*Entries in the book are ordered alphabetically…* [OPPOSITE] disarrange
[NOUN] 1 = <u>instruction</u>, ruling, demand, direction, command, say-so (*informal*), dictate, decree, mandate, directive, injunction, behest, stipulation …*They were arrested and executed on the orders of Stalin…*
2 = <u>request</u>, booking, demand, commission, application, reservation, requisition …*The company

say they can't supply our order…*
3 = <u>sequence</u>, grouping, ordering, line, series, structure, chain, arrangement, line-up, succession, disposal, array, placement, classification, layout, progression, disposition, setup (*informal*), categorization, codification …*List the key headings and sort them in a logical order…*
4 = <u>organization</u>, system, method, plan, pattern, arrangement, harmony, symmetry, regularity, propriety, neatness, tidiness, orderliness …*The wish to impose order upon confusion is a kind of intellectual instinct…* [OPPOSITE] chaos
5 = <u>peace</u>, control, law, quiet, calm, discipline, law and order, tranquillity, peacefulness, lawfulness …*He has the power to use force to maintain public order…*
6 = <u>society</u>, company, group, club, union, community, league, association, institute, organization, circle, corporation, lodge, guild, sect, fellowship, fraternity, brotherhood, sisterhood, sodality …*the Benedictine order of monks…*
7 = <u>class</u>, set, rank, degree, grade, sphere, caste …*He maintained that the higher orders of society must rule the lower…*
8 = <u>kind</u>, group, class, family, form, sort, type, variety, cast, species, breed, strain, category, tribe, genre, classification, genus, ilk, subdivision, subclass, taxonomic group …*the order of insects Coleoptera, better known as beetles…*
[PHRASES] **in order** 1 = <u>tidy</u>, ordered, neat, arranged, trim, orderly, spruce, well-kept, well-ordered, shipshape, spick-and-span, trig (*archaic or dialect*), in apple-pie order (*informal*) …*We tried to keep the room in order…* 2 = <u>appropriate</u>, right, fitting, seemly, called for, correct, suitable, acceptable, proper, to the point, apt, applicable, pertinent, befitting, well-suited, well-timed, apposite, germane, to the purpose, meet (*archaic*), O.K. or okay (*informal*) …*I think an apology would be in order…* ◆ **out of order** 1 = <u>not working</u>, broken, broken-down, ruined, bust (*informal*), defective, wonky (*Brit. slang*), not functioning, out of commission, on the blink (*slang*), on its last legs, inoperative, kaput (*informal*), in disrepair, gone haywire (*informal*), nonfunctional, on the fritz (*U.S. slang*), gone phut (*informal*), U.S. (*informal*) …*The phone is out of order…* 2 = <u>improper</u>, wrong, unsuitable, not done, not on (*informal*), unfitting, vulgar, out of place, unseemly, untoward, unbecoming, impolite, off-colour, out of turn, uncalled-for, not cricket (*informal*), indelicate, indecorous …*Don't you think that remark was a bit out of order?…*

orderly 1 = <u>well-behaved</u>, controlled, disciplined, quiet, restrained, law-abiding, nonviolent, peaceable, decorous …*The organizers guided them in orderly fashion out of the building…* [OPPOSITE] disorderly
2 = <u>well-organized</u>, ordered, regular, in order, organized, trim, precise, neat, tidy, systematic, businesslike, methodical, well-kept, shipshape, systematized, well-regulated, in apple-pie order (*informal*) …*The vehicles were parked in orderly rows…* [OPPOSITE] disorganized

ordinance = <u>rule</u>, order, law, ruling, standard, guide, direction, principle, command, regulation, guideline, criterion, decree, canon, statute, fiat, edict, dictum, precept

ordinarily = <u>usually</u>, generally, normally, commonly, regularly, routinely, in general, as a rule, habitually, customarily, in the usual way, as is usual, as is the custom, in the general run (of things) OPPOSITE> seldom

ordinary ADJECTIVE 1 = <u>usual</u>, standard, normal, common, established, settled, regular, familiar, household, typical, conventional, routine, stock, everyday, prevailing, accustomed, customary, habitual, quotidian, wonted ...*It was just an ordinary day for us*...
2 = <u>commonplace</u>, plain, modest, humble, stereotyped, pedestrian, mundane, vanilla (*slang*), stale, banal, unremarkable, prosaic, run-of-the-mill, humdrum, homespun, uninteresting, workaday, common or garden (*informal*), unmemorable ...*My life seems pretty ordinary compared to yours*...
3 = <u>average</u>, middling, fair, indifferent, not bad, mediocre, so-so (*informal*), unremarkable, tolerable, run-of-the-mill, passable, undistinguished, uninspired, unexceptional, bog-standard (*Brit. & Irish slang*), no great shakes (*informal*), dime-a-dozen (*informal*) ...*The food here is cheap, but very ordinary*... OPPOSITE> extraordinary
PHRASES **out of the ordinary** = <u>unusual</u>, different, odd, important, special, striking, surprising, significant, strange, exciting, rare, impressive, extraordinary, outstanding, remarkable, bizarre, distinguished, unexpected, curious, exceptional, notable, unfamiliar, abnormal, queer, uncommon, singular, unconventional, noteworthy, atypical ...*Have you noticed anything out of the ordinary about him?*...

ordnance = <u>weapons</u>, arms, guns, artillery, cannon, firearms, weaponry, big guns, armaments, munitions, materiel, instruments of war

organ 1 = <u>body part</u>, part of the body, member, element, biological structure ...*damage to the muscles and internal organs*...
2 = <u>newspaper</u>, paper, medium, voice, agency, channel, vehicle, journal, publication, rag (*informal*), gazette, periodical, mouthpiece ...*the People's Daily, the official organ of the Chinese Commmunist Party*...

organic 1 = <u>natural</u>, biological, living, live, vital, animate, biotic ...*Oxygen is vital to all organic life on Earth*...
2 = <u>systematic</u>, ordered, structured, organized, integrated, orderly, standardized, methodical, well-ordered, systematized ...*City planning treats the city as an organic whole*...
3 = <u>integral</u>, fundamental, constitutional, structural, inherent, innate, immanent ...*The history of Russia is an organic part of European history*...

organism = <u>creature</u>, being, thing, body, animal, structure, beast, entity, living thing, critter (*U.S. dialect*)

organization 1 = <u>group</u>, company, party, body, concern, league, association, band, institution, gathering, circle, corporation, federation, outfit (*informal*), faction, consortium, syndicate, combine, congregation, confederation ...*Most of the funds are provided by voluntary organizations*...
2 = <u>management</u>, running, planning, making, control, operation, handling, structuring, administration, direction, regulation, construction, organizing, supervision, governance, formulation, coordination, methodology, superintendence ...*the work that goes into the organization of this event*...
3 = <u>structure</u>, grouping, plan, system, form, design, method, pattern, make-up, arrangement, construction, constitution, format, formation, framework, composition, chemistry, configuration, conformation, interrelation of parts ...*the internal organization of the department*...

organize 1 = <u>arrange</u>, run, plan, form, prepare, establish, set up, shape, schedule, frame, look after, be responsible for, construct, constitute, devise, put together, take care of, see to (*informal*), get together, marshal, contrive, get going, coordinate, fix up, straighten out, lay the foundations of, lick into shape, jack up (*N.Z. informal*) ...*We need someone to help organize our campaign*... OPPOSITE> disrupt
2 = <u>put in order</u>, arrange, group, list, file, index, catalogue, classify, codify, pigeonhole, tabulate, inventory, systematize, dispose ...*He began to organize his papers*... OPPOSITE> muddle

orgasm = <u>climax</u>, coming (*taboo slang*), pleasure, the big O (*informal*), (sexual) satisfaction

orgy 1 = <u>party</u>, celebration, rave (*Brit. slang*), revel, festivity, bender (*informal*), debauch, revelry, carouse, Saturnalia, bacchanal, rave-up (*Brit. slang*), bacchanalia, carousal, hooley or hoolie (*chiefly Irish & N.Z.*) ...*a drunken orgy*...
2 = <u>spree</u>, fit, spell, run, session, excess, bout, indulgence, binge (*informal*), splurge, surfeit, overindulgence ...*He blew £43,000 in an 18-month orgy of spending*...

orient *or* **orientate** 1 = <u>adjust</u>, settle, adapt, tune, convert, alter, compose, accommodate, accustom, reconcile, align, harmonize, familiarize, acclimatize, find your feet (*informal*) ...*It will take some time to orient yourself to this new way of thinking*...
2 = <u>get your bearings</u>, get the lie of the land, establish your location ...*She lay still for a few seconds, trying to orient herself*...

orientation 1 = <u>inclination</u>, tendency, bias, leaning, bent, disposition, predisposition, predilection, proclivity, partiality, turn of mind ...*The party is liberal and democratic in orientation*...
2 = <u>induction</u>, introduction, breaking in, adjustment, settling in, adaptation, initiation, assimilation, familiarization, acclimatization ...*the company's policy on recruiting and orientation*...
3 = <u>position</u>, situation, location, site, bearings, direction, arrangement, whereabouts, disposition, coordination ...*The orientation of the church is such that the front faces the square*...

orifice = <u>opening</u>, space, hole, split, mouth, gap, rent, breach, vent, pore, rupture, aperture, cleft, chink, fissure, perforation, interstice

origin 1 = <u>beginning</u>, start, birth, source, launch, foundation, creation, dawning, early stages, emergence, outset, starting point, onset, genesis, initiation, inauguration, inception, font (*poetic*), commencement, fountain, fount, origination, fountainhead, mainspring …*theories about the origin of life…* OPPOSITE end
2 = <u>root</u>, source, basis, beginnings, base, cause, spring, roots, seed, foundation, nucleus, germ, provenance, derivation, wellspring, fons et origo (*Latin*) …*What is the origin of the word 'honeymoon'?…*
3 = <u>ancestry</u>, family, race, beginnings, stock, blood, birth, heritage, ancestors, descent, pedigree, extraction, lineage, forebears, antecedents, parentage, forefathers, genealogy, derivation, progenitors, stirps …*people of Asian origin…*

original ADJECTIVE 1 = <u>first</u>, earliest, early, initial, aboriginal, primitive, pristine, primordial, primeval, autochthonous …*The Dayaks were the original inhabitants of Borneo…*
2 = <u>initial</u>, first, starting, opening, primary, inaugural, commencing, introductory …*Let's stick to the original plan…* OPPOSITE final
3 = <u>authentic</u>, real, actual, genuine, legitimate, first generation, bona fide, the real McCoy …*The company specializes in selling original movie posters…* OPPOSITE copied
4 = <u>new</u>, fresh, novel, different, unusual, unknown, unprecedented, innovative, unfamiliar, unconventional, seminal, ground-breaking, untried, innovatory, newfangled …*an original idea…* OPPOSITE unoriginal
5 = <u>creative</u>, inspired, imaginative, artistic, fertile, ingenious, visionary, inventive, resourceful …*a chef with an original touch and a measure of inspiration…* NOUN 1 = <u>prototype</u>, master, pattern …*Photocopy the form and send the original to your employer…* OPPOSITE copy
2 = <u>character</u>, eccentric, case (*informal*), card (*informal*), nut (*slang*), flake (*slang, chiefly U.S.*), anomaly, oddity, oddball (*informal*), nonconformist, wacko (*slang*), odd bod (*informal*), queer fish (*Brit. informal*), weirdo *or* weirdie (*informal*) …*He's an original, this one, and a good storyteller…*

originality = <u>novelty</u>, imagination, creativity, innovation, new ideas, individuality, ingenuity, freshness, uniqueness, boldness, inventiveness, cleverness, resourcefulness, break with tradition, newness, unfamiliarity, creative spirit, unorthodoxy, unconventionality, creativeness, innovativeness, imaginativeness OPPOSITE conventionality

originally = <u>initially</u>, first, firstly, at first, primarily, at the start, in the first place, to begin with, at the outset, in the beginning, in the early stages

originate 1 = <u>begin</u>, start, emerge, come, issue, happen, rise, appear, spring, flow, be born, proceed, arise, dawn, stem, derive, commence, emanate, crop up (*informal*), come into being, come into existence …*The disease originated in Africa…* OPPOSITE end
2 = <u>invent</u>, produce, create, form, develop, design,

launch, set up, introduce, imagine, institute, generate, come up with (*informal*), pioneer, evolve, devise, initiate, conceive, bring about, formulate, give birth to, contrive, improvise, dream up (*informal*), inaugurate, think up, set in motion …*No-one knows who originated this story…*

originator = <u>creator</u>, father *or* mother, founder, author, maker, framer, designer, architect, pioneer, generator, inventor, innovator, prime mover, initiator, begetter

ornament NOUN 1 = <u>decoration</u>, trimming, accessory, garnish, frill, festoon, trinket, bauble, flounce, gewgaw, knick-knack, furbelow, falderal …*Christmas tree ornaments…*
2 = <u>embellishment</u>, trimming, decoration, embroidery, elaboration, adornment, ornamentation …*Her dress was plain and without ornament…*
VERB = <u>decorate</u>, trim, adorn, enhance, deck, array, dress up, enrich, brighten, garnish, gild, do up (*informal*), embellish, emblazon, festoon, bedeck, beautify, prettify, bedizen (*archaic*), engarland …*The Egyptians ornamented their mirrors with carved handles of ivory, gold, or wood…*

ornamental = <u>decorative</u>, pretty, attractive, fancy, enhancing, for show, embellishing, showy, beautifying, nonfunctional

ornamentation = <u>decoration</u>, trimming, frills, garnishing, embroidery, enrichment, elaboration, embellishment, adornment, beautification, ornateness

ornate = <u>elaborate</u>, fancy, decorated, detailed, beautiful, complex, busy, complicated, elegant, extravagant, baroque, ornamented, fussy, flowery, showy, ostentatious, rococo, florid, bedecked, overelaborate, high-wrought, aureate OPPOSITE plain

orthodox 1 = <u>established</u>, official, accepted, received, common, popular, traditional, normal, regular, usual, ordinary, approved, familiar, acknowledged, conventional, routine, customary, well-established, kosher (*informal*) …*These ideas are now being incorporated into orthodox medical treatment…* OPPOSITE unorthodox
2 = <u>conformist</u>, conservative, traditional, strict, devout, observant, doctrinal …*orthodox Jews…* OPPOSITE nonconformist

orthodoxy 1 = <u>doctrine</u>, teaching, opinion, principle, belief, convention, canon, creed, dogma, tenet, precept, article of faith …*He departed from prevailing orthodoxies and broke new ground…*
2 = <u>conformity</u>, received wisdom, traditionalism, inflexibility, conformism, conventionality …*a return to political orthodoxy…* OPPOSITE nonconformity

oscillate 1 = <u>fluctuate</u>, swing, vary, sway, waver, veer, rise and fall, vibrate, undulate, go up and down, seesaw …*The needle indicating volume was oscillating wildly…*
2 = <u>waver</u>, change, swing, shift, vary, sway, alternate, veer, ebb and flow, vacillate, seesaw …*She oscillated between elation and despair…* OPPOSITE settle

oscillation 1 = <u>fluctuation</u>, swing, variation,

instability, imbalance, wavering, volatility, variability, unpredictability, seesawing, disequilibrium, capriciousness, mutability, inconstancy, changeableness ...*a slight oscillation in world temperature*...

2 = wavering, swing, shift, swaying, alteration, veering, seesawing, vacillation ...*his oscillation between skepticism and credulity*...

ostensible = apparent, seeming, supposed, alleged, so-called, pretended, exhibited, manifest, outward, superficial, professed, purported, avowed, specious

ostensibly = apparently, seemingly, supposedly, outwardly, on the surface, on the face of it, superficially, to all intents and purposes, professedly, speciously, for the ostensible purpose of

ostentatious = pretentious, extravagant, flamboyant, flash (*informal*), loud, dashing, inflated, conspicuous, vulgar, brash, high-flown, flashy, pompous, flaunted, flaunting, grandiose, crass, gaudy, showy, swanky (*informal*), snobbish, puffed up, specious, boastful, obtrusive, highfalutin (*informal*), arty-farty (*informal*), magniloquent OPPOSITE modest

ostracism = exclusion, boycott, isolation, exile, rejection, expulsion, avoidance, cold-shouldering, renunciation, banishment OPPOSITE acceptance

other **1** = additional, more, further, new, added, extra, fresh, spare, supplementary, auxiliary ...*No other details are available at the moment*...

2 = different, alternative, contrasting, distinct, diverse, dissimilar, separate, alternative, substitute, alternate, unrelated, variant ...*Try to find other words and phrases to give variety to your writing*...

3 = remaining, left-over, residual, extant ...*The other pupils were taken to an exhibition*...

otherwise **1** = or else, or, if not, or then ...*Write it down, otherwise you'll forget it*...

2 = apart from that, in other ways, in (all) other respects ...*a caravan slightly dented but otherwise in good condition*...

3 = differently, any other way, in another way, contrarily, contrastingly, in contrary fashion ...*I believed he would be home soon – I had no reason to think otherwise*...

ounce = shred, bit, drop, trace, scrap, grain, particle, fragment, atom, crumb, snippet, speck, whit, iota

oust = expel, turn out, dismiss, exclude, exile, discharge, throw out, relegate, displace, topple, banish, eject, depose, evict, dislodge, unseat, dispossess, send packing, turf out (*informal*), disinherit, drum out, show someone the door, give the bum's rush (*slang*), throw out on your ear (*informal*)

out ADJECTIVE **1** = not in, away, elsewhere, outside, gone, abroad, from home, absent, not here, no there, not at home ...*I tried to phone you last night, but you were out*...

2 = extinguished, ended, finished, dead, cold, exhausted, expired, used up, doused, at an end ...*There was an occasional spark but the fire was out*... OPPOSITE alight

3 = in bloom, opening, open, flowering, blooming, in flower, in full bloom ...*The daffodils are out now*...

4 = available, on sale, in the shops, at hand, to be had, purchasable, procurable ...*Their new album is out next week*...

5 = not allowed, banned, forbidden, ruled out, vetoed, not on (*informal*), unacceptable, prohibited, taboo, verboten (*German*) ...*Drinking is bad enough, but smoking is right out*... OPPOSITE allowed

6 = out of date, dead, square (*informal*), old-fashioned, dated, outdated, unfashionable, antiquated, outmoded, passé, old hat, behind the times, out of style, démodé (*French*), not with it (*informal*) ...*Romance is making a comeback. Cynicism is out*... OPPOSITE fashionable

7 = inaccurate, wrong, incorrect, faulty, off the mark, erroneous, off target, wide of the mark ...*Our calculations were only slightly out*... OPPOSITE accurate

8 = revealed, exposed, common knowledge, public knowledge, (out) in the open ...*The secret about his drug addiction is out*... OPPOSITE kept secret

VERB = expose, uncover, unmask ...*The New York gay action group recently outed an American Congressman*...

out-and-out = absolute, complete, total, perfect, sheer, utter, outright, thorough, downright, consummate, unqualified, unmitigated, dyed-in-the-wool, thoroughgoing, unalloyed, arrant, deep-dyed (*usually derogatory*)

outbreak **1** = eruption, burst, explosion, epidemic, rash, outburst, flare-up, flash, spasm, upsurge ...*This outbreak of flu is no worse than normal*...

2 = onset, beginning, outset, opening, dawn, commencement ...*On the outbreak of war he had expected to be called up*...

outburst = explosion, fit, storm, surge, attack, outbreak, gush, flare-up, eruption, spasm, outpouring, paroxysm

outcast = pariah, exile, outlaw, undesirable, untouchable, leper, vagabond, wretch, persona non grata (*Latin*)

outclass = surpass, top, beat, cap (*informal*), exceed, eclipse, overshadow, excel, transcend, outstrip, outdo, outshine, leave standing (*informal*), tower above, go one better than (*informal*), be a cut above (*informal*), run rings around (*informal*), outdistance, outrank, put in the shade, leave *or* put in the shade

outcome = result, end, consequence, conclusion, end result, payoff (*informal*), upshot

outcry = protest, complaint, objection, cry, dissent, outburst, disapproval, clamour, uproar, commotion, protestation, exclamation, formal complaint, hue and cry, hullaballoo, demurral

outdated = old-fashioned, dated, obsolete, out of date, passé, antique, archaic, unfashionable, antiquated, outmoded, behind the times, out of style, obsolescent, démodé (*French*), out of the ark (*informal*), oldfangled OPPOSITE modern

outdo = surpass, best, top, beat, overcome, exceed, eclipse, overshadow, excel, transcend, outstrip, get the better of, outclass, outshine, tower above, outsmart (*informal*), outmanoeuvre, go one better than (*informal*), run rings around (*informal*), outfox, outdistance, be one up on, score points off, put in the shade, outjockey

outdoor = <u>open-air</u>, outside, out-of-door(s), alfresco OPPOSITE indoor

outer 1 = <u>external</u>, outside, outward, exterior, exposed, outermost ...*Peel away the outer skin of the onion*... OPPOSITE inner
2 = <u>surface</u>, external, outward, exterior, superficial ...*Our preoccupation with appearance goes much deeper than the outer image*...
3 = <u>outlying</u>, remote, distant, provincial, out-of-the-way, peripheral, far-flung ...*the outer suburbs of the city*... OPPOSITE central

outfit NOUN 1 = <u>costume</u>, dress, clothes, clothing, suit, gear (*informal*), get-up (*informal*), kit, ensemble, apparel, attire, garb, togs (*informal*), threads (*slang*), schmutter (*slang*), rigout (*informal*) ...*She was wearing an outfit we'd bought the previous day*...
2 (*Informal*) = <u>group</u>, company, team, set, party, firm, association, unit, crowd, squad, organization, crew, gang, corps, setup (*informal*), galère (*French*) ...*He works for a private security outfit*...
VERB 1 = <u>equip</u>, stock, supply, turn out, appoint, provision, furnish, fit out, deck out, kit out, fit up, accoutre ...*Homes can be outfitted with security lights for a few hundred dollars*...
2 = <u>dress</u>, clothe, attire, deck out, kit out, rig out ...*The travel company outfitted their staff in coloured jerseys*...

outfitter (*Old-fashioned*) = <u>clothier</u>, tailor, couturier, dressmaker, seamstress, haberdasher (*U.S.*), costumier, garment maker, modiste

outflow 1 = <u>stream</u>, issue, flow, rush, emergence, spate, deluge, outpouring, effusion, emanation, efflux ...*an increasing outflow of refugees from the country*...
2 = <u>discharge</u>, flow, jet, cascade, ebb, gush, drainage, torrent, deluge, spurt, spout, outpouring, outfall, efflux, effluence, debouchment ...*an outflow of fresh water from a river*...

outgoing 1 = <u>leaving</u>, last, former, past, previous, retiring, withdrawing, prior, departing, erstwhile, late, ex- ...*the outgoing director of the Edinburgh International Festival*... OPPOSITE incoming
2 = <u>sociable</u>, open, social, warm, friendly, accessible, expansive, cordial, genial, affable, extrovert, approachable, gregarious, communicative, convivial, demonstrative, unreserved, companionable ...*She is very friendly and outgoing*... OPPOSITE reserved

outgoings = <u>expenses</u>, costs, payments, expenditure, overheads, outlay

outgrowth 1 = <u>product</u>, result, development, fruit, consequence, outcome, legacy, emergence, derivative, spin-off, by-product, end result, offshoot, upshot ...*Her first book is an outgrowth of an art project she began in 1988*...
2 = <u>offshoot</u>, shoot, branch, limb, projection, sprout, node, outcrop, appendage, scion, protuberance, excrescence ...*a new organism develops as an outgrowth or bud*...

outing = <u>journey</u>, run, trip, tour, expedition, excursion, spin (*informal*), ramble, jaunt, pleasure trip

outlandish = <u>strange</u>, odd, extraordinary, wonderful, funny, bizarre, fantastic, astonishing, curious, weird, foreign, alien, exotic, exceptional, peculiar, eccentric, abnormal, out-of-the-way, queer, irregular, singular, grotesque, far-out (*slang*), unheard-of, preposterous, off-the-wall (*slang*), left-field (*informal*), freakish, barbarous, outré OPPOSITE normal

outlast = <u>outlive</u>, survive, live after, outstay, live on after, endure beyond, outwear, remain alive after

outlaw VERB 1 = <u>ban</u>, bar, veto, forbid, condemn, exclude, embargo, suppress, prohibit, banish, disallow, proscribe, make illegal, interdict ...*The German government has outlawed some fascist groups*... OPPOSITE legalise
2 = <u>banish</u>, excommunicate, ostracize, put a price on (someone's) head ...*He should be outlawed for his crimes against the state*...
NOUN (*History*) = <u>bandit</u>, criminal, thief, crook, robber, fugitive, outcast, delinquent, felon, highwayman, desperado, marauder, brigand, lawbreaker, footpad (*archaic*) ...*a band of desperate outlaws*...

outlay = <u>expenditure</u>, cost, spending, charge, investment, payment, expense(s), outgoings, disbursement

outlet 1 = <u>shop</u>, store, supermarket, market, mart, boutique, emporium, hypermarket ...*the largest retail outlet in the city*...
2 = <u>channel</u>, release, medium, avenue, vent, conduit, safety valve, means of expression ...*He found an outlet for his emotions in his music*...
3 = <u>pipe</u>, opening, channel, passage, tube, exit, canal, way out, funnel, conduit, duct, orifice, egress ...*The leak was caused by a fracture in the cooling water outlet*...

outline VERB 1 = <u>summarize</u>, review, draft, plan, trace, sketch (in), sum up, encapsulate, delineate, rough out, adumbrate ...*The methods outlined in this book are only suggestions*...
2 = <u>silhouette</u>, etch, delineate ...*The building was a beautiful sight, outlined against the starry sky*...
NOUN 1 = <u>summary</u>, review, résumé, abstract, summing-up, digest, rundown, compendium, main features, synopsis, rough idea, précis, bare facts, thumbnail sketch, recapitulation, abridgment ...*There follows an outline of the survey findings*...
2 = <u>draft</u>, plan, drawing, frame, tracing, rough, framework, sketch, skeleton, layout, delineation, preliminary form ...*an outline of a plan to reduce the country's national debt*...
3 = <u>shape</u>, lines, form, figure, profile, silhouette, configuration, contour(s), delineation, lineament(s) ...*He could see only the hazy outline of the trees*...

outlive = <u>survive</u>, outlast, live on after, endure beyond, remain alive after

outlook 1 = <u>attitude</u>, views, opinion, position, approach, mood, perspective, point of view, stance,

viewpoint, disposition, standpoint, frame of mind ...*The illness had a profound effect on his outlook*...
2 = prospect(s), future, expectations, forecast, prediction, projection, probability, prognosis ...*The economic outlook is one of rising unemployment*...
3 = view, prospect, scene, aspect, perspective, panorama, vista ...*The house has an expansive southern outlook over the valley*...

outlying = remote, isolated, distant, outer, provincial, out-of-the-way, peripheral, far-off, secluded, far-flung, faraway, in the middle of nowhere, off the beaten track, backwoods, godforsaken

outmanoeuvre = outwit, outdo, get the better of, circumvent, outflank, outsmart (*informal*), steal a march on (*informal*), put one over on (*informal*), outfox, run rings round (*informal*), outthink, outgeneral, outjockey

outmoded = old-fashioned, passé, dated, out, dead, square (*informal*), ancient, antique, outdated, obsolete, out-of-date, old-time, archaic, unfashionable, superseded, bygone, antiquated, anachronistic, olden (*archaic*), behind the times, superannuated, fossilized, out of style, antediluvian, outworn, obsolescent, démodé (*French*), out of the ark (*informal*), not with it (*informal*), oldfangled
OPPOSITE> modern

out of date 1 = old-fashioned, ancient, dated, discarded, extinct, outdated, stale, obsolete, démodé (*French*), archaic, unfashionable, superseded, antiquated, outmoded, passé, old hat, behind the times, superannuated, out of style, outworn, obsolescent, out of the ark (*informal*), oldfangled ...*processes using out-of-date technology and very old equipment*... OPPOSITE> modern
2 = invalid, expired, lapsed, void, superseded, elapsed, null and void ...*These tax records are now out of date*...

out-of-the-way 1 = remote, far, distant, isolated, lonely, obscure, far-off, secluded, inaccessible, far-flung, faraway, outlying, in the middle of nowhere, off the beaten track, backwoods, godforsaken, unfrequented ...*I like travelling to out-of-the-way places*... OPPOSITE> nearby
2 = unusual, surprising, odd, strange, extraordinary, remarkable, bizarre, unexpected, curious, exceptional, notable, peculiar, abnormal, queer, uncommon, singular, unconventional, outlandish, out of the ordinary, left-field (*informal*), atypical ...*He did not seem to think her behaviour at all out of the way*...

outpouring = outburst, storm, stream, explosion, surge, outbreak, deluge, eruption, spasm, paroxysm, effusion, issue

output = production, manufacture, manufacturing, yield, productivity, outturn (*rare*)

outrage VERB = offend, shock, upset, pain, wound, provoke, insult, infuriate, incense, gall, madden, vex, affront, displease, rile, scandalize, give offence, nark (*Brit., Austral., & N.Z. slang*), cut to the quick, make your blood boil, put (someone's) nose out of joint, put (someone's) back up, disgruntle ...*Many people have been outraged by these comments*...
NOUN 1 = indignation, shock, anger, rage, fury, hurt, resentment, scorn, wrath, ire (*literary*), exasperation, umbrage, righteous anger ...*The decision has provoked outrage from human rights groups*...
2 = atrocity, crime, horror, evil, cruelty, brutality, enormity, barbarism, inhumanity, abomination, barbarity, villainy, act of cruelty ...*The terrorists' latest outrage is a bomb attack on a busy station*...

outrageous 1 = atrocious, shocking, terrible, violent, offensive, appalling, cruel, savage, horrible, beastly, horrifying, vicious, ruthless, infamous, disgraceful, scandalous, wicked, barbaric, unspeakable, inhuman, diabolical, heinous, flagrant, egregious, abominable, infernal, fiendish, villainous, nefarious, iniquitous, execrable, godawful (*slang*), hellacious (*U.S. slang*) ...*I must apologize for my friend's outrageous behaviour*...
OPPOSITE> mild
2 = unreasonable, unfair, excessive, steep (*informal*), shocking, over the top (*slang*), extravagant, too great, scandalous, preposterous, unwarranted, exorbitant, extortionate, immoderate, O.T.T. (*slang*) ...*Charges for long-distance telephone calls are absolutely outrageous*... OPPOSITE> reasonable

outright ADJECTIVE 1 = absolute, complete, total, direct, perfect, pure, sheer, utter, thorough, wholesale, unconditional, downright, consummate, unqualified, undeniable, out-and-out, unadulterated, unmitigated, thoroughgoing, unalloyed, arrant, deep-dyed (*usually derogatory*) ...*He told me an outright lie*...
2 = definite, clear, certain, straight, flat, absolute, black-and-white, decisive, straightforward, clear-cut, unmistakable, unequivocal, unqualified, unambiguous, cut-and-dried (*informal*), incontrovertible, uncontestable ...*She failed to win an outright victory*...
ADVERB 1 = openly, frankly, plainly, face to face, explicitly, overtly, candidly, unreservedly, unhesitatingly, forthrightly, straight from the shoulder (*informal*) ...*Why are you being so mysterious? Why can't you just tell me outright?*...
2 = absolutely, completely, totally, fully, entirely, thoroughly, wholly, utterly, to the full, without hesitation, to the hilt, one hundred per cent, straightforwardly, without restraint, unmitigatedly, lock, stock and barrel ...*His plan was rejected outright*...
3 = instantly, immediately, at once, straight away, cleanly, on the spot, right away, there and then, instantaneously ...*The driver was killed outright in the crash*...

outset = beginning, start, opening, early days, starting point, onset, inauguration, inception, commencement, kickoff (*informal*) OPPOSITE> finish

outside NOUN = exterior, face, front, covering, skin, surface, shell, coating, finish, façade, topside ...*the outside of the building*... ...*Grill until the outsides are browned*...
ADJECTIVE 1 = external, outer, exterior, surface, extreme, outdoor, outward, superficial, extraneous, outermost, extramural ...*Cracks are beginning to*

appear on the outside wall... OPPOSITE inner

2 = remote, small, unlikely, slight, slim, poor, distant, faint, marginal, doubtful, dubious, slender, meagre, negligible, inconsiderable ...*I thought I had an outside chance of winning*...

ADVERB = outdoors, out, out of the house, out-of-doors ...*I went outside and sat on the steps*...

Word Power

outside – The use of *outside of* and *inside of*, although fairly common, is generally thought to be incorrect or nonstandard: *She waits outside* (not *outside of*) *the school.*

---

outsider = stranger, incomer, visitor, foreigner, alien, newcomer, intruder, new arrival, unknown, interloper, odd one out, nonmember, outlander

outsize 1 = huge, great, large, giant, massive, enormous, monster, immense, mega (*slang*), jumbo (*informal*), gigantic, monumental, mammoth, bulky, colossal, mountainous, oversized, stupendous, gargantuan, elephantine, ginormous (*informal*), Brobdingnagian, humongous *or* humungous (*U.S. slang*) ...*An outsize teddy bear sat on the bed*... OPPOSITE tiny

2 = extra-large, large, generous, ample, roomy ...*Often outsize clothes are made from cheap fabric*...

outskirts = edge, borders, boundary, suburbs, fringe, perimeter, vicinity, periphery, suburbia, environs, purlieus, faubourgs

outsmart (*Informal*) = outwit, trick, take in (*informal*), cheat, deceive, defraud, dupe, gull (*archaic*), get the better of, swindle, circumvent, outperform, make a fool of (*informal*), outmanoeuvre, go one better than (*informal*), put one over on (*informal*), outfox, run rings round (*informal*), pull a fast one on (*informal*), outthink, outjockey

outspan (*S. African*) = relax, chill out (*slang, chiefly U.S.*), take it easy, loosen up, laze, lighten up (*slang*), put your feet up, hang loose (*slang*), let yourself go (*informal*), let your hair down (*informal*), mellow out (*informal*), make yourself at home

outspoken = forthright, open, free, direct, frank, straightforward, blunt, explicit, downright, candid, upfront (*informal*), unequivocal, undisguised, plain-spoken, unreserved, unconcealed, unceremonious, free-spoken, straight from the shoulder (*informal*), undissembling OPPOSITE reserved

outstanding 1 = excellent, good, great, important, special, fine, noted, champion, celebrated, brilliant, impressive, superb, distinguished, well-known, prominent, superior, first-class, exceptional, notable, world-class, exquisite, admirable, eminent, exemplary, first-rate, stellar (*informal*), superlative, top-notch (*informal*), mean (*slang*), pre-eminent, meritorious, estimable, tiptop, A1 *or* A-one (*informal*), booshit (*Austral. slang*), exo (*Austral. slang*), sik (*Austral. slang*) ...*an outstanding tennis player*... OPPOSITE mediocre

2 = conspicuous, marked, striking, arresting, signal, remarkable, memorable, notable, eye-catching,

salient, noteworthy ...*an area of outstanding natural beauty*...

3 = unpaid, remaining, due, owing, ongoing, pending, payable, unsettled, unresolved, uncollected ...*The total debt outstanding is $70 billion*...

4 = undone, left, not done, omitted, unfinished, incomplete, passed over, unfulfilled, not completed, unperformed, unattended to ...*Complete any work outstanding from yesterday*...

outstrip 1 = exceed, eclipse, overtake, top, cap (*informal*), go beyond, surpass, outdo ...*In 1989 and 1990 demand outstripped supply*...

2 = surpass (*informal*), beat, leave behind, eclipse, overtake, best, top, better, overshadow, outdo, outclass, outperform, outshine, leave standing (*informal*), tower above, get ahead of, go one better than (*informal*), run rings around, knock spots off (*informal*), put in the shade ...*In pursuing her ambition she outstripped everyone else*...

3 = outdistance, shake off, outrun, outpace ...*He soon outstripped the other runners*...

outward = apparent, seeming, outside, surface, external, outer, superficial, ostensible OPPOSITE inward

outwardly = apparently, externally, seemingly, it seems that, on the surface, it appears that, ostensibly, on the face of it, superficially, to the eye, to all intents and purposes, to all appearances, as far as you can see, professedly

outweigh = override, cancel (out), eclipse, offset, make up for, compensate for, redeem, supersede, neutralize, counterbalance, nullify, take precedence over, prevail over, obviate, balance out, preponderate, outbalance

outwit = outsmart (*informal*), get the better of, circumvent, outperform, outmanoeuvre, go one better than (*informal*), put one over on (*informal*), outfox, run rings round (*informal*), pull a fast one on (*informal*), outthink, outjockey

oval = elliptical, egg-shaped, ovoid, ovate, ellipsoidal, oviform

ovation = applause, hand, cheering, cheers, praise, tribute, acclaim, clapping, accolade, plaudits, big hand, commendation, hand-clapping, acclamation, laudation OPPOSITE derision

over PREPOSITION **1** = above, on top of, atop ...*He looked at himself in the mirror over the fireplace*...

2 = on top of, on, across, upon ...*His coat was thrown over a chair*...

3 = across, past, (looking) onto ...*a room with a wonderful view over the river*...

4 = more than, above, exceeding, in excess of, upwards of ...*Smoking kills over 100,000 people in Britain a year*...

5 = about, regarding, relating to, with respect to, re, concerning, apropos of, anent (*Scot.*) ...*You're making a lot of fuss over nothing*...

ADVERB **1** = above, overhead, in the sky, on high, aloft, up above ...*Planes flew over every 15 minutes or so*...

2 = extra, more, other, further, beyond, additional, in

addition, surplus, in excess, left over, unused, supplementary, auxiliary ...*There were two for each of us, and one over...*
ADJECTIVE = finished, by, done (with), through, ended, closed, past, completed, complete, gone, in the past, settled, concluded, accomplished, wrapped up (*informal*), bygone, at an end, ancient history (*informal*), over and done with ...*I think the worst is over now...*
PHRASES **over and above** = in addition to, added to, on top of, besides, plus, let alone, not to mention, as well as, over and beyond ...*Costs have gone up 7% over and above inflation...* ♦ **over and over (again)** = repeatedly, frequently, again and again, often, many times, time and (time) again, time after time, ad nauseam ...*He plays the same song over and over again...*

(*Related Words*)
prefixes: hyper-, super-, supra-, sur-

overall **ADJECTIVE** = total, full, whole, general, complete, long-term, entire, global, comprehensive, gross, blanket, umbrella, long-range, inclusive, all-embracing, overarching ...*Cut down your overall intake of calories...*
ADVERB = in general, generally, mostly, all things considered, on average, in (the) large, on the whole, predominantly, in the main, in the long term, by and large, all in all, on balance, generally speaking, taking everything into consideration ...*Overall, I was disappointed with the result...*

overawed = intimidated, threatened, alarmed, frightened, scared, terrified, cowed, put off, daunted, unnerved

overbearing = domineering, lordly, superior, arrogant, authoritarian, oppressive, autocratic, masterful, dictatorial, coercive, bossy (*informal*), imperious, haughty, tyrannical, magisterial, despotic, high-handed, peremptory, supercilious, officious, overweening, iron-handed **OPPOSITE** submissive

overblown 1 = excessive, exaggerated, over the top (*slang*), too much, inflated, extravagant, overdone, disproportionate, undue, fulsome, intemperate, immoderate, O.T.T. (*slang*) ...*The reporting of the story was fair, though a little overblown...*
2 = inflated, rhetorical, high-flown, pompous, pretentious, flowery, florid, turgid, bombastic, windy, grandiloquent, fustian, magniloquent, aureate, euphuistic ...*The book contains a heavy dose of overblown lyrical description...*

overcast = cloudy, grey, dull, threatening, dark, clouded, dim, gloomy, dismal, murky, dreary, leaden, clouded over, sunless, louring *or* lowering **OPPOSITE** bright

overcharge = cheat, con (*informal*), do (*slang*), skin (*slang*), stiff (*slang*), sting (*informal*), rip off (*slang*), fleece, defraud, surcharge, swindle, stitch up (*slang*), rook (*slang*), short-change, diddle (*informal*), take for a ride (*informal*), cozen

overcome **VERB** 1 = defeat, beat, conquer, master, tank (*slang*), crush, overwhelm, overthrow, lick

(*informal*), undo, subdue, rout, overpower, quell, triumph over, best, get the better of, trounce, worst, clobber (*slang*), stuff (*slang*), vanquish, surmount, subjugate, prevail over, wipe the floor with (*informal*), make mincemeat of (*informal*), blow (someone) out of the water (*slang*), come out on top of (*informal*), bring (someone) to their knees (*informal*), render incapable, render powerless, be victorious over, render helpless ...*the satisfaction of overcoming a rival...*
2 = conquer, beat, master, survive, weather, curb, suppress, subdue, rise above, quell, triumph over, get the better of, vanquish ...*I have fought to overcome my fear of spiders...*
ADJECTIVE = overwhelmed, moved, affected, emotional, choked, speechless, bowled over (*informal*), unable to continue, at a loss for words, visibly moved, swept off your feet ...*I don't know what to say! I'm quite overcome...*

overdo **VERB** = exaggerate, overstate, overuse, overplay, do to death (*informal*), belabour, carry *or* take too far, make a production (out) of (*informal*), lay (something) on thick (*informal*) ...*He overdid his usually quite funny vitriol...* **OPPOSITE** minimize
PHRASES **overdo it** = overwork, go too far, go overboard, strain *or* overstrain yourself, burn the midnight oil, burn the candle at both ends (*informal*), wear yourself out, bite off more than you can chew, have too many irons in the fire, overtire yourself, drive yourself too far, overburden yourself, overload yourself, overtax your strength, work your fingers to the bone ...*When you start your running programme, don't be tempted to overdo it...*

overdone 1 = overcooked, burnt, spoiled, dried up, charred, burnt to a crisp *or* cinder ...*The meat was overdone and the vegetables disappointing...*
2 = excessive, too much, unfair, unnecessary, exaggerated, over the top (*slang*), needless, unreasonable, disproportionate, undue, hyped, preposterous, inordinate, fulsome, immoderate, overelaborate, beyond all bounds, O.T.T. (*slang*) ...*In fact, all the panic about the drought in Britain was overdone...* **OPPOSITE** minimized

overdue 1 = delayed, belated, late, late in the day, long delayed, behind schedule, tardy, not before time (*informal*), behind time, unpunctual, behindhand ...*I'll go and pay an overdue visit to my mother...* **OPPOSITE** early
2 = unpaid, owing ...*a strike aimed at forcing the government to pay overdue salaries...*

overflow **VERB** 1 = spill over, discharge, well over, run over, pour over, pour out, bubble over, brim over, surge over, slop over, teem over ...*the sickening stench of raw sewage overflowing from toilets...*
2 = flood, swamp, submerge, cover, drown, soak, immerse, inundate, deluge, pour over ...*The river has overflowed its banks in several places...*
NOUN 1 = flood, flooding, spill, discharge, spilling over, inundation ...*Carpeting is damaged from the overflow of water from a bathtub...*
2 = surplus, extra, excess, overspill, inundation,

overabundance, additional people *or* things …*Tents have been set up next to hospitals to handle the overflow…*

overflowing = <u>full</u>, abounding, swarming, rife, plentiful, thronged, teeming, copious, bountiful, profuse, brimful, overfull, superabundant OPPOSITE deficient

overhang = <u>project (over)</u>, extend (over), loom (over), stand out (over), bulge (over), stick out (over), protrude (over), jut (over), impend (over)

overhaul VERB 1 = <u>check</u>, service, maintain, examine, restore, tune (up), repair, go over, inspect, fine tune, do up (*informal*), re-examine, recondition …*The plumbing was overhauled a year ago…*
2 = <u>overtake</u>, pass, leave behind, catch up with, get past, outstrip, get ahead of, draw level with, outdistance …*Beattie led for several laps before he was overhauled by Itoh…*
NOUN = <u>check</u>, service, examination, going-over (*informal*), inspection, once-over (*informal*), checkup, reconditioning …*The study says there must be a complete overhaul of air traffic control systems…*

overhead ADJECTIVE = <u>raised</u>, suspended, elevated, aerial, overhanging …*people who live under or near overhead cables…*
ADVERB = <u>above</u>, in the sky, on high, aloft, up above …*planes passing overhead…* OPPOSITE underneath

overheads = <u>running costs</u>, expenses, outgoings, operating costs, oncosts

overjoyed = <u>delighted</u>, happy, pleased, thrilled, ecstatic, jubilant, joyous, joyful, elated, over the moon (*informal*), euphoric, rapturous, rapt, only too happy, gladdened, on cloud nine (*informal*), transported, cock-a-hoop, blissed out, in raptures, tickled pink (*informal*), deliriously happy, in seventh heaven, floating on air OPPOSITE heartbroken

overlay VERB = <u>cover</u>, coat, blanket, adorn, mantle, ornament, envelop, veneer, encase, inlay, superimpose, laminate, overspread …*a very large dark wood table overlaid in glass… …The floor was overlaid with rugs of Oriental design…*
NOUN = <u>covering</u>, casing, wrapping, decoration, veneer, adornment, ornamentation, appliqué …*Silver overlay is bonded to the entire surface…*

overlook 1 = <u>look over</u> *or* <u>out on</u>, have a view of, command a view of, front on to, give upon, afford a view of …*The rooms overlooked the garden…*
2 = <u>miss</u>, forget, neglect, omit, disregard, pass over, fail to notice, leave undone, slip up on, leave out of consideration …*We overlook all sorts of warning signals about our health…* OPPOSITE notice
3 = <u>ignore</u>, excuse, forgive, pardon, disregard, condone, turn a blind eye to, wink at, blink at, make allowances for, let someone off with, let pass, let ride, discount, pass over, take no notice of, be oblivious to, pay no attention to, turn a deaf ear to, shut your eyes to …*satisfying relationships that enable them to overlook each other's faults…*

overly = <u>too</u>, very, extremely, exceedingly, unduly, excessively, unreasonably, inordinately, immoderately,

over-

overpower 1 = <u>overcome</u>, master, overwhelm, overthrow, subdue, quell, get the better of, subjugate, prevail over, immobilize, bring (someone) to their knees (*informal*), render incapable, render powerless, render helpless, get the upper hand over …*It took four policemen to overpower him…*
2 = <u>beat</u>, defeat, tank (*slang*), crush, lick (*informal*), triumph over, best, clobber (*slang*), stuff (*slang*), vanquish, be victorious (over), wipe the floor with (*informal*), make mincemeat of (*informal*), worst …*Britain's tennis No.1 yesterday overpowered his American rival…*
3 = <u>overwhelm</u>, overcome, bowl over (*informal*), stagger …*I was so overpowered by shame that I was unable to speak…*

overpowering 1 = <u>overwhelming</u>, powerful, extreme, compelling, irresistible, breathtaking, compulsive, invincible, uncontrollable …*The desire for revenge can be overpowering…*
2 = <u>strong</u>, marked, powerful, distinct, sickening, unbearable, suffocating, unmistakable, nauseating …*There was an overpowering smell of garlic…*
3 = <u>forceful</u>, powerful, overwhelming, dynamic, compelling, persuasive, overbearing …*his overpowering manner…*

overrate = <u>overestimate</u>, glorify, overvalue, oversell, make too much of, rate too highly, assess too highly, overpraise, exaggerate the worth of, overprize, think *or* expect too much of, think too highly of, attach to much importance to

override 1 = <u>outweigh</u>, overcome, eclipse, supersede, take precedence over, prevail over, outbalance …*His work frequently overrides all other considerations…*
2 = <u>overrule</u>, reverse, cancel, overturn, set aside, repeal, quash, revoke, disallow, rescind, upset, rule against, invalidate, annul, nullify, ride roughshod over, outvote, countermand, trample underfoot, make null and void …*The senate failed by one vote to override the President's veto…*
3 = <u>ignore</u>, reject, discount, overlook, set aside, disregard, pass over, take no notice of, take no account of, pay no attention to, turn a deaf ear to …*He overrode all opposition to his plans…*

overriding = <u>major</u>, chief, main, prime, predominant, leading, controlling, final, ruling, determining, primary, supreme, principal, ultimate, dominant, compelling, prevailing, cardinal, sovereign, paramount, prevalent, pivotal, top-priority, overruling, preponderant, number one OPPOSITE minor

overrule = <u>reverse</u>, alter, cancel, recall, discount, overturn, set aside, override, repeal, quash, revoke, disallow, rescind, rule against, invalidate, annul, nullify, outvote, countermand, make null and void OPPOSITE approve

overrun 1 = <u>overwhelm</u>, attack, assault, occupy, raid, invade, penetrate, swamp, rout, assail, descend upon, run riot over …*A group of rebels overran the port… …A military group overran them and took four of them off…*

2 = <u>spread over</u>, overwhelm, choke, swamp, overflow, infest, inundate, permeate, spread like wildfire, swarm over, surge over, overgrow ...*The flower beds were overrun with weeds*...

3 = <u>exceed</u>, go beyond, surpass, overshoot, outrun, run over *or* on ...*Costs overran the budget by about 30%*...

overseer = <u>supervisor</u>, manager, chief, boss (*informal*), master, inspector, superior, administrator, steward, superintendent, gaffer (*informal, chiefly Brit.*), foreman, super (*informal*), baas (*S. African*)

overshadow 1 = <u>spoil</u>, ruin, mar, wreck, scar, blight, crool *or* cruel (*Austral. slang*), mess up, take the edge off, put a damper on, cast a gloom upon, take the pleasure *or* enjoyment out of ...*Her mother's illness overshadowed her childhood*...

2 = <u>outshine</u>, eclipse, surpass, dwarf, rise above, take precedence over, tower above, steal the limelight from, leave *or* put in the shade, render insignificant by comparison, throw into the shade ...*I'm sorry to say that she overshadowed her less attractive sister*...

3 = <u>shade</u>, cloud, eclipse, darken, overcast, adumbrate ...*one of the towers that overshadow the square*...

oversight 1 = <u>mistake</u>, error, slip, fault, misunderstanding, blunder, lapse, omission, boob (*Brit. slang*), gaffe, slip-up (*informal*), delinquency, inaccuracy, carelessness, howler (*informal*), goof (*informal*), bloomer (*Brit. informal*), clanger (*informal*), miscalculation, error of judgment, faux pas, inattention, laxity, boo-boo (*informal*), erratum ...*By an unfortunate oversight, full instructions do not come with the product*...

2 = <u>supervision</u>, keeping, control, charge, care, management, handling, administration, direction, custody, stewardship, superintendence ...*I had the oversight of their collection of manuscripts*...

overt = <u>open</u>, obvious, plain, public, clear, apparent, visible, patent, evident, manifest, noticeable, blatant, downright, avowed, flagrant, observable, undisguised, barefaced, unconcealed OPPOSITE hidden

overtake 1 = <u>pass</u>, leave behind, overhaul, catch up with, get past, draw level with, outdistance, go by *or* past ...*He overtook the truck and pulled into the inside lane*...

2 = <u>outdo</u>, top, exceed, eclipse, surpass, outstrip, get the better of, outclass, outshine, best, go one better than (*informal*), outdistance, be one up on ...*Japan has overtaken Britain as the Mini's biggest market*...

3 = <u>befall</u>, hit, happen to, come upon, take by surprise, catch off guard, catch unawares, catch unprepared ...*Tragedy was about to overtake him*...

4 = <u>engulf</u>, overwhelm, hit, strike, consume, swamp, envelop, swallow up ...*A sudden flood of panic overtook me*...

overthrow VERB = <u>defeat</u>, beat, master, overcome, crush, overwhelm, conquer, bring down, oust, lick (*informal*), topple, subdue, rout, overpower, do away with, depose, trounce, unseat, vanquish, subjugate, dethrone ...*The government was overthrown in a military coup three years ago*... OPPOSITE uphold

NOUN = <u>downfall</u>, end, fall, defeat, collapse, ruin, destruction, breakdown, ousting, undoing, rout, suppression, displacement, subversion, deposition, unseating, subjugation, dispossession, disestablishment, dethronement ...*They were charged with plotting the overthrow of the state*... OPPOSITE preservation

overtone *often plural* = <u>connotation</u>, association, suggestion, sense, hint, flavour, implication, significance, nuance, colouring, innuendo, undercurrent, intimation

overture 1 (*Music*) = <u>prelude</u>, opening, introduction, introductory movement ...*the William Tell Overture*... OPPOSITE finale

2 *usually plural* = <u>approach</u>, offer, advance, proposal, appeal, invitation, tender, proposition, opening move, conciliatory move ...*He had begun to make clumsy yet endearing overtures of friendship*... OPPOSITE rejection

overturn 1 = <u>tip over</u>, spill, topple, upturn, capsize, upend, keel over, overbalance ...*The lorry went out of control, overturned and smashed into a wall*... ...*Two salmon fishermen died when their boat overturned*...

2 = <u>knock over</u> *or* <u>down</u>, upset, upturn, tip over, upend ...*Alex jumped up so violently that he overturned the table*...

3 = <u>reverse</u>, change, alter, cancel, abolish, overthrow, set aside, repeal, quash, revoke, overrule, override, negate, rescind, invalidate, annul, nullify, obviate, countermand, declare null and void, overset ...*The Russian parliament overturned his decision*...

4 = <u>overthrow</u>, defeat, destroy, overcome, crush, bring down, oust, topple, do away with, depose, unseat, dethrone ...*He accused his opponents of wanting to overturn the government*...

overweight = <u>fat</u>, heavy, stout, huge, massive, solid, gross, hefty, ample, plump, bulky, chunky, chubby, obese, fleshy, beefy (*informal*), tubby (*informal*), portly, outsize, buxom, roly-poly, rotund, podgy, corpulent, elephantine, well-padded (*informal*), well-upholstered (*informal*), broad in the beam (*informal*), on the plump side OPPOSITE underweight

overwhelm 1 = <u>overcome</u>, overpower, devastate, stagger, get the better of, bowl over (*informal*), prostrate, knock (someone) for six (*informal*), render speechless, render incapable, render powerless, render helpless, sweep (someone) off his *or* her feet, take (someone's) breath away ...*He was overwhelmed by a longing for times past*...

2 = <u>destroy</u>, beat, defeat, overcome, smash, crush, massacre, conquer, wipe out, overthrow, knock out, lick (*informal*), subdue, rout, eradicate, overpower, quell, annihilate, put paid to, vanquish, subjugate, immobilize, make mincemeat of (*informal*), cut to pieces ...*One massive Allied offensive would overwhelm the weakened enemy*...

3 = <u>swamp</u>, bury, flood, crush, engulf, submerge, beset, inundate, deluge, snow under ...*The small Pacific island could be overwhelmed by rising sea levels*...

overwhelming 1 = <u>overpowering</u>, strong, powerful, towering, vast, stunning, extreme, crushing, devastating, shattering, compelling, irresistible,

breathtaking, compulsive, forceful, unbearable, uncontrollable ...*She felt an overwhelming desire to have another child*... OPPOSITE> negligible
2 = <u>vast</u>, huge, massive, enormous, tremendous, immense, very large, astronomic, humongous *or* humungous (*U.S. slang*) ...*An overwhelming majority of small businesses fail within the first two years*... OPPOSITE> insignificant

overwork 1 = <u>wear yourself out</u>, burn the midnight oil, burn the candle at both ends, bite off more than you can chew, strain yourself, overstrain yourself, work your fingers to the bone, overtire yourself, drive yourself too far, overburden yourself, overload yourself, overtax yourself ...*You've been overworking – you need a holiday*...
2 = <u>exploit</u>, exhaust, fatigue, weary, oppress, wear out, prostrate, overtax, drive into the ground, be a slave-driver *or* hard taskmaster to ...*He overworks his staff*...

overwrought 1 = <u>distraught</u>, upset, excited, desperate, wired (*slang*), anxious, distressed, tense, distracted, frantic, in a state, hysterical, wound up (*informal*), worked up (*informal*), agitated, uptight (*informal*), on edge, strung out (*informal*), out of your mind, keyed up, overexcited, in a tizzy (*informal*), at the end of your tether, wrought-up, beside yourself, in a twitter (*informal*), tooshie (*Austral. slang*) ...*When I'm feeling overwrought, I try to take some time out to relax*... OPPOSITE> calm
2 = <u>overelaborate</u>, contrived, overdone, flamboyant, baroque, high-flown, ornate, fussy, flowery, busy, rococo, florid, grandiloquent, euphuistic, overembellished, overornate ...*He writes pretentious, overwrought poetry*...

owe = <u>be in debt (to)</u>, be in arrears (to), be overdrawn (by), be beholden to, be under an obligation to, be obligated *or* indebted (to)

owing = <u>unpaid</u>, due, outstanding, owed, payable, unsettled, overdue

owing to = <u>because of</u>, thanks to, as a result of, on account of, by reason of

own ADJECTIVE = <u>personal</u>, special, private, individual, particular, exclusive ...*She insisted on having her own room*...
VERB = <u>possess</u>, have, keep, hold, enjoy, retain, be responsible for, be in possession of, have to your name ...*His father owns a local pub*...
PHRASES **hold your own** = <u>keep going</u>, compete, get on, get along, stand your ground, keep your head above water, keep your end up, maintain your position ...*Placed in brilliant company at Eton, he more than held his own*... ◆ **on your own 1** = <u>alone</u>, by yourself, all alone, unaccompanied, on your tod (*Brit. slang*) ...*I need some time on my own*... **2** = <u>independently</u>, alone, singly, single-handedly, by yourself, unaided, without help, unassisted, left to your own devices, under your own steam, off your own bat, by your own efforts, (standing) on your own two feet ...*I work best on my own*...

owner = <u>possessor</u>, holder, proprietor, freeholder, titleholder, proprietress, proprietrix, landlord *or* landlady, master *or* mistress, deed holder

ownership = <u>possession</u>, occupation, tenure, dominion, occupancy, proprietorship, proprietary rights, right of possession

ox

Related Words
adjective: bovine
male: bull
female: cow
young: calf
collective nouns: yoke, drove, team, herd

P p

pace NOUN **1** = <u>speed</u>, rate, momentum, tempo, progress, motion, clip (*informal*), lick (*informal*), velocity …*driving at a steady pace*…
2 = <u>step</u>, walk, stride, tread, gait …*Their pace quickened as they approached their cars*…
3 = <u>footstep</u>, step, stride …*I took a pace backwards*…
VERB = <u>stride</u>, walk, pound, patrol, walk up and down, march up and down, walk back and forth …*He paced the room nervously*…

pacific 1 = <u>nonaggressive</u>, pacifist, nonviolent, friendly, gentle, mild, peace-loving, peaceable, dovish, nonbelligerent, dovelike …*a country with a pacific policy*… OPPOSITE aggressive
2 (*Formal*) = <u>peacemaking</u>, diplomatic, appeasing, conciliatory, placatory, propitiatory, irenic, pacificatory …*He spoke in a pacific voice*…

pacifist = <u>peace lover</u>, dove, conscientious objector, peacenik (*informal*), conchie (*informal*), peacemonger, satyagrahi (*rare*), passive resister

pacify 1 = <u>calm (down)</u>, appease, placate, still, content, quiet, moderate, compose, soften, soothe, allay, assuage, make peace with, mollify, ameliorate, conciliate, propitiate, tranquillize, smooth someone's ruffled feathers, clear the air with, restore harmony to …*Is this just something to pacify the critics?*…
2 = <u>quell</u>, silence, crush, put down, tame, subdue, repress, chasten, impose peace upon …*Government forces have found it difficult to pacify the rebels*…

pack VERB **1** = <u>package</u>, load, store, bundle, batch, stow …*They offered me a job packing goods in a warehouse*…
2 = <u>cram</u>, charge, crowd, press, fill, stuff, jam, compact, mob, ram, wedge, compress, throng, tamp …*All her possessions were packed into the back of her car*… …*Thousands of people packed into the mosque*…
NOUN **1** = <u>packet</u>, box, package, carton …*a pack of cigarettes*…
2 = <u>bundle</u>, kit, parcel, load, burden, bale, rucksack, truss, knapsack, back pack, kitbag, fardel (*archaic*) …*I hid the money in my pack*…
3 = <u>group</u>, crowd, collection, company, set, lot, band, troop, crew, drove, gang, deck, bunch, mob, flock, herd, assemblage …*a pack of journalists who wanted to interview him*…
PHRASES **pack someone in 1** = <u>cram</u>, squeeze in, fill to capacity …*The prisons pack in as many inmates as possible*… **2** = <u>attract</u>, draw …*The show is still packing audiences in*… ◆ **pack someone off** = <u>send away</u>, dismiss, send packing (*informal*), bundle out, hustle out …*The children were packed off to bed*… ◆ **pack something in 1** (*Brit. informal*) = <u>resign from</u>, leave, give up, quit (*informal*), chuck (*informal*), jack in (*informal*) …*I've just packed in my job*… **2** = <u>stop</u>, give up, kick (*informal*), cease, chuck (*informal*), leave off, jack in, desist from …*He's trying to pack in smoking*… ◆ **pack something up 1** = <u>put away</u>, store, tidy up …*He began packing up his things*… **2** (*Informal*) = <u>stop</u>, finish, give up, pack in (*Brit. informal*), call it a day (*informal*), call it a night (*informal*) …*He's packed up coaching and retired*… ◆ **pack up** = <u>break down</u>, stop, fail, stall, give out, conk out (*informal*) …*Our car packed up*… ◆ **send someone packing** = <u>send away</u>, dismiss, discharge, give someone the bird (*informal*), give someone the brushoff (*slang*), send someone about his *or* her business, send someone away with a flea in his *or* her ear (*informal*) …*He was sent packing in disgrace*…

package NOUN **1** = <u>parcel</u>, box, container, packet, carton …*I tore open the package*…
2 = <u>collection</u>, lot, unit, combination, compilation …*A complete package of teaching aids, course notes and case studies had been drawn up*…
VERB = <u>pack</u>, box, wrap up, parcel (up), batch …*The coffee beans are ground and packaged for sale*…

packaging = <u>wrapping</u>, casing, covering, cover, box, packing, wrapper

packed = <u>filled</u>, full, crowded, jammed, crammed, swarming, overflowing, overloaded, seething, congested, jam-packed, chock-full, bursting at the seams, cram-full, brimful, chock-a-block, packed like sardines, hoatching (*Scot.*), loaded *or* full to the gunwales OPPOSITE empty

packet 1 = <u>container</u>, box, package, wrapping, poke (*dialect*), carton, wrapper …*He wrote the number on the back of a cigarette packet*…
2 = <u>package</u>, parcel …*the cost of sending letters and packets abroad*…
3 (*Slang*) = <u>a fortune</u>, lot(s), pot(s) (*informal*), a bomb (*Brit. slang*), a pile (*informal*), big money, a bundle (*slang*), big bucks (*informal, chiefly U.S.*), a small fortune, a mint, a wad (*U.S. & Canad. slang*), megabucks (*U.S. & Canad. slang*), an arm and a leg (*informal*), a bob or two (*Brit. informal*), a tidy sum (*informal*), a king's ransom (*informal*), a pretty penny (*informal*) …*You could save yourself a packet*…

pact = <u>agreement</u>, contract, alliance, treaty, deal, understanding, league, bond, arrangement, bargain, convention, compact, protocol, covenant, concord, concordat

pad¹ NOUN **1** = <u>wad</u>, dressing, pack, padding, compress, wadding …*He placed a pad of cotton wool over the cut*…
2 = <u>cushion</u>, filling, stuffing, pillow, bolster, upholstery …*Seat-pad covers which tie to the backs of your chairs*…
3 = <u>notepad</u>, block, tablet, notebook, jotter, writing pad …*Have a pad and pencil ready*…
4 (*Slang*) = <u>home</u>, flat, apartment, place, room,

quarters, hang-out (*informal*) ...*He's bought himself a bachelor pad...*

5 = <u>paw</u>, foot, sole ...*My cat has an infection in the pad of its foot...*

VERB = <u>pack</u>, line, fill, protect, shape, stuff, cushion ...*Pad the seat with a pillow...*

PHRASES **pad something out** = <u>lengthen</u>, stretch, elaborate, inflate, fill out, amplify, augment, spin out, flesh out, eke out, protract ...*He padded out his article with a lot of quotations...*

pad² = <u>sneak</u>, creep, steal, pussyfoot (*informal*), go barefoot ...*He padded around in his slippers...*

padding 1 = <u>filling</u>, stuffing, packing, wadding ...*the chair's foam rubber padding...*

2 = <u>waffle</u> (*informal, chiefly Brit.*), hot air (*informal*), verbiage, wordiness, verbosity, prolixity ...*Politicians fill their speeches with a lot of padding...*

paddle¹ NOUN = <u>oar</u>, sweep, scull ...*He used a piece of driftwood as a paddle...*

VERB = <u>row</u>, pull, scull ...*paddling around the South Pacific in a kayak...*

paddle² = <u>wade</u>, splash (about), slop, plash ...*The children were paddling in the stream...*

paddy (*Brit. slang*) = <u>temper</u>, tantrum, bad mood, passion, rage, pet, fit of pique, fit of temper, foulie (*Austral. slang*)

paean (*Literary*) = <u>eulogy</u>, tribute, panegyric, hymn of praise, encomium

pagan ADJECTIVE = <u>heathen</u>, infidel, irreligious, polytheistic, idolatrous, heathenish ...*Britain's ancient pagan heritage...*

NOUN = <u>heathen</u>, infidel, unbeliever, polytheist, idolater ...*He has been a practising pagan for years...*

page¹ 1 = <u>folio</u>, side, leaf, sheet ...*Turn to page four of your books...*

2 (*Literary*) = <u>period</u>, chapter, phase, era, episode, time, point, event, stage, incident, epoch ...*a new page in the country's history...*

page² VERB = <u>call</u>, seek, summon, call out for, send for ...*He was paged repeatedly as the flight was boarding...*

NOUN **1** = <u>attendant</u>, bellboy (*U.S.*), pageboy, footboy ...*He worked as a page in a hotel...*

2 = <u>servant</u>, attendant, squire, pageboy, footboy ...*He served as page to a noble lord...*

pageant 1 = <u>show</u>, display, parade, ritual, spectacle, procession, extravaganza, tableau ...*a traditional Christmas pageant...*

2 = <u>contest</u>, competition ...*the Miss World beauty pageant...*

pageantry = <u>spectacle</u>, show, display, drama, parade, splash (*informal*), state, glitter, glamour, grandeur, splendour, extravagance, pomp, magnificence, theatricality, showiness

pain NOUN **1** = <u>suffering</u>, discomfort, trouble, hurt, irritation, tenderness, soreness ...*a disease that causes excruciating pain...*

2 = <u>ache</u>, smarting, stinging, aching, cramp, cramp, throb, throbbing, spasm, pang, twinge, shooting pain ...*I felt a sharp pain in my lower back...*

3 = <u>sorrow</u>, suffering, torture, distress, despair, grief, misery, agony, sadness, torment, hardship, bitterness, woe, anguish, heartache, affliction, tribulation, desolation, wretchedness ...*Her eyes were filled with pain...*

PLURAL NOUN = <u>trouble</u>, labour, effort, industry, care, bother, diligence, special attention, assiduousness ...*He got little thanks for his pains...*

VERB **1** = <u>distress</u>, worry, hurt, wound, torture, grieve, torment, afflict, sadden, disquiet, vex, agonize, cut to the quick, aggrieve ...*It pains me to think of an animal being in distress...*

2 = <u>hurt</u>, chafe, cause pain to, cause discomfort to ...*His ankle still pained him...*

pained = <u>distressed</u>, worried, hurt, injured, wounded, upset, unhappy, stung, offended, aggrieved, anguished, miffed (*informal*), reproachful

painful 1 = <u>sore</u>, hurting, smarting, aching, raw, tender, throbbing, inflamed, excruciating ...*Her glands were swollen and painful...* OPPOSITE painless

2 = <u>distressing</u>, unpleasant, harrowing, saddening, grievous, distasteful, agonizing, disagreeable, afflictive ...*His remark brought back painful memories...* OPPOSITE pleasant

3 = <u>difficult</u>, arduous, trying, hard, severe, troublesome, laborious, vexatious ...*the long and painful process of getting divorced...* OPPOSITE easy

4 (*Informal*) = <u>terrible</u>, awful, dreadful, dire, excruciating, abysmal, gut-wrenching, godawful, extremely bad ...*The interview was painful to watch...*

painfully = <u>distressingly</u>, clearly, sadly, unfortunately, markedly, excessively, alarmingly, woefully, dreadfully, deplorably

painkiller = <u>analgesic</u>, drug, remedy, anaesthetic, sedative, palliative, anodyne

painless 1 = <u>pain-free</u>, without pain ...*The operation is a brief, painless procedure...*

2 = <u>simple</u>, easy, fast, quick, no trouble, effortless, trouble-free ...*There are no painless solutions to the problem...*

painstaking = <u>thorough</u>, careful, meticulous, earnest, exacting, strenuous, conscientious, persevering, diligent, scrupulous, industrious, assiduous, thoroughgoing, punctilious, sedulous OPPOSITE careless

paint NOUN = <u>colouring</u>, colour, stain, dye, tint, pigment, emulsion ...*a pot of red paint...*

VERB **1** = <u>colour</u>, cover, coat, decorate, stain, whitewash, daub, distemper, apply paint to ...*They painted the walls yellow...*

2 = <u>depict</u>, draw, portray, figure, picture, represent, sketch, delineate, catch a likeness ...*He was painting a portrait of his wife...*

3 = <u>describe</u>, capture, portray, depict, evoke, recount, bring to life, make you see, conjure up a vision, put graphically, tell vividly ...*The report paints a grim picture of life in the city...*

PHRASES **paint the town red** (*Informal*) = <u>celebrate</u>, revel, carouse, live it up (*informal*), make merry, make whoopee (*informal*), go on a binge

(*informal*), go on a spree, go on the town
…*Thousands of football fans painted the town red after the match*…

pair NOUN **1** = set, match, combination, doublet, matched set, two of a kind …*a pair of socks*…
2 = couple, brace, duo, twosome …*A pair of teenage boys were arrested*…
VERB = team, match (up), join, couple, marry, wed, twin, put together, bracket, yoke, pair off …*Each trainee is paired with an experienced worker*…

> ### *Word Power*
> **pair** – Like other collective nouns, *pair* takes a singular or a plural verb according to whether it is seen as a unit or as a collection of two things: *the pair are said to dislike each other; a pair of good shoes is essential.*

pal (*Informal*) = friend, companion, mate (*informal*), buddy (*informal*), comrade, chum (*informal*), crony, cock (*Brit. informal*), main man (*slang, chiefly U.S.*), homeboy (*slang, chiefly U.S.*), cobber (*Austral. or old-fashioned N.Z. informal*), boon companion

palatable **1** = delicious, tasty, luscious, savoury, delectable, mouthwatering, appetizing, toothsome, yummo (*Austral. slang*) …*flavourings designed to make the food more palatable*… OPPOSITE unpalatable
2 = acceptable, pleasant, agreeable, fair, attractive, satisfactory, enjoyable …*There is no palatable way of sacking someone*…

palate = taste, heart, stomach, appetite

> ### *Word Power*
> **palate** – This word is occasionally confused with *palette*: *This wine is too sweet for my palate* (not *palette*).

palatial = magnificent, grand, imposing, splendid, gorgeous, luxurious, spacious, majestic, regal, stately, sumptuous, plush (*informal*), illustrious, grandiose, opulent, de luxe, splendiferous (*facetious*)

pale¹ ADJECTIVE **1** = light, soft, faded, subtle, muted, bleached, pastel, light-coloured …*a pale blue dress*…
2 = dim, weak, faint, feeble, thin, wan, watery …*A pale light seeped through the window*…
3 = white, pasty, bleached, washed-out, wan, bloodless, colourless, pallid, anaemic, ashen, sallow, whitish, ashy, like death warmed up (*informal*) …*She looked pale and tired*… OPPOSITE rosy-cheeked
4 = poor, weak, inadequate, pathetic, feeble …*a pale imitation of the real thing*…
VERB **1** = fade, dull, diminish, decrease, dim, lessen, grow dull, lose lustre …*My problems paled in comparison with his*…
2 = become pale, blanch, whiten, go white, lose colour …*Her face paled at the news*…

pale² NOUN = post, stake, paling, upright, picket, slat, palisade …*the pales of the fence*…

PHRASES **beyond the pale** = unacceptable, not done, forbidden, irregular, indecent, unsuitable, improper, barbaric, unspeakable, out of line, unseemly, inadmissible …*His behaviour was beyond the pale*…

palette
➤ palate

pall¹ = become boring, become dull, become tedious, become tiresome, jade, cloy, become wearisome …*The glamour of her job soon palled*…

pall² **1** = cloud, shadow, veil, mantle, shroud …*A pall of black smoke drifted over the cliff-top*…
2 = gloom, damp, dismay, melancholy, damper, check …*His depression cast a pall on the proceedings*…

pallid **1** = pale, wan, pasty, colourless, anaemic, ashen, sallow, whitish, cadaverous, waxen, ashy, like death warmed up (*informal*), wheyfaced …*His thin, pallid face broke into a smile*…
2 = insipid, boring, tired, tame, sterile, lifeless, bloodless, colourless, anaemic, uninspired, vapid, spiritless …*pallid romantic fiction*…

pallor = paleness, whiteness, lack of colour, wanness, bloodlessness, ashen hue, pallidness

palm NOUN = hand, hook, paw (*informal*), mitt (*slang*), meathook (*slang*) …*He wiped his sweaty palm*…
PHRASES **have someone in the palm of your hand** = in your power, in your control, in your clutches, have someone at your mercy …*He had the board of directors in the palm of his hand*… ◆ **palm someone off** = fob someone off, dismiss, disregard, pooh-pooh (*informal*) …*Mark was palmed off with a series of excuses*… ◆ **palm something off on someone** = foist something on, force something upon, impose something upon, pass something off, thrust something upon, unload something upon …*They palm a lot of junk off on the tourists*…

palpable = obvious, apparent, patent, clear, plain, visible, evident, manifest, open, blatant, conspicuous, unmistakable, salient

paltry **1** = meagre, petty, trivial, trifling, beggarly, derisory, measly, piddling (*informal*), inconsiderable …*He was fined the paltry sum of $50*… OPPOSITE considerable
2 = insignificant, trivial, worthless, unimportant, small, low, base, minor, slight, petty, trifling, Mickey Mouse (*slang*), piddling (*informal*), toytown (*slang*), poxy (*slang*), nickel-and-dime (*U.S. slang*), picayune (*U.S.*), twopenny-halfpenny (*Brit. informal*) …*She had no interest in such paltry concerns*… OPPOSITE important

pamper = spoil, indulge, gratify, baby, pet, humour, pander to, fondle, cosset, coddle, mollycoddle, wait on (someone) hand and foot, cater to your every whim

pamphlet = booklet, leaflet, brochure, circular, tract, folder

pan¹ NOUN = pot, vessel, container, saucepan …*Heat the butter in a large pan*…
VERB **1** (*Informal*) = criticize, knock, blast, hammer (*Brit. informal*), slam (*slang*), rubbish (*informal*), roast

(*informal*), put down, slate (*informal*), censure, slag (off) (*slang*), tear into (*informal*), flay, lambast(e), throw brickbats at (*informal*) ...*His first movie was panned by the critics*...

2 = sift out, look for, wash, search for ...*People came westward in the 1800s to pan for gold in Sierra Nevada*...

PHRASES **pan out** (*Informal*) = work out, happen, result, come out, turn out, culminate, come to pass (*archaic*), eventuate ...*None of his ideas panned out*...

pan² = move along *or* across, follow, track, sweep, scan, traverse, swing across ...*A television camera panned the crowd*...

panacea = cure-all, elixir, nostrum, heal-all, sovereign remedy, universal cure

panache = style, spirit, dash, flair, verve, swagger, flourish, élan, flamboyance, brio

pandemonium = uproar, confusion, chaos, turmoil, racket, clamour, din, commotion, rumpus, bedlam, babel, tumult, hubbub, ruction (*informal*), hullabaloo, hue and cry, ruckus (*informal*) OPPOSITE order

pander

PHRASES **pander to something** *or* **someone** = indulge, please, satisfy, gratify, cater to, play up to (*informal*), fawn on

pang 1 = pain, stab, sting, stitch, ache, wrench, prick, spasm, twinge, throe (*rare*) ...*pangs of hunger*...

2 = twinge, stab, prick, spasm, qualm, gnawing ...*She felt a pang of guilt about the way she was treating him*...

panic NOUN = fear, alarm, horror, terror, anxiety, dismay, hysteria, fright, agitation, consternation, trepidation, a flap (*informal*) ...*The earthquake has caused panic among the population*...

VERB **1** = go to pieces, overreact, become hysterical, have kittens (*informal*), lose your nerve, be terror-stricken, lose your bottle (*Brit. slang*) ...*The guests panicked and screamed when the bomb went off*...

2 = alarm, scare, terrify, startle, unnerve ...*The dogs were panicked by the noise*...

panicky = frightened, worried, afraid, nervous, distressed, fearful, frantic, frenzied, hysterical, worked up, windy (*slang*), agitated, jittery (*informal*), in a flap (*informal*), antsy (*informal*), in a tizzy (*informal*) OPPOSITE calm

panic-stricken = frightened, alarmed, scared, terrified, startled, horrified, fearful, frenzied, hysterical, agitated, unnerved, petrified, aghast, panicky, scared stiff, in a cold sweat (*informal*), frightened to death, terror-stricken, horror-stricken, frightened out of your wits

panoply 1 = array, range, display, collection ...*The film features a vast panoply of special effects*...

2 = trappings, show, dress, get-up (*informal*), turnout, attire, garb, insignia, regalia, raiment (*archaic or poetic*) ...*all the panoply of a royal wedding*...

panorama 1 = view, prospect, scenery, vista, bird's-eye view, scenic view ...*He looked out over a panorama of hills and valleys*...

2 = survey, perspective, overview, overall picture

...*The play presents a panorama of the history of communism*...

panoramic 1 = wide, overall, extensive, scenic, bird's-eye ...*I had a panoramic view of the city*...

2 = comprehensive, general, extensive, sweeping, inclusive, far-reaching, all-embracing ...*the panoramic sweep of his work*...

pant VERB = puff, blow, breathe, gasp, throb, wheeze, huff, heave, palpitate ...*He was panting with the effort of the climb*...

NOUN = gasp, puff, wheeze, huff ...*His breath was coming in short pants*...

PHRASES **pant for something** = long for, want, desire, crave for, covet, yearn for, thirst for, hunger for, pine for, hanker after, ache for, sigh for, set your heart on, eat your heart out over, suspire for (*archaic or poetic*) ...*They left the audience panting for more*...

panting 1 = out of breath, winded, gasping, puffed, puffing, breathless, puffed out, short of breath, out of puff, out of whack (*informal*) ...*She collapsed, panting, at the top of the stairs*...

2 = eager, raring, anxious, impatient, champing at the bit (*informal*), all agog ...*He came down here panting to be rescued from the whole ghastly mess*...

pants 1 (*Brit.*) = underpants, briefs, drawers, knickers, panties, boxer shorts, Y-fronts (*trademark*), broekies (*S. African*), underdaks (*Austral. slang*) ...*a matching set of bra and pants*...

2 (*U.S.*) = trousers, slacks ...*He was wearing brown corduroy pants and a white shirt*...

pap = rubbish, trash, trivia, drivel

paper NOUN **1** = newspaper, news, daily, journal, organ, rag (*informal*), tabloid, gazette, broadsheet ...*The story is in all the papers*...

2 = essay, study, article, analysis, script, composition, assignment, thesis, critique, treatise, dissertation, monograph ...*He has just written a paper on the subject*...

3 = examination, test, exam ...*the applied mathematics paper*...

4 = report, study, survey, inquiry ...*a new government paper on European policy*...

PLURAL NOUN **1** = letters, records, documents, file, diaries, archive, paperwork, dossier ...*After her death, her papers were collected and published*...

2 = documents, records, certificates, identification, deeds, identity papers, I.D. (*informal*) ...*people who were trying to leave the country with forged papers*...

VERB = wallpaper, line, hang, paste up, cover with paper ...*We have papered this room in grey*...

PHRASES **on paper 1** = in writing, written down, on (the) record, in print, in black and white ...*It is important to get something down on paper*... **2** = in theory, ideally, theoretically, in the abstract ...*On paper, he is the best man for the job*...

par

PHRASES **above par** = excellent, outstanding, superior, exceptional, first-rate (*informal*) ...*Their performance was way above par for an amateur production*... ♦ **below** *or* **under par 1** = inferior, poor, lacking, imperfect, second-rate, wanting, below average, substandard, two-bit (*U.S. & Canad. slang*), off form, not up to scratch (*informal*), dime-a-dozen (*informal*), bush-league (*Austral. & N.Z. informal*), not up to snuff (*informal*), tinhorn (*U.S. slang*), bodger *or* bodgie (*Austral. slang*) ...*His playing is below par this season*... **2** = <u>unwell</u>, sick, poorly (*informal*), funny (*informal*), crook (*Austral. & N.Z. informal*), queer, unfit, unhealthy, queasy, out of sorts (*informal*), dicky (*Brit. informal*), off colour (*chiefly Brit.*), under the weather (*informal*), off form, indisposed, not yourself, green about the gills ...*If you have been feeling below par for a while, consult your doctor*... ◆ **on a par with** = <u>equal to</u>, the same as, much the same as, well-matched with ...*Parts of the city are on a par with New York for street crime*... ◆ **par for the course** = <u>usual</u>, expected, standard, average, ordinary, typical, predictable ...*Long hours are par for the course in this job*... ◆ **up to par** = <u>satisfactory</u>, acceptable, good enough, adequate, up to scratch (*informal*), passable, up to the mark ...*The service is not up to par here*...

parable = <u>lesson</u>, story, fable, allegory, moral tale, exemplum

parade NOUN **1** = <u>procession</u>, march, ceremony, pageant, train, review, column, spectacle, tattoo, motorcade, cavalcade, cortège ...*A military parade marched slowly through the streets*...
2 = <u>show</u>, display, exhibition, spectacle, array ...*A glittering parade of celebrities attended the event*...
VERB **1** = <u>march</u>, process, file, promenade ...*More than four thousand people paraded down the Champs Elysées*...
2 = <u>flaunt</u>, show, display, exhibit, show off (*informal*), air, draw attention to, brandish, vaunt, make a show of ...*He was a modest man who never paraded his wealth*...
3 = <u>strut</u>, show off (*informal*), swagger, swank ...*She loves to parade around in designer clothes*...

paradigm = <u>model</u>, example, original, pattern, ideal, norm, prototype, archetype, exemplar

paradise 1 = <u>heaven</u>, Promised Land, Zion (*Christianity*), Happy Valley (*Islam*), City of God, Elysian fields, garden of delights, divine abode, heavenly kingdom ...*They believe they will go to paradise when they die*...
2 = <u>Garden of Eden</u>, Eden ...*Adam and Eve's expulsion from Paradise*...
3 = <u>bliss</u>, delight, heaven, felicity, utopia, seventh heaven ...*This job is paradise compared to my last one*...

paradox = <u>contradiction</u>, mystery, puzzle, ambiguity, anomaly, inconsistency, enigma, oddity, absurdity

paradoxical = <u>contradictory</u>, inconsistent, impossible, puzzling, absurd, baffling, riddling, ambiguous, improbable, confounding, enigmatic, illogical, equivocal, oracular

paragon = <u>model</u>, standard, pattern, ideal, criterion, norm, jewel, masterpiece, prototype, paradigm, archetype, epitome, exemplar, apotheosis, quintessence, nonesuch (*archaic*), nonpareil, best *or* greatest thing since sliced bread (*informal*), cynosure

paragraph = <u>section</u>, part, notice, item, passage, clause, portion, subdivision

parallel NOUN **1** = <u>equivalent</u>, counterpart, match, equal, twin, complement, duplicate, analogue, likeness, corollary ...*It is an ecological disaster with no parallel in the modern era*... OPPOSITE opposite
2 = <u>similarity</u>, correspondence, correlation, comparison, analogy, resemblance, likeness, parallelism ...*Detectives realised there were parallels between the two murders*... OPPOSITE difference
VERB **1** = <u>correspond to</u>, compare with, agree with, complement, conform to, be alike, chime with, correlate to ...*His remarks paralleled those of the president*... OPPOSITE differ from
2 = <u>match</u>, equal, duplicate, keep pace (with), measure up to ...*His achievements have never been paralleled*...
ADJECTIVE **1** = <u>matching</u>, correspondent, corresponding, like, similar, uniform, resembling, complementary, akin, analogous ...*He describes the rise in tuberculosis as an epidemic parallel to that of AIDS*... OPPOSITE different
2 = <u>equidistant</u>, alongside, aligned, side by side, coextensive ...*seventy-two ships, drawn up in two parallel lines*... OPPOSITE divergent

paralyse 1 = <u>disable</u>, cripple, lame, debilitate, incapacitate ...*Her sister had been paralysed in a road accident*...
2 = <u>freeze</u>, stun, numb, petrify, transfix, stupefy, halt, stop dead, immobilize, anaesthetize, benumb ...*He was paralysed with fear*...
3 = <u>immobilize</u>, freeze, halt, disable, cripple, arrest, incapacitate, bring to a standstill ...*The strike has virtually paralysed the country*...

paralysis 1 = <u>immobility</u>, palsy, paresis (*Pathology*) ...*paralysis of the legs*...
2 = <u>standstill</u>, breakdown, stoppage, shutdown, halt, stagnation, inactivity ...*The unions have brought about a total paralysis of trade*...

parameter (*Informal*) *usually plural* = <u>limit</u>, constant, restriction, guideline, criterion, framework, limitation, specification

paramount = <u>principal</u>, prime, first, chief, main, capital, primary, supreme, outstanding, superior, dominant, cardinal, foremost, eminent, predominant, pre-eminent OPPOSITE secondary

paranoid 1 (*Informal*) = <u>suspicious</u>, worried, nervous, fearful, apprehensive, antsy (*informal*) ...*We live in an increasingly paranoid and fearful society*...
2 = <u>obsessive</u>, disturbed, unstable, manic, neurotic, mentally ill, psychotic, deluded, paranoiac ...*his increasingly paranoid delusions*...

paraphernalia = <u>equipment</u>, things, effects, material, stuff, tackle, gear, baggage, apparatus, belongings, clobber (*Brit. slang*), accoutrements, impedimenta, appurtenances, equipage

paraphrase VERB = <u>reword</u>, interpret, render, restate, rehash, rephrase, express in other words *or* your own words ...*Baxter paraphrased the contents of the press release*...

NOUN = <u>rewording</u>, version, interpretation, rendering, translation, rendition, rehash, restatement, rephrasing …*The following is a paraphrase of his remarks*…

parasite = <u>sponger</u> (*informal*), sponge (*informal*), drone (*Brit.*), leech, hanger-on, scrounger (*informal*), bloodsucker (*informal*), cadger, quandong (*Austral. slang*)

parasitic *or* **parasitical** = <u>scrounging</u> (*informal*), sponging (*informal*), cadging, bloodsucking (*informal*), leechlike

parcel NOUN 1 = <u>package</u>, case, box, pack, packet, bundle, carton …*They sent parcels of food and clothing*…
2 = <u>plot</u>, area, property, section, patch, tract, allotment, piece of land …*These small parcels of land were sold to the local people*…
3 = <u>group</u>, crowd, pack, company, lot, band, collection, crew, gang, bunch, batch …*He described them, quite rightly, as a parcel of rogues*…
VERB *often with* ***up*** = <u>wrap</u>, pack, package, tie up, do up, gift-wrap, box up, fasten together …*We parcelled up our unwanted clothes to take to the charity shop*…
PHRASES **parcel something out** = <u>distribute</u>, divide, portion, allocate, split up, dispense, allot, carve up, mete out, dole out, share out, apportion, deal out …*The inheritance was parcelled out equally among the three brothers*…

parched 1 = <u>dried out</u> *or* up, dry, withered, scorched, arid, torrid, shrivelled, dehydrated, waterless …*Showers poured down upon the parched earth*…
2 = <u>thirsty</u>, dry, dehydrated, drouthy (*Scot.*) …*After all that exercise, I was parched*…

pardon VERB 1 = <u>forgive</u>, excuse …*Pardon me for asking, but what business is it of yours?*… OPPOSITE condemn
2 = <u>acquit</u>, free, release, liberate, reprieve, remit, amnesty, let off (*informal*), exonerate, absolve, exculpate …*Hundreds of political prisoners were pardoned and released*… OPPOSITE punish
NOUN 1 = <u>forgiveness</u>, mercy, indulgence, absolution, grace …*He asked God's pardon for his sins*… OPPOSITE condemnation
2 = <u>acquittal</u>, release, discharge, amnesty, reprieve, remission, exoneration …*They lobbied the government on his behalf and he was granted a pardon*… OPPOSITE punishment

pare 1 = <u>peel</u>, cut, skin, trim, clip, shave …*Pare the rind thinly from the lemon*…
2 = <u>cut back</u>, cut, reduce, crop, decrease, dock, prune, shear, lop, retrench …*Local authorities must pare down their budgets*…

parent 1 = <u>father</u> *or* mother, sire, progenitor, begetter, procreator, old (*Austral. & N.Z. informal*), patriarch …*Both her parents were killed in a car crash*…
2 = <u>source</u>, cause, author, root, origin, architect, creator, prototype, forerunner, originator, wellspring …*He is regarded as one of the parents of modern classical music*…

parentage = <u>family</u>, birth, origin, descent, line, race, stock, pedigree, extraction, ancestry, lineage, paternity, derivation

parenthood = <u>fatherhood</u> *or* motherhood, parenting, rearing, bringing up, nurturing, upbringing, child rearing, baby *or* child care, fathering *or* mothering

pariah = <u>outcast</u>, exile, outlaw, undesirable, untouchable, leper, unperson

parings = <u>peelings</u>, skins, slices, clippings, peel, fragments, shavings, shreds, flakes, rind, snippets, slivers

parish 1 = <u>district</u>, community …*the vicar of a small parish in a West Country town*…
2 = <u>community</u>, fold, flock, church, congregation, parishioners, churchgoers …*The whole parish will object if he is appointed as priest*…
(**Related Words**)
adjective: parochial

parity = <u>equality</u>, correspondence, consistency, equivalence, quits (*informal*), par, unity, similarity, likeness, uniformity, equal terms, sameness, parallelism, congruity

park NOUN 1 = <u>recreation ground</u>, garden, playground, pleasure garden, playpark, domain (*N.Z.*) …*We went for a brisk walk round the park*…
2 = <u>parkland</u>, grounds, estate, lawns, woodland, grassland …*a manor house in six acres of park and woodland*…
3 = <u>field</u>, pitch, playing field …*Chris was the best player on the park*…
VERB 1 = <u>leave</u>, stop, station, position …*He found a place to park the car*…
2 = <u>put (down)</u>, leave, place, stick, deposit, dump, shove, plonk (*informal*) …*Just park your bag on the floor*…

parlance = <u>language</u>, talk, speech, tongue, jargon, idiom, lingo (*informal*), phraseology, manner of speaking

parliament 1 = <u>assembly</u>, council, congress, senate, convention, legislature, talking shop (*informal*), convocation …*The Bangladesh Parliament has approved the policy*…
2 = <u>sitting</u>, diet …*The legislation will be passed in the next parliament*…
3 *with cap.* = <u>Houses of Parliament</u>, the House, Westminster, Mother of Parliaments, the House of Commons and the House of Lords …*Questions have been raised in Parliament regarding this issue*…

parliamentary = <u>governmental</u>, congressional, legislative, law-making, law-giving, deliberative

parlour *or* (*U.S.*) **parlor** 1 (*Old-fashioned*) = <u>sitting room</u>, lounge, living room, drawing room, front room, reception room, best room …*The guests were shown into the parlour*…
2 = <u>establishment</u>, shop, store, salon …*a funeral parlour*…

parlous (*Archaic or humorous*) = <u>dangerous</u>, difficult, desperate, risky, dire, hazardous, hairy (*slang*), perilous, chancy (*informal*)

parochial = <u>provincial</u>, narrow, insular, limited, restricted, petty, narrow-minded, inward-looking,

parody NOUN 1 = takeoff (*informal*), imitation, satire, caricature, send-up (*Brit. informal*), spoof (*informal*), lampoon, skit, burlesque ...*a parody of a well-know soap opera*...
2 = travesty, farce, caricature, mockery, apology for ...*His trial was a parody of justice*...
VERB = take off (*informal*), mimic, caricature, send up (*Brit. informal*), spoof (*informal*), travesty, lampoon, poke fun at, burlesque, satirize, do a takeoff of (*informal*) ...*It was easy to parody his rather pompous manner of speaking*...

paroxysm = outburst, attack, fit, seizure, flare-up (*informal*), eruption, spasm, convulsion

parrot = repeat, echo, imitate, copy, reiterate, mimic

parry 1 = evade, avoid, fence off, dodge, duck (*informal*), shun, sidestep, circumvent, fight shy of ...*He parried questions about his involvement in the affair*...
2 = ward off, block, deflect, repel, rebuff, fend off, stave off, repulse, hold at bay ...*My opponent parried every blow I got close enough to attempt*...

parsimonious = mean, stingy, penny-pinching (*informal*), miserly, near (*informal*), saving, sparing, grasping, miserable, stinting, frugal, niggardly, penurious, tightfisted, close-fisted, mingy (*Brit. informal*), cheeseparing, skinflinty, snoep (*S. African informal*) OPPOSITE extravagant

parson = clergyman, minister, priest, vicar, divine, incumbent, reverend (*informal*), preacher, pastor, cleric, rector, curate, churchman, man of God, man of the cloth, ecclesiastic

part NOUN 1 = piece, share, proportion, percentage, lot, bit, section, sector, slice, scrap, particle, segment, portion, fragment, lump, fraction, chunk, wedge ...*A large part of his earnings went on repaying the bank loan*... OPPOSITE entirety
2 *often plural* = region, area, district, territory, neighbourhood, quarter, vicinity, neck of the woods (*informal*), airt (*Scot.*) ...*It's a beautiful part of the country*... ...*That kind of behaviour doesn't go down too well round these parts*...
3 = component, bit, piece, unit, element, ingredient, constituent, module ...*The engine only has three moving parts*...
4 = branch, department, division, office, section, wing, subdivision, subsection ...*He works in a different part of the company*...
5 = organ, member, limb ...*hands, feet, and other body parts*...
6 (*Theatre*) = role, representation, persona, portrayal, depiction, character part ...*the actor who played the part of the doctor in the soap*...
7 (*Theatre*) = lines, words, script, dialogue ...*She's having a lot of trouble learning her part*...
8 = duty, say, place, work, role, hand, business, share, charge, responsibility, task, function, capacity, involvement, participation ...*He felt a sense of relief now that his part in this business was over*...
9 = side, behalf ...*There's no hurry on my part*...

VERB 1 = divide, separate, break, tear, split, rend, detach, sever, disconnect, cleave, come apart, disunite, disjoin ...*The clouds parted and a shaft of sunlight broke through*... ...*He parted the bushes with his stick*... OPPOSITE join
2 = part company, separate, break up, split up, say goodbye, go (their) separate ways ...*We parted on bad terms*... OPPOSITE meet
PHRASES **for the most part** = mainly, largely, generally, chiefly, mostly, principally, on the whole, in the main ...*For the most part, they try to keep out of local disputes*... ◆ **in good part** = good-naturedly, well, cheerfully, cordially, without offence ...*He took their jokes in good part*... ◆ **in part** = partly, a little, somewhat, slightly, partially, to some degree, to a certain extent, in some measure ...*His reaction was due, in part, to his fear of rejection*... ◆ **on the part of** = by, in, from, made by, carried out by ...*There was a change of mood on the part of the government*...
◆ **part with something** = give up, abandon, yield, sacrifice, surrender, discard, relinquish, renounce, let go of, forgo ...*He was reluctant to part with his money, even in such a good cause*... ◆ **take part in** = participate in, be involved in, join in, play a part in, be instrumental in, have a hand in, partake in, take a hand in, associate yourself with, put your twopence-worth in ...*Thousands of students have taken part in the demonstrations*...

partake
PHRASES **partake in something** = participate in, share in, take part in, engage in, enter into ...*Do you partake in dangerous sports?*... ◆ **partake of something** 1 = consume, take, share, receive, eat ...*They were happy to partake of our food and drink*...
2 = display, exhibit, evoke, hint at, be characterized by ...*These groups generally partake of a common characteristic*...

Word Power

partake – The phrase *partake of* is sometimes inappropriately used as if it were a synonym of *eat* or *drink*. In strict usage, you can only *partake of* food or drink which is available for several people to share.

---

partial ADJECTIVE 1 = incomplete, limited, unfinished, imperfect, fragmentary, uncompleted ...*Their policy only met with partial success*... OPPOSITE complete
2 = biased, prejudiced, discriminatory, partisan, influenced, unfair, one-sided, unjust, predisposed, tendentious ...*Some of the umpiring in the tournament was partial*... OPPOSITE unbiased
PHRASES **be partial to** = have a liking for, care for, be fond of, be keen on, be taken with, have a soft spot for, have a weakness for ...*I am partial to red wine*...

partially = partly, somewhat, moderately, in part, halfway, piecemeal, not wholly, fractionally, incompletely, to a certain extent *or* degree
➤ partly

participant = participator, party, member, player,

associate, shareholder, contributor, stakeholder, partaker

participate = <u>take part</u>, be involved, engage, perform, join, enter into, partake, have a hand, get in on the act, be a party to, be a participant [OPPOSITE] refrain from

participation = <u>taking part</u>, contribution, partnership, involvement, assistance, sharing in, joining in, partaking

particle = <u>bit</u>, piece, scrap, grain, molecule, atom, shred, crumb, mite, jot, speck, mote, whit, tittle, iota

particular [ADJECTIVE] 1 = <u>specific</u>, special, express, exact, precise, distinct, peculiar ...*What particular aspects of the job are you interested in?*... [OPPOSITE] general
2 = <u>special</u>, exceptional, notable, uncommon, marked, unusual, remarkable, singular, noteworthy, especial ...*Stress is a particular problem for women*... ...*This is a question of particular importance for us*...
3 = <u>fussy</u>, demanding, critical, exacting, discriminating, meticulous, fastidious, dainty, choosy (*informal*), picky (*informal*), finicky, pernickety (*informal*), overnice ...*Ted was very particular about the colours he used*... [OPPOSITE] indiscriminate
4 = <u>detailed</u>, minute, precise, thorough, selective, painstaking, circumstantial, itemized, blow-by-blow ...*a very particular account of the history of sociology*...
[NOUN] *usually plural* = <u>detail</u>, fact, feature, item, circumstance, specification ...*The nurses at the admission desk asked for her particulars*...
[PHRASES] **in particular** = <u>especially</u>, particularly, expressly, specifically, exactly, distinctly ...*Why should he have noticed me in particular?*...

particularly 1 = <u>specifically</u>, expressly, explicitly, especially, in particular, distinctly ...*I particularly asked for a seat by the window*...
2 = <u>especially</u>, surprisingly, notably, unusually, exceptionally, decidedly, markedly, peculiarly, singularly, outstandingly, uncommonly ...*The number of fatal road accidents has been particularly high*...

parting [NOUN] 1 = <u>farewell</u>, departure, goodbye, leave-taking, adieu, valediction ...*It was a dreadfully emotional parting*...
2 = <u>division</u>, breaking, split, separation, rift, partition, detachment, rupture, divergence ...*Through a parting in the mist, we saw a huddle of buildings*...
[ADJECTIVE] = <u>farewell</u>, last, final, departing, valedictory ...*Her parting words made him feel empty and alone*...

partisan [ADJECTIVE] 1 = <u>prejudiced</u>, one-sided, biased, partial, sectarian, factional, tendentious ...*He is too partisan to be a referee*... [OPPOSITE] unbiased
2 = <u>underground</u>, resistance, guerrilla, irregular ...*the hide-out of a Bulgarian partisan leader*...
[NOUN] 1 = <u>supporter</u>, champion, follower, backer, disciple, stalwart, devotee, adherent, upholder, votary ...*At first the young poet was a partisan of the Revolution*... [OPPOSITE] opponent
2 = <u>underground fighter</u>, guerrilla, irregular, freedom fighter, resistance fighter ...*He was rescued by some*

Italian partisans...

partition [NOUN] 1 = <u>screen</u>, wall, barrier, divider, room divider ...*offices divided only by a glass partition*...
2 = <u>division</u>, splitting, dividing, separation, segregation, severance ...*the fighting which followed the partition of India*...
[VERB] 1 = <u>separate</u>, screen, divide, fence off, wall off ...*Two rooms have been created by partitioning a single larger room*...
2 = <u>divide</u>, separate, segment, split up, share, section, portion, cut up, apportion, subdivide, parcel out ...*Korea was partitioned in 1945*...

partly = <u>partially</u>, relatively, somewhat, slightly, in part, halfway, not fully, in some measure, incompletely, up to a certain point, to a certain degree *or* extent [OPPOSITE] completely

---

Word Power

partly – *Partly* and *partially* are to some extent interchangeable, but *partly* should be used when referring to a part or parts of something: *the building is partly* (not *partially*) *made of stone*, while *partially* is preferred for the meaning *to some extent*: *his mother is partially* (not *partly*) *sighted*.

---

partner 1 = <u>spouse</u>, consort, bedfellow, significant other (*U.S. informal*), mate, better half (*Brit. informal*), helpmate, husband *or* wife ...*Wanting other friends doesn't mean you don't love your partner*...
2 = <u>companion</u>, collaborator, accomplice, ally, colleague, associate, mate, team-mate, participant, comrade, confederate, bedfellow, copartner ...*They were partners in crime*...
3 = <u>associate</u>, colleague, collaborator, copartner ...*He is a partner in a Chicago law firm*...

partnership 1 = <u>cooperation</u>, association, alliance, sharing, union, connection, participation, copartnership ...*the partnership between Germany's banks and its businesses*...
2 = <u>company</u>, firm, corporation, house, interest, society, conglomerate, cooperative ...*As the partnership prospered, the employees shared in the benefits*...

party 1 = <u>faction</u>, association, alliance, grouping, set, side, league, camp, combination, coalition, clique, coterie, schism, confederacy, cabal ...*opposing political parties*...
2 = <u>get-together</u> (*informal*), celebration, do (*informal*), social, at-home, gathering, function, reception, bash (*informal*), rave (*Brit. slang*), festivity, knees-up (*Brit. informal*), beano (*Brit. slang*), social gathering, shindig (*informal*), soirée, rave-up (*Brit. slang*), hooley *or* hoolie (*chiefly Irish & N.Z.*) ...*We threw a huge birthday party*...
3 = <u>group</u>, team, band, company, body, unit, squad, gathering, crew, gang, bunch (*informal*), detachment (*Military*) ...*a party of explorers*...
4 (*Law*) = <u>litigant</u>, defendant, participant, contractor (*Law*), plaintiff ...*It has to be proved that he is the guilty party*...

pass `VERB` **1** = <u>go by</u> or <u>past</u>, overtake, drive past, lap, leave behind, pull ahead of ...*A car passed me going quite fast...* `OPPOSITE` stop

2 = <u>go</u>, move, travel, roll, progress, flow, proceed, move onwards ...*He passed through the doorway to ward B...*

3 = <u>run</u>, move, stroke ...*He passed a hand through her hair...*

4 = <u>give</u>, hand, send, throw, exchange, transfer, deliver, toss, transmit, convey, chuck (*informal*), let someone have ...*He passed the books to the librarian...*

5 = <u>be left</u>, come, be bequeathed, be inherited by ...*His mother's estate passed to him after her death...*

6 = <u>kick</u>, hit, loft, head, lob ...*Their team passed the ball better than ours did...*

7 = <u>elapse</u>, progress, go by, lapse, wear on, go past, tick by ...*As the years passed, he grew discontented with his marriage...*

8 = <u>end</u>, go, die, disappear, fade, cease, vanish, dissolve, expire, terminate, dwindle, evaporate, wane, ebb, melt away, blow over ...*This crisis will pass eventually... ...Her feelings lightened as the storm passed...*

9 = <u>spend</u>, use (up), kill, fill, waste, employ, occupy, devote, beguile, while away ...*The children passed the time playing in the streets...*

10 = <u>exceed</u>, beat, overtake, go beyond, excel, surpass, transcend, outstrip, outdo, surmount ...*They were the first company in their field to pass the £2 billion turnover mark...*

11 = <u>be successful in</u>, qualify (in), succeed (in), graduate (in), get through, do, pass muster (in), come up to scratch (in) (*informal*), gain a pass in ...*Kevin has just passed his driving test...* `OPPOSITE` fail

12 = <u>approve</u>, accept, establish, adopt, sanction, decree, enact, authorize, ratify, ordain, validate, legislate (for) ...*The Senate passed the bill by a vote of seventy-three to twenty-four...* `OPPOSITE` ban

13 = <u>pronounce</u>, deliver, issue, set forth ...*Passing sentence, the judge described the crime as odious...*

14 = <u>utter</u>, speak, voice, express, declare ...*We passed a few remarks about the weather...*

15 = <u>discharge</u>, release, expel, evacuate, emit, let out, eliminate (*rare*) ...*The first symptom is extreme pain when passing urine...*

`NOUN` **1** = <u>licence</u>, ticket, permit, permission, passport, warrant, identification, identity card, authorization ...*Can I see your boarding pass, please?...*

2 = <u>gap</u>, route, canyon, col, gorge, ravine, defile ...*The monastery is in a remote mountain pass...*

3 = <u>predicament</u>, condition, situation, state, stage, pinch, plight, straits, state of affairs, juncture ...*Things have come to a pretty pass when people are afraid to go out after dark...*

`PHRASES` **make a pass at someone** = <u>make advances to</u>, proposition, hit on (*U.S. & Canad. slang*), come on to (*informal*), make a play for (*informal*), make an approach to, make sexual overtures to ...*Was he just being friendly, or was he making a pass at her?...* ◆ **pass as** or **for something** or **someone** = <u>be mistaken for</u>, be taken for, impersonate, be accepted as, be regarded as ...*He*

was trying to pass as one of the locals... ◆ **pass away** or **on** (*Euphemistic*) = <u>die</u>, pass on, depart (this life), buy it (*U.S. slang*), expire, check out (*U.S. slang*), pass over, kick it (*slang*), croak (*slang*), go belly-up (*slang*), snuff it (*informal*), peg out (*informal*), kick the bucket (*slang*), buy the farm (*U.S. slang*), peg it (*informal*), decease, shuffle off this mortal coil, cark it (*Austral. & N.Z. informal*), pop your clogs (*informal*) ...*He unfortunately passed away last year...* ◆ **pass by** = <u>go past</u>, pass, move past, walk by or past ...*He gave me a nod as he passed by... ...I passed by your house last night...* ◆ **pass off 1** = <u>take place</u>, happen, occur, turn out, go down (*U.S. & Canad.*), be completed, go off, fall out, be finished, pan out ...*The event passed off without any major incidents...* **2** = <u>come to an end</u>, disappear, vanish, die away, fade out or away ...*The effects of the anaesthetic gradually passed off...* ◆ **pass out** (*Informal*) = <u>faint</u>, drop, black out (*informal*), swoon (*literary*), lose consciousness, keel over (*informal*), flake out (*informal*), become unconscious ...*She got drunk and passed out...* ◆ **pass someone over** = <u>overlook</u>, ignore, discount, pass by, disregard, not consider, take no notice of, not take into consideration, pay not attention to ...*She claimed she was repeatedly passed over for promotion...* ◆ **pass something** or **someone off as something** or **someone** = <u>misrepresent as</u>, palm something or someone off as, falsely represent as, disguise something or someone as, dress something or someone up as ...*horse meat being passed off as ground beef...* ◆ **pass something out** = <u>hand out</u>, distribute, dole out, deal out ...*They were passing out leaflets in the street...* ◆ **pass something over** = <u>disregard</u>, forget, ignore, skip, omit, pass by, not dwell on ...*Let's pass over that subject...* ◆ **pass something up** (*Informal*) = <u>miss</u>, ignore, let slip, refuse, decline, reject, neglect, forgo, abstain from, let (something) go by, give (something) a miss (*informal*) ...*It's too good a chance to pass up...* ◆ **pass yourself off as someone** = <u>pretend to be</u>, fake being, feign being, make a pretence of being ...*He tried to pass himself off as a doctor...*

Word Power

pass – The past participle of *pass* is sometimes wrongly spelt *past*: *the time for recriminations has passed* (not *past*).

---

passable 1 = <u>adequate</u>, middling, average, fair, all right, ordinary, acceptable, moderate, fair enough, mediocre, so-so (*informal*), tolerable, not too bad, allowable, presentable, admissible, unexceptional, half-pie (*N.Z. informal*) ...*The meal was passable, but nothing special...* `OPPOSITE` unsatisfactory

2 = <u>clear</u>, open, navigable, unobstructed, traversable, crossable ...*muddy mountain roads that are barely passable...* `OPPOSITE` impassable

passage 1 = <u>corridor</u>, hallway, passageway, hall, lobby, entrance, exit, doorway, aisle, entrance hall, vestibule ...*The toilets are up the stairs and along the* *passage to your right…*

2 = alley, way, opening, close (*Brit.*), course, road, channel, route, path, lane, avenue, thoroughfare …*He spotted someone lurking in the passage between the two houses…*

3 = extract, reading, piece, section, sentence, text, clause, excerpt, paragraph, verse, quotation …*He read a passage from the Bible…*

4 = movement, passing, advance, progress, flow, motion, transit, progression …*the passage of troops through Spain…*

5 = transition, change, move, development, progress, shift, conversion, progression, metamorphosis …*the passage from school to college…*

6 = establishment, passing, legislation, sanction, approval, acceptance, adoption, ratification, enactment, authorization, validation, legalization …*It has been 200 years since the passage of the Bill of Rights…*

7 = passing, course, march, advance, flow, moving on …*Its value increases with the passage of time…*

8 = journey, crossing, tour, trip, trek, voyage …*We arrived after a 10-hour passage by ship…*

9 = safe-conduct, right to travel, freedom to travel, permission to travel, authorization to travel …*They were granted safe passage to Baghdad…*

passageway = corridor, passage, hallway, hall, lane, lobby, entrance, exit, alley, aisle, wynd (*Scot.*)

passé = out-of-date, old-fashioned, dated, outdated, obsolete, unfashionable, antiquated, outmoded, old hat, outworn, démodé (*French*)

passenger = traveller, rider, fare, commuter, hitchhiker, pillion rider, fare payer

passer-by = bystander, witness, observer, viewer, spectator, looker-on, watcher, onlooker, eyewitness

passing ADJECTIVE **1** = momentary, fleeting, short-lived, transient, ephemeral, short, brief, temporary, transitory, evanescent, fugacious (*rare*) …*people who dismissed mobile phones as a passing fad…*

2 = superficial, short, quick, slight, glancing, casual, summary, shallow, hasty, cursory, perfunctory, desultory …*He only gave us a passing glance…*

NOUN **1** = end, finish, loss, vanishing, disappearance, termination, dying out, expiry, expiration …*the passing of an era…*

2 = death, demise, decease, passing on *or* away …*His passing will be mourned by many people…*

3 = passage, course, process, advance, progress, flow …*The passing of time brought a sense of emptiness…*

PHRASES **in passing** = incidentally, on the way, by the way, accidentally, en passant, by the bye …*She only mentioned you in passing…*

passion **1** = love, desire, affection, lust, the hots (*slang*), attachment, itch, fondness, adoration, infatuation, ardour, keenness, concupiscence …*Romeo's passion for Juliet…*

2 = emotion, feeling, fire, heat, spirit, transport, joy, excitement, intensity, warmth, animation, zeal, zest, fervour, eagerness, rapture, ardour …*Her eyes were blazing with passion…* OPPOSITE indifference

3 = mania, fancy, enthusiasm, obsession, bug

(*informal*), craving, fascination, craze, infatuation …*She has a passion for gardening… …Television is his passion…*

4 = rage, fit, storm, anger, fury, resentment, outburst, frenzy, wrath, indignation, flare-up (*informal*), ire, vehemence, paroxysm …*Sam flew into a passion at the suggestion… …He killed the woman in a fit of passion…*

passionate **1** = emotional, excited, eager, enthusiastic, animated, strong, warm, wild, intense, flaming, fierce, frenzied, ardent, fervent, heartfelt, impassioned, zealous, impulsive, vehement, impetuous, fervid …*He made a passionate speech about his commitment to peace…* OPPOSITE unemotional

2 = loving, erotic, hot, sexy (*informal*), aroused, sensual, ardent, steamy (*informal*), wanton, amorous, lustful, desirous …*a passionate embrace…* OPPOSITE cold

passionately **1** = emotionally, eagerly, enthusiastically, vehemently, excitedly, strongly, warmly, wildly, fiercely, intensely, fervently, impulsively, ardently, zealously, animatedly, with all your heart, frenziedly, impetuously, fervidly …*He spoke passionately about the country's moral crisis…* OPPOSITE unemotionally

2 = lovingly, with passion, erotically, ardently, sexily (*informal*), sensually, lustfully, amorously, steamily (*informal*), libidinously, desirously …*She kissed him passionately…* OPPOSITE coldly

passive **1** = submissive, resigned, compliant, receptive, lifeless, docile, nonviolent, quiescent, acquiescent, unassertive, unresisting …*their passive acceptance of the new regime…* OPPOSITE spirited

2 = inactive, inert, uninvolved, non-participating …*He took a passive role in the interview…* OPPOSITE active

password = watchword, key word, magic word (*informal*), open sesame

past NOUN **1** = former times, history, long ago, antiquity, the good old days, yesteryear (*literary*), times past, the old times, days gone by, the olden days, days of yore …*In the past, things were very different…* OPPOSITE future

2 = background, life, experience, history, past life, life story, career to date …*shocking revelations about his past…*

ADJECTIVE **1** = former, late, early, recent, previous, ancient, prior, long-ago, preceding, foregoing, erstwhile, bygone, olden …*a return to the turbulence of past centuries…* OPPOSITE future

2 = previous, former, one-time, sometime, erstwhile, quondam, ex- …*I was still longing for my past lover…*

3 = last, recent, previous, preceding …*the events of the past few days…*

4 = over, done, ended, spent, finished, completed, gone, forgotten, accomplished, extinct, elapsed, over and done with …*The great age of exploration is past…*

PREPOSITION **1** = after, beyond, later than, over, outside, farther than, in excess of, subsequent to …*It's well past your bedtime…*

2 = <u>by</u>, across, in front of ...*She dashed past me and ran out of the room...*
ADVERB = <u>on</u>, by, along ...*The ambulance drove past...*

> ## Word Power
>
> **pass** – The past participle of *pass* is sometimes wrongly spelt *past: the time for recrimination has passed* (not *past*).

paste NOUN **1** = <u>adhesive</u>, glue, cement, gum, mucilage ...*wallpaper paste...*
2 = <u>purée</u>, pâté, spread ...*tomato paste...*
VERB = <u>stick</u>, fix, glue, cement, gum, fasten ...*pasting labels on bottles...*

pastel = <u>pale</u>, light, soft, delicate, muted, soft-hued **OPPOSITE** bright

pastiche **1** = <u>medley</u>, mixture, blend, motley, mélange (*French*), miscellany, farrago, hotchpotch, gallimaufry ...*The world menu may be a pastiche of dishes from many countries...*
2 = <u>parody</u>, take off, imitation ...*a pastiche of Botticelli's Birth of Venus...*

pastime = <u>activity</u>, game, sport, entertainment, leisure, hobby, relaxation, recreation, distraction, amusement, diversion

pastor = <u>clergyman</u>, minister, priest, vicar, divine, parson, rector, curate, churchman, ecclesiastic

pastoral **1** = <u>ecclesiastical</u>, priestly, ministerial, clerical ...*the pastoral duties of bishops...*
2 = <u>rustic</u>, country, simple, rural, idyllic, bucolic, Arcadian, georgic (*literary*), agrestic ...*a tranquil pastoral scene...*

pasture = <u>grassland</u>, grass, meadow, grazing, lea (*poetic*), grazing land, pasturage, shieling (*Scot.*)

pasty = <u>pale</u>, unhealthy, wan, sickly, pallid, anaemic, sallow, like death warmed up (*informal*), wheyfaced

pat¹ VERB = <u>stroke</u>, touch, tap, pet, slap, dab, caress, fondle ...*She patted me on the knee...*
NOUN **1** = <u>tap</u>, stroke, slap, clap, dab, light blow ...*He gave her an encouraging pat on the shoulder...*
2 = <u>lump</u>, cake, portion, dab, small piece ...*a pat of butter...*

pat² ADJECTIVE = <u>glib</u>, easy, ready, smooth, automatic, slick, simplistic, facile ...*There's no pat answer to your question...*
PHRASES **off pat** = <u>perfectly</u>, precisely, exactly, flawlessly, faultlessly ...*He doesn't have the answer off pat...*

patch NOUN **1** = <u>spot</u>, bit, stretch, scrap, shred, small piece ...*a damp patch on the carpet...*
2 = <u>plot</u>, area, ground, land, tract ...*the little vegetable patch in her backyard...*
3 = <u>reinforcement</u>, piece of fabric, piece of cloth, piece of material, piece sewn on ...*jackets with patches on the elbows...*
VERB *often with* **up** = <u>mend</u>, cover, fix, repair, reinforce, stitch (up), sew (up) ...*They patched the barn roof... ...elaborately patched blue jeans...*
PHRASES **patch something up** **1** = <u>settle</u>, make friends, placate, bury the hatchet, conciliate, settle

differences, smooth something over ...*He's trying to patch things up with his wife...* **2** = <u>mend</u>, fix, repair ...*We can patch up those holes in the roof...*

patchwork = <u>mixture</u>, confusion, jumble, medley, hash, pastiche, mishmash, hotchpotch

patchy **1** = <u>uneven</u>, irregular, variegated, spotty, mottled, dappled ...*Bottle tans can make your legs look a patchy orange colour...* **OPPOSITE** even
2 = <u>irregular</u>, varying, variable, random, erratic, uneven, sketchy, fitful, bitty, inconstant ...*The response to the strike call has been patchy...* **OPPOSITE** constant

patent NOUN = <u>copyright</u>, licence, franchise, registered trademark ...*He had a number of patents for his inventions...*
ADJECTIVE = <u>obvious</u>, apparent, evident, blatant, open, clear, glaring, manifest, transparent, conspicuous, downright, unmistakable, palpable, unequivocal, flagrant, indisputable, unconcealed ...*This was a patent lie...*

paternal **1** = <u>fatherly</u>, concerned, protective, benevolent, vigilant, solicitous, fatherlike ...*He has always taken a paternal interest in her...*
2 = <u>patrilineal</u>, patrimonial ...*my paternal grandparents...*

paternity = <u>fatherhood</u>, fathership (*rare*)

path **1** = <u>way</u>, road, walk, track, trail, avenue, pathway, footpath, walkway (*chiefly U.S.*), towpath, footway ...*We followed the path along the clifftops...*
2 = <u>route</u>, way, course, direction, passage ...*A group of reporters blocked his path... ...The tornado wrecked everything in its path...*
3 = <u>course</u>, way, road, track, route, procedure ...*The country is on the path to economic recovery...*

pathetic **1** = <u>sad</u>, moving, touching, affecting, distressing, tender, melting, poignant, harrowing, heartbreaking, plaintive, heart-rending, gut-wrenching, pitiable ...*It was a pathetic sight, watching the people queue for food...* **OPPOSITE** funny
2 = <u>inadequate</u>, useless, feeble, poor, sorry, wet (*Brit. informal*), pants (*informal*), miserable, petty, worthless, meagre, pitiful, woeful, deplorable, lamentable, trashy, measly, crummy (*slang*), crappy (*slang*), rubbishy, poxy (*slang*) ...*That's the most pathetic excuse I've ever heard...*

pathfinder = <u>pioneer</u>, guide, scout, explorer, discoverer, trailblazer

pathos = <u>sadness</u>, poignancy, plaintiveness, pitifulness, pitiableness

patience **1** = <u>forbearance</u>, tolerance, composure, serenity, cool (*slang*), restraint, calmness, equanimity, toleration, sufferance, even temper, imperturbability ...*She lost her patience and shrieked, 'Just shut up, will you?'...* **OPPOSITE** impatience
2 = <u>endurance</u>, resignation, submission, fortitude, persistence, long-suffering, perseverance, stoicism, constancy ...*a burden which he has borne with great patience...*

patient NOUN = <u>sick person</u>, case, sufferer, invalid ...*He specialized in the treatment of cancer patients...*

ADJECTIVE **1** = <u>forbearing</u>, understanding, forgiving, mild, accommodating, tolerant, indulgent, lenient, even-tempered ...*He was endlessly kind and patient with children...* OPPOSITE impatient

2 = <u>long-suffering</u>, resigned, calm, enduring, quiet, composed, persistent, philosophical, serene, persevering, stoical, submissive, self-possessed, uncomplaining, untiring ...*years of patient devotion to her family...*

patois 1 = <u>dialect</u>, vernacular ...*In France patois was spoken in rural regions...*

2 = <u>jargon</u>, slang, vernacular, patter, cant, lingo (*informal*), argot ...*people from the ghetto who speak street patois...*

patriarch = <u>father</u>, old man, elder, grandfather, sire, paterfamilias, greybeard

patrician NOUN = <u>aristocrat</u>, peer, noble, nobleman, aristo (*informal*) ...*He was a patrician, born to wealth...* ADJECTIVE = <u>aristocratic</u>, noble, lordly, high-class, blue-blooded, highborn ...*a member of a patrician German family...*

patriot = <u>nationalist</u>, loyalist, chauvinist, flag-waver (*informal*), lover of your country

patriotic = <u>nationalistic</u>, loyal, flag-waving (*informal*), chauvinistic, jingoistic

patriotism = <u>nationalism</u>, loyalty, flag-waving (*informal*), jingoism, love of your country

patrol VERB = <u>police</u>, guard, keep watch (on), pound, range (over), cruise, inspect, safeguard, make the rounds (of), keep guard (on), walk *or* pound the beat (of) ...*Prison officers continued to patrol the grounds...* NOUN = <u>guard</u>, watch, garrison, watchman, sentinel, patrolman ...*Gunmen opened fire after they were challenged by a patrol...* PHRASES **on patrol** = <u>during a vigil</u>, policing, watching, protecting, guarding, safeguarding, beat-pounding, on your rounds ...*a soldier shot while on patrol...*

patron 1 = <u>supporter</u>, friend, champion, defender, sponsor, guardian, angel (*informal*), advocate, backer, helper, protagonist, protector, benefactor, philanthropist ...*Catherine the Great was a patron of the arts and sciences...*

2 = <u>customer</u>, client, buyer, frequenter, shopper, habitué ...*Like so many of its patrons, he could not resist the food at the Savoy...*

patronage = <u>support</u>, promotion, sponsorship, backing, help, aid, championship, assistance, encouragement, espousal, benefaction

patronize 1 = <u>talk down to</u>, look down on, treat as inferior, treat like a child, be lofty with, treat condescendingly ...*a doctor who does not patronize his patients...*

2 = <u>support</u>, promote, sponsor, back, help, fund, maintain, foster, assist, subscribe to, befriend ...*Some believe it is not the job of the government to patronize the arts...*

3 = <u>be a customer</u> *or* <u>client of</u>, deal with, frequent, buy from, trade with, shop at, do business with ...*the record stores he patronized...*

patronizing = <u>condescending</u>, superior, stooping, lofty, gracious, contemptuous, haughty, snobbish, disdainful, supercilious, toffee-nosed (*slang, chiefly Brit.*) OPPOSITE respectful

patter¹ VERB = <u>tap</u>, beat, pat, pelt, spatter, rat-a-tat, pitter-patter, pitapat ...*All night the sleet pattered on the tin roof...* NOUN = <u>tapping</u>, pattering, pitter-patter, pitapat ...*the patter of the driving rain on the window...*

patter² **1** = <u>spiel</u> (*informal*), line, pitch, monologue ...*Don't be taken in by the sales patter...*

2 = <u>chatter</u>, prattle, nattering, jabber, gabble, yak (*slang*) ...*the cheery patter of DJs...*

3 = <u>jargon</u>, slang, vernacular, cant, lingo (*informal*), patois, argot ...*the famous Glasgow patter...*

pattern 1 = <u>order</u>, plan, system, method, arrangement, sequence, orderliness ...*All three attacks followed the same pattern...*

2 = <u>design</u>, arrangement, motif, figure, device, decoration, ornament, decorative design ...*curtains in a light floral pattern...*

3 = <u>plan</u>, design, original, guide, instructions, diagram, stencil, template ...*a sewing pattern...*

4 = <u>model</u>, example, standard, original, guide, par, criterion, norm, prototype, paradigm, archetype, paragon, exemplar, cynosure ...*the ideal pattern of a good society...*

paucity (*Formal*) = <u>scarcity</u>, lack, poverty, shortage, deficiency, rarity, dearth, smallness, insufficiency, slenderness, sparseness, slightness, sparsity, meagreness, paltriness, scantiness

paunch = <u>belly</u>, beer-belly (*informal*), spread (*informal*), corporation (*informal*), pot, spare tyre (*Brit. slang*), middle-age spread (*informal*), potbelly, large abdomen

pauper = <u>down-and-out</u>, have-not, bankrupt, beggar, insolvent, indigent, poor person, mendicant

pause VERB = <u>stop briefly</u>, delay, hesitate, break, wait, rest, halt, cease, interrupt, deliberate, waver, take a break, discontinue, desist, have a breather (*informal*) ...*He paused briefly before answering...* OPPOSITE continue NOUN = <u>stop</u>, break, delay, interval, hesitation, stay, wait, rest, gap, halt, interruption, respite, lull, stoppage, interlude, cessation, let-up (*informal*), breathing space, breather (*informal*), intermission, discontinuance, entr'acte, caesura ...*There was a brief pause in the conversation...* OPPOSITE continuance

pave = <u>cover</u>, floor, surface, flag, concrete, tile, tar, asphalt, macadamize

paw (*Informal*) = <u>manhandle</u>, grab, maul, molest, handle roughly

pawn¹ = <u>hock</u> (*informal, chiefly U.S.*), pop (*Brit. informal*), stake, mortgage, deposit, pledge, hazard, wager ...*He pawned his wedding ring...*

pawn² = <u>tool</u>, instrument, toy, creature, puppet, dupe, stooge (*slang*), plaything, cat's-paw ...*He is being used as a political pawn by the President...*

pay VERB **1** = <u>reward</u>, compensate, reimburse, recompense, requite, remunerate ...*They are paid well*

for doing such a difficult job...
2 = spend, offer, give, fork out (*informal*), remit, cough up (*informal*), shell out (*informal*) *...I was prepared to pay anything for that car...*
3 = settle, meet, clear, foot, honour, discharge, liquidate, square up *...If you cannot pay your debts, you can file for bankruptcy...*
4 = bring in, earn, return, net, yield *...This job pays $500 a week...*
5 = be profitable, make money, make a return, provide a living, be remunerative *...She took over her husband's restaurant and made it pay...*
6 = benefit, serve, repay, be worthwhile, be advantageous *...It pays to invest in protective clothing...*
7 = give, extend, present with, grant, render, hand out, bestow, proffer *...My husband never pays me compliments or says he loves me...*
NOUN = wages, income, payment, earnings, fee, reward, hire, salary, compensation, allowance, remuneration, takings, reimbursement, hand-outs, recompense, stipend, emolument, meed (*archaic*) *...the workers' complaints about pay and conditions...*
PHRASES **pay for something** = suffer for, compensate for, answer for, be punished for, atone for, make amends for, suffer the consequences of, get your just deserts *...Don't you think criminals should pay for their crimes?...* ◆ **pay off** = succeed, work, be successful, be effective, be profitable *...Her persistence paid off in the end...* ◆ **pay someone back** = get even with (*informal*), punish, repay, retaliate, hit back at, reciprocate, recompense, get revenge on, settle a score with, get your own back on, revenge yourself on, avenge yourself for *...It was her chance to pay him back for humiliating her...*
◆ **pay someone off** (*Informal*) **1** = bribe, corrupt, oil (*informal*), get at, buy off, suborn, grease the palm of (*slang*) *...corrupt societies where officials have to be paid off...* **2** = dismiss, fire, sack (*informal*), discharge, let go, lay off *...Most of the staff are being paid off at the end of the month...* ◆ **pay something back** = repay, return, square, refund, reimburse, settle up *...I'll pay you back that money tomorrow...* ◆ **pay something off** = settle, clear, square, discharge, liquidate, pay in full *...It would take him the rest of his life to pay off that loan...* ◆ **pay something out** = spend, lay out (*informal*), expend, cough up (*informal*), shell out (*informal*), disburse, fork out *or* over *or* up (*slang*) *...football clubs who pay out millions of pounds for players...* ◆ **pay up** = pay, fork out (*informal*), stump up (*Brit. informal*), make payment, pay in full, settle up, come up with the money *...We claimed a refund, but the company wouldn't pay up...*

payable = due, outstanding, owed, owing, mature, to be paid, obligatory, receivable

payment 1 = remittance, advance, deposit, premium, portion, instalment *...a deposit of £50, followed by three monthly payments of £15...*
2 = settlement, paying, discharge, outlay, remittance, defrayal *...He sought payment of a sum which he claimed was owed to him...*

3 = wages, fee, reward, hire, remuneration *...It is reasonable to expect proper payment for this work...*

payoff 1 = bribe, incentive, cut (*informal*), payment, sweetener (*informal*), bung (*Brit. informal*), inducement, kick-back (*informal*), backhander (*informal*), hush money (*informal*) *...payoffs from drugs exporters...*
2 = settlement, payment, reward, payout, recompense *...a $1m divorce payoff...*
3 (*Informal*) = outcome, result, consequence, conclusion, climax, finale, culmination, the crunch (*informal*), upshot, moment of truth, clincher (*informal*), punch line *...The payoff of the novel is patently predictable...*

peace 1 = truce, ceasefire, treaty, armistice, pacification, conciliation, cessation of hostilities *...They hope the treaty will bring peace to Southeast Asia...* **OPPOSITE** war
2 = stillness, rest, quiet, silence, calm, hush, tranquillity, seclusion, repose, calmness, peacefulness, quietude, restfulness *...All I want is a bit of peace and quiet...*
3 = serenity, calm, relaxation, composure, contentment, repose, equanimity, peacefulness, placidity, harmoniousness *...People always felt a sense of peace in her company...*
4 = harmony, accord, agreement, concord, amity *...a period of relative peace in the country's industrial relations...*

peaceable = peace-loving, friendly, gentle, peaceful, mild, conciliatory, amiable, pacific, amicable, placid, inoffensive, dovish, unwarlike, nonbelligerent

peaceful 1 = at peace, friendly, harmonious, amicable, cordial, nonviolent, without hostility, free from strife, on friendly *or* good terms *...Their relations with most of these people were peaceful...* **OPPOSITE** hostile
2 = peace-loving, conciliatory, peaceable, placatory, irenic, pacific, unwarlike *...warriors who killed or enslaved the peaceful farmers...* **OPPOSITE** belligerent
3 = calm, still, quiet, gentle, pleasant, soothing, tranquil, placid, restful *...a peaceful scene...* **OPPOSITE** agitated
4 = serene, placid, undisturbed, untroubled, unruffled *...I felt relaxed and peaceful...*

peacemaker = mediator, appeaser, arbitrator, conciliator, pacifier, peacemonger

peak **NOUN 1** = high point, crown, climax, culmination, zenith, maximum point, apogee, acme, ne plus ultra (*Latin*) *...His career was at its peak when he died...*
2 = point, top, tip, summit, brow, crest, pinnacle, apex, aiguille *...the snow-covered peaks of the Alps...*
VERB = culminate, climax, come to a head, be at its height, reach its highest point, reach the zenith *...Temperatures have peaked at over 30 degrees Celsius...*

peal **VERB** = ring, sound, toll, resound, chime, resonate, tintinnabulate *...The church bells pealed at the stroke of midnight...*
NOUN 1 = ring, sound, ringing, clamour, chime, clang, carillon, tintinnabulation *...the great peals of the*

Abbey bells…

2 = <u>clap</u>, sound, crash, blast, roar, rumble, resounding, reverberation *…great peals of thunder…*

3 = <u>roar</u>, fit, shout, scream, gale, howl, shriek, hoot *…She burst into peals of laughter…*

pearly 1 = <u>iridescent</u>, mother-of-pearl, opalescent, nacreous, margaric, margaritic *…a suit covered with pearly buttons…*

2 = <u>ivory</u>, creamy, milky, silvery *…pearly white teeth…*

peasant 1 = <u>rustic</u>, countryman, hind (*obsolete*), swain (*archaic*), son of the soil, churl (*archaic*) *…land given to peasants for food production…*

2 (*Informal*) = <u>boor</u>, provincial, hick (*informal, chiefly U.S. & Canad.*), lout, yokel, country bumpkin, hayseed (*U.S. & Canad. informal*), churl *…Why should I let a lot of peasants traipse over my property?…*

peck ▌VERB▐ **1** = <u>pick</u>, bite, hit, strike, tap, poke, jab, prick, nibble *…The crow pecked his hand…*

2 = <u>kiss</u>, plant a kiss, give someone a smacker, give someone a peck *or* kiss *…She walked up to him and pecked him on the cheek…*

▌NOUN▐ = <u>kiss</u>, smacker, osculation (*rare*) *…He gave me a peck on the lips…*

peculiar 1 = <u>odd</u>, strange, unusual, bizarre, funny, extraordinary, curious, weird, exceptional, eccentric, abnormal, out-of-the-way, queer, uncommon, singular, unconventional, far-out (*slang*), quaint, off-the-wall (*slang*), outlandish, offbeat, freakish, wacko (*slang*), outré *…He has a very peculiar sense of humour…* ▌OPPOSITE▐ ordinary

2 = <u>special</u>, private, individual, personal, particular, unique, characteristic, distinguishing, distinct, idiosyncratic *…He has his own peculiar way of doing things…* ▌OPPOSITE▐ common

3 *with* **to** = <u>specific to</u>, characteristic of, restricted to, appropriate to, special to, unique to, particular to, endemic to, distinctive of *…surnames peculiar to this area…*

peculiarity 1 = <u>oddity</u>, abnormality, eccentricity, weirdness, queerness, bizarreness, freakishness *…the peculiarity of her behaviour…*

2 = <u>quirk</u>, caprice, mannerism, whimsy, foible, idiosyncrasy, odd trait *…He had many little peculiarities…*

3 = <u>characteristic</u>, mark, feature, quality, property, attribute, trait, speciality, singularity, distinctiveness, particularity *…a strange peculiarity of the Soviet system…*

pecuniary = <u>monetary</u>, economic, financial, capital, commercial, fiscal, budgetary

pedantic 1 = <u>hairsplitting</u>, particular, formal, precise, fussy, picky (*informal*), nit-picking (*informal*), punctilious, priggish, pedagogic, overnice *…all his pedantic quibbles about grammar…*

2 = <u>academic</u>, pompous, schoolmasterly, stilted, erudite, scholastic, didactic, bookish, abstruse, donnish, sententious *…His lecture was pedantic and uninteresting…*

peddle = <u>sell</u>, trade, push (*informal*), market, hawk, flog (*slang*), vend, huckster, sell door to door

peddler *or* **pedlar** = <u>seller</u>, vendor, hawker, duffer

(*dialect*), huckster, door-to-door salesman, cheap-jack (*informal*), colporteur

pedestal ▌NOUN▐ = <u>support</u>, stand, base, foot, mounting, foundation, pier, plinth, dado (*Architecture*) *…a bronze statue on a granite pedestal…*

▌PHRASES▐ **put someone on a pedestal** = <u>worship</u>, dignify, glorify, exalt, idealize, ennoble, deify, apotheosize *…Since childhood, I put my parents on a pedestal…*

pedestrian ▌NOUN▐ = <u>walker</u>, foot-traveller, footslogger *…In Los Angeles, a pedestrian is a rare spectacle…* ▌OPPOSITE▐ driver

▌ADJECTIVE▐ = <u>dull</u>, flat, ordinary, boring, commonplace, mundane, mediocre, plodding, banal, prosaic, run-of-the-mill, humdrum, unimaginative, uninteresting, uninspired, ho-hum (*informal*), no great shakes (*informal*), half-pie (*N.Z. informal*) *…His style is so pedestrian that the book is really boring…* ▌OPPOSITE▐ exciting

pedigree ▌ADJECTIVE▐ = <u>purebred</u>, thoroughbred, full-blooded *…A pedigree dog will never cost less than a three-figure sum…*

▌NOUN▐ = <u>lineage</u>, family, line, race, stock, blood, breed, heritage, descent, extraction, ancestry, family tree, genealogy, derivation *…a countess of impeccable pedigree…*

pedlar
➤ **peddler**

peek ▌VERB▐ = <u>glance</u>, look, peer, spy, take a look, peep, eyeball (*slang*), sneak a look, keek (*Scot.*), snatch a glimpse, take *or* have a gander (*informal*) *…She peeked at him through a crack in the wall…*

▌NOUN▐ = <u>glance</u>, look, glimpse, blink, peep, butcher's (*Brit. slang*), gander (*informal*), look-see (*slang*), shufti (*Brit. slang*), keek (*Scot.*) *…I had a quick peek into the bedroom…*

peel ▌NOUN▐ = <u>rind</u>, skin, peeling, epicarp, exocarp *…grated lemon peel…*

▌VERB▐ = <u>skin</u>, scale, strip, pare, shuck, flake off, decorticate (*rare*), take the skin *or* rind off *…She sat down and began peeling potatoes…*

peep ▌VERB▐ **1** = <u>peek</u>, look, peer, spy, eyeball (*slang*), sneak a look, steal a look, keek (*Scot.*), look surreptitiously, look from hiding *…Now and then she peeped to see if he was watching her…*

2 = <u>appear briefly</u>, emerge, pop up, spring up, issue from, peer out, peek from, show partially *…Purple and yellow flowers peeped between the rocks…*

▌NOUN▐ = <u>look</u>, glimpse, peek, butcher's (*Brit. slang*), gander (*informal*), look-see (*slang*), shufti (*Brit. slang*), keek (*Scot.*) *…He took a peep at his watch…*

peer¹ = <u>squint</u>, look, spy, gaze, scan, inspect, peep, peek, snoop, scrutinize, look closely *…She peered at him sleepily over the bedclothes…*

peer² 1 = <u>noble</u>, lord, count, duke, earl, baron, aristocrat, viscount, marquess, marquis, nobleman, aristo (*informal*) *…He was made a life peer in 1981…*

2 = <u>equal</u>, like, match, fellow, contemporary, coequal, compeer *…His personality made him popular with his peers…*

peerage = <u>aristocracy</u>, peers, nobility, lords and ladies, titled classes

peerless = <u>unequalled</u>, excellent, unique, outstanding, unparalleled, superlative, unrivalled, second to none, incomparable, unmatched, unsurpassed, matchless, beyond compare, nonpareil <u>OPPOSITE</u> mediocre

peeved = <u>irritated</u>, upset, annoyed, put out, hacked off (*U.S. slang*), sore, galled, exasperated, nettled, vexed, irked, riled, piqued, tooshie (*Austral. slang*)

peg NOUN = <u>pin</u>, spike, rivet, skewer, dowel, spigot *...He builds furniture using wooden pegs instead of nails...*
VERB 1 = <u>fasten</u>, join, fix, secure, attach, make fast *...trying to peg a sheet on to the washing line...*
2 = <u>fix</u>, set, control, limit, freeze *...The bank wants to peg interest rates at 9%...*

pejorative = <u>derogatory</u>, negative, slighting, unpleasant, belittling, disparaging, debasing, deprecatory, uncomplimentary, depreciatory, detractive, detractory

pelt[1] = <u>coat</u>, fell, skin, hide *...mink which had been bred for their pelts...*

pelt[2] 1 = <u>shower</u>, beat, strike, pepper, batter, thrash, bombard, wallop (*informal*), assail, pummel, hurl at, cast at, belabour, sling at *...Crowds started to pelt police cars with stones...*
2 = <u>pour</u>, teem, rain hard, bucket down (*informal*), rain cats and dogs (*informal*) *...It's pelting down with rain out there...*
3 = <u>rush</u>, charge, shoot, career, speed, tear, belt (*slang*), dash, hurry, barrel (along) (*informal, chiefly U.S. & Canad.*), whizz (*informal*), stampede, run fast, burn rubber (*informal*) *...She pelted down the stairs in her nightgown...*

pen[1] = <u>write (down)</u>, draft, compose, pencil, draw up, scribble, take down, inscribe, scrawl, jot down, dash off, commit to paper *...She penned a short memo to his private secretary...*

pen[2] NOUN = <u>enclosure</u>, pound, fold, cage, coop, hutch, corral (*chiefly U.S. & Canad.*), sty *...a holding pen for sheep...*
VERB = <u>enclose</u>, confine, cage, pound, mew (up), fence in, impound, hem in, coop up, hedge in, shut up or in *...The cattle had been milked and penned for the night...*

penal = <u>disciplinary</u>, punitive, corrective, penalizing, retributive

penalize 1 = <u>punish</u>, discipline, correct, handicap, award a penalty against (*Sport*), impose a penalty on *...Players who break the rules will be penalized...*
2 = <u>put at a disadvantage</u>, handicap, cause to suffer, unfairly disadvantage, inflict a handicap on *...Old people are being penalized for being pensioners...*

penalty = <u>punishment</u>, price, fine, handicap, forfeit, retribution, forfeiture

penance NOUN = <u>atonement</u>, punishment, penalty, reparation, expiation, sackcloth and ashes, self-punishment, self-mortification *...carrying out acts of penance for his sins... ...The penance imposed on him*

proved light...
PHRASES **do penance** = <u>atone</u>, suffer, make amends, make reparation, accept punishment, show contrition, mortify yourself *...He is doing penance for a lifetime of crime...*

penchant = <u>liking</u>, taste, tendency, turn, leaning, bent, bias, inclination, affinity, disposition, fondness, propensity, predisposition, predilection, proclivity, partiality, proneness

pending ADJECTIVE 1 = <u>undecided</u>, unsettled, in the balance, up in the air, undetermined *...The cause of death was listed as pending...*
2 = <u>forthcoming</u>, imminent, prospective, impending, in the wind, in the offing *...Customers have been inquiring about the pending price rises...*
PREPOSITION = <u>awaiting</u>, until, waiting for, till *...The judge has suspended the ban, pending a full inquiry...*

penetrate 1 = <u>pierce</u>, enter, go through, bore, probe, stab, prick, perforate, impale *...The needle penetrated the skin...*
2 = <u>pervade</u>, enter, permeate, filter through, suffuse, seep through, get in through, percolate through *...A cool breeze penetrated the mosquito netting...*
3 = <u>infiltrate</u>, enter, get in to, make inroads into, sneak in to (*informal*), work or worm your way into *...They had managed to penetrate Soviet defences...*
4 = <u>grasp</u>, understand, work out, figure out (*informal*), unravel, discern, comprehend, fathom, decipher, suss (out) (*slang*), get to the bottom of *...long answers that were often difficult to penetrate...*
5 = <u>be understood by</u>, touch, affect, impress on, come across to, become clear to, get through to *...His words penetrated her fuddled brain...*

penetrating 1 = <u>sharp</u>, harsh, piercing, carrying, piping, loud, intrusive, strident, shrill, high-pitched, ear-splitting *...Her voice was nasal and penetrating...* OPPOSITE sweet
2 = <u>pungent</u>, biting, strong, powerful, sharp, heady, pervasive, aromatic *...a most wonderful penetrating smell and taste...*
3 = <u>piercing</u>, cutting, biting, sharp, freezing, fierce, stinging, frosty, bitterly cold, artic *...A raw, penetrating wind was blowing in off the plain...*
4 = <u>intelligent</u>, quick, sharp, keen, critical, acute, profound, discriminating, shrewd, discerning, astute, perceptive, incisive, sharp-witted, perspicacious, sagacious *...a penetrating mind...* OPPOSITE dull
5 = <u>perceptive</u>, searching, sharp, keen, alert, probing, discerning *...a penetrating stare...* OPPOSITE unperceptive

penetration 1 = <u>piercing</u>, entry, entrance, invasion, puncturing, incision, perforation *...the penetration of eggs by more than one sperm...*
2 = <u>entry</u>, entrance, inroad *...US penetration of Japanese markets...*

pennant = <u>flag</u>, jack, banner, ensign, streamer, burgee (*Nautical*), pennon, banderole

penniless = <u>poor</u>, broke (*informal*), bankrupt, impoverished, short, ruined, strapped (*slang*), needy, cleaned out (*slang*), destitute, poverty-stricken, down and out, skint (*Brit. slang*), indigent, down at heel, impecunious, dirt-poor (*informal*), on the breadline, flat broke (*informal*), penurious, on your uppers, stony-broke (*Brit. slang*), necessitous, in queer street, moneyless, without two pennies to rub together (*informal*), without a penny to your name OPPOSITE> rich

penny-pinching = <u>mean</u>, close, near (*informal*), frugal, stingy, scrimping, miserly, niggardly, tightfisted, Scrooge-like, mingy (*Brit. informal*), cheeseparing, snoep (*S. African informal*) OPPOSITE> generous

pension = <u>allowance</u>, benefit, welfare, annuity, superannuation

pensioner = <u>senior citizen</u>, retired person, retiree (*U.S.*), old-age pensioner, O.A.P.

pensive = <u>thoughtful</u>, serious, sad, blue (*informal*), grave, sober, musing, preoccupied, melancholy, solemn, reflective, dreamy, wistful, mournful, contemplative, meditative, sorrowful, ruminative, in a brown study (*informal*), cogitative OPPOSITE> carefree

pent-up = <u>suppressed</u>, checked, curbed, inhibited, held back, stifled, repressed, smothered, constrained, bridled, bottled up

penury = <u>poverty</u>, want, need, privation, destitution, straitened circumstances, beggary, indigence, pauperism

people PLURAL NOUN 1 = <u>persons</u>, humans, individuals, folk (*informal*), men and women, human beings, humanity, mankind, mortals, the human race, Homo sapiens ...*People should treat the planet with respect*...
2 = <u>the public</u>, the crowd, the masses, the general public, the mob, the herd, the grass roots, the rank and file, the multitude, the populace, the proletariat, the rabble, the plebs, the proles (*derogatory slang, chiefly Brit.*), the commonalty, (the) hoi polloi ...*the will of the people*...
3 = <u>nation</u>, public, community, subjects, population, residents, citizens, folk, inhabitants, electors, populace, tax payers, citizenry, (general) public ...*the people of Rome*...
4 = <u>race</u>, tribe, ethnic group ...*the native peoples of Central and South America*...
5 = <u>family</u>, parents, relations, relatives, folk, folks (*informal*), clan, kin, next of kin, kinsmen, nearest and dearest, kith and kin, your own flesh and blood ...*My people still live in Ireland*...
VERB = <u>inhabit</u>, occupy, settle, populate, colonize ...*a small town peopled by workers and families*...
➤ **peoples**

pep NOUN = <u>energy</u>, life, spirit, zip (*informal*), vitality, animation, vigour, verve, high spirits, gusto, get-up-and-go (*informal*), brio, vivacity, liveliness, vim (*slang*) ...*They need something to put the pep back in their lives*...
PHRASES **pep something** or **someone up** = <u>enliven</u>, inspire, stimulate, animate, exhilarate, quicken, invigorate, jazz up (*informal*), vitalize, vivify ...*an attempt to pep up your sex life*...

pepper NOUN = <u>seasoning</u>, flavour, spice ...*Season the mixture with salt and pepper*...

VERB 1 = <u>pelt</u>, hit, shower, scatter, blitz, riddle, rake, bombard, assail, strafe, rain down on ...*He was peppered with shrapnel*...
2 = <u>sprinkle</u>, spot, scatter, dot, stud, fleck, intersperse, speck, spatter, freckle, stipple, bespatter ...*The road was peppered with glass*...

peppery = <u>hot</u>, fiery, spicy, pungent, highly seasoned, piquant OPPOSITE> mild

perceive 1 = <u>see</u>, notice, note, identify, discover, spot, observe, remark, recognize, distinguish, glimpse, make out, pick out, discern, behold, catch sight of, espy, descry ...*I perceived a number of changes*...
2 = <u>understand</u>, sense, gather, get (*informal*), know, see, feel, learn, realize, conclude, appreciate, grasp, comprehend, get the message about, deduce, apprehend, suss (out) (*slang*), get the picture about ...*He was beginning to perceive the true nature of their relationship*...
3 = <u>consider</u>, believe, judge, suppose, rate, deem, adjudge ...*How real do you perceive this threat to be?*...

perceptible = <u>noticeable</u>, clear, obvious, apparent, visible, evident, distinct, tangible, blatant, conspicuous, palpable, discernible, recognizable, detectable, observable, appreciable, perceivable OPPOSITE> imperceptible

perception 1 = <u>awareness</u>, understanding, sense, impression, feeling, idea, taste, notion, recognition, observation, consciousness, grasp, sensation, conception, apprehension ...*how our perception of death affects the way we live*...
2 = <u>understanding</u>, intelligence, observation, discrimination, insight, sharpness, cleverness, keenness, shrewdness, acuity, discernment, perspicacity, astuteness, incisiveness, perceptiveness, quick-wittedness, perspicuity ...*It did not require a great deal of perception to realise what he meant*...

perceptive = <u>observant</u>, acute, intelligent, discerning, quick, aware, sharp, sensitive, alert, penetrating, discriminating, shrewd, responsive, astute, intuitive, insightful, percipient, perspicacious OPPOSITE> obtuse

perch VERB 1 = <u>sit</u>, rest, balance, settle ...*He perched on the corner of the desk*...
2 = <u>place</u>, put, rest, balance ...*His glasses were perched precariously on his head*...
3 = <u>land</u>, alight, roost ...*A blackbird perched on the parapet outside the window*...
NOUN = <u>resting place</u>, post, branch, pole, roost ...*The canary fell off its perch*...

percolate 1 = <u>penetrate</u>, filter, seep, pervade, permeate, transfuse ...*These truths begin to percolate through our minds*...
2 = <u>filter</u>, brew, perk (*informal*) ...*the machine I use to percolate my coffee*...
3 = <u>seep</u>, strain, drain, filter, penetrate, drip, leach, ooze, pervade, permeate, filtrate ...*Water cannot percolate through the clay*...

perennial = <u>continual</u>, lasting, continuing, permanent, constant, enduring, chronic, persistent,

Peoples http://www.aaanet.org/

African peoples

Bantu
Barotse
Basotho
Berber
Bushman
Chewa
Damara
Dinka
Duala
Edo
Eritrean
Ethiopian
Ewe
Gabonese
Galla
Gambian
Ghanaian *or* Ghanian
Griqua *or* Grikwa
Hausa
Herero
Hottentot
Hutu
Ibibio
Ibo *or* Igbo

Kabyle
Kikuyu
Kongo
Luba
Luo
Malinke *or* Maninke
Masai
Matabele
Moor
Mosotho
Mossi
Nama *or* Namaqua
Ndebele
Negrillo
Negro
Nguni
Nuba
Nupe
Nyanja
Nyoro
Ovambo
Pondo
Pygmy *or* Pigmy
Rif, Riff, *or* Rifi

Shangaan
Shluh
Shona
Somali
Songhai
Sotho
Strandloper
Susu
Swahili
Swazi
Temne
Tiv
Tsonga
Tswana
Tuareg
Tunisian
Tutsi
Venda
Watusi *or* Watutsi
Wolof
Xhosa
Yoruba
Zulu

Asian peoples

Adivasi
Ainu
Akkadian *or* Accadian
Amalekite
Amorite
Andamanese
Arab
Babylonian
Bakhtyari
Baluchi *or* Balochi
Bashkir
Bedouin *or* Beduin
Bengali
Bihari
Burmese
Buryat
Chaldean *or* Chaldaean
Cham
Chinese
Chukchee *or* Chukchi
Chuvash
Cossack
Cumans
Dani
Dard
Dyak *or* Dayak
Elamite
Ephesian
Ephraimite
Essene
Evenki
Fulani
Gond
Gujarati *or* Gujerati

Gurkha
Hittite
Hui
Hun
Hurrian
Igorot *or* Igorrote
Israeli
Jat
Jewish
Kabardian
Kalmuck *or* Kalmyk
Kanarese *or* Canarese
Kara-Kalpak
Karen
Kashmiri
Kassite
Kazakh *or* Kazak
Khmer
Kurd
Lao
Lepcha
Lycian
Lydian
Malay
Maratha *or* Mahratta
Mede
Mishmi
Mon
Mongol
Montagnard
Moro
Motu
Munda
Naga

Negrito
Nogay
Nuri *or* Kafir
Palestinian
Pathan, Pashto, Pushto, *or* Pushtu
Phoenician
Punjabi *or* Panjabi
Sabaean *or* Sabean
Samoyed
Saracen
Semite
Shan
Sherpa
Sindhi
Sinhalese
Sogdian
Sumerian
Tadzhik, Tadjik, *or* Tajik
Tagalog
Talaing
Tamil
Tatar *or* Tartar
Thai
Tocharian *or* Tokharian
Tongan
Tungus
Turanian
Turk
Turkmen
Uigur *or* Uighur
Uzbek
Vedda *or* Veddah
Visayan *or* Bisayan
Yakut

Peoples (continued)

Australasian peoples

Aborigine	Gurindji	Polynesian
Aranda	Maori	Tagalog
Dayak	Melanesian	

Central and South American Indian peoples

Araucanian	Chimú	Nahuatl
Arawakan	Ge	Quechua, Kechua, *or* Quichua
Aymara	Guarani	Toltec
Aztec	Inca	Tupi
Carib	Makuna	Zapotec
Cashinahua	Maya	
Chibca	Mixtec	

Eskimo peoples

Aleut *or* Aleutian	Inuit *or* Innuit
Caribou Eskimo	Yupik

European peoples

Achaean *or* Achaian	Ephesian	Ostrogoth
Aeolian *or* Eolian	Estonian *or* Esthonian	Ostyak
Albanian	Etruscan *or* Etrurian	Pict
Alemanni	Fleming	Pole
Andalusian	Frank	Portuguese
Angle	French	Provençal
Anglo-Norman	Frisian	Prussian
Anglo-Saxon	Gaelic	Romanian
Aragonese	Galician	Russian
Armenian	Gascon	Sabellian
Aryan	Gaul	Sabine
Ashkenazi	Georgian	Salain
Austrian	German	Samnite
Azerbaijani *or* Azeri	Goidel	Samoyed
Azorean	Goth	Sardinian
Basque	Greek	Saxon
Bavarian	Gypsy *or* Gipsy	Scot
Belgae	Hellenic	Scythian
Belorussian	Iberian *or* Celtiberian	Sephardi
Bosnian Muslim	Icelandic	Serbian
Breton	Iceni	Sicilian
Briton	Illyrian	Silures
Brython	Indo-European	Slav
Bulgar	Ingush	Slovak
Bulgarian	Ionian	Slovene
Burgundian	Irish	Sorb
Carinthian	Jute	Swabian
Castilian	Karelian	Swede
Catalan	Komi	Swiss
Celt	Latin	Teuton
Celtiberi	Lapp	Thracian
Chechen	Latvian	Turk
Cheremis *or* Cheremiss	Lithuanian	Tyrolese
Cimbri	Lombard *or* Langobard	Ugrian
Cornish	Lusatian	Ukrainian
Corsican	Luxembourger	Vandal
Croatian *or* Croat	Macedonian	Viking
Cymry *or* Kymry	Magyar	Visigoth
Czech	Maltese	Vlach *or* Walach
Dane	Manx	Volsci
Dorian	Montenegrin	Votyak
Dutch	Mordvin	Walloon
English	Norman	Welsh
Faeroese	Norse	Wend
Finn	Norwegian	

Peoples (continued)

Native American tribes

Abnaki	Hopi	Ostiak
Aguaruna	Hupa	Ottawa
Algonquian *or* Algonkian	Huron	Paiute
Algonquin *or* Algonkin	Illinois	Pasamaquoddy
Apache	Inca	Pawnee
Apalachee	Iowa	Penobscot
Arapaho	Iroquois	Pequot
Araucan	Kansa	Pericu
Arikara	Karankawa	Piegan
Ashochimi	Kichai	Pima
Assiniboine	Kickapoo	Powhatan
Athabascan	Kiowa	Pueblo
Aymara	Kootenay	Quakaw
Aztec	Kwakiutl	Quechua, Quichua, *or* Kechua
Bella Coola	Leni-Lenapé	Root-digger
Biloxi	Lipan	Salish
Blackfoot	Mandan	Santee
Blood	Mapuche	Sarcee
Caddo	Maya	Sauk
Campa	Menomini *or* Menominee	Seminole
Carib	Miami	Seneca
Catawba	Micmac	Shawnee
Cayuga	Minnetaree	Shoshoni
Cherokee	Mixtec	Shushwap
Cheyenne	Mohave *or* Mojave	Sioux
Chickasaw	Mohawk	Stonies
Chilcal	Mohegan	Susquehanna
Chinook	Mohican *or* Mahican	Teton
Chippewa *or* Chippeway	Moki *or* Moqui	Tlingit
Choctaw	Montagnard	Toltec
Cocopa	Muskogean *or* Muskhogean	Tonkawa
Comanche	Nahuatl	Tuscarora
Cree	Narraganset	Ute
Creek	Natchez	Wappo
Crow	Navaho *or* Navajo	Warrau
Dakota	Nez Percé	Wichita
Delaware	Nootka	Winnebago
Dene	Ojibwa *or* Ojibway	Wyandot
Dogrib	Omaha	Yaqui
Flathead	Oneida	Yuchi
Fox	Onondaga	Yuma
Haida	Orejone	Yunca
Hidatsa	Osage	Zuni

abiding, lifelong, perpetual, recurrent, never-ending, incessant, unchanging, inveterate

perfect [ADJECTIVE] **1** = <u>faultless</u>, correct, pure, accurate, faithful, impeccable, exemplary, flawless, foolproof, blameless ...*Nobody's perfect*... ...*He spoke perfect English*... [OPPOSITE] deficient
2 = <u>excellent</u>, ideal, supreme, superb, splendid, sublime, superlative ...*This is a perfect time to buy a house*...
3 = <u>immaculate</u>, impeccable, flawless, spotless, unblemished, untarnished, unmarred ...*The car is in perfect condition*... [OPPOSITE] flawed
4 = <u>complete</u>, absolute, sheer, utter, consummate, out-and-out, unadulterated, unmitigated, unalloyed ...*She behaved like a perfect fool*... [OPPOSITE] partial
5 = <u>exact</u>, true, accurate, precise, right, close, correct, strict, faithful, spot-on (*Brit. informal*), on the money (*U.S.*), unerring ...*She spoke in a perfect imitation of*

her father's voice...
[VERB] = <u>improve</u>, develop, polish, elaborate, refine, cultivate, hone ...*He worked hard to perfect his drawing technique*... [OPPOSITE] mar

Word Power

perfect – For most of its meanings, the adjective *perfect* describes an absolute state, so that something either is or is not *perfect*, and cannot be referred to in terms of degree – thus, one thing should not be described as *more perfect* or *less perfect* than another thing. However, when *perfect* is used in the sense of 'excellent in all respects', *more* and *most* are acceptable, for example *the next day the weather was even more perfect.*

perfection 1 = <u>excellence</u>, integrity, superiority, purity, wholeness, sublimity, exquisiteness, faultlessness, flawlessness, perfectness, immaculateness ...*the quest for physical perfection*...
2 = <u>the ideal</u>, the crown, the last word, one in a million (*informal*), a paragon, the crème de la crème, the acme, a nonpareil, the beau idéal ...*She seems to be perfection itself*...
3 = <u>accomplishment</u>, achieving, achievement, polishing, evolution, refining, completion, realization, fulfilment, consummation ...*the woman credited with the perfection of this technique*...

perfectionist = <u>stickler</u>, purist, formalist, precisionist, precisian

perfectly 1 = <u>completely</u>, totally, entirely, absolutely, quite, fully, altogether, thoroughly, wholly, utterly, consummately, every inch ...*These mushrooms are perfectly safe to eat*... [OPPOSITE] partially
2 = <u>flawlessly</u>, ideally, wonderfully, superbly, admirably, supremely, to perfection, exquisitely, superlatively, impeccably, like a dream, faultlessly ...*The system worked perfectly*... [OPPOSITE] badly

perforate = <u>pierce</u>, hole, bore, punch, drill, penetrate, puncture, honeycomb

perform 1 = <u>do</u>, achieve, carry out, effect, complete, satisfy, observe, fulfil, accomplish, execute, bring about, pull off, act out, transact ...*people who have performed outstanding acts of bravery*...
2 = <u>fulfil</u>, carry out, execute, discharge ...*Each part of the engine performs a different function*...
3 = <u>present</u>, act (out), stage, play, produce, represent, put on, render, depict, enact, appear as ...*students performing Shakespeare's Macbeth*...
4 = <u>appear on stage</u>, act ...*He began performing in the early fifties*...
5 = <u>function</u>, go, work, run, operate, handle, respond, behave ...*This car performs well*...

performance 1 = <u>presentation</u>, playing, acting (out), staging, production, exhibition, interpretation, representation, rendering, portrayal, rendition ...*They are giving a performance of Bizet's Carmen*...
2 = <u>show</u>, appearance, concert, gig (*informal*), recital ...*The band did three performances at the Royal Albert Hall*...
3 = <u>work</u>, acts, conduct, exploits, feats ...*The study looked at the performance of 18 surgeons*...
4 = <u>functioning</u>, running, operation, working, action, behaviour, capacity, efficiency, capabilities ...*What is the car's performance like?*...
5 = <u>carrying out</u>, practice, achievement, discharge, execution, completion, accomplishment, fulfilment, consummation ...*the performance of his duties*...
6 (*Informal*) = <u>carry-on</u> (*informal, chiefly Brit.*), business, to-do, act, scene, display, bother, fuss, pantomime (*informal, chiefly Brit.*), song and dance (*informal*), palaver, rigmarole, pother ...*She made a big performance of cooking the dinner*...

performer = <u>artiste</u>, player, Thespian, trouper, play-actor, actor *or* actress

perfume 1 = <u>fragrance</u>, scent, essence, incense, cologne, eau de toilette, eau de cologne, attar ...*The room smelled of her mother's perfume*...
2 = <u>scent</u>, smell, fragrance, bouquet, aroma, odour, sweetness, niff (*Brit. slang*), redolence, balminess ...*the perfume of roses*...

perfunctory = <u>offhand</u>, routine, wooden, automatic, stereotyped, mechanical, indifferent, careless, superficial, negligent, sketchy, unconcerned, cursory, unthinking, slovenly, heedless, slipshod, inattentive [OPPOSITE] thorough

perhaps = <u>maybe</u>, possibly, it may be, it is possible (that), conceivably, as the case may be, perchance (*archaic*), feasibly, for all you know, happen (*Northern English dialect*)

peril 1 = <u>danger</u>, risk, threat, hazard, menace, jeopardy, perilousness ...*sailors in peril on the sea*...
2 *often plural* = <u>pitfall</u>, problem, risk, hazard ...*the perils of starring in a TV commercial*... [OPPOSITE] safety

perilous = <u>dangerous</u>, threatening, exposed, vulnerable, risky, unsure, hazardous, hairy (*slang*), unsafe, precarious, parlous (*archaic*), fraught with danger, chancy (*informal*)

perimeter = <u>boundary</u>, edge, border, bounds, limit, margin, confines, periphery, borderline, circumference, ambit [OPPOSITE] centre

period 1 = <u>time</u>, term, season, space, run, stretch, spell, phase, patch (*Brit. informal*), interval, span ...*a period of a few months*...
2 = <u>age</u>, generation, years, time, days, term, stage, date, cycle, era, epoch, aeon ...*the Victorian period*...

periodic = <u>recurrent</u>, regular, repeated, occasional, periodical, seasonal, cyclical, sporadic, intermittent, every so often, infrequent, cyclic, every once in a while, spasmodic, at fixed intervals

periodical 1 = <u>publication</u>, paper, review, magazine, journal, weekly, monthly, organ, serial, quarterly, zine (*informal*) ...*The walls were lined with books and periodicals*...
2 = <u>recurrent</u>, regular, repeated, occasional, seasonal, cyclical, sporadic, intermittent, every so often, infrequent, cyclic, every once in a while, spasmodic, at fixed intervals ...*periodical fits of depression*...

peripheral 1 = <u>secondary</u>, beside the point, minor, marginal, irrelevant, superficial, unimportant, incidental, tangential, inessential ...*That information is peripheral to the main story*...
2 = <u>outermost</u>, outside, external, outer, exterior, borderline, perimetric ...*development in the peripheral areas of large towns*...

periphery = <u>boundary</u>, edge, border, skirt, fringe, verge, brink, outskirts, rim, hem, brim, perimeter, circumference, outer edge, ambit

perish 1 = <u>die</u>, be killed, be lost, expire, pass away, lose your life, decease, cark it (*Austral. & N.Z. slang*) ...*the ferry disaster in which 193 passengers perished*...
2 = <u>be destroyed</u>, fall, decline, collapse, disappear, vanish, go under ...*Civilizations do eventually decline and perish*...
3 = <u>rot</u>, waste away, break down, decay, wither, disintegrate, decompose, moulder ...*The rubber lining*

had perished…

perishable = <u>short-lived</u>, biodegradable, easily spoilt, decomposable, liable to rot <u>OPPOSITE</u> non-perishable

perjury = <u>lying under oath</u>, false statement, forswearing, bearing false witness, giving false testimony, false oath, oath breaking, false swearing, violation of an oath, wilful falsehood

perk (*Brit. informal*) = <u>bonus</u>, benefit, extra, plus, dividend, icing on the cake, fringe benefit, perquisite

perk up **VERB** = <u>cheer up</u>, recover, rally, revive, look up, brighten, take heart, recuperate, buck up (*informal*) *…She perked up and began to laugh…*

PHRASES **perk something** *or* **someone up** = <u>liven someone up</u>, revive someone, cheer someone up, pep someone up *…A brisk stroll will perk you up…*

perky = <u>lively</u>, spirited, bright, sunny, cheerful, animated, upbeat (*informal*), buoyant, bubbly, cheery, bouncy, genial, jaunty, chirpy (*informal*), sprightly, vivacious, in fine fettle, full of beans (*informal*), gay, bright-eyed and bushy-tailed (*informal*)

permanence = <u>continuity</u>, survival, stability, duration, endurance, immortality, durability, finality, perpetuity, constancy, continuance, dependability, permanency, fixity, indestructibility, fixedness, lastingness, perdurability (*rare*)

permanent 1 = <u>lasting</u>, fixed, constant, enduring, persistent, eternal, abiding, perennial, durable, perpetual, everlasting, unchanging, immutable, indestructible, immovable, invariable, imperishable, unfading *…Heavy drinking can cause permanent damage to the brain…* <u>OPPOSITE</u> temporary
2 = <u>long-term</u>, established, secure, stable, steady, long-lasting *…a permanent job…* <u>OPPOSITE</u> temporary

permanently = <u>for ever</u>, constantly, continually, always, invariably, perennially, persistently, eternally, perpetually, steadfastly, indelibly, in perpetuity, enduringly, unwaveringly, immutably, lastingly, immovably, abidingly, unchangingly, unfadingly <u>OPPOSITE</u> temporarily

permeable = <u>penetrable</u>, porous, absorbent, spongy, absorptive, pervious

permeate 1 = <u>infiltrate</u>, fill, pass through, pervade, filter through, spread through, diffuse throughout *…Bias against women permeates every level of the judicial system…*
2 = <u>pervade</u>, saturate, charge, fill, pass through, penetrate, infiltrate, imbue, filter through, spread through, impregnate, seep through, percolate, soak through, diffuse throughout *…The water will eventually permeate through the surrounding concrete…*

permissible = <u>permitted</u>, acceptable, legitimate, legal, all right, sanctioned, proper, authorized, lawful, allowable, kosher (*informal*), admissible, legit (*slang*), licit, O.K. *or* okay (*informal*) <u>OPPOSITE</u> forbidden

permission = <u>authorization</u>, sanction, licence, approval, leave, freedom, permit, go-ahead (*informal*), liberty, consent, allowance, tolerance, green light, assent, dispensation, carte blanche, blank cheque, sufferance <u>OPPOSITE</u> prohibition

permissive = <u>tolerant</u>, liberal, open-minded, indulgent, easy-going, free, lax, lenient, forbearing, acquiescent, latitudinarian, easy-oasy (*slang*) <u>OPPOSITE</u> strict

permit **VERB** 1 = <u>allow</u>, admit, grant, sanction, let, suffer, agree to, entitle, endure, license, endorse, warrant, tolerate, authorize, empower, consent to, give the green light to, give leave *or* permission *…I was permitted to bring my camera into the concert… …The German constitution does not permit the sending of troops…* <u>OPPOSITE</u> forbid
2 = <u>enable</u>, let, allow, cause *…This method of cooking permits the heat to penetrate evenly…*
NOUN = <u>licence</u>, pass, document, certificate, passport, visa, warrant, authorization *…He has to apply for a permit before looking for a job…* <u>OPPOSITE</u> prohibition

permutation = <u>transformation</u>, change, shift, variation, modification, alteration, mutation, transmutation, transposition

pernicious (*Formal*) = <u>wicked</u>, bad, damaging, dangerous, evil, offensive, fatal, deadly, destructive, harmful, poisonous, malicious, malign, malignant, detrimental, hurtful, malevolent, noxious, venomous, ruinous, baleful, deleterious, injurious, noisome, baneful (*archaic*), pestilent, maleficent

perpendicular 1 = <u>upright</u>, straight, vertical, plumb, on end *…the perpendicular wall of sandstone…*
2 = <u>at right angles</u>, at 90 degrees *…The left wing dipped until it was perpendicular to the ground…*

perpetrate = <u>commit</u>, do, perform, carry out, effect, be responsible for, execute, inflict, bring about, enact, wreak

---

Word Power

perpetrate – *Perpetrate* and *perpetuate* are sometimes confused: *he must answer for the crimes he has perpetrated* (not *perpetuated*); *the book helped to perpetuate* (not *perpetrate*) *some of the myths surrounding his early life.*

---

perpetual 1 = <u>everlasting</u>, permanent, endless, eternal, lasting, enduring, abiding, perennial, infinite, immortal, never-ending, unending, unchanging, undying, sempiternal (*literary*) *…the regions of perpetual night at the lunar poles…* <u>OPPOSITE</u> temporary
2 = <u>continual</u>, repeated, constant, endless, continuous, persistent, perennial, recurrent, never-ending, uninterrupted, interminable, incessant, ceaseless, unremitting, unfailing, unceasing *…her perpetual complaints…* <u>OPPOSITE</u> brief

perpetuate = <u>maintain</u>, preserve, sustain, keep up, keep going, continue, keep alive, immortalize, eternalize <u>OPPOSITE</u> end
➤ **perpetrate**

perplex = <u>puzzle</u>, confuse, stump, baffle, bewilder, muddle, confound, beset, mystify, faze, befuddle, flummox, bemuse, dumbfound, nonplus, mix you up

perplexing = <u>puzzling</u>, complex, confusing, complicated, involved, hard, taxing, difficult, strange, weird, mysterious, baffling, bewildering, intricate, enigmatic, mystifying, inexplicable, thorny, paradoxical, unaccountable, knotty, labyrinthine

perplexity 1 = <u>puzzlement</u>, confusion, bewilderment, incomprehension, bafflement, mystification, stupefaction ...*There was utter perplexity in both their expressions*...
2 *usually plural* = <u>complexity</u>, difficulty, mystery, involvement, puzzle, paradox, obscurity, enigma, intricacy, inextricability ...*the perplexities of quantum mechanics*...

per se = <u>in itself</u>, essentially, as such, in essence, by itself, of itself, by definition, intrinsically, by its very nature

persecute 1 = <u>victimize</u>, hunt, injure, pursue, torture, hound, torment, martyr, oppress, pick on, molest, ill-treat, maltreat ...*They have been persecuted for their beliefs*... OPPOSITE mollycoddle
2 = <u>harass</u>, bother, annoy, bait, tease, worry, hassle (*informal*), badger, pester, vex, be on your back (*slang*) ...*He described his first wife as constantly persecuting him*... OPPOSITE leave alone

perseverance = <u>persistence</u>, resolution, determination, dedication, stamina, endurance, tenacity, diligence, constancy, steadfastness, doggedness, purposefulness, pertinacity, indefatigability, sedulity

persevere = <u>keep going</u>, continue, go on, carry on, endure, hold on (*informal*), hang on, persist, stand firm, plug away (*informal*), hold fast, remain firm, stay the course, keep your hand in, pursue your goal, be determined *or* resolved, keep on *or* at, stick at *or* to OPPOSITE give up

persist 1 = <u>continue</u>, last, remain, carry on, endure, keep up, linger, abide ...*Consult your doctor if the symptoms persist*...
2 = <u>persevere</u>, continue, go on, carry on, hold on (*informal*), keep on, keep going, press on, not give up, stand firm, soldier on (*informal*), stay the course, plough on, be resolute, stick to your guns (*informal*), show determination ...*He urged them to persist with their efforts to bring about peace*...

persistence = <u>determination</u>, resolution, pluck, stamina, grit, endurance, tenacity, diligence, perseverance, constancy, steadfastness, doggedness, pertinacity, indefatigability, tirelessness

persistent 1 = <u>continuous</u>, constant, relentless, lasting, repeated, endless, perpetual, continual, never-ending, interminable, unrelenting, incessant, unremitting ...*flooding caused by persistent rain*... OPPOSITE occasional
2 = <u>determined</u>, dogged, fixed, steady, enduring, stubborn, persevering, resolute, tireless, tenacious, steadfast, obstinate, indefatigable, immovable, assiduous, obdurate, stiff-necked, unflagging, pertinacious ...*He phoned again this morning – he's very persistent*... OPPOSITE irresolute

person NOUN = <u>individual</u>, being, body, human, soul, creature, human being, mortal, living soul, man *or* woman ...*He's the only person who can do the job*...
PHRASES **in person** 1 = <u>personally</u>, yourself ...*She collected the award in person*... 2 = <u>in the flesh</u>, actually, physically, bodily ...*It was the first time she had seen him in person*...

persona = <u>personality</u>, part, face, front, role, character, mask, façade, public face, assumed role

personable = <u>pleasant</u>, pleasing, nice, attractive, charming, handsome, good-looking, winning, agreeable, amiable, affable, presentable, likable *or* likeable OPPOSITE unpleasant

personage = <u>personality</u>, celebrity, big name, somebody, worthy, notable, public figure, dignitary, luminary, celeb (*informal*), big shot (*informal*), megastar (*informal*), big noise (*informal*), well-known person, V.I.P.

personal 1 = <u>own</u>, special, private, individual, particular, peculiar, privy ...*That's my personal property!*...
2 = <u>individual</u>, special, particular, exclusive ...*I'll give it my personal attention*...
3 = <u>private</u>, intimate, confidential ...*prying into his personal life*...
4 = <u>offensive</u>, critical, slighting, nasty, insulting, rude, belittling, disparaging, derogatory, disrespectful, pejorative ...*a series of personal comments about my family*...
5 = <u>physical</u>, intimate, bodily, corporal, corporeal ...*personal hygiene*...

personality 1 = <u>nature</u>, character, make-up, identity, temper, traits, temperament, psyche, disposition, individuality ...*She has such a kind, friendly personality*...
2 = <u>character</u>, charm, attraction, charisma, attractiveness, dynamism, magnetism, pleasantness, likableness *or* likeableness ...*a woman of great personality and charm*...
3 = <u>celebrity</u>, star, big name, notable, household name, famous name, celeb (*informal*), personage, megastar (*informal*), well-known face, well-known person ...*a radio and television personality*...

personalized = <u>customized</u>, special, private, individual, distinctive, tailor-made, individualized, monogrammed

personally 1 = <u>in your opinion</u>, for yourself, in your book, for your part, from your own viewpoint, in your own view ...*Personally, I think it's a waste of time*...
2 = <u>by yourself</u>, alone, independently, solely, on your own, in person, in the flesh ...*The minister will answer the allegations personally*...
3 = <u>individually</u>, specially, subjectively, individualistically ...*This topic interests me personally*...
4 = <u>privately</u>, in private, off the record ...*Personally he was quiet, modest and unobtrusive*...

personification = <u>embodiment</u>, image, representation, recreation, portrayal, incarnation, likeness, semblance, epitome

personify = <u>embody</u>, represent, express, mirror,

exemplify, symbolize, typify, incarnate, image (*rare*), epitomize, body forth

personnel = <u>employees</u>, people, members, staff, workers, men and women, workforce, human resources, helpers, liveware

perspective 1 = <u>outlook</u>, attitude, context, angle, overview, way of looking, frame of reference, broad view ...*The death of my mother gave me a new perspective on life*...
2 = <u>objectivity</u>, proportion, relation, relativity, relative importance ...*helping her to get her problems into perspective*...
3 = <u>view</u>, scene, prospect, outlook, panorama, vista ...*stretching away along the perspective of a tree-lined, wide avenue*...

perspiration = <u>sweat</u>, moisture, wetness, exudation

perspire = <u>sweat</u>, glow, swelter, drip with sweat, break out in a sweat, pour with sweat, secrete sweat, be damp *or* wet *or* soaked with sweat, exude sweat

persuade 1 = <u>talk (someone) into</u>, urge, advise, prompt, influence, counsel, win (someone) over, induce, sway, entice, coax, incite, prevail upon, inveigle, bring (someone) round (*informal*), twist (someone's) arm, argue (someone) into ...*My husband persuaded me to come*... OPPOSITE> dissuade
2 = <u>cause</u>, prompt, lead, move, influence, motivate, induce, incline, dispose, impel, actuate ...*the event which persuaded the United States to enter the war*...
3 = <u>convince</u>, satisfy, assure, prove to, convert to, cause to believe ...*Derek persuaded me of the feasibility of the idea*...

persuasion 1 = <u>urging</u>, influencing, conversion, inducement, exhortation, wheedling, enticement, cajolery, blandishment, inveiglement ...*It took all her powers of persuasion to induce them to stay*...
2 = <u>belief</u>, views, opinion, party, school, side, camp, faith, conviction, faction, cult, sect, creed, denomination, tenet, school of thought, credo, firm belief, certitude, fixed opinion ...*people who are of a different political persuasion*...

persuasive = <u>convincing</u>, telling, effective, winning, moving, sound, touching, impressive, compelling, influential, valid, inducing, logical, credible, plausible, forceful, eloquent, weighty, impelling, cogent OPPOSITE> unconvincing

pertain to = <u>relate to</u>, concern, refer to, regard, be part of, belong to, apply to, bear on, befit, be relevant to, be appropriate to, appertain to

pertinent = <u>relevant</u>, fitting, fit, material, appropriate, pat, suitable, proper, to the point, apt, applicable, apposite, apropos, admissible, germane, to the purpose, ad rem (*Latin*) OPPOSITE> irrelevant

perturb = <u>disturb</u>, worry, trouble, upset, alarm, bother, unsettle, agitate, ruffle, unnerve, disconcert, disquiet, vex, fluster, faze, discountenance, discompose

perturbed = <u>disturbed</u>, worried, troubled, shaken, upset, alarmed, nervous, anxious, uncomfortable, uneasy, fearful, restless, flurried, agitated, disconcerted, disquieted, flustered, ill at ease, antsy

(*informal*) OPPOSITE> relaxed

peruse = <u>read</u>, study, scan, check, examine, inspect, browse, look through, eyeball (*slang*), work over, scrutinize, run your eye over

pervade = <u>spread through</u>, fill, affect, penetrate, infuse, permeate, imbue, suffuse, percolate, extend through, diffuse through, overspread

pervasive = <u>widespread</u>, general, common, extensive, universal, prevalent, ubiquitous, rife, pervading, permeating, inescapable, omnipresent

perverse 1 = <u>stubborn</u>, contrary, unreasonable, dogged, contradictory, troublesome, rebellious, wayward, delinquent, intractable, wilful, unyielding, obstinate, intransigent, headstrong, unmanageable, cussed (*informal*), obdurate, stiff-necked, disobedient, wrong-headed, refractory, pig-headed, miscreant, mulish, cross-grained, contumacious ...*You're just being perverse*... OPPOSITE> cooperative
2 = <u>ill-natured</u>, cross, surly, petulant, crabbed, fractious, spiteful, churlish, ill-tempered, stroppy (*Brit. slang*), cantankerous, peevish, shrewish ...*He seems to take a perverse pleasure in being disagreeable*... OPPOSITE> good-natured
3 = <u>abnormal</u>, incorrect, unhealthy, improper, deviant, depraved ...*perverse sexual practices*...

perversion 1 = <u>deviation</u>, vice, abnormality, aberration, kink (*Brit. informal*), wickedness, depravity, immorality, debauchery, unnaturalness, kinkiness (*slang*), vitiation ...*The most frequent sexual perversion is fetishism*...
2 = <u>distortion</u>, twisting, corruption, misuse, misrepresentation, misinterpretation, falsification ...*a monstrous perversion of justice*...

perversity = <u>contrariness</u>, intransigence, obduracy, waywardness, contradictoriness, wrong-headedness, refractoriness, contumacy, contradictiveness, frowardness (*archaic*)

pervert VERB 1 = <u>distort</u>, abuse, twist, misuse, warp, misinterpret, misrepresent, falsify, misconstrue ...*officers attempting to pervert the course of justice*...
2 = <u>corrupt</u>, degrade, subvert, deprave, debase, desecrate, debauch, lead astray ...*He was accused of perverting the nation's youth*...
NOUN = <u>deviant</u>, degenerate, sicko (*informal*), sleazeball (*slang*), debauchee, weirdo *or* weirdie (*informal*) ...*You're nothing but a sick pervert*...

perverted = <u>unnatural</u>, sick, corrupt, distorted, abnormal, evil, twisted, impaired, warped, misguided, unhealthy, immoral, deviant, wicked, kinky (*slang*), depraved, debased, debauched, aberrant, vitiated, pervy (*slang*), sicko (*slang*)

pessimism = <u>gloominess</u>, depression, despair, gloom, cynicism, melancholy, hopelessness, despondency, dejection, glumness

pessimist = <u>defeatist</u>, cynic, melancholic, worrier, killjoy, prophet of doom, misanthrope, wet blanket (*informal*), gloom merchant (*informal*), doomster

pessimistic = <u>gloomy</u>, dark, despairing, bleak, resigned, sad, depressed, cynical, hopeless, melancholy, glum, dejected, foreboding, despondent, morose, fatalistic, distrustful, downhearted, misanthropic OPPOSITE optimistic

pest 1 = infection, bug, insect, plague, epidemic, blight, scourge, bane, pestilence, gogga (*S. African informal*) ...*bacterial, fungal, and viral pests of the plants themselves... ...all kinds of pests like flies and mosquitoes...*
2 = nuisance, bore, trial, pain (*informal*), drag (*informal*), bother, irritation, gall, annoyance, bane, pain in the neck (*informal*), vexation, thorn in your flesh ...*My neighbour's a real pest...*

pester = annoy, worry, bother, disturb, bug (*informal*), plague, torment, get at, harass, nag, hassle (*informal*), harry, aggravate (*informal*), fret, badger, pick on, irk, bedevil, chivvy, get on your nerves (*informal*), bend someone's ear (*informal*), drive you up the wall (*slang*), be on your back (*slang*), get in your hair (*informal*)

pestilence = plague, epidemic, visitation, pandemic

pet ADJECTIVE 1 = favourite, chosen, special, personal, particular, prized, preferred, favoured, dearest, cherished, fave (*informal*), dear to your heart ...*The proceeds will be split between her pet charities...*
2 = tame, trained, domestic, house, domesticated, house-trained (*Brit.*), house-broken ...*One in four households owns a pet dog...*
NOUN = favourite, treasure, darling, jewel, idol, fave (*informal*), apple of your eye, blue-eyed boy *or* girl (*Brit. informal*) ...*They taunted her about being the teacher's pet...*
VERB 1 = fondle, pat, stroke, caress ...*A woman sat petting a cocker spaniel...*
2 = pamper, spoil, indulge, cosset, baby, dote on, coddle, mollycoddle, wrap in cotton wool ...*She had petted her son all his life...*
3 (*Informal*) = cuddle, kiss, snog (*Brit. slang*), smooch (*informal*), neck (*informal*), canoodle (*slang*) ...*They were kissing and petting on the couch...*

peter out = die out, stop, fail, run out, fade, dwindle, evaporate, wane, give out, ebb, come to nothing, run dry, taper off

petite = small, little, slight, delicate, dainty, dinky (*Brit. informal*), elfin

petition NOUN 1 = appeal, round robin, list of signatures ...*We presented the government with a petition signed by 4,500 people...*
2 = entreaty, appeal, address, suit, application, request, prayer, plea, invocation, solicitation, supplication ...*a humble petition to Saint Anthony...*
VERB = appeal, press, plead, call (upon), ask, urge, sue, pray, beg, crave, solicit, beseech, entreat, adjure, supplicate ...*She is petitioning to regain custody of the child...*

petrified 1 = terrified, horrified, shocked, frozen, stunned, appalled, numb, dazed, speechless, aghast, dumbfounded, stupefied, scared stiff, terror-stricken ...*He was petrified at the thought of having to make a speech...*
2 = fossilized, ossified, rocklike ...*a block of petrified wood...*

petrify 1 = terrify, horrify, amaze, astonish, stun, appal, paralyse, astound, confound, transfix, stupefy, immobilize, dumbfound ...*His story petrified me...*
2 = fossilize, set, harden, solidify, ossify, turn to stone, calcify ...*Bird and bat guano petrifies into a mineral called taranakite...*

petty 1 = trivial, inferior, insignificant, little, small, slight, trifling, negligible, unimportant, paltry, measly (*informal*), contemptible, piddling (*informal*), inconsiderable, inessential, nickel-and-dime (*U.S. slang*) ...*Rows would start over petty things...* OPPOSITE important
2 = small-minded, mean, cheap, grudging, shabby, spiteful, stingy, ungenerous, mean-minded ...*I think that attitude is a bit petty...* OPPOSITE broad-minded
3 = minor, lower, junior, secondary, lesser, subordinate, inferior ...*Wilson was not a man who dealt with petty officials...*

petulance = sulkiness, bad temper, irritability, spleen, pique, sullenness, ill-humour, peevishness, querulousness, crabbiness, waspishness, pettishness

petulant = sulky, cross, moody, sour, crabbed, impatient, pouting, perverse, irritable, crusty, sullen, bad-tempered, ratty (*Brit. & N.Z. informal*), fretful, waspish, querulous, peevish, ungracious, cavilling, huffy, fault-finding, snappish, ill-humoured, captious OPPOSITE good-natured

phantasy
➤ **fantasy**

phantom = spectre, ghost, spirit, shade (*literary*), spook (*informal*), apparition, wraith, revenant, phantasm

phase NOUN = stage, time, state, point, position, step, development, condition, period, chapter, aspect, juncture ...*The crisis is entering a crucial phase...*
PHRASES **phase something in** = introduce, incorporate, ease in, start ...*Reforms will be phased in over the next three years...* ◆ **phase something out** = eliminate, close, pull, remove, replace, withdraw, pull out, axe (*informal*), wind up, run down, terminate, wind down, ease off, taper off, deactivate, dispose of gradually ...*The present system of military conscription should be phased out...*

phenomenal = extraordinary, outstanding, remarkable, fantastic, unique, unusual, marvellous, exceptional, notable, sensational, uncommon, singular, miraculous, stellar (*informal*), prodigious, unparalleled, wondrous (*archaic or literary*) OPPOSITE unremarkable

phenomenon 1 = occurrence, happening, fact, event, incident, circumstance, episode ...*scientific explanations of this natural phenomenon...*
2 = wonder, sensation, spectacle, sight, exception, miracle, marvel, prodigy, rarity, nonpareil ...*The Loch Ness monster is not the only bizarre phenomenon that bookmakers take bets on...*

Word Power

phenomenon – Although *phenomena* is often treated as a singular, this is not grammatically correct. *Phenomenon* is the singular form of this word, and *phenomena* the plural; so *several new phenomena were recorded in his notes* is correct, but *that is an interesting phenomena* is not.

philanthropic = <u>humanitarian</u>, generous, charitable, benevolent, kind, humane, gracious, altruistic, public-spirited, beneficent, kind-hearted, munificent, almsgiving, benignant OPPOSITE> selfish

philanthropist = <u>humanitarian</u>, patron, benefactor, giver, donor, contributor, altruist, almsgiver

philanthropy = <u>humanitarianism</u>, charity, generosity, patronage, bounty, altruism, benevolence, munificence, beneficence, liberality, public-spiritedness, benignity, almsgiving, brotherly love, charitableness, kind-heartedness, generousness, open-handedness, largesse *or* largess

philistine NOUN = <u>boor</u>, barbarian, yahoo, lout, bourgeois, hoon (*Austral. & N.Z.*), ignoramus, lowbrow, vulgarian, cougan (*Austral. slang*), scozza (*Austral. slang*), bogan (*Austral. slang*) ...*The man's a total philistine when it comes to the arts...*
ADJECTIVE = <u>uncultured</u>, ignorant, crass, tasteless, bourgeois, uneducated, boorish, unrefined, uncultivated, anti-intellectual, lowbrow, inartistic ...*the country's philistine, consumerist mentality...*

philosopher = <u>thinker</u>, theorist, sage, wise man, logician, metaphysician, dialectician, seeker after truth

philosophical *or* **philosophic** 1 = <u>theoretical</u>, abstract, learned, wise, rational, logical, thoughtful, erudite, sagacious ...*a philosophical discourse...* OPPOSITE> practical
2 = <u>stoical</u>, calm, composed, patient, cool, collected, resigned, serene, tranquil, sedate, impassive, unruffled, imperturbable ...*He was remarkably philosophical about his failure...* OPPOSITE> emotional

philosophy 1 = <u>thought</u>, reason, knowledge, thinking, reasoning, wisdom, logic, metaphysics ...*He studied philosophy and psychology at Cambridge...*
2 = <u>outlook</u>, values, principles, convictions, thinking, beliefs, doctrine, ideology, viewpoint, tenets, world view, basic idea, attitude to life, Weltanschauung (*German*) ...*his philosophy of non-violence...*

phlegmatic = <u>unemotional</u>, indifferent, cold, heavy, dull, sluggish, matter-of-fact, placid, stoical, lethargic, bovine, apathetic, frigid, lymphatic, listless, impassive, stolid, unfeeling, undemonstrative OPPOSITE> emotional

phobia = <u>fear</u>, horror, terror, thing about (*informal*), obsession, dislike, dread, hatred, loathing, distaste, revulsion, aversion to, repulsion, irrational fear, detestation, overwhelming anxiety about OPPOSITE> liking
➤ types of phobia

phone NOUN 1 = <u>telephone</u>, blower (*informal*), dog and bone (*slang*) ...*I spoke to her on the phone only yesterday...*
2 = <u>call</u>, ring (*informal, chiefly Brit.*), bell (*Brit. slang*), buzz (*informal*), tinkle (*Brit. informal*) ...*If you need anything, give me a phone...*
VERB = <u>call</u>, telephone, ring (up) (*informal, chiefly Brit.*), give someone a call, give someone a ring (*informal, chiefly Brit.*), make a call, give someone a buzz (*informal*), give someone a bell (*Brit. slang*), give someone a tinkle (*Brit. informal*), get on the blower (*informal*) ...*I got more and more angry as I waited for her to phone...*

phoney (*Informal*) ADJECTIVE 1 = <u>fake</u>, affected, assumed, trick, put-on, false, forged, imitation, sham, pseudo (*informal*), counterfeit, feigned, spurious ...*He used a phoney accent...* OPPOSITE> genuine
2 = <u>bogus</u>, false, fake, pseudo (*informal*), ersatz ...*phoney 'experts'...*
NOUN 1 = <u>faker</u>, fraud, fake, pretender, humbug, impostor, pseud (*informal*) ...*He was a liar, a cheat, and a phoney...*
2 = <u>fake</u>, sham, forgery, counterfeit ...*This passport is a phoney...*

photograph NOUN = <u>picture</u>, photo (*informal*), shot, image, print, slide, snap (*informal*), snapshot, transparency, likeness ...*He wants to take some photographs of the house...*
VERB = <u>take a picture of</u>, record, film, shoot, snap (*informal*), take (someone's) picture, capture on film, get a shot of ...*I hate being photographed...*

photographic 1 = <u>pictorial</u>, visual, graphic, cinematic, filmic ...*The bank is able to use photographic evidence of who used the machine...*
2 = <u>accurate</u>, minute, detailed, exact, precise, faithful, retentive ...*a photographic memory...*

phrase NOUN = <u>expression</u>, saying, remark, motto, construction, tag, quotation, maxim, idiom, utterance, adage, dictum, way of speaking, group of words, locution ...*the Latin phrase, 'mens sana in corpore sano'...*
VERB = <u>express</u>, say, word, put, term, present, voice, frame, communicate, convey, utter, couch, formulate, put into words ...*The speech was carefully phrased...*

physical 1 = <u>corporal</u>, fleshly, bodily, carnal, somatic, corporeal ...*the physical problems caused by the illness...*
2 = <u>earthly</u>, fleshly, mortal, incarnate, unspiritual ...*They were still aware of the physical world around them...*
3 = <u>material</u>, real, substantial, natural, solid, visible, sensible, tangible, palpable ...*There is no physical evidence to support the story...*

physician = <u>doctor</u>, specialist, doc (*informal*), healer, medic (*informal*), general practitioner, medical practitioner, medico (*informal*), doctor of medicine, sawbones (*slang*), G.P., M.D.

physique = <u>build</u>, form, body, figure, shape, structure, make-up, frame, constitution

pick VERB 1 = <u>select</u>, choose, identify, elect, nominate, sort out, specify, opt for, single out, mark

Types of phobia   http://www.rcpsych.ac.uk/info/anxpho.htm

Phobia	Meaning	Phobia	Meaning
achluophobia	darkness	laliophobia	stuttering
acrophobia	heights	maniaphobia	insanity
agoraphobia	open spaces	mechanophobia	machinery
ailurophobia	cats	meteorophobia	meteors
algophobia	pain	misophobia	contamination
androphobia	men	musophobia	mice
anthropophobia	man	necrophobia	corpses
aquaphobia	water	neophobia	newness
arachnophobia	spiders	nosophobia	disease
astraphobia	lightning	nyctophobia	night
belonephobia	needles	ochlophobia	crowds
brontophobia	thunder	ommatophobia	eyes
cheimaphobia	cold	ophidiophobia	snakes
claustrophobia	closed spaces	ornithophobia	birds
cnidophobia	stings	panphobia	everything
cyberphobia	computers	parthenophobia	girls
cynophobia	dogs	peniaphobia	poverty
demophobia	crowds	phasmophobia	ghosts
demonophobia	demons	phobophobia	fears
entomophobia	insects	photophobia	light
eremophobia	solitude	poinephobia	punishment
ergasiophobia	work	potophobia	drink
genophobia	sex	pteronophobia	feathers
gymnophobia	nudity	pyrophobia	fire
gynophobia	women	sitophobia	food
haematophobia	blood	spermaphobia	germs
haptophobia	touch	spermatophobia	germs
hedonophobia	pleasure	taphephobia	being buried alive
helminthophobia	worms	technophobia	technology
hodophobia	travel	thalassophobia	sea
homichlophobia	fog	thanatophobia	death
homophobia	homosexuals	thermophobia	heat
hydrophobia	water	tonitrophobia	thunder
hypegiaphobia	responsibility	toxiphobia	poison
hypnophobia	sleep	triskaidekaphobia	thirteen
kakorraphiaphobia	failure	xenophobia	strangers or foreigners
katagelophobia	ridicule	zelophobia	jealousy
kleptophobia	stealing	zoophobia	animals

out, plump for, hand-pick, decide upon, cherry-pick, fix upon, settle on *or* upon, sift out ...*He had picked ten people to interview for the jobs...* OPPOSITE⟩ reject **2** = gather, cut, pull, collect, take in, harvest, pluck, garner, cull ...*He helped his mother pick fruit...* **3** = provoke, start, cause, stir up, incite, instigate, foment ...*He picked a fight with a waiter and landed in jail...* **4** = open, force, crack (*informal*), break into, break open, prise open, jemmy (*informal*) ...*He picked the lock, and rifled the papers in each drawer...* NOUN **1** = choice, decision, choosing, option, selection, preference ...*We had the pick of winter coats from the shop...* **2** = best, prime, finest, tops (*slang*), choicest, flower, prize, elect, pride, elite, cream, jewel in the crown, crème de la crème (*French*) ...*These boys are the pick of the under-15 cricketers in the country...* PHRASES **pick at something** = nibble, peck at, have no appetite for, play *or* toy with, push round the plate, eat listlessly ...*She picked at her breakfast...* ◆ **pick on someone 1** = torment, bully, bait, tease, get at (*informal*), badger, persecute, hector, goad, victimize, have it in for (*informal*), tyrannize, have a down on (*informal*) ...*Bullies pick on smaller children...* **2** = choose, select, prefer, elect, single out, fix on, settle upon ...*He needed to confess to someone – he just happened to pick on me...* ◆ **pick someone up** (*Informal*) = arrest, nick (*slang, chiefly Brit.*), bust (*informal*), do (*slang*), lift (*slang*), run in (*slang*), nail (*informal*), collar (*informal*), pinch (*informal*), pull in (*Brit. slang*), nab (*informal*), apprehend, take someone into custody, feel your collar (*slang*) ...*The police picked him up within the hour...* ◆ **pick something** *or* **someone out 1** = identify, notice, recognize, distinguish, perceive, discriminate, make someone *or* something out, tell someone *or* something apart, single someone *or* something out ...*He wasn't difficult to pick out when the bus drew in...* **2** = select, choose, decide on, take, sort out, opt for, cull, plump for, hand-pick ...*Pick out a painting you think she'd like...* ◆ **pick something** *or* **someone up 1** = lift, raise, gather, take up, grasp, uplift, hoist ...*He picked his cap up from the floor... ...They had to pick him up* *and carry on...* **2** = <u>collect</u>, get, call for, go for, go to get, fetch, uplift (*Scot.*), go and get, give someone a lift *or* a ride ...*We drove to the airport to pick her up...* ...*He went to Miami where he had arranged to pick up the money...* ◆ **pick something up 1** = <u>learn</u>, master, acquire, get the hang of (*informal*), become proficient in ...*Where did you pick up your English?...* **2** = <u>obtain</u>, get, find, buy, score (*slang*), discover, purchase, acquire, locate, come across, come by, unearth, garner, stumble across, chance upon, happen upon ...*Auctions can be great places to pick up a bargain...* ◆ **pick up 1** = <u>improve</u>, recover, rally, get better, bounce back, make progress, make a comeback (*informal*), perk up, turn the corner, gain ground, take a turn for the better, be on the road to recovery ...*Industrial production is beginning to pick up...* **2** = <u>recover</u>, improve, rally, get better, mend, perk up, turn the corner, be on the mend, take a turn for the better ...*A good dose of tonic will help you to pick up...* ◆ **pick your way** = <u>tread carefully</u>, work through, move cautiously, walk tentatively, find *or* make your way ...*I picked my way among the rubble...*

picket VERB = <u>blockade</u>, boycott, demonstrate outside ...*The miners went on strike and picketed the power station...*
NOUN **1** = <u>demonstration</u>, strike, blockade ...*Demonstrators have set up a twenty-four-hour picket...*
2 = <u>protester</u>, demonstrator, picketer, flying picket ...*Ten hotels were damaged by pickets in the weekend strike...*
3 = <u>lookout</u>, watch, guard, patrol, scout, spotter, sentry, sentinel, vedette (*Military*) ...*Troops are still manning pickets and patrolling the area...*
4 = <u>stake</u>, post, pale, paling, peg, upright, palisade, stanchion ...*The area was fenced in with pickets to keep out the animals...*

pickings = <u>profits</u>, returns, rewards, earnings, yield, proceeds, spoils, loot, plunder, gravy (*slang*), booty, ill-gotten gains

pickle VERB = <u>preserve</u>, marinade, keep, cure, steep ...*Herrings can be salted, smoked and pickled...* ...*Pickle your favourite vegetables while they're still fresh...*
NOUN **1** = <u>chutney</u>, relish, piccalilli ...*jars of pickle...*
2 (*Informal*) = <u>predicament</u>, spot (*informal*), fix (*informal*), difficulty, bind (*informal*), jam (*informal*), dilemma, scrape (*informal*), hot water (*informal*), uphill (*S. African*), quandary, tight spot ...*Connie had got herself into a real pickle this time...*

pick-me-up (*Informal*) = <u>tonic</u>, drink, pick-up (*slang*), bracer (*informal*), refreshment, stimulant, shot in the arm (*informal*), restorative

pick-up = <u>improvement</u>, recovery, rise, gain, rally, strengthening, revival, upturn, change for the better, upswing

picky (*Informal*) = <u>fussy</u>, particular, critical, carping, fastidious, dainty, choosy, finicky, cavilling, pernickety (*informal*), fault-finding, captious

picnic 1 = <u>excursion</u>, fête champêtre (*French*), barbecue, barbie (*informal*), cookout (*U.S. & Canad.*),

alfresco meal, déjèuner sur l'herbe (*French*), clambake (*U.S. & Canad.*), outdoor meal, outing ...*We're going on a picnic tomorrow...*
2 (*Informal*) (In this sense, the construction is always negative) = <u>walkover</u> (*informal*), breeze (*U.S. & Canad. informal*), pushover (*slang*), snap (*informal*), child's play (*informal*), piece of cake (*Brit. informal*), cinch (*slang*), cakewalk (*informal*), duck soup (*U.S. slang*) ...*Emigrating is no picnic...*

pictorial = <u>graphic</u>, striking, illustrated, vivid, picturesque, expressive, scenic, representational

picture NOUN **1** = <u>representation</u>, drawing, painting, portrait, image, print, illustration, sketch, portrayal, engraving, likeness, effigy, delineation, similitude ...*drawing a small picture with coloured chalks...*
2 = <u>photograph</u>, photo, still, shot, image, print, frame, slide, snap, exposure, portrait, snapshot, transparency, enlargement ...*I saw his picture in the paper...*
3 = <u>film</u>, movie (*U.S. informal*), flick (*slang*), feature film, motion picture ...*a director of epic pictures...*
4 = <u>idea</u>, vision, concept, impression, notion, visualization, mental picture, mental image ...*I'm trying to get a picture of what kind of person you are...*
5 = <u>description</u>, impression, explanation, report, account, image, sketch, depiction, re-creation ...*I want to give you a clear picture of what we are trying to do...*
6 = <u>personification</u>, model, embodiment, soul, essence, archetype, epitome, perfect example, exemplar, quintessence, living example ...*Six years after the operation, he remains a picture of health...*
VERB **1** = <u>imagine</u>, see, envision, visualize, conceive of, fantasize about, conjure up an image of, see in the mind's eye ...*She pictured herself working with animals...*
2 = <u>represent</u>, show, describe, draw, paint, illustrate, portray, sketch, render, depict, delineate ...*The goddess Demeter is pictured holding an ear of wheat...*
3 = <u>show</u>, photograph, capture on film ...*Betty is pictured here with her award...*

⟨ **Related Words** ⟩
adjective: pictorial

picturesque 1 = <u>interesting</u>, pretty, beautiful, attractive, charming, scenic, quaint ...*the Algarve's most picturesque village...* OPPOSITE> unattractive
2 = <u>vivid</u>, striking, graphic, colourful, memorable ...*Every inn had a quaint and picturesque name...* OPPOSITE> dull

piddling (*Informal*) = <u>trivial</u>, little, petty, worthless, insignificant, pants (*informal*), useless, fiddling, trifling, unimportant, paltry, Mickey Mouse (*slang*), puny, derisory, measly (*informal*), crappy (*slang*), toytown (*slang*), piffling, poxy (*slang*), nickel-and-dime (*U.S. slang*) OPPOSITE> significant

piece NOUN **1** = <u>bit</u>, section, slice, part, share, division, block, length, quantity, scrap, segment, portion, fragment, fraction, chunk, wedge, shred, slab, mouthful, morsel, wodge (*Brit. informal*) ...*a piece of wood...* ...*Another piece of cake?...*
2 = <u>component</u>, part, section, bit, unit, segment, constituent, module ...*The equipment was taken*

down the shaft in pieces...

3 = instance, case, example, sample, specimen, occurrence *...a highly complex piece of legislation...*

4 = item, report, story, bit (*informal*), study, production, review, article *...There was a piece about him on television...*

5 = composition, work, production, opus *...an orchestral piece...*

6 = work of art, work, creation *...The cabinets display a wide variety of porcelain pieces...*

7 = share, cut (*informal*), slice, percentage, quantity, portion, quota, fraction, allotment, subdivision *...They got a small piece of the net profits...*

PHRASES **go** *or* **fall to pieces** = break down, fall apart, disintegrate, lose control, crumple, crack up (*informal*), have a breakdown, lose your head *...She went to pieces when her husband died...* ♦ **in pieces** = smashed, broken, shattered, damaged, ruined, bust (*informal*), disintegrated, in bits, in smithereens *...The bowl was lying in pieces on the floor...* ♦ **of a piece (with)** = like, the same (as), similar (to), consistent (with), identical (to), analogous (to), of the same kind (as) *...These essays are of a piece with his earlier work... ...Thirties design and architecture was all of a piece...* ♦ **piece something together 1** = work out, understand, figure out, make out, see, suss out (*slang*), fathom out *...Frank was beginning to piece together what had happened...* **2** = mend, unite, join, fix, restore, repair, patch (together), assemble, compose *...Doctors painstakingly pieced together the broken bones...*

piecemeal ADJECTIVE = unsystematic, interrupted, partial, patchy, intermittent, spotty, fragmentary *...piecemeal changes to the constitution...*
ADVERB = bit by bit, slowly, gradually, partially, intermittently, at intervals, little by little, fitfully, by degrees, by fits and starts *...It was built piecemeal over some 130 years...*

pied = variegated, spotted, streaked, irregular, flecked, motley, mottled, dappled, multicoloured, piebald, parti-coloured, varicoloured

pier 1 = jetty, wharf, quay, promenade, landing place *...The lifeboats were moored at the pier...*
2 = pillar, support, post, column, pile, piling, upright, buttress *...the cross-beams bracing the piers of the jetty...*

pierce 1 = penetrate, stab, spike, enter, bore, probe, drill, run through, lance, puncture, prick, transfix, stick into, perforate, impale *...Pierce the skin of the potato with a fork...*
2 = hurt, cut, wound, strike, touch, affect, pain, move, excite, stir, thrill, sting, rouse, cut to the quick *...Her words pierced Lydia's heart like an arrow...*

piercing 1 (*of sound*) = penetrating, sharp, loud, shattering, shrill, high-pitched, ear-splitting *...a piercing whistle...* OPPOSITE low
2 = perceptive, searching, aware, bright (*informal*), sharp, keen, alert, probing, penetrating, shrewd, perspicacious, quick-witted *...He fixes you with a piercing stare...* OPPOSITE unperceptive
3 = sharp, shooting, powerful, acute, severe, intense,

painful, stabbing, fierce, racking, exquisite, excruciating, agonizing *...I felt a piercing pain in my abdomen...*
4 (*of weather*) = cold, biting, keen, freezing, bitter, raw, arctic, nipping, numbing, frosty, wintry, nippy *...a piercing wind...*

piety = holiness, duty, faith, religion, grace, devotion, reverence, sanctity, veneration, godliness, devoutness, dutifulness, piousness

pig 1 = hog, sow, boar, piggy, swine, grunter, piglet, porker, shoat *...He keeps poultry, pigs and goats...*
2 (*Informal*) = slob, hog (*informal*), guzzler (*slang*), glutton, gannet (*informal*), sloven, greedy guts (*slang*) *...He's just a greedy pig...*
3 (*Informal*) = brute, monster, scoundrel, animal, beast, rogue, swine, rotter, boor *...Her ex-husband was a real pig to her...*

(Related Words)
adjective: porcine
male: boar
female: sow
young: piglet
collective noun: litter
habitation: sty

Breeds of pig

http://www.ansi.okstate.edu/breeds/swine/

Berkshire	Middle White
Cheshire	Pietrain
Chester White	Saddleback
Duroc	Small White
Gloucester Old Spot	Tamworth
Hampshire	Welsh
Landrace	Vietnamese pot-
Large Black	bellied
Large White	

---

pigeon = squab, bird, dove, culver (*archaic*)
(Related Words)
young: squab
collective nouns: flock, flight

pigment = colour, colouring, paint, stain, dye, tint, tincture, colouring matter, colorant, dyestuff

piker (*Aust. & N.Z. slang*) = slacker, shirker, skiver (*Brit. slang*), loafer, layabout, idler, passenger, do-nothing, dodger, good-for-nothing, bludger (*Austral. & N.Z. informal*), gold brick (*U.S. slang*), scrimshanker (*Brit. Military slang*)

pile¹ NOUN **1** = heap, collection, mountain, mass, stack, rick, mound, accumulation, stockpile, hoard, assortment, assemblage *...a pile of books...*
2 (*Informal*) often *plural* = lot(s), mountain(s), load(s) (*informal*), oceans, wealth, great deal, stack(s), abundance, large quantity, oodles (*informal*), shedload (*Brit. informal*) *...I've got piles of questions for you...*
3 = mansion, building, residence, manor, country house, seat, big house, stately home, manor house *...a stately pile in the country...*
4 (*Informal*) = fortune, bomb (*Brit. slang*), pot, packet (*slang*), mint, big money, wad (*U.S. & Canad. slang*), big bucks (*informal, chiefly U.S.*), megabucks (*U.S. &*

Canad. slang), tidy sum (*informal*), pretty penny (*informal*) ...*He made a pile in various business ventures*...
VERB 1 = <u>load</u>, stuff, pack, stack, charge, heap, cram, lade ...*He was piling clothes into the case*...
2 = <u>crowd</u>, pack, charge, rush, climb, flood, stream, crush, squeeze, jam, flock, shove ...*They all piled into the car*...
PHRASES **pile something up** 1 = <u>gather (up)</u>, collect, assemble, stack (up), mass, heap (up), load up ...*Bulldozers piled up huge mounds of dirt*... 2 = <u>collect</u>, accumulate, gather in, pull in, amass, hoard, stack up, store up, heap up ...*Their aim is to pile up the points and aim for a qualifying place*... ♦ **pile up** = <u>accumulate</u>, collect, gather (up), build up, amass ...*Her mail had piled up inside the front door*...

pile² = <u>foundation</u>, support, post, column, piling, beam, upright, pier, pillar ...*wooden houses set on piles along the shore*...

pile³ = <u>nap</u>, fibre, down, hair, surface, fur, plush, shag, filament ...*the carpet's thick pile*...

piles = <u>haemorrhoids</u> ...*More women than men suffer from piles*...

pile-up (*Informal*) = <u>collision</u>, crash, accident, smash, smash-up (*informal*), multiple collision

pilfer = <u>steal</u>, take, rob, lift (*informal*), nick (*slang, chiefly Brit.*), appropriate, rifle, pinch (*informal*), swipe (*slang*), embezzle, blag (*slang*), walk off with, snitch (*slang*), purloin, filch, snaffle (*Brit. informal*), thieve

pilgrim = <u>traveller</u>, crusader, wanderer, devotee, palmer, haji (*Islam*), wayfarer

pilgrimage = <u>journey</u>, tour, trip, mission, expedition, crusade, excursion, hajj (*Islam*)

pill **NOUN** = <u>tablet</u>, capsule, pellet, bolus, pilule ...*a sleeping pill*...
PHRASES **a bitter pill (to swallow)** = <u>trial</u>, pain (*informal*), bore, drag (*informal*), pest, nuisance, pain in the neck (*informal*) ...*You're too old to be given a job. That's a bitter pill to swallow*...

pillage **VERB** = <u>plunder</u>, strip, sack, rob, raid, spoil (*archaic*), rifle, loot, ravage, ransack, despoil, maraud, reive (*dialect*), depredate (*rare*), freeboot, spoliate ...*Soldiers went on a rampage, pillaging stores and shooting*...
NOUN = <u>plundering</u>, sacking, robbery, plunder, sack, devastation, marauding, depredation, rapine, spoliation ...*There were no signs of violence or pillage*...

pillar 1 = <u>support</u>, post, column, piling, prop, shaft, upright, pier, obelisk, stanchion, pilaster ...*the pillars supporting the roof*...
2 = <u>supporter</u>, leader, rock, worthy, mainstay, leading light (*informal*), tower of strength, upholder, torchbearer ...*My father had been a pillar of the community*...

pillory = <u>ridicule</u>, denounce, stigmatize, brand, lash, show someone up, expose someone to ridicule, cast a slur on, heap *or* pour scorn on, hold someone up to shame

pilot **NOUN** 1 = <u>airman</u>, captain, flyer, aviator, aeronaut

...*He spent seventeen years as an airline pilot*...
2 = <u>helmsman</u>, guide, navigator, leader, director, conductor, coxswain, steersman ...*The pilot steered the ship safely inside the main channel*...
VERB 1 = <u>fly</u>, control, operate, be at the controls of ...*the first person to pilot an aircraft across the Pacific*...
2 = <u>navigate</u>, drive, manage, direct, guide, handle, conduct, steer ...*Local fishermen piloted the boats*...
3 = <u>direct</u>, lead, manage, conduct, steer ...*We are piloting the strategy through Parliament*...
ADJECTIVE = <u>trial</u>, test, model, sample, experimental ...*a pilot show for a new TV series*...

pimp **NOUN** = <u>procurer</u>, go-between, bawd (*archaic*), white-slaver, pander, panderer, whoremaster (*archaic*) ...*Every hooker I ever met had a pimp*...
VERB = <u>procure</u>, sell, tout, solicit, live off immoral earnings ...*He sold drugs, and also did a bit of pimping on the side*...

pimple = <u>spot</u>, boil, swelling, pustule, zit (*slang*), papule (*Pathology*), plook (*Scot.*)

pin **NOUN** 1 = <u>tack</u>, nail, needle, safety pin ...*Use pins to keep the material in place as you work*...
2 = <u>peg</u>, rod, brace, bolt ...*the steel pin holding his left leg together*...
VERB 1 = <u>fasten</u>, stick, attach, join, fix, secure, nail, clip, staple, tack, affix ...*They pinned a notice to the door*...
2 = <u>hold fast</u>, hold down, press, restrain, constrain, immobilize, pinion ...*I pinned him against the wall*...
PHRASES **pin someone down** 1 = <u>force</u>, pressure, compel, put pressure on, pressurize, nail someone down, make someone commit themselves ...*She couldn't pin him down to a decision*... ♦ **pin something down** 1 = <u>determine</u>, identify, locate, name, specify, designate, pinpoint, home in on ...*It has taken until now to pin down its exact location*...
2 = <u>trap</u>, confine, constrain, bind, squash, tie down, nail down, immobilize ...*The wreckage of the cockpit had pinned down my legs*...

pinch **VERB** 1 = <u>nip</u>, press, squeeze, grasp, compress, tweak ...*She pinched his arm as hard as she could*...
2 = <u>hurt</u>, crush, squeeze, pain, confine, cramp, chafe ...*shoes which pinch our toes*...
3 (*Brit. informal*) = <u>steal</u>, rob, snatch, lift (*informal*), nick (*slang, chiefly Brit.*), swipe (*slang*), knock off (*slang*), blag (*slang*), pilfer, snitch (*slang*), purloin, filch, snaffle (*Brit. informal*) ...*pickpockets who pinched his wallet*...
NOUN 1 = <u>nip</u>, squeeze, tweak ...*She gave him a little pinch*...
2 = <u>dash</u>, bit, taste, mite, jot, speck, small quantity, smidgen (*informal*), soupçon (*French*) ...*a pinch of salt*...
3 = <u>emergency</u>, crisis, difficulty, plight, scrape (*informal*), strait, uphill (*S. African*), predicament, extremity, hardship ...*I'd trust her in a pinch*...

pinched = <u>thin</u>, starved, worn, drawn, gaunt, haggard, careworn, peaky **OPPOSITE** plump

pine **VERB** = <u>waste</u>, decline, weaken, sicken, sink, flag, fade, decay, dwindle, wither, wilt, languish, droop

…*While away from her children, she pined dreadfully…*
PHRASES **pine for something** or **someone** **1** = long, ache, crave, yearn, sigh, carry a torch, eat your heart out over, suspire (*archaic or poetic*) …*She was pining for her lost husband…* **2** = hanker after, crave, covet, wish for, yearn for, thirst for, hunger for, lust after …*pining for a mythical past…*

pink **NOUN** or **ADJECTIVE** = rosy, rose, salmon, flushed, reddish, flesh coloured, roseate
➤ **shades of red**

pinnacle **1** = summit, top, height, peak, eminence …*He plunged 80 ft from a rocky pinnacle…*
2 = height, top, crown, crest, meridian, zenith, apex, apogee, acme, vertex …*He had reached the pinnacle of his career…*

pinpoint **1** = identify, discover, spot, define, distinguish, put your finger on …*It was impossible to pinpoint the cause of death…*
2 = locate, find, spot, identify, home in on, zero in on, get a fix on …*trying to pinpoint his precise location…*

pint (*Brit. informal*) = beer, jar (*Brit. informal*), jug (*Brit. informal*), ale

pint-sized (*Informal*) = small, little, tiny, wee, pocket-sized, miniature, diminutive, midget, teeny-weeny, teensy-weensy, pygmy or pigmy

pioneer **NOUN** **1** = founder, leader, developer, innovator, founding father, trailblazer …*one of the pioneers in embryology work…*
2 = settler, explorer, colonist, colonizer, frontiersman …*abandoned settlements of early European pioneers…*
VERB = develop, create, launch, establish, start, prepare, discover, institute, invent, open up, initiate, originate, take the lead on, instigate, map out, show the way on, lay the groundwork on …*the scientist who invented and pioneered DNA tests…*

pious **1** = religious, godly, devoted, spiritual, holy, dedicated, righteous, devout, saintly, God-fearing, reverent …*He was brought up by pious female relatives…* **OPPOSITE** irreligious
2 = self-righteous, hypocritical, sanctimonious, goody-goody, unctuous, holier-than-thou, pietistic, religiose …*They were derided as pious, self-righteous bores…* **OPPOSITE** humble

pipe **NOUN** **1** = tube, drain, canal, pipeline, line, main, passage, cylinder, hose, conduit, duct, conveyor …*The liquid is conveyed along a pipe…*
2 = clay (pipe), briar, calabash (*rare*), meerschaum, hookah (*rare*) …*He gave up cigarettes and started smoking a pipe…*
3 = whistle, horn, recorder, fife, flute, wind instrument, penny whistle …*Pan is often pictured playing a reed pipe…*
VERB = convey, channel, supply, conduct, bring in, transmit, siphon …*The gas is piped through a coil surrounded by water…*
PHRASES **pipe down** (*Informal*) = be quiet, shut up (*informal*), hush, stop talking, quieten down, shush, button it (*slang*), belt up (*slang*), shut your mouth, hold your tongue, put a sock in it (*Brit. slang*), button

your lip (*slang*) …*Just pipe down and I'll tell you what I want…* ◆ **pipe up** = speak, volunteer, speak up, have your say, raise your voice, make yourself heard, put your oar in …*'That's right, mister,' another child piped up…*

pipe dream = daydream, dream, notion, fantasy, delusion, vagary, reverie, chimera, castle in the air

pipeline **NOUN** = tube, passage, pipe, line, conduit, duct, conveyor …*a natural-gas pipeline…*
PHRASES **in the pipeline** = on the way, expected, coming, close, near, being prepared, anticipated, forthcoming, under way, brewing, imminent, in preparation, in production, in process, in the offing …*A 2.9 per cent pay increase is already in the pipeline…*

piquant **1** = spicy, biting, sharp, stinging, tart, savoury, pungent, tangy, highly-seasoned, peppery, zesty, with a kick (*informal*), acerb …*a mixed salad with a piquant dressing…* **OPPOSITE** mild
2 = interesting, spirited, stimulating, lively, sparkling, provocative, salty, racy, scintillating …*There was a piquant novelty about her books…* **OPPOSITE** dull

pique **NOUN** = resentment, offence, irritation, annoyance, huff, displeasure, umbrage, hurt feelings, vexation, wounded pride …*In a fit of pique, he threw down his bag…*
VERB **1** = arouse, excite, stir, spur, stimulate, provoke, rouse, goad, whet, kindle, galvanize …*This phenomenon piqued Dr. Morris' interest…*
2 = displease, wound, provoke, annoy, get (*informal*), sting, offend, irritate, put out, incense, gall, nettle, vex, affront, mortify, irk, rile, peeve (*informal*), nark (*Brit., Austral., & N.Z. slang*), put someone's nose out of joint (*informal*), miff (*informal*) …*She was piqued by his lack of enthusiasm…*

piracy **1** = robbery, stealing, theft, hijacking, infringement, buccaneering, rapine, freebooting …*Seven of the fishermen have been formally charged with piracy…*
2 = illegal copying, bootlegging, plagiarism, copyright infringement, illegal reproduction …*Video piracy is a criminal offence…*

pirate **NOUN** = buccaneer, raider, rover, filibuster, marauder, corsair, sea wolf, freebooter, sea robber, sea rover …*In the nineteenth century, pirates roamed the seas…*
VERB = copy, steal, reproduce, bootleg, lift (*informal*), appropriate, borrow, poach, crib (*informal*), plagiarize …*pirated copies of music tapes…*

pirouette **NOUN** = spin, turn, whirl, pivot, twirl …*a ballerina famous for her pirouettes…*
VERB = spin, turn, whirl, pivot, twirl …*She pirouetted in front of the mirror…*

pit **NOUN** **1** = coal mine, mine, shaft, colliery, mine shaft …*Up to ten pits and ten-thousand jobs could be lost…*
2 = hole, gulf, depression, hollow, trench, crater, trough, cavity, abyss, chasm, excavation, pothole …*He lost his footing and began to slide into the pit…*
VERB = scar, mark, hole, nick, notch, dent, gouge,

indent, dint, pockmark …*The plaster was pitted and the paint scuffed…*

> **PHRASES** **pit something** *or* **someone against something** *or* **someone** = set against, oppose, match against, measure against, put in competition with, put in opposition to …*You will be pitted against people as good as you are…*

pitch **NOUN** **1** = sports field, ground, stadium, arena, park, field of play …*a cricket pitch…*
2 = tone, sound, key, frequency, timbre, modulation …*He raised his voice to a higher pitch…*
3 = level, point, degree, summit, extent, height, intensity, high point …*Tensions have reached such a pitch in the area that the army have been called in…*
4 = talk, line, patter, spiel (*informal*) …*He was impressed with her hard sales pitch…*

> **VERB** **1** = throw, launch, cast, toss, hurl, fling, chuck (*informal*), sling, lob (*informal*), bung (*Brit. slang*), heave …*Simon pitched the empty bottle into the lake…*
> **2** = fall, drop, plunge, dive, stagger, tumble, topple, plummet, fall headlong, (take a) nosedive …*He pitched head-first over the low wall…*
> **3** = set up, place, station, locate, raise, plant, settle, fix, put up, erect …*He had pitched his tent in the yard…*
> **4** = toss (about), roll, plunge, flounder, lurch, wallow, welter, make heavy weather …*The ship was pitching and rolling as if in mid-ocean…*

> **PHRASES** **pitch in** = help, contribute, participate, join in, cooperate, chip in (*informal*), get stuck in (*Brit. informal*), lend a hand, muck in (*Brit. informal*), do your bit, lend a helping hand …*Everyone pitched in to help…*

pitch-black *or* **pitch-dark** = dark, black, jet, raven, ebony, sable, unlit, jet-black, inky, Stygian, pitchy, unilluminated

pitfall *usually plural* = danger, difficulty, peril, catch, trap, hazard, drawback, snag, uphill (*S. African*), banana skin (*informal*)

pithy = succinct, pointed, short, brief, to the point, compact, meaningful, forceful, expressive, concise, terse, laconic, trenchant, cogent, epigrammatic, finely honed OPPOSITE long-winded

pitiful **1** = pathetic, distressing, miserable, harrowing, heartbreaking, grievous, sad, woeful, deplorable, lamentable, heart-rending, gut-wrenching, wretched, pitiable, piteous …*It was the most pitiful sight I had ever seen…* OPPOSITE funny
2 = inadequate, mean, low, miserable, dismal, beggarly, shabby, insignificant, paltry, despicable, measly, contemptible …*Many of them work as farm labourers for pitiful wages…* OPPOSITE adequate
3 = worthless, base, sorry, vile, abject, scurvy …*a pitiful performance…* OPPOSITE admirable

pitiless = merciless, ruthless, heartless, harsh, cruel, brutal, relentless, callous, inhuman, inexorable, implacable, unsympathetic, cold-blooded, uncaring, unfeeling, cold-hearted, unmerciful, hardhearted OPPOSITE merciful

pittance = peanuts (*slang*), trifle, modicum, drop, mite, chicken feed (*slang*), slave wages, small

allowance

pitted = scarred, marked, rough, scratched, dented, riddled, blemished, potholed, indented, eaten away, holey, pockmarked, rutty

pity **NOUN** **1** = compassion, understanding, charity, sympathy, distress, sadness, sorrow, kindness, tenderness, condolence, commiseration, fellow feeling …*He felt a sudden tender pity for her…* OPPOSITE mercilessness
2 = shame, crime (*informal*), sin (*informal*), misfortune, bad luck, sad thing, bummer (*slang*), crying shame, source of regret …*It's a pity you couldn't come…*
3 = mercy, kindness, clemency, leniency, forbearance, quarter …*a killer who had no pity for his victims…*

> **VERB** = feel sorry for, feel for, sympathize with, grieve for, weep for, take pity on, empathize with, bleed for, commiserate with, have compassion for, condole with …*I don't know whether to hate him or pity him…*

> **PHRASES** **take pity on something** *or* **someone** – have mercy on, spare, forgive, pity, pardon, reprieve, show mercy to, feel compassion for, put out of your misery, relent against …*She took pity on him because he was homeless…*

pivot **NOUN** **1** = hub, centre, heart, hinge, focal point, kingpin …*A large group of watercolours forms the pivot of the exhibition…*
2 = axis, swivel, axle, spindle, fulcrum …*The pedal had sheared off at the pivot…*

> **VERB** = turn, spin, revolve, rotate, swivel, twirl …*The boat pivoted on its central axis…*

> **PHRASES** **pivot on something** = rely on, depend on, hang on, hinge on, be contingent on, revolve round …*the economic problems that pivoted on overseas trade…*

pivotal = crucial, central, determining, vital, critical, decisive, focal, climactic

pixie = elf, fairy, brownie, sprite, peri

placard = notice, bill, advertisement, poster, sticker, public notice, affiche (*French*)

placate = calm, satisfy, humour, soothe, appease, assuage, pacify, mollify, win someone over, conciliate, propitiate

place **NOUN** **1** = spot, point, position, site, area, situation, station, location, venue, whereabouts, locus …*the place where the temple actually stood…*
2 = region, city, town, quarter, village, district, neighbourhood, hamlet, vicinity, locality, locale, dorp (*S. African*) …*the opportunity to visit new places…*
3 = position, point, spot, location …*He returned the album to its place on the shelf…*
4 = space, position, seat, chair …*There was a single empty place left at the table…*
5 = rank, standing, position, footing, station, status, grade, niche …*a society where everyone knows their place…*
6 = situation, position, circumstances, shoes (*informal*) …*If I were in your place I'd see a lawyer as soon as possible…*
7 = job, position, post, situation, office, employment,

appointment, berth (*informal*), billet (*informal*) ...*All the candidates won places on the ruling council*...

8 = <u>home</u>, house, room, property, seat, flat, apartment, accommodation, pad (*slang*), residence, mansion, dwelling, manor, abode, domicile ...*Let's all go back to my place!*...

9 (In this context, the construction is always negative) = <u>duty</u>, right, job, charge, concern, role, affair, responsibility, task, function, prerogative ...*It is not my place to comment*...

▸ VERB **1** = <u>lay (down)</u>, leave, put (down), set (down), stand, sit, position, rest, plant, station, establish, stick (*informal*), settle, fix, arrange, lean, deposit, locate, set out, install, prop, dispose, situate, stow, bung (*Brit. slang*), plonk (*informal*), array ...*Chairs were placed in rows for the parents*...

2 = <u>put</u>, lay, set, invest, pin ...*Children place their trust in us*...

3 = <u>classify</u>, class, group, put, order, sort, rank, arrange, grade, assign, categorize ...*The authorities have placed the drug in Class A*...

4 = <u>entrust to</u>, give to, assign to, appoint to, allocate to, find a home for ...*The twins were placed in a foster home*...

5 = <u>identify</u>, remember, recognize, pin someone down, put your finger on, put a name to, set someone in context ...*I know we've met, but I can't place you*...

▸ PHRASES **in place of** = <u>instead of</u>, rather than, in exchange for, as an alternative to, taking the place of, in lieu of, as a substitute for, as a replacement for ...*Cooked kidney beans can be used in place of French beans*... ◆ **put someone in their place** = <u>humble</u>, humiliate, deflate, crush, mortify, take the wind out of someone's sails, cut someone down to size (*informal*), take someone down a peg (*informal*), make someone eat humble pie, bring someone down to size (*informal*), make someone swallow their pride, settle someone's hash (*informal*) ...*She put him in his place with just a few words*... ◆ **take place** = <u>happen</u>, occur, go on, go down (*U.S. & Canad.*), arise, come about, crop up, transpire (*informal*), befall, materialize, come to pass (*archaic*), betide ...*Similar demonstrations also took place elsewhere*...

➤ **WORD POWER SUPPLEMENT places and their nicknames**

placement 1 = <u>positioning</u>, stationing, arrangement, location, ordering, distribution, locating, installation, deployment, disposition, emplacement ...*The treatment involves the placement of electrodes in the inner ear*...

2 = <u>appointment</u>, employment, engagement, assignment ...*He had a six-month work placement with the Japanese government*...

piacid 1 = <u>calm</u>, cool, quiet, peaceful, even, collected, gentle, mild, composed, serene, tranquil, undisturbed, unmoved, untroubled, unfazed (*informal*), unruffled, self-possessed, imperturbable, equable, even-tempered, unexcitable ...*She was a placid child who rarely cried*... OPPOSITE excitable

2 = <u>still</u>, quiet, calm, peaceful, serene, tranquil, undisturbed, halcyon, unruffled ...*the placid waters of Lake Erie*... OPPOSITE rough

plagiarism = <u>copying</u>, borrowing, theft, appropriation, infringement, piracy, lifting (*informal*), cribbing (*informal*)

plague NOUN **1** = <u>disease</u>, infection, epidemic, contagion, pandemic, pestilence, lurgy (*informal*) ...*A cholera plague had killed many prisoners of war*...

2 = <u>infestation</u>, invasion, epidemic, influx, host, swarm, multitude ...*The city is under threat from a plague of rats*...

3 (*Informal*) = <u>bane</u>, trial, cancer, evil, curse, torment, blight, calamity, scourge, affliction ...*the cynicism which is the plague of our generation*...

4 (*Informal*) = <u>nuisance</u>, problem, pain (*informal*), bother, pest, hassle (*informal*), annoyance, irritant, aggravation (*informal*), vexation, thorn in your flesh ...*Those children can be a real plague at times*...

▸ VERB **1** = <u>torment</u>, trouble, pain, torture, haunt, afflict (*informal*) ...*She was plagued by weakness, fatigue, and dizziness*...

2 = <u>pester</u>, trouble, bother, disturb, annoy, tease, harry, harass, hassle, fret, badger, persecute, molest, vex, bedevil, get on your nerves (*informal*), give someone grief (*Brit. & S. African*), be on your back (*slang*), get in your hair (*informal*) ...*I'm not going to plague you with a lot of questions*...

plain ADJECTIVE **1** = <u>unadorned</u>, simple, basic, severe, pure, bare, modest, stark, restrained, muted, discreet, austere, spartan, unfussy, unvarnished, unembellished, unornamented, unpatterned ...*a plain grey stone house, distinguished by its unspoilt simplicity*... ...*Her dress was plain, but it hung well on her*... OPPOSITE ornate

2 = <u>clear</u>, obvious, patent, evident, apparent, visible, distinct, understandable, manifest, transparent, overt, unmistakable, lucid, unambiguous, comprehensible, legible ...*It was plain to me that he was having a nervous breakdown*... OPPOSITE hidden

3 = <u>straightforward</u>, open, direct, frank, bold, blunt, sincere, outspoken, honest, downright, candid, forthright, upfront (*informal*), artless, ingenuous, guileless ...*his reputation for plain speaking*... OPPOSITE roundabout

4 = <u>ugly</u>, ordinary, unattractive, homely (*U.S. & Canad.*), not striking, unlovely, unprepossessing, not beautiful, no oil painting (*informal*), ill-favoured, unalluring ...*a shy, rather plain girl with a pale complexion*... OPPOSITE attractive

5 = <u>ordinary</u>, homely, common, simple, modest, everyday, commonplace, lowly, unaffected, unpretentious, frugal, workaday ...*We are just plain people*... OPPOSITE sophisticated

▸ NOUN = <u>flatland</u>, plateau, prairie, grassland, mesa, lowland, steppe, open country, pampas, tableland, veld, llano ...*Once there were 70 million buffalo on the plains*...

plain-spoken = <u>blunt</u>, direct, frank, straightforward, open, explicit, outright, outspoken, downright, candid, forthright, upfront (*informal*), unequivocal OPPOSITE tactful

plaintive = <u>sorrowful</u>, sad, pathetic, melancholy, grievous, pitiful, woeful, wistful, mournful, heart-rending, rueful, grief-stricken, disconsolate, doleful, woebegone, piteous

plan NOUN **1** = <u>scheme</u>, system, design, idea, programme, project, proposal, strategy, method, suggestion, procedure, plot, device, scenario, proposition, contrivance ...*She met her creditors to propose a plan for making repayments...*
2 = <u>diagram</u>, map, drawing, chart, illustration, representation, sketch, blueprint, layout, delineation, scale drawing ...*Draw a plan of the garden...*
VERB **1** = <u>devise</u>, arrange, prepare, scheme, frame, plot, draft, organize, outline, invent, formulate, contrive, think out, concoct ...*I had been planning a trip to the West Coast...*
2 = <u>intend</u>, aim, mean, propose, purpose, contemplate, envisage, foresee ...*The rebel soldiers plan to strike again...*
3 = <u>design</u>, outline, draw up a plan of ...*The company is planning a theme park on the site...*

plane NOUN **1** = <u>aeroplane</u>, aircraft, jet, airliner, jumbo jet ...*He had plenty of time to catch his plane...*
2 = <u>flat surface</u>, the flat, horizontal, level surface ...*a building with angled planes...*
3 = <u>level</u>, position, stage, footing, condition, standard, degree, rung, stratum, echelon ...*life on a higher plane of existence...*
ADJECTIVE = <u>level</u>, even, flat, regular, plain, smooth, uniform, flush, horizontal ...*a plane surface...*
VERB = <u>skim</u>, sail, skate, glide ...*The boats planed across the lake with the greatest of ease...*

planet

Planets

http://www.nineplanets.org/

Earth	Pluto
Jupiter	Saturn
Mars	Uranus
Mercury	Venus
Neptune	

---

plant[1] NOUN = <u>flower</u>, bush, vegetable, herb, weed, shrub ...*Water each plant as often as required...*
VERB **1** = <u>sow</u>, scatter, set out, transplant, implant, put in the ground ...*He intends to plant fruit and vegetables...*
2 = <u>seed</u>, sow, implant ...*They are going to plant the area with grass and trees...*
3 = <u>place</u>, put, set, settle, fix ...*She planted her feet wide and bent her knees slightly...*
4 = <u>hide</u>, put, place, conceal ...*So far no-one has admitted to planting the bomb in the hotel...*
5 = <u>place</u>, put, establish, found, fix, institute, root, lodge, insert, sow the seeds of, imbed ...*Sir Eric had evidently planted the idea in her mind...*

(*Related Words*)
fondness for: florimania
➤ **flowers** ➤ **shrubs** ➤ **trees**

plant[2] **1** = <u>factory</u>, works, shop, yard, mill, foundry ...*The plant provides forty per cent of the country's electricity...*

2 = <u>machinery</u>, equipment, gear, apparatus ...*Firms may invest in plant and equipment abroad where costs are cheaper...*

plaque = <u>plate</u>, panel, medal, tablet, badge, slab, brooch, medallion, cartouch(e)

plaster NOUN **1** = <u>mortar</u>, stucco, gypsum, plaster of Paris, gesso ...*a sculpture in plaster by Rodin...*
2 = <u>bandage</u>, dressing, sticking plaster, Elastoplast (*trademark*), adhesive plaster ...*Put a piece of plaster on the graze...*
VERB = <u>cover</u>, spread, coat, smear, overlay, daub, besmear, bedaub ...*She gets sunburn even when she plasters herself in lotion...*

plastic **1** (*Slang*) = <u>false</u>, artificial, synthetic, superficial, sham, pseudo (*informal*), spurious, specious, meretricious, phoney *or* phony (*informal*) ...*When girls wear too much make-up, they look plastic...* OPPOSITE natural
2 = <u>pliant</u>, soft, flexible, supple, pliable, tensile, ductile, mouldable, fictile ...*The mud is as soft and plastic as butter...* OPPOSITE rigid

plate NOUN **1** = <u>platter</u>, dish, dinner plate, salver, trencher (*archaic*) ...*Scott piled his plate with food...*
2 = <u>helping</u>, course, serving, dish, portion, platter, plateful ...*a huge plate of bacon and eggs...*
3 = <u>layer</u>, panel, sheet, slab ...*The beam is strengthened by a steel plate 6 millimetres thick...*
4 = <u>illustration</u>, picture, photograph, print, engraving, lithograph ...*The book has 55 colour plates...*
VERB = <u>coat</u>, gild, laminate, face, cover, silver, nickel, overlay, electroplate, anodize, platinize ...*small steel balls plated with chrome or gold...*

plateau **1** = <u>upland</u>, table, highland, mesa, tableland ...*a high, flat plateau of cultivated land...*
2 = <u>levelling off</u>, level, stage, stability ...*The economy is stuck on a plateau of slow growth...*

platform **1** = <u>stage</u>, stand, podium, rostrum, dais, soapbox ...*Nick finished his speech and jumped down from the platform...*
2 = <u>policy</u>, programme, principle, objective(s), manifesto, tenet(s), party line ...*The party has announced a platform of economic reforms... ...They won a landslide victory on a nationalist platform...*

platitude = <u>cliché</u>, stereotype, commonplace, banality, truism, bromide, verbiage, inanity, trite remark, hackneyed saying

platonic = <u>nonphysical</u>, ideal, intellectual, spiritual, idealistic, transcendent

platoon = <u>squad</u>, company, group, team, outfit (*informal*), patrol, squadron

platter = <u>plate</u>, dish, tray, charger, salver, trencher (*archaic*)

plaudits = <u>approval</u>, acclaim, applause, praise, clapping, ovation, kudos, congratulation, round of applause, commendation, approbation, acclamation

plausible **1** = <u>believable</u>, possible, likely, reasonable, credible, probable, persuasive, conceivable, tenable, colourable, verisimilar ...*That explanation seems entirely plausible to me...* OPPOSITE unbelievable
2 = <u>glib</u>, smooth, specious, smooth-talking, smooth-

tongued, fair-spoken ...*He was so plausible he conned us all...*

play VERB **1** = amuse yourself, have fun, frolic, sport, fool, romp, revel, trifle, caper, frisk, gambol, entertain yourself, engage in games ...*The children played in the garden...*

2 = take part in, be involved in, engage in, participate in, compete in, be in a team for ...*I used to play basketball...*

3 = compete against, challenge, take on, rival, oppose, vie with, contend against ...*Northern Ireland will play Latvia tomorrow...*

4 = perform, carry out, execute ...*Someone had played a trick on her...*

5 = act, portray, represent, perform, impersonate, act the part of, take the part of, personate ...*His ambition is to play the part of Dracula...*

6 = perform on, strum, make music on ...*Do you play the guitar?...*

NOUN **1** = amusement, pleasure, leisure, games, sport, fun, entertainment, relaxation, a good time, recreation, enjoyment, romping, larks, capering, frolicking, junketing, fun and games, revelry, skylarking, living it up (*informal*), gambolling, horseplay, merrymaking ...*Try to strike a balance between work and play... ...a few hours of play until you go to bed...*

2 = drama, show, performance, piece, comedy, entertainment, tragedy, farce, soap opera, soapie (*Austral. slang*), pantomime, stage show, television drama, radio play, masque, dramatic piece ...*The company put on a play about the homeless...*

PHRASES **in play** = in or for fun, for sport, for a joke, for a lark (*informal*), as a prank, for a jest ...*It was done only in play, but they got a ticking-off from the police...* ◆ **play around 1** = fool around, toy, fiddle, trifle, mess around, take something lightly ...*He's not working, he's just playing around...* **2** = philander, have an affair, carry on (*informal*), fool around, dally, sleep around (*informal*), womanize, play away from home (*informal*) ...*Up to 75 per cent of married men may be playing around...* ◆ **play at something** = pretend to be, pose as, impersonate, make like (*U.S. & Canad. informal*), profess to be, assume the role of, give the appearance of, masquerade as, pass yourself off as ...*rich people just playing at being farmers...* ◆ **play on** or **upon something** = take advantage of, abuse, exploit, impose on, trade on, misuse, milk, make use of, utilize, profit by, capitalize on, turn to your account ...*I felt as if I was playing on her generosity...* ◆ **play something down** = minimize, make light of, gloss over, talk down, underrate, underplay, pooh-pooh (*informal*), soft-pedal (*informal*), make little of, set no store by ...*Western diplomats have played down the significance of the reports...* ◆ **play something up** = emphasize, highlight, underline, magnify, stress, accentuate, point up, call attention to, turn the spotlight on, bring to the fore ...*This increase in crime is definitely being played up by the media...* ◆ **play up 1** (*Brit. informal*) = hurt, be painful, bother you, trouble you, be sore,

pain you, give you trouble, give you gyp (*Brit. & N.Z. slang*) ...*My bad back is playing up again...* **2** (*Brit. informal*) = malfunction, not work properly, be on the blink (*slang*), be wonky (*Brit. slang*) ...*The engine has started playing up...* **3** (*Brit. informal*) = be awkward, misbehave, give trouble, be disobedient, give someone grief (*Brit. & S. African*), be stroppy (*Brit. slang*), be bolshie (*Brit. informal*) ...*The kids always play up in his class...* ◆ **play up to someone** (*Informal*) = butter up, flatter, pander to, crawl to, get in with, suck up to (*informal*), curry favour with, toady, fawn over, keep someone sweet, bootlick (*informal*), ingratiate yourself to ...*She plays up to journalists in the media...* ◆ **play with something** = toy with, wiggle, fiddle with, jiggle, waggle, mess about with, fidget with ...*She played idly with the strap of her handbag...*

playboy = womanizer, philanderer, rake, socialite, man about town, pleasure seeker, lady-killer (*informal*), roué, lover boy (*slang*), ladies' man

player 1 = sportsman or sportswoman, competitor, participant, contestant, team member ...*top chess players...*

2 = musician, artist, performer, virtuoso, instrumentalist, music maker ...*a professional trumpet player...*

3 = performer, entertainer, Thespian, trouper, actor or actress ...*Oscar nominations went to all five leading players...*

playful 1 = joking, humorous, jokey, arch, teasing, coy, tongue-in-cheek, jesting, flirtatious, good-natured, roguish, waggish ...*She gave her husband a playful slap...*

2 = lively, spirited, cheerful, merry, mischievous, joyous, sprightly, vivacious, rollicking, impish, frisky, puckish, coltish, kittenish, frolicsome, ludic (*literary*), sportive, gay, larkish (*informal*) ...*They tumbled around like playful children...* OPPOSITE sedate

playmate = friend, companion, comrade, chum (*informal*), pal (*informal*), cobber (*Austral. or old-fashioned N.Z. informal*), playfellow

plaything = toy, amusement, game, pastime, trifle, trinket, bauble, gimcrack, gewgaw

playwright = dramatist, scriptwriter, tragedian, dramaturge, dramaturgist

plea 1 = appeal, request, suit, prayer, begging, petition, overture, entreaty, intercession, supplication ...*an impassioned plea to mankind to act to save the planet...*

2 (*Law*) = suit, cause, action, allegation ...*We will enter a plea of not guilty...*

3 = excuse, claim, defence, explanation, justification, pretext, vindication, extenuation ...*He murdered his wife, but got off on a plea of insanity...*

plead 1 = appeal, ask, request, beg, petition, crave, solicit, implore, beseech, entreat, importune, supplicate ...*He was kneeling on the floor pleading for mercy...*

2 = allege, claim, argue, maintain, assert, put forward, adduce, use as an excuse ...*The guards pleaded that *they were only obeying orders…*

pleasant 1 = pleasing, nice, welcome, satisfying, fine, lovely, acceptable, amusing, refreshing, delightful, enjoyable, gratifying, agreeable, pleasurable, delectable, lekker (*S. African slang*) …*a pleasant surprise…* OPPOSITE> horrible
2 = friendly, nice, agreeable, likable *or* likeable, engaging, charming, cheerful, cheery, good-humoured, amiable, genial, affable, congenial …*He was most anxious to seem agreeable and pleasant…* OPPOSITE> disagreeable

pleasantry *usually plural* = comment, remark, casual remark, polite remark

please 1 = delight, entertain, humour, amuse, suit, content, satisfy, charm, cheer, indulge, tickle, gratify, gladden, give pleasure to, tickle someone pink (*informal*) …*This comment pleased her immensely…* OPPOSITE> annoy
2 = want, like, choose, wish, will, prefer, desire, opt, be inclined, see fit …*Women should be able to dress as they please…*

pleased = happy, delighted, contented, satisfied, thrilled, glad, tickled, gratified, over the moon (*informal*), chuffed (*Brit. slang*), euphoric, rapt, in high spirits, tickled pink (*informal*), pleased as punch (*informal*)

pleasing 1 = enjoyable, satisfying, attractive, charming, entertaining, delightful, gratifying, agreeable, pleasurable …*a pleasing view…* OPPOSITE> unpleasant
2 = likable *or* likeable, attractive, engaging, charming, winning, entertaining, amusing, delightful, polite, agreeable, amiable …*a pleasing personality…* OPPOSITE> disagreeable

pleasurable = enjoyable, pleasant, diverting, good, nice, welcome, fun, lovely, entertaining, delightful, gratifying, agreeable, congenial

pleasure 1 = happiness, delight, satisfaction, enjoyment, bliss, gratification, contentment, gladness, delectation …*We exclaimed with pleasure when we saw them…* OPPOSITE> displeasure
2 = amusement, joy, recreation, diversion, solace, jollies (*slang*), beer and skittles (*informal*) …*Watching TV is our only pleasure…* OPPOSITE> duty
3 = wish, choice, desire, will, mind, option, preference, inclination …*Let me get you a drink. What's your pleasure?…*

pledge NOUN **1** = promise, vow, assurance, word, undertaking, warrant, oath, covenant, word of honour …*a pledge to step up cooperation between the states…*
2 = guarantee, security, deposit, bail, bond, collateral, earnest, pawn, gage, surety …*items held in pledge for loans…*
VERB **1** = promise, vow, vouch, swear, contract, engage, undertake, give your word, give your word of honour, give your oath …*I pledge that by next year we will have the problem solved…*
2 = bind, guarantee, mortgage, engage, gage (*archaic*) …*He asked her to pledge the house as security*

for the loan…

plenary 1 (*of assemblies, councils, etc.*) = full, open, general, whole, complete, entire …*a plenary session of the Central Committee…*
2 = complete, full, sweeping, absolute, thorough, unlimited, unconditional, unqualified, unrestricted …*The president has plenary power in some areas of foreign policy…*

plentiful 1 = abundant, liberal, generous, lavish, complete, ample, infinite, overflowing, copious, inexhaustible, bountiful, profuse, thick on the ground, bounteous (*literary*), plenteous …*a plentiful supply…* OPPOSITE> scarce
2 = productive, bumper, fertile, prolific, fruitful, luxuriant, plenteous …*a celebration that gives thanks for a plentiful harvest…*

plenty 1 = abundance, wealth, luxury, prosperity, fertility, profusion, affluence, opulence, plenitude, fruitfulness, copiousness, plenteousness, plentifulness …*You are fortunate to be growing up in a time of peace and plenty…*
2 *usually with of* = lots of (*informal*), enough, a great deal of, masses of, quantities of, piles of (*informal*), mountains of, a good deal of, stacks of, heaps of (*informal*), a mass of, a volume of, an abundance of, a plethora of, a quantity of, a fund of, oodles of (*informal*), a store of, a mine of, a sufficiency of …*There was still plenty of time…*

plethora = excess, surplus, glut, profusion, surfeit, overabundance, superabundance, superfluity OPPOSITE> shortage

pliable 1 = flexible, plastic, supple, lithe, limber, malleable, pliant, tensile, bendy, ductile, bendable …*The baskets are made with young, pliable spruce roots…* OPPOSITE> rigid
2 = compliant, susceptible, responsive, manageable, receptive, yielding, adaptable, docile, impressionable, easily led, pliant, tractable, persuadable, influenceable, like putty in your hands …*His young queen was pliable and easily influenced…* OPPOSITE> stubborn

plight = difficulty, condition, state, situation, trouble, circumstances, dilemma, straits, predicament, extremity, perplexity

plod 1 = trudge, drag, tread, clump, lumber, tramp, stomp (*informal*), slog …*He plodded slowly up the hill…*
2 = slog away, labour, grind away (*informal*), toil, grub, persevere, soldier on, plough through, plug away (*informal*), drudge, peg away …*He is still plodding away at the same job…*

plot¹ NOUN **1** = plan, scheme, intrigue, conspiracy, cabal, stratagem, machination, covin (*Law*) …*a plot to overthrow the government…*
2 = story, action, subject, theme, outline, scenario, narrative, thread, story line …*the plot of a cheap spy novel…*
VERB **1** = plan, scheme, conspire, intrigue, manoeuvre, contrive, collude, cabal, hatch a plot, machinate …*They are awaiting trial for plotting*

against the state…

2 = <u>devise</u>, design, project, lay, imagine, frame, conceive, brew, hatch, contrive, concoct, cook up (*informal*) …*a meeting to plot the survival strategy of the party…*

3 = <u>chart</u>, mark, draw, map, draft, locate, calculate, outline, compute …*We were trying to plot the course of the submarine…*

plot² = <u>patch</u>, lot, area, ground, parcel, tract, allotment …*a small plot of land for growing vegetables…*

plotter = <u>conspirator</u>, architect, intriguer, planner, conspirer, strategist, conniver, Machiavellian, schemer, cabalist

plough VERB = <u>turn over</u>, dig, till, ridge, cultivate, furrow, break ground …*They ploughed 100,000 acres of virgin moorland…*

PHRASES **plough into something** or **someone** = <u>plunge into</u>, crash into, smash into, career into, shove into, hurtle into, bulldoze into …*The car veered off the road and ploughed into a culvert…* ♦ **plough through something** = <u>forge</u>, cut, drive, press, push, plunge, surge, stagger, wade, flounder, trudge, plod …*Mr Dambar watched her plough through the grass…*

ploy = <u>tactic</u>, move, trick, device, game, scheme, manoeuvre, dodge, ruse, gambit, subterfuge, stratagem, contrivance, wile

pluck VERB **1** = <u>pull out</u> or off, pick, draw, collect, gather, harvest …*I plucked a lemon from the tree…*

2 = <u>tug</u>, catch, snatch, clutch, jerk, yank, tweak, pull at …*He plucked the cigarette from his mouth…*

3 = <u>strum</u>, pick, finger, twang, thrum, plunk …*Nell was plucking a harp…*

NOUN = <u>courage</u>, nerve, heart, spirit, bottle (*Brit. slang*), resolution, determination, guts (*informal*), grit, bravery, backbone, mettle, boldness, spunk (*informal*), intrepidity, hardihood …*Cynics might sneer at him but you have to admire his pluck…*

plucky = <u>courageous</u>, spirited, brave, daring, bold, game, hardy, heroic, gritty, feisty (*informal, chiefly U.S. & Canad.*), gutsy (*slang*), intrepid, valiant, doughty, undaunted, unflinching, spunky (*informal*), mettlesome OPPOSITE cowardly

plug NOUN **1** = <u>stopper</u>, cork, bung, spigot, stopple …*A plug had been inserted in the drill hole…*

2 (*Informal*) = <u>mention</u>, advertisement, advert (*Brit. informal*), push, promotion, publicity, puff, hype, good word …*The show was little more than a plug for her new film…*

VERB **1** = <u>seal</u>, close, stop, fill, cover, block, stuff, pack, cork, choke, stopper, bung, stop up, stopple …*Crews are working to plug a major oil leak…*

2 (*Informal*) = <u>mention</u>, push, promote, publicize, advertise, build up, puff, hype, write up …*If I hear another actor plugging his latest book I will scream…*

PHRASES **plug away** (*Informal*) = <u>slog away</u>, labour, toil away, grind away (*informal*), peg away, plod away, drudge away …*I just keep plugging away at this job, although I hate it…*

plum = <u>choice</u>, prize, first-class

plumb VERB = <u>delve into</u>, measure, explore, probe,

sound out, search, go into, penetrate, gauge, unravel, fathom …*her attempts to plumb my innermost emotions…*

ADVERB = <u>exactly</u>, precisely, bang, slap, spot-on (*Brit. informal*) …*The hotel is set plumb in the middle of the High Street…*

plume = <u>feather</u>, crest, quill, pinion, aigrette

plummet **1** = <u>drop</u>, fall, crash, nose-dive, descend rapidly …*Share prices have plummeted…*

2 = <u>plunge</u>, fall, drop, crash, tumble, swoop, stoop, nose-dive, descend rapidly …*The car plummeted off a cliff…*

plummy (*of a voice*) = <u>deep</u>, posh (*informal, chiefly Brit.*), refined, upper-class, fruity, resonant

plump¹ = <u>chubby</u>, fat, stout, full, round, burly, obese, fleshy, beefy (*informal*), tubby, portly, buxom, dumpy, roly-poly, well-covered, rotund, podgy, corpulent, well-upholstered (*informal*) …*Maria was small and plump with a mass of curly hair…* OPPOSITE scrawny

plump² VERB = <u>flop</u>, fall, drop, sink, dump, slump …*Breathlessly, she plumped down next to Katrina…*

PHRASES **plump for something** or **someone** = <u>choose</u>, favour, go for, back, support, opt for, side with, come down in favour of …*In the end, we plumped for an endowment mortgage…*

plunder VERB **1** = <u>loot</u>, strip, sack, rob, raid, devastate, spoil, rifle, ravage, ransack, pillage, despoil …*They plundered and burned the town…*

2 = <u>steal</u>, rob, take, nick (*informal*), pinch (*informal*), embezzle, pilfer, thieve …*a settlement to recover money plundered from government coffers…*

NOUN **1** = <u>pillage</u>, sacking, robbery, marauding, rapine, spoliation …*a guerrilla group infamous for torture and plunder…*

2 = <u>loot</u>, spoils, prey, booty, swag (*slang*), ill-gotten gains …*Pirates swarmed the seas in search of easy plunder…*

plunge VERB **1** = <u>descend</u>, fall, drop, crash, pitch, sink, go down, dive, tumble, plummet, nose-dive …*50 people died when a bus plunged into a river…*

2 = <u>hurtle</u>, charge, career, jump, tear, rush, dive, dash, swoop, lurch …*I plunged forward, calling her name…*

3 = <u>submerge</u>, sink, duck, dip, immerse, douse, dunk …*She plunged her face into a bowl of cold water…*

4 = <u>throw</u>, cast, pitch, propel …*conflicts which threaten to plunge the country into chaos…*

5 = <u>fall steeply</u>, drop, crash (*informal*), go down, slump, plummet, take a nosedive (*informal*) …*Net profits plunged 73% last year…*

NOUN **1** = <u>dive</u>, jump, duck, swoop, descent, immersion, submersion …*a refreshing plunge into cold water…*

2 = <u>fall</u>, crash (*informal*), slump, drop, tumble …*the stock market plunge…*

plurality = <u>multiplicity</u>, variety, diversity, profusion, numerousness

plus PREPOSITION = <u>and</u>, with, added to, coupled with, with the addition of …*Send a cheque for £18.99 plus £2 for postage and packing…*

NOUN (*Informal*) = <u>advantage</u>, benefit, asset, gain,

extra, bonus, perk (*Brit. informal*), good point, icing on the cake ...*A big plus is that the data can be stored on a PC*...

ADJECTIVE = <u>additional</u>, added, extra, positive, supplementary, add-on ...*Accessibility is the other plus point of the borough*...

Word Power

plus – When you have a sentence with more than one subject linked by *and*, this makes the subject plural and means it should take a plural verb: *the doctor and all the nurses were* (not *was*) *waiting for the patient*. However, where the subjects are linked by *plus*, *together with*, or *along with*, the number of the verb remains just as it would have been if the extra subjects had not been mentioned. Therefore you would say *the doctor, together with all the nurses, was* (not *were*) *waiting for the patient*.

---

plush = <u>luxurious</u>, luxury, costly, lavish, rich, sumptuous, opulent, palatial, ritzy (*slang*), de luxe
OPPOSITE cheap

ply[1] **1** = <u>provide</u>, supply, shower, lavish, regale ...*Elsie plied her with food and drink*...
2 = <u>bombard</u>, press, harass, besiege, beset, assail, importune ...*Giovanni plied him with questions*...
3 = <u>work at</u>, follow, exercise, pursue, carry on, practise ...*streetmarkets with stallholders plying their trade*...
4 = <u>travel</u>, go, ferry, shuttle ...*The brightly-coloured boats ply between the islands*...
5 = <u>use</u>, handle, employ, swing, manipulate, wield, utilize ...*With startling efficiency, the chef plied his knives*...

ply[2] = <u>thickness</u>, leaf, sheet, layer, fold, strand ...*The plastic surfaces are covered with teak ply*...

poach 1 = <u>steal</u>, rob, plunder, hunt *or* fish illegally ...*Many national parks are invaded by people poaching game*...
2 = <u>take</u>, steal, appropriate, snatch (*informal*), nab (*informal*), purloin ...*allegations that it had poached members from other unions*...

pocket **NOUN** = <u>pouch</u>, bag, sack, hollow, compartment, receptacle ...*a canvas container with customised pockets for each tool*...
ADJECTIVE = <u>small</u>, compact, miniature, portable, little, potted (*informal*), concise, pint-size(d) (*informal*), abridged ...*a pocket dictionary*...
VERB = <u>steal</u>, take, lift (*informal*), appropriate, pilfer, purloin, filch, help yourself to, snaffle (*Brit. informal*) ...*He pocketed a wallet from the bedside of a dead man*...

pod = <u>shell</u>, case, hull, husk, shuck

podium = <u>platform</u>, stand, stage, rostrum, dais

poem = <u>verse</u>, song, lyric, rhyme, sonnet, ode, verse composition

poet = <u>bard</u>, rhymer, lyricist, lyric poet, versifier, maker (*archaic*), elegist
➤ **WORD POWER SUPPLEMENT poets**

poetic 1 = <u>figurative</u>, creative, lyric, symbolic, lyrical,

rhythmic, rhythmical, songlike ...*Heidegger's interest in the poetic, evocative uses of language*...
2 = <u>lyrical</u>, lyric, rhythmic, elegiac, rhythmical, metrical ...*There's a very rich poetic tradition in Gaelic*...

poetry = <u>verse</u>, poems, rhyme, rhyming, poesy (*archaic*), verse composition, metrical composition
➤ **WORD POWER SUPPLEMENT poetry**

po-faced = <u>humourless</u>, disapproving, solemn, prim, puritanical, narrow-minded, stolid, prudish, strait-laced

poignancy = <u>sadness</u>, emotion, sentiment, intensity, feeling, tenderness, pathos, emotionalism, plaintiveness, evocativeness, piteousness

poignant = <u>moving</u>, touching, affecting, upsetting, sad, bitter, intense, painful, distressing, pathetic, harrowing, heartbreaking, agonizing, heart-rending, gut-wrenching

point **NOUN** **1** = <u>essence</u>, meaning, subject, question, matter, heart, theme, import, text, core, burden, drift, thrust, proposition, marrow, crux, gist, main idea, nub, pith ...*You have missed the main point of my argument*...
2 = <u>purpose</u>, aim, object, use, end, reason, goal, design, intention, objective, utility, intent, motive, usefulness ...*What's the point of all these questions?*...
3 = <u>aspect</u>, detail, feature, side, quality, property, particular, respect, item, instance, characteristic, topic, attribute, trait, facet, peculiarity, nicety ...*The most interesting point about the village is its religion*...
4 = <u>place</u>, area, position, station, site, spot, location, locality, locale ...*The town square is a popular meeting point for tourists*...
5 = <u>moment</u>, time, stage, period, phase, instant, juncture, moment in time, very minute ...*At this point, Diana arrived*...
6 = <u>stage</u>, level, position, condition, degree, pitch, circumstance, extent ...*It got to the point where he had to leave*...
7 = <u>end</u>, tip, sharp end, top, spur, spike, apex, nib, tine, prong ...*the point of a knife*...
8 = <u>score</u>, tally, mark ...*Sort the answers out and add up the points*...
9 = <u>headland</u>, head, bill, cape, ness (*archaic*), promontory, foreland ...*a long point of land reaching southwards into the sea*...
10 = <u>pinpoint</u>, mark, spot, dot, fleck, speck ...*a point of light in an otherwise dark world*...
VERB **1** = <u>aim</u>, level, train, direct ...*A man pointed a gun at them and pulled the trigger*...
2 = <u>indicate</u>, show, signal, point to, gesture towards ...*They asked for directions and I pointed the way*...
3 = <u>face</u>, look, direct ...*He controlled the car until it was pointing forwards again*...
PHRASES **beside the point** = <u>irrelevant</u>, inappropriate, pointless, peripheral, unimportant, incidental, unconnected, immaterial, inconsequential, nothing to do with it, extraneous, neither here nor there, off the subject, inapplicable, not to the point, inapposite, without connection, inconsequent, not pertinent, not germane, not to the purpose ...*Brian didn't like it, but that was beside the point*... ◆ **point**

at *or* **to something** *or* **someone** = <u>indicate</u>, point out, specify, designate, gesture towards …*I pointed at the boy sitting nearest me…* ◆ **point of view 1** = <u>opinion</u>, view, attitude, belief, feeling, thought, idea, approach, judgment, sentiment, viewpoint, way of thinking, way of looking at it …*His point of view is that money isn't everything…* **2** = <u>perspective</u>, side, position, stance, stand, angle, outlook, orientation, viewpoint, slant, standpoint, frame of reference …*Try to look at it from my point of view…* ◆ **point something** *or* **someone out 1** = <u>identify</u>, show, point to, indicate, finger (*informal, chiefly U.S.*), single out, call attention to, draw *or* call attention to …*She pointed him out to me as we drove past…* **2** = <u>allude to</u>, reveal, mention, identify, indicate, bring up, specify, draw *or* call attention to …*We all too easily point out other people's failings…* ◆ **point something up** = <u>emphasize</u>, stress, highlight, underline, make clear, accent, spotlight, draw attention to, underscore, play up, accentuate, foreground, focus attention on, give prominence to, turn the spotlight on, bring to the fore, put emphasis on …*Politicians pointed up the differences between the two countries…* ◆ **point to something 1** = <u>denote</u>, reveal, indicate, show, suggest, evidence, signal, signify, be evidence of, bespeak (*literary*) …*All the evidence pointed to his guilt…* **2** = <u>refer to</u>, mention, indicate, specify, single out, touch on, call attention to …*Gooch pointed to their bowling as the key to their success…* ◆ **to the point** = <u>relevant</u>, appropriate, apt, pointed, short, fitting, material, related, brief, suitable, applicable, pertinent, terse, pithy, apposite, apropos, germane …*The description he gave was brief and to the point…*

point-blank ADJECTIVE = <u>direct</u>, plain, blunt, explicit, abrupt, express, downright, categorical, unreserved, straight-from-the-shoulder …*He gave a point-blank refusal…*
ADVERB = <u>directly</u>, openly, straight, frankly, plainly, bluntly, explicitly, overtly, candidly, brusquely, straightforwardly, forthrightly …*Mr Patterson was asked point-blank if he would resign…*

pointed 1 = <u>sharp</u>, edged, acute, barbed …*the pointed end of the chisel…*
2 = <u>cutting</u>, telling, biting, sharp, keen, acute, accurate, penetrating, pertinent, incisive, trenchant …*a pointed remark…*

pointer 1 = <u>hint</u>, tip, suggestion, warning, recommendation, caution, piece of information, piece of advice …*Here are a few pointers to help you make a choice…*
2 = <u>indicator</u>, hand, guide, needle, arrow …*The pointer indicates the pressure on the dial…*

pointless = <u>senseless</u>, meaningless, futile, fruitless, unproductive, stupid, silly, useless, absurd, irrelevant, in vain, worthless, ineffectual, unprofitable, nonsensical, aimless, inane, unavailing, without rhyme or reason OPPOSITE worthwhile

poise 1 = <u>composure</u>, cool (*slang*), presence, assurance, dignity, equilibrium, serenity, coolness, aplomb, calmness, equanimity, presence of mind,

sang-froid, savoir-faire, self-possession …*It took a moment for Mark to recover his poise…*
2 = <u>grace</u>, balance, equilibrium, elegance …*Ballet classes are important for poise…*

poised 1 = <u>ready</u>, waiting, prepared, standing by, on the brink, in the wings, all set …*US forces are poised for a massive air, land and sea assault…*
2 = <u>composed</u>, calm, together (*informal*), collected, dignified, graceful, serene, suave, urbane, self-confident, unfazed (*informal*), debonair, unruffled, nonchalant, self-possessed …*Rachel appeared poised and calm…* OPPOSITE agitated

poison NOUN **1** = <u>toxin</u>, venom, bane (*archaic*) …*Poison from the weaver fish causes paralysis and swelling…*
2 = <u>contamination</u>, corruption, contagion, cancer, virus, blight, bane, malignancy, miasma, canker …*the poison of crime and violence spreading through the city…*
VERB **1** = <u>murder</u>, kill, give someone poison, administer poison to …*There were rumours that she had poisoned her husband…*
2 = <u>contaminate</u>, foul, infect, spoil, pollute, blight, taint, adulterate, envenom, befoul …*The land has been completely poisoned by chemicals…*
3 = <u>corrupt</u>, colour, undermine, bias, sour, pervert, warp, taint, subvert, embitter, deprave, defile, jaundice, vitiate, envenom …*ill-feeling that will poison further negotiations…*
ADJECTIVE = <u>poisonous</u>, deadly, toxic, lethal, venomous …*a cloud of poison gas…*

(**Related Words**)
adjective: toxic

poisonous 1 = <u>toxic</u>, fatal, deadly, lethal, mortal, virulent, noxious, venomous, baneful (*archaic*), mephitic …*All parts of the yew tree are poisonous…*
2 = <u>evil</u>, vicious, malicious, corrupting, pernicious, baleful, baneful (*archaic*), pestiferous …*poisonous attacks on the Church…*

poke VERB **1** = <u>jab</u>, hit, push, stick, dig, punch, stab, thrust, butt, elbow, shove, nudge, prod …*Lindy poked him in the ribs…*
2 = <u>protrude</u>, stick, thrust, jut …*His fingers poked through the worn tips of his gloves…*
NOUN = <u>jab</u>, hit, dig, punch, thrust, butt, nudge, prod …*John smiled and gave Richard a playful poke…*

polar 1 = <u>freezing</u>, frozen, extreme, furthest, cold, terminal, Arctic, icy, Antarctic, glacial …*the rigours of life in the polar regions…*
2 = <u>opposite</u>, opposed, contrary, contradictory, antagonistic, antithetical, diametric, antipodal …*economists at polar ends of the politico-economic spectrum…*

polarity = <u>opposition</u>, contradiction, paradox, ambivalence, dichotomy, duality, contrariety

pole[1] = <u>rod</u>, post, support, staff, standard, bar, stick, stake, paling, shaft, upright, pillar, mast, picket, spar, stave …*The sign hung at the top of a large pole…*

pole[2] NOUN = <u>extremity</u>, limit, terminus, antipode …*The two mayoral candidates represent opposite poles*

of the political spectrum…
PHRASES **poles apart** = <u>at opposite extremes</u>, incompatible, irreconcilable, worlds apart, miles apart, like chalk and cheese (*Brit.*), like night and day, widely separated, completely different, at opposite ends of the earth …*Her views on Europe are poles apart from those of her successor…*

polemic = <u>argument</u>, attack, debate, dispute, controversy, rant, tirade, diatribe, invective, philippic (*rare*)

polemics = <u>dispute</u>, debate, argument, discussion, controversy, contention, wrangling, disputation, argumentation

police **NOUN** = <u>the law</u> (*informal*), police force, constabulary, fuzz (*slang*), law enforcement agency, boys in blue (*informal*), the Old Bill (*slang*), rozzers (*slang*) …*The police have arrested twenty people following the disturbances…*
VERB **1** = <u>control</u>, patrol, guard, watch, protect, regulate, keep the peace, keep in order …*the UN force whose job it is to police the border…*
2 = <u>monitor</u>, check, observe, oversee, supervise …*the body which polices the investment management business…*

police officer = <u>cop</u> (*slang*), officer, pig (*offensive slang*), bobby (*informal*), copper (*slang*), constable, peeler (*Irish and obsolete Brit. slang*), gendarme (*slang*), fuzz (*slang*), woodentop (*slang*), bizzy (*informal*), flatfoot (*slang*), rozzer (*slang*), policeman *or* policewoman

policy **1** = <u>procedure</u>, plan, action, programme, practice, scheme, theory, code, custom, stratagem …*plans which include changes in foreign policy…*
2 = <u>line</u>, rules, approach, guideline, protocol …*significant changes in Britain's policy on global warming…*

polish **NOUN** **1** = <u>varnish</u>, wax, glaze, lacquer, japan …*The air smelt of furniture polish…*
2 = <u>sheen</u>, finish, sparkle, glaze, gloss, brilliance, brightness, veneer, lustre, smoothness …*I admired the high polish of his boots…*
3 = <u>style</u>, class (*informal*), finish, breeding, grace, elegance, refinement, finesse, urbanity, suavity, politesse …*She was enormously popular for her charm and polish…*
VERB **1** = <u>shine</u>, wax, clean, smooth, rub, buff, brighten, burnish, furbish …*Every morning he polished his shoes…*
2 *often with* **up** = <u>perfect</u>, improve, enhance, refine, finish, correct, cultivate, brush up, touch up, emend …*Polish up your writing skills on a one-week course…*
PHRASES **polish someone off** = <u>eliminate</u>, take out (*slang*), get rid of, dispose of, do away with, blow away (*slang, chiefly U.S.*), beat someone once and for all …*a chance to polish off their bitter local rivals…*
♦ **polish something off** (*Informal*) = <u>finish</u>, down, shift (*informal*), wolf, consume, put away, eat up, swill …*He polished off the whole box of truffles on his own…*

polished **1** = <u>elegant</u>, sophisticated, refined, polite, cultivated, civilized, genteel, suave, finished, urbane, courtly, well-bred …*He is polished, charming and articulate…* **OPPOSITE** unsophisticated
2 = <u>accomplished</u>, professional, masterly, fine, expert, outstanding, skilful, adept, impeccable, flawless, superlative, faultless …*a polished performance…* **OPPOSITE** amateurish
3 = <u>shining</u>, bright, smooth, gleaming, glossy, slippery, burnished, glassy, furbished …*a highly polished surface…* **OPPOSITE** dull

polite **1** = <u>mannerly</u>, civil, courteous, affable, obliging, gracious, respectful, well-behaved, deferential, complaisant, well-mannered …*He was a quiet and very polite young man…* **OPPOSITE** rude
2 = <u>refined</u>, cultured, civilized, polished, sophisticated, elegant, genteel, urbane, courtly, well-bred …*Certain words are not acceptable in polite society…* **OPPOSITE** uncultured

politeness = <u>courtesy</u>, decency, correctness, etiquette, deference, grace, civility, graciousness, common courtesy, complaisance, courteousness, respectfulness, mannerliness, obligingness

politic = <u>wise</u>, diplomatic, sensible, discreet, prudent, advisable, expedient, judicious, tactful, sagacious, in your best interests

political **1** = <u>governmental</u>, government, state, parliamentary, constitutional, administrative, legislative, civic, ministerial, policy-making, party political …*a democratic political system…*
2 = <u>factional</u>, party, militant, partisan …*I'm not political, I take no interest in politics…*

politician = <u>statesman</u> *or* <u>stateswoman</u>, representative, senator (*U.S.*), congressman (*U.S.*), Member of Parliament, legislator, public servant, congresswoman (*U.S.*), politico (*informal, chiefly U.S.*), lawmaker, office bearer, M.P., elected offical

politics **1** = <u>affairs of state</u>, government, government policy, public affairs, civics …*He quickly involved himself in politics…*
2 = <u>political beliefs</u>, party politics, political allegiances, political leanings, political sympathies …*My politics are well to the left of centre…*
3 = <u>political science</u>, polity, statesmanship, civics, statecraft …*He studied politics and medieval history…*
4 = <u>power struggle</u>, machinations, opportunism, realpolitik, Machiavellianism …*He doesn't know how to handle office politics…*
➤ **WORD POWER SUPPLEMENT political parties**

poll **NOUN** **1** = <u>survey</u>, figures, count, sampling, returns, ballot, tally, census, canvass, Gallup Poll, (public) opinion poll …*Polls show that the party is losing support…*
2 = <u>election</u>, vote, voting, referendum, ballot, plebiscite …*In 1945, Churchill was defeated at the polls…*
VERB **1** = <u>question</u>, interview, survey, sample, ballot, canvass …*More than 18,000 people were polled…*
2 = <u>gain</u>, return, record, register, tally …*He had polled enough votes to force a second ballot…*

pollute **1** = <u>contaminate</u>, dirty, mar, poison, soil, foul, infect, spoil, stain, taint, adulterate, make filthy, smirch, befoul ...*beaches polluted by sewage pumped into the sea...* OPPOSITE decontaminate

2 = defile, violate, corrupt, sully, deprave, debase, profane, desecrate, dishonour, debauch, besmirch ...*a man accused of polluting the minds of children...* OPPOSITE honour

pollution 1 = contamination, dirtying, corruption, taint, adulteration, foulness, defilement, uncleanness, vitiation ...*environmental pollution...*

2 = waste, poisons, dirt, impurities ...*the level of pollution in the river...*

pomp 1 = ceremony, grandeur, splendour, state, show, display, parade, flourish, pageant, magnificence, solemnity, pageantry, ostentation, éclat ...*the pomp and splendour of the English aristocracy...*

2 = show, pomposity, grandiosity, vainglory ...*The band have trawled new depths of pomp and self-indulgence...*

pomposity 1 = self-importance, vanity, arrogance, pretension, airs, flaunting, presumption, affectation, pretentiousness, grandiosity, haughtiness, portentousness, vainglory, pompousness ...*He was modest and simple, without a trace of pomposity...*

2 = grandiloquence, rant, hot air (*informal*), bombast, fustian, loftiness, turgidity, magniloquence ...*She has no time for political jargon and pomposity...*

pompous 1 = self-important, affected, arrogant, pretentious, bloated, grandiose, imperious, showy, overbearing, ostentatious, puffed up, portentous, magisterial, supercilious, pontifical, vainglorious ...*What a pompous little man he is...* OPPOSITE unpretentious

2 = grandiloquent, high-flown, inflated, windy, overblown, turgid, bombastic, boastful, flatulent, arty-farty (*informal*), fustian, orotund, magniloquent ...*She winced at his pompous phraseology...* OPPOSITE simple

pond = pool, tarn, small lake, fish pond, duck pond, millpond, lochan (*Scot.*), dew pond

ponder = think about, consider, study, reflect on, examine, weigh up, contemplate, deliberate about, muse on, brood on, meditate on, mull over, puzzle over, ruminate on, give thought to, cogitate on, rack your brains about, excogitate

ponderous 1 = dull, laboured, pedestrian, dreary, heavy, tedious, plodding, tiresome, lifeless, stilted, stodgy, pedantic, long-winded, verbose, prolix ...*He had a dense, ponderous writing style...*

2 = clumsy, awkward, lumbering, laborious, graceless, elephantine, heavy-footed, unco (*Austral. slang*) ...*He strolled about with a ponderous, heavy gait...* OPPOSITE graceful

pontificate = expound, preach, sound off, pronounce, declaim, lay down the law, hold forth, dogmatize, pontify

pool¹ 1 = swimming pool, lido, swimming bath(s) (*Brit.*), bathing pool (*archaic*) ...*a heated indoor pool...*

2 = pond, lake, mere, tarn ...*Beautiful gardens filled with pools and fountains...*

3 = puddle, drop, patch, splash ...*There were pools of water on the gravel drive...*

pool² NOUN 1 = supply, reserve, fall-back ...*the available pool of manpower...*

2 = kitty, bank, fund, stock, store, pot, jackpot, stockpile, hoard, cache ...*a reserve pool of cash...*

VERB = combine, share, merge, put together, amalgamate, lump together, join forces on ...*We pooled our savings to start up a new business...*

poor 1 = impoverished, broke (*informal*), badly off, hard up (*informal*), short, in need, needy, on the rocks, penniless, destitute, poverty-stricken, down and out, skint (*Brit. slang*), in want, indigent, down at heel, impecunious, dirt-poor (*informal*), on the breadline, flat broke (*informal*), penurious, on your uppers, stony-broke (*Brit. slang*), necessitous, in queer street, without two pennies to rub together (*informal*), on your beam-ends ...*He was one of thirteen children from a poor family...* OPPOSITE rich

2 = unfortunate, pathetic, miserable, unlucky, hapless, pitiful, luckless, wretched, ill-starred, pitiable, ill-fated ...*I feel sorry for that poor child...* OPPOSITE fortunate

3 = inferior, unsatisfactory, mediocre, second-rate, sorry, weak, pants (*informal*), rotten (*informal*), faulty, feeble, worthless, shabby, shoddy, low-grade, below par, substandard, low-rent (*informal*), crappy (*slang*), valueless, no great shakes (*informal*), rubbishy, poxy (*slang*), not much cop (*Brit. slang*), half-pie (*N.Z. informal*), bodger *or* bodgie (*Austral. slang*) ...*He was a poor actor... ...The wine is very poor...* OPPOSITE excellent

4 = meagre, inadequate, insufficient, reduced, lacking, slight, miserable, pathetic, incomplete, scant, sparse, deficient, skimpy, measly, scanty, pitiable, niggardly, straitened, exiguous ...*poor wages and terrible working conditions... ...A poor crop has sent vegetable prices spiralling...* OPPOSITE ample

5 = unproductive, barren, fruitless, bad, bare, exhausted, depleted, impoverished, sterile, infertile, unfruitful ...*Mix in some planting compost to improve poor soil when you dig...* OPPOSITE productive

poorly ADVERB = badly, incompetently, inadequately, crudely, inferiorly, unsuccessfully, insufficiently, shabbily, unsatisfactorily, inexpertly ...*poorly built houses...* OPPOSITE well

ADJECTIVE (*Informal*) = ill, sick, ailing, unwell, crook (*Austral. & N.Z. informal*), seedy (*informal*), below par, out of sorts, off colour, under the weather (*informal*), indisposed, feeling rotten (*informal*) ...*I've just phoned Julie and she's still poorly...* OPPOSITE healthy

pop NOUN 1 (*Informal*) = soft drink, ginger (*Scot.*), soda (*U.S. & Canad.*), fizzy drink, cool drink (*S. African*) ...*He still visits the village shop for buns and fizzy pop...*

2 = bang, report, crack, noise, burst, explosion ...*Each corn kernel will make a loud pop when cooked...*

VERB 1 = burst, crack, snap, bang, explode, report, go off (with a bang) ...*The champagne cork popped and shot to the ceiling...*

2 = protrude, bulge, stick out ...*My eyes popped at the sight of so much food...*

3 = <u>put</u>, insert, push, stick, slip, thrust, tuck, shove …*He plucked a grape from the bunch and popped it into his mouth*…
4 (*Informal*) often with **in, out,** etc. = <u>call</u>, visit, appear, drop in (*informal*), leave quickly, come *or* go suddenly, nip in *or* out (*Brit. informal*) …*Wendy popped in for a quick visit on Monday night*…

pope = <u>Holy Father</u>, pontiff, His Holiness, Bishop of Rome, Vicar of Christ
(Related Words)
adjective : papal

populace = <u>people</u>, crowd, masses, mob, inhabitants, general public, multitude, throng, rabble, hoi polloi, Joe Public (*slang*), Joe Six-Pack (*U.S. slang*), commonalty

popular 1 = <u>well-liked</u>, liked, favoured, celebrated, in, accepted, favourite, famous, approved, in favour, fashionable, in demand, sought-after, fave (*informal*) …*This is the most popular game ever devised*…
[OPPOSITE] unpopular
2 = <u>common</u>, general, standard, widespread, prevailing, stock, current, public, conventional, universal, prevalent, ubiquitous …*the popular misconception that dinosaurs were all lumbering giants*… [OPPOSITE] rare

popularity 1 = <u>favour</u>, fame, esteem, acclaim, regard, reputation, approval, recognition, celebrity, vogue, adoration, renown, repute, idolization, lionization …*His authority and popularity have declined*…
2 = <u>currency</u>, acceptance, circulation, vogue, prevalence …*This theory has enjoyed tremendous popularity among sociologists*…

popularize 1 = <u>make something popular</u>, spread the word about, disseminate, universalize, give mass appeal to …*the first person to popularize rock 'n' roll in China*…
2 = <u>simplify</u>, make available to all, give currency to, give mass appeal to …*a magazine devoted to popularizing science*…

popularly = <u>generally</u>, commonly, widely, usually, regularly, universally, traditionally, ordinarily, conventionally, customarily

populate 1 = <u>inhabit</u>, people, live in, occupy, reside in, dwell in (*formal*) …*the native people who populate areas around the city*…
2 = <u>settle</u>, people, occupy, pioneer, colonize …*North America was populated largely by Europeans*…

population = <u>inhabitants</u>, people, community, society, residents, natives, folk, occupants, populace, denizens, citizenry

populous = <u>populated</u>, crowded, packed, swarming, thronged, teeming, heavily populated, overpopulated

pore = <u>opening</u>, hole, outlet, orifice, stoma

pore over *or* **through** = <u>study</u>, read, examine, go over, contemplate, ponder, brood, dwell on, work over, scrutinize, peruse
➤ **pour**

pornographic = <u>obscene</u>, erotic, indecent, blue, dirty, offensive, rude, sexy, filthy, lewd, risqué, X-rated (*informal*), salacious, prurient, smutty

pornography = <u>obscenity</u>, porn (*informal*), erotica, dirt, filth, indecency, porno (*informal*), smut

porous = <u>permeable</u>, absorbent, spongy, absorptive, penetrable, pervious [OPPOSITE] impermeable

port = <u>harbour</u>, haven, anchorage, seaport, roadstead
➤ **WORD POWER SUPPLEMENT ports**

portable = <u>light</u>, compact, convenient, handy, lightweight, manageable, movable, easily carried, portative

portal (*Literary*) = <u>doorway</u>, door, entry, way in, entrance, gateway, entrance way

portent = <u>omen</u>, sign, warning, threat, indication, premonition, foreshadowing, foreboding, harbinger, presage, forewarning, prognostication, augury, presentiment, prognostic

portentous 1 = <u>pompous</u>, solemn, ponderous, self-important, pontifical …*There was nothing portentous or solemn about him*…
2 = <u>significant</u>, alarming, sinister, ominous, important, threatening, crucial, forbidding, menacing, momentous, fateful, minatory, bodeful …*portentous prophecies of doom*…

porter¹ (*Chiefly Brit.*) = <u>doorman</u>, caretaker, janitor, concierge, gatekeeper …*a porter at the block of flats*…

porter² = <u>baggage attendant</u>, carrier, bearer, baggage-carrier …*A porter slammed the baggage compartment doors*…

portion 1 = <u>part</u>, bit, piece, section, scrap, segment, fragment, fraction, chunk, wedge, hunk, morsel …*I have spent a large portion of my life here*…
2 = <u>helping</u>, serving, piece, plateful …*fish and chips at about £2.70 a portion*…
3 = <u>share</u>, division, allowance, lot, measure, quantity, quota, ration, allocation, allotment …*his portion of the inheritance*…

portly = <u>stout</u>, fat, overweight, plump, large, heavy, ample, bulky, burly, obese, fleshy, beefy (*informal*), tubby (*informal*), rotund, corpulent

portrait 1 = <u>picture</u>, painting, image, photograph, representation, sketch, likeness, portraiture …*Lucian Freud has been asked to paint a portrait of the Queen*…
2 = <u>description</u>, account, profile, biography, portrayal, depiction, vignette, characterization, thumbnail sketch …*a beautifully written and sensitive portrait of a great woman*…

portray 1 = <u>play</u>, take the role of, act the part of, represent, personate (*rare*) …*He portrayed the king in a revival of 'Camelot'*…
2 = <u>describe</u>, present, depict, evoke, delineate, put in words …*the novelist accurately portrays provincial domestic life*…
3 = <u>represent</u>, draw, paint, illustrate, sketch, figure, picture, render, depict, delineate …*the landscape as portrayed by painters such as Poussin*…
4 = <u>characterize</u>, describe, represent, depict, paint a mental picture of …*complaints about the way women are portrayed in adverts*…

portrayal 1 = <u>performance</u>, interpretation, enacting, take (*informal, chiefly U.S.*), acting, impersonation,

performance as, characterization, personation (*rare*)
…*He is well known for his portrayal of a prison guard in
'The Last Emperor'*…
2 = <u>depiction</u>, picture, representation, sketch,
rendering, delineation …*a near-monochrome
portrayal of a wood infused with silvery light*…
3 = <u>description</u>, account, representation …*an often
funny portrayal of a friendship between two boys*…
4 = <u>characterization</u>, representation, depiction …*The
media persists in its portrayal of us as muggers and
dope sellers*…

pose VERB **1** = <u>present</u>, cause, produce, create, lead
to, result in, constitute, give rise to …*His ill health
poses serious problems*…
2 = <u>ask</u>, state, advance, put, set, submit, put forward,
posit, propound …*When I posed the question 'Why?',
he merely shrugged*…
3 = <u>position yourself</u>, sit, model, strike a pose, arrange
yourself …*The six foreign ministers posed for
photographs*…
4 = <u>put on airs</u>, affect, posture, show off (*informal*),
strike an attitude, attitudinize …*He criticized them for
posing pretentiously*…
NOUN **1** = <u>posture</u>, position, bearing, attitude, stance,
mien (*literary*) …*We have had several sittings in
various poses*…
2 = <u>act</u>, role, façade, air, front, posturing, pretence,
masquerade, mannerism, affectation, attitudinizing
…*In many writers modesty is a pose, but in him it seems
to be genuine*…
PHRASES **pose as something** or **someone** =
<u>impersonate</u>, pretend to be, sham, feign, profess to
be, masquerade as, pass yourself off as …*The team
posed as drug dealers to trap the ringleaders*…

poser = <u>puzzle</u>, problem, question, riddle, enigma,
conundrum, teaser, tough one, vexed question, brain-
teaser (*informal*), knotty point

poser or **poseur** = <u>show-off</u> (*informal*), posturer,
masquerader, hot dog (*chiefly U.S.*), impostor,
exhibitionist, self-publicist, mannerist, attitudinizer

posh (*Informal, chiefly Brit.*) **1** = <u>smart</u>, grand,
exclusive, luxury, elegant, fashionable, stylish,
luxurious, classy (*slang*), swish (*informal, chiefly Brit.*),
up-market, swanky (*informal*), ritzy (*slang*) …*I took
her to a posh hotel for a cocktail*…
2 = <u>upper-class</u>, high-class, top-drawer, plummy, high-
toned, la-di-da (*informal*) …*He sounded very posh on
the phone*…

posit = <u>put forward</u>, advance, submit, state, assume,
assert, presume, predicate, postulate, propound

position NOUN **1** = <u>location</u>, place, point, area, post,
situation, station, site, spot, bearings, reference,
orientation, whereabouts, locality, locale …*The ship's
position was reported to the coastguard*…
2 = <u>posture</u>, attitude, arrangement, pose, stance,
disposition …*He had raised himself into a sitting
position*…
3 = <u>status</u>, place, standing, class, footing, station, rank,
reputation, importance, consequence, prestige, caste,
stature, eminence, repute …*their changing role and
position in society*…

4 = <u>job</u>, place, post, opening, office, role, situation,
duty, function, employment, capacity, occupation,
berth (*informal*), billet (*informal*) …*He took up a
position with the Arts Council*…
5 = <u>place</u>, standing, rank, status …*The players
resumed their battle for the no. 1 position*…
6 = <u>situation</u>, state, condition, set of circumstances,
plight, strait(s), predicament …*He's going to be in a
difficult position if things go badly*…
7 = <u>attitude</u>, view, perspective, point of view,
standing, opinion, belief, angle, stance, outlook,
posture, viewpoint, slant, way of thinking, standpoint
…*He usually takes a moderate position*…
VERB = <u>place</u>, put, set, stand, stick (*informal*), settle,
fix, arrange, locate, sequence, array, dispose, lay out
…*Position trailing plants near the edges of the
basket*…

positive 1 = <u>beneficial</u>, effective, useful, practical,
helpful, progressive, productive, worthwhile,
constructive, pragmatic, efficacious …*Working abroad
should be a positive experience*… OPPOSITE harmful
2 = <u>certain</u>, sure, convinced, confident, satisfied,
assured, free from doubt …*I'm positive she said she'd
be here*… OPPOSITE uncertain
3 = <u>definite</u>, real, clear, firm, certain, direct, express,
actual, absolute, concrete, decisive, explicit,
affirmative, clear-cut, unmistakable, conclusive,
unequivocal, indisputable, categorical,
incontrovertible …*there was no positive evidence*…
OPPOSITE inconclusive
4 (*Informal*) = <u>absolute</u>, complete, perfect, right (*Brit.
informal*), real, total, rank, sheer, utter, thorough,
downright, consummate, veritable, unqualified, out-
and-out, unmitigated, thoroughgoing, unalloyed
…*He was in a positive fury*…

positively 1 = <u>definitely</u>, surely, firmly, certainly,
absolutely, emphatically, unquestionably, undeniably,
categorically, unequivocally, unmistakably, with
certainty, assuredly, without qualification …*This is
positively the worst thing I can imagine*…
2 = <u>really</u>, completely, simply, plain (*informal*),
absolutely, thoroughly, utterly, downright …*He was
positively furious*…

possess 1 = <u>own</u>, have, hold, be in possession of, be
the owner of, have in your possession, have to your
name …*He is said to possess a huge fortune*…
2 = <u>be endowed with</u>, have, enjoy, benefit from, be
born with, be blessed with, be possessed of, be gifted
with …*individuals who possess the qualities of sense
and discretion*…
3 = <u>control</u>, influence, dominate, consume, obsess,
bedevil, mesmerize, eat someone up, fixate, put
under a spell …*Absolute terror possessed her*…
4 = <u>seize</u>, hold, control, dominate, occupy, haunt, take
someone over, bewitch, take possession of, have
power over, have mastery over …*It was as if the spirit
of his father possessed him*…

possessed = <u>crazed</u>, haunted, cursed, obsessed,
raving, frenzied, consumed, enchanted, maddened,
demented, frenetic, berserk, bewitched, bedevilled,
under a spell, hag-ridden

possession NOUN 1 = <u>ownership</u>, control, custody, hold, hands, tenure, occupancy, proprietorship ...*These documents are now in the possession of the authorities...*
2 = <u>province</u>, territory, colony, dominion, protectorate ...*All of these countries were once French possessions...*
PLURAL NOUN = <u>property</u>, things, effects, estate, assets, wealth, belongings, chattels, goods and chattels ...*People had lost their homes and all their possessions...*

possessive 1 = <u>jealous</u>, controlling, dominating, domineering, proprietorial, overprotective ...*Danny could be very jealous and possessive of me...*
2 = <u>selfish</u>, grasping, acquisitive ...*He's very possessive about his car...*

possibility 1 = <u>feasibility</u>, likelihood, plausibility, potentiality, practicability, workableness ...*a debate about the possibility of political reform...*
2 = <u>likelihood</u>, chance, risk, odds, prospect, liability, hazard, probability ...*There is still a possibility of unrest in the country...*
3 *often plural* = <u>potential</u>, promise, prospects, talent, capabilities, potentiality ...*This situation has great possibilities...*

possible 1 = <u>feasible</u>, viable, workable, achievable, within reach, on (*informal*), practicable, attainable, doable, realizable ...*Everything is possible if we want it enough...* OPPOSITE unfeasible
2 = <u>likely</u>, potential, anticipated, probable, odds-on, on the cards ...*One possible solution is to take legal action...* OPPOSITE improbable
3 = <u>conceivable</u>, likely, credible, plausible, hypothetical, imaginable, believable, thinkable ...*It's just possible that he was trying to put me off the trip...* OPPOSITE inconceivable
4 = <u>aspiring</u>, would-be, promising, hopeful, prospective, wannabe (*informal*) ...*a possible presidential contender...*

> ### Word Power
>
> **possible** – Although it is very common to talk about something's being *very possible* or *more possible*, many people object to such uses, claiming that *possible* describes an absolute state, and therefore something can only be either *possible* or *not possible*. If you want to refer to different degrees of probability, a word such as *likely* or *easy* may be more appropriate than *possible*, for example *it is very likely that he will resign* (not *very possible*).

possibly 1 = <u>perhaps</u>, maybe, God willing, perchance (*archaic*), mayhap (*archaic*), peradventure (*archaic*), haply (*archaic*) ...*Exercise may possibly protect against heart attacks...*
2 = <u>at all</u>, in any way, conceivably, by any means, under any circumstances, by any chance ...*I couldn't possibly answer that...*

post[1] NOUN 1 = <u>mail</u>, collection, delivery, postal service, snail mail (*informal*) ...*rushing to catch the post...* ...*You'll receive your book through the post...*

2 = <u>correspondence</u>, letters, cards, mail ...*He flipped through the post without opening any of it...*
VERB = <u>send (off)</u>, forward, mail, get off, transmit, dispatch, consign ...*I'm posting you a cheque tonight...*
PHRASES **keep someone posted** = <u>notify</u>, brief, advise, inform, report to, keep someone informed, keep someone up to date, apprise, fill someone in on (*informal*) ...*Keep me posted on your progress...*

post[2] NOUN 1 = <u>job</u>, place, office, position, situation, employment, appointment, assignment, berth (*informal*), billet (*informal*) ...*Sir Peter has held several senior military posts...*
2 = <u>position</u>, place, base, beat, station ...*Quick, men, back to your posts!...*
VERB = <u>station</u>, assign, put, place, position, establish, locate, situate, put on duty ...*After training she was posted to Brixton...*

post[3] NOUN = <u>support</u>, stake, pole, stock, standard, column, pale, shaft, upright, pillar, picket, palisade, newel ...*Eight wooden posts were driven into the ground...*
VERB = <u>put something up</u>, announce, publish, display, advertise, proclaim, publicize, promulgate, affix, stick something up, make something known, pin something up ...*Officials began posting warning notices...*

poster = <u>notice</u>, bill, announcement, advertisement, sticker, placard, public notice, affiche (*French*)

posterior NOUN = <u>bottom</u>, behind (*informal*), bum (*Brit. slang*), seat, rear, tail (*informal*), butt (*U.S. & Canad. informal*), buns (*U.S. slang*), buttocks, backside, rump, rear end, derrière (*euphemistic*), tush (*U.S. slang*), fundament, jacksy (*Brit. slang*) ...*her curvaceous posterior...*
ADJECTIVE = <u>rear</u>, back, hinder, hind ...*the posterior lobe of the pituitary gland...*

posterity = <u>the future</u>, future generations, succeeding generations

postpone = <u>put off</u>, delay, suspend, adjourn, table, shelve, defer, put back, hold over, put on ice (*informal*), put on the back burner (*informal*), take a rain check on (*U.S. & Canad. informal*) OPPOSITE go ahead with

postponement = <u>delay</u>, stay, suspension, moratorium, respite, adjournment, deferment, deferral

postscript = <u>P.S.</u>, addition, supplement, appendix, afterthought, afterword

postulate (*Formal*) = <u>presuppose</u>, suppose, advance, propose, assume, put forward, take for granted, predicate, theorize, posit, hypothesize

posture NOUN 1 = <u>bearing</u>, set, position, attitude, pose, stance, carriage, disposition, mien (*literary*) ...*She walked haltingly and her posture was stooped...*
2 = <u>attitude</u>, feeling, mood, point of view, stance, outlook, inclination, disposition, standpoint, frame of mind ...*None of the banks changed their posture on the deal as a result of the inquiry...*
VERB = <u>show off</u> (*informal*), pose, affect, hot-dog

(*chiefly U.S.*), make a show, put on airs, try to attract attention, attitudinize, do something for effect

posy = <u>bouquet</u>, spray, buttonhole, corsage, nosegay, boutonniere

pot NOUN **1** = <u>container</u>, bowl, pan, vessel, basin, vase, jug, cauldron, urn, utensil, crock, skillet *...metal cooking pots... ...use a large terracotta pot or a wooden tub...*
2 = <u>jackpot</u>, bank, prize, stakes, purse *...The pot for this Saturday's draw stands at over £18 million...*
3 = <u>kitty</u>, funds, pool *...If there is more money in the pot, all the members will benefit proportionally...*
4 = <u>paunch</u>, beer belly *or* gut (*informal*), spread (*informal*), corporation (*informal*), gut, bulge, spare tyre (*Brit. slang*), potbelly *...He's already developing a pot from all the beer he drinks...*
PHRASES **go to pot** = <u>decline</u>, slump, deteriorate, worsen, go downhill (*informal*), go to the dogs (*informal*), run to seed, go to rack and ruin *...This neighbourhood is really going to pot...*

pot-bellied = <u>fat</u>, overweight, bloated, obese, distended, corpulent, paunchy

pot belly = <u>paunch</u>, beer belly *or* gut (*informal*), spread (*informal*), corporation (*informal*), pot, gut, spare tyre (*Brit. slang*), middle-age spread (*informal*)

potency 1 = <u>influence</u>, might, force, control, authority, energy, potential, strength, capacity, mana (*N.Z.*) *...the extraordinary potency of his personality...*
2 = <u>persuasiveness</u>, force, strength, muscle, effectiveness, sway, forcefulness, cogency, impressiveness *...His remarks have added potency given the current situation...*
3 = <u>power</u>, force, strength, effectiveness, efficacy *...The potency of the wine increases with time...*
4 = <u>vigour</u>, puissance *...Alcohol abuse in men can reduce sexual potency...*

potent 1 = <u>powerful</u>, commanding, dynamic, dominant, influential, authoritative *...a potent political force...*
2 = <u>persuasive</u>, telling, convincing, effective, impressive, compelling, forceful, cogent *...a potent electoral message...* OPPOSITE unconvincing
3 = <u>strong</u>, powerful, mighty, vigorous, forceful, efficacious, puissant *...The drug is extremely potent, but can have unpleasant side-effects...* OPPOSITE weak

potentate = <u>ruler</u>, king, prince, emperor, monarch, sovereign, mogul, overlord

potential ADJECTIVE **1** = <u>possible</u>, future, likely, promising, budding, embryonic, undeveloped, unrealized, probable *...potential customers...*
2 = <u>hidden</u>, possible, inherent, dormant, latent *...We are aware of the potential dangers...*
NOUN = <u>ability</u>, possibilities, capacity, capability, the makings, what it takes (*informal*), aptitude, wherewithal, potentiality *...The boy has potential...*

potion = <u>concoction</u>, mixture, brew, tonic, cup, dose, draught, elixir, philtre

potter *usually with **around** or **about*** = <u>mess about</u>, fiddle (*informal*), tinker, dabble, fritter, footle (*informal*), poke along, fribble

pottery = <u>ceramics</u>, terracotta, crockery, earthenware, stoneware

potty (*Brit. informal*) = <u>crazy</u>, eccentric, crackers (*Brit. slang*), barmy (*slang*), touched, soft (*informal*), silly, foolish, daft (*informal*), off-the-wall (*slang*), oddball (*informal*), off the rails, dotty (*slang, chiefly Brit.*), loopy (*informal*), crackpot (*informal*), out to lunch (*informal*), dippy (*slang*), gonzo (*slang*), doolally (*slang*), off your trolley (*slang*), up the pole (*informal*), off your chump (*slang*), wacko *or* whacko (*informal*), off the air (*Austral. slang*)

pouch = <u>bag</u>, pocket, sack, container, purse, poke (*dialect*)

pounce VERB = <u>attack</u>, strike, jump, leap, swoop *...Before I could get to the pigeon, the cat pounced...*
PHRASES **pounce on something** *or* **someone 1** = <u>attack</u>, ambush, leap at, take someone by surprise, take someone unawares *...At that moment, a guard pounced on him...* **2** = <u>spring on</u>, attack, snatch, jump on, drop on, swoop on, fall upon, leap at, dash at, bound onto *...like a tiger pouncing on its prey...*

pound¹ = <u>enclosure</u>, yard, pen, compound, kennels, corral (*chiefly U.S. & Canad.*) *...The dog has been sent to the pound...*

pound² 1 *sometimes with **on*** = <u>beat</u>, strike, hammer, batter, thrash, thump, pelt, clobber (*slang*), pummel, belabour, beat the living daylights out of *...He pounded the table with his fist...*
2 = <u>crush</u>, powder, bruise, bray (*dialect*), pulverize *...She paused as she pounded the maize grains...*
3 = <u>pulsate</u>, beat, pulse, throb, palpitate, pitapat *...I'm sweating and my heart is pounding...*
4 *often with **out*** = <u>thump</u>, beat, hammer, bang *...A group of tribal drummers pounded out an unrelenting beat...*
5 = <u>stomp</u>, tramp, march, thunder (*informal*), clomp *...I pounded up the stairs to my room and slammed the door...*

pour 1 = <u>let flow</u>, spill, splash, dribble, drizzle, slop (*informal*), slosh (*informal*), decant *...Francis poured a generous measure of whisky into the glass...*
2 = <u>flow</u>, stream, run, course, rush, emit, cascade, gush, spout, spew *...Blood was pouring from his broken nose...*
3 = <u>rain</u>, sheet, pelt (down), teem, bucket down (*informal*), rain cats and dogs (*informal*), come down in torrents, rain hard *or* heavily *...It has been pouring all week...*
4 = <u>stream</u>, crowd, flood, swarm, gush, throng, teem *...The northern forces poured across the border...*

> ## *Word Power*
>
> **pour** – The spelling of *pour* (as in *she poured cream on her strudel*) should be carefully distinguished from that of *pore over* or *through* (as in *she pored over the manuscript*).

pout VERB = <u>sulk</u>, glower, mope, look sullen, purse your lips, look petulant, pull a long face, lour *or* lower, make a moue, turn down the corners of your mouth …*He whined and pouted like a kid when he didn't get what he wanted*…

NOUN = <u>sullen look</u>, glower, long face, moue (*French*) …*She jutted her lower lip out in a pout*…

poverty 1 = <u>pennilessness</u>, want, need, distress, necessity, hardship, insolvency, privation, penury, destitution, hand-to-mouth existence, beggary, indigence, pauperism, necessitousness …*41 per cent of Brazilians live in absolute poverty*… OPPOSITE wealth
2 = <u>scarcity</u>, lack, absence, want, deficit, shortage, deficiency, inadequacy, dearth, paucity, insufficiency, sparsity …*a poverty of ideas*… OPPOSITE abundance
3 = <u>barrenness</u>, deficiency, infertility, sterility, aridity, bareness, poorness, meagreness, unfruitfulness …*the poverty of the soil*… OPPOSITE fertility

poverty-stricken = <u>penniless</u>, broke (*informal*), bankrupt, impoverished, short, poor, distressed, beggared, needy, destitute, down and out, skint (*Brit. slang*), indigent, down at heel, impecunious, dirt poor (*informal*), on the breadline, flat broke (*informal*), penurious, on your uppers, stony-broke (*Brit. slang*), in queer street, without two pennies to rub together (*informal*), on your beam-ends

powder **NOUN** = <u>dust</u>, pounce (*rare*), talc, fine grains, loose particles …*a fine white powder*…
VERB 1 = <u>dust</u>, cover, scatter, sprinkle, strew, dredge …*Powder the puddings with icing sugar*…
2 = <u>grind</u>, crush, pound, pestle, pulverize, granulate …*Mix all the powdered ingredients together*…

powdery = <u>fine</u>, dry, sandy, dusty, loose, crumbling, grainy, chalky, crumbly, granular, pulverized, friable

power 1 = <u>control</u>, authority, influence, command, sovereignty, sway, dominance, domination, supremacy, mastery, dominion, ascendancy, mana (*N.Z.*) …*women who have reached positions of great power and influence*…
2 = <u>ability</u>, capacity, faculty, property, potential, capability, competence, competency …*He was so drunk that he had lost the power of speech*… OPPOSITE inability
3 = <u>authority</u>, right, licence, privilege, warrant, prerogative, authorization …*The Prime Minister has the power to dismiss senior ministers*…
4 = <u>strength</u>, might, energy, weight, muscle, vigour, potency, brawn …*He had no power in his left arm*… OPPOSITE weakness
5 = <u>forcefulness</u>, force, strength, punch (*informal*), intensity, potency, eloquence, persuasiveness, cogency, powerfulness …*the power of his rhetoric*…

powerful 1 = <u>influential</u>, dominant, controlling, commanding, supreme, prevailing, sovereign, authoritative, puissant …*You're a powerful woman – people will listen to you*… OPPOSITE powerless
2 = <u>strong</u>, strapping, mighty, robust, vigorous, potent, energetic, sturdy, stalwart …*a big, powerful man*… OPPOSITE weak
3 = <u>persuasive</u>, convincing, effective, telling, moving, striking, storming, dramatic, impressive, compelling, authoritative, forceful, weighty, forcible, cogent,

effectual …*a powerful drama about a corrupt city leader*…

powerfully = <u>strongly</u>, hard, vigorously, forcibly, forcefully, mightily, with might and main

powerless 1 = <u>defenceless</u>, vulnerable, dependent, subject, tied, ineffective, unarmed, disenfranchised, over a barrel (*informal*), disfranchised …*political systems that keep women poor and powerless*…
2 = <u>weak</u>, disabled, helpless, incapable, paralysed, frail, feeble, debilitated, impotent, ineffectual, incapacitated, prostrate, infirm, etiolated …*His leg muscles were powerless with lack of use*… OPPOSITE strong

practicable = <u>feasible</u>, possible, viable, workable, achievable, attainable, doable, within the realm of possibility, performable OPPOSITE unfeasible
➤ practical

practical 1 = <u>functional</u>, efficient, realistic, pragmatic …*practical suggestions on how to improve your diet*… OPPOSITE impractical
2 = <u>empirical</u>, real, applied, actual, hands-on, in the field, experimental, factual …*theories based on practical knowledge*… OPPOSITE theoretical
3 = <u>sensible</u>, ordinary, realistic, down-to-earth, mundane, matter-of-fact, no-nonsense, businesslike, hard-headed, workaday …*She is always so practical and full of common sense*… OPPOSITE impractical
4 = <u>feasible</u>, possible, sound, viable, constructive, workable, practicable, doable …*We do not yet have any practical way to prevent cancer*… OPPOSITE impractical
5 = <u>useful</u>, ordinary, appropriate, sensible, everyday, functional, utilitarian, serviceable …*clothes which are practical as well as stylish*…
6 = <u>skilled</u>, working, seasoned, trained, experienced, qualified, veteran, efficient, accomplished, proficient …*people with practical experience of running businesses*… OPPOSITE inexperienced

---

Word Power

practical – A distinction is usually made between *practical* and *practicable*. *Practical* refers to a person, idea, project, etc., as being more concerned with or relevant to practice than theory: *he is a very practical person*; *the idea had no practical application*. *Practicable* refers to a project or idea as being capable of being done or put into effect: *the plan was expensive, yet practicable*.

---

practically 1 = <u>almost</u>, nearly, close to, essentially, virtually, basically, fundamentally, all but, just about, in effect, very nearly, to all intents and purposes, well-nigh …*He'd known the old man practically all his life*…
2 = <u>sensibly</u>, reasonably, matter-of-factly, realistically, rationally, pragmatically, with common sense, unsentimentally …*'Let me help you to bed,' Helen said, practically*…

practice 1 = <u>custom</u>, use, way, system, rule, method, tradition, habit, routine, mode, usage, wont, praxis, usual procedure …*a public inquiry into bank *practices…*

2 = <u>training</u>, study, exercise, work-out, discipline, preparation, drill, rehearsal, repetition …*netball practice…*

3 = <u>profession</u>, work, business, career, occupation, pursuit, vocation …*improving his skills in the practice of medicine…*

4 = <u>business</u>, company, office, firm, enterprise, partnership, outfit (*informal*) …*He worked in a small legal practice…*

5 = <u>use</u>, experience, action, effect, operation, application, enactment …*attempts to encourage the practice of safe sex…*

practise **1** = <u>rehearse</u>, study, prepare, perfect, repeat, go through, polish, go over, refine, run through …*Lauren practises the concerto every day…*

2 = <u>do</u>, train, exercise, work out, drill, warm up, keep your hand in …*practising for a gym display…*

3 = <u>carry out</u>, follow, apply, perform, observe, engage in, live up to, put into practice …*Astronomy continued to be practised in Byzantium…*

4 = <u>work at</u>, pursue, carry on, undertake, specialize in, ply your trade …*He practised as a lawyer for thirty years…*

practised = <u>skilled</u>, trained, experienced, seasoned, able, expert, qualified, accomplished, versed, proficient OPPOSITE> inexperienced

pragmatic = <u>practical</u>, efficient, sensible, realistic, down-to-earth, matter-of-fact, utilitarian, businesslike, hard-headed OPPOSITE> idealistic

praise VERB **1** = <u>acclaim</u>, approve of, honour, cheer, admire, applaud, compliment, congratulate, pay tribute to, laud, extol, sing the praises of, pat someone on the back, cry someone up, big up (*slang, chiefly Caribbean*), eulogize, take your hat off to, crack someone up (*informal*) …*Many praised him for taking a strong stand…* OPPOSITE> criticize

2 = <u>give thanks to</u>, bless, worship, adore, magnify (*archaic*), glorify, exalt, pay homage to …*She asked the congregation to praise God…*

NOUN **1** = <u>approval</u>, acclaim, applause, cheering, tribute, compliment, congratulations, ovation, accolade, good word, kudos, eulogy, commendation, approbation, acclamation, panegyric, encomium, plaudit, laudation …*I have nothing but praise for the police…* OPPOSITE> criticism

2 = <u>thanks</u>, glory, worship, devotion, homage, adoration …*Hindus were singing hymns in praise of the god Rama…*

prance **1** = <u>dance</u>, bound, leap, trip, spring, jump, skip, romp, caper, cavort, frisk, gambol, cut a rug (*informal*) …*The cheerleaders pranced on the far side of the pitch…*

2 = <u>strut</u>, parade, stalk, show off (*informal*), swagger, swank (*informal*) …*models prancing around on the catwalk…*

prank = <u>trick</u>, lark (*informal*), caper, frolic, escapade, practical joke, skylarking (*informal*), antic, jape

prattle VERB = <u>chatter</u>, babble, waffle (*informal, chiefly Brit.*), run on, rabbit on (*Brit. informal*), witter on

(*informal*), patter, drivel, clack, twitter, jabber, gabble, rattle on, blather, blether, run off at the mouth (*slang*) …*She prattled on until I wanted to scream…*

NOUN = <u>chatter</u>, talk, babble, waffle (*informal*), rambling, wittering (*informal*), prating, drivel, jabber, gabble, blather, blether …*I had had enough of his mindless prattle…*

pray **1** = <u>say your prayers</u>, offer a prayer, recite the rosary …*He spent his time in prison praying and studying…*

2 = <u>beg</u>, ask, plead, petition, urge, request, sue, crave, invoke, call upon, cry, solicit, implore, beseech, entreat, importune, adjure, supplicate …*They prayed for help…*

prayer **1** = <u>supplication</u>, devotion, communion …*The night was spent in prayer and meditation…*

2 = <u>orison</u>, litany, invocation, intercession …*prayers of thanksgiving…*

3 = <u>plea</u>, appeal, suit, request, petition, entreaty, supplication …*Say a quick prayer I don't get stopped for speeding…*

preach VERB **1** *often with* **to** = <u>deliver a sermon</u>, address, exhort, evangelize, preach a sermon, orate …*The bishop preached to a huge crowd…*

2 = <u>urge</u>, teach, champion, recommend, advise, counsel, advocate, exhort …*the movement preaches revolution…*

PHRASES **preach at someone** = <u>lecture</u>, admonish, harangue, sermonize, moralize against, preachify …*I can't stand being preached at…*

preacher = <u>clergyman</u>, minister, parson, missionary, evangelist, revivalist

preamble = <u>introduction</u>, prelude, preface, foreword, overture, opening move, proem, prolegomenon, exordium, opening statement *or* remarks

precarious **1** = <u>insecure</u>, dangerous, uncertain, tricky, risky, doubtful, dubious, unsettled, dodgy (*Brit., Austral., & N.Z. informal*), unstable, unsure, hazardous, shaky, hairy (*slang*), perilous, touch and go, dicey (*informal, chiefly Brit.*), chancy (*informal*), built on sand …*Our financial situation had become precarious…* OPPOSITE> secure

2 = <u>dangerous</u>, unstable, shaky, slippery, insecure, unsafe, unreliable, unsteady …*They crawled up a precarious rope ladder…* OPPOSITE> stable

precaution **1** = <u>safeguard</u>, insurance, protection, provision, safety measure, preventative measure, belt and braces (*informal*) …*This is purely a safety precaution…*

2 = <u>forethought</u>, care, caution, anticipation, prudence, foresight, providence, wariness, circumspection …*Exercise adequate precaution when out in public…*

precede **1** = <u>go before</u>, introduce, herald, pave the way for, usher in, antedate, antecede, forerun …*Intensive negotiations preceded the vote…*

2 = <u>go ahead of</u>, lead, head, go before, take precedence …*Alice preceded them from the room…*

3 = <u>preface</u>, introduce, go before, launch, prefix …*the information that precedes the paragraph in question…*

precedence = <u>priority</u>, lead, rank, preference,

superiority, supremacy, seniority, primacy, pre-eminence, antecedence

precedent = <u>instance</u>, example, authority, standard, model, pattern, criterion, prototype, paradigm, antecedent, exemplar, previous example

preceding 1 = <u>previous</u>, earlier, former, above, foregoing, aforementioned, anterior, aforesaid ...*Please refer back to the preceding chapter...*
2 = <u>past</u>, earlier, former, prior, foregoing ...*the student revolution of the preceding years...*

precept 1 = <u>rule</u>, order, law, direction, principle, command, regulation, instruction, decree, mandate, canon, statute, ordinance, commandment, behest, dictum ...*the precepts of Buddhism...*
2 = <u>maxim</u>, saying, rule, principle, guideline, motto, dictum, axiom, byword ...*the precept, 'If a job's worth doing, it's worth doing well'...*

precinct NOUN = <u>area</u>, quarter, section, sector, district, zone ...*a pedestrian precinct...*
PLURAL NOUN = <u>district</u>, limits, region, borders, bounds, boundaries, confines, neighbourhood, milieu, surrounding area, environs, purlieus ...*No-one carrying arms is allowed within the precincts of the temple...*

precious 1 = <u>valuable</u>, expensive, rare, fine, choice, prized, dear, costly, high-priced, exquisite, invaluable, priceless, recherché, inestimable ...*jewellery and precious objects belonging to her mother...* OPPOSITE> worthless
2 = <u>loved</u>, valued, favourite, prized, dear, dearest, treasured, darling, beloved, adored, cherished, fave (*informal*), idolized, worth your *or* its weight in gold ...*her most precious possession...*
3 = <u>affected</u>, artificial, fastidious, twee (*Brit. informal*), chichi, overrefined, overnice ...*Actors, he decided, were all precious and neurotic...*

precipice = <u>cliff</u>, crag, rock face, cliff face, height, brink, bluff, sheer drop, steep cliff, scarp

precipitate VERB 1 = <u>quicken</u>, trigger, accelerate, further, press, advance, hurry, dispatch, speed up, bring on, hasten, push forward, expedite ...*The killings in the city have precipitated the worst crisis yet...*
2 = <u>throw</u>, launch, cast, discharge, hurl, fling, let fly, send forth ...*Dust was precipitated into the air...*
ADJECTIVE 1 = <u>hasty</u>, hurried, frantic, rash, reckless, impulsive, madcap, ill-advised, precipitous, impetuous, indiscreet, heedless, harum-scarum ...*I don't think we should make any precipitate decisions...*
2 = <u>sudden</u>, quick, brief, rushing, violent, plunging, rapid, unexpected, swift, abrupt, without warning, headlong, breakneck ...*the precipitate collapse of European communism...*

precipitous 1 = <u>sheer</u>, high, steep, dizzy, abrupt, perpendicular, falling sharply ...*a steep, precipitous cliff...*
2 = <u>hasty</u>, sudden, hurried, precipitate, abrupt, harum-scarum ...*the stock market's precipitous drop...*

> ### *Word Power*
> **precipitous** – Some people think the use of *precipitous* to mean 'hasty' is incorrect, and that *precipitate* should be used instead.

---

precise 1 = <u>exact</u>, specific, actual, particular, express, fixed, correct, absolute, accurate, explicit, definite, clear-cut, literal, unequivocal ...*We will never know the precise details of his death...* OPPOSITE> vague
2 = <u>strict</u>, particular, exact, nice, formal, careful, stiff, rigid, meticulous, inflexible, scrupulous, fastidious, prim, puritanical, finicky, punctilious, ceremonious ...*They speak very precise English...* OPPOSITE> inexact

precisely 1 = <u>exactly</u>, bang on, squarely, correctly, absolutely, strictly, accurately, plumb (*informal*), slap on (*informal*), square on, on the dot, smack on (*informal*) ...*The meeting began at precisely 4.00 p.m...*
2 = <u>just so</u>, yes, absolutely, exactly, quite so, you bet (*informal*), without a doubt, on the button (*informal*), indubitably ...*'Is that what you meant?' – 'Precisely.'...*
3 = <u>just</u>, entirely, absolutely, altogether, exactly, in all respects ...*That is precisely what I suggested...*
4 = <u>word for word</u>, literally, exactly, to the letter, neither more nor less ...*Please repeat precisely what she said...*

precision = <u>exactness</u>, care, accuracy, fidelity, correctness, rigour, nicety, particularity, exactitude, meticulousness, definiteness, dotting the i's and crossing the t's, preciseness

preclude 1 = <u>rule out</u>, put a stop to, obviate, make impossible, make impracticable ...*At 84, John feels his age precludes much travelling...*
2 = <u>prevent</u>, stop, check, exclude, restrain, prohibit, inhibit, hinder, forestall, debar ...*Poor English precluded them from ever finding a job...*

precocious = <u>advanced</u>, developed, forward, quick, bright, smart OPPOSITE> backward

preconceived = <u>presumed</u>, premature, predetermined, presupposed, prejudged, forejudged

preconception = <u>preconceived idea</u> *or* notion, notion, prejudice, bias, presumption, predisposition, presupposition, prepossession

precondition = <u>necessity</u>, essential, requirement, prerequisite, must, sine qua non (*Latin*)

precursor 1 = <u>forerunner</u>, pioneer, predecessor, forebear, antecedent, originator ...*Real tennis, a precursor of the modern game, originated in the eleventh century...*
2 = <u>herald</u>, usher, messenger, vanguard, forerunner, harbinger ...*The deal should not be seen as a precursor to a merger...*

predatory 1 = <u>hunting</u>, ravening, carnivorous, rapacious, raptorial, predacious ...*predatory birds like the eagle...*
2 = <u>plundering</u>, ravaging, pillaging, marauding, thieving, despoiling ...*predatory gangs...*
3 = <u>rapacious</u>, greedy, voracious, vulturous, vulturine ...*predatory business practices...*

predecessor 1 = <u>previous job holder</u>, precursor, forerunner, antecedent, former job holder, prior job holder …*He learned everything he knew from his predecessor*…
2 = <u>ancestor</u>, forebear, antecedent, forefather …*opportunities our predecessors never had*…

predetermined 1 = <u>fated</u>, predestined, preordained, meant, doomed, foreordained, pre-elected, predestinated …*our predetermined fate*…
2 = <u>prearranged</u>, set, agreed, set up, settled, fixed, cut and dried (*informal*), preplanned, decided beforehand, arranged in advance …*The capsules release the drug at a predetermined time*…

predicament = <u>fix</u> (*informal*), state, situation, spot (*informal*), corner, hole (*slang*), emergency, mess, jam (*informal*), dilemma, pinch, plight, scrape (*informal*), hot water (*informal*), pickle (*informal*), how-do-you-do (*informal*), quandary, tight spot

predicate
PHRASES **be predicated on** = <u>be based on</u>, rest on, be founded on, be built on, be established on, be grounded on

predict = <u>foretell</u>, forecast, divine, foresee, prophesy, call, augur, presage, portend, prognosticate, forebode, soothsay, vaticinate (*rare*)

predictable = <u>likely</u>, expected, sure, certain, anticipated, reliable, foreseen, on the cards, foreseeable, sure-fire (*informal*), calculable OPPOSITE unpredictable

prediction = <u>prophecy</u>, forecast, prognosis, divination, prognostication, augury, soothsaying, sortilege

predilection = <u>liking</u>, love, taste, weakness, fancy, leaning, tendency, preference, bias, inclination, penchant, fondness, propensity, predisposition, proclivity, partiality, proneness

predispose = <u>incline</u>, influence, prepare, prompt, lead, prime, affect, prejudice, bias, induce, dispose, sway, make you of a mind to

predisposed 1 = <u>inclined</u>, willing, given, minded, ready, agreeable, amenable …*Franklin was predisposed to believe him*…
2 = <u>susceptible</u>, subject, prone, liable …*Some people are genetically predisposed to diabetes*…

predisposition 1 = <u>inclination</u>, tendency, disposition, bent, bias, willingness, likelihood, penchant, propensity, predilection, proclivity, potentiality, proneness …*the predisposition to behave in a certain way*…
2 = <u>susceptibility</u>, tendency, proneness …*a hereditary predisposition to the disease*…

predominance 1 = <u>prevalence</u>, weight, preponderance, greater number …*An interesting note was the predominance of London club players*…
2 = <u>dominance</u>, hold, control, edge, leadership, sway, supremacy, mastery, dominion, upper hand, ascendancy, paramountcy …*their economic predominance*…

predominant 1 = <u>main</u>, chief, prevailing, notable, paramount, prevalent, preponderant …*Amanda's predominant emotion was one of confusion*…
2 = <u>principal</u>, leading, important, prime, controlling, ruling, chief, capital, primary, supreme, prominent, superior, dominant, sovereign, top-priority, ascendant …*He played a predominant role in shaping French economic policy*… OPPOSITE minor

predominantly = <u>mainly</u>, largely, chiefly, mostly, generally, principally, primarily, on the whole, in the main, for the most part, to a great extent, preponderantly

predominate 1 = <u>be in the majority</u>, dominate, prevail, stand out, be predominant, be most noticeable, preponderate …*All nationalities were represented, but the English and American predominated*…
2 = <u>prevail</u>, rule, reign, hold sway, get the upper hand, carry weight …*a society where Islamic principles predominate*…

pre-eminence = <u>superiority</u>, distinction, excellence, supremacy, prestige, prominence, transcendence, renown, predominance, paramountcy

pre-eminent = <u>outstanding</u>, supreme, paramount, chief, excellent, distinguished, superior, renowned, foremost, consummate, predominant, transcendent, unrivalled, incomparable, peerless, unsurpassed, unequalled, matchless

pre-empt = <u>forestall</u>, anticipate, prevent, steal a march on, get in before

preen VERB 1 *often reflexive* = <u>smarten</u>, admire, dress up, doll up (*slang*), trim, array, deck out, spruce up, prettify, primp, trig (*archaic or dialect*), titivate, prink …*He spent half an hour preening in front of the mirror*… …*20 minutes preening themselves every morning*…
2 (*of birds*) = <u>clean</u>, smooth, groom, tidy, plume …*The linnet shook herself and preened a few feathers on her breast*…
PHRASES **preen yourself** = <u>pride yourself</u>, congratulate yourself, give yourself a pat on the back, pique yourself, plume yourself …*His only negative feature is the desire to brag and preen himself over his abilities*…

preface NOUN = <u>introduction</u>, preliminary, prelude, preamble, foreword, prologue, proem, prolegomenon, exordium …*the preface to the English edition of the novel*…
VERB = <u>introduce</u>, precede, open, begin, launch, lead up to, prefix …*I will preface what I am going to say with a few lines from Shakespeare*…

prefer 1 = <u>like better</u>, favour, go for, pick, select, adopt, fancy, opt for, single out, plump for, incline towards, be partial to …*Do you prefer a particular sort of music?*…
2 = <u>choose</u>, elect, opt for, pick, wish, desire, would rather, would sooner, incline towards …*I prefer to go on self-catering holidays*…

> ### Word Power
>
> **prefer** – Normally, *to* (not *than*) is used after *prefer* and *preferable*. Therefore, you would say *I prefer skating to skiing*, and *a small income is preferable to no income at all*. However, when expressing a preference between two activities stated as infinitive verbs, for example *to skate* and *to ski*, use *than*, as in *I prefer to skate than to ski*.

preferable = <u>better</u>, best, chosen, choice, preferred, recommended, favoured, superior, worthier, more suitable, more desirable, more eligible OPPOSITE undesirable
➤ **prefer**

> ### Word Power
>
> **preferable** – Since *preferable* already means 'more desirable', it is better when writing not to say something is *more preferable* or *most preferable*.

preferably = <u>ideally</u>, if possible, rather, sooner, much rather, by choice, much sooner, as a matter of choice, in *or* for preference

preference 1 = <u>liking</u>, wish, taste, desire, bag (*slang*), leaning, bent, bias, cup of tea (*informal*), inclination, penchant, fondness, predisposition, predilection, proclivity, partiality …*Whatever your preference, we have a product to suit you…*
2 = <u>first choice</u>, choice, favourite, election, pick, option, selection, top of the list, fave (*informal*) …*He enjoys all styles of music, but his preference is opera…*
3 = <u>priority</u>, first place, precedence, advantage, favouritism, pride of place, favoured treatment …*Candidates with the right qualifications should be given preference…*

preferential = <u>privileged</u>, favoured, superior, better, special, partial, partisan, advantageous

prefigure = <u>foreshadow</u>, suggest, indicate, intimate, presage, portend, shadow forth, adumbrate, foretoken

pregnancy = <u>gestation</u>, gravidity
(Related Words)
adjectives: antenatal, postnatal, maternity

pregnant 1 = <u>expectant</u>, expecting (*informal*), with child, in the club (*Brit. slang*), in the family way (*informal*), gravid, preggers (*Brit. informal*), enceinte, in the pudding club (*slang*), big *or* heavy with child …*Tina was pregnant with their first child…*
2 = <u>meaningful</u>, pointed, charged, significant, telling, loaded, expressive, eloquent, weighty, suggestive …*There was a long, pregnant silence…*
3 *with* **with** = <u>full of</u>, rich in, fraught with, teeming with, replete with, abounding in, abundant in, fecund with …*The songs are pregnant with irony and insight…*

prehistoric = <u>earliest</u>, early, primitive, primordial, primeval

prejudice NOUN 1 = <u>discrimination</u>, racism, injustice, sexism, intolerance, bigotry, unfairness, chauvinism, narrow-mindedness …*a victim of racial prejudice…*
2 = <u>bias</u>, preconception, partiality, preconceived notion, warp, jaundiced eye, prejudgment …*the male prejudices which Dr Greer identifies…*
3 = <u>harm</u>, damage, hurt, disadvantage, loss, mischief, detriment, impairment …*I feel sure it can be done without prejudice to anybody's principles…*
VERB 1 = <u>bias</u>, influence, colour, poison, distort, sway, warp, slant, predispose, jaundice, prepossess …*I think your upbringing has prejudiced you…*
2 = <u>harm</u>, damage, hurt, injure, mar, undermine, spoil, impair, hinder, crool *or* cruel (*Austral. slang*) …*He claimed that the media coverage had prejudiced his chance of a fair trial…*

prejudiced = <u>biased</u>, influenced, unfair, one-sided, conditioned, partial, partisan, discriminatory, bigoted, intolerant, opinionated, narrow-minded, jaundiced, prepossessed OPPOSITE unbiased

prejudicial = <u>harmful</u>, damaging, undermining, detrimental, hurtful, unfavourable, counterproductive, deleterious, injurious, inimical, disadvantageous

preliminary ADJECTIVE 1 = <u>first</u>, opening, trial, initial, test, pilot, prior, introductory, preparatory, exploratory, initiatory, prefatory, precursory …*Preliminary talks began yesterday…*
2 = <u>qualifying</u>, eliminating …*the last match of the preliminary rounds…*
NOUN = <u>introduction</u>, opening, beginning, foundation, start, preparation, first round, prelude, preface, overture, initiation, preamble, groundwork, prelims …*Today's survey is a preliminary to a more detailed one…*

prelude 1 = <u>introduction</u>, beginning, preparation, preliminary, start, commencement, curtain-raiser …*The protests are now seen as the prelude to last year's uprising…*
2 = <u>overture</u>, opening, introduction, introductory movement …*the third-act Prelude of Parsifal…*

premature 1 = <u>early</u>, untimely, before time, unseasonable …*a twenty-four-year-old man suffering from premature baldness…*
2 = <u>hasty</u>, rash, too soon, precipitate, impulsive, untimely, ill-considered, jumping the gun, ill-timed, inopportune, overhasty …*It now seems their optimism was premature…*
3 = <u>preterm</u>, prem (*informal*), preemie (*U.S. & Canad. informal*) …*a greater risk of having a premature baby…*

prematurely 1 = <u>too early</u>, too soon, before your time, preterm …*Danny was born prematurely…*
2 = <u>overhastily</u>, rashly, too soon, precipitately, too hastily, half-cocked, at half-cock …*He may have spoken just a little prematurely…*

premeditated = <u>planned</u>, calculated, deliberate, considered, studied, intended, conscious, contrived, intentional, wilful, aforethought, prepense OPPOSITE unplanned

premier NOUN = head of government, prime minister, chancellor, chief minister, P.M. ....*Australia's premier Paul Keating*...
ADJECTIVE = chief, leading, top, first, highest, head, main, prime, primary, principal, arch, foremost ...*the country's premier opera company*...

premiere = first night, opening, debut, first showing, first performance

premise NOUN = assumption, proposition, thesis, ground, argument, hypothesis, assertion, postulate, supposition, presupposition, postulation ...*the premise that men and women are on equal terms in this society*...
VERB = predicate, found, build, ground, establish, posit ...*The plan is premised on continuing abundant tax returns*...

premises = building(s), place, office, property, site, establishment

premium NOUN 1 = fee, charge, payment, instalment ...*an increase in insurance premiums*...
2 = surcharge, extra charge, additional fee *or* charge ...*Customers are not willing to pay a premium*...
3 = bonus, reward, prize, percentage (*informal*), perk (*Brit. informal*), boon, bounty, remuneration, recompense, perquisite ...*Shareholders did not receive a premium on the price of their shares*...
PHRASES **at a premium** = in great demand, valuable, expensive, rare, costly, scarce, in short supply, hard to come by, like gold dust, beyond your means, not to be had for love or money ...*Tickets to the game are at a premium*... ◆ **put** *or* **place a (high) premium on something** = hold in high regard, value, appreciate, set great store by, put a high value on ...*I place a high premium on what someone is like as a person*...

premonition = feeling, idea, intuition, suspicion, hunch, apprehension, misgiving, foreboding, funny feeling (*informal*), presentiment, feeling in your bones

preoccupation 1 = obsession, concern, hang-up (*informal*), fixation, pet subject, hobbyhorse, idée fixe (*French*), bee in your bonnet ...*Her main preoccupation from an early age was boys*...
2 = absorption, musing, oblivion, abstraction, daydreaming, immersion, reverie, absent-mindedness, brown study, inattentiveness, absence of mind, pensiveness, engrossment, prepossession, woolgathering ...*He kept sinking back into gloomy preoccupation*...

preoccupied 1 = absorbed, taken up, caught up, lost, intent, wrapped up, immersed, engrossed, rapt ...*They were preoccupied with their own concerns*...
2 = lost in thought, abstracted, distracted, unaware, oblivious, faraway, absent-minded, heedless, distrait, in a brown study ...*He was too preoccupied to notice what was going on*...

preparation 1 = groundwork, development, preparing, arranging, devising, getting ready, thinking-up, putting in order ...*Behind any successful event lies months of preparation*...
2 = readiness, expectation, provision, safeguard, precaution, anticipation, foresight, preparedness, alertness ...*a military build-up in preparation for war*...
3 *usually plural* = arrangement, plan, measure, provision ...*Final preparations are under way for the celebration*...
4 = mixture, cream, medicine, compound, composition, lotion, concoction, amalgam, ointment, tincture ...*a specially formulated natural skin preparation*...

preparatory ADJECTIVE = introductory, preliminary, opening, basic, primary, elementary, prefatory, preparative ...*At least a year's preparatory work will be needed*...
PHRASES **preparatory to** = before, prior to, in preparation for, in advance of, in anticipation of ...*Sloan cleared his throat preparatory to speaking*...

prepare 1 = make *or* get ready, arrange, draw up, form, fashion, get up (*informal*), construct, assemble, contrive, put together, make provision, put in order ...*He said the government must prepare an emergency plan for evacuation*...
2 = equip, fit, adapt, adjust, outfit, furnish, fit out, accoutre ...*The crew has been preparing the ship for storage*...
3 = train, guide, prime, direct, coach, brief, discipline, groom, put someone in the picture ...*It is a school's job to prepare students for university studies*...
4 = make, cook, put together, get, produce, assemble, muster, concoct, fix up, dish up, rustle up (*informal*) ...*She found him in the kitchen, preparing dinner*...
5 = get ready, plan, anticipate, make provision, lay the groundwork, make preparations, arrange things, get everything set ...*They were not given enough time to prepare for the election battle*...
6 = practise, get ready, train, exercise, warm up, get into shape ...*giving the players a chance to prepare for the match*...
7 *usually reflexive* = brace, ready, strengthen, fortify, steel, gird ...*I began to prepare myself for the worst*...

prepared 1 = willing, minded, able, ready, inclined, disposed, in the mood, predisposed, of a mind ...*Are you prepared to take industrial action?*...
2 = ready, set, all set ...*I was prepared for a long wait*...
3 = fit, primed, in order, arranged, in readiness, all systems go (*informal*) ...*The country is fully prepared for war*...

preparedness = readiness, order, preparation, fitness, alertness

preponderance 1 = predominance, instance, dominance, prevalence ...*the huge preponderance of males among homeless people*...
2 = greater part, mass, bulk, weight, lion's share, greater numbers, extensiveness ...*The preponderance of the evidence strongly supports his guilt*...
3 = domination, power, sway, superiority, supremacy, dominion, ascendancy ...*In 1965, the preponderance of West Germany over East had become even greater*...

preposterous = <u>ridiculous</u>, bizarre, incredible, outrageous, shocking, impossible, extreme, crazy, excessive, absurd, foolish, ludicrous, extravagant, unthinkable, unreasonable, insane, irrational, monstrous, senseless, out of the question, laughable, exorbitant, nonsensical, risible, asinine, cockamamie (*slang, chiefly U.S.*)

prerequisite NOUN = <u>requirement</u>, must, essential, necessity, condition, qualification, imperative, precondition, requisite, sine qua non (*Latin*) ...*Good self-esteem is a prerequisite for a happy life...*
ADJECTIVE = <u>required</u>, necessary, essential, called for, vital, mandatory, imperative, indispensable, obligatory, requisite, of the essence, needful ...*Young children can be taught the prerequisite skills necessary to learn to read...*

prerogative = <u>right</u>, choice, claim, authority, title, due, advantage, sanction, liberty, privilege, immunity, exemption, birthright, droit, perquisite

presage VERB = <u>portend to</u>, point to, warn of, signify, omen, bode, foreshadow, augur, betoken, adumbrate, forebode, foretoken ...*Diplomats fear the incidents presage a new chapter in the conflict...*
NOUN = <u>omen</u>, sign, warning, forecast, prediction, prophecy, portent, harbinger, intimation, forewarning, prognostication, augury, prognostic, auspice ...*Soldiers used to believe a raven was a presage of coming battle...*

prescient = <u>foresighted</u>, psychic, prophetic, divining, discerning, perceptive, clairvoyant, far-sighted, divinatory, mantic

prescribe 1 = <u>specify</u>, order, direct, stipulate, write a prescription for ...*Our doctor prescribed antibiotics for her throat infection...*
2 = <u>ordain</u>, set, order, establish, rule, require, fix, recommend, impose, appoint, command, define, dictate, assign, lay down, decree, stipulate, enjoin ...*The judge said he was passing the sentence prescribed by law...*

prescription 1 = <u>instruction</u>, direction, formula, script (*informal*), recipe ...*These drugs are freely available without a prescription...*
2 = <u>medicine</u>, drug, treatment, preparation, cure, mixture, dose, remedy ...*I'm not sleeping, even with that new prescription the doctor gave me...*

prescriptive = <u>dictatorial</u>, rigid, authoritarian, legislating, dogmatic, didactic, preceptive

presence NOUN 1 = <u>being</u>, existence, company, residence, attendance, showing up, companionship, occupancy, habitation, inhabitance ...*His presence in the village could only stir up trouble... ...the presence of a carcinogen in the water...*
2 = <u>proximity</u>, closeness, vicinity, nearness, neighbourhood, immediate circle, propinquity ...*conscious of being in the presence of a great man...*
3 = <u>personality</u>, bearing, appearance, aspect, air, ease, carriage, aura, poise, demeanour, self-assurance, mien (*literary*), comportment ...*Hendrix's stage presence appealed to thousands of teenage rebels...*
4 = <u>spirit</u>, ghost, manifestation, spectre, apparition,

shade (*literary*), wraith, supernatural being, revenant, eidolon ...*The house was haunted by shadows and unseen presences...*
PHRASES **presence of mind** = <u>level-headedness</u>, assurance, composure, poise, cool (*slang*), wits, countenance, coolness, aplomb, alertness, calmness, equanimity, self-assurance, phlegm, quickness, sang-froid, self-possession, unflappability (*informal*), imperturbability, quick-wittedness, self-command, collectedness ...*Someone had the presence of mind to call for an ambulance...*

present[1] ADJECTIVE 1 = <u>current</u>, existing, immediate, contemporary, instant, present-day, existent, extant ...*the government's present economic difficulties...*
2 = <u>here</u>, there, near, available, ready, nearby, accounted for, to hand, at hand, in attendance ...*The whole family was present...* OPPOSITE> absent
3 = <u>in existence</u>, existing, existent, extant ...*This vitamin is naturally present in breast milk...*
PHRASES **at present** = <u>just now</u>, now, presently, currently, at the moment, right now, nowadays, at this time, at the present time, in this day and age ...*At present, children under 14 are not permitted in bars...*
◆ **for the present** = <u>for now</u>, for a while, in the meantime, temporarily, for the moment, for the time being, provisionally, not for long, for the nonce ...*The minsters agreed that sanctions should remain in place for the present...* ◆ **the present** = <u>now</u>, today, the time being, here and now, this day and age, the present moment ...*His struggle to reconcile the past with the present...*

present[2] NOUN = <u>gift</u>, offering, grant, favour, donation, hand-out, endowment, boon, bounty, gratuity, prezzie (*informal*), benefaction, bonsela (*S. African*), largesse *or* largess ...*The vase was a wedding present...*
VERB 1 = <u>give</u>, award, hand over, offer, grant, donate, hand out, furnish, confer, bestow, entrust, proffer, put at someone's disposal ...*The queen presented the prizes to the winning captain...*
2 = <u>put forward</u>, offer, suggest, raise, state, produce, introduce, advance, relate, declare, extend, pose, submit, tender, hold out, recount, expound, proffer, adduce ...*We presented three options to the unions for discussion...*
3 = <u>put on</u>, stage, perform, give, show, mount, render, put before the public ...*The theatre is presenting a new production of 'Hamlet'...*
4 = <u>launch</u>, display, demonstrate, parade, exhibit, unveil ...*presenting a new product or service to the market-place...*
5 = <u>introduce</u>, make known, acquaint someone with ...*Fox stepped forward and presented him to Jack...*

presentable 1 = <u>tidy</u>, elegant, well groomed, becoming, trim, spruce, dapper, natty (*informal*), smartly dressed, fit to be seen ...*She managed to make herself presentable in time for work...* OPPOSITE> unpresentable
2 = <u>satisfactory</u>, suitable, decent, acceptable, proper, good enough, respectable, not bad (*informal*), tolerable, passable, O.K. *or* okay (*informal*) ...*His score*

had reached a presentable total… OPPOSITE
unsatisfactory

presentation 1 = <u>giving</u>, award, offering, donation,
investiture, bestowal, conferral …*at the presentation
ceremony*…
2 = <u>demonstration</u>, show, talk, launch, address,
display, speech, exhibition, lecture, unveiling,
exposition …*a business presentation*…
3 = <u>appearance</u>, look, display, packaging,
arrangement, layout, delivery …*Keep the presentation
of the dish simple*…
4 = <u>performance</u>, staging, production, show,
arrangement, representation, portrayal, rendition
…*Scottish Opera's presentation of Das Rheingold*…

present-day = <u>current</u>, modern, present, recent,
contemporary, up-to-date, latter-day, newfangled

presently 1 = <u>at present</u>, currently, now, today, these
days, nowadays, at the present time, in this day and
age, at the minute (*Brit. informal*) …*The island is
presently uninhabited*…
2 = <u>soon</u>, shortly, directly, before long, momentarily
(*U.S. & Canad.*), in a moment, in a minute, pretty soon
(*informal*), anon (*archaic*), by and by, in a short while,
in a jiffy (*informal*), erelong (*archaic or poetic*) …*Just
take it easy and you'll feel better presently*…

preservation 1 = <u>upholding</u>, keeping, support,
security, defence, maintenance, perpetuation …*the
preservation of the status quo*…
2 = <u>protection</u>, safety, maintenance, conservation,
salvation, safeguarding, safekeeping …*the
preservation of buildings of historic interest*…
3 = <u>storage</u>, smoking, drying, bottling, freezing,
curing, chilling, candying, pickling, conserving, tinning
…*the preparation, cooking and preservation of food*…

preserve VERB 1 = <u>maintain</u>, keep, continue, retain,
sustain, keep up, prolong, uphold, conserve,
perpetuate, keep alive …*We will do everything we can
to preserve peace*… OPPOSITE end
2 = <u>protect</u>, keep, save, maintain, guard, defend,
secure, shelter, shield, care for, safeguard, conserve
…*We need to preserve the rainforests*… OPPOSITE
attack
3 = <u>keep</u>, save, store, can, dry, bottle, salt, cure, candy,
pickle, conserve …*ginger preserved in syrup*…
NOUN 1 *often plural* = <u>jam</u>, jelly, conserve, marmalade,
confection, sweetmeat, confiture …*jars of pear and
blackberry preserves*…
2 = <u>area</u>, department, field, territory, province, arena,
orbit, sphere, realm, domain, specialism …*The
conduct of foreign policy is largely the preserve of the
president*…
3 = <u>reserve</u>, reservation, sanctuary, game reserve
…*one of the world's great wildlife preserves*…

preside VERB = <u>officiate</u>, chair, moderate, be
chairperson …*He presided at the closing ceremony*…
PHRASES **preside over something** *or* **someone**
= <u>run</u>, lead, head, control, manage, direct, conduct,
govern, administer, supervise, be at the head of, be in
authority …*The question of who should preside over
the next full commission was being debated*…

president
► WORD POWER SUPPLEMENT Presidents

press VERB 1 = <u>push (down)</u>, depress, lean on, bear
down, press down, force down …*her hands pressing
down on the desk*… …*He pressed a button and the
door closed*…
2 = <u>push</u>, squeeze, jam, thrust, ram, wedge, shove
…*He pressed his back against the door*…
3 = <u>hug</u>, squeeze, embrace, clasp, crush, encircle,
enfold, hold close, fold in your arms …*I pressed my
child closer to my heart and shut my eyes*…
4 = <u>urge</u>, force, beg, petition, sue, enforce, insist on,
compel, constrain, exhort, implore, enjoin, pressurize,
entreat, importune, supplicate …*The trade unions are
pressing him to stand firm*…
5 = <u>plead</u>, present, lodge, submit, tender, advance
insistently …*mass strikes and demonstrations to press
their demands*…
6 = <u>steam</u>, finish, iron, smooth, flatten, put the creases
in …*Vera pressed his shirt*…
7 = <u>compress</u>, grind, reduce, mill, crush, pound,
squeeze, tread, pulp, mash, trample, condense,
pulverize, tamp, macerate …*The grapes are hand-
picked and pressed*…
8 = <u>crowd</u>, push, gather, rush, surge, mill, hurry,
cluster, flock, herd, swarm, hasten, seethe, throng …*As
the music stopped, the crowd pressed forward*…
PHRASES **be pressed for** = <u>be short of</u>, be pushed
for, be hard put to, have too little …*I'm pressed for
time right now*… ♦ **the press** 1 = <u>newspapers</u>, the
papers, journalism, news media, Fleet Street, fourth
estate …*Today the British press is full of articles on the
subject*… 2 = <u>journalists</u>, correspondents, reporters,
photographers, columnists, pressmen, newsmen,
journos (*slang*), gentlemen of the press …*He looked
relaxed and calm as he faced the press*…

pressing = <u>urgent</u>, serious, burning, vital, crucial,
imperative, important, constraining, high-priority,
now or never, importunate, exigent OPPOSITE
unimportant

pressure 1 = <u>force</u>, crushing, squeezing,
compressing, weight, compression, heaviness …*The
pressure of his fingers had relaxed*…
2 = <u>power</u>, influence, force, obligation, constraint,
sway, compulsion, coercion …*He may be putting
pressure on her to agree*…
3 = <u>stress</u>, demands, difficulty, strain, press, heat, load,
burden, distress, hurry, urgency, hassle (*informal*),
uphill (*S. African*), adversity, affliction, exigency …*The
pressures of modern life are great*…

pressurize = <u>force</u>, drive, compel, intimidate, coerce,
dragoon, breathe down someone's neck, browbeat,
press-gang, twist someone's arm (*informal*), turn on
the heat (*informal*), put the screws on (*slang*)

prestige = <u>status</u>, standing, authority, influence,
credit, regard, weight, reputation, honour,
importance, fame, celebrity, distinction, esteem,
stature, eminence, kudos, cachet, renown, Brownie
points, mana (*N.Z.*)

prestigious = <u>celebrated</u>, respected, prominent,
great, important, imposing, impressive, influential,

esteemed, notable, renowned, eminent, illustrious, reputable, exalted OPPOSITE unknown

presumably = it would seem, probably, likely, apparently, most likely, seemingly, doubtless, on the face of it, in all probability, in all likelihood, doubtlessly

presume VERB 1 = believe, think, suppose, assume, guess (*informal, chiefly U.S. & Canad.*), take it, take for granted, infer, conjecture, postulate, surmise, posit, presuppose ...*I presume you're here on business...*
2 = dare, venture, undertake, go so far as, have the audacity, take the liberty, make bold, make so bold as ...*I wouldn't presume to question your judgement...*
PHRASES **presume on something** or **someone** = depend on, rely on, exploit, take advantage of, count on, bank on, take liberties with, trust in *or* to ...*He's presuming on your good nature...*

presumption 1 = assumption, opinion, belief, guess, hypothesis, anticipation, conjecture, surmise, supposition, presupposition, premiss ...*the presumption that a defendant is innocent until proved guilty...*
2 = cheek (*informal*), front, neck (*informal*), nerve (*Informal*), assurance, brass (*Informal*), gall (*informal*), audacity, boldness, temerity, chutzpah (*U.S. & Canad. informal*), insolence, impudence, effrontery, brass neck (*Brit. informal*), sassiness (*U.S. informal*), presumptuousness, forwardness ...*He had the presumption to answer me back...*

presumptuous = pushy (*informal*), forward, bold, arrogant, presuming, rash, audacious, conceited, foolhardy, insolent, overweening, overconfident, overfamiliar, bigheaded (*informal*), uppish (*Brit. informal*), too big for your boots OPPOSITE shy

presuppose = presume, consider, accept, suppose, assume, take it, imply, take for granted, postulate, posit, take as read

presupposition = assumption, theory, belief, premise, hypothesis, presumption, preconception, supposition, preconceived idea

pretence 1 = deception, invention, sham, fabrication, acting, faking, simulation, deceit, feigning, charade, make-believe, trickery, falsehood, subterfuge, fakery ...*struggling to keep up the*

pretence that all was well... OPPOSITE candour
2 = show, posturing, artifice, affectation, display, appearance, posing, façade, veneer, pretentiousness, hokum (*slang, chiefly U.S. & Canad.*) ...*She was completely without guile or pretence...* OPPOSITE reality
3 = pretext, claim, excuse, show, cover, mask, veil, cloak, guise, façade, masquerade, semblance, ruse, garb, wile ...*He claimed the police beat him up under the pretence that he was resisting arrest...*

pretend 1 = feign, affect, assume, allege, put on, fake, make out, simulate, profess, sham, counterfeit, falsify, impersonate, dissemble, dissimulate, pass yourself off as ...*He pretended to be asleep...*
2 = make believe, suppose, imagine, play, act, make up, play the part of ...*She can sunbathe and pretend she's in Spain... ...The children pretended to be animals...*
3 = lay claim, claim, allege, aspire, profess, purport ...*I cannot pretend to understand the problem...*

pretended = feigned, alleged, so-called, phoney *or* phony (*informal*), false, pretend (*informal*), fake, imaginary, bogus, professed, sham, purported, pseudo (*informal*), counterfeit, spurious, fictitious, avowed, ostensible

pretender = claimant, claimer, aspirant

pretension 1 = affectation, hypocrisy, conceit, show, airs, vanity, snobbery, pomposity, self-importance, ostentation, pretentiousness, snobbishness, vainglory, showiness ...*We liked him for his honesty and lack of pretension...*
2 *usually plural* = aspiration, claim, demand, profession, assumption, assertion, pretence ...*one of the few fashion designers who does not have pretensions to be an artist...*

pretentious = affected, mannered, exaggerated, pompous, assuming, hollow, inflated, extravagant, high-flown, flaunting, grandiose, conceited, showy, ostentatious, snobbish, puffed up, bombastic, specious, grandiloquent, vainglorious, high-sounding, highfalutin (*informal*), overambitious, arty-farty (*informal*), magniloquent OPPOSITE unpretentious

pretext = guise, excuse, veil, show, cover, appearance, device, mask, ploy, cloak, simulation, pretence,

---

Birds of prey

accipiter	eagle-hawk *or* wedge-	kestrel	owl
Australian goshawk *or*	tailed eagle	kite	peregrine falcon
chicken hawk	falcon	lammergeier,	red kite *or* (*archaic*)
bald eagle	falconet	lammergeyer, bearded	gled(e)
barn owl	golden eagle	vulture, *or* (*archaic*)	rough-legged buzzard
bateleur eagle	goshawk	ossifrage	saker
boobook	gyrfalcon *or* gerfalcon	lanner	screech owl
brown owl	harrier	little owl	sea eagle, erne, *or* ern
buzzard	hawk	long-eared owl	secretary bird
caracara	hawk owl	merlin	snowy owl
condor	hobby	Montagu's harrier	sparrowhawk
Cooper's hawk	honey buzzard	mopoke *or* (*N.Z.*) ruru	tawny owl
duck hawk	hoot owl	osprey, fish eagle, *or*	turkey buzzard *or*
eagle	horned owl	(*archaic*) ossifrage	vulture

semblance, ruse, red herring, alleged reason

pretty ADJECTIVE **1** = <u>attractive</u>, appealing, beautiful, sweet, lovely, charming, fair, fetching, good-looking, cute, graceful, bonny, personable, comely, prepossessing …*She's a charming and pretty girl…* OPPOSITE⟩ plain

2 = <u>pleasant</u>, fine, pleasing, nice, elegant, trim, delicate, neat, tasteful, dainty, bijou …*comfortable sofas covered in a pretty floral print…*
ADVERB (*Informal*) = <u>fairly</u>, rather, quite, kind of (*informal*), somewhat, moderately, reasonably …*I had a pretty good idea what she was going to do…*

prevail VERB **1** = <u>win</u>, succeed, triumph, overcome, overrule, be victorious, carry the day, prove superior, gain mastery …*We hoped that common sense would prevail…*

2 = <u>be widespread</u>, abound, predominate, be current, be prevalent, preponderate, exist generally …*A similar situation prevails in America…*
PHRASES **prevail on** *or* **upon someone** = <u>persuade</u>, influence, convince, prompt, win over, induce, incline, dispose, sway, talk into, bring round …*Do you think she can be prevailed upon to do it?…*

prevailing 1 = <u>widespread</u>, general, established, popular, common, set, current, usual, ordinary, fashionable, in style, customary, prevalent, in vogue …*individuals who have gone against the prevailing opinion…*

2 = <u>predominating</u>, ruling, main, existing, principal …*the prevailing weather conditions in the area…*

prevalence = <u>commonness</u>, frequency, regularity, currency, universality, ubiquity, common occurrence, pervasiveness, extensiveness, widespread presence, rampancy, rifeness

prevalent = <u>common</u>, accepted, established, popular, general, current, usual, widespread, extensive, universal, frequent, everyday, rampant, customary, commonplace, ubiquitous, rife, habitual OPPOSITE⟩ rare

prevent = <u>stop</u>, avoid, frustrate, restrain, check, bar, block, anticipate, hamper, foil, inhibit, head off, avert, thwart, intercept, hinder, obstruct, preclude, impede, counteract, ward off, balk, stave off, forestall, defend against, obviate, nip in the bud …*These methods prevent pregnancy… …We took steps to prevent it happening…* OPPOSITE⟩ help

prevention = <u>elimination</u>, safeguard, precaution, anticipation, thwarting, avoidance, deterrence, forestalling, prophylaxis, preclusion, obviation

preventive *or* **preventative 1** = <u>precautionary</u>, protective, hampering, hindering, deterrent, impeding, pre-emptive, obstructive, inhibitory …*They accused the police of failing to take adequate preventive measures…*

2 = <u>prophylactic</u>, protective, precautionary, counteractive …*preventive medicine…*

> ## *Word Power*
>
> **preventive** – In all contexts, *preventive* is commoner than, and generally used in preference to, *preventative*.

preview NOUN = <u>sample</u>, sneak preview, trailer, sampler, taster, foretaste, advance showing …*He had gone to see a preview of the play…*
VERB = <u>sample</u>, taste, give a foretaste of …*We preview this season's collections from Paris…*

previous 1 = <u>earlier</u>, former, past, prior, one-time, preceding, sometime, erstwhile, antecedent, anterior, quondam, ex- …*He had a daughter from a previous marriage…* OPPOSITE⟩ later

2 = <u>preceding</u>, past, prior, foregoing …*He recalled what Bob had told him the previous night…*

previously = <u>before</u>, earlier, once, in the past, formerly, back then, until now, at one time, hitherto, beforehand, a while ago, heretofore, in days *or* years gone by

prey NOUN **1** = <u>quarry</u>, game, kill …*These animals were the prey of hyenas…*

2 = <u>victim</u>, target, mark, mug (*Brit. slang*), dupe, fall guy (*informal*) …*Old people are easy prey for con men…*
PHRASES **prey on something** *or* **someone 1** = <u>hunt</u>, live off, eat, seize, devour, feed upon …*The larvae prey on small aphids…* **2** = <u>victimize</u>, bully, intimidate, exploit, take advantage of, bleed (*informal*), blackmail, terrorize …*unscrupulous men who preyed on young runaways…* **3** = <u>worry</u>, trouble, burden, distress, haunt, hang over, oppress, weigh down, weigh heavily …*This was the question that preyed on his mind…*
➤ **birds of prey**

price NOUN **1** = <u>cost</u>, value, rate, charge, bill, figure, worth, damage (*informal*), amount, estimate, fee, payment, expense, assessment, expenditure, valuation, face value, outlay, asking price …*a sharp increase in the price of petrol… …What's the price on that one?…*

2 = <u>consequences</u>, penalty, cost, result, sacrifice, toll, forfeit …*He's paying the price for pushing his body so hard…*

3 = <u>reward</u>, bounty, compensation, premium, recompense …*He is still at large despite the high price on his head…*
VERB = <u>evaluate</u>, value, estimate, rate, cost, assess, put a price on …*The shares are priced at 330p…*
PHRASES **at any price** = <u>whatever the cost</u>, regardless, no matter what the cost, anyhow, cost what it may, expense no object …*We want the hostages home at any price…* ◆ **beyond price** = <u>priceless</u>, treasured, precious, invaluable, inestimable, without price, of incalculable value …*a treasure that was beyond price…*

priceless = <u>valuable</u>, expensive, precious, invaluable, rich, prized, dear, rare, treasured, costly, cherished, incomparable, irreplaceable, incalculable, inestimable, beyond price, worth a king's ransom, worth your *or* its weight in gold OPPOSITE▷ worthless

pricey *or* **pricy** = <u>expensive</u>, dear, steep (*informal*), costly, high-priced, exorbitant, over the odds (*Brit. informal*), extortionate

prick VERB 1 = <u>pierce</u>, stab, puncture, bore, pink, punch, lance, jab, perforate, impale ...*She pricked her finger with a needle...*
2 = <u>move</u>, trouble, touch, pain, wound, distress, grieve ...*Most were sympathetic once we had pricked their consciences...*
NOUN 1 = <u>pang</u>, smart, sting, spasm, gnawing, twinge, prickle ...*She felt a prick on the back of her neck...*
2 = <u>puncture</u>, cut, hole, wound, gash, perforation, pinhole ...*a tiny hole no bigger than a pin prick...*
PHRASES **prick up** = <u>raise</u>, point, rise, stand erect ...*The dog's ears pricked up at the sound...*

prickle VERB 1 = <u>tingle</u>, smart, sting, twitch, itch ...*His scalp prickled under his wig...*
2 = <u>prick</u>, stick into, nick, jab ...*The pine needles prickled her skin...*
NOUN 1 = <u>tingling</u>, smart, chill, tickle, tingle, pins and needles (*informal*), goose bumps, goose flesh ...*a prickle at the nape of my neck reminds me of my fears...*
2 = <u>spike</u>, point, spur, needle, spine, thorn, barb ...*an erect stem covered at the base with prickles...*

prickly 1 = <u>spiny</u>, barbed, thorny, bristly, brambly, briery ...*The grass was prickly and damp...*
2 = <u>itchy</u>, sharp, smarting, stinging, crawling, pricking, tingling, scratchy, prickling ...*a hot prickly feeling at the back of her eyes...*
3 = <u>irritable</u>, edgy, grumpy, touchy, bad-tempered, fractious, petulant, stroppy (*Brit. slang*), cantankerous, tetchy, ratty (*Brit. & N.Z. informal*), waspish, shirty (*slang, chiefly Brit.*), peevish, snappish, liverish, pettish ...*You know how prickly she can be...*
4 = <u>difficult</u>, complicated, tricky, trying, involved, intricate, troublesome, thorny, knotty, ticklish ...*The issue is likely to prove a prickly one...*

pride NOUN 1 = <u>satisfaction</u>, achievement, fulfilment, delight, content, pleasure, joy, gratification ...*the sense of pride in a job well done...*
2 = <u>self-respect</u>, honour, ego, dignity, self-esteem, self-image, self-worth, amour-propre (*French*) ...*Her rejection was a severe blow to his pride...*
3 = <u>conceit</u>, vanity, arrogance, pretension, presumption, snobbery, morgue (*French*), hubris, smugness, self-importance, egotism, self-love, hauteur, pretentiousness, haughtiness, loftiness, vainglory, superciliousness, bigheadedness (*informal*) ...*His pride may still be his downfall...* OPPOSITE▷ humility
4 = <u>elite</u>, pick, best, choice, flower, prize, cream, glory, boast, treasure, jewel, gem, pride and joy ...*This glittering dress is the pride of her collection...*
PHRASES **pride yourself on something** = <u>be proud of</u>, revel in, boast of, glory in, vaunt, take pride in, brag about, crow about, exult in, congratulate yourself on, flatter yourself, pique yourself, plume yourself ...*He prides himself on being able to organise his own life...*

priest = <u>clergyman</u>, minister, father, divine, vicar, pastor, cleric, curate, churchman, padre (*informal*), holy man, man of God, man of the cloth, ecclesiastic, father confessor

priestly = <u>ecclesiastic</u>, pastoral, clerical, canonical, hieratic, sacerdotal, priestlike

prim = <u>prudish</u>, particular, formal, proper, precise, stiff, fussy, fastidious, puritanical, demure, starchy (*informal*), prissy (*informal*), strait-laced, priggish, schoolmarmish (*Brit. informal*), old-maidish (*informal*), niminy-piminy OPPOSITE▷ liberal

primacy = <u>supremacy</u>, leadership, command, dominance, superiority, dominion, ascendancy, pre-eminence

prima donna = <u>diva</u>, star, leading lady, female lead

primal 1 = <u>basic</u>, prime, central, first, highest, greatest, major, chief, main, most important, principal, paramount ...*the most primal of human fears...*
2 = <u>earliest</u>, prime, original, primary, first, initial, primitive, pristine, primordial ...*Yeats's remarks about folklore and the primal religion...*

primarily 1 = <u>chiefly</u>, largely, generally, mainly, especially, essentially, mostly, basically, principally, fundamentally, above all, on the whole, for the most part ...*Public order is primarily an urban problem...*
2 = <u>at first</u>, originally, initially, in the first place, in the beginning, first and foremost, at *or* from the start ...*These machines were primarily intended for use in editing...*

primary 1 = <u>chief</u>, leading, main, best, first, highest, greatest, top, prime, capital, principal, dominant, cardinal, paramount ...*His primary aim in life is to be happy...* OPPOSITE▷ subordinate
2 = <u>basic</u>, essential, radical, fundamental, ultimate, underlying, elemental, bog-standard (*informal*) ...*our primary needs of air, food and water...*
3 = <u>major</u>, chief, main, principal, key, foremost ...*the primary cause of the disease...* OPPOSITE▷ secondary

primate
➤ **monkeys, apes and other primates**

prime ADJECTIVE 1 = <u>main</u>, leading, chief, central, major, ruling, key, senior, primary, supreme, principal, ultimate, cardinal, paramount, overriding, foremost, predominant, pre-eminent, number-one (*informal*) ...*Political stability is a prime concern...*
2 = <u>best</u>, top, select, highest, capital, quality, choice, selected, excellent, superior, first-class, first-rate, grade-A ...*It was one of the City's prime locations...*
3 = <u>fundamental</u>, original, basic, primary, underlying ...*A prime cause of deforestation was the burning of charcoal to melt ore into iron...*
NOUN = <u>peak</u>, flower, bloom, maturity, height, perfection, best days, heyday, zenith, full flowering ...*She was in her intellectual prime...*
VERB 1 = <u>inform</u>, tell, train, coach, brief, fill in (*informal*), groom (*informal*), notify, clue in (*informal*), gen up (*Brit. informal*), give someone the lowdown, clue up (*informal*) ...*The press corps has been primed to avoid this topic...*
2 = <u>prepare</u>, set up, load, equip, get ready, make ready

…They had primed the bomb to go off in an hour's time…

prime minister

➤ WORD POWER SUPPLEMENT prime ministers

primeval *or* **primaeval** 1 = earliest, old, original, ancient, primitive, first, early, pristine, primal, prehistoric, primordial *…a vast expanse of primeval swamp…*

2 = primal, primitive, natural, basic, inherited, inherent, hereditary, instinctive, innate, congenital, primordial, inborn, inbred *…a primeval urge…*

primitive 1 = uncivilized, savage, barbarian, barbaric, undeveloped, uncultivated *…studies of primitive societies…* OPPOSITE civilized

2 = early, first, earliest, original, primary, elementary, pristine, primordial, primeval *…primitive birds from the dinosaur era…* OPPOSITE modern

3 = simple, naive, childlike, untrained, undeveloped, unsophisticated, untutored *…primitive art…* OPPOSITE sophisticated

4 = crude, simple, rough, rude, rudimentary, unrefined *…primitive tools…* OPPOSITE elaborate

primordial 1 = primeval, primitive, first, earliest, pristine, primal, prehistoric *…Twenty million years ago this was dense primordial forest…*

2 = fundamental, original, basic, radical, elemental *…primordial particles generated by the Big Bang…*

prince = ruler, lord, monarch, sovereign, crown prince, liege, potentate, prince regent, crowned head, dynast

princely 1 = substantial, considerable, goodly, large, huge, massive, enormous, tidy (*informal*), whopping (great) (*informal*), sizable *or* sizeable *…It cost them the princely sum of seventy-five pounds…*

2 = regal, royal, imposing, magnificent, august, grand, imperial, noble, sovereign, majestic, dignified, stately, lofty, high-born *…the embodiment of princely magnificence…*

princess = ruler, lady, monarch, sovereign, liege, crowned head, crowned princess, dynast, princess regent

principal ADJECTIVE = main, leading, chief, prime, first, highest, controlling, strongest, capital, key, essential, primary, most important, dominant, arch, cardinal, paramount, foremost, pre-eminent *…their principal concern is that of winning the next election…* OPPOSITE minor

NOUN 1 = headmaster *or* headmistress, head (*informal*), director, dean, head teacher, rector, master *or* mistress *…the principal of the local high school…*

2 = boss, head, leader, director, chief (*informal*), master, ruler, superintendent, baas (*S. African*) *…the principal of the company…*

3 = star, lead, leader, prima ballerina, first violin, leading man *or* lady, coryphée *…soloists and principals of The Scottish Ballet orchestra…*

4 = capital, money, assets, working capital, capital funds *…Use the higher premiums to pay the interest and principal on the debt…*

➤ principle

principally = mainly, largely, chiefly, especially, particularly, mostly, primarily, above all, predominantly, in the main, for the most part, first and foremost

principle NOUN 1 = morals, standards, ideals, honour, virtue, ethics, integrity, conscience, morality, decency, scruples, probity, rectitude, moral standards, sense of duty, moral law, sense of honour, uprightness *…He would never compromise his principles… …They had great trust in him as a man of principle…*

2 = belief, rule, standard, attitude, code, notion, criterion, ethic, doctrine, canon, creed, maxim, dogma, tenet, dictum, credo, axiom *…a violation of the basic principles of Marxism…*

3 = rule, idea, law, theory, basis, truth, concept, formula, fundamental, assumption, essence, proposition, verity, golden rule, precept *…the principles of quantum theory…*

PHRASES **in principle** 1 = in general, generally, all things considered, on the whole, in the main, by and large, in essence, all in all, on balance *…I agree with this plan in principle…* 2 = in theory, ideally, on paper, theoretically, in an ideal world, en principe (*French*) *…In principle, it should be possible…*

> ## *Word Power*
>
> **principle** – *Principle* and *principal* are often confused: *the principal* (not *principle*) *reason for his departure; the plan was approved in principle* (not *principal*).

principled = moral, ethical, upright, honourable, just, correct, decent, righteous, conscientious, virtuous, scrupulous, right-minded, high-minded

print VERB 1 = run off, publish, copy, reproduce, issue, engrave, go to press, put to bed (*informal*) *…It costs far less to press a CD than to print a book…*

2 = publish, release, circulate, issue, disseminate *…a questionnaire printed in the magazine…*

3 = mark, impress, stamp, imprint *…printed with a paisley pattern…*

NOUN 1 = photograph, photo, snap *…a black and white print of the children…*

2 = picture, plate, etching, engraving, lithograph, woodcut, linocut *…Hogarth's famous series of prints…*

3 = copy, photo (*informal*), picture, reproduction, replica *…There was a huge print of 'Dejeuner Sur l'Herbe' on the wall…*

4 = type, lettering, letters, characters, face, font (*chiefly U.S.*), fount, typeface *…columns of tiny print…*

PHRASES **in print** 1 = published, printed, on the streets, on paper, in black and white, out *…the appearance of his poems in print…* 2 = available, current, on the market, in the shops, on the shelves, obtainable *…The book has been in print for over 40 years…* ◆ **out of print** = unavailable, unobtainable, no longer published, o.p. *…The book is now out of print, but can be found in libraries…*

prior ADJECTIVE = earlier, previous, former, preceding, foregoing, antecedent, aforementioned, pre-existing, anterior, pre-existent …*He claimed he had no prior knowledge of the protest…*

PHRASES **prior to** = before, preceding, earlier than, in advance of, previous to …*A man was seen in the area prior to the shooting…*

priority 1 = prime concern, first concern, primary issue, most pressing matter …*The government's priority should be better health care…*

2 = precedence, preference, greater importance, primacy, predominance …*The school gives priority to science and maths…*

3 = supremacy, rank, the lead, superiority, precedence, prerogative, seniority, right of way, pre-eminence …*the premise that economic development has priority over the environment…*

priory = monastery, abbey, convent, cloister, nunnery, religious house

prise
> prize³

prison = jail, confinement, can (*slang*), pound, nick (*Brit. slang*), stir (*slang*), cooler (*slang*), jug (*slang*), dungeon, clink (*slang*), glasshouse (*Military informal*), gaol, penitentiary (*U.S.*), slammer (*slang*), lockup, quod (*slang*), penal institution, calaboose (*U.S. informal*), choky (*slang*), poky or pokey (*U.S. & Canad. slang*), boob (*Austral. slang*)

prisoner 1 = convict, con (*slang*), lag (*slang*), jailbird …*the large number of prisoners sharing cells…*

2 = captive, hostage, detainee, internee …*wartime hostages and concentration-camp prisoners…*

prissy = prim, precious, fussy, fastidious, squeamish, prudish, finicky, strait-laced, schoolmarmish (*Brit. informal*), old-maidish (*informal*), niminy-piminy, overnice, prim and proper

pristine = new, pure, virgin, immaculate, untouched, unspoiled, virginal, unsullied, uncorrupted, undefiled

---

Word Power

pristine – The use of *pristine* to mean 'fresh, clean, and unspoiled' used to be considered incorrect by some people, but it is now generally accepted.

---

privacy = seclusion, isolation, solitude, retirement, retreat, separateness, sequestration, privateness

private **ADJECTIVE** 1 = nonpublic, independent, commercial, privatised, private-enterprise, denationalized …*a joint venture with private industry…*

2 = exclusive, individual, privately owned, own, special, particular, reserved …*He has had to sell his private plane…* **OPPOSITE** public

3 = secret, confidential, covert, inside, closet, unofficial, privy (*archaic*), clandestine, off the record, hush-hush (*informal*), in camera …*He held a private meeting with the country's political party leaders…* **OPPOSITE** public

4 = personal, individual, secret, intimate, undisclosed, unspoken, innermost, unvoiced …*I've always kept my private and professional life separate… …He hardly*

ever betrayed his private thoughts…*

5 = secluded, secret, separate, isolated, concealed, retired, sequestered, not overlooked …*It was the only reasonably private place they could find to talk…* **OPPOSITE** busy

6 = solitary, reserved, retiring, withdrawn, discreet, secretive, self-contained, reclusive, reticent, insular, introvert, uncommunicative …*Gould was an intensely private individual…* **OPPOSITE** sociable

NOUN = enlisted man (*U.S.*), tommy (*Brit. informal*), private soldier, Tommy Atkins (*Brit. informal*), squaddie or squaddy (*Brit. slang*) …*The rest of the gunners in the battery were privates…*

PHRASES **in private** = in secret, privately, personally, behind closed doors, in camera, between ourselves, confidentially …*I think we should discuss this in private…*

privation (*Formal*) = want, poverty, need, suffering, loss, lack, distress, misery, necessity, hardship, penury, destitution, neediness, indigence

privilege = right, benefit, due, advantage, claim, freedom, sanction, liberty, concession, franchise, entitlement, prerogative, birthright

privileged 1 = special, powerful, advantaged, favoured, ruling, honoured, entitled, elite, indulged …*They were a wealthy and privileged elite…*

2 = confidential, special, inside, exceptional, privy, off the record, not for publication …*This data is privileged information…*

privy **NOUN** (*Obsolete*) = lavatory, closet, bog (*slang*), latrine, outside toilet, earth closet, pissoir (*French*), bogger (*Austral. slang*), brasco (*Austral. slang*) …*an outside privy…*

ADJECTIVE with **to** = informed of, aware of, in on, wise to (*slang*), hip to (*slang*), in the loop, apprised of, cognizant of, in the know about (*informal*) …*Only three people were privy to the facts…*

prize¹ **NOUN** 1 = reward, cup, award, honour, premium, medal, trophy, accolade …*He won a prize in the Leeds Piano Competition…*

2 = winnings, haul, jackpot, stakes, purse, windfall …*A single winner is in line for a jackpot prize of £8 million…*

3 = goal, hope, gain, aim, desire, ambition, conquest, Holy Grail (*informal*) …*A settlement of the dispute would be a great prize…*

ADJECTIVE = champion, best, winning, top, outstanding, award-winning, first-rate, top-notch (*informal*) …*a prize bull…*

prize² = value, appreciate, treasure, esteem, cherish, hold dear, regard highly, set store by …*Those items are greatly prized by collectors…*

prize³ or **prise** 1 = force, pull, lever …*He tried to prize the dog's jaws open…*

2 = drag, force, draw, wring, extort …*We had to prize the story out of him…*

probability 1 = likelihood, prospect, chance, odds, expectation, liability, presumption, likeliness …*There is a high probability of success…*

2 = chance, odds, possibility, likelihood …*the probability of life on other planets…*

probable = <u>likely</u>, possible, apparent, reasonable to think, most likely, presumed, credible, plausible, feasible, odds-on, on the cards, presumable OPPOSITE unlikely

probably = <u>likely</u>, perhaps, maybe, possibly, presumably, most likely, doubtless, in all probability, in all likelihood, perchance (*archaic*), as likely as not

probation = <u>trial period</u>, test, trial, examination, apprenticeship, initiation, novitiate

probe VERB 1 *often with into* = <u>examine</u>, research, go into, investigate, explore, test, sound, search, look into, query, verify, sift, analyze, dissect, delve into, work over, scrutinize ...*The more they probed into his background, the more suspicious they became...* 2 = <u>explore</u>, examine, poke, prod, feel around ...*A doctor probed deep in his shoulder wound for shrapnel...* NOUN = <u>investigation</u>, study, research, inquiry, analysis, examination, exploration, scrutiny, inquest, scrutinization ...*a federal grand-jury probe into corruption within the FDA...*

probity (*Formal*) = <u>integrity</u>, worth, justice, honour, equity, virtue, goodness, morality, honesty, fairness, fidelity, sincerity, righteousness, rectitude, truthfulness, trustworthiness, uprightness

problem NOUN 1 = <u>difficulty</u>, trouble, dispute, plight, obstacle, dilemma, headache (*informal*), disagreement, complication, predicament, quandary ...*the economic problems of the inner city...* 2 = <u>puzzle</u>, question, riddle, enigma, conundrum, teaser, poser, brain-teaser (*informal*) ...*a mathematical problem...* ADJECTIVE = <u>difficult</u>, disturbed, troublesome, unruly, delinquent, uncontrollable, intractable, recalcitrant, intransigent, unmanageable, disobedient, ungovernable, refractory, maladjusted ...*Sometimes a problem child is placed in a special school...*

problematic = <u>tricky</u>, puzzling, uncertain, doubtful, dubious, unsettled, questionable, enigmatic, debatable, moot, problematical, chancy (*informal*), open to doubt OPPOSITE clear

procedure = <u>method</u>, policy, process, course, system, form, action, step, performance, operation, practice, scheme, strategy, conduct, formula, custom, routine, transaction, plan of action, modus operandi

proceed 1 = <u>begin</u>, go ahead, get going, make a start, get under way, set something in motion ...*I had no idea how to proceed...* 2 = <u>continue</u>, go on, progress, carry on, go ahead, get on, press on ...*The defence is not yet ready to proceed with the trial...* OPPOSITE discontinue 3 = <u>go on</u>, continue, advance, progress, carry on, go ahead, move on, move forward, press on, push on, make your way ...*She proceeded along the hallway...* OPPOSITE stop 4 = <u>arise</u>, come, follow, issue, result, spring, flow, stem, derive, originate, ensue, emanate ...*Does Othello's downfall proceed from a flaw in his character?...*

proceeding = <u>action</u>, process, procedure, move, act, step, measure, venture, undertaking, deed,

occurrence, course of action

proceeds = <u>income</u>, profit, revenue, returns, produce, products, gain, earnings, yield, receipts, takings

process NOUN 1 = <u>procedure</u>, means, course, system, action, performance, operation, measure, proceeding, manner, transaction, mode, course of action ...*The best way to find out is by a process of elimination...* 2 = <u>development</u>, growth, progress, course, stage, step, movement, advance, formation, evolution, unfolding, progression ...*the evolutionary process of Homo sapiens...* 3 = <u>method</u>, system, practice, technique, procedure ...*the cost of the production process...* 4 (*Law*) = <u>action</u>, case, trial, suit ...*steps in the impeachment process against the president...* VERB 1 = <u>prepare</u>, treat, convert, transform, alter, refine ...*silicon chips process electrical signals...* ...*facilities to process the beans before export...* 2 = <u>handle</u>, manage, action, deal with, fulfil, take care of, dispose of ...*A number of applications are being processed at the moment...*

procession 1 = <u>parade</u>, train, march, file, column, motorcade, cavalcade, cortege ...*a funeral procession...* 2 = <u>sequence</u>, run, course, train, series, cycle, string, succession ...*a seemingly endless procession of corruption cases...*

proclaim 1 = <u>announce</u>, declare, advertise, show, publish, indicate, blaze (abroad), herald, circulate, trumpet, affirm, give out, profess, promulgate, make known, enunciate, blazon (abroad), shout from the housetops (*informal*) ...*He continues to proclaim his innocence...* OPPOSITE keep secret 2 = <u>pronounce</u>, announce, declare ...*He launched a coup and proclaimed himself president...*

proclamation 1 = <u>declaration</u>, notice, announcement, decree, manifesto, edict, pronouncement, pronunciamento ...*A formal proclamation of independence was issued eight days ago...* 2 = <u>publishing</u>, broadcasting, announcement, publication, declaration, notification, pronouncement, promulgation ...*his proclamation of the good news...*

proclivity (*Formal*) = <u>tendency</u>, liking, leaning, inclination, bent, weakness, bias, disposition, penchant, propensity, kink, predisposition, predilection, partiality, proneness, liableness

procrastinate = <u>delay</u>, stall, postpone, prolong, put off, defer, adjourn, retard, dally, play for time, gain time, temporize, play a waiting game, protract, drag your feet (*informal*), be dilatory OPPOSITE hurry (up)

procrastination = <u>delay</u>, hesitation, slowness, slackness, dilatoriness, temporization *or* temporisation

procure = <u>obtain</u>, get, find, buy, win, land, score (*slang*), gain, earn, pick up, purchase, secure, appropriate, acquire, manage to get, get hold of, come by, lay hands on

prod `VERB` 1 = <u>poke</u>, push, dig, shove, propel, nudge, jab, prick ...*He prodded Murray with the shotgun...*
2 = <u>prompt</u>, move, urge, motivate, spur, stimulate, rouse, stir up, incite, egg on, goad, impel, put a bomb under (*informal*) ...*a tactic to prod the government into spending more on the Health Service...*
`NOUN` 1 = <u>poke</u>, push, boost, dig, elbow, shove, nudge, jab ...*He gave the donkey a prod in the backside...*
2 = <u>prompt</u>, boost, signal, cue, reminder, stimulus ...*She won't do it without a prod from you...*
3 = <u>goad</u>, stick, spur, poker ...*a cattle prod...*

prodigal 1 = <u>extravagant</u>, excessive, reckless, squandering, wasteful, wanton, profligate, spendthrift, intemperate, immoderate, improvident ...*his prodigal habits...* `OPPOSITE` thrifty
2 *often with* **of** = <u>lavish</u>, bountiful, unstinting, unsparing, bounteous, profuse with ...*You are prodigal of both your toil and your talent...* `OPPOSITE` generous

prodigious 1 – <u>huge</u>, giant, massive, vast, enormous, tremendous, immense, gigantic, monumental, monstrous, mammoth, colossal, stellar (*informal*), stupendous, inordinate, immeasurable ...*This business generates cash in prodigious amounts...* `OPPOSITE` tiny
2 = <u>wonderful</u>, striking, amazing, unusual, dramatic, impressive, extraordinary, remarkable, fantastic (*informal*), fabulous, staggering, marvellous, startling, exceptional, abnormal, phenomenal, astounding, miraculous, stupendous, flabbergasting (*informal*) ...*He impressed everyone with his prodigious memory...* `OPPOSITE` ordinary

prodigy = <u>genius</u>, talent, wizard, mastermind, whizz (*informal*), whizz kid (*informal*), wunderkind, brainbox, child genius, wonder child

produce `VERB` 1 – <u>cause</u>, lead to, result in, effect, occasion, generate, trigger, make for, provoke, set off, induce, bring about, give rise to, engender ...*The drug is known to produce side-effects...*
2 = <u>make</u>, build, create, develop, turn out, manufacture, construct, invent, assemble, put together, originate, fabricate, mass-produce ...*The company produces circuitry for communications systems...*
3 = <u>create</u>, develop, write, turn out, compose, originate, churn out (*informal*) ...*So far he has produced only one composition he deems suitable for performance...*
4 = <u>yield</u>, provide, grow, bear, give, supply, afford, render, furnish ...*The plant produces sweet fruit with deep red flesh...*
5 = <u>bring forth</u>, bear, deliver, breed, give birth to, beget, bring into the world ...*Some species of snake produce live young...*
6 = <u>show</u>, provide, present, advance, demonstrate, offer, come up with, exhibit, put forward, furnish, bring forward, set forth, bring to light ...*They challenged him to produce evidence to support his allegations...*
7 = <u>display</u>, show, present, proffer ...*You must produce

your passport upon re-entering the country...*
8 = <u>present</u>, stage, direct, put on, do, show, mount, exhibit, put before the public ...*He produced Broadway's longest show...*
`NOUN` = <u>fruit and vegetables</u>, goods, food, products, crops, yield, harvest, greengrocery (*Brit.*) ...*I buy organic produce whenever possible...*

producer 1 = <u>director</u>, promoter, impresario, régisseur (*French*) ...*a freelance film producer...*
2 = <u>maker</u>, manufacturer, builder, creator, fabricator ...*producers of precision instruments and electrical equipment...*
3 = <u>grower</u>, farmer ...*They are producers of high-quality wines...*

product 1 = <u>goods</u>, produce, production, creation, commodity, invention, merchandise, artefact, concoction ...*Try to get the best products at the lowest price...*
2 = <u>result</u>, fruit, consequence, yield, returns, issue, effect, outcome, legacy, spin-off, end result, offshoot, upshot ...*The company is the product of a merger...*

production 1 = <u>producing</u>, making, manufacture, manufacturing, construction, assembly, preparation, formation, fabrication, origination ...*two companies involved in the production of the steel pipes...*
2 = <u>creation</u>, development, fashioning, composition, origination ...*the apparent lack of skill in the production of much new modern art...*
3 = <u>management</u>, administration, direction ...*the story behind the show's production...*
4 = <u>presentation</u>, staging, mounting ...*a critically acclaimed production of Othello...*

productive 1 = <u>fertile</u>, rich, producing, prolific, plentiful, fruitful, teeming, generative, fecund ...*fertile and productive soil...* `OPPOSITE` barren
2 = <u>creative</u>, dynamic, vigorous, energetic, inventive ...*a highly productive writer of fiction...*
3 = <u>useful</u>, rewarding, valuable, profitable, effective, worthwhile, beneficial, constructive, gratifying, fruitful, advantageous, gainful ...*a productive relationship...* `OPPOSITE` useless

productivity = <u>output</u>, production, capacity, yield, efficiency, mass production, work rate, productive capacity, productiveness

profane `ADJECTIVE` 1 = <u>sacrilegious</u>, wicked, irreverent, sinful, disrespectful, heathen, impure, godless, ungodly, irreligious, impious, idolatrous ...*a hard-drinking, profane Irishman...* `OPPOSITE` religious
2 = <u>crude</u>, foul, obscene, abusive, coarse, filthy, vulgar, blasphemous ...*a campaign against suggestive and profane lyrics in country songs...*
3 = <u>secular</u>, lay, temporal, unholy, worldly, unconsecrated, unhallowed, unsanctified ...*Churches should not be used for profane or secular purposes...*
`VERB` = <u>desecrate</u>, violate, abuse, prostitute, contaminate, pollute, pervert, misuse, debase, defile, vitiate, commit sacrilege ...*They have profaned the traditions of the Church...*

profess 1 = <u>claim</u>, allege, pretend, fake, make out, sham, purport, feign, act as if, let on, dissemble ...*'I don't know,' he replied, professing innocence...*

2 = <u>state</u>, admit, announce, maintain, own, confirm, declare, acknowledge, confess, assert, proclaim, affirm, certify, avow, vouch, aver, asseverate ...*He professed that he was content with the arrangements...*

professed 1 = <u>supposed</u>, would-be, alleged, so-called, apparent, pretended, purported, self-styled, ostensible, soi-disant (*French*) ...*their professed concern for justice...*
2 = <u>declared</u>, confirmed, confessed, proclaimed, certified, self-confessed, avowed, self-acknowledged ...*He was a professed anarchist...*

profession = <u>occupation</u>, calling, business, career, employment, line, office, position, sphere, vocation, walk of life, line of work, métier

professional ADJECTIVE **1** = <u>qualified</u>, trained, skilled, white-collar ...*professional people like doctors and engineers...*
2 = <u>expert</u>, experienced, finished, skilled, masterly, efficient, crack (*slang*), polished, practised, ace (*informal*), accomplished, slick, competent, adept, proficient ...*She told me we'd done a really professional job...* OPPOSITE amateurish
NOUN = <u>expert</u>, authority, master, pro (*informal*), specialist, guru, buff (*informal*), wizard, adept, whizz (*informal*), maestro, virtuoso, hotshot (*informal*), past master, dab hand (*Brit. informal*), wonk (*informal*), maven (*U.S.*), fundi (*S. African*) ...*a dedicated professional...*

professor = <u>don</u> (*Brit.*), fellow (*Brit.*), prof (*informal*), head of faculty

proffer (*Formal*) **1** = <u>offer</u>, hand over, present, extend, hold out ...*He proffered a box of cigarettes...*
2 = <u>suggest</u>, propose, volunteer, submit, tender, propound ...*They have not yet proffered an explanation of how the accident happened...*

proficiency = <u>skill</u>, ability, know-how (*informal*), talent, facility, craft, expertise, competence, accomplishment, mastery, knack, aptitude, dexterity, expertness, skilfulness

proficient = <u>skilled</u>, trained, experienced, qualified, able, expert, masterly, talented, gifted, capable, efficient, clever, accomplished, versed, competent, apt, skilful, adept, conversant OPPOSITE unskilled

profile 1 = <u>outline</u>, lines, form, figure, shape, silhouette, contour, side view ...*His handsome profile was turned away from us...*
2 = <u>biography</u>, sketch, vignette, characterization, thumbnail sketch, character sketch ...*The newspaper published comparative profiles of the candidates...*
3 = <u>analysis</u>, study, table, review, survey, chart, examination, diagram, graph ...*a profile of the hospital's catchment area...*

profit NOUN **1** *often plural* = <u>earnings</u>, winnings, return, revenue, gain, boot (*dialect*), yield, proceeds, percentage (*informal*), surplus, receipts, bottom line, takings, emoluments ...*The bank made pre-tax profits of £3.5 million...* OPPOSITE loss
2 = <u>benefit</u>, good, use, interest, value, gain, advantage, advancement, mileage (*informal*), avail ...*They saw little profit in risking their lives to capture the militants...* OPPOSITE disadvantage
VERB **1** = <u>make money</u>, clear up, gain, earn, clean up (*informal*), rake in (*informal*), make a killing (*informal*), make a good thing of (*informal*) ...*The dealers profited shamelessly at my family's expense...*
2 = <u>benefit</u>, help, serve, aid, gain, promote, contribute to, avail, be of advantage to ...*So far the French alliance has profited the rebels very little...*
PHRASES **profit from something** = <u>capitalize on</u>, take advantage of, learn from, use, exploit, make the most of, cash in on (*informal*), utilize, make good use of, reap the benefit of, put to good use, make capital of, turn to advantage *or* account ...*One can profit from that example and try to follow it...*

profitable 1 = <u>money-making</u>, lucrative, paying, commercial, rewarding, worthwhile, cost-effective, fruitful, gainful, remunerative ...*Drug manufacturing is the most profitable business in America...*
2 = <u>beneficial</u>, useful, rewarding, valuable, productive, worthwhile, fruitful, advantageous, expedient, serviceable ...*a profitable exchange of ideas...* OPPOSITE useless

profligacy = <u>extravagance</u>, excess, squandering, waste, recklessness, wastefulness, lavishness, prodigality, improvidence

profligate = <u>extravagant</u>, reckless, squandering, wasteful, prodigal, spendthrift, immoderate, improvident

profound 1 = <u>sincere</u>, acute, intense, great, keen, extreme, hearty, heartfelt, abject, deeply felt, heartrending ...*The overwhelming feeling is profound shock and anger...* OPPOSITE insincere
2 = <u>wise</u>, learned, serious, deep, skilled, subtle, penetrating, philosophical, thoughtful, sage, discerning, weighty, insightful, erudite, abstruse, recondite, sagacious ...*a book full of profound and challenging insights...* OPPOSITE uninformed
3 = <u>complete</u>, intense, absolute, serious (*informal*), total, extreme, pronounced, utter, consummate, unqualified, out-and-out ...*A profound silence fell...* OPPOSITE slight
4 = <u>radical</u>, extensive, thorough, far-reaching, exhaustive, thoroughgoing ...*the profound changes brought about by World War I...*

profoundly = <u>greatly</u>, very, deeply, seriously, keenly, extremely, thoroughly, sincerely, intensely, acutely, heartily, to the core, abjectly, to the nth degree, from the bottom of your heart

profundity = <u>insight</u>, intelligence, depth, wisdom, learning, penetration, acumen, erudition, acuity, perspicacity, sagacity, perceptiveness, perspicuity

profuse 1 = <u>plentiful</u>, ample, prolific, abundant, overflowing, teeming, copious, bountiful, luxuriant ...*This plant produces profuse bright-blue flowers...* OPPOSITE sparse
2 = <u>extravagant</u>, liberal, generous, excessive, lavish, exuberant, prodigal, fulsome, open-handed, unstinting, immoderate ...*Helena's profuse thanks were met with only a nod...* OPPOSITE moderate

profusion = <u>abundance</u>, wealth, excess, quantity,

surplus, riot, multitude, bounty, plethora, exuberance, glut, extravagance, cornucopia, oversupply, plenitude, superabundance, superfluity, lavishness, luxuriance, prodigality, copiousness

progenitor 1 = <u>ancestor</u>, parent, forebear, forefather, begetter, procreator, primogenitor ...*the Arabian stallions which were the progenitors of all modern thoroughbreds...*
2 = <u>originator</u>, source, predecessor, precursor, forerunner, antecedent, instigator ...*the man who is considered the progenitor of modern drama...*

progeny 1 = <u>children</u>, family, young, issue, offspring, descendants ...*They set aside funds to ensure the welfare of their progeny...*
2 = <u>race</u>, stock, breed, posterity (*archaic*), seed (*chiefly biblical*), lineage, scions ...*They claimed to be the progeny of Genghis Khan...*

prognosis = <u>forecast</u>, prediction, diagnosis, expectation, speculation, projection, surmise, prognostication

programme NOUN 1 = <u>plan</u>, scheme, strategy, procedure, project, plan of action ...*the programme for reform outlined by the Soviet President...*
2 = <u>schedule</u>, plan, agenda, timetable, listing, list, line-up, calendar, order ...*the programme of events for the forthcoming year...*
3 = <u>course</u>, curriculum, syllabus ...*a detailed ten-step programme of study with attainment targets...*
4 = <u>show</u>, performance, production, broadcast, episode, presentation, transmission, telecast ...*a series of TV programmes on global warming...*
VERB 1 = <u>schedule</u>, plan, timetable, book, bill, list, design, arrange, work out, line up, organize, lay on, formulate, map out, itemize, prearrange ...*His homework is more manageable now because it is programmed into his schedule...*
2 = <u>set</u>, fix ...*Most VCRs can be programmed using a remote control handset...*

progress NOUN 1 = <u>development</u>, increase, growth, advance, gain, improvement, promotion, breakthrough, step forward, advancement, progression, headway, betterment, amelioration ...*The two sides made little progress towards agreement... ...The doctors say they are pleased with her progress...* OPPOSITE regression
2 = <u>movement forward</u>, passage, advancement, progression, course, advance, headway, onward movement ...*The road was too rough for further progress in the car...* OPPOSITE movement backward
VERB 1 = <u>move on</u>, continue, travel, advance, proceed, go forward, gain ground, forge ahead, make inroads (into), make headway, make your way, cover ground, make strides, gather way ...*He progressed slowly along the coast in an easterly direction...* OPPOSITE move back
2 = <u>develop</u>, improve, advance, better, increase, grow, gain, get on, come on, mature, blossom, ameliorate ...*He came round to see how our work was progressing...* OPPOSITE get behind
PHRASES **in progress** = <u>going on</u>, happening, continuing, being done, occurring, taking place,

proceeding, under way, ongoing, being performed, in operation ...*The game was already in progress when we took our seats...*

progression 1 = <u>progress</u>, advance, advancement, gain, headway, furtherance, movement forward ...*Both drugs slow the progression of HIV...*
2 = <u>sequence</u>, course, order, series, chain, cycle, string, succession ...*the steady progression of events in my life...*

progressive 1 = <u>enlightened</u>, liberal, modern, advanced, radical, enterprising, go-ahead, revolutionary, dynamic, avant-garde, reformist, up-and-coming, forward-looking ...*The children go to a progressive school...*
2 = <u>growing</u>, continuing, increasing, developing, advancing, accelerating, ongoing, continuous, intensifying, escalating ...*One symptom of the disease is a progressive loss of memory...*

prohibit 1 = <u>forbid</u>, ban, rule out, veto, outlaw, disallow, proscribe, debar, interdict ...*the law which prohibits trading on Sunday...* OPPOSITE permit
2 = <u>prevent</u>, restrict, rule out, stop, hamper, hinder, constrain, obstruct, preclude, impede, make impossible ...*The contraption prohibited any movement...* OPPOSITE allow

prohibited = <u>forbidden</u>, barred, banned, illegal, not allowed, vetoed, taboo, off limits, proscribed, verboten (*German*)

prohibition = <u>ban</u>, boycott, embargo, bar, veto, prevention, exclusion, injunction, disqualification, interdiction, interdict, proscription, disallowance, forbiddance

prohibitive 1 = <u>exorbitant</u>, excessive, steep (*informal*), high-priced, preposterous, sky-high, extortionate, beyond your means ...*The cost of private treatment can be prohibitive...*
2 = <u>prohibiting</u>, forbidding, restraining, restrictive, repressive, suppressive, proscriptive ...*prohibitive regulations...*

project NOUN 1 = <u>scheme</u>, plan, job, idea, design, programme, campaign, operation, activity, proposal, venture, enterprise, undertaking, occupation, proposition, plan of action ...*a local development project...*
2 = <u>assignment</u>, task, homework, piece of research ...*Students complete their projects at their own pace...*
VERB 1 = <u>forecast</u>, expect, estimate, predict, reckon, calculate, gauge, extrapolate, predetermine ...*Africa's population is projected to double by 2025...*
2 = <u>plan</u>, propose, design, scheme, purpose, frame, draft, outline, devise, contemplate, contrive, map out ...*His projected visit to Washington had to be postponed...*
3 = <u>launch</u>, shoot, throw, cast, transmit, discharge, hurl, fling, propel ...*The hardware can be used for projecting nuclear missiles...*
4 = <u>stick out</u>, extend, stand out, bulge, beetle, protrude, overhang, jut ...*A piece of metal projected out from the side...*

projectile = <u>missile</u>, shell, bullet, rocket

projection = <u>forecast</u>, estimate, reckoning, prediction, calculation, estimation, computation, extrapolation

proletarian [ADJECTIVE] = <u>working-class</u>, common, cloth-cap (*informal*), plebeian, blue-singlet (*Austral. slang*) …*the issue of proletarian world solidarity*… [NOUN] = <u>worker</u>, commoner, Joe Bloggs (*Brit. informal*), pleb, plebeian, prole (*derogatory slang, chiefly Brit.*) …*The proletarians have nothing to lose but their chains*…

proletariat = <u>working class</u>, the masses, lower classes, commoners, the herd, wage-earners, lower orders, the common people, hoi polloi, plebs, the rabble, the great unwashed (*derogatory*), labouring classes, proles (*derogatory slang, chiefly Brit.*), commonalty [OPPOSITE] ruling class

proliferate = <u>increase</u>, expand, breed, mushroom, escalate, multiply, burgeon, snowball, run riot, grow rapidly

proliferation = <u>multiplication</u>, increase, spread, build-up, concentration, expansion, extension, step-up (*informal*), escalation, intensification

prolific 1 = <u>productive</u>, creative, fertile, inventive, copious …*a prolific writer of novels and short stories*… 2 = <u>fruitful</u>, fertile, abundant, rich, rank, teeming, bountiful, luxuriant, generative, profuse, fecund …*Closer planting will give you a more prolific crop*… [OPPOSITE] unproductive

prologue = <u>introduction</u>, preliminary, prelude, preface, preamble, foreword, proem, exordium

prolong = <u>lengthen</u>, continue, perpetuate, draw out, extend, delay, stretch out, carry on, spin out, drag out, make longer, protract [OPPOSITE] shorten

promenade [NOUN] 1 = <u>walkway</u>, parade, boulevard, prom, esplanade, public walk …*a fine promenade running past the boathouses*… 2 = <u>stroll</u>, walk, turn, airing, constitutional, saunter …*Take a tranquil promenade along a stretch of picturesque coastline*… [VERB] 1 = <u>stroll</u>, walk, saunter, take a walk, perambulate, stretch your legs …*People came out to promenade along the front*… 2 = <u>parade</u>, strut, swagger, flaunt …*attracting attention as he promenaded up and down the street in his flashy clothes*…

prominence 1 = <u>fame</u>, name, standing, rank, reputation, importance, celebrity, distinction, prestige, greatness, eminence, pre-eminence, notability, outstandingness …*He came to prominence during the World Cup in Italy*… 2 = <u>conspicuousness</u>, weight, precedence, top billing, specialness, salience, markedness …*Many papers give prominence to reports of the latest violence*… 3 = <u>protrusion</u>, swelling, projection, bulge, jutting, protuberance …*Birds have a prominence on the breast bone called a keel*…

prominent 1 = <u>famous</u>, leading, top, chief, important, main, noted, popular, respected, celebrated, outstanding, distinguished, well-known, notable, renowned, big-time (*informal*), foremost, eminent, major league (*informal*), pre-eminent, well-thought-of …*a prominent member of the Law Society*… [OPPOSITE] unknown 2 = <u>noticeable</u>, striking, obvious, outstanding, remarkable, pronounced, blatant, conspicuous, to the fore, unmistakable, eye-catching, salient, in the foreground, easily seen, obtrusive …*the lighthouses that are still a prominent feature of the Scottish coast*… [OPPOSITE] inconspicuous 3 = <u>jutting</u>, projecting, standing out, bulging, hanging over, protruding, protuberant, protrusive …*a low forehead and prominent eyebrows*… [OPPOSITE] indented

promiscuity = <u>licentiousness</u>, profligacy, sleeping around (*informal*), permissiveness, abandon, incontinence, depravity, immorality, debauchery, laxity, dissipation, looseness, amorality, lechery, laxness, wantonness, libertinism, promiscuousness

promiscuous = <u>licentious</u>, wanton, profligate, debauched, fast, wild, abandoned, loose, immoral, lax, dissipated, unbridled, dissolute, libertine, of easy virtue, unchaste [OPPOSITE] chaste

promise [VERB] 1 = <u>guarantee</u>, pledge, vow, swear, contract, assure, undertake, warrant, plight, stipulate, vouch, take an oath, give an undertaking to, cross your heart, give your word …*They promised they would deliver it on Friday*… 2 = <u>seem likely</u>, look like, hint at, show signs of, bespeak, augur, betoken, lead you to expect, hold out hopes of, give hope of, bid fair, hold a probability of …*The seminar promises to be most instructive*… [NOUN] 1 = <u>guarantee</u>, word, bond, vow, commitment, pledge, undertaking, assurance, engagement, compact, oath, covenant, word of honour …*If you make a promise, you should keep it*… 2 = <u>potential</u>, ability, talent, capacity, capability, flair, aptitude …*He first showed promise as an athlete in grade school*…

promising 1 = <u>encouraging</u>, likely, bright, reassuring, hopeful, favourable, rosy, auspicious, propitious, full of promise …*a new and promising stage in the negotiations*… [OPPOSITE] unpromising 2 = <u>talented</u>, able, gifted, rising, likely, up-and-coming …*one of the school's brightest and most promising pupils*…

promontory = <u>point</u>, cape, head, spur, ness (*archaic*), headland, foreland

promote 1 = <u>help</u>, back, support, further, develop, aid, forward, champion, encourage, advance, work for, urge, boost, recommend, sponsor, foster, contribute to, assist, advocate, stimulate, endorse, prescribe, speak for, nurture, push for, espouse, popularize, gee up …*His country will do everything possible to promote peace*… [OPPOSITE] impede 2 = <u>advertise</u>, sell, hype, publicize, push, plug (*informal*), puff, call attention to, beat the drum for (*informal*) …*He has announced a full British tour to promote his new album*… 3 = <u>raise</u>, upgrade, elevate, honour, dignify, exalt, kick upstairs (*informal*), aggrandize …*I was promoted to editor and then editorial director*… [OPPOSITE] demote

promoter 1 = <u>organizer</u>, arranger, entrepreneur, impresario ...*one of the top boxing promoters in Britain...*
2 = <u>supporter</u>, champion, advocate, campaigner, helper, proponent, stalwart, mainstay, upholder ...*Aaron Copland was a most energetic promoter of American music...*

promotion 1 = <u>rise</u>, upgrading, move up, advancement, elevation, exaltation, preferment, aggrandizement, ennoblement ...*rewarding outstanding employees with promotion...*
2 = <u>publicity</u>, advertising, hype, pushing, plugging (*informal*), propaganda, advertising campaign, hard sell, media hype, ballyhoo (*informal*), puffery (*informal*), boosterism ...*The company spent a lot of money on advertising and promotion...*
3 = <u>encouragement</u>, backing, support, development, progress, boosting, advancement, advocacy, cultivation, espousal, furtherance, boosterism ...*dedicated to the promotion of new ideas and research...*

prompt VERB 1 = <u>cause</u>, move, inspire, stimulate, occasion, urge, spur, provoke, motivate, induce, evoke, give rise to, elicit, incite, instigate, impel, call forth ...*The recession has prompted consumers to cut back on buying cars...* OPPOSITE discourage
2 = <u>remind</u>, assist, cue, help out, prod, jog the memory, refresh the memory ...*'What was that you were saying about a guided tour?' he prompted her...*
ADJECTIVE 1 = <u>immediate</u>, quick, rapid, instant, timely, early, swift, on time, speedy, instantaneous, punctual, pdq (*slang*), unhesitating ...*an inflammation of the eyeball which needs prompt treatment...* OPPOSITE slow
2 = <u>quick</u>, ready, efficient, eager, willing, smart, alert, brisk, responsive, expeditious ...*I was impressed by the prompt service I received...* OPPOSITE inefficient
ADVERB (*Informal*) = <u>exactly</u>, sharp, promptly, on the dot, punctually ...*The invitation specifies eight o'clock prompt...*
NOUN = <u>reminder</u>, hint, cue, help, spur, stimulus, jog, prod, jolt ...*Her blushes were saved by a prompt from her host...*

promptly 1 = <u>immediately</u>, instantly, swiftly, directly, quickly, at once, speedily, by return, pronto (*informal*), unhesitatingly, hotfoot, pdq (*slang*), posthaste ...*She lay down and promptly fell asleep...*
2 = <u>punctually</u>, on time, spot on (*informal*), bang on (*informal*), on the dot, on the button (*U.S.*), on the nail ...*We left the hotel promptly at seven...*

promulgate 1 = <u>make known</u>, issue, announce, publish, spread, promote, advertise, broadcast, communicate, proclaim, circulate, notify, make public, disseminate ...*Such behaviour promulgates a negative image of the British...*
2 = <u>make official</u>, pass, declare, decree ...*bills limiting the FDA's authority to promulgate such regulations...*

prone 1 = <u>liable</u>, given, subject, inclined, tending, bent, disposed, susceptible, apt, predisposed ...*For all her experience, she was still prone to nerves...* OPPOSITE disinclined

2 = <u>face down</u>, flat, lying down, horizontal, prostrate, recumbent, procumbent ...*Bob slid from his chair and lay prone on the floor...* OPPOSITE face up

pronounce 1 = <u>say</u>, speak, voice, stress, sound, utter, articulate, enunciate, vocalize ...*Have I pronounced your name correctly?...*
2 = <u>declare</u>, announce, judge, deliver, assert, proclaim, decree, affirm ...*A specialist has pronounced him fully fit... ...They took time to pronounce their verdict...*

pronounced = <u>noticeable</u>, clear, decided, strong, marked, striking, obvious, broad, evident, distinct, definite, conspicuous, unmistakable, salient OPPOSITE imperceptible

pronouncement = <u>announcement</u>, statement, declaration, judgment, decree, manifesto, proclamation, notification, edict, dictum, promulgation, pronunciamento

pronunciation = <u>intonation</u>, accent, speech, stress, articulation, inflection, diction, elocution, enunciation, accentuation

> ## Word Power
>
> **pronunciation** – The *-un-* in *pronunciation* should be written and pronounced in the same way as the *-un-* in *unkind*. It is incorrect to add an *o* after the *u* to make this word look and sound more like *pronounce*.

proof NOUN 1 = <u>evidence</u>, demonstration, testimony, confirmation, verification, certification, corroboration, authentication, substantiation, attestation ...*You must have proof of residence in the state...*
2 (*Printing*) = <u>trial print</u>, pull, slip, galley, page proof, galley proof, trial impression ...*I'm correcting the proofs of the Spanish edition right now...*
ADJECTIVE = <u>impervious</u>, strong, tight, resistant, impenetrable, repellent ...*The fortress was proof against attack...*

prop VERB 1 = <u>lean</u>, place, set, stand, position, rest, lay, balance, steady ...*He propped his bike against the fence...*
2 often with **up** = <u>support</u>, maintain, sustain, shore, hold up, brace, uphold, bolster, truss, buttress ...*Plaster ceilings are propped with scaffolding...*
NOUN 1 = <u>support</u>, stay, brace, mainstay, truss, buttress, stanchion ...*The timber is reinforced with three steel props on a concrete foundation...*
2 = <u>mainstay</u>, support, sustainer, anchor, backbone, cornerstone, upholder ...*The army is one of the main props of the government...*
PHRASES **prop something** or **someone up** 1 = <u>rest</u>, place, set, stand, lean ...*He slouched back and propped his elbows up on the bench behind him...* 2 = <u>subsidize</u>, support, fund, finance, maintain, underwrite, shore up, buttress, bolster up ...*Investments in the US money markets have propped up the American dollar...*

propaganda = <u>information</u>, advertising, promotion, publicity, hype, brainwashing, disinformation, ballyhoo (*informal*), agitprop, newspeak, boosterism

propagandist = <u>publicist</u>, advocate, promoter, proponent, evangelist, proselytizer, pamphleteer, indoctrinator

propagate 1 = <u>spread</u>, publish, promote, broadcast, proclaim, transmit, circulate, diffuse, publicize, disseminate, promulgate, make known ...*They propagated subversive political doctrines...* [OPPOSITE] suppress
2 = <u>produce</u>, generate, engender, increase ...*The easiest way to propagate a vine is to take cuttings...*
3 = <u>reproduce</u>, breed, multiply, proliferate, beget, procreate ...*Tomatoes rot in order to transmit their seed and propagate the species...*

propagation 1 = <u>spreading</u>, spread, promotion, communication, distribution, circulation, transmission, diffusion, dissemination, promulgation ...*working towards the propagation of true Buddhism...*
2 = <u>reproduction</u>, generation, breeding, increase, proliferation, multiplication, procreation ...*the successful propagation of a batch of new plants...*

propel 1 = <u>drive</u>, launch, start, force, send, shoot, push, thrust, shove, set in motion ...*The rocket is designed to propel the spacecraft...* [OPPOSITE] stop
2 = <u>impel</u>, drive, push, prompt, spur, motivate ...*He is propelled by the need to avenge his father...* [OPPOSITE] hold back

propensity = <u>tendency</u>, leaning, weakness, inclination, bent, liability, bias, disposition, penchant, susceptibility, predisposition, proclivity, proneness, aptness

proper 1 = <u>real</u>, actual, genuine, true, bona fide, kosher (*informal*), dinkum (*Austral. & N.Z. informal*) ...*Two out of five people do not have a proper job...*
2 = <u>correct</u>, accepted, established, appropriate, right, formal, conventional, accurate, exact, precise, legitimate, orthodox, apt ...*Please ensure that the proper procedures are followed...* [OPPOSITE] improper
3 = <u>polite</u>, right, becoming, seemly, fitting, fit, mannerly, suitable, decent, gentlemanly, refined, respectable, befitting, genteel, de rigueur (*French*), ladylike, meet (*archaic*), decorous, punctilious, comme il faut (*French*) ...*In those days it was not thought proper for a woman to be on the stage...* [OPPOSITE] unseemly
4 = <u>characteristic</u>, own, special, individual, personal, particular, specific, peculiar, respective ...*Make sure everything is in its proper place...*

properly 1 = <u>correctly</u>, rightly, fittingly, appropriately, legitimately, accurately, suitably, aptly, deservedly, as intended, in the true sense, in the accepted *or* approved manner ...*The debate needs to be conducted properly...* [OPPOSITE] incorrectly
2 = <u>politely</u>, respectfully, ethically, decently, respectably, decorously, punctiliously ...*It's about time that brat learned to behave properly...* [OPPOSITE] badly

property 1 = <u>possessions</u>, goods, means, effects, holdings, capital, riches, resources, estate, assets, wealth, belongings, chattels ...*Security forces confiscated weapons and stolen property...*
2 = <u>land</u>, holding, title, estate, acres, real estate, freehold, realty, real property ...*He inherited a family property near Stamford...*
3 = <u>quality</u>, feature, characteristic, mark, ability, attribute, virtue, trait, hallmark, peculiarity, idiosyncrasy ...*A radio signal has both electrical and magnetic properties...*

prophecy 1 = <u>prediction</u>, forecast, revelation, prognosis, foretelling, prognostication, augury, sortilege, vaticination (*rare*) ...*Nostradamus's prophecy of the end of the world...*
2 = <u>second sight</u>, divination, augury, telling the future, soothsaying ...*a child born with the gift of prophecy...*

prophesy = <u>predict</u>, forecast, divine, foresee, augur, presage, foretell, forewarn, prognosticate, soothsay, vaticinate (*rare*)

prophet *or* **prophetess** = <u>soothsayer</u>, forecaster, diviner, oracle, seer, clairvoyant, augur, sibyl, prognosticator, prophesier

prophetic = <u>predictive</u>, foreshadowing, presaging, prescient, divinatory, oracular, sibylline, prognostic, mantic, vatic (*rare*), augural, fatidic (*rare*)

propitious = <u>favourable</u>, timely, promising, encouraging, bright, lucky, fortunate, prosperous, rosy, advantageous, auspicious, opportune, full of promise

proponent = <u>supporter</u>, friend, champion, defender, advocate, patron, enthusiast, subscriber, backer, partisan, exponent, apologist, upholder, vindicator, spokesman *or* spokeswoman

proportion [NOUN] 1 = <u>part</u>, share, cut (*informal*), amount, measure, division, percentage, segment, quota, fraction ...*A proportion of the rent is met by the city council...*
2 = <u>relative amount</u>, relationship, distribution, ratio ...*the proportion of women in the profession... ...the proportion of length to breadth...*
3 = <u>balance</u>, agreement, harmony, correspondence, symmetry, concord, congruity ...*an artist with a special feel for colour and proportion...*
[PLURAL NOUN] = <u>dimensions</u>, size, volume, capacity, extent, range, bulk, scope, measurements, magnitude, breadth, expanse, amplitude ...*In the tropics, plants grow to huge proportions...*

proportional *or* **proportionate** = <u>correspondent</u>, equivalent, corresponding, even, balanced, consistent, comparable, compatible, equitable, in proportion, analogous, commensurate [OPPOSITE] disproportionate

proposal = <u>suggestion</u>, plan, programme, scheme, offer, terms, design, project, bid, motion, recommendation, tender, presentation, proposition, overture

propose 1 = <u>put forward</u>, present, suggest, advance, come up with, submit, tender, proffer, propound ...*We are about to propose some changes to the system...*
2 = <u>intend</u>, mean, plan, aim, design, scheme, purpose,

have in mind, have every intention …*I propose to spend my entire life travelling…*

3 = <u>nominate</u>, name, present, introduce, invite, recommend, put up …*He was proposed for renomination as party chairman…*

4 = <u>offer marriage</u>, pop the question (*informal*), ask for someone's hand (in marriage), pay suit …*Merton proposed to her on bended knee…*

proposition NOUN **1** = <u>task</u>, problem, activity, job, affair, venture, undertaking …*Designing his own flat was quite a different proposition to designing for clients…*

2 = <u>theory</u>, idea, argument, concept, thesis, hypothesis, theorem, premiss, postulation …*the proposition that monarchs derived their authority by divine right…*

3 = <u>proposal</u>, plan, suggestion, scheme, bid, motion, recommendation …*I want to make you a business proposition…*

4 = <u>advance</u>, pass (*informal*), proposal, overture, improper suggestion, come-on (*informal*) …*unwanted sexual propositions…*

VERB = <u>make a pass at</u>, solicit, accost, make an indecent proposal to, make an improper suggestion to …*He had allegedly tried to proposition Miss Hawes…*

propound = <u>put forward</u>, present, advance, propose, advocate, submit, suggest, lay down, contend, postulate, set forth

proprietor *or* **proprietress** = <u>owner</u>, landowner, freeholder, possessor, titleholder, deed holder, landlord *or* landlady

propriety NOUN **1** = <u>decorum</u>, manners, courtesy, protocol, good form, decency, breeding, delicacy, modesty, respectability, etiquette, refinement, politeness, good manners, rectitude, punctilio, seemliness …*Their sense of social propriety is eroded…* OPPOSITE indecorum

2 = <u>correctness</u>, fitness, appropriateness, rightness, aptness, seemliness, suitableness …*They questioned the propriety of the corporation's use of public money…* PLURAL NOUN = <u>etiquette</u>, niceties, civilities, amenities, the done thing, social graces, rules of conduct, social conventions, social code, accepted conduct …*respectable couples who observe the proprieties but loathe each other…*

propulsion = <u>power</u>, pressure, push, thrust, momentum, impulse, impetus, motive power, impulsion, propelling force

prosaic = <u>dull</u>, ordinary, boring, routine, flat, dry, everyday, tame, pedestrian, commonplace, mundane, matter-of-fact, stale, banal, uninspiring, humdrum, trite, unimaginative, hackneyed, workaday, vapid OPPOSITE exciting

proscribe 1 = <u>prohibit</u>, ban, forbid, boycott, embargo, interdict …*They are proscribed by federal law from owning guns…* OPPOSITE permit

2 = <u>condemn</u>, reject, damn, denounce, censure …*Slang is reviled and proscribed by pedants and purists…*

3 = <u>outlaw</u>, exclude, exile, expel, banish, deport,

expatriate, excommunicate, ostracize, blackball, attaint (*archaic*) …*He was proscribed in America, where his estate was put up for sale…*

prosecute 1 (*Law*) = <u>take someone to court</u>, try, sue, summon, indict, do (*slang*), arraign, seek redress, put someone on trial, litigate, bring suit against, bring someone to trial, put someone in the dock, bring action against, prefer charges against …*The police have decided not to prosecute him…*

2 = <u>conduct</u>, continue, manage, direct, pursue, work at, carry on, practise, engage in, discharge, persist, see through, follow through, persevere, carry through …*To prosecute this war is costing the country fifteen million pounds a day…*

prospect NOUN **1** = <u>likelihood</u>, chance, possibility, plan, hope, promise, proposal, odds, expectation, probability, anticipation, presumption …*There is little prospect of having these questions answered…*

2 = <u>idea</u>, thought, outlook, contemplation …*the pleasant prospect of a quiet night in…*

3 = <u>view</u>, perspective, landscape, scene, sight, vision, outlook, spectacle, panorama, vista …*The windows overlooked the superb prospect of the hills…* PLURAL NOUN = <u>possibilities</u>, openings, chances, future, potential, expectations, outlook, scope …*I chose to work abroad to improve my career prospects…*

VERB = <u>look</u>, search, seek, survey, explore, drill, go after, dowse …*The companies are prospecting for oil not far from here…*

PHRASES **in prospect** = <u>in view</u>, planned, projected, on the way, in sight, in store, on the cards, in the wind, on the horizon, coming soon, likely to happen, in the offing …*Further defence cuts are now in prospect…*

prospective 1 = <u>potential</u>, possible, to come, about to be, upcoming, soon-to-be …*The story is a warning to other prospective buyers…*

2 = <u>expected</u>, coming, future, approaching, likely, looked-for, intended, awaited, hoped-for, anticipated, forthcoming, imminent, destined, eventual, on the cards …*The terms of the prospective deal are spelled out clearly…*

prospectus = <u>catalogue</u>, plan, list, programme, announcement, outline, brochure, handbook, syllabus, synopsis, conspectus

prosper = <u>succeed</u>, advance, progress, thrive, make it (*informal*), flower, get on, do well, flourish, bloom, make good, be fortunate, grow rich, fare well

prosperity = <u>success</u>, riches, plenty, ease, fortune, wealth, boom, luxury, well-being, good times, good fortune, the good life, affluence, life of luxury, life of Riley (*informal*), prosperousness OPPOSITE poverty

prosperous 1 = <u>wealthy</u>, rich, affluent, well-off, in the money (*informal*), blooming, opulent, well-heeled (*informal*), well-to-do, moneyed, in clover (*informal*) …*the youngest son of a prosperous family…* OPPOSITE poor

2 = <u>successful</u>, booming, thriving, flourishing, doing well, prospering, on a roll, on the up and up (*Brit.*), palmy …*He has developed a prosperous business…* OPPOSITE unsuccessful

prostitute NOUN = whore, hooker (*U.S. slang*), pro (*slang*), brass (*slang*), tart (*informal*), hustler (*U.S. & Canad. slang*), moll (*slang*), call girl, courtesan, working girl (*facetious slang*), harlot, streetwalker, camp follower, loose woman, fallen woman, scrubber (*Brit. & Austral. slang*), strumpet, trollop, white slave, bawd (*archaic*), cocotte, fille de joie (*French*) ...*He admitted that he had paid for sex with a prostitute...*
VERB = cheapen, sell out, pervert, degrade, devalue, squander, demean, debase, profane, misapply ...*His friends said that he had prostituted his talents...*

prostitution = harlotry, the game (*slang*), vice, the oldest profession, whoredom, streetwalking, harlot's trade, Mrs. Warren's profession

prostrate ADJECTIVE 1 = prone, fallen, flat, horizontal, abject, bowed low, kowtowing, procumbent ...*Percy was lying prostrate with his arms outstretched...*
2 = exhausted, overcome, depressed, drained, spent, worn out, desolate, dejected, inconsolable, at a low ebb, fagged out (*informal*) ...*After my mother's death, I was prostrate with grief...*
3 = helpless, overwhelmed, disarmed, paralysed, powerless, reduced, impotent, defenceless, brought to your knees ...*Gaston was prostrate on his sickbed...*
VERB = exhaust, tire, drain, fatigue, weary, sap, wear out, fag out (*informal*) ...*patients who have been prostrated by fatigue...*
PHRASES **prostrate yourself** = bow down to, submit to, kneel to, cringe before, grovel before, fall at someone's feet, bow before, kowtow to, bend the knee to, abase yourself before, cast yourself before, fall on your knees before ...*They prostrated themselves before the king in awe and fear...*

protagonist 1 = supporter, leader, champion, advocate, exponent, mainstay, prime mover, standard-bearer, moving spirit, torchbearer ...*an active protagonist of his country's membership of the EU...*
2 = leading character, lead, principal, central character, hero *or* heroine ...*the protagonist of J.D. Salinger's novel...*

protean = changeable, variable, volatile, versatile, temperamental, ever-changing, mercurial, many-sided, mutable, polymorphous, multiform

protect = keep someone safe, defend, keep, support, save, guard, secure, preserve, look after, foster, shelter, shield, care for, harbour, safeguard, watch over, stick up for (*informal*), cover up for, chaperon, give someone sanctuary, take someone under your wing, mount *or* stand guard over OPPOSITE> endanger

protection 1 = safety, charge, care, defence, protecting, security, guarding, custody, safeguard, preservation, aegis, guardianship, safekeeping ...*The primary duty of parents is the protection of their children...*
2 = safeguard, cover, guard, shelter, screen, barrier, shield, refuge, buffer, bulwark ...*Innocence is no protection from the evils in our society...*
3 = armour, cover, screen, barrier, shelter, shield, bulwark ...*Riot shields acted as protection against the*

attack...

protective 1 = protecting, covering, sheltering, shielding, safeguarding, insulating ...*Protective gloves reduce the absorption of chemicals through the skin...*
2 = caring, defensive, motherly, fatherly, warm, careful, maternal, vigilant, watchful, paternal, possessive ...*He is very protective towards his sisters...*

protector 1 = defender, champion, guard, guardian, counsel, advocate, patron, safeguard, bodyguard, benefactor, guardian angel, tower of strength, knight in shining armour ...*Many mothers see their son as a protector and provider...*
2 = guard, screen, protection, shield, pad, cushion, buffer ...*Ear protectors must be worn when operating this equipment...*

protégé *or* **protégée** = charge, student, pupil, ward, discovery, dependant

protest VERB 1 = object, demonstrate, oppose, complain, disagree, cry out, disapprove, say no to, demur, take exception, remonstrate, kick against (*informal*), expostulate, take up the cudgels, express disapproval ...*Women took to the streets to protest against the arrests...*
2 = assert, argue, insist, maintain, declare, vow, testify, contend, affirm, profess, attest, avow, asseverate ...*'I never said that,' he protested...*
NOUN 1 = demonstration, march, rally, sit-in, demo (*informal*) ...*The opposition staged a protest against the government...*
2 = objection, complaint, declaration, dissent, outcry, disapproval, protestation, demur, formal complaint, remonstrance, demurral ...*a protest against people's growing economic hardship...*

protestation 1 (*Formal*) = declaration, pledge, vow, oath, profession, affirmation, avowal, asseveration ...*his constant protestations of love and devotion...*
2 = objection, protest, complaint, disagreement, dissent, remonstrance, expostulation, remonstration ...*Graham's protestation that he has been unjustly treated...*

protester 1 = demonstrator, rebel, dissident, dissenter, agitator, picketers, protest marcher ...*anti-abortion protesters...*
2 = objector, opposer, complainer, opponent, dissident, dissenter ...*Protesters say the government is corrupt...*

protocol 1 = code of behaviour, manners, courtesies, conventions, customs, formalities, good form, etiquette, propriety, decorum, rules of conduct, politesse, p's and q's ...*He is a stickler for royal protocol...*
2 = agreement, contract, treaty, convention, pact, compact, covenant, concordat ...*the Montreal Protocol to phase out use and production of CFCs...*

prototype = original, model, precedent, first, example, standard, paradigm, archetype, mock-up

protracted = extended, long, prolonged, lengthy, time-consuming, never-ending, drawn-out, interminable, spun out, dragged out, long-drawn-out, overlong

protrude = <u>stick out</u>, start (from), point, project, pop (*of eyes*), extend, come through, stand out, bulge, shoot out, jut, stick out like a sore thumb, obtrude

proud 1 = <u>satisfied</u>, pleased, content, contented, honoured, thrilled, glad, gratified, joyful, appreciative, well-pleased ...*I am proud to be a Scot...* OPPOSITE> dissatisfied
2 = <u>glorious</u>, rewarding, memorable, pleasing, satisfying, illustrious, gratifying, exalted, red-letter ...*My daughter's graduation was a proud moment for me...*
3 = <u>distinguished</u>, great, grand, imposing, magnificent, noble, august, splendid, eminent, majestic, stately, illustrious ...*The American Indians were a proud and noble people...* OPPOSITE> lowly
4 = <u>conceited</u>, vain, arrogant, stuck-up (*informal*), lordly, imperious, narcissistic, overbearing, snooty (*informal*), haughty, snobbish, egotistical, self-satisfied, disdainful, self-important, presumptuous, boastful, supercilious, high and mighty (*informal*), toffee-nosed (*slang, chiefly Brit.*), too big for your boots *or* breeches ...*She has a reputation for being proud and arrogant...* OPPOSITE> humble

prove 1 = <u>turn out</u>, come out, end up, be found to be ...*In the past this process has proved difficult...*
2 = <u>verify</u>, establish, determine, show, evidence, confirm, demonstrate, justify, ascertain, bear out, attest, substantiate, corroborate, authenticate, evince, show clearly ...*new evidence that could prove their innocence...* OPPOSITE> disprove

proven = <u>established</u>, accepted, proved, confirmed, tried, tested, checked, reliable, valid, definite, authentic, certified, verified, attested, undoubted, dependable, trustworthy

provenance = <u>origin</u>, source, birthplace, derivation

proverb = <u>saying</u>, saw, maxim, gnome, adage, dictum, aphorism, byword, apophthegm

proverbial = <u>conventional</u>, accepted, traditional, famous, acknowledged, typical, well-known, legendary, notorious, customary, famed, archetypal, time-honoured, self-evident, unquestioned, axiomatic

provide VERB 1 = <u>supply</u>, give, contribute, provision, distribute, outfit, equip, accommodate, donate, furnish, dispense, part with, fork out (*informal*), stock up, cater to, purvey ...*I will be happy to provide you with a copy of the report... ...They did not provide any food...* OPPOSITE> withhold
2 = <u>give</u>, bring, add, produce, present, serve, afford, yield, lend, render, impart ...*The summit will provide an opportunity for discussions on the crisis...*
3 = <u>stipulate</u>, state, require, determine, specify, lay down ...*The treaty provides that, by 2000, the US must have removed its military bases...*
PHRASES **provide for someone** = <u>support</u>, look after, care for, keep, maintain, sustain, take care of, fend for ...*He can't even provide for his family...*
♦ **provide for something** = <u>take precautions against</u>, plan for, prepare for, anticipate, arrange for, get ready for, make plans for, make arrangements for, plan ahead for, take measures against, forearm for ...*James had provided for just such an emergency...*

provided *often with* ***that*** = <u>if</u>, given, subject to, in case, in the event, on condition, on the assumption, with the understanding, with the proviso, contingent upon, as long as, if and only if, upon these terms

providence = <u>fate</u>, fortune, destiny, God's will, divine intervention, predestination

provider 1 = <u>supplier</u>, giver, source, donor, benefactor ...*Japan is the largest provider of foreign aid in the world...*
2 = <u>breadwinner</u>, supporter, earner, mainstay, wage earner ...*A husband's job is to be a good provider...*

providing *often with* ***that*** = <u>on condition that</u>, subject to, given that, on the assumption that, in the event that, with the proviso that, contingent upon, with the understanding that, as long as, if and only if

province 1 = <u>region</u>, section, county, district, territory, zone, patch, colony, domain, dependency, tract ...*the Algarve, Portugal's southernmost province...*
2 = <u>area</u>, business, concern, responsibility, part, line, charge, role, post, department, field, duty, function, employment, capacity, orbit, sphere, turf (*U.S. slang*), pigeon (*Brit. informal*) ...*Industrial research is the province of the Department of Trade and Industry...*
➤ **WORD POWER SUPPLEMENT Canadian provinces**
➤ **WORD POWER SUPPLEMENT South African provinces and provincial capitals**

provincial ADJECTIVE 1 = <u>regional</u>, state, local, county, district, territorial, parochial ...*The local and provincial elections take place in June...*
2 = <u>rural</u>, country, local, home-grown, rustic, homespun, hick (*informal, chiefly U.S. & Canad.*), backwoods ...*My accent gave away my provincial roots...* OPPOSITE> urban
3 = <u>parochial</u>, insular, narrow-minded, unsophisticated, limited, narrow, small-town (*chiefly U.S.*), uninformed, inward-looking, small-minded, parish-pump, upcountry ...*The audience was dull and very provincial...* OPPOSITE> cosmopolitan
NOUN = <u>yokel</u>, hick (*informal, chiefly U.S. & Canad.*), rustic, country cousin, hayseed (*U.S. & Canad. informal*) ...*French provincials looking for work in Paris...*

provision NOUN 1 = <u>supplying</u>, giving, providing, supply, delivery, distribution, catering, presentation, equipping, furnishing, allocation, fitting out, purveying, accoutrement ...*the provision of military supplies to the Khmer Rouge...*
2 = <u>arrangement</u>, plan, planning, preparation, precaution, contingency, prearrangement ...*There is no provision for funding performance-related pay increases...*
3 = <u>facilities</u>, services, funds, resources, means, opportunities, arrangements, assistance, concession(s), allowance(s), amenities ...*Special provision should be made for single mothers...*
4 = <u>condition</u>, term, agreement, requirement, demand, rider, restriction, qualification, clause, reservation, specification, caveat, proviso, stipulation ...*a provision that would allow existing regulations to*

be reviewed…

PLURAL NOUN = <u>food</u>, supplies, stores, feed, fare, rations, eats (*slang*), groceries, tack (*informal*), grub (*slang*), foodstuff, kai (*N.Z. informal*), sustenance, victuals, edibles, comestibles, provender, nosebag (*slang*), vittles (*obsolete or dialect*), viands, eatables …*On board were enough provisions for two weeks…*

provisional 1 = <u>temporary</u>, interim, transitional, stopgap, pro tem …*the possibility of setting up a provisional coalition government…* **OPPOSITE** permanent
2 = <u>conditional</u>, limited, qualified, contingent, tentative, provisory …*The times stated are provisional and subject to confirmation…* **OPPOSITE** definite

proviso = <u>condition</u>, requirement, provision, strings, rider, restriction, qualification, clause, reservation, limitation, stipulation

provocation 1 = <u>cause</u>, reason, grounds, motivation, justification, stimulus, inducement, incitement, instigation, casus belli (*Latin*) …*The soldiers fired without provocation…*
2 = <u>offence</u>, challenge, insult, taunt, injury, dare, grievance, annoyance, affront, indignity, red rag, vexation …*They kept their tempers in the face of severe provocation…*

provocative 1 = <u>offensive</u>, provoking, insulting, challenging, disturbing, stimulating, annoying, outrageous, aggravating (*informal*), incensing, galling, goading …*Their behaviour was called provocative and antisocial…*
2 = <u>suggestive</u>, tempting, stimulating, exciting, inviting, sexy (*informal*), arousing, erotic, seductive, alluring, tantalizing …*sexually provocative behaviour…*

provoke 1 = <u>anger</u>, insult, annoy, offend, irritate, infuriate, hassle (*informal*), aggravate (*informal*), incense, enrage, gall, put someone out, madden, exasperate, vex, affront, chafe, irk, rile, pique, get on someone's nerves (*informal*), get someone's back up, put someone's back up, try someone's patience, nark (*Brit., Austral., & N.Z. slang*), make someone's blood boil, get in someone's hair (*informal*), rub someone up the wrong way (*informal*), take a rise out of …*I didn't want to do anything to provoke him…* **OPPOSITE** pacify
2 = <u>rouse</u>, cause, produce, lead to, move, fire, promote, occasion, excite, inspire, generate, prompt, stir, stimulate, motivate, induce, bring about, evoke, give rise to, precipitate, elicit, inflame, incite, instigate, kindle, foment, call forth, draw forth, bring on *or* down …*His comments have provoked a shocked reaction…* **OPPOSITE** curb

prowess 1 = <u>skill</u>, ability, talent, expertise, facility, command, genius, excellence, accomplishment, mastery, attainment, aptitude, dexterity, adroitness, adeptness, expertness …*He's always bragging about his prowess as a cricketer…* **OPPOSITE** inability
2 = <u>bravery</u>, daring, courage, heroism, mettle, boldness, gallantry, valour, fearlessness, intrepidity, hardihood, valiance, dauntlessness, doughtiness …*a race of people noted for their fighting prowess…*

OPPOSITE cowardice

prowl = <u>move stealthily</u>, hunt, patrol, range, steal, cruise, stalk, sneak, lurk, roam, rove, scavenge, slink, skulk, nose around

proximity = <u>nearness</u>, closeness, vicinity, neighbourhood, juxtaposition, contiguity, propinquity, adjacency

proxy = <u>representative</u>, agent, deputy, substitute, factor, attorney, delegate, surrogate

prudence 1 = <u>caution</u>, care, discretion, vigilance, wariness, circumspection, canniness, heedfulness …*He urged prudence rather than haste on any new resolution…*
2 = <u>wisdom</u>, common sense, good sense, good judgment, sagacity, judiciousness …*acting with prudence and judgement…*
3 = <u>thrift</u>, economy, planning, saving, precaution, foresight, providence, preparedness, good management, husbandry, frugality, forethought, economizing, far-sightedness, careful budgeting …*A lack of prudence may lead to financial problems…*

prudent 1 = <u>cautious</u>, careful, wary, discreet, canny, vigilant, circumspect …*He is taking a prudent and cautious approach…* **OPPOSITE** careless
2 = <u>wise</u>, politic, sensible, sage, shrewd, discerning, judicious, sagacious …*We believed ours was the prudent and responsible course of action…* **OPPOSITE** unwise
3 = <u>thrifty</u>, economical, sparing, careful, canny, provident, frugal, far-sighted …*In private, she is prudent and even frugal…* **OPPOSITE** extravagant

prudish = <u>prim</u>, formal, proper, stuffy, puritanical, demure, squeamish, narrow-minded, starchy (*informal*), prissy (*informal*), strait-laced, Victorian, priggish, schoolmarmish (*Brit. informal*), old-maidish (*informal*), niminy-piminy, overmodest, overnice **OPPOSITE** broad-minded

prune 1 = <u>cut</u>, trim, clip, dock, shape, cut back, shorten, snip, lop, pare down …*You have to prune the bushes if you want fruit…*
2 = <u>reduce</u>, cut, cut back, trim, cut down, pare down, make reductions in …*Economic hard times are forcing the company to prune their budget…*

prurient 1 = <u>lecherous</u>, longing, lewd, salacious, lascivious, itching, hankering, voyeuristic, lustful, libidinous, desirous, concupiscent …*our prurient fascination with sexual scandals…*
2 = <u>indecent</u>, dirty, erotic, obscene, steamy (*informal*), pornographic, X-rated (*informal*), salacious, smutty …*the film's harshly prurient and cynical sex scenes…*

pry = <u>be inquisitive</u>, peer, interfere, poke, peep, meddle, intrude, snoop (*informal*), nose into, be nosy (*informal*), be a busybody, ferret about, poke your nose in *or* into (*informal*)

prying = <u>inquisitive</u>, spying, curious, interfering, meddling, intrusive, eavesdropping, snooping (*informal*), snoopy (*informal*), impertinent, nosy (*informal*), meddlesome

psalm = <u>hymn</u>, carol, chant, paean, song of praise

pseudonym = <u>false name</u>, alias, incognito, stage

name, pen name, assumed name, nom de guerre, nom de plume, professional name

psyche = <u>soul</u>, mind, self, spirit, personality, individuality, subconscious, true being, anima, essential nature, pneuma (*Philosophy*), innermost self, inner man

psychedelic 1 = <u>hallucinogenic</u>, mind-blowing (*informal*), psychoactive, hallucinatory, mind-bending (*informal*), psychotropic, mind-expanding, consciousness-expanding, psychotomimetic ...*experimenting with psychedelic drugs*...
2 = <u>multicoloured</u>, wild, crazy, freaky (*slang*), kaleidoscopic ...*psychedelic patterns*...

psychiatrist = <u>psychotherapist</u>, analyst, therapist, psychologist, shrink (*slang*), psychoanalyst, psychoanalyser, headshrinker (*slang*)

psychic ADJECTIVE **1** = <u>supernatural</u>, mystic, occult, clairvoyant, telepathic, extrasensory, preternatural, telekinetic ...*Trevor helped police by using his psychic powers*...
2 = <u>mystical</u>, spiritual, magical, other-worldly, paranormal, preternatural ...*He declared his total disbelief in psychic phenomena*...
3 = <u>psychological</u>, emotional, mental, spiritual, inner, psychiatric, cognitive, psychogenic ...*Childhood mistreatment is the primary cause of every kind of psychic disorder*...
NOUN = <u>clairvoyant</u>, fortune teller ...*a natural psychic who used Tarot as a focus for his intuition*...

psychological 1 = <u>mental</u>, emotional, intellectual, inner, cognitive, cerebral ...*the treatment of psychological disorders*...
2 = <u>imaginary</u>, psychosomatic, unconscious, subconscious, subjective, irrational, unreal, all in the mind ...*My GP dismissed my back pains as purely psychological*...

psychology 1 = <u>behaviourism</u>, study of personality, science of mind ...*He is Professor of Psychology at Bedford Community College*...
2 (*Informal*) = <u>way of thinking</u>, attitude, behaviour, temperament, mentality, thought processes, mental processes, what makes you tick, mental make-up ...*a fascination with the psychology of serial killers*...

psychopath = <u>madman</u>, lunatic, maniac, psychotic, nutter (*Brit. slang*), nutcase (*slang*), sociopath, headcase (*informal*), mental case (*slang*), headbanger (*informal*), insane person
➤ **mad**

psychotic ADJECTIVE = <u>mad</u>, mental (*slang*), insane, lunatic, demented, unbalanced, deranged, psychopathic, round the bend (*Brit. slang*), certifiable, off your head (*slang*), off your trolley (*slang*), not right in the head, non compos mentis (*Latin*), off your rocker (*slang*), off your chump ...*He was diagnosed as psychotic and schizophrenic*...
NOUN = <u>lunatic</u>, maniac, psychopath, nut (*slang*), psycho (*slang*), loony (*slang*), nutter (*Brit. slang*), nutcase (*slang*), headcase (*informal*), mental case (*slang*), headbanger (*informal*)
➤ **mad**

pub or **public house** = <u>tavern</u>, bar, inn, local (*Brit. informal*), saloon, watering hole (*facetious slang*), boozer (*Brit., Austral., & N.Z. informal*), roadhouse, hostelry (*archaic or facetious*), alehouse (*archaic*), taproom

puberty = <u>adolescence</u>, teenage, teens, young adulthood, pubescence, awkward age, juvenescence

public NOUN **1** = <u>people</u>, society, country, population, masses, community, nation, everyone, citizens, voters, electorate, multitude, populace, hoi polloi, Joe Public (*slang*), Joe Six-Pack (*U.S. slang*), commonalty ...*The poll is a test of the public's confidence in the government*...
2 = <u>clientele</u>, fans, supporters, following, followers, audience, buyers, patrons ...*She won't do anything that makes her look bad to her public*...
ADJECTIVE **1** = <u>civic</u>, government, state, national, local, official, community, social, federal, civil, constitutional, municipal ...*a substantial part of public spending*...
2 = <u>general</u>, popular, national, shared, common, widespread, universal, collective ...*Parliament's decision was in line with public opinion*...
3 = <u>open</u>, community, accessible, communal, open to the public, unrestricted, free to all, not private ...*a public library*... OPPOSITE private
4 = <u>well-known</u>, leading, important, respected, famous, celebrated, recognized, distinguished, prominent, influential, notable, renowned, eminent, famed, noteworthy, in the public eye ...*He hit out at public figures who commit adultery*...
5 = <u>known</u>, published, exposed, open, obvious, acknowledged, recognized, plain, patent, notorious, overt, in circulation ...*She was reluctant to make her views public*... OPPOSITE secret
PHRASES **in public** = <u>openly</u>, publicly, overtly, for all to see, in full view, coram populo (*Latin*) ...*by-laws to make it illegal to smoke in public*...

publication 1 = <u>pamphlet</u>, book, newspaper, magazine, issue, title, leaflet, brochure, booklet, paperback, hardback, periodical, zine (*informal*), handbill ...*a renewed campaign against pornographic publications*...
2 = <u>announcement</u>, publishing, broadcasting, reporting, airing, appearance, declaration, advertisement, disclosure, proclamation, notification, dissemination, promulgation ...*We have no comment regarding the publication of these photographs*...

publicity 1 = <u>advertising</u>, press, promotion, hype, boost, build-up, plug (*informal*), puff, ballyhoo (*informal*), puffery (*informal*), boosterism ...*Much advance publicity was given to the talks*...
2 = <u>attention</u>, exposure, fame, celebrity, fuss, public interest, limelight, notoriety, media attention, renown, public notice ...*The case has generated enormous publicity*...

publicize 1 = <u>advertise</u>, promote, plug (*informal*), hype, push, spotlight, puff, play up, write up, spread about, beat the drum for (*informal*), give publicity to, bring to public notice ...*The author appeared on TV to publicize her latest book*...
2 = <u>make known</u>, report, reveal, publish, broadcast,

leak, disclose, proclaim, circulate, make public, divulge …*He never publicized his plans…* OPPOSITE keep secret

public-spirited = <u>altruistic</u>, generous, humanitarian, charitable, philanthropic, unselfish, community-minded

publish 1 = <u>put out</u>, issue, produce, print, bring out …*His latest book will be published in May…*
2 = <u>announce</u>, reveal, declare, spread, advertise, broadcast, leak, distribute, communicate, disclose, proclaim, circulate, impart, publicize, divulge, promulgate, shout from the rooftops (*informal*), blow wide open (*slang*) …*The paper did not publish his name for legal reasons…*

pucker VERB = <u>wrinkle</u>, tighten, purse, pout, contract, gather, knit, crease, compress, crumple, ruffle, furrow, screw up, crinkle, draw together, ruck up, ruckle …*She puckered her lips and kissed him on the nose…*
NOUN = <u>wrinkle</u>, fold, crease, crumple, ruck, crinkle, ruckle …*small puckers in the material…*

pudding = <u>dessert</u>, afters (*Brit. informal*), sweet, pud (*informal*), second course, last course

puerile = <u>childish</u>, juvenile, naive, weak, silly, ridiculous, foolish, petty, trivial, irresponsible, immature, infantile, inane, babyish, jejune OPPOSITE mature

puff VERB 1 = <u>smoke</u>, draw, drag (*slang*), suck, inhale, pull at *or* on …*He gave a wry smile as he puffed on his cigarette…*
2 = <u>breathe heavily</u>, pant, exhale, blow, gasp, gulp, wheeze, fight for breath, puff and pant …*I could see he was unfit, because he was puffing…*
3 = <u>promote</u>, push, plug (*informal*), hype, publicize, advertise, praise, crack up (*informal*), big up (*slang, chiefly Caribbean*), overpraise …*TV correspondents puffing the new digital channels…*
NOUN 1 = <u>drag</u>, pull (*slang*), moke …*She was taking quick puffs at her cigarette…*
2 = <u>blast</u>, breath, flurry, whiff, draught, gust, emanation …*an occasional puff of air stirring the brittle leaves…*
3 = <u>advertisement</u>, ad (*informal*), promotion, plug (*informal*), good word, commendation, sales talk, favourable mention, piece of publicity …*an elaborate puff for his magazine…*
PHRASES **puff out** *or* **up** = <u>swell</u>, expand, enlarge, inflate, dilate, distend, bloat …*His chest puffed out with pride…* ♦ **puff something out** *or* **up** = <u>expand</u>, inflate, stick out, dilate, distend …*He puffed out his cheeks and let out his breath…*

puffy = <u>swollen</u>, enlarged, inflated, inflamed, bloated, puffed up, distended

pugnacious = <u>aggressive</u>, contentious, irritable, belligerent, combative, petulant, antagonistic, argumentative, bellicose, irascible, quarrelsome, hot-tempered, choleric, disputatious, aggers (*Austral. slang*), biffo (*Austral. slang*) OPPOSITE peaceful

puke (*Slang*) = <u>vomit</u>, be sick, throw up (*informal*),

spew, heave, regurgitate, disgorge, retch, be nauseated, chuck (*Austral. & N.Z. informal*), barf (*U.S. slang*), chunder (*slang, chiefly Austral.*), upchuck (*U.S. slang*), do a technicolour yawn (*slang*), toss your cookies (*U.S. slang*)

pull VERB 1 = <u>draw</u>, haul, drag, trail, tow, tug, jerk, yank, prise, wrench, lug, wrest …*I helped pull him out of the water…* OPPOSITE push
2 = <u>extract</u>, pick, remove, gather, take out, weed, pluck, cull, uproot, draw out …*Wes was in the yard pulling weeds when we drove up…* OPPOSITE insert
3 (*Informal*) = <u>attract</u>, draw, bring in, tempt, lure, interest, entice, pull in, magnetize …*The organizers have to employ performers to pull a crowd…* OPPOSITE repel
4 = <u>strain</u>, tear, stretch, rend, rip, wrench, dislocate, sprain …*Dave pulled a back muscle and could hardly move…*
NOUN 1 = <u>tug</u>, jerk, yank, twitch, heave …*The tooth must be removed with a firm, straight pull…* OPPOSITE shove
2 = <u>attraction</u>, appeal, lure, fascination, force, draw, influence, magnetism, enchantment, drawing power, enticement, allurement …*No matter how much you feel the pull of the past, try to look to the future…*
3 = <u>force</u>, exertion, magnetism, forcefulness …*the pull of gravity…*
4 = <u>puff</u>, drag (*slang*), inhalation …*He took a deep pull of his cigarette…*
5 (*Informal*) = <u>influence</u>, power, authority, say, standing, weight, advantage, muscle, sway, prestige, clout (*informal*), leverage, kai (*N.Z. informal*) …*Using all his pull in parliament, he obtained the necessary papers…*
PHRASES **pull a fast one on someone** (*Informal*) = <u>trick</u>, cheat, con (*informal*), take advantage of, deceive, defraud, swindle, bamboozle (*informal*), hoodwink, take for a ride (*informal*), put one over on (*informal*) …*Someone had pulled a fast one on her over a procedural matter…* ♦ **pull in** = <u>draw in</u>, stop, park, arrive, come in, halt, draw up, pull over, come to a halt …*He pulled in at the side of the road…* ♦ **pull out (of)** 1 = <u>withdraw</u>, retire from, abandon, quit, step down from, back out, bow out, stop participating in …*An injury forced him to pull out of the race…* 2 = <u>leave</u>, abandon, get out, quit, retreat from, depart, evacuate …*The militia has agreed to pull out of Beirut…* ♦ **pull someone in** (*Brit. slang*) = <u>arrest</u>, nail (*informal*), bust (*informal*), lift (*slang*), run in (*slang*), collar (*informal*), pinch (*informal*), nab (*informal*), take someone into custody, feel someone's collar (*slang*) …*The police pulled him in for questioning…* ♦ **pull someone up** = <u>reprimand</u>, lecture, rebuke, reproach, carpet (*informal*), censure, scold, berate, castigate, admonish, chastise, tear into (*informal*), read the riot act to, tell someone off (*informal*), reprove, upbraid, take someone to task, tick someone off (*informal*), read someone the riot act, bawl someone out (*informal*), dress someone down (*informal*), lambaste, give someone an earful, chew someone out (*U.S. & Canad. informal*), tear

someone off a strip (*Brit. informal*), haul someone over the coals, give someone a dressing down, give someone a rocket (*Brit. & N.Z. informal*), slap someone on the wrist, rap someone over the knuckles ...*My boss pulled me up about my timekeeping...* ◆ **pull something apart** or **to pieces** 1 = dismantle, strip down, disassemble, take something apart, break something up, take something to bits ...*You'll have to pull it apart and start all over again...* 2 = criticize, attack, blast, pan (*informal*), slam (*slang*), put down, run down, slate (*informal*), tear into (*informal*), lay into (*informal*), flay, diss (*slang, chiefly U.S.*), find fault with, lambast(e), pick holes in ...*The critics pulled his new book to pieces...* ◆ **pull something down** = demolish, level, destroy, dismantle, remove, flatten, knock down, take down, tear down, bulldoze, raze, lay waste, raze to the ground ...*They'd pulled the school down...* ◆ **pull something in** 1 = attract, draw, pull, bring in, lure ...*his ability to pull in a near capacity crowd for a match...* 2 = earn, make, clear, gain, net, collect, be paid, pocket, bring in, gross, take home, rake in ...*I only pull in £15,000 a year as a social worker...* ◆ **pull something off** 1 (*Informal*) = succeed in, manage, establish, effect, complete, achieve, engineer, carry out, crack (*informal*), fulfil, accomplish, execute, discharge, clinch, bring about, carry off, perpetrate, bring off ...*Labour might just pull off its third victory in a row...* 2 = remove, detach, rip off, tear off, doff, wrench off ...*He pulled off his shirt...* ◆ **pull something out** = produce, draw, bring out, draw out ...*He pulled out a gun and threatened us...* ◆ **pull something up** = uproot, raise, lift, weed, dig up, dig out, rip up ...*Pull up weeds by hand and put them on the compost heap...* ◆ **pull through** = survive, improve, recover, rally, come through, get better, be all right, recuperate, turn the corner, pull round, get well again ...*Everyone waited to see whether he would pull through or not...* ◆ **pull up** = stop, park, halt, arrive, brake, draw up, come to a halt, reach a standstill ...*The cab pulled up and the driver jumped out...* ◆ **pull yourself together** (*Informal*) = get a grip on yourself, recover, get over it, buck up (*informal*), snap out of it (*informal*), get your act together, regain your composure ...*He pulled himself together and got back to work...*

pulp NOUN 1 = paste, mash, pap, mush, semisolid, pomace, semiliquid ...*The olives are crushed to a pulp by stone rollers...*
2 = flesh, meat, marrow, soft part ...*Use the whole fruit, including the pulp, which is high in fibre...*
ADJECTIVE = cheap, sensational, lurid, mushy (*informal*), trashy, rubbishy ...*lurid '50s pulp fiction...*
VERB = crush, squash, mash, pulverize ...*Onions can be boiled and pulped to a puree...*

pulsate = throb, pound, beat, hammer, pulse, tick, thump, quiver, vibrate, thud, palpitate

pulse NOUN = beat, rhythm, vibration, beating, stroke, throb, throbbing, oscillation, pulsation ...*the repetitive pulse of the music...*
VERB = beat, tick, throb, vibrate, pulsate ...*Her feet pulsed with pain...*

pummel = beat, punch, pound, strike, knock, belt (*informal*), hammer, bang, batter, thump, clobber (*slang*), lambast(e), beat the living daylights out of, rain blows upon

pump VERB 1 = drive out, empty, drain, force out, bail out, siphon, draw off ...*drill rigs that are busy pumping natural gas...*
2 = supply, send, pour, inject ...*The government must pump more money into community care...*
3 = interrogate, probe, quiz, cross-examine, grill (*informal*), worm out of, give someone the third degree, question closely ...*He ran in every five minutes to pump me for details...*
4 = fire, shoot, discharge, let off ...*A gunman burst in and pumped five bullets into her head...*
PHRASES **pump something up** = inflate, blow up, fill up, dilate, puff up, aerate ...*I was trying to pump up my back tyre...*

pun = play on words, quip, double entendre, witticism, paronomasia (*Rhetoric*), equivoque

punch[1] VERB = hit, strike, box, smash, belt (*informal*), slam, plug (*slang*), bash (*informal*), sock (*slang*), clout (*informal*), slug, swipe (*informal*), biff (*slang*), bop (*informal*), wallop (*informal*), pummel ...*After punching him on the chin, she hit him over the head...*
NOUN 1 = blow, hit, knock, bash (*informal*), plug (*slang*), sock (*slang*), thump, clout (*informal*), jab, swipe (*informal*), biff (*slang*), bop (*informal*), wallop (*informal*) ...*He's asking for a punch on the nose...*
2 (*Informal*) = effectiveness, force, bite, impact, point, drive, vigour, verve, forcefulness ...*The film lacks punch and pace...*

punch[2] = pierce, cut, bore, drill, pink, stamp, puncture, prick, perforate ...*I took a pen and punched holes in the carton...*

punch-up (*Brit. informal*) = fight, row, argument, set-to (*informal*), scrap (*informal*), brawl, free-for-all (*informal*), dust-up (*informal*), shindig (*informal*), battle royal, stand-up fight (*informal*), dingdong, shindy (*informal*), bagarre (*French*), biffo (*Austral. slang*)

punchy (*Informal*) = effective, spirited, dynamic, lively, storming (*informal*), aggressive, vigorous, forceful, incisive, in-your-face (*slang*)

punctual = on time, timely, early, prompt, strict, exact, precise, in good time, on the dot, seasonable
OPPOSITE late

punctuality = promptness, readiness, regularity, promptitude

punctuate = interrupt, break, pepper, sprinkle, intersperse, interject

puncture NOUN 1 = flat tyre, flat ...*Someone helped me to mend the puncture...*
2 = hole, opening, break, cut, nick, leak, slit, rupture, perforation ...*an instrument used to make a puncture in the abdominal wall...*
VERB 1 = pierce, cut, nick, penetrate, prick, rupture, perforate, impale, bore a hole ...*The bullet punctured his stomach...*

2 = <u>deflate</u>, go down, go flat ...*The tyre is guaranteed never to puncture...*

3 = <u>humble</u>, discourage, disillusion, flatten, deflate, take down a peg (*informal*) ...*a witty column which punctures celebrity egos...*

pundit = <u>expert</u>, guru, maestro, buff (*informal*), wonk (*informal*), fundi (*S. African*), one of the cognoscenti, (self-appointed) expert *or* authority

pungent 1 = <u>strong</u>, hot, spicy, seasoned, sharp, acid, bitter, stinging, sour, tart, aromatic, tangy, acrid, peppery, piquant, highly flavoured, acerb ...*The more herbs you use, the more pungent the sauce will be...* OPPOSITE mild

2 = <u>cutting</u>, pointed, biting, acute, telling, sharp, keen, stinging, piercing, penetrating, poignant, stringent, scathing, acrimonious, barbed, incisive, sarcastic, caustic, vitriolic, trenchant, mordant, mordacious ...*He enjoyed the play's shrewd and pungent social analysis...* OPPOSITE dull

punish = <u>discipline</u>, correct, castigate, chastise, beat, sentence, whip, lash, cane, flog, scourge, chasten, penalize, bring to book, slap someone's wrist, throw the book at, rap someone's knuckles, give someone the works (*slang*), give a lesson to

punishable = <u>culpable</u>, criminal, chargeable, indictable, blameworthy, convictable

punishing = <u>hard</u>, taxing, demanding, grinding, wearing, tiring, exhausting, uphill, gruelling, strenuous, arduous, burdensome, backbreaking OPPOSITE easy

punishment 1 = <u>penalizing</u>, discipline, correction, retribution, what for (*informal*), chastening, just deserts, chastisement, punitive measures ...*The man is guilty and he deserves punishment...*

2 = <u>penalty</u>, reward, sanction, penance, comeuppance (*slang*) ...*The usual punishment is a fine...*

3 (*Informal*) = <u>beating</u>, abuse, torture, pain, victimization, manhandling, maltreatment, rough treatment ...*He took a lot of punishment in the first few rounds of the fight...*

4 = <u>rough treatment</u>, abuse, maltreatment ...*This bike isn't designed to take that kind of punishment...*

punitive = <u>retaliatory</u>, in retaliation, vindictive, in reprisal, revengeful, retaliative, punitory

punk = <u>delinquent</u>, rebel, offender, wrongdoer, juvenile delinquent, miscreant

punt VERB = <u>bet</u>, back, stake, gamble, lay, wager ...*He punted the lot on Little Nell in the third race...* NOUN = <u>bet</u>, stake, gamble, wager ...*I like to take the odd punt on the stock exchange...*

punter 1 = <u>gambler</u>, better, backer, punt (*chiefly Brit.*) ...*Punters are expected to gamble £70m on the Grand National...*

2 (*Informal*) = <u>customer</u>, guest, client, patron, member of the audience ...*The show ended when an irate punter punched one of the performers...*

3 (*Informal*) = <u>person</u>, guy (*informal*), fellow, bloke (*Brit. informal*), man in the street ...*Most of these artists are not known to the ordinary punter...*

puny 1 = <u>feeble</u>, weak, frail, little, tiny, weakly, stunted, diminutive, sickly, undeveloped, pint-sized (*informal*), undersized, underfed, dwarfish, pygmy *or* pigmy ...*Our Kevin has always been a puny lad...* OPPOSITE strong

2 = <u>insignificant</u>, minor, petty, inferior, trivial, worthless, trifling, paltry, inconsequential, piddling (*informal*) ...*the puny resources at our disposal...*

pup *or* **puppy** = <u>whippersnapper</u>, braggart, whelp, jackanapes, popinjay

(*Related Words*)
collective noun: litter

pupil 1 = <u>student</u>, scholar, schoolboy *or* schoolgirl, schoolchild ...*a school with over 1,000 pupils...* OPPOSITE teacher

2 = <u>learner</u>, student, follower, trainee, novice, beginner, apprentice, disciple, protégé, neophyte, tyro, catechumen ...*Goldschmidt became a pupil of the composer Franz Schreker...* OPPOSITE instructor

puppet 1 = <u>marionette</u>, doll, glove puppet, finger puppet ...*The show features huge inflatable puppets...*

2 = <u>pawn</u>, tool, instrument, creature, dupe, gull (*archaic*), figurehead, mouthpiece, stooge, cat's-paw ...*The ministers have denied that they are puppets of a foreign government...*

purchase VERB = <u>buy</u>, pay for, obtain, get, score (*slang*), gain, pick up, secure, acquire, invest in, shop for, get hold of, come by, procure, make a purchase ...*She purchased a tuna sandwich and a carton of orange juice... ...Most of the shares were purchased by brokers...* OPPOSITE sell

NOUN **1** = <u>acquisition</u>, buy, investment, property, gain, asset, possession ...*She opened the bag and looked at her purchases...*

2 = <u>grip</u>, hold, support, footing, influence, edge, advantage, grasp, lever, leverage, foothold, toehold ...*I got a purchase on the rope and pulled...*

purchaser = <u>buyer</u>, customer, consumer, vendee (*Law*) OPPOSITE seller

pure 1 = <u>unmixed</u>, real, clear, true, simple, natural, straight, perfect, genuine, neat, authentic, flawless, unalloyed ...*The ancient alchemists tried to transmute base metals into pure gold...* OPPOSITE adulterated

2 = <u>clean</u>, immaculate, sterile, wholesome, sanitary, spotless, sterilized, squeaky-clean, unblemished, unadulterated, untainted, disinfected, uncontaminated, unpolluted, pasteurized, germ-free ...*Demands for pure and clean river water...* OPPOSITE contaminated

3 = <u>theoretical</u>, abstract, philosophical, speculative, academic, conceptual, hypothetical, conjectural, non-practical ...*Physics isn't just about pure science with no practical applications...* OPPOSITE practical

4 = <u>complete</u>, total, perfect, absolute, mere, sheer, patent, utter, outright, thorough, downright, palpable, unqualified, out-and-out, unmitigated ...*The old man turned to give her a look of pure surprise...* OPPOSITE qualified

5 = <u>innocent</u>, virgin, modest, good, true, moral, maidenly, upright, honest, immaculate, impeccable, righteous, virtuous, squeaky-clean, blameless, chaste, virginal, unsullied, guileless, uncorrupted, unstained, undefiled, unspotted …*a pure and chaste maiden*… OPPOSITE> corrupt

purely = <u>absolutely</u>, just, only, completely, simply, totally, entirely, exclusively, plainly, merely, solely, wholly

purgatory = <u>torment</u>, agony, murder (*informal*), hell (*informal*), torture, misery, hell on earth

purge VERB 1 = <u>rid</u>, clear, cleanse, strip, empty, void …*They voted to purge the party of 'hostile and anti-party elements'*…
2 = <u>get rid of</u>, kill, remove, dismiss, axe (*informal*), expel, wipe out, oust, eradicate, eject, do away with, liquidate, exterminate, sweep out, rout out, wipe from the face of the earth, rid somewhere of …*They have purged thousands from the upper levels of the civil service*… …*They purged any individuals suspected of loyalty to the king*…
3 = <u>cleanse</u>, clear, purify, wash, clean out, expiate …*He lay still, trying to purge his mind of anxiety*…
NOUN = <u>removal</u>, elimination, crushing, expulsion, suppression, liquidation, cleanup, witch hunt, eradication, ejection …*a thorough purge of people associated with the late ruler*…

purify 1 = <u>clean</u>, filter, cleanse, refine, clarify, disinfect, fumigate, decontaminate, sanitize …*Plants can filter and purify the air in your office*… OPPOSITE> contaminate
2 = <u>absolve</u>, cleanse, redeem, exonerate, sanctify, exculpate, shrive, lustrate …*They believe that bathing in the Ganges at certain holy places purifies the soul*… OPPOSITE> sully

purist = <u>stickler</u>, traditionalist, perfectionist, classicist, pedant, formalist, literalist

puritan NOUN = <u>moralist</u>, fanatic, zealot, prude, pietist, rigorist …*He delighted in dealing with subjects that enraged puritans*…
ADJECTIVE = <u>strict</u>, austere, puritanical, narrow, severe, intolerant, ascetic, narrow-minded, moralistic, prudish, hidebound, strait-laced …*Paul has always had a puritan streak*…

puritanical = <u>strict</u>, forbidding, puritan, stuffy, narrow, severe, proper, stiff, rigid, disapproving, austere, fanatical, bigoted, prim, ascetic, narrow-minded, prudish, strait-laced OPPOSITE> liberal

puritanism = <u>strictness</u>, austerity, severity, zeal, piety, rigidity, fanaticism, narrowness, asceticism, moralism, prudishness, rigorism, piousness

purity 1 = <u>cleanness</u>, clarity, cleanliness, brilliance, genuineness, wholesomeness, fineness, clearness, pureness, faultlessness, immaculateness, untaintedness …*the purity of the air in your working environment*… OPPOSITE> impurity
2 = <u>innocence</u>, virtue, integrity, honesty, decency, sincerity, virginity, piety, chastity, rectitude, guilelessness, virtuousness, chasteness, blamelessness …*The American Female Reform Society promoted sexual purity*… OPPOSITE> immorality

purple

Shades of purple

amethyst	magenta
aubergine	mauve
burgundy	mulberry
carmine	pansy
claret	peach-blow
dubonnet	periwinkle
gentian	plum
gentian blue	puce
heather	royal purple
heliotrope	Tyrian purple
indigo	violet
lavender	wine
lilac	

purport = <u>claim</u>, allege, proclaim, maintain, declare, pretend, assert, pose as, profess

purpose NOUN 1 = <u>reason</u>, point, idea, goal, grounds, design, aim, basis, principle, function, object, intention, objective, motive, motivation, justification, impetus, the why and wherefore …*The purpose of the occasion was to raise money for charity*…
2 = <u>aim</u>, end, plan, hope, view, goal, design, project, target, wish, scheme, desire, object, intention, objective, ambition, aspiration, Holy Grail (*informal*) …*They are prepared to go to any lengths to achieve their purpose*…
3 = <u>determination</u>, commitment, resolve, will, resolution, initiative, enterprise, ambition, conviction, motivation, persistence, tenacity, firmness, constancy, single-mindedness, steadfastness …*The teachers are enthusiastic and have a sense of purpose*…
4 = <u>use</u>, good, return, result, effect, value, benefit, profit, worth, gain, advantage, outcome, utility, merit, mileage (*informal*), avail, behoof (*archaic*) …*Talking about it will serve no purpose*…
PHRASES **on purpose** = <u>deliberately</u>, purposely, consciously, intentionally, knowingly, wilfully, by design, wittingly, calculatedly, designedly …*Was it an accident, or did she do it on purpose?*…

Word Power

purpose – The two concepts *purposeful* and *on purpose* should be carefully distinguished. *On purpose* and *purposely* have roughly the same meaning, and imply that a person's action is deliberate, rather than accidental. However, *purposeful* and its related adverb *purposefully* refer to the way that someone acts as being full of purpose or determination.

purposeful = <u>determined</u>, resolved, resolute, decided, firm, settled, positive, fixed, deliberate, single-minded, tenacious, strong-willed, steadfast, immovable, unfaltering OPPOSITE> undecided
➤ **purpose**

purposely = <u>deliberately</u>, expressly, consciously, intentionally, knowingly, with intent, on purpose, wilfully, by design, calculatedly, designedly OPPOSITE> accidentally
➤ **purpose**

purse NOUN **1** = <u>pouch</u>, wallet, money-bag ...*I dug the money out of my purse...*
2 (*U.S.*) = <u>handbag</u>, bag, shoulder bag, pocket book, clutch bag ...*She reached into her purse for her cigarettes...*
3 = <u>funds</u>, means, money, resources, treasury, wealth, exchequer, coffers, wherewithal ...*The money will go into the public purse, helping to lower taxes...*
4 = <u>prize</u>, winnings, award, gift, reward ...*She is tipped to win the biggest purse in women's pro volleyball history...*
VERB = <u>pucker</u>, close, contract, tighten, knit, wrinkle, pout, press together ...*She pursed her lips in disapproval...*

pursue **1** = <u>engage in</u>, follow, perform, conduct, wage, tackle, take up, work at, carry on, practise, participate in, prosecute, ply, go in for, apply yourself to ...*Japan would continue to pursue the policies laid down at the summit...*
2 = <u>try for</u>, seek, desire, search for, aim for, aspire to, work towards, strive for, have as a goal ...*Mr Menendez has aggressively pursued success...*
3 = <u>continue</u>, maintain, carry on, keep on, hold to, see through, adhere to, persist in, proceed in, persevere in ...*If your request is denied, don't be afraid to pursue the matter...*
4 = <u>follow</u>, track, hunt, chase, dog, attend, shadow, accompany, harry, tail (*informal*), haunt, plague, hound, stalk, harass, go after, run after, hunt down, give chase to ...*She pursued the man who had stolen her bag...* OPPOSITE flee
5 = <u>court</u>, woo, pay attention to, make up to (*informal*), chase after, pay court to, set your cap at ...*He had pursued her, and within weeks they had become lovers...* OPPOSITE fight shy of

pursuit **1** = <u>quest</u>, seeking, search, aim of, aspiration for, striving towards ...*individuals in pursuit of their dreams... ...the pursuit of happiness...*
2 = <u>pursuing</u>, seeking, tracking, search, hunt, hunting, chase, trail, trailing ...*Police had obstructed justice by hindering the pursuit of terrorists...*
3 = <u>occupation</u>, activity, interest, line, pleasure, hobby, pastime, vocation ...*They both love outdoor pursuits...*

push VERB **1** = <u>shove</u>, force, press, thrust, drive, knock, sweep, plunge, elbow, bump, ram, poke, propel, nudge, prod, jostle, hustle, bulldoze, impel, manhandle ...*They pushed him into the car...* OPPOSITE pull
2 = <u>press</u>, operate, depress, squeeze, activate, hold down ...*He got into the lift and pushed the button for the second floor...*
3 = <u>make</u> or <u>force your way</u>, move, shoulder, inch, squeeze, thrust, elbow, shove, jostle, work your way, thread your way ...*I pushed through the crowds and on to the escalator...*
4 = <u>urge</u>, encourage, persuade, spur, drive, press, influence, prod, constrain, incite, coerce, egg on, impel, browbeat, exert influence on ...*Her parents kept her in school and pushed her to study...* OPPOSITE discourage

5 = <u>promote</u>, advertise, hype, publicize, boost, plug (*informal*), puff, make known, propagandize, cry up ...*Advertisers often use scientific doublespeak to push their products...*
NOUN **1** = <u>shove</u>, thrust, butt, elbow, poke, nudge, prod, jolt ...*He gave me a sharp push...* OPPOSITE pull
2 (*Informal*) = <u>effort</u>, charge, attack, campaign, advance, assault, raid, offensive, sally, thrust, blitz, onset ...*All that was needed was one final push, and the enemy would be vanquished once and for all...*
3 (*Informal*) = <u>drive</u>, go (*informal*), energy, initiative, enterprise, ambition, determination, pep, vitality, vigour, dynamism, get-up-and-go (*informal*), gumption (*informal*) ...*He lacked the push to succeed in his chosen vocation...*
PHRASES **push off** (*Informal*) = <u>go away</u>, leave, get lost (*informal*), clear off (*informal*), take off (*informal*), depart, beat it (*slang*), light out (*informal*), hit the road (*slang*), hook it (*slang*), slope off, pack your bags (*informal*), make tracks, buzz off (*informal*), hop it (*informal*), shove off (*informal*), skedaddle (*informal*), naff off (*informal*), be off with you, sling your hook (*informal*), make yourself scarce (*informal*), voetsek (*S. African offensive*) ...*Do me a favour and push off, will you?...* ♦ **push something forward** = <u>speed (up)</u>, advance, promote, accelerate, forward, rush, assist, hurry, facilitate, hasten, precipitate, quicken, expedite, gee up ...*They will use their influence to push forward the peace process...* ♦ **the push** (*Informal, chiefly Brit.*) = <u>dismissal</u>, the sack (*informal*), discharge, the boot (*slang*), your cards (*informal*), your books (*informal*), marching orders (*informal*), the kiss-off (*slang, chiefly U.S. & Canad.*), the (old) heave-ho (*informal*), the order of the boot (*slang*) ...*Two cabinet ministers also got the push...*

pushed (*Informal*) often with **for** = <u>short of</u>, pressed, rushed, tight, hurried, under pressure, in difficulty, up against it (*informal*)

pushover **1** = <u>sucker</u> (*slang*), mug (*Brit. slang*), stooge (*slang*), soft touch (*slang*), chump (*informal*), walkover (*informal*), easy game (*informal*), easy or soft mark (*informal*) ...*He's a tough negotiator – you won't find him a pushover...*
2 (*Informal*) = <u>piece of cake</u> (*Brit. informal*), breeze (*U.S. & Canad. informal*), picnic (*informal*), child's play (*informal*), plain sailing, doddle (*Brit. slang*), walkover (*informal*), cinch (*slang*), cakewalk (*informal*), duck soup (*U.S. slang*) ...*You might think Hungarian is a pushover to learn, but it isn't...* OPPOSITE challenge

pushy = <u>forceful</u>, aggressive, assertive, brash, loud, offensive, ambitious, bold, obnoxious, presumptuous, obtrusive, officious, bumptious, self-assertive OPPOSITE shy

put VERB **1** = <u>place</u>, leave, set, position, rest, park (*informal*), plant, establish, lay, stick (*informal*), settle, fix, lean, deposit, dump (*informal*), prop, lay down, put down, situate, set down, stow, bung (*informal*), plonk (*informal*) ...*She put her bag on the floor...*
2 = <u>consign to</u>, place, commit to, doom to, condemn to ...*She was put in prison for her beliefs...*
3 = <u>impose</u>, subject, levy, inflict ...*The government has

put a big tax on beer, wine and spirits…

4 = lay, place, set, pin, attach to, attribute to, ascribe to, impute to …It's no good putting all the blame on me…

5 = express, state, word, phrase, set, pose, utter …To put it bluntly, he doesn't give a damn…

6 = present, suggest, advance, propose, offer, forward, submit, tender, bring forward, proffer, posit, set before, lay before …He sat there listening as we put our suggestions to him…

PHRASES **put someone away** (Informal) = commit, confine, cage (informal), imprison, certify, institutionalize, incarcerate, put in prison, put behind bars, lock up or away …He's insane! He should be put away for life… ◆ **put someone down** (Slang) = humiliate, shame, crush, show up, reject, dismiss, condemn, slight, criticize, snub, have a go at (informal), deflate, denigrate, belittle, disparage, deprecate, mortify, diss (slang, chiefly U.S.) …She's always putting her husband down in public… ◆ **put someone off** **1** = discourage, intimidate, deter, daunt, dissuade, demoralize, scare off, dishearten …We tried to visit the abbey but were put off by the queues… **2** = disconcert, confuse, unsettle, throw (informal), distress, rattle (informal), dismay, perturb, faze, discomfit, take the wind out of someone's sails, nonplus, abash …All this noise is putting me off… ◆ **put someone out** **1** = inconvenience, trouble, upset, bother, disturb, impose upon, discomfit, discommode, incommode …Thanks for the offer, but I couldn't put you out like that… **2** = annoy, anger, provoke, irritate, disturb, harass, confound, exasperate, disconcert, nettle, vex, perturb, irk, put on the spot, take the wind out of someone's sails, discountenance, discompose …They were quite put out to find me in charge… ◆ **put someone up** **1** = accommodate, house, board, lodge, quarter, entertain, take someone in, billet, give someone lodging …She asked if I could put her up for a few days… **2** = nominate, put forward, offer, present, propose, recommend, float, submit …The new party is putting up 15 candidates for 22 seats… ◆ **put someone up to something** = encourage, urge, persuade, prompt, incite, egg on, goad, put the idea into someone's head …How do you know he asked me out? Did you put him up to it?… ◆ **put something across** or **over** = communicate, explain, clarify, express, get through, convey, make clear, spell out, get across, make yourself understood …The opposition parties were hampered from putting across their message… ◆ **put something aside** or **by** **1** = save, store, stockpile, deposit, hoard, cache, lay by, stow away, salt away, keep in reserve, squirrel away …Encourage children to put some money aside each week… **2** = disregard, forget, ignore, bury, discount, set aside, pay no heed to …We should put aside our differences and discuss this sensibly… ◆ **put something away** **1** = store away, replace, put back, tidy up, clear away, tidy away, return to its place …She began putting away the dishes… **2** = save, set aside, put aside, keep, deposit, put by, stash away, store away …He had been able to put away money, to

insure against old age… **3** (Informal) = consume, devour, eat up, demolish (informal), gobble, guzzle, polish off (informal), gulp down, wolf down, pig out on (informal) …The food was superb, and we put away a fair amount of it… ◆ **put something down** **1** = record, write down, list, enter, log, take down, inscribe, set down, transcribe, put in black and white …Never put anything down on paper which might be used in evidence… **2** = repress, crush, suppress, check, silence, overthrow, squash, subdue, quash, quell, stamp out …Soldiers went in to put down a rebellion… **3** = put to sleep, kill, destroy, do away with, put away, put out of its misery …Magistrates ordered that the dog should be put down at once… ◆ **put something down to something** = attribute to, blame on, ascribe to, set down to, impute to, chalk up to …You may be a sceptic and put it down to coincidence… ◆ **put something forward** = recommend, present, suggest, introduce, advance, propose, press, submit, tender, nominate, prescribe, move for, proffer …He has put forward new peace proposals… ◆ **put something off** = postpone, delay, defer, adjourn, put back, hold over, reschedule, put on ice, put on the back burner (informal), take a rain check on (U.S. & Canad. Informal) …The Association has put the event off until December… ◆ **put something on** **1** = don, dress in, slip into, pull on, climb into, change into, throw on, get dressed in, fling on, pour yourself into, doll yourself up in …She put on her coat and went out… **2** = present, stage, perform, do, show, produce, mount …The band are putting on a UK show before the end of the year… **3** = add, gain, increase by …I've put on a stone since I stopped training… **4** = bet, back, place, chance, risk, lay, stake, hazard, wager …They put £20 on Matthew scoring the first goal… **5** = fake, affect, assume, simulate, feign, make believe, play-act …Anything becomes funny if you put on an American accent… ◆ **put something out** **1** = issue, release, publish, broadcast, bring out, circulate, make public, make known …The French news agency put out a statement from the Trade Minister… **2** = extinguish, smother, blow out, stamp out, douse, snuff out, quench …Firemen tried to free the injured and put out the blaze… ◆ **put something up** **1** = build, raise, set up, construct, erect, fabricate …He was putting up a new fence round the garden… **2** = offer, present, mount, put forward …In the end they surrendered without putting up any resistance… **3** = provide, advance, invest, contribute, give, pay up, supply, come up with, pledge, donate, furnish, fork out (informal), cough up (informal), shell out (informal) …The state agreed to put up the money to start his company… ◆ **put up with something** or or **someone** (Informal) = stand, suffer, bear, take, wear (Brit. informal), stomach, endure, swallow, brook, stand for, lump (informal), tolerate, hack (slang), abide, countenance …I won't put up with this kind of behaviour from you… ◆ **put upon someone** = take advantage of, trouble, abuse, harry, exploit, saddle, take for granted, put someone out, inconvenience, beset, overwork, impose upon, take for a fool …Don't allow people to put upon you or take you for granted…

putative (*Formal*) = <u>supposed</u>, reported, assumed, alleged, presumed, reputed, imputed, presumptive, commonly believed

put-down = <u>humiliation</u>, slight, snub, knock (*informal*), dig, sneer, rebuff, barb, sarcasm, kick in the teeth (*slang*), gibe, disparagement, one in the eye (*informal*)

puzzle VERB = <u>perplex</u>, beat (*slang*), confuse, baffle, stump, bewilder, confound, mystify, faze, flummox, bemuse, nonplus ...*What puzzles me is why nobody has complained before now*...
NOUN **1** = <u>problem</u>, riddle, maze, labyrinth, question, conundrum, teaser, poser, brain-teaser (*informal*) ...*a word puzzle*...
2 = <u>mystery</u>, problem, paradox, enigma, conundrum ...*the puzzle of why there are no Stone Age cave paintings in Britain*...
PHRASES **puzzle over something** = <u>think about</u>, study, wonder about, mull over, muse on, think hard about, ponder on, brood over, ask yourself about, cudgel *or* rack your brains ...*puzzling over the complexities of Shakespeare's verse*... ◆ **puzzle something out** = <u>solve</u>, work out, figure out, unravel, see, get, crack, resolve, sort out, clear up, decipher, think through, suss (out) (*slang*), get the answer of, find the key to, crack the code of ...*I stared at the symbols, trying to puzzle out their meaning*...

puzzled = <u>perplexed</u>, beaten, confused, baffled, lost, stuck, stumped, doubtful, at sea, bewildered, mixed up, at a loss, mystified, clueless, nonplussed, flummoxed, in a fog, without a clue

puzzlement = <u>perplexity</u>, questioning, surprise, doubt, wonder, confusion, uncertainty, bewilderment, disorientation, bafflement, mystification, doubtfulness

puzzling = <u>perplexing</u>, baffling, bewildering, hard, involved, misleading, unclear, ambiguous, enigmatic, incomprehensible, mystifying, inexplicable, unaccountable, knotty, unfathomable, labyrinthine, full of surprises, abstruse, beyond you, oracular
OPPOSITE> simple

pygmy *or* **pigmy** ADJECTIVE = <u>small</u>, miniature, dwarf, tiny, wee, stunted, diminutive, minuscule, midget, elfin, undersized, teeny-weeny, Lilliputian, dwarfish, teensy-weensy, pygmean ...*The pygmy hippopotamus is less than 6 ft long*...
NOUN **1** = <u>midget</u>, dwarf, shrimp (*informal*), Lilliputian, Tom Thumb, munchkin (*informal, chiefly U.S.*), homunculus, manikin ...*an encounter with the Ituri Forest pygmies*...
2 = <u>nonentity</u>, nobody, lightweight (*informal*), mediocrity, cipher, small fry, pipsqueak (*informal*) ...*He saw the politicians of his day as pygmies, not as giants*...

Q q

quack NOUN = <u>charlatan</u>, fraud, fake, pretender, humbug, impostor, mountebank, phoney *or* phony (*informal*) …*The man was a quack after all, just as Rosalinda had warned*…
ADJECTIVE = <u>fake</u>, fraudulent, phoney *or* phony (*informal*), pretended, sham, counterfeit …*Why do intelligent people find quack remedies so appealing?*…

quaff = <u>drink</u>, gulp, swig (*informal*), have, down, swallow, slug, guzzle, imbibe, partake of

quagmire 1 = <u>predicament</u>, difficulty, quandary, pass, fix (*informal*), jam (*informal*), dilemma, pinch, plight, scrape (*informal*), muddle, pickle (*informal*), impasse, entanglement, imbroglio …*a political quagmire*…
2 = <u>bog</u>, marsh, swamp, slough, fen, mire, morass, quicksand …*Overnight rain had turned the grass airstrip into a quagmire*…

quail = <u>shrink</u>, cringe, flinch, shake, faint, tremble, quake, shudder, falter, droop, blanch, recoil, cower, blench, have cold feet (*informal*)

quaint 1 = <u>unusual</u>, odd, curious, original, strange, bizarre, fantastic, old-fashioned, peculiar, eccentric, queer, rum (*Brit. slang*), singular, fanciful, whimsical, droll …*When visiting restaurants, be prepared for some quaint customs*… OPPOSITE ordinary
2 = <u>old-fashioned</u>, charming, picturesque, antique, gothic, old-world, antiquated …*Whisky-making is treated as a quaint cottage industry*… OPPOSITE modern

quake = <u>shake</u>, tremble, quiver, move, rock, shiver, throb, shudder, wobble, waver, vibrate, pulsate, quail, totter, convulse

qualification 1 = <u>eligibility</u>, quality, ability, skill, capacity, fitness, attribute, capability, endowment(s), accomplishment, achievement, aptitude, suitability, suitableness …*That time with him is my qualification to write the book*…
2 = <u>condition</u>, restriction, proviso, requirement, rider, exception, criterion, reservation, allowance, objection, limitation, modification, exemption, prerequisite, caveat, stipulation …*The empirical evidence is subject to many qualifications*…

qualified 1 = <u>capable</u>, trained, experienced, seasoned, able, fit, expert, talented, chartered, efficient, practised, licensed, certificated, equipped, accomplished, eligible, competent, skilful, adept, knowledgeable, proficient …*Demand has far outstripped supply of qualified teachers*… OPPOSITE untrained
2 = <u>restricted</u>, limited, provisional, conditional, reserved, guarded, bounded, adjusted, moderated, adapted, confined, modified, tempered, cautious, refined, amended, contingent, tentative, hesitant, circumscribed, equivocal …*He answers both questions with a qualified yes*… OPPOSITE unconditional

qualify 1 = <u>certify</u>, equip, empower, train, ground, condition, prepare, fit, commission, ready, permit, sanction, endow, capacitate …*The course does not qualify you to practise as a therapist*… OPPOSITE disqualify
2 = <u>be described</u>, count, be considered as, be named, be counted, be eligible, be characterized, be designated, be distinguished …*13 percent of households qualify as poor*…
3 = <u>restrict</u>, limit, reduce, vary, ease, moderate, adapt, modify, regulate, diminish, temper, soften, restrain, lessen, mitigate, abate, tone down, assuage, modulate, circumscribe …*I would qualify that by putting it into context*…

quality 1 = <u>standard</u>, standing, class, condition, value, rank, grade, merit, classification, calibre …*high quality paper and plywood*…
2 = <u>excellence</u>, status, merit, position, value, worth, distinction, virtue, superiority, calibre, eminence, pre-eminence …*a college of quality*…
3 = <u>characteristic</u>, feature, attribute, point, side, mark, property, aspect, streak, trait, facet, quirk, peculiarity, idiosyncrasy …*He wanted to introduce mature people with leadership qualities*…
4 = <u>nature</u>, character, constitution, make, sort, kind, worth, description, essence …*The pretentious quality of the poetry*…

qualm = <u>misgiving</u>, doubt, uneasiness, regret, anxiety, uncertainty, reluctance, hesitation, remorse, apprehension, disquiet, scruple, compunction, twinge *or* pang of conscience

quandary = <u>difficulty</u>, dilemma, predicament, puzzle, uncertainty, embarrassment, plight, strait, impasse, bewilderment, perplexity, delicate situation, cleft stick

quantity 1 = <u>amount</u>, lot, total, sum, part, portion, quota, aggregate, number, allotment …*a vast quantity of food*…
2 = <u>size</u>, measure, mass, volume, length, capacity, extent, bulk, magnitude, greatness, expanse …*the sheer quantity of data can cause problems*…

Word Power

quantity – The use of a plural noun after *quantity of*, as in *a large quantity of bananas*, used to be considered incorrect, the objection being that the word *quantity* should only be used to refer to an uncountable amount, which was grammatically regarded as a singular concept. Nowadays, however, most people consider the use of *quantity* with a plural noun to be acceptable.

---

quarrel NOUN = <u>disagreement</u>, fight, row, difference

(of opinion), argument, dispute, controversy, breach, scrap (*informal*), disturbance, misunderstanding, contention, feud, fray, brawl, spat, squabble, strife, wrangle, skirmish, vendetta, discord, fracas, commotion, tiff, altercation, broil, tumult, dissension, affray, shindig (*informal*), disputation, dissidence, shindy (*informal*), bagarre (*French*), biffo (*Austral. slang*) ...*I had a terrible quarrel with my other brothers...* OPPOSITE> accord
VERB = disagree, fight, argue, row, clash, dispute, scrap (*informal*), differ, fall out (*informal*), brawl, squabble, spar, wrangle, bicker, be at odds, lock horns, cross swords, fight like cat and dog, go at it hammer and tongs, altercate ...*My brother quarrelled with my father...* OPPOSITE> get on *or* along (with)

quarrelsome = argumentative, belligerent, pugnacious, cross, contentious, irritable, combative, fractious, petulant, ill-tempered, irascible, cantankerous, litigious, querulous, peevish, choleric, disputatious OPPOSITE> easy-going

quarry = prey, victim, game, goal, aim, prize, objective

quarter NOUN 1 = district, region, neighbourhood, place, point, part, side, area, position, station, spot, territory, zone, location, province, colony, locality ...*He wandered through the Chinese quarter...*
2 = mercy, pity, compassion, favour, charity, sympathy, tolerance, kindness, forgiveness, indulgence, clemency, leniency, forbearance, lenity ...*It is bloody brutal work, with no quarter given...*
PLURAL NOUN = lodgings, rooms, accommodation, post, station, chambers, digs (*Brit. informal*), shelter, lodging, residence, dwelling, barracks, abode, habitation, billet, domicile, cantonment (*Military*) ...*Mckinnon went down from the deck to the officers' quarters...*
VERB = accommodate, house, lodge, place, board, post, station, install, put up, billet, give accommodation, provide with accommodation ...*Our soldiers are quartered in Peredelkino...*

quash 1 = annul, overturn, reverse, cancel, overthrow, set aside, void, revoke, overrule, rescind, invalidate, nullify, declare null and void ...*The Appeal Court has quashed the convictions...*
2 = suppress, crush, put down, beat, destroy, overthrow, squash, subdue, repress, quell, extinguish, quench, extirpate ...*an attempt to quash regional violence...*

quaver = tremble, shake, quiver, thrill, quake, shudder, flicker, flutter, waver, vibrate, pulsate, oscillate, trill, twitter

queasy 1 = sick, ill, nauseous, squeamish, upset, uncomfortable, crook (*Austral. & N.Z. informal*), queer, unwell, giddy, nauseated, groggy (*informal*), off colour, bilious, indisposed, green around the gills (*informal*), sickish ...*He was prone to sickness and already felt queasy...*
2 = uneasy, concerned, worried, troubled, disturbed, anxious, uncertain, restless, ill at ease, fidgety ...*Some people feel queasy about how their names and addresses have been obtained...*

queen 1 = sovereign, ruler, monarch, leader, Crown, princess, majesty, head of state, Her Majesty, empress, crowned head ...*the time she met the Queen...*
2 = leading light, star, favourite, celebrity, darling, mistress, idol, big name, doyenne ...*the queen of crime writing...*

queer 1 = strange, odd, funny, unusual, extraordinary, remarkable, curious, weird, peculiar, abnormal, rum (*Brit. slang*), uncommon, erratic, singular, eerie, unnatural, unconventional, uncanny, disquieting, unorthodox, outlandish, left-field (*informal*), anomalous, droll, atypical, outré ...*If you ask me, there's something queer going on...* OPPOSITE> normal
2 = faint, dizzy, giddy, queasy, light-headed, reeling ...*Wine before beer and you'll feel queer...*

> ### *Word Power*
>
> **queer** – Although the term *queer* meaning 'gay' is still considered derogatory when used by non-gays, it is now being used by gay people themselves as a positive term in certain contexts, such as *queer politics*, *queer cinema*. Nevertheless, many gay people would not wish to have the term applied to them, nor would they use it of themselves.

quell 1 = suppress, crush, put down, defeat, overcome, conquer, subdue, stifle, overpower, quash, extinguish, stamp out, vanquish, squelch ...*Troops eventually quelled the unrest...*
2 = calm, quiet, silence, moderate, dull, soothe, alleviate, appease, allay, mitigate, assuage, pacify, mollify, deaden ...*He is trying to quell fears of a looming crisis...*

quench 1 = satisfy, appease, allay, satiate, slake, sate ...*He stopped to quench his thirst at a stream...*
2 = put out, extinguish, douse, end, check, destroy, crush, suppress, stifle, smother, snuff out, squelch ...*Fire crews struggled to quench the fire...*

query NOUN 1 = question, inquiry, problem, demand ...*If you have any queries, please contact us...*
2 = doubt, suspicion, reservation, objection, hesitation, scepticism ...*I read the query in the guide's eyes...*
VERB 1 = question, challenge, doubt, suspect, dispute, object to, distrust, mistrust, call into question, disbelieve, feel uneasy about, throw doubt on, harbour reservations about ...*No one queried my decision...*
2 = ask, inquire *or* enquire, question ...*'Is there something else?' he queried...*

quest 1 = search, hunt, mission, enterprise, undertaking, exploration, crusade ...*his quest to find true love...*
2 = expedition, journey, adventure, voyage, pilgrimage ...*Sir Guy the Seeker came on his quest to Dunstanburgh Castle...*

question NOUN 1 = inquiry, enquiry, query, investigation, examination, interrogation ...*He refused to answer further questions on the subject...*

OPPOSITE answer
2 = <u>difficulty</u>, problem, doubt, debate, argument, dispute, controversy, confusion, uncertainty, query, contention, misgiving, can of worms (*informal*), dubiety ...*There's no question about their success*...
3 = <u>issue</u>, point, matter, subject, problem, debate, proposal, theme, motion, topic, proposition, bone of contention, point at issue ...*the whole question of aid is a tricky political one*...
VERB **1** = <u>interrogate</u>, cross-examine, interview, examine, investigate, pump (*informal*), probe, grill (*informal*), quiz, ask questions, sound out, catechize ...*A man is being questioned by police*...
2 = <u>dispute</u>, challenge, doubt, suspect, oppose, query, distrust, mistrust, call into question, disbelieve, impugn, cast aspersions on, cast doubt upon, controvert ...*It never occurs to them to question the doctor's decisions*... OPPOSITE accept
PHRASES **in question** = <u>under discussion</u>, at issue, under consideration, in doubt, on the agenda, to be discussed, for debate, open to debate ...*The film in question detailed allegations about party corruption*...
♦ **out of the question** = <u>impossible</u>, unthinkable, inconceivable, not on (*informal*), hopeless, unimaginable, unworkable, unattainable, unobtainable, not feasible, impracticable, unachievable, unrealizable, not worth considering, not to be thought of ...*Is a tax increase still out of the question?*...

questionable = <u>dubious</u>, suspect, doubtful, controversial, uncertain, suspicious, dodgy (*Brit., Austral., & N.Z. informal*), unreliable, shady (*informal*), debatable, unproven, fishy (*informal*), moot, arguable, iffy (*informal*), equivocal, problematical, disputable, controvertible, dubitable OPPOSITE indisputable

queue = <u>line</u>, row, file, train, series, chain, string, column, sequence, succession, procession, crocodile (*Brit. informal*), progression, cavalcade, concatenation

quibble VERB = <u>split hairs</u>, carp, cavil, prevaricate, beat about the bush, equivocate ...*Let's not quibble*...
NOUN = <u>objection</u>, complaint, niggle, protest, criticism, nicety, equivocation, prevarication, cavil, quiddity, sophism ...*These are minor quibbles*...

quick 1 = <u>fast</u>, swift, speedy, express, active, cracking (*Brit. informal*), smart, rapid, fleet, brisk, hasty, headlong, nippy (*informal*), pdq (*slang*) ...*Europe has moved a long way at a quick pace*... OPPOSITE slow
2 = <u>brief</u>, passing, hurried, flying, fleeting, summary, lightning, short-lived, hasty, cursory, perfunctory ...*I just popped in for a quick chat*... OPPOSITE long
3 = <u>immediate</u>, instant, prompt, sudden, abrupt, instantaneous, expeditious ...*The President has admitted there is no quick end in sight*...
4 = <u>excitable</u>, passionate, impatient, abrupt, hasty, irritable, touchy, curt, petulant, irascible, testy ...*She had inherited her father's quick temper*... OPPOSITE calm
5 = <u>intelligent</u>, bright (*informal*), alert, sharp, acute, smart, clever, all there (*informal*), shrewd, discerning, astute, receptive, perceptive, quick-witted, quick on the uptake (*informal*), nimble-witted ...*The older

adults are not as quick in their thinking... OPPOSITE stupid

quicken 1 = <u>speed up</u>, hurry, accelerate, hasten, gee up (*informal*) ...*He quickened his pace a little*...
2 = <u>stimulate</u>, inspire, arouse, excite, strengthen, revive, refresh, activate, animate, rouse, incite, resuscitate, energize, revitalize, kindle, galvanize, invigorate, reinvigorate, vitalize, vivify ...*Thank you for quickening my spiritual understanding*...

quickly 1 = <u>swiftly</u>, rapidly, hurriedly, speedily, fast, quick, hastily, briskly, at high speed, apace, at full speed, hell for leather (*informal*), like lightning, at the speed of light, at full tilt, hotfoot, at a rate of knots (*informal*), like the clappers (*Brit. informal*), pdq (*slang*), like nobody's business (*informal*), with all speed, posthaste, lickety-split (*U.S. informal*), like greased lightning (*informal*), at *or* on the double ...*She turned and ran quickly up the stairs to the flat above*... OPPOSITE slowly
2 = <u>soon</u>, speedily, as soon as possible, momentarily (*U.S.*), instantaneously, pronto (*informal*), a.s.a.p. (*informal*) ...*You can become fitter quickly and easily*...
3 = <u>immediately</u>, instantly, at once, directly, promptly, abruptly, without delay, expeditiously ...*The meeting quickly adjourned*...

quick-witted = <u>clever</u>, bright (*informal*), sharp, keen, smart, alert, shrewd, astute, perceptive OPPOSITE slow

quid pro quo = <u>exchange</u>, interchange, tit for tat, equivalent, compensation, retaliation, reprisal, substitution

quiet ADJECTIVE **1** = <u>soft</u>, low, muted, lowered, whispered, faint, suppressed, stifled, hushed, muffled, inaudible, indistinct, low-pitched ...*A quiet murmur passed through the classroom*... OPPOSITE loud
2 = <u>peaceful</u>, silent, hushed, soundless, noiseless ...*She was received in a small, quiet office*... OPPOSITE noisy
3 = <u>calm</u>, peaceful, tranquil, contented, gentle, mild, serene, pacific, placid, restful, untroubled ...*She wanted a quiet life*... OPPOSITE exciting
4 = <u>still</u>, motionless, calm, peaceful, tranquil, untroubled ...*a look of quiet satisfaction*... OPPOSITE troubled
5 = <u>undisturbed</u>, isolated, secluded, private, secret, retired, sequestered, unfrequented ...*a quiet rural backwater*... OPPOSITE crowded
6 = <u>silent</u>, dumb ...*I told them to be quiet and go to sleep*...
7 = <u>reserved</u>, retiring, shy, collected, gentle, mild, composed, serene, sedate, meek, placid, docile, unflappable (*informal*), phlegmatic, peaceable, imperturbable, equable, even-tempered, unexcitable ...*He's a nice quiet man*... OPPOSITE excitable
8 = <u>subdued</u>, conservative, plain, sober, simple, modest, restrained, unassuming, unpretentious, unobtrusive ...*They dress in quiet colours*... OPPOSITE bright
NOUN = <u>peace</u>, rest, tranquillity, ease, silence, solitude, serenity, stillness, repose, calmness, quietness, peacefulness, restfulness ...*He wants some peace and

quiet... OPPOSITE noise

quieten 1 = silence, subdue, stifle, still, stop, quiet, mute, hush, quell, muffle, shush (*informal*) *...She tried to quieten her breathing...*
2 = soothe, calm, allay, dull, blunt, alleviate, appease, lull, mitigate, assuage, mollify, deaden, tranquillize, palliate *...a long time to quieten the paranoia of the West...* OPPOSITE provoke

quietly 1 = noiselessly, silently *...She closed the door quietly...*
2 = softly, in hushed tones, in a low voice *or* whisper, inaudibly, in an undertone, under your breath *...'This is goodbye, isn't it?' she said quietly...*
3 = privately, secretly, confidentially *...quietly planning their next move...*
4 = calmly, serenely, placidly, patiently, mildly, meekly, contentedly, dispassionately, undemonstratively *...She sat quietly watching all that was going on around her...*
5 = silently, in silence, mutely, without talking, dumbly *...Amy stood quietly in the door watching him...*
6 = modestly, humbly, unobtrusively, diffidently, unpretentiously, unassumingly, unostentatiously *...He is quietly confident about the magazine's chances...*

quilt = bedspread, duvet, comforter (*U.S.*), downie (*informal*), coverlet, eiderdown, counterpane, doona (*Austral.*), continental quilt

quintessential = ultimate, essential, typical, fundamental, definitive, archetypal, prototypical

quip = joke, sally, jest, riposte, wisecrack (*informal*), retort, counterattack, pleasantry, repartee, gibe, witticism, bon mot, badinage

quirk = peculiarity, eccentricity, mannerism, foible, idiosyncrasy, habit, fancy, characteristic, trait, whim, oddity, caprice, fetish, aberration, kink, vagary, singularity, idée fixe (*French*)

quirky = odd, unusual, eccentric, idiosyncratic, curious, peculiar, unpredictable, rum (*Brit. slang*), singular, fanciful, whimsical, capricious, offbeat

quit 1 = resign (from), leave, retire (from), pull out (of), surrender, chuck (*informal*), step down (from) (*informal*), relinquish, renounce, pack in (*informal*), abdicate *...He figured he would quit his job before he was fired...*
2 = stop, give up, cease, end, drop, abandon, suspend, halt, discontinue, belay (*Nautical*) *...I was trying to quit smoking at the time...* OPPOSITE continue
3 = leave, depart from, go out of, abandon, desert, exit, withdraw from, forsake, go away from, pull out

from, decamp from *...Police were called when he refused to quit the building...*

quite 1 = somewhat, rather, fairly, reasonably, kind of (*informal*), pretty (*informal*), relatively, moderately, to some extent, comparatively, to some degree, to a certain extent *...I was doing quite well, but I wasn't earning a lot of money...*
2 = absolutely, perfectly, completely, totally, fully, entirely, precisely, considerably, wholly, in all respects, without reservation *...It is quite clear that we were firing in self defence...*

quiver VERB = shake, tremble, shiver, quake, shudder, agitate, vibrate, pulsate, quaver, convulse, palpitate *...Her bottom lip quivered and big tears rolled down her cheeks...*
NOUN = shake, tremble, shiver, throb, shudder, tremor, spasm, vibration, tic, convulsion, palpitation, pulsation *...I felt a quiver of panic...*

quixotic = unrealistic, idealistic, romantic, absurd, imaginary, visionary, fanciful, impractical, dreamy, Utopian, impulsive, fantastical, impracticable, chivalrous, unworldly, chimerical

quiz NOUN = examination, questioning, interrogation, interview, investigation, grilling (*informal*), cross-examination, cross-questioning, the third degree (*informal*) *...Man faces quiz over knife death...*
VERB = question, ask, interrogate, examine, investigate, pump (*informal*), grill (*informal*), catechize *...Sybil quizzed her about life as a working girl...*

quizzical = mocking, questioning, inquiring, curious, arch, teasing, bantering, sardonic, derisive, supercilious

quota = share, allowance, ration, allocation, part, cut (*informal*), limit, proportion, slice, quantity, portion, assignment, whack (*informal*), dispensation

quotation 1 = passage, quote (*informal*), excerpt, cutting, selection, reference, extract, citation *...He illustrated his argument with quotations from Pasternak...*
2 (*Commerce*) = estimate, price, tender, rate, cost, charge, figure, quote (*informal*), bid price *...Get several written quotations and check exactly what's included in the cost...*

quote 1 = repeat, recite, reproduce, recall, echo, extract, excerpt, proclaim, parrot, paraphrase, retell *...Then suddenly he quoted a line from the play...*
2 = refer to, cite, give, name, detail, relate, mention, instance, specify, spell out, recount, recollect, make reference to, adduce *...Most newspapers quote the warning...*

R r

rabbit

> **Related Words**
>
> *male*: buck
> *female*: doe
> *collective noun*: nest
> *habitation*: warren

> **Rabbits and hares**
> http://animaldiversity.ummz.umich.edu/site/
> accounts/information/Lagomorpha.html
>
> | | |
> |---|---|
> | Angora rabbit | jack rabbit |
> | arctic hare | pika *or* cony |
> | Belgian hare | rabbit *or* cottontail |
> | coney *or* cony | snowshoe hare *or* |
> | hare | snowshoe rabbit |

rabble 1 = <u>mob</u>, crowd, herd, swarm, horde, throng, canaille ...*a rabble of gossip columnists*...
2 (*Derogatory*) = <u>commoners</u>, proletariat, common people, riffraff, crowd, masses, trash (*chiefly U.S. & Canad.*), scum, lower classes, populace, peasantry, dregs, hoi polloi, the great unwashed (*derogatory*), canaille, lumpenproletariat, commonalty ...*They are forced to socialise with the rabble*... OPPOSITE upper classes

rabid 1 = <u>fanatical</u>, extreme, irrational, fervent, zealous, bigoted, intolerant, narrow-minded, intemperate ...*the rabid state media*... OPPOSITE moderate
2 = <u>crazed</u>, wild, violent, mad, raging, furious, frantic, frenzied, infuriated, berserk, maniacal, berko (*Austral. slang*) ...*The tablets gave him the look of a rabid dog*...

race¹ NOUN 1 = <u>competition</u>, contest, chase, dash, pursuit, contention ...*a running race in a Cambridge quadrangle*...
2 = <u>contest</u>, competition, rivalry, contention ...*the race for the White House*...
VERB 1 = <u>compete against</u>, run against ...*They may even have raced each other*...
2 = <u>compete</u>, run, contend, take part in a race ...*He, too, will be racing here again soon*...
3 = <u>run</u>, fly, career, speed, tear, dash, hurry, barrel (along) (*informal, chiefly U.S. & Canad.*), dart, gallop, zoom, hare (*Brit. informal*), hasten, burn rubber (*informal*), go like a bomb (*Brit. & N.Z. informal*), run like mad (*informal*) ...*They raced away out of sight*...

race² = <u>people</u>, ethnic group, nation, blood, house, family, line, issue, stock, type, seed (*chiefly biblical*), breed, folk, tribe, offspring, clan, kin, lineage, progeny, kindred ...*We welcome students of all races, faiths and nationalities*...

racial = <u>ethnic</u>, ethnological, national, folk, genetic, tribal, genealogical

rack NOUN = <u>frame</u>, stand, structure, framework ...*a luggage rack*...
VERB = <u>torture</u>, distress, torment, harass, afflict, oppress, harrow, crucify, agonize, pain, excruciate ...*a teenager racked with guilt*...

> ## *Word Power*
>
> **rack** – The use of the spelling *wrack* rather than *rack* in sentences such as *she was wracked by grief* or *the country was wracked by civil war* is very common, but is thought by many people to be incorrect.

racket 1 = <u>noise</u>, row, shouting, fuss, disturbance, outcry, clamour, din, uproar, commotion, pandemonium, rumpus, babel, tumult, hubbub, hullaballoo, ballyhoo (*informal*) ...*The racket went on past midnight*...
2 = <u>fraud</u>, scheme, criminal activity, illegal enterprise ...*a drugs racket*...

racy 1 = <u>risqué</u>, naughty, indecent, bawdy, blue, broad, spicy (*informal*), suggestive, smutty, off colour, immodest, indelicate, near the knuckle (*informal*) ...*Her novels may be racy but they don't fight shy of larger issues*...
2 = <u>lively</u>, spirited, exciting, dramatic, entertaining, stimulating, sexy (*informal*), sparkling, vigorous, energetic, animated, heady, buoyant, exhilarating, zestful ...*very high-quality wines with quite a racy character*...

radiance 1 = <u>happiness</u>, delight, pleasure, joy, warmth, rapture, gaiety ...*There was a new radiance about her*...
2 = <u>brightness</u>, light, shine, glow, glitter, glare, gleam, brilliance, lustre, luminosity, incandescence, resplendence, effulgence ...*The dim bulb cast a soft radiance over his face*...

radiant 1 = <u>happy</u>, glowing, ecstatic, joyful, sent (*informal*), gay, delighted, beaming, joyous, blissful, rapturous, rapt, on cloud nine (*informal*), beatific, blissed out (*informal*), floating on air ...*On her wedding day the bride looked truly radiant*... OPPOSITE miserable
2 = <u>bright</u>, brilliant, shining, glorious, beaming, glowing, sparkling, sunny, glittering, gleaming, luminous, resplendent, incandescent, lustrous, effulgent ...*Out on the bay the morning is radiant*... OPPOSITE dull

radiate 1 = <u>emit</u>, spread, send out, disseminate, pour, shed, scatter, glitter, gleam ...*Thermal imagery will show up objects radiating heat*...
2 = <u>shine</u>, emanate, be diffused ...*From here contaminated air radiates out to the open countryside*...

3 = <u>show</u>, display, demonstrate, exhibit, emanate, give off *or* out …*She radiates happiness and health*…
4 = <u>spread out</u>, diverge, branch out …*the narrow streets which radiate from the Cathedral Square*…

radiation = <u>emission</u>, rays, emanation

radical ADJECTIVE **1** = <u>extreme</u>, complete, entire, sweeping, violent, severe, excessive, thorough, drastic …*periods of radical change*…
2 = <u>revolutionary</u>, extremist, fanatical …*political tension between radical and conservative politicians*…
3 = <u>fundamental</u>, natural, basic, essential, native, constitutional, organic, profound, innate, deep-seated, thoroughgoing …*the radical differences between them*… OPPOSITE superficial
NOUN = <u>extremist</u>, revolutionary, militant, fanatic …*a former left-wing radical who was involved with the civil rights movement*… OPPOSITE conservative

raffle = <u>draw</u>, lottery, sweepstake, sweep

rage NOUN **1** = <u>fury</u>, temper, frenzy, rampage, tantrum, foulie (*Austral. slang*) …*I flew into a rage*… OPPOSITE calmness
2 = <u>anger</u>, violence, passion, obsession, madness, raving, wrath, mania, agitation, ire, vehemence, high dudgeon …*The people are full of fear and rage*…
3 = <u>craze</u>, fashion, enthusiasm, vogue, fad (*informal*), latest thing …*the latest technological rage*…
VERB **1** = <u>be at its height</u>, surge, rampage, be uncontrollable, storm …*The war rages on and the time has come to take sides*…
2 = <u>be furious</u>, rave, blow up (*informal*), fume, lose it (*informal*), fret, seethe, crack up (*informal*), see red (*informal*), chafe, lose the plot (*informal*), go ballistic (*slang, chiefly U.S.*), rant and rave, foam at the mouth, lose your temper, blow a fuse (*slang, chiefly U.S.*), fly off the handle (*informal*), be incandescent, go off the deep end (*informal*), throw a fit (*informal*), wig out (*slang*), go up the wall (*slang*), blow your top, lose your rag (*slang*), be beside yourself, flip your lid (*slang*) …*He was annoyed, no doubt, but not raging*… OPPOSITE stay calm

ragged 1 = <u>tatty</u>, worn, poor, torn, rent, faded, neglected, run-down, frayed, shabby, worn-out, seedy, scruffy, in tatters, dilapidated, tattered, threadbare, unkempt, in rags, down at heel, the worse for wear, in holes, having seen better days, scraggy …*I am usually happiest in ragged jeans and a t-shirt*… OPPOSITE smart
2 = <u>rough</u>, fragmented, crude, rugged, notched, irregular, unfinished, uneven, jagged, serrated …*She tore her tights on the ragged edge of a desk*…

raging = <u>furious</u>, mad, raving, fuming, frenzied, infuriated, incensed, enraged, seething, fizzing (*Scot.*), incandescent, foaming at the mouth, fit to be tied (*slang*), boiling mad (*informal*), beside yourself, doing your nut (*Brit. slang*), off the air (*Austral. slang*)

raid VERB **1** = <u>steal from</u>, break into, plunder, pillage, sack …*The guerrillas raided banks and destroyed a police barracks*…
2 = <u>attack</u>, invade, assault, rifle, forage (*Military*), fall upon, swoop down upon, reive (*dialect*) …*8th century Vikings set off to raid the coasts of Europe*…
3 = <u>make a search of</u>, search, bust (*informal*), descend on, make a raid on, make a swoop on …*Fraud squad officers raided the firm's offices*…
NOUN **1** = <u>attack</u>, invasion, seizure, onset, foray, sortie, incursion, surprise attack, hit-and-run attack, sally, inroad, irruption …*The rebels attempted a surprise raid on a military camp*…
2 = <u>bust</u> (*informal*), swoop, descent, surprise search …*a raid on a house by thirty armed police*…
3 = <u>robbery</u>, sacking, break-in …*He carried out a series of bank raids*…

raider = <u>attacker</u>, thief, robber, plunderer, invader, forager (*Military*), marauder, reiver (*dialect*)

rail = <u>complain</u>, attack, abuse, blast, put down, criticize, censure, scold, castigate, revile, tear into (*informal*), fulminate, inveigh, upbraid, lambast(e), vituperate, vociferate

railing = <u>fence</u>, rails, barrier, paling, balustrade

rain NOUN **1** = <u>rainfall</u>, fall, showers, deluge, drizzle, downpour, precipitation, raindrops, cloudburst …*You'll get soaked standing out in the rain*…
2 = <u>shower</u>, flood, stream, hail, volley, spate, torrent, deluge …*A rain of stones descended on the police*…
VERB **1** = <u>pour</u>, pelt (down), teem, bucket down (*informal*), fall, shower, drizzle, rain cats and dogs (*informal*), come down in buckets (*informal*) …*It rained the whole weekend*…
2 = <u>fall</u>, shower, be dropped, sprinkle, be deposited …*Rockets, mortars and artillery rained on buildings*…
3 = <u>bestow</u>, pour, shower, lavish …*Banks rained money on commercial real estate developers*…

(**Related Words**)
adjectives: pluvial, pluvious

rainy = <u>wet</u>, damp, drizzly, showery OPPOSITE dry

raise 1 = <u>lift</u>, move up, elevate, uplift, heave …*He raised his hand to wave*…
2 = <u>set upright</u>, lift, elevate …*She raised herself on one elbow*…
3 = <u>increase</u>, reinforce, intensify, heighten, advance, boost, strengthen, enhance, put up, exaggerate, hike (up) (*informal*), enlarge, escalate, inflate, aggravate, magnify, amplify, augment, jack up …*Two incidents in recent days have raised the level of concern*… OPPOSITE reduce
4 = <u>make louder</u>, heighten, amplify, louden …*Don't you raise your voice to me!*…
5 = <u>collect</u>, get, gather, obtain …*events held to raise money*…
6 = <u>mobilize</u>, form, mass, rally, recruit, assemble, levy, muster …*Landed nobles provided courts of justice and raised troops*…
7 = <u>cause</u>, start, produce, create, occasion, provoke, bring about, originate, give rise to, engender …*a joke that raised a smile*…
8 = <u>put forward</u>, suggest, introduce, advance, bring up, broach, moot …*He had been consulted and had raised no objections*…

9 = <u>bring up</u>, develop, rear, nurture ...*the house where she was raised...*

10 = <u>grow</u>, produce, rear, cultivate, propagate ...*He raises 2,000 acres of wheat and hay...*

11 = <u>breed</u>, keep ...*She raised chickens and pigs...*

12 = <u>build</u>, construct, put up, erect ...*They raised a church in the shape of a boat...* OPPOSITE demolish

13 = <u>promote</u>, upgrade, elevate, advance, prefer, exalt, aggrandize ...*He was to be raised to the rank of ambassador...* OPPOSITE demote

rake¹ 1 = <u>scrape</u>, break up, scratch, scour, harrow, hoe ...*The beach is raked and cleaned daily...*

2 = <u>gather</u>, collect, scrape together, scrape up, remove ...*I watched the men rake leaves into heaps...*

3 = <u>strafe</u>, pepper, enfilade ...*The caravan was raked with bullets...*

4 = <u>graze</u>, scratch, scrape ...*Ragged fingernails raked her skin...*

5 *with* **through** = <u>search</u>, hunt, examine, scan, comb, scour, ransack, forage, scrutinize, fossick (*Austral. & N.Z.*) ...*Many can only survive by raking through dustbins...*

rake² = <u>libertine</u>, playboy, swinger (*slang*), profligate, lecher, roué, sensualist, voluptuary, debauchee, rakehell (*archaic*), dissolute man, lech *or* letch (*informal*) ...*As a young man I was a rake...* OPPOSITE puritan

rakish = <u>dashing</u>, smart, sporty, flashy, breezy, jaunty, dapper, natty (*informal*), debonair, snazzy (*informal*), raffish, devil-may-care

rally NOUN **1** = <u>gathering</u>, mass meeting, convention, convocation, meeting, conference, congress, assembly, congregation, muster, hui (*N.Z.*) ...*They held a rally to mark international human rights day...*

2 = <u>recovery</u>, improvement, comeback (*informal*), revival, renewal, resurgence, recuperation, turn for the better ...*After a brief rally, shares returned to 126p...* OPPOSITE relapse

VERB **1** = <u>gather together</u>, unite, bring together, regroup, reorganize, reassemble, re-form ...*He rallied his own supporters for a fight...*

2 = <u>recover</u>, improve, pick up, revive, get better, come round, perk up, recuperate, turn the corner, pull through, take a turn for the better, regain your strength, get your second wind ...*He rallied enough to thank his doctor...* OPPOSITE get worse

PHRASES **rally around** *or* **round** = <u>gather</u>, unite, collect, organize, assemble, get together, convene, mobilize, bond together, come together ...*So many people have rallied round to help the family...*

ram 1 = <u>hit</u>, force, drive into, strike, crash, impact, smash, slam, dash, run into, butt, collide with ...*They used a lorry to ram the main gate...*

2 = <u>cram</u>, pound, force, stuff, pack, hammer, jam, thrust, tamp ...*He rammed the key into the lock and kicked the front door open...*

ramble NOUN = <u>walk</u>, tour, trip, stroll, hike, roaming, excursion, roving, saunter, traipse (*informal*), peregrination, perambulation ...*an hour's ramble*

through the woods...

VERB **1** = <u>walk</u>, range, drift, wander, stroll, stray, roam, rove, amble, saunter, straggle, traipse (*informal*), go walkabout (*Austral.*), perambulate, stravaig (*Scot. & Northern English dialect*), peregrinate ...*freedom to ramble across the moors...*

2 *often with* **on** = <u>babble</u>, wander, rabbit (on) (*Brit. informal*), chatter, waffle (*informal, chiefly Brit.*), digress, rattle on, maunder, witter on (*informal*), expatiate, run off at the mouth (*slang*) ...*Sometimes she tended to ramble...*

rambler = <u>walker</u>, roamer, wanderer, rover, hiker, drifter, stroller, wayfarer

rambling 1 = <u>sprawling</u>, spreading, trailing, irregular, straggling ...*that rambling house with its bizarre contents...*

2 = <u>long-winded</u>, incoherent, disjointed, prolix, irregular, diffuse, disconnected, desultory, wordy, circuitous, discursive, digressive, periphrastic ...*He wrote a rambling letter to his wife...* OPPOSITE concise

ramification = <u>consequences</u>, results, developments, complications, sequel, upshot

ramp = <u>slope</u>, grade, incline, gradient, inclined plane, rise

rampage VERB = <u>go berserk</u>, tear, storm, rage, run riot, run amok, run wild, go ballistic (*slang*), go ape (*slang*) ...*He used a sword to defend his shop from a rampaging mob...*

PHRASES **on the rampage** = <u>berserk</u>, wild, violent, raging, destructive, out of control, rampant, amok, riotous, berko (*Austral. slang*) ...*a bull that went on the rampage...*

rampant 1 = <u>widespread</u>, rank, epidemic, prevalent, rife, exuberant, uncontrolled, unchecked, unrestrained, luxuriant, profuse, spreading like wildfire ...*the rampant corruption of the administration...*

2 = <u>unrestrained</u>, wild, violent, raging, aggressive, dominant, excessive, outrageous, out of control, rampaging, out of hand, uncontrollable, flagrant, unbridled, vehement, wanton, riotous, on the rampage, ungovernable ...*rampant civil and military police atrocities...*

3 (*Heraldry*) = <u>upright</u>, standing, rearing, erect ...*a shield with a lion rampant...*

rampart = <u>defence</u>, wall, parapet, fortification, security, guard, fence, fort, barricade, stronghold, bastion, embankment, bulwark, earthwork, breastwork

ramshackle = <u>rickety</u>, broken-down, crumbling, shaky, unsafe, derelict, flimsy, tottering, dilapidated, decrepit, unsteady, tumbledown, jerry-built OPPOSITE stable

rancid = <u>rotten</u>, sour, foul, bad, off, rank, tainted, stale, musty, fetid, putrid, fusty, strong-smelling, frowsty OPPOSITE fresh

rancour = <u>hatred</u>, hate, spite, hostility, resentment, bitterness, grudge, malice, animosity, venom, antipathy, spleen, enmity, ill feeling, bad blood, ill will, animus, malevolence, malignity, chip on your shoulder (*informal*), resentfulness

random ADJECTIVE **1** = chance, spot, casual, stray, accidental, arbitrary, incidental, indiscriminate, haphazard, unplanned, fortuitous, aimless, desultory, hit or miss, purposeless, unpremeditated, adventitious ...*The competitors will be subject to random drug testing...* OPPOSITE planned
2 = casual, arbitrary, indiscriminate, unplanned, aimless, purposeless, unpremeditated ...*random violence against innocent children...*
PHRASES **at random** = haphazardly, randomly, arbitrarily, casually, accidentally, irregularly, by chance, indiscriminately, aimlessly, willy-nilly, unsystematically, purposelessly, adventitiously ...*We received several answers and we picked one at random...*

randy (*Informal*) = lustful, hot, sexy (*informal*), turned-on (*slang*), aroused, raunchy (*slang*), horny (*slang*), amorous, lascivious, lecherous, sexually excited, concupiscent, satyric

range NOUN **1** = series, variety, selection, assortment, lot, collection, gamut ...*The two men discussed a range of issues...*
2 = limits, reach, distance, sweep, extent, pale, confines, parameters (*informal*), ambit ...*The average age range is between 35 and 55...*
3 = scope, area, field, bounds, province, orbit, span, domain, compass, latitude, radius, amplitude, purview, sphere ...*The trees on the mountain within my range of vision had all been felled...*
4 = row, series, line, file, rank, chain, string, sequence, tier ...*the massive mountain ranges to the north...*
VERB **1** = vary, run, reach, extend, go, stretch, fluctuate ...*offering merchandise ranging from the everyday to the esoteric...*
2 = arrange, order, line up, sequence, array, dispose, draw up, align ...*More than 1,500 police are ranged against them...*
3 = roam, explore, wander, rove, sweep, cruise, stroll, ramble, traverse ...*They range widely in search of carrion...*
4 = group, class, file, rank, arrange, grade, catalogue, classify, bracket, categorize, pigeonhole ...*The pots are all ranged in neat rows...*

rank¹ NOUN **1** = status, level, position, grade, order, standing, sort, quality, type, station, division, degree, classification, echelon ...*He eventually rose to the rank of captain...*
2 = class, dignity, caste, nobility, stratum ...*Each rank of the peerage was respected...*
3 = row, line, file, column, group, range, series, formation, tier ...*Ranks of police in riot gear stood nervously by...*
VERB **1** = order, class, grade, classify, dispose ...*Universities were ranked according to marks scored in seven areas...*
2 = arrange, sort, position, range, line up, locate, sequence, array, marshal, align ...*Daffodils were ranked along a crazy paving path...*

rank² **1** = absolute, complete, total, gross, sheer, excessive, utter, glaring, thorough, extravagant, rampant, blatant, downright, flagrant, egregious, unmitigated, undisguised, arrant ...*He accused his rival of rank hypocrisy...*
2 = foul, off, bad, offensive, disgusting, revolting, stinking, stale, pungent, noxious, disagreeable, musty, rancid, fetid, putrid, fusty, strong-smelling, gamey, noisome, mephitic, olid, yucky *or* yukky (*slang*), yucky *or* yukky (*slang*), festy (*Austral. slang*) ...*the rank smell of unwashed clothes...*
3 = abundant, flourishing, lush, luxuriant, productive, vigorous, dense, exuberant, profuse, strong-growing ...*brambles and rank grass...*

rank and file **1** = general public, body, majority, mass, masses, Joe (and Eileen) Public (*slang*), Joe Six-Pack (*U.S. slang*) ...*There was widespread support for him among the rank and file...*
2 = lower ranks, men, troops, soldiers, other ranks, private soldiers ...*the rank and file of the Red Army...*

rankle = annoy, anger, irritate, gall, fester, embitter, chafe, irk, rile, get on your nerves (*informal*), get your goat (*slang*)

ransack **1** = search, go through, rummage through, rake through, explore, comb, scour, forage, turn inside out, fossick (*Austral. & N.Z.*) ...*Why should they be allowed to ransack your bag?...*
2 = plunder, raid, loot, pillage, strip, sack, gut, rifle, ravage, despoil ...*Demonstrators ransacked and burned the house where he was staying...*

ransom NOUN **1** = payment, money, price, payoff ...*The demand for the ransom was made by telephone...*
2 = release, rescue, liberation, redemption, deliverance ...*the eventual ransom of the victim...*
VERB = buy the freedom of, release, deliver, rescue, liberate, buy (someone) out (*informal*), redeem, set free, obtain *or* pay for the release of ...*The same system was used for ransoming or exchanging captives...*

rant VERB = shout, roar, yell, rave, bellow, cry, spout (*informal*), bluster, declaim, vociferate ...*I don't rant and rave or throw tea cups...*
NOUN = tirade, rhetoric, bluster, diatribe, harangue, bombast, philippic, vociferation, fanfaronade (*rare*) ...*As the boss began his rant, I stood up and went out...*

rap VERB **1** = hit, strike, knock, crack, tap ...*A guard raps his stick on a metal hand rail...*
2 = reprimand, knock (*informal*), blast, pan (*informal*), carpet (*informal*), criticize, censure, scold, tick off (*informal*), castigate, diss (*slang, chiefly U.S.*), read the riot act, lambast(e), chew out (*U.S. & Canad. informal*), give a rocket (*Brit. & N.Z. informal*) ...*The minister rapped the banks over their treatment of small businesses...*
3 (*Slang, chiefly U.S.*) = talk, chat, discourse, converse, shoot the breeze (*slang, chiefly U.S.*), confabulate ...*Today we're going to rap about relationships...*
NOUN **1** = blow, knock, crack, tap, clout (*informal*)

...*There was a light rap on the door*...

2 (*Slang*) = <u>rebuke</u>, sentence, blame, responsibility, punishment, censure, chiding ...*You'll be facing a federal rap for aiding and abetting an escaped convict*...

rapacious = <u>greedy</u>, grasping, insatiable, ravenous, preying, plundering, predatory, voracious, marauding, extortionate, avaricious, wolfish, usurious

rape VERB **1** = <u>sexually assault</u>, violate, abuse, ravish, force, outrage ...*A young woman was brutally raped in her own home*...

2 = <u>pillage</u>, plunder, ransack, despoil, sack, loot, spoliate ...*There is no guarantee that companies will not rape the environment*...

NOUN **1** = <u>sexual assault</u>, violation, ravishment, outrage ...*Ninety per cent of all rapes and violent assaults went unreported*...

2 = <u>plundering</u>, pillage, depredation, despoliation, rapine, spoliation, despoilment, sack ...*the rape of the environment*...

rapid 1 = <u>sudden</u>, prompt, speedy, precipitate, express, fleet, swift, quickie (*informal*), expeditious ...*the country's rapid economic growth*... OPPOSITE gradual

2 = <u>quick</u>, fast, hurried, swift, brisk, hasty, flying, pdq (*slang*) ...*He walked at a rapid pace along Charles Street*... OPPOSITE slow

rapidity = <u>speed</u>, swiftness, promptness, speediness, rush, hurry, expedition, dispatch, velocity, haste, alacrity, quickness, briskness, fleetness, celerity, promptitude, precipitateness

rapidly = <u>quickly</u>, fast, swiftly, briskly, promptly, hastily, precipitately, in a hurry, at speed, hurriedly, speedily, apace, in a rush, in haste, like a shot, pronto (*informal*), hell for leather, like lightning, expeditiously, hotfoot, like the clappers (*Brit. informal*), pdq (*slang*), like nobody's business (*informal*), posthaste, with dispatch, like greased lightning (*informal*)

rapport = <u>bond</u>, understanding, relationship, link, tie, sympathy, harmony, affinity, empathy, interrelationship

rapprochement = <u>reconciliation</u>, softening, reunion, détente, reconcilement, restoration of harmony OPPOSITE dissension

rapt 1 = <u>spellbound</u>, entranced, enthralled, engrossed, held, gripped, fascinated, absorbed, intent, preoccupied, carried away ...*I noticed that everyone was watching me with rapt attention*... OPPOSITE uninterested

2 = <u>rapturous</u>, enchanted, captivated, bewitched, sent, transported, delighted, charmed, ecstatic, blissful, ravished, enraptured, blissed out ...*He played to a rapt audience*...

rapture = <u>ecstasy</u>, delight, enthusiasm, joy, transport, spell, happiness, bliss, euphoria, felicity, rhapsody, exaltation, cloud nine (*informal*), seventh heaven, delectation, beatitude, ravishment

rapturous = <u>ecstatic</u>, delighted, enthusiastic, rapt, sent (*informal*), happy, transported, joyous, exalted, joyful, over the moon (*informal*), overjoyed, blissful, ravished, euphoric, on cloud nine (*informal*), blissed out (*informal*), rhapsodic, in seventh heaven, floating on air

rare¹ 1 = <u>priceless</u>, rich, precious, invaluable ...*She collects rare plants*...

2 = <u>uncommon</u>, unusual, exceptional, out of the ordinary, few, strange, scarce, singular, sporadic, sparse, infrequent, thin on the ground, recherché ...*I think big families are extremely rare nowadays*... OPPOSITE common

3 = <u>superb</u>, great, fine, excellent, extreme, exquisite, admirable, superlative, choice, incomparable, peerless ...*She has a rare ability to record her observations on paper*...

rare² = <u>underdone</u>, bloody, undercooked, half-cooked, half-raw ...*Waiter, I specifically asked for this steak rare*...

rarefied = <u>exclusive</u>, select, esoteric, cliquish, private, occult, clannish

rarely = <u>seldom</u>, hardly, almost never, hardly ever, little, once in a while, infrequently, on rare occasions, once in a blue moon, only now and then, scarcely ever ...*I rarely wear a raincoat because I spend most of my time in a car*... OPPOSITE often

---

Word Power

rarely – Since the meaning of *rarely* is 'hardly ever', the combination *rarely ever* is repetitive and should be avoided in careful writing, even though you may sometimes hear this phrase used in informal speech.

---

raring (in construction *raring to do something*) = <u>eager</u>, impatient, longing, yearning, willing, ready, keen, desperate, enthusiastic, avid, champing at the bit (*informal*), keen as mustard, athirst

rarity 1 = <u>curio</u>, find, treasure, pearl, one-off, curiosity, gem, collector's item ...*Other rarities include an interview with Presley*...

2 = <u>uncommonness</u>, scarcity, infrequency, unusualness, shortage, strangeness, singularity, sparseness ...*This indicates the rarity of such attacks*...

rascal = <u>rogue</u>, devil, villain, scoundrel, disgrace, rake, pickle (*Brit. informal*), imp, scally (*Northwest English dialect*), wretch, knave (*archaic*), ne'er-do-well, reprobate, scallywag (*informal*), good-for-nothing, miscreant, scamp, wastrel, bad egg (*old-fashioned informal*), blackguard, varmint (*informal*), rapscallion, caitiff (*archaic*), nointer (*Austral. slang*)

rash¹ = <u>reckless</u>, hasty, impulsive, imprudent, premature, adventurous, careless, precipitate, brash, audacious, headlong, madcap, ill-advised, foolhardy, unwary, thoughtless, unguarded, headstrong, impetuous, indiscreet, unthinking, helter-skelter, ill-considered, hot-headed, heedless, injudicious, incautious, venturesome, harebrained, harum-scarum ...*Don't do anything rash until the feelings subside*...

OPPOSITE > cautious

rash² 1 = <u>outbreak of spots</u>, (skin) eruption ...*I noticed a rash on my leg...*
2 = <u>spate</u>, series, wave, flood, succession, plague, outbreak, epidemic ...*a rash of internet-related companies...*

rasp VERB = <u>scrape</u>, grind, rub, scour, excoriate, abrade ...*The blade rasped over his skin...*
NOUN = <u>grating</u>, grinding, scratch, scrape ...*the rasp of something being drawn across the sand...*

rasping or **raspy** = <u>harsh</u>, rough, hoarse, gravelly, jarring, grating, creaking, husky, croaking, gruff, croaky

rat (*Informal*) NOUN 1 = <u>traitor</u>, grass (*Brit. informal*), betrayer, deceiver, informer, defector, deserter, double-crosser, quisling, stool pigeon, nark (*Brit., Austral., & N.Z. slang*), snake in the grass, two-timer (*informal*), fizgig (*Austral. slang*) ...*He was known as 'The Rat', even before the bribes had come to light...*
2 = <u>rogue</u>, scoundrel, heel (*slang*), cad (*old-fashioned Brit. informal*), bounder (*old-fashioned Brit. slang*), rotter (*slang, chiefly Brit.*), bad lot, shyster (*informal, chiefly U.S.*), ratfink (*slang, chiefly U.S. & Canad.*) ...*What did you do with the gun you took from that little rat?...*
PHRASES **rat on someone** = <u>betray</u>, denounce, tell on, shop (*slang, chiefly Brit.*), grass (*Brit. slang*), peach (*slang*), squeal (*slang*), incriminate (*informal*), blow the whistle on (*informal*), spill the beans (*informal*), snitch (*slang*), blab, let the cat out of the bag, blow the gaff (*Brit. slang*), nark (*Brit., Austral., & N.Z. slang*), put the finger on (*informal*), spill your guts (*slang*), inculpate, clype (*Scot.*), dob in (*Austral. slang*) ...*They were accused of encouraging children to rat on their parents...*

rate NOUN 1 = <u>speed</u>, pace, tempo, velocity, time, measure, gait, frequency ...*The rate at which hair grows can be agonisingly slow...*
2 = <u>degree</u>, standard, scale, proportion, percentage, ratio ...*bank accounts paying above the average rate of interest...*
3 = <u>charge</u>, price, cost, fee, tax, figure, dues, duty, hire, toll, tariff ...*specially reduced rates...*
VERB 1 = <u>evaluate</u>, consider, rank, reckon, class, value, measure, regard, estimate, count, grade, assess, weigh, esteem, classify, appraise, adjudge ...*The film was rated excellent by 90 per cent of children...*
2 (*Slang*) = <u>think highly of</u>, value, respect, admire, esteem ...*It's flattering to know other clubs seem to rate me...*
3 = <u>deserve</u>, merit, be entitled to, be worthy of ...*Her attire did not rate a second glance...*
PHRASES **at any rate** = <u>in any case</u>, anyway, nevertheless, anyhow, at all events ...*Well, at any rate, let me thank you for all you did...*

rather 1 = <u>preferably</u>, sooner, instead, more readily, more willingly ...*I'd rather stay at home than fight against the holiday crowds...*
2 = <u>to some extent</u>, quite, sort of (*informal*), kind of (*informal*), a little, a bit, pretty (*informal*), fairly,

relatively, somewhat, slightly, moderately, to some degree ...*I'm afraid it's rather a long story...*

> ### Word Power
> **rather** – It is acceptable to use either *would rather* or *had rather* in sentences such as *I would rather* (or *had rather*) *see a film than a play. Had rather*, however, is less common than *would rather*, and sounds a little old-fashioned nowadays.

ratify = <u>approve</u>, sign, establish, confirm, bind, sanction, endorse, uphold, authorize, affirm, certify, consent to, validate, bear out, corroborate, authenticate OPPOSITE > annul

rating = <u>position</u>, evaluation, classification, placing, rate, order, standing, class, degree, estimate, rank, status, grade, designation

ratio = <u>proportion</u>, rate, relationship, relation, arrangement, percentage, equation, fraction, correspondence, correlation

ration NOUN = <u>allowance</u>, quota, allotment, provision, helping, part, share, measure, dole, portion ...*The meat ration was down to one pound per person per week...*
VERB 1 = <u>limit</u>, control, restrict, save, budget, conserve ...*Staples such as bread, rice and tea are already being rationed...*
2 = <u>distribute</u>, issue, deal, dole, allocate, give out, allot, mete, apportion, measure out, parcel out ...*I had a flask so I rationed out cups of tea...*

rational 1 = <u>sensible</u>, sound, wise, reasonable, intelligent, realistic, logical, enlightened, sane, lucid, judicious, sagacious ...*a rational decision...*
2 = <u>reasoning</u>, thinking, cognitive, cerebral, ratiocinative ...*Man, as a rational being, may act against his impulses...*
3 = <u>sane</u>, balanced, normal, all there (*informal*), lucid, of sound mind, compos mentis (*Latin*), in your right mind ...*Rachel looked calmer and more rational now...* OPPOSITE > insane

rationale = <u>reason</u>, grounds, theory, principle, philosophy, logic, motivation, exposition, raison d'être (*French*)

rationalize 1 = <u>justify</u>, excuse, account for, vindicate, explain away, make allowances for, make excuses for, extenuate ...*It's easy to rationalize gambling...*
2 = <u>reason out</u>, resolve, think through, elucidate, apply logic to ...*an attempt to rationalize my feelings...*
3 = <u>streamline</u>, trim, make more efficient, make cuts in ...*They have been unable or unwilling to modernize and rationalize the business...*

rattle VERB 1 = <u>clatter</u>, bang, jangle ...*She slams the kitchen door so hard I hear dishes rattle...*
2 = <u>shake</u>, jiggle, jolt, vibrate, bounce, jar, jounce ...*He gently rattled the cage and whispered to the canary...*
3 (*Informal*) = <u>fluster</u>, shake, upset, frighten, scare, disturb, disconcert, perturb, faze, discomfit,

discountenance, put (someone) off his stride, discompose, put (someone) out of countenance …*She refused to be rattled by his lawyer*…
PHRASES **rattle on** = <u>prattle</u>, rabbit (on) (*Brit. informal*), chatter, witter (*informal*), cackle, yak (away) (*slang*), gibber, jabber, gabble, blether, prate, run on …*He listened in silence as she rattled on*… ♦ **rattle something off** = <u>recite</u>, list, run through, rehearse, reel off, spiel off (*informal*) …*He could rattle off yards of poetry*…

ratty = <u>irritable</u>, cross, angry, annoyed, crabbed, impatient, snappy, touchy, tetchy, testy, short-tempered, tooshie (*Austral. slang*)

raucous = <u>harsh</u>, rough, loud, noisy, grating, strident, rasping, husky, hoarse **OPPOSITE** quiet

raunchy (*Slang*) = <u>sexy</u>, sexual, steamy (*informal*), earthy, suggestive, lewd, lusty, bawdy, salacious, smutty, lustful, lecherous, ribald, coarse

ravage **VERB** = <u>destroy</u>, ruin, devastate, wreck, shatter, gut, spoil, loot, demolish, plunder, desolate, sack, ransack, pillage, raze, lay waste, wreak havoc on, despoil, leave in ruins …*The soldiers had ravaged the village*…
PLURAL NOUN = <u>damage</u>, destruction, devastation, desolation, waste, ruin, havoc, demolition, plunder, pillage, depredation, ruination, rapine, spoliation …*the ravages of a cold, wet climate*…

rave **VERB** 1 = <u>rant</u>, rage, roar, thunder, fume, go mad (*informal*), babble, splutter, storm, be delirious, talk wildly …*She cried and raved for weeks*…
2 (*Informal*) = <u>enthuse</u>, praise, gush, be delighted by, be mad about (*informal*), big up (*slang, chiefly Caribbean*), rhapsodize, be wild about (*informal*), cry up …*She raved about the new foods she ate while she was there*…
NOUN (*Brit. slang*) = <u>party</u>, rave-up (*Brit. slang*), do (*informal*), affair, celebration, bash (*informal*), blow-out (*slang*), beano (*Brit. slang*), hooley or hoolie (*chiefly Irish & N.Z.*) …*an all-night rave*…
ADJECTIVE (*Informal*) = <u>enthusiastic</u>, excellent, favourable, ecstatic, laudatory …*The show has drawn rave reviews from the critics*…

ravenous 1 = <u>starving</u>, starved, very hungry, famished, esurient …*a pack of ravenous animals*… **OPPOSITE** sated
2 = <u>greedy</u>, insatiable, avaricious, covetous, grasping, insatiate …*He had moderated his ravenous appetite*…

ravine = <u>canyon</u>, pass, gap (*U.S.*), gorge, clough (*dialect*), gully, defile, linn (*Scot.*), gulch (*U.S.*), flume

raving = <u>mad</u>, wild, raging, crazy, furious, frantic, frenzied, hysterical, insane, irrational, crazed, berserk, delirious, rabid, out of your mind, gonzo (*slang*), berko (*Austral. slang*), off the air (*Austral. slang*)

ravish 1 (*Literary*) = <u>rape</u>, sexually assault, violate, abuse, force, outrage …*Her ravished body was found a week later*…
2 = <u>enchant</u>, transport, delight, charm, fascinate, entrance, captivate, enrapture, spellbind, overjoy …*an eerie power to ravish the eye and seduce the soul*…

ravishing = <u>enchanting</u>, beautiful, lovely, stunning (*informal*), charming, entrancing, gorgeous, dazzling, delightful, radiant, drop-dead (*slang*), bewitching

raw 1 = <u>unrefined</u>, natural, crude, unprocessed, basic, rough, organic, coarse, unfinished, untreated, unripe …*two ships carrying raw sugar*… **OPPOSITE** refined
2 = <u>uncooked</u>, natural, fresh, bloody (*of meat*), undressed, unprepared …*a popular dish made of raw fish*… **OPPOSITE** cooked
3 = <u>sore</u>, open, skinned, sensitive, tender, scratched, grazed, chafed, abraded …*the drag of the rope against the raw flesh of my shoulder*…
4 = <u>frank</u>, plain, bare, naked, realistic, brutal, blunt, candid, unvarnished, unembellished …*the raw passions of nationalism*… **OPPOSITE** embellished
5 = <u>inexperienced</u>, new, green, ignorant, immature, unskilled, callow, untrained, untried, undisciplined, unseasoned, unpractised …*He is still raw but his potential shows*… **OPPOSITE** experienced
6 = <u>chilly</u>, biting, cold, freezing, bitter, wet, chill, harsh, piercing, damp, unpleasant, bleak, parky (*Brit. informal*) …*a raw December morning*…

ray 1 = <u>beam</u>, bar, flash, shaft, gleam …*The first rays of light spread over the horizon*…
2 = <u>trace</u>, spark, flicker, glimmer, hint, indication, scintilla …*I can offer you a slender ray of hope*…

raze = <u>destroy</u>, level, remove, ruin, demolish, flatten, knock down, pull down, tear down, throw down, bulldoze

re = <u>concerning</u>, about, regarding, respecting, with regard to, on the subject of, in respect of, with reference to, apropos, anent (*Scot.*)

> ### Word Power
> **re** – In contexts such as *re your letter, your remarks have been noted* or *he spoke to me re your complaint*, *re* is common in business or official correspondence. In spoken and in general written English *with reference to* is preferable in the former case and *about* or *concerning* in the latter. Even in business correspondence, the use of *re* is often restricted to the letter heading.

reach **VERB** 1 = <u>arrive at</u>, get to, get as far as, make, attain, land at …*He did not stop until he reached the door*…
2 = <u>attain</u>, get to, amount to …*We're told the figure could reach 100,000 next year*…
3 = <u>touch</u>, grasp, extend to, get (a) hold of, stretch to, go as far as, contact …*Can you reach your toes with your fingertips?*…
4 = <u>contact</u>, get in touch with, get through to, make contact with, get, find, communicate with, get hold of, establish contact with …*I'll tell her you've been trying to reach her*…
5 = <u>come to</u>, move to, rise to, fall to, drop to, sink to …*a nightshirt that reached to his knees*…
6 = <u>achieve</u>, come to, arrive at …*They are meeting in

Lusaka in an attempt to reach a compromise…
NOUN 1 = grasp, range, distance, stretch, sweep, capacity, extent, extension, scope …*The clothes they model are in easy reach of every woman…*
2 = jurisdiction, power, influence, command, compass, mastery, ambit …*The elite are no longer beyond the reach of the law…*

react = respond, act, proceed, behave, conduct yourself

reaction 1 = response, acknowledgment, feedback, answer, reply …*He showed no reaction when the judge pronounced his sentence…*
2 = counteraction, compensation, backlash, recoil, counterbalance, counterpoise …*All new fashion starts out as a reaction against existing convention…*
3 = conservatism, the right, counter-revolution, obscurantism …*their victory against the forces of reaction and conservatism…*

Word Power

reaction – Some people say that *reaction* should always refer to an instant response to something (as in *his reaction was one of amazement*), and that this word should not be used to refer to a considered response given in the form of a statement (as in *the Minister gave his reaction to the court's decision*). Use *response* instead.

---

reactionary **ADJECTIVE** = conservative, right-wing, counter-revolutionary, obscurantist, blimpish …*narrow and reactionary ideas about family life…*
NOUN = conservative, die-hard, right-winger, rightist, counter-revolutionary, obscurantist, Colonel Blimp …*Critics viewed him as a reactionary, even a monarchist…* **OPPOSITE** radical

read 1 = scan, study, look at, refer to, glance at, pore over, peruse, run your eye over …*He read through the pages slowly and carefully…*
2 = recite, deliver, utter, declaim, speak, announce …*Jay reads poetry so beautifully…*
3 = understand, interpret, comprehend, construe, decipher, perceive the meaning of, see, discover …*He could read words at 18 months…*
4 = register, show, record, display, indicate …*The sign on the bus read 'Private: Not in Service'…*

readable 1 = enjoyable, interesting, gripping, entertaining, pleasant, enthralling, easy to read, worth reading …*This is an impeccably researched and very readable book…* **OPPOSITE** dull
2 = legible, clear, plain, understandable, comprehensible, intelligible, decipherable …*a typewritten and readable script…* **OPPOSITE** illegible

readily 1 = willingly, freely, quickly, gladly, eagerly, voluntarily, cheerfully, with pleasure, with good grace, lief (*rare*) …*When I was invited to the party, I readily accepted…* **OPPOSITE** reluctantly
2 = promptly, quickly, easily, smoothly, at once, straight away, right away, effortlessly, in no time,

speedily, without delay, without hesitation, without difficulty, unhesitatingly, hotfoot, without demur, pdq (*slang*) …*I don't readily make friends…* **OPPOSITE** with difficulty

readiness **NOUN** 1 = willingness, inclination, eagerness, keenness, aptness, gameness (*informal*) …*their readiness to co-operate with the new US envoy…*
2 = preparedness, preparation, fitness, maturity, ripeness …*a constant state of readiness for war…*
3 = promptness, facility, ease, skill, dexterity, rapidity, quickness, adroitness, handiness, promptitude …*the warmth of his personality and the readiness of his wit…*
PHRASES in readiness = prepared, set, waiting, primed, ready, all set, waiting in the wings, at the ready, at *or* on hand, fit …*Everything was in readiness for the President's arrival…*

reading 1 = perusal, study, review, examination, inspection, scrutiny …*This knowledge makes the second reading as enjoyable as the first…*
2 = learning, education, knowledge, scholarship, erudition, edification, book-learning …*a man of great imagination, of wide reading and deep learning…*
3 = recital, performance, rendering, rendition, lesson, lecture, sermon, homily …*a poetry reading…*
4 = interpretation, take (*informal, chiefly U.S.*), understanding, treatment, version, construction, impression, grasp, conception …*There is a reading of this situation which upsets people…*

ready **ADJECTIVE** 1 = prepared, set, primed, organized, all set, in readiness …*It took her a long time to get ready for church…* **OPPOSITE** unprepared
2 = completed, arranged …*Everything's ready for the family to move in…*
3 = mature, ripe, mellow, ripened, fully developed, fully grown, seasoned …*In a few days' time the sprouts will be ready to eat…*
4 = willing, happy, glad, disposed, game (*informal*), minded, keen, eager, inclined, prone, have-a-go (*informal*), apt, agreeable, predisposed …*She was always ready to give interviews…* **OPPOSITE** reluctant
5 = prompt, smart, quick, bright, sharp, keen, acute, rapid, alert, clever, intelligent, handy, apt, skilful, astute, perceptive, expert, deft, resourceful, adroit, quick-witted, dexterous …*I didn't have a ready answer for this dilemma…* **OPPOSITE** slow
6 = available, handy, at the ready, at your fingertips, present, near, accessible, convenient, on call, on tap (*informal*), close to hand, at *or* on hand …*I'm afraid I don't have much ready cash…* **OPPOSITE** unavailable
7 with **to** = on the point of, close to, about to, on the verge of, likely to, in danger of, liable to, on the brink of …*She looked ready to cry…*
VERB = prepare, get set, organize, get ready, order, arrange, equip, fit out, make ready …*John's soldiers were readying themselves for the final assault…*
PHRASES at the ready = poised, waiting, prepared, in readiness, ready for action, all systems go …*Soldiers came charging through the forest, guns at the ready…*

real ADJECTIVE **1** = <u>true</u>, genuine, sincere, honest, factual, existent, dinkum (*Austral. & N.Z. informal*), unfeigned ...*No, it wasn't a dream. It was real*...
2 = <u>genuine</u>, authentic, bona fide, dinkum (*Austral. & N.Z. informal*) ...*the smell of real leather*... OPPOSITE fake
3 = <u>proper</u>, true, valid, legitimate ...*His first real girlfriend*...
4 = <u>actual</u>, true ...*This was the real reason for her call*...
5 = <u>typical</u>, true, genuine, sincere, unaffected, dinkum (*Austral. & N.Z. informal*), unfeigned ...*Their expressions of regret did not smack of real sorrow*...
6 = <u>complete</u>, right, total, perfect, positive, absolute, utter, thorough, veritable, out-and-out ...*You must think I'm a real idiot*...
ADVERB (*U.S. informal*) = <u>extremely</u>, very, really, particularly, seriously (*informal*), terribly, remarkably, unusually, jolly (*Brit.*), awfully (*informal*), uncommonly ...*He's been trying real hard*...

realistic **1** = <u>practical</u>, real, sensible, rational, common-sense, sober, pragmatic, down-to-earth, matter-of-fact, businesslike, level-headed, hard-headed, unsentimental, unromantic ...*a realistic view of what we can afford*... OPPOSITE impractical
2 = <u>attainable</u>, reasonable, sensible ...*Establish deadlines that are more realistic*...
3 = <u>lifelike</u>, true to life, authentic, naturalistic, true, natural, genuine, graphic, faithful, truthful, representational, vérité ...*The language is foul and the violence horribly realistic*...

reality NOUN **1** = <u>fact</u>, truth, certainty, realism, validity, authenticity, verity, actuality, materiality, genuineness, verisimilitude, corporeality ...*Fiction and reality were increasingly blurred*...
2 = <u>truth</u>, fact, actuality ...*the harsh reality of top international competition*...
PHRASES **in reality** = <u>in fact</u>, really, actually, in truth, as a matter of fact, in actuality, in point of fact ...*He came across as streetwise, but in reality he was not*...

realization **1** = <u>awareness</u>, understanding, recognition, perception, imagination, consciousness, grasp, appreciation, conception, comprehension, apprehension, cognizance ...*There is a growing realization that things cannot go on like this for much longer*...
2 = <u>achievement</u>, carrying-out, completion, accomplishment, fulfilment, consummation, effectuation ...*the realization of his worst fears*...

realize **1** = <u>become aware of</u>, understand, recognize, appreciate, take in, grasp, conceive, catch on (*informal*), comprehend, twig (*Brit. informal*), get the message, apprehend, become conscious of, be cognizant of ...*As soon as we realized what was going on, we moved the children away*...
2 = <u>fulfil</u>, achieve, accomplish, make real ...*Realize your dreams! Pursue your passions!*...
3 = <u>achieve</u>, do, effect, complete, perform, fulfil, accomplish, bring about, consummate, incarnate, bring off, make concrete, bring to fruition, actualize,

make happen, effectuate, reify, carry out *or* through ...*The kaleidoscopic quality of the book is brilliantly realized on stage*...
4 = <u>sell for</u>, go for, bring *or* take in, make, get, clear, produce, gain, net, earn, obtain, acquire ...*A selection of correspondence from P.G. Wodehouse realized £1,232*...

really **1** = <u>certainly</u>, absolutely, undoubtedly, genuinely, positively, categorically, without a doubt, assuredly, verily, surely ...*I really do feel that some people are being unfair*...
2 = <u>truly</u>, actually, in fact, indeed, in reality, in actuality ...*My father didn't really love her*...

realm **1** = <u>field</u>, world, area, province, sphere, department, region, branch, territory, zone, patch, orbit, turf (*U.S. slang*) ...*the realm of politics*...
2 = <u>kingdom</u>, state, country, empire, monarchy, land, province, domain, dominion, principality ...*Defence of the realm is crucial*...

reap **1** = <u>get</u>, win, gain, obtain, acquire, derive ...*We are not in this to reap immense financial rewards*...
2 = <u>collect</u>, gather, bring in, harvest, garner, cut ...*a group of peasants reaping a harvest of fruit and vegetables*...

rear¹ NOUN **1** = <u>back part</u>, back ...*He settled back in the rear of the taxi*... OPPOSITE front
2 = <u>back</u>, end, tail, rearguard, tail end, back end ...*Musicians played at the front and rear of the procession*...
ADJECTIVE = <u>back</u>, aft, hind, hindmost, after (*Nautical*), last, following, trailing ...*the rear end of a tractor*... OPPOSITE front

rear² **1** = <u>bring up</u>, raise, educate, care for, train, nurse, foster, nurture ...*I was reared in east Texas*...
2 = <u>breed</u>, keep ...*She spends a lot of time rearing animals*...
3 = <u>rise</u>, tower, soar, loom ...*The exhibition hall reared above me behind a high fence*...

reason NOUN **1** = <u>cause</u>, grounds, purpose, motive, end, goal, design, target, aim, basis, occasion, object, intention, incentive, warrant, impetus, inducement, why and wherefore (*informal*) ...*There is a reason for every important thing that happens*...
2 = <u>justification</u>, case, grounds, defence, argument, explanation, excuse, apology, rationale, exposition, vindication, apologia ...*I hope you have a good reason for your actions*...
3 = <u>sense</u>, mind, reasoning, understanding, brains, judgment, logic, mentality, intellect, comprehension, apprehension, sanity, rationality, soundness, sound mind, ratiocination ...*a conflict between emotion and reason*... OPPOSITE emotion
VERB = <u>deduce</u>, conclude, work out, solve, resolve, make out, infer, draw conclusions, think, ratiocinate, syllogize ...*I reasoned that changing my diet would lower my cholesterol level*...
PHRASES **in** *or* **within reason** = <u>within limits</u>, within reasonable limits, within bounds ...*I will take any job that comes along, within reason*... ♦ **reason**

with someone = <u>persuade</u>, debate with, remonstrate with, bring round, urge, win over, argue with, dispute with, dissuade, prevail upon (*informal*), expostulate with, show (someone) the error of his ways, talk into *or* out of …*All he wanted was to reason with one of them*…

Word Power

reason – Many people object to the expression *the reason is because*, on the grounds that it is repetitive. It is therefore advisable to use either *this is because* or *the reason is that*.

---

reasonable 1 = <u>sensible</u>, reasoned, sound, practical, wise, intelligent, rational, logical, sober, credible, plausible, sane, judicious …*He's a reasonable sort of chap*… OPPOSITE⟩ irrational
2 = <u>fair</u>, just, right, acceptable, moderate, equitable, justifiable, well-advised, well-thought-out, tenable …*a perfectly reasonable decision*… OPPOSITE⟩ unfair
3 = <u>within reason</u>, fit, proper …*It seems reasonable to expect rapid urban growth*… OPPOSITE⟩ impossible
4 = <u>low</u>, cheap, competitive, moderate, modest, inexpensive, tolerable …*His fees were quite reasonable*…
5 = <u>average</u>, fair, moderate, modest, tolerable, O.K. *or* okay (*informal*) …*The boy answered him in reasonable French*…

reasoned = <u>sensible</u>, clear, logical, systematic, judicious, well-thought-out, well-presented, well-expressed

reasoning 1 = <u>thinking</u>, thought, reason, analysis, logic, deduction, cogitation, ratiocination …*the reasoning behind the decision*…
2 = <u>case</u>, argument, proof, interpretation, hypothesis, exposition, train of thought …*She was not really convinced by their line of reasoning*…

reassure = <u>encourage</u>, comfort, bolster, hearten, cheer up, buoy up, gee up, restore confidence to, inspirit, relieve (someone) of anxiety, put *or* set your mind at rest

rebate = <u>refund</u>, discount, reduction, bonus, allowance, deduction

rebel NOUN 1 = <u>revolutionary</u>, resistance fighter, insurgent, secessionist, mutineer, insurrectionary, revolutionist …*fighting between rebels and government forces*…
2 = <u>nonconformist</u>, dissenter, heretic, apostate, schismatic …*She had been a rebel at school*…
VERB 1 = <u>revolt</u>, resist, rise up, mutiny, take to the streets, take up arms, man the barricades …*Poverty-stricken citizens could rise up and rebel*…
2 = <u>defy</u>, dissent, disobey, come out against, refuse to obey, dig your heels in (*informal*) …*The child who rebels against his parents is unlikely to be overlooked*…
3 = <u>recoil</u>, shrink, shy away, flinch, show repugnance …*His free spirit rebelled at this demand*…
ADJECTIVE = <u>rebellious</u>, revolutionary, insurgent, mutinous, insubordinate, insurrectionary …*Many*

soldiers in this rebel platoon joined as teenagers…

rebellion 1 = <u>resistance</u>, rising, revolution, revolt, uprising, mutiny, insurrection, insurgency, insurgence …*They soon put down the rebellion*…
2 = <u>nonconformity</u>, dissent, defiance, heresy, disobedience, schism, insubordination, apostasy …*He engaged in a small act of rebellion against his heritage*…

rebellious 1 = <u>defiant</u>, difficult, resistant, intractable, recalcitrant, obstinate, unmanageable, incorrigible, refractory, contumacious …*a rebellious teenager*…
OPPOSITE⟩ obedient
2 = <u>revolutionary</u>, rebel, disorderly, unruly, turbulent, disaffected, insurgent, recalcitrant, disloyal, seditious, mutinous, disobedient, ungovernable, insubordinate, insurrectionary …*a rebellious and dissident territory*…
OPPOSITE⟩ obedient

rebirth = <u>revival</u>, restoration, renaissance, renewal, resurrection, reincarnation, regeneration, resurgence, new beginning, revitalization, renascence

rebound 1 = <u>bounce</u>, ricochet, spring back, return, resound, recoil …*His shot rebounded from a post*…
2 = <u>misfire</u>, backfire, recoil, boomerang …*Mia realised her trick had rebounded on her*…

rebuff VERB = <u>reject</u>, decline, refuse, turn down, cut, check, deny, resist, slight, discourage, put off, snub, spurn, knock back (*slang*), brush off (*slang*), repulse, cold-shoulder …*He wanted to go out with Julie but she rebuffed him*… OPPOSITE⟩ encourage
NOUN = <u>rejection</u>, defeat, snub, knock-back, check, opposition, slight, refusal, denial (*slang*), brush-off (*slang*), repulse, thumbs down, cold shoulder, slap in the face (*informal*), kick in the teeth (*slang*), discouragement …*The results of the poll dealt a humiliating rebuff to Mr Jones*… OPPOSITE⟩ encouragement

rebuke VERB = <u>scold</u>, censure, reprimand, reproach, blame, lecture, carpet (*informal*), berate, tick off (*informal*), castigate, chide, dress down (*informal*), admonish, tear into (*informal*), tell off (*informal*), take to task, read the riot act, reprove, upbraid, bawl out (*informal*), haul (someone) over the coals (*informal*), chew out (*U.S. & Canad. informal*), tear (someone) off a strip (*informal*), give a rocket (*Brit. & N.Z. informal*), reprehend …*He has been seriously rebuked*…
OPPOSITE⟩ praise
NOUN = <u>scolding</u>, censure, reprimand, reproach, blame, row, lecture, wigging (*Brit. slang*), ticking-off (*informal*), dressing down (*informal*), telling-off (*informal*), admonition, tongue-lashing, reproof, castigation, reproval …*'Silly little boy' was his favourite expression of rebuke*… OPPOSITE⟩ praise

rebut = <u>disprove</u>, defeat, overturn, quash, refute, negate, invalidate, prove wrong, confute

rebuttal = <u>disproof</u>, negation, refutation, invalidation, confutation, defeat

recalcitrant = <u>disobedient</u>, contrary, unwilling, defiant, stubborn, wayward, unruly, uncontrollable, intractable, wilful, obstinate, unmanageable, ungovernable, refractory, insubordinate, contumacious OPPOSITE obedient

recall VERB 1 = recollect, remember, call up, evoke, reminisce about, call to mind, look *or* think back to, mind (*dialect*) ...*I recalled the way they had been dancing together...*
2 = call back ...*Parliament was recalled from its summer recess...*
3 = annul, withdraw, call in, take back, cancel, repeal, call back, revoke, retract, rescind, nullify, countermand, abjure ...*The order was recalled...*
NOUN 1 = recollection, memory, remembrance ...*He had a total recall of her spoken words...*
2 = annulment, withdrawal, repeal, cancellation, retraction, revocation, nullification, rescission, rescindment ...*The appellant sought a recall of the order...*

recant = withdraw, take back, retract, disclaim, deny, recall, renounce, revoke, repudiate, renege, disown, disavow, forswear, abjure, unsay, apostatize OPPOSITE maintain

recede 1 = fall back, withdraw, retreat, draw back, return, go back, retire, back off, regress, retrogress, retrocede ...*As she receded into the distance he waved goodbye...*
2 = lessen, decline, subside, abate, sink, fade, shrink, diminish, dwindle, wane, ebb ...*The illness began to recede...*

receipt NOUN 1 = sales slip, proof of purchase, voucher, stub, acknowledgment, counterfoil ...*I wrote her a receipt for the money...*
2 = receiving, delivery, reception, acceptance, recipience ...*the receipt of your order...*
PLURAL NOUN = takings, return, profits, gains, income, gate, proceeds ...*He was tallying the day's receipts...*

receive 1 = get, accept, be given, pick up, collect, obtain, acquire, take, derive, be in receipt of, accept delivery of ...*I received your letter...*
2 = experience, suffer, bear, go through, encounter, meet with, sustain, undergo, be subjected to ...*He received a blow to the head...*
3 = greet, meet, admit, welcome, entertain, take in, accommodate, be at home to ...*The following evening the duchess was again receiving guests...*

recent = new, modern, contemporary, up-to-date, late, young, happening (*informal*), current, fresh, novel, latter, present-day, latter-day OPPOSITE old

recently = not long ago, newly, lately, currently, freshly, of late, latterly

receptacle = container, holder, repository

reception 1 = party, gathering, get-together, social gathering, do (*informal*), social, function, entertainment, celebration, bash (*informal*) (*informal*), festivity, knees-up (*Brit. informal*), shindig (*informal*), soirée, levee, rave-up (*Brit. slang*) ...*a glittering wedding reception...*
2 = response, reaction, acknowledgment, recognition, treatment, welcome, greeting ...*He received a cool reception to his speech...*

3 = receiving, admission, acceptance, receipt, recipience ...*the production, distribution and reception of medical knowledge...*

receptive 1 = open, sympathetic, favourable, amenable, interested, welcoming, friendly, accessible, susceptible, open-minded, hospitable, approachable, open to suggestions ...*The voters had seemed receptive to his ideas...* OPPOSITE narrow-minded
2 = responsive, sensitive ...*The patient was not at all receptive to treatment...* OPPOSITE unresponsive

recess NOUN 1 = break, rest, holiday, closure, interval, vacation, respite, intermission, cessation of business ...*Parliament returns to work today after its summer recess...*
2 = alcove, corner, bay, depression, hollow, niche, cavity, nook, oriel, indentation ...*a discreet recess next to a fireplace...*
PLURAL NOUN = depths, reaches, heart, retreats, bowels, innards (*informal*), secret places, innermost parts, penetralia ...*He emerged from the dark recesses of the garage...*

recession = depression, drop, decline, slump, downturn OPPOSITE boom

recherché = refined, rare, exotic, esoteric, arcane, far-fetched, choice

recipe NOUN = directions, instructions, ingredients, receipt (*obsolete*) ...*I can give you the recipe for these biscuits...*
PHRASES **a recipe for something** = method, formula, prescription, process, programme, technique, procedure, modus operandi ...*Large-scale inflation is a recipe for disaster...*

reciprocal = mutual, corresponding, reciprocative, reciprocatory, exchanged, equivalent, alternate, complementary, interchangeable, give-and-take, interdependent, correlative OPPOSITE unilateral

reciprocate = return, requite, feel in return, match, respond, equal, return the compliment

recital 1 = performance, rendering, rehearsal, reading ...*a solo recital...*
2 = account, telling, story, detailing, statement, relation, tale, description, narrative, narration, enumeration, recapitulation ...*It was a depressing recital of childhood abuse...*
3 = recitation, repetition ...*The album features a recital of 13th century Latin prayers...*

recitation = recital, reading, performance, piece, passage, lecture, rendering, narration, telling

recite = perform, relate, deliver, repeat, rehearse, declaim, recapitulate, do your party piece (*informal*)

reckless = careless, wild, rash, irresponsible, precipitate, hasty, mindless, negligent, headlong, madcap, ill-advised, regardless, foolhardy, daredevil, thoughtless, indiscreet, imprudent, heedless, devil-may-care, inattentive, incautious, harebrained, harum-scarum, overventuresome OPPOSITE cautious

reckon VERB 1 (*Informal*) = think, believe, suppose, imagine, assume, guess (*informal, chiefly U.S. & Canad.*), fancy, conjecture, surmise, be of the opinion

…He reckoned he was still fond of her…

2 = <u>consider</u>, hold, rate, account, judge, think of, regard, estimate, count, evaluate, esteem, deem, gauge, look upon, appraise *…The sale has been held up because the price is reckoned to be too high…*

3 = <u>count</u>, figure, total, calculate, compute, add up, tally, number, enumerate *…The 'normal' by-election swing against a government is reckoned at about 5 per cent…*

PHRASES **reckon on** or **upon something** = <u>rely on</u>, count on, bank on, depend on, hope for, calculate, trust in, take for granted *…He reckons on being world heavyweight champion…* ◆ **reckon with something** or **someone** (usually in negative construction) = <u>take into account</u>, expect, plan for, anticipate, be prepared for, bear in mind, foresee, bargain for, take cognizance of *…He had not reckoned with the strength of her feelings for him…* ◆ **to be reckoned with** = <u>powerful</u>, important, strong, significant, considerable, influential, weighty, consequential *…This act was a signal that he was someone to be reckoned with…*

reckoning 1 = <u>count</u>, working, estimate, calculation, adding, counting, addition, computation, summation *…By my reckoning we were seven or eight kilometers away…*

2 = <u>day of retribution</u>, doom, judgment day, last judgment *…the day of reckoning…*

reclaim 1 = <u>retrieve</u>, get or take back, rescue, regain, reinstate *…I've come to reclaim my property…*

2 = <u>regain</u>, restore, salvage, recapture, regenerate *…The Netherlands has been reclaiming farmland from water…*

3 = <u>rescue</u>, reform, redeem *…He set out to fight the drug infestation by reclaiming a youth from the local gangs…*

recline = <u>lean</u>, lie (down), stretch out, rest, lounge, sprawl, loll, repose, be recumbent OPPOSITE> stand up

recluse = <u>hermit</u>, solitary, ascetic, anchoress, monk, anchorite, eremite

reclusive = <u>solitary</u>, retiring, withdrawn, isolated, secluded, cloistered, monastic, recluse, ascetic, sequestered, hermit-like, hermitic, eremitic OPPOSITE> sociable

recognition NOUN **1** = <u>identification</u>, recall, recollection, discovery, detection, remembrance *…He searched for a sign of recognition on her face…*

2 = <u>acceptance</u>, acknowledgement, understanding, admission, perception, awareness, concession, allowance, confession, realization, avowal *…They welcomed his recognition of the recession…*

3 = <u>acknowledgment</u>, approval *…His government did not receive full recognition until July…*

4 = <u>approval</u>, honour, appreciation, salute, gratitude, acknowledgment *…At last, her father's work has received popular recognition…*

PHRASES **in recognition of** = <u>in appreciation of</u>, in respect of, in cognizance of *…He had just received a doctorate in recognition of his contributions to*

seismology…

recognize 1 = <u>identify</u>, know, place, remember, spot, notice, recall, make out, recollect, know again, put your finger on *…The receptionist recognized him at once…*

2 = <u>acknowledge</u>, see, allow, understand, accept, admit, grant, realize, concede, perceive, confess, be aware of, take on board, avow *…I recognize my own shortcomings…* OPPOSITE> ignore

3 = <u>approve</u>, acknowledge, appreciate, greet, honour *…Most doctors appear to recognize homeopathy as a legitimate form of medicine…*

4 = <u>appreciate</u>, respect, notice, salute *…He had the insight to recognize their talents…*

recoil VERB **1** = <u>jerk back</u>, kick, react, rebound, spring back, resile *…I recoiled in horror…*

2 = <u>draw back</u>, shrink, falter, shy away, flinch, quail, balk at *…People used to recoil from the idea of getting into debt…*

NOUN **1** = <u>jerking back</u>, reaction, springing back *…His reaction was as much a rebuff as a physical recoil…*

2 = <u>kickback</u>, kick *…The policeman fires again, tensed against the recoil…*

recollect = <u>remember</u>, mind (*dialect*), recall, reminisce, summon up, call to mind, place

recollection = <u>memory</u>, recall, impression, remembrance, reminiscence, mental image

recommend 1 = <u>advocate</u>, suggest, propose, approve, endorse, commend *…Ask your doctor to recommend a suitable treatment…* OPPOSITE> disapprove of

2 = <u>put forward</u>, approve, endorse, commend, vouch for, praise, big up (*slang, chiefly Caribbean*), speak well of, put in a good word for *…He recommended me for a promotion…*

3 = <u>advise</u>, suggest, advance, propose, urge, counsel, advocate, prescribe, put forward, exhort, enjoin *…I recommend that you consult your doctor…*

4 = <u>make attractive</u>, make interesting, make appealing, make acceptable *…These qualities recommended him to Olivier…*

recommendation 1 = <u>advice</u>, proposal, suggestion, counsel, urging *…The committee's recommendations are unlikely to be made public…*

2 = <u>commendation</u>, reference, praise, sanction, approval, blessing, plug (*informal*), endorsement, advocacy, testimonial, good word, approbation, favourable mention *…The best way of finding a solicitor is by personal recommendation…*

recompense NOUN = <u>compensation</u>, pay, payment, satisfaction, amends, repayment, remuneration, reparation, indemnity, restitution, damages, emolument, indemnification, requital *…He demands no financial recompense for his troubles…*

VERB = <u>compensate</u>, reimburse, redress, repay, pay for, satisfy, make good, make up for, make amends for, indemnify, requite, make restitution for *…If they succeed in court, they will be fully recompensed for their loss…*

reconcile VERB 1 = <u>resolve</u>, settle, square, adjust, compose, rectify, patch up, harmonize, put to rights ...*It is possible to reconcile these apparently opposing perspectives...*
2 = <u>reunite</u>, bring back together, make peace between, pacify, conciliate ...*He never believed he and Susan would be reconciled...*
3 = <u>make peace between</u>, reunite, propitiate, bring to terms, restore harmony between, re-establish friendly relations between ...*my attempt to reconcile him and Toby...*
PHRASES **reconcile yourself to something** = <u>accept</u>, resign yourself to, get used to, put up with (*informal*), submit to, yield to, make the best of, accommodate yourself to ...*She had reconciled herself to never seeing him again...*

reconciliation 1 = <u>reunion</u>, conciliation, rapprochement (*French*), appeasement, détente, pacification, propitiation, understanding, reconcilement ...*The couple have separated but he wants a reconciliation...* OPPOSITE> separation
2 = <u>accommodation</u>, settlement, compromise ...*the reconciliation of our differences...*

reconnaissance = <u>inspection</u>, survey, investigation, observation, patrol, scan, exploration, scouting, scrutiny, recce (*slang*), reconnoitring

reconsider = <u>rethink</u>, review, revise, think again, think twice, reassess, re-examine, have second thoughts, change your mind, re-evaluate, think over, think better of, take another look at

reconstruct 1 = <u>rebuild</u>, reform, restore, recreate, remake, renovate, remodel, re-establish, regenerate, reorganize, reassemble ...*The government must reconstruct the shattered economy...*
2 = <u>build up a picture of</u>, build up, piece together, deduce ...*Elaborate efforts were made to reconstruct what had happened...*

record NOUN 1 = <u>document</u>, file, register, log, report, minute, account, entry, journal, diary, memorial, archives, memoir, chronicle, memorandum, annals ...*Keep a record of all the payments...*
2 = <u>evidence</u>, trace, documentation, testimony, witness, memorial, remembrance ...*There's no record of any marriage or children...*
3 = <u>disc</u>, recording, single, release, album, waxing (*informal*), LP, vinyl, EP, forty-five, platter (*U.S. slang*), seventy-eight, gramophone record, black disc ...*This is one of my favourite records...*
4 = <u>background</u>, history, performance, career, track record (*informal*), curriculum vitae ...*His record reveals a tough streak...*
VERB 1 = <u>set down</u>, report, minute, note, enter, document, register, preserve, log, put down, chronicle, write down, enrol, take down, inscribe, transcribe, chalk up (*informal*), put on record, put on file ...*In her letters she records the domestic and social details of life in China...*
2 = <u>make a recording of</u>, cut, video, tape, lay down (*slang*), wax (*informal*), video-tape, tape-record, put on wax (*informal*) ...*She recorded a new album in Nashville...*
3 = <u>register</u>, show, read, contain, indicate, give evidence of ...*The test records the electrical activity of the brain...*
PHRASES **off the record** 1 = <u>confidentially</u>, in private, in confidence, unofficially, sub rosa, under the rose ...*May I speak off the record?...* 2 = <u>confidential</u>, private, unofficial, not for publication ...*Those remarks were supposed to be off the record...*

recorder = <u>chronicler</u>, archivist, historian, scorer, clerk, registrar, scribe, diarist, scorekeeper, annalist

recording = <u>record</u>, video, tape, disc, gramophone record, cut (*informal*)

recount = <u>tell</u>, report, detail, describe, relate, repeat, portray, depict, rehearse, recite, tell the story of, narrate, delineate, enumerate, give an account of

recoup = <u>regain</u>, recover, make good, retrieve, redeem, win back

recourse = <u>option</u>, choice, alternative, resort, appeal, resource, remedy, way out, refuge, expedient

recover 1 = <u>get better</u>, improve, get well, recuperate, pick up, heal, revive, come round, bounce back, mend, turn the corner, pull through, convalesce, be on the mend, take a turn for the better, get back on your feet, feel yourself again, regain your health *or* strength ...*He is recovering after sustaining a knee injury...* OPPOSITE> relapse
2 = <u>rally</u> ...*The stockmarket index fell by 80% before it began to recover...*
3 = <u>save</u>, rescue, retrieve, salvage, reclaim ...*Rescue teams recovered a few more survivors from the rubble...* OPPOSITE> abandon
4 = <u>recoup</u>, restore, repair, get back, regain, make good, retrieve, reclaim, redeem, recapture, win back, take back, repossess, retake, find again ...*Legal action is being taken to try and recover the money...* OPPOSITE> lose

recovery 1 = <u>improvement</u>, return to health, rally, healing, revival, mending, recuperation, convalescence, turn for the better ...*He made a remarkable recovery from a shin injury...*
2 = <u>revival</u>, improvement, rally, restoration, rehabilitation, upturn, betterment, amelioration ...*In many sectors of the economy the recovery has started...*
3 = <u>retrieval</u>, repossession, reclamation, restoration, repair, redemption, recapture ...*the recovery of a painting by Turner...*

recreation = <u>leisure</u>, play, sport, exercise, fun, relief, pleasure, entertainment, relaxation, enjoyment, distraction, amusement, diversion, refreshment, beer and skittles (*informal*)

recrimination = <u>bickering</u>, retaliation, counterattack, mutual accusation, retort, quarrel, squabbling, name-calling, countercharge

recruit VERB 1 = <u>gather</u>, take on, obtain, engage, round up, enrol, procure, proselytize ...*He helped to recruit volunteers to go to Pakistan...*
2 = <u>assemble</u>, raise, levy, muster, mobilize ...*He's

Shades of red

auburn	coral	maroon	ruby
baby pink	crimson	mulberry	russet
bay	cyclamen	old rose	rust
burgundy	damask	oxblood	salmon pink
burnt sienna	dubonnet	oyster pink	sandy
cardinal red	flame	peach	scarlet
carmine	flesh	peach-blow	shell pink
carnation	foxy	pink	strawberry
carroty	fuchsia	plum	tea rose
cerise	ginger	poppy	terracotta
cherry	grenadine	puce	Titian
chestnut	gules	raspberry	Turkey red
cinnabar	henna	rose	vermeil
claret	liver	roseate	vermilion
copper *or* coppery	magenta	rosy	wine

---

managed to recruit an army of crooks...
3 = <u>enlist</u>, draft, impress, enrol ...*He had the forlorn job of trying to recruit soldiers...* OPPOSITE> dismiss
NOUN = <u>beginner</u>, trainee, apprentice, novice, convert, initiate, rookie (*informal*), helper, learner, neophyte, tyro, greenhorn (*informal*), proselyte ...*A new recruit could well arrive later this week...*

rectify = <u>correct</u>, right, improve, reform, square, fix, repair, adjust, remedy, amend, make good, mend, redress, put right, set the record straight, emend

rectitude 1 = <u>morality</u>, principle, honour, virtue, decency, justice, equity, integrity, goodness, honesty, correctness, righteousness, probity, incorruptibility, scrupulousness, uprightness ...*people of the utmost rectitude...* OPPOSITE> immorality
2 = <u>correctness</u>, justice, accuracy, precision, verity, rightness, soundness, exactness ...*Has the rectitude of this principle ever been formally contested?...*

recuperate = <u>recover</u>, improve, pick up, get better, mend, turn the corner, convalesce, be on the mend, get back on your feet, regain your health

recur = <u>happen again</u>, return, come back, repeat, persist, revert, reappear, come and go, come again

recurrent = <u>periodic</u>, continued, regular, repeated, frequent, recurring, repetitive, cyclical, habitual OPPOSITE> one-off

recycle = <u>reprocess</u>, reuse, salvage, reclaim, save

red NOUN *or* ADJECTIVE **1** = <u>crimson</u>, scarlet, ruby, vermilion, rose, wine, pink, cherry, cardinal, coral, maroon, claret, carmine ...*a bunch of red roses...*
2 = <u>flushed</u>, embarrassed, blushing, suffused, florid, shamefaced, rubicund ...*She was red with shame...*
3 (*of hair*) = <u>chestnut</u>, flaming, reddish, flame-coloured, bay, sandy, foxy, Titian, carroty ...*Her red hair flowed out in the wind...*
4 = <u>bloodshot</u>, inflamed, red-rimmed ...*He rubbed his red eyes...*
5 = <u>rosy</u>, healthy, glowing, blooming, ruddy, roseate ...*rosy red cheeks...*
PHRASES **in the red** (*Informal*) = <u>in debt</u>, bankrupt, on the rocks, insolvent, in arrears, overdrawn, owing money, in deficit, showing a loss, in debit ...*The*

theatre is in the red... ◆ **see red** (*Informal*) = <u>lose your temper</u>, boil, lose it (*informal*), seethe, go mad (*informal*), crack up (*informal*), lose the plot (*informal*), go ballistic (*slang, chiefly U.S.*), blow a fuse (*slang, chiefly U.S.*), fly off the handle (*informal*), become enraged, go off the deep end (*informal*), wig out (*slang*), go up the wall (*slang*), blow your top, lose your rag (*slang*), be beside yourself with rage (*informal*), be *or* get very angry, go off your head (*slang*) ...*I didn't mean to break his nose. I just saw red...*

(Related Words)
adjectives: rubicund, ruddy
➤ **shades of red**

red-blooded (*Informal*) = <u>vigorous</u>, manly, lusty, virile, strong, vital, robust, hearty

redden = <u>flush</u>, colour (up), blush, crimson, suffuse, go red, go beetroot (*informal*)

redeem 1 = <u>reinstate</u>, absolve, restore to favour, rehabilitate ...*He had realized the mistake he had made and wanted to redeem himself...*
2 = <u>make up for</u>, offset, make good, compensate for, outweigh, redress, atone for, make amends for, defray ...*Work is the way people seek to redeem their sins...*
3 = <u>trade in</u>, cash (in), exchange, change ...*The voucher will be redeemed for one toy...*
4 = <u>buy back</u>, recover, regain, retrieve, reclaim, win back, repossess, repurchase, recover possession of ...*the date upon which you plan to redeem the item...*
5 = <u>save</u>, free, deliver, rescue, liberate, ransom, set free, extricate, emancipate, buy the freedom of, pay the ransom of ...*a new female spiritual force to redeem the world...*
6 = <u>fulfil</u>, meet, keep, carry out, satisfy, discharge, make good, hold to, acquit, adhere to, abide by, keep faith with, be faithful to, perform ...*They must redeem that pledge...*

redemption 1 = <u>compensation</u>, amends, reparation, atonement, expiation ...*trying to make some redemption for his actions...*
2 = <u>salvation</u>, release, rescue, liberation, ransom, emancipation, deliverance ...*offering redemption*

from our sins…
3 = <u>paying-off</u>, paying back …*redemption of the loan…*
4 = <u>trade-in</u>, recovery, retrieval, repurchase, repossession, reclamation, quid pro quo …*cash redemptions and quota payments…*

red-handed = <u>in the act</u>, with your pants down (*U.S. slang*), (in) flagrante delicto, with your fingers *or* hand in the till (*informal*), bang to rights (*slang*)

redolent 1 = <u>reminiscent</u>, evocative, suggestive, remindful …*a sad tale, redolent with regret…*
2 = <u>scented</u>, perfumed, fragrant, aromatic, sweet-smelling, odorous …*The air was redolent of cinnamon and apple…*

redoubtable = <u>formidable</u>, strong, powerful, terrible, awful, mighty, dreadful, fearful, fearsome, resolute, valiant, doughty

redress **VERB** **1** = <u>make amends for</u>, pay for, make up for, compensate for, put right, recompense for, make reparation for, make restitution for …*Victims are turning to litigation to redress wrongs done to them…*
2 = <u>put right</u>, reform, balance, square, correct, ease, repair, relieve, adjust, regulate, remedy, amend, mend, rectify, even up, restore the balance …*To redress the economic imbalance…*
NOUN = <u>amends</u>, payment, compensation, reparation, restitution, atonement, recompense, requital, quittance …*a legal battle to seek some redress from the government…*

reduce **VERB** **1** = <u>lessen</u>, cut, contract, lower, depress, moderate, weaken, diminish, turn down, decrease, slow down, cut down, shorten, dilute, impair, curtail, wind down, abate, tone down, debase, truncate, abridge, downsize …*Consumption is being reduced by 25 per cent…* **OPPOSITE** increase
2 = <u>degrade</u>, downgrade, demote, lower in rank, break, humble, humiliate, bring low, take down a peg (*informal*), lower the status of …*They wanted the army reduced to a police force…* **OPPOSITE** promote
3 = <u>drive</u>, force, bring, bring to the point of …*He was reduced to begging for a living…*
4 = <u>cheapen</u>, cut, lower, discount, slash, mark down, bring down the price of …*Companies should reduce prices today…*
PHRASES **in reduced circumstances** = <u>impoverished</u>, penniless, destitute, poverty-stricken, broke (*informal*), short, ruined, in need, bankrupt, needy, badly off, on the rocks, hard up (*informal*), down and out, skint (*Brit. slang*), in want, indigent, down at heel, impecunious, dirt-poor (*informal*), on the breadline, flat broke (*informal*), penurious, on your uppers, stony-broke (*Brit. slang*), necessitous, in queer street, pauperized, without two pennies to rub together (*informal*), on your beam-ends …*living in reduced circumstances…*

redundancy 1 = <u>layoff</u>, sacking, dismissal …*They hope to avoid future redundancies…*
2 = <u>unemployment</u>, the sack (*informal*), the axe

(*informal*), joblessness …*Thousands of employees are facing redundancy…*
3 = <u>superfluity</u>, surplus, surfeit, superabundance …*the redundancy of its two main exhibits…*

redundant 1 = <u>superfluous</u>, extra, surplus, excessive, unnecessary, unwanted, inordinate, inessential, supernumerary, de trop (*French*), supererogatory …*the conversion of redundant buildings to residential use…* **OPPOSITE** essential
2 = <u>tautological</u>, wordy, repetitious, verbose, padded, diffuse, prolix, iterative, periphrastic, pleonastic …*The last couplet collapses into redundant adjectives…*

reek **VERB** **1** = <u>stink</u>, smell, pong (*Brit. informal*), smell to high heaven, hum (*slang*) …*Your breath reeks…*
2 *with of* = <u>be redolent of</u>, suggest, smack of, testify to, be characterized by, bear the stamp of, be permeated by, be suggestive *or* indicative of …*The whole thing reeks of hypocrisy…*
NOUN = <u>stink</u>, smell, odour, stench, pong (*Brit. informal*), effluvium, niff (*Brit. slang*), malodour, mephitis, fetor …*He smelt the reek of whisky…*

reel 1 = <u>stagger</u>, rock, roll, pitch, stumble, sway, falter, lurch, wobble, waver, totter …*He lost his balance and reeled back…*
2 = <u>whirl</u>, swim, spin, revolve, swirl, twirl, go round and round …*The room reeled and he jammed his head down…*

refer **VERB** **1** = <u>pass on</u>, transfer, deliver, commit, hand over, submit, turn over, consign …*He could refer the matter to the high court…*
2 = <u>direct</u>, point, send, guide, recommend …*He referred me to a book on the subject…*
PHRASES **refer to something** *or* **someone 1** = <u>allude to</u>, mention, cite, speak of, bring up, invoke, hint at, touch on, make reference to, make mention of …*He referred to a recent trip to Canada…* **2** = <u>relate to</u>, concern, apply to, pertain to, be relevant to …*The term 'electronics' refers to electrically-induced action…*
3 = <u>consult</u>, go, apply, turn to, look up, have recourse to, seek information from …*He referred briefly to his notebook…*

Word Power

refer – It is usually unnecessary to add *back* to the verb *refer*, since the sense of *back* is already contained in the *re-* part of this word. For example, you might say *This refers to* (not *refers back to*) *what has already been said. Refer back* is only considered acceptable when used to mean 'return a document or question to the person it came from for further consideration', as in *he referred the matter back to me.*

---

referee **NOUN** = <u>umpire</u>, judge, ref (*informal*), arbiter, arbitrator, adjudicator …*The referee stopped the fight…*
VERB = <u>umpire</u>, judge, mediate, adjudicate, arbitrate …*He has refereed in two World Cups…*

reference **NOUN** **1** = <u>allusion</u>, note, mention, remark, quotation ...*He summed up his philosophy, with reference to Calvin*...

2 = <u>citation</u> ...*I would have found a brief list of references useful*...

3 = <u>testimonial</u>, recommendation, credentials, endorsement, certification, good word, character reference ...*The firm offered to give her a reference*...

PHRASES **with reference to** = <u>concerning</u>, regarding, relating to, in connection with, with respect to ...*I'm calling with reference to your series on prejudice*...

referendum = <u>public vote</u>, popular vote, plebiscite

refine **1** = <u>purify</u>, process, filter, cleanse, clarify, distil, rarefy ...*Oil is refined so as to remove naturally occurring impurities*...

2 = <u>improve</u>, perfect, polish, temper, elevate, hone ...*Surgical techniques are constantly being refined*...

refined **1** = <u>purified</u>, processed, pure, filtered, clean, clarified, distilled ...*refined sugar*... **OPPOSITE** unrefined

2 = <u>cultured</u>, civil, polished, sophisticated, gentlemanly, elegant, polite, cultivated, gracious, civilized, genteel, urbane, courtly, well-bred, ladylike, well-mannered ...*His speech and manner are refined*... **OPPOSITE** coarse

3 = <u>discerning</u>, fine, nice, sensitive, exact, subtle, delicate, precise, discriminating, sublime, fastidious, punctilious ...*refined tastes*...

refinement **1** = <u>subtlety</u>, nuance, nicety, fine point ...*the refinements of the game*...

2 = <u>sophistication</u>, finish, style, culture, taste, breeding, polish, grace, discrimination, courtesy, civilization, precision, elegance, delicacy, cultivation, finesse, politeness, good manners, civility, gentility, good breeding, graciousness, urbanity, fastidiousness, fineness, courtliness, politesse ...*a girl who possessed both dignity and refinement*...

3 = <u>purification</u>, processing, filtering, cleansing, clarification, distillation, rectification, rarefaction ...*the refinement of crude oil*...

reflect **1** = <u>show</u>, reveal, express, display, indicate, demonstrate, exhibit, communicate, manifest, bear out, bespeak, evince ...*Concern was reflected in the government's budget*...

2 = <u>throw back</u>, return, mirror, echo, reproduce, imitate, give back ...*The glass appears to reflect light naturally*...

3 = <u>consider</u>, think, contemplate, deliberate, muse, ponder, meditate, mull over, ruminate, cogitate, wonder ...*I reflected on the child's future*...

reflection **1** = <u>image</u>, echo, counterpart, mirror image ...*Meg stared at her reflection in the mirror*...

2 = <u>criticism</u>, censure, slur, reproach, imputation, derogation, aspersion ...*Infection with head lice is no reflection on personal hygiene*...

3 = <u>consideration</u>, thinking, pondering, deliberation, thought, idea, view, study, opinion, impression, observation, musing, meditation, contemplation, rumination, perusal, cogitation, cerebration ...*After days of reflection she decided to write back*...

reflective = <u>thoughtful</u>, contemplative, meditative, pensive, reasoning, pondering, deliberative, ruminative, cogitating

reform **NOUN** = <u>improvement</u>, amendment, correction, rehabilitation, renovation, betterment, rectification, amelioration ...*a programme of economic reform*...

VERB **1** = <u>improve</u>, better, correct, restore, repair, rebuild, amend, reclaim, mend, renovate, reconstruct, remodel, rectify, rehabilitate, regenerate, reorganize, reconstitute, revolutionize, ameliorate, emend ...*his plans to reform the country's economy*...

2 = <u>mend your ways</u>, go straight (*informal*), shape up (*informal*), get it together (*informal*), turn over a new leaf, get your act together (*informal*), clean up your act (*informal*), pull your socks up (*Brit. informal*), get back on the straight and narrow (*informal*) ...*Under such a system where is the incentive to reform?*...

refrain¹ = <u>stop</u>, avoid, give up, cease, do without, renounce, abstain, eschew, leave off, desist, forbear, kick (*informal*) ...*She refrained from making any comment*...

refrain² = <u>chorus</u>, song, tune, melody ...*a refrain from an old song*...

refresh **1** = <u>revive</u>, cool, freshen, revitalize, cheer, stimulate, brace, rejuvenate, kick-start (*informal*), enliven, breathe new life into, invigorate, revivify, reanimate, inspirit ...*The lotion cools and refreshes the skin*...

2 = <u>replenish</u>, restore, repair, renew, top up, renovate ...*She appeared, her make-up refreshed*...

3 = <u>stimulate</u>, prompt, renew, jog, prod, brush up (*informal*) ...*Allow me to refresh your memory*...

refreshing **1** = <u>new</u>, different, original, novel ...*refreshing new ideas*...

2 = <u>stimulating</u>, fresh, cooling, bracing, invigorating, revivifying, thirst-quenching, inspiriting ...*Herbs have been used for centuries to make refreshing drinks*... **OPPOSITE** tiring

refreshment **NOUN** = <u>revival</u>, restoration, renewal, stimulation, renovation, freshening, reanimation, enlivenment, repair ...*a place where city dwellers come to find spiritual refreshment*...

PLURAL NOUN = <u>food and drink</u>, drinks, snacks, titbits, kai (*N.Z. informal*) ...*Some refreshments would be nice*...

refrigerate = <u>cool</u>, freeze, chill, keep cold

refuge **1** = <u>protection</u>, security, shelter, harbour, asylum ...*They took refuge in a bomb shelter*...

2 = <u>haven</u>, resort, retreat, sanctuary, hide-out, bolt hole ...*We climbed up a winding track towards a mountain refuge*...

refugee = <u>exile</u>, émigré, displaced person, runaway, fugitive, escapee

refund **NOUN** = <u>repayment</u>, reimbursement, return ...*They plan to demand a refund*...

VERB = <u>repay</u>, return, restore, make good, pay back, reimburse, give back ...*She will refund you the* *purchase price…*

refurbish = <u>renovate</u>, restore, repair, clean up, overhaul, revamp, mend, remodel, do up (*informal*), refit, fix up (*informal, chiefly U.S. & Canad.*), spruce up, re-equip, set to rights

refusal NOUN = <u>rejection</u>, denial, defiance, rebuff, knock-back (*slang*), thumbs down, repudiation, kick in the teeth (*slang*), negation, no …*a refusal of planning permission…*
PHRASES **first refusal** = <u>option</u>, choice, opportunity, consideration …*A tenant may have a right of first refusal if a property is offered for sale…*

refuse[1] 1 = <u>decline</u>, reject, turn down, say no to, repudiate …*I could hardly refuse his invitation…*
2 = <u>deny</u>, decline, withhold …*She was refused access to her children…* OPPOSITE allow

refuse[2] = <u>rubbish</u>, waste, sweepings, junk (*informal*), litter, garbage, trash, sediment, scum, dross, dregs, leavings, dreck (*slang, chiefly U.S.*), offscourings, lees …*a weekly collection of refuse…*

refute = <u>disprove</u>, counter, discredit, prove false, silence, overthrow, negate, rebut, give the lie to, blow out of the water (*slang*), confute OPPOSITE prove

Word Power

refute – The use of *refute* to mean *deny* as in *I'm not refuting the fact that* is thought by some people to be incorrect. In careful writing it may be advisable to use *refute* only where there is an element of disproving something through argument and evidence, as in *we haven't got evidence to refute their hypothesis.*

regain 1 = <u>recover</u>, get back, retrieve, redeem, recapture, win back, take back, recoup, repossess, retake …*Troops have regained control of the city…*
2 = <u>get back to</u>, return to, reach again, reattain …*Davis went to regain his carriage…*

regal = <u>royal</u>, majestic, kingly *or* queenly, noble, princely, proud, magnificent, sovereign, fit for a king *or* queen

regale 1 = <u>entertain</u>, delight, amuse, divert, gratify …*He was constantly regaled with amusing stories…*
2 = <u>serve</u>, refresh, ply …*On Sunday evenings we were usually regaled with a roast dinner…*

regalia = <u>trappings</u>, gear, decorations, finery, apparatus, emblems, paraphernalia, garb, accoutrements, rigout (*informal*)

regard VERB 1 = <u>consider</u>, see, hold, rate, view, value, account, judge, treat, think of, esteem, deem, look upon, adjudge …*I regard creativity as both a gift and a skill…*
2 = <u>look at</u>, view, eye, watch, observe, check, notice, clock (*Brit. slang*), remark, check out (*informal*), gaze at, behold, eyeball (*U.S. slang*), scrutinize, get a load of (*informal*), take a dekko at (*Brit. slang*) …*She regarded him curiously for a moment…*
NOUN 1 = <u>respect</u>, esteem, deference, store, thought, love, concern, care, account, note, reputation, honour, consideration, sympathy, affection, attachment …*I have a very high regard for him and what he has achieved…*
2 = <u>look</u>, gaze, scrutiny, stare, glance …*This gave an air of calculated menace to his regard…*
PLURAL NOUN = <u>good wishes</u>, respects, greetings, compliments, best wishes, salutations, devoirs …*Give my regards to your family…*
PHRASES **as regards** = <u>concerning</u>, regarding, relating to, pertaining to …*As regards the war, he believed in victory at any price…* ♦ **in this regard** = <u>on this point</u>, on this matter, on this detail, in this respect …*In this regard nothing has changed…*
♦ **with regard to** = <u>concerning</u>, regarding, relating to, with respect to, as regards …*The UN has urged sanctions with regard to trade in arms…*

Word Power

regard – The word *regard* in the expression *with regard to* is singular, and has no *s* at the end. People often make the mistake of saying *with regards to*, perhaps being influenced by the phrase *as regards.*

regarding = <u>concerning</u>, about, as to, on the subject of, re, respecting, in respect of, as regards, with reference to, in re, in the matter of, apropos, in *or* with regard to

regardless 1 = <u>in spite of everything</u>, anyway, nevertheless, nonetheless, in any case, no matter what, for all that, rain or shine, despite everything, come what may …*Despite her recent surgery she has been carrying on regardless…*
2 with *of* = <u>irrespective of</u>, disregarding, unconcerned about, heedless of, unmindful of …*It takes in anybody regardless of religion, colour or creed…*

regenerate = <u>renew</u>, restore, revive, renovate, change, reproduce, uplift, reconstruct, re-establish, rejuvenate, kick-start (*informal*), breathe new life into, invigorate, reinvigorate, reawaken, revivify, give a shot in the arm, inspirit OPPOSITE degenerate

regime 1 = <u>government</u>, rule, management, administration, leadership, establishment, reign …*the collapse of the fascist regime…*
2 = <u>plan</u>, course, system, policy, programme, scheme, regimen …*a drastic regime of economic reform…*

region NOUN = <u>area</u>, country, place, part, land, quarter, division, section, sector, district, territory, zone, province, patch, turf (*U.S. slang*), tract, expanse, locality …*a remote mountain region…*
PHRASES **in the region of** 1 = <u>around</u>, almost, nearing, nearly, approaching, close to, roughly, more or less, approximately …*There are still somewhere in the region of 18 million members…* 2 = <u>in the vicinity of</u>, in the area of, in the range of, in the scope of, in the neighbourhood of, in the sphere of …*a series of battles in the region of Matebete…*
➤ **WORD POWER SUPPLEMENT administrative regions**

regional = <u>local</u>, district, provincial, parochial, sectional, zonal

register NOUN = <u>list</u>, record, roll, file, schedule, diary, catalogue, log, archives, chronicle, memorandum, roster, ledger, annals ...*registers of births, deaths and marriages...*
VERB **1** = <u>enrol</u>, sign on *or* up, enlist, list, note, enter, check in, inscribe, set down ...*Have you come to register at the school?...*
2 = <u>record</u>, catalogue, chronicle, take down ...*We registered his birth...*
3 = <u>indicate</u>, show, record, read ...*The meter registered loads of 9 and 10 kg...*
4 = <u>show</u>, mark, record, reflect, indicate, betray, manifest, bespeak ...*Many people registered no symptoms when they became infected...*
5 = <u>express</u>, say, show, reveal, display, exhibit ...*Workers stopped work to register their protest...*
6 (*Informal*) = <u>have an effect</u>, get through, sink in, make an impression, tell, impress, come home, dawn on ...*What I said sometimes didn't register in her brain...*

regress = <u>revert</u>, deteriorate, return, go back, retreat, lapse, fall back, wane, recede, ebb, degenerate, relapse, lose ground, turn the clock back, backslide, retrogress, retrocede, fall away *or* off OPPOSITE progress

regret VERB **1** = <u>be</u> *or* <u>feel sorry about</u>, feel remorse about, be upset about, rue, deplore, bemoan, repent (of), weep over, bewail, cry over spilt milk ...*She regrets having given up her home...* OPPOSITE be satisfied with
2 = <u>mourn</u>, miss, grieve for *or* over ...*I regret the passing of the old era...*
NOUN **1** = <u>remorse</u>, compunction, self-reproach, pang of conscience, bitterness, repentance, contrition, penitence, ruefulness ...*He has no regrets about retiring...*
2 = <u>sorrow</u>, disappointment, grief, lamentation ...*He expressed great regret...* OPPOSITE satisfaction

regretful = <u>sorry</u>, disappointed, sad, ashamed, apologetic, mournful, rueful, contrite, sorrowful, repentant, remorseful, penitent

---

Word Power

regretful – *Regretful* and *regretfully* are sometimes wrongly used where *regrettable* and *regrettably* are meant. A simple way of making the distinction is that when you regret something YOU have done, you are *regretful*: *he gave a regretful smile; he smiled regretfully.* In contrast, when you are sorry about an occurrence you did not yourself cause, you view the occurrence as *regrettable*: *this is a regrettable* (not *regretful*) *mistake; regrettably* (not *regretfully*, i.e. because of circumstances beyond my control) *I shall be unable to attend.*

---

regrettable = <u>unfortunate</u>, wrong, disappointing, sad, distressing, unhappy, shameful, woeful, deplorable, ill-advised, lamentable, pitiable
➤ **regretful**

regular 1 = <u>frequent</u>, daily ...*Take regular exercise...*
2 = <u>normal</u>, common, established, usual, ordinary, typical, routine, everyday, customary, commonplace, habitual, unvarying ...*Children are encouraged to make reading a regular routine...* OPPOSITE infrequent
3 = <u>steady</u>, consistent ...*a very regular beat...*
4 = <u>even</u>, level, balanced, straight, flat, fixed, smooth, uniform, symmetrical ...*regular rows of wooden huts...* OPPOSITE uneven
5 = <u>methodical</u>, set, ordered, formal, steady, efficient, systematic, orderly, standardized, dependable, consistent ...*an unfailingly regular procedure...* OPPOSITE inconsistent
6 = <u>official</u>, standard, established, traditional, classic, correct, approved, formal, sanctioned, proper, prevailing, orthodox, time-honoured, bona fide ...*The regular method is to take your cutting, and insert it into the compost...*

regulate 1 = <u>control</u>, run, order, rule, manage, direct, guide, handle, conduct, arrange, monitor, organize, govern, administer, oversee, supervise, systematize, superintend ...*a powerful body to regulate the stock market...*
2 = <u>moderate</u>, control, modulate, settle, fit, balance, tune, adjust ...*He breathed deeply, trying to regulate the pound of his heartbeat...*

regulation NOUN **1** = <u>rule</u>, order, law, direction, procedure, requirement, dictate, decree, canon, statute, ordinance, commandment, edict, precept, standing order ...*new safety regulations...*
2 = <u>control</u>, government, management, administration, direction, arrangement, supervision, governance, rule ...*They also have responsibility for the regulation of nurseries...*
ADJECTIVE = <u>conventional</u>, official, standard, required, normal, usual, prescribed, mandatory, customary ...*He wears the regulation dark suit of corporate America...*

regurgitate = <u>disgorge</u>, throw up (*informal*), chuck up (*slang, chiefly U.S.*), puke up (*slang*), sick up (*informal*), spew out *or* up

rehabilitate 1 = <u>reintegrate</u> ...*Considerable efforts have been made to rehabilitate patients...*
2 = <u>restore</u>, convert, renew, adjust, rebuild, make good, mend, renovate, reconstruct, reinstate, re-establish, fix up (*informal, chiefly U.S. & Canad.*), reconstitute, recondition, reinvigorate ...*a program for rehabilitating low-income housing...*

rehash NOUN = <u>reworking</u>, rewrite, new version, rearrangement ...*It was a rehash of an old script...*
VERB = <u>rework</u>, rewrite, rearrange, change, alter, reshuffle, make over, reuse, rejig (*informal*), refashion ...*The tour seems to rely heavily on rehashed old favourites...*

rehearsal = <u>practice</u>, rehearsing, practice session, run-through, reading, preparation, drill, going-over (*informal*)

rehearse 1 = <u>practise</u>, prepare, run through, go over, train, act, study, ready, repeat, drill, try out, recite ...*A group of actors are rehearsing a play about Joan of Arc...*
2 = <u>recite</u>, practice, go over, run through, tell, list, detail, describe, review, relate, depict, spell out, recount, narrate, trot out (*informal*), delineate, enumerate ...*Anticipate any tough questions and rehearse your answers...*

reign VERB 1 = <u>be supreme</u>, prevail, predominate, hold sway, be rife, be rampant ...*A relative calm reigned over the city...*
2 = <u>rule</u>, govern, be in power, occupy *or* sit on the throne, influence, command, administer, hold sway, wear the crown, wield the sceptre ...*Henry II, who reigned from 1154 to 1189...*
NOUN = <u>rule</u>, sovereignty, supremacy, power, control, influence, command, empire, monarchy, sway, dominion, hegemony, ascendancy ...*Queen Victoria's reign...*

> ## Word Power
>
> **reign** – The words *rein* and *reign* should not be confused; note the correct spellings in *he gave full rein to his feelings* (not *reign*); and *it will be necessary to rein in public spending* (not *reign in*).

reimburse = <u>pay back</u>, refund, repay, recompense, return, restore, compensate, indemnify, remunerate

rein NOUN = <u>control</u>, harness, bridle, hold, check, restriction, brake, curb, restraint ...*He wrapped his horse's reins round his left wrist...*
PHRASES **give (a) free rein to something** *or* **someone** = <u>give a free hand (to)</u>, give carte blanche (to), give a blank cheque (to), remove restraints (from), indulge, let go, give way to, give (someone) his or her head ...*They gave him a free rein with time to mould a decent side...* ◆ **rein something in** *or* **back** = <u>check</u>, control, limit, contain, master, curb, restrain, hold back, constrain, bridle, keep in check ...*He promised the government would rein back inflation...*
➤ **reign**

reincarnation = <u>rebirth</u>, metempsychosis, transmigration of souls

reinforce 1 = <u>support</u>, strengthen, fortify, toughen, stress, prop, supplement, emphasize, underline, harden, bolster, stiffen, shore up, buttress ...*They had to reinforce the walls with exterior beams...*
2 = <u>increase</u>, extend, add to, strengthen, supplement, augment ...*Troops and police have been reinforced...*

reinforcement NOUN 1 = <u>strengthening</u>, increase, supplement, enlargement, fortification, amplification, augmentation ...*the reinforcement of peace and security around the world...*
2 = <u>support</u>, stay, shore, prop, brace, buttress ...*There are reinforcements on all doors...*
PLURAL NOUN = <u>reserves</u>, support, auxiliaries, additional

or fresh troops ...*troop reinforcements...*

reinstate = <u>restore</u>, recall, bring back, re-establish, return, rehabilitate

reiterate (*Formal*) = <u>repeat</u>, restate, say again, retell, do again, recapitulate, iterate

reject VERB 1 = <u>rebuff</u>, drop, jilt, desert, turn down, ditch (*slang*), break with, spurn, refuse, say no to, repulse, throw over ...*people who have been rejected by their lovers...* OPPOSITE accept
2 = <u>deny</u>, decline, abandon, exclude, veto, discard, relinquish, renounce, spurn, eschew, leave off, throw off, disallow, forsake, retract, repudiate, cast off, disown, forgo, disclaim, forswear, swear off, wash your hands of ...*They are rejecting the values on which Thatcherism was built...* OPPOSITE approve
3 = <u>discard</u>, decline, eliminate, scrap, bin, jettison, cast aside, throw away *or* out ...*Seventeen publishers rejected the manuscript...* OPPOSITE accept
NOUN 1 = <u>castoff</u>, second, discard, flotsam, clunker (*informal*) ...*a hat that looks like a reject from an army patrol...* OPPOSITE treasure
2 = <u>failure</u>, loser, flop ...*I'm an outsider, a reject, a social failure... ...a reject of Real Madrid...*

rejection 1 = <u>denial</u>, veto, dismissal, exclusion, abandonment, spurning, casting off, disowning, thumbs down, renunciation, repudiation, eschewal ...*his rejection of our values...* OPPOSITE approval
2 = <u>rebuff</u>, refusal, knock-back (*slang*), kick in the teeth (*slang*), bum's rush (*slang*), the (old) heave-ho (*informal*), brushoff (*slang*) ...*These feelings of rejection and hurt remain...* OPPOSITE acceptance

rejoice = <u>be glad</u>, celebrate, delight, be happy, joy, triumph, glory, revel, be overjoyed, exult, jump for joy, make merry OPPOSITE lament

rejoicing = <u>happiness</u>, delight, joy, triumph, celebration, cheer, festivity, elation, gaiety, jubilation, revelry, exultation, gladness, merrymaking

rejoin = <u>reply</u>, answer, respond, retort, come back with, riposte, return

rejuvenate = <u>revitalize</u>, restore, renew, refresh, regenerate, breathe new life into, reinvigorate, revivify, give new life to, reanimate, make young again, restore vitality to

relapse VERB 1 = <u>lapse</u>, revert, degenerate, slip back, fail, weaken, fall back, regress, backslide, retrogress ...*He was relapsing into his usual gloom...*
2 = <u>worsen</u>, deteriorate, sicken, weaken, fail, sink, fade ...*In 90 per cent of cases the patient will relapse within six months...* OPPOSITE recover
NOUN 1 = <u>lapse</u>, regression, fall from grace, reversion, backsliding, recidivism, retrogression ...*a relapse into the nationalism of the nineteenth century...*
2 = <u>worsening</u>, setback, deterioration, recurrence, turn for the worse, weakening ...*The sufferer can experience frequent relapses...* OPPOSITE recovery

relate VERB = <u>tell</u>, recount, report, present, detail, describe, chronicle, rehearse, recite, impart, narrate, set forth, give an account of ...*He was relating a story he had once heard...*

PHRASES **relate to something** or **someone** 1 = concern, refer to, apply to, have to do with, pertain to, be relevant to, bear upon, appertain to, have reference to ...*papers relating to the children*... 2 = connect with, associate with, link with, couple with, join with, ally with, correlate to, coordinate with ...*how language relates to particular cultural codes*...

related 1 = associated, linked, allied, joint, accompanying, connected, affiliated, akin, correlated, interconnected, concomitant, cognate, agnate ...*equipment and accessories for diving and related activities*... **OPPOSITE** unconnected
2 = akin, kin, kindred, cognate, consanguineous, agnate ...*He is related by marriage to some of the complainants*... **OPPOSITE** unrelated

relation **NOUN** 1 = similarity, link, bearing, bond, application, comparison, tie-in, correlation, interdependence, pertinence, connection ...*This theory bears no relation to reality*...
2 = relative, kin, kinsman or kinswoman ...*I call him Uncle though he's no relation*...
PLURAL NOUN 1 = dealings, relationship, rapport, communications, meetings, terms, associations, affairs, contact, connections, interaction, intercourse, liaison ...*The company has a track record of good employee relations*...
2 = family, relatives, tribe, clan, kin, kindred, kinsmen, kinsfolk ...*all my relations come from the place*...
PHRASES **in relation to** = concerning, regarding, respecting, in connection with, with regard to, on the subject of, in respect of, with reference to, apropos ...*He is the sixth person to be arrested in relation to the coup plot*...

relationship 1 = association, bond, communications, connection, conjunction, affinity, rapport, kinship ...*Money problems place great stress on close family relationships*...
2 = affair, romance, liaison, amour, intrigue ...*She likes to have a relationship with her leading men*...
3 = connection, link, proportion, parallel, ratio, similarity, tie-up, correlation ...*the relationship between culture and power*...

relative **NOUN** = relation, connection, kinsman or kinswoman, member of your or the family ...*Do relatives of yours still live in Siberia?*...
ADJECTIVE 1 = comparative ...*a period of relative calm*...
2 = corresponding, respective, reciprocal ...*the relative importance of education in 50 countries*...
3 with **to** = in proportion to, corresponding to, proportionate to, proportional to ...*The satellite remains in one spot relative to the earth's surface*...

relatively = comparatively, rather, somewhat, to some extent, in or by comparison

relax 1 = be or feel at ease, chill out (*slang, chiefly U.S.*), take it easy, loosen up, laze, lighten up (*slang*), put your feet up, hang loose (*slang*), let yourself go (*informal*), let your hair down (*informal*), mellow out (*informal*), make yourself at home, outspan (*S.*

African), take your ease ...*I ought to relax and stop worrying about it*... **OPPOSITE** be alarmed
2 = calm down, calm, unwind, loosen up, tranquillize ...*Do something that you know relaxes you*...
3 = make less tense, soften, loosen up, unbend, rest ...*Massage is used to relax muscles*...
4 = lessen, reduce, ease, relieve, weaken, loosen, let up, slacken ...*He gradually relaxed his grip on the arms of the chair*... **OPPOSITE** tighten
5 = moderate, ease, relieve, weaken, diminish, mitigate, slacken ...*Rules governing student conduct have been relaxed in recent years*... **OPPOSITE** tighten up

relaxation 1 = leisure, rest, fun, pleasure, entertainment, recreation, enjoyment, amusement, refreshment, beer and skittles (*informal*) ...*You should be able to find the odd moment for relaxation*...
2 = lessening, easing, reduction, weakening, moderation, let-up (*informal*), slackening, diminution, abatement ...*There will be no relaxation of army pressure*...

relaxed 1 = easy-going, easy, casual, informal, laid-back (*informal*), mellow, leisurely, downbeat (*informal*), unhurried, nonchalant, free and easy, mild, insouciant, untaxing ...*Try to adopt a more relaxed manner*...
2 = comfortable, easy-going, casual, laid-back (*informal*), informal ...*The atmosphere at lunch was relaxed*...

relay = broadcast, carry, spread, communicate, transmit, send out

release **VERB** 1 = set free, free, discharge, liberate, drop, deliver, loose, let go, undo, let out, extricate, untie, disengage, emancipate, unchain, unfasten, turn loose, unshackle, unloose, unfetter, unbridle, manumit ...*He was released from custody the next day*...
OPPOSITE imprison
2 = acquit, excuse, exempt, let go, dispense, let off, exonerate, absolve ...*He wants to be released from any promise between us*...
3 = issue, publish, make public, make known, break, present, launch, distribute, unveil, put out, circulate, disseminate ...*They're not releasing any more details yet*... **OPPOSITE** withhold
NOUN 1 = liberation, freedom, delivery, liberty, discharge, emancipation, deliverance, manumission, relief ...*the secret negotiations necessary to secure the release of the hostages*... **OPPOSITE** imprisonment
2 = acquittal, exemption, let-off (*informal*), dispensation, absolution, exoneration, acquittance ...*a blessed release from the obligation to work*...
3 = issue, announcement, publication, proclamation, offering ...*a meeting held after the release of the report*...

relegate 1 = demote, degrade, downgrade, declass ...*Other newspapers relegated the item to the middle pages*...
2 = banish, exile, expel, throw out, oust, deport, eject, expatriate ...*a team about to be relegated to the second division*...

relent 1 = be merciful, yield, give in, soften, give way, come round, capitulate, acquiesce, change your mind, unbend, forbear, show mercy, have pity, melt, give quarter ...*Finally his mother relented...* OPPOSITE> show no mercy
2 = ease, die down, let up, fall, drop, slow, relax, weaken, slacken ...*If the bad weather relents the game will be finished today...* OPPOSITE> intensify

relentless 1 = merciless, hard, fierce, harsh, cruel, grim, ruthless, uncompromising, unstoppable, inflexible, unrelenting, unforgiving, inexorable, implacable, unyielding, remorseless, pitiless, undeviating ...*He was the most relentless enemy I have ever known...* OPPOSITE> merciful
2 = unremitting, sustained, punishing, persistent, unstoppable, unbroken, unrelenting, incessant, unabated, nonstop, unrelieved, unflagging, unfaltering ...*The pressure now was relentless...*

relevant = significant, appropriate, proper, related, fitting, material, suited, relative, to the point, apt, applicable, pertinent, apposite, admissible, germane, to the purpose, appurtenant, ad rem (*Latin*) OPPOSITE> irrelevant

reliable 1 = dependable, trustworthy, honest, responsible, sure, sound, true, certain, regular, stable, faithful, predictable, upright, staunch, reputable, trusty, unfailing, tried and true ...*She was efficient and reliable...* OPPOSITE> unreliable
2 = safe, dependable ...*Japanese cars are so reliable...*
3 = definitive, sound, dependable, trustworthy ...*There is no reliable evidence...*

reliance 1 = dependency, dependence ...*the country's increasing reliance on foreign aid...*
2 = trust, confidence, belief, faith, assurance, credence, credit ...*If you respond immediately, you will guarantee people's reliance on you...*

relic = remnant, vestige, memento, trace, survival, scrap, token, fragment, souvenir, remembrance, keepsake

relief 1 = ease, release, comfort, cure, remedy, solace, balm, deliverance, mitigation, abatement, alleviation, easement, palliation, assuagement ...*The news will come as a great relief...*
2 = rest, respite, let-up, relaxation, break, diversion, refreshment (*informal*), remission, breather (*informal*) ...*a self-help programme which can give lasting relief...*
3 = aid, help, support, assistance, sustenance, succour ...*famine relief...*

relieve 1 = ease, soothe, alleviate, allay, relax, comfort, calm, cure, dull, diminish, soften, console, appease, solace, mitigate, abate, assuage, mollify, salve, palliate ...*Drugs can relieve much of the pain...* OPPOSITE> intensify
2 = free, release, deliver, discharge, exempt, unburden, disembarrass, disencumber ...*He felt relieved of a burden...*
3 = take over from, substitute for, stand in for, take the place of, give (someone) a break *or* rest ...*At*

seven o'clock the night nurse came in to relieve her...
4 = help, support, aid, sustain, assist, succour, bring aid to ...*a programme to relieve poor countries...*

religion = belief, faith, theology, creed
➤ **Bible** ➤ **Buddhism** ➤ **Christianity**
➤ **Hinduism** ➤ **Islam** ➤ **Judaism** ➤ **religion**

religious 1 = spiritual, holy, sacred, divine, theological, righteous, sectarian, doctrinal, devotional, scriptural ...*different religious beliefs...*
2 = conscientious, exact, faithful, rigid, rigorous, meticulous, scrupulous, fastidious, unerring, unswerving, punctilious ...*The clientele turned up, with religious regularity, every night...*

relinquish (*Formal*) = give up, leave, release, drop, abandon, resign, desert, quit, yield, hand over, surrender, withdraw from, let go, retire from, renounce, waive, vacate, say goodbye to, forsake, cede, repudiate, cast off, forgo, abdicate, kiss (something) goodbye, lay aside

relish VERB 1 = enjoy, like, prefer, taste, appreciate, savour, revel in, luxuriate in ...*He ate quietly, relishing his meal...* OPPOSITE> dislike
2 = look forward to, fancy, delight in, lick your lips over ...*She is not relishing the prospect of another spell in prison...*
NOUN 1 = enjoyment, liking, love, taste, fancy, stomach, appetite, appreciation, penchant, zest, fondness, gusto, predilection, zing (*informal*), partiality ...*The three men ate with relish...* OPPOSITE> distaste
2 = condiment, seasoning, sauce, appetizer ...*pots of spicy relish...*

reluctance = unwillingness, dislike, loathing, distaste, aversion, backwardness, hesitancy, disinclination, repugnance, indisposition, disrelish

reluctant = unwilling, slow, backward, grudging, hesitant, averse, recalcitrant, loath, disinclined, unenthusiastic, indisposed OPPOSITE> willing

---

Word Power

reluctant – *Reticent* is quite commonly used nowadays as a synonym of *reluctant* and followed by *to* and a verb. In careful writing it is advisable to avoid this use, since many people would regard it as mistaken.

---

rely on 1 = depend on, lean on ...*They relied heavily on the advice of their advisors...*
2 = be confident of, bank on, trust, count on, bet on, reckon on, lean on, be sure of, have confidence in, swear by, repose trust in ...*I know I can rely on you to sort it out...*

remain 1 = stay, continue, go on, stand, dwell, bide ...*The three men remained silent...*
2 = stay behind, wait, delay, stay put (*informal*), tarry ...*He remained at home with his family...* OPPOSITE> go
3 = continue, be left, endure, persist, linger, hang in the air, stay ...*There remains deep mistrust of his government...*

Religion   http://www.bbc.co.uk/religion/religions/

Religions

animism	Jainism	Satanism
Babi *or* Babism	Judaism	Scientology
Baha'ism	Macumba	shamanism
Buddhism	Manichaeism *or* Manicheism	Shango
Christianity	Mithraism *or* Mithraicism	Shembe
Confucianism	Orphism	Shinto
druidism	paganism	Sikhism
heliolatry	Rastafarianism	Taoism
Hinduism *or* Hindooism	Ryobu Shinto	voodoo *or* voodooism
Islam	Santeria	Yezidis

Religious books

Adi Granth	Koran *or* Quran	Shi Ching
Apocrypha	Li Chi	Siddhanta
Atharveda	Lu	Su Ching
Ayurveda	Mahabharata	Talmud
Bhagavad-Gita	New Testament	Tipitaka
Bible	Old Testament	Torah
Book of Mormon	Ramayana	Tripitaka
Granth *or* Guru Granth Sahib	Rigveda	Veda
I Ching	Samaveda	Yajurveda

Religious festivals

Advent	Feast of Tabernacles	Purim
Al Hijrah	Good Friday	Quadragesima
Ascension Day	Guru Nanak's Birthday	Quinquagesima
Ash Wednesday	Hirja	Raksha Bandhan
Baisakhi	Hola Mohalla	Ramadan
Bodhi Day	Holi	Rama Naumi
Candlemas	Janamashtami	Rogation
Chanukah *or* Hanukkah	Lailat ul-Barah	Rosh Hashanah
Ching Ming	Lailat ul-Isra Wal Mi'raj	Septuagesima
Christmas	Lailat ul-Qadr	Sexagesima
Corpus Christi	Lent	Shavuot
Day of Atonement	Mahashivaratri	Shrove Tuesday
Dhammacakka	Maundy Thursday	Sukkoth *or* Succoth
Diwali	Michaelmas	Trinity
Dragon Boat Festival	Moon Festival	Wesak
Dussehra	Palm Sunday	Whitsun
Easter	Passion Sunday	Winter Festival
Eid ul-Adha *or* Id-ul-Adha	Passover	Yom Kippur
Eid ul-Fitr *or* Id-ul-Fitr	Pentecost	Yuan Tan
Epiphany	Pesach	

---

remainder = <u>rest</u>, remains, balance, trace, excess, surplus, butt, remnant, relic, residue, stub, vestige(s), tail end, dregs, oddment, leavings, residuum

remaining 1 = <u>left-over</u>, surviving, outstanding, lingering, unfinished, residual ...*Stir in the remaining ingredients...*
2 = <u>surviving</u>, lasting, persisting, abiding, extant ...*They wanted to purge remaining memories of his reign...*

remains 1 = <u>remnants</u>, leftovers, remainder, scraps, rest, pieces, balance, traces, fragments, debris, residue, crumbs, vestiges, detritus, dregs, odds and ends, oddments, leavings ...*the remains of their picnic...*
2 = <u>corpse</u>, body, carcass, cadaver ...*The remains of a man had been found...*
3 = <u>relics</u> ...*There are Roman remains all around us...*

remark VERB **1** = <u>comment</u>, say, state, reflect, mention, declare, observe, pass comment, animadvert ...*I remarked that I would go shopping that afternoon...*
2 = <u>notice</u>, note, observe, perceive, see, mark, regard, make out, heed, espy, take note *or* notice of ...*Everyone has remarked what a lovely lady she is...*
NOUN **1** = <u>comment</u>, observation, reflection, statement, thought, word, opinion, declaration, assertion, utterance ...*She has made outspoken remarks on the issue...*
2 = <u>notice</u>, thought, comment, attention, regard, mention, recognition, consideration, observation, heed, acknowledgment ...*He had never found the situation worthy of remark...*

remarkable = <u>extraordinary</u>, striking, outstanding, famous, odd, strange, wonderful, signal, rare, unusual, impressive, surprising, distinguished, prominent, notable, phenomenal, uncommon, conspicuous, singular, miraculous, noteworthy, pre-eminent OPPOSITE ordinary

remedy NOUN 1 = solution, relief, redress, antidote, corrective, panacea, countermeasure …*a remedy for economic ills…*
2 = cure, treatment, specific, medicine, therapy, antidote, panacea, restorative, relief, nostrum, physic (*rare*), medicament, counteractive …*natural remedies to overcome winter infections…*
VERB 1 = put right, redress, rectify, reform, fix, correct, solve, repair, relieve, ameliorate, set to rights …*A great deal has been done to remedy the situation…*
2 = cure, treat, heal, help, control, ease, restore, relieve, soothe, alleviate, mitigate, assuage, palliate …*He's been remedying a hamstring injury…*

remember 1 = recall, think back to, recollect, reminisce about, retain, recognize, call up, summon up, call to mind …*He was remembering the old days…* OPPOSITE forget
2 = bear in mind, keep in mind …*Remember that each person reacts differently…*
3 = look back (on), commemorate …*He is remembered for being bad at games…*

remembrance 1 = commemoration, memorial, testimonial …*They wore black in remembrance of those who had died…*
2 = souvenir, token, reminder, monument, relic, remembrancer (*archaic*), memento, keepsake …*As a remembrance, he left a photo album…*
3 = memory, recollection, thought, recall, recognition, retrospect, reminiscence, anamnesis …*He had clung to the remembrance of things past…*

remind VERB = jog your memory, prompt, refresh your memory, make you remember …*Can you remind me to buy a bottle of milk?…*
PHRASES **remind someone of something** or **someone** = bring to mind, call to mind, put in mind, awaken memories of, call up, bring back to …*She reminds me of the wife of the pilot…*

reminisce = recall, remember, look back, hark back, review, think back, recollect, live in the past, go over in the memory

reminiscences = recollections, memories, reflections, retrospections, reviews, recalls, memoirs, anecdotes, remembrances

reminiscent = suggestive, evocative, redolent, remindful, similar

remission 1 = lessening, abatement, abeyance, lull, relaxation, ebb, respite, moderation, let-up (*informal*), alleviation, amelioration …*The disease is in remission…*
2 = pardon, release, discharge, amnesty, forgiveness, indulgence, exemption, reprieve, acquittal, absolution, exoneration, excuse …*I've got 10 years and there's no remission for drug offenders…*
3 = reduction, lessening, suspension, decrease,

diminution …*It had been raining hard all day, without remission…*

remit NOUN = instructions, brief, guidelines, authorization, terms of reference, orders …*That issue is not within the remit of the group…*
VERB 1 = send, post, forward, mail, transmit, dispatch …*Many immigrants regularly remit money to their families…*
2 = cancel, stop, halt, repeal, rescind, desist, forbear …*Every creditor shall remit the claim that is held against a neighbour…*
3 = lessen, diminish, abate, ease up, reduce, relax, moderate, weaken, decrease, soften, dwindle, alleviate, wane, fall away, mitigate, slacken …*an episode of 'baby blues' which eventually remitted…*

remittance = payment, fee, consideration, allowance

remnant = remainder, remains, trace, fragment, end, bit, rest, piece, balance, survival, scrap, butt, shred, hangover, residue, rump, leftovers, stub, vestige, tail end, oddment, residuum

remonstrate (*Formal*) = protest, challenge, argue, take issue, object, complain, dispute, dissent, take exception, expostulate

remorse = regret, shame, guilt, pity, grief, compassion, sorrow, anguish, repentance, contrition, compunction, penitence, self-reproach, pangs of conscience, ruefulness, bad *or* guilty conscience

remorseless 1 = relentless, unstoppable, unrelenting, inexorable, unremitting …*the remorseless pressure of financial constraint…*
2 = pitiless, hard, harsh, cruel, savage, ruthless, callous, merciless, unforgiving, implacable, inhumane, unmerciful, hardhearted, uncompassionate …*the capacity for quick, remorseless violence…*

remote 1 = distant, far, isolated, lonely, out-of-the-way, far-off, secluded, inaccessible, faraway, outlying, in the middle of nowhere, off the beaten track, backwoods, godforsaken …*a remote farm in the hills…* OPPOSITE nearby
2 = far, distant, obscure, far-off …*particular events in the remote past…*
3 = irrelevant, foreign, outside, removed, alien, unrelated, unconnected, immaterial, extraneous, extrinsic …*subjects that seem remote from their daily lives…* OPPOSITE relevant
4 = slight, small, outside, poor, unlikely, slim, faint, doubtful, dubious, slender, meagre, negligible, implausible, inconsiderable …*The chances of his surviving are pretty remote…* OPPOSITE strong
5 = aloof, cold, removed, reserved, withdrawn, distant, abstracted, detached, indifferent, faraway, introspective, uninterested, introverted, uninvolved, unapproachable, uncommunicative, standoffish …*She looked so remote…* OPPOSITE outgoing

removal 1 = extraction, stripping, withdrawal, purging, abstraction, uprooting, displacement, eradication, erasure, subtraction, dislodgment, expunction, taking away *or* off *or* out …*the removal* *of a small lump…*

2 = <u>dismissal</u>, expulsion, elimination, ejection, dispossession …*His removal from power was illegal…*

3 = <u>move</u>, transfer, departure, relocation, flitting (*Scot. & Northern English dialect*) …*Home removals are best done in cool weather…*

remove 1 = <u>take out</u>, withdraw, extract, abstract …*Remove the cake from the oven…* OPPOSITE⟩ insert

2 = <u>take off</u>, doff …*He removed his jacket…* OPPOSITE⟩ put on

3 = <u>erase</u>, eliminate, take out …*This treatment removes the most stubborn stains…*

4 = <u>dismiss</u>, eliminate, get rid of, discharge, abolish, expel, throw out, oust, relegate, purge, eject, do away with, depose, unseat, see the back of, dethrone, show someone the door, give the bum's rush (*slang*), throw out on your ear (*informal*) …*The senate voted to remove him…* OPPOSITE⟩ appoint

5 = <u>get rid of</u>, wipe out, erase, eradicate, blow away (*slang, chiefly U.S.*), blot out, expunge …*Most of her fears have been removed…*

6 = <u>take away</u>, move, pull, transfer, detach, displace, do away with, dislodge, cart off (*slang*), carry off *or* away …*They tried to remove the barricades which had been erected…* OPPOSITE⟩ put back

7 = <u>delete</u>, shed, get rid of, erase, excise, strike out, efface, expunge …*They intend to remove up to 100 offensive words…*

8 = <u>amputate</u>, cut off …*When you remove the branches, cut beyond the trunk ridge…* OPPOSITE⟩ join

9 = <u>move</u>, transfer, transport, shift, quit, depart, move away, relocate, vacate, flit (*Scot. & Northern English dialect*) …*They removed to America…*

10 = <u>kill</u>, murder, do in (*slang*), eliminate, take out (*slang*), get rid of, execute, wipe out, dispose of, assassinate, do away with, liquidate, bump off (*slang*), wipe from the face of the earth …*If someone irritates you, remove him, destroy him…*

remuneration = <u>payment</u>, income, earnings, salary, pay, return, profit, fee, wages, reward, compensation, repayment, reparation, indemnity, retainer, reimbursement, recompense, stipend, emolument, meed (*archaic*)

renaissance *or* **renascence** = <u>rebirth</u>, revival, restoration, renewal, awakening, resurrection, regeneration, resurgence, reappearance, new dawn, re-emergence, reawakening, new birth

rend (*Literary*) = <u>tear</u>, break, split, rip, pull, separate, divide, crack, burst, smash, disturb, shatter, pierce, fracture, sever, wrench, splinter, rupture, cleave, lacerate, rive, tear to pieces, sunder (*literary*), dissever

render 1 = <u>make</u>, cause to become, leave …*It has so many errors as to render it useless…*

2 = <u>provide</u>, give, show, pay, present, supply, deliver, contribute, yield, submit, tender, hand out, furnish, turn over, make available …*Any assistance you can render him will be helpful…*

3 = <u>deliver</u>, give, return, announce, pronounce …*The Board was slow to render its verdict…*

4 = <u>translate</u>, put, explain, interpret, reproduce, transcribe, construe, restate …*150 Psalms rendered into English…*

5 = <u>give up</u>, give, deliver, yield, hand over, surrender, turn over, relinquish, cede …*I render up my soul to God…*

6 = <u>represent</u>, interpret, portray, depict, do, give, play, act, present, perform …*a powerful, bizarre, and beautifully rendered story…*

rendezvous NOUN **1** = <u>appointment</u>, meeting, date, engagement, tryst (*archaic*), assignation …*I had decided to keep my rendezvous with him…*

2 = <u>meeting place</u>, venue, gathering point, place of assignation, trysting-place (*archaic*) …*Their rendezvous would be the hotel at the airport…*

VERB = <u>meet</u>, assemble, get together, come together, collect, gather, rally, muster, converge, join up, be reunited …*The plan was to rendezvous on Sunday afternoon…*

rendition (*Formal*) **1** = <u>performance</u>, arrangement, interpretation, rendering, take (*informal, chiefly U.S.*), reading, version, delivery, presentation, execution, portrayal, depiction …*The musicians broke into a rousing rendition of the song…*

2 = <u>translation</u>, reading, version, construction, explanation, interpretation, transcription …*a rendition of the works of Conrad…*

renegade NOUN = <u>deserter</u>, rebel, betrayer, dissident, outlaw, runaway, traitor, defector, mutineer, turncoat, apostate, backslider, recreant (*archaic*) …*He was a renegade – a traitor…*

ADJECTIVE = <u>traitorous</u>, rebel, dissident, outlaw, runaway, rebellious, unfaithful, disloyal, backsliding, mutinous, apostate, recreant (*archaic*) …*The renegade policeman supplied details of the murder…*

renege = <u>break your word</u>, go back, welsh (*slang*), default, back out, repudiate, break a promise

renew 1 = <u>recommence</u>, continue, extend, repeat, resume, prolong, reopen, recreate, reaffirm, re-establish, rejuvenate, regenerate, restate, begin again, revitalize, bring up to date …*He renewed his attack on government policy…*

2 = <u>reaffirm</u>, resume, breathe new life into, recommence …*They renewed their friendship…*

3 = <u>replace</u>, refresh, replenish, restock …*Cells are constantly renewed…*

4 = <u>restore</u>, repair, transform, overhaul, mend, refurbish, renovate, refit, fix up (*informal, chiefly U.S. & Canad.*), modernize …*the cost of renewing the buildings…*

renounce 1 = <u>disown</u>, reject, abandon, quit, discard, spurn, eschew, leave off, throw off, forsake, retract, repudiate, cast off, abstain from, recant, forswear, abjure, swear off, wash your hands of …*She renounced terrorism…*

2 = <u>disclaim</u>, deny, decline, give up, resign, relinquish, waive, renege, forgo, abdicate, abjure, abnegate …*He renounced his claim to the throne…* OPPOSITE⟩ assert

renovate = <u>restore</u>, repair, refurbish, do up (*informal*), reform, renew, overhaul, revamp, recreate, remodel, rehabilitate, refit, fix up (*informal, chiefly U.S. & Canad.*), modernize, reconstitute, recondition

renown = <u>fame</u>, note, distinction, repute, mark, reputation, honour, glory, celebrity, acclaim, stardom, eminence, lustre, illustriousness

renowned = <u>famous</u>, noted, celebrated, well-known, distinguished, esteemed, acclaimed, notable, eminent, famed, illustrious OPPOSITE unknown

rent¹ VERB 1 = <u>hire</u>, lease ...*He rented a car*...
2 = <u>let</u>, lease ...*She rented rooms to university students*...
NOUN = <u>hire</u>, rental, lease, tariff, fee, payment ...*She worked to pay the rent*...

rent² 1 = <u>tear</u>, split, rip, slash, slit, gash, perforation, hole ...*a small rent in the silk*...
2 = <u>opening</u>, break, hole, crack, breach, flaw, chink ...*welling up from a rent in the ground*...

renunciation 1 = <u>rejection</u>, giving up, denial, abandonment, spurning, abstention, repudiation, forswearing, disavowal, abnegation, eschewal, abjuration ...*a renunciation of terrorism*...
2 = <u>giving up</u>, resignation, surrender, waiver, disclaimer, abdication, relinquishment, abjuration ...*the renunciation of territory*...

repair¹ VERB 1 = <u>mend</u>, fix, recover, restore, heal, renew, patch, make good, renovate, patch up, put back together, restore to working order ...*He has repaired the roof*... OPPOSITE damage
2 = <u>put right</u>, make up for, compensate for, rectify, square, retrieve, redress ...*They needed to repair the damage done by the interview*...
NOUN 1 = <u>mend</u>, restoration, overhaul, adjustment ...*Many of the buildings are in need of repair*...
2 = <u>darn</u>, mend, patch ...*She spotted a couple of obvious repairs in the dress*...
3 = <u>condition</u>, state, form, shape (*informal*), nick (*informal*), fettle ...*The road was in bad repair*...

repair² = <u>go</u>, retire, withdraw, head for, move, remove, leave for, set off for, betake yourself ...*We repaired to the pavilion for lunch*...

reparation = <u>compensation</u>, damages, repair, satisfaction, amends, renewal, redress, indemnity, restitution, atonement, recompense, propitiation, requital

repay 1 = <u>pay back</u>, refund, settle up, return, square, restore, compensate, reimburse, recompense, requite, remunerate ...*It will take 30 years to repay the loan*...
2 = <u>reward</u>, make restitution ...*How can I ever repay such kindness?*...

repeal VERB = <u>abolish</u>, reverse, revoke, annul, recall, withdraw, cancel, set aside, rescind, invalidate, nullify, obviate, abrogate, countermand, declare null and void ...*The government has just repealed that law*...
OPPOSITE pass
NOUN = <u>abolition</u>, withdrawal, cancellation, rescinding, annulment, revocation, nullification, abrogation, rescission, invalidation, rescindment ...*a repeal of the age of consent law*... OPPOSITE passing

repeat VERB 1 = <u>reiterate</u>, restate, recapitulate,

iterate ...*He repeated that he had been misquoted*...
2 = <u>retell</u>, relate, quote, renew, echo, replay, reproduce, rehearse, recite, duplicate, redo, rerun, reshow ...*I repeated the story to a delighted audience*...
NOUN 1 = <u>repetition</u>, echo, duplicate, reiteration, recapitulation ...*a repeat of Wednesday's massive protests*...
2 = <u>rerun</u>, replay, reproduction, reshowing ...*There's nothing except repeats on TV*...

Word Power

repeat – Since the sense of *again* is already contained within the *re-* part of the word *repeat*, it is unnecessary to say that something is *repeated again*.

---

repeatedly = <u>over and over</u>, often, frequently, many times, again and again, time and (time) again, time after time, many a time and oft (*archaic or poetic*)

repel 1 = <u>drive off</u>, fight, refuse, check, decline, reject, oppose, resist, confront, parry, hold off, rebuff, ward off, beat off, repulse, keep at arm's length, put to flight ...*troops ready to repel an attack*... OPPOSITE submit to
2 = <u>disgust</u>, offend, revolt, sicken, nauseate, put you off, make you sick, gross out (*U.S. slang*), turn you off (*informal*), make you shudder, turn your stomach, give you the creeps (*informal*) ...*excitement which frightened and repelled her*... OPPOSITE delight
➤ repulse

repellent 1 = <u>disgusting</u>, offensive, revolting, obscene, sickening, distasteful, horrid, obnoxious, repulsive, noxious, nauseating, odious, hateful, repugnant, off-putting (*Brit. informal*), loathsome, abhorrent, abominable, cringe-making (*Brit. informal*), yucky *or* yukky (*slang*), yucko (*Austral. slang*), discouraging ...*She still found the place repellent*...
2 = <u>proof</u>, resistant, repelling, impermeable ...*a shower repellent jacket*...

repent = <u>regret</u>, lament, rue, sorrow, be sorry about, deplore, be ashamed of, relent, atone for, be contrite about, feel remorse about, reproach yourself for, see the error of your ways, show penitence

repentance = <u>regret</u>, guilt, grief, sorrow, remorse, contrition, compunction, penitence, self-reproach, sackcloth and ashes, sorriness

repercussions = <u>consequences</u>, result, side effects, backlash, sequel

repertoire = <u>range</u>, list, stock, supply, store, collection, repertory, repository

repertory = <u>repertoire</u>, list, range, stock, supply, store, collection, repository

repetition 1 = <u>recurrence</u>, repeating, reappearance, duplication, echo ...*He wants to avoid repetition of the confusion*...
2 = <u>repeating</u>, redundancy, replication, duplication, restatement, iteration, reiteration, tautology, recapitulation, repetitiousness ...*He could have cut*

much of the repetition and saved pages...

repetitive = <u>monotonous</u>, boring, dull, mechanical, tedious, recurrent, unchanging, samey (*informal*), unvaried

replace 1 = <u>take the place of</u>, follow, succeed, oust, take over from, supersede, supplant, stand in lieu of, fill (someone's) shoes *or* boots, step into (someone's) shoes *or* boots ...*the man who deposed and replaced him...*
2 = <u>substitute</u>, change, exchange, switch, swap, commute ...*Replace that liquid with salt, sugar and water...*
3 = <u>put back</u>, restore ...*Replace the caps on the bottles...*

replacement 1 = <u>replacing</u> ...*the replacement of damaged or lost books...*
2 = <u>successor</u>, double, substitute, stand-in, fill-in, proxy, surrogate, understudy ...*a replacement for the injured player...*

replenish 1 = <u>fill</u>, top up, refill, replace, renew, furnish ...*He went to replenish her glass...* OPPOSITE> empty
2 = <u>refill</u>, provide, stock, supply, fill, make up, restore, top up, reload, restock ...*stock to replenish the shelves...*

replete 1 = <u>filled</u>, stuffed, jammed, crammed, abounding, brimming, teeming, glutted, well-stocked, jam-packed, well-provided, chock-full, brimful, full to bursting, charged ...*The harbour was replete with boats...* OPPOSITE> empty
2 = <u>sated</u>, full, gorged, full up, satiated ...*replete after a heavy lunch...* OPPOSITE> hungry

replica 1 = <u>reproduction</u>, model, copy, imitation, facsimile, carbon copy ...*It was a replica, for display only...* OPPOSITE> original
2 = <u>duplicate</u>, copy, carbon copy ...*The child was a replica of her mother...*

replicate = <u>copy</u>, follow, repeat, reproduce, recreate, ape, mimic, duplicate, reduplicate

reply VERB = <u>answer</u>, respond, retort, return, come back, counter, acknowledge, react, echo, rejoin, retaliate, write back, reciprocate, riposte, make answer ...*He replied that this was absolutely impossible...* NOUN = <u>answer</u>, response, reaction, counter, echo, comeback (*informal*), retort, retaliation, acknowledgment, riposte, counterattack, return, rejoinder, reciprocation ...*They went ahead without waiting for a reply...*

report VERB 1 = <u>inform of</u>, communicate, announce, mention, declare, recount, give an account of, bring word on ...*I reported the theft to the police...*
2 *often with* **on** = <u>communicate</u>, publish, record, announce, tell, state, air, detail, describe, note, cover, document, give an account of, relate, broadcast, pass on, proclaim, circulate, relay, recite, narrate, write up ...*Several newspapers reported the decision...*
3 = <u>present yourself</u>, come, appear, arrive, turn up, be present, show up (*informal*), clock in *or* on ...*None of them had reported for duty...*

NOUN 1 = <u>article</u>, story, dispatch, piece, message, communiqué, write-up ...*Press reports vary dramatically...*
2 = <u>account</u>, record, detail, note, statement, relation, version, communication, tale, description, declaration, narrative, summary, recital ...*a full report of what happened here tonight...*
3 *often plural* = <u>news</u>, word, information, announcement, tidings ...*There were no reports of casualties...*
4 = <u>bang</u>, sound, crash, crack, noise, blast, boom, explosion, discharge, detonation, reverberation ...*There was a loud report as the fuel tanks exploded...*
5 = <u>rumour</u>, talk, buzz, gossip, hearsay, scuttlebutt (*U.S. slang*) ...*According to report, she made an impact at the party...*
6 = <u>repute</u>, character, regard, reputation, fame, esteem, eminence ...*He is true, manly, and of good report...*

reporter = <u>journalist</u>, writer, correspondent, newscaster, hack (*derogatory*), announcer, pressman, journo (*slang*), newshound (*informal*), newspaperman *or* newspaperwoman

repose¹ NOUN 1 = <u>rest</u>, relaxation, inactivity, restfulness ...*He had a still, almost blank face, in repose...*
2 = <u>peace</u>, rest, quiet, ease, relaxation, respite, tranquillity, stillness, inactivity, quietness, quietude, restfulness ...*The atmosphere is one of repose...*
3 = <u>composure</u>, dignity, peace of mind, poise, serenity, tranquillity, aplomb, calmness, equanimity, self-possession ...*She has a great deal of natural repose...*
4 = <u>sleep</u>, rest, doze, slumber, kip (*Brit. slang*), dormancy, beauty sleep (*informal*), forty winks (*informal*) ...*So you'll be ready for a night's repose?...*
VERB 1 = <u>rest</u>, lie, be set, be placed, rest upon ...*China soup dishes reposed on silver plates...*
2 = <u>lie</u>, rest, sleep, relax, lie down, recline, take it easy, slumber, rest upon, lie upon, drowse, outspan (*S. African*), take your ease ...*They repose on couches...*

repose² = <u>place</u>, put, store, invest, deposit, lodge, confide, entrust ...*Little trust can be reposed in such promises...*

repository 1 = <u>store</u>, archive, storehouse, depository, magazine, treasury, warehouse, vault, depot, emporium, receptacle ...*The church became a repository for police files...*
2 = <u>storehouse</u> ...*He was the repository of all important information...*

reprehensible = <u>blameworthy</u>, bad, disgraceful, shameful, delinquent, errant, unworthy, objectionable, culpable, ignoble, discreditable, remiss, erring, opprobrious, condemnable, censurable OPPOSITE> praiseworthy

represent VERB 1 = <u>act for</u>, speak for ...*the lawyers representing the victims...*
2 = <u>stand for</u>, substitute for, play the part of, assume the role of, serve as ...*He will represent the president at

ceremonies…

3 = express, equal, correspond to, symbolize, equate with, mean, betoken …*Circle the letter that represents the sound…*

4 = exemplify, embody, symbolize, typify, personify, epitomize …*You represent everything British racing needs…*

5 = depict, show, describe, picture, express, illustrate, outline, portray, sketch, render, designate, reproduce, evoke, denote, delineate …*God is represented as male…*

PHRASES **represent someone as something** *or* **someone** = make out to be, describe as …*They tend to represent him as a guru…* ◆ **represent yourself as something** *or* **someone** = pass yourself off as, pose as, pretend to be …*He represented himself as an upright community member…*

representation **1** = body of representatives, committee, embassy, delegates, delegation …*They have no representation in congress…*

2 = picture, model, image, portrait, illustration, sketch, resemblance, likeness …*a life-like representation of Christ…*

3 = portrayal, depiction, account, relation, description, narrative, narration, delineation …*the representation of women in film and literature…*

4 *often plural* = statement, argument, explanation, exposition, remonstrance, expostulation, account …*We have made representations to ministers…*

representative NOUN **1** = delegate, member, agent, deputy, commissioner, councillor, proxy, depute (*Scot.*), spokesman *or* spokeswoman …*trade union representatives…*

2 = member, congressman *or* congresswoman (*U.S.*), member of parliament, Member of Congress (*U.S.*), M.P. …*the representative for Eastleigh…*

3 = agent, salesman, rep, traveller, commercial traveller …*She was a sales representative…*

ADJECTIVE **1** = chosen, elected, delegated, elective …*a representative government…*

2 = typical, characteristic, archetypal, exemplary, illustrative …*fairly representative groups of adults…* OPPOSITE uncharacteristic

3 = symbolic, evocative, emblematic, typical …*images chosen as representative of English life…*

repress **1** = control, suppress, hold back, bottle up, check, master, hold in, overcome, curb, restrain, inhibit, overpower, keep in check …*People who repress their emotions risk having nightmares…* OPPOSITE release

2 = hold back, suppress, stifle, smother, silence, swallow, muffle …*I couldn't repress a sigh of admiration…*

3 = subdue, abuse, crush, quash, wrong, persecute, quell, subjugate, maltreat, trample underfoot, tyrannize over, rule with an iron hand …*They have been repressed for decades…* OPPOSITE liberate

repression **1** = subjugation, control, constraint, domination, censorship, tyranny, coercion, authoritarianism, despotism …*a society conditioned*

by violence and repression…

2 = suppression, crushing, prohibition, quashing, dissolution …*extremely violent repression of opposition…*

3 = inhibition, control, holding in, restraint, suppression, bottling up …*the repression of intense feelings…*

repressive = oppressive, tough, severe, absolute, harsh, authoritarian, dictatorial, coercive, tyrannical, despotic OPPOSITE democratic

reprieve VERB = grant a stay of execution to, pardon, let off the hook (*slang*), postpone *or* remit the punishment of …*Fourteen people, waiting to be hanged, have been reprieved…*

NOUN = stay of execution, suspension, amnesty, pardon, remission, abeyance, deferment, postponement of punishment …*a reprieve for eight people waiting to be hanged…*

reprimand VERB = blame, censure, rebuke, reproach, check, lecture, carpet (*informal*), scold, tick off (*informal*), castigate, chide, dress down (*informal*), admonish, tear into (*informal*), tell off (*informal*), take to task, read the riot act, tongue-lash, reprove, upbraid, slap on the wrist (*informal*), bawl out (*informal*), rap over the knuckles, haul over the coals (*informal*), chew out (*U.S. & Canad. informal*), tear (someone) off a strip (*Brit. informal*), give a rocket (*Brit. & N.Z. informal*), reprehend, give (someone) a row (*informal*), send someone away with a flea in his or her ear (*informal*) …*He was reprimanded by a teacher…* OPPOSITE praise

NOUN = blame, talking-to (*informal*), row, lecture, wigging (*Brit. slang*), censure, rebuke, reproach, ticking-off (*informal*), dressing-down (*informal*), telling-off (*informal*), admonition, tongue-lashing, reproof, castigation, reprehension, flea in your ear (*informal*) …*He has been given a severe reprimand…* OPPOSITE praise

reprisal = retaliation, revenge, vengeance, retribution, an eye for an eye, counterstroke, requital

reproach VERB = blame, criticize, rebuke, reprimand, abuse, blast, condemn, carpet (*informal*), discredit, censure, have a go at (*informal*), scold, disparage, chide, tear into (*informal*), diss (*slang, chiefly U.S.*), defame, find fault with, take to task, read the riot act to, reprove, upbraid, lambast(e), bawl out (*informal*), chew out (*U.S. & Canad. informal*), tear (someone) off a strip (*Brit. informal*), give a rocket (*Brit. & N.Z. informal*), reprehend …*She is quick to reproach anyone…*

NOUN **1** = rebuke, lecture, wigging (*Brit. slang*), censure, reprimand, scolding, ticking-off (*informal*), dressing down (*informal*), telling-off (*informal*), admonition, tongue-lashing, reproof, castigation, reproval …*Her reproach was automatic…*

2 = censure, blame, abuse, contempt, condemnation, scorn, disapproval, opprobrium, odium, obloquy …*He looked at her with reproach…*

3 = disgrace, shame, slight, stain, discredit, stigma, slur, disrepute, blemish, indignity, ignominy,

Reptiles http://nationalzoo.si.edu/Animals/ReptilesAmphibians/

adder	diamondback,	horned viper	rock snake, rock
agama	diamondback terrapin,	iguana	python, amethystine
agamid	*or* diamondback turtle	indigo snake	python, *or* Schneider
alligator	diamond snake *or*	jew lizard, bearded	python
amphisbaena	diamond python	lizard, *or* bearded	saltwater crocodile *or*
anaconda *or* (*Caribbean*)	dugite *or* dukite	dragon	(*Austral. informal*) saltie
camoodi	elapid	kabaragoya *or* Malayan	sand lizard
anole	fer-de-lance	monitor	sand viper
asp	flying lizard *or* flying	king cobra *or*	sea snake
bandy-bandy	dragon	hamadryad	sidewinder
black snake *or* red-	freshwater crocodile *or*	king snake	skink
bellied black snake	(*Austral. informal*) freshy	Komodo dragon *or*	slowworm *or*
blind snake	frill-necked lizard,	Komodo lizard	blindworm
blue racer	frilled lizard, bicycle	krait	smooth snake
blue tongue	lizard, cycling lizard, *or*	leatherback *or* (*Brit.*)	snake
boa	(*Austral. informal*) frillie	leathery turtle	snapping turtle
boa constrictor	gaboon viper	leguan	soft-shelled turtle
boomslang	galliwasp	lizard	swift
box turtle	garter snake	loggerhead *or*	taipan
brown snake *or* (*Austral.*)	gavial, gharial, *or* garial	loggerhead turtle	terrapin
mallee snake	gecko	mamba	tiger snake
bull snake *or* gopher	giant tortoise	massasauga	tokay
snake	Gila monster	milk snake	tortoise
bushmaster	glass snake	moloch, thorny devil,	tree snake
carpet snake *or* python	goanna, bungarra	thorn lizard, *or*	tuatara *or* (*technical*)
cayman *or* caiman	(*Austral.*), *or* go (*Austral.*	mountain devil	sphenodon
cerastes	*informal*)	monitor	turtle
chameleon	grass snake	mud turtle	viper
chuckwalla	green turtle	perentie *or* perenty	wall lizard
cobra	habu	pit viper	water moccasin,
cobra de capello	harlequin snake	puff adder	moccasin, *or*
constrictor	hawksbill *or* hawksbill	python	cottonmouth
copperhead	turtle	racer	water snake
coral snake	hognose snake *or* puff	rat snake	whip snake
crocodile	adder	rattlesnake *or* (*U.S. &*	worm lizard
death adder *or* deaf	hoop snake	*Canad. informal*) rattler	
adder	horned toad *or* lizard	ringhals	

dishonour …*The shootings were a reproach to all of us*…

reproduce 1 = copy, recreate, replicate, duplicate, match, represent, mirror, echo, parallel, imitate, emulate …*The effect has proved hard to reproduce*…
2 = print, copy, transcribe …*permission to reproduce this article*…
3 (*Biology*) = breed, produce young, procreate, generate, multiply, spawn, propagate, proliferate …*Women are defined by their ability to reproduce*…

reproduction 1 = copy, picture, print, replica, imitation, duplicate, facsimile …*a reproduction of a religious painting*… OPPOSITE> original
2 (*Biology*) = breeding, procreation, propagation, increase, generation, proliferation, multiplication …*what doctors call 'assisted human reproduction'*…

reptile
➤ **reptiles**

Republican ADJECTIVE = right-wing, Conservative …*Senator John McCain, Mr Bush's rival for the Republican nomination*…
NOUN = right-winger, Conservative …*President Clinton is under pressure from Republicans in Congress*…

repudiate 1 = reject, renounce, retract, disown, abandon, desert, reverse, cut off, discard, revoke, forsake, cast off, rescind, disavow, turn your back on, abjure, wash your hands of …*He repudiated any form of nationalism*… OPPOSITE> assert
2 = deny, oppose, disagree with, rebuff, refute, disprove, rebut, disclaim, gainsay (*archaic or literary*) …*He repudiated the charges*…

repugnant 1 = distasteful, offensive, foul, disgusting, revolting, sickening, vile, horrid, repellent, obnoxious, objectionable, nauseating, odious, hateful, loathsome, abhorrent, abominable, yucky *or* yukky (*slang*), yucko (*Austral. slang*) …*His actions were improper and repugnant*… OPPOSITE> pleasant
2 = incompatible, opposed, hostile, adverse, contradictory, inconsistent, averse, antagonistic, inimical, antipathetic …*It is repugnant to the values of our society*… OPPOSITE> compatible

repulse VERB 1 = disgust, offend, revolt, put off, sicken, repel, nauseate, gross out (*U.S. slang*), turn your stomach, fill with loathing …*The thought of it repulsed me*…
2 = drive back, check, defeat, fight off, repel, rebuff, ward off, beat off, throw back …*The army were*

prepared to repulse any attack…

3 = <u>reject</u>, refuse, turn down, snub, disregard, disdain, spurn, rebuff, give the cold shoulder to …*She repulsed him with undisguised venom…*

NOUN 1 = <u>defeat</u>, check …*the repulse of invaders in 1785…*

2 = <u>rejection</u>, refusal, snub, spurning, rebuff, knockback (*slang*), cold shoulder, kick in the teeth (*slang*), the (old) heave-ho (*informal*) …*If he meets with a repulse he will not be cast down…*

> ### *Word Power*
>
> **repulse** – Some people think that the use of *repulse* in sentences such as *he was repulsed by what he saw* is incorrect and that the correct word is *repel*.

repulsive = <u>disgusting</u>, offensive, foul, ugly, forbidding, unpleasant, revolting, obscene, sickening, hideous, vile, distasteful, horrid, repellent, obnoxious, objectionable, disagreeable, nauseating, odious, hateful, loathsome, abhorrent, abominable, yucky *or* yukky (*slang*), yucko (*Austral. slang*) OPPOSITE delightful

reputable = <u>respectable</u>, good, excellent, reliable, worthy, legitimate, upright, honourable, honoured, trustworthy, creditable, estimable, well-thought-of, of good repute OPPOSITE disreputable

reputation = <u>name</u>, standing, credit, character, honour, fame, distinction, esteem, stature, eminence, renown, repute

repute 1 = <u>reputation</u>, standing, fame, celebrity, distinction, esteem, stature, eminence, estimation, renown …*The UN's repute has risen immeasurably…*

2 = <u>name</u>, character, reputation …*a house of ill-repute…*

reputed 1 = <u>supposed</u>, said, seeming, held, believed, thought, considered, accounted, regarded, estimated, alleged, reckoned, rumoured, deemed …*a man reputed to be in his nineties…*

2 = <u>apparent</u>, supposed, putative, ostensible …*They booked the ballroom for a reputed $15,000 last year…*

reputedly = <u>supposedly</u>, apparently, allegedly, seemingly, ostensibly

request VERB 1 = <u>ask for</u>, apply for, appeal for, put in for, demand, desire, pray for, beg for, requisition, beseech …*I requested a copy of the form…*

2 = <u>invite</u>, call for, beg, petition, beseech, entreat, supplicate …*They requested him to leave…*

3 = <u>seek</u>, ask (for), sue for, solicit …*the right to request a divorce…*

NOUN 1 = <u>appeal</u>, call, demand, plea, desire, application, prayer, petition, requisition, solicitation, entreaty, supplication, suit …*They agreed to his request for help…*

2 = <u>asking</u>, plea, begging …*At his request, they attended some of the meetings…*

require 1 = <u>need</u>, crave, depend upon, have need of, want, miss, lack, wish, desire, stand in need of …*A*

baby requires warmth and physical security…

2 = <u>demand</u>, take, involve, call for, entail, necessitate …*This requires thought, effort, and a certain ruthlessness…*

3 = <u>order</u>, demand, direct, command, compel, exact, oblige, instruct, call upon, constrain, insist upon …*The rules require employers to provide safety training…*

4 = <u>ask</u>, enjoin …*She was required to take to the stage…*

> ### *Word Power*
>
> **require** – The use of *require to* as in *I require to see the manager* or *you require to complete a special form* is thought by many people to be incorrect. Useful alternatives are: *I need to see the manager* and *you are required to complete a special form*.

required = <u>obligatory</u>, prescribed, compulsory, mandatory, needed, set, demanded, necessary, called for, essential, recommended, vital, unavoidable, requisite, de rigueur (*French*) OPPOSITE optional

requirement = <u>necessity</u>, demand, specification, stipulation, want, need, must, essential, qualification, precondition, requisite, prerequisite, sine qua non (*Latin*), desideratum

requisite ADJECTIVE = <u>necessary</u>, needed, required, called for, essential, vital, mandatory, indispensable, obligatory, prerequisite, needful …*She filled in the requisite paperwork…*

NOUN = <u>necessity</u>, condition, requirement, precondition, need, must, essential, prerequisite, sine qua non (*Latin*), desideratum …*a major requisite for the work of the analysts…*

requisition VERB 1 = <u>take over</u>, appropriate, occupy, seize, commandeer, take possession of …*The vessel was requisitioned by the British Navy…*

2 = <u>demand</u>, call for, request, apply for, put in for …*the task of requisitioning men and supplies…*

NOUN 1 = <u>demand</u>, request, call, application, summons …*a requisition for a replacement typewriter…*

2 = <u>takeover</u>, occupation, seizure, appropriation, commandeering …*They are against the requisition of common land…*

rescind = <u>annul</u>, recall, reverse, cancel, overturn, set aside, void, repeal, quash, revoke, retract, invalidate, obviate, abrogate, countermand, declare null and void OPPOSITE confirm

rescue VERB 1 = <u>save</u>, get out, save the life of, extricate, free, release, deliver, recover, liberate, set free, save (someone's) bacon (*Brit. informal*) …*Helicopters rescued nearly 20 people…* OPPOSITE desert

2 = <u>salvage</u>, deliver, redeem, come to the rescue of …*He rescued a 14th century barn from demolition…*

NOUN = <u>saving</u>, salvage, deliverance, extrication, release, relief, recovery, liberation, salvation, redemption …*the rescue of the crew of a ship…*

research NOUN = investigation, study, inquiry, analysis, examination, probe, exploration, scrutiny, experimentation, delving, groundwork, fact-finding …*His groundbreaking research will be vital in future developments…*

VERB = investigate, study, examine, experiment, explore, probe, analyse, look into, work over, scrutinize, make inquiries, do tests, consult the archives …*They research the needs of both employers and staff…*

resemblance = similarity, correspondence, conformity, semblance, image, comparison, parallel, counterpart, analogy, affinity, closeness, parity, likeness, kinship, facsimile, sameness, comparability, similitude OPPOSITE dissimilarity

resemble = be like, look like, favour (*informal*), mirror, echo, parallel, be similar to, duplicate, take after, remind you of, bear a resemblance to, put you in mind of

resent = be bitter about, dislike, object to, grudge, begrudge, take exception to, be offended by, be angry about, take offence at, take umbrage at, harbour a grudge against, take as an insult, bear a grudge about, be in a huff about, take amiss to, have hard feelings about OPPOSITE be content with

resentful = bitter, hurt, wounded, angry, offended, put out, jealous, choked, incensed, grudging, exasperated, aggrieved, indignant, irate, miffed (*informal*), embittered, unforgiving, peeved (*informal*), in a huff, piqued, huffy, in high dudgeon, revengeful, huffish, tooshie (*Austral. slang*) OPPOSITE content

resentment = bitterness, indignation, ill feeling, ill will, hurt, anger, rage, fury, irritation, grudge, wrath, malice, animosity, huff, ire, displeasure, pique, rancour, bad blood, umbrage, vexation, chip on your shoulder (*informal*)

reservation 1 *often plural* = doubt, scepticism, scruples, demur, hesitancy …*Their demands were met with some reservations…*
2 = reserve, territory, preserve, homeland, sanctuary, tract, enclave …*a Navaho Indian from a North American reservation…*

reserve VERB 1 = book, prearrange, pre-engage, engage, bespeak …*I'll reserve a table for five…*
2 = put by, secure, retain …*Ask your newsagent to reserve your copy today…*
3 = keep, hold, save, husband, store, retain, preserve, set aside, withhold, hang on to, conserve, stockpile, hoard, lay up, put by, keep back …*Strain and reserve the cooking liquor…*
4 = delay, postpone, withhold, put off, defer, keep back …*The Court has reserved its judgement…*
NOUN 1 = store, fund, savings, stock, capital, supply, reservoir, fall-back, stockpile, hoard, backlog, cache …*The country's reserves of petrol are running very low…*
2 = park, reservation, preserve, sanctuary, tract

…*monkeys at the wildlife reserve…*
3 = shyness, silence, restraint, constraint, reluctance, formality, modesty, reticence, coolness, aloofness, secretiveness, taciturnity …*I hope you'll overcome your reserve…*
4 = reservation, doubt, delay, uncertainty, indecision, hesitancy, vacillation, irresolution, dubiety …*I committed myself without reserve…*
ADJECTIVE = substitute, extra, spare, secondary, alternative, fall-back, auxiliary …*You always have to have reserve players…*

reserved 1 = uncommunicative, cold, cool, retiring, formal, silent, modest, shy, cautious, restrained, secretive, aloof, reticent, prim, demure, taciturn, unresponsive, unapproachable, unsociable, undemonstrative, standoffish, close-mouthed, unforthcoming …*He was unemotional and reserved…*
OPPOSITE uninhibited
2 = set aside, taken, kept, held, booked, retained, engaged, restricted, spoken for …*Three coaches were reserved for us boys…*

reservoir 1 = lake, pond, basin …*Torrents of water gushed into the reservoir…*
2 = repository, store, tank, holder, container, receptacle …*It was on his desk next to the ink reservoir…*
3 = store, stock, source, supply, reserves, fund, pool, accumulation, stockpile …*the body's short-term reservoir of energy…*

reside 1 (*Formal*) = live, lodge, dwell, have your home, remain, stay, settle, abide, hang out (*informal*), sojourn …*She resides with her invalid mother…*
OPPOSITE visit
2 = be present, lie, exist, consist, dwell, abide, rest with, be intrinsic to, inhere, be vested …*Happiness does not reside in money…*

residence 1 = home, house, household, dwelling, place, quarters, flat, lodging, pad (*slang*), abode, habitation, domicile …*There was a stabbing at a residence next door…*
2 = mansion, seat, hall, palace, villa, manor …*She's staying at her country residence…*
3 = stay, tenancy, occupancy, occupation, sojourn …*He returned to his place of residence…*

resident NOUN 1 = inhabitant, citizen, denizen, indweller, local …*Ten per cent of residents live below the poverty line…* OPPOSITE nonresident
2 = tenant, occupant, lodger …*Council house residents purchasing their own homes…*
3 = guest, lodger …*Bar closed on Sunday except to hotel residents…*
ADJECTIVE 1 = inhabiting, living, settled, dwelling …*He had been resident in Brussels since 1967…* OPPOSITE nonresident
2 = local, neighbourhood …*The resident population of the inner city has risen…*

residual = remaining, net, unused, leftover, vestigial, nett, unconsumed

residue = remainder, remains, remnant, leftovers, rest, extra, balance, excess, surplus, dregs, residuum

resign VERB **1** = <u>quit</u>, leave, step down (*informal*), vacate, abdicate, call it a day *or* night, give *or* hand in your notice …*He has resigned after only ten weeks in office*…

2 = <u>give up</u>, abandon, yield, hand over, surrender, turn over, relinquish, renounce, forsake, cede, forgo …*He has resigned his seat in parliament*…

PHRASES **resign yourself to something** = <u>accept</u>, reconcile yourself to, succumb to, submit to, bow to, give in to, yield to, acquiesce to …*I simply resigned myself to staying indoors*…

resignation 1 = <u>leaving</u>, notice, retirement, departure, surrender, abandonment, abdication, renunciation, relinquishment …*He has withdrawn his letter of resignation*…

2 = <u>acceptance</u>, patience, submission, compliance, endurance, fortitude, passivity, acquiescence, forbearing, sufferance, nonresistance …*He sighed with profound resignation*… OPPOSITE resistance

resigned = <u>stoical</u>, patient, subdued, long-suffering, compliant, submissive, acquiescent, unresisting, unprotesting

resilient 1 = <u>flexible</u>, plastic, elastic, supple, bouncy, rubbery, pliable, springy, whippy …*some resilient plastic material*… OPPOSITE rigid

2 = <u>tough</u>, strong, hardy, buoyant, feisty (*informal, chiefly U.S. & Canad.*), bouncy, irrepressible, quick to recover …*I'm a resilient kind of person*… OPPOSITE weak

resist 1 = <u>oppose</u>, fight, battle against, refuse, check, weather, dispute, confront, combat, defy, curb, thwart, stand up to, hinder, contend with, counteract, hold out against, put up a fight (against), countervail …*They resisted our attempts to modernize distribution*… OPPOSITE accept

2 = <u>fight against</u>, fight, struggle against, put up a fight (against) …*He tried to resist arrest*…

3 = <u>refrain from</u>, refuse, avoid, turn down, leave alone, keep from, forgo, abstain from, forbear, prevent yourself from …*Try to resist giving him advice*… OPPOSITE indulge in

4 = <u>withstand</u>, repel, be proof against …*bodies trained to resist the cold*…

resistance 1 = <u>opposition</u>, hostility, aversion …*In remote villages there is a resistance to change*…

2 = <u>fighting</u>, fight, battle, struggle, combat, contention, defiance, obstruction, impediment, intransigence, hindrance, counteraction …*The protesters offered no resistance*…

Resistance = <u>freedom fighters</u>, underground, guerrillas, partisans, irregulars, maquis

resistant 1 = <u>opposed</u>, hostile, dissident, unwilling, defiant, intractable, combative, recalcitrant, antagonistic, intransigent …*Some people are resistant to the idea of exercise*…

2 = <u>impervious</u>, hard, strong, tough, unaffected, unyielding, insusceptible …*The body may be less resistant if it is cold*…

resolute = <u>determined</u>, set, firm, dogged, fixed, constant, bold, relentless, stubborn, stalwart, staunch, persevering, inflexible, purposeful, tenacious, undaunted, strong-willed, steadfast, obstinate, unwavering, immovable, unflinching, unbending, unshakable, unshaken OPPOSITE irresolute

resolution 1 = <u>declaration</u>, motion, verdict, judgment …*The UN had passed two major resolutions*…

2 = <u>decision</u>, resolve, intention, aim, purpose, determination, intent …*It had been her resolution to lose weight*…

3 = <u>determination</u>, energy, purpose, resolve, courage, dedication, fortitude, sincerity, tenacity, perseverance, willpower, boldness, firmness, staying power, stubbornness, constancy, earnestness, obstinacy, steadfastness, doggedness, relentlessness, resoluteness, staunchness …*He implemented policy with resolution and single-mindedness*…

4 = <u>solution</u>, end, settlement, outcome, finding, answer, working out, solving, sorting out, unravelling, upshot …*a peaceful resolution to the crisis*…

resolve VERB **1** = <u>work out</u>, answer, solve, find the solution to, clear up, crack, fathom, suss (out) (*slang*), elucidate …*We must find a way to resolve these problems*…

2 = <u>decide</u>, determine, undertake, make up your mind, agree, design, settle, purpose, intend, fix, conclude …*She resolved to report the matter*…

3 = <u>change</u>, convert, transform, alter, metamorphose, transmute …*The spirals of light resolved into points*…

4 = <u>dispel</u>, explain, remove, clear up, banish …*Many years of doubt were finally resolved*…

NOUN **1** = <u>determination</u>, resolution, courage, willpower, boldness, firmness, earnestness, steadfastness, resoluteness …*He doesn't weaken in his resolve*… OPPOSITE indecision

2 = <u>decision</u>, resolution, undertaking, objective, design, project, purpose, conclusion, intention …*the resolve to enforce a settlement using troops*…

resonant 1 = <u>sonorous</u>, full, rich, ringing, booming, vibrant …*He responded with a resonant laugh*…

2 = <u>echoing</u>, resounding, reverberating, reverberant …*a hall, resonant with the sound of violins*…

resort NOUN **1** = <u>course</u>, hope, chance, alternative, possibility, expedient …*the option of force as a last resort*…

2 = <u>holiday centre</u>, spot, retreat, haunt, refuge, tourist centre, watering place (*Brit.*) …*a genteel resort on the south coast*…

3 = <u>recourse to</u>, reference to …*without resort to illegal methods*…

PHRASES **resort to something** = <u>have recourse to</u>, turn to, fall back on, bring into play, use, exercise, employ, look to, make use of, utilize, avail yourself of …*We were forced to resort to violence*…

resound 1 = <u>echo</u>, resonate, reverberate, fill the air, re-echo …*The soldiers' boots resounded in the street*…

2 = <u>ring</u> …*The whole place resounded with music*…

resounding = <u>echoing</u>, full, sounding, rich, ringing, powerful, booming, vibrant, reverberating, resonant, sonorous

resource NOUN 1 = <u>supply</u>, source, reserve, stockpile, hoard …*a great resource of teaching materials*…
2 = <u>facility</u> …*The directory is a valuable resource*…
3 = <u>means</u>, course, resort, device, expedient …*The only resource left to allay her husband's pain was opium*…
PLURAL NOUN 1 = <u>funds</u>, means, holdings, money, capital, wherewithal, riches, materials, assets, wealth, property …*They do not have the resources to feed themselves properly*…
2 = <u>reserves</u>, supplies, stocks …*We are overpopulated, straining the earth's resources*…

resourceful = <u>ingenious</u>, able, bright, talented, sharp, capable, creative, clever, imaginative, inventive, quick-witted OPPOSITE unimaginative

respect VERB 1 = <u>think highly of</u>, value, regard, honour, recognize, appreciate, admire, esteem, adore, revere, reverence, look up to, defer to, venerate, set store by, have a good *or* high opinion of …*I want him to respect me as a career woman*…
2 = <u>show consideration for</u>, regard, notice, honour, observe, heed, attend to, pay attention to …*Trying to respect her wishes, I said I'd leave*…
3 = <u>abide by</u>, follow, observe, comply with, obey, heed, keep to, adhere to …*It's about time they respected the law*… OPPOSITE disregard
NOUN 1 = <u>regard</u>, honour, recognition, esteem, appreciation, admiration, reverence, estimation, veneration, approbation …*I have tremendous respect for him*… OPPOSITE contempt
2 = <u>consideration</u>, kindness, deference, friendliness, tact, thoughtfulness, solicitude, kindliness, considerateness …*They should be treated with respect*…
3 = <u>particular</u>, way, point, matter, sense, detail, feature, aspect, characteristic, facet …*He's simply wonderful in every respect*…
PLURAL NOUN = <u>greetings</u>, regards, compliments, good wishes, salutations, devoirs …*He visited the hospital to pay his respects to her*…
PHRASES **in respect of** *or* **with respect to** = <u>concerning</u>, in relation to, in connection with, with regard to, with reference to, apropos of …*The system is not working in respect of training*…

respectable 1 = <u>honourable</u>, good, respected, decent, proper, worthy, upright, admirable, honest, dignified, venerable, reputable, decorous, estimable …*He came from a respectable middle-class family*… OPPOSITE disreputable
2 = <u>decent</u>, neat, tidy (*informal*), spruce …*At last I have something respectable to wear*…
3 = <u>reasonable</u>, considerable, substantial, fair, tidy (*informal*), ample, tolerable, presentable, appreciable, fairly good, sizable *or* sizeable, goodly …*respectable and highly attractive rates of return*… OPPOSITE small

respectful = <u>polite</u>, civil, mannerly, humble, gracious, courteous, obedient, submissive, self-effacing, dutiful, courtly, deferential, reverential, solicitous, reverent, regardful, well-mannered

respective = <u>specific</u>, own, several, individual, personal, particular, various, separate, relevant, corresponding

respite 1 = <u>pause</u>, break, rest, relief, halt, interval, relaxation, recess, interruption, lull, cessation, let-up (*informal*), breathing space, breather (*informal*), hiatus, intermission …*I rang home during a brief respite at work*…
2 = <u>reprieve</u>, stay, delay, suspension, moratorium, postponement, adjournment …*Devaluation would only give the economy brief respite*…

resplendent = <u>brilliant</u>, radiant, splendid, glorious, bright, shining, beaming, glittering, dazzling, gleaming, luminous, lustrous, refulgent (*literary*), effulgent, irradiant

respond 1 = <u>answer</u>, return, reply, come back, counter, acknowledge, retort, rejoin …*'Of course,' she responded scornfully*… OPPOSITE remain silent
2 *often with* **to** = <u>reply to</u>, answer …*He was quick to respond to questions*…
3 = <u>react</u>, retaliate, reciprocate, take the bait, rise to the bait, act in response …*He responded to the attacks by exacting suitable retribution*…

response = <u>answer</u>, return, reply, reaction, comeback (*informal*), feedback, retort, acknowledgment, riposte, counterattack, rejoinder, counterblast

responsibility 1 = <u>duty</u>, business, job, role, task, accountability, answerability …*The 600 properties were his responsibility*…
2 = <u>fault</u>, blame, liability, guilt, culpability, burden …*They have admitted responsibility for the accident*…
3 = <u>obligation</u>, duty, liability, charge, care …*This helps employees balance work and family responsibilities*…
4 = <u>authority</u>, power, importance, mana (*N.Z.*) …*a better-paying job with more responsibility*…
5 = <u>job</u>, task, function, role, pigeon (*informal*) …*I'm glad it's not my responsibility to be their guardian*…
6 = <u>level-headedness</u>, stability, maturity, reliability, rationality, dependability, trustworthiness, conscientiousness, soberness, sensibleness …*I think she's shown responsibility*…

responsible 1 = <u>to blame</u>, guilty, at fault, culpable …*He felt responsible for her death*…
2 = <u>in charge</u>, in control, at the helm, in authority, carrying the can (*informal*) …*the minister responsible for the environment*…
3 = <u>accountable</u>, subject, bound, liable, amenable, answerable, duty-bound, chargeable, under obligation …*I'm responsible to my board of directors*… OPPOSITE unaccountable
4 = <u>sensible</u>, sound, adult, stable, mature, reliable, rational, sober, conscientious, dependable, trustworthy, level-headed …*He's a very responsible sort of person*… OPPOSITE unreliable

5 = <u>authoritative</u>, high, important, executive, decision-making ...*demoted to less responsible jobs*...

responsive = <u>sensitive</u>, open, aware, sharp, alive, forthcoming, sympathetic, awake, susceptible, receptive, reactive, perceptive, impressionable, quick to react |OPPOSITE⟩ unresponsive

rest¹ |VERB| **1** = <u>relax</u>, sleep, take it easy, lie down, idle, nap, be calm, doze, sit down, slumber, kip (*Brit. slang*), snooze (*informal*), laze, lie still, be at ease, put your feet up, take a nap, drowse, mellow out (*informal*), have a snooze (*informal*), refresh yourself, outspan (*S. African*), zizz (*Brit. informal*), have forty winks (*informal*), take your ease ...*He has been advised to rest for two weeks*... |OPPOSITE⟩ work
2 = <u>stop</u>, have a break, break off, take a breather (*informal*), stay, halt, cease, discontinue, knock off (*informal*), desist, come to a standstill ...*They rested only once that morning*... |OPPOSITE⟩ keep going
3 = <u>depend</u>, turn, lie, be founded, hang, be based, rely, hinge, reside ...*Such a view rests on incorrect assumptions*...
4 = <u>place</u>, lay, repose, stretch out, stand, sit, lean, prop ...*He rested his arms on the back of the chair*...
5 = <u>be placed</u>, sit, lie, be supported, recline ...*Matt's elbow rested on the table*...
|NOUN| **1** = <u>sleep</u>, snooze (*informal*), lie-down, nap, doze, slumber, kip (*Brit. slang*), siesta, forty winks (*informal*), zizz (*Brit. informal*) ...*Go home and have a rest*...
2 = <u>relaxation</u>, repose, leisure, idleness ...*I feel in need of some rest*... |OPPOSITE⟩ work
3 = <u>pause</u>, break, breather, time off, stop, holiday, halt, interval, vacation, respite, lull, interlude, cessation, breathing space (*informal*), intermission ...*He took a rest from teaching*...
4 = <u>refreshment</u>, release, relief, ease, comfort, cure, remedy, solace, balm, deliverance, mitigation, abatement, alleviation, easement, palliation, assuagement ...*some rest from the intense concentration*...
5 = <u>inactivity</u>, a halt, a stop, a standstill, motionlessness ...*The plane came to rest in a field*...
6 = <u>support</u>, stand, base, holder, shelf, prop, trestle ...*Keep your elbow on the arm rest*...
7 = <u>calm</u>, tranquillity, stillness, somnolence ...*a remote part of the valley for those seeking rest and relaxation*...
|PHRASES| **at rest 1** = <u>motionless</u>, still, stopped, at a standstill, unmoving ...*When you are at rest you breathe with your tummy muscles*... **2** = <u>calm</u>, still, cool, quiet, pacific, peaceful, composed, serene, tranquil, at peace, sedate, placid, undisturbed, restful, untroubled, unperturbed, unruffled, unexcited ...*with your mind at rest*... **3** = <u>asleep</u>, resting, sleeping, napping, dormant, crashed out (*slang*), dozing, slumbering, snoozing (*informal*), fast asleep, sound asleep, out for the count, dead to the world (*informal*) ...*She is at rest; don't disturb her*...

rest² |NOUN| = <u>remainder</u>, remains, excess, remnants, others, balance, surplus, residue, rump, leftovers,

residuum ...*The rest is thrown away*...
|VERB| = <u>continue being</u>, keep being, remain, stay, be left, go on being ...*Of one thing we may rest assured*...

restaurant = <u>café</u>, diner (*chiefly U.S. & Canad.*), bistro, cafeteria, trattoria, tearoom, eatery *or* eaterie

restful = <u>relaxing</u>, quiet, relaxed, comfortable, pacific, calm, calming, peaceful, soothing, sleepy, serene, tranquil, placid, undisturbed, languid, unhurried, tranquillizing |OPPOSITE⟩ busy

restitution 1 (*Law*) = <u>compensation</u>, satisfaction, amends, refund, repayment, redress, remuneration, reparation, indemnity, reimbursement, recompense, indemnification, requital ...*The victims are demanding full restitution*...
2 = <u>return</u>, return, replacement, restoration, reinstatement, re-establishment, reinstallation ...*the restitution of their equal rights as citizens*...

restive = <u>restless</u>, nervous, uneasy, impatient, agitated, unruly, edgy, jittery (*informal*), recalcitrant, on edge, fractious, ill at ease, jumpy, fretful, fidgety, refractory, unquiet, antsy (*informal*) |OPPOSITE⟩ calm

restless 1 = <u>unsettled</u>, worried, troubled, nervous, disturbed, anxious, uneasy, agitated, unruly, edgy, fidgeting, on edge, ill at ease, restive, jumpy, fitful, fretful, fidgety, unquiet, antsy (*informal*) ...*My father seemed very restless and excited*... |OPPOSITE⟩ relaxed
2 = <u>sleepless</u>, disturbed, wakeful, unsleeping, insomniac, tossing and turning ...*He had spent a restless few hours on the plane*...
3 = <u>moving</u>, active, wandering, unsettled, unstable, bustling, turbulent, hurried, roving, transient, nomadic, unsteady, changeable, footloose, irresolute, inconstant, having itchy feet ...*He led a restless life*... |OPPOSITE⟩ settled

restlessness 1 = <u>movement</u>, activity, turmoil, unrest, instability, bustle, turbulence, hurry, transience, inconstancy, hurry-scurry, unsettledness ...*increasing sounds of restlessness*...
2 = <u>restiveness</u>, anxiety, disturbance, nervousness, disquiet, agitation, insomnia, jitters (*informal*), uneasiness, edginess, heebie-jeebies (*slang*), jumpiness, fretfulness, ants in your pants (*slang*), fitfulness, inquietude, worriedness ...*She complained of hyperactivity and restlessness*...

restoration 1 = <u>reinstatement</u>, return, revival, restitution, re-establishment, reinstallation, replacement ...*the restoration of diplomatic relations*... |OPPOSITE⟩ abolition
2 = <u>repair</u>, recovery, reconstruction, renewal, rehabilitation, refurbishing, refreshment, renovation, rejuvenation, revitalization ...*I specialized in the restoration of old houses*... |OPPOSITE⟩ demolition

restore 1 = <u>reinstate</u>, re-establish, reintroduce, reimpose, re-enforce, reconstitute ...*The army has been brought in to restore order*... |OPPOSITE⟩ abolish
2 = <u>revive</u>, build up, strengthen, bring back, refresh, rejuvenate, revitalize, revivify, reanimate ...*We will restore her to health*... |OPPOSITE⟩ make worse

3 = <u>re-establish</u>, replace, reinstate, give back, reinstall, retrocede ...*Civil rights were restored in a matter of days*...
4 = <u>repair</u>, refurbish, renovate, reconstruct, fix (up), recover, renew, rebuild, mend, rehabilitate, touch up, recondition, retouch, set to rights ...*They partly restored a local castle*... OPPOSITE demolish
5 = <u>return</u>, replace, recover, bring back, send back, hand back ...*Their horses and goods were restored*...

restrain **1** = <u>hold back</u>, hold, control, check, contain, prevent, restrict, handicap, confine, curb, hamper, rein, harness, subdue, hinder, constrain, curtail, bridle, debar, keep under control, have on a tight leash, straiten ...*He grabbed my arm, partly to restrain me*... OPPOSITE encourage
2 = <u>control</u>, keep in, limit, govern, suppress, inhibit, repress, muzzle, keep under control ...*She was unable to restrain her desperate anger*...
3 = <u>imprison</u>, hold, arrest, jail, bind, chain, confine, detain, tie up, lock up, fetter, manacle, pinion ...*Police restrained her on July 28*... OPPOSITE release

restrained **1** = <u>controlled</u>, reasonable, moderate, self-controlled, soft, calm, steady, mild, muted, reticent, temperate, undemonstrative ...*He felt he'd been very restrained*... OPPOSITE hot-headed
2 = <u>unobtrusive</u>, discreet, subdued, tasteful, quiet ...*Her black suit was restrained and expensive*... OPPOSITE garish

restraint **1** = <u>limitation</u>, limit, check, ban, boycott, embargo, curb, rein, taboo, bridle, disqualification, interdict ...*Criminals could cross into the country without restraint*... OPPOSITE freedom
2 = <u>self-control</u>, self-discipline, self-restraint, self-possession, pulling your punches ...*They behaved with more restraint than I'd expected*... OPPOSITE self-indulgence
3 = <u>constraint</u>, limitation, inhibition, moderation, hold, control, restriction, prevention, suppression, hindrance, curtailment ...*A Bill of Rights would act as a restraint on judicial power*...
4 = <u>confinement</u>, arrest, detention, imprisonment, captivity, bondage, fetters ...*There was a meeting and he was put under restraint*...

restrict **1** = <u>limit</u>, fix, regulate, specify, curb, ration, keep within bounds *or* limits ...*a move to restrict the number of students on campus at any one time*... OPPOSITE widen
2 = <u>hamper</u>, impede, handicap, restrain, cramp, inhibit, straiten ...*The shoulder straps restrict movement*...

restriction **1** = <u>control</u>, rule, condition, check, regulation, curb, restraint, constraint, confinement, containment, demarcation, stipulation ...*the relaxation of travel restrictions*...
2 = <u>limitation</u>, handicap, inhibition ...*the restrictions of urban living*...

result NOUN **1** = <u>consequence</u>, effect, outcome, end result, issue, event, development, product, reaction, fruit, sequel, upshot ...*This is the result of eating too*

much fatty food... OPPOSITE cause
2 = <u>outcome</u>, conclusion, end, decision, termination ...*They were surprised by the result of their trials*...
VERB = <u>arise</u>, follow, issue, happen, appear, develop, spring, flow, turn out, stem, derive, ensue, emanate, eventuate ...*Many hair problems result from what you eat*...
PHRASES **result in something** = <u>end in</u>, bring about, cause, lead to, wind up, finish with, culminate in, terminate in ...*Fifty per cent of road accidents result in head injuries*...

resume **1** = <u>begin again</u>, continue, go on with, proceed with, carry on, reopen, restart, recommence, reinstitute, take up *or* pick up where you left off ...*They are expected to resume the search early today*... OPPOSITE discontinue
2 = <u>take up again</u>, assume again ...*After the war he resumed his duties at the college*...
3 = <u>occupy again</u>, take back, reoccupy ...*She resumed her seat*...

résumé **1** = <u>summary</u>, synopsis, abstract, précis, review, digest, epitome, rundown, recapitulation ...*I will leave you a résumé of his speech*...
2 (*U.S.*) = <u>curriculum vitae</u>, CV, career history, details, biography ...*I mailed him my résumé this week*...

resumption = <u>continuation</u>, carrying on, reopening, renewal, restart, resurgence, new beginning, re-establishment, fresh outbreak

resurgence = <u>revival</u>, return, renaissance, resurrection, resumption, rebirth, re-emergence, recrudescence, renascence

resurrect **1** = <u>revive</u>, renew, bring back, kick-start (*informal*), reintroduce, breathe new life into ...*Attempts to resurrect the ceasefire have failed*...
2 = <u>restore to life</u>, raise from the dead ...*Only the True Cross was able to resurrect a dead youth*...

resurrection **1** = <u>revival</u>, restoration, renewal, resurgence, return, comeback (*informal*), renaissance, rebirth, reappearance, resuscitation, renascence ...*This is a resurrection of an old story*... OPPOSITE killing off
2 *usually caps* = <u>raising</u> *or* <u>rising from the dead</u>, return from the dead ...*the Resurrection of Jesus Christ*... OPPOSITE demise

resuscitate **1** = <u>give artificial respiration to</u>, save, quicken, bring to life, bring round, give the kiss of life to ...*A paramedic tried to resuscitate her*...
2 = <u>revive</u>, rescue, restore, renew, resurrect, revitalize, breathe new life into, revivify, reanimate ...*his promise to resuscitate the failing economy*...

retain **1** = <u>maintain</u>, keep, reserve, preserve, keep up, uphold, nurture, continue to have, hang *or* hold onto ...*He retains a deep respect for the profession*...
2 = <u>keep</u>, keep possession of, hang *or* hold onto, save ...*They want to retain a strip 33ft wide on the eastern shore*... OPPOSITE let go
3 = <u>remember</u>, recall, bear in mind, keep in mind, memorize, recollect, impress on the memory ...*She needs tips on how to retain facts*... OPPOSITE forget

retainer 1 = <u>fee</u>, advance, deposit ...*I'll need a five-hundred-dollar retainer...*
2 = <u>servant</u>, domestic, attendant, valet, supporter, dependant, henchman, footman, lackey, vassal, flunky ...*the ever-faithful family retainer...*

retaliate = <u>pay someone back</u>, hit back, strike back, reciprocate, take revenge, get back at someone, get even with (*informal*), even the score, get your own back (*informal*), wreak vengeance, exact retribution, give as good as you get (*informal*), take an eye for an eye, make reprisal, give (someone) a taste of his *or* her own medicine, give tit for tat, return like for like [OPPOSITE] turn the other cheek

retaliation = <u>revenge</u>, repayment, vengeance, reprisal, retribution, tit for tat, an eye for an eye, reciprocation, counterstroke, requital, counterblow, a taste of your own medicine

retard = <u>slow down</u>, check, arrest, delay, handicap, stall, brake, detain, defer, clog, hinder, obstruct, impede, set back, encumber, decelerate, hold back *or* up [OPPOSITE] speed up

retch = <u>gag</u>, be sick, vomit, regurgitate, chuck (*Austral. & N.Z. informal*), throw up (*informal*), spew, heave, puke (*slang*), disgorge, barf (*U.S. slang*), chunder (*slang, chiefly Austral.*), upchuck (*U.S. slang*), do a technicolour yawn (*slang*), toss your cookies (*U.S. slang*)

reticence = <u>silence</u>, reserve, restraint, quietness, secretiveness, taciturnity, uncommunicativeness, unforthcomingness

reticent = <u>uncommunicative</u>, reserved, secretive, unforthcoming, quiet, silent, restrained, taciturn, tight-lipped, unspeaking, close-lipped, mum [OPPOSITE] communicative
➤ **reluctant**

retinue = <u>attendants</u>, entourage, escort, servants, following, train, suite, aides, followers, cortege

retire 1 = <u>stop working</u>, give up work, be pensioned off, (be) put out to grass (*informal*) ...*In 1974 he retired...*
2 = <u>withdraw</u>, leave, remove, exit, go away, depart, absent yourself, betake yourself ...*He retired from the room with his colleagues...*
3 = <u>go to bed</u>, turn in (*informal*), go to sleep, hit the sack (*slang*), go to your room, kip down (*Brit. slang*), hit the hay (*slang*) ...*She retires early most nights...*
4 = <u>retreat</u>, withdraw, pull out, give way, recede, pull back, back off, decamp, give ground ...*He was wounded, but did not retire from the field...*

retirement = <u>withdrawal</u>, retreat, privacy, loneliness, obscurity, solitude, seclusion

retiring = <u>shy</u>, reserved, quiet, modest, shrinking, humble, timid, coy, meek, reclusive, reticent, unassuming, self-effacing, demure, diffident, bashful, timorous, unassertive [OPPOSITE] outgoing

retort [VERB] = <u>reply</u>, return, answer, respond, counter, rejoin, retaliate, come back with, riposte, answer back ...*'Who do you think you're talking to?' she retorted...*
[NOUN] = <u>reply</u>, answer, response (*informal*), comeback, riposte, rejoinder ...*His sharp retort made an impact...*

retract 1 = <u>withdraw</u>, take back, revoke, disown, deny, recall, reverse, cancel, repeal, renounce, go back on, repudiate, rescind, renege on, back out of, disavow, recant, disclaim, abjure, eat your words, unsay ...*He hurriedly sought to retract the statement...*
2 = <u>draw in</u>, pull in, pull back, reel in, sheathe ...*A cat in ecstasy will extend and retract his claws...*

retreat [VERB] = <u>withdraw</u>, retire, back off, draw back, leave, go back, shrink, depart, fall back, recede, pull back, back away, recoil, give ground, turn tail ...*They were forced to retreat...* [OPPOSITE] advance
[NOUN] **1** = <u>flight</u>, retirement, departure, withdrawal, evacuation ...*The army was in full retreat...* [OPPOSITE] advance
2 = <u>refuge</u>, haven, resort, retirement, shelter, haunt, asylum, privacy, den, sanctuary, hideaway, seclusion ...*He spent yesterday in his country retreat...*

retrenchment = <u>cutback</u>, cuts, economy, reduction, pruning, contraction, cost-cutting, rundown, curtailment, tightening your belt [OPPOSITE] expansion

retribution = <u>punishment</u>, retaliation, reprisal, redress, justice, reward, reckoning, compensation, satisfaction, revenge, repayment, vengeance, Nemesis, recompense, an eye for an eye, requital

retrieve 1 = <u>get back</u>, regain, repossess, fetch back, recall, recover, restore, recapture ...*He retrieved his jacket from the seat...*
2 = <u>redeem</u>, save, rescue, repair, salvage, win back, recoup ...*He could retrieve the situation...*

retro = <u>old-time</u>, old, former, past, period, antique, old-fashioned, nostalgia, old-world, bygone, of yesteryear

retrograde = <u>deteriorating</u>, backward, regressive, retrogressive, declining, negative, reverse, retreating, worsening, downward, waning, relapsing, inverse, degenerative

retrospect = <u>hindsight</u>, review, afterthought, re-examination, survey, recollection, remembrance, reminiscence [OPPOSITE] foresight

return [VERB] **1** = <u>come back</u>, go back, repair, retreat, turn back, revert, reappear ...*More than 350,000 people have returned home...* [OPPOSITE] depart
2 = <u>put back</u>, replace, restore, render, transmit, convey, send back, reinstate, take back, give back, carry back, retrocede ...*The car was not returned on time...* [OPPOSITE] keep
3 = <u>give back</u>, repay, refund, pay back, remit, reimburse, recompense ...*They promised to return the money...* [OPPOSITE] keep
4 = <u>reciprocate</u>, requite, feel in return, respond to ...*Her feelings are not returned...*
5 = <u>recur</u>, come back, repeat, persist, revert, happen again, reappear, come and go, come again ...*The pain returned in waves...*
6 = <u>announce</u>, report, come to, deliver, arrive at, bring in, submit, render ...*They returned a verdict of not guilty...*
7 = <u>earn</u>, make, net, yield, bring in, repay ...*The*

business returned a handsome profit… OPPOSITE> lose
8 = <u>elect</u>, choose, pick, vote in …*He has been returned as leader of the party…*
NOUN **1** = <u>reappearance</u> …*his sudden return to London…* OPPOSITE> departure
2 = <u>restoration</u>, replacement, reinstatement, re-establishment …*Their demand was for the return of acres of forest…* OPPOSITE> removal
3 = <u>recurrence</u>, repetition, reappearance, reversion, persistence …*It was like the return of his youth…*
4 = <u>profit</u>, interest, benefit, gain, income, advantage, revenue, yield, proceeds, takings, boot (*dialect*) …*They have seen no return on their investment…*
5 = <u>repayment</u>, reward, compensation, reparation, reimbursement, recompense, reciprocation, requital, retaliation, meed (*archaic*) …*What do I get in return for taking part in your experiment?…*
6 = <u>statement</u>, report, form, list, account, summary …*a new analysis of the census returns…*

revamp = <u>renovate</u>, restore, overhaul, refurbish, rehabilitate, do up (*informal*), patch up, refit, repair, fix up (*informal, chiefly U.S. & Canad.*), recondition, give a face-lift to

reveal 1 = <u>make known</u>, disclose, give away, make public, tell, announce, publish, broadcast, leak, communicate, proclaim, betray, give out, let out, impart, divulge, let slip, let on, take the wraps off (*informal*), blow wide open (*slang*), get off your chest (*informal*) …*She has refused to reveal her daughter's whereabouts…* OPPOSITE> keep secret
2 = <u>show</u>, display, bare, exhibit, unveil, uncover, manifest, unearth, unmask, lay bare, bring to light, expose to view …*A grey carpet was removed to reveal the pine floor…* OPPOSITE> hide

revel VERB = <u>celebrate</u>, rave (*Brit. slang*), carouse, live it up (*informal*), push the boat out (*Brit. informal*), whoop it up (*informal*), make merry, paint the town red (*informal*), go on a spree, roister …*I'm afraid I revelled the night away…*
NOUN *often plural* = <u>merrymaking</u>, party, celebration, rave (*Brit. slang*), gala, spree, festivity, beano (*Brit. slang*), debauch, saturnalia, bacchanal, rave-up (*Brit. slang*), jollification, carousal, hooley *or* hoolie (*chiefly Irish & N.Z.*), carouse …*The revels often last until dawn…*
PHRASES **revel in something** = <u>enjoy</u>, relish, indulge in, delight in, savour, thrive on, bask in, wallow in, lap up, take pleasure in, drool over, luxuriate in, crow about, rejoice over, gloat about, rub your hands …*She revelled in her freedom…*

revelation 1 = <u>disclosure</u>, discovery, news, broadcast, exposé, announcement, publication, exposure, leak, uncovering, confession, divulgence …*revelations about his private life…*
2 = <u>exhibition</u>, telling, communication, broadcasting, discovery, publication, exposure, leaking, unveiling, uncovering, manifestation, unearthing, giveaway, proclamation, exposition …*the revelation of his private life…*

reveller = <u>merrymaker</u>, carouser, pleasure-seeker, partygoer, roisterer, celebrator

revelry = <u>merrymaking</u>, partying, fun, celebration, rave (*Brit. slang*), spree, festivity, beano (*Brit. slang*), debauch, debauchery, carouse, jollity, saturnalia, roistering, rave-up (*Brit. slang*), jollification, carousal, hooley *or* hoolie (*chiefly Irish & N.Z.*)

revenge NOUN = <u>retaliation</u>, satisfaction, vengeance, reprisal, retribution, vindictiveness, an eye for an eye, requital …*in revenge for the murder of her lover…*
VERB = <u>avenge</u>, repay, vindicate, pay (someone) back, take revenge for, requite, even the score for, get your own back for (*informal*), make reprisal for, take an eye for an eye for …*The relatives wanted to revenge the dead man's murder…*

revenue = <u>income</u>, interest, returns, profits, gain, rewards, yield, proceeds, receipts, takings OPPOSITE> expenditure

reverberate = <u>echo</u>, ring, resound, vibrate, re-echo

reverberation = <u>echo</u>, ringing, resonance, resounding, vibration, re-echoing

revere = <u>be in awe of</u>, respect, honour, worship, adore, reverence, exalt, look up to, defer to, venerate, have a high opinion of, put on a pedestal, think highly of OPPOSITE> despise

reverence NOUN = <u>respect</u>, honour, worship, admiration, awe, devotion, homage, deference, adoration, veneration, high esteem …*in mutual support and reverence for the dead…* OPPOSITE> contempt
VERB = <u>revere</u>, respect, honour, admire, worship, adore, pay homage to, venerate, be in awe of, hold in awe …*Some men even seem to reverence them…*

reverent = <u>respectful</u>, awed, solemn, deferential, loving, humble, adoring, devout, pious, meek, submissive, reverential OPPOSITE> disrespectful

reverie = <u>daydream</u>, musing, preoccupation, trance, abstraction, daydreaming, inattention, absent-mindedness, brown study, woolgathering, castles in the air *or* Spain

reverse VERB **1** (*Law*) = <u>change</u>, alter, cancel, overturn, overthrow, set aside, undo, repeal, quash, revoke, overrule, retract, negate, rescind, invalidate, annul, obviate, countermand, declare null and void, overset, upset …*They have made it clear they will not reverse the decision…* OPPOSITE> implement
2 = <u>turn round</u>, turn over, turn upside down, upend …*The curve of the spine may be reversed under such circumstances…*
3 = <u>transpose</u>, change, move, exchange, transfer, switch, shift, alter, swap, relocate, rearrange, invert, interchange, reorder …*He reversed the position of the two stamps…*
4 = <u>go backwards</u>, retreat, back up, turn back, backtrack, move backwards, back …*He reversed and drove away…* OPPOSITE> go forward
NOUN **1** = <u>opposite</u>, contrary, converse, antithesis, inverse, contradiction …*There is absolutely no evidence. Quite the reverse…*

2 = <u>misfortune</u>, check, defeat, blow, failure, disappointment, setback, hardship, reversal, adversity, mishap, affliction, repulse, trial, misadventure, vicissitude ...*They have suffered a major reverse...*
3 = <u>back</u>, rear, other side, wrong side, underside, flip side, verso ...*on the reverse of the coin...* OPPOSITE front
ADJECTIVE **1** = <u>opposite</u>, contrary, converse, inverse ...*The wrong attitude will have the reverse effect...*
2 = <u>backward</u>, inverted, back to front ...*We will take them in reverse order...*

revert 1 = <u>go back</u>, return, come back, resume, lapse, recur, relapse, regress, backslide, take up where you left off ...*He reverted to smoking heavily...*
2 = <u>return</u> ...*The property reverts to the freeholder...*

> ### Word Power
>
> **revert** – Since the concept *back* is already contained in the *re-* part of the word *revert*, it is unnecessary to say that someone *reverts back* to a particular type of behaviour.

review NOUN **1** = <u>re-examination</u>, revision, rethink, retrospect, another look, reassessment, fresh look, second look, reconsideration, re-evaluation, recapitulation ...*She has announced a review of adoption laws...*
2 = <u>survey</u>, report, study, analysis, examination, scrutiny, perusal ...*a review on the training and education of over-16s...*
3 = <u>critique</u>, commentary, evaluation, critical assessment, study, notice, criticism, judgment ...*We've never had a good review in the press...*
4 = <u>inspection</u>, display, parade, procession, march past ...*an early morning review of the troops...*
5 = <u>magazine</u>, journal, periodical, zine (*informal*) ...*He was recruited to write for the Edinburgh Review...*
VERB **1** = <u>reconsider</u>, revise, rethink, run over, reassess, re-examine, re-evaluate, think over, take another look at, recapitulate, look at again, go over again ...*The next day we reviewed the previous day's work...*
2 = <u>assess</u>, write a critique of, study, judge, discuss, weigh, evaluate, criticize, read through, give your opinion of ...*I see that no papers have reviewed my book...*
3 = <u>inspect</u>, check, survey, examine, vet, check out (*informal*), scrutinize, give (something *or* someone) the once-over (*informal*) ...*He reviewed the troops...*
4 = <u>look back on</u>, remember, recall, reflect on, summon up, recollect, call to mind ...*Review all the information you need...*

reviewer = <u>critic</u>, judge, commentator, connoisseur, arbiter, essayist

revile = <u>malign</u>, abuse, knock (*informal*), rubbish (*informal*), run down, smear, libel, scorn, slag (off) (*slang*), reproach, denigrate, vilify, slander, defame, bad-mouth (*slang, chiefly U.S. & Canad.*), traduce, calumniate, vituperate, asperse

revise 1 = <u>change</u>, review, modify, reconsider, re-examine ...*He soon came to revise his opinion...*
2 = <u>edit</u>, correct, alter, update, amend, rewrite, revamp, rework, redo, emend ...*Three editors handled revising the articles...*
3 = <u>study</u>, go over, run through, cram (*informal*), memorize, reread, swot up on (*Brit. informal*) ...*I have to revise maths tonight...*

revision 1 = <u>emendation</u>, editing, updating, correction, rewriting ...*The phase of writing that is important is revision...*
2 = <u>change</u>, review, amendment, modification, alteration, re-examination ...*The government will make a number of revisions...*
3 = <u>studying</u>, cramming (*informal*), memorizing, swotting (*Brit. informal*), rereading, homework ...*They prefer to do their revision at home...*

revitalize = <u>reanimate</u>, restore, renew, refresh, resurrect, rejuvenate, breathe new life into, bring back to life, revivify

revival 1 = <u>resurgence</u> ...*There is no chance of a revival in car sales...* OPPOSITE decline
2 = <u>reawakening</u>, restoration, renaissance, renewal, awakening, resurrection, refreshment, quickening, rebirth, resuscitation, revitalization, recrudescence, reanimation, renascence, revivification ...*a revival of nationalism and the rudiments of democracy...*

revive 1 = <u>revitalize</u>, restore, rally, renew, renovate, rekindle, kick-start (*informal*), breathe new life into, invigorate, reanimate ...*an attempt to revive the economy...*
2 = <u>bring round</u>, awaken, animate, rouse, resuscitate, bring back to life ...*They tried in vain to revive him...*
3 = <u>come round</u>, recover, quicken, spring up again ...*After three days in a coma, he revived...*
4 = <u>refresh</u>, restore, comfort, cheer, renew, resurrect, rejuvenate, revivify ...*Superb food and drink revived our little band...* OPPOSITE exhaust

revoke = <u>cancel</u>, recall, withdraw, reverse, abolish, set aside, repeal, renounce, quash, take back, call back, retract, repudiate, negate, renege, rescind, invalidate, annul, nullify, recant, obviate, disclaim, abrogate, countermand, declare null and void OPPOSITE endorse

revolt NOUN = <u>uprising</u>, rising, revolution, rebellion, mutiny, defection, insurrection, insurgency, putsch, sedition ...*a revolt by ordinary people against the leaders...*
VERB **1** = <u>rebel</u>, rise up, resist, defect, mutiny, take to the streets, take up arms (against) ...*The townspeople revolted...*
2 = <u>disgust</u>, offend, turn off (*informal*), sicken, repel, repulse, nauseate, gross out (*U.S. slang*), shock, turn your stomach, make your flesh creep, give you the creeps (*informal*) ...*He entirely revolts me...*

revolting = <u>disgusting</u>, shocking, offensive, appalling, nasty, foul, horrible, obscene, sickening, distasteful, horrid, repellent, obnoxious, repulsive, nauseating, repugnant, loathsome, abhorrent, abominable, nauseous, cringe-making (*Brit. informal*), noisome, yucky *or* yukky (*slang*), yucko (*Austral. slang*) OPPOSITE delightful

revolution 1 = revolt, rising, coup, rebellion, uprising, mutiny, insurgency, coup d'état, putsch ...*after the French Revolution*...
2 = transformation, shift, innovation, upheaval, reformation, metamorphosis, sea change, drastic *or* radical change ...*a revolution in ship design and propulsion*...
3 = rotation, turn, cycle, circle, wheel, spin, lap, circuit, orbit, whirl, gyration, round ...*The gear drives a wheel 1/10th revolution per cycle*...

revolutionary ADJECTIVE 1 = rebel, radical, extremist, subversive, insurgent, seditious, mutinous, insurrectionary ...*Do you know anything about the revolutionary movement?*... OPPOSITE reactionary
2 = innovative, new, different, novel, radical, fundamental, progressive, experimental, drastic, avant-garde, ground-breaking, thoroughgoing ...*His trumpet-playing was quite revolutionary*... OPPOSITE conventional
NOUN = rebel, insurgent, mutineer, insurrectionary, revolutionist, insurrectionist ...*The revolutionaries laid down their arms*... OPPOSITE reactionary

revolutionize = transform, reform, revamp, modernize, metamorphose, break with the past

revolve 1 = go round, circle, orbit, gyrate ...*The satellite revolves around the earth*...
2 = rotate, turn, wheel, spin, twist, whirl ...*The entire circle revolved slowly*...
3 = consider, study, reflect, think about, deliberate, ponder, turn over (in your mind), meditate, mull over, think over, ruminate ...*He revolved the new notion dizzily in his mind*...

revulsion = disgust, loathing, distaste, aversion, recoil, abomination, repulsion, abhorrence, repugnance, odium, detestation OPPOSITE liking

reward NOUN 1 = prize ...*He earned his reward for contributions to the struggle*...
2 = punishment, desert, retribution, comeuppance (*slang*), just deserts, requital ...*He'll get his reward before long*...
3 = payment, return, benefit, profit, gain, prize, wages, honour, compensation, bonus, premium, merit, repayment, bounty, remuneration, recompense, meed (*archaic*), requital ...*They last night offered a £10,000 reward*... OPPOSITE penalty
VERB = compensate, pay, honour, repay, recompense, requite, remunerate, make it worth your while ...*Their generosity will be rewarded*... OPPOSITE penalize

rewarding = satisfying, fulfilling, gratifying, edifying, economic, pleasing, valuable, profitable, productive, worthwhile, beneficial, enriching, fruitful, advantageous, gainful, remunerative OPPOSITE unrewarding

rewrite = revise, correct, edit, recast, touch up, redraft, emend

rhetoric 1 = hyperbole, rant, hot air (*informal*),

pomposity, bombast, wordiness, verbosity, fustian, grandiloquence, magniloquence ...*He has continued his warlike rhetoric*...
2 = oratory, eloquence, public speaking, speech-making, elocution, declamation, speechifying, grandiloquence, spieling (*informal*) ...*the noble institutions, such as political rhetoric*...

rhetorical 1 = oratorical, verbal, linguistic, stylistic ...*a rhetorical device used to emphasize moments in the text*...
2 = high-flown, flamboyant, windy, flashy, pompous, pretentious, flowery, showy, florid, bombastic, hyperbolic, verbose, oratorical, grandiloquent, high-sounding, declamatory, arty-farty (*informal*), silver-tongued, magniloquent ...*He disgorges a stream of rhetorical flourishes*...

rhyme NOUN = poem, song, verse, ode ...*He has taught her a little rhyme*...
PHRASES **rhyme or reason** (usually in negative construction) = sense, meaning, plan, planning, system, method, pattern, logic ...*He picked people without rhyme or reason*...

rhythm 1 = beat, swing, accent, pulse, tempo, cadence, lilt ...*His music fused the rhythms of jazz and classical music*...
2 = metre, time, measure (*Prosody*) ...*the rhythm and rhyme inherent in nursery rhymes*...
3 = pattern, movement, flow, periodicity ...*This is the rhythm of the universe*...

rhythmic *or* **rhythmical** = cadenced, throbbing, periodic, pulsating, flowing, musical, harmonious, lilting, melodious, metrical

rich 1 = wealthy, affluent, well-off, opulent, propertied, rolling (*slang*), loaded (*slang*), flush (*informal*), prosperous, well-heeled (*informal*), well-to-do, moneyed, filthy rich, stinking rich (*informal*), made of money (*informal*) ...*You're going to be a very rich man*... OPPOSITE poor
2 = well-stocked, full, productive, ample, abundant, plentiful, copious, well-provided, well-supplied, plenteous ...*a rich supply of fresh, clean water*... OPPOSITE scarce
3 = full-bodied, heavy, sweet, delicious, fatty, tasty, creamy, spicy, juicy, luscious, savoury, succulent, flavoursome, highly-flavoured ...*the hearty rich foods of Gascony*... OPPOSITE bland
4 = fruitful, productive, fertile, prolific, fecund ...*Farmers grow rice in the rich soil*... OPPOSITE barren
5 = abounding, full, luxurious, lush, abundant, exuberant, well-endowed ...*The bees buzzed around a garden rich with flowers*...
6 = resonant, full, deep, mellow, mellifluous, dulcet ...*He spoke in that deep rich voice which made them all swoon*... OPPOSITE high-pitched
7 = vivid, strong, deep, warm, bright, intense, vibrant, gay ...*an attractive, glossy rich red colour*... OPPOSITE dull
8 = costly, fine, expensive, valuable, superb, elegant, precious, elaborate, splendid, gorgeous, lavish, exquisite, sumptuous, priceless, palatial, beyond price

…*This is a Baroque church with a rich interior*…
OPPOSITE⟩ cheap
9 = <u>funny</u>, amusing, ridiculous, hilarious, ludicrous, humorous, laughable, comical, risible, side-splitting …*That's rich, coming from him*…

riches 1 = <u>wealth</u>, money, property, gold, assets, plenty, fortune, substance, treasure, abundance, richness, affluence, opulence …*Some people want fame or riches*… OPPOSITE⟩ poverty
2 = <u>resources</u>, treasures …*Russia's vast natural riches*…

richly 1 = <u>elaborately</u>, lavishly, elegantly, splendidly, exquisitely, expensively, luxuriously, gorgeously, sumptuously, opulently, palatially …*The rooms are richly decorated*…
2 = <u>fully</u>, well, thoroughly, amply, appropriately, properly, suitably, in full measure …*He achieved the success he so richly deserved*…

rickety = <u>shaky</u>, broken, weak, broken-down, frail, insecure, feeble, precarious, derelict, flimsy, wobbly, imperfect, tottering, ramshackle, dilapidated, decrepit, unsteady, unsound, infirm, jerry-built

rid VERB = <u>free</u>, clear, deliver, relieve, purge, lighten, unburden, disabuse, make free, disembarrass, disencumber, disburden …*an attempt to rid the country of corruption*…
PHRASES **get rid of something** *or* **someone** = <u>dispose of</u>, throw away *or* out, dispense with, dump, remove, eliminate, expel, unload, shake off, eject, do away with, jettison, weed out, see the back of, wipe from the face of the earth, give the bum's rush to (*slang*) …*The owner needs to get rid of the car*…

riddle¹ 1 = <u>puzzle</u>, problem, conundrum, teaser, poser, rebus, brain-teaser (*informal*), Chinese puzzle …*Tell me a riddle*…
2 = <u>enigma</u>, question, secret, mystery, puzzle, conundrum, teaser, problem …*a riddle of modern architecture*…

riddle² 1 = <u>pierce</u>, pepper, puncture, perforate, honeycomb …*Attackers riddled two homes with gunfire*…
2 = <u>pervade</u>, fill, spread through …*She was found to be riddled with cancer*…

riddled = <u>filled</u>, marred, spoilt, corrupted, impaired, pervaded, infested, permeated …*The report was riddled with errors*…

ride VERB **1** = <u>control</u>, handle, sit on, manage …*I saw a girl riding a horse*…
2 = <u>travel</u>, be carried, be supported, be borne, go, move, sit, progress, journey …*I was riding on the back of a friend's bicycle*…
NOUN = <u>journey</u>, drive, trip, lift, spin (*informal*), outing, whirl (*informal*), jaunt …*Would you like to go for a ride?*…

ridicule VERB = <u>laugh at</u>, mock, make fun of, make a fool of, humiliate, taunt, sneer at, parody, caricature, jeer at, scoff at, deride, send up (*Brit. informal*), lampoon, poke fun at, chaff, take the mickey out of (*informal*), satirize, pooh-pooh, laugh out of court,

make a monkey out of, make someone a laughing stock, laugh to scorn …*I admire her for allowing them to ridicule her*…
NOUN = <u>mockery</u>, scorn, derision, laughter, irony, rib, taunting, sneer, satire, jeer, banter, sarcasm, chaff, gibe, raillery …*He was subjected to public ridicule*…

ridiculous = <u>laughable</u>, stupid, incredible, silly, outrageous, absurd, foolish, unbelievable, hilarious, ludicrous, preposterous, farcical, comical, zany, nonsensical, derisory, inane, risible, contemptible, cockamamie (*slang, chiefly U.S.*) OPPOSITE⟩ sensible

rife 1 = <u>widespread</u>, abundant, plentiful, rampant, general, common, current, raging, universal, frequent, prevailing, epidemic, prevalent, ubiquitous …*Speculation is rife that he'll be sacked*…
2 *usually with* **with** = <u>abounding</u>, seething, teeming …*Hollywood soon became rife with rumours*…

rifle 1 = <u>rummage</u>, go, rake, fossick (*Austral. & N.Z.*) …*The men rifled through his clothing*…
2 = <u>ransack</u>, rob, burgle, loot, strip, sack, gut, plunder, pillage, despoil …*The child rifled the till while her mother distracted the postmistress*…

rift 1 = <u>breach</u>, difference, division, split, separation, falling out (*informal*), disagreement, quarrel, alienation, schism, estrangement …*They hope to heal the rift with their father*…
2 = <u>split</u>, opening, space, crack, gap, break, fault, breach, fracture, flaw, cleavage, cleft, chink, crevice, fissure, cranny …*In the open bog are many rifts and potholes*…

rig VERB **1** = <u>fix</u>, doctor, engineer (*informal*), arrange, fake, manipulate, juggle, tamper with, fiddle with (*informal*), falsify, trump up, gerrymander …*She accused her opponents of rigging the vote*…
2 (*Nautical*) = <u>equip</u>, fit out, kit out, outfit, supply, turn out, provision, furnish, accoutre …*He had rigged the dinghy for a sail*…
PHRASES **rig something up** = <u>set up</u>, build, construct, put up, arrange, assemble, put together, erect, improvise, fix up, throw together, cobble together …*I rigged up a shelter with a tarpaulin*…

right ADJECTIVE **1** = <u>correct</u>, true, genuine, accurate, exact, precise, valid, authentic, satisfactory, spot-on (*Brit. informal*), factual, on the money (*U.S.*), unerring, admissible, dinkum (*Austral. & N.Z. informal*), veracious, sound …*That's absolutely right!*… OPPOSITE⟩ wrong
2 = <u>proper</u>, done, becoming, seemly, fitting, fit, appropriate, suitable, desirable, comme il faut (*French*) …*Make sure you approach it in the right way*… OPPOSITE⟩ inappropriate
3 = <u>favourable</u>, due, ideal, convenient, rightful, advantageous, opportune, propitious …*at the right time in the right place*… OPPOSITE⟩ disadvantageous
4 = <u>just</u>, good, fair, moral, proper, ethical, upright, honourable, honest, equitable, righteous, virtuous, lawful …*It's not right, leaving her like this*… OPPOSITE⟩ unfair
5 = <u>sane</u>, sound, balanced, normal, reasonable,

rational, all there (*informal*), lucid, unimpaired, compos mentis (*Latin*) ...*I think he's not right in the head actually*...

6 = <u>healthy</u>, well, fine, fit, in good health, in the pink, up to par ...*He just didn't look right*... OPPOSITE unwell

7 = <u>complete</u>, real, pure, absolute, utter, outright, thorough, out-and-out, thoroughgoing ...*He gave them a right telling off*...

ADVERB **1** = <u>correctly</u>, truly, precisely, exactly, genuinely, accurately, factually, aright ...*He guessed right about some things*... OPPOSITE wrongly

2 = <u>suitably</u>, fittingly, appropriately, properly, aptly, satisfactorily, befittingly ...*They made sure I did everything right*... OPPOSITE improperly

3 = <u>exactly</u>, squarely, precisely, bang, slap-bang (*informal*) ...*It caught me right in the middle of the forehead*...

4 = <u>directly</u>, straight, precisely, exactly, unswervingly, without deviation, by the shortest route, in a beeline ...*It was taken right there on a conveyor belt*...

5 = <u>all the way</u>, completely, totally, perfectly, entirely, absolutely, altogether, thoroughly, wholly, utterly, quite ...*The candle had burned right down*...

6 = <u>straight</u>, directly, immediately, quickly, promptly, instantly, straightaway, without delay ...*She'll be right down*... OPPOSITE indirectly

7 = <u>properly</u>, fittingly, fairly, morally, honestly, justly, ethically, honourably, righteously, virtuously ...*If you're not treated right, let us know*...

8 = <u>favourably</u>, well, fortunately, for the better, to advantage, beneficially, advantageously ...*I hope things will turn out right*... OPPOSITE badly

NOUN **1** = <u>prerogative</u>, interest, business, power, claim, authority, title, due, freedom, licence, permission, liberty, privilege ...*a woman's right to choose*...

2 = <u>justice</u>, good, reason, truth, honour, equity, virtue, integrity, goodness, morality, fairness, legality, righteousness, propriety, rectitude, lawfulness, uprightness ...*a fight between right and wrong*... OPPOSITE injustice

VERB = <u>rectify</u>, settle, fix, correct, repair, sort out, compensate for, straighten, redress, vindicate, put right ...*We've made progress in righting the wrongs of the past*...

PHRASES **by rights** = <u>in fairness</u>, properly, justly, equitably ...*Negotiations should, by rights, have been conducted by him*... ♦ **put something to rights** = <u>order</u>, arrange, straighten out ...*He decided to put matters to rights*...

(**Related Words**)
adjective: dextral

right away = <u>immediately</u>, now, directly, promptly, instantly, at once, right off, straightaway, without delay, without hesitation, straight off (*informal*), forthwith, pronto (*informal*), this instant, posthaste

righteous = <u>virtuous</u>, good, just, fair, moral, pure, ethical, upright, honourable, honest, equitable, law-abiding, squeaky-clean, blameless OPPOSITE wicked

righteousness = <u>virtue</u>, justice, honour, equity, integrity, goodness, morality, honesty, purity, probity, rectitude, faithfulness, uprightness, blamelessness, ethicalness

rightful = <u>lawful</u>, just, real, true, due, legal, suitable, proper, valid, legitimate, authorized, bona fide, de jure

right-wing = <u>conservative</u>, Tory, reactionary OPPOSITE left-wing

rigid 1 = <u>strict</u>, set, fixed, exact, rigorous, stringent, austere, severe ...*Hospital routines for nurses are very rigid*... OPPOSITE flexible

2 = <u>inflexible</u>, harsh, stern, adamant, uncompromising, unrelenting, unyielding, intransigent, unbending, invariable, unalterable, undeviating ...*My father is very rigid in his thinking*...

3 = <u>stiff</u>, inflexible, inelastic ...*rigid plastic containers*... OPPOSITE pliable

rigorous 1 = <u>strict</u>, hard, firm, demanding, challenging, tough, severe, exacting, harsh, stern, rigid, stringent, austere, inflexible ...*rigorous military training*... OPPOSITE soft

2 = <u>thorough</u>, meticulous, painstaking, scrupulous, nice, accurate, exact, precise, conscientious, punctilious ...*He is rigorous in his control of expenditure*... OPPOSITE careless

rigour 1 *often plural* = <u>ordeal</u>, suffering, trial, hardship, privation ...*the rigours of childbirth*...

2 = <u>strictness</u>, austerity, rigidity, firmness, hardness, harshness, inflexibility, stringency, asperity, sternness ...*We need to address such challenging issues with rigour*...

3 = <u>thoroughness</u>, accuracy, precision, exactitude, exactness, conscientiousness, meticulousness, punctiliousness, preciseness ...*His work is built round academic rigour and years of insight*...

rile = <u>anger</u>, upset, provoke, bug (*informal*), annoy, irritate, aggravate (*informal*), gall, nettle, vex, irk, pique, peeve (*informal*), get under your skin (*informal*), get on your nerves (*informal*), nark (*Brit., Austral., & N.Z. slang*), get your goat (*slang*), try your patience, rub you up the wrong way, get *or* put your back up

rim 1 = <u>edge</u>, lip, brim, flange ...*She looked at him over the rim of her glass*...

2 = <u>border</u>, edge, trim, circumference ...*a round mirror with white metal rim*...

3 = <u>margin</u>, border, verge, brink ...*round the eastern rim of the Mediterranean*...

rind 1 = <u>skin</u>, peel, outer layer, epicarp ...*grated lemon rind*...

2 = <u>crust</u>, husk, integument ...*Cut off the rind of the cheese*...

ring[1] VERB **1** = <u>phone</u>, call, telephone, buzz (*informal, chiefly Brit.*) ...*He rang me at my mother's*...

2 = <u>chime</u>, sound, toll, resound, resonate, reverberate, clang, peal ...*He heard the school bell ring*...

3 = <u>reverberate</u>, resound, resonate ...*The whole place was ringing with music*...

NOUN **1** = <u>call</u>, phone call, buzz (*informal, chiefly Brit.*)

…We'll give him a ring as soon as we get back…
2 = <u>chime</u>, knell, peal *…There was a ring of the bell…*

Word Power

ring – *Rang* is the past tense of the verb *ring*, as in *he rang the bell*. *Rung* is the past participle, as in *he has already rung the bell*, and care should be taken not to use it as if it were a variant form of the past tense.

---

ring² NOUN **1** = <u>circle</u>, round, band, circuit, loop, hoop, halo *…a ring of blue smoke…*
2 = <u>arena</u>, enclosure, circus, rink *…The fight continued in the ring…*
3 = <u>gang</u>, group, association, band, cell, combine, organization, circle, crew (*informal*), knot, mob, syndicate, cartel, junta, clique, coterie, cabal *…investigation of an international crime ring…*
VERB = <u>encircle</u>, surround, enclose, encompass, seal off, girdle, circumscribe, hem in, gird *…The area is ringed by troops…*

rinse VERB = <u>wash</u>, clean, wet, dip, splash, cleanse, bathe, wash out *…After washing always rinse the hair in clear water…*
NOUN = <u>wash</u>, wetting, dip, splash, bath *…plenty of lather followed by a rinse with cold water…*

riot NOUN **1** = <u>disturbance</u>, row, disorder, confusion, turmoil, quarrel, upheaval, fray, strife, uproar, turbulence, commotion, lawlessness, street fighting, tumult, donnybrook, mob violence *…Twelve inmates have been killed during a riot…*
2 = <u>display</u>, show, splash, flourish, extravaganza, profusion *…The garden was a riot of colour…*
3 = <u>laugh</u>, joke, scream (*informal*), blast (*U.S. slang*), hoot (*informal*), lark *…It was a riot when I introduced my two cousins!…*
VERB = <u>rampage</u>, take to the streets, run riot, go on the rampage, fight in the streets, raise an uproar *…They rioted in protest against the government…*
PHRASES **run riot 1** = <u>rampage</u>, go wild, be out of control, raise hell, let yourself go, break *or* cut loose, throw off all restraint *…Rampaging prisoners ran riot through the jail…* **2** = <u>grow profusely</u>, luxuriate, spread like wildfire, grow like weeds *…Virginia creeper ran riot up the walls…*

riotous 1 = <u>reckless</u>, wild, outrageous, lavish, rash, luxurious, extravagant, wanton, unrestrained, intemperate, heedless, immoderate *…They wasted their lives in riotous living…*
2 = <u>unrestrained</u>, wild, loud, noisy, boisterous, rollicking, uproarious, orgiastic, side-splitting, rambunctious (*informal*), saturnalian, roisterous *…Dinner was often a riotous affair…*
3 = <u>unruly</u>, violent, disorderly, rebellious, rowdy, anarchic, tumultuous, lawless, mutinous, ungovernable, uproarious, refractory, insubordinate, rampageous *…a riotous mob of hooligans…* OPPOSITE orderly

rip VERB **1** = <u>tear</u>, cut, score, split, burst, rend, slash,

hack, claw, slit, gash, lacerate *…I tried not to rip the paper…*
2 = <u>be torn</u>, tear, split, burst, be rent *…I felt the banner rip as we were pushed in opposite directions…*
NOUN = <u>tear</u>, cut, hole, split, rent, slash, slit, cleavage, gash, laceration *…She looked at the rip in her new dress…*
PHRASES **rip someone off** (*Slang*) = <u>cheat</u>, trick, rob, con (*informal*), skin (*slang*), stiff (*slang*), steal from, fleece, defraud, dupe, swindle, diddle (*informal*), do the dirty on (*Brit. informal*), gyp (*slang*), cozen *…Ticket touts ripped them off…* ◆ **rip something off** (*Slang*) = <u>steal</u>, pinch (*informal*), swipe (*slang*), thieve, lift (*informal*), cabbage (*Brit. slang*), pilfer, filch *…He ripped off a camera and a Game Boy…*

ripe 1 = <u>ripened</u>, seasoned, ready, mature, mellow, fully developed, fully grown *…Always choose firm, but ripe fruit…* OPPOSITE unripe
2 = <u>right</u>, suitable *…Conditions are ripe for an outbreak of cholera…*
3 = <u>mature</u> *…He lived to the ripe old age of 65…*
4 = <u>suitable</u>, timely, ideal, favourable, auspicious, opportune *…The time is ripe for high-level dialogue…* OPPOSITE unsuitable
5 with *for* = <u>ready for</u>, prepared for, eager for, in readiness for *…Do you think she's ripe for romance again?…*

ripen = <u>mature</u>, season, develop, get ready, burgeon, come of age, come to fruition, grow ripe, make ripe

rip-off *or* **ripoff** (*Slang*) = <u>cheat</u>, con (*informal*), scam (*slang*), con trick (*informal*), fraud, theft, sting (*informal*), robbery, exploitation, swindle, daylight robbery (*informal*)

riposte NOUN = <u>retort</u>, return, answer, response, reply, sally, comeback (*informal*), counterattack, repartee, rejoinder *…He glanced at her, expecting a cheeky riposte…*
VERB = <u>retort</u>, return, answer, reply, respond, come back, rejoin, reciprocate *…'You look kind of funny,' she riposted blithely…*

ripple 1 = <u>wave</u>, tremor, oscillation, undulation *…the ripples on the sea's calm surface…*
2 usually plural = <u>consequence</u>, result, side effect, backlash, sequel, repercussion, reverberation *…The problem has created economic ripples…*
3 = <u>flutter</u>, thrill, tremor, tingle, vibration, frisson *…The news sent a ripple of excitement through the Security Council…*

rise VERB **1** = <u>get up</u>, stand up, get to your feet *…He rose slowly from his chair…*
2 = <u>arise</u>, surface, get out of bed, rise and shine *…He had risen early and gone to work…*
3 = <u>go up</u>, climb, move up, ascend *…The sun had risen high in the sky…* OPPOSITE descend
4 = <u>loom</u>, tower *…The building rose before him…*
5 = <u>get steeper</u>, mount, climb, ascend, go uphill, slope upwards *…the slope of land that rose from the house…* OPPOSITE drop
6 = <u>increase</u>, mount, soar *…We need to increase our*

charges in order to meet rising costs... OPPOSITE decrease

7 = grow, go up, intensify ...*His voice rose almost to a scream...*

8 = rebel, resist, revolt, mutiny, take up arms, mount the barricades ...*The people wanted to rise against the oppression...*

9 = advance, progress, get on, be promoted, prosper, go places (*informal*), climb the ladder, work your way up ...*She has risen to the top of her organisation...*

NOUN **1** = upward slope, incline, elevation, ascent, hillock, rising ground, acclivity, kopje *or* koppie (*S. African*) ...*I climbed to the top of the rise...*

2 = increase, climb, upturn, upswing, advance, improvement, ascent, upsurge, upward turn ...*the prospect of another rise in interest rates...* OPPOSITE decrease

3 = pay increase, raise (*U.S.*), increment ...*He will get a rise of nearly £4,000...*

4 = advancement, progress, climb, promotion, aggrandizement ...*They celebrated the regime's rise to power...*

PHRASES **give rise to something** = cause, produce, effect, result in, provoke, bring about, bring on ...*The picture gave rise to speculation...*

risible (*Formal*) = ridiculous, ludicrous, laughable, farcical, funny, amusing, absurd, hilarious, humorous, comical, droll, side-splitting, rib-tickling (*informal*)

risk NOUN **1** = danger, chance, possibility, speculation, uncertainty, hazard ...*There is a small risk of brain damage...*

2 = gamble, chance, venture, speculation, leap in the dark ...*This was one risk that paid off...*

3 = peril, jeopardy ...*He would not put their lives at risk...*

VERB **1** = stand a chance of ...*Those who fail to register risk severe penalties...*

2 = dare, endanger, jeopardize, imperil, venture, gamble, hazard, take a chance on, put in jeopardy, expose to danger ...*She risked her life to help a woman...*

risky = dangerous, hazardous, unsafe, perilous, uncertain, tricky, dodgy (*Brit., Austral., & N.Z. informal*), precarious, touch-and-go, dicey (*informal, chiefly Brit.*), fraught with danger, chancy (*informal*) OPPOSITE safe

risqué = suggestive, blue, daring, naughty, improper, racy, bawdy, off colour, ribald, immodest, indelicate, near the knuckle (*informal*), Rabelaisian

rite = ceremony, custom, ritual, act, service, form, practice, procedure, mystery, usage, formality, ceremonial, communion, ordinance, observance, sacrament, liturgy, solemnity

ritual NOUN **1** = ceremony, rite, ceremonial, sacrament, service, mystery, communion, observance, liturgy, solemnity ...*This is the most ancient and holiest of the rituals...*

2 = custom, tradition, routine, convention, form, practice, procedure, habit, usage, protocol, formality, ordinance ...*Italian culture revolves around the ritual*

of eating...

ADJECTIVE = ceremonial, formal, conventional, routine, prescribed, stereotyped, customary, procedural, habitual, ceremonious ...*Here, the conventions required me to make the ritual noises...*

ritzy (*Slang*) = luxurious, grand, luxury, elegant, glittering, glamorous, stylish, posh (*informal, chiefly Brit.*), sumptuous, plush (*informal*), high-class, opulent, swanky (*informal*), de luxe

rival NOUN **1** = opponent, competitor, contender, challenger, contestant, adversary, antagonist, emulator ...*He finished two seconds ahead of his rival...* OPPOSITE supporter

2 = equal, match, fellow, equivalent, peer, compeer ...*He is a pastry chef without rival...*

VERB = compete with, match, equal, oppose, compare with, contend, come up to, emulate, vie with, measure up to, be a match for, bear comparison with, seek to displace ...*Cassettes cannot rival the sound quality of CDs...*

ADJECTIVE = competing, conflicting, opposed, opposing, competitive, emulating ...*It would be no use having two rival companies...*

rivalry = competition, competitiveness, vying, opposition, struggle, conflict, contest, contention, duel, antagonism, emulation

river 1 = stream, brook, creek, beck, waterway, tributary, rivulet, watercourse, burn (*Scot.*) ...*boating on the river...*

2 = flow, rush, flood, spate, torrent ...*a river of lava was flowing down the mountainside towards the village...*

(*Related Words*)

adjective: fluvial

➤ **WORD POWER SUPPLEMENT rivers**

riveting = enthralling, arresting, gripping, fascinating, absorbing, captivating, hypnotic, engrossing, spellbinding

road 1 = roadway, street, highway, motorway, track, direction, route, path, lane, avenue, pathway, thoroughfare, course ...*There was very little traffic on the roads...*

2 = way, path ...*on the road to recovery...*

roam = wander, walk, range, travel, drift, stroll, stray, ramble, prowl, meander, rove, stravaig (*Scot. & Northern English dialect*), peregrinate

roar VERB **1** = thunder, crash, rumble ...*the roaring waters of Niagara Falls...*

2 = guffaw, laugh heartily, hoot, crack up (*informal*), bust a gut (*informal*), split your sides (*informal*) ...*He threw back his head and roared...*

3 = cry, shout, yell, howl, bellow, clamour, bawl, bay, vociferate ...*'I'll kill you for that,' he roared...*

NOUN **1** = rumble, thunder ...*the roar of traffic...*

2 = guffaw, hoot, belly laugh (*informal*) ...*There were roars of laughter as he stood up...*

3 = cry, crash, shout, yell, howl, outcry, bellow, clamour ...*the roar of lions in the distance...*

rob 1 = steal from, hold up, rifle, mug (*informal*), stiff (*slang*) ...*Police said he had robbed a man hours earlier...*

2 = <u>raid</u>, hold up, sack, loot, plunder, burgle, ransack, pillage ...*A man who tried to rob a bank was sentenced yesterday...*

3 = <u>dispossess</u>, con (*informal*), rip off, skin (*slang*), cheat (*slang*), defraud, swindle, despoil, gyp (*slang*) ...*I was robbed by a used-car dealer...*

4 = <u>deprive</u>, strip, do out of (*informal*) ...*I can't forgive him for robbing me of an Olympic gold...*

robber = <u>thief</u>, raider, burglar, looter, stealer, fraud, cheat, pirate, bandit, plunderer, mugger (*informal*), highwayman, con man (*informal*), fraudster, swindler, brigand, grifter (*slang, chiefly U.S. & Canad.*), footpad (*archaic*)

robbery 1 = <u>burglary</u>, raid, hold-up, rip-off (*slang*), stick-up (*slang, chiefly U.S.*) ...*He committed dozens of armed robberies...*

2 = <u>theft</u>, stealing, fraud, steaming (*informal*), mugging (*informal*), plunder, swindle, pillage, embezzlement, larceny, depredation, filching, thievery, rapine, spoliation ...*He was serving a sentence for robbery...*

robe 1 = <u>gown</u>, costume, vestment, habit ...*a fur-lined robe of green silk...*

2 = <u>dressing gown</u>, wrapper, bathrobe, negligée, housecoat, peignoir ...*She put on a robe and went down to the kitchen...*

robot = <u>machine</u>, automaton, android, mechanical man

robust 1 = <u>strong</u>, tough, powerful, athletic, well, sound, fit, healthy, strapping, hardy, rude, vigorous, rugged, muscular, sturdy, hale, stout, staunch, hearty, husky (*informal*), in good health, lusty, alive and kicking, fighting fit, sinewy, brawny, in fine fettle, thickset, fit as a fiddle (*informal*), able-bodied ...*His robust physique counts for much in the modern game...* OPPOSITE> weak

2 = <u>rough</u>, raw, rude, coarse, raunchy (*slang*), earthy, boisterous, rollicking, unsubtle, indecorous, roisterous ...*a robust sense of humour...* OPPOSITE> refined

3 = <u>straightforward</u>, practical, sensible, realistic, pragmatic, down-to-earth, hard-headed, common-sensical ...*She has a robust attitude to children, and knows how to deal with them...*

rock¹ 1 = <u>stone</u>, boulder ...*She sat cross-legged on the rock...*

2 = <u>tower of strength</u>, foundation, cornerstone, mainstay, support, protection, anchor, bulwark ...*She was the rock of the family...*

rock² 1 = <u>sway</u>, pitch, swing, reel, toss, lurch, wobble, roll ...*His body rocked from side to side...*

2 = <u>shock</u>, surprise, shake, stun, astonish, stagger, jar, astound, daze, dumbfound, set you back on your heels (*informal*) ...*His death rocked the fashion business...*

rocky¹ = <u>rough</u>, rugged, stony, craggy, pebbly, boulder-strewn ...*The paths are often very rocky...*

rocky² = <u>unstable</u>, weak, uncertain, doubtful, shaky, unreliable, wobbly, rickety, unsteady, undependable ...*Their relationship had gotten off to a rocky start...*

rod 1 = <u>stick</u>, bar, pole, shaft, switch, crook, cane, birch, dowel ...*reinforced with steel rods...*

2 = <u>staff</u>, baton, mace, wand, sceptre ...*It was a witch-doctor's rod...*

rodent
> **rodents**

rogue 1 = <u>scoundrel</u>, crook (*informal*), villain, fraudster, sharper, fraud, cheat, devil, deceiver, charlatan, con man (*informal*), swindler, knave (*archaic*), ne'er-do-well, reprobate, scumbag (*slang*), blackguard, mountebank, grifter (*slang, chiefly U.S. & Canad.*), skelm (*S. African*), rorter (*Austral. slang*) ...*He wasn't a rogue at all...*

2 = <u>scamp</u>, rascal, scally (*Northwest English dialect*), rapscallion, nointer (*Austral. slang*) ...*a loveable rogue...*

role 1 = <u>job</u>, part, position, post, task, duty, function, capacity ...*His role in the events has been pivotal...*

2 = <u>part</u>, character, representation, portrayal, impersonation ...*Shakespearean women's roles...*

roll VERB **1** = <u>turn</u>, wheel, spin, reel, go round, revolve, rotate, whirl, swivel, pivot, twirl, gyrate ...*The*

Rodents   http://animaldiversity.ummz.umich.edu/site/accounts/information/Rodentia.html

acouchi *or* acouchy	flying squirrel	jerboa rat	rat
agouti	fox squirrel	house mouse	red squirrel *or* chickaree
beaver	gerbil, gerbille, *or* jerbil	jerboa	spinifex hopping mouse
black rat	gopher *or* pocket gopher	jumping mouse	*or* (*Austral.*) dargawarra
brown rat *or* Norway	gopher *or* ground	kangaroo rat	springhaas
rat	squirrel	lemming	squirrel
cane rat	grey squirrel	Maori rat *or* (*N.Z.*) kiore	suslik *or* souslik
capybara	groundhog *or*	mara	taguan
cavy	woodchuck	marmot	tucotuco
chinchilla	ground squirrel *or*	mole rat	viscacha *or* vizcacha
chipmunk	gopher	mouse	vole
coypu *or* nutria	guinea pig *or* cavy	muskrat *or* musquash	water rat
deer mouse	hamster	paca	water vole *or* water rat
desert rat	harvest mouse	pack rat	white-footed mouse
dormouse	hedgehog	pocket mouse	white rat
fieldmouse	hopping mouse *or*	porcupine	

car went off the road and rolled over into a ditch…

2 = <u>trundle</u>, go, move …*The lorry slowly rolled forward…*

3 = <u>flow</u>, run, course, slide, glide, purl …*Tears rolled down her cheeks…*

4 *often with* ***up*** = <u>wind</u>, bind, wrap, twist, curl, coil, swathe, envelop, entwine, furl, enfold …*He took off his sweater and rolled it into a pillow…*

5 = <u>level</u>, even, press, spread, smooth, flatten …*Rub in and roll out the pastry…*

6 = <u>toss</u>, rock, lurch, reel, tumble, sway, wallow, billow, swing, welter …*The ship was still rolling in the troughs…*

7 = <u>rumble</u>, boom, echo, drum, roar, thunder, grumble, resound, reverberate …*guns firing, drums rolling, cymbals clashing…*

8 = <u>sway</u>, reel, stagger, lurch, lumber, waddle, swagger …*They rolled about in hysterics…*

9 = <u>pass</u>, go past, elapse …*The years roll by and look at us now…*

NOUN **1** = <u>reel</u>, ball, bobbin, cylinder …*a roll of blue insulated wire…*

2 = <u>spool</u>, reel, scroll …*a dozen rolls of film…*

3 = <u>rumble</u>, boom, drumming, roar, thunder, grumble, resonance, growl, reverberation …*They heard the roll of drums…*

4 = <u>register</u>, record, list, table, schedule, index, catalogue, directory, inventory, census, chronicle, scroll, roster, annals …*A new electoral roll should be drawn up…*

5 = <u>tossing</u>, rocking, rolling, pitching, swell, lurching, wallowing …*despite the roll of the boat…*

6 = <u>turn</u>, run, spin, rotation, cycle, wheel, revolution, reel, whirl, twirl, undulation, gyration …*Control the roll of the ball…*

rollicking¹ = <u>boisterous</u>, spirited, lively, romping, merry, hearty, playful, exuberant, joyous, carefree, jaunty, cavorting, sprightly, jovial, swashbuckling, frisky, rip-roaring (*informal*), devil-may-care, full of beans (*informal*), frolicsome, sportive OPPOSITE⟩ sedate …*outrageous, and a rollicking good read…*

rollicking² (*Brit. informal*) = <u>scolding</u>, lecture, reprimand, telling-off, roasting (*informal*), wigging (*Brit. slang*), ticking off (*informal*), dressing-down (*informal*), tongue-lashing (*informal*) …*Whoever was responsible got a rollicking…*

romance **1** = <u>love affair</u>, relationship, affair, intrigue, attachment, liaison, amour, affair of the heart, affaire (du coeur) (*French*) …*a holiday romance…*

2 = <u>love</u> …*He still finds time for romance…*

3 = <u>excitement</u>, colour, charm, mystery, adventure, sentiment, glamour, fascination, nostalgia, exoticness …*We want to recreate the romance of old train journeys…*

4 = <u>story</u>, novel, tale, fantasy, legend, fiction, fairy tale, love story, melodrama, idyll, tear-jerker (*informal*) …*Her taste in fiction was for historical romances…*

romantic ADJECTIVE **1** = <u>loving</u>, tender, passionate, fond, sentimental, sloppy (*informal*), amorous, mushy (*informal*), soppy (*Brit. informal*), lovey-dovey, icky

(*informal*) …*They enjoyed a romantic dinner for two…* OPPOSITE⟩ unromantic

2 = <u>idealistic</u>, unrealistic, visionary, high-flown, impractical, dreamy, utopian, whimsical, quixotic, starry-eyed …*He has a romantic view of rural society…* OPPOSITE⟩ realistic

3 = <u>exciting</u>, charming, fascinating, exotic, mysterious, colourful, glamorous, picturesque, nostalgic …*romantic images from travel brochures…* OPPOSITE⟩ unexciting

4 = <u>fictitious</u>, made-up, fantastic, fabulous, legendary, exaggerated, imaginative, imaginary, extravagant, unrealistic, improbable, fairy-tale, idyllic, fanciful, wild, chimerical …*Both figures have become the stuff of romantic legends…* OPPOSITE⟩ realistic

NOUN = <u>idealist</u>, romancer, visionary, dreamer, utopian, Don Quixote, sentimentalist …*You're a hopeless romantic…*

Rome

The seven hills of Rome

Aventine	Palatine
Caelian	Quirinal
Capitoline	Viminal
Esquiline	

---

romp VERB = <u>frolic</u>, sport, skip, have fun, revel, caper, cavort, frisk, gambol, make merry, rollick, roister, cut capers …*Dogs romped happily in the garden…*

NOUN = <u>frolic</u>, lark (*informal*), caper …*a romp in the snow and slush…*

PHRASES **romp home** *or* **in** = <u>win easily</u>, walk it (*informal*), win hands down, run away with it, win by a mile (*informal*) …*He romped home with 141 votes…*

room **1** = <u>chamber</u>, office, apartment …*He excused himself and left the room…*

2 = <u>space</u>, area, territory, volume, capacity, extent, expanse, elbow room …*There wasn't enough room for all the gear…*

3 = <u>opportunity</u>, scope, leeway, play, chance, range, occasion, margin, allowance, compass, latitude …*There's a lot of room for you to express yourself…*

roomy = <u>spacious</u>, large, wide, broad, extensive, generous, ample, capacious, commodious, sizable *or* sizeable OPPOSITE⟩ cramped

root¹ NOUN **1** = <u>stem</u>, tuber, rhizome, radix, radicle …*the twisted roots of an apple tree…*

2 = <u>source</u>, cause, heart, bottom, beginnings, base, seat, occasion, seed, foundation, origin, core, fundamental, essence, nucleus, starting point, germ, crux, nub, derivation, fountainhead, mainspring …*We got to the root of the problem…*

PLURAL NOUN = <u>sense of belonging</u>, origins, heritage, birthplace, home, family, cradle …*I am proud of my Brazilian roots…*

PHRASES **root and branch** **1** = <u>complete</u>, total, entire, radical, thorough …*in need of root and branch reform…* **2** = <u>completely</u>, finally, totally, entirely, radically, thoroughly, wholly, utterly, without exception, to the last man …*They want to deal with the problem root and branch*… ◆ **root something** or **someone out** 1 = <u>get rid of</u>, remove, destroy, eliminate, abolish, cut out, erase, eradicate, do away with, uproot, weed out, efface, exterminate, extirpate, wipe from the face of the earth …*The generals have to root out traitors*… 2 = <u>discover</u>, find, expose, turn up, uncover, unearth, bring to light, ferret out …*It shouldn't take long to root out the cause of the problem*…

(**Related Words**)
adjective : radical

root² = <u>dig</u>, hunt, nose, poke, burrow, delve, ferret, pry, rummage, forage, rootle …*She rooted through the bag*…

rooted = <u>deep-seated</u>, firm, deep, established, confirmed, fixed, radical, rigid, entrenched, ingrained, deeply felt

rootless = <u>footloose</u>, homeless, roving, transient, itinerant, vagabond

rope NOUN = <u>cord</u>, line, cable, strand, hawser …*He tied the rope around his waist*…
VERB = <u>tie</u>, bind, moor, lash, hitch, fasten, tether, pinion, lasso …*I roped myself to the chimney*…
PHRASES **know the ropes** = <u>be experienced</u>, know the score (*informal*), be knowledgeable, know what's what, be an old hand, know your way around, know where it's at (*slang*), know all the ins and outs …*She got to know the ropes*… ◆ **rope someone in** or **into something** (*Brit.*) = <u>persuade</u>, involve, engage, enlist, talk into, drag in, inveigle …*I got roped into helping*…

roster = <u>rota</u>, listing, list, table, roll, schedule, register, agenda, catalogue, inventory, scroll

rostrum = <u>stage</u>, stand, platform, podium, dais

rosy ADJECTIVE 1 = <u>glowing</u>, fresh, blooming, flushed, blushing, radiant, reddish, ruddy, healthy-looking, roseate, rubicund …*She had bright, rosy cheeks*…
OPPOSITE pale
2 = <u>promising</u>, encouraging, bright, reassuring, optimistic, hopeful, sunny, cheerful, favourable, auspicious, rose-coloured, roseate …*Is the future really so rosy?*… OPPOSITE gloomy
NOUN = <u>pink</u>, red, rose-coloured, roseate …*the rosy brick buildings*…
➤ **shades of red**

rot VERB 1 = <u>decay</u>, break down, spoil, corrupt, deteriorate, taint, perish, degenerate, fester, decompose, corrode, moulder, go bad, putrefy …*The grain will start rotting in the silos*…
2 = <u>crumble</u>, disintegrate, become rotten …*It is not true to say that this wood never rots*…
3 = <u>deteriorate</u>, decline, languish, degenerate, wither away, waste away …*I was left to rot nine years for a crime I didn't commit*…
NOUN 1 = <u>decay</u>, disintegration, corrosion, decomposition, corruption, mould, blight, deterioration, canker, putrefaction, putrescence …*Investigations revealed rot in the beams*…

2 (*Informal*) = <u>nonsense</u>, rubbish, drivel, twaddle, pants (*slang*), crap (*slang*), garbage (*chiefly U.S.*), trash, bunk (*informal*), hot air (*informal*), tosh (*slang, chiefly Brit.*), pap, bilge (*informal*), tripe (*informal*), guff (*slang*), moonshine, claptrap (*informal*), hogwash, hokum (*slang, chiefly U.S. & Canad.*), codswallop (*Brit. slang*), piffle (*informal*), poppycock (*informal*), balderdash, bosh (*informal*), eyewash (*informal*), stuff and nonsense, flapdoodle (*slang*), tommyrot, horsefeathers (*U.S. slang*), bunkum or buncombe (*chiefly U.S.*), bizzo (*Austral. slang*), bull's wool (*Austral. & N.Z. slang*) …*You do talk rot!*…

(**Related Words**)
adjective : putrid

rotary = <u>revolving</u>, turning, spinning, rotating, rotational, gyratory, rotatory

rotate 1 = <u>revolve</u>, turn, wheel, spin, reel, go round, swivel, pivot, gyrate, pirouette …*The earth rotates round the sun*…
2 = <u>follow in sequence</u>, switch, alternate, interchange, take turns …*The members of the club can rotate*…

rotation 1 = <u>revolution</u>, turning, turn, wheel, spin, spinning, reel, orbit, pirouette, gyration …*the daily rotation of the earth upon its axis*…
2 = <u>sequence</u>, switching, cycle, succession, interchanging, alternation …*crop rotation and integration of livestock*…

rotten 1 = <u>decaying</u>, bad, rank, foul, corrupt, sour, stinking, tainted, perished, festering, decomposed, decomposing, mouldy, mouldering, fetid, putrid, putrescent, festy (*Austral. slang*) …*The smell is like rotten eggs*… OPPOSITE fresh
2 = <u>crumbling</u>, decayed, disintegrating, perished, corroded, unsound …*The bay window is rotten*…
3 (*Informal*) = <u>bad</u>, disappointing, unfortunate, unlucky, regrettable, deplorable …*What rotten luck!*…
4 (*Informal*) = <u>despicable</u>, mean, base, dirty, nasty, unpleasant, filthy, vile, wicked, disagreeable, contemptible, scurrilous …*You rotten swine!*…
5 (*Informal*) = <u>unwell</u>, poorly (*informal*), ill, sick, rough (*informal*), bad, crook (*Austral. & N.Z. informal*), below par, off colour, under the weather (*informal*), ropey or ropy (*Brit. informal*) …*I felt rotten with the flu*…
6 (*Informal*) = <u>inferior</u>, poor, sorry, inadequate, unacceptable, punk, duff (*Brit. informal*), unsatisfactory, lousy (*slang*), low-grade, substandard, ill-considered, crummy (*slang*), ill-thought-out, poxy (*slang*), of a sort or of sorts, ropey or ropy (*Brit. informal*), bodger or bodgie (*Austral. slang*) …*I thought it was a rotten idea*…
7 = <u>corrupt</u>, immoral, deceitful, untrustworthy, bent (*slang*), crooked (*informal*), vicious, degenerate, mercenary, treacherous, dishonest, disloyal, faithless, venal, dishonourable, perfidious …*There was something rotten in our legal system*… OPPOSITE honourable

rotund 1 = <u>plump</u>, rounded, heavy, fat, stout, chubby, obese, fleshy, tubby, portly, roly-poly, podgy, corpulent …*A rotund gentleman appeared*…

OPPOSITE> skinny

2 = <u>pompous</u>, orotund, magniloquent, full ...*writing rotund passages of purple prose...*

3 = <u>round</u>, rounded, spherical, bulbous, globular, orbicular ...*rotund towers, moats and drawbridges...*

4 = <u>sonorous</u>, round, rich, resonant, orotund ...*the wonderfully rotund tones of the presenter...*

rough ADJECTIVE **1** = <u>uneven</u>, broken, rocky, rugged, irregular, jagged, bumpy, stony, craggy ...*She made her way across the rough ground...* OPPOSITE> even

2 = <u>coarse</u>, disordered, tangled, hairy, fuzzy, bushy, shaggy, dishevelled, uncut, unshaven, tousled, bristly, unshorn ...*people who looked rough and stubbly...* OPPOSITE> smooth

3 = <u>boisterous</u>, hard, tough, rugged, arduous ...*Rugby's a rough game...*

4 = <u>ungracious</u>, blunt, rude, coarse, bluff, curt, churlish, bearish, brusque, uncouth, unrefined, inconsiderate, impolite, loutish, untutored, discourteous, unpolished, indelicate, uncivil, uncultured, unceremonious, ill-bred, unmannerly, ill-mannered ...*He was rough and common...* OPPOSITE> refined

5 = <u>unpleasant</u>, hard, difficult, tough, uncomfortable, drastic, unjust ...*Women have a rough time in our society...* OPPOSITE> easy

6 (*Informal*) = <u>unwell</u>, poorly (*informal*), ill, upset, sick, crook (*Austral. & N.Z. informal*), rotten (*informal*), below par, off colour, under the weather (*informal*), not a hundred per cent (*informal*), ropey or ropy (*Brit. informal*) ...*The lad is still feeling a bit rough...*

7 = <u>approximate</u>, estimated ...*We were only able to make a rough estimate...* OPPOSITE> exact

8 = <u>vague</u>, general, sketchy, imprecise, hazy, foggy, amorphous, inexact ...*I've got a rough idea of what he looks like...*

9 = <u>basic</u>, quick, raw, crude, unfinished, incomplete, hasty, imperfect, rudimentary, sketchy, cursory, shapeless, rough-and-ready, unrefined, formless, rough-hewn, untutored, unpolished ...*Make a rough plan of the space...* OPPOSITE> complete

10 = <u>rough-hewn</u>, crude, uncut, unpolished, raw, undressed, unprocessed, unhewn, unwrought ...*a rough wooden table...*

11 = <u>stormy</u>, wild, turbulent, agitated, choppy, tempestuous, inclement, squally ...*The ships collided in rough seas...* OPPOSITE> calm

12 = <u>grating</u>, harsh, jarring, raucous, rasping, husky, discordant, gruff, cacophonous, unmusical, inharmonious ...*'Wait!' a rough voice commanded...* OPPOSITE> soft

13 = <u>harsh</u>, tough, sharp, severe, nasty, cruel, rowdy, curt, unfeeling ...*I was a bit rough with you this morning...* OPPOSITE> gentle

NOUN **1** = <u>outline</u>, draft, mock-up, preliminary sketch, suggestion ...*Editors are always saying that the roughs are better...*

2 (*Informal*) = <u>thug</u>, tough, casual, rowdy, hoon (*Austral. & N.Z.*), bully boy, bruiser, ruffian, lager lout, roughneck (*slang*), ned (*slang*), cougan (*Austral.*

slang), scozza (*Austral. slang*), bogan (*Austral. slang*) ...*The roughs of the town are out...*

PHRASES **rough and ready 1** = <u>makeshift</u>, adequate, crude, provisional, improvised, sketchy, thrown together, cobbled together, stopgap ...*Here is a rough and ready measurement...* **2** = <u>unrefined</u>, shabby, untidy, unkempt, unpolished, ungroomed, ill-groomed ...*The soldiers were a bit rough and ready...*

♦ **rough and tumble 1** = <u>fight</u>, struggle, scrap (*informal*), brawl, scuffle, punch-up (*Brit. informal*), fracas, affray (*Law*), dust-up (*informal*), shindig (*informal*), donnybrook, scrimmage, roughhouse (*slang*), shindy (*informal*), melee or mêlée, biffo (*Austral. slang*) ...*the rough and tumble of political combat...* **2** = <u>disorderly</u>, rough, scrambled, scrambling, irregular, rowdy, boisterous, haphazard, indisciplined ...*He enjoys rough and tumble play...*

♦ **rough someone up** (*Informal*) = <u>beat up</u>, batter, thrash, do over (*Brit., Austral., & N.Z. slang*), work over (*slang*), mistreat, manhandle, maltreat, bash up (*informal*), beat the living daylights out of (*informal*), knock about or around ...*They roughed him up a bit...*

♦ **rough something out** = <u>outline</u>, plan, draft, sketch, suggest, block out, delineate, adumbrate ...*He roughed out a framework for their story...*

round NOUN **1** = <u>series</u>, session, cycle, sequence, succession, bout ...*This is the latest round of job cuts...*

2 = <u>stage</u>, turn, level, period, division, session, lap ...*in the third round of the cup...*

3 = <u>sphere</u>, ball, band, ring, circle, disc, globe, orb ...*small fresh rounds of goat's cheese...*

4 = <u>course</u>, turn, tour, circuit, beat, series, schedule, routine, compass, ambit ...*The consultant did his morning round...*

5 = <u>bullet</u>, shot, shell, discharge, cartridge ...*live rounds of ammunition...*

ADJECTIVE **1** = <u>spherical</u>, rounded, bowed, curved, circular, cylindrical, bulbous, rotund, globular, curvilinear, ball-shaped, ring-shaped, disc-shaped, annular, discoid, orbicular ...*the round church known as The New Temple...*

2 = <u>complete</u>, full, whole, entire, solid, unbroken, undivided ...*a round dozen...*

3 = <u>plump</u>, full, rounded, ample, fleshy, roly-poly, rotund, full-fleshed ...*She was a small, round person in her early sixties...*

4 = <u>considerable</u>, large, liberal, substantial, generous, ample, bountiful, bounteous ...*She had a nice, round figure...*

VERB = <u>go round</u>, circle, skirt, flank, bypass, encircle, turn, circumnavigate ...*The boats rounded the Cape...*

PHRASES **round on someone** = <u>attack</u>, abuse, turn on, retaliate against, have a go at (*Brit. slang*), snap at, wade into, lose your temper with, bite (someone's) head off (*informal*) ...*He has rounded on his critics...*

♦ **round something or someone up** = <u>gather</u>, assemble, bring together, muster, group, drive, collect, rally, herd, marshal ...*The police rounded up a number of suspects...* ♦ **round something off** = <u>complete</u>, close, settle, crown, cap, conclude, finish off, put the finishing touch to, bring to a close ...*A fireworks display rounded off the day...*

roundabout 1 = <u>indirect</u>, meandering, devious, tortuous, circuitous, evasive, discursive, circumlocutory ...*a roundabout route...* OPPOSITE▷ direct

2 = <u>oblique</u>, implied, indirect, evasive, circuitous, circumlocutory, periphrastic ...*indirect or roundabout language...*

roundly = <u>thoroughly</u>, sharply, severely, bitterly, fiercely, bluntly, intensely, violently, vehemently, rigorously, outspokenly, frankly

roundup 1 (*Informal*) = <u>summary</u>, survey, collation ...*a roundup of the day's news...*

2 = <u>muster</u>, collection, rally, assembly, herding ...*What keeps a cowboy ready for another roundup?...*

rouse 1 = <u>wake up</u>, call, wake, awaken ...*She roused him at 8.30...*

2 = <u>excite</u>, move, arouse, stir, disturb, provoke, anger, startle, animate, prod, exhilarate, get going, agitate, inflame, incite, whip up, galvanize, bestir ...*He did more to rouse the crowd than anybody else...*

3 = <u>stimulate</u>, provoke, arouse, incite, instigate ...*It roused a feeling of rebellion in him...*

rousing = <u>lively</u>, moving, spirited, exciting, inspiring, stirring, stimulating, vigorous, brisk, exhilarating, inflammatory, electrifying OPPOSITE▷ dull

rout VERB = <u>defeat</u>, beat, overthrow, thrash, stuff (*slang*), worst, destroy, chase, tank (*slang*), crush, scatter, conquer, lick (*informal*), dispel, drive off, overpower, clobber (*slang*), wipe the floor with (*informal*), cut to pieces, put to flight, drub, put to rout, throw back in confusion ...*The Norman army routed the English opposition...*

NOUN = <u>defeat</u>, beating, hiding (*informal*), ruin, overthrow, thrashing, licking (*informal*), pasting (*slang*), shambles, debacle, drubbing, overwhelming defeat, headlong flight, disorderly retreat ...*The retreat turned into a rout...*

➤ **route**

route NOUN 1 = <u>way</u>, course, road, direction, path, journey, passage, avenue, itinerary ...*the most direct route to the town centre...*

2 = <u>beat</u>, run, round, circuit ...*They would go out on his route and check him...*

VERB 1 = <u>direct</u>, lead, guide, steer, convey ...*Approaching cars will be routed into two lanes...*

2 = <u>send</u>, forward, dispatch ...*plans to route every emergency call through three exchanges...*

Word Power

route – When adding -*ing* to the verb *route* to form the present participle, it is more conventional, and clearer, to keep the final *e* from the end of the verb stem: *routeing*. The spelling *routing* in this sense is also possible, but keeping the *e* distinguishes it from *routing*, which is the participle formed from the verb *rout* meaning 'to defeat'.

routine NOUN 1 = <u>procedure</u>, programme, way, order, practice, method, pattern, formula, custom, usage, wont ...*The players had to change their daily routine...*

2 = <u>grind</u> (*informal*), monotony, banality, groove, boredom, chore, the doldrums, dullness, sameness, ennui, drabness, deadness, dreariness, tediousness, lifelessness ...*the mundane routine of her life...*

3 (*Informal*) = <u>performance</u>, line, act, bit (*informal*), piece, spiel (*informal*) ...*like a Marx Brothers routine...*

ADJECTIVE 1 = <u>usual</u>, standard, normal, customary, ordinary, familiar, typical, conventional, everyday, habitual, workaday, wonted ...*a series of routine medical tests...* OPPOSITE▷ unusual

2 = <u>boring</u>, dull, predictable, tedious, tiresome, run-of-the-mill, humdrum, unimaginative, clichéd, uninspired, mind-numbing, hackneyed, unoriginal, shtick (*slang*) ...*So many days are routine and uninteresting...*

rove = <u>wander</u>, range, cruise, drift, stroll, stray, roam, ramble, meander, traipse (*informal*), gallivant, gad about, stravaig (*Scot. & Northern English dialect*)

rover = <u>wanderer</u>, traveller, gypsy, rolling stone, rambler, transient, nomad, itinerant, ranger, drifter, vagrant, stroller, bird of passage, gadabout (*informal*)

row¹ NOUN = <u>line</u>, bank, range, series, file, rank, string, column, sequence, queue, tier ...*a row of pretty little cottages...*

PHRASES **in a row** = <u>consecutively</u>, running, in turn, one after the other, successively, in sequence ...*They have won five championships in a row...*

row² NOUN (*Informal*) 1 = <u>quarrel</u>, dispute, argument, squabble, tiff, trouble, controversy, scrap (*informal*), fuss, falling-out (*informal*), fray, brawl, fracas, altercation, slanging match (*Brit.*), shouting match (*informal*), shindig (*informal*), ruction (*informal*), ruckus (*informal*), shindy (*informal*), bagarre (*French*) ...*A man was stabbed to death in a family row...*

2 = <u>disturbance</u>, noise, racket, uproar, commotion, rumpus, tumult ...*'Whatever is that row?' she demanded...*

3 = <u>telling-off</u>, talking-to (*informal*), lecture, reprimand, ticking-off (*informal*), dressing-down (*informal*), rollicking (*Brit. informal*) (*informal*), tongue-lashing, reproof, castigation, flea in your ear (*informal*) ...*I can't give you a row for scarpering off...*

VERB = <u>quarrel</u>, fight, argue, dispute, scrap (*informal*), brawl, squabble, spar, wrangle, go at it hammer and tongs ...*They rowed all the time...*

rowdy ADJECTIVE = <u>disorderly</u>, rough, loud, noisy, unruly, boisterous, loutish, wild, uproarious, obstreperous ...*He has complained about rowdy neighbours...* OPPOSITE▷ orderly

NOUN *often plural* = <u>hooligan</u>, tough, rough (*informal*), casual, ned (*Scot. slang*), brawler, yahoo, lout, troublemaker, tearaway (*Brit.*), ruffian, lager lout, yob *or* yobbo (*Brit. slang*), cougan (*Austral. slang*), scozza (*Austral. slang*), bogan (*Austral. slang*) ...*The owner kept a baseball bat to deal with rowdies...*

royal 1 = <u>regal</u>, kingly, queenly, princely, imperial, sovereign, monarchical, kinglike ...*an invitation to a royal garden party*...

2 = splendid, august, grand, impressive, superb, magnificent, superior, majestic, stately ...*She was given a royal welcome on her first visit to Britain*...

rub VERB **1** = stroke, smooth, massage, caress, knead ...*He rubbed his arms and stiff legs*...

2 = polish, clean, shine, wipe, scour ...*She took off her glasses and rubbed them*...

3 = spread, put, apply, smear ...*He rubbed oil into my aching back*...

4 = chafe, scrape, grate, abrade ...*Smear cream on to prevent it from rubbing*...

NOUN **1** = massage, caress, kneading ...*She sometimes asks if I want a back rub*...

2 = polish, stroke, shine, wipe ...*Give them a rub with a clean, dry cloth*...

PHRASES **rub something out** = erase, remove, cancel, wipe out, excise, delete, obliterate, efface, expunge ...*She began rubbing out the pencilled marks*... ◆ **the rub** = difficulty, problem, catch, trouble, obstacle, hazard, hitch, drawback, snag, uphill (*S. African*), impediment, hindrance ...*And therein lies the rub*...

rubbish 1 = waste, refuse, scrap, junk (*informal*), litter, debris, crap (*slang*), garbage (*chiefly U.S.*), trash, lumber, offal, dross, dregs, flotsam and jetsam, grot (*slang*), dreck (*slang, chiefly U.S.*), offscourings ...*unwanted household rubbish*...

2 = nonsense, garbage (*chiefly U.S.*), drivel, twaddle, pants (*slang*), rot, crap (*slang*), trash, hot air (*informal*), tosh (*slang, chiefly Brit.*), pap, bilge (*informal*), tripe (*informal*), gibberish, guff (*slang*), havers (*Scot.*), moonshine, claptrap (*informal*), hogwash, hokum (*slang, chiefly U.S. & Canad.*), codswallop (*Brit. slang*), piffle (*informal*), poppycock (*informal*), balderdash, bosh (*informal*), wack (*U.S. slang*), eyewash (*informal*), stuff and nonsense, flapdoodle (*slang*), tommyrot, horsefeathers (*U.S. slang*), bunkum *or* buncombe (*chiefly U.S.*), bizzo (*Austral. slang*), bull's wool (*Austral. & N.Z. slang*) ...*He's talking rubbish*...

ruddy 1 = rosy, red, fresh, healthy, glowing, blooming, flushed, blushing, radiant, reddish, sanguine, florid, sunburnt, rosy-cheeked, rubicund ...*He had a naturally ruddy complexion*... OPPOSITE pale

2 = red, pink, scarlet, ruby, crimson, reddish, roseate ...*barges, with their sails ruddy brown*...

➤ **shades of red**

rude 1 = impolite, insulting, cheeky, abrupt, short, blunt, abusive, curt, churlish, disrespectful, brusque, offhand, impertinent, insolent, inconsiderate, peremptory, impudent, discourteous, uncivil, unmannerly, ill-mannered ...*He's rude to her friends*... OPPOSITE polite

2 = uncivilized, low, rough, savage, ignorant, coarse, illiterate, uneducated, brutish, barbarous, scurrilous, boorish, uncouth, unrefined, loutish, untutored, graceless, ungracious, unpolished, oafish, uncultured ...*a rude barbarian*...

3 = vulgar, gross, crude ...*He made a rude gesture with*

his finger... OPPOSITE refined

4 = unpleasant, sharp, violent, sudden, harsh, startling, abrupt ...*It came as a rude shock*...

5 = roughly-made, simple, rough, raw, crude, primitive, makeshift, rough-hewn, artless, inelegant, inartistic ...*He had already constructed a rude cabin*... OPPOSITE well-made

rudimentary 1 = primitive, undeveloped ...*It had been extended into a kind of rudimentary kitchen*...

2 = basic, fundamental, elementary, early, primary, initial, introductory ...*He had only a rudimentary knowledge of French*...

3 = undeveloped, embryonic, vestigial ...*a rudimentary backbone called a notochord*... OPPOSITE complete

rudiments = basics, elements, essentials, fundamentals, beginnings, foundation, nuts and bolts, first principles

rue (*Literary*) = regret, mourn, grieve, lament, deplore, bemoan, repent, be sorry for, weep over, sorrow for, bewail, kick yourself for, reproach yourself for

rueful = regretful, sad, dismal, melancholy, grievous, pitiful, woeful, sorry, mournful, plaintive, lugubrious, contrite, sorrowful, repentant, doleful, remorseful, penitent, pitiable, woebegone, conscience-stricken, self-reproachful OPPOSITE unrepentant

ruffle 1 = disarrange, disorder, wrinkle, mess up, rumple, tousle, derange, discompose, dishevel ...*She let the wind ruffle her hair*...

2 = annoy, worry, trouble, upset, confuse, stir, disturb, rattle (*informal*), irritate, put out, unsettle, shake up (*informal*), harass, hassle (*informal*), agitate, unnerve, disconcert, disquiet, nettle, vex, fluster, perturb, faze, peeve (*informal*) ...*My refusal to let him ruffle me infuriated him*... OPPOSITE calm

rugby
➤ **rugby terms**

rugged 1 = rocky, broken, rough, craggy, difficult, ragged, stark, irregular, uneven, jagged, bumpy ...*a rugged mountainous terrain*... OPPOSITE even

2 = strong-featured, lined, worn, weathered, wrinkled, furrowed, leathery, rough-hewn, weather-beaten ...*A look of disbelief crossed his rugged face*... OPPOSITE delicate

3 = well-built, strong, tough, robust, sturdy ...*this rugged all-steel design*...

4 = tough, strong, hardy, robust, vigorous, muscular, sturdy, hale, burly, husky (*informal*), beefy (*informal*), brawny ...*He's rugged and durable, but not the best technical boxer*... OPPOSITE delicate

5 = uncompromising, decided, firm, tough, strict, rigid, stubborn, hardline, die-hard, inflexible, inexorable, steadfast, unyielding, obstinate, intransigent, unbending, obdurate, stiff-necked ...*Rugged individualism forged America's frontier society*...

6 = difficult, trying, hard, taxing, demanding, tough, exacting, harsh, stern, rigorous, strenuous, arduous, laborious ...*enjoying rugged sports like mountain*

Rugby terms http://www.irb.com/

back	flanker *or* wing forward	maul	ruck
back row	forward	number eight forward	scrum half
ball	front row	scrum *or* scrummage	second row
centre	full back	stand-off half, fly half,	tackle
conversion	garryowen	*or* outside half	three-quarter
crossbar	goalpost	pack	tight head
drop goal	half back	pass	touch judge
lock forward	hooker	penalty	try
loose forward	knock on	prop forward	up and under
loose head	line-out	punt	winger
five-eighth	mark	referee	

biking… OPPOSITE easy

7 = <u>stern</u>, hard, severe, rough, harsh, sour, rude, crabbed, austere, dour, surly, gruff …*a fairly rugged customer*…

ruin VERB **1** = <u>destroy</u>, devastate, wreck, trash (*slang*), break, total (*slang*), defeat, smash, crush, overwhelm, shatter, overturn, overthrow, bring down, demolish, raze, lay waste, lay in ruins, wreak havoc upon, bring to ruin, bring to nothing …*Roads have been destroyed and crops ruined*… OPPOSITE create
2 = <u>bankrupt</u>, break, impoverish, beggar, pauperize …*She accused him of ruining her financially*…
3 = <u>spoil</u>, damage, mar, mess up, blow (*slang*), injure, undo, screw up (*informal*), botch, mangle, cock up (*Brit. slang*), disfigure, make a mess of, bodge (*informal*), crool *or* cruel (*Austral. slang*) …*The original decor was all ruined during renovation*… OPPOSITE improve
NOUN **1** = <u>bankruptcy</u>, insolvency, destitution …*Recent inflation has driven them to the brink of ruin*…
2 = <u>disrepair</u>, decay, disintegration, ruination, wreckage …*The vineyards were falling into ruin*…
3 = <u>destruction</u>, fall, the end, breakdown, damage, defeat, failure, crash, collapse, wreck, overthrow, undoing, havoc, Waterloo, downfall, devastation, dissolution, subversion, nemesis, crackup (*informal*) …*It is the ruin of society*… OPPOSITE preservation

ruinous 1 = <u>extravagant</u>, crippling, wasteful, immoderate …*the ruinous costs of the legal system*…
2 = <u>destructive</u>, devastating, shattering, fatal, deadly, disastrous, dire, withering, catastrophic, murderous, pernicious, noxious, calamitous, baleful, deleterious, injurious, baneful (*archaic*) …*the ruinous effects of the conflict*…
3 = <u>ruined</u>, broken-down, derelict, ramshackle, dilapidated, in ruins, decrepit …*They passed by the ruinous building*…

rule NOUN **1** = <u>regulation</u>, order, law, ruling, guide, direction, guideline, decree, ordinance, dictum …*the rule against retrospective prosecution*…
2 = <u>precept</u>, principle, criterion, canon, maxim, tenet, axiom …*An important rule is to drink plenty of water*…
3 = <u>procedure</u>, policy, standard, method, way, course, formula …*according to the rules of quantum theory*…
4 = <u>custom</u>, procedure, practice, routine, form, condition, tradition, habit, convention, wont, order *or*

way of things …*The usual rule is to start as one group*…
5 = <u>government</u>, power, control, authority, influence, administration, direction, leadership, command, regime, empire, reign, sway, domination, jurisdiction, supremacy, mastery, dominion, ascendancy, mana (*N.Z.*) …*the winding-up of British rule over the territory*…
VERB **1** = <u>govern</u>, lead, control, manage, direct, guide, regulate, administer, oversee, preside over, have power over, reign over, command over, have charge of …*the feudal lord who ruled this land*…
2 = <u>reign</u>, govern, be in power, hold sway, wear the crown, be in authority, be number one (*informal*) …*He ruled for eight years*…
3 = <u>control</u>, dominate, monopolize, tyrannize, be pre-eminent, have the upper hand over …*Fear can rule our lives*…
4 = <u>decree</u>, find, decide, judge, establish, determine, settle, resolve, pronounce, lay down, adjudge …*The court ruled that laws passed by the assembly remained valid*…
5 = <u>be prevalent</u>, prevail, predominate, hold sway, be customary, preponderate, obtain …*A ferocious form of anarchy ruled here*…
PHRASES **as a rule** = <u>usually</u>, generally, mainly, normally, on the whole, for the most part, ordinarily, customarily …*As a rule, these tourists take far too many souvenirs with them*… ♦ **rule someone out** = <u>exclude</u>, eliminate, disqualify, ban, prevent, reject, dismiss, forbid, prohibit, leave out, preclude, proscribe, obviate, debar …*a suspension which ruled him out of the grand final*… ♦ **rule something out** = <u>reject</u>, exclude, eliminate …*Local detectives have ruled out foul play*…

ruler 1 = <u>governor</u>, leader, lord, commander, controller, monarch, sovereign, head of state, potentate, crowned head, emperor *or* empress, king *or* queen, prince *or* princess …*He was an indecisive ruler*…
2 = <u>measure</u>, rule, yardstick, straight edge …*taking measurements with a ruler*…

ruling ADJECTIVE **1** = <u>governing</u>, upper, reigning, controlling, leading, commanding, dominant, regnant …*the domination of the ruling class*…
2 = <u>predominant</u>, dominant, prevailing, preponderant, chief, main, current, supreme,

principal, prevalent, pre-eminent, regnant ...*a ruling passion for liberty and equality*... OPPOSITE minor NOUN = decision, finding, resolution, verdict, judgment, decree, adjudication, pronouncement ...*He tried to have the court ruling overturned*...

rum (*Brit. slang*) = strange, odd, suspect, funny, unusual, curious, weird, suspicious, peculiar, dodgy (*Brit., Austral., & N.Z. informal*), queer, singular

ruminate = ponder, think, consider, reflect, contemplate, deliberate, muse, brood, meditate, mull over things, chew over things, cogitate, rack your brains, turn over in your mind

rummage = search, hunt, root, explore, delve, examine, ransack, forage, fossick (*Austral. & N.Z.*), rootle

rumour NOUN = story, news, report, talk, word, whisper, buzz, gossip, dirt (*U.S. slang*), hearsay, canard, tidings, scuttlebutt (*U.S. slang*), bush telegraph, bruit (*archaic*) ...*There's a strange rumour going around*... PHRASES **be rumoured** = be said, be told, be reported, be published, be circulated, be whispered, be passed around, be put about, be noised abroad ...*It was rumoured that he'd been interned in an asylum*...

rump = buttocks, bottom, rear, backside (*informal*), tail (*informal*), seat, butt (*U.S. & Canad. informal*), bum (*Brit. slang*), buns (*U.S. slang*), rear end, posterior, haunch, hindquarters, derrière (*euphemistic*), croup, jacksy (*Brit. slang*)

rumple = ruffle, crush, disorder, dishevel, wrinkle, crease, crumple, screw up, mess up, pucker, crinkle, scrunch, tousle, derange

rumpus = commotion, row, noise, confusion, fuss, disturbance, disruption, furore, uproar, tumult, brouhaha, shindig (*informal*), hue and cry, kerfuffle (*informal*), shindy (*informal*)

run VERB **1** = race, speed, rush, dash, hurry, career, barrel (along) (*informal, chiefly U.S. & Canad.*), sprint, scramble, bolt, dart, gallop, hare (*Brit. informal*), jog, scud, hasten, scurry, stampede, scamper, leg it (*informal*), lope, hie, hotfoot ...*I excused myself and ran back to the telephone*... OPPOSITE dawdle
2 = flee, escape, take off (*informal*), depart, bolt, clear out, beat it (*slang*), leg it (*informal*), make off, abscond, decamp, take flight, do a runner (*slang*), scarper (*Brit. slang*), slope off, cut and run (*informal*), make a run for it, fly the coop (*U.S. & Canad. informal*), beat a retreat, show a clean pair of heels, skedaddle (*informal*), take a powder (*U.S. & Canad. slang*), take it on the lam (*U.S. & Canad. slang*), take to your heels ...*As they closed in on him, he turned and ran*... OPPOSITE stay
3 = take part, compete ...*I was running in the marathon*...
4 = continue, go, stretch, last, reach, lie, range, extend, proceed ...*the trail which ran through the beech woods*... OPPOSITE stop
5 (*Chiefly U.S. & Canad.*) = compete, stand, contend, be a candidate, put yourself up for, take part, challenge

...*He announced he would run for president*...
6 = manage, lead, direct, be in charge of, own, head, control, boss (*informal*), operate, handle, conduct, look after, carry on, regulate, take care of, administer, oversee, supervise, mastermind, coordinate, superintend ...*His father ran a prosperous business*...
7 = go, work, operate, perform, function, be in business, be in action, tick over ...*the staff who have kept the bank running*...
8 = perform, carry out ...*He ran a lot of tests*...
9 = work, go, operate, function ...*The tape recorder was still running*...
10 = drive ...*I ran a 1960 Rover 100*...
11 = operate, go ...*A shuttle bus runs frequently*...
12 = give a lift to, drive, carry, transport, convey, bear, manoeuvre, propel ...*Can you run me to work?*...
13 = pass, go, move, roll, slide, glide, skim ...*He winced as he ran his hand over his ribs*...
14 = flow, pour, stream, cascade, go, move, issue, proceed, leak, spill, discharge, gush, spout, course ...*cisterns to catch rainwater as it ran off the walls*...
15 = spread, mix, bleed, be diffused, lose colour ...*The ink had run on the wet paper*...
16 = circulate, spread, creep, go round ...*A buzz of excitement ran through the crowd*...
17 = publish, feature, display, print ...*The paper ran a series of scathing editorials*...
18 = melt, dissolve, liquefy, go soft, turn to liquid ...*The pitch between the planks of the deck melted and ran*...
19 = unravel, tear, ladder, come apart, come undone ...*ladders in your tights gradually running all the way up your leg*...
20 = smuggle, deal in, traffic in, bootleg, ship, sneak ...*I started running guns again*...
NOUN **1** = race, rush, dash, sprint, gallop, jog, spurt ...*a six mile run*...
2 = ride, drive, trip, lift, journey, spin (*informal*), outing, excursion, jaunt, joy ride (*informal*) ...*Take them for a run in the car*...
3 = round, journey ...*doing the morning school run*...
4 = sequence, period, stretch, spell, course, season, round, series, chain, cycle, string, passage, streak ...*Their run of luck is holding*...
5 = type, sort, kind, class, variety, category, order ...*outside the common run of professional athletes*...
6 = tear, rip, ladder, snag ...*She had a huge run in her tights*...
7 = enclosure, pen, coop ...*My mother had a little chicken run*...
8 = direction, way, course, current, movement, progress, flow, path, trend, motion, passage, stream, tendency, drift, tide, tenor ...*The only try came against the run of play*...
9 with **on** = sudden demand for, pressure for, rush for ...*A run on sterling has killed hopes of a rate cut*...
PHRASES **in the long run** = in the end, eventually, in time, ultimately, at the end of the day, in the final analysis, when all is said and done, in the fullness of time ...*Things could get worse in the long run*... ◆ **on**

the run 1 = <u>escaping</u>, fugitive, in flight, at liberty, on the loose, on the lam (*U.S. slang*) ...*The four men still on the run are Rule 43 prisoners*... 2 = <u>in retreat</u>, defeated, fleeing, retreating, running away, falling back, in flight ...*I knew I had him on the run*... 3 = <u>hurrying</u>, hastily, in a hurry, at speed, hurriedly, in a rush, in haste ...*We ate lunch on the run*... ◆ **run across something** or **someone** = <u>meet</u>, encounter, meet with, come across, run into, bump into, come upon, chance upon ...*We ran across some old friends*... ◆ **run away** = <u>flee</u>, escape, take off, bolt, run off, clear out, beat it (*slang*), abscond, decamp, take flight, hook it (*slang*), do a runner (*slang*), scarper (*Brit. slang*), cut and run (*informal*), make a run for it, turn tail, do a bunk (*Brit. slang*), scram (*informal*), fly the coop (*U.S. & Canad. informal*), show a clean pair of heels, skedaddle (*informal*), take a powder (*U.S. & Canad. slang*), take it on the lam (*U.S. & Canad. slang*), take to your heels ...*I ran away from home when I was sixteen*... ◆ **run away with something** or **someone** 1 = <u>abscond with</u>, run off with, elope with ...*She ran away with a man called Allen*... 2 = <u>win easily</u>, walk it (*informal*), romp home, win hands down, win by a mile (*informal*) ...*She ran away with the gold medal*... ◆ **run for it** = <u>flee</u>, fly, escape, take off, bolt, make off, abscond, decamp, take flight, do a runner (*slang*), scarper (*Brit. slang*), cut and run (*informal*), do a bunk (*Brit. slang*), scram (*informal*), fly the coop (*U.S. & Canad. informal*), make a break for it, show a clean pair of heels, skedaddle (*informal*), take a powder (*U.S. & Canad. slang*), take it on the lam (*U.S. & Canad. slang*) ...*Get out, run for it!*... ◆ **run into someone** = <u>meet</u>, encounter, bump into, run across, chance upon, come across or upon ...*He ran into him in the corridor*... ◆ **run into something** 1 = <u>be beset by</u>, encounter, meet with, come across or upon, face, experience, be confronted by, happen on or upon ...*They ran into financial problems*... 2 = <u>collide with</u>, hit, strike, ram, bump into, crash into, dash against ...*The driver ran into a tree*... ◆ **run off** = <u>flee</u>, escape, bolt, run away, clear out, make off, decamp, take flight, hook it (*slang*), do a runner (*slang*), scarper (*Brit. slang*), cut and run (*informal*), turn tail, fly the coop (*U.S. & Canad. informal*), show a clean pair of heels, skedaddle (*informal*), take a powder (*U.S. & Canad. slang*), take it on the lam (*U.S. & Canad. slang*), take to your heels ...*He then ran off towards a nearby underground railway station*... ◆ **run off with someone** = <u>run away with</u>, elope with, abscond with ...*He ran off with a younger woman*... ◆ **run off with something** = <u>steal</u>, take, lift (*informal*), nick (*slang, chiefly Brit.*), pinch (*informal*), swipe (*slang*), run away with, make off with, embezzle, misappropriate, purloin, filch, walk or make off with ...*Who ran off with the money?*... ◆ **run out** 1 = <u>be used up</u>, dry up, give out, peter out, fail, finish, cease, be exhausted ...*Supplies are running out*... 2 = <u>expire</u>, end, terminate ...*the day my visa ran out*... ◆ **run out of something** = <u>exhaust your supply of</u>, be out of, be cleaned out, have no

more, have none left, have no remaining ...*The plane ran out of fuel*... ◆ **run out on someone** (*Informal*) = <u>desert</u>, abandon, strand, run away from, forsake, rat on (*informal*), leave high and dry, leave holding the baby, leave in the lurch ...*You can't run out on your wife and children like that*... ◆ **run over** = <u>overflow</u>, spill over, brim over ...*Water ran over the sides and trickled down on to the floor*... ◆ **run over something** 1 = <u>exceed</u>, overstep, go over the top of, go beyond the bounds of, go over the limit of ...*Phase one has run over budget*... 2 = <u>review</u>, check, survey, examine, go through, go over, run through, rehearse, reiterate ...*Let's run over the instructions again*... ◆ **run over something** or **someone** = <u>knock down</u>, hit, strike, run down, knock over ...*He ran over a six-year-old child*... ◆ **run someone in** (*Informal*) = <u>arrest</u>, apprehend, pull in (*Brit. slang*), take into custody, lift (*slang*), pick up, jail, nail (*informal*), bust (*informal*), collar (*informal*), pinch (*informal*), nab (*informal*), throw in jail, take to jail, feel your collar (*slang*) ...*They had run him in on a petty charge*... ◆ **run someone through** = <u>pierce</u>, stab, spit, transfix, impale, stick ...*He threatened to run him through with his sword*... ◆ **run something** or **someone down** 1 = <u>criticize</u>, denigrate, belittle, revile, knock (*informal*), rubbish (*informal*), put down, slag (off) (*slang*), disparage, decry, vilify, diss (*slang, chiefly U.S.*), defame, bad-mouth (*slang, chiefly U.S. & Canad.*), speak ill of, asperse ...*He was running down state schools*... 2 = <u>downsize</u>, cut, drop, reduce, trim, decrease, cut back, curtail, pare down ...*The property business could be sold or run down*... 3 = <u>knock down</u>, hit, strike, run into, run over, knock over ...*He was in the roadway and I nearly ran him down*... ◆ **run something in** = <u>break in gently</u>, run gently ...*He hardly had the time to run the car in*... ◆ **run something off** = <u>produce</u>, print, duplicate, churn out (*informal*) ...*They ran off some copies for me*... ◆ **run through something** 1 = <u>review</u>, check, survey, examine, go through, look over, run over ...*I ran through the options with him*... 2 = <u>rehearse</u>, read, practise, go over, run over ...*I ran through the handover procedure*... 3 = <u>squander</u>, waste, exhaust, throw away, dissipate, fritter away, spend like water, blow (*slang*) ...*The country had run through its public food stocks*...

runaway ADJECTIVE 1 = <u>easily won</u>, easy, effortless ...*a runaway success*...
2 = <u>out of control</u>, uncontrolled ...*The runaway car careered into a bench*...
3 = <u>escaped</u>, wild, fleeing, loose, fugitive ...*a runaway horse*...
NOUN = <u>fugitive</u>, escaper, refugee, deserter, truant, escapee, absconder ...*a teenage runaway*...

run-down or **rundown** ADJECTIVE 1 = <u>exhausted</u>, weak, tired, drained, fatigued, weary, unhealthy, worn-out, debilitated, below par, under the weather (*informal*), enervated, out of condition, peaky ...*She started to feel run-down last December*... OPPOSITE > fit
2 = <u>dilapidated</u>, broken-down, shabby, worn-out,

seedy, ramshackle, dingy, decrepit, tumbledown …*a run-down block of flats*…
NOUN = summary, review, briefing, résumé, outline, sketch, run-through, synopsis, recap (*informal*), précis …*Here's a rundown of the options*…

run-in (*Informal*) = fight, row, argument, dispute, set-to (*informal*), encounter, brush, confrontation, quarrel, skirmish, tussle, altercation, face-off (*slang*), dust-up (*informal*), contretemps, biffo (*Austral. slang*)

runner 1 = athlete, miler, sprinter, harrier, jogger …*a marathon runner*…
2 = messenger, courier, errand boy, dispatch bearer …*a bookie's runner*…
3 (*Botany*) = stem, shoot, sprout, sprig, offshoot, tendril, stolon (*Botany*) …*strawberry runners*…

running **NOUN** 1 = management, control, administration, direction, conduct, charge, leadership, organization, regulation, supervision, coordination, superintendency …*in charge of the day-to-day running of the party*…
2 = working, performance, operation, functioning, maintenance …*the smooth running of the machine*…
ADJECTIVE 1 = continuous, constant, perpetual, uninterrupted, incessant, unceasing …*The song turned into a running joke between them*…
2 = in succession, together, unbroken, on the trot (*informal*) …*She never seems the same woman two days running*…
3 = flowing, moving, streaming, coursing …*Wash the lentils under cold, running water*…

runny = flowing, liquid, melted, fluid, diluted, watery, streaming, liquefied

run-of-the-mill = ordinary, middling, average, fair, modest, commonplace, common, vanilla (*informal*), mediocre, banal, tolerable, passable, undistinguished, unimpressive, unexciting, unexceptional, bog-standard (*Brit. & Irish slang*), no great shakes (*informal*), dime-a-dozen (*informal*) **OPPOSITE** exceptional

run up *or* **run-up** = time leading up to, approach, build-up, preliminaries

rupture **NOUN** 1 = hernia (*Medical*) …*a rupture of the abdominal aorta*…
2 = breach, split, hostility, falling-out (*informal*), disagreement, contention, feud, disruption, quarrel, rift, break, bust-up (*informal*), dissolution, altercation, schism, estrangement …*a major rupture between the two countries*…
3 = break, tear, split, crack, rent, burst, breach, fracture, cleavage, cleft, fissure …*ruptures in a 60-mile pipeline on the island*…
VERB 1 = break, separate, tear, split, crack, burst, rend, fracture, sever, puncture, cleave …*Tanks can rupture and burn in a collision*…
2 = cause a breach, split, divide, disrupt, break off, come between, dissever …*an accident which ruptured the bond between them*…

rural 1 = agricultural, country, agrarian, upcountry, agrestic …*These plants grow in the more rural areas*…
2 = rustic, country, hick (*informal, chiefly U.S. & Canad.*), pastoral, bucolic, sylvan, Arcadian, countrified …*the old rural way of life*… **OPPOSITE** urban

ruse = trick, deception, ploy, hoax, device, manoeuvre, dodge, sham, artifice, blind, subterfuge, stratagem, wile, imposture

rush **VERB** 1 = hurry, run, race, shoot, fly, career, speed, tear, dash, sprint, scramble, bolt, dart, hasten, scurry, stampede, lose no time, make short work of, burn rubber (*informal*), make haste, hotfoot …*Someone inside the building rushed out*… **OPPOSITE** dawdle
2 = push, hurry, accelerate, dispatch, speed up, quicken, press, hustle, expedite …*The Act was rushed through after a legal loophole was discovered*…
3 = attack, storm, capture, overcome, charge at, take by storm …*They rushed the entrance*…
NOUN 1 = dash, charge, race, scramble, stampede, expedition, speed, dispatch …*The explosion caused panic and a mad rush for the doors*…
2 = hurry, urgency, bustle, haste, hustle, helter-skelter, hastiness …*the rush not to be late for school*…
3 = surge, flood, gush …*A rush of affection swept over him*…
4 = attack, charge, push, storm, assault, surge, onslaught …*Throw something noisy and feign a rush at him*…
ADJECTIVE = hasty, fast, quick, hurried, emergency, prompt, rapid, urgent, swift, brisk, cursory, expeditious …*I guess you could call it a rush job*… **OPPOSITE** leisurely

rust **NOUN** 1 = corrosion, oxidation …*a decaying tractor, red with rust*…
2 = mildew, must, mould, rot, blight …*canker, rust, mildew or insect attack*…
VERB 1 = corrode, tarnish, oxidize …*The bolt on the door had rusted*…
2 = deteriorate, decline, decay, stagnate, atrophy, go stale …*If you rest, you rust*…

rustic **ADJECTIVE** 1 = rural, country, pastoral, bucolic, sylvan, Arcadian, countrified, upcountry, agrestic …*the rustic charms of a country lifestyle*… **OPPOSITE** urban
2 = simple, homely, plain, homespun, unsophisticated, unrefined, artless, unpolished …*wonderfully rustic old log cabins*… **OPPOSITE** grand
NOUN = yokel, peasant, hick (*informal, chiefly U.S. & Canad.*), bumpkin, swain (*archaic*), hillbilly, country boy, clod, boor, country cousin, hayseed (*U.S. & Canad. informal*), clodhopper (*informal*), son of the soil, clown, countryman *or* countrywoman …*rustics in from the country*… **OPPOSITE** sophisticate

rustle **VERB** = crackle, whisper, swish, whoosh, crinkle, whish, crepitate, susurrate (*literary*) …*The leaves rustled in the wind*…
NOUN = crackle, whisper, rustling, crinkling, crepitation, susurration *or* susurrus (*literary*) …*with a rustle of her frilled petticoats*…

rusty 1 = corroded, rusted, oxidized, rust-covered

…travelling around in a rusty old van…

2 = <u>out of practice</u>, weak, impaired, sluggish, stale, deficient, not what it was, unpractised *…Your French is a bit rusty…*

3 = <u>reddish-brown</u>, chestnut, reddish, russet, coppery, rust-coloured *…Her hair was rusty brown…*

4 = <u>croaking</u>, cracked, creaking, hoarse, croaky *…his mild, rusty voice…*

➤ **shades of red**

rut 1 = <u>habit</u>, routine, dead end, humdrum existence, system, pattern, groove *…I don't like being in a rut…*

2 = <u>groove</u>, score, track, trough, furrow, gouge, pothole, indentation, wheel mark *…deep ruts left by the truck's heavy wheels…*

ruthless = <u>merciless</u>, hard, severe, fierce, harsh, cruel, savage, brutal, stern, relentless, adamant, ferocious, callous, heartless, unrelenting, inhuman, inexorable, remorseless, barbarous, pitiless, unfeeling, hard-hearted, without pity, unmerciful, unpitying OPPOSITE> merciful

rutted = <u>grooved</u>, cut, marked, scored, holed, furrowed, gouged, indented

S s

sable NOUN *or* ADJECTIVE **1** = black, jet, raven, jetty, ebony, ebon (*poetic*) …*thick sable lashes*…
➤ **shades from black to white**
2 = dark, black, dim, gloomy, dismal, dreary, sombre, shadowy …*Night enveloped me in its sable mantle*…

sabotage VERB **1** = damage, destroy, wreck, undermine, disable, disrupt, cripple, subvert, incapacitate, vandalize, throw a spanner in the works (*Brit. informal*) …*The main pipeline was sabotaged by rebels*…
2 = disrupt, ruin, wreck, spoil, interrupt, interfere with, obstruct, intrude, crool *or* cruel (*Austral. slang*) …*My ex-wife deliberately sabotages my access to the children*…
NOUN **1** = damage, destruction, wrecking, vandalism, deliberate damage …*The bombing was a spectacular act of sabotage*…
2 = disruption, ruining, wrecking, spoiling, interference, intrusion, interruption, obstruction …*political sabotage of government policy*…

saboteur = demonstrator, rebel, dissident, hooligan, vandal, delinquent, dissenter, agitator, protest marcher

sac = pouch, bag, pocket, bladder, pod, cyst, vesicle

saccharine = sickly, honeyed, sentimental, sugary, nauseating, soppy (*Brit. informal*), cloying, maudlin, syrupy (*informal*), mawkish, icky (*informal*), treacly, oversweet

sack¹ NOUN **1** = bag, pocket, poke (*Scot.*), sac, pouch, receptacle …*A sack of potatoes*…
2 = dismissal, discharge, the boot (*slang*), the axe (*informal*), the chop (*Brit. slang*), the push (*slang*), the (old) heave-ho (*informal*), termination of employment, the order of the boot (*slang*) …*People who make mistakes can be given the sack the same day*…
VERB (*Informal*) = dismiss, fire (*informal*), axe (*informal*), discharge, kick out (*informal*), give (someone) the boot (*slang*), give (someone) his marching orders, kiss off (*slang, chiefly U.S. & Canad.*), give (someone) the push (*informal*), give (someone) the bullet (*Brit. slang*), give (someone) his books (*informal*), give (someone) the elbow, give (someone) his cards …*He was sacked for slapping a schoolboy*…
PHRASES **hit the sack** (*Slang*) = go to bed, retire, turn in (*informal*), bed down, hit the hay (*slang*) …*I hit the sack early*…

sack² VERB = plunder, loot, pillage, destroy, strip, rob, raid, ruin, devastate, spoil, rifle, demolish, ravage, lay waste, despoil, maraud, depredate (*rare*) …*Imperial troops sacked the French ambassador's residence in Rome*…
NOUN = plundering, looting, pillage, waste, rape, ruin, destruction, ravage, plunder, devastation, depredation, despoliation, rapine …*the sack of Troy*…

sacred **1** = holy, hallowed, consecrated, blessed, divine, revered, venerable, sanctified …*shrines and sacred places*… OPPOSITE secular
2 = religious, holy, ecclesiastical, hallowed, venerated …*the awe-inspiring sacred art of the Renaissance masters*… OPPOSITE unconsecrated
3 = inviolable, protected, sacrosanct, secure, hallowed, inalienable, invulnerable, inviolate, unalterable …*My memories are sacred*…

sacrifice VERB **1** = offer, offer up, immolate …*The priest sacrificed a chicken*…
2 = give up, abandon, relinquish, lose, surrender, let go, do without, renounce, forfeit, forego, say goodbye to …*She sacrificed family life when her career took off*…
NOUN **1** = offering, immolation, oblation, hecatomb …*animal sacrifices to the gods*…
2 = surrender, loss, giving up, resignation, rejection, waiver, abdication, renunciation, repudiation, forswearing, relinquishment, eschewal, self-denial …*They have not suffered any sacrifice of identity*…

sacrificial = propitiatory, atoning, reparative, expiatory, oblatory

sacrilege = desecration, violation, blasphemy, mockery, heresy, irreverence, profanity, impiety, profanation, profaneness OPPOSITE reverence

sacrosanct = inviolable, sacred, inviolate, untouchable, hallowed, sanctified, set apart

sad **1** = unhappy, down, low, blue, depressed, gloomy, grieved, dismal, melancholy, sombre, glum, wistful, mournful, dejected, downcast, grief-stricken, tearful, lugubrious, pensive, disconsolate, doleful, heavy-hearted, down in the dumps (*informal*), cheerless, lachrymose, woebegone, down in the mouth (*informal*), low-spirited, triste (*archaic*), sick at heart …*The loss left me feeling sad and empty*…
OPPOSITE happy
2 = tragic, moving, upsetting, dark, sorry, depressing, disastrous, dismal, pathetic, poignant, harrowing, grievous, pitiful, calamitous, heart-rending, pitiable …*the sad news that he had been killed in a motor-cycle accident*…
3 = deplorable, bad, sorry, terrible, distressing, unfortunate, miserable, dismal, shabby, heartbreaking, regrettable, lamentable, wretched, to be deplored …*It's a sad truth that children are the biggest victims of passive smoking*… OPPOSITE good
4 = regrettable, disappointing, distressing, unhappy, unfortunate, unsatisfactory, woeful, deplorable, lamentable …*a sad state of affairs*… OPPOSITE fortunate

sadden = <u>upset</u>, depress, distress, grieve, desolate, cast down, bring tears to your eyes, make sad, dispirit, make your heart bleed, aggrieve, deject, cast a gloom upon

saddle = <u>burden</u>, load, lumber (*Brit. informal*), charge, tax, task, encumber

sadism = <u>cruelty</u>, savagery, brutality, severity, ferocity, spite, ruthlessness, depravity, harshness, inhumanity, barbarity, callousness, viciousness, bestiality, heartlessness, brutishness, spitefulness, bloodthirstiness, murderousness, mercilessness, fiendishness, hardheartedness

sadistic = <u>cruel</u>, savage, brutal, beastly, vicious, ruthless, perverted, perverse, inhuman, barbarous, fiendish

sadness = <u>unhappiness</u>, sorrow, grief, tragedy, depression, the blues, misery, melancholy, poignancy, despondency, bleakness, heavy heart, dejection, wretchedness, gloominess, mournfulness, dolour (*poetic*), dolefulness, cheerlessness, sorrowfulness OPPOSITE> happiness

safe ADJECTIVE 1 = <u>protected</u>, secure, in safety, impregnable, out of danger, safe and sound, in safe hands, out of harm's way, free from harm ...*Keep your camera safe from sand*... OPPOSITE> endangered
2 = <u>all right</u>, fine, intact, unscathed, unhurt, unharmed, undamaged, out of the woods, O.K. *or* okay (*informal*) ...*Where is Sophie? Is she safe?*...
3 = <u>cautious</u>, prudent, sure, conservative, reliable, realistic, discreet, dependable, trustworthy, circumspect, on the safe side, unadventurous, tried and true ...*I shall conceal myself at a safe distance from the battlefield*... OPPOSITE> risky
4 = <u>risk-free</u>, sound, secure, certain, impregnable, riskless ...*We are assured by our engineers that the building is safe*...
5 = <u>harmless</u>, wholesome, innocuous, pure, tame, unpolluted, nontoxic, nonpoisonous ...*a clean, inexpensive and safe fuel*... OPPOSITE> dangerous
NOUN = <u>strongbox</u>, vault, coffer, repository, deposit box, safe-deposit box ...*The files are now in a safe*...
PHRASES **be on the safe side** = <u>be cautious</u>, be careful, be prudent, be alert, be tentative, be circumspect, be judicious, be heedful ...*Let's say two-thirty to be on the safe side*...

safeguard VERB = <u>protect</u>, guard, defend, save, screen, secure, preserve, look after, shield, watch over, keep safe ...*international action to safeguard the ozone layer*...
NOUN = <u>protection</u>, security, defence, guard, shield, armour, aegis, bulwark, surety ...*A system like ours lacks adequate safeguards for civil liberties*...

safe haven = <u>refuge</u>, security, haven, protection, resort, shelter, retreat, harbour, asylum, sanctuary, hide-out, bolt hole

safely = <u>in safety</u>, securely, with impunity, without risk, with safety, safe and sound

safety 1 = <u>security</u>, protection, safeguards, assurance, precautions, immunity, safety measures,

impregnability ...*The report makes recommendations to improve safety on aircraft*... OPPOSITE> risk
2 = <u>shelter</u>, haven, protection, cover, retreat, asylum, refuge, sanctuary ...*the safety of your own home*...

sag 1 = <u>sink</u>, bag, droop, fall, drop, seat (*of skirts, etc.*), settle, slump, dip, give way, bulge, swag, hang loosely, fall unevenly ...*The shirts cuffs won't sag and lose their shape after washing*...
2 = <u>drop</u>, sink, slump, flop, droop, loll ...*He shrugged and sagged into a chair*...
3 = <u>decline</u>, fall, slip, tire, slide, flag, slump, weaken, wilt, wane, cave in, droop ...*Some of the tension he builds up begins to sag*...

saga 1 = <u>carry-on</u> (*informal, chiefly Brit.*), to-do, performance (*informal*), rigmarole, soap opera, pantomime (*informal*) ...*the whole saga of Hoddle's dismissal*...
2 = <u>epic</u>, story, tale, legend, adventure, romance, narrative, chronicle, yarn, fairy tale, folk tale, roman-fleuve (*French*) ...*a Nordic saga of giants and trolls*...

sage NOUN = <u>wise man</u>, philosopher, guru, authority, expert, master, elder, pundit, Solomon, mahatma, Nestor, savant, Solon, man of learning ...*ancient Chinese sages*...
ADJECTIVE = <u>wise</u>, learned, intelligent, sensible, politic, acute, discerning, prudent, canny, judicious, perspicacious, sagacious, sapient ...*He was famous for his sage advice to young painters*...

sail NOUN = <u>sheet</u>, canvas ...*The white sails billow with the breezes they catch*...
VERB 1 = <u>go by water</u>, cruise, voyage, ride the waves, go by sea ...*We sailed upstream*...
2 = <u>set sail</u>, embark, get under way, put to sea, put off, leave port, hoist sail, cast *or* weigh anchor ...*The boat is due to sail tonight*...
3 = <u>pilot</u>, steer, navigate, captain, skipper ...*I shall get myself a little boat and sail her around the world*...
4 = <u>glide</u>, sweep, float, shoot, fly, wing, soar, drift, skim, scud, skirr ...*We got into the lift and sailed to the top floor*...
PHRASES **sail through something** = <u>cruise through</u>, walk through, romp through, pass easily, succeed easily at ...*She sailed through her maths exams*... ◆ **set sail** = <u>put to sea</u>, embark, get under way, put off, leave port, hoist sail, cast *or* weigh anchor ...*He loaded his vessel with another cargo and set sail*...

sailor = <u>mariner</u>, marine, seaman, salt, tar (*informal*), hearty (*informal*), navigator, sea dog, seafarer, matelot (*slang, chiefly Brit.*), Jack Tar, seafaring man, lascar, leatherneck (*slang*)

saint
➤ saints

saintly = <u>virtuous</u>, godly, holy, religious, sainted, blessed, worthy, righteous, devout, pious, angelic, blameless, god-fearing, beatific, sinless, saintlike, full of good works

sake NOUN = <u>purpose</u>, interest, cause, reason, end, aim, principle, objective, motive ...*For the sake of*

Saints

Saint	Feast day	Saint	Feast day
Agatha	5 February	Gilbert of Sempringham	4 February
Agnes	31 January	Giles (cripples, beggars, and lepers)	1 September
Aidan	31 August		
Alban	22 June	Gregory I (the Great)	3 September
Albertus Magnus	15 November	Gregory VII or Hildebrand	25 May
Aloysius (patron saint of youth)	21 June	Gregory of Nazianzus	2 January
Ambrose	7 December	Gregory of Nyssa	9 March
Andrew (Scotland)	30 November	Gregory of Tours	17 November
Anne	26 July	Hilary of Poitiers	13 January
Anselm	21 April	Hildegard of Bingen	17 September
Anthony or Antony	17 January	Helen or Helena	18 August
Anthony or Antony of Padua	13 June	Helier	16 July
Athanasius	2 May	Ignatius	17 October
Augustine of Hippo	28 August	Ignatius of Loyola	31 July
Barnabas	11 June	Isidore of Seville	4 April
Bartholomew	24 August	James	23 October
Basil	2 January	James the Less	3 May
Bede	25 May	Jane Frances de Chantal	12 December
Benedict	11 July	Jerome	30 September
Bernadette of Lourdes	16 April	Joachim	26 July
Bernard of Clairvaux	20 August	Joan of Arc	30 May
Bernard of Menthon	28 May	John	27 December
Bonaventura or Bonaventure	15 July	John Bosco	31 January
Boniface	5 June	John Chrysostom	13 September
Brendan	16 May	John Ogilvie	10 March
Bridget, Bride or Brigid (Ireland)	1 February	John of Damascus	4 December
Bridget or Birgitta (Sweden)	23 July	John of the Cross	14 December
Catherine of Alexandria	25 November	John the Baptist	24 June
Catherine of Siena (the Dominican Order)	29 April	Joseph	19 March
		Joseph of Arimathaea	17 March
Cecilia (music)	22 November	Joseph of Copertino	18 September
Charles Borromeo	4 November	Jude	28 October
Christopher (travellers)	25 July	Justin	1 June
Clare of Assisi	11 August	Kentigern or Mungo	14 January
Clement I	23 November	Kevin	3 June
Clement of Alexandria	5 December	Lawrence	10 August
Columba or Colmcille	9 June	Lawrence O'Toole	14 November
Crispin (shoemakers)	25 October	Leger	2 October
Crispinian (shoemakers)	25 October	Leo I (the Great)	10 November
Cuthbert	20 March	Leo II	3 July
Cyprian	16 September	Leo III	12 June
Cyril	14 February	Leo IV	17 July
Cyril of Alexandria	27 June	Leonard	6 November
David (Wales)	1 March	Lucy	13 December
Denis (France)	9 October	Luke	18 October
Dominic	7 August	Malachy	3 November
Dorothy	6 February	Margaret	20 July
Dunstan	19 May	Margaret of Scotland	10 June, 16 November (in Scotland)
Edmund	20 November		
Edward the Confessor	13 October		
Edward the Martyr	18 March	Maria Goretti	6 July
Elizabeth	5 November	Mark	25 April
Elizabeth of Hungary	17 November	Martha	29 July
Elmo	2 June	Martin de Porres	3 November
Ethelbert or Æthelbert	25 February	Martin of Tours (France)	11 November
Francis of Assisi	4 October	Mary	15 August
Francis of Sales	24 January	Mary Magdalene	22 July
Francis Xavier	3 December	Matthew or Levi	21 September
Geneviève (Paris)	3 January	Matthias	14 May
George (England)	23 April	Methodius	14 February
Gertrude	16 November	Michael	29 September

Saints (continued)

Saint	Feast day	Saint	Feast day
Neot	31 July	Simon Zelotes	28 October
Nicholas (Russia, children, sailors, merchants, and pawnbrokers)	6 December	Stanislaw *or* Stanislaus (Poland)	11 April
		Stanislaus Kostka	13 November
		Stephen	26 *or* 27 December
Nicholas I (the Great)	13 November		
Ninian	16 September	Stephen of Hungary	16 *or* 20 August
Olaf *or* Olav (Norway)	29 July	Swithin *or* Swithun	15 July
Oliver Plunket *or* Plunkett	1 July	Teresa *or* Theresa of Avila	15 October
Oswald	28 February	Thérèse de Lisieux	1 October
Pachomius	14 May	Thomas	3 July
Patrick (Ireland)	17 March	Thomas à Becket	29 December
Paul	29 June	Thomas Aquinas	28 January
Paulinus	10 October	Thomas More	22 June
Paulinus of Nola	22 June	Timothy	26 January
Peter *or* Simon Peter	29 June	Titus	26 January
Philip	3 May	Ursula	21 October
Philip Neri	26 May	Valentine	14 February
Pius V	30 April	Veronica	12 July
Pius X	21 August	Vincent de Paul	27 September
Polycarp	26 January *or* 23 February	Vitus	15 June
		Vladimir	15 July
Rose of Lima	23 August	Wenceslaus *or* Wenceslas	28 September
Sebastian	20 January	Wilfrid	12 October
Silas	13 July		

historical accuracy, permit us to state the true facts...

PHRASES **for someone's sake** = <u>in someone's interests</u>, to someone's advantage, on someone's account, for the benefit of, for the good of, for the welfare of, out of respect for, out of consideration for, out of regard for ...*I trust you to do a good job for Stan's sake...*

salacious = <u>obscene</u>, indecent, pornographic, blue, erotic, steamy (*informal*), lewd, X-rated (*informal*), bawdy, smutty, lustful, ribald, ruttish

salary = <u>pay</u>, income, wage, fee, payment, wages, earnings, allowance, remuneration, recompense, stipend, emolument

sale **NOUN** 1 = <u>selling</u>, marketing, dealing, trading, transaction, disposal, vending ...*Efforts were made to limit the sale of alcohol...*
2 = <u>auction</u>, fair, mart, bazaar ...*The Old Master was bought at the Christie's sale...*
PHRASES **for sale** = <u>available to buy</u>, on sale, on offer, on the market, in stock, obtainable ...*His former home is for sale...* ◆ **on sale** = <u>going cheap</u>, reduced, at a discount, at a reduced price ...*He bought a sports jacket on sale at the shop...*

salient = <u>prominent</u>, outstanding, important, marked, striking, arresting, signal, remarkable, pronounced, noticeable, conspicuous

saliva = <u>spit</u>, dribble, drool, slaver, spittle, sputum

sallow = <u>wan</u>, pale, sickly, pasty, pallid, unhealthy, yellowish, anaemic, bilious, jaundiced-looking, peely-wally (*Scot.*) **OPPOSITE** rosy

sally **NOUN** = <u>witticism</u>, joke, quip, crack (*informal*), retort, jest, riposte, wisecrack (*informal*), bon mot, smart remark ...*He had thus far succeeded in fending*

off my conversational sallies...

VERB = <u>go forth</u>, set out, rush, issue, surge, erupt ...*She would sally out on a bitter night to keep her appointments...*

salon 1 = <u>shop</u>, store, establishment, parlour, boutique ...*a beauty salon...*
2 = <u>sitting room</u>, lounge, living room, parlour, drawing room, front room, reception room, morning room ...*His apartment was the most famous literary salon in Russia...*

salt **NOUN** 1 = <u>seasoning</u>, sodium chloride, table salt, rock salt ...*a pinch of salt...*
2 = <u>sailor</u>, marine, seaman, mariner, tar (*informal*), hearty (*informal*), navigator, sea dog, seafarer, matelot (*slang, chiefly Brit.*), Jack Tar, seafaring man, lascar, leatherneck (*slang*) ...*'Did he look like an old sea salt?' I asked, laughing...*
ADJECTIVE = <u>salty</u>, salted, saline, brackish, briny ...*Put a pan of salt water on to boil...*
PHRASES **rub salt into the wound** = <u>make something worse</u>, add insult to injury, fan the flames, aggravate matters, magnify a problem ...*I had no intention of rubbing salt into his wounds...* ◆ **with a grain** *or* **pinch of salt** = <u>sceptically</u>, suspiciously, cynically, doubtfully, with reservations, disbelievingly, mistrustfully ...*You have to take these findings with a pinch of salt...*

salty = <u>salt</u>, salted, saline, brackish, briny, over-salted, brak (*S. African*)

salubrious 1 = <u>healthy</u>, beneficial, good for you, wholesome, invigorating, salutary, healthful, health-giving ...*your salubrious lochside hotel...*
2 = <u>agreeable</u>, respectable, grand, pleasant, nice, posh

(*informal*), luxurious, classy, upmarket, high-class, glitzy, swanky ...*London's less salubrious quarters...*

salutary = <u>beneficial</u>, useful, valuable, helpful, profitable, good, practical, good for you, advantageous

salute VERB 1 = <u>greet</u>, welcome, acknowledge, address, kiss, hail, salaam, accost, pay your respects to, doff your cap to ...*He stepped out and saluted the general...*
2 = <u>honour</u>, acknowledge, recognize, take your hat off to (*informal*), pay tribute or homage to ...*The statement salutes the changes of the past year...*
NOUN 1 = <u>greeting</u>, recognition, salutation, address, kiss, salaam, obeisance ...*He raised his hand in salute...*
2 = <u>homage</u>, recognition, tribute, toast, compliment, testimonial, acknowledgment, eulogy ...*a special salute to her for her protest...*

salvage VERB = <u>save</u>, recover, rescue, restore, repair, get back, retrieve, redeem, glean, repossess, fetch back ...*They studied flight recorders salvaged from the wreckage...*
NOUN 1 = <u>rescue</u>, saving, recovery, release, relief, liberation, salvation, deliverance, extrication ...*The salvage of the ship went on...*
2 = <u>scrap</u>, remains, waste, junk, offcuts ...*They climbed up on the rock with their salvage...*

salvation 1 = <u>saving</u>, rescue, recovery, restoration, salvage, redemption, deliverance ...*those whose marriages are beyond salvation...* OPPOSITE ruin
2 = <u>lifeline</u>, escape, relief, preservation ...*I consider books my salvation...*

salve VERB = <u>ease</u>, soothe, appease, still, allay, pacify, mollify, tranquillize, palliate ...*I give myself treats and justify them to salve my conscience...*
NOUN = <u>balm</u>, cream, medication, lotion, lubricant, ointment, emollient, liniment, dressing, unguent ...*a soothing salve for sore, dry lips...*

salvo = <u>barrage</u>, storm, bombardment, strafe, cannonade

same ADJECTIVE 1 = <u>identical</u>, similar, alike, equal, twin, equivalent, corresponding, comparable, duplicate, indistinguishable, interchangeable ...*The houses were all the same...* OPPOSITE different
2 = <u>the very same</u>, very, one and the same, selfsame ...*Bernard works at the same institution as Arlette...*
3 = <u>aforementioned</u>, aforesaid, selfsame ...*Wrist watches: £5. Inscription of same: £25...*
4 = <u>unchanged</u>, consistent, constant, uniform, unaltered, unfailing, invariable, unvarying, changeless ...*Always taking the ingredients from here means the beers stay the same...* OPPOSITE altered
PHRASES **all the same** 1 = <u>nevertheless</u>, still, regardless, nonetheless, after all, in any case, for all that, notwithstanding, in any event, anyhow, just the same, be that as it may ...*She didn't understand the joke but laughed all the same...* 2 = <u>unimportant</u>, insignificant, immaterial, inconsequential, of no consequence, of little account, not worth mentioning

...*It's all the same to me whether he goes or not...*

> ## Word Power
>
> **same** –The use of *same* as in *if you send us your order for the materials, we will deliver same tomorrow* is common in business and official English. In general English, however, this use of the word is best avoided, as it may sound rather stilted: *may I borrow your book? I will return it* (not *same*) *tomorrow.*

sameness = <u>similarity</u>, resemblance, uniformity, likeness, oneness, standardization, indistinguishability, identicalness

sample NOUN 1 = <u>specimen</u>, example, model, pattern, instance, representative, indication, illustration, exemplification ...*We're giving away 2000 free samples...*
2 = <u>cross section</u>, test, sampling ...*We based our analysis on a random sample of more than 200 males...*
VERB = <u>test</u>, try, check out (*informal*), experience, taste, examine, evaluate, inspect, experiment with, appraise, partake of ...*We sampled a selection of different bottled waters...*
ADJECTIVE 1 = <u>test</u>, trial, specimen, representative, pilot, illustrative ...*Nearly 65 per cent of the sample population agreed with this statement...*
2 = <u>specimen</u>, test, trial, pilot, dummy ...*Let's go through one more sample study to make sure you understand...*

sanctify 1 = <u>consecrate</u>, bless, anoint, set apart, hallow, make sacred ...*Their marriage has not been sanctified in a Christian church...*
2 = <u>cleanse</u>, redeem, purify, absolve ...*May the God of peace sanctify you entirely...*

sanctimonious = <u>pious</u>, smug, hypocritical, pi (*Brit. slang*), too good to be true, self-righteous, self-satisfied, goody-goody (*informal*), unctuous, holier-than-thou, priggish, pietistic, canting, pharisaical

sanction VERB 1 = <u>permit</u>, back, support, allow, approve, entitle, endorse, authorize, countenance, vouch for, lend your name to ...*He may seem ready to sanction the use of force...* OPPOSITE forbid
2 = <u>punish</u>, discipline, penalize, chastise, bring to book, slap someone's wrist, throw the book at, rap someone's knuckles ...*failure to sanction countries for butchering whales...*
NOUN 1 *often plural* = <u>ban</u>, restriction, boycott, embargo, exclusion, penalty, deterrent, prohibition, coercive measures ...*He expressed his opposition to lifting the sanctions...* OPPOSITE permission
2 = <u>permission</u>, backing, support, authority, approval, allowance, confirmation, endorsement, countenance, ratification, authorization, approbation, O.K. *or* okay (*informal*), stamp *or* seal of approval ...*The king could not enact laws without the sanction of parliament...* OPPOSITE ban

sanctity = <u>sacredness</u>, inviolability, inalienability, hallowedness, sacrosanctness

sanctuary 1 = <u>protection</u>, shelter, refuge, haven, retreat, asylum …*Some of them have sought sanctuary in the church*…
2 = <u>reserve</u>, park, preserve, reservation, national park, tract, nature reserve, conservation area …*a bird sanctuary*…

sanctum 1 = <u>refuge</u>, retreat, den, private room …*His bedroom is his inner sanctum*…
2 = <u>sanctuary</u>, shrine, altar, holy place, Holy of Holies …*the inner sanctum of the mosque*…

sand VERB = <u>smooth</u>, file, scrape, scour, wear down, grind down, wear away, abrade …*Sand the surface softly and carefully*…
PLURAL NOUN = <u>beach</u>, shore, strand (*literary*), dunes …*miles of golden sands*…

sane 1 = <u>rational</u>, normal, all there (*informal*), lucid, of sound mind, compos mentis (*Latin*), in your right mind, mentally sound, in possession of all your faculties …*He seemed perfectly sane*… OPPOSITE insane
2 = <u>sensible</u>, sound, reasonable, balanced, moderate, sober, judicious, level-headed …*a sane and safe energy policy*… OPPOSITE foolish

sanguine = <u>cheerful</u>, confident, optimistic, assured, hopeful, buoyant, in good heart OPPOSITE gloomy

sanitary = <u>hygienic</u>, clean, healthy, wholesome, salubrious, unpolluted, germ-free

sanitation = <u>hygiene</u>, cleanliness, sewerage

sanity 1 = <u>mental health</u>, reason, rationality, stability, normality, right mind (*informal*), saneness …*He and his wife finally had to move, just to preserve their sanity*… OPPOSITE insanity
2 = <u>common sense</u>, sense, good sense, rationality, level-headedness, judiciousness, soundness of judgment …*He's been looking at ways of introducing some sanity into the market*… OPPOSITE stupidity

sap¹ 1 = <u>juice</u>, essence, vital fluid, secretion, lifeblood, plant fluid …*The leaves, bark and sap are common ingredients of herbal remedies*…
2 (*Slang*) = <u>fool</u>, jerk (*slang, chiefly U.S. & Canad.*), idiot, noodle, wally (*slang*), wet (*Brit. informal*), charlie (*Brit. informal*), drip (*informal*), gull (*archaic*), prat (*slang*), plonker (*slang*), noddy, twit (*informal*), chump (*informal*), oaf, simpleton, nitwit (*informal*), ninny, nincompoop, dweeb (*U.S. slang*) (*U.S. slang*), wuss (*slang*), Simple Simon, weenie (*U.S. informal*), muggins (*Brit. slang*), eejit (*Scot. & Irish*), dumb-ass (*slang*), numpty (*Scot. informal*), doofus (*slang, chiefly U.S.*), nerd *or* nurd (*slang*), numskull *or* numbskull, dorba *or* dorb (*Austral. slang*), bogan (*Austral. slang*) …*her poor sap of a husband*…

sap² = <u>weaken</u>, drain, undermine, rob, exhaust, bleed, erode, deplete, wear down, enervate, devitalize …*I was afraid the sickness had sapped my strength*…

sarcasm = <u>irony</u>, satire, cynicism, contempt, ridicule, bitterness, scorn, sneering, mockery, venom, derision, vitriol, mordancy, causticness

sarcastic = <u>ironical</u>, cynical, satirical, cutting, biting, sharp, acid, mocking, taunting, sneering, acrimonious, backhanded, contemptuous, disparaging, sardonic, caustic, bitchy (*informal*), vitriolic, acerbic, derisive, ironic, mordant, sarky (*Brit. informal*), mordacious, acerb

sardonic = <u>mocking</u>, cynical, dry, bitter, sneering, jeering, malicious, wry, sarcastic, derisive, ironical, mordant, mordacious

sash = <u>belt</u>, girdle, waistband, cummerbund

Satan = <u>The Devil</u>, Lucifer, Prince of Darkness, Lord of the Flies, Mephistopheles, Beelzebub, Old Nick (*informal*), The Evil One, Apollyon, Old Scratch (*informal*)

satanic = <u>evil</u>, demonic, hellish, black, malignant, wicked, inhuman, malevolent, devilish, infernal, fiendish, accursed, iniquitous, diabolic, demoniac, demoniacal OPPOSITE godly

sated = <u>satisfied</u>, satiated, slaked, indulged to the full

satellite 1 = <u>spacecraft</u>, communications satellite, sputnik, space capsule …*The rocket launched two satellites*…
2 = <u>moon</u>, secondary planet …*the satellites of Jupiter*…

satire 1 = <u>mockery</u>, wit, irony, ridicule, sarcasm …*It's an easy target for satire*…
2 = <u>parody</u>, mockery, caricature, send-up (*Brit. informal*), spoof (*informal*), travesty, takeoff (*informal*), lampoon, skit, burlesque …*A sharp satire on the American political process*…

satirical *or* **satiric** = <u>mocking</u>, ironical, cynical, cutting, biting, bitter, taunting, pungent, incisive, sarcastic, sardonic, caustic, vitriolic, burlesque, mordant, Rabelaisian, mordacious

satisfaction 1 = <u>fulfilment</u>, pleasure, achievement, joy, relish, glee, gratification, pride, complacency …*She felt a small glow of satisfaction*… OPPOSITE dissatisfaction
2 = <u>compensation</u>, damages, justice, amends, settlement, redress, remuneration, reparation, vindication, restitution, reimbursement, atonement, recompense, indemnification, requital …*Buyers have the right to go to court and demand satifaction*… OPPOSITE injury
3 = <u>contentment</u>, content, comfort, ease, pleasure, well-being, happiness, enjoyment, peace of mind, gratification, satiety, repletion, contentedness …*a state of satisfaction*… OPPOSITE discontent

satisfactory = <u>adequate</u>, acceptable, good enough, average, fair, all right, suitable, sufficient, competent, up to scratch, passable, up to standard, up to the mark OPPOSITE unsatisfactory

satisfied 1 = <u>contented</u>, happy, content, pacified, pleased …*our satisfied customers*… OPPOSITE dissatisfied
2 = <u>smug</u>, complacent, like the cat that swallowed the canary (*informal*), pleased …*a satisfied look*…
3 = <u>sure</u>, smug, convinced, positive, easy in your mind …*People must be satisfied that the treatment is safe*…

satisfy 1 = <u>content</u>, please, indulge, fill, feed,

appease, gratify, pander to, assuage, pacify, quench, mollify, surfeit, satiate, slake, sate …*The pace of change has not been quick enough to satisfy everyone*… OPPOSITE dissatisfy
2 = convince, persuade, assure, reassure, dispel (someone's) doubts, put (someone's) mind at rest …*He has to satisfy us that real progress will be made*… OPPOSITE dissuade
3 = comply with, meet, fulfil, answer, serve, fill, observe, obey, conform to …*The procedures should satisfy certain basic requirements*… OPPOSITE fail to meet

satisfying = satisfactory, pleasing, gratifying, pleasurable, cheering

saturate 1 = flood, overwhelm, swamp, overrun, deluge, glut …*Both sides are saturating the airwaves*…
2 = soak, steep, drench, seep, imbue, douse, impregnate, suffuse, ret (*used of flax, etc.*), wet through, waterlog, souse, drouk (*Scot.*) …*If the filter has been saturated with motor oil, discard it*…

saturated = soaked, soaking (wet), drenched, sodden, dripping, waterlogged, sopping (wet), wet through, soaked to the skin, wringing wet, droukit *or* drookit (*Scot.*)

sauce = dressing, dip, relish, condiment

saucy = impudent, cheeky (*informal*), impertinent, forward, fresh (*informal*), flip (*informal*), rude, sassy (*U.S. informal*), pert, disrespectful, flippant, presumptuous, insolent, lippy (*U.S. & Canad. slang*), smart-alecky (*informal*)

saunter VERB = stroll, wander, amble, roam, ramble, meander, rove, take a stroll, mosey (*informal*), stravaig (*Scot. & Northern English dialect*) …*We watched our fellow students saunter into the building*…
NOUN = stroll, walk, amble, turn, airing, constitutional, ramble, promenade, breather, perambulation …*She began a slow saunter towards the bonfire*…

savage ADJECTIVE **1** = cruel, brutal, vicious, bloody, fierce, harsh, beastly, ruthless, ferocious, murderous, ravening, sadistic, inhuman, merciless, diabolical, brutish, devilish, bloodthirsty, barbarous, pitiless, bestial …*This was a savage attack on a defenceless young girl*… OPPOSITE gentle
2 = wild, fierce, ferocious, unbroken, feral, untamed, undomesticated …*a strange and savage animal encountered at the zoo*… OPPOSITE tame
3 = primitive, undeveloped, uncultivated, uncivilized, in a state of nature, nonliterate …*a savage people*…
4 = uncultivated, rugged, unspoilt, uninhabited, waste, rough, uncivilized, unfrequented …*stunning images of a wild and savage land*… OPPOSITE cultivated
NOUN **1** = native, barbarian, heathen, indigene, primitive person, autochthon …*a frozen desert peopled by uncouth savages*…
2 = lout, yob (*Brit. slang*), brute, bear, monster, beast, barbarian, fiend, yahoo, hoon (*Austral. & N.Z.*), yobbo (*Brit. slang*), roughneck (*slang*), boor, cougan (*Austral.*

slang), scozza (*Austral. slang*), bogan (*Austral. slang*) …*Our orchestra is a bunch of savages*…
VERB **1** = maul, tear, claw, attack, mangle, lacerate, mangulate (*Austral. slang*) …*The animal turned on him and he was savaged to death*…
2 = criticize, attack, knock (*informal*), blast, pan (*informal*), slam (*slang*), put down, slate (*informal*), have a go (at) (*informal*), disparage, tear into (*informal*), find fault with, lambast(e), pick holes in, pick to pieces, give (someone *or* something) a bad press …*The show had already been savaged by the critics*… OPPOSITE praise

savagery = cruelty, brutality, ferocity, ruthlessness, sadism, inhumanity, barbarity, viciousness, bestiality, fierceness, bloodthirstiness

save 1 = rescue, free, release, deliver, recover, get out, liberate, salvage, redeem, bail out, come to someone's rescue, set free, save the life of, extricate, save someone's bacon (*British informal*) …*She could have saved him from this final disaster*… OPPOSITE endanger
2 = keep, reserve, set aside, store, collect, gather, hold, hoard, hide away, lay by, put by, salt away, treasure up, keep up your sleeve (*informal*), put aside for a rainy day …*I thought we were saving money for a holiday*… OPPOSITE spend
3 = protect, keep, guard, preserve, look after, take care of, safeguard, salvage, conserve, keep safe …*a final attempt to save 40,000 jobs*…
4 = budget, be economical, economize, scrimp and save, retrench, be frugal, make economies, be thrifty, tighten your belt (*informal*) …*The majority of people intend to save*…
5 = put aside, keep, reserve, collect, retain, set aside, amass, put by …*Scraps of material were saved, cut up and pieced together for quilts*…
6 = prevent, avoid, spare, rule out, avert, obviate …*This will save the expense and trouble of buying two pairs*…

saving NOUN = economy, discount, reduction, bargain, cut …*Use these vouchers for some great savings on holidays*…
PLURAL NOUN = nest egg, fund, store, reserves, resources, fall-back, provision for a rainy day …*Many people lost all their savings when the bank collapsed*…

saviour = rescuer, deliverer, defender, guardian, salvation, protector, liberator, Good Samaritan, redeemer, preserver, knight in shining armour, friend in need

Saviour = Christ, Jesus, the Messiah, the Redeemer

savour VERB **1** = relish, like, delight in, revel in, luxuriate in, gloat over …*We won't pretend we savour the prospect of a month in prison*…
2 = enjoy, appreciate, relish, delight in, revel in, partake of, drool over, luxuriate in, enjoy to the full, smack your lips over …*Savour the flavour of each mouthful*…
NOUN **1** = flavour, taste, smell, relish, smack, zest, tang, zing (*informal*), piquancy …*The rich savour of the

beans give this dish its character...

2 = <u>zest</u>, interest, spice, excitement, salt, flavour ...*Life without Anna had no savour...*

savoury ADJECTIVE **1** = <u>spicy</u>, rich, delicious, tasty, luscious, palatable, tangy, dainty, delectable, mouthwatering, piquant, full-flavoured, scrumptious (*informal*), appetizing, toothsome, yummo (*Austral. slang*) ...*Italian cooking is best known for its savoury dishes...* OPPOSITE tasteless

2 = <u>wholesome</u>, decent, respectable, honest, reputable, apple-pie (*informal*) ...*He does not have a particularly savoury reputation...* OPPOSITE disreputable

PLURAL NOUN = <u>appetizers</u>, nibbles, apéritifs, canapés, titbits, hors d'oeuvres ...*I'll make some cheese straws or savouries...*

savvy (*Slang*) NOUN = <u>understanding</u>, perception, grasp, ken, comprehension, apprehension ...*He is known for his political savvy...*

ADJECTIVE = <u>shrewd</u>, sharp, astute, knowing, fly (*slang*), keen, smart, clever, intelligent, discriminating, discerning, canny, perceptive, artful, far-sighted, far-seeing, long-headed, perspicacious, sagacious ...*She was a pretty savvy woman...*

say VERB **1** = <u>state</u>, declare, remark, add, announce, maintain, mention, assert, affirm, asseverate ...*She said she was very impressed...*

2 = <u>speak</u>, utter, voice, express, pronounce, come out with (*informal*), put into words, give voice *or* utterance to ...*I hope you didn't say anything about me...*

3 = <u>make known</u>, reveal, disclose, divulge, answer, reply, respond, give as your opinion ...*I must say that that rather shocked me, too...*

4 = <u>read</u>, show, display, indicate ...*The clock said four minutes past eleven...*

5 = <u>suggest</u>, express, imply, communicate, disclose, give away, convey, divulge ...*That says a lot about the power of their marketing people...*

6 = <u>suppose</u>, supposing, imagine, assume, presume ...*Say you lived in Boston, Massachusetts...*

7 = <u>estimate</u>, suppose, guess, conjecture, surmise, dare say, hazard a guess ...*I'd say she must be at least a size 20...*

8 = <u>recite</u>, perform, deliver, do, read, repeat, render, rehearse, orate ...*How am I going to go on and say those lines tonight?...*

9 = <u>allege</u>, report, claim, hold, suggest, insist, maintain, rumour, assert, uphold, profess, put about that ...*He says he did it after the police pressured him...*

NOUN **1** = <u>influence</u>, power, control, authority, weight, sway, clout (*informal*), predominance, mana (*N.Z.*) ...*The students wanted more say in the running of the university...*

2 = <u>chance to speak</u>, vote, voice, crack (*informal*), opportunity to speak, turn to speak ...*Let him have his say...*

PHRASES **to say the least** = <u>at the very least</u>, without any exaggeration, to put it mildly ...*The*

result was, to say the least, fascinating...

saying NOUN = <u>proverb</u>, maxim, adage, saw, slogan, gnome, dictum, axiom, aphorism, byword, apophthegm ...*that old saying: 'Charity begins at home'...*

PHRASES **go without saying** = <u>be obvious</u>, be understood, be taken for granted, be accepted, be self-evident, be taken as read, be a matter of course ...*It should go without saying that you shouldn't smoke...*

say-so (*Informal*) = <u>assertion</u>, authority, agreement, word, guarantee, sanction, permission, consent, assurance, assent, authorization, dictum, asseveration, O.K. *or* okay (*informal*)

scalding = <u>burning</u>, boiling, searing, blistering, piping hot

scale¹ = <u>flake</u>, plate, layer, lamina ...*a thing with scales all over its body...*

scale² NOUN **1** = <u>degree</u>, size, range, spread, extent, dimensions, scope, magnitude, breadth ...*He underestimates the scale of the problem...*

2 = <u>system of measurement</u>, register, measuring system, graduated system, calibration, calibrated system ...*an earthquake measuring five-point-five on the Richter scale...*

3 = <u>ranking</u>, ladder, spectrum, hierarchy, series, sequence, progression, pecking order (*informal*) ...*This has become a reality for increasing numbers across the social scale...*

4 = <u>ratio</u>, proportion, relative size ...*The map, on a scale of 1:10,000, shows over 5,000 individual paths...*

VERB = <u>climb up</u>, mount, go up, ascend, surmount, scramble up, clamber up, escalade ...*The men scaled a wall and climbed down scaffolding on the other side...*

PHRASES **scale something down** = <u>reduce</u>, cut, moderate, slow down, cut down, wind down, tone down, downsize ...*The air rescue operation has now been scaled down...* ◆ **scale something up** = <u>expand</u>, extend, blow up, enlarge, lengthen, magnify, amplify, augment ...*Simply scaling up a size 10 garment often leads to disaster...*

scaly 1 = <u>squamous</u>, squamate, lamellose, lamelliform ...*The brown rat has prominent ears and a long scaly tail...*

2 = <u>flaky</u>, scabrous, scurfy, furfuraceous (*Medical*), squamous *or* squamose (*Biology*), squamulose ...*If your skin becomes red, sore or very scaly, consult your doctor...*

scam (*Slang*) = <u>swindle</u>, fiddle, racket, stratagem, diddle

scamper = <u>run</u>, dash, dart, fly, hurry, sprint, romp, beetle, hasten, scuttle, scurry, scoot

scan VERB **1** = <u>glance over</u>, skim, look over, eye, check, clock (*Brit. slang*), examine, check out (*informal*), run over, eyeball (*slang*), size up (*informal*), get a load of (*informal*), look someone up and down, run your eye over, take a dekko at (*Brit. slang*) ...*She scanned the advertisement pages of the newspaper...*

2 = <u>survey</u>, search, investigate, sweep, con (*archaic*), scour, scrutinize, take stock of, recce (*slang*) ...*The officer scanned the room...*

NOUN 1 = <u>look</u>, glance, skim, browse, flick, squint, butcher's (*Brit. slang*), brief look, dekko (*Brit. slang*), shufti (*Brit. slang*) ...*I've had a quick scan through your book again...*

2 = <u>examination</u>, scanning, ultrasound ...*He was rushed to hospital for a brain scan...*

scandal 1 = <u>disgrace</u>, crime, offence, sin, embarrassment, wrongdoing, skeleton in the cupboard, dishonourable behaviour, discreditable behaviour ...*a financial scandal...*

2 = <u>gossip</u>, talk, rumours, dirt, slander, tattle, dirty linen (*informal*), calumny, backbiting, aspersion ...*He loved gossip and scandal...*

3 = <u>shame</u>, offence, disgrace, stigma, infamy, opprobrium, obloquy ...*She braved the scandal of her husband's love child...*

4 = <u>outrage</u>, shame, insult, disgrace, injustice, crying shame ...*It is a scandal that a person can be stopped for no reason by the police...*

scandalous 1 = <u>shocking</u>, disgraceful, outrageous, offensive, appalling, foul, dreadful, horrifying, obscene, monstrous, unspeakable, atrocious, frightful, abominable ...*They would be sacked for criminal or scandalous behaviour...* **OPPOSITE** decent

2 = <u>slanderous</u>, gossiping, scurrilous, untrue, defamatory, libellous ...*Newspaper columns were full of scandalous tales...* **OPPOSITE** laudatory

3 = <u>outrageous</u>, shocking, infamous, disgraceful, monstrous, shameful, atrocious, unseemly, odious, disreputable, opprobrious, highly improper ...*a scandalous waste of money...* **OPPOSITE** proper

scant 1 = <u>inadequate</u>, insufficient, meagre, sparse, little, limited, bare, minimal, deficient, barely sufficient ...*There is scant evidence of strong economic growth to come...* **OPPOSITE** adequate

2 = <u>small</u>, limited, inadequate, insufficient, meagre, measly, scanty, inconsiderable ...*The hole was a scant 0.23 inches in diameter...*

scanty 1 = <u>meagre</u>, sparse, poor, thin, narrow, sparing, restricted, bare, inadequate, pathetic, insufficient, slender, scant, deficient, exiguous ...*So far, what scanty evidence we have points to two subjects...*

2 = <u>skimpy</u>, short, brief, tight, thin ...*a model in scanty clothing...*

scapegoat = <u>fall guy</u> (*informal*), whipping boy

scar **NOUN** 1 = <u>mark</u>, injury, wound, trauma (*Pathology*), blemish, cicatrix ...*He had a scar on his forehead...*

2 = <u>trauma</u>, suffering, pain, strain, torture, disturbance, anguish ...*emotional scars that come from having been abused...*

VERB 1 = <u>mark</u>, disfigure, damage, brand, mar, mutilate, maim, blemish, deface, traumatize, disfeature ...*He was scarred for life during a pub fight...*

2 = <u>damage</u>, ruin, mar, spoil, mutilate, deface ...*The*

table top was scarred and dented...

3 = <u>traumatize</u>, distress, afflict, worry, trouble, pain, wound, upset, bother, disturb, torment, harrow, agonize ...*This is something that is going to scar him forever...*

scarce 1 = <u>in short supply</u>, wanting, insufficient, deficient, at a premium, thin on the ground ...*Food was scarce and expensive...* **OPPOSITE** plentiful

2 = <u>rare</u>, few, unusual, uncommon, few and far between, infrequent, thin on the ground ...*I'm unemployed, so luxuries are scarce...* **OPPOSITE** common

scarcely 1 = <u>hardly</u>, barely, only just, scarce (*archaic*) ...*He could scarcely breathe...*

2 (*Often used ironically*) = <u>by no means</u>, hardly, not at all, definitely not, under no circumstances, on no account ...*It can scarcely be coincidence...*

3 = <u>rarely</u>, seldom, not often, infrequently, occasionally, once in a blue moon (*informal*), hardly ever ...*I scarcely ever re-read my published writings...*

> ## *Word Power*
>
> **scarcely** – Since *scarcely*, *hardly*, and *barely* already have negative force, it is unnecessary to use another negative word with them. Therefore, say *he had hardly had time to think* (not *he hadn't hardly had time to think*); and *there was scarcely any bread left* (not *there was scarcely no bread left*). When *scarcely*, *hardly*, and *barely* are used at the beginning of a sentence, as in *scarcely had I arrived*, the following clause should start with *when*: *scarcely had I arrived when I was asked to chair a meeting*. The word *before* can be used in place of *when* in this context, but the word *than* used in the same way is considered incorrect by many people, though this use is becoming increasingly common.

scarcity = <u>shortage</u>, lack, deficiency, poverty, want, dearth, paucity, insufficiency, infrequency, undersupply, rareness **OPPOSITE** abundance

scare **VERB** = <u>frighten</u>, alarm, terrify, panic, shock, startle, intimidate, dismay, daunt, terrorize, put the wind up (someone) (*informal*), give (someone) a fright, give (someone) a turn (*informal*), affright (*archaic*) ...*She's just trying to scare me...*

NOUN 1 = <u>fright</u>, shock, start ...*We got a bit of a scare...*

2 = <u>panic</u>, hysteria ...*the doctor at the centre of an Aids scare...*

3 = <u>alert</u>, warning, alarm ...*a security scare over a suspect package...*

scared = <u>afraid</u>, alarmed, frightened, terrified, shaken, cowed, startled, fearful, unnerved, petrified, panicky, terrorized, panic-stricken, scared stiff, terror-stricken

scarf = <u>muffler</u>, stole, headscarf, comforter, cravat, neckerchief, headsquare

scary (*Informal*) = <u>frightening</u>, alarming, terrifying, shocking, chilling, horrifying, intimidating, horrendous, hairy (*slang*), unnerving, spooky (*informal*), creepy (*informal*), hair-raising, spine-chilling, bloodcurdling

scathing = <u>critical</u>, cutting, biting, harsh, savage, brutal, searing, withering, belittling, sarcastic, caustic, scornful, vitriolic, trenchant, mordant, mordacious

scatter 1 = <u>throw about</u>, spread, sprinkle, strew, broadcast, shower, fling, litter, sow, diffuse, disseminate ...*He began by scattering seed and putting in plants...* OPPOSITE gather
2 = <u>disperse</u>, separate, break up, dispel, disband, dissipate, disunite, put to flight ...*After dinner, everyone scattered...* OPPOSITE assemble
3 = <u>dot</u>, spot, sprinkle, pepper, litter, fleck, stipple ...*bays picturesquely scattered with rocky islets...*

scattering = <u>sprinkling</u>, few, handful, scatter, smattering, smatter

scavenge = <u>search</u>, hunt, forage, rummage, root about, fossick (*Austral. & N.Z.*)

scenario 1 = <u>situation</u>, sequence of events, chain of events, course of events, series of developments ...*That apocalyptic scenario cannot be ruled out...*
2 = <u>story line</u>, résumé, outline, sketch, summary, rundown, synopsis ...*I will write an outline of the scenario...*

scene 1 = <u>act</u>, part, division, episode ...*the opening scene...*
2 = <u>setting</u>, set, background, location, backdrop, mise en scène (*French*) ...*The lights go up, revealing a scene of chaos...*
3 = <u>incident</u>, happening, event, episode ...*There were emotional scenes as the refugees enjoyed their first breath of freedom...*
4 = <u>site</u>, place, setting, area, position, stage, situation, spot, whereabouts, locality ...*Riot vans were on the scene in minutes...*
5 (*Informal*) = <u>world</u>, business, environment, preserve, arena, realm, domain, milieu, thing, field of interest ...*the local music scene... ...Sport just isn't my scene...*
6 = <u>view</u>, prospect, panorama, vista, landscape, tableau, outlook ...*James Lynch's country scenes...*
7 = <u>fuss</u>, to-do, row, performance, upset, drama, exhibition, carry-on (*informal, chiefly Brit.*), confrontation, tantrum, commotion, hue and cry, display of emotion ...*I'm sorry I made such a scene...*
8 = <u>section</u>, part, sequence, segment, clip ...*She was told to cut some scenes from her new series...*

scenery 1 = <u>landscape</u>, view, surroundings, terrain, vista ...*Sometimes they just drive slowly down the lane enjoying the scenery...*
2 (*Theatre*) = <u>set</u>, setting, backdrop, flats, décor, stage set ...*There was a break while the scenery was changed...*

scenic = <u>picturesque</u>, beautiful, spectacular, striking, grand, impressive, breathtaking, panoramic

scent NOUN 1 = <u>fragrance</u>, smell, perfume, bouquet, aroma, odour, niff (*Brit. slang*), redolence ...*She could smell the scent of her mother's lacquer...*

2 = <u>trail</u>, track, spoor ...*A police dog picked up the murderer's scent...*
3 = <u>perfume</u>, fragrance, cologne, eau de toilette (*French*), eau de cologne (*French*), toilet water ...*a bottle of scent...*
VERB = <u>smell</u>, sense, recognize, detect, sniff, discern, sniff out, nose out, get wind of (*informal*), be on the track *or* trail of ...*dogs which scent the hidden birds...*

scented = <u>fragrant</u>, perfumed, aromatic, sweet-smelling, redolent, ambrosial, odoriferous

sceptic 1 = <u>doubter</u>, cynic, scoffer, disbeliever, Pyrrhonist ...*He was a born sceptic...*
2 = <u>agnostic</u>, doubter, unbeliever, doubting Thomas ...*a lifelong religious sceptic...*

sceptical = <u>doubtful</u>, cynical, dubious, questioning, doubting, hesitating, scoffing, unconvinced, disbelieving, incredulous, quizzical, mistrustful, unbelieving OPPOSITE convinced

scepticism = <u>doubt</u>, suspicion, disbelief, cynicism, incredulity

schedule NOUN 1 = <u>plan</u>, programme, agenda, calendar, timetable, itinerary, list of appointments ...*He has been forced to adjust his schedule...*
2 = <u>list</u>, catalogue, inventory, syllabus ...*a detailed written schedule...*
VERB = <u>plan</u>, set up, book, programme, arrange, organize, timetable ...*No new talks are scheduled...*

schematic = <u>graphic</u>, representational, illustrative, diagrammatic, diagrammatical

scheme NOUN 1 = <u>plan</u>, programme, strategy, system, design, project, theory, proposal, device, tactics, course of action, contrivance ...*a private pension scheme...*
2 = <u>plot</u>, dodge, ploy, ruse, game (*informal*), shift, intrigue, conspiracy, manoeuvre, machinations, subterfuge, stratagem ...*a quick money-making scheme...*
VERB = <u>plot</u>, plan, intrigue, manoeuvre, conspire, contrive, collude, wheel and deal, machinate ...*Everyone's always scheming and plotting...*

scheming = <u>calculating</u>, cunning, sly, designing, tricky, slippery, wily, artful, conniving, Machiavellian, foxy, deceitful, underhand, duplicitous OPPOSITE straightforward

schism = <u>division</u>, break, split, breach, separation, rift, splintering, rupture, discord, disunion

scholar 1 = <u>intellectual</u>, academic, man of letters, bookworm, egghead (*informal*), savant, bluestocking (*usually disparaging*), acca (*Austral. slang*) ...*The library attracts thousands of scholars and researchers...*
2 = <u>student</u>, pupil, learner, schoolboy *or* schoolgirl ...*She could be a good scholar if she didn't let her mind wander so much...*

scholarly = <u>learned</u>, academic, intellectual, lettered, erudite, scholastic, well-read, studious, bookish, swotty (*Brit. informal*) OPPOSITE uneducated

scholarship 1 = <u>grant</u>, award, payment, exhibition, endowment, fellowship, bursary ...*scholarships for* *women over 30...*

2 = <u>learning</u>, education, culture, knowledge, wisdom, accomplishments, attainments, lore, erudition, academic study, book-learning *...I want to take advantage of your lifetime of scholarship...*

scholastic = <u>learned</u>, academic, scholarly, lettered, literary, bookish

school `NOUN` **1** = <u>academy</u>, college, institution, institute, discipline, seminary, educational institution, centre of learning, alma mater *...a boy who was in my class at school...*

2 = <u>group</u>, set, circle, following, class, faction, followers, disciples, sect, devotees, denomination, clique, adherents, schism *...the Chicago school of economists...*

3 = <u>way of life</u>, creed, faith, outlook, persuasion, school of thought *...He was never a member of any school...*

`VERB` = <u>train</u>, prime, coach, prepare, discipline, educate, drill, tutor, instruct, verse, indoctrinate *...He is schooled to spot trouble...*

schooling **1** = <u>teaching</u>, education, tuition, formal education, book-learning *...normal schooling has been severely disrupted...*

2 = <u>training</u>, coaching, instruction, grounding, preparation, drill, guidance *...the schooling of horses...*

schoolteacher = <u>schoolmaster</u> or <u>schoolmistress</u>, instructor, pedagogue, schoolmarm (*informal*), dominie (*Scot.*)

science = <u>discipline</u>, body of knowledge, branch of knowledge

scientific **1** = <u>technological</u>, technical, chemical, biological, empirical, factual *...scientific research...*

2 = <u>systematic</u>, accurate, exact, precise, controlled, mathematical *...the scientific study of capitalist development...*

scientist = <u>researcher</u>, inventor, boffin (*informal*), technophile

scintillating = <u>brilliant</u>, exciting, stimulating, lively, sparkling, bright, glittering, dazzling, witty, animated

scion = <u>descendant</u>, child, offspring, successor, heir

scoff¹ = <u>scorn</u>, mock, laugh at, ridicule, knock (*informal*), taunt, despise, sneer, jeer, deride, slag (off) (*slang*), flout, belittle, revile, make light of, poke fun at, twit, gibe, pooh-pooh, make sport of *...At first I scoffed at the notion...*

scoff² = <u>gobble (up)</u>, wolf, devour, bolt, cram, put away, guzzle, gulp down, gorge yourself on, gollop, stuff yourself with, cram yourself on, make a pig of yourself on (*informal*) *...I scoffed the lot!...*

scold = <u>reprimand</u>, censure, rebuke, rate, blame, lecture, carpet (*informal*), slate (*informal, chiefly Brit.*), nag, go on at, reproach, berate, tick off (*informal*), castigate, chide, tear into (*informal*), tell off (*informal*), find fault with, remonstrate with, bring (someone) to book, take (someone) to task, read the riot act, reprove, upbraid, bawl out (*informal*), give (someone)

a talking-to (*informal*), haul (someone) over the coals (*informal*), chew out (*U.S. & Canad. informal*), give (someone) a dressing-down, tear (someone) off a strip (*Brit. informal*), give a rocket (*Brit. & N.Z. informal*), vituperate, give (someone) a row, have (someone) on the carpet (*informal*) `OPPOSITE` praise

scolding = <u>ticking-off</u>, row, lecture, wigging (*Brit. slang*), rebuke (*informal*), dressing-down (*informal*), telling-off (*informal*), tongue-lashing, piece of your mind, (good) talking-to (*informal*)

scoop `VERB` = <u>win</u>, get, receive, land, gain, achieve, net, earn, pick up, bag (*informal*), secure, collect, obtain, procure, come away with *...films which scooped awards around the world...*

`NOUN` **1** = <u>ladle</u>, spoon, dipper *...a small ice-cream scoop...*

2 = <u>spoonful</u>, lump, dollop (*informal*), ball, ladleful *...She gave him an extra scoop of clotted cream...*

3 = <u>exclusive</u>, exposé, coup, revelation, sensation, inside story *...one of the biggest scoops in the history of newspapers...*

`PHRASES` **scoop something** *or* **someone up** = <u>gather up</u>, lift, pick up, take up, sweep up *or* away *...He began to scoop his things up frantically... ...I wanted to scoop him up in my arms and give him a hug...* ♦ **scoop something out** **1** = <u>take out</u>, empty, dig out, scrape out, spoon out, bail *or* bale out *...Cut a marrow in half and scoop out the seeds...* **2** = <u>dig</u>, shovel, excavate, gouge, hollow out *...A hole had been scooped out next to the house...*

scoot = <u>dash</u>, run, dart, sprint, bolt, zip, scuttle, scurry, scamper, skitter, skedaddle (*informal*), skirr

scope **1** = <u>opportunity</u>, room, freedom, space, liberty, latitude, elbowroom, leeway *...He believed in giving his staff scope for initiative...*

2 = <u>range</u>, capacity, reach, area, extent, outlook, orbit, span, sphere, ambit, purview, field of reference *...the scope of a novel...*

scorch = <u>burn</u>, sear, char, roast, blister, wither, blacken, shrivel, parch, singe

scorching = <u>burning</u>, boiling, baking, flaming, tropical, roasting, searing, fiery, sizzling, red-hot, torrid, sweltering, broiling, unbearably hot

score `VERB` **1** = <u>gain</u>, win, achieve, make, get, net, bag, obtain, bring in, attain, amass, notch up (*informal*), chalk up (*informal*) *...They scored 282 points in their first innings...*

2 = <u>go down well with (someone)</u>, impress, triumph, make a hit (*informal*), make a point, gain an advantage, put yourself across, make an impact *or* impression *...He told them he had scored with the girl...*

3 (*Music*) = <u>arrange</u>, set, orchestrate, adapt *...He scored a piece for a chamber music ensemble...*

4 = <u>cut</u>, scratch, nick, mark, mar, slash, scrape, notch, graze, gouge, deface, indent, crosshatch *...Lightly score the surface of the steaks with a sharp cook's knife...*

`NOUN` **1** = <u>rating</u>, mark, grade, percentage *...low* maths scores...

2 = <u>points</u>, result, total, outcome ...*The final score was 4-1...*

3 = <u>composition</u>, soundtrack, arrangement, orchestration ...*the composer of classic film scores...*

4 = <u>grievance</u>, wrong, injury, injustice, grudge, bone of contention, bone to pick ...*They had a score to settle with each other...*

5 = <u>charge</u>, bill, account, total, debt, reckoning, tab (*U.S. informal*), tally, amount due ...*So what is the score anyway?...*

PLURAL NOUN = <u>lots</u>, loads, many, millions, hundreds, hosts, crowds, masses, droves, an army, legions, swarms, multitudes, myriads, very many, a flock, a throng, a great number ...*Campaigners lit scores of bonfires...*

PHRASES **score points off someone** = <u>get the better of</u>, make a fool of, be one up on (*informal*), worst, humiliate, have the laugh on, make (someone) look silly ...*They kept trying to score points off each other...* ◆ **score something out** or **through** = <u>cross out</u>, delete, strike out, cancel, obliterate, put a line through ...*Words and sentences had been scored out and underlined...* ◆ **settle a score** (*Informal*) = <u>get your own back on someone</u>, retaliate, repay someone, hit back (at someone), pay (someone) back (in their own coin), get even with someone (*informal*), give (someone) a taste of their own medicine, avenge something, give an eye for an eye, give like for like or tit for tat, requite someone's actions ...*Attempting to settle the score can provide us with temporary satisfaction...*

scorn NOUN = <u>contempt</u>, disdain, mockery, derision, despite, slight, sneer, sarcasm, disparagement, contumely, contemptuousness, scornfulness ...*They greeted the proposal with scorn...* OPPOSITE respect
VERB = <u>despise</u>, reject, disdain, slight, snub, shun, be above, spurn, rebuff, deride, flout, look down on, scoff at, make fun of, sneer at, hold in contempt, turn up your nose at (*informal*), contemn, curl your lip at, consider beneath you ...*People scorn me as a single parent... ...people who scorned traditional methods...* OPPOSITE respect

scornful = <u>contemptuous</u>, insulting, mocking, defiant, withering, sneering, slighting, jeering, scoffing, scathing, sarcastic, sardonic, haughty, disdainful, insolent, derisive, supercilious, contumelious

scornfully = <u>contemptuously</u>, with contempt, dismissively, disdainfully, with disdain, scathingly, witheringly, with a sneer, slightingly, with lip curled

scotch = <u>put an end to</u>, destroy, smash, devastate, wreck, thwart, scupper, extinguish, put paid to, nip in the bud, bring to an end, put the lid on, put the kibosh on

scoundrel (*Old-fashioned*) = <u>rogue</u>, villain, heel (*slang*), cheat, swine, rascal, son-of-a-bitch (*slang, chiefly U.S. & Canad.*), scally (*Northwest English dialect*), wretch, incorrigible, knave (*archaic*), rotter (*slang, chiefly Brit.*), ne'er-do-well, reprobate, scumbag

(*slang*), good-for-nothing, miscreant, scamp, bad egg (*old-fashioned informal*), blackguard, scapegrace, caitiff (*archaic*), dastard (*archaic*), skelm (*S. African*)

scour[1] = <u>scrub</u>, clean, polish, rub, cleanse, buff, burnish, whiten, furbish, abrade ...*He decided to scour the sink...*

scour[2] = <u>search</u>, hunt, comb, ransack, forage, look high and low, go over with a fine-tooth comb ...*We scoured the telephone directory for clues...*

scourge NOUN **1** = <u>affliction</u>, plague, curse, terror, pest, torment, misfortune, visitation, bane, infliction ...*Drugs are a scourge that is devastating our society...* OPPOSITE benefit
2 = <u>whip</u>, lash, thong, switch, strap, cat-o'-nine-tails ...*a heavy scourge with a piece of iron lashed into its knot...*
VERB **1** = <u>afflict</u>, plague, curse, torment, harass, terrorize, excoriate ...*Economic anarchy scourged the post-war world...*
2 = <u>whip</u>, beat, lash, thrash, discipline, belt (*informal*), leather, punish, whale, cane, flog, trounce, castigate, wallop (*informal*), chastise, lather (*informal*), horsewhip, tan (someone's) hide (*slang*), take a strap to ...*They were scourging him severely...*

scout NOUN **1** = <u>vanguard</u>, lookout, precursor, outrider, reconnoitrer, advance guard ...*They set off, two men out in front as scouts...*
2 = <u>recruiter</u>, talent scout ...*We've had scouts watching him for some time...*
VERB = <u>reconnoitre</u>, investigate, check out, case (*slang*), watch, survey, observe, spy, probe, recce (*slang*), spy out, make a reconnaissance, see how the land lies ...*I have people scouting the hills already...*
PHRASES **scout around** or **round** = <u>search</u>, look for, hunt for, fossick (*Austral. & N.Z.*), cast about or around, ferret about or around ...*They scouted around for more fuel...*

scowl VERB = <u>glower</u>, frown, look daggers, grimace, lour or lower ...*She scowled at the two men as they entered the room...*
NOUN = <u>glower</u>, frown, dirty look, black look, grimace ...*He met the remark with a scowl...*

scrabble = <u>scrape</u>, scratch, scramble, dig, claw, paw, grope, clamber

scramble VERB **1** = <u>struggle</u>, climb, clamber, push, crawl, swarm, scrabble, move with difficulty ...*He scrambled up a steep bank...*
2 = <u>strive</u>, rush, contend, vie, run, push, hasten, jostle, jockey for position, make haste ...*More than a million fans are expected to scramble for tickets...*
3 = <u>jumble</u>, mix up, muddle, shuffle, entangle, disarrange ...*The latest machines scramble the messages...*
NOUN **1** = <u>clamber</u>, ascent ...*the scramble to the top of the cliffs...*
2 = <u>race</u>, competition, struggle, rush, confusion, hustle, free-for-all (*informal*), commotion, melee or mêlée ...*the scramble for jobs...*

scrap[1] NOUN **1** = <u>piece</u>, fragment, bit, trace, grain,

particle, portion, snatch, part, atom, remnant, crumb, mite, bite, mouthful, snippet, sliver, morsel, modicum, iota …*a fire fuelled by scraps of wood*…
2 = <u>waste</u>, junk, off cuts …*cut up for scrap*…
PLURAL NOUN = <u>leftovers</u>, remains, bits, scrapings, leavings …*children foraging for scraps of food*…
VERB = <u>get rid of</u>, drop, abandon, shed, break up, ditch (*slang*), junk (*informal*), chuck (*informal*), discard, write off, demolish, trash (*slang*), dispense with, jettison, toss out, throw on the scrapheap, throw away *or* out …*We should scrap nuclear and chemical weapons*… **OPPOSITE** bring back

scrap² (*Informal*) **NOUN** = <u>fight</u>, battle, row, argument, dispute, set-to (*informal*), disagreement, quarrel, brawl, squabble, wrangle, scuffle, tiff, dust-up (*informal*), shindig (*informal*), scrimmage, shindy (*informal*), bagarre (*French*), biffo (*Austral. slang*) …*He has never been one to avoid a scrap*…
VERB = <u>fight</u>, argue, row, fall out (*informal*), barney (*informal*), squabble, spar, wrangle, bicker, have words, come to blows, have a shouting match (*informal*) …*They are always scrapping*…

scrape **VERB** **1** = <u>rake</u>, sweep, drag, brush …*She went round the car scraping the frost off the windows*…
2 = <u>grate</u>, grind, scratch, screech, squeak, rasp …*The only sound is that of knives and forks scraping against china*…
3 = <u>graze</u>, skin, scratch, bark, scuff, rub, abrade …*She stumbled and fell, scraping her palms and knees*…
4 = <u>clean</u>, remove, scour …*She scraped food off the plates into the bin*…
NOUN (*Informal*) = <u>predicament</u>, trouble, difficulty, spot (*informal*), fix (*informal*), mess, distress, dilemma, plight, tight spot, awkward situation, pretty pickle (*informal*) …*We got into terrible scrapes*…
PHRASES **scrape something together** = <u>collect</u>, save, muster, get hold of, amass, hoard, glean, dredge up, rake up *or* together …*They only just managed to scrape the money together*…

scrapheap
PHRASES **on the scrapheap** = <u>discarded</u>, ditched (*slang*), redundant, written off, jettisoned, put out to grass (*informal*)

scrappy = <u>incomplete</u>, sketchy, piecemeal, disjointed, perfunctory, thrown together, fragmentary, bitty

scratch **VERB** **1** = <u>rub</u>, scrape, claw at …*The old man lifted his cardigan to scratch his side*…
2 = <u>mark</u>, cut, score, damage, grate, graze, etch, lacerate, incise, make a mark on …*Knives will scratch the worktop*…
NOUN = <u>mark</u>, scrape, graze, blemish, gash, laceration, claw mark …*I pointed to a number of scratches on the tile floor*…
PHRASES **scratch something out** = <u>erase</u>, eliminate, delete, cancel, strike off, annul, cross out …*She scratched out the word 'frightful'*… ♦ **up to scratch** (*Informal*) = <u>adequate</u>, acceptable, satisfactory, capable, sufficient, competent, up to standard, up to snuff (*informal*) …*She made me feel I*

wasn't up to scratch…

scrawl **VERB** = <u>scribble</u>, doodle, squiggle …*graffiti scrawled on school walls*…
NOUN = <u>scribble</u>, doodle, squiggle …*a hasty, barely decipherable scrawl*…

scrawny = <u>thin</u>, lean, skinny, angular, gaunt, skeletal, bony, lanky, undernourished, skin-and-bones (*informal*), scraggy, rawboned, macilent (*rare*)

scream **VERB** = <u>cry</u>, yell, shriek, screech, squeal, shrill, bawl, howl, holler (*informal*), sing out …*If I hear one more joke about my hair, I shall scream*…
NOUN **1** = <u>cry</u>, yell, howl, wail, outcry, shriek, screech, yelp …*Hilda let out a scream*…
2 (*Informal*) = <u>laugh</u>, card (*informal*), riot (*slang*), comic, character (*informal*), caution (*informal*), sensation, wit, comedian, entertainer, wag, joker, hoot (*informal*) …*He's a scream, isn't he?*…

screech **VERB** = <u>shriek</u>, scream, yell, howl, wail, squeal, holler …*She was screeching at them*…
NOUN = <u>cry</u>, scream, shriek, squeal, squawk, yelp …*The figure gave a screech*…

screen **NOUN** = <u>cover</u>, guard, shade, shelter, shield, hedge, partition, cloak, mantle, shroud, canopy, awning, concealment, room divider …*They put a screen in front of me*…
VERB **1** = <u>broadcast</u>, show, put on, present, air, cable, beam, transmit, relay, televise, put on the air …*The series is likely to be screened in January*…
2 = <u>cover</u>, hide, conceal, shade, mask, veil, cloak, shroud, shut out …*The road is screened by a block of flats*…
3 = <u>investigate</u>, test, check, examine, scan …*They need to screen everyone at risk of contracting the illness*…
4 = <u>process</u>, sort, examine, grade, filter, scan, evaluate, gauge, sift …*It was their job to screen information for their bosses*…
5 = <u>protect</u>, guard, shield, defend, shelter, safeguard …*They deliberately screened him from knowledge of their operations*…

screw **NOUN** = <u>nail</u>, pin, tack, rivet, fastener, spike …*Each bracket is fixed to the wall with just three screws*…
VERB **1** = <u>fasten</u>, fix, attach, bolt, clamp, rivet …*I like the sort of shelving that you screw on the wall*…
2 = <u>turn</u>, twist, tighten, work in …*Screw down the lid fairly tightly*…
3 (*Informal*) = <u>contort</u>, twist, distort, contract, wrinkle, warp, crumple, deform, pucker …*He screwed his face into an expression of mock pain*…
4 (*Informal*) = <u>cheat</u>, do (*slang*), rip (someone) off (*slang*), skin (*slang*), trick, con, stiff (*slang*), sting (*informal*), deceive, fleece, dupe, overcharge, rook (*slang*), bamboozle (*informal*), diddle (*informal*), take (someone) for a ride (*informal*), put one over on (someone) (*informal*), pull a fast one (on someone) (*informal*), take to the cleaners (*informal*), sell a pup (to) (*slang*), hornswoggle (*slang*) …*We've been screwed*…

5 (*Informal*) *often with **out of*** = squeeze, wring, extract, wrest, bleed someone of something ...*rich nations screwing money out of poor nations...*

PHRASES **put the screws on someone** (*Informal*) = coerce, force, compel, drive, squeeze, intimidate, constrain, oppress, pressurize, browbeat, press-gang, bring pressure to bear on, hold a knife to someone's throat ...*They had to put the screws on Harper to get the information they needed...* ◆ **screw something up 1** = contort, contract, wrinkle, knot, knit, distort, crumple, pucker ...*She screwed up her eyes...* **2** (*Informal*) = bungle, botch, mess up, spoil, bitch (up) (*slang*), queer (*informal*), cock up (*Brit. slang*), mishandle, make a mess of (*slang*), mismanage, make a hash of (*informal*), make a nonsense of, bodge (*informal*), flub (*U.S. slang*), louse up (*slang*), crool or cruel (*Austral. slang*) ...*Get out. Haven't you screwed things up enough already!...*

scribble = scrawl, write, jot, pen, scratch, doodle, dash off

scribe = secretary, clerk, scrivener (*archaic*), notary (*archaic*), amanuensis, copyist

script **NOUN 1** = text, lines, words, book, copy, dialogue, manuscript, libretto ...*Jenny's writing a film script...*

2 = handwriting, writing, hand, letters, calligraphy, longhand, penmanship ...*She wrote the letter in an elegant script...*

VERB = write, draft, compose, author ...*I scripted and directed both films...*

scripture = The Bible, The Word, The Gospels, The Scriptures, The Word of God, The Good Book, Holy Scripture, Holy Writ, Holy Bible, The Book of Books

Scrooge = miser, penny-pincher (*informal*), skinflint, cheapskate (*informal*), tightwad (*U.S. & Canad. slang*), niggard, money-grubber (*informal*), meanie or meany (*informal, chiefly Brit.*)

scrounge (*Informal*) = cadge, beg, sponge (*informal*), bum (*informal*), touch (someone) for (*slang*), blag (*slang*), wheedle, mooch (*slang*), forage for, hunt around (for), sorn (*Scot.*), freeload (*slang*), bludge (*Austral. & N.Z. informal*)

scrounger = parasite, freeloader (*slang*), sponger (*informal*), bum (*informal*), cadger, bludger (*Austral. & N.Z. informal*), sorner (*Scot.*), quandong (*Austral. slang*)

scrub 1 = scour, clean, polish, rub, wash, cleanse, buff ...*The corridors are scrubbed clean...*

2 (*Informal*) = cancel, drop, give up, abandon, abolish, forget about, call off, delete, do away with, discontinue ...*The whole thing had to be scrubbed...*

scruff = nape, scrag (*informal*)

scruffy = shabby, untidy, ragged, run-down, messy, sloppy (*informal*), seedy, squalid, tattered, tatty, unkempt, disreputable, scrubby (*Brit. informal*), grungy, slovenly, mangy, sluttish, slatternly, ungroomed, frowzy, ill-groomed, draggletailed (*archaic*) **OPPOSITE** neat

scrum = crowd, group, mob, lot, body, host, band, troop, mass, bunch (*informal*), number, horde, throng,

assemblage

scrumptious (*Informal*) = delicious, delectable, inviting, magnificent, exquisite, luscious, succulent, mouthwatering, yummy (*slang*), appetizing, moreish (*informal*), yummo (*Austral. slang*)

scrunch = crumple, crush, squash, crunch, mash, ruck up

scruple = misgiving, hesitation, qualm, doubt, difficulty, caution, reluctance, second thoughts, uneasiness, perplexity, compunction, squeamishness, twinge of conscience

scrupulous 1 = moral, principled, upright, honourable, conscientious ...*I have been scrupulous about telling them the truth...* **OPPOSITE** unscrupulous **2** = careful, strict, precise, minute, nice, exact, rigorous, meticulous, painstaking, fastidious, punctilious ...*scrupulous attention to detail...* **OPPOSITE** careless

scrutinize = examine, study, inspect, research, search, investigate, explore, probe, analyse, scan, sift, dissect, work over, pore over, peruse, inquire into, go over with a fine-tooth comb

scrutiny = examination, study, investigation, search, inquiry, analysis, inspection, exploration, sifting, once-over (*informal*), perusal, close study

scud = fly, race, speed, shoot, blow, sail, skim

scuffle **NOUN** = fight, set-to (*informal*), scrap (*informal*), disturbance, fray, brawl, barney (*informal*), ruck (*slang*), skirmish, tussle, commotion, rumpus, affray (*Law*), shindig (*informal*), ruction (*informal*), ruckus (*informal*), scrimmage, shindy (*informal*), bagarre (*French*), biffo (*Austral. slang*) ...*Violent scuffles broke out...*

VERB = fight, struggle, clash, contend, grapple, jostle, tussle, come to blows, exchange blows ...*Police scuffled with some of the protesters...*

sculpture **NOUN** = statue, figure, model, bust, effigy, figurine, statuette ...*a collection of 20th-century sculptures...*

VERB = carve, form, cut, model, fashion, shape, mould, sculpt, chisel, hew, sculp ...*He sculptured the figure in marble...*

scum 1 = rabble, trash (*chiefly U.S. & Canad.*), riffraff, rubbish, dross, lowest of the low, dregs of society, canaille (*French*), ragtag and bobtail ...*They're cultureless scum drifted from elsewhere...*

2 = impurities, film, crust, froth, scruff, dross, offscourings ...*scum around the bath...*

scungy (*Austral. & N.Z. slang*) = sordid, seedy, sleazy, squalid, mean, dirty, foul, filthy, unclean, wretched, seamy, slovenly, skanky (*slang*), slummy, festy (*Austral. slang*)

scupper (*Brit. slang*) = destroy, ruin, wreck, defeat, overwhelm, disable, overthrow, demolish, undo, torpedo, put paid to, discomfit

scurrilous = slanderous, scandalous, defamatory, low, offensive, gross, foul, insulting, infamous, obscene, abusive, coarse, indecent, vulgar, foul-mouthed, salacious, ribald, vituperative, scabrous,

Rabelaisian

scurry `VERB` = <u>hurry</u>, race, dash, fly, sprint, dart, whisk, skim, beetle, scud, scuttle, scoot, scamper …*The attack began, sending residents scurrying for cover…* `OPPOSITE` amble
`NOUN` = <u>flurry</u>, race, bustle, whirl, scampering …*a mad scurry for a suitable venue…*

scuttle = <u>run</u>, scurry, scamper, rush, hurry, scramble, hare (*Brit. informal*), bustle, beetle, scud, hasten, scoot, scutter (*Brit. informal*)

sea `NOUN` 1 = <u>ocean</u>, the deep, the waves, the drink (*informal*), the briny (*informal*), main …*Most of the kids have never seen the sea…*
2 = <u>mass</u>, lot, lots (*informal*), army, host, crowd, collection, sheet, assembly, mob, congregation, legion, abundance, swarm, horde, multitude, myriad, throng, expanse, plethora, profusion, concourse, assemblage, vast number, great number …*Down below them was the sea of upturned faces…*
`ADJECTIVE` = <u>marine</u>, ocean, maritime, aquatic, oceanic, saltwater, ocean-going, seagoing, pelagic, briny, salt …*a sea vessel…*
`PHRASES` **at sea** = <u>bewildered</u>, lost, confused, puzzled, uncertain, baffled, adrift, perplexed, disconcerted, at a loss, mystified, disoriented, bamboozled (*informal*), flummoxed, at sixes and sevens …*I'm totally at sea with popular culture…*

(*Related Words*)
adjective : marine

➤ **WORD POWER SUPPLEMENT seas and oceans**

sea bird
➤ **sea birds**

seafaring = <u>nautical</u>, marine, naval, maritime, oceanic

seal `VERB` = <u>settle</u>, clinch, conclude, consummate, finalize, shake hands on (*informal*) …*McLaren are close to sealing a deal with Renault…*
`NOUN` 1 = <u>sealant</u>, sealer, adhesive …*Wet the edges where the two crusts join, to form a seal…*
2 = <u>authentication</u>, stamp, confirmation, assurance, ratification, notification, insignia, imprimatur, attestation …*the President's seal of approval…*
`PHRASES` **set the seal on something** = <u>confirm</u>, establish, assure, stamp, ratify, validate, attest, authenticate …*Such a visit may set the seal on a new relationship between them…*

seam 1 = <u>joint</u>, closure, suture (*Surgery*) …*The seam of her tunic was split from armpit to hem…*
2 = <u>layer</u>, vein, stratum, lode …*The average UK coal seam is one metre thick…*

sea mammal

Sea mammals
http://nmml.afsc.noaa.gov/education/marinemammals.htm

dugong	manatee
eared seal	sea cow
earless seal	seal
elephant seal	sea lion
harp seal	walrus *or* (*archaic*) sea
hooded seal	horse

sear = <u>wither</u>, burn, blight, brand, scorch, sizzle, shrivel, cauterize, desiccate, dry up *or* out

search `VERB` = <u>examine</u>, check, investigate, explore, probe, inspect, comb, inquire, sift, scour, ferret, pry, ransack, forage, scrutinize, turn upside down, rummage through, frisk (*informal*), cast around, rifle through, leave no stone unturned, turn inside out, fossick (*Austral. & N.Z.*), go over with a fine-tooth comb …*Armed troops searched the hospital yesterday…*
`NOUN` = <u>hunt</u>, look, inquiry, investigation, examination, pursuit, quest, going-over (*informal*), inspection, exploration, scrutiny, rummage …*There was no chance of him being found alive and the search was abandoned…*
`PHRASES` **search for something** *or* **someone** = <u>look for</u>, seek, hunt for, pursue, go in search of, cast around for, go in pursuit of, go in quest of, ferret around for, look high and low for …*The Turkish security forces have started searching for the missing men…*

searching = <u>keen</u>, sharp, probing, close, severe, intent, piercing, penetrating, thorough, quizzical
`OPPOSITE` superficial

searing 1 = <u>acute</u>, sharp, intense, shooting, violent, severe, painful, distressing, stabbing, fierce, stinging, piercing, sore, excruciating, gut-wrenching …*She woke to a searing pain in her feet…*
2 = <u>cutting</u>, biting, severe, bitter, harsh, scathing,

Sea birds http://www.deh.gov.au/coasts/species/seabirds/

albatross *or* (*informal*) gooney bird	fish hawk	murrelet	short-tailed shearwater, (*Tasmanian*) mutton
auk	fulmar	old squaw *or* oldwife	bird, *or* (*N.Z.*) titi
auklet	gannet	oystercatcher	skua
black-backed gull	glaucous gull	petrel	storm petrel, stormy
black guillemot	guillemot	prion	petrel, *or* Mother
booby (*Austral.*)	gull *or* (*archaic or dialect*) cob(b)	razorbill *or* razor-billed auk	Carey's chicken
coot	herring gull	scoter	surf scoter *or* surf duck
cormorant	ivory gull	sea duck	takapu (*N.Z.*)
fairy penguin, little penguin, *or* (*N.Z.*)	kittiwake	sea eagle, erne, *or* ern	velvet scoter
korora	man-of-war bird *or* frigate bird	seagull	wandering albatross
		shearwater	Wilson's petrel

acrimonious, barbed, hurtful, sarcastic, sardonic, caustic, vitriolic, trenchant, mordant, mordacious, acerb ...*They have long been subject to searing criticism*...

season NOUN = period, time, term, spell, time of year ...*birds arriving for the breeding season*...
VERB **1** = flavour, salt, spice, lace, salt and pepper, enliven, pep up, leaven ...*Season the meat with salt and pepper*...
2 = mature, age, condition, prime, prepare, temper, mellow, ripen, acclimatize ...*Ensure that the new wood has been seasoned*...
3 = make experienced, train, mature, prepare, discipline, harden, accustom, toughen, inure, habituate, acclimatize, anneal ...*Both actors seem to have been seasoned by experience*...

Seasons

Season	Related adjective
spring	vernal
summer	aestival *or* estival
autumn	autumnal
winter	hibernal *or* hiemal

seasoned = experienced, veteran, mature, practised, old, weathered, hardened, long-serving, battle-scarred, time-served, well-versed OPPOSITE inexperienced

seasoning = flavouring, spice, salt and pepper, condiment

seat NOUN **1** = chair, bench, stall, throne, stool, pew, settle ...*Stephen returned to his seat*...
2 = membership, place, constituency, chair, incumbency ...*He lost his seat to the Tories*...
3 = centre, place, site, heart, capital, situation, source, station, location, headquarters, axis, cradle, hub ...*Gunfire broke out around the seat of government*...
4 = mansion, house, residence, abode, ancestral hall ...*her family's ancestral seat in Scotland*...
VERB **1** = sit, place, settle, set, fix, deposit, locate, install ...*He waved towards a chair, and seated himself at the desk*...
2 = hold, take, accommodate, sit, contain, cater for, have room *or* capacity for ...*The theatre seats 570*...

seating = accommodation, room, places, seats, chairs

secede = withdraw, leave, resign, separate, retire, quit, pull out, break with, split from, disaffiliate, apostatize

secession = withdrawal, break, split, defection, seceding, apostasy, disaffiliation

secluded = private, sheltered, isolated, remote, lonely, cut off, solitary, out-of-the-way, tucked away, cloistered, sequestered, off the beaten track, unfrequented OPPOSITE public

seclusion = privacy, isolation, solitude, hiding, retirement, shelter, retreat, remoteness, ivory tower, concealment, purdah

second¹ ADJECTIVE **1** = next, following, succeeding, subsequent ...*the second day of his visit to Delhi*...

2 = additional, other, further, extra, alternative, repeated ...*Her second attempt proved disastrous*...
3 = spare, duplicate, alternative, additional, back-up ...*The suitcase contained clean shirts and a second pair of shoes*...
4 = inferior, secondary, subordinate, supporting, lower, lesser ...*They have to rely on their second string strikers*...
NOUN = supporter, assistant, aide, partner, colleague, associate, backer, helper, collaborator, henchman, right-hand man, cooperator ...*He shouted to his seconds, 'I did it!'*...
VERB = support, back, endorse, forward, promote, approve, go along with, commend, give moral support to ...*He seconded the motion against fox hunting*...

second² = moment, minute, instant, flash, tick (*Brit. informal*), sec (*informal*), twinkling, split second, jiffy (*informal*), trice, twinkling of an eye, two shakes of a lamb's tail (*informal*), bat of an eye (*informal*) ...*For a few seconds nobody said anything*...

secondary **1** = subordinate, minor, lesser, lower, inferior, unimportant, second-rate ...*Refugee problems remained of secondary importance*...
OPPOSITE main
2 = resultant, resulting, contingent, derived, derivative, indirect, second-hand, consequential ...*There was evidence of secondary tumours*...
OPPOSITE original

second-class **1** = inferior, lesser, second-best, unimportant, second-rate, low-class ...*Too many airlines treat our children as second-class citizens*...
2 = mediocre, second-rate, mean, middling, ordinary, inferior, indifferent, commonplace, insignificant, so-so (*informal*), outclassed, uninspiring, undistinguished, uninspired, bog-standard (*Brit. & Irish slang*), no great shakes (*informal*), déclassé, half-pie (*N.Z. informal*), fair to middling (*informal*) ...*a second-class education*...

second-hand = used, old, handed down, hand-me-down (*informal*), nearly new, reach-me-down (*informal*)

secondly = next, second, moreover, furthermore, also, in the second place

second-rate = inferior, mediocre, poor, cheap, pants (*slang*), commonplace, tacky (*informal*), shoddy, low-grade, tawdry, low-quality, substandard, low-rent (*informal, chiefly U.S.*), for the birds (*informal*), two-bit (*U.S. & Canad. slang*), end-of-the-pier (*Brit. informal*), no great shakes (*informal*), cheap and nasty (*informal*), rubbishy, dime-a-dozen (*informal*), bush-league (*Austral. & N.Z. informal*), not much cop (*Brit. slang*), tinhorn (*U.S. slang*), strictly for the birds (*informal*), bodger *or* bodgie (*Austral. slang*) OPPOSITE first-rate

secrecy **1** = mystery, stealth, concealment, furtiveness, cloak and dagger, secretiveness, huggermugger (*rare*), clandestineness, covertness ...*He shrouded his business dealings in secrecy*...

2 = <u>confidentiality</u>, privacy ...*The secrecy of the confessional...*

3 = <u>privacy</u>, silence, retirement, solitude, seclusion ...*These problems had to be dealt with in the secrecy of your own cell...*

secret ADJECTIVE 1 = <u>undisclosed</u>, unknown, confidential, underground, undercover, unpublished, under wraps, unrevealed ...*Soldiers have been training at a secret location...*

2 = <u>concealed</u>, hidden, disguised, covered, camouflaged, unseen ...*It has a secret compartment hidden behind the magical mirror...* OPPOSITE> unconcealed

3 = <u>undercover</u>, covert, furtive, shrouded, behind someone's back, conspiratorial, hush-hush (*informal*), surreptitious, cloak-and-dagger, backstairs ...*I was heading on a secret mission that made my flesh crawl...* OPPOSITE> open

4 = <u>secretive</u>, reserved, withdrawn, close, deep, discreet, enigmatic, reticent, cagey (*informal*), unforthcoming ...*the secret man behind the masks...* OPPOSITE> frank

5 = <u>mysterious</u>, cryptic, abstruse, classified, esoteric, occult, clandestine, arcane, recondite, cabbalistic ...*a secret code...* OPPOSITE> straightforward

NOUN 1 = <u>private affair</u>, confidence, skeleton in the cupboard ...*I can't tell you; it's a secret...*

2 = <u>key</u>, answer, formula, recipe ...*The secret of success is honesty and fair dealing...*

PHRASES **in secret** = <u>secretly</u>, surreptitiously, slyly, behind closed doors, incognito, by stealth, in camera, huggermugger (*archaic*) ...*Dan found out that I'd been meeting my ex-boyfriend in secret...*

> **Related Words**
> *adjective*: cryptic

secret agent = <u>spy</u>, undercover agent, spook (*U.S. & Canad. informal*), nark (*Brit., Austral., & N.Z. slang*), cloak-and-dagger man

secrete[1] = <u>give off</u>, emit, emanate, exude, extrude ...*The sweat glands secrete water...*

secrete[2] = <u>hide</u>, conceal, stash (*informal*), cover, screen, secure, bury, harbour, disguise, veil, shroud, stow, cache, stash away (*informal*) OPPOSITE> display ...*She secreted the gun in the kitchen cabinet...*

secretion = <u>discharge</u>, emission, excretion, exudation, extravasation (*Medical*)

secretive = <u>reticent</u>, reserved, withdrawn, close, deep, enigmatic, cryptic, cagey (*informal*), uncommunicative, unforthcoming, tight-lipped, playing your cards close to your chest, clamlike OPPOSITE> open

secretly = <u>in secret</u>, privately, surreptitiously, quietly, covertly, behind closed doors, in confidence, in your heart, furtively, in camera, confidentially, on the fly (*slang, chiefly Brit.*), stealthily, under the counter, clandestinely, unobserved, on the sly, in your heart of hearts, behind (someone's) back, in your innermost thoughts, on the q.t. (*informal*)

sect = <u>group</u>, division, faction, party, school, camp, wing, denomination, school of thought, schism, splinter group

sectarian ADJECTIVE = <u>narrow-minded</u>, partisan, fanatic, fanatical, limited, exclusive, rigid, parochial, factional, bigoted, dogmatic, insular, doctrinaire, hidebound, clannish, cliquish ...*sectarian religious groups...* OPPOSITE> tolerant

NOUN = <u>bigot</u>, extremist, partisan, disciple, fanatic, adherent, zealot, true believer, dogmatist ...*He remains a sectarian...*

section 1 = <u>part</u>, piece, portion, division, sample, slice, passage, component, segment, fragment, fraction, instalment, cross section, subdivision ...*a geological section of a rock...*

2 = <u>district</u>, area, region, sector, zone ...*Kolonarai is a lovely residential section of Athens...*

sectional = <u>regional</u>, local, separate, divided, exclusive, partial, separatist, factional, localized

sector 1 = <u>part</u>, division, category, stratum, subdivision ...*the nation's manufacturing sector...*

2 = <u>area</u>, part, region, district, zone, quarter ...*Officers were going to retake sectors of the city...*

secular = <u>worldly</u>, state, lay, earthly, civil, temporal, profane, laic, nonspiritual, laical OPPOSITE> religious

secure VERB 1 = <u>obtain</u>, get, acquire, land (*informal*), score (*slang*), gain, pick up, get hold of, come by, procure, make sure of, win possession of ...*His achievements helped him to secure the job...* OPPOSITE> lose

2 = <u>attach</u>, stick, fix, bind, pin, lash, glue, fasten, rivet ...*The frames are secured by horizontal rails to the back wall...* OPPOSITE> detach

3 = <u>guarantee</u>, insure, ensure, assure ...*The loan is secured against your home...* OPPOSITE> endanger

ADJECTIVE 1 = <u>safe</u>, protected, shielded, sheltered, immune, unassailable, impregnable ...*We shall make sure our home is as secure as possible...* OPPOSITE> unprotected

2 = <u>fast</u>, firm, fixed, tight, stable, steady, fortified, fastened, dependable, immovable ...*Shelves are only as secure as their fixings...* OPPOSITE> insecure

3 = <u>reliable</u>, definite, solid, absolute, conclusive, in the bag (*informal*) ...*demands for secure wages and employment...*

4 = <u>confident</u>, sure, easy, certain, assured, reassured ...*She felt secure and protected when she was with him...* OPPOSITE> uneasy

security 1 = <u>precautions</u>, defence, safeguards, guards, protection, surveillance, safety measures ...*under pressure to tighten airport security...*

2 = <u>assurance</u>, confidence, conviction, certainty, reliance, sureness, positiveness, ease of mind, freedom from doubt ...*He loves the security of a happy home life...* OPPOSITE> insecurity

3 = <u>pledge</u>, insurance, guarantee, hostage, collateral, pawn, gage, surety ...*The banks will pledge the land as security...*

4 = <u>protection</u>, cover, safety, retreat, asylum, custody, refuge, sanctuary, immunity, preservation,

safekeeping …*He could not remain long in a place of security…* OPPOSITE vulnerability

sedate ADJECTIVE **1** = <u>calm</u>, collected, quiet, seemly, serious, earnest, cool, grave, proper, middle-aged, composed, sober, dignified, solemn, serene, tranquil, placid, staid, demure, unflappable (*informal*), unruffled, decorous, imperturbable …*She took them to visit her sedate, elderly cousins…* OPPOSITE wild
2 = <u>unhurried</u>, easy, relaxed, comfortable, steady, gentle, deliberate, leisurely, slow-moving …*We set off again at a more sedate pace…*
VERB = <u>drug</u>, knock out, dope, anaesthetize, tranquillize, put under sedation, give a sedative to …*The patient was sedated…*

sedative ADJECTIVE = <u>calming</u>, relaxing, soothing, allaying, anodyne, soporific, sleep-inducing, tranquillizing, calmative, lenitive …*Amber bath oil has a sedative effect…*
NOUN = <u>tranquillizer</u>, narcotic, sleeping pill, opiate, anodyne, calmative, downer *or* down (*slang*) …*They use opium as a sedative…*

sedentary = <u>inactive</u>, sitting, seated, desk, motionless, torpid, desk-bound OPPOSITE active

sediment = <u>dregs</u>, grounds, residue, lees, deposit, precipitate, settlings

sedition = <u>rabble-rousing</u>, treason, subversion, agitation, disloyalty, incitement to riot

seduce 1 = <u>tempt</u>, attract, lure, entice, mislead, deceive, beguile, allure, decoy, ensnare, lead astray, inveigle …*The view of the lake and plunging cliffs seduces visitors…*
2 = <u>corrupt</u>, ruin (*archaic*), betray, deprave, dishonour, debauch, deflower …*a fifteen-year-old seduced by a man twice her age…*

seduction 1 = <u>temptation</u>, lure, snare, allure, enticement …*The seduction of the show is the fact that the kids are in it…*
2 = <u>corruption</u>, ruin (*archaic*), defloration …*his seduction of a minor…*

seductive = <u>tempting</u>, inviting, attractive, sexy (*informal*), irresistible, siren, enticing, provocative, captivating, beguiling, alluring, bewitching, ravishing, flirtatious, come-to-bed (*informal*), come-hither (*informal*)

see VERB **1** = <u>perceive</u>, note, spot, notice, mark, view, eye, check, regard, identify, sight, witness, clock (*Brit. slang*), observe, recognize, distinguish, glimpse, check out (*informal*), make out, heed, discern, behold, eyeball (*slang*), catch a glimpse of, catch sight of, espy, get a load of (*slang*), descry, take a dekko at (*Brit. slang*), lay *or* clap eyes on (*informal*) …*I saw a man making his way towards me…*
2 = <u>understand</u>, get, follow, realize, know, appreciate, take in, grasp, make out, catch on (*informal*), comprehend, fathom, get the hang of (*informal*), get the drift of …*Oh, I see what you're saying…*
3 = <u>foresee</u>, picture, imagine, anticipate, divine, envisage, visualize, foretell …*We can see a day when all people live side by side…*

4 = <u>find out</u>, learn, discover, determine, investigate, verify, ascertain, make inquiries …*I'd better go and see if she's all right…*
5 = <u>consider</u>, decide, judge, reflect, deliberate, mull over, think over, make up your mind, give some thought to …*We'll see what we can do, Miss…*
6 = <u>make sure</u>, mind, ensure, guarantee, take care, make certain, see to it …*See that you take care of him…*
7 = <u>accompany</u>, show, escort, lead, walk, attend, usher …*He didn't offer to see her to her car…*
8 = <u>speak to</u>, receive, interview, consult, confer with …*The doctor can see you now…*
9 = <u>meet</u>, encounter, come across, run into, happen on, bump into, run across, chance on …*I saw her last night at Monica's…*
10 = <u>go out with</u>, court, date (*informal, chiefly U.S.*), walk out with (*obsolete*), keep company with, go steady with (*informal*), consort *or* associate with …*My husband was still seeing her…*
PHRASES **see about something** = <u>take care of</u>, deal with, look after, see to, attend to …*I must see about selling the house…* ♦ **see something through** = <u>persevere (with)</u>, keep at, persist, stick out (*informal*), see out, stay to the bitter end …*He will not be credited with seeing the project through…*
♦ **see through something** *or* **someone** = <u>be undeceived by</u>, penetrate, be wise to (*informal*), fathom, get to the bottom of, not fall for, have (someone's) number (*informal*), read (someone) like a book …*I saw through your little ruse from the start…*
♦ **see to something** *or* **someone** = <u>take care of</u>, manage, arrange, look after, organize, be responsible for, sort out, attend to, take charge of, do …*Franklin saw to the luggage…* ♦ **seeing as** = <u>since</u>, as, in view of the fact that, inasmuch as …*Seeing as he is a doctor, I would assume he has a modicum of intelligence…*

> ## Word Power
>
> **see** – It is common to hear *seeing as how*, as in *seeing as how the bus is always late, I don't need to hurry*. However, the use of *how* here is considered incorrect or nonstandard, and should be avoided.

seed NOUN **1** = <u>grain</u>, pip, germ, kernel, egg, embryo, spore, ovum, egg cell, ovule …*a packet of cabbage seed…*
2 = <u>beginning</u>, start, suspicion, germ, inkling …*His questions were meant to plant seeds of doubt in our minds…*
3 = <u>origin</u>, source, nucleus …*the seed of an idea…*
4 (*Chiefly Bible*) = <u>offspring</u>, children, descendants, issue, race, successors, heirs, spawn, progeny, scions …*a curse on my seed…*
PHRASES **go** *or* **run to seed** = <u>decline</u>, deteriorate, degenerate, decay, go downhill (*informal*), go to waste, go to pieces, let yourself go, go to pot, go to rack and ruin, retrogress …*If unused, winter radishes*

run to seed in spring…

seedy 1 = <u>sleazy</u>, sordid, squalid, low, nasty …*They suck you into their seedy world…*
2 = <u>shabby</u>, run-down, scruffy, old, worn, faded, decaying, grubby, dilapidated, tatty, unkempt, grotty (*slang*), crummy (*slang*), down at heel, slovenly, mangy, manky (*Scot. dialect*), scungy (*Austral. & N.Z.*) …*a seedy hotel close to the red light district…* OPPOSITE> smart
3 (*Informal*) = <u>unwell</u>, ill, poorly (*informal*), crook (*Austral. & N.Z. informal*), ailing, sickly, out of sorts, off colour, under the weather (*informal*), peely-wally (*Scot.*) …*All right, are you? Not feeling seedy?…*

seek 1 = <u>look for</u>, pursue, search for, be after, hunt, go in search of, go in pursuit of, go gunning for, go in quest of …*They have had to seek work as labourers…*
2 = <u>request</u>, invite, ask for, petition, plead for, solicit, beg for, petition for …*The couple have sought help from marriage guidance counsellors…*
3 = <u>try</u>, attempt, aim, strive, endeavour, essay, aspire to, have a go at (*informal*) …*He also denied that he would seek to annex the country…*

seem = <u>appear</u>, give the impression of being, look, look to be, sound as if you are, look as if you are, look like you are, strike you as being, have the *or* every appearance of being

seeming = <u>apparent</u>, appearing, outward, surface, illusory, ostensible, specious, quasi-

seemingly = <u>apparently</u>, outwardly, on the surface, ostensibly, on the face of it, to all intents and purposes, to all appearances, as far as anyone could tell

seep = <u>ooze</u>, well, leak, soak, bleed, weep, trickle, leach, exude, permeate, percolate

seer = <u>prophet</u>, augur, predictor, soothsayer, sibyl

see-saw = <u>alternate</u>, swing, fluctuate, teeter, oscillate, go from one extreme to the other

seethe 1 = <u>be furious</u>, storm, rage, fume, simmer, be in a state (*informal*), see red (*informal*), be incensed, be livid, go ballistic (*slang, chiefly U.S.*), foam at the mouth, be incandescent, get hot under the collar (*informal*), wig out (*slang*), breathe fire and slaughter …*Under the surface she was seething…*
2 = <u>teem</u>, be full of, abound, swarm, bristle, brim, be abundant, be alive with, be crawling with …*The forest below him seethed and teemed with life…*
3 = <u>boil</u>, bubble, foam, churn, fizz, ferment, froth …*a seething cauldron of broth…*

segment = <u>section</u>, part, piece, division, slice, portion, wedge, compartment

segregate = <u>set apart</u>, divide, separate, isolate, single out, discriminate against, dissociate OPPOSITE> unite

segregation = <u>separation</u>, discrimination, apartheid, isolation

seize 1 = <u>grab</u>, grip, grasp, take, snatch, clutch, snap up, pluck, fasten, latch on to, lay hands on, catch *or* take hold of …*an otter seizing a fish…* OPPOSITE> let

go
2 = <u>take by storm</u>, take over, acquire, occupy, conquer, annex, usurp …*Troops have seized the airport and radio terminals…*
3 = <u>confiscate</u>, appropriate, commandeer, impound, take possession of, requisition, sequester, expropriate, sequestrate …*Police were reported to have seized all copies the newspaper…* OPPOSITE> hand back
4 = <u>capture</u>, catch, arrest, get, nail (*informal*), grasp, collar (*informal*), hijack, abduct, nab (*informal*), apprehend, take captive …*Men carrying sub-machine guns seized the five soldiers…* OPPOSITE> release

seizure 1 = <u>attack</u>, fit, spasm, convulsion, paroxysm …*I was prescribed drugs to control seizures…*
2 = <u>taking</u>, grabbing, annexation, confiscation, commandeering …*the seizure of territory through force…*
3 = <u>capture</u>, arrest, apprehension, abduction …*a mass seizure of hostages…*

seldom = <u>rarely</u>, occasionally, not often, infrequently, once in a blue moon (*informal*), hardly ever, scarcely ever OPPOSITE> often

select VERB = <u>choose</u>, take, pick, prefer, opt for, decide on, single out, adopt, single out, fix on, cherry-pick, settle upon …*They selected only bright pupils…* OPPOSITE> reject
ADJECTIVE 1 = <u>choice</u>, special, prime, picked, selected, excellent, rare, superior, first-class, posh (*informal, chiefly Brit.*), first-rate, hand-picked, top-notch (*informal*), recherché …*a select group of French cheeses…* OPPOSITE> ordinary
2 = <u>exclusive</u>, elite, privileged, limited, cliquish …*a meeting of a very select club…* OPPOSITE> indiscriminate

selection 1 = <u>choice</u>, choosing, pick, option, preference …*Make your selection from the list…*
2 = <u>anthology</u>, collection, medley, choice, line-up, mixed bag (*informal*), potpourri, miscellany …*this selection of popular songs…*

selective = <u>particular</u>, discriminating, critical, careful, discerning, astute, discriminatory, tasteful, fastidious OPPOSITE> indiscriminate

self-assurance = <u>confidence</u>, self-confidence, poise, nerve, assertiveness, self-possession, positiveness

self-centred = <u>selfish</u>, narcissistic, self-absorbed, inward looking, self-seeking, egotistic, wrapped up in yourself

self-confidence = <u>self-assurance</u>, confidence, poise, nerve, self-respect, aplomb, self-reliance, high morale

self-confident = <u>self-assured</u>, confident, assured, secure, poised, fearless, self-reliant, sure of yourself

self-conscious = <u>embarrassed</u>, nervous, uncomfortable, awkward, insecure, diffident, ill at ease, sheepish, bashful, shamefaced, like a fish out of water, out of countenance

self-control = <u>willpower</u>, restraint, self-discipline, cool, coolness, calmness, self-restraint, self-mastery, strength of mind *or* will

self-denial = <u>self-sacrifice</u>, renunciation, asceticism, abstemiousness, selflessness, unselfishness, self-abnegation

self-esteem = <u>self-respect</u>, confidence, courage, vanity, boldness, self-reliance, self-assurance, self-regard, self-possession, amour-propre (*French*), faith in yourself, pride in yourself

self-evident = <u>obvious</u>, clear, undeniable, inescapable, written all over (something), cut-and-dried (*informal*), incontrovertible, axiomatic, manifestly *or* patently true

self-government = <u>independence</u>, democracy, sovereignty, autonomy, devolution, self-determination, self-rule, home rule

self-important = <u>conceited</u>, arrogant, pompous, strutting, swaggering, cocky, pushy (*informal*), overbearing, presumptuous, bumptious, swollen-headed, bigheaded, full of yourself

self-indulgence = <u>extravagance</u>, excess, incontinence, dissipation, self-gratification, intemperance, sensualism

selfish = <u>self-centred</u>, self-interested, greedy, mercenary, self-seeking, ungenerous, egoistic *or* egoistical, egotistic *or* egoistical, looking out for number one (*informal*) OPPOSITE> unselfish

selfless = <u>unselfish</u>, generous, altruistic, self-sacrificing, magnanimous, self-denying, ungrudging

self-reliant = <u>independent</u>, capable, self-sufficient, self-supporting, able to stand on your own two feet (*informal*) OPPOSITE> dependent

self-respect = <u>pride</u>, dignity, self-esteem, morale, amour-propre (*French*), faith in yourself

self-restraint = <u>self-control</u>, self-discipline, willpower, patience, forbearance, abstemiousness, self-command

self-righteous = <u>sanctimonious</u>, smug, pious, superior, complacent, hypocritical, pi (*Brit. slang*), too good to be true, self-satisfied, goody-goody (*informal*), holier-than-thou, priggish, pietistic, pharisaic

self-sacrifice = <u>selflessness</u>, altruism, self-denial, generosity, self-abnegation

self-satisfied = <u>smug</u>, complacent, proud of yourself, well-pleased, puffed up, self-congratulatory, flushed with success, pleased with yourself, like a cat that has swallowed the canary, too big for your boots *or* breeches

self-styled = <u>so-called</u>, would-be, professed, self-appointed, soi-disant (*French*), quasi-

sell VERB **1** = <u>trade</u>, dispose of, exchange, barter, put up for sale ...*I sold everything I owned except for my car and books...* OPPOSITE> buy
2 = <u>deal in</u>, market, trade in, stock, handle, retail, hawk, merchandise, peddle, traffic in, vend, be in the business of ...*It sells everything from hair ribbons to oriental rugs...* OPPOSITE> buy
3 = <u>promote</u>, put across, gain acceptance for ...*She is*

hoping she can sell the idea to clients...
PHRASES **sell out of something** = <u>run out of</u>, be out of stock of ...*Hardware stores have sold out of water pumps and tarpaulins...*

seller = <u>dealer</u>, merchant, vendor, agent, representative, rep, retailer, traveller, supplier, shopkeeper, purveyor, tradesman, salesman *or* saleswoman

semblance = <u>appearance</u>, show, form, air, figure, front, image, bearing, aspect, mask, similarity, resemblance, guise, façade, pretence, veneer, likeness, mien

semen = <u>sperm</u>, seed (*archaic or dialect*), scum (*U.S. slang*), seminal fluid, spermatic fluid

seminal = <u>influential</u>, important, ground-breaking, original, creative, productive, innovative, imaginative, formative

seminary = <u>college</u>, school, high school, academy, institution, institute

send VERB **1** = <u>dispatch</u>, forward, direct, convey, consign, remit ...*He sent a basket of exotic fruit and a card...*
2 = <u>transmit</u>, broadcast, communicate ...*The space probe Voyager sent back pictures of Triton...*
3 = <u>propel</u>, hurl, fling, shoot, fire, deliver, cast, let fly ...*He let me go with a thrust of his wrist that sent me flying...*
PHRASES **send something** *or* **someone up** (*Brit. informal*) = <u>mock</u>, mimic, parody, spoof (*informal*), imitate, take off (*informal*), make fun of, lampoon, burlesque, take the mickey out of (*informal*), satirize ...*a spoof that sends up the macho world of fighter pilots...*

send-off = <u>farewell</u>, departure, leave-taking, valediction, going-away party

send-up = <u>parody</u>, take-off (*informal*), satire, mockery, spoof (*informal*), imitation, skit, mickey-take (*informal*)

senile = <u>doddering</u>, doting, decrepit, failing, imbecile, gaga (*informal*), in your dotage, in your second childhood

---

Word Power

senile – Words such as *senile* and *geriatric* are only properly used as medical terms. They are very insulting when used loosely to describe a person of advanced years. Care should be taken when using *old* and its synonyms, as they can all potentially cause offence.

---

senility = <u>dotage</u>, Alzheimer's disease, infirmity, senile dementia, decrepitude, senescence, second childhood, caducity, loss of your faculties

senior 1 = <u>higher ranking</u>, superior ...*Television and radio needed many more women in senior jobs...* OPPOSITE> subordinate
2 = <u>the elder</u>, major (*Brit.*) ...*George Bush Senior...* OPPOSITE> junior

senior citizen = <u>pensioner</u>, retired person, old age pensioner, O.A.P., elder, old *or* elderly person

seniority = <u>superiority</u>, rank, priority, precedence, longer service

sensation 1 = <u>feeling</u>, sense, impression, perception, awareness, consciousness …*A sensation of burning or tingling may be felt in the hands*…
2 = <u>excitement</u>, surprise, thrill, stir, scandal, furore, agitation, commotion …*she caused a sensation at the Montreal Olympics*…
3 (*informal*) = <u>hit</u>, wow (*slang, chiefly U.S.*), crowd puller (*informal*) …*the film that turned her into an overnight sensation*…

sensational 1 = <u>amazing</u>, dramatic, thrilling, revealing, spectacular, staggering, startling, horrifying, breathtaking, astounding, lurid, electrifying, hair-raising …*The world champions suffered a sensational defeat*… OPPOSITE dull
2 = <u>shocking</u>, scandalous, exciting, yellow (*of the press*), melodramatic, shock-horror (*facetious*), sensationalistic …*sensational tabloid newspaper reports*… OPPOSITE unexciting
3 (*Informal*) = <u>excellent</u>, brilliant, superb, mean (*slang*), topping (*Brit. slang*), cracking (*Brit. informal*), crucial (*slang*), impressive, smashing (*informal*), fabulous (*informal*), first class, marvellous, exceptional, mega (*slang*), sovereign, awesome (*slang*), def (*slang*), brill (*informal*), out of this world (*informal*), mind-blowing (*informal*), bodacious (*slang, chiefly U.S.*), boffo (*slang*), jim-dandy (*slang*), chillin' (*U.S. slang*), booshit (*Austral. slang*), exo (*Austral. slang*), sik (*Austral. slang*) …*Her voice is sensational*… OPPOSITE ordinary

sense NOUN 1 = <u>faculty</u>, sensibility …*a keen sense of smell*…
2 = <u>feeling</u>, impression, perception, awareness, consciousness, atmosphere, aura, intuition, premonition, presentiment …*There is no sense of urgency on either side*…
3 = <u>understanding</u>, awareness, appreciation …*He has an impeccable sense of timing*…
4 *sometimes plural* = <u>intelligence</u>, reason, understanding, brains (*informal*), smarts (*slang, chiefly U.S.*), judgment, discrimination, wisdom, wit(s), common sense, sanity, sharpness, tact, nous (*Brit. slang*), cleverness, quickness, discernment, gumption (*Brit. informal*), sagacity, clear-headedness, mother wit …*When he was younger he had a bit more sense*… OPPOSITE foolishness
5 = <u>point</u>, good, use, reason, value, worth, advantage, purpose, logic …*There's no sense in pretending this doesn't happen*…
6 = <u>meaning</u>, definition, interpretation, significance, message, import, substance, implication, drift, purport, nuance, gist, signification, denotation …*a noun which has two senses*…
VERB = <u>perceive</u>, feel, understand, notice, pick up, suspect, realize, observe, appreciate, grasp, be aware of, divine, discern, just know, have a (funny) feeling (*informal*), get the impression, apprehend, have a

hunch …*He had sensed what might happen*… OPPOSITE be unaware of

senseless 1 = <u>pointless</u>, mad, crazy, stupid, silly, ridiculous, absurd, foolish, daft (*informal*), ludicrous, meaningless, unreasonable, irrational, inconsistent, unwise, mindless, illogical, incongruous, idiotic, nonsensical, inane, fatuous, moronic, unintelligent, asinine, imbecilic, dumb-ass (*slang*), without rhyme or reason, halfwitted …*acts of senseless violence*… OPPOSITE sensible
2 = <u>unconscious</u>, stunned, insensible, out, cold, numb, numbed, deadened, unfeeling, out cold, anaesthetized, insensate …*Then I saw my boy lying senseless on the floor*… OPPOSITE conscious

sensibility 1 = <u>awareness</u>, insight, intuition, taste, appreciation, delicacy, discernment, perceptiveness …*Everything he writes demonstrates the depths of his sensibility*… OPPOSITE lack of awareness
2 *often plural* = <u>feelings</u>, emotions, sentiments, susceptibilities, moral sense …*The challenge offended their sensibilities*…

sensible 1 = <u>wise</u>, practical, prudent, shrewd, well-informed, judicious, well-advised …*It might be sensible to get a solicitor*… OPPOSITE foolish
2 = <u>intelligent</u>, practical, reasonable, rational, sound, realistic, sober, discriminating, discreet, sage, shrewd, down-to-earth, matter-of-fact, prudent, sane, canny, judicious, far-sighted, sagacious …*She was a sensible girl and did not panic*… OPPOSITE senseless

sensitive 1 = <u>thoughtful</u>, kind, kindly, concerned, patient, attentive, tactful, unselfish …*He was always so sensitive and caring*…
2 = <u>delicate</u>, tender …*gentle cosmetics for sensitive skin*…
3 = <u>susceptible to</u>, responsive to, reactive to, easily affected by …*My eyes are overly sensitive to bright light*…
4 = <u>touchy</u>, oversensitive, easily upset, easily offended, easily hurt, umbrageous (*rare*) …*Young people are very sensitive about their appearance*… OPPOSITE insensitive
5 = <u>precise</u>, fine, acute, keen, responsive, perceptive …*an extremely sensitive microscope*… OPPOSITE imprecise

sensitivity 1 = <u>susceptibility</u>, responsiveness, reactivity, receptiveness, sensitiveness, reactiveness …*the sensitivity of cells to chemotherapy*…
2 = <u>consideration</u>, patience, thoughtfulness …*concern and sensitivity for each other's feelings*…
3 = <u>touchiness</u>, oversensitivity …*an atmosphere of extreme sensitivity over the situation*…
4 = <u>responsiveness</u>, precision, keenness, acuteness …*the sensitivity of the detector*…

sensual 1 = <u>sexual</u>, sexy (*informal*), erotic, randy (*informal, chiefly Brit.*), steamy (*informal*), raunchy (*slang*), lewd, lascivious, lustful, lecherous, libidinous, licentious, unchaste …*He was a very sensual person*…
2 = <u>physical</u>, bodily, voluptuous, animal, luxurious, fleshly, carnal, epicurean, unspiritual …*sensual*

pleasure...

sensuality = <u>eroticism</u>, sexiness (*informal*), voluptuousness, prurience, licentiousness, carnality, lewdness, salaciousness, lasciviousness, animalism, libidinousness, lecherousness

sensuous = <u>pleasurable</u>, pleasing, sensory, gratifying

sentence NOUN **1** = <u>punishment</u>, prison term, condemnation ...*He was given a four-year sentence...* **2** = <u>verdict</u>, order, ruling, decision, judgment, decree, pronouncement ...*When she heard of the sentence, she said: 'Is that all?'...*
▸ VERB **1** = <u>condemn</u>, doom ...*A military court sentenced him to death in his absence...* **2** = <u>convict</u>, condemn, penalize, pass judgment on, mete out justice to ...*They sentenced him for punching a policewoman...*

sentient = <u>feeling</u>, living, conscious, live, sensitive, reactive

sentiment **1** = <u>feeling</u>, thought, idea, view, opinion, attitude, belief, judgment, persuasion, way of thinking ...*The Foreign Secretary echoed this sentiment...* **2** = <u>sentimentality</u>, emotion, tenderness, romanticism, sensibility, slush (*informal*), emotionalism, tender feeling, mawkishness, soft-heartedness, overemotionalism ...*Laura kept that letter out of sentiment...*

sentimental = <u>romantic</u>, touching, emotional, tender, pathetic, nostalgic, sloppy (*informal*), tearful, corny (*slang*), impressionable, mushy (*informal*), maudlin, simpering, weepy (*informal*), slushy (*informal*), mawkish, tear-jerking (*informal*), drippy (*informal*), schmaltzy (*slang*), icky (*informal*), gushy (*informal*), soft-hearted, overemotional, dewy-eyed, three-hankie (*informal*) OPPOSITE unsentimental

sentimentality = <u>romanticism</u>, nostalgia, tenderness, gush (*informal*), pathos, slush (*informal*), mush (*informal*), schmaltz (*slang*), sloppiness (*informal*), emotionalism, bathos, mawkishness, corniness (*slang*), play on the emotions, sob stuff (*informal*)

sentinel = <u>guard</u>, watch, lookout, sentry, picket, watchman

separate ADJECTIVE **1** = <u>unconnected</u>, individual, particular, divided, divorced, isolated, detached, disconnected, discrete, unattached, disjointed ...*The two things are separate and mutually irrelevant...* OPPOSITE connected **2** = <u>individual</u>, independent, apart, distinct, autonomous ...*We both live our separate lives...* OPPOSITE joined
▸ VERB **1** = <u>divide</u>, detach, disconnect, come between, disentangle, keep apart, disjoin ...*Police moved in to separate the two groups...* OPPOSITE combine **2** = <u>come apart</u>, split, break off, come away ...*The nose section separates from the fuselage...* OPPOSITE connect **3** = <u>sever</u>, disconnect, break apart, split in two, divide in two, uncouple, bifurcate ...*Separate the garlic into*

cloves... OPPOSITE join **4** = <u>split up</u>, part, divorce, break up, part company, get divorced, be estranged, go different ways ...*Her parents separated when she was very young...* **5** = <u>distinguish</u>, mark, single out, set apart, make distinctive, set at variance *or* at odds ...*What separates terrorism from other acts of violence?...* OPPOSITE link

separated **1** = <u>estranged</u>, parted, split up, separate, apart, broken up, disunited, living apart *or* separately ...*Most single parents are either separated or divorced...* **2** = <u>disconnected</u>, parted, divided, separate, disassociated, disunited, sundered, put asunder ...*They're trying their best to bring together separated families...*

separately **1** = <u>alone</u>, independently, apart, personally, not together, severally ...*Chris had insisted that we went separately to the club...* OPPOSITE together **2** = <u>individually</u>, singly, one by one, one at a time ...*Cook the stuffing separately...*

separation **1** = <u>division</u>, break, segregation, detachment, severance, disengagement, dissociation, disconnection, disjunction, disunion ...*a permanent separation from his son...* **2** = <u>split-up</u>, parting, split, divorce, break-up, farewell, rift, estrangement, leave-taking ...*They agreed to a trial separation...*

septic = <u>infected</u>, poisoned, toxic, festering, pussy, putrid, putrefying, suppurating, putrefactive

sequel **1** = <u>follow-up</u>, continuation, development ...*She is currently writing a sequel...* **2** = <u>consequence</u>, result, outcome, conclusion, end, issue, payoff (*informal*), upshot ...*The arrests were a direct sequel to the investigations...*

sequence **1** = <u>succession</u>, course, series, order, chain, cycle, arrangement, procession, progression ...*the sequence of events that led to the murder...* **2** = <u>order</u>, structure, arrangement, ordering, placement, layout, progression ...*The chronological sequence gives the book an element of structure...*

serene = <u>calm</u>, peaceful, tranquil, composed, sedate, placid, undisturbed, untroubled, unruffled, imperturbable

serenity = <u>calm</u>, peace, tranquillity, composure, peace of mind, stillness, calmness, quietness, peacefulness, quietude, placidity

serf = <u>vassal</u>, servant, slave, thrall, bondsman, varlet (*archaic*), helot, villein, liegeman

series **1** = <u>sequence</u>, course, chain, succession, run, set, line, order, train, arrangement, string, progression ...*a series of explosions...* **2** = <u>drama</u>, serial, soap (*informal*), sitcom (*informal*), soap opera, soapie (*Austral. slang*), situation comedy ...*Channel 4's 'GBH' won best drama series...*

serious ADJECTIVE **1** = <u>grave</u>, bad, critical, worrying, dangerous, acute, alarming, severe, extreme, grievous ...*His condition was serious but stable...*

2 = <u>important</u>, crucial, urgent, pressing, difficult, worrying, deep, significant, grim, far-reaching, momentous, fateful, weighty, no laughing matter, of moment *or* consequence ...*I regard this as a serious matter...* OPPOSITE unimportant

3 = <u>thoughtful</u>, detailed, careful, deep, profound, in-depth ...*It was a question which deserved serious consideration...*

4 = <u>deep</u>, sophisticated, highbrowed ...*a serious novel...*

5 = <u>solemn</u>, earnest, grave, stern, sober, thoughtful, sedate, glum, staid, humourless, long-faced, pensive, unsmiling ...*He's quite a serious person...* OPPOSITE light-hearted

6 = <u>sincere</u>, determined, earnest, resolved, genuine, deliberate, honest, resolute, in earnest ...*You really are serious about this, aren't you?...* OPPOSITE insincere

seriously 1 = <u>truly</u>, no joking (*informal*), in earnest, all joking aside ...*Seriously, though, something must be done about it...*

2 = <u>badly</u>, severely, gravely, critically, acutely, sorely, dangerously, distressingly, grievously ...*Three people were seriously injured in the blast...*

seriousness 1 = <u>importance</u>, gravity, urgency, moment, weight, danger, significance ...*the seriousness of the crisis...*

2 = <u>solemnity</u>, gravity, earnestness, sobriety, gravitas, sternness, humourlessness, staidness, sedateness ...*They had shown a commitment and a seriousness of purpose...*

sermon = <u>homily</u>, address, exhortation

serpentine = <u>twisting</u>, winding, snaking, crooked, coiling, meandering, tortuous, sinuous, twisty, snaky

serrated = <u>notched</u>, toothed, sawtoothed, serrate, serrulate, sawlike, serriform (*Biology*)

servant = <u>attendant</u>, domestic, slave, maid, help, helper, retainer, menial, drudge, lackey, vassal, skivvy (*chiefly Brit.*), servitor (*archaic*), varlet (*archaic*), liegeman

serve VERB **1** = <u>work for</u>, help, aid, assist, be in the service of ...*soldiers who have served their country well...*

2 = <u>perform</u>, do, complete, go through, fulfil, pass, discharge ...*He had served an apprenticeship as a bricklayer...*

3 = <u>be adequate</u>, do, suffice, answer, suit, content, satisfy, be good enough, be acceptable, fill the bill (*informal*), answer the purpose ...*This little book should serve...*

4 = <u>present</u>, provide, supply, deliver, arrange, set out, distribute, dish up, purvey ...*Serve it with French bread...*

PHRASES **serve as something** *or* **someone** = <u>act as</u>, function as, do the work of, do duty as ...*She ushered me into the front room, which served as her office...*

service NOUN **1** = <u>facility</u>, system, resource, utility, amenity ...*a campaign for better social services...*

2 = <u>ceremony</u>, worship, rite, function, observance ...*The President was attending the morning service...*

3 = <u>work</u>, labour, employment, business, office, duty, employ ...*If a young woman did not have a dowry, she went into domestic service...*

4 = <u>check</u>, servicing, maintenance check ...*The car needs a service...*

VERB = <u>overhaul</u>, check, maintain, tune (up), repair, go over, fine tune, recondition ...*Make sure that all gas fires are serviced annually...*

serviceable = <u>useful</u>, practical, efficient, helpful, profitable, convenient, operative, beneficial, functional, durable, usable, dependable, advantageous, utilitarian, hard-wearing OPPOSITE useless

servile = <u>subservient</u>, cringing, grovelling, mean, low, base, humble, craven, fawning, abject, submissive, menial, sycophantic, slavish, unctuous, obsequious, toadying, bootlicking (*informal*), toadyish

serving = <u>portion</u>, helping, plateful

servitude (*Formal*) = <u>slavery</u>, bondage, enslavement, bonds, chains, obedience, thrall, subjugation, serfdom, vassalage, thraldom

session = <u>meeting</u>, hearing, sitting, term, period, conference, congress, discussion, assembly, seminar, get-together (*informal*)

set¹ VERB **1** = <u>put</u>, place, lay, park (*informal*), position, rest, plant, station, stick, deposit, locate, lodge, situate, plump, plonk ...*He took the case out of her hand and set it on the floor...*

2 = <u>switch on</u>, turn on, activate, programme ...*I forgot to set my alarm and I overslept...*

3 = <u>adjust</u>, regulate, coordinate, rectify, synchronize ...*He set his watch, then waited for five minutes...*

4 = <u>embed</u>, fix, mount, install, fasten ...*a gate set in a high wall...*

5 = <u>arrange</u>, decide (upon), settle, name, establish, determine, fix, schedule, appoint, specify, allocate, designate, ordain, fix up, agree upon ...*A date will be set for a future meeting...*

6 = <u>assign</u>, give, allot, prescribe ...*We will train you first before we set you a task...*

7 = <u>harden</u>, stiffen, condense, solidify, cake, thicken, crystallize, congeal, jell, gelatinize ...*Lower the heat and allow the omelet to set on the bottom...*

8 = <u>go down</u>, sink, dip, decline, disappear, vanish, subside ...*The sun sets at about 4pm in winter...*

9 = <u>prepare</u>, lay, spread, arrange, make ready ...*She had set the table and was drinking coffee at the hearth...*

ADJECTIVE **1** = <u>established</u>, planned, decided, agreed, usual, arranged, rigid, definite, inflexible, hard and fast, immovable ...*A set period of fasting is supposed to bring us closer to godliness...*

2 = <u>strict</u>, firm, rigid, hardened, stubborn, entrenched, inflexible, hidebound ...*They have very set ideas about how to get the message across...* OPPOSITE flexible

3 = <u>conventional</u>, stock, standard, traditional, formal, routine, artificial, stereotyped, rehearsed, hackneyed, unspontaneous ...*Use the subjunctive in some set*

phrases and idioms…

NOUN 1 = <u>scenery</u>, setting, scene, stage setting, stage set, mise-en-scène (*French*) …*a movie set*…

2 = <u>position</u>, bearing, attitude, carriage, turn, fit, hang, posture …*the set of his shoulders*…

PHRASES **be set on** *or* **upon something** = <u>be determined to</u>, be intent on, be bent on, be resolute about …*She was set on going to an all-girls school*…

◆ **set about someone** = <u>assault</u>, attack, mug (*informal*), assail, sail into (*informal*), lambast(e), belabour …*Several thugs set about him with clubs*…

◆ **set about something** = <u>begin</u>, start, get down to, attack, tackle, set to, get to work, sail into (*informal*), take the first step, wade into, get cracking (*informal*), make a start on, roll up your sleeves, get weaving (*informal*), address yourself to, put your shoulder to the wheel (*informal*) …*He set about proving she was completely wrong*… ◆ **set off** = <u>leave</u>, set out, depart, embark, start out, sally forth …*I set off, full of optimism*… ◆ **set on** *or* **upon someone** = <u>attack</u>, beat up, assault, turn on, mug (*informal*), set about, ambush, go for, sic, pounce on, fly at, work over (*slang*), assail, sail into (*informal*), fall upon, lay into (*informal*), put the boot in (*slang*), pitch into (*informal*), let fly at …*We were set upon by three youths*… ◆ **set out** = <u>embark</u>, set off, start out, begin, get under way, hit the road (*slang*), take to the road, sally forth …*When setting out on a long walk, always wear suitable boots*… ◆ **set someone against someone** = <u>alienate</u>, oppose, divide, drive a wedge between, disunite, estrange, set at odds, make bad blood between, make mischief between, set at cross purposes, set by the ears (*informal*), sow dissension amongst …*The case has set neighbour against neighbour in the village*… ◆ **set something against something** = <u>balance</u>, compare, contrast, weigh, juxtapose …*a considerable sum when set against the maximum wage*… ◆ **set something aside** 1 = <u>reserve</u>, keep, save, separate, select, single out, earmark, keep back, set apart, put on one side …*£130 million would be set aside for repairs to schools*… 2 = <u>reject</u>, dismiss, reverse, cancel, overturn, discard, quash, overrule, repudiate, annul, nullify, abrogate, render null and void …*The decision was set aside because one of the judges had links with the defendant*… ◆ **set something back** = <u>hold up</u>, slow, delay, hold back, hinder, obstruct, retard, impede, slow up …*a risk of public protest that could set back reforms*… ◆ **set something off** 1 = <u>detonate</u>, trigger (off), explode, ignite, light, set in motion, touch off …*Who set off the bomb?*… 2 = <u>cause</u>, start, produce, generate, prompt, trigger (off), provoke, bring about, give rise to, spark off, set in motion …*It set off a storm of speculation*… 3 = <u>enhance</u>, show off, throw into relief, bring out the highlights in …*Blue suits you – it sets off the colour of your hair*… ◆ **set something out** 1 = <u>arrange</u>, present, display, lay out, exhibit, array, dispose, set forth, expose to view …*Set out the cakes attractively*… 2 = <u>explain</u>, list, describe, detail,

elaborate, recount, enumerate, elucidate, itemize, particularize …*He has written a letter setting out his views*… ◆ **set something up** 1 = <u>arrange</u>, organize, prepare, make provision for, prearrange …*an organization that sets up meetings*… 2 = <u>establish</u>, begin, found, institute, install, initiate …*He set up the company four years ago*… 3 = <u>build</u>, raise, construct, put up, assemble, put together, erect, elevate …*The activists set up a peace camp at the border*… 4 = <u>assemble</u>, put up …*I set up the computer so that they could work from home*…

set² 1 = <u>series</u>, collection, assortment, kit, outfit, batch, compendium, assemblage, coordinated group, ensemble …*Only she and Mr Cohen had complete sets of keys to the shop*…

2 = <u>group</u>, company, crowd, circle, class, band, crew (*informal*), gang, outfit, faction, sect, posse (*informal*), clique, coterie, schism …*the popular watering hole for the literary set*…

setback = <u>hold-up</u>, check, defeat, blow, upset, reverse, disappointment, hitch, misfortune, rebuff, whammy (*informal, chiefly U.S.*), bummer (*slang*), bit of trouble

setting = <u>surroundings</u>, site, location, set, scene, surround, background, frame, context, perspective, backdrop, scenery, locale, mise en scène (*French*)

settle **VERB** 1 = <u>resolve</u>, work out, put an end to, straighten out, set to rights …*They agreed to try and settle their dispute by negotiation*…

2 = <u>pay</u>, clear, square (up), discharge …*I settled the bill for my coffee and his two glasses of wine*…

3 = <u>move to</u>, take up residence in, live in, dwell in, inhabit, reside in, set up home in, put down roots in, make your home in …*He visited Paris and eventually settled there*…

4 = <u>colonize</u>, populate, people, pioneer …*This was one of the first areas to be settled by Europeans*…

5 = <u>make comfortable</u>, bed down …*Albert settled himself on the sofa*…

6 = <u>subside</u>, fall, sink, decline …*Once its impurities had settled, the oil could be graded*…

7 = <u>land</u>, alight, descend, light, come to rest …*The birds settled less than two hundred paces away*…

8 = <u>calm</u>, quiet, relax, relieve, reassure, compose, soothe, lull, quell, allay, sedate, pacify, quieten, tranquillize …*They needed a win to settle their nerves*… **OPPOSITE** disturb

PHRASES **settle on** *or* **upon something** *or* **someone** = <u>decide on</u>, choose, pick, select, adopt, agree on, opt for, fix on, elect for …*We finally settled on a Mercedes estate*…

settlement 1 = <u>agreement</u>, arrangement, resolution, working out, conclusion, establishment, adjustment, confirmation, completion, disposition, termination …*Our objective must be to secure a peace settlement*…

2 = <u>payment</u>, clearing, discharge, clearance, defrayal …*ways to delay the settlement of debts*…

3 = <u>colony</u>, community, outpost, peopling, hamlet, encampment, colonization …*a Muslim settlement*…

settler = <u>colonist</u>, immigrant, pioneer, colonizer, frontiersman

set-up (*Informal*) = <u>arrangement</u>, system, structure, organization, conditions, circumstances, regime

sever 1 = <u>cut</u>, separate, split, part, divide, rend, detach, disconnect, cleave, bisect, disunite, cut in two, sunder, disjoin ...*Oil was still gushing from the severed fuel line...* OPPOSITE> join
2 = <u>discontinue</u>, terminate, break off, abandon, dissolve, put an end to, dissociate ...*He was able to sever all emotional bonds to his family...* OPPOSITE> continue

several ADJECTIVE = <u>some</u>, a few, a number of, a handful of, many, manifold ...*I had lived two doors away from his family for several years...*
PRONOUN = <u>various</u>, different, diverse, divers (*archaic*), assorted, disparate, indefinite, sundry ...*one of several failed attempts...*

severe 1 = <u>serious</u>, critical, terrible, desperate, alarming, extreme, awful, distressing, appalling, drastic, catastrophic, woeful, ruinous ...*a business with severe cash flow problems...*
2 = <u>acute</u>, extreme, intense, burning, violent, piercing, racking, searing, tormenting, exquisite, harrowing, unbearable, agonizing, insufferable, torturous, unendurable ...*He woke up blinded and in severe pain...*
3 = <u>tough</u>, hard, difficult, taxing, demanding, fierce, punishing, exacting, rigorous, stringent, arduous, unrelenting ...*He had faced an appallingly severe task in the jungle...* OPPOSITE> easy
4 = <u>strict</u>, hard, harsh, cruel, rigid, relentless, drastic, oppressive, austere, Draconian, unrelenting, inexorable, pitiless, unbending, iron-handed ...*This was a dreadful crime and a severe sentence is necessary...* OPPOSITE> lenient
5 = <u>grim</u>, serious, grave, cold, forbidding, stern, sober, disapproving, dour, unsmiling, flinty, strait-laced, tight-lipped ...*He had a severe look that disappeared when he smiled...* OPPOSITE> genial
6 = <u>plain</u>, simple, austere, classic, restrained, functional, Spartan, ascetic, unadorned, unfussy, unembellished ...*wearing her felt hats and severe grey suits...* OPPOSITE> fancy
7 = <u>harsh</u>, cutting, biting, scathing, satirical, caustic, astringent, vitriolic, mordant, unsparing, mordacious ...*The team has suffered severe criticism from influential figures...* OPPOSITE> kind

severely 1 = <u>seriously</u>, badly, extremely, gravely, hard, sorely, dangerously, critically, acutely ...*the severely depressed construction industry...*
2 = <u>strictly</u>, harshly, sternly, rigorously, sharply, like a ton of bricks (*informal*), with an iron hand, with a rod of iron ...*They should punish these drivers more severely...*

severity = <u>strictness</u>, seriousness, harshness, austerity, rigour, toughness, hardness, stringency, sternness, severeness

sew = <u>stitch</u>, tack, seam, hem

sex 1 = <u>gender</u> ...*differences between the sexes...*
2 = <u>facts of life</u>, sexuality, reproduction, the birds and the bees (*informal*) ...*a campaign to help parents talk about sex with their children...*
3 (*Informal*) = <u>lovemaking</u>, sexual relations, copulation, the other (*informal*), screwing (*taboo slang*), intimacy, going to bed (with someone), shagging (*Brit. taboo slang*), nookie (*slang*), fornication, coitus, rumpy-pumpy (*slang*), legover (*slang*), coition ...*The entire film revolves around sex and drugs...*

sex appeal = <u>desirability</u>, attractiveness, allure, glamour, sensuality, magnetism, sexiness (*informal*), oomph (*informal*), it (*informal*), voluptuousness, seductiveness

sexual 1 = <u>carnal</u>, erotic, intimate, of the flesh, coital ...*Men's sexual fantasies often have little to do with their sexual desire...*
2 = <u>sexy</u>, erotic, sensual, inviting, bedroom, provoking, arousing, naughty, provocative, seductive, sensuous, suggestive, voluptuous, slinky, titillating, flirtatious, come-hither (*informal*), kissable, beddable ...*exchanging sexual glances...*

sexual intercourse = <u>copulation</u>, sex (*informal*), the other (*informal*), union, coupling, congress, mating, commerce (*archaic*), screwing (*taboo slang*), intimacy, penetration, shagging (*Brit. taboo slang*), nookie (*slang*), consummation, bonking (*informal*), coitus, carnal knowledge, rumpy-pumpy (*slang*), legover (*slang*), coition

sexuality = <u>desire</u>, lust, eroticism, sensuality, virility, sexiness (*informal*), voluptuousness, carnality, bodily appetites ...*the growing discussion of human sexuality...*

sexy = <u>erotic</u>, sensual, seductive, inviting, bedroom, provoking, arousing, naughty, provocative, sensuous, suggestive, voluptuous, slinky, titillating, flirtatious, come-hither (*informal*), kissable, beddable

shabby 1 = <u>tatty</u>, worn, ragged, scruffy, faded, frayed, worn-out, tattered, threadbare, down at heel, the worse for wear, having seen better days ...*His clothes were old and shabby...* OPPOSITE> smart
2 = <u>run-down</u>, seedy, mean, neglected, dilapidated ...*a rather shabby Naples hotel...*
3 = <u>mean</u>, low, rotten (*informal*), cheap, dirty, shameful, low-down (*informal*), shoddy, unworthy, despicable, contemptible, scurvy, dishonourable, ignoble, ungentlemanly ...*It was hard to know why the man deserved such shabby treatment...* OPPOSITE> fair

shack = <u>hut</u>, cabin, shanty, lean-to, dump (*informal*), hovel, shiel (*Scot.*), shieling (*Scot.*)

shackle VERB 1 = <u>hamper</u>, limit, restrict, restrain, hamstring, inhibit, constrain, obstruct, impede, encumber, tie (someone's) hands ...*The trade unions are shackled by the law...*
2 = <u>fetter</u>, chain, handcuff, secure, bind, hobble, manacle, trammel, put in irons ...*She was shackled to a wall...*

NOUN *often plural* = <u>fetter</u>, chain, iron, bond, handcuff, hobble, manacle, leg-iron, gyve (*archaic*) ...*He unbolted the shackles on Billy's hands...*

shade NOUN **1** = <u>hue</u>, tone, colour, tint ...*The walls were painted in two shades of green...*

2 = <u>shadow</u>, screen, shadows, coolness, shadiness ...*Exotic trees provide welcome shade...*

3 = <u>dash</u>, trace, hint, suggestion, suspicion, small amount, semblance ...*There was a shade of irony in her voice...*

4 = <u>nuance</u>, difference, degree, graduation, subtlety ...*the capacity to convey subtle shades of meaning...*

5 = <u>screen</u>, covering, cover, blind, curtain, shield, veil, canopy ...*She left the shades down and the lights off...*

6 (*Literary*) = <u>ghost</u>, spirit, shadow, phantom, spectre, manes, apparition, eidolon ...*His writing benefits from the shade of Lincoln hovering over his shoulder...*

VERB **1** = <u>darken</u>, shadow, cloud, dim, cast a shadow over, shut out the light ...*a health resort whose beaches are shaded by palm trees...*

2 = <u>cover</u>, protect, screen, hide, shield, conceal, obscure, veil, mute ...*You've got to shade your eyes or close them altogether...*

PHRASES **put something** *or* **someone in the shade** = <u>outshine</u>, exceed, eclipse, outdo, overshadow, surpass, transcend, outclass, outshine, make pale by comparison ...*a run that put every other hurdler's performance in the shade...*

shadow NOUN **1** = <u>silhouette</u>, shape, outline, profile ...*All he could see was his shadow...*

2 = <u>shade</u>, dimness, darkness, gloom, cover, protection, shelter, dusk, obscurity, gloaming (*Scot. or poetic*), gathering darkness ...*Most of the lake was in shadow...*

VERB **1** = <u>shade</u>, screen, shield, darken, overhang, cast a shadow over ...*The hood shadowed her face...*

2 = <u>follow</u>, dog, tail (*informal*), trail, stalk, spy on ...*shadowed by a large and highly visible body of police...*

shadowy 1 = <u>dark</u>, shaded, dim, gloomy, shady, obscure, murky, dusky, funereal, crepuscular, tenebrous, tenebrious ...*I watched him from a shadowy corner...*

2 = <u>vague</u>, indistinct, faint, ghostly, obscure, dim, phantom, imaginary, unreal, intangible, illusory, spectral, undefined, nebulous, dreamlike, impalpable, unsubstantial, wraithlike ...*the shadowy shape of a big barge loaded with logs...*

shady 1 = <u>shaded</u>, cool, shadowy, dim, leafy, bowery, bosky (*literary*), umbrageous ...*After flowering, place the pot in a shady spot...* OPPOSITE sunny

2 (*Informal*) = <u>crooked</u>, dodgy (*Brit., Austral., & N.Z. informal*), unethical, suspect, suspicious, dubious, slippery, questionable, unscrupulous, fishy (*informal*), shifty, disreputable, untrustworthy ...*Be wary of people who try to talk you into shady deals...* OPPOSITE honest

shaft 1 = <u>tunnel</u>, hole, passage, burrow, passageway, channel ...*old mine shafts...*

2 = <u>handle</u>, staff, pole, rod, stem, upright, baton, shank

...*a drive shaft...*

3 = <u>ray</u>, beam, gleam, streak ...*A brilliant shaft of sunlight burst through the doorway...*

shaggy = <u>unkempt</u>, rough, tousled, hairy, long-haired, hirsute, unshorn OPPOSITE smooth

shake VERB **1** = <u>jiggle</u>, agitate, joggle ...*Shake the rugs well and hang them out...*

2 = <u>tremble</u>, shiver, quake, shudder, quiver ...*I stood there, crying and shaking with fear...*

3 = <u>rock</u>, sway, shudder, wobble, waver, totter, oscillate ...*The plane shook frighteningly as it hit the high, drenching waves...*

4 = <u>wave</u>, wield, flourish, brandish ...*They shook clenched fists...*

5 = <u>upset</u>, shock, frighten, disturb, distress, move, rattle (*informal*), intimidate, unnerve, discompose, traumatize ...*The news of his escape had shaken them all...*

6 = <u>undermine</u>, threaten, disable, weaken, impair, sap, debilitate, subvert, pull the rug out from under (*informal*) ...*It won't shake the football world if we beat them...*

NOUN = <u>vibration</u>, trembling, quaking, shock, jar, disturbance, jerk, shiver, shudder, jolt, tremor, agitation, convulsion, pulsation, jounce ...*blurring of photos caused by camera shake...*

PHRASES **shake someone off** = <u>leave behind</u>, lose, get rid of, get away from, elude, get rid of, throw off, get shot of (*slang*), rid yourself of, give the slip ...*He had shaken off his pursuers...* ◆ **shake someone up** (*Informal*) = <u>upset</u>, shock, frighten, disturb, distress, rattle (*informal*), unsettle, unnerve, discompose ...*He was shaken up when he was thrown from his horse...* ◆ **shake something off** = <u>get rid of</u>, lose, recuperate from ...*He just couldn't shake off that cough...* ◆ **shake something up** = <u>restructure</u>, reorganize, mix, overturn, churn (up), turn upside down ...*Directors and shareholders are preparing to shake things up...*

Shakespeare
➤ **Shakespeare**

shaky 1 = <u>unstable</u>, weak, precarious, tottering, rickety ...*Our house will remain on shaky foundations unless the architect sorts out the basement...* OPPOSITE stable

2 = <u>unsteady</u>, faint, trembling, faltering, wobbly, tremulous, quivery, all of a quiver (*informal*) ...*Even small operations can leave you feeling a bit shaky...*

3 = <u>uncertain</u>, suspect, dubious, questionable, unreliable, unsound, iffy (*informal*), unsupported, undependable ...*We knew we may have to charge them on shaky evidence...* OPPOSITE reliable

shallow = <u>superficial</u>, surface, empty, slight, foolish, idle, trivial, meaningless, flimsy, frivolous, skin-deep OPPOSITE deep

sham NOUN = <u>fraud</u>, imitation, hoax, pretence, forgery, counterfeit, pretender, humbug, impostor, feint, pseud (*informal*), wolf in sheep's clothing, imposture, phoney *or* phony (*informal*) ...*Their*

Shakespeare http://www.shakespeare-online.com/

Characters in Shakespeare

Character	Play	Character	Play
Sir Andrew Aguecheek	Twelfth Night	Iago	Othello
Antonio	The Merchant of Venice	Jaques	As You Like It
Antony	Antony and Cleopatra, Julius Caesar	John of Gaunt	Richard II
		Juliet	Romeo and Juliet
Ariel	The Tempest	Julius Caesar	Julius Caesar
Aufidius	Coriolanus	Katharina or Kate	The Taming of the Shrew
Autolycus	The Winter's Tale		
Banquo	Macbeth	Kent	King Lear
Bassanio	The Merchant of Venice	Laertes	Hamlet
Beatrice	Much Ado About Nothing	Lear	King Lear
		Lysander	A Midsummer Night's Dream
Sir Toby Belch	Twelfth Night		
Benedick	Much Ado About Nothing	Macbeth	Macbeth
		Lady Macbeth	Macbeth
Bolingbroke	Richard II	Macduff	Macbeth
Bottom	A Midsummer Night's Dream	Malcolm	Macbeth
		Malvolio	Twelfth Night
Brutus	Julius Caesar	Mercutio	Romeo and Juliet
Caliban	The Tempest	Miranda	The Tempest
Casca	Julius Caesar	Oberon	A Midsummer Night's Dream
Cassio	Othello		
Cassius	Julius Caesar	Octavius	Antony and Cleopatra
Claudio	Much Ado About Nothing, Measure for Measure	Olivia	Twelfth Night
		Ophelia	Hamlet
		Orlando	As You Like It
Claudius	Hamlet	Orsino	Twelfth Night
Cleopatra	Antony and Cleopatra	Othello	Othello
Cordelia	King Lear	Pandarus	Troilus and Cressida
Coriolanus	Coriolanus	Perdita	The Winter's Tale
Cressida	Troilus and Cressida	Petruchio	The Taming of the Shrew
Demetrius	A Midsummer Night's Dream		
		Pistol	Henry IV Part II, Henry V, The Merry Wives of Windsor
Desdemona	Othello		
Dogberry	Much Ado About Nothing		
		Polonius	Hamlet
Edmund	King Lear	Portia	The Merchant of Venice
Enobarbus	Antony and Cleopatra	Prospero	The Tempest
Falstaff	Henry IV Parts I and II, The Merry Wives of Windsor	Puck	A Midsummer Night's Dream
		Mistress Quickly	The Merry Wives of Windsor
Ferdinand	The Tempest		
Feste	Twelfth Night	Regan	King Lear
Fluellen	Henry V	Romeo	Romeo and Juliet
Fool	King Lear	Rosalind	As You Like It
Gertrude	Hamlet	Rosencrantz	Hamlet
Gloucester	King Lear	Sebastian	The Tempest, Twelfth Night
Goneril	King Lear		
Guildenstern	Hamlet	Shylock	The Merchant of Venice
Hamlet	Hamlet	Thersites	Troilus and Cressida
Helena	All's Well that Ends Well, A Midsummer Night's Dream	Timon	Timon of Athens
		Titania	A Midsummer Night's Dream
Hermia	A Midsummer Night's Dream	Touchstone	As You Like It
		Troilus	Troilus and Cressida
Hero	Much Ado About Nothing	Tybalt	Romeo and Juliet
		Viola	Twelfth Night
Hotspur	Henry IV Part I		

Shakespeare (continued)

Plays of Shakespeare

All's Well that Ends Well	Henry VIII	Richard II
Antony and Cleopatra	Julius Caesar	Richard III
As You Like It	King John	Romeo and Juliet
The Comedy of Errors	King Lear	The Taming of the Shrew
Coriolanus	Love's Labour's Lost	The Tempest
Cymbeline	Macbeth	Timon of Athens
Hamlet	Measure for Measure	Titus Andronicus
Henry IV Part I	The Merchant of Venice	Troilus and Cressida
Henry IV Part II	The Merry Wives of Windsor	Twelfth Night
Henry V	A Midsummer Night's Dream	The Two Gentlemen of Verona
Henry VI Part I	Much Ado About Nothing	The Winter's Tale
Henry VI Part II	Othello	
Henry VI Part III	Pericles, Prince of Tyre	

---

promises were exposed as a hollow sham… OPPOSITE ▷ the real thing
ADJECTIVE = <u>false</u>, artificial, bogus, pretended, mock, synthetic, imitation, simulated, pseudo (*informal*), counterfeit, feigned, spurious, ersatz, pseud (*informal*), phoney *or* phony (*informal*) *…a sham marriage…* OPPOSITE ▷ real

shambles 1 = <u>chaos</u>, mess, disorder, confusion, muddle, havoc, anarchy, disarray, madhouse, disorganization *…The economy is a shambles…*
2 = <u>mess</u>, state, jumble, untidiness *…The boat's interior was an utter shambles…*

shambling = <u>clumsy</u>, awkward, shuffling, lurching, lumbering, unsteady, ungainly, unco (*Austral. slang*)

shambolic (*Informal*) = <u>disorganized</u>, disordered, chaotic, confused, muddled, inefficient, anarchic, topsy-turvy, at sixes and sevens, in total disarray, unsystematic

shame NOUN 1 = <u>embarrassment</u>, humiliation, chagrin, ignominy, compunction, mortification, loss of face, abashment *…I was, to my shame, a coward…* OPPOSITE ▷ shamelessness
2 = <u>disgrace</u>, scandal, discredit, contempt, smear, degradation, disrepute, reproach, derision, dishonour, infamy, opprobrium, odium, ill repute, obloquy *…I don't want to bring shame on the family name…* OPPOSITE ▷ honour
VERB 1 = <u>embarrass</u>, disgrace, humiliate, humble, disconcert, mortify, take (someone) down a peg (*informal*), abash *…Her son's affair had humiliated and shamed her…* OPPOSITE ▷ make proud
2 = <u>dishonour</u>, discredit, degrade, stain, smear, blot, debase, defile *…I wouldn't shame my family by trying that…* OPPOSITE ▷ honour
PHRASES **put something** *or* **someone to shame** = <u>show up</u>, disgrace, eclipse, surpass, outstrip, outclass *…His playing really puts me to shame…*

shameful = <u>disgraceful</u>, outrageous, scandalous, mean, low, base, infamous, indecent, degrading, vile, wicked, atrocious, unworthy, reprehensible, ignominious, dastardly, unbecoming, dishonourable OPPOSITE ▷ admirable

shameless = <u>brazen</u>, audacious, flagrant, abandoned, corrupt, hardened, indecent, brash, improper, depraved, wanton, unabashed, profligate, unashamed, incorrigible, insolent, unprincipled, impudent, dissolute, reprobate, immodest, barefaced, unblushing

shanty = <u>shack</u>, shed, cabin, hut, lean-to, hovel, shiel (*Scot.*), bothy (*Scot.*), shieling (*Scot.*)

shape NOUN 1 = <u>appearance</u>, form, aspect, guise, likeness, semblance *…The glass bottle is the shape of a woman's torso…*
2 = <u>form</u>, profile, outline, lines, build, cut, figure, silhouette, configuration, contours *…the shapes of the trees against the sky…*
3 = <u>pattern</u>, model, frame, mould *…Carefully cut round the shape of the design you wish to use…*
4 = <u>condition</u>, state, health, trim, kilter, fettle *…He was still in better shape than many young men…*
VERB 1 = <u>form</u>, make, produce, create, model, fashion, mould *…Like it or not, our families shape our lives…*
2 = <u>mould</u>, form, make, fashion, model, frame *…Cut the dough in half and shape each half into a loaf…*

shapeless = <u>formless</u>, irregular, amorphous, unstructured, misshapen, asymmetrical OPPOSITE ▷ well-formed

shapely = <u>well-formed</u>, elegant, trim, neat, graceful, well-turned, curvaceous, sightly, comely, well-proportioned

share NOUN = <u>part</u>, portion, quota, ration, lot, cut (*informal*), due, division, contribution, proportion, allowance, whack (*informal*), allotment *…I have had more than my share of adventures…*
VERB 1 = <u>divide</u>, split, distribute, assign, apportion, parcel out, divvy up (*informal*) *…the small income he has shared with his brother…*
2 = <u>go halves on</u>, go fifty-fifty on (*informal*), go Dutch on (*informal*) *…Share the cost of the flowers…*

shark
➤ **sharks**

sharp ADJECTIVE 1 = <u>keen</u>, cutting, sharpened, honed, jagged, knife-edged, razor-sharp, serrated, knifelike *…Using a sharp knife, cut away the pith and peel from*

Sharks http://www.flmnh.ufl.edu/fish/Sharks/sharks.htm

angel shark, angelfish, *or* monkfish	grey nurse shark	seven-gill shark
basking shark *or* sailfish	gummy (shark)	shovelhead
blue pointer	hammerhead	soupfin *or* soupfin shark
bronze whaler	mako	thrasher *or* thresher shark
carpet shark *or* (*Austral.*) wobbegong	nursehound	tiger shark
	nurse shark	tope
cow shark *or* six-gilled shark	porbeagle *or* mackerel shark	whale shark
dogfish *or* (*Austral.*) dog shark	requiem shark	whaler shark
	school shark	

both fruits... OPPOSITE blunt

2 = quick-witted, clever, astute, knowing, ready, quick, bright, alert, subtle, penetrating, apt, discerning, on the ball (*informal*), perceptive, observant, long-headed *...He is very sharp and swift with repartee...* OPPOSITE dim

3 = cutting, biting, severe, bitter, harsh, scathing, acrimonious, barbed, hurtful, sarcastic, sardonic, caustic, vitriolic, trenchant, mordant, mordacious, acerb *...'Don't criticize your mother,' was his sharp reprimand...* OPPOSITE gentle

4 = sudden, marked, abrupt, extreme, distinct *...There's been a sharp rise in the rate of inflation...* OPPOSITE gradual

5 = clear, distinct, clear-cut, well-defined, crisp *...All the footmarks are quite sharp and clear...* OPPOSITE indistinct

6 = sour, tart, pungent, hot, burning, acid, acerbic, acrid, piquant, acetic, vinegary, acerb *...a colourless, almost odourless liquid with a sharp, sweetish taste...* OPPOSITE bland

7 (*Informal*) = stylish, smart, fashionable, trendy (*informal*), chic, classy (*slang*), snappy, natty (*informal*), dressy *...Now politics is all about the right haircut and a sharp suit...*

8 = acute, violent, severe, intense, painful, shooting, distressing, stabbing, fierce, stinging, piercing, sore, excruciating, gut-wrenching *...I felt a sharp pain in my lower back...*

ADVERB 1 = promptly, precisely, exactly, on time, on the dot, punctually *...She planned to unlock the store at 8.00 sharp...* OPPOSITE approximately

2 = suddenly, unexpectedly, abruptly, without warning *...Events mid-month should pull you up sharp...* OPPOSITE gradually

sharpen = make sharp, hone, whet, grind, edge, strop, put an edge on

shatter 1 = smash, break, burst, split, crack, crush, explode, demolish, shiver, implode, pulverize, crush to smithereens *...Safety glass won't shatter if it's broken...*

2 = destroy, ruin, wreck, blast, disable, overturn, demolish, impair, blight, torpedo, bring to nought *...Something like that really shatters your confidence...*

3 = devastate, shock, stun, crush, overwhelm, upset, break (someone's) heart, knock the stuffing out of (someone) (*informal*), traumatize *...the tragedy which had shattered him...*

shattered 1 = devastated, crushed, upset, gutted (*slang*) *...I am absolutely shattered to hear the news...*

2 (*Informal*) = exhausted, drained, worn out, spent, done in (*informal*), all in (*slang*), wiped out (*informal*), weary, knackered (*slang*), clapped out (*Brit., Austral., & N.Z. informal*), tired out, ready to drop, dog-tired (*informal*), zonked (*slang*), dead tired (*informal*), dead beat (*informal*), shagged out (*Brit. slang*), jiggered (*informal*) *...He was shattered and too tired to concentrate...*

shattering = devastating, stunning, severe, crushing, overwhelming, paralysing

shave 1 = trim, crop *...It's a pity you shaved your moustache off...*

2 = scrape, plane, trim, shear, pare *...I set the log on the ground and shaved off the bark...*

3 = underline{brush past}, touch, graze *...The ball shaved the goalpost...*

shed¹ 1 = hut, shack, lean-to, outhouse, lockup, bothy (*chiefly Scot.*) *...a garden shed...*

shed² 1 = drop, spill, scatter *...Some of the trees were already beginning to shed their leaves...*

2 = cast off, discard, moult, slough off, exuviate *...a snake who has shed its skin...*

3 = give out, cast, emit, give, throw, afford, radiate, diffuse, pour forth *...as dawn sheds its first light...*

sheen = shine, gleam, gloss, polish, brightness, lustre, burnish, patina, shininess

sheep

(Related Words)

adjective: ovine
male: ram, tup
female: ewe
young: lamb, yeanling
collective noun: flock

➤ breeds of sheep

sheepish = embarrassed, uncomfortable, ashamed, silly, foolish, self-conscious, chagrined, mortified, abashed, shamefaced OPPOSITE unembarrassed

sheer 1 = total, complete, absolute, utter, rank, pure, downright, unqualified, out-and-out, unadulterated, unmitigated, thoroughgoing, unalloyed, arrant *...acts of sheer desperation...* OPPOSITE moderate

2 = steep, abrupt, perpendicular, precipitous *...There was a sheer drop just outside my window...* OPPOSITE gradual

3 = fine, thin, transparent, see-through, gossamer,

Breeds of sheep   http://www.ansi.okstate.edu/breeds/sheep/

Beulah Speckled-face	Dorset Horn	Rambouillet
bighorn *or* mountain sheep	East Friesland	Romney Marsh
Blackface	English Halfbred	Rouge de l'Ouest
Black Welsh Mountain	Exmoor Horn	Rough Fell
Blue-faced *or* Hexham Leicester	Hampshire Down	Ryeland
Border Leicester	Hebridian *or* St. Kilda	Scottish Blackface
Boreray	Herdwick	Scottish Halfbred
Brecknock Hill Cheviot	Hill Radnor	Shetland
British Bleu du Maine	Île de France	Shropshire
British Charollais	Jacob	Soay
British Friesland	karakul, caracul, *or* broadtail	Southdown
British Milksheep	Kerry Hill	South Wales Mountain
British Oldenburg	Leicester Longwool	Suffolk
British Texel	Lincoln Longwool	Swaledale
British Vendéen	Llanwenog	Teeswater
Cambridge	Lleyn	Texel
Cheviot	Lonk	Welsh Halfbred
Clun Forest	Manx Loghtan	Welsh Hill Speckled
Colbred	Masham	Welsh Mountain
Corriedale	Merino	Welsh Mountain Badger Faced
Cotswold	Mule	Welsh Mule
Dalesbred	Norfolk Horn	Wensleydale Longwool
Dartmoor	North Country Cheviot	White Face Dartmoor
Derbyshire Gritstone	Orkney *or* North Ronaldsay	Whitefaced Woodland
Devon and Cornwall Longwool	Oxford *or* Oxfordshire Down	Wiltshire Horn
Devon Closewool	Polwarth	
Dorset Down	Portland	

diaphanous, gauzy ...*sheer black tights...* OPPOSITE > thick

sheet **1** = page, leaf, folio, piece of paper ...*I was able to fit it all on one sheet...*
2 = plate, piece, panel, slab, pane ...*a cracked sheet of glass...*
3 = coat, film, layer, membrane, surface, stratum, veneer, overlay, lamina ...*a sheet of ice...*
4 = expanse, area, stretch, sweep, covering, blanket ...*Sheets of rain slanted across the road...*

shell NOUN **1** = husk, case, pod, shuck ...*They cracked the nuts and removed their shells...*
2 = carapace, armour ...*The baby tortoise tucked his head in his shell...*
3 = frame, structure, hull, framework, skeleton, chassis ...*The solid feel of the car's shell is impressive...*
VERB **1** = remove the shells from, husk, shuck ...*She shelled and ate a few nuts...*
2 = bomb, barrage, bombard, attack, strike, blitz, strafe ...*The rebels shelled the densely-populated suburbs near the port...*
PHRASES **shell something out** (with money or a specified sum of money as object) = pay out, fork out (*slang*), expend, give, hand over, lay out (*informal*), disburse, ante up (*informal, chiefly U.S.*) ...*You won't have to shell out a fortune for it...*

shelter NOUN **1** = cover, screen, awning, shiel (*Scot.*) ...*a bus shelter...*
2 = protection, safety, refuge, cover, security, defence, sanctuary ...*the hut where they were given food and shelter...*

3 = refuge, haven, sanctuary, retreat, asylum ...*a shelter for homeless women...*
VERB **1** = take shelter, hide, seek refuge, take cover ...*a man sheltering in a doorway...*
2 = protect, shield, harbour, safeguard, cover, hide, guard, defend, take in ...*A neighbour sheltered the boy for seven days...* OPPOSITE > endanger

sheltered **1** = screened, covered, protected, shielded, secluded ...*a shallow-sloping beach next to a sheltered bay...* OPPOSITE > exposed
2 = protected, screened, shielded, quiet, withdrawn, isolated, secluded, cloistered, reclusive, ensconced, hermitic, conventual ...*She had a sheltered upbringing...*

shelve = postpone, put off, defer, table (*U.S.*), dismiss, freeze, suspend, put aside, hold over, mothball, pigeonhole, lay aside, put on ice, put on the back burner (*informal*), hold in abeyance, take a rain check on (*U.S. & Canad. informal*)

shepherd NOUN = drover, stockman, herdsman, grazier ...*The shepherd was filled with terror...*
VERB = guide, conduct, steer, convoy, herd, marshal, usher ...*She was shepherded by her guards up the rear ramp of the aircraft...*
(**Related Words**)
adjective: pastoral

shield NOUN **1** = protection, cover, defence, screen, guard, ward (*archaic*), shelter, safeguard, aegis, rampart, bulwark ...*innocents used as a human shield against attack...*

2 = buckler, escutcheon (*Heraldry*), targe (*archaic*) ...*a warrior with sword and shield...*
VERB = protect, cover, screen, guard, defend, shelter, safeguard ...*He shielded his head from the sun with an old sack...*

shift **VERB** **1** = move, drift, move around, veer, budge, swerve, change position ...*The entire pile shifted and slid, thumping onto the floor...*
2 = remove, move, transfer, displace, relocate, rearrange, transpose, reposition ...*We shifted the vans and used the area for skateboarding...*
NOUN **1** = change, switch, shifting, modification, alteration, displacement, about-turn, permutation, fluctuation ...*a shift in policy...*
2 = move, transfer, removal, veering, rearrangement ...*There has been a shift of the elderly to this state...*

shifty (*Informal*) = untrustworthy, sly, devious, scheming, tricky, slippery, contriving, wily, crafty, evasive, furtive, deceitful, underhand, unprincipled, duplicitous, fly-by-night (*informal*) [OPPOSITE] honest

shimmer **VERB** = gleam, twinkle, glimmer, dance, glisten, scintillate ...*The lights shimmered on the water...*
NOUN = gleam, glimmer, iridescence, unsteady light ...*a shimmer of starlight...*

shine **VERB** **1** = gleam, flash, beam, glow, sparkle, glitter, glare, shimmer, radiate, twinkle, glimmer, glisten, emit light, give off light, scintillate ...*It is a mild morning and the sun is shining...*
2 = polish, buff, burnish, brush, rub up ...*Let him dust and shine the furniture...*
3 = be outstanding, stand out, excel, star, be distinguished, steal the show, be conspicuous, be pre-eminent, stand out in a crowd ...*He conspicuously failed to shine academically...*
NOUN **1** = polish, gloss, sheen, glaze, lustre, patina ...*The wood has been recently polished to bring back the shine...*
2 = brightness, light, sparkle, radiance ...*There was a sparkle about her, a shine of anticipation...*

shining **1** = outstanding, glorious, splendid, leading, celebrated, brilliant, distinguished, eminent, conspicuous, illustrious ...*She is a shining example to us all...*
2 = bright, brilliant, gleaming, beaming, sparkling, glittering, shimmering, radiant, luminous, glistening, resplendent, aglow, effulgent, incandescent ...*shining brass buttons...*

shiny = bright, gleaming, glossy, glistening, polished, burnished, lustrous, satiny, sheeny, agleam

ship = vessel, boat, craft
➤ **boats and ships**

shirk **1** = dodge, avoid, evade, get out of, duck (out of) (*informal*), shun, sidestep, body-swerve (*Scot.*), bob off (*Brit. slang*), scrimshank (*Brit. military slang*) ...*We will not shirk the task of considering the need for further action...*
2 = skive (*Brit. slang*), slack, idle, malinger, swing the lead, gold-brick (*U.S. slang*), bob off (*Brit. slang*),

bludge (*Austral. & N.Z. informal*), scrimshank (*Brit. military slang*) ...*He was sacked for shirking...*

shiver **VERB** = shudder, shake, tremble, quake, quiver, palpitate ...*He shivered in the cold...*
NOUN = tremble, shudder, quiver, thrill, trembling, flutter, tremor, frisson (*French*) ...*Alice gave a shiver of delight...*
PHRASES **the shivers** = the shakes, a chill (*informal*), goose pimples, goose flesh, chattering teeth ...*My boss gives me the shivers...*

shock **NOUN** **1** = upset, blow, trauma, bombshell, turn (*informal*), distress, disturbance, consternation, whammy (*informal, chiefly U.S.*), state of shock, rude awakening, bolt from the blue, prostration ...*The extent of the violence came as a shock...*
2 = impact, blow, jolt, clash, encounter, jarring, collision ...*Steel barriers can bend and absorb the shock...*
3 = start, scare, fright, turn, jolt ...*It gave me quite a shock to see his face on the screen...*
VERB **1** = shake, stun, stagger, jar, shake up (*informal*), paralyse, numb, jolt, stupefy, shake out of your complacency ...*Relief workers were shocked by what they saw...*
2 = horrify, appal, disgust, outrage, offend, revolt, unsettle, sicken, agitate, disquiet, nauseate, raise someone's eyebrows, scandalize, gross out (*U.S. slang*), traumatize, give (someone) a turn (*informal*) ...*They were easily shocked in those days...*

shocking **1** (*Informal*) = terrible, appalling, dreadful, bad, fearful, dire, horrendous, ghastly, from hell (*informal*), deplorable, abysmal, frightful, godawful (*slang*) ...*I must have been in a shocking state last night...*
2 = appalling, outrageous, disgraceful, offensive, distressing, disgusting, horrible, dreadful, horrifying, revolting, obscene, sickening, ghastly, hideous, monstrous, scandalous, disquieting, unspeakable, atrocious, repulsive, nauseating, odious, loathsome, abominable, stupefying, hellacious (*U.S. slang*) ...*This was a shocking invasion of privacy...* [OPPOSITE] wonderful

shoddy = inferior, poor, second-rate, cheap, tacky (*informal*), tawdry, tatty, trashy, low-rent (*informal, chiefly U.S.*), slipshod, cheapo (*informal*), rubbishy, junky (*informal*), cheap-jack (*informal*), bodger or bodgie (*Austral. slang*) [OPPOSITE] excellent

shoemaker = cobbler, bootmaker, souter (*Scot.*)

shoot **VERB** **1** = open fire on, blast (*slang*), hit, kill, bag, plug (*slang*), bring down, blow away (*slang, chiefly U.S.*), zap (*slang*), pick off, pump full of lead (*slang*) ...*The police had orders to shoot anyone who attacked them...*
2 = fire, launch, discharge, project, hurl, fling, propel, emit, let fly ...*He shot an arrow into the air...*
3 = speed, race, rush, charge, fly, spring, tear, flash, dash, barrel (along) (*informal, chiefly U.S. & Canad.*), bolt, streak, dart, whisk, whizz (*informal*), hurtle, scoot, burn rubber (*informal*) ...*They had almost reached the*

boat when a figure shot past them…

NOUN = sprout, branch, bud, twig, sprig, offshoot, scion, slip …*This week saw the first pink shoots of the new season's crop…*

shop = store, market, supermarket, mart, boutique, emporium, hypermarket

shore = beach, coast, sands, strand (*poetic*), lakeside, waterside, seaboard (*chiefly U.S.*), foreshore, seashore

shore up = support, strengthen, reinforce, prop, brace, underpin, augment, buttress

short ADJECTIVE 1 = brief, fleeting, short-term, short-lived, momentary …*We had a short meeting…*
OPPOSITE〉 long
2 = concise, brief, succinct, clipped, summary, compressed, curtailed, terse, laconic, pithy, abridged, compendious, sententious …*This is a short note to say thank you…* OPPOSITE〉 lengthy
3 = small, little, wee, squat, diminutive, petite, dumpy, knee high to a grasshopper, fubsy (*archaic or dialect*), knee high to a gnat …*I'm tall and thin and he's short and fat…* OPPOSITE〉 tall
4 = abrupt, sharp, terse, curt, blunt, crusty, gruff, brusque, offhand, testy, impolite, discourteous, uncivil …*She was definitely short with me…* OPPOSITE〉 polite
5 (*of pastry*) = crumbly, crisp, brittle, friable …*a crisp short pastry…*
6 = direct, straight, undeviating, through …*a short route through the town…*
7 = scarce, wanting, low, missing, limited, lacking, tight, slim, inadequate, insufficient, slender, scant, meagre, sparse, deficient, scanty …*Money was short in those days…* OPPOSITE〉 plentiful
ADVERB = abruptly, suddenly, unaware, by surprise, without warning …*He had no insurance and was caught short when his house was burgled…* OPPOSITE〉 gradually
PHRASES **cut someone short** = stop, interrupt, cut in on, butt in on …*His father cut him short…* ◆ **in short** = briefly, in essence, in a word, in a nutshell, to cut a long story short, to come to the point, to put it briefly …*In short, it is a treaty that everyone should be pleased with…*

shortage = deficiency, want, lack, failure, deficit, poverty, shortfall, inadequacy, scarcity, dearth, paucity, insufficiency OPPOSITE〉 abundance

shortcoming = failing, fault, weakness, defect, flaw, drawback, imperfection, frailty, foible, weak point

shorten 1 = cut, reduce, decrease, cut down, trim, diminish, dock, cut back, prune, lessen, curtail, abbreviate, truncate, abridge, downsize …*The day surgery will help to shorten waiting lists…* OPPOSITE〉 increase
2 = turn up, trim …*It's a simple matter to shorten trouser legs…*

short-lived = brief, short, temporary, fleeting, passing, transient, ephemeral, transitory, impermanent

shortly 1 = soon, presently, before long, anon (*archaic*), in a little while, any minute now, erelong

(*archaic or poetic*) …*Their trial will begin shortly…*
2 = curtly, sharply, abruptly, tartly, tersely, succinctly, briefly, concisely, in a few words …*'I don't know you,' he said shortly, 'and I'm in a hurry.'…*

short-sighted 1 = near-sighted, myopic, blind as a bat …*Testing showed her to be very short-sighted…*
2 = imprudent, injudicious, ill-advised, unthinking, careless, impractical, ill-considered, improvident, impolitic, seeing no further than (the end of) your nose …*I think we're being very short-sighted…*

shot NOUN 1 = discharge, report, gunfire, crack, blast, explosion, bang …*Guards at the training base heard the shots…*
2 = ammunition, bullet, slug, pellet, projectile, lead, ball …*These guns are lighter and take more shot for their size…*
3 = marksman, shooter, markswoman …*He was not a particularly good shot because of his eyesight…*
4 (*Informal*) = strike, throw, lob …*He had only one shot at goal…*
5 = attempt, go (*informal*), try, turn, chance, effort, opportunity, crack (*informal*), essay, stab (*informal*), endeavour …*He will be given a shot at the world title…*
PHRASES **a shot in the arm** (*Informal*) = boost, lift, encouragement, stimulus, impetus, fillip, geeing-up …*A win would provide a much-needed shot in the arm for the team…* ◆ **by a long shot** 1 = by far, undoubtedly, without doubt, far and away, indubitably …*He's missed the mark by a long shot…*
2 = by any means, in any circumstances, on any account …*This isn't over by a long shot…* ◆ **have a shot** (*Informal*) = make an attempt, have a go, try, have a crack (*informal*), try your luck, have a stab (*informal*), have a bash (*informal*), tackle …*Why don't you have a shot at it?…* ◆ **like a shot** = at once, immediately, in a flash, quickly, eagerly, unhesitatingly, like a bat out of hell (*slang*) …*I heard the key in the front door and I was out of bed like a shot…* ◆ **long shot** = outsider, outside chance, slim chance, fat chance (*informal*), remote possibility, chance in a million …*The prospect of them being freed is not such a long shot…*

shoulder VERB 1 = bear, carry, take on, accept, assume, be responsible for, take upon yourself …*He has to shoulder the responsibilities of his father's mistakes…*
2 = push, thrust, elbow, shove, jostle, press …*He shouldered past her and opened the door…*
PHRASES **give someone the cold shoulder** = snub, ignore, blank (*slang*), put down, shun, rebuff, kick in the teeth (*slang*), ostracize, send someone to Coventry, cut (*informal*) …*He was given the cold shoulder by his former friends…* ◆ **rub shoulders with someone** (*Informal*) = mix with, associate with, consort with, hobnob with, socialize with, fraternize with …*I was destined to rub shoulders with the most unexpected people…* ◆ **shoulder to shoulder** 1 = side by side, abreast, next to each other …*walking shoulder to shoulder with their heads*

bent against the rain... **2** = <u>together</u>, united, jointly, as one, in partnership, in cooperation, in unity ...*My party will stand shoulder to shoulder with the Prime Minister and his Government*... ◆ **straight from the shoulder** = <u>frankly</u>, directly, straight, plainly, candidly, outright, unequivocally, man to man, pulling no punches (*informal*), with no holds barred ...*I want you to give me the truth, straight from the shoulder*...

shout VERB = <u>cry (out)</u>, call (out), yell, scream, roar, shriek, bellow, bawl, holler (*informal*), raise your voice ...*We began to shout for help*...
NOUN = <u>cry</u>, call, yell, scream, roar, shriek, bellow ...*I heard a distant shout*...
PHRASES **shout someone down** = <u>drown out</u>, overwhelm, drown, silence ...*The hecklers began to shout down the speakers*...

shove VERB **1** = <u>push</u>, shoulder, thrust, elbow, drive, press, crowd, propel, jostle, impel ...*He shoved her out of the way*...
2 = <u>stick</u>, push, thrust, ram, plonk, park ...*He shoved a cloth into my hand*...
NOUN = <u>push</u>, knock, thrust, elbow, bump, nudge, jostle ...*She gave Gracie a shove in the back*...
PHRASES **shove off** (*Informal*) = <u>go away</u>, leave, clear off (*informal*), depart, go to hell (*informal*), push off (*informal*), slope off, pack your bags (*informal*), scram (*informal*), get on your bike (*Brit. slang*), take yourself off, vamoose (*slang, chiefly U.S.*), sling your hook (*Brit. slang*) ...*Why don't you just shove off and leave me alone?*...

shovel NOUN = <u>spade</u>, scoop ...*She dug the foundation with a pick and shovel*...
VERB **1** = <u>move</u>, scoop, dredge, shift, load, heap ...*He had to get out and shovel snow*...
2 = <u>stuff</u>, spoon, ladle ...*shovelling food into his mouth*...

show VERB **1** = <u>indicate</u>, demonstrate, prove, reveal, display, evidence, point out, manifest, testify to, evince ...*These figures show an increase in unemployment*... OPPOSITE disprove
2 = <u>display</u>, exhibit, put on display, present, put on show, put before the public ...*What made you decide to show your paintings?*...
3 = <u>guide</u>, lead, conduct, accompany, direct, steer, escort ...*Let me show you to my study*...
4 = <u>demonstrate</u>, describe, explain, teach, illustrate, instruct ...*Claire showed us how to make a chocolate roulade*...
5 = <u>be visible</u> ...*I'd driven both ways down this road, but the tracks didn't show*... OPPOSITE be invisible
6 = <u>express</u>, display, reveal, indicate, register, demonstrate, disclose, manifest, divulge, make known, evince ...*She had enough time to show her gratitude*... OPPOSITE hide
7 = <u>turn up</u>, come, appear, arrive, attend, show up (*informal*), put in *or* make an appearance ...*There was always a chance he wouldn't show*...
8 = <u>broadcast</u>, transmit, air, beam, relay, televise, put on the air ...*The drama will be shown on American TV*...

NOUN **1** = <u>display</u>, view, sight, spectacle, array ...*Spring brings a lovely show of green and yellow striped leaves*...
2 = <u>exhibition</u>, fair, display, parade, expo (*informal*), exposition, pageant, pageantry ...*the Chelsea flower show*...
3 = <u>appearance</u>, display, pose, profession, parade, ostentation ...*The change in government is more for show than for real*...
4 = <u>pretence</u>, appearance, semblance, illusion, pretext, likeness, affectation ...*We need to make a show of acknowledging their expertise*...
5 = <u>programme</u>, broadcast, presentation, production ...*I had my own TV show*...
6 = <u>entertainment</u>, performance, play, production, drama, musical, presentation, theatrical performance ...*How about going to see a show in London?*...
PHRASES **show off** (*Informal*) = <u>boast</u>, brag, blow your own trumpet, swagger, hot-dog (*chiefly U.S.*), strut your stuff (*chiefly U.S.*), make a spectacle of yourself ...*He had been showing off at the poker table*... ◆ **show someone up** (*Informal*) = <u>embarrass</u>, shame, let down, mortify, put to shame, show in a bad light ...*He wanted to teach her a lesson for showing him up*... ◆ **show something off** = <u>exhibit</u>, display, parade, advertise, demonstrate, spread out, flaunt ...*She was showing off her engagement ring*... ◆ **show something up** = <u>reveal</u>, expose, highlight, pinpoint, unmask, lay bare, put the spotlight on ...*The awards showed up the fact that TV has been a washout this year*...

showdown (*Informal*) = <u>confrontation</u>, crisis, clash, moment of truth, face-off (*slang*)

shower NOUN **1** = <u>deluge</u>, downpour ...*a shower of rain*...
2 = <u>profusion</u>, plethora ...*They were reunited in a shower of kisses and tears*...
VERB **1** = <u>cover</u>, dust, spray, sprinkle ...*They were showered with rice in the traditional manner*...
2 = <u>inundate</u>, load, heap, lavish, pour, deluge ...*He showered her with emeralds and furs*... ...*She showered gifts on us*...

showing **1** = <u>display</u>, staging, presentation, exhibition, demonstration ...*a private showing of the hit film*...
2 = <u>performance</u>, demonstration, track record, show, appearance, impression, account of yourself ...*On this showing he has a big job ahead of him*...

showman = <u>performer</u>, entertainer, artiste, player, Thespian, trouper, play-actor, actor *or* actress

show-off (*Informal*) = <u>exhibitionist</u>, boaster, swaggerer, hot dog (*chiefly U.S.*), poseur, egotist, braggart, braggadocio, peacock

showy = <u>ostentatious</u>, flamboyant, flashy, flash (*informal*), loud, over the top (*informal*), brash, pompous, pretentious, gaudy, garish, tawdry, splashy (*informal*), tinselly OPPOSITE tasteful

shred **1** = <u>strip</u>, bit, piece, scrap, fragment, rag, ribbon, snippet, sliver, tatter ...*Cut the cabbage into fine long shreds...*

2 = particle, trace, scrap, grain, atom, jot, whit, iota ...*There is not a shred of truth in this story...*

shrew¹ = nag, fury, dragon (*informal*), spitfire, virago, vixen, harpy, harridan, termagant (*rare*), scold, Xanthippe ...*After the first visit he announced that his stepmother was a shrew...*

shrew²

Shrews and other insectivores

http://www.bbc.co.uk/nature/wildfacts/factfiles/260.shtml

desman	shrew mole
elephant shrew	solenodon
mole	star-nosed mole
moon rat	tenrec
shrew *or*	tree shrew
shrewmouse	water shrew

---

shrewd = astute, clever, sharp, knowing, fly (*slang*), keen, acute, smart, calculated, calculating, intelligent, discriminating, cunning, discerning, sly, canny, perceptive, wily, crafty, artful, far-sighted, far-seeing, long-headed, perspicacious, sagacious OPPOSITE⟩ naive

shrewdly = astutely, perceptively, cleverly, knowingly, artfully, cannily, with consummate skill, sagaciously, far-sightedly, perspicaciously, with all your wits about you

shriek VERB = scream, cry, yell, howl, wail, whoop, screech, squeal, holler ...*She shrieked and leapt from the bed...*
NOUN = scream, cry, yell, howl, wail, whoop, screech, squeal, holler ...*a shriek of joy...*

shrill = piercing, high, sharp, acute, piping, penetrating, screeching, high-pitched, ear-splitting, ear-piercing OPPOSITE⟩ deep

shrink = decrease, dwindle, lessen, grow *or* get smaller, contract, narrow, diminish, fall off, shorten, wrinkle, wither, drop off, deflate, shrivel, downsize OPPOSITE⟩ grow

shrivel = wither, dry (up), wilt, shrink, wrinkle, dwindle, dehydrate, desiccate, wizen

shrivelled = withered, dry, dried up, wrinkled, shrunken, wizened, desiccated, sere (*archaic*)

shroud NOUN **1** = winding sheet, grave clothes, cerecloth, cerement ...*a burial shroud...*
2 = covering, veil, mantle, screen, cloud, pall ...*a parked car huddled under a shroud of grey snow...*
VERB = conceal, cover, screen, hide, blanket, veil, cloak, swathe, envelop ...*Mist shrouded the outline of the palace...*

shrub
➤ shrubs

shudder VERB = shiver, shake, tremble, quake, quiver, convulse ...*She shuddered with cold...*
NOUN = shiver, trembling, tremor, quiver, spasm, convulsion ...*She recoiled with a shudder...*

Shrubs

acacia	tawine, tarwine, *or* tauhinu	lilac
acanthus	cranberry	liquorice
arbutus	crowea	magnolia
banksia	crown-of-thorns	mistletoe
bauera	daphne	mock orange
bilberry	dogwood	myrtle
black boy, yacca (bush), *or* yacka	emu bush	oleander
blackcurrant	eriostemon	olearia *or* daisy bush
blackthorn	forsythia	pittosporum
blueberry	frangipani	pituri
bluebush	fuchsia	poinsettia
boronia	gardenia	poison ivy
bottlebrush	geebung, geebong, *or* jibbong	poison oak
box	Geraldton waxflower	potentilla
bramble	gooseberry	privet
briar *or* brier	gorse	pyracantha
broom	grevillea	raspberry
buckthorn	hakea	redcurrant
buddleia	hawthorn	rhododendron
camellia	heath	rose
caper	heather	rosemary
Christmas bush	honeysuckle	rue
clematis	hydrangea	saltbush
coca	jasmine	strawberry
correa	juniper	tea
cotton	kerrawang	thyme
cottonbush	laburnum	waratah
cottonwood, blanket bush,	laurel	wax(flower)

shuffle 1 = <u>shamble</u>, stagger, stumble, dodder …*She shuffled across the kitchen…*
2 = <u>scuffle</u>, drag, scrape, scuff …*He shuffled his feet along the gravel path…*
3 = <u>rearrange</u>, jumble, mix, shift, disorder, disarrange, intermix …*The silence lengthened as he unnecessarily shuffled some papers…*

shun = <u>avoid</u>, steer clear of, keep away from, evade, eschew, shy away from, cold-shoulder, have no part in, fight shy of, give (someone *or* something) a wide berth, body-swerve (*Scot.*)

shut VERB = <u>close</u>, secure, fasten, bar, seal, slam, push to, draw to …*Just make sure you shut the gate after you…* OPPOSITE open
ADJECTIVE = <u>closed</u>, fastened, sealed, locked …*A smell of burning came from behind the shut door…* OPPOSITE open
PHRASES **shut down** = <u>stop work</u>, halt work, cease operating, close down, cease trading, discontinue …*Smaller constructors had been forced to shut down…*
♦ **shut someone out** = <u>exclude</u>, bar, keep out, black, lock out, ostracize, debar, blackball …*I was set to shut out anyone else who came knocking…* ♦ **shut someone up** 1 (*Informal*) = <u>silence</u>, gag, hush, muzzle, fall silent, button it (*slang*), pipe down (*slang*), hold your tongue, put a sock in it (*Brit. slang*), keep your trap shut (*slang*), cut the cackle (*informal*), button your lip (*slang*) …*A sharp put-down was the only way he knew of shutting her up…* 2 = <u>confine</u>, cage, imprison, keep in, box in, intern, incarcerate, coop up, immure …*They shut him up in a windowless tower…* ♦ **shut something in** = <u>confine</u>, cage, enclose, imprison, impound, pound, wall off *or* up …*The door enables us to shut the birds in in bad weather…* ♦ **shut something out** = <u>block out</u>, screen, hide, cover, mask, veil …*I shut out the memory that was too painful to dwell on…* ♦ **shut up** (*Informal*) = <u>be quiet</u>, hush, fall silent, button it (*slang*), pipe down (*slang*), hold your tongue, put a sock in it (*Brit. slang*), keep your trap shut (*slang*), cut the cackle (*informal*), button your lip (*slang*) …*Why don't you just shut up for a minute?…*

shuttle = <u>go back and forth</u>, commute, go to and fro, alternate, ply, shunt, seesaw

shy ADJECTIVE 1 = <u>timid</u>, self-conscious, bashful, reserved, retiring, nervous, modest, shrinking, backward, coy, reticent, self-effacing, diffident, mousy …*He is painfully shy when it comes to talking to women…* OPPOSITE confident
2 = <u>cautious</u>, wary, hesitant, suspicious, reticent, distrustful, chary …*You should not be shy of having your say…* OPPOSITE reckless
VERB *sometimes with* **off** *or* **away** = <u>recoil</u>, flinch, draw back, start, rear, buck, wince, swerve, balk, quail, take fright …*The horse shied as the wind sent sparks flying…*

shyness = <u>timidity</u>, self-consciousness, bashfulness, modesty, nervousness, lack of confidence, reticence, diffidence, timorousness, mousiness, timidness

sick 1 = <u>unwell</u>, ill, poorly (*informal*), diseased, weak, crook (*Austral. & N.Z. informal*), under par (*informal*), ailing, feeble, laid up (*informal*), under the weather, indisposed, on the sick list (*informal*) …*He's very sick…* OPPOSITE well
2 = <u>nauseous</u>, ill, queasy, nauseated, green about the gills (*informal*), qualmish …*The very thought of food made him feel sick…*
3 = <u>tired</u>, bored, fed up, weary, jaded, blasé, satiated …*I am sick of hearing all these people moaning…*
4 (*Informal*) = <u>morbid</u>, cruel, sadistic, black, macabre, ghoulish …*a sick joke about a cat…*

sicken 1 = <u>disgust</u>, revolt, nauseate, repel, gross out (*U.S. slang*), turn your stomach, make your gorge rise …*What he saw there sickened him, despite years of police work…*
2 = <u>fall ill</u>, take sick, ail, go down with something, contract something, be stricken by something …*Many of them sickened and died…*

sickening = <u>disgusting</u>, revolting, vile, offensive, foul, distasteful, repulsive, nauseating, loathsome, nauseous, gut-wrenching, putrid, stomach-turning (*informal*), cringe-making (*Brit. informal*), noisome, yucky *or* yukky (*slang*), yucko (*Austral. slang*) OPPOSITE delightful

sickly 1 = <u>unhealthy</u>, weak, delicate, ailing, feeble, infirm, in poor health, indisposed …*He had been a sickly child…*
2 = <u>pale</u>, wan, pasty, bloodless, pallid, sallow, ashen-faced, waxen, peaky …*his pale, sickly face and woebegone expression…*
3 = <u>nauseating</u>, revolting (*informal*), cloying, icky (*informal*) …*the sickly smell of rum…*
4 = <u>sentimental</u>, romantic, sloppy (*informal*), corny (*slang*), mushy (*informal*), weepy (*informal*), slushy (*informal*), mawkish, tear-jerking (*informal*), schmaltzy (*slang*), gushy (*informal*) …*a sickly sequel to the flimsy series…*

sickness 1 = <u>illness</u>, disorder, ailment, disease, complaint, bug (*informal*), affliction, malady, infirmity, indisposition, lurgy (*informal*) …*a sickness that affects children…*
2 = <u>nausea</u>, queasiness …*He felt a great rush of sickness…*
3 = <u>vomiting</u>, nausea, upset stomach, throwing up, puking (*slang*), retching, barfing (*U.S. slang*) …*Symptoms include sickness and diarrhoea…*

side NOUN 1 = <u>border</u>, margin, boundary, verge, flank, rim, perimeter, periphery, edge …*Park at the side of the road…* OPPOSITE middle
2 = <u>face</u>, surface, facet …*The copier only copies onto one side of the paper…*
3 = <u>half</u>, part …*the right side of your face…*
4 = <u>district</u>, area, region, quarter, sector, neighbourhood, vicinity, locality, locale, neck of the woods (*informal*) …*He lives on the south side of Edinburgh…*
5 = <u>party</u>, camp, faction, cause …*Both sides appealed for a new ceasefire…*

6 = <u>point of view</u>, viewpoint, position, opinion, angle, slant, standpoint ...*those with the ability to see all sides of a question*...

7 = <u>team</u>, squad, crew, line-up ...*Italy were the better side*...

8 = <u>aspect</u>, feature, angle, facet ...*He is in charge of the civilian side of the UN mission*...

ADJECTIVE = <u>subordinate</u>, minor, secondary, subsidiary, lesser, marginal, indirect, incidental, ancillary ...*The refugees were treated as a side issue*... OPPOSITE⟩ main

PHRASES **side with someone** = <u>support</u>, back, champion, agree with, stand up for, second, favour, defend, team up with (*informal*), go along with, befriend, join with, sympathize with, be loyal to, take the part of, associate yourself with, ally yourself with ...*They side with the forces of evil*...

⟨ Related Words ⟩
adjective: lateral

sidestep = <u>avoid</u>, dodge, evade, duck (*informal*), skirt, skip, bypass, elude, circumvent, find a way round, body-swerve (*Scot.*)

sidetrack = <u>distract</u>, divert, lead off the subject, deflect

sidewalk (*U.S. & Canad.*) = <u>pavement</u>, footpath (*Austral.*)

sideways ADVERB **1** = <u>indirectly</u>, obliquely ...*He glanced sideways at her*...

2 = <u>to the side</u>, laterally, crabwise ...*They moved sideways, their arms still locked together*...

ADJECTIVE = <u>sidelong</u>, side, slanted, oblique ...*Alfred shot him a sideways glance*...

sidle = <u>edge</u>, steal, slink, inch, creep, sneak

siesta = <u>nap</u>, rest, sleep, doze, kip (*Brit. slang*), snooze (*informal*), catnap, forty winks (*informal*), zizz (*Brit. informal*)

sieve NOUN = <u>strainer</u>, sifter, colander, screen, riddle, tammy cloth ...*Press the raspberries through a fine sieve to form a puree*...

VERB = <u>sift</u>, filter, strain, separate, pan, bolt, riddle ...*Sieve the icing sugar into the bowl*...

sift 1 = <u>part</u>, filter, strain, separate, pan, bolt, riddle, sieve ...*Sift the flour and baking powder into a medium-sized mixing bowl*...

2 = <u>examine</u>, investigate, go through, research, screen, probe, analyse, work over, pore over, scrutinize ...*He has sifted the evidence and summarised it clearly*...

sigh VERB **1** = <u>breathe out</u>, exhale, moan, suspire (*archaic*) ...*Dad sighed and stood up*...

2 = <u>moan</u>, complain, groan, grieve, lament, sorrow ...*'Everyone forgets,' she sighed*...

PHRASES **sigh for something** or **someone** = <u>long for</u>, yearn for, pine for, mourn for, languish over, eat your heart out over ...*sighing for the good old days*...

sight NOUN **1** = <u>vision</u>, eyes, eyesight, seeing, eye ...*My sight is failing and I can't see to read any more*...

2 = <u>spectacle</u>, show, scene, display, exhibition, vista, pageant ...*Among the most spectacular sights are the*

great sea-bird colonies...

3 = <u>view</u>, field of vision, range of vision, eyeshot, viewing, ken, visibility ...*The Queen's carriage came into sight*...

4 (*Informal*) = <u>eyesore</u>, mess, spectacle, fright (*informal*), monstrosity, blot on the landscape (*informal*) ...*She looked a sight in the street-lamps*...

VERB = <u>spot</u>, see, observe, distinguish, perceive, make out, discern, behold ...*A fleet of ships was sighted in the North Sea*...

PHRASES **catch sight of something** or **someone** = <u>see</u>, spot, glimpse, view, clock (*Brit. informal*), recognize, spy, espy, descry ...*Every time I catch sight of myself in the mirror, I feel so disappointed*...

⟨ Related Words ⟩
adjectives: optical, visual

sign NOUN **1** = <u>symbol</u>, mark, character, figure, device, representation, logo, badge, emblem, ensign, cipher ...*Equations are generally written with a two-bar equals sign*...

2 = <u>figure</u>, form, shape, outline ...*The priest made the sign of the cross over him*...

3 = <u>gesture</u>, signal, motion, indication, cue, gesticulation ...*They gave him the thumbs-up sign*...

4 = <u>notice</u>, board, warning, signpost, placard ...*a sign saying that the highway was closed*...

5 = <u>indication</u>, evidence, trace, mark, note, signal, suggestion, symptom, hint, proof, gesture, clue, token, manifestation, giveaway, vestige, spoor ...*His face and movements rarely betrayed any sign of nerves*...

6 = <u>omen</u>, warning, portent, foreboding, presage, forewarning, writing on the wall, augury, auspice ...*It is a sign of things to come*...

VERB **1** = <u>gesture</u>, indicate, signal, wave, beckon, gesticulate, use sign language ...*She signed to me to go out*...

2 = <u>autograph</u>, initial, inscribe, subscribe, set your hand to ...*I got him to sign my copy of his book*...

PHRASES **sign someone up** = <u>engage</u>, recruit, employ, take on, hire, contract, take on board (*informal*), put on the payroll, take into service ...*Spalding wants to sign you up*... ♦ **sign something away** = <u>give up</u>, relinquish, renounce, lose, transfer, abandon, surrender, dispose of, waive, forgo ...*The Duke signed away his inheritance*... ♦ **sign up** = <u>enlist</u>, join, volunteer, register, enrol, join up ...*He signed up as a steward*...

signal NOUN **1** = <u>flare</u>, rocket, beam, beacon, smoke signal, signal fire ...*They fired three distress signals*...

2 = <u>cue</u>, sign, nod, prompting, go-ahead (*informal*), reminder, green light ...*You mustn't fire without my signal*...

3 = <u>sign</u>, gesture, indication, mark, note, evidence, expression, proof, token, indicator, manifestation ...*The event was seen as a signal of support*...

VERB = <u>gesture</u>, sign, wave, indicate, nod, motion, beckon, gesticulate, give a sign to ...*She signalled a passing taxi*...

significance = <u>importance</u>, import, consequence,

matter, moment, weight, consideration, gravity, relevance, magnitude, impressiveness

significant 1 = <u>important</u>, notable, serious, material, vital, critical, considerable, momentous, weighty, noteworthy ...*It is the first drug that seems to have a significant effect on this disease...* OPPOSITE insignificant
2 = <u>meaningful</u>, expressive, eloquent, knowing, meaning, expressing, pregnant, indicative, suggestive ...*The old woman gave her a significant glance...* OPPOSITE meaningless

signify = <u>indicate</u>, show, mean, matter, suggest, announce, evidence, represent, express, imply, exhibit, communicate, intimate, stand for, proclaim, convey, be a sign of, symbolize, denote, connote, portend, betoken

silence NOUN 1 = <u>quiet</u>, peace, calm, hush, lull, stillness, quiescence, noiselessness ...*They stood in silence...* OPPOSITE noise
2 = <u>reticence</u>, dumbness, taciturnity, speechlessness, muteness, uncommunicativeness ...*The court ruled that his silence should be entered as a plea of not guilty...* OPPOSITE speech
VERB = <u>quieten</u>, still, quiet, cut off, subdue, stifle, cut short, quell, muffle, deaden, strike dumb ...*The shock silenced him completely...* OPPOSITE make louder

silent 1 = <u>mute</u>, dumb, speechless, wordless, mum, struck dumb, voiceless, unspeaking ...*They both fell silent...* OPPOSITE noisy
2 = <u>uncommunicative</u>, quiet, taciturn, tongue-tied, unspeaking, nonvocal, not talkative ...*He was a serious, silent man...*
3 = <u>quiet</u>, still, hushed, soundless, noiseless, muted, stilly (*poetic*) ...*The heavy guns have again fallen silent...* OPPOSITE loud
4 = <u>unspoken</u>, implied, implicit, tacit, understood, unexpressed ...*He watched with silent contempt...*

silently 1 = <u>quietly</u>, in silence, soundlessly, noiselessly, inaudibly, without a sound ...*as silently as a mouse...*
2 = <u>mutely</u>, dumbly, in silence, wordlessly, speechlessly ...*He could no longer stand by silently while these rumours persisted...*

silhouette NOUN = <u>outline</u>, form, shape, profile, delineation ...*The dark silhouette of the castle ruins...* VERB = <u>outline</u>, delineate, etch ...*firefighters silhouetted against the burning wreckage...*

silky = <u>smooth</u>, soft, sleek, velvety, silken

silly ADJECTIVE 1 = <u>stupid</u>, ridiculous, absurd, daft, inane, childish, immature, senseless, frivolous, preposterous, giddy, goofy (*informal*), idiotic, dozy (*Brit. informal*), fatuous, witless, puerile, brainless, asinine, dumb-ass (*slang*), dopy (*slang*) ...*That's a silly thing to say...* OPPOSITE clever
2 = <u>foolish</u>, stupid, unwise, inappropriate, rash, irresponsible, reckless, foolhardy, idiotic, thoughtless, imprudent, inadvisable ...*Don't go doing anything silly, now, will you?...* OPPOSITE sensible
NOUN (*Informal*) = <u>fool</u>, twit (*informal*), goose

(*informal*), clot (*Brit. informal*), wally (*slang*), prat (*slang*), plonker (*slang*), duffer (*informal*), simpleton, ignoramus, nitwit (*informal*), ninny, silly-billy (*informal*), dweeb (*U.S. slang*), putz (*U.S. slang*), eejit (*Scot. & Irish*), doofus (*slang, chiefly U.S.*), nerd *or* nurd (*slang*), dorba *or* dorb (*Austral. slang*), bogan (*Austral. slang*) ...*Come on, silly, we'll miss all the fun...*

silt NOUN = <u>sediment</u>, deposit, residue, ooze, sludge, alluvium ...*The lake was almost solid with silt and vegetation...*
PHRASES **silt something up** = <u>clog up</u>, block up, choke up, obstruct, stop up, jam up, dam up, bung up, occlude, congest ...*The soil washed from the hills is silting up the dams...*

silver NOUN = <u>silverware</u>, silver plate ...*He beat the rugs and polished the silver...*
ADJECTIVE = <u>snowy</u>, white, grey, silvery, greyish-white, whitish-grey ...*He had thick silver hair which needed cutting...*

similar 1 = <u>alike</u>, uniform, resembling, corresponding, comparable, much the same, homogeneous, of a piece, homogenous, cut from the same cloth, congruous ...*The sisters looked very similar...* OPPOSITE different
2 *with* **to** = <u>like</u>, much the same as, comparable to, analogous to, close to, cut from the same cloth as ...*The accident was similar to one that happened in 1973...*

> ## *Word Power*
>
> **similar** – *As* should not be used after *similar* – so *Wilson held a similar position to Jones* is correct, but not *Wilson held a similar position as Jones*); and *the system is similar to the one in France* is correct, but not *the system is similar as in France*).

similarity = <u>resemblance</u>, likeness, sameness, agreement, relation, correspondence, analogy, affinity, closeness, concordance, congruence, comparability, point of comparison, similitude OPPOSITE difference

similarly 1 = <u>in the same way</u>, the same, identically, in a similar fashion, uniformly, homogeneously, undistinguishably ...*Most of the men who now gathered round him were similarly dressed...*
2 = <u>likewise</u>, in the same way, by the same token, correspondingly, in like manner ...*Similarly a baby's cry is instantly identified by the mother...*

simmer VERB 1 = <u>bubble</u>, stew, boil gently, seethe, cook gently ...*Turn the heat down so the sauce simmers gently...*
2 = <u>fume</u>, seethe, smoulder, burn, smart, rage, boil, be angry, see red (*informal*), be tense, be agitated, be uptight (*informal*) ...*He simmered with rage...*
PHRASES **simmer down** (*Informal*) = <u>calm down</u>, grow quieter, control yourself, unwind (*informal*), contain yourself, collect yourself, cool off *or* down, get down off your high horse (*informal*) ...*After an hour*

or so, she finally managed to simmer down...

simper = smile coyly, smirk, smile self-consciously, smile affectedly

simpering = coy, affected, flirtatious, coquettish, kittenish

simple 1 = uncomplicated, clear, plain, understandable, coherent, lucid, recognizable, unambiguous, comprehensible, intelligible, uninvolved ...*simple pictures and diagrams...* OPPOSITE > complicated
2 = easy, straightforward, not difficult, light, elementary, manageable, effortless, painless, uncomplicated, undemanding, easy-peasy (*slang*) ...*The job itself had been simple enough...*
3 = plain, natural, basic, classic, severe, Spartan, uncluttered, unadorned, unfussy, unembellished ...*She's shunned Armani for a simple blouse and jeans...* OPPOSITE > elaborate
4 = pure, mere, sheer, unalloyed ...*His refusal to talk was simple stubborness...*
5 = artless, innocent, naive, natural, frank, green, sincere, simplistic, unaffected, childlike, unpretentious, unsophisticated, ingenuous, guileless ...*He was as simple as a child...* OPPOSITE > sophisticated
6 = unpretentious, modest, humble, homely, lowly, rustic, uncluttered, unfussy, unembellished ...*It was a simple home...* OPPOSITE > fancy

simple-minded = stupid, simple, foolish, backward, idiot, retarded, idiotic, moronic, brainless, feeble-minded, addle-brained, dead from the neck up (*informal*), a bit lacking (*informal*), dim-witted

simplicity 1 = straightforwardness, ease, clarity, obviousness, easiness, clearness, absence of complications, elementariness ...*The apparent simplicity of his plot is deceptive...* OPPOSITE > complexity
2 = plainness, restraint, purity, clean lines, naturalness, lack of adornment ...*fussy details that ruin the simplicity of the design...* OPPOSITE > elaborateness

simplify = make simpler, facilitate, streamline, disentangle, dumb down, make intelligible, reduce to essentials

simplistic = oversimplified, shallow, facile, naive, oversimple

---

Word Power

simplistic – Since *simplistic* already has 'too' as part of its meaning, some people object to something being referred to as *too simplistic* or *oversimplistic*, and it is best to avoid such uses in serious writing.

---

simply 1 = just, only, merely, purely, solely ...*The table is simply a chip-board circle on a base...*
2 = totally, really, completely, absolutely, altogether, wholly, utterly, unreservedly ...*He's simply wonderful in every respect...*
3 = clearly, straightforwardly, directly, plainly, intelligibly, unaffectedly ...*The book is clearly and simply written...*
4 = plainly, naturally, modestly, with restraint, unpretentiously, without any elaboration ...*He dressed simply and led a quiet family life...*
5 = without doubt, surely, certainly, definitely, unquestionably, undeniably, unmistakably, beyond question, beyond a shadow of (a) doubt ...*It was simply the greatest night any of us ever had...*

simulate = pretend, act, feign, affect, assume, put on, reproduce, imitate, sham, fabricate, counterfeit, make believe

simulated 1 = pretended, put-on, feigned, assumed, artificial, make-believe, insincere, phoney *or* phony (*informal*) ...*He performed a simulated striptease...*
2 = synthetic, artificial, fake, substitute, mock, imitation, man-made, sham, pseudo (*informal*) ...*a necklace of simulated pearls...*

simultaneous = coinciding, concurrent, contemporaneous, coincident, synchronous, happening at the same time

simultaneously = at the same time, together, all together, in concert, in unison, concurrently, in the same breath, in chorus

sin NOUN **1** = wickedness, wrong, evil, crime, error, trespass, immorality, transgression, iniquity, sinfulness, unrighteousness, ungodliness ...*Sin can be forgiven, but never condoned...*
2 = crime, offence, misdemeanour, error, wrongdoing, misdeed, transgression, act of evil, guilt ...*Was it a sin to have believed too much in themselves?...*
VERB = transgress, offend, lapse, err, trespass (*archaic*), fall from grace, go astray, commit a sin, do wrong ...*They charged him with sinning against God and man...*

Seven deadly sins

anger	lust
covetousness *or*	pride
avarice	sloth
envy	
gluttony	

---

sincere = honest, genuine, real, true, serious, natural, earnest, frank, open, straightforward, candid, unaffected, no-nonsense, heartfelt, upfront (*informal*), bona fide, wholehearted, dinkum (*Austral. & N.Z. informal*), artless, guileless, unfeigned OPPOSITE > false

sincerely = honestly, really, truly, genuinely, seriously, earnestly, wholeheartedly, in good faith, in earnest, in all sincerity, from the bottom of your heart

sincerity = honesty, truth, candour, frankness, seriousness, good faith, probity, bona fides, genuineness, straightforwardness, artlessness, guilelessness, wholeheartedness

sinewy = muscular, strong, powerful, athletic, robust, wiry, brawny

sinful = wicked, bad, criminal, guilty, corrupt, immoral, erring, unholy, depraved, iniquitous,

ungodly, irreligious, unrighteous, morally wrong
OPPOSITE> virtuous

sing VERB **1** = <u>croon</u>, carol, chant, warble, yodel, pipe, vocalize ...*Go on, then, sing us a song!...*
2 = <u>trill</u>, chirp, warble, make melody ...*Birds were already singing in the garden...*
PHRASES **sing out** = <u>call (out)</u>, cry (out), shout, yell, holler (*informal*), halloo ...*'See you,' Jeff sang out...*

> ### Word Power
>
> **sing** – *Sang* is the past tense of the verb *sing*, as in *she sang sweetly*. *Sung* is the past participle, as in *we have sung our song*, and care should be taken not to use it as if it were a variant form of the past tense.

singe = <u>burn</u>, sear, scorch, char

singer = <u>vocalist</u>, crooner, minstrel, soloist, cantor, troubadour, chorister, chanteuse (*fem.*), balladeer, songster *or* songstress

single ADJECTIVE **1** = <u>one</u>, sole, lone, solitary, only, only one, unique, singular ...*A single shot rang out...*
2 = <u>individual</u>, particular, separate, distinct ...*Every single house had been damaged...*
3 = <u>unmarried</u>, free, unattached, a bachelor, unwed, a spinster ...*The last I heard she was still single, still out there...*
4 = <u>separate</u>, individual, exclusive, undivided, unshared ...*A single room at the hotel costs £36 a night...*
5 = <u>simple</u>, unmixed, unblended, uncompounded ...*single malt whisky...*
PHRASES **single something** *or* **someone out** = <u>pick</u>, choose, select, separate, distinguish, fix on, set apart, winnow, put on one side, pick on *or* out ...*He singled me out for special attention...*

single-handed = <u>unaided</u>, on your own, by yourself, alone, independently, solo, without help, unassisted, under your own steam

single-minded = <u>determined</u>, dogged, fixed, dedicated, stubborn, tireless, steadfast, unwavering, unswerving, hellbent (*informal*), undeviating, monomaniacal

singly = <u>one by one</u>, individually, one at a time, separately, one after the other

singular 1 = <u>single</u>, individual ...*The pronoun 'you' can be singular or plural...*
2 = <u>remarkable</u>, unique, extraordinary, outstanding, exceptional, rare, notable, eminent, uncommon, conspicuous, prodigious, unparalleled, noteworthy ...*a smile of singular sweetness...* OPPOSITE> ordinary
3 = <u>unusual</u>, odd, strange, extraordinary, puzzling, curious, peculiar, eccentric, out-of-the-way, queer, oddball (*informal*), atypical, wacko (*slang*), outré ...*He was without doubt a singular character...* OPPOSITE> conventional

singularity = <u>oddity</u>, abnormality, eccentricity, peculiarity, strangeness, idiosyncrasy, irregularity, particularity, oddness, queerness, extraordinariness, curiousness

singularly = <u>remarkably</u>, particularly, exceptionally, especially, seriously (*informal*), surprisingly, notably, unusually, extraordinarily, conspicuously, outstandingly, uncommonly, prodigiously

sinister = <u>threatening</u>, evil, menacing, forbidding, dire, ominous, malign, disquieting, malignant, malevolent, baleful, injurious, bodeful OPPOSITE> reassuring

sink NOUN = <u>basin</u>, washbasin, hand basin, wash-hand basin ...*The sink was full of dirty dishes...*
VERB **1** = <u>scupper</u>, scuttle ...*In a naval battle your aim is to sink the enemy's ship...*
2 = <u>go down</u>, founder, go under, submerge, capsize ...*The boat was beginning to sink fast...*
3 = <u>slump</u>, drop, flop, collapse, droop ...*Kate laughed, and sank down again to her seat...*
4 = <u>fall</u>, drop, decline, slip, plunge, plummet, subside, relapse, abate, retrogress ...*Pay increases have sunk to around seven per cent...*
5 = <u>drop</u>, fall ...*Her voice had sunk to a whisper...*
6 = <u>stoop</u>, descend, be reduced to, succumb, lower yourself, debase yourself, demean yourself ...*You know who you are, be proud of it and don't sink to his level...*
7 = <u>decline</u>, die, fade, fail, flag, weaken, diminish, decrease, deteriorate, decay, worsen, dwindle, lessen, degenerate, depreciate, go downhill (*informal*) ...*He's still alive, but sinking fast...* OPPOSITE> improve
8 = <u>dig</u>, bore, drill, drive, lay, put down, excavate ...*the site where Stephenson sank his first mineshaft...*

sinner = <u>wrongdoer</u>, offender, evildoer, trespasser (*archaic*), reprobate, miscreant, malefactor, transgressor

sinuous = <u>curving</u>, winding, meandering, crooked, coiling, tortuous, undulating, serpentine, curvy, lithe, twisty, mazy

sip VERB = <u>drink</u>, taste, sample, sup ...*Jessica sipped her drink thoughtfully...*
NOUN = <u>swallow</u>, mouthful, swig, drop, taste, thimbleful ...*Harry took a sip of bourbon...*

siren 1 = <u>alert</u>, warning, signal, alarm ...*It sounds like an air raid siren...*
2 = <u>seductress</u>, vamp (*informal*), femme fatale (*French*), witch, charmer, temptress, Lorelei, Circe ...*She's a voluptuous siren with a husky voice...*

sissy *or* **cissy** NOUN = <u>wimp</u>, softie (*informal*), weakling, baby, wet (*Brit. informal*), coward (*informal*), jessie (*Scot. slang*), pansy, pussy (*slang, chiefly U.S.*), mummy's boy, mollycoddle, namby-pamby, wuss (*slang*), milksop, milquetoast (*U.S.*), sisspot (*informal*) ...*They were rough kids and thought we were sissies...*
ADJECTIVE = <u>wimpish</u> *or* <u>wimpy</u> (*informal*) = <u>wimp</u>, soft (*informal*), weak, wet (*Brit. informal*), cowardly, feeble, unmanly, effeminate, namby-pamby, wussy (*slang*), sissified (*informal*) ...*Far from being sissy, it takes a real man to admit he's not perfect...*

sit 1 = <u>take a seat</u>, perch, settle down, be seated, take the weight off your feet ...*Eva pulled up a chair and* sat beside her husband...

2 = <u>place</u>, set, put, position, rest, lay, settle, deposit, situate ...*She found her chair and sat it in the usual spot...*

3 = <u>be a member of</u>, serve on, have a seat on, preside on ...*He was asked to sit on numerous committees...*

4 = <u>convene</u>, meet, assemble, officiate, be in session ...*Parliament sits for only 28 weeks out of 52...*

site NOUN **1** = <u>area</u>, ground, plot, patch, tract ...*He became a hod carrier on a building site...*

2 = <u>location</u>, place, setting, point, position, situation, spot, whereabouts, locus ...*the site of Moses' tomb...*

VERB = <u>locate</u>, put, place, set, position, establish, install, situate ...*He said chemical weapons had never been sited in Germany...*

sitting **1** = <u>session</u>, period ...*Dinner was in two sittings...*

2 = <u>meeting</u>, hearing, session, congress, consultation, get-together (*informal*) ...*the recent emergency sittings...*

situation **1** = <u>position</u>, state, case, condition, circumstances, equation, plight, status quo, state of affairs, ball game (*informal*), kettle of fish (*informal*) ...*We are in a difficult financial situation...*

2 = <u>scenario</u>, the picture (*informal*), the score (*informal*), state of affairs, lie of the land ...*They looked at each other and weighed up the situation...*

3 = <u>location</u>, place, setting, position, seat, site, spot, locality, locale ...*The garden is in a beautiful situation...*

Word Power

situation – It is common to hear the word *situation* used in sentences such as *the company is in a crisis situation*. This use of *situation* is considered bad style and the word should be left out, since it adds nothing to the sentence's meaning.

---

sixth sense = <u>intuition</u>, second sight, clairvoyance

size NOUN = <u>dimensions</u>, extent, measurement(s), range, amount, mass, length, volume, capacity, proportions, bulk, width, magnitude, greatness, vastness, immensity, bigness, largeness, hugeness ...*books of various sizes...*

PHRASES **size something** *or* **someone up** (*Informal*) = <u>assess</u>, evaluate, appraise, take stock of, eye up, get the measure of, get (something) taped (*Brit. informal*) ...*He spent the evening sizing me up intellectually...*

sizeable *or* **sizable** = <u>large</u>, considerable, substantial, goodly, decent, respectable, tidy (*informal*), decent-sized, largish

sizzle = <u>hiss</u>, spit, crackle, sputter, fry, frizzle

skeletal = <u>emaciated</u>, wasted, gaunt, skin-and-bone (*informal*), cadaverous, hollow-cheeked, lantern-jawed, fleshless, worn to a shadow

skeleton NOUN **1** = <u>bones</u>, bare bones ...*a human skeleton...*

2 = <u>frame</u>, shell, framework, basic structure ...*Only skeletons of buildings remained in the area...*

3 = <u>plan</u>, structure, frame, draft, outline, framework, sketch, abstract, blueprint, main points ...*a skeleton of policy guidelines...*

ADJECTIVE = <u>minimum</u>, reduced, minimal, essential ...*Only a skeleton staff remains to see anyone interested around the site...*

sketch NOUN **1** = <u>drawing</u>, design, draft, delineation ...*a sketch of a soldier...*

2 = <u>draft</u>, outline, framework, plan, frame, rough, skeleton, layout, lineament(s) ...*I had a basic sketch of a plan...*

3 = <u>skit</u>, piece, scene, turn, act, performance, item, routine, number ...*a five-minute humorous sketch...*

VERB = <u>draw</u>, paint, outline, represent, draft, portray, depict, delineate, rough out ...*I sketched the scene with my pen and paper...*

sketchy = <u>incomplete</u>, rough, vague, slight, outline, inadequate, crude, superficial, unfinished, skimpy, scrappy, cursory, perfunctory, cobbled together, bitty OPPOSITE complete

skid = <u>slide</u>, slip, slither, coast, glide, skim, veer, toboggan

skilful = <u>expert</u>, skilled, masterly, trained, experienced, able, professional, quick, clever, practised, accomplished, handy, competent, apt, adept, proficient, adroit, dexterous OPPOSITE clumsy

skill = <u>expertise</u>, ability, proficiency, experience, art, technique, facility, talent, intelligence, craft, competence, readiness, accomplishment, knack, ingenuity, finesse, aptitude, dexterity, cleverness, quickness, adroitness, expertness, handiness, skilfulness OPPOSITE clumsiness

skilled = <u>expert</u>, professional, accomplished, trained, experienced, able, masterly, practised, skilful, proficient, a dab hand at (*Brit. informal*) OPPOSITE unskilled

skim **1** = <u>remove</u>, separate, cream, take off ...*Skim off the fat...*

2 = <u>glide</u>, fly, coast, sail, float, brush, dart ...*seagulls skimming over the waves...*

3 *usually with* **over** *or* **through** = <u>scan</u>, glance, run your eye over, thumb *or* leaf through ...*I only had time to skim over the script before I came here...*

skimp = <u>stint</u>, scrimp, be sparing with, pinch, withhold, scant, cut corners, scamp, be mean with, be niggardly, tighten your belt OPPOSITE be extravagant

skimpy = <u>inadequate</u>, insufficient, scant, meagre, short, tight, thin, sparse, scanty, miserly, niggardly, exiguous

skin NOUN **1** = <u>complexion</u>, colouring, skin tone ...*His skin is clear and smooth...*

2 = <u>hide</u>, fleece, pelt, fell, integument, tegument ...*That was real crocodile skin...*

3 = <u>peel</u>, rind, husk, casing, outside, crust ...*banana skins...*

4 = <u>film</u>, coating, coat, membrane ...*Stir the custard occasionally to prevent a skin forming...*

VERB 1 = peel, pare, hull …*two tomatoes, skinned, peeled and chopped…*

2 = scrape, graze, bark, flay, excoriate, abrade …*He fell down and skinned his knee…*

PHRASES **by the skin of your teeth** = narrowly, only just, by a whisker (*informal*), by a narrow margin, by a hair's-breadth …*He won, but only by the skin of his teeth…* ◆ **get under your skin** (*Informal*) = annoy, irritate, aggravate (*informal*), needle (*informal*), nettle, irk, grate on, get on your nerves (*informal*), get in your hair (*informal*), rub you up the wrong way …*Her mannerisms can just get under your skin and needle you…*

skin-deep = superficial, surface, external, artificial, shallow, on the surface, meaningless

skinny = thin, lean, scrawny, skeletal, emaciated, twiggy, undernourished, skin-and-bone (*informal*), scraggy **OPPOSITE** fat

skip 1 = hop, dance, bob, trip, bounce, caper, prance, cavort, frisk, gambol …*She was skipping along the pavement…*

2 = miss out, omit, leave out, overlook, pass over, eschew, forego, skim over, give (something) a miss …*It is important not to skip meals…*

3 (*Informal*) = miss, cut (*informal*), bunk off (*slang*), play truant from, wag (*dialect*), dog it *or* dog off (*dialect*) …*Her daughter started skipping school…*

skirmish **NOUN** = fight, battle, conflict, incident, clash, contest, set-to (*informal*), encounter, brush, combat, scrap (*informal*), engagement, spat, tussle, fracas, affray (*Law*), dust-up (*informal*), scrimmage, biffo (*Austral. slang*) …*Border skirmishes are common…*

VERB = fight, clash, come to blows, scrap (*informal*), collide, grapple, wrangle, tussle, lock horns, cross swords …*Police skirmished with youths on a council estate last Friday…*

skirt **VERB** 1 = border, edge, lie alongside, line, fringe, flank …*We raced across a large field that skirted the slope of the hill…*

2 often with **around** or **round** = go round, bypass, walk round, circumvent …*She skirted around the edge of the room to the door…*

3 often with **around** or **round** = avoid, evade, steer clear of, sidestep, circumvent, detour, body-swerve (*Scot.*) …*They have, until now, skirted around the issue…*

NOUN often plural = border, edge, margin, fringe, outskirts, rim, hem, periphery, purlieus …*the skirts of the hill…*

skit = parody, spoof (*informal*), travesty, takeoff (*informal*), burlesque, turn, sketch

skittish = nervous, lively, excitable, jumpy, restive, fidgety, highly strung, antsy (*informal*) **OPPOSITE** calm

skulduggery (*Informal*) = trickery, swindling, machinations, duplicity, double-dealing, fraudulence, shenanigan(s) (*informal*), unscrupulousness, underhandedness

skulk 1 = creep, sneak, slink, pad, prowl …*He skulked*

off…

2 = lurk, hide, lie in wait, loiter …*skulking in the safety of the car…*

sky = heavens, firmament, upper atmosphere, azure (*poetic*), welkin (*archaic*), vault of heaven

(*Related Words*)

adjective: celestial

slab = piece, slice, lump, chunk, wedge, hunk, portion, nugget, wodge (*Brit. informal*)

slack **ADJECTIVE** 1 = limp, relaxed, loose, lax, flaccid, not taut …*The electronic pads work slack muscles to astounding effect…*

2 = loose, hanging, flapping, baggy …*The wind had gone, leaving the sails slack…* **OPPOSITE** taut

3 = slow, quiet, inactive, dull, sluggish, slow-moving …*busy times and slack periods…* **OPPOSITE** busy

4 = negligent, lazy, lax, idle, easy-going, inactive, tardy, slapdash, neglectful, slipshod, inattentive, remiss, asleep on the job (*informal*) …*Many publishers have simply become far too slack…* **OPPOSITE** strict

VERB = shirk, idle, relax, flag, neglect, dodge, skive (*Brit. slang*), bob off (*Brit. slang*), bludge (*Austral. & N.Z. informal*) …*He had never let a foreman see him slacking…*

NOUN 1 = surplus, excess, overflow, leftover, glut, surfeit, overabundance, superabundance, superfluity …*Buying-to-let could stimulate the housing market by reducing the slack…*

2 = room, excess, leeway, give (*informal*), play, looseness …*He cranked in the slack, and the ship was moored…*

slacken often with **off** = lessen, reduce, decrease, ease (off), moderate, diminish, slow down, drop off, abate, let up, slack off

slacker = layabout, shirker, loafer, skiver (*Brit. slang*), idler, passenger, do-nothing, piker (*Austral. & N.Z. slang*), dodger, good-for-nothing, bludger (*Austral. & N.Z. informal*), gold brick (*U.S. slang*), scrimshanker (*Brit. military slang*)

slag **NOUN** (*Brit. slang*) = tart (*informal*), scrubber (*Brit. & Austral. slang*), whore, pro (*slang*), brass (*slang*), prostitute, hooker (*U.S. slang*), hustler (*U.S. & Canad. slang*), moll (*slang*), call girl, courtesan, working girl (*facetious slang*), harlot, slapper (*Brit. informal*), streetwalker, camp follower, loose woman, fallen woman, strumpet, trollop, white slave, bawd (*archaic*), cocotte, fille de joie (*French*) …*She became a slag, a tart, a hustler, a lost girl…*

PHRASES **slag something** or **someone off** (*Slang*) = criticize, abuse, malign, slam, insult, mock, slate, slang, deride, berate, slander, diss (*slang, chiefly U.S.*), lambast(e), flame (*informal*) …*People keep slagging me off…*

slam 1 = bang, crash, smash, thump, shut with a bang, shut noisily …*She slammed the door and locked it behind her…*

2 = throw, dash, hurl, fling …*They slammed him up against a wall…*

3 (*Slang*) = criticize, attack, blast, pan (*informal*),

damn, slate (*informal*), shoot down (*informal*), castigate, vilify, pillory, tear into (*informal*), diss (*slang, chiefly U.S.*), lambast(e), excoriate ...*The director slammed the claims as an outrageous lie...*

slander NOUN = defamation, smear, libel, scandal, misrepresentation, calumny, backbiting, muckraking, obloquy, aspersion, detraction ...*He is now suing the company for slander...* OPPOSITE praise
VERB = defame, smear, libel, slur, malign, detract, disparage, decry, vilify, traduce, backbite, blacken (someone's) name, calumniate, muckrake ...*He has been questioned on suspicion of slandering the politician...* OPPOSITE praise

slang = colloquialisms, jargon, idioms, argot, informal language

slant VERB 1 = slope, incline, tilt, list, bend, lean, heel, shelve, skew, cant, bevel, angle off ...*The morning sun slanted through the glass roof...*
2 = bias, colour, weight, twist, angle, distort ...*The coverage was deliberately slanted to make the home team look good...*
NOUN 1 = slope, incline, tilt, gradient, pitch, ramp, diagonal, camber, declination ...*The house is on a slant...*
2 = bias, emphasis, prejudice, angle, leaning, point of view, viewpoint, one-sidedness ...*They give a slant to every single news item that's put on the air...*

slanting = sloping, angled, inclined, tilted, tilting, sideways, slanted, bent, diagonal, oblique, at an angle, canted, on the bias, aslant, slantwise, atilt, cater-cornered (*U.S. informal*)

slap VERB 1 = smack, hit, strike, beat, bang, clap, clout (*informal*), cuff, whack, swipe, spank, clobber (*slang*), wallop (*informal*), lay one on (*slang*) ...*He would push and slap her once in a while...*
2 (*Informal, chiefly Brit.*) = plaster, apply, spread, daub ...*We now routinely slap sun screen on ourselves before venturing out...*
NOUN = smack, blow, whack, wallop (*informal*), bang, clout (*informal*), cuff, swipe, spank ...*He reached forward and gave her a slap...*
PHRASES **a slap in the face** = insult, humiliation, snub, affront, blow, rejection, put-down, rebuke, rebuff, repulse ...*They treated any pay rise of less than 5% as a slap in the face...*

slapstick = farce, horseplay, buffoonery, knockabout comedy

slap-up (*Brit. informal*) = luxurious, lavish, sumptuous, princely, excellent, superb, magnificent, elaborate, splendid, first-rate, no-expense-spared, fit for a king

slash VERB 1 = cut, slit, gash, lacerate, score, rend, rip, hack ...*He nearly bled to death after slashing his wrists...*
2 = reduce, cut, decrease, drop, lower, moderate, diminish, cut down, lessen, curtail ...*Everyone agrees that subsidies have to be slashed...*
NOUN = cut, slit, gash, rent, rip, incision, laceration ...*deep slashes in the meat...*

slate (*Informal, chiefly Brit.*) = criticize, blast, pan (*informal*), slam (*slang*), blame, roast (*informal*), censure, rebuke, slang, scold, berate, castigate, rail against, tear into (*informal*), lay into (*informal*), pitch into (*informal*), take to task, lambast(e), flame (*informal*), excoriate, haul over the coals (*informal*), tear (someone) off a strip (*informal*), rap (someone's) knuckles

slaughter VERB 1 = kill, murder, massacre, destroy, do in (*slang*), execute, dispatch, assassinate, blow away (*slang, chiefly U.S.*), annihilate, bump off (*slang*) ...*Thirty-four people were slaughtered while queueing up to cast their votes...*
2 = butcher, kill, slay, destroy, massacre, exterminate ...*Whales and dolphins are still being slaughtered for commercial gain...*
3 (*Informal*) = defeat, thrash, vanquish, stuff (*slang*), tank (*slang*), hammer (*informal*), crush, overwhelm, lick (*informal*), undo, rout, trounce, wipe the floor with (*informal*), blow out of the water (*slang*) ...*He slaughtered his opponent in three sets...*
NOUN = slaying, killing, murder, massacre, holocaust, bloodshed, carnage, liquidation, extermination, butchery, blood bath ...*The annual slaughter of wildlife is horrific...*

slaughterhouse = abattoir, butchery, shambles

slave NOUN 1 = servant, serf, vassal, bondsman, slavey (*Brit. informal*), varlet (*archaic*), villein, bondservant ...*still living as slaves in the desert...*
2 = drudge, skivvy (*chiefly Brit.*), scullion (*archaic*) ...*Mum says to Dad, 'I'm not your slave, you know!'...*
VERB = toil, labour, grind (*informal*), drudge, sweat, graft, slog, skivvy (*Brit.*), work your fingers to the bone ...*slaving over a hot stove...*

slaver = dribble, drool, salivate, slobber

slavery = enslavement, servitude, subjugation, captivity, bondage, thrall, serfdom, vassalage, thraldom OPPOSITE freedom

slavish 1 = imitative, unimaginative, unoriginal, conventional, second-hand, uninspired ...*a slavish follower of fashion...* OPPOSITE original
2 = servile, cringing, abject, submissive, grovelling, mean, low, base, fawning, despicable, menial, sycophantic, obsequious ...*slavish devotion...* OPPOSITE rebellious

slay 1 (*Archaic or literary*) = kill, destroy, slaughter, eliminate, massacre, butcher, dispatch, annihilate, exterminate ...*the hill where he slew the dragon...*
2 = murder, kill, assassinate, do in (*slang*), eliminate, massacre, slaughter, do away with, exterminate, mow down, rub out (*U.S. slang*) ...*Two Australian tourists were slain...*

sleaze (*Informal*) = corruption, fraud, dishonesty, fiddling (*informal*), bribery, extortion, venality, shady dealings (*informal*), crookedness (*informal*), unscrupulousness

sleazy = squalid, seedy, sordid, low, run-down, tacky (*informal*), disreputable, crummy, scungy (*Austral. & N.Z.*)

sleek = <u>glossy</u>, shiny, lustrous, smooth, silky, velvety, well-groomed [OPPOSITE] shaggy

sleep [NOUN] = <u>slumber(s)</u>, rest, nap, doze, kip (*Brit. slang*), snooze (*informal*), repose, hibernation, siesta, dormancy, beauty sleep (*informal*), forty winks (*informal*), shuteye (*slang*), zizz (*Brit. informal*) ...*Try and get some sleep*...
[VERB] = <u>slumber</u>, drop off (*informal*), doze, kip (*Brit. slang*), snooze (*informal*), snore, hibernate, nod off (*informal*), take a nap, catnap, drowse, go out like a light, take forty winks (*informal*), zizz (*Brit. informal*), be in the land of Nod, rest in the arms of Morpheus ...*I've not been able to sleep for the last few nights*...

sleepless 1 = <u>wakeful</u>, disturbed, restless, insomniac, unsleeping ...*I have sleepless nights worrying about her*...
2 (*Chiefly poetic*) = <u>alert</u>, vigilant, watchful, wide awake, unsleeping ...*his sleepless vigilance*...

sleepwalking = <u>somnambulism</u>, noctambulation, noctambulism, somnambulation

sleepy 1 = <u>drowsy</u>, sluggish, lethargic, heavy, dull, inactive, somnolent, torpid ...*I was beginning to feel amazingly sleepy*... [OPPOSITE] wide-awake
2 = <u>soporific</u>, hypnotic, somnolent, sleep-inducing, slumberous ...*How long we spent there in that sleepy heat, I don't know*...
3 = <u>quiet</u>, peaceful, dull, tranquil, inactive ...*a sleepy little town*... [OPPOSITE] busy

slender 1 = <u>slim</u>, narrow, slight, lean, svelte, willowy, sylphlike ...*He gazed at her slender neck*... [OPPOSITE] chubby
2 = <u>faint</u>, slight, remote, slim, thin, weak, fragile, feeble, flimsy, tenuous ...*the first slender hope of peace*... [OPPOSITE] strong
3 = <u>meagre</u>, little, small, inadequate, insufficient, scant, scanty, inconsiderable ...*the Government's slender 21-seat majority*... [OPPOSITE] large

sleuth (*Informal*) = <u>detective</u>, private eye (*informal*), (private) investigator, tail (*informal*), dick (*slang, chiefly U.S.*), gumshoe (*U.S. slang*), sleuthhound (*informal*)

slice [NOUN] = <u>piece</u>, segment, portion, wedge, sliver, helping, share, cut ...*water flavoured with a slice of lemon*...
[VERB] = <u>cut</u>, divide, carve, segment, sever, dissect, cleave, bisect ...*She sliced the cake*...

slick [ADJECTIVE] 1 = <u>efficient</u>, professional, smart, smooth, streamlined, masterly, sharp, deft, well-organized, adroit ...*His style is slick and visually exciting*...
2 = <u>skilful</u>, deft, adroit, dextrous, dexterous, professional, polished ...*a slick gear change*... [OPPOSITE] clumsy
3 = <u>glib</u>, smooth, sophisticated, plausible, polished, specious, meretricious ...*a slick, suit-wearing detective*...
4 = <u>glossy</u>, smooth, shiny, greasy, oily, silky, lustrous ...*his greasy, slick hair-do*...
[VERB] = <u>smooth</u>, oil, grease, sleek, plaster down, make glossy, smarm down (*Brit. informal*) ...*She had slicked*

her hair...

slide [VERB] = <u>slip</u>, slither, glide, skim, coast, toboggan, glissade ...*She slipped and slid downhill on her backside*...
[PHRASES] **let something slide** = <u>neglect</u>, forget, ignore, pass over, turn a blind eye to, gloss over, push to the back of your mind, let ride ...*The company had let environmental standards slide*...

slight [ADJECTIVE] 1 = <u>small</u>, minor, insignificant, negligible, weak, modest, trivial, superficial, feeble, trifling, meagre, unimportant, paltry, measly, insubstantial, scanty, inconsiderable ...*It's only made a slight difference*... [OPPOSITE] large
2 = <u>slim</u>, small, delicate, spare, fragile, lightly-built ...*a man of slight build*... [OPPOSITE] sturdy
[VERB] = <u>snub</u>, insult, ignore, rebuff, affront, neglect, put down, despise, scorn, disdain, disparage, cold-shoulder, treat with contempt, show disrespect for, give offence *or* umbrage to ...*They felt slighted by not being adequately consulted*... [OPPOSITE] compliment
[NOUN] = <u>insult</u>, snub, affront, contempt, disregard, indifference, disdain, rebuff, disrespect, slap in the face (*informal*), inattention, discourtesy, (the) cold shoulder ...*a child weeping over an imagined slight*...
[OPPOSITE] compliment

slightly = <u>a little</u>, a bit, somewhat, moderately, marginally, a shade, to some degree, on a small scale, to some extent *or* degree

slim [ADJECTIVE] 1 = <u>slender</u>, slight, trim, thin, narrow, lean, svelte, willowy, sylphlike ...*She is pretty, of slim build, with blue eyes*... [OPPOSITE] chubby
2 = <u>slight</u>, remote, faint, distant, slender ...*a slim chance*... [OPPOSITE] strong
[VERB] = <u>lose weight</u>, diet, get thinner, get into shape, slenderize (*chiefly U.S.*) ...*Some people will gain weight no matter how hard they try to slim*... [OPPOSITE] put on weight

slimy 1 = <u>viscous</u>, clammy, glutinous, muddy, mucous, gloopy (*informal*), oozy, miry ...*Her hand touched something cold and slimy*...
2 (*Chiefly Brit.*) = <u>obsequious</u>, creepy, unctuous, smarmy (*Brit. informal*), oily, grovelling, soapy (*slang*), sycophantic, servile, toadying ...*his slimy business partner*...

sling [VERB] 1 (*Informal*) = <u>throw</u>, cast, toss, hurl, fling, chuck (*informal*), lob (*informal*), heave, shy ...*She slung her coat over the desk chair*...
2 = <u>hang</u>, swing, suspend, string, drape, dangle ...*We slept in hammocks slung beneath the roof*...
[NOUN] = <u>harness</u>, support, bandage, strap ...*She was back at work with her arm in a sling*...

slink = <u>creep</u>, steal, sneak, slip, prowl, skulk, pussyfoot (*informal*)

slinky = <u>figure-hugging</u>, clinging, sleek, close-fitting, skintight

slip¹ [VERB] 1 = <u>fall</u>, trip (over), slide, skid, lose your balance, miss *or* lose your footing ...*Be careful not to slip*...
2 = <u>slide</u>, fall, drop, slither ...*The hammer slipped out*

of her grasp...
3 = <u>sneak</u>, creep, steal, insinuate yourself ...*She slipped downstairs and out of the house...*
NOUN = <u>mistake</u>, failure, error, blunder, lapse, omission, boob (*Brit. slang*), oversight, slip-up (*informal*), indiscretion, bloomer (*Brit. informal*), faux pas, slip of the tongue, imprudence ...*There must be no slips...*
PHRASES **give someone the slip** = <u>escape from</u>, get away from, evade, shake (someone) off, elude, lose (someone), flee, dodge, outwit, slip through someone's fingers ...*He gave reporters the slip by leaving by the back door at midnight...* ◆ **let something slip** = <u>give away</u>, reveal, disclose, divulge, leak, come out with (*informal*), let out (*informal*), blurt out, let the cat out of the bag ...*I bet he'd let slip that I'd gone to America...* ◆ **slip away** = <u>get away</u>, escape, disappear, break away, break free, get clear of, take French leave ...*He slipped away in the early hours to exile in France...* ◆ **slip up** = <u>make a mistake</u>, go wrong, blunder, mistake, boob (*Brit. slang*), err, misjudge, miscalculate, drop a brick *or* clanger (*informal*) ...*You will see exactly where you are slipping up...*

slip² – <u>strip</u>, piece, sliver ...*little slips of paper...*

slippery 1 = <u>smooth</u>, icy, greasy, glassy, slippy (*informal or dialect*), unsafe, lubricious (*rare*), skiddy (*informal*) ...*The floor was wet and slippery...*
2 = <u>untrustworthy</u>, tricky, cunning, false, treacherous, dishonest, devious, crafty, evasive, sneaky, two-faced, shifty, foxy, duplicitous ...*a slippery customer...*

slit **VERB** = <u>cut (open)</u>, rip, slash, knife, pierce, lance, gash, split open ...*They say somebody slit her throat...*
NOUN **1** = <u>cut</u>, gash, incision, tear, rent, fissure ...*Make a slit in the stem...*
2 = <u>opening</u>, split, crack, aperture, chink, space ...*She watched them through a slit in the curtain...*

slither = <u>slide</u>, slip, glide, snake, undulate, slink, skitter

sliver = <u>shred</u>, fragment, splinter, slip, shaving, flake, paring

slob (*Informal*) = <u>layabout</u>, lounger, loafer, couch potato (*slang*), idler, good-for-nothing

slog **VERB** **1** = <u>work</u>, labour, toil, slave, plod, persevere, plough through, sweat blood (*informal*), apply yourself to, work your fingers to the bone, peg away at, keep your nose to the grindstone ...*While slogging at your work, have you neglected your marriage?...*
2 = <u>trudge</u>, tramp, plod, trek, hike, traipse (*informal*), yomp, walk heavily, footslog ...*The men had to slog up a muddy incline...*
NOUN **1** = <u>work</u>, labour, toil, industry, grind (*informal*), effort, struggle, pains, sweat (*informal*), painstaking, exertion, donkey-work, blood, sweat, and tears (*informal*) ...*There is little to show for two years of hard slog...*
2 = <u>trudge</u>, tramp, trek, hike, traipse (*informal*), yomp, footslog ...*a slog through heather and bracken...*

slogan = <u>catch phrase</u>, motto, jingle, rallying cry, tag-line, catchword

slop = <u>spill</u>, splash, overflow, splatter, spatter, slosh (*informal*)

slope **NOUN** = <u>inclination</u>, rise, incline, tilt, descent, downgrade (*chiefly U.S.*), slant, ramp, gradient, brae (*Scot.*), scarp, declination, declivity ...*a mountain slope...*
VERB = <u>slant</u>, incline, drop away, fall, rise, pitch, lean, tilt ...*The garden sloped quite steeply...*
PHRASES **slope off** (*Informal*) = <u>slink away</u>, slip away, steal away, skulk, creep away, make yourself scarce ...*She sloped off quietly on Saturday afternoon...*

sloping = <u>slanting</u>, leaning, inclined, inclining, oblique, atilt

sloppy 1 (*Informal*) = <u>careless</u>, slovenly, slipshod, messy, clumsy, untidy, amateurish, hit-or-miss (*informal*), inattentive ...*I won't accept sloppy work from my students...*
2 (*Informal*) = <u>sentimental</u>, mushy (*informal*), soppy (*Brit. informal*), slushy (*informal*), wet (*Brit. informal*), gushing, banal, trite, mawkish, icky (*informal*), overemotional, three-hankie (*informal*) ...*some sloppy love-story...*
3 = <u>wet</u>, watery, slushy, splashy, sludgy ...*sloppy foods...*

slosh 1 = <u>splash</u>, wash, slop, break, plash ...*The water sloshed around the bridge...*
2 = <u>wade</u>, splash, flounder, paddle, dabble, wallow, swash ...*We sloshed through the mud together...*

slot **NOUN** **1** = <u>opening</u>, hole, groove, vent, slit, aperture, channel ...*He dropped a coin in the slot and dialled...*
2 (*Informal*) = <u>place</u>, time, space, spot, opening, position, window, vacancy, niche ...*Visitors can book a time slot a week or more in advance...*
VERB = <u>fit</u>, slide, insert, put, place ...*She slotted a fresh filter into the machine...*

sloth = <u>laziness</u>, inactivity, idleness, inertia, torpor, sluggishness, slackness, indolence

slouch = <u>lounge</u>, slump, flop, sprawl, stoop, droop, loll, lean

slouching = <u>shambling</u>, lumbering, ungainly, awkward, uncouth, loutish

slow **ADJECTIVE** **1** = <u>unhurried</u>, sluggish, leisurely, easy, measured, creeping, deliberate, lagging, lazy, plodding, slow-moving, loitering, ponderous, leaden, dawdling, laggard, lackadaisical, tortoise-like, sluggardly ...*He moved in a slow, unhurried way...*
OPPOSITE quick
2 = <u>prolonged</u>, time-consuming, protracted, long-drawn-out, lingering, gradual ...*The distribution of passports has been a slow process...*
3 = <u>unwilling to</u>, reluctant to, loath to, averse to, hesitant to, disinclined to, indisposed to ...*He was not slow to take up the offer...*
4 = <u>late</u>, unpunctual, behindhand, behind, tardy ...*My watch is slow...*
5 = <u>stupid</u>, dim, dense, thick, dull, dumb (*informal*), retarded, bovine, dozy (*Brit. informal*), unresponsive,

obtuse, slow on the uptake (*informal*), braindead (*informal*), dull-witted, blockish, slow-witted ...*He got hit in the head and he's been a bit slow since...* OPPOSITE bright

6 = <u>dull</u>, quiet, boring, dead, tame, slack, sleepy, sluggish, tedious, stagnant, unproductive, inactive, one-horse (*informal*), uneventful, uninteresting, wearisome, dead-and-alive (*Brit.*), unprogressive ...*Island life is too slow for her liking...* OPPOSITE exciting

VERB **1** *often with* **down** = <u>decelerate</u>, brake, lag ...*The car slowed down as they passed customs...*
2 *often with* **down** = <u>delay</u>, hold up, hinder, check, restrict, handicap, detain, curb, retard, rein in ...*Damage to the turbine slowed the work down...* OPPOSITE speed

> ### Word Power
>
> **slow** – While not as unkind as *thick* or *stupid*, words like *slow* and *backward*, when used to talk about a person's mental abilities, are both unhelpful and likely to cause offence. It is preferable to say that a person has *special educational needs* or *learning difficulties*.

slowly = <u>gradually</u>, steadily, by degrees, unhurriedly, taking your time, at your leisure, at a snail's pace, in your own (good) time, ploddingly, inchmeal OPPOSITE quickly

sludge = <u>sediment</u>, ooze, silt, mud, muck, residue, slop, mire, slime, slush, slob (*Irish*), dregs, gloop (*informal*)

slug
➤ **snails, slugs and other gastropods**

sluggish = <u>inactive</u>, slow, lethargic, listless, heavy, dull, lifeless, inert, slow-moving, unresponsive, phlegmatic, indolent, torpid, slothful OPPOSITE energetic

sluice = <u>drain</u>, cleanse, flush, drench, wash out, wash down

slum = <u>hovel</u>, ghetto, shanty

slumber NOUN = <u>sleep</u>, nap, doze, rest, kip (*Brit. informal*), snooze (*informal*), siesta, catnap, forty winks (*informal*) ...*He had fallen into exhausted slumber...*
VERB = <u>sleep</u>, nap, doze, kip (*Brit. slang*), snooze (*informal*), lie dormant, drowse, zizz (*Brit. informal*) ...*The older three girls are still slumbering peacefully...*

slump VERB **1** = <u>fall</u>, decline, sink, plunge, crash, collapse, slip, deteriorate, fall off, plummet, go downhill (*informal*) ...*Net profits slumped...* OPPOSITE increase
2 = <u>sag</u>, bend, hunch, droop, slouch, loll ...*I closed the door and slumped into a chair...*
NOUN **1** = <u>fall</u>, drop, decline, crash, collapse, reverse, lapse, falling-off, downturn, depreciation, trough, meltdown (*informal*) ...*a slump in property prices...* OPPOSITE increase
2 = <u>recession</u>, depression, stagnation, inactivity, hard

or bad times ...*the slump of the early 1980s...*

slur NOUN = <u>insult</u>, stain, smear, stigma, disgrace, discredit, blot, affront, innuendo, calumny, insinuation, aspersion ...*yet another slur on the integrity of the police...*
VERB = <u>mumble</u>, stammer, stutter, stumble over, falter, mispronounce, garble, speak unclearly ...*He repeated himself and slurred his words more than usual...*

slut = <u>tart</u>, slag (*Brit. slang*), slapper (*Brit. slang*), scrubber (*Brit. & Austral. slang*), trollop, drab (*archaic*), sloven, slattern

sly ADJECTIVE **1** = <u>roguish</u>, knowing, arch, mischievous, impish ...*His lips were spread in a sly smile...*
2 = <u>cunning</u>, scheming, devious, secret, clever, subtle, tricky, covert, astute, wily, insidious, crafty, artful, furtive, conniving, Machiavellian, shifty, foxy, underhand, stealthy, guileful ...*She is devious, sly and manipulative...* OPPOSITE open
3 = <u>secret</u>, furtive, surreptitious, stealthy, sneaking, covert, clandestine ...*They were giving each other sly looks across the room...*
PHRASES **on the sly** = <u>secretly</u>, privately, covertly, surreptitiously, under the counter (*informal*), on the quiet, behind (someone's) back, like a thief in the night, underhandedly, on the q.t. (*informal*) ...*Was she meeting some guy on the sly?...*

smack VERB **1** = <u>slap</u>, hit, strike, pat, tap, sock (*slang*), clap, cuff, swipe, box, spank ...*She smacked me on the side of the head...*
2 = <u>drive</u>, hit, strike, thrust, impel ...*He smacked the ball against the post...*
NOUN = <u>slap</u>, blow, whack, clout (*informal*), cuff, crack, swipe, spank, wallop (*informal*) ...*I end up shouting at him or giving him a smack...*
ADVERB (*Informal*) = <u>directly</u>, right, straight, squarely, precisely, exactly, slap (*informal*), plumb, point-blank ...*smack in the middle of the city...*
PHRASES **smack of something** = <u>be suggestive</u> or <u>indicative of</u>, suggest, smell of, testify to, reek of, have all the hallmarks of, betoken, be redolent of, bear the stamp of ...*His comments smacked of racism...*

small 1 = <u>little</u>, minute, tiny, slight, mini, miniature, minuscule, diminutive, petite, teeny, puny, pint-sized (*informal*), pocket-sized, undersized, teeny-weeny, Lilliputian, teensy-weensy, pygmy or pigmy ...*She is small for her age...* OPPOSITE big
2 = <u>intimate</u>, close, private ...*a small select group of friends...*
3 = <u>young</u>, little, growing up, junior, wee, juvenile, youthful, immature, unfledged, in the springtime of life ...*What were you like when you were small?...*
4 = <u>unimportant</u>, minor, trivial, insignificant, little, lesser, petty, trifling, negligible, paltry, piddling (*informal*) ...*No detail was too small to escape her attention...* OPPOSITE important
5 = <u>modest</u>, small-scale, humble, unpretentious ...*shops, restaurants and other small businesses...* OPPOSITE grand
6 = <u>soft</u>, low, inaudible, low-pitched, noiseless ...*a*

very small voice...

7 = <u>foolish</u>, uncomfortable, humiliated, crushed, stupid, ashamed, deflated, mortified ...*This may be just another of her schemes to make me feel small...*
8 = <u>meagre</u>, inadequate, insufficient, scant, measly, scanty, limited, inconsiderable ...*a diet of one small meal a day...* OPPOSITE ample

small-minded = <u>petty</u>, mean, rigid, grudging, envious, bigoted, intolerant, narrow-minded, hidebound, ungenerous OPPOSITE broad-minded

small-time = <u>minor</u>, insignificant, unimportant, petty, no-account (*U.S. informal*), piddling (*informal*), of no consequence, of no account

smart ADJECTIVE **1** = <u>chic</u>, trim, neat, fashionable, stylish, fine, elegant, trendy (*Brit. informal*), spruce, snappy, natty (*informal*), modish, well turned-out ...*I was dressed in a smart navy-blue suit...* OPPOSITE scruffy
2 = <u>clever</u>, bright, intelligent, quick, sharp, keen, acute, shrewd, apt, ingenious, astute, canny, quick-witted ...*He thinks he's much smarter than Sarah...* OPPOSITE stupid
3 = <u>fashionable</u>, stylish, chic, genteel, in vogue, voguish (*informal*) ...*smart dinner parties...*
4 = <u>brisk</u>, quick, lively, vigorous, spirited, cracking (*informal*), spanking, jaunty ...*We set off at a smart pace...*
     VERB = <u>sting</u>, burn, tingle, pain, hurt, throb ...*My eyes smarted from the smoke...*

smarten *often with* ***up*** = <u>tidy</u>, spruce up, groom, beautify, put in order, put to rights, gussy up (*slang, chiefly U.S.*)

smash VERB **1** = <u>break</u>, crush, shatter, crack, demolish, shiver, disintegrate, pulverize, crush to smithereens ...*A crowd of youths started smashing windows...*
2 = <u>shatter</u>, break, disintegrate, split, crack, explode, splinter ...*The bottle smashed against a wall...*
3 = <u>collide</u>, crash, meet head-on, clash, come into collision ...*The train smashed into the car at 40 mph...*
4 = <u>destroy</u>, ruin, wreck, total (*slang*), defeat, overthrow, trash (*slang*), lay waste ...*Police staged a raid to smash one of Britain's biggest crack factories...*
     NOUN **1** = <u>success</u>, hit, winner, triumph (*informal*), belter (*slang*), sensation, smash hit, sellout ...*It is the public who decide if a film is a smash or a flop...*
2 = <u>collision</u>, crash, accident, pile-up (*informal*), smash-up (*informal*) ...*He was near to death after a car smash...*
3 = <u>crash</u>, smashing, clatter, clash, bang, thunder, racket, din, clattering, clang ...*the smash of falling crockery...*

smashing (*Informal, chiefly Brit.*) = <u>excellent</u>, mean (*slang*), great (*informal*), wonderful, topping (*Brit. slang*), brilliant (*informal*), cracking (*Brit. informal*), crucial (*slang*), superb, fantastic (*informal*), magnificent, fabulous (*informal*), first-class, marvellous, terrific (*informal*), sensational (*informal*), mega (*slang*), sovereign, awesome (*slang*), world-class, exhilarating, fab (*informal, chiefly Brit.*), super (*informal*), first-rate, def (*slang*), superlative, brill (*informal*), stupendous, out of this world (*informal*), bodacious (*slang, chiefly U.S.*), boffo (*slang*), jim-dandy (*slang*), chillin' (*U.S. slang*), booshit (*Austral. slang*), exo (*Austral. slang*), sik (*Austral. slang*) OPPOSITE awful

smattering = <u>modicum</u>, dash, rudiments, bit, elements, sprinkling, passing acquaintance, nodding acquaintance, smatter

smear VERB **1** = <u>spread over</u>, daub, rub on, cover, coat, plaster, bedaub ...*Smear a little olive oil over the inside of the salad bowl...*
2 = <u>slander</u>, tarnish, malign, vilify, blacken, sully, besmirch, traduce, calumniate, asperse, drag (someone's) name through the mud ...*a crude attempt to smear her...*
3 = <u>smudge</u>, soil, dirty, stain, sully, besmirch, smirch ...*a face covered by a heavy beard, smeared with dirt...*
     NOUN **1** = <u>smudge</u>, daub, streak, blot, blotch, splotch, smirch ...*a smear of gravy...*
2 = <u>slander</u>, libel, defamation, vilification, whispering campaign, calumny, mudslinging ...*a smear by his rivals...*

smell NOUN **1** = <u>odour</u>, scent, fragrance, perfume, bouquet, aroma, whiff, niff (*Brit. slang*), redolence ...*the smell of freshly baked bread...*
2 = <u>stink</u>, stench, reek, pong (*Brit. informal*), niff (*Brit. slang*), malodour, fetor ...*horrible smells...*
     VERB **1** = <u>stink</u>, reek, pong (*Brit. informal*), hum (*slang*), whiff (*Brit. slang*), stink to high heaven (*informal*), niff (*Brit. slang*), be malodorous ...*Do my feet smell?...*
2 = <u>sniff</u>, scent, get a whiff of, nose ...*We could smell the gas...*

  Related Words
adjective: olfactory

smelly = <u>stinking</u>, reeking, fetid, foul-smelling, high, strong, foul, putrid, strong-smelling, stinky (*informal*), malodorous, evil-smelling, noisome, whiffy (*Brit. slang*), pongy (*Brit. informal*), mephitic, niffy (*Brit. slang*), olid, festy (*Austral. slang*) OPPOSITE fragrant

smile VERB = <u>grin</u>, beam, smirk, twinkle, grin from ear to ear ...*He smiled and waved...*
     NOUN = <u>grin</u>, beam, smirk ...*She gave a wry smile...*

smirk = <u>give a smug look</u>, grin, simper

smitten **1** = <u>infatuated</u>, charmed, captivated, beguiled, bewitched, bowled over (*informal*), enamoured, swept off your feet ...*They were totally smitten with each other...*
2 = <u>afflicted</u>, struck, beset, laid low, plagued ...*smitten with yellow fever...*

smoky *or* **smokey** = <u>thick</u>, murky, hazy

smooth ADJECTIVE **1** = <u>even</u>, level, flat, plane, plain, flush, horizontal, unwrinkled ...*a smooth surface...* OPPOSITE uneven
2 = <u>sleek</u>, polished, shiny, glossy, silky, velvety, glassy, mirror-like ...*The flagstones were worn smooth by centuries of use...* OPPOSITE rough
3 = <u>mellow</u>, pleasant, mild, soothing, bland, agreeable

…This makes the flavour much smoother…

4 = <u>flowing</u>, steady, fluent, regular, uniform, rhythmic *…This exercise is done in one smooth motion…*

5 = <u>calm</u>, peaceful, serene, tranquil, undisturbed, unruffled, equable *…This was only a brief upset in their smooth lives…* OPPOSITE troubled

6 = <u>easy</u>, effortless, untroubled, well-ordered *…A number of problems marred the smooth running of this event…*

7 = <u>suave</u>, slick, persuasive, urbane, silky, glib, facile, ingratiating, debonair, unctuous, smarmy (*Brit. informal*) *…Twelve extremely good-looking, smooth young men have been picked as finalists…*

VERB **1** = <u>flatten</u>, level, press, plane, iron *…She stood up and smoothed down her frock…*

2 = <u>ease</u>, aid, assist, facilitate, pave the way, make easier, help along, iron out the difficulties of *…smoothing the path towards a treaty…* OPPOSITE hinder

smoothness 1 = <u>evenness</u>, regularity, levelness, flushness, unbrokenness *…The lawn was rich, weed-free, and trimmed to smoothness…*

2 = <u>fluency</u>, finish, flow, ease, polish, rhythm, efficiency, felicity, smooth running, slickness, effortlessness *…the strength and smoothness of his movements…*

3 = <u>sleekness</u>, softness, smooth texture, silkiness, velvetiness *…the smoothness of her skin…*

4 = <u>suavity</u>, urbanity, oiliness, glibness, smarminess (*Brit. informal*) *…His cleverness, smoothness even, made his relationships uneasy…*

smother 1 = <u>extinguish</u>, put out, stifle, snuff *…They tried to smother the flames…*

2 = <u>suffocate</u>, choke, strangle, stifle *…He had attempted to smother his sixteen-week-old son…*

3 = <u>suppress</u>, stifle, repress, hide, conceal, muffle, keep back *…She tried to smother her feelings of panic…*

4 = <u>overwhelm</u>, cover, shower, surround, heap, shroud, inundate, envelop, cocoon *…He smothered her with kisses…*

5 = <u>stifle</u>, suppress, hold in, restrain, hold back, repress, muffle, bottle up, keep in check *…trying to smother our giggles…*

6 = <u>smear</u>, cover, spread *…Luckily, it wasn't smothered in creamy sauce…*

smoulder 1 = <u>smoke</u>, burn slowly *…Whole blocks had been turned into smouldering rubble…*

2 = <u>seethe</u>, rage, fume, burn, boil, simmer, fester, be resentful, smart *…He smouldered as he drove home for lunch…*

smudge NOUN = <u>smear</u>, blot, smut, smutch *…smudges of blood…*

VERB **1** = <u>smear</u>, blur, blot *…Smudge the outline using a cotton-wool bud…*

2 = <u>mark</u>, soil, dirty, daub, smirch *…She kissed me, careful not to smudge me with her fresh lipstick…*

smug = <u>self-satisfied</u>, superior, complacent, conceited, self-righteous, holier-than-thou, priggish, self-opinionated

smuggler = <u>trafficker</u>, runner, bootlegger, moonshiner (*U.S.*), rum-runner, contrabandist

snack = <u>light meal</u>, bite, refreshment(s), nibble, titbit, bite to eat, elevenses (*Brit. informal*)

snag NOUN = <u>difficulty</u>, hitch, problem, obstacle, catch, hazard, disadvantage, complication, drawback, inconvenience, downside, stumbling block, the rub *…A police crackdown hit a snag when villains stole one of their cars…*

VERB = <u>catch</u>, tear, rip, hole *…He snagged his suit…*

snail

Snails, slugs and other gastropods

http://www.gardensafari.net/english/snails.htm

abalone *or* ear shell	ramshorn snail
conch	Roman snail
cowrie *or* cowry	sea hare
limpet	slug
murex	snail
nudibranch *or* sea slug	top-shell
	triton
ormer *or* sea-ear	wentletrap
periwinkle *or* winkle	whelk

---

snake NOUN = <u>serpent</u> *…He was caught with his pet snake in his pocket…*

VERB = <u>wind</u>, twist, curve, turn, bend, ramble, meander, deviate, zigzag *…The road snaked through the forested mountains…*

(*Related Words*)

adjective: serpentine

► **reptiles**

snap VERB **1** = <u>break</u>, split, crack, separate, fracture, give way, come apart *…The brake pedal had just snapped…*

2 = <u>pop</u>, click, crackle *…He snapped the cap on his ballpoint…*

3 = <u>speak sharply</u>, bark, lash out at, flash, retort, snarl, growl, fly off the handle at (*informal*), jump down (someone's) throat (*informal*) *…I'm sorry, I didn't mean to snap at you…*

4 = <u>bite at</u>, bite, nip *…The poodle yapped and snapped at our legs…*

NOUN **1** = <u>crack</u>, pop, crash, report, burst, explosion, clap *…Every minute or so I could hear a snap, a crack and a crash as another tree went down…*

2 = <u>pop</u>, crack, smack, whack *…He shut the book with a snap and stood up…*

ADJECTIVE = <u>instant</u>, immediate, sudden, abrupt, spur-of-the-moment, unpremeditated *…I think this is too important for a snap decision…*

PHRASES **snap out of it** (*Informal*) = <u>get over it</u>, recover, cheer up, perk up, liven up, pull yourself together (*informal*), get a grip on yourself *…Come on, snap out of it!…* ♦ **snap something up** = <u>grab</u>, seize, take advantage of, swoop down on, pounce upon, avail yourself of *…a queue of people waiting to snap up the bargains…*

snappy ADJECTIVE **1** = <u>succinct</u>, brief, concise, to the point, crisp, witty, condensed, incisive, pithy, short and sweet, in a few well-chosen words ...*Each film gets a snappy two-line summary*...

2 = smart, fashionable, stylish, trendy (*Brit. informal*), chic, dapper, up-to-the-minute, natty (*informal*), modish, voguish ...*snappy sports jackets*...

3 = irritable, cross, bad-tempered, tart, impatient, edgy, touchy, tetchy, ratty (*Brit. & N.Z. informal*), testy, waspish, quick-tempered, snappish, like a bear with a sore head (*informal*), apt to fly off the handle (*informal*) ...*He wasn't irritable or snappy*...

PHRASES **make it snappy** = hurry (up), be quick, get a move on (*informal*), buck up (*informal*), make haste, look lively, get your skates on ...*Look at the pamphlets, and make it snappy*...

snare **NOUN** = trap, net, wire, gin, pitfall, noose, springe ...*an animal caught in a snare*...
VERB = trap, catch, net, wire, seize, entrap, springe ...*He'd snared a rabbit earlier in the day*...

snarl[1] 1 = growl, show your teeth (*of an animal*) ...*The dogs snarled at the intruders*...

2 = snap, bark, lash out, speak angrily, jump down someone's throat, speak roughly ...*'Call that a good performance?' he snarled*...

snarl[2]

PHRASES **snarl something up** = tangle, complicate, muddle, embroil, entangle, entwine, ravel, enmesh ...*The group had succeeded in snarling up rush-hour traffic throughout the country*...

snatch **VERB** 1 = grab, seize, wrench, wrest, take, grip, grasp, clutch, take hold of ...*He snatched the telephone from me*...

2 = steal, take, nick (*slang, chiefly Brit.*), pinch (*informal*), swipe (*slang*), lift (*informal*), pilfer, filch, shoplift, thieve, walk *or* make off with ...*He snatched her bag and threw her to the ground*...

3 = win, take, score, gain, secure, obtain ...*They snatched a third goal*...

4 = save, free, rescue, pull, recover, get out, salvage, extricate ...*He was snatched from the jaws of death at the last minute*...

NOUN = bit, part, fragment, piece, spell, snippet, smattering ...*I heard snatches of the conversation*...

snazzy (*Informal*) = stylish, smart, dashing, with it (*informal*), attractive, sophisticated, flamboyant, sporty, flashy, jazzy (*informal*), showy, ritzy (*slang*), raffish

sneak **VERB** 1 = slink, slip, steal, pad, sidle, skulk ...*Don't sneak away and hide*...

2 = slip, smuggle, spirit ...*He snuck me a cigarette*...
NOUN = informer, grass (*Brit. slang*), betrayer, telltale, squealer (*slang*), Judas, accuser, stool pigeon, snake in the grass, nark (*Brit., Austral., & N.Z. slang*), fizgig (*Austral. slang*) ...*He is disloyal, distrustful and a sneak*...
ADJECTIVE = secret, quick, clandestine, furtive, stealthy ...*We can give you this exclusive sneak preview*...

sneaking 1 = nagging, worrying, persistent, niggling, uncomfortable ...*a sneaking suspicion*...

2 = secret, private, hidden, suppressed, unexpressed, unvoiced, unavowed, unconfessed, undivulged ...*a sneaking admiration*...

sneaky = sly, dishonest, devious, mean, low, base, nasty, cowardly, slippery, unreliable, malicious, unscrupulous, furtive, disingenuous, shifty, snide, deceitful, contemptible, untrustworthy, double-dealing

sneer **VERB** 1 = scorn, mock, ridicule, laugh, jeer, disdain, scoff, deride, look down on, snigger, sniff at, gibe, hold in contempt, hold up to ridicule, turn up your nose (*informal*) ...*There is too great a readiness to sneer at anything they do*...

2 = say contemptuously, snigger ...*'I wonder what you people do with your lives,' he sneered*...
NOUN 1 = scorn, ridicule, mockery, derision, jeer, disdain, snigger, gibe, snidery ...*Best-selling authors may have to face the sneers of the literati*...

2 = contemptuous smile, snigger, curl of the lip ...*His mouth twisted in a contemptous sneer*...

snide *or* **snidey** = nasty, sneering, malicious, mean, cynical, unkind, hurtful, sarcastic, disparaging, spiteful, insinuating, scornful, shrewish, ill-natured

sniff 1 = breathe in, inhale, snuffle, snuff ...*She wiped her face and sniffed loudly*...

2 = smell, nose, breathe in, scent, get a whiff of ...*Suddenly, he stopped and sniffed the air*...

3 = inhale, breathe in, suck in, draw in ...*He'd been sniffing glue*...

sniffy (*Informal*) = contemptuous, superior, condescending, haughty, scornful, disdainful, supercilious

snigger **VERB** = laugh, giggle, sneer, snicker, titter ...*The tourists snigger at the locals' outdated ways and dress*...
NOUN = laugh, giggle, sneer, snicker, titter ...*trying to suppress a snigger*...

snip **VERB** = cut, nick, clip, crop, trim, dock, notch, nip off ...*Snip the corners off the card*...
NOUN (*Informal, chiefly Brit.*) = bargain, steal (*informal*), good buy, giveaway ...*a snip at £74.25*...

snipe = criticize, knock (*informal*), put down, carp, bitch, have a go (at) (*informal*), jeer, denigrate, disparage

snippet = piece, scrap, fragment, part, particle, snatch, shred

snob = elitist, highbrow, social climber

snobbery = arrogance, airs, pride, pretension, condescension, snobbishness, snootiness (*informal*), side (*Brit. slang*), uppishness (*Brit. informal*)

snobbish = superior, arrogant, stuck-up (*informal*), patronizing, condescending, snooty (*informal*), pretentious, uppity, high and mighty (*informal*), toffee-nosed (*slang, chiefly Brit.*), hoity-toity (*informal*), high-hat (*informal, chiefly U.S.*), uppish (*Brit. informal*) **OPPOSITE** humble

snooker
➤ **snooker and billiards terms**

snoop **VERB** 1 = investigate, explore, have a good

Snooker and billiards terms http://www.easb.co.uk/

baize	drop cannon	plain ball
ball	fluke	plant
baulk	foul	pocket
baulkline	frame	pot
black	free ball	red
blue	green	rest
bouclée	half-butt	safety
break	hazard	scratch
bricole	headrail	screw
bridge	in-off	short jenny
brown	jenny	side *or* (*U.S. & Canad.*) English
cannon	kick	snooker
carom	kiss	spider
chalk	lag	spot
clearance	long jenny	spot ball
cue ball	massé	stun
cue extension	maximum break *or* 147	top
cue tip	miscue	triangle *or* (*U.S. & Canad.*) rack
cushion	nurse	white
D *or* d	nursery cannon	Whitechapel
double	object ball	yellow
draw	pink	

look at, prowl around, nose around, peer into ...*He's been snooping around her hotel...*
2 = spy, poke your nose in, nose, interfere, pry (*informal*) ...*Governments have been known to snoop into innocent citizens' lives...*
NOUN = look, search, nose, prowl, investigation ...*He had a snoop around...*

snooty (*Informal*) = snobbish, superior, aloof, pretentious, stuck-up (*informal*), condescending, proud, haughty, disdainful, snotty, uppity, supercilious, high and mighty (*informal*), toffee-nosed (*slang, chiefly Brit.*), hoity-toity (*informal*), high-hat (*informal, chiefly U.S.*), uppish (*Brit. informal*), toplofty (*informal*) OPPOSITE> humble

snooze (*Informal*) NOUN = doze, nap, kip (*Brit. slang*), siesta, catnap, forty winks (*informal*) ...*The bird is enjoying a snooze...*
VERB = doze, drop off (*informal*), nap, kip (*Brit. slang*), nod off (*informal*), catnap, drowse, take forty winks (*informal*) ...*He snoozed in front of the television...*

snub VERB = insult, slight, put down, humiliate, cut (*informal*), shame, humble, rebuff, mortify, cold-shoulder, kick in the teeth (*slang*), give (someone) the cold shoulder, give (someone) the brush-off (*slang*), cut dead (*informal*) ...*He snubbed her in public and made her feel an idiot...*
NOUN = insult, put-down, humiliation, affront, slap in the face, brush-off (*slang*) ...*He took it as a snub...*

snug 1 = cosy, warm, comfortable, homely, sheltered, intimate, comfy (*informal*) ...*a snug log cabin...*
2 = tight, close, trim, neat ...*a snug black T-shirt and skin-tight black jeans...*

snuggle = nestle, cuddle up

so = therefore, thus, hence, consequently, then, as a result, accordingly, for that reason, whence, thence, ergo

soak VERB 1 = steep, immerse, submerge, infuse, marinate (*Cookery*), dunk, submerse ...*Soak the beans for two hours...*
2 = wet, damp, saturate, drench, douse, moisten, suffuse, wet through, waterlog, souse, drouk (*Scot.*) ...*Soak the soil around each bush with at least 4 gallons of water...*
3 = penetrate, pervade, permeate, enter, get in, infiltrate, diffuse, seep, suffuse, make inroads (into) ...*Rain had soaked into the sand...*
PHRASES **soak something up** = absorb, suck up, take in *or* up, drink in, assimilate ...*Wrap in absorbent paper after frying to soak up excess oil...*

soaking = soaked, dripping, saturated, drenched, sodden, waterlogged, streaming, sopping, wet through, soaked to the skin, wringing wet, like a drowned rat, droukit *or* drookit (*Scot.*)

soar 1 = rise, increase, grow, mount, climb, go up, rocket, swell, escalate, shoot up ...*soaring unemployment...*
2 = fly, rise, wing, climb, ascend, fly up ...*Buzzards soar overhead at a great height...* OPPOSITE> plunge
3 = tower, rise, climb, go up ...*The steeple soars skyward...*

sob VERB = cry, weep, blubber, greet (*Scot. or archaic*), howl, bawl, snivel, shed tears, boohoo ...*She began to sob again, burying her face in the pillow...*
NOUN = cry, whimper, howl ...*Her body was racked by violent sobs...*

sober ADJECTIVE 1 = abstinent, temperate, abstemious, moderate, on the wagon (*informal*) ...*He was dour and uncommunicative when stone sober...* OPPOSITE> drunk
2 = serious, practical, realistic, sound, cool, calm, grave, reasonable, steady, composed, rational, solemn, lucid, sedate, staid, level-headed, dispassionate, unruffled, clear-headed, unexcited ...*We are now far

more sober and realistic... OPPOSITE frivolous

3 = plain, dark, sombre, quiet, severe, subdued, drab ...*He dresses in sober grey suits...* OPPOSITE bright

VERB 1 *usually with* **up** = come to your senses ...*He was left to sober up in a police cell...* OPPOSITE get drunk

2 *usually with* **up** = clear your head ...*These events sobered him up considerably...*

sobriety 1 = abstinence, temperance, abstemiousness, moderation, self-restraint, soberness, nonindulgence ...*the boredom of a lifetime of sobriety...*

2 = seriousness, gravity, steadiness, restraint, composure, coolness, calmness, solemnity, reasonableness, level-headedness, staidness, sedateness ...*the values society depends upon, such as honesty, sobriety and trust...*

so-called = alleged, supposed, professed, pretended, self-styled, ostensible, soi-disant (*French*)

sociability = friendliness, conviviality, cordiality, congeniality, neighbourliness, affability, gregariousness, companionability

sociable = friendly, social, outgoing, warm, neighbourly, accessible, cordial, genial, affable, approachable, gregarious, convivial, companionable, conversable OPPOSITE unsociable

social ADJECTIVE **1** = communal, community, collective, group, public, general, common, societal ...*the tightly woven social fabric of small towns...*

2 = sociable, friendly, companionable, neighbourly ...*We ought to organize more social events...*

3 = organized, gregarious ...*social insects like bees and ants...*

NOUN = get-together (*informal*), party, gathering, function, do (*informal*), reception, bash (*informal*), social gathering ...*church socials...*

socialize = mix, interact, mingle, be sociable, meet, go out, entertain, get together, fraternize, be a good mixer, get about *or* around

society 1 = the community, social order, people, the public, the population, humanity, civilization, mankind, the general public, the world at large ...*This reflects attitudes and values prevailing in society...*

2 = culture, community, population ...*those responsible for destroying our African heritage and the fabric of our society...*

3 = organization, group, club, union, league, association, institute, circle, corporation, guild, fellowship, fraternity, brotherhood *or* sisterhood ...*the historical society...*

4 = upper classes, gentry, upper crust (*informal*), elite, the swells (*informal*), high society, the top drawer, polite society, the toffs (*Brit. slang*), the smart set, beau monde, the nobs (*slang*), the country set, haut monde (*French*) ...*The couple tried to secure themselves a position in society...*

5 (*Old-fashioned*) = companionship, company, fellowship, friendship, camaraderie ...*I largely withdrew from the society of others...*

sodden = soaked, saturated, sopping, drenched, soggy, waterlogged, marshy, boggy, miry, droukit *or* drookit (*Scot.*)

sodomy = anal intercourse, anal sex, buggery

sofa = couch, settee, divan, chaise longue, chesterfield, ottoman

soft 1 = velvety, smooth, silky, furry, feathery, downy, fleecy, like a baby's bottom (*informal*) ...*Regular use of a body lotion will keep the skin soft and supple...* OPPOSITE rough

2 = yielding, flexible, pliable, cushioned, elastic, malleable, spongy, springy, cushiony ...*She lay down on the soft, comfortable bed...* OPPOSITE hard

3 = soggy, swampy, marshy, boggy, squelchy, quaggy ...*The horse didn't handle the soft ground very well...*

4 = squashy, sloppy, mushy, spongy, squidgy (*Brit. informal*), squishy, gelatinous, squelchy, pulpy, doughy ...*a simple bread made with a soft dough...*

5 = pliable, flexible, supple, malleable, plastic, elastic, tensile, ductile (*of metals*), bendable, mouldable, impressible ...*Aluminium is a soft metal...*

6 = quiet, low, gentle, sweet, whispered, soothing, murmured, muted, subdued, mellow, understated, melodious, mellifluous, dulcet, soft-toned ...*When he woke again he could hear soft music... ...She spoke in a soft whisper...* OPPOSITE loud

7 = lenient, easy-going, lax, liberal, weak, indulgent, permissive, spineless, boneless, overindulgent ...*He says the measure is soft and weak on criminals...* OPPOSITE harsh

8 = kind, tender, sentimental, compassionate, sensitive, gentle, pitying, sympathetic, tenderhearted, touchy-feely (*informal*) ...*a very soft and sensitive heart...*

9 (*Informal*) = easy, comfortable, undemanding, cushy (*informal*), easy-peasy (*slang*) ...*a soft option...*

10 = pale, light, subdued, pastel, pleasing, bland, mellow ...*The room was tempered by the soft colours...* OPPOSITE bright

11 = dim, faint, dimmed ...*His skin looked golden in the soft light...* OPPOSITE bright

12 = mild, delicate, caressing, temperate, balmy ...*a soft breeze...*

13 (*Informal*) = feeble-minded, simple, silly, foolish, daft (*informal*), soft in the head (*informal*), a bit lacking (*informal*) ...*They were wary of him, thinking he was soft in the head...*

soften 1 = melt, tenderize ...*Soften the butter mixture in a small saucepan...*

2 = lessen, moderate, diminish, temper, lower, relax, ease, calm, modify, cushion, soothe, subdue, alleviate, lighten, quell, muffle, allay, mitigate, abate, tone down, assuage ...*He could not think how to soften the blow of what he had to tell her...*

soggy = sodden, saturated, moist, heavy, soaked, dripping, waterlogged, sopping, mushy, spongy, pulpy

soil¹ 1 = earth, ground, clay, dust, dirt, loam ...*regions with sandy soils...*

2 = territory, country, land, region, turf (*U.S. slang*), terrain ...*The issue of foreign troops on Turkish soil is a sensitive one...*

soil² = dirty, foul, stain, smear, muddy, pollute, tarnish, spatter, sully, defile, besmirch, smirch, bedraggle, befoul, begrime ...*Young people don't want to do things that soil their hands...* OPPOSITE clean

sojourn (*Literary*) = stay, visit, stop, rest, stopover

solace NOUN = comfort, consolation, help, support, relief, succour, alleviation, assuagement ...*I found solace in writing when my father died...*
VERB = comfort, console, soothe ...*They solaced themselves with their fan mail...*

soldier = fighter, serviceman, trooper, warrior, Tommy (*Brit. informal*), GI (*U.S. informal*), military man, redcoat, enlisted man (*U.S.*), man-at-arms, squaddie *or* squaddy (*Brit. slang*)

sole = only, one, single, individual, alone, exclusive, solitary, singular, one and only

solely = only, completely, entirely, exclusively, alone, singly, merely, single-handedly

solemn 1 = serious, earnest, grave, sober, thoughtful, sedate, glum, staid, portentous ...*His solemn little face broke into smiles...* OPPOSITE cheerful
2 = formal, august, grand, imposing, impressive, grave, majestic, dignified, ceremonial, stately, momentous, awe-inspiring, ceremonious ...*This is a solemn occasion...* OPPOSITE informal
3 = sacred, religious, holy, ritual, venerable, hallowed, sanctified, devotional, reverential ...*a solemn religious ceremony...* OPPOSITE irreligious

solemnity 1 = seriousness, gravity, formality, grandeur, gravitas, earnestness, portentousness, momentousness, impressiveness ...*the solemnity of the occasion...*
2 *often plural* = ritual, proceedings, ceremony, rite, formalities, ceremonial, observance, celebration ...*the constitutional solemnities...*

solicit 1 (*Formal*) = request, seek, ask for, petition, crave, pray for, plead for, canvass, beg for ...*He's already solicited their support on health care reform...*
2 (*Formal*) = appeal to, ask, call on, lobby, press, beg, petition, plead with, implore, beseech, entreat, importune, supplicate ...*They were soliciting Nader's supporters to re-register as Republicans...*

solicitous = concerned, caring, attentive, careful

solid 1 = firm, hard, compact, dense, massed, concrete ...*a tunnel carved through 50ft of solid rock...* OPPOSITE unsubstantial
2 = strong, stable, sturdy, sound, substantial, unshakable ...*I stared up at the square, solid house...* OPPOSITE unstable
3 = pure, unalloyed, unmixed, complete ...*The taps appeared to be made of solid gold...*
4 = continuous, unbroken, uninterrupted ...*a solid line...*
5 = reliable, decent, dependable, upstanding, serious, constant, sensible, worthy, upright, sober, law-abiding, trusty, level-headed, estimable ...*a good, solid*

member of the community... OPPOSITE unreliable
6 = sound, real, reliable, good, genuine, dinkum (*Austral. & N.Z. informal*) ...*Some solid evidence was what was required...* OPPOSITE unsound

solidarity = unity, harmony, unification, accord, stability, cohesion, team spirit, camaraderie, unanimity, soundness, concordance, esprit de corps, community of interest, singleness of purpose, like-mindedness

solidify = harden, set, congeal, cake, jell, coagulate, cohere

soliloquy = monologue, address, speech, aside, oration, dramatic monologue

Word Power

soliloquy – Although *soliloquy* and *monologue* are close in meaning, you should take care when using one as a synonym of the other. Both words refer to a long speech by one person, but a *monologue* can be addressed to other people, whereas in a *soliloquy* the speaker is always talking to himself or herself.

solitary 1 = unsociable, retiring, reclusive, unsocial, isolated, lonely, cloistered, lonesome, friendless, companionless ...*Paul was a shy, pleasant, solitary man...* OPPOSITE sociable
2 = lone, alone ...*His evenings were spent in solitary drinking...*
3 = isolated, remote, out-of-the-way, desolate, hidden, sequestered, unvisited, unfrequented ...*a boy of eighteen in a solitary house in the Ohio countryside...* OPPOSITE busy

solitude 1 = isolation, privacy, seclusion, retirement, loneliness, ivory tower, reclusiveness ...*Imagine long golden beaches where you can wander in solitude...*
2 (*Poetic*) = wilderness, waste, desert, emptiness, wasteland ...*travelling by yourself in these vast solitudes...*

solution 1 = answer, resolution, key, result, solving, explanation, unfolding, unravelling, clarification, explication, elucidation ...*the ability to sort out effective solutions to practical problems...*
2 (*Chemistry*) = mixture, mix, compound, blend, suspension, solvent, emulsion ...*a warm solution of liquid detergent...*

solve = answer, work out, resolve, explain, crack, interpret, unfold, clarify, clear up, unravel, decipher, expound, suss (out) (*slang*), get to the bottom of, disentangle, elucidate

solvent = financially sound, secure, in the black, solid, profit-making, in credit, debt-free, unindebted

sombre 1 = gloomy, sad, sober, grave, dismal, melancholy, mournful, lugubrious, joyless, funereal, doleful, sepulchral ...*The pair were in sombre mood...* OPPOSITE cheerful
2 = dark, dull, gloomy, sober, drab ...*a worried official in sombre black...* OPPOSITE bright

somebody = celebrity, big name, public figure,

name, star, heavyweight (*informal*), notable, superstar, household name, dignitary, luminary, bigwig (*informal*), celeb (*informal*), big shot (*informal*), personage, megastar (*informal*), big wheel (*slang*), big noise (*informal*), big hitter (*informal*), heavy hitter (*informal*), person of note, V.I.P., someone OPPOSITE> nobody

some day *or* **someday** = one day, eventually, ultimately, sooner or later, one of these (fine) days, in the fullness of time

somehow = one way or another, come what may, come hell or high water (*informal*), by fair means or foul, by hook or (by) crook, by some means or other

sometime ADVERB = some day, one day, at some point in the future, sooner or later, one of these days, by and by ...*Why don't you come and see me sometime?*...
ADJECTIVE = former, one-time, erstwhile, ex-, late, past, previous ...*She was in her early thirties, a sometime actress, dancer and singer*...

sometimes = occasionally, at times, now and then, from time to time, on occasion, now and again, once in a while, every now and then, every so often, off and on OPPOSITE> always

son = male child, boy, lad (*informal*), descendant, son and heir

(**Related Words**)
adjective: filial

song = ballad, air, tune, lay, strain, carol, lyric, chant, chorus, melody, anthem, number, hymn, psalm, shanty, pop song, ditty, canticle, canzonet

song and dance (*Brit. informal*) = fuss, to-do, flap (*informal*), performance (*informal*), stir, pantomime (*informal*), commotion, ado, shindig (*informal*), kerfuffle (*informal*), hoo-ha, pother, shindy (*informal*)

soon = before long, shortly, in the near future, in a minute, anon (*archaic*), in a short time, in a little while, any minute now, betimes (*archaic*), in two shakes of a lamb's tail, erelong (*archaic or poetic*), in a couple of shakes

sooner 1 = earlier, before, already, beforehand, ahead of time ...*I thought she would have recovered sooner*...
2 = rather, more readily, by preference, more willingly ...*They would sooner die than stay in London*...

soothe 1 = calm, still, quiet, hush, settle, calm down, appease, lull, mitigate, pacify, mollify, smooth down, tranquillize ...*He would take her in his arms and soothe her*... OPPOSITE> upset
2 = relieve, ease, alleviate, dull, diminish, assuage ...*Lemon tisanes with honey can soothe sore throats*... OPPOSITE> irritate

soothing 1 = calming, relaxing, peaceful, quiet, calm, restful ...*Put on some nice soothing music*...
2 = emollient, palliative, balsamic, demulcent, easeful, lenitive ...*Cold tea is very soothing for burns*...

sophisticated 1 = complex, advanced, complicated, subtle, delicate, elaborate, refined, intricate, multifaceted, highly-developed ...*a large and sophisticated new telescope*... OPPOSITE> simple
2 = cultured, refined, cultivated, worldly, cosmopolitan, urbane, jet-set, world-weary, citified, worldly-wise ...*Recently her tastes have become more sophisticated*... OPPOSITE> unsophisticated

sophistication = poise, worldliness, savoir-faire, urbanity, finesse, savoir-vivre (*French*), worldly wisdom

soporific = sleep-inducing, hypnotic, sedative, sleepy, somnolent, tranquillizing, somniferous (*rare*)

soppy (*Brit. informal*) = sentimental, corny (*slang*), slushy (*informal*), soft (*informal*), silly, daft (*informal*), weepy (*informal*), mawkish, drippy (*informal*), lovey-dovey, schmaltzy (*slang*), icky (*informal*), gushy (*informal*), overemotional, three-hankie (*informal*)

sorcerer *or* **sorceress** = magician, witch, wizard, magus, warlock, mage (*archaic*), enchanter, necromancer

sorcery = black magic, witchcraft, black art, necromancy, spell, magic, charm, wizardry, enchantment, divination, incantation, witchery

sordid 1 = base, degraded, shameful, low, vicious, shabby, vile, degenerate, despicable, disreputable, debauched ...*He put his head in his hands as his sordid life was exposed*... OPPOSITE> honourable
2 = dirty, seedy, sleazy, squalid, mean, foul, filthy, unclean, wretched, seamy, slovenly, slummy, scungy (*Austral. & N.Z.*), festy (*Austral. slang*) ...*the attic windows of their sordid little rooms*... OPPOSITE> clean

sore ADJECTIVE 1 = painful, smarting, raw, tender, burning, angry, sensitive, irritated, inflamed, chafed, reddened ...*My chest is still sore from the surgery*...
2 = annoyed, cross, angry, pained, hurt, upset, stung, irritated, grieved, resentful, aggrieved, vexed, irked, peeved (*informal*), tooshie (*Austral. slang*) ...*The result of it is that they are all feeling very sore at you*...
3 = annoying, distressing, troublesome, harrowing, grievous ...*Timing is frequently a sore point*...

4 (*Literary*) = <u>urgent</u>, desperate, extreme, dire, pressing, critical, acute ...*The prime minister is in sore need of friends*...
[NOUN] = <u>abscess</u>, boil, ulcer, inflammation, gathering ...*All of us had long sores on our backs*...

sorrow [NOUN] **1** = <u>grief</u>, sadness, woe, regret, distress, misery, mourning, anguish, unhappiness, heartache, heartbreak, affliction ...*It was a time of great sorrow*... [OPPOSITE] joy
2 = <u>hardship</u>, trial, tribulation, affliction, worry, trouble, blow, woe, misfortune, bummer (*slang*) ...*the joys and sorrows of family life*... [OPPOSITE] good fortune
[VERB] = <u>grieve</u>, mourn, lament, weep, moan, be sad, bemoan, agonize, eat your heart out, bewail ...*She was lamented by a large circle of sorrowing friends and acquaintances*... [OPPOSITE] rejoice

sorrowful = <u>sad</u>, unhappy, miserable, sorry, depressed, painful, distressed, grieving, dismal, afflicted, melancholy, tearful, heartbroken, woeful, mournful, dejected, rueful, lugubrious, wretched, disconsolate, doleful, heavy-hearted, down in the dumps (*informal*), woebegone, piteous, sick at heart

sorry 1 = <u>regretful</u>, apologetic, contrite, repentant, guilt-ridden, remorseful, penitent, shamefaced, conscience-stricken, in sackcloth and ashes, self-reproachful ...*She was very sorry about all the trouble she'd caused*... [OPPOSITE] unapologetic
2 = <u>sympathetic</u>, moved, full of pity, pitying, compassionate, commiserative ...*I am very sorry for the family*... [OPPOSITE] unsympathetic
3 = <u>sad</u>, distressed, unhappy, grieved, melancholy, mournful, sorrowful, disconsolate ...*What he must not do is sit around at home feeling sorry for himself*... [OPPOSITE] happy
4 = <u>wretched</u>, miserable, pathetic, mean, base, poor, sad, distressing, dismal, shabby, vile, paltry, pitiful, abject, deplorable, pitiable, piteous ...*She is in a sorry state*...

sort [NOUN] = <u>kind</u>, type, class, make, group, family, order, race, style, quality, character, nature, variety, brand, species, breed, category, stamp, description, denomination, genus, ilk ...*What sort of person is he?*...
[VERB] **1** = <u>arrange</u>, group, order, class, separate, file, rank, divide, grade, distribute, catalogue, classify, categorize, tabulate, systematize, put in order ...*He sorted the materials into their folders*...
2 = <u>resolve</u>, answer, work out, clear up, crack, fathom, suss (out) (*slang*), find the solution to ...*These problems have now been sorted*...
[PHRASES] **out of sorts 1** = <u>irritable</u>, cross, edgy, tense, crabbed, snarling, prickly, snappy, touchy, bad-tempered, petulant, ill-tempered, irascible, cantankerous, tetchy, ratty (*Brit. & N.Z. informal*), testy, fretful, grouchy (*informal*), peevish, crabby, dyspeptic, choleric, crotchety, oversensitive, snappish, ill-humoured, narky (*Brit. slang*), out of humour ...*Lack of sleep can leave us feeling jaded and out of sorts*...
2 = <u>depressed</u>, miserable, in low spirits, down, low, blue, sad, unhappy, gloomy, melancholy, mournful, dejected, despondent, dispirited, downcast, long-faced, sorrowful, disconsolate, crestfallen, down in the dumps (*informal*), down in the mouth (*informal*), mopy ...*You are feeling out of sorts and unable to see the wood for the trees*... **3** = <u>unwell</u>, ill, sick, poorly (*informal*), funny (*informal*), crook (*Austral. & N.Z. informal*), ailing, queer, unhealthy, seedy (*informal*), laid up (*informal*), queasy, infirm, dicky (*Brit. informal*), off colour, under the weather (*informal*), at death's door, indisposed, on the sick list (*informal*), not up to par, valetudinarian, green about the gills, not up to snuff (*informal*) ...*At times, he has seemed lifeless and out of sorts*... ♦ **sort of** = <u>rather</u>, somewhat, as it were, slightly, moderately, in part, reasonably ...*I sort of made my own happiness*...

> ## *Word Power*
>
> **sort** – It is common in informal speech to combine singular and plural in sentences like *these sort of distinctions are becoming blurred*. This is not acceptable in careful writing, where the plural must be used consistently: *these sorts of distinctions are becoming blurred.*

so-so (*Informal*) = <u>average</u>, middling, fair, ordinary, moderate, adequate, respectable, indifferent, not bad (*informal*), tolerable, run-of-the-mill, passable, undistinguished, fair to middling (*informal*), O.K. *or* okay (*informal*)

soul 1 = <u>spirit</u>, essence, psyche, life, mind, reason, intellect, vital force, animating principle ...*Such memories stirred in his soul*...
2 = <u>embodiment</u>, essence, incarnation, epitome, personification, quintessence, type ...*With such celebrated clients, she necessarily remains the soul of discretion*...
3 = <u>person</u>, being, human, individual, body, creature, mortal, man *or* woman ...*a tiny village of only 100 souls*...
4 = <u>feeling</u>, force, energy, vitality, animation, fervour, ardour, vivacity ...*an ice goddess without soul*...

soulful = <u>expressive</u>, sensitive, eloquent, moving, profound, meaningful, heartfelt, mournful

soulless 1 = <u>characterless</u>, dull, bland, mundane, ordinary, grey, commonplace, dreary, mediocre, drab, uninspiring, colourless, featureless, unexceptional ...*a clean but soulless hotel*...
2 = <u>unfeeling</u>, dead, cold, lifeless, inhuman, harsh, cruel, callous, unkind, unsympathetic, spiritless ...*He was big and brawny with soulless eyes*...

sound¹ [NOUN] **1** = <u>noise</u>, racket, din, report, tone, resonance, hubbub, reverberation ...*Peter heard the sound of gunfire*...
2 = <u>idea</u>, impression, implication(s), drift ...*Here's a new idea we like the sound of*...
3 = <u>cry</u>, noise, peep, squeak ...*She didn't make a sound*...
4 = <u>tone</u>, music, note, chord ...*the soulful sound of the*

violin…

5 = <u>earshot</u>, hearing, hearing distance …*I was born and bred within the sound of the cathedral bells…* VERB 1 = <u>toll</u>, set off …*A young man sounds the bell to start the Sunday service…*

2 = <u>resound</u>, echo, go off, toll, set off, chime, resonate, reverberate, clang, peal …*A silvery bell sounded somewhere…*

3 = <u>express</u>, declare, utter, announce, signal, pronounce, articulate, enunciate …*Others consider the move premature and have sounded a note of caution…*

4 = <u>seem</u>, seem to be, appear to be, give the impression of being, strike you as being …*She sounded a bit worried…*

(**Related Words**)
adjectives: sonic, acoustic

sound² 1 = <u>fit</u>, healthy, robust, firm, perfect, intact, vigorous, hale, unhurt, undamaged, uninjured, unimpaired, hale and hearty …*His body was still sound…* OPPOSITE frail

2 = <u>sturdy</u>, strong, solid, stable, substantial, durable, stout, well-constructed …*a perfectly sound building…*

3 = <u>safe</u>, secure, reliable, proven, established, recognized, solid, stable, solvent, reputable, tried-and-true …*a sound financial proposition…* OPPOSITE unreliable

4 = <u>sensible</u>, wise, reasonable, right, true, responsible, correct, proper, reliable, valid, orthodox, rational, logical, prudent, trustworthy, well-founded, level-headed, right-thinking, well-grounded …*They are trained nutritionists who can give sound advice on diets…* OPPOSITE irresponsible

5 = <u>deep</u>, peaceful, unbroken, undisturbed, untroubled …*She has woken me out of a sound sleep…* OPPOSITE troubled

sound³

PHRASES **sound someone out** = <u>question</u>, interview, survey, poll, examine, investigate, pump (*informal*), inspect, canvass, test the opinion of …*Sound him out gradually…* ◆ **sound something out** = <u>investigate</u>, research, examine, probe, look into, test the water, put out feelers to, see how the land lies, carry out an investigation of …*They are discreetly sounding out blue-chip American banks…*

sound⁴ = <u>channel</u>, passage, strait, inlet, fjord, voe, arm of the sea …*a blizzard blasting great drifts of snow across the sound…*

sour ADJECTIVE 1 = <u>sharp</u>, acid, tart, bitter, unpleasant, pungent, acetic, acidulated, acerb …*The stewed apple was sour even with honey…* OPPOSITE sweet

2 = <u>rancid</u>, turned, gone off, fermented, unsavoury, curdled, unwholesome, gone bad, off …*tiny fridges full of sour milk…* OPPOSITE fresh

3 = <u>bitter</u>, cynical, crabbed, tart, discontented, grudging, acrimonious, embittered, disagreeable, churlish, ill-tempered, jaundiced, waspish, grouchy (*informal*), ungenerous, peevish, ill-natured …*He became a sour, lonely old man…* OPPOSITE good-natured

VERB = <u>embitter</u>, disenchant, alienate, envenom …*The experience, she says, has soured her…*

source 1 = <u>cause</u>, origin, derivation, beginning, author …*This gave me a clue as to the source of the problem…*

2 = <u>informant</u>, authority, documentation …*a major source of information about the arts…*

3 = <u>origin</u>, spring, fount, fountainhead, wellspring, rise …*the source of the Tiber…*

souvenir = <u>keepsake</u>, token, reminder, relic, remembrancer (*archaic*), memento

sovereign ADJECTIVE 1 = <u>supreme</u>, ruling, absolute, chief, royal, principal, dominant, imperial, unlimited, paramount, regal, predominant, monarchal, kingly *or* queenly …*No contract can absolutely restrain a sovereign power…*

2 = <u>excellent</u>, efficient, efficacious, effectual …*wild garlic, a sovereign remedy in any healer's chest…* NOUN = <u>monarch</u>, ruler, king *or* queen, chief, shah, potentate, supreme ruler, emperor *or* empress, prince *or* princess, tsar *or* tsarina …*the first British sovereign to set foot on Spanish soil…*

sovereignty = <u>supreme power</u>, domination, supremacy, primacy, sway, ascendancy, kingship, suzerainty

sow = <u>scatter</u>, plant, seed, lodge, implant, disseminate, broadcast, inseminate

space 1 = <u>room</u>, volume, capacity, extent, margin, extension, scope, play, expanse, leeway, amplitude, spaciousness, elbowroom …*The furniture proved impractical because it took up too much space…*

2 = <u>gap</u>, opening, interval, gulf, cavity, aperture …*The space underneath could be used as a storage area…*

3 = <u>period</u>, interval, time, while, span, duration …*They've come a long way in a short space of time…*

4 = <u>outer space</u>, the universe, the galaxy, the solar system, the cosmos …*launching satellites into space…*

5 = <u>blank</u>, gap, interval …*Affix your stamps on the space provided…*

(**Related Words**)
adjective : spatial

spaceman *or* **spacewoman** = <u>astronaut</u>, cosmonaut, space cadet, space traveller

spacious = <u>roomy</u>, large, huge, broad, vast, extensive, ample, expansive, capacious, uncrowded, commodious, comfortable, sizable *or* sizeable OPPOSITE limited

Spain

(**Related Words**)
adjective : Spanish
➤ **administrative regions**

span NOUN 1 = <u>period</u>, term, duration, spell …*The batteries had a life span of six hours…*

2 = <u>extent</u>, reach, spread, length, distance, stretch …*With a span of 6ft, her wings dominated the stage…* VERB = <u>extend across</u>, cross, bridge, cover, link, vault, traverse, range over, arch across …*the humped iron*

bridge spanning the railway…

spank = <u>smack</u>, slap, whack, belt (*informal*), tan (*slang*), slipper (*informal*), cuff, wallop (*informal*), give (someone) a hiding (*informal*), put (someone) over your knee

spanking `NOUN` = <u>smacking</u>, hiding (*informal*), whacking, slapping, walloping (*informal*) …*Andrea gave her son a sound spanking…*
`ADJECTIVE` 1 (*Informal*) = <u>smart</u>, brand-new, fine, gleaming …*a spanking new car…*
2 = <u>fast</u>, quick, brisk, lively, smart, vigorous, energetic, snappy …*The film moves along at a spanking pace…*

spar = <u>argue</u>, row, squabble, dispute, scrap (*informal*), fall out (*informal*), spat (*U.S.*), wrangle, skirmish, bicker, have a tiff

spare `ADJECTIVE` 1 = <u>back-up</u>, reserve, second, extra, relief, emergency, additional, substitute, fall-back, auxiliary, in reserve …*He could have taken a spare key…*
2 = <u>extra</u>, surplus, leftover, over, free, odd, unwanted, in excess, unused, superfluous, supernumerary …*They don't have a lot of spare cash…* `OPPOSITE` necessary
3 = <u>free</u>, leisure, unoccupied …*In her spare time she raises funds for charity…*
4 = <u>thin</u>, lean, slim, slender, slight, meagre, gaunt, wiry, lank …*She was thin and spare, with a shapely intelligent face…* `OPPOSITE` plump
5 = <u>meagre</u>, sparing, modest, economical, frugal, scanty …*The two rooms were spare and neat, stripped bare of ornaments…*
`VERB` 1 = <u>afford</u>, give, grant, do without, relinquish, part with, allow, bestow, dispense with, manage without, let someone have …*He suggested that his country could not spare the troops…*
2 = <u>have mercy on</u>, pardon, have pity on, leave, release, excuse, let off (*informal*), go easy on (*informal*), be merciful to, grant pardon to, deal leniently with, refrain from hurting, save (from harm) …*Not a man was spared…* `OPPOSITE` show no mercy to
`PHRASES` **go spare** (*Brit. slang*) = <u>become angry</u>, become upset, go mental (*slang*), become distracted, become enraged, become mad (*informal*), go up the wall (*slang*), become distraught, blow your top (*informal*), do your nut (*Brit. slang*), have *or* throw a fit (*informal*) …*She went spare when we told her what had happened…*

sparing = <u>economical</u>, frugal, thrifty, saving, careful, prudent, cost-conscious, chary, money-conscious `OPPOSITE` lavish

spark `NOUN` 1 = <u>flicker</u>, flash, gleam, glint, spit, flare, scintillation …*Sparks flew in all directions…*
2 = <u>trace</u>, hint, scrap, atom, jot, vestige, scintilla …*Even Oliver felt a tiny spark of excitement…*
`VERB` often with *off* = <u>start</u>, stimulate, provoke, excite, inspire, stir, trigger (off), set off, animate, rouse, prod, precipitate, kick-start, set in motion, kindle, touch off …*What was it that sparked your interest in*

motoring?…

sparkle `VERB` = <u>glitter</u>, flash, spark, shine, beam, glow, gleam, wink, shimmer, twinkle, dance, glint, glisten, glister (*archaic*), scintillate …*His bright eyes sparkled…*
`NOUN` 1 = <u>glitter</u>, flash, gleam, spark, dazzle, flicker, brilliance, twinkle, glint, radiance …*There was a sparkle in her eye that could not be hidden…*
2 = <u>vivacity</u>, life, spirit, dash, zip (*informal*), vitality, animation, panache, gaiety, élan, brio, liveliness, vim (*slang*) …*There was little sparkle in their performance…*

sparse = <u>scattered</u>, scarce, meagre, sporadic, few and far between, scanty `OPPOSITE` thick

spartan = <u>austere</u>, severe, frugal, ascetic, plain, disciplined, extreme, strict, stern, bleak, rigorous, stringent, abstemious, self-denying

spasm 1 = <u>convulsion</u>, contraction, paroxysm, twitch, throe (*rare*) …*A lack of magnesium causes muscles to go into spasm…*
2 = <u>burst</u>, fit, outburst, seizure, frenzy, eruption, access …*He felt a spasm of fear…*

spasmodic = <u>sporadic</u>, irregular, erratic, intermittent, jerky, fitful, convulsive

spat = <u>quarrel</u>, dispute, squabble, controversy, contention, bickering, tiff, altercation

spate = <u>flood</u>, flow, torrent, rush, deluge, outpouring

spatter = <u>splash</u>, spray, sprinkle, soil, dirty, scatter, daub, speckle, splodge, bespatter, bestrew

spawn `NOUN` (*Often derogatory*) = <u>offspring</u>, issue, product, seed (*chiefly biblical*), progeny, yield …*They are the spawn of Bible-belting repression…*
`VERB` = <u>generate</u>, produce, give rise to, start, prompt, provoke, set off, bring about, spark off, set in motion …*His novels spawned both movies and television shows…*

speak `VERB` 1 = <u>talk</u>, say something …*The President spoke of the need for territorial compromise…*
2 = <u>articulate</u>, say, voice, pronounce, utter, tell, state, talk, express, communicate, make known, enunciate …*The very act of speaking the words gave him comfort…*
3 = <u>converse</u>, talk, chat, discourse, confer, commune, exchange views, shoot the breeze (*slang, chiefly U.S. & Canad.*) …*It was very emotional when we spoke again…*
4 = <u>lecture</u>, talk, discourse, spout (*informal*), make a speech, pontificate, give a speech, declaim, hold forth, spiel (*informal*), address an audience, deliver an address, speechify …*Last month I spoke in front of two thousand people in Birmingham…*
`PHRASES` **speak for something** *or* **someone** 1 = <u>represent</u>, act for *or* on behalf of, appear for, hold a brief for, hold a mandate for …*It was the job of the church to speak for the underprivileged…* 2 = <u>support</u>, back, champion, defend, promote, advocate, fight for, uphold, commend, espouse, stick up for (*informal*) …*a role in which he would be seen as speaking for the Government…*

speaker = <u>orator</u>, public speaker, lecturer, spokesperson, mouthpiece, spieler (*informal*), word-spinner, spokesman *or* spokeswoman

spearhead = <u>lead</u>, head, pioneer, launch, set off, initiate, lead the way, set in motion, blaze the trail, be in the van, lay the first stone

special 1 = <u>exceptional</u>, important, significant, particular, unique, unusual, extraordinary, distinguished, memorable, gala, festive, uncommon, momentous, out of the ordinary, one in a million, red-letter, especial …*I usually reserve these outfits for special occasions*… OPPOSITE ordinary
2 = <u>major</u>, chief, main, primary …*He is a special correspondent for Newsweek magazine*…
3 = <u>specific</u>, particular, distinctive, certain, individual, appropriate, characteristic, precise, peculiar, specialized, especial …*It requires a very special brand of courage to fight dictators*… OPPOSITE general

specialist = <u>expert</u>, authority, professional, master, consultant, guru, buff (*informal*), whizz (*informal*), connoisseur, boffin (*Brit. informal*), hotshot (*informal*), wonk (*informal*), maven (*U.S.*), fundi (*S. African*)

speciality 1 = <u>forte</u>, strength, special talent, métier, specialty, bag (*slang*), claim to fame, pièce de résistance (*French*), distinctive *or* distinguishing feature …*His speciality was creating rich, creamy sauces*…
2 = <u>special subject</u>, specialty, field of study, branch of knowledge, area of specialization …*His speciality was the history of Germany*…

species = <u>kind</u>, sort, type, group, class, variety, breed, category, description, genus

specific 1 = <u>particular</u>, special, characteristic, distinguishing, peculiar, definite, especial …*the specific needs of the individual*… OPPOSITE general
2 = <u>precise</u>, exact, explicit, definite, limited, express, clear-cut, unequivocal, unambiguous …*I asked him to be more specific*… OPPOSITE vague
3 = <u>peculiar</u>, appropriate, individual, particular, personal, unique, restricted, idiosyncratic, endemic …*Send your resume with a covering letter that is specific to that particular job*…

specification = <u>requirement</u>, detail, particular, stipulation, condition, qualification

specify = <u>state</u>, designate, spell out, stipulate, name, detail, mention, indicate, define, cite, individualize, enumerate, itemize, be specific about, particularize

specimen 1 = <u>sample</u>, example, individual, model, type, pattern, instance, representative, exemplar, exemplification …*a perfect specimen of a dinosaur fossil*…
2 = <u>example</u>, model, exhibit, embodiment, type …*a fine specimen of manhood*…

specious = <u>fallacious</u>, misleading, deceptive, plausible, unsound, sophistic, sophistical, casuistic

speck 1 = <u>mark</u>, spot, dot, stain, blot, fleck, speckle, mote …*There is a speck of blood by his ear*…
2 = <u>particle</u>, bit, grain, dot, atom, shred, mite, jot, modicum, whit, tittle, iota …*He leaned forward and

brushed a speck of dust off his shoes*…

speckled = <u>flecked</u>, spotted, dotted, sprinkled, spotty, freckled, mottled, dappled, stippled, brindled, speckledy

spectacle NOUN 1 = <u>show</u>, display, exhibition, event, performance, sight, parade, extravaganza, pageant …*a director passionate about music and spectacle*…
2 = <u>sight</u>, wonder, scene, phenomenon, curiosity, marvel, laughing stock …*the bizarre spectacle of an actor desperately demanding an encore*…
PLURAL NOUN = <u>glasses</u>, specs (*informal*), eyeglasses (*U.S.*), eyewear …*He looked at me over the tops of his spectacles*…

spectacular ADJECTIVE = <u>impressive</u>, striking, dramatic, stunning (*informal*), marked, grand, remarkable, fantastic (*informal*), magnificent, staggering, splendid, dazzling, sensational, breathtaking, eye-catching …*The results have been spectacular*… OPPOSITE unimpressive
NOUN = <u>show</u>, display, spectacle, extravaganza …*a television spectacular*…

spectator = <u>onlooker</u>, observer, viewer, witness, looker-on, watcher, eyewitness, bystander, beholder OPPOSITE participant

spectral = <u>ghostly</u>, unearthly, eerie, supernatural, weird, phantom, shadowy, uncanny, spooky (*informal*), insubstantial, incorporeal, wraithlike

spectre = <u>ghost</u>, spirit, phantom, presence, vision, shadow, shade (*literary*), apparition, wraith

speculate 1 = <u>conjecture</u>, consider, wonder, guess, contemplate, deliberate, muse, meditate, surmise, theorize, hypothesize, cogitate …*The reader can speculate about what will happen next*…
2 = <u>gamble</u>, risk, venture, hazard, have a flutter (*informal*), take a chance with, play the market …*They speculated in property whose value has now dropped*…

speculation 1 = <u>theory</u>, opinion, hypothesis, conjecture, guess, consideration, deliberation, contemplation, surmise, guesswork, supposition …*I had published my speculations about the future of the universe*…
2 = <u>gamble</u>, risk, gambling, hazard …*speculation on the Stock Exchange*…

speculative 1 = <u>hypothetical</u>, academic, theoretical, abstract, tentative, notional, conjectural, suppositional …*He has written a speculative biography of Christopher Marlowe*…
2 = <u>risky</u>, uncertain, hazardous, unpredictable, dicey (*informal, chiefly Brit.*), chancy (*informal*) …*a speculative venture*…

speech 1 = <u>communication</u>, talk, conversation, articulation, discussion, dialogue, intercourse …*the development of speech in children*…
2 = <u>diction</u>, pronunciation, articulation, delivery, fluency, inflection, intonation, elocution, enunciation …*His speech became increasingly thick and nasal*…
3 = <u>language</u>, tongue, utterance, jargon, dialect, idiom, parlance, articulation, diction, lingo (*informal*),

enunciation ...*the way common letter clusters are pronounced in speech*...

4 = <u>talk</u>, address, lecture, discourse, harangue, homily, oration, spiel (*informal*), disquisition ...*He delivered his speech in French*...

speechless = <u>dumb</u>, dumbfounded, lost for words, dumbstruck, astounded, shocked, mum, amazed, silent, mute, dazed, aghast, inarticulate, tongue-tied, wordless, thunderstruck, unable to get a word out (*informal*)

speed NOUN **1** = <u>rate</u>, pace, momentum, tempo, velocity ...*He drove off at high speed*...

2 = <u>velocity</u>, swiftness, acceleration, precipitation, rapidity, quickness, fastness, briskness, speediness, precipitateness ...*Speed is the essential ingredient of all athletics*...

3 = <u>swiftness</u>, rush, hurry, expedition, haste, rapidity, quickness, fleetness, celerity ...*I was amazed at his speed of working*... OPPOSITE> slowness

VERB **1** = <u>race</u>, rush, hurry, zoom, career, bomb (along), tear, flash, belt (along) (*slang*), barrel (along) (*informal, chiefly U.S. & Canad.*), sprint, gallop, hasten, press on, quicken, lose no time, get a move on (*informal*), burn rubber (*informal*), bowl along, put your foot down (*informal*), step on it (*informal*), make haste, go hell for leather (*informal*), exceed the speed limit, go like a bomb (*Brit. & N.Z. informal*), go like the wind, go like a bat out of hell ...*The engine noise rises only slightly as I speed along*... OPPOSITE> crawl

2 = <u>help</u>, further, advance, aid, promote, boost, assist, facilitate, impel, expedite ...*Invest in low-cost language courses to speed your progress*... OPPOSITE> hinder

PHRASES **speed something up** = <u>accelerate</u>, promote, hasten, help along, further, forward, advance ...*Excessive drinking will speed up the ageing process*...

Word Power

speed – The past tense of *speed up* is *speeded up* (not *sped up*), for example *I speeded up to overtake the lorry.* The past participle is also *speeded up*, for example *I had already speeded up when I spotted the police car.*

---

speedy = <u>quick</u>, fast, rapid, swift, express, winged, immediate, prompt, fleet, hurried, summary, precipitate, hasty, headlong, quickie (*informal*), expeditious, fleet of foot, pdq (*slang*) OPPOSITE> slow

spell¹ VERB = <u>indicate</u>, mean, signify, suggest, promise, point to, imply, amount to, herald, augur, presage, portend ...*The report spells more trouble*...

PHRASES **spell something out** = <u>make clear</u> or <u>plain</u>, specify, make explicit, clarify, elucidate, explicate ...*How many times do I have to spell it out?*...

spell² **1** = <u>incantation</u>, charm, sorcery, exorcism, abracadabra, witchery, conjuration ...*Vile witch! She cast a spell on me!*...

2 = <u>enchantment</u>, magic, fascination, glamour, allure,

---

bewitchment ...*The King also falls under her spell*...

spell³ = <u>period</u>, time, term, stretch, turn, course, season, patch, interval, bout, stint ...*There has been a spell of dry weather*...

spellbound = <u>entranced</u>, gripped, fascinated, transported, charmed, hooked, possessed, bemused, captivated, enthralled, bewitched, transfixed, rapt, mesmerized, under a spell

spelling = <u>orthography</u>

spend **1** = <u>pay out</u>, fork out (*slang*), expend, lay out, splash out (*Brit. informal*), shell out (*informal*), disburse ...*They have spent £23m on new players*... OPPOSITE> save

2 = <u>apply</u>, use, employ, concentrate, invest, put in, devote, lavish, exert, bestow ...*This energy could be much better spent taking some positive action*...

3 = <u>pass</u>, fill, occupy, while away ...*We spent the night in a hotel*...

4 = <u>use up</u>, waste, squander, blow (*slang*), empty, drain, exhaust, consume, run through, deplete, dissipate, fritter away ...*My stepson was spending money like it grew on trees*... OPPOSITE> save

spendthrift NOUN = <u>squanderer</u>, spender, profligate, prodigal, big spender, waster, wastrel ...*I was a natural spendthrift when I was single*... OPPOSITE> miser

ADJECTIVE = <u>wasteful</u>, extravagant, prodigal, profligate, improvident ...*his father's spendthrift ways*... OPPOSITE> economical

spent **1** = <u>used up</u>, finished, gone, consumed, expended ...*The money was spent*...

2 = <u>exhausted</u>, drained, worn out, bushed (*informal*), all in (*slang*), shattered (*informal*), weakened, wiped out (*informal*), wearied, weary, played out (*informal*), burnt out, fagged (out) (*informal*), whacked (*Brit. informal*), debilitated, knackered (*slang*), prostrate, clapped out (*Brit., Austral., & N.Z. informal*), tired out, ready to drop (*informal*), dog-tired (*informal*), zonked (*informal*), dead beat (*informal*), shagged out (*Brit. slang*), done in or up (*informal*) ...*After all that exertion, we were completely spent*...

sperm **1** = <u>spermatozoon</u>, reproductive cell, male gamete ...*Conception occurs when a single sperm fuses with an egg*...

2 = <u>semen</u>, seed (*archaic or dialect*), spermatozoa, scum (*U.S. slang*), come or cum (*taboo*), jism or jissom (*taboo*) ...*the ejaculation of sperm*...

spew **1** = <u>shed</u>, discharge, send out, issue, throw out, eject, diffuse, emanate, exude, cast out ...*An oil tanker spewed its cargo into the sea*...

2 = <u>vomit</u>, throw up (*informal*), puke (*slang*), chuck (*Austral. & N.Z. informal*), spit out, regurgitate, disgorge, barf (*U.S. slang*), chunder (*slang, chiefly Austral.*), belch forth, upchuck (*U.S. slang*), do a technicolour yawn (*slang*), toss your cookies (*U.S. slang*) ...*Let's get out of his way before he starts spewing*...

sphere **1** = <u>ball</u>, globe, orb, globule, circle ...*The cactus will form a large sphere crested with golden thorns*...

2 = field, range, area, department, function, territory, capacity, province, patch, scope, turf (*U.S. slang*), realm, domain, compass, walk of life ...*the sphere of international politics*...

3 = rank, class, station, status, stratum ...*life outside academic spheres of society*...

spherical = round, globular, globe-shaped, rotund, orbicular

spice 1 = seasoning, condiment ...*herbs and spices*...
2 = excitement, kick (*informal*), zest, colour, pep, zip (*informal*), tang, zap (*slang*), gusto, zing (*informal*), piquancy ...*The spice of danger will add to the lure*...

spicy 1 = hot, seasoned, pungent, aromatic, savoury, tangy, piquant, flavoursome ...*Thai food is hot and spicy*...
2 (*Informal*) = risqué, racy, off-colour, ribald, hot (*informal*), broad, improper, suggestive, unseemly, titillating, indelicate, indecorous ...*spicy anecdotes about his sexual adventures*...

spider

(*Related Words*)
fear of: arachnophobia
➤ **spiders and other arachnids**

spiel = patter, speech, pitch, recital, harangue, sales talk, sales patter

spike NOUN **1** = point, stake, spur, pin, nail, spine, barb, tine, prong ...*a 15-foot wall topped with iron spikes*...
2 = prickle, spine, bristle, thorn ...*Its skin is covered with spikes*...
VERB **1** = drug, lace, dope, cut, contaminate, adulterate ...*drinks spiked with tranquillizers*...
2 = impale, spit, spear, stick ...*She was spiked on a railing after a 20ft plunge*...

spill VERB **1** = tip over, upset, overturn, capsize, knock over, topple over ...*He always spilled the drinks*...
2 = shed, scatter, discharge, throw off, disgorge, spill or run over ...*A number of bags had split and were spilling their contents*...
3 = slop, flow, pour, run, overflow, slosh, splosh ...*It doesn't matter if red wine spills on this floor*...
4 = emerge, flood, pour, mill, stream, surge, swarm, crowd, teem ...*When the bell rings, more than 1,000 children spill from the classrooms*...
NOUN = spillage, flood, leak, leakage, overspill ...*An oil spill could be devastating for wildlife*...

spin VERB **1** = revolve, turn, rotate, wheel, twist, reel, whirl, twirl, gyrate, pirouette, birl (*Scot.*) ...*The Earth spins on its own axis*...
2 = reel, swim, whirl, be giddy, be in a whirl, grow dizzy ...*My head was spinning from the wine*...
3 = tell, relate, recount, develop, invent, unfold, concoct, narrate ...*She had spun a story that was too good to be true*...
NOUN **1** (*Informal*) = drive, ride, turn, hurl (*Scot.*), whirl, joy ride (*informal*) ...*Think twice about going for a spin by the light of the silvery moon*...
2 = revolution, roll, whirl, twist, gyration ...*a spin of the roulette wheel*...
PHRASES **spin something out** = prolong, extend, lengthen, draw out, drag out, delay, amplify, pad out, protract, prolongate ...*They will try to spin out the conference into next autumn*...

spindly = lanky, gangly, spidery, leggy, twiggy, attenuated, gangling, spindle-shanked

spine 1 = backbone, vertebrae, spinal column, vertebral column ...*fractures of the hip and spine*...
2 = barb, spur, needle, spike, ray, quill ...*Carry a pair of thick gloves to protect you from hedgehog spines*...
3 = determination, resolution, backbone, resolve, drive, conviction, fortitude, persistence, tenacity, perseverance, willpower, firmness, constancy, single-mindedness, steadfastness, doggedness, resoluteness, indomitability ...*If you had any spine, you wouldn't let her walk all over you like that*...

spineless = weak, soft, cowardly, ineffective, feeble, yellow (*informal*), inadequate, pathetic, submissive, squeamish, vacillating, boneless, gutless (*informal*), weak-willed, weak-kneed (*informal*), faint-hearted, irresolute, spiritless, lily-livered, without a will of your own OPPOSITE brave

spiral ADJECTIVE = coiled, winding, corkscrew, circular, scrolled, whorled, helical, cochlear, voluted, cochleate (*Biology*) ...*a spiral staircase*...
NOUN = coil, helix, corkscrew, whorl, screw, curlicue ...*Larks were rising in spirals from the ridge*...

spirit NOUN **1** = soul, life, psyche, essential being ...*The human spirit is virtually indestructable*...
2 = life force, vital spark, breath ...*His spirit left him during the night*...
3 = ghost, phantom, spectre, vision, shadow, shade (*literary*), spook (*informal*), apparition, sprite ...*Do you believe in the existence of evil spirits?*...

Spiders and other arachnids http://bubl.ac.uk/link/s/spiders.htm

bird spider	harvestman *or* (*U.S. & Canad.*)	spider
black widow	daddy-longlegs	spider mite
book scorpion	house spider	tarantula
cardinal spider	itch mite	tick
cheese mite	jumping spider	trap-door spider
chigger, chigoe, *or* (*U.S. & Canad.*) redbug	katipo	vinegarroon
chigoe, chigger, jigger, *or* sand flea	mite	water spider
	money spider	whip scorpion
funnel-web	red-back (spider) (*Austral.*)	wolf spider *or* hunting spider
	jockey spider	

4 = <u>courage</u>, guts (*informal*), grit, balls (*taboo slang*), backbone, spunk (*informal*), gameness, ballsiness (*taboo slang*), dauntlessness, stoutheartedness ...*She was a very brave girl and everyone admired her spirit...*

5 = <u>liveliness</u>, energy, vigour, life, force, fire, resolution, enterprise, enthusiasm, sparkle, warmth, animation, zest, mettle, ardour, earnestness, brio ...*They played with spirit...*

6 = <u>attitude</u>, character, quality, humour, temper, outlook, temperament, complexion, disposition ...*They approached the talks in a conciliatory spirit...*

7 = <u>heart</u>, sense, nature, soul, core, substance, essence, lifeblood, quintessence, fundamental nature ...*the real spirit of the Labour movement...*

8 = <u>intention</u>, meaning, purpose, substance, intent, essence, purport, gist ...*the spirit of the treaty...*

9 = <u>feeling</u>, atmosphere, character, feel, quality, tone, mood, flavour, tenor, ambience, vibes (*slang*) ...*I appreciate the sounds, smells and the spirit of the place...*

10 = <u>resolve</u>, will, drive, resolution, conviction, motivation, dedication, backbone, fortitude, persistence, tenacity, perseverance, willpower, firmness, constancy, single-mindedness, steadfastness, doggedness, resoluteness, indomitability ...*It takes a lot of spirit to win with 10 men...*

PLURAL NOUN = <u>mood</u>, feelings, morale, humour, temper, tenor, disposition, state of mind, frame of mind ...*A bit of exercise will help lift his spirits...*

spirited = <u>lively</u>, vigorous, energetic, animated, game, active, bold, sparkling, have-a-go (*informal*), courageous, ardent, feisty (*informal, chiefly U.S. & Canad.*), plucky, high-spirited, sprightly, vivacious, spunky (*informal*), mettlesome OPPOSITE lifeless

spirits = <u>strong alcohol</u>, liquor, the hard stuff (*informal*), firewater, strong liquor

spiritual 1 = <u>nonmaterial</u>, immaterial, incorporeal ...*She lived entirely by spiritual values...* OPPOSITE material

2 = <u>sacred</u>, religious, holy, divine, ethereal, devotional, otherworldly ...*A man in priestly clothes offered spiritual guidance...*

spit VERB **1** = <u>expectorate</u>, sputter ...*They spat at me and taunted me...*

2 = <u>eject</u>, discharge, throw out ...*I spat it on to my plate...*

NOUN = <u>saliva</u>, dribble, spittle, drool, slaver, sputum ...*When he took a corner kick he was showered with spit...*

spite NOUN = <u>malice</u>, malevolence, ill will, hate, hatred, gall, animosity, venom, spleen, pique, rancour, bitchiness (*slang*), malignity, spitefulness ...*Never had she met such spite and pettiness...* OPPOSITE kindness

VERB = <u>annoy</u>, hurt, injure, harm, provoke, offend, needle (*informal*), put out, gall, nettle, vex, pique, discomfit, put someone's nose out of joint (*informal*) ...*He was giving his art collection away for nothing, to spite them...* OPPOSITE benefit

PHRASES **in spite of** = <u>despite</u>, regardless of, notwithstanding, in defiance of, (even) though ...*Their love of life comes in spite of considerable hardship...*

spiteful = <u>malicious</u>, nasty, vindictive, cruel, malignant, barbed, malevolent, venomous, bitchy (*informal*), snide, rancorous, catty (*informal*), splenetic, shrewish, ill-disposed, ill-natured

spitting image = <u>double</u>, lookalike, (dead) ringer (*slang*), picture, spit (*informal, chiefly Brit.*), clone, replica, likeness, living image, spit and image (*informal*)

splash VERB **1** = <u>paddle</u>, plunge, bathe, dabble, wade, wallow ...*A lot of people were in the water, splashing about...*

2 = <u>scatter</u>, shower, spray, sprinkle, spread, wet, strew, squirt, spatter, slop, slosh (*informal*) ...*He closed his eyes tight, and splashed the water on his face...*

3 = <u>spatter</u>, mark, stain, smear, speck, speckle, blotch, splodge, bespatter ...*The carpet was splashed with beer stains...*

4 = <u>dash</u>, break, strike, wash, batter, surge, smack, buffet, plop, plash ...*waves splashing against the side of the boat...*

NOUN **1** = <u>splashing</u>, dashing, plash, beating, battering, swashing ...*I would sit alone and listen to the splash of water on the rocks...*

2 = <u>dash</u>, touch, spattering, splodge ...*Add a splash of lemon juice to flavour the butter...*

3 = <u>spot</u>, burst, patch, stretch, spurt ...*splashes of colour...*

4 = <u>blob</u>, spot, smudge, stain, smear, fleck, speck ...*splashes of ink over a glowing white surface...*

PHRASES **make a splash** (*Informal*) = <u>cause a stir</u>, make an impact, cause a sensation, cut a dash, be ostentatious ...*He knows how to make a splash in the House of Lords...*

spleen = <u>spite</u>, anger, bitterness, hostility, hatred, resentment, wrath, gall, malice, animosity, venom, bile, bad temper, acrimony, pique, rancour, ill will, animus, malevolence, vindictiveness, malignity, spitefulness, ill humour, peevishness

splendid 1 = <u>excellent</u>, wonderful, marvellous, mean (*slang*), great (*informal*), topping (*Brit. slang*), fine, cracking (*Brit. informal*), crucial (*slang*), fantastic (*informal*), first-class, glorious, mega (*slang*), sovereign, awesome (*slang*), def (*slang*), brill (*informal*), bodacious (*slang, chiefly U.S.*), boffo (*slang*), chillin' (*U.S. slang*), booshit (*Austral. slang*), exo (*Austral. slang*), sik (*Austral. slang*) ...*The book includes a wealth of splendid photographs...* OPPOSITE poor

2 = <u>magnificent</u>, grand, imposing, impressive, rich, superb, costly, gorgeous, dazzling, lavish, luxurious, sumptuous, ornate, resplendent, splendiferous (*facetious*) ...*a splendid Victorian mansion...* OPPOSITE squalid

3 = <u>glorious</u>, superb, magnificent, grand, brilliant, rare, supreme, outstanding, remarkable, sterling, exceptional, renowned, admirable, sublime, illustrious

...*a splendid career in publishing*... OPPOSITE⟩ ignoble

splendour 1 = <u>magnificence</u>, glory, grandeur, show, display, ceremony, luxury, spectacle, majesty, richness, nobility, pomp, opulence, solemnity, éclat, gorgeousness, sumptuousness, stateliness, resplendence, luxuriousness ...*They met in the splendour of the hotel*... OPPOSITE⟩ squalor
2 = <u>brilliance</u>, brightness, radiance, dazzle, lustre, effulgence, refulgence ...*We were led through the fairy-lit splendour of the centre*... OPPOSITE⟩ dullness

splice = <u>join</u>, unite, graft, marry, wed, knit, mesh, braid, intertwine, interweave, yoke, plait, entwine, interlace, intertwist

splinter NOUN = <u>sliver</u>, fragment, chip, needle, shaving, flake, paring ...*a splinter in the finger*...
VERB = <u>shatter</u>, split, fracture, shiver, disintegrate, break into fragments ...*The ruler cracked and splintered into pieces*...

split VERB 1 = <u>break</u>, crack, burst, snap, break up, open, give way, splinter, gape, come apart, come undone ...*In a severe gale the ship split in two*...
2 = <u>cut</u>, break, crack, snap, chop, cleave, hew ...*He started on the main course while she split the avocados*...
3 = <u>divide</u>, separate, disunite, disrupt, disband, cleave, pull apart, set at odds, set at variance ...*It is feared they could split the government*...
4 = <u>diverge</u>, separate, branch, fork, part, go separate ways ...*that place where the road split in two*...
5 = <u>tear</u>, rend, rip, slash, slit ...*The seat of his short grey trousers split*...
6 = <u>share out</u>, divide, distribute, halve, allocate, partition, allot, carve up, dole out, apportion, slice up, parcel out, divvy up (*informal*) ...*Split the wages between you*...
NOUN 1 = <u>division</u>, break, breach, rift, difference, disruption, rupture, discord, divergence, schism, estrangement, dissension, disunion ...*a split in the party*...
2 = <u>separation</u>, break, divorce, break-up, split-up, disunion ...*The split from her husband was acrimonious*...
3 = <u>crack</u>, tear, rip, damage, gap, rent, breach, slash, slit, fissure ...*The seat had a few small splits around the corners*...
ADJECTIVE 1 = <u>divided</u>, ambivalent, bisected ...*The Kremlin is deeply split in its approach to foreign policy*...
2 = <u>broken</u>, cracked, snapped, fractured, splintered, ruptured, cleft ...*a split finger nail*...
PHRASES **split on someone** (*Slang*) = <u>betray</u>, tell on, shop (*slang, chiefly Brit.*), sing (*slang, chiefly U.S.*), grass (*Brit. slang*), give away, squeal (*slang*), inform on, spill your guts (*slang*), dob in (*Austral. slang*) ...*If I wanted to tell, I'd have split on you before now*...
◆ **split up** = <u>break up</u>, part, separate, divorce, disband, part company, go separate ways ...*I was beginning to think that we would never split up*...

spoil VERB 1 = <u>ruin</u>, destroy, wreck, damage, total

(*slang*), blow (*slang*), injure, upset, harm, mar, scar, undo, trash (*slang*), impair, mess up, blemish, disfigure, debase, deface, put a damper on, crool *or* cruel (*Austral. slang*) ...*It is important not to let mistakes spoil your life*... OPPOSITE⟩ improve
2 = <u>overindulge</u>, indulge, pamper, baby, cosset, coddle, spoon-feed, mollycoddle, kill with kindness ...*Grandparents are often tempted to spoil their grandchildren*... OPPOSITE⟩ deprive
3 = <u>indulge</u>, treat, pamper, satisfy, gratify, pander to, regale ...*Spoil yourself with a new perfume this summer*...
4 = <u>go bad</u>, turn, go off (*Brit. informal*), rot, decay, decompose, curdle, mildew, addle, putrefy, become tainted ...*Fats spoil by becoming tainted*...
PLURAL NOUN = <u>booty</u>, loot, plunder, gain, prizes, prey, pickings, pillage, swag (*slang*), boodle (*slang, chiefly U.S.*), rapine ...*Competing warlords and foreign powers scrambled for political spoils*...

spoken ADJECTIVE = <u>verbal</u>, voiced, expressed, uttered, oral, said, told, unwritten, phonetic, by word of mouth, put into words, viva voce ...*written and spoken communication skills*...
PHRASES **spoken for** 1 = <u>reserved</u>, booked, claimed, chosen, selected, set aside ...*The top jobs in the party are already spoken for*... 2 = <u>engaged</u>, taken, going out with someone, betrothed (*archaic*), going steady ...*Both girls, I remind him, are spoken for*...

spokesperson = <u>speaker</u>, official, spokesman *or* spokeswoman, voice, spin doctor (*informal*), mouthpiece

spongy = <u>porous</u>, light, absorbent, springy, cushioned, elastic, cushiony

sponsor VERB = <u>back</u>, fund, finance, promote, subsidize, patronize, put up the money for, lend your name to ...*They are sponsoring a major pop art exhibition*...
NOUN = <u>backer</u>, patron, promoter, angel (*informal*), guarantor ...*the new sponsors of the League Cup*...

spontaneous = <u>unplanned</u>, impromptu, unprompted, willing, free, natural, voluntary, instinctive, impulsive, unforced, unbidden, unconstrained, unpremeditated, extempore, uncompelled OPPOSITE⟩ planned

spontaneously = <u>voluntarily</u>, freely, instinctively, impromptu, off the cuff (*informal*), on impulse, impulsively, in the heat of the moment, extempore, off your own bat, of your own accord, quite unprompted

spoof (*Informal*) = <u>parody</u>, take-off (*informal*), satire, caricature, mockery, send-up (*Brit. informal*), travesty, lampoon, burlesque

spook NOUN = <u>ghost</u>, spirit, phantom, spectre, soul, shade (*literary*), manes, apparition, wraith, revenant, phantasm, eidolon ...*She woke up to see a spook hovering over her bed*...
VERB = <u>frighten</u>, alarm, scare, terrify, startle, intimidate, daunt, unnerve, petrify, scare (someone) stiff, put the wind up (someone) (*informal*), scare the

living daylights out of (someone) (*informal*), make your hair stand on end (*informal*), get the wind up, make your blood run cold, throw into a panic, scare the bejesus out of (*informal*), affright (*archaic*), freeze your blood, make (someone) jump out of his skin (*informal*), throw into a fright ...*But was it the wind that spooked her?*...

spooky = <u>eerie</u>, frightening, chilling, ghostly, weird, mysterious, scary (*informal*), unearthly, supernatural, uncanny, creepy (*informal*), spine-chilling

sporadic = <u>intermittent</u>, occasional, scattered, isolated, random, on and off, irregular, infrequent, spasmodic OPPOSITE> steady

sport NOUN 1 = <u>game</u>, exercise, recreation, play, entertainment, amusement, diversion, pastime, physical activity ...*I'd say football is my favourite sport*...
2 = <u>fun</u>, kidding (*informal*), joking, teasing, ridicule, joshing (*slang, chiefly U.S. & Canad.*), banter, frolic, jest, mirth, merriment, badinage, raillery ...*Had themselves a bit of sport first, didn't they?*...

VERB (*Informal*) = <u>wear</u>, display, flaunt, boast, exhibit, flourish, show off, vaunt ...*He was fat-faced, heavily-built and sported a red moustache*...

➤ **athletic events** ➤ **ballgames** ➤ **boxing weights** ➤ **cricket terms** ➤ **equestrianism** ➤ **football** ➤ **golf terms** ➤ **gymnastic events** ➤ **martial arts rugby terms** ➤ **snooker and billiards terms** ➤ **sports** ➤ **tennis terms** ➤ **water sports** ➤ **winter sports**

sporting = <u>fair</u>, sportsmanlike, game (*informal*), gentlemanly OPPOSITE> unfair

sporty 1 = <u>athletic</u>, outdoor, energetic, hearty ...*He would go to the ballgames with his sporty friends*...
2 = <u>casual</u>, stylish, jazzy (*informal*), loud, informal, trendy (*Brit. informal*), flashy, jaunty, showy, snazzy (*informal*), raffish, rakish, gay ...*The moustache gave him a certain sporty air*...

spot NOUN 1 = <u>mark</u>, stain, speck, scar, flaw, taint, blot, smudge, blemish, daub, speckle, blotch, discoloration ...*The floorboards were covered with white spots*...
2 = <u>pimple</u>, blackhead, pustule, zit (*slang*), plook

Sports

Team sports

American football	football	roller hockey
association football *or* soccer	Gaelic football	rounders
Australian Rules *or* Australian Rules football	goalball	rugby *or* rugby football
baseball	handball	rugby league
bandy	hockey	rugby union
basketball	hurling *or* hurley	shinty
camogie	ice hockey	softball
Canadian football	kabbadi	stool ball
cricket	korfball	tug-of-war
curling	lacrosse	volleyball
five-a-side football	netball	water polo
	polo	

Combat sports

boxing	sambo *or* sambo wrestling	wrestling
fencing	savate	

Other sports http://dmoz.org/Sports/

angling *or* fishing	fox-hunting	quoits
archery	gliding	rackets
badminton	golf	real tennis
ballooning	greyhound racing	rhythmic gymnastics
billiards	gymnastics	rock climbing
boules	hang gliding	roller skating
bowls	jai alai	shooting
bullfighting	lawn tennis	skeet
candlepins	modern pentathlon	skittles
clay pigeon shooting	mountaineering	skydiving
cockfighting	paddleball	snooker
coursing	parachuting	squash *or* squash rackets
croquet	paragliding	table tennis
cycling	parascending	tennis
cyclo-cross	paraskiing	tenpin bowling
darts	pelota	trampolining
decathlon	pétanque	trapshooting
falconry	pigeon racing	triathlon
fives	pool	weightlifting
fly-fishing	potholing	

(*Scot.*), acne ...*Never squeeze blackheads, spots or pimples*...

3 (*Informal, chiefly Brit.*) = <u>bit</u>, little, drop, bite, splash, small amount, tad, morsel ...*We've given all the club members tea, coffee and a spot of lunch*...

4 = <u>place</u>, situation, site, point, position, scene, location, locality ...*They returned to the remote spot where they had left him*...

5 (*Informal*) = <u>predicament</u>, trouble, difficulty, mess, plight, hot water (*informal*), quandary, tight spot ...*In a tight spot there is no one I would sooner see than Frank*...

VERB 1 = <u>see</u>, observe, catch sight of, identify, sight, recognize, detect, make out, pick out, discern, behold (*archaic or literary*), espy, descry ...*He left the party seconds before smoke was spotted coming up the stairs*...

2 = <u>mark</u>, stain, dot, soil, dirty, scar, taint, tarnish, blot, fleck, spatter, sully, speckle, besmirch, splodge, splotch, mottle, smirch ...*a brown shoe spotted with paint*...

PHRASES a soft spot for = <u>fondness for</u>, liking for, attachment to, love of, taste for, preference for, penchant for, weakness for, predilection for, fancy for, partiality for ...*You've still got a soft spot for red-haired colleens*...

spotless 1 = <u>clean</u>, immaculate, impeccable, white, pure, virgin, shining, gleaming, snowy, flawless, faultless, unblemished, virginal, unsullied, untarnished, unstained ...*Every morning cleaners make sure everything is spotless*... OPPOSITE> dirty

2 = <u>blameless</u>, squeaky-clean, unimpeachable, innocent, chaste, irreproachable, above reproach ...*He was determined to leave a spotless record behind him*... OPPOSITE> reprehensible

spotlight NOUN 1 = <u>search light</u>, headlight, floodlight, headlamp, foglamp ...*the light of a powerful spotlight from a police helicopter*...

2 = <u>attention</u>, limelight, public eye, interest, fame, notoriety, public attention ...*Webb is back in the spotlight*...

VERB = <u>highlight</u>, feature, draw attention to, focus attention on, accentuate, point up, give prominence to, throw into relief ...*a new book spotlighting female entrepreneurs*...

spot-on (*Informal*) = <u>accurate</u>, exact, precise, right, correct, on the money (*U.S.*), unerring, punctual (to the minute), hitting the nail on the head (*informal*), on the bull's-eye (*informal*)

spotted = <u>speckled</u>, dotted, flecked, pied, specked, mottled, dappled, polka-dot

spotty 1 = <u>pimply</u>, pimpled, blotchy, poor-complexioned, plooky-faced (*Scot.*) ...*She was rather fat, and her complexion was muddy and spotty*...

2 = <u>inconsistent</u>, irregular, erratic, uneven, fluctuating, patchy, sporadic ...*His attendance record was spotty*...

spouse = <u>partner</u>, mate, husband *or* wife, companion, consort, significant other (*U.S. informal*), better half (*humorous*), her indoors (*Brit. slang*),

helpmate

spout 1 = <u>stream</u>, shoot, gush, spurt, jet, spray, surge, discharge, erupt, emit, squirt ...*In a storm, water spouts out of the blowhole just like a whale*...

2 (*Informal*) = <u>hold forth</u>, talk, rant, go on (*informal*), rabbit (on) (*Brit. informal*), ramble (on), pontificate, declaim, spiel (*informal*), expatiate, orate, speechify ...*She would go red in the face and start to spout*...

sprawl = <u>loll</u>, slump, lounge, flop, slouch

spray¹ NOUN 1 = <u>droplets</u>, moisture, fine mist, drizzle, spindrift, spoondrift ...*The moon was casting a rainbow through the spray of the waterfall*...

2 = <u>aerosol</u>, sprinkler, atomizer ...*an insect-repellent spray*...

VERB = <u>scatter</u>, shower, sprinkle, diffuse ...*A shower of seeds sprayed into the air and fell on the grass*... ...*We sprayed the area with weedkiller*...

spray² = <u>sprig</u>, floral arrangement, branch, bough, shoot, corsage ...*a small spray of freesias*...

spread VERB 1 = <u>open (out)</u>, extend, stretch, unfold, sprawl, unfurl, fan out, unroll ...*He spread his coat over the bed*...

2 = <u>extend</u>, open, stretch ...*He stepped back and spread his hands wide*...

3 = <u>coat</u>, cover, smear, smother ...*Spread the bread with the cream cheese*...

4 = <u>smear</u>, apply, rub, put, smooth, plaster, daub ...*Spread the cream over the skin and allow it to remain for 12 hours*...

5 = <u>grow</u>, increase, develop, expand, widen, mushroom, escalate, proliferate, multiply, broaden ...*The sense of fear is spreading in residential neighbourhoods*...

6 = <u>space out</u>, stagger ...*The course is spread over a five-week period*...

7 = <u>circulate</u>, publish, broadcast, advertise, distribute, scatter, proclaim, transmit, make public, publicize, propagate, disseminate, promulgate, make known, blazon, bruit ...*Someone has been spreading rumours about us*... OPPOSITE> suppress

8 = <u>diffuse</u>, cast, shed, radiate ...*The overall flaring tends to spread light*...

NOUN 1 = <u>increase</u>, development, advance, spreading, expansion, transmission, proliferation, advancement, escalation, diffusion, dissemination, dispersal, suffusion ...*The greatest hope for reform is the gradual spread of information*...

2 = <u>extent</u>, reach, span, stretch, sweep, compass ...*The rhododendron grows to 18 inches with a spread of 24 inches*...

3 (*Informal*) = <u>feast</u>, banquet, blowout (*slang*), repast, array ...*They put on a spread of sandwiches for us*...

spree 1 = <u>fling</u>, binge (*informal*), orgy, splurge ...*They went on a spending spree*...

2 = <u>binge</u>, bender (*informal*), orgy, revel (*informal*), jag (*slang*), junketing, beano (*Brit. slang*), debauch, carouse, bacchanalia, carousal ...*They attacked two London shops after a drinking spree*...

sprightly = <u>lively</u>, spirited, active, energetic,

animated, brisk, nimble, agile, jaunty, gay, perky, vivacious, spry, bright-eyed and bushy-tailed OPPOSITE inactive

spring NOUN **1** = springtime, springtide (*literary*) …*We met again in the spring of 1977…*
2 = source, root, origin, well, beginning, cause, fount, fountainhead, wellspring …*the hidden springs of consciousness…*
3 = flexibility, give (*informal*), bounce, resilience, elasticity, recoil, buoyancy, springiness, bounciness …*Put some spring back into your old sofa…*
VERB **1** = jump, bound, leap, bounce, hop, rebound, vault, recoil …*The lion roared once and sprang…*
2 *often with* **from** = originate, come, derive, start, issue, grow, emerge, proceed, arise, stem, descend, be derived, emanate, be descended …*The art springs from the country's Muslim heritage…*
ADJECTIVE **1** = vernal, springlike …*Walking carefree through the fresh spring rain…*
2 = geyser, hot spring, fount (*literary*), well head, thermal spring …*To the north are the hot springs…*
⟮ **Related Words** ⟯
adjective : vernal

springy = flexible, elastic, resilient, bouncy, rubbery, spongy

sprinkle = scatter, dust, strew, pepper, shower, spray, powder, dredge

sprinkling = scattering, dusting, scatter, few, dash, handful, sprinkle, smattering, admixture

sprint = run, race, shoot, tear, dash, barrel (along) (*informal, chiefly U.S. & Canad.*), dart, hare (*Brit. informal*), whizz (*informal*), scamper, hotfoot, go like a bomb (*Brit. & N.Z. informal*), put on a burst of speed, go at top speed

sprite = spirit, fairy, elf, nymph, brownie, pixie, apparition, imp, goblin, leprechaun, peri, dryad, naiad, sylph, Oceanid (*Greek myth*)

sprout 1 = germinate, bud, shoot, push, spring, vegetate …*It only takes a few days for beans to sprout…*
2 = grow, develop, blossom, ripen …*Leaf-shoots were beginning to sprout on the hawthorn…*

spruce = smart, trim, neat, elegant, dainty, dapper, natty (*informal*), well-groomed, well turned out, trig (*archaic or dialect*), as if you had just stepped out of a bandbox, soigné *or* soignée OPPOSITE untidy

spry = active, sprightly, quick, brisk, supple, nimble, agile, nippy (*Brit. informal*) OPPOSITE inactive

spur VERB = incite, drive, prompt, press, urge, stimulate, animate, prod, prick, goad, impel …*His friend's plight had spurred him into taking part…*
NOUN = stimulus, incentive, impetus, motive, impulse, inducement, incitement, kick up the backside (*informal*) …*Redundancy is the spur for many to embark on new careers…*
PHRASES **on the spur of the moment** = on impulse, without thinking, impulsively, on the spot, impromptu, unthinkingly, without planning, impetuously, unpremeditatedly …*They admitted they*

had taken a vehicle on the spur of the moment…

spurious = false, bogus, sham, pretended, artificial, forged, fake, mock, imitation, simulated, contrived, pseudo (*informal*), counterfeit, feigned, ersatz, specious, unauthentic, phoney *or* phony (*informal*) OPPOSITE genuine

spurn = reject, slight, scorn, rebuff, put down, snub, disregard, despise, disdain, repulse, cold-shoulder, kick in the teeth (*slang*), turn your nose up at (*informal*), contemn (*formal*) OPPOSITE accept

spurt VERB = gush, shoot, burst, jet, surge, erupt, spew, squirt …*I saw flames spurt from the roof…*
NOUN **1** = gush, jet, burst, spray, surge, eruption, squirt …*A spurt of diesel came from one valve and none from the other…*
2 = burst, rush, surge, fit, access, spate …*I flushed bright red as a spurt of anger flashed through me…*

spy NOUN = undercover agent, secret agent, double agent, secret service agent, foreign agent, mole, fifth columnist, nark (*Brit., Austral., & N.Z. slang*) …*He was jailed for five years as an alleged British spy…*
VERB **1** = be a spy, snoop (*informal*), gather intelligence …*I never agreed to spy for the United States…*
2 *usually with* **on** = watch, follow, shadow, tail (*informal*), trail, keep watch on, keep under surveillance …*He had his wife spied on for evidence in a divorce case…*
3 = catch sight of, see, spot, notice, sight, observe, glimpse, behold (*archaic or literary*), set eyes on, espy, descry …*He was walking down the street when he spied an old freind…*

spying = espionage, reconnaissance, infiltration, undercover work

squabble VERB = quarrel, fight, argue, row, clash, dispute, scrap (*informal*), fall out (*informal*), brawl, spar, wrangle, bicker, have words, fight like cat and dog, go at it hammer and tongs …*Mother is devoted to Dad although they squabble all the time…*
NOUN = quarrel, fight, row, argument, dispute, set-to (*informal*), scrap (*informal*), disagreement, barney (*informal*), spat, difference of opinion, tiff, bagarre (*French*) …*There have been minor squabbles about phone bills…*

squad = team, group, band, company, force, troop, crew, gang

squalid 1 = dirty, filthy, seedy, sleazy, sordid, low, nasty, foul, disgusting, run-down, decayed, repulsive, poverty-stricken, unclean, fetid, slovenly, skanky (*slang*), slummy, yucky *or* yukky (*slang*), yucko (*Austral. slang*), festy (*Austral. slang*) …*The migrants have been living in squalid conditions…* OPPOSITE hygienic
2 = unseemly, sordid, inappropriate, unsuitable, out of place, improper, undignified, disreputable, unbecoming, unrefined, out of keeping, discreditable, indelicate, in poor taste, indecorous, unbefitting …*the squalid pursuit of profit…*

squalor = filth, wretchedness, sleaziness, decay,

foulness, slumminess, squalidness, meanness OPPOSITE> luxury

squander = <u>waste</u>, spend, fritter away, blow (*slang*), consume, scatter, run through, lavish, throw away, misuse, dissipate, expend, misspend, be prodigal with, frivol away, spend like water OPPOSITE> save

square NOUN 1 = <u>town square</u>, close, quad, market square, quadrangle, village square ...*The house is located in one of Pimlico's prettiest squares...*
2 (*Informal*) = <u>conservative</u>, dinosaur, traditionalist, die-hard, stick-in-the-mud (*informal*), fuddy-duddy (*informal*), old buffer (*Brit. informal*), antediluvian, back number (*informal*), (old) fogey ...*I'm a square, man. I adore Steely Dan...*
ADJECTIVE 1 = <u>fair</u>, just, straight, genuine, decent, ethical, straightforward, upright, honest, equitable, upfront (*informal*), on the level (*informal*), kosher (*informal*), dinkum (*Austral. & N.Z. informal*), above board, fair and square, on the up and up ...*We are asking for a square deal...*
2 (*Informal*) = <u>old-fashioned</u>, straight (*slang*), conservative, conventional, dated, bourgeois, out of date, stuffy, behind the times, strait-laced, out of the ark (*informal*), Pooterish ...*I felt so square in my three-piece suit...* OPPOSITE> fashionable
VERB *often with* **with** = <u>agree</u>, match, fit, accord, correspond, tally, conform, reconcile, harmonize ...*His dreams did not square with reality...*

squash 1 = <u>crush</u>, press, flatten, mash, pound, smash, distort, pulp, compress, stamp on, trample down ...*She made clay models and squashed them flat again...*
2 = <u>suppress</u>, put down (*slang*), quell, silence, sit on (*informal*), crush, quash, annihilate ...*The troops would stay in position to squash the first murmur of trouble...*
3 = <u>embarrass</u>, put down, humiliate, shame, disgrace, degrade, mortify, debase, discomfit, take the wind out of someone's sails, put (someone) in his (*or* her) place, take down a peg (*informal*) ...*Worried managers would be sacked or simply squashed...*

squawk VERB 1 = <u>cry</u>, crow, screech, hoot, yelp, cackle ...*I threw pebbles at the hens, and that made them jump and squawk...*
2 (*Informal*) = <u>complain</u>, protest, squeal (*informal, chiefly Brit.*), kick up a fuss (*informal*), raise Cain (*slang*) ...*He squawked that the deal was a double cross...*
NOUN 1 = <u>cry</u>, crow, screech, hoot, yelp, cackle ...*rising steeply into the air with an angry squawk...*
2 = <u>scream</u>, cry, yell, wail, shriek, screech, squeal, yelp, yowl ...*She gave a loud squawk when the water was poured on her...*

squeak = <u>squeal</u>, pipe, peep, shrill, whine, yelp

squeal VERB 1 = <u>scream</u>, yell, shriek, screech, yelp, wail, yowl ...*Jennifer squealed with delight and hugged me...*
2 (*Informal, chiefly Brit.*) = <u>complain</u>, protest, moan, squawk (*informal*), kick up a fuss (*informal*) ...*They*

went squealing to the European Commission...
3 (*Slang*) = <u>inform on</u>, grass (*Brit. slang*), betray, shop (*slang, chiefly Brit.*), sing (*slang, chiefly U.S.*), peach (*slang*), tell all, spill the beans (*informal*), snitch (*slang*), blab, rat on (*informal*), sell (someone) down the river (*informal*), blow the gaff (*Brit. slang*), spill your guts (*slang*), dob in (*Austral. slang*) ...*There was no question of squealing to the police...*
NOUN = <u>scream</u>, shriek, screech, yell, scream, shriek, wail, yelp, yowl ...*At that moment there was a squeal of brakes... ...the squeal of piglets...*

squeamish 1 = <u>queasy</u>, sick, nauseous, queer, sickish, qualmish ...*I feel squeamish at the sight of blood...* OPPOSITE> strong-stomached
2 = <u>fastidious</u>, particular, delicate, nice (*rare*), scrupulous, prudish, prissy (*informal*), finicky, strait-laced, punctilious ...*A meeting with this man is not for the socially squeamish...* OPPOSITE> coarse

squeeze VERB 1 = <u>press</u>, crush, squash, pinch ...*Dip the bread in the water and squeeze it dry...*
2 = <u>clutch</u>, press, grip, crush, pinch, squash, nip, compress, wring ...*He squeezed her arm reassuringly...*
3 = <u>extract</u>, force, press, express ...*Joe squeezed some juice from the oranges...*
4 = <u>cram</u>, press, crowd, force, stuff, pack, jam, thrust, ram, wedge, jostle ...*Somehow they managed to squeeze into the tight space...*
5 = <u>pressurize</u>, lean on (*informal*), bring pressure to bear on, milk, bleed (*informal*), oppress, wrest, extort, put the squeeze on (*informal*), put the screws on (*informal*) ...*The investigators are accused of squeezing the residents for information...*
6 = <u>hug</u>, embrace, cuddle, clasp, enfold, hold tight ...*He longed to just scoop her up and squeeze her...*
NOUN 1 = <u>press</u>, grip, clasp, crush, pinch, squash, nip, wring
2 = <u>crush</u>, jam, squash, press, crowd, congestion ...*The lift holds six people, but it's a bit of a squeeze...*
3 = <u>hug</u>, embrace, cuddle, hold, clasp, handclasp ...*She gave her teddy bear a squeeze...*

squint VERB = <u>peer</u>, screw up your eyes, narrow your eyes, look through narrowed eyes ...*The girl squinted at the photograph...*
NOUN = <u>cross eyes</u>, strabismus ...*she had a bad squint in her right eye...*

squirm = <u>wriggle</u>, twist, writhe, shift, flounder, wiggle, fidget

squirt VERB = <u>spurt</u>, shoot, gush, burst, jet, surge, erupt, spew ...*The water squirted from its throat...*
NOUN = <u>spurt</u>, jet, burst, gush, surge, eruption ...*a squirt of air freshener...*

stab VERB = <u>pierce</u>, cut, gore, run through, stick, injure, wound, knife, thrust, spear, jab, puncture, bayonet, transfix, impale, spill blood ...*Somebody stabbed him in the stomach...*
NOUN 1 (*Informal*) = <u>attempt</u>, go, try, shot (*informal*), crack (*informal*), essay (*informal*), endeavour ...*Several times tennis stars have had a stab at*

acting…

2 = twinge, prick, pang, ache …*a stab of pain just above his eye…*

PHRASES **stab someone in the back** = betray, double-cross (*informal*), sell out (*informal*), sell, let down, inform on, do the dirty on (*Brit. slang*), break faith with, play false, give the Judas kiss to, dob in (*Austral. slang*) …*She has been stabbed in the back by her supposed 'friends'…*

stability = firmness, strength, soundness, durability, permanence, solidity, constancy, steadiness, steadfastness OPPOSITE instability

stable 1 = secure, lasting, strong, sound, fast, sure, established, permanent, constant, steady, enduring, reliable, abiding, durable, deep-rooted, well-founded, steadfast, immutable, unwavering, invariable, unalterable, unchangeable …*a stable marriage…* OPPOSITE insecure
2 = well-balanced, balanced, sensible, reasonable, rational, mentally sound …*Their characters are fully formed and they are both very stable children…*
3 = solid, firm, secure, fixed, substantial, sturdy, durable, well-made, well-built, immovable, built to last …*This structure must be stable…* OPPOSITE unstable

stack NOUN **1** = pile, heap, mountain, mass, load, cock, rick, clamp (*Brit. agriculture*), mound …*There were stacks of books on the bedside table and floor…*
2 = lot, mass, load (*informal*), ton (*informal*), heap (*informal*), large quantity, great amount …*If the job's that good, you'll have stacks of money…*
VERB = pile, heap up, load, assemble, accumulate, amass, stockpile, bank up …*They are stacked neatly in piles of three…*

staff 1 = workers, employees, personnel, workforce, team, organization …*The staff were very good…*
2 = stick, pole, rod, prop, crook, cane, stave, wand, sceptre …*We carried a staff that was notched at various lengths…*

stage NOUN = step, leg, phase, point, level, period, division, length, lap, juncture …*the final stage of the tour…*
VERB **1** = present, produce, perform, put on, do, give, play …*She staged her first play in the late 1970s…*
2 = organize, mount, arrange, lay on, orchestrate, engineer …*At the middle of this year the government staged a huge military parade…*

stagger 1 = totter, reel, sway, falter, lurch, wobble, waver, teeter …*He was staggering and had to lean on the bar…*
2 = astound, amaze, stun, surprise, shock, shake, overwhelm, astonish, confound, take (someone) aback, bowl over (*informal*), stupefy, strike (someone) dumb, throw off balance, give (someone) a shock, dumbfound, nonplus, flabbergast, take (someone's) breath away …*The whole thing staggers me…*

stagnant 1 = stale, still, standing, quiet, sluggish, motionless, brackish …*Mosquitoes have been thriving in stagnant water on building sites…* OPPOSITE flowing

2 = inactive, declining, stagnating, slow, depressed, sluggish, slow-moving …*Mass movements are often a factor in the awakening of stagnant societies…*

stagnate 1 = vegetate, decline, deteriorate, rot, decay, idle, rust, languish, stand still, fester, go to seed, lie fallow …*His career had stagnated…*
2 = fester, become stale, become stagnant, become trapped, putrefy, stop flowing, become foul …*They do not like water gathering round their roots and stagnating…*

staid = sedate, serious, sober, quiet, calm, grave, steady, composed, solemn, demure, decorous, self-restrained, set in your ways OPPOSITE wild

stain NOUN **1** = mark, spot, blot, blemish, discoloration, smirch …*a black stain…*
2 = stigma, shame, disgrace, slur, reproach, blemish, dishonour, infamy, blot on the escutcheon …*a stain on the honour of its war dead…*
3 = dye, colour, tint …*Give each surface two coats of stain…*
VERB **1** = mark, soil, discolour, dirty, tarnish, tinge, spot, blot, blemish, smirch …*Some foods can stain teeth, as of course can smoking…*
2 = dye, colour, tint …*a technique biologists use to stain proteins…*
3 = disgrace, taint, blacken, sully, corrupt, contaminate, deprave, defile, besmirch, drag through the mud …*It was too late. Their reputation had been stained…*

stake¹ NOUN = pole, post, spike, stick, pale, paling, picket, stave, palisade …*Drive in a stake before planting the tree…*
VERB = support, secure, prop, brace, tie up, tether …*The plants are susceptible to wind, and should be well staked…*
PHRASES **stake something out** = lay claim to, define, outline, mark out, demarcate, delimit …*The time has come for Hindus to stake out their claim to their own homeland…*

stake² NOUN = bet, ante, wager, chance, risk, venture, hazard …*The game was usually played for high stakes between two large groups…*
VERB **1** = bet, gamble, wager, chance, risk, venture, hazard, jeopardize, imperil, put on the line …*He has staked his reputation on the outcome…*
2 = interest, share, involvement, claim, concern, investment …*a stake in the plot…*
PHRASES **at stake** = to lose, at risk, being risked …*The tension was naturally high for a game with so much at stake…*

stale 1 = old, hard, dry, decayed, fetid …*a lump of stale bread…* OPPOSITE fresh
2 = musty, stagnant, fusty …*the smell of stale sweat…*
3 = tasteless, flat, sour, insipid …*The place smelled of stale beer and dusty carpets…*
4 = unoriginal, banal, trite, common, flat, stereotyped, commonplace, worn-out, antiquated, threadbare, old hat, insipid, hackneyed, overused, repetitious, platitudinous, cliché-ridden …*repeating stale jokes to*

kill the time… OPPOSITE ▷ original

stalemate = <u>deadlock</u>, draw, tie, impasse, standstill

stalk 1 = <u>pursue</u>, follow, track, hunt, shadow, tail (*informal*), haunt, creep up on …*He stalks his victims like a hunter after a deer…*
2 = <u>march</u>, pace, stride, strut, flounce …*If his patience is tried at meetings he has been known to stalk out…*

stall VERB 1 = <u>hinder</u>, obstruct, impede, block, check, arrest, halt, slow down, hamper, thwart, sabotage …*an attempt to stall the negotiations…*
2 = <u>play for time</u>, delay, hedge, procrastinate, stonewall, beat about the bush (*informal*), temporize, drag your feet …*Thomas had spent all week stalling over a decision…*
3 = <u>hold up</u>, delay, detain, divert, distract …*Shop manager Brian Steel stalled the man until the police arrived…*
4 = <u>stop dead</u>, jam, seize up, catch, stick, stop short …*The engine stalled…*
NOUN 1 = <u>stand</u>, table, counter, booth, kiosk …*market stalls selling local fruits…*
2 = <u>enclosure</u>, pen, coop, corral, sty …*mucking out the animal stalls…*

stalwart 1 = <u>loyal</u>, faithful, strong, firm, true, constant, resolute, dependable, steadfast, true-blue, tried and true …*a stalwart supporter of the colonial government…*
2 = <u>strong</u>, strapping, robust, athletic, vigorous, rugged, manly, hefty (*informal*), muscular, sturdy, stout, husky (*informal*), beefy (*informal*), lusty, sinewy, brawny …*I was never in any danger with my stalwart bodyguard around me…* OPPOSITE ▷ puny

stamina = <u>staying power</u>, endurance, resilience, force, power, energy, strength, resistance, grit, vigour, tenacity, power of endurance, indefatigability, lustiness

stammer VERB = <u>stutter</u>, falter, splutter, pause, hesitate, hem and haw, stumble over your words …*She stammered her way through an introduction…*
NOUN = <u>speech impediment</u>, stutter, speech defect …*A speech-therapist cured his stammer…*

stamp NOUN 1 = <u>imprint</u>, mark, brand, cast, mould, signature, earmark, hallmark …*You may live only where the stamp in your passport says you may…*
2 = <u>stomp</u>, stump, clump, tramp, clomp …*the stamp of feet on the stairs…*
3 = <u>type</u>, sort, kind, form, cut, character, fashion, cast, breed, description …*Montgomerie's style is of a different stamp…*
VERB 1 = <u>print</u>, mark, fix, impress, mould, imprint, engrave, inscribe …*'Eat before July 14' was stamped on the label…*
2 = <u>stomp</u>, stump, clump, tramp, clomp …*She stamped her feet on the pavement to keep out the cold…*
3 = <u>trample</u>, step, tread, crush …*He received a ban last week after stamping on the referee's foot…*
4 = <u>identify</u>, mark, brand, label, reveal, exhibit, betray, pronounce, show to be, categorize, typecast …*They had stamped me as a bad woman…*
PHRASES **stamp something out** = <u>eliminate</u>, destroy, eradicate, crush, suppress, put down, put out, scotch, quell, extinguish, quench, extirpate …*on-the-spot fines to stamp the problems out…*

stampede NOUN = <u>rush</u>, charge, flight, scattering, rout …*There was a stampede for the exit…*
VERB = <u>bolt</u>, run, charge, race, career, rush, dash …*The crowd stampeded and many were crushed or trampled underfoot…*

stance 1 = <u>attitude</u>, stand, position, viewpoint, standpoint …*They have maintained a consistently neutral stance…*
2 = <u>posture</u>, carriage, bearing, deportment …*The woman detective shifted her stance from one foot to another…*

stand VERB 1 = <u>be upright</u>, be erect, be vertical …*She was standing beside my bed staring down at me…*
2 = <u>get to your feet</u>, rise, stand up, straighten up …*Becker stood and shook hands with Ben…*
3 = <u>be located</u>, be, sit, perch, nestle, be positioned, be sited, be perched, be situated *or* located …*The house stands alone on top of a small hill…*
4 = <u>be valid</u>, be in force, continue, stay, exist, prevail, remain valid …*The supreme court says the convictions still stand…*
5 = <u>put</u>, place, position, set, mount …*Stand the plant in the open in a sunny, sheltered place…*
6 = <u>sit</u>, rest, mellow, maturate …*The salad improves if made in the open and left to stand…*
7 = <u>resist</u>, endure, withstand, wear (*Brit. slang*), weather, undergo, defy, tolerate, stand up to, hold out against, stand firm against …*Ancient wisdom has stood the test of time…*
8 = <u>tolerate</u>, bear, abide, suffer, stomach, endure, brook, hack (*slang*), submit to, thole (*dialect*) …*He hates vegetables and can't stand curry…*
9 = <u>take</u>, bear, handle, cope with, experience, sustain, endure, undergo, put up with (*informal*), withstand, countenance …*I can't stand any more. I'm going to run away…*
NOUN 1 = <u>position</u>, attitude, stance, opinion, determination, standpoint, firm stand …*His tough stand won some grudging admiration…*
2 = <u>stall</u>, booth, kiosk, table …*She bought a hot dog from a stand on a street corner…*
3 = <u>grandstand</u> …*The people in the stands are cheering with all their might…*
4 = <u>support</u>, base, platform, place, stage, frame, rack, bracket, tripod, dais, trivet …*The teapot came with a stand to catch the drips…*
PHRASES **stand by** 1 = <u>be prepared</u>, wait, stand ready, prepare yourself, wait in the wings …*Stand by for details…* 2 = <u>look on</u>, watch, not lift a finger, wait, turn a blind eye …*The police just stood by and watched as the missiles rained down on us…* ◆ **stand by someone** = <u>support</u>, back, champion, defend, take (someone's) part, uphold, befriend, be loyal to, stick up for (*informal*) …*I wouldn't break the law for a*

friend, but I would stand by her if she did… ◆ **stand by something** = <u>support</u>, maintain, defend, champion, justify, sustain, endorse, assert, uphold, vindicate, stand up for, espouse, speak up for, stick up for (*informal*) *…The decision has been made and I have got to stand by it…* ◆ **stand for something** 1 = <u>represent</u>, mean, signify, denote, indicate, exemplify, symbolize, betoken *…What does EEC stand for?…* 2 (*Informal*) = <u>tolerate</u>, suffer, bear, endure, put up with, wear (*Brit. informal*), brook, lie down under (*informal*) *…It's outrageous, and we won't stand for it any more…* ◆ **stand in for someone** = <u>be a substitute for</u>, represent, cover for, take the place of, replace, understudy, hold the fort for, do duty for, deputize for *…I had to stand in for her on Tuesday when she didn't show up…* ◆ **stand out** 1 = <u>be conspicuous</u>, be striking, be prominent, be obvious, be highlighted, attract attention, catch the eye, be distinct, stick out like a sore thumb (*informal*), stare you in the face (*informal*), be thrown into relief, bulk large, stick out a mile (*informal*), leap to the eye *…Every tree, wall and fence stood out against dazzling white fields…* 2 = <u>project</u>, protrude, bristle *…Her hair stood out in spikes…* ◆ **stand up for something** or **someone** = <u>support</u>, champion, defend, uphold, side with, stick up for (*informal*), come to the defence of *…They stood up for what they believed to be right…* ◆ **stand up to something** or **someone** 1 = <u>withstand</u>, take, bear, weather, cope with, resist, endure, tolerate, hold out against, stand firm against *…Is this building going to stand up to the strongest gales?…* 2 = <u>resist</u>, oppose, confront, tackle, brave, defy *…Women are now aware of their rights and are prepared to stand up to their employers…*

standard NOUN 1 = <u>level</u>, grade *…There will be new standards of hospital cleanliness…*
2 = <u>criterion</u>, measure, guideline, example, model, average, guide, pattern, sample, par, norm, gauge, benchmark, yardstick, touchstone *…systems that were by later standards absurdly primitive…*
3 *often plural* = <u>principles</u>, ideals, morals, rule, ethics, canon, moral principles, code of honour *…My father has always had high moral standards…*
4 = <u>flag</u>, banner, pennant, colours, ensign, pennon *…a gleaming limousine bearing the royal standard…* ADJECTIVE 1 = <u>usual</u>, normal, customary, set, stock, average, popular, basic, regular, typical, prevailing, orthodox, staple *…It was standard practice for them to advise in cases of murder…* OPPOSITE⟩ unusual
2 = <u>accepted</u>, official, established, classic, approved, recognized, definitive, authoritative *…a standard text in several languages…* OPPOSITE⟩ unofficial

standardize = <u>bring into line</u>, stereotype, regiment, assimilate, mass-produce, institutionalize

stand-in = <u>substitute</u>, deputy, replacement, reserve, surrogate, understudy, locum, stopgap

standing NOUN 1 = <u>status</u>, position, station, footing, condition, credit, rank, reputation, eminence, estimation, repute *…He has improved his country's standing abroad…*

2 = <u>duration</u>, existence, experience, continuance *…My girlfriend of long standing left me…* ADJECTIVE 1 = <u>permanent</u>, lasting, fixed, regular, repeated, perpetual *…a standing offer…*
2 = <u>upright</u>, erect, vertical, rampant (*Heraldry*), perpendicular, upended *…standing stones…*

standpoint = <u>point of view</u>, position, angle, viewpoint, stance, vantage point

staple = <u>principal</u>, chief, main, key, basic, essential, primary, fundamental, predominant

star NOUN 1 = <u>heavenly body</u>, sun, celestial body *…The nights were pure with cold air and lit with stars…*
2 = <u>celebrity</u>, big name, celeb (*informal*), megastar (*informal*), name, draw, idol, luminary *…Not all football stars are ill-behaved louts…*
3 = <u>leading man</u> *or* <u>lady</u>, lead, hero *or* heroine, principal, main attraction *…She could play opposite the other star of the film…* PLURAL NOUN = <u>horoscope</u>, forecast, astrological chart *…There was nothing in my stars to say I'd have problems…*
VERB = <u>play the lead</u>, appear, feature, perform *…He's starred in dozens of films…*
ADJECTIVE = <u>leading</u>, major, principal, celebrated, brilliant, well-known, prominent, paramount, illustrious *…He was the school's star pupil…*

(*Related Words*)
adjectives: astral, sidereal, stellar
➤ **stars and constellations**

starchy = <u>formal</u>, stiff, stuffy, conventional, precise, prim, punctilious, ceremonious

stare = <u>gaze</u>, look, goggle, watch, gape, eyeball (*slang*), ogle, gawp (*Brit. slang*), gawk, rubberneck (*slang*)

stark ADJECTIVE 1 = <u>plain</u>, simple, harsh, basic, bare, grim, straightforward, blunt, bald *…The stark truth is that we are paying more now than we ever were…*
2 = <u>sharp</u>, clear, striking, distinct, clear-cut *…in stark contrast…*
3 = <u>austere</u>, severe, plain, bare, harsh, unadorned *…the stark, white, characterless fireplace in the drawing room…*
4 = <u>bleak</u>, grim, barren, hard, cold, depressing, dreary, desolate, forsaken, godforsaken, drear (*literary*) *…a stark landscape of concrete, wire and utility equipment…*
5 = <u>absolute</u>, pure, sheer, utter, downright, patent, consummate, palpable, out-and-out, flagrant, unmitigated, unalloyed, arrant *…They are motivated, he said, by stark fear…*
ADVERB = <u>absolutely</u>, quite, completely, clean, entirely, altogether, wholly, utterly *…I gasped again. He must have gone stark staring mad…*

start VERB 1 = <u>set about</u>, begin, proceed, embark upon, take the plunge (*informal*), take the first step, make a beginning, put your hand to the plough (*informal*) *…She started cleaning the kitchen…* OPPOSITE⟩ stop
2 = <u>begin</u>, arise, originate, issue, appear, commence,

Stars and constellations http://www.astro.wisc.edu/~dolan/constellations/

Stars

Aldebaran	Sirius, the Dog Star, Canicula, *or* Sothis
Betelgeuse *or* Betelgeux	the Sun
Polaris, the Pole Star, *or* the North Star	

Constellations

Latin name	*English name*	*Latin name*	*English name*
Andromeda	Andromeda	Leo	Lion
Antila	Air Pump	Leo Minor	Little Lion
Apus	Bird of Paradise	Lepus	Hare
Aquarius	Water Bearer	Libra	Scales
Aquila	Eagle	Lupus	Wolf
Ara	Altar	Lynx	Lynx
Aries	Ram	Lyra	Harp
Auriga	Charioteer	Mensa	Table
Boötes	Herdsman	Microscopium	Microscope
Caelum	Chisel	Monoceros	Unicorn
Camelopardalis	Giraffe	Musca	Fly
Cancer	Crab	Norma	Level
Canes Venatici	Hunting Dogs	Octans	Octant
Canis Major	Great Dog	Ophiuchus	Serpent Bearer
Canis Minor	Little Dog	Orion	Orion
Capricornus	Sea Goat	Pavo	Peacock
Carina	Keel	Pegasus	Winged Horse
Cassiopeia	Cassiopeia	Perseus	Perseus
Centaurus	Centaur	Phoenix	Phoenix
Cepheus	Cepheus	Pictor	Easel
Cetus	Whale	Pisces	Fishes
Chamaeleon	Chameleon	Piscis Austrinus	Southern Fish
Circinus	Compasses	Puppis	Ship's Stern
Columba	Dove	Pyxis	Mariner's Compass
Coma Bernices	Bernice's Hair	Reticulum	Net
Corona Australis	Southern Crown	Sagitta	Arrow
Corona Borealis	Northern Crown	Sagittarius	Archer
Corvus	Crow	Scorpius	Scorpion
Crater	Cup	Sculptor	Sculptor
Crux	Southern Cross	Scutum	Shield
Cygnus	Swan	Serpens	Serpent
Delphinus	Dolphin	Sextans	Sextant
Dorado	Swordfish	Taurus	Bull
Draco	Dragon	Telescopium	Telescope
Equuleus	Little Horse	Triangulum	Triangle
Eridanus	River Eridanus	Triangulum Australe	Southern Triangle
Fornax	Furnace	Tucana	Toucan
Gemini	Twins	Ursa Major	Great Bear (contains the Plough *or* (*U.S.*) Big Dipper)
Grus	Crane		
Hercules	Hercules	Ursa Minor	Little Bear *or* (*U.S.*) Little Dipper
Horologium	Clock		
Hydra	Sea Serpent	Vela	Sails
Hydrus	Water Snake	Virgo	Virgin
Indus	Indian	Volans	Flying Fish
Lacerta	Lizard	Vulpecula	Fox

get under way, come into being, come into existence, first see the light of day ...*The fire is thought to have started in an upstairs room...* OPPOSITE end

3 = set in motion, initiate, instigate, open, trigger, kick off (*informal*), originate, get going, engender, kick-start, get (something) off the ground (*informal*), enter upon, get *or* set *or* start the ball rolling ...*Who started the fight?...* OPPOSITE stop

4 = establish, begin, found, father, create, launch, set

up, introduce, institute, pioneer, initiate, inaugurate, lay the foundations of ...*Now is probably as good a time as any to start a business...* OPPOSITE terminate

5 = start up, activate, get something going ...*He started the car, which hummed smoothly...* OPPOSITE turn off

6 = jump, shy, jerk, twitch, flinch, recoil ...*Rachel started at his touch...*

NOUN 1 = beginning, outset, opening, birth,

foundation, dawn, first step(s), onset, initiation, inauguration, inception, commencement, kickoff (*informal*), opening move ...*She demanded to know why she had not been told from the start...* OPPOSITE end

2 = jump, jerk, twitch, spasm, convulsion ...*He gave a start of surprise and astonishment...*

startle = surprise, shock, alarm, frighten, scare, agitate, take (someone) aback, make (someone) jump, give (someone) a turn (*informal*)

startling = surprising, shocking, alarming, extraordinary, sudden, unexpected, staggering, unforeseen, jaw-dropping

starving = hungry, starved, ravenous, famished, hungering, sharp-set, esurient, faint from lack of food, ready to eat a horse (*informal*)

stash (*Informal*) VERB = store, stockpile, save up, hoard, hide, secrete, stow, cache, lay up, salt away, put aside for a rainy day ...*He had stashed money away in secret offshore bank accounts...*

NOUN = hoard, supply, store, stockpile, cache, collection ...*A large stash of drugs had been found aboard the yacht...*

state NOUN **1** = country, nation, land, republic, territory, federation, commonwealth, kingdom, body politic ...*Mexico is a secular state...*

2 = province, region, district, area, territory, federal state ...*Leaders of the Southern States are meeting in Louisville...*

3 = government, ministry, administration, executive, regime, powers-that-be ...*The state does not collect enough revenue to cover its expenditure...*

4 = condition, shape, state of affairs ...*When we moved here the walls and ceiling were in an awful state...*

5 = frame of mind, condition, spirits, attitude, mood, humour ...*When you left our place, you weren't in a fit state to drive...*

6 = ceremony, glory, grandeur, splendour, dignity, majesty, pomp ...*Nelson's body lay in state in the Painted Hall after the battle of Trafalgar...*

7 = circumstances, situation, position, case, pass, mode, plight, predicament ...*You shouldn't be lifting heavy things in your state...*

VERB = say, report, declare, specify, put, present, explain, voice, express, assert, utter, articulate, affirm, expound, enumerate, propound, aver, asseverate ...*Clearly state your address and telephone number...*

PHRASES **in a state** (*Informal*) **1** = distressed, upset, agitated, disturbed, anxious, ruffled, uptight (*informal*), flustered, panic-stricken, het up, all steamed up (*slang*) ...*I was in a terrible state because nobody could understand why I had this illness...*

2 = untidy, disordered, messy, muddled, cluttered, jumbled, in disarray, topsy-turvy, higgledy-piggledy (*informal*) ...*The living room was in a dreadful state...*

➤ **WORD POWER SUPPLEMENT US states**
➤ **WORD POWER SUPPLEMENT Australian states and territories**

stately = grand, majestic, dignified, royal, august, imposing, impressive, elegant, imperial, noble, regal, solemn, lofty, pompous, ceremonious OPPOSITE lowly

statement **1** = announcement, declaration, communication, explanation, communiqué, proclamation, utterance ...*He now disowns that statement, saying he was depressed when he made it...*

2 = account, report, testimony, evidence ...*statements from witnesses to the event...*

state-of-the-art = latest, newest, up-to-date, up-to-the-minute OPPOSITE old-fashioned

static = stationary, still, motionless, fixed, constant, stagnant, inert, immobile, unmoving, stock-still, unvarying, changeless OPPOSITE moving

station NOUN **1** = railway station, stop, stage, halt, terminal, train station, terminus ...*She went with him to the station to see him off...*

2 = headquarters, base, depot ...*He was taken to the police station for questioning...*

3 = channel, wavelength, broadcasting company ...*Which radio station do you usually listen to?...*

4 = position, rank, status, standing, post, situation, grade, sphere ...*The vast majority knew their station in life and kept to it...*

5 = post, place, location, position, situation, seat ...*Police said the bomb was buried in the sand near a lifeguard station...*

VERB = assign, post, locate, set, establish, fix, install, garrison ...*I was stationed there just after the war...*

stationary = motionless, standing, at a standstill, parked, fixed, moored, static, inert, unmoving, stock-still OPPOSITE moving

---

Word Power

stationary – This word, which is always an adjective, is occasionally wrongly used where 'paper products' are meant: *in the stationery* (not *stationary*) *cupboard*.

---

statuesque = well-proportioned, stately, Junoesque, imposing, majestic, dignified, regal

stature **1** = height, build, size ...*She was a little short in stature...*

2 = importance, standing, prestige, size, rank, consequence, prominence, eminence, high station ...*This club has grown in stature over the last 20 years...*

status **1** = position, rank, grade, degree ...*promoted to the status of foreman...*

2 = prestige, standing, authority, influence, weight, reputation, honour, importance, consequence, fame, distinction, eminence, renown, mana (*N.Z.*) ...*She cheated banks to satisfy her desire for money and status...*

3 = state of play, development, progress, condition, evolution, progression ...*Please keep us informed of the status of this project...*

statute = law, act, rule, regulation, decree, ordinance, enactment, edict

staunch = loyal, faithful, stalwart, sure, strong, firm, sound, true, constant, reliable, stout, resolute, dependable, trustworthy, trusty, steadfast, true-blue, immovable, tried and true

stay VERB **1** = remain, continue to be, linger, stand, stop, wait, settle, delay, halt, pause, hover, abide, hang around (*informal*), reside, stay put, bide, loiter, hang in the air, tarry, put down roots, establish yourself ...*Hundreds of people defied army orders to stay at home...* OPPOSITE go
2 *often with **at*** = lodge, visit, sojourn, put up at, be accommodated at ...*He tried to stay at the hotel a few days every year...*
3 = continue, remain, go on, survive, endure ...*Nothing stays the same for long...*
4 = suspend, put off, defer, adjourn, hold over, hold in abeyance, prorogue ...*The finance ministry stayed the execution to avoid upsetting a nervous market...*
NOUN **1** = visit, stop, holiday, stopover, sojourn ...*An experienced Italian guide is provided during your stay...*
2 = postponement, delay, suspension, stopping, halt, pause, reprieve, remission, deferment ...*The court dismissed defence appeals for a permanent stay of execution...*

staying power = endurance, strength, stamina, toughness

steadfast 1 = loyal, faithful, stalwart, staunch, constant, steady, dedicated, reliable, persevering, dependable ...*a steadfast friend...* OPPOSITE undependable
2 = resolute, firm, fast, fixed, stable, intent, single-minded, unwavering, immovable, unflinching, unswerving, unfaltering ...*He remained steadfast in his belief that he had done the right thing...* OPPOSITE irresolute

steady 1 = continuous, even, regular, constant, consistent, persistent, rhythmic, unbroken, habitual, uninterrupted, incessant, ceaseless, unremitting, unwavering, nonstop, unvarying, unfaltering, unfluctuating ...*the steady beat of the drums...* OPPOSITE irregular
2 = stable, fixed, secure, firm, safe, immovable, on an even keel ...*Make sure the camera is steady...* OPPOSITE unstable
3 = regular, established ...*a steady boyfriend...*
4 = dependable, sensible, reliable, balanced, settled, secure, calm, supportive, sober, staunch, serene, sedate, staid, steadfast, level-headed, serious-minded, imperturbable, equable, unchangeable, having both feet on the ground ...*He was firm and steady, unlike other men she knew...* OPPOSITE undependable

steal 1 = take, nick (*slang, chiefly Brit.*), pinch (*informal*), lift (*informal*), cabbage (*Brit. slang*), swipe (*slang*), half-inch (*old-fashioned slang*), heist (*U.S. slang*), embezzle, blag (*slang*), pilfer, misappropriate, snitch (*slang*), purloin, filch, prig (*Brit. slang*), shoplift, thieve, be light-fingered, peculate, walk *or* make off with ...*People who are drug addicts come in and steal stuff...*
2 = copy, take, plagiarize, appropriate, pinch (*informal*), pirate, poach ...*They solved the problem by stealing an idea from nature...*
3 = sneak, slip, creep, flit, tiptoe, slink, insinuate yourself ...*They can steal away at night and join us...*

stealth = secrecy, furtiveness, slyness, sneakiness, unobtrusiveness, stealthiness, surreptitiousness

stealthy = secret, secretive, furtive, sneaking, covert, sly, clandestine, sneaky, skulking, underhand, surreptitious

steamy 1 (*Informal*) = erotic, hot (*slang*), sexy (*informal*), sensual, raunchy (*slang*), lewd, carnal, titillating, prurient, lascivious, lustful, lubricious (*formal or literary*) ...*He'd had a steamy affair with an office colleague...*
2 = muggy, damp, humid, sweaty, like a sauna ...*a steamy café...*

steel yourself = brace yourself, make up your mind, grit your teeth, fortify yourself, harden yourself

steep¹ 1 = sheer, precipitous, perpendicular, abrupt, headlong, vertical ...*a narrow, steep-sided valley...* OPPOSITE gradual
2 = sharp, sudden, abrupt, marked, extreme, distinct ...*Unemployment has shown a steep rise...*
3 (*Informal*) = high, excessive, exorbitant, extreme, stiff, unreasonable, overpriced, extortionate, uncalled-for ...*The annual premium can be a little steep...* OPPOSITE reasonable

steep² = soak, immerse, marinate (*Cookery*), damp, submerge, drench, moisten, macerate, souse, imbrue (*rare*) ...*green beans steeped in olive oil...*

steeped = saturated, pervaded, permeated, filled, infused, imbued, suffused

steer VERB **1** = drive, control, direct, handle, conduct, pilot, govern, be in the driver's seat ...*What is it like to steer a ship of this size?...*
2 = direct, lead, guide, conduct, escort, show in *or* out ...*Nick steered them into the nearest seats...*
PHRASES **steer clear of something** *or* **someone** = avoid, evade, fight shy of, shun, eschew, circumvent, body-swerve (*Scot.*), give a wide berth to, sheer off ...*A lot of people steer clear of these sensitive issues...*

stem¹ NOUN = stalk, branch, trunk, shoot, stock, axis, peduncle ...*He cut the stem for her with his knife and handed her the flower...*
PHRASES **stem from something** = originate from, be caused by, derive from, arise from, flow from, emanate from, develop from, be generated by, be brought about by, be bred by, issue forth from ...*Much of the instability stems from the economic effects of the war...*

stem² = stop, hold back, staunch, stay (*archaic*), check, contain, dam, curb, restrain, bring to a standstill, stanch ...*He was still conscious, trying to stem the bleeding with his right hand...*

stench = stink, whiff (*Brit. slang*), reek, pong (*Brit. informal*), foul smell, niff (*Brit. slang*), malodour, mephitis, noisomeness

step NOUN **1** = pace, stride, footstep ...*I took a step *towards him*…

2 = <u>footfall</u> …*He heard steps in the corridor*…

3 = <u>stair</u>, tread, rung …*He slowly climbed the steps*…

4 = <u>doorstep</u> …*Leave empty milk bottles on the step*…

5 = <u>move</u>, measure, action, means, act, proceeding, procedure, manoeuvre, deed, expedient …*He greeted the agreement as the first step towards peace*…

6 = <u>stage</u>, point, phase …*Aristotle took the scientific approach a step further*…

7 = <u>gait</u>, walk …*He quickened his step*…

8 = <u>level</u>, rank, remove, degree …*This is the final step in the career ladder*…

VERB **1** = <u>walk</u>, pace, tread, move …*the first man to step on the moon*…

2 = <u>stand</u>, stamp, tread, walk …*One of them accidentally stepped on my hand*…

PHRASES **in step** (*Informal*) = <u>in agreement</u>, in harmony, in unison, in line, coinciding, conforming, in conformity …*Now they are more in step and more in love with each other*… ◆ **mind** or **watch your step** (*Informal*) = <u>be careful</u>, take care, look out, be cautious, be discreet, take heed, tread carefully, be canny, be on your guard, mind how you goes, have your wits about you, mind your p's and q's …*Hey! she thought. Watch your step, girl!*… ◆ **out of step** (*Informal*) = <u>in disagreement</u>, out of line, out of phase, out of harmony, incongruous, pulling different ways …*They jogged in silence a while, faces lowered, out of step*… ◆ **step down** or **aside** (*Informal*) = <u>resign</u>, retire, quit, leave, give up, pull out, bow out, abdicate …*Many would prefer to see him step aside in favour of a younger man*… ◆ **step in** (*Informal*) = <u>intervene</u>, take action, become involved, chip in (*informal*), intercede, take a hand …*If no agreement was reached, the army would step in*… ◆ **step something up** = <u>increase</u>, boost, intensify, up, raise, accelerate, speed up, escalate, augment …*Security is being stepped up to deal with the increase in violence*… ◆ **take steps** = <u>take action</u>, act, intervene, move in, take the initiative, take measures …*They agreed to take steps to avoid confrontation*…

stereotype NOUN = <u>formula</u>, cliché, pattern, mould, received idea …*Accents can reinforce a stereotype*… VERB = <u>categorize</u>, typecast, pigeonhole, dub, standardize, take to be, ghettoize, conventionalize …*He was stereotyped by some as a renegade*…

stereotyped = <u>unoriginal</u>, stock, standard, tired, conventional, played out, stale, banal, standardized, mass-produced, corny (*slang*), threadbare, trite, hackneyed, overused, platitudinous, cliché-ridden

sterile 1 = <u>germ-free</u>, antiseptic, sterilized, disinfected, aseptic …*He always made sure that any cuts were protected by sterile dressings*… OPPOSITE unhygienic

2 = <u>barren</u>, infertile, unproductive, childless, infecund …*a sterile male*… OPPOSITE fertile

3 = <u>bare</u>, dry, unproductive, waste, empty, desert, barren, desolate, arid, infertile, unfruitful …*a sterile and barren wasteland*…

sterilize 1 = <u>disinfect</u>, purify, fumigate,

decontaminate, autoclave, sanitize …*Sulphur is also used to sterilize equipment*…

2 = <u>make infertile</u>, hysterectomize, vasectomize …*Just after a birth may seem a logical time to be sterilized*…

sterling = <u>excellent</u>, sound, fine, first-class, superlative

stern 1 = <u>strict</u>, harsh, rigorous, hard, cruel, grim, rigid, relentless, drastic, authoritarian, austere, inflexible, unrelenting, unyielding, unsparing …*He said stern measures would be taken against the killers*… OPPOSITE lenient

2 = <u>severe</u>, serious, forbidding, steely, flinty …*Her father was stern and hard to please*… OPPOSITE friendly

stew NOUN = <u>hash</u>, goulash, ragout, olla, olio, olla podrida …*She served him a bowl of beef stew*… VERB = <u>braise</u>, boil, simmer, casserole …*Stew the apple and blackberries to make a thick pulp*… PHRASES **in a stew** (*Informal*) = <u>troubled</u>, concerned, anxious, worried, fretting, in a panic, in a lather (*informal*) …*Highly charged emotions have you in a stew*…

stick¹ 1 = <u>twig</u>, branch, birch, offshoot …*people carrying bundles of dry sticks to sell for firewood*…

2 = <u>cane</u>, staff, pole, rod, stake, switch, crook, baton, wand, sceptre …*Crowds armed with sticks and stones took to the streets*…

3 (*Slang*) = <u>abuse</u>, criticism, flak (*informal*), blame, knocking (*informal*), hostility, slagging (*slang*), denigration, critical remarks, fault-finding …*It's not motorists who give you the most stick, it's the general public*…

stick² 1 (*Informal*) = <u>put</u>, place, set, position, drop, plant, store, lay, stuff, fix, deposit, install, plonk …*He folded the papers and stuck them in a drawer*…

2 = <u>poke</u>, dig, stab, insert, thrust, pierce, penetrate, spear, prod, jab, transfix …*They stuck a needle in my back*… …*The knife stuck in his chest*…

3 = <u>fasten</u>, fix, bind, hold, bond, attach, hold on, glue, fuse, paste, adhere, affix …*Stick down any loose bits of flooring*…

4 = <u>adhere</u>, cling, cleave, become joined, become cemented, become welded …*The soil sticks to the blade and blocks the plough*…

5 = <u>stay</u>, remain, linger, persist …*That song has stuck in my head for years*…

6 = <u>catch</u>, lodge, jam, stop, clog, snag, be embedded, be bogged down, come to a standstill, become immobilized …*The dagger stuck tightly in the silver scabbard*…

7 (*Slang*) = <u>tolerate</u>, take, stand, stomach, endure, hack (*slang*), abide, bear up under …*How long did you stick that abuse for?*…

PHRASES **stick out** = <u>protrude</u>, stand out, jut out, show, project, bulge, obtrude …*Your label's sticking out*… ◆ **stick something out 1** = <u>offer</u>, present, extend, hold out, advance, reach out, stretch out, proffer …*He stuck his hand out in welcome*…

2 (*Informal*) = <u>endure</u>, bear, put up with (*informal*), weather, take it (*informal*), see through, soldier on, last out, grin and bear it (*informal*) ...*I know the job's tough, but try to stick it out a bit longer*... ◆ **stick to something 1** = keep to, persevere in, cleave to ...*Stick to well-lit roads*... **2** = adhere to, honour, hold to, keep to, abide by, stand by ...*We must stick to the rules*... ◆ **stick up for someone** (*Informal*) = defend, support, champion, uphold, stand up for, take the part *or* side of ...*Thanks for sticking up for me*...

stickler = fanatic, nut (*slang*), maniac (*informal*), purist, perfectionist, pedant, martinet, hard taskmaster, fusspot (*Brit. informal*)

sticky 1 = adhesive, gummed, adherent ...*Peel away the sticky paper*...
2 = gooey, tacky (*informal*), syrupy, viscous, glutinous, gummy, icky (*informal*), gluey, clinging, claggy (*dialect*), viscid ...*a weakness for rich meat dishes and sticky puddings*...
3 (*Informal*) = difficult, awkward, tricky, embarrassing, painful, nasty, delicate, unpleasant, discomforting, hairy (*slang*), thorny, barro (*Austral. slang*) ...*He found himself in a not inconsiderably sticky situation*...
4 = humid, close, sultry, oppressive, sweltering, clammy, muggy ...*sticky days in the middle of August*...

stiff 1 = inflexible, rigid, unyielding, hard, firm, tight, solid, tense, hardened, brittle, taut, solidified, unbending, inelastic ...*The film is crammed with corsets, bustles and stiff collars*... OPPOSITE flexible
2 = unsupple, arthritic, creaky (*informal*), rheumaticky ...*I'm stiff all over right now*... OPPOSITE supple
3 = formal, constrained, forced, laboured, cold, mannered, wooden, artificial, uneasy, chilly, unnatural, austere, pompous, prim, stilted, starchy (*informal*), punctilious, priggish, standoffish, ceremonious, unrelaxed ...*They always seemed a little awkward with each other, a bit stiff and formal*... OPPOSITE informal
4 = vigorous, great, strong ...*The film faces stiff competition for the nomination*...
5 = severe, strict, harsh, hard, heavy, sharp, extreme, cruel, drastic, rigorous, stringent, oppressive, austere, inexorable, pitiless ...*stiff anti-drugs laws*...
6 = strong, fresh, powerful, vigorous, brisk ...*a stiff breeze rustling the trees*...
7 = difficult, hard, tough, exacting, formidable, trying, fatiguing, uphill, arduous, laborious ...*the stiff climb to the finish*...

stifle 1 = suppress, repress, prevent, stop, check, silence, curb, restrain, cover up, gag, hush, smother, extinguish, muffle, choke back ...*Critics have accused them of trying to stifle debate*...
2 = restrain, suppress, repress, smother ...*She makes no attempt to stifle a yawn*...

stigma = disgrace, shame, dishonour, mark, spot, brand, stain, slur, blot, reproach, imputation, smirch

stigmatize = brand, label, denounce, mark, discredit, pillory, defame, cast a slur upon

still ADJECTIVE **1** = motionless, stationary, at rest, calm, smooth, peaceful, serene, tranquil, lifeless, placid,

undisturbed, inert, restful, unruffled, unstirring ...*He sat very still for several minutes*... OPPOSITE moving
2 = silent, quiet, hushed, noiseless, stilly (*poetic*) ...*The night air was very still*... OPPOSITE noisy
VERB = quieten, calm, subdue, settle, quiet, silence, soothe, hush, alleviate, lull, tranquillize ...*Her crying slowly stilled*... ...*The people's voice has been stilled*... OPPOSITE get louder
NOUN (*Poetic*) = stillness, peace, quiet, silence, hush, tranquillity ...*It was the only noise in the still of the night*... OPPOSITE noise
ADVERB **1** = continue to, yet, even now, up until now, up to this time ...*I still dream of home*...
2 = however, but, yet, nevertheless, for all that, notwithstanding ...*Despite the ruling, he was still found guilty*... ...*It won't be easy. Still, I'll do my best*...

stilted = stiff, forced, wooden, laboured, artificial, inflated, constrained, unnatural, high-flown, pompous, pretentious, pedantic, bombastic, grandiloquent, high-sounding, arty-farty (*informal*), fustian OPPOSITE natural

stimulant = pick-me-up, tonic, restorative, upper (*slang*), reviver, bracer (*informal*) (*informal*), energizer, pep pill (*informal*), excitant, analeptic OPPOSITE sedative

stimulate = encourage, inspire, prompt, fire, fan, urge, spur, provoke, turn on (*slang*), arouse, animate, rouse, prod, quicken, inflame, incite, instigate, goad, whet, impel, foment, gee up

stimulating = exciting, inspiring, stirring, provoking, intriguing, rousing, provocative, exhilarating, thought-provoking, galvanic OPPOSITE boring

stimulus = incentive, spur, encouragement, impetus, provocation, inducement, goad, incitement, fillip, shot in the arm (*informal*), clarion call, geeing-up

sting VERB **1** = hurt, burn, wound ...*The nettles stung their legs*...
2 = smart, burn, pain, hurt, tingle ...*His cheeks were stinging from the icy wind*...
3 = anger, provoke, infuriate, incense, gall, inflame, nettle, rile, pique ...*Some of the criticism has really stung him*...
NOUN = smarting, pain, stinging, pricking, soreness, prickling ...*This won't hurt – you will just feel a little sting*...

stingy 1 = mean, penny-pinching (*informal*), miserly, near, parsimonious, scrimping, illiberal, avaricious, niggardly, ungenerous, penurious, tightfisted, close-fisted, mingy (*Brit. informal*), cheeseparing, snoep (*S. African informal*) ...*The West is stingy with aid*...
2 = insufficient, inadequate, meagre, small, pathetic, scant, skimpy, measly (*informal*), scanty, on the small side ...*Many people may consider this a rather stingy amount*...

stink VERB **1** = reek, pong (*Brit. informal*), whiff (*Brit. slang*), stink to high heaven (*informal*), offend the nostrils ...*We all stank and nobody minded*...
2 (*Slang*) = be bad, be no good, be rotten, be offensive, be abhorrent, have a bad name, be

detestable, be held in disrepute ...*I think their methods stink...*

NOUN **1** = <u>stench</u>, pong (*Brit. informal*), foul smell, foulness, malodour, fetor, noisomeness ...*The stink was overpowering...*

2 (*Slang*) = <u>fuss</u>, to-do, row, upset, scandal, stir, disturbance, uproar, commotion, rumpus, hubbub, brouhaha, deal of trouble (*informal*) ...*The family's making a hell of a stink...*

stinker (*Slang*) = <u>scoundrel</u>, heel, sod (*slang*), cad (*Brit. informal*), swine, bounder (*old-fashioned Brit. slang*), cur, rotter (*slang, chiefly Brit.*), nasty piece of work (*informal*), dastard (*archaic*)

stinking 1 (*Informal*) = <u>rotten</u>, disgusting, unpleasant, vile, contemptible, wretched ...*I had a stinking cold...*

2 = <u>foul-smelling</u>, smelly, reeking, fetid, malodorous, noisome, whiffy (*Brit. slang*), pongy (*Brit. informal*), mephitic, ill-smelling, niffy (*Brit. slang*), olid, festy (*Austral. slang*), yucko (*Austral. slang*) ...*They were locked up in a stinking cell...*

stint NOUN = <u>term</u>, time, turn, bit, period, share, tour, shift, stretch, spell, quota, assignment ...*a five-year stint in Hong Kong...*

VERB = <u>be mean</u>, hold back, be sparing, scrimp, skimp on, save, withhold, begrudge, economize, be frugal, be parsimonious, be mingy (*Brit. informal*), spoil the ship for a ha'porth of tar ...*He didn't stint on the special effects...*

stipulate = <u>specify</u>, agree, require, promise, contract, settle, guarantee, engage, pledge, lay down, covenant, postulate, insist upon, lay down *or* impose conditions

stipulation = <u>condition</u>, requirement, provision, term, contract, agreement, settlement, rider, restriction, qualification, clause, engagement, specification, precondition, prerequisite, proviso, sine qua non (*Latin*)

stir VERB **1** = <u>mix</u>, beat, agitate ...*Stir the soup for a few seconds...*

2 = <u>move</u>, change position ...*The two women lay on their backs, not stirring...*

3 = <u>get moving</u>, move, get a move on (*informal*), hasten, budge, make an effort, be up and about (*informal*), look lively (*informal*), shake a leg (*informal*), exert yourself, bestir yourself ...*Stir yourself! We've got a visitor...*

4 = <u>stimulate</u>, move, excite, fire, raise, touch, affect, urge, inspire, prompt, spur, thrill, provoke, arouse, awaken, animate, rouse, prod, quicken, inflame, incite, instigate, electrify, kindle ...*I was intrigued by him, stirred by his intellect...* OPPOSITE inhibit

5 = <u>spur</u>, drive, prompt, stimulate, prod, press, urge, animate, prick, incite, goad, impel ...*The sight of them stirred him into action...*

NOUN = <u>commotion</u>, to-do, excitement, activity, movement, disorder, fuss, disturbance, bustle, flurry, uproar, ferment, agitation, ado, tumult ...*His film has caused a stir in America...*

stirring = <u>exciting</u>, dramatic, thrilling, moving, spirited, inspiring, stimulating, lively, animating, rousing, heady, exhilarating, impassioned, emotive, intoxicating

stock NOUN **1** = <u>shares</u>, holdings, securities, investments, bonds, equities ...*Stock prices have dropped...*

2 = <u>property</u>, capital, assets, funds ...*The Fisher family holds 40% of the stock...*

3 = <u>goods</u>, merchandise, wares, range, choice, variety, selection, commodities, array, assortment ...*We took a decision to withdraw a quantity of stock from sale...*

4 = <u>supply</u>, store, reserve, fund, reservoir, stockpile, hoard, cache ...*a stock of ammunition...*

5 = <u>lineage</u>, descent, extraction, ancestry, house, family, line, race, type, variety, background, breed, strain, pedigree, forebears, parentage, line of descent ...*We are both from working-class stock...*

6 = <u>livestock</u>, cattle, beasts, domestic animals ...*I am carefully selecting the breeding stock...*

VERB **1** = <u>sell</u>, supply, handle, keep, trade in, deal in ...*The shop stocks everything from cigarettes to recycled loo paper...*

2 = <u>fill</u>, supply, provide with, provision, equip, furnish, fit out, kit out ...*I worked stocking shelves in a grocery store...*

ADJECTIVE **1** = <u>hackneyed</u>, standard, usual, set, routine, stereotyped, staple, commonplace, worn-out, banal, run-of-the-mill, trite, overused ...*National security is the stock excuse for keeping things confidential...*

2 = <u>regular</u>, traditional, usual, basic, ordinary, conventional, staple, customary ...*They supply stock sizes outside the middle range...*

PHRASES **stock up with something** = <u>store (up)</u>, lay in, hoard, save, gather, accumulate, amass, buy up, put away, replenish supplies of ...*New Yorkers have been stocking up with bottled water...* ◆ **take stock** = <u>review the situation</u>, weigh up, appraise, estimate, size up (*informal*), see how the land lies ...*It was time to take stock of my life...*

stocky = <u>thickset</u>, solid, sturdy, chunky, stubby, dumpy, stumpy, mesomorphic

stodgy 1 = <u>heavy</u>, filling, substantial, leaden, starchy ...*He was disgusted by the stodgy pizzas on sale in London...* OPPOSITE light

2 = <u>dull</u>, boring, stuffy, formal, tedious, tiresome, staid, unimaginative, turgid, uninspired, unexciting, ho-hum, heavy going, fuddy-duddy (*informal*), dull as ditchwater ...*stodgy old fogies...* OPPOSITE exciting

stoical = <u>resigned</u>, long-suffering, phlegmatic, philosophic, cool, calm, indifferent, stoic, dispassionate, impassive, stolid, imperturbable

stoicism = <u>resignation</u>, acceptance, patience, indifference, fortitude, long-suffering, calmness, fatalism, forbearance, stolidity, dispassion, impassivity, imperturbability

stolen = <u>hot</u> (*slang*), bent (*slang*), hooky (*slang*)

stolid = <u>apathetic</u>, unemotional, dull, heavy, slow, wooden, stupid, bovine, dozy (*Brit. informal*), obtuse, lumpish, doltish OPPOSITE> lively

stomach NOUN **1** = belly, inside(s) (*informal*), gut (*informal*), abdomen, tummy (*informal*), puku (*N.Z.*) ...*My stomach is completely full*...

2 = tummy, pot, spare tyre (*informal*), paunch, breadbasket (*slang*), potbelly ...*This exercise strengthens the stomach, buttocks and thighs*...

3 = inclination, taste, desire, appetite, relish, mind ...*They have no stomach for a fight*...

VERB = bear, take, tolerate, suffer, endure, swallow, hack (*slang*), abide, put up with (*informal*), submit to, reconcile *or* resign yourself to ...*I could never stomach the cruelty involved in the wounding of animals*...

(*Related Words*)

adjective : gastric

stone 1 = masonry, rock ...*He could not tell if the floor was wood or stone*...

2 = rock, pebble ...*The crowd began throwing stones*...

3 = pip, seed, pit, kernel ...*Old men sat beneath the plane trees and spat cherry stones at my feet*...

stony 1 = rocky, rough, gritty, gravelly, rock-strewn, pebble ...*a stony track*...

2 = cold, icy, hostile, hard, harsh, blank, adamant, indifferent, chilly, callous, heartless, merciless, unforgiving, inexorable, frigid, expressionless, unresponsive, pitiless, unfeeling, obdurate ...*The stony look he was giving her made it hard to think*...

stooge = pawn, puppet, fall guy (*informal*), butt, foil, patsy (*slang, chiefly U.S. & Canad.*), dupe, henchman, lackey

stoop VERB **1** = hunch, be bowed *or* round-shouldered ...*She was taller than he was and stooped slightly*...

2 = bend, lean, bow, duck, descend, incline, kneel, crouch, squat ...*He stooped to pick up the carrier bag of groceries*...

NOUN = slouch, slump, droop, sag, bad posture, round-shoulderedness ...*He was a tall, thin fellow with a slight stoop*...

PHRASES **stoop to something** = resort to, sink to, descend to, deign to, condescend to, demean yourself by, lower yourself by ...*How could anyone stoop to doing such a thing?*...

stop VERB **1** = quit, cease, refrain, break off, put an end to, pack in (*Brit. informal*), discontinue, leave off, call it a day (*informal*), desist, belay (*Nautical*), bring *or* come to a halt *or* standstill ...*I've been told to lose weight and stop smoking*... OPPOSITE> start

2 = prevent, suspend, cut short, close, break, check, bar, arrest, silence, frustrate, axe (*informal*), interrupt, restrain, hold back, intercept, hinder, repress, impede, rein in, forestall, nip (something) in the bud ...*I think she really would have liked to stop everything right there*... OPPOSITE> facilitate

3 = end, conclude, finish, be over, cut out (*informal*), terminate, come to an end, peter out ...*The music stopped and the lights were turned up*... OPPOSITE> continue

4 = cease, shut down, discontinue, desist ...*His heart stopped three times*... OPPOSITE> continue

5 = halt, pause, stall, draw up, pull up ...*The car failed to stop at an army checkpoint*... OPPOSITE> keep going

6 = pause, wait, rest, hesitate, deliberate, take a break, have a breather (*informal*), stop briefly ...*She doesn't stop to think about what she's saying*...

7 = stay, rest, put up, lodge, sojourn, tarry, break your journey ...*He insisted we stop at a small restaurant just outside Atlanta*...

NOUN **1** = halt, standstill ...*He slowed the car almost to a stop*...

2 = station, stage, halt, destination, depot, termination, terminus ...*They waited at a bus stop*...

3 = stay, break, visit, rest, stopover, sojourn ...*The last stop in his lengthy tour was Paris*...

stopgap NOUN = makeshift, improvisation, temporary expedient, shift, resort, substitute ...*It is not an acceptable long term solution, just a stopgap*...

ADJECTIVE = makeshift, emergency, temporary, provisional, improvised, impromptu, rough-and-ready ...*It was only ever intended as a stopgap solution*...

stoppage 1 = stopping, halt, standstill, close, arrest, lay-off, shutdown, cutoff, abeyance, discontinuance ...*a seven-hour stoppage by air-traffic controllers*...

2 = blockage, obstruction, stopping up, occlusion ...*The small traffic disturbance will soon grow into a complete stoppage*...

store NOUN **1** = shop, outlet, department store, market, supermarket, mart, emporium, chain store, hypermarket ...*Bombs were planted in stores in Manchester and Blackpool*...

2 = supply, stock, reserve, lot, fund, mine, plenty, provision, wealth, quantity, reservoir, abundance, accumulation, stockpile, hoard, plethora, cache ...*I handed over my store of chocolate biscuits*...

3 = repository, warehouse, depot, storehouse, depository, storeroom ...*a grain store*...

VERB **1** *often with* **away** *or* **up** = put by, save, hoard, keep, stock, husband, reserve, deposit, accumulate, garner, stockpile, put aside, stash (*informal*), salt away, keep in reserve, put aside for a rainy day, lay by *or* in ...*storing away cash that will come in useful later on*...

2 = put away, put in storage, put in store, lock away ...*Some types of garden furniture must be stored inside in the winter*...

3 = keep, hold, preserve, maintain, retain, conserve ...*chips for storing data*...

PHRASES **set great store by something** = value, prize, esteem, appreciate, hold in high regard, think highly of ...*a retail group that sets great store by traditional values*...

storm NOUN **1** = tempest, blast, hurricane, gale, tornado, cyclone, blizzard, whirlwind, gust, squall ...*the violent storms which whipped America's East Coast*...

2 = outburst, row, stir, outcry, furore, violence, anger, passion, outbreak, turmoil, disturbance, strife, clamour, agitation, commotion, rumpus, tumult, hubbub ...*The photos caused a storm when they were* first published…

3 = <u>roar</u>, thunder, clamour, din …*His speech was greeted with a storm of applause…*

4 = <u>barrage</u>, volley, salvo, rain, shower, spray, discharge, fusillade …*a storm of missiles…*

VERB **1** = <u>rush</u>, stamp, flounce, fly, stalk, stomp (*informal*) …*After a bit of an argument, he stormed out…*

2 = <u>rage</u>, fume, rant, complain, thunder, rave, scold, bluster, go ballistic (*slang, chiefly U.S.*), fly off the handle (*informal*), wig out (*slang*) …*'It's a fiasco,' he stormed…*

3 = <u>attack</u>, charge, rush, assault, beset, assail, take by storm …*The refugees decided to storm the embassy…*

stormy **1** = <u>wild</u>, rough, tempestuous, raging, dirty, foul, turbulent, windy, blustering, blustery, gusty, inclement, squally …*the long stormy winter of 1942…*

2 = <u>rough</u>, wild, turbulent, tempestuous, raging …*the stormy waters that surround the British Isles…*

3 = <u>angry</u>, heated, fierce, passionate, fiery, impassioned, tumultuous …*The letter was read at a stormy meeting…*

story **1** = <u>tale</u>, romance, narrative, record, history, version, novel, legend, chronicle, yarn, recital, narration, urban myth, urban legend, fictional account …*a popular love story with a happy ending…*

2 = <u>anecdote</u>, account, tale, report, detail, relation …*The parents all shared interesting stories about their children…*

3 (*Informal*) = <u>lie</u>, falsehood, fib, fiction, untruth, porky (*Brit. slang*), pork pie (*Brit. slang*), white lie …*He invented some story about a cousin…*

4 = <u>report</u>, news, article, feature, scoop, news item …*Those are some of the top stories in the news…*

storyteller = <u>raconteur</u>, author, narrator, romancer, novelist, chronicler, bard, fabulist, spinner of yarns, anecdotist

stout **1** = <u>fat</u>, big, heavy, overweight, plump, bulky, substantial, burly, obese, fleshy, tubby, portly, rotund, corpulent, on the large *or* heavy side …*exercises ideal for stout women of maturer years…* **OPPOSITE** slim

2 = <u>strong</u>, strapping, muscular, tough, substantial, athletic, hardy, robust, vigorous, sturdy, stalwart, husky (*informal*), hulking, beefy (*informal*), lusty, brawny, thickset, able-bodied …*a great stout fellow, big in brawn and bone…* **OPPOSITE** puny

3 = <u>brave</u>, bold, courageous, fearless, resolute, gallant, intrepid, valiant, plucky, doughty, indomitable, dauntless, lion-hearted, valorous …*The invasion was held up by unexpectedly stout resistance…* **OPPOSITE** timid

stow = <u>pack</u>, load, put away, store, stuff, deposit, jam, tuck, bundle, cram, stash (*informal*), secrete

straggle = <u>trail</u>, drift, wander, range, lag, stray, roam, ramble, rove, loiter, string out

straggly = <u>spread out</u>, spreading, rambling, untidy, loose, drifting, random, straying, irregular, aimless, disorganized, straggling

straight **ADJECTIVE** **1** = <u>direct</u>, unswerving,

undeviating …*Keep the boat in a straight line…* **OPPOSITE** indirect

2 = <u>level</u>, even, right, square, true, smooth, in line, aligned, horizontal …*There wasn't a single straight wall in the building…* **OPPOSITE** crooked

3 = <u>frank</u>, plain, straightforward, blunt, outright, honest, downright, candid, forthright, bold, point-blank, upfront (*informal*), unqualified …*a straight answer to a straight question…* **OPPOSITE** evasive

4 = <u>successive</u>, consecutive, continuous, through, running, solid, sustained, uninterrupted, nonstop, unrelieved …*They'd won twelve straight games before they lost…* **OPPOSITE** discontinuous

5 (*Slang*) = <u>conventional</u>, conservative, orthodox, traditional, square (*informal*), bourgeois, Pooterish …*Dorothy was described as a very straight woman…* **OPPOSITE** fashionable

6 = <u>honest</u>, just, fair, decent, reliable, respectable, upright, honourable, equitable, law-abiding, trustworthy, above board, fair and square …*You need to be straight with them to gain their respect…* **OPPOSITE** dishonest

7 = <u>undiluted</u>, pure, neat, unadulterated, unmixed …*a large straight whisky, with ice…*

8 = <u>in order</u>, organized, arranged, sorted out, neat, tidy, orderly, shipshape, put to rights …*We need to get the house straight again before they come home…* **OPPOSITE** untidy

ADVERB **1** = <u>directly</u>, precisely, exactly, as the crow flies, unswervingly, by the shortest route, in a beeline …*Straight ahead were the low cabins of the motel…*

2 = <u>immediately</u>, directly, promptly, instantly, at once, straight away, without delay, without hesitation, forthwith, unhesitatingly, before you could say Jack Robinson (*informal*) …*As always, we went straight to the experts for advice…*

3 = <u>frankly</u>, honestly, point-blank, candidly, pulling no punches (*informal*), in plain English, with no holds barred …*I told him straight that I had been looking for another job…*

straight away = <u>immediately</u>, now, at once, directly, instantly, on the spot, right away, there and then, this minute, straightway (*archaic*), without more ado, without any delay

straighten **VERB** = <u>neaten</u>, arrange, tidy (up), order, spruce up, smarten up, put in order, set *or* put to rights …*She looked in the mirror and straightened her hair…*

PHRASES **straighten something out** = <u>sort out</u>, resolve, put right, settle, correct, work out, clear up, rectify, disentangle, unsnarl …*My sister had come in with her common sense and straightened things out…*

straightforward **1** (*Chiefly Brit.*) = <u>simple</u>, easy, uncomplicated, routine, elementary, clear-cut, undemanding, easy-peasy (*slang*) …*The question seemed straightforward enough…* **OPPOSITE** complicated

2 = <u>honest</u>, open, direct, genuine, sincere, candid, truthful, forthright, upfront (*informal*), dinkum (*Austral. & N.Z. informal*), above board, guileless …*I*

was impressed by his straightforward intelligent manner... OPPOSITE devious

strain¹ NOUN **1** = <u>pressure</u>, stress, difficulty, demands, burden, adversity ...*The prison service is already under considerable strain...*

2 = <u>stress</u>, pressure, anxiety, difficulty, distress, nervous tension ...*She was tired and under great strain...*

3 = <u>worry</u>, effort, struggle, tension, hassle ...*the strain of being responsible for the mortgage...* OPPOSITE ease

4 = <u>burden</u>, tension ...*Place your hands under your buttocks to take some of the strain off your back...*

5 = <u>injury</u>, wrench, sprain, pull, tension, tautness, tensity (*rare*) ...*a groin strain...*

6 = <u>tune</u>, air, melody, measure (*poetic*), lay, song, theme ...*She could hear the tinny strains of a chamber orchestra...*

VERB **1** = <u>stretch</u>, test, tax, overtax, push to the limit ...*Resources will be further strained by new demands for housing...*

2 = <u>injure</u>, wrench, sprain, damage, pull, tear, hurt, twist, rick ...*He strained his back during a practice session...*

3 = <u>strive</u>, struggle, endeavour, labour, go for it (*informal*), bend over backwards (*informal*), go for broke (*slang*), go all out for (*informal*), bust a gut (*informal*), give it your best shot (*informal*), make an all-out effort (*informal*), knock yourself out (*informal*), do your damnedest (*informal*), give it your all (*informal*), break your back *or* neck (*informal*), rupture yourself (*informal*) ...*Several thousand supporters strained to catch a glimpse of the new president...* OPPOSITE relax

4 = <u>sieve</u>, filter, sift, screen, separate, riddle, purify ...*Strain the stock and put it back in the pan...*

strain² **1** = <u>trace</u>, suggestion, suspicion, tendency, streak, trait ...*There was a strain of bitterness in his voice...*

2 = <u>breed</u>, type, stock, family, race, blood, descent, pedigree, extraction, ancestry, lineage ...*a particularly beautiful strain of Swiss pansies...*

strained **1** = <u>tense</u>, difficult, uncomfortable, awkward, embarrassed, stiff, uneasy, constrained, self-conscious, unrelaxed ...*a period of strained relations...* OPPOSITE relaxed

2 = <u>forced</u>, put on, false, artificial, unnatural, laboured ...*His laughter seemed a little strained...* OPPOSITE natural

strait NOUN *often plural* = <u>channel</u>, sound, narrows, stretch of water, sea passage ...*Thousands of vessels pass through the straits annually...*

PLURAL NOUN = <u>difficulty</u>, crisis, mess, pass, hole (*slang*), emergency, distress, dilemma, embarrassment, plight, hardship, uphill (*S. African*), predicament, extremity, perplexity, panic stations (*informal*), pretty *or* fine kettle of fish (*informal*) ...*If we had a child, we'd be in really dire straits...*

strand = <u>filament</u>, fibre, thread, length, lock, string, twist, rope, wisp, tress

stranded **1** = <u>beached</u>, grounded, marooned, ashore, shipwrecked, aground, cast away ...*He returned to his stranded vessel yesterday afternoon...*

2 = <u>helpless</u>, abandoned, high and dry, left in the lurch ...*He left me stranded by the side of the road...*

strange **1** = <u>odd</u>, unusual, curious, weird, wonderful, rare, funny, extraordinary, remarkable, bizarre, fantastic, astonishing, marvellous, exceptional, peculiar, eccentric, abnormal, out-of-the-way, queer, irregular, rum (*Brit. slang*), uncommon, singular, perplexing, uncanny, mystifying, unheard-of, off-the-wall (*slang*), oddball (*informal*), unaccountable, left-field (*informal*), outré, curiouser and curiouser ...*There was something strange about the flickering blue light...* OPPOSITE ordinary

2 = <u>out of place</u>, lost, uncomfortable, awkward, bewildered, disoriented, ill at ease, like a fish out of water ...*I felt strange in his office, realizing how absurd it was...* OPPOSITE comfortable

3 = <u>unfamiliar</u>, new, unknown, foreign, novel, alien, exotic, untried, unexplored, outside your experience ...*I ended up alone in a strange city...* OPPOSITE familiar

4 = <u>unwell</u>, ill, sick, poorly (*informal*), funny (*informal*), crook (*Austral. & N.Z. informal*), ailing, queer, queasy, out of sorts (*informal*), dicky (*Brit. informal*), off-colour, under the weather (*informal*), indisposed, green about the gills, not up to snuff (*informal*) ...*I felt all dizzy and strange...*

stranger **1** = <u>unknown person</u> ...*Sometimes I feel like I'm living with a stranger...*

2 = <u>newcomer</u>, incomer, foreigner, guest, visitor, unknown, alien, new arrival, outlander ...*Being a stranger in town can be a painful experience...*

3 = <u>unaccustomed to</u>, new to, unused to, ignorant of, a stranger to, inexperienced in, unversed in, unpractised in, unseasoned in ...*He is no stranger to controversy...*

(*Related Words*)
fear of: xenophobia

strangle **1** = <u>throttle</u>, choke, asphyxiate, garrotte, strangulate, smother, suffocate ...*He was almost strangled by his parachute harness straps...*

2 = <u>suppress</u>, inhibit, subdue, stifle, gag, repress, overpower, quash, quell, quench ...*His creative drive has been strangled by his sense of guilt...*

strap NOUN = <u>tie</u>, thong, leash, belt ...*Nancy gripped the strap of her beach bag...*

VERB = <u>fasten</u>, tie, secure, bind, lash, buckle, truss ...*She strapped the gun belt around the middle...*

strapping = <u>well-built</u>, big, powerful, robust, hefty (*informal*), sturdy, stalwart, burly, husky (*informal*), hulking, beefy (*informal*), brawny, well set-up

stratagem = <u>trick</u>, scheme, manoeuvre, plan, plot, device, intrigue, dodge, ploy, ruse, artifice, subterfuge, feint, wile

strategic **1** = <u>tactical</u>, calculated, deliberate, planned, politic, diplomatic ...*a strategic plan for reducing the rate of infant mortality...*

2 = <u>crucial</u>, important, key, vital, critical, decisive, cardinal ...*an operation to take the strategic island*...

strategy **1** = <u>policy</u>, procedure, planning, programme, approach, scheme, manoeuvring, grand design ...*Community involvement is now integral to company strategy*...
2 = <u>plan</u>, approach, scheme, manoeuvring, grand design ...*the basic principles of my strategy*...

stratum **1** = <u>class</u>, group, level, station, estate, rank, grade, category, bracket, caste ...*It was an enormous task that affected every stratum of society*...
2 = <u>layer</u>, level, seam, table, bed, vein, tier, stratification, lode ...*The rock strata shows that the region was intensely dry 15,000 years ago*...

> ## Word Power
>
> **stratum** – The word *strata* is the plural form of *stratum*, and should not be used as if it is a singular form: so you would say *this stratum of society is often disregarded*, or *these strata of society are often disregarded*, but not *this strata of society is often disregarded*.

stray VERB **1** = <u>wander</u>, roam, go astray, range, drift, meander, rove, straggle, lose your way, be abandoned or lost ...*A railway line crosses the park so children must not be allowed to stray*...
2 = <u>drift</u>, wander, roam, meander, rove ...*She could not keep her eyes from straying towards him*...
3 = <u>digress</u>, diverge, deviate, ramble, get sidetracked, go off at a tangent, get off the point ...*Anyway, as usual, we seem to have strayed from the point*...
ADJECTIVE **1** = <u>lost</u>, abandoned, homeless, roaming, vagrant ...*A stray dog came up to him*...
2 = <u>random</u>, chance, freak, accidental, odd, scattered, erratic ...*An 8-year-old boy was killed by a stray bullet*...

streak NOUN **1** = <u>band</u>, line, strip, stroke, layer, slash, vein, stripe, smear ...*There are these dark streaks on the surface of the moon*...
2 = <u>trace</u>, touch, element, strain, dash, vein ...*He's still got a mean streak*...
VERB **1** = <u>fleck</u>, smear, daub, band, slash, stripe, striate ...*Rain had begun to streak the window pains*...
2 = <u>speed</u>, fly, tear, sweep, flash, barrel (along) (*informal, chiefly U.S. & Canad.*), whistle, sprint, dart, zoom, whizz (*informal*), hurtle, burn rubber (*informal*), move like greased lightning (*informal*) ...*A meteorite streaked across the sky*...

stream NOUN **1** = <u>river</u>, brook, creek (*U.S.*), burn (*Scot.*), beck, tributary, bayou, rivulet, rill, freshet ...*a mountain stream*...
2 = <u>flow</u>, current, rush, run, course, drift, surge, tide, torrent, outpouring, tideway ...*a continuous stream of lava*...
3 = <u>succession</u>, series, flood, chain, battery, volley, avalanche, barrage, torrent ...*a never-ending stream of jokes*...
VERB **1** = <u>flow</u>, run, pour, course, issue, flood, shed,

spill, emit, glide, cascade, gush, spout ...*Tears streamed down their faces*...
2 = <u>rush</u>, fly, speed, tear, flood, pour ...*The traffic streamed past him*...

streamer = <u>banner</u>, flag, pennant, standard, colours, ribbon, ensign, pennon

streamlined = <u>efficient</u>, organized, modernized, rationalized, smooth, slick, sleek, well-run, time-saving, smooth-running

street NOUN = <u>road</u>, lane, avenue, terrace, row, boulevard, roadway, thoroughfare ...*a small, quaint town with narrow streets*...
PHRASES **up your street** (*Informal*) = <u>to your liking</u>, to your taste, your cup of tea (*informal*), pleasing, familiar, suitable, acceptable, compatible, congenial ...*She loved it, this was right up her street*...

strength **1** = <u>might</u>, muscle, brawn, sinew, brawniness ...*He threw it forward with all his strength*... OPPOSITE weakness
2 = <u>will</u>, spirit, resolution, resolve, courage, character, nerve, determination, pluck, stamina, grit, backbone, fortitude, toughness, tenacity, willpower, mettle, firmness, strength of character, steadfastness, moral fibre ...*Something gave me the strength to overcome the difficulty*...
3 = <u>health</u>, fitness, vigour, lustiness ...*It'll take a while before you regain full strength*...
4 = <u>mainstay</u>, anchor, tower of strength, security, succour ...*He was my strength during that terrible time*...
5 = <u>toughness</u>, soundness, robustness, sturdiness, stoutness ...*He checked the strength of the cables*...
6 = <u>force</u>, power, intensity, energy, vehemence, intenseness ...*He was surprised at the strength of his own feeling*... OPPOSITE weakness
7 = <u>potency</u>, effectiveness, concentration, efficacy ...*maximum strength migraine tablets*...
8 = <u>strong point</u>, skill, asset, advantage, talent, forte, speciality, aptitude ...*Take into account your own strengths and weaknesses*... OPPOSITE failing

strengthen **1** = <u>fortify</u>, encourage, harden, toughen, consolidate, stiffen, hearten, gee up, brace up, give new energy to ...*Such antagonism, he has asserted, strengthened his resolve*... OPPOSITE weaken
2 = <u>reinforce</u>, support, confirm, establish, justify, enhance, intensify, bolster, substantiate, buttress, corroborate, give a boost to ...*Research would strengthen the case for socialist reform*...
3 = <u>bolster</u>, harden, reinforce, give a boost to ...*Any experience can teach and strengthen you*...
4 = <u>heighten</u>, intensify ...*Every day of sunshine strengthens the feeling of optimism*...
5 = <u>make stronger</u>, build up, invigorate, restore, nourish, rejuvenate, give strength to ...*Yoga can be used to strengthen the immune system*...
6 = <u>support</u>, brace, steel, reinforce, consolidate, harden, bolster, augment, buttress ...*The builders will have to strengthen the existing joists with additional timber*...
7 = <u>become stronger</u>, intensify, heighten, gain

strength ...*As it strengthened, the wind was veering southerly...*

strenuous 1 = demanding, hard, tough, exhausting, taxing, uphill, arduous, laborious, Herculean, tough going, toilsome, unrelaxing ...*Avoid strenuous exercise in the evening...* OPPOSITE easy

2 = tireless, determined, zealous, strong, earnest, spirited, active, eager, bold, persistent, vigorous, energetic, resolute ...*Strenuous efforts have been made to improve conditions in the jail...*

stress VERB 1 = emphasize, highlight, underline, repeat, draw attention to, dwell on, underscore, accentuate, point up, rub in, harp on, belabour ...*He stressed the need for new measures...*

2 = place the emphasis on, emphasize, give emphasis to, place the accent on, lay emphasis upon ...*She stresses the syllables as though teaching a child...*
NOUN 1 = emphasis, importance, significance, force, weight, urgency ...*Japanese car makers are laying ever more stress on European sales...*

2 = strain, pressure, worry, tension, burden, anxiety, trauma, oppression, hassle (*informal*), nervous tension ...*Katy could not think clearly when under stress...*

3 = accent, beat, emphasis, accentuation, ictus ...*the misplaced stress on the first syllable...*

stressful = worrying, anxious, tense, taxing, demanding, tough, draining, exhausting, exacting, traumatic, agitating, nerve-racking

stretch VERB 1 = extend, cover, spread, reach, unfold, put forth, unroll ...*an artificial reef stretching the length of the coast...*

2 = last, continue, go on, extend, carry on, reach ...*Protests stretched into their second week...*

3 = expand, lengthen, be elastic, be stretchy ...*The cables are designed not to stretch...*

4 = pull, distend, pull out of shape, strain, swell, tighten, rack, inflate, lengthen, draw out, elongate ...*Make sure you don't stretch the pastry as you ease it into the corners...*

5 = hold out, offer, present, extend, proffer ...*She stretched out her hand and slowly led him upstairs...*
NOUN 1 = expanse, area, tract, spread, distance, sweep, extent ...*It's a very dangerous stretch of road...*

2 = period, time, spell, stint, run, term, bit, space ...*He would study for eight to ten hour stretches...*

strew = scatter, spread, litter, toss, sprinkle, disperse, bestrew

stricken = affected, hit, afflicted, struck, injured, struck down, smitten, laid low

strict 1 = severe, harsh, stern, firm, rigid, rigorous, stringent, austere ...*French privacy laws are very strict...* OPPOSITE easy-going

2 = stern, firm, severe, harsh, authoritarian, austere, no-nonsense ...*My parents were very strict...*

3 = exact, accurate, precise, close, true, particular, religious, faithful, meticulous, scrupulous ...*the strictest sense of the word...*

4 = devout, religious, orthodox, pious, pure, reverent, prayerful ...*a strict Catholic...*

5 = absolute, complete, total, perfect, utter ...*Your enquiry will be handled in strict confidence...*

stricture (*Formal*) = criticism, censure, stick (*slang*), blame, rebuke, flak (*informal*), bad press, animadversion

strident = harsh, jarring, grating, clashing, screeching, raucous, shrill, rasping, jangling, discordant, clamorous, unmusical, stridulant, stridulous OPPOSITE soft

strife = conflict, battle, struggle, row, clash, clashes, contest, controversy, combat, warfare, rivalry, contention, quarrel, friction, squabbling, wrangling, bickering, animosity, discord, dissension

strike NOUN = walkout, industrial action, mutiny, revolt ...*a call for a strike...*
VERB 1 = walk out, take industrial action, down tools, revolt, mutiny ...*their recognition of the worker's right to strike...*

2 = hit, smack, thump, pound, beat, box, knock, punch, hammer, deck (*slang*), slap, sock (*slang*), chin (*slang*), buffet, clout (*informal*), cuff, clump (*slang*), swipe, clobber (*slang*), smite, wallop (*informal*), lambast(e), lay a finger on (*informal*), lay one on (*slang*) ...*She took two steps forward and struck him across the mouth...*

3 = drive, propel, force, hit, smack, wallop (*informal*) ...*He struck the ball straight into the hospitality tents...*

4 = collide with, hit, run into, bump into, touch, smash into, come into contact with, knock into, be in collision with ...*He was killed when a car struck him...*

5 = knock, bang, smack, thump, beat, smite ...*He fell and struck his head on the stone floor...*

6 = affect, move, hit, touch, devastate, overwhelm, leave a mark on, make an impact *or* impression on ...*He was suddenly struck with a sense of loss...*

7 = attack, assault someone, fall upon someone, set upon someone, lay into someone (*informal*) ...*The killer says he will strike again...*

8 = occur to, hit, come to, register (*informal*), come to the mind of, dawn on *or* upon ...*At this point, it suddenly struck me that I was wasting my time...*

9 = seem to, appear to, look to, give the impression to ...*He struck me as a very serious but friendly person...*

10 = move, touch, impress, hit, affect, overcome, stir, disturb, perturb, make an impact on ...*She was struck by his simple, spellbinding eloquence...*

11 = achieve, arrive at, attain, reach, effect, arrange ...*You have to strike a balance between sleep and homework...*

12 *sometimes with* **upon** = discover, find, come upon *or* across, reach, encounter, turn up, uncover, unearth, hit upon, light upon, happen *or* chance upon, stumble upon *or* across ...*He realized he had just struck oil...*

PHRASES **strike out** = set out, set off, start out, sally forth ...*They left the car and struck out along the muddy track...* ♦ **strike someone down** = kill, destroy, slay, ruin, afflict, smite, bring low, deal a deathblow to ...*a great sporting hero, struck down at*

49... ◆ **strike something out** *or* **off** *or* **through** = <u>score out</u>, delete, cross out, remove, cancel, erase, excise, efface, expunge ...*The censor struck out the next two lines...*

striking 1 = <u>distinct</u>, noticeable, conspicuous, clear, obvious, evident, manifest, unmistakable, observable, perceptible, appreciable ...*He bears a striking resemblance to Lenin...*
2 = <u>impressive</u>, dramatic, stunning (*informal*), wonderful, extraordinary, outstanding, astonishing, memorable, dazzling, noticeable, conspicuous, drop-dead (*slang*), out of the ordinary, forcible, jaw-dropping ...*She was a striking woman with long blonde hair...* OPPOSITE> unimpressive

string NOUN 1 = <u>cord</u>, yarn, twine, strand, fibre, thread ...*He held out a small bag tied with string...*
2 = <u>series</u>, line, row, file, sequence, queue, succession, procession ...*The landscape is broken only by a string of villages...*
3 = <u>sequence</u>, run, series, chain, succession, streak ...*The incident was the latest in a string of attacks...* PLURAL NOUN 1 = <u>stringed instruments</u> ...*The strings provided a melodic background...*
2 = <u>conditions</u>, catches (*informal*), provisos, stipulations, requirements, riders, obligations, qualifications, complications, prerequisites ...*an offer made in good faith, with no strings attached...* VERB = <u>hang</u>, stretch, suspend, sling, thread, loop, festoon ...*He had strung a banner across the wall...* PHRASES **string along with someone** = <u>accompany</u>, go with, go along with, chaperon ...*Can I string along with you for a while?...* ◆ **string someone along** = <u>deceive</u>, fool, take (someone) for a ride (*informal*), kid (*informal*), bluff, hoax, dupe, put one over on (someone) (*informal*), play fast and loose with (someone) (*informal*), play (someone) false ...*She was stringing him along even after they were divorced...* ◆ **string something out** = <u>prolong</u>, extend, lengthen, protract ...*Do you want to get it over with, or do you want to string it out?...*

stringent = <u>strict</u>, tough, rigorous, demanding, binding, tight, severe, exacting, rigid, inflexible OPPOSITE> lax

stringy = <u>fibrous</u>, tough, chewy, sinewy, gristly, wiry

strip¹ 1 = <u>undress</u>, disrobe, unclothe, uncover yourself ...*Women residents stripped naked in protest...*
2 = <u>plunder</u>, rob, loot, empty, sack, deprive, ransack, pillage, divest, denude ...*The soldiers have stripped the civilians of their passports...*

strip² 1 = <u>piece</u>, shred, bit, band, slip, belt, tongue, ribbon, fillet, swathe ...*Serve with strips of fresh raw vegetables...*
2 = <u>stretch</u>, area, tract, expanse, extent ...*a short boat ride across a narrow strip of water...*

striped = <u>banded</u>, stripy, barred, striated

stripy *or* **stripey** = <u>banded</u>, striped, streaky

strive = <u>try</u>, labour, struggle, fight, attempt, compete, strain, contend, endeavour, go for it (*informal*), try

hard, toil, make every effort, go all out (*informal*), bend over backwards (*informal*), do your best, go for broke (*slang*), leave no stone unturned, bust a gut (*informal*), do all you can, give it your best shot (*informal*), jump through hoops (*informal*), break your neck (*informal*), exert yourself, make an all-out effort (*informal*), knock yourself out (*informal*), do your utmost, do your damnedest (*informal*), give it your all (*informal*), rupture yourself (*informal*)

stroke VERB = <u>caress</u>, rub, fondle, pat, pet ...*She was smoking a cigarette and stroking her cat...*
NOUN 1 = <u>apoplexy</u>, fit, seizure, attack, shock, collapse ...*He had a minor stroke in 1987, which left him partly paralysed...*
2 = <u>mark</u>, line, slash ...*Fill in gaps by using short, upward strokes of the pencil...*
3 = <u>movement</u>, action, motion ...*I turned and swam a few strokes further out to sea...*
4 = <u>blow</u>, hit, knock, pat, rap, thump, swipe ...*He was sending the ball into the net with each stroke...*
5 = <u>feat</u>, move, achievement, accomplishment, movement ...*At the time, his appointment seemed a stroke of genius...*

stroll VERB = <u>walk</u>, ramble, amble, wander, promenade, saunter, stooge (*slang*), take a turn, toddle, make your way, mooch (*slang*), mosey (*informal*), stretch your legs ...*We strolled back, put the kettle on and settled down...*
NOUN = <u>walk</u>, promenade, turn, airing, constitutional, excursion, ramble, breath of air ...*After dinner, I took a stroll around the city...*

strong 1 = <u>powerful</u>, muscular, tough, capable, athletic, strapping, hardy, sturdy, stout, stalwart, burly, beefy (*informal*), virile, Herculean, sinewy, brawny ...*I'm not strong enough to carry him...* OPPOSITE> weak
2 = <u>fit</u>, sound, healthy, robust, hale, in good shape, in good condition, lusty, fighting fit, fit as a fiddle ...*It took me a long while to feel well and strong again...*
3 = <u>self-confident</u>, determined, tough, brave, aggressive, courageous, high-powered, forceful, resilient, feisty (*informal, chiefly U.S. & Canad.*), resolute, resourceful, tenacious, plucky, hard-nosed (*informal*), steadfast, unyielding, hard as nails, self-assertive, stouthearted, firm in spirit ...*Eventually I felt strong enough to look at him...* OPPOSITE> timid
4 = <u>durable</u>, substantial, sturdy, reinforced, heavy-duty, well-built, well-armed, hard-wearing, well-protected, on a firm foundation ...*Around its summit, a strong wall had been built...* OPPOSITE> flimsy
5 = <u>forceful</u>, powerful, intense, vigorous ...*A strong current seemed to be moving the whole boat...*
6 = <u>extreme</u>, radical, drastic, strict, harsh, rigid, forceful, uncompromising, Draconian, unbending ...*She is known to hold strong views on Cuba...*
7 = <u>decisive</u>, firm, forceful, decided, determined, severe, resolute, incisive ...*The government will take strong action against any further strikes...*
8 = <u>persuasive</u>, convincing, compelling, telling, great, clear, sound, effective, urgent, formidable, potent, well-established, clear-cut, overpowering, weighty,

well-founded, redoubtable, trenchant, cogent …*The evidence that such investment promotes growth is strong…*

9 = pungent, powerful, concentrated, pure, undiluted …*strong aftershave…* OPPOSITE bland

10 = highly-flavoured, hot, spicy, piquant, biting, sharp, heady, overpowering, intoxicating, highly-seasoned …*It's a good strong flavour, without being overpowering…*

11 = keen, deep, acute, eager, fervent, zealous, vehement …*He has a strong interest in paintings and owns a fine collection…*

12 = intense, deep, passionate, ardent, fierce, profound, forceful, fervent, deep-rooted, vehement, fervid …*Having strong unrequited feelings for someone is hard…*

13 = staunch, firm, keen, dedicated, fierce, ardent, eager, enthusiastic, passionate, fervent …*The Deputy Prime Minister is a strong supporter of the plan…*

14 = distinct, marked, clear, unmistakable …*'Good, Mr Royle,' he said in English with a strong French accent…* OPPOSITE slight

15 = bright, brilliant, dazzling, loud, bold, stark, glaring …*strong colours…* OPPOSITE dull

strong-arm (*Informal*) = bullying, threatening, aggressive, violent, terror, forceful, high-pressure, coercive, terrorizing, thuggish

stronghold 1 = bastion, fortress, bulwark, fastness …*The seat was a stronghold of the labour party…*

2 = refuge, haven, retreat, sanctuary, hide-out, bolt hole …*Shetland is the last stronghold of otters in the British Isles…*

strong-minded = determined, resolute, strong willed, firm, independent, uncompromising, iron-willed, unbending

strong point = forte, strength, speciality, advantage, asset, strong suit, métier, long suit (*informal*)

stroppy (*Brit. informal*) = awkward, difficult, obstreperous, destructive, perverse, unhelpful, cantankerous, bloody-minded (*Brit. informal*), quarrelsome, litigious, uncooperative

structure NOUN **1** = arrangement, form, make-up, make, design, organization, construction, fabric, formation, configuration, conformation, interrelation of parts …*The chemical structure of this particular molecule is very unusual…*

2 = building, construction, erection, edifice, pile …*The house was a handsome four-storey brick structure…* VERB = arrange, organize, design, shape, build up, assemble, put together …*You have begun to structure your time…*

struggle VERB **1** = strive, labour, toil, work, strain, go for it (*informal*), make every effort, go all out (*informal*), bend over backwards (*informal*), go for broke (*slang*), bust a gut (*informal*), give it your best shot (*informal*), break your neck (*informal*), exert yourself, make an all-out effort (*informal*), work like a Trojan, knock yourself out (*informal*), do your damnedest (*informal*), give it your all (*informal*),

rupture yourself (*informal*) …*They had to struggle against all kinds of adversity…*

2 = fight, battle, wrestle, grapple, compete, contend, scuffle, lock horns …*We were struggling for the gun when it went off…*

3 = have trouble, have problems, have difficulties, fight, come unstuck …*The company is struggling to find visitors…*

NOUN **1** = problem, battle, effort, trial, strain …*Life became a struggle…*

2 = effort, labour, toil, work, grind (*informal*), pains, scramble, long haul, exertion …*a young lad's struggle to support his poverty-stricken family…*

3 = fight, battle, conflict, clash, contest, encounter, brush, combat, hostilities, strife, skirmish, tussle, biffo (*Austral. slang*) …*He died in a struggle with prison officers…*

strut = swagger, parade, stalk, peacock, prance

stub 1 = butt, end, stump, tail, remnant, tail end, fag end (*informal*), dog-end (*informal*) …*an ashtray of cigarette stubs…*

2 = counterfoil …*Those who still have their ticket stubs, please contact the arena…*

stubborn = obstinate, dogged, inflexible, fixed, persistent, intractable, wilful, tenacious, recalcitrant, unyielding, headstrong, unmanageable, unbending, obdurate, stiff-necked, unshakeable, self-willed, refractory, pig-headed, bull-headed, mulish, cross-grained, contumacious OPPOSITE compliant

stubby = stumpy, short, squat, stocky, chunky, dumpy, thickset, fubsy (*archaic or dialect*)

stuck ADJECTIVE **1** = fastened, fast, fixed, joined, glued, cemented …*She had got something stuck between her teeth…*

2 = trapped, caught, ensnared …*I don't want to get stuck in another job like that…*

3 = burdened, saddled, lumbered, landed, loaded, encumbered …*Many people are now stuck with fixed-rate mortgages…*

4 (*Informal*) = baffled, stumped, at a loss, beaten, nonplussed, at a standstill, bereft of ideas, up against a brick wall (*informal*), at your wits' end …*They will be there to help if you're stuck…*

PHRASES **be stuck on something** or **someone** (*Slang*) = be infatuated with, be obsessed with, be keen on, be enthusiastic about, be mad about, be wild about (*informal*), be hung up on (*slang*), be crazy about, for, or over (*informal*) …*She's stuck on him because he was her first lover…* ♦ **get stuck into something** (*Informal*) = set about, tackle, get down to, make a start on, take the bit between your teeth …*The sooner we get stuck into this, the sooner we'll finish…*

stuck-up (*Informal*) = snobbish, arrogant, conceited, proud, patronizing, condescending, snooty (*informal*), haughty, uppity (*informal*), high and mighty (*informal*), toffee-nosed (*slang, chiefly Brit.*), hoity-toity (*informal*), swollen-headed, bigheaded (*informal*), uppish (*Brit. informal*)

student 1 = <u>undergraduate</u>, scholar ...*a 23-year-old medical student...*
2 = <u>pupil</u>, scholar, schoolchild, schoolboy *or* schoolgirl ...*She's a former student of the school...*
3 = <u>learner</u>, observer, trainee, apprentice, disciple ...*a passionate student of history...*

studied = <u>planned</u>, calculated, deliberate, conscious, intentional, wilful, purposeful, premeditated, well-considered OPPOSITE unplanned

studio = <u>workshop</u>, shop, workroom, atelier

studious 1 = <u>scholarly</u>, academic, intellectual, serious, earnest, hard-working, thoughtful, reflective, diligent, meditative, bookish, assiduous, sedulous ...*I was a very quiet, studious little girl...* OPPOSITE unacademic
2 = <u>intent</u>, attentive, watchful, listening, concentrating, careful, regardful ...*He had a look of studious concentration on his face...* OPPOSITE careless
3 = <u>deliberate</u>, planned, conscious, calculated, considered, studied, designed, thoughtful, intentional, wilful, purposeful, premeditated, prearranged ...*the studious refusal of most of these firms to get involved in politics...*

study VERB 1 = <u>learn</u>, cram (*informal*), swot (up) (*Brit. informal*), read up, hammer away at, bone up on (*informal*), burn the midnight oil, mug up (*Brit. slang*) ...*The rehearsals make it difficult for her to study for her law exams...*
2 = <u>examine</u>, survey, look at, scrutinize, peruse ...*Debbie studied her friend's face for a moment...*
3 = <u>contemplate</u>, read, examine, consider, go into, con (*archaic*), pore over, apply yourself (to) ...*I invite every citizen to carefully study the document...*
NOUN 1 = <u>examination</u>, investigation, analysis, consideration, inspection, scrutiny, contemplation, perusal, cogitation ...*the use of maps and visual evidence in the study of local history...*
2 = <u>piece of research</u>, survey, report, paper, review, article, inquiry, investigation ...*the first study of English children's attitudes...*
3 = <u>learning</u>, lessons, school work, academic work, reading, research, cramming (*informal*), swotting (*Brit. informal*), book work ...*She gave up her studies to have a family...*
4 = <u>office</u>, room, studio, workplace, den, place of work, workroom ...*I went through the papers in his study...*

stuff NOUN 1 = <u>things</u>, gear, possessions, effects, materials, equipment, objects, tackle, kit, junk, luggage, belongings, trappings, bits and pieces, paraphernalia, clobber (*Brit. slang*), impedimenta, goods and chattels ...*He pointed to a duffle bag. 'That's my stuff.'...*
2 = <u>nonsense</u>, rubbish, rot, trash, bunk (*informal*), foolishness, humbug, twaddle, tripe (*informal*), baloney (*informal*), verbiage, claptrap (*informal*), bunkum, poppycock (*informal*), balderdash, pants (*slang*), bosh (*informal*), stuff and nonsense, tommyrot, bizzo (*Austral. slang*), bull's wool (*Austral. &*

N.Z. slang) ...*Don't tell me you believe in all that stuff...*
3 = <u>substance</u>, material, essence, matter, staple, pith, quintessence ...*The idea that we can be what we want has become the stuff of TV commercials...*
VERB 1 = <u>shove</u>, force, push, squeeze, jam, ram, wedge, compress, stow ...*His trousers were stuffed inside the tops of his boots...*
2 = <u>cram</u>, fill, pack, load, crowd ...*wallets stuffed with dollars...*
PHRASES **stuff yourself** = <u>gorge</u>, gobble, guzzle, satiate, pig out (*slang*), sate, overindulge, make a pig of yourself (*informal*), gormandize ...*I could stuff myself with ten chocolate bars and still feel hungry...*

stuffing 1 = <u>filling</u>, forcemeat ...*a stuffing for turkey, guinea fowl or chicken...*
2 = <u>wadding</u>, filling, packing, quilting, kapok ...*She made a wig from pillow stuffing...*

stuffy 1 (*Informal*) = <u>staid</u>, conventional, dull, old-fashioned, deadly, dreary, pompous, formal, prim, stilted, musty, stodgy, uninteresting, humourless, fusty, strait-laced, priggish, as dry as dust, old-fogeyish, niminy-piminy, prim and proper ...*stuffy attitudes...*
2 = <u>airless</u>, stifling, oppressive, close, heavy, stale, suffocating, sultry, fetid, muggy, unventilated, fuggy, frowsty ...*It was hot and stuffy in the classroom...*
OPPOSITE airy

stumble VERB 1 = <u>trip</u>, fall, slip, reel, stagger, falter, flounder, lurch, come a cropper (*informal*), lose your balance, blunder about ...*The smoke was so thick that I stumbled on the first step...*
2 = <u>totter</u>, reel, stagger, blunder, falter, lurch, wobble, teeter ...*I stumbled into the telephone box and dialled 999...*
3 = <u>falter</u>, hesitate, stammer, stutter, fluff (*informal*) ...*His voiced wavered and he stumbled over his words...*
PHRASES **stumble across** *or* **on** *or* **upon something** *or* **someone** = <u>discover</u>, find, come across, encounter, run across, chance upon, happen upon, light upon, blunder upon ...*History relates that they stumbled on a magnificent waterfall...*

stumbling block = <u>obstacle</u>, difficulty, bar, barrier, hurdle, hazard, snag, uphill (*S. African*), obstruction, impediment, hindrance

stump NOUN = <u>tail end</u>, end, remnant, remainder ...*The tramp produced a stump of candle from his pocket...*
VERB 1 = <u>baffle</u>, confuse, puzzle, snooker, foil, bewilder, confound, perplex, mystify, outwit, stymie, flummox, bring (someone) up short, dumbfound, nonplus ...*Well, maybe I stumped you on that one...*
2 = <u>stamp</u>, clump, stomp (*informal*), trudge, plod, clomp ...*The marshal stumped out of the room...*
PHRASES **stump something up** (*Brit. informal*) (with money or a sum of money as object) = <u>pay</u>, fork out (*slang*), shell out (*informal*), contribute, hand over, donate, chip in (*informal*), cough up (*informal*), come across with (*informal*) ...*Customers do not have to stump up cash for at least four weeks...*

stumped = <u>baffled</u>, perplexed, at a loss, floored (*informal*), at sea, stymied, nonplussed, flummoxed, brought to a standstill, uncertain which way to turn, at your wits' end

stun 1 = <u>overcome</u>, shock, amaze, confuse, astonish, stagger, bewilder, astound, overpower, confound, stupefy, strike (someone) dumb, knock (someone) for six (*informal*), dumbfound, flabbergast (*informal*), hit (someone) like a ton of bricks (*informal*), take (someone's) breath away ...*Many cinema-goers were stunned by the film's violent and tragic end...*
2 = <u>daze</u>, knock out, stupefy, numb, benumb ...*He stood his ground and took a heavy blow that stunned him...*

stung = <u>hurt</u>, wounded, angered, roused, incensed, exasperated, resentful, nettled, goaded, piqued

stunned = <u>staggered</u>, shocked, devastated, numb, astounded, bowled over (*informal*), gobsmacked (*Brit. slang*), dumbfounded, flabbergasted (*informal*), struck dumb, at a loss for words

stunner (*Informal*) = <u>beauty</u>, looker (*informal, chiefly U.S.*), lovely (*slang*), dish (*informal*), sensation, honey (*informal*), good-looker, dazzler, peach (*informal*), wow (*slang, chiefly U.S.*), dolly (*slang*), knockout (*informal*), heart-throb, charmer, eyeful (*informal*), smasher (*informal*), humdinger (*slang*), glamour puss

stunning (*Informal*) = <u>wonderful</u>, beautiful, impressive, great (*informal*), striking, brilliant, dramatic, lovely, remarkable, smashing (*informal*), heavenly, devastating (*informal*), spectacular, marvellous, splendid, gorgeous, dazzling, sensational (*informal*), drop-dead (*slang*), ravishing, out of this world (*informal*), jaw-dropping [OPPOSITE] unimpressive

stunt = <u>feat</u>, act, trick, exploit, deed, tour de force (*French*)

stunted = <u>undersized</u>, dwarfed, little, small, tiny, diminutive, dwarfish

stupefy = <u>astound</u>, shock, amaze, stun, stagger, bewilder, numb, daze, confound, knock senseless, dumbfound

stupendous 1 = <u>wonderful</u>, brilliant, amazing, stunning (*informal*), superb, overwhelming, fantastic (*informal*), tremendous (*informal*), fabulous (*informal*), surprising, staggering, marvellous, sensational (*informal*), breathtaking, phenomenal, astounding, prodigious, wondrous (*archaic or literary*), mind-boggling (*informal*), out of this world (*informal*), mind-blowing (*informal*), jaw-dropping, surpassing belief ...*This stupendous novel keeps you gripped to the end...* [OPPOSITE] unremarkable
2 = <u>huge</u>, vast, enormous, mega (*slang*), gigantic, colossal ...*a stupendous amount of money...* [OPPOSITE] tiny

stupid 1 = <u>unintelligent</u>, thick, dumb (*informal*), simple, slow, dull, dim, dense, sluggish, deficient, crass, gullible, simple-minded, dozy (*Brit. informal*), witless, stolid, dopey (*informal*), moronic, obtuse, brainless, cretinous, half-witted, slow on the uptake (*informal*),

braindead (*informal*), dumb-ass (*slang*), doltish, dead from the neck up, thickheaded, slow-witted, Boeotian, thick as mince (*Scot. informal*), woodenheaded (*informal*) ...*I'm not stupid, you know...* [OPPOSITE] intelligent
2 = <u>silly</u>, foolish, daft (*informal*), rash, trivial, ludicrous, meaningless, irresponsible, pointless, futile, senseless, mindless, laughable, short-sighted, ill-advised, idiotic, fatuous, nonsensical, half-baked (*informal*), inane, crackpot (*informal*), unthinking, puerile, unintelligent, asinine, imbecilic, crackbrained ...*I wouldn't call it art. It's just stupid and tasteless... ...You won't go and do anything stupid, will you?...* [OPPOSITE] sensible
3 = <u>senseless</u>, dazed, groggy, punch-drunk, insensate, semiconscious, into a daze ...*She would drink herself stupid...*

stupidity 1 = <u>lack of intelligence</u>, imbecility, obtuseness, simplicity, thickness, slowness, dullness, dimness, dumbness (*informal*), feeble-mindedness, lack of brain, denseness, brainlessness, doziness (*Brit. informal*), asininity, dopiness (*slang*), thickheadedness ...*I stared at him, astonished by his stupidity...*
2 = <u>silliness</u>, folly, foolishness, idiocy, madness, absurdity, futility, lunacy, irresponsibility, pointlessness, inanity, rashness, impracticality, foolhardiness, senselessness, bêtise (*rare*), ludicrousness, puerility, fatuousness, fatuity ...*I can't get over the stupidity of their decision...*

stupor = <u>daze</u>, numbness, unconsciousness, trance, coma, inertia, lethargy, torpor, stupefaction, insensibility

sturdy 1 = <u>robust</u>, hardy, vigorous, powerful, athletic, muscular, stalwart, staunch, hearty, lusty, brawny, thickset ...*She was a short, sturdy woman in her early sixties...* [OPPOSITE] puny
2 = <u>substantial</u>, secure, solid, durable, well-made, well-built, built to last ...*The camera was mounted on a sturdy tripod...* [OPPOSITE] flimsy

stutter [NOUN] = <u>stammer</u>, faltering, speech impediment, speech defect, hesitance ...*He spoke with a pronounced stutter...*
[VERB] = <u>stammer</u>, stumble, falter, hesitate, splutter, speak haltingly ...*I was trembling so hard, I though I would stutter when I spoke...*

style [NOUN] **1** = <u>manner</u>, way, method, approach, technique, custom, mode ...*Our children's different learning styles created many problems...*
2 = <u>elegance</u>, taste, chic, flair, polish, grace, dash, sophistication, refinement, panache, élan, cosmopolitanism, savoir-faire, smartness, urbanity, stylishness, bon ton (*French*), fashionableness, dressiness (*informal*) ...*She has not lost her grace and style...*
3 = <u>design</u>, form, cut ...*Several styles of hat were available...*
4 = <u>type</u>, sort, kind, spirit, pattern, variety, appearance, tone, strain, category, characteristic, genre, tenor ...*six scenes in the style of a classical Greek tragedy...*
5 = <u>fashion</u>, trend, mode, vogue, rage ...*The longer length of skirt is the style at the moment...*

6 = <u>luxury</u>, ease, comfort, elegance, grandeur, affluence, gracious living ...*The £17 million settlement allowed her to live in style to the end...*

7 = <u>mode of expression</u>, phrasing, turn of phrase, wording, treatment, expression, vein, diction, phraseology ...*The author's style is wonderfully anecdotal...*

VERB **1** = <u>design</u>, cut, tailor, fashion, shape, arrange, adapt ...*classically styled clothes...*

2 = <u>call</u>, name, term, address, label, entitle, dub, designate, christen, denominate ...*people who would like to style themselves as arms dealers...*

stylish = <u>smart</u>, chic, polished, fashionable, trendy (*Brit. informal*), classy (*slang*), in fashion, snappy, in vogue, dapper, natty (*informal*), snazzy (*informal*), modish, well turned-out, dressy (*informal*), à la mode, voguish **OPPOSITE** scruffy

stymie = <u>frustrate</u>, defeat, foil, thwart, puzzle, stump, snooker, hinder, confound, mystify, balk, flummox, throw a spanner in the works (*Brit. informal*), nonplus, spike (someone's) guns

suave = <u>smooth</u>, charming, urbane, debonair, worldly, cool (*informal*), sophisticated, polite, gracious, agreeable, courteous, affable, smooth-tongued

subconscious **NOUN** = <u>mind</u>, psyche ...*the hidden power of the subconscious...*
ADJECTIVE = <u>hidden</u>, inner, suppressed, repressed, intuitive, latent, innermost, subliminal ...*a subconscious cry for affection...* **OPPOSITE** conscious

subdue **1** = <u>overcome</u>, defeat, master, break, control, discipline, crush, humble, put down, conquer, tame, overpower, overrun, trample, quell, triumph over, get the better of, vanquish, beat down, get under control, get the upper hand over, gain ascendancy over ...*They admit they have not been able to subdue the rebels...*

2 = <u>moderate</u>, control, check, suppress, soften, repress, mellow, tone down, quieten down ...*He forced himself to subdue and overcome his fears...* **OPPOSITE** arouse

subdued **1** = <u>quiet</u>, serious, sober, sad, grave, restrained, repressed, solemn, chastened, dejected, downcast, crestfallen, repentant, down in the mouth, sadder and wiser, out of spirits ...*He faced the press, initially, in a somewhat subdued mood...* **OPPOSITE** lively

2 = <u>hushed</u>, soft, quiet, whispered, murmured, muted ...*The conversation around them was resumed, but in subdued tones...* **OPPOSITE** loud

3 = <u>dim</u>, soft, subtle, muted, shaded, low-key, understated, toned down, unobtrusive ...*The lighting was subdued...* **OPPOSITE** bright

subject **NOUN** **1** = <u>topic</u>, question, issue, matter, point, business, affair, object, theme, substance, subject matter, field of inquiry *or* reference ...*It was I who first raised the subject of plastic surgery...*

2 = <u>branch of study</u>, area, field, discipline, speciality, branch of knowledge ...*a tutor in maths and science subjects...*

3 = <u>participant</u>, case, patient, victim, client, guinea pig (*informal*) ...*Subjects in the study were forced to follow a modified diet...*

4 = <u>citizen</u>, resident, native, inhabitant, national ...*Roughly half of them are British subjects...*

5 = <u>dependant</u>, subordinate, vassal, liegeman ...*His subjects regard him as a great and wise monarch...*
ADJECTIVE = <u>subordinate</u>, dependent, satellite, inferior, captive, obedient, enslaved, submissive, subservient, subjugated ...*colonies and other subject territories...*
VERB = <u>put through</u>, expose, submit, lay open, make liable ...*He had subjected her to four years of beatings and abuse...*

PHRASES **subject to** **1** = <u>liable to</u>, open to, exposed to, vulnerable to, prone to, susceptible to, disposed to ...*Prices may be subject to alteration...* **2** = <u>bound by</u>, under the control of, constrained by ...*It could not be subject to another country's laws...* **3** = <u>dependent on</u>, contingent on, controlled by, conditional on ...*The merger is subject to certain conditions...*

subjective = <u>personal</u>, emotional, prejudiced, biased, instinctive, intuitive, idiosyncratic, nonobjective **OPPOSITE** objective

subjugate = <u>conquer</u>, master, overcome, defeat, crush, suppress, put down, overthrow, tame, lick (*informal*), subdue, overpower, quell, rule over, enslave, vanquish, hold sway over, bring to heel, bring (someone) to his knees, bring under the yoke

sublimate = <u>channel</u>, transfer, divert, redirect, turn

sublime = <u>noble</u>, magnificent, glorious, high, great, grand, imposing, elevated, eminent, majestic, lofty, exalted, transcendent **OPPOSITE** lowly

subliminal = <u>subconscious</u>, unconscious

submerge **1** = <u>flood</u>, swamp, engulf, drown, overflow, inundate, deluge ...*The river burst its banks, submerging an entire village...*

2 = <u>immerse</u>, plunge, dip, duck, dunk ...*Submerge the pieces of fish in the poaching liquid and simmer...*

3 = <u>sink</u>, plunge, go under water ...*Just as I shot at it, the crocodile submerged again...*

4 = <u>overwhelm</u>, swamp, engulf, overload, inundate, deluge, snow under, overburden ...*He was suddenly submerged in an avalanche of scripts and offers...*

submerged = <u>immersed</u>, sunk, underwater, drowned, submarine, sunken, undersea, subaqueous, submersed, subaquatic

submission **1** = <u>surrender</u>, yielding, giving in, cave-in (*informal*), capitulation, acquiescence ...*The army intends to take the city or force it into submission...*

2 = <u>presentation</u>, submitting, handing in, entry, tendering ...*the submission of a dissertation...*

3 = <u>proposal</u>, argument, contention ...*A written submission has to be prepared...*

4 = <u>compliance</u>, obedience, submissiveness, meekness, resignation, deference, passivity, docility, tractability, unassertiveness ...*She nodded her head in submission...*

submissive = <u>meek</u>, passive, obedient, compliant,

patient, resigned, yielding, accommodating, humble, subdued, lowly, abject, amenable, docile, dutiful, ingratiating, malleable, deferential, pliant, obsequious, uncomplaining, tractable, acquiescent, biddable, unresisting, bootlicking (*informal*), obeisant OPPOSITE> obstinate

submit 1 = surrender, yield, give in, agree, bend, bow, endure, tolerate, comply, put up with (*informal*), succumb, defer, stoop, cave in (*informal*), capitulate, accede, acquiesce, toe the line, knuckle under, resign yourself, lay down arms, hoist the white flag, throw in the sponge ...*If I submitted to their demands, they would not press the allegations...*
2 = present, hand in, tender, put forward, table, commit, refer, proffer ...*They submitted their reports to the Chancellor yesterday...*
3 = suggest, claim, argue, propose, state, put, move, advance, volunteer, assert, contend, propound ...*I submit that you knew exactly what you were doing...*

subordinate NOUN = inferior, junior, assistant, aide, second, attendant, dependant, underling, subaltern ...*Nearly all her subordinates adored her...* OPPOSITE> superior
ADJECTIVE 1 = inferior, lesser, lower, junior, subject, minor, secondary, dependent, subservient ...*Sixty of his subordinate officers followed his example...* OPPOSITE> superior
2 = subsidiary, supplementary, auxiliary, ancillary ...*It was an art in which words were subordinate to images...*

subordination = inferiority, servitude, subjection, inferior *or* secondary status

subscribe 1 = support, agree, advocate, consent, endorse, countenance, acquiesce ...*I've personally never subscribed to the view...*
2 = contribute, give, donate, chip in (*informal*) ...*I subscribe to a few favourable charities...*

subscription (*Chiefly Brit.*) = membership fee, charge, dues, annual payment

subsequent = following, later, succeeding, after, successive, ensuing, consequent OPPOSITE> previous

subsequently = later, afterwards, in the end, consequently, in the aftermath (of), at a later date

subservient 1 = servile, submissive, deferential, subject, inferior, abject, sycophantic, slavish, obsequious, truckling, bootlicking (*informal*) ...*Her willingness to be subservient to her children isolated her...* OPPOSITE> domineering
2 = subordinate, subsidiary, accessory, auxiliary, conducive, ancillary ...*The individual's needs are seen as subservient to the group's...*

subside 1 = decrease, diminish, lessen, ease, moderate, dwindle, wane, recede, ebb, abate, let up, peter out, slacken, melt away, quieten, level off, de-escalate ...*The pain had subsided during the night...* OPPOSITE> increase
2 = collapse, sink, cave in, drop, lower, settle ...*Does that mean that the whole house is subsiding?...*
3 = drop, fall, decline, ebb, descend ...*Local officials

say the flood waters have subsided...*

subsidence = sinking, settling, collapse, settlement

subsidiary NOUN = branch, division, section, office, department, wing, subdivision, subsection, local office ...*a subsidiary of the American multinational...*
ADJECTIVE = secondary, lesser, subordinate, minor, supplementary, auxiliary, supplemental, contributory, ancillary, subservient ...*a subsidiary position...* OPPOSITE> main

subsidize = fund, finance, support, promote, sponsor, underwrite, put up the money for

subsidy = aid, help, support, grant, contribution, assistance, allowance, financial aid, stipend, subvention

subsist = stay alive, survive, keep going, make ends meet, last, live, continue, exist, endure, eke out an existence, keep your head above water, sustain yourself

subsistence = living, maintenance, upkeep, keep, support, existence, survival, livelihood

substance 1 = material, body, stuff, element, fabric, texture ...*The substance that causes the problem comes from the barley...*
2 = importance, significance, concreteness ...*It is questionable whether anything of substance has been achieved...*
3 = meaning, main point, gist, matter, subject, theme, import, significance, essence, pith, burden, sum and substance ...*The substance of his discussions doesn't really matter...*
4 = truth, fact, reality, certainty, validity, authenticity, verity, verisimilitude ...*There is no substance in any of these allegations...*
5 = wealth, means, property, assets, resources, estate, affluence ...*mature men of substance...*

substandard = inferior, inadequate, unacceptable, damaged, imperfect, second-rate, shoddy

substantial 1 = big, significant, considerable, goodly, large, important, generous, worthwhile, tidy (*informal*), ample, sizable *or* sizeable ...*That is a very substantial improvement in the current situation...* OPPOSITE> small
2 = solid, sound, sturdy, strong, firm, massive, hefty, durable, bulky, well-built ...*those fortunate enough to have a fairly substantial property to sell...* OPPOSITE> insubstantial

substantially 1 = considerably, significantly, very much, greatly, seriously (*informal*), remarkably, markedly, noticeably, appreciably ...*The price was substantially higher than had been expected...*
2 = essentially, largely, mainly, materially, in the main, in essence, to a large extent, in substance, in essentials ...*He checked the details given and found them substantially correct...*

substantiate = support, prove, confirm, establish, affirm, verify, validate, bear out, corroborate, attest to, authenticate OPPOSITE> disprove

substitute VERB 1 = replace, exchange, swap, change, switch, commute, interchange ...*They were *substituting violence for dialogue…*

2 with **for** = <u>stand in for</u>, cover for, take over from, relieve, act for, double for, fill in for, hold the fort for, be in place of, deputize for …*Her parents are trying to be supportive but they can't substitute for Jackie as a mother…*

NOUN = <u>replacement</u>, reserve, equivalent, surrogate, deputy, relief, representative, sub, temporary, stand-by, makeshift, proxy, temp (*informal*), expedient, locum, depute (*Scot.*), stopgap, locum tenens …*She is seeking a substitute for the man who broke her heart…*

ADJECTIVE = <u>replacement</u>, reserve, temporary, surrogate, second, acting, alternative, additional, fall-back, proxy …*They had fallen for their substitute teacher…*

> ## Word Power
>
> **substitute** – Although *substitute* and *replace* have the same meaning, the structures they are used in are different. You replace A *with* B, while you substitute B *for* A. Accordingly, *he replaced the worn tyre with a new one*, and *he substituted a new tyre for the worn one* are both correct ways of saying the same thing.

substitution = <u>replacement</u>, exchange, switch, swap, change, interchange

subterfuge = <u>trick</u>, dodge, ploy, shift, manoeuvre, deception, evasion, pretence, pretext, ruse, artifice, duplicity, stratagem, deviousness, machination

subtle 1 = <u>faint</u>, slight, implied, delicate, indirect, understated, insinuated …*a subtle hint…* OPPOSITE> obvious

2 = <u>crafty</u>, cunning, sly, designing, scheming, intriguing, shrewd, ingenious, astute, devious, wily, artful, Machiavellian …*He is a subtle character, you know…* OPPOSITE> straightforward

3 = <u>muted</u>, soft, subdued, low-key, toned down …*subtle shades of brown…*

4 = <u>fine</u>, minute, narrow, tenuous, hair-splitting …*There was, however, a subtle distinction between the two lawsuits…*

subtlety 1 = <u>fine point</u>, refinement, nicety, sophistication, delicacy, intricacy, discernment …*All those linguistic subtleties get lost when a book goes into translation…*

2 = <u>delicacy</u>, softness, delicateness, subtleness …*Many of the resulting wines lack the subtlety of the original model…*

3 = <u>skill</u>, acumen, astuteness, ingenuity, guile, cleverness, deviousness, sagacity, acuteness, craftiness, artfulness, slyness, wiliness …*She analyses herself with great subtlety…*

4 = <u>sensitivity</u>, diplomacy, discretion, delicacy, understanding, skill, consideration, judgment, perception, finesse, thoughtfulness, discernment, savoir-faire, adroitness …*They had obviously been hoping to approach the topic with more subtlety…*

subtract = <u>take away</u>, take off, deduct, remove,

withdraw, diminish, take from, detract OPPOSITE> add

suburb = <u>residential area</u>, neighbourhood, outskirts, precincts, suburbia, environs, purlieus, dormitory area (*Brit.*), faubourgs

subversive ADJECTIVE = <u>seditious</u>, inflammatory, incendiary, underground, undermining, destructive, overthrowing, riotous, insurrectionary, treasonous, perversive …*The play was promptly banned as subversive and possibly treasonous…*

NOUN = <u>dissident</u>, terrorist, saboteur, insurrectionary, quisling, fifth columnist, deviationist, seditionary, seditionist …*Agents regularly rounded up suspected subversives…*

subvert 1 = <u>overturn</u>, destroy, undermine, upset, ruin, wreck, demolish, sabotage …*an alleged plot to subvert the state…*

2 = <u>corrupt</u>, pervert, deprave, poison, contaminate, confound, debase, demoralize, vitiate …*an attempt to subvert culture from within…*

succeed 1 = <u>triumph</u>, win, prevail …*Some people will succeed in their efforts to stop smoking…*

2 = <u>work out</u>, work, be successful, come off (*informal*), do the trick (*informal*), turn out well, go like a bomb (*Brit. & N.Z. informal*), go down a bomb (*informal, chiefly Brit.*) …*a move which would make any future talks even more unlikely to succeed…*

3 = <u>make it</u> (*informal*), do well, be successful, arrive (*informal*), triumph, thrive, flourish, make good, prosper, cut it (*informal*), make the grade (*informal*), get to the top, crack it (*informal*), hit the jackpot (*informal*), bring home the bacon (*informal*), make your mark (*informal*), gain your end, carry all before you, do all right for yourself …*the skills and qualities needed to succeed…* OPPOSITE> fail

4 = <u>take over from</u>, replace, assume the office of, fill (someone's) boots, step into (someone's) boots …*He is almost certain to succeed him as chairman…*

5 with **to** = <u>take over</u>, assume, attain, acquire, come into, inherit, accede to, come into possession of …*He eventually succeeded to the post in 1998…*

6 = <u>follow</u>, come after, follow after, replace, be subsequent to, supervene …*He succeeded Trajan as emperor in AD 117…* OPPOSITE> precede

success 1 = <u>victory</u>, triumph, positive result, favourable outcome …*the success of European business in building a stronger partnership…* OPPOSITE> failure

2 = <u>prosperity</u>, fortune, luck, fame, eminence, ascendancy …*Nearly all of them believed work was the key to success…*

3 = <u>hit</u> (*informal*), winner, smash (*informal*), triumph, sensation, wow (*slang*), best seller, market leader, smash hit (*informal*) …*We hope it will be a commercial success…* OPPOSITE> flop

4 = <u>big name</u>, star, hit (*informal*), somebody, celebrity, sensation, megastar (*informal*), V.I.P. …*Everyone who knows her says she will be a great success…* OPPOSITE> nobody

successful 1 = <u>triumphant</u>, victorious, lucky,

fortunate …*The successful candidate will be announced in June…*

2 = thriving, profitable, productive, paying, effective, rewarding, booming, efficient, flourishing, unbeaten, lucrative, favourable, fruitful, efficacious, moneymaking …*One of the keys to successful business is careful planning…* OPPOSITE unprofitable

3 = top, prosperous, acknowledged, wealthy, out in front (*informal*), going places, at the top of the tree …*She is a successful lawyer…*

successfully = well, favourably, in triumph, with flying colours, famously (*informal*), swimmingly, victoriously

succession NOUN **1** = series, run, sequence, course, order, train, flow, chain, cycle, procession, continuation, progression …*He took a succession of jobs which have stood him in good stead…*

2 = taking over, assumption, inheritance, elevation, accession, entering upon …*She is now seventh in line of succession to the throne…*

PHRASES **in succession** = one after the other, running, successively, consecutively, on the trot (*informal*), one behind the other …*They needed to reach the World Cup final for the third time in succession…*

successive = consecutive, following, succeeding, in a row, in succession, sequent

succinct = brief, to the point, concise, compact, summary, condensed, terse, laconic, pithy, gnomic, compendious, in a few well-chosen words OPPOSITE rambling

succour NOUN = help, support, aid, relief, comfort, assistance …*Have you offered comfort and succour to your friend?…*

VERB = help, support, aid, encourage, nurse, comfort, foster, assist, relieve, minister to, befriend, render assistance to, give aid and encouragement to …*They had left nothing to succour a dung beetle, let alone a human…*

succulent = juicy, moist, luscious, rich, lush, mellow, mouthwatering

succumb 1 *often with* **to** = surrender, yield, submit, give in, give way, go under, cave in (*informal*), capitulate, knuckle under …*Don't succumb to the temptation to have just one cigarette…* OPPOSITE beat

2 *with* **to** (with an *illness* as object) = catch, fall victim to, fall ill with …*I was determined not to succumb to the virus…*

suck VERB **1** = drink, sip, draw …*They waited in silence and sucked their drinks through straws…*

2 = take, draw, pull, extract …*The air is sucked out by a high-powered fan…*

PHRASES **suck up to someone** (*Informal*) = ingratiate yourself with, play up to (*informal*), curry favour with, flatter, pander to, toady, butter up, keep in with (*informal*), fawn on, truckle, lick someone's boots, dance attendance on, get on the right side of, worm yourself into (someone's) favour …*She kept sucking up to the teachers…*

sucker (*Slang*) = fool, mug (*Brit. slang*), dupe, victim, butt, sap (*slang*), pushover (*slang*), sitting duck (*informal*), sitting target, putz (*U.S. slang*), cat's paw, easy game *or* mark (*informal*), nerd *or* nurd (*slang*), dorba *or* dorb (*Austral. slang*), bogan (*Austral. slang*)

sudden = quick, rapid, unexpected, swift, hurried, abrupt, hasty, impulsive, unforeseen OPPOSITE gradual

suddenly = abruptly, all of a sudden, all at once, unexpectedly, out of the blue (*informal*), without warning, on the spur of the moment

sue 1 (*Law*) = take (someone) to court, prosecute, bring an action against (someone), charge, summon, indict, have the law on (someone) (*informal*), prefer charges against (someone), institute legal proceedings against (someone) …*The company could be sued for damages…*

2 = appeal for, plead, beg, petition, solicit, beseech, entreat, supplicate …*He realized that suing for peace was the only option…*

suffer 1 = be in pain, hurt, ache, be racked, have a bad time, go through a lot (*informal*), go through the mill (*informal*), feel wretched …*Can you assure me that my father is not suffering?…*

2 = be affected, have trouble with, be afflicted, be troubled with …*I realized he was suffering from shock…*

3 = undergo, experience, sustain, feel, bear, go through, endure …*The peace process has suffered a serious blow now…*

4 = deteriorate, decline, get worse, fall off, be impaired …*I'm not surprised that your studies are suffering…*

5 = tolerate, stand, put up with (*informal*), support, bear, endure, hack (*Brit. informal*), abide …*She doesn't suffer fools gladly and, in her view, most people are fools…*

suffering = pain, torture, distress, agony, misery, ordeal, discomfort, torment, hardship, anguish, affliction, martyrdom

suffice = be enough, do, be sufficient, be adequate, answer, serve, content, satisfy, fill the bill (*informal*), meet requirements

sufficient = adequate, enough, ample, satisfactory, enow (*archaic*) OPPOSITE insufficient

suffocate 1 = choke, stifle, smother, asphyxiate …*They were suffocated as they slept…*

2 = be choked, be stifled, be smothered, be asphyxiated …*He either suffocated, or froze to death…*

suffuse = spread through *or* over, flood, infuse, cover, steep, bathe, mantle, pervade, permeate, imbue, overspread, transfuse

suggest 1 = recommend, propose, advise, move, advocate, prescribe, put forward, offer a suggestion …*I suggest you ask him some specific questions about his past…*

2 = indicate, lead you to believe …*The figures suggest that their success is conditional on this restriction…*

3 = hint at, imply, insinuate, intimate, get at, drive at (*informal*) …*What exactly are you suggesting?…*

4 = <u>bring to mind</u>, evoke, remind you of, connote, make you think of, put you in mind of ...*Its hairy body suggests a mammal...*

suggestion 1 = <u>recommendation</u>, proposal, proposition, plan, motion ...*I have lots of suggestions for the park's future...*
2 = <u>hint</u>, implication, insinuation, intimation ...*There is absolutely no suggestion of any mainstream political party involvement...*
3 = <u>trace</u>, touch, hint, breath, indication, whisper, suspicion, intimation ...*that fashionably faint suggestion of a tan...*

suggestive ADJECTIVE = <u>smutty</u>, rude, indecent, improper, blue, provocative, spicy (*informal*), racy, unseemly, titillating, risqué, bawdy, prurient, off colour, ribald, immodest, indelicate ...*A female employee claimed he made suggestive remarks to her...*
PHRASES **suggestive of** = <u>reminiscent of</u>, indicative of, redolent of, evocative of ...*These headaches were most suggestive of raised blood pressure...*

suit NOUN **1** = <u>outfit</u>, costume, ensemble, dress, clothing, habit ...*a smart suit and tie...*
2 = <u>lawsuit</u>, case, trial, proceeding, cause, action, prosecution, industrial tribunal ...*The judge dismissed the suit...*
VERB **1** = <u>be acceptable to</u>, please, satisfy, do, answer, gratify ...*They will only release information if it suits them...*
2 = <u>agree with</u>, become, match, go with, correspond with, conform to, befit, harmonize with ...*I don't think a sedentary life would altogether suit me...*
3 = <u>look attractive on</u>, become, flatter, look good on, enhance the appearance of, show to advantage ...*Green suits you...*
4 = <u>adjust</u>, adapt, modify, fit, fashion, proportion, accommodate, tailor, customize ...*'I'm off.' He suited the action to the word and left...*
PHRASES **follow suit** = <u>copy someone</u>, emulate someone, accord with someone, take your cue from someone, run with the herd ...*The Dutch seem set to follow suit...*

suitability = <u>appropriateness</u>, fitness, rightness, aptness

suitable 1 = <u>appropriate</u>, right, fitting, fit, suited, acceptable, becoming, satisfactory, apt, befitting ...*She had no other dress suitable for the occasion...* OPPOSITE > inappropriate
2 = <u>seemly</u>, fitting, becoming, due, proper, correct ...*Was it really suitable behaviour for someone who wants to be taken seriously?...* OPPOSITE > unseemly
3 = <u>suited</u>, appropriate, in keeping with, in character, cut out for ...*a resort where the slopes are more suitable for young children...* OPPOSITE > out of keeping
4 = <u>pertinent</u>, relevant, applicable, fitting, appropriate, to the point, apt, apposite, germane ...*Give a few people an idea of suitable questions to ask...* OPPOSITE > irrelevant
5 = <u>convenient</u>, timely, appropriate, well-timed, opportune, commodious ...*He could think of no less suitable moment to mention the idea...* OPPOSITE > inopportune

suite 1 = <u>rooms</u>, apartment, set of rooms, living quarters ...*a suite at the Paris Hilton...*
2 = <u>set</u>, series, collection ...*We will run a suite of checks...*
3 = <u>attendants</u>, escorts, entourage, train, followers, retainers, retinue ...*Fox and his suite sat there, looking uncertain...*

suitor (*Old-fashioned*) = <u>admirer</u>, young man, beau, follower (*obsolete*), swain (*archaic*), wooer

sulk = <u>be sullen</u>, brood, be in a huff, pout, be put out, have the hump (*Brit. informal*)

sulky = <u>huffy</u>, sullen, petulant, cross, put out, moody, perverse, disgruntled, aloof, resentful, vexed, churlish, morose, querulous, ill-humoured, in the sulks

sullen = <u>morose</u>, cross, moody, sour, gloomy, brooding, dour, surly, glowering, sulky, unsociable, out of humour OPPOSITE > cheerful

sully 1 = <u>dishonour</u>, ruin, disgrace, besmirch, smirch ...*Reputations are easily sullied and business lost...*
2 = <u>defile</u>, dirty, stain, spot, spoil, contaminate, pollute, taint, tarnish, blemish, befoul ...*I felt loath to sully the gleaming brass knocker by handling it...*

sultry 1 = <u>humid</u>, close, hot, sticky, stifling, oppressive, stuffy, sweltering, muggy ...*The climax came one sultry August evening...* OPPOSITE > cool
2 = <u>seductive</u>, sexy (*informal*), sensual, voluptuous, passionate, erotic, provocative, amorous, come-hither (*informal*) ...*a dark-haired sultry woman...*

sum NOUN **1** = <u>amount</u>, quantity, volume ...*Large sums of money were lost...*
2 = <u>calculation</u>, figures, arithmetic, problem, numbers, reckonings, mathematics, maths (*Brit. informal*), tally, math (*U.S. informal*), arithmetical problem ...*I can't do my sums...*
3 = <u>total</u>, aggregate, entirety, sum total ...*The sum of all the angles of a triangle is 180 degrees...*
4 = <u>totality</u>, whole ...*The sum of evidence points to the crime resting on them...*
PHRASES **sum something** or **someone up** = <u>size up</u>, estimate (*informal*), get the measure of, form an opinion of ...*My mother probably summed her up better than I ever could...*

summarily = <u>immediately</u>, promptly, swiftly, on the spot, speedily, without delay, arbitrarily, at short notice, forthwith, expeditiously, peremptorily, without wasting words

summarize = <u>sum up</u>, recap, review, outline, condense, encapsulate, epitomize, abridge, précis, recapitulate, give a rundown of, put in a nutshell, give the main points of

summary NOUN = <u>synopsis</u>, résumé, précis, recapitulation, review, outline, extract, essence, abstract, summing-up, digest, epitome, rundown, compendium, abridgment ...*Here's a summary of the day's news...*
ADJECTIVE **1** = <u>hasty</u>, cursory, perfunctory, arbitrary ...*The four men were killed after a summary trial...*

2 = <u>concise</u>, brief, compact, condensed, laconic, succinct, pithy, compendious ...*a summary profit and loss statement*...

summit 1 = <u>meeting</u>, talks, conference, discussion, negotiation, dialogue ...*a NATO summit held in Rome*...
2 = <u>peak</u>, top, tip, pinnacle, apex, head, crown, crest ...*the first man to reach the summit of Mount Everest*... OPPOSITE base
3 = <u>height</u>, pinnacle, culmination, peak, high point, zenith, acme, crowning point ...*This is just a molehill on the way to the summit of her ambitions*... OPPOSITE depths

summon 1 = <u>send for</u>, call, bid, invite, rally, assemble, convene, call together, convoke ...*Howe summoned a doctor and hurried over*...
2 *often with* **up** = <u>gather</u>, muster, draw on, invoke, mobilize, call into action ...*We couldn't even summon up the energy to open the envelope*...

sumptuous = <u>luxurious</u>, rich, grand, expensive, superb, magnificent, costly, splendid, posh (*Informal, chiefly Brit.*), gorgeous, lavish, extravagant, plush (*informal*), opulent, palatial, ritzy (*slang*), de luxe, splendiferous (*facetious*) OPPOSITE plain

sun NOUN = <u>Sol</u> (*Roman myth*), Helios (*Greek myth*), Phoebus (*Greek myth*), daystar (*poetic*), eye of heaven, Phoebus Apollo (*Greek myth*) ...*The sun was now high in the southern sky*...
PHRASES **sun yourself** = <u>sunbathe</u>, tan, bask ...*She was last seen sunning herself in a riverside park*...
(Related Words)
adjective: solar

sundry = <u>various</u>, several, varied, assorted, some, different, divers (*archaic*), miscellaneous

sunk = <u>ruined</u>, lost, finished, done for (*informal*), on the rocks, all washed up (*informal*), up the creek without a paddle (*informal*)

sunken 1 = <u>submerged</u>, immersed, submersed ...*Try diving for sunken treasure*...
2 = <u>lowered</u>, buried, depressed, recessed, below ground, at a lower level ...*Steps led down to the sunken bath*...
3 = <u>hollow</u>, drawn, haggard, hollowed, concave ...*an elderly man with sunken cheeks*...

sunny 1 = <u>bright</u>, clear, fine, brilliant, radiant, luminous, sunlit, summery, unclouded, sunshiny, without a cloud in the sky ...*The weather was surprisingly warm and sunny*... OPPOSITE dull
2 = <u>cheerful</u>, happy, cheery, smiling, beaming, pleasant, optimistic, buoyant, joyful, genial, chirpy (*informal*), blithe, light-hearted ...*The staff wear big sunny smiles*... OPPOSITE gloomy

sunrise = <u>dawn</u>, daybreak, break of day, daylight, aurora (*poetic*), sunup, cockcrow, dayspring (*poetic*)

sunset = <u>nightfall</u>, dusk, sundown, eventide, gloaming (*Scot. or poetic*), close of (the) day

super (*Informal*) = <u>excellent</u>, wonderful, marvellous, mean (*slang*), topping (*Brit. slang*), cracking (*Brit. informal*), crucial (*slang*), outstanding, smashing

(*informal*), superb, magnificent, glorious, terrific (*informal*), sensational (*informal*), mega (*slang*), sovereign, awesome (*slang*), def (*slang*), top-notch (*informal*), brill (*informal*), incomparable, out of this world (*informal*), peerless, matchless, boffo (*slang*), jim-dandy (*slang*), chillin' (*U.S. slang*), booshit (*Austral. slang*), exo (*Austral. slang*), sik (*Austral. slang*)

superb 1 = <u>splendid</u>, excellent, magnificent, topping (*Brit. slang*), fine, choice, grand, superior, divine, marvellous, gorgeous, mega (*slang*), awesome (*slang*), world-class, exquisite, breathtaking, first-rate, superlative, unrivalled, brill (*informal*), bodacious (*slang, chiefly U.S.*), boffo (*slang*), splendiferous (*facetious*), of the first water, chillin' (*U.S. slang*), booshit (*Austral. slang*), exo (*Austral. slang*), sik (*Austral. slang*) ...*a superb 18-hole golf course*... OPPOSITE inferior
2 = <u>magnificent</u>, superior, marvellous, exquisite, breathtaking, admirable, superlative, unrivalled, splendiferous (*facetious*) ...*With superb skill he managed to make a perfect landing*... OPPOSITE terrible

superficial 1 = <u>shallow</u>, frivolous, empty-headed, empty, silly, lightweight, trivial ...*a superficial yuppie with no intellect whatsoever*... OPPOSITE serious
2 = <u>hasty</u>, cursory, perfunctory, passing, nodding, hurried, casual, sketchy, facile, desultory, slapdash, inattentive ...*He only gave it a superficial glance through*... OPPOSITE thorough
3 = <u>slight</u>, surface, external, cosmetic, on the surface, exterior, peripheral, skin-deep ...*It may well look different but the changes are only superficial*... OPPOSITE profound

superficially = <u>at first glance</u>, apparently, on the surface, ostensibly, externally, at face value, to the casual eye

superfluous = <u>excess</u>, surplus, redundant, remaining, extra, spare, excessive, unnecessary, in excess, needless, left over, on your hands, surplus to requirements, uncalled-for, unneeded, residuary, supernumerary, superabundant, pleonastic (*Rhetoric*), unrequired, supererogatory OPPOSITE necessary

superhuman = <u>heroic</u>, phenomenal, prodigious, stupendous, herculean

superintend = <u>supervise</u>, run, oversee, control, manage, direct, handle, look after, overlook, administer, inspect

superintendent 1 = <u>supervisor</u>, director, manager, chief, governor, inspector, administrator, conductor, controller, overseer ...*He became superintendent of the bank's East African branches*...
2 (*U.S.*) = <u>warden</u>, caretaker, curator, keeper, porter, custodian, watchman, janitor, concierge ...*He lost his job as a building superintendent*...

superior ADJECTIVE **1** = <u>better</u>, higher, greater, grander, preferred, prevailing, paramount, surpassing, more advanced, predominant, unrivalled, more extensive, more skilful, more expert, a cut above (*informal*), streets ahead (*informal*), running rings around (*informal*) …*a woman greatly superior to her husband in education*… OPPOSITE inferior

2 = first-class, excellent, first-rate, good, fine, choice, exclusive, distinguished, exceptional, world-class, good quality, admirable, high-class, high calibre, de luxe, of the first order, booshit (*Austral. slang*), exo (*Austral. slang*), sik (*Austral. slang*) …*He's got a superior car, and it's easy to win races that way*… OPPOSITE average

3 = higher-ranking, senior, higher-level, upper-level …*negotiations between mutineers and their superior officers*…

4 = supercilious, patronizing, condescending, haughty, disdainful, lordly, lofty, airy, pretentious, stuck-up (*informal*), snobbish, on your high horse (*informal*) …*Finch gave a superior smile*…

NOUN = boss, senior, director, manager, chief (*informal*), principal, supervisor, baas (*S. African*) …*my immediate superior*… OPPOSITE subordinate

---

Word Power

superior – *Superior should not be used with* than: *he is a better* (not *a superior*) *poet than his brother; his poetry is superior to* (not *than*) *his brother's.*

---

superiority = supremacy, lead, advantage, excellence, prevalence, ascendancy, pre-eminence, preponderance, predominance

superlative = supreme, excellent, outstanding, highest, greatest, crack (*slang*), magnificent, surpassing, consummate, stellar (*informal*), unparalleled, transcendent, unrivalled, peerless, unsurpassed, matchless, of the highest order, of the first water OPPOSITE average

supernatural = paranormal, mysterious, unearthly, uncanny, dark, hidden, ghostly, psychic, phantom, abnormal, mystic, miraculous, unnatural, occult, spectral, preternatural, supranatural

➤ **supernatural creatures**

supersede = replace, displace, usurp, supplant, remove, take over, oust, take the place of, fill or step

into (someone's) boots

supervise 1 = observe, guide, monitor, oversee, keep an eye on …*He supervised and trained more than 400 volunteers*…

2 = oversee, run, manage, control, direct, handle, conduct, look after, be responsible for, administer, inspect, preside over, keep an eye on, be on duty at, superintend, have or be in charge of …*One of his jobs was supervising the dining room*…

supervision = superintendence, direction, instruction, control, charge, care, management, administration, guidance, surveillance, oversight, auspices, stewardship

supervisor = boss (*informal*), manager, superintendent, chief, inspector, administrator, steward, gaffer (*informal, chiefly Brit.*), foreman, overseer, baas (*S. African*)

supervisory = managerial, administrative, overseeing, superintendent, executive

supine 1 = flat on your back, flat, horizontal, recumbent …*a statue of a supine dog*… OPPOSITE prone

2 = lethargic, passive, lazy, idle, indifferent, careless, sluggish, negligent, inert, languid, uninterested, apathetic, lymphatic, listless, indolent, heedless, torpid, slothful, spiritless …*a willing and supine executive*…

supplant = replace, oust, displace, supersede, remove, take over, undermine, overthrow, unseat, take the place of

supple 1 = pliant, flexible, pliable, plastic, bending, elastic …*The leather is supple and sturdy enough to last for years*… OPPOSITE rigid

2 = flexible, lithe, limber, lissom(e), loose-limbed …*Paul was incredibly supple and strong*… OPPOSITE stiff

supplement VERB = add to, reinforce, complement, augment, extend, top up, fill out …*I suggest supplementing your diet with vitamins E and A*…

NOUN **1** = pull-out, insert, magazine section, added feature …*a special supplement to a monthly financial*

Supernatural creatures http://www.pantheon.org/

angel	gnome	ogre
banshee	goblin	peri
brownie	god or goddess	phantom
demon	golem	pixie
devil	gremlin	poltergeist
dwarf	guardian angel	sandman
dybbuk	hobgoblin	selkie or silkie
elf	imp	spectre
fairy	incubus	sprite
fairy godmother	jinni, jinnee, djinni, or djinny	succubus
familiar	kachina	sylph
fay	kelpie	troll
genie	lamia	vampire
ghost	leprechaun	werewolf or lycanthrope
ghoul	little people or folk	wraith
giant	monster	zombie or zombi

magazine…

2 = appendix, sequel, add-on, complement, postscript, addendum, codicil …*the supplement to the Encyclopedia Britannica…*

3 = addition, extra, surcharge …*The single room supplement is £11 a night…*

supplementary = additional, extra, complementary, accompanying, secondary, auxiliary, add-on, supplemental, ancillary

supply `VERB` **1** = provide, give, furnish, produce, stock, store, grant, afford, contribute, yield, come up with, outfit, endow, purvey, victual …*an agreement not to supply chemical weapons to these countries…*

2 = furnish, provide, equip, endow …*a pipeline which will supply the city with natural gas…*

3 = meet, provide for, fill, satisfy, fulfil, be adequate for, cater to *or* for …*a society that looks to the government to supply their needs…*

`NOUN` = store, fund, stock, source, reserve, quantity, reservoir, stockpile, hoard, cache …*The brain requires a constant supply of oxygen…*

`PLURAL NOUN` = provisions, necessities, stores, food, materials, items, equipment, rations, foodstuff, provender …*The country's only supplies are those it can import by lorry…*

support `VERB` **1** = help, back, champion, second, aid, forward, encourage, defend, promote, take (someone's) part, strengthen, assist, advocate, uphold, side with, go along with, stand up for, espouse, stand behind, hold (someone's) hand, stick up for (*informal*), succour, buoy up, boost (someone's) morale, take up the cudgels for, be a source of strength to …*He supported the hardworking people…* `OPPOSITE` oppose

2 = provide for, maintain, look after, keep, fund, finance, sustain, foster, take care of, subsidize …*I have children to support, and a home to be maintained…* `OPPOSITE` live off

3 = bear out, confirm, verify, substantiate, corroborate, document, endorse, attest to, authenticate, lend credence to …*The evidence does not support the argument…* `OPPOSITE` refute

4 = bear, hold up, carry, sustain, prop (up), reinforce, hold, brace, uphold, bolster, underpin, shore up, buttress …*the thick wooden posts that supported the ceiling…*

`NOUN` **1** = furtherance, backing, promotion, championship, approval, assistance, encouragement, espousal …*They are prepared to resort to violence in support of their views…*

2 = help, protection, comfort, friendship, assistance, blessing, loyalty, patronage, moral support, succour …*We hope to continue to have her close support and friendship…* `OPPOSITE` opposition

3 = aid, help, benefits, relief, assistance …*the EC's proposal to cut agricultural support…*

4 = prop, post, foundation, back, lining, stay, shore, brace, pillar, underpinning, stanchion, stiffener, abutment …*Rats had been gnawing at the supports of the house…*

5 = supporter, prop, mainstay, tower of strength, second, stay, backer, backbone, comforter …*Andrew is terrific. He's been such a support to me…* `OPPOSITE` antagonist

6 = upkeep, maintenance, keep, livelihood, subsistence, sustenance …*He failed to send child support…*

supporter = follower, fan, advocate, friend, champion, ally, defender, sponsor, patron, helper, protagonist, adherent, henchman, apologist, upholder, well-wisher `OPPOSITE` opponent

supportive = helpful, caring, encouraging, understanding, reassuring, sympathetic

(**Related Words**)

prefix: pro-

suppose 1 = imagine, believe, consider, conclude, fancy, conceive, conjecture, postulate, hypothesize …*Where do you suppose he's got to?…*

2 = think, imagine, expect, judge, assume, guess (*informal, chiefly U.S. & Canad.*), calculate (*U.S. dialect*), presume, take for granted, infer, conjecture, surmise, dare say, opine, presuppose, take as read …*The problem was more complex than he supposed…*

supposed 1 *usually with* **to** = meant, expected, required, obliged …*He produced a handwritten note of nine men he was supposed to kill…*

2 = presumed, alleged, professed, reputed, accepted, assumed, rumoured, hypothetical, putative, presupposed …*What is it his son is supposed to have said?…*

supposedly = presumably, allegedly, ostensibly, theoretically, by all accounts, purportedly, avowedly, hypothetically, at a guess, professedly `OPPOSITE` actually

supposition = belief, idea, notion, view, theory, speculation, assumption, hypothesis, presumption, conjecture, surmise, guesswork

suppress 1 = stamp out, stop, check, crush, conquer, overthrow, subdue, put an end to, overpower, quash, crack down on, quell, extinguish, clamp down on, snuff out, quench, beat down, trample on, drive underground …*drug traffickers who flourish despite attempts to suppress them…* `OPPOSITE` encourage

2 = check, inhibit, subdue, stop, quell, quench …*strong evidence that ultraviolet light can suppress immune responses…*

3 = restrain, cover up, withhold, stifle, contain, silence, conceal, curb, repress, smother, keep secret, muffle, muzzle, hold in check, hold in *or* back …*Liz thought of Barry and suppressed a smile…*

4 = conceal, hide, keep secret, hush up, stonewall, sweep under the carpet, draw a veil over, keep silent about, keep dark, keep under your hat (*informal*) …*At no time did they try to persuade me to suppress the information…*

suppression 1 = elimination, crushing, crackdown, check, extinction, prohibition, quashing, dissolution, termination, clampdown …*They were imprisoned after the suppression of pro-democracy protests…*

2 = <u>inhibition</u>, blocking, restriction, restraint, smothering ...*suppression of the immune system...*
3 = <u>concealment</u>, covering, hiding, disguising, camouflage ...*A mother's suppression of her own feelings can cause problems...*
4 = <u>hiding</u>, hushing up, stonewalling ...*suppression of official documents...*

supremacy = <u>domination</u>, dominance, ascendancy, sovereignty, sway, lordship, mastery, dominion, primacy, pre-eminence, predominance, supreme power, absolute rule, paramountcy

supreme 1 = <u>paramount</u>, surpassing, superlative, prevailing, sovereign, predominant, incomparable, mother of all (*informal*), unsurpassed, matchless ...*The lady conspired to seize supreme power...*
OPPOSITE> least
2 = <u>chief</u>, leading, principal, first, highest, head, top, prime, cardinal, foremost, pre-eminent, peerless ...*He proposes to make himself the supreme overlord...*
OPPOSITE> lowest
3 = <u>ultimate</u>, highest, greatest, utmost, final, crowning, extreme, culminating ...*My oldest son made the supreme sacrifice in Vietnam...*

supremo (*Brit. informal*) = <u>head</u>, leader, boss (*informal*), director, master, governor, commander, principal, ruler, baas (*S. African*)

sure 1 = <u>certain</u>, positive, clear, decided, convinced, persuaded, confident, satisfied, assured, definite, free from doubt ...*She was no longer sure how she felt about him...* OPPOSITE> uncertain
2 = <u>inevitable</u>, guaranteed, bound, assured, in the bag (*slang*), inescapable, irrevocable, ineluctable ...*Another victory is now sure...* OPPOSITE> unsure
3 = <u>reliable</u>, accurate, dependable, effective, precise, honest, unmistakable, undoubted, undeniable, trustworthy, never-failing, trusty, foolproof, infallible, indisputable, sure-fire (*informal*), unerring, well-proven, unfailing, tried and true ...*a sure sign of rain...* OPPOSITE> unreliable
4 = <u>secure</u>, firm, steady, fast, safe, solid, stable ...*A doctor's sure hands may perform surgery...*

surely 1 = <u>it must be the case that</u>, assuredly ...*If I can accept this situation, surely you can?...*
2 = <u>undoubtedly</u>, certainly, definitely, inevitably, doubtless, for certain, without doubt, unquestionably, inexorably, come what may, without fail, indubitably, doubtlessly, beyond the shadow of a doubt ...*He knew that under the surgeon's knife he would surely die...*

surety 1 = <u>security</u>, guarantee, deposit, insurance, bond, safety, pledge, bail, warranty, indemnity ...*a surety of £2,500...*
2 = <u>guarantor</u>, sponsor, hostage, bondsman, mortgagor ...*I agreed to stand surety for Arthur to be bailed out...*

surface NOUN **1** = <u>covering</u>, face, exterior, side, top, skin, plane, facet, veneer ...*The road surface had started breaking up...*
2 = <u>façade</u>, outward appearance ...*A much wider controversy was bubbling under the surface...*
ADJECTIVE = <u>superficial</u>, external, outward, exterior ...*Doctors believed it was just a surface wound...*
VERB **1** = <u>emerge</u>, come up, come to the surface ...*He surfaced, gasping for air...*
2 = <u>appear</u>, emerge, arise, come to light, crop up (*informal*), transpire, materialize ...*The emotions will surface at some point in life...*
PHRASES **on the surface** = <u>at first glance</u>, apparently, outwardly, seemingly, ostensibly, superficially, to all appearances, to the casual eye ...*On the surface the elections appear to be democratic...*

surfeit = <u>excess</u>, plethora, glut, satiety, overindulgence, superabundance, superfluity
OPPOSITE> shortage

surge NOUN **1** = <u>rush</u>, flood, upsurge, sudden increase, uprush ...*a new surge of interest in Dylan's work...*
2 = <u>flow</u>, wave, rush, roller, breaker, gush, upsurge, outpouring, uprush ...*The bridge was destroyed in a tidal surge during a storm...*
3 = <u>tide</u>, roll, rolling, swell, swirling, billowing ...*the beating and surge of the sea...*
4 = <u>rush</u>, wave, storm, outburst, torrent, eruption ...*He was overcome by a sudden surge of jealousy...*
VERB **1** = <u>rush</u>, pour, stream, rise, swell, spill, swarm, seethe, gush, well forth ...*The crowd surged out from the church...*
2 = <u>roll</u>, rush, billow, heave, swirl, eddy, undulate ...*Fish and seaweed rose, caught motionless in the surging water...*
3 = <u>sweep</u>, rush, storm ...*Panic surged through her...*

surly = <u>ill-tempered</u>, cross, churlish, crabbed, perverse, crusty, sullen, gruff, bearish, sulky, morose, brusque, testy, grouchy (*informal*), curmudgeonly, ungracious, uncivil, shrewish OPPOSITE> cheerful

surmise VERB = <u>guess</u>, suppose, imagine, presume, consider, suspect, conclude, fancy, speculate, infer, deduce, come to the conclusion, conjecture, opine, hazard a guess ...*He surmised that he had discovered one of the illegal streets...*
NOUN = <u>guess</u>, speculation, assumption, thought, idea, conclusion, notion, suspicion, hypothesis, deduction, inference, presumption, conjecture, supposition ...*His surmise proved correct...*

surmount = <u>overcome</u>, master, conquer, pass, exceed, surpass, overpower, triumph over, vanquish, prevail over

surpass = <u>outdo</u>, top, beat, best, cap (*informal*), exceed, eclipse, overshadow, excel, transcend, outstrip, outshine, tower above, go one better than (*informal*), put in the shade

surpassing = <u>supreme</u>, extraordinary, outstanding, exceptional, rare, phenomenal, stellar (*informal*), transcendent, unrivalled, incomparable, matchless

surplus NOUN = <u>excess</u>, surfeit, superabundance, superfluity ...*Germany suffers from a surplus of teachers...* OPPOSITE> shortage

ADJECTIVE = <u>extra</u>, spare, excess, remaining, odd, in excess, left over, unused, superfluous ...*Few people have large sums of surplus cash...* **OPPOSITE** insufficient

surprise **NOUN** 1 = <u>shock</u>, start (*informal*), revelation, jolt, bombshell, eye-opener (*informal*), bolt from the blue, turn-up for the books (*informal*) ...*It is perhaps no surprise to see her attempting a comeback...*
2 = <u>amazement</u>, astonishment, wonder, incredulity, stupefaction ...*To my surprise I am in a room where I see one of my mother's sisters...*
VERB 1 = <u>amaze</u>, astonish, astound, stun, startle, stagger, disconcert, take aback, bowl over (*informal*), leave open-mouthed, nonplus, flabbergast (*informal*), take (someone's) breath away ...*We'll solve the case ourselves and surprise everyone...*
2 = <u>catch unawares</u> or <u>off-guard</u>, catch napping, catch on the hop (*informal*), burst in on, spring upon, catch in the act or red-handed, come down on like a bolt from the blue ...*The army surprised their enemy near the village of Blenheim...*

surprised = <u>amazed</u>, astonished, startled, disconcerted, at a loss, taken aback, speechless, incredulous, open-mouthed, nonplussed, thunderstruck, unable to believe your eyes

surprising = <u>amazing</u>, remarkable, incredible, astonishing, wonderful, unusual, extraordinary, unexpected, staggering, marvellous, startling, astounding, jaw-dropping, unlooked-for

surrender **VERB** 1 = <u>give in</u>, yield, submit, give way, quit, succumb, cave in (*informal*), capitulate, throw in the towel, lay down arms, give yourself up, show the white flag ...*We'll never surrender to the terrorists...* **OPPOSITE** resist
2 = <u>give up</u>, abandon, relinquish, resign, yield, concede, part with, renounce, waive, forego, cede, deliver up ...*She had to surrender all rights to her property...*
NOUN = <u>submission</u>, yielding, cave-in (*informal*), capitulation, resignation, renunciation, relinquishment ...*the unconditional surrender of the rebels...*

surreptitious = <u>secret</u>, clandestine, furtive, sneaking, veiled, covert, sly, fraudulent, unauthorized, underhand, stealthy **OPPOSITE** open

surrogate = <u>substitute</u>, deputy, representative, stand-in, proxy

surround 1 = <u>enclose</u>, ring, encircle, encompass, envelop, close in on, fence in, girdle, hem in, environ, enwreath ...*The church was surrounded by a rusted wrought-iron fence...*
2 = <u>besiege</u>, beset, lay siege to, invest (*rare*) ...*When the car stopped it was surrounded by police and militiamen...*

surrounding **ADJECTIVE** = <u>nearby</u>, neighbouring ...*Aerial bombing of the surrounding area is continuing...*
PLURAL NOUN = <u>environment</u>, setting, background, location, neighbourhood, milieu, environs ...*a*

peaceful holiday home in beautiful surroundings...

surveillance = <u>observation</u>, watch, scrutiny, supervision, control, care, direction, inspection, vigilance, superintendence

survey **NOUN** 1 = <u>poll</u>, study, research, review, inquiry, investigation, opinion poll, questionnaire, census ...*According to the survey, overall world trade has also slackened...*
2 = <u>examination</u>, inspection, scrutiny, overview, once-over (*informal*), perusal ...*He sniffed the perfume she wore, then gave her a quick survey...*
3 = <u>valuation</u>, estimate, assessment, appraisal ...*a structural survey undertaken by a qualified surveyor...*
VERB 1 = <u>interview</u>, question, poll, study, research, investigate, sample, canvass ...*Only 18 percent of those surveyed opposed the idea...*
2 = <u>look over</u>, view, scan, examine, observe, contemplate, supervise, inspect, eyeball (*slang*), scrutinize, size up, take stock of, eye up, recce (*slang*), reconnoitre ...*He pushed himself to his feet and surveyed the room...*
3 = <u>measure</u>, estimate, prospect, assess, appraise, triangulate ...*Geological experts were commissioned to survey the land...*

survive 1 = <u>remain alive</u>, live, pull through, last, exist, live on, endure, hold out, subsist, keep body and soul together (*informal*), be extant, fight for your life, keep your head above water ...*Drugs that dissolve blood clots can help heart-attack victims survive...*
2 = <u>continue</u>, last, live on, pull through ...*Rejected by the people, can the organization survive at all?...*
3 = <u>live longer than</u>, outlive, outlast ...*Most women will survive their spouses...*

susceptibility = <u>vulnerability</u>, weakness, liability, propensity, predisposition, proneness

susceptible 1 = <u>responsive</u>, sensitive, receptive, alive to, impressionable, easily moved, suggestible ...*He was unusually susceptible to flattery...* **OPPOSITE** unresponsive
2 *usually with* **to** = <u>liable</u>, inclined, prone, given, open, subject, vulnerable, disposed, predisposed ...*Walking with weights makes the shoulders susceptible to injury...* **OPPOSITE** resistant

suspect **VERB** 1 = <u>believe</u>, feel, guess, consider, suppose, conclude, fancy, speculate, conjecture, surmise, hazard a guess, have a sneaking suspicion, think probable ...*I suspect they were right...* **OPPOSITE** know
2 = <u>distrust</u>, doubt, mistrust, smell a rat (*informal*), harbour suspicions about, have your doubts about ...*You don't really think he suspects you, do you?...* **OPPOSITE** trust
ADJECTIVE = <u>dubious</u>, doubtful, dodgy (*Brit., Austral., & N.Z. informal*), questionable, fishy (*informal*), iffy (*informal*), open to suspicion ...*Delegates evacuated the building when a suspect package was found...* **OPPOSITE** innocent

suspend 1 = <u>postpone</u>, delay, put off, arrest, cease, interrupt, shelve, withhold, defer, adjourn, hold off, cut short, discontinue, lay aside, put in cold storage ...*The union suspended strike action this week...* OPPOSITE continue

2 = remove, expel, eject, debar ...*Julie was suspended from her job shortly after the incident...* OPPOSITE reinstate

3 = hang, attach, dangle, swing, append ...*chandeliers suspended on heavy chains from the ceiling...*

suspense NOUN = uncertainty, doubt, tension, anticipation, expectation, anxiety, insecurity, expectancy, apprehension ...*a writer who holds the suspense throughout her tale...*

PHRASES **in suspense** = on tenterhooks, anxious, on edge, keyed up, in an agony of doubt, with bated breath ...*'Go on, don't leave us in suspense,' Dennis said...*

suspension = postponement, delay, break, stay, breaking off, interruption, moratorium, respite, remission, adjournment, abeyance, deferment, discontinuation, disbarment

suspicion NOUN **1** = feeling, theory, impression, intuition, conjecture, surmise (*informal*), presentiment ...*Police had suspicions that it was not a natural death...*

2 = distrust, scepticism, mistrust, doubt, misgiving, qualm, lack of confidence, wariness, bad vibes (*slang*), dubiety, chariness ...*Our culture harbours deep suspicions of big-time industry...*

3 = idea, notion, hunch, guess, impression, conjecture, surmise, gut feeling (*informal*), supposition ...*I have a sneaking suspicion that they are going to succeed...*

4 = trace, touch, hint, shadow, suggestion, strain, shade, streak, tinge, glimmer, soupçon (*French*) ...*large blooms of white with a suspicion of pale pink...*

PHRASES **above suspicion** = blameless, unimpeachable, above reproach, pure, honourable, virtuous, sinless, like Caesar's wife ...*he was a respected academic and above suspicion...*

suspicious 1 = distrustful, suspecting, sceptical, doubtful, apprehensive, leery (*slang*), mistrustful, unbelieving, wary ...*He has his father's suspicious nature...* OPPOSITE trusting

2 = suspect, dubious, questionable, funny, doubtful, dodgy (*Brit., Austral., & N.Z. informal*), queer, irregular, shady (*informal*), fishy (*informal*), of doubtful honesty, open to doubt *or* misconstruction ...*two suspicious-looking characters...* OPPOSITE beyond suspicion

3 = odd, strange, mysterious, dark, dubious, irregular, questionable, murky (*informal*), shady (*informal*), fishy ...*Four people have died in suspicious circumstances...*

sustain 1 = maintain, continue, keep up, prolong, keep going, keep alive, protract ...*He has sustained his fierce social conscience...*

2 = suffer, experience, undergo, feel, bear, endure, withstand, bear up under ...*Every aircraft in there has sustained some damage...*

3 = help, aid, comfort, foster, assist, relieve, nurture ...*I am sustained by letters of support...*

4 = keep alive, nourish, provide for ...*not enough food*

to sustain a mouse...

5 = support, carry, bear, keep up, uphold, keep from falling ...*The magnets have lost the capacity to sustain the weight...*

6 = uphold, confirm, endorse, approve, ratify, verify, validate ...*The court sustained his objection...*

sustained = continuous, constant, steady, prolonged, perpetual, unremitting, nonstop OPPOSITE periodic

sustenance 1 = nourishment, food, provisions, rations, refreshments, kai (*N.Z. informal*), daily bread, victuals, edibles, comestibles, provender, aliment, eatables, refection ...*The state provided a basic quantity of food for daily sustenance...*

2 = support, maintenance, livelihood, subsistence ...*everything that is necessary for the sustenance of the offspring...*

svelte = slender, lithe, willowy, graceful, slinky, lissom(e), sylphlike

swagger VERB **1** = stride, parade, strut, prance ...*The burly brute swaggered forward, towering over me, and shouted...*

2 = show off, boast, brag, hot-dog (*chiefly U.S.*), bluster, swank (*informal*), gasconade (*rare*) ...*It's bad manners to swagger about how rich you are...*

NOUN **1** = strut ...*He walked with something of a swagger...*

2 = ostentation, show, display, showing off (*informal*), bluster, swashbuckling, swank (*informal*), braggadocio, gasconade (*rare*) ...*What he needed was confidence and a bit of swagger...*

swallow VERB **1** = eat, down (*informal*), consume, devour, absorb, swig (*informal*), swill, wash down, ingest ...*Polly took a bite of the apple, chewed and swallowed it...*

2 = gulp, drink ...*He took a glass of Scotch and swallowed it down...*

3 (*Informal*) = believe, accept, buy (*slang*), fall for, take (something) as gospel ...*I too found this story a little hard to swallow...*

4 = suppress, hold in, restrain, contain, hold back, stifle, repress, bottle up, bite back, choke back ...*Gordon swallowed the anger he felt...*

PHRASES **swallow something** *or* **someone up** **1** = engulf, overwhelmed, overrun, consume ...*Weeds had swallowed up the garden...* **2** = absorb, assimilate, envelop ...*Wage costs swallow up two-thirds of the turnover...*

swamp NOUN = bog, marsh, quagmire, moss (*Scot. & Northern English dialect*), slough, fen, mire, morass, everglade(s) (*U.S.*) ...*Much of the land is desert or swamp...*

VERB **1** = flood, engulf, submerge, inundate, deluge ...*The Ventura river burst its banks, swamping a mobile home park...*

2 = overload, overwhelm, inundate, besiege, beset, snow under ...*We swamp them with praise, make them think that they are important...*

swampy = boggy, waterlogged, marshy, wet, fenny,

miry, quaggy, marish (*obsolete*)

swan

> **Related Words**

male : cob
female : pen
young : cygnet
collective nouns : herd, bevy

swank (*Informal*) **VERB** = <u>show off</u>, swagger, give yourself airs, posture (*informal*), hot-dog (*chiefly U.S.*), put on side (*Brit. slang*) ...*I never swank about the things I have been lucky enough to win...*
NOUN = <u>boastfulness</u>, show, ostentation, display, swagger, vainglory ...*There was no swank in Martin...*

swanky (*Informal*) = <u>ostentatious</u>, grand, posh (*informal, chiefly Brit.*), rich, expensive, exclusive, smart, fancy, flash, fashionable, glamorous, stylish, gorgeous, lavish, luxurious, sumptuous, plush (*informal*), flashy, swish (*informal, chiefly Brit.*), glitzy (*slang*), showy, ritzy (*slang*), de luxe, swank (*informal*), plushy (*informal*) **OPPOSITE** modest

swap *or* **swop** = <u>exchange</u>, trade, switch, traffic, interchange, barter

swarm **NOUN** = <u>multitude</u>, crowd, mass, army, host, drove, flock, herd, horde, myriad, throng, shoal, concourse, bevy ...*A swarm of people encircled the hotel...*
VERB 1 = <u>crowd</u>, flock, throng, mass, stream, congregate ...*People swarmed to the shops, buying up everything in sight...*
2 = <u>teem</u>, crawl, be alive, abound, bristle, be overrun, be infested ...*Within minutes the area was swarming with officers...*

swarthy = <u>dark-skinned</u>, black, brown, dark, tawny, dusky, swart (*archaic*), dark-complexioned

swashbuckling = <u>dashing</u>, spirited, bold, flamboyant, swaggering, gallant, daredevil, mettlesome, roisterous

swastika = <u>crooked cross</u>, fylfot

swathe **NOUN** = <u>area</u>, section, stretch, patch, tract ...*On May 1st the army took over another swathe of territory...*
VERB = <u>wrap</u>, drape, envelop, bind, lap, fold, bandage, cloak, shroud, swaddle, furl, sheathe, enfold, bundle up, muffle up, enwrap ...*She swathed her enormous body in thin black fabrics...*

sway **VERB** 1 = <u>move from side to side</u>, rock, wave, roll, swing, bend, lean, incline, lurch, oscillate, move to and fro ...*The people swayed back and forth with arms linked...*
2 = <u>influence</u>, control, direct, affect, guide, dominate, persuade, govern, win over, induce, prevail on ...*Don't ever be swayed by fashion...*
NOUN = <u>power</u>, control, influence, government, rule, authority, command, sovereignty, jurisdiction, clout (*informal*), dominion, predominance, ascendency ...*How can mothers keep daughters under their sway?...*
PHRASES **hold sway** = <u>prevail</u>, rule, predominate, reign ...*Here, a completely different approach seems to*

hold sway...

swear **VERB** 1 = <u>curse</u>, cuss (*informal*), blaspheme, turn the air blue (*informal*), be foul-mouthed, take the Lord's name in vain, utter profanities, imprecate ...*It is wrong to swear and shout...*
2 = <u>vow</u>, promise, take an oath, warrant, testify, depose, attest, avow, give your word, state under oath, pledge yourself ...*Alan swore that he would do everything in his power to help us...*
3 = <u>declare</u>, assert, affirm, swear blind, asseverate ...*I swear I've told you all I know...*
PHRASES **swear by something** = <u>believe in</u>, trust, depend on, rely on, have confidence in ...*Many people swear by vitamin C's ability to ward off colds...*

swearing = <u>bad language</u>, cursing, profanity, blasphemy, cussing (*informal*), foul language, imprecations, malediction

swear word *usually plural* = <u>oath</u>, curse, obscenity, expletive, four-letter word, cuss (*informal*), profanity

sweat **NOUN** 1 = <u>perspiration</u>, moisture, dampness ...*He wiped the sweat off his face and looked around...*
2 (*Informal*) = <u>panic</u>, anxiety, state (*informal*), worry, distress, flap (*informal*), agitation, fluster, lather (*informal*), tizzy (*informal*), state of anxiety ...*She was in a sweat about the exam...*
VERB 1 = <u>perspire</u>, swelter, break out in a sweat, exude moisture, glow ...*Already they were sweating as the sun beat down upon them...*
2 (*Informal*) = <u>worry</u>, fret, agonize, lose sleep over, be on tenterhooks, torture yourself, be on pins and needles (*informal*) ...*It gives sales chiefs something to sweat about...*
PHRASES **sweat something out** (*Informal*) = <u>endure</u>, see (something) through, stick it out (*informal*), stay the course ...*I just had to sweat it out and hope...*

sweaty = <u>perspiring</u>, sweating, sticky, clammy, bathed *or* drenched *or* soaked in perspiration, glowing

sweep **VERB** 1 = <u>brush</u>, clean ...*She was in the kitchen sweeping the floor...*
2 = <u>clear</u>, remove, brush, clean ...*I swept rainwater off the flat top of a gravestone...*
3 = <u>carry</u>, pull, drag, drive ...*Suddenly, she was swept along by the crowd...*
4 = <u>sail</u>, pass, fly, tear, zoom, glide, skim, scud, hurtle ...*The car swept past the gate house...*
5 = <u>swagger</u>, sail, breeze, stride, stroll, glide, flounce ...*She swept into the conference room...*
NOUN 1 = <u>movement</u>, move, swing, stroke, gesture ...*She indicated the garden with a sweep of her hand...*
2 = <u>arc</u>, bend, curve ...*the great sweep of the bay...*
3 = <u>extent</u>, range, span, stretch, scope, compass ...*the whole sweep of German social and political history...*

sweeping 1 = <u>indiscriminate</u>, blanket, across-the-board, wholesale, exaggerated, overstated, unqualified, overdrawn ...*sweeping generalizations about ability based on gender...*
2 = <u>wide-ranging</u>, global, comprehensive, wide,

broad, radical, extensive, all-inclusive, all-embracing, overarching, thoroughgoing ...*sweeping economic reforms*... OPPOSITE limited

sweet ADJECTIVE **1** = <u>sugary</u>, sweetened, cloying, honeyed, saccharine, syrupy, icky (*informal*), treacly ...*a mug of sweet tea*... OPPOSITE sour

2 = <u>fragrant</u>, perfumed, aromatic, redolent, sweet-smelling ...*the sweet smell of a summer garden*... OPPOSITE stinking

3 = <u>fresh</u>, clean, pure, wholesome ...*I gulped a breath of sweet air*...

4 = <u>melodious</u>, musical, harmonious, soft, mellow, silvery, tuneful, dulcet, sweet-sounding, euphonious, silver-toned, euphonic ...*the sweet sounds of Mozart*... OPPOSITE harsh

5 = <u>charming</u>, kind, gentle, tender, affectionate, agreeable, amiable, sweet-tempered ...*He was a sweet man but when he drank he tended to quarrel*... OPPOSITE nasty

6 = <u>delightful</u>, appealing, cute, taking, winning, fair, beautiful, attractive, engaging, lovable, winsome, cutesy (*informal, chiefly U.S.*), likable *or* likeable ...*a sweet little baby girl*... OPPOSITE unpleasant

7 = <u>beloved</u>, dear, darling, dearest, pet, treasured, precious, cherished ...*my dear, sweet mother*...

NOUN **1** *usually plural* = <u>confectionery</u>, candy (*U.S.*), sweetie, lolly (*Austral. & N.Z.*), sweetmeat, bonbon ...*They've always enjoyed fish and chips – and sweets and cakes*...

2 (*Brit.*) = <u>dessert</u>, pudding, afters (*Brit. informal*), sweet course ...*The sweet was a mousse flavoured with whisky*...

PHRASES **sweet on** = <u>in love with</u>, keen on, infatuated with, gone on (*slang*), fond of, taken with, enamoured of, head over heels in love with, obsessed *or* bewitched by, wild *or* mad about (*informal*) ...*It was rumoured that she was sweet on him*...

sweeten 1 = <u>sugar</u> ...*He liberally sweetened his coffee*...

2 = <u>soften</u>, ease, alleviate, relieve, temper, cushion, mellow, make less painful ...*They sweetened the deal with a rather generous cash payment*...

3 = <u>mollify</u>, appease, soothe, pacify, soften up, sugar the pill ...*He is likely to try to sweeten them with pledges of fresh aid*...

sweetheart 1 = <u>dearest</u>, beloved, sweet, angel, treasure, honey, dear, sweetie (*informal*) ...*Happy birthday, sweetheart!*...

2 = <u>love</u>, boyfriend *or* girlfriend, beloved, lover, steady (*informal*), flame (*informal*), darling, follower (*obsolete*), valentine, admirer, suitor, beau, swain (*archaic*), truelove, leman (*archaic*), inamorata *or* inamorato ...*I married my childhood sweetheart, in Liverpool*...

swell VERB **1** = <u>increase</u>, rise, grow, mount, expand, accelerate, escalate, multiply, grow larger ...*The human population swelled as migrants moved south*... OPPOSITE decrease

2 = <u>expand</u>, increase, grow, rise, extend, balloon, belly, enlarge, bulge, protrude, well up, billow, fatten, dilate,

puff up, round out, be inflated, become larger, distend, bloat, tumefy, become bloated *or* distended ...*The limbs swell to an enormous size*... OPPOSITE shrink

NOUN = <u>wave</u>, rise, surge, billow ...*the swell of the incoming tide*...

swelling = <u>enlargement</u>, lump, puffiness, bump, blister, bulge, inflammation, dilation, protuberance, distension, tumescence

(Related Words)

adjective : tumescent

sweltering = <u>hot</u>, burning, boiling, steaming, baking, roasting, stifling, scorching, oppressive, humid, torrid, sultry, airless

swerve = <u>veer</u>, turn, swing, shift, bend, incline, deflect, depart from, skew, diverge, deviate, turn aside, sheer off

swift 1 = <u>quick</u>, immediate, prompt, rapid, instant, abrupt, ready, expeditious ...*We need to make a swift decision*...

2 = <u>fast</u>, quick, rapid, flying, express, winged, sudden, fleet, hurried, speedy, spanking, nimble, quickie (*informal*), nippy (*Brit. informal*), fleet-footed, pdq (*slang*) ...*a swift runner*... OPPOSITE slow

swiftly 1 = <u>quickly</u>, rapidly, speedily, without losing time ...*They have acted swiftly and decisively*...

2 = <u>fast</u>, promptly, hurriedly, apace, pronto (*informal*), double-quick, hell for leather, like lightning, hotfoot, like the clappers (*Brit. informal*), posthaste, like greased lightning (*informal*), nippily (*Brit. informal*), in less than no time, as fast as your legs can carry you, (at) full tilt ...*Lenny moved swiftly and silently across the front lawn*...

swill VERB **1** = <u>drink</u>, gulp, swig (*informal*), guzzle, drain, consume, swallow, imbibe, quaff, bevvy (*dialect*), toss off, bend the elbow (*informal*), pour down your gullet ...*A crowd of men were standing around swilling beer*...

2 (*Chiefly Brit.*) *often with* **out** = <u>rinse</u>, wash out, sluice, flush, drench, wash down ...*He swilled out the mug and left it on the draining board*...

NOUN = <u>waste</u>, slops, mash, mush, hogwash, pigswill, scourings ...*The porker ate swill from a trough*...

swindle VERB = <u>cheat</u>, do (*slang*), con, skin (*slang*), trick, stiff (*slang*), sting (*informal*), rip (someone) off (*slang*), deceive, fleece, defraud, dupe, overcharge, rook (*slang*), bamboozle (*informal*), diddle (*informal*), take (someone) for a ride (*informal*), put one over on (someone) (*informal*), pull a fast one (on someone) (*informal*), bilk (of), take to the cleaners (*informal*), sell a pup (to) (*slang*), cozen, hornswoggle (*slang*) ...*He swindled investors out of millions of pounds*...

NOUN = <u>fraud</u>, fiddle (*Brit. informal*), rip-off (*slang*), racket, scam (*slang*), sting (*informal*), deception, imposition, deceit, trickery, double-dealing, con trick (*informal*), sharp practice, swizzle (*Brit. informal*), knavery, swizz (*Brit. informal*), roguery ...*He fled to Switzerland rather than face trial for a tax swindle*...

swing VERB **1** = <u>brandish</u>, wave, shake, flourish, wield, dangle …*She was swinging a bottle of wine by its neck*…

2 = <u>sway</u>, rock, wave, veer, vibrate, oscillate, move back and forth, move to and fro …*The sail of the little boat swung from one side to the other*…

3 *usually with* **round** = <u>turn</u>, veer, swivel, twist, curve, rotate, pivot, turn on your heel …*The canoe found the current and swung around*…

4 = <u>hit out</u>, strike, swipe, lash out at, slap …*I picked up his baseball bat and swung at the man's head*…

5 = <u>hang</u>, dangle, be suspended, suspend, move back and forth …*He looks cute swinging from a branch*…

NOUN **1** = <u>swaying</u>, sway …*a woman walking with a slight swing to her hips*…

2 = <u>fluctuation</u>, change, shift, switch, variation …*Dieters can suffer from violent mood swings*…

PHRASES **in full swing** = <u>at its height</u>, under way, on the go (*informal*) …*The international rugby season was in full swing*…

swingeing (*Chiefly Brit.*) = <u>severe</u>, heavy, drastic, huge, punishing, harsh, excessive, daunting, stringent, oppressive, Draconian, exorbitant

swinging (*Old-fashioned informal*) = <u>trendy</u>, happening (*informal*), with it (*informal*), hip (*slang*), fashionable (*Brit. informal*), up-to-date, groovy (*dated slang*), up to the minute, in the swim (*informal*), full of go *or* pep (*informal*)

swipe **VERB** **1** (*Informal*) = <u>hit out</u>, strike, slap, lash out at …*She swiped at him as though he were a fly*…

2 (*Slang*) = <u>steal</u>, nick (*slang, chiefly Brit.*), pinch (*informal*), lift (*informal*), appropriate, cabbage (*Brit. slang*), make off with, pilfer, purloin, filch, snaffle (*Brit. informal*) …*People kept trying to swipe my copy of the New York Times*…

NOUN = <u>blow</u>, slap, smack, clip (*informal*), thump, clout (*informal*), cuff, clump (*slang*), wallop (*informal*) …*He gave Andrew a swipe on the ear*…

swirl = <u>whirl</u>, churn, spin, twist, boil, surge, agitate, eddy, twirl

swish (*Informal, chiefly Brit.*) = <u>smart</u>, grand, posh (*informal, chiefly Brit.*), exclusive, elegant, swell (*informal*), fashionable, sumptuous, ritzy (*slang*), de luxe, plush *or* plushy (*informal*)

switch **NOUN** **1** = <u>control</u>, button, lever, on/off device …*a light switch*…

2 = <u>change</u>, shift, transition, conversion, reversal, alteration, about-turn, change of direction …*New technology made the switch to oil possible*…

VERB **1** = <u>change</u>, shift, convert, divert, deviate, change course …*I'm switching to a new gas supplier*…

2 = <u>exchange</u>, trade, swap, replace, substitute, rearrange, interchange …*The ballot boxes have been switched*…

PHRASES **switch something off** = <u>turn off</u>, shut off, deactivate, cut …*She switched off the coffee-machine*… ♦ **switch something on** = <u>turn on</u>, put on, set off, activate, set in motion …*He pointed the light at his feet and tried to switch it on*…

swivel = <u>turn</u>, spin, revolve, rotate, pivot, pirouette, swing round

swollen = <u>enlarged</u>, bloated, puffy, inflamed, puffed up, distended, tumescent, oedematous, dropsical, tumid, edematous

swoop **VERB** **1** = <u>pounce</u>, attack, charge, rush, descend …*The terror ended when armed police swooped on the car*…

2 = <u>drop</u>, plunge, dive, sweep, descend, plummet, pounce, stoop …*The hawk swooped and soared away carrying something*…

NOUN = <u>raid</u>, attack, assault, surprise search …*a swoop on a German lorry*…

swop
➤ **swap**

sword **NOUN** = <u>blade</u>, brand (*archaic*), trusty steel …*The stubby sword used by ancient Roman gladiators*…

PHRASES **cross swords** = <u>fight</u>, argue, dispute, disagree, spar, wrangle, come to blows …*the last time they crossed swords was during the 1980s*…
➤ **swords and other weapons with blades**

swot (*Informal*) = <u>study</u>, revise, cram (*informal*), work, get up (*informal*), pore over, bone up on (*informal*), burn the midnight oil, mug up (*Brit. slang*), toil over, apply yourself to, lucubrate (*rare*)

sycophant = <u>crawler</u>, yes man, toady, slave, parasite,

Swords and other weapons with blades

http://www.myarmoury.com/feature_swordintro1.html

assegai *or* assagai	hatchet	sgian-dhu
backsword	jackknife	sheath knife
battle-axe	jerid, jereed, *or* jerreed	skean
bayonet	knife *or* (*slang*) chiv	smallsword
bill	kris	snickersnee
bowie knife	kukri	spear
broadsword	machete	spontoon
claymore	parang	stiletto
cutlass	partisan	stone axe
dagger	pike	sword *or* (*archaic*) glaive
dirk	poleaxe	sword bayonet
épée	poniard	swordstick
falchion	rapier	tomahawk
foil	sabre *or* saber	trench knife
halberd	scimitar	yataghan *or* ataghan

cringer, fawner, hanger-on, sponger, flatterer, truckler, lickspittle, apple polisher (*U.S. slang*), bootlicker (*informal*), toadeater (*rare*)

sycophantic = <u>obsequious</u>, grovelling, ingratiating, servile, crawling, flattering, cringing, fawning, slimy, slavish, unctuous, smarmy (*Brit. informal*), toadying, parasitical, bootlicking (*informal*), timeserving

syllabus = <u>course of study</u>, curriculum

symbol 1 = <u>metaphor</u>, image, sign, representation, token ...*To them the monarchy is a special symbol of nationhood*...
2 = <u>representation</u>, sign, figure, mark, type, image, token, logo, badge, emblem, glyph ...*I frequently use sunflowers as symbols of strength*...

symbolic 1 = <u>representative</u>, token, emblematic, allegorical ...*The move today was largely symbolic*...
2 = <u>representative</u>, figurative ...*symbolic representations of landscape*...

symbolize = <u>represent</u>, signify, stand for, mean, exemplify, denote, typify, personify, connote, betoken, body forth

symmetrical = <u>balanced</u>, regular, proportional, in proportion, well-proportioned OPPOSITE unbalanced

symmetry = <u>balance</u>, proportion, regularity, form, order, harmony, correspondence, evenness

sympathetic 1 = <u>caring</u>, kind, understanding, concerned, feeling, interested, kindly, warm, tender, pitying, supportive, responsive, affectionate, compassionate, commiserating, warm-hearted, condoling ...*It may be that he sees you only as a sympathetic friend*... OPPOSITE uncaring
2 = <u>supportive</u>, encouraging, pro, approving of, friendly to, in sympathy with, well-disposed towards, favourably disposed towards ...*They were sympathetic to our cause*...
3 = <u>like-minded</u>, compatible, agreeable, friendly, responsive, appreciative, congenial, companionable, well-intentioned ...*She sounds a most sympathetic character*... OPPOSITE uncongenial

sympathetically = <u>feelingly</u>, kindly, understandingly, warmly, with interest, with feeling, sensitively, with compassion, appreciatively, perceptively, responsively, warm-heartedly

sympathize 1 = <u>feel for</u>, pity, empathize, commiserate, bleed for, have compassion, grieve with, offer consolation, condole, share another's sorrow, feel your heart go out to ...*I must tell you how much I sympathize with you for your loss*... OPPOSITE

have no feelings for
2 = <u>agree</u>, support, side with, understand, identify with, go along with, be in accord, be in sympathy ...*Some Europeans sympathize with the Americans over the issue*... OPPOSITE disagree

sympathizer = <u>supporter</u>, partisan, protagonist, fellow traveller, well-wisher

sympathy 1 = <u>compassion</u>, understanding, pity, empathy, tenderness, condolence(s), thoughtfulness, commiseration ...*We expressed our sympathy for her loss*... OPPOSITE indifference
2 = <u>affinity</u>, agreement, rapport, union, harmony, warmth, correspondence, fellow feeling, congeniality ...*I still have sympathy with this point of view*... OPPOSITE opposition

symptom 1 = <u>sign</u>, mark, indication, warning ...*patients with flu symptoms*...
2 = <u>manifestation</u>, sign, indication, mark, evidence, expression, proof, token ...*Your problem with sleep is just a symptom of a larger problem*...

symptomatic = <u>indicative</u>, characteristic, suggestive

synonymous = <u>equivalent</u>, the same, identical, similar, identified, equal, tantamount, interchangeable, one and the same

synopsis = <u>summary</u>, review, résumé, outline, abstract, digest, epitome, rundown, condensation, compendium, précis, aperçu (*French*), abridgment, conspectus, outline sketch

synthesis = <u>combining</u>, integration, amalgamation, unification, welding, coalescence

synthetic = <u>artificial</u>, manufactured, fake, man-made, mock, simulated, sham, pseudo (*informal*), ersatz OPPOSITE real

system 1 = <u>arrangement</u>, structure, organization, scheme, combination, classification, coordination, setup (*informal*) ...*a multi-party system of government*...
2 = <u>network</u>, organization, web, grid, set of channels ...*a news channel on a local cable system*...
3 = <u>method</u>, practice, technique, procedure, routine, theory, usage, methodology, frame of reference, modus operandi, fixed order ...*the decimal system of metric weights and measures*...

systematic = <u>methodical</u>, organized, efficient, precise, orderly, standardized, businesslike, well-ordered, systematized OPPOSITE unmethodical

T t

tab = <u>flap</u>, tag, label, ticket, flag, marker, sticker

table NOUN **1** = <u>counter</u>, bench, stand, board, surface, slab, work surface ...*I placed his drink on the small table...*
2 = <u>list</u>, chart, tabulation, record, roll, index, register, digest, diagram, inventory, graph, synopsis, itemization ...*Consult the table on page 104...*
3 (*Formal*) = <u>food</u>, spread (*informal*), board, diet, fare, kai (*N.Z. informal*), victuals ...*She always sets a marvellous table...*
VERB (*Brit.*) = <u>submit</u>, propose, put forward, move, suggest, enter, file, lodge, moot ...*They've tabled a motion criticising the government for inaction...*

tableau = <u>picture</u>, scene, representation, arrangement, spectacle

taboo NOUN = <u>prohibition</u>, ban, restriction, disapproval, anathema, interdict, proscription ...*Not all men respect the taboo against bedding a friend's woman...*
ADJECTIVE = <u>forbidden</u>, banned, prohibited, ruled out, not allowed, unacceptable, outlawed, unthinkable, not permitted, disapproved of, anathema, off limits, frowned on, proscribed, beyond the pale, unmentionable ...*Cancer is a taboo subject...*
OPPOSITE> permitted

tacit = <u>implied</u>, understood, implicit, silent, taken for granted, unspoken, inferred, undeclared, wordless, unstated, unexpressed OPPOSITE> stated

taciturn = <u>uncommunicative</u>, reserved, reticent, unforthcoming, quiet, withdrawn, silent, distant, dumb, mute, aloof, antisocial, tight-lipped, close-lipped OPPOSITE> communicative

tack NOUN = <u>nail</u>, pin, stud, staple, rivet, drawing pin, thumbtack (*U.S.*), tintack ...*Use a staple gun or upholstery tacks...*
VERB **1** = <u>fasten</u>, fix, attach, pin, nail, staple, affix ...*He had tacked this note to the door...*
2 (*Brit.*) = <u>stitch</u>, sew, hem, bind, baste ...*Tack the cord around the cushion...*
PHRASES **tack something on to something** = <u>append</u>, add, attach, tag, annex ...*The child-care bill is to be tacked on to the budget plan...*

tackle VERB **1** = <u>deal with</u>, take on, set about, wade into, get stuck into (*informal*), sink your teeth into, apply yourself to, come *or* get to grips with ...*We need to tackle these problems and save people's lives...*
2 = <u>undertake</u>, deal with, attempt, try, begin, essay, engage in, embark upon, get stuck into (*informal*), turn your hand to, have a go *or* stab at (*informal*) ...*My husband is quite good at DIY and wants to tackle the job himself...*
3 = <u>intercept</u>, block, bring down, stop, challenge ...*He tackled the quarter-back...*

NOUN **1** = <u>block</u>, stop, challenge ...*a tackle by a full-back...*
2 = <u>rig</u>, rigging, apparatus ...*I finally hoisted him up with a block and tackle...*

tacky¹ = <u>sticky</u>, wet, adhesive, gummy, icky (*informal*), gluey ...*If the finish is still tacky, leave to harden...*

tacky² (*Informal*)
1 = <u>vulgar</u>, cheap, tasteless, nasty, sleazy, naff (*Brit. slang*) ...*tacky red sunglasses...*
2 = <u>seedy</u>, shabby, shoddy ...*The whole thing is dreadfully tacky...*

tact = <u>diplomacy</u>, understanding, consideration, sensitivity, delicacy, skill, judgment, perception, discretion, finesse, thoughtfulness, savoir-faire, adroitness OPPOSITE> tactlessness

tactful = <u>diplomatic</u>, politic, discreet, prudent, understanding, sensitive, polished, careful, subtle, delicate, polite, thoughtful, perceptive, considerate, judicious OPPOSITE> tactless

tactic NOUN = <u>policy</u>, approach, course, way, means, move, line, scheme, plans, method, trick, device, manoeuvre, tack, ploy, stratagem ...*His tactic to press on paid off...*
PLURAL NOUN = <u>strategy</u>, campaigning, manoeuvres, generalship ...*guerrilla tactics...*

tactical = <u>strategic</u>, politic, shrewd, smart, diplomatic, clever, cunning, skilful, artful, foxy, adroit OPPOSITE> impolitic

tactician = <u>strategist</u>, campaigner, planner, mastermind, general, director, brain (*informal*), coordinator, schemer

tag NOUN = <u>label</u>, tab, sticker, note, ticket, slip, flag, identification, marker, flap, docket ...*Staff wore name tags and called inmates by their first names...*
VERB **1** = <u>label</u>, mark, flag, ticket, identify, earmark ...*Important trees were tagged to protect them from machinery...*
2 = <u>name</u>, call, label, term, style, dub, nickname, christen ...*The critics still tagged him with his old name...*
PHRASES **tag something on** = <u>add</u>, tack on, append, adjoin, fasten, annex, affix ...*It's worth tagging on an extra day or two to see the capital...*

tail NOUN **1** = <u>extremity</u>, appendage, brush, rear end, hindquarters, hind part, empennage ...*The cattle were swinging their tails to disperse the flies...*
2 = <u>train</u>, end, trail, tailpiece ...*a comet tail...*
3 (*Informal*) = <u>buttocks</u>, behind (*informal*), bottom, butt (*U.S. & Canad. informal*), bum (*Brit. slang*), rear (*informal*), buns (*U.S. slang*), backside (*informal*), rump, rear end, posterior, derrière (*euphemistic*), jacksy (*Brit. slang*) ...*He desperately needs a kick in the*

tail…

4 (used of hair) = <u>ponytail</u>, braid, plait, tress, pigtail …*She wore bleached denims with her golden tail of hair swinging…*

VERB (*Informal*) = <u>follow</u>, track, shadow, trail, stalk, keep an eye on, dog the footsteps of …*Officers had tailed the gang in an undercover inquiry…*

PHRASES **tail away** *or* **off** = <u>decrease</u>, fade, die out, fail, drop, dwindle, wane, fall away, peter out …*His voice tailed away in the bitter cold air…* ◆ **turn tail** = <u>run away</u>, flee, run off, escape, take off (*informal*), retreat, make off, hook it (*slang*), run for it (*informal*), scarper (*Brit. slang*), cut and run, show a clean pair of heels, skedaddle (*informal*), take to your heels …*I turned tail and fled in the direction of the house…*

> **Related Words**
adjective : caudal

tailor **NOUN** = <u>outfitter</u>, couturier, dressmaker, seamstress, clothier, costumier, garment maker …*He's the grandson of an East End tailor…*

VERB = <u>adapt</u>, adjust, modify, cut, style, fit, fashion, shape, suit, convert, alter, accommodate, mould, customize …*scripts tailored to American comedy audiences…*

> **Related Words**
adjective : sartorial

tailor-made **1** = <u>custom-made</u>, personalized, customized …*Each client's portfolio is tailor-made…*
2 = <u>perfect</u>, right, ideal, suitable, just right, right up your street (*informal*), up your alley …*This job was tailor-made for me…*
3 = <u>made-to-measure</u>, fitted, cut to fit, made to order …*his expensive tailor-made shirt…*

taint **VERB** **1** = <u>disgrace</u>, shame, dishonour, brand, ruin, blacken, stigmatize …*They said that the elections had been tainted by corruption…*
2 = <u>spoil</u>, ruin, contaminate, damage, soil, dirty, poison, foul, infect, stain, corrupt, smear, muddy, pollute, blight, tarnish, blot, blemish, sully, defile, adulterate, besmirch, vitiate, smirch …*Rancid oil will taint the flavour…* **OPPOSITE** purify
NOUN = <u>disgrace</u>, shame, stigma, dishonour …*Her government never really shook off the taint of corruption…*

take **VERB** **1** = <u>grip</u>, grab, seize, catch, grasp, clutch, get hold of, clasp, take hold of, lay hold of …*He took her by the shoulders and shook her…*
2 = <u>carry</u>, bring, bear, transport, ferry, haul, convey, fetch, cart, tote (*informal*) …*I'll take these papers home and read them…* **OPPOSITE** send
3 = <u>accompany</u>, lead, bring, guide, conduct, escort, convoy, usher …*She was taken to hospital…*
4 = <u>remove</u>, draw, pull, fish, withdraw, extract, abstract …*He took a handkerchief from his pocket…*
5 = <u>steal</u>, nick (*slang, chiefly Brit.*), appropriate, pocket, pinch (*informal*), carry off, swipe (*slang*), run off with, blag (*slang*), walk off with, misappropriate, cart off (*slang*), purloin, filch, help yourself to, gain possession of …*The burglars took just about anything they could*

carry… **OPPOSITE** return
6 = <u>capture</u>, arrest, seize, abduct, take into custody, ensnare, entrap, lay hold of …*Marines went in and took 15 prisoners…* **OPPOSITE** release
7 = <u>tolerate</u>, stand, bear, suffer, weather, go through, brave, stomach, endure, undergo, swallow, brook, hack (*slang*), abide, put up with (*informal*), withstand, submit to, countenance, pocket, thole (*Scot.*) …*His rudeness was becoming hard to take…* **OPPOSITE** avoid
8 = <u>require</u>, need, involve, demand, call for, entail, necessitate …*Walking across the room took all her strength…*
9 = <u>accept</u>, assume, take on, undertake, adopt, take up, enter upon …*When I took the job, I thought I could change the system…* **OPPOSITE** reject
10 = <u>understand</u>, follow, comprehend, get, see, grasp, apprehend …*They've turned sensible, if you take my meaning…*
11 = <u>regard as</u>, see as, believe to be, consider to be, think of as, deem to be, perceive to be, hold to be, judge to be, reckon to be, presume to be, look on as …*Do you take me for an idiot?…*
12 = <u>hire</u>, book, rent, lease, reserve, pay for, engage, make a reservation for …*My wife and I have taken the cottage for a month…*
13 = <u>perform</u>, have, do, make, effect, accomplish, execute …*She took her driving test last week…*
14 = <u>ingest</u>, consume, swallow, inhale …*She's been taking sleeping pills…*
15 = <u>consume</u>, have, drink, eat, imbibe …*She took tea with Nanny every day…*
16 = <u>have room for</u>, hold, contain, accommodate, accept …*The place could just about take 2000 people…*
17 = <u>work</u>, succeed, do the trick (*informal*), have effect, be efficacious …*If the cortisone doesn't take, I may have to have surgery…* **OPPOSITE** fail
NOUN = <u>takings</u>, profits, revenue, return, gate, yield, proceeds, haul, receipts …*It added another $11.8 million to the take…*
PHRASES **take it** = <u>assume</u>, suppose, presume, expect, imagine, guess (*informal, chiefly U.S. & Canad.*) …*I take it you're a friend of theirs…* ◆ **take off 1** = <u>lift off</u>, leave the ground, take to the air, become airborne …*We eventually took off at 11am and arrived in Venice at 1.30pm…* **2** (*Informal*) = <u>depart</u>, go, leave, split (*slang*), disappear, set out, strike out, beat it (*slang*), hit the road (*slang*), abscond, decamp, hook it (*slang*), slope off, pack your bags (*informal*) …*He took off at once and headed home…* ◆ **take on** (*Informal*) = <u>get upset</u>, get excited, make a fuss, break down, give way …*Please don't take on so. I'll help you…* ◆ **take someone in 1** = <u>let in</u>, receive, admit, board, welcome, harbour, accommodate, take care of, put up, billet …*The monastery has taken in 26 refugees…*
2 = <u>deceive</u>, fool, con (*informal*), do (*slang*), trick, cheat, mislead, dupe, gull (*archaic*), swindle, hoodwink, pull the wool over someone's eyes (*informal*), bilk, cozen …*He was a real charmer who totally took me in…* ◆ **take someone off** (*Informal*)

= <u>parody</u>, imitate, mimic, mock, ridicule, ape, caricature, send up (*Brit. informal*), spoof (*informal*), travesty, impersonate, lampoon, burlesque, satirize ...*He can take off his father to perfection*... ◆ **take someone on 1** = <u>compete against</u>, face, contend with, fight, oppose, vie with, pit yourself against, enter the lists against, match yourself against ...*I knew I couldn't take him on if it came to a fight*... **2** = <u>engage</u>, employ, hire, retain, enlist, enrol ...*A publishing firm agreed to take him on*... ◆ **take something back 1** = <u>return</u>, bring something back, send something back, hand something back ...*I'm going to take it back and ask for a refund*... **2** = <u>give a refund for</u>, exchange, accept something back ...*The store wouldn't take damaged goods back*... **3** = <u>retract</u>, withdraw, renounce, renege on, disavow, recant, disclaim, unsay ...*Take back what you said about Jeremy!*... **4** = <u>regain</u>, get back, reclaim, recapture, repossess, retake, reconquer ...*The government took back control of the city*... ◆ **take something down 1** = <u>remove</u>, take off, extract ...*He went to the bookcase and took down a volume*... **2** = <u>lower</u>, drop, let down, pull down, haul down ...*The flag was taken down from the flag pole*... **3** = <u>dismantle</u>, demolish, take apart, disassemble, level, tear down, raze, take to pieces ...*They took down the barricades that had been erected*... **4** = <u>make a note of</u>, record, write down, minute, note, set down, transcribe, put on record ...*I took down his comments in shorthand*... ◆ **take something in 1** = <u>understand</u>, absorb, grasp, digest, comprehend, assimilate, get the hang of (*informal*) ...*She seemed to take in all he said*... **2** = <u>include</u>, contain, comprise, cover, embrace, encompass ...*The constituency takes in a population of more than 4 million people*... ◆ **take something off 1** = <u>remove</u>, discard, strip off, drop, peel off, doff, divest yourself of ...*She took off her spectacles*... **2** = <u>subtract</u>, deduct, take something away, remove, eliminate ...*Take off the price of the house; that's another five thousand*... ◆ **take something on 1** = <u>accept</u>, tackle, undertake, shoulder, have a go at (*informal*), agree to do, address yourself to ...*No one was able or willing to take on the job*... **2** (with a quality or identity as object) = <u>acquire</u>, assume, come to have ...*His writing took on a feverish intensity*... ◆ **take something over** = <u>gain control of</u>, take command of, assume control of, come to power in, become leader of ...*They took over Rwanda under a League of Nations mandate*... ◆ **take something up 1** = <u>start</u>, begin, engage in, assume, adopt, become involved in ...*He didn't want to take up a competitive sport*... **2** = <u>occupy</u>, absorb, consume, use up, cover, fill, waste, squander, extend over ...*I don't want to take up too much of your time*... **3** = <u>resume</u>, continue, go on with, pick up, proceed with, restart, carry on with, recommence, follow on with, begin something again ...*His wife takes up the story*... ◆ **take to someone** = <u>like</u>, get on with, warm to, be taken with, be pleased by, become friendly with, conceive an affection for ...*Did the children take to

him?*... ◆ **take to something 1** = <u>start</u>, resort to, make a habit of, have recourse to ...*They had taken to aimlessly wandering through the streets*... **2** = <u>head for</u>, make for, run for, flee to ...*He took to the roof of his home when police officers came round*...

takeoff 1 = <u>departure</u>, launch, liftoff ...*The aircraft crashed soon after takeoff*...
2 (*Informal*) = <u>parody</u>, imitation, send-up (*Brit. informal*), mocking, satire, caricature, spoof (*informal*), travesty, lampoon ...*an inspired takeoff of the two sisters*...

takeover = <u>merger</u>, coup, change of leadership, incorporation

tale 1 = <u>story</u>, narrative, anecdote, account, relation, novel, legend, fiction, romance, saga, short story, yarn (*informal*), fable, narration, conte (*French*), spiel (*informal*), urban myth, urban legend ...*a collection of poems and folk tales*...
2 = <u>lie</u>, fabrication, falsehood, fib, untruth, spiel (*informal*), tall story (*informal*), rigmarole, cock-and-bull story (*informal*) ...*He's always ready to spin a tall tale about the one that got away*...

talent = <u>ability</u>, gift, aptitude, power, skill, facility, capacity, bent, genius, expertise, faculty, endowment, forte, flair, knack

talented = <u>gifted</u>, able, expert, master, masterly, brilliant, ace (*informal*), artistic, consummate, first-rate, top-notch (*informal*), adroit

talisman = <u>charm</u>, mascot, amulet, lucky charm, fetish, juju

talk VERB 1 = <u>speak</u>, chat, chatter, converse, communicate, rap (*slang*), articulate, witter (*informal*), gab (*informal*), express yourself, prattle, natter, shoot the breeze (*U.S. slang*), prate, run off at the mouth (*slang*) ...*The boys all began to talk at once*...
2 = <u>discuss</u>, confer, hold discussions, negotiate, palaver, parley, confabulate, have a confab (*informal*), chew the rag *or* fat (*slang*) ...*Let's talk about these new ideas of yours*...
3 = <u>inform</u>, shop (*slang, chiefly Brit.*), grass (*Brit. slang*), sing (*slang, chiefly U.S.*), squeal (*slang*), squeak (*informal*), tell all, spill the beans (*informal*), give the game away, blab, let the cat out of the bag, reveal information, spill your guts (*slang*) ...*They'll talk; they'll implicate me*...
NOUN 1 = <u>speech</u>, lecture, presentation, report, address, seminar, discourse, sermon, symposium, dissertation, harangue, oration, disquisition ...*The guide gave us a brief talk on the history of the site*...
2 = <u>discussion</u>, tête-à-tête, conference, dialogue, consultation, heart-to-heart, confabulation, confab (*informal*), powwow ...*I think it's time we had a talk*...
3 = <u>conversation</u>, chat, natter, crack (*Scot. & Irish*), rap (*slang*), jaw (*slang*), chatter, gab (*informal*), chitchat, blether, blather ...*We had a long talk about her father*...
4 = <u>gossip</u>, rumour, hearsay, tittle-tattle ...*There has been a lot of talk about me getting married*...
5 = <u>language</u>, words, speech, jargon, slang, dialect,

lingo (*informal*), patois, argot ...*children babbling on in baby talk*...

PLURAL NOUN = <u>meeting</u>, conference, discussions, negotiations, congress, summit, mediation, arbitration, conciliation, conclave, palaver, parley ...*Talks between strikers and government have broken down*...

PHRASES **talk big** = <u>boast</u>, exaggerate, brag, crow, vaunt, bluster, blow your own trumpet ...*men who talk big and drive fast cars*... ◆ **talk someone into something** = <u>persuade</u>, convince, win someone over, sway, bring round (*informal*), sweet-talk someone into, prevail on *or* upon ...*He talked me into marrying him*...

talkative = <u>loquacious</u>, chatty, garrulous, long-winded, big-mouthed (*slang*), wordy, effusive, gabby (*informal*), voluble, gossipy, verbose, mouthy, prolix **OPPOSITE** reserved

talker = <u>speaker</u>, lecturer, orator, conversationalist, chatterbox, speechmaker

talking-to (*Informal*) = <u>reprimand</u>, lecture, rebuke, scolding, row, criticism, wigging (*Brit. slang*), slating (*informal*), reproach, ticking-off (*informal*), dressing-down (*informal*), telling-off (*informal*), reproof, rap on the knuckles **OPPOSITE** praise

tall **1** = <u>lofty</u>, big, giant, long-legged, lanky, leggy ...*Being tall can make you incredibly self-confident*...
2 = <u>high</u>, towering, soaring, steep, elevated, lofty ...*a lawn of tall, waving grass*... **OPPOSITE** short
3 (*Informal*) = <u>implausible</u>, incredible, far-fetched, steep (*Brit. informal*), exaggerated, absurd, unbelievable, preposterous, embellished, overblown, cock-and-bull (*informal*) ...*a tall story*... **OPPOSITE** plausible
4 = <u>difficult</u>, hard, demanding, unreasonable, exorbitant, well-nigh impossible ...*Financing your studies can be a tall order*...

tally **NOUN** = <u>record</u>, score, total, count, reckoning, running total ...*They do not keep a tally of visitors to the palace*...
VERB **1** = <u>agree</u>, match, accord, fit, suit, square, parallel, coincide, correspond, conform, concur, harmonize ...*The figures didn't seem to tally*... **OPPOSITE** disagree
2 = <u>count up</u>, total, compute, keep score ...*When the final numbers are tallied, sales will probably have fallen*...

tame **ADJECTIVE** **1** = <u>domesticated</u>, unafraid, docile, broken, gentle, fearless, obedient, amenable, tractable, used to human contact ...*tame animals at a children's zoo or farm*... **OPPOSITE** wild
2 = <u>submissive</u>, meek, compliant, subdued, manageable, obedient, docile, spiritless, unresisting ...*a tame and gullible newspaper journalist*... **OPPOSITE** stubborn
3 = <u>unexciting</u>, boring, dull, bland, tedious, flat, tiresome, lifeless, prosaic, uninspiring, humdrum, uninteresting, insipid, vapid, wearisome ...*The report was pretty tame stuff*... **OPPOSITE** exciting

VERB **1** = <u>domesticate</u>, train, break in, gentle, pacify, house-train, make tame ...*They were the first to tame horses*... **OPPOSITE** make fiercer
2 = <u>subdue</u>, suppress, master, discipline, curb, humble, conquer, repress, bridle, enslave, subjugate, bring to heel, break the spirit of ...*Two regiments were called out to tame the crowds*... **OPPOSITE** arouse

tamper with **1** = <u>interfere with</u>, tinker with, meddle with, alter, fiddle with (*informal*), mess about with, muck about with (*Brit. slang*), monkey around with, fool about with (*informal*) ...*He found his computer had been tampered with*...
2 = <u>influence</u>, fix (*informal*), rig, corrupt, manipulate ...*I don't want to be accused of tampering with the evidence*...

tang **1** = <u>scent</u>, smell, odour, perfume, fragrance, aroma, reek, redolence ...*She could smell the salty tang of the sea*...
2 = <u>taste</u>, bite, flavour, edge, relish, smack, savour, zest, sharpness, piquancy, spiciness, zestiness ...*Some liked its strong, fruity tang*...
3 = <u>trace</u>, touch, tinge, suggestion, hint, whiff, smattering ...*His criticism seemed to have acquired a tang of friendliness*...

tangible = <u>definite</u>, real, positive, solid, material, physical, actual, substantial, objective, concrete, evident, manifest, palpable, discernible, tactile, perceptible, corporeal, touchable **OPPOSITE** intangible

tangle **NOUN** **1** = <u>knot</u>, mass, twist, web, jungle, mat, coil, snarl, mesh, ravel, entanglement ...*a tangle of wires*...
2 = <u>mess</u>, jam, fix (*informal*), confusion, complication, maze, mix-up, shambles, labyrinth, entanglement, imbroglio ...*I was thinking what a tangle we had got ourselves into*...
VERB **1** = <u>twist</u>, knot, mat, coil, snarl, mesh, entangle, interlock, kink, interweave, ravel, interlace, enmesh, intertwist ...*a huge mass of hair, all tangled together*... **OPPOSITE** disentangle
2 *sometimes with* **up** = <u>entangle</u>, catch, ensnare, entrap ...*Animals get tangled in fishing nets and drown*...
3 = <u>confuse</u>, mix up, muddle, jumble, scramble ...*Themes get tangled in his elliptical storytelling*...
PHRASES **tangle something** *or* **someone up** *usually passive* **1** = <u>entangle</u>, catch, trap, snare, ensnare ...*Sheep keep getting tangled up in the wire*...
2 = <u>mix up</u>, involve, implicate, embroil, drag into, mire ...*He tried to avoid getting tangled up in any awkward situations*... ◆ **tangle with someone** = <u>come into conflict with</u>, come up against, cross swords with, dispute with, contend with, contest with, lock horns with ...*They are not the first bank to tangle with the taxman recently*...

tangled **1** = <u>knotted</u>, twisted, matted, messy, snarled, jumbled, entangled, knotty, tousled ...*tugging a comb through her tangled hair*...
2 = <u>complicated</u>, involved, complex, confused, messy, mixed-up, convoluted, knotty ...*His personal life has*

become more tangled than ever…

tangy = sharp, tart, piquant, biting, fresh, spicy, pungent, briny, acerb

tantalize = torment, tease, taunt, torture, provoke, entice, lead on, titillate, make someone's mouth water, keep someone hanging on

tantamount
> **PHRASES** **tantamount to** = equivalent to, equal to, as good as, synonymous with, the same as, commensurate with

tantrum = outburst, temper, hysterics, fit, storm, paddy (*Brit. informal*), wax (*informal, chiefly Brit.*), flare-up, paroxysm, bate (*Brit. slang*), ill humour, foulie (*Austral. slang*)

tap[1] **VERB** = knock, strike, pat, rap, beat, touch, drum …*Tap the egg lightly with a teaspoon…*
> **NOUN** = knock, pat, rap, beat, touch, drumming, light blow …*A tap on the door interrupted him…*

tap[2] **NOUN** 1 = valve, spout, faucet (*U.S.*), spigot, stopcock …*She turned on the taps…*
2 = bug (*informal*), listening device, wiretap, bugging device, hidden microphone …*Ministers are not subject to phone taps…*
> **VERB** 1 = listen in on, monitor, bug (*informal*), spy on, eavesdrop on, wiretap …*laws allowing the police to tap telephones…*
2 = use, draw on, make use of, mine, milk, exploit, utilize, put to use, turn to account …*She tapped her own experiences for her novels…*
> **PHRASES** **on tap** 1 (*Informal*) = available, ready, standing by, to hand, on hand, at hand, in reserve …*He's already got surveyors on tap to measure for the road…* 2 = on draught, cask-conditioned, from barrels, not bottled *or* canned …*They only have one beer on tap…*

tape **NOUN** = binding, strip, band, string, ribbon …*The books were all tied up with tape…*
> **VERB** 1 = record, video, tape-record, make a recording of …*She has just taped an interview…*
2 *sometimes with* **up** = bind, secure, stick, seal, wrap …*I taped the base of the feather onto the velvet…*

taper **VERB** = narrow, thin, attenuate, come to a point, become thinner, become narrow …*The trunk doesn't taper very much…* **OPPOSITE** widen
> **PHRASES** **taper off** = decrease, dwindle, lessen, reduce, fade, weaken, wane, subside, wind down, die out, die away, thin out …*Immigration is beginning to taper off…*

tardy 1 = late, overdue, unpunctual, belated, dilatory, behindhand …*He was as tardy as ever for our appointment…*
2 = slow, belated, delayed …*the agency's tardy response to the hurricane…*

target 1 = mark, goal, bull's-eye …*We threw knives at targets…*
2 = goal, aim, objective, end, mark, object, intention, ambition, Holy Grail (*informal*) …*school leavers who fail to reach their targets…*
3 = victim, butt, prey, quarry, scapegoat …*In the past

they have been the targets of racist abuse…

tariff 1 = tax, rate, duty, toll, levy, excise, impost, assessment …*America wants to eliminate tariffs on items such as electronics…*
2 = price list, charges, schedule …*electricity tariffs and telephone charges…*

tarnish **VERB** 1 = damage, taint, blacken, sully, drag through the mud, smirch …*His image was tarnished by the savings and loans scandal…* **OPPOSITE** enhance
2 = stain, dull, discolour, spot, soil, dim, rust, darken, blot, blemish, befoul, lose lustre *or* shine …*It never rusts or tarnishes…* **OPPOSITE** brighten
> **NOUN** = stain, taint, discoloration, spot, rust, blot, blemish …*The tarnish lay thick on the inside of the ring…*

tarry (*Old-fashioned*) = linger, remain, loiter, wait, delay, pause, hang around (*informal*), lose time, bide, dally, take your time, dawdle, drag your feet *or* heels **OPPOSITE** hurry

tart[1] = pie, pastry, pasty, tartlet, patty …*a slice of home-made tart…*

tart[2] 1 = sharp, acid, sour, bitter, pungent, tangy, astringent, piquant, vinegary, acidulous, acerb …*a slightly tart wine…* **OPPOSITE** sweet
2 = cutting, biting, sharp, short, wounding, nasty, harsh, scathing, acrimonious, barbed, hurtful, caustic, astringent, vitriolic, trenchant, testy, mordant, snappish, mordacious …*The words were more tart than she had intended…* **OPPOSITE** kind

tart[3] (*Informal*) = slut, prostitute, hooker (*U.S. slang*), whore, slag (*Brit. slang*), call girl, working girl (*facetious slang*), harlot, streetwalker, loose woman, fallen woman, scrubber (*Brit. & Austral. slang*), strumpet, trollop, floozy (*slang*), woman of easy virtue, fille de joie (*French*) …*He said I looked like a tart…*

task **NOUN** = job, duty, assignment, work, business, charge, labour, exercise, mission, employment, enterprise, undertaking, occupation, chore, toil …*He had the unenviable task of breaking the bad news…*
> **VERB** = charge, assign to, entrust …*The minister was tasked with checking that aid was spent wisely…*
> **PHRASES** **take someone to task** = criticize, blame, blast, lecture, carpet (*informal*), censure, rebuke, reprimand, reproach, scold, tear into (*informal*), tell off (*informal*), diss (*slang, chiefly U.S.*), read the riot act, reprove, upbraid, lambast(e), bawl out (*informal*), chew out (*U.S. & Canad. informal*), tear (someone) off a strip (*Brit. informal*), give a rocket (*Brit. & N.Z. informal*) …*The country's intellectuals are being taken to task…*

taste **NOUN** 1 = flavour, savour, relish, smack, tang …*Nettles have a surprisingly sweet taste…* **OPPOSITE** blandness
2 = bit, bite, drop, swallow, sip, mouthful, touch, sample, dash, nip, spoonful, morsel, titbit, soupçon (*French*) …*He took another small taste…*
3 = liking, preference, penchant, fondness, partiality, desire, fancy, leaning, bent, appetite, relish,

inclination, palate, predilection ...*She developed a taste for journeys to hazardous regions*... OPPOSITE> dislike

4 = refinement, style, judgment, culture, polish, grace, discrimination, perception, appreciation, elegance, sophistication, cultivation, discernment ...*She has very good taste in clothes*... OPPOSITE> lack of judgment

5 = propriety, discretion, correctness, delicacy, tact, politeness, nicety, decorum, tactfulness ...*I do not feel your actions were in good taste*... OPPOSITE> impropriety

VERB **1** = have a flavour of, smack of, savour of ...*The drink tastes like chocolate*...

2 = sample, try, test, relish, sip, savour, nibble ...*Cut off a small piece of meat and taste it*...

3 = distinguish, perceive, discern, differentiate ...*You can taste the chilli in the dish*...

4 = experience, know, undergo, partake of, feel, encounter, meet with, come up against, have knowledge of ...*He had tasted outdoor life, and didn't want to come home*... OPPOSITE> miss

(*Related Words*)
noun: gustation

tasteful = refined, stylish, elegant, cultured, beautiful, smart, charming, polished, delicate, artistic, handsome, cultivated, discriminating, exquisite, graceful, harmonious, urbane, fastidious, aesthetically pleasing, in good taste OPPOSITE> tasteless

tasteless 1 = gaudy, cheap, vulgar, tacky (*informal*), flashy, naff (*Brit. slang*), garish, inelegant, tawdry ...*spectacularly tasteless objets d'art*... OPPOSITE> tasteful

2 = vulgar, crude, improper, low, gross, rude, coarse, crass, unseemly, indiscreet, tactless, uncouth, impolite, graceless, indelicate, indecorous ...*a tasteless remark*...

3 = insipid, bland, flat, boring, thin, weak, dull, mild, tame, watered-down, uninteresting, uninspired, vapid, flavourless ...*The fish was mushy and tasteless*... OPPOSITE> tasty

tasty = delicious, luscious, palatable, delectable, good-tasting, savoury, full-flavoured, yummy (*slang*), flavoursome, scrumptious (*informal*), appetizing, toothsome, flavourful, sapid, lekker (*S. African slang*), yummo (*Austral. slang*) OPPOSITE> bland

tatters PLURAL NOUN = rags, scraps, shreds, bits, pieces, fragments ...*The walls are bare with a few tatters of wallpaper here and there*...

PHRASES **in tatters** = ragged, torn, ripped, tattered, in rags, in shreds ...*His jersey was left in tatters*...

tatty (*Chiefly Brit.*) = shabby, seedy, scruffy, worn, poor, neglected, ragged, run-down, frayed, worn out, dilapidated, tattered, tawdry, threadbare, rumpled, bedraggled, unkempt, down at heel, the worse for wear, having seen better days OPPOSITE> smart

taunt VERB = jeer, mock, tease, ridicule, provoke, insult, torment, sneer, deride, revile, twit, guy (*informal*), gibe ...*Other youths taunted him about his*

clothes...

NOUN = jeer, dig, insult, ridicule, cut, teasing, provocation, barb, derision, sarcasm, gibe ...*For years they suffered racist taunts*...

taut 1 = tense, rigid, tight, stressed, stretched, strained, flexed ...*When muscles are taut or cold, there is more chance of injury*... OPPOSITE> relaxed

2 = tight, stretched, rigid, tightly stretched ...*The clothes line is pulled taut and secured*... OPPOSITE> slack

tavern = inn, bar, pub (*informal, chiefly Brit.*), public house, watering hole (*facetious slang*), boozer (*Brit., Austral., & N.Z. informal*), hostelry, alehouse (*archaic*), taproom

tawdry = vulgar, cheap, tacky (*informal*), flashy, tasteless, plastic (*slang*), glittering, naff (*Brit. slang*), gaudy, tatty, showy, tinsel, raffish, gimcrack, meretricious, tinselly, cheap-jack (*informal*) OPPOSITE> stylish

tax NOUN **1** = charge, rate, duty, toll, levy, tariff, excise, contribution, assessment, customs, tribute, imposition, tithe, impost ...*a cut in tax on new cars*...

2 = strain, demand, burden, pressure, weight, load, drain ...*less of a tax on her bodily resources*...

VERB **1** = charge, impose a tax on, levy a tax on, rate, demand, assess, extract, exact, tithe ...*The government taxes profits of corporations at a high rate*...

2 = strain, push, stretch, try, test, task, load, burden, drain, exhaust, weaken, weary, put pressure on, sap, wear out, weigh heavily on, overburden, make heavy demands on, enervate ...*Overcrowding has taxed the city's ability to deal with waste*...

3 = accuse, charge, blame, confront, impeach, incriminate, arraign, impugn, lay at your door ...*Writers to the letters column taxed me with shallowness*... OPPOSITE> acquit

taxing = demanding, trying, wearing, heavy, tough, tiring, punishing, exacting, stressful, sapping, onerous, burdensome, wearisome, enervating OPPOSITE> easy

teach 1 = instruct, train, coach, school, direct, advise, inform, discipline, educate, drill, tutor, enlighten, impart, instil, inculcate, edify, give lessons in ...*a programme to teach educational skills*... ...*She taught me to read*...

2 = show, train, demonstrate ...*George had taught him how to ride a horse*...

teacher = instructor, coach, tutor, don, guide, professor, trainer, lecturer, guru, mentor, educator, handler, schoolteacher, pedagogue, dominie (*Scot.*), master *or* mistress, schoolmaster *or* schoolmistress

team NOUN **1** = side, squad, troupe ...*The team failed to qualify for the final*...

2 = group, company, set, body, band, crew, gang, line-up, bunch, posse (*informal*) ...*Mr Hunter and his management team*...

3 = pair, span, yoke ...*Ploughing is no longer done with a team of oxen*...

PHRASES **team up** = join, unite, work together, cooperate, couple, link up, get together, yoke, band

together, collaborate, join forces …*He suggested that we team up for a working holiday in France…*
> **family**

teamwork = <u>cooperation</u>, collaboration, unity, concert, harmony, fellowship, coordination, joint action, esprit de corps

tear VERB 1 = <u>rip</u>, split, rend, shred, rupture, sunder …*She very nearly tore my overcoat…*
2 = <u>run</u>, rip, ladder, snag …*Too fine a material may tear…*
3 = <u>scratch</u>, cut (open), gash, lacerate, injure, mangle, cut to pieces, cut to ribbons, mangulate (*Austral. slang*) …*He'd torn his skin trying to do it barehanded…*
4 = <u>pull apart</u>, claw, lacerate, sever, mutilate, mangle, mangulate (*Austral. slang*) …*Canine teeth are for tearing flesh…*
5 = <u>rush</u>, run, charge, race, shoot, fly, career, speed, belt (*slang*), dash, hurry, barrel (along) (*informal, chiefly U.S. & Canad.*), sprint, bolt, dart, gallop, zoom, burn rubber (*informal*) …*The door flew open and she tore into the room…*
6 = <u>pull</u>, seize, rip, grab, snatch, pluck, yank, wrench, wrest …*She tore the windscreen wipers from his car…*
NOUN = <u>hole</u>, split, rip, run, rent, snag, rupture …*I peered through a tear in the van's curtains…*

tearaway (*Brit.*) = <u>hooligan</u>, delinquent, tough, rough (*informal*), rowdy, ruffian, roughneck (*slang*), good-for-nothing

tearful 1 = <u>weeping</u>, crying, sobbing, in tears, whimpering, blubbering, weepy (*informal*), lachrymose …*She was tearful when asked to talk about it…*
2 = <u>sad</u>, pathetic, poignant, upsetting, distressing, harrowing, pitiful, woeful, mournful, lamentable, sorrowful, pitiable, dolorous …*a tearful farewell…*

tears PLURAL NOUN = <u>crying</u>, weeping, sobbing, wailing, whimpering, blubbering, lamentation …*She was very near to tears…*
PHRASES **in tears** = <u>weeping</u>, crying, sobbing, whimpering, blubbering, visibly moved …*He was in tears at the funeral…*
(Related Words)
adjectives: lacrimal, lachrymal, *or* lacrymal

tease 1 = <u>mock</u>, bait, wind up (*Brit. slang*), worry, bother, provoke, annoy, needle (*informal*), plague (*informal*), rag, rib (*informal*), torment, ridicule, taunt, aggravate (*informal*), badger, pester, vex, goad, bedevil, take the mickey out of (*informal*), twit, chaff, guy (*informal*), gibe, pull someone's leg (*informal*), make fun of …*He teased me mercilessly about going there…*
2 = <u>tantalize</u>, lead on, flirt with, titillate …*When did you last flirt with him or tease him?…*

technical = <u>scientific</u>, technological, skilled, specialist, specialized, hi-tech *or* high-tech

technique 1 = <u>method</u>, way, system, approach, means, course, style, fashion, manner, procedure, mode, MO, modus operandi …*tests performed using a new technique…*

2 = <u>skill</u>, art, performance, craft, touch, know-how (*informal*), facility, delivery, execution, knack, artistry, craftsmanship, proficiency, adroitness …*He went abroad to improve his tennis technique…*

tedious = <u>boring</u>, dull, dreary, monotonous, tiring, annoying, fatiguing, drab, banal, tiresome, lifeless, prosaic, laborious, humdrum, uninteresting, long-drawn-out, mind-numbing, irksome, unexciting, soporific, ho-hum (*informal*), vapid, wearisome, deadly dull, prosy, dreich (*Scot.*) OPPOSITE exciting

tedium = <u>boredom</u>, monotony, dullness, routine, the doldrums, banality, sameness, ennui, drabness, deadness, dreariness, tediousness, lifelessness OPPOSITE excitement

teem¹ = <u>be full of</u>, abound, swarm, bristle, brim, overflow, be abundant, burst at the seams, be prolific, be crawling, pullulate …*The forest below him seethed and teemed with life…*

teem² = <u>pour</u>, lash, pelt (down), sheet, stream, belt (*slang*), bucket down (*informal*), rain cats and dogs (*informal*) …*The wedding was supposed to be outside but it teemed with rain…*

teeming¹ = <u>full</u>, packed, crowded, alive, thick, bursting, numerous, crawling, swarming, abundant, bristling, brimming, overflowing, fruitful, replete, chock-full, brimful, chock-a-block …*The area is usually teeming with tourists…* OPPOSITE lacking

teeming² = <u>pouring</u>, lashing, pelting, sheeting, streaming, belting (*slang*), bucketing down (*informal*) …*I arrived early to find it teeming with rain…*

teenage = <u>youthful</u>, adolescent, juvenile, immature

teenager = <u>youth</u>, minor, adolescent, juvenile, girl, boy

teeny (*Informal*) = <u>tiny</u>, minute, wee, miniature, microscopic, diminutive, minuscule, teeny-weeny, teensy-weensy

teeter = <u>wobble</u>, rock, totter, balance, stagger, sway, tremble, waver, pivot, seesaw

teeth
> **teeth**

telegram = <u>cable</u>, wire (*informal*), telegraph, telex, radiogram

telegraph = <u>cable</u>, wire (*informal*), transmit, telex, send

telepathy = <u>mind-reading</u>, ESP, sixth sense, clairvoyance, extra sensory perception, psychometry, thought transference

telephone NOUN = <u>phone</u>, blower (*informal*), mobile (phone), handset, dog and bone (*slang*) …*They usually exchanged messages by telephone…*
VERB = <u>call</u>, phone, ring (*chiefly Brit.*), buzz (*informal*), dial, call up, give someone a call, give someone a ring (*informal, chiefly Brit.*), give someone a buzz (*informal*), give someone a bell (*Brit. slang*), put a call through to, give someone a tinkle (*Brit. informal*), get on the blower to (*informal*) …*I had to telephone him to say I was sorry…*

telescope NOUN = <u>glass</u>, scope (*informal*), spyglass

...*The telescope enables us to see deeper into the universe than ever*...

VERB = <u>shorten</u>, contract, compress, cut, trim, shrink, tighten, condense, abbreviate, abridge, capsulize ...*Film naturally tends to telescope time*... OPPOSITE lengthen

television = <u>TV</u>, telly (*Brit. informal*), small screen (*informal*), the box (*Brit. informal*), receiver, the tube (*slang*), TV set, gogglebox (*Brit. slang*), idiot box (*slang*)

tell **VERB** 1 = <u>inform</u>, notify, make aware, say to, state to, warn, reveal to, express to, brief, advise, disclose to, proclaim to, fill in, speak about to, confess to, impart, alert to, divulge, announce to, acquaint with, communicate to, mention to, make known to, apprise, utter to, get off your chest (*informal*), let know ...*I called her to tell her how spectacular it looked*...
2 = <u>describe</u>, relate, recount, report, portray, depict, chronicle, rehearse, narrate, give an account of ...*He told his story to the Sunday Times*...
3 = <u>instruct</u>, order, command, direct, bid, enjoin ...*She told me to come and help clean the house*...
4 = <u>see</u>, make out, discern, understand, discover, be certain, comprehend ...*It was impossible to tell where the bullet had entered*...
5 = <u>distinguish</u>, discriminate, discern, differentiate, identify ...*I can't really tell the difference between their policies and ours*...
6 = <u>have</u> or <u>take effect</u>, register, weigh, have force, count, take its toll, carry weight, make its presence felt ...*The pressure began to tell as rain closed in after 20 laps*...
PHRASES **tell someone off** = <u>reprimand</u>, rebuke, scold, lecture, carpet (*informal*), censure, reproach, berate, chide, tear into (*informal*), read the riot act, reprove, upbraid, take someone to task, tick someone off (*informal*), bawl someone out (*informal*), chew someone out (*U.S. & Canad. informal*), tear someone off a strip (*Brit. informal*), give someone a piece of your mind, haul someone over the coals (*informal*), give someone a rocket (*Brit. & N.Z. informal*) ...*He never listened to us when we told him off*...

telling = <u>effective</u>, significant, considerable, marked, striking, powerful, solid, impressive, influential, decisive, potent, forceful, weighty, forcible, trenchant, effectual OPPOSITE unimportant

telling-off = <u>reprimand</u>, talking-to, row, criticism, lecture, rocket (*Brit. & N.Z. informal*), wigging (*Brit. slang*), slating (*informal*), censure, rebuke, reproach, scolding, ticking-off (*informal*), dressing-down (*informal*), reproof, rap on the knuckles

temerity = <u>audacity</u>, nerve (*informal*), cheek, gall (*informal*), front, assurance, pluck, boldness, recklessness, chutzpah (*U.S. & Canad. informal*), impudence, effrontery, impulsiveness, rashness, brass neck (*Brit. informal*), foolhardiness, sassiness (*U.S. informal*), forwardness, heedlessness

temper **NOUN** 1 = <u>irritability</u>, anger, irascibility, passion, resentment, irritation, annoyance, petulance, surliness, ill humour, peevishness, hot-headedness ...*I hope he can control his temper*... OPPOSITE good humour
2 = <u>frame of mind</u>, character, nature, attitude, mind, mood, constitution, humour, vein, temperament, tenor, disposition ...*He's known for his placid temper*...
3 = <u>rage</u>, fury, bad mood, passion, paddy (*Brit. informal*), wax (*informal, chiefly Brit.*), tantrum, bate (*Brit. slang*), fit of pique, foulie (*Austral. slang*) ...*She was still in a temper when I arrived*...
4 = <u>self-control</u>, composure, cool (*slang*), calm, good humour, tranquillity, coolness, calmness, equanimity ...*I've never seen him lose his temper*... OPPOSITE anger
VERB 1 = <u>moderate</u>, restrain, tone down, calm, soften, soothe, lessen, allay, mitigate, abate, assuage, mollify, soft-pedal (*informal*), palliate, admix ...*He had to learn to temper his enthusiasm*... OPPOSITE intensify
2 = <u>strengthen</u>, harden, toughen, anneal ...*a new way of tempering glass*... OPPOSITE soften

temperament 1 = <u>nature</u>, character, personality, quality, spirit, make-up, soul, constitution, bent, stamp, humour, tendencies, tendency, temper, outlook, complexion, disposition, frame of mind, mettle, cast of mind ...*His impulsive temperament regularly got him into difficulties*...
2 = <u>moods</u>, anger, volatility, impatience, petulance, excitability, moodiness, explosiveness, hot-headedness, mercurialness ...*Some of the models were given to fits of temperament*...

temperamental 1 = <u>moody</u>, emotional, touchy, sensitive, explosive, passionate, volatile, fiery, impatient, erratic, neurotic, irritable, mercurial, excitable, capricious, petulant, hot-headed, hypersensitive, highly strung, easily upset, unstable ...*a man given to temperamental outbursts and paranoia*... OPPOSITE even-tempered
2 (*Informal*) = <u>unreliable</u>, unpredictable, undependable, inconsistent, erratic, inconstant, unstable ...*The machine guns could be temperamental*... OPPOSITE reliable
3 = <u>natural</u>, inherent, innate, constitutional, ingrained, congenital, inborn ...*Some temperamental qualities are not easily detected by parents*...

temperance 1 = <u>teetotalism</u>, abstinence, sobriety, abstemiousness ...*a reformed alcoholic extolling the joys of temperance*...
2 = <u>moderation</u>, restraint, self-control, self-discipline, continence, self-restraint, forbearance ...*The age of hedonism was replaced by a new era of temperance*... OPPOSITE excess

temperate 1 = <u>mild</u>, moderate, balmy, fair, cool, soft, calm, gentle, pleasant, clement, agreeable ...*The valley keeps a temperate climate throughout the year*... OPPOSITE extreme
2 = <u>moderate</u>, dispassionate, self-controlled, calm, stable, reasonable, sensible, mild, composed, equable, even-tempered, self-restrained ...*His final report was*

more temperate than earlier ones… OPPOSITE
unrestrained
3 = abstemious, continent, sober, abstinent, moderate
…*He lived a temperate and contented life with his
wife…* OPPOSITE excessive

tempest 1 (*Literary*) = storm, hurricane, gale,
tornado, cyclone, typhoon, squall …*torrential rain and
howling tempest…*
2 storm, furore, disturbance, upheaval = uproar,
ferment, commotion, tumult …*I hadn't foreseen the
tempest my request would cause…* OPPOSITE calm

tempestuous 1 = passionate, intense, turbulent,
heated, wild, excited, emotional, violent, flaming,
hysterical, stormy, impassioned, uncontrolled,
boisterous, feverish …*the couple's tempestuous
relationship…* OPPOSITE peaceful
2 = stormy, turbulent, inclement, raging, windy,
boisterous, blustery, gusty, squally …*adverse winds
and tempestuous weather…*

temple = shrine, church, sanctuary, holy place, place
of worship, house of God

tempo = pace, time, rate, beat, measure (*Prosody*),
speed, metre, rhythm, cadence, pulse

temporal 1 = secular, worldly, lay, earthly, mundane,
material, civil, fleshly, mortal, terrestrial, carnal,
profane, sublunary …*Clergy should not be preoccupied with temporal matters…*
2 = temporary, passing, transitory, fleeting, short-
lived, fugitive, transient, momentary, evanescent,
impermanent, fugacious …*The temporal gifts that
Fortune grants in this world are finally worthless…*

temporarily = briefly, for the moment, for the time
being, momentarily, for a moment, for a short time,
for a little while, fleetingly, for a short while, pro tem,
for the nonce

temporary 1 = impermanent, passing, transitory,
brief, fleeting, interim, short-lived, fugitive, transient,
momentary, ephemeral, evanescent, pro tem, here
today and gone tomorrow, pro tempore (*Latin*),
fugacious …*a temporary loss of memory…* OPPOSITE
permanent
2 = short-term, acting, interim, supply, stand-in, fill-in,
caretaker, provisional, stopgap …*She was working as
a temporary teacher at a Belfast school…*

tempt 1 = attract, draw, appeal to, allure, whet the
appetite of, make your mouth water …*Can I tempt
you with a little puff pastry?…*
2 = entice, lure, lead on, invite, woo, seduce, coax,
decoy, inveigle …*Don't let credit tempt you to buy
something you can't afford…* OPPOSITE discourage
3 = provoke, try, test, risk, dare, bait, fly in the face of
…*As soon as you talk about never losing, it's tempting
fate…*

temptation 1 = enticement, lure, inducement, pull,
come-on (*informal*), invitation, bait, coaxing, snare,
seduction, decoy, allurement, tantalization …*the
many temptations to which they will be exposed…*
2 = appeal, draw, attraction, attractiveness …*The thrill
and the temptation of crime is very strong…*

tempting = inviting, enticing, seductive, alluring,
attractive, mouthwatering, appetizing OPPOSITE
uninviting

tenacious 1 = stubborn, dogged, determined,
persistent, sure, firm, adamant, staunch, resolute,
inflexible, strong-willed, steadfast, unyielding,
obstinate, intransigent, immovable, unswerving,
obdurate, stiff-necked, pertinacious …*He is regarded
as a persistent and tenacious interviewer…* OPPOSITE
irresolute
2 = firm, dogged, persistent, unyielding, unswerving
…*a tenacious belief…*
3 = strong, firm, fast, iron, tight, clinging, forceful,
immovable, unshakeable …*He has a particularly
tenacious grip on life…*
4 = retentive, good, photographic, unforgetful …*her
analytical mind and tenacious memory…*
5 = adhesive, clinging, sticky, glutinous, gluey,
mucilaginous …*tenacious catarrh in the nasal
passages and lungs…*

tenacity = perseverance, resolution, determination,
application, resolve, persistence, diligence,
intransigence, firmness, stubbornness, inflexibility,
obstinacy, steadfastness, obduracy, doggedness,
strength of will, strength of purpose, resoluteness,
pertinacity, staunchness

tenancy 1 = lease, residence, occupancy, holding,
renting, possession, occupation …*Check the terms of
your tenancy closely…*
2 = period of office, tenure, incumbency, time in
office …*Baroness Thatcher's nine year tenancy…*

tenant = leaseholder, resident, renter, occupant,
holder, inhabitant, occupier, lodger, boarder, lessee

tend¹ 1 = be inclined, be likely, be liable, have a
tendency, be apt, be prone, trend, lean, incline, be
biased, be disposed, gravitate, have a leaning, have an
inclination …*Lighter cars tend to be noisy…*

tend² 1 = take care of, look after, care for, keep,
watch, serve, protect, feed, handle, attend, guard,
nurse, see to, nurture, minister to, cater for, keep an
eye on, wait on, watch over …*For years he tended her
in her illness…* OPPOSITE neglect
2 = maintain, take care of, nurture, cultivate, manage
…*The grey-haired lady dug and tended her garden…*
OPPOSITE neglect

tendency 1 = trend, drift, movement, turning,
heading, course, drive, bearing, direction, bias …*the
government's tendency towards secrecy in recent years…*
2 = inclination, leaning, bent, liability, readiness,
disposition, penchant, propensity, susceptibility,
predisposition, predilection, proclivity, partiality,
proneness …*He has a tendency towards snobbery…*

tender¹ 1 = gentle, loving, kind, caring, warm,
sympathetic, fond, sentimental, humane, affectionate,
compassionate, benevolent, considerate, merciful,
amorous, warm-hearted, tenderhearted, softhearted,
touchy-feely (*informal*) …*tender, loving care…*
OPPOSITE harsh
2 = romantic, moving, touching, emotional,

sentimental, poignant, evocative, soppy (*Brit. informal*) …*a tragic, tender love story*…

3 = <u>vulnerable</u>, young, sensitive, new, green, raw, youthful, inexperienced, immature, callow, impressionable, unripe, wet behind the ears (*informal*) …*He had become attracted to the game at the tender age of seven*… OPPOSITE experienced

4 = <u>sensitive</u>, painful, sore, smarting, raw, bruised, irritated, aching, inflamed …*My tummy felt very tender*…

5 = <u>fragile</u>, delicate, frail, soft, weak, feeble, breakable …*The newborn looked so fragile and tender*…

6 = <u>difficult</u>, sensitive, tricky, dangerous, complicated, risky, touchy, ticklish …*Even his continuing presence remains a tender issue*…

tender² NOUN = <u>offer</u>, bid, estimate, proposal, suggestion, submission, proffer …*Builders will be asked to submit a tender for the work*…

▪ VERB = <u>offer</u>, present, submit, give, suggest, propose, extend, volunteer, hand in, put forward, proffer …*She quickly tendered her resignation*…

tenderness 1 = <u>gentleness</u>, love, affection, liking, care, consideration, sympathy, pity, humanity, warmth, mercy, attachment, compassion, devotion, kindness, fondness, sentimentality, benevolence, humaneness, amorousness, warm-heartedness, softheartedness, tenderheartedness …*She smiled, politely, rather than with tenderness*… OPPOSITE harshness

2 = <u>soreness</u>, pain, sensitivity, smart, bruising, ache, aching, irritation, inflammation, rawness, sensitiveness, painfulness …*There is still some tenderness on her tummy*…

3 = <u>fragility</u>, vulnerability, weakness, sensitivity, softness, feebleness, sensitiveness, frailness, delicateness …*the vulnerability and tenderness he brings to the role*…

tenet = <u>principle</u>, rule, doctrine, creed, view, teaching, opinion, belief, conviction, canon, thesis, maxim, dogma, precept, article of faith

tennis
▶ **tennis terms**

tenor = <u>meaning</u>, trend, drift, way, course, sense, aim, purpose, direction, path, theme, substance, burden, tendency, intent, purport

tense ADJECTIVE **1** = <u>strained</u>, uneasy, stressful, fraught, charged, difficult, worrying, exciting, uncomfortable, knife-edge, nail-biting, nerve-racking …*the tense atmosphere of the talks*…

2 = <u>nervous</u>, wound up (*informal*), edgy, strained, wired (*slang*), anxious, under pressure, restless, apprehensive, jittery (*informal*), uptight (*informal*), on edge, jumpy, twitchy (*informal*), overwrought, strung up (*informal*), on tenterhooks, fidgety, keyed up, antsy (*informal*), wrought up …*He had been very tense, but he finally relaxed*… OPPOSITE calm

3 = <u>rigid</u>, strained, taut, stretched, tight …*She lay, eyes shut, body tense*… OPPOSITE relaxed

▪ VERB = <u>tighten</u>, strain, brace, tauten, stretch, flex, stiffen …*His stomach muscles tensed*… OPPOSITE relax

tension 1 = <u>strain</u>, stress, nervousness, pressure, anxiety, unease, apprehension, suspense, restlessness, the jitters (*informal*), edginess …*Smiling relieves tension and stress*… OPPOSITE calmness

2 = <u>friction</u>, hostility, unease, antagonism, antipathy, enmity, ill feeling …*The tension between the two countries is likely to remain*…

3 = <u>rigidity</u>, tightness, stiffness, pressure, stress, stretching, straining, tautness …*Slowly, the tension in his face dispersed*…

tentative 1 = <u>unconfirmed</u>, provisional, indefinite, test, trial, pilot, preliminary, experimental, unsettled, speculative, pencilled in, exploratory, to be confirmed, TBC, conjectural …*They have reached a tentative agreement to hold talks next month*… OPPOSITE confirmed

2 = <u>hesitant</u>, cautious, uncertain, doubtful, backward, faltering, unsure, timid, undecided, diffident, iffy (*informal*) …*My first attempts at complaining were very tentative*… OPPOSITE confident

tenuous 1 = <u>slight</u>, weak, dubious, shaky, doubtful, questionable, insignificant, flimsy, sketchy, insubstantial, nebulous …*Links between the provinces were seen to be tenuous*… OPPOSITE strong

2 = <u>fine</u>, slim, delicate, attenuated, gossamer …*She was holding onto life by a tenuous thread*…

Tennis terms http://www.itftennis.com/

ace	double fault	linesman	service line
advantage	doubles	lob	set
approach shot	drop shot	love	set point
backhand	fault	love game	sideline
ball	foot fault	match	singles
baseline	forecourt	mixed doubles	slice
break of serve	forehand	net	smash
break point	game	net cord	tie-break *or* tiebreaker
cannonball	grass court	passing shot	topspin
centre line	ground stroke	racket *or* racquet	tramline
centre mark	half-volley	rally	umpire
chip	hard court	receiver	undercut
clay court	lawn tennis	return	volley
court	let	server	
deuce	line call	service	

tenure 1 = <u>occupancy</u>, holding, occupation, residence, tenancy, possession, proprietorship ...*Lack of security of tenure meant that many became homeless...*
2 = <u>term of office</u>, term, incumbency, period in office, time ...*his short tenure of the Labour leadership...*

tepid 1 = <u>lukewarm</u>, warmish, slightly warm ...*She bent to the tap and drank the tepid water...*
2 = <u>unenthusiastic</u>, half-hearted, indifferent, cool, lukewarm, apathetic ...*His nomination has received tepid support in the Senate...* OPPOSITE> enthusiastic

term NOUN 1 = <u>word</u>, name, expression, title, label, phrase, denomination, designation, appellation, locution ...*What's the medical term for a heart attack?...*
2 = <u>session</u>, course, quarter (U.S.), semester, trimester (U.S.) ...*the summer term...*
3 = <u>period</u>, time, spell, while, season, space, interval, span, duration, incumbency ...*a 12 month term of service...*
4 = <u>conclusion</u>, end, close, finish, culmination, fruition ...*Older women are just as capable of carrying a baby to term...*
PLURAL NOUN 1 = <u>language</u>, terminology, phraseology, manner of speaking ...*The video explains in simple terms how the tax works...*
2 = <u>conditions</u>, particulars, provisions, provisos, stipulations, qualifications, premises (Law), specifications ...*the terms of the Helsinki agreement...*
3 = <u>relationship</u>, standing, footing, relations, position, status ...*We shook hands and parted on good terms...*
4 = <u>price</u>, rates, charges, fee, payment ...*They provide favourable terms to shops that invest in their services...*
VERB = <u>call</u>, name, label, style, entitle, tag, dub, designate, describe as, denominate ...*He had been termed a temporary employee...*
PHRASES **come to terms** = <u>come to an agreement</u>, reach agreement, come to an understanding, conclude agreement ...*Even if they came to terms, investors would object to the merger...* ◆ **come to terms with something** = <u>learn to live with</u>, come to accept, be reconciled to, reach acceptance of ...*She had come to terms with the fact that she would always be ill...*

> ### Word Power
>
> **term** – Many people object to the use of *in terms of* as an all-purpose preposition replacing phrases such as 'as regards', 'about', and so forth in a context such as the following: *in terms of trends in smoking habits, there is good news*. They would maintain that in strict usage it should be used to specify a relationship, as in: *obesity is defined in terms of body mass index, which involves a bit of cumbersome maths.* Nevertheless, despite objections, it is very commonly used as a link word, particularly in speech.

terminal ADJECTIVE 1 = <u>fatal</u>, deadly, lethal, killing, mortal, incurable, inoperable, untreatable ...*terminal cancer...*

2 = <u>final</u>, last, closing, finishing, concluding, ultimate, terminating ...*Endowments pay a terminal bonus at maturity...* OPPOSITE> initial
NOUN = <u>terminus</u>, station, depot, end of the line ...*Only the original ochre facade of the nearby railway terminal remains...*

terminate 1 = <u>end</u>, stop, conclude, finish, complete, axe (*informal*), cut off, wind up, put an end to, discontinue, pull the plug on (*informal*), belay (*Nautical*), bring *or* come to an end ...*Her next remark abruptly terminated the conversation...* OPPOSITE> begin
2 = <u>cease</u>, end, close, finish, run out, expire, lapse ...*His contract terminates at the end of the season...*
3 = <u>abort</u>, end ...*She finally decided to terminate the pregnancy...*

termination 1 = <u>ending</u>, end, close, finish, conclusion, wind-up, completion, cessation, expiry, cut-off point, finis, discontinuation ...*a dispute which led to the abrupt termination of trade...* OPPOSITE> beginning
2 = <u>abortion</u>, ending, discontinuation ...*You should have a medical after the termination of a pregnancy...*

terminology = <u>language</u>, terms, vocabulary, jargon, cant, lingo (*informal*), nomenclature, patois, phraseology, argot

terminus = <u>end of the line</u>, terminal, station, depot, last stop, garage

terrain = <u>ground</u>, country, land, landscape, topography, going

terrestrial = <u>earthly</u>, worldly, global, mundane, sublunary, tellurian, terrene

terrible 1 = <u>awful</u>, shocking, appalling, terrifying, horrible, dreadful, horrifying, dread, dreaded, fearful, horrendous, monstrous, harrowing, gruesome, horrid, unspeakable, frightful, hellacious (*U.S. slang*) ...*Thousands suffered terrible injuries in the disaster...*
2 (*Informal*) = <u>bad</u>, awful, dreadful, beastly (*informal*), dire, abysmal, abhorrent, poor, offensive, foul, unpleasant, revolting, rotten (*informal*), obscene, hideous, vile, from hell (*informal*), obnoxious, repulsive, frightful, odious, hateful, loathsome, godawful (*slang*) ...*I have the most terrible nightmares...* OPPOSITE> wonderful
3 = <u>serious</u>, desperate, severe, extreme, bad, dangerous, insufferable ...*He claimed that he had a terrible pain in his head... ...We are in terrible trouble...* OPPOSITE> mild

terribly 1 = <u>very much</u>, greatly, very, much, dreadfully, seriously, extremely, gravely, desperately, thoroughly, decidedly, awfully (*informal*), exceedingly ...*He has suffered terribly in losing his best friend...*
2 = <u>extremely</u>, very, much, greatly, dreadfully, seriously, desperately, thoroughly, decidedly, awfully (*informal*), exceedingly ...*I'm terribly sorry to bother you at this hour...*

terrific 1 (*Informal*) = <u>excellent</u>, great (*informal*), wonderful, mean (*slang*), topping (*Brit. slang*), fine, brilliant, very good, cracking (*Brit. informal*), amazing,

outstanding, smashing (*informal*), superb, fantastic (*informal*), ace (*informal*), magnificent, fabulous (*informal*), marvellous, sensational (*informal*), sovereign, awesome (*slang*), breathtaking, super (*informal*), brill (*informal*), stupendous, bodacious (*slang, chiefly U.S.*), boffo (*slang*), jim-dandy (*slang*), chillin' (*U.S. slang*), booshit (*Austral. slang*), exo (*Austral. slang*), sik (*Austral. slang*) ...*What a terrific idea!...* OPPOSITE awful
2 = intense, great, huge, terrible, enormous, severe, extreme, awful, tremendous, fierce, harsh, excessive, dreadful, horrific, fearful, awesome, gigantic, monstrous ...*There was a terrific bang and a great cloud of smoke...*

terrified = frightened, scared, petrified, alarmed, intimidated, awed, panic-stricken, scared to death, scared stiff, terror-stricken, horror-struck, frightened out of your wits

terrify = frighten, scare, petrify, alarm, intimidate, terrorize, scare to death, put the fear of God into, make your hair stand on end, fill with terror, make your flesh creep, make your blood run cold, frighten out of your wits

territory = district, area, land, region, state, country, sector, zone, province, patch, turf (*U.S. slang*), domain, terrain, tract, bailiwick
➤ **WORD POWER SUPPLEMENT New Zealand territories**

terror 1 = fear, alarm, dread, fright, panic, anxiety, intimidation, fear and trembling ...*I shook with terror whenever I flew in an aeroplane...*
2 = nightmare, monster, bogeyman, devil, fiend, bugbear, scourge ...*the many obscure terrors that haunted the children of that period...*

terrorize 1 = bully, menace, intimidate, threaten, oppress, coerce, strong-arm (*informal*), browbeat ...*In his childhood he liked to terrorize his young siblings...*
2 = terrify, alarm, frighten, scare, intimidate, petrify, scare to death, strike terror into, put the fear of God into, fill with terror, frighten out of your wits, inspire panic in ...*The government had the helicopter gunships to terrorize the population...*

terse 1 = curt, abrupt, brusque, short, rude, tart, snappy, gruff ...*His tone was terse as he asked the question...* OPPOSITE polite
2 = concise, short, brief, clipped, neat, to the point, crisp, compact, summary, condensed, incisive, elliptical, laconic, succinct, pithy, monosyllabic, gnomic, epigrammatic, aphoristic, sententious ...*He issued a terse statement, saying the decision will be made on Monaday...* OPPOSITE lengthy

test VERB **1** = check, try, investigate, assess, research, prove, analyse, experiment with, try out, verify, assay, put something to the proof, put something to the test ...*Test the temperature of the water with your wrist...*
2 = examine, put someone to the test, put someone through their paces ...*He tested him on verbs and gave him a forfeit for each one he got wrong...*

NOUN **1** = trial, research, check, investigation, attempt, analysis, assessment, proof, examination, evaluation, acid test ...*High levels of dioxin were confirmed by scientific tests...*
2 = examination, paper, assessment, evaluation ...*Only 922 pupils passed the test...*

testament 1 = proof, evidence, testimony, witness, demonstration, tribute, attestation, exemplification ...*His house is a testament to his Gothic tastes...*
2 = will, last wishes ...*a codicil to my will and testament...*

testify = bear witness, state, swear, certify, declare, witness, assert, affirm, depose (*Law*), attest, corroborate, vouch, evince, give testimony, asseverate OPPOSITE disprove

testimonial = reference, recommendation, credential, character, tribute, certificate, endorsement, commendation

Word Power
testimonial – *Testimonial* is sometimes wrongly used where *testimony* is meant: *his re-election is a testimony* (not *a testimonial*) *to his popularity with his constituents.*

testimony 1 = evidence, information, statement, witness, profession, declaration, confirmation, submission, affirmation, affidavit, deposition, corroboration, avowal, attestation ...*His testimony was an important element of the case...*
2 = proof, evidence, demonstration, indication, support, manifestation, verification, corroboration ...*Her living room piled with documents is a testimony to her dedication to her work...*
➤ **testimonial**

testing = difficult, trying, demanding, taxing, challenging, searching, tough, exacting, formidable, rigorous, strenuous, arduous OPPOSITE undemanding

testy = irritable, cross, grumpy, crabbed, impatient, snappy, sullen, touchy, bad-tempered, petulant, irascible, cantankerous, peppery, tetchy, ratty (*Brit. & N.Z. informal*), quarrelsome, fretful, short-tempered, waspish, peevish, quick-tempered, splenetic, snappish, liverish, captious

tetchy = irritable, cross, grumpy, crabbed, impatient, snappy, sullen, touchy, bad-tempered, petulant, irascible, cantankerous, peppery, ratty (*Brit. & N.Z. informal*), testy, quarrelsome, fretful, short-tempered, waspish, peevish, quick-tempered, splenetic, snappish, liverish, captious

tether NOUN = leash, rope, lead, bond, chain, restraint, fastening, shackle, fetter, halter ...*The eagle sat on a tether, looking fierce...*
VERB = tie, secure, bind, chain, rope, restrain, fasten, shackle, leash, fetter, manacle ...*He dismounted, tethering his horse to a tree...*
PHRASES **at the end of your tether** = exasperated, exhausted, at your wits' end, finished, out of patience, at the limit of your endurance ...*She*

was emotionally at the end of her tether...

text 1 = <u>contents</u>, words, content, wording, body, matter, subject matter, main body ...*The photographs enhance the clarity of the text...*
2 = <u>words</u>, wording ...*A CD-ROM can store up to 250,000 pages of text...*
3 = <u>transcript</u>, script ...*the text of Dr. Runcie's speech...*
4 = <u>reference book</u>, textbook, source, reader ...*reluctant readers of GCSE set texts...*
5 = <u>passage</u>, extract, line, sentence, paragraph, verse ...*I'll read the text aloud first...*
6 = <u>subject</u>, matter, topic, argument, theme, thesis, motif ...*His work served as the text of secret debates...*
➤ text messaging abbreviations and symbols

texture = <u>feel</u>, quality, character, consistency, structure, surface, constitution, fabric, tissue, grain, weave, composition

thank = <u>say thank you to</u>, express gratitude to, show gratitude to, show your appreciation to

thankful = <u>grateful</u>, pleased, relieved, obliged, in (someone's) debt, indebted, appreciative, beholden `OPPOSITE` ungrateful

thankless = <u>unrewarding</u>, unappreciated `OPPOSITE` rewarding

thanks `PLURAL NOUN` = <u>gratitude</u>, appreciation, thanksgiving, credit, recognition, acknowledgment, gratefulness ...*They accepted their certificates with words of thanks...*
`PHRASES` **thanks to** = <u>because of</u>, through, due to, as a result of, owing to, by reason of ...*Thanks to recent research, effective treatment is available...*

thaw = <u>melt</u>, dissolve, soften, defrost, warm, liquefy, unfreeze `OPPOSITE` freeze

theatrical 1 = <u>dramatic</u>, stage, Thespian, dramaturgical ...*major theatrical productions...*
2 = <u>exaggerated</u>, dramatic, melodramatic, histrionic, affected, camp (*informal*), mannered, artificial, overdone, unreal, pompous, stilted, showy, ostentatious, hammy (*informal*), ceremonious, stagy, actorly *or* actressy ...*In a theatrical gesture he clamped his hand over his eyes...* `OPPOSITE` natural

theft = <u>stealing</u>, robbery, thieving, fraud, rip-off (*slang*), swindling, embezzlement, pilfering, larceny, purloining, thievery

theme 1 = <u>motif</u>, leitmotif, recurrent image, unifying idea ...*The need to strengthen the family has become a recurrent theme...*
2 = <u>subject</u>, idea, topic, matter, argument, text, burden, essence, thesis, subject matter, keynote, gist ...*The novel's central theme is the conflict between men and women...*

theological = <u>religious</u>, ecclesiastical, doctrinal, divine

theorem = <u>proposition</u>, statement, formula, rule, principle, thesis, hypothesis, deduction, dictum

theoretical 1 = <u>abstract</u>, pure, speculative, ideal, impractical ...*theoretical physics...* `OPPOSITE` practical

2 = <u>hypothetical</u>, academic, notional, unproven, conjectural, postulatory ...*There is a theoretical risk, but there is seldom a problem...*

theorize = <u>speculate</u>, conjecture, hypothesize, project, suppose, guess, formulate, propound

theory 1 = <u>hypothesis</u>, philosophy, system of ideas, plan, system, science, scheme, proposal, principles, ideology, thesis ...*He produced a theory about historical change...* `OPPOSITE` fact
2 = <u>belief</u>, feeling, speculation, assumption, guess, hunch, presumption, conjecture, surmise, supposition ...*There was a theory that he wanted to marry her...*

therapeutic = <u>beneficial</u>, healing, restorative, good, corrective, remedial, salutary, curative, salubrious, ameliorative, analeptic, sanative `OPPOSITE` harmful

therapist = <u>psychologist</u>, analyst, psychiatrist, shrink (*informal*), counsellor, healer, psychotherapist, psychoanalyst, trick cyclist (*informal*)

therapy = <u>remedy</u>, treatment, cure, healing, method of healing, remedial treatment

therefore = <u>consequently</u>, so, thus, as a result, hence, accordingly, for that reason, whence, thence, ergo

thesaurus = <u>wordbook</u>, wordfinder

thesis 1 = <u>proposition</u>, theory, hypothesis, idea, view, opinion, proposal, contention, line of argument ...*This thesis does not stand up to close inspection...*
2 = <u>dissertation</u>, paper, treatise, essay, composition, monograph, disquisition ...*He was awarded his PhD for a thesis on industrial robots...*
3 (*Logic*) = <u>premise</u>, subject, statement, proposition, theme, topic, assumption, postulate, surmise, supposition ...*His central thesis is that crime is up because children do not learn self-control...*

thick `ADJECTIVE` 1 = <u>bulky</u>, broad, big, large, fat, solid, substantial, hefty, plump, sturdy, stout, chunky, stocky, meaty, beefy, thickset ...*He folded his thick arms across his chest...* `OPPOSITE` thin
2 = <u>wide</u>, across, deep, broad, in extent *or* diameter ...*The folder was two inches thick...*
3 = <u>dense</u>, close, heavy, deep, compact, impenetrable, lush ...*He led the rescuers through the thick undergrowth...*
4 = <u>heavy</u>, heavyweight, dense, chunky, bulky, woolly ...*She wore a thick tartan skirt...*
5 = <u>opaque</u>, heavy, dense, impenetrable ...*The smoke was blueish-black and thick...*
6 = <u>viscous</u>, concentrated, stiff, condensed, clotted, coagulated, gelatinous, semi-solid, viscid ...*The sauce is thick and rich...* `OPPOSITE` runny
7 = <u>crowded</u>, full, packed, covered, filled, bursting, jammed, crawling, choked, crammed, swarming, abundant, bristling, brimming, overflowing, seething, thronged, teeming, congested, replete, chock-full, bursting at the seams, chock-a-block ...*The area is so thick with people that the police close the streets...* `OPPOSITE` empty
8 = <u>husky</u>, rough, hoarse, distorted, muffled, croaking, inarticulate, throaty, indistinct, gravelly, guttural,

Text messaging abbreviations and symbols

www.collins.co.uk/wordexchange

2	to, too, *or* two	MSG	message
2DAY	today	MT	empty
2MORO	tomorrow	Ndls$	endless
4	for *or* four	NE	any
al2gethr	altogether	NE1	anyone
ALrlt	all right	NEhng	anything
aQr8	accurate	NEwer	anywhere
ATB	all the best	Njoy	enjoy
ATTN	attention	no1	no one
B	be	NtRtain	entertain
B4	before	OB	obligatory
BCNU	be seeing you	ofN	often
b%k	book	OIC	oh I see
BK *or* COZ	because	oper8n	operation
bf, b/f, *or* boyf	boyfriend	opN	open
BR	bathroom	opRtunET	opportunity
BRB	be right back	PCM	please call me
BS	bullshit	PLS	please
Butiful	beautiful	Po$Ebl	possible
BWD	backward	PPL	people
BY	busy	QL	cool
C	see	QT	quiet
CU	see you	R	are
c%d	could	r%m	room
c%dNt	couldn't	reCv	receive
ca$et	cassette	RGDS	regards
centR	centre	RUOK	are you OK?
CIAO	goodbye	S	smile
Cngrtultns	congratulations	SA	essay
DEp	deep	SEC	second
dubl	double	sh%d	should
duz	does	S/O *or* SUM1	someone
duzNt	doesn't	Sopa	superstar
Enuf	enough	S/TH	something
Esp	especially	stra	stray
evr	ever	THNQ, TY, *or* T/Y	thank you
EZ	easy	THX *or* TNZ	thanks
F%D	food	U	you
f%t	foot	unl$	unless
F2T	free to talk	unppl&	unplanned
fwd	forward	USU	usually
GEnys	genius	v	very
GF	girlfriend	w/ *or* WIV	with
GGG *or* GGL	giggle	w8	wait
GR8	great	WADYA	what do you
H8	hate	WAN2	want to
H&	hand	w%d	would
HD	hold	w%dNt	wouldn't
hevE	heavy	wknd	weekend
IDD	indeed	w/o	without
K	okay	WOT	what
L	laugh	x	extra *or* kiss
l%k	look	XOXO	hugs and kisses
l&	land	xample	example
L8	late		
L8R	later	:-)	smiley face
LUV	love	d:-)	baseball cap
LZ	loser	:-o	surprised face
M8	mate	;-)	winking face
MergNC	emergency	;-(	sad face
MLO	mellow	:@)	pig
MLOD	melody		
mRvLS	marvellous		

raspy, croaky …*His voice was thick with bitterness*… OPPOSITE clear

9 = <u>strong</u>, marked, broad, decided, rich, distinct, pronounced …*He answered questions in a thick accent*… OPPOSITE slight

10 (*Informal*) = <u>stupid</u>, slow, dull, dense, insensitive, dozy (*Brit. informal*), dopey (*informal*), moronic, obtuse, brainless, blockheaded, braindead (*informal*), dumb-ass (*informal*), thickheaded, dim-witted (*informal*), slow-witted …*How could she have been so thick?*… OPPOSITE clever

11 (*Informal*) = <u>friendly</u>, close, intimate, familiar, pally (*informal*), devoted, well in (*informal*), confidential, inseparable, on good terms, chummy (*informal*), hand in glove, buddy-buddy (*slang, chiefly U.S. & Canad.*), palsy-walsy (*informal*), matey *or* maty (*Brit. informal*) …*You're thick with the girl, aren't you?*… OPPOSITE unfriendly

NOUN = <u>middle</u>, centre, heart, focus, core, midst, hub …*I enjoy being in the thick of things*…

thicken = <u>set</u>, condense, congeal, cake, gel, clot, jell, coagulate, inspissate (*archaic*) OPPOSITE thin

thicket = <u>wood</u>, grove, woodland, brake, clump, covert, hurst (*archaic*), copse, coppice, spinney (*Brit.*)

thick-skinned = <u>insensitive</u>, tough, callous, hardened, hard-boiled (*informal*), impervious, stolid, unfeeling, case-hardened, unsusceptible OPPOSITE sensitive

thief = <u>robber</u>, crook (*informal*), burglar, stealer, bandit, plunderer, mugger (*informal*), shoplifter, embezzler, pickpocket, pilferer, swindler, purloiner, housebreaker, footpad (*archaic*), cracksman (*slang*), larcenist

thin ADJECTIVE **1** = <u>narrow</u>, fine, attenuate, attenuated, threadlike …*A thin cable carries the signal to a computer*… OPPOSITE thick

2 = <u>slim</u>, spare, lean, slight, slender, skinny, light, meagre, skeletal, bony, lanky, emaciated, spindly, underweight, scrawny, lank, undernourished, skin and bone, scraggy, thin as a rake …*a tall, thin man with grey hair*… OPPOSITE fat

3 = <u>watery</u>, weak, diluted, dilute, runny, rarefied, wishy-washy (*informal*) …*The soup was thin and clear*… OPPOSITE viscous

4 = <u>meagre</u>, sparse, scanty, poor, scattered, inadequate, insufficient, deficient, paltry …*The crowd had been thin for the first half of the match*… OPPOSITE plentiful

5 = <u>fine</u>, delicate, flimsy, sheer, transparent, see-through, translucent, skimpy, gossamer, diaphanous, filmy, unsubstantial …*Her gown was thin and she shivered from the cold*… OPPOSITE thick

6 = <u>unconvincing</u>, inadequate, feeble, poor, weak, slight, shallow, insufficient, superficial, lame, scant, flimsy, scanty, unsubstantial …*The evidence is thin, and to some extent, ambiguous*… OPPOSITE convincing

7 = <u>wispy</u>, thinning, sparse, scarce, scanty …*She had pale thin yellow hair*…

VERB **1** = <u>prune</u>, trim, cut back, weed out …*It would*

have been better to thin the trees over several winters…

2 = <u>dilute</u>, water down, weaken, attenuate …*Aspirin thins the blood, letting it flow more easily*…

thing NOUN **1** = <u>object</u>, article, implement, machine, device, tool, instrument, mechanism, apparatus, gadget, gizmo (*informal*), contrivance, whatsit (*informal*), doo-dah (*informal*), thingummy (*informal*), thingummyjig (*informal*) …*What's that thing in the middle of the fountain?*…

2 = <u>substance</u>, stuff, element, being, body, material, fabric, texture, entity …*The Earth is mainly made of iron and silicon and things like that*…

3 = <u>concept</u>, idea, notion, conception …*Literacy isn't the same thing as intelligence*…

4 = <u>matter</u>, issue, subject, thought, concern, worry, topic, preoccupation …*There were far more serious things on my mind*…

5 = <u>affair</u>, situation, state of affairs, state, circumstance, scenario …*This war thing is upsetting me*…

6 = <u>fact</u>, detail, particular, point, factor, piece of information …*The first thing parents want to know is what sex the baby is*…

7 = <u>feature</u>, point, detail, something, particular, factor, item, aspect, facet …*If you could change one thing about yourself, what would it be?*…

8 = <u>happening</u>, event, incident, proceeding, phenomenon, occurrence, eventuality …*A strange thing happened*…

9 (*Informal*) = <u>phobia</u>, fear, complex, horror, terror, hang-up (*informal*), aversion, neurosis, bee in your bonnet (*informal*) …*She had a thing about spiders*…

10 (*Informal*) = <u>obsession</u>, liking, preoccupation, mania, quirk, fetish, fixation, soft spot, predilection, idée fixe (*French*) …*He's got a thing about red hair*…

11 = <u>remark</u>, comment, statement, observation, declaration, utterance, pronouncement …*No, some things are better left unsaid*…

PLURAL NOUN **1** = <u>possessions</u>, stuff, gear, belongings, goods, effects, clothes, luggage, baggage, bits and pieces, paraphernalia, clobber (*Brit. slang*), odds and ends, chattels, impedimenta …*She told him to take his things and not come back*…

2 = <u>equipment</u>, gear, tools, stuff, tackle, implements, kit, apparatus, utensils, accoutrements …*He forgot his shaving things*…

3 = <u>circumstances</u>, the situation, the state of affairs, matters, life, affairs …*Everyone agrees things are getting better*…

think VERB **1** = <u>believe</u>, hold that, be of the opinion, conclude, esteem, conceive, be of the view …*I think there should be a ban on tobacco advertising*…

2 = <u>anticipate</u>, expect, figure (*U.S. informal*), suppose, imagine, guess (*informal, chiefly U.S. & Canad.*), reckon (*informal*), presume, envisage, foresee, surmise …*I think he'll do a great job for us*…

3 = <u>judge</u>, consider, estimate, reckon, deem, regard as …*She thought he was about seventeen years old*…

4 = <u>ponder</u>, reflect, contemplate, deliberate, brood, meditate, ruminate, cogitate, rack your brains, be lost in thought, cerebrate …*She closed her eyes for a moment, trying to think…*

5 = remember, recall, recollect, review, think back to, bring to mind, call to mind …*I was trying to think what else we had to do…*

NOUN (*Informal*) = ponder, consideration, muse, assessment, reflection, deliberation, contemplation …*I'll have a think about that…*

PHRASES **think about something** or **someone** = ponder, consider, mull over, have in mind, weigh up, chew over (*informal*), reason over, turn over in your mind, revolve in your mind …*I have often thought about this problem…* ◆ **think better of something** = change your mind about, reconsider, decide against, think again, go back on, think twice about, repent, have second thoughts about …*He opened his mouth to protest. Then he thought better of it…* ◆ **think much of** or **a lot of something** or **someone** = have a high opinion of, value, respect, admire, esteem, rate (*slang*), hold in high regard, attach importance to, set store by, think highly of …*We think a lot of him, and believe he could go a long way…* ◆ **think nothing of something** 1 = have no compunction about, have no hesitation about, take in your stride …*I thought nothing of betting £1,000 on a horse…* 2 = consider unimportant, set no store by, regard as routine …*One of his friends kept coming to the house, but I thought nothing of it…* ◆ **think something over** = consider, contemplate, ponder, reflect upon, give thought to, consider the pros and cons of, weigh up, rack your brains about, chew over (*informal*), mull over, turn over in your mind …*She says she needs time to think it over…* ◆ **think something up** = devise, create, imagine, manufacture, come up with, invent, contrive, improvise, visualize, concoct, dream something up, trump something up …*'Where did you get that idea?' 'I just thought it up.'…*

thinker = philosopher, intellect (*informal*), wise man, sage, brain (*informal*), theorist, mastermind, mahatma

thinking NOUN = reasoning, thoughts, philosophy, idea, view, position, theory, opinion, conclusions, assessment, judgment, outlook, conjecture …*There was a strong theoretical dimension to his thinking…* ADJECTIVE = thoughtful, intelligent, cultured, reasoning, sophisticated, rational, philosophical, reflective, contemplative, meditative, ratiocinative …*Thinking people on both sides will applaud this book…*

third-rate = mediocre, bad, inferior, indifferent, poor, duff (*Brit. informal*), shoddy, poor-quality, low-grade, no great shakes (*informal*), not much cop (*informal*), cheap-jack, half-pie (*N.Z. informal*), of a sort or of sorts, ropey or ropy (*Brit. informal*), bodger or bodgie (*Austral. slang*)

thirst 1 = dryness, thirstiness, drought, craving to drink …*Instead of tea or coffee, drink water to quench your thirst…* 2 = craving, hunger, appetite, longing, desire, passion, yen (*informal*), ache, lust, yearning, eagerness, hankering, keenness …*their ever-growing thirst for cash…* OPPOSITE aversion

thirsty 1 = parched, dry, dehydrated …*If a baby is thirsty, it feeds more often…* 2 *with* **for** = eager for, longing for, hungry for, dying for, yearning for, lusting for, craving for, thirsting for, burning for, hankering for, itching for, greedy for, desirous of, avid for, athirst for …*People should understand how thirsty for revenge they are…*

thorn NOUN = prickle, spike, spine, barb …*Roses will always have thorns, but with care they can be avoided…* PHRASES **thorn in your side** = irritation, nuisance, annoyance, trouble, bother, torture, plague, curse, pest, torment, hassle (*informal*), scourge, affliction, irritant, bane …*She's a real thorn in his side…*

thorny 1 = prickly, spiky, spiny, pointed, sharp, barbed, bristly, spinous, bristling with thorns …*thorny hawthorn trees…* 2 = troublesome, difficult, problematic(al), trying, hard, worrying, tough, upsetting, awkward, unpleasant, sticky (*informal*), harassing, irksome, ticklish, vexatious …*the thorny issue of immigration policy…*

thorough 1 = comprehensive, full, complete, sweeping, intensive, in-depth, exhaustive, all-inclusive, all-embracing, leaving no stone unturned …*We are making a thorough investigation…* OPPOSITE cursory 2 = careful, conscientious, painstaking, efficient, meticulous, exhaustive, scrupulous, assiduous …*The men were expert, thorough and careful…* OPPOSITE careless 3 = complete, total, absolute, utter, perfect, entire, pure, sheer, outright, downright, unqualified, out-and-out, unmitigated, arrant, deep-dyed (*usually derogatory*) …*I was a thorough little academic snob…* OPPOSITE partial

thoroughbred = purebred, pedigree, pure-blooded, blood, full-blooded, of unmixed stock OPPOSITE mongrel

thoroughfare = road, way, street, highway, passageway, roadway, access, passage, avenue

thoroughly 1 = carefully, completely, fully, comprehensively, sweepingly, efficiently, inside out, meticulously, painstakingly, scrupulously, assiduously, intensively, from top to bottom, conscientiously, exhaustively, leaving no stone unturned …*a thoroughly researched and illuminating biography…* OPPOSITE carelessly 2 = fully, completely, throughout, inside out, through and through …*Food must be reheated thoroughly…* 3 = completely, quite, totally, perfectly, entirely, absolutely, utterly, to the full, downright, to the hilt, without reservation …*We returned home thoroughly contented…* OPPOSITE partly

though CONJUNCTION = although, while, even if, despite the fact that, allowing, granted, even though, albeit, notwithstanding, even supposing, tho' (*U.S. or* *poetic*) *…He's very attractive, though he certainly isn't a ladykiller…*

ADVERB = nevertheless, still, however, yet, nonetheless, all the same, for all that, notwithstanding *…I like him. He makes me angry sometimes, though…*

thought 1 = thinking, consideration, reflection, deliberation, regard, musing, meditation, contemplation, introspection, rumination, navel-gazing (*slang*), cogitation, brainwork, cerebration *…After much thought I decided to end my marriage…*
2 = opinion, view, belief, idea, thinking, concept, conclusion, assessment, notion, conviction, judgment, conception, conjecture, estimation *…It is my thought that the situation will be resolved…*
3 = consideration, study, attention, care, regard, scrutiny, heed *…He had given some thought to what she had told him…*
4 = intention, plan, idea, design, aim, purpose, object, notion *…They had no thought of surrendering…*
5 = hope, expectation, dream, prospect, aspiration, anticipation *…He had now banished all thought of retirement…*
6 = concern, care, regard, anxiety, sympathy, compassion, thoughtfulness, solicitude, attentiveness *…They had no thought for others who might get hurt…*

thoughtful 1 = reflective, pensive, contemplative, meditative, thinking, serious, musing, wistful, introspective, rapt, studious, lost in thought, deliberative, ruminative, in a brown study *…He was looking very thoughtful…* **OPPOSITE** shallow
2 = considerate, kind, caring, kindly, helpful, attentive, unselfish, solicitous *…a thoughtful and caring man…* **OPPOSITE** inconsiderate

thoughtless 1 = inconsiderate, rude, selfish, insensitive, unkind, uncaring, indiscreet, tactless, impolite, undiplomatic *…a minority of thoughtless and inconsiderate people…* **OPPOSITE** considerate
2 = unthinking, stupid, silly, careless, regardless, foolish, rash, reckless, mindless, negligent, inadvertent, ill-considered, tactless, absent-minded, imprudent, slapdash, neglectful, heedless, slipshod, inattentive, injudicious, remiss, unmindful, unobservant, ditsy *or* ditzy (*slang*) *…It was thoughtless of her to mention it…* **OPPOSITE** wise

thrall = slavery, bondage, servitude, enslavement, subjugation, serfdom, subjection, vassalage, thraldom

thrash **VERB** 1 = defeat, beat, hammer (*informal*), stuff (*slang*), tank (*slang*), crush, overwhelm, slaughter (*informal*), lick (*informal*), paste (*slang*), rout, maul, trounce, clobber (*slang*), run rings around (*informal*), wipe the floor with (*informal*), make mincemeat of (*informal*), blow someone out of the water (*slang*), drub, beat someone hollow (*Brit. informal*) *…They thrashed their opponents 5-nil…*
2 = beat, wallop, whip, hide (*informal*), belt (*informal*), leather, tan (*slang*), cane, lick (*informal*), paste (*slang*), birch, flog, scourge, spank, clobber (*slang*), lambast(e), flagellate, horsewhip, give someone a (good) hiding (*informal*), drub, take a stick to *…'Liar!' she screamed,*

as she thrashed the child…
3 = thresh, flail, jerk, plunge, toss, squirm, writhe, heave, toss and turn *…He collapsed on the floor, thrashing his legs about…*

PHRASES **thrash something out** = settle, resolve, discuss, debate, solve, argue out, have something out, talk something over *…an effort to thrash out differences about which they have strong feelings…*

thrashing 1 = defeat, beating, hammering (*informal*), hiding (*informal*), pasting (*slang*), rout, mauling, trouncing, drubbing *…She dropped only 8 points in her thrashing of the former champion…*
2 = beating, hiding (*informal*), belting (*informal*), whipping, tanning (*slang*), lashing, caning, pasting (*slang*), flogging, drubbing, chastisement *…She knew if she was caught she would get a thrashing…*

thread **NOUN** 1 = strand, fibre, yarn, filament, line, string, cotton, twine *…a hat embroidered with golden threads…*
2 = theme, motif, train of thought, course, direction, strain, plot, drift, tenor, story line *…the thread running through the book…*
VERB = move, pass, inch, ease, thrust, meander, squeeze through, pick your way *…She threaded her way back through the crowd…*

threadbare 1 = shabby, worn, frayed, old, ragged, worn-out, scruffy, tattered, tatty, down at heel *…She sat cross-legged on a square of threadbare carpet…* **OPPOSITE** new
2 = hackneyed, common, tired, stale, corny (*slang*), stock, familiar, conventional, stereotyped, commonplace, well-worn, trite, clichéd, overused, cliché-ridden *…the government's threadbare domestic policies…* **OPPOSITE** original

threat 1 = danger, risk, hazard, menace, peril *…the threat of tropical storms…*
2 = threatening remark, menace, commination, intimidatory remark *…He may be forced to carry out his threat to resign…*
3 = warning, foreshadowing, foreboding *…The people who lived there felt a permanent sense of threat…*

threaten 1 = intimidate, bully, menace, terrorize, warn, cow, lean on (*slang*), pressurize, browbeat, make threats to *…He tied her up and threatened her with a knife…* **OPPOSITE** defend
2 = endanger, jeopardize, put at risk, imperil, put in jeopardy, put on the line *…The newcomers directly threaten the livelihood of current workers…* **OPPOSITE** protect
3 = be imminent, hang over, be in the air, loom, be in the offing, hang over someone's head, impend *…Plants must be covered with a leaf-mould if frost threatens…*

threatening 1 = menacing, bullying, intimidatory, terrorizing, minatory, comminatory *…The police should have charged them with threatening behaviour…*
2 = ominous, sinister, forbidding, grim, baleful,

inauspicious, bodeful …*a threatening atmosphere of rising tension and stress…* OPPOSITE promising

threesome = trio, trinity, trilogy, triplet, triad, triumvirate, troika, triptych, triplex, trine, triune

threshold 1 = entrance, doorway, door, doorstep, sill, doorsill …*He stopped at the threshold of the bedroom…*
2 = start, beginning, opening, dawn, verge, brink, outset, starting point, inception …*We are on the threshold of a new era in astronomy…* OPPOSITE end
3 = limit, margin, starting point, minimum …*She has a low threshold of boredom, and needs constant stimulation…*

thrift = economy, prudence, frugality, saving, parsimony, carefulness, good husbandry, thriftiness OPPOSITE extravagance

thrifty = economical, prudent, provident, frugal, saving, sparing, careful, parsimonious OPPOSITE extravagant

thrill NOUN 1 = pleasure, charge (*slang*), kick (*informal*), glow, sensation, buzz (*slang*), high, stimulation, tingle, titillation, flush of excitement …*I remember the thrill of opening presents on Christmas morning…* OPPOSITE tedium
2 = trembling, throb, shudder, flutter, fluttering, tremor, quiver, vibration …*He felt a thrill of fear, of adrenaline…*
VERB = excite, stimulate, arouse, move, send (*slang*), stir, flush, tingle, electrify, titillate, give someone a kick …*The electric atmosphere both thrilled and terrified him…*

thrilling = exciting, gripping, stimulating, stirring, sensational, rousing, riveting, electrifying, hair-raising, rip-roaring (*informal*) OPPOSITE boring

thrive = prosper, do well, flourish, increase, grow, develop, advance, succeed, get on, boom, bloom, wax, burgeon, grow rich OPPOSITE decline

thriving = successful, doing well, flourishing, growing, developing, healthy, booming, wealthy, blooming, prosperous, burgeoning, going strong OPPOSITE unsuccessful

throaty = hoarse, husky, gruff, low, deep, thick, guttural

throb VERB 1 = pulsate, pound, beat, pulse, thump, palpitate …*His head throbbed…*
2 = vibrate, pulse, resonate, pulsate, reverberate, shake, judder (*informal*) …*The engines throbbed…*
NOUN 1 = pulse, pounding, beat, thump, thumping, pulsating, palpitation …*The bruise on his stomach ached with a steady throb…*
2 = vibration, pulse, throbbing, resonance, reverberation, judder (*informal*), pulsation …*His head jerked up at the throb of the engine…*

throes PLURAL NOUN = pains, spasms, pangs, fit, stabs, convulsions, paroxysm …*The animal twitched in its final death throes…*
PHRASES **in the throes of something** = in the midst of, in the process of, suffering from, struggling with, wrestling with, toiling with, anguished by,

agonized by, in the pangs of …*The country is in the throes of a general election…*

throng NOUN = crowd, mob, horde, press, host, pack, mass, crush, jam, congregation, swarm, multitude, concourse, assemblage …*An official pushed through the throng…*
VERB 1 = crowd, flock, congregate, troop, bunch, herd, cram, converge, hem in, mill around, swarm around …*the multitudes that throng around the Pope…* OPPOSITE disperse
2 = pack, fill, crowd, press, jam …*They throng the beaches in July and August…*

throttle 1 = strangle, choke, garrotte, strangulate …*He tried to throttle her with wire…*
2 = suppress, inhibit, stifle, control, silence, gag …*The over-valuation of sterling is throttling industry…*

through PREPOSITION 1 = via, by way of, by, between, past, in and out of, from end to end of, from one side to the other of …*The path continues through a tunnel of trees…*
2 = because of, by way of, by means of, by virtue of, with the assistance of, as a consequence *or* result of …*the thought of someone suffering through a mistake of mine…*
3 = using, via, by way of, by means of, by virtue of, with the assistance of …*I got it cheap through a friend in the trade…*
4 = during, throughout, in the middle of, for the duration of, in …*trips at home and abroad all through the year…*
ADJECTIVE 1 often with **with** = finished with, done with, having had enough of …*I'm through with women…*
2 = completed, done, finished, ended, terminated …*It would guarantee employment once her schooling was through…*
PHRASES **through and through** = completely, totally, fully, thoroughly, entirely, altogether, wholly, utterly, to the core, unreservedly …*People assume they know me through and through as soon as we meet…*

throughout PREPOSITION 1 = right through, all through, everywhere in, for the duration of, during the whole of, through the whole of, from end to end of …*The same themes are repeated throughout the film…*
2 = all over, all through, everywhere in, through the whole of, over the length and breadth of …*He now runs projects throughout Africa…*
ADVERB 1 = from start to finish, right through, the whole time, all the time, from the start, all through, from beginning to end …*The concert wasn't bad, but people talked throughout…*
2 = all through, right through, in every nook and cranny …*Throughout, the walls are white…*

throw VERB 1 = hurl, toss, fling, send, project, launch, cast, pitch, shy, chuck (*informal*), propel, sling, lob (*informal*), heave, put …*He spent hours throwing a tennis ball against a wall…*
2 = toss, fling, chuck (*informal*), cast, hurl, sling, heave,

put …*He threw his jacket onto the back seat*…
3 = dislodge, unseat, upset, overturn, hurl to the ground …*The horse reared, throwing its rider*…
4 (*Informal*) = confuse, baffle, faze, astonish, confound, unnerve, disconcert, perturb, throw you out, throw you off, dumbfound, discompose, put your off your stroke, throw you off your stride, unsettle …*He threw me by asking if I went in for martial arts*…
NOUN = toss, pitch, fling, put, cast, shy, sling, lob (*informal*), heave …*One of the judges thought it was a foul throw*…
PHRASES **throw someone off** **1** = disconcert, unsettle, faze, throw (*informal*), upset, confuse, disturb, put you off your stroke, throw you off your stride …*I lost my first serve in the first set; it threw me off a bit*… **2** = escape from, lose, leave behind, get away from, evade, shake off, elude, outrun, outdistance, give someone the slip, show a clean pair of heels to …*He threw off his pursuers by pedalling across the state line*… ◆ **throw someone out** = expel, eject, evict, dismiss, get rid of, oust, kick someone out (*informal*), show someone the door, turf someone out (*Brit. informal*), give someone the bum's rush (*slang*), kiss someone off (*slang, chiefly U.S. & Canad.*) …*I wanted to kill him, but instead I just threw him out*… ◆ **throw something away** **1** = discard, dump (*informal*), get rid of, reject, scrap, axe (*informal*), bin (*informal*), ditch (*slang*), junk (*informal*), chuck (*informal*), throw out, dispose of, dispense with, jettison, cast off …*I never throw anything away*… **2** = waste, lose, blow (*slang*), squander, fritter away, fail to make use of, make poor use of …*Failing to tackle the problem would be throwing away an opportunity*… ◆ **throw something off** (*Literary*) = cast off, shake off, rid yourself of, free yourself of, drop, abandon, discard …*a country ready to throw off the shackles of its colonial past*… ◆ **throw something out** **1** = discard, dump (*informal*), get rid of, reject, scrap, bin (*informal*), ditch (*slang*), junk (*informal*), chuck (*informal*), throw away, dispose of, dispense with, jettison, cast off …*Never throw out milk that is about to go off*… **2** = emit, radiate, give off, diffuse, disseminate, put forth …*a workshop throwing out a pool of light*… ◆ **throw something up** **1** = throw together, jerry-build, run up, slap together …*Scrap metal dwellings are thrown up in any available space*… **2** = produce, reveal, bring to light, bring forward, bring to the surface, bring to notice …*These studies have throw up some interesting results*… **3** = give up, leave, abandon, quit, chuck (*informal*), resign from, relinquish, renounce, step down from (*informal*), jack in …*He threw up his job as party chairman*… ◆ **throw up** (*Informal*) = vomit, be sick, spew, puke (*slang*), chuck (*Austral. & N.Z. informal*), heave, regurgitate, disgorge, retch, barf (*U.S. slang*), chunder (*slang, chiefly Austral.*), upchuck (*U.S. slang*), do a technicolour yawn (*slang*), toss your cookies (*U.S. slang*) …*He threw up over a seat next to me*…
throwaway (*Chiefly Brit.*) = casual, passing, offhand,

careless, understated, unthinking, ill-considered
thrust **VERB** **1** = push, force, shove, drive, press, plunge, jam, butt, ram, poke, propel, prod, impel …*They thrust him into the back of a jeep*…
2 = shove, push, shoulder, lunge, jostle, elbow *or* shoulder your way …*She thrust her way into the crowd*…
3 = stab, stick, jab, pierce …*How can I thrust a knife into my son's heart?*…
NOUN **1** = stab, pierce, lunge …*Two of the knife thrusts were fatal*…
2 = push, shove, poke, prod …*a thrust of his hand that sent the lad reeling*…
3 = momentum, impetus, drive, motive power, motive force, propulsive force …*It provides the thrust that makes the craft move forward*…
thud **NOUN** = thump, crash, knock, smack, clump, wallop (*informal*), clunk, clonk …*She tripped and fell with a sickening thud*…
VERB = thump, crash, knock, smack, clump, wallop (*informal*), clunk, clonk …*She ran upstairs, her bare feet thudding on the wood*…
thug = ruffian, hooligan, tough, heavy (*slang*), killer, murderer, robber, gangster, assassin, bandit, mugger (*informal*), cut-throat, bully boy, bruiser (*informal*), tsotsi (*S. African*)
thumb **NOUN** = digit …*She bit her thumb, not looking at me*…
VERB **1** = handle, finger, mark, soil, maul, mess up, dog-ear …*a well-thumbed copy of Who's Who*…
2 = hitch, request (*informal*), signal for, hitchhike …*Thumbing a lift once had a carefree image*…
PHRASES **all thumbs** = clumsy, inept, cack-handed (*informal*), maladroit, butterfingered (*informal*), ham-fisted (*informal*), unco (*Austral. slang*) …*Can you open this? I'm all thumbs*… ◆ **thumb through something** = flick through, browse through, leaf through, glance at, turn over, flip through, skim through, riffle through, scan the pages of, run your eye over …*He had the drawer open and was thumbing through files*… ◆ **thumbs down** = disapproval, refusal, rejection, no, rebuff, negation …*Brokers have given the firm the thumbs down*… ◆ **thumbs up** = approval, go-ahead (*informal*), acceptance, yes, encouragement, green light, affirmation, O.K. *or* okay (*informal*) …*The film got a general thumbs up from the critics*…
thumbnail = brief, short, concise, quick, compact, succinct, pithy
thump **VERB** **1** = strike, hit, punch, pound, beat, knock, deck (*slang*), batter, rap, chin (*slang*), smack, thrash, clout (*informal*), whack, swipe, clobber (*slang*), wallop (*informal*), lambast(e), belabour, lay one on (*slang*) …*He thumped me, nearly knocking me over*…
2 = thud, crash, bang, thwack …*She thumped her hand on the witness box*…
3 = throb, pound, beat, pulse, pulsate, palpitate …*My heart was thumping wildly*…
NOUN **1** = blow, knock, punch, rap, smack, clout

(*informal*), whack, swipe, wallop (*informal*) ...*He felt a thump on his shoulder*...
2 = thud, crash, bang, clunk, thwack ...*There was a loud thump as the horse crashed into the van*...

thumping (*Slang*) = huge, massive, enormous, great, impressive, tremendous, excessive, terrific, thundering (*slang*), titanic, gigantic, monumental, mammoth, colossal, whopping (*informal*), stellar (*informal*), exorbitant, gargantuan, elephantine, humongous *or* humungous (*U.S. slang*) OPPOSITE> insignificant

thunder NOUN = rumble, crash, crashing, boom, booming, explosion, rumbling, pealing, detonation, cracking ...*The thunder of the sea on the rocks*...
VERB **1** = rumble, crash, blast, boom, explode, roar, clap, resound, detonate, reverberate, crack, peal ...*the sound of the guns thundering in the fog*...
2 = shout, roar, yell, bark, bellow, declaim ...*'It's your money. Ask for it!' she thundered*...
3 = rail, curse, fulminate ...*He started thundering about feminists and liberals*...

thunderous = loud, noisy, deafening, booming, roaring, resounding, tumultuous, ear-splitting

thus 1 = therefore, so, hence, consequently, accordingly, for this reason, ergo, on that account ...*women's access to the basic means of production, and thus to political power*...
2 = in this way, so, like this, as follows, like so, in this manner, in this fashion, to such a degree ...*She explained her mistake thus*...

thwart = frustrate, stop, foil, check, defeat, prevent, oppose, snooker, baffle, hinder, obstruct, impede, balk, outwit, stymie, cook someone's goose (*informal*), put a spoke in someone's wheel (*informal*) OPPOSITE> assist

tic = twitch, jerk, spasm

tick NOUN **1** = check mark, mark, line, stroke, dash ...*Place a tick in the appropriate box*...
2 = click, tap, tapping, clicking, clack, ticktock ...*He sat listening to the tick of the grandfather clock*...
3 (*Brit. informal*) = moment, second, minute, shake (*informal*), flash, instant, sec (*informal*), twinkling, split second, jiffy (*informal*), trice, half a mo (*Brit. informal*), two shakes of a lamb's tail (*informal*), bat of an eye (*informal*) ...*I'll be back in a tick*...
VERB **1** = mark, indicate, mark off, check off, choose, select ...*Please tick here if you do not want to receive such mailings*...
2 = click, tap, clack, ticktock ...*A clock ticked busily from the kitchen counter*...
PHRASES **tick someone off** (*Informal*) = scold, rebuke, tell someone off (*informal*), lecture, carpet (*informal*), censure, reprimand, reproach, berate, chide, tear into (*informal*), reprove, upbraid, take someone to task, read someone the riot act, bawl someone out (*informal*), chew someone out (*U.S. & Canad. informal*), tear someone off a strip (*Brit. informal*), haul someone over the coals (*informal*), give someone a rocket (*Brit. & N.Z. informal*) ...*His mum ticked him off when they got home*... ◆ **tick**

something off = mark off, check off, put a tick at ...*He ticked off my name on a piece of paper*...

ticket 1 = voucher, pass, coupon, card, slip, certificate, token, chit ...*They were queueing to get tickets for the football match*...
2 = label, tag, marker, sticker, card, slip, tab, docket ...*a price ticket*...

tickle = amuse, delight, entertain, please, divert, gratify, titillate OPPOSITE> bore

tide NOUN **1** = current, flow, stream, course, ebb, undertow, tideway ...*They used to sail with the tide*...
2 = course, direction, trend, current, movement, tendency, drift ...*They talked of reversing the tide of events*...
PHRASES **tide someone over** = keep you going, see you through, keep the wolf from the door, keep your head above water, bridge the gap for ...*He wanted to borrow some money to tide him over*...

tidings = news, report, word, message, latest (*informal*), information, communication, intelligence, bulletin, gen (*Brit. informal*)

tidy ADJECTIVE **1** = neat, orderly, ordered, clean, trim, systematic, spruce, businesslike, well-kept, well-ordered, shipshape, spick-and-span, trig (*archaic or dialect*), in apple-pie order (*informal*) ...*Having a tidy desk can sometimes seem impossible*... OPPOSITE> untidy
2 = organized, neat, fastidious, methodical, smart, efficient, spruce, businesslike, well-groomed, well turned out ...*She wasn't a tidy person*...
3 (*Informal*) = considerable, large, substantial, good, goodly, fair, healthy, generous, handsome, respectable, ample, largish, sizable *or* sizeable ...*The opportunities are there to make a tidy profit*...
OPPOSITE> small
VERB = neaten, straighten, put in order, order, clean, groom, spruce up, put to rights, put in trim ...*She made her bed and tidied her room*... OPPOSITE> disorder

tie VERB **1** = fasten, bind, join, unite, link, connect, attach, knot, truss, interlace ...*He tied the ends of the plastic bag together*... OPPOSITE> unfasten
2 = tether, secure, rope, moor, lash, make fast ...*She tied her horse to a fence post*...
3 = restrict, limit, confine, hold, bind, restrain, hamper, hinder ...*I wouldn't like to be tied to catching the last train home*... OPPOSITE> free
4 = draw, be even, be level, be neck and neck, match, equal ...*Both teams had tied on points and goal difference*...
NOUN **1** = fastening, binding, link, band, bond, joint, connection, string, rope, knot, cord, fetter, ligature ...*little empire-line coats with ribbon ties*...
2 = bond, relationship, connection, duty, commitment, obligation, liaison, allegiance, affinity, affiliation, kinship ...*She had family ties in France*...
3 = draw, dead heat, deadlock, stalemate ...*The first game ended in a tie*...
4 (*Brit.*) = match, game, contest, fixture, meeting,

event, trial, bout …*They'll meet the winners of the first round tie*…

5 = encumbrance, restriction, limitation, check, handicap, restraint, hindrance, bind (*informal*) …*It's a bit of a tie, going there every Sunday*…

[PHRASES] **tie in with something** **1** = link, relate to, connect, be relevant to, come in to, have bearing on …*subjects which tie in with whatever you enjoy about painting*… **2** = fit in with, coincide with, coordinate with, harmonize with, occur simultaneously with …*Our wedding date had to tie in with Dave's leaving the army*… ♦ **tie something** or **someone up** = bind, restrain, pinion, truss someone or something up …*Don't you think we should tie him up and put a guard over him?*… ♦ **tie something up** **1** = secure, lash, tether, make fast, moor, attach, rope …*I had tied the boat up in the marina and furled my sail*… **2** = conclude, settle, wrap up (*informal*), end, wind up, terminate, finish off, bring to a close …*They hope to tie up a deal within the next few weeks*…

tie in or **tie-in** = link, connection, relation, relationship, association, tie-up, liaison, coordination, hook-up

tier = row, bank, layer, line, order, level, series, file, rank, storey, stratum, echelon

tie-up = link, association, connection, relationship, relation, liaison, tie-in, coordination, hook-up, linkup

tiff = quarrel, row, disagreement, words, difference, dispute, scrap (*informal*), falling-out (*informal*), squabble, petty quarrel

tight **1** = close-fitting, narrow, cramped, snug, constricted, close …*His jeans were too tight*… [OPPOSITE] loose

2 = secure, firm, fast, fixed …*Keep a tight grip on my hand*…

3 = underline{taut}, stretched, tense, rigid, stiff …*Pull the elastic tight and knot the ends*… [OPPOSITE] slack

4 = strict, stringent, severe, tough, harsh, stern, rigid, rigorous, uncompromising, inflexible, unyielding …*tight control of media coverage*… [OPPOSITE] easy-going

5 = sealed, watertight, impervious, sound, proof, hermetic …*Cover with foil and the lid to ensure a tight seal*… [OPPOSITE] open

6 = close, even, well-matched, near, hard-fought, evenly-balanced …*It was a very tight match*… [OPPOSITE] uneven

7 (*Informal*) = miserly, mean, stingy, close, sparing, grasping, parsimonious, niggardly, penurious, tightfisted …*Are you so tight you won't even spend a few quid?*… [OPPOSITE] generous

8 = difficult, tough, dangerous, tricky, sticky (*informal*), hazardous, troublesome, problematic, precarious, perilous, worrisome, ticklish …*They teach you to use your head and get out of a tight spot*…

9 (*Informal*) = drunk, intoxicated, flying (*slang*), bombed (*slang*), stoned (*slang*), wasted (*slang*), smashed (*slang*), steaming (*slang*), wrecked (*slang*), out of it (*slang*), plastered (*slang*), blitzed (*slang*), lit up (*slang*), stewed (*slang*), pickled (*informal*), bladdered

(*slang*), under the influence (*informal*), tipsy, legless (*informal*), paralytic (*informal*), sozzled (*informal*), steamboats (*Scot. slang*), tiddly (*slang, chiefly Brit.*), half cut (*Brit. slang*), zonked (*slang*), blotto (*slang*), inebriated, out to it (*Austral. & N.Z. slang*), three sheets to the wind (*slang*), in your cups, half seas over (*Brit. informal*), bevvied (*dialect*), pie-eyed (*slang*) …*He laughed loudly. There was no doubt he was tight*… [OPPOSITE] sober

tighten **1** = close, narrow, strengthen, squeeze, harden, constrict …*He answered by tightening his grip on her shoulder*… [OPPOSITE] slacken

2 = stretch, strain, tense, tauten, stiffen, rigidify …*He flung his whole weight back, tightening the rope*… [OPPOSITE] slacken

3 = fasten, secure, screw, fix …*I used my thumbnail to tighten the screw*… [OPPOSITE] unfasten

tight-lipped = secretive, reticent, uncommunicative, reserved, quiet, silent, mute, taciturn, close-mouthed, unforthcoming, close-lipped

till¹ = cultivate, dig, plough, work, turn over …*freshly tilled fields*…

till² = cash register, cash box, cash drawer …*He checked the register. There was money in the till*…

tilt [VERB] = slant, tip, slope, list, lean, heel, incline, cant …*The boat instantly tilted, filled and sank*… [NOUN] **1** = slope, angle, inclination, list, pitch, incline, slant, cant, camber, gradient …*the tilt of the earth's axis*…

2 (*Medieval history*) = joust, fight, tournament, lists, clash, set-to (*informal*), encounter, combat, duel, tourney …*The crowd cheered and the tilt began*…

timber **1** = beams, boards, planks …*a bird nestling in the timbers of the roof*…

2 = wood, logs …*These forests have been exploited for timber since Saxon times*…

timbre = tone, sound, ring, resonance, colour, tonality, tone colour, quality of sound

time [NOUN] **1** = period, while, term, season, space, stretch, spell, phase, interval, span, period of time, stint, duration, length of time …*For a long time I didn't tell anyone*…

2 = occasion, point, moment, stage, instance, point in time, juncture …*It seemed like a good time to tell her*…

3 = age, days, era, year, date, generation, duration, epoch, chronology, aeon …*The design has remained unchanged since the time of the pharaohs*…

4 = tempo, beat, rhythm, measure, metre …*A reel is in four-four time*…

5 = lifetime, day, life, season, duration, life span, allotted span …*I wouldn't change anything if I had my time again*…

6 = heyday, prime, peak, hour, springtime, salad days, best years or days …*He was a very good jockey in his time*…

[VERB] **1** = underline{measure}, judge, clock, count …*He timed each performance with a stop-watch*…

2 = schedule, set, plan, book, programme, set up, fix, arrange, line up, organize, timetable, slate (*U.S.*), fix up, prearrange …*We had timed our visit for March 7…* 3 = regulate, control, calculate …*an alarm timed to go off every hour on the hour…*

PHRASES **all the time** = constantly, always, continually, ever, throughout, continuously, at all times, for the duration, perpetually, ceaselessly, without a break …*She keeps nagging me about my smoking all the time…* ◆ **at one time** = once, previously, formerly, for a while, hitherto, once upon a time …*At one time, 400 people lived in the village…* ◆ **at times** = sometimes, occasionally, from time to time, now and then, on occasion, once in a while, every now and then, every so often …*The debate was highly emotional at times…* ◆ **behind the times** = out of date, old-fashioned, outdated, square (*informal*), dated, obsolete, out of fashion, antiquated, outmoded, passé, old hat, out of style …*That idea is about 20 years behind the times…* ◆ **for the time being** = for now, meanwhile, meantime, in the meantime, temporarily, for the moment, for the present, pro tem, for the nonce …*The situation is calm for the time being…* ◆ **from time to time** = occasionally, sometimes, now and then, at times, on occasion, once in a while, every now and then, every so often …*Her daughters visited her from time to time…* ◆ **in good time** 1 = on time, early, ahead of schedule, ahead of time, with time to spare …*We always make sure we're home in good time for the programme…* 2 = promptly, quickly, rapidly, swiftly, speedily, with dispatch …*Ninety-three per cent of the students received their loans in good time…* ◆ **in no time** = quickly, rapidly, swiftly, in a moment, in a flash, speedily, in an instant, apace, before you know it, in a trice, in a jiffy (*informal*), in two shakes of a lamb's tail (*informal*), before you can say Jack Robinson …*At his age he'll heal in no time…* ◆ **in time** 1 = on time, on schedule, in good time, at the appointed time, early, with time to spare …*I arrived in time for my flight to London…* 2 = eventually, one day, ultimately, sooner or later, someday, in the fullness of time, by and by …*He would sort out his own problems in time…* ◆ **on time** 1 = punctual, prompt, on schedule, in good time …*Don't worry, she'll be on time…* 2 = punctually, promptly, on schedule, on the dot …*The train arrived on time and she stepped out…* ◆ **time after time** = repeatedly, many times, over and over again, often, frequently, persistently, on many occasions …*He escaped from jail time after time…* ◆ **time and again** = over and over again, repeatedly, time after time …*Time and again political parties have failed to tackle this issue…*

(Related Words)

adjective: temporal

➤ **time**

time-honoured = long-established, traditional, customary, old, established, fixed, usual, ancient, conventional, venerable, age-old

timeless = eternal, lasting, permanent, enduring, abiding, immortal, everlasting, ceaseless, immutable, indestructible, undying, ageless, imperishable, deathless, changeless OPPOSITE temporary

timely = opportune, appropriate, well-timed, prompt, suitable, convenient, at the right time, judicious, punctual, propitious, seasonable OPPOSITE untimely

timetable 1 = schedule, programme, agenda, list,

Time

Gregorian calendar

January	May	September
February	June	October
March	July	November
April	August	December

Jewish calendar

Tishri	Shevat *or* Shebat	Sivan
Cheshvan *or* Heshvan	Adar	Tammuz
Kislev	Nisan	Av *or* Ab
Tevet	Iyar *or* Iyyar	Elul

Muslim calendar

Muharram *or* Moharram	Jumada II	Shawwal
Safar *or* Saphar	Rajab	Dhu'l-Qa'dah
Rabia I	Shaban *or* Shaaban	Dhu'l-Hijjah
Rabia II	Ramadan, Rhamadhan, *or*	
Jumada I	Ramazan	

French revolutionary calendar

Vendémiaire	Pluviôse	Prairial
Brumaire	Ventôse	Messidor
Frimaire	Germinal	Thermidor *or* Fervidor
Nivôse	Floréal	Fructidor

diary, calendar, order of the day ...*The timetable was hopelessly optimistic...*

2 = syllabus, course, curriculum, programme, teaching programme ...*Latin was not included on the timetable...*

timid = nervous, shy, retiring, modest, shrinking, fearful, cowardly, apprehensive, coy, diffident, bashful, mousy, timorous, pusillanimous, faint-hearted, irresolute OPPOSITE bold

tincture = tinge, trace, hint, colour, touch, suggestion, shade, flavour, dash, stain, smack, aroma, tint, hue, soupçon (*French*)

tinge NOUN **1** = tint, colour, shade, cast, wash, stain, dye, tincture ...*His skin had an unhealthy greyish tinge...*

2 = trace, bit, drop, touch, suggestion, dash, pinch, smack, sprinkling, smattering, soupçon (*French*) ...*Could there have been a slight tinge of envy in her voice?...*

VERB = tint, colour, shade, stain, dye ...*The living room was tinged yellow by the sunlight...*

tingle VERB = prickle, sting, itch, tickle, have goose pimples ...*The backs of her thighs tingled...*

NOUN **1** = prickling, stinging, itch, itching, tickle, tickling, pins and needles (*informal*) ...*I felt a sudden tingle in my fingers...*

2 = thrill, quiver, shiver ...*a sudden tingle of excitement...*

tinker = meddle, play, toy, monkey, potter, fiddle (*informal*), dabble, mess about, muck about (*Brit. slang*)

tinsel = showy, flashy, gaudy, cheap, plastic (*slang*), superficial, sham, tawdry, ostentatious, trashy, specious, gimcrack, meretricious, pinchbeck

tint NOUN **1** = shade, colour, tone, hue, cast ...*Its large leaves often show a delicate purple tint...*

2 = dye, wash, stain, rinse, tinge, tincture ...*You've had a tint on your hair...*

3 = hint, touch, trace, suggestion, shade, tinge ...*His words had more than a tint of truth to them...*

VERB = dye, colour, stain, rinse, tinge, tincture ...*Eyebrows can be tinted with the same dye...*

tiny = small, little, minute, slight, mini, wee, miniature, trifling, insignificant, negligible, microscopic, diminutive, petite, puny, pint-sized (*informal*), infinitesimal, teeny-weeny, Lilliputian, dwarfish, teensy-weensy, pygmy *or* pigmy OPPOSITE huge

tip¹ NOUN **1** = end, point, head, extremity, sharp end, nib, prong ...*She poked and shifted things with the tip of her walking stick...*

2 = peak, top, summit, pinnacle, crown, cap, zenith, apex, spire, acme, vertex ...*After dusk, the tip of the cone will light up...*

VERB = cap, top, crown, surmount, finish ...*a missile tipped with three war-heads...*

tip² VERB **1** = reward, remunerate, give a tip to, sweeten (*informal*) ...*Do you think it's customary to tip the waiters?...*

2 = predict, back, recommend, think of ...*He was

widely tipped for success...*

NOUN **1** = gratuity, gift, reward, present, sweetener (*informal*), perquisite, baksheesh, pourboire (*French*) ...*I gave the barber a tip...*

2 = hint, suggestion, piece of information, piece of advice, gen (*Brit. informal*), pointer, piece of inside information ...*A good tip is to buy the most expensive lens you can afford...*

tip³ VERB **1** = pour, drop, empty, dump, drain, spill, discharge, unload, jettison, offload, slop (*informal*), slosh (*informal*), decant ...*She took the plate and tipped the contents into the bin...*

2 (*Brit.*) = dump, empty, ditch (*slang*), unload, pour out ...*the costs of tipping rubbish in landfills...*

NOUN (*Brit.*) = dump, midden, rubbish heap, refuse heap ...*I took a load of rubbish and grass cuttings to the tip...*

PHRASES **tip someone off** = advise, warn, caution, forewarn, give a clue to, give a hint to, tip someone the wink (*Brit. informal*) ...*He tipped police off on his carphone...*

tip-off = hint, word, information, warning, suggestion, clue, pointer, inside information, word of advice

tipple NOUN = alcohol, drink, booze (*informal*), poison (*informal*), liquor, John Barleycorn ...*My favourite tipple is a glass of port...*

VERB = drink, imbibe, tope, indulge (*informal*), swig, quaff, take a drink, bevvy (*dialect*), bend the elbow (*informal*) ...*You may be tempted to tipple unobserved...*

tipsy = tiddly (*slang, chiefly Brit.*), fuddled, slightly drunk, happy (*informal*), merry (*Brit. informal*), mellow, woozy (*slang, chiefly Brit.*)

tirade = outburst, diatribe, harangue, abuse, lecture, denunciation, invective, fulmination, philippic

tire 1 = exhaust, drain, fatigue, weary, fag (*informal*), whack (*Brit. informal*), wear out, wear down, take it out of (*informal*), knacker (*slang*), enervate ...*If driving tires you, take the train...* OPPOSITE refresh

2 = flag, become tired, fail, droop ...*He tired easily, and was unable to sleep well at night...*

3 = bore, weary, exasperate, annoy, irritate, harass, hassle (*informal*), aggravate (*informal*), irk, get on your nerves (*informal*) ...*That subject tires me...*

tired 1 = exhausted, fatigued, weary, spent, done in (*informal*), flagging, all in (*slang*), drained, sleepy, fagged (*informal*), whacked (*Brit. informal*), worn out, drooping, knackered (*slang*), drowsy, clapped out (*Brit., Austral., & N.Z. informal*), enervated, ready to drop, dog-tired (*informal*), zonked (*slang*), dead beat (*informal*), tuckered out (*Austral. & N.Z. informal*), asleep *or* dead on your feet (*informal*) ...*He is tired and he has to rest after his long trip...* OPPOSITE energetic

2 = bored, fed up, weary, sick, annoyed, irritated, exasperated, irked ...*I was tired of being a bookkeeper...* OPPOSITE enthusiastic about

3 = hackneyed, stale, well-worn, old, stock, familiar,

conventional, corny (*slang*), threadbare, trite, clichéd, outworn …*I didn't want to hear one of his tired excuses…* OPPOSITE original

tireless = energetic, vigorous, industrious, determined, resolute, indefatigable, unflagging, untiring, unwearied OPPOSITE exhausted

tiresome = boring, annoying, irritating, trying, wearing, dull, tedious, exasperating, monotonous, laborious, uninteresting, irksome, wearisome, vexatious OPPOSITE interesting

tiring = exhausting, demanding, wearing, tough, exacting, fatiguing, wearying, strenuous, arduous, laborious, enervative

tissue 1 = matter, material, substance, stuff, structure …*As we age we lose muscle tissue…*
2 = paper, wipe, paper handkerchief, wrapping paper …*a box of tissues…*
3 = series, pack, collection, mass, network, chain, combination, web, accumulation, fabrication, conglomeration, concatenation …*It was all a tissue of lies which ended in his resignation…*

titan = giant, superman, colossus, leviathan

titanic = gigantic, huge, giant, massive, towering, vast, enormous, mighty, immense, jumbo (*informal*), monstrous, mammoth, colossal, mountainous, stellar (*informal*), prodigious, stupendous, herculean, elephantine, humongous *or* humungous (*U.S. slang*)

titbit = delicacy, goody, dainty, morsel, treat, snack, choice item, juicy bit, bonne bouche (*French*)

tit for tat NOUN = retaliation, like for like, measure for measure, an eye for an eye, a tooth for a tooth, blow for blow, as good as you get …*a dangerous game of tit for tat…*
ADJECTIVE = retaliatory, revenge, reciprocal …*a round of tit-for-tat expulsions…*

tithe = tax, levy, duty, assessment, tribute, toll, tariff, tenth, impost

titillate = excite, stimulate, arouse, interest, thrill, provoke, turn on (*slang*), tease, tickle, tantalize

titillating = exciting, stimulating, interesting, thrilling, arousing, sensational, teasing, provocative, lurid, suggestive, lewd

title NOUN 1 = heading, name, caption, label, legend, inscription …*The book was first published under the title 'A Place for Us'…*
2 = name, designation, epithet, term, handle (*slang*), nickname, denomination, pseudonym, appellation, sobriquet, nom de plume, moniker *or* monicker (*slang*) …*Her husband was honoured with the title 'Sir Denis'…*
3 (*Sport*) = championship, trophy, laurels, bays, crown, honour …*He has retained his title as world chess champion…*
4 (*Law*) = ownership, right, claim, privilege, entitlement, tenure, prerogative, freehold …*He never had title to the property…*
VERB = name, call, term, style, label, tag, designate …*a new book titled 'The Golden Thirteen'…*

titter = snigger, laugh, giggle, chuckle, chortle (*informal*), tee-hee, te-hee

toad
(*Related Words*)
adjective: batrachian
young: tadpole
➤ **amphibians**

toast[1] 1 = brown, grill, crisp, roast …*Toast the bread lightly on both sides…*
2 = warm (up), heat (up), thaw, bring back to life …*a bar with an open fire for toasting feet after a day skiing…*

toast[2] NOUN 1 = tribute, drink, compliment, salute, health, pledge, salutation …*We drank a toast to Miss Jacobs…*
2 = favourite, celebrity, darling, talk, pet, focus of attention, hero *or* heroine, blue-eyed boy *or* girl (*Brit. informal*) …*She was the toast of Paris…*
VERB = drink to, honour, pledge to, salute, drink (to) the health of …*They toasted her with champagne…*

to-do = fuss, performance (*informal*), disturbance, bother, stir, turmoil, unrest, flap (*informal*), quarrel, upheaval, bustle, furore, uproar, agitation, commotion, rumpus, tumult, brouhaha, ruction (*informal*), hue and cry, hoo-ha

together ADVERB 1 = collectively, jointly, closely, as one, with each other, in conjunction, side by side, mutually, hand in hand, as a group, in partnership, in concert, in unison, shoulder to shoulder, cheek by jowl, in cooperation, in a body, hand in glove …*Together they swam to the ship…* OPPOSITE separately
2 = at the same time, simultaneously, in unison, as one, (all) at once, en masse, concurrently, contemporaneously, with one accord, at one fell swoop …*'Yes,' they said together…*
ADJECTIVE (*Informal*) = self-possessed, calm, composed, well-balanced, cool, stable, well-organized, well-adjusted …*She was very headstrong, and very together…*

toil VERB 1 = labour, work, struggle, strive, grind (*informal*), sweat (*informal*), slave, graft (*informal*), go for it (*informal*), slog, grub, bend over backwards (*informal*), drudge, go for broke (*slang*), push yourself, bust a gut (*informal*), give it your best shot (*informal*), break your neck (*informal*), work like a dog, make an all-out effort (*informal*), work like a Trojan, knock yourself out (*informal*), do your damnedest (*informal*), give it your all (*informal*), work your fingers to the bone, rupture yourself (*informal*) …*Boys toiled in the hot sun to finish the wall…*
2 = struggle, trek, slog, trudge, push yourself, fight your way, drag yourself, footslog …*He had his head down as he toiled up the hill…*
NOUN = hard work, industry, labour, effort, pains, application, sweat, graft (*informal*), slog, exertion, drudgery, travail, donkey-work, elbow grease (*informal*), blood, sweat, and tears (*informal*) …*It is only toil which gives meaning to things…* OPPOSITE

idleness

toilet 1 = <u>lavatory</u>, bathroom, loo (*Brit. informal*), bog (*slang*), gents *or* ladies, can (*U.S. & Canad. slang*), john (*slang, chiefly U.S. & Canad.*), head(s) (*Nautical slang*), throne (*informal*), closet, privy, cloakroom (*Brit.*), urinal, latrine, washroom, powder room, ablutions (*Military informal*), dunny (*Austral. & old-fashioned N.Z. informal*), water closet, khazi (*slang*), pissoir (*French*), little boy's room *or* little girl's room (*informal*), (public) convenience, W.C., bogger (*Austral. slang*), brasco (*Austral. slang*) ...*She made him flush the pills down the toilet...*
2 = <u>bathroom</u>, washroom, gents *or* ladies (*Brit. informal*), privy, outhouse, latrine, powder room, water closet, pissoir (*French*), ladies' room, little boy's *or* little girl's room, W.C. ...*I ran to the toilet, vomiting...*

token NOUN = <u>symbol</u>, mark, sign, note, evidence, earnest, index, expression, demonstration, proof, indication, clue, representation, badge, manifestation ...*He sent her a gift as a token of his appreciation...*
ADJECTIVE = <u>nominal</u>, symbolic, minimal, hollow, superficial, perfunctory ...*weak token gestures with no real consequences...*

tolerable 1 = <u>bearable</u>, acceptable, allowable, supportable, endurable, sufferable ...*He described their living conditions as tolerable...* OPPOSITE intolerable
2 (*Informal*) = <u>fair</u>, O.K. *or* okay (*informal*), middling, average, all right, ordinary, acceptable, reasonable, good enough, adequate, indifferent, not bad (*informal*), mediocre, so-so (*informal*), run-of-the-mill, passable, unexceptional, fairly good, fair to middling ...*Is there anywhere tolerable to eat in town?...* OPPOSITE dreadful

tolerance 1 = <u>broad-mindedness</u>, charity, sympathy, patience, indulgence, forbearance, permissiveness, magnanimity, open-mindedness, sufferance, lenity ...*his tolerance and understanding of diverse human nature...* OPPOSITE intolerance
2 = <u>endurance</u>, resistance, stamina, fortitude, resilience, toughness, staying power, hardness, hardiness ...*She has a high tolerance for pain...*
3 = <u>resistance</u>, immunity, resilience, non-susceptibility ...*Your body will build up a tolerance to most drugs...*

tolerant = <u>broad-minded</u>, understanding, sympathetic, open-minded, patient, fair, soft, catholic, charitable, indulgent, easy-going, long-suffering, lax, lenient, permissive, magnanimous, free and easy, forbearing, kind-hearted, unprejudiced, complaisant, latitudinarian, unbigoted, easy-oasy (*slang*) OPPOSITE intolerant

tolerate 1 = <u>endure</u>, stand, suffer, bear, take, stomach, undergo, swallow, hack (*slang*), abide, put up with (*informal*), submit to, thole (*Scot.*) ...*She can no longer tolerate the position that she's in...*
2 = <u>allow</u>, accept, permit, sanction, take, receive, admit, brook, indulge, put up with (*informal*), condone, countenance, turn a blind eye to, wink at

...*I will not tolerate breaches of the code of conduct...* OPPOSITE forbid

toleration 1 = <u>acceptance</u>, endurance, indulgence, sanction, allowance, permissiveness, sufferance, condonation ...*They urged toleration of mixed marriages...*
2 = <u>religious freedom</u>, freedom of conscience, freedom of worship ...*his views on religious toleration, education and politics...*

toll[1] VERB 1 = <u>ring</u>, sound, strike, chime, knell, clang, peal ...*Church bells tolled and black flags fluttered...*
2 = <u>announce</u>, call, signal, warn of ...*Big Ben tolled the midnight hour...*
NOUN = <u>ringing</u>, ring, tolling, chime, knell, clang, peal ...*the insistent toll of the bell in the church tower...*

toll[2] 1 = <u>charge</u>, tax, fee, duty, rate, demand, payment, assessment, customs, tribute, levy, tariff, impost ...*Opponents of motorway tolls say they would force cars onto smaller roads...*
2 = <u>damage</u>, cost, loss, roll, penalty, sum, number, roster, inroad ...*There are fears that the death toll may be higher...*
3 = <u>adverse effects</u>, price, cost, suffering, damage, penalty, harm...*Winter takes its toll on your health...*

tomb = <u>grave</u>, vault, crypt, mausoleum, sarcophagus, catacomb, sepulchre, burial chamber

tombstone = <u>gravestone</u>, memorial, monument, marker, headstone

tome = <u>book</u>, work, title, volume, opus, publication

tone NOUN 1 = <u>pitch</u>, stress, volume, accent, force, strength, emphasis, inflection, intonation, timbre, modulation, tonality ...*He spoke in a low tone to her...*
2 = <u>volume</u>, timbre, tonality ...*the clear tone of the bell...*
3 = <u>character</u>, style, approach, feel, air, effect, note, quality, spirit, attitude, aspect, frame, manner, mood, drift, grain, temper, vein, tenor ...*The tone of the letter was very friendly...*
4 = <u>colour</u>, cast, shade, tint, tinge, hue ...*Each brick also varies slightly in tone...*
VERB = <u>harmonize</u>, match, blend, suit, go well with ...*Her sister toned with her in a turquoise print dress...*
PHRASES **tone something down** 1 = <u>moderate</u>, temper, soften, restrain, subdue, play down, dampen, mitigate, modulate, soft-pedal (*informal*) ...*He toned down his militant statement after the meeting...* 2 = <u>reduce</u>, moderate, soften, lessen ...*He was asked to tone down the spices and garlic in his recipes...* ◆ **tone something up** = <u>get into condition</u>, trim, shape up, freshen, tune up, sharpen up, limber up, invigorate, get in shape ...*Regular exercise will tone up your stomach muscles...*

tongue 1 = <u>language</u>, speech, vernacular, talk, dialect, idiom, parlance, lingo (*informal*), patois, argot ...*They feel passionately about their native tongue...*
2 = <u>utterance</u>, voice, speech, articulation, verbal expression ...*her sharp wit and quick tongue...*

Related Words
adjective: lingual

tongue-tied = <u>speechless</u>, dumb, mute, inarticulate, dumbstruck, struck dumb, at a loss for words
OPPOSITE> talkative

tonic = <u>stimulant</u>, boost, bracer (*informal*), refresher, cordial, pick-me-up (*informal*), fillip, shot in the arm (*informal*), restorative, livener, analeptic, roborant

too 1 = <u>also</u>, as well, further, in addition, moreover, besides, likewise, to boot, into the bargain …*Depression may be expressed physically too…*
2 = <u>excessively</u>, very, extremely, overly, unduly, unreasonably, inordinately, exorbitantly, immoderately, over- …*I'm afraid you're too late; she's gone…*
➤ **very**

tool NOUN 1 = <u>implement</u>, device, appliance, apparatus, machine, instrument, gadget, utensil, contraption, contrivance …*The best tool for the purpose is a pair of shears…*
2 = <u>means</u>, agency, vehicle, medium, agent, intermediary, wherewithal …*The video has become an invaluable teaching tool…*
3 = <u>puppet</u>, creature, pawn, dupe, stooge (*slang*), jackal, minion, lackey, flunkey, hireling, cat's-paw …*He became the tool of the security services…*
VERB = <u>make</u>, work, cut, shape, chase, decorate, ornament …*We have a beautifully tooled glass replica of it…*

tooth

(Related Words)
adjective : dental

Teeth
http://www.tooth.net/info/oralcavity.htm
canine   premolar
incisor *or* foretooth   wisdom tooth
molar

top NOUN 1 = <u>peak</u>, summit, head, crown, height, ridge, brow, crest, high point, pinnacle, culmination, meridian, zenith, apex, apogee, acme, vertex …*I came down alone from the top of the mountain…* OPPOSITE> bottom
2 = <u>lid</u>, cover, cap, cork, plug, stopper, bung …*the plastic tops from aerosol containers…*
3 = <u>first place</u>, head, peak, lead, highest rank, high point …*The US will be at the top of the medals table…*
ADJECTIVE 1 = <u>highest</u>, upper, loftiest, furthest up, uppermost, topmost …*Our new flat was on the top floor…*
2 = <u>leading</u>, best, first, highest, greatest, lead, head, prime, finest, crowning, crack (*informal*), elite, superior, dominant, foremost, pre-eminent …*He was the top student in physics…* OPPOSITE> lowest
3 = <u>chief</u>, most important, principal, most powerful, highest, lead, head, ruling, leading, main, commanding, prominent, notable, sovereign, eminent, high-ranking, illustrious …*I need to have the top people in this company work together…*
4 = <u>prime</u>, best, select, first-class, capital, quality, choice, excellent, premier, superb, elite, superior, top-

class, A1 (*informal*), top-quality, first-rate, top-notch (*informal*), grade A, top-grade …*a candlelit dinner at a top restaurant…*
VERB 1 = <u>lead</u>, head, command, be at the top of, be first in …*What happens if the socialists top the poll?…*
2 = <u>cover</u>, coat, garnish, finish, crown, cap, overspread …*To serve, top the fish with cooked leeks…*
3 = <u>surpass</u>, better, beat, improve on, cap, exceed, best, eclipse, go beyond, excel, transcend, outstrip, outdo, outshine …*How are you ever going to top that?…* OPPOSITE> not be as good as
4 = <u>reach the top of</u>, scale, mount, climb, conquer, crest, ascend, surmount …*As they topped the hill he saw the town in the distance…*
PHRASES **over the top** = <u>excessive</u>, too much, going too far, inordinate, over the limit, a bit much (*informal*), uncalled-for, immoderate …*The special effects are a bit over the top, but I enjoyed it…* ◆ **top something up** 1 = <u>fill (up)</u>, refresh, recharge, refill, replenish, freshen …*He topped her glass up, complaining that she was a slow drinker…* 2 = <u>supplement</u>, boost, add to, enhance, augment …*The bank topped up their loan to £5000…*

topic = <u>subject</u>, point, question, issue, matter, theme, text, thesis, subject matter

topical = <u>current</u>, popular, contemporary, up-to-date, up-to-the-minute, newsworthy

topple 1 = <u>fall over</u>, fall, collapse, tumble, overturn, capsize, totter, tip over, keel over, overbalance, fall headlong …*He released his hold and toppled slowly backwards…*
2 = <u>knock over</u>, upset, knock down, tip over …*Wind and rain toppled trees and electricity lines…*
3 = <u>overthrow</u>, overturn, bring down, oust, unseat, bring low …*the revolution which toppled the regime…*

topsy-turvy = <u>confused</u>, upside-down, disorderly, chaotic, messy, mixed-up, jumbled, inside-out, untidy, disorganized, disarranged OPPOSITE> orderly

torment NOUN 1 = <u>suffering</u>, distress, misery, pain, hell, torture, agony, anguish …*He spent days in torment while they searched for her…* OPPOSITE> bliss
2 = <u>trouble</u>, worry, bother, plague, irritation, hassle (*informal*), nuisance, annoyance, bane, pain in the neck (*informal*) …*the torments of being a writer…*
VERB 1 = <u>torture</u>, pain, distress, afflict, rack, harrow, crucify, agonize, excruciate …*At times, memories returned to torment her…* OPPOSITE> comfort
2 = <u>tease</u>, annoy, worry, trouble, bother, provoke, devil (*informal*), harry, plague, irritate, hound, harass, hassle (*informal*), aggravate (*informal*), persecute, pester, vex, bedevil, chivvy, give someone grief (*Brit. & S. African*), lead someone a merry dance (*Brit. informal*) …*My older brother used to torment me by singing it to me…*

torn 1 = <u>cut</u>, split, rent, ripped, ragged, slit, lacerated …*a torn photograph…*
2 = <u>undecided</u>, divided, uncertain, split, unsure, wavering, vacillating, in two minds (*informal*), irresolute …*I know the administration was very torn on*

tornado = <u>whirlwind</u>, storm, hurricane, gale, cyclone, typhoon, tempest, squall, twister (*U.S. informal*), windstorm

torpor = <u>inactivity</u>, apathy, inertia, lethargy, passivity, laziness, numbness, sloth, stupor, drowsiness, dullness, sluggishness, indolence, languor, listlessness, somnolence, inertness, stagnancy, accidie (*Theology*), inanition, torpidity [OPPOSITE] vigour

torrent 1 = <u>stream</u>, flow, rush, flood, tide, spate, cascade, gush, effusion, inundation ...*A torrent of water rushed into the reservoir...*
2 = <u>downpour</u>, flood, shower, deluge, rainstorm ...*The rain came down in torrents...*
3 = <u>outburst</u>, stream, barrage, hail, spate, outpouring, effusion ...*He directed a torrent of abuse at me...*

torrid 1 = <u>hot</u>, tropical, burning, dry, boiling, flaming, blistering, stifling, fiery, scorched, scorching, sizzling, arid, sultry, sweltering, parched, parching, broiling ...*the torrid heat of a Spanish summer...*
2 = <u>passionate</u>, intense, sexy (*informal*), hot, flaming, erotic, ardent, steamy (*informal*), fervent ...*He is locked in a torrid affair with a mystery older woman...*

tortoise
➤ **reptiles**

tortuous 1 = <u>winding</u>, twisting, meandering, bent, twisted, curved, crooked, indirect, convoluted, serpentine, zigzag, sinuous, circuitous, twisty, mazy ...*a tortuous mountain route...*
2 = <u>complicated</u>, involved, misleading, tricky, indirect, ambiguous, roundabout, deceptive, devious, convoluted, mazy ...*long and tortuous negotiations...* [OPPOSITE] straightforward

---

Word Power

tortuous – The adjective *tortuous* is sometimes confused with *torturous*. A *tortuous* road is one that winds or twists, while a *torturous* experience is one that involves pain, suffering, or discomfort.

---

torture [VERB] 1 = <u>torment</u>, abuse, persecute, afflict, martyr, scourge, molest, crucify, mistreat, ill-treat, maltreat, put on the rack ...*Police are convinced she was tortured and killed...* [OPPOSITE] comfort
2 = <u>distress</u>, torment, worry, trouble, , pain, rack, afflict, harrow, agonize, give someone grief (*Brit. & S. African*), inflict anguish on ...*He would not torture her further by arguing...*
[NOUN] 1 = <u>ill-treatment</u>, abuse, torment, persecution, martyrdom, maltreatment, harsh treatment ...*alleged cases of torture and murder by security forces...*
2 = <u>agony</u>, suffering, misery, anguish, hell, distress, torment, heartbreak ...*Waiting for the result was torture...* [OPPOSITE] bliss

torturous
➤ **tortuous**

toss [VERB] 1 = <u>throw</u>, pitch, hurl, fling, project, launch, cast, shy, chuck (*informal*), flip, propel, sling, lob

(*informal*) ...*He screwed the paper up and tossed it into the fire...*
2 = <u>shake</u>, turn, mix, stir, tumble, agitate, jiggle ...*Toss the apple slices in the mixture...*
3 = <u>heave</u>, labour, rock, roll, pitch, lurch, jolt, wallow ...*The small boat tossed about in the high seas like a cork...*
4 = <u>thrash (about)</u>, twitch, wriggle, squirm, writhe ...*I felt as though I'd been tossing and turning all night...*
[NOUN] = <u>throw</u>, cast, pitch, shy, fling, lob (*informal*) ...*Decisions are almost made with the toss of a die...*

tot [NOUN] 1 = <u>infant</u>, child, baby, toddler, mite, wean (*Scot.*), little one, sprog (*slang*), munchkin (*informal, chiefly U.S.*), rug rat (*slang*), littlie (*Austral. informal*), ankle-biter (*Austral. slang*), tacker (*Austral. slang*) ...*They may hold a clue to the missing tot...*
2 = <u>measure</u>, shot (*informal*), finger, nip, slug, dram, snifter (*informal*), toothful ...*a tot of dark rum...*
[PHRASES] **tot something up** = <u>add up</u>, calculate, sum (up), total, reckon, compute, tally, enumerate, count up ...*Now tot up the points you've scored...*

total [NOUN] = <u>sum</u>, mass, entirety, grand total, whole, amount, aggregate, totality, full amount, sum total ...*The companies have a total of 1,776 employees...* [OPPOSITE] part
[ADJECTIVE] = <u>complete</u>, absolute, utter, whole, perfect, entire, sheer, outright, all-out, thorough, unconditional, downright, undisputed, consummate, unqualified, out-and-out, undivided, overarching, unmitigated, thoroughgoing, arrant, deep-dyed (*usually derogatory*) ...*The car was in a total mess...* ...*I mean I'm not a total idiot...* [OPPOSITE] partial
[VERB] 1 = <u>amount to</u>, make, come to, reach, equal, run to, number, add up to, correspond to, work out as, mount up to, tot up to ...*Their exports will total £85 million this year...*
2 = <u>add up</u>, work out, sum up, compute, reckon, tot up ...*They haven't totalled the exact figures...* [OPPOSITE] subtract

totalitarian = <u>dictatorial</u>, authoritarian, one-party, oppressive, undemocratic, monolithic, despotic, tyrannous [OPPOSITE] democratic

totality 1 = <u>entirety</u>, unity, fullness, wholeness, completeness, entireness ...*He did not want to reform the system in its totality...*
2 = <u>aggregate</u>, whole, entirety, all, total, sum, sum total ...*We must take into consideration the totality of the evidence...*

totally = <u>completely</u>, entirely, absolutely, quite, perfectly, fully, comprehensively, thoroughly, wholly, utterly, consummately, wholeheartedly, unconditionally, to the hilt, one hundred per cent, unmitigatedly [OPPOSITE] partly

totter 1 = <u>stagger</u>, stumble, reel, sway, falter, lurch, wobble, walk unsteadily ...*He tottered to the fridge to get another beer...*
2 = <u>shake</u>, sway, rock, tremble, quake, shudder, lurch, waver, quiver, vibrate, teeter, judder ...*The balconies begin to tremble and totter in the smoke and fumes...*

touch VERB 1 = <u>feel</u>, handle, finger, stroke, brush, make contact with, graze, caress, fondle, lay a finger on, palpate …*Her tiny hand gently touched my face…*
2 = <u>come into contact</u>, meet, contact, border, brush, come together, graze, adjoin, converge, be in contact, abut, impinge upon …*Their knees were touching…*
3 = <u>tap</u>, hit, strike, push, pat …*As the aeroplane came down, the wing touched a pile of rubble…*
4 = <u>affect</u>, mark, involve, strike, get to (*informal*), influence, inspire, impress, get through to, have an effect on, make an impression on …*a guilt that in some way touches everyone…*
5 = <u>consume</u>, take, drink, eat, partake of …*He doesn't drink much, and he never touches drugs…*
6 = <u>move</u>, upset, stir, disturb, melt, soften, tug at someone's heartstrings (*often facetious*), leave an impression on …*It has touched me deeply to see how these people live…*
7 = <u>match</u>, rival, equal, compare with, parallel, come up to, come near, be on a par with, be a match for, hold a candle to (*informal*), be in the same league as …*No one can touch these girls for professionalism…*
8 = <u>get involved in</u>, use, deal with, handle, have to do with, utilize, be a party to, concern yourself with …*Some sports wouldn't touch tobacco advertising…*
9 = <u>reach</u>, hit (*informal*), come to, rise to, arrive at, attain, get up to …*The winds had touched storm-force the day before…*
NOUN 1 = <u>contact</u>, push, stroke, brush, press, tap, poke, nudge, prod, caress, fondling …*Even a light touch on the face can trigger this pain…*
2 = <u>feeling</u>, feel, handling, physical contact, palpation, tactility …*Our sense of touch is programmed to diminish with age…*
3 = <u>bit</u>, spot, trace, drop, taste, suggestion, hint, dash, suspicion, pinch, smack, small amount, tinge, whiff, jot, speck, smattering, intimation, tincture …*She thought she might have a touch of flu…*
4 = <u>style</u>, approach, method, technique, way, manner, characteristic, trademark, handiwork …*The striker was unable to find his scoring touch…*
5 = <u>awareness</u>, understanding, acquaintance, familiarity …*They've lost touch with what is happening in the country…*
6 = <u>communication</u>, contact, association, connection, correspondence …*In my job one tends to lose touch with friends…*
7 = <u>skill</u>, ability, flair, art, facility, command, craft, mastery, knack, artistry, virtuosity, deftness, adroitness …*You don't want to lose your touch. You should get some practice…*
8 = <u>influence</u>, hand, effect, management, direction …*This place is crying out for a woman's touch…*
PHRASES **touch and go** = <u>risky</u>, close, near, dangerous, critical, tricky, sticky (*informal*), hazardous, hairy (*slang*), precarious, perilous, nerve-racking, parlous …*It was touch and go whether we'd go bankrupt…* ◆ **touch on** or **upon something** = <u>refer to</u>, cover, raise, deal with, mention, bring in, speak of, hint at, allude to, broach, make allusions to

…*The film touches on these issues, but only superficially…* ◆ **touch something off** 1 = <u>trigger (off)</u>, start, begin, cause, provoke, set off, initiate, arouse, give rise to, ignite, stir up, instigate, spark off, set in motion, foment …*The massacre touched off a new round of violence…* 2 = <u>ignite</u>, light, fire, set off, detonate, put a match to …*set enormous fuel fires raging, or touch off explosions…* ◆ **touch something up** 1 = <u>enhance</u>, revamp, renovate, patch up, brush up, gloss over, polish up, retouch, titivate, give a face-lift to …*He got up regularly to touch up the painting…* 2 = <u>improve</u>, perfect, round off, enhance, dress up, finish off, embellish, put the finishing touches to …*Use these tips to touch up your image…*

(**Related Words**)
adjectives: haptic, tactile, tactual

touched 1 = <u>moved</u>, affected, upset, impressed, stirred, disturbed, melted, softened, swayed …*I was touched to hear that he finds me engaging…*
2 = <u>mad</u>, crazy, nuts (*slang*), daft (*informal*), batty (*slang*), cuckoo (*informal*), barmy (*slang*), nutty (*slang*), bonkers (*slang, chiefly Brit.*), loopy (*informal*), crackpot (*informal*), out to lunch (*informal*), gonzo (*slang*), not all there, doolally (*slang*), off your trolley (*slang*), up the pole (*informal*), soft in the head (*informal*), not right in the head, off your rocker (*slang*), nutty as a fruitcake (*slang*), wacko *or* whacko (*informal*), off the air (*Austral. slang*) …*They thought I was a bit touched…*

touching = <u>moving</u>, affecting, sad, stirring, tender, melting, pathetic, poignant, heartbreaking, emotive, pitiful, pitiable, piteous

touchstone = <u>standard</u>, measure, par, criterion, norm, gauge, yardstick

touchy 1 = <u>oversensitive</u>, irritable, bad-tempered, cross, crabbed, grumpy, surly, petulant, irascible, tetchy, ratty (*Brit. & N.Z. informal*), testy, thin-skinned, grouchy (*informal*), querulous, peevish, quick-tempered, splenetic, easily offended, captious, pettish, toey (*N.Z. slang*) …*She is very touchy about her past…* OPPOSITE thick-skinned
2 = <u>delicate</u>, sensitive, tricky, risky, sticky (*informal*), thorny, knotty, ticklish …*a touchy subject…*

tough ADJECTIVE 1 = <u>strong</u>, determined, aggressive, high-powered, feisty (*informal, chiefly U.S. & Canad.*), hard-nosed (*informal*), self-confident, unyielding, hard as nails, self-assertive, badass (*slang, chiefly U.S.*) …*She is tough and ambitious…* OPPOSITE weak
2 = <u>hardy</u>, strong, seasoned, fit, strapping, hardened, vigorous, sturdy, stout, stalwart, resilient, brawny, hard as nails …*He's small, but he's tough, and I expect him to do well in the match…*
3 = <u>violent</u>, rough, vicious, ruthless, pugnacious, hard-bitten, ruffianly …*He shot three people, earning his reputation as a tough guy…*
4 = <u>strict</u>, severe, stern, hard, firm, exacting, adamant, resolute, draconian, intractable, inflexible, merciless, unforgiving, unyielding, unbending …*He announced

tough measures to limit the money supply... OPPOSITE> lenient

5 = hard, difficult, exhausting, troublesome, uphill, strenuous, arduous, thorny, laborious, irksome ...*Whoever wins the election is going to have a tough job*...

6 = resilient, hard, resistant, durable, strong, firm, solid, stiff, rigid, rugged, sturdy, inflexible, cohesive, tenacious, leathery, hard-wearing, robust ...*tough leather boots and trousers*... OPPOSITE> fragile

NOUN = ruffian, heavy (*slang*), rough (*informal*), bully, thug, hooligan, brute, rowdy, bravo, bully boy, bruiser (*informal*), roughneck (*slang*), tsotsi (*S. African*) ...*Three burly toughs elbowed their way to the front*...

tour NOUN **1** = circuit, course, round ...*the first official cricket tour of South Africa for 22 years*...
2 = journey, expedition, excursion, trip, progress, outing, jaunt, junket, peregrination ...*week five of my tour of European cities*...
VERB **1** = travel round, holiday in, travel through, journey round, trek round, go on a trip through ...*A few years ago they toured the country in a roadshow*...
2 = visit, explore, go round, inspect, walk round, drive round, sightsee ...*You can tour the site in modern coaches fitted with videos*...

tourist = traveller, journeyer, voyager, tripper, globetrotter, holiday-maker, sightseer, excursionist

tournament **1** = competition, meeting, match, event, series, contest ...*Here is a player capable of winning a world tournament*...
2 (*Medieval*) = joust, the lists, tourney ...*a medieval tournament with displays of archery, armour and combat*...

tousled = dishevelled, disordered, tangled, ruffled, messed up, rumpled, disarranged, disarrayed

tout VERB **1** (*Informal*) = recommend, promote, endorse, support, tip, urge, approve, praise, commend, speak well of ...*the advertising practice of using performers to tout products*...
2 (*Informal*) = praise, tip, promote, urge, endorse, big up (*slang, chiefly Caribbean*) ...*He was being touted as the most interesting thing in pop*...
3 = solicit, canvass, drum up, bark (*U.S. informal*), spiel ...*He visited several foreign countries to tout for business*...
NOUN = seller, solicitor, barker, canvasser, spieler ...*a ticket tout*...

tow = drag, draw, pull, trail, haul, tug, yank, hale, trawl, lug

towards **1** = in the direction of, to, for, on the way to, on the road to, en route for ...*She walked down the corridor towards the foyer*...
2 = regarding, about, concerning, respecting, in relation to, with regard to, with respect to, apropos ...*You must develop your own attitude towards religion*...
3 = just before, nearing, close to, coming up to, almost at, getting on for, shortly before ...*There's a forecast of cooler weather towards the end of the

week*...

tower NOUN **1** = column, pillar, turret, belfry, steeple, obelisk ...*an eleventh century house with 120-foot high towers*...
2 = stronghold, castle, fort, refuge, keep, fortress, citadel, fortification ...*troops occupied the first two floors of the tower*...
VERB *usually with* **over** = rise, dominate, loom, top, mount, rear, soar, overlook, surpass, transcend, ascend, be head and shoulders above, overtop ...*He stood up and towered over her*...

towering **1** = tall, high, great, soaring, elevated, gigantic, lofty, colossal ...*towering cliffs of black granite*...
2 = impressive, imposing, supreme, striking, extraordinary, outstanding, magnificent, superior, paramount, surpassing, sublime, stellar (*informal*), prodigious, transcendent ...*a towering figure in British politics*...
3 = intense, violent, extreme, excessive, burning, passionate, mighty, fiery, vehement, inordinate, intemperate, immoderate ...*I saw her in a towering rage only once*...

toxic = poisonous, deadly, lethal, harmful, pernicious, noxious, septic, pestilential, baneful (*archaic*) OPPOSITE> harmless

toy NOUN **1** = plaything, game, doll ...*He was really too old for children's toys*...
2 = trinket, trifle, bauble, gimcrack, gewgaw, knick-knack ...*Computers have become household toys*...
PHRASES **toy with something** = play with, consider, trifle with, flirt with, dally with, entertain the possibility of, amuse yourself with, think idly of ...*He toyed with the idea of going to China*...

trace VERB **1** = search for, follow, seek out, track, determine, pursue, unearth, ascertain, hunt down ...*I first went there to trace my roots*...
2 = find, track (down), discover, trail, detect, unearth, hunt down, ferret out, locate ...*Police are anxious to trace a man seen leaving the house*...
3 = outline, chart, sketch, draw, map out, depict, mark out, delineate ...*I traced the course of the river on the map*...
4 = copy, map, draft, outline, sketch, reproduce, draw over ...*She learnt to draw by tracing pictures from story books*...
NOUN **1** = bit, drop, touch, shadow, suggestion, hint, dash, suspicion, tinge, trifle, whiff, jot, tincture, iota ...*Wash them in cold water to remove all traces of sand*...
2 = remnant, remains, sign, record, mark, evidence, indication, token, relic, vestige ...*The church has traces of fifteenth-century frescoes*...
3 = track, trail, footstep, path, slot, footprint, spoor, footmark ...*He disappeared mysteriously without a trace*...

track NOUN **1** = path, way, road, route, trail, pathway, footpath ...*We set off once more, over a rough mountain track*...

2 = <u>course</u>, line, path, orbit, trajectory, flight path
…*following the track of a hurricane*…
3 = <u>line</u>, rail, tramline …*A woman fell onto the railway track*…
PLURAL NOUN = <u>trail</u>, marks, impressions, traces, imprints, prints …*He suddenly noticed tyre tracks on the bank ahead*… …*The killer returned to the scene to cover his tracks*…
VERB = <u>follow</u>, pursue, chase, trace, tail (*informal*), dog, shadow, trail, stalk, hunt down, follow the trail of …*He thought he had better track this creature and kill it*…
PHRASES **keep track of something** or **someone** = <u>keep up with</u>, follow, monitor, watch, keep an eye on, keep in touch with, keep up to date with …*It's hard to keep track of time here*… ♦ **lose track of something** or **someone** = <u>lose</u>, lose sight of, misplace …*It's so easy to lose track of who's playing who and when*… ♦ **stop something** or **someone in its** or **their tracks** = <u>bring to a standstill</u>, freeze, petrify, transfix, immobilize, stop someone dead, rivet to the spot …*His remark stopped me in my tracks*…
♦ **track something** or **someone** or **down** = <u>find</u>, catch, capture, apprehend, discover, expose, trace, unearth, dig up, hunt down, sniff out, bring to light, ferret out, run to earth or ground …*They are doing all they can to track down terrorists*…

tract¹ = <u>area</u>, lot, region, estate, district, stretch, quarter, territory, extent, zone, plot, expanse …*A vast tract of land is ready for development*…

tract² = <u>treatise</u>, essay, leaflet, brochure, booklet, pamphlet, dissertation, monograph, homily, disquisition, tractate …*She produced a feminist tract, 'Comments on birth control'*…

traction = <u>grip</u>, resistance, friction, adhesion, purchase

trade NOUN **1** = <u>commerce</u>, business, transactions, buying and selling, dealing, exchange, traffic, truck, barter …*The ministry has control over every aspect of foreign trade*…
2 = <u>job</u>, employment, calling, business, line, skill, craft, profession, occupation, pursuit, line of work, métier, avocation …*He was a jeweller by trade*…
3 = <u>exchange</u>, deal, swap, interchange …*It wouldn't exactly have been a fair trade*…
VERB **1** = <u>deal</u>, do business, buy and sell, exchange, traffic, truck, bargain, peddle, barter, transact, cut a deal, have dealings …*They had years of experience trading with the west*…
2 = <u>exchange</u>, switch, swap, barter …*They traded land for goods and money*…
3 = <u>operate</u>, run, deal, do business …*The company is thought to be trading at a loss*…
(*Related Words*)
adjective : mercantile

trader = <u>dealer</u>, marketer, buyer, broker, supplier, merchant, seller, purveyor, merchandiser

tradesman = <u>craftsman</u>, workman, artisan, journeyman, skilled worker

tradition 1 = <u>customs</u>, institution, ritual, folklore, lore, praxis …*a country steeped in tradition*…
2 = <u>established practice</u>, custom, convention, habit, ritual, unwritten law …*She has carried on the family tradition of giving away plants*…

traditional 1 = <u>old-fashioned</u>, old, established, conventional, fixed, usual, transmitted, accustomed, customary, ancestral, long-established, unwritten, time-honoured …*Traditional teaching methods can put students off learning*… OPPOSITE revolutionary
2 = <u>folk</u>, old, historical …*traditional Indian music*…

traffic NOUN **1** = <u>transport</u>, movement, vehicles, transportation, freight, coming and going …*There was heavy traffic on the roads*…
2 = <u>trade</u>, dealing, commerce, buying and selling, business, exchange, truck, dealings, peddling, barter, doings …*traffic in illicit drugs*…
VERB = <u>trade</u>, market, deal, exchange, truck, bargain, do business, buy and sell, peddle, barter, cut a deal, have dealings, have transactions …*Anyone who trafficked in illegal drugs was brought to justice*…

tragedy = <u>disaster</u>, catastrophe, misfortune, adversity, calamity, affliction, whammy (*informal, chiefly U.S.*), bummer (*slang*), grievous blow OPPOSITE fortune

tragic 1 = <u>distressing</u>, shocking, sad, awful, appalling, fatal, deadly, unfortunate, disastrous, dreadful, dire, catastrophic, grievous, woeful, lamentable, ruinous, calamitous, wretched, ill-starred, ill-fated …*the tragic loss of so many lives*… OPPOSITE fortunate
2 = <u>sad</u>, miserable, dismal, pathetic, heartbreaking, anguished, mournful, heart-rending, sorrowful, doleful, pitiable …*She is a tragic figure*… OPPOSITE happy

trail NOUN **1** = <u>path</u>, track, route, way, course, road, pathway, footpath, beaten track …*He was following a broad trail through the trees*…
2 = <u>tracks</u>, path, mark, marks, wake, trace, scent, footsteps, footprints, spoor …*They would take no action except that of following her trail*…
3 = <u>wake</u>, stream, tail, slipstream …*the high vapour trail of an aircraft*…
VERB **1** = <u>follow</u>, track, chase, pursue, dog, hunt, shadow, trace, tail (*informal*), hound, stalk, keep an eye on, keep tabs on (*informal*), run to ground …*Two detectives were trailing him*…
2 = <u>drag</u>, draw, pull, sweep, stream, haul, tow, dangle, droop …*She came down the stairs, trailing the coat behind her*…
3 = <u>lag</u>, follow, drift, wander, linger, trudge, fall behind, plod, meander, amble, loiter, straggle, traipse (*informal*), dawdle, hang back, tag along (*informal*), bring up the rear, drag yourself …*I spent a long afternoon trailing behind him*…
PHRASES **trail away** or **off** = <u>fade away</u> or <u>out</u>, sink, weaken, diminish, decrease, dwindle, shrink, lessen, subside, fall away, peter out, die away, tail off, taper off, grow weak, grow faint …*'But he of all men…' her voice trailed away*…

train `VERB` 1 = <u>instruct</u>, school, prepare, improve, coach, teach, guide, discipline, rear, educate, drill, tutor, rehearse ...*We train them in bricklaying and other building techniques...*
2 = <u>exercise</u>, prepare, work out, practise, do exercise, get into shape ...*They have spent a year training for the race...*
3 = <u>aim</u>, point, level, position, direct, focus, sight, line up, turn on, fix on, zero in, bring to bear ...*She trained her binoculars on the horizon...*
`NOUN` 1 = <u>convoy</u>, file, rank, string, column, queue, succession, caravan, procession, progression, cavalcade ...*a long train of oil tankers...*
2 = <u>sequence</u>, series, chain, string, set, course, order, cycle, trail, succession, progression, concatenation ...*a train of events which would culminate in tragedy...*
3 = <u>tail</u>, trail, appendage ...*a velvet dress, bias cut with a train...*
4 = <u>retinue</u>, following, entourage, court, staff, household, suite, cortège ...*Toby arrived with his train of medical students...*

trainer = <u>coach</u>, manager, guide, adviser, tutor, instructor, counsellor, guru, handler

training 1 = <u>instruction</u>, schooling, grounding, education, tutelage ...*He had no formal training as a decorator...*
2 = <u>practice</u>, exercise, working out, preparation, body building ...*He will soon be back in training for next year...*

traipse (*Informal*) `VERB` = <u>trudge</u>, trail, tramp, slouch, drag yourself, footslog ...*He traipsed from one doctor to another...*
`NOUN` – <u>trudge</u>, trek, tramp, slog, long walk ...*It's rather a long traipse from here. Let's take a bus...*

trait = <u>characteristic</u>, feature, quality, attribute, quirk, peculiarity, mannerism, idiosyncrasy, lineament

traitor = <u>betrayer</u>, deserter, turncoat, deceiver, informer, renegade, defector, Judas, double-crosser (*informal*), quisling, apostate, miscreant, fifth columnist, snake in the grass (*informal*), back-stabber, fizgig (*Austral. slang*) `OPPOSITE` loyalist

trajectory = <u>path</u>, line, course, track, flight, route, flight path

tramp `VERB` 1 = <u>trudge</u>, march, stamp, stump, toil, plod, traipse (*informal*), walk heavily ...*They put on their coats and tramped through the fallen snow...*
2 = <u>hike</u>, walk, trek, roam, march, range, ramble, slog, rove, yomp, footslog ...*He spent a month tramping in the hills around Balmoral...*
`NOUN` 1 = <u>vagrant</u>, bum (*informal*), derelict, drifter, down-and-out, hobo (*chiefly U.S.*), vagabond, bag lady (*chiefly U.S.*), dosser (*Brit. slang*), derro (*Austral. slang*) ...*an old tramp who slept rough in our neighbourhood...*
2 = <u>tread</u>, stamp, footstep, footfall ...*the slow, heavy tramp of feet on the staircase...*
3 = <u>hike</u>, march, trek, ramble, slog ...*He had just come from a day-long tramp on some wild moor...*

trample *often with **on*** = <u>stamp</u>, crush, squash, tread, flatten, run over, walk over

trance = <u>daze</u>, dream, spell, ecstasy, muse, abstraction, rapture, reverie, stupor, unconsciousness, hypnotic state

tranquil 1 = <u>peaceful</u>, quiet, calm, serene, still, cool, pacific, composed, at peace, sedate, placid, undisturbed, restful, untroubled, unperturbed, unruffled, unexcited ...*The place was tranquil and appealing...*
2 = <u>calm</u>, quiet, peaceful, serene, still, cool, pacific, composed, sedate, placid, undisturbed, restful, untroubled, unperturbed, unruffled, unexcited ...*She settled into a life of tranquil celibacy...* `OPPOSITE` troubled

tranquillity 1 = <u>peace</u>, calm, quiet, hush, composure, serenity, stillness, coolness, repose, rest, calmness, equanimity, quietness, peacefulness, quietude, placidity, restfulness, sedateness ...*The hotel is a haven of peace and tranquillity...*
2 = <u>calm</u>, peace, composure, serenity, stillness, coolness, repose, calmness, equanimity, quietness, peacefulness, quietude, placidity, imperturbability, restfulness, sedateness ...*He has a tranquillity and maturity that I desperately need...* `OPPOSITE` agitation

tranquillizer = <u>sedative</u>, opiate, barbiturate, downer (*slang*), red (*slang*), bromide

transact = <u>carry out</u>, handle, conduct, do, manage, perform, settle, conclude, negotiate, carry on, accomplish, execute, take care of, discharge, see to, prosecute, enact

transaction `NOUN` = <u>deal</u>, matter, affair, negotiation, business, action, event, proceeding, enterprise, bargain, coup, undertaking, deed, occurrence ...*plans to disclose a business transaction with British Telecommunications...*
`PLURAL NOUN` = <u>records</u>, minutes, affairs, proceedings, goings-on (*informal*), annals, doings ...*the transactions of the Metallurgical Society of Great Britain...*

transcend = <u>surpass</u>, exceed, go beyond, rise above, leave behind, eclipse, excel, outstrip, outdo, outshine, overstep, go above, leave in the shade (*informal*), outrival, outvie

transcendence *or* **transcendency** = <u>greatness</u>, excellence, superiority, supremacy, ascendancy, pre-eminence, sublimity, paramountcy, incomparability, matchlessness

transcendent = <u>unparalleled</u>, unique, extraordinary, superior, exceeding, sublime, consummate, unrivalled, second to none, pre-eminent, transcendental, incomparable, peerless, unequalled, matchless

transcribe 1 = <u>write out</u>, reproduce, take down, copy out, note, transfer, set out, rewrite ...*Every telephone call will be recorded and transcribed...*
2 = <u>translate</u>, interpret, render, transliterate ...*He decided to transcribe the work for piano...*

transcript = <u>copy</u>, record, note, summary, notes, version, carbon, log, translation, manuscript, reproduction, duplicate, transcription, carbon copy, transliteration, written version

transfer VERB = <u>move</u>, carry, remove, transport, shift, transplant, displace, relocate, transpose, change ...*The person can be transferred from wheelchair to seat with relative ease...*
NOUN = <u>transference</u>, move, removal, handover, change, shift, transmission, translation, displacement, relocation, transposition ...*Arrange for the transfer of medical records to your new doctor...*

transfix = <u>stun</u>, hold, fascinate, paralyse, petrify, mesmerize, hypnotize, stop dead, root to the spot, engross, rivet the attention of, spellbind, halt or stop in your tracks OPPOSITE> bore

transform 1 = <u>change</u>, convert, alter, translate, reconstruct, metamorphose, transmute, renew, transmogrify (*jocular*) ...*the speed at which your body transforms food into energy...*
2 = <u>make over</u>, overhaul, revamp, remake, renovate, remodel, revolutionize, redo, transfigure, restyle ...*A cheap table can be transformed by an attractive cover...*

transformation 1 = <u>change</u>, conversion, alteration, metamorphosis, transmutation, renewal, transmogrification (*jocular*) ...*the transformation of an attic room into a study...*
2 = <u>revolution</u>, radical change, sea change, revolutionary change, transfiguration ...*He has undergone a personal transformation...*

transgress (*Formal*) 1 = <u>misbehave</u>, sin, offend, break the law, err, lapse, fall from grace, go astray, be out of order, do or go wrong ...*If a politician transgresses, it is his own fault...*
2 = <u>go beyond</u>, exceed, infringe, overstep, break, defy, violate, trespass, contravene, disobey, encroach upon ...*He had transgressed the boundaries of good taste...*

transgression = <u>crime</u>, wrong, fault, error, offence, breach, sin, lapse, violation, wrongdoing, infringement, trespass, misdemeanour, misdeed, encroachment, misbehaviour, contravention, iniquity, peccadillo, infraction

transient = <u>brief</u>, passing, short-term, temporary, short, flying, fleeting, short-lived, fugitive, momentary, ephemeral, transitory, evanescent, impermanent, here today and gone tomorrow, fugacious OPPOSITE> lasting

transit NOUN = <u>movement</u>, transfer, transport, passage, travel, crossing, motion, transportation, carriage, shipment, traverse, conveyance, portage ...*They halted transit of EU livestock...*
VERB = <u>pass</u>, travel, cross, journey, traverse, move ...*They have been allowed back into Kuwait by transitting through Baghdad...*
PHRASES **in transit** = <u>en route</u>, on the way, on the road, on the move, in motion, on the go (*informal*), on the journey, while travelling, during transport, during passage ...*We cannot be held responsible for goods lost in transit...*

transition = <u>change</u>, passing, development, shift,

passage, conversion, evolution, transit, upheaval, alteration, progression, flux, metamorphosis, changeover, transmutation, metastasis

transitional 1 = <u>changing</u>, passing, fluid, intermediate, unsettled, developmental, transitionary ...*a transitional period following a decade of civil war...*
2 = <u>temporary</u>, working, acting, short-term, interim, fill-in, caretaker, provisional, makeshift, make-do, stopgap, pro tem ...*a meeting to set up a transitional government...*

transitory = <u>short-lived</u>, short, passing, brief, short-term, temporary, fleeting, transient, flying, momentary, ephemeral, evanescent, impermanent, here today and gone tomorrow, fugacious OPPOSITE> lasting

translate 1 = <u>render</u>, put, change, convert, interpret, decode, transcribe, construe, paraphrase, decipher, transliterate ...*Only a small number of his books have been translated into English...*
2 = <u>put in plain English</u>, explain, make clear, clarify, spell out, simplify, gloss, unravel, decode, paraphrase, decipher, elucidate, rephrase, reword, state in layman's language ...*Translating IT jargon is the key to the IT director's role...*
3 = <u>convert</u>, change, turn, transform, alter, render, metamorphose, transmute, transfigure ...*Your decision must be translated into specific actions...*
4 = <u>transfer</u>, move, send, relocate, carry, remove, transport, shift, convey, transplant, transpose ...*The local-government minister was translated to Wales...*

translation 1 = <u>interpretation</u>, version, rendering, gloss, rendition, decoding, transcription, paraphrase, transliteration ...*his excellent English translation of 'Faust'...*
2 = <u>conversion</u>, change, rendering, transformation, alteration, metamorphosis, transfiguration, transmutation ...*the translation of these goals into classroom activities...*

translator = <u>interpreter</u>, transcriber, paraphraser, decipherer, linguist, metaphrast, paraphrast, transliterator

translucent = <u>semitransparent</u>, clear, limpid, lucent, diaphanous, pellucid

transmission 1 = <u>transfer</u>, spread, spreading, communication, passing on, circulation, dispatch, relaying, mediation, imparting, diffusion, transference, dissemination, conveyance, channeling ...*the transmission of knowledge and skills...*
2 = <u>broadcasting</u>, showing, putting out, relaying, sending ...*The transmission of the programme was brought forward...*
3 = <u>programme</u>, broadcast, show, production, telecast ...*A webcast is a transmission using the internet...*

transmit 1 = <u>broadcast</u>, put on the air, televise, relay, send, air, radio, send out, disseminate, beam out ...*letters begging them to transmit the programme daily...*
2 = <u>pass on</u>, carry, spread, communicate, take, send,

forward, bear, transfer, transport, hand on, convey, dispatch, hand down, diffuse, remit, impart, disseminate …*mosquitoes that transmit disease to humans*…

transmute = transform, change, convert, alter, metamorphose, transfigure, alchemize

transparency 1 = photograph, slide, exposure, photo, picture, image, print, plate, still …*The first colour photo was a transparency of a tartan ribbon*…
2 = clarity, translucency, translucence, clearness, limpidity, transparence, diaphaneity, filminess, diaphanousness, gauziness, limpidness, pellucidity, pellucidness, sheerness …*It is a condition that affects the transparency of the lenses*… [OPPOSITE] opacity
3 = frankness, openness, candour, directness, forthrightness, straightforwardness …*openness and transparency in the government's decision-making*… [OPPOSITE] ambiguity
4 = obviousness, explicitness, plainness, distinctness, unambiguousness, apparentness, patentness, perspicuousness …*the transparency of pricing with the euro*… [OPPOSITE] vagueness

transparent 1 = clear, sheer, see-through, lucid, translucent, crystal clear, crystalline, limpid, lucent, diaphanous, gauzy, filmy, pellucid …*a sheet of transparent coloured plastic*… [OPPOSITE] opaque
2 = frank, open, direct, straight, straightforward, candid, forthright, unequivocal, unambiguous, plain-spoken …*striving to establish a transparent parliamentary democracy*… [OPPOSITE] unclear
3 = obvious, plain, apparent, visible, bold, patent, evident, distinct, explicit, easy, understandable, manifest, recognizable, unambiguous, undisguised, as plain as the nose on your face (*informal*), perspicuous …*The meaning of their actions is transparent*… [OPPOSITE] uncertain

transpire 1 = become known, emerge, come out, be discovered, come to light, be disclosed, be made public …*It transpired that he had left his driving licence at home*…
2 = happen, occur, take place, arise, turn up, come about, come to pass (*archaic*) …*Nothing is known about what transpired at the meeting*…

Word Power

transpire – It is sometimes maintained that *transpire* should not be used to mean 'happen' or 'occur', as in *the event transpired late in the evening*, and that the word is properly used to mean 'become known', as in *it transpired later that the thief had been caught*. The word is, however, widely used in the first sense, especially in spoken English.

---

transplant 1 = implant, transfer, graft …*The operation to transplant a kidney is now fairly routine*…
2 = transfer, take, bring, carry, remove, transport, shift, convey, fetch, displace, relocate, uproot …*Marriage had transplanted her from London to Manchester*…

transport [NOUN] 1 = vehicle, wheels (*informal*), transportation, conveyance …*Have you got your own transport?*…
2 = transference, carrying, shipping, delivery, distribution, removal, transportation, carriage, shipment, freight, haulage, conveyance, freightage …*Safety rules had been breached during transport of radioactive fuel*…
3 often plural = ecstasy, delight, heaven, happiness, bliss, euphoria, rapture, enchantment, cloud nine (*informal*), seventh heaven, ravishment …*transports of joy*… [OPPOSITE] despondency
[VERB] 1 = convey, take, run, move, bring, send, carry, bear, remove, ship, transfer, deliver, conduct, shift, ferry, haul, fetch …*There's no petrol so it's difficult to transport goods*…
2 = enrapture, move, delight, entrance, enchant, carry away, captivate, electrify, ravish, spellbind …*I have never seen any man so completely transported by excitement*…
3 (*History*) = exile, banish, deport, sentence to transportation …*He was transported to Italy and interned*…

transpose 1 = transplant, move, transfer, shift, displace, relocate, reposition …*Genetic engineers transpose bits of material from one organism to another*…
2 = interchange, switch, swap, reorder, change, move, exchange, substitute, alter, rearrange …*Many people inadvertently transpose the digits of the code*…

transverse = crossways, diagonal, oblique, crosswise, athwart

trap [NOUN] 1 = snare, net, booby trap, gin, toils (*old-fashioned*), pitfall, noose, springe …*He came across a bird caught in a trap*…
2 = ambush, set-up (*informal*), device, lure, bait, honey trap, ambuscade (*old-fashioned*) …*He failed to keep the appointment after sensing a police trap*…
3 = trick, set-up (*informal*), deception, ploy, ruse, artifice, trickery, subterfuge, stratagem, wile, device …*He was trying to decide whether the question was a trap*…
[VERB] 1 = catch, snare, ensnare, entrap, take, corner, bag, lay hold of, enmesh, lay a trap for, run to earth *or* ground …*The locals were trying to trap and kill the birds*…
2 = trick, fool, cheat, lure, seduce, deceive, dupe, beguile, gull, cajole, ensnare, hoodwink, wheedle, inveigle …*Were you trying to trap her into making an admission?*…
3 = capture, catch, arrest, seize, take, lift (*slang*), secure, nail (*informal*), collar (*informal*), nab (*informal*), apprehend, take prisoner, take into custody …*To trap the killer they had to play him at his own game*…

trapped = caught, cornered, snared, ensnared, stuck (*informal*), netted, surrounded, cut off, at bay, in a tight corner, in a tight spot, with your back to the wall

trappings = accessories, trimmings, paraphernalia, finery, things, fittings, dress, equipment, gear, fixtures, decorations, furnishings, ornaments, livery, adornments, panoply, accoutrements, fripperies, bells and whistles, raiment (*archaic or poetic*)

trash 1 = <u>nonsense</u>, rubbish, garbage (*informal*), rot, pants (*slang*), crap (*slang*), hot air (*informal*), tosh (*slang, chiefly Brit.*), pap, bilge (*informal*), drivel, twaddle, tripe (*informal*), guff (*slang*), moonshine, hogwash, hokum (*slang, chiefly U.S. & Canad.*), piffle (*informal*), poppycock (*informal*), inanity, balderdash, bosh (*informal*), eyewash (*informal*), kak (*S. African taboo slang*), trumpery, tommyrot, foolish talk, horsefeathers (*U.S. slang*), bunkum *or* buncombe (*chiefly U.S.*), bizzo (*Austral. slang*), bull's wool (*Austral. & N.Z. slang*) ...*Don't read that awful trash...* OPPOSITE sense

2 (*Chiefly U.S. & Canad.*) = <u>litter</u>, refuse, waste, rubbish, sweepings, junk (*informal*), garbage, dross, dregs, dreck (*slang, chiefly U.S.*), offscourings ...*The yards are overgrown and cluttered with trash...*

trashy = <u>worthless</u>, cheap, inferior, shabby, flimsy, shoddy, tawdry, tinsel, thrown together, crappy (*slang*), meretricious, rubbishy, poxy (*slang*), catchpenny, cheap-jack (*informal*), of a sort *or* of sorts OPPOSITE excellent

trauma 1 = <u>shock</u>, suffering, worry, pain, stress, upset, strain, torture, distress, misery, disturbance, ordeal, anguish, upheaval, jolt ...*I'd been through the trauma of losing a house...*

2 = <u>injury</u>, damage, hurt, wound, agony ...*spinal trauma...*

traumatic = <u>shocking</u>, upsetting, alarming, awful, disturbing, devastating, painful, distressing, terrifying, scarring, harrowing OPPOSITE calming

travel VERB 1 = <u>go</u>, journey, proceed, make a journey, move, walk, cross, tour, progress, wander, trek, voyage, roam, ramble, traverse, rove, take a trip, make your way, wend your way ...*You can travel to Helsinki tomorrow...*

2 = <u>be transmitted</u>, move, advance, proceed, get through ...*Light travels at around 300 million metres per second...*

NOUN *usually plural* = <u>journey</u>, wandering, expedition, globetrotting, walk, tour, touring, movement, trip, passage, voyage, excursion, ramble, peregrination ...*He collects things for the house on his travels...*

(*Related Words*)
adjective: itinerant

traveller *or* (*U.S.*) **traveler** 1 = <u>voyager</u>, tourist, passenger, journeyer, explorer, hiker, tripper, globetrotter, holiday-maker, wayfarer, excursionist ...*Many air travellers suffer puffy ankles during long flights...*

2 = <u>travelling salesman</u>, representative, rep, salesman, sales rep, commercial traveller, agent ...*My father was a commercial traveller who migrated from Scotland...*

travelling = <u>itinerant</u>, moving, touring, mobile, wandering, unsettled, roaming, migrant, restless, roving, nomadic, migratory, peripatetic, wayfaring

traverse 1 = <u>cross</u>, go across, travel over, make your

way across, cover, range, bridge, negotiate, wander, go over, span, roam, ply ...*I traversed the narrow pedestrian bridge...*

2 = <u>cut across</u>, pass over, stretch across, extend across, lie across ...*a steep-sided valley traversed by streams...*

travesty = <u>mockery</u>, distortion, parody, caricature, sham, send-up (*Brit. informal*), spoof (*informal*), perversion, takeoff (*informal*), lampoon, burlesque

treacherous 1 = <u>disloyal</u>, deceitful, untrustworthy, duplicitous, false, untrue, unreliable, unfaithful, faithless, double-crossing (*informal*), double-dealing, perfidious, traitorous, treasonable, recreant (*archaic*) ...*The President spoke of the treacherous intentions of the enemy...* OPPOSITE loyal

2 = <u>dangerous</u>, tricky, risky, unstable, hazardous, icy, slippery, unsafe, unreliable, precarious, deceptive, perilous, slippy (*informal or dialect*) ...*The current of the river is fast-flowing and treacherous...* OPPOSITE safe

treachery = <u>betrayal</u>, infidelity, treason, duplicity, disloyalty, double-cross (*informal*), double-dealing, stab in the back, perfidy, faithlessness, perfidiousness OPPOSITE loyalty

tread VERB = <u>step</u>, walk, march, pace, stamp, stride, hike, tramp, trudge, plod ...*She trod casually, enjoying the sensation of bare feet on grass...*

NOUN = <u>step</u>, walk, pace, stride, footstep, gait, footfall ...*We could hear their heavy tread and an occasional coarse laugh...*

PHRASES **tread on something** 1 = <u>crush</u> underfoot, step on, stamp on, trample (on), stomp on, squash, flatten ...*Oh sorry, I didn't mean to tread on your foot...* 2 = <u>repress</u>, crush, suppress, subdue, oppress, quell, bear down on, subjugate, ride roughshod over ...*Paid lawyers would tread on the farmers' interests...*

treason = <u>disloyalty</u>, mutiny, treachery, subversion, disaffection, duplicity, sedition, perfidy, lese-majesty, traitorousness OPPOSITE loyalty

treasure NOUN 1 = <u>riches</u>, money, gold, fortune, wealth, valuables, jewels, funds, cash ...*It was here, the buried treasure, she knew it was...*

2 (*Informal*) = <u>angel</u>, darling, find, star (*informal*), prize, pearl, something else (*informal*), jewel, gem, paragon, one in a million (*informal*), one of a kind (*informal*), nonpareil ...*Charlie? Oh he's a treasure, loves children...*

VERB = <u>prize</u>, value, worship, esteem, adore, cherish, revere, venerate, hold dear, love, idolize, set great store by, dote upon, place great value on ...*She treasures her memories of those joyous days...*

treasury 1 = <u>funds</u>, money, capital, finances, resources, assets, revenues, exchequer, coffers ...*reconciling accounts with the central bank and its treasury...*

2 = <u>storehouse</u>, bank, store, vault, hoard, cache, repository ...*He had been compiling a treasury of jokes...*

treat `VERB` **1** = <u>behave towards</u>, deal with, handle, act towards, use, consider, serve, manage, regard, look upon ...*He treated most women with indifference...*
2 = <u>take care of</u>, minister to, attend to, give medical treatment to, doctor (*informal*), nurse, care for, medicate, prescribe medicine for, apply treatment to ...*An experienced nurse treats all minor injuries...*
3 = <u>provide</u>, give, buy, stand (*informal*), pay for, entertain, feast, lay on, regale, wine and dine, take out for, foot *or* pay the bill ...*She was always treating him to ice cream...*
4 = <u>negotiate</u>, bargain, consult, have talks, confer, come to terms, parley, make a bargain, make terms ...*They assumed we were treating with the rebels...*
`NOUN` **1** = <u>entertainment</u>, party, surprise, gift, celebration, feast, outing, excursion, banquet, refreshment ...*a birthday treat...*
2 = <u>pleasure</u>, delight, joy, thrill, satisfaction, enjoyment, gratification, source of pleasure, fun ...*It's a real treat to see someone doing justice to the film...*
`PHRASES` **treat of something** = <u>deal with</u>, discuss, go into, be concerned with, touch upon, discourse upon ...*part of Christian theology that treats of the afterlife...*

treatise = <u>paper</u>, work, writing, study, essay, thesis, tract, pamphlet, exposition, dissertation, monograph, disquisition

treatment **1** = <u>care</u>, medical care, nursing, medicine, surgery, therapy, healing, medication, therapeutics, ministrations ...*Many patients are not getting the treatment they need...*
2 = <u>cure</u>, remedy, medication, medicine ...*a new treatment for eczema...*
3 *often with* **of** = <u>handling</u>, dealings with, behaviour towards, conduct towards, management, reception, usage, manipulation, action towards ...*She was shocked at his treatment of her...*

treaty = <u>agreement</u>, pact, contract, bond, alliance, bargain, convention, compact, covenant, entente, concordat

tree
(*Related Words*)
adjective: arboreal
➤ **trees**

trek `VERB` **1** = <u>journey</u>, march, range, hike, roam, tramp, rove, go walkabout (*Austral.*) ...*trekking through the jungles...*
2 = <u>trudge</u>, plod, traipse (*informal*), footslog, slog ...*They trekked from shop to shop looking for knee-length socks...*
`NOUN` **1** = <u>slog</u>, tramp, long haul, footslog ...*It's a bit of a trek, but it's worth it...*
2 = <u>journey</u>, hike, expedition, safari, march, odyssey ...*He is on a trek through the South Gobi desert...*

tremble `VERB` **1** = <u>shake</u>, shiver, quake, shudder, quiver, teeter, totter, quake in your boots, shake in your boots *or* shoes ...*He began to tremble all over...*
2 = <u>vibrate</u>, rock, shake, quake, wobble, oscillate ...*He felt the earth tremble under him...*

`NOUN` = <u>shake</u>, shiver, quake, shudder, wobble, tremor, quiver, vibration, oscillation ...*I'll never forget the tremble in his hand...*

tremendous **1** = <u>huge</u>, great, towering, vast, enormous, terrific, formidable, immense, awesome, titanic, gigantic, monstrous, mammoth, colossal, whopping (*informal*), stellar (*informal*), prodigious, stupendous, gargantuan ...*I felt a tremendous pressure on my chest...* `OPPOSITE` tiny
2 = <u>excellent</u>, great, wonderful, brilliant, mean (*slang*), topping (*Brit. slang*), cracking (*Brit. informal*), amazing, extraordinary, fantastic (*informal*), ace (*informal*), incredible, fabulous (*informal*), marvellous, exceptional, terrific (*informal*), sensational (*informal*), sovereign, awesome (*slang*), super (*informal*), brill (*informal*), bodacious (*slang, chiefly U.S.*), boffo (*slang*), jim-dandy (*slang*), chillin' (*U.S. slang*), booshit (*Austral. slang*), exo (*Austral. slang*), sik (*Austral. slang*) ...*I thought it was absolutely tremendous...* `OPPOSITE` terrible

tremor **1** = <u>shake</u>, shaking, tremble, trembling, shiver, quaking, wobble, quiver, quivering, agitation, vibration, quaver ...*He felt a tremor in his arm...*
2 = <u>earthquake</u>, shock, quake (*informal*), tremblor (*U.S. informal*) ...*The minute-long tremor measured 6.8 on the Richter Scale...*

trench = <u>ditch</u>, cut, channel, drain, pit, waterway, gutter, trough, furrow, excavation, earthwork, fosse, entrenchment

trenchant **1** = <u>scathing</u>, pointed, cutting, biting, sharp, keen, acute, severe, acid, penetrating, tart, pungent, incisive, hurtful, sarcastic, caustic, astringent, vitriolic, acerbic, piquant, mordant, acidulous, mordacious ...*He was shattered by the trenchant criticism...* `OPPOSITE` kind
2 = <u>clear</u>, driving, strong, powerful, effective, distinct, crisp, explicit, vigorous, potent, energetic, clear-cut, forceful, emphatic, unequivocal, salient, well-defined, effectual, distinctly defined ...*His comment was trenchant and perceptive...* `OPPOSITE` vague

trend `NOUN` **1** = <u>tendency</u>, swing, drift, inclination, current, direction, flow, leaning, bias ...*a trend towards part-time employment...*
2 = <u>fashion</u>, craze, fad (*informal*), mode, look, thing, style, rage, vogue, mania ...*The record may well start a trend...*
`VERB` = <u>tend</u>, turn, head, swing, flow, bend, lean, incline, veer, run ...*Unemployment is still trending down...*

trendy `ADJECTIVE` (*Brit. informal*) = <u>fashionable</u>, in (*slang*), now (*informal*), latest, with it (*informal*), flash (*informal*), stylish, in fashion, in vogue, up to the minute, modish, voguish ...*a trendy London night club...*
`NOUN` (*Brit. informal*) = <u>poser</u> (*informal*), pseud (*informal*) ...*an example of what happens when you get a few trendies in power...*

trepidation (*Formal*) = <u>anxiety</u>, fear, worry, alarm, emotion, excitement, dread, butterflies (*informal*),

Trees http://www.british-trees.com/

acacia	camphor laurel	hornbeam	peach
akee	carbeen, carbean,	horse chestnut	pear
alder	karbeen, *or* Moreton	huon pine	peppermint gum
almond	Bay ash	ilex	persimmon
aloe	carob	ironbark	pine
angophora	cashew	iron gum	plane
Antarctic beech	cassia	ironwood	plum
apple	casuarina *or* native oak	jacaranda	pomegranate
apricot	cedar	jarrah	poplar
ash	cedar of Lebanon	Judas tree	pussy willow
aspen	celery pine *or* celery-top	juniper	quandong *or* quondong
balsa	pine	karri	quince
banana	cherry	kauri	radiata pine, insignis
bangalay *or* bastard	chestnut	kentia palm	pine, *or* Monterey pine
mahogany	cinnamon	kurrajong *or* currajong	raffia
bangalow (palm) *or*	citrus	laburnum	redwood
piccabean	coachwood	larch	rivergum *or* river red
banyalla *or* tallowwood	coco	laurel	gum
banyan	coconut	lemon	rosewood
baobab *or* boab	coolabah *or* coolibah	lilac	rowan
bat's wing coral-tree	coral tree	lilly pilly *or* lilli pilli	sandalwood
bay	cork oak	lime	sassafras
beech	corkwood *or* cork tree	lind	Scots fir
beefwood	cypress	linden	Scots pine
belah, belar, billar, *or*	date palm	lotus	scribbly gum
black oak	deal	macadamia, bauple nut,	sequoia
berrigan *or* bitterbush	dogwood	*or* Queensland nut	silky oak
bimble box	Douglas fir	macrocarpa	silver birch
birch	ebony	magnolia	snow gum
bitterbark	elder	mahogany	spotted gum
black bean *or* Moreton	elm	mallee	spruce
Bay chestnut	eucalyptus *or* eucalypt	mango	stinging tree
blackbutt	eumung *or* eumong	mangrove	stringy-bark
black pine *or* matai	fig	manuka, kahikatoa, *or*	sycamore
black wattle	fir	kanuka	tamarind
blackwood *or*	firewheel tree	maple	Tasmanian blue gum
mudgerabah	flame tree *or* Illawarra	marri	teak
blanket-leaf	flame tree	melaleuca	tea-tree
bloodwood	flooded gum	mimosa	umbrella tree
bonsai	ghost gum	monkey puzzle *or* Chile	walnut
boree	gidgee *or* stinking wattle	pine	wandoo
bottle tree	golden wattle	Moreton Bay fig	wattle
box	grapefruit	mountain ash	weeping willow
brazil	grasstree *or* black boy	mugga	white ash
brigalow	grey gum	mulberry	whitebeam
bulwaddy, bullwaddy,	ground ash	myall	wilga
bullwaddie, *or*	ground oak	Norfolk Island pine	willow
bulwaddee	guava	nutmeg	wirilda
bunya *or* bunya-bunya	gum (tree)	oak	witch
(pine)	gympie	olive	witch elm
burrawang *or* zamia	hawthorn	orange	yellow box (*Austral.*)
butternut	hazel	osier	yew
cabbage tree (palm)	hemlock	palm	ylang-ylang
cacao	hickory	papaya	yucca
cadagi *or* cadaga	holly	paperbark	
cajuput *or* cajeput	hoop pine	pawpaw *or* papaw	

shaking, disturbance, dismay, trembling, fright, apprehension, tremor, quivering, nervousness, disquiet, agitation, consternation, jitters (*informal*), cold feet (*informal*), uneasiness, palpitation, cold sweat (*informal*), perturbation, the heebie-jeebies (*slang*) OPPOSITE> composure

trespass VERB **1** = intrude, infringe, encroach, enter without permission, invade, poach, obtrude ...*They were trespassing on private property*...
2 (*Archaic*) = underline{sin}, offend, transgress, commit a sin ...*Forgive those who trespass against us*...
NOUN **1** = intrusion, infringement, encroachment,

unlawful entry, invasion, poaching, wrongful entry
…*You could be prosecuted for trespass*…
2 (*Old-fashioned*) = <u>sin</u>, crime, fault, error, offence,
breach, misconduct, wrongdoing, misdemeanour,
delinquency, misdeed, transgression, misbehaviour,
iniquity, infraction, evildoing, injury …*Forgive us our
trespasses*…

tresses = <u>hair</u>, locks, curls, braid, plait, pigtail, ringlets

triad = <u>threesome</u>, triple, trio, trinity, trilogy, triplet,
triumvirate, triptych, trine, triune

trial NOUN **1** (*Law*) = <u>hearing</u>, case, court case, inquiry,
contest, tribunal, lawsuit, appeal, litigation, industrial
tribunal, court martial, legal proceedings, judicial
proceedings, judicial examination …*New evidence
showed that he lied at the trial*…
2 = <u>test</u>, testing, experiment, evaluation, check,
examination, audition, assay, dry run (*informal*),
assessment, proof, probation, appraisal, try-out, test-
run, pilot study, dummy run …*They have been treated
with drugs in clinical trials*…
3 = <u>hardship</u>, suffering, trouble, pain, load, burden,
distress, grief, misery, ordeal, hard times, woe,
unhappiness, adversity, affliction, tribulation,
wretchedness, vexation, cross to bear …*the trials of
adolescence*…
4 = <u>nuisance</u>, drag (*informal*), bother, plague
(*informal*), pest, irritation, hassle (*informal*), bane, pain
in the neck (*informal*), vexation, thorn in your flesh *or*
side …*The whole affair has been a terrible trial for us
all*…
ADJECTIVE = <u>experimental</u>, probationary, testing, pilot,
provisional, exploratory …*a trial period*…

tribe = <u>race</u>, ethnic group, people, family, class, stock,
house, division, blood, seed (*chiefly biblical*), sept,
gens, clan, caste, dynasty

tribulation = <u>trouble</u>, care, suffering, worry, trial,
blow, pain, burden, distress, grief, misery, curse,
ordeal, hardship, sorrow, woe, hassle (*informal*),
misfortune, bad luck, unhappiness, heartache,
adversity, affliction, bummer (*slang*), wretchedness,
vexation, ill fortune, cross to bear OPPOSITE> joy

tribunal = <u>hearing</u>, court, trial, bar, bench, industrial
tribunal, judgment seat, judicial examination

tribute = <u>accolade</u>, testimonial, eulogy, recognition,
respect, gift, honour, praise, esteem, applause,
compliment, gratitude, acknowledgment,
commendation, panegyric, encomium, laudation
OPPOSITE> criticism

trick NOUN **1** = <u>joke</u>, put-on (*slang*), gag (*informal*),
stunt, spoof (*informal*), caper, prank, frolic, practical
joke, antic, jape, leg-pull (*Brit. informal*), cantrip (*Scot.*)
…*We are playing a trick on a man who keeps bothering
me*…
2 = <u>deception</u>, trap, fraud, con (*slang*), sting
(*informal*), manoeuvre, dodge, ploy, scam (*slang*),
imposition, gimmick, device, hoax, deceit, swindle,
ruse, artifice, subterfuge, canard, feint, stratagem, wile,
imposture …*That was a really mean trick*…
3 = <u>sleight of hand</u>, device, feat, stunt, juggle,

legerdemain …*He shows me card tricks*…
4 = <u>secret</u>, skill, device, knack, art, hang (*informal*),
technique, know-how (*informal*), gift, command, craft,
expertise …*She showed me all the tricks of the trade*…
5 = <u>mannerism</u>, habit, characteristic, trait, quirk,
peculiarity, foible, idiosyncrasy, practice, crotchet …*all
her little tricks and funny voices*…
VERB = <u>deceive</u>, trap, have someone on, take
someone in (*informal*), fool, cheat, con (*informal*), kid
(*informal*), stiff (*slang*), sting (*informal*), mislead, hoax,
defraud, dupe, gull (*archaic*), delude, swindle, impose
upon, bamboozle (*informal*), hoodwink, put one over
on (*informal*), pull the wool over someone's eyes, pull
a fast one on (*informal*) …*He'll be upset when he finds
out how you tricked him*…
PHRASES **do the trick** (*Informal*) = <u>work</u>, fit the bill,
have effect, achieve the desired result, produce the
desired result, take care of the problem, be effective
or effectual …*Sometimes a few choice words will do
the trick*…

trickery = <u>deception</u>, fraud, cheating, con (*informal*),
hoax, pretence, deceit, dishonesty, swindling, guile,
double-dealing, skulduggery (*informal*), chicanery,
hanky-panky (*informal*), hokum (*slang, chiefly U.S. &
Canad.*), monkey business (*informal*), funny business,
jiggery-pokery (*informal, chiefly Brit.*), imposture
OPPOSITE> honesty

trickle VERB = <u>dribble</u>, run, drop, stream, creep,
crawl, drip, ooze, seep, exude, percolate …*A tear
trickled down his cheek*…
NOUN = <u>dribble</u>, drip, seepage, thin stream …*There
was not so much as a trickle of water*…

trickster = <u>deceiver</u>, fraud, cheat, joker, hoaxer,
pretender, hustler (*U.S. informal*), con man (*informal*),
impostor, fraudster, swindler, practical joker, grifter
(*slang, chiefly U.S. & Canad.*), chiseller (*informal*), rorter
(*Austral. slang*)

tricky 1 = <u>difficult</u>, sensitive, complicated, delicate,
risky, sticky (*informal*), hairy (*informal*), problematic,
thorny, touch-and-go, knotty, dicey (*informal*), ticklish
…*This could be a very tricky problem*… OPPOSITE>
simple
2 = <u>crafty</u>, scheming, subtle, cunning, slippery, sly,
deceptive, devious, wily, artful, foxy, deceitful …*They
could encounter some tricky political manoevring*…
OPPOSITE> open

trifle 1 = <u>little</u>, bit, touch, spot, trace, dash, pinch, jot,
drop …*He found both locations just a trifle
disappointing*…
2 = <u>knick-knack</u>, nothing, toy, plaything, bauble,
triviality, bagatelle, gewgaw …*He had no money to
spare on trifles*…

trifling = <u>insignificant</u>, small, tiny, empty, slight, silly,
shallow, petty, idle, trivial, worthless, negligible,
unimportant, frivolous, paltry, minuscule, puny,
measly, piddling (*informal*), inconsiderable, valueless,
nickel-and-dime (*U.S. slang*), footling (*informal*)
OPPOSITE> significant

trigger = <u>bring about</u>, start, cause, produce,

generate, prompt, provoke, set off, activate, give rise to, elicit, spark off, set in motion OPPOSITE> prevent

trim ADJECTIVE **1** = <u>neat</u>, nice, smart, compact, tidy, orderly, spruce, dapper, natty (*informal*), well-groomed, well-ordered, well turned-out, shipshape, spick-and-span, trig (*archaic or dialect*), soigné *or* soignée ...*The neighbour's gardens were trim and neat...* OPPOSITE> untidy
2 = <u>slender</u>, fit, slim, sleek, streamlined, shapely, svelte, willowy, lissom ...*The driver was a trim young woman of about thirty...*
VERB **1** = <u>cut</u>, crop, clip, dock, shave, barber, tidy, prune, shear, pare, lop, even up, neaten ...*My friend trims my hair every eight weeks...*
2 = <u>decorate</u>, dress, array, adorn, embroider, garnish, ornament, embellish, deck out, bedeck, beautify, trick out ...*jackets trimmed with crocheted flowers...*
NOUN **1** = <u>decoration</u>, edging, border, piping, trimming, fringe, garnish, frill, embellishment, adornment, ornamentation ...*a white satin scarf with black trim...*
2 = <u>condition</u>, form, health, shape (*informal*), repair, fitness, wellness, order, fettle ...*He is already getting in trim for the big day...*
3 = <u>cut</u>, crop, trimming, clipping, shave, pruning, shearing, tidying up ...*His hair needed a trim...*

trimming NOUN = <u>decoration</u>, edging, border, piping, fringe, garnish, braid, frill, festoon, embellishment, adornment, ornamentation ...*the lace trimming on her satin nightgown...*
PLURAL NOUN **1** = <u>extras</u>, accessories, garnish, ornaments, accompaniments, frills, trappings, paraphernalia, appurtenances ...*a Thanksgiving dinner of turkey and all the trimmings...*
2 = <u>clippings</u>, ends, cuttings, shavings, brash, parings ...*Use any pastry trimmings to decorate the apples...*

trinity = <u>threesome</u>, triple, trio, trilogy, triplet, triad, triumvirate, triptych, trine, triune

trinket = <u>ornament</u>, bauble, knick-knack, piece of bric-a-brac, nothing, toy, trifle, bagatelle, gimcrack, gewgaw, bibelot, kickshaw

trio = <u>threesome</u>, triple, trinity, trilogy, triplet, triad, triumvirate, triptych, trine, triune

trip NOUN **1** = <u>journey</u>, outing, excursion, day out, run, drive, travel, tour, spin (*informal*), expedition, voyage, ramble, foray, jaunt, errand, junket (*informal*) ...*On the Thursday we went out on a day trip...*
2 = <u>stumble</u>, fall, slip, blunder, false move, misstep, false step ...*Slips, trips and falls were monitored using a daily calendar...*
VERB **1** = <u>stumble</u>, fall, fall over, slip, tumble, topple, stagger, misstep, lose your balance, make a false move, lose your footing, take a spill ...*She tripped and broke her hip...*
2 = <u>skip</u>, dance, spring, hop, caper, flit, frisk, gambol, tread lightly ...*They tripped along without a care in the world...*
3 (*Informal*) = <u>take drugs</u>, get high (*informal*), get stoned (*slang*), turn on (*slang*) ...*One night I was tripping on acid...*
4 = <u>activate</u>, turn on, flip, release, pull, throw, engage, set off, switch on ...*He set the timer, then tripped the switch...*
PHRASES **trip someone up** = <u>catch out</u>, trap, confuse, unsettle, disconcert, throw you off, wrongfoot, put you off your stride ...*Your own lies will trip you up...*

tripe (*Informal*) = <u>nonsense</u>, rot, trash, twaddle, rubbish, pants (*slang*), crap (*slang*), garbage (*informal*), hot air (*informal*), tosh (*slang, chiefly Brit.*), pap, bilge (*informal*), drivel, guff (*slang*), moonshine, claptrap (*informal*), hogwash, hokum (*slang, chiefly U.S. & Canad.*), piffle (*informal*), poppycock (*informal*), inanity, balderdash, bosh (*informal*), eyewash (*informal*), trumpery, tommyrot, foolish talk, horsefeathers (*U.S. slang*), bunkum *or* buncombe (*chiefly U.S.*), bizzo (*Austral. slang*), bull's wool (*Austral. & N.Z. slang*)

triple ADJECTIVE **1** = <u>treble</u>, three times, three times as much as ...*The kitchen is triple the size it used to be...*
2 = <u>three-way</u>, threefold, tripartite ...*Germany, Austria and Italy formed the Triple Alliance...*
VERB = <u>treble</u>, triplicate, increase threefold ...*I got a great new job and my salary tripled...*

triplet = <u>threesome</u>, triple, trio, trinity, trilogy, triad, triumvirate, trine, triune

tripper (*Chiefly Brit.*) = <u>tourist</u>, holiday-maker, sightseer, excursionist, journeyer, voyager

trite = <u>unoriginal</u>, worn, common, stock, ordinary, tired, routine, dull, stereotyped, hack, pedestrian, commonplace, stale, banal, corny (*slang*), run-of-the-mill, threadbare, clichéd, uninspired, hackneyed, bromidic OPPOSITE> original

triumph NOUN **1** = <u>success</u>, victory, accomplishment, mastery, hit (*informal*), achievement, smash (*informal*), coup, sensation, feat, conquest, attainment, smash hit (*informal*), tour de force (*French*), walkover (*informal*), feather in your cap, smasheroo (*slang*) ...*Cataract operations are a triumph of modern surgery...* OPPOSITE> failure
2 = <u>joy</u>, pride, happiness, rejoicing, elation, jubilation, exultation ...*Her sense of triumph was short-lived...*
VERB **1** *often with* **over** = <u>succeed</u>, win, overcome, prevail, best, dominate, overwhelm, thrive, flourish, subdue, prosper, get the better of, vanquish, come out on top (*informal*), carry the day, take the honours ...*a symbol of good triumphing over evil...* OPPOSITE> fail
2 = <u>rejoice</u>, celebrate, glory, revel, swagger, drool, gloat, exult, jubilate, crow ...*the euphoria, the sense of triumphing together as a nation...*

triumphant 1 = <u>victorious</u>, winning, successful, dominant, conquering, undefeated ...*the triumphant team...* OPPOSITE> defeated
2 = <u>celebratory</u>, rejoicing, jubilant, triumphal, proud, glorious, swaggering, elated, exultant, boastful, cock-a-hoop ...*his triumphant return home...*

trivia = <u>minutiae</u>, details, trifles, trivialities, petty details OPPOSITE essentials

trivial = unimportant, little, small, minor, slight, everyday, petty, meaningless, commonplace, worthless, trifling, insignificant, negligible, frivolous, paltry, incidental, puny, inconsequential, trite, inconsiderable, valueless, nickel-and-dime (*U.S. slang*) OPPOSITE important

triviality 1 = insignificance, frivolity, smallness, pettiness, worthlessness, meaninglessness, unimportance, littleness, slightness, triteness, paltriness, inconsequentiality, valuelessness, negligibility, much ado about nothing …*news items of quite astonishing triviality*… OPPOSITE importance
2 = trifle, nothing, detail, technicality, petty detail, no big thing, no great matter …*He accused me of making a great fuss about trivialities*… OPPOSITE essential

troop NOUN = group, company, team, body, unit, band, crowd, pack, squad, gathering, crew (*informal*), drove, gang, bunch (*informal*), flock, herd, contingent, swarm, horde, multitude, throng, posse (*informal*), bevy, assemblage …*She was aware of a little troop of travellers watching them*…
PLURAL NOUN = soldiers, men, armed forces, servicemen, fighting men, military, army, soldiery …*the deployment of more than 35,000 troops from a dozen countries*…
VERB = flock, march, crowd, stream, parade, swarm, throng, traipse (*informal*) …*The VIPs trooped into the hall and sat down*…

trophy 1 = prize, cup, award, bays, laurels …*They could win a trophy this year*…
2 = souvenir, spoils, relic, memento, booty, keepsake …*lines of stuffed animal heads, trophies of his hunting hobby*…

tropical = hot, stifling, lush, steamy, humid, torrid, sultry, sweltering OPPOSITE cold

trot VERB = run, jog, scamper, lope, go briskly, canter …*I trotted down the steps and out to the shed*…
NOUN = run, jog, lope, brisk pace, canter …*He walked briskly, but without breaking into a trot*…
PHRASES **on the trot** (*Informal*) = one after the other, in a row, in succession, without break, without interruption, consecutively …*She lost five games on the trot*… ♦ **trot something out** (*Informal*) = repeat, relate, exhibit, bring up, reiterate, recite, come out with, bring forward, drag up …*Was it really necessary to trot out the same old stereotypes?*…

troubadour = minstrel, singer, poet, balladeer, lyric poet, jongleur

trouble NOUN 1 = bother, problems, concern, worry, stress, difficulty (*informal*), anxiety, distress, grief (*Brit. & S. African*), irritation, hassle (*informal*), strife, inconvenience, unease, disquiet, annoyance, agitation, commotion, unpleasantness, vexation …*You've caused a lot of trouble*…
2 *usually plural* = distress, problem, suffering, worry, pain, anxiety, grief, torment, hardship, sorrow, woe, irritation, hassle (*informal*), misfortune, heartache, disquiet, annoyance, agitation, tribulation, bummer

(*slang*), vexation …*She tells me her troubles. I tell her mine*… OPPOSITE pleasure
3 = ailment, disease, failure, complaint, upset, illness, disorder, disability, defect, malfunction …*He had never before had any heart trouble*…
4 = disorder, fighting, row, conflict, bother, grief (*Brit. & S. African*), unrest, disturbance, to-do (*informal*), discontent, dissatisfaction, furore, uproar, scuffling, discord, fracas, commotion, rumpus, breach of the peace, tumult, affray (*Law*), brouhaha, ructions, hullabaloo (*informal*), kerfuffle (*Brit. informal*), hoo-ha (*informal*), biffo (*Austral. slang*) …*Riot police are being deployed to prevent any trouble*… OPPOSITE peace
5 = problem, bother, concern, pest, irritation, hassle (*informal*), nuisance, inconvenience, irritant, cause of annoyance …*He's no trouble at all, but his brother is rude and selfish*…
6 = effort, work, thought, care, labour, struggle, pains, bother, grief (*Brit. & S. African*), hassle (*informal*), inconvenience, exertion …*You've saved us a lot of trouble by helping*… OPPOSITE convenience
7 = difficulty, hot water (*informal*), predicament, deep water (*informal*), spot (*informal*), danger, mess, dilemma, scrape (*informal*), pickle (*informal*), dire straits, tight spot …*a charity that helps women in trouble with the law*…
VERB 1 = bother, worry, upset, disturb, distress, annoy, plague, grieve, torment, harass, hassle (*informal*), afflict, pain, fret, agitate, sadden, perplex, disconcert, disquiet, pester, vex, perturb, faze, give someone grief (*Brit. & S. African*), discompose, put *or* get someone's back up …*Is anything troubling you?*… OPPOSITE please
2 = afflict, hurt, bother, cause discomfort to, cause discomfort to, pain, grieve …*The ulcer had been troubling her for several years*…
3 = inconvenience, disturb, burden, put out, impose upon, discommode, incommode …*'Good morning. I'm sorry to trouble you.'*… OPPOSITE relieve
4 = underline{take pains}, take the time, make an effort, go to the effort of, exert yourself …*He yawns, not troubling to cover his mouth*… OPPOSITE avoid

troublemaker = mischief-maker, firebrand, instigator, agitator, bad apple (*U.S. informal*), rabble-rouser, agent provocateur (*French*), stirrer (*informal*), incendiary, rotten apple (*Brit. informal*), meddler, stormy petrel OPPOSITE peace-maker

troublesome 1 = bothersome, trying, taxing, demanding, difficult, worrying, upsetting, annoying, irritating, tricky, harassing, oppressive, arduous, tiresome, inconvenient, laborious, burdensome, hard, worrisome, irksome, wearisome, vexatious, importunate, pestilential, plaguy (*informal*) …*The economy has become a troublesome problem for the party*… OPPOSITE simple
2 = disorderly, violent, turbulent, rebellious, unruly, rowdy, recalcitrant, undisciplined, uncooperative, refractory, insubordinate …*Parents may find that a troublesome teenager becomes unmanageable*… OPPOSITE well-behaved

trough = <u>manger</u>, crib, water trough

trounce = <u>defeat someone heavily</u> *or* <u>utterly</u>, beat, thrash, slaughter (*informal*), stuff (*slang*), tank (*slang*), hammer (*informal*), crush, overwhelm, lick (*informal*), paste (*slang*), rout, walk over (*informal*), clobber (*slang*), run rings around (*informal*), wipe the floor with (*informal*), make mincemeat of, blow someone out of the water (*slang*), give someone a hiding (*informal*), drub, beat someone hollow (*Brit. informal*), give someone a pasting (*slang*)

troupe = <u>company</u>, group, band, cast, ensemble

truancy = <u>absence</u>, shirking, skiving (*Brit. slang*), malingering, absence without leave

truant NOUN = <u>absentee</u>, skiver (*Brit. slang*), shirker, dodger, runaway, delinquent, deserter, straggler, malingerer ...*She became a truant at the age of ten*... ADJECTIVE = <u>absent</u>, missing, skiving (*Brit. slang*), absent without leave, A.W.O.L. ...*Neither the parents nor the truant students showed up at court*... VERB = <u>absent yourself</u>, play truant, skive (*Brit. slang*), bunk off (*slang*), desert, run away, dodge, wag (*dialect*), go missing, shirk, malinger, bob off (*Brit. slang*) ...*In his fourth year he was truanting regularly*...

truce = <u>ceasefire</u>, break, stay, rest, peace, treaty, interval, moratorium, respite, lull, cessation, let-up (*informal*), armistice, intermission, cessation of hostilities

truculent = <u>hostile</u>, defiant, belligerent, bad-tempered, cross, violent, aggressive, fierce, contentious, combative, sullen, scrappy (*informal*), antagonistic, pugnacious, ill-tempered, bellicose, obstreperous, itching *or* spoiling for a fight (*informal*), aggers (*Austral. slang*) OPPOSITE amiable

trudge VERB = <u>plod</u>, trek, tramp, traipse (*informal*), march, stump, hike, clump, lumber, slog, drag yourself, yomp, walk heavily, footslog ...*We had to trudge up the track back to the station*... NOUN = <u>tramp</u>, march, haul, trek, hike, slog, traipse (*informal*), yomp, footslog ...*We were reluctant to start the long trudge home*...

true ADJECTIVE 1 = <u>correct</u>, right, accurate, exact, precise, valid, legitimate, factual, truthful, veritable, bona fide, veracious ...*Everything I had heard about him was true*... OPPOSITE false
2 = <u>actual</u>, real, natural, pure, genuine, proper, authentic, dinkum (*Austral. & N.Z. informal*) ...*I allowed myself to acknowledge my true feelings*...
3 = <u>faithful</u>, loyal, devoted, dedicated, firm, fast, constant, pure, steady, reliable, upright, sincere, honourable, honest, staunch, trustworthy, trusty, dutiful, true-blue, unswerving ...*He was always true to his wife*... OPPOSITE unfaithful
4 = <u>exact</u>, perfect, correct, accurate, proper, precise, spot-on (*Brit. informal*), on target, unerring ...*The score is usually a true reflection of events on the pitch*... OPPOSITE inaccurate
ADVERB 1 = <u>truthfully</u>, honestly, veritably, veraciously, rightly ...*Does the lad speak true?*...
2 = <u>precisely</u>, accurately, on target, perfectly, correctly,

properly, unerringly ...*Most of the bullets hit true*...
PHRASES **come true** = <u>happen</u>, be realized, come to pass, become reality, occur, be granted ...*Many of his predictions are coming true*...

true-blue = <u>staunch</u>, confirmed, constant, devoted, dedicated, loyal, faithful, orthodox, uncompromising, trusty, unwavering, dyed-in-the-wool

truism = <u>cliché</u>, commonplace, platitude, axiom, stock phrase, trite saying

truly 1 = <u>genuinely</u>, really, correctly, truthfully, rightly, in fact, precisely, exactly, legitimately, accurately, in reality, in truth, beyond doubt, without a doubt, authentically, beyond question, factually, in actuality, veritably, veraciously ...*a truly democratic system*... OPPOSITE falsely
2 = <u>really</u>, very, greatly, indeed, seriously (*informal*), extremely, to be sure, exceptionally, verily ...*a truly splendid man*...
3 = <u>faithfully</u>, firmly, constantly, steadily, honestly, sincerely, staunchly, dutifully, loyally, honourably, devotedly, with all your heart, with dedication, with devotion, confirmedly ...*He truly loved his children*...

trump VERB = <u>outdo</u>, top, cap, surpass, score points off, excel ...*The Socialists tried to trump this with their slogan*...
PHRASES **trump something up** = <u>invent</u>, create, make up, manufacture, fake, contrive, fabricate, concoct, cook up (*informal*) ...*He insists that charges against him have been trumped up*...

trumped up = <u>invented</u>, made-up, manufactured, false, fake, contrived, untrue, fabricated, concocted, falsified, cooked-up (*informal*), phoney *or* phony (*informal*) OPPOSITE genuine

trumpet NOUN 1 = <u>horn</u>, clarion, bugle ...*Picking up his trumpet, he gave it a quick blow*...
2 = <u>roar</u>, call, cry, bay, bellow ...*The elephants trumpeted and stamped their feet*... VERB = <u>proclaim</u>, advertise, extol, tout (*informal*), announce, publish, broadcast, crack up (*informal*), sound loudly, shout from the rooftops, noise abroad ...*He is trumpeted as the dance talent of his generation*... OPPOSITE keep secret
PHRASES **blow your own trumpet** = <u>boast</u>, crow, brag, vaunt, sing your own praises, big yourself up (*slang, chiefly Caribbean*) ...*The cameramen have good reason to blow their own trumpets*...

truncate = <u>shorten</u>, cut, crop, trim, clip, dock, prune, curtail, cut short, pare, lop, abbreviate OPPOSITE lengthen

truncheon (*Chiefly Brit.*) = <u>club</u>, staff, stick, baton, cudgel

trunk 1 = <u>stem</u>, stock, stalk, bole ...*toadstools growing on fallen tree trunks*...
2 = <u>chest</u>, case, box, crate, bin, suitcase, locker, coffer, casket, portmanteau, kist (*Scot. & Northern English dialect*) ...*He had left most of his records in a trunk in the attic*...
3 = <u>body</u>, torso ...*Simultaneously, raise your trunk 6 inches above the ground*...

4 = <u>snout</u>, nose, proboscis …*It could exert the suction power of an elephant's trunk…*

truss `VERB` *often with* **up** = <u>tie</u>, secure, bind, strap, fasten, tether, pinion, make fast …*She trussed him with the bandage and gagged his mouth…* `NOUN` **1** (*Medical*) = <u>support</u>, pad, bandage …*For a hernia he introduced the simple solution of a truss…* **2** = <u>joist</u>, support, stay, shore, beam, prop, brace, strut, buttress, stanchion …*the bridge's arched, lightweight steel truss…*

trust `VERB` **1** = <u>believe in</u>, have faith in, depend on, count on, bank on, lean on, rely upon, swear by, take at face value, take as gospel, place reliance on, place your trust in, pin your faith on, place *or* have confidence in …*'I trust you completely,' he said…* `OPPOSITE` distrust
2 = <u>entrust</u>, commit, assign, confide, consign, put into the hands of, allow to look after, hand over, turn over, sign over, delegate …*I'd been willing to trust my life to him…*
3 = <u>expect</u>, believe, hope, suppose, assume, guess (*informal*), take it, presume, surmise, think likely …*We trust that they are considering our suggestion…* `NOUN` **1** = <u>confidence</u>, credit, belief, faith, expectation, conviction, assurance, certainty, reliance, credence, certitude …*There's a feeling of warmth and trust here…* `OPPOSITE` distrust
2 = <u>responsibility</u>, duty, obligation …*She held a position of trust, which was generously paid…*
3 = <u>custody</u>, care, guard, protection, guardianship, safekeeping, trusteeship …*The British Library holds its collection in trust for the nation…*
Related Words
adjective : fiducial

trusting *or* **trustful** = <u>unsuspecting</u>, simple, innocent, optimistic, naïve, confiding, gullible, unwary, unguarded, credulous, unsuspicious `OPPOSITE` suspicious

trustworthy = <u>dependable</u>, responsible, principled, mature, sensible, reliable, ethical, upright, true, honourable, honest, staunch, righteous, reputable, truthful, trusty, steadfast, level-headed, to be trusted `OPPOSITE` untrustworthy

trusty = <u>reliable</u>, dependable, trustworthy, responsible, solid, strong, firm, true, steady, faithful, straightforward, upright, honest, staunch `OPPOSITE` unreliable

truth **1** = <u>reality</u>, fact(s), real life, actuality …*Is it possible to separate truth from fiction?…* `OPPOSITE` unreality
2 = <u>truthfulness</u>, fact, accuracy, honesty, precision, validity, legitimacy, authenticity, correctness, sincerity, verity, candour, veracity, rightness, genuineness, exactness, factuality, factualness …*There is no truth in this story…* `OPPOSITE` inaccuracy
3 = <u>fact</u>, law, reality, certainty, maxim, verity, axiom, truism, proven principle …*It's a universal truth that we all die eventually…*
4 = <u>honesty</u>, principle, honour, virtue, integrity,

goodness, righteousness, candour, frankness, probity, rectitude, incorruptibility, uprightness …*His mission is to uphold truth, justice and the American way…* `OPPOSITE` dishonesty
Related Words
adjectives : veritable, veracious

truthful **1** = <u>honest</u>, frank, candid, upfront (*informal*), true, straight, reliable, faithful, straightforward, sincere, forthright, trustworthy, plain-spoken, veracious …*We are all fairly truthful about our personal lives…* `OPPOSITE` dishonest
2 = <u>true</u>, correct, accurate, exact, realistic, precise, literal, veritable, naturalistic …*They had not given a truthful account of what actually happened…* `OPPOSITE` untrue

try `VERB` **1** = <u>attempt</u>, seek, aim, undertake, essay, strive, struggle, endeavour, have a go, go for it (*informal*), make an effort, have a shot (*informal*), have a crack (*informal*), bend over backwards (*informal*), do your best, go for broke (*slang*), make an attempt, move heaven and earth, bust a gut (*informal*), give it your best shot (*informal*), have a stab (*informal*), break your neck (*informal*), exert yourself, make an all-out effort (*informal*), knock yourself out (*informal*), have a whack (*informal*), do your damnedest (*informal*), give it your all (*informal*), rupture yourself (*informal*) …*He secretly tried to block her advancement in the Party…*
2 = <u>experiment with</u>, try out, put to the test, test, taste, examine, investigate, sample, evaluate, check out, inspect, appraise …*It's best not to try a new recipe on such an important occasion…*
3 = <u>judge</u>, hear, consider, examine, adjudicate, adjudge, pass judgement on …*The case was tried in Tampa, a changed venue with an all-white jury…*
4 = <u>tax</u>, test, trouble, pain, stress, upset, tire, strain, drain, exhaust, annoy, plague, irritate, weary, afflict, sap, inconvenience, wear out, vex, irk, make demands on, give someone grief (*Brit. & S. African*) …*She really tried my patience…* `NOUN` = <u>attempt</u>, go (*informal*), shot (*informal*), effort, crack (*informal*), essay, stab (*informal*), bash (*informal*), endeavour, whack (*informal*) …*I didn't really expect anything, but it was worth a try…* `PHRASES` **try something out** = <u>test</u>, experiment with, appraise, put to the test, taste, sample, evaluate, check out, inspect, put into practice …*She knew I wanted to try the boat out at the weekend…*

trying = <u>annoying</u>, hard, taxing, difficult, tough, upsetting, irritating, fatiguing, stressful, aggravating (*informal*), troublesome, exasperating, arduous, tiresome, vexing, irksome, wearisome, bothersome `OPPOSITE` straightforward

tsar *or* **czar** **1** = <u>ruler</u>, leader, emperor, sovereign, tyrant, despot, overlord, autocrat …*Princess Anne is related to the Tsar of Russia…*
2 (*Informal*) = <u>head</u>, chief, boss, big cheese (*informal*), baas (*S. African*), head honcho (*informal*) …*He was appointed 'drugs tsar' by Bill Clinton…*

tubby = <u>fat</u>, overweight, plump, stout, chubby, obese, portly, roly-poly, podgy, corpulent, paunchy

tuck `VERB` = <u>push</u>, stick, stuff, slip, ease, insert, pop (*informal*) …*He tried to tuck his shirt inside his trousers*…
`NOUN` 1 (*Brit. informal*) = <u>food</u>, eats (*slang*), tack (*informal*), scoff (*slang*), grub (*slang*), kai (*N.Z. informal*), nosh (*slang*), victuals, comestibles, nosebag (*slang*), vittles (*obsolete or dialect*) …*The wags from the rival house were ready to snaffle his tuck*…
2 = <u>fold</u>, gather, pleat, pinch …*a tapered tuck used to take in fullness and control shape in a garment*…
`PHRASES` **tuck in** (*Informal*) = <u>eat up</u>, get stuck in (*informal*), eat heartily, fall to, chow down (*slang*) …*Tuck in, it's the last hot food you'll get for a while*…
♦ **tuck someone in** = <u>make someone snug</u>, wrap someone up, put someone to bed, bed someone down, swaddle …*I read her a story and tucked her in*…

tuft = <u>clump</u>, bunch, shock, collection, knot, cluster, tussock, topknot

tug `VERB` 1 = <u>pull</u>, drag, pluck, jerk, yank, wrench, lug …*A little boy tugged at her sleeve excitedly*…
2 = <u>drag</u>, pull, haul, tow, lug, heave, draw …*She tugged him along by his arm*…
`NOUN` = <u>pull</u>, jerk, yank, wrench, drag, haul, tow, traction, heave …*My head was snapped backwards by a tug on my air hose*…

tuition = <u>training</u>, schooling, education, teaching, lessons, instruction, tutoring, tutelage

tumble `VERB` = <u>fall</u>, drop, topple, plummet, roll, pitch, toss, stumble, flop, trip up, fall head over heels, fall headlong, fall end over end …*The dog had tumbled down the cliff*…
`NOUN` = <u>fall</u>, drop, roll, trip, collapse, plunge, spill, toss, stumble, flop, headlong fall …*He injured his knee in a tumble from his horse*…

tummy (*Informal*) = <u>stomach</u>, belly, abdomen, corporation (*informal*), pot, gut (*informal*), paunch, tum (*informal*), spare tyre (*informal*), breadbasket (*slang*), potbelly

tumour = <u>growth</u>, cancer, swelling, lump, carcinoma (*Pathology*), sarcoma (*Medical*), neoplasm (*Medical*)

tumult 1 = <u>disturbance</u>, trouble, chaos, turmoil, storms, upset, stir, disorder, excitement, unrest, upheaval, havoc, mayhem, strife, disarray, turbulence, ferment, agitation, convulsions, bedlam …*the recent tumult in global financial markets*…
2 = <u>clamour</u>, row, outbreak, racket, din, uproar, fracas, commotion, pandemonium, babel, hubbub, hullabaloo …*Round one ended to a tumult of whistles, screams and shouts*… `OPPOSITE` silence

tumultuous 1 = <u>turbulent</u>, exciting, confused, disturbed, hectic, stormy, agitated …*the tumultuous changes in Eastern Europe*… `OPPOSITE` quiet
2 = <u>wild</u>, excited, riotous, unrestrained, violent, raging, disorderly, fierce, passionate, noisy, restless, unruly, rowdy, boisterous, full-on (*informal*), lawless, vociferous, rumbustious, uproarious, obstreperous, clamorous …*Delegates greeted the news with*

tumultuous applause…

tune `NOUN` 1 = <u>melody</u>, air, song, theme, strain(s), motif, jingle, ditty, melody line …*She was humming a merry little tune*…
2 = <u>harmony</u>, pitch, euphony …*It was an ordinary voice, but he sang in tune*…
`VERB` 1 = <u>tune up</u>, adjust, bring into harmony …*They were quietly tuning their instruments*…
2 = <u>regulate</u>, adapt, modulate, harmonize, attune, pitch …*He will rapidly be tuned to the keynote of his associates*…
`PHRASES` **change your tune** = <u>change your attitude</u>, reconsider, think again, change your mind, have a change of heart, take a different tack, do an about-face …*He changed his tune, saying that the increase was experimental*…

tuneful = <u>melodious</u>, musical, pleasant, harmonious, melodic, catchy, consonant (*Music*), symphonic, mellifluous, easy on the ear (*informal*), euphonious, euphonic `OPPOSITE` discordant

tunnel `NOUN` = <u>passage</u>, underpass, passageway, subway, channel, hole, shaft …*two new railway tunnels through the Alps*…
`VERB` = <u>dig</u>, dig your way, burrow, mine, bore, drill, excavate …*The rebels tunnelled out of a maximum security jail*…

turbulence = <u>confusion</u>, turmoil, unrest, instability, storm, boiling, disorder, upheaval, agitation, commotion, pandemonium, tumult, roughness `OPPOSITE` peace

turbulent 1 = <u>wild</u>, violent, disorderly, agitated, rebellious, unruly, rowdy, boisterous, anarchic, tumultuous, lawless, unbridled, riotous, undisciplined, seditious, mutinous, ungovernable, uproarious, refractory, obstreperous, insubordinate …*six turbulent years of rows and reconciliations*…
2 = <u>stormy</u>, rough, raging, tempestuous, boiling, disordered, furious, unsettled, foaming, unstable, agitated, tumultuous, choppy, blustery …*I had to have a boat that could handle turbulent seas*… `OPPOSITE` calm

turf `NOUN` 1 = <u>grass</u>, green, sward …*They shuffled slowly down the turf towards the cliff's edge*…
2 = <u>sod</u>, divot, clod …*Lift the turfs carefully – they can be re-used elsewhere*…
`PHRASES` **the turf** = <u>horse-racing</u>, the flat, racecourse, racetrack, racing …*He has sent out only three winners on the turf this year*… ♦ **turf someone out** (*Brit. informal*) = <u>throw someone out</u>, evict, cast out, kick out (*informal*), fire (*informal*), dismiss, sack (*informal*), bounce (*slang*), discharge, expel, oust, relegate, banish, eject, dispossess, chuck out (*informal*), fling out, kiss off (*slang, chiefly U.S. & Canad.*), show someone the door, give someone the sack (*informal*), give someone the bum's rush (*slang*) …*stories of people being turfed out and ending up on the streets*…

turgid = <u>pompous</u>, inflated, windy, high-flown, pretentious, grandiose, flowery, overblown, stilted, ostentatious, fulsome, bombastic, grandiloquent, arty-farty (*informal*), fustian, orotund, magniloquent, sesquipedalian, tumid

turmoil = underline(confusion), trouble, violence, row, noise, stir, disorder, chaos, disturbance, upheaval, bustle, flurry, strife, disarray, uproar, turbulence, ferment, agitation, commotion, pandemonium, bedlam, tumult, hubbub, brouhaha OPPOSITE peace

turn VERB **1** = change course, swing round, wheel round, veer, move, return, go back, switch, shift, reverse, swerve, change position ...*He turned abruptly and walked away...*
2 = rotate, spin, go round (and round), revolve, roll, circle, wheel, twist, spiral, whirl, swivel, pivot, twirl, gyrate, go round in circles, move in a circle ...*As the wheel turned, the potter shaped the clay...*
3 = go round, come round, negotiate, pass, corner, pass around, take a bend ...*The taxi turned the corner of the lane and stopped...*
4 = change, transform, fashion, shape, convert, alter, adapt, mould, remodel, form, mutate, refit, metamorphose, transmute, transfigure ...*She turned the house into a beautiful home...*
5 = shape, form, fashion, cast, frame, construct, execute, mould, make ...*finely-turned metal...*
6 = sicken, upset, nauseate ...*The true facts will turn your stomach...*
7 = go bad, go off (*Brit. informal*), curdle, go sour, become rancid ...*milk starting to turn in the refrigerator...*
8 = make rancid, spoil, sour, taint ...*They are stupid and ugly enough to turn milk...*
NOUN **1** = rotation, turning, cycle, circle, revolution, spin, twist, reversal, whirl, swivel, pivot, gyration ...*The rear sprocket will turn only twice for one turn of the pedals...*
2 = change of direction, bend, curve, change of course, shift, departure, deviation ...*You can't do a right-hand turn here...*
3 = direction, course, tack, swing, tendency, drift, bias ...*The scandal took a new turn today...*
4 = opportunity, go, spell, shot (*informal*), time, try, round, chance, period, shift, crack (*informal*), succession, fling, stint, whack (*informal*) ...*Let each child have a turn at fishing...*
5 = stroll, airing, walk, drive, ride, spin (*informal*), circuit, constitutional, outing, excursion, promenade, jaunt, saunter ...*I think I'll just go up and take a turn round the deck...*
6 = deed, service, act, action, favour, gesture ...*He did you a good turn by resigning...*
7 (*Informal*) = shock, start, surprise, scare, jolt, fright ...*It gave me quite a turn...*
8 = inclination, talent, gift, leaning, bent, bias, flair, affinity, knack, propensity, aptitude ...*She has a turn for gymnastic exercises...*
PHRASES **by turns** = alternately, in succession, turn and turn about, reciprocally ...*His tone was by turns angry and aggrieved...* ◆ **to a turn** (*Informal*) = perfectly, correctly, precisely, exactly, just right

...*sweet tomatoes roasted to a turn...* ◆ **turn off** = branch off, leave, quit, depart from, deviate, change direction, take a side road, take another road ...*He turned off only to find that he was trapped in the main square... ...The truck turned off the main road along the gravelly track...* ◆ **turn on someone** = attack, assault, fall on, round on, lash out at, assail, lay into (*informal*), let fly at, lose your temper with ...*The demonstrators turned on the police...* ◆ **turn on something** = depend on, hang on, rest on, hinge on, be decided by, balance on, be contingent on, pivot on ...*It all turns on what his real motives are...* ◆ **turn out 1** = prove to be, transpire, become apparent, happen, emerge, become known, develop, come to light, crop up (*informal*) ...*It turned out that I knew the person who got shot...* **2** = end up, happen, result, work out, evolve, come to be, come about, transpire, pan out (*informal*), eventuate ...*Things don't always turn out the way we expect...* **3** = come, be present, turn up, show up (*informal*), go, appear, attend, gather, assemble, put in an appearance ...*Thousands of people turned out for the funeral...* ◆ **turn over** = overturn, tip over, flip over, upend, be upset, reverse, capsize, keel over ...*The buggy turned over and she was thrown out...* ◆ **turn someone off** (*Informal*) = repel, bore, put someone off, disgust, offend, irritate, alienate, sicken, displease, nauseate, gross someone out (*U.S. slang*), disenchant, lose your interest ...*Aggressive men turn me off completely...* ◆ **turn someone on** (*Informal*) = arouse, attract, excite, thrill, stimulate, please, press someone's buttons (*slang*), work someone up, titillate, ring someone's bell (*U.S. slang*), arouse someone's desire ...*The body that turns men on doesn't have to be perfect...* ◆ **turn someone on to something** (*Slang*) = introduce to, show, expose, inform about, initiate into, get you started with ...*She turned me on to this really interesting website...* ◆ **turn someone out** = expel, drive out, evict, throw out, fire (*informal*), dismiss, sack (*informal*), axe (*informal*), discharge, oust, relegate, banish, deport, put out, cashier, unseat, dispossess, kick out (*informal*), cast out, drum out, show the door, turf out (*Brit. informal*), give someone the sack (*informal*), give someone the bum's rush (*slang*), kiss off (*slang, chiefly U.S. & Canad.*) ...*It was a monastery but the authorities turned all the monks out...* ◆ **turn something down 1** = refuse, decline, reject, spurn, rebuff, say no to, repudiate, abstain from, throw something out ...*I thanked him for the offer but turned it down...* **2** = lower, soften, reduce the volume of, mute, lessen, muffle, quieten, diminish ...*The police told the DJs to turn down the music...* ◆ **turn something in** = hand in, return, deliver, give back, give up, hand over, submit, surrender, tender ...*He told her to turn in her library books...* ◆ **turn something off** = switch off, turn out, put out, stop, kill, cut out, shut down, unplug, flick off ...*She had turned off the light to go to sleep...* ◆ **turn something on** = switch on, put on, activate, start, start up, ignite, kick-start, set in motion, energize

…Why haven't you turned the lights on?… ◆ **turn something out** 1 = <u>turn off</u>, put out, switch off, extinguish, disconnect, unplug, flick off *…I'll play till they come round to turn the lights out…* 2 = <u>produce</u>, make, process, finish, manufacture, assemble, put together, put out, bring out, fabricate, churn out *…They have been turning out great furniture for 400 years…* ◆ **turn something over** 1 = <u>flip over</u>, flick through, leaf through *…She was turning over the pages of the directory…* 2 = <u>consider</u>, think about, contemplate, ponder, reflect on, wonder about, mull over, think over, deliberate on, give thought to, ruminate about, revolve *…You could see her turning things over in her mind…* 3 = <u>hand over</u>, transfer, deliver, commit, give up, yield, surrender, pass on, render, assign, commend, give over *…The lawyer turned over the release papers…* 4 = <u>start up</u>, warm up, activate, switch on, crank, set something in motion, set something going, switch on the ignition of *…I squeezed into the seat and turned the engine over…* ◆ **turn something up** 1 = <u>find</u>, reveal, discover, expose, come up with, disclose, unearth, dig up, bring to light *…Investigations have never turned up any evidence…* 2 = <u>increase</u>, raise, boost, enhance, intensify, amplify, increase the volume of, make louder *…I turned the volume up…* ◆ **turn to someone** = <u>appeal to</u>, go to, approach, apply to, look to, resort to, have recourse to *…There was no one to turn to, no one to tell…* ◆ **turn up** 1 = <u>arrive</u>, come, appear, show up (*informal*), show (*informal*), attend, put in an appearance, show your face *…He turned up on Christmas Day with a friend…* 2 = <u>come to light</u>, be found, show up, pop up, materialize, appear *…The rare spoon turned up in an old house in Devon…*

turned out *or* **turned-out** = <u>dressed</u>, clothed, fitted out, attired, rigged out, apparelled (*archaic*), accoutred

turning = <u>turn-off</u>, turn, bend, curve, junction, crossroads, side road, exit

turning point = <u>crossroads</u>, critical moment, decisive moment, change, crisis, crux, moment of truth, point of no return, moment of decision, climacteric

turn-off *or* **turnoff** = <u>turning</u>, turn, branch, exit, side road

turnout = <u>attendance</u>, crowd, audience, gate, assembly, congregation, number, throng, assemblage

turnover 1 = <u>output</u>, business, production, flow, volume, yield, productivity, outturn (*rare*) *…The company had a turnover of £3.8 million…* 2 = <u>movement</u>, replacement, coming and going, change *…Short-term contracts increase staff turnover…*

turtle
➤ **reptiles**

tussle VERB = <u>fight</u>, battle, struggle, scrap (*informal*), contend, wrestle, vie, brawl, grapple, scuffle *…They ended up tussling with the security staff…* NOUN = <u>fight</u>, scrap (*informal*), brawl, scuffle, battle,

competition, struggle, conflict, contest, set-to (*informal*), bout, contention, fray, punch-up (*Brit. informal*), fracas, shindig (*informal*), scrimmage, shindy (*informal*), bagarre (*French*), biffo (*Austral. slang*) *…The referee booked him for a tussle with the goalie…*

tutelage (*Formal*) = <u>guidance</u>, education, instruction, preparation, schooling, charge, care, teaching, protection, custody, tuition, dependence, patronage, guardianship, wardship

tutor NOUN = <u>teacher</u>, coach, instructor, educator, guide, governor, guardian, lecturer, guru, mentor, preceptor, master *or* mistress, schoolmaster *or* schoolmistress *…He surprised his tutors by failing the exam…* VERB = <u>teach</u>, educate, school, train, coach, guide, discipline, lecture, drill, instruct, edify, direct *…She was at home, being tutored with her brothers…*

tutorial NOUN = <u>seminar</u>, lesson, individual instruction *…Methods of study include lectures, tutorials and practical work…* ADJECTIVE = <u>teaching</u>, coaching, guiding, instructional *…Students may seek tutorial guidance…*

TV = <u>television</u>, telly (*Brit. informal*), the box (*Brit. informal*), receiver, the tube (*slang*), television set, TV set, small screen (*informal*), gogglebox (*Brit. slang*), idiot box (*slang*)

twaddle = <u>nonsense</u>, rubbish, rot, garbage (*informal*), pants (*slang*), gossip, crap (*slang*), trash (*slang*), hot air (*informal*), tosh (*slang, chiefly Brit.*), waffle (*informal, chiefly Brit.*), pap, bilge (*informal*), drivel, tripe (*informal*), guff (*slang*), tattle, moonshine, verbiage, gabble, claptrap (*informal*), gobbledegook (*informal*), hogwash, hokum (*slang, chiefly U.S. & Canad.*), rigmarole, blather, piffle (*informal*), poppycock (*informal*), inanity, balderdash, bosh (*informal*), eyewash (*informal*), trumpery, tommyrot, foolish talk, horsefeathers (*U.S. slang*), bunkum *or* buncombe (*chiefly U.S.*), bizzo (*Austral. slang*), bull's wool (*Austral. & N.Z. slang*)

tweak VERB = <u>twist</u>, pull, pinch, jerk, squeeze, nip, twitch *…He tweaked my ear roughly…* NOUN = <u>twist</u>, pull, squeeze, pinch, jerk, nip, twitch *…a tweak on the ear…*

twee (*Informal*) 1 = <u>sweet</u>, pretty, cute, sentimental, quaint, dainty, cutesy (*informal, chiefly U.S.*), bijou, precious *…twee musical boxes shaped like cottages…* 2 = <u>sentimental</u>, over-sentimental, soppy (*Brit. informal*), mawkish, affected, precious *…Although twee at times, the script is well-constructed…*

twiddle = <u>fiddle with</u>, adjust, finger, play with, juggle, wiggle (*informal*), twirl, jiggle, monkey with (*informal*)

twig[1] = <u>branch</u>, stick, sprig, offshoot, shoot, spray, withe *…There was a slight sound of a twig breaking underfoot…*

twig[2] (*Brit. informal*) = <u>understand</u>, get, see, find out, grasp, make out, rumble (*Brit. informal*), catch on (*informal*), comprehend, fathom, tumble to (*informal*) *…By the time she'd twigged what it was all about, it* *was too late…*

twilight NOUN **1** = <u>dusk</u>, evening, sunset, early evening, nightfall, sundown, gloaming (*Scot. or poetic*), close of day, evo (*Austral. slang*) …*They returned at twilight and set off for the bar…* OPPOSITE dawn

2 = <u>half-light</u>, gloom, dimness, semi-darkness …*the deepening autumn twilight…*

3 = <u>decline</u>, last years, final years, closing years, autumn, downturn, ebb, last phase …*Now they are both in the twilight of their careers…* OPPOSITE height ADJECTIVE **1** = <u>evening</u>, dim, darkening, evo (*Austral. slang*) …*the summer twilight sky…*

2 = <u>declining</u>, last, final, dying, ebbing …*the twilight years of the Hapsburg Empire…*

twin NOUN = <u>double</u>, counterpart, mate, match, fellow, clone, duplicate, lookalike, likeness, ringer (*slang*), corollary …*the twin of the chair she had at the cottage…*
VERB = <u>pair</u>, match, join, couple, link, yoke …*The borough is twinned with Kasel in Germany…*
ADJECTIVE = <u>identical</u>, matched, matching, double, paired, parallel, corresponding, dual, duplicate, twofold, geminate …*the twin spires of the cathedral…*

twine NOUN = <u>string</u>, cord, yarn, strong thread …*a ball of twine…*
VERB **1** = <u>twist together</u>, weave, knit, braid, splice, interweave, plait, entwine, interlace, twist …*He twined his fingers into hers…*

2 = <u>coil</u>, wind, surround, bend, wrap, twist, curl, loop, spiral, meander, encircle, wreathe …*These strands of molecules twine around each other…*

twinge 1 = <u>pang</u>, twitch, tweak, throe (*rare*), twist …*I would have twinges of guilt occasionally…*

2 = <u>pain</u>, sharp pain, gripe, stab, bite, twist, stitch, pinch, throb, twitch, prick, spasm, tweak, tic …*the occasional twinge of indigestion…*

twinkle VERB = <u>sparkle</u>, flash, shine, glitter, gleam, blink, flicker, wink, shimmer, glint, glisten, scintillate, coruscate …*At night, lights twinkle in distant villages across the valleys…*
NOUN **1** = <u>sparkle</u>, light, flash, spark, shine, glittering, gleam, blink, flicker, wink, shimmer, glimmer, glistening, scintillation, coruscation …*a kindly twinkle came into his eyes…*

2 = <u>moment</u>, second, shake (*informal*), flash, instant, tick (*Brit. informal*), twinkling, split second, jiffy (*informal*), trice, two shakes of a lamb's tail (*informal*) …*Hours can pass in a twinkle…*

twinkling = <u>moment</u>, second, flash, instant, tick (*Brit. informal*), twinkle, split second, jiffy (*informal*), trice, two shakes of a lamb's tail (*informal*), shake (*informal*), bat of an eye (*informal*)

twirl VERB **1** = <u>twiddle</u>, turn, rotate, wind, spin, twist, revolve, whirl …*She twirled an empty glass in her fingers…*

2 = <u>turn</u>, whirl, wheel, spin, twist, pivot, gyrate, pirouette, turn on your heel …*Several hundred people twirl around the dance floor…*

NOUN = <u>turn</u>, spin, rotation, whirl, wheel, revolution, twist, pirouette, gyration …*with a twirl of his silver-handled cane…*

twist VERB **1** = <u>coil</u>, curl, wind, plait, wrap, screw, twirl …*She twisted her hair into a bun…*

2 = <u>intertwine</u>, wind, weave, braid, interweave, plait, entwine, twine, wreathe, interlace …*The fibres are twisted together during spinning…*

3 = <u>distort</u>, screw up, contort, mangle, mangulate (*Austral. slang*) …*The car was left a mess of twisted metal…* OPPOSITE straighten

4 = <u>sprain</u>, turn, rick, wrench …*He fell and twisted his ankle…*

5 = <u>misrepresent</u>, distort, misquote, alter, change, pervert, warp, falsify, garble …*It's a shame the way the media can twist your words…*

6 = <u>squirm</u>, wriggle, writhe …*He tried to twist out of my grasp…*
NOUN **1** = <u>surprise</u>, change, turn, development, revelation …*This little story has a twist in its tail…*

2 = <u>development</u>, emphasis, variation, slant …*The battle of the sexes took on a new twist…*

3 = <u>wind</u>, turn, spin, swivel, twirl …*The bag is resealed with a simple twist of the valve…*

4 = <u>coil</u>, roll, curl, hank, twine …*the bare bulb hanging from a twist of flex…*

5 = <u>curve</u>, turn, bend, loop, arc, kink, zigzag, convolution, dog-leg, undulation …*the twists and turns of the existing track…*

6 = <u>trait</u>, fault, defect, peculiarity, bent, characteristic, flaw, deviation, quirk, eccentricity, oddity, aberration, imperfection, kink, foible, idiosyncrasy, proclivity, crotchet …*If only she could alter this personality twist…*

7 = <u>sprain</u>, turn, pull, jerk, wrench …*A twist of the ankle denied him a place on the substitutes bench…*

twit (*Informal, chiefly Brit.*) = <u>fool</u>, idiot, jerk (*slang, chiefly U.S. & Canad.*), charlie (*Brit. informal*), dope (*informal*), clown, ass, plank (*Brit. slang*), berk (*Brit. slang*), wally (*slang*), prat (*slang*), plonker (*slang*), geek (*slang*), chump (*informal*), oaf, simpleton, airhead (*slang*), dipstick (*Brit. slang*), gonzo (*slang*), schmuck (*U.S. slang*), dork (*slang*), nitwit (*informal*), blockhead, ninny, divvy (*Brit. slang*), pillock (*Brit. slang*), halfwit, silly-billy (*informal*), nincompoop, dweeb (*U.S. slang*), putz (*U.S. slang*), weenie (*U.S. informal*), eejit (*Scot. & Irish*), dumb-ass (*slang*), numpty (*Scot. informal*), doofus (*slang, chiefly U.S.*), juggins (*Brit. informal*), dickwit (*slang*), nerd *or* nurd (*slang*), numbskull *or* numskull, twerp *or* twirp (*informal*), dorba *or* dorb (*Austral. slang*), bogan (*Austral. slang*)

twitch VERB **1** = <u>jerk</u>, blink, flutter, jump, squirm …*His left eyelid twitched involuntarily…*

2 = <u>pull (at)</u>, snatch (at), tug (at), pluck (at), yank (at) …*He twitched his curtains to check on callers…*
NOUN = <u>jerk</u>, tic, spasm, twinge, jump, blink, flutter, tremor …*He developed a nervous twitch…*

twitter VERB **1** = <u>chirrup</u>, whistle, chatter, trill, chirp, warble, cheep, tweet …*There were birds twittering in the trees…*

2 = <u>chatter</u>, chat, rabbit (on) (*Brit. informal*), gossip, babble, gab (*informal*), prattle, natter, jabber, blather, prate ...*They were twittering excitedly about their new dresses*...

NOUN = <u>chirrup</u>, call, song, cry, whistle, chatter, trill, chirp, warble, cheep, tweet ...*She would waken to the twitter of birds*...

two-faced = <u>hypocritical</u>, false, deceiving, treacherous, deceitful, untrustworthy, insincere, double-dealing, duplicitous, dissembling, perfidious, Janus-faced OPPOSITE honest

tycoon = <u>magnate</u>, capitalist, baron, industrialist, financier, fat cat (*slang, chiefly U.S.*), mogul, captain of industry, potentate, wealthy businessman, big cheese (*slang, old-fashioned*), plutocrat, big noise (*informal*), merchant prince

type 1 = <u>kind</u>, sort, class, variety, group, form, order, style, species, breed, strain, category, stamp, kidney, genre, classification, ilk, subdivision ...*There are various types of the disease*...

2 = <u>print</u>, printing, face, case, characters, font, fount ...*The correction has already been set in type*...

typhoon = <u>storm</u>, tornado, cyclone, tempest, squall, tropical storm

typical 1 = <u>archetypal</u>, standard, model, normal, classic, stock, essential, representative, usual, conventional, regular, characteristic, orthodox, indicative, illustrative, archetypical, stereotypical ...*such typical schoolgirl pastimes as horse-riding and reading*... OPPOSITE unusual

2 = <u>characteristic</u>, in keeping, in character, true to type ...*That's just typical of you, isn't it?*...

3 = <u>average</u>, normal, usual, conventional, routine, regular, orthodox, predictable, run-of-the-mill, bog-standard (*Brit. & Irish slang*) ...*not exactly your typical Sunday afternoon stroll*...

typify = <u>represent</u>, illustrate, sum up, characterize, embody, exemplify, personify, incarnate, epitomize

tyrannical = <u>oppressive</u>, cruel, authoritarian, dictatorial, severe, absolute, unreasonable, arbitrary, unjust, autocratic, inhuman, coercive, imperious, domineering, overbearing, magisterial, despotic, high-handed, peremptory, overweening, tyrannous OPPOSITE liberal

tyranny = <u>oppression</u>, cruelty, dictatorship, authoritarianism, reign of terror, despotism, autocracy, absolutism, coercion, high-handedness, harsh discipline, unreasonableness, imperiousness, peremptoriness OPPOSITE liberality

tyrant = <u>dictator</u>, bully, authoritarian, oppressor, despot, autocrat, absolutist, martinet, slave-driver, Hitler

tyro = <u>beginner</u>, novice, apprentice, learner, neophyte, rookie (*informal*), greenhorn (*informal*), catechumen

U u

ubiquitous = <u>ever-present</u>, pervasive, omnipresent, all-over, everywhere, universal

ugly 1 = <u>unattractive</u>, homely (*chiefly U.S.*), plain, unsightly, unlovely, unprepossessing, not much to look at, no oil painting (*informal*), ill-favoured, hard-featured, hard-favoured ...*She makes me feel dowdy and ugly*... OPPOSITE beautiful
2 = <u>unpleasant</u>, shocking, terrible, offensive, nasty, disgusting, revolting, obscene, hideous, monstrous, vile, distasteful, horrid, repulsive, frightful, objectionable, disagreeable, repugnant ...*an ugly scene*... OPPOSITE pleasant
3 = <u>bad-tempered</u>, nasty, sullen, surly, threatening, dangerous, angry, forbidding, menacing, sinister, ominous, malevolent, spiteful, baleful, bodeful ...*He's in an ugly mood today*... OPPOSITE good-natured

ulcer = <u>sore</u>, abscess, gathering, peptic ulcer, gumboil

ulterior = <u>hidden</u>, secret, concealed, personal, secondary, selfish, covert, undisclosed, unexpressed OPPOSITE obvious

ultimate ADJECTIVE 1 = <u>final</u>, eventual, conclusive, last, end, furthest, extreme, terminal, decisive ...*He said it is still not possible to predict the ultimate outcome*...
2 = <u>fundamental</u>, basic, primary, radical, elemental ...*the ultimate cause of what's happened*...
3 = <u>supreme</u>, highest, greatest, maximum, paramount, most significant, superlative, topmost ...*Of course the ultimate authority remained the presidency*...
4 = <u>worst</u>, greatest, utmost, extreme ...*Treachery was the ultimate sin*...
5 = <u>best</u>, greatest, supreme, optimum, quintessential ...*the ultimate luxury foods*...
NOUN = <u>epitome</u>, height, greatest, summit, peak, extreme, perfection, the last word ...*This hotel is the ultimate in luxury*...

ultimately 1 = <u>finally</u>, eventually, in the end, after all, at last, at the end of the day, sooner or later, in the fullness of time, in due time ...*a tough but ultimately worthwhile struggle*...
2 = <u>fundamentally</u>, essentially, basically, primarily, at heart, deep down ...*Ultimately, Bismarck's revisionism scarcely affected British interests*...

ultra-modern = <u>advanced</u>, progressive, avant-garde, futuristic, ahead of its time, modernistic, neoteric (*rare*)

umbrella 1 = <u>brolly</u> (*Brit. informal*), parasol, sunshade, gamp ...*Harry held an umbrella over Dawn*...
2 = <u>cover</u>, protection, guardianship, backing, support, charge, care, agency, responsibility, guidance, patronage, auspices, aegis, safe keeping, protectorship ...*under the moral umbrella of the United Nations*...

umpire NOUN = <u>referee</u>, judge, ref (*informal*), arbiter, arbitrator, moderator, adjudicator ...*The umpire's decision is final*...
VERB = <u>referee</u>, judge, adjudicate, arbitrate, call (*Sport*), moderate, mediate ...*He umpired for school football matches*...

umpteen (*Informal*) = <u>very many</u>, numerous, countless, millions, considerable, a good many, a thousand and one, ever so many

unable = <u>incapable</u>, inadequate, powerless, unfit, unfitted, not able, impotent, not up to, unqualified, ineffectual, not equal to OPPOSITE able

unaccountable 1 = <u>inexplicable</u>, mysterious, baffling, odd, strange, puzzling, peculiar, incomprehensible, inscrutable, unfathomable, unexplainable ...*He had an unaccountable change of mind*... OPPOSITE understandable
2 = <u>not answerable</u>, exempt, not responsible, free, unliable ...*Economic policy should not be run by an unaccountable committee*...

unaccustomed 1 = <u>unfamiliar</u>, unusual, unexpected, new, special, surprising, strange, remarkable, unprecedented, uncommon, out of the ordinary, unwonted ...*He comforted me with unaccustomed gentleness*... OPPOSITE familiar
2 with **to** = <u>not used to</u>, unfamiliar with, unused to, not given to, a newcomer to, a novice at, inexperienced at, unversed in, unpractised in ...*They were unaccustomed to such military setbacks*... OPPOSITE used to

unaffected[1] = <u>natural</u>, genuine, unpretentious, simple, plain, straightforward, naive, sincere, honest, unassuming, unspoilt, unsophisticated, dinkum (*Austral. & N.Z. informal*), artless, ingenuous, without airs, unstudied ...*this unaffected, charming couple*... OPPOSITE pretentious

unaffected[2] often with **by** = <u>impervious to</u>, unchanged, untouched, unimpressed, unmoved, unaltered, not influenced, unresponsive to, unstirred ...*She seemed totally unaffected by what she'd drunk*... OPPOSITE affected

unanimity = <u>agreement</u>, accord, consensus, concert, unity, harmony, chorus, unison, assent, concord, one mind, concurrence, like-mindedness OPPOSITE disagreement

unanimous 1 = <u>agreed</u>, united, in agreement, agreeing, at one, harmonious, like-minded, concordant, of one mind, of the same mind, in complete accord ...*Editors were unanimous in their condemnation of the proposals*... OPPOSITE divided

2 = <u>united</u>, common, concerted, solid, consistent, harmonious, undivided, congruent, concordant, unopposed ...*the unanimous vote for Hungarian membership...* OPPOSITE> split

unanimously = <u>without exception</u>, by common consent, without opposition, with one accord, unitedly, nem. con.

unarmed = <u>defenceless</u>, helpless, unprotected, without arms, unarmoured, weaponless OPPOSITE> armed

unassailable 1 = <u>undeniable</u>, indisputable, irrefutable, sound, proven, positive, absolute, conclusive, incontrovertible, incontestable ...*His legal position is unassailable...* OPPOSITE> doubtful
2 = <u>invincible</u>, impregnable, invulnerable, secure, well-defended ...*Liverpool football club are still looking unassailable...*

unassuming = <u>modest</u>, quiet, humble, meek, simple, reserved, retiring, unpretentious, unobtrusive, self-effacing, diffident, unassertive, unostentatious OPPOSITE> conceited

unattached 1 = <u>single</u>, available, unmarried, on your own, by yourself, a free agent, not spoken for, left on the shelf, footloose and fancy-free, unengaged ...*Those who are unattached may find that a potential mate is very close...*
2 *often with* **to** = <u>independent (from)</u>, unaffiliated (to), nonaligned (to), free (from), autonomous (from), uncommitted (to) ...*There's one nursery which is unattached to any school...* OPPOSITE> attached (to)

unavoidable = <u>inevitable</u>, inescapable, inexorable, sure, certain, necessary, fated, compulsory, obligatory, bound to happen, ineluctable

unaware = <u>ignorant</u>, unconscious, oblivious, in the dark (*informal*), unsuspecting, uninformed, unknowing, heedless, unenlightened, unmindful, not in the loop (*informal*), incognizant OPPOSITE> aware

unawares 1 = <u>by surprise</u>, unprepared, off guard, suddenly, unexpectedly, abruptly, aback, without warning, on the hop (*Brit. informal*), caught napping ...*The suspect was taken unawares...* OPPOSITE> prepared
2 = <u>unknowingly</u>, unwittingly, unconsciously ...*They were entertaining an angel unawares...* OPPOSITE> knowingly

unbalanced 1 = <u>deranged</u>, disturbed, unstable, touched, mad, crazy, barking (*slang*), eccentric, insane, irrational, erratic, lunatic, demented, unsound, unhinged, loopy (*informal*), out to lunch (*informal*), barking mad (*slang*), gonzo (*slang*), not all there, doolally (*slang*), off your trolley (*slang*), up the pole (*informal*), non compos mentis (*Latin*), not the full shilling (*informal*), wacko *or* whacko (*informal*), off the air (*Austral. slang*) ...*He was shown to be mentally unbalanced...*
2 = <u>biased</u>, one-sided, prejudiced, unfair, partial, partisan, unjust, inequitable ...*unbalanced and unfair reporting...*
3 = <u>irregular</u>, not balanced, lacking ...*unbalanced and uncontrolled diets...*
4 = <u>shaky</u>, unstable, wobbly ...*The Logan Air BAe 46 was noticeably unbalanced...* OPPOSITE> stable

unbearable = <u>intolerable</u>, insufferable, unendurable, too much (*informal*), unacceptable, oppressive, insupportable OPPOSITE> tolerable

unbeatable 1 = <u>unsurpassed</u>, matchless, unsurpassable ...*These resorts remain unbeatable in terms of price...*
2 = <u>invincible</u>, unstoppable, indomitable, unconquerable ...*The opposition was unbeatable...*

unbeaten = <u>undefeated</u>, winning, triumphant, victorious, unsurpassed, unbowed, unvanquished, unsubdued

unbelievable 1 = <u>wonderful</u>, excellent, superb, fantastic (*informal*), mean (*slang*), great (*informal*), topping (*Brit. slang*), bad (*slang*), cracking (*Brit. informal*), crucial (*slang*), smashing (*informal*), magnificent, fabulous (*informal*), divine (*informal*), glorious, terrific (*informal*), splendid, sensational (*informal*), mega (*slang*), sovereign, awesome (*slang*), colossal, super (*informal*), wicked (*informal*), def (*slang*), brill (*informal*), stupendous, bodacious (*slang, chiefly U.S.*), boffo (*slang*), jim-dandy (*slang*), chillin' (*U.S. slang*), booshit (*Austral. slang*), exo (*Austral. slang*), sik (*Austral. slang*) ...*His guitar solos are just unbelievable...* OPPOSITE> terrible
2 = <u>incredible</u>, impossible, unthinkable, astonishing, staggering, questionable, improbable, inconceivable, preposterous, unconvincing, unimaginable, outlandish, far-fetched, implausible, beyond belief, jaw-dropping, cock-and-bull (*informal*) ...*I find it unbelievable that people can accept this sort of behaviour...* OPPOSITE> believable

unbeliever = <u>atheist</u>, sceptic, disbeliever, agnostic, infidel, doubting Thomas

unborn = <u>expected</u>, awaited, embryonic, in utero (*Latin*)

unbridled = <u>unrestrained</u>, uncontrolled, unchecked, violent, excessive, rampant, unruly, full-on (*informal*), wanton, riotous, intemperate, ungovernable, unconstrained, licentious, ungoverned, uncurbed

unbroken 1 = <u>intact</u>, whole, undamaged, complete, total, entire, solid, untouched, unscathed, unspoiled, unimpaired ...*Against all odds her glasses remained unbroken after the explosion...* OPPOSITE> broken
2 = <u>continuous</u>, uninterrupted, constant, successive, endless, progressive, incessant, ceaseless, unremitting ...*The ruling party has governed the country for an unbroken thirty years...* OPPOSITE> interrupted
3 = <u>undisturbed</u>, uninterrupted, sound, fast, deep, profound, untroubled, unruffled ...*We maintained an almost unbroken silence...*
4 = <u>untamed</u>, wild, undomesticated ...*The car plunged like an unbroken horse...*

unburden VERB **1** = <u>reveal</u>, confide, disclose, lay bare, unbosom ...*He had to unburden his soul to somebody...*
2 = <u>unload</u>, relieve, discharge, lighten, disencumber,

disburden, ease the load of …*The human touch is one of the surest ways of unburdening stresses…*

PHRASES **unburden yourself** = <u>confess</u>, come clean about (*informal*), get something off your chest (*informal*), tell all about, empty yourself, spill your guts about (*slang*), make a clean breast of something …*Many came to unburden themselves of emotional problems…*

uncanny 1 = <u>weird</u>, strange, mysterious, queer, unearthly, eerie, supernatural, unnatural, spooky (*informal*), creepy (*informal*), eldritch (*poetic*), preternatural …*I had this uncanny feeling that Alice was warning me…*
2 = <u>extraordinary</u>, remarkable, incredible, unusual, fantastic, astonishing, exceptional, astounding, singular, miraculous, unheard-of, prodigious …*The hero bears an uncanny resemblance to Kirk Douglas…*

uncertain 1 = <u>unsure</u>, undecided, at a loss, vague, unclear, doubtful, dubious, ambivalent, hazy, hesitant, vacillating, in two minds, undetermined, irresolute …*He stopped, uncertain how to put the question tactfully…* OPPOSITE> sure
2 = <u>doubtful</u>, undetermined, unpredictable, insecure, questionable, ambiguous, unreliable, precarious, indefinite, indeterminate, incalculable, iffy (*informal*), changeable, indistinct, chancy, unforeseeable, unsettled, unresolved, in the balance, unconfirmed, up in the air, unfixed, conjectural …*Students all over the country are facing an uncertain future…* OPPOSITE> decided

uncertainty 1 = <u>unpredictability</u>, precariousness, state of suspense, ambiguity, unreliability, fickleness, inconclusiveness, chanciness, changeableness …*a period of political uncertainty…* OPPOSITE> predictability
2 = <u>doubt</u>, confusion, dilemma, misgiving, qualm, bewilderment, quandary, puzzlement, perplexity, mystification …*The magazine ignores all the uncertainties males currently face…* OPPOSITE> confidence
3 = <u>hesitancy</u>, hesitation, indecision, lack of confidence, vagueness, irresolution …*There was a hint of uncertainty in his voice…*

uncharted = <u>unexplored</u>, unknown, undiscovered, strange, virgin, unfamiliar, unplumbed, not mapped

Word Power

uncharted – *Unchartered* is sometimes mistakenly used where *uncharted* is meant: *We did not want to pioneer in completely uncharted* (not *unchartered*) *territory.*

unclean 1 = <u>dirty</u>, soiled, foul, contaminated, polluted, nasty, filthy, defiled, impure, scuzzy (*slang, chiefly U.S.*) …*By bathing in unclean water, they expose themselves to contamination…* OPPOSITE> clean
2 = <u>immoral</u>, corrupt, impure, evil, dirty, nasty, foul, polluted, filthy, scuzzy (*slang, chiefly U.S.*) …*unclean thoughts…*

uncomfortable 1 = <u>uneasy</u>, troubled, disturbed, embarrassed, distressed, awkward, out of place, self-conscious, disquieted, ill at ease, discomfited, like a fish out of water …*The request for money made them feel uncomfortable…* OPPOSITE> comfortable
2 = <u>painful</u>, awkward, irritating, hard, rough, troublesome, disagreeable, causing discomfort …*Wigs are hot and uncomfortable to wear constantly…*

uncommitted = <u>undecided</u>, uninvolved, nonpartisan, nonaligned, free, floating, neutral, not involved, unattached, free-floating, (sitting) on the fence

uncommon 1 = <u>rare</u>, unusual, odd, novel, strange, bizarre, curious, peculiar, unfamiliar, scarce, queer, singular, few and far between, out of the ordinary, infrequent, thin on the ground …*Cancer of the breast in young women is uncommon…* OPPOSITE> common
2 = <u>extraordinary</u>, rare, remarkable, special, outstanding, superior, distinctive, exceptional, unprecedented, notable, singular, unparalleled, noteworthy, inimitable, incomparable …*Both are blessed with an uncommon ability to fix things…* OPPOSITE> ordinary

uncommonly 1 = <u>exceptionally</u>, very, extremely, remarkably, particularly, strangely, seriously (*informal*), unusually, peculiarly, to the nth degree …*Mary was uncommonly good at tennis…*
2 (always used in a negative construction) = <u>rarely</u>, occasionally, seldom, not often, infrequently, hardly ever, only now and then, scarcely ever …*Not uncommonly, family strains may remain hidden behind complaints…*

uncompromising = <u>inflexible</u>, strict, rigid, decided, firm, tough, stubborn, hardline, die-hard, inexorable, steadfast, unyielding, obstinate, intransigent, unbending, obdurate, stiff-necked

unconcerned = <u>untroubled</u>, relaxed, unperturbed, nonchalant, easy, careless, not bothered, serene, callous, carefree, unruffled, blithe, insouciant, unworried, not giving a toss (*informal*) OPPOSITE> concerned

unconditional = <u>absolute</u>, full, complete, total, positive, entire, utter, explicit, outright, unlimited, downright, unqualified, unrestricted, out-and-out, plenary, categorical, unreserved OPPOSITE> qualified

unconscious 1 = <u>senseless</u>, knocked out, out cold (*informal*), out, stunned, numb, dazed, blacked out (*informal*), in a coma, comatose, stupefied, asleep, out for the count (*informal*), insensible, dead to the world (*informal*) …*By the time ambulancemen arrived he was unconscious…* OPPOSITE> awake
2 = <u>unaware</u>, ignorant, oblivious, unsuspecting, lost to, blind to, in ignorance, unknowing …*Mr Battersby was apparently quite unconscious of their presence…* OPPOSITE> aware
3 = <u>unintentional</u>, unwitting, unintended, inadvertent, accidental, unpremeditated …*'You're well out of it,' he said with unconscious brutality…*

OPPOSITE> intentional

4 = <u>subconscious</u>, automatic, suppressed, repressed, inherent, reflex, instinctive, innate, involuntary, latent, subliminal, unrealized, gut (*informal*) ...*an unconscious desire expressed solely during sleep...*

unconventional 1 = <u>unusual</u>, unorthodox, odd, eccentric, different, individual, original, bizarre, way-out (*informal*), informal, irregular, bohemian, far-out (*slang*), idiosyncratic, off-the-wall (*slang*), oddball (*informal*), individualistic, out of the ordinary, offbeat, left-field (*informal*), freakish, atypical, nonconformist, wacko (*slang*), outré, uncustomary ...*He was known for his unconventional behaviour...* OPPOSITE> conventional

2 = <u>unorthodox</u>, original, unusual, irregular, atypical, different, uncustomary ...*The vaccine had been produced by an unconventional technique...* OPPOSITE> normal

uncover 1 = <u>reveal</u>, find, discover, expose, encounter, turn up, detect, disclose, unveil, come across, unearth, dig up, divulge, chance on, root out, unmask, lay bare, make known, blow the whistle on (*informal*), bring to light, smoke out, take the wraps off, blow wide open (*slang*), stumble on *or* across ...*Auditors said they had uncovered evidence of fraud...* OPPOSITE> conceal

2 = <u>open</u>, unveil, unwrap, show, strip, expose, bare, lay bare, lift the lid, lay open ...*When the seedlings sprout, uncover the tray...*

undaunted = <u>undeterred</u>, unflinching, not discouraged, not put off, brave, bold, courageous, gritty, fearless, resolute, gallant, intrepid, steadfast, indomitable, dauntless, undismayed, unfaltering, nothing daunted, undiscouraged, unshrinking

undecided 1 = <u>unsure</u>, uncertain, uncommitted, torn, doubtful, dubious, wavering, hesitant, ambivalent, dithering (*chiefly Brit.*), in two minds, irresolute, swithering (*Scot.*) ...*She was still undecided as to what career she wanted to pursue...* OPPOSITE> sure

2 = <u>unsettled</u>, open, undetermined, vague, pending, tentative, in the balance, indefinite, debatable, up in the air, moot, iffy (*informal*), unconcluded ...*The release date for his record is still undecided...* OPPOSITE> settled

undeniable = <u>certain</u>, evident, undoubted, incontrovertible, clear, sure, sound, proven, obvious, patent, manifest, beyond (a) doubt, unassailable, indisputable, irrefutable, unquestionable, beyond question, incontestable, indubitable OPPOSITE> doubtful

under PREPOSITION **1** = <u>below</u>, beneath, underneath, on the bottom of ...*A path runs under the trees...* OPPOSITE> over

2 = <u>subordinate to</u>, subject to, reporting to, directed by, governed by, inferior to, secondary to, subservient to, junior to ...*I am the new manager and you will be working under me...*

3 = <u>included in</u>, belonging to, subsumed under, comprised in ...*under section 4 of the Family Law Reform Act...*

ADVERB = <u>below</u>, down, beneath, downward, to the bottom ...*A hand came from behind and pushed his head under...* OPPOSITE> up

(Related Words)
prefix: sub-

undercover = <u>secret</u>, covert, clandestine, private, hidden, intelligence, underground, spy, concealed, confidential, hush-hush (*informal*), surreptitious OPPOSITE> open

undercurrent 1 = <u>undertone</u>, feeling, atmosphere, sense, suggestion, trend, hint, flavour, tendency, drift, murmur, tenor, aura, tinge, vibes (*slang*), vibrations, overtone, hidden feeling ...*a deep undercurrent of racism in British society...*

2 = <u>undertow</u>, tideway, riptide, rip, rip current, crosscurrent, underflow ...*He tried to swim after him but the strong undercurrent swept them apart...*

undercut = <u>underprice</u>, sell cheaply, sell at a loss, undersell, sacrifice, undercharge

underdog = <u>weaker party</u>, victim, loser, little fellow (*informal*), outsider, fall guy (*informal*)

underestimate 1 = <u>undervalue</u>, understate, underrate, diminish, play down, minimize, downgrade, miscalculate, trivialize, rate too low, underemphasize, hold cheap, misprize ...*Never underestimate what you can learn from a group of like-minded people...* OPPOSITE> overestimate

2 = <u>underrate</u>, undervalue, belittle, sell short (*informal*), not do justice to, rate too low, set no store by, hold cheap, think too little of ...*The first lesson I learnt was never to underestimate the enemy...* OPPOSITE> overrate

Word Power

underestimate – *Underestimate* is sometimes wrongly used where *overestimate* is meant: *the importance of his work cannot be overestimated* (not *cannot be underestimated*).

undergo = <u>experience</u>, go through, be subjected to, stand, suffer, bear, weather, sustain, endure, withstand, submit to

underground ADJECTIVE **1** = <u>subterranean</u>, basement, lower-level, sunken, covered, buried, below the surface, below ground, subterrestrial ...*a run-down shopping area with an underground car park...*

2 = <u>secret</u>, undercover, covert, hidden, guerrilla, revolutionary, concealed, confidential, dissident, closet, subversive, clandestine, renegade, insurgent, hush-hush (*informal*), surreptitious, cloak-and-dagger, hugger-mugger, insurrectionist, hole-and-corner, radical ...*accused of organising and financing an underground youth movement...*

PHRASES **the underground 1** = <u>the tube</u> (*Brit.*), the subway, the metro ...*The underground is ideal for getting to work in Milan...* **2** = <u>the Resistance</u>, partisans, freedom fighters, the Maquis ...*US dollars were smuggled into the country to aid the* *underground…*

undergrowth = <u>scrub</u>, brush, underwood, bracken, brambles, briars, underbrush, brushwood, underbush

underhand = <u>sly</u>, secret, crooked (*informal*), devious, sneaky, secretive, fraudulent, treacherous, dishonest, deceptive, clandestine, unscrupulous, crafty, unethical, furtive, deceitful, surreptitious, stealthy, dishonourable, below the belt (*informal*), underhanded OPPOSITE honest

underline 1 = <u>emphasize</u>, stress, highlight, bring home, accentuate, point up, give emphasis to, call *or* draw attention to …*The report underlined his concern that standards were at risk*… OPPOSITE minimize
2 = <u>underscore</u>, mark, italicize, rule a line under …*Take two pens and underline the positive and negative words…*

underling (*Derogatory*) = <u>subordinate</u>, inferior, minion, servant, slave, cohort (*chiefly U.S.*), retainer, menial, nonentity, lackey, hireling, flunky, understrapper

underlying 1 = <u>fundamental</u>, basic, essential, root, prime, primary, radical, elementary, intrinsic, basal …*To stop a problem you have to understand its underlying causes…*
2 = <u>hidden</u>, concealed, lurking, veiled, latent …*hills with the hard underlying rock poking through the turf…*

undermine = <u>weaken</u>, sabotage, subvert, compromise, disable, debilitate OPPOSITE reinforce

underpinning = <u>support</u>, base, foundation, footing, groundwork, substructure

underprivileged = <u>disadvantaged</u>, poor, deprived, in need, impoverished, needy, badly off, destitute, in want, on the breadline

underrate = <u>underestimate</u>, discount, undervalue, belittle, disparage, fail to appreciate, not do justice to, set (too) little store by, misprize OPPOSITE overestimate

understand 1 = <u>comprehend</u>, get, take in, perceive, grasp, know, see, follow, realize, recognize, appreciate, be aware of, penetrate, make out, discern, twig (*Brit. informal*), fathom, savvy (*slang*), apprehend, conceive of, suss (*Brit. informal*), get to the bottom of, get the hang of (*informal*), tumble to (*informal*), catch on to (*informal*), cotton on to (*informal*), make head or tail of (*informal*), get your head round …*I think you understand my meaning…*
2 = <u>sympathize with</u>, appreciate, be aware of, be able to see, take on board (*informal*), empathize with, commiserate with, show compassion for …*Trish had not exactly understood his feelings…*
3 = <u>believe</u>, hear, learn, gather, think, see, suppose, notice, assume, take it, conclude, fancy, presume, be informed, infer, surmise, hear tell, draw the inference …*I understand you've heard about David…*

understandable = <u>reasonable</u>, natural, normal, justified, expected, inevitable, legitimate, logical, predictable, accountable, on the cards (*informal*), foreseeable, to be expected, justifiable, unsurprising, excusable, pardonable

understanding NOUN 1 = <u>perception</u>, knowledge, grasp, sense, know-how (*informal*), intelligence, judgment, awareness, appreciation, insight, skill, penetration, mastery, comprehension, familiarity with, discernment, proficiency …*They have to have a basic understanding of computers…* OPPOSITE ignorance
2 = <u>agreement</u>, deal, promise, arrangement, accord, contract, bond, pledge, bargain, pact, compact, concord, gentlemen's agreement …*We had not set a date but there was an understanding between us…* OPPOSITE disagreement
3 = <u>belief</u>, view, opinion, impression, interpretation, feeling, idea, conclusion, notion, conviction, judgment, assumption, point of view, perception, suspicion, viewpoint, hunch, way of thinking, estimation, supposition, sneaking suspicion, funny feeling …*It is my understanding that this has been going on for many years…*
ADJECTIVE = <u>sympathetic</u>, kind, compassionate, considerate, kindly, accepting, patient, sensitive, forgiving, discerning, tolerant, responsive, perceptive, forbearing …*Her boss, who was very understanding, gave her time off…* OPPOSITE unsympathetic

understood 1 = <u>assumed</u>, presumed, accepted, taken for granted …*The management is understood to be very unwilling to agree…*
2 = <u>implied</u>, implicit, unspoken, inferred, tacit, unstated …*The technical equality of all officers was understood…*

understudy = <u>stand-in</u>, reserve, substitute, double, sub, replacement, fill-in

undertake 1 = <u>take on</u>, embark on, set about, commence, try, begin, attempt, tackle, enter upon, endeavour to do …*She undertook the arduous task of monitoring the elections…*
2 = <u>agree</u>, promise, contract, guarantee, engage, pledge, covenant, commit yourself, take upon yourself …*He undertook to edit the text himself…*

undertaker = <u>funeral director</u>, mortician (*U.S.*)

undertaking 1 = <u>task</u>, business, operation, project, game, attempt, effort, affair, venture, enterprise, endeavour …*Organizing the show has been a massive undertaking…*
2 = <u>promise</u>, commitment, pledge, word, vow, assurance, word of honour, solemn word …*British Coal gave an undertaking that it was maintaining the pits…*

undertone 1 = <u>murmur</u>, whisper, low tone, subdued voice …*Well-dressed clients were talking in polite undertones as they ate…*
2 = <u>undercurrent</u>, suggestion, trace, hint, feeling, touch, atmosphere, flavour, tinge, vibes (*slang*) …*The sobbing voice had an undertone of anger…*

undervalue = <u>underrate</u>, underestimate, minimize, look down on, misjudge, depreciate, make light of, set no store by, hold cheap, misprize OPPOSITE overrate

underwater = <u>submerged</u>, submarine, immersed,

sunken, undersea, subaqueous, subaquatic

underway = <u>in progress</u>, going on, started, begun, in business, in motion, in operation, afoot

underwear = <u>underclothes</u>, lingerie, undies (*informal*), smalls (*informal*), undergarments, unmentionables (*humorous*), underclothing, underthings, underlinen, broekies (*S. African informal*), underdaks (*Austral. slang*)

underweight = <u>skinny</u>, puny, emaciated, undernourished, skin and bone (*informal*), undersized, half-starved, underfed

underworld 1 = <u>criminals</u>, gangsters, organized crime, gangland (*informal*), criminal element ...*a wealthy businessman with underworld connections...* 2 = <u>nether world</u>, hell, Hades, the inferno, nether regions, infernal region, abode of the dead ...*Persephone, goddess of the underworld...*

underwrite = <u>finance</u>, back, fund, guarantee, sponsor, insure, ratify, subsidize, bankroll (*U.S. informal*), provide security, provide capital for

undesirable = <u>unwanted</u>, unwelcome, disagreeable, objectionable, offensive, disliked, unacceptable, dreaded, unpopular, unsuitable, out of place, unattractive, distasteful, unsavoury, obnoxious, repugnant, unpleasing, unwished-for OPPOSITE: desirable

undo 1 = <u>open</u>, unfasten, loose, loosen, unlock, unwrap, untie, disengage, unbutton, disentangle, unstrap, unclasp ...*I managed to undo a corner of the parcel...* 2 = <u>reverse</u>, cancel, offset, wipe out, neutralize, invalidate, annul, nullify ...*It would be difficult to undo the damage that had been done...* 3 = <u>ruin</u>, defeat, destroy, wreck, shatter, upset, mar, undermine, overturn, quash, subvert, bring to naught ...*Their hopes of a victory were undone by a goal from John Barnes...*

undoing = <u>downfall</u>, weakness, curse, trouble, trial, misfortune, blight, affliction, the last straw, fatal flaw

undone[1] = <u>unfinished</u>, left, outstanding, not done, neglected, omitted, incomplete, passed over, unfulfilled, not completed, unperformed, unattended to ...*She left nothing undone that needed attention...* OPPOSITE: finished

undone[2] (*Literary*) = <u>ruined</u>, destroyed, overcome, hapless, forlorn, prostrate, wretched ...*He is undone by his lack of inner substance...*

undoubted = <u>certain</u>, sure, definite, confirmed, positive, obvious, acknowledged, patent, evident, manifest, transparent, clear-cut, undisputed, indisputable, unquestioned, unquestionable, incontrovertible, indubitable

undoubtedly = <u>certainly</u>, definitely, undeniably, surely, of course, doubtless, without doubt, unquestionably, unmistakably, assuredly, beyond question, beyond a shadow of (a) doubt

undress VERB = <u>strip</u>, strip naked, disrobe, take off your clothes, peel off, doff your clothes ...*She went out, leaving Rachel to undress and have her shower...* NOUN = <u>nakedness</u>, nudity, disarray, deshabille ...*Every cover showed a woman in a state of undress...*

undue = <u>excessive</u>, too much, inappropriate, extreme, unnecessary, extravagant, needless, unsuitable, improper, too great, disproportionate, unjustified, unwarranted, unseemly, inordinate, undeserved, intemperate, uncalled-for, overmuch, immoderate OPPOSITE: appropriate

undulate = <u>wave</u>, roll, surge, swell, ripple, rise and fall, billow, heave

unduly = <u>excessively</u>, overly, too much, unnecessarily, disproportionately, improperly, unreasonably, extravagantly, out of all proportion, inordinately, unjustifiably, overmuch, immoderately OPPOSITE: reasonably

undying = <u>eternal</u>, everlasting, perpetual, continuing, permanent, constant, perennial, infinite, unending, indestructible, undiminished, imperishable, deathless, inextinguishable, unfading, sempiternal (*literary*) OPPOSITE: short-lived

unearth 1 = <u>discover</u>, find, reveal, expose, turn up, uncover, bring to light, ferret out, root up ...*No evidence has yet been unearthed...* 2 = <u>dig up</u>, excavate, exhume, dredge up, disinter ...*Fossil hunters have unearthed the bones of an elephant...*

unearthly 1 = <u>eerie</u>, strange, supernatural, ghostly, weird, phantom, uncanny, spooky (*informal*), nightmarish, spectral, eldritch (*poetic*), preternatural ...*The sound was so serene that it seemed unearthly...* 2 = <u>unreasonable</u>, ridiculous, absurd, strange, extraordinary, abnormal, unholy (*informal*), ungodly (*informal*) ...*They arranged to meet at the unearthly hour of seven in the morning...*

uneasiness = <u>anxiety</u>, apprehension, misgiving, worry, doubt, alarm, suspicion, nervousness, disquiet, agitation, qualms, trepidation, perturbation, apprehensiveness, dubiety OPPOSITE: ease

uneasy 1 = <u>anxious</u>, worried, troubled, upset, wired (*slang*), nervous, disturbed, uncomfortable, unsettled, impatient, restless, agitated, apprehensive, edgy, jittery (*informal*), perturbed, on edge, ill at ease, restive, twitchy (*informal*), like a fish out of water, antsy (*informal*), discomposed ...*He looked uneasy and refused to answer questions...* OPPOSITE: relaxed 2 = <u>precarious</u>, strained, uncomfortable, tense, awkward, unstable, shaky, insecure, constrained ...*An uneasy calm has settled over Los Angeles...* 3 = <u>disturbing</u>, upsetting, disquieting, worrying, troubling, bothering, dismaying ...*This is an uneasy book...*

uneconomic = <u>unprofitable</u>, loss-making, non-profit-making, nonpaying, nonviable OPPOSITE: profitable

unemployed = <u>out of work</u>, redundant, laid off, jobless, idle, on the dole (*Brit. informal*), out of a job, workless, resting (*of an actor*) OPPOSITE: working

unequal 1 = <u>disproportionate</u>, uneven, unbalanced, unfair, irregular, unjust, inequitable, ill-matched ...*the unequal power relationships between men and women...*

2 = <u>different</u>, differing, dissimilar, unlike, varying, variable, disparate, unmatched, not uniform ...*These pipes appear to me to be all of unequal length...* OPPOSITE identical

3 *with* **to** = <u>not up to</u>, not qualified for, inadequate for, insufficient for, found wanting in, not cut out for (*informal*), incompetent at ...*Her critics say that she has proved unequal to the task...*

unequalled = <u>incomparable</u>, supreme, unparalleled, paramount, transcendent, unrivalled, second to none, pre-eminent, inimitable, unmatched, peerless, unsurpassed, matchless, beyond compare, without equal, nonpareil

unequivocal = <u>clear</u>, absolute, definite, certain, direct, straight, positive, plain, evident, black-and-white, decisive, explicit, manifest, clear-cut, unmistakable, unambiguous, cut-and-dried (*Informal*), Incontrovertible, indubitable, uncontestable OPPOSITE vague

unerring = <u>accurate</u>, sure, certain, perfect, exact, impeccable, faultless, infallible, unfailing

uneven **1** = <u>rough</u>, bumpy, not flat, not level, not smooth ...*He staggered on the uneven surface of the car park...* OPPOSITE level

2 = <u>irregular</u>, unsteady, fitful, variable, broken, fluctuating, patchy, intermittent, jerky, changeable, spasmodic, inconsistent ...*He could hear that her breathing was uneven...*

3 = <u>unequal</u>, unfair, one-sided, ill-matched ...*It was an uneven contest...*

4 = <u>lopsided</u>, unbalanced, asymmetrical, odd, out of true, not parallel ...*a flat head accentuated by a short, uneven crew-cut...*

uneventful = <u>humdrum</u>, ordinary, routine, quiet, boring, dull, commonplace, tedious, monotonous, unremarkable, uninteresting, unexciting, unexceptional, ho-hum (*informal*), unmemorable, unvaried OPPOSITE exciting

unexpected = <u>unforeseen</u>, surprising, unanticipated, chance, sudden, astonishing, startling, unpredictable, accidental, abrupt, out of the blue, unannounced, fortuitous, unheralded, unlooked-for, not bargained for OPPOSITE expected

unfailing **1** = <u>continuous</u>, endless, persistent, unlimited, continual, never-failing, boundless, bottomless, ceaseless, inexhaustible, unflagging ...*He continued to appear in the office with unfailing regularity...*

2 = <u>reliable</u>, constant, dependable, sure, true, certain, loyal, faithful, staunch, infallible, steadfast, tried and true ...*He had the unfailing care and support of Erica, his wife...* OPPOSITE unreliable

unfair **1** = <u>biased</u>, prejudiced, unjust, one-sided, partial, partisan, arbitrary, discriminatory, bigoted, inequitable ...*Some have been sentenced to long prison terms after unfair trials...*

2 = <u>unscrupulous</u>, crooked (*informal*), dishonest, unethical, wrongful, unprincipled, dishonourable, unsporting ...*nations involved in unfair trade practices...* OPPOSITE ethical

unfaithful **1** = <u>faithless</u>, untrue, two-timing (*informal*), adulterous, fickle, inconstant, unchaste ...*She was frequently left alone by her unfaithful husband...* OPPOSITE faithful

2 = <u>disloyal</u>, false, treacherous, deceitful, faithless, perfidious, traitorous, treasonable, false-hearted, recreant (*archaic*) ...*They denounced him as unfaithful to the traditions of the Society...* OPPOSITE loyal

unfamiliar **1** = <u>strange</u>, new, unknown, different, novel, unusual, curious, alien, out-of-the-way, uncommon, little known, unaccustomed, beyond your ken ...*She grew many plants that were unfamiliar to me...* OPPOSITE familiar

2 *with* **with** = <u>unacquainted with</u>, a stranger to, unaccustomed to, inexperienced in, uninformed about, unversed in, uninitiated in, unskilled at, unpractised in, unconversant with ...*She speaks no Japanese and is unfamiliar with Japanese culture...* OPPOSITE acquainted with

unfathomable **1** = <u>baffling</u>, incomprehensible, inexplicable, deep, profound, esoteric, impenetrable, unknowable, abstruse, indecipherable ...*How unfathomable and odd is life!...*

2 = <u>immeasurable</u>, bottomless, unmeasured, unplumbed, unsounded ...*Her eyes were black, unfathomable pools...*

unfavourable **1** = <u>adverse</u>, bad, unfortunate, disadvantageous, threatening, contrary, unlucky, ominous, untlmely, untoward, unpromising, unsuited, inauspicious, ill-suited, inopportune, unseasonable, unpropitious, infelicitous ...*Unfavourable economic conditions were blocking a recovery...*

2 = <u>hostile</u>, negative, unfriendly, inimical ...*First reactions have been distinctly unfavourable...* OPPOSITE positive

unfinished **1** = <u>incomplete</u>, uncompleted, half-done, lacking, undone, in the making, imperfect, unfulfilled, unaccomplished ...*Jane Austen's unfinished novel...*

2 = <u>natural</u>, rough, raw, bare, crude, unrefined, unvarnished, unpolished ...*unfinished wood ready for you to varnish or paint...* OPPOSITE polished

unfit **1** = <u>out of shape</u>, feeble, unhealthy, debilitated, flabby, decrepit, in poor condition, out of trim, out of kilter ...*Many children are so unfit they are unable to do basic exercises...* OPPOSITE healthy

2 = <u>incapable</u>, inadequate, incompetent, no good, useless, not up to, unprepared, ineligible, unqualified, untrained, ill-equipped, not equal, not cut out ...*They were utterly unfit to govern America...* OPPOSITE capable

3 = <u>unsuitable</u>, inadequate, inappropriate, useless, not fit, not designed, unsuited, ill-adapted ...*I can show them plenty of houses unfit for human habitation...* OPPOSITE suitable

unflappable (*Informal*) = <u>imperturbable</u>, cool, collected, calm, composed, level-headed, unfazed (*informal*), impassive, unruffled, self-possessed, not given to worry OPPOSITE> excitable

unflinching = <u>determined</u>, firm, steady, constant, bold, stalwart, staunch, resolute, steadfast, unwavering, immovable, unswerving, unshaken, unfaltering, unshrinking OPPOSITE> wavering

unfold 1 = <u>develop</u>, happen, progress, grow, emerge, occur, take place, expand, work out, mature, evolve, blossom, transpire, bear fruit ...*The outcome depends on conditions as well as how events unfold*...
2 = <u>reveal</u>, tell, present, show, describe, explain, illustrate, disclose, uncover, clarify, divulge, narrate, make known ...*Mr Wills unfolds his story with evident enjoyment*...
3 = <u>open</u>, spread out, undo, expand, flatten, straighten, stretch out, unfurl, unwrap, unroll ...*He quickly unfolded the blankets and spread them on the mattress*...

unfortunate 1 = <u>disastrous</u>, calamitous, inopportune, adverse, untimely, unfavourable, untoward, ruinous, ill-starred, infelicitous, ill-fated ...*Through some unfortunate accident, the information reached me a day late*... OPPOSITE> opportune
2 = <u>regrettable</u>, deplorable, lamentable, inappropriate, unsuitable, ill-advised, unbecoming ...*the unfortunate incident of the upside-down Canadian flag*... OPPOSITE> becoming
3 = <u>unlucky</u>, poor, unhappy, doomed, cursed, hopeless, unsuccessful, hapless, luckless, out of luck, wretched, star-crossed, unprosperous ...*charity days to raise money for unfortunate people*... OPPOSITE> fortunate

unfounded = <u>groundless</u>, false, unjustified, unproven, unsubstantiated, idle, fabricated, spurious, trumped up, baseless, without foundation, without basis OPPOSITE> justified

unfriendly 1 = <u>hostile</u>, cold, distant, sour, chilly, aloof, surly, antagonistic, disagreeable, quarrelsome, unsociable, ill-disposed, unneighbourly ...*She spoke in a loud, rather unfriendly voice*... OPPOSITE> friendly
2 = <u>unfavourable</u>, hostile, inhospitable, alien, inauspicious, inimical, uncongenial, unpropitious, unkind ...*We got an unfriendly reception from the hotel-owner*... OPPOSITE> congenial

ungainly = <u>awkward</u>, clumsy, inelegant, lumbering, slouching, gawky, uncouth, gangling, loutish, uncoordinated, ungraceful, lubberly, unco (*Austral. slang*) OPPOSITE> graceful

unguarded 1 = <u>unprotected</u>, vulnerable, defenceless, undefended, open to attack, unpatrolled ...*The U-boat entered in through a narrow unguarded eastern entrance*...
2 = <u>careless</u>, rash, unwary, foolhardy, thoughtless, indiscreet, unthinking, ill-considered, imprudent, heedless, incautious, undiplomatic, impolitic, uncircumspect ...*He was tricked by a reporter into an unguarded comment*... OPPOSITE> cautious

unhappiness 1 = <u>sadness</u>, depression, misery, gloom, sorrow, melancholy, heartache, despondency, blues, dejection, wretchedness, low spirits ...*There was a lot of unhappiness in my adolescence*...
2 = <u>discontent</u>, dissatisfaction, displeasure, uneasiness, vexation, discontentment ...*He has signalled his unhappiness with the government's decision*...

unhappy 1 = <u>sad</u>, depressed, miserable, down, low, blue, gloomy, melancholy, mournful, dejected, despondent, dispirited, downcast, long-faced, sorrowful, disconsolate, crestfallen, down in the dumps (*informal*) ...*Her marriage is in trouble and she is desperately unhappy*... OPPOSITE> happy
2 = <u>unlucky</u>, unfortunate, hapless, luckless, cursed, wretched, ill-omened, ill-fated ...*I have already informed your unhappy father of your expulsion*... OPPOSITE> fortunate
3 = <u>inappropriate</u>, awkward, clumsy, unsuitable, inept, ill-advised, tactless, ill-timed, injudicious, infelicitous, malapropos, untactful ...*The legislation represents in itself an unhappy compromise*... OPPOSITE> apt

unhealthy 1 = <u>harmful</u>, detrimental, unwholesome, noxious, deleterious, insanitary, noisome, insalubrious ...*the unhealthy environment of a coal mine*... OPPOSITE> beneficial
2 = <u>sick</u>, sickly, unwell, poorly (*informal*), weak, delicate, crook (*Austral. & N.Z. informal*), ailing, frail, feeble, invalid, unsound, infirm, in poor health ...*a poorly dressed, unhealthy looking fellow with a poor complexion*... OPPOSITE> well
3 = <u>weak</u>, unsound, ailing ...*a clear sign of an unhealthy economy*... OPPOSITE> strong
4 = <u>unwholesome</u>, morbid, bad, negative, corrupt, corrupting, degrading, undesirable, demoralizing, baneful (*archaic*) ...*an unhealthy obsession with secrecy*... OPPOSITE> wholesome

unheard-of 1 = <u>unprecedented</u>, inconceivable, undreamed of, new, novel, unique, unusual, unbelievable, singular, ground-breaking, never before encountered, unexampled ...*In those days, it was unheard-of for a woman to work after marriage*...
2 = <u>shocking</u>, extreme, outrageous, offensive, unacceptable, unthinkable, disgraceful, preposterous, outlandish ...*the unheard-of rate of a bottle of rum for $30*...
3 = <u>obscure</u>, unknown, undiscovered, unfamiliar, little known, unsung, unremarked, unregarded ...*an unheard-of comic waiting for his big break to come along*...

unhinge = <u>unbalance</u>, confuse, derange, disorder, unsettle, madden, craze, confound, distemper (*archaic*), dement, drive you out of your mind

unholy 1 (*Informal*) = <u>shocking</u>, awful, appalling, dreadful, outrageous, horrendous, unearthly, ungodly (*informal*) ...*The economy is still in an unholy mess*...
2 = <u>evil</u>, vile, wicked, base, corrupt, immoral, dishonest, sinful, heinous, depraved, profane, iniquitous, ungodly, irreligious ...*He screamed unholy

things at me... OPPOSITE> holy

unification = <u>union</u>, uniting, alliance, combination, coalition, merger, federation, confederation, fusion, amalgamation, coalescence

uniform NOUN 1 = <u>regalia</u>, suit, livery, colours, habit, regimentals ...*He was dressed in his uniform for parade...*
2 = <u>outfit</u>, dress, costume, attire, gear (*informal*), get-up (*informal*), ensemble, garb ...*Mark's is the uniform of the young male traveller...*
ADJECTIVE 1 = <u>consistent</u>, unvarying, similar, even, same, matching, regular, constant, equivalent, identical, homogeneous, unchanging, equable, undeviating ...*Chips should be cut into uniform size and thickness...* OPPOSITE> varying
2 = <u>alike</u>, similar, identical, like, same, equal, selfsame ...*Along each wall stretched uniform green metal filing cabinets...*

uniformity 1 = <u>regularity</u>, similarity, sameness, constancy, homogeneity, evenness, invariability ...*Caramel was used to maintain uniformity of color in the brandy...*
2 = <u>monotony</u>, sameness, tedium, dullness, flatness, drabness, lack of diversity ...*the dull uniformity of the houses...*

unify = <u>unite</u>, join, combine, merge, consolidate, bring together, fuse, confederate, amalgamate, federate OPPOSITE> divide

uninterested = <u>indifferent</u>, unconcerned, apathetic, bored, distant, listless, impassive, blasé, unresponsive, uninvolved, incurious OPPOSITE> concerned
▶ **disinterested**

union 1 = <u>joining</u>, uniting, unification, combination, coalition, merger, mixture, blend, merging, integration, conjunction, fusion, synthesis, amalgamating, amalgam, amalgamation ...*The Romanian majority in the province voted for union with Romania...*
2 = <u>alliance</u>, league, association, coalition, federation, confederation, confederacy, Bund ...*the question of which countries should join the currency union...*
3 = <u>marriage</u>, match, wedlock, matrimony ...*Even Louis began to think their union was not blessed...*
4 = <u>intercourse</u>, coupling, copulation, the other (*informal*), nookie (*slang*), coitus, rumpy-pumpy (*slang*), coition ...*the joys of sexual union...*

unique 1 = <u>distinct</u>, special, exclusive, peculiar, only, single, lone, solitary, one and only, sui generis ...*The area has its own unique language, Catalan...*
2 = <u>unparalleled</u>, unrivalled, incomparable, inimitable, unmatched, peerless, unequalled, matchless, without equal, nonpareil, unexampled ...*She was a woman of unique talent and determination...*

> ### *Word Power*
>
> **unique** – *Unique* with the meaning 'being the only one' or 'having no equal' describes an absolute state: *a case unique in British law*. In this use it cannot therefore be qualified; something is either *unique* or *not unique*. However, *unique* is also very commonly used in the sense of 'remarkable' or 'exceptional', particularly in the language of advertising, and in this meaning it can be used with qualifying words such as *rather*, *quite*, etc. Since many people object to this use, it is best avoided in formal and serious writing.

unit 1 = <u>entity</u>, whole, item, feature, piece, portion, module ...*Agriculture was based in the past on the family as a unit...*
2 = <u>section</u>, company, group, force, detail, division, cell, squad, crew, outfit, faction, corps, brigade, regiment, battalion, legion, contingent, squadron, garrison, detachment, platoon ...*a secret military unit...*
3 = <u>measure</u>, quantity, measurement ...*The liver can only burn up one unit of alcohol in an hour...*
4 = <u>part</u>, section, segment, class, element, component, constituent, tutorial ...*designed for teachers to plan a study unit on marine mammals...*

unite 1 = <u>join</u>, link, combine, couple, marry, wed, blend, incorporate, merge, consolidate, unify, fuse, amalgamate, coalesce, meld ...*They have agreed to unite their efforts to bring peace...* OPPOSITE> separate
2 = <u>cooperate</u>, ally, join forces, league, band, associate, pool, collaborate, confederate, pull together, join together, close ranks, club together ...*The two parties have been trying to unite since the New Year...* OPPOSITE> split

united 1 = <u>in agreement</u>, agreed, unanimous, one, like-minded, in accord, of like mind, of one mind, of the same opinion ...*Every party is united on the need for parliamentary democracy...*
2 = <u>combined</u>, leagued, allied, unified, pooled, concerted, collective, affiliated, in partnership, banded together ...*the first elections in a united Germany for fifty eight years...*

unity 1 = <u>union</u>, unification, coalition, federation, integration, confederation, amalgamation ...*the future of European economic unity...*
2 = <u>wholeness</u>, integrity, oneness, union, unification, entity, singleness, undividedness ...*The deer represents the unity of the universe...* OPPOSITE> disunity
3 = <u>agreement</u>, accord, consensus, peace, harmony, solidarity, unison, assent, unanimity, concord, concurrence ...*Speakers at the rally mouthed sentiments of unity...* OPPOSITE> disagreement

universal 1 = <u>widespread</u>, general, common, whole, total, entire, catholic, unlimited, ecumenical, omnipresent, all-embracing, overarching ...*proposals for universal health care...*
2 = <u>global</u>, worldwide, international, pandemic

...universal diseases...

> ## Word Power
>
> **universal** – The use of *more universal* as in *his writings have long been admired by fellow scientists, but his latest book should have more universal appeal* is acceptable in modern English usage.

universality = <u>comprehensiveness</u>, generalization, generality, totality, completeness, ubiquity, all-inclusiveness

universally = <u>without exception</u>, uniformly, everywhere, always, invariably, across the board, in all cases, in every instance

universe = <u>cosmos</u>, space, creation, everything, nature, heavens, the natural world, macrocosm, all existence

unjust = <u>unfair</u>, prejudiced, biased, wrong, one-sided, partial, partisan, unjustified, wrongful, undeserved, inequitable, unmerited OPPOSITE fair

unkempt 1 = <u>uncombed</u>, tousled, shaggy, ungroomed *...His hair was unkempt and filthy...*
2 = <u>untidy</u>, scruffy, dishevelled, disordered, messy, sloppy (*informal*), shabby, rumpled, bedraggled, slovenly, blowsy, sluttish, slatternly, disarranged, ungroomed, disarrayed, frowzy *...an unkempt old man...* OPPOSITE tidy

unkind = <u>cruel</u>, mean, nasty, spiteful, harsh, malicious, insensitive, unfriendly, inhuman, unsympathetic, uncaring, thoughtless, unfeeling, inconsiderate, uncharitable, unchristian, hardhearted OPPOSITE kind

unknown 1 = <u>strange</u>, new, undiscovered, uncharted, unexplored, virgin, remote, alien, exotic, outlandish, unmapped, untravelled, beyond your ken *...a perilous expedition, through unknown terrain...*
2 = <u>unidentified</u>, mysterious, anonymous, unnamed, nameless, incognito *...Unknown thieves had forced their way into the apartment...*
3 = <u>obscure</u>, little known, minor, humble, unfamiliar, insignificant, lowly, unimportant, unheard-of, unsung, inconsequential, undistinguished, unrenowned *...He was an unknown writer...* OPPOSITE famous

unleash = <u>release</u>, let go, let loose, free, untie, unloose, unbridle

unlike 1 = <u>different from</u>, dissimilar to, not resembling, far from, not like, distinct from, incompatible with, unrelated to, distant from, unequal to, far apart from, divergent from, not similar to, as different as chalk and cheese from (*informal*) *...She was unlike him in every way except her eyes...* OPPOSITE similar to
2 = <u>contrasted with</u>, not like, in contradiction to, in contrast with *or* to, as opposed to, differently from, opposite to *...Unlike aerobics, walking entails no expensive fees...*

unlikely 1 = <u>improbable</u>, doubtful, remote, slight, faint, not likely, unimaginable *...A military coup seems

unlikely...* OPPOSITE probable
2 = <u>unbelievable</u>, incredible, unconvincing, implausible, questionable, cock-and-bull (*informal*) *...I smiled sincerely, to encourage him to buy this unlikely story...* OPPOSITE believable

unlimited 1 = <u>infinite</u>, endless, countless, great, vast, extensive, immense, stellar (*informal*), limitless, boundless, incalculable, immeasurable, unbounded, illimitable *...An unlimited number of copies can be made from the original...* OPPOSITE finite
2 = <u>total</u>, full, complete, absolute, unconditional, unqualified, unfettered, unrestricted, all-encompassing, unconstrained *...You'll also have unlimited access to the swimming pool...* OPPOSITE restricted

unload 1 = <u>empty</u>, clear, unpack, dump, discharge, off-load, disburden, unlade *...Unload everything from the boot and clean it thoroughly...*
2 = <u>unburden</u>, relieve, lighten, disburden *...He unloaded the horse where the track dead-ended...*

unlock = <u>open</u>, undo, unfasten, release, unbolt, unlatch, unbar

unlucky 1 = <u>unfortunate</u>, unhappy, disastrous *...Argentina's unlucky defeat by Ireland...* OPPOSITE fortunate
2 = <u>ill-fated</u>, doomed, inauspicious, ominous, untimely, unfavourable, cursed, ill-starred, ill-omened *...13 was to prove an unlucky number...*

unmask = <u>reveal</u>, expose, uncover, discover, disclose, unveil, show up, lay bare, bring to light, uncloak

unmistakable = <u>clear</u>, certain, positive, decided, sure, obvious, plain, patent, evident, distinct, pronounced, glaring, manifest, blatant, conspicuous, palpable, unequivocal, unambiguous, indisputable OPPOSITE doubtful

unmitigated 1 = <u>unrelieved</u>, relentless, unalleviated, intense, harsh, grim, persistent, oppressive, unbroken, unqualified, unabated, undiminished, unmodified, unredeemed *...She leads a life of unmitigated misery...*
2 = <u>complete</u>, absolute, utter, perfect, rank, sheer, total, outright, thorough, downright, consummate, out-and-out, thoroughgoing, arrant, deep-dyed (*usually derogatory*) *...A senior policeman had called him an unmitigated liar...*

unnatural 1 = <u>abnormal</u>, odd, strange, unusual, extraordinary, bizarre, perverted, queer, irregular, perverse, supernatural, uncanny, outlandish, unaccountable, anomalous, freakish, aberrant *...The altered landscape looks unnatural and weird...* OPPOSITE normal
2 = <u>false</u>, forced, artificial, studied, laboured, affected, assumed, mannered, strained, stiff, theatrical, contrived, self-conscious, feigned, stilted, insincere, factitious, stagy, phoney *or* phony (*informal*) *...She gave him a bright, determined smile which seemed unnatural...* OPPOSITE genuine
3 = <u>inhuman</u>, evil, monstrous, wicked, savage, brutal, ruthless, callous, heartless, cold-blooded, fiendish,

unfeeling ...*Murder is an unnatural act...* OPPOSITE humane

unnecessary = <u>needless</u>, excessive, unwarranted, useless, pointless, not needed, redundant, wasteful, gratuitous, superfluous, wanton, expendable, surplus to requirements, uncalled-for, dispensable, unneeded, nonessential, inessential, unmerited, to no purpose, unrequired, supererogatory OPPOSITE essential

unnerve = <u>shake</u>, upset, disconcert, disturb, intimidate, frighten, rattle (*informal*), discourage, dismay, daunt, disarm, confound, fluster, faze, unman, demoralize, unhinge, psych out (*informal*), throw off balance, dishearten, dispirit OPPOSITE strengthen

unoccupied 1 = <u>empty</u>, vacant, uninhabited, untenanted, tenantless ...*The house was unoccupied at the time of the explosion...*
2 = <u>idle</u>, unemployed, inactive, disengaged, at leisure, at a loose end ...*Portraits of unoccupied youths and solitary females predominate...*

unofficial 1 = <u>unconfirmed</u>, off the record, unsubstantiated, private, personal, unauthorized, undocumented, uncorroborated ...*Unofficial estimates speak of at least two hundred dead...*
2 = <u>unauthorized</u>, informal, unsanctioned, casual, wildcat ...*Rail workers have voted to continue their unofficial strike...*

unparalleled = <u>unequalled</u>, exceptional, unprecedented, rare, unique, singular, consummate, superlative, unrivalled, incomparable, unmatched, peerless, unsurpassed, matchless, beyond compare, without equal

unpleasant 1 = <u>nasty</u>, bad, horrid, distressing, annoying, irritating, miserable, troublesome, distasteful, obnoxious, unpalatable, displeasing, repulsive, objectionable, disagreeable, abhorrent, irksome, unlovely, execrable ...*They tolerated what they felt was an unpleasant situation...* OPPOSITE nice
2 = <u>obnoxious</u>, disagreeable, vicious, malicious, rude, mean, cruel, poisonous, unattractive, unfriendly, vindictive, venomous, mean-spirited, inconsiderate, impolite, unloveable, ill-natured, unlikable *or* unlikeable ...*He was very unpleasant indeed...*
OPPOSITE likable *or* likeable

unpleasantness 1 = <u>hostility</u>, animosity, antagonism, bad feeling, malice, rudeness, offensiveness, abrasiveness, argumentativeness, unfriendliness, quarrelsomeness, ill humour *or* will ...*Most offices are riddled with sniping and general unpleasantness...* OPPOSITE friendliness
2 = <u>nastiness</u>, awfulness, grimness, trouble, misery, woe, ugliness, unacceptability, dreadfulness, disagreeableness, horridness ...*the unpleasantness of surgery and chemotherapy...* OPPOSITE pleasantness

unpopular = <u>disliked</u>, rejected, unwanted, avoided, shunned, unwelcome, undesirable, unattractive, detested, out of favour, unloved, out in the cold, cold-shouldered, not sought out, sent to Coventry (*Brit.*) OPPOSITE popular

unprecedented 1 = <u>unparalleled</u>, unheard-of, exceptional, new, original, novel, unusual, abnormal, singular, ground-breaking, unrivalled, freakish, unexampled ...*Such a move is unprecedented...*
2 = <u>extraordinary</u>, amazing, remarkable, outstanding, fantastic, marvellous, exceptional, phenomenal, uncommon ...*The scheme has been hailed as an unprecedented success...*

unprofessional 1 = <u>unethical</u>, unfitting, improper, lax, negligent, unworthy, unseemly, unprincipled ...*He was also fined $150 for unprofessional conduct...*
2 = <u>amateurish</u>, amateur, incompetent, inefficient, cowboy (*informal*), inexperienced, untrained, slapdash, slipshod, inexpert ...*He rubbished his team for another unprofessional performance...* OPPOSITE skilful

unqualified 1 = <u>unfit</u>, incapable, incompetent, not up to, unprepared, ineligible, ill-equipped, not equal to ...*She was unqualified for the job...*
2 = <u>unconditional</u>, complete, total, absolute, utter, outright, thorough, downright, consummate, unrestricted, out-and-out, categorical, unmitigated, unreserved, thoroughgoing, without reservation, arrant, deep-dyed (*usually derogatory*) ...*The event was an unqualified success...*

unquestionable = <u>certain</u>, undeniable, indisputable, clear, sure, perfect, absolute, patent, definite, manifest, unmistakable, conclusive, flawless, unequivocal, faultless, self-evident, irrefutable, incontrovertible, incontestable, indubitable, beyond a shadow of doubt OPPOSITE doubtful

unravel 1 = <u>solve</u>, explain, work out, resolve, interpret, figure out (*informal*), make out, clear up, suss (out) (*slang*), get to the bottom of, get straight, puzzle out ...*She wanted to unravel the mystery of her husband's disappearance...*
2 = <u>undo</u>, separate, disentangle, free, unwind, extricate, straighten out, untangle, unknot ...*He could unravel knots that others could not even attempt...*

unreadable 1 = <u>turgid</u>, heavy going, badly written, dry as dust ...*Most computer ads used to be unreadable...*
2 = <u>illegible</u>, undecipherable, crabbed ...*She scribbled an unreadable address on the receipt...*

unreal = <u>imaginary</u>, make-believe, illusory, fabulous, visionary, mythical, fanciful, fictitious, intangible, immaterial, storybook, insubstantial, nebulous, dreamlike, impalpable, chimerical, phantasmagoric

unreasonable 1 = <u>biased</u>, arbitrary, irrational, illogical, blinkered, opinionated, headstrong ...*The strikers were being unreasonable in their demands...* OPPOSITE open-minded
2 = <u>excessive</u>, steep (*informal*), exorbitant, unfair, absurd, extravagant, unjust, too great, undue, preposterous, unwarranted, far-fetched, extortionate, uncalled-for, immoderate ...*unreasonable increases in the price of petrol...* OPPOSITE moderate

unrelenting 1 = <u>merciless</u>, tough, ruthless, relentless, cruel, stern, inexorable, implacable, intransigent, remorseless, pitiless, unsparing ...*in the*

face of severe opposition and unrelenting criticism…
2 = <u>steady</u>, constant, continuous, endless, perpetual, continual, unbroken, incessant, unabated, ceaseless, unremitting, unwavering …*an unrelenting downpour of rain…*

unremitting = <u>constant</u>, continuous, relentless, perpetual, continual, unbroken, incessant, diligent, unabated, unwavering, indefatigable, remorseless, assiduous, unceasing, sedulous, unwearied

unrest = <u>discontent</u>, rebellion, dissatisfaction, protest, turmoil, upheaval, strife, agitation, discord, disaffection, sedition, tumult, dissension [OPPOSITE] peace

unrivalled = <u>unparalleled</u>, incomparable, unsurpassed, supreme, unmatched, peerless, unequalled, matchless, beyond compare, without equal, nonpareil, unexcelled

unruffled **1** = <u>calm</u>, cool, collected, peaceful, composed, serene, tranquil, sedate, placid, undisturbed, unmoved, unfazed (*informal*), unperturbed, unflustered …*Anne had remained unruffled, very cool and controlled…*
2 = <u>smooth</u>, even, level, flat, unbroken …*the unruffled surface of the pool…*

unruly = <u>uncontrollable</u>, wild, unmanageable, disorderly, turbulent, rebellious, wayward, rowdy, intractable, wilful, lawless, fractious, riotous, headstrong, mutinous, disobedient, ungovernable, refractory, obstreperous, insubordinate [OPPOSITE] manageable

unsafe = <u>dangerous</u>, risky, hazardous, threatening, uncertain, unstable, insecure, unreliable, precarious, treacherous, perilous, unsound [OPPOSITE] safe

unsavoury **1** = <u>unpleasant</u>, nasty, obnoxious, offensive, revolting, distasteful, repellent, repulsive, objectionable, repugnant …*The sport has long been associated with unsavoury characters…*
2 = <u>unappetizing</u>, unpalatable, distasteful, sickening, disagreeable, nauseating …*unsavoury school meals…*
[OPPOSITE] appetizing

unscathed = <u>unharmed</u>, unhurt, uninjured, whole, sound, safe, untouched, unmarked, in one piece, unscarred, unscratched

unscrupulous = <u>unprincipled</u>, corrupt, crooked (*informal*), ruthless, improper, immoral, dishonest, unethical, exploitative, dishonourable, roguish, unconscionable, knavish, conscienceless, unconscientious [OPPOSITE] honourable

unseat **1** = <u>depose</u>, overthrow, oust, remove, dismiss, discharge, displace, dethrone …*It is not clear who was behind the attempt to unseat the President…*
2 = <u>throw</u>, unsaddle, unhorse …*She was unseated on her first ride…*

unseemly = <u>improper</u>, inappropriate, unsuitable, out of place, undignified, disreputable, unbecoming, unrefined, out of keeping, discreditable, indelicate, in poor taste, indecorous, unbefitting [OPPOSITE] proper

unseen **1** = <u>unobserved</u>, undetected, unperceived,

lurking, unnoticed, unobtrusive …*I can now accept that there are unseen forces at work…*
2 = <u>hidden</u>, concealed, invisible, veiled, obscure …*playing computer games against unseen opponents…*

unselfish = <u>generous</u>, selfless, noble, kind, liberal, devoted, humanitarian, charitable, disinterested, altruistic, self-sacrificing, magnanimous, self-denying

unsettle = <u>disturb</u>, trouble, upset, throw (*informal*), bother, confuse, disorder, rattle (*informal*), agitate, ruffle, unnerve, disconcert, unbalance, fluster, perturb, faze, throw into confusion, throw off balance, discompose, throw into disorder, throw into uproar

unsettled **1** = <u>unstable</u>, shaky, insecure, disorderly, unsteady …*Britain's unsettled political scene also worries some investors…*
2 = <u>restless</u>, tense, uneasy, troubled, shaken, confused, wired (*slang*), disturbed, anxious, agitated, unnerved, flustered, perturbed, on edge, restive …*To tell the truth, I'm a bit unsettled tonight…*
3 = <u>unresolved</u>, undecided, undetermined, open, doubtful, debatable, up in the air, moot …*They were in the process of resolving all the unsettled issues…*
4 = <u>uninhabited</u>, unoccupied, unpopulated, unpeopled …*Until very recently Texas was an unsettled frontier…*
5 = <u>inconstant</u>, changing, unpredictable, variable, uncertain, changeable …*Despite the unsettled weather, we had a marvellous weekend…*
6 = <u>owing</u>, due, outstanding, pending, payable, in arrears …*Liabilities related to unsettled transactions are recorded…*

unsightly = <u>ugly</u>, unattractive, repulsive, unpleasant, revolting (*informal*), hideous, horrid, disagreeable, unprepossessing [OPPOSITE] attractive

unskilled = <u>unprofessional</u>, inexperienced, unqualified, untrained, uneducated, amateurish, cowboy (*informal*), untalented [OPPOSITE] skilled

unsophisticated **1** = <u>simple</u>, plain, uncomplicated, straightforward, unrefined, uninvolved, unspecialized, uncomplex …*music of a crude kind which unsophisticated audiences enjoyed…* [OPPOSITE] advanced
2 = <u>naive</u>, innocent, inexperienced, unworldly, unaffected, childlike, natural, artless, ingenuous, guileless …*She was quite unsophisticated in the ways of the world…*

unsound **1** = <u>flawed</u>, faulty, weak, false, shaky, unreliable, invalid, defective, illogical, erroneous, specious, fallacious, ill-founded …*The thinking is muddled and fundamentally unsound…*
2 = <u>unstable</u>, shaky, insecure, unsafe, unreliable, flimsy, wobbly, tottering, rickety, unsteady, not solid …*The church was structurally unsound…* [OPPOSITE] stable
3 = <u>unhealthy</u>, unstable, unbalanced, diseased, ill, weak, delicate, ailing, frail, defective, unwell, deranged, unhinged …*He was rejected as an army conscript as being of unsound mind…*

unspeakable = <u>dreadful</u>, shocking, appalling, evil, awful, overwhelming, horrible, unbelievable, monstrous, from hell (*informal*), inconceivable, unimaginable, repellent, abysmal, frightful, heinous, odious, indescribable, loathsome, abominable, ineffable, beyond words, execrable, unutterable, inexpressible, beyond description, hellacious (*U.S. slang*), too horrible for words

unstable 1 = <u>changeable</u>, volatile, unpredictable, variable, fluctuating, unsteady, fitful, inconstant ...*The situation is unstable and potentially dangerous...* OPPOSITE constant
2 = <u>insecure</u>, shaky, precarious, unsettled, wobbly, tottering, rickety, unsteady, not fixed ...*a house built on unstable foundations...*
3 = <u>unpredictable</u>, irrational, erratic, inconsistent, unreliable, temperamental, capricious, changeable, untrustworthy, vacillating ...*He was emotionally unstable...* OPPOSITE level-headed

unsteady 1 = <u>unstable</u>, shaky, insecure, unsafe, precarious, treacherous, rickety, infirm ...*a slightly unsteady item of furniture...*
2 = <u>reeling</u>, wobbly, tottering ...*The boy was unsteady, staggering around the room...*
3 = <u>erratic</u>, unpredictable, volatile, unsettled, wavering, unreliable, temperamental, changeable, vacillating, flighty, inconstant ...*She knew the impact an unsteady parent could have on a young girl...*

unsung = <u>unacknowledged</u>, unrecognized, unappreciated, unknown, neglected, anonymous, disregarded, unnamed, uncelebrated, unhonoured, unacclaimed, unhailed

unswerving = <u>firm</u>, staunch, steadfast, constant, true, direct, devoted, steady, dedicated, resolute, single-minded, unwavering, unflagging, untiring, unfaltering, undeviating

untangle 1 = <u>disentangle</u>, unravel, sort out, extricate, straighten out, untwist, unsnarl ...*trying to untangle several reels of film...* OPPOSITE entangle
2 = <u>solve</u>, clear up, straighten out, understand, explain, figure out (*informal*), clarify, unravel, fathom, get to the bottom of, elucidate, suss out (*informal*), puzzle out ...*Lawyers began trying to untangle the complex affairs of the bank...* OPPOSITE complicate

untenable = <u>unsustainable</u>, indefensible, unsound, groundless, weak, flawed, shaky, unreasonable, illogical, fallacious, insupportable OPPOSITE justified

unthinkable 1 = <u>impossible</u>, out of the question, inconceivable, unlikely, not on (*informal*), absurd, unreasonable, improbable, preposterous, illogical ...*Her strong Catholic beliefs made abortion unthinkable...*
2 = <u>inconceivable</u>, incredible, unbelievable, unimaginable, beyond belief, beyond the bounds of possibility ...*Monday's unthinkable tragedy...*

unthinking 1 = <u>thoughtless</u>, insensitive, tactless, rude, blundering, inconsiderate, undiplomatic ...*He doesn't say those silly things that unthinking people say...*

2 = <u>impulsive</u>, senseless, unconscious, mechanical, rash, careless, instinctive, oblivious, negligent, unwitting, witless, inadvertent, heedless, unmindful ...*Bruce was no unthinking vandal...* OPPOSITE deliberate

untidy 1 = <u>messy</u>, disordered, chaotic, littered, muddled, cluttered, jumbled, rumpled, shambolic, bedraggled, unkempt, topsy-turvy, higgledy-piggledy (*informal*), mussy (*U.S. informal*), muddly, disarrayed ...*Clothes were thrown in the luggage in an untidy heap...* OPPOSITE neat
2 = <u>unkempt</u>, dishevelled, tousled, disordered, messy, ruffled, scruffy, rumpled, bedraggled, ratty (*informal*), straggly, windblown, disarranged, mussed up (*informal*) ...*a thin man with untidy hair...*
3 = <u>sloppy</u>, messy (*informal*), slovenly, slipshod, slatternly ...*I'm untidy in most ways...* OPPOSITE methodical

untie = <u>undo</u>, free, release, loosen, unfasten, unbind, unstrap, unclasp, unlace, unknot, unmoor, unbridle

until

Word Power

until – The use of *until such time as* (as in *industrial action will continue until such time as our demands are met*) is unnecessary and should be avoided: *industrial action will continue until our demands are met*. The use of *up* before *until* is also redundant and should be avoided: *the talks will continue until* (not *up until*) *23rd March*.

---

untimely 1 = <u>early</u>, premature, before time, unseasonable ...*His mother's untimely death had a catastrophic effect on him...* OPPOSITE timely
2 = <u>ill-timed</u>, inappropriate, badly timed, inopportune, unfortunate, awkward, unsuitable, inconvenient, mistimed, inauspicious ...*Your readers would have seen the article as at best untimely...* OPPOSITE well-timed

untold 1 = <u>indescribable</u>, unthinkable, unimaginable, unspeakable, undreamed of, unutterable, inexpressible ...*This might do untold damage to her health...*
2 = <u>countless</u>, incalculable, innumerable, myriad, numberless, uncounted, uncountable, unnumbered, measureless ...*the glittering prospect of untold riches...*
3 = <u>undisclosed</u>, unknown, unrevealed, private, secret, hidden, unrelated, unpublished, unrecounted ...*the untold story of children's suffering...*

untoward = <u>unfavourable</u>, unfortunate, disastrous, adverse, contrary, annoying, awkward, irritating, unlucky, inconvenient, untimely, inauspicious, inimical, ill-timed, vexatious, inopportune

untrue 1 = <u>false</u>, lying, wrong, mistaken, misleading, incorrect, inaccurate, sham, dishonest, deceptive, spurious, erroneous, fallacious, untruthful ...*The allegations were completely untrue...* OPPOSITE true
2 = <u>unfaithful</u>, disloyal, deceitful, treacherous, two-

faced, faithless, false, untrustworthy, perfidious, forsworn, traitorous, inconstant …*untrue to the basic tenets of socialism*… OPPOSITE faithful

untruth 1 = <u>lie</u>, fabrication, falsehood, fib, story, tale, fiction, deceit, whopper (*informal*), porky (*Brit. slang*), pork pie (*Brit. slang*), falsification, prevarication …*The Authority accused estate agents of using blatant untruths*…
2 = <u>lying</u>, perjury, duplicity, falsity, mendacity, deceitfulness, untruthfulness, inveracity (*rare*), truthlessness …*I have never uttered one word of untruth*…

unused 1 = <u>new</u>, untouched, remaining, fresh, intact, immaculate, pristine …*unused containers of food and drink*…
2 = <u>remaining</u>, leftover, unconsumed, left, available, extra, unutilized …*Throw away any unused cream when it has reached the expiry date*…
3 *with* **to** = <u>unaccustomed to</u>, new to, unfamiliar with, not up to, not ready for, a stranger to, inexperienced in, unhabituated to …*Mother was entirely unused to such hard work*…

unusual 1 = <u>rare</u>, odd, strange, extraordinary, different, surprising, novel, bizarre, unexpected, curious, weird (*informal*), unfamiliar, abnormal, queer, phenomenal, uncommon, out of the ordinary, left-field (*informal*), unwonted …*rare and unusual plants*… OPPOSITE common
2 = <u>extraordinary</u>, unique, remarkable, exceptional, notable, phenomenal, uncommon, singular, unconventional, out of the ordinary, atypical …*He was an unusual man with great business talents*… OPPOSITE average

unveil = <u>reveal</u>, publish, launch, introduce, release, display, broadcast, demonstrate, expose, bare, parade, exhibit, disclose, uncover, bring out, make public, flaunt, divulge, lay bare, make known, bring to light, put on display, lay open, put on show, put on view OPPOSITE conceal

unwarranted = <u>unnecessary</u>, unjustified, indefensible, wrong, unreasonable, unjust, gratuitous, unprovoked, inexcusable, groundless, uncalled-for

unwary = <u>careless</u>, rash, reckless, hasty, thoughtless, unguarded, indiscreet, imprudent, heedless, incautious, uncircumspect, unwatchful OPPOSITE cautious

unwell = <u>ill</u>, poorly (*informal*), sick, crook (*Austral. & N.Z. informal*), ailing, unhealthy, sickly, out of sorts, off colour, under the weather (*informal*), in poor health, at death's door, indisposed, green about the gills OPPOSITE well

unwieldy 1 = <u>bulky</u>, massive, hefty, clumsy, weighty, ponderous, ungainly, clunky (*informal*) …*They came panting up to his door with their unwieldy baggage*…
2 = <u>awkward</u>, cumbersome, inconvenient, burdensome, unmanageable, unhandy …*His firm must contend with the unwieldy Russian bureaucracy*…

unwilling 1 = <u>disinclined</u>, reluctant, averse, loath, slow, opposed, resistant, not about, not in the mood,

indisposed …*Initially the government was unwilling to accept the defeat*… OPPOSITE willing
2 = <u>reluctant</u>, grudging, unenthusiastic, resistant, involuntary, averse, demurring, laggard (*rare*) …*He finds himself an unwilling participant in school politics*… OPPOSITE eager

unwind 1 = <u>relax</u>, wind down, take it easy, slow down, sit back, calm down, take a break, loosen up, quieten down, let yourself go, mellow out (*informal*), make yourself at home, outspan (*S. African*) …*It helps them to unwind after a busy day at work*…
2 = <u>unravel</u>, undo, uncoil, slacken, disentangle, unroll, unreel, untwist, untwine …*One of them unwound a length of rope from around his waist*…

unwise = <u>foolish</u>, stupid, silly, rash, irresponsible, reckless, senseless, short-sighted, ill-advised, foolhardy, inane, indiscreet, ill-judged, ill-considered, imprudent, inadvisable, asinine, injudicious, improvident, impolitic OPPOSITE wise

unwitting 1 = <u>unintentional</u>, involuntary, inadvertent, chance, accidental, unintended, unplanned, undesigned, unmeant …*It had been an unwitting blunder on his part*… OPPOSITE deliberate
2 = <u>unknowing</u>, innocent, unsuspecting, unconscious, unaware, ignorant …*We're unwitting victims of the system*… OPPOSITE knowing

unworthy 1 = <u>undeserving</u>, not good enough, not fit, not worth, ineligible, not deserving …*You may feel unworthy of the attention and help people offer you*… OPPOSITE deserving
2 = <u>dishonourable</u>, base, contemptible, degrading, disgraceful, shameful, disreputable, ignoble, discreditable …*Aren't you amazed by how loving the father is to his unworthy son?*… OPPOSITE commendable
3 *with* **of** = <u>unbefitting</u>, beneath, unfitting to, unsuitable for, inappropriate to, improper to, out of character with, out of place with, unbecoming to …*His accusations are unworthy of a prime minister*…

unwritten 1 = <u>oral</u>, word-of-mouth, unrecorded, vocal …*the unwritten stories of his infancy and childhood*…
2 = <u>understood</u>, accepted, tacit, traditional, conventional, silent, customary, implicit, unformulated …*They obey the one unwritten rule that binds them all – no talking*…

up
PHRASES **ups and downs** = <u>fluctuations</u>, changes, vicissitudes, moods, ebb and flow

up-and-coming = <u>promising</u>, ambitious, go-getting (*informal*), pushing, eager

upbeat (*Informal*) = <u>cheerful</u>, positive, optimistic, promising, encouraging, looking up, hopeful, favourable, rosy, buoyant, heartening, cheery, forward-looking

upbringing = <u>education</u>, training, breeding, rearing, care, raising, tending, bringing-up, nurture, cultivation

update = <u>bring up to date</u>, improve, correct, renew, revise, upgrade, amend, overhaul, streamline, modernize, rebrand

upgrade 1 = <u>improve</u>, better, update, reform, add to, enhance, refurbish, renovate, remodel, make better, modernize, spruce up, ameliorate ...*Medical facilities are being reorganized and upgraded*...
2 = <u>promote</u>, raise, advance, boost, move up, elevate, kick upstairs (*informal*), give promotion to ...*He was upgraded to security guard*... OPPOSITE> demote

upheaval = <u>disturbance</u>, revolution, disorder, turmoil, overthrow, disruption, eruption, cataclysm, violent change

uphill ADJECTIVE **1** = <u>ascending</u>, rising, upward, mounting, climbing ...*a long, uphill journey*... OPPOSITE> descending
2 = <u>arduous</u>, hard, taxing, difficult, tough, exhausting, punishing, gruelling, strenuous, laborious, wearisome, Sisyphean ...*It had been an uphill struggle to achieve what she wanted*...
NOUN (*S. African*) = <u>difficulty</u>, problem, trouble, dilemma, headache (*informal*), hassle (*informal*), can of worms (*informal*) ...*This job has been a real uphill*...

uphold 1 = <u>support</u>, back, defend, aid, champion, encourage, maintain, promote, sustain, advocate, stand by, stick up for (*informal*) ...*upholding the artist's right to creative freedom*...
2 = <u>confirm</u>, support, sustain, endorse, approve, justify, hold to, ratify, vindicate, validate ...*The crown court upheld the magistrate's decision*...

upkeep 1 = <u>maintenance</u>, running, keep, subsistence, support, repair, conservation, preservation, sustenance ...*The money will be used for the estate's upkeep*...
2 = <u>running costs</u>, expenses, overheads, expenditure, outlay, operating costs, oncosts (*Brit.*) ...*subsidies for the upkeep of kindergartens and orphanages*...

uplift VERB = <u>improve</u>, better, raise, advance, inspire, upgrade, refine, cultivate, civilize, ameliorate, edify ...*Art was created to uplift the mind and the spirit*...
NOUN = <u>improvement</u>, enlightenment, advancement, cultivation, refinement, enhancement, enrichment, betterment, edification ...*literature intended for the uplift of the soul*...

upper 1 = <u>topmost</u>, top ...*There is a smart restaurant on the upper floor*... OPPOSITE> bottom
2 = <u>higher</u>, high ...*the muscles of the upper back and chest*... OPPOSITE> lower
3 = <u>superior</u>, senior, higher-level, greater, top, important, chief, most important, elevated, eminent, higher-ranking ...*the upper echelons of the Army*... OPPOSITE> inferior

upper class = <u>aristocratic</u>, upper-class, noble, high-class, patrician, top-drawer, blue-blooded, highborn

uppermost 1 = <u>top</u>, highest, topmost, upmost, loftiest, most elevated ...*John was on the uppermost floor of the three-storey gatehouse*... OPPOSITE> bottom
2 = <u>supreme</u>, greatest, chief, leading, main, primary, principal, dominant, paramount, foremost, predominant, pre-eminent ...*Protection of sites is of uppermost priority*... OPPOSITE> least

upright 1 = <u>vertical</u>, straight, standing up, erect, on end, perpendicular, bolt upright ...*He moved into an upright position*... OPPOSITE> horizontal
2 = <u>honest</u>, good, principled, just, true, faithful, ethical, straightforward, honourable, righteous, conscientious, virtuous, trustworthy, high-minded, above board, incorruptible, unimpeachable ...*a very upright, trustworthy man*... OPPOSITE> dishonourable

uprising = <u>rebellion</u>, rising, revolution, outbreak, revolt, disturbance, upheaval, mutiny, insurrection, putsch, insurgence

uproar 1 = <u>commotion</u>, noise, racket, riot, confusion, turmoil, brawl, mayhem, clamour, din, turbulence, pandemonium, rumpus, hubbub, hurly-burly, brouhaha, ruction (*informal*), hullabaloo, ruckus (*informal*), bagarre (*French*) ...*The announcement caused uproar in the crowd*...
2 = <u>protest</u>, outrage, complaint, objection, fuss, stink (*informal*), outcry, furore, hue and cry ...*The announcement could cause an uproar in the United States*...

uproot 1 = <u>displace</u>, remove, exile, disorient, deracinate ...*the trauma of uprooting them from their homes*...
2 = <u>pull up</u>, dig up, root out, weed out, rip up, grub up, extirpate, deracinate, pull out by the roots ...*fallen trees which have been uprooted by the storm*...

upset ADJECTIVE **1** = <u>distressed</u>, shaken, disturbed, worried, troubled, hurt, bothered, confused, unhappy, gutted (*Brit. informal*), put out, dismayed, choked (*informal*), grieved, frantic, hassled (*informal*), agitated, ruffled, cut up (*informal*), disconcerted, disquieted, overwrought, discomposed ...*They are terribly upset by the breakup of their parents' marriage*...
2 = <u>sick</u>, queasy, bad, poorly (*informal*), ill, gippy (*slang*) ...*Larry is suffering from an upset stomach*...
3 = <u>overturned</u>, toppled, upside down, capsized, spilled, tumbled, tipped over ...*an upset cart with one wheel off*...
VERB **1** = <u>distress</u>, trouble, disturb, worry, alarm, bother, dismay, grieve, hassle (*informal*), agitate, ruffle, unnerve, disconcert, disquiet, fluster, perturb, faze, throw someone off balance (*Brit. & S. African*), discompose ...*She warned me not to say anything to upset him*...
2 = <u>tip over</u>, overturn, capsize, knock over, spill, topple over ...*bumping into him, and almost upsetting the ginger ale*...
3 = <u>mess up</u>, spoil, disturb, change, confuse, disorder, unsettle, mix up, disorganize, turn topsy-turvy, put out of order, throw into disorder ...*I was wondering whether that might upset my level of concentration*...
4 = <u>defeat</u>, overcome, conquer, overthrow, triumph over, get the better of, be victorious over ...*Chang upset world No 1 Pete Sampras in Saturday's semi-finals*...
NOUN **1** = <u>distress</u>, worry, trouble, shock, bother, disturbance, hassle (*informal*), disquiet, agitation,

discomposure ...*a source of continuity in times of worry and upset...*

2 = <u>reversal</u>, surprise, shake-up (*informal*), defeat, sudden change ...*She caused a major upset when she beat last year's finalist...*

3 = <u>illness</u>, complaint, disorder, bug (*informal*), disturbance, sickness, malady, queasiness, indisposition ...*Paul was unwell last night with a stomach upset...*

upshot = <u>result</u>, consequence, outcome, end, issue, event, conclusion, sequel, finale, culmination, end result, payoff (*informal*)

upside down *or* **upside-down** ADVERB = <u>wrong side up</u>, bottom up, on its head ...*The painting was hung upside down...*

ADJECTIVE **1** = <u>inverted</u>, overturned, upturned, on its head, bottom up, wrong side up ...*Tony had an upside-down map of Britain on his wall...*

2 (*Informal*) = <u>confused</u>, disordered, chaotic, muddled, jumbled, in disarray, in chaos, topsy-turvy, in confusion, higgledy-piggledy (*informal*), in disorder ...*the upside-down sort of life that we've had...*

upstanding = <u>honest</u>, principled, upright, honourable, good, moral, ethical, trustworthy, incorruptible, true OPPOSITE immoral

upstart = <u>social climber</u>, nobody, nouveau riche (*French*), parvenu, arriviste, status seeker

uptight (*Informal*) = <u>tense</u>, wired (*slang*), anxious, neurotic, uneasy, prickly, edgy, on the defensive, on edge, nervy (*Brit. informal*)

up-to-date = <u>modern</u>, fashionable, trendy (*Brit. informal*), in, newest, now (*informal*), happening (*informal*), current, with it (*informal*), stylish, in vogue, all the rage, up-to-the-minute, having your finger on the pulse OPPOSITE out of date

upturn = <u>rise</u>, increase, boost, improvement, recovery, revival, advancement, upsurge, upswing

urban = <u>civic</u>, city, town, metropolitan, municipal, dorp (*S. African*), inner-city

urbane = <u>sophisticated</u>, cultured, polished, civil, mannerly, smooth, elegant, refined, cultivated, cosmopolitan, civilized, courteous, suave, well-bred, debonair, well-mannered OPPOSITE boorish

urchin (*Old-fashioned*) = <u>ragamuffin</u>, waif, guttersnipe, brat, mudlark (*slang*), gamin, young rogue

urge VERB **1** = <u>beg</u>, appeal to, exhort, press, prompt, plead, put pressure on, lean on, solicit, goad, implore, enjoin, beseech, pressurize, entreat, twist someone's arm (*informal*), put the heat on (*informal*), put the screws on (*informal*) ...*They urged parliament to approve plans for their reform programme...*

2 = <u>advocate</u>, suggest, recommend, advise, back, support, champion, counsel, insist on, endorse, push for ...*He urged restraint on the security forces...* OPPOSITE discourage

NOUN = <u>impulse</u>, longing, wish, desire, fancy, drive, yen (*informal*), hunger, appetite, craving, yearning, itch

(*informal*), thirst, compulsion, hankering ...*He had an urge to open a shop of his own...* OPPOSITE reluctance

PHRASES **urge someone on** = <u>drive on</u>, push, encourage, force, press, prompt, stimulate, compel, induce, propel, hasten, constrain, incite, egg on, goad, spur on, impel, gee up ...*She had a strong and supportive sister who urged her on...*

urgency = <u>importance</u>, need, necessity, gravity, pressure, hurry, seriousness, extremity, exigency, imperativeness

urgent 1 = <u>crucial</u>, desperate, pressing, great, important, crying, critical, immediate, acute, grave, instant, compelling, imperative, top-priority, now or never, exigent, not to be delayed ...*There is an urgent need for food and water...* OPPOSITE unimportant

2 = <u>insistent</u>, earnest, determined, intense, persistent, persuasive, resolute, clamorous, importunate ...*His mother leaned forward and spoke to him in urgent undertones...* OPPOSITE casual

urinate = <u>pee</u>, wee, leak (*slang*) (*slang*), tinkle (*Brit. informal*), piddle (*informal*), spend a penny (*Brit. informal*), make water, pass water, wee-wee (*informal*), micturate, take a whizz (*slang, chiefly U.S.*)

usable = <u>serviceable</u>, working, functional, available, current, practical, valid, at your disposal, ready for use, in running order, fit for use, utilizable

usage 1 = <u>use</u>, operation, employment, running, control, management, treatment, handling ...*Parts of the motor wore out because of constant usage...*

2 = <u>practice</u>, method, procedure, form, rule, tradition, habit, regime, custom, routine, convention, mode, matter of course, wont ...*a fruitful convergence with past usage and custom...*

use VERB **1** = <u>employ</u>, utilize, make use of, work, apply, operate, exercise, practise, resort to, exert, wield, ply, put to use, bring into play, find a use for, avail yourself of, turn to account ...*Officials used loud hailers to call for calm...*

2 *sometimes with* **up** = <u>consume</u>, go through, exhaust, spend, waste, get through, run through, deplete, dissipate, expend, fritter away ...*You used all the ice cubes and didn't put the ice trays back...*

3 = <u>take advantage of</u>, exploit, manipulate, abuse, milk, profit from, impose on, misuse, make use of, cash in on (*informal*), walk all over (*informal*), take liberties with ...*Be careful she's not just using you...*

NOUN **1** = <u>usage</u>, employment, utilization, operation, application ...*research related to microcomputers and their use in classrooms...*

2 = <u>service</u>, handling, wear and tear, treatment, practice, exercise ...*Holes had developed, the result of many years of use...*

3 = <u>purpose</u>, call, need, end, point, cause, reason, occasion, object, necessity ...*You will no longer have a use for the car...*

4 = <u>good</u>, point, help, service, value, benefit, profit, worth, advantage, utility, mileage (*informal*), avail, usefulness ...*There's no use you asking me any more questions about that...*

PHRASES **use something up** = <u>consume</u>, drain, exhaust, finish, waste, absorb, run through, deplete, squander, devour, swallow up, burn up, fritter away …*They aren't the ones who use up the world's resources*…

used = <u>second-hand</u>, worn, not new, cast-off, hand-me-down (*informal*), nearly new, shopsoiled, reach-me-down (*informal*) OPPOSITE> new

used to = <u>accustomed to</u>, familiar with, in the habit of, given to, at home in, attuned to, tolerant of, wont to, inured to, hardened to, habituated to

useful = <u>helpful</u>, effective, valuable, practical, of use, profitable, of service, worthwhile, beneficial, of help, fruitful, advantageous, all-purpose, salutary, general-purpose, serviceable OPPOSITE> useless

usefulness = <u>helpfulness</u>, value, worth, use, help, service, benefit, profit, utility, effectiveness, convenience, practicality, efficacy

useless 1 = <u>worthless</u>, of no use, valueless, pants (*slang*), ineffective, impractical, fruitless, unproductive, ineffectual, unworkable, disadvantageous, unavailing, bootless, unsuitable …*He realised that their money was useless in this country*… OPPOSITE> useful
2 = <u>pointless</u>, hopeless, futile, vain, idle, profitless …*She knew it was useless to protest*… OPPOSITE> worthwhile
3 (*Informal*) = <u>inept</u>, no good, hopeless, weak, stupid, pants (*slang*), incompetent, ineffectual …*He was useless at any game with a ball*…

usher **VERB** = <u>escort</u>, lead, direct, guide, conduct, pilot, steer, show …*They were quickly ushered away*…
NOUN = <u>attendant</u>, guide, doorman, usherette, escort, doorkeeper …*He did part-time work as an usher in a theatre*…
PHRASES **usher something in** = <u>introduce</u>, launch, bring in, precede, initiate, herald, pave the way for, ring in, open the door to, inaugurate …*a unique opportunity to usher in a new era of stability in Europe*…

usual = <u>normal</u>, customary, regular, expected, general, common, stock, standard, fixed, ordinary, familiar, typical, constant, routine, everyday, accustomed, habitual, bog-standard (*Brit. & Irish slang*), wonted OPPOSITE> unusual

usually = <u>normally</u>, generally, mainly, commonly, regularly, mostly, routinely, on the whole, in the main, for the most part, by and large, most often, ordinarily, as a rule, habitually, as is usual, as is the custom

usurp = <u>seize</u>, take over, assume, take, appropriate, wrest, commandeer, arrogate, infringe upon, lay hold of

utility = <u>usefulness</u>, use, point, benefit, service, profit, fitness, convenience, mileage (*informal*), avail, practicality, efficacy, advantageousness, serviceableness

utilize = <u>use</u>, employ, deploy, take advantage of, resort to, make the most of, make use of, put to use, bring into play, have recourse to, avail yourself of, turn to account

utmost **ADJECTIVE 1** = <u>greatest</u>, highest, maximum, supreme, extreme, paramount, pre-eminent …*Security matters are treated with the utmost seriousness*…
2 = <u>farthest</u>, extreme, last, final, outermost, uttermost, farthermost …*The break-up tested our resolve to its utmost limits*…
NOUN = <u>best</u>, greatest, maximum, most, highest, hardest …*I'm going to do my utmost to climb as fast and as far as I can*…

utopia = <u>paradise</u>, heaven, Eden, bliss, perfect place, Garden of Eden, Shangri-la, Happy Valley, seventh heaven, ideal life, Erewhon

utopian **ADJECTIVE** = <u>perfect</u>, ideal, romantic, dream, fantasy, imaginary, visionary, airy, idealistic, fanciful, impractical, illusory, chimerical …*He was pursuing a utopian dream of world prosperity*…
NOUN = <u>dreamer</u>, visionary, idealist, Don Quixote, romanticist …*Kennedy had no patience with dreamers or liberal utopians*…

utter¹ = <u>say</u>, state, speak, voice, express, deliver, declare, mouth, breathe, pronounce, articulate, enunciate, put into words, verbalize, vocalize …*They departed without uttering a word*…

utter² = <u>absolute</u>, complete, total, perfect, positive, pure, sheer, stark, outright, all-out, thorough, downright, real, consummate, veritable, unqualified, out-and-out, unadulterated, unmitigated, thoroughgoing, arrant, deep-dyed (*usually derogatory*) …*A look of utter confusion swept across his handsome face*…

utterance 1 = <u>speech</u>, words, statement, comment, opinion, remark, expression, announcement, observation, declaration, reflection, pronouncement …*the Queen's public utterances*…
2 = <u>speaking</u>, voicing, expression, breathing, delivery, ejaculation, articulation, enunciation, vocalization, verbalization, vociferation …*the simple utterance of a few platitudes*…

utterly = <u>totally</u>, completely, absolutely, just, really, quite, perfectly, fully, entirely, extremely, altogether, thoroughly, wholly, downright, categorically, to the core, one hundred per cent, in all respects, to the nth degree, unqualifiedly

V v

vacancy 1 = <u>opening</u>, job, post, place, position, role, situation, opportunity, slot, berth (*informal*), niche, job opportunity, vacant position, situation vacant …*They had a vacancy for a temporary secretary…*
2 = <u>room</u>, space, available accommodation, unoccupied room …*The hotel only has a few vacancies left…*

vacant 1 = <u>empty</u>, free, available, abandoned, deserted, to let, for sale, on the market, void, up for grabs, disengaged, uninhabited, unoccupied, not in use, unfilled, untenanted …*They came upon a vacant house…* OPPOSITE occupied
2 = <u>unfilled</u>, unoccupied …*The post has been vacant for some time…* OPPOSITE taken
3 = <u>blank</u>, vague, dreamy, dreaming, empty, abstracted, idle, thoughtless, vacuous, inane, expressionless, unthinking, absent-minded, incurious, ditzy *or* ditsy (*slang*) …*She had a dreamy, vacant look on her face…* OPPOSITE thoughtful

vacate 1 = <u>leave</u>, quit, move out of, give up, withdraw from, evacuate, depart from, go away from, leave empty, relinquish possession of …*He vacated the flat and went back to stay with his parents…*
2 = <u>quit</u>, leave, resign from, give up, withdraw from, chuck (*informal*), retire from, relinquish, renounce, walk out on, pack in (*informal*), abdicate, step down from (*informal*), stand down from …*He recently vacated his post as Personnel Director…*

vacillate = <u>waver</u>, hesitate, dither (*chiefly Brit.*), haver, sway, falter, be doubtful, fluctuate, be uncertain, be unsure, teeter, oscillate, be undecided, chop and change, seesaw, blow hot and cold (*informal*), temporize, hum and haw, be unable to decide, keep changing your mind, shillyshally (*informal*), be irresolute *or* indecisive, swither (*Scot.*), be unable to make up your mind (*chiefly Brit.*), dillydally

vacuous = <u>vapid</u>, stupid, inane, blank, vacant, unintelligent

vacuum 1 = <u>gap</u>, lack, absence, space, deficiency, void …*The collapse of the army left a vacuum in the area…*
2 = <u>emptiness</u>, space, void, gap, empty space, nothingness, vacuity …*The spinning turbine creates a vacuum…*

vagabond NOUN = <u>tramp</u>, bum (*informal*), drifter, vagrant, migrant, rolling stone, wanderer, beggar, outcast, rover, nomad, itinerant, down-and-out, hobo (*U.S.*), bag lady (*chiefly U.S.*), wayfarer, dosser (*Brit. slang*), knight of the road, person of no fixed address, derro (*Austral. slang*) …*He had lived as a vagabond, begging for food…*
ADJECTIVE = <u>vagrant</u>, drifting, wandering, homeless, journeying, unsettled, roaming, idle, roving, nomadic,

destitute, itinerant, down and out, rootless, footloose, fly-by-night (*informal*), shiftless …*his impoverished, vagabond existence…*

vagary *usually plural* = <u>whim</u>, caprice, unpredictability, sport, urge, fancy, notion, humour, impulse, quirk, conceit, whimsy, crotchet, sudden notion

vagrant NOUN = <u>tramp</u>, bum (*informal*), drifter, vagabond, rolling stone, wanderer, beggar, derelict, itinerant, down-and-out, hobo (*U.S.*), bag lady (*chiefly U.S.*), dosser (*Brit. slang*), person of no fixed address, derro (*Austral. slang*) …*He lived on the street as a vagrant…*
ADJECTIVE = <u>vagabond</u>, drifting, wandering, homeless, journeying, unsettled, roaming, idle, roving, nomadic, destitute, itinerant, down and out, rootless, footloose, fly-by-night (*informal*), shiftless …*the terrifying sub-culture of vagrant alcoholics…* OPPOSITE settled

vague 1 = <u>unclear</u>, indefinite, hazy, confused, loose, uncertain, doubtful, unsure, superficial, incomplete, woolly, imperfect, sketchy, cursory …*Her description of her attacker was very vague…* OPPOSITE clear
2 = <u>imprecise</u>, unspecified, generalized, rough, loose, ambiguous, hazy, equivocal, ill-defined, non-specific, inexact, obfuscatory, inexplicit …*His answer was deliberately vague…*
3 = <u>absent-minded</u>, absorbed, abstracted, distracted, unaware, musing, vacant, preoccupied, bemused, oblivious, dreamy, daydreaming, faraway, unthinking, heedless, inattentive, unheeding …*She had married a charming but rather vague Englishman…*
4 = <u>indistinct</u>, blurred, unclear, dim, fuzzy, unknown, obscure, faint, shadowy, indefinite, misty, hazy, indistinguishable, amorphous, indeterminate, bleary, nebulous, out of focus, ill-defined, indiscernible …*He could just make out a vague shape in the distance…* OPPOSITE distinct

vaguely 1 = <u>slightly</u>, rather, sort of (*informal*), kind of (*informal*), a little, a bit, somewhat, moderately, faintly, dimly, to some extent, kinda (*informal*) …*The voice was vaguely familiar…*
2 = <u>absent-mindedly</u>, evasively, abstractedly, obscurely, vacantly, inattentively …*'What did you talk about?' 'Oh, this and that,' she replied vaguely…*
3 = <u>roughly</u>, loosely, indefinitely, carelessly, in a general way, imprecisely …*'She's back there,' he said, waving vaguely behind him…*

vagueness 1 = <u>impreciseness</u>, ambiguity, obscurity, looseness, inexactitude, woolliness, undecidedness, lack of preciseness …*the vagueness of the language used in the text…* OPPOSITE preciseness
2 = <u>absent-mindedness</u>, abstraction, forgetfulness, confusion, inattention, disorganization, giddiness,

dreaminess, befuddlement, empty-headedness ...*her deliberately affected vagueness*...

vain `ADJECTIVE` **1** = <u>futile</u>, useless, pointless, unsuccessful, empty, hollow, idle, trivial, worthless, trifling, senseless, unimportant, fruitless, unproductive, abortive, unprofitable, time-wasting, unavailing, nugatory ...*They worked all night in a vain attempt to finish on schedule*... `OPPOSITE` successful
2 = <u>conceited</u>, narcissistic, proud, arrogant, inflated, swaggering, stuck-up (*informal*), cocky, swanky (*informal*), ostentatious, egotistical, self-important, overweening, vainglorious, swollen-headed (*informal*), pleased with yourself, bigheaded (*informal*), peacockish ...*She's a shallow, vain and self-centred woman*... `OPPOSITE` modest
`PHRASES` **in vain** **1** = <u>useless</u>, to no avail, unsuccessfu, fruitless, useless, unsuccessful, fruitless, wasted, vain, ineffectual, without success, to no purpose, bootless ...*All her complaints were in vain*...
2 = <u>uselessly</u>, to no avail, unsuccessfully, fruitlessly, vainly, ineffectually, without success, to no purpose, bootlessly ...*He hammered the door, trying in vain to attract her attention*...

valiant = <u>brave</u>, heroic, courageous, bold, worthy, fearless, gallant, intrepid, plucky, doughty, indomitable, redoubtable, dauntless, lion-hearted, valorous, stouthearted `OPPOSITE` cowardly

valid **1** = <u>sound</u>, good, reasonable, just, telling, powerful, convincing, substantial, acceptable, sensible, rational, logical, viable, credible, sustainable, plausible, conclusive, weighty, well-founded, cogent, well-grounded ...*Both sides have made valid points*... `OPPOSITE` unfounded
2 = <u>legal</u>, official, legitimate, correct, genuine, proper, in effect, authentic, in force, lawful, bona fide, legally binding, signed and sealed ...*For foreign holidays you will need a valid passport*... `OPPOSITE` invalid

validate **1** = <u>confirm</u>, prove, certify, substantiate, corroborate ...*The evidence has been validated by historians*...
2 = <u>authorize</u>, endorse, ratify, legalize, authenticate, make legally binding, set your seal on *or* to ...*Give the retailer your winning ticket to validate*...

validity **1** = <u>soundness</u>, force, power, grounds, weight, strength, foundation, substance, point, cogency ...*Some people deny the validity of this claim*...
2 = <u>legality</u>, authority, legitimacy, right, lawfulness ...*They now want to challenge the validity of the vote*...

valley = <u>hollow</u>, dale, glen, vale, depression, dell, dingle, strath (*Scot.*), cwm (*Welsh*), coomb

valour = <u>bravery</u>, courage, heroism, spirit, boldness, gallantry, derring-do (*archaic*), fearlessness, intrepidity, doughtiness, lion-heartedness `OPPOSITE` cowardice

valuable `ADJECTIVE` **1** = <u>useful</u>, important, profitable, worthwhile, beneficial, valued, helpful, worthy, of use, of help, invaluable, serviceable, worth its weight in gold ...*The experience was very valuable*... `OPPOSITE` useless
2 = <u>treasured</u>, esteemed, cherished, prized, precious, held dear, estimable, worth your weight in gold ...*She was a valuable friend and an excellent teacher*...
3 = <u>precious</u>, expensive, costly, dear, high-priced, priceless, irreplaceable ...*valuable old books*... `OPPOSITE` worthless
`PLURAL NOUN` = <u>treasures</u>, prized possessions, precious items, heirlooms, personal effects, costly article ...*Leave your valuables in the hotel safe*...

value `NOUN` **1** = <u>importance</u>, use, benefit, worth, merit, point, help, service, sense, profit, advantage, utility, significance, effectiveness, mileage (*informal*), practicality, usefulness, efficacy, desirability, serviceableness ...*Studies are needed to see if these therapies have any value*... `OPPOSITE` worthlessness
2 = <u>cost</u>, price, worth, rate, equivalent, market price, face value, asking price, selling price, monetary worth ...*The value of his investment has risen by more than 100%*...
`PLURAL NOUN` = <u>principles</u>, morals, ethics, mores, standards of behaviour, code of behaviour, (moral) standards ...*a return to traditional family values*...
`VERB` **1** = <u>appreciate</u>, rate, prize, regard highly, respect, admire, treasure, esteem, cherish, think much of, hold dear, have a high opinion of, set store by, hold in high regard *or* esteem ...*Do you value your best friend enough?*... `OPPOSITE` undervalue
2 = <u>evaluate</u>, price, estimate, rate, cost, survey, assess, set at, appraise, put a price on ...*I have had my jewellery valued for insurance purposes*... ...*cocaine valued at $53 million*...

valued = <u>appreciated</u>, prized, esteemed, highly regarded, loved, dear, treasured, cherished

vandal = <u>hooligan</u>, ned (*Scot. slang*), delinquent, rowdy, lager lout, graffiti artist, yob *or* yobbo (*Brit. slang*), cougan (*Austral. slang*), scozza (*Austral. slang*), bogan (*Austral. slang*)

vanguard = <u>forefront</u>, front line, cutting edge, leaders, front, van, spearhead, forerunners, front rank, trailblazers, advance guard, trendsetters `OPPOSITE` rearguard

vanish **1** = <u>disappear</u>, become invisible, be lost to sight, dissolve, evaporate, fade away, melt away, disappear from sight, exit, evanesce ...*The aircraft vanished without trace*... `OPPOSITE` appear
2 = <u>die out</u>, disappear, pass away, end, fade, dwindle, cease to exist, become extinct, disappear from the face of the earth ...*Dinosaurs vanished from the earth millions of years ago*...

vanity **1** = <u>pride</u>, arrogance, conceit, airs, showing off (*informal*), pretension, narcissism, egotism, self-love, ostentation, vainglory, self-admiration, affected ways, bigheadedness (*informal*), conceitedness, swollen-headedness (*informal*) ...*Men who use steroids are motivated by sheer vanity*... `OPPOSITE` modesty
2 = <u>futility</u>, uselessness, worthlessness, emptiness, frivolity, unreality, triviality, hollowness, pointlessness,

inanity, unproductiveness, fruitlessness, unsubstantiality, profitlessness ...*the futility of human existence and the vanity of wealth...* OPPOSITE value

vanquish (*Literary*) = defeat, beat, conquer, reduce, stuff (*slang*), master, tank (*slang*), overcome, crush, overwhelm, put down, lick (*informal*), undo, subdue, rout, repress, overpower, quell, triumph over, clobber (*slang*), subjugate, run rings around (*informal*), wipe the floor with (*informal*), blow out of the water (*slang*), put to flight, get the upper hand over, put to rout

vapour = mist, fog, haze, smoke, breath, steam, fumes, dampness, miasma, exhalation

variable = changeable, unstable, fluctuating, shifting, flexible, wavering, uneven, fickle, temperamental, mercurial, capricious, unsteady, protean, vacillating, fitful, mutable, inconstant, chameleonic OPPOSITE constant

variance NOUN = difference, contrast, discrepancy, variation, disagreement, contradiction, inconsistency, deviation, divergence, incongruity, dissimilarity ...*the variances in the stock price...* OPPOSITE agreement
PHRASES **at variance** = in disagreement, conflicting, at odds, in opposition, out of line, at loggerheads, at sixes and sevens (*informal*), out of harmony ...*Many of his statements are at variance with the facts...*

variant NOUN = variation, form, version, development, alternative, adaptation, revision, modification, permutation, transfiguration, aberration, derived form ...*Bulimia was once seen as a variant of anorexia...*
ADJECTIVE = different, alternative, modified, derived, exceptional, divergent ...*There are so many variant spellings of this name...*

variation 1 = alternative, variety, modification, departure, innovation, variant ...*This delicious variation on an omelette is easy to prepare...*
2 = variety, change, deviation, difference, diversity, diversion, novelty, alteration, discrepancy, diversification, departure from the norm, break in routine ...*Every day without variation my grandfather ate a plate of ham...* OPPOSITE uniformity

varied = different, mixed, various, diverse, assorted, miscellaneous, sundry, motley, manifold, heterogeneous OPPOSITE unvarying

variegated = mottled, pied, streaked, motley, many-coloured, parti-coloured, varicoloured

variety 1 = diversity, change, variation, difference, diversification, heterogeneity, many-sidedness, multifariousness ...*people who like variety in their lives and enjoy trying new things...* OPPOSITE uniformity
2 = range, selection, assortment, mix, collection, line-up, mixture, array, cross section, medley, multiplicity, mixed bag (*informal*), miscellany, motley collection, intermixture ...*a store selling a wide variety of goods...*
3 = type, sort, kind, make, order, class, brand, species, breed, strain, category ...*She grows 12 varieties of old-*

fashioned roses...

various 1 = different, assorted, miscellaneous, varied, differing, distinct, diverse, divers (*archaic*), diversified, disparate, sundry, heterogeneous ...*He plans to spread his capital between various bank accounts...* OPPOSITE similar
2 = many, numerous, countless, several, abundant, innumerable, sundry, manifold, profuse ...*The methods employed are many and various...*

> ## *Word Power*
>
> **various** – The use of *different* after *various*, which seems to be most common in speech, is unnecessary and should be avoided in serious writing: *the disease exists in various forms* (not *in various different forms*).

varnish NOUN = lacquer, polish, glaze, japan, gloss, shellac ...*The varnish comes in six natural shades...*
VERB 1 = lacquer, polish, glaze, japan, gloss, shellac ...*The painting still has to be varnished...*
2 = polish, decorate, glaze, adorn, gild, lacquer, embellish ...*The floors have all been varnished...*

vary 1 = differ, be different, be dissimilar, disagree, diverge, be unlike ...*As the rugs are all handmade, each one varies slightly...*
2 = change, shift, swing, transform, alter, fluctuate, oscillate, see-saw ...*women whose moods vary according to their menstrual cycle...*
3 = alternate, mix, diversify, reorder, intermix, bring variety to, permutate, variegate ...*Try to vary your daily diet to include all the major food groups...*
4 = modify, change, alter, adjust ...*The colour can be varied by adding filters...*

varying 1 = different, contrasting, inconsistent, varied, distinct, diverse, assorted, disparate, dissimilar, distinguishable, discrepant, streets apart ...*Reporters gave varying figures on the number of casualties...*
2 = changing, variable, irregular, inconsistent, fluctuating ...*The green table lamp flickered with varying intensity...* OPPOSITE unchanging

vassal = serf, slave, bondsman, subject, retainer, thrall, varlet (*archaic*), bondservant, liegeman

vast = huge, massive, enormous, great, wide, sweeping, extensive, tremendous, immense, mega (*slang*), unlimited, gigantic, astronomical, monumental, monstrous, mammoth, colossal, never-ending, prodigious, limitless, boundless, voluminous, immeasurable, unbounded, elephantine, ginormous (*informal*), vasty (*archaic*), measureless, illimitable, humongous *or* humungous (*U.S. slang*) OPPOSITE tiny

vault[1] 1 = strongroom, repository, depository ...*The money was in storage in bank vaults...*
2 = crypt, tomb, catacomb, cellar, mausoleum, charnel house, undercroft ...*He ordered that Matilda's body should be buried in the family vault...*
3 = arch, roof, ceiling, span ...*the vault of a magnificent cathedral...*

vault[2] = jump, spring, leap, clear, bound, hurdle

...Ned vaulted over the low wall...

vaunted = <u>boasted about</u>, flaunted, paraded, shown off, made much of, bragged about, crowed about, exulted in, made a display of, prated about

veer = <u>change direction</u>, turn, swerve, shift, sheer, tack, be deflected, change course

vehemence = <u>forcefulness</u>, force, violence, fire, energy, heat, passion, emphasis, enthusiasm, intensity, warmth, vigour, zeal, verve, fervour, eagerness, ardour, earnestness, keenness, fervency OPPOSITE indifference

vehement = <u>strong</u>, fierce, forceful, earnest, powerful, violent, intense, flaming, eager, enthusiastic, passionate, ardent, emphatic, fervent, impassioned, zealous, forcible, fervid OPPOSITE half-hearted

vehicle 1 = <u>conveyance</u>, machine, motor vehicle, means of transport *...a vehicle which was somewhere between a tractor and a truck...*
2 = <u>medium</u>, means, channel, mechanism, organ, apparatus, means of expression *...Her art became a vehicle for her political beliefs...*

➤ boats and ships ➤ carriages and carts
➤ types of vehicle

veil NOUN 1 = <u>mask</u>, cover, shroud, film, shade, curtain, cloak *...She swathed her face in a veil of decorative muslin...*
2 = <u>screen</u>, mask, disguise, blind *...the chilling facts behind this veil of secrecy...*
3 = <u>film</u>, cover, curtain, cloak, shroud *...He recognized the coast of England through the veil of mist...*
VERB = <u>cover</u>, screen, hide, mask, shield, disguise, conceal, obscure, dim, cloak, mantle *...Her hair swept across her face, as if to veil it...* OPPOSITE reveal

veiled = <u>disguised</u>, implied, hinted at, covert, masked, concealed, suppressed

vein 1 = <u>blood vessel</u> *...Many veins are found just under the skin...*
2 = <u>mood</u>, style, spirit, way, turn, note, key, character, attitude, atmosphere, tone, manner, bent, stamp, humour, tendency, mode, temper, temperament, tenor, inclination, disposition, frame of mind *...He also wrote several works in a lighter vein...*

Types of vehicle

aircraft	dustcart or (*U.S. &*	motor scooter	stagecoach
ambulance	*Canad.*) garbage truck	motor vehicle	steamroller
articulated lorry or	estate car	off-road vehicle	sulky
(*informal*) artic	fire engine	omnibus	tandem
autocycle	fork-lift truck	paddock-basher	tank
autorickshaw	gritter	panda car	tank engine or
barrow	hansom or hansom cab	pantechnicon	locomotive
bicycle or (*informal*) bike	hatchback or hatch	pick-up (*Austral. &*	tanker
Black Maria	hog	*N.Z.*), utility truck, or	tarantass
boat	jaunting car or jaunty	(*informal*) ute	taxi
breakdown van or truck,	car	police car	telega
tow truck, or (*Austral.*	JCB	postbus	three-wheeler
slang) towie	Jeep	post chaise	tipper truck or lorry
bulldozer	jet ski	pram	toboggan
bus	jinricksha, jinrickshaw,	racing car	tonga
cab	jinrikisha or jinriksha	railcar	tourer or (*especially U.S.*)
cabriolet	jitney	ratha	touring car
camion	kart, go-cart, or go-kart	rickshaw	traction engine
camper	kibitka	roadroller	tractor
camper van	komatik	road train	trail bike
car	koneke	rocket	trailer
caravan	landaulet or landaulette	scooter	train
carriage	light engine or (*U.S.*)	scout car	tram, tramcar, or (*U.S.*
Caterpillar	wildcat	shandydan	*& Canad.*) streetcar or
chaise	limousine	ship	trolley car
charabanc	litter	single-decker	travois
chariot	locomotive	skibob	tricycle
coach	lorry	sledge or (*especially U.S.*	troika
combine harvester	low-loader	*& Canad.*) sled	trolley
Conestoga wagon	luge	sleigh	trolleybus
coupé	milk float	Sno-Cat	troop carrier
cycle	minibus	snowmobile	truck
delivery van or (*U.S. &*	moped	snow plough	tumbrel or tumbril
Canad.) panel truck	motorbicycle	space capsule	unicycle
Dormobile	motorbike	spacecraft	van
double-decker	motorbus	space probe	wagon or waggon
dray	motorcar	spaceship	wagonette or
dump truck or dumper-	motor caravan	space shuttle	waggonette
truck	motorcycle	sports car	wheelbarrow

3 = <u>streak</u>, element, thread, suggestion, strain, trace, hint, dash, trait, sprinkling, nuance, smattering ...*The song has a vein of black humour running through it...*
4 = <u>seam</u>, layer, stratum, course, current, bed, deposit, streak, stripe, lode ...*a rich deep vein of copper in the rock...*

(Related Words)
adjective: venous

velocity = <u>speed</u>, pace, rapidity, quickness, swiftness, fleetness, celerity

velvety = <u>soft</u>, smooth, downy, delicate, mossy, velvet-like

venal = <u>corrupt</u>, bent (*slang*), crooked (*informal*), prostituted, grafting (*informal*), mercenary, sordid, rapacious, unprincipled, dishonourable, corruptible, purchasable OPPOSITE honest

vendetta = <u>feud</u>, dispute, quarrel, enmity, bad blood, blood feud

veneer **1** = <u>mask</u>, show, façade, front, appearance, guise, pretence, semblance, false front ...*He was able to fool people with his veneer of intellectuality...*
2 = <u>layer</u>, covering, finish, facing, film, gloss, patina, laminate, cladding, lamination ...*bath panels fitted with a mahogany veneer...*

venerable = <u>respected</u>, august, sage, revered, honoured, wise, esteemed, reverenced

venerate = <u>respect</u>, honour, esteem, revere, worship, adore, reverence, look up to, hold in awe OPPOSITE scorn

veneration = <u>respect</u>, esteem, reverence, worship, awe, deference, adoration

vengeance NOUN = <u>revenge</u>, retaliation, reprisal, retribution, avenging, an eye for an eye, settling of scores, requital, lex talionis ...*She wanted vengeance for the loss of her daughter...* OPPOSITE forgiveness
PHRASES **with a vengeance** = <u>to the utmost</u>, greatly, extremely, to the full, and no mistake, to the nth degree, with no holds barred ...*The problem has returned with a vengeance...*

vengeful = <u>unforgiving</u>, relentless, avenging, vindictive, punitive, implacable, spiteful, retaliatory, rancorous, thirsting for revenge, revengeful

venom **1** = <u>malice</u>, hate, spite, bitterness, grudge, gall, acidity, spleen, acrimony, rancour, ill will, malevolence, virulence, pungency, malignity, spitefulness, maliciousness ...*There was no mistaking the venom in his voice...* OPPOSITE benevolence
2 = <u>poison</u>, toxin, bane ...*snake handlers who grow immune to snake venom...*

venomous **1** = <u>malicious</u>, vindictive, spiteful, hostile, savage, vicious, malignant, virulent, baleful, rancorous ...*He made a venomous personal attack on his opponent...* OPPOSITE benevolent
2 = <u>poisonous</u>, poison, toxic, virulent, noxious, baneful (*archaic*), envenomed, mephitic ...*The adder is Britain's only venomous snake...* OPPOSITE harmless

vent NOUN = <u>outlet</u>, opening, hole, split, aperture, duct, orifice ...*There was a small air vent in the ceiling...*
VERB = <u>express</u>, release, voice, air, empty, discharge, utter, emit, come out with, pour out, give vent to, give expression to ...*She telephoned her best friend to vent her frustration...* OPPOSITE hold back

ventilate **1** = <u>aerate</u>, fan, cool, refresh, air-condition, freshen, oxygenate ...*The pit is ventilated by a steel fan...*
2 = <u>discuss</u>, air, bring out into the open, talk about, debate, examine, broadcast, sift, scrutinize, make known ...*Following a bereavement, people need a safe place to ventilate their feelings...*

venture NOUN = <u>undertaking</u>, project, enterprise, chance, campaign, risk, operation, activity, scheme, task, mission, speculation, gamble, adventure, exploit, pursuit, fling, hazard, crusade, endeavour ...*a Russian-American joint venture...*
VERB **1** = <u>go</u>, travel, journey, set out, wander, stray, plunge into, rove, set forth ...*Few Europeans had ventured beyond the Himalayas...*
2 = <u>dare</u>, presume, have the courage to, be brave enough to, hazard, go out on a limb (*informal*), take the liberty, stick your neck out (*informal*), go so far as, make so bold as, have the temerity *or* effrontery *or* nerve ...*Each time I ventured to speak, I was ignored...*
3 = <u>put forward</u>, offer, suggest, present, air, table, advance, propose, volunteer, submit, bring up, postulate, proffer, broach, posit, moot, propound, dare to say ...*We were warned not to make fools of ourselves by venturing an opinion...*

veracity **1** = <u>accuracy</u>, truth, credibility, precision, exactitude ...*We have total confidence in the veracity of our research...*
2 = <u>truthfulness</u>, integrity, honesty, candour, frankness, probity, rectitude, trustworthiness, uprightness ...*He was shocked to find his veracity being questioned...*

verbal = <u>spoken</u>, oral, word-of-mouth, unwritten, verbatim, literal

verbally = <u>orally</u>, vocally, in words, in speech, by word of mouth

verbatim ADVERB = <u>exactly</u>, to the letter, word for word, closely, precisely, literally, faithfully, rigorously, in every detail, letter for letter ...*The president's speeches are reproduced verbatim in the state-run newspapers...*
ADJECTIVE = <u>word for word</u>, exact, literal, close, precise, faithful, line by line, unabridged, unvarnished, undeviating, unembellished ...*He gave me a verbatim report of the entire conversation...*

verdant (*Literary*) = <u>green</u>, lush, leafy, grassy, fresh, flourishing

verdict = <u>decision</u>, finding, judgment, opinion, sentence, conclusion, conviction, adjudication, pronouncement

verge NOUN **1** = <u>brink</u>, point, edge, threshold ...*Carole was on the verge of tears...*
2 = <u>border</u>, edge, margin, limit, extreme, lip, boundary, threshold, roadside, brim ...*The car pulled over on to the verge off the road...*

PHRASES **verge on something** = <u>come near to</u>, approach, border on, resemble, incline to, be similar to, touch on, be more or less, be tantamount to, tend towards, be not far from, incline towards ...*a fury that verges on madness*...

verification = <u>proof</u>, confirmation, validation, corroboration, authentication, substantiation

verify 1 = <u>check</u>, confirm, make sure, examine, monitor, check out (*informal*), inspect ...*A clerk simply verifies that the payment and invoice amount match*...
2 = <u>confirm</u>, prove, substantiate, support, validate, bear out, attest, corroborate, attest to, authenticate ...*The government has not verified any of these reports*... **OPPOSITE** disprove

vernacular **NOUN** = <u>speech</u>, jargon, idiom, parlance, cant, native language, dialect, patois, argot, vulgar tongue ...*To use the vernacular of the day, Peter was square*...
ADJECTIVE = <u>colloquial</u>, popular, informal, local, common, native, indigenous, vulgar ...*dialects such as black vernacular English*...

versatile 1 = <u>adaptable</u>, flexible, all-round, resourceful, protean, multifaceted, many-sided, all-singing, all-dancing ...*He stood out as one of the game's most versatile athletes*... **OPPOSITE** unadaptable
2 = <u>all-purpose</u>, handy, functional, variable, adjustable, all-singing, all-dancing ...*a versatile piece of equipment*... **OPPOSITE** limited

versed = <u>knowledgeable</u>, experienced, skilled, seasoned, qualified, familiar, practised, accomplished, competent, acquainted, well-informed, proficient, well up (*informal*), conversant **OPPOSITE** ignorant

version 1 = <u>form</u>, variety, variant, sort, kind, class, design, style, model, type, brand, genre ...*Ludo is a version of an ancient Indian racing game*...
2 = <u>adaptation</u>, edition, interpretation, form, reading, copy, rendering, translation, reproduction, portrayal ...*The English version is far inferior to the original French text*...
3 = <u>account</u>, report, side, description, record, reading, story, view, understanding, history, statement, analysis, take (*informal, chiefly U.S.*), construction, tale, impression, explanation, interpretation, rendering, narrative, chronicle, rendition, narration, construal ...*She went public with her version of events*...

vertical = <u>upright</u>, sheer, perpendicular, straight (up and down), erect, plumb, on end, precipitous, vertiginous, bolt upright **OPPOSITE** horizontal

vertigo = <u>dizziness</u>, giddiness, light-headedness, fear of heights, loss of balance, acrophobia, loss of equilibrium, swimming of the head

verve = <u>enthusiasm</u>, energy, spirit, life, force, punch (*informal*), dash, pep, sparkle, zip (*informal*), vitality, animation, vigour, zeal, gusto, get-up-and-go (*informal*), élan, brio, vivacity, liveliness, vim (*slang*) **OPPOSITE** indifference

very **ADVERB** = <u>extremely</u>, highly, greatly, really, deeply, particularly, seriously (*informal*), truly, absolutely, terribly, remarkably, unusually, jolly (*Brit.*), wonderfully, profoundly, decidedly, awfully (*informal*), acutely, exceedingly, excessively, noticeably, eminently, superlatively, uncommonly, surpassingly ...*I am very grateful to you for all your help*...
ADJECTIVE 1 = <u>exact</u>, actual, precise, same, real, express, identical, unqualified, selfsame ...*Those were his very words to me*...
2 = <u>ideal</u>, perfect, right, fitting, appropriate, suitable, spot on (*Brit. informal*), apt, just the job (*Brit. informal*) ...*the very person we need for the job*...

Word Power

very – In strict usage, adverbs of degree such as *very*, *too*, *quite*, *really*, and *extremely* are used only to qualify adjectives: *he is very happy*; *she is too sad*. By this rule, these words should not be used to qualify past participles that follow the verb *to be*, since they would then be technically qualifying verbs. With the exception of certain participles, such as *tired* or *disappointed*, that have come to be regarded as adjectives, all other past participles are qualified by adverbs such as *much*, *greatly*, *seriously*, or *excessively*: *he has been much* (not *very*) *inconvenienced*; *she has been excessively* (not *too*) *criticized*.

vessel 1 = <u>ship</u>, boat, craft, barque (*poetic*) ...*a Moroccan fishing vessel*...
2 = <u>container</u>, receptacle, can, bowl, tank, pot, drum, barrel, butt, vat, bin, jar, basin, tub, jug, pitcher, urn, canister, repository, cask ...*plastic storage vessels*...
➤ boats and ships

vest
PHRASES **vest in something** or **someone** *usually passive* = <u>place</u>, invest, entrust, settle, lodge, confer, endow, bestow, consign, put in the hands of, be devolved upon ...*All the authority was vested in one man*... ♦ **vest with something** *usually passive* = <u>endow with</u>, furnish with, entrust with, empower with, authorize with ...*The mass media has been vested with considerable power*...

vestibule = <u>hall</u>, lobby, foyer, porch, entrance hall, portico, anteroom

vestige 1 = <u>remnant</u>, remains, trace, relic, track, token, remainder, residue ...*the last vestiges of a great and ancient kingdom*...
2 = <u>trace</u>, sign, hint, scrap, evidence, indication, suspicion, glimmer ...*She had lost every vestige of her puppy fat*...

vet = <u>check</u>, examine, investigate, check out, review, scan, look over, appraise, scrutinize, size up (*informal*), give someone or something the once-over (*informal*), pass under review

veteran **NOUN** = <u>old hand</u>, master, pro (*informal*), old-timer, past master, trouper, warhorse (*informal*), old stager ...*Graf was already a tennis veteran at the age of 21*... **OPPOSITE** novice
ADJECTIVE = <u>long-serving</u>, seasoned, experienced, old,

established, expert, qualified, mature, practised, hardened, adept, proficient, well trained, battle-scarred, worldly-wise ...*Tony Benn, the veteran Labour MP and former Cabinet Minister...*

veto `VERB` = <u>ban</u>, block, reject, rule out, kill (*informal*), negative, turn down, forbid, boycott, prohibit, disallow, put a stop to, refuse permission to, interdict, give the thumbs down to, put the kibosh on (*slang*) ...*De Gaulle vetoed Britain's application to join the EEC...* `OPPOSITE` pass

`NOUN` = <u>ban</u>, dismissal, rejection, vetoing, boycott, embargo, prohibiting, prohibition, suppression, knock-back (*informal*), interdict, declination, preclusion, nonconsent ...*congressmen who tried to override the president's veto of the bill...* `OPPOSITE` ratification

vex = <u>annoy</u>, bother, irritate, worry, trouble, upset, disturb, distress, provoke, bug (*informal*), offend, needle (*informal*), plague, put out, tease, torment, harass, hassle (*informal*), aggravate (*informal*), afflict, fret, gall, agitate, exasperate, nettle, pester, displease, rile, pique, peeve (*informal*), grate on, get on your nerves (*informal*), nark (*Brit., Austral., & N.Z. slang*), give someone grief (*Brit. & S. African*), get your back up, put your back up `OPPOSITE` soothe

vexed 1 = <u>annoyed</u>, upset, irritated, worried, troubled, bothered, confused, disturbed, distressed, provoked, put out, fed up, tormented, harassed, aggravated (*informal*), afflicted, agitated, ruffled, exasperated, perplexed, nettled, miffed (*informal*), displeased, riled, peeved (*informal*), hacked off (*U.S. slang*), out of countenance, tooshie (*Austral. slang*) ...*He was vexed by the art establishment's rejection of his work...*
2 = <u>controversial</u>, disputed, contested, moot, much debated ...*Later the minister raised the vexed question of refugees...*

viable = <u>workable</u>, practical, feasible, suitable, realistic, operational, applicable, usable, practicable, serviceable, operable, within the bounds of possibility `OPPOSITE` unworkable

vibes (*Informal*) *sometimes singular* 1 = <u>feelings</u>, emotions, response, reaction ...*I don't like the guy – I have bad vibes about him...*
2 = <u>atmosphere</u>, aura, vibrations, feeling, emanation ...*a club with really good vibes...*

vibrant 1 = <u>energetic</u>, dynamic, sparkling, vivid, spirited, storming, alive, sensitive, colourful, vigorous, animated, responsive, electrifying, vivacious, full of pep (*informal*) ...*Tom was drawn to her by her vibrant personality...*
2 = <u>vivid</u>, bright, brilliant, intense, clear, rich, glowing, colourful, highly-coloured ...*His shirt was a vibrant shade of green...*

vibrate 1 = <u>shake</u>, tremble, shiver, fluctuate, quiver, oscillate, judder (*informal*) ...*Her whole body seemed to vibrate with terror...*
2 = <u>throb</u>, pulse, resonate, pulsate, reverberate ...*The noise vibrated through the whole house...*

vibration 1 = <u>shaking</u>, shake, trembling, quake, quaking, shudder, shuddering, quiver, oscillation, judder (*informal*) ...*The vibration dislodged the pins from the plane's rudder...*
2 = <u>throbbing</u>, pulse, thumping, hum, humming, throb, resonance, tremor, drone, droning, reverberation, pulsation ...*They heard a distant low vibration in the distance...*

vicarious = <u>indirect</u>, substitute, surrogate, by proxy, empathetic, at one remove

vice 1 = <u>fault</u>, failing, weakness, limitation, defect, deficiency, flaw, shortcoming, blemish, imperfection, frailty, foible, weak point, infirmity ...*Having the odd flutter on the horses is his only vice...* `OPPOSITE` good point
2 = <u>wickedness</u>, evil, corruption, sin, depravity, immorality, iniquity, profligacy, degeneracy, venality, turpitude, evildoing ...*offences connected with vice, gaming and drugs...* `OPPOSITE` virtue

vice versa = <u>the other way round</u>, conversely, in reverse, contrariwise

vicinity = <u>neighbourhood</u>, area, district, precincts, locality, environs, neck of the woods (*informal*), purlieus

vicious 1 = <u>savage</u>, brutal, violent, bad, dangerous, foul, cruel, ferocious, monstrous, vile, atrocious, diabolical, heinous, abhorrent, barbarous, fiendish ...*He suffered a vicious attack by a gang of youths...* `OPPOSITE` gentle
2 = <u>depraved</u>, corrupt, wicked, infamous, degraded, worthless, degenerate, immoral, sinful, debased, profligate, unprincipled ...*a vicious criminal incapable of remorse...* `OPPOSITE` virtuous
3 = <u>malicious</u>, vindictive, spiteful, mean, cruel, venomous, bitchy (*informal*), defamatory, rancorous, backbiting, slanderous ...*a vicious attack on an innocent woman's character...* `OPPOSITE` complimentary

vicissitudes = <u>variations</u>, changes, shifts, changes of fortune, life's ups and downs (*informal*)

victim 1 = <u>casualty</u>, sufferer, injured party, fatality ...*an organisation representing victims of the accident...* `OPPOSITE` survivor
2 = <u>prey</u>, patsy (*slang, chiefly U.S. & Canad.*), sucker (*slang*), dupe, gull (*archaic*), stooge, sitting duck (*informal*), sitting target, innocent ...*the victim of a particularly cruel hoax...* `OPPOSITE` culprit
3 = <u>scapegoat</u>, sacrifice, martyr, fall guy (*informal*), whipping boy ...*A sacrificial victim was thrown to the judicial authorities...*

victimize = <u>persecute</u>, bully, pick on, abuse, harass, discriminate against, lean on, have it in for (*informal*), push someone around, give someone a hard time, demonize, have a down on (*informal*), have your knife into

victor = <u>winner</u>, champion, conqueror, first, champ (*informal*), vanquisher, top dog (*informal*), prizewinner, conquering hero `OPPOSITE` loser

victorious = <u>winning</u>, successful, triumphant, first,

champion, conquering, vanquishing, prizewinning
OPPOSITE> losing

victory = <u>win</u>, success, triumph, the prize, superiority, conquest, laurels, mastery, walkover (*informal*)
OPPOSITE> defeat

vie = <u>compete</u>, struggle, contend, contest, strive, be rivals, match yourself against

view NOUN **1** *sometimes plural* = <u>opinion</u>, thought, idea, belief, thinking, feeling, attitude, reckoning, impression, notion, conviction, judgment, point of view, sentiment, viewpoint, persuasion, way of thinking, standpoint ...*You should make your views known to your local MP*...
2 = <u>scene</u>, picture, sight, prospect, aspect, perspective, landscape, outlook, spectacle, panorama, vista ...*The view from our window was one of beautiful countryside*...
3 = <u>vision</u>, sight, visibility, perspective, eyeshot, range or field of vision ...*A group of riders came into view*...
4 = <u>study</u>, review, survey, assessment, examination, scan, inspection, look, scrutiny, contemplation ...*a concise but comprehensive view of basic economics*...
VERB **1** = <u>regard</u>, see, consider, judge, perceive, treat, estimate, reckon, deem, look on, adjudge, think about or of ...*America was viewed as a land of golden opportunity*...
2 = <u>look at</u>, see, inspect, gaze at, eye, watch, check, regard, survey, witness, clock (*Brit. slang*), examine, observe, explore, stare at, scan, contemplate, check out (*informal*), behold, eyeball (*slang*), gawp at, recce (*slang*), get a load of (*informal*), spectate, take a dekko at (*Brit. slang*) ...*The mourners filed past to view the body*...
PHRASES **with a view to** = <u>with the aim</u> or <u>intention of</u>, in order to, so as to, in the hope of ...*She joined a dating agency with a view to finding a husband*...

viewer = <u>watcher</u>, observer, spectator, onlooker, couch potato (*informal*), TV watcher, one of an audience

viewpoint = <u>point of view</u>, perspective, angle, position, attitude, stance, slant, belief, conviction, feeling, opinion, way of thinking, standpoint, vantage point, frame of reference

vigilance = <u>watchfulness</u>, alertness, caution, observance, circumspection, attentiveness, carefulness

vigilant = <u>watchful</u>, alert, on the lookout, careful, cautious, attentive, circumspect, wide awake, on the alert, on your toes, wakeful, on your guard, on the watch, on the qui vive, keeping your eyes peeled or skinned (*informal*) OPPOSITE> inattentive

vigorous 1 = <u>strenuous</u>, energetic, arduous, hard, taxing, active, intense, exhausting, rigorous, brisk ...*Avoid vigorous exercise for a few weeks*...
2 = <u>spirited</u>, lively, energetic, active, intense, dynamic, sparkling, animated, forceful, feisty (*informal*), spanking, high-spirited, sprightly, vivacious, forcible, effervescent, full of energy, zippy (*informal*), spunky

(*informal*) ...*The choir and orchestra gave a vigorous performance of Haydn's oratorio*... OPPOSITE> lethargic
3 = <u>strong</u>, powerful, robust, sound, healthy, vital, lively, flourishing, hardy, hale, hearty, lusty, virile, alive and kicking, red-blooded, fighting fit, full of energy, full of beans (*informal*), hale and hearty, fit as a fiddle (*informal*) ...*He was a vigorous, handsome young man*... OPPOSITE> weak

vigorously 1 = <u>energetically</u>, hard, forcefully, strongly, all out, eagerly, with a vengeance, strenuously, like mad (*slang*), lustily, hammer and tongs, with might and main ...*She shivered and rubbed her arms vigorously*...
2 = <u>forcefully</u>, strongly, vehemently, strenuously ...*The police vigorously denied that excessive force had been used*...

vigour or (*U.S.*) **vigor** = <u>energy</u>, might, force, vitality, power, activity, spirit, strength, snap (*informal*), punch (*informal*), dash, pep, zip (*informal*), animation, verve, gusto, dynamism, oomph (*informal*), brio, robustness, liveliness, vim (*slang*), forcefulness OPPOSITE> weakness

vile 1 = <u>wicked</u>, base, evil, mean, bad, low, shocking, appalling, ugly, corrupt, miserable, vicious, humiliating, perverted, coarse, degrading, worthless, disgraceful, vulgar, degenerate, abject, sinful, despicable, depraved, debased, loathsome, contemptible, impure, wretched, nefarious, ignoble ...*a vile and despicable crime*... OPPOSITE> honourable
2 = <u>disgusting</u>, foul, revolting, offensive, nasty, obscene, sickening, horrid, repellent, repulsive, noxious, nauseating, repugnant, loathsome, yucky or yukky (*slang*), yucko (*Austral. slang*) ...*the vile smell of his cigar smoke*... OPPOSITE> pleasant

vilification = <u>denigration</u>, abuse, defamation, invective, calumny, mudslinging, disparagement, vituperation, contumely, aspersion, scurrility, calumniation

vilify = <u>malign</u>, abuse, denigrate, knock (*informal*), rubbish (*informal*), run down, smear, slag (off) (*slang*), berate, disparage, decry, revile, slander, dump on (*slang, chiefly U.S.*), debase, defame, bad-mouth (*slang, chiefly U.S. & Canad.*), traduce, speak ill of, pull to pieces (*informal*), calumniate, vituperate, asperse OPPOSITE> praise

villain 1 = <u>evildoer</u>, criminal, rogue, profligate, scoundrel, wretch, libertine, knave (*archaic*), reprobate, miscreant, malefactor, blackguard, rapscallion, caitiff (*archaic*) ...*As a copper, I've spent my life putting villains like him away*...
2 = <u>baddy</u> (*informal*), antihero ...*Darth Vader, the villain of the Star Wars trilogy*... OPPOSITE> hero

villainous = <u>wicked</u>, evil, depraved, mean, bad, base, criminal, terrible, cruel, vicious, outrageous, infamous, vile, degenerate, atrocious, inhuman, sinful, diabolical, heinous, debased, hateful, scoundrelly, fiendish, ruffianly, nefarious, ignoble, detestable, blackguardly, thievish OPPOSITE> virtuous

vindicate 1 = <u>clear</u>, acquit, exonerate, absolve, let off the hook, exculpate, free from blame …*The director said he had been vindicated by the expert's report…* OPPOSITE condemn

2 = <u>support</u>, uphold, ratify, defend, excuse, justify, substantiate …*Subsequent events vindicated his policy…*

vindication 1 = <u>exoneration</u>, pardon, acquittal, dismissal, discharge, amnesty, absolution, exculpating, exculpation …*He insisted on a complete vindication from the libel jury…*

2 = <u>support</u>, defence, ratification, excuse, apology, justification, assertion, substantiation …*He called the success a vindication of his party's economic policy…*

vindictive = <u>vengeful</u>, malicious, spiteful, relentless, resentful, malignant, unrelenting, unforgiving, implacable, venomous, rancorous, revengeful, full of spleen OPPOSITE merciful

vintage NOUN **1** (always used of wines) = <u>harvest</u>, year, crop, yield …*This wine is from one of the best vintages of the decade…*

2 = <u>era</u>, period, origin, sort, type, generation, stamp, epoch, ilk, time of origin …*a Jeep of World War Two vintage…*

ADJECTIVE **1** (always used of wines) = <u>high-quality</u>, best, prime, quality, choice, select, rare, superior …*Gourmet food and vintage wines are also part of the service…*

2 = <u>classic</u>, old, veteran, historic, heritage, enduring, antique, timeless, old-world, age-old, ageless …*vintage, classic and racing cars… …This is vintage comedy at its best…*

violate 1 = <u>break</u>, infringe, disobey, transgress, ignore, defy, disregard, flout, rebel against, contravene, fly in the face of, overstep, not comply with, take no notice of, encroach upon, pay no heed to, infract …*They violated the ceasefire agreement…* OPPOSITE obey

2 = <u>invade</u>, infringe on, disturb, upset, shatter, disrupt, impinge on, encroach on, intrude on, trespass on, obtrude on …*These journalists were violating her family's privacy…*

3 = <u>desecrate</u>, profane, defile, abuse, outrage, pollute, deface, dishonour, vandalize, treat with disrespect, befoul …*Police are still searching for the people who violated the graves…* OPPOSITE honour

4 = <u>rape</u>, molest, sexually assault, ravish, abuse, assault, interfere with, sexually abuse, indecently assault, force yourself on …*He broke into a woman's home and attempted to violate her…*

violation 1 = <u>breach</u>, abuse, infringement, contravention, abuse, trespass, transgression, infraction …*This is a flagrant violation of state law…*

2 = <u>invasion</u>, intrusion, trespass, breach, disturbance, disruption, interruption, encroachment …*Legal action will be initiated for defamation and violation of privacy…*

3 = <u>desecration</u>, sacrilege, defilement, profanation, spoliation …*This violation of the church is not the first such incident…*

4 = <u>rape</u>, sexual assault, molesting, ravishing (old-

fashioned), abuse, sexual abuse, indecent assault, molestation …*the violation of women in war…*

violence 1 = <u>brutality</u>, bloodshed, savagery, fighting, terrorism, frenzy, thuggery, destructiveness, bestiality, strong-arm tactics (*informal*), rough handling, bloodthirstiness, murderousness …*Twenty people were killed in the violence…*

2 = <u>force</u>, power, strength, might, ferocity, brute force, fierceness, forcefulness, powerfulness …*The violence of the blow forced the hammer through his skull…*

3 = <u>intensity</u>, passion, fury, force, cruelty, severity, fervour, sharpness, harshness, vehemence …*'There's no need,' she snapped with sudden violence…*

4 = <u>power</u>, turbulence, wildness, raging, tumult, roughness, boisterousness, storminess …*The house was destroyed in the violence of the storm…*

violent 1 = <u>brutal</u>, aggressive, savage, wild, rough, fierce, bullying, cruel, vicious, destructive, ruthless, murderous, maddened, berserk, merciless, bloodthirsty, homicidal, pitiless, hot-headed, thuggish, maniacal, hot-tempered …*He was a violent man with a drink and drugs problem…* OPPOSITE gentle

2 = <u>sharp</u>, hard, powerful, forceful, strong, fierce, fatal, savage, deadly, brutal, vicious, lethal, hefty, ferocious, death-dealing …*She had died from a violent blow to the head…*

3 = <u>intense</u>, acute, severe, biting, sharp, extreme, painful, harsh, excruciating, agonizing, inordinate …*He had violent stomach pains…*

4 = <u>passionate</u>, intense, extreme, strong, wild, consuming, uncontrollable, vehement, unrestrained, tempestuous, ungovernable …*his violent, almost pathological jealousy…*

5 = <u>fiery</u>, raging, fierce, flaming, furious, passionate, peppery, ungovernable …*I had a violent temper and was always in fights…*

6 = <u>powerful</u>, wild, devastating, strong, storming, raging, turbulent, tumultuous, tempestuous, gale force, blustery, ruinous, full of force …*That night a violent storm arose and wrecked most of the ships…* OPPOSITE mild

VIP = <u>celebrity</u>, big name, public figure, star, somebody, lion, notable, luminary, bigwig (*informal*), leading light (*informal*), big shot (*informal*), personage, big noise (*informal*), big hitter (*informal*), heavy hitter (*informal*), man *or* woman of the hour

virago = <u>harridan</u>, fury, shrew, vixen, scold, battle-axe (*informal*), termagant (*rare*)

virgin NOUN = <u>maiden</u>, maid (*archaic*), damsel (*archaic*), girl (*archaic*), celibate, vestal, virgo intacta …*I was a virgin until I was twenty-four years old…*

ADJECTIVE **1** = <u>untouched</u>, immaculate, fresh, new, pure, unused, pristine, flawless, unblemished, unadulterated, unsullied …*Within 40 years there will be no virgin forest left…* OPPOSITE spoiled

2 = <u>pure</u>, maidenly, chaste, immaculate, virginal, unsullied, vestal, uncorrupted, undefiled …*a society in which men still prize virgin brides…* OPPOSITE corrupted

virginal 1 = <u>chaste</u>, pure, maidenly, virgin, immaculate, celibate, uncorrupted, undefiled ...*She had always been a child in his mind, pure and virginal...*
2 = <u>immaculate</u>, fresh, pristine, white, pure, untouched, snowy, undisturbed, spotless ...*linen tablecloths of virginal white...*

virginity = <u>chastity</u>, maidenhead, maidenhood

virile = <u>manly</u>, masculine, macho, strong, male, robust, vigorous, potent, forceful, lusty, red-blooded, manlike [OPPOSITE] effeminate

virility = <u>masculinity</u>, manhood, potency, vigour, machismo [OPPOSITE] effeminacy

virtual = <u>practical</u>, near, essential, implied, indirect, implicit, tacit, near enough, unacknowledged, in all but name

virtually = <u>practically</u>, almost, nearly, in effect, in essence, as good as, to all intents and purposes, in all but name, for all practical purposes, effectually

virtue [NOUN] **1** = <u>goodness</u>, honour, integrity, worth, dignity, excellence, morality, honesty, decency, respectability, nobility, righteousness, propriety, probity, rectitude, worthiness, high-mindedness, incorruptibility, uprightness, virtuousness, ethicalness ...*His mother was held up to the family as a paragon of virtue...* [OPPOSITE] vice
2 = <u>merit</u>, strength, asset, plus (*informal*), attribute, good quality, good point, strong point ...*His chief virtue is patience...* [OPPOSITE] failing
3 = <u>advantage</u>, benefit, merit, credit, usefulness, efficacy ...*There is no virtue in overexercising...*
4 = <u>chastity</u>, honour, virginity, innocence, purity, maidenhood, chasteness ...*His many attempts on her virtue were all unavailing...* [OPPOSITE] unchastity
[PHRASES] **by virtue of** = <u>because of</u>, in view of, on account of, based on, thanks to, as a result of, owing to, by reason of, by dint of ...*Mr Olaechea has British residency by virtue of his marriage...*

virtuosity = <u>mastery</u>, skill, brilliance, polish, craft, expertise, flair, panache, éclat

virtuoso [NOUN] = <u>master</u>, artist, genius, maestro, magician, grandmaster, maven (*U.S.*), master hand ...*Canada's foremost piano virtuoso, Glenn Gould...*
[ADJECTIVE] = <u>masterly</u>, brilliant, dazzling, bravura (*Music*) ...*a virtuoso performance by a widely respected musician...*

virtuous 1 = <u>good</u>, moral, ethical, upright, honourable, excellent, pure, worthy, honest, righteous, exemplary, squeaky-clean, blameless, praiseworthy, incorruptible, high-principled ...*The president is portrayed as a virtuous family man...* [OPPOSITE] corrupt
2 = <u>chaste</u>, pure, innocent, celibate, spotless, virginal, clean-living ...*a prince who falls in love with a beautiful and virtuous maiden...* [OPPOSITE] promiscuous
3 = <u>self-righteous</u>, pleased with yourself, smug ...*I cleaned the flat, which left me feeling very virtuous...*

virulent 1 = <u>vicious</u>, vindictive, bitter, hostile, malicious, resentful, acrimonious, malevolent, spiteful, venomous, rancorous, splenetic, envenomed ...*A virulent personal campaign is being waged against him...* [OPPOSITE] benign
2 = <u>deadly</u>, lethal, toxic, poisonous, malignant, pernicious, venomous, septic, infective, injurious, baneful (*archaic*) ...*A virulent form of the disease has appeared in Belgium...* [OPPOSITE] harmless

viscous = <u>thick</u>, sticky, gooey (*informal*), adhesive, tenacious, clammy, syrupy, glutinous, gummy, gelatinous, icky (*informal*), gluey, treacly, mucilaginous, viscid

visible = <u>perceptible</u>, noticeable, observable, clear, obvious, plain, apparent, bold, patent, to be seen, evident, manifest, in sight, in view, conspicuous, unmistakable, palpable, discernible, salient, detectable, not hidden, distinguishable, unconcealed, perceivable, discoverable, anywhere to be seen [OPPOSITE] invisible

vision 1 = <u>image</u>, idea, dream, plans, hopes, prospect, ideal, concept, fancy, fantasy, conception, delusion, daydream, reverie, flight of fancy, mental picture, pipe dream, imago (*Psychoanalysis*), castle in the air, fanciful notion ...*I have a vision of a society free of exploitation and injustice...*
2 = <u>hallucination</u>, illusion, apparition, revelation, ghost, phantom, delusion, spectre, mirage, wraith, chimera, phantasm, eidolon ...*She heard voices and saw visions of her ancestors...*
3 = <u>sight</u>, seeing, eyesight, view, eyes, perception ...*The disease causes blindness or serious loss of vision...*
4 = <u>foresight</u>, imagination, perception, insight, awareness, inspiration, innovation, creativity, intuition, penetration, inventiveness, shrewdness, discernment, prescience, perceptiveness, farsightedness, breadth of view ...*The government's lack of vision could have profound economic consequences...*
5 = <u>picture</u>, dream, sight, delight, beauty, joy, sensation, spectacle, knockout (*informal*), beautiful sight, perfect picture, feast for the eyes, sight for sore eyes, pearler (*Austral. slang*) ...*The girl was a vision in crimson organza...*

visionary [NOUN] **1** = <u>idealist</u>, romantic, dreamer, daydreamer, utopian, enthusiast (*archaic*), theorist, zealot, Don Quixote ...*Visionaries see the world not as it is but as it could be...* [OPPOSITE] realist
2 = <u>prophet</u>, diviner, mystic, seer, soothsayer, sibyl, scryer, spaewife (*Scot.*) ...*shamans, mystics and religious visionaries...*
[ADJECTIVE] **1** = <u>idealistic</u>, romantic, unrealistic, utopian, dreaming, speculative, impractical, dreamy, unworkable, quixotic, starry-eyed, with your head in the clouds ...*His ideas were dismissed as mere visionary speculation...* [OPPOSITE] realistic
2 = <u>prophetic</u>, mystical, divinatory, predictive, oracular, sibylline, mantic, vatic (*rare*), fatidic (*rare*) ...*visionary experiences and contact with spirit beings...*

3 = <u>imaginary</u>, fantastic, unreal, fanciful, ideal, idealized, illusory, imaginal (*Psychoanal.*), chimerical, delusory …*the visionary worlds created by fantasy writers…* OPPOSITE> real

visit VERB **1** = <u>call on</u>, go to see, drop in on (*informal*), stay at, stay with, stop by, spend time with, look someone up, go see (*U.S.*), pay a visit to, be the guest of, call in on, pop in on (*informal*), pay a call on …*I want to visit my relatives in Scotland…*
2 = <u>stay in</u>, see, tour, explore, take in (*informal*), holiday in, go to see, stop by, spend time in, vacation in (*U.S.*), stop over in …*He'll be visiting four cities, including Cagliari in Sardinia…*
NOUN **1** = <u>call</u>, social call …*Helen recently paid me a visit…*
2 = <u>trip</u>, stop, stay, break, tour, holiday, vacation (*informal*), stopover, sojourn …*the Pope's visit to Canada…*

visitation **1** = <u>apparition</u>, vision, manifestation, appearance, materialization …*He claims to have had a visitation from the Virgin Mary…*
2 = <u>inspection</u>, survey, examination, visit, review, scrutiny …*House-to-house visitation has been authorized by the Board of Health…*

visitor = <u>guest</u>, caller, company, visitant

vista = <u>view</u>, scene, prospect, landscape, panorama, perspective

visual **1** = <u>optical</u>, optic, ocular …*the way our brain processes visual information…*
2 = <u>observable</u>, visible, perceptible, discernible …*There was no visual evidence to support his claim…* OPPOSITE> imperceptible

visualize = <u>picture</u>, imagine, think about, envisage, contemplate, conceive of, see in the mind's eye, conjure up a mental picture of

vital **1** = <u>essential</u>, important, necessary, key, basic, significant, critical, radical, crucial, fundamental, urgent, decisive, cardinal, imperative, indispensable, requisite, life-or-death …*a blockade which could cut off vital oil and gas supplies…* OPPOSITE> unnecessary
2 = <u>lively</u>, vigorous, energetic, spirited, dynamic, animated, vibrant, forceful, sparky, vivacious, full of beans (*informal*), zestful, full of the joy of living …*It is tragic to see how the disease has diminished a once vital person…* OPPOSITE> lethargic

vitality = <u>energy</u>, vivacity, sparkle, go (*informal*), life, strength, pep, stamina, animation, vigour, exuberance, brio, robustness, liveliness, vim (*slang*), lustiness, vivaciousness OPPOSITE> lethargy

vitriolic = <u>venomous</u>, scathing, malicious, acid, bitter, destructive, withering, virulent, sardonic, caustic, bitchy (*informal*), acerbic, envenomed, dripping with malice

vivacious = <u>lively</u>, spirited, vital, gay, bubbling, sparkling, cheerful, jolly, animated, merry, upbeat (*informal*), high-spirited, ebullient, chirpy (*informal*), sparky, scintillating, sprightly, effervescent, full of life, full of beans (*informal*), frolicsome, sportive, light-hearted OPPOSITE> dull

vivid **1** = <u>clear</u>, detailed, realistic, telling, moving, strong, affecting, arresting, powerful, sharp, dramatic, stirring, stimulating, haunting, graphic, distinct, lively, memorable, unforgettable, evocative, lucid, lifelike, true to life, sharply-etched …*Last night I had a vivid dream which really upset me…* OPPOSITE> vague
2 = <u>bright</u>, brilliant, intense, clear, rich, glowing, colourful, highly-coloured …*a vivid blue sky…* OPPOSITE> dull
3 = <u>lively</u>, strong, dynamic, striking, spirited, powerful, quick, storming, active, vigorous, energetic, animated, vibrant, fiery, flamboyant, expressive, vivacious, zestful …*one of the most vivid personalities in tennis…* OPPOSITE> quiet

vixen = <u>shrew</u>, fury, spitfire, virago, harpy, scold, harridan, termagant (*rare*), hellcat

viz = <u>namely</u>, that is to say, to wit, videlicet

vocabulary **1** = <u>language</u>, words, lexicon, word stock, word hoard …*Children need to read to improve their vocabularies…*
2 = <u>wordbook</u>, dictionary, glossary, lexicon …*I could not find this word in my small Italian-English vocabulary…*

vocal **1** = <u>outspoken</u>, frank, blunt, forthright, strident, vociferous, noisy, articulate, expressive, eloquent, plain-spoken, clamorous, free-spoken …*He has been very vocal in his displeasure over the decision…* OPPOSITE> quiet
2 = <u>spoken</u>, voiced, uttered, oral, said, articulate, articulated, put into words …*a child's ability to imitate rhythms and vocal sounds…*

vocation = <u>profession</u>, calling, job, business, office, trade, role, post, career, mission, employment, pursuit, life work, métier

vociferous = <u>outspoken</u>, vocal, strident, noisy, shouting, loud, ranting, vehement, loudmouthed (*informal*), uproarious, obstreperous, clamorous OPPOSITE> quiet

vogue NOUN = <u>fashion</u>, trend, craze, style, the latest, the thing (*informal*), mode, last word, the rage, passing fancy, dernier cri (*French*) …*the new vogue for herbal medicines…*
ADJECTIVE = <u>fashionable</u>, trendy (*Brit. informal*), in, now (*informal*), popular, with it (*informal*), prevalent, up-to-the-minute, modish, voguish …*The word 'talisman' has become a vogue word in sports writing…*
PHRASES **in vogue** = <u>popular</u>, big, fashionable, all the rage, happening, accepted, current, cool, in favour, stylish, up to date, in use, prevalent, up to the minute, modish, trendsetting …*Pale colours are in vogue this season…*

voice NOUN **1** = <u>tone</u>, sound, language, articulation, power of speech …*Miriam's voice was strangely calm…*
2 = <u>utterance</u>, expression, words, airing, vocalization, verbalization …*The crowd gave voice to their anger…*
3 = <u>opinion</u>, will, feeling, wish, desire …*the voice of the opposition…*
4 = <u>say</u>, part, view, decision, vote, comment, input

...Our employees have no voice in how our company is run...

5 = instrument, medium, spokesman or spokeswoman, agency, channel, vehicle, organ, spokesperson, intermediary, mouthpiece ...He claims to be the voice of the people...

VERB = express, say, declare, air, raise, table, reveal, mention, mouth, assert, pronounce, utter, articulate, come out with (informal), divulge, ventilate, enunciate, put into words, vocalize, give expression or utterance to ...Scientists have voiced concern that the disease could be passed to humans...

(*Related Words*)

adjective: vocal

void NOUN **1** = gap, space, lack, want, hole, blank, emptiness ...His death has created a void which will never be filled...

2 = emptiness, space, vacuum, oblivion, blankness, nullity, vacuity ...the limitless void of outer space...

ADJECTIVE **1** = invalid, null and void, inoperative, useless, ineffective, worthless, ineffectual, unenforceable, nonviable ...The elections were declared void by the former military ruler...

2 with **of** = devoid of, without, lacking, free from, wanting, bereft of, empty of, bare of, destitute of, vacant of ...His face was void of emotion as he left the room...

VERB = invalidate, nullify, cancel, withdraw, reverse, undo, repeal, quash, revoke, disallow, retract, repudiate, negate, rescind, annul, abrogate, countermand, render invalid, abnegate ...The Supreme Court voided his conviction for murder...

volatile 1 = changeable, shifting, variable, unsettled, unstable, explosive, unreliable, unsteady, inconstant ...There have been riots before and the situation is volatile... OPPOSITE stable

2 = temperamental, erratic, mercurial, up and down (informal), fickle, whimsical, giddy, flighty, over-emotional, inconstant ...She has a volatile temperament... OPPOSITE calm

volcano
➤ **WORD POWER SUPPLEMENT volcanoes**

volition = free will, will, choice, election, choosing, option, purpose, resolution, determination, preference, discretion

volley = barrage, blast, burst, explosion, shower, hail, discharge, bombardment, salvo, fusillade, cannonade

voluble = talkative, garrulous, loquacious, forthcoming, articulate, fluent, glib, blessed with the gift of the gab OPPOSITE reticent

volume 1 = amount, quantity, level, body, total, measure, degree, mass, proportion, bulk, aggregate ...the sheer volume of traffic on our motorways...

2 = capacity, size, mass, extent, proportions, dimensions, bulk, measurements, magnitude, compass, largeness, cubic content ...When water is frozen it increases in volume...

3 = book, work, title, opus, publication, manual, tome, treatise, almanac, compendium ...a slim volume of English poetry...

4 = loudness, sound, amplification ...He came round to complain about the volume of the music...

(*Related Words*)

adjective: cubical

voluminous 1 = large, big, full, massive, vast, ample, bulky, billowing, roomy, cavernous, capacious ...She was swathed in a voluminous cloak... OPPOSITE small

2 = copious, extensive, prolific, abundant, plentiful, profuse ...this author's voluminous writings and correspondence... OPPOSITE scanty

voluntarily = willingly, freely, by choice, without being asked, without prompting, lief (rare), on your own initiative, of your own free will, off your own bat, of your own accord, of your own volition

voluntary 1 = intentional, intended, deliberate, planned, studied, purposed, calculated, wilful, done on purpose ...a voluntary act undertaken in full knowledge of the consequences... OPPOSITE unintentional

2 = optional, discretionary, up to the individual, open, unforced, unconstrained, unenforced, at your discretion, discretional, open to choice, uncompelled ...The extra course in Commercial French is voluntary... OPPOSITE obligatory

3 = unpaid, volunteer, free, willing, honorary, gratuitous, pro bono (Law) ...In her spare time she does voluntary work for the homeless...

volunteer 1 = offer, step forward, offer your services, propose, let yourself in for (informal), need no invitation, present your services, proffer your services, put yourself at someone's disposal ...Aunt Mary volunteered to clean up the kitchen... OPPOSITE refuse

2 = suggest, advance, put forward, venture, tender ...His wife volunteered an ingenious suggestion...

voluptuous 1 = buxom, shapely, curvaceous, erotic, ample, enticing, provocative, seductive (informal), well-stacked (Brit. slang), full-bosomed ...a voluptuous, well-rounded lady with glossy red hair...

2 = sensual, luxurious, self-indulgent, hedonistic, sybaritic, epicurean, licentious, bacchanalian, pleasure-loving ...a life of voluptuous decadence... OPPOSITE abstemious

vomit 1 = be sick, throw up (informal), spew, chuck (Austral. & N.Z. informal), heave (slang), puke (slang), retch, barf (U.S. slang), chunder (slang, chiefly Austral.), belch forth, upchuck (U.S. slang), do a technicolour yawn, toss your cookies (U.S. slang) ...Any dairy product made him vomit...

2 often with **up** = bring up, throw up, regurgitate, chuck (up) (slang, chiefly U.S.), emit (informal), eject, puke (slang), disgorge, sick up (informal), spew out or up ...She vomited up all she had just eaten...

voracious 1 = gluttonous, insatiable, ravenous, hungry, greedy, ravening, devouring ...For their size, stoats are voracious predators...

2 = avid, prodigious, insatiable, uncontrolled, rapacious, unquenchable ...He was a voracious reader... OPPOSITE moderate

vortex = <u>whirlpool</u>, eddy, maelstrom, gyre, countercurrent

vote NOUN **1** = <u>poll</u>, election, ballot, referendum, popular vote, plebiscite, straw poll, show of hands …*They took a vote and decided not to do it*…
2 = <u>right to vote</u>, franchise, voting rights, suffrage, say, voice, enfranchisement …*Before that, women did not even have the vote*…
VERB **1** = <u>cast your vote</u>, go to the polls, mark your ballot paper …*Over half of the electorate did not vote in the last general election*…
2 = <u>judge</u>, declare, pronounce, decree, adjudge …*They voted him Player of the Year*…
3 (*Informal*) = <u>suggest</u>, propose, recommend, move, table, advocate, submit …*I vote that we ask him to come with us*…
PHRASES **vote someone in** = <u>elect</u>, choose, select, appoint, return, pick, opt for, designate, decide on, settle on, fix on, plump for, put in power …*The Prime Minister was voted in by a huge majority*…

voucher = <u>ticket</u>, token, coupon, pass, slip, chit, chitty (*Brit. informal*), docket

vouch for 1 = <u>guarantee</u>, back, certify, answer for, swear to, stick up for (*informal*), stand witness, give assurance of, asseverate, go bail for …*Kim's mother agreed to vouch for Maria and get her a job*…
2 = <u>confirm</u>, support, affirm, attest to, assert, uphold …*I cannot vouch for the accuracy of the story*…

vow VERB = <u>promise</u>, pledge, swear, commit, engage, affirm, avow, bind yourself, undertake solemnly …*She vowed that some day she would return to live in France*…
NOUN = <u>promise</u>, commitment, pledge, oath, profession, troth (*archaic*), avowal …*Most people still take their marriage vows seriously*…

voyage NOUN = <u>journey</u>, travels, trip, passage, expedition, crossing, sail, cruise, excursion …*He aims to follow Columbus's voyage to the West Indies*…
VERB = <u>travel</u>, journey, tour, cruise, steam, take a trip, go on an expedition …*The boat is currently voyaging through the Barents Sea*…

vulgar 1 = <u>tasteless</u>, common, flashy, low, gross, nasty, gaudy, tawdry, cheap and nasty, common as muck …*The decor is ugly, tasteless and vulgar*…
OPPOSITE tasteful
2 = <u>crude</u>, dirty, rude, low, blue, nasty, naughty, coarse, indecent, improper, suggestive, tasteless, risqué, off colour, ribald, indelicate, indecorous …*an oaf with a taste for racist and vulgar jokes*…
3 = <u>uncouth</u>, boorish, unrefined, impolite, ill-bred, unmannerly …*He was a vulgar old man, but he never swore in front of women*… OPPOSITE refined
4 = <u>vernacular</u>, native, common, general, ordinary …*translated from Latin into the vulgar tongue*…

vulgarity 1 = <u>tastelessness</u>, bad taste, grossness, tawdriness, gaudiness, lack of refinement …*I hate the vulgarity of this room*… OPPOSITE tastefulness
2 = <u>crudeness</u>, rudeness, coarseness, crudity, ribaldry, suggestiveness, indelicacy, indecorum …*a comedian famous for his vulgarity and irreverence*… OPPOSITE decorum
3 = <u>coarseness</u>, roughness, boorishness, rudeness, loutishness, oafishness, uncouthness …*For all his apparent vulgarity, Todd had a certain raw charm*… OPPOSITE refinement

vulnerable 1 = <u>susceptible</u>, helpless, unprotected, defenceless, exposed, weak, sensitive, tender, unguarded, thin-skinned …*criminals who prey on the more vulnerable members of our society*… OPPOSITE immune
2 = <u>exposed</u>, open, unprotected, defenceless, accessible, wide open, open to attack, assailable …*Their tanks would be vulnerable to attack from the air*… OPPOSITE well-protected

W w

wacky = <u>unusual</u>, odd, wild, strange, crazy, silly, weird, way-out (*informal*), eccentric, unpredictable, daft (*informal*), irrational, erratic, Bohemian, unconventional, far-out (*slang*), loony (*slang*), kinky (*informal*), off-the-wall (*slang*), unorthodox, nutty (*slang*), oddball, zany, goofy (*informal*), offbeat (*informal*), freaky (*slang*), outré, gonzo (*slang*), screwy (*informal*), wacko or whacko (*informal*), off the air (*Austral. slang*)

wad **1** = <u>bundle</u>, roll, bankroll (*U.S. & Canad.*), pocketful ...*a wad of banknotes*...
2 = <u>mass</u>, ball, lump, hunk, piece, block, plug, chunk ...*a wad of cotton wool*...

waddle = <u>shuffle</u>, shamble, totter, toddle, rock, stagger, sway, wobble

wade **VERB** **1** = <u>paddle</u>, splash, splash about, slop ...*The boys were wading in the cold pool nearby*...
2 = <u>walk through</u>, cross, ford, pass through, go across, travel across, make your way across ...*We had to wade the river and then climb out of the valley*...
PHRASES **wade in** = <u>move in</u>, pitch in, dive in (*informal*), set to work, advance, set to, get stuck in (*informal*), buckle down ...*I waded in to help, but I got pushed aside*... ◆ **wade into someone** = <u>launch yourself at</u>, charge at, attack, rush, storm, tackle, go for, set about, strike at, assail, tear into (*informal*), fall upon, set upon, lay into (*informal*), light into (*informal*) ...*The troops waded into the protesters with batons*... ◆ **wade into something** = <u>get involved in</u>, tackle, pitch in, interfere in, dive in, plunge in, get stuck into ...*The Stock Exchange yesterday waded into the debate on stamp duty*... ◆ **wade through something** = <u>plough through</u>, trawl through, labour at, work your way through, toil at, drudge at, peg away at ...*scientists who have to wade through tons of data*...

waffle **VERB** = <u>chatter</u>, rabbit (on) (*Brit. informal*), babble, drivel, prattle, jabber, gabble, rattle on, verbalize, blather, witter on (*informal*), blether, run off at the mouth (*slang*), prate ...*some guy on TV waffling about political correctness*...
NOUN = <u>prattle</u>, nonsense, hot air (*informal*), twaddle, padding, prating, gibberish, jabber, verbiage, blather, wordiness, verbosity, prolixity, bunkum or buncombe (*chiefly U.S.*), bizzo (*Austral. slang*), bull's wool (*Austral. & N.Z. slang*) ...*I'm tired of his smug, sanctimonious waffle*...

waft **VERB** **1** = <u>drift</u>, float, be carried, be transported, coast, flow, stray, glide, be borne, be conveyed ...*The scent of roses wafted through the open window*...
2 = <u>transport</u>, bring, carry, bear, guide, conduct, transmit, convey ...*A slight breeze wafted the heavy scent of flowers past her*...

NOUN = <u>current</u>, breath, puff, whiff, draught, breeze ...*A waft of perfume reached Ingrid's nostrils*...

wag[1] **VERB** **1** = <u>wave</u>, shake, swing, waggle, stir, sway, flutter, waver, quiver, vibrate, wiggle, oscillate ...*The dog was barking and wagging its tail wildly*...
2 = <u>waggle</u>, wave, shake, flourish, brandish, wobble, wiggle ...*He wagged a disapproving finger at me*...
3 = <u>shake</u>, bob, nod ...*She wagged her head in agreement*...
NOUN **1** = <u>wave</u>, shake, swing, toss, sway, flutter, waver, quiver, vibration, wiggle, oscillation, waggle ...*The dog gave a responsive wag of his tail*...
2 = <u>nod</u>, bob, shake ...*a wag of the head*...

wag[2] = <u>joker</u>, comic, wit, comedian, clown, card (*informal*), kidder (*informal*), jester, dag (*N.Z. informal*), prankster, buffoon, trickster, humorist, joculator or (*fem.*) joculatrix ...*My dad's always been a bit of a wag*...

wage **NOUN** often plural = <u>payment</u>, pay, earnings, remuneration, fee, reward, compensation, income, allowance, recompense, stipend, emolument ...*efforts to set a minimum wage well above the poverty line*...
VERB = <u>engage in</u>, conduct, pursue, carry on, undertake, practise, prosecute, proceed with ...*the three factions that had been waging a civil war*...

wager **VERB** = <u>bet</u>, chance, risk, stake, lay, venture, put on, pledge, gamble, hazard, speculate, punt (*chiefly Brit.*) ...*People had wagered a good deal of money on his winning the championship*...
NOUN = <u>bet</u>, stake, pledge, gamble, risk, flutter (*Brit. informal*), ante, punt (*chiefly Brit.*), long shot ...*punters placing wagers on the day's racing*...

waggle = <u>wag</u>, wiggle, wave, shake, flutter, wobble, oscillate

waif = <u>stray</u>, orphan, outcast, urchin, foundling

wail **VERB** = <u>cry</u>, weep, grieve, lament, keen, greet (*Scot. or archaic*), howl, whine, deplore, bemoan, bawl, bewail, yowl, ululate ...*The woman began to wail for her lost child*...
NOUN = <u>cry</u>, moan, sob, howl, keening, lament, bawl, lamentation, yowl, ululation ...*Wails of grief were heard as visitors filed past the site of the disaster*...

wait **VERB** **1** = <u>stay</u>, remain, stop, pause, rest, delay, linger, hover, hang around (*informal*), dally, loiter, tarry ...*I waited at the corner for the lights to go green*...
OPPOSITE go
2 = <u>stand by</u>, delay, hold on (*informal*), hold back, wait in the wings, mark time, hang fire, bide your time, kick your heels, cool your heels ...*Let's wait and see what happens*...
3 = <u>be postponed</u>, be suspended, be delayed, be put off, be put back, be deferred, be put on hold (*informal*), be shelved, be tabled, be held over, be put

on ice (*informal*), be put on the back burner (*informal*) ...*I want to talk to you but it can wait...*
NOUN = <u>delay</u>, gap, pause, interval, stay, rest, halt, hold-up, lull, stoppage, hindrance, hiatus, entr'acte ...*After a long wait, someone finally picked up the phone...*
PHRASES **wait for** or **on something** or **someone** = <u>await</u>, expect, look forward to, hope for, anticipate, look for ...*I'm still waiting for a reply from him...*
♦ **wait on** or **upon someone** = <u>serve</u>, tend to, look after, take care of, minister to, attend to, cater to ...*The owner of the restaurant himself waited on us...*
♦ **wait up** = <u>stay awake</u>, stay up, keep vigil ...*I waited up for you till three in the morning...*

waiter or **waitress** = <u>attendant</u>, server, flunkey, steward or stewardess, servant

waive 1 = <u>give up</u>, relinquish, renounce, forsake, drop, abandon, resign, yield, surrender, set aside, dispense with, cede, forgo ...*He pled guilty to the charges and waived his right to appeal...* OPPOSITE claim
2 = <u>disregard</u>, ignore, discount, overlook, set aside, pass over, dispense with, brush aside, turn a blind eye to, forgo ...*The council has agreed to waive certain statutory planning regulations...*

waiver = <u>renunciation</u>, surrender, remission, abdication, giving up, resignation, denial, setting aside, abandonment, disclaimer, disavowal, relinquishment, eschewal, abjuration

wake¹ VERB 1 = <u>awake</u>, stir, awaken, come to, arise, get up, rouse, get out of bed, waken, bestir, rouse from sleep, bestir yourself ...*It was still dark when I woke...* OPPOSITE fall asleep
2 = <u>awaken</u>, arouse, rouse, waken, rouse someone from sleep ...*She went upstairs at once to wake the children...*
3 = <u>evoke</u>, recall, excite, renew, stimulate, revive, induce, arouse, call up, awaken, rouse, give rise to, conjure up, stir up, rekindle, summon up, reignite ...*Seeing him again upset her, because it woke painful memories...*
NOUN = <u>vigil</u>, watch, funeral, deathwatch ...*A funeral wake was in progress...*
PHRASES **wake someone up** = <u>activate</u>, stimulate, enliven, galvanize, fire, excite, provoke, motivate, arouse, awaken, animate, rouse, mobilize, energize, kindle, switch someone on, stir someone up ...*He needs a shock to wake him up a bit...*

> ### Word Power
>
> **wake** – Both *wake* and its synonym *waken* can be used either with or without an object: *I woke/wakened my sister*, and also *I woke/wakened (up) at noon*. Wake, wake up, and occasionally *waken*, can also be used in a figurative sense, for example *seeing him again woke painful memories*; and *it's time he woke up to his responsibilities*. The verbs *awake* and *awaken* are more commonly used in the figurative than the literal sense, for example *he awoke to the danger he was in*.

wake² NOUN = <u>slipstream</u>, wash, trail, backwash, train, track, waves, path ...*Dolphins sometimes play in the wake of the boats...*
PHRASES **in the wake of** = <u>in the aftermath of</u>, following, because of, as a result of, on account of, as a consequence of ...*The move comes in the wake of new measures brought in by the government...*

waken 1 = <u>awaken</u>, wake, stir, wake up, stimulate, revive, awake, arouse, activate, animate, rouse, enliven, galvanize ...*Have a cup of coffee to waken you...*
2 = <u>wake up</u>, come to, get up, awake, awaken, be roused, come awake ...*I dozed off and I only wakened when she came in...* OPPOSITE fall asleep

Wales = <u>Cymru</u> (*Welsh*), Cambria (*Latin*)

walk VERB 1 = <u>stride</u>, wander, stroll, trudge, go, move, step, march, advance, pace, trek, hike, tread, ramble, tramp, promenade, amble, saunter, take a turn, traipse (*informal*), toddle, make your way, mosey (*informal*), plod on, perambulate, footslog ...*They walked in silence for a while...*
2 = <u>travel on foot</u>, go on foot, hoof it (*slang*), foot it, go by shanks's pony (*informal*) ...*When I was your age I walked five miles to school...*
3 = <u>escort</u>, take, see, show, partner, guide, conduct, accompany, shepherd, convoy, usher, chaperon ...*He offered to walk me home...*
NOUN 1 = <u>stroll</u>, hike, ramble, tramp, turn, march, constitutional, trek, outing, trudge, promenade, amble, saunter, traipse (*informal*), breath of air, perambulation ...*He often took long walks in the hills...*
2 = <u>gait</u>, manner of walking, step, bearing, pace, stride, carriage, tread ...*Despite his gangling walk, George was a good dancer...*
3 = <u>path</u>, pathway, footpath, track, way, road, lane, trail, avenue, pavement, alley, aisle, sidewalk (*chiefly U.S.*), walkway (*chiefly U.S.*), promenade, towpath, esplanade, footway ...*a covered walk consisting of a roof supported by columns...*
PHRASES **walk of life** = <u>area</u>, calling, business, line, course, trade, class, field, career, rank, employment, province, profession, occupation, arena, sphere, realm, domain, caste, vocation, line of work, métier ...*In this job you meet people from all walks of life...* ♦ **walk out** 1 = <u>leave suddenly</u>, storm out, get up and go, flounce out, vote with your feet, make a sudden departure, take off (*informal*) ...*Mr Mason walked out during the performance...* 2 = <u>go on strike</u>, strike, revolt, mutiny, stop work, take industrial action, down tools, withdraw your labour ...*Industrial action began this week, when most of the staff walked out...* ♦ **walk out on someone** = <u>abandon</u>, leave, desert, strand, betray, chuck (*informal*), run away from, forsake, jilt, run out on (*informal*), throw over, leave high and dry, leave in the lurch ...*Her husband walked out on her...*

walker = <u>hiker</u>, rambler, backpacker, wayfarer, footslogger, pedestrian

walkout = <u>strike</u>, protest, revolt, stoppage, industrial action

wall NOUN **1** = partition, divider, room divider, screen, panel, barrier, enclosure …*We're going to knock down the dividing wall to give us one big room…*

2 = barricade, rampart, fortification, bulwark, blockade, embankment, parapet, palisade, stockade, breastwork …*The Romans breached the city walls and captured the city…*

3 = barrier, obstacle, barricade, obstruction, check, bar, block, fence, impediment, hindrance …*I appealed for help but met the usual wall of silence…*

PHRASES **drive someone up the wall** (*Informal*) = infuriate, madden, exasperate, get on your nerves (*informal*), anger, provoke, annoy, irritate, aggravate (*informal*), incense, enrage, gall, rile, drive you crazy (*informal*), nark (*Brit., Austral., & N.Z. slang*), be like a red rag to a bull, make your blood boil, get your goat (*slang*), drive you insane, make your hackles rise, raise your hackles, send off your head (*slang*), get your back up, make you see red (*informal*), put your back up …*That tuneless humming of his drives me up the wall…* ◆ **go to the wall** (*Informal*) = fail, close down, go under, go out of business, fall, crash, collapse, fold (*Informal*), be ruined, go bust (*informal*), go bankrupt, go broke (*informal*), go into receivership, become insolvent …*Even big companies are going to the wall these days…*

(Related Words)

adjective : mural

wallet = purse, pocketbook, notecase, pouch, case, holder, money-bag

wallop (*Informal*) VERB **1** = hit, beat, strike, knock, belt (*informal*), deck (*slang*), bang, batter, bash (*informal*), pound, chin (*slang*), smack, thrash, thump, paste (*slang*), buffet, clout (*informal*), slug, whack, swipe, clobber (*slang*), pummel, tonk (*slang*), lambast(e), lay one on (*slang*) …*Once she walloped me over the head with a frying pan…*

2 = beat, defeat, slaughter, thrash, best, stuff (*slang*), worst, tank, hammer (*informal*), crush, overwhelm, lick (*informal*), paste (*slang*), rout, walk over (*informal*), trounce, clobber (*slang*), vanquish, run rings around (*informal*), wipe the floor with (*informal*), make mincemeat of, blow out of the water (*slang*), drub, beat hollow (*Brit. informal*), defeat heavily *or* utterly …*England were walloped by Brazil in the finals…*

NOUN = blow, strike, punch, thump, belt (*informal*), bash, sock (*slang*), smack, clout (*informal*), slug, whack, swipe, thwack, haymaker (*slang*) …*With one brutal wallop, Clarke sent him flying…*

wallow 1 = revel, indulge, relish, savour, delight, glory, thrive, bask, take pleasure, luxuriate, indulge yourself …*All he wants to do is wallow in self-pity…* OPPOSITE refrain from

2 = roll about, lie, tumble, wade, slosh, welter, splash around …*Hippos love to wallow in mud…*

wan 1 = pale, white, washed out, pasty, faded, bleached, ghastly, sickly, bloodless, colourless, pallid, anaemic, discoloured, ashen, sallow, whitish, cadaverous, waxen, like death warmed up (*informal*), wheyfaced …*He looked wan and tired…* OPPOSITE glowing

2 = dim, weak, pale, faint, feeble …*The lamp cast a wan light through the swirls of fog…*

wand = stick, rod, cane, baton, stake, switch, birch, twig, sprig, withe, withy

wander VERB = roam, walk, drift, stroll, range, cruise, stray, ramble, prowl, meander, rove, straggle, traipse (*informal*), mooch around (*slang*), stravaig (*Scot. & Northern English dialect*), knock about *or* around, peregrinate …*He wandered aimlessly around the garden…*

NOUN = excursion, turn, walk, stroll, cruise, ramble, meander, promenade, traipse (*informal*), mosey (*informal*), peregrination …*Let's go for a wander round the shops…*

PHRASES **wander off** = stray, roam, go astray, lose your way, drift, depart, rove, straggle …*The child wandered off and got lost…* ◆ **wander off something** = deviate from, diverge from, veer from, swerve from, digress from, go off at a tangent from, go off course from, lapse from …*He has a tendency to wander off the point when he's talking…*

wanderer = traveller, rover, nomad, drifter, ranger, journeyer, gypsy, explorer, migrant, rolling stone, rambler, voyager, tripper, itinerant, globetrotter, vagrant, stroller, vagabond, wayfarer, bird of passage

wandering = itinerant, travelling, journeying, roving, drifting, homeless, strolling, voyaging, unsettled, roaming, rambling, nomadic, migratory, vagrant, peripatetic, vagabond, rootless, wayfaring

wane VERB **1** = decline, flag, weaken, diminish, fall, fail, drop, sink, fade, decrease, dim, dwindle, wither, lessen, subside, ebb, wind down, die out, fade away, abate, draw to a close, atrophy, taper off …*His interest in her began to wane…* OPPOSITE grow

2 = diminish, decrease, dwindle …*The sliver of a waning moon was high in the sky…* OPPOSITE wax

PHRASES **on the wane** = declining, dropping, fading, weakening, dwindling, withering, lessening, subsiding, ebbing, dying out, on the way out, on the decline, tapering off, obsolescent, on its last legs, at its lowest ebb …*His career prospects were clearly on the wane…*

want VERB **1** = wish for, desire, fancy, long for, crave, covet, hope for, yearn for, thirst for, hunger for, pine for, hanker after, set your heart on, feel a need for, have a yen for (*informal*), have a fancy for, eat your heart out over, would give your eyeteeth for …*My husband really wants a new car…* OPPOSITE have

2 = need, demand, require, call for, have need of, stand in need of …*The grass wants cutting…*

3 = should, need, must, ought …*You want to look where you're going, mate…*

4 = desire, fancy, long for, crave, wish for, yearn for, thirst for, hanker after, burn for …*Come on, darling. I want you…*

5 = lack, need, require, be short of, miss, be deficient

in, be without, fall short in ...*Our team still wants one more player...*
NOUN **1** = <u>lack</u>, need, absence, shortage, deficiency, famine, default, shortfall, inadequacy, scarcity, dearth, paucity, shortness, insufficiency, non-existence, scantiness ...*The men were daily becoming weaker for want of rest...* OPPOSITE abundance
2 = <u>poverty</u>, need, hardship, privation, penury, destitution, neediness, hand-to-mouth existence, indigence, pauperism, pennilessness, distress ...*He said they were fighting for freedom from want...* OPPOSITE wealth
3 = <u>wish</u>, will, need, demand, desire, requirement, fancy, yen (*informal*), longing, hunger, necessity, appetite, craving, yearning, thirst, whim, hankering ...*The company needs to respond to the wants of our customers...*

wanting **1** = <u>deficient</u>, poor, disappointing, inadequate, pathetic, inferior, insufficient, faulty, not good enough, defective, patchy, imperfect, sketchy, unsound, substandard, leaving much to be desired, not much cop (*Brit. slang*), not up to par, not up to expectations, bodger *or* bodgie (*Austral. slang*) ...*He examined her work and found it wanting...* OPPOSITE adequate
2 = <u>lacking</u>, missing, absent, incomplete, needing, short, shy ...*I feel as if something important is wanting in my life...* OPPOSITE complete

wanton **1** = <u>wilful</u>, needless, senseless, unjustified, willed, evil, cruel, vicious, deliberate, arbitrary, malicious, wicked, purposeful, gratuitous, malevolent, spiteful, unprovoked, groundless, unjustifiable, uncalled-for, motiveless ...*the unnecessary and wanton destruction of our environment...* OPPOSITE justified
2 = <u>promiscuous</u>, immoral, shameless, licentious, fast, wild, abandoned, loose, dissipated, lewd, profligate, debauched, lustful, lecherous, dissolute, libertine, libidinous, of easy virtue, unchaste ...*Women behaving with the same sexual freedom as men are considered wanton...* OPPOSITE puritanical

war **NOUN** **1** = <u>conflict</u>, drive, attack, fighting, fight, operation, battle, movement, push, struggle, clash, combat, offensive, hostilities, hostility, warfare, expedition, crusade, strife, bloodshed, jihad, enmity, armed conflict ...*matters of war and peace...* OPPOSITE peace
2 = <u>campaign</u>, drive, attack, operation, movement, push, mission, offensive, crusade ...*the war against organized crime...*
VERB = <u>fight</u>, battle, clash, wage war, campaign, struggle, combat, contend, go to war, do battle, make war, take up arms, bear arms, cross swords, conduct a war, engage in hostilities, carry on hostilities ...*The two tribes warred to gain new territory...* OPPOSITE make peace
(Related Words)
adjectives: belligerent, martial

warble **VERB** = <u>sing</u>, trill, chirp, twitter, chirrup, make melody, pipe, quaver ...*A flock of birds was warbling in the trees...*
NOUN = <u>song</u>, trill, quaver, twitter, call, cry, chirp, chirrup ...*the soft warble of her speaking voice...*

ward **NOUN** **1** = <u>room</u>, department, unit, quarter, division, section, apartment, cubicle ...*A toddler was admitted to the emergency ward...*
2 = <u>district</u>, constituency, area, division, zone, parish, precinct ...*Canvassers are focusing on marginal wards in this election...*
3 = <u>dependant</u>, charge, pupil, minor, protégé ...*Richard became Burton's legal ward and took his name by deed poll...*
PHRASES **ward someone off** = <u>drive off</u>, resist, confront, fight off, block, oppose, thwart, hold off, repel, fend off, beat off, keep someone at bay, keep someone at arm's length ...*She may have tried to ward off her assailant...* ♦ **ward something off** **1** = <u>avert</u>, turn away, fend off, stave off, avoid, block, frustrate, deflect, repel, forestall ...*A rowan cross was hung over the door to ward off evil...* **2** = <u>parry</u>, avert, deflect, fend off, avoid, block, repel, turn aside ...*He lifted his hands as if to ward off a blow...*

warden **1** = <u>steward</u>, guardian, administrator, superintendent, caretaker, curator, warder, custodian, watchman, janitor ...*He was a warden at the local parish church...*
2 = <u>jailer</u>, prison officer, guard, screw (*slang*), keeper, captor, turnkey (*archaic*), gaoler ...*The prisoners seized three wardens...*
3 = <u>governor</u>, head, leader, director, manager, chief, executive, boss (*informal*), commander, ruler, controller, overseer, baas (*S. African*) ...*A new warden took over the prison...*
4 = <u>ranger</u>, keeper, guardian, protector, custodian, official ...*a safari park warden...*

warder *or* **wardress** = <u>jailer</u>, guard, screw (*slang*), warden, prison officer, keeper, captor, custodian, turnkey (*archaic*), gaoler

wardrobe **1** = <u>clothes cupboard</u>, cupboard, closet (*U.S.*), clothes-press, cabinet ...*Hang your dress up in the wardrobe...*
2 = <u>clothes</u>, outfit, apparel, clobber (*Brit. slang*), attire, collection of clothes ...*splurging on an expensive new wardrobe of clothes...*

warehouse = <u>store</u>, depot, storehouse, repository, depository, stockroom

wares = <u>goods</u>, produce, stock, products, stuff, commodities, merchandise, lines

warfare = <u>war</u>, fighting, campaigning, battle, struggle, conflict, combat, hostilities, strife, bloodshed, jihad, armed struggle, discord, enmity, armed conflict, clash of arms, passage of arms OPPOSITE peace

warily **1** = <u>cautiously</u>, carefully, discreetly, with care, tentatively, gingerly, guardedly, circumspectly, watchfully, vigilantly, cagily (*informal*), heedfully ...*He backed warily away from the animal...* OPPOSITE carelessly
2 = <u>suspiciously</u>, uneasily, guardedly, sceptically, cagily (*informal*), distrustfully, mistrustfully, charily

…The two men eyed each other warily…

wariness 1 = <u>caution</u>, care, attention, prudence, discretion, deliberation, foresight, vigilance, alertness, forethought, circumspection, mindfulness, watchfulness, carefulness, caginess (*informal*), heedfulness …*Extreme wariness is the safest policy when dealing with these substances…* OPPOSITE carelessness

2 = <u>suspicion</u>, scepticism, distrust, mistrust …*the country's obsessive wariness of foreigners…*

warlike = <u>belligerent</u>, military, aggressive, hostile, martial, combative, unfriendly, antagonistic, pugnacious, argumentative, bloodthirsty, hawkish, bellicose, quarrelsome, militaristic, inimical, sabre-rattling, jingoistic, warmongering, aggers (*Austral. slang*), biffo (*Austral. slang*) OPPOSITE peaceful

warm ADJECTIVE **1** = <u>balmy</u>, mild, temperate, pleasant, fine, bright, sunny, agreeable, sultry, summery, moderately hot …*The weather was so warm I had to take off my jacket…* OPPOSITE cool

2 = <u>cosy</u>, snug, toasty (*informal*), comfortable, homely, comfy (*informal*) …*Nothing beats coming home to a warm house…*

3 = <u>moderately hot</u>, heated …*A warm bath will help to relax you…* OPPOSITE cool

4 = <u>thermal</u>, winter, thick, chunky, woolly …*Some people can't afford warm clothes…* OPPOSITE cool

5 = <u>mellow</u>, relaxing, pleasant, agreeable, restful …*The basement hallway is painted a warm yellow…*

6 = <u>affable</u>, kindly, friendly, affectionate, loving, happy, tender, pleasant, cheerful, hearty, good-humoured, amiable, amicable, cordial, sociable, genial, congenial, hospitable, approachable, amorous, good-natured, likable *or* likeable …*We were instantly attracted by his warm personality…* OPPOSITE unfriendly

7 = <u>near</u>, close, hot, near to the truth …*Am I getting warm? Am I right?…*

VERB = <u>warm up</u>, heat, thaw (out), heat up …*She went to warm her hands by the fire…* OPPOSITE cool down

PHRASES **warm something** *or* **someone up 1** = <u>heat</u>, thaw, heat up …*He blew on his hands to warm them up…* **2** = <u>rouse</u>, stimulate, stir up, animate, interest, excite, provoke, turn on (*slang*), arouse, awaken, exhilarate, incite, whip up, galvanize, put some life into, get something *or* someone going, make something *or* someone enthusiastic …*They went on before us to warm up the audience…*

warm-hearted = <u>kindly</u>, loving, kind, warm, gentle, generous, tender, pleasant, mild, sympathetic, affectionate, compassionate, hearty, cordial, genial, affable, good-natured, kind-hearted, tender-hearted OPPOSITE cold-hearted

warmth 1 = <u>heat</u>, snugness, warmness, comfort, homeliness, hotness …*She went in, drawn by the warmth of the fire…* OPPOSITE coolness

2 = <u>affection</u>, feeling, love, goodwill, kindness, tenderness, friendliness, cheerfulness, amity, cordiality, affability, kindliness, heartiness, amorousness, hospitableness, fondness …*He greeted*

us both with warmth… OPPOSITE hostility

warn 1 = <u>notify</u>, tell, remind, inform, alert, tip off, give notice, make someone aware, forewarn, apprise, give fair warning …*They warned him of the dangers of sailing alone…*

2 = <u>advise</u>, urge, recommend, counsel, caution, commend, exhort, admonish, put someone on his *or* her guard …*My mother warned me not to interfere…*

warning NOUN **1** = <u>caution</u>, information, advice, injunction, notification, caveat, word to the wise …*health warnings on cigarette packets…*

2 = <u>notice</u>, notification, word, sign, threat, tip, signal, alarm, announcement, hint, alert, tip-off (*informal*) …*The soldiers opened fire without warning…*

3 = <u>omen</u>, sign, forecast, indication, token, prediction, prophecy, premonition, foreboding, portent, presage, augury, foretoken …*a warning of impending doom…*

4 = <u>reprimand</u>, talking-to (*informal*), caution, censure, counsel, carpeting (*Brit. informal*), rebuke, reproach, scolding, berating, ticking-off (*informal*), chiding, dressing down (*informal*), telling-off (*informal*), admonition, upbraiding, reproof, remonstrance …*He was given a severe warning from the referee…*

ADJECTIVE = <u>cautionary</u>, threatening, ominous, premonitory, admonitory, monitory, bodeful …*Pain can act as a warning signal that something is wrong…*

warp VERB **1** = <u>distort</u>, bend, twist, buckle, deform, disfigure, contort, misshape, malform …*Rainwater had warped the door's timber…*

2 = <u>become distorted</u>, bend, twist, contort, become deformed, become misshapen …*Plastic can warp in the sun…*

3 = <u>pervert</u>, twist, corrupt, degrade, deprave, debase, desecrate, debauch, lead astray …*Their minds have been warped by their experiences…*

NOUN = <u>twist</u>, turn, bend, defect, flaw, distortion, deviation, quirk, imperfection, kink, contortion, deformation …*small warps in the planking…*

warrant VERB **1** = <u>call for</u>, demand, require, merit, rate, commission, earn, deserve, permit, sanction, excuse, justify, license, authorize, entail, necessitate, be worthy of, give ground for …*The allegations are serious enough to warrant an investigation…*

2 = <u>guarantee</u>, declare, assure, pledge, promise, maintain, ensure, secure, swear, uphold, underwrite, affirm, certify, attest, vouch, avouch …*The ship owner must warrant that his vessel is seaworthy…*

NOUN **1** = <u>authorization</u>, permit, licence, permission, security, authority, commission, sanction, pledge, warranty, carte blanche …*Police have issued a warrant for his arrest…*

2 = <u>justification</u>, reason, grounds, defence, basis, licence, rationale, vindication, authority …*There is some warrant for his behaviour…*

warranty = <u>guarantee</u>, promise, contract, bond, pledge, certificate, assurance, covenant

warring = <u>hostile</u>, fighting, conflicting, opposed, contending, at war, embattled, belligerent, combatant, antagonistic, warlike, bellicose, ill-disposed

warrior = <u>soldier</u>, combatant, fighter, gladiator, champion, brave, trooper, military man, fighting man, man-at-arms

wary 1 = <u>suspicious</u>, sceptical, mistrustful, suspecting, guarded, apprehensive, cagey (*informal*), leery (*slang*), distrustful, on your guard, chary, heedful ...*My mother always told me to be wary of strangers...*
2 = <u>watchful</u>, careful, alert, cautious, prudent, attentive, vigilant, circumspect, heedful ...*Keep a wary eye on children when they are playing near water...*
OPPOSITE careless

wash VERB 1 = <u>clean</u>, scrub, sponge, rinse, scour, cleanse ...*He got a job washing dishes in a pizza parlour...*
2 = <u>launder</u>, clean, wet, rinse, dry-clean, moisten ...*The colours will fade a little each time you wash the shirt...*
3 = <u>rinse</u>, clean, scrub, lather ...*It took a long time to wash the mud out of his hair...*
4 = <u>bathe</u>, bath, shower, take a bath *or* shower, clean yourself, soak, sponge, douse, freshen up, lave (*archaic*), soap, scrub yourself down ...*There was a sour smell about him, as if he had not washed for days...*
5 = <u>lap</u>, break, dash, roll, flow, surge, splash, slap, ripple, swish, splosh ...*The force of the water washed him back into the cave...*
6 = <u>move</u>, overcome, touch, upset, stir, disturb, perturb, surge through, tug at someone's heartstrings (*often facetious*) ...*A wave of despair washed over him...*
7 (*Informal*) (always used in negative constructions) = <u>be plausible to</u>, stand up, hold up, pass muster, hold water, stick, carry weight, be convincing to, bear scrutiny ...*All those excuses simply won't wash with me...*
NOUN 1 = <u>laundering</u>, cleaning, clean, cleansing ...*That coat could do with a good wash...*
2 = <u>bathe</u>, bath, shower, dip, soak, scrub, shampoo, rinse, ablution ...*She had a wash and changed her clothes...*
3 = <u>backwash</u>, slipstream, path, trail, train, track, waves, aftermath ...*The wash from a passing ship overturned their dinghy...*
4 = <u>splash</u>, roll, flow, sweep, surge, swell, rise and fall, ebb and flow, undulation ...*The steady wash of waves on the shore calmed me...*
5 = <u>coat</u>, film, covering, layer, screen, coating, stain, overlay, suffusion ...*He painted a wash of colour over the entire surface...*
PHRASES **wash something** *or* **someone away** = <u>sweep away</u>, carry off, bear away ...*Flood waters washed him away...* ◆ **wash something away** = <u>erode</u>, corrode, eat into, wear something away, eat something away ...*The topsoil is washed away by flood rains...*

washed out 1 = <u>pale</u>, light, flat, mat, muted, drab, lacklustre, watery, lustreless ...*The room was now dull and flat with washed-out colours...*
2 = <u>wan</u>, drawn, pale, pinched, blanched, haggard, bloodless, colourless, pallid, anaemic, ashen, chalky, peaky, deathly pale ...*She tried to hide her washed-out face behind large, dark glasses...*
3 = <u>faded</u>, bleached, blanched, colourless, stonewashed ...*a washed-out blue denim jacket...*
4 = <u>exhausted</u>, drained, worn-out, tired-out, spent, drawn, done in (*informal*), all in (*slang*), fatigued, wiped out (*informal*), weary, knackered (*slang*), clapped out (*Austral. & N.Z. informal*), dog-tired (*informal*), zonked (*slang*), dead on your feet (*informal*) ...*She looked washed-out and listless...*
OPPOSITE lively

washout 1 = <u>failure</u>, disaster, disappointment, flop (*informal*), mess, fiasco, dud (*informal*), clunker (*informal*) ...*The concert was a total washout...*
OPPOSITE success
2 = <u>loser</u>, failure, incompetent, no-hoper ...*As a husband, he's a complete washout...*

wasp
➤ **ants, bees, and wasps**

waste VERB 1 = <u>squander</u>, throw away, blow (*slang*), run through, lavish, misuse, dissipate, fritter away, frivol away (*informal*) ...*We can't afford to waste money on another holiday...* OPPOSITE save
2 = <u>wear out</u>, wither, deplete, debilitate, drain, undermine, exhaust, disable, consume, gnaw, eat away, corrode, enfeeble, sap the strength of, emaciate ...*a cruel disease which wastes the muscles...*
NOUN 1 = <u>squandering</u>, misuse, loss, expenditure, extravagance, frittering away, lost opportunity, dissipation, wastefulness, misapplication, prodigality, unthriftiness ...*The whole project is a complete waste of time and resources...* OPPOSITE saving
2 = <u>rubbish</u>, refuse, debris, sweepings, scrap, litter, garbage, trash, leftovers, offal, dross, dregs, leavings, offscourings ...*This country produces 10 million tonnes of toxic waste every year...*
PLURAL NOUN = <u>desert</u>, wilds, wilderness, void, solitude, wasteland ...*the barren wastes of the Sahara...*
ADJECTIVE 1 = <u>unwanted</u>, useless, worthless, unused, leftover, superfluous, unusable, supernumerary ...*suitable locations for the disposal of waste products...* OPPOSITE necessary
2 = <u>uncultivated</u>, wild, bare, barren, empty, devastated, dismal, dreary, desolate, unproductive, uninhabited ...*Yarrow can be found growing wild on waste ground...* OPPOSITE cultivated
PHRASES **lay something waste** = <u>devastate</u>, destroy, ruin, spoil, total (*slang*), sack, undo, trash (*slang*), ravage, raze, despoil, wreak havoc upon, depredate (*rare*) ...*The war has laid waste large regions of the country...* ◆ **waste away** = <u>decline</u>, dwindle, wither, perish, sink, fade, crumble, decay, wane, ebb, wear out, atrophy ...*People dying from cancer grow thin and visibly waste away...*

Word Power

waste – *Waste* and *wastage* are to some extent interchangeable, but many people think that *wastage* should not be used to refer to loss resulting from human carelessness, inefficiency, etc.: *a waste* (not *a wastage*) *of time, money, effort*, etc.

wasteful = <u>extravagant</u>, lavish, prodigal, profligate, ruinous, spendthrift, uneconomical, improvident, unthrifty, thriftless OPPOSITE> thrifty

wasteland = <u>wilderness</u>, waste, wild, desert, void

waster = <u>layabout</u>, loser, good-for-nothing, shirker, piker (*Austral. & N.Z. slang*), drone, loafer, skiver (*Brit. slang*), idler, ne'er-do-well, wastrel, malingerer, bludger (*Austral. & N.Z. informal*)

watch VERB **1** = <u>look at</u>, observe, regard, eye, see, mark, view, note, check, clock (*Brit. slang*), stare at, contemplate, check out (*informal*), look on, gaze at, pay attention to, eyeball (*slang*), peer at, leer at, get a load of (*informal*), feast your eyes on, take a butcher's at (*Brit. informal*), take a dekko at (*Brit. slang*) …*The man was standing in the doorway watching him*…
2 = <u>spy on</u>, follow, track, monitor, keep an eye on, stake out, keep tabs on (*informal*), keep watch on, keep under observation, keep under surveillance …*I had the feeling we were being watched*…
3 = <u>guard</u>, keep, mind, protect, tend, look after, shelter, take care of, safeguard, superintend …*Parents can't be expected to watch their children 24 hours a day*…
4 = <u>be careful about</u>, mind, consider, be aware of, take into account, bear in mind, attend to, pay attention to, keep in mind, pay heed to, exercise caution over …*Watch your diet and try to avoid too much salt*…
NOUN **1** = <u>wristwatch</u>, timepiece, pocket watch, clock, chronometer …*He looked at his watch and checked the time*…
2 = <u>guard</u>, eye, attention, supervision, surveillance, notice, observation, inspection, vigil, lookout, vigilance …*Keep a close watch on him while I'm gone*…
PHRASES **watch out** or **watch it** or **watch yourself** = <u>be careful</u>, look out, be wary, be alert, be on the lookout, be vigilant, take heed, have a care, be on the alert, watch yourself, keep your eyes open, be watchful, be on your guard, mind out, be on (the) watch, keep a sharp lookout, keep a weather eye open, keep your eyes peeled or skinned (*informal*), pay attention …*Watch out if you're walking home after dark*… ◆ **watch out for something** or **someone** = <u>keep a sharp lookout for</u>, look out for, be alert for, be on the alert for, keep your eyes open for, be on your guard for, be on (the) watch for, be vigilant for, keep a weather eye open for, be watchful for, keep your eyes peeled or skinned for (*informal*) …*We had to watch out for unexploded mines*…

watchdog **1** = <u>guardian</u>, monitor, inspector, protector, custodian, scrutineer …*the government's consumer watchdog, the Office of Fair Trading*…
2 = <u>guard dog</u> …*A good watchdog can be a faithful friend as well as a deterrent to intruders*…

watcher = <u>viewer</u>, witness, observer, spy, spectator, looker-on, onlooker, lookout, fly on the wall

watchful = <u>alert</u>, attentive, vigilant, observant, guarded, suspicious, wary, on the lookout, circumspect, wide awake, on your toes, on your guard, on the watch, on the qui vive, heedful
OPPOSITE> careless

watchman = <u>guard</u>, security guard, security man, custodian, caretaker

watchword = <u>motto</u>, slogan, maxim, byword, rallying cry, battle cry, catch phrase, tag-line, catchword

water NOUN = <u>liquid</u>, aqua, Adam's ale or wine, H_2O …*Could I have a glass of water, please?*…
PLURAL NOUN = <u>sea</u>, main, waves, ocean, depths, briny …*the open waters of the Arctic Ocean*…
VERB **1** = <u>sprinkle</u>, spray, soak, irrigate, damp, hose, dampen, drench, douse, moisten, souse …*Water the plants once a week*…
2 = <u>get wet</u>, cry, weep, become wet, exude water …*His eyes were watering from the smoke*…
PHRASES **hold water** = <u>be sound</u>, work, stand up, be convincing, hold up, make sense, be logical, ring true, be credible, pass the test, be plausible, be tenable, bear examination or scrutiny …*This argument simply doesn't hold water*… ◆ **water something down**
1 = <u>dilute</u>, add water to, put water in, weaken, water, doctor, thin, adulterate …*He always waters his whisky down before drinking it*… **2** = <u>moderate</u>, weaken, temper, curb, soften, qualify, tame, mute, play down, mitigate, tone down, downplay, adulterate, soft-pedal …*The government has no intention of watering down its social security reforms*…

(Related Words)
adjectives: aquatic, aqueous
combining form: hydro-
fear of: hydrophobia

Water sports

aquabobbing	skin diving
canoeing	surfing
canoe polo	swimming
diving	synchronized
parasailing	swimming
powerboating *or*	water polo
powerboat racing	water-skiing
rowing	windsurfing
sailing	yachting

waterfall = <u>cascade</u>, fall, cataract, chute, linn (*Scot.*), force (*Northern English dialect*)
➤ WORD POWER SUPPLEMENT waterfalls

waterlogged = <u>soaked</u>, saturated, drenched, sodden, streaming, dripping, sopping, wet through, wringing wet, droukit or drookit (*Scot.*)

watertight **1** = <u>waterproof</u>, hermetically sealed, sealed, water-resistant, sound, coated, impermeable,

weatherproof, water-repellent, damp-proof, rubberized …*The batteries are enclosed in a watertight compartment…* OPPOSITE leaky
2 = foolproof, firm, sound, perfect, conclusive, flawless, undeniable, unassailable, airtight, indisputable, impregnable, irrefutable, unquestionable, incontrovertible …*The police had a watertight case against their suspect…* OPPOSITE weak

watery 1 = pale, thin, weak, faint, feeble, washed-out, wan, colourless, anaemic, insipid, wishy-washy (*informal*) …*A watery light began to show through the branches…*
2 = diluted, thin, weak, dilute, watered-down, tasteless, runny, insipid, washy, adulterated, wishy-washy (*informal*), flavourless, waterish …*a plateful of watery cabbage soup…* OPPOSITE concentrated
3 = wet, damp, moist, soggy, humid, marshy, squelchy …*a wide watery sweep of marshland…*
4 = liquid, fluid, aqueous, hydrous …*There was a watery discharge from her ear…*
5 = tearful, moist, weepy, lachrymose (*formal*), tear-filled, rheumy …*Emma's eyes were red and watery…*

wave VERB **1** = signal, sign, gesture, gesticulate …*He waved to us from across the street…*
2 = guide, point, direct, indicate, signal, motion, gesture, nod, beckon, point in the direction …*The policeman waved to us to go on…*
3 = brandish, swing, flourish, wield, wag, move something to and fro, shake …*The protesters were waving banners and shouting…*
4 = flutter, flap, stir, waver, shake, swing, sway, ripple, wag, quiver, undulate, oscillate, move to and fro …*Flags were waving gently in the breeze…*
NOUN **1** = gesture, sign, signal, indication, gesticulation …*Paddy spotted Mary Anne and gave her a cheery wave…*
2 = ripple, breaker, sea surf, swell, ridge, roller, comber, billow …*the sound of waves breaking on the shore…*
3 = surge, welling up, rush, flood, thrill, stab, shiver, feeling, tingle, spasm, upsurge, frisson …*She felt a wave of grief flood over her…*
4 = outbreak, trend, rash, upsurge, sweep, flood, tendency, surge, ground swell …*the current wave of violence in schools…*
5 = stream, flood, surge, spate, current, movement, flow, rush, tide, torrent, deluge, upsurge …*the wave of immigrants flooding into the country…*

waver 1 = hesitate, dither (*chiefly Brit.*), vacillate, be irresolute, falter, fluctuate, seesaw, blow hot and cold (*informal*), be indecisive, hum and haw, be unable to decide, shillyshally (*informal*), be unable to make up your mind, swither (*Scot.*) …*Some military commanders wavered over whether to support the coup…* OPPOSITE be decisive
2 = flicker, wave, shake, vary, reel, weave, sway, tremble, wobble, fluctuate, quiver, undulate, totter …*The shadows of the dancers wavered on the wall…*

wax 1 = increase, rise, grow, develop, mount, expand, swell, enlarge, fill out, magnify, get bigger, dilate, become larger …*Portugal and Spain had vast empires*

which waxed and waned… OPPOSITE wane
2 = become fuller, become larger, enlarge, get bigger …*One should plant seeds and cuttings when the moon is waxing…*

way NOUN **1** = method, means, system, process, approach, practice, scheme, technique, manner, plan, procedure, mode, course of action …*Freezing is a great way to preserve most foods…*
2 = manner, style, fashion, mode …*He had a strange way of talking…*
3 = aspect, point, sense, detail, feature, particular, regard, respect, characteristic, facet …*In some ways, we are better off than we were before…*
4 *often plural* = custom, manner, habit, idiosyncrasy, style, practice, nature, conduct, personality, characteristic, trait, usage, wont …*You'll have to get used to my mother's odd little ways…*
5 = route, direction, course, road, path …*Can you tell me the way to the station?…*
6 = access, street, road, track, channel, route, path, lane, trail, avenue, highway, pathway, thoroughfare …*He came round the back way…*
7 = journey, approach, advance, progress, passage …*She said she'd pick me up on her way to work…*
8 = room, opening, space, elbowroom …*The ranks of soldiers parted and made way for her…*
9 = distance, length, stretch, journey, trail …*We've a long way to go yet…*
10 = condition, state, shape (*informal*), situation, status, circumstances, plight, predicament, fettle …*He's in a bad way, but he'll live…*
11 = will, demand, wish, desire, choice, aim, pleasure, ambition …*It's bad for a child to get its own way all the time…*
PHRASES **by the way** = incidentally, in passing, in parenthesis, en passant, by the bye …*By the way, how did your seminar go?…* ◆ **give way** = collapse, give, fall, crack, break down, subside, cave in, crumple, fall to pieces, go to pieces …*The whole ceiling gave way and fell in on us…* ◆ **give way to something 1** = be replaced by, be succeeded by, be supplanted by …*The numbness gave way to anger…* **2** = concede, yield, back down, make concessions, accede, acquiesce, acknowledge defeat …*The President has given way to pressure from his opponents…* ◆ **under way** = in progress, going, started, moving, begun, on the move, in motion, afoot, on the go (*informal*) …*A full-scale security operation is now under way…*
◆ **ways and means** = capability, methods, procedure, way, course, ability, resources, capacity, tools, wherewithal …*discussing ways and means of improving productivity…*

way-out = outlandish, eccentric, unconventional, unorthodox, advanced, wild, crazy, bizarre, weird, progressive, experimental, avant-garde, far-out (*slang*), off-the-wall (*slang*), oddball (*informal*), offbeat, freaky (*slang*), outré, wacko *or* whacko (*informal*), off the air (*Austral. slang*)

wayward = erratic, unruly, wilful, unmanageable, disobedient, contrary, unpredictable, stubborn, perverse, rebellious, fickle, intractable, capricious, obstinate, headstrong, changeable, flighty, incorrigible, obdurate, ungovernable, self-willed, refractory, insubordinate, undependable, inconstant, mulish, cross-grained, contumacious, froward (*archaic*) OPPOSITE> obedient

weak ADJECTIVE **1** = feeble, exhausted, frail, debilitated, spent, wasted, weakly, tender, delicate, faint, fragile, shaky, sickly, languid, puny, decrepit, unsteady, infirm, anaemic, effete, enervated ...*I was too weak to move my arms and legs*... OPPOSITE> strong **2** = deficient, wanting, poor, lacking, inadequate, pathetic, faulty, substandard, under-strength ...*His eyesight had always been weak*... OPPOSITE> effective **3** = ineffectual, pathetic, cowardly, powerless, soft, impotent, indecisive, infirm, spineless, boneless, timorous, weak-kneed (*informal*), namby-pamby, irresolute ...*a weak man who let his wife walk all over him*... OPPOSITE> firm **4** = slight, faint, feeble, pathetic, shallow, hollow ...*He managed a weak smile and said, 'Don't worry about me.'*... **5** = faint, soft, quiet, slight, small, low, poor, distant, dull, muffled, imperceptible ...*Her voice was so weak we could hardly hear her*... OPPOSITE> loud **6** = fragile, brittle, flimsy, unsound, fine, delicate, frail, dainty, breakable ...*The animals escaped through a weak spot in the fence*... **7** = unsafe, exposed, vulnerable, helpless, wide open, unprotected, untenable, defenceless, unguarded ...*The trade unions are in a very weak position*... OPPOSITE> secure **8** = unconvincing, unsatisfactory, lame, invalid, flimsy, inconclusive, pathetic ...*The evidence against him was too weak to hold up in court*... OPPOSITE> convincing **9** = tasteless, thin, diluted, watery, runny, insipid, wishy-washy (*informal*), under-strength, milk-and-water, waterish ...*a weak cup of tea*... OPPOSITE> strong

weaken 1 = reduce, undermine, moderate, diminish, temper, impair, lessen, sap, mitigate, invalidate, soften up, take the edge off ...*Her opponents believe that her authority has been fatally weakened*... OPPOSITE> boost **2** = wane, fail, diminish, dwindle, lower, flag, fade, give way, lessen, abate, droop, ease up ...*Family structures are weakening and breaking up*... ...*The storm was finally beginning to weaken*... OPPOSITE> grow **3** = sap the strength of, tire, exhaust, debilitate, depress, disable, cripple, incapacitate, enfeeble, enervate ...*Malnutrition weakens the patient*... OPPOSITE> strengthen

weakness 1 = frailty, fatigue, exhaustion, fragility, infirmity, debility, feebleness, faintness, decrepitude, enervation ...*Symptoms of anaemia include weakness and fatigue*... OPPOSITE> strength **2** = liking, appetite, penchant, soft spot, passion, inclination, fondness, predilection, proclivity, partiality, proneness ...*Carol has a great weakness for ice cream*... OPPOSITE> aversion **3** = powerlessness, vulnerability, impotence,

meekness, irresolution, spinelessness, ineffectuality, timorousness, cravenness, cowardliness ...*People are always taking advantage of his weakness*... **4** = inadequacy, deficiency, transparency, lameness, hollowness, implausibility, flimsiness, unsoundness, tenuousness ...*She was quick to spot the weakness in his argument*... **5** = failing, fault, defect, deficiency, flaw, shortcoming, blemish, imperfection, Achilles' heel, chink in your armour, lack ...*His main weakness was his violent temper*... OPPOSITE> strong point

wealth 1 = riches, fortune, prosperity, affluence, goods, means, money, funds, property, cash, resources, substance, possessions, big money, big bucks (*informal, chiefly U.S.*), opulence, megabucks (*U.S. & Canad. slang*), lucre, pelf ...*The discovery of oil brought untold wealth to the island*... OPPOSITE> poverty **2** = property, funds, capital, estate, assets, fortune, possessions ...*His personal wealth is estimated at over 50 million dollars*... **3** = abundance, store, plenty, richness, bounty, profusion, fullness, cornucopia, plenitude, copiousness ...*The city boasts a wealth of beautiful churches*... OPPOSITE> lack

(**Related Words**)
fondness for: plutomania

wealthy = rich, prosperous, affluent, well-off, loaded (*slang*), comfortable, flush (*informal*), in the money (*informal*), opulent, well-heeled (*informal*), well-to-do, moneyed, quids in (*slang*), filthy rich, rolling in it (*slang*), on Easy Street (*informal*), stinking rich (*slang*), made of money (*informal*) OPPOSITE> poor

weapon
➤ **guns** ➤ **swords and other weapons with blades** ➤ **weapons**

wear VERB **1** = be dressed in, have on, dress in, be clothed in, carry, sport (*informal*), bear, put on, clothe yourself in ...*He was wearing a dark green uniform*... **2** = show, present, bear, display, assume, put on, exhibit ...*Millson's face wore a smug expression*... **3** = deteriorate, fray, wear thin, become threadbare ...*The living room carpet is beginning to wear*... **4** = accept (*Brit. informal*), take, allow, permit, stomach, swallow (*informal*), brook, stand for, fall for, put up with (*informal*), countenance ...*I asked if I could work part-time, but the company wouldn't wear it*... NOUN **1** = clothes, things, dress, gear (*informal*), attire, habit, outfit, costume, threads (*slang*), garments, apparel, garb, raiments ...*The shops stock an extensive range of beach wear*... **2** = usefulness, use, service, employment, utility, mileage (*informal*) ...*You'll get more wear out of a car if you look after it properly*... **3** = damage, wear and tear, use, erosion, friction, deterioration, depreciation, attrition, corrosion, abrasion ...*a large, well-upholstered armchair which showed signs of wear*... OPPOSITE> repair PHRASES **wear down** = be eroded, erode, be

---

Weapons http://www.royalarmouries.org/

Projectile weapons

ballista	fléchette	quarrel
bazooka	grapeshot	rifle grenade
blowpipe	gun	torpedo
catapult	longbow	trebuchet *or* trebucket
crossbow	onager	

Miscellaneous weapons

biological warfare	flame-thrower	Mace
bomb	germ warfare *or* bacteriological	mustard gas
chemical warfare	warfare	napalm
club	Greek fire	poison gas
death ray	knuckle-duster	

---

consumed, wear away ...*Eventually the parts start to wear down...* ◆ **wear off 1** = <u>subside</u>, disappear, fade, weaken, diminish, decrease, dwindle, wane, ebb, abate, peter out, lose strength, lose effect ...*Her initial excitement soon began to wear off...* **2** = <u>rub away</u>, disappear, fade, abrade ...*The paint is discoloured and little bits have worn off...* ◆ **wear out** = <u>deteriorate</u>, become worn, become useless, wear through, fray ...*Eventually the artificial joint wears out and has to be replaced...* ◆ **wear someone down** = <u>undermine</u>, reduce, chip away at (*informal*), fight a war of attrition against, overcome gradually ...*his sheer persistence in wearing down the opposition...* ◆ **wear someone out** (*Informal*) = <u>exhaust</u>, tire, fatigue, weary, impair, sap, prostrate, knacker (*slang*), frazzle (*informal*), fag someone out (*informal*), enervate ...*The past few days had really worn him out...*
◆ **wear something down** = <u>erode</u>, grind down, consume, impair, corrode, grind down, rub away, abrade ...*Rabbits wear down their teeth with constant gnawing...* ◆ **wear something out** = <u>erode</u>, go through, consume, use up, wear holes in, make worn ...*He wore his shoes out wandering around the streets...* ◆ **wear well** = <u>last</u>, stand up, endure, hold up, bear up, be durable ...*These shoes haven't worn very well...*

weariness = <u>tiredness</u>, fatigue, exhaustion, lethargy, drowsiness, lassitude, languor, listlessness, prostration, enervation OPPOSITE energy

wearing = <u>tiresome</u>, trying, taxing, tiring, exhausting, fatiguing, oppressive, exasperating, irksome, wearisome OPPOSITE refreshing

weary ADJECTIVE **1** = <u>tired</u>, exhausted, drained, worn out, spent, done in (*informal*), flagging, all in (*slang*), fatigued, wearied, sleepy, fagged (*informal*), whacked (*Brit. informal*), jaded, drooping, knackered (*slang*), drowsy, clapped out (*Austral. & N.Z. informal*), enervated, ready to drop, dog-tired (*informal*), zonked (*slang*), dead beat (*informal*), asleep *or* dead on your feet (*informal*) ...*She sank to the ground, too weary to walk another step...* OPPOSITE energetic
2 = <u>fed up</u>, bored, sick (*informal*), discontented, impatient, indifferent, jaded, sick and tired (*informal*), browned-off (*informal*) ...*He was growing weary of his wife's constant complaints...* OPPOSITE excited
3 = <u>tiring</u>, taxing, wearing, arduous, tiresome, laborious, irksome, wearisome, enervative ...*a long, weary journey in search of food and water...* OPPOSITE refreshing
VERB **1** = <u>grow tired</u>, tire, sicken, have had enough, become bored ...*He had wearied of teaching in state universities...*
2 = <u>bore</u>, annoy, plague, sicken, jade, exasperate, vex, irk, try the patience of, make discontented ...*Her nagging and criticism wearied him so much that he left her...* OPPOSITE excite
3 = <u>tire</u>, tax, burden, drain, fatigue, fag (*informal*), sap, wear out, debilitate, take it out of (*informal*), tire out, enervate ...*Her pregnancy wearied her to the point of exhaustion...* OPPOSITE invigorate

weather NOUN = <u>climate</u>, conditions, temperature, forecast, outlook, meteorological conditions, elements ...*I don't like hot weather much...*
VERB **1** = <u>toughen</u>, season, worn, expose, harden ...*The stones have been weathered by centuries of wind and rain...*
2 = <u>withstand</u>, stand, suffer, survive, overcome, resist, brave, endure, come through, get through, rise above, live through, ride out, make it through (*informal*), surmount, pull through, stick it out (*informal*), bear up against ...*The company has weathered the recession...* OPPOSITE surrender to
PHRASES **under the weather** = <u>ill</u>, unwell, poorly (*informal*), sick, rough (*informal*), crook (*Austral. & N.Z. informal*), ailing, not well, seedy (*informal*), below par, queasy, out of sorts, nauseous, off-colour (*Brit.*), indisposed, peaky, ropy (*Brit. informal*), wabbit (*Scot. informal*) ...*I'm feeling a bit under the weather today...*
➤ **regions of the atmosphere** ➤ **types of cloud** ➤ **weather** ➤ **winds**

weave 1 = <u>knit</u>, twist, intertwine, plait, unite, introduce, blend, incorporate, merge, mat, fuse, braid, entwine, intermingle, interlace ...*She then weaves the fibres together to make the traditional Awatum basket...*
2 = <u>zigzag</u>, wind, move in and out, crisscross, weave your way ...*The cyclists wove in and out of the traffic...*
3 = <u>create</u>, tell, recount, narrate, make, build, relate,

Weather   http://www.bbc.co.uk/weather/

Weather descriptions

arctic	dull	parky
baking	filthy	perishing
balmy	fine	rainy
bland	foggy	raw
blistering	foul	scorching
blustery	freezing	showery
breezy	fresh	snowy
clammy	hazy	sticky
clear	hot	stormy
clement	humid	sultry
close	icy	sunny
cloudy	inclement	thundery
cold	mild	tropical
dirty	misty	wet
dreich	muggy	windy
drizzly	nippy	wintry
dry	overcast	

Weather phenomena

acid rain	heatwave	squall
ball lightning	hurricane	storm
breeze	ice	sunshine
cloud	lightning	tempest
cold snap	mist	thaw
cyclone	peasouper	thunder
drizzle	precipitation	tidal wave
dust devil	pressure	tornado
dust storm	rain	tsunami
fog	sandstorm	typhoon
freeze	sheet lightning	waterspout
gale	shower	whirlwind
gust	sleet	wind
haar	smirr	willy-willy
hail	snow	zephyr

Meteorological terms

anticyclone	isallobar	synoptic chart
cold front	isobar	thermal
cyclone	lee wave	trough
depression	occluded front	virga
front	ridge	warm front
heat-island	scud	

---

make up, spin, construct, invent, put together, unfold, contrive, fabricate …*The author weaves a compelling tale of life in London during the war*…

web 1 = <u>cobweb</u>, spider's web …*He was caught like a fly in a web*…

2 = <u>mesh</u>, net, netting, screen, webbing, weave, lattice, latticework, interlacing, lacework …*a delicate web of fine lace*…

3 = <u>tangle</u>, series, network, mass, chain, knot, maze, toils, nexus …*a complex web of financial dealings*…

wed 1 = <u>get married to</u>, espouse, get hitched to (*slang*), be united to, plight your troth to (*old-fashioned*), get spliced to (*informal*), take as your husband *or* wife …*In 1952 he wed his childhood sweetheart*… OPPOSITE▷ divorce

2 = <u>get married</u>, marry, be united, tie the knot

(*informal*), take the plunge (*informal*), get hitched (*slang*), get spliced (*informal*), become man and wife, plight your troth (*old-fashioned*) …*The pair wed in a secret ceremony in front of just nine guests*… OPPOSITE▷ divorce

3 = <u>unite</u>, combine, bring together, amalgamate, join, link, marry, ally, connect, blend, integrate, merge, unify, make one, fuse, weld, interweave, yoke, coalesce, commingle …*a film which weds stunning visuals and a first-class score*… OPPOSITE▷ divide

wedding = <u>marriage</u>, nuptials, wedding ceremony, marriage ceremony, marriage service, wedding service, nuptial rite, espousals

wedge VERB = <u>squeeze</u>, force, lodge, jam, crowd, block, stuff, pack, thrust, ram, cram, stow …*He wedged himself between the door and the radiator*…

NOUN = block, segment, lump, chunk, triangle, slab, hunk, chock, wodge (*Brit. informal*) …*a wedge of cheese*…

wedlock = marriage, matrimony, holy matrimony, married state, conjugal bond

wee = little, small, minute, tiny, miniature, insignificant, negligible, microscopic, diminutive, minuscule, teeny, itsy-bitsy (*informal*), teeny-weeny, titchy (*Brit. informal*), teensy-weensy, pygmy *or* pigmy

weedy = weak, thin, frail, skinny, feeble, ineffectual, puny, undersized, weak-kneed (*informal*), namby-pamby, nerdy *or* nurdy (*slang*)

weekly **ADJECTIVE** = once a week, hebdomadal, hebdomadary …*her weekly visit to her parents' house*…
ADVERB = every week, once a week, by the week, hebdomadally …*The group meets weekly*…

weep = cry, shed tears, sob, whimper, complain, keen, greet (*Scot. or archaic*), moan, mourn, grieve, lament, whinge (*informal*), blubber, snivel, ululate, blub (*slang*), boohoo **OPPOSITE** rejoice

weepy **ADJECTIVE** = tearful, crying, weeping, sobbing, whimpering, close to tears, blubbering, lachrymose, on the verge of tears …*After her mother's death she was depressed and weepy for months*…
NOUN = tear-jerker (*informal*) …*The film is an old-fashioned weepy with fine performances by both stars*…

weigh **VERB** 1 = have a weight of, tip the scales at (*informal*) …*His wife weighs over 22 stone*…
2 = measure the weight of, put someone *or* something on the scales, measure how heavy someone *or* something is …*They counted and weighed the fruits*…
3 *often with* **up** = consider, study, examine, contemplate, evaluate, ponder, mull over, think over, eye up, reflect upon, give thought to, meditate upon, deliberate upon …*He is weighing the possibility of filing charges against the doctor*…
4 = compare, balance, contrast, juxtapose, place side by side …*We must weigh the pros and cons of each method*…
5 = matter, carry weight, cut any ice (*informal*), impress, tell, count, have influence, be influential …*His opinion doesn't weigh much with me, I'm afraid*…
PHRASES **weigh on someone** = oppress, burden, depress, distress, plague, prey, torment, hang over, bear down, gnaw at, cast down, take over …*The separation weighed on both of them*… ◆ **weigh someone down** 1 = burden, overload, encumber, overburden, tax, weight, strain, handicap, saddle, hamper …*The soldiers were weighed down by their heavy packs*… 2 = oppress, worry, trouble, burden, depress, haunt, plague, get down, torment, take control of, hang over, beset, prey on, bear down, gnaw at, cast down, press down on, overburden, weigh upon, lie heavy on …*He could not shake off the guilt that weighed him down*… ◆ **weigh someone**

up = assess, judge, gauge, appraise, eye someone up, size someone up (*informal*) …*As soon as I walked into his office I could see him weighing me up*… ◆ **weigh something out** = measure, dole out, apportion, deal out …*I weighed out portions of tea and sugar*…

weight **NOUN** 1 = heaviness, mass, burden, poundage, pressure, load, gravity, tonnage, heft (*informal*), avoirdupois …*Try to reduce the weight of the load*…
2 = load, mass, ballast, heavy object …*Straining to lift heavy weights can cause back injury*…
3 = importance, force, power, moment, value, authority, influence, bottom, impact, import, muscle, consequence, substance, consideration, emphasis, significance, sway, clout (*informal*), leverage, efficacy, mana (*N.Z.*), persuasiveness …*That argument no longer carries much weight*…
4 = burden, pressure, load, strain, oppression, albatross, millstone, encumbrance …*He heaved a sigh of relief. 'That's a great weight off my mind.'*…
5 = preponderance, mass, bulk, main body, most, majority, onus, lion's share, greatest force, main force, best *or* better part …*The weight of evidence suggests that he is guilty*…
VERB 1 *often with* **down** = load, ballast, make heavier …*The body was weighted down with bricks*…
2 = bias, load, slant, unbalance …*The electoral law is still heavily weighted in favour of the ruling party*…
3 = burden, handicap, oppress, impede, weigh down, encumber, overburden …*His life was a struggle, weighted with failures and disappointments*…
► **weights and measures**

weighty 1 = important, serious, significant, critical, crucial, considerable, substantial, grave, solemn, momentous, forcible, consequential, portentous …*Surely such weighty matters merit a higher level of debate?*… **OPPOSITE** unimportant
2 = heavy, massive, dense, hefty (*informal*), cumbersome, ponderous, burdensome …*Simon lifted a weighty volume from the shelf*…
3 = onerous, taxing, demanding, difficult, worrying, crushing, exacting, oppressive, burdensome, worrisome, backbreaking …*the weighty responsibility of organizing the entire event*…

weird 1 = strange, odd, unusual, bizarre, ghostly, mysterious, queer, unearthly, eerie, grotesque, supernatural, unnatural, far-out (*slang*), uncanny, spooky (*informal*), creepy (*informal*), eldritch (*poetic*) …*I had such a weird dream last night*… **OPPOSITE** normal
2 = bizarre, odd, strange, unusual, queer, grotesque, unnatural, creepy (*informal*), outlandish, freakish …*I don't like that guy – he's really weird*… **OPPOSITE** ordinary

weirdo *or* **weirdie** = eccentric, nut (*slang*), freak (*informal*), crank (*informal*), loony (*slang*), nutter (*Brit. slang*), oddball (*informal*), crackpot (*informal*), nutcase (*slang*), headcase (*informal*), headbanger (*informal*), queer fish (*Brit. informal*)

welcome **VERB** 1 = greet, meet, receive, embrace,

Weights and measures

Imperial system			Metric system		
Linear	**Square**	**Weight**	**Linear**	**Square**	**Weight**
mile	square mile	ton	kilometre	square kilometre	tonne
furlong	acre	hundredweight	metre	square metre	kilogram
rod	square rod	stone	centimetre	square centimetre	gram
yard	square yard	pound	millimetre	square millimetre	–
foot	square foot	ounce			
inch	square inch	–			
mil	–	–			

Land	**Volume**	**Liquid volume**	**Land**	**Volume**	**Liquid volume**
square mile	cubic yard	gallon	square kilometre	cubic metre	litre
acre	cubic foot	quart	hectare	cubic decimetre	millilitre
square rod	cubic inch	pint	are	cubic centimetre	–
square yard	–	fluid ounce	–	cubic millimetre	–

hail, usher in, say hello to, roll out the red carpet for, offer hospitality to, receive with open arms, bid welcome …*Several people came out to welcome me*… OPPOSITE⟩ reject
2 = <u>accept gladly</u>, appreciate, embrace, approve of, be pleased by, give the thumbs up to (*informal*), be glad about, express pleasure *or* satisfaction at …*They welcomed the move but felt it did not go far enough*… NOUN = <u>greeting</u>, welcoming, entertainment, reception, acceptance, hail, hospitality, salutation …*There was a wonderful welcome waiting for him when he arrived*… OPPOSITE⟩ rejection
ADJECTIVE **1** = <u>pleasing</u>, wanted, accepted, appreciated, acceptable, pleasant, desirable, refreshing, delightful, gratifying, agreeable, pleasurable, gladly received …*a welcome change from the usual routine*… OPPOSITE⟩ unpleasant
2 = <u>wanted</u>, at home, invited …*I was really made to feel welcome*… OPPOSITE⟩ unwanted
3 = <u>free</u>, invited …*Non-residents are welcome to use our facilities*…

weld VERB **1** = <u>join</u>, link, bond, bind, connect, cement, fuse, solder, braze …*It's possible to weld stainless steel to ordinary steel*…
2 = <u>unite</u>, combine, blend, consolidate, unify, fuse, meld …*The miracle was that Rose had welded them into a team*… NOUN = <u>joint</u>, bond, seam, juncture …*The weld on the outlet pipe was visibly fractured*…

welfare 1 = <u>wellbeing</u>, good, interest, health, security, benefit, success, profit, safety, protection, fortune, comfort, happiness, prosperity, prosperousness …*Above all we must consider the welfare of the children*…
2 = <u>state benefit</u>, support, benefits, pensions, dole (*slang*), social security, unemployment benefit, state benefits …*proposed cuts in welfare*…

well¹ ADVERB **1** = <u>skilfully</u>, expertly, adeptly, with skill, professionally, correctly, properly, effectively, efficiently, adequately, admirably, ably, conscientiously, proficiently …*All the team members played well*… OPPOSITE⟩ badly

2 = <u>satisfactorily</u>, nicely, smoothly, successfully, capitally, pleasantly, happily, famously (*informal*), splendidly, agreeably, like nobody's business (*informal*), in a satisfactory manner …*I thought the interview went very well*… OPPOSITE⟩ badly
3 = <u>thoroughly</u>, completely, fully, carefully, effectively, efficiently, rigorously …*Mix all the ingredients well*…
4 = <u>intimately</u>, closely, completely, deeply, fully, personally, profoundly …*How well do you know him?*… OPPOSITE⟩ slightly
5 = <u>carefully</u>, closely, minutely, fully, comprehensively, accurately, in detail, in depth, extensively, meticulously, painstakingly, rigorously, scrupulously, assiduously, intensively, from top to bottom, methodically, attentively, conscientiously, exhaustively …*This is obviously a man who's studied his subject well*…
6 = <u>favourably</u>, highly, kindly, warmly, enthusiastically, graciously, approvingly, admiringly, with admiration, appreciatively, with praise, glowingly, with approbation …*He speaks very well of you*… OPPOSITE⟩ unfavourably
7 = <u>considerably</u>, easily, very much, significantly, substantially, markedly …*Franklin did not turn up until well after midnight*…
8 = <u>fully</u>, highly, greatly, completely, amply, very much, thoroughly, considerably, sufficiently, substantially, heartily, abundantly …*I am well aware of how much she has suffered*…
9 = <u>possibly</u>, probably, certainly, reasonably, conceivably, justifiably …*The murderer may well be someone who was close to the victim*…
10 = <u>decently</u>, right, kindly, fittingly, fairly, easily, correctly, properly, readily, politely, suitably, generously, justly, in all fairness, genially, civilly, hospitably …*My parents always treated me well*… OPPOSITE⟩ unfairly
11 = <u>prosperously</u>, comfortably, splendidly, in comfort, in (the lap of) luxury, flourishingly, without hardship …*We manage to live very well on our combined salaries*…
ADJECTIVE **1** = <u>healthy</u>, strong, sound, fit, blooming,

robust, hale, hearty, in good health, alive and kicking, fighting fit (*informal*), in fine fettle, up to par, fit as a fiddle, able-bodied, in good condition ...*I hope you're well...* OPPOSITE ill

2 = satisfactory, good, right, fine, happy, fitting, pleasing, bright, useful, lucky, proper, thriving, flourishing, profitable, fortunate ...*He was satisfied that all was well...* OPPOSITE unsatisfactory

3 = advisable, useful, proper, prudent, agreeable ...*It would be well to check the facts before you speak out...* OPPOSITE inadvisable

PHRASES **as well** = also, too, in addition, moreover, besides, to boot, into the bargain ...*I like the job, and the people I work with are very nice as well...* ◆ **as well as** = including, along with, in addition to, not to mention, at the same time as, over and above ...*food and other goods, as well as energy supplies such as gas and oil...*

well² NOUN **1** = hole, bore, pit, shaft ...*the cost of drilling an oil well...*

2 = waterhole, source, spring, pool, fountain, fount ...*I had to fetch water from the well...*

3 = source, fund, mine, treasury, reservoir, storehouse, repository, fount, wellspring ...*a man with a well of experience and insight...*

VERB **1** = flow, trickle, seep, run, issue, spring, pour, jet, burst, stream, surge, discharge, trickle, gush, ooze, seep, exude, spurt, spout ...*Blood welled from a gash in his thigh...*

2 = rise, increase, grow, mount, surge, swell, intensify ...*He could feel the anger welling inside him...*

well-balanced 1 = sensible, rational, level-headed, well-adjusted, together (*slang*), sound, reasonable, sober, sane, judicious ...*a sensible, well-balanced individual...* OPPOSITE unbalanced

2 = well-proportioned, proportional, graceful, harmonious, symmetrical ...*Intervals of depth are essential to a well-balanced composition...*

well-bred 1 = polite, ladylike, well-brought-up, well-mannered, cultured, civil, mannerly, polished, sophisticated, gentlemanly, refined, cultivated, courteous, gallant, genteel, urbane, courtly ...*She was too well-bred to make personal remarks...* OPPOSITE ill-bred

2 = aristocratic, gentle, noble, patrician, blue-blooded, well-born, highborn ...*He was clearly of well-bred stock...*

well-groomed = smart, trim, neat, tidy, spruce, well-dressed, dapper, well turned out, soigné *or* soignée

well-heeled (*Informal*) = prosperous, rich, wealthy, affluent, loaded (*slang*), comfortable, flush (*informal*), well-off, in the money (*informal*), opulent, well-to-do, moneyed, well-situated, in clover (*informal*)

well-informed = educated, aware, informed, acquainted, knowledgeable *or* knowledgable, understanding, well-educated, in the know (*informal*), well-read, conversant, au fait (*French*), in the loop (*informal*), well-grounded, au courant (*French*), clued-up (*informal*), cognizant *or* cognisant,

well-versed

well-known 1 = famous, important, celebrated, prominent, great, leading, noted, august, popular, familiar, distinguished, esteemed, acclaimed, notable, renowned, eminent, famed, illustrious, on the map, widely known ...*He liked to surround himself with attractive or well-known people...*

2 = familiar, common, established, popular, everyday, widely known ...*It is a well-known fact that smoking can cause lung cancer...*

well-mannered = polite, civil, mannerly, gentlemanly, gracious, respectful, courteous, genteel, well-bred, ladylike

well-nigh = almost, nearly, virtually, practically, next to, all but, just about, more or less

well-off 1 = rich, wealthy, comfortable, affluent, loaded (*slang*), flush (*informal*), prosperous, well-heeled (*informal*), well-to-do, moneyed ...*My family was quite well-off...* OPPOSITE poor

2 = fortunate, lucky, comfortable, thriving, flourishing, successful ...*Compared to some of the people in my ward, I feel quite well off...*

well-to-do = rich, wealthy, affluent, well-off, loaded (*slang*), comfortable, flush (*informal*), prosperous, well-heeled (*informal*), moneyed OPPOSITE poor

well-worn 1 = stale, tired, stereotyped, commonplace, banal, trite, hackneyed, overused, timeworn ...*To use a well-worn cliché, she does not suffer fools gladly...*

2 = shabby, worn, faded, ragged, frayed, worn-out, scruffy, tattered, tatty, threadbare ...*He was dressed casually in a sweater and well-worn jeans...*

welter = jumble, confusion, muddle, hotchpotch, web, mess, tangle

wend

PHRASES **wend your way** = go, move, travel, progress, proceed, make for, direct your course

wet ADJECTIVE **1** = damp, soaked, soaking, dripping, saturated, moist, drenched, watery, soggy, sodden, waterlogged, moistened, dank, sopping, aqueous, wringing wet ...*He rubbed his wet hair with a towel...* OPPOSITE dry

2 = rainy, damp, drizzly, showery, raining, pouring, drizzling, misty, teeming, humid, dank, clammy ...*It was a miserable wet day...* OPPOSITE sunny

3 (*Informal*) = feeble, soft, weak, silly, foolish, ineffectual, weedy (*informal*), spineless, effete, boneless, timorous, namby-pamby, irresolute, wussy (*slang*), nerdy *or* nurdy (*slang*) ...*I despised him for being so wet and spineless...*

VERB = moisten, spray, damp, dampen, water, dip, splash, soak, steep, sprinkle, saturate, drench, douse, irrigate, humidify ...*Wet the fabric with a damp sponge before ironing...* OPPOSITE dry

NOUN **1** = rain, rains, damp, drizzle, wet weather, rainy season, rainy weather, damp weather ...*They had come in from the cold and the wet...* OPPOSITE fine weather

2 = moisture, water, liquid, damp, humidity,

condensation, dampness, wetness, clamminess …*splashing around in the wet of the puddles…* OPPOSITE dryness

whack (*Informal*) VERB = strike, hit, beat, box, belt (*informal*), deck (*slang*), bang, rap, slap, bash (*informal*), sock (*slang*), chin (*slang*), smack, thrash, thump, buffet, clout (*informal*), slug, cuff, swipe, clobber (*slang*), wallop (*informal*), thwack, lambast(e), lay one on (*slang*) …*Someone whacked him on the head with a baseball bat…*
NOUN **1** = blow, hit, box, stroke, belt (*informal*), bang, rap, slap, bash (*informal*), sock (*slang*), smack, thump, buffet, clout (*informal*), slug, cuff, swipe, wallop (*informal*), wham, thwack …*He gave the donkey a whack across the back with a stick…*
2 (*Informal*) = share, part, cut (*informal*), bit, portion, quota, allotment …*I pay a sizeable whack of capital gains tax…*
3 (*Informal*) = attempt, go (*informal*), try, turn, shot (*informal*), crack (*informal*), stab (*informal*), bash (*informal*) …*Let me have a whack at trying to fix the car…*

whacking (*Informal*) = huge, big, large, giant, enormous, extraordinary, tremendous, gigantic, great, monstrous, mammoth, whopping (*informal*), prodigious, elephantine, humongous *or* humungous (*U.S. slang*)

whale
(**Related Words**)
adjective : cetacean
male : bull
female : cow
young : calf
collective nouns : school, gam, run
➤ **whales and dolphins**

wharf = dock, pier, berth, quay, jetty, landing stage

wheedle = coax, talk, court, draw, persuade, charm, worm, flatter, entice, cajole, inveigle

wheel NOUN = disc, ring, hoop …*a bicycle wheel…*
VERB **1** = push, trundle, roll …*He wheeled his bike into the alley beside the house…*
2 = turn, swing, spin, revolve, rotate, whirl, swivel …*He wheeled around to face her…*
3 = circle, orbit, go round, twirl, gyrate …*A flock of crows wheeled overhead…*
PHRASES **at** *or* **behind the wheel** = driving, steering, in the driving seat, in the driver's seat …*He persuaded his wife to say she was at the wheel when the car crashed…*

wheeze VERB = gasp, whistle, cough, hiss, rasp, catch your breath, breathe roughly …*His chest problems made him wheeze constantly…*
NOUN **1** = gasp, whistle, cough, hiss, rasp …*He puffed up the stairs, emitting a wheeze at every breath…*
2 (*Brit. slang*) = trick, plan, idea, scheme, stunt, ploy, expedient, ruse …*He came up with a clever wheeze to get round the problem…*

whereabouts = position, situation, site, location

wherewithal = resources, means, money, funds, capital, supplies, ready (*informal*), essentials, ready money

whet = stimulate, increase, excite, stir, enhance, provoke, arouse, awaken, animate, rouse, quicken, incite, kindle, pique OPPOSITE suppress

whiff NOUN = smell, hint, scent, sniff, aroma, odour, draught, niff (*Brit. slang*) …*He caught a whiff of her perfume…*
VERB **1** (*Brit. slang*) = stink, stench, reek, pong (*Brit. informal*), niff (*Brit. slang*), malodour, hum (*slang*) …*the nauseating whiff of rotting flesh…*
2 = trace, suggestion, hint, suspicion, bit, drop, note, breath, whisper, shred, crumb, tinge, jot, smidgen (*informal*), soupçon …*Not a whiff of scandal has ever tainted his private life…*
3 = puff, breath, flurry, waft, rush, blast, draught, gust …*At the first whiff of smoke, the alarm will go off…*

whim = impulse, sudden notion, caprice, fancy, sport, urge, notion, humour, freak, craze, fad (*informal*), quirk, conceit, vagary, whimsy, passing thought, crotchet

whimper VERB = cry, moan, sob, weep, whine, whinge (*informal*), grizzle (*informal, chiefly Brit.*), blubber, snivel, blub (*slang*), mewl …*She lay at the bottom of the stairs, whimpering in pain…*
NOUN = sob, moan, whine, snivel …*David's crying subsided to a whimper…*

whimsical = fanciful, odd, funny, unusual, fantastic, curious, weird, peculiar, eccentric, queer, flaky (*slang, chiefly U.S.*), singular, quaint, playful, mischievous, capricious, droll, freakish, fantastical, crotchety, chimerical, waggish

whine VERB **1** = cry, sob, wail, whimper, sniffle, snivel, moan …*He could hear a child whining in the background…*
2 = complain, grumble, gripe (*informal*), whinge (*informal*), moan, cry, beef (*slang*), carp, sob, wail, grouse, whimper, bleat, grizzle (*informal, chiefly Brit.*),

---

Whales and dolphins http://www.ucmp.berkeley.edu/mammal/cetacea/cetacean.html

beluga	humpback whale	sei whale
baleen whale	killer whale, grampus, *or* orc	sperm whale *or* cachalot
blue whale *or* sulphur-bottom	minke whale	toothed whale
bottlenose dolphin	narwhal	whalebone whale
bowhead	porpoise	white whale
dorado	right whale *or* (*Austral.*) bay	
Greenland whale	whale	
greyback *or* grey whale	rorqual	

grouch (*informal*), bellyache (*slang*), kvetch (*U.S. slang*) …*She's always calling me to whine about her problems…*
NOUN **1** = <u>cry</u>, moan, sob, wail, whimper, plaintive cry …*His voice became a pleading whine…*
2 = <u>drone</u>, note, hum …*the whine of air-raid sirens…*
3 = <u>complaint</u>, moan, grumble, grouse, gripe (*informal*), whinge (*informal*), grouch (*informal*), beef (*slang*) …*Her conversation is one long whine about her husband…*

whinge (*Informal*) VERB = <u>complain</u>, moan, grumble, grouse, gripe (*informal*), beef (*slang*), carp, bleat, grizzle (*informal, chiefly Brit.*), grouch (*informal*), bellyache (*slang*), kvetch (*U.S. slang*) …*people who whinge about their alleged misfortunes…*
NOUN = <u>complaint</u>, moan, grumble, whine, grouse, gripe (*informal*), grouch, beef (*slang*) …*It must be depressing having to listen to everyone's whinges…*

whip NOUN = <u>lash</u>, cane, birch, switch, crop, scourge, thong, rawhide, riding crop, horsewhip, bullwhip, knout, cat-o'-nine-tails …*Prisoners were regularly beaten with a whip…*
VERB **1** = <u>lash</u>, cane, flog, beat, switch, leather, punish, strap, tan (*slang*), thrash, lick (*informal*), birch, scourge, spank, castigate, lambast(e), flagellate, give a hiding (*informal*) …*He was whipped with a studded belt…*
2 (*Informal*) = <u>dash</u>, shoot, fly, tear, rush, dive, dart, whisk, flit …*I whipped into a parking space…*
3 = <u>whisk</u>, beat, mix vigorously, stir vigorously …*Whip the cream until it is thick…*
4 = <u>incite</u>, drive, push, urge, stir, spur, provoke, compel, hound, prod, work up, get going, agitate, prick, inflame, instigate, goad, foment …*an accomplished orator who could whip a crowd into hysteria…*
5 (*Informal*) = <u>beat</u>, thrash, trounce, wipe the floor with (*informal*), best, defeat, stuff (*slang*), worst, overcome, hammer (*informal*), overwhelm, conquer, lick (*informal*), rout, overpower, outdo, clobber (*slang*), take apart (*slang*), run rings around (*informal*), blow out of the water (*slang*), make mincemeat out of (*informal*), drub …*Our school can whip theirs at football and rugby…*
PHRASES **whip someone up** = <u>rouse</u>, excite, provoke, arouse, stir up, work up, agitate, inflame …*McCarthy whipped up Americans into a frenzy of anti-Communist activity…* ♦ **whip something out** = <u>pull out</u>, produce, remove, jerk out, show, flash, seize, whisk out, snatch out …*Bob whipped out his notebook…* ♦ **whip something up** = <u>instigate</u>, trigger, provoke, rouse, stir up, incite, kindle, foment …*He accused his opponent of whipping up anti-foreign sentiments…*

whipping = <u>beating</u>, lashing, thrashing, caning, hiding (*informal*), punishment, tanning (*slang*), birching, flogging, spanking, the strap, flagellation, castigation, leathering

whirl VERB **1** = <u>spin</u>, turn, circle, wheel, twist, reel, rotate, pivot, twirl …*Hearing a sound behind her, she whirled round…*

2 = <u>rotate</u>, roll, twist, revolve, swirl, twirl, gyrate, pirouette …*The smoke whirled and grew into a monstrous column…*
3 = <u>feel dizzy</u>, swim, spin, reel, go round …*My head whirled in a giddiness like that of intoxication…*
NOUN **1** = <u>revolution</u>, turn, roll, circle, wheel, spin, twist, reel, swirl, rotation, twirl, pirouette, gyration, birl (*Scot.*) …*the whirl of snowflakes in the wind…*
2 = <u>bustle</u>, round, series, succession, flurry, merry-go-round …*Her life is one long whirl of parties…*
3 = <u>confusion</u>, daze, dither (*chiefly Brit.*), giddiness …*My thoughts are in a complete whirl…*
4 = <u>tumult</u>, spin, stir, agitation, commotion, hurly-burly …*I was caught up in a terrible whirl of emotion…*
PHRASES **give something a whirl** (*Informal*) = <u>attempt</u>, try, have a go at (*informal*), have a crack at (*informal*), have a shot at (*informal*), have a stab at (*informal*), have a bash at, have a whack at (*informal*) …*Why not give acupuncture a whirl?…*

whirlwind NOUN **1** = <u>tornado</u>, hurricane, cyclone, typhoon, twister (*U.S.*), dust devil, waterspout …*They scattered like leaves in a whirlwind…*
2 = <u>turmoil</u>, chaos, swirl, mayhem, uproar, maelstrom, welter, bedlam, tumult, hurly-burly, madhouse …*a whirlwind of frenzied activity…*
ADJECTIVE = <u>rapid</u>, short, quick, swift, lightning, rash, speedy, hasty, impulsive, headlong, impetuous …*He got married after a whirlwind romance…* OPPOSITE⟩ unhurried

whisk VERB **1** = <u>rush</u>, sweep, hurry …*I was whisked away in a police car…*
2 = <u>pull</u>, whip (*informal*), snatch, take …*The waiter whisked our plates away…*
3 = <u>speed</u>, race, shoot, fly, career, tear, rush, sweep, dash, hurry, barrel (along) (*informal, chiefly U.S. & Canad.*), sprint, dart, hasten, burn rubber (*informal*), go like the clappers (*Brit. informal*), hightail it (*U.S. informal*), wheech (*Scot. informal*) …*She whisked out of the room…*
4 = <u>flick</u>, whip, sweep, brush, wipe, twitch …*The dog whisked its tail around in excitement…*
5 = <u>beat</u>, mix vigorously, stir vigorously, whip, fluff up …*Whisk together the sugar and the egg yolks…*
NOUN **1** = <u>flick</u>, sweep, brush, whip, wipe …*With one whisk of its tail, the horse brushed the flies off…*
2 = <u>beater</u>, mixer, blender …*Using a whisk, beat the mixture until it thickens…*

whisky = <u>Scotch</u>, malt, rye, bourbon, firewater, John Barleycorn, usquebaugh (*Gaelic*), barley-bree (*Scot.*)

whisper VERB **1** = <u>murmur</u>, breathe, mutter, mumble, purr, speak in hushed tones, say softly, say sotto voce, utter under the breath …*'Keep your voice down,' I whispered…* OPPOSITE⟩ shout
2 = <u>gossip</u>, hint, intimate, murmur, insinuate, spread rumours …*People started whispering that the pair were having an affair…*
3 = <u>rustle</u>, sigh, moan, murmur, hiss, swish, sough, susurrate (*literary*) …*The leaves whispered and rustled in the breeze…*
NOUN **1** = <u>murmur</u>, mutter, mumble, undertone, low

voice, soft voice, hushed tone …*Men were talking in whispers in the corridor…*
2 (*Informal*) = rumour, report, word, story, hint, buzz, gossip, dirt (*U.S. slang*), innuendo, insinuation, scuttlebutt (*U.S. slang*) …*I've heard a whisper that he is planning to resign…*
3 = rustle, sigh, sighing, murmur, hiss, swish, soughing, susurration *or* susurrus (*literary*) …*the slight whisper of the wind in the grass…*
4 = hint, shadow, suggestion, trace, breath, suspicion, fraction, tinge, whiff …*There is a whisper of conspiracy about the whole affair…*

whit = bit, drop, piece, trace, scrap, dash, grain, particle, fragment, atom, pinch, shred, crumb, mite, jot, speck, modicum, least bit, iota

white ADJECTIVE **1** = pale, grey, ghastly, wan, pasty, bloodless, pallid, ashen, waxen, like death warmed up (*informal*), wheyfaced …*He turned white and began to stammer…*
2 = (only used of *hair*) silver, grey, snowy, grizzled, hoary …*an old man with white hair…*
PHRASES **whiter than white** = immaculate, innocent, virtuous, saintly, clean, pure, worthy, noble, stainless, impeccable, exemplary, spotless, squeaky-clean, unblemished, untainted, unsullied, irreproachable, uncorrupted …*A man in his position has to be seen as being whiter than white…*
➤ **shades from black to white**

white-collar = clerical, office, executive, professional, salaried, nonmanual

whiten **1** = pale, blanch, go white, turn pale, blench, fade, etiolate …*His face whitened as he heard the news…* OPPOSITE darken
2 = bleach, lighten …*toothpastes that whiten the teeth…* OPPOSITE darken

whitewash VERB = cover up, conceal, suppress, camouflage, make light of, gloss over, extenuate …*The administration is whitewashing the regime's actions…* OPPOSITE expose
NOUN = cover-up, deception, camouflage, concealment, extenuation …*The report's findings were condemned as total whitewash…*

whittle VERB = carve, cut, hew, shape, trim, shave, pare …*Chitty sat in his rocking chair whittling a piece of wood…*
PHRASES **whittle something** *or* **someone down** = reduce, cut down, cut, decrease, prune, scale down …*He had whittled the twenty interviewees down to two…* ◆ **whittle something away** = undermine, reduce, destroy, consume, erode, eat away, wear away …*I believe the Government's aim is to whittle away the Welfare State…*

whole NOUN **1** = total, all, lot, everything, aggregate, sum total, the entire amount …*Taken as a percentage of the whole, it has to be a fairly minor part…*
2 = unit, body, piece, object, combination, unity, entity, ensemble, entirety, fullness, totality …*The different components combine to form a complete whole…* OPPOSITE part

ADJECTIVE **1** = complete, full, total, entire, integral, uncut, undivided, unabridged, unexpurgated, uncondensed …*I have now read the whole book…* OPPOSITE partial
2 = undamaged, intact, unscathed, unbroken, good, sound, perfect, mint, untouched, flawless, unhurt, faultless, unharmed, in one piece, uninjured, inviolate, unimpaired, unmutilated …*I struck the glass with all my might, but it remained whole…* OPPOSITE damaged
ADVERB = in one piece, in one …*Snakes swallow their prey whole…*
PHRASES **on the whole 1** = all in all, altogether, all things considered, by and large, taking everything into consideration …*On the whole, I think it's better if I don't come with you…* **2** = generally, in general, for the most part, as a rule, chiefly, mainly, mostly, principally, on average, predominantly, in the main, to a large extent, as a general rule, generally speaking …*On the whole, women are having children much later these days…*

wholehearted = sincere, complete, committed, genuine, real, true, determined, earnest, warm, devoted, dedicated, enthusiastic, emphatic, hearty, heartfelt, zealous, unqualified, unstinting, unreserved, unfeigned OPPOSITE half-hearted

wholesale ADJECTIVE = extensive, total, mass, sweeping, broad, comprehensive, wide-ranging, blanket, outright, far-reaching, indiscriminate, all-inclusive …*the wholesale destruction of life on this planet…* OPPOSITE limited
ADVERB = extensively, comprehensively, across the board, all at once, indiscriminately, without exception, on a large scale …*The army was burning down houses and killing villagers wholesale…*

wholesome 1 = moral, nice, clean, pure, decent, innocent, worthy, ethical, respectable, honourable, uplifting, righteous, exemplary, virtuous, apple-pie (*informal*), squeaky-clean, edifying …*It was all good, wholesome fun…* OPPOSITE corrupt
2 = healthy, good, strengthening, beneficial, nourishing, nutritious, sanitary, invigorating, salutary, hygienic, healthful, health-giving …*The food was filling and wholesome…* OPPOSITE unhealthy

wholly 1 = completely, totally, perfectly, fully, entirely, comprehensively, altogether, thoroughly, utterly, heart and soul, one hundred per cent (*informal*), in every respect …*The accusation is wholly without foundation…* OPPOSITE partly
2 = solely, only, exclusively, without exception, to the exclusion of everything else …*societies which rely wholly on farming to survive…*

whoop VERB = cry, shout, scream, cheer, yell, shriek, hoot, holler (*informal*) …*The audience whooped and cheered with delight…*
NOUN = cry, shout, scream, cheer, yell, shriek, hoot, holler (*informal*), hurrah, halloo …*A wild frenzy of whoops and yells arose outside…*

whopper 1 = big lie, fabrication, falsehood, untruth, tall story (*informal*), fable …*He's always telling

whoppers about his sex life…
2 = giant, monster, jumbo (*informal*), mammoth, colossus, leviathan, crackerjack (*informal*) …*As comets go, it is a whopper…*

whopping = gigantic, great, big, large, huge, giant, massive, enormous, extraordinary, tremendous, monstrous, whacking (*informal*), mammoth, prodigious, elephantine, humongous *or* humungous (*U.S. slang*)

whore NOUN = prostitute, hooker (*U.S. slang*), tart (*informal*), streetwalker, tom (*Brit. slang*), brass (*slang*), slag (*Brit. slang*), hustler (*U.S. & Canad. slang*), call girl, courtesan, working girl (*facetious slang*), harlot, loose woman, fallen woman, scrubber (*Brit. & Austral. slang*), strumpet, trollop, lady of the night, cocotte, woman of easy virtue, demimondaine, woman of ill repute, fille de joie (*French*), demirep (*rare*) …*There were pimps and whores standing on every street corner…*
VERB = sleep around, womanize, wanton (*informal*), wench (*archaic*), fornicate, lech *or* letch (*informal*) …*His eldest son gambled, whored and drank…*

whorl = swirl, spiral, coil, twist, vortex, helix, corkscrew

wicked **1** = bad, evil, corrupt, vile, guilty, abandoned, foul, vicious, worthless, shameful, immoral, scandalous, atrocious, sinful, heinous, depraved, debased, devilish, amoral, egregious, abominable, fiendish, villainous, unprincipled, nefarious, dissolute, iniquitous, irreligious, black-hearted, impious, unrighteous, maleficent, flagitious …*She flew at me, shouting how evil and wicked I was…* OPPOSITE virtuous
2 = mischievous, playful, impish, devilish, arch, teasing, naughty, cheeky, rascally, incorrigible, raffish, roguish, rakish, tricksy, puckish, waggish …*She has a delightfully wicked sense of humour…* OPPOSITE well-behaved
3 = agonizing, terrible, acute, severe, intense, awful, painful, fierce, mighty, dreadful, fearful, gut-wrenching …*A wicked pain shot through his injured elbow…*
4 = harmful, terrible, intense, mighty, crashing, dreadful, destructive, injurious …*The wind gets so wicked you want to stay indoors while the sea rages…* OPPOSITE harmless
5 (*Slang*) = expert, great (*informal*), strong, powerful, masterly, wonderful, outstanding, remarkable, ace (*informal*), first-class, marvellous, mighty, dazzling, skilful, A1 (*informal*), adept, deft, adroit …*John's a wicked tennis player. He always wins…*

wide ADJECTIVE **1** = spacious, broad, extensive, ample, roomy, commodious …*The doorway should be wide enough to allow wheelchair access…* OPPOSITE confined
2 = baggy, full, loose, ample, billowing, roomy, voluminous, capacious, oversize, generously cut …*Wear the shirt loose over wide trousers…*
3 = expanded, dilated, fully open, distended …*His eyes were wide with disbelief…* OPPOSITE shut
4 = broad, comprehensive, extensive, wide-ranging,

large, catholic, expanded, sweeping, vast, immense, ample, inclusive, expansive, exhaustive, encyclopedic, far-ranging, compendious …*The brochure offers a wide choice of hotels and holiday homes…* OPPOSITE restricted
5 = extensive, general, far-reaching, overarching …*The case has attracted wide publicity…*
6 = large, broad, vast, immense …*the wide variation in the ages and backgrounds of the candidates…*
7 = distant, off, away, remote, off course, off target …*The shot was several feet wide…*
ADVERB **1** = fully, completely, right out, as far as possible, to the furthest extent …*He opened his mouth wide…* OPPOSITE partly
2 = off target, nowhere near, astray, off course, off the mark …*The big striker fired wide and missed an easy goal…*
PHRASES **wide awake 1** = conscious, fully awake, roused, wakened …*I could not relax and was still wide awake after midnight…* **2** = alert, vigilant, on the ball (*informal*), aware, keen, wary, watchful, observant, on the alert, on your toes, on the qui vive, heedful …*You need to stay alert and wide awake to avoid accidents as you drive…* OPPOSITE inattentive

wide-eyed 1 = naive, green, trusting, credulous, simple, innocent, impressionable, unsophisticated, ingenuous, wet behind the ears (*informal*), unsuspicious, as green as grass …*He told tall stories to a wide-eyed group of tourists…*
2 = staring, spellbound, gobsmacked (*Brit. slang*), dumbfounded, agog, agape, thunderstruck, goggle-eyed, awe-stricken …*She was wide-eyed in astonishment…*

widen 1 = broaden, expand, enlarge, dilate, spread, extend, stretch, open wide, open out *or* up …*He had an operation to widen an artery in his heart…* OPPOSITE narrow
2 = get wider, spread, extend, expand, broaden, open wide, open out *or* up …*The river widens considerably as it begins to turn east…* OPPOSITE narrow

wide-open 1 = outspread, spread, outstretched, splayed, fully open, fully extended, gaping …*He came towards her with his arms wide open in welcome…*
2 = unprotected, open, exposed, vulnerable, at risk, in danger, susceptible, defenceless, in peril …*The virus leaves the body wide open to infection…*
3 = uncertain, unsettled, unpredictable, up for grabs (*informal*), indeterminate, anybody's guess (*informal*) …*The match was still wide open at half-time…*

widespread = common, general, popular, sweeping, broad, extensive, universal, epidemic, wholesale, far-reaching, prevalent, rife, pervasive, far-flung OPPOSITE limited

width = breadth, extent, span, wideness, reach, range, measure, scope, diameter, compass, thickness, girth

wield 1 = brandish, flourish, manipulate, swing, use, manage, handle, employ, ply …*He was attacked by an assailant wielding a kitchen knife…*
2 = exert, hold, maintain, exercise, have, control,

manage, apply, command, possess, make use of, utilize, put to use, be possessed of, have at your disposal …*He remains chairman, but wields little power in the company*…

wife = <u>spouse</u>, woman (*informal*), partner, mate, bride, old woman (*informal*), old lady (*informal*), little woman (*informal*), significant other (*U.S. informal*), better half (*humorous*), her indoors (*Brit. slang*), helpmate, helpmeet, (the) missis *or* missus (*informal*), vrou (*S. African*)

(**Related Words**)
adjective: uxorial

wiggle VERB **1** = <u>jerk</u>, shake, twitch, wag, jiggle, waggle …*She wiggled her fingers to attract his attention*…
2 = <u>squirm</u>, twitch, writhe, shimmy …*A little worm was wiggling on the pavement*…
NOUN = <u>jerk</u>, shake, twitch, wag, squirm, writhe, jiggle, waggle, shimmy …*With a wiggle of her hips, she slid out of her skirt*…

wild ADJECTIVE **1** = <u>untamed</u>, fierce, savage, ferocious, unbroken, feral, undomesticated, free, warrigal (*Austral. literary*) …*The organization is calling for a total ban on the trade of wild animals*… OPPOSITE tame
2 = <u>uncultivated</u>, natural, native, indigenous …*The lane was lined with wild flowers*… OPPOSITE cultivated
3 = <u>desolate</u>, empty, desert, deserted, virgin, lonely, uninhabited, godforsaken, uncultivated, uncivilized, trackless, unpopulated …*one of the few wild areas remaining in the South East*… OPPOSITE inhabited
4 = <u>stormy</u>, violent, rough, intense, raging, furious, howling, choppy, tempestuous, blustery …*The recent wild weather has caused millions of pounds' worth of damage*…
5 = <u>excited</u>, mad (*informal*), crazy (*informal*), eager, nuts (*slang*), enthusiastic, raving, frantic, daft (*informal*), frenzied, hysterical, avid, potty (*Brit. informal*), delirious, agog …*The children were wild with excitement*… OPPOSITE unenthusiastic
6 = <u>uncontrolled</u>, violent, rough, disorderly, noisy, chaotic, turbulent, wayward, unruly, rowdy, boisterous, lawless, unfettered, unbridled, riotous, unrestrained, unmanageable, impetuous, undisciplined, ungovernable, self-willed, uproarious …*When drunk, he became wild and violent*… OPPOSITE calm
7 = <u>mad</u> (*informal*), furious, fuming, infuriated, incensed, enraged, very angry, irate, livid (*informal*), in a rage, on the warpath (*informal*), hot under the collar (*informal*), beside yourself, tooshie (*Austral. slang*), off the air (*Austral. slang*) …*When I told him what I had done, he was wild*…
8 = <u>outrageous</u>, fantastic, foolish, rash, extravagant, reckless, preposterous, giddy, madcap, foolhardy, flighty, ill-considered, imprudent, impracticable …*I was just a kid and full of wild ideas*… OPPOSITE practical
9 = <u>dishevelled</u>, disordered, untidy, unkempt, tousled, straggly, windblown …*They were alarmed by his wild*

hair and staring eyes…
10 = <u>passionate</u>, mad (*informal*), ardent, fervent, zealous, fervid …*She's just wild about him*…
11 = <u>uncivilized</u>, fierce, savage, primitive, rude, ferocious, barbaric, brutish, barbarous …*the wild tribes which still roam the northern plains with their horse herds*… OPPOSITE civilized
PLURAL NOUN = <u>wilderness</u>, desert, wasteland, middle of nowhere (*informal*), backwoods, back of beyond (*informal*), uninhabited area …*They went canoeing in the wilds of Canada*…
PHRASES **run wild 1** = <u>grow unchecked</u>, spread, ramble, straggle …*The front garden is running wild*…
2 = <u>go on the rampage</u>, stray, rampage, run riot, cut loose, run free, kick over the traces, be undisciplined, abandon all restraint …*She lets her children run wild*…

wilderness 1 = <u>wilds</u>, waste, desert, wasteland, uncultivated region …*He looked out over a wilderness of mountain, lake and forest*…
2 = <u>tangle</u>, confusion, maze, muddle, clutter, jumble, welter, congeries, confused mass …*The neglected cemetery was a wilderness of crumbling gravestones and parched grass*…

wildlife = <u>flora and fauna</u>, animals, fauna

wiles 1 = <u>ploys</u>, tricks, devices, lures, manoeuvres, dodges, ruses, artifices, subterfuges, stratagems, contrivances, impositions …*She never hesitated to use her feminine wiles to get her own way*…
2 = <u>cunning</u>, craft, fraud, cheating, guile, artifice, trickery, chicanery, craftiness, artfulness, slyness …*His wit and wiles have made him one of the sharpest politicians in the Cabinet*…

wilful 1 = <u>intentional</u>, willed, intended, conscious, voluntary, deliberate, purposeful, volitional …*Wilful neglect of the environment has caused this problem*… OPPOSITE unintentional
2 = <u>obstinate</u>, dogged, determined, persistent, adamant, stubborn, perverse, uncompromising, intractable, inflexible, unyielding, intransigent, headstrong, obdurate, stiff-necked, self-willed, refractory, pig-headed, bull-headed, mulish, froward (*archaic*) …*a spoilt and wilful teenager*… OPPOSITE obedient

will NOUN **1** = <u>determination</u>, drive, aim, purpose, commitment, resolution, resolve, intention, spine, backbone, tenacity, willpower, single-mindedness, doggedness, firmness of purpose …*He lacked the will to confront her*…
2 = <u>wish</u>, mind, desire, pleasure, intention, fancy, preference, inclination …*He was forced to leave the country against his will*…
3 = <u>choice</u>, decision, option, prerogative, volition …*the concept of free will*…
4 = <u>decree</u>, wish, desire, command, dictate, ordinance …*He has submitted himself to the will of God*…
5 = <u>testament</u>, declaration, bequest(s), last wishes, last will and testament …*Attached to his will was a letter he had written just before his death*…
VERB **1** = <u>decree</u>, order, cause, effect, direct,

determine, bid, intend, command, resolve, bring about, ordain …*They believed they would win because God had willed it…*

2 = <u>wish</u>, want, choose, prefer, desire, elect, opt, see fit …*Say what you will about him, but he's always been a good provider…*

3 = <u>bequeath</u>, give, leave, transfer, gift, hand on, pass on, confer, hand down, settle on …*She had willed all her money to her brother, Frank…*

PHRASES **at will** = <u>as you please</u>, at your discretion, as you think fit, at your pleasure, at your desire, at your whim, at your inclination, at your wish …*Some yoga practitioners can slow their heart-rates down at will…*

(Related Words)

adjectives : voluntary, volitive

willing 1 = <u>inclined</u>, prepared, happy, pleased, content, in favour, consenting, disposed, favourable, agreeable, in the mood, compliant, amenable, desirous, so-minded, nothing loath …*There are some questions which they will not be willing to answer…* OPPOSITE unwilling

2 = <u>ready</u>, game (*informal*), eager, enthusiastic …*He had plenty of willing volunteers to help him clear up…* OPPOSITE reluctant

willingly = <u>readily</u>, freely, gladly, happily, eagerly, voluntarily, cheerfully, with pleasure, without hesitation, by choice, with all your heart, lief (*rare*), of your own free will, of your own accord OPPOSITE unwillingly

willingness = <u>inclination</u>, will, agreement, wish, favour, desire, enthusiasm, consent, goodwill, disposition, volition, agreeableness OPPOSITE reluctance

willowy = <u>slender</u>, slim, graceful, supple, lithe, limber, svelte, lissom(e), sylphlike

willpower = <u>self-control</u>, drive, resolution, resolve, determination, grit, self-discipline, single-mindedness, fixity of purpose, firmness of purpose *or* will, force *or* strength of will OPPOSITE weakness

willy-nilly 1 = <u>whether you like it or not</u>, necessarily, of necessity, perforce, whether or no, whether desired or not, nolens volens (*Latin*) …*We were dragged willy-nilly into the argument…*

2 = <u>haphazardly</u>, at random, randomly, without order, without method, without planning, any old how (*informal*) …*The papers were just bundled into the drawers willy-nilly…*

wilt 1 = <u>droop</u>, wither, sag, shrivel, become limp *or* flaccid …*The roses wilted the day after she bought them…*

2 = <u>weaken</u>, sag, languish, droop …*She began to wilt in the morning heat…*

3 = <u>wane</u>, fail, sink, flag, fade, diminish, dwindle, wither, ebb, melt away, lose courage …*Their resolution wilted in the face of such powerful opposition…*

wily = <u>cunning</u>, designing, scheming, sharp, intriguing, arch, tricky, crooked, shrewd, sly, astute,

deceptive, crafty, artful, shifty, foxy, cagey (*informal*), deceitful, underhand, guileful, fly (*slang*) OPPOSITE straightforward

wimp (*Informal*) = <u>weakling</u>, wet (*Brit. slang*), mouse, drip (*informal*), coward, jessie (*Scot. slang*), pussy (*slang, chiefly U.S.*), jellyfish (*informal*), sissy, doormat (*slang*), wuss (*slang*), milksop, softy *or* softie

win VERB **1** = <u>be victorious in</u>, succeed in, prevail in, come first in, finish first in, be the victor in, gain victory in, achieve first place in …*He does not have any reasonable chance of winning the election…* OPPOSITE lose

2 = <u>be victorious</u>, succeed, triumph, overcome, prevail, conquer, come first, finish first, carry the day, sweep the board, take the prize, gain victory, achieve mastery, achieve first place, carry all before you …*Our team is confident of winning again this year…* OPPOSITE lose

3 = <u>gain</u>, get, receive, land, catch, achieve, net, earn, pick up, bag (*informal*), secure, collect, obtain, acquire, accomplish, attain, procure, come away with …*The first correct entry will win the prize…* OPPOSITE forfeit

NOUN = <u>victory</u>, success, triumph, conquest …*Arsenal's run of eight games without a win…* OPPOSITE defeat

PHRASES **win someone over** *or* **round** = <u>convince</u>, influence, attract, persuade, convert, charm, sway, disarm, allure, prevail upon, bring *or* talk round …*He had won over a significant number of his opponents…*

wince VERB = <u>flinch</u>, start, shrink, cringe, quail, recoil, cower, draw back, blench …*He tightened his grip on her arm until she winced in pain…*

NOUN = <u>flinch</u>, start, cringe …*She gave a wince at the memory of their first date…*

wind¹ NOUN **1** = <u>air</u>, blast, breath, hurricane, breeze, draught, gust, zephyr, air-current, current of air …*During the night the wind had blown down the fence…*

2 = <u>flatulence</u>, gas, flatus …*tablets to treat trapped wind…*

3 = <u>breath</u>, puff, respiration …*A punch in the stomach knocked the wind out of me…*

4 = <u>nonsense</u>, talk, boasting, hot air, babble, bluster, humbug, twaddle (*informal*), gab (*informal*), verbalizing, blather, codswallop (*informal*), eyewash (*informal*), idle talk, empty talk, bizzo (*Austral. slang*), bull's wool (*Austral. & N.Z. slang*) …*You're just talking a lot of wind…*

PHRASES **get wind of something** = <u>hear about</u>, learn of, find out about, become aware of, be told about, be informed of, be made aware of, hear tell of, have brought to your notice, hear something on the grape vine (*informal*) …*I don't want the press to get wind of our plans at this stage…* ◆ **in the wind** = <u>imminent</u>, coming, near, approaching, on the way, looming, brewing, impending, on the cards (*informal*), in the offing, about to happen, close at hand …*By the mid-1980s, economic change was in the*

Winds

Wind	Location	Wind force	Beaufort number	Speed (kph)
berg wind	South Africa	Calm	0	less than 1
bise	Switzerland	Light air	1	1–5
bora	Adriatic Sea	Light breeze	2	6–11
buran *or* bura	central Asia	Gentle breeze	3	12–19
Cape doctor	Cape Town, South Africa	Moderate breeze	4	20–28
chinook	Washington & Oregon coasts	Fresh	5	29–38
		Strong	6	39–49
föhn *or* foehn	N slopes of the Alps	Near gale	7	50–61
harmattan	W African coast	Gale	8	62–74
khamsin, kamseen, *or* kamsin	Egypt	Strong gale	9	75–88
levanter	W Mediterranean	Storm	10	89–102
libeccio *or* libecchio	Corsica	Violent storm	11	103–117
meltemi *or* etesian wind	NE Mediterranean	Hurricane	12	118 and over
mistral	S France to Mediterranean			
monsoon	S Asia			
nor'wester	Southern Alps, New Zealand			
pampero	S America			
simoom *or* simoon	Arabia & N Africa			
sirocco	N Africa to S Europe			
tramontane *or* tramontana	W coast of Italy			

wind again... ◆ **put the wind up someone** (*Informal*) = scare, alarm, frighten, panic, discourage, unnerve, scare off, frighten off ...*I had an anonymous letter that really put the wind up me*...

➤ **winds**

wind² VERB **1** = meander, turn, bend, twist, curve, snake, ramble, twist and turn, deviate, zigzag ...*The Moselle winds through some 160 miles of tranquil countryside*...
2 = wrap, twist, reel, curl, loop, coil, twine, furl, wreathe ...*She wound the sash round her waist*...
3 = coil, curl, spiral, encircle, twine ...*The snake wound around my leg*...
PHRASES **wind down 1** = calm down, unwind, take it easy, unbutton (*informal*), put your feet up, de-stress (*informal*), outspan (*S. African*), cool down *or* off ...*I need a drink to help me wind down*... **2** = subside, decline, diminish, come to an end, dwindle, tail off, taper off, slacken off ...*The relationship was winding down by more or less mutual agreement*... ◆ **wind someone up** (*Informal*) **1** = irritate, excite, anger, annoy, exasperate, nettle, work someone up, pique, make someone nervous, put someone on edge, make someone tense ...*This woman kept winding me up by talking over me*... **2** = tease, kid (*informal*), have someone on (*informal*), annoy, rag (*informal*), rib (*informal*), josh (*informal*), vex, make fun of, take the mickey out of (*informal*), send someone up (*informal*), pull someone's leg (*informal*) ...*You're joking. Come on, you're just winding me up*... ◆ **wind something down** = coil, reduce, relax, lessen, slacken, bring something to a close *or* end, wind something up ...*Foreign aid workers have already begun to wind down their operation*... ◆ **wind something up 1** = end, finish, settle, conclude, tie up, wrap up, finalize, bring to a close, tie up the loose ends of (*informal*) ...*The President is about to wind up his visit to Somalia*... **2** = close down, close, dissolve, terminate, liquidate, put something into liquidation ...*The bank seems determined to wind up the company*... ◆ **wind up** = end up, be left, find yourself, finish up, fetch up (*informal*), land up, end your days ...*You're going to wind up a bitter and lonely old man*...

winded = out of breath, panting, puffed, breathless, gasping for breath, puffed out, out of puff, out of whack (*informal*)

windfall = godsend, find, jackpot, bonanza, stroke of luck, manna from heaven, pot of gold at the end of the rainbow OPPOSITE> misfortune

winding = twisting, turning, bending, curving, crooked, spiral, indirect, roundabout, meandering, tortuous, convoluted, serpentine, sinuous, circuitous, twisty, anfractuous, flexuous OPPOSITE> straight

windy = breezy, wild, stormy, boisterous, blustering, windswept, tempestuous, blustery, gusty, inclement, squally, blowy OPPOSITE> calm

wing NOUN **1** = organ of flight, pinion (*poetic*), pennon (*poetic*) ...*The bird flapped its wings furiously*...
2 = annexe, part, side, section, extension, adjunct, ell (*U.S.*) ...*We were given an office in the empty west wing of the building*...
3 = faction, grouping, group, set, side, arm, section, camp, branch, circle, lobby, segment, caucus, clique,

coterie, schism, cabal ...*the liberal wing of the Democratic party*...

VERB **1** = <u>fly</u>, soar, glide, take wing ...*Several birds broke cover and went winging over the lake*...

2 = <u>hurry</u>, fly, race, speed, streak, zoom, hasten, hurtle ...*He was soon winging his way home to rejoin his family*...

3 = <u>wound</u>, hit, nick, clip, graze ...*He shot at the bird but only managed to wing it*...

wink **VERB** **1** = <u>blink</u>, bat, flutter, nictate, nictitate ...*Brian winked an eye at me, giving me his seal of approval*...

2 = <u>twinkle</u>, flash, shine, sparkle, gleam, shimmer, glimmer ...*From the hotel window, they could see lights winking on the bay*...

NOUN **1** = <u>blink</u>, flutter, nictation, nictitation ...*Diana gave me a reassuring wink*...

2 = <u>twinkle</u>, flash, sparkle, gleam, blink, glimmering, glimmer ...*In the distance, he noticed the wink of a red light*...

PHRASES **in the wink of an eye** (*Informal*) = <u>quickly</u>, in a moment, in a second, in a flash, in an instant, in a split second, in the blink of an eye (*informal*), in a jiffy (*informal*), in a twinkling, in two shakes of a lambs tail (*informal*) ...*It was all over in the wink of an eye*... ◆ **wink at something** = <u>condone</u>, allow, ignore, overlook, tolerate, put up with (*informal*), disregard, turn a blind eye to, blink at, connive at, pretend not to notice, shut your eyes to ...*Corrupt police have been known to wink at crimes in return for bribes*...

winner = <u>victor</u>, first, champion, master, champ (*informal*), conqueror, vanquisher, prizewinner, conquering hero **OPPOSITE** loser

winning **ADJECTIVE** **1** = <u>victorious</u>, first, top, successful, unbeaten, conquering, triumphant, undefeated, vanquishing, top-scoring, unvanquished ...*The winning team returned home to a heroes' welcome*...

2 = <u>charming</u>, taking, pleasing, sweet, attractive, engaging, lovely, fascinating, fetching, delightful, cute, disarming, enchanting, endearing, captivating, amiable, alluring, bewitching, delectable, winsome, prepossessing, likable *or* likeable ...*She had great charm and a winning personality*... **OPPOSITE** unpleasant

PLURAL NOUN = <u>spoils</u>, profits, gains, prize, proceeds, takings, booty ...*The poker player collected his winnings and left*...

winsome = <u>charming</u>, taking, winning, pleasing, pretty, fair, sweet, attractive, engaging, fascinating, pleasant, fetching, cute, disarming, enchanting, endearing, captivating, agreeable, amiable, alluring, bewitching, delectable, comely, likable *or* likeable

winter sport

Winter sports	
Alpine skiing	skating
biathlon	skibobbing
bobsleigh	skiing
curling	skijoring
downhill racing	ski jumping
ice dancing	slalom
ice hockey	snowboarding
ice skating *or* figure	speed skating
skating	super-G
luge	tobogganing
Nordic skiing	

wintry **1** = <u>cold</u>, freezing, frozen, harsh, icy, chilly, snowy, frosty, hibernal ...*The wintry weather continues to sweep across the country*... **OPPOSITE** warm

2 = <u>unfriendly</u>, cold, cool, remote, distant, bleak, chilly, frigid, cheerless ...*Melissa gave him a wintry smile and walked on without a word*...

wipe **VERB** **1** = <u>clean</u>, dry, polish, brush, dust, rub, sponge, mop, swab ...*She wiped her hands on the towel*...

2 = <u>erase</u>, remove, take off, get rid of, take away, rub off, efface, clean off, sponge off ...*Gleb wiped the sweat from his face*...

NOUN = <u>rub</u>, clean, polish, brush, lick, sponge, mop, swab ...*I'll give the surfaces a wipe with some disinfectant*...

PHRASES **wipe something** *or* **someone out** = <u>destroy</u>, eliminate, take out (*slang*), massacre, slaughter, erase, eradicate, blow away (*slang, chiefly U.S.*), obliterate, liquidate (*informal*), annihilate, efface, exterminate, expunge, extirpate, wipe from the face of the earth (*informal*), kill to the last man ...*a fanatic who is determined to wipe out anyone who opposes him*...

wiry **1** = <u>lean</u>, strong, tough, thin, spare, skinny, stringy, sinewy ...*a wiry and athletic young man*... **OPPOSITE** flabby

2 = <u>stiff</u>, rough, coarse, curly, kinky, bristly ...*wiry black hair*...

wisdom **1** = <u>understanding</u>, learning, knowledge, intelligence, smarts (*slang, chiefly U.S.*), judgment, insight, enlightenment, penetration, comprehension, foresight, erudition, discernment, sagacity, sound judgment, sapience ...*a man respected for his wisdom and insight*... **OPPOSITE** foolishness

2 = <u>prudence</u>, reason, sense, intelligence, logic, circumspection, astuteness, judiciousness ...*Many have expressed doubts about the wisdom of the decision*... **OPPOSITE** folly

Related Words

adjective: sagacious

wise **1** = <u>sage</u>, knowing, understanding, aware, informed, clever, intelligent, sensible, enlightened, shrewd, discerning, perceptive, well-informed, erudite, sagacious, sapient, clued-up (*informal*) ...*She has the air of a wise woman*... **OPPOSITE** foolish

2 = <u>sensible</u>, sound, politic, informed, reasonable, clever, intelligent, rational, logical, shrewd, prudent, judicious, well-advised ...*She had made a very wise decision...* OPPOSITE⟩ unwise

wisecrack = joke, sally, gag (*informal*), quip, jibe, barb, jest, witticism, smart remark, pithy remark, sardonic remark

wish NOUN 1 = desire, liking, want, longing, hope, urge, intention, fancy (*informal*), ambition, yen (*informal*), hunger, aspiration, craving, lust, yearning, inclination, itch (*informal*), thirst, whim, hankering ...*Clearly she had no wish for his company...* OPPOSITE⟩ aversion

2 = request, will, want, order, demand, desire, command, bidding, behest (*literary*) ...*The decision was made against the wishes of the party leader...*

VERB 1 = want, feel, choose, please, desire, think fit ...*We can dress as we wish nowadays...*

2 = require, ask, order, direct, bid, desire, command, instruct ...*I will do as you wish...*

3 = bid, greet with ...*He wished me a good morning...*

PHRASES **wish for something** = desire, want, need, hope for, long for, crave, covet, aspire to, yearn for, thirst for, hunger for, hanker for, sigh for, set your heart on, desiderate ...*They both wished for a son to carry on the family business...*

wisp = piece, twist, strand, thread, shred, snippet

wispy 1 = straggly, fine, thin, frail, wisplike ...*Grey wispy hair straggled down to her shoulders...*

2 = thin, light, fine, delicate, fragile, flimsy, ethereal, insubstantial, gossamer, diaphanous, wisplike ...*a wispy chiffon dress...*

wistful = melancholy, longing, dreaming, sad, musing, yearning, thoughtful, reflective, dreamy, forlorn, mournful, contemplative, meditative, pensive, disconsolate

wit NOUN 1 = humour, fun, quips, banter, puns, pleasantry, repartee, wordplay, levity, witticisms, badinage, jocularity, facetiousness, drollery, raillery, waggishness, wittiness ...*Bill was known for his biting wit...* OPPOSITE⟩ seriousness

2 = humorist, card (*informal*), comedian, wag, joker, dag (*N.Z. informal*), punster, epigrammatist ...*a man who fancied himself as a great wit...*

3 *often plural* = cleverness, mind, reason, understanding, sense, brains, smarts (*slang, chiefly U.S.*), judgment, perception, wisdom, insight, common sense, intellect, comprehension, ingenuity, acumen, nous (*Brit. slang*), discernment, practical intelligence ...*The information is there for anyone with the wit to use it...* OPPOSITE⟩ stupidity

PHRASES **at your wits' end** = in despair, lost, stuck (*informal*), stumped, baffled, bewildered, at a loss, at the end of your tether ...*I just can't think what to do – I'm at my wits' end...*

witch = enchantress, magician, hag, crone, occultist, sorceress, Wiccan, necromancer

witchcraft = magic, spell, witching, voodoo, the occult, wizardry, black magic, enchantment, occultism, sorcery, incantation, Wicca, the black art,

witchery, necromancy, sortilege

withdraw 1 = remove, pull, take off, pull out, extract, take away, pull back, draw out, draw back ...*Cassandra withdrew her hand from Roger's...* ...*He reached into his pocket and withdrew a piece of paper...*

2 = take out, extract, draw out ...*They withdrew 100 dollars from their bank account...*

3 = retreat, go, leave (*informal*), retire, depart, pull out of, fall back, pull back, back out, back off, cop out (*slang*), disengage from ...*Troops withdrew from the country last March...* OPPOSITE⟩ advance

4 = go, leave, retire, retreat, depart, make yourself scarce, absent yourself ...*The waiter poured the wine and then withdrew...*

5 = pull out, leave, drop out, secede, disengage, detach yourself, absent yourself ...*The African National Congress threatened to withdraw from the talks...*

6 = retract, recall, take back, revoke, rescind, disavow, recant, disclaim, abjure, unsay ...*He withdrew his remarks and said he had not intended to cause offence...*

withdrawal 1 = removal, ending, stopping, taking away, abolition, elimination, cancellation, termination, extraction, discontinuation ...*the withdrawal of foreign aid...*

2 = exit, retirement, departure, pull-out, retreat, exodus, evacuation, disengagement ...*the withdrawal of troops from Eastern Europe...*

3 = departure, retirement, exit, secession ...*his withdrawal from government in 1946...*

4 = retraction, recall, disclaimer, repudiation, revocation, disavowal, recantation, rescission, abjuration ...*The charity insists on a withdrawal of the accusations...*

withdrawn = uncommunicative, reserved, retiring, quiet, silent, distant, shy, shrinking, detached, aloof, taciturn, introverted, timorous, unforthcoming OPPOSITE⟩ outgoing

wither 1 = wilt, dry, decline, shrink, decay, disintegrate, perish, languish, droop, shrivel, desiccate ...*Farmers have watched their crops wither because of the drought...* OPPOSITE⟩ flourish

2 = waste, decline, shrink, shrivel, atrophy ...*His leg muscles had withered from lack of use...*

3 = fade, decline, wane, perish ...*His dream of being a famous footballer withered and died...* OPPOSITE⟩ increase

4 = humiliate, blast, shame, put down, snub, mortify, abash ...*Mary withered me with a glance...*

withering = scornful, blasting, devastating, humiliating, snubbing, blighting, hurtful, mortifying

withhold 1 = keep secret, keep, refuse, hide, reserve, retain, sit on (*informal*), conceal, suppress, hold back, keep back ...*Police withheld the victim's name until her relatives had been informed...* OPPOSITE⟩ reveal

2 = hold back, check, resist, suppress, restrain, repress, keep back ...*She could not withhold a scornful

comment as he passed… OPPOSITE> release

with it = <u>fashionable</u>, in (*informal*), happening (*informal*), the latest (*informal*), modern, swinging (*slang*), progressive, stylish, trendy (*Brit. informal*), up-to-date, in vogue, up-to-the-minute, modish

withstand = <u>resist</u>, take, face, suffer, bear, weather, oppose, take on, cope with, brave, confront, combat, endure, defy, tolerate, put up with (*informal*), thwart, stand up to, hold off, grapple with, hold out against, stand firm against OPPOSITE> give in to

witless = <u>foolish</u>, crazy, stupid, silly, dull, daft (*informal*), senseless, goofy (*informal*), idiotic, dozy (*Brit. informal*), inane, loopy (*informal*), crackpot (*informal*), moronic, obtuse, unintelligent, empty-headed, asinine, imbecilic, braindead (*informal*), dumb-ass (*slang*), halfwitted, rattlebrained (*slang*)

witness NOUN 1 = <u>observer</u>, viewer, spectator, looker-on, watcher, onlooker, eyewitness, bystander, beholder …*No witnesses of the crash have come forward…*
2 = <u>testifier</u>, deponent, attestant …*Eleven witnesses were called to testify…*
VERB 1 = <u>see</u>, mark, view, watch, note, notice, attend, observe, perceive, look on, be present at, behold (*archaic or literary*) …*Anyone who witnessed the attack is urged to contact the police…*
2 = <u>countersign</u>, sign, endorse, validate …*Ask a friend to witness your signature on the application…*
PHRASES **bear witness** 1 = <u>confirm</u>, show, prove, demonstrate, bear out, testify to, be evidence of, corroborate, attest to, be proof of, vouch for, evince, betoken, be a monument to, constitute proof of …*Many of his poems bear witness to the years he spent in India…* 2 = <u>give evidence</u>, testify, depose, give testimony, depone …*His mother bore witness in court that he had been at home that night…*

(**Related Words**)
adjective: testimonial

witter = <u>chatter</u>, chat, rabbit (on) (*Brit. informal*), babble, waffle (*informal, chiefly Brit.*), cackle, twaddle, clack, burble, gab (*informal*), prattle, tattle, jabber, blab, gabble, blather, blether, prate

witty = <u>humorous</u>, gay, original, brilliant, funny, clever, amusing, lively, sparkling, ingenious, fanciful, whimsical, droll, piquant, facetious, jocular, epigrammatic, waggish OPPOSITE> dull

wizard 1 = <u>magician</u>, witch, shaman, sorcerer, occultist, magus, conjuror, warlock, mage (*archaic*), enchanter, necromancer, thaumaturge (*rare*) …*Merlin, the legendary wizard who worked magic for King Arthur…*
2 = <u>genius</u>, star, expert, master, ace (*informal*), guru, buff (*informal*), adept, whizz (*informal*), prodigy, maestro, virtuoso, hotshot (*informal*), rocket scientist (*informal, chiefly U.S.*), wiz (*informal*), whizz kid (*informal*), wonk (*informal*), maven (*U.S.*), fundi (*S. African*) …*a mathematical wizard at Harvard University…*

wizardry 1 = <u>expertise</u>, skill, know-how (*informal*),

craft, mastery, cleverness, expertness …*a piece of technical wizardry…*
2 = <u>magic</u>, witching, witchcraft, voodoo, enchantment, occultism, sorcery, the black art, witchery, necromancy, conjuration, sortilege …*Hogwarts School of Witchcraft and Wizardry…*

wizened = <u>wrinkled</u>, lined, worn, withered, dried up, shrivelled, gnarled, shrunken, sere (*archaic*) OPPOSITE> rounded

wobble VERB 1 = <u>shake</u>, rock, sway, tremble, quake, waver, teeter, totter, seesaw …*The ladder wobbled on the uneven ground…*
2 = <u>tremble</u>, shake, vibrate …*My voice wobbled with nerves…*
3 = <u>hesitate</u>, waver, fluctuate, dither (*chiefly Brit.*), be undecided, vacillate, shillyshally (*informal*), be unable to make up your mind, swither (*Scot.*) …*He dithered and wobbled when questioned on his policies…*
NOUN 1 = <u>unsteadiness</u>, shake, tremble, quaking …*He rode off on his bicycle with only a slight wobble…*
2 = <u>unsteadiness</u>, shake, tremor, vibration …*There was a distinct wobble in her voice when she replied…*

wobbly 1 = <u>unstable</u>, shaky, unsafe, uneven, teetering, unbalanced, tottering, rickety, unsteady, wonky (*Brit. slang*) …*I was sitting on a wobbly plastic chair…*
2 = <u>unsteady</u>, weak, unstable, shaky, quivery, all of a quiver (*informal*) …*His legs felt wobbly after the long flight…*
3 = <u>shaky</u>, unsteady, tremulous …*'I want to go home,' she said in a wobbly voice…*

woe 1 = <u>misery</u>, suffering, trouble, pain, disaster, depression, distress, grief, agony, gloom, sadness, hardship, sorrow, anguish, misfortune, unhappiness, heartache, heartbreak, adversity, dejection, wretchedness …*He listened to my tale of woe…*
OPPOSITE> happiness
2 = <u>problem</u>, trouble, trial, burden, grief, misery, curse, hardship, sorrow, misfortune, heartache, heartbreak, affliction, tribulation …*He did not tell his friends about all his woes…*

woeful 1 = <u>wretched</u>, sad, unhappy, tragic, miserable, gloomy, grieving, dismal, pathetic, afflicted, pitiful, anguished, agonized, disconsolate, doleful, pitiable …*those woeful people to whom life had dealt a bad hand…* OPPOSITE> happy
2 = <u>sad</u>, distressing, tragic, miserable, gloomy, dismal, pathetic, harrowing, heartbreaking, grievous, mournful, plaintive, heart-rending, sorrowful, doleful, piteous …*a woeful ballad about lost love…* OPPOSITE> happy
3 = <u>pitiful</u>, mean, bad, poor, shocking, sorry, disappointing, terrible, awful, appalling, disastrous, inadequate, dreadful, miserable, hopeless, rotten (*informal*), pathetic, catastrophic, duff (*Brit. informal*), feeble, disgraceful, lousy (*slang*), grievous, paltry, deplorable, abysmal, lamentable, calamitous, wretched, pitiable, godawful (*slang*), not much cop (*Brit. slang*) …*the team's recent woeful performance…*

wolf VERB *often with* **down** = <u>devour</u>, stuff, bolt, cram, scoff (*slang*), gulp, gobble, pack away (*informal*), gorge on, gollop …*I was in the changing-room wolfing down tea and sandwiches…* OPPOSITE nibble
NOUN (*Informal*) = <u>womanizer</u>, seducer, Don Juan, Casanova, philanderer, Lothario, lecher, lady-killer, lech *or* letch (*informal*) …*My grandfather is still an old wolf…*

(Related Words)

adjective : lupine
female : bitch
young : cub, whelp
collective nouns : pack, rout, herd

woman 1 = <u>lady</u>, girl, miss, female, bird (*slang*), dame (*slang*), ho (*U.S. derogatory slang*), sheila (*Austral. & N.Z. informal*), vrou (*S. African*), maiden (*archaic*), chick (*slang*), maid (*archaic*), gal (*slang*), lass, lassie (*informal*), wench (*facetious*), adult female, she, charlie (*Austral. slang*), chook (*Austral. slang*) …*No woman in her right mind would ever want to go out with you…* OPPOSITE man
2 (*Informal*) = <u>girlfriend</u>, girl, wife, partner, mate, lover, bride, mistress, spouse, old lady (*informal*), sweetheart, significant other (*U.S. informal*), ladylove …*I know my woman will never leave me, whatever I do…*
3 = <u>maid</u>, domestic, char (*informal*), housekeeper, lady-in-waiting, chambermaid, handmaiden, charwoman, maidservant, female servant …*Catriona had been nagging him to get a woman in to clean once a week…*

(Related Words)

combining forms : gyn(o)-, gynaeco-

womanly 1 = <u>feminine</u>, motherly, female, warm, tender, matronly, ladylike …*the accepted womanly qualities of compassion and unselfishness…*
2 = <u>curvaceous</u>, ample, voluptuous, shapely, curvy (*informal*), busty (*informal*), buxom, full-figured, Rubenesque, Junoesque …*a womanly figure…*

wonder VERB 1 = <u>think</u>, question, doubt, puzzle, speculate, query, ponder, inquire, ask yourself, meditate, be curious, conjecture, be inquisitive …*I wonder what he's up to… …We were wondering where you were…*
2 = <u>be amazed</u>, stare, marvel, be astonished, gape, boggle, be awed, be flabbergasted (*informal*), gawk, be dumbstruck, stand amazed …*I wondered at the arrogance of the man…*
NOUN 1 = <u>amazement</u>, surprise, curiosity, admiration, awe, fascination, astonishment, bewilderment, wonderment, stupefaction …*'How did you know that?' Bobby exclaimed in wonder…*
2 = <u>phenomenon</u>, sight, miracle, spectacle, curiosity, marvel, prodigy, rarity, portent, wonderment, nonpareil …*a fascinating lecture on the wonders of nature…*

Seven wonders of the ancient world
Colossus of Rhodes
Hanging Gardens of Babylon
mausoleum of Halicarnassus
Pharos of Alexandria
Phidias' statue of Zeus at Olympia
Pyramids of Egypt
temple of Artemis at Ephesus

wonderful 1 = <u>excellent</u>, mean (*slang*), great (*informal*), topping (*Brit. slang*), brilliant, cracking (*Brit. informal*), outstanding, smashing (*informal*), superb, fantastic (*informal*), tremendous, ace (*informal*), magnificent, fabulous (*informal*), marvellous, terrific, sensational (*informal*), sovereign, awesome (*slang*), admirable, super (*informal*), brill (*informal*), stupendous, out of this world (*informal*), tiptop, bodacious (*slang, chiefly U.S.*), boffo (*slang*), jim-dandy (*slang*), chillin' (*U.S. slang*), booshit (*Austral. slang*), exo (*Austral. slang*), sik (*Austral. slang*) …*I've always thought he was a wonderful actor…* OPPOSITE terrible
2 = <u>remarkable</u>, surprising, odd, strange, amazing, extraordinary, fantastic, incredible, astonishing, staggering, marvellous, startling, peculiar, awesome, phenomenal, astounding, miraculous, unheard-of, wondrous (*archaic or literary*), awe-inspiring, jaw-dropping …*This is a wonderful achievement for one so young…* OPPOSITE ordinary

wonky 1 = <u>askew</u>, squint (*informal*), awry, out of alignment, skewwhiff (*Brit. informal*) …*The wheels of the trolley kept going wonky…*
2 = <u>shaky</u>, weak, wobbly, unsteady, infirm …*He's got a wonky knee…*

wont ADJECTIVE = <u>accustomed</u>, used, given, in the habit of …*Both have made mistakes, as human beings are wont to do…*
NOUN = <u>habit</u>, use, way, rule, practice, custom …*Keith woke early, as was his wont…*

woo 1 = <u>seek</u>, cultivate, try to attract, curry favour with, seek to win, solicit the goodwill of …*The bank wooed customers by offering low interest rates…*
2 = <u>court</u>, chase, pursue, spark (*rare*), importune, seek to win, pay court to, seek the hand of, set your cap at (*old-fashioned*), pay your addresses to, pay suit to, press your suit with …*The penniless author successfully wooed and married Roxanne…*

wood NOUN 1 = <u>timber</u>, planks, planking, lumber (*U.S.*) …*The floor is made of polished wood…*
2 *Also* **woods** = <u>woodland</u>, trees, forest, grove, hurst (*archaic*), thicket, copse, coppice …*After dinner they went for a walk through the wood…*
3 = <u>firewood</u>, fuel, logs, kindling …*We gathered wood for the fire…*
PHRASES **out of the wood(s)** (*usually used in a negative construction*) = <u>safe</u>, clear, secure, in the clear, out of danger, home and dry (*Brit. slang*), safe and sound …*The nation's economy is not out of the woods yet…*

Related Words

adjectives : ligneous, sylvan

wooded = tree-covered, forested, timbered, woody, sylvan (*poetic*), tree-clad

wooden 1 = made of wood, timber, woody, of wood, ligneous …*the shop's bare brick walls and wooden floorboards*…

2 = awkward, stiff, rigid, clumsy, lifeless, stilted, ungainly, gauche, gawky, inelegant, graceless, maladroit …*The film is marred by the wooden acting of the star*… OPPOSITE graceful

3 = expressionless, empty, dull, blank, vacant, lifeless, deadpan, colourless, glassy, unresponsive, unemotional, emotionless, spiritless …*It's hard to tell from his wooden expression whether he's happy or sad*…

wool NOUN **1** = fleece, hair, coat …*These shawls are made from the wool of mountain goats*…

2 = yarn …*a ball of wool*…

PHRASES **dyed in the wool** = hardened, confirmed, settled, fixed, uncompromising, inflexible, diehard, inveterate, unshakeable, unchangeable …*He is a dyed-in-the-wool socialist*… ◆ **pull the wool over someone's eyes** = deceive, kid (*informal*), trick, fool, take in (*informal*), con (*slang*), dupe, delude, bamboozle (*informal*), hoodwink, put one over on (*slang*), pull a fast one on someone (*informal*), lead someone up the garden path (*informal*) …*a phony psychic who pulled the wool over everyone's eyes*…

woolly or (U.S. (*sometimes*)) **wooly** ADJECTIVE **1** = woollen, fleecy, made of wool …*She wore a woolly hat with pompoms*…

2 = vague, confused, clouded, blurred, unclear, muddled, fuzzy, indefinite, hazy, foggy, nebulous, ill-defined, indistinct …*It is no good setting vague, woolly goals – we need a specific aim*… OPPOSITE precise

3 = downy, hairy, shaggy, flocculent …*The plant has silvery, woolly leaves*…

NOUN = sweater, jersey, jumper, pullover …*Bring a woolly – it can get cold here at night*…

word NOUN **1** = term, name, expression, designation, appellation (*formal*), locution, vocable …*The word 'ginseng' comes from the Chinese word 'Shen-seng'*…

2 = chat, tête-à-tête, talk, discussion, consultation, chitchat, brief conversation, colloquy, confabulation, confab (*informal*), heart-to-heart, powwow (*informal*) …*James, could I have a quick word with you?*…

3 = comment, remark, expression, declaration, utterance, brief statement …*I'd like to say a word of thanks to everyone who helped me*…

4 = message, news, latest (*informal*), report, information, account, notice, advice, communication, intelligence, bulletin, dispatch, gen (*Brit. informal*), communiqué, intimation, tidings …*There is no word from the authorities on the reported attack*…

5 = promise, guarantee, pledge, undertaking, vow, assurance, oath, parole, word of honour, solemn oath, solemn word …*He simply cannot be trusted to keep his word*…

6 = command, will, order, go-ahead (*informal*), decree, bidding, mandate, commandment, edict, ukase (*rare*) …*I want nothing said about this until I give the word*…

PLURAL NOUN **1** = remark, comment, statement, observation, declaration, utterance, pronouncement …*I was devastated when her words came true*…

2 = text, script, lyrics …*Can you hear the words on the album?*…

VERB = express, say, state, put, phrase, utter, couch, formulate …*If I had written the letter, I might have worded it differently*…

PHRASES **in a word** = briefly, in short, in a nutshell, to sum up, succinctly, concisely, not to put too fine a point on it, to put it briefly …*'Don't you like her?' 'In a word – no.'*… ◆ **the last word 1** = final say, ultimatum …*Our manager has the last word on all major decisions*… **2** = summation, finis …*We'll let this gentleman have the last word*… ◆ **the last word in something** = epitome, newest, best, latest, crown, cream, rage, ultimate, vogue, perfection, mother of all (*informal*), quintessence, crème de la crème (*French*), ne plus ultra (*French*), dernier cri (*French*) …*The spa is the last word in luxury*…

Related Words

adjective : lexical, verbal

wording = phraseology, words, language, phrasing, terminology, choice of words, mode of expression

wordy = long-winded, rambling, windy, diffuse, garrulous, discursive, loquacious, verbose, prolix, pleonastic (*rare*) OPPOSITE brief

work VERB **1** = be employed, do business, have a job, earn a living, be in work, hold down a job …*I want to work, I don't want to be on welfare*…

2 = labour, sweat, slave, toil, slog (away), drudge, peg away, exert yourself, break your back …*My father worked hard all his life*… OPPOSITE relax

3 = function, go, run, operate, perform, be in working order …*The pump doesn't work and we have no running water*… OPPOSITE be out of order

4 = succeed, work out, pay off (*informal*), be successful, be effective, do the trick (*informal*), do the business (*informal*), get results, turn out well, have the desired result, go as planned …*Most of these diets don't work*…

5 = accomplish, cause, create, effect, achieve, carry out, implement, execute, bring about, encompass, contrive …*Modern medicine can work miracles*…

6 = handle, move, excite, manipulate, rouse, stir up, agitate, incite, whip up, galvanize …*a performer with the ability to work an audience*…

7 = cultivate, farm, dig, till, plough …*Farmers worked the fertile valleys*…

8 = operate, use, move, control, drive, manage, direct, handle, manipulate, wield, ply …*I learnt how to work the forklift*…

9 = manipulate, make, form, process, fashion, shape, handle, mould, knead …*Work the dough with your hands until it is very smooth*…

10 = progress, move, force, manoeuvre, make your

way …*Rescuers were still working their way towards the trapped men*…

11 = <u>move</u>, twitch, writhe, convulse, be agitated …*His face was working in his sleep*…

12 (*Informal*) = <u>contrive</u>, handle, fix (*informal*), swing (*informal*), arrange, exploit, manipulate, pull off, fiddle (*informal*), bring off …*Some clever people work it so that they never have to pay taxes*…

NOUN **1** = <u>employment</u>, calling, business, job, line, office, trade, duty, craft, profession, occupation, pursuit, livelihood, métier …*What kind of work do you do?*… OPPOSITE> play

2 = <u>effort</u>, industry, labour, grind (*informal*), sweat, toil, slog, exertion, drudgery, travail (*literary*), elbow grease (*facetious*) …*This needs time and a lot of hard work*… OPPOSITE> leisure

3 = <u>task</u>, jobs, projects, commissions, duties, assignments, chores, yakka (*Austral. & N.Z. informal*) …*I used to take work home, but I don't do it any more*…

4 = <u>handiwork</u>, doing, act, feat, deed …*Police say the bombing was the work of extremists*…

5 = <u>creation</u>, performance, piece, production, opus, achievement, composition, oeuvre (*French*), handiwork …*In my opinion, this is Rembrandt's greatest work*…

PLURAL NOUN **1** = <u>factory</u>, shop, plant, mill, workshop …*the belching chimneys of the steel-works at Corby*…

2 = <u>writings</u>, productions, output, canon, oeuvre (*French*) …*the complete works of Milton*…

3 = <u>deeds</u>, acts, actions, doings …*a religious order who dedicated their lives to prayer and good works*…

4 = <u>mechanism</u>, workings, parts, action, insides (*informal*), movement, guts (*informal*), machinery, moving parts, innards (*informal*) …*The box held what looked like the works of a large clock*…

PHRASES **out of work** = <u>unemployed</u>, on the street, jobless, idle, on the dole (*Brit. informal*), out of a job …*A third of the population is out of work*… ◆ **work out 1** = <u>happen</u>, go, result, develop, come out, turn out, evolve, pan out (*informal*) …*Things didn't work out as planned*… **2** = <u>succeed</u>, flourish, go well, be effective, prosper, go as planned, prove satisfactory …*I hope everything works out for you in your new job*… **3** = <u>exercise</u>, train, practise, drill, warm up, do exercises …*I work out at a gym twice a week*… ◆ **work out at something** = <u>amount to</u>, come to, reach, add up to, reach a total of …*The price per pound works out at £3.20*… ◆ **work someone up** = <u>excite</u>, move, spur, wind up (*informal*), arouse, animate, rouse, stir up, agitate, inflame, incite, instigate, get someone all steamed up (*slang*) …*By now she had worked herself up so much that she couldn't sleep*… ◆ **work something out 1** = <u>solve</u>, find out, resolve, calculate, figure out, clear up, suss (out) (*slang*), puzzle out …*It took me some time to work out what was going on*… **2** = <u>plan</u>, form, develop, arrange, construct, evolve, devise, elaborate, put together, formulate, contrive …*Negotiators are due to meet today to work out a compromise*…

◆ **work something up** = <u>generate</u>, rouse, instigate, foment, enkindle …*Malcolm worked up the courage to ask his grandfather for help*…

workable = <u>viable</u>, possible, practical, feasible, practicable, doable OPPOSITE> unworkable

workaday = <u>ordinary</u>, common, familiar, practical, routine, everyday, commonplace, mundane, prosaic, run-of-the-mill, humdrum, bog-standard (*Brit. & Irish slang*) OPPOSITE> extraordinary

worker = <u>employee</u>, hand, labourer, workman, craftsman, artisan, tradesman, wage earner, proletarian, working man *or* working woman

working ADJECTIVE **1** = <u>employed</u>, labouring, in work, in a job …*Like most working women, I use a lot of convenience foods*…

2 = <u>functioning</u>, going, running, operating, active, operative, operational, functional, usable, serviceable, in working order …*the oldest working steam engine in the world*…

3 = <u>effective</u>, useful, practical, sufficient, adequate …*I used to have a good working knowledge of French*… PLURAL NOUN **1** = <u>operation</u>, running, action, method, functioning, manner, mode of operation …*computer systems which mimic the workings of the human brain*…

2 = <u>mine</u>, pit, shaft, quarry, excavations, diggings …*housing which was built over old mine workings*…

workman = <u>labourer</u>, hand, worker, employee, mechanic, operative, craftsman, artisan, tradesman, journeyman, artificer (*rare*)

workmanlike = <u>efficient</u>, professional, skilled, expert, masterly, careful, satisfactory, thorough, skilful, adept, painstaking, proficient OPPOSITE> amateurish

workmanship = <u>skill</u>, work, art, technique, manufacture, craft, expertise, execution, artistry, craftsmanship, handiwork, handicraft

workout = <u>exercise</u>, training, drill, warm-up, training session, practice session, exercise session

workshop 1 = <u>seminar</u>, class, discussion group, study group, masterclass …*She runs a writing workshop for women*…

2 = <u>factory</u>, works, shop, plant, mill …*a small workshop for repairing secondhand motorcycles*…

3 = <u>workroom</u>, studio, atelier …*He got a job in the workshop of a local tailor*…

world NOUN **1** = <u>earth</u>, planet, globe, earthly sphere …*It's a beautiful part of the world*…

2 = <u>mankind</u>, man, men, everyone, the public, everybody, humanity, human race, humankind, the race of man …*The world was shocked by this heinous crime*…

3 = <u>sphere</u>, system, area, field, environment, province, kingdom, realm, domain …*The publishing world had never seen an event quite like this*…

4 = <u>life</u>, nature, existence, creation, universe, cosmos …*Be happy, in this world and the next!*…

5 = <u>planet</u>, star, orb, heavenly body …*conditions which would support life on other worlds*…

6 = <u>period</u>, times, days, age, era, epoch …*What was

life like for the ordinary man in the medieval world?...
7 = (usually used in phrase *a world of difference*) <u>huge amount</u>, mountain, wealth, great deal, good deal, abundance, enormous amount, vast amount ...*They may look alike but there's a world of difference between them...*

PHRASES **for all the world** = <u>exactly</u>, just like, precisely, in every way, to all intents and purposes, just as if, in every respect ...*He looked for all the world as if he was dead...* ◆ **on top of the world** (*Informal*) = <u>overjoyed</u>, happy, ecstatic, elated, over the moon (*informal*), exultant, on cloud nine (*informal*), cock-a-hoop, in raptures, beside yourself with joy ...*After his win, he was on top of the world...*
◆ **out of this world** (*Informal*) = <u>wonderful</u>, great (*informal*), excellent, superb, fantastic (*informal*), incredible, fabulous (*informal*), marvellous, unbelievable, awesome (*slang*), indescribable, bodacious (*slang, chiefly U.S.*), booshit (*Austral. slang*), exo (*Austral. slang*), sik (*Austral. slang*) ...*The food in this place is simply out of this world...*

worldly 1 = <u>earthly</u>, lay, physical, fleshly, secular, mundane, terrestrial, temporal, carnal, profane, sublunary ...*It is time you woke up and focused your thoughts on more worldly matters...* OPPOSITE spiritual
2 = <u>materialistic</u>, grasping, selfish, greedy, avaricious, covetous, worldly-minded ...*He has repeatedly criticized Western churches as being too worldly...* OPPOSITE nonmaterialistic
3 = <u>worldly-wise</u>, knowing, experienced, politic, sophisticated, cosmopolitan, urbane, blasé, well versed in the ways of the world ...*He was worldly and sophisticated, quite unlike me...* OPPOSITE naive

worldwide = <u>global</u>, general, international, universal, ubiquitous, omnipresent, pandemic OPPOSITE limited

worn 1 = <u>ragged</u>, shiny, frayed, shabby, tattered, tatty, threadbare, the worse for wear ...*an elderly man in well-cut but worn clothes...*
2 = <u>haggard</u>, lined, drawn, pinched, wizened, careworn ...*A sudden smile lit up his worn face...*
3 = <u>exhausted</u>, spent, tired, fatigued, wearied, weary, played-out (*informal*), worn-out, jaded, tired out ...*She looked tired and worn...*

worn out 1 = <u>worn</u>, done, used, broken-down, ragged, useless, run-down, frayed, used-up, shabby, tattered, tatty, threadbare, decrepit, clapped out (*Brit., Austral., & N.Z. informal*), moth-eaten ...*Always replace worn out tyres with the same brand...*
2 = <u>exhausted</u>, spent, done in (*informal*), tired, all in (*slang*), fatigued, wiped out (*informal*), weary, played-out, knackered (*slang*), prostrate, clapped out (*Austral. & N.Z. informal*), tired out, dog-tired (*informal*), zonked (*slang*), shagged out (*Brit. slang*), fit to drop, jiggered (*dialect*), dead *or* out on your feet (*informal*) ...*I was exhausted – worn out by the strain I'd been under...* OPPOSITE refreshed

worried = <u>anxious</u>, concerned, troubled, upset, afraid, bothered, frightened, wired (*slang*), nervous, disturbed, distressed, tense, distracted, uneasy, fearful, tormented, distraught, apprehensive, perturbed, on edge, ill at ease, overwrought, fretful, hot and bothered, unquiet, antsy (*informal*) OPPOSITE unworried

worrisome = <u>disturbing</u>, worrying, upsetting, distressing, troublesome, disquieting, vexing, perturbing, irksome, bothersome

worry VERB **1** = <u>be anxious</u>, be concerned, be worried, obsess, brood, fret, agonize, feel uneasy, get in a lather (*informal*), get in a sweat (*informal*), get in a tizzy (*informal*), get overwrought ...*I worry about my daughter constantly...* OPPOSITE be unconcerned
2 = <u>trouble</u>, upset, harry, bother, disturb, distress, annoy, plague, irritate, tease, unsettle, torment, harass, hassle (*informal*), badger, hector, disquiet, pester, vex, perturb, tantalize, importune, make anxious ...*'Why didn't you tell us?' 'I didn't want to worry you.'...* OPPOSITE soothe
NOUN **1** = <u>anxiety</u>, concern, care, fear, trouble, misery, disturbance, torment, woe, irritation, unease, apprehension, misgiving, annoyance, trepidation, perplexity, vexation ...*His last years were overshadowed by financial worry...* OPPOSITE peace of mind
2 = <u>problem</u>, care, trouble, trial, bother, plague, pest, torment, irritation, hassle (*informal*), annoyance, vexation ...*Robert's health had always been a worry to his wife...*

worsen 1 = <u>deteriorate</u>, decline, sink, decay, get worse, degenerate, go downhill (*informal*), go from bad to worse, take a turn for the worse, retrogress ...*The security forces had to intervene to prevent the situation from worsening...* OPPOSITE improve
2 = <u>aggravate</u>, damage, exacerbate, make worse ...*These options would actually worsen the economy and add to the deficit...* OPPOSITE improve

worship VERB **1** = <u>revere</u>, praise, respect, honour, adore, glorify, reverence, exalt, laud, pray to, venerate, deify, adulate ...*people who still worship the pagan gods...* OPPOSITE dishonour
2 = <u>love</u>, adore, idolize, put on a pedestal ...*The children worship their father...* OPPOSITE despise
NOUN = <u>reverence</u>, praise, love, regard, respect, honour, glory, prayer(s), devotion, homage, adulation, adoration, admiration, exaltation, glorification, deification, laudation ...*The temple had been a centre of worship of the goddess Hathor...*

worth 1 = <u>value</u>, price, rate, cost, estimate, valuation ...*The total worth of the Australian sharemarket is now close to $520 billion...* OPPOSITE worthlessness
2 = <u>merit</u>, value, quality, importance, desert(s), virtue, excellence, goodness, estimation, worthiness ...*She did not appreciate her husband's true worth until he was gone...* OPPOSITE unworthiness
3 = <u>usefulness</u>, value, benefit, quality, importance, utility, excellence, goodness ...*The client has little means of judging the worth of the advice he is given...* OPPOSITE uselessness

worthless 1 = <u>valueless</u>, poor, miserable, trivial, trifling, paltry, trashy, measly, wretched, two a penny (*informal*), rubbishy, poxy (*slang*), nickel-and-dime (*U.S. slang*), wanky (*taboo slang*), a dime a dozen, nugatory, negligible …*This piece of old junk is totally worthless…* OPPOSITE valuable

2 = useless, meaningless, pointless, futile, no use, insignificant, unimportant, ineffectual, unusable, unavailing, not much cop (*Brit. slang*), inutile, not worth a hill of beans (*chiefly U.S.*), negligible, pants (*slang*) …*Training is worthless unless there is proof that it works…* OPPOSITE useful

3 = good-for-nothing, base, abandoned, useless, vile, abject, despicable, depraved, contemptible, ignoble …*Murphy was an evil, worthless man…* OPPOSITE honourable

worthwhile = useful, good, valuable, helpful, worthy, profitable, productive, beneficial, meaningful, constructive, justifiable, expedient, gainful OPPOSITE useless

worthy ADJECTIVE = praiseworthy, good, excellent, deserving, valuable, decent, reliable, worthwhile, respectable, upright, admirable, honourable, honest, righteous, reputable, virtuous, dependable, commendable, creditable, laudable, meritorious, estimable …*worthy members of the community…* OPPOSITE disreputable
NOUN = dignitary, notable, luminary, bigwig (*informal*), big shot (*informal*), personage, big hitter (*informal*), heavy hitter (*informal*) …*The event brought together worthies from many fields…* OPPOSITE nobody

would-be = budding, potential, so-called, professed, dormant, self-styled, latent, wannabe (*informal*), unfulfilled, undeveloped, self-appointed, unrealized, manqué, soi-disant (*French*), quasi-

wound NOUN **1** = injury, cut, damage, hurt, harm, slash, trauma (*Pathology*), gash, lesion, laceration …*Six soldiers are reported to have died of their wounds…*
2 *often plural* = trauma, injury, shock, pain, offence, slight, torture, distress, insult, grief, torment, anguish, heartbreak, pang, sense of loss …*Her experiences have left deep psychological wounds…*
VERB **1** = injure, cut, hit, damage, wing, hurt, harm, slash, pierce, irritate, gash, lacerate …*The driver of the bus was wounded by shrapnel…*
2 = offend, shock, pain, hurt, distress, annoy, sting, grieve, mortify, cut to the quick, hurt the feelings of, traumatize …*He was deeply wounded by the treachery of his closest friends…*

wounding = hurtful, pointed, cutting, damaging, acid, bitter, slighting, offensive, distressing, insulting, cruel, savage, stinging, destructive, harmful, malicious, scathing, grievous, barbed, unkind, pernicious, caustic, spiteful, vitriolic, trenchant, injurious, maleficent

wrangle VERB = argue, fight, row, dispute, scrap, disagree, fall out (*informal*), contend, quarrel, brawl, squabble, spar, bicker, have words, altercate …*The*

two parties are still wrangling over the timing of the election…
NOUN = argument, row, clash, dispute, contest, set-to (*informal*), controversy, falling-out (*informal*), quarrel, brawl, barney (*informal*), squabble, bickering, tiff, altercation, slanging match (*Brit.*), angry exchange, argy-bargy (*Brit. informal*), bagarre (*French*) …*He was involved in a legal wrangle with the Health Secretary…*

wrap VERB **1** = cover, surround, fold, enclose, roll up, cloak, shroud, swathe, muffle, envelop, encase, sheathe, enfold, bundle up …*She wrapped the baby in a blanket…* OPPOSITE uncover
2 = pack, package, parcel (up), tie up, gift-wrap …*Harry had wrapped some presents for the children…* OPPOSITE unpack
3 = bind, wind, fold, swathe …*She wrapped a handkerchief round her bleeding hand…* OPPOSITE unwind
NOUN = cloak, cape, stole, mantle, shawl …*a model wearing a leopard-print wrap…*
PHRASES **wrap something up 1** = giftwrap, pack, package, enclose, bundle up, enwrap …*We spent the evening wrapping up Christmas presents…*
2 (*Informal*) = end, conclude, wind up, terminate, finish off, round off, tidy up, polish off, bring to a close …*NATO defence ministers wrap up their meeting in Brussels today…* ♦ **wrap up** = dress warmly, muffle up, wear something warm, put warm clothes on …*Make sure you wrap up warmly before you go out…*

wrapper = cover, case, paper, packaging, wrapping, jacket, envelope, sleeve, sheath

wrath = anger, passion, rage, temper, fury, resentment, irritation, indignation, ire, displeasure, exasperation, choler OPPOSITE satisfaction

wreak 1 = create, work, cause, visit, effect, exercise, carry out, execute, inflict, bring about …*Violent storms wreaked havoc on the coast…*
2 = unleash, express, indulge, vent, gratify, give vent to, give free rein to …*He wreaked vengeance on the men who had betrayed him…*

wreath = garland, band, ring, crown, loop, festoon, coronet, chaplet

wreathe 1 = surround, envelop, encircle, enfold, coil around, writhe around, enwrap …*Cigarette smoke wreathed her face…*
2 = festoon, wind, crown, wrap, twist, coil, adorn, intertwine, interweave, entwine, twine, engarland …*The temple's huge columns were wreathed in laurels…*

wreck VERB **1** = destroy, break, total (*slang*), smash, ruin, devastate, mar, shatter, spoil, demolish, sabotage, trash (*slang*), ravage, dash to pieces …*Vandals wrecked the garden…* OPPOSITE build
2 = spoil, blow (*slang*), ruin, devastate, shatter, undo, screw up (*informal*), cock up (*Brit. slang*), play havoc with, crool *or* cruel (*Austral. slang*) …*His life has been wrecked by the tragedy…* OPPOSITE save
3 = run aground, strand, shipwreck, run onto the rocks …*His ship was wrecked off the coast of Ireland…*

NOUN **1** = <u>shipwreck</u>, derelict, hulk, sunken vessel *…the wreck of a sailing ship…*

2 = <u>ruin</u>, mess, destruction, overthrow, undoing, disruption, devastation, desolation *…a broken man contemplating the wreck of his life…* OPPOSITE preservation

3 = <u>accident</u>, smash, pile-up *…He was killed in a car wreck…*

wreckage = <u>remains</u>, pieces, ruin, fragments, debris, rubble, hulk, wrack

wrench VERB **1** = <u>twist</u>, force, pull, tear, rip, tug, jerk, yank, wring, wrest *…They wrenched open the passenger door and got into the car…*

2 = <u>sprain</u>, strain, rick, distort *…He had wrenched his ankle badly in the fall…*

NOUN **1** = <u>twist</u>, pull, rip, tug, jerk, yank *…The rope stopped his fall with a wrench that broke his neck…*

2 = <u>sprain</u>, strain, twist *…We are hoping the injury is just a wrench…*

3 = <u>blow</u>, shock, pain, ache, upheaval, uprooting, pang *…I knew it would be a wrench to leave home…*

4 = <u>spanner</u>, adjustable spanner, shifting spanner *…He took a wrench from his toolbox…*

wrest 1 = <u>seize</u>, take, win, extract *…He has been trying to wrest control from the central government…*

2 = <u>pull</u>, force, strain, seize, twist, extract, wrench, wring *…She wrested the suitcase from the chauffeur's grasp…*

wrestle = <u>fight</u>, battle, struggle, combat, contend, strive, grapple, tussle, scuffle

wretch 1 = <u>poor thing</u>, unfortunate, poor soul, poor devil (*informal*), miserable creature *…Before the wretch had time to reply, he was shot…*

2 = <u>scoundrel</u>, rat (*informal*), worm, villain, rogue, outcast, swine, rascal, son-of-a-bitch (*slang, chiefly U.S. & Canad.*), profligate, vagabond, ruffian, cur, rotter (*slang, chiefly Brit.*), scumbag (*slang*), good-for-nothing, miscreant, bad egg (*old-fashioned informal*), blackguard *…I think he's a mean-minded, vindictive old wretch…*

wretched 1 = <u>unfortunate</u>, poor, sorry, hapless, pitiful, luckless, star-crossed, pitiable *…wretched people living in abject poverty…*

2 = <u>unhappy</u>, depressed, distressed, miserable, gloomy, hopeless, dismal, pathetic, worthless, melancholy, pitiful, forlorn, abject, woeful, dejected, downcast, disconsolate, funereal, crestfallen, doleful, down in the dumps (*informal*), pitiable, cheerless, woebegone, comfortless, brokenhearted *…The wretched look on the little girl's face melted his heart…* OPPOSITE happy

3 = <u>worthless</u>, poor, sorry, miserable, pathetic, inferior, paltry, deplorable *…What a wretched excuse!…* OPPOSITE excellent

4 = <u>shameful</u>, mean, low, base, shabby, vile, low-down (*informal*), paltry, despicable, contemptible, scurvy, crappy (*slang*), poxy (*slang*) *…Politicians – I hate the whole wretched lot of them…* OPPOSITE admirable

5 = <u>ill</u>, poorly, sick, crook (*Austral. & N.Z. informal*), sickly, unwell, off colour (*Brit. informal*), under the weather (*informal*) *…The flu was making him feel absolutely wretched…*

wriggle VERB **1** = <u>jiggle</u>, turn, twist, jerk, squirm, writhe *…The audience were fidgeting and wriggling in their seats…*

2 = <u>wiggle</u>, jerk, wag, jiggle, waggle *…She pulled off her shoes and stockings and wriggled her toes…*

3 = <u>crawl</u>, snake, worm, twist and turn, zigzag, slink *…Bauman wriggled along the passage on his stomach…*

NOUN = <u>twist</u>, turn, jerk, wag, squirm, wiggle, jiggle, waggle *…With a wriggle, he freed himself from her grasp and ran off…*

PHRASES **wriggle out of something** = <u>twist</u>, avoid, duck, dodge, extricate yourself from, talk your way out of, worm your way out of *…The government is trying to wriggle out of its responsibilities…*

wring = <u>twist</u>, force, squeeze, extract, screw, wrench, coerce, wrest, extort

wrinkle NOUN **1** = <u>line</u>, fold, crease, furrow, pucker, crow's-foot, corrugation *…His face was covered with wrinkles…*

2 = <u>crease</u>, gather, fold, crumple, furrow, rumple, pucker, crinkle, corrugation *…He noticed a wrinkle in the material…*

VERB = <u>crease</u>, line, gather, fold, crumple, ruck, furrow, rumple, pucker, crinkle, corrugate *…I wrinkled the velvet… …The skin around her eyes had begun to wrinkle…* OPPOSITE smooth

writ = <u>summons</u>, document, decree, indictment, court order, subpoena, arraignment

write VERB **1** = <u>record</u>, copy, scribble, take down, inscribe, set down, transcribe, jot down, put in writing, commit to paper, indite, put down in black and white *…Write your name and address at the top of the page…*

2 = <u>compose</u>, create, author, draft, pen, draw up *…She wrote articles for magazines in Paris…*

3 = <u>correspond</u>, get in touch, keep in touch, write a letter, drop a line, drop a note *…Why didn't you write and let me know you were coming?…*

PHRASES **write something** or **someone off** = <u>disregard</u>, ignore, dismiss, regard something or someone as finished, consider something or someone as unimportant *…He is fed up with people writing him off because of his age…* ◆ **write something off 1** (*Informal*) = <u>wreck</u>, total (*slang*), crash, destroy, trash (*slang*), smash up, damage beyond repair *…John's written off four cars. Now he sticks to public transport…* **2** = <u>cancel</u>, shelve, forget about, cross out, score out, give up for lost *…The President persuaded the West to write off Polish debts…*

writer = <u>author</u>, novelist, hack, columnist, scribbler, scribe, essayist, penman, wordsmith, man of letters, penpusher, littérateur, penny-a-liner (*rare*)

➤ **WORD POWER SUPPLEMENT writers**

writhe = <u>squirm</u>, struggle, twist, toss, distort, thrash, jerk, wriggle, wiggle, contort, convulse, thresh

writing 1 = <u>script</u>, hand, print, printing, fist (*informal*), scribble, handwriting, scrawl, calligraphy, longhand, penmanship, chirography *...It's a little difficult to read your writing...*
2 = <u>documents</u>, works, books, letters, titles, opuses, publications, literature, compositions, belles-lettres *...Althusser's writings are focused mainly on France...*

wrong ADJECTIVE **1** = <u>amiss</u>, faulty, unsatisfactory, not right, defective, awry *...Pain is the body's way of telling us that something is wrong...*
2 = <u>incorrect</u>, mistaken, false, faulty, inaccurate, untrue, erroneous, off target, unsound, in error, wide of the mark, fallacious, off base (*U.S. & Canad. informal*), off beam (*informal*), way off beam (*informal*) *...That was the wrong answer – try again...*
3 = <u>inappropriate</u>, incorrect, unfitting, unsuitable, unhappy, not done, unacceptable, undesirable, improper, unconventional, incongruous, unseemly, unbecoming, indecorous, inapt, infelicitous, malapropos *...I'm always embarrassing myself by saying the wrong thing...* OPPOSITE correct
4 = <u>bad</u>, criminal, illegal, evil, unfair, crooked, unlawful, illicit, immoral, unjust, dishonest, wicked, sinful, unethical, wrongful, under-the-table, reprehensible, dishonourable, iniquitous, not cricket (*informal*), felonious, blameworthy *...It was wrong of you to leave her alone in the house...* OPPOSITE moral
5 = <u>defective</u>, not working, faulty, out of order, awry, askew, out of commission *...We think there's something wrong with the computer...*
6 = <u>opposite</u>, inside, reverse, inverse *...Iron the t-shirt on the wrong side to prevent damage to the design...*
ADVERB **1** = <u>incorrectly</u>, badly, wrongly, mistakenly, erroneously, inaccurately *...You've spelled my name wrong...* OPPOSITE correctly
2 = <u>amiss</u>, astray, awry, askew *...Where did we go wrong with our children?...*
NOUN **1** = <u>wickedness</u>, injustice, unfairness, inequity, immorality, iniquity, sinfulness *...He doesn't seem to know the difference between right and wrong...* OPPOSITE morality
2 = <u>offence</u>, injury, crime, abuse, error, sin, injustice, grievance, infringement, trespass, misdeed, transgression, infraction, bad *or* evil deed *...I intend to right the wrong done to you...* OPPOSITE good deed
VERB = <u>mistreat</u>, abuse, hurt, injure, harm, cheat, take advantage of, discredit, oppress, malign, misrepresent, dump on (*slang, chiefly U.S.*), impose upon, dishonour, ill-treat, maltreat, ill-use *...She felt she had been wronged...* OPPOSITE treat well
PHRASES **go wrong 1** = <u>fail</u>, flop (*informal*), fall through, come to nothing, miscarry, misfire, come to grief (*informal*), go pear-shaped (*informal*) *...Nearly everything that could go wrong has gone wrong...* **2** = <u>make a mistake</u>, boob (*Brit. slang*), err, slip up (*informal*), go astray *...I think I've gone wrong somewhere in my calculations...* **3** = <u>break down</u>, fail, malfunction, misfire, cease to function, conk out (*informal*), go on the blink (*slang*), go kaput (*informal*), go phut (*informal*) *...If your video recorder goes wrong, you can have it repaired...* **4** = <u>lapse</u>, sin, err, fall from grace, go astray, go to the bad, go off the straight and narrow (*informal*) *...We condemn teenagers who go wrong and punish those who step out of line...* ◆ **in the wrong** = <u>guilty</u>, mistaken, at fault, off course, off target, in error, to be blamed, off beam (*informal*), blameworthy *...He didn't argue because he knew he was in the wrong...*

wrongful = <u>improper</u>, illegal, unfair, inappropriate, unlawful, illicit, immoral, unjust, illegitimate, unethical, groundless OPPOSITE rightful

wry 1 = <u>ironic</u>, dry, mocking, sarcastic, sardonic, droll, pawky (*Scot.*), mordacious *...a wry sense of humour...*
2 = <u>contorted</u>, twisted, crooked, distorted, warped, uneven, deformed, awry, askew, aslant, skewwhiff (*Brit. informal*) *...She cast a wry grin in his direction...* OPPOSITE straight

Xmas = <u>Christmas</u>, Noel, festive season, Yule (*archaic*), Yuletide (*archaic*), Christmastime, Christmastide, Crimbo (*Brit. informal*)

X-ray = <u>radiograph</u>, x-ray image

Y y

ya (*S. African*) = <u>yes</u>, yeah (*informal*), sure, okay, aye (*Scot. informal*), affirmative (*formal*), uh-huh (*slang*), yebo (*S. African informal*)

yahoo = <u>philistine</u>, savage, lout, beast, barbarian, brute, rowdy, hoon (*Austral. & N.Z.*), roughneck (*slang*), boor, churl, yob *or* yobbo (*Brit. slang*), cougan (*Austral. slang*), scozza (*Austral. slang*), bogan (*Austral. slang*)

yak = <u>gossip</u>, go on, gab (*informal*), rabbit (on) (*Brit. Informal*), run on, jaw (*slang*), chatter, spout, waffle (*informal, chiefly Brit.*), yap (*informal*), tattle, jabber, blather, chew the fat (*slang*), witter on (*informal*), run off at the mouth

yank VERB = <u>pull</u>, tug, jerk, seize, snatch, pluck, hitch, wrench ...*She yanked the child back into the house...* NOUN = <u>pull</u>, tug, jerk, snatch, hitch, wrench, tweak ...*Grabbing his ponytail, Shirley gave it a yank...*

yap 1 = <u>yelp</u>, bark, woof, yip (*chiefly U.S.*) ...*The little dog yapped frantically...* 2 (*Informal*) = <u>talk</u>, go on, rabbit (on) (*Brit. informal*), gossip, jaw (*slang*), chatter, spout, babble, waffle (*informal, chiefly Brit.*), prattle, jabber, blather, run off at the mouth (*slang*) ...*She keeps yapping at me about Joe...*

yardstick = <u>standard</u>, measure, criterion, gauge, benchmark, touchstone, par

yarn 1 = <u>thread</u>, fibre, cotton, wool ...*vegetable-dyed yarn...* 2 (*Informal*) = <u>story</u>, tale, anecdote, account, narrative, fable, reminiscence, urban myth, tall story, urban legend, cock-and-bull story (*informal*) ...*Doug has a yarn or two to tell me about his trips into the bush...*

yawning = <u>gaping</u>, wide, huge, vast, wide-open, cavernous

year

Word Power

year – In writing spans of years, it is important to avoid ambiguity. A common style with four-figure dates is to write the first date in full and the last two digits of the second date: *1860–73* , except where the two dates fall in different centuries, in which case both dates are given in full: *1850–1916*. In three- and two-figure dates, the first and last dates of the span are both written in full to avoid ambiguity: *636–612* B.C. It is advisable to specify B.C. or A.D. in years under 1000, unless this is self-evident from the context.

yearly ADJECTIVE = <u>annual</u>, each year, every year, once a year ...*a yearly meeting...* ADVERB = <u>annually</u>, every year, by the year, once a year, per annum ...*interest is paid yearly...*

yearn *often with* **for** = <u>long</u>, desire, pine, pant, hunger, ache, lust, crave, covet, itch, languish, hanker after, have a yen for (*informal*), eat your heart out over, set your heart upon, suspire (*archaic or poetic*), would give your eyeteeth for

yell VERB = <u>scream</u>, shout, cry out, howl, call out, wail, shriek, screech, squeal, bawl, holler (*informal*), yelp, call at the top of your voice ...*He was out there shouting and yelling...* OPPOSITE whisper
NOUN = <u>scream</u>, cry, shout, roar, howl, shriek, whoop, screech, squeal, holler (*informal*), yelp, yowl ...*He let out a yell...* OPPOSITE whisper

yellow

Shades of yellow

almond	gold *or* golden
amber	jasmine
beige	lemon
bisque	magnolia
bistre	maize
buff	mustard
butternut	nankeen
canary yellow	oatmeal
champagne	ochre
cinnamon	old gold
citron	primrose
daffodil	saffron
eau de nil	straw
ecru	tea rose
eggshell	topaz
gamboge	tortoiseshell

yelp VERB = <u>bark</u>, howl, yap, yip (*chiefly U.S.*), yowl ...*Her dog yelped and came to heel...* NOUN = <u>cry</u>, squeal ...*She gave a yelp of pain...*

yen = <u>longing</u>, desire, craving, yearning, passion, hunger, ache, itch, thirst, hankering

yet ADVERB 1 = <u>so far</u>, until now, up to now, still, as yet, even now, thus far, up till now, up to the present time ...*They haven't finished yet...* 2 = <u>now</u>, right now, just now, so soon, already ...*Don't get up yet...* 3 = <u>still</u>, further, in addition, as well, moreover, besides, to boot, additionally, over and above, into the bargain ...*This weekend yet more uniformed soldiers were posted at official buildings...* CONJUNCTION = <u>nevertheless</u>, still, however, for all that, notwithstanding, just the same, be that as it may ...*I don't eat much, yet I am a size 16...*

yield VERB 1 = <u>bow</u>, submit, give in, surrender, give way, succumb, cave in (*informal*), capitulate, knuckle under, resign yourself ...*She yielded to general pressure...* 2 = <u>relinquish</u>, resign, hand over, surrender, turn over,

part with, make over, cede, give over, bequeath, abdicate, deliver up …*He may yield control*…
OPPOSITE retain

3 = surrender, give up, give in, concede defeat, cave in (*informal*), throw in the towel, admit defeat, accept defeat, give up the struggle, knuckle under, raise the white flag, lay down your arms, cry quits …*Their leader refused to yield*… OPPOSITE resist

4 = produce, give, provide, pay, return, supply, bear, net, earn, afford, generate, bring in, furnish, bring forth …*400,000 acres of land yielded a crop worth $1.75 billion*… OPPOSITE use up

NOUN **1** = produce, crop, harvest, output …*improving the yield of the crop*…

2 = profit, return, income, revenue, earnings, takings …*the yield on a bank's investment*… OPPOSITE loss

PHRASES **yield to something** = comply with, agree to, concede, allow, grant, permit, go along with, bow to, consent to, accede to …*Television officials had yielded to demands*…

yielding 1 = soft, pliable, springy, elastic, resilient, supple, spongy, unresisting, quaggy …*the soft yielding cushions*…

2 = submissive, obedient, compliant, docile, easy, flexible, accommodating, pliant, tractable, acquiescent, biddable …*women's yielding nature*… OPPOSITE obstinate

yob or **yobbo** = thug, hooligan, lout, heavy (*slang*), tough, rough (*informal*), rowdy, yahoo, hoon (*Austral. & N.Z. slang*), hoodlum, ruffian, roughneck (*slang*), tsotsi (*S. African*), cougan (*Austral. slang*), scozza (*Austral. slang*), bogan (*Austral. slang*)

yoke NOUN **1** = oppression, slavery, bondage, servitude, service, burden, enslavement, serfdom, servility, vassalage, thraldom …*People are suffering under the yoke of capitalism*…

2 = harness, coupling, tackle, chain, collar, tack …*He

put a yoke around his body and pulled along the cart*…
VERB **1** = unite, join, link, tie, bond, bind, connect …*They are yoked by money and votes*…

2 = harness, join, couple, link, tie, connect, bracket, hitch …*a plough team of eight oxen yoked in pairs*…

young ADJECTIVE **1** = immature, juvenile, youthful, little, growing, green, junior, infant, adolescent, callow, unfledged, in the springtime of life …*I was still too young to understand what was going on*… OPPOSITE old

2 = early, new, undeveloped, fledgling, newish, not far advanced …*the larvae, the young stages of the worm*… OPPOSITE advanced

PLURAL NOUN = offspring, babies, litter, family, issue, brood, little ones, progeny …*The hen may not be able to feed its young*… OPPOSITE parents

youngster = youth, girl, boy, kid (*informal*), lad, teenager, juvenile, cub, young person, lass, young adult, pup (*informal, chiefly Brit.*), urchin, teenybopper (*slang*), young shaver (*informal*), young 'un (*informal*)

youth 1 = immaturity, adolescence, early life, young days, boyhood or girlhood, salad days, juvenescence …*the comic books of my youth*… OPPOSITE old age

2 = boy, lad, youngster, kid (*informal*), teenager, young man, adolescent, teen (*informal*), stripling, young shaver (*informal*) …*gangs of youths who broke windows and looted shops*… OPPOSITE adult

3 = young people, the young, the younger generation, teenagers, the rising generation …*He represents the opinions of the youth of today*… OPPOSITE old people

youthful 1 = young, juvenile, childish, immature, boyish, pubescent, girlish, puerile …*youthful enthusiasm and high spirits*… OPPOSITE elderly

2 = vigorous, fresh, active, young looking, young at heart, spry …*I'm a very youthful 50*… OPPOSITE tired

Z z

zany = comical, crazy, nutty (*slang*), funny, eccentric, wacky (*slang*), loony (*slang*), oddball (*informal*), madcap, goofy (*informal*), kooky (*U.S. informal*), clownish, wacko or whacko (*informal*), off the air (*Austral. slang*)

zeal = enthusiasm, passion, zest, fire, spirit, warmth, devotion, verve, fervour, eagerness, gusto, militancy, fanaticism, ardour, earnestness, keenness, fervency [OPPOSITE] apathy

zealot = fanatic, enthusiast, extremist, militant, maniac, fiend (*informal*), bigot

zealous = enthusiastic, passionate, earnest, burning, spirited, keen, devoted, eager, militant, ardent, fanatical, fervent, impassioned, rabid, fervid [OPPOSITE] apathetic

zenith = height, summit, peak, top, climax, crest, high point, pinnacle, meridian, apex, high noon, apogee, acme, vertex [OPPOSITE] lowest point

zero [NOUN] 1 = nought, nothing, nil, naught, cipher ...*a scale ranging from zero to seven...*
2 = rock bottom, the bottom, an all-time low, a nadir, as low as you can get, the lowest point or ebb ...*My spirits were at zero...*
[PHRASES] **zero in on something** 1 = zoom in on, focus on, aim at, train on, home in on ...*He raised the binoculars again and zeroed in on an eleventh-floor room...* 2 = focus on, concentrate on, home in on, pinpoint, converge on ...*Critics have zeroed in on his weakness...*

zest 1 = enjoyment, love, appetite, relish, interest, joy, excitement, zeal, gusto, keenness, zing (*informal*), delectation ...*He has a zest for life and a quick intellect...* [OPPOSITE] aversion
2 = flavour, taste, savour, kick (*informal*), spice, relish, smack, tang, piquancy, pungency ...*Lemon oil adds zest to your cuppa...*
3 = rind, skin, peel, outer layer ...*the zest and juice of the lemon...*

zip [VERB] = speed, shoot, fly, tear, rush, flash, dash, hurry, barrel (along) (*informal, chiefly U.S. & Canad.*), buzz, streak, hare (*Brit. informal*), zoom, whizz (*informal*), hurtle, pelt, burn rubber (*informal*) ...*My craft zipped along the bay...*

[NOUN] (*Informal*) = energy, go (*informal*), life, drive, spirit, punch (*informal*), pep, sparkle, vitality, vigour, verve, zest, gusto, get-up-and-go (*informal*), oomph (*informal*), brio, zing (*informal*), liveliness, vim (*slang*), pizzazz or pizazz (*informal*) ...*He gave the choreography his usual class and zip...* [OPPOSITE] lethargy

zodiac

Signs of the zodiac
http://www.geocities.com/astrologyzodiacs/

♒	Aquarius (the Water Carrier)
♈	Aries (the Ram)
♋	Cancer (the Crab)
♑	Capricorn (the Goat)
♊	Gemini (the Twins)
♌	Leo (the Lion)
♎	Libra (the Scales)
♓	Pisces (the Fishes)
♐	Sagittarius (the Archer)
♏	Scorpio (the Scorpion)
♉	Taurus (the Bull)
♍	Virgo (the Virgin)

Chinese animal years
http://www.c-c-c.org/chineseculture/zodiac/zodiac.html

Chinese	English	Years
Shu	Rat	1960 1972 1984 1996 2008
Niu	Ox	1961 1973 1985 1997 2009
Hu	Tiger	1962 1974 1986 1998 2010
Tu	Hare	1963 1975 1987 1999 2011
Long	Dragon	1964 1976 1988 2000 2012
She	Serpent	1965 1977 1989 2001 2013
Ma	Horse	1966 1978 1990 2002 2014
Yang	Sheep	1967 1979 1991 2003 2015
Hou	Monkey	1968 1980 1992 2004 2016
Ji	Cock	1969 1981 1993 2005 2017
Gou	Dog	1970 1982 1994 2006 2018
Zhu	Boar	1971 1983 1995 2007 2019

zone = area, region, section, sector, district, territory, belt, sphere, tract

zoom = speed, shoot, fly, tear, rush, flash, dash, barrel (along) (*informal, chiefly U.S. & Canad.*), buzz, streak, hare (*Brit. informal*), zip (*informal*), whizz (*informal*), hurtle, pelt, burn rubber (*informal*)

WORD
POWER
Supplement

CONTENTS

WORD POWER

CONTENTS

WORD POWER

WORD POWER

Male

Woody Allen (*U.S.*)
Fred Astaire (*U.S.*)
Richard Attenborough
(*English*)
Jean-Louis Barrault (*French*)
John Barrymore (*U.S.*)
Alan Bates (*English*)
Warren Beatty (*U.S.*)
Jean-Paul Belmondo
(*French*)
Alan Bennett (*English*)
Dirk Bogarde (*English*)
Humphrey Bogart (*U.S.*)
Charles Boyer (*French*)
Kenneth Branagh (*English*)
Marlon Brando (*U.S.*)
Adrien Brody (*U.S.*)
Mel Brooks (*U.S.*)
Richard Burbage (*English*)
Richard Burton (*Welsh*)
Glen Byam Shaw (*English*)
James Cagney (*U.S.*)
Michael Caine (*English*)
Simon Callow (*English*)
Robert Carlyle (*Scottish*)
Jim Carrey (*U.S.*)
Charlie Chaplin (*English*)
Maurice Chevalier (*French*)
John Cleese (*English*)
George Clooney (*U.S.*)
Sean Connery (*Scottish*)
Peter Cook (*English*)
Chris Cooper (*U.S.*)
Gary Cooper (*U.S.*)
Kevin Costner (*U.S.*)
Noel Coward (*English*)
Michael Crawford (*English*)
Tom Cruise (*U.S.*)
James Dean (*U.S.*)
Robert De Niro (*U.S.*)
Gerard Depardieu (*French*)
Vittorio de Sica (*Italian*)
John Dexter (*English*)
Leonardo DiCaprio (*U.S.*)
Kirk Douglas (*U.S.*)
Michael Douglas (*U.S.*)
Clint Eastwood (*U.S.*)
Douglas Fairbanks Jr. (*U.S.*)
Douglas Fairbanks Snr.
(*U.S.*)
WC Fields (*U.S.*)
Albert Finney (*English*)

Errol Flynn (*Australian*)
Henry Fonda (*U.S.*)
Harrison Ford (*U.S.*)
Jean Gabin (*France*)
Clark Gable (*U.S.*)
David Garrick (*English*)
Mel Gibson (*Australian*)
John Gielgud (*English*)
Cary Grant (*English-U.S.*)
Alec Guinness (*English*)
Gene Hackman (*U.S.*)
Tom Hanks (*U.S.*)
Oliver Hardy (*U.S.*)
Rex Harrison (*English*)
Dustin Hoffman (*U.S.*)
Bob Hope (*U.S.*)
Anthony Hopkins (*Welsh*)
Michael Hordern (*English*)
Leslie Howard (*English*)
Trevor Howard (*English*)
Rock Hudson (*U.S.*)
Barry Humphries
(*Australian*)
John Hurt (*English*)
Jeremy Irons (*English*)
Henry Irving (*English*)
Derek Jacobi (*English*)
Al Jolson (*U.S.*)
Boris Karloff (*English*)
Edmund Kean (*English*)
Buster Keaton (*U.S.*)
Harvey Keitel (*U.S.*)
Gene Kelly (*U.S.*)
John Kemble (*English*)
Ben Kingsley (*English*)
Burt Lancaster (*U.S.*)
Charles Laughton (*English-
U.S.*)
Stan Laurel (*English-U.S.*)
Bruce Lee (*U.S.*)
Christopher Lee (*English*)
Harold Lloyd (*U.S.*)
Bela Lugosi (*Hungarian*)
Ewan McGregor (*Scottish*)
Ian McKellen (*English*)
Steve McQueen (*U.S.*)
William Macready (*English*)
James Mason (*English*)
Raymond Massey
(*Canadian*)
Marcello Mastroianni
(*Italian*)

Bernard Miles (*English*)
John Mills (*English*)
Robert Mitchum (*U.S.*)
Dudley Moore (*English*)
Robert Morley (*English*)
Sam Neill (*N.Z.*)
Paul Newman (*U.S.*)
Jack Nicholson (*U.S.*)
Liam Neeson (*Irish*)
David Niven (*English*)
Gary Oldman (*English*)
Laurence Olivier (*English*)
Peter O'Toole (*Irish-British*)
Al Pacino (*U.S.*)
Gregory Peck (*U.S.*)
Donald Pleasence (*English*)
Anthony Quayle (*English*)
Anthony Quinn (*U.S.*)
Daniel Radcliffe (*English*)
Ronald Reagan (*U.S.*)
Robert Redford (*U.S.*)
Michael Redgrave (*English*)
Fernando Rey (*Spanish*)
Ralph Richardson (*English*)
Paul Robeson (*U.S.*)
Edward G Robinson (*U.S.*)
Tim Roth (*English*)
Arnold Schwarzenegger
(*Austrian-U.S.*)
Paul Scofield (*English*)
Peter Sellers (*English*)
Sam Shepard (*U.S.*)
Sylvester Stallone (*U.S.*)
Konstantin Stanislavsky
(*Russian*)
James Stewart (*U.S.*)
Donald Sutherland
(*Canadian*)
Jacques Tati (*French*)
Spencer Tracy (*U.S.*)
John Travolta (*U.S.*)
Peter Ustinov (*English*)
Rudolph Valentino (*Italian-
U.S.*)
Max Von Sydow (*Swedish*)
John Wayne (*U.S.*)
Johnny Weissmuller (*U.S.*)
Orson Welles (*U.S.*)
Elijah Wood (*U.S.*)

ACTORS

Female

Yvonne Arnaud (*French*)
Peggy Ashcroft (*English*)
Tallulah Bankhead (*U.S.*)
Brigitte Bardot (*French*)
Ingrid Bergman (*Swedish-U.S.*)
Sarah Bernhardt (*French*)
Clara Bow (*U.S.*)
Fanny Brice (*U.S.*)
Glenn Close (*U.S.*)
Claudette Colbert (*French-U.S.*)
Joan Crawford (*U.S.*)
Bette Davis (*U.S.*)
Geena Davis (*U.S.*)
Judy Davis (*Australian*)
Judi Dench (*English*)
Catherine Deneuve (*French*)
Marlene Dietrich (*German*)
Faye Dunaway (*U.S.*)
Edith Evans (*English*)
Jane Fonda (*U.S.*)
Jodie Foster (*U.S.*)
Greta Garbo (*Swedish*)
Ava Gardner (*U.S.*)
Judy Garland (*U.S.*)
Lillian Gish (*U.S.*)
Joyce Grenfell (*English*)
Jean Harlow (*U.S.*)
Audrey Hepburn (*Belgian-U.S.*)

Katharine Hepburn (*U.S.*)
Wendy Hiller (*English*)
Holly Hunter (*U.S.*)
Isabelle Huppert (*French*)
Glenda Jackson (*English*)
Diane Keaton (*U.S.*)
Grace Kelly (*U.S.*)
Fanny Kemble (*English-U.S.*)
Nicole Kidman (*Australian*)
Jessica Lange (*U.S.*)
Gertrude Lawrence (*English*)
Vivien Leigh (*English*)
Lotte Lenya (*Austrian*)
Margaret Lockwood (*English*)
Jennifer Lopez (*Puerto Rican*)
Sophia Loren (*Italian*)
Siobhan McKenna (*Irish*)
Shirley MacLaine (*U.S.*)
Melina Mercouri (*Greek*)
Liza Minnelli (*U.S.*)
Helen Mirren (*English*)
Marilyn Monroe (*U.S.*)
Jeanne Moreau (*French*)
Michelle Pfeiffer (*U.S.*)
Mary Pickford (*U.S.*)
Joan Plowright (*English*)
Jian Qing (*Chinese*)
Vanessa Redgrave (*English*)
Julia Roberts (*U.S.*)

Flora Robson (*English*)
Ginger Rogers (*U.S.*)
Margaret Rutherford (*English*)
Susan Sarandon (*U.S.*)
Delphine Seyrig (*French*)
Sarah Siddons (*English*)
Simone Signoret (*French*)
Maggie Smith (*English*)
Meryl Streep (*U.S.*)
Barbra Streisand (*U.S.*)
Janet Suzman (*South African*)
Elizabeth Taylor (*English-U.S.*)
Shirley Temple (*U.S.*)
Ellen Terry (*English*)
Emma Thompson (*English*)
Sybil Thorndike (*English*)
Sigourney Weaver (*U.S.*)
Raquel Welch (*U.S.*)
Mae West (*U.S.*)
Billie Whitelaw (*English*)
Kate Winslet (*English*)
Peg Woffington (*Irish*)
Catherine Zeta-Jones (*Welsh*)

WORD POWER

French regions

Alsace	Corsica	Nord-Pas-de-Calais
Aquitaine	Franche-Comté	Pays de Loire
Auvergne	Haute-Normandie	Picardie
Basse-Normandie	Île-de-France	Poitou-Charentes
Brittany	Languedoc-Roussillon	Provence-Alpes-Côte
Burgundy	Limousin	d'Azur
Centre	Lorraine	Rhône-Alpes
Champagne-Ardenne	Midi-Pyrénées	

French départements

Ain	Gers	Morbihan
Aisne	Gironde	Moselle
Allier	Guadeloupe	Niveres
Alpes de Haute Provence	Haut Rhin	Nord
Alpes Maritimes	Haute Garonne	Oise
Ardèche	Haute Loire	Orne
Ardennes	Haute Marne	Paris
Ariège	Haute Savoie	Pas de Calais
Aube	Haute Vienne	Puy de Dôme
Aude	Hautes Alpes	Pyrénées Atlantiques
Aveyron	Hautes Pyrénées	Pyrénées Orientales
Bas Rhin	Hauts de Seine	Réunion
Bouches du Rhône	Hérault	Rhône
Calvados	Ille et Vilaine	Saône
Cantal	Indre	Saône et Loire
Charente	Indre et Loire	Sarthe
Charente Maritime	Isère	Savoie
Cher	Jura	Seine et Marne
Corrèze	Landes	Seine Maritime
Corse	Loir et Cher	Seine Saint Denis
Cote d'Or	Loire	Somme
Côtes du Nord	Loire Atlantique	Tarn
Creuse	Loiret	Tarn et Garonne
Deux Sèvres	Lot	Territoire de Belfort
Dordogne	Lot et Garonne	Val d'Oise
Doubs	Lozère	Val de Marne
Drôme	Maine et Loire	Var
Essone	Manche	Vaucluse
Eure	Marne	Vendée
Eure et Loir	Martinique	Vienne
Finistère	Mayenne	Vosges
Gard	Meurthe et Moselle	Yonne
Gayane	Meuse	Yvelines

German states

Baden-Württemberg	Hessen	Saarland
Bavaria	Lower Saxony	Saxony
Berlin	Mecklenburg-West	Saxony-Anhalt
Brandenburg	Pomerania	Schleswig-Holstein
Bremen	North Rhine-Westphalia	Thuringia
Hamburg	Rhineland-Palatinate	

Italian regions

Abruzzo	Friuli-Venezia Giulia	Molise	Trentino-Alto Adige
Basilicata	Lazio	Piedmont	Tuscany
Calabria	Liguria	Puglia	Umbria
Campania	Lombardy	Sardinia	Valle d'Aosta
Emilia-Romagna	Marche	Sicily	Veneto

Italian provinces

Agrigento	Catanzaro	Lecce	Pesaro	Siracusa
Alessandria	Chieti	Lecco	Pescara	Sondrio
Ancona	Como	Livorno	Piacenza	Taranto
Aosta	Cosenza	Lodi	Pisa	Teramo
Arezzo	Cremona	Lucca	Pistoia	Terni
Ascoli Piceno	Crotone	Macerata	Pordenone	Torino
Asti	Cuneo	Mantova	Potenza	Trapani
Avellino	Enna	Massa Carrara	Prato	Trento
Bari	Ferrara	Matera	Ragusa	Treviso
Belluno	Firenze	Messina	Ravenna	Trieste
Benevento	Foggia	Milano	Reggio di	Udine
Bergamo	Forlì	Modena	Calabria	Varese
Bologna	Frosinone	Napoli	Reggio Emilia	Venezia
Bolzano	Genova	Novara	Rieti	Verbania
Brescia	Gorizia	Nuoro	Rimini	Vercelli
Brindisi	Grosseto	Oristano	Roma	Verona
Cagliari	Imperia	Padova	Rovigo	Vibo Valentia
Caltanissetta	Isernia	Palermo	Salerno	Vicenza
Campobasso	L'Aquila	Parma	Sassari	Viterbo
Caserta	La Spezia	Pavia	Savona	Repubblica di
Catania	Latina	Perugia	Siena	San Marino

Spanish regions

Andalucía	Castilla-La Mancha	Murcia
Aragón	Castilla-León	Navarra
Asturias	Catalonia	Valencian Community
Balearic Islands	Extremadura	Ceuta
Basque Country	Galicia	Melilla
Canary Islands	La Rioja	
Cantabria	Madrid	

Spanish provinces

Álava	Cádiz	Huelva	Murcia	Teruel
Albacete	Cantabria	Huesca	Navarra	Toledo
Alhucemas	Castellón	Jaén	Orense	Valencia
Alicante	Chafarinas	La Coruna	Palencia	Valladolid
Almerìa	Cordoba	La Rioja	Pontevedra	Vélez de la
Asturias	Cuenca	Las Palmas	Salamanca	Gomera
Ávila	Ceuta	León	Santa Cruz de	Vizcaya
Badajoz	Ciudad Real	Lleida	Tenerife	Zamora
Balearics	Girona	Lugo	Segovia	Zaragoza
Barcelona	Granada	Madrid	Sevilla	
Burgos	Gualalajara	Málaga	Soria	
Cácares	Guipúzcoa	Melilla	Tarragona	

WORD POWER

Agostino di Duccio (*Italian*)
Josef Albers (*German-U.S.*)
Leon Battista Alberti
  (*Italian*)
Washington Allston (*U.S.*)
Lawrence Alma-Tadema
  (*Dutch-English*)
Albrecht Altdorfer (*German*)
Fra Angelico (*Italian*)
Pietro Annigoni (*Italian*)
Antonello da Messina
  (*Italian*)
Apelles (*Greek*)
Karel Appel (*Dutch*)
Aleksandr Porfiryevich
  Archipenko (*Russian*)
Giuseppe Arcimboldo
  (*Italian*)
Jean *or* Hans Arp (*French*)
John James Audubon (*U.S.*)
Frank Auerbach (*English-
  German*)
Francis Bacon (*Irish*)
Leon Nikolayevich Bakst
  (*Russian*)
Balthus (*Polish-French*)
Frédéric August Bartholdi
  (*French*)
Fra Bartolommeo (*Italian*)
Max Beckmann (*German*)
Vanessa Bell (*English*)
Giovanni Bellini (*Italian*)
Thomas Hart Benton
  (*U.S.*)
Gian Lorenzo Bernini
  (*Italian*)
Joseph Beuys (*German*)
Peter Blake (*English*)
William Blake (*English*)
Umberto Boccioni (*Italian*)
David Bomberg (*English*)
Rosa Bonheur (*French*)
Pierre Bonnard (*French*)
Richard Parkes Bonnington
  (*English*)
Gutzon Borglum (*U.S.*)
Hieronymus Bosch (*Dutch*)
Sandro Botticelli (*Italian*)
Francois Boucher (*French*)
Eugène Boudin (*French*)
Arthur Boyd (*Australian*)
Donato Bramante (*Italian*)
Constantin Brancusi
  (*Romanian*)
Georges Braque (*French*)
Brassaï (*French*)
Agnolo Bronzino (*Italian*)

Ford Madox Brown
  (*English*)
Jan Brueghel (*Flemish*)
Pieter Brueghel the Elder
  (*Flemish*)
Pieter Brueghel the Younger
  (*Flemish*)
Bernard Buffet (*French*)
Edward Burne-Jones
  (*English*)
Edward Burra (*English*)
Reg Butler (*English*)
Alexander Calder (*U.S.*)
Callimachus (*Greek*)
Robert Campin (*Flemish*)
Antonio Canova (*Italian*)
Michelangelo Merisi da
  Caravaggio (*Italian*)
Anthony Caro (*English*)
Vittore Carpaccio (*Italian*)
Agostino Carracci (*Italian*)
Annibale Carracci (*Italian*)
Ludovico Carracci (*Italian*)
Mary Cassatt (*U.S.*)
Pietro Cavallini (*Italian*)
Benvenuto Cellini (*Italian*)
Lynn Chadwick (*English*)
Marc Chagall (*Russian-
  French*)
Philippe de Champaigne
  (*French*)
Jean-Baptiste Siméon
  Chardin (*French*)
Giorgio de Chirico (*Italian*)
Giovanni Cimabue (*Italian*)
Claude Lorrain (*French*)
François Clouet (*French*)
Jean Clouet (*French*)
John Constable (*English*)
John Copley (*U.S.*)
Jean Baptiste Camille Corot
  (*French*)
Antonio Allegri da
  Corregio (*Italian*)
Gustave Courbet (*French*)
David Cox (*English*)
Antoine Coypel (*French*)
Lucas Cranach (*German*)
Walter Crane (*English*)
John Crome (*English*)
Aelbert Cuyp *or* Kuyp (*Dutch*)
Paul Cézanne (*French*)
Richard Dadd (*English*)
Salvador Dalí (*Spanish*)
Francis Danby (*Irish*)
Charles François Daubigny
  (*French*)

Honoré Daumier (*French*)
Jacques Louis David
  (*French*)
Peter de Wint (*English*)
Hilaire Germain Edgar
  Degas (*French*)
Eugène Delacroix (*French*)
Paul Delaroche (*French*)
Robert Delaunay (*French*)
Paul Delvaux (*Belgian*)
Maurice Denis (*French*)
André Derain (*French*)
William Dobell (*Australian*)
Domenichino (*Italian*)
Domenico del Barbiere
  (*Italian*)
Donatello (*Italian*)
Gerrit Dou (*Dutch*)
George Russell Drysdale
  (*Australian*)
Jean Dubuffet (*French*)
Duccio di Buoninsegna
  (*Italian*)
Marcel Duchamp (*French-
  U.S.*)
Raoul Dufy (*French*)
Albrecht Dürer (*German*)
Thomas Eakins (*U.S.*)
El Greco (*Greek-Spanish*)
James Ensor (*Belgian*)
Jacob Epstein (*British*)
Max Ernst (*German*)
Henri Fantin-Latour (*French*)
Lyonel Feininger (*U.S.*)
John Flaxman (*English*)
Jean Fouquet (*French*)
Jean Honoré Fragonard
  (*French*)
Lucian Freud (*English*)
Caspar David Friedrich
  (*German*)
Roger Fry (*English*)
Henry Fuseli (*Swiss*)
Naum Gabo (*Russian-U.S.*)
Thomas Gainsborough
  (*English*)
Henri Gaudier-Brzeska
  (*French*)
Paul Gauguin (*French*)
Gentile da Fabriano (*Italian*)
Lorenzo Ghiberti (*Italian*)
Domenico Ghirlandaio
  (*Italian*)
Alberto Giacometti (*Swiss*)
Giambologna (*Italian*)
Grinling Gibbons (*Dutch*)
Gilbert (Proesch) and

George (Passmore) (*English*)
Eric Gill (*English*)
Giorgione da Castelfranco (*Italian*)
Giotto di Bondone (*Italian*)
Giulio Romano (*Italian*)
Hugo van der Goes (*Flemish*)
Julio González (*Spanish*)
Arshile Gorky (*U.S.*)
Francisco de Goya (*Spanish*)
Jan van Goyen (*Dutch*)
Duncan Grant (*Scottish*)
Jean Baptiste Greuze (*French*)
Juan Gris (*Spanish*)
Antoine Jean Gros (*French*)
George Grosz (*German-U.S.*)
Grünewald (*German*)
Francesco Guardi (*Italian*)
François Gérard (*French*)
Théodore Géricault (*French*)
Frans Hals (*Dutch*)
Richard Hamilton (*English*)
Ando Hiroshige (*Japanese*)
Damien Hirst (*English*)
Meindert Hobbema (*Dutch*)
David Hockney (*English*)
Hans Hofmann (*German-U.S.*)
William Hogarth (*English*)
Katsushika Hokusai (*Japanese*)
Hans Holbein (*German*)
Winslow Homer (*U.S.*)
Pieter de Hooch *or* Hoogh (*Dutch*)
Edward Hopper (*U.S.*)
Jean Antoine Houdon (*French*)
William Holman Hunt (*English*)
Jean Auguste Dominique Ingres (*French*)
Augustus John (*Welsh*)
Gwen John (*Welsh*)
Jasper Johns (*U.S.*)
Johan Barthold Jongkind (*Dutch*)
Jacob Jordaens (*Flemish*)
Wassily Kandinsky (*Russian*)
Angelica Kauffmann (*Swiss*)
Ernst Ludwig Kirchner (*German*)
Ron B. Kitaj (*U.S.*)

Paul Klee (*Swiss*)
Gustav Klimt (*Austrian*)
Franz Kline (*U.S.*)
Godfrey Kneller (*German-English*)
Laura Knight (*English*)
Oscar Kokoschka (*Austrian*)
Willem de Kooning (*Dutch-U.S.*)
Leon Kossoff (*English*)
Georges de La Tour (*French*)
Edwin Landseer (*English*)
Thomas Lawrence (*English*)
Charles Lebrun (*French*)
Fernand Léger (*French*)
Wilhelm Lehmbruck (*German*)
Frederic Leighton (*English*)
Peter Lely (*Dutch-English*)
Leonardo da Vinci (*Italian*)
Wyndham Lewis (*British*)
Roy Lichtenstein (*U.S.*)
Norman Alfred William Lindsay (*Australian*)
Jacques Lipchitz (*Lithuanian-U.S.*)
Filippino Lippi (*Italian*)
L(awrence) S(tephen) Lowry (*English*)
Lysippus (*Greek*)
Jan Mabuse (*Flemish*)
Charles Rennie Mackintosh (*Scottish*)
René Magritte (*Belgian*)
Aristide Maillol (*French*)
Kasimir Severinovich Malevich (*Russian*)
Edouard Manet (*French*)
Andrea Mantegna (*Italian*)
Franz Marc (*German*)
John Martin (*English*)
Simone Martini (*Italian*)
Masaccio (*Italian*)
Quentin Massys (*Flemish*)
Henri Matisse (*French*)
Hans Memling *or* Memlinc (*Flemish*)
Franz Xavier Messerschmidt (*Austrian*)
Ivan Mestrovic (*Yugoslav-U.S.*)
Michelangelo Buonarroti (*Italian*)
Michelozzi Michelozzo (*Italian*)
John Everett Millais (*English*)

Jean François Millet (*French*)
Joan Miró (*Spanish*)
Amedeo Modigliani (*Italian*)
László Moholy-Nagy (*Hungarian*)
Piet Mondrian (*Dutch*)
Claude Oscar Monet (*French*)
Henry Moore (*British*)
Gustave Moreau (*French*)
Berthe Morisot (*French*)
William Morris (*English*)
Samuel Finley Breese Morse (*U.S.*)
Grandma Moses (*U.S.*)
Edvard Munch (*Norwegian*)
Alfred Munnings (*English*)
Bartolomé Esteban Murillo (*Spanish*)
Myron (*Greek*)
Paul Nash (*English*)
Ernst Wilhelm Nay (*German*)
Barnett Newman (*U.S.*)
Ben Nicholson (*English*)
Sidney Nolan (*Australian*)
Emil Nolde (*German*)
Joseph Nollekens (*Dutch-English*)
Georgia O'Keefe (*U.S.*)
Claes Oldenburg (*Swedish-U.S.*)
Orcagna (*Italian*)
José Clemente Orozco (*Mexican*)
Jean Baptiste Oudry (*French*)
Palma Vecchio (*Italian*)
Samuel Palmer (*English*)
Eduardo Paolozzi (*Scottish*)
Parmigianino (*Italian*)
Victor Pasmore (*English*)
Joachim Patinir *or* Patenier (*Flemish*)
Perugino (*Italian*)
Baldassare Peruzzi (*Italian*)
Antoine Pevsner (*Russian-French*)
Phidias (*Greek*)
Francis Picabia (*French*)
Pablo Picasso (*Spanish*)
Piero della Francesca (*Italian*)
Piero di Cosimo (*Italian*)
Pietro da Cortona (*Italian*)
Jean Baptiste Pigalle (*French*)
Germain Pilon (*French*)
Pinturicchio (*Italian*)

John Piper (*English*)
Pisanello (*Italian*)
Andrea Pisano (*Italian*)
Giovanni Pisano (*Italian*)
Nicola Pisano (*Italian*)
Camille Pissarro (*French*)
Antonio del Pollaiuolo (*Italian*)
Piero del Pollaiuolo (*Italian*)
Jackson Pollock (*U.S.*)
Polyclitus (*Greek*)
Polygnotus (*Greek*)
Pontormo (*Italian*)
Paulus Potter (*Dutch*)
Nicolas Poussin (*French*)
Praxiteles (*Greek*)
Pierre Paul Prud'hon (*French*)
Pierre Puget (*French*)
Pierre Puvis de Chavannes (*French*)
Jacopa della Quercia (*Italian*)
Arthur Rackham (*English*)
Henry Raeburn (*Scottish*)
Allan Ramsay (*Scottish*)
Raphael (*Italian*)
Robert Rauschenberg (*U.S.*)
Man Ray (*U.S.*)
Odilon Redon (*French*)
Rembrandt Harmensz van Rijn (*Dutch*)
Guido Reni (*Italian*)
Pierre Auguste Renoir (*French*)
Joshua Reynolds (*English*)
José de Ribera (*Spanish*)
Bridget Riley (*English*)
Diego Rivera (*Mexican*)
Andrea della Robbia (*Italian*)
Luca della Robbia (*Italian*)
Alexander Mikhailovich Rodchenko (*Russian*)
Auguste Rodin (*French*)
George Romney (*English*)
Salvator Rosa (*Italian*)
Dante Gabriel Rossetti (*English*)
Mark Rothko (*U.S.*)
Geroges Rouault (*French*)
Louis-François Roubiliac *or* Roubillac (*French*)
Henri Julien Rousseau (*French*)

Théodore Rousseau (*French*)
Peter Paul Rubens (*Flemish*)
Rublyov *or* Rublev Andrei (*Russian*)
Jacob van Ruisdael (*Dutch*)
Philipp Otto Runge (*German*)
Salomen van Ruysdael (*Dutch*)
John Singer Sargent (*U.S.*)
Egon Schiele (*Austrian*)
Martin Schongauer (*German*)
Kurt Schwitters (*German*)
Scopas (*Greek*)
Maurice Sendak (*U.S.*)
Sesshu (*Japanese*)
Georges Seurat (*French*)
Ben Shahn (*U.S.*)
Walter Richard Sickert (*British*)
Paul Signac (*French*)
Luca Signorelli (*Italian*)
David Alfaro Siqueiros (*Mexican*)
Alfred Sisley (*French*)
John Sloan (*U.S.*)
Claus Sluter (*Dutch*)
David Smith (*U.S.*)
Chaim Soutine (*Lithuanian-French*)
Stanley Spencer (*English*)
Jan Steen (*Dutch*)
Veit Stoss (*German*)
George Stubbs (*English*)
Graham Sutherland (*English*)
Yves Tanguy (*French*)
Vladimir Tatlin (*Russian*)
David Teniers the Elder (*Flemish*)
David Teniers the Younger (*Flemish*)
Gerard Ter Borch *or* Terborch (*Dutch*)
Hendrik Terbrugghen (*Dutch*)
James Thornhill (*English*)
Bertel Thorvaldsen (*Danish*)
Giambattista Tiepolo (*Italian*)
Jacopo Tintoretto (*Italian*)
James Jacques Joseph Tissot (*French*)
Titian (*Italian*)

Henri Marie Raymond de Toulouse-Lautrec (*French*)
J(oseph) M(allord) W(illiam) Turner (*English*)
Paolo Uccello (*Italian*)
Utagawa Kuniyoshi (*Japanese*)
Maurice Utrillo (*French*)
Adriaen van de Velde (*Dutch*)
Willem van de Velde the Elder (*Dutch*)
Willem van de Velde the Younger (*Dutch*)
Rogier van der Weyden (*Flemish*)
Anthony Van Dyck (*Flemish*)
Jan van Eyck (*Flemish*)
Vincent van Gogh (*Dutch*)
Victor Vasarely (*Hungarian-French*)
Giorgio Vasari (*Italian*)
Diego Rodríguez de Silva y Velázquez (*Spanish*)
Jan Vermeer (*Dutch*)
Paolo Veronese (*Italian*)
Andrea del Verrocchio (*Italian*)
Élisabeth Vigée-Lebrun (*French*)
Jacques Villon (*French*)
Maurice de Vlaminck (*French*)
Andy Warhol (*U.S.*)
Jean Antoine Watteau (*French*)
George Frederick Watts (*English*)
Benjamin West (*U.S.*)
James Abbott McNeill Whistler (*U.S.*)
Richard Wilson (*Welsh*)
Joseph Wright (*English*)
Xia Gui *or* Hsia Kuei (*Chinese*)
Zeuxis (*Greek*)
Johann Zoffany (*German*)
Anders Zorn (*Swedish*)
Gaetano Giulio Zumbo (*Italian*)
Francisco Zurbarán (*Spanish*)

WORD POWER

AUSTRALIAN STATES AND TERRITORIES

Australian Capital Territory
New South Wales
Northern Territory

Queensland
South Australia
Tasmania

Victoria
Western Australia

BAYS

Aboukir *or* Abukir Bay
Bay of Acre
Algoa Bay
Ariake Bay
Baffin Bay
Bay of Bengal
Bay of Biscay
Biscayne Bay
Bombetoka Bay
Botany Bay
Buzzards Bay
Bay of Cádiz
Caernarvon Bay
Callao Bay
Bay of Campeche
Cape Cod Bay
Cardigan Bay
Carmarthen Bay
Casco Bay
Chesapeake Bay
Cienfuegos Bay
Colwyn Bay
Corpus Christi Bay
Delagoa Bay
Delaware Bay
Discovery Bay
Dublin Bay
Dundalk Bay
Dvina Bay
Encounter Bay
Bay of Espírito Santo
False Bay
Famagusta Bay

Florida Bay
Bay of Fundy
Galway Bay
Bay of Gdansk
Georgian Bay
Bay of Gibraltar
Guanabara Bay
Guantánamo Bay
Hangzhou Bay
Hawke Bay
Hudson Bay
Inhambane Bay
Ise Bay
James Bay
Jervis Bay
Jiazhou Bay
Bay of Kaválla
Korea Bay
Kuskokwim Bay
Lobito Bay
Lützow-Holm Bay
Magdalena Bay
Manila Bay
Massachusetts Bay
Milne Bay
Mobile Bay
Montego Bay
Morecambe Bay
Moreton Bay
Narragansett Bay
Newark Bay
Bay of Naples
New York Bay

Omura Bay
Osaka Bay
Passamaquoddy Bay
Bay of Pigs
Bay of Plenty
Port Phillip Bay
Poverty Bay
Quiberon Bay
San Francisco Bay
San Pedro Bay
Santiago Bay
Setúbal Bay
Sligo Bay
St Austell Bay
Bay of St Michel
Swansea Bay
Table Bay
Tampa Bay
Tasman Bay
Thunder Bay
Tokyo Bay
Toyama Bay
Tralee Bay
Bay of Trincomalee
Ungava Bay
Urado Bay
Vigo Bay
Bay of Vlorë
Vyborg Bay
Walvis *or* Walfish Bay
Whitley Bay
Wick Bay

CANADIAN PROVINCES

Province	Abbreviation	Province	Abbreviation
Alberta	AB	Nunavut	NU
British Columbia	BC	Ontario	ON
Manitoba	MB	Prince Edward Island	PE
New Brunswick	NB	Quebec	PQ
Newfoundland	NF	Saskatchewan	SK
Northwest Territories	NWT	Yukon Territory	YT
Nova Scotia	NS		

CANALS

Berezina Canal
Bridgewater Canal
Caledonian Canal
Champlain Canal
Corinth Canal
Dortmund-Ems Canal
Erie Canal
Göta Canal
Grand Canal

Grand Union Canal
Houston Ship Canal
Kiel Canal
Manchester Ship Canal
Canal du Midi
Mittelland Canal
Moscow Canal
New York State Barge
  Canal

Canal do Norte
Panama Canal
Rhine-Herne Canal
Canal de São Gonçalo
Suez Canal
Twente Canal
Welland Canal

CAPITAL CITIES

City	Country	City	Country
Abu Dhabi Emirates	United Arab	Caracas	Venezuela
		Cardiff	Wales
Abuja	Nigeria	Castries	St. Lucia
Accra	Ghana	Cayenne	French Guiana
Addis Ababa	Ethiopia	Colombo	Sri Lanka
Astana	Kazakhstan	Conakry or Konakry	Guinea
Algiers	Algeria	Copenhagen	Denmark
Amman	Jordan	Dakar	Senegal
Amsterdam	Netherlands	Damascus	Syria
Andorra la Vella	Andorra	Delhi	India
Ankara	Turkey	Dhaka or Dacca	Bangladesh
Antananarivo	Madagascar	Dili	East Timor
Apia	Samoa	Djibouti or Jibouti	Djibouti or Jibouti
Ashkhabad	Turkmenistan	Dodoma	Tanzania
Asmara	Eritrea	Doha	Qatar
Asunción	Paraguay	Douglas	Isle of Man
Athens	Greece	Dublin	Republic of Ireland
Baghdad	Iraq	Dushanbe	Tajikistan
Baku	Azerbaijan	Edinburgh	Scotland
Bamako	Mali	Fort-de-France	Martinique
Bandar Seri Begawan	Brunei	Freetown	Sierra Leone
Bangkok	Thailand	Funafuti	Tuvalu
Bangui	Central African Republic	Gaborone	Botswana
		Georgetown	Guyana
Banjul	Gambia	Guatemala City	Guatemala
Basseterre	St. Kitts and Nevis	Hanoi	Vietnam
Beijing	People's Republic of China	Harare	Zimbabwe
		Havana	Cuba
Beirut or Beyrouth	Lebanon	Helsinki	Finland
Belfast	Northern Ireland	Honiara	Solomon Islands
Belgrade	Yugoslavia (Serbia and Montenegro)	Islamabad	Pakistan
		Jakarta or Djakarta	Indonesia
Belmopan	Belize	Jerusalem	Israel
Berlin	Germany	Kabul	Afghanistan
Berne	Switzerland	Kampala	Uganda
Bishkek	Kyrgyzstan	Katmandu or Kathmandu	Nepal
Bissau	Guinea-Bissau		
Bloemfontein	judicial capital of South Africa	Khartoum or Khartum	Sudan
		Kiev	Ukraine
Bogotá	Colombia	Kigali	Rwanda
Brasília	Brazil	Kingston	Jamaica
Bratislava	Slovakia	Kingstown	St. Vincent and the Grenadines
Brazzaville	Congo (Republic of)		
Bridgetown	Barbados	Kinshasa	Congo (Democratic Republic of)
Brussels	Belgium		
Bucharest	Romania		
Budapest	Hungary	Kishinev	Moldova
Buenos Aires	Argentina	Palikir	Micronesia
Bujumbura	Burundi	Koror	Palau
Cairo	Egypt	Kuala Lumpur	Malaysia
Canberra	Australia	Kuwait	Kuwait
Cape Town	legislative capital of South Africa	La Paz	administrative capital of Bolivia

WORD POWER

13

CAPITAL CITIES

WORD POWER

City	Country	City	Country
Libreville	Gabon	Prague	Czech Republic
Lilongwe	Malawi	Praia	Cape Verde
Lima	Peru	Pretoria	administrative capital of South Africa
Lisbon	Portugal		
Ljubljana	Slovenia		
Lomé	Togo	Pristina	Kosovo (Federal Republic of Yugoslavia)
London	United Kingdom		
Luanda	Angola		
Lusaka	Zambia	Pyongyang	North Korea
Luxembourg	Luxembourg	Quito	Ecuador
Madrid	Spain	Rabat	Morocco
Majuro	Marshall Islands	Reykjavik	Iceland
Malabo	Equatorial Guinea	Riga	Latvia
Malé	Maldives	Riyadh	Saudi Arabia
Managua	Nicaragua	Rome	Italy
Manama	Bahrain	Roseau	Dominica
Manila	Philippines	San`a	Yemen
Maputo	Mozambique	San José	Costa Rica
Maseru	Lesotho	San Juan	Puerto Rico
Mbabane	Swaziland	San Marino	San Marino
Mexico City	Mexico	San Salvador	El Slavador
Minsk	Belarus	Santiago	Chile
Mogadishu	Somalia	Santo Domingo	Dominican Republic
Monaco-Ville	Monaco		
Monrovia	Liberia	São Tomé	São Tomé and Principe
Montevideo	Uruguay		
Moroni	Comoros	Sarajevo	Bosnia and Herzegovina
Moscow	Russia		
Muscat	Oman	Seoul	South Korea
Nairobi	Kenya	Singapore	Singapore
Nassau	Bahamas	Skopje	Macedonia
Ndjamena	Chad	Sofia	Bulgaria
Niamey	Niger	St. George's	Grenada
Nicosia	Cyprus	St. John's	Antigua and Barbuda
Nouakchott	Mauritania		
Nuku'alofa	Tonga	Stockholm	Sweden
Nuuk	Greenland	Sucre	legislative and judicial capital of Bolivia
Oslo	Norway		
Ottawa	Canada		
Ouagadougou	Burkina-Faso	Suva	Fiji
Panama City	Panama	Taipei	Taiwan
Paramaribo	Suriname	Tallinn	Estonia
Paris	France	Tarawa	Kiribati
Phnom Penh	Cambodia	Tashkent	Uzbekistan
Pishpek	Kirghizia	Tbilisi	Georgia
Port-au-Prince	Haiti	Tegucigalpa	Honduras
Port Louis	Mauritius	Tehran	Iran
Port Moresby	Papua New Guinea	Tel Aviv	Israel
		Thimphu	Bhutan
Port of Spain	Trinidad and Tobago	Tirana	Albania
		Tokyo	Japan
Porto Novo	Benin	Tripoli	Libya

CAPITAL CITIES

City	Country	City	Country
Tunis	Tunisia	Washington DC	United States of America
Ulan Bator	Mongolia		
Vaduz	Liechtenstein	Wellington	New Zealand
Valletta	Malta	Windhoek	Namibia
Vatican City	Vatican City	Yamoussoukro	Côte d'Ivoire
Victoria	Seychelles	Yangon (Rangoon)	Myanmar (Burma)
Vienna	Austria	Yaoundé *or* Yaunde	Cameroon
Vientiane	Laos	Yaren	Nauru
Port Vila	Vanuatu	Yerevan	Armenia
Vilnius	Lithuania	Zagreb	Croatia
Warsaw	Poland		

CASTLES

Aberystwyth	Chillon	Leeds
Amboise	Colditz	Leicester
Arundel	Conwy	Lincoln
Ashby de la Zouch	Crathes	Ludlow
Ashford	Culzean	Malahide
Aydon	Darnaway	Monmouth
Ballindalloch	Dinan	Otranto
Balmoral	Drum	Pembroke
Balvenie	Dublin	Pendennis
Barnard	Dunnottar	Pontefract
Beaumaris	Dunsinane	Portlick
Beeston	Dunstaffnage	Rait
Belvoir	Durham	Restormel
Berkeley	Edinburgh	Richmond
Berkhamstead	Eilean Donan	Rock of Cashel
Berwick-upon-Tweed	Esterháza	Rithes
Blarney	Farney	St Mawes
Blois	Forfar	Sherborne
Braemar	Fotheringhay	Scarborough
Brodie	Glamis	Skipton
Bunraity	Harlech	Stirling
Cabra	Heidelberg	Stuart
Caerlaverock	Herstmonceux	Taymouth
Caernarfon	Inverness	Tintagel
Caerphilly	Kenilworth	Torún
Cahir	Kilkea	Trausnitz
Canossa	Kilkenny	Trim
Carisbrooke	Killaghy	Urquhart
Carmarthen	Kilravock	Vaduz
Carrickfergus	Lancaster	Vincennes
Château-Raoul	Leamaneh	Wartburg
Cheb	Launceston	Warwick

Classical composers

Adolphe Adam (*French*)
John Adams (*U.S.*)
Isaac Albéniz (*Spanish*)
Tomaso Albinoni (*Italian*)
Gregorio Allegri (*Italian*)
William Alwyn (*British*)
George Antheil (*U.S.*)
Thomas Arne (*English*)
Malcolm Arnold (*British*)
Daniel François Espirit Auber (*French*)
Georges Auric (*French*)
Carl Philipp Emanuel Bach (*German*)
Johann Christian Bach (*German*)
Johann Christoph Friedrich Bach (*German*)
Johann Sebastian Bach (*German*)
Wilhelm Friedemann Bach (*German*)
Mily Alexeyevich Balakirev (*Russian*)
Granville Bantock (*British*)
Samuel Barber (*U.S.*)
Béla Bartók (*Hungarian*)
Arnold Bax (*British*)
Ludwig van Beethoven (*German*)
Vincenzo Bellini (*Italian*)
Arthur Benjamin (*Australian*)
Richard Rodney Bennett (*British*)
Alban Berg (*Austrian*)
Luciano Berio (*Italian*)
Lennox Berkeley (*British*)
Hector Berlioz (*French*)
Leonard Bernstein (*U.S.*)
Heinrich Biber (*German*)
Harrison Birtwhistle (*British*)
Georges Bizet (*French*)
Arthur Bliss (*British*)
Ernest Bloch (*U.S.*)
Luigi Bocherini (*Italian*)
Arrigo Boito (*Italian*)
Francesco Antonio Bonporti (*Italian*)
Aleksandr Porfirevich Borodin (*Russian*)
Pierre Boulez (*French*)
William Boyce (*English*)
Johannes Brahms (*German*)
Havergal Brian (*British*)
Frank Bridge (*British*)
Benjamin Britten (*British*)
Max Bruch (*German*)
Anton Bruckner (*Austrian*)
John Bull (*English*)
George Butterworth (*British*)
Dietrich Buxtehude (*Danish*)
William Byrd (*English*)
John Cage (*U.S.*)

Joseph Canteloube (*French*)
John Alden Carpenter (*U.S.*)
Eliot Carter (*U.S.*)
Robert Carver (*Scottish*)
Pablo Casals (*Spanish*)
Emmanuel Chabrier (*French*)
Gustave Charpentier (*French*)
Marc-Antoine Charpentier (*French*)
Ernest Chausson (*French*)
Luigi Cherubini (*Italian*)
Frédéric Chopin (*Polish-French*)
Domenico Cimarosa (*Italian*)
Jeremiah Clarke (*English*)
Samuel Coleridge-Taylor (*British*)
Aaron Copland (*U.S.*)
Arcangelo Corelli (*Italian*)
François Couperin (*French*)
Karl Czerny (*Austrian*)
Luigi Dallapiccola (*Italian*)
Peter Maxwell Davies (*British*)
Claude Debussy (*French*)
Léo Delibes (*French*)
Frederick Delius (*British*)
Josquin des Prés (*Flemish*)
Vincent d'Indy (*French*)
Ernst von Dohnányi (*Hungarian*)
Gaetano Donizetti (*Italian*)
Antal Doráti (*U.S.*)
John Dowland (*English*)
Paul Dukas (*French*)
John Dunstable (*English*)
Henri Duparc (*French*)
Marcel Dupré (*French*)
Maurice Duruflé (*French*)
Henri Dutilleux (*French*)
Antonín Dvořák (*Czech*)
Edward Elgar (*British*)
Georges Enesco (*Romanian*)
Manuel de Falla (*Spanish*)
John Farmer (*English*)
Gabriel Fauré (*French*)
John Field (*Irish*)
Gerald Finzi (*British*)
Friedrich von Flotow (*German*)
César Franck (*Belgian-French*)
Girolamo Frescobaldi (*Italian*)
Wilhelm Fürtwangler (*German*)
Andrea Gabrieli (*Italian*)
Giovanni Gabrieli (*Italian*)
George Gershwin (*U.S.*)
Carlo Gesualdo (*Italian*)
Orlando Gibbons (*English*)

Classical composers (continued)

Alberto Ginastera (*Argentinian*)
Philip Glass (*U.S.*)
Aleksandr Konstantinovich Glazunov (*Russian*)
Mikhail Ivanovich Glinka (*Russian*)
Christoph Willibald Gluck (*German*)
Eugene Goossens (*Belgian-British*)
Henryk Górecki (*Polish*)
Charles François Gounod (*French*)
Percy Grainger (*Australian*)
Enrique Granados (*Spanish*)
Edvard Grieg (*Norwegian*)
Ivor Gurney (*British*)
Fromental Halévy (*French*)
George Frederick Handel (*German*)
Roy Harris (*U.S.*)
Franz Joseph Haydn (*Austrian*)
Michael Haydn (*Austrian*)
Hans Werner Henze (*German*)
Hildegard of Bingen (*German*)
Paul Hindemith (*German*)
Heinz Holliger (*Swiss*)
Gustav Holst (*British*)
Arthur Honegger (*French*)
Johann Nepomuk Hummel (*German*)
Englebert Humperdinck (*German*)
Jacques Ibert (*French*)
John Ireland (*British*)
Charles Ives (*U.S.*)
Leoš Janáček (*Czech*)
Émile Jaques-Dalcroze (*Swiss*)
Joseph Joachim (*Hungarian*)
Daniel Jones (*British*)
Aram Ilich Khachaturian (*Armenian*)
Otto Klemperer (*German*)
Oliver Knussen (*British*)
Zoltán Kodály (*Hungarian*)
Erich Korngold (*Austrian*)
Franz Krommer (*Moravian*)
Raphael Kubelik (*Czech*)
Édouard Lalo (*French*)
Constant Lambert (*British*)
Roland de Lassus (*Flemish*)
Henry Lawes (*English*)
William Lawes (*English*)
Franz Lehár (*Hungarian*)
Ruggiero Leoncavallo (*Italian*)
György Ligeti (*Hungarian*)
Franz Liszt (*Hungarian*)
George Lloyd (*British*)
Matthew Locke (*English*)
Karl Loewe (*German*)

Jean Baptiste Lully (*Italian-French*)
Witold Lutosławski (*Polish*)
Elisabeth Lutyens (*British*)
Guillaume de Machaut (*French*)
James MacMillan (*British*)
Elizabeth Maconchy (*British*)
Gustav Mahler (*Austrian*)
Luca Marenzio (*Italian*)
Frank Martin (*Swiss*)
Bohuslav Martinů (*Czech*)
Steve Martland (*British*)
Pietro Mascagni (*Italian*)
Jules Émile Frédéric Massenet (*French*)
Fanny Mendelssohn (*German*)
Felix Mendelssohn (*German*)
Gian Carlo Menotti (*Italian*)
André Messager (*French*)
Olivier Messiaen (*French*)
Giacomo Meyerbeer (*German*)
Darius Milhaud (*French*)
Claudio Monteverdi (*Italian*)
Thomas Morley (*English*)
Leopold Mozart (*Austrian*)
Wolfgang Amadeus Mozart (*Austrian*)
Thea Musgrave (*British*)
Modest Petrovich Mussorgsky (*Russian*)
Carl Otto Ehrenfried Nicolai (*German*)
Carl Nielsen (*Danish*)
Luigi Nono (*Italian*)
Michael Nyman (*British*)
Johannes Ockeghem (*Flemish*)
Jacques Offenbach (*German-French*)
John Ogdon (*British*)
Carl Orff (*German*)
Johann Pachelbel (*German*)
Ignace Jan Paderewski (*Polish*)
Niccolò Paganini (*Italian*)
Giovanni Pierluigi da Palestrina (*Italian*)
Andrzej Panufnik (*Polish-British*)
Hubert Parry (*British*)
Arvo Pärt (*Estonian*)
Krzystof Penderecki (*Polish*)
Giovanni Battista Pergolesi (*Italian*)
Francis Poulenc (*French*)
Michael Praetorius (*German*)
Sergei Sergeyevich Prokofiev (*Russian*)
Giacomo Puccini (*Italian*)
Henry Purcell (*English*)
Sergei Vassilievich Rachmaninov (*Russian*)
Jean Philippe Rameau (*French*)
Maurice Ravel (*French*)
Alan Rawsthorne (*British*)

WORD POWER

17

Classical composers (continued)

Max Reger (*German*)
Steve Reich (*U.S.*)
Ottorino Respighi (*Italian*)
Vittorio Rieti (*Italian*)
Nikolai Andreyevich Rimsky-Korsakov (*Russian*)
Joaquín Rodrigo (*Spanish*)
Sigmund Romberg (*U.S.*)
Gioacchino Antonio Rossini (*Italian*)
Mstislav Leopoldovich Rostropovich (*Russian*)
Claude Joseph Rouget de Lisle (*French*)
Albert Roussel (*French*)
Edmund Rubbra (*British*)
Anton Grigorevich Rubinstein (*Russian*)
Camille Saint-Saëns (*French*)
Antonio Salieri (*Italian*)
Erik Satie (*French*)
Alessandro Scarlatti (*Italian*)
Domenico Scarlatti (*Italian*)
Artur Schnabel (*Austrian-U.S.*)
Alfred Schnittke (*Russian*)
Arnold Schoenberg (*Austrian*)
Franz Schubert (*Austrian*)
William Schuman (*U.S.*)
Clara Schumann (*German*)
Robert Schumann (*German*)
Heinrich Schütz (*German*)
Aleksandr Nikolayvich Scriabin (*Russian*)
Peter Sculthorpe (*Australian*)
Roger Sessions (*U.S.*)
Dmitri Dmitriyevich Shostakovich (*Russian*)
Jean Sibelius (*Finnish*)
Robert Simpson (*English*)
Bedřich Smetana (*Czech*)
Ethel Smyth (*British*)
John Philip Sousa (*U.S.*)
John Stainer (*British*)
Charles Stanford (*Irish*)
Karlheinz Stockhausen (*German*)

Oscar Straus (*French*)
Johann Strauss, the elder (*Austrian*)
Johann Strauss, the younger (*Austrian*)
Richard Strauss (*German*)
Igor Fyodorovich Stravinsky (*Russian-U.S.*)
Jan Pieterszoon Sweelinck (*Dutch*)
Karol Szymanowski (*Polish*)
Toru Takemitsu (*Japanese*)
Thomas Tallis (*English*)
John Tavener (*British*)
John Taverner (*English*)
Pyotr Ilyich Tchaikovsky (*Russian*)
Georg Philipp Telemann (*German*)
Mikis Theodorakis (*Greek*)
Ambroise Thomas (*French*)
Virgil Thomson (*U.S.*)
Michael Tippett (*British*)
Paul Tortelier (*French*)
Edgar Varèse (*French-U.S.*)
Ralph Vaughan Williams (*British*)
Giuseppi Verdi (*Italian*)
Tomás Luis de Victoria (*Spanish*)
Heitor Villa-Lobos (*Brazilian*)
Antonio Vivaldi (*Italian*)
Richard Wagner (*German*)
William Walton (*British*)
David Ward (*British*)
Peter Warlock (*British*)
Carl Maria von Weber (*German*)
Anton Webern (*Austrian*)
Thomas Weelkes (*English*)
Judith Weir (*British*)
Egon Wellesz (*Austrian-British*)
Gillian Whitehead (*New Zealand*)
Malcolm Williamson (*Australian*)
Hugo Wolf (*Austrian*)
Ermanno Wolf-Ferrari (*Italian*)
Yannis Xenakis (*Romanian-Greek*)
Alexander Zemlinsky (*Austrian*)

WORD POWER

Popular composers, songwriters and lyricists

Harold Arlen (*U.S.*)
Burt Bacharach (*U.S.*)
Joan Baez (*U.S.*)
John Barry (*British*)
Lionel Bart (*British*)
Irving Berlin (*Russian-U.S.*)
Leonard Bernstein (*U.S.*)
David Bowie (*English*)
Jacques Brel (*Belgian*)
Nacio Herb Brown (*U.S.*)
Sammy Cahn (*U.S.*)
Hoagy Carmichael (*U.S.*)
George Cohan (*U.S.*)
Leonard Cohen (*Canadian*)
Noel Coward (*English*)
Willie Dixon (*U.S.*)
Lamont Dozier (*U.S.*)
Vernon Duke (*Russian-U.S.*)
Bob Dylan (*U.S.*)
Duke Ellington (*U.S.*)
Stephen Foster (*U.S.*)
George Gershwin (*U.S.*)
W(illiam) S(chwenck) Gilbert (*British*)
Gerry Goffin (*U.S.*)
Elliot Goldenthal (*U.S.*)
Jerry Goldsmith (*U.S.*)
Woody Guthrie (*U.S.*)
W(illiam) C(hristopher) Handy (*U.S.*)
Marvin Hamlisch (*U.S.*)
Oscar Hammerstein (*U.S.*)
Lorenz Hart (*U.S.*)
Jerry Herman (*U.S.*)
Brian Holland (*U.S.*)
Eddie Holland (*U.S.*)
Mick Jagger (*British*)
Maurice Jarre (*French*)
Antonio Carlos Jobim (*Brazilian*)
Elton John (*British*)
Robert Johnson (*U.S.*)
Jerome (David) Kern (*U.S.*)
Carole King (*U.S.*)
Kris Kristofferson (*U.S.*)
Huddie 'Leadbelly' Ledbetter (*U.S.*)
Tom Lehrer (*U.S.*)
John Lennon (*British*)

Alan Jay Lerner (*U.S.*)
Jerry Lieber (*U.S.*)
Jay Livingston (*U.S.*)
Andrew Lloyd-Webber (*British*)
Frank Loesser (*U.S.*)
Frederick Loewe (*Austrian-U.S.*)
Paul McCartney (*British*)
Ewan McColl (*British*)
Kirsty McColl (*British*)
Jimmy McHugh (*U.S.*)
Henry Mancini (*U.S.*)
Barry Manilow (*U.S.*)
Barry Mann (*U.S.*)
Joni Mitchell (*Canadian*)
Thelonious (Sphere) Monk (*U.S.*)
Van Morrison (*Irish*)
Willie Nelson (*U.S.*)
Ivor Novello (*British*)
Doc Pomus (*U.S.*)
Cole Porter (*U.S.*)
Keith Richards (*British*)
William 'Smokey' Robinson (*U.S.*)
Tim Rice (*British*)
Richard Rodgers (*U.S.*)
Sigmund Romberg (*Hungarian-U.S.*)
Howard Shore (*Canadian*)
Paul Simon (*U.S.*)
Stephen Sondheim (*U.S.*)
Mike Stoller (*U.S.*)
Billy Strayhorn (*U.S.*)
Barrett Strong (*U.S.*)
Jule Styne (*U.S.*)
Arthur Sullivan (*British*)
Allen Toussaint (*U.S.*)
Johnny Van Heusen (*U.S.*)
Tom Waites (*U.S.*)
Harry Warren (*U.S.*)
Jimmy Webb (*U.S.*)
Cynthia Weil (*U.S.*)
Kurt Weill (*German-U.S.*)
Norman Whitfield (*U.S.*)
Hank Williams (*U.S.*)
John Williams (*U.S.*)
Brian Wilson (*U.S.*)
Vincent Youmans (*U.S.*)

WORD POWER

——— CONTINENTS ———

Africa
Antarctica
Asia

Australia
Europe
North America

South America

WORD POWER

English counties

Bedfordshire	Greater London	Oxfordshire
Berkshire	Greater Manchester	Rutland
Bristol	Hampshire	Shropshire
Buckinghamshire	Herefordshire	Somerset
Cambridgeshire	Hertfordshire	South Yorkshire
Cheshire	Isle of Wight	Staffordshire
Cornwall	Kent	Suffolk
Cumbria	Lancashire	Surrey
Derbyshire	Leicestershire	Tyne and Wear
Devon	Lincolnshire	Warwickshire
Dorset	Merseyside	West Midlands
Durham	Norfolk	West Sussex
East Riding of Yorkshire	Northamptonshire	West Yorkshire
East Sussex	Northumberland	Wiltshire
Essex	North Yorkshire	Worcestershire
Gloucestershire	Nottinghamshire	

Scottish counties

Aberdeen City	East Renfrewshire	Perth and Kinross
Aberdeenshire	Falkirk	Renfrewshire
Angus	Fife	Scottish Borders
Argyll and Bute	Glasgow City	Shetland
City of Edinburgh	Highland	South Ayrshire
Clackmannanshire	Inverclyde	South Lanarkshire
Dumfries and Galloway	Midlothian	Stirling
Dundee City	Moray	West Dunbartonshire
East Ayrshire	North Ayrshire	Western Isles (Eilean Siar)
East Dunbartonshire	North Lanarkshire	West Lothian
East Lothian	Orkney	

Welsh counties

Clwyd	Gwynedd	South Glamorgan
Dyfed	Mid Glamorgan	West Glamorgan
Gwent	Powys	

Northern Irish counties

Antrim	Down	Londonderry City
Armagh	Fermanagh	Tyrone
Belfast City	Londonderry	

Republic of Ireland counties

Carlow	Kilkenny	Offaly
Cavan	Laois	Roscommon
Clare	Leitrim	Sligo
Cork	Limerick	Tipperary
Donegal	Longford	Waterford
Dublin	Louth	Westmeath
Galway	Mayo	Wexford
Kerry	Meath	Wicklow
Kildare	Monaghan	

Afghanistan
Albania
Algeria
American Samoa
Andorra
Angola
Antigua and Barbuda
Argentina
Armenia
Australia
Austria
Azerbaijan
Bahamas
Bahrain
Bangladesh
Barbados
Belarus
Belau
Belgium
Belize
Benin
Bhutan
Bolivia
Bosnia and Herzegovina
Botswana
Brazil
Brunei
Bulgaria
Burkina-Faso
Burundi
Cambodia
Cameroon
Canada
Cape Verde
Central African Republic
Chad
Chile
Colombia
Comoros
Congo (Republic of)
Congo (Democratic
  Republic of)
Costa Rica
Côte d'Ivoire
Croatia
Cuba
Cyprus
Czech Republic
Denmark
Djibouti
Dominica
Dominican Republic
East Timor
Ecuador

Egypt
El Salvador
England
Equatorial Guinea
Eritrea
Estonia
Ethiopia
Fiji
Finland
France
Gabon
Gambia
Georgia
Germany
Ghana
Greece
Greenland
Grenada
Guatemala
Guinea
Guinea-Bissau
Guyana
Haiti
Honduras
Hungary
Iceland
India
Indonesia
Iran
Iraq
Israel
Italy
Jamaica
Japan
Jordan
Kazakhstan
Kenya
Kirghizia
Kiribati
Kuwait
Laos
Latvia
Lebanon
Lesotho
Liberia
Libya
Liechtenstein
Lithuania
Luxembourg
Macedonia
Madagascar
Malawi
Malaysia
Mali

Malta
Marshall Islands
Mauritania
Mauritius
Mexico
Micronesia
Moldova
Monaco
Mongolia
Morocco
Mozambique
Myanmar
Namibia
Nauru
Nepal
Netherlands
New Zealand
Nicaragua
Niger
Nigeria
Northern Ireland
North Korea
Norway
Oman
Pakistan
Panama
Papua New Guinea
Paraguay
People's Republic of China
Peru
Philippines
Poland
Portugal
Puerto Rico
Qatar
Republic of Ireland
Republic of Maldives
Romania
Russia
Rwanda
St Kitts and Nevis
St Lucia
St Vincent and the
  Grenadines
Samoa
San Marino
São Tomé and Principe
Saudi Arabia
Scotland
Senegal
Seychelles
Sierra Leone
Singapore
Slovakia

WORD POWER

Slovenia
Solomon Islands
Somalia
South Africa
South Korea
Spain
Sri Lanka
Sudan
Surinam
Swaziland
Sweden
Switzerland
Syria
Taiwan

Tajikistan
Tanzania
Thailand
Togo
Tonga
Trinidad and Tobago
Tunisia
Turkey
Turkmenistan
Tuvalu
Uganda
Ukraine
United Arab Emirates
United Kingdom

United States of America
Uruguay
Uzbekistan
Vanuatu
Vatican City
Venezuela
Vietnam
Wales
Yemen
Yugoslavia (Serbia and
 Montenegro)
Zambia
Zimbabwe

WORD POWER

CURRENCIES

Country	Currency	Country	Currency
Afghanistan	afghani	Dominican Republic	peso
Albania	lek	East Timor	US dollar
Algeria	Algerian dinar	Ecuador	US dollar
Andorra	euro	Egypt	pound
Angola	kwanza	El Salvador	cólon
Antigua and Barbuda	East Caribbean dollar	Equatorial Guinea	CFA franc
		Eritrea	nakfa
Argentina	peso	Estonia	kroon
Armenia	dram	Ethiopia	birr
Australia	Australian dollar	Fiji	Fiji dollar
Austria	euro	Finland	euro
Azerbaijan	manat	France	euro
Bahamas	Bahamian dollar	French Guiana	French franc
Bahrain	dinar	Gabon	CFA franc
Bangladesh	taka	Gambia	dalasi
Barbados	Barbados dollar	Germany	euro
Belarus	rouble	Ghana	cedi
Belgium	euro	Greece	euro
Belize	Belize dollar	Greenland	Danish krone
Benin	CFA franc	Grenada	East Caribbean dollar
Bhutan	ngultrum		
Bolivia	boliviano	Guatemala	quetzal
Bosnia-Herzegovina	convertible marka	Guinea	Guinea franc
Botswana	pula	Guinea-Bissau	CFA franc
Brazil	real	Guyana	Guyana dollar
Brunei	Brunei dollar	Haiti	gourde
Bulgaria	lev	Honduras	lempira
Burkina-Faso	CFA franc	Hungary	forint
Burundi	Burundi franc	Iceland	krona
Cambodia	riel	India	rupee
Cameroon	CFA franc	Indonesia	rupiah
Canada	Canadian dollar	Iran	rial
Cape Verde	escudo	Iraq	dinar
Central African Republic	CFA franc	Ireland (Republic of)	euro
		Israel	shekel
Chad	CFA franc	Italy	euro
Chile	peso	Jamaica	Jamaican dollar
China	yuan	Japan	yen
Colombia	peso	Jordan	dinar
Comoros	Comorian franc	Kazakhstan	tenge
Congo (Republic of)	CFA franc	Kenya	shilling
Congo (Democratic Republic of)	Congolese franc	Kirghizia	som
		Kiribati	Australian dollar
Costa Rica	cólon	Kosovo	dinar; euro
Côte d'Ivoire	CFA franc	Kuwait	dinar
Croatia	kuna	Kyrgyzstan	som
Cuba	peso	Laos	kip
Cyprus	pound	Latvia	lat
Czech Republic	koruna	Lebanon	pound
Denmark	krone	Lesotho	loti
Djibouti	Djibouti franc	Liberia	Liberian dollar
Dominica	East Caribbean dollar	Libya	dinar
		Liechtenstein	Swiss franc

Country	Currency	Country	Currency
Lithuania	litas	Samoa	tala
Luxembourg	euro	San Marino	euro
Macedonia	denar	São Tomé and Principe	dobra
Madagascar	Malagasy franc	Saudi Arabia	riyal
Malawi	kwacha	Senegal	CFA franc
Malaysia	ringgit	Seychelles	rupee
Maldives (Republic of)	rufiyaa	Sierra Leone	leone
Mali	CFA franc	Singapore	Singapore dollar
Malta	lira	Slovakia	koruna
Marshall Islands	U.S. dollar	Slovenia	tolar
Mauritania	ouguiya	Solomon Islands	Solomon Islands dollar
Mauritius	rupee		
Mexico	peso	Somalia	shilling
Micronesia	U.S. dollar	South Africa	rand
Moldova	leu	South Korea	won
Monaco	French franc	Spain	euro
Mongolia	tugrik	Sri Lanka	rupee
Montenegro	euro	Sudan	dinar
Montserrat	East Caribbean dollar	Surinam	guilder
		Swaziland	lilangeni
Morocco	dirham	Sweden	krona
Mozambique	metical	Switzerland	Swiss franc
Myanmar	kyat	Syria	pound
Namibia	Namibian dollar	Taiwan	Taiwan dollar
Nauru	Australian dollar	Tajikistan	somoni
Nepal	rupee	Tanzania	shilling
Netherlands	euro	Thailand	baht
New Zealand	New Zealand dollar	Togo	CFA franc
Nicaragua	córdoba	Tonga	pa'anga
Niger	CFA franc	Trinidad and Tobago	Trinidad and Tobago dollar
Nigeria	naira		
North Korea	won	Tunisia	dinar
Norway	krone	Turkey	Turkish lira
Oman	rial	Turkmenistan	manat
Pakistan	rupee	Tuvalu	Australian dollar
Palau	U.S. dollar	Uganda	shilling
Panama	balboa	Ukraine	hryvna
Papua New Guinea	kina	United Arab Emirates	dirham
Paraguay	guarani	United Kingdom	pound sterling
Peru	new sol	United States of America	U.S. dollar
Philippines	Philippine peso		
Poland	zloty	Uruguay	peso
Portugal	euro	Uzbekistan	sum
Qatar	riyal	Vanuatu	vatu
Romania	leu	Vatican City	euro
Russia	rouble	Venezuela	bolívar
Rwanda	Rwanda franc	Vietnam	dong
St. Kitts and Nevis	East Caribbean dollar	Yemen	riyal
		Yugoslavia (Serbia)	dinar
St. Lucia	East Caribbean dollar	Zambia	kwacha
		Zimbabwe	Zimbabwe dollar
St. Vincent and the Grenadines	East Caribbean dollar		

WORD POWER

DESERTS

Arabian
Atacama
Dasht-i-Lut *or* Dasht-e-Lut
Death Valley
Gibson
Gobi

Great Sandy
Great Victoria
Kalahari
Kara Kum
Kyzyl Kum
Libyan

Mohave *or* Mojave
Nubian
Rub'al Khali
Sahara
Taklimakan Shama
Thar

DIRECTORS

Robert Aldrich (*U.S.*)
Woody Allen (*U.S.*)
Pedro Almódovar (*Spanish*)
Robert Altman (*U.S.*)
Lindsay Anderson (*British*)
Michelangelo Antonioni (*Italian*)
Gillian Armstrong (*Australian*)
Anthony Asquith (*English*)
Richard Attenborough (*British*)
John Badham (*U.S.*)
Warren Beatty (*U.S.*)
Ingmar Bergman (*Swedish*)
Bernardo Bertolucci (*Italian*)
Luc Besson *French*)
Peter Bogdanovich (*U.S.*)
John Boorman (*English*)
Robert Bresson *French*)
Peter Brook (*British*)
Mel Brooks (*U.S.*)
Luis Buñuel *Spanish*)
Tim Burton (*U.S.*)
James Cameron (*U.S.*)
Jane Campion (*New Zealander*)
Frank Capra (*U.S.*)
John Carpenter (*U.S.*)
Marcel Carné (*French*)
Claude Chabrol (*French*)
Christopher Columbus (*U.S.*)
René Clair (*French*)
Jean Cocteau (*French*)
Ethan Coen (*U.S.*)
Joel Coen (*U.S.*)
Francis Ford Coppola (*U.S.*)
Roger Corman (*U.S.*)
David Cronenberg (*Canadian*)
Alfonso Cuarón (*Mexican*)
Michael Curtiz (*American-Hungarian*)
Joe Dante (*U.S.*)
Cecil B. de Mille (*U.S.*)
Johnathan Demme (*U.S.*)

Brian de Palma (*U.S.*)
Vittoria De Sicca (*Italian*)
Richard Donner (*U.S.*)
Aleksandr Petrovitch Dovzhenko (*Russian*)
Clint Eastwood (*U.S.*)
Blake Edwards (*U.S.*)
Sergei Mikhailovich Eisenstein (*Russian*)
Rainer Werner Fassbinder (*German*)
Federico Fellini (*Italian*)
Victor Fleming (*U.S.*)
Bryan Forbes (*English*)
John Ford (*U.S.*)
Milös Forman (*Czech*)
Bill Forsyth (*Scottish*)
Stephen Frears (*English*)
William Friedkin (*U.S.*)
Abel Gance (*French*)
Terry Gilliam (*U.S.*)
Jean-Luc Godard (*French*)
Peter Greenaway (*English*)
John Grierson (*Scottish*)
D(avid) W(ark) Griffith (*U.S.*)
Sacha Guitry (*French*)
Peter Hall (*English*)
Howard Hawks (*U.S.*)
Werner Herzog (*German*)
George Roy Hill (*U.S.*)
Alfred Hitchcock (*English*)
John Huston (*U.S.*)
James Ivory (*U.S.*)
Peter Jackson (*New Zealander*)
Derek Jarman (*English*)
Neil Jordan (*Irish*)
Chen Kaige (*China*)
Lawrence Kasdan (*U.S.*)
Philip Kaufman (*U.S.*)
Elia Kazan (*U.S.*)
Krzysztof Kieslowski (*Polish*)
Stanley Kubrick (*U.S.*)
Akira Kurosawa (*Japanese*)
John Landis (*U.S.*)

Fritz Lang (*Austrian*)
David Lean (*English*)
Spike Lee (*U.S.*)
Mike Leigh (*English*)
Richard Lester (*U.S.*)
Barry Levinson (*U.S.*)
Ken Loach (*English*)
George Lucas (*U.S.*)
Sidney Lumet (*U.S.*)
David Lynch (*U.S.*)
Jim McBride (*U.S.*)
Alexander Mackendrick (*Scottish*)
Louis Malle (*French*)
Joseph Mankiewicz (*U.S.*)
Georges Méliès (*French*)
Sam Mendes (*English*)
Ismail Merchant (*Indian*)
George Miller (*Australian*)
Jonathon Wolfe Miller (*English*)
Vincente Minnelli (*U.S.*)
Kenji Mizoguchi (*Japanese*)
Mike Nichols (*American-German*)
Laurence Olivier *English*)
Max Ophüls (*German*)
G(eorge) W(ilhelm) Pabst (*German*)
Marcel Pagnol (*French*)
Alan Parker (*English*)
Pier Paolo Pasolini (*Italian*)
Sam Peckinpah (*U.S.*)
Arthur Penn (*U.S.*)
Roman Polanski (*Polish*)
Sydney Pollack (*U.S.*)
Michael Powell (*English*)
Otto Preminger (*Austrian-U.S.*)
Emeric Pressburger (*Hungarian*)
Vsevolod Pudovkin (*Russian*)
David Puttnam (*English*)
Satyajit Ray (*Indian*)
Robert Redford (*U.S.*)
Carol Reed (*English*)

Directors (continued)

Carl Reiner (*U.S.*)
Rob Reiner (*U.S.*)
Edgar Reitz (*German*)
Jean Renoir (*French*)
Alain Resnais (*French*)
Leni Riefenstahl (*German*)
Guy Ritchie (*English*)
Hal Roach (*U.S.*)
Tim Robbins (*U.S.*)
Nicholas Roeg (*English*)
Eric Rohmer (*France*)
George Romero (*U.S.*)
Roberto Rossellini (*Italian*)
Ken Russell (*English*)
John Schlesinger (*English*)
Martin Scorsese (*U.S.*)

Ridley Scott (*British*)
Don Siegal (*U.S.*)
Steven Soderbergh (*U.S.*)
Steven Spielberg (*U.S.*)
Robert Stevenson (*English*)
Oliver Stone (*U.S.*)
Preston Sturges (*U.S.*)
Quentin Tarantino (*U.S.*)
Andrei Tarkovsky (*Russian*)
Jacques Tati (*French*)
Bertrand Tavernier (*French*)
François Truffaut (*French*)
Roger Vadim (*French*)
Luchino Visconti (*Italian*)
Joseph von Sternberg
 (*Austrian-U.S.*)

Erich von Stroheim
 (*Austrian-U.S.*)
Andrei Wajda (*Polish*)
Peter Weir (*Australian*)
Orson Welles (*U.S.*)
Wim Wenders (*German*)
Billy Wilder (*Austrian-U.S.*)
Michael Winner (*English*)
Robert Wise (*U.S.*)
Zhang Yimou (*Chinese*)
Franco Zeffirelli (*Italian*)
Robert Zemeckis (*U.S.*)
Fred Zinnemann (*Austrian-British*)

WORD POWER

DRAMA

Types of Drama

comedy
comedy of manners
commedia dell'arte
costume piece *or* costume
  drama
farce
Grand Guignol
Jacobean
kabuki

Kathakali
kitchen sink
melodrama
morality play
mystery play
No *or* Noh
passion play
Restoration Comedy
revenge tragedy

shadow play
situation comedy *or* sitcom
sketch
soap opera
street theatre
theatre of cruelty
theatre of the absurd
tragedy
tragicomedy

Dramatists

Aeschylus (*Greek*)
Edward Albee (*U.S.*)
Robert Amos (*Australian*)
Jean Anouilh (*French*)
Aristophanes (*Greek*)
Alan Ayckbourn (*English*)
Pierre Augustin Caron de Beaumarchais
  (*French*)
Francis Beaumont (*English*)
Samuel Beckett (*Irish*)
Brendan Behan (*Irish*)
Richard Beynon (*Australian*)
Alan Bleasdale (*English*)
Edward Bond (*English*)
Bertolt Brecht (*German*)
Eugene Brieux (*French*)
Pedro Calderón de la Barca (*Spanish*)
George Chapman (*English*)
Anton Pavlovich Chekhov (*Russian*)
William Congreve (*English*)
Pierre Corneille (*French*)
Noël (Pierce) Coward (*English*)
Thomas Dekker (*English*)
John Dryden (*English*)
T(homas) S(tearns) Eliot (*U.S.-British*)
Louis Esson (*Australian*)
Euripides (*Greek*)
John Fletcher (*English*)
Dario Fo (*Italian*)
John Ford (*English*)
Brian Friel (*Irish*)
John Galsworthy (*English*)
Jean Genet (*French*)
W(illiam) S(chwenk) Gilbert (*English*)
(Hippolyte) Jean Giraudoux (*French*)
Johann Wolfgang von Goethe (*German*)
Nikolai Gogol (*Russian*)
Oliver Goldsmith (*Irish*)
Oriel Gray (*Australian*)
Robert Greene (*English*)

David Hare (*English*)
Gerhart Johann Robert Hauptmann
  (*German*)
Václav Havel (*Czech*)
Alfred Hayes (*U.S.*)
(Christian) Friedrich Hebbel (*German*)
Dorthy Hewett (*Australian*)
Thomas Heywood (*English*)
Jack Hibberd (*Australian*)
Sidney Howard (*U.S.*)
Henrik Ibsen (*Norwegian*)
William Motter Inge (*U.S.*)
Eugène Ionesco (*Romanian-French*)
Ben Jonson (*English*)
George Kaiser (*German*)
Tony Kushner (*U.S.*)
Thomas Kyd (*English*)
Ray Lawler (*Australian*)
Liz Lochhead (*Scottish*)
Lope de Vega (*Spanish*)
Federico Garcia Lorca (*Spanish*)
Maurice Maeterlinck (*Belgian*)
David Mamet (*U.S.*)
Christopher Marlowe (*English*)
John Marston (*English*)
Menander (*Greek*)
Arthur Miller (*U.S.*)
Molière (*French*)
Barry Oakley (*Australian*)
Sean O'Casey (*Irish*)
Eugene (Gladstone) O'Neill (*U.S.*)
Joe Orton (*English*)
John Osborne (*English*)
Thomas Otway (*English*)
John Patrick (*U.S.*)
Arthur Wing Pinero (*English*)
Harold Pinter (*English*)
Luigi Pirandello (*Italian*)
Titus Maccius Plautus (*Roman*)
Hal Porter (*Australian*)

Dramatists (continued)

Aleksander Sergeyevich Pushkin (*Russian*)
Jean Baptiste Racine (*French*)
Terence Mervyn Rattigan (*English*)
John Romeril (*Australian*)
Willy Russell (*English*)
Thomas Sackville (*English*)
Jean-Paul Sartre (*French*)
Johann Christoph Friedrich von Schiller
   (*German*)
Lucius Annaeus Seneca (*Roman*)
Alan Seymour (*Australian*)
Peter Shaffer (*English*)
William Shakespeare (*English*)
George Bernard Shaw (*Irish*)

Sam Shepard (*U.S.*)
Richard Brinsley Sheridan (*Irish*)
Robert Sherwood (*U.S.*)
Sophocles (*Greek*)
Wole Soyinka (*Nigerian*)
Tom Stoppard (*Czech-English*)
August Strindberg (*Swedish*)
John Millington Synge (*Irish*)
John Webster (*English*)
Oscar Wilde (*Irish*)
Thornton Wilder (*U.S.*)
Tennessee Williams (*U.S.*)
David Keith Williamson (*Australian*)
William Wycherly (*English*)

EUROPEAN UNION

EU *member states*

1958 Belgium	1958 The Netherlands	1986 Portugal
1958 France	1973 Denmark	1986 Spain
1958 Germany	1973 Republic of Ireland	1995 Finland
1958 Italy	1973 United Kingdom	1995 Sweden
1958 Luxembourg	1981 Greece	1995 Austria

EU *applications under consideration*

Cyprus	Hungary	Switzerland
Estonia	Poland	Czech Republic

INHABITANTS

WORD POWER

Place	Inhabitant	Place	Inhabitant
Aberdeen	Aberdonian	Bolivia	Bolivian
Afghanistan	Afghan	Bordeaux	Bordelais
Alabama	Alabaman *or* Alabamian	the Borders	Borderer
		Bosnia	Bosnian
Alaska	Alaskan	Boston	Bostonian *or (U.S. slang)* Bean-eater
Albania	Albanian		
Alberta	Albertan	Botswana	Botswanan
Algeria	Algerian	Brazil	Brazilian
Alsace	Alsatian	Bristol	Bristolian
American continent	American	Brittany	Breton
American Samoa	American Samoan	British Columbia	British Columbian
Amsterdam	Amsterdammer	Bulgaria	Bulgarian
Anatolia	Anatolian	Burgundy	Burgundian
Andorra	Andorran	Burkina-Faso	Burkinabe
Angola	Angolan	Burma	Burmese
Anjou	Angevin	Burundi	Burundian
Antigua	Antiguan	Byzantium	Byzantine
Argentina	Argentine *or* Argentinian	California	Californian
		Cambridge	Cantabrigian
Arizona	Arizonan	Cambodia	Cambodian
Arkansas	Arkansan *or (informal)* Arkie	Cameroon	Cameroonian
		Canada	Canadian *or (informal)* Canuck
Armenia	Armenian		
Asia	Asian	Canada, Maritime Provinces	Downeaster
Assam	Assamese		
Assyria	Assyrian	Cape Verde	Cape Verdean
Australia	Australian *or (informal)* Aussie	Castile	Castilian
		Catalonia	Catalan
Austria	Austrian	the Caucasus	Caucasian
Azerbaijan	Azerbaijani *or* Azeri	Cayman Islands	Cayman Islander
		Chad	Chadian *or* Chadean
Babylon	Babylonian		
Bahamas	Bahamian	Chicago	Chicagoan
Bahrain	Bahraini	Chile	Chilean
Bangladesh	Bangladeshi	China	Chinese
Bali	Balinese	Circassia	Circassian
Barbados	Barbadian, Bajan *(informal), or* Bim *(informal)*	Colombia	Colombian
		Colorado	Coloradan
		Connecticut	Nutmegger
Barbuda	Barbudan *or* Barbudian	Cork	Corkonian
		Comoros Islands	Comorian
Bavaria	Bavarian	Congo Republic	Congolese
Belarus *or* Byelorussia	Belarussian *or* Byelorussian	Cornwall	Cornishman, Cornishwoman
Belau	Belauan	Corsica	Corsican
Belgium	Belgian	Costa Rica	Costa Rican
Benin	Beninese *or* Beninois	Côte d'Ivoire	Ivorian *or* Ivorean
		Croatia	Croat *or* Croatian
Berlin	Berliner	Cuba	Cuban
Bhutan	Bhutanese	Cumbria	Cumbrian
Birmingham	Brummie	Cyprus	Cypriot
Bohemia	Bohemian	Czech Republic	Czech

Place	Inhabitant	Place	Inhabitant
Czechoslovakia	Czechoslovak *or* Czechoslovakian	Gascony	Gascon
		Genoa	Genoese
Delaware	Delawarean	Georgia (country)	Georgian
Denmark	Dane	Georgia (U.S. state)	Georgian
Delphi	Pythian	Germany	German
Devon	Devonian	Ghana	Ghanaian *or* Ghanian
Djibouti	Djiboutian *or* Djiboutien	Glasgow	Glaswegian
Dominica	Dominican	Greece	Greek
Dominican Republic	Dominican	Greenland	Greenlander
Dublin	Dubliner	Grenada	Grenadian
Dundee	Dundonian	Guam	Guamanian
East Timor	East Timorese	Guatemala	Guatemalan
Ecuador	Ecuadorean *or* Ecuadoran	Guinea	Guinean
		Guyana	Guyanese *or* Guyanan
Edinburgh	Edinburgher		
Egypt	Egyptian	Haiti	Haitian
El Salvador	Salvadoran, Salvadorean, *or* Salvadorian	Hawaii	Hawaiian
		Havana	Habanero
		Hesse	Hessian
England	Englishman, Englishwoman	Hungary	Hungarian *or* Magyar
Ephesus	Ephesian	Honduras	Honduran
Estonia	Estonian	Hyderabad state	Mulki
Eritrea	Eritrean	Ibiza	Ibizan
Ethiopia	Ethiopian	Iceland	Icelander
Equatorial Guinea	Equatorian	Idaho	Idahoan
Eritrea	Eritrean	Illinois	Illinoian *or* Illinoisian
Estonia	Estonian		
Ethiopia	Ethiopian	India	Indian
Europe	European	Indiana	Indianan, Indianian, *or* (*informal*) Hoosier
Euzkadi	Basque		
Faeroe Islands	Faeroese		
Falkland Islands	Falkland Islanders *or* Falklander	Indonesia	Indonesian
		Iowa	Iowan
Fife	Fifer	Iran	Iranian
Fiji	Fijian	Iraq	Iraqi
Finland	Finn	Ireland	Irishman, Irishwoman
Flanders	Fleming		
Florence	Florentine	Israel	Israeli
Florida	Floridian	Italy	Italian
France	Frenchman, Frenchwoman	Jamaica	Jamaican
		Japan	Japanese
French Guiana	Guianese	Java	Javanese
Friesland	Frisian	Jordan	Jordanian
Friuili	Friulian	Kansas	Kansan
Gabon	Gabonese	Karelia	Karelian
Galicia	Galician	Kazakhstan	Kazakh
Galilee	Galilean	Kent (East)	Man, Woman of Kent
Galloway	Gallovidian		
Galway	Galwegian	Kent (West)	Kentish Man, Woman
Gambia	Gambian		

31

Place	Inhabitant	Place	Inhabitant
Kentucky	Kentuckian	Mauritania	Mauritanian
Kenya	Kenyan	Mauritius	Mauritian
Kirghizia	Kirghiz	Melanesia	Melanesian
Korea	Korean	Melbourne	Melburnian
Kuwait	Kuwaiti	Mexico	Mexican
Lancashire	Lancastrian	Michigan	Michigander,
Lancaster	Lancastrian		Michiganite, *or*
Laos	Laotian		Michiganian
Latvia	Latvian *or* Lett	Micronesia	Micronesian
Lebanon	Lebanese	Milan	Milanese
Liberia	Liberian	Minnesota	Minnesotan
Libya	Libyan	Mississippi	Mississippian
Liechtenstein	Liechtensteiner	Missouri	Missourian
Lincolnshire	yellow belly	Moldavia	Moldavian
	(*dialect*)	Monaco	Monegasque
Lithuania	Lithuanian	Mongolia	Mongolian
Liverpool	Liverpudlian *or*	Montana	Montanan
	(*informal*) Scouse	Montenegro	Montenegrin
	or Scouser	Montserrat	Montserratian
Lombardy	Lombard	Moravia	Moravian
London	Londoner *or*	Morocco	Moroccan
	Cockney	Moscow	Muscovite
Los Angeles	Angeleno	Mozambique	Mozambican
Louisiana	Louisianan *or*	Namibia	Namibian
	Louisianian	Nauru	Nauruan
Luxembourg	Luxembourger	Naples	Neapolitan
Lyon	Lyonnais	Nebraska	Nebraskan
Macao	Macaonese	the Netherlands	Dutchman,
Macedonia	Macedonian		Dutchwoman
Madagascar	Madagascan *or*	New Brunswick	New Brunswicker
	Malagasy	Newcastle upon Tyne	Geordie
Madrid	Madrileño,	New England	New Englander *or*
	Madrileña		(*informal*) Yankee
Maine	Mainer *or*		*or* Downeaster
	Downeaster	Newfoundland	Newfoundlander
Majorca	Majorcan		*or* (*informal*)
Malawi	Malawian		Newfie
Malaya	Malayan	Newfoundland fishing	Outporter
Malaysia	Malaysian	village	
Maldive Islands	Maldivian	New Hampshire	New Hampshirite
Malta	Maltese	New Jersey	New Jerseyan *or*
Man, Isle of	Manxman,		New Jerseyite
	Manxwoman	New Mexico	New Mexican
Manchester	Mancunian	New South Wales	New South
Manitoba	Manitoban		Welshman, New
Marquesas Islands	Marquesan		South
Mars	Martian		Welshwoman
Marseilles	Marsellais	New York	New Yorker *or*
Marshall Islands	Marshall Islander		Knickerbocker
Martinique	Martiniquean	New Zealand	New Zealander *or*
Maryland	Marylander		(*informal*) Kiwi *or*
Massachusetts	Bay Stater		Enzedder

Place	Inhabitant	Place	Inhabitant
Nicaragua	Nicaraguan	Queensland	Queenslander
Niger	Nigerien	Rhode Island	Rhode Islander
Nigeria	Nigerian	Rhodes	Rhodian
Normandy	Norman	Rhodesia	Rhodesian
North Carolina	North Carolinian or Tarheel	Rio de Janeiro	Cariocan
		Romania	Romanian
North Dakota	North Dakotan	Rome	Roman
Northern Ireland	Northern Irishman, Northern Irishwoman	Russian Federation	Russian
		Ruthenia	Ruthenian
		Rwanda	Rwandan
		Samaria	Samaritan
Northern Territory	Territorian	San Marino	San Marinese or Sammarinese
Northern Territory, northern part of	Top Ender		
		Sardinia	Sardinian
North Korea	North Korean	Saskatchewan	Saskatchewanian
Northumbria	Northumbrian	Saxony	Saxon
Norway	Norwegian	Saudi Arabia	Saudi or Saudi Arabian
Nova Scotia	Nova Scotian or (informal) Bluenose	Savoy	Savoyard
Ohio	Ohioan	Scandinavia	Scandinavian
Okinawa	Okinawan	Scotland	Scot, Scotsman, Scotswoman, or Caledonian
Oklahoma	Oklahoman or (slang) Okie		
Oman	Omani	Scottish Highlands	Highlander or (old-fashioned) Hielanman
Ontario	Ontarian or Ontarioan		
Oregon	Oregonian	Senegal	Senegalese
Orkney	Orcadian	Serbia	Serb or Serbian
Oxford	Oxonian	Seychelles	Seychellois
Pakistan	Pakistani	Shetland	Shetlander
Palestine	Palestinian	Sierra Leone	Sierra Leonean
Panama	Panamanian	Sind	Sindhi
Papua New Guinea	Papua	Singapore	Singaporean
Paraguay	Paraguayan	Slovakia	Slovak
Paris	Parisian or Parisienne	Slovenia	Slovene or Slovenian
		Solomon Islands	Solomon Islander
Pennsylvania	Pennsylvanian	South Africa	South African
Persia	Persian	South Australia	South Australian or (informal) Croweater
Perth	Perthite		
Peru	Peruvian		
the Philippines	Filipino	South Carolina	South Carolinian
Poland	Pole	South Dakota	South Dakota
Pomerania	Pomeranian	South Korea	South Korean
Portugal	Portuguese	Spain	Spaniard
Prince Edward Island	Prince Edward Islander	Sri Lanka	Sri Lankan
		Sudan	Sudanese
Provence	Provençal	Suriname	Surinamese
Prussia	Prussian	Swaziland	Swazi
Puerto Rico	Puerto Rican	Switzerland	Swiss
Qatar	Qatari	Sweden	Swede
Quebec	Quebecer, Quebecker, or Quebecois	Sydney	Sydneysider
		Sydney, Western suburbs of	Westie (informal)

WORD POWER

WORD POWER

Place	Inhabitant	Place	Inhabitant
Syria	Syrian	Uruguay	Uruguayan
Taiwan	Taiwanese	Utah	Utahan *or* Utahn
Tajikistan	Tajik	Uzbekistan	Uzbek
Tanzania	Tanzanian	Venezuela	Venezuelan
Tasmania	Tasmanian *or* (*informal*) Tassie *or* Apple Islander	Venice	Venetian
		Vermont	Vermonter
		Victoria	Victorian
Tennessee	Tennessean	Vienna	Viennese
Texas	Texan	Vietnam	Vietnamese
Thailand	Thai	Virginia	Virginian
Thessalonika	Thessalonian	Wales	Welshman, Welshwoman
Tibet	Tibetan		
Togo	Togolese	Washington	Washingtonian
Tonga	Tongan	Wearside	Mackem
Trinidad	Trinidadian	Wessex	West Saxon
Tobago	Tobagan *or* Tobagonian	Western Australia	Western Australian, Westralian, *or* (*informal*) Sandgroper
Troy	Trojan		
Tuscany	Tuscan		
Tunisia	Tunisian		
Turkey	Turk	Western Sahara	Sahwari
Turkmenistan	Turkmen	West Virginia	West Virginian
Tuvalu	Tuvaluan	Winnipeg	Winnipegger
Tyneside	Geordie	Wisconsin	Wisconsinite
Tyre	Tyrian	Wyoming	Wyomingite
Uganda	Ugandan	Yemen	Yemeni
Ukraine	Ukrainian	Yorkshire	Yorkshireman, Yorkshirewoman
Ulster	Ulsterman, Ulsterwoman		
		the Yukon	Yukoner
Umbria	Umbrian	Zaire	Zairean
United Kingdom	Briton, Brit (*informal*), *or* Britisher	Zambia	Zambian
		Zanzibar	Zanzibari
		Zimbabwe	Zimbabwean
United States of America	American *or* (*informal*) Yank *or* Yankee		

Achill
Admiralty
Aegean
Aegina
Alcatraz
Aldabra
Alderney
Aleutian
Alexander
Amboina
Andaman
Andaman and Nicobar
Andreanof
Andros
Anglesey
Anguilla
Anticosti
Antigua
Antilles
Antipodes
Aran
Arran
Aru or Arru
Aruba
Ascension
Auckland
Azores
Baffin
Bahamas
Balearic
Bali
Banaba
Bangka
Banks
Baranof
Barbados
Barbuda
Bardsey
Barra
Basilan
Basse-Terre
Batan
Belau
Belle
Benbecula
Bermuda
Biak
Billiton
Bioko
Bohol
Bonaire
Bonin
Bora Bora
Borneo

Bornholm
Bougainville
British
Bute
Butung
Caicos
Caldy
Calf of Man
Campobello
Canary
Canna
Canvey
Cape Breton
Capri
Caroline
Cayman
Cebú
Ceylon
Channel
Chatham
Cheju
Chichagof
Chiloé
Chios
Choiseul
Christmas
Cocos
Coll
Colonsay
Coney
Cook
Corfu
Corregidor
Corsica
Crete
Cuba
Curaçao
Cyclades
Cyprus
Cythera
Delos
D'Entrecasteaux
Diomede
Disko
Diu
Djerba or Jerba
Dodecanese
Dominica
Dry Tortugas
Easter
Eigg
Elba
Ellesmere
Espíritu Santo

Euboea
Faeroes
Faial or Fayal
Fair
Falkland
Falster
Farquhar
Fernando de Noronha
Fiji
Flannan
Flinders
Flores
Florida Keys
Foula
Foulness
Franz Josef Land
French West Indies
Frisian
Fyn
Galápagos
Gambier
Gigha
Gilbert
Gotland, Gothland, or
  Gottland
Grand Bahama
Grand Canary
Grande-Terre
Grand Manan
Greater Antilles
Greater Sunda
Greenland
Grenada
Grenadines
Guadalcanal
Guam
Guernsey
Hainan or Hainan Tao
Handa
Hawaii
Hayling
Heard and McDonald
Hebrides
Heimaey
Heligoland
Herm
Hispaniola
Hokkaido
Holy
Hong Kong
Honshu
Hormuz or Ormuz
Howland
Ibiza

WORD POWER

WORD POWER

Icaria	Lundy	New Caledonia
Iceland	Luzon	Newfoundland
Imbros	Mackinac	New Georgia
Iona	Macquarie	New Guinea
Ionian	Madagascar	New Ireland
Ireland	Madeira	New Providence
Ischia	Madura	New Siberian
Islay	Maewo	Nicobar
Isle Royale	Mahé	Niue
Ithaca	Mainland	Norfolk
Iwo Jima	Majorca	North
Jamaica	Maldives	North Uist
Jan Mayen	Malé	Nusa Tenggara
Java	Malta	Oahu
Jersey	Man	Oceania
Jolo	Manhattan	Okinawa
Juan Fernández	Manitoulin	Orkneys or Orkney
Jura	Marajó	Palawan
Kangaroo	Margarita	Palmyra
Kauai	Marie Galante	Panay
Keos	Marinduque	Pantelleria
Kerrera	Marquesas	Páros
Kiritimati	Marshall	Patmos
Kodiak	Martinique	Pelagian
Kos or Cos	Masbate	Pemba
Kosrae	Mascarene	Penang
Krakatoa or Krakatau	Matsu or Mazu	Pescadores
Kuril or Kurile	Maui	Philae
Kyushu or Kiushu	Mauritius	Philippines
La Palma	May	Phoenix
Labuan	Mayotte	Pitcairn
Lakshadweep	Melanesia	Polynesia
Lampedusa	Melos	Ponape
Lanai	Melville	Pribilof
Lavongai	Mersea	Prince Edward
Leeward	Micronesia	Prince of Wales
Lemnos	Mindanao	Principe
Lesbos	Mindoro	Qeshm or Qishm
Lesser Antilles	Minorca	Queen Charlotte
Levkás, Leukas, or Leucas	Miquelon	Queen Elizabeth
Lewis with Harris or Lewis and Harris	Molokai	Quemoy
	Moluccas	Raasay
Leyte	Montserrat	Ramsey
Liberty	Mount Desert	Rarotonga
Lindisfarne	Muck	Rathlin
Line	Mull	Réunion
Lipari	Mykonos	Rhodes
Lismore	Nantucket	Rhum
Lolland or Laaland	Nauru	Rialto
Lombok	Naxos	Roanoke
Long	Negros	Robben
Longa	Netherlands Antilles	Rockall
Lord Howe	Nevis	Rona
Luing	New Britain	Ross

Ryukyu
Saba
Safety
Saipan
Sakhalin
Salamis
Saltee
Samar
Samoa
Samos
Samothrace
San Cristóbal
San Juan
San Salvador
Santa Catalina
Sao Miguel
Sao Tomé
Sardinia
Sark
Savaii
Scalpay
Schouten
Scilly
Sea
Seil
Seram *or* Ceram
Seychelles
Sheppey
Shetland
Sicily
Singapore
Sjælland
Skikoku
Skokholm
Skomer
Skye
Skyros *or* Scyros
Society
Socotra
South
Southampton

South Georgia
South Orkney
South Shetland
South Uist
Spitsbergen
Sporades
Sri Lanka
St. Croix
St. Helena
St. John
St. Kilda
St. Kitts *or* St. Christopher
St. Lucia
St. Martin
St. Tudwal's
St. Vincent
Staffa
Staten
Stewart
Stroma
Stromboli
Sulawesi
Sumatra
Sumba *or* Soemba
Sumbawa *or* Soembawa
Summer
Sunda *or* Soenda
Tahiti
Taiwan
Tasmania
Tenedos
Tenerife
Terceira
Thanet
Thásos
Thera
Thousand
Thursday
Timor
Tiree
Tobago

Tokelau
Tombo
Tonga
Tortola
Tortuga
Trinidad
Tristan da Cunha
Trobriand
Truk
Tsushima
Tuamotu
Tubuai
Turks
Tutuila
Tuvalu
Ulva
Unimak
Upolu
Ushant
Vancouver
Vanua Levu
Vanuatu
Vestmannaeyjar
Victoria
Virgin
Visayan
Viti Levu
Volcano
Walcheren
Walney
West Indies
Western
Wight
Windward
Wrangel
Yap
Youth
Zante
Zanzibar

WORD POWER

WORD POWER

Allen
Annecy
Aral Sea *or* Lake Aral
Ard
Athabaska
Averno
Awe
Baikal
Bala
Balaton
Balkhash
Bangweulu
Bassenthwaite
Belfast
Biel
Bodensee
Buttermere
Caspian Sea
Chad
Champlain
Como
Coniston Water
Constance
Crummock Water
Dead Sea
Derwentwater
Dongting
Earn
Edward
Ennerdale Water
Erie
Erne
Eyre
Frome
Fyne
Garda
Gatún
Geneva
Grasmere
Great Bear
Great Bitter
Great Lakes
Great Salt
Great Slave
Hawes Water
Huron
Ijsselmeer *or* Ysselmeer
Iliamna

Ilmen
Issyk-Kul
Kariba
Katrine
Kivu
Koko Nor *or* Kuku Nor
Kootenay
Ladoga
Laggan
Lake of the Woods
Leven
Linnhe
Little Bitter
Lochy
Lomond
Lucerne
Lugano
Léman
Maggiore
Malawi
Managua
Manitoba
Maracaibo
Mead
Meech
Memphremagog
Menteith
Michigan
Miraflores
Mistassini
Mobutu
Morar
Mweru
Nam Co *or* Nam Tso
Nasser
Neagh
Ness
Neuchâtel
Nicaragua
Nipigon
Nipissing
No
Nyasa
Okanagan
Okeechobee
Onega
Oneida
Onondaga

Ontario
Patos
Peipus
Pontchartrain
Poopó
Poyang *or* P'o-yang
Pskov
Rannoch
Reindeer
Rudolf
Saint Clair
Saint John
Sea of Galilee
Sevan
Stanley Pool
Superior
Sween
Taal
Tahoe
Tana
Tanganyika
Taupo
Tay
Thirlmere
Thun
Tien
Titicaca
Tonle Sap
Torrens
Torridon
Trasimene
Tummel
Turkana
Ullswater
Urmia
Van
Victoria
Volta
Waikaremoana
Washington
Wast Water
Windermere
Winnebago
Winnipeg
Zug
Zürich

Aconcagua
Adams
Albert Edward
Anai Mudi
Aneto
Annapurna
Apo
Aragats
Aran Fawddwy
Ararat
Arber
Argentera
Belukha
Ben Lomond
Ben Macdhui
Ben Nevis
Blackburn
Blanca Peak
Blue Mountain Peak
Bona
Brocken
Carmarthen Van
Carmel
Cerro de Mulhacén
Citlaltépetl
Clingman's Dome
Cook
Corcovado
Corno
Croagh Patrick
Demavend
Dhaulagiri
Eiger
Elbert
Elbrus
El Capitan
Emi Koussi
Estrella
Everest
Finsteraarhorn
Fuji
Gannet Peak
Gerlachovka
Grand Teton
Gran Paradiso
Harney Peak
Helicon
Helvellyn
Hermon

Humphreys Peak
Hymettus
Ida
Illimani
Isto
Jebel Musa
Jungfrau
K2 *or* Godwin Austen
Kamet
Kangchenjunga
Kenya
Kilimanjaro
Kinabalu
Kings Peak
Klínovec
Kommunizma Peak
Kongur Shan
Kosciusko
Lenin Peak
Leone
Logan
Longs Peak
Mansfield
Marcy
Markham
Marmolada
Masharbrum
Matterhorn
McKinley
Mitchell
Mont Blanc
Mount of Olives
Mulhacén
Munku-Sardyk
Musala
Nanda Devi
Nanga Parbat
Narodnaya
Nebo
Negoiu
Olympus
Ossa
Palomar
Parnassus
Pelion
Pentelikon
Perdido
Petermann Peak
Pikes Peak

Pilatus
Piz Bernina
Pobeda Peak
Puy de Dôme
Rainier
Rigi
Robson
Rock Creek
Rosa
Rushmore
Scafell Pike
Schneekoppe
Scopus
Sinai
Siple
Sir Sandford
Sir Wilfrid Laurier
Skalitsy
Slide Mountain
Smólikas
Snowdon
Sorata
Stanley
Sugar Loaf Mountain
Table Mountain
Tabor
Teide
Tengri Khan
Thabana Ntlenyana
Timpanogos
Tirich Mir
Toubkal
Troglav
Ulugh Muztagh
Uncompahgre Peak
Venusberg
Victoria
Viso
Waddington
Washington
Waun Fach
Weisshorn
White Mountain
Whitney
Wrangell
Zard Kuh
Zugspitze

WORD POWER

NEW ZEALAND TERRITORIES

Cook Islands   the Ross Dependency
Niue   Tokelau *or* Union Islands

Peter Abrahams (*South African*)
Chinua Achebe (*Nigerian*)
Peter Ackroyd (*English*)
Douglas Adams (*English*)
Richard Adams (*English*)
Alain-Fournier (*French*)
Brian Aldiss (*English*)
James Aldridge (*Australian*)
Al Alvarez (*English*)
Eric Ambler (*English*)
Kingsley Amis (*English*)
Martin Amis (*English*)
Mulk Raj Anand (*Indian*)
Maya Angelou (*U.S.*)
Lucius Apuleius (*Roman*)
Jeffrey Archer (*English*)
Isaac Asimov (*U.S.*)
Margaret Atwood (*Canadian*)
Louis Auchincloss (*U.S.*)
Jane Austen (*English*)
Beryl Bainbridge (*English*)
R M Ballantyne (*Scottish*)
J G Ballard (*English*)
Honoré de Balzac (*French*)
Iain Banks (*Scottish*)
Lynne Reid Banks (*English*)
Elspeth Barker (*Scottish*)
Pat Barker (*English*)
Julian Barnes (*English*)
Stanley Barstow (*English*)
John Barth (*U.S.*)
H E Bates (*English*)
Nina Bawden (*English*)
Simone de Beauvoir (*French*)
Sybille Bedford (*British*)
Max Beerbohm (*English*)
Aphra Behn (*English*)
Saul Bellow (*Canadian*)
Andrei Bely (*Russian*)
David Benedictus (*English*)
(Enoch) Arnold Bennett (*English*)
John Berger (*English*)
Thomas Berger (*U.S.*)
Maeve Binchy (*Irish*)
R(ichard) D(oddridge) Blackmore (*English*)
Alan Bleasdale (*English*)
Heinrich Böll (*German*)
Elizabeth Bowen (*Irish*)
Paul Bowles (*U.S.*)

William Boyd (*Scottish*)
Malcolm Bradbury (*English*)
Barbara Taylor Bradford (*English*)
Melvin Bragg (*English*)
John Braine (*English*)
André Brink (*South African*)
Vera Brittain (*English*)
Louis Bromfield (*U.S.*)
Anne Brontë (*English*)
Charlotte Brontë (*English*)
Emily (Jane) Brontë (*English*)
Christina Brooke-Rose (*English*)
Anita Brookner (*English*)
Brigid Brophy (*English*)
George Douglas Brown (*Scottish*)
George Mackay Brown (*Scottish*)
John Buchan (*Scottish*)
Pearl Buck (*U.S.*)
Mikhail Afanaseyev Bulgakov (*Russian*)
John Bunyan (*English*)
Anthony Burgess (*British*)
Fanny Burney (*English*)
Edgar Rice Burrows (*U.S.*)
William Burroughs (*U.S.*)
Samuel Butler (*English*)
A S Byatt (*English*)
Italo Calvino (*Italian*)
Albert Camus (*French*)
Elias Canetti (*Bulgarian*)
Truman Capote (*U.S.*)
Peter Carey (*Australian*)
Angela Carter (*English*)
Barbara Cartland (*English*)
Willa Cather (*U.S.*)
Camilo José Cela (*Spanish*)
Miguel de Cervantes (*Spanish*)
Raymond Chandler (*U.S.*)
G K Chesterton (*English*)
Agatha (Mary Clarissa) Christie (*English*)
Arthur C Clarke (*English*)
James Clavell (*U.S.*)
Jon Cleary (*Australian*)
J M Coatzee (*South African*)
Colette (*French*)
(William) Wilkie Collins (*English*)

Ivy Compton-Burnett (*English*)
Richard Condon (*U.S.*)
Evan Connell (*U.S.*)
Joseph Conrad (*Polish-British*)
Catherine Cookson (*English*)
James Fenimore Cooper (*U.S.*)
Jilly Cooper (*English*)
William Cooper (*English*)
Maria Correlli (*English*)
Stephen Crane (*U.S.*)
Lionel Davidson (*English*)
(William) Robertson Davies (*Canadian*)
Daniel Defoe (*English*)
Len Deighton (*English*)
E M Delafield (*English*)
Don DeLillo (*U.S.*)
Thomas de Quincy (*English*)
Anita Desai (*Indian*)
Peter De Vries (*U.S.*)
Charles (John Huffam) Dickens (*English*)
Monica Dickens (*English*)
Joan Didion (*U.S.*)
Isak Dinesen (*Danish*)
Benjamin Disraeli (*English*)
J P Donleavy (*Irish*)
John Roderigo Dos Passos (*U.S.*)
Fyodor Mikhailovich Dostoevsky (*Russian*)
Arthur Conan Doyle (*Scottish*)
Roddy Doyle (*Irish*)
Margaret Drabble (*English*)
Maureen Duffy (*English*)
Alexandre Dumas (*French*)
Daphne Du Maurier (*English*)
Nell Dunn (*English*)
Gerald Durrell (*English*)
Laurence Durrell (*English*)
Umberto Eco (*Italian*)
Maria Edgeworth (*English*)
George Eliot (*English*)
Stanley Elkin (*U.S.*)
Alice Thomas Ellis (*English*)
Ben Elton (*English*)
Zöe Fairbairns (*English*)

Philip José Farmer (*U.S.*)
Howard Fast (*U.S.*)
William Faulkner (*U.S.*)
Elaine Feinstein (*English*)
Helen Fielding (*English*)
Henry Fielding (*English*)
Eva Figes (*British*)
F(rancis) Scott (Key) Fitzgerald (*U.S.*)
Penelope Fitzgerald (*English*)
Gustave Flaubert (*French*)
Ian Fleming (*English*)
Ford Madox Ford (*English*)
Richard Ford (*U.S.*)
C S Forester (*English*)
E M Forster (*English*)
Frederick Forsyth (*English*)
John Fowles (*English*)
Janet Paterson Frame (*New Zealand*)
Dick Francis (*English*)
Antonia Fraser (*English*)
Michael Frayn (*English*)
Nicholas Freeling (*English*)
Marilyn French (*U.S.*)
Roy Fuller (*English*)
William Gaddis (*U.S.*)
Janice Galloway (*Scottish*)
John Galsworthy (*English*)
Gabriel García Márquez (*Colombian*)
Helen Garner (*Australian*)
Elizabeth Gaskell (*English*)
William Alexander Gerhardie (*English*)
Lewis Grassic Gibbon (*Scottish*)
Stella Gibbons (*English*)
André Gide (*French*)
Penelope Gilliat (*English*)
George Gissing (*English*)
Ellen Glasgow (*U.S.*)
(Margaret) Rumer Godden (*English*)
William Godwin (*English*)
Johann Wolfgang von Goethe (*German*)
Nikolai Vasilievich Gogol (*Russian*)
Herbert Gold (*U.S.*)
William (Gerald) Golding (*English*)
William Goldman (*U.S.*)

Oliver Goldsmith (*Anglo-Irish*)
Ivan Aleksandrovich Goncharov (*Russian*)
Nadine Gordimer (*South African*)
Maxim Gorky (*Russian*)
Edmund Gosse (*English*)
Winston Graham (*English*)
Günter (Wilhelm) Grass (*German*)
Robert Graves (*English*)
Alasdair Gray (*Scottish*)
Graham Greene (*English*)
John Grisham (*U.S.*)
George Grossmith (*English*)
Weedon Grossmith (*English*)
David Guterson (*U.S.*)
Rider Haggard (*English*)
Arthur Hailey (*Anglo-Canadian*)
Thomas Hardy (*English*)
L(eslie) P(oles) Hartley (*English*)
Nathaniel Hawthorne (*U.S.*)
Shirley Hazzard (*U.S.*)
Robert A Heinlein (*U.S.*)
Joseph Heller (*U.S.*)
Ernest Hemingway (*U.S.*)
Hermann Hesse (*German*)
Georgette Heyer (*English*)
Patricia Highsmith (*U.S.*)
Susan Hill (*English*)
James Hilton (*English*)
Barry Hines (*English*)
Russell Hoban (*U.S.*)
James Hogg (*Scottish*)
Winifred Holtby (*English*)
Anthony Hope (*English*)
Paul Horgan (*U.S.*)
Elizabeth Jane Howard (*English*)
Thomas Hughes (*English*)
Victor (Marie) Hugo (*French*)
Keri Hulme (*New Zealand*)
Evan Hunter (*U.S.*)
Zora Neale Hurston (*U.S.*)
Aldous Huxley (*English*)
Hammond Innes (*English*)
John Irving (*U.S.*)
Christopher Isherwood (*English-U.S.*)

Kazuo Ishiguro (*British*)
Henry James (*U.S.-British*)
P D James (*English*)
Ruth Prawer Jhabvala (*Anglo-Polish*)
Erica Jong (*U.S.*)
James Joyce (*Irish*)
Franz Kafka (*Czech*)
Johanna Kaplan (*U.S.*)
Nikos Kazantazakis (*Greek*)
Molly Keane (*Anglo-Irish*)
James Kelman (*Scottish*)
Thomas Keneally (*Australian*)
Margaret Kennedy (*English*)
Jack Kerouac (*U.S.*)
Ken Kesey (*U.S.*)
Francis King (*English*)
Stephen King (*U.S.*)
Charles Kingsley (*English*)
Rudyard Kipling (*English*)
Milan Kundera (*French-Czech*)
Pierre Choderlos de Laclos (*French*)
George Lamming (*Barbadian*)
Guiseppe Tomasi di Lampedusa (*Italian*)
D H Lawrence (*English*)
John Le Carré (*English*)
Harper Lee (*U.S.*)
Laurie Lee (*English*)
Sheridan Le Fanu (*Irish*)
Ursula Le Guin (*U.S.*)
Rosamond Lehmann (*English*)
Mikhail Yurievich Lermontov (*Russian*)
Doris Lessing (*Rhodesian*)
Primo Levi (*Italian*)
(Harry) Sinclair Lewis (*U.S.*)
Penelope Lively (*English*)
David Lodge (*English*)
Jack London (*U.S.*)
(Clarence) Malcolm Lowry (*English*)
Alison Lurie (*U.S.*)
Rose Macauley (*English*)
Carson McCullers (*U.S.*)
George MacDonald (*Scottish*)
Ian McEwan (*English*)

William McIlvanney (*Scottish*)

Colin MacInnes (*English*)

Compton MacKenzie (*English*)

Henry MacKenzie (*Scottish*)

Bernard McLaverty (*Irish*)

Alistair MacLean (*Scottish*)

Naguib Mahfouz (*Egyptian*)

Norman Mailer (*U.S.*)

Bernard Malamud (*U.S.*)

David Malouf (*Australian*)

(Cyril) Wolf Mankowitz (*English*)

Thomas Mann (*German*)

Olivia Manning (*English*)

Kamala Markandaya (*Indian*)

Frederick Marryat (*English*)

Ngaio Marsh (*New Zealand*)

Allan Massie (*Scottish*)

Somerset Maugham (*English*)

Guy de Maupassant (*French*)

Francois Mauriac (*French*)

Herman Melville (*U.S.*)

George Meredith (*English*)

James A Michener (*U.S.*)

Henry Miller (*U.S.*)

Yukio Mishima (*Japanese*)

Julian Mitchell (*English*)

Margaret Mitchell (*U.S.*)

Naomi Mitchison (*Scottish*)

Nancy Mitford (*English*)

Timothy Mo (*British*)

Nicholas Monsarrat (*English*)

Michael Moorcock (*English*)

Brian Moore (*Irish-Canadian*)

Toni Morrison (*U.S.*)

John Mortimer (*English*)

Penelope Mortimer (*Welsh*)

Nicholas Mosley (*English*)

Iris Murdoch (*Irish*)

Vladimir Vladimirovich Nabokov (*Russian-U.S.*)

V S Naipaul (*Trinidadian*)

P H Newby (*English*)

Ngugi wa Thiong'o (*Kenyan*)

Robert Nye (*English*)

Joyce Carol Oates (*U.S.*)

Edna O'Brien (*Irish*)

Kenzaburo Oë (*Japanese*)

Liam O'Flaherty (*Irish*)

John O'Hara (*U.S.*)

Ben Okri (*Nigerian*)

Margaret Oliphant (*Scottish*)

Michael Ondaatje (*Canadian*)

Baroness Emmuska Orczy (*Hungarian-British*)

George Orwell (*English*)

Ouida (*English*)

Cynthia Ozick (*U.S.*)

Boris Leonidovich Pasternak (*Russian*)

Allan Paton (*South African*)

Thomas Love Peacock (*English*)

Mervyn Peake (*English*)

Harold Porter (*Australian*)

Katherine Anne Porter (*U.S.*)

Anthony Powell (*English*)

John Cowper Powys (*English*)

Terry Pratchett (*English*)

J B Priestley (*English*)

V S Pritchett (*English*)

E Annie Proulx (*U.S.*)

Marcel Proust (*French*)

Mario Puzo (*U.S.*)

Thomas Pynchon (*U.S.*)

Ellery Queen (*U.S.*)

Ann Radcliffe (*English*)

Raja Rao (*Indian*)

Frederic Raphael (*U.S.*)

Piers Paul Read (*English*)

Erich Maria Remarque (*German*)

Mary Renault (*English*)

Ruth Rendell (*English*)

Jean Rhys (*British*)

Dorothy Richardson (*English*)

Samuel Richardson (*English*)

Mordecai Richler (*Canadian*)

Harold Robbins (*U.S.*)

Frederick William Rolfe (*English*)

Henry Roth (*U.S.*)

(Ahmed) Salman Rushdie (*Indian-British*)

Vita Sackville-West (*English*)

Marquis de Sade (*French*)

Antoine de Saint-Exupéry (*French*)

Saki (*British*)

J D Salinger (*U.S.*)

George Sand (*French*)

William Saroyan (*U.S.*)

Jean-Paul Sartre (*French*)

Dorothy L Sayers (*English*)

Olive Schreiner (*South African*)

Walter Scott (*Scottish*)

Hubert Selby Jr (*U.S.*)

Tom Sharpe (*English*)

Mary Shelley (*English*)

Carol Shields (*Canadian-American*)

Mikhail Alexandrovich Sholokhov (*Russian*)

Nevil Shute (*Anglo-Austrian*)

Alan Sillitoe (*English*)

Georges Simenon (*Belgian*)

Claude Simon (*French*)

Isaac Bashevis Singer (*U.S.*)

Iain Crichton Smith (*Scottish*)

Zadie Smith (*British*)

Tobias George Smollett (*Scottish*)

C P Snow (*English*)

Alexander Isayevich Solzhenitsyn (*Russian*)

Muriel Spark (*Scottish*)

Howard Spring (*Welsh*)

C K Stead (*New Zealand*)

Gertrude Stein (*U.S.*)

John Steinbeck (*U.S.*)

Stendhal (*French*)

Laurence Sterne (*Irish-British*)

Robert Louis Stevenson (*Scottish*)

J I M Stewart (*Scottish*)

Mary Stewart (*English*)

Bram Stoker (*Irish*)

Robert Stone (*U.S.*)

David Storey (*English*)

Harriet Elizabeth Beecher Stowe (*U.S.*)

William Styron (*U.S.*)

Patrick Süskind (*German*)

Graham Swift (*English*)

Jonathan Swift (*Irish*)

WORD POWER

Julian Symons (*English*)
Emma Tennant (*English*)
William Makepeace
  Thackeray (*English*)
Paul Theroux (*U.S.*)
J(ohn) R(onald) R(euel)
  Tolkien (*English*)
Leo Tolstoy (*Russian*)
John Kennedy Toole (*U.S.*)
Nigel Tranter (*Scottish*)
Rose Tremain (*English*)
William Trevor (*Irish*)
Anthony Trollope (*English*)
Joanna Trollope (*English*)
Frank Tuohy (*English*)
Ivan Sergeyevich Turgenev
  (*Russian*)
Amos Tutuola (*Nigerian*)
Mark Twain (*U.S.*)
Anne Tyler (*U.S.*)
John Updike (*U.S.*)
Edward (Falaise) Upward
  (*English*)
Leon Uris (*U.S.*)
Laurens Van der Post (*South
  African*)

Peter Vansittart (*English*)
Mario Vargos Llosa
  (*Peruvian*)
Jules Verne (*French*)
Gore Vidal (*U.S.*)
Voltaire (*French*)
Kurt Vonnegut (*U.S.*)
John Wain (*English*)
Alice Walker (*U.S.*)
Horace Walpole (*English*)
Marina Warner (*English*)
Robert Penn Warren (*U.S.*)
Keith Waterhouse
  (*English*)
Evelyn Waugh (*English*)
Fay Weldon (*English*)
H G Wells (*English*)
Irvine Welsh (*Scottish*)
Eudora Welty (*U.S.*)
Mary Wesley (*English*)
Morris West (*Australian*)
Rebecca West (*Irish*)
Edith Wharton (*U.S.*)
Antonia White (*English*)
Patrick White
  (*Australian*)

T H White (*English*)
Oscar Wilde (*Irish*)
Thornton Wilder (*U.S.*)
Michael Wilding
  (*Australian*)
A(ndrew) N(orman) Wilson
  (*English*)
Jeanette Winterson (*English*)
P(elham) G(renville)
  Wodehouse (*English-U.S.*)
Thomas Clayton Wolfe
  (*U.S.*)
Tom Wolfe (*U.S.*)
Tobias Wolff (*U.S.*)
Virginia Woolf (*English*)
Herman Wouk (*U.S.*)
Richard Nathaniel Wright
  (*U.S.*)
Frank Yerby (*U.S.*)
Marguerite Yourcenar
  (*French*)
Evgeny Ivanovich
  Zamyatin (*Russian*)
Emile Zola (*French*)

WORD POWER

PLACES AND THEIR NICKNAMES

Place	Nickname	Place	Nickname
Aberdeen	the Granite City	London	the Big Smoke or the Great Wen
Adelaide	the City of Churches		
Amsterdam	the Venice of the North	Los Angeles	L.A.
		New Jersey	the Garden State
Birmingham	Brum or the Venice of the North	New Orleans	the Crescent City or the Big Easy
Boston	Bean Town	New South Wales	Ma State
Bruges	the Venice of the North	New York (City)	the Big Apple
		New York (State)	the Empire State
California	the Golden State	New Zealand	Pig Island
Chicago	the Windy City	North Carolina	the Tarheel State
Dallas	the Big D	Nottingham	Queen of the Midlands
Detroit	the Motor City		
Dresden	Florence on the Elbe	Oklahoma	the Sooner State
Dublin	the Fair City	Pennsylvania	the Keystone State
Dumfries	Queen of the South	Philadelphia	Philly
Edinburgh	Auld Reekie or the Athens of the North	Portsmouth	Pompey
		Prince Edward Island	Spud Island
Florida	the Sunshine State		
Fraserburgh	the Broch	Queensland	Bananaland or the Deep North (both derogatory)
Fremantle	Freo		
Glasgow	the Dear Green Place		
Hamburg	the Venice of the North	Rome	the Eternal City
		San Francisco	Frisco
Indiana	the Hoosier State	Southeastern U.S.A.	Dixie, Dixieland, or the Deep South
Iowa	the Hawkeye State		
Ireland	the Emerald Isle	Tasmania	Tassie or the Apple Isle
Jamaica	J.A. or the Yard		
Jerusalem	the Holy City	Texas	the Lone Star State
Kentucky	the Bluegrass State	Utah	the Beehive State
Kuala Lumpur	K.L.	Venice	La Serenissima

Poetry and prosody terms

accentual metre
accentual-syllabic metre *or*
  stress-syllabic metre
Adonic
Alcaic
Alexandrine
alliteration
amoebaean *or* amoebean
amphibrach
amphimacer
anacrusis
arsis
anapaest *or* anapest
anapaestic *or* anapestic
antistrophe
assonance
bacchius
ballad stanza
blank verse
bob
cadence *or* cadency
caesura *or* cesura
canto
catalectic
choriamb *or* choriambus
closed couplet
common measure
common metre
consonance *or* consonancy
couplet
cretic *or* amphimacer
dactyl
dactylic
diaeresis *or* dieresis
dipody
distich
elision
end-stopped

enjambement
envoy *or* envoi
epode
eye rhyme
feminine ending
feminine rhyme
foot
free verse *or* vers libre
half-rhyme
hemistich
heptameter
heptastich
heroic couplet
hexameter
hypermeter
iamb *or* iambus
iambic
ictus
internal rhyme
ionic
jabberwocky
leonine rhyme
long metre
macaronic
masculine ending
masculine rhyme
metre
octameter
octave *or* octet
onomatopoeia
ottava rima
paeon
paeonic
pararhyme
pentameter
pentastich
perfect rhyme *or* full rhyme
Pindaric

pyhrric
quantitative metre
quatrain
quintain *or* quintet
refrain
rhyme
rhyme royal
rhyme scheme
rhythm
rime riche
Sapphic
scansion
septet
sestet
sestina *or* sextain
short metre
Spenserian stanza
spondee
spondaic
sprung rhythm
stanza
stichic
strophe
syllabic metre
tercet
terza rima
tetrabrach
tetrameter
tetrapody
tetrastich
triplet
trochaic
trochee
unstopped
verse paragraph
wheel

Poetry movements and groupings

Alexandrians
Decadents
Georgian Poets
imagists

Lake Poets
Liverpool Poets
Metaphysical Poets
the Movement

Petrarchans
Romantics
Scottish Chaucerians
symbolists

POETS

Dannie Abse (*Welsh*)
(Karen) Fleur Adcock (*New Zealander*)
Conrad (Potter) Aiken (*U.S.*)
Anna Akhamatova (*Russian*)
Maya Angelou (*U.S.*)
Guillaume Apollinaire (*French*)
Ludovico Ariosto (*Italian*)
Matthew Arnold (*English*)
W(ystan) H(ugh) Auden (*English-U.S.*)
Charles Pierre Baudelaire (*French*)
Patricia Beer (*English*)
Hilaire Belloc (*British*)
John Berryman (*U.S.*)
John Betjeman (*English*)
Elizabeth Bishop (*U.S.*)
William Blake (*English*)
Edmund Blunden (*English*)
Joseph Brodsky (*Russian-American*)
Rupert (Chawner) Brooke (*English*)
Gwendolyn Brooks (*U.S.*)
Elizabeth Barrett Browning (*English*)
Robert Browning (*English*)
Robert Burns (*Scottish*)
(George Gordon) Byron (*British*)
Callimachus (*Greek*)
Luis Vaz de Camoëns (*Portuguese*)
Thomas Campion (*English*)
Raymond Carver (*U.S.*)
Gaius Valerius Catullus (*Roman*)
Charles Causley (*English*)
Geoffrey Chaucer (*English*)
Amy Clampitt (*U.S.*)
John Clare (*English*)
Samuel Taylor Coleridge (*English*)
William Cowper (*English*)
George Crabbe (*English*)
e(dward) e(stlin) cummings (*U.S.*)
Dante (Alighieri) (*Italian*)
Cecil Day Lewis (*Irish*)
Walter de la Mare (*English*)
Emily Dickinson (*U.S.*)
John Donne (*English*)
H D (Hilda Doolittle) (*U.S.*)
John Dryden (*English*)
Carol Ann Duffy (*Scottish*)
William Dunbar (*Scottish*)
Douglas Dunn (*Scottish*)
Geoffrey Dutton (*Australian*)
T(homas) S(tearns) Eliot (*U.S.-British*)
Ebenezer Elliot (the Corn Law Rhymer) (*English*)
Paul Éluard (*French*)
Ralph Waldo Emerson (*U.S.*)
William Empson (*English*)

Edward Fitzgerald (*English*)
Robert Fitzgerald (*Australian*)
Robert (Lee) Frost (*U.S.*)
Allen Ginsberg (*U.S.*)
Johann Wolfgang von Goethe (*German*)
Robert Graves (*English*)
Thomas Gray (*English*)
Thom Gunn (*English*)
Seamus Heaney (*Irish*)
Adrian Henri (*English*)
Robert Henryson (*Scottish*)
George Herbert (*English*)
Robert Herrick (*English*)
Hesiod (*Greek*)
Geoffrey Hill (*English*)
Ralph Hodgson (*English*)
Homer (*Greek*)
Thomas Hood (*English*)
Gerard Manley Hopkins (*English*)
Horace (*Roman*)
A(lfred) E(dward) Housman (*English*)
Ted Hughes (*English*)
Elizabeth Jennings (*English*)
Samuel Johnson (*English*)
Ben Jonson (*English*)
Juvenal (*Roman*)
Patrick Kavanagh (*Irish*)
John Keats (*English*)
Sidney Keyes (*English*)
(Joseph) Rudyard Kipling (*English*)
Jean de La Fontaine (*French*)
Alphonse Marie Louis de Prat de Lamartine (*French*)
Walter Savage Landor (*English*)
William Langland (*English*)
Philip Larkin (*English*)
Tom Leonard (*Scottish*)
Henry Wadsworth Longfellow (*U.S.*)
Amy Lowell (*U.S.*)
Robert Lowell (*U.S.*)
Richard Lovelace (*English*)
Lucretius (*Roman*)
Thomas Macauley (*English*)
Norman MacCaig (*Scottish*)
Hugh MacDiarmid (*Scottish*)
Roger McGough (*English*)
Sorley MacLean (*Scottish*)
Louis MacNeice (*Irish*)
Stéphane Mallarmé (*French*)
Martial (*Roman*)
Andrew Marvell (*English*)
John Masefield (*English*)
Edna St Vincent Millay (*U.S.*)
John Milton (*English*)

Marianne Moore (*U.S.*)
Edwin Morgan (*Scottish*)
Andrew Motion (*English*)
Edwin Muir (*Scottish*)
Ogden Nash (*U.S.*)
Pablo Neruda (*Chilean*)
Frank O'Hara (*U.S.*)
Omar Khayyam (*Persian*)
Ovid (*Roman*)
Wilfred Owen (*British*)
Brian Patten (*English*)
Octavio Paz (*Mexican*)
Petrarch (*Italian*)
Pindar (*Greek*)
Sylvia Plath (*U.S.*)
Alexander Pope (*English*)
Peter Porter (*Australian*)
Ezra (Loomis) Pound (*U.S.*)
Sextus Propertius (*Roman*)
Aleksander Sergeyevich Pushkin (*Russian*)
Kathleen Raine (*English*)
Adrienne Rich (*U.S.*)
Laura Riding (*U.S.*)
Rainer Maria Rilke (*Austro-German*)
Arthur Rimbaud (*French*)
(John Wilmot) Rochester (*English*)
Theodore Huebner Roethke (*U.S.*)
Isaac Rosenberg (*English*)
Christina Georgina Rossetti (*English*)
Dante Gabriel Rossetti (*English*)
Saint-John Perse (*French*)
Sappho (*Greek*)
Siegfried Sassoon (*English*)
Johann Christoph Friedrich von Schiller (*German*)

Delmore Schwarz (*U.S.*)
Sir Walter Scott (*Scottish*)
Jaroslav Seifert (*Czech*)
William Shakespeare (*English*)
Percy Bysshe Shelley (*English*)
Sir Philip Sidney (*English*)
Edith Sitwell (*English*)
John Skelton (*English*)
Christopher Smart (*English*)
Stevie Smith (*English*)
Robert Southey (*English*)
Stephen Spender (*English*)
Edmund Spenser (*English*)
Wallace Stevens (*U.S.*)
Algernon Charles Swinburne (*English*)
Wislawa Szymborska (*Polish*)
Torquato Tasso (*Italian*)
Alfred, Lord Tennyson (*English*)
Dylan (Marlais) Thomas (*Welsh*)
Edward Thomas (*English*)
R(onald) S(tuart) Thomas (*Welsh*)
James Thomson (*Scottish*)
Paul Verlaine (*French*)
Alfred Victor de Vigny (*French*)
François Villon (*French*)
Virgil (*Roman*)
Derek Walcott (*West Indian*)
Francis Charles Webb (*Australian*)
Walt Whitman (*U.S.*)
William Wordsworth (*English*)
Judith Wright (*Australian*)
Thomas Wyatt (*English*)
W(illiam) B(utler) Yeats (*Irish*)

WORD POWER

POLITICAL PARTIES

Australia
Australian Labor Party
Liberal Party of Australia
National Party of Australia

Austria
Freedom Party (FPÖ)
People's Party (ÖVP)
Socialist Party (SPÖ)

Belgium
Flemish Bloc (VB)
Flemish Green Party (Agalev)
French Green Party (Ecolo)
Flemish Liberal Party (PVV)
French Liberal Reform Party (PRL)
Flemish Social Christian Party (CVP)
French Social Christian Party (PSC)
Flemish Socialist Party (SP)
French Socialist Party (PS)

Canada
Bloc Quebecois
Liberal Party
New Democratic Party
Progressive Conservative
Reform Party
Social Credit Party

Denmark
Centre Democrats (CD)
Christian People's Party (KrF)
Conservative People's Party (KF)
Left Socialists
Liberals (V)
Progress Party (FP)
Radical Liberals (RV)
Social Democrats (SD)
Socialist People's Party (SF)

Finland
Centre Party (KP)
Democratic Alternative
Finnish People's Democratic League (SKDL)
Finnish Rural Party (SMP)
Green Party
National Coalition Party (KOK)
Social Democratic Party (SD)
Swedish People's Party (SFP)

France
Communist Party (PC)
National Front
Rally for the Republic (RDR)
Republican Party (PR)
Socialist Party (PS)
Union for French Democracy (UDF)

Germany
Christian-Democratic Union (CDU)
Christian-Social Union (CSU)
Free Democratic Party (FDP)
Green Party
Party of Democratic Socialism (PDS)
Social Democratic Party (SPD)

Greece
Greek Communist Party
New Democracy (ND)
Pan-Hellenic Socialist Movement (PASOK)
Political Spring (Politiki Aniksi)

India
Congress (I)
Janata Dal
Bharitiya Janata Party (BJP)

Irish Republic
Democratic Left
Fianna Fáil
Fine Gael
Labour Party
Progressive Democrats

Israel
Labour Party
Likud

Italy
Centre Union
Christian Democrat Party
Democratic Party of the Left (PDS)
Forza Italia
National Alliance
Northern League

Japan
Democratic Socialist Party
Liberal Democratic Party
Komeito
Social Democratic Party

WORD POWER

POLITICAL PARTIES

WORD POWER

Luxembourg
Communist Party
Democratic Party (PD)
Luxembourg Socialist Workers' Party
  (POSL)
Christian Social Party (PCS)

Malta
Malta Labour Party
Nationalist Party

Mexico
Institutional Revolutionary Party (PRI)
National Action Party (PAN)
Party of the Democratic Revolution (PRD)
Revolutionary Workers' Party

the Netherlands
Christian Democratic Appeal (CDA)
Labour Party (PvdA)
People's Party for Freedom and Democracy
  (VVD)

New Zealand
Labour Party
National Party

Northern Ireland
Democratic Unionist Party
Official Ulster Unionist Party
Sinn Féin
Social Democratic and Labour Party (SDLP)

Portugal
Democratic Renewal Party (PRD)
Democratic Social Centre Party (CDS)
Social Democratic Party (PSD)
Socialist Party (PS)

South Africa
African National Congress (ANC)
Inkatha Freedom Party
National Party
Pan-Africanist Congress (PAC)

Spain
Basque Nationalist Party (PNV)
Convergencia i Uni (CiU)
Herri Batasuna (HB)
People's Party (PP)
Socialist Workers' Party (PSOE)
United Left (IU)

Sweden
Centre Party
Christian Democratic Party
Green Party
Left Party
Liberal Party
Moderate Party
Social Democratic Labour Party (SAP)

Turkey
Motherland Party (ANAP)
Kurdish Workers' Party (PKK)
Social Democratic Populist Party
True Path Party

United Kingdom (mainland)
Conservative and Unionist Party
Labour Party
Liberal Democrats
Plaid Cymru
Scottish National Party

United States of America
Democratic Party
Republican Party

Major world ports

Abidjan	Chicago	Kingston
Accra	Chittagong	Kobe
Aden	Colombo	Kowloon
Alexandria	Colón	Kuwait
Algiers	Conakry	La Coruña
Alicante	Copenhagen	Lagos
Amsterdam	Corinth	La Guaira
Anchorage	Dakar	Las Palmas
Antwerp	Dar es Salaam	Launceston
Apia	Darwin	Le Havre
Aqaba	Dieppe	Limassol
Archangel	Djibouti	Lisbon
Ashdod	Dubrovnik	Liverpool
Auckland	Duluth	Livorno
Baku	Dunedin	Lomé
Baltimore	Dunkerque	London
Bangkok	Durban	Los Angeles
Barcelona	East London	Luanda
Basra	Eilat or Elat	Lübeck
Bathurst	Esbjerg	Macao
Batum	Europoort	Madras
Beira	Fray Bentos	Malmo
Beirut	Freetown	Manama
Belize	Fremantle	Manaus
Benghazi	Gdańsk	Manila
Bergen	Genoa	Maputo
Bilbao	Georgetown	Mar del Plata
Bissau	Gijón	Marseille
Bombay	Göteborg or Gothenburg	Melbourne
Bordeaux	Guayaquil	Mobile
Boston	Haifa	Mogadiscio or Mogadishu
Boulogne	Halifax	Mombasa
Bridgetown	Hamburg	Monrovia
Brindisi	Hamilton	Montego Bay
Brisbane	Havana	Montevideo
Bristol	Helsinki	Montreal
Buenaventura	Hobart	Murmansk
Buenos Aires	Ho Chi Minh City	Muscat
Cádiz	Honolulu	Nagasaki
Cagliari	Hook of Holland	Naples
Calais	Inchon	Nassau
Calcutta	Istanbul	New Orleans
Callao	Izmir	New York
Cannes	Jacksonville	Oakland
Canton	Jaffa	Odense
Cape Town	Jidda or Jedda	Odessa
Cap-Haitien	Juneau	Oporto
Casablanca	Kaohsiung or Kao-hsiung	Osaka
Catania	Karachi	Oslo
Cebu	Kawasaki	Ostend
Charleston	Keflavik	Phnom Penh
Cherbourg	Kiel	Piraeus

WORD POWER

Major world ports (continued)

Port Adelaide
Port au Prince
Port Elizabeth
Portland
Port Louis
Port Moresby
Port Said
Portsmouth
Port Sudan
Punta Arenas
Pusan
Recife
Reykjavik
Riga
Rimini
Rio de Janeiro
Rostock
Rotterdam
Saint Petersburg
Salvador
San Diego
San Francisco
San Juan

San Sebastian
Santander
Santo Domingo
Santos
Savannah
Seattle
Sevastopol
Seville
Shanghai
Singapore
Southampton
Split
Stavanger
Stockholm
Suez
Suva
Sydney
Szczecin
Takoradi
Tallinn *or* Tallin
Tampa
Tandjungpriok
Tangier

Tokyo
Townsville
Trieste
Tripoli
Trondheim
Tunis
Turku
Tyre
Valencia
Valparaíso
Vancouver
Venice
Veracruz
Vigo
Vishakhapatnam
Vladivostok
Volgograd
Walvis Bay
Wellington
Yangon
Yokohama
Zeebrugge

Major British and Irish ports

Aberdeen
Arbroath
Ayr
Barry
Belfast
Birkenhead
Bristol
Caernarfon
Cardiff
Cóbh
Cork
Dover
Dundee
Dún Laoghaire
Ellesmere Port
Fishguard
Fleetwood
Folkestone
Galway
Glasgow
Grangemouth
Gravesend
Great Yarmouth

Greenock
Grimsby
Harwich
Holyhead
Hull
Immingham
Kirkcaldy
Larne
Leith
Lerwick
Limerick
Liverpool
London
Londonderry *or* Derry
Lowestoft
Milford Haven
Morecambe
Newcastle upon Tyne
Newhaven
Newport
Newry
Oban
Penzance

Plymouth
Poole
Portsmouth
Port Talbot
Ramsgate
Rosslare
Scarborough
Sheerness
Sligo
Southampton
South Shields
Stornoway
Stranraer
Sunderland
Swansea
Tynemouth
Waterford
Wexford
Weymouth
Whitby
Wicklow

PRIME MINISTERS

British Prime Ministers

Prime Minister	Party	Term of office
Robert Walpole	Whig	1721–42
Earl of Wilmington	Whig	1742–43
Henry Pelham	Whig	1743–54
Duke of Newcastle	Whig	1754–56
Duke of Devonshire	Whig	1756–57
Duke of Newcastle	Whig	1757–62
Earl of Bute	Tory	1762–63
George Grenville	Whig	1763–65
Marquess of Rockingham	Whig	1765–66
Duke of Grafton	Whig	1766–70
Lord North	Tory	1770–82
Marquess of Rockingham	Whig	1782
Earl of Shelburne	Whig	1782–83
Duke of Portland	Coalition	1783
William Pitt	Tory	1783–1801
Henry Addington	Tory	1801–04
William Pitt	Tory	1804–06
Lord Grenville	Whig	1806–07
Duke of Portland	Tory	1807–09
Spencer Perceval	Tory	1809–12
Earl of Liverpool	Tory	1812–27
George Canning	Tory	1827
Viscount Goderich	Tory	1827–28
Duke of Wellington	Tory	1828–30
Earl Grey	Whig	1830–34
Viscount Melbourne	Whig	1834
Robert Peel	Conservative	1834–35
Viscount Melbourne	Whig	1835–41
Robert Peel	Conservative	1841–46
Lord John Russell	Liberal	1846–52
Earl of Derby	Conservative	1852
Lord Aberdeen	Peelite	1852–55
Viscount Palmerston	Liberal	1855–58
Earl of Derby	Conservative	1858–59
Viscount Palmerston	Liberal	1859–65
Lord John Russell	Liberal	1865–66
Earl of Derby	Conservative	1866–68
Benjamin Disraeli	Conservative	1868
William Gladstone	Liberal	1868–74
Benjamin Disraeli	Conservative	1874–80
William Gladstone	Liberal	1880–85
Marquess of Salisbury	Conservative	1885–86
William Gladstone	Liberal	1886
Marquess of Salisbury	Conservative	1886–92
William Gladstone	Liberal	1892–94
Earl of Rosebery	Liberal	1894–95
Marquess of Salisbury	Conservative	1895–1902
Arthur James Balfour	Conservative	1902–05
Henry Campbell-Bannerman	Liberal	1905–08
Herbert Henry Asquith	Liberal	1908–15

WORD POWER

British Prime Ministers (continued)

Prime Minister	Party	Term of office
Herbert Henry Asquith	Coalition	1915–16
David Lloyd George	Coalition	1916–22
Andrew Bonar Law	Conservative	1922–23
Stanley Baldwin	Conservative	1923–24
James Ramsay MacDonald	Labour	1924
Stanley Baldwin	Conservative	1924–29
James Ramsay MacDonald	Labour	1929–31
James Ramsay MacDonald	Nationalist	1931–35
Stanley Baldwin	Nationalist	1935–37
Arthur Neville Chamberlain	Nationalist	1937–40
Winston Churchill	Coalition	1940–45
Clement Attlee	Labour	1945–51
Winston Churchill	Conservative	1951–55
Anthony Eden	Conservative	1955–57
Harold Macmillan	Conservative	1957–63
Alec Douglas-Home	Conservative	1963–64
Harold Wilson	Labour	1964–70
Edward Heath	Conservative	1970–74
Harold Wilson	Labour	1974–76
James Callaghan	Labour	1976–79
Margaret Thatcher	Conservative	1979–90
John Major	Conservative	1990–97
Tony Blair	Labour	1997–2007
Gordon Brown	Labour	2007–

Australian Prime Ministers

Prime Minister	Party	Term of office
Edmund Barton	Protectionist	1901–03
Alfred Deakin	Protectionist	1903–04
John Christian Watson	Labor	1904
George Houston Reid	Free Trade	1904–05
Alfred Deakin	Protectionist	1905–08
Andrew Fisher	Labor	1908–09
Alfred Deakin	Fusion	1909–10
Andrew Fisher	Labor	1910–13
Joseph Cook	Liberal	1913–14
Andrew Fisher	Labor	1914–15
William Morris Hughes	National Labor	1915–17
William Morris Hughes	Nationalist	1917–23
Stanley Melbourne Bruce	Nationalist	1923–29
James Henry Scullin	Labor	1929–31
Joseph Aloysius Lyons	United	1931–39
Earle Christmas Page	Country	1939
Robert Gordon Menzies	United	1939–41
Arthur William Fadden	Country	1941
John Joseph Curtin	Labor	1941–45
Joseph Benedict Chifley	Labor	1945–49
Robert Gordon Menzies	Liberal	1949–66
Harold Edward Holt	Liberal	1966–67

Australian Prime Ministers (continued)

Prime Minister	Party	Term of office
John McEwen	Country	1967–68
John Grey Gorton	Liberal	1968–71
William McMahon	Liberal	1971–72
Edward Gough Whitlam	Labor	1972–75
John Malcolm Fraser	Liberal	1975–83
Robert James Lee Hawke	Labor	1983–91
Paul Keating	Labor	1991–96
John Howard	Liberal	1996–2007
Kevin Rudd	Labor	2007–

Canadian Prime Ministers

Prime Minister	Party	Term of office
John A. MacDonald	Conservative	1867–73
Alexander Mackenzie	Liberal	1873–78
John A. MacDonald	Conservative	1878–91
John J.C. Abbot	Conservative	1891–92
John S.D. Thompson	Conservative	1892–94
Mackenzie Bowell	Conservative	1894–96
Charles Tupper	Conservative	1896
Wilfrid Laurier	Liberal	1896–1911
Robert Borden	Conservative	1911–20
Arthur Meighen	Conservative	1920–21
William Lyon Mackenzie King	Liberal	1921–1926
Arthur Meighen	Conservative	1926
William Lyon Mackenzie King	Liberal	1926–30
Richard Bedford Bennet	Conservative	1930–35
William Lyon Mackenzie King	Liberal	1935–48
Louis St. Laurent	Liberal	1948–57
John George Diefenbaker	Conservative	1957–63
Lester Bowles Pearson	Liberal	1963–68
Pierre Elliott Trudeau	Liberal	1968–79
Joseph Clark	Conservative	1979–80
Pierre Elliott Trudeau	Liberal	1968–79
Joseph Clark	Conservative	1979–80
Pierre Elliott Trudeau	Liberal	1980–84
John Turner	Liberal	1984
Brian Mulroney	Conservative	1984–93
Kim Campbell	Conservative	1993
Joseph Jacques Jean Chrétien	Liberal	1993–2003
Paul Martin	Liberal	2003–2006
Stephen Harper	Conservative	2006–

New Zealand Prime Ministers

Prime Minister	Party	Term of office
Henry Sewell	–	1856
William Fox	–	1856
Edward William Stafford	–	1856–61
William Fox	–	1861–62

WORD POWER

New Zealand Prime Ministers (continued)

Prime Minister	Party	Term of office
Alfred Domett	–	1862–63
Frederick Whitaker	–	1863–64
Frederick Aloysius Weld	–	1864–65
Edward William Stafford	–	1865–69
William Fox	–	1869–72
Edward William Stafford	–	1872
William Fox	–	1873
Julius Vogel	–	1873–75
Daniel Pollen	–	1875–76
Julius Vogel	–	1876
Harry Albert Atkinson	–	1876–77
George Grey	–	1877–79
John Hall	–	1879–82
Frederic Whitaker	–	1882–83
Harry Albert Atkinson	–	1883–84
Robert Stout	–	1884
Harry Albert Atkinson	–	1884
Robert Stout	–	1884–87
Harry Albert Atkinson	–	1887–91
John Ballance	–	1891–93
Richard John Seddon	Liberal	1893–1906
William Hall-Jones	Liberal	1906
Joseph George Ward	Liberal/National	1906–12
Thomas Mackenzie	National	1912
William Ferguson Massey	Reform	1912–25
Francis Henry Dillon Bell	Reform	1925
Joseph Gordon Coates	Reform	1925–28
Joseph George Ward	Liberal/National	1928–30
George William Forbes	United	1930–35
Michael Joseph Savage	Labour	1935–40
Peter Fraser	Labour	1940–49
Sidney George Holland	National	1949–57
Keith Jacka Holyoake	National	1957
Walter Nash	Labour	1957–60
Keith Jacka Holyoake	National	1960–72
John Ross Marshall	National	1972
Norman Eric Kirk	Labour	1972–74
Wallace Edward Rowling	Labour	1974–75
Robert David Muldoon	National	1975–84
David Russell Lange	Labour	1984–89
Geoffrey Palmer	Labour	1989–90
Mike Moore	Labour	1990
Jim Bolger	National	1990–97
Jenny Shipley	National	1997–99
Helen Clark	Labour	1999–

RIVERS

Adige
Ain
Aire
Aisne
Alabama
Albany
Aldan
Allier
Amazon
Amu Darya
Amur
Anadyr
Anderson
Angara
Apure
Apurimac
Araguaia
Aras
Arkansas
Arno
Aruwimi
Assiniboine
Atbara
Athabaska
Aube
Avon
Back
Barrow
Beni
Benue
Berezina
Bermejo
Bío-Bío
Black Volta
Blue Nile
Bomu
Boyne
Brahmaputra
Bug
Cam
Canadian
Caquetá
Cauca
Cauvery *or* Kaveri
Chagres
Chao Phraya
Charente
Chari *or* Shari
Chenab
Cher
Chindwin
Churchill
Clutha
Clyde

Colorado
Columbia
Congo
Connecticut
Cooper's Creek
Courantyne
Cuiaba
Damodar
Danube
Darling
Dee
Delaware
Demerara
Derwent
Des Moines
Detroit
Dnieper
Dniester
Don
Donets
Dordogne
Doubs
Douro
Drava *or* Drave
Drin
Durance
Dvina
Ebro
Elbe
Ems
Erne
Essequibo
Euphrates
Fly
Forth
Fraser
Ganges
Garonne
Glomma
Godavari
Gogra
Göta
Granta
Green
Guadalquivir
Guadiana
Guaporé
Han
Havel
Helmand
Hooghly
Hudson
Iguaçú *or* Iguassú
IJssel *or* Yssel

Illinois
Indus
Inn
Irrawaddy
Irtysh *or* Irtish
Isar
Isère
Isis
Japurá
Javari
Jhelum
Jordan
Juba
Jumna
Juruá
Kabul
Kagera
Kama
Kasai
Kentucky
Kizil Irmak
Klondike
Kolyma
Komati
Kootenay *or*
   Kootenai
Krishna
Kuban
Kura
Kuskokwim
Lachlan
Lech
Lee
Lena
Liao
Liard
Liffey
Limpopo
Lippe
Little Bighorn
Loire
Lot
Lualaba
Mackenzie
Macquarie
Madeira
Madre de Dios
Magdalena
Mahanadi
Main
Mamoré
Marañón
Maritsa
Marne

Medway
Mekong
Menderes
Mersey
Meta
Meuse
Minnesota
Miño
Mississippi
Missouri
Mohawk
Molopo
Monongahela
Morava
Moselle
Moskva
Murray
Murrumbidgee
Narmada
Neckar
Negro
Neisse
Nelson
Neman *or* Nyeman
Neva
Niagara
Niger
Nile
Ob
Oder
Ogooué *or* Ogowe
Ohio
Oise
Okanagan
Okavango
Orange
Ord
Orinoco
Orontes
Ottawa
Ouachita *or*
   Washita
Ouse
Paraguay
Paraíba
Paraná
Parnaíba *or*
   Parnahiba
Peace
Pearl
Pechora
Pecos
Piave
Pilcomayo

Plate
Po
Potomac
Pripet
Prut
Purús
Putamayo
Red
Rhine *or* Rhein
Rhône
Ribble
Richelieu
Rio Branco
Rio Grande
Rubicon
Saar
Sacramento
Safid Rud
Saguenay
Saint Croix
Saint John
Saint Lawrence
Salado
Salambria
Salween
Sambre
San
Santee
Saône
Saskatchewan

Sava *or* Save
Savannah
Scheldt
Seine
Severn
Shannon
Shatt-al-Arab
Shiré
Siret
Skien
Slave
Snake
Snowy
Somme
Songhua
Spey
Struma
Susquehanna
Sutlej
Suwannee *or* Swanee
Swan
Swat
Syr Darya
Tagus
Tana
Tanana
Tapajós
Tarim
Tarn

Tarsus
Tay
Tees
Tennessee
Thames
Tiber
Ticino
Tigris
Tisza
Tobol
Tocantins
Trent
Tugela
Tunguska
Tweed
Tyne
Ubangi
Ucayali
Uele
Ural
Usk
Ussuri
Vaal
Var
Vardar
Vienne
Vistula
Vltava
Volga
Volta

Volturno
Waal
Wabash
Waikato
Warta
Wear
Weser
White Volta
Wisconsin
Xi, Hsi, *or* Si
Xiang, Hsiang, *or* Siang
Xingú
Wye
Yalu
Yangtze
Yaqui
Yarra
Yellow
Yellowstone
Yenisei
Yonne
Yser
Yüan *or* Yüen
Yukon
Zambezi *or* Zambese
Zhu Jiang

SEAS AND OCEANS

Seas

Adriatic
Aegean
Amundsen
Andaman
Arabian
Arafura
Aral
Azov
Baltic
Banda
Barents
Beaufort
Bellingshausen
Bering
Bismarck
Black *or* Euxine
Caribbean
Caspian
Celebes

Ceram
China
Chukchi
Coral
East China
East Siberian
Flores
Icarian
Inland
Ionian
Irish
Japan
Java
Kara
Laptev
Ligurian
Lincoln
Marmara *or* Marmora
Mediterranean

Nordenskjöld
North
Norwegian
Okhotsk
Philippine
Red
Ross
Sargasso
Scotia
Solomon
South China
Sulu
Tasman
Timor
Tyrrhenian
Weddell
White
Yellow *or* Hwang Hai

Oceans

Antarctic *or* Southern
Arctic

Atlantic
Indian

Pacific

SOUTH AFRICAN PROVINCES

Province	Capital	Province	Capital
Eastern Cape	Bisho	Mpumalanga	Nelspruit
Free State	Bloemfontein	North-West	Mafikeng
Gauteng	Johannesburg	Northern Cape	Kimberley
KwaZulu-Natal	Pietermaritzburg	Western Cape	Cape Town
Limpopo	Pietersburg		

WORD POWER

U.S. PRESIDENTS

President	Party	Term of office
1. George Washington	Federalist	1789–97
2. John Adams	Federalist	1797–1801
3. Thomas Jefferson	Democratic Republican	1801–1809
4. James Madison	Democratic Republican	1809–1817
5. James Monroe	Democratic Republican	1817–25
6. John Quincy Adams	Democratic Republican	1825–29
7. Andrew Jackson	Democrat	1829–37
8. Martin Van Buren	Democrat	1837–41
9. William Henry Harrison	Whig	1841
10. John Tyler	Whig	1841–45
11. James K. Polk	Democrat	1845–49
12. Zachary Taylor	Whig	1849–50
13. Millard Fillmore	Whig	1850–53
14. Franklin Pierce	Democrat	1853–57
15. James Buchanan	Democrat	1857–61
16. Abraham Lincoln	Republican	1861–65
17. Andrew Johnson	Republican	1865–69
18. Ulysses S. Grant	Republican	1869–77
19. Rutherford B. Hayes	Republican	1877–81
20. James A. Garfield	Republican	1881
21. Chester A. Arthur	Republican	1881–85
22. Grover Cleveland	Democrat	1885–89
23. Benjamin Harrison	Republican	1889–93
24. Grover Cleveland	Democrat	1893–97
25. William McKinley	Republican	1897–1901
26. Theodore Roosevelt	Republican	1901–1909
27. William Howard Taft	Republican	1909–13
28. Woodrow Wilson	Democrat	1913–21
29. Warren G. Harding	Republican	1921–23
30. Calvin Coolidge	Republican	1923–29
31. Herbert C. Hoover	Republican	1929–33
32. Franklin D. Roosevelt	Democrat	1933–45
33. Harry S. Truman	Democrat	1945–53
34. Dwight D. Eisenhower	Republican	1953–61
35. John F. Kennedy	Democrat	1961–63
36. Lyndon B. Johnson	Democrat	1963–69
37. Richard M. Nixon	Republican	1969–74
38. Gerald R. Ford	Republican	1974–77
39. James E. Carter, Jr	Democrat	1977–81
40. Ronald W. Reagan	Republican	1981–89
41. George H. W. Bush	Republican	1989–93
42. William J. Clinton	Democrat	1993–2001
43. George W. Bush	Republican	2001–

WORD POWER

WORD POWER

State	Abbreviation	Zip code
Alabama	Ala.	AL
Alaska	Alas.	AK
Arizona	Ariz.	AZ
Arkansas	Ark.	AR
California	Cal.	CA
Colorado	Colo.	CO
Connecticut	Conn.	CT
Delaware	Del.	DE
District of Columbia	D.C.	DC
Florida	Fla.	FL
Georgia	Ga.	GA
Hawaii	Haw.	HI
Idaho	Id. *or* Ida.	ID
Illinois	Ill.	IL
Indiana	Ind.	IN
Iowa	Ia. *or* Io.	IA
Kansas	Kan. *or* Kans.	KS
Kentucky	Ken.	KY
Louisiana	La.	LA
Maine	Me.	ME
Maryland	Md.	MD
Massachusetts	Mass.	MA
Michigan	Mich.	MI
Minnesota	Minn.	MN
Mississippi	Miss.	MS
Missouri	Mo.	MO
Montana	Mont.	MT
Nebraska	Neb.	NE
Nevada	Nev.	NV
New Hampshire	N.H.	NH
New Jersey	N.J.	NJ
New Mexico	N.M. *or* N.Mex.	NM
New York	N.Y.	NY
North Carolina	N.C.	NC
North Dakota	N.D. *or* N.Dak.	ND
Ohio	O.	OH
Oklahoma	Okla.	OK
Oregon	Oreg.	OR
Pennsylvania	Pa., Penn., *or* Penna.	PA
Rhode Island	R.I.	RI
South Carolina	S.C.	SC
South Dakota	S.Dak.	SD
Tennessee	Tenn.	TN
Texas	Tex.	TX
Utah	Ut.	UT
Vermont	Vt.	VT
Virginia	Va.	VA
Washington	Wash.	WA
West Virginia	W.Va.	WV
Wisconsin	Wis.	WI
Wyoming	Wyo.	WY

VOLCANOES

Antisana
Apo
Askja
Cameroon
Chimborazo
Citlaltépetl
Corcovado
Cotopaxi
Egmont
Elgon
El Misti
Erciyas Dagi
Erebus
Etna
Fuji
Haleakala

Hekla
Helgafell
Huascarán *or* Huascán
Iliamna
Ixtaccihuatl *or* Iztaccihuatl
Katmai
Kazbek
Kenya
Krakatoa *or* Krakatau
Lassen Peak
Mauna Kea
Mauna Loa
Mayon
Mount St. Helens
Nevado de Colima
Nevado de Toluca

Paricutín
Pelée
Popocatépetl
Santa Maria
Semeru *or* Semeroe
Soufrière
Stromboli
Suribachi
Taal
Tambora
Teide *or* Teyde
Tolima
Tristan da Cunha
Vesuvius

WATERFALLS

Angel Falls
Churchill Falls
Cleve-Garth
Cuquenan
Iguaçú Falls
Itatinga

Kaieteur Falls
Niagara Falls
Ormeli
Pilao
Ribbon
Roraima

Sutherland Falls
Tysse
Vestre Mardola
Victoria Falls
Yellowstone Falls
Yosemite Falls

WORD POWER

WRITERS

Children's writers

Louisa May Alcott (*U.S.*)
Hans Christian Andersen (*Danish*)
Lynn Reid Banks (*English*)
J(ames) M(atthew) Barrie (*Scottish*)
Judy Blume (*U.S.*)
Enid (Mary) Blyton (*English*)
Elinor M(ary) Brent-Dyer (*English*)
Lewis Carroll (*English*)
Babette Cole (*British*)
Eoin Colfer (*Irish*)
Susan Coolidge (*U.S.*)
Karen Cushman (*U.S.*)
Roald Dahl (*British*)
Anne Digby (*English*)
Dr Seuss (*U.S.*)
Ann Fine (*English*)
Kenneth Grahame (*Scottish*)
Laura Ingalls Wilder (*U.S.*)

Mike Inkpen (*English*)
Robin Jarvis (*English*)
Diana Wynne Jones (*Welsh*)
C(live) S(taples) Lewis (*English*)
A(lan) A(lexander) Milne (*English*)
Michael Morpurgo (*English*)
Jill Murphy (*English*)
E(dith) Nesbit (*English*)
Terry Pratchett (*English*)
Philip Pullman (*English*)
Chris Riddell (*English*)
J K Rowling (*British*)
Louis Sachar (*U.S.*)
Dick King Smith (*English*)
Paul Stewart (*English*)
Noel Streatfield (*English*)
Jacqueline Wilson (*English*)

Short story writers

Giovanni Boccaccio (*Italian*)
Jorge Luis Borges (*Argentinian*)
Stephen Crane (*U.S.*)
Arthur Conan Doyle (*British*)
Joel Chandler Harris (*U.S.*)
Nathaniel Hawthorne (*U.S.*)
Washington Irving (*U.S.*)
Carson McCullers (*U.S.*)
Katherine Mansfield (*N.Z.-British*)

Herman Melville (*U.S.*)
W(illiam) Somerset Maugham (*English*)
(Henri René Albert) Guy de Maupassant
  (*French*)
H(ector) H(ugh) Munro (*Scottish*)
O. Henry (*U.S.*)
Dorothy Parker (*U.S.*)
Edgar Allan Poe (*U.S.*)

Non-fiction writers

Joseph Addison (*English*)
Aesop (*Greek*)
Roger Ascham (*English*)
James Boswell (*Scottish*)
John Bunyan (*English*)
Edmund Burke (*British*)
Jane Welsh Carlyle (*Scottish*)
Thomas Carlyle (*Scottish*)
William Godwin (*English*)
Marcus Tullius Cicero (*Roman*)
William Cobbett (*English*)
Desiderius Erasmus (*Dutch*)
Edward Gibbon (*English*)
William Hazlitt (*English*)
R.H. Hutton (*English*)
Thomas Jefferson (*U.S.*)

Jerome K(lapka) Jerome (*English*)
Samuel Johnson (*English*)
Margery Kempe (*English*)
Lord Chesterfield (*English*)
John Lyly (*English*)
Thomas Malory (*English*)
Michel Eyquem de Montaigne (*French*)
Tom Paine (*English-U.S.*)
Samuel Pepys (*English*)
François Rabelais (*French*)
John Ruskin (*English*)
Richard Steele (*English*)
Leslie Stephen (*English*)
Thomas Traherne (*English*)
Izaac Walton (*English*)
Mary Wollstonecraft (*English*)